Life-Span

Human Development 9e

Carol K. Sigelman
The George Washington University

Elizabeth A. Rider
Elizabethtown College

© Documentary Foundations

CENGAGE
Learning

Australia • Brazil • Mexico • Singapore • United Kingdom • United States

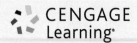

Life-Span Human Development,
Ninth Edition
Carol K. Sigelman and Elizabeth A. Rider

Product Director: Marta Lee-Perriard

Product Manager: Nedah Rose

Content Developer: Stefanie Chase

Product Assistant: Katie Chen

Digital Content Specialist: Jaclyn Hermesmeyer

Marketing Manager: James Finlay

Content Project Manager: Ruth Sakata Corley

Art Director: Vernon Boes

Manufacturing Planner: Karen Hunt

Production and Composition: SPi Global

Photo and Text Research: Lumina
    Datamatics, Ltd.

Text and Cover Designer: Jeanne Calabrese

Cover Image: Paul Giamou/Aurora Photos

For product information and technology assistance, contact us at
Cengage Learning Customer & Sales Support, 1-800-354-9706.
For permission to use material from this text or product,
submit all requests online at **www.cengage.com/permissions.**
Further permissions questions can be e-mailed to
permissionrequest@cengage.com.

Library of Congress Control Number: 2017930382

Student Edition:
ISBN: 978-1-337-10073-1

Loose-leaf Edition:
ISBN: 978-1-337-10075-5

Cengage Learning
20 Channel Center Street
Boston, MA 02210
USA

Cengage Learning is a leading provider of customized learning solutions with employees residing in nearly 40 different countries and sales in more than 125 countries around the world. Find your local representative at **www.cengage.com.**

Cengage Learning products are represented in Canada by Nelson Education, Ltd.

To learn more about Cengage Learning Solutions, visit **www.cengage.com.**

Purchase any of our products at your local college store or at our preferred online store **www.cengagebrain.com.**

Printed in the United States of America
Print Number: 02   Print Year: 2017

Dedication

To the students who have inspired us

Brief Contents

Contents

3 Genes, Environment, and Development 59

4 Prenatal Development and Birth 89

5 Body, Brain, and Health 127

6 Sensation, Perception, and Action 165

7 Cognition 201

8 Memory and Information Processing 233

9 Intelligence and Creativity 265

10 Language and Education 299

11 Self and Personality 333

12 Gender Roles and Sexuality 365

13 Social Cognition and Moral Development 399

14 Emotions, Attachment, and Social Relationships 433

15 The Family 467

16 Developmental Psychopathology 501

17 The Final Challenge: Death and Dying **533**

Appendix Careers in Human Development 562

Preface

This book is about the development of human beings—from their start as fertilized eggs to their dying days. It explores regularities as well as differences in development, and it asks fundamental questions about why we humans develop as we do. This ninth edition of *Life-Span Human Development* retains four core features valued by students and instructors over the years: (1) our unique integrated topical-chronological approach, (2) a presentation that is both research-based and relevant to students, (3) an emphasis on ideas—on the different theoretical perspectives that guide thinking about human development and research, and (4) an in-depth exploration of the all-important nature–nurture issue. In addition, we introduce exciting new topics and controversies in life-span human development, update coverage throughout, and offer new pedagogical features and supplements to enhance the teaching-learning process.

Topical and Chronological Approach

The most distinctive feature of this book is its unique integrated topical-chronological approach. Almost all other life-span development textbooks adopt a chronological or "age-stage" approach, carving the life span into age ranges and describing the prominent characteristics of individuals within each age range. In contrast, we adopt a topical approach for the overall organization of the book blended with a chronological approach within chapters. Each chapter focuses on a domain of development, such as cognition, personality, or social relationships, and traces developmental trends and influences in that domain from infancy to old age. At the same time, each chapter highlights the special qualities of different age groups through major sections on infancy, childhood, adolescence, and adulthood.

Why Topical?

Why have we fought the tide? Like many other instructors, we have typically favored topically organized textbooks when teaching child, adolescent, or adult development. As a result, it seemed natural to extend that same topical approach to the whole life span. It also bothered us that chronologically organized texts often have to repeat themselves to remind readers of where development left off in an earlier age period that was covered much earlier in the book.

More important, a topic-by-topic organization conveys the flow of development in each area—the systematic, and often dramatic, transformations we undergo as well as the ways in which we continue to be the same individuals. The topical approach also helps us emphasize the processes behind development. Finally, a topical approach captures the spirit of a life-span perspective on development: It encourages us—indeed obliges us—to view each period of life in relation to what comes before and what comes after. In chronologically organized textbooks, many topics are taken up only in connection with the age group to which they seem most relevant and are then dropped. A topical organization stimulates us to ask intriguing questions we might otherwise not ask, such as these about close relationships:

- What do infants' attachments to their parents have in common with, and how do they differ from, attachments between childhood friends or between adult romantic partners?
- Do securely attached infants later have a greater capacity to form and sustain close relationships than infants whose early social experiences are less favorable?
- What are the consequences at different points in the life span of lacking a close relationship?

Attachments are important throughout the life span and evolve over the life span; a topical organization helps make that clear.

Why Chronological?

We also appreciate the strengths of the chronological approach, particularly its ability to portray the whole person in each period of the life span. For this reason, we integrated the age-stage approach with the topical organization, aiming to have the best of both worlds.

Each topical chapter contains major sections on infancy, childhood, adolescence, and adulthood. These age-stage sections call attention to the distinctive qualities of each phase of life and make it easier for students to find material on an age period of particular interest to them. In short, we believe that our integrated topical-chronological approach gives students exactly what they deserve: an understanding of the flow of life-span development in particular areas and the factors influencing it along with an appreciation of the flavor of each developmental period.

Adaptability of the Integrated Topical-Chronological Approach

Even though links across chapters are noted throughout the book, instructors who are teaching condensed courses or who are otherwise pressed for time can omit a chapter without fear of rendering other chapters incomprehensible. For example:

- A cognitively oriented course might omit one or more of the socially oriented chapters (Chapters 11, 12, 14, 15, 16, and 17).

- A socially oriented course might omit one or more of the cognitively oriented chapters (Chapters 6, 7, 8, 9, and 10).

Moreover, this approach gives instructors the flexibility to cover infancy, childhood, and adolescence in the first portion of the course, if they prefer, and to save the material on adulthood for the end.

Research-Oriented and Relevant Coverage

We have worked hard to create a text that is rigorous yet readable—research-oriented yet "real" to students. The ninth edition of *Life-Span Human Development* tackles complex theoretical controversies and presents both classic and contemporary research from multiple disciplines. We aim to make developmental science accessible and relevant to students' lives and career goals but we do not "dumb it down."

Students need to understand how we know what we know about development—to appreciate the research process. With that in mind, we describe illustrative studies and present data in graphs and tables, and we cite the authors and dates of publication for a large number of books and articles, all fully referenced in the bibliography at the end of the book. Some students may wonder why they are there. It is because we are committed to the value of systematic research, because we are bound to give credit where credit is due, and because we want students and their professors to have the resources they need to pursue their interest in a topic during and after the course.

We also appreciate that solid scholarship is of little good to students unless they want to read it, can understand it, and see its relevance. To make the material more "real," we clarify developmental concepts through examples, analogies, and visuals; we connect topics in the text to topics in the news, and highlight the practical implications of research findings. This book contains a wealth of applied material relevant to students' current and future roles as parents, teachers, psychologists, health professionals, and other human service professionals. It helps students see that major theories of human development do not just guide researchers but can guide them—for example, in raising, educating, or treating infants, children, or adolescents, understanding themselves and making important life decisions, appreciating that their parents and grandparents are also developing persons, and coping with developmental challenges.

Theoretical Grounding

Theories are critical in any science, guiding scientists on what to study, how to study it, and how to interpret their findings. We want students to leave the study of life-span human development with more than facts alone; we want them to appreciate the major issues of interest to developmental scientists and how the leading theories in the field have shaped our thinking about development. Most important, we want students to learn to use these theoretical perspectives to guide their thinking and action when they encounter a question about human development outside the course.

With this in mind, we have devoted Chapter 2 to laying out in broad strokes the psychoanalytic, learning, cognitive developmental, and systems perspectives on human development. In later chapters, we draw on these and other perspectives as we explore different aspects of development; see, for example, treatment of the dynamic systems view of motor development in Chapter 6; Jean Piaget's groundbreaking cognitive-developmental theory in comparison to Lev Vygotsky's sociocultural perspective and Kurt Fischer's dynamic skill theory in Chapter 7; the information-processing perspective in Chapter 8; alternative views of intelligence in Chapter 9; nativist, learning, and interactionist theories of language development in Chapter 10; alternative theories of personality development in Chapter 11; theories of gender identity in chapter 12; theories of moral development, including evolutionary theory, in Chapter 13; attachment theory in Chapter 14; and family systems theory in Chapter 15.

Nature–Nurture Theme

Finally, we want students to gain a deeper understanding of the nature–nurture issue and of the many interacting forces affecting the developing person. We want students to appreciate that human development is an incredibly complex process that grows out of transactions between a changing person and a changing world and out of dynamic relationships among biological, psychological, and social influences. No contributor to development—a gene, a temperament, a parent, a culture—acts alone and is unaffected by other influences on development.

We introduce the nature–nurture issue in Chapter 1, compare theorists' stands on the issue in Chapter 2, and give the issue extended treatment in Chapter 3 on genes and environment. Each subsequent chapter includes one or more illustrations of the intertwined contributions of nature and nurture to development and aging, and Chapter 16 looks at their roles in the development of psychological disorders. Along the way, we describe exciting studies that bring home what it means to say that genes and environment interact to influence development—as when genes predisposing an individual to depression combine with stressful life events to produce depression. We also illustrate the many ways in which genes and environment affect one another—for instance, ways in which genetic makeup influences the experiences an individual has, and ways in which experience can affect the activation or expression of genes in ways that alter development.

In this edition, we have tried to convey how much more today's developmental scientists know about the intricacies of nature and nurture. We have incorporated new discoveries about genes, hormones, neural networks, and other biological forces in development. We have also strengthened coverage of contextual influences on development—ways in which developmental pathways can differ, sometimes dramatically, depending on the individual's family, school, neighborhood, social class, and subcultural and cultural contexts. Most important, we illuminate the interplay between biological and environmental influences that is at the heart of the developmental process—and that makes it difficult to leave this course as either an extreme nativist or an extreme environmentalist.

Organization of the Text

Core Concepts: Chapters 1 to 4

The book begins by orienting students to the life-span perspective on human development and to approaches to the scientific study of development (Chapter 1), as well as to the central issues and theoretical perspectives that have dominated the field (Chapter 2). Next it explores developmental processes in some depth, examining genetic and environmental influences on development (Chapter 3) and then focusing on important environmental influences during the critical prenatal and perinatal periods (Chapter 4).

Development of Basic Human Capacities: Chapters 5 to 10

Chapters on the growth and aging of the body and nervous system and on health (Chapter 5) and on the development of sensory, perceptual, and motor capacities (Chapter 6) launch our examination of the development of basic human capacities. Chapter 7 turns to cognitive development, starting with the influential theory of Jean Piaget and then moving on to Vygotsky's and Fischer's perspectives; Chapter 8 views memory and problem solving from an information-processing perspective; Chapter 9 highlights the psychometric approach to cognition, exploring individual differences in intelligence and creativity; and Chapter 10 explores language development and the roles of language, cognition, and motivation in educational achievement.

Development of Self in Society: Chapters 11 to 17

The next three chapters concern the development of the self: changes in self-conceptions and personality and their relationships to vocational identity and development (Chapter 11); in gender roles and sexuality (Chapter 12); and in social cognition, morality, and prosocial and antisocial behavior (Chapter 13). The self is set more squarely in a social context as we trace life-span changes in attachment relationships (Chapter 14) and in roles and relationships within the family (Chapter 15). Finally, we offer a life-span perspective on developmental problems and disorders (Chapter 16) and examine how humans of different ages cope with dying and bereavement (Chapter 17).

Getting the Big Picture

To help students pull together the "big picture" of life-span human development at the end of the course, we remind students of some of the major themes of the book at the end of

Chapter 17 and offer a chart inside the back cover that summarizes major developments in each of seven periods of the life span. Finally, an appendix, Careers in Human Development, lays out possibilities for translating an interest in human development into a career in research, teaching, or professional practice.

Engaging Students

The ninth edition provides learning objectives for each major numbered section and continues to use a variety of other strategies to increase students' engagement with the material and, more importantly, their learning.

Learning Objectives

Each major numbered section starts with two to five learning objectives to focus students' reading and give it purpose.

Checking Mastery Questions

To encourage students to actively check their command of the material as they progress through the chapter, we pose two to four Checking Mastery questions at the end of each numbered chapter section. Instructors can find the answers in the *Instructor's Manual* and can decide whether they want to use the questions as assignments or test items or give the answers to students so that they can test their own mastery.

Making Connections Questions

Also at the end of each major section, Making Connections questions invite students to reflect on the material—to weigh in on a debate in the field, evaluate the material's implications for public policy, apply the material to a case example, or explore the material's relevance to their own development. These questions can serve as the basis for writing assignments, essay questions, or class discussions.

Boxes

The topics we address in boxes sprinkled throughout the chapters were chosen because they struck us as both interesting and important; they are not fluff to be skipped! This edition continues to include three kinds of boxes, each with a different purpose:

- **Exploration boxes** allow more in-depth investigation of research or thinking on a topic.
- **Application boxes** examine how knowledge has been applied to optimize development.
- **Engagement boxes** provide opportunities for students to engage personally and actively with the material—to assess their own knowledge, beliefs, traits, and attitudes by completing personality scales, test items, surveys, and short quizzes.

To see the titles of these boxes, scan the table of contents.

Content Updates in This Edition

As always, the book has been thoroughly updated to convey the most recent discoveries and insights developmental scientists have to offer. We have added some exciting new topics and revised and updated coverage of many other topics for this edition. A few examples:

Chapter 1. Understanding Life-Span Human Development

- New illustrations of how the digital age may be affecting development
- Discussion of the criticism that most psychological research is about "WEIRD people" (such as American college students) who are not representative of people around the globe—and a call for understanding development in its cultural context

Chapter 2. Theories of Human Development

- Application of each major theoretical perspective to understanding and changing sexual risk behavior in adolescence
- A deeper dive into Bronfenbrenner's bioecological systems theory

Chapter 3. Genes, Environment, and Development

- Coverage of the differential susceptibility hypothesis and research suggesting that so-called risk genes that predispose some children to psychological problems in unsupportive environments may also help them benefit from supportive environments
- More on epigenetic effects of the environment on gene expression and examples of key findings and their implications

Chapter 4. Prenatal Development and Birth

- The latest research on fetal programming in response to the prenatal environment and its implications for later health and development
- New studies of the effects of exposure to radiation, pollution, and maternal stress on prenatal development
- A box on parenting tiny, low birth weight babies

Chapter 5. Body, Brain, and Health

- A timely discussion of sports-related concussions and brain development
- The latest on centenarians and why they live so long

Chapter 6. Sensation, Perception, and Action

- New twists in the study of how infants learn to avoid drop-offs
- Discussion of our limited capacity for multitasking
- An updated discussion of driving in later life

Chapter 7. Cognition

- Introduction of the theories of Piaget, Vygotsky, and Fischer and reminders of their themes in the chapter's survey of milestones in cognitive development
- New attempts to relate theories to classroom learning

Chapter 8. Memory and Information Processing

- Discussion of cases of amnesia to bring home the importance of memory processes in development
- More on the neural bases of memory

Chapter 9. Intelligence and Creativity

- A new report on the implications of socioeconomic status for IQ and changes in intellectual abilities with age
- Research on why even intelligent people sometimes make "dumb" decisions

Chapter 10. Language and Education

- The latest on bilingualism and its implications for cognitive development and aging
- A reworked discussion of nature and nurture in language acquisition, including a discussion of how the quantity and quality of speech to young language learners affects their progress

Chapter 11. Self and Personality

- A new box on culture and personality to supplement the chapter's contrasts of development in individualistic and collectivist cultures
- Recent multicultural research on changes in self-esteem and personality in adulthood

Chapter 12. Gender Roles and Sexuality

- An updated account of significant similarities and differences between the sexes
- A new section on transgender youth
- An exploration of sexual assaults on college campuses

Chapter 13. Social Cognition and Moral Development

- Exciting research on the roots of morality in infancy and early childhood, as illustrated by a sense of fairness, evaluation of good guys and bad guys, and a motivation to help
- A look at moral thinking in India and the role of religious and spiritual beliefs in moral thinking

Chapter 14. Emotions, Attachment, and Social Relationships

- More on the quality of adolescents' attachments to parents, friends, and romantic partners
- New coverage of dating among LGBT youth
- A box examining loneliness as a public health threat through the life span

Chapter 15. The Family

- More on the family as a system and the importance of supportive coparenting
- Research on the implications of helicopter parenting for the development of college students
- Challenges facing older adults in a rapidly changing China

Chapter 16. Developmental Psychopathology

- Highlights of the Great Smoky Mountains Study of the origin and course of psychological disorders.
- Research on identifying through brain imaging children at risk for depression and treating preschool children suffering from depression
- A new section on how adolescent problem behavior grows out of the normal developmental tasks of adolescence

Chapter 17. The Final Challenge: Death and Dying

- Coverage of the Brittany Maynard right-to-die case
- Recent research questioning findings of widespread resilience among bereaved adults
- An exploration of bereavement among partners of gay men with HIV/AIDS

Chapter Organization

The chapters of this book use a consistent format and contain the following:

- A chapter outline that orients students to what lies ahead
- A chapter opener that engages student interest

- Introductory material that lays out the plan for the chapter and introduces key concepts, theories, and issues relevant to the area of development to be explored
- Learning objectives at the start of each major numbered section
- Developmental sections (in Chapters 5–17) highlighting four developmental periods: infancy, childhood, adolescence, and adulthood
- Checking Mastery and Making Connections questions after each major section
- A Chapter Summary reviewing the chapter's main messages
- A Key Terms section listing new terms introduced in the chapter in the order in which they were introduced and with the page number on which they were introduced. Printed in blue, bold font, key terms are defined when they are first presented in a chapter and are included in the glossary at the end of the book.

Supplements

The ninth edition of *Life-Span Human Development* is accompanied by an outstanding array of supplements for both the instructor and the student that are intended to enrich the student's learning experience inside and outside the classroom. All the supplements have been thoroughly revised and updated. We invite instructors and students to examine and take advantage of the teaching and learning tools available.

Online Instructor's Manual

The *Instructor's Manual* contains chapter-specific outlines; a list of print, video, and online resources; and student learning objectives. The manual has a special emphasis on active learning, offering suggested student activities and projects for each chapter.

Cengage Learning Testing, Powered by Cognero®

Cengage Learning Testing Powered by Cognero® is a flexible, online system that allows you to import, edit, and manipulate content from the text's test bank or elsewhere, including your own favorite test questions; create multiple test versions in an instant; and deliver tests from your learning management system, your classroom, or wherever you want.

Online PowerPoint® Lecture Slide Decks

The *Online PowerPoint® Lecture Slides* are designed to facilitate an instructor's use of PowerPoint in lectures. Slides are provided for each chapter; they contain main concepts with figures, graphics, and tables to visually illustrate main points from the text. Slides have been designed to be easily modifiable so instructors are able to customize them with their own materials.

MindTap

MindTap for *Life-Span: Human Development* creates a unique learning path that fosters increased comprehension and efficiency of learning. It engages students and empowers them to produce their best work—consistently. In MindTap, course material is seamlessly integrated with videos, activities, apps, and more.

In MindTap, instructors can:

- Control the content. Instructors select what students see and when they see it.
- Create a unique learning path. In MindTap, your textbook is enhanced with multimedia and activities to encourage and motivate learning and retention, moving students up the learning taxonomy. Materials can be used as is or modified to match an instructor's syllabus exactly.
- Integrate their own content. Instructors can modify the MindTap Reader using their own documents or by pulling from sources like RSS feeds, YouTube videos, websites, Google docs, and more.
- Follow student progress. Powerful analytics and reports provide a snapshot of class progress, the time students spend logging into the course, and information on assignment completion to help instructors assess levels of engagement and identify problem areas.

Acknowledgments

We would like to express our continuing debt to David Shaffer of the University of Georgia for allowing his child development textbook to inform the first and second editions of this book.

Credit for excellent supplementary materials goes to Bradley Caskey, who revised the *Instructor's Manual with Test Bank*.

Producing this book required the joint efforts of Cengage Learning and SPi Global. We thank our product manager, Star Barruto, for her leadership of the project, and Stefanie Chase, our content developer, for her superb efforts to keep the project moving, support us cheerfully throughout, and make this edition the most visually appealing and pedagogically effective edition yet. We thank Phil Scott at SPi Global for outstanding management of the book's production and Padmarekha Madhukannan and Carly Bergey for photo research. We are grateful, as well, for the able assistance of Ruth Sakata Corley, production project manager; Vernon Boes, art director; and Deanna Ettinger, IP analyst. We also appreciate the strong support of James Finlay, marketing manager.

We remain deeply indebted to sponsoring editors past—to C. Deborah Laughton, who insisted that this project be undertaken, and to Vicki Knight, who skillfully shepherded the first edition through its final stages and oversaw the second edition. Finally, Patrick Sheehan deserves thanks for his help with referencing, and Corby Rider deserves appreciation for his support and understanding of his workaholic mother.

Reviewers

We are very grateful to nine "cohorts" of reviewers for the constructive criticism and great suggestions that have helped us make each edition of this book better than the one before:

Jeanie Allen, *Drury University*
Nina Banerjee, *Delaware State University*
Barinder Bhavra, *Macomb Community College*
David Beach, *University of Wisconsin–Parkside*
Howard Bierenbaum, *College of William & Mary*
Fredda Blanchard-Fields, *Louisiana State University*
Cheryl Bluestone, *Queensborough Community College*
Tracie Blumentritt, *University of Wisconsin–La Crosse*
Denise Ann Bodman, *Arizona State University*
Bob Bornstein, *Miami University–Oxford*
Janet Boseovski, *University of North Carolina–Greensboro*
Kim G. Brenneman, *Eastern Mennonite University*
Donna Brent, *Hartwick College*
Mary Ann Bush, *Western Michigan University*
Elaine H. Cassel, *Lord Fairfax Community College*
Yiwei Chen, *Bowling Green State University*
Bonny K. Dillon, *Bluefield College*
David R. Donnelly, *Monroe Community College–Rochester*
Shelley Drazen, *Binghamton University (SUNY)*
Michelle R. Dunlap, *Connecticut College*
Marion Eppler, *East Carolina University*
Dan Florell, *Eastern Kentucky University*
James N. Forbes, *Angelo State University*
Claire Ford, *Bridgewater State College*
Carie Forden, *Clarion University*
Jody S. Fournier, *Capital University*
Janet Fritz, *Colorado State University*
Rebecca J. Glover, *University of North Texas*
Cheryl Hale, *Jefferson College*
Charles Harris, *James Madison University*
Karen Hartlep, *California State University–Bakersfield*
Abby Harvey, *Temple University*
Christina Hawkey, *Arizona Western College*
Jay E. Hillis, *Bevill State Community College–Brewer*
Debra L. Hollister, *Valencia Community College*
Amy Holmes, *Davidson County Community College*
Stephen Hoyer, *Pittsburg State University*
Malia Huchendorf, *Normandale Community College*
David P. Hurford, *Pittsburg State University*
Vivian Jenkins, *University of Southern Indiana*
Wayne G. Joosse, *Calvin College*

John Klein, *Castleton State College*

Franz Klutschkowski, *North Central Texas College*

Jim Korcuska, *University of San Diego*

Suzanne Krinsky, *University of Southern Colorado*

Brett Laursen, *Florida Atlantic University*

Sherry Loch, *Paradise Valley Community College*

Becky White Loewy, *San Francisco State University*

Rosanne Lorden, *Eastern Kentucky University*

Carolyn Cass Lorente, *Northern Virginia Community College–Alexandria*

Nancy Macdonald, *University of South Carolina–Sumter*

Susan Magun-Jackson, *University of Memphis*

Robert F. Marcus, *University of Maryland*

Gabriela A. Martorell, *Portland State University*

Rebecca Kang McGill, *Temple University*

Russell Miars, *Portland State University*

Ann K. Mullis, *Florida State University*

Ronald L. Mullis, *Florida State University*

Bridget C. Murphy-Kelsey, *Metropolitan State College*

Susan L. O'Donnell, *George Fox University*

Shirley M. Ogletree, *Southwest Texas State University*

Jim O'Neill, *Wayne State University*

Rob Palkovitz, *University of Delaware*

Suzanne Pasch, *University of Wisconsin–Milwaukee*

Louise Perry, *Florida Atlantic University*

Sharon Presley, *California State University–East Bay*

Mark Rafter, *College of the Canyons*

Lakshmi Raman, *Oakland University*

Marjorie Reed, *Oregon State University*

Elizabeth Rhodes, *Florida International University*

Eileen Rogers, *University of Texas–San Antonio*

Mark Runco, *California State University–Fullerton*

Pamela Schuetze, *Buffalo State College*

Matt Scullin, *West Virginia University*

Lisa Sethre-Hofstad, *Concordia College*

Timothy Shearon, *Albertson College of Idaho*

Dawn Taylor-Wright, *Meridian Community College*

Luis Terrazas, *California State University–San Marcos*

Brooke Thompson, *Gardner-Webb University*

Polly Trnavsky, *Appalachian State University*

Katherine Van Giffen, *California State University–Long Beach*

Nancy L. Voorhees, *Ivy Tech Community College–Lafayette*

Catherine Weir, *Colorado College*

Kyle Weir, *California State University–Fresno*

Diane E. Wille, *Indiana University–Southeast*

Ruth Wilson, *Idaho State University*

Robin Yaure, *Penn State Mont Alto*

About the Authors

CAROL K. SIGELMAN is professor and chair of psychology at George Washington University, where she also served as an associate vice president for 13 years. She earned her bachelor's degree from Carleton College and a double-major doctorate in English and psychology from George Peabody College for Teachers, now part of Vanderbilt University. She has been on the faculty at Texas Tech University, Eastern Kentucky University (where she won her college's outstanding teacher award), and the University of Arizona. She has taught courses in child, adolescent, adult, and life-span development and has published research on such topics as the communication skills of individuals with developmental disabilities, the development of stigmatizing reactions to children and adolescents who are different, and children's emerging understandings of diseases and psychological disorders. She is a Fellow of the Association for Psychological Science. For fun, she enjoys hiking, biking, and discovering good movies.

ELIZABETH A. RIDER is professor of psychology and associate provost at Elizabethtown College in Pennsylvania. She has also been on the faculty at the University of North Carolina at Asheville. She earned her undergraduate degree from Gettysburg College and her doctorate from Vanderbilt University. She has taught courses on child and life-span development, women and gender issues, applied developmental psychology, and genetic and environmental influences on development. She has published research on children's and adults' spatial perception, orientation, and ability to find their way. Through a grant from the Pennsylvania State System for Higher Education, she studied factors associated with academic success. The second edition of her text on the psychology of women, Our Voices, was published by John Wiley & Sons in 2005. When she is not working, her life revolves around her son and a fun-loving springer spaniel.

1 Understanding Life-Span Human Development

In a middle-class neighborhood in Los Angeles, California, 8-year-old Ben's father asks him to get his jacket so they can leave the house. Ben ignores him, trying to put his feet into shoes that are already tied. Ben's father, expressing his annoyance, tells Ben again to get his jacket. Instead, Ben sits down and says, "Seriously, it's like you're always a control freak," then asking his father to untie his shoes and, that accomplished, asking his father to tie them—after getting Ben's jacket for him. After more resistance from Ben, Ben's father finally insists, "No, son, *go* get your own jacket and *you* tie your shoes and let's *go*" (Ochs & Izquierdo, 2009, p. 400). The boy finally goes for his jacket.

This sounds like pretty typical child behavior until we contrast it with the behavior of Matsigenka children in Peru. The Matsigenka live by fishing, hunting, and growing vegetables and children contribute to the work of the family and community from an early age. Thus 6-year-old Yanira, invited to travel down the Amazon with another family from her village, pulls her weight the whole time without ever being asked—stacking and carrying leaves to be used for roofing, sweeping sand off the sleeping mats, fishing for crustaceans and cleaning and boiling them to serve to the group, taking care of her own needs without prompts or help. Like other children in her culture, she probably experimented with heating her own food on the fire as a toddler—expected to learn, even if by burning herself, how to do it well. She was probably told folk stories about characters whose laziness had terrible consequences. By the age of 6 or 7, Matsigenka girls are cooking alongside their mothers while boys are hunting and fishing with their fathers.

Anthropologists Elinor Ochs and Carolina Izquierdo (2009) have been struck by these and other examples of how children in many societies of the world are far more responsible and self-sufficient far earlier in life than children in the United States are. Their observations of family life suggest that American parents, rather than expecting and counting on children to contribute to the family's work, load their children with toys and perform what in other cultures would be viewed as basic self-care tasks such as shoe tying for their children—or at least prod them at every step of the way (see Arnold, Graesch, & Ochs, 2012).

This book is about the development of humans like Ben and Yanira—and yes, you—from conception to death. The lives of Ben and Yanira raise questions: What will be the later effects on them of their very different childhood experiences? Will Yanira grow up to be more responsible and independent as an adult than Ben because she was expected to learn self-care and responsibility to other people from an early age, or will Ben benefit from all the help and guidance his parents are providing him? How much can human development be bent this way or that depending on a person's experiences in his or her family and culture?

We address questions like these and others in this book. We tackle fundamental questions: How in the world does a single fertilized egg cell turn into a unique human being? How do

Life on the Amazon for a Matsigenka family in Peru.

Takahiro Igarashi/Image Source/Getty Images

genetic and environmental forces shape development? What can be done to optimize development? We also ask questions about different periods of the life span—for example, about how infants perceive the world, how preschool children think, how life events such as divorce affect an adolescent's adjustment, why some college students have more trouble than others deciding on a major, whether most adults experience a midlife crisis, and how people typically change as they age.

Do any of these questions intrigue you? Probably so, because we are all developing persons interested in ourselves and the other developing people around us. Most college students want to understand how they and those they know have been affected by their experiences, how they have changed over the years, and where they may be headed. Many students also have practical motivations for learning about human development—for example, a desire to be a good parent or to pursue a career as a psychologist, nurse, teacher, or other human services professional.

This introductory chapter lays the groundwork for the remainder of the book by addressing some basic questions: How should we think about development and the influences on it? What is the science of life-span development? How is development studied? And what are some of the special challenges in studying human development?

1.1 How Should We Think about Development?

LEARNING OBJECTIVES

- Define development, aging, and their relationship to each other.
- Explain and illustrate the role played by age grades, age norms, and the social clock in making human development different in different historical, cultural, and subcultural contexts.
- Summarize the extreme positions one can take on the "nature–nurture" issue and the position most developmental scientists today take.

We begin by asking what it means to say that humans "develop" or "age" over the life span, how we can conceptualize the life span and its cultural and historical diversity, and how we can approach the single biggest issue in the study of development, the nature–nurture issue.

Defining Development

Development can be defined as systematic changes and continuities in the individual that occur between conception and death, or from "womb to tomb." By describing developmental

changes as systematic, we imply that they are orderly, patterned, and relatively enduring—not fleeting and unpredictable like mood swings. The changes can be gains, losses, or just differences from what we were like before. Development also involves continuities, ways in which we remain the same or continue to reflect our past selves.

The systematic changes and continuities of interest to students of human development fall into three broad domains:

1. **Physical development.** The growth of the body and its organs, the functioning of physiological systems including the brain, physical signs of aging, changes in motor abilities, and so on.

2. **Cognitive development.** Changes and continuities in perception, language, learning, memory, problem solving, and other mental processes.
3. **Psychosocial development.** Changes and carryover in personal and interpersonal aspects of development, such as motives, emotions, personality traits, interpersonal skills and relationships, and roles played in the family and in the larger society.

Even though developmentalists often specialize in one of these three aspects of development, they appreciate that humans are whole beings and that changes in one area affect the others. The baby who develops the ability to crawl, for example, has new opportunities to develop her mind by exploring kitchen cabinets and to hone her social skills by trailing her parents from room to room. And the older adult who joins an exercise group may not only become fitter but sharpen his cognitive skills and strengthen his social network.

How would you portray, as a line on a graph, typical changes from birth to old age? Many people picture tremendous positive gains in capacity from infancy to young adulthood, a flat line reflecting little change during early adulthood and middle age, and a steep decline of capacities in the later years. This stereotyped view of the life span is largely false, but it also has some truth in it, especially with respect to biological development. Traditionally, biologists have defined growth as the physical changes that occur from conception to maturity. We indeed become biologically mature and physically competent during the early part of the life span. Biological aging is the deterioration of organisms (including humans) that leads inevitably to their death. Biologically, then, development *does* involve growth in early life, stability in early and middle adulthood, and declines associated with now-accumulated effects of aging in later life.

Many aspects of development do not follow this "gain–stability–loss" model, however. Modern developmental scientists have come to appreciate that developmental change at any age involves both gains and losses. For example, although children gain many cognitive abilities as they get older and become more efficient at solving problems, they also become less flexible in their thinking, less open to considering unusual solutions (Gopnik, Griffiths, & Lucas, 2015). They also lose self-esteem and become more prone to depression (Gotlib & Hammen, 2002).

Nor should we associate aging only with loss: Some cognitive abilities do decline over the adult years. However, adults aged 50 and older typically score higher on vocabulary tests and on tests of mental ability that draw on a person's accumulated knowledge than young adults do (Hartshorne & Germine, 2015; Salthouse, 2012). They also sometimes show more wisdom when given social problems to ponder (Grossmann et al., 2010). Gerontologist Margaret Cruikshank (2009) conveyed the gains associated with aging this way: "Decline is thought to be the main theme of aging, and yet for many old age is a time of ripening, of becoming most ourselves" (p. 207).

In addition, people do not always improve or worsen but instead just become different than they were (as when a child who once feared loud noises comes to fear hairy monsters under the bed instead, or an adult who was worried about career success becomes more concerned about her children's futures). Development clearly means more than positive growth during infancy,

childhood, and adolescence. And aging, as developmental scientists define it, involves more than biological aging; it refers to a range of physical, cognitive, and psychosocial changes, *positive and negative*, in the mature organism (Overton, 2010). In short, development involves gains, losses, neutral changes, and continuities in each phase of the life span, and aging is part of it.

Conceptualizing the Life Span

If you were to divide the human life span into periods, how would you do it? ● **Table 1.1** lists the periods that many of today's developmentalists regard as distinct. You will want to keep them in mind as you read this book, because we will constantly be speaking of infants, preschoolers, school-age children, adolescents, emerging adults, and young, middle-aged, and older adults. Note, however, that the given ages are approximate. Age is only a rough indicator of developmental status. Improvements in standards of living and health, for example, have meant that today's 65-year-olds are not as "old" physically, cognitively, or psychosocially as 65-year-olds a few decades ago were. There are also huge differences in functioning and personality among individuals of the same age; while some adults are bedridden at age 90, others are swimming laps.

The most recent addition to this list of periods of the life span—the one you may not have heard of—is emerging adulthood, a transitional period between adolescence and full-fledged adulthood that extends from about age 18 to age 25 and maybe as late as 29. After World War II, as jobs became more complex and required more education, more adolescents began to attend college in large numbers to prepare for work and postponed marriage and parenthood in the process (Keniston, 1970). As a result, psychologist Jeffrey Arnett and others began to describe emerging adulthood as a distinct phrase of the life span in which college-aged youth spend years getting educated and saving money in order to launch their adult lives (Arnett, 2000, 2011, 2015). Emerging adulthood is a distinct developmental period primarily in developed countries but the phenomenon is

What periods of the life span do these four females, representing four generations of the same family, fall in?

Takahiro Igarashi/Image Source/Getty Images

Period of Life	Age Range
Prenatal period	Conception to birth
Infancy	First 2 years of life (the first month is the neonatal or newborn period)
Preschool period	2–5 (some prefer to describe as *toddlers* children who have begun to walk and are age 1–3)
Middle childhood	6 to about 10 (or until the onset of puberty)
Adolescence	Approximately 10–18 (or from puberty to when the individual becomes relatively independent)
Emerging adulthood	18–25 or even 29 (transitional period between adolescence and adulthood)
Early adulthood	25–40 years (adult roles are established)
Middle adulthood	40–65 years
Late adulthood	65 years and older (some break out subcategories such as the young-old, old-old, and very old based on differences in functioning)

spreading to developing ones, especially in urban areas (Arnett, 2015). According to Arnett (2004), emerging adults (maybe you?):

- explore their identities;
- lead unstable lives filled with job changes, new relationships, and moves;
- are self-focused, relatively free of obligations to others, and therefore free to focus on their own psychological needs;
- feel in between—adultlike in some ways but not others; and
- believe they have limitless possibilities ahead.

Do you believe you are truly an adult rather than an "emerging" adult? Why or why not? There are many ways to define adulthood, but sociologist Frank Furstenberg and his colleagues (2004) looked at five traditional, objective markers of adulthood: completing an education, being financially independent, leaving home, marrying, and having children. In 1960, 65% of men and 77% of women in the United States had achieved these milestones by age 30. By 2000, only 31% of men and 46% of women had achieved them by age 30.

Not everyone agrees that emerging adulthood is a truly distinct period of development (Epstein, 2013). However, it is clear that adolescents in modern societies are taking longer and longer to enter adult roles. Knowing that many youth do not yet have adult responsibilities and knowing too that brain development is not complete in our 20s, some European countries and some states in the United States are questioning the notion that 18-year-olds should be treated as adults under the law. For example, they are raising legal ages or creating special provisions to protect emerging adults from the adult criminal system (Schiraldi & Western, 2015).

Cultural Differences

● **Table 1.1** represents only one view of the periods of the life span. Age—like gender, race, and other significant human characteristics—means different things in different societies (Fry, 2009). **Culture** is often defined as the shared understandings and way of life of a people (see Mistry & Dutta, 2015; Packer & Cole, 2015). It includes beliefs, values, and practices concerning the nature of humans in different phases of the life span, what children need to be taught to function in

their society, and how people should lead their lives as adults. Different cultures can lead us along different developmental pathways, as we saw in the case of Ben and Yanira, but we all participate in a culture. That culture becomes part of us, influencing how we live and how we experience our lives (Packer & Cole, 2015).

Each culture has its own ways of carving up the life span and of treating the people in different age groups. Each socially defined age group in a society—called an **age grade**—is assigned different statuses, roles, privileges, and responsibilities. Separating children into grades in school based on age is one form of age grading. Just as high schools have "elite" seniors and "lowly" freshmen, whole societies are layered into age grades.

Our society, for example, grants "adults" (18-year-olds by law in the United States) a voting privilege not granted to children. Legal definitions of the boundary between adolescence and adulthood vary, though. In most states in the United States, the legal age for marrying is lower than the legal ages for voting or serving in the military, and the right to drink alcohol is granted last, commonly at age 21 (Settersten, 2005). Similarly, although we seem to define age 65 as the boundary between middle age and old age, in fact the ages at which people become eligible for Medicare, Social Security benefits, and "senior discounts" at restaurants and stores differ.

We define old age as age 65 or older, but the !Kung San of Botswana often don't know people's chronological ages and define old age instead in terms of functioning (Rosenberg, 2009). They distinguish between the *na* or "old" (an honorary title meaning big and great granted to all older people starting at around age 50); the "old/dead" (older but still able to function); and the "old to the point of helplessness," who are ailing and need care. The St. Lawrence Eskimo simply distinguish between boys and men (or between girls and women), whereas the Arusha people of East Africa devised six socially meaningful age grades for males: youths, junior warriors, senior warriors, junior elders, senior elders, and retired elders (Keith, 1985). In certain other cultures, the recognized periods of the life span include a period before birth and an afterlife (Fry, 1985; Kojima, 2003).

Cultures differ not only in the age grades they recognize but in how they mark the transition from one age grade to another. A **rite of passage** is a ritual that marks a person's "passage" from one status to another, usually in reference to the transition from

Each January 15 in Japan, 20-year-olds are officially pronounced adults in a national celebration and enter a new age grade. Young women receive kimonos, young men receive suits, and all are reminded of their responsibilities to society. Young adults also gain the right to drink, smoke, and vote. The modern ceremony grew out of an ancient one in which young samurai became recognized as warriors (Reid, 1993). The age-grading system in Japanese culture clearly marks the beginning of adulthood with this rite of passage.

AP Photo/Shizuo Kambayashi

childhood to adulthood. Rites of passage can involve such varied practices as body painting, circumcision, beatings, instruction by elders in adult sexual practices, tests of physical prowess, and gala celebrations (see Schlegel & Barry, 2015).

Adolescent rites of passage were more common in traditional societies than they are in modern industrial societies. Yes, Jewish youth experience a clear rite of passage when they have their *bar* or *bat mitzvahs*, and 15-year-old Hispanic American girls in some communities participate in a *quinceañera* (meaning "fifteen years ceremony") to signify that they have become women. But often coming-of-age ceremonies do not have the broader meaning for the whole society that they used to have. Modern societies are more diverse than traditional societies, are not so clearly organized around distinct male and female roles, and tend to move us from childhood to adolescence and on to adulthood more gradually (Schlegel & Barry, 2015). About the clearest rite of passage to adulthood in our society, unfortunately, is a night of binge drinking at age 21. In one study, four of five college students reported that they drank on their 21st birthday to celebrate—12% of them an extremely dangerous 21 drinks (Rutledge, Park, & Sher, 2008). Perhaps because we lack a clear, society-wide rite of passage, adolescents in our society end up less sure than adolescents in many other societies of when they are adults.

Once a society has established age grades, it defines what people should and should not do at different points in the life span (Elder & Shanahan, 2006). According to pioneering gerontologist Bernice Neugarten and her colleagues (Neugarten, Moore, & Lowe, 1965), these expectations, or **age norms**, are society's way of telling people how to act their age. In our culture, for example, most people agree that 6-year-olds are too young to date or drink beer but

are old enough to attend school. We also tend to agree that adults should think about marrying around age 25 (although in some segments of society earlier or later is better) and should retire around age 65 (Neugarten et al., 1965; Settersten, 1998). In less industrialized countries, age norms often call for starting work in childhood, marrying and having children in one's teens and often remaining in the family home, and stopping work earlier than 65 in response to illness and disability (Juárez & Gayer, 2014; Shanahan, 2000).

Why are age norms important? First, they influence people's decisions about how to lead their lives. They are the basis for what Neugarten (1968) called the **social clock**—a person's sense of when things should be done and when he or she is ahead of or behind the schedule dictated by age norms. Prompted by the social clock, for example, an unmarried 30-year-old may feel that he should propose to his girlfriend before she gives up on him, or a 70-year-old who loves her job may feel she should start planning for retirement. Second, age norms affect how easily people adjust to life transitions. Normal life events such as having children tend to affect us more negatively when they occur "off time" than when they occur "on time" (McLanahan & Sorensen, 1985). It can be challenging to experience puberty at either age 8 or age 18 or to become a new parent at 13 or 45. However, as Neugarten could see even in the 1960s, age norms in our society have been weakening for some time. It's less clear now what one should be doing at what age and so people do things like marry and retire at a wide range of ages (Settersten & Trauten, 2009). Witness Madonna adopting a child at 50 or Elton John becoming a first-time father at 62 (Mayer, 2011).

Subcultural Differences

Age grades, age norms, and social clocks differ not only from culture to culture but also from subculture to subculture. Our own society is diverse with respect to race and **ethnicity**, or people's affiliation with a group based on common heritage or traditions. It is also diverse with respect to **socioeconomic status (SES)**, or standing in society based on such indicators as occupational prestige, education, and income. African American, Hispanic American, Native American, Asian American, and European American individuals, and individuals of high versus low SES, sometimes have very different developmental experiences. Within these broad groups, of course, there are immense variations associated with a host of other factors. We must be careful not to overgeneralize.

To illustrate, age norms tend to differ in higher-SES and lower-SES communities: Youth from lower-income families tend to reach milestones of adulthood such as starting work, marrying, and having children earlier and to feel like adults sooner (Benson & Elder, 2011; Elder & Shanahan, 2006; Mollborn, 2009). When sociologist Linda Burton (1990, 1996, 2007) studied a low-SES African American community, she found it was common for young women to become mothers at about age 16—earlier than in most middle-class communities, white or black. Teenage mothers in this community looked to their own mothers and grandmothers to help them care for their children. Meanwhile, children were asked to grow up fast; they often tended younger siblings and helped their mothers with household tasks. Although age norms in middle-class communities in the United States call for postponing parenthood (Mollborn, 2009), it is common in cultures around the world for females to become mothers in their teens and for grandmothers and older children to help them with child care responsibilities (Ochs & Izquierdo, 2009; Rogoff, 2003).

Perhaps the most important message about socioeconomic status is that, regardless of race and ethnicity, poverty can be very damaging to human development. About one in five children—and more like one of every three children of color—lives in poverty in the United States today, defined as an income of $24,250 for a family of four (Children's Defense Fund, 2014). Parents and children living in poverty experience more stress than higher-SES parents and children owing to noise, crowding, family disruption, hunger, exposure to violence, and other factors (Evans & Kim, 2013). Under these conditions, parents may have difficulty providing a safe, stable, stimulating, and supportive home environment for their children (Duncan, Magnuson, & Votruba-Drzal, 2015; and see Chapter 15). As a result, the developmental experiences and trajectories of children who grow up in poverty and children who grow up in affluence are significantly different. The damaging effects of poverty can be seen in measurable differences in brain development between high- and low-SES children that grow wider over the critical months of infancy and early childhood (Hanson et al., 2013) and that are linked to lower school achievement in adolescence (Mackey et al., 2015). Indeed, the negative impacts of poverty show themselves in a host of ways: not only in lower average academic achievement but in poorer mental health and well-being and even poorer physical health in adulthood (Aber, Morris, & Raver, 2012; Conger & Dogan, 2007; Evans & Kim, 2012).

Historical Changes

The nature and meanings of periods of the life span also change from one historical period to another. In Europe and North America, they have changed along these lines:

- **Childhood as an age of innocence.** Although it is not quite this simple (Stearns, 2015), it has been claimed that not until the 17th century in Western cultures did children come to be viewed as distinctly different from adults, as innocents to be protected and nurtured. In medieval Europe (A.D. 500–1500), for example, 6-year-olds were dressed in miniature versions of adult clothing, treated much like adults under the law, and expected to contribute to the family's survival as soon as possible (Ariès, 1962). Today the goal in Western families is for children to be happy and self-fulfilled rather than economically useful, as illustrated by the case of Ben at the start of the chapter (Stearns, 2015).
- **Adolescence.** Not until the late 19th century and early 20th century was adolescence—the transitional period between childhood and adulthood that begins with puberty and involves significant physical, cognitive, and psychosocial changes—given a name and recognized as a distinctive phase of the life span (Kett, 1977). As farming decreased and industrialization advanced, an educated labor force was needed, so laws were passed restricting child labor, making schooling compulsory, and separating youths attending school from the adult world (Furstenberg, 2000).
- **Emerging adulthood.** As you saw earlier, the transition period from adolescence to adulthood has become so long in modern societies that a new period of the life span, *emerging adulthood*, has been defined in the late 20th and early 21st centuries.

Although medieval children were pressured to abandon their childish ways as soon as possible and were dressed like miniature adults, it is doubtful that they were really viewed as miniature adults. Still, the modern concept of children as innocents to be nurtured and protected did not begin to take hold until the 17th century.

PAINTING/Alamy Stock Photo

- **Middle age as an emptying of the nest.** This distinct life phase emerged in the 20th century as parents began to bear fewer children and live long enough to see their children grow up and leave home (Moen & Wethington, 1999).
- **Old age as retirement.** Not until the 20th century did our society come to define old age as a period of retirement. In earlier eras, adults who survived to old age literally worked until they dropped. Starting in the last half of the 20th century, thanks to Social Security, pensions, Medicare, and other support programs, working adults began to retire in their 60s with many years ahead of them (Schulz & Binstock, 2006).

Projecting the Future

What will the life span look like in the future? In the early 21st century, the average life expectancy for a newborn in the United States—the average number of years a newborn who is born now can be expected to live—is almost 79 years, compared with 47 years in 1900 (National Center for Health Statistics, 2015). As ■ Figure 1.1 shows, that life expectancy is generally greater for females than for males and

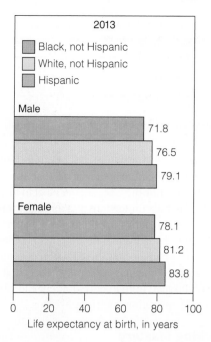

2013

- ◼ Black, not Hispanic
- ◻ White, not Hispanic
- ◼ Hispanic

Male
71.8
76.5
79.1

Female
78.1
81.2
83.8

Life expectancy at birth, in years

◼ **Figure 1.1** Life expectancy for non-Hispanic white, African American, and Hispanic males and females at birth in the United States.

Source: National Center for Health Statistics

is highest among Hispanic Americans, lowest among African Americans, and in-between among European Americans. In each group, wealth is associated with longer life than poverty.

To put these numbers in a global context, the average life expectancy of 79 in the United States is quite a bit lower than life expectancies in the longest-lived countries, Japan (84) and Singapore (83), but considerably higher than life expectancies in Central African Republic (51), Chad (52) and other African nations that have been hurt by widespread poverty and disease, including the HIV/AIDS epidemic (World Health Organization, 2015). By 2030, when most members of the baby boom generation will have retired, adults 65 and older will represent not the 13% of the U.S. population they represented in 2010 but over 20% (Ortman, Velkoff, & Hogan, 2014). As a result, an increasingly large group of elderly people will depend on a smaller generation of younger, working adults to support them. Although these elders will be healthier, wealthier, and better educated than the generations that preceded them, they will also need a lot of services—and health and mental health professionals trained in aging to serve them—as more of them reach very old ages (Schaie, 2011; Treas & Hill, 2009). How will policy makers address these issues? Conflict between the generations over resources and resentful attitudes toward aging adults could become problems (North & Fiske, 2012). This "graying of America," and indeed of the world's population, along with societal changes we cannot yet anticipate, will make the aging experience by the end of the 21st century different than it is today.

In sum, age—whether it is 7, 17, or 70—has had different meanings in different historical eras and most likely will mean something different in the 21st century than it did in the 20th. The broader message is clear: *We must view development in its historical, cultural, and subcultural context.* We must bear in mind that each social group settles on its own definitions of the life span, the age grades within it, and the age norms appropriate to each age range, and that each social group experiences development differently. We must also appreciate that in Western cultures it was only in the 17th century that children came to be seen as innocents; in the late 19th century that adolescence emerged as a distinct phase; and in the 20th century that our society recognized emerging adulthood, a middle-aged "empty nest" period, and an old age retirement period. One of the most fascinating challenges in the study of human development is to understand which aspects of development are universal and which differ across social and historical contexts—and why.

Framing the Nature–Nurture Issue

Understanding human development means grappling with *the* major issue in the study of human development—the nature–nurture issue, or the question of how biological forces and environmental forces act and interact to make us what we are (see Goldhaber, 2012). We will highlight this central and always fascinating issue throughout this book.

Nature

On the nature side of the debate are those who emphasize the influence of heredity, universal maturational processes guided by the genes, biologically based or innate predispositions produced by evolution, and biological influences on us every day of hormones, neurotransmitters, and other biochemicals. To those who emphasize nature, some aspects of development are inborn or innate, others are the product of maturation, the biological unfolding of the individual as sketched out in the genes (the hereditary material passed from parents to child at conception). Just as seeds turn into mature plants through a predictable process, humans "unfold" within the womb (assuming that they receive the necessary nourishment from

Today's older adults are healthier, wealthier, and more educated than older adults of previous generations. However, as more of them reach advanced ages, they will need more services from people trained in gerontology and geriatrics.

AAriel Skelly/Blend Images/Getty Images

their environment). Their genetic code then makes it likely that they will walk and utter their first words at about 1 year of age, achieve sexual maturity between 10 and 14, and gray in their 40s and 50s. Maturational changes in the brain contribute to cognitive changes such as increased memory and problem-solving skills and to psychosocial changes such as increased understanding of other people's feelings. Genetically influenced maturational processes guide all of us through many of the same developmental changes at about the same points in our lives. Meanwhile, *individual* hereditary endowment is making each person's development unique.

Nurture

On the nurture side of the nature–nurture debate are those who emphasize change in response to environment—all the external physical and social conditions, stimuli, and events that can affect us, from crowded living quarters and polluted air, to social interactions with family members, peers, and teachers, to the neighborhood and broader cultural context in which we develop. We know that the physical environment matters—for example, that exposure to lead in the paint in old buildings or in water pipes can stunt children's intellectual development or that living near a noisy airport can interfere with their progress in learning to read (Evans, 2004). And we will see countless examples in this book of how the social environment—the behavior of other people—shapes development. Rather than seeing biological maturation as the process driving development, those on the nurture side of the nature–nurture debate emphasize learning—the process through which experience brings about relatively permanent changes in thoughts, feelings, or behavior. A certain degree of maturation is clearly necessary before a child can dribble a basketball, but careful instruction and long, hard hours of practice are just as clearly required if the child is to excel in basketball. In some ways, humans around the world have similar experiences at similar ages but in many ways their experiences differ dramatically, as suggested by the stories of Yanira and Ben at the start of the chapter.

The Interplay of Nature and Nurture

● **Table 1.2** summarizes the terms of the nature–nurture debate. But let's settle the nature–nurture debate right now: Developmental changes are the products of a complex interplay between nature and nurture. It is not nature *or* nurture; it is nature *and* nurture (Plomin et al., 2013). To make matters more complex, it is nature affecting

● **Table 1.2** The Language of Nature and Nurture

Nature	Nurture
Heredity	Environment
Maturation	Learning
Genes	Experience
Innate or biologically based predispositions	Cultural influences

nurture and nurture affecting nature! For example, biology (nature) provides us with the beginnings of a brain that allows us to learn from our experiences (nurture), experiences that in turn change our brains by altering neural connections and that can even change our genes by activating or deactivating them (see Chapter 3). Much of the fascination of studying human development comes from trying to understand more precisely how these two forces combine to make us what we are and become. It is appropriate, then, that we look next at the science of life-span human development and whether it is up to the challenge of answering questions like this.

● Checking Mastery

1. How does the concept of aging differ from the concept of biological aging?
2. What is the difference between an age grade and an age norm?

● Making Connections

1. Many observers, starting with Bernice Neugarten, believe that age norms for transitions in adult development such as marriage, parenthood, peak career achievement, and retirement have weakened in our society. Do you think such age norms could ever disappear entirely? Why or why not?
2. Returning to the chapter opener, how might your life and development be different if you had been born to a Matsigenka family in the rain forest of Peru? Speculate a bit.
3. We know that men are much more likely to commit murder than women are. How might you explain this in terms of "nature" and how might you explain it in terms of "nurture"?

1.2
What Is the Science of Life-Span Development?

LEARNING OBJECTIVES
- Summarize the four goals of the science of life-span development and describe how the study of human development began.
- List and illustrate the seven key assumptions of the modern life-span perspective.

If development consists of systematic changes and continuities from conception to death, the science of development consists of the study of those changes and continuities and their causes.

In this section we consider the goals of the science of life-span development, its origins, and the modern life-span perspective on development.

Goals and Uses of Studying Development

The goals driving the study of life-span development are:

describing,

predicting,

explaining, and

optimizing development (Baltes, Reese, & Lipsitt, 1980).

To achieve the goal of *description*, developmentalists characterize the functioning of humans of different ages and trace how it changes with age. They describe both normal development and individual differences, or variations, in development. Although average trends in human development across the life span can be described, it is clear that no two people (even identical twins) develop along precisely the same pathways.

Description is the starting point in any science, but scientists ultimately strive to achieve their second and third goals, *prediction* and *explanation*. Developmentalists seek to identify factors that predict development and establish that these factors actually cause humans to develop as they typically do or cause some individuals to develop differently than others. To do so, developmentalists often address nature-nurture issues. A first step is often finding a relationship between a possible influence on development and an aspect of development—for example, a relationship between whether or not an adolescent's friends use drugs and whether or not the adolescent does. If there is a relationship, knowing whether an adolescent's friends use drugs allows us to *predict* whether the adolescent uses drugs. But is this a causal relationship? That's what must be established before the goal of *explanation* is achieved. Maybe it's not that friends cause adolescents to use drugs by exposing them to drugs and encouraging them to try them. Maybe it's just that adolescents who use drugs pick friends who also use drugs (see Chapter 16 for evidence that both possibilities may be true).

The fourth goal of developmental science is *optimization* of human development. How can humans be helped to develop in positive directions? How can their capacities be enhanced, how can developmental difficulties be prevented, and how can any developmental problems that emerge be overcome? Pursuing the goal of optimizing development might involve evaluating ways to stimulate intellectual growth in preschool programs, to prevent binge drinking among college students, or to support elderly adults after the death of a spouse.

To those who are or aspire to be teachers, psychologists or counselors, nurses or occupational therapists, or other helping professionals, applied research aimed at optimizing development is especially relevant. Today's educators and human service and health professionals are being asked to engage in **evidence-based practice**, grounding what they do in research and ensuring that the curricula and treatments they provide have been demonstrated to be effective. Too often, these professionals go with what their personal experience tells them works rather than using what scientific research establishes to be the most effective approaches (Baker, McFall, & Shoham, 2009; Williams et al., 2012). We can all probably agree that we would rather have interventions of proven effectiveness than interventions that are ineffective or even harmful.

Early Beginnings

Just as human development has changed through the ages, attempts to understand it have evolved over time. Although philosophers have long expressed their views on the nature of humans and the proper methods of raising children, it was not until the late 19th century that the first scientific investigations of development were undertaken. Several scholars began to carefully observe the growth and development of their own children and to publish their findings in the form of **baby biographies**. Perhaps the most influential baby biographer was Charles Darwin (1809–1882), who made daily records of his son's development (Darwin, 1877). Darwin's curiosity about child development stemmed from his interest in evolution. He believed that infants share many characteristics with their nonhuman ancestors and that understanding the development of the embryo and child can offer insights into the evolution of the species. Darwin's evolutionary perspective strongly influenced early theories of human development, which emphasized universal, biologically based maturational changes (Cairns & Cairns, 2006; Parke et al., 1994).

Baby biographies left much to be desired as works of science, however. Can you see why? Because different baby biographers emphasized different aspects of their children's behavior, baby biographies were difficult to compare. Moreover, parents are not entirely objective observers of their own children, and early baby biographers may have let their assumptions about evolution bias their observations. Finally, because each baby biography was based on a single child—often the child of a distinguished family—its findings were not necessarily generalizable to other children.

Darwin greatly influenced the man most often cited as the founder of developmental psychology, G. Stanley Hall (1846–1924), the first president of the American Psychological Association (see Lepore, 2011, for an interesting view of the man). Well aware of the shortcomings of baby biographies, Hall attempted to collect more objective data from larger samples of individuals. He developed a now all-too-familiar research tool—the questionnaire—to explore "the contents of children's minds" at different ages (Hall, 1891).

G. Stanley Hall, regarded as the founder of developmental psychology and first president of the American Psychological Association, did pioneering research on childhood, adolescence, and old age. He is perhaps best known for characterizing adolescence as a period of "storm and stress."

Library of Congress, Prints & Photographs Division, Reproduction number LC-DIG-ggbain-05209 (digital file from original neg.)

Hall went on to write an influential book, *Adolescence* (1904). Inspired by Darwin's evolutionary theory, Hall drew parallels between adolescence and the turbulent period in the evolution of human society during which barbarism gave way to modern civilization. Adolescence, then, was a tempestuous period of the life span, a time of emotional ups and downs and rapid changes—a time of what Hall characterized as storm and stress. Thus, we have Hall to thank for the idea that most teenagers are emotionally unstable—a largely inaccurate idea, as it turns out (see Chapter 16). Yet as this book will reveal, Hall was right to mark adolescence as a time of dramatic changes.

Hall capped his remarkable career by turning his attention to the end of the life span in *Senescence* (1922), an analysis of how society treats (or, really, mistreats) its older members. Among other things, he recognized that aging involves more than just decline (Thompson, 2009). Clearly G. Stanley Hall deserves much credit for stimulating scientific research on the entire human life span and for raising many important questions about it.

The Modern Life-Span Perspective

Although a few early pioneers of the study of human development like G. Stanley Hall viewed all phases of the life span as worthy of study, the science of human development began to break into age-group specialty areas during the 20th century. Some researchers focused on infant or child development, others specialized in adolescence, and still others formed the specialization of gerontology, the study of aging and old age. Development was often viewed as something that happened in infancy, childhood, and adolescence, that proceeded through universal stages, and that led toward one outcome: mature adult functioning.

In the 1960s and 1970s, however, a true life-span perspective on human development began to emerge. In an influential paper, Paul Baltes (1939–2006) laid out seven key assumptions of the life-span perspective (Baltes, 1987; also see Baltes, Lindenberger, & Staudinger, 2006). These are important themes that you will see echoed throughout this book. They will also give you a good sense of the challenges facing researchers who study human development.

1. **Development is a lifelong process.** Today's developmentalists appreciate that human development is not just "kid stuff," that we change throughout the life span. They also believe that development in any period of life is best seen in the context of the whole life span. For instance, our understanding of adolescent career choices is bound to be richer if we concern ourselves with how those choices took shape during childhood and whether and how they affect adult career development and success.

2. **Development is multidirectional.** To many pioneers of its study, development was a universal process leading in one direction—toward more "mature" functioning. Today's developmentalists recognize that different capacities show different patterns of change over time. For example, some intellectual abilities peak in adolescence while others do not peak until a person's 40s or 50s; some decline in late adulthood, some don't change much, and some, such as command

Developmentalist Paul Baltes is credited with encouraging adoption of a life-span perspective on development.

Christine Windbichler

of vocabulary, continue to improve (Hartshorne & Germine, 2015; and see Chapters 7, 8, and 9). Different aspects of human functioning have different trajectories of change.

3. **Development involves both gain and loss.** Building on the theme that development is multidirectional and that it is not all gain in childhood and loss in old age, Baltes maintained that both gain and loss are evident in each phase of the life span. Moreover, he believed that gain inevitably brings with it loss of some kind, and loss brings gain—that gain and loss occur jointly. Examples? As infants become more able to discriminate the sounds of the language they hear spoken around them, they lose their ability to discriminate sounds used in other languages of the world (Werker et al., 2012; and see Chapter 6). Similarly, choosing to hone certain skills in one's education or career often means losing command of other skills (see Chapter 11).

4. **Development is characterized by lifelong plasticity.** Plasticity refers to the capacity to change in response to experience, whether positive or negative. Developmental scholars have long appreciated that child development can be damaged by a deprived environment and optimized by an enriched one. It is now understood that this plasticity continues into later life—that the aging process is not fixed but rather can take many forms depending on the individual's environment and experiences. For example, older adults can maintain or regain some of their intellectual abilities and even enhance them with the help of physical exercise, a mentally and socially active lifestyle, or training designed to improve specific cognitive skills (Hertzog et al., 2009; Park et al., 2014; and see Chapter 9). Such cognitive benefits are rooted in neuroplasticity, the brain's remarkable ability to change in response to experience throughout the life span (see Chapter 5).

5. **Development is shaped by its historical-cultural context.** This theme was illustrated in Section 1.1 of this chapter and is illustrated beautifully by the pioneering work of Glen Elder and his colleagues. They researched how the Great Depression of the 1930s affected the later life courses and development of the era's children and adolescents (Elder, 1998; Elder, Liker, & Cross, 1984). This work gives us insights into the many effects of the economic crisis called the Great Recession that began in 2008 (see Chapter 15). A few years after the stock market crashed in 1929, one of three workers was unemployed and many families were tossed into poverty. Although many families survived the Great Depression nicely, this economic crisis proved to be especially difficult for children if their

out-of-work and demoralized fathers became less affectionate and less consistent in disciplining them. When this happened, children displayed behavior problems and had low aspirations and poor records in school. They turned into men who had erratic careers and unstable marriages and women who were seen by their own children as ill tempered. Adolescents generally fared better than children did. Less dependent on their parents than children, adolescents were pushed into working to help support their families and developed a strong sense of responsibility from their experience. No question about it: Our development is shaped by how our lives play out over time in the social contexts and historical times in which we develop (see Elder, Shanahan, & Jennings, 2015). See Exploration 1.1

for a look at how adolescent development is being changed by today's innovations in digital media and communication technologies.

6. **Development is multiply influenced.** Today's developmental scientists believe that human development is the product of nature and nurture, of many interacting causes both inside and outside the person, and both biological and environmental (see Chapter 3). It is the often-unpredictable outcome of ongoing interactions between a changing person and her changing world.

7. **Development must be studied by multiple disciplines.** Because human development is influenced by everything from biochemical reactions to historical events, it is impossible for one discipline to have all the answers. A full

● **EXPLORATION 1.1**

Growing Up Online

How is adolescent development affected by the fact that teens today spend many hours a week with media—everything from TV and videos to Facebook, texting, Twitter, and Skype? When baby boomers grew up, there were no cell phones or home computers, much less an Internet. The Internet came into being in the early 1980s, around the time that home computers were becoming common (see, for example, Cotten et al., 2011). Facebook was launched in 2004, Twitter in 2006, Snapchat in 2011.

Media are now a big part of the daily lives of children and teens (Calvert, 2015; Lenhart et al., 2015). In a national survey, it was found that 8- to 18-year-olds spent an average of 7½ hours a day using media—from most to least frequently used, TV, music, computers, video games, print, and movies (Rideout, Foehr, & Roberts, 2010). And the researchers did not even ask about texting! Of teens aged 13 to 17, 88% text with friends and 55% do it daily (Lenhart et al., 2015).

How are these technologies affecting adolescent development? Researchers are beginning to address the question (see Calvert, 2015). For example, early research suggested that heavy Internet use was turning adolescents into social isolates with few friends and low well-being. However, that may have been because the first adolescent users were surfing the web and talking to strangers in chat rooms (Valkenburg & Peter, 2009). Now most adolescents use the Internet and use it primarily to interact with their friends—mainly through Facebook and other social media sites if they are girls, often through video game sites if they

are boys (Lenhart et al., 2015). And now that teens are spending much of their online time interacting with friends, studies seem to be showing more positive correlations between Internet use and social adjustment and well-being (Reich, Subrahmanyam, & Espinoza, 2012; Valkenburg & Peter, 2009). For emerging adults who have gone away to college, for example, social networking sites can be a way to hold on to the social support offered by their high school friends (Manago et al., 2012).

However, questions about the effects of digital media on adolescents are far from resolved. For example, Roy Pea and his colleagues (2012), studying a young sample of girls aged 8 to 12, found that heavy media use—especially spending large amounts of time watching videos, communicating online, and multitasking by using multiple media at once—was negatively associated with feeling good about one's close relationships and social acceptance. By contrast, spending time in face-to-face conversations was positively

The creation of the Internet is an historical change with many implications for the social lives of teens and for human development more generally.

Rawpixel.com/Shutterstock.com

related to these aspects of social well-being. Then there are the negative effects of cyberbullying to consider. Cyberbullying, which has increased in recent years (Jones, Mitchell, & Finkelhor, 2013), is linked to stress, depression, and suicidal thoughts among its victims (Hamm et al., 2015; Kowalski et al., 2014).

We have much to learn about the effects of digital media. It is becoming clear that these effects can be good or bad depending on what adolescents are doing with media, how much time they are spending with it, and whether it is crowding out other more developmentally important activities. In the meantime, there is much to be said for interacting with friends the old-fashioned way: offline.

understanding of human development will come only when many disciplines, each with its own perspectives and tools of study, join forces. Not only psychologists but also biologists, neuroscientists, historians, economists, sociologists, anthropologists, and many others have something to contribute to our understanding. Some universities have established interdisciplinary human development programs that bring members of different disciplines together to forge more integrated perspectives on development.

In sum, Baltes's modern life-span perspective assumes that development occurs throughout the life span, is multidirectional, involves gains and interlinked losses at every age, is characterized by plasticity, is affected by its historical and cultural context, is influenced by multiple, interacting causes, and is best studied by multiple disciplines.

● **Checking Mastery**

1. Focusing on the development over childhood of self-esteem, state a research question that illustrates each of four main goals of the study of life-span development.

2. Which three of the seven assumptions in Baltes's life-span perspective concern the nature-nurture issue?

● **Making Connections**

1. How does the developmental psychology of Paul Baltes improve on the developmental psychology of Charles Darwin?

2. Create examples to show how four of the assumptions of the life-span perspective might apply to your development.

1.3

How Is Development Studied?

LEARNING OBJECTIVES

- Summarize the scientific method and the choices involved in selecting a sample and choosing data collection methods.

- Evaluate the strengths and weaknesses of the case study, experimental, and correlational methods.

- Evaluate the strengths and weaknesses of the cross-sectional, longitudinal, and sequential designs.

How do developmental scholars gain understanding of life-span development? Let us review for you, briefly, some basic concepts of scientific research and then turn to research strategies devised specifically for describing, predicting, explaining, and optimizing development (see Miller, 2013). Even if you have no desire to do developmental research yourself, it is important for you to understand how the knowledge of development represented in this book was generated.

The Scientific Method

There is nothing mysterious about the scientific method. It is both a method and an attitude—a belief that investigators should allow their systematic observations (or data) to determine the merits of their thinking. For example, for every "expert" who believes that psychological differences between males and females are largely biological in origin, there is likely to be another expert who just as firmly insists that boys and girls differ because they are raised differently. Whom should we believe? It is in the spirit of the scientific method to believe the data—the findings of research. The scientist is willing to abandon a pet theory if the data contradict it. Ultimately, then, the scientific method can help the scientific community and society at large weed out flawed ideas.

The scientific method involves generating ideas and testing them by making observations. Often, preliminary observations provide ideas for a theory—a set of concepts and propositions

intended to describe and explain certain phenomena. Jean Piaget, for instance, formulated his influential theory of cognitive development by closely observing how French children of different ages responded to items on the Binet IQ test when he worked on the test's development, as well as by watching his own children's development (see Chapters 2 and 7).

Theories generate specific predictions, or hypotheses, regarding a particular set of observations. Consider, for example, a theory claiming that psychological differences between males and females are largely caused by differences in their experiences in the family. Based on this theory, a researcher might hypothesize that if parents grant boys and girls the same freedoms, the two sexes will be similarly independent, whereas if parents give boys more freedom than girls, boys will be more independent than girls. Suppose that the study designed to test this hypothesis indicates that boys are more independent than girls no matter how their parents treat them. Then the hypothesis would be disconfirmed by the findings, and the researcher would want to rethink this theory of gender differences. If other hypotheses based on this theory were inconsistent with the facts, the theory would have to be significantly revised or abandoned in favor of a better theory.

This, then, is the heart of the scientific method: Theories generate hypotheses, which are tested through observation of behavior, and new observations indicate which theories are worth keeping and which are not (■ **Figure 1.2**). It should be clear that theories are not just speculations, hunches, or unsupported opinions. A good theory should be:

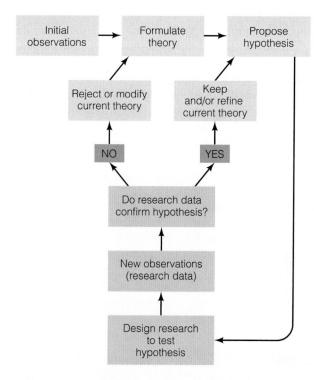

■ Figure 1.2 The scientific method in action.

- **Internally consistent.** Its different parts and propositions should hang together and should not generate contradictory hypotheses.
- **Falsifiable.** It can be proved wrong; that is, it can generate specific hypotheses that can be tested and either supported or not supported by the data collected. If a theory is vague or does not generate clear hypotheses, it cannot be tested and will not be useful in advancing knowledge.
- **Supported by data.** A good theory should help us better describe, predict, and explain human development; that is, its hypotheses should be confirmed by research results.

Sample Selection

Any study of development focuses on a particular research **sample** (the group of individuals studied) with the intention of generalizing the results to a larger **population**, a well-defined group (such as premature infants, American high school students, or Chinese elders) from which the sample is drawn and about which we want to draw conclusions. Although it is advocated more than it is used, the best approach is to study a **random sample** of the population of interest—a sample formed by identifying all members of the larger population and then, by a random means (such as drawing names blindly), selecting a portion of that population to study. Why do this? Random sampling increases confidence that the sample studied is representative of the larger population of interest and therefore that conclusions based on studying the sample will be true of the whole population.

In practice, developmentalists often draw their samples—sometimes random, sometimes not—from their local communities. Thus, researchers might survey students at a local high school about their drug use but then be unable to draw firm conclusions about American teenagers in general if, for example, the school is in a suburb where drug-use patterns are different than they might be in an inner-city or rural area. They would certainly be unable to generalize about Kenyan or Brazilian high school students. All researchers must therefore be careful to describe the characteristics of the sample they studied and to avoid overgeneralizing their findings to populations that might be socioeconomically or culturally different from their research sample.

Data Collection

No matter what aspect of human development we are interested in, we must find appropriate ways to measure what interests us. The methods used to study human development are varied, depending on the age group and aspect of development of interest (Miller, 2013). Here we will focus on three major methods of data collection used by developmental researchers: verbal reports, behavioral observations, and physiological measurements.

Verbal Reports

Interviews, written questionnaires or surveys, ability and achievement tests, and personality scales all involve asking people questions, either about themselves (self-report measures) or about someone else (for example, child behavior as reported by informants such as parents or teachers). These verbal report measures usually ask the same questions in precisely the same order of everyone so that the responses of different individuals can be directly compared. Increasingly, verbal report measures are administered via websites and smart phones (Wilt, Condon, & Revelle, 2012).

Although self-report and other verbal report methods are widely used to study human development, they have shortcomings. First, self-report measures typically cannot be used with infants, young children, cognitively impaired elders, or other individuals who cannot read or understand speech well. Informant surveys, questionnaires, or interviews are often used in these situations instead. Second, because individuals of different ages may not understand questions in the same way, age differences in responses may reflect age differences in comprehension or interpretation rather than age differences in the quality of interest to the researcher. Finally, respondents may try to present themselves (or those they are providing information about) in a positive or socially desirable light.

Behavioral Observations

Naturalistic observation involves observing people in their everyday (that is, natural) surroundings (Miller, 2013; Pellegrini, 1996). Ongoing behavior is observed in homes, schools, playgrounds, workplaces, nursing homes, or wherever people are going about their lives. Naturalistic observation has been used to study child development more often than adult development, largely because infants and young children often cannot be studied through self-report techniques that demand verbal skills. It is the only data collection technique that can reveal what children or adults do in everyday life.

However, naturalistic observation has its limitations as well. First, some behaviors (for example, heroic efforts to help in emergencies) occur too infrequently and unexpectedly to be studied through naturalistic observation. Second, it is difficult to pinpoint the causes of the behavior observed, because in a natural setting many events are usually happening at the same time, any of which may affect behavior. Finally, the presence of an observer can sometimes make people behave differently than they otherwise would. Children may "ham it up" when they have an audience; parents may be on their best behavior. Therefore, researchers sometimes videotape the proceedings from a hidden location or spend time in the setting before they collect their "real" data so that the individuals they are observing become used to their presence and behave more naturally.

To achieve greater control over the conditions under which they gather behavioral data, and to capture rarely occurring events, researchers often use structured observation; that is, they create special stimuli, tasks, or situations designed to elicit the behavior of interest. To study moral development and cheating among college students, for example, researchers might arrange a situation in which students take a cognitive test after having been led to believe that any cheating on their part could not possibly be detected. By exposing all research participants to the same stimuli, this approach increases the investigator's ability to compare the effects of these stimuli on different individuals. Concerns about this method center on whether research participants will behave naturally and whether conclusions based on their behavior in specially designed settings will generalize to their behavior in the real world.

Physiological Measurements

Finally, developmental scientists sometimes take physiological measurements to assess variables of interest to them. For example, they use electrodes to measure electrical activity in the brain, chart changes in hormone levels in menopausal women, or measure heart rate and other indicators of arousal to assess emotions.

Today, exciting breakthroughs are being made in understanding relationships between brain and behavior through the use of functional magnetic resonance imaging (fMRI), a brain-scanning technique that uses magnetic forces to measure the increase in blood flow to an area of the brain that occurs when that brain area is active. By having children and adults perform cognitive tasks while lying very still in an fMRI scanner, researchers can determine which parts of the brain are involved in particular cognitive activities. Sometimes fMRI studies reveal that children and adults, or young adults and older adults, rely on different areas of the brain to perform the same tasks, providing new insights into typical and atypical brain development and aging and its implications (see, for example, Goh & Park, 2009; Matthews & Fair, 2015; Wittmann & D'Esposito, 2012; and see Chapter 5).

Physiological measurements have the advantage of being hard to fake; the person who tells you she is not angry may be physiologically aroused, and the adolescent who claims not to take drugs may be given away by a blood test. Physiological measurements are also particularly useful in the study of infants because infants cannot tell us verbally what they are thinking or feeling. The main limitation of physiological measurements is that it is not always clear exactly what they are assessing. For example, physiological arousal can signal other emotions besides anger.

These, then, are the most commonly used techniques of collecting data about human development: verbal report measures (interviews, questionnaires, and tests), behavioral observation (both naturalistic and structured), and physiological measures. **Exploration 1.2** illustrates the use of the three techniques in a study of anger and aggression. Because each method has its limitations, knowledge is advanced the most when *multiple* methods and measures are used to study the same aspect of human development and these different methods lead to similar conclusions.

The Case Study, Experimental, and Correlational Methods

Once developmental scientists have formulated hypotheses, chosen a sample, and figured out what to measure and how to measure it, they can test their hypotheses. As we have seen, developmental science got its start with baby biographies, and on occasion today's researchers still study the development of particular individuals through case studies. More often they use the experimental and correlational methods to examine relationships between one variable and another—and, where possible,

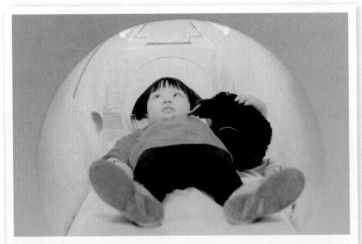

Functional magnetic resonance imaging is increasingly being used to study which parts of the brain are activated when humans of different ages perform various cognitive tasks. Testing children is challenging, however; they may fear entering the tube of the MRI scanner and, once there, may have difficulty staying still as required.

Stephan Elleringmann/laif/Redux

Data Collection Methods in Action: Measuring Anger

We can illustrate the primary methods of data collection by considering a study by Julie Hubbard and her colleagues (2002) that used all three approaches. Hubbard was interested in the relationship between anger and two styles of aggression in 8-year-olds, as determined by teachers' responses to questions about children's behavior in the classroom: a "hot" kind of aggression in which children hit, pinch, and otherwise abuse other children when provoked, and a cooler, more calculating style of aggression in which children use aggression to get what they want. The researchers hypothesized that aggressive children of the first type would be more likely than aggressive children of the second type to become angry in a laboratory situation in which another child (a confederate of the researchers) cheated shamelessly in a board game about astronauts and won. The researchers needed a way to measure anger. What would you suggest?

Behavioral observation. Hubbard used *structured observation* by setting up the astronaut game situation, having the confederate cheat to provoke children's anger, and then observing signs of anger in facial expressions and nonverbal behavior. The confederate was carefully trained to behave the same way with each of the 272 participants in the study. Sessions were videotaped; trained graduate and undergraduate students then coded second by second whether the participants' facial expressions were angry, sad, happy, or neutral and whether they showed any nonverbal signs of anger (for example, slamming game pieces on the table). Two students independently coded a subsample of the videotapes to ensure that their codings agreed.

Verbal report. The researchers also had each participant watch a videotape of the game he or she played with the cheating confederate, stopped the tape at each turn in the game, and asked each child, "How angry did you feel now?" The child responded on a four-point scale ranging from 1 (not at all) to 4 (a lot). The researchers used these ratings to calculate for each child an average degree of self-reported anger during the game.

Physiological measure. The researchers collected data on two physiological indicators of anger by attaching electrodes to children's hands and chests (after convincing the children that astronauts normally wear sensors when they go into space). Emotionally aroused individuals, including angry ones, often have sweaty palms and low electrical resistance of the skin, which can be measured by electrodes attached to their hands. Emotional arousal is also given away by a high heart rate, measured through electrodes on the chest.

Using these measures, Hubbard and her colleagues found that, as hypothesized, children who engaged in "hot" aggression in the classroom showed more anger during the game than "cool" aggressors. Their anger was clearest in the skin resistance and nonverbal behavior measures. Because all data collection methods have their weaknesses, and because different measures often yield different results, as in this study, use of multiple methods in the same study is a wise research strategy.

---

to establish that one variable causes another. We will illustrate these methods by sampling research on the implications of digital media for human development.

The Case Study

A **case study** is an in-depth examination of an individual (or a small number of individuals), typically carried out by compiling and analyzing information from a variety of sources, such as observation, testing, and interviewing the person or people who know her (see Flyvbjerg, 2011; Miller, 2013). The case study method can provide rich information about the complexities of an individual's development and the influences on it. It is particularly useful in studying people with rare conditions, disorders, and developmental experiences when it is not possible to assemble a large sample of people to study or when an unusual case can say something important about typical development. To illustrate, the case study method was used by Matthew Bowen and Marvin Firestone (2011) to describe four individuals, all European American males, who have what has come to be called "Internet addiction." One of the four men that they studied spent all afternoon and night until 8 or 9 A.M. online, mostly in chat rooms and at blogs or playing video games. He enjoyed disguising his identity and making other participants in chat rooms think that he knew of their most painful experiences. All four men in the study had psychological problems and difficulties in interpersonal relationships.

The case study method can complement correlational and experimental research (Flyvbjerg, 2011). It can be a good source of hypotheses that can be examined further in larger-scale studies, and it can provide a rich picture of atypical development. However, conclusions based on a single case (or four) may not generalize to other individuals, and inferences about what may have caused a person to develop as he or she did often need further study.

The Experimental Method

In an **experiment**, an investigator manipulates or alters some aspect of the environment to see how this affects the behavior of the sample of individuals studied. Consider the effects of watching videos or DVDs on infants. Many of today's parents, wanting to get their children off to a great start, not only set their babies in front of *Sesame Street* and other television programs and let them play with iPhones and iPads but buy them special baby videos that claim they will advance infants' cognitive and language development—products such as Baby Einstein's Baby Wordsworth, Intellectual Baby (which promises to teach babies to read), and many others. Do such infant videos actually speed infant language development?

Judy DeLoache and her colleagues (2010) decided to find out by conducting an experiment with 72 infants ranging in age from 12 to 18 months. The DVD they studied showed scenes of a house and yard while a voice labeled 25 different household objects, each shown three different times. Each family in the study was randomly assigned to one of four experimental groups: (1) *parent teaching* (in this old-fashioned condition, no video was provided; rather, parents were given the 25 words featured in the video and asked to teach as many as possible to their babies however they wished), (2) *video-with-interaction* (child and parent watched the video together five or more times a week for four weeks and interacted as they did), (3) *video-with-no-interaction* (infants watched the video by themselves; their parents were usually nearby but did not interact with them), and (4) a *no-intervention* control (these babies got no video and no parent training; this control group was needed to determine how many words infants might learn naturally, without any training). After the training period, babies took a test of their knowledge of the target words. For example, an infant would be presented with replicas of a table (a target word in the video) and a fan (not a target word) and asked to point to the right object: "Can you show me the table?"

The goal of an experiment is to see whether the different treatments that form the **independent variable**—the variable manipulated so that its causal effects can be assessed—have different effects on the behavior expected to be affected, the **dependent variable** in the experiment. The independent variable in DeLoache's experiment was the type of training babies received, as defined by the four different experimental conditions. The dependent variable of interest was vocabulary learning (the percentage of words taught in the video that were correctly identified by the infant during the vocabulary test). When cause-effect relationships are studied in an experiment, the independent variable is the hypothesized cause and the dependent variable is the effect. For example, if researchers were testing drugs to improve memory function in elderly adults with Alzheimer's disease, the type of drug administered (for example, a new drug versus a placebo with no active ingredients) would be the independent variable, and performance on a memory task would be the dependent variable.

So, in DeLoache's experiment, did vocabulary learning "depend on" the independent variable, the type of training received? Did infants learn from the baby video? The mean or average word learning scores for the four treatment groups are shown in ■ **Figure 1.3**. Babies did no better on the vocabulary learning test if they had seen the video than if they were in the control condition and received no training at all. The only group that did better on the test than what would be expected by chance was the group of babies taught the old-fashioned

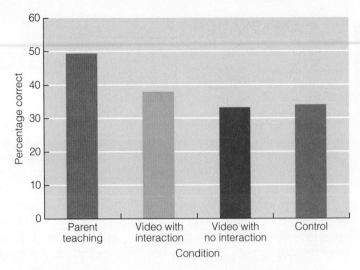

■ **Figure 1.3** Infants' mean scores on the vocabulary test after training in the DeLoache et al. (2010) experiment. Only infants taught words by their parents did better than chance on the test; exposure to baby videos that taught the words had no effect.

Source: Adapted from DeLoache, J. S. Chiong, C. S., Sherman, K. Islam, N., Vanderborght, M., Troseth, G. L., Strouse, G. A., & O'Doherty, K. (2010). "Do babies learn from baby media?" *Psychological Science*, 21, 1570–1574 (Figure 1 on p. 1572).

way—those in the parent teaching group. And it wasn't that babies or mothers were unenthusiastic about the video. As one mother exclaimed, "She loves the blasted thing. It's crack for babies!" (p. 1572).

The DeLoache study has the three critical features shared by any true experiment:

1. **Random assignment.** **Random assignment** of participants to different experimental conditions (for example, by drawing names blindly to determine who gets which treatment) is critical in experiments. It helps ensure that the treatment groups are similar in all respects at the outset (for example, in the baby video study, similar in socioeconomic status, ethnicity, previous level of cognitive and language development, and any other characteristics that could affect infants' performance). Only if experimental groups are similar in all respects initially can researchers be confident that differences among groups at the end of the experiment were caused by differences in which experimental treatment they received. Some studies, such as those evaluating already-started interventions, cannot randomly assign participants to groups; instead they compare the group receiving the intervention to a control group. Such studies are sometimes called "quasi experiments" because uncontrolled differences between the two groups could influence the results.

2. **Manipulation of the independent variable.** Investigators must arrange the experiences that different groups in the experiment have so that the effects of those experiences can be assessed. If investigators merely compare infants who already watch baby videos with infants who do not, they cannot establish whether video watching *causes* an increase in word

knowledge. For example, it could be that more-educated parents buy these videos more often than less-educated parents and also talk and read more to their children.

3. **Experimental control.** In a true experiment with proper **experimental control**, all factors other than the independent variable are controlled or held constant so that they cannot contribute to differences among the treatment groups. In a laboratory study, for example, all experimental groups may be tested in the same room by the same experimenter reading the same instructions. It is hard in a field experiment like DeLoache's, where the experimental conditions are implemented in children's homes by their parents, to control all extraneous factors. However, DeLoache and her colleagues asked parents to keep a log of their use of the video (or of the time they spent teaching vocabulary words if they were in the parent teaching condition). This allowed the experimenters to check that parents were following instructions and not using other materials or departing from the study plan. They were trying their best to ensure that infants in the four treatment conditions were treated similarly except for the type of training they received.

The greatest strength of the experimental method is its ability to establish unambiguously that one thing causes another—that manipulating the independent variable causes a change in the dependent variable. When experiments are properly conducted, they contribute to our ability to *explain* human development and sometimes to *optimize* it. In the DeLoache study, the results suggest that parent-infant interaction may contribute more to vocabulary growth than baby videos. Does the experimental method have limitations? Absolutely! First, because experiments are often conducted in laboratory settings or under unusual conditions, the results may not always hold true in the real world. Noted developmental psychologist Urie Bronfenbrenner (1979) was critical of the fact that so many developmental studies are contrived experiments. He once charged that developmental psychology had become "the science of the strange behavior of children in strange situations with strange adults" (p. 19). Experiments often show what can cause development but not necessarily what most strongly shapes development in natural settings (McCall, 1977).

A second limitation of the experimental method is that it often cannot be used for ethical reasons. How would you conduct a true experiment to determine how older women are affected by their husbands' deaths, for example? You would need to identify a sample of elderly women, randomly assign them to either the experimental group or the control group, and then manipulate the independent variable by killing the husbands of all the members of the experimental group! Ethical principles obviously demand that developmentalists use methods other than true experimental ones to study questions about the effect of widowhood—and a host of other significant questions about development.

The Correlational Method

Largely because it is unethical to manipulate people's lives, most developmental research is correlational rather than experimental. The **correlational method** generally involves determining whether two or more variables are related in a systematic way. Researchers do not randomly assign participants to treatment conditions and manipulate the independent variable as in an experiment. Instead, researchers take people as they are and attempt to determine whether there are relationships among their experiences, characteristics, and developmental outcomes.

Like DeLoache and her colleagues, Frederick Zimmerman and his colleagues (2007) were interested in the effects of media viewing on the language development of infants. They conducted a correlational study that involved telephone surveys with 1008 parents of children 8–24 months of age. They asked about infants' exposure to several types of media—not only videos and DVDs especially for babies, but children's educational programs, children's noneducational programs, and grownup TV. They used an established measure of language development in which parents report on their children's understanding of various words, and they correlated frequency of exposure to the different types of media with infants' vocabulary scores. Appreciating that there could be uncontrolled differences between families high and low in media use, they used statistical control techniques to adjust vocabulary scores to make it "as if" families were equal in potentially confounding characteristics such as race/ethnicity, parent education, family income, the presence of two parents in the home, day care participation, and other factors that they believed might be related to both media use and language development. They also asked about and controlled for the amount of time parents spent interacting with their infants by reading books and telling stories.

In correlational studies, researchers often determine the strength of the relationship between two variables of interest by calculating a **correlation coefficient**—an index of the extent to which individuals' scores on one variable are systematically associated with their scores on another variable. A correlation coefficient (symbolized as *r*) can range in value from -1.00 to $+1.00$. A positive correlation between video viewing time and language development

Is this infant really building her vocabulary as she watches baby videos? Both experimental and correlational research suggest that infants learn more from face-to-face interactions than from videos.

Peopleimages/E+/Getty Images

would indicate that as time spent watching videos increases, so does an infant's language development score. (■ Figure 1.4, Panel A). A positive correlation of *r* = +.90 would indicate a stronger, more predictable positive relationship than a smaller positive correlation such as *r* = +.30. A negative correlation would result if the heaviest video viewers consistently had the lowest language development scores and the lightest viewers had the highest language development scores (■ Figure 1.4, Panel B). A correlation near 0.00 would be obtained if there was no relationship between the two variables—if one cannot predict how advanced in language development infants are based on knowing how much they watch baby videos (■ Figure 1.4, Panel C).

The findings of Zimmerman's study were quite surprising. Among the youngest infants (8–16 months), each hour of viewing baby DVDs or videos per day was associated with *fewer* words known; the correlation was negative. By contrast, parent reading and storytelling were positively correlated with language development scores. Among older infants (ages 17–24 months), baby video viewing was not associated one way or the other with language development scores, as the DeLoache et al. (2010) experimental study also found. However, reading, and to a lesser extent storytelling, continued to be positively correlated with language development.

Should we conclude from the Zimmerman study, then, that reading to infants and toddlers advances their language development but that giving babies under 17 months of age baby videos and DVDs impedes their language development? Not so fast. Because this is a correlational study, we cannot draw firm cause-effect conclusions the way we can in an experiment. Does watching baby videos really delay language development among young infants, or could there be other reasons for the negative relationship between watching baby videos and vocabulary?

One important rival interpretation in most correlational studies is the **directionality problem**: The direction of the cause-effect relationship could be the reverse of what the researcher thinks it is. That is, exposure to baby videos may not *cause* infants to be delayed in language development; rather, as Zimmerman et al. (2007) acknowledge, slow language development could cause video viewing. That is, parents who fear that their infant is delayed in language development may buy baby videos in the hope that the videos will speed language development.

A second rival interpretation in correlational studies is the **third variable problem**: The association between the two variables of interest may be caused by some third variable. Zimmerman and his colleagues measured and tried to control for a number of possible third variables. For example, it could be that parents who are not very motivated to interact with their babies rely more on videos to entertain or babysit them and that it is the lack of parent-infant interaction, not increased time watching baby videos, that hurts young infants' language development. To rule out this possibility, Zimmerman and his colleagues showed that babies' video watching was negatively correlated with vocabulary score even when the amount of parent interaction through reading and storytelling, as well as a number of other potential "third variables," such as parent education and income, were controlled. However, as they admit, they did not control for the quality of parent-infant interactions and for additional, unmeasured factors that could explain why some infants both watch more baby videos than other infants and have lower language development scores.

Thus, the correlational method has one major limitation: It cannot unambiguously establish a causal relationship between one variable and another the way an experiment can. Correlational studies can only *suggest* that a causal relationship exists. Although Zimmerman's team used statistical control techniques to make it as if other factors were equal, they could not completely rule out the directionality problem and the third variable problem to establish a cause-effect relationship between baby video viewing and delayed language development. It's a rule every researcher knows by heart: "Correlation is not causation."

Despite this key limitation, the correlational method is extremely valuable. First, as already noted, most important

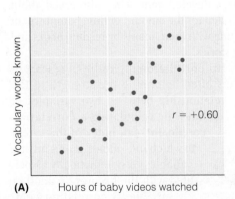
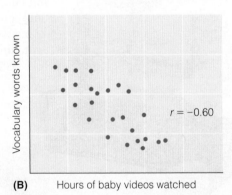
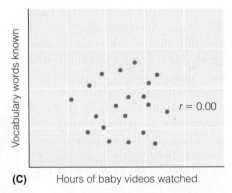

(A) Hours of baby videos watched (B) Hours of baby videos watched (C) Hours of baby videos watched

■ **Figure 1.4** Plots of hypothetical correlations between the time babies spend watching infant videos and their knowledge of vocabulary words. Each dot represents a specific child who watches a certain amount of baby videos and has a certain score on a vocabulary test. Panel A shows a positive correlation between video watching and vocabulary: The more infants watch infant videos, the more vocabulary words they know. Panel B shows a negative correlation: The more infants watch videos, the fewer vocabulary words they know. Finally, Panel C shows zero correlation: The amount of time watching baby videos is unrelated to an infant's knowledge of vocabulary words.

questions about human development can be addressed only through the correlational method because it would be unethical to manipulate people's experiences in experiments. Second, complex correlational studies and statistical analyses allow researchers to learn about how multiple factors operating in the "real world" may combine to influence development. We just have to be on the lookout for the directionality problem and the third variable problem in interpreting correlational relationships. See • **Table 1.3** for a comparison of experimental and correlational methods.

In the end, understanding of why humans develop as they do is best advanced when the results of different kinds of studies *converge*—when experiments demonstrate a clear cause-effect relationship and correlational studies reveal that the same relationship seems to operate in everyday life. One study's findings are not enough to go on; indeed, very often in psychology as well as in other sciences the findings of a particular study are not consistently confirmed when other researchers try to replicate the study (Open Science Collaboration, 2015). When we have the results of multiple studies addressing the same question, they can be synthesized to produce overall conclusions through the research method of meta-analysis (Glass, McGaw, & Smith, 1981; van IJzendoorn, Bakermans-Kranenburg, & Alink, 2012). In our baby DVDs example, this might involve comparing, across many studies, the language development scores of infants who were exposed to baby videos and infants who were not.

We do not yet have enough studies to say whether baby videos are helpful or worthless as a tool of language development. However, the experimental study and correlational study we have highlighted here, as well as other studies, do not support the claims of the makers of these products. They mostly say that baby DVDs neither help nor hurt infants (see, for example, Ferguson & Donnellan, 2014; Neuman et al., 2014; Richert et al., 2010). It's still the case that the best way for infants and toddlers to learn language is the old-fashioned way: by conversing with their caregivers as they go about their daily activities (Golinkoff et al., 2015; and see Chapter 7). Researchers are discovering that infants have a video deficit, a difficulty learning as much from video presentations as they do from face-to-face presentations (Anderson & Pempek, 2005; Strouse & Troseth, 2014). Interestingly, they seem to need to

perceive an adult on a screen as a real social partner who is talking with them personally in order to learn from that adult (Roseberry, Hirsh-Pasek, & Golinkoff, 2014; Troseth, Saylor, & Archer, 2006). Partly because of findings like these, the American Academy of Pediatrics (2010) recommends that children younger than 2 not watch television or other media on the grounds that they are likely to develop better if they spend that time interacting with adults.

Developmental Research Designs

Along with the experimental and correlational methods they use to study relationships between variables, developmental researchers need specialized research designs to study how people change and remain the same as they get older (Schaie, 2000). To describe development, researchers have relied extensively on two types of research designs: the cross-sectional design and the longitudinal design. A third type of design, the sequential study, has come into use in an attempt to overcome the limitations of the other two techniques.

Cross-Sectional Designs

In a cross-sectional design, the performances of people of different age groups, or cohorts, are compared. A cohort is a group of individuals born at the same time, either in the same year or within a specified span of years (for example, a generation is a cohort). A researcher interested in the development of vocabulary might gather samples of speech from several 2-, 3-, and 4-year-olds; calculate the mean (or average) number of distinct words used per child for each age group; and compare these means to describe how the vocabulary sizes of children age 2, 3, and 4 differ. The cross-sectional study provides information about *age differences*. By seeing how age groups differ, researchers can attempt to draw conclusions about how performance changes with age.

Suppose we are interested in learning about how people's use of computers, the Internet, and other communication technologies changes as they get older. Psychologists Patricia Tun and Margie Lachman (2010) conducted a cross-sectional study of computer use and its relationship to cognitive functioning in

• **Table 1.3** A Comparison of the Experimental Method and the Correlational Method

Experimental Method	Correlational Method
Manipulation by the investigator of an independent variable to observe effect on a dependent variable	Study of the relationship between one variable and another (without investigator manipulation and control of people's experiences)
Random assignment to treatment groups (to ensure similarity of groups except for the experimental manipulation)	No random assignment (so comparison groups may not be similar in all respects)
Experimental control of extraneous variables	Lack of control over extraneous variables
Can establish a cause-effect relationship between independent variable and dependent variable	Can suggest but not firmly establish that one variable causes another owing to directionality and third variable problems
May not be possible for ethical reasons	Can be used to study many important issues that cannot be studied experimentally for ethical reasons
May be artificial (findings from contrived experiments may not generalize to the "real world")	Can study multiple influences operating in natural settings (findings may generalize better to the "real world")

adulthood. They surveyed a national sample of adults ranging in age from 32 to 84 about how often they used computers and then compared computer use across age groups. ■ **Figure** 1.5 shows the percentage of each age group using computers to some extent. Clearly computer use was more common among younger adults than among elderly adults. But can we conclude that computer use normally declines with age as people get older? Not really.

People who are in their 70s not only are older than people in their 50s and 30s but they also belong to a different cohort or generation and have had different formative experiences. The 70-year-olds in Tun and Lachman's study did not have computers when they were children, whereas the 30-year-olds did. Do 70-year-olds use computers less because people lose interest in computers as they age, or is it that 70-year-olds were never as heavily into computers even when they were younger? Tun and Lachman's study cannot tell us.

In cross-sectional studies, such as Tun and Lachman's, *age effects and cohort effects are confounded, or entangled.* **Age effects** are relationships between age (a rough proxy for changes brought about by nature and nurture) and an aspect of development. **Cohort effects** are the effects of being born as a member of a particular cohort or generation in a particular historical context. Cross-sectional studies tell how people of different ages (cohorts) differ, but they do not necessarily tell how people normally *change* as they get older. In Tun and Lachman's study, for example, what initially looked like a developmental trend toward declining computer use in later life (an age effect) could actually be a cohort effect resulting from differences in the formative experiences of the different generations studied.

Indeed, the Pew Research Center (2014) has found through yearly surveys that Internet use among U.S. adults has in fact been steadily *increasing* from year to year. And this is just as true

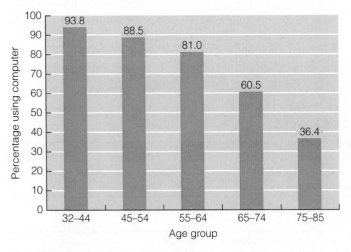

among adults age 65 and older as among younger adults. The percentage of adults aged 65 and older who report Internet use climbed from only 14% in 2000 to 59% by 2013. This is quite a different picture than we got from the cross-sectional study shown in **Figure** 1.5, where Internet use seemed to *decrease* with age.

The discovery of cohort effects tells us that it can make a difference whether you are born into one generation or another (see **Exploration 1.3** on the millennial and baby boom generations). However, the presence of cohort effects poses a problem in cross-sectional research whenever the growing-up experiences of the cohorts being compared differ. As you will see in Chapter 9, it was once believed, based on cross-sectional studies of performance on intelligence tests, that people experience significant declines in intellectual functioning starting in middle age. However, later longitudinal studies suggested that intellectual declines were much less steep and came later in life (Schaie, 2000). Why the discrepancy? The elderly adults in cross-sectional studies probably performed less well than younger cohorts not because they experienced steep losses of intellectual abilities during adulthood (a true developmental or age effect) but because they had received less education in their youth (a cohort effect). They probably always had lower intellectual abilities than younger cohorts as a result.

The second major limitation of the cross-sectional design besides the entanglement of age effects and cohorts is this: Because each person is observed at only one point, researchers learn nothing about how individuals change with age. Returning to our computer-use example, researchers cannot see whether different people show similar or different patterns of change in computer use as they get older or whether people's levels of computer use at age 30 predict whether they are heavy or light users at 70. To address issues like these, researchers need to do longitudinal research.

Despite the limitations of the cross-sectional design, it is a very important approach and developmentalists rely heavily on it. It has the great advantage of being quick and easy: Researchers can go out this year, sample individuals of different ages, and be done with it. Moreover, cross-sectional studies should yield valid conclusions about age effects if the cohorts studied are likely to have had similar growing-up experiences—as when 3- and 4-year-olds rather than 30- and 40-year-olds are compared. It is when researchers attempt to make inferences about development over the span of many years that cohort effects in cross-sectional studies can yield a misleading picture of development.

Longitudinal Designs

In a **longitudinal design**, one cohort of individuals is assessed repeatedly over time. A study of the development of vocabulary would be longitudinal rather than cross-sectional if a researcher identified a group of 2-year-olds and measured their vocabulary sizes, then measured their vocabularies again at age 3 and then again at age 4, and compared the children's mean scores at ages 2, 3, and 4. In any longitudinal study, whether it covers only a few months in infancy or 50 years, the same individuals are studied as they develop. Thus, the longitudinal design provides information about *age changes* rather than age differences.

Imagine that we had had the foresight to design a longitudinal study of computer use back in 1970 and had surveyed 30-year-olds about their computer use in 1970, and again every 20 years since,

■ **Figure 1.5** Percentage of American adults of different ages who used computers in 2005–2006. Do you think that computer use normally declines with age during adulthood? Read about age effects vs. cohort effects in cross-sectional studies.

Source: Adapted from Tun, P. A. & Lachman, M. E. (2010). "The association between computer use and cognition across adulthood: Use it so you won't lose it?" *Psychology and Aging, 25,* 560–568.

Millennials and Boomers: Cohort Effects

For baby boomers growing up in the 1950s, gender roles were more traditional than they are now. Fewer women worked outside the home, and more parents dressed and treated girls and boys differently.

Liu Liqun/Corbis Documentary/Getty Images

Does it make a difference in your development what generation, or cohort, you belong to? Whether you are part of the Silent Generation (the World War II and Korean War generation born between 1925 and 1946), the **baby boom generation** (the huge cohort born after World War II between 1946 and 1964), Generation X (the small generation born between 1964 and 1982), or the **millennials** (also called Generation Y or the "baby boomlet," the generation born from the early 1980s to the early 2000s)?

We seem to believe that different cohorts or generations not only have different formative experiences but also develop different characters. Popular writing on the subject often presents overgeneralized portraits of different generations—call it stereotyping—based on little solid data. The first wave of baby boomers turned 65 in 2011: George W. and Laura Bush, Bill Clinton, Dolly Parton, Donald Trump, and Cher. They were a year old when Howdy Doody first appeared on the first home TVs and 17 when John F. Kennedy was assassinated; they grew up fearing nuclear bombs and Russians and listening to rock and roll; and many of them protested the Vietnam War or fought in it (Adler, 2005). In the 1960s, boomers were stereotyped as antiestablishment, antiwar rebels who were into drugs and sexual freedom.

Millennials (born from the early 1980s to the early 2000s) have also gotten a lot of attention. They grew up in a digital world, are close to their parents, and appear to be less committed to traditional institutions like marriage and organized religion, less trusting, and more liberal on social issues like gay marriage than older generations (Pew Research Center, 2014). They also have been characterized quite uncharitably as a self-absorbed, narcissistic, "pampered, over-praised, relentlessly self-confident generation" (Matchar, 2012,

p. B1; and see Twenge, 2006; Twenge et al., 2008).

Should we believe this profile? There are more psychological differences within than between generations, so this description surely doesn't apply to all millennials. Some surveys do suggest, though, that the millennials as a group score higher on personality scales measuring narcissism, or self-absorption, than earlier generations (Twenge & Foster, 2010; Twenge et al., 2008).

But are these generational differences (cohort effects) or are they developmental differences (age effects)? Jean Twenge and her colleagues conclude from their studies that these are real generational differences. But what if millennials appear to be more narcissistic than older adults only because they do not yet have spouses, children, jobs, and other adult responsibilities that require thinking beyond their own needs, whereas older generations do? Perhaps we would see signs of self-absorption in emerging and young adults *regardless of the era in which they live*. After finding evidence to support this possibility, Roberts, Edmonds, and Grijalva (2010) concluded that high narcissism in emerging adulthood may be a normal developmental phenomenon, speculating that "every generation is Generation Me. That is, until they grow up" (p. 101). Here, then, is another example of how, in cross-sectional studies comparing different age groups, we cannot easily separate cohort effects and age effects. Understanding how people typically change with age and understanding how they are affected by the historical-cultural context in which they develop are both important goals of the science of life-span development. We must be careful, though, not to stereotype whole generations based on ambiguous findings.

---

until 2010 (when they would have been 70). The study would have shown that very few adults used computers in 1970 but that rates of computer use increased with age as more and more people gained access to computers. ■ **Figure 1.6** compares a cross-sectional and a longitudinal design for studying 30-, 50-, and 70-year-olds.

Because the longitudinal design traces changes in individuals as they age, it can tell whether most people change in the same direction or whether different individuals travel different developmental paths. It can indicate whether the characteristics and behaviors measured remain consistent over time—for example,

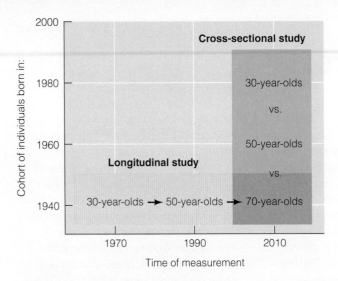

■ **Figure 1.6** Cross-sectional and longitudinal studies of development from age 30 to age 70. The longitudinal study involves repeated assessment every 20 years starting in 1970, whereas in the cross-sectional study, the three age groups of interest are compared in 2010.

whether people who used computers a lot at age 30 were still among the heaviest users at age 70. And it can tell whether experiences earlier in life predict traits and behaviors later in life. The cross-sectional design can do none of these.

What, then, are the limitations of the longitudinal design? Our hypothetical longitudinal study of computer use centered on *one cohort* of individuals: members of the 1940 birth cohort. These people were raised in an historical context in which computers were scarce and lived through a time when they became a fixture in almost every American home (Cotten, McCullough, & Adams, 2011). Their computer use probably increased over time from 1970 to 2010 as a result—a developmental trend precisely the opposite of the "decline" with age in computer use in Tun and Lachman's (2010) cross-sectional study (shown in **Figure 1.5**). However, this does not necessarily mean that computer use *typically* increases with age. The technological advances that occurred from one time of measurement to the next during the time frame of this particular study could be responsible for the observed increase. Time-of-measurement effects in developmental research are the effects of historical events and trends occurring when the data are being collected and that can affect anyone alive at the time (for example, effects of an economic recession, a traumatic event like 9/11, advances in health care, or, here, the invention of personal computers and the Internet). In a longitudinal study, then, *age effects and time-of-measurement effects are confounded.*

Because of time-of-measurement effects, we may not know whether the age-related changes observed in a longitudinal study are generalizable to people developing in other sociohistorical contexts. Perhaps we would obtain different "developmental" trends if we were to conduct a longitudinal study about computer use starting today, when computer use is already widespread, rather than in 1970. Our research example was chosen to highlight problems in both cross-sectional studies (where cohort effects

are tangled with age effects) and longitudinal studies (where time-of-measurement effects are tangled with age effects). Moral: It can be challenging to identify true developmental or age effects.

The longitudinal design has other disadvantages (Pulkkinen & Kokko, 2012): It is costly and time-consuming; its methods and measures may seem outdated or incomplete by the end of the study; its participants may drop out because they move, lose interest, or die; and participants may be affected by being tested repeatedly (for example, become more test wise).

Are both the cross-sectional and the longitudinal designs hopelessly flawed, then? Not at all. Cross-sectional studies are very efficient and informative, especially when the cohorts studied are not widely different in age or formative experiences. Longitudinal studies are extremely valuable for what they can reveal about how people change as they get older—even though it must be recognized that we may not be able to generalize to people living during other times in history. Still, in an attempt to overcome the limitations of both cross-sectional and longitudinal designs, developmentalists have devised a more powerful method of describing developmental change: the sequential design.

Sequential Designs: The Best of Both Worlds

A sequential design combines the cross-sectional approach and the longitudinal approach in a single study (Schaie, 1994; Schaie & Caskie, 2005). In Chapter 9, you will read about an ambitious and important sequential study of changes in mental abilities during adulthood conducted by psychologist and gerontologist K. Warner Schaie and his colleagues (1996, 2005). Adults ranging in age from 22 to 70 and grouped into age groups (cohorts) were tested on a battery of mental ability tests (in a cross-sectional design), and then they were retested every 7 years (to create a longitudinal design). At each testing point, new cohorts of adults in their 20s–70s were added to the study and those age groups were then retested. Some of the adults in the study were followed for as long as 45 years. This elaborate study has yielded many insights into intellectual aging. Not only were systematic changes with age in mental abilities identified, but cohort and time-of-measurement effects were revealed, suggesting that intellectual functioning is indeed influenced by the times in which people develop.

Sequential designs, by combining the cross-sectional and longitudinal approaches, improve on both. They can tell researchers

1. which age-related trends are truly developmental in nature and reflect how most people, *regardless of cohort*, can be expected to change over time (age effects);
2. which age trends differ from cohort to cohort and suggest that each generation is affected by its distinct growing-up experiences (cohort effects); and
3. which trends suggest that events during a specific period of history affect all cohorts alive at the time (time-of-measurement effects).

In short, sequential designs can begin to untangle the effects of age, cohort, and time of measurement. Yet they are complex and expensive. Generally, the study of life-span human development has progressed from early (and sometimes misleading) cross-sectional studies to more long-term longitudinal studies and, increasingly, to more complex sequential studies, especially of adult development (Baltes, Lindenberger, & Staudinger, 2006). See ● Table 1.4 for a summary of the three basic developmental designs.

Now that you have encountered examples of the various data collection methods and research designs used to study development, we challenge you to identify the research examples in Engagement 1.1.

● **Table 1.4** Cross-sectional, Longitudinal, and Sequential Developmental Designs

	Cross-Sectional Design	**Longitudinal Design**	**Sequential Design**
Procedure	Observe people of different cohorts at one point in time	Observe people of one age group repeatedly over time	Combine cross-sectional and longitudinal approaches; observe different cohorts on multiple occasions
Information Gained	Describes age differences	Describes age changes	Describes age differences and age changes
Advantages	Demonstrates age differences in behavior and hints at developmental trends Takes little time to conduct and is inexpensive	Indicates how individuals are alike and different in the way they change over time Can reveal links between early behavior or experiences and later behavior	Helps separate the effects of age, cohort, and time of measurement Indicates whether developmental changes are similar in different cohorts
Disadvantages	Age trends may reflect cohort effects rather than true developmental change Provides no information about change in individuals over time	Age trends may reflect time of measurement effects during the study rather than true developmental change Relatively time-consuming and expensive Measures may later prove inadequate Participants drop out Participants can be affected by repeated testing	Complex, time-consuming, and expensive Despite being the strongest method, may still leave questions unresolved

● **ENGAGEMENT 1.1**

Recognizing Research Strategies

For each research example, identify the most appropriate descriptive term. Answers are printed upside down below. Testing yourself is a great way to learn!

1. To study prejudice, a researcher gives some children red T-shirts and others blue T-shirts to see how children interact with members of the "in-group" and members of the "out-group."
   a. meta-analysis
   b. structured observation
   c. case study
   d. naturalistic observation

2. Every 10 years, a researcher assesses the religious participation of a group of adults who were age 20 in 2000, at the start of the study, and does the same with a similar group of adults who were age 20 in 2010.
   a. cross-sectional
   b. quasi-experimental
   c. correlational
   d. sequential

3. A new program to encourage teenage fathers to support their partners during labor and delivery is compared to a standard childbirth education program to see what effect it has on pain during labor and delivery. The independent variable is:
   a. gender of parent
   b. type of program
   c. pain during labor and delivery
   d. support given by fathers

4. A researcher finds that adults who were college age when 9/11 occurred in 2001 view the world as a scarier place than adults who were older at that time. This is a(n):
   a. time-of-measurement effect
   b. age effect
   c. cohort effect
   d. sequential effect

5. A researcher finds a small or modest relationship indicating that the greater a child's weight, the less he or she is liked by peers. The correlation coefficient calculated is probably around:
   a. +.70   b. +.20
   c. −.70   d. −.20

Answers: 1. b, 2. d, 3. b, 4. c, 5. d

1. Design an experiment to determine whether listening to music while studying a chapter helps or hurts performance on a test on the chapter material compared to studying the chapter in silence. Make it clear that your experiment has the key features of an experiment and label the independent and dependent variables.

2. You conduct a longitudinal study of the development of self-esteem in college students from age 18 to age 22. What would you be able to learn that you could not learn by conducting a cross-sectional study of the same topic?

1. Explain how a cross-sectional study of age differences over the adult years in attitudes about gender roles could suggest that attitudes become more traditional with age, but a longitudinal study could suggest that gender attitudes become *less* traditional with age.

2. Professor Feelgood conducts a study that reveals a correlation of +.50 between self-esteem and academic achievement (grade point average) among college students. He then argues, based on this finding, that his college should launch a self-esteem-boosting program if it wants its students to gain more from their college experience. Convince the professor that there are at least two rival explanations for this correlation and suggest how he could do research to try to determine which explanation is most correct.

1.4

What Special Challenges Do Developmental Scientists Face?

LEARNING OBJECTIVES

- Discuss the challenges in conducting culturally sensitive research.
- Explain the four major ethical obligations of investigators to their research participants.

We hope we have convinced you that human development is worthy of study and requires serious and thoughtful research. We conclude this chapter by discussing two additional challenges in the study of human development: being sensitive to cultural and subcultural differences and protecting the rights of research participants.

Conducting Culturally Sensitive Research

Baltes's life-span perspective emphasizes that development is shaped by its cultural context. This implies that we need to study development in a variety of contexts using culturally sensitive research methods and measurements to understand both what is universal and what is culturally specific about human development (Cole & Packer, 2011). Easier said than done!

By one count, two-thirds of the research samples in studies published in American psychology journals were American, yet 95% of the world's population is *not* American (Arnett, 2008). Joseph Henrich and his colleagues have gone so far as to characterize psychology as the study of WEIRD people: people living in societies that are Western, Educated, Industrialized, Rich, and Democratic (Henrich, Heine, & Norenzayan, 2010). They go on to suggest that American undergraduate students are especially WEIRD, unrepresentative of the human species. They give many examples, some of which you will encounter in this book, of psychological differences between WEIRD samples and samples from other types of societies. For example, it has been found that in Western societies, people tend to define themselves as individuals and want to stand out, whereas in Eastern societies, such as Japan, they tend to define themselves in relation to other people and want to fit in (Henrich et al., 2010).

Developmentalists appreciate the importance of studying samples of developing persons from a variety of ecological settings, not just white middle-class America. However, carrying out research in a variety of cultures and subcultures and ensuring that questionnaire, interview, and test questions and testing and observation procedures are meaningful in each culture and allow meaningful comparisons across different subcultural or cultural groups can be extremely challenging (Gardner et al., 2012; Rogoff, 2003). Language differences pose a problem: When one organization translated a survey into 63 languages and then had the questions translated back into English, for example, "married or living with a partner" was translated as "married but have a girlfriend" (Morin, 2003). And when a team of researchers sought to conduct a cross-cultural study of caregiver-infant interactions, they faced a dilemma: Should they observe such interactions when the caregiver and infant were alone (typical in American homes) or when the caregiver and infant were in a group (typical in Micronesia)? They settled on observing in both social contexts

Only cross-cultural research can tell us whether the findings of research conducted in our society hold true in societies very different from ours.

Bettmann/Getty Images

Many ethical issues arise in developmental research. For example, is it ethical to tell children that they performed poorly on a test to create a temporary sense of failure? Is it an invasion of a family's privacy to ask adolescents questions about conversations they have had with their parents about sex? If a drug to treat memory loss in elderly adults with Alzheimer's disease appears to be working, should it be withheld from the control group in the study? Concepts of consent, privacy, and harm also differ from society to society, so researchers must be sensitive to ethical values in the culture they will be studying (Miller, Goyal, & Wice, 2015).

The federal government (through the Office for Human Research Protections) and a variety of professional organizations such as the American Psychological Association have established guidelines for ethical research with humans. Federal regulations require universities and other organizations that conduct research with humans to have institutional review boards (IRBs) that determine whether proposed research projects conform to ethical standards and to approve projects only if they comply.

Deciding whether a proposed study is on safe ethical ground involves weighing the possible benefits of the research (gains in knowledge and potential benefits to humanity or to the participants) against the potential risks to participants. If the potential benefits greatly outweigh the potential risks, and if there are no other, less risky procedures that could produce these same benefits, the investigation is likely to be viewed as ethical. The investigator's ethical responsibilities boil down to respecting the rights of research participants by (1) allowing them to freely give their informed consent, (2) debriefing them afterward if they are not told everything in advance or are deceived, (3) protecting them from harm, and (4) treating any information they provide as confidential.

to avoid findings that might be biased toward one cultural group or the other (Sostek et al., 1981). To make their research more culturally sensitive, many researchers involve community members in the planning and design of their studies (Karlawish et al., 2009; Martin & Lantos, 2005).

In addition, researchers who study cultural or racial, ethnic, or socioeconomic differences in development must work hard to keep their own cultural values from biasing their perceptions of other groups and interpretations of their data. Too often, Western researchers have let ethnocentrism—the belief that one's own group and its culture are superior—creep into their research designs, procedures, and measures. And too often, researchers have judged minority group children and adults according to white middle-class standards, have labeled them "deficient" when they would better be described as "different," and have looked more at their vulnerabilities than at their strengths (Ogbu, 1981; Spencer, 2006). Also too often, researchers have assumed that all African Americans or Asian Americans or Hispanic Americans are alike psychologically, when in fact there is immense diversity within each racial or ethnic group (Helms, Jernigan, & Mascher, 2005). Today's developmentalists appreciate the importance of understanding human development in its cultural and subcultural context, but actually doing so is a tremendous challenge.

Protecting the Rights of Research Participants

Developmental researchers must also be sensitive to research ethics—the standards of conduct that investigators are ethically bound to honor to protect their research participants from physical or psychological harm (see, for example, Buchanan, Fisher, & Gable, 2009; Kodish, 2005; Pimple, 2008).

Informed Consent

Researchers generally should inform potential participants of all aspects of the research that might affect their decision to participate so that they can make a voluntary decision based on full knowledge of what the research involves. But are young children or mentally impaired people, such as older adults with Alzheimer's disease, capable of understanding what they are being asked to do and of giving their *informed* consent? Often they are not or it can be challenging to tell if they are (for example, see Drotar, 2008; Dunn & Misra, 2009; Kodish, 2005; Miller, 2013). Therefore, researchers who study such "vulnerable" populations should obtain at least the "assent" or agreement of the individual (if possible) as well as the informed consent from someone who can decide on the individual's behalf—for example, the parent or guardian of a child or the legal representative of a cognitively impaired nursing home resident. Investigators also must take care not to pressure anyone to participate and must respect participants' right to refuse to participate, to drop out during the study, and to refuse to have their data used by the investigator.

Debriefing

Researchers generally tell participants about the purposes of the study in advance, but in some cases doing so would ruin the study. If you told college students in advance that you were studying moral development and then gave them an opportunity to cheat on a test, do you think anyone would cheat? Instead, you might set up a situation in which students believe they can cheat without being detected, see who cheats, and then debrief them afterward, explaining the true purpose of the study. You would also have an obligation to make sure that participants do not leave feeling upset about cheating.

Protection from Harm

Researchers are bound not to harm research participants either physically or psychologically. Infants may cry if they are left in a room with a stranger. Adolescents may become embarrassed if they are asked about their sex lives. Investigators must try to anticipate and prepare to deal with such consequences (for example, by having a counselor on call). If physical or psychological harm to participants seems likely, the researcher may need to find another way of answering the research question. Federal regulations provide extra protection from harm to children (Kodish, 2005).

Confidentiality

Researchers also have an ethical responsibility to keep confidential the information they collect. It would be unacceptable, for example, to tell a child's teacher that the child performed poorly on an intelligence test or to let an adult's employer know that he revealed a drinking problem in an interview. Only if participants give explicit permission to have information about them shared with someone else or, in rare cases, if the law requires disclosure

of information (such as when a researcher learns that a child is being abused) can that information be passed on.

Clearly, developmental researchers have some challenging issues to weigh if they want their research to be well designed, culturally sensitive, and ethically responsible. Understanding life-span human development would be downright impossible, though, if researchers merely conducted study after study without guiding ideas. Theories of human development provide those guiding ideas and are the subject of Chapter 2.

● Checking Mastery

1. How many of the characteristics of WEIRD people do you have?
2. A researcher deceives research participants into thinking they are in a study of learning when the real purpose is to determine whether they are willing to inflict harm on people who make learning errors if told to do so by an authority figure. What ethical responsibilities does this researcher have? (Yes, this is about the famous obedience research conducted by Stanley Milgram, featured in the recent film *The Experimenter*.)

● Making Connections

1. Now that you have earned your PhD in life-span developmental psychology, you want to interview elderly widows in Japan and in the United States about their emotional reactions to widowhood shortly after the deaths of their husbands. What ethical issues should you consider, and what steps should you take to make your study as ethical as possible?
2. What might you do to make this research as culturally sensitive as possible?

Chapter Summary

1.1 How Should We Think about Development?

- Development is systematic changes and continuities over the life span, involving gains, losses, and neutral changes in physical, cognitive, and psychosocial functioning; it is more than growth in childhood and biological aging in adulthood.
- Development takes place in an historical, cultural, and subcultural context and is influenced by age grades, age norms, and social clocks.
- Concepts of the life span and its distinctive periods have changed over history in Europe and North America and differ from culture to culture. Starting in the 17th century, children came to be seen as innocents; in the late 19th century, adolescence emerged as a distinct phase; and only in the 20th century did our society recognize emerging adulthood, a middle-aged "empty nest" period, and an old age characterized by retirement.

- Understanding the nature-nurture issue means understanding the interaction of biology and maturation with environment and learning.

1.2 What Is the Science of Life-Span Development?

- The study of life-span development, guided by the goals of description, prediction, explanation, and optimization, began with the baby biographies written by Charles Darwin and others.
- Through his use of questionnaires and attention to all phases of the life span, including the storm and stress of adolescence, American psychologist G. Stanley Hall came to be regarded as the founder of developmental psychology.
- The modern life-span perspective on human development set forth by Paul Baltes assumes that development (1) occurs throughout the life span, (2) can take many different directions,

(3) involves gains and interlinked losses at every age, (4) is characterized by plasticity, (5) is affected by its historical and cultural context, (6) is influenced by multiple interacting causal factors, and (7) can best be understood if scholars from multiple disciplines join forces to study it.

1.3 How Is Development Studied?

- The scientific method involves formulating theories and testing hypotheses derived from a theory by conducting research with a sample (ideally a random sample) representative of a larger population of interest. Good theories should be internally consistent, falsifiable, and, ultimately, supported by the data.
- Common data collection methods include verbal reports, behavioral observations (naturalistic and structured), and physiological measures.
- The goal of explaining development is best achieved through experiments, which involve random assignments to conditions, manipulation of the independent variable, and experimental control. However, not all developmental issues can be studied with experiments for ethical reasons. Case studies may have limited generalizability, and in correlational studies, one faces the directionality and third variable problems in attempting to draw cause-effect conclusions. Developmentalists use meta-analyses to synthesize the results of multiple studies of the same issue.
- Developmental research designs seek to describe age effects on development. Cross-sectional studies compare different age groups but confound age effects and cohort effects. Longitudinal studies study age change but confound age effects and time-of-measurement effects. Sequential studies combine the cross-sectional and longitudinal approaches.

1.4 What Special Challenges Do Developmental Scientists Face?

- To understand human development, researchers must study it in a variety of ecological contexts, develop culturally sensitive methods and measures, and keep their own cultural values and ethnocentrism from biasing their conclusions.
- Researchers must adhere to standards of ethical research practice, with attention to ensuring informed consent, debriefing individuals from whom information has been withheld, protecting research participants from harm, and maintaining confidentiality of data.

Key Terms

development 4	maturation 9	population 15	third variable problem 20
growth 5	genes 9	random sample 15	meta-analysis 21
biological aging 5	environment 10	naturalistic observation 15	video deficit 21
aging 5	learning 10	structured observation 16	cross-sectional design 21
emerging adulthood 5	evidence-based practice 11	functional magnetic resonance imaging (fMRI) 16	cohort 21
culture 6	baby biographies 11	case study 17	age effects 22
age grade 6	storm and stress 12	experiment 17	cohort effects 22
rite of passage 6	gerontology 12	independent variable 18	longitudinal design 22
age norms 7	life-span perspective 12	dependent variable 18	baby boom generation 23
social clock 7	plasticity 12	random assignment 18	millennials 23
ethnicity 7	neuroplasticity 12	experimental control 19	time-of-measurement effects 24
socioeconomic status (SES) 7	scientific method 14	correlational method 19	sequential design 24
adolescence 8	theory 14	correlation coefficient 19	WEIRD people 26
life expectancy 8	hypotheses 14	directionality problem 20	ethnocentrism 27
nature–nurture issue 9	sample 15		research ethics 27

2

Theories of Human Development

For over a year now, Jared, age 15, has been spending a few nights a week out with his new friend Damien, who is two years older and has a driver's license. Often they drive around town looking for action. Often they find it, hooking up with girls they know from school or town hangouts and taking them back to Damien's basement for a few beers and sometimes more. Jared has had sex by now with about ten different partners and he has not used a condom every time—or even most times. After he complained to his doctor about genital sores, he was diagnosed with a case of genital herpes. He will not tell his parents if he can avoid it. They have been on his case lately about doing poorly in school and staying out too late.

Having sex at an early age, having many sexual partners, and having unprotected sex—all part of Jared's developmental story—are common examples of sexual risk behavior. In the United States, 44% of females and 47% of males in the 15–19 age range (18% of those age 15 like Jared) have had sexual intercourse at least once (Martinez & Abma, 2015). Only about 60% of sexually active American teens used a condom during their last experience of intercourse (Kann et al., 2014). Teenagers have higher rates of sexually transmitted infections such as herpes than adults (Abma, Martinez, & Copen, 2010; and see Chapter 12). And, although teenage pregnancy rates have decreased considerably since a mid-1950s peak, the current pregnancy rate in the United States, 57 of every 1,000 females aged 15–19, is higher than that of most other Western nations (Abma et al., 2010; Sedgh et al., 2015). Why is there so much sexual risk taking among American teens, and what might we do if we want to reduce it?

What is your explanation? What explanations might the leading theories of human development offer? In this chapter we will illustrate that different theories of human development provide different lenses through which to view developmental phenomena, such as teen sexual risk behavior.

LEARNING OBJECTIVES

- Explain why theories are needed in developmental science.
- Outline the four issues addressed by theories of human development.

Teenagers who start having sex early, with multiple partners and little protection, put themselves at risk for sexually transmitted infections and pregnancy.

Hybrid Images/Cultura/Getty Images

- what is most important to study,
- what can be hypothesized or predicted about it,
- how it should be studied, and
- how findings should be interpreted.

Because different theorists often have different views on these critical matters, what is learned in any science greatly depends on which theoretical perspectives become dominant, which largely depends on how well they account for the facts.

In this chapter, we examine four major theoretical viewpoints, each with important messages about the nature of human development:

1. The *psychoanalytic* viewpoint developed by Sigmund Freud and revised by Erik Erikson and other neo-Freudians
2. The *learning* perspective developed by such pioneers as Ivan Pavlov, John Watson, B. F. Skinner, and Albert Bandura
3. The *cognitive developmental* viewpoint associated with Jean Piaget
4. The *systems theory* approach, exemplified by Urie Bronfenbrenner's bioecological model

As noted in Chapter 1, a theory is a set of ideas proposed to describe and explain certain phenomena—in this book, human development. In science, it is not enough simply to catalog facts without organizing this information around some set of concepts and propositions. Researchers would soon be overwhelmed by trivia and would lack "the big picture." A theory of human development provides needed organization, offering a lens through which researchers can interpret and explain any number of specific facts or observations. A theory also guides the collection of new facts or observations, making clear

We will be asking as we go whether these theoretical perspectives meet the criteria of good theories introduced in Chapter 1—that is, whether they are internally consistent (coherent), falsifiable (testable), and supported by data (confirmed by research). To further aid you in comparing the theories, we outline four key developmental issues on which theorists—and people in general—often disagree (Miller, 2016; Lerner et al., 2015;

Newman & Newman, 2016): nature–nurture, activity–passivity, continuity–discontinuity, and universality–context specificity. All of us hold some basic beliefs about human development—for example, about the importance of genes versus good parenting in healthy development. Reading this chapter will make you more aware of your own assumptions about human development and how they compare with those of the major theorists. We therefore invite you to clarify your stands on these issues by completing **Engagement 2.1**. ● **Table 2.5** at the end of the chapter indicates how the major developmental theorists might answer the questions, so you can compare your assumptions with theirs.

In Exploration boxes throughout this chapter, we imagine some major points each theorist might make about the causes of sexual risk behavior in adolescence. We suggest that you predict what each theorist would say before you read each of these boxes to see whether you can successfully apply each theory. At the end of the chapter (**Application 2.1**), we'll invite you to apply the different theories to understanding and preventing risky sexual behavior in adolescence. It is our hope that when you master the major theories of human development, you will be able to draw on their concepts and propositions to make better sense of—and perhaps to guide in more positive directions—your own and other people's development. Now to the four major issues addressed by theories of human development: nature–nurture, activity–passivity, continuity–discontinuity, and universality–context specificity.

Nature–Nurture

Is development primarily the product of nature (biological forces) or nurture (environmental forces)? As you saw in Chapter 1, the nature–nurture issue has been resolved in the sense that the two forces always "co-act" to produce development. However, different theories have taken different positions on the issue and it remains centrally important in the study of human development (Goldhaber, 2012). Strong believers in nature stress the importance of individual genetic makeup, universal maturational processes guided by genes, biologically based predispositions built into genes over the course of evolution, and other biological influences. They are likely to claim that children will typically achieve the same developmental milestones at similar times because of maturational forces, that major changes in functioning associated with aging are largely biologically based, and that differences among individuals are largely because of differences in their genetic makeup and physiology.

By contrast, strong believers in nurture emphasize environment—influences outside the person. Nurture includes influences of the physical environment (crowding, climate, and the like) as well as the social environment (for example, learning experiences, child-rearing methods, peer influence, societal trends, and the cultural context in which the person develops). A strong believer in nurture is likely to argue that human development can take many paths depending on the individual's experiences over a lifetime.

● **ENGAGEMENT 2.1**

Where Do You Stand on Major Developmental Issues?

Choose one option for each statement, and write down the corresponding letter or fill it in at the end of the box. See **Table 2.5** to compare your results with how the theorists described in this chapter view development.

1. Biological influences (heredity and maturational forces) and environmental influences (culture, parenting styles, and learning experiences) are thought to contribute to development. Overall,
    a. biological factors contribute far more than environmental factors.
    b. biological factors contribute somewhat more than environmental factors.
    c. biological and environmental factors are equally important.
    d. environmental factors contribute somewhat more than biological factors.

e. environmental factors contribute far more than biological factors.

2. People are basically
    a. active beings who are the prime determiners of their own abilities and traits.
    b. passive beings whose characteristics are molded either by social influences (parents, other significant people, experiences) or by biological changes beyond their control.

3. Development proceeds
    a. through stages so that the individual changes into a different kind of person than she was in an earlier stage.
    b. in a variety of ways—some stage-like and some gradual or continuous.

c. continuously—in small increments without abrupt changes or distinct stages.

4. When you compare the development of different individuals, you see
    a. many similarities; children and adults develop along universal paths and experience similar changes at similar ages.
    b. many differences; different people often undergo different sequences of change and have widely different timetables of development.

Statement

1   2   3   4

Your pattern of choices:

___   ___   ___   ___

Activity–Passivity

The activity–passivity issue focuses on the extent to which human beings are active in creating and influencing their own environments and, in the process, in producing their own development, or are passively shaped by forces beyond their control. Some theorists believe that humans are curious, active creatures who orchestrate their own development by exploring the world around them and shaping their environments. The girl who asks for dolls at the toy store and the boy who clamors instead for a toy machine gun are actively contributing to their own gender-role development. Both the budding scientist who experiments with chemicals in the basement and the sociable adolescent who spends hours text messaging are seeking out and creating a niche that suits their emerging traits and abilities—and that further develops those traits in the process (Plomin et al., 2013).

Other theorists view humans as passively shaped by forces beyond their control—usually environmental influences but possibly strong biological forces. From this vantage point, children's academic failings might be blamed on the failure of their parents and teachers to provide them with appropriate learning experiences, and the problems of socially isolated older adults might be attributed to societal neglect of the elderly.

Continuity–Discontinuity

Do you believe that humans change gradually, in ways that leave them not so different from the way they were before, or do you believe humans change abruptly and dramatically? The continuity–discontinuity issue focuses in part on whether the changes people undergo over the life span are gradual or abrupt. Continuity theorists view human development as a process that occurs in small steps, without sudden changes, as when grade school children gradually gain weight from year to year. In contrast, discontinuity theorists tend to picture the course of development as more like a series of stair steps, each of which elevates the individual to a new (and often more advanced) level of functioning. When an adolescent boy rapidly shoots up 6 inches in height, gains a bass voice, and grows a beard, the change seems discontinuous.

The continuity–discontinuity issue also concerns whether changes are quantitative or qualitative in nature. Quantitative changes are changes in *degree* and indicate continuity: a person grows taller, knows more vocabulary words, gains more wrinkles, or interacts with friends less frequently. Or there is continuity when people stay much the same. By contrast, qualitative changes are changes in *kind* and suggest discontinuity. They are changes that make the individual fundamentally different in some way (■ Figure 2.1). The transformations of a caterpillar into a butterfly rather than just a bigger caterpillar, of a nonverbal infant into a toddler who uses language, or of a prepubertal

Continuity in development | Discontinuity in development

Little frog | Bigger frog | Tadpole | Frog
(A) | | (B)

■ **Figure 2.1** Is development continuous (A) or discontinuous (B)? That is, do people change quantitatively, becoming different in degree (as shown in Panel A with a size increase), or do they change qualitatively, becoming different in kind (as shown in Panel B, where a tadpole becomes a frog)?

child into a sexually mature adolescent are examples of qualitative changes.

So continuity theorists typically hold that developmental changes are gradual and quantitative, whereas discontinuity theorists hold that changes are more abrupt and qualitative. Discontinuity theorists often propose that people progress through **developmental stages**. A stage is a distinct phase of development characterized by a particular set of abilities, motives, emotions, or behaviors that form a coherent pattern. Development is said to involve transitions from one stage to another, each stage being qualitatively different from the stage before or the stage after. Thus, the adolescent may be able to grasp abstract concepts like human rights and justice in a way that the school-aged child cannot, or the middle-aged adult may be said to be concerned with fundamentally different life issues or conflicts than the young adult or older adult.

To what extent is human development universal and to what extent is it culture specific? Only cross-cultural research can tell us.

Imagno/Hulton Archive/Getty Images

Issue	Description
1. Nature–Nurture	Is development primarily the product of genes, biology, and maturation—or of experience, learning, and social influences?
2. Activity–Passivity	Do humans actively shape their own environments and contribute to their own development—or are they passively shaped by forces beyond their control?
3. Continuity–Discontinuity	Do humans change gradually and in quantitative ways—or do they progress through qualitatively different stages and develop very different competencies and characteristics?
4. Universality–Context Specificity	Is development similar from person to person and from culture to culture—or do pathways of development vary considerably depending on the social context?

Universality–Context Specificity

Finally, developmental theorists often disagree on the universality–context specificity issue—or the extent to which developmental changes are common to all humans (universal) or are different across cultures, subcultures, task contexts, and individuals (context specific). Stage theorists typically believe that the stages they propose are universal. For example, a stage theorist might claim that virtually all children enter a new stage in their intellectual development as they enter adolescence or that most adults, sometime around age 40, experience a midlife crisis in which they raise major questions about their lives. From this perspective, development proceeds in certain universal directions.

But other theorists believe that human development is far more varied because it is so influenced by contextual factors. Paths of development followed in one culture may be quite different from paths followed in another culture (or subculture, neighborhood, or even situational context). For example, preschool children in the United States sometimes believe that dreams are real but give up this belief as they get older. By contrast, children raised in the Atayal culture of Taiwan have been observed to become more and more convinced as they get older that dreams are real, most likely because that is what adults in their culture believe (Kohlberg, 1966b). Within a particular culture, developmental change may also differ from subcultural group to subcultural group, from family to family, and from individual to individual. The issue is this: How alike—or how diverse—are the developmental pathways we travel?

As we survey the major theories of human development, starting with Freud's well-known psychoanalytic perspective, look to see what stands each theory takes on these four key issues (● **Table 2.1**).

● Checking Mastery

1. What are the two meanings of discontinuity in development?
2. Stage theorists can disagree about a lot, but they are all likely to take certain stands on the issues of nature–nurture, continuity–discontinuity, and universality–context specificity. What stands?

● Making Connections

1. See if you can apply the four main issues in human development to aging and issues in old age. What questions would be raised about nature and nurture, continuity and discontinuity, and so on?

2.2
Psychoanalytic Theory

LEARNING OBJECTIVES

- Summarize the three parts of the personality and the five psychosexual stages in Freud's psychoanalytic theory.
- Analyze how Erikson's psychosocial theory differs from and expands on Freud's theory.
- Explain the conflicts humans face as they move through Erikson's eight psychosocial stages.
- Evaluate the strengths and weaknesses of Freud's and Erikson's theories.

It is difficult to think of a theorist who has had a greater effect on Western thought than Sigmund Freud, the Viennese physician who lived from 1856 to 1939. This revolutionary thinker's psychoanalytic theory, which focused on the development and dynamics of the personality, revolutionized thinking about human nature and human development. It proposed that people are driven by motives and emotional conflicts of which they are largely unaware and that they are shaped by their earliest experiences in the family (Hall, 1954; Newman & Newman, 2016; Westen, Gabbard, & Ortigo, 2008). Freud's ideas continue to influence thinking about human development, even though they are far less influential today than they once were. We introduce this historically important theorist briefly to set the stage for one of his most influential followers, neo-Freudian Erik Erikson.

Freud's Legacy

Freud's hugely influential theory emphasized biological instincts and unconscious motivation, the dynamics of three parts of the personality, and five stages of psychosexual development.

Instincts and Unconscious Motivation

Central to Freudian psychoanalytic theory is the notion that humans have basic biological urges or drives that must be satisfied. Freud viewed the newborn as an inherently selfish and aggressive creature driven by instincts—inborn biological forces that motivate behavior. These biological instincts are the source of the psychic (or mental) energy that fuels human behavior and that is channeled in new directions over the course of human development.

Freud strongly believed in unconscious motivation—the power of instincts and other inner forces to influence our behavior without our awareness. A preadolescent girl, for example, may not realize that she is acting in babyish ways in order to regain the security of her mother's love; a teenage boy may not realize that his devotion to body building is a way of channeling his sexual and aggressive urges. You immediately see that Freud's theory tilts toward the nature side of the nature–nurture issue: Development is shaped by biological forces that provide an unconscious motivation for behavior. Nevertheless, his theory also includes environmental influences on development, mostly in the form of experiences in the family during the first 5 years of life.

Sigmund Freud's psychoanalytic theory was one of the first, and one of the most influential, theories of how the personality develops from childhood to adulthood. Here, Freud poses with his grandsons, Heinz and Ernst (and a lighted cigar).

Imagno/Hulton Archive/Getty Images

Id, Ego, and Superego

According to Freud (1933), the child's psychic energy is divided among three components of the personality as she develops: the id, the ego, and the superego. At birth, there is only the id—the impulsive, irrational, and selfish part of the personality whose mission is to satisfy the instincts. The id seeks immediate gratification, even when biological needs cannot be realistically or appropriately met. If you think about it, young infants do seem to be "all id" in many ways. When they are hungry or wet, they fuss and cry until their needs are met. They are not known for their patience.

The second component of the personality is the ego, the rational side of the individual that tries to find realistic ways of gratifying the instincts. According to Freud (1933), the ego begins to emerge during infancy and takes the form of cognitive processes such as perception, learning, and problem solving. The hungry toddler may be able to do more than merely cry when she is hungry; she may be able to draw on the resources of the ego to hunt down Dad, lead him to the kitchen, and say "cookie." As the ego matures further, children become more capable of postponing pleasures until a more appropriate time and of devising logical and realistic strategies for meeting their needs.

The third part of the Freudian personality is the superego, the individual's internalized moral standards. The superego develops from the ego as 3- to 6-year-old children internalize (take on as their own) the moral standards and values of their parents. Once the superego emerges, children have a parental voice in their heads that keeps them from violating society's rules and makes them feel guilty or ashamed if they do. The superego insists that people find socially acceptable or ethical outlets for the id's undesirable impulses.

Conflict among the id, ego, and superego is inevitable, Freud said. In the mature, healthy personality, a dynamic balance operates: The id communicates its basic needs, the ego restrains the impulsive id long enough to find realistic ways to satisfy these needs, and the superego decides whether the ego's problem-solving strategies are morally acceptable (Freud, 1940/1964). The ego has to balance the opposing demands of id and superego while taking into account the realities of the person's environment. Psychological problems often arise if there is imbalance among the three parts of the personality. For example, a salesman with an antisocial personality who routinely lies and cheats may have a strong id but a weak superego, whereas a married woman who cannot undress in front of her husband may have an overly strong superego that makes it difficult for her to fulfill her sexual needs. Through analysis of the dynamics operating among the id, ego, and superego, Freud and his followers attempted to describe and understand individual differences in personality and the origins of psychological disorders.

Psychosexual Stages

Freud (1940/1964) maintained that as the child matures biologically, the psychic energy of the sex instinct, which he called libido, shifts from one part of the body to another, seeking to gratify different biological needs. In the process, as outlined in ● Table 2.2, the child moves through five psychosexual stages: oral, anal, phallic, latency, and genital. Harsh child-rearing

Freud's Psychosexual Theory		Erikson's Psychosocial Theory	
Stage (Age Range) / Description		Stage (Age Range) / Description	
Oral stage (birth–1 year)	Libido is focused on the mouth as a source of pleasure. Obtaining oral gratification from a mother figure is critical to later development.	Trust vs. mistrust (birth–1 year)	Infants must learn to trust their caregivers to meet their needs. Responsive parenting is critical.
Anal stage (1–3 years)	Libido is focused on the anus, and toilet training creates conflicts between the child's biological urges and the society's demands.	Autonomy vs. shame and doubt (1–3 years)	Children must learn to be autonomous—to assert their wills and do things for themselves—or they will doubt their abilities.
Phallic stage (3–6 years)	Libido centers on the genitals. Resolution of the Oedipus or the Electra complex, which involves desire for the other-sex parent, results in identification with the same-sex parent and development of the superego.	Initiative vs. guilt (3–6 years)	Preschoolers develop initiative by devising and carrying out bold plans, but they must learn not to impinge on the rights of others.
Latent period (6–12 years)	Libido is quiet; psychic energy is invested in schoolwork and play with same-sex friends.	Industry vs. inferiority (6–12 years)	Children must master important social and academic skills and keep up with their peers; otherwise, they will feel inferior.
Genital stage (12 years and older)	Puberty reawakens the sexual instincts as youths seek to establish mature sexual relationships and pursue the biological goal of reproduction.	Identity vs. role confusion (12–20 years)	Adolescents ask who they are and must establish social and vocational identities; otherwise, they will remain confused about the roles they should play as adults.
		Intimacy vs. isolation (20–40 years)	Young adults seek to form a shared identity with another person, but may fear intimacy and experience loneliness and isolation.
		Generativity vs. stagnation (40–65 years)	Middle-aged adults must feel that they are producing something that will outlive them, either as parents or as workers; otherwise, they will become stagnant and self-centered.
		Integrity vs. despair (65 years and older)	Older adults must come to view their lives as meaningful to face death without worries and regrets.

methods—punishing babies for mouthing paychecks and other interesting objects around the house, or toddlers for their toileting accidents, or preschoolers for taking interest in their genitals—can heighten these biologically based psychic conflicts—and the child's anxiety.

The baby in the *oral stage* of psychosexual development focuses on the mouth as a source of sexual pleasure and can, according to Freud, experience anxiety and need to defend against it if denied oral gratification—for example, by being weaned too early. Through fixation, arrested development in which part of the libido remains tied to an earlier stage of development, an infant deprived of oral gratification might become "stuck" in the oral stage. He might become a chronic thumb sucker and then an adult who chain smokes and is overdependent on other people. How the child copes with the challenges of a stage and what parents do to help or hurt can leave a lasting imprint on the personality.

Similarly, the toddler in the *anal stage* must cope with new demands when toilet training begins. Parents who are impatient and punitive as their children learn to delay the gratification of relieving themselves can create high levels of anxiety and a personality that resists demands from authority figures. The parent's goal should be to allow some (but not too much) gratification of impulses while helping the child achieve reasonable (but not too much) control over these impulses.

The *phallic* stage from age 3 to age 6 is an especially treacherous time. Children, Freud claimed, develop an incestuous desire for the parent of the other sex and must defend against it. A boy experiencing an "Oedipus complex" loves his mother, fears that his father will retaliate against him, and resolves this conflict through identification with his father—by taking on his father's attitudes and behaviors. Meanwhile, a girl experiencing an "Electra complex" is said to desire her father, view her mother as a rival, and ultimately resolve her conflict by identifying with her

Freud and Erikson: Notes on Sexual Risk Behavior

(We suggest you read this and subsequent boxes on sexual risk behavior in adolescence after you read about each theory; it will make more sense and you'll be able to test your ability to apply the theory.)

I, Freud, believe teenagers engage in sexual risk-taking because they experience intense emotional conflicts during the genital stage of psychosexual development. Their new sexual urges are anxiety-provoking. From a psycho-analytic perspective, teenagers who engage in risky sex may not have developed strong enough egos and superegos to keep their ids in check. Psychological conflicts stemming from early childhood—for example, conflicts rooted

in a boy's unresolved and unconscious Oedipal desire to possess his mother—can contribute to an adolescent's premature and promiscuous sex (Harris, 2011; Schofield, Bierman, & Heinrichs, 2008). Perhaps Jared is unconsciously acting out his sexual fantasies. His behavior may also be a sign of underlying mental health problems such as depression or conduct disorder (Parkes et al., 2014; Pilgrim & Blum, 2012).

I, Erikson, agree with Dr. Freud that unre-solved conflicts from earlier stages of devel-opment could contribute to Jared's behavior. If he never developed a sense of trust as an infant, for example, he could fear abandon-ment and drop one girl for the next so that

he won't be dumped first. But let's focus on my adolescent psychosocial conflict: identity versus role confusion (Erikson, 1968). Adoles-cents seek a sense of identity by experiment-ing with different roles and behaviors to see what suits them. They try drugs, dye their hair orange, join radical groups, change majors every semester, and yes, have sex, sometimes with multiple partners. Like Freud, I would also look into the parent–child relationship, but I would recognize that other relation-ships count too. Something may be going on in Jared's relationships with his friends or teachers, or even in the wider culture, that is influencing him.

mother. When boys and girls resolve their emotional conflicts by identifying with the same-sex parent, they incorporate their same-sex parent's values into their superego and also adopt their gender role, so Freud viewed the preschool period as important in both moral development and gender-role development.

During the *latency period*, sexual urges are tame and 6-to 12-year-olds invest psychic energy in schoolwork and play. However, adolescents experience new psychic conflicts as they reach puberty and enter the final stage of psychosexual development, the *genital stage*. Adolescents may have difficulty accepting their new sexuality, may reexperience the conflicting feelings toward their parents that they felt during the preschool phallic stage, and may distance themselves from their parents to defend themselves against these anxiety-provoking feelings. Freud believed that psychosexual development stops with ado-lescence and that the individual remains in the genital stage throughout adulthood.

To defend itself against all the anxiety that can arise as these psychic conflicts play out, the ego adopts unconscious coping devices called **defense mechanisms** (Freud, 1940/1964). One well-known example (besides identification, which we already discussed) is **repression**, or removing unacceptable thoughts or traumatic memories from consciousness. Through repression, a young woman who was raped may have no memory at all of it. Or through the defense mechanism of **regression**, or retreating to an earlier, less traumatic stage of development, a preschool girl, threatened by her new baby brother, may revert to infantile behavior and want to be rocked.

We learn these and other defense mechanisms to cope with inner conflicts of which we are largely unaware, deceiving our-selves in order to save ourselves. Defense mechanisms can be

healthy in that they allow us to function despite anxiety, but they can also spell trouble if they involve too much distortion of reality.

Erikson's Psychosocial Theory

A sign of Freud's immense influence is that he inspired so many disciples and descendants to make their own contributions to the understanding of human development (Bergen, 2008). Among these well-known neo-Freudians were Alfred Adler, who suggested that siblings (and rivalries among siblings) are significant in devel-opment; Carl Jung, a pioneer in the study of adult development who claimed that adults experience a midlife crisis and then become freer to express both the "masculine" and the "feminine" sides of their personalities; Karen Horney, who challenged Freud's ideas about gender differences; Harry Stack Sullivan, who argued that close friendships in childhood set the stage for romantic rela-tionships later in life; and Freud's daughter Anna, who developed techniques of psychoanalysis appropriate for children.

But the neo-Freudian psychoanalytic theorist who most influ-enced thinking about life-span development was Erik Erikson (1902–1994), whom we will revisit in more detail in Chapter 11. Erikson studied with Anna Freud and emigrated from Germany to the United States when Hitler rose to power (Friedman, 1999). Like Sigmund Freud, Erikson (1963, 1968, 1982) concerned himself with the inner dynamics of personality and proposed that the personality evolves through systematic stages. However, compared with Freud, Erikson:

- Placed less emphasis on sexual urges as the drivers of devel-opment and more emphasis on social influences—not just parents but peers, teachers, schools, and the broader culture— claiming that nature and nurture are equally important.

Erik Erikson built on Freudian theory and proposed that people experience eight psychosexual crises over their life span.

Bettmann/Getty Images

- Placed less emphasis on the unconscious, irrational, and selfish id and more on the rational ego and its adaptive powers.
- Held a more positive view of human nature, seeing people as active in their development, largely rational, and able to overcome the effects of harmful early experiences.
- Put more emphasis on development after adolescence.

Eight Psychosocial Stages

Erikson believed that humans everywhere experience eight major **psychosocial stages**, or conflicts, during their lives. (Erikson's psychosocial stages are matched up with Freud's psychosexual stages in **Table 2.2**.) Whether the conflict of a particular stage is successfully resolved or not, the individual is pushed by both biological maturation and social demands into the next stage. However, the unsuccessful resolution of a conflict will affect how later stages play out.

For example, the first conflict, *trust versus mistrust*, revolves around whether or not infants become able to rely on other people to be responsive to their needs. To develop a sense of trust, infants must be able to count on their primary caregivers not only to feed them (Freud's emphasis) but to relieve their discomfort, come when beckoned, and return their smiles and babbles—to be responsive to all their needs. If caregivers neglect, reject, or respond inconsistently to infants, infants will mistrust others. A healthy balance between the terms of the conflict must be struck for development to proceed optimally. Trust should outweigh mistrust, but an element of skepticism is also needed: an overindulged infant may become too trusting (a gullible "sucker").

So it goes for the remaining stages of childhood. If all goes well as children confront and resolve each conflict, they will gain a sense of self and develop *autonomy* (rather than shame and doubt) about their ability to act independently, develop the *initiative* (as opposed to guilt) that allows them to plan and tackle big projects, and acquire the sense of *industry* (rather than inferiority) that will enable them to master important academic and social skills in school.

This growth will position adolescents to successfully resolve the conflict for which Erikson (1968) is best known, *identity versus role confusion*. Erikson characterized adolescence as a time of "identity crisis" in which youth attempt to define who they are (in terms of career, religion, sexual identity, and so on), where they are heading, and how they fit into society. As part of their search, they often change their minds and experiment with new looks, new career plans, and new relationships. Erikson should know: He was the tall, blond stepson of a Jewish doctor and wandered all over Europe after high school, trying out a career as an artist and other possibilities before he ended up studying child psychoanalysis under Anna Freud and finally found his calling in his mid-20s (Friedman, 1999).

Whereas Freud's stages stopped with adolescence, Erikson believed that psychosocial growth continues during the adult years. Successfully resolving the adolescent conflict of identity versus role confusion paves the way for resolving the early adulthood conflict of *intimacy versus isolation* and for becoming ready to form a shared identity with someone else in a committed, long-term relationship. Successful resolution of the middle-age conflict of *generativity versus stagnation* involves adults gaining a sense that they have produced something that will outlive them, whether by successfully raising children or by contributing something meaningful to the world through work or volunteer activities. Finally, elderly adults who resolve the psychosocial conflict of *integrity versus despair* find a sense of meaning in their lives that will help them face death.

Erikson clearly did not agree with Freud that the personality is essentially "set in stone" during the first 5 years of life. Yet he, like Freud and other psychoanalytic theorists, believed that people progress through systematic stages of development, undergoing similar personality changes at similar ages. Individual differences in personality reflect the different experiences individuals have, not only in the family but beyond, as they struggle to cope with the challenges of each life stage. Both biological maturation and demands of the social and cultural environment influence the individual's progress through Erikson's sequence of psychosocial stages. As an illustration, in **Exploration 2.1**, we imagine the notes that Freud and Erikson might have scribbled down to explain Jared's sexual behavior, as described at the start of the chapter. What might you say if you were Freud and Erikson?

Strengths and Weaknesses

Sigmund Freud is a giant in the history of psychology. Many of his general insights have stood up well and have profoundly influenced theories of human development, personality, and psychotherapy (Fonagy & Target, 2000; Newman & Newman, 2016; Westen et al., 2008). Consider these three major contributions:

- Freud called attention to *unconscious processes* underlying human behavior, a fundamental insight supported by modern psychological and neuropsychological research (Bargh & Morsella, 2008; Westen et al., 2008).
- Freud was one of the first to stress the importance for later development of *early experiences* in the family, which, as we will see throughout this book, can be tremendously important.

- Freud emphasized the importance of *emotions* and emotional conflicts in development and the inner workings of personality; most other developmental theories have been more interested in observable behavior or rational thought.

Erikson too has made important contributions. Many people find Erikson's emphasis on our rational, adaptive nature and his interactionist position emphasizing both biological and social influences easier to accept than Freud's emphasis on unconscious, irrational motivations based in biological needs. Erikson also captured important developmental issues in his eight stages. He has had an especially great impact on research on adolescence and adulthood (see Berzoff, 2008; Newman & Newman, 2016; and Chapter 11).

What are the limitations of psychoanalytic theories? Developmentalists fault Freud for proposing a theory that is ambiguous, internally inconsistent, difficult to pin down and test, and therefore not easily falsifiable (Fonagy & Target, 2000; Newman & Newman, 2016). Testing hypotheses that require studying unconscious motivations and the workings of the unseen id, ego, and superego has been challenging. Moreover, when the theory has been tested, many of its specific ideas—for example, ideas about the lasting importance of early feeding practices or the preschool child's Oedipus and Electra conflicts—have not been well supported (Crews, 1996; Fisher & Greenberg, 1977).

Erikson's theory has some of the same shortcomings as Freud's. It is sometimes vague and difficult to test. And although it provides a useful *description* of human personality development, it does not provide an adequate *explanation* of how this development comes about. Important psychoanalytic theorists such as Erikson continue to shape understanding of human development, but many developmentalists have left psychoanalytic theory behind in favor of theories that are more precise and testable.

Checking Mastery

1. Jaime believes that people have both a moral side and a selfish side that work against each other. According to Freud's psychoanalytic theory, what are these "sides" called and when do they arise in development?

2. What are three major ways in which Erikson's ideas differ from Freud's?

3. Wanda, at age 40, is depressed. She seems to doubt her ability to assert herself and take charge of situations at work, and she always fears other people will let her down. What Eriksonian stages might have been problematic for her in childhood, and how might her parents have contributed to her current problems?

Making Connections

1. When Brenda was only 12, her stepfather started sexually abusing her and continued doing so for the next two years. What might Freud hypothesize about Brenda's personality development? What might Erikson hypothesize?

2. Thinking about yourself, your parents, and your grandparents, can you see any evidence that Erikson's conflicts of adolescence and adulthood are relevant in your family?

2.3
Learning Theories

LEARNING OBJECTIVES

- Explain how the learning theory perspective on development differs from stage theory perspectives like Freud's and Erikson's.

- Using examples, differentiate between Watson's classical conditioning, Skinner's operant conditioning, and Bandura's observational learning with regard to what learning involves and what can be learned.

- Evaluate the strengths and weaknesses of learning theories in general and discuss how Bandura overcame some of the weaknesses of earlier learning theories.

Give me a dozen healthy infants, well formed, and my own specified world to bring them up in, and I'll guarantee to take any one at random and train him to become any type of specialist I might select—doctor, lawyer, artist, merchant, chief, and yes, even beggar-man and thief, regardless of his talents, penchants, tendencies, abilities, vocations, and race of his ancestors. (Watson, 1925, p. 82)

This bold statement—that nurture is everything and that nature, or genetic endowment, counts for nothing—was made by John B. Watson, a pioneer of learning theory perspectives on human development. Watson and other early learning theorists believed that children have no inborn tendencies; how they turn out depends entirely on the environment in which they grow up and the ways in which their parents and other people in their lives treat them.

Early learning theorists such as Watson (1878–1958) and B. F. Skinner (1905–1990) emphasized that human behavior changes in direct response to environmental stimuli. Later learning theorists such as Albert Bandura (born in 1925) grant humans a more active and cognitive role in their own development but still believe that their development can take very different directions depending on their learning experiences. All these learning theorists have provided us with important and practical tools for understanding how human behavior changes through learning and how learning principles can be applied to optimize development. We will lay out the basics of learning theory here and illustrate its significance throughout this book.

Watson: Classical Conditioning

Watson's (1913) behaviorism rested on his belief that conclusions about human development and functioning should be based on observations of overt behavior rather than on speculations about unobservable cognitive and emotional processes. Watson rejected psychoanalytic theory and demonstrated that some of Freud's fascinating discoveries about human behavior could be explained as learned associations between stimuli and responses (Rilling, 2000).

In his most famous study, Watson and colleague Rosalie Raynor (1920) set out to demonstrate that fears can be learned—that fears are not necessarily inborn, as was commonly thought. They used the principles of classical conditioning, a simple form of learning in which a stimulus that initially had no effect on the individual comes to elicit a response through its association with a stimulus that already elicits the response. The Russian physiologist Ivan Pavlov first discovered classical conditioning quite accidentally while studying the digestive systems of dogs. In a famous experiment, Pavlov demonstrated how dogs, who have an innate (unlearned) tendency to salivate at the sight of food, could learn to salivate at the sound of a tone if, during a training period, the tone was sounded each time a dog was given meat powder.

In their demonstration of classical conditioning, Watson and Raynor presented a gentle white rat to a now-famous infant named Albert, who showed no fear of it. However, every time the rat was presented, Watson would slip behind Albert and bang a steel rod with a hammer. Babies are naturally scared by loud noises and, through conditioning—through the pairing of the white rat and the loud noise—Albert learned to whimper and cry in response to the white rat alone. Through learning, an initially neutral stimulus, the white rat, had become a stimulus for fear. This conditioned or learned fear response generalized to other furry items such as a rabbit and a Santa Claus mask. By today's standards, Watson's experiment would be viewed as unethical. However, he had made his point: *emotional responses can be learned*. Fortunately, fears learned through classical conditioning can be unlearned if the feared stimulus is paired with a stimulus for happy emotions (Jones, 1924).

Many emotional associations and attitudes, both positive and negative, are acquired through classical conditioning. Classical conditioning is undoubtedly involved when infants learn to love their parents, who become associated with the positive sensations of drinking milk, being rocked, and being comforted. And classical conditioning helps explain why adults find that certain songs, scents, or articles of clothing "turn them on." It also explains why so many of us have odd phobias (in the case of one of the authors, an aversion to antiseptic cotton, which arose as a learned association between cotton and having a skinned knee daubed with cotton soaked with iodine, a disinfectant that burns when it hits a fresh wound). When a humor columnist polled his colleagues about their phobias, he found one who, like the author, cannot stand the tearing of cotton balls, another whose arm hair stands up if he touches peach fuzz, and another who feels "daggers shooting up my spine" when someone rubs pieces of Styrofoam together

(Weingarten, 2011, p. 29). If you have your own unusual phobia, perhaps you can trace it to classical conditioning.

According to the learning theory perspective, it is a mistake to assume that children advance through a series of distinct stages guided by biological maturation, as Freud, Erikson, and other stage theorists have argued. Instead, learning theorists view development as nothing more than learning. For them, development is a continuous process of behavior change that is context specific and can differ enormously from person to person. Watson's basic view was further advanced by B. F. Skinner.

Skinner: Operant Conditioning

B. F. Skinner, probably the most famous American psychologist, had a long, distinguished career at Harvard University and a huge impact on approaches to behavior change (Rutherford, 2009). Through his research with animals, Skinner (1953) gained

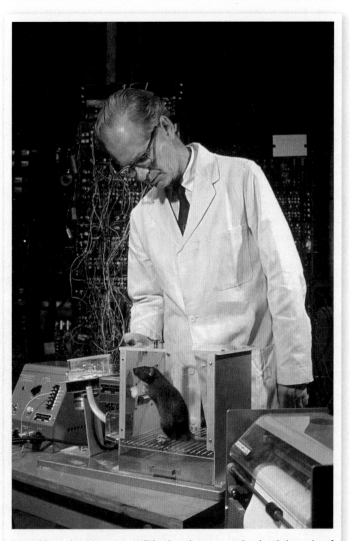

B. F. Skinner's operant conditioning theory emphasized the role of environment in controlling behavior. Here he delivers food pellets (reinforcers) to a rat each time the rat presses a bar in what we now know as a "Skinner box."

understanding of another important form of learning, **operant conditioning**, in which a learner's behavior becomes either more or less probable depending on the consequences it produces. In operant conditioning, a learner first behaves in some way (rather than reacting automatically to a stimulus, as in classical conditioning) and then comes to associate this behavior with the positive or negative consequences that follow it. The basic principle behind operant conditioning makes sense: People tend to repeat behaviors that have desirable consequences and cut down on behaviors that have undesirable consequences. Through operant conditioning, individuals can learn new skills and all kinds of habits, good and bad.

In the language of operant conditioning, *reinforcement* occurs when a consequence strengthens a response, or makes it more likely to occur. If a preschool child cleans his room, receives a hug, and then cleans his room more frequently thereafter, the hug provided **positive reinforcement** for room cleaning. *Positive* here means that something pleasant or desirable has been added to the situation, and *reinforcement* means that the behavior is strengthened. Thus, a positive reinforcer is a desirable event that, when introduced following a behavior, makes that behavior more probable. (Note that the effect on the child's behavior, not the parent's belief about what might be reinforcing, defines what is reinforcing.)

Negative reinforcement (which is *not*, we repeat *not*, a fancy term for punishment, as so many people wrongly believe) occurs when a behavior is strengthened because something unpleasant or undesirable is removed from the situation or is escaped or avoided after the behavior occurs. Consider the annoying sound that goes off in the car until you fasten your seat belt. The idea is that your buckling-up behavior will become a habit through negative reinforcement: Buckling your seat belt allows you to escape the unpleasant sound.

Bad habits can also develop because they allow people to avoid or escape unpleasant consequences. Teenagers may learn to lie to avoid lectures from their parents about their misdeeds or to drink alcohol because it allows them to escape their feelings of social anxiety at parties. In each case, a behavior is strengthened through negative reinforcement—because it results in the removal or elimination of something undesirable like a lecture or social anxiety.

Contrast reinforcement, whether it is positive or negative, with punishment: Whereas reinforcement increases the strength of the behavior that preceded it, *punishment* decreases the strength of the behavior or weakens it. Two forms of punishment parallel the two forms of reinforcement. **Positive punishment** occurs when an unpleasant stimulus is the consequence of a behavior (for example, a child is spanked for misbehaving, or a cashier is criticized for coming up short of cash at the end of the day). **Negative punishment** occurs when a desirable stimulus is removed following the behavior (a misbehaving child loses the privilege of watching TV, or the amount the cashier was short is deducted from her pay). By definition, both positive and negative punishments decrease the likelihood that the punished behavior will be repeated.

The four possible consequences of a behavior are summarized in ■ **Figure 2.2**. In addition, some behavior has no consequence. Behavior that is ignored, or no longer reinforced, tends to become less frequent through the process of **extinction**. Indeed, a good alternative to punishing a child's misbehavior is ignoring it and instead reinforcing desirable behavior that is incompatible with it. Too often, the well-behaved child is ignored and the misbehaving child gets the attention—attention that can backfire because it serves as positive reinforcement for the misbehavior.

Leading learning theorists emphasize the importance of setting up conditions that will prompt desired behaviors and reinforcing that behavior rather than telling kids what not to do all the time, as so many parents do (Kazdin & Rotella, 2013). Their child-rearing advice is, "Catch them being good," and they generally discourage the use of physical punishment. Yet, despite trends suggesting less acceptance of physical punishment today than in the past, most parents of young children in the United States believe that physical punishment of bad behavior is sometimes necessary and spank their children on occasion (Gershoff, 2008; Reeves & Cuddy, 2014). What does research tell us about the effects of physical punishment?

It is generally best to use more positive approaches instead of or before resorting to punishment. Mild physical punishment can be effective in changing behavior if it (1) is administered immediately after the act (not hours later, when the child is being an angel), (2) is administered consistently after each offense, (3) is not overly harsh, (4) is accompanied by explanations, (5) is administered by an otherwise affectionate person, and (6) is used sparingly and combined with efforts to reinforce more acceptable behavior (Benjet & Kazdin, 2003; Domjan, 1993; Gershoff, 2002).

	PLEASANT STIMULUS	UNPLEASANT STIMULUS
ADMINISTERED	**Positive reinforcement, adding a pleasant stimulus** (strengthens the behavior) Dad gives in to the whining and lets Moosie play Nintendo, making whining more likely in the future.	**Positive punishment, adding an unpleasant stimulus** (weakens the behavior) Dad calls Moosie a "baby." Moosie does not like this at all and is less likely to whine in the future.
WITHDRAWN	**Negative punishment, withdrawing a pleasant stimulus** (weakens the behavior) Dad confiscates Moosie's favorite Nintendo game to discourage whining in the future.	**Negative reinforcement, withdrawing an unpleasant stimulus** (strengthens the behavior) Dad stops joking with Lulu. Moosie gets very jealous when Dad pays attention to Lulu, so his whining enables him to bring this unpleasant state of affairs to an end.

■ **Figure 2.2** Possible consequences of whining behavior. Moosie comes into the TV room and sees his father talking and joking with his sister, Lulu, as the two watch a football game. Soon Moosie begins to whine, louder and louder, that he wants them to turn off the television so he can play Nintendo. If you were Moosie's father, how would you react? Above are four possible consequences of Moosie's behavior. Consider both the type of consequence—whether it is a pleasant or aversive stimulus—and whether it is administered ("added to" the situation) or withdrawn (taken away). Notice that reinforcement, by definition, always strengthens whining behavior, or makes it more likely in the future, whereas punishment weakens it.

However, research is clear: Physical punishment, especially if it is harsh, can have a number of undesirable effects. It has been shown repeatedly to be linked to increased aggression, and in some studies it is also associated with mental health problems such as anxiety, depression, and substance use, and with poorer intellectual and moral functioning (Durrant & Ensom, 2012; Gershoff, 2008; Österman, Björkqvist, & Wahlbeck, 2014). For example, Lisa Berlin and her colleagues (2009) studied low-income African-American, Mexican-American, and Euro-American toddlers longitudinally when they were ages 1, 2, and 3. Spanking, but not verbal punishment, at age 1 was associated with more aggressive behavior at age 2 and lower mental development scores at age 3. Moreover, the researchers showed that physical punishment led to later aggressive behavior and intellectual delay even with early behavior and mental development controlled (see also Lee, Altschul, & Gershoff, 2015; Maguire-Jack, Gromoske, & Berger, 2012).

Especially worrisome is evidence that episodes of physical punishment sometimes turn into child abuse (Benjet & Kazdin, 2003; Gershoff, 2002). Especially encouraging is evidence that training in positive parenting based on Skinnerian principles of reinforcement can have long-lasting, positive effects on both child behavior and parent adjustment (Patterson, Forgatch, & DeGarmo, 2010; Reed et al., 2013). Perhaps this is why more and more countries are banning spanking and other forms of physical punishment, not only in schools and child care settings but in homes (Durrant & Ensom, 2012; Reeves & Cuddy, 2014). In Finland, for example, physical punishment, even by parents, was outlawed in 1983. Numbers of adults reporting being slapped or beaten with objects have declined since, as have numbers of children murdered, and adults who had not been punished as children report fewer mental health problems than those who had (Österman et al., 2014).

In sum, Skinner, like Watson, believed that the course of human development depends on the individual's learning experiences. One boy's aggressive behavior may be reinforced over time because he gets his way with other children or because his parents reinforce his "tough" behavior. Another boy may quickly learn that aggression is prohibited and punished. The two may develop in different directions based on their different histories of reinforcement and punishment.

Skinner's operant conditioning principles can help explain many aspects of human development and behavior. And they are still widely applied in educational and psychotherapeutic settings. Indeed, there are now smart-phone apps based on Skinnerian principles to help people lose weight, exercise more, overcome addictions, and otherwise improve their health and well-being (Freedman, 2012). Yet many developmentalists fault Skinner for not examining the role of cognitive processes in learning. Therefore, today's developmental scholars are more attracted to Albert Bandura's cognitive brand of learning theory than to Skinner's operant conditioning approach.

Bandura: Social Cognitive Theory

In his **social cognitive theory** (also called **social learning theory**), Stanford psychologist Albert Bandura (1977, 1986, 1989, 2000, 2006) claims that humans are cognitive beings

Albert Bandura's social cognitive theory highlighted the role of cognition in human learning. He is on the faculty at Stanford University. Behind him is a film shot from his famous "Bobo doll" study, in which children learned aggressive behaviors through observational learning.

Jon Brenneis/Life Magazine/The Life Images Collection/Getty Images

whose active processing of information plays a critical role in their learning, behavior, and development. Bandura argues that human learning is very different from rat learning because humans have far more sophisticated cognitive capabilities. He agrees with Skinner that operant conditioning is an important type of learning, but he notes that people think about the connections between their behavior and its consequences, anticipate the consequences likely to follow from their behavior, and often are more affected by what they believe will happen than by the consequences they actually encounter. Individuals also reinforce or punish themselves with mental pats on the back and self-criticism, and these cognitions also affect behavior. Bandura prefers to call his position social cognitive theory rather than social learning theory for a reason: to distance himself from behavioral learning theories like Watson's and Skinner's and to emphasize that his theory is about the motivating and self-regulating role of cognition in human behavior (Bandura, 1986).

Observational Learning

By highlighting observational learning as the most important mechanism through which human behavior changes, Bandura made his cognitive emphasis clear. **Observational learning** is simply learning by observing the behavior of other people (called *models*). By learning from and imitating other people, children can master computer skills and math problems, as well as how to swear, sing, or smoke. Observational learning is regarded as a more cognitive form of learning than conditioning because learners must pay attention, construct and remember mental representations (images and verbal summaries) of what they saw, retrieve these representations from memory later, and use them to guide behavior.

In his classic "Bobo doll" experiment, Bandura (1965) set out to demonstrate that children could learn a response neither elicited by a conditioned stimulus (as in classical conditioning) nor performed and then strengthened by a reinforcer (as in operant conditioning). He had nursery school children watch a short film in which an adult model attacked an inflatable "Bobo" doll: hitting the doll with a mallet while shouting "Sockeroo," throwing rubber balls at the doll while shouting "Bang, bang, bang," and so on. Some children saw the model praised, others saw the model punished, and still others saw no consequences follow the model's violent attack. After the film ended, children were observed in a playroom with the Bobo doll and many of the props the model had used to work Bobo over.

Humans can learn almost anything through observational learning.

Hello Lovely/Blend Images/Getty Images

What did the children learn? The children who saw the model rewarded and the children in the no-consequences condition imitated more of the model's aggressive acts than did the children who had seen the model punished. But interestingly, when the children who had seen the model punished were asked to reproduce all of the model's behavior they could remember, it turned out that they had learned just as much as the other children about how to treat a Bobo doll. Apparently, then, through a process termed **latent learning** in which learning occurs but is not evident in behavior, children can learn from observation even though they do not imitate (perform) the learned responses. Whether they will perform what they learn depends partly on **vicarious reinforcement** (or punishment), a process in which learners become more or less likely to perform a behavior based on whether consequences experienced by the model they observe are reinforcing or punishing. You are more likely to imitate someone who is rewarded for their behavior than someone who is punished.

Research since Bandura's demonstrations has revealed just how important observational learning is in making us human. Consider the discovery that, across cultures, children display **overimitation**, a tendency to imitate every detail of what they see a model do, even actions that are useless in achieving a goal. In an interesting demonstration of this by Mark Nielsen and Keyan Tomaselli (2010), children in both urban Australia and the Kalahari bush of Africa watched an adult demonstrate how to open a box. Children in both cultures—and both younger and older children within the 2-to-13 age range studied—readily imitated the adult model's action of pushing a stick down on a knob on the front of the box, even though a more direct and effective way to open the box was to simply pull the knob with one's hand. More surprisingly, children also faithfully copied completely irrelevant actions such as waving the stick three times over the box like a magic wand before opening the box. Such overimitation is not as evident among chimpanzees, who tend to imitate only the actions that are actually required to open the box (Horner & Whiten, 2005).

Why do humans overimitate when it makes us look pretty dumb compared to chimps? Possibly because overimitation has proven adaptive for our species, helping us learn "how we do things" in our culture—helping us acquire the many, often arbitrary, skills, rituals, and rules important in our culture, including new ways of solving problems (Nielsen et al., 2014; Nielsen & Tomaselli, 2010; Whiten, 2013). Overimitation also helps us fit in. Thus, after 2-year-olds had learned on their own a perfectly good method of getting rewards by dropping balls in one of three boxes, about half switched to dropping balls in a different box after seeing a peer do so (Haun, Rekers, & Tomasello, 2014). Almost none of the chimpanzees and orangutans tested switched methods. And if you let 3-year-old children learn their own methods of opening a puzzle box to get a reward and then put them all in the same room with the box, the children will soon converge on the same method of opening the box after observing one another for a while (Flynn & Whiten, 2010). Our human tendency to imitate members of our group remains strong later in life and appears to be a critical means of transmitting cultural ways from one person to another and from one generation to the next.

Human Agency

In his later work, Bandura (2000, 2006) moved beyond the study of observational learning to emphasize ways in which people deliberately and actively exercise cognitive control over themselves, their environments, and their lives. From the time they are infants discovering that they can make things happen in their worlds, people form intentions, foresee what will happen, evaluate and regulate their actions as they pursue plans, and reflect on their functioning. These cognitions play a real causal role in influencing their behavior. For example, individuals develop a high or low sense of **self-efficacy**, or belief that they can effectively produce a particular desired outcome. Whether you are trying to lose 10 pounds or get an A on a test, Bandura and colleagues have shown, your success depends greatly on whether you have a sense of self-efficacy concerning your ability to achieve your goal.

Watson and Skinner may have believed that people are passively shaped by parents and other socialization agents, but Bandura does not. Because he views humans as active, cognitive beings, he holds that human development occurs through a continuous reciprocal interaction among the person (the individual's biological and psychological characteristics and cognitions), his or her behavior, and his or her environment—a perspective he calls **reciprocal determinism** (■ Figure 2.3). As Bandura sees it, environment does not rule, as it did in Skinner's thinking: People choose, build, and change their environments;

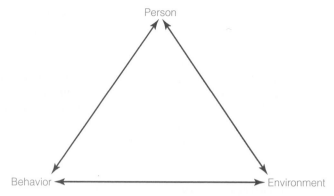

Figure 2.3 Bandura's reciprocal determinism involves mutual influence of the person, the person's behavior, and the environment.

they are not just shaped by them. And people's personal characteristics and behaviors affect the people around them, just as other people are influencing their personal characteristics and future behaviors.

Like Watson and Skinner, however, Bandura doubts that there are universal stages of human development. Indeed, he did research to demonstrate that young children could pass some of Piaget's cognitive development tasks if they were trained to do so (Bandura, 1986). Like other learning theorists, Bandura maintains that development is context specific and can proceed along many paths. It is also continuous, occurring gradually through a lifetime of learning. Bandura acknowledges that children's cognitive capacities mature, so they can remember more about what they have seen and can imitate a greater variety of novel behaviors. Yet he also believes that children of the same age will be dissimilar if their learning experiences have differed considerably.

Obviously there is a fundamental disagreement between stage theorists such as Freud and Erikson and learning theorists such as Watson, Skinner, and Bandura (see ● **Table 2.3** for a summary of the three men's distinct contributions to the learning perspective on development). We imagine what Watson, Skinner, and Bandura would say about sexual risk behavior in **Exploration 2.2**.

● **Table 2.3** A Summary of the Three Major Types of Learning

Learning Theorist	Type of Learning	What It Involves	What Is Learned
John Watson	Classical conditioning	A stimulus comes to elicit a response through its association with an unconditioned stimulus.	Emotional reactions (e.g., pleasant associations, phobias)
B. F. Skinner	Operant conditioning	Learning involves reacting to the consequences of one's behavior (reinforcement and punishment).	Skills; good and bad habits
Albert Bandura	Observational learning	Learning involves watching a model and, through vicarious reinforcement or punishment, the consequences of the model's behavior.	Skills, cognitions, and behaviors, including ones that the learner has not been directly reinforced for displaying

● **EXPLORATION 2.2**

Learning Theorists: Notes on Sexual Risk Behavior

We would all agree that patterns of sexual behavior are learned—and can be learned in a variety of ways:

I, John Watson, would argue that, through classical conditioning, a teenager may learn to associate the very presence of potential sexual partners with the pleasurable sensations associated with sexual activity. These learned emotional reactions are part of the picture in Jared's case.

I, B. F. Skinner, maintain that teenagers probably have unprotected sex because having sex is reinforcing, whereas using contraceptives may not be. Jared's friend Damien may also be reinforcing Jared for joining him in his attempts to hook up with girls. Through simple operant conditioning, then, Jared's sexual risk taking increases.

I, Albert Bandura, think observational learning is at work here. Jared may be imitating the behavior of his older friend Damien, especially if, through what I call vicarious reinforcement, he sees Damien reinforced by other kids when he tells them of his sexual exploits. Consider observational learning

from the media too. Teens who are exposed to lots of sexually explicit material through the media begin having sex earlier in life and engage in more risky sexual behavior than other teens (Bleakley, Hennessy, & Fishbein, 2011; Brown et al., 2006; Chandra et al., 2008; O'Hara et al., 2012). Finally, I want to know more about how Jared perceives the consequences of his behavior, as perceptions of the likelihood of positive or negative consequences are often more important than their actual likelihood.

Strengths and Weaknesses

Pavlov's and Watson's demonstrations of classical conditioning, Skinner's work on operant conditioning, and Bandura's modern social cognitive theory with its highlighting of observational learning have contributed immensely to our understanding of development and continue to be influential. Learning theories are precise and testable. Carefully controlled experiments have shown how people might learn everything from altruism to alcoholism. Moreover, learning principles operate across the life span and can be used to understand behavior at any age. Finally, learning theories have incredibly important applications; principles of classical conditioning, operant conditioning, and observational learning have been the basis for many highly effective techniques for optimizing development and treating developmental problems (Newman & Newman, 2016).

Still, behavioral learning theories, and even Bandura's more recent social cognitive theory, leave something to be desired as theories of human development. First, they do not provide a clear description of the typical course of human development; they have been more focused on describing mechanisms of learning. Second, although they offer a rich account of the mechanisms through which behavior can change, they do not show that learning is responsible for the changes we normally see in developing humans. For instance, Skinnerians have shown that reinforcing 3-month-old infants whenever they happen to make babbling sounds, such as "bababa," causes them to babble more often than infants who are not reinforced (Weisberg, 1963). But does this mean that infants normally begin to babble *because* babbling is reinforced by their caregivers? Probably not. All normal infants, even deaf ones, even infants whose parents do not reinforce their babbling, babble around 4 months of age, probably because that is when they have the neural and muscular control required for babbling.

Third and finally, learning theorists, even Bandura, probably put too little emphasis on biological influences on development, such as genetic endowment and maturational processes. We may well learn to fear snakes, for example. However, probably because snakes were a threat to our ancestors, we have evolved so that we are biologically prepared to be wary of these critters. Thus, we learn to fear snakes far more easily than we learn to fear bunnies or flowers (Ohman & Mineka, 2003). Today's learning theorists appreciate more than Watson and Skinner did that factors such as genetic endowment, personality, and social context affect how humans react to learning experiences (Mineka & Zinbarg, 2006).

Checking Mastery

1. The Foxes try to control their teenage daughter's behavior by (a) giving her an allowance only if she does her weekly chores, (b) setting her weekend curfew earlier if she stayed out later than she was supposed to the weekend before, and (c) allowing her to get out of the distasteful task of cleaning the bathroom if she spends time with her grandmother. What specific consequences, using operant conditioning language, are illustrated by these three parenting tactics, and in each case, what effect do the parents hope to have on their daughter's behavior?

2. What are two main criticisms Albert Bandura might make of earlier behavioral learning theories?

Making Connections

1. Marge, age 78, fell and broke her hip a year ago and has become overly dependent on her daughter for help ever since she left the rehabilitation hospital, even though she can get around quite well now. How might Skinner and Bandura explain her old-age dependency?

2.4
Piaget: Cognitive Developmental Theory

LEARNING OBJECTIVES

- Explain the concept of constructivism and the differences in modes of thinking captured in the four stages in Piaget's cognitive developmental theory.

- Evaluate the strengths and weaknesses of Piaget's theory, noting how the sociocultural and information-processing approaches have attempted to correct for its limitations.

After behavioral learning theories dominated the study of development in the 1950s and 1960s, many developmentalists began to look for a theory that was both more cognitive and more clearly developmental. They found what they wanted in the groundbreaking work of Jean Piaget. No theorist has contributed more to the understanding of children's minds than Piaget (1896–1980), a Swiss scholar who began to study children's intellectual development during the 1920s. This remarkable man developed quickly himself, publishing his first scientific work (a letter to the editor about an albino sparrow) at age 11. Eventually, Piaget blended his interest in zoology and animals' adaptation to their environments with his interest in philosophy. He then devoted his career to the study of how humans acquire knowledge and use it to adapt to their world. His big insight was that children think in a qualitatively different way than adults do. His stage theory describes the development of thought from infancy to adolescence; we will explore it more thoroughly in Chapter 7 but introduce some basic concepts here.

Constructivism

Influenced by his background in biology, Piaget (1950) viewed intelligence as a process that helps an organism adapt to its environment. The infant who grasps a cookie and brings it to her mouth is behaving adaptively, as is the adolescent who solves algebra problems or the mechanic who fixes cars. As humans mature, they acquire ever more complex cognitive structures, or organized patterns of thought or action, that aid them in adapting to their environments.

Piaget insisted that children are not born with innate ideas about reality, as some philosophers have claimed. Nor did he think children are simply filled with information by adults, as learning theorists believe. Piaget's position, called **constructivism**, was that children actively construct their own understandings of the world based on their interactions with it. Thus preschool children may invent ideas that were not taught to them by adults, saying that the sun is alive because it moves across the sky, that children get diseases if they tell lies, or that babies are bought at the baby store and then put in their mommies' tummies. If you've ever marveled over what comes out of the mouths of preschool children, you can appreciate constructivism!

How do children construct more accurate understandings of the world? By being curious and active explorers: watching what is going on around them, seeing what happens when they experiment on the objects they encounter, and recognizing instances in which their current understandings are inadequate to explain events. Children use their current understandings of the world to help them solve problems, but they also revise their understandings to make them better fit reality (Piaget, 1952). Piaget was an interactionist: The interaction between biological maturation (most importantly, a developing brain) and experience (especially discrepancies between the child's current understanding and new experiences) is responsible for the child's progress from one stage of cognitive development to a new, qualitatively different stage.

Stages of Cognitive Development

Piaget proposed four major periods of cognitive development: the sensorimotor stage (birth to age 2), the preoperational stage (ages 2–7), the concrete operations stage (ages 7–11), and the formal

Swiss psychologist Jean Piaget revolutionized the field of human development with his cognitive developmental theory of intellectual growth.

Bettmann/Getty Images

operations stage (ages 11–12 or older). These stages form what Piaget called an *invariant sequence*; that is, all children everywhere progress through the stages in the order they are listed without skipping stages or regressing to earlier stages (Inhelder & Piaget, 1958). The ages given are only average ages; different children progress at different rates. The key features of each stage are summarized in ● **Table 2.4**.

Infants in the **sensorimotor stage** deal with the world directly through their perceptions (senses) and actions (motor skills). They

● **Table 2.4** Jean Piaget's Four Stages of Cognitive Development

Stage (Age Range)	Description
Sensorimotor (birth–2 years)	Infants use their senses and motor actions to explore and understand the world. At the start, they have only innate reflexes, but they develop increasingly "intelligent" actions. By the end, they are capable of symbolic thought using images or words and can therefore plan solutions to problems mentally.
Preoperational (2–7 years)	Preschoolers use their capacity for symbolic thought to develop language, engage in pretend play, and solve problems. But their thinking is not yet logical; they are egocentric (unable to take others' perspectives) and are easily fooled by perceptions, failing conservation problems because they cannot rely on logical operations.
Concrete operations (7–11 years)	School-age children acquire concrete logical operations that allow them to mentally classify, add, and otherwise act on concrete objects in their heads. They can solve practical, real-world problems through a trial-and-error approach but have difficulty with hypothetical and abstract problems.
Formal operations (11–12 years and older)	Adolescents can think about abstract concepts and purely hypothetical possibilities. With age and experience, they can trace the long-range consequences of possible actions, and they can form hypotheses and systematically test them using the scientific method.

Note: Piaget's theory is elaborated upon in Chapter 7.

are unable to use symbols (gestures, images, or words representing real objects and events) to help them solve problems mentally. However, they learn a great deal about the world by exploring it, and they acquire tools for solving problems through their sensory and motor experiences.

The preschooler who has entered the **preoperational stage** of cognitive development has now developed the capacity for symbolic thought but is not yet capable of logical problem solving. The 4- or 5-year-old can use words as symbols to talk about a problem and can mentally imagine doing something before actually doing it. However, according to Piaget, preschool children are egocentric thinkers who have difficulty adopting perspectives other than their own and who may cling to incorrect ideas simply because they want them to be true. Lacking the tools of logical thought, preoperational children must also rely on their perceptions and as a result are easily fooled by appearances. Piaget demonstrated this with his famous conservation of liquid quantity task, in which preschool children believe that water poured before their eyes from a short, wide glass into a tall, narrow glass has become "more" water because it looks like more (see Chapter 7).

School-age children who have advanced to the **concrete operations stage** are more logical than preschoolers. They use a trial-and-error approach to problem solving and do well on problems that involve thinking about concrete objects. These children can perform many important logical actions, or operations, on concrete objects in their heads (hence, the term *concrete operations*, and Piaget's description of the preschool child as preoperational). For example, they can mentally categorize or mentally add and subtract objects, and they can mentally coordinate the height and width of glasses in order to solve conservation problems correctly and appreciate that there is not more water in the tall glass. They can also draw sound, general conclusions based on their concrete or specific observations. However, they have difficulty dealing with abstract and hypothetical problems.

Adolescents who reach the **formal operations stage** are able to think more abstractly and hypothetically than school-age children. They can define *justice* abstractly, in terms of fairness, rather than concretely, in terms of the cop on the corner or the judge in the courtroom. They can formulate hypotheses or predictions in their heads, plan how to systematically test their ideas in experiments, and imagine the results of their experiments. It often takes

Cognitive growth occurs when there is a discrepancy between a child's current understanding of the world and a new experience—here, a butterfly.

Denniro/Shutterstock.com

some years beyond age 11 or 12 before adolescents fully master formal operations and can adopt a thoroughly scientific method of solving problems or think logically about the implications of purely hypothetical ideas. Then they may be able to devise grand theories about what is wrong with their parents or the federal government or analyze the long-term consequences of choosing a particular career or trying drugs.

Obviously, children's cognitive capacities change dramatically between infancy and adolescence as they progress through Piaget's four stages of cognitive development. Infants, young children, school-age children, and adolescents and adults simply do not think the same way. What, then, do you suppose Piaget would have said about sexual risk behavior in adolescence? **Exploration 2.3** sketches his possible thoughts.

Strengths and Weaknesses

Like Freud, Piaget was a true pioneer whose work has left a deep and lasting imprint on thinking about human development. You will see his influence throughout this text, for the mind that

● **EXPLORATION 2.3**

Piaget: Notes on Sexual Risk Behavior

Cognition is an important influence on behavior. I agree with Bandura that we need to understand how Jared is thinking about things, but I would go at this by interviewing him and assessing his stage of cognitive development. Cognitive limitations, failure to anticipate consequences, and lack of

knowledge all influence adolescents' sexual decision making.

Teens who are slow to develop cognitively and are not yet solidly into the stage of formal operations may not be able to plan out how to acquire and make use of condoms and may not think through the long-range consequences of

unprotected sex (Holmbeck et al., 1994). And misconceptions (pun intended!) about sex and contraception are rampant among teens (Aarons & Jenkins, 2002; Cohn & Richters, 2013). In one study of 13- to 15-year-olds, more than 60% did not know that urinating after sex will not prevent pregnancy (Carrera et al., 2000).

"constructs" understanding of the physical world also comes, with age, to understand gender, moral values, emotions, death, and a range of other important aspects of the human experience. Piaget's cognitive developmental perspective dominated the study of child development for about three decades, until the 1980s.

Most developmentalists today continue to accept and to build on Piaget's basic beliefs that children construct their own understandings of the world and that their thinking changes in fundamental and qualitative ways as they get older (see, for example, Carey, Zaitchik, & Bascandziev, 2015). Developmentalists simply assume that children are active in their own development and that development occurs through an interaction of nature and nurture. Piaget's description of intellectual development has been tested and has been largely, although not wholly, supported. Finally, Piaget's ideas have influenced education and child rearing by encouraging teachers and parents to pitch their educational programs to children's levels of understanding and to stimulate children to discover new concepts through their own direct grappling with problems.

Still, Piaget has had his share of criticism (Lourenco & Machado, 1996; Newman & Newman, 2016; and see Chapter 7). For example, critics question whether Piaget's stages really hang together as general modes of thinking that are applied to a variety of types of problems. Research suggests that cognitive development proceeds at different rates for different types of problems. Critics also conclude that Piaget underestimated the cognitive abilities of infants and young children; if tasks are simplified, they are often mastered earlier than Piaget believed (Desrochers, 2008). Piaget is also charged with putting too little emphasis on social and cultural influences on cognitive development. He said little about the role of parents and other more knowledgeable people in nurturing cognitive development and did not appreciate enough that it can go differently in different cultures (see Chapter 7). As a result, developmentalists began to seek theoretical perspectives that allowed more diversity in the pathways that cognitive development could take.

Other Perspectives on Cognitive Development

Two important approaches to cognitive development that challenged some of Piaget's thinking are Vygotsky's *sociocultural perspective* (discussed in Chapter 7) and the *information-processing approach* (discussed in Chapter 8). We will briefly mention them here to elaborate on limitation of Piaget's cognitive developmental theory.

The **sociocultural perspective** on cognitive development offered by a contemporary of Piaget, Russian psychologist Lev Vygotsky (1896–1934), has become quite influential in recent years.

Disagreeing with Piaget's notion of universal stages of cognitive development, Vygotsky maintained that cognitive development is shaped by the sociocultural context in which it occurs and grows out of children's interactions with members of their culture (Vygotsky, 1962, 1978). Each culture provides its members with certain tools of thought—most notably a language, but also tools such as pencils, art media, mathematical systems, and computers. The ways in which people in a particular culture approach and solve problems are passed from generation to generation through oral and written communication. Hence culture, especially as it is embodied in language, shapes thought. As a result, cognitive development is not the same universally. Whereas Piaget tended to see children as independent explorers, Vygotsky saw them as social beings who develop their minds through their interactions with more knowledgeable members of their culture.

Other challenges to Piaget came from scholars who saw a need to look more closely than Piaget did at the processes involved in thinking and factors affecting those processes. Factors like failing to notice or pay attention to key aspects of the problem or being unable, because of working memory limitations, to keep in mind two dimensions at once (like the height *and* width of a glass) can help explain why young children fail Piagetian problems like conservation tasks. The **information-processing approach** to cognitive development, which became the dominant perspective starting in the 1980s, likens the human mind to a computer with hardware and software and examines the fundamental mental processes, such as attention, memory, decision making, and the like, involved in performing cognitive tasks. Development involves changes in the capacity and speed of the information-processing machine we call the brain, in the strategies used to process information, and in the information stored in memory.

This Oglala Lakota girl in South Dakota is learning a traditional skill of her Native American culture with the help of an adult mentor. As Vygotsky emphasized, development is shaped by the cultural environment in which it occurs.

AARON HUEY/National Geographic Creative

1. Distinguish between concrete operational thinking and formal operational thinking in terms of what is operated upon mentally, using specific examples if you can.

2. What one major criticism would advocates of (a) the sociocultural perspective on cognitive development and (b) the information-processing approach to cognition make of Piaget's cognitive developmental theory?

1. Although we will look at the implications of Piaget's theory for education more closely in Chapter 7, based on what you know so far, what recommendations might Piaget make to teachers of (a) 4-year-olds, (b) 9-year-olds, and (c) 14-year-olds to help them recognize the strengths and limitations of children of these ages?

2.5
Systems Theories

LEARNING OBJECTIVES

- Explain how systems theorists such as Urie Bronfenbrenner have changed the way developmentalists think about the roles of biological and environmental forces in development.

- Define and give an example of each of the four main environmental systems in Bronfenbrenner's bioecological theory.

- Explain what the PPCT model says are the four ingredients of good research on human development.

- Evaluate the strengths and weaknesses of Bronfenbrenner's theory.

Systems theories of development, sometimes called contextual theories, claim that changes over the life span arise from ongoing transactions in which a changing organism and a changing environment affect one another (see, for example, Lerner, 2006; Newman & Newman, 2016; Overton & Molenaar, 2015). The individual and the physical and social contexts with which he interacts are inseparable parts of a larger system in which everything affects everything else. Development can take a variety of paths, and some surprising turns, depending on the complex interplay of multiple influences. Nature and nurture cannot be separated easily because they are part of a dynamic system, continually influencing one another, "co-acting" to produce development.

Bronfenbrenner's Bioecological Model

To help you think about a changing person in a changing environment, consider an influential conceptual model formulated by Russian-born American psychologist Urie Bronfenbrenner (1917–2005). Bronfenbrenner became disturbed that many early developmental scientists were studying human development out of context, expecting it to be universal and failing to appreciate how much it could vary from culture to culture, from neighborhood to neighborhood, and from home to home. He charged that developmental psychology had become the study of ". . . the strange behavior of children in strange situations with strange adults for the briefest possible periods of time" (Bronfenbrenner, 1977, p. 519) and called for more research in natural settings. Bronfenbrenner formulated an ecological model to describe how the environment is organized and how it affects development. He later renamed his framework a **bioecological model** of development to get the "person" back into the picture and to convey how it is really

the transactions between person and environment that produce development (Bronfenbrenner, 1979, 1989; Bronfenbrenner & Morris, 2006; Rosa & Tudge, 2013; Wachs, 2015).

In Bronfenbrenner's view, the developing person, with his or her genetic makeup and biological and psychological characteristics, is embedded in a series of environmental systems. These nested systems interact with one another and with the individual over time to influence development. There are many bidirectional or reciprocal influences at work. The four environmental systems that influence and are influenced by the developing person are shown in ■ **Figure 2.4**.

1. A **microsystem** is an immediate physical and social environment in which the person interacts face-to-face with other people and influences and is affected by them. The

Urie Bronfenbrenner sought to understand how a person and the environmental systems in which the person is embedded interact over time to produce development.

AP Images

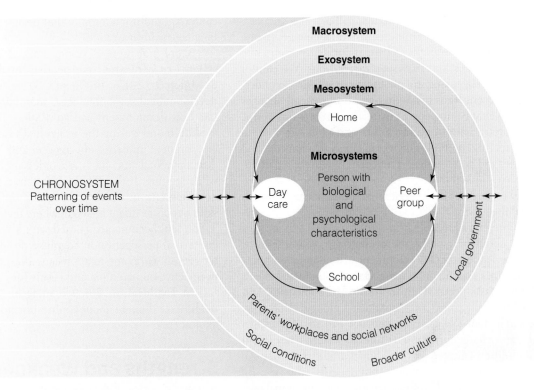

Macrosystem

Exosystem

Mesosystem

Home

Microsystems

Person with biological and psychological characteristics

Day care

Peer group

School

CHRONOSYSTEM
Patterning of events over time

Local government

Parents' workplaces and social networks

Social conditions

Broader culture

■ **Figure 2.4** Urie Bronfenbrenner's bioecological model of development pictures environment as a series of nested structures in which the person is embedded. A microsystem is an immediate environment, such as the family, in which the person interacts. The mesosystem is connections among microsystems, the exosystem is settings that affect but do not contain the individual, and the macrosystem is the broader cultural context of development. The chronosystem is the patterning over time of historical and life events taking place in these systems. All the systems influence and are influenced by the developing person. Source: Adapted from Kopp & Krakow (1982)

primary microsystem for a firstborn infant is likely to be the family—perhaps infant, mother, and father, all reciprocally influencing one another. The developing child may also experience other microsystems, such as a day care center or peer group. We have much evidence that the family environment is an important influence on child development and have also come to appreciate the importance of other microsystems such as peer groups, schools, workplaces, and the like.

2. The **mesosystem** consists of the interrelationships between two or more microsystems. For example, teenagers from Mexican, Chinese, and European American backgrounds who experience stressful events such as arguments in the family, one microsystem, show increased problems of poor attendance and difficulty learning at school, a second microsystem (Flook & Fuligni, 2008). Similarly, problems at school can spill over to the family if adolescents take their bad moods home with them. For any developing person, what happens in one microsystem can have implications, good or bad, for what happens in another microsystem—and for development.

3. The **exosystem** involves social settings that individuals do not experience directly but that can still influence their development. For example, children can be affected by their parents' experiences of stress at work, by how strong their parents' social support network is, or by what kind of neighborhood

they live in. They can also be affected by a decision by the local school board to eliminate health education from the curriculum or a decision by the police department to enforce underage drinking laws more aggressively.

4. The **macrosystem** is the larger cultural or societal context in which the microsystem, mesosystem, and exosystem are embedded. It includes a society's cultural values, laws, political and economic systems, and institutions. To illustrate, although the United States has a high standard of living, it is not a very family-friendly cultural environment in many ways, as Bronfenbrenner himself often lamented (Bronfenbrenner & Morris, 2006). For example, modern nations typically offer paid leave from work to new parents, whereas the United States is among only three countries in the world out of 185 countries reporting that do not; the others are Oman and Papua New Guinea (International Labor Organization, 2014). Policies regarding paid family leave to care for sick children or ailing parents, affordable child care, and flexible work hours are also far behind those of other countries and have negative implications for American families and their children (Schulte, 2014).

In addition to the microsystem, mesosystem, exosystem, and macrosystem levels, Bronfenbrenner introduced the concept of the **chronosystem** ("chrono" means time) to capture the idea that people and their environments and the relations between the two change over time and unfold in particular patterns or sequences. This time dimension captures minute-by-minute changes (while learning a new skill, for example), changes during a person's life, and historical changes that may span generations. We cannot study development by taking still photos; we need video to understand how one event leads to another and how societal changes intertwine with changes in people's lives. Thus an economic crisis may precipitate a chain of events: a husband's job loss, marital conflict, divorce, and multiple changes in family relationships and children's lives and development. Each of us functions in particular microsystems linked through the mesosystem and embedded in the larger contexts of the exosystem and the macrosystem, all in continual flux.

Bronfenbrenner's bioecological model suggests that answers to questions about how child abuse, marriage, retirement, or other life experiences affect development will often be complex because outcomes depend on so many factors. Contextual effects on development can occur at any of the levels. To illustrate, Ann Crouter and her colleagues (2007) conducted a longitudinal study of changes in gender-role attitudes from age 7 to age 19 during a period of major changes in women's roles in society. They found that most children adopted less traditional attitudes as they got older. However, the attitudes of boys (but not girls) who grew up with traditional parents and brothers became more traditional over the years. In other words, both the child's personal characteristics (here, the child's gender) and the child's social context (parent and sibling characteristics) made for differences in developmental paths.

As Bronfenbrenner continued to think about environmental influences, he became disenchanted with contextual studies that merely compared the development of children who lived at different "social addresses"—in different cultures, in low versus high SES neighborhoods, in different ethnic or racial groups, and so on (Bronfenbrenner, 1979). He wanted to know what was going on at these social addresses. He began to call for the study of what he called **proximal processes**: recurring, reciprocal interactions between the individual and other people, objects, or symbols that move development forward toward more effective functioning (Bronfenbrenner & Ceci, 1994). A proximal process in the family microsystem might be reading bedtime stories together, an activity that is likely to become more complex as the child gets older and helps the child master language skills. Playing with other children as a preschool child or interacting with peers as an adolescent are other examples of proximal processes that happen often, become more complex over time, and build social competence.

According to Bronfenbrenner and Morris (2006), researchers who want to understand development need to do research guided by a **PPCT model**, in which, rather than simply comparing children at different social addresses, they examine development as a function of four factors: *process, person, context, and time*. Thus a researcher interested in parent influences on the development of language skills might examine how parents converse with their children in everyday life (*process*), compare this important proximal process for hearing impaired and hearing children (a *person* factor), examine whether conversations differ for families in the United States and families in China (different

contexts), and use a longitudinal design to examine changes in language skills over *time*.

More and more developmental scientists are adopting a systems or contextual perspective on development (Overton & Molenaar, 2015). In Chapter 3, you will learn that modern developmental psychobiologists maintain that genes do not dictate how development will go. Rather, both over the course of evolution and during the individual's development, genes and environment influence one another and "co-act" to make certain developmental outcomes more or less probable. In Chapter 5, you will encounter Esther Thelen's dynamic systems theory of motor development, in which a process of self-organization of motor skills occurs as infant try to get where they want to go. In Chapter 7, you will become acquainted with Vygotsky's sociocultural or contextual perspective on cognitive development, and in Chapter 15 you will come to appreciate the value of a family systems perspective on parenting and family life.

In **Exploration 2.4**, we imagine what Bronfenbrenner might have thought about contributors to sexual risk behavior in adolescence.

Strengths and Weaknesses

Systems theories of development are complex, but that is one of their great strengths: They capture the complexity of life-span human development. We can applaud Bronfenbrenner and like-minded theorists for conceptualizing development as the product of many biological and environmental forces interacting within a complex system and for challenging us to look closely at ongoing transactions, including proximal processes, involving person and environment (Newman & Newman, 2016).

Yet systems theories can be faulted for not yet providing a clear picture of the course of human development and for being only partially formulated and tested at this point (Newman & Newman, 2016). Indeed, an even more serious criticism can be made: Systems perspectives may never provide a coherent picture of development. Why? If we take seriously the idea that development can take any number of paths depending on a range of interacting influences both within and outside the person, how can we ever state generalizations about development that will hold up for most people? If change over a lifetime depends on the ongoing transactions between a unique person and a unique environment, does each life require its own theory? The problem is this: "For the contextual or systems theorist, often the only generalization that holds is, 'It depends'" (Goldhaber, 2000, p. 33).

Human development may be more predictable than Bronfenbrenner's bioecological model implies, though. When children with typical human biological endowments grow up in typical human environments, they may change in similar directions at similar ages, much as stage theorists like Piaget and Erikson maintain (Hoare, 2009; Lerner & Kauffman, 1985). Perhaps it is still possible to see humans as moving in orderly and similar directions in many aspects of their development while also appreciating the tremendous diversity of human development and the many contextual influences on it (Goldhaber, 2012).

Bronfenbrenner: Notes on Sexual Risk Behavior

I, Urie Bronfenbrenner, would look for multiple, interacting causes of adolescent sexual risk behavior, analyzing the ongoing interactions between developing adolescents and the environmental systems in which they are developing.

Although I'm best known for describing the ecology of human development, I also look at biological and psychological characteristics of the person who interacts with the environment. We know, for example, that puberty and the hormonal changes associated with it activate certain genes. Among them are genes that contribute to some teens having stronger sensation-seeking tendencies than others; like Jared, they seek new and exciting experiences (Harden & Mann, 2015). Sensation seeking, in turn, contributes to a number of adolescent problem behaviors, including sexual risk behavior (Harden & Mann, 2015; Voisin et al., 2013).

I would definitely assess Jared's environment. I would analyze important adolescent microsystems such as the family, peer group, and school and the processes that go on in them. Stressful relationships with parents, involvement with peers who are having sex, and lack of connectedness to school can all increase the likelihood of risky sexual behavior (Henrich et al., 2006; James et al., 2012; Lansford et al., 2010; Pilgrim & Blum, 2012).

I would suspect influences of key microsystems on one another—that is, the mesosystem—may be important. For example, Jared may be coping with tensions with his parents by becoming more dependent on his older friend Damien; in turn, that friendship may be aggravating problems in Jared's relationship with his parents.

I would consider the exosystem—for example, the possibility that Jared comes from a disadvantaged neighborhood in which early sex and sex with multiple partners are common (Carlson et al., 2014), or the possibility that a shortage of job training programs for youth and jobs in the area could be contributing to a sense that it is pointless to postpone a sex life in order to pursue an education (Cowan, 2011).

I would also wonder whether the broader cultural environment—the macrosystem—is one that views teenage sexual behavior a normal developmental milestone or a social problem. In some cultures of the world, and in some low-SES subcultures in the United States, early sexual initiation and parenthood are viewed as adaptive (Davies et al., 2003). The fact is that some teens view having sex at an early age as an important step in becoming a "man" or becoming a parent as a desired goal (Abma et al., 2010; Pilgrim & Blum, 2012).

Mainly, I believe that there is not one cause of teenage sexual risk behavior; there is a whole system of interacting causes. Moreover, there are changes in these interactions between person and environment over time (in the chronosystem).

● Checking Mastery

1. Describe how being given a big raise at work might affect a mother's parenting and which of Bronfenbrenner's systems would be involved if it did.

2. Describe the relationship between nature and nurture in Bronfenbrenner's bioecological model.

● Making Connections

1. Applying Bronfenbrenner's bioecological model to yourself, give an example of how each of Bronfenbrenner's four environmental systems may have affected you and your development within the past year.

2. How might Bronfenbrenner explain the high prevalence of binge drinking on college campuses today? (Give examples of how each of his four different environmental systems might contribute.)

2.6
Theories in Perspective

LEARNING OBJECTIVES
- Compare and contrast the major theories in this chapter in terms of their stands on the four major issues in human development.

Just as developmental scientists need theories such as the ones we have surveyed in this chapter to guide their work, every parent, teacher, human services professional, and observer of humans is guided by some set of basic assumptions about how humans develop and why they develop as they do. We hope that you will think about your own assumptions about human development by comparing the answers you gave to the questions in **Engagement 2.1** at the start of the chapter with the summary information in ● **Table 2.5** and seeing which theorists' views are most compatible with your own.

Theories of human development can be grouped into categories based on the broad assumptions they make (P. H. Miller, 2016; Pepper, 1942; Reese & Overton, 1970). Stage theorists such as Freud, Erikson, and Piaget form one broad group. They believe that development is guided in certain universal directions by biological-maturational forces, assuming the child also experiences a reasonably nurturing environment. Humans everywhere progress through distinct or discontinuous stages that are universal and lead to the same final state of maturity.

● **Table 2.5** Compare Yourself with the Theorists

In **Engagement 2.1**, you were asked to indicate your position on basic issues in human development by answering four questions. If you transcribe your answers (a, b, c, d, or e) in the appropriate boxes at the bottom of the table below, you can compare your stands with those of the major theorists described in this chapter—and review the theories. With whom do you seem to agree the most?

Theory:Theorist	Message	Nature–Nurture	Activity–Passivity	Continuity–Discontinuity	Universality–Context Specificity
Psychoanalytic Theory: Freud's Psychosexual Theory	Biologically based sexual instincts motivate behavior and steer development through five psychosexual stages, oral to genital.	b. More nature (biology drives development; early experience in the family influences it, too)	b. Passive (humans are influenced by forces beyond their control)	a. Discontinuous (stagelike)	a. Universal
Psychoanalytic Theory: Erikson's Psychosocial Theory	Humans progress through eight psychosocial conflicts, from trust vs. mistrust to integrity vs. despair.	c. Interactionist; nature and nurture equally	a. Active	a. Discontinuous (stagelike)	a. Universal (although stages may be expressed differently in different cultures)
Learning Theory: Skinner's Behavioral Theory	Development is the product of learning from the consequences of one's behavior through operant conditioning.	e. Mostly nurture	b. Passive (humans are shaped by environment)	c. Continuous (habits gradually increase or decrease in strength)	b. Context specific (direction of development depends on experiences)
Learning Theory: Bandura's Social Cognitive Theory	Development is the product of cognition, as illustrated by observational learning and human agency.	d. More nurture	a. Active (humans influence their environments)	c. Continuous	b. Context specific
Cognitive Developmental Theory: Piaget's Constructivism	Development proceeds through four stages of cognitive development, from sensorimotor to formal operations.	c. Interactionist (maturation interacting with experience guides all through the same stages)	a. Active	a. Discontinuous (stagelike)	a. Universal
Systems Theories: Bronfenbrenner's Bioecological Model	Development takes many directions depending on transactions between a changing person and a changing environment.	c. Nature and nurture co-acting, influencing one another	a. Active	b. Both continuous and discontinuous	b. Context specific
Your Answers: (From Engagement 2.1)	Question 1:	Question 2:	Question 3:	Question 4:	

By contrast, learning theorists such as Watson, Skinner, and Bandura emphasize the role of environment more than the role of biological forces in development. Children cannot be expected to develop in healthy directions (or at least will never be Harvard material) unless they are exposed to particular learning experiences and shaped in certain directions.

Finally, systems theorists such as Bronfenbrenner view biology and environment as inseparable components of a larger system. Children contribute actively to the developmental process (as stage theorists such as Piaget maintain), but the environment is also an active participant in the developmental drama (as learning theorists maintain). The potential exists for both qualitative (stagelike) change and quantitative change. Development can proceed along many paths depending on the intricate interplay of nature and nurture.

Our understanding of human development has changed, and will continue to change, as one prevailing view gives way to another. From the beginning of the study of human development at the beginning of the 20th century through the heyday of Freud's psychoanalytic theory, a stage theory perspective with an emphasis on biological forces prevailed (Parke et al., 1994). In the 1950s and 1960s, learning theories came to the fore, and attention shifted from biology toward environment. Then, with the rising influence of cognitive psychology and Piaget's theory of cognitive development in the late 1960s and 1970s, a stage theory emphasizing an *interaction* of nature and nurture gained prominence. Finally, in the 1980s and 1990s, we gained a fuller appreciation of how multiple biological and environmental forces influence one another.

Where are we today? The broad perspective on key developmental issues taken by systems theorists such as Bronfenbrenner is the perspective that most 21st-century developmentalists have adopted. The field has moved beyond the black-or-white positions taken by many of its pioneers. We now appreciate that human development is always the product of ongoing transactions between nature and nurture; that both humans and their environments are active in the developmental process; that development is both continuous and discontinuous in form; and that development has both universal aspects and aspects particular to certain cultures, times, and individuals. In short, the assumptions and theories that guide the study of human development have become increasingly complex as the incredible complexity of human development has become more apparent.

As we have emphasized, a main function of theories is to guide research. Thus, Freud stimulated researchers to study inner personality conflicts, Skinner inspired them to analyze how behavior changes when its consequences change, and Piaget inspired them to explore children's modes of thinking. Different theories make different assumptions, stimulate different kinds of research, and yield different kinds of facts about development and explanations of them, as you will see throughout this book. Theorists who view the world through different lenses not only study different things in different ways but are likely to disagree even when the same "facts" are set before them, because they will interpret those facts differently (Miller, 2016). This is the nature of science.

Theories also guide practice. As you have seen, each theory of human development represents a particular way of defining developmental issues and problems. Now that we have surveyed the major theories and seen how each might explain sexual risk taking in adolescence, how do you think each would go about trying to reduce it? **Application 2.1** offers some ideas and evidence and will serve, too, as a review of the theories. You might think the problem through yourself before you read the box.

You need not choose one favored developmental theory and reject others. Because different theories often highlight different aspects of development, one may be more relevant to a particular issue or to a particular age group than another. Many developmentalists today are theoretical eclectics who rely on many theories, recognizing that no major theory of human development can explain everything but that each has something to contribute to our understanding.

● **APPLICATION 2.1**

Using Developmental Theories to Reduce Sexual Risk Behavior among Teens

Often how you define a problem determines how you attempt to solve it. So how would psychoanalytic, cognitive developmental, learning, and bioecological theorists approach reducing sexual risk behavior in adolescence?

Psychoanalytic Theory

Psychoanalytic theorists tend to locate the causes of problems within the person—in their personality dynamics. They would want to identify teenagers who are at risk because they are experiencing especially difficult psychic conflicts and treat them through psychoanalysis aimed at helping them resolve their conflicts. Freud might focus on anxieties related to developing as a sexual being, Erikson on broader identity issues. Although the psychoanalytic approach might work with teenagers who are indeed psychologically disturbed, most teenagers who become sexually active are not.

Cognitive Developmental Theory

According to Piaget's cognitive developmental perspective, the solution is improved sex education programs—programs that correct teens' many misconceptions, provide them with accurate information and strategies for avoiding unwanted and unprotected sex, and help them think through the long-range consequences of their sexual decisions. For teens who are still primarily in Piaget's concrete operational stage rather than the formal operational stage, this education might need to involve concrete examples and demonstrations.

Carefully designed, comprehensive sex education programs can indeed delay teens from having sex, decrease the number of sexual partners and frequency of sex, and increase contraception use without having unintended negative effects such as increasing sexual activity

(continued)

Using Developmental Theories to Reduce Sexual Risk Behavior among Teens (continued)

(Chin et al., 2012; Franklin & Corcoran, 2000; Kirby & Laris, 2009). In fact, simply completing more years of school is associated with lower levels of sexual risk taking, sexually transmitted infections, and other unintended consequences of sex (De Graaf, Vanwesenbeeck, & Meijer, 2015). However, education alone is often not enough, so we need to consider solutions that locate the causes of teenage pregnancy in the environment rather than in the individual's psychological weaknesses or cognitive limitations.

Learning Theories

Learning theorists believe that changing the environment will change the person. In support of this belief, it appears that one effective approach to preventing the negative consequences of teen sex is to make contraceptives readily available to teens and teach them how to use them (Franklin & Corcoran, 2000). This approach reflects a Skinnerian philosophy of encouraging desired behavior by making it more reinforcing and less punishing. Albert Bandura's social cognitive theory suggests that it would also help to provide teenagers with more role models of responsible sexual behavior and fewer models of risky sexual behavior (Finnerty-Myers, 2011; Unger, Molina, & Teran,

2000). And it would help to change teens' perceptions of the consequences of using condoms in a positive direction (Balassone, 1991).

Bioecological Theory

Systems theorists such as Bronfenbrenner would recommend comprehensive programs that attempt to change *both* the person and the environment—or really, the whole system of interacting influences on development (Arbeit, 2014; Pilgrim & Blum, 2012). Interventions may need to address teenagers' broader needs as sexual and social beings and empower them to take charge of their own development (Allen, Seitz, & Apfel, 2007; Arbeit, 2014). Interventions may also need to alter contextual influences—for example, to change how adolescents and their parents, peers, and partners interact with each other, address problems associated with poverty and family instability, and enable youth in disadvantaged segments of society to perceive opportunities to succeed in life if they focus on

Sex education can combat the many misconceptions children and adolescents have about sex and can even change their behavior—but it is not the only answer.

Colin McConnell/Toronto Star/Getty Images

education and vocational preparation (Cowan, 2011; Jordahl & Lohman, 2009; Tanner et al., 2013).

You can see, then, that the theoretical position one takes has a profound effect on how one attempts to optimize development. In all likelihood, multiple approaches will be needed to address complex problems such teen sexual risk behavior—and to achieve the larger goal of understanding human development.

● Checking Mastery

1. How have stands on the nature–nurture issue changed during the 20th century from (a) Freud to (b) Skinner to (c) Bronfenbrenner?
2. Of the theorists discussed in this chapter, who is the only one with something specific to say about development during adulthood?

● Making Connections

1. You have decided to become an eclectic. What would you identify as the one greatest insight from each of the four major perspectives in this chapter (psychoanalytic, learning, cognitive developmental, and systems theory)—and why?
2. We like to think that there is progress in science. Looking at the theories in this chapter, to what extent do you see progress over the 20th century?

Chapter Summary

2.1 Developmental Theories and the Issues They Raise

- Theories organize and explain the facts of human development and should be internally consistent, falsifiable, and supported by data.
- The four major issues in the study of human development are nature and nurture, activity and passivity, continuity and discontinuity, and universality and context specificity.

2.2 Psychoanalytic Theory

- In Freud's psychoanalytic theory, humans are irrational beings primarily driven by inborn biological instincts of which they are largely unconscious. The personality is partitioned into the id, ego, and superego (which emerge in that order).
- Libido is rechanneled across five psychosexual stages—oral, anal, phallic, latent, and genital. Each stage involves psychic conflicts that can result in fixation at a stage, create the need for defense mechanisms, and have lasting effects on personality.

- Biological needs drive development, but parents affect a child's success in dealing with conflicts and can contribute to emotional problems, especially if they are overly restrictive or punitive.
- Compared with Freud, neo-Freudian Erik Erikson emphasized biological urges less and social influences more; emphasized id less and ego more; held a more optimistic view of human nature; and theorized about the whole life span.
- According to Erikson's psychosocial theory, development proceeds through eight psychosocial stages involving issues of trust, autonomy, initiative, industry, identity, intimacy, generativity, and integrity. Parents, peers, and the larger culture influence how conflicts are resolved.
- Although Freud made huge contributions by calling attention to the unconscious, early experiences in the family, and emotional aspects of development, his theory is not easily falsifiable and many of its specifics lack support. Although Erikson deserves credit for broadening Freud's theory and considering the whole life span, aspects of his theory have also been difficult to test.

2.3 Learning Theories

- Learning theorists maintain that humans change gradually and can develop in many directions depending on environmental influences.
- Behaviorist Watson focused on the role of Pavlov's classical conditioning in the learning of emotional responses, and Skinner highlighted operant conditioning and the roles of reinforcement and punishment.
- Bandura's social cognitive theory emphasizes the importance of cognitive processes in learning, observational learning as the most important type of human learning, and self-efficacy; reciprocal determinism among person, behavior, and environment shapes development.
- Learning theories are well supported and applicable across the life span, but they do not necessarily explain normal developmental changes and they underemphasize biological influences on development.

2.4 Piaget: Cognitive Developmental Theory

- Piaget's cognitive developmental perspective holds that humans adapt to and create new understandings of the world through their active interactions with it (constructivism).

- The interaction of biological maturation and experience causes children to progress through four universal, invariant, and qualitatively different stages of thinking: sensorimotor, preoperational, concrete operational, and formal operational.
- Despite Piaget's immense influence, critics think his concept of broad stages is flawed, that he underestimated young children, and that he put too little emphasis on social and cultural influences on development (according to Vygotsky's sociocultural perspective) and on cognitive processes such as attention and memory (according to the information-processing approach).

2.5 Systems Theories

- Systems and contextual theories view development as the product of ongoing transactions and mutual influence between the individual and the environment.
- Bronfenbrenner's bioecological model portrays person and environment (at the microsystem, mesosystem, exosystem, and macrosystem levels) as mutually influencing each other over time (chronosystem).
- Bronfenbrenner called attention to development-producing proximal processes and asked developmental scientists to study process, person, context, and time in his PPCT model.
- Systems theories are incomplete, however, and do not provide a coherent picture of human development.

2.6 Theories in Perspective

- During the 20th century, stage theories such as Freud's emphasizing biological forces gave way to learning theories emphasizing environmental influences and then to Piaget's cognitive developmental theory and an emphasis on the interaction of nature and nurture.
- Today's developmentalists prefer the perspective of complex systems theories, such as Bronfenbrenner's bioecological theory, in which developmental outcomes are more or less probable depending on the ongoing transactions between person and the environment.
- Theories influence both research and practice, and many developmentalists are theoretical eclectics.

Key Terms

activity–passivity issue **34**
continuity–discontinuity issue **34**
developmental stage **34**
universality–context-specificity issue **35**
psychoanalytic theory **35**
instinct **36**
unconscious motivation **36**
id **36**
ego **36**
superego **36**
libido **36**
psychosexual stages **36**

fixation **37**
identification **37**
defense mechanisms **38**
repression **38**
regression **38**
psychosocial stages **39**
behaviorism **41**
classical conditioning **41**
operant conditioning **42**
positive reinforcement **42**
negative reinforcement **42**
positive punishment **42**
negative punishment **42**

extinction **42**
social cognitive theory (social learning theory) **43**
observational learning **43**
latent learning **44**
vicarious reinforcement **44**
overimitation **44**
self-efficacy **44**
reciprocal determinism **44**
constructivism **47**
sensorimotor stage **47**
preoperational stage **48**
concrete operations stage **48**

formal operations stage **48**
sociocultural perspective **49**
information-processing approach **49**
systems theories **50**
bioecological model **50**
microsystem **50**
mesosystem **51**
exosystem **51**
macrosystem **51**
chronosystem **51**
proximal processes **52**
PPCT model **52**
eclectic **55**

3

Genes, Environment, and Development

A newspaper story about Jim Lewis and Jim Springer inspired Thomas Bouchard Jr. and his associates at the University of Minnesota to undertake a study in which they reunited identical twins who had been separated soon after birth and asked them to complete a 50–hour battery of tests (Bouchard, 1984; Bouchard et al., 1990; and see Segal, 2012, for a summary of this study's many findings). Together after spending all but the first 4 weeks of their 39 years apart, Jim and Jim discovered that they had both married women named Linda—and then women named Betty. They named their first sons James Alan and James Allan, had dogs named Toy, and liked Miller Lite beer and Salem cigarettes. They liked math and hated spelling and enjoyed the same vacation spot in Florida.

Yet identical twins Jessica and Rachel Wessell, despite having the same genes, growing up together, and being close, are far from identical. One excels in math, the other in English. One has cerebral palsy and is in a wheelchair, possibly because of lack of oxygen to her brain at birth; the other was in the marching band in high school (Helderman, 2003).

Do similarities between identical twins arise mainly because identical twins have identical genes, or is it because people treat individuals who look so alike the same way? How can we explain differences between individuals who have identical genes and grow up in the same environment?

The influence of genes on development must be taken seriously—but so must the influence of environment. How do nature and nurture, heredity and environment, contribute to the shaping of our physical and psychological characteristics? That is the complex puzzle we grapple with in this chapter—and throughout the book. Reading this chapter should increase your appreciation of genetic contributions to development, give you new insights into the importance of environmental influences, and most importantly, reveal the fascinating ways in which nature and nurture

work together to guide development. We invite you to take the short quiz in **Engagement 3.1** to find out whether you come to this chapter with any misconceptions about genetic influence. The correct answers will become clear as you read and are also provided in the box.

We begin with a brief look at evolution and ways in which genes make humans similar. Then we turn to what each individual inherits at conception and how this genetic endowment, in combination with environmental factors, influences the individual's traits. Then the chapter explores research findings on how genes and environment contribute to differences among people in intelligence, personality, and other important characteristics. Finally, we examine key ways in which genes and environment work together—and influence one another—over the life span.

3.1
Evolution and Species Heredity

LEARNING OBJECTIVES

- Summarize the basic argument of Darwin's theory of evolution and the significance of the theory for the study of development.

- Compare and contrast biological evolution and cultural evolution.

Most descriptions of heredity focus on its role in creating differences among people. Some individuals inherit genes for blue eyes, others genes for brown eyes; some inherit genes for blood type O, others genes for blood type A or B. But isn't it remarkable that almost every one of us has two eyes and that we all have blood coursing through our veins? Virtually all of us also develop in similar ways at similar ages—walking and talking around 1 year, maturing sexually from 10 to 14, watching our skin wrinkle in our 40s and 50s. Such similarities in development and aging are a product of species heredity—the genetic endowment that members of a species have in common, including genes that influence development and aging processes. Humans can feel guilty but cannot fly; birds can fly but cannot feel guilty. Each species has a distinct heredity. Species heredity is one reason certain patterns of development and aging are universal.

To understand where we got our species heredity, we must turn to evolutionary theory—to the pathblazing work of Charles Darwin (1809–1882; see Dewsbury, 2009). Darwin's theory of evolution sought to explain how the characteristics of a species change over time and how new species evolve from earlier ones (Darwin, 1859). The theory has been and continues to be controversial, but it is strongly supported by a wealth of evidence

and guides scientific research not only in biology but in psychology and other fields (D. M. Buss, 2012). Darwin's theory makes these main arguments:

1. **There is genetic variation in a species.** Some members of the species have different genes than other members of the species do. If all members of the species were genetically identical, there would be no way for the genetic makeup of the species to change over time in response to changes in the environment.

2. **Some genes aid adaptation more than others do.** Suppose that some genes contribute to strength and intelligence whereas other genes tend to make people weak and dull. People with the genes for strength and intelligence would likely be better able to adapt to their environment—for example, to win fights for survival or to figure out how to obtain food.

3. **Genes that aid their bearers in adapting to their environment will be passed to future generations more frequently than genes that do not.** This is the key principle of natural selection—the idea that nature "selects," or allows to survive and reproduce, those members of a species

Each species has evolved through natural selection to be adapted to its environment. What will happen to polar bears as global warming melts their icebergs?

Stock Connection Blue/Alamy Stock Photo

Genetic Influence: What is Myth, What is Reality?

Answer each of the following questions True or False to identify, before reading this chapter, any misconceptions about genetic influences you may have. Then watch for the correct answers and their explanations throughout the chapter and return to review the answers (printed upside down in this box).

1. The most important reason that identical twins are similar psychologically is that they are treated similarly.
2. The father, not the mother, determines the sex of a child.
3. If a trait is highly influenced by genes, it is generally extremely hard for environmental forces to change it.
4. Most important psychological traits, such as intelligence and extraversion, are influenced by a single pair of genes.

5. Environmental influences such as stress and a poor diet can cause certain genes to become inactive.
6. Homosexuality is genetically influenced, although environment plays an important role in its development too.
7. Prenatal experiences can change the functioning of an individual's genes.
8. The contribution of genes to differences in intelligence typically decreases with age during childhood and adolescence as the effects of learning experiences become more evident.
9. Biological siblings turn out about as similar in personality if they grow up apart as if they grow up in the same home.
10. People's social attitudes and interests are influenced by environment rather than heredity.

Answers: 1. F (twins are treated similarly because they are so similar) 2. T (because sperm have either an X or a Y chromosome) 3. F (for example, genetically influenced IQ scores can be raised by enriched environments) 4. F (most are influenced by multiple genes) 5. T (environment influences gene expression) 6. T (genes and environment both contribute to homosexuality) 7. T (through what are called epigenetic effects, environmental factors such as stress can alter gene expression) 8. F (heritability, a measure of the magnitude of genetic influence on individual differences, often increases from childhood to adulthood as intellectually inclined children seek out more intellectual stimulation than their less intellectually inclined peers) 9. T (shared environment has little effect on personality) 10. T (attitudes and interests are modestly influenced by genetic makeup)

whose genes help them adapt to their environment. Genes that increase the chances of surviving and reproducing will become more common over time because they will be passed to many offspring. Through natural selection, then, the genetic makeup of a species slowly changes—and will continue to change as long as individuals with certain genetic makeups reproduce more frequently than individuals with other genetic makeups. Change can eventually be sufficient to produce a new species. The result is what Darwin marveled at when he conducted observations in the Galapagos Islands: the incredible diversity of species on earth, each well adapted to its environment.

Consider a classic example of evolution in action. H. B. D. Kettlewell (1959) carefully studied moths in England. There is genetic variation among moths that makes some dark and others light. By placing light and dark moths in several sites, Kettlewell found that in rural areas light-colored moths were more likely to survive but that in industrial areas dark moths were more likely to survive. The explanation? In rural areas, light-colored moths blend in well with light-colored trees and are therefore better protected from predators. Natural selection favors them. However, in sooty industrial areas, light-colored moths are easy pickings against the darkened trees, whereas dark moths are well disguised. When industry came to England, the proportion of dark moths increased; as pollution was brought under control in some highly industrialized areas, light-colored moths became more common again (Bishop & Cooke, 1975).

Notice, then, that evolution is not just about genes. It is about the *interaction between genes and environment*. A particular genetic makeup may enhance survival in one kind of environment but prove maladaptive in another. Which genes are advantageous, and therefore which become more common in future generations, depends on what environment a group experiences and what traits that environment demands. Genes that helped our ancestors hunt prey may not be as important in today's world as genes that help people master iPhone apps and Excel spreadsheets.

According to evolutionary theory, then, humans, like any other species, are as they are and develop as they do partly because they have a shared species heredity that evolved through natural selection. But modern evolutionary theorists and developmental scientists understand that we need to get away from "nature versus nurture" thinking. The two forces are completely intertwined over the course of evolution as well as over the course of an individual's development (Lickliter & Honeycutt, 2015).

Modern **evolutionary psychology** is the application of evolutionary theory to understanding why humans think and behave as they do. Evolutionary psychologists ask important questions about how the characteristics and behaviors we observe in humans today may have helped our ancestors adapt to their environments and consequently may have become part of the shared genetic endowment of our species (Bjorklund & Pellegrini, 2002; D. M. Buss, 2012). They ask, for example, whether humans are basically cooperative and helpful or selfish and aggressive, whether we have evolved special brain modules to handle critical cognitive functions such as recognizing faces, whether gender differences have origins in evolution, why humans mate and raise children as they do, and why human children develop as they do.

Not all human similarity is because of genes, however. Through the process of **cultural evolution**, we "inherit" from previous generations a characteristically human environment and tried and true ways of adapting to it, invent better ways of adapting and adjusting to changing conditions, and pass on what we learn to the next generation (Bjorklund & Pellegrini, 2002). We teach others methods of building igloos or building condos, cooking over fires or cooking in microwaves, sending smoke signals or sending text messages. Cultural evolution through learning and socialization of the young works much more quickly than biological evolution, especially in our age of globalization and instant communication. In the end, the most significant legacy of biological evolution may be a powerful and very flexible brain that allows humans to learn from their experiences, to devise better ways of adapting to their environments and even changing their environments to suit them better, and to communicate what they have learned (Bjorklund & Pellegrini, 2002).

● **Checking Mastery**

1. Biological evolution will not necessarily make humans better and better over time, but it *will* make them _____.
2. For natural selection to work and for a species to evolve, what must be true of the genetic makeup of a species?
3. What does evolutionary psychology try to explain?

● **Making Connections**

1. Think of two human behaviors that you believe are so universal that they are probably built into the heredity of our species. Now, why might genes underlying these behaviors have been selected for in the course of evolution?
2. Think about people with a slow metabolism. Can you imagine an environment in which it would be beneficial to have a slow metabolism and another environment in which it could be harmful? What does this tell you about the "adaptiveness" of this human trait?

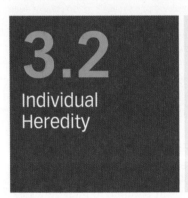

3.2
Individual Heredity

LEARNING OBJECTIVES

- Describe the basics of the genetic code and what we inherit from our parents.

- Distinguish and give examples of the major mechanisms of inheritance (single gene-pair, sex-linked, and polygenic inheritance), mutations, copy number variations (CNVs), and chromosome abnormalities.

- Summarize what we know about the nature, inheritance, diagnosis, and treatment of selected genetic diseases such as sickle-cell disease, Huntington's disease, and phenylketonuria (PKU) and compare the major techniques of prenatal diagnosis of diseases and disorders.

To begin to understand how genes contribute to *differences* among humans, we must start at **conception**—the moment when an egg is fertilized by a sperm—look at the workings of genes, and then consider the mechanisms through which genes can influence traits.

The Genetic Code

A sperm cell and an ovum each contribute 23 chromosomes to the **zygote**, or fertilized egg, to give it 46 chromosomes total, organized into 23 pairs. **Chromosomes** are threadlike bodies in the nucleus of each cell and contain stretches called *genes*, the basic units of heredity (■ **Figure 3.1**). Thus, of each chromosome pair—and of each pair of genes located on corresponding sites on a chromosome pair—one member came from the father and one member came from the mother.

Sperm and ova, unlike other cells, have only 23 chromosomes because they are produced through the specialized process of cell division called **meiosis**. At the start of this process, a reproductive cell in the ovary of a female or the testis of a male that contains the usual 46 chromosomes splits to form two 46-chromosome cells,

and then these two cells each split again to form a total of four cells. In this last step, though, each resulting cell receives only 23 chromosomes. The end product is one egg (and three nonfunctional cells that play no role in reproduction) in a female or four sperm in a male. Each resulting sperm cell or ovum thus has only one member of each of the parent's 23 pairs of chromosomes. Ova are formed prenatally and later ripen one by one during menstrual cycles; sperm production starts in puberty and continues throughout adulthood.

A few hours after a sperm cell penetrates an ovum, the sperm cell begins to disintegrate, releasing its genetic material. The nucleus of the ovum releases its own genetic material, and a new cell nucleus is created from the genetic material provided by mother and father. This new cell, called a zygote and only the size of a pin-head, is the beginning of a human. Conception has occurred.

The single-celled zygote formed at conception becomes a multiple-celled organism through the more usual process of cell division, **mitosis**. During mitosis, a cell (and each of its 46 chromosomes) divides to produce two identical cells, each containing the same 46 chromosomes. As the zygote moves through the fallopian

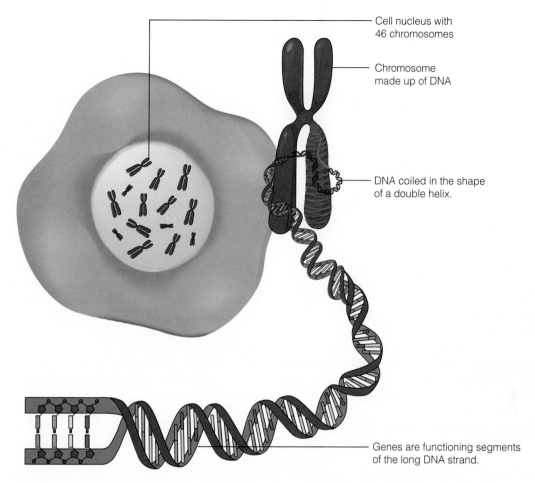

Cell nucleus with
46 chromosomes

Chromosome
made up of DNA

DNA coiled in the shape
of a double helix.

Genes are functioning segments
of the long DNA strand.

Figure 3.1 The chromosomes in each cell consist of strands of DNA made up of sequences of the base chemicals A, T, C, and G. Some sequences are functional units called genes.

Source: National Institute of General Medical Sciences, publications.nigms.nih.gov/insidelifescience/genetics-numbers.html

tube toward its prenatal home in the uterus, it first divides into two cells. The two then become four, the four become eight, and so on, all through mitosis. Except for sperm and ova, all normal human cells contain copies of the 46 chromosomes provided at conception. Mitosis continues throughout life, creating new cells that enable growth and the replacement of old cells that are damaged. (● **Table 3.1** compares mitosis and meiosis.)

Both members of a chromosome pair—one from the mother and one from the father—influence the same characteristics. Each chromosome consists of strands of deoxyribonucleic acid (**DNA**), the double helix molecule whose chemical code is our genetic endowment. DNA is made up of sequences of four chemicals known by the letters A (adenine), C (cytosine), G (guanine), and T (thymine). Some of these sequences are functional units called genes. There are 20,000–25,000 genes (International Human Genome Sequencing Consortium, 2004). Each gene, of which there can be two or more different versions or variants, provides instructions for the production of particular proteins, the building blocks of all bodily tissues and of essential substances such as hormones, neurotransmitters, and enzymes.

The Human Genome Project

Through the federally funded **Human Genome Project**, completed in 2003, researchers mapped the sequence of the chemical units or "letters" that make up the strands of DNA in a full set of 46 human chromosomes (Weiss, 2003; and see www.genome.gov/10001772). The human genome has about 3.1 billion of the chemical constituents A, C, G, and T. However, it turns out that only about 3% of the human genome consists of what has traditionally been defined as genes: stretches of DNA that are transcribed into RNA (ribonucleic acid), which then serves as a template for the production of particular proteins (Brown & Boytchev, 2012; Plomin, 2013). The remaining stretches of DNA were at first called "junk DNA," but it soon became clear that they are not junk at all. These other segments of DNA play critical roles in regulating the activity of genes, helping to choreograph, along with environmental influences, how genes turn on and off in different types of cells at different times.

The Human Genome Project and the massive genome analysis projects that have followed it are yielding astounding new discoveries like this every year. One project, for example, described

	Mitosis	Meiosis in Males	Meiosis in Females
Begins	Conception	Puberty	Early in prenatal period when unripened ova form
Continues	Throughout life span	Throughout adolescence and adulthood	Throughout reproductive years; an ovum ripens each month of the menstrual cycle
Produces	Two identical daughter cells, each with 46 chromosomes like its parent	Four sperm, each with 23 chromosomes	One ovum and three nonfunctional polar bodies, each with 23 chromosomes
Accomplishes	Growth of human from fertilized egg, renewal of the body's cells	Formation of male reproductive cells	Formation of female reproductive cells

the genetic similarities and differences among 270 people from a variety of racial and ethnic groups around the world (Turnpenny & Ellard, 2012). It turns out that about 999 of 1,000 base chemicals are identical in all humans; it is the remaining 1 of 1,000 that makes us each unique. Analysis of DNA samples is also shedding light on evolution. For example, it has revealed that gene variants that allow people to tolerate lactose in milk spread quite rapidly among Europeans as dairy farming became common in Europe, presumably because tolerating milk enhanced survival (McCabe & McCabe, 2008; Voight et al., 2006). Through such studies, researchers are gaining new insights into how the human species evolved and how humans are similar to and different from one another.

Genetic Uniqueness and Relatedness

People are both different from and like their relatives genetically because when a pair of parental chromosomes separates during meiosis, which of the two chromosomes ends up in a particular sperm or ovum is a matter of chance. And because each chromosome pair separates independently of all other pairs and each sperm or ovum contains 23 pairs of chromosomes, a single parent can produce 2^{23}—more than 8 million—genetically different sperm or ova. Any couple could theoretically have at least 64 trillion babies without producing 2 children with identical genes.

The genetic uniqueness of children of the same parents is even greater than this because of a quirk of meiosis known as **crossing over**. When pairs of chromosomes line up before they separate, they cross each other and parts of them are exchanged, much as if you were to exchange a couple of fingers with a friend at the end of a handshake. In short, it is incredibly unlikely that there ever was or ever will be another human exactly like you genetically. The one exception is **identical twins** (or identical triplets, and so on), also called monozygotic twins because they result when one fertilized ovum divides to form two or more genetically identical individuals. This happens in about 1 of every 250 births (Segal, 2005).

How genetically alike are parent and child or brother and sister? You have 50% of your genes in common with your mother and 50% in common with your father because you received half of your chromosomes (and genes) from each parent. But if you have followed our mathematics, you will see that siblings may have many genes in common or few depending on the luck of the draw during meiosis. Because siblings receive half of their genes from the same mother and half from the same father, their average genetic resemblance to each other is 50%, the same genetic resemblance as that of parent and child. The critical difference is that they share half of their genes *on average*; some siblings share more and others fewer. Indeed, we have all known some siblings who are almost like twins and others who could not be more different if they tried.

Fraternal twins (also called dizygotic twins because two eggs are involved) result when two ova are released at approximately the same time and each is fertilized by a different sperm, as happens in about 1 of every 125 births (Plomin, 1990). Fraternal twins are no more alike genetically than brothers and sisters born at different times and can be of different sexes. Fraternal twins tend to run in families and have become more common in recent years because more couples are taking fertility drugs and undergoing in vitro fertilization (Segal, 2005).

Grandparent and grandchild, aunt or uncle and niece or nephew, and half brothers and half sisters share 25% of their genes in common on average. Thus, everyone except an identical twin is genetically unique, but each person also shares genes with kin that contribute to family resemblances.

Determination of Sex

Of the 23 pairs of chromosomes that each individual inherits, 22 are similar in males and females. The chromosomes of the 23rd pair are the sex chromosomes. A male child has one long chromosome called an **X chromosome** and a shorter companion with far fewer genes called a **Y chromosome**. Females have two X chromosomes. The photos on page 65 show male and female chromosomes that have been photographed through a powerful microscope, then arranged in pairs and rephotographed in a pattern called a *karyotype*, which allows their number and form to be studied.

Because a mother's egg has only X chromosomes and a father's sperm cell has either an X chromosome or a Y chromosome (depending on which sex chromosome a sperm receives during meiosis), it is the father who determines a child's gender. If an ovum with its one X chromosome is fertilized by a sperm bearing a Y chromosome, the product is an XY zygote—a genetic male.

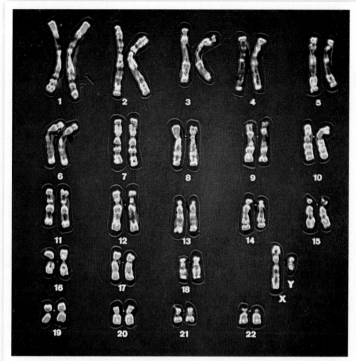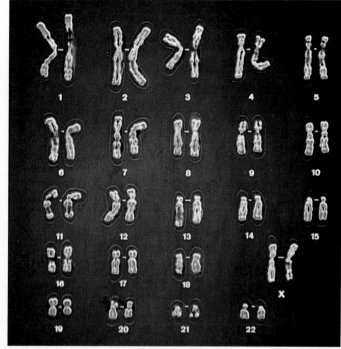

The male karyotype (*left*) shows the 22 pairs of autosomal chromosomes and the 2 sex chromosomes—an elongated X and a shorter Y chromosome. The photographic arrangement of a female's chromosomes (*right*) shows 2 X chromosomes.

CNRI/Science Source

A gene on the Y chromosome then sets in motion the biological events that result in male sexual development (see Chapter 12). If a sperm carrying an X chromosome reaches the ovum first, the result is an XX zygote—a genetic female. Perhaps if these facts had been known in earlier eras, women would not have been criticized, tortured, divorced, and even beheaded for failing to bear male heirs.

So a genetically unique boy or girl has a genome in each of its cells with 20,000–25,000 protein-coding genes and lots of regulatory DNA on 46 chromosomes arranged in 23 pairs. How do these genes, along with environmental factors, influence the individual's characteristics and development? The mystery is far from solved, but knowledge is expanding by leaps and bounds.

From Genotype to Phenotype

One does not have to understand cell biology to appreciate that environmental factors help determine how genetic codes translate into physical and psychological characteristics. For example, some people inherit genes calling for exceptional height, and others inherit genes calling for a short stature. But genotype, the genetic makeup a person inherits, is different from phenotype, the characteristic or trait the person eventually has (for example, a height of 5 feet 8 inches). An individual whose genotype calls for exceptional height may or may not be tall. Indeed, a child who is severely malnourished from the prenatal period onward may have the genetic potential to be a basketball center but may end up too short to make the team. Genes and environment combine to determine how a particular genotype is translated into a particular phenotype—the way a person looks, thinks, feels, or behaves.

As you have seen, genes provide information that is used in the production of particular proteins. For example, genes help set in motion a process that lays a pigment called *melanin* in the iris of the eye. Some people's genes call for much of this pigment, and the result is brown eyes; other people's genes call for less of it, and the result is blue eyes. Genetically coded proteins also guide the formation of cells that become neurons in the brain, influencing potential intelligence and personality. But genes both influence and are influenced by the biochemical environment surrounding them (Gottlieb & Halpern, 2008; Lickliter & Honeycutt, 2015; Meaney, 2010). During embryonic development, a particular cell can become part of an eyeball or part of a kneecap depending on what cells are next to it and what they are doing. Because all of a person's cells have the same genes on the same chromosomes, what makes neurons, blood cells, and other cells of the body different from each other is not what genes they contain but which of those genes are *expressed*.

Gene expression is the activation of particular genes in particular cells of the body at particular times; only if a gene is "turned on" is it influential. Gene expression, then, is what ultimately influences our traits. And gene expression is guided by genetic influences (the action of regulatory DNA) and by environmental influences. As we will see at the end of the chapter (see **Section 3.5**, Epigenetic Effects on Gene Expression), great excitement now surrounds the discovery that gene expression can be altered, starting prenatally but throughout the life span, and sometimes in lasting ways, by environmental factors such as diet, stress, drugs, toxins, early parenting, and more (Moore, 2015; Zhang & Meaney, 2010). You should therefore think of the genetic "code" as sketched in erasable pencil rather than in indelible ink. Genes do not "determine" anything. Rather, genes and environment interact and coact to influence gene expression and, in turn, development and behavior throughout the life span.

Mechanisms of Inheritance

Let us now consider the major mechanisms of inheritance—how parents' genes influence their children's genotypes and phenotypes. There are three main mechanisms of inheritance: single gene-pair inheritance, sex-linked inheritance, and polygenic (or multiple gene) inheritance (Nussbaum, McInnes, & Willard, 2016; Turnpenny & Ellard, 2012).

Single Gene-Pair Inheritance

Through single gene-pair inheritance, each of thousands of human characteristics are influenced by only one pair of genes—one from the mother, one from the father. Although he knew nothing of genes, the 19th-century monk Gregor Mendel contributed greatly to our knowledge of single gene-pair inheritance and earned his place as the father of genetics by cross-breeding different strains of peas and carefully observing the outcomes (Henig, 2000). As an illustration of the principles of Mendelian inheritance, consider the remarkable fact that about three-fourths of us can curl our tongues upward into a tubelike shape, whereas

one-fourth of us cannot. (We have no idea why.) It happens that there is a gene associated with tongue curling; it is a **dominant gene**, meaning that it will be expressed when paired with a **recessive gene**, a weaker gene that can be dominated (like one associated with the absence of tongue-curling ability).

The person who inherits one "tongue-curl" gene (label it *U*) and one "no-curl" gene (call it -) would be able to curl his tongue (that is, would have a tongue-curling phenotype) because the dominant tongue-curl gene overpowers the recessive no-curl gene. Using ■ **Figure 3.2** as a guide, you can calculate the odds that parents with various genotypes for tongue curling will have children who can or cannot curl their tongues. Each of the nine cells of the figure shows the four possible types of children that can result when a father contributes one of his two genes to a sperm and a mother contributes one of her two genes to an ovum and a child is conceived.

If a father with the genotype *UU* (a tongue curler) and a mother with the genotype - - (a non–tongue curler) have children, each child they produce will have one dominant gene for tongue curling and one recessive gene for a lack of tongue curling (genotype *U-*) and each will be a tongue curler because the tongue-curl gene will rule. You can say that this couple has a 100% chance of having a tongue-curling child. Notice that two different genotypes, *UU* and *U-*, both produce the same phenotype: an acrobatic tongue.

A tongue-curling man and a tongue-curling woman can surprise everyone and have a child who lacks this amazing talent.

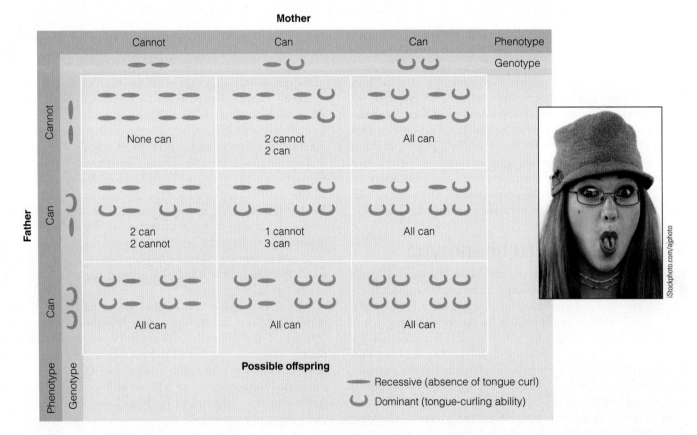

■ **Figure 3.2** Can you curl your tongue as shown? Tongue-curling ability is determined by a dominant gene. If you can curl your tongue, then either your mother or your father can, because one of them must have the dominant gene. All possibilities are shown in the figure; each of the nine boxes shows the gene combinations of the four possible children a particular mother and a particular father can have.

These two parents both must have the *U-* genotype. If the father's recessive gene and the mother's recessive gene happen to unite in the zygote, they will have a non–tongue-curling child (with the genotype - -). The chances are 25%—one out of four—that this couple will have such a child. Of course, the laws of conception are much like the laws of cards. This couple could beat the odds and have a whole family of non–tongue-curling children, or they could have none. Because people who cannot curl their tongues must have the - - genotype, two non–tongue-curling parents will have only non–tongue-curling (- -) children.

● **Table 3.2** lists a few examples of dominant and recessive traits associated with single gene-pair inheritance. In some cases, a dominant gene incompletely dominates a recessive partner gene and the result is a blend of the parents' traits—as when crossing red and white flowers produces pink ones or when dark-skinned and light-skinned parents have a child with light brown skin. In other cases, two genes influence a trait but each is expressed in the product because they codominate, as when crossing red and white flowers produces flowers with red and white streaks. For example, an AB blood type is a mix of A and B blood types. So, Gregor Mendel, despite not knowing about the existence of genes, got the basics of single gene-pair inheritance mostly right.

Sex-Linked Inheritance

In **sex-linked inheritance**, a characteristic is influenced by single genes located on the sex chromosomes rather than on the other 22 pairs of chromosomes. Indeed, you could say *X-linked* rather than *sex-linked* because most of these attributes are associated with genes located on X but not Y chromosomes.

Why do far more males than females display red–green color blindness? The inability to distinguish red from green is caused by a recessive gene that appears only on X chromosomes. Recall that Y chromosomes are shorter than X chromosomes and have fewer genes. If a boy inherits the recessive color-blindness gene on the X chromosome his mother provides to him, there is no color-vision gene on his Y chromosome that could dominate the color-blindness gene. He will be color blind. By contrast, a girl who inherits the gene usually has a normal color-vision gene on her other X chromosome that can dominate the color-blindness gene. She would have to inherit two of the recessive color-blindness genes to be color blind. **Hemophilia**, a deficiency in the blood's ability to clot, is also far more common among males than females because it is a sex-linked disorder associated with a recessive gene on X chromosomes.

Polygenic Inheritance

So far we have considered only the influence of single genes or gene pairs on human traits. Every week, it seems, we read in the newspaper that researchers have identified "the gene" for high blood pressure, happiness, or some other human trait. In fact, most important human characteristics are influenced by **polygenic inheritance**—by multiple pairs of genes, interacting with multiple environmental factors, rather than by a single pair of genes. Examples of polygenic traits include height, weight, intelligence, personality, susceptibility to cancer and depression, and much more.

When a trait like intelligence is influenced by multiple genes, many degrees of it are possible, depending on how many of the genes associated with high levels of the trait individuals

● **Table 3.2** Examples of Traits Influenced by Dominant and Recessive Genes

Dominant Trait	Recessive Trait
Brown eyes	Gray green, hazel, or blue eyes
Dark hair	Blond hair
Nonred hair	Red hair
Curly hair	Straight hair
Normal vision	Nearsightedness
Farsightedness	Normal vision
Broad lips	Thin lips
Double jointed	Normal joints
Pigmented skin	Albinism
Type A blood	Type O blood
Type B blood	Type O blood

Source: Burns & Bottino, 1989; McKusick, 1990

inherit. Most people will get some "high IQ" genes and some "low IQ" genes, so are likely to have pretty average IQs. A few at the extremes will inherit only "low IQ" genes or only "high IQ" genes. The trait will therefore tend to be distributed in the population according to the familiar bell-shaped or normal curve: Many people are near the average of the distribution; fewer are at the extremes. This is in fact the way intelligence and most other measurable human traits are distributed. At this point, we do not know how many gene pairs influence intelligence or other polygenic traits. What we can say is that many, many genes, interacting with many environmental forces, create a range of individual differences in most important human traits (Plomin et al., 2013).

Mutations

So far, we have described the three major mechanisms by which the genes inherited at conception influence traits: single gene-pair, sex-linked, and polygenic inheritance. Occasionally, however, a new gene appears as if out of nowhere; neither parent has it. A **mutation** is a change in the structure or arrangement of one or more genes. Mutations can be either beneficial or harmful, depending on their nature and on the environment in which their bearers live.

Experts believe that the recessive gene for the sex-linked disorder hemophilia was a mutation first introduced into the royal families of Europe by Queen Victoria and then passed on to some of her descendants. New cases of hemophilia, then, can be caused by either sex-linked inheritance or spontaneous mutations. The odds that mutations will occur are increased by environmental hazards such as radiation and toxic industrial waste, but most mutations are just spontaneous errors during cell division (Lewis, 2015). Recently it has been discovered that fathers contribute about four times the number of new mutations as mothers do overall and that the odds of mutations increase steadily as fathers get older because more errors are made during sperm production, or meiosis (Kong et al., 2012). Mutations associated with autism (O'Roak et al., 2012), schizophrenia (Frans et al., 2011), and other disorders become more likely as a father's age increases.

Copy Number Variations

Still another major discovery of the Human Genome Project is the importance of **copy number variations (CNVs)**, instances in which part of the genome is either deleted or duplicated (Gershon & Alliey-Rodriguez, 2013; Lewis, 2015). A CNV is more extensive than a mutation, which is typically just a different version of a particular gene. CNVs can extend over a large stretch of DNA containing multiple genes and they can mean that, instead of having two paired genes, the person may have only one gene (due to a deletion) or three or four copies of the gene (due to a duplication). Like mutations of specific genes, CNVs are errors that can either be inherited from a parent or arise spontaneously.

Increasingly, researchers are discovering that CNVs happen quite often and can significantly increase the risks of a number of polygenic disorders involving the nervous system, among them autism, schizophrenia, bipolar disorder, attention deficit hyperactivity disorder (ADHD), and Alzheimer's disease (Gershon & Alliey-Rodriguez, 2013; Hohmann et al., 2015; Swaminathan et al., 2012). As a result, genetic tests now check for CNVs.

Chromosome Abnormalities

Genetic endowment can also influence human development through **chromosome abnormalities**, in which a child receives too many or too few chromosomes (or abnormal chromosomes) at conception (Gardner, Sutherland, & Shaffer, 2012). Most such abnormalities are caused by errors in chromosome division during meiosis. Through an accident of nature, an ovum or sperm cell may be produced with more or fewer than the usual 23 chromosomes. In most cases, a zygote with the wrong number of chromosomes is spontaneously aborted; chromosome abnormalities are the main cause of pregnancy loss.

The most familiar chromosome abnormality is **Down syndrome**, also known as *trisomy 21* because it is associated with three rather than two 21st chromosomes. Children with Down syndrome have distinctive eyelid folds, short stubby limbs, and thick tongues. Their levels of intellectual functioning vary widely, but most have some degree of *intellectual disability* (formerly called mental retardation and associated with an IQ of below 70). They therefore develop and learn at a slower pace than most children, but they can benefit greatly from early stimulation programs, special education, and

Children with Down syndrome have distinctive eyelid folds, short limbs, and thick tongues.

Peter Casolino/Alamy Stock Photo

vocational training (Hazlett, Hammer, Hooper, & Kamphaus, 2011; Roizen & Patterson, 2003). Witness Lauren Potter, the young woman with Down syndrome who played a cheerleader on the TV program *Glee*, and others of her generation who are working and even attending college (Rochman, 2012). In some parts of the world, over half of children with Down syndrome die in infancy, most often because of heart defects (Christianson, Howson, & Modell, 2006). However, in the United States and other wealthy nations, many people with Down syndrome are now living into middle age and beyond, when many of them show signs of premature aging, including early Alzheimer's disease (Berney, 2009; Zigman, 2013).

Overall, the chances of having a baby with Down syndrome are about 12 births in 10,000 in the United States (Zigman, 2013). What determines who has a child with Down syndrome and who does not? Chance, partly. The errors in meiosis responsible for Down syndrome can occur in any mother—or father. However, the odds increase with a mother's age, especially from about age 35 on, as well as with a father's age (■ **Figure 3.3**). Indeed, couples older than 40 have about six times the risk of having a child with Down syndrome as couples younger than 35 (Fisch et al., 2003).

Most other chromosome abnormalities involve a child's receiving either too many or too few sex chromosomes. Like Down syndrome, these **sex chromosome abnormalities** can be attributed mainly to errors in meiosis, errors that become increasingly likely in older parents and parents whose chromosomes have been damaged by environmental hazards such as radiation (Wodrich, 2006). Examples:

- In Turner syndrome, a female (about 1 in 2,000–3,000) is born with a single X chromosome rather than two (XO). These girls are small and underdeveloped, typically favor traditionally feminine activities, and often have lower-than-average spatial and mathematical abilities (Downey et al., 1991; Powell & Schulte, 2011).
- In Klinefelter syndrome, a male (1 in 500–1,000) is born with one or more extra X chromosomes (XXY). Klinefelter males tend to have long limbs and sometimes big ears and long faces, and, at puberty, they may show feminine characteristics such as enlarged breasts. Most have normal IQs, but many have language learning disabilities (Hazlett, De Alba, & Hooper, 2011; Mandoki et al., 1991).
- In XYY syndrome, a male (as many as 1 in 1,000) is born with an extra Y chromosome (XYY). These males tend to be tall and strong and often have learning disabilities. The common belief that XYY syndrome results in aggression and criminal behavior is not well-supported (Re & Birkhoff, 2015).

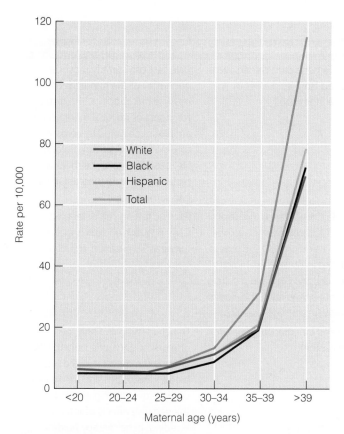

■ Figure 3.3 The rate of Down syndrome births increases steeply as the mother's age increases. (Father's age is also a factor.)

Source: "Down Syndrome Prevalence at Birth"—United States, 1983–1990 (1994, August 26). *Mortality and Morbidity Weekly Reports, 43*, 617–622.

Genetic Diseases and their Diagnosis

Diseases and disorders associated with a single gene or pair of genes, polygene disorders, mutations and copy number variations, and chromosome abnormalities, although rare, can profoundly affect human development. Today's genetic counselors have more information than ever about genetic disorders and can quickly and quite inexpensively collect and analyze DNA samples by swabbing the inside of people's cheeks or drawing small samples of their blood and informing people of what the results mean.

Examples of Genetic Diseases

To illustrate issues in genetic diagnosis and the workings of important genetic disorders, consider sickle-cell disease, Huntington's disease, and PKU. **Sickle-cell disease**, a blood disease, common among African Americans, in which red blood cells take on a sickle shape, become entangled, and distribute less oxygen through the circulatory system than round blood cells do, causing breathing problems and pain (Serjeant, 2010; Smith & Baker, 2011). The gene responsible probably started as a mutation which, because it protected its bearers from malaria, became

more common through natural selection over many generations in Africa, Central America, and other tropical areas. The life expectancy of children with sickle-cell disease used to be around 14 years; they often died early as a result of blood clots, strokes, and heart or kidney failure. Now improved treatment is prolonging lives; average life expectancy is more like 50 years (Hambleton, 2014; National Human Genome Research Institute, 2015).

About 9% of African Americans in the United States have the genotype we will call Ss; they carry one dominant gene (S) that calls for round blood cells and one recessive gene (s) that calls for sickle-shaped blood cells. Such people are **carriers**; although they do not have the disease, they can transmit the gene for it to their children. The child who inherits two recessive sickle-cell genes (ss) will have sickle-cell disease. An Ss father and an Ss mother (two carriers) have a one-in-four, or 25%, chance of having a child with sickle-cell disease (ss). Two carriers also have a two-in-four, or 50%, chance of having a child who will be a carrier like themselves.

A blood test is used to screen all newborns in the United States for sickle-cell disease. Affected children begin a life of treatment with blood transfusions, antibiotics to prevent infections, and more recently a drug called hydroxyurea that prevents the sickling of blood cells. Early interventions can help optimize children's intellectual development (Smith & Baker, 2011). In less developed areas of sub-Saharan Africa and central India, where rates of sickle-cell disease are high, screening of newborns could do much good but is lacking (Serjeant, 2010).

Now consider **Huntington's disease**, a famous (and terrifying) example of a genetic disorder associated with a single dominant gene. This disease typically strikes in middle age—after a person has typically had children—and disrupts the expression of genes in the nervous system, resulting in motor problems, personality changes, and dementia or loss of cognitive abilities (Anderson et al., 2008; Bishop & Waldholz, 1990; Sutton-Brown & Suchowersky, 2003). The child of a parent with the dominant (and fortunately rare) Huntington's gene has a 50%

Sickle-shaped (elongated) and normal (round) blood cells from a carrier of the sickle-cell gene.

● Table 3.3 Some Genetic Disorders

Disease	Description	Genetic Mechanism	Diagnosis and Treatment
Cystic fibrosis	Glandular problem results in mucus buildup in lungs that makes breathing difficult and shortens life; common among Caucasians	Recessive gene pair; carriers were protected from epidemics of diarrhea in Europe	DNA test can identify most carriers, but not all of the hundreds of possible mutations can be tested for; hours of physical therapy and antibiotics delivered by aerosol spray to keep lungs clear can prolong life; experimental gene therapy replacing genes in lung tissue has had some success
Fragile X syndrome	Most common inherited cause of intellectual disability; associated with an X chromosome in which an arm looks ready to break off	Sex-linked inheritance (dominant gene on X chromosome); a copy number variation (CNV) in a gene important in brain development is involved; the CNV and resulting intellectual disability can become worse over family generations	Genetic testing can detect the CNV involved; no cure is available but special education and other treatments can help
Hemophilia	Deficiency in blood's ability to clot; more common in males than in females	Sex-linked inheritance (gene on X chromosome)	Genetic testing can find the disease-causing gene variant; DNA analysis can detect it in the fetus; blood transfusions and medication can improve clotting and reduce the negative effects of internal bleeding; gene therapy holds promise
Huntington's disease	Deterioration of the nervous system in middle age; associated with dementia, jerky movements, personality changes	Dominant gene; a CNV, an abnormal number of repetitions of a DNA sequence, implicated	Genetic test can tell relatives whether they have the gene; preimplantation genetic diagnosis of embryonic cells may be used to ensure a healthy child
Phenylketonuria (PKU)	Lack of enzyme needed to metabolize phenylalanine in milk results in conversion of phenylalanine into an acid that attacks the nervous system and causes intellectual disability	Recessive gene pair	Genetic test can identify carriers; routinely screened for with a blood test at birth; special diet low in phenylalanine prevents brain damage, must be maintained for life
Sickle-cell disease	Blood cells are sickle-shaped rather than round; stick together, make breathing difficult; and cause painful swelling of joints and blood clots; common in African Americans	Recessive gene pair; carriers were protected from malaria in Africa	Blood test can identify carriers; newborns in most states of the U.S. are screened with a blood test; antibiotics, the drug hydroxyurea, and blood transfusions prevent infections and relieve symptoms; gene therapy holds promise
Tay–Sachs disease	Metabolic defect results in accumulation of fat in a child's brain, degeneration of the nervous system, and early death; common in Jewish people from Eastern Europe	Recessive gene pair	Blood test can identify carriers; fetal DNA analysis can determine whether a child is affected; medication may help, but most victims die in childhood

Sources: Goldstein & Reynolds, 2011; Kingston, 2008; Nussbaum, McInnes, & Willard, 2016; Pritchard & Korf, 2008; Turnpenny & Ellard, 2012. Also consult the website of the National Human Genome Research Institute: www.genome.gov/10001204

chance of inheriting the gene and developing Huntington's disease later in life. A genetic test can enable the relatives of Huntington's victims to find out whether or not they inherited the gene, but some prefer to live with uncertainty rather than with the knowledge that they will develop this awful and incurable disease (Bombard, 2009; Sutton-Brown & Suchowersky, 2003).

Finally, a success story. **Phenylketonuria (PKU)** is a metabolic disorder caused by a single pair of recessive genes that results in brain damage and intellectual disability (Waisbren, 2011; Widaman, 2009). About 1 in 50 people in the United States are carriers of the PKU gene (Waisbren, 2011). Two carriers have a one-in-four, or 25%, chance of having a child with PKU. Affected children lack a critical enzyme needed to metabolize phenylalanine, a component of many foods, including milk. As phenylalanine accumulates in the body, it is converted to a harmful acid that attacks the nervous system and causes intellectual disability and hyperactivity.

Today, newborn infants are routinely screened for PKU with a blood test, and affected children are immediately placed on a special (and, unfortunately, distasteful) diet low in phenylalanine. They are advised to stay on the diet, at least to some extent, for the rest of their lives to prevent deterioration of their intellectual functioning (Waisbren, 2011; Widaman, 2009). Sickle-cell disease, Huntington's disease, PKU, and a few other genetic diseases are summarized in ● **Table 3.3** (and see www.genome.gov/10001204 for more).

Prenatal Diagnosis

Individuals who have a disorder in their family history or have been tested and know they carry the gene for one, as well as older parents concerned about mutations, copy number variations, and chromosome abnormalities may wish to use prenatal diagnosis procedures that can detect many genetic abnormalities prenatally. Three widely used techniques—ultrasound, amniocentesis, and chorionic villus sampling—as well as the newer methods of maternal blood sampling and preimplantation genetic diagnosis are described in ● **Application 3.1**.

● **APPLICATION 3.1**

Prenatal Detection of Abnormalities

Pregnant women, especially those over 35 or 40, turn to a variety of medical techniques to tell them in advance whether their babies are likely to be normal (Nussbaum et al., 2016; Turnpenny & Ellard, 2012; Winerman, 2013). How much can they learn? And what are the pros and cons of various prenatal diagnostic techniques?

Ultrasound

The easiest and most commonly used method is **ultrasound**, the use of sound waves to scan the womb and create a visual image of the fetus on a monitor screen. Ultrasound can indicate how many fetuses are in the uterus, their sex, and whether they are alive, and it can detect genetic defects that produce visible physical abnormalities. Ultrasound is widely used even when abnormalities are not suspected because it is considered very safe.

Amniocentesis

To detect chromosome abnormalities such as Down syndrome and to determine, through DNA analysis, whether the genes for a particular single gene-pair disorder or some other genetic variation are present, **amniocentesis** is used. A needle is inserted into the abdomen,

a sample of amniotic fluid is withdrawn, and fetal cells that have been shed are analyzed. A risk of miscarriage exists but it is very low, making the procedure relatively safe and advisable for pregnant women over age 35. Its main disadvantage is that it is not considered safe until the fifteenth week of pregnancy.

Chorionic Villus Sampling

Chorionic villus sampling (CVS) involves inserting a catheter through the mother's vagina and cervix (or, less commonly, through her abdomen) into the membrane called the *chorion* that surrounds the fetus, and then extracting tiny hair cells from the chorion that contain genetic material from the fetus. Sample cells are then analyzed for the same genetic conditions that can be detected using amniocentesis. The difference is that chorionic villus sampling can be performed as early as the tenth week of pregnancy. The risks of CVS are only slightly greater than those of amniocentesis.

Maternal Blood Sampling

Maternal blood sampling has been used for a number of years to test the mother's blood for various chemicals that can indicate

abnormalities in the fetus. However, now it can also be used to obtain loose embryonic DNA that has slipped through the placenta into the mother's blood—DNA that can then be analyzed for chromosome abnormalities and genetic diseases *with no risk at all to the fetus* (Benn & Chapman, 2009; Fan et al., 2012; Winerman, 2013). Methods for detecting Down syndrome with high accuracy at around 9 or 10 weeks after conception are now available (Rubin, 2012; Verweij et al., 2012). Maternal blood sampling of fetal DNA has the tremendous advantages of being noninvasive and usable early in the pregnancy, but it is normally followed up with amniocentesis or CVS to be 100% certain (Winerman, 2013).

Preimplantation Genetic Diagnosis

Finally, parents who know they are at high risk to have a baby with a serious condition can minimize their risk through **preimplantation genetic diagnosis**. This involves fertilizing a mother's eggs with a father's sperm in the laboratory using *in vitro fertilization (IVF) techniques* (see Chapter 4), conducting DNA tests on the first cells that result from mitosis of each fertilized egg, and implanting in the mother's uterus only eggs that do not have

(continued)

Prenatal Detection of Abnormalities (continued)

chromosome abnormalities or genes associated with disorders (Geddes, 2013). Although costly, this option may appeal to couples who would not consider abortion but do not want to have a child with a serious defect.

Pros and Cons

Prenatal diagnostic techniques such as ultrasound, amniocentesis, CVS, maternal blood sampling, and preimplantation genetic diagnosis can provide tremendously important information when there is reason to suspect a problem. They can prevent serious disorders and diseases and open the door to early interventions that can save the lives of babies with problems or set them on a healthier developmental path. DNA sequencing of the genomes of newborns is already being used to help pinpoint what is wrong with babies in neonatal intensive care units in order to treat them more effectively (Saunders et al., 2012).

However, the prospect that all pregnant women may soon have their blood analyzed for evidence of genetic abnormalities is raising ethical red flags, especially about the possibility that abortion rates will increase if more parents decide that they do not want babies with Down syndrome or other "undesirable" characteristics or if parents try to create through in vitro fertilization "designer" babies who are likely to be healthy, smart, and of the desired gender (Benn & Chapman, 2009). There is much for society and prospective parents to weigh here.

For the parents whose tests reveal a normal embryo or fetus, there is relief. For the parents who learn that their fetus may develop a serious defect, the choice between abortion and bearing a child with a serious disorder can be agonizing. For the many conditions that are polygenic in origin, it is usually not possible to do a definitive test or even give solid odds, but genetic counselors can educate families and attempt to correct their misunderstandings (Gershon & Alliey-Rodriguez, 2013). It makes sense for all of us to become educated about any genetic conditions in our family trees.

● Checking Mastery

1. Ted and Ned, fraternal twins, are not very alike at all. Give both a "nature" explanation and a "nurture" explanation of their differences.

2. Huge nose syndrome (we made it up) is caused by a single dominant gene, *H*. Using diagrams such as those in Figure 3.2, figure out the odds that Herb (who has the genotype *Hh*) and Harriet (who also has the genotype *Hh*) will have a child with huge nose syndrome. Now repeat the exercise, but assume that huge nose syndrome is caused by a recessive gene, *h*, and that both parents again have an *Hh* genotype.

3. Juan has red–green color blindness. Knowing that he is color blind, what can you infer about his parents?

● Making Connections

1. A DNA sample taken by swabbing a person's cheek can now reveal the person's entire genome. What do you think will be the positive and negative consequences of this scientific breakthrough for society?

2. Are you aware of any genetically influenced diseases that run in your family? If so, what are they and what do you know (or what can you learn) about the mechanism involved?

3.3

Studying Genetic and Environmental Influences

LEARNING OBJECTIVES

- Define the main goal and research methods of behavioral genetics and the meaning of *heritability*.

- Distinguish among the effects of genes, shared environmental influences, and nonshared environmental influences, and explain how a study of identical and fraternal twin pairs raised together versus raised apart can shed light on the importance of each of these influences.

- Explain what molecular genetics studies tell us that behavioral genetics studies cannot.

We now ask a critical question: How do researchers learn about the contributions of genes and environment to variation among us in physical and psychological traits? **Behavioral genetics** is the scientific study of the extent to which genetic and environmental differences among people or animals are responsible for differences in their physical and psychological traits (Plomin et al., 2013; Rutter, 2006). It is impossible to say that a given person's intelligence test score is the result of, say, 80%, 50%, or 20% heredity and the rest environment. The individual would have no intelligence without both genetic makeup and experiences, and their contributions cannot be separated. It is, however, possible for behavioral geneticists to estimate the heritability of measured IQ and of other traits or behaviors. Heritability is the proportion of all the variability in the trait within a large sample of people that can be linked to genetic differences among those individuals. To say that measured intelligence is *heritable*, then, is to say that differences in tested IQ among the individuals studied are to some degree attributable to the different genetic endowments of these individuals (Plomin et al., 2013).

It may seem from their name that *behavioral geneticists* would tell us only about genetic contributions to development, but in fact their work tells us about the contributions of both genetic and environmental factors to differences among people. The variability in a trait that is not associated with genetic differences is associated with differences in environment.

Behavioral geneticists who study animals can gather evidence through experimental breeding studies. For example, if a trait like learning ability is genetically influenced, breeding animals with high learning ability with each other should produce more offspring with high learning ability over several generations than breeding animals with low learning ability together does (Plomin et al., 2013). Experimental breeding studies have shown that genes contribute to learning ability, activity level, emotionality, aggressiveness, sex drive, and many other attributes in rats, mice, and chickens (Plomin et al., 2013).

But people do not take kindly to the idea of being selectively bred. So how can researchers try to separate the contributions of genes and environment to human differences? How can they tell whether family resemblances are due to common genes or common experiences? Behavioral genetics research in humans has relied primarily on determining whether the degree of genetic similarity between pairs of people is associated with the degree of physical or psychological similarity between them. Twin, adoption, and other family studies provide this information. More recently, molecular genetics techniques that allow studying the effects of specific genes have expanded our knowledge (see Plomin et al., 2013).

Twin, Adoption, and Family Studies

Twins have long been recognized as important sources of evidence about the effects of heredity. A simple type of twin study to untangle genetic and environmental influences involves determining whether identical twins reared together are more similar to each other in traits of interest than fraternal twins reared together. If genes matter, identical twins should be more similar because they have 100% of their genes in common, whereas fraternal twins share only 50% on average.

More complex twin studies include not only identical and fraternal twin pairs raised together but also identical and fraternal twins reared apart—four groups in all, differing in both whether they share 100% or 50% of their genes and whether they shared the same home environment. Identical twins separated near birth and raised in different environments—like the twins introduced at the beginning of the chapter—are particularly informative because any similarities between them cannot be attributed to common family experiences.

Although it is basically sound and widely used, the twin method has some limitations (Brendgen, Vitaro, & Girard, 2012; Lickliter & Honeycutt, 2015). First, identical twins could be more psychologically similar than fraternal twins, even if they were separated at birth, because they shared a more similar prenatal environment than fraternal twins did. Second, the fact that identical twins are often treated more similarly than fraternal twins could explain their greater psychological similarity. As it turns out, though, there appears to be little relationship between how similarly twins are treated and how similar they turn out to be psychologically. More likely, twins' similarities result in their being treated similarly (Loehlin, 1992; Brendgen et al., 2012).

A second commonly used method in behavioral genetics research is the adoption study. Are children adopted early in life psychologically similar to their biological parents, whose genes they share, or are they similar to their adoptive parents, whose environment they share? If adopted children resemble their biological parents in intelligence or personality, even though those parents did not raise them, genes must be influential. If they resemble their adoptive parents, even though they are genetically unrelated to them, a good case can be made for environmental influence.

Like the twin method, the adoption method has proved useful but has its limitations (Lickliter & Honeycutt, 2015). Researchers must appreciate that not only the genes of a biological mother but also the prenatal environment she provided influence how an adopted child turns out. Researchers must also be careful to correct for the tendency of adoption agencies to place children in homes similar to those they were adopted from. Finally, researchers must recognize that because adoptive homes are generally above-average environments, adoption studies may underestimate the effects of the full range of environments children can experience.

Finally, today's researchers are conducting complex family studies that include pairs of siblings who have a variety of different degrees of genetic similarity—for example, identical twins, fraternal twins, full biological siblings, half siblings, and unrelated stepsiblings who live together in stepfamilies (Plomin et al., 2013; Reiss et al., 2000). They are also measuring qualities of these family members' experiences to determine how similar or different the environments of siblings are. Finally, they are looking at twins and other pairs of relatives in longitudinal studies to assess the contributions of genes and environment to continuity and change in traits as individuals develop.

Estimating Influences

Having conducted a twin, adoption, or family study, behavioral geneticists use statistical calculations to estimate the degree to which heredity and environment account for individual differences in a trait of interest. When they study traits that a person either has or does not have (for example, a smoking habit or diabetes), researchers calculate and compare concordance rates—the percentage of pairs of people studied (for example, pairs of identical twins or adoptive parents and children) in which if one member of a pair displays the trait, the other does too. If concordance rates are higher for more genetically related than for less genetically related pairs of people, the trait is heritable.

Is homosexuality heritable? Researchers interested in this question might locate men who are gay and are twins, either identical or fraternal, locate their twin siblings, and find out whether they, too, are gay. In one study of this type (Bailey & Pillard, 1991), the concordance rate for identical twins was 52% (29 of the 56 twins of gay men were also gay), whereas the concordance rate for fraternal twins was much lower, 22% (12 of 54 twins of gay men were also gay). Studies like this indicate that genes contribute to both men's and women's sexual orientation (Bailey, Dunne, & Martin, 2000; Dawood, Bailey, & Martin, 2009). Importantly, though, identical twins are *not* perfectly concordant, so environmental factors must also affect sexual orientation. After all, Bailey and Pillard found that in 48% of the identical twin pairs, one twin was gay but the other was not, despite their identical genes.

When a trait can be present in varying degrees, as is true of height or intelligence, correlation coefficients rather than concordance rates are calculated. In a behavioral genetics study of IQ scores, a correlation would indicate whether the IQ score of one twin is systematically related to the IQ score of the other, such that if one twin is bright, the other is bright, and if one is not so bright, the other is not so bright. The larger the correlation for a group of twins, the closer the resemblance between members of twin pairs.

To better appreciate what can be learned from behavioral genetics studies, consider what Robert Plomin and his colleagues (1988) found when they assessed aspects of personality among twins in Sweden whose ages averaged 59. One of their measures assessed an aspect of emotionality—the tendency to be angry or quick tempered. The scale was given to many pairs of identical twins and fraternal twins—some pairs raised together, others separated near birth and raised apart. Correlations reflecting the degree of similarity between twins are presented in ● Table 3.4. From such data, behavioral geneticists—and you too—can estimate the contributions of three factors to individual differences in angry emotionality: genes (heritability), shared environmental influences, and nonshared environmental influences.

1. **Genes (heritability).** In the example in **Table 3.4**, genetic influences are clearly evident, for identical twins are consistently more similar in angry emotionality than fraternal twins are. (Remember, these correlations tell us how similar twin pairs are—not how high or low they score in angry emotionality.) The greater-than-zero correlation of 0.33 for identical twins reared apart also testifies to the role of genetic makeup. These data suggest that angry emotionality is heritable. Specifically, Plomin et al. (1988) estimated that about a third of

Twins are concordant for a trait of interest such as smoking if they both display it.

Anna Peisl/Corbis/Getty Images

the variation in emotionality in the sample they studied can be linked to variations in genetic makeup.

2. **Shared environmental influences.** Individuals growing up in the same environment experience shared environmental influences, common experiences that work to make them similar—for example, a common parenting style or exposure to the same toys, peers, schools, and neighborhood. In **Table 3.4**, notice that both identical and fraternal twins are slightly more similar in angry emotionality if they are raised together than if they are raised apart. These correlations tell us that shared environmental influences are evident but are weak: Twins are almost as similar when they grow up in different homes as when they grow up in the same home.

3. **Nonshared environmental influences.** Experiences unique to the individual—those that are not shared by other members of the family and that work to make individuals different from each other—are referred to as nonshared environmental influences. Whether they involve being treated differently by parents, having different friends or teachers, undergoing different life crises, or even being affected differently by the same life events, nonshared environmental influences make members of the same family different (Rowe, 1994). Notice in **Table 3.4** that identical twins raised together are not identical in angry emotionality, even though they share 100% of their genes *and* the same family environment. The fact that the correlation of 0.37 for identical twins raised together is much lower than a perfect correlation of 1.00 tells us that nonshared environmental influences are at work—making identical twins raised together different from each other.

● **Table 3.4** Correlations from a Twin Study of the Heritability of Angry Emotionality

	Raised Together	Raised Apart
Identical twin pairs	0.37	0.33
Fraternal twin pairs	0.17	0.09

Pointing to specific correlations in this table, can you find evidence that genes, shared environment, and nonshared environment all contribute to individual differences in angry emotionality?

Source: From Plomin, R. et al. (1988). EAS temperaments during the last half of the life span: Twins reared apart and twins reared together. *Psychology and Aging, 3,* 43–50.

If you have brothers and sisters, do you think your parents treated you and your siblings differently? If so, what might have been the effects of these nonshared environmental influences on your development?

Tetra Images/Getty Images

Molecular Genetics

Behavioral genetics studies do not tell us which genes are responsible when they find that a trait is heritable. The Human Genome Project, by providing a map of the human genome, has opened the door to exciting new approaches to studying genetic and environmental influence. **Molecular genetics** is the analysis of particular genes and their effects (Plomin et al., 2013). It involves identification of specific variants of genes that influence particular traits and comparisons of animals or humans who have these genes with those who do not. It also allows researchers to study the effects of specific genes in combination with the effects of specific environmental influences.

If researchers are not sure which genes contribute to a trait, they can analyze research participants' entire genomes to identify which genes distinguish individuals who do or do not have the trait (Butcher et al., 2008; Plomin & Davis, 2009). Molecular genetics can therefore help identify the multiple genes that contribute to polygenic traits—the genes behind evidence from twin and adoption studies that these traits are heritable (Plomin et al., 2013). The goal is to be able to say, for instance, "This gene accounts for 20% of the variation, and these two other genes each account for 10% of the variation" in a phenotype or trait of interest. So far, molecular genetics studies have failed to identify genes that account for large percentages of the variation in psychological traits like intelligence. Rather, large numbers of genes seem to contribute to each polygenic trait or disorder and each gene's contribution is very small (Chabris et al., 2012; Davis et al., 2010).

If a specific gene's location and function are already known, researchers may test people's DNA for the presence of the gene and study how people who have a particular variant of a gene differ from those who have other variants. Consider Alzheimer's disease,

the most common cause of dementia in later life (to be discussed in Chapter 16). Twin studies indicate that it is heritable (Gatz et al., 2006), but what genes are behind it? One variant of a gene called *Apolipoprotein E, APOE4,* has been linked to a higher-than-average risk of Alzheimer's. Although *APOE4* is only one of many contributors to Alzheimer's disease, researchers have been busily studying the brains and cognitive functioning of individuals with the gene compared to individuals without it (Fouquet et al., 2014). For example, they find that elderly adults with the *APOE4* gene show greater deterioration in memory and reasoning over the years than do individuals without it—long before some develop diagnosable Alzheimer's disease (Hofer et al., 2002; Schiepers et al., 2012). Moreover, having the *APOE4* gene *and* experiencing an environmental risk factor for dementia such as a traumatic brain injury increases the odds of Alzheimer's disease still further—something college football and soccer players and boxers might want to note (Chauhan, 2014). Such research can help make possible early identification and help for people likely to develop Alzheimer's disease and other conditions that are genetically influenced.

Despite its limitations, behavioral genetics research involving experimental breeding studies of animals and twin, adoption, and family studies of humans has revealed a great deal about the contributions of genes (heritability), shared environment, and nonshared environment to similarities and differences among us. Molecular genetics research is now leading to important discoveries about which specific genes, interacting with which environmental factors, are involved.

Checking Mastery

1. What does the following (hypothetical) table of correlations tell you about the contributions of genes, shared environment, and nonshared environment to frequency of use of marijuana?

	Raised Together	Raised Apart
Identical twins	+0.70	+0.40
Fraternal twins	+0.40	+0.10

2. What are two problems with adoption studies of genetic influence?

3. If twin studies show that depression is heritable, what good would it do to conduct molecular genetics studies of the disorder?

1. Design both a twin study and an adoption study to examine the contributions of genes and environment to creativity. Explain what patterns of results would provide evidence of genetic and environmental influence.

2. Speculate about how genes, shared environmental influences, and nonshared environmental influences could each help explain why some teenagers abuse alcohol and others do not. Then design a study to find out which of these factors are most important.

3.4

Selected Behavioral Genetics Findings

LEARNING OBJECTIVES

*   Summarize the main messages of behavioral genetics research on intelligence, personality, and psychological disorder about the roles of genes, shared environment, and nonshared environment.

*   Compare the average heritabilities of physical traits, intelligence, personality, psychological disorder, and attitudes and interests.

Findings from behavioral genetics studies have challenged and changed our understandings of human development, as you will see throughout this book. We give a few examples here to illustrate major themes in this research, drawing from studies of intellectual abilities, temperament and personality, and psychological disorders (see Plomin et al., 2013). Expect some surprises.

Intellectual Abilities

How do genes and environment contribute to individual differences in intellectual functioning? Consider the average correlations between the IQ scores of different pairs of relatives presented in ● **Table 3.5**. Clearly, correlations are higher when pairs of people are closely related genetically than when they are not and are highest when they are identical twins. Overall, the heritability of IQ scores is about 0.50, meaning that genetic differences account for about 50% of the variation in IQ scores and environmental differences account for the other half of the variation in the samples studied (Plomin et al., 2013; Segal & Johnson, 2009).

Can you detect the workings of environment in the table? Notice that (1) pairs of family members reared together are somewhat more similar in IQ than pairs reared apart; (2) fraternal twins, who should have especially similar family experiences because they grow up at the same time, tend to be more alike than siblings born at different times; and (3) the IQs of adopted individuals are related to those of their adoptive parents (that is, the correlation is greater than 0). All these findings suggest that *shared* environmental influences tend to make individuals more alike. Notice, however, that even genetically identical twins reared together are not perfectly similar. This is evidence that their unique or *nonshared* experiences have made them different.

Do the contributions of genes and environment to differences in intellectual ability change over the life span? Might genetic influence on individual differences decrease as we accumulate learning experiences? It seems logical, but it's wrong. Genetic endowment appears to *gain* rather than lose importance from infancy to adulthood as a source of individual differences in intellectual performance (McCartney, Harris, & Bernieri, 1990; Tucker-Drob, Briley, & Harden, 2013). The change is large: from a heritability of under 25% of the variation in intelligence in infancy to a heritability of more like 70% by adolescence (Tucker-Drob et al., 2013). Genetic influences on individual

● **Table 3.5** Average Correlations Between the IQ Scores of Pairs of Individuals

Family Pairs	Raised Together	Raised Apart
Identical twins	0.86	0.72
Fraternal twins	0.60	0.52
Biological siblings	0.47	0.24
Biological parent and child	0.42	0.22
Half siblings	0.31	—
Adopted siblings	0.34	—
Adoptive parent and adopted child	0.19	—
Unrelated siblings (same age, same home)	0.26	—

Source: All but two of these averages were calculated by Bouchard and McGue (1981) from studies of both children and adults. The correlation for fraternal twins reared apart is based on data reported by Pedersen et al. (1985); that for unrelated children in the same home is based on data reported by Segal (2000).

differences in intellectual functioning remain evident in old age (Finkel & Reynolds, 2010; Sachdev et al., 2013).

Whereas the heritability of intelligence test performance increases with age, shared environmental influences tend to become less significant with age, explaining about 30% of the variation in IQ in childhood but much less in adulthood (Tucker-Drob et al., 2013). Siblings are probably exposed to similar (shared) learning experiences when they are young and spend a good deal of time with their parents. As they age, they seek and have different (nonshared) life experiences. Partly because of their different genetic makeups, they may elicit different reactions from their parents, join different peer groups, encounter different teachers, develop different hobbies, go on to different colleges or universities and careers, and so on.

Estimates of heritability and environmental influence not only differ depending on the ages of the individuals studied but also vary quite dramatically depending on their socioeconomic background. Eric Turkheimer and his colleagues (2003) studied the heritability of IQ among children from very low-income families and children from affluent homes. As shown in

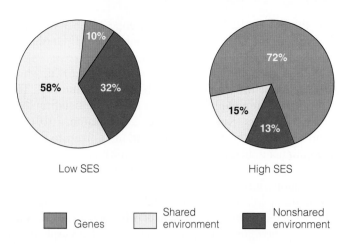

Figure 3.4 The proportions of variance in child IQ scores explained by genes, shared environment, and nonshared environment differ for children from low versus high socioeconomic status (SES) environments.

Source: From Turkheimer, E., Haley, M., D'Onofrio, B., & Gottesman, I. I. (2003). Socioeconomic status modifies heritability of IQ in young children, *Psychological Science, 14*(6), 623–628. Reprinted by permission of Sage Publications.

Figure 3.4, among children from wealthy (high SES) families, genes accounted for 72% of the variation in IQ, whereas shared environment was not very important—as in most previous studies. By contrast, genes explained only about 10% of the variation in IQ among children from poor (low SES) families, whereas shared environmental influences accounted for almost 60% of the variation (see also Harden, Turkheimer, & Loehlin, 2007; Tucker-Drob et al., 2013).

Why might this be? In affluent environments, it is likely that children have plenty of opportunities to build niches that allow them to develop whatever genetically based potentials and interests they have, intellectual or otherwise (Tucker-Drob et al., 2013). By contrast, deprived and unstimulating environments may drag many poor children down, regardless of their genetic potential. However, some parents may be more able than others to offer a home environment that helps their children thrive intellectually despite economic disadvantage.

Interestingly, this pattern of higher heritability in more affluent samples is seen in other studies done in the United States but is not evident in Western Europe and Australia. There, heritability is quite similar for low- and high-SES individuals, possibly because social welfare programs in those countries protect families from extreme poverty (Tucker-Drob & Bates, 2016). The point is this:

The temperament of infants is genetically influenced. These identical twins seem like easy babies, eager to socialize.

Stu Monk Images/Alamy Stock Photo

The heritability of a trait is not one number written in stone. It can differ greatly depending on the age, socioeconomic status, culture, and other characteristics of the sample studied.

Does evidence of the heritability of IQ scores mean that we cannot improve children's intellectual development by enriching their environment? Not at all. True, the IQs of adopted children are, by adolescence, correlated more strongly with the IQs of their biological parents than with the IQs of their adoptive parents. However, the *level* of intellectual performance that adopted children reach can increase dramatically (by 20 points on an IQ test) if they are adopted into more intellectually stimulating homes than those provided by their biological parents (Scarr & Weinberg, 1978, 1983; van IJzendoorn & Juffer, 2005). It is critical for parents, teachers, and others concerned with optimizing development to understand that they can make a difference—that genetically influenced qualities can very often be altered.

Temperament and Personality

As parents know well, different babies have different personalities. In trying to describe infant personality, researchers have focused on aspects of **temperament**—tendencies to respond in predictable ways, such as sociability and emotional reactivity, that serve as the building blocks of later personality (see Chapter 11). Genes contribute to individual differences in both early temperament and later personality (Davis et al., 2015; Krueger & Johnson, 2008; Saudino & Micalizzi, 2015).

Arnold Buss and Robert Plomin (1984) reported average correlations of around 0.50 to 0.60 between the temperament scores of identical twins. The corresponding correlations for fraternal twins were not much greater than zero. Think about that: A zero correlation is what you would expect if fraternal twins were strangers living in different homes rather than siblings who, on average, share half their genes, the same home, and often the same bedroom! It does not seem to matter whether researchers look at fraternal twin pairs, ordinary siblings, or unrelated children adopted into the same family: *Living in the same home generally does not do much to make children more similar in temperament and personality* (Plomin et al., 2013). This does not mean that the family is unimportant. It means that family influences do more to make children different from each other than to make them alike—that nonshared environment is more influential than shared environment.

As shown in Figure 3.5, about 40% of the variation among adults in major dimensions of personality is attributable to genetic differences among them (Loehlin, 1985; Vukasović & Bratko, 2015). Only about 5% of the variation reflects the

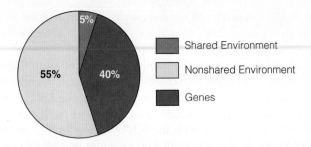

Figure 3.5 Average contributions of genes, nonshared environment, and shared environment to differences in adult personality. Growing up in the same home does not do much to make children alike in personality. Based on data from Loehlin (1985).

effects of shared family environment. The remaining 55% of the variability in adult personalities is associated with nonshared environmental influences that make siblings different from each other.

Shared environmental influences sometimes prove more important than these summary statistics would suggest. Yet behavioral geneticists have discovered repeatedly that for many aspects of temperament and personality, unique, nonshared environmental influences seems to be more significant than shared ones (Plomin et al., 2013; Reiss et al., 2000). There is little evidence that parents mold all their children's personalities in similar directions. There is plenty of evidence that parents treat different children differently, guided in part by their children's personality tendencies and behavior.

Psychological Disorders

Both genes and environment contribute to psychological disorders across the life span—to alcohol and drug abuse, autism, depression, attention deficit hyperactivity disorder, eating disorders, aggressive and criminal behavior, Alzheimer's disease, and every other psychological disorder that has been studied (Plomin et al., 2013; and see Chapter 16). Usually it's a matter of multiple genes, along with multiple environmental influences, each making small contributions to the development of a disorder.

Consider just one example. **Schizophrenia** is a serious mental illness that involves disturbances in logical thinking, emotional expression, and social behavior. It typically emerges in late adolescence or early adulthood. Genes contribute substantially to this disorder (Gottesman & Hanson, 2005). The average concordance rate for schizophrenia in identical twin pairs is 48%; that is, if one twin has the disorder, in 48% of the cases the other has it too (Gottesman, 1991; Owen & O'Donovan, 2003). By comparison, the concordance rate for fraternal twins is only 17%. As a result, the heritability of schizophrenia is estimated to be 80% or higher (Cardno & Pepper, 2014). What's more, children who have at least one biological parent with the disorder have an increased risk of schizophrenia *even if they are adopted away early in life* (Heston, 1970). Thus, the increased risk these children face has more to do with their genes than with being brought up by a schizophrenic adult.

But not all children of a parent with schizophrenia develop it. Here are the facts: Whereas about 1% of people in the general population develop schizophrenia, about 10% of children who have a schizophrenic parent become schizophrenic (Gottesman,

1991; Plomin et al., 2013). If certain copy number variations are involved, the odds can become much higher (Gershon & Alliey-Rodriguez, 2013; Hall et al., 2015).

Notice, though, that the odds for an identical twin whose twin develops schizophrenia are not 100% but around 50%. This means that environmental factors also contribute significantly to this mental illness (King, St. Hilaire, & Heidkamp, 2010). For example, genetically at-risk children are more likely to develop schizophrenia if their mothers come down with an infectious illness during pregnancy, such as the flu, if their mothers experience complications during delivery that deprive the fetus of oxygen, or if they grow up in a dysfunctional family after birth (Laurens et al., 2015). Differences in the expression of twins' genes caused by differences in their prenatal experiences may also help explain why one twin develops schizophrenia but the other does not (Debnath, Venkatasubramanian, & Berk, 2015).

In short, children do not inherit psychological disorders. Some inherit genetically based *predispositions* to develop disorders, but their experiences will interact with their genetic makeup to determine how well adjusted they turn out to be.

The Heritability of Different Traits

Genes contribute to variation in virtually all the human traits that have been studied, yet some traits are more heritable than others (Polderman et al., 2015; Segal, 2012). ■ **Figure 3.6** presents, by way of summary, correlations obtained in the Minnesota Study of Twins Reared Apart between the traits of identical twins raised apart and reunited as adults.

Observable physical characteristics, from eye color to height, are strongly associated with individual genetic endowment. Even weight is highly heritable; genes explain about 70% of variation in weight (Plomin et al., 2013), and adopted children resemble their biological parents but not their adoptive parents in weight, even though their adoptive parents feed them (Grilo & Pogue-Geile, 1991). Certain aspects of physiology, such as measured brain activity and reactions to alcohol, are highly heritable, too (Lykken, Tellegen, & Iacono, 1982; Neale & Martin, 1989).

In addition, genetic differences among older adults contribute to differences in their physical functioning and aging processes (Finkel & Reynolds, 2010). Genes also contribute to susceptibilities to many chronic diseases associated with aging. In the end, genes account for about 35–40% of the variation in longevity, leaving plenty of room for lifestyle and other environmental factors to make a difference (Finkel et al., 2014).

If physical and physiological characteristics are typically strongly heritable, general intelligence is moderately heritable: 50% or more of the variation in IQ scores is attributable to genes. Temperament and personality are somewhat less heritable. Many psychological disorders are also at least moderately heritable, with degree of heritability varying from condition to condition. Finally, and most surprisingly, differences in genetic endowment even contribute, though modestly, to differences in attitudes and interests—for example, religiousness, political conservatism or liberalism, political party identification, and vocational interests (Bell & Kandler, 2015; Segal, 2012). As you can see, it has proven difficult to find a human characteristic that is *not* to some degree heritable.

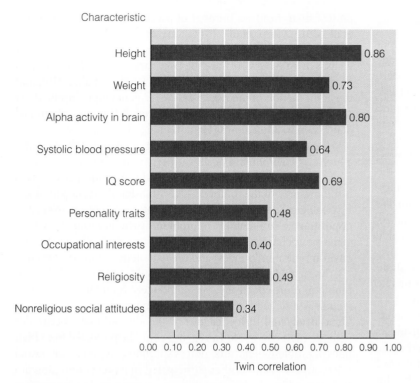

Characteristic

	Twin correlation
Height	0.86
Weight	0.73
Alpha activity in brain	0.80
Systolic blood pressure	0.64
IQ score	0.69
Personality traits	0.48
Occupational interests	0.40
Religiosity	0.49
Nonreligious social attitudes	0.34

0.00 0.10 0.20 0.30 0.40 0.50 0.60 0.70 0.80 0.90 1.00

Twin correlation

■ **Figure 3.6** Correlations between the traits of middle-aged identical twins raised apart in the Minnesota Study of Twins.

Source: From Bouchard, T. J., Jr., Lykken, D. T., McGue, M., Segal, N. L, & Tellegen, A. Sources of psychological differences: The Minnesota Study of Twins Reared Apart, *Science*, 250, 223–228. Copyright © 1990, The American Association for the Advancement of Science. Reprinted with permission.

Checking Mastery

1. Professor Gene Ohm is studying genetic and environmental influences on individual differences in extraversion/introversion. Based on previous behavioral genetics studies, what should he expect?

2. Ayaan's biological mother had schizophrenia, so he was placed in an adoptive home when he was only 2 months old. He grew up with his adoptive parents (neither of whom had any psychological disorders) in a stable, loving family. What would you tell Ayaan, now age 18, about his chances of developing schizophrenia if you were a genetic counselor?

Making Connections

1. There's surely no single gene that directly makes people politically liberal or politically conservative, yet political liberalism/conservatism is heritable. Develop an explanation of how genes could influence it. While you're at it, how might shared environment and nonshared environment influence it?

2. What in the behavioral genetics evidence we have reviewed in this section most convinces you of the importance of genes—and what most convinces you of the importance of environment?

3.5

Gene–Environment Interplay

LEARNING OBJECTIVES

- Distinguish between gene-environment interaction (and the diathesis-stress and differential susceptibility concepts) and gene-environment correlation (and passive, evocative, and active types of gene-environment correlations).

- Explain how genetic makeup can affect measures of environment and how genetically informed studies can help determine whether parenting and other environmental influences on development really matter.

- Explain what epigenetic effects are and what they say about the relationship between genes and environment.

- Explain why genetic research and behavioral genetic research are controversial.

Genes do not orchestrate our growth before birth and then leave us alone. Instead, they are "turning on" and "turning off" in patterned ways throughout the life span, helping shape our characteristics and behavior. No less important are ever-changing environmental influences, from conception to death. But genes and environment do not operate independently; they are interrelated in important ways.

As you have seen throughout this chapter, behavioral geneticists try to establish how much of the variation in human traits such as intelligence can be attributed to individual differences in genetic makeup and how much can be attributed to individual differences in experience. Useful as that research is, it does not take us far in understanding the complex interplay between genes and environment over the life span (Meaney, 2010). As Ann Anastasi (1958) noted many years ago, instead of asking *how much* is because of genes and how much is because of environment, researchers should be asking *how* heredity and environment work together to make us what we are. With that in mind, let's examine the workings of three tremendously important forms of gene–environment interplay: gene–environment interactions, gene-environment correlations, and epigenetic effects on gene expression (Brendgen et al., 2012; Plomin et al., 2013).

Gene–Environment Interactions

Genes provide us with potentials that are or are not realized depending on our experiences. You have encountered some examples already but consider another one. Using the molecular genetics approach, Avshalom Caspi and his colleagues (2003) sought to understand why stressful life experiences cause some people but not others to become depressed. They performed DNA analysis on a large sample of New Zealanders to determine which variants of a now famous gene called *5-HTTLPR* each person had. They knew that this gene affects stress reactivity by affecting levels of the neurotransmitter serotonin in the brain, and they knew that a low serotonin level is linked to depression. Caspi and colleagues also administered surveys to measure the stressful events each person had experienced between ages 21 and 26, and whether at age 26 each person had experienced a diagnosable episode of depression in the past year.

In ■ **Figure 3.7**, you can see the results, which illustrate wonderfully the concept of **gene–environment interaction**: The effects of our genes depend on what kind of environment we experience, and how we respond to the environment depends on what genes we have. In **Figure 3.7**, you see that individuals with two of the high-risk variants of the *5-HTTLPR* gene are more vulnerable to depression than people with two of the protective variants of the gene—but only if they experience multiple stressful events. By comparison, even multiple stressful events will not easily cause people with the protective variants of the gene to become depressed. Thus, the genes people have make a difference only when their environment is stressful, and a stressful environment has an effect only on individuals with a genotype that predisposes them to depression. Genes and environment interact.

Both human and animal studies indicate that the *5-HTTLPR* gene affects stress reactivity and can put individuals at risk for—or

protect them from—a number of psychological disorders (Booij et al., 2015; Caspi et al., 2011; Karg et al., 2011). For example, bullying is more likely to be linked to emotional problems in victims of bullying who have the risky variants of *5-HTTLPR* than in victims with the protective variants (Sugden et al., 2010), and the combination of the risky *5-HTTLPR* genes and chronic stress stemming from peer relationships increases the odds of clinical depression in adolescents (Hankin et al., 2015).

Generally, it often takes a combination of high-risk genes and a high-risk environment or stressful experiences to trigger psychological problems (Dick et al., 2011; Dodge & Rutter, 2011). This is the message of the **diathesis–stress model** of psychopathology: Psychological disorder results from an interaction of a person's predisposition or vulnerability to problems (whether rooted solely in genes or in characteristics that have arisen from both genetic and environmental influences) and the experience of stressful events.

From an applied standpoint, we could prevent psychological problems more effectively if we could identify and help those individuals whose genes predispose them to problems. For example, Gene Brody and his colleagues (2009) showed that 11-year-olds with the high-risk *5-HTTLPR* genes could be protected from high rates of problem behaviors such as substance use and early sexual intercourse if their families participated in a prevention program that stressed good parenting skills and parent–child communication. Control group youth who had the high-risk genes but did not receive the prevention program engaged in problem behaviors at twice the rate of youth with the high-risk genes who participated in the prevention program and peers who did not have high-risk genes (see also Brody, Yu, & Beach, 2015).

More and more evidence of gene–environment interactions involving the *5-HTTLPR* gene and a number of other important genes affecting neurotransmitter activity in the brain is emerging as researchers use the molecular genetics approach to study interactions between specific genes and specific experiences. But another fascinating discovery has been made: The diathesis-stress model of psychopathology may be only part of the story. Some of the very genes that have been labeled as "risk genes" are turning out to be genes that not only make people more susceptible to the damaging effects of stressful environments but also allow them to benefit more than others from nurturing environments. **Exploration 3.1** examines this **differential susceptibility hypothesis**, which says that some people's genetic makeup makes them more reactive than other people to environmental influences, whether good or bad. Our knowledge of forms of gene-environment interaction such as diathesis-stress and differential susceptibility is expanding rapidly.

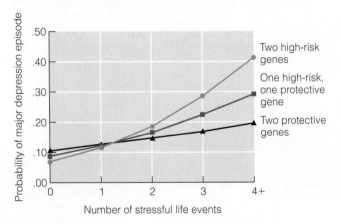

■ **Figure 3.7** The odds of a depressive episode at age 26 are highest for individuals who: (1) inherit two *5-HTTLPR* gene variants known to increase the risk of depression rather than a pair known to protect against depression, and (2) experience four or more stressful life events between ages 21 and 26. This is an example of gene-environment interaction: The effects of genetic makeup on depression depend on how stressful a person's environment is, and the effects of stressful life events depend on the person's genotype.

Source: From Caspi et al., Influences of Life Stress on Depression, *Science*, July 18, 2003, Fig. 1B. Copyright © 2003. Reprinted by permission of AAAS.

Gene–Environment Correlations

Not only do genes and environment interact, but each person's genetic makeup influences the kinds of experiences she seeks and has. Sandra Scarr and Kathleen McCartney (1983), drawing on the theorizing of Robert Plomin, John DeFries, and John Loehlin (1977), proposed three kinds of **gene–environment correlations**, or ways in which a person's genes and his environment or experiences are interrelated: passive, evocative, and active. The concept of gene–environment *interactions* tells us that people with different genes react differently to the experiences they have.

Differential Susceptibility: Orchids and Dandelions

Something interesting happened when researchers Bruce Ellis, Thomas Boyce, Jay Belsky, and others looked more closely at some of the genes like *5-HTTLPR* that had been identified as "risk genes" for disorders such as depression and antisocial behavior. They discovered that individuals with these genes not only displayed more psychological problems if they were exposed to stressful, negative environments but responded better than individuals without the genes to positive environments. According to the *differential susceptibility hypothesis*, some individuals, by virtue of their genetic makeup, are simply more responsive than other people to environment influences—good or bad. The "susceptible to environmental influence" individuals have been likened to orchids, which thrive in just the right conditions but wilt in poor conditions; the less environmentally responsive individuals have been likened to dandelions, which grow pretty well almost anywhere (Boyce & Ellis, 2005).

Consider a study by Jay Belsky and Kevin Beaver (2011) of self-control among eleventh-grade students raised by more or less supportive mothers. These researchers focused on variants of five genes, including *5-HTTLPR*, that had previously been identified as risk genes and counted how many of the risky versions each teen had. They also assessed the extent to which teens' mothers were involved with and attached to them. Finally, self-regulation was assessed with a 23-item scale completed by both teens and their mothers that asked about such behaviors as having a temper and being reliable or trustworthy.

The results supported the differential susceptibility hypothesis for males but not for females. As shown in ■ Figure 3.8, males with a large number of risk genes (which Belsky and Beaver relabeled "plasticity" genes), had the highest level of self-control when they had supportive mothers but the lowest self-control when they had unsupportive mothers. Among the "dandelion" youth who had 0 or only 1 of these genes, the degree of self-regulation was unrelated to how supportive their mothers were. Researchers were not sure why the differential susceptibility effect was evident only among males, as other studies suggest it works in both sexes (Buil et al., 2015; DiLalla et al., 2015; Sumner et al., 2015).

The message is clear: The diathesis-stress model tells only part of the story. The "risk" genes that combine with stressful and negative experiences to put some individuals on a path to psychopathology do just that in unsupportive environments but also help the same individuals thrive in highly supportive environments (see Ellis et al., 2011, for more examples). It

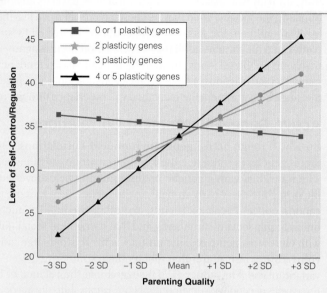

Figure 3.8 Male adolescents who had 4 or 5 of the "risk" genes identified in previous research (the black line) showed very low self-control if their mothers were unsupportive—support for the diathesis-stress model. However, they also showed exceptionally good self-control if raised by supportive mothers—support for the differential susceptibility hypothesis, and a good reason to relabel these genes "plasticity" genes rather than "risk" genes.

Source: Belsky, J., & Beaver, K. M. (2011). Cumulative-genetic plasticity, parenting and adolescent self-regulation. *Journal of Child Psychology and Psychiatry*, 52(5), 619–626. Figure 1, p. 624.

makes good sense, then, to identify children who may be at risk for problems and target them for interventions such as positive parenting training so that these orchids have a chance to blossom (as in the Brody, 2009, study described in the text).

By contrast, the concept of gene–environment *correlations* says that people with different genes have different experiences (Loehlin, 1992). As an illustration, imagine children with a genetic potential to be highly sociable and other children whose genes are likely to make them shy.

Passive Gene–Environment Correlations

The kind of home environment that parents provide for their children is influenced partly by the parents' genotypes. **Passive gene–environment correlations** work like this: Because parents provide children with both their genes and a home environment

compatible with those genes, the home environments to which children are exposed are correlated with (and are typically likely to reinforce) their genotypes.

For instance, sociable parents not only transmit their "sociable" genes to their children but also, because they have "sociable" genes themselves, create a highly social home environment—inviting their friends over, taking their children to social gatherings, and so on. The combination of genes for sociability and a sociable environment may make their children more sociable than they would otherwise be. By contrast, the child with shy parents may receive genes for shyness *and* a correlated environment without as much social stimulation.

Evocative Gene–Environment Correlations

In evocative gene–environment correlations, a child's genotype also *evokes* certain kinds of reactions from other people. The smiley, sociable baby is likely to get more smiles, hugs, and social stimulation—and more opportunities to build social skills—than the wary, shy baby who makes you worry he will howl if you try anything. Similarly, the sociable child may be chosen more often as a playmate by other children, the sociable adolescent may be invited to more parties, and the sociable adult may be given more work assignments involving public relations. In short, genetically based tendencies may affect the reactions of other people to an individual and, hence, the kind of environment the individual will experience through life.

Active Gene–Environment Correlations

Finally, through active gene–environment correlations, children's genotypes influence the kinds of environments they *seek*. The individual with a genetic predisposition to be extraverted is likely to go to every party in sight, invite friends over, join organizations, collect Facebook friends, and otherwise build a "niche" that is highly socially stimulating and that strengthens social skills. The child with genes for shyness may actively avoid large group activities and instead develop solitary interests.

Scarr and McCartney (1983) suggest that the balance of the three types of genotype–environment correlations shifts during development. Because infants are at home a good deal and are dependent on their caregivers, their environment is largely influenced by their parents through passive influences. Evocative influences operate throughout life; our genetically influenced traits consistently evoke certain reactions from other people. Finally, as humans develop, they become increasingly able to build their own niches, so active gene–environment correlations become increasingly important.

Implications of Gene–Environment Correlations

How much evidence is there for Scarr and McCartney's claim that people's genes are correlated with, and possibly influence, their experiences in life? A good deal. It turns out that many measures of aspects of the environment are heritable (Butcher & Plomin, 2008). What this means is that identical twins are more similar than fraternal twins, and biological siblings are more similar than adoptive siblings, in the environments they experience and in their perceptions of those environments. For example, genetic makeup is related to the following:

- Aspects of parenting, such as the warmth and quality of the parent–child relationship (Plomin & Bergeman, 1991; Reiss, 2005)
- Time spent watching television (Plomin et al., 1990)
- Number of stressful life events experienced (Kendler et al., 1993)

If our genetically influenced personality traits affect how others treat us and what experiences we seek and have, these findings make sense. For example, identical twins who are irritable and difficult could help create a conflict-ridden family environment, whereas calm, self-controlled twins could help create a cohesive family environment (Krueger, Markon, & Bouchard, 2003).

Such findings challenge our usual assumptions about human development. They say that what we thought were purely environmental influences on development partly reflect the workings of heredity (Reiss et al., 2000; Rowe, 1994). Leading behavioral geneticist Robert Plomin (1990) gives us this example to ponder: Suppose we find that parents who read to their children have brighter children than parents who do not read to their children. In the not-so-distant past, most developmentalists would have interpreted this finding rather uncritically as evidence that parents make important contributions to their children's intellectual development by reading to them. Without denying the importance of parents, consider this alternative interpretation: Parents and children whose genes predispose them to be highly intelligent are more likely to seek opportunities to read than parents and children who are less intellectually inclined. If this is the case, can we be so sure that reading to children *causes* them to be brighter? Would we be able to show that reading to children is beneficial even when the parents and children involved are genetically unrelated?

Some of the strongest evidence of the importance of gene–environment correlations comes from an ambitious family study by David Reiss, Jenae Neiderhiser, E. Mavis Hetherington, and Robert Plomin (2000). These researchers studied 720 pairs of same-sex adolescents who differed in their degree of biological relationship, from identical twins to biological siblings to unrelated stepsiblings. They measured environmental variables such as quality of parent–child interaction and adolescent adjustment variables such as self-esteem, sociability, depression, and antisocial behavior.

Repeatedly, genes shared by parents and adolescents partly or even largely accounted for relationships between children's experiences in the family and their developmental outcomes—for example, between a negative parenting style and antisocial behavior on the part of adolescents. Taking this and other evidence into account, we must conclude that *reciprocal influences* are at work in human development. For example, harsh, negative parenting contributes to antisocial behavior in children, but children genetically predisposed to be antisocial also provoke and bring out the worst in their parents (Larsson et al., 2008; O'Connor et al., 1998).

In short, simple correlational studies that show a relationship between some aspect of experience and some aspect of development cannot establish that experience really affects development. As a result, more and more researchers are conducting **genetically informed studies**, like the Reiss et al. (2000) study just described, that try to determine whether there are genetic explanations for apparent environmental effects and establish more firmly whether environment matters (Johnson et al., 2009; Plomin et al., 2013).

One approach to genetically informed research is to determine whether an environmental influence is just as evident among adoptive children—that is, with genetic resemblance between parent and child out of the picture—as among biological children. For instance, Amato and Cheadle (2008) showed that the relationship between marital conflict and child behavior problems was equally strong in biological and adoptive families, suggesting a true environmental effect.

Another genetically informed research tactic is to study identical twins to see if differences in their development are systematically related to differences in their experiences. Since they have identical genes and grew up in similar prenatal and postnatal environments, differences in their behavior or development can be credited to differences in their experiences—to nonshared environmental influences. So, for example, identical twins who

If the child of a top athlete turns out to be a good athlete, is it because of genetic endowment or experience? We cannot say because genes and environment are correlated. How might passive, evocative, and active gene-environment correlation influence this child's development as an athlete?

Jeff Greenberg/Alamy Stock Photo

"birth or origin") is a term for the general process through which nature and nurture co-act to bring about development (Moore, 2015). Think of it as what happens as a fertilized egg becomes a human being. It is now abundantly clear that genes do not dictate development (Lickliter & Honeycutt, 2015; Moore, 2015). Rather, genes and environment interact with and influence each other from conception on to shape development, to the point that their influences cannot be separated.

Nowhere is this clearer than in what are now called **epigenetic effects**, ways in which environmental factors influence the expression of particular genes in particular cells (Boyce & Kobor, 2015; Champagne, 2013; Meaney, 2010; Moore, 2015). Through epigenetic effects, factors such as diet, stress, alcohol and drugs, environmental toxins, and early parental care leave records, chemical codings on top of certain genes that affect whether those genes are turned on or off. Analysis of RNA can now reveal these patterns of gene expression.

So, on top of the complex genome in each cell, we also have a complex "epigenome" consisting of all kinds of these epigenetic markings. The genes themselves are not altered when epigenetic effects occur. Rather, their expression is altered—in ways that can affect cognition, emotion, behavior, health, and mental health. Epigenetic markings can be long-lasting and can lead to continuity in development (as when these codings cause a blood cell or liver cell to continue to act like a blood cell or liver cell for life), but they can also produce change in response to changes in the environment, acting as a source of plasticity or flexibility in development (Boyce & Kobor, 2015).

Epigenetic effects are especially important during prenatal development, when regulatory DNA and environmental influences orchestrate early development (see Chapter 4 on fetal programming in response to factors such as maternal diet). However, epigenetic effects continue throughout the life span. A temporary rise in the most well-studied type of epigenetic coding, DNA methylation, has been observed in the cells of adults who complete a social stress test in the laboratory (Unternaehrer et al., 2012). And epigenetic changes involving genes associated with neurotransmitters in the brain happen every time we learn something, and are critical in brain development and aging (Mather et al., 2014; Moore, 2015). Let's look at three examples of some of the remarkable discoveries about epigenetic effects that have been made recently: a study of differences between identical twins, a study of the implications of early parenting for rat pup development, and research on the implications of a father's overeating for his children's health.

Epigenetic Effects and Differences Between Twins

Epigenetic effects may help explain why, despite their identical genes, identical twins often differ. Mario Fraga and his colleagues (2005) conducted analyses of the DNA and RNA of 40 pairs of identical twins ranging in age from 3 to 74. Analysis of the RNA of 3-year-old twins showed that the genes of these young children had very similar patterns of expression. If a gene was turned on in one twin, it was turned on in the other; if it was turned off in one twin, it was turned off in the other. By contrast, the genes of 50-year-old twins were expressed very differently; many genes that were activated in one twin were deactivated in the other.

What's more, those adult twins who had spent less of their lives together and had led quite different lifestyles—for example, who

receive more negative discipline from their parents at age 7 than their co-twins turn out to have more conduct problems at age 12 (Viding et al., 2009). And twins who are bullied by peers have more atypical hormonal responses to stressful experiences and are more likely to develop emotional problems than their non-bullied co-twins (Ouellet-Morin et al., 2011; Sugden et al., 2010).

These kinds of genetically informed studies often offer the most convincing evidence we have that environment truly matters. We end up appreciating that, through gene–environment correlations, genes influence how parents, peers, and others treat us and that how we are treated then contributes on its own to our development, often reinforcing our genetically based predispositions.

Epigenetic Effects on Gene Expression

Having seen that genes can influence one's environment through gene-environment correlations, let's now look at how environment can influence genes. **Epigenesis** (*epi-* = "over and above" + *genesis* =

Identical but not identical. "We think the same. We've even bought each other the same birthday cards," says Geraldine (*right*) about herself and her identical twin, Christine. Yet Christine has arthritis and Geraldine does not. Could epigenetic effects be one way in which environmental influences make these identical twins different?

Karen Kasmauski/Science Faction/Getty Images

Rats turned out to be stress resistant if raised by nurturant mothers and stress reactive if raised by neglectful mothers, regardless of their biological parentage.

But these styles of responding to stress also were not acquired through learning, either—for example, by watching a stressed-out mother. Rather, Meaney and his colleagues discovered that early licking and grooming affect the development of the stress response system through epigenetic effects. In nurtured pups, certain genes in cells in the hippocampus of the brain that influence the regulation of stress hormones stayed turned on, whereas in neglected pups these genes were turned off by DNA methylation, making the hippocampus less able to tone down stress hormone responses. Early caregiving therefore had a lasting effect on development by altering gene expression.

Too little licking and grooming in infancy also turns off genes that affect sensitivity to female hormones and later maternal behavior (Champagne, 2013). As a result, the daughters of neglectful mothers turn into neglectful mothers themselves! Here, then, we see epigenetic transmission of neglectful (or nurturing) parenting styles across generations.

Epigenetic effects like this example represent no less than a whole new way in which parents influence their children besides genetic inheritance and social learning: *environmental influence on gene expression*. And there's now suggestive evidence that epigenetic marks similar to those observed in rat pups may help explain the transmission from mother to daughter of abusive and neglectful parenting in both monkeys and humans, as well as the increased susceptibility to mental health problems associated with early abuse and neglect (Maestripieri, Lindell, & Higley, 2007; McGowan, 2013; McGowan et al., 2009). But the cycle of neglect and abuse may be breakable: Meaney and his colleagues showed that epigenetic effects of neglectful parenting on stress response and parenting style in rats can be reversed if young animals are raised by sensitive, nurturing mothers or if drugs that affect gene expression in critical parts of the brain are administered (McGowan, Meaney, & Szyf, 2008; Zhang & Meaney, 2010).

had different diets, levels of physical activity, and use of tobacco, alcohol, and drugs—showed greater differences in their patterns of gene expression than did twins who had led similar lives. Some differences in the epigenetic markings of identical twins are detectable from birth, suggesting that differences in identical twins' prenatal experiences, recorded in their epigenomes, may also help explain why they often differ (Moore, 2015; and see Chapter 4).

Epigenetic Effects of Nurturing and Neglect

Now consider the groundbreaking work on the epigenetic effects of early caregiving on the development of rat pups by Michael Meaney, Frances Champagne, and their colleagues. These researchers have shown through a series of elegant studies how the early experience of rat pups can affect the activity of their genes and, in turn, not only their own development but that of their offspring (see Champagne, 2013; Francis et al., 1999; Kaffman & Meaney, 2007).

Here's how it goes: If mother rats are nurturant—if they regularly lick and groom their pups and nurse them with an arched back in the first week of life—the pups grow up able to handle stress well. If rat moms are neglectful and do not provide this tender tactile care, rat pups become timid and easily stressed adults. But how? The differences in pups' reactivity to stress were not due to heredity. Raising the pups of nurturant mothers with neglectful mothers and the pups of neglectful mothers with nurturant mothers demonstrated that it was rearing that mattered, not heredity.

A mother rat's nurturing—or neglect—influences her pups' reactions to stress, through epigenetic effects, and later their parenting behavior.

Eric Isselee/Shutterstock.com

Epigenetic Effects and Obesity

Finally, consider another study of rats that appears to have implications for humans too. It seems that feeding a *father* rat a high-fat diet and making him overweight changes epigenetic marks on genes in his sperm (Ng et al., 2010; and see Chapter 4 on fetal programming). The marks then become part of his daughter's epigenetic profile and change her physiology in ways that make her more prone to obesity and diabetes—*even though both she and her mother ate healthy diets!* There's now suggestive evidence that overweight human fathers can also pass on epigenetic marks through their sperm that are likely to increase their children's odds of obesity and related problems—and that in men who lose weight after undergoing gastric bypass surgery, many of the markings associated with obesity are reversed (Donkin et al.,

2016). Findings like this are truly astonishing; they are giving new life to an idea that was discredited in Charles Darwin's time: the notion that characteristics acquired during an individual's lifetime can be inherited by the individual's descendants (Moore, 2015).

So, although the chromosomes are generally wiped clean of epigenetic marks soon after conception, *some* epigenetic codings etched on top of genes during a parent's life can affect his or her offspring (Boyce & Kobor, 2015; Moore, 2015). As we have seen, this can happen in two ways: (a) through social transmission (illustrated when the caregiving behavior of mother rats affects their pups' epigenetic codings and later behavior), and (b) through epigenetic inheritance, in which epigenetic codings in a parent's sperm or egg are inherited by an embryo. Remarkably, some epigenetic marks have been shown to survive in animals across multiple generations (Moore, 2015).

It's not yet clear where epigenetic research will lead, how often epigenetic marks are inherited by our children and grandchildren, or how often they actually cause later physical and mental health problems. However, it *is* clear that environment can influence gene expression and, in turn, traits and behavior. By altering gene expression, some epigenetic effects may contribute to greater plasticity, helping organisms and their offspring adapt flexibly to whatever environmental conditions they encounter rather than wait generations for biological evolution to do its work (Champagne, 2013; Meaney, 2010).

In the end, no one completely understands the remarkable epigenetic process that transforms a single cell with its genetic endowment into millions of diverse cells—blood cells, nerve cells, skin cells, and so on—all organized into a living, behaving human. However, we are learning a tremendous amount from studies of gene–environment interactions, gene–environment correlations, and epigenetic effects (see ● **Table 3.6** for a summary). Genes and environment are active partners in the developmental process at every step.

Controversies Surrounding Genetic Research

Our society is grappling with the complex and troubling public policy and ethical issues that have arisen as geneticists have gained the capacity to identify the carriers and potential victims of diseases and disorders, to give parents information that might prompt them to abort a fetus that is not of the desired health status or intellect, and to experiment with techniques for altering an individual's genetic makeup through gene therapy (Lewis, 2012, 2015; Nussbaum et al., 2016). Gene therapy to treat such genetic disorders as hemophilia (through infusions of normal genes into the blood), the lung disease cystic fibrosis, and recently sickle-cell disease have had some success and are likely to have more. New techniques for "editing" the genome and inserting new genes in patients' bodies promise to revolutionize gene therapy—and raise all kinds of ethical issues and concerns about unintended consequences (Achenbach, 2015). Now, of course, researchers are also studying the epigenetic markings of individuals who have diseases and disorders and scrambling to develop drugs and dietary treatments to alter these codings (Boyce & Kobor, 2015; Moore, 2015).

If you think about it, though, it may be simpleminded to think that gene therapies will ever prevent or cure most diseases and disorders. Why? Because, as you now understand, most conditions are the product of the interaction of multiple genes and multiple environmental influences, including epigenetic effects on genes. Researchers not only must deliver the right genes to the body in sufficient number to have the desired effect but also must get them to turn on and off when they should and control important environmental influences as well. No "quick fixes" such as the PKU diet are likely for most conditions, especially those that are polygenic in origin. Still, genetic and epigenetic diagnosis and

● **Table 3.6** Types of Gene-Environment Interplay

Type	Meaning	Example	Significance
Gene–environment interaction	People with different genes are affected differently by environmental influences	Stress triggers depression only if a person has high-risk genes	Nature and nurture combine. *Diathesis-stress model* of psychopathology (vulnerability + stress leads to problems) and *differential susceptibility hypothesis* (some individuals are more sensitive to both good and bad environments)
Gene–environment correlation	People with different genes experience different environments—environments correlated with their genes (through passive, evocative, and active G–E correlations)	Children who have genes associated with sociability have sociable parents, evoke sociable responses from others, and actively seek social interaction	Nature affects nurture. Genetic predispositions influence experiences, which often strengthen genetically based tendencies. Measures of environment are not purely environmental; they are genetically influenced
Epigenetic effects	Environment affects gene expression through chemical codings on genes, e.g., DNA methylation	Early abuse/neglect results in an overly reactive stress response system and later psychological disorders	Nurture affects nature. Environmental influences alter the functioning of genes; some epigenetic marks are passed on to offspring

therapy techniques will improve, and we as a society will have to decide how—and how not—to use them.

Likewise, behavioral genetics research is controversial. On the one hand, it has provided truly important insights into human development: that differences in genetic makeup between us contribute to differences in virtually all of our physical and psychological characteristics, that our unique experiences are often more influential than those we share with siblings, that gene–environment interactions mean that we differ in our responses to the same experiences, that gene–environment correlations mean that we create our own environments, and that experiences get "under our skin" through epigenetic effects to shape the way our genes and physiologies function.

Nonetheless, some developmentalists question the whole idea of trying to separate the influences of genes and environment on differences between individuals when the two are so inseparable in each individual's development. They insist that behavioral genetics research will never tell us about what we should really want to understand: *epigenesis*, that long and complex process through which the interplay of genes and environment brings about development. Our best bet as parents and practitioners is to be sensitive to each child's genetically based predispositions as well as knowledgeable about ways to optimize development so that we can strengthen each child's adaptive tendencies and weaken or work around the maladaptive ones. Providing children with optimal experiences, of course, depends on knowing which environments stimulate healthy development and which do not. It is fitting, then, that the next chapter looks more closely at the critical importance of early environmental influences on development.

Checking Mastery

Label each example below as an example of (a) gene–environment interaction, (b) passive gene-environment correlation, (c) evocative gene–environment correlation, (d) active gene–environment correlation, or (e) epigenetic effects.

1. Roger inherited genes for artistic creativity from his parents and grew up watching them sketch and paint.
2. Tamara was abused as a child and this seems to have made her stress response system overly reactive.
3. Kayla inherited genes for mathematical ability and has been taking extra math and science courses in college.
4. Sydney inherited a gene that can cause intellectual disability but only in children who do not receive enough folic acid in their diet.
5. Jorge got genes for anxiety, and his anxious behavior makes his parents overprotective of him.

Making Connections

1. Assume that genes predispose some people to be highly religious and some people to be unreligious and that some environments nurture religiousness and others do not. Explain how a gene–environment interaction and a gene–environment correlation could each help make Peter more religious than Paul.
2. What information in this chapter makes you think you will turn out very much like your parents—and what information suggests that this may not be the case at all?

Chapter Summary

3.1 Evolution and Species Heredity

- As humans, we develop similarly in part because we share a species heredity, the product of evolution.
- According to Darwin's theory of biological evolution, if there is genetic variation in a species—and if some genes aid members of the species in adapting to their environment and reproducing—those genes will become more common in the population over time through natural selection.
- Humans also adapt to changes in their environments through the faster process of cultural evolution.

3.2 Individual Heredity

- Each human has an individual heredity provided at conception, when sperm and ovum, each with 23 chromosomes (thanks to meiosis), unite to form a single-cell zygote with 46 chromosomes. Parent and child share 50% of their genes in common; siblings share 50% on average.
- The chromosomes contain some 20,000–25,000 protein-building genes, along with regulatory DNA; the Human Genome Project and related studies have mapped these genes and revealed similarities and differences between the genes of different human groups and species.

- Environmental factors influence how a genotype (genetic makeup) is translated into a phenotype (actual traits); regulatory DNA and environmental factors influence the important process of gene expression.
- The three main mechanisms of inheritance are single gene-pair inheritance, sex-linked inheritance, and polygenic (multiple gene) inheritance. Some children are also affected by new or inherited changes in gene structure (mutations, copy number variations); others, because of errors in meiosis, have chromosome abnormalities such as Down syndrome or a sex chromosome abnormality.
- Couples can obtain information about genetic diseases such as sickle-cell disease, Huntington's disease, and PKU from genetic counselors, and many genetic abnormalities can be detected prenatally through ultrasound, amniocentesis, chorionic villus sampling, maternal blood sampling, and preimplantation genetic diagnosis.

3.3 Studying Genetic and Environmental Influences

- Behavioral geneticists conduct twin, adoption, and other family studies that describe resemblances between pairs of people using concordance rates and correlation coefficients. They then estimate the heritability of traits and the contributions of shared (with siblings) and nonshared (unique) environmental influences.

- Techniques of molecular genetics are used to identify and study particular gene variants and to compare people who do and do not have them.

3.4 Selected Behavioral Genetics Findings

- Performance on measures of intelligence is a heritable trait. From infancy to adulthood, individual differences in mental ability more strongly reflect both individual genetic makeup and non-shared environmental influences, whereas shared environmental influences wane.
- Aspects of temperament and personality are also genetically influenced, and nonshared environmental influences are significant whereas shared environmental influences are typically not.
- Similarly, psychological disorders such as schizophrenia have a genetic basis, but it often takes an interaction of genes and environmental stressors to produce disorder.
- Overall, physical and physiological characteristics are more strongly influenced by genetic endowment than are intellectual abilities and, in turn, temperament and personality, psychological disorders, and finally, attitudes and interests.

3.5 Gene–Environment Interplay

- Gene–environment interactions mean that genes influence how people react to the environment, as illustrated by the diathesis-stress model and differential susceptibility hypothesis.
- Passive, evocative, and active gene–environment correlations suggest that people experience and seek out environments that often match and reinforce their genetic predispositions. As a result, measures meant to assess environmental influences partly reflect genetic makeup, and we need genetically informed studies.
- Epigenetic effects, effects of the environment on gene expression, further illustrate how completely intertwined nature and nurture are in development.
- Genetic research is controversial, as illustrated by issues in gene therapy and by criticisms of behavioral genetics.

Key Terms

4

Prenatal Development and Birth

4.1 Prenatal Development	**4.2 The Prenatal Environment and Fetal Programming**	**4.3 The Perinatal Environment**	**4.4 The Neonatal Environment**
Conception	Teratogens	Possible Hazards	Breast or Bottle?
Prenatal Stages	The Mother's State	The Mother's Experience	Identifying At-Risk Newborns
	The Father's State	The Father's Experience	Risk and Resilience

At age 26, Serena was not thinking about getting pregnant. She and her boyfriend, Tony, were both getting adjusted to new jobs and working long hours. Serena tried to keep up with her regular exercise routine and struggled through a nasty sinus infection requiring treatment with antibiotics. She wasn't too concerned when she gained a few pounds but began to worry when she missed several menstrual periods. A visit to her doctor revealed that she was nearly 5 months pregnant, probably a result of the antibiotics decreasing the effectiveness of her birth control. Serena's mind raced as she considered all the things she had—or had not—done during recent months that might have influenced her unborn baby. Did she drink too much alcohol? Had she eaten a healthy diet? These thoughts were quickly followed by concerns about what the childbirth experience would be like and how she and Tony would adjust to this rather unexpected change in their lives.

We will answer these questions and more in this chapter on prenatal development, the birth experience, and the first hours and days of life. You will learn why the environment of the womb is so important and how it can set the stage for healthy development across the entire life span. The material in this chapter is a good illustration of how developmentalists seek to optimize development by using research to guide practices before, during, and after pregnancy.

LEARNING OBJECTIVES

- Summarize the main events and three phases of the prenatal period.

- Explain the major changes in brain development during the prenatal period.

Perhaps at no time in the life span does development occur faster, or is environment more important, than between conception and birth. What maturational milestones normally occur during this period?

Conception

Midway through the menstrual cycle, every 28 days or so, females ovulate: A follicle that has been growing inside the ovary erupts and releases an egg, thanks, in part, to follicle-stimulating hormone (FSH) and luteinizing hormone (LH). Once released, the egg cell, called an ovum, begins its journey through the nearest fallopian tube to the uterus. Usually the egg disintegrates and leaves the body as part of the menstrual flow. However, if the woman has intercourse with a fertile man around the time of ovulation, the 300 million or so sperm cells in his seminal fluid swim, tadpole style, in all directions. Of the approximately 300 sperm that survive the 6-hour journey into the fallopian tubes, one may meet and penetrate the ovum on its descent from the ovary (Sadler, 2015; see also ■ **Figure 4.1**). Although fertilization usually takes place within 12 hours of ovulation, sperm can

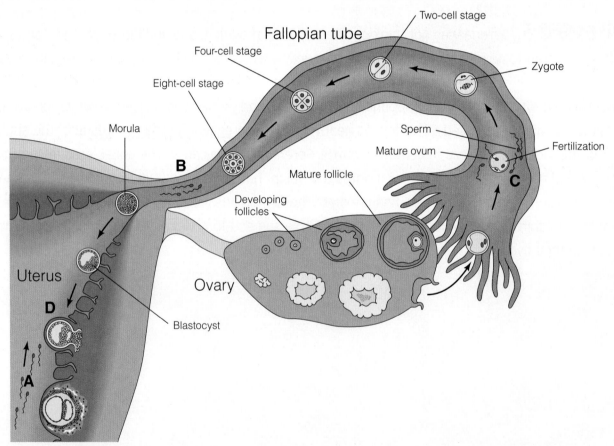

■ **Figure 4.1** Fertilization and implantation. (A) Millions of sperm cells have entered the vagina and are finding their way into the uterus. (B) Some sperm are moving up the fallopian tube (there is a similar tube on the other side) toward the ovum. (C) Fertilization occurs. The fertilized ovum drifts down the tube, dividing and forming new cells as it goes, until it implants itself in the wall of the uterus (D) by the seventh or eighth day after fertilization.

survive for up to 6 days in the reproductive tract, which means pregnancy can result from intercourse that has occurred as much as 6 days prior to ovulation (Sadler, 2015). Once a single sperm penetrates the egg cell, a biochemical reaction occurs that repels other sperm and keeps them from entering the already fertilized egg. As explained in Chapter 3, conception, the beginning of life, occurs when the genetic material of the sperm and egg unite to form a single-celled zygote.

For many couples, the process proceeds smoothly and swiftly leads to a pregnancy, but for as many as one in four couples, the experience of conceiving is fraught with difficulties. **Infertility**—not being able to get pregnant after a year of trying—is equally likely to be traced to the man as to the woman and stems from a variety of causes. For example, adolescents and adults—both male and female—who have contracted sexually transmitted infections (STIs) may become infertile. Some men have a condition called *varicocele* in which enlarged veins on their testicles raises the temperature in the testes, interfering with sperm production (Sohrabvand, et al., 2015). Infertility traced to women may be related to problems with ovulation, blocked fallopian tubes, or **endometriosis**, a condition arising when bits of tissue lining the uterus grow outside the uterus. Depending on the suspected cause of infertility, couples may be helped to conceive with simple solutions. A man may be advised to wear loose boxer shorts rather than tighter briefs that might elevate testicular temperature. A woman may be able to track her morning body temperature to determine when she ovulates and is therefore most likely to become pregnant. As **Figure 4.2** shows, ovulation is accompanied by a rise in body temperature along with a spike in follicle-stimulating hormone (FSH) and luteinizing hormone (LH).

When simpler methods fail, some couples move on to more elaborate (and expensive) assisted reproductive technologies (ARTs), medical techniques used to increase fertility. ART techniques typically start with or include prescription drugs for the woman to stimulate her ovaries to ripen multiple follicles, leading to the release of several eggs. If this is unsuccessful, couples and their doctors may proceed to **artificial insemination** (also called intrauterine insemination), which involves injecting sperm, either from a woman's partner or from a donor, into her uterus. Or they may use **in vitro fertilization (IVF)**, in which several eggs are removed from a woman's ovary and manually combined with sperm in a laboratory dish before being returned to a woman's uterus in hopes that one egg will implant on the wall of the uterus. We should note that there are many variations of IVF, depending on who provides the eggs and the sperm. A couple wanting to have a child could donate both eggs and sperm and have the biological mother carry the baby to term. At the other end of the spectrum, an infant conceived through IVF could wind up with five "parents": a sperm donor, an egg donor, a surrogate mother in whom the fertilized egg is implanted, and a caregiving mother and father. This raises intriguing issues about the meaning of family, which we will return to in a later chapter.

Infertility is costly, both economically and emotionally. Worldwide, the cost of IVF is highest in the United States, where each attempt runs between $12,000 and $15,000. The success rate for women who use their own fresh (rather than frozen) eggs is about 1 in 4 overall, but decreases as mothers get older. IVF results in a live birth in 40% of women under 35 years but in only 5% of women 43–44 years of age (CDC, 2015). Several recent advances in selecting eggs based on their mitochondria or energy levels (an indication of egg health), changing the time of when eggs are harvested for fertilization, and even augmenting egg cells with a bath of mitochondrial cells retrieved from the ovaries show promise for increasing the success rates of IVF (Fragouli et al., 2015; Tilly & Sinclair, 2013; Wu et al., 2015).

Couples report that infertility is stressful as they are going through it, but most couples do not regret going through the process, regardless of outcome. In one study, researchers in Germany followed up with couples 10 years after their fertility treatments. Couples with children showed somewhat greater growth in self-esteem over the 10 years relative to couples without children, but women without children reported greater job satisfaction and indicated that there were positive aspects to not having children (Wischmann et al., 2012). All couples, with and without children, reported similar levels of satisfaction with their friendships, their sex lives, and life in general. A study conducted in Sweden 20 years after women had undergone IVF treatment found somewhat negative outcomes, such as higher rates of depression, for women whose treatment was unsuccessful (Vikström et al., 2015). The authors noted that, 20 years after IVF treatment, many women were in a peer group beginning to experience or anticipate grandparenthood, which may have contributed to elevated depression levels.

Coping skills contribute to how successfully individuals and couples readjust their thinking from possible parenthood to parenthood not being a likely life outcome. Those women who maintain a strong desire for children in the years following infertility treatment are more likely to experience adjustment or mental health problems, but

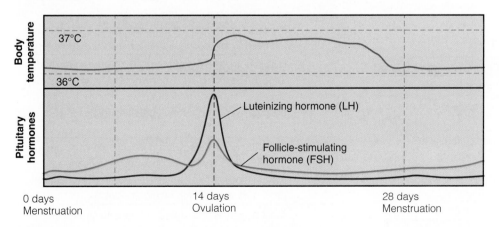

Figure 4.2 Levels of luteinizing hormone and follicle-stimulating hormone spike and there is a rise in body temperature at about the midpoint of a woman's cycle, signaling ovulation.

these women represent only a small minority of those who go through infertility treatments (Gamiero et al., 2014; Wischmann et al., 2012). Finally, women seem to fare better when they know that the cause of infertility is not directly attributable to them (Gamiero et al., 2014). Overall, then, despite the stress experienced during treatment for infertility, there does not seem to be significant or long-lasting negative outcomes for most women or couples.

Prenatal Stages

The zygote contains the 46 chromosomes that are the genetic blueprint for the individual's development. It takes about 266 days, or roughly 9 months, for the zygote to become a fetus of billions of cells that is ready to be born. Experts called **embryologists**, who study early growth and development, divide prenatal development into three stages or periods: the germinal period, the embryonic period, and the fetal period. More commonly, parents-to-be and their obstetricians organize pregnancy into trimesters corresponding to the first 3 months, the middle 3 months, and the last 3 months of the prenatal period.

The Germinal Period

The first trimester begins with the **germinal period**, which lasts approximately 2 weeks; the important events of this period are outlined in ● **Table 4.1**. For the first week or two, the zygote divides many times through mitosis, forming the **blastocyst**, a hollow ball of about 150 cells that is the size of the head of a pin. When the blastocyst reaches the uterus around day 6, it implants tendrils from its outer layer into the blood vessels of the uterine wall. This is quite an accomplishment; only about half of all fertilized ova are successfully implanted in the uterus. In addition, not all implanted embryos survive the early phases of prenatal development. Although estimates vary widely, somewhere between as few as 8% and as many as 50% of pregnancies are short-lived, ending in **miscarriage** (also called spontaneous abortion) before survival outside the womb is possible, with many of these losses occurring before the pregnancy has even been detected (Sadler, 2015; Tulandi, 2015). Many such early losses are because of genetic defects and are, perhaps, the body's natural way of eliminating an embryo or fetus that will not survive.

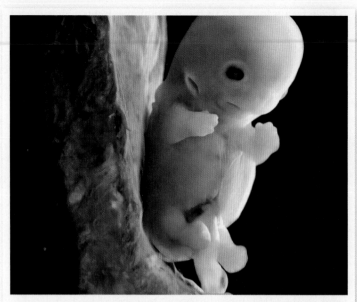

About a month after conception, this embryo is shown up against a cross-section of the placenta. The umbilical cord is shown at the bottom of the photo, connecting the embryo to its vital source of life in the womb. The eyes are clearly visible, as are the arms, legs, and ear buds. The fingers are just beginning to differentiate, and the mouth is formed.

Mark Alberhasky/RGB Ventures LLC dba SuperStock/Alamy Stock Photo

The Embryonic Period

The first trimester continues with the **embryonic period**, which occurs from the third to the eighth week after conception. During this short time, every major organ takes shape, in at least a primitive form, in a process called **organogenesis** (● **Table 4.2**). The layers of the blastocyst

● **Table 4.1** Events of the Germinal Period

Day	Event
1	Fertilization usually occurs within 24 hours of ovulation.
2	The single-celled zygote begins to divide 24–36 hours after fertilization.
3	The mass has 12–16 cells and is called a morula; it is traveling down the fallopian tube to the uterus.
4–5	An inner cell mass forms; the entire mass is called a blastocyst and is the size of a pinhead.
6–7	The blastocyst attaches to the wall of the uterus.
8–14	During the second week, the blastocyst becomes fully embedded in the wall of the uterus. It now has about 250 cells.

● **Table 4.2** Events of the Embryonic Period

Week	Event
3	Now an embryo, the person-to-be is just 1/10 of an inch (2 mm) long. It has become elongated, and three layers emerge—the ectoderm, mesoderm, and endoderm.
4	The embryo is so curved that the two ends almost touch. The outer layer (ectoderm) folds into the neural tube. From the mesoderm, a tiny heart forms and begins to beat. The endoderm differentiates into a gastrointestinal tract and lungs. Between days 21 and 28, eyes develop.
5	Ears, mouth, and throat take shape. Arm and leg buds appear. The handplate, from which fingers will emerge, appears. The heart divides into two regions, and the brain differentiates into forebrain, midbrain, and hindbrain.
6–7	The embryo is almost 1 inch long. The heart divides into four chambers. Fingers emerge from the handplate, and primitive facial features are evident. The important process of sexual differentiation begins.
8	Most structures and organs are present. Ovaries and testes are evident. The embryo begins to straighten and assumes a more human appearance.

differentiate, forming structures that sustain development. The outer layer becomes both the **amnion**, a watertight membrane that fills with fluid that cushions and protects the embryo, and the **chorion**, a membrane that surrounds the amnion and attaches rootlike extensions called *villi* to the uterine lining to gather nourishment for the embryo. The chorion eventually becomes the lining of the **placenta**, a tissue fed by blood vessels from the mother and connected to the embryo by the umbilical cord. Through the placenta and umbilical cord, the embryo receives oxygen and nutrients from the mother and eliminates carbon dioxide and metabolic wastes into the mother's bloodstream. A membrane called the *placental barrier* allows these small molecules to pass through, but it prevents the large blood cells of embryo and mother from mingling. It also protects the developing child from many harmful substances, but as you will see shortly, it is not infallible; some dangerous substances slip through.

Meanwhile, the cells in the interior of the blastocyst give rise to the ectoderm, mesoderm, and endoderm. These will eventually evolve into specific tissues and organ systems, including the central nervous system (brain and spinal cord) from the ectoderm; muscles, bones, cartilage, heart, arteries, kidneys, and gonads from the mesoderm; and gastrointestinal tract, lungs, and bladder from the endoderm (Sadler, 2015).

Development proceeds at a breathtaking pace. The beginnings of a brain are apparent after only 3–4 weeks, when the neural plate folds up to form the neural tube (■Figure 4.3). The bottom of the tube becomes the spinal cord. "Lumps" emerge at the top of the tube and form the forebrain, midbrain, and hindbrain (■Figure 4.4). The so-called primitive or lower portions of the brain develop earliest. They regulate such biological functions as digestion, respiration, and elimination; they also control sleep–wake states and permit simple motor reactions. These are the parts of the brain that make life possible.

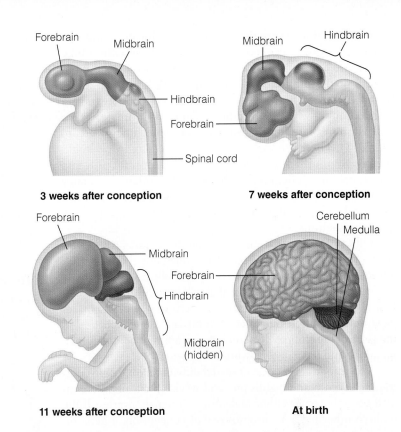

3 weeks after conception

7 weeks after conception

11 weeks after conception

At birth

■ **Figure 4.4** The brain at four stages of development, showing hindbrain, midbrain, and forebrain.

In approximately 1 out of 2,000 pregnancies, the neural tube fails to fully close (Liptak, 2013). When this happens at the bottom of the tube, it can lead to **spina bifida**, in which part of the spinal cord is not fully encased in the protective covering of the spinal column (■ **Figure 4.5**). Children with spina bifida typically have neurological problems ranging

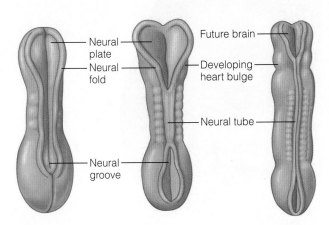

■ **Figure 4.3** The nervous system emerges from the neural plate, which thickens and folds to form the neural groove. When the edges of the groove meet, the neural tube is formed. All this takes place between 18 and 26 days after conception.

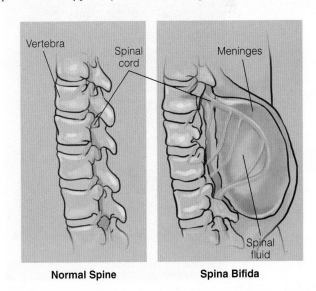

Normal Spine

Spina Bifida

■ **Figure 4.5** Unlike the normal spine, spina bifida is characterized by an opening in the spinal cord that may be relatively small and invisible, or may be large enough to allow part of the spinal cord and nerves to bulge out of the protective spinal column.

from very mild to severe depending on the location and size of the opening. Failure to close at the top of the neural tube can lead to **anencephaly**, a lethal defect in which the main portion of the brain above the brain stem fails to develop. Neural tube defects occur by 26 days after conception and are more common when the mother is deficient in folate, a type of B vitamin that is critical for normal gene function (Liptak, 2013). There are various reasons why folate levels might become diminished, including use of birth control pills and poor nutrition (deRegnier & Desai, 2010). Folate deficiency has helped highlight the importance of good maternal nutrition for development, about which we will have more to say in a later section.

Other critical organs are also taking shape. Just 4 weeks after conception, a tiny heart not only has formed but also has begun to beat. The eyes, ears, nose, and mouth rapidly take shape in the second month, and buds appear that will become arms and legs. During the second month, a primitive nervous system also makes newly formed muscles contract. Only 60 days after conception, at the close of the embryonic period, the organism is a little over an inch long and has a distinctly human appearance.

The important process of sexual differentiation begins during the seventh and eighth prenatal weeks. First, undifferentiated tissue becomes either male testes or female ovaries: If the embryo inherited a Y chromosome at conception, a gene on it calls for the construction of testes; in a genetic female with two X chromosomes, ovaries form instead. The testes of a male embryo secrete **testosterone**, the primary male sex hormone that stimulates the development of a male internal reproductive system, and another hormone that inhibits the development of a female internal reproductive system. In the absence of these hormones, the embryo develops the internal reproductive system of a female.

Clearly the embryonic period is dramatic and highly important because it is when the structures that make us human evolve. Yet many pregnant women, either because they do not yet know they are pregnant—like Serena from the chapter opening story— or because they do not appreciate the value of early prenatal care, do not go to a doctor until *after* the eighth week of prenatal development. By this time, it may be too late to prevent the damage that can be caused by an unhealthy lifestyle.

The Fetal Period

The fetal period lasts from the ninth week of pregnancy until birth, which means it encompasses part of the first trimester and all of the middle and last trimesters (● **Table 4.3**). It is a critical

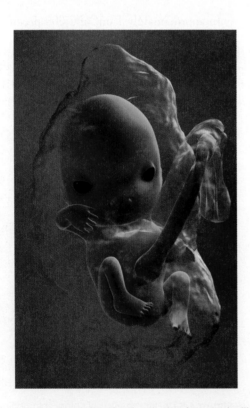

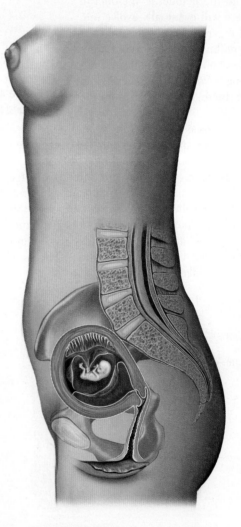

Here we see what the developing fetus looks like in the womb at 10 weeks after conception. Right, we see how things look at this same time on the outside: a "baby bump" is just barely visible on the mother, despite the amazing changes that have been taking place inside.

Week	Event
9	Bone tissue emerges, and the embryo becomes a fetus. The head of the fetus looks huge relative to the rest of the body—it takes up about half the total length of the fetus. The fetus can open and close its mouth and turn its head.
10–12	Fingers and toes are clearly formed. External genitalia have developed. Movements have increased substantially—arms and legs kick vigorously, but the fetus is still too small for the mother to feel all these movements. The fetus also shows "breathing" movements with its chest and some reflexes.
13–16	The heartbeat should be audible with a stethoscope. Fetal movements may become apparent to the mother. The fetus is about 4½ inches long, and the skeleton is becoming harder.
17–22	Fingernails and toenails, hair, teeth buds, and eyelashes grow. Brain development is phenomenal, and brainwaves are detectable.
23–25	These weeks mark the age of viability, when the fetus has a *chance* of survival outside the womb. It is about 12 inches long and weighs about 1 pound.
26–32	The fetus gains weight, and its brain grows. The nervous system becomes better organized.
33–38	The last 6 weeks of a full-term pregnancy bring further weight gain and brain activity. The lungs mature and begin to expand and contract.

period for brain development, which involves three processes: proliferation, migration, and differentiation. **Proliferation** of neurons involves their multiplying at a staggering rate during this period; by one estimate, the number of neurons increases by hundreds of thousands every minute throughout all of pregnancy, with a concentrated period of proliferation occurring between 6 and 17 weeks after conception (du Plessis, 2013; McDonald, 2007). As a result of this rapid proliferation, the young infant has around 100 billion neurons. Another period of proliferation takes place after birth, but this produces an increase in glial cells, not nerve cells. Glial cells function primarily as support cells for neurons.

In **migration**, the neurons move from their place of origin in the center of the brain to particular locations throughout the brain where they will become part of specialized functioning units. Migration is influenced by genetic instructions and by the biochemical environment in which brain cells find themselves. Some neurons migrate passively by getting pushed out of the way to make room for other neurons being born (Johnson & de Haan, 2015). This form of migration is typical for neurons that will end up in the brain stem and thalamus. Other neurons, such as those that will form the cerebral cortex, take a more active role: They travel along the surface of glial cells and detach at programmed destinations in the developing brain (■ **Figure 4.6**). The first neurons to migrate stop at the closest or innermost layer of what will be the cerebral cortex. Other groups of neurons follow suit but need to travel farther until all six layers of the cerebral cortex have been formed. Although this process occurs throughout the prenatal period, much of it occurs between 8 and 15 weeks after conception (McDonald, 2007). Once a neuron reaches its "home," it begins to communicate with the surrounding neurons.

Along with proliferation and migration of cells, a third process of **differentiation**, or transformation of cells, is occurring (● **Table 4.4** summarizes these events). Neurons may evolve into a particular type or function based on where they land following migration. Alternatively, another theory is that cells may "know" what they are supposed to be and where they are intended to go on their migratory path *before* reaching their final destination (Johnson & de Haan, 2015). Under normal circumstances, this proliferation-migration-differentiation process proceeds smoothly and everything ends up where it should be. In some cases, though, as we'll see later in this chapter, cells get slowed down or sidetracked along their migratory path or they do not properly differentiate at their endpoint. This can lead to a nervous system that does not function as well as it could (McDonald, 2007).

Organ systems that formed during the embryonic period continue to grow and begin to function. Harmful agents will no longer cause major malformations because organs have already

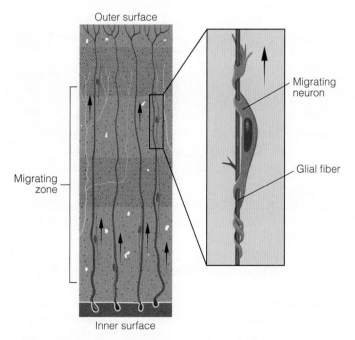

■ **Figure 4.6** Neurons move to their final destinations in the brain by attaching themselves to strands of glial fiber and then slowly progressing along the surface of the glial fiber.

● **Table 4.4** Processes of Prenatal Brain Development

Process	Explanation
Proliferation	An intense period of cell growth, originating from stem cells undergoing rapid cell division.
Migration	Cells move or travel to their intended location in the nervous system. Chemical signals may serve as a neural GPS, guiding cells to their destination.
Differentiation	Cells change or transform into a particular type. At their destination, they set up camp and begin to communicate with surrounding neurons.

formed, but they can stunt the growth of the fetus and interfere with the wiring of its rapidly developing nervous system.

In the third month of pregnancy, distinguishable external sex organs appear, the bones and muscles develop, and the fetus becomes frisky: By the end of the first trimester of pregnancy, it moves its arms, kicks its legs, makes fists, and even turns somersaults in its own little amniotic fluid-filled gymnasium. The mother probably does not yet feel all this activity because the fetus is still only about 3 inches long. Nonetheless, all of this moving around and bumping into the walls of the uterus may help create a "body sense" that will later evolve into a meaningful sense of self (Piontelli, 2015). Other behaviors are also evident at this stage: swallowing, yawning, hiccupping, and urinating. These early actions contribute to the proper development of the nervous system, respiratory system, digestive system, and other systems of the body, and they are consistent with the behaviors that we observe *after* birth (Piontelli, 2015).

During the second trimester, more refined activities such as occasional thumb sucking appear and fetuses spend more time touching themselves, especially their faces (Piontelli, 2015). By the end of this period the sensory organs are functioning: Premature infants as young as 25 weeks respond to loud noises and bright lights (Allen & Capute, 1986; Sadler, 2015). At about 23 weeks after conception, midway through the fifth month, the fetus reaches the **age of viability**, when survival outside the uterus is possible *if* the brain and respiratory system are sufficiently developed. The age of viability is earlier today than at any time in the past because medical techniques for keeping fragile babies alive have improved considerably over the past few decades. Although there are cases of "miracle babies" who survive severely premature birth, many infants born at 22–25 weeks do not survive, and of those who do, many experience chronic health or neurological problems. Among infants born at the cusp of survivability—22–23 weeks— 92% do not survive beyond a few hours or

days despite the use of aggressive medical therapies (Swamy et al., 2010). At 23 weeks, 25% of preemies survive, and with just one more week in the womb, the survival rate jumps to 55% (Berger et al., 2012). Thus, the age of viability is an indicator of when survival *may be possible*, but it is by no means a guarantee of life or health. Further, as ■ **Figure 4.7** shows, the odds of survival may also depend on the country where you live and even the birthing location within a country. Such differences likely reflect variations in how aggressively premature infants are resuscitated and treated, something we will say more about later in this chapter (Berger et al., 2012; Serenius et al., 2013).

In terms of growth, it is primarily all about length during the second trimester and then weight during the third trimester. Not surprisingly, this increased size of the fetus means the little bundle of joy gradually makes its presence known to mom as it tries to move within the increasingly tight space of the womb. The third trimester is also critical in the development of the brain, as is the entire prenatal period (more on this in Chapter 5). Early in pregnancy, the basic architecture of the nervous system is developed. During the second half of pregnancy, neurons not only multiply at an astonishing rate (proliferation) but they also increase in size and develop an insulating cover, myelin, that improves their ability to transmit signals rapidly. Most importantly, guided by both a genetic blueprint and early sensory experiences, neurons connect with one another and organize into working groups that control vision, memory, motor behavior, and other functions. For good reason, parents should be concerned about damage to the developing human during the first trimester, when the brain and other organs are forming. However, they should not overlook the significance of the second and third trimesters,

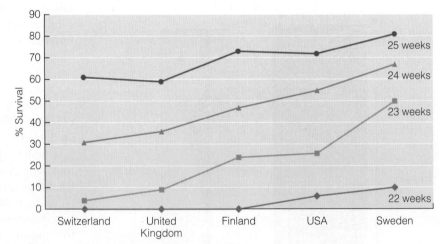

■ **Figure 4.7** Percentage survival at 22, 23, 24, and 25 weeks gestation. At 22 weeks gestational age, the chances of survival are very bleak. But with each additional week in the womb, the odds of survival improve. There are also cross-national variations: Babies born very prematurely in Sweden have the best chances of survival relative to similarly premature babies born in one of the other countries shown here.

Source: Berger, T. M., Steurer, M. A., Woerner, A., Meyer-Schiffer, P., & Adams, M. (2012). Trends and centre-to-centre variability in survival rates of very preterm infants (<32 weeks) over a 10-year-period in Switzerland. *Archives of Disease in Childhood-Fetal and Neonatal Edition*, 97, F323–F328.

which are critical to normal brain functioning and therefore to normal development.

As the brain develops, the behavior of the fetus becomes more like the organized and adaptive behavior seen in the newborn. For example, Janet DiPietro and her colleagues (2006, 2007) assessed heart rates and activity levels at various points prenatally and postnatally. Heart rate was relatively stable from the prenatal period into early childhood. By 36 weeks of gestation, heart rate activity and movement become increasingly organized into coherent patterns known as *infant states*. Fetuses whose heart rates and movements were concordant (that is, matched) at 36 weeks showed better regulation of their behavioral states at 2 weeks old. They were more alert, less irritable, better able to sustain their attention, and more likely to maintain control even during stressful parts of a postnatal examination. Beyond this, fetal heart rate variability was associated with mental development at age 2 and language development at age 2½. In particular, fetuses with slower and more variable heart rates had higher levels of mental and language development in early childhood compared with those who had faster and less variable heart rates. The researchers speculate that slow and variable heart rates may reflect optimal regulation of the nervous system.

With age, fetal heart rates also become increasingly responsive to such stimuli as a vibrator placed on the mother's abdomen or loud noises (DiPietro et al., 1996b). While it might be tempting to conclude that these fetal reactions and movements signify being awake, experts argue that fetuses are never truly awake (see Piontelli, 2015). Instead, they spend most of their time snoozing, either in quiet sleep or active sleep. As pregnancy progresses, fetuses experience "micro-awakenings," when they might briefly open their eyes or grimace, but even these are short-lived and cannot be equated directly to the awake state of an infant. Most fetuses settle into a predictable pattern of quiet sleep-active sleep by 27–30 weeks. Such findings are important because they point to greater organization of the nervous system at about the time when premature infants are typically well equipped to survive. As the nervous system becomes more organized, so does behavior.

Interestingly, different fetuses display consistent differences in their patterns of heart rate and movement, and researchers have detected correlations between measures of fetal physiology and behavior and measures of infant temperament (DiPietro et al., 1996a, 2007; Werner et al., 2007). For example, active fetuses turn out to be active, difficult, and unpredictable babies, and fetuses whose states are better organized are also better regulated at 3 months old, as indicated by their waking fewer times during the night. This shows that newborn behavior does not spring from nowhere; it emerges long before birth. There is

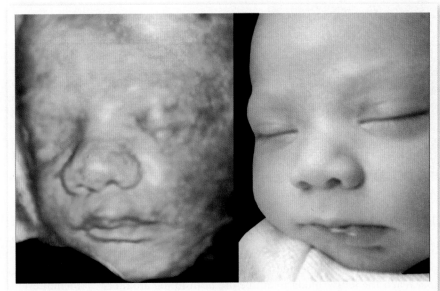

The behaviors and facial expressions of the fetus (*left*, from 3D ultrasound) are remarkably similar to those exhibited by the infant after birth (*right*).

Thierry Berrod/Mona Lisa Production/Science Source

a good deal of continuity between prenatal behavior and postnatal behavior.

By the middle of the ninth month, the fetus is so large that its most comfortable position in cramped quarters is head down with limbs curled in (the "fetal position"). The mother's uterus contracts at irregular intervals during the last month of pregnancy. When these contractions are strong, frequent, and regular, the mother is in the first stage of labor and the prenatal period is drawing to a close. Under normal circumstances, birth will occur within hours.

Checking Mastery

1. What is conception, and what techniques can be used to assist conception?
2. How does the development of the brain and nervous system unfold during the embryonic and fetal periods?
3. When is survival outside the womb possible?

Making Connections

1. What ethical concerns should be considered with the use of artificial reproductive technologies? As technologies become more advanced in the future, what additional concerns may arise?
2. Based on what you know about the developments during the prenatal period, where would you focus attempts to optimize prenatal care and why?

LEARNING OBJECTIVES

- Discuss the concept of fetal programming, and evaluate its usefulness in understanding connections between prenatal events and postnatal outcomes.

- Organize teratogens according to the seriousness of their impact on development (that is, from major structural abnormalities to small or undetermined effects).

- Summarize characteristics of the parents-to-be that may influence pregnancy and its outcomes.

The mother's womb is the prenatal environment for the unborn child. Just as children are influenced by their physical and social environments, so too is the fetus affected by its surroundings. The physical environment includes everything from the molecules that reach the fetus's bloodstream before birth to the architecture of a home to the climate outside it. The social environment includes all the people who can influence and be influenced by the developing person and the broader culture. Although early theorists tended to view environment as a set of forces that shaped the individual, as though a person were just a lump of clay to be molded, we now know this is not the case. Recall the concept in Chapter 2's discussion of the bioecological model of *reciprocal influences*: People shape their physical and social environments and are, in turn, affected by the environments they have helped create. For example, if a woman uses cocaine during pregnancy, her newborn may be extraordinarily fussy: Environment has affected development. But a fussy baby is likely to affect his environment by irritating his mother, who then expresses her tenseness in her interactions with him; this makes him fussier, which aggravates his mother even more, and her aggravation, in turn, makes him even crankier. Such transactions between person and environment begin at the moment of conception. When all is right, the prenatal environment provides just the stimulation and support needed for the fetus to mature physically and to develop a repertoire of behaviors that allow it to seek more stimulation, which in turn contributes to the development of more sophisticated behavior.

The developing embryo-then-fetus is a vulnerable little creature. Where it was once believed that the placenta served as a screen to protect the fetus from harmful substances, we now know that this is not the case. Research increasingly shows that events of the prenatal period can have lifelong effects on physical health and mental development. In Chapter 3, we introduced the idea of *epigenetic effects* whereby gene expression may be modified by environmental factors. The period of greatest environmental influence is during the prenatal period when growth and changes are occurring at an astonishingly fast rate. During this time, factors originating inside the mother, such as her hormone levels or immune system functioning, as well as factors originating outside the mother, such as exposure to pollution, can alter the expression of genes throughout life (see Boyce & Kobor, 2015). As we explained in Chapter 3, experience leaves its "fingerprint" on top of certain genes in certain cells, which influences whether those genes are turned on or not.

A growing body of research indicates that developmental outcomes may be influenced by **fetal programming** brought about by such epigenetic effects of the environment (Boyce & Kobor, 2015). The general idea of fetal programming is that environmental events and maternal conditions during pregnancy may alter the expected genetic unfolding of the embryo/fetus or reset its physiologic functions. As a result of these alterations, prenatal experience can change a person's physiology and the wiring of the brain and influence how the individual responds to postnatal events. Conditions of the prenatal period, then, set the stage for susceptibility to later health and mental health problems, perhaps decades down the road. But that's not all.

As ■ **Figure** 4.8 illustrates, it is not only the unborn child who may be affected by prenatal environmental factors: The offspring of the unborn child may also be affected. Through epigenetic codings carried on the DNA of the reproductive cells of the developing fetus, a pregnant woman's health, diet, and environment may adversely affect her future grandchildren

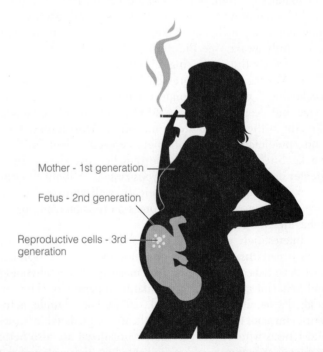

Mother - 1st generation

Fetus - 2nd generation

Reproductive cells - 3rd generation

■ **Figure 4.8** A woman's experiences during pregnancy can impact not only her own health, but that of her unborn baby *and* her future grandchildren.

(Shrivastava et al., 2012). Epigenetics is a critical component in understanding fetal programming (Barouki et al., 2012; Sookoian et al., 2013). According to research with animals and increasingly humans, prenatal imbalances in nutrition and exposure to environmental toxins may alter molecular pathways in ways leading to disease and health challenges later in life. Adult health and mental health conditions such as obesity, heart disease, and schizophrenia may arise, in part, from the prenatal environment and fetal programming (Boyce & Kobor, 2015). Unfortunately, adverse prenatal conditions such as poor nutrition and exposure to pollution disproportionately affect women—and their children—who live in poverty. The growing body of research showing life-long effects of epigenetic processes helps contribute to our understanding of the oft-seen multigenerational impacts of poverty (Boyce & Kobor, 2015). On the bright side, though, *good* health may also have its origins in the prenatal period, suggesting that this is a period of opportunity, not just a period of vulnerability.

How then can development during this period be optimized? What hazards does the fetus face? In the next sections, your main mission is to discover the extent to which early environmental influences, interacting with genetic influences, make or break later development. The nature–nurture issue, then, is the central question to consider when thinking about prenatal development and its influence on the developing person. Early exposure to certain environmental factors interacts with genetic makeup throughout the life span to make us who we are. If a common genetic heritage (species heredity) can make different human beings alike in some respects, so can similar environments. If unique genes make one person different from another, so do unique experiences.

Teratogens

A teratogen is any disease, drug, or other environmental agent that can harm a developing fetus (for example, by causing deformities, blindness, brain damage, or even death). The list of teratogens has grown frighteningly long, and the environment contains many potential teratogens whose effects on development have not yet been assessed. Before considering the effects of some major teratogens, however, let us emphasize that *only 15% of newborns have minor problems, and even fewer—perhaps 3%—have more significant anomalies due to teratogens* (Sadler, 2015). We will start with a few generalizations about the effects of teratogens, which we will then illustrate with examples:

- **Critical period.** The effects of a teratogenic agent are worst during the critical period when an organ system grows most rapidly.
- **Dosage and duration.** The greater the level of exposure and the longer the exposure to a teratogen, the more likely it is that serious damage will occur.
- **Genetic makeup.** Susceptibility to harm is influenced by the genetic makeup of the unborn child as well as the mother's genotype. Some fetuses are more (or less) resistant to teratogens and some mothers are more (or less) able to detoxify teratogens (Cassina et al., 2012). Therefore, not all embryos and fetuses are affected, nor are they affected equally, by a teratogen.

- **Environment.** The effects of a teratogen depend on the quality of both the prenatal and the postnatal environments.

Look more closely at the first generalization, which is particularly important. A period of rapid growth is a critical period for an organ system—a time during which the developing organism is especially sensitive to environmental influences, positive or negative. As you will recall, organogenesis takes place during the embryonic period (weeks 3–8 of prenatal development). As ■ Figure 4.9 shows, it is during this time—before many women even realize they are pregnant—that most organ systems are most vulnerable to damage. Moreover, each organ has a critical period that corresponds to its own time of most rapid development (for example, weeks 3–6 for the heart and weeks 4–7 for the arms and fingers). Once an organ or body part is fully formed, it is usually less susceptible to damage. However, because some organ systems—above all, the nervous system—can be damaged throughout pregnancy, *sensitive periods* might be a better term than *critical periods*.

Drugs

The principles of teratology can be illustrated by surveying just a few of the many drugs—prescription, over-the-counter, and social—that can disrupt prenatal development. As many as 80% of pregnant women take either prescription or over-the-counter medications during pregnancy (Mitchell et al., 2011; Sadler, 2015). Women from lower socioeconomic backgrounds are especially likely to have a prescription during the time they are pregnant, with antibiotics the most commonly prescribed drug (Palmsten et al., 2015). Under a doctor's close supervision, medications used to treat ailments and medical conditions are usually safe for mother and fetus. However, certain individuals exposed to certain drugs in certain doses at certain times during the prenatal period are damaged for life.

Thalidomide. There is perhaps no more striking example of drug effects on prenatal development than thalidomide (Martinez-Frias, 2012). Approximately 50 years ago, this mild tranquilizer was widely used in Europe to relieve morning sickness (the periodic nausea and vomiting many women experience during pregnancy). Presumably, the drug was safe; it had no ill effects in tests on pregnant rats. Tragically, however, the drug had adverse effects on humans.

Thousands of women who used thalidomide during the first 2 months of pregnancy gave birth to babies with all or parts of their limbs missing, with the feet or hands attached directly to the torso like flippers, or with deformed eyes, ears, noses, and hearts. It soon became clear that there were critical periods for different deformities. If the mother had taken thalidomide 20–22 days after conception (34–36 days after the first day of a woman's last menstrual period), her baby was likely to be born without ears. If she had taken it 22–27 days after conception, the baby often had missing or small thumbs; if thalidomide was taken between 27 and 33 days after conception, the child was likely to have stunted legs or no legs. And if the mother waited until 35 or 36 days after conception before using thalidomide, her baby was usually not affected. Thus, thalidomide had specific effects on development,

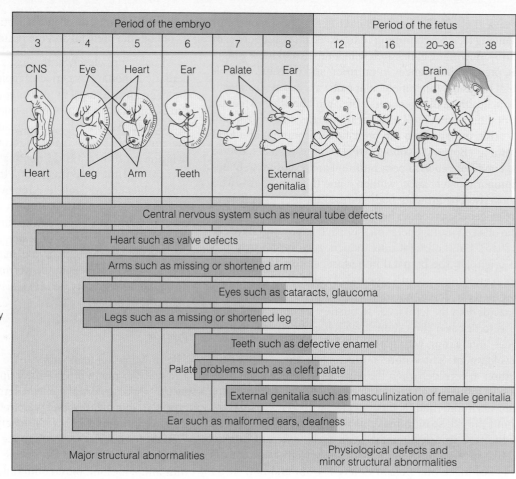

	Period of the embryo						Period of the fetus			
Prenatal week	3	4	5	6	7	8	12	16	20–36	38

Figure 4.9 Sensitive periods of prenatal development. Teratogens are more likely to produce major structural abnormalities during the third through the eighth prenatal week. Note, however, that many organs and body parts remain sensitive to teratogenic agents throughout the 9-month prenatal period.

Source: Adapted from Moore, K. L. (2013). *The developing human: Clinically oriented embryology*. Philadelphia: W. B. Saunders.

This child was born with some of the characteristic limb defects associated with thalidomide, a drug prescribed in the late 1950s and early 1960s to relieve the nausea some women experience during pregnancy.

depending on which structures were developing when the drug was taken.

Thalidomide had been banned for years, but it is again being prescribed by physicians, this time for treatment of conditions associated with leprosy, acquired immunodeficiency syndrome (AIDS), tuberculosis, and some forms of cancer. Given its tragic past association with birth defects, the manufacturers of thalidomide have taken significant steps to ensure it is used safely, including stamping each pill with a drawing of a pregnant woman inside a circle with a diagonal line through it (the universal "no" symbol) and including a picture of a baby with the characteristic stunted limbs on the packaging accompanying the pills. In addition, the prescribing physician and the patient must both abide by guidelines developed specifically for this drug (Celgene Corporation, 2016).

Tobacco. Warning labels on cigarette packages that smoking may damage fetuses have resulted in a decline, but not an absence, of smoking during pregnancy. During the first trimester, about 20% of mothers smoke, but by the third semester, this has dipped to 13% of pregnant women. Roughly 25% of non-pregnant women smoke, so clearly some women adjust their smoking behavior during their pregnancies (CDC, 2015;

Substance Abuse & Mental Health Services Administration, 2014). Rates of smoking during pregnancy vary by age and the race or Hispanic origin of the mother, with young white women most likely to smoke, and Asian and Hispanic women of any age least likely to smoke during pregnancy (Yang et al., 2014). Interestingly, the more that Asian and Hispanic women interact with white women, the more likely they—Asian and Hispanic women—are to smoke during pregnancy (Yang et al., 2014).

The effects of smoking during pregnancy are varied and may include:

- increased risk of miscarriage
- prematurity, growth retardation, and small size
- respiratory problems
- cleft lips (an opening in the top lip) and cleft palates (an opening in the roof of the mouth)
- central nervous system (CNS) impairment
- later health problems such as inflammatory bowel disease

Whether, and to what extent, infants experience ill effects from prenatal exposure to smoking depends, as our teratogenic principles would predict, on the length of exposure and the "dose." For example, more than half of infants born to heavy smokers (20 or more cigarettes a day) end up in neonatal intensive care and experience some degree of CNS impairment. Infants born to lighter smokers (5 cigarettes a day) may not have the same degree of CNS impairment, but they are more irritable and score lower on standard assessments of behavioral functioning than infants born to nonsmokers (Behnke et al., 2013). The more a woman smokes during pregnancy, the more likely it is that her infant will experience growth retardation and neurological problems (see Behnke et al., 2013). Heavier smoking also raises the risk of **sudden infant death syndrome (SIDS)**, in which a sleeping baby suddenly stops breathing and dies. Further, the odds that problems from prenatal cigarette exposure will persist into childhood are greater when the mother was a heavier smoker (Burstyn et al., 2012; Duijts et al., 2012).

Smoking causes these effects by restricting blood flow to the fetus, which in turn reduces the levels of growth factors, oxygen, and nutrients that reach the fetus, leading to a variety of outcomes. It's not just the nicotine in cigarettes that contributes to the poorer outcomes for exposed infants. Cigarettes contain more than 4,000 other chemicals and smoking cigarettes produces carbon monoxide, which reduces the flow of blood and oxygen to the fetus.

A rather alarming conclusion from some researchers is that chronic prenatal exposure to nicotine—a legal substance—may have more negative effects on CNS development than sporadic exposure to the illegal drug cocaine (Bada et al., 2005; Slotkin, 1998). But there is good news: Even women who start their pregnancies as smokers can improve the outcome for their babies by quitting smoking during their pregnancy (Polakowski, Akinbami, & Mendola, 2009). The benefits are greatest for those women who quit during their first trimester but are also apparent for the babies of mothers who quit during their second trimester. Thus, women should be encouraged and supported to stop or reduce smoking during pregnancy.

Finally, we must consider that women who smoke during pregnancy are likely to be white or American Indians or Alaska Natives, young, low-income, and less educated than women who do not smoke during pregnancy (Substance Abuse & Mental Health Services Administration, 2014). It may be that some of these other factors act independently or in conjunction with cigarette smoking to create the less-than-ideal outcomes seen among these exposed infants. A clever study by British researchers Frances Rice, Anita Thapar, and their colleagues (2007, 2009) helps clarify the connection between maternal smoking during pregnancy and genetic influences on some of the outcomes observed in infants and young children. They studied two groups of children conceived through in vitro fertilization: children who were the biological offspring of the mother (that is, the mother's own eggs were retrieved, fertilized, and then implanted in her womb) and children who were not biologically related to the mother (that is, a donor egg was fertilized and then implanted in a woman's uterus). The researchers looked at two dependent variables: birth weight and antisocial behavior at around age 6. Their findings were clear: Low birth weight occurred among infants whose mothers smoked during pregnancy regardless of whether the infant was biologically related to the mother or not (own egg versus donor egg). In contrast, elevated antisocial behaviors occurred among children whose mothers smoked during pregnancy only when they were biologically related to their mother (i.e., her own egg had been used), not when they were biologically unrelated to their mother (i.e., a donor egg had been used). Thus, a prenatal environment of smoke by-products does not increase antisocial behavior, but the mother's genetic contribution to her child does. There may be, for example, certain genetically influenced personality characteristics that make it more likely that a woman will smoke and that also contribute to antisocial behaviors in her offspring.

Alcohol. Alcohol consumed by the mother readily crosses the placenta, where it can directly affect fetal development in various ways. For one, prenatal alcohol exposure disrupts the normal process of neuronal migration, leading to cells that do not end

A young child with fetal alcohol syndrome, showing some of the characteristic facial features such as thin upper lip, low nasal bridge, short nose, and somewhat flat midface.

Rick's Photography/Shutterstock.com

up at their proper final destination in the nervous system. Prenatal alcohol exposure can also lead to neuronal death and impair the function of the glial cells—those nonneuronal cells that are needed to support and nourish neurons (Goodlett & Horn, 2001).

The most severe outcome of fetal alcohol exposure is a cluster of symptoms dubbed **fetal alcohol syndrome (FAS)**, with noticeable physical symptoms such as a small head and distinctive facial abnormalities including thin upper lip, short nose, and flat midface. Children with FAS are smaller and lighter than normal, and their physical growth lags behind that of their age-mates. Most importantly, children with FAS also show signs of CNS damage. As newborns, they are likely to display excessive irritability, hyperactivity, seizures, or tremors. Most children with FAS score well below average on IQ tests throughout childhood and adolescence, and many also exhibit hyperactive behavior and attention deficits (Bhatara, Loudenberg, & Ellis, 2006). As adults, many continue to experience problems, with higher rates of unemployment and psychiatric disorders compared to their peers who had not been diagnosed with FAS (Rangmar et al., 2015). Importantly, though, not every child with FAS exhibits problems in adulthood, raising the intriguing question of what factors may lead to the different outcomes. Before considering this question, though, how widespread is alcohol use during pregnancy?

Estimates of alcohol use during pregnancy vary widely from country to country, as well as across different regions within a country. Most surveys indicate approximately 10% of pregnant women in the United States drink some alcohol during pregnancy, about 3% admit to binge drinking, and less than 1% report heavy drinking (Substance Abuse & Mental Health Services Administration, 2014). As a result, as many as 3 in 1,000 babies in the United States are born with FAS and suffer its symptoms all their lives. In Italy, where many people partake in daily alcohol consumption with meals, the incidence of FAS and its milder forms may be as high as 37–47 out of 1,000 children (May et al., 2011). South Africa's Western Cape province region has as many as 70–80 FAS cases per 1,000 babies, but perhaps the highest FAS rates are found in some remote Aboriginal regions of western Australia, where the prevalence has been found to be 120 of 1000 children (Fitzpatrick et al., 2015).

Children who were exposed prenatally to alcohol but do not have FAS experience milder alcohol-related effects labeled either *fetal alcohol effects* or *alcohol-related neurodevelopmental disorder* (Nulman et al., 2007). These individuals do not have all the features of FAS but have physical, behavioral, or cognitive problems or a combination of these. How much drinking does it take to harm an unborn baby? In keeping with the dosage principle of teratology, mothers who consume larger quantities of alcohol are at greater risk for having children with alcohol-related complications (Roccella & Testa, 2003; Streissguth et al., 1999). The pattern of drinking is also important. Binge drinking (for women, consuming four or more drinks during a single session) has more negative effects on fetal development than consuming the same number of drinks across multiple sessions (Fraser et al., 2012; Jacobson & Jacobson, 1999). This makes sense when you consider that consuming four drinks in one evening results in higher blood alcohol levels for both mother and fetus than consuming one drink on each of four evenings. Finally, in keeping with the critical-period principle of teratogens, the effects of alcohol depend on which systems are developing at the time of exposure. The facial abnormalities associated with FAS result from consumption during the first trimester, more precisely the second half of the first trimester, when the face and skull bones are forming (Feldman et al., 2012). During the second and third trimesters, there is much fetal growth as well as rapid brain development; thus, alcohol consumption during this latter part of pregnancy is likely to stunt growth and brain development.

No amount of drinking seems to be entirely safe, leading the American Academy of Pediatrics to issue a statement that pregnant women and those considering pregnancy should refrain from all alcohol consumption (see *Light Drinking During Pregnancy*, 2015). Even a mother who drinks less than an ounce a day is at risk to have a sluggish or placid newborn whose mental development is slightly below average (Jacobson et al., 1993). Other research shows that exposure to less than one drink per week during pregnancy is associated with mental health problems during childhood, at least among girls (Sayal et al., 2007). What is more, there is no well-defined critical period before or after which fetal alcohol effects cannot occur; drinking late in pregnancy can be as risky as drinking soon after conception.

Let's go back, now, to that intriguing question of why some offspring of drinking mothers suffer ill effects but others do not. To answer this, you need to consider the nature–nurture issue again. First, the chances of damage depend partly on the mother's physiology—for example, on how efficiently she metabolizes alcohol and therefore how much is passed to the fetus (Shepard & Lemire, 2010). Complicating the situation, problem drinkers often have other issues that can aggravate the effects of alcohol on the fetus or cause independent damage that can be difficult to disentangle from the effects of alcohol alone (Rodriguez et al., 2009). Women who consume unsafe levels of alcohol during pregnancy are also more likely to use drugs other than alcohol, smoke cigarettes, have inadequate prenatal care, and be young and single. Combining alcohol use with other risky behaviors increases the odds of pregnancy complications (Odendaal et al., 2009). In addition, consistent with the third principle of teratogenic effects, the embryo's genetic makeup and physical condition influence its ability to resist and recover from damage. Fraternal twins are 64% concordant (i.e., matched) for signs of FAS, whereas identical twins are 100% concordant (Streissguth & Dehaene, 1993). Thus, for example, one fraternal twin may show all the physical abnormalities associated with FAS, but the other twin, although exposed to the same prenatal environment, may show almost none; by contrast, identical twins respond very similarly when exposed to alcohol prenatally (Eberhart & Harris, 2013). As the third principle of teratology states, then, both the child's and the mother's characteristics influence the extent to which a given teratogen proves damaging. Thus, the genetic makeup of both the mother and the child interact with environmental forces to determine the effects of alcohol on development.

Finally, note that it is not just the mother's use of alcohol that can adversely affect development. Some research suggests that a father's use of alcohol can influence fetal development through transmission of the father's genes to his offspring (Knopik et al., 2009). How might this occur? There are two possibilities. One is that a man's use of alcohol, as well as other substances, may cause mutations of some DNA that is then passed to the offspring. A second possibility is that epigenetic effects are the culprit. That is, a father's alcohol use may alter the epigenome that "sits" on top of the genome, altering the expression of the gene, which may then be transmitted to the offspring through the father's sperm (Champagne, 2010; Curley, Mashoodh, &

Champagne, 2011). We should also note, however, that other research suggests that paternal drinking affects development indirectly through poor parenting (Knopik et al., 2009; Leonard & Das Eiden, 2002). Fathers who use or abuse alcohol may have parenting styles that differ from those of fathers who do not use or abuse alcohol. Thus, further research needs to be done to determine the pathways through which a father's alcohol use relates to his offspring's development.

Cocaine. Although there is no "cocaine syndrome" with characteristic physical abnormalities such as those associated with FAS, cocaine use can damage the fetus. It can cause spontaneous abortion in the first trimester of pregnancy and premature detachment of the placenta or fetal strokes later in pregnancy. Cocaine also contributes to fetal malnourishment, retarded growth, and low birth weight (Gouin et al., 2011; March of Dimes, 2015). At birth, a small proportion of babies born to cocaine users experience withdrawal-like symptoms such as tremors and extreme irritability and have respiratory difficulties (Patrick et al., 2012).

Cocaine–exposed infants show increased activity levels as well as greater reactivity in response to stimulation during their first year (Fallone et al., 2014). Infants may also show deficits on measures of information processing. Some of the consequences of prenatal cocaine exposure persist into adolescence, with higher rates of delinquent behavior and continued deficits on problem solving and abstract reasoning tasks (Richardson et al., 2015). For problems that persist, it is unclear whether they are caused by the prenatal exposure to cocaine or by other prenatal or postnatal risk factors that affected infants may experience as the children of substance-abusing parents (Bandstra et al., 2010). For instance, as noted earlier for women who consume alcohol during pregnancy, women who use cocaine during pregnancy also tend to engage in more than one risky behavior. In addition, cocaine-using mothers are less attentive to their babies and engage in fewer interactions with them during the first year than non–drug-using mothers or mothers who use drugs other than cocaine (Minnes et al., 2005). Mother–child interactions continue to be of lower quality throughout early childhood (Mansoor et al., 2012). Children exposed to prenatal cocaine who are raised by adoptive or foster parents display fewer language problems at age 10 than those raised by their biological mother, suggesting that the quality of the postnatal environment matters (Lewis et al., 2011).

● **Table 4.5** catalogs several substances and their known or suspected effects on the child. What should you make of these

● **Table 4.5** Some Drugs Taken by the Mother that Affect the Fetus or Newborn (in addition to alcohol and tobacco, discussed in the chapter)

Drug	Effects
Accutane	Prescribed as an acne treatment, Accutane can result in small, abnormally shaped ears, cleft palate, facial defects, and small lower jaw.
Antiepileptic drugs	Drugs such as phenytoin (Dilantin), phenobarbital (Luminal), and carbamazepine (Tegretol), used to treat seizures, increase the incidence of cleft lip and palate, neural tube defects, kidney disease, and restricted growth (Wlodarczyk et al., 2012). Approximately 1 in 12 infants exposed prenatally to antiepileptic drugs will develop a birth defect.
Antidepressant drugs	Treating pregnant women with antidepressant drugs such as Prozac or Zoloft (selective serotonin reuptake inhibitors) may place their infants at greater risk for heart malformations, neural tube defects, low-birth weight, and respiratory distress.
Over-the-counter pain/fever reducers (acetaminophen, aspirin, and ibuprofen)	An occasional low dose may be okay, but used in large quantities, such drugs may cause neonatal bleeding and gastrointestinal discomfort. Large amounts of these over-the-counter pain relievers have been associated with low birth weight, prematurity, and increased risk of miscarriage (Hernandez et al., 2012).
Chemotherapy drugs	Such drugs cross the placenta and attack rapidly dividing cells. They can increase malformations and lead to miscarriage, particularly when administered to the mother during the first trimester.
Marijuana	Heavy use of marijuana has been linked to premature birth, low birth weight, and mild behavioral abnormalities such as irritability at birth (Janisse et al., 2014). It may lead to small deficits in general intelligence as well as increased risk of hyperactivity (Brown & Graves, 2013).
Narcotics	Addiction to heroin, codeine, methadone, or morphine increases the risk of premature delivery and low birth weight. The newborn is often addicted and experiences potentially fatal withdrawal symptoms (e.g., vomiting and convulsions). Longer-term cognitive deficits are sometimes evident.
Sex hormones	Birth control pills containing female hormones have been known to produce heart defects and cardiovascular problems, but today's pill formulas are safer. Progesterone in drugs used to prevent miscarriage may masculinize the fetus. Diethylstilbestrol—the first synthetic estrogen—was once prescribed to prevent miscarriage, but it led to increased risk of cervical cancer and created infertility and pregnancy problems in exposed offspring (DESAction, 2015).
Stimulants	Caffeine, found in coffees, teas, and many sodas, is a stimulant and diuretic. As such, it can increase blood pressure, heart rate, and urination. Heavy caffeine use has been linked to miscarriages, higher heart rates, growth restriction, and irritability at birth, but it does not seem to have long-lasting effects on development (Loomans et al., 2012). Cocaine is an illegal stimulant that can cause premature delivery, spontaneous abortion, and low birth weight, and it may result in later learning and behavioral problems (see main text).

Sources: Modified from Creasy et al., 2013; Paulson, 2013; Liptak, 2013; Sadler, 2015; Shepard & Lemire, 2010.

findings? You now understand that drugs do not damage all fetuses exposed to them in a simple, direct way. Instead, complex transactions between an individual with a certain genetic makeup and the prenatal, perinatal, and postnatal environments influence whether or not prenatal drug exposure does lasting damage. Still, women who are planning to become pregnant or who are pregnant should avoid all drugs unless they are prescribed by a physician and essential to health. Fortunately, most women have gotten the message and significantly alter their behavior during pregnancy to eliminate or reduce such unhealthy practices as drinking alcohol and smoking cigarettes and to increase healthy behaviors such as eating nutritious foods and getting regular prenatal care.

Diseases and Infections

Just as drugs can jeopardize the prenatal environment, so can diseases and infections. Here we take a look at four problems—rubella, diabetes, AIDS, and syphilis—that illustrate principles of teratogens. ● **Table 4.6** summarizes several other maternal conditions that may affect prenatal development.

Rubella. In the early 1940s, a doctor discovered that many infants born to women affected by rubella (German measles) during pregnancy had one or more of a variety of defects, including blindness, deafness, heart defects, and intellectual disability. Because rubella was fairly common, there were enough cases for doctors to see that the environment of the womb leaves the fetus vulnerable to outside influences. Rubella is most dangerous during the first trimester, a critical period in which the eyes, ears, heart, and brain are rapidly forming. Nearly 25% of pregnant women with rubella miscarry or experience a fetal death and some may choose to terminate the pregnancy out of concern

for harmful consequences of the virus on the developing fetus (Andrade et al., 2006; Thompson et al., 2014). Yet not all babies whose mothers had rubella, even during the most critical period of prenatal development, will have problems. Birth defects occur in two-thirds of babies whose mothers had the disease in the first 2 months of pregnancy, in about half of those infected in the third month, and in relatively few of those infected in the fourth or fifth months (Waldorf & McAdams, 2013). Consistent with the critical-period principle, damage to the nervous system, eyes, and heart is most likely during that part of the first 8 weeks of pregnancy (the period of the embryo) when each of these organs is forming, whereas deafness is more likely when the mother contracts rubella in weeks 6–13 of the pregnancy. Today, doctors stress that a woman should not try to become pregnant unless she has been immunized against rubella or has already had it. As a result of successful immunization programs, many women are now immune to this previously common infection. Nevertheless, recent outbreaks of rubella have been reported in in various spots around the world, including Italy and Netherlands in 2013 and Germany in 2015, among others (European Centre for Disease Prevention and Control, 2015).

Diabetes. Diabetes is a fairly common pregnancy complication, with most cases arising during pregnancy (gestational diabetes) rather than from preexisting diabetes. Diabetes results from elevated blood glucose levels. When glucose levels are well controlled with diet, there are few ill effects on the developing fetus. But in poorly controlled maternal diabetes, there is increased risk of premature delivery, stillbirth or miscarriage, immature lung development, congenital heart defects, and neural tube defects. Maternal diabetes is also associated with large-for-date fetuses,

● **Table 4.6** Maternal Illnesses and Conditions that May Affect an Embryo, Fetus, or Newborn

Disease or Condition	Effects
Chickenpox	Chickenpox can cause spontaneous abortion, premature delivery, and slow growth, although fewer than 2% of exposed fetuses develop limb, facial, or skeletal malformations.
Chlamydia	Chlamydia can lead to premature birth, low birth weight, eye inflammation, or pneumonia in newborns. This most common STI is easily treatable.
Cytomegalovirus (CMV)	This common infection shows mild flulike symptoms in adults. About 25% of infected newborns develop hearing or vision loss, mental retardation, or other impairments, and 10% develop severe neurological problems or even die.
Gonorrhea	This STI attacks the eyes of the infant during birth; blindness is prevented by administering silver nitrate eyedrops to newborns.
Herpes simplex (genital herpes)	This disease may cause eye and brain damage or death in the first trimester. Mothers with active herpes may be advised to undergo cesarean deliveries to avoid infecting their babies during delivery, because 85% of infants born with herpes acquire the virus during birth through the birth canal.
Influenza (flu)	The more powerful strains can cause spontaneous abortions or neural abnormalities early in pregnancy that may lead to decreased intelligence scores in adulthood (Eriksen, Sundet, & Tambs, 2009).
Toxemia	Affecting about 5% of mothers in the third trimester, its mildest form, preeclampsia, causes high blood pressure and rapid weight gain in the mother. Untreated, preeclampsia may become eclampsia and cause maternal convulsions, coma, and death of the mother, the unborn child, or both. Surviving infants may be brain damaged.
Toxoplasmosis	This illness, caused by a parasite in raw meat and cat feces, leads to blindness, deafness, and mental retardation in approximately 40% of infants born to infected mothers.

Sources: Reproductive Health, 2015; Sadler, 2015; Waldorf & McAdams, 2013.

which can complicate delivery. These complications arise from the abnormal glucose levels associated with diabetes and not from the insulin used to control this disease. This highlights why it is important to ensure that women who are, or may become, pregnant have access to good medical care.

Sexually Transmitted Infections.   Several sexually transmitted infections (STIs) can affect development prenatally and beyond. The sexually transmitted infection of greatest concern in recent decades is **acquired immunodeficiency syndrome (AIDS)**, the life-threatening illness caused by the **human immunodeficiency virus (HIV)**. AIDS destroys the immune system and makes victims susceptible to "opportunistic" infections that eventually kill them unless they are treated with multiple drugs. HIV-infected mothers can transmit the virus to their babies (1) prenatally, if the virus passes through the placenta; (2) perinatally, when blood may be exchanged between mother and child as the umbilical cord separates from the placenta; or (3) postnatally, if the virus is transmitted during breast-feeding. Without treatment, somewhere between 15% and 35% of babies born to HIV-infected mothers will become infected (Avert, 2016). The rate is much lower if these mothers are treated with antiretroviral drugs, or if they and their newborns are given a drug called nevirapine, which helps block transmission of HIV at birth (Avert, 2016; Stringer et al., 2004). Bottle-feeding further reduces the rate of HIV transmission from affected mothers to their infants but breast-feeding can be safe if managed effectively with treatment (Becquet et al., 2012). Infected infants now live longer than they did at the outset of the AIDS epidemic because of the development of appropriate treatments—50–75% in the United States are alive at age 5, and some survive into adolescence (Greenfield, 2012).

Although mother-to-child transmission of HIV in the United States has decreased significantly since peaking in 1992, it continues to be a tremendous problem in Africa and other parts of the world with AIDS epidemics. In 2010, for example, an estimated

390,000 infants worldwide became infected with HIV from their mothers, most in sub-Saharan Africa (Avert, 2016).

Another sexually transmitted infection of concern is syphilis. Syphilis during pregnancy can cause miscarriage or stillbirth in as many as 25% of cases where the mother is infected with syphilis and does not receive treatment (Qin et al., 2014). Babies born alive to mothers who have syphilis and who do not receive treatment in a timely manner can end up suffering blindness, deafness, heart problems or brain damage, like those babies born to mothers who have rubella. This shows that different teratogens—here, syphilis and rubella—can be responsible for the same problem. However, whereas rubella is most damaging in the early stage of pregnancy, syphilis is most damaging in the middle and later stages of pregnancy. This is because syphilitic organisms cannot cross the placental barrier until the eighteenth prenatal week, providing a window of opportunity for treating the mother-to-be who finds out she has the disease. Even with appropriate treatment—penicillin—some infants are infected or die, although treatment substantially lowers this risk (Blencowe et al., 2011).

Environmental Hazards

A mother can control what she ingests, but sometimes she cannot avoid a hazardous external environment. Next we discuss two environmental conditions—radiation and pollutants—that may endanger the unborn child.

Radiation.   Throughout the 20th century, there have been several notable events associated with the release of large quantities of radiation, allowing researchers to study the potential impact on unborn children. Perhaps the most dramatic radiological event was when atomic bombs were dropped on Hiroshima and Nagasaki in 1945: Not one pregnant woman who was within one-half mile of the blasts gave birth to a live child, and 75% of those who were within a mile and a quarter of the blasts had stillborn infants or seriously handicapped infants who died soon after birth (Apgar & Beck, 1974). Surviving children of these mothers had a higher-than-normal rate of intellectual disability and greater incidence of leukemia and cancers later in life (CDC, 2012b; Kodama, Mabuchi, & Shigematsu, 1996). Autopsies of these individuals would later reveal thinner-than-normal layers of cerebral cortex, an indication that neuronal migration had been disrupted (McDonald, 2007).

The Chernobyl nuclear disaster in 1986 similarly led to increased congenital defects among infants born to women who were in the area of exposure (Marples, 1996). Even across the Bay of Bothnia, in Sweden, women who were pregnant during the fallout from the Chernobyl accident experienced higher rates of congenital abnormalities among their babies despite much lower levels of radiation exposure (Almond, Edlund, & Palme, 2009).

Other research has examined exposure to radiation released during nuclear weapon testing (Black et al., 2014). This, too, is associated with lower IQ scores among those who were exposed in utero. In all cases, the greatest damage was during prenatal weeks 8–25, illustrating that timing is important. What's happening during this time? Neurons are migrating and differentiating, a complex process that is disrupted by radiation. Dosage is important as well; children whose mothers were exposed to higher levels

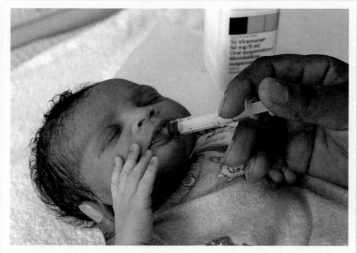

An infant of an HIV-infected mother receives nevirapine syrup to help protect this little one from mother-to-infant transmission of HIV.

of radiation experienced more significant deficits. Even clinical doses of radiation, such as those used in X-rays and cancer treatment, are capable of causing mutations, spontaneous abortions, and a variety of birth defects, especially if the mother is exposed between weeks 8 and 25. Therefore, expectant mothers are routinely advised to avoid X-rays or radiation unless they are essential to their own survival, as might be the case with women undergoing certain cancer treatments.

Pollutants. The air we breathe contains numerous pollutants, including ozone, carbon monoxide, nitrogen oxides, sulpher dioxides, and lead. Some of these originate from natural events such as volcanic eruptions, but others are by-products of fuel combustion from engines. Researchers seeking to understand the effects of pollutants on the developing fetus have evaluated pregnancy outcomes in select areas of the world such as Delhi, India, which has the dubious distinction of being the most polluted city in the world (Kumar et al., 2015). Sometimes, researchers have an opportunity to study the consequences of pollutants following an unexpected event, such as the tragic 9/11 attacks and collapse of the World Trade Centers in New York City, which exposed those living in the vicinity to large amounts of potentially toxic pollutants. These sorts of studies consistently show a connection between the by-products of pollution, measured in maternal blood and umbilical cord blood collected at birth, and such birth complications as prematurity and low birth weight (e.g., Lederman et al., 2004; van den Hooven et al., 2012). And that's not all. Three years after birth, some of the children exposed to pollution in utero show decreased cognitive abilities (Perera et al., 2007). In a large study conducted in various locations throughout Europe, children exposed to pollution in utero, specifically nitrogen oxides, showed delays in psychomotor development, although not in cognitive development (Guxens et al., 2014). It is important to note that those children who were exposed to multiple risk factors in utero experienced more problems than those exposed to a single factor. In particular, prenatal exposure to pollution *in combination with* cigarette smoke led to further complications that were not present in the children who were exposed to just one of these prenatal risk factors. (Lederman et al., 2004; Perera et al., 2007). As we'll see later in this chapter, the more hazards that a child faces, the more likely it is that she will struggle to get back on track. Thus, with good postnatal care, children might overcome negative consequences of prenatal exposure to pollution or to cigarette smoke, but overcoming multiple risk factors is more of a challenge.

Exposure to heavy metals, such as lead in the air we breathe and the water we drink, is an ongoing concern. Children exposed prenatally to lead are smaller at birth and may be born preterm. They also show impaired intellectual functioning as children in proportion to the amount of lead in their umbilical cords (Canfield et al., 2003; Yorifuji et al., 2011). This finding holds true even after controlling for other differences among children, such as socioeconomic status. Postnatal lead exposure, usually from living in a home with lead dust from old paint or old lead water pipes, is also dangerous. Exposure to even very low levels of lead—lower than previously thought to be safe—is associated with lowered mental function during childhood (Jedrychowski et al., 2009).

Mercury exposure typically results from eating certain long-lived fish such as tuna, mackerel, and swordfish that have higher levels of mercury than shorter-lived fish such as salmon. Studies looking at prenatal exposure to mercury from maternal consumption of fish suggest adverse consequences, including delayed development and memory, attention, and language problems, with the effects related to the amount of mercury exposure (Paulson, 2013). As for whether mercury from vaccines that used to contain the mercury-based preservative thimerosal had toxic effects on development, the vast majority of the research concludes that it did not (Paulson, 2013; Waterhouse, 2013). Some parents whose children developed autism around the time of a vaccination continue to question whether there might be a link between the two events, but there is no credible evidence of this (see Chapter 16).

Finally, prenatal exposure to pesticides, dioxins, and polychlorinated biphenyls (PCBs) has also been associated with perinatal and postnatal problems (see Govarts et al., 2012). For example, prenatal exposure to PCBs from maternal consumption of contaminated foods is associated with poor reflexes in infants and later learning difficulties, including lower IQ scores at age 9 (Paulson, 2013; Stewart et al., 2008). PCBs were produced in various locations around the world, well after researchers had raised the alarm regarding toxicity of the substance. Another synthetic compound that has come under scrutiny is bisphenol-A (BPA), which is found in many plastics, including baby bottles.

Exposure to high levels of pollution during pregnancy can lead to preterm births and other adverse infant outcomes.

PRAKASH SINGH/Getty Images

Many companies began banning BPA in bottles in 2009, but now even the 'safe' alternative has come under fire for its connection to hyperactivity (Nutt, 2015; Tavernise, 2012). And then there are those pesticides. Children whose mothers were exposed to pesticides during pregnancy have greater body fat relative to children not exposed (Wohlfahrt-Veje et al., 2011). Boys exposed in utero to pesticides have smaller genitals than nonexposed boys and, consistent with the dose principle, the greater the exposure the smaller the genitals (Wohlfahrt-Veje et al., 2012a). And in girls, in utero exposure to pesticides is associated with earlier breast development, suggesting changes in hormone levels (Wohlfahrt-Veje et al., 2012b).

Clearly there is a critical need for more research aimed at identifying a huge number of chemicals, wastes, and other environmental hazards that may affect unborn children. There are more than 80,000 chemicals "out there" to which children may be exposed, but fewer than 3% of these have been evaluated for toxicity (Grandjean & Landigan, 2006; Paulson, 2013).

The message is unmistakable: The chemistry of the prenatal environment often determines whether an embryo or fetus survives and how it looks and functions after birth. A variety of teratogens can affect development; although, as you have learned, the influence of teratogens varies. Effects are worst in critical periods when organ systems are growing most rapidly, and effects are more serious with greater exposure to teratogens. Not all embryos or fetuses are equally affected by the same teratogen; the genetic makeup of both the mother and her unborn child and the quality of the prenatal and postnatal environments all play a role in determining the effects (Cassina et al., 2012). By becoming familiar with the information here and by keeping up with new knowledge, parents-to-be can do much to increase the already high odds that their unborn child will be normal as it approaches its next challenge: the birth process.

The Mother's State

What can parents, especially the mother-to-be, do to sustain a healthy pregnancy? **Application 4.1** explores how parents can set the stage for a healthy pregnancy. Here we describe several characteristics of the mother—her age and race/ethnicity, emotional state, and nutritional status—that can affect the quality of the prenatal environment.

Age and Race/Ethnicity

At one end of the age spectrum, 11- and 12-year-old girls have given birth; at the other end of the spectrum, a 70-year-old woman from rural India made it to the record book by giving birth to twins after IVF. These are, however, unusual cases. The safest, and more typical, time to bear a child appears to be from about age 20 to age 40, as shown by the fetal mortality rates in ■ **Figure** 4.10.

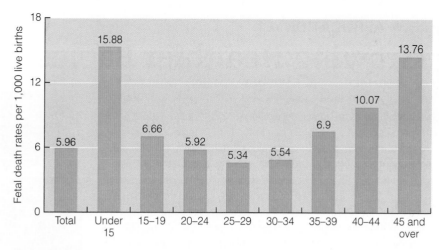

■ **Figure 4.10** Fetal mortality varies with the mother's age: Very young and very old mothers are at greater risk for fetal mortality. The best time to have a baby, if all other variables are the same, is when a woman is in her 20s or early 30s.

Source: CDC/NCHS, National Vital Statistics System, fetal mortality data, 2016.

Very young mothers have higher-than-normal rates of birth complications, including premature deliveries and **stillbirths**—fetal deaths late in pregnancy (20 or more weeks gestational age). The reproductive system of the teenager (19 years or younger) may not be physically mature enough to sustain a fetus to full term, making this group more vulnerable to having a low-birth-weight baby. However, the greater problem appears to be that teenagers often do not seek prenatal care and they are more likely to live in poverty and drink alcohol than mothers in their 20s and older (Substance Abuse and Mental Health Services Administration, 2014). Unfortunately, these conditions are likely to persist after the birth, leading to increased death rates before their first birthday among infants born to mothers 20 years or younger (Mathews, MacDorman, & Thoma, 2015).

As for older women, they are more likely to experience trouble getting pregnant. For those who do conceive, there is an increased risk of miscarriage, stillbirth, and low-birth-weight babies (Kenny et al., 2013; Laopaiboon et al., 2014). In the past, many fetal deaths in older women were caused by genetic abnormalities or defects arising during the first weeks after conception, when the major organs are forming. With today's extensive prenatal testing of women older than 35, however, fewer babies are dying from genetic problems, partly because many such fetuses are identified early and aborted. Still, as Figure 4.10 shows, fetal death rates remain higher for older women, particularly for those over age 45 (MacDorman & Gregory, 2015). Compared with younger women, women over age 35 are more likely to release more than a single egg during ovulation, which increases their chances of conceiving fraternal twins (Beemsterboer et al., 2006). Though some women may be thrilled to learn that they are carrying twins, any multiple pregnancy and delivery carries additional health risks for the mother and the babies. Fetal mortality for higher-order pregnancies (three or more fetuses) is more than four times the rate for single pregnancies (MacDorman & Gregory, 2015). Finally, keep in mind that despite the increased risks older women face in childbearing, most have normal pregnancies and healthy babies.

Growing Healthier Babies

The more we learn about important environmental influences on human development, the better able we are to optimize environment and therefore to optimize development. Although the quality of an individual's environment matters throughout the life span, it seems sensible to do as much as possible to get a baby's life off to a good start because events of the prenatal period help set the stage for a lifetime of good (or poor) health. Ideally, pregnancies are planned rather than "discovered" after the fact, when it may be too late to make certain lifestyle changes. All women of childbearing age, for example, should eat a diet that contains the recommended amount of folic acid and should try to quit or reduce their smoking. Women who are thinking about getting pregnant should talk to their doctor about any prescription drugs they may be taking for ongoing medical conditions such as depression, high blood pressure, or diabetes. Doctors and mothers-to-be can develop a plan for how best to manage any preexisting conditions during a pregnancy.

Once a woman is pregnant, she should seek good prenatal care as quickly as possible so that she will learn how to optimize the well-being of both herself and her unborn child and so that any problems during the pregnancy can be managed appropriately. Prenatal care varies tremendously around the world, with some mothers-to-be seeing a health-care professional or midwife only once prior to delivery. Although the recommendations for pregnant women are not complicated, they are not always followed. They boil down to such practices as eating a good diet, taking prenatal vitamins, protecting oneself against diseases, and avoiding drugs and alcohol. Women who become ill during pregnancy should always

check with their doctor before taking even seemingly safe over-the-counter drugs. Women should avoid eating undercooked meat because of the risks of toxoplasmosis and *Escherichia coli* (*E. coli*) contamination, and they should be cautious of eating some fish, namely those larger fish that consume lots of little fish. These tend to have higher concentrations of mercury.

AMELIE-BENOIST/BSIP SA/Alamy Stock Photo

Most women can continue to engage in all their regular activities, including exercise, during pregnancy unless advised against it by their health-care provider. Exercise can help keep muscles toned for the rigors of childbirth and also provides a sense of positive well-being. Exercise and a healthy diet during pregnancy may also influence the baby's metabolism and could set the stage for normal adult weight. In addition, researchers are beginning to find that prenatal exposure to certain environmental toxins may "program" the endocrine system in ways that lead to obesity across all stages of the life span (see, for example, Newbold et al., 2009).

Women who want to do some home renovations in preparation for the baby's arrival should be careful of lead paint that may be present in older homes and avoid inhaling paint fumes in poorly ventilated rooms. They may also want to have someone else clean the cat's

litter box, because cat feces is another source of the parasite that causes toxoplasmosis. For women who can't avoid litter box duty, having cats tested and treated before pregnancy can eliminate potential exposure to parasites.

Finally, many couples today also enroll in classes that prepare them for childbirth. These classes started in the 1940s to help reduce the fear and pain experienced by many women during labor and delivery. The **Lamaze method** of prepared childbirth teaches women to associate childbirth with pleasant feelings and to ready themselves for the process by learning exercises, breathing and pushing methods, and relaxation techniques that make childbirth easier. Couples who participate in childbirth preparation classes report a greater sense of control during labor and delivery, and this sense of control is associated with higher levels of satisfaction with the childbirth experience (Hart & Foster, 1997).

Does the mother's race/ethnicity impact pregnancy success? As ■ **Figure 4.11** shows, fetal mortality rates do vary with the race/ethnicity of the mother. Most notable is that non-Hispanic black women have fetal mortality rates that are more than twice the rates experienced by other women. The reasons for this disparity are not completely understood but include poorer preconception health of the mother and less prenatal care. In addition, non-Hispanic black mothers are more susceptible to premature labor,

which creates numerous health concerns that we will discuss in a later section.

Emotional Condition

Is the prenatal environment affected by how the mother feels about being pregnant or how her life is going while she is pregnant? Life is filled with many stressors—both chronic (poverty, for example, or ongoing job stress) and acute (experiencing a serious

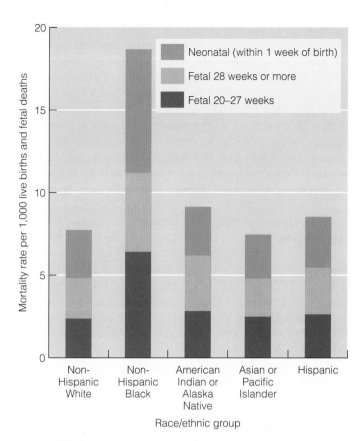

Figure 4.11 Fetal and neonatal mortality rates by race/ethnicity of mother. What factors might contribute to the markedly higher mortality rates for black infants (and fetuses)?

Source: Adapted from Figures 5 and 6 in MacDorman, M. F., Kirmeyer, S. E., & Wilson, E. D. (2012). Fetal and perinatal mortality, United States, 2006. *National Vital Statistics Reports*, 60 (8). Centers for Disease Control and Prevention/National Center for Health Statistics, National Vital Statistics System.

car accident, for example, or the unexpected death of a loved one). Being pregnant does not make stress disappear; indeed, for some women with unintended or mistimed pregnancies, pregnancy may increase stress levels. How might the fetus be affected by the mother's experience of stress?

When a woman becomes emotionally aroused, her glands secrete powerful hormones such as adrenaline (also called epinephrine) that may cross the placental barrier and enter the fetus's bloodstream. At the least, these hormones temporarily increase the fetus's motor activity. A temporarily stressful experience such as falling or receiving a scare will generally not damage mother or fetus. It is only when a mother experiences *prolonged and severe* emotional stress and anxiety during her pregnancy (as a result, for example, of the death of her husband, chronic illness of another child, or unemployment) that long-lasting damage may be done. The most immediate effects on the fetus are a faster and more irregular heart rate and stunted prenatal growth, which can lower birth weight, cause premature birth, and lead to birth complications (Bussières et al., 2015). There is some evidence that female fetuses may be more susceptible to maternal stress than their male counterparts (Wainstock et al., 2015). Following birth, babies whose mothers had been highly stressed during pregnancy tend to be smaller, more active, more irritable, and more prone to crying than other

babies (de Weerth, van Hees, & Buitelaar, 2003; Wurmser et al., 2006). They may experience delays in cognitive development, exhibit greater fearfulness as young children, and have higher rates of depression at age 11 (Bergman et al., 2007; Laplante et al., 2008; Slykerman, et al., 2015). Finally, severe maternal stress during the first trimester has been linked to an increased likelihood of developing *schizophrenia*, a serious mental disorder whose symptoms typically emerge in adolescence or early adulthood (Barouki et al., 2012; Susser et al., 2008). Still, it is clear that not all stressed mothers have babies who are small and arrive early. The outcomes may depend on the effect that the stressful event has on the woman's daily life. If the event significantly disrupts daily life, child outcomes may be worse than if the mother's daily life is affected very little by the event.

Maternal stress likely stunts fetal growth and contributes to the offspring's irritability and anxiety through fetal programming involving epigenetic effects of the environment on gene expression, as discussed earlier (Gudsnuk & Champagne, 2011). Prenatal exposure to maternal stress hormones may program the developing fetal nervous system in such a way as to alter the postnatal stress response (Davis et al., 2011). Stress elevates levels of maternal cortisol, which crosses the placenta and influences, or sensitizes, developing fetal "stress" receptors in the brain. After birth, when a prenatally stressed infant is exposed to stressful events, their prenatally sensitized nervous system is more reactive, leading to poor stress regulation. This prenatal environmental influence does not rule out that there might also be a genetic component to infant stress response. But children who are conceived through IVF and are genetically unrelated to the mother who bore them also show this connection between prenatal stress and their own stress response, supporting the epigenetic connection between prenatal stress and infant-child outcomes (Rice et al., 2010). Also interesting to consider is research showing that significant *preconception* maternal stress is associated with higher rates of infant mortality (Class et al., 2013). Analyzing infant mortality rates in Sweden over a 30-year period in relation to preconception maternal stress, defined as the death of a close family member, revealed that stress experienced by the mother-to-be prior to pregnancy was associated with higher odds of infant mortality. The authors speculate that poor preconception nutrition of the mother, during the period of stress, may set in motion epigenetic effects that influence infant mortality.

Stress and anxiety are not the only maternal emotional states to consider. Maternal depression during pregnancy may contribute to preterm delivery and motor delays in newborns (Suri et al., 2014). Depression affects levels of neurotransmitters (brain chemicals) in both mothers and their newborns. Depression during pregnancy poses a challenge for women and their physicians because, left untreated, depression can affect fetal development, but some treatments for depression, namely prescription antidepressant medication, have also been found to negatively influence prenatal development (Suri et al., 2014).

Nutritional Condition

There was a time when doctors advised mothers to gain a mere 10–15 pounds while pregnant. With better understanding of nutrition and pregnancy, most doctors now recommend a well-balanced diet with about 300 additional calories per day, and a total weight gain of 25–35 pounds for normal-weight women. Healthy eating, including consuming lots of milk and leafy green vegetables, during pregnancy can help reduce the risk of having low-birth-weight babies. Doctors know that inadequate prenatal nutrition and lack of weight gain can be harmful. It is perhaps surprising, then, that fewer than half of pregnant women report that their practitioner talked to them about weight guidelines (Phelan et al., 2011). Clearly, then, there is room for improvement here as the consequences can be significant.

Severe maternal malnutrition, which occurs during famine, stunts prenatal growth and produces small, underweight babies (Barouki et al., 2012). The effects of malnutrition depend on when it occurs. During the first trimester, malnutrition can disrupt the formation of the spinal cord, result in fewer brain cells, and even cause stillbirth. Restrictive dieting, use of diuretics, and disordered eating behaviors during the first trimester can also cause serious problems, such as neural tube defects (Carmichael et al., 2003). During the third trimester, malnutrition is most likely to result in smaller neurons, a smaller brain, and a smaller child overall.

The offspring of malnourished mothers sometimes show cognitive deficits as infants and children. Through fetal programming, poor prenatal nutrition may also put some children at risk for certain diseases in adulthood, including hypertension, coronary heart disease, diabetes, and even the serious mental disorder schizophrenia (Barouki et al., 2012; Susser, St. Clair, & He, 2008). But let's be clear: There may be latent effects of prenatal malnutrition on some children and adults, but because of the complicated interplay of genetics, epigenetics, and environment, other children and adults will show no apparent ill effects.

Among women who are adequately nourished, it is even more difficult to establish a connection between specific nutrients and birth outcome or later behaviors (Langley-Evans & Langley-Evans, 2003; Mathews, Youngman, & Neil, 2004). One exception to this is a deficiency of folate, a water-soluble B vitamin occurring naturally in some foods such as leafy green vegetables (see ■ Figure 4.12), which has been linked to neural

tube defects. In the mid-1990's, the United States and Canada initiated mandatory enrichment of cereal products with folic acid, the synthetic version of folate, in an effort to increase folate levels of women of childbearing age. These fortification programs have been associated with a decrease in the incidence of neural tube defects such as spina bifida, although some have questioned whether the benefits of such programs for women of child-bearing age come at some cost to others who may not need to ingest higher levels of folic acid (see Kim, 2007; Powers, 2007). Even with such fortification programs, it is often difficult to consume the "perfect" combination of foods to provide the full measure of recommended vitamins and minerals. Consequently, most health-care professionals prescribe prenatal vitamins for their pregnant patients.

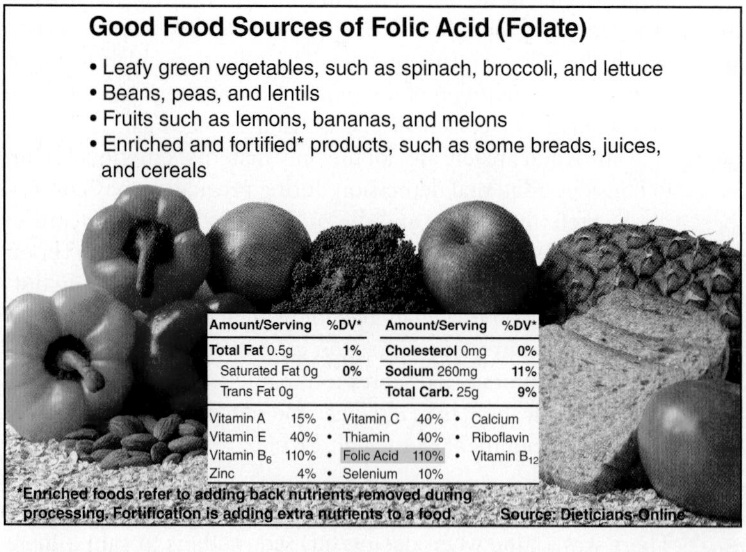

Just as maternal malnutrition can lead to developmental issues, so too can maternal conditions associated with overeating. Maternal obesity, as well as excessive weight gain during pregnancy, is associated with offspring obesity and diabetes (Barouki et al., 2012). And we now have evidence from research with animals that paternal obesity is also associated with offspring obesity and diabetes. In Chapter 3, we described some research with male rats that became overweight from being fed a high-fat diet. This caused epigenetic changes in their sperm, which led to increased rates of obesity and diabetes indicators when passed on to female offspring, even when the daughters—and their mothers—ate healthy diets (Ng et al., 2010). Prenatal environmental conditions as well as preconception conditions of the parents help to build the architecture of the developing fetus and set the stage for how its body will react and respond to events postnatally. Still, much depends on whether a child receives an adequate diet and good care after birth. Best, of course, is appropriate nourishment before conception for the parents, as well as good nutrition before *and* after birth for the offspring.

Now that we have had a chance to review the major teratogens that affect development during the prenatal period, go to **Engagement 4.1** to check your understanding of this material.

The Father's State

Does the father's state have any influence on the quality of the prenatal environment or the outcome of a pregnancy? Unfortunately, there is not a lot of research on the father's contributions to prenatal development beyond his genetic contribution. But researchers know that the father's age, just like the mother's age, can influence development (Sadler, 2015). We noted earlier that teenagers and women older than 35 are at greater risk of miscarriage than women in their 20s and 30s. Similarly, the odds of miscarriage increase with paternal age and are approximately twice the rate when fathers are in their 40s or 50s than when they are in their 20s or 30s (Belloc et al., 2008; Frattarelli et al., 2008). Children born to older fathers also face elevated risk of congenital heart defects, neural tube defects, and kidney problems, as well as preterm delivery and low birth weight (Alio et al., 2012; Shah, 2010). Like the risk of miscarriage, the odds of Down syndrome

Good Food Sources of Folic Acid (Folate)

- Leafy green vegetables, such as spinach, broccoli, and lettuce
- Beans, peas, and lentils
- Fruits such as lemons, bananas, and melons
- Enriched and fortified* products, such as some breads, juices, and cereals

Amount/Serving		%DV*	Amount/Serving		%DV*
Total Fat 0.5g		1%	Cholesterol 0mg		0%
Saturated Fat 0g		0%	Sodium 260mg		11%
Trans Fat 0g			Total Carb. 25g		9%

Vitamin A	15%	•	Vitamin C	40%	•	Calcium	
Vitamin E	40%	•	Thiamin	40%	•	Riboflavin	
Vitamin B₆	110%	•	Folic Acid	110%	•	Vitamin B₁₂	
Zinc	4%	•	Selenium	10%			

*Enriched foods refer to adding back nutrients removed during processing. Fortification is adding extra nutrients to a food. Source: Dieticians Online

■ **Figure 4.12** Women who are pregnant or considering pregnancy need to consume a healthy diet that includes foods rich in naturally occurring folate or foods that have been enriched with folic acid, the synthetic version of folate.

Hannamariah/Shutterstock.com

Understanding Effects of Teratogens

Check your understanding of how teratogens can influence the health and development of an unborn child by answering the following true–false questions.

1. Most teratogens have their most devastating effects during the third trimester.
2. Women should monitor their fish consumption during pregnancy.
3. The fetus is protected from most environmental insults once it has fully implanted in the uterus and the umbilical cord has been completely established.
4. Women who drink any amount of alcohol at any time during pregnancy will give birth to a baby with fetal alcohol syndrome.
5. A woman's age and race/ethnicity affect the odds of a healthy pregnancy.

Answers: 1. F (The most serious problems occur during the first trimester when most major organs are forming.) 2. T (Some fish, such as swordfish, can contain high levels of the heavy metal mercury and should be avoided or eaten in small quantities.) 3. F (The umbilical cord is not a very good filter for many harmful substances. Carbon monoxide from cigarette smoke, for example, is actually "allowed" to cross the placenta before oxygen.) 4. F (Although FAS is a possibility, there are many variables that determine how an individual child will fare if exposed prenatally to alcohol. Certainly, the dosage generalization is important here: The more alcohol a woman drinks during pregnancy, the more likely it is that her child will have FAS. FAS is also more likely to arise when alcohol consumption occurs during the time when neurons are migrating to their proper final destination or when organs are forming in the first trimester.) 5. T (Women between the ages of 20 and 35 have the lowest rates of fetal mortality. Non-Hispanic black women have some of the highest rates of fetal mortality and premature labor.)

and genetic conditions caused by mutations are greater when both mother and father are older (Fisch et al., 2003; and see Chapter 3). As well, the offspring of *young* fathers (less than 20 years) are at greater risk for Down syndrome and some other anomalies (Wiener-Megnazi, Auslender, & Dirnfeld, 2012). Finally, researchers have consistently identified advanced paternal age (that is, 50 and older) as a risk factor for schizophrenia (see Chapter 3; Crystal et al., 2011).

A father's exposure to environmental toxins can also affect a couple's children. A father's prolonged exposure to radiation, anesthetic gases used in operating rooms, pesticides, or other environmental toxins can damage the genetic material in his sperm and cause genetic defects in his children (Soubry et al., 2014). We pointed out the adverse effects of maternal smoking. Paternal smoking also has an adverse effect that is independent of mother's smoking (Langley et al., 2012). In short, fathers, like mothers, should assess and, if need be, change their lifestyles and exposure to risk factors to optimize their chances of a healthy child.

● Checking Mastery

1. What principles can help us understand the effects of teratogens?
2. What have researchers learned about the effects on the child of alcohol consumption during pregnancy?
3. What effects are likely to be seen among babies born to mothers who smoked throughout their pregnancies?

● Making Connections

1. Consider Serena, whose story was summarized at the start of the chapter. What disadvantages might her child face, given Serena's lack of awareness of her pregnancy for the first 4–5 months?
2. A close friend of yours has just gotten a positive reading on a home pregnancy test. What information would you give her about her activities during pregnancy and the potential impact of these on the development and health of her child?

4.3
The Perinatal Environment

LEARNING OBJECTIVES

- Examine current childbirth practices and analyze the use of various interventions during delivery on neonatal outcomes.

- Compare cultural practices surrounding labor, delivery, and neonatal life and predict how these differences might affect later child development.

The **perinatal environment** is the environment surrounding birth; it includes influences such as drugs given to the mother during labor, delivery practices, and the social environment shortly after birth. Like the prenatal environment, the perinatal environment can greatly affect human development.

In most Western cultures, a dramatic shift in birthing practices occurred during the 20th century. In 1930, 8 out of 10 births took place at home; by 1990, this figure had plummeted to just 1 out of 100 births before creeping back up to 1 in 90 births in recent years (MacDorman, Mathews, & Declercq, 2014). This change in birth setting was accompanied by a shift from thinking about birth as a natural family event that occurred at home to thinking about it as a medical problem to be solved with high technology (Cassidy, 2006). There is a small increase in mortality rates for home births, but the higher risk may be more related to the mother's income level than to location of the birth (Daysal et al., 2015; MacDorman et al., 2014). In the United States, women who give birth at home—or try to do so—often report that their decision is met with horror and disgust from others who believe the women are jeopardizing the well-being of their unborn baby (Cunha, 2015). In other parts of the world, home births are the norm.

What can couples do when they want the comfort and control of a home birth as well as the technology and modern interventions of a hospital? Many hospitals have restructured their labor and delivery rooms and practices to give parents greater flexibility and control when it comes time to deliver. Mothers-to-be have several choices when it comes to who will assist with their delivery, including family physicians, obstetricians, specialists in maternal–fetal medicine, and midwives. For high-risk pregnancies associated with delivery complications, a maternal–fetal specialist, or **perinatologist**, is recommended. However, for the majority of women, personal preference can determine the best caregiver for pregnancy and delivery. In many countries, such as England and France, midwives have been the traditional pregnancy caregivers. For the past century, most (around 90%) women in the United States have relied on physicians or obstetricians for pregnancy care, but the use of midwives is slowly increasing, from 4% in 1990 to 8% more recently (Declercq, 2012). In general, midwives view pregnancy and delivery as natural life events rather than as medical events requiring medical intervention. They partner with the laboring mother-to-be to assist her with delivery but do not dictate the conditions of labor and delivery.

Another change in the delivery room is the presence of a spouse, partner, mother, sister, and/or friend to provide support and share in the miracle of birth. Most women find the support provided by this familiar person helpful and reassuring. Some women have the support of a *doula*—an individual trained to provide continuous physical and emotional support throughout the childbirth process. Such support tends to shorten labor by as much as half and to reduce the need for pain medication and assisted delivery such as use of forceps or vacuum (Hodnett et al., 2013). The rate of cesarean sections is lower among women continuously supported by a doula, midwife, or other labor support person (Hodnett et al., 2013). Mothers with continuous labor support also report more positive feelings about the birth experience, fewer symptoms of postnatal depression, and greater likelihood of breast-feeding than nonsupported mothers. Clearly, then, the social context surrounding labor and delivery is important: Women who receive more support during childbirth have more positive experiences.

Childbirth is a three-stage process (■ Figure 4.13). The first stage of labor begins as the mother experiences regular contractions of the uterus and ends when her cervix has fully dilated (widened) so that the fetus's head can pass through. This stage of labor lasts an average of 9 hours for firstborn children and 5 hours for later-born children, but these figures represent averages and may not be representative of a particular woman's experience. Approximately one-third of laboring women receive some assistance with this stage, usually the administration of **oxytocin** (brand name Pitocin), a hormone released by

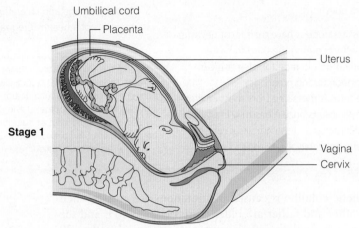

Stage 1

(A) Contractions occur and the cervix opens (dilates)

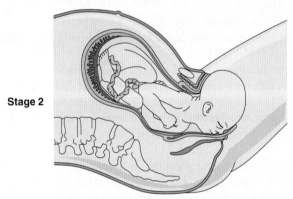

Stage 2

(B) After the head appears (crowns), the baby passes through the vagina

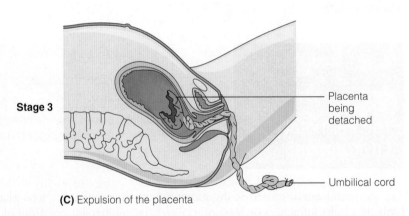

Stage 3

(C) Expulsion of the placenta

■ **Figure 4.13** The three stages of labor. Stage 1: Contractions of the uterus cause dilation of the cervix. Stage 2: The mother pushes with each contraction, forcing the baby down the birth canal, and the head appears, followed by the shoulders and then the rest of the baby's body. Stage 3: With a few final pushes, the placenta is delivered.

the pituitary gland that can initiate and speed up contractions, moving labor along more quickly. The body naturally produces low levels of oxytocin throughout pregnancy, and administering synthetic oxytocin to assist delivery is considered very safe. In Chapter 14, we'll examine some of the other functions of oxytocin, which some have dubbed the "love hormone." Just to be clear, though, oxytocin may speed up labor, but it speeds up what is typically a stalled or very slow-to-progress labor, so that women whose labor is assisted in this manner spend, on average, as much as 6–7 more hours in this stage than women who not need to be assisted (Harper, et al., 2012). This first stage of labor ends when the cervix has dilated to 10 centimeters.

The second stage of labor is delivery, which begins as the fetus's head passes through the cervix into the vagina and ends when the baby emerges from the mother's body. This is when the mother is often told to "bear down" (push) with each contraction to assist her baby through the birth canal. For first deliveries, this stage may take about 1 hour; for later deliveries, it can be 15–20 minutes. Finally, the third stage of the birth process is the delivery of the placenta, which lasts only a few minutes.

When the birth process is completed, the mother (and often the father, if he is present) is typically physically exhausted, relieved to be through the ordeal of giving birth, and exhilarated all at once. Meanwhile, the fetus has been thrust from its carefree but cramped existence into a strange new world.

Possible Hazards

In most births the entire process goes smoothly, and parents and newborn quickly begin their relationship. Occasionally, however, problems arise.

Anoxia

One clear hazard during the birth process is **anoxia**, or oxygen shortage (also called *asphyxia*). Anoxia can occur for any number of reasons—for example, because the umbilical cord becomes pinched or tangled during birth, because sedatives given to the mother reach the fetus and interfere with the baby's breathing, because mucus lodged in the baby's throat prevents normal breathing, or because the baby is in a **breech presentation** (feet or buttocks first) during a vaginal delivery. If identified in advance, fetuses in breech position can be safely delivered by cesarean section to avoid possible anoxia that may occur with a vaginal delivery. Anoxia is dangerous primarily because brain cells die if they are starved of oxygen for more than a few minutes. Severe anoxia can initially cause poor reflexes, seizures, heart rate irregularities, and breathing difficulties. In the long run, severe anoxia can lead to memory impairment or **cerebral palsy**, a neurological disability primarily associated with difficulty controlling muscle movements; it also increases the risk of learning or intellectual disabilities and speech difficulties (Fehlings, Hunt, & Rosenbaum, 2007). Milder anoxia makes some infants irritable at birth or delays their motor and cognitive development but usually does not lead to permanent problems.

Fetal monitoring procedures during labor and delivery can alert caregivers to the possibility of anoxia and allow them to take preventive measures. For example, a vaginal delivery is nearly impossible for the 1 fetus in 100 that is found lying sideways in the uterus. The fetus must be turned to assume a head-down position or be delivered by **cesarean section**, a surgical procedure in which an incision is made in the mother's abdomen and uterus so that the baby can be removed.

Complicated Delivery

In some cases, mothers may need assistance with delivery, possibly because labor has proceeded too long with too little to show for it or because of concern about the well-being of the baby or mother. For years, doctors frequently used forceps (an instrument resembling an oversized pair of salad tongs) to assist with a vaginal delivery. However, forceps on the soft skull of the newborn occasionally caused serious problems, including cranial bleeding and brain damage, leading to a sharp decline in use of this instrument over the past 50 years (Laughon et al., 2012). Alternatively, doctors may use vacuum extraction ("suction") to assist difficult deliveries. This procedure has fewer risks associated with it, although it is not risk free. In a vacuum extraction, a cup is inserted through the opening of the birth canal and attached to the baby's head. Suction is applied to make the cup adhere to the baby's scalp; during each contraction and with the mother bearing down, the doctor uses the traction created by the suction to help deliver the baby.

From the mother's point of view, vacuum extraction is less painful than forceps because the vacuum extractor takes up less space in the birth canal (and therefore is felt less) than forceps (Shekhar, Rana, & Jaswal, 2012). For the baby, however, there is likely to be swelling of the scalp and some marking where the vacuum cup was attached. Bleeding under the scalp is also possible, which may lead to a condition called jaundice. More serious injuries are possible if the vacuum is not properly used (Schot et al., 2013). Thus, relative to forceps, vacuum extraction may be less traumatic for the mother but just as traumatic for the infant. This illustrates the complexity of perinatal issues that need to be considered to ensure a safe outcome for both mother and infant.

Cesarean sections, too, have been controversial. Use of this alternative to normal vaginal delivery has prevented the death of many babies—for example, when the baby is too large or the mother is too small to permit normal delivery, when a fetus out of position cannot be repositioned, when the placenta prematurely separates from the uterus, or when fetal monitoring reveals that a birth complication is likely. Still, overall rates of fetal/neonatal death have not improved with all these Cesareans (Blanchette, 2011). Medical advances have made Cesarean sections about as safe as vaginal deliveries, and few ill effects on mothers and infants have been observed. But mothers who have "C-sections" do take longer to recover from the surgery than from a vaginal delivery, and they are sometimes less positive toward and involved with their babies during the recovery period. The start of breast-feeding may also be delayed in women who have delivered by C-section (Prior et al., 2012; Sakalidis et al., 2013). Nonetheless, the development of babies born by cesarean appears to be perfectly normal and early observed differences in mother–infant interaction disappear by 6 months (Durik, Hyde, & Clark, 2000).

Many observers have questioned why cesarean deliveries have become so much more common—to the point that they accounted for about one-third of all births in the United States. By one estimate, 11% of first-time cesarean sections are unnecessary and 65% of second-time cesareans are unnecessary (Kabir et al., 2005). Some obstetricians readily opt for C-section deliveries because it may help protect them from the costly malpractice suits that might arise from complications in vaginal deliveries (Childbirth Connection, 2012). C-sections also generate more revenue for physicians and medical practices than vaginal deliveries. Contributing to the high rate of C-sections is the strong likelihood (90%) for women who have had one C-section to deliver subsequent babies by C-section rather than attempting a vaginal delivery (Menacker, MacDorman, & Declercq, 2010). Although there is a very small risk of complications with a vaginal delivery following a C-section, it is safe for the large majority of women and having multiple C-sections carries its own set of risks (Blanchette, 2011). Finally, the high rate of C-section deliveries also reflects the fact that some mothers—and their doctors—prefer having a scheduled birth rather than contending with an unscheduled vaginal delivery (Fuglenes et al., 2012). In one study, 55% of repeat C-sections were elective, not medically necessary (Tita et al., 2009). In some instances, anxiety about a vaginal delivery may lead mothers-to-be to lobby for a C-section delivery (Ramvi & Tangerud, 2011). Women who have planned C-sections, as opposed to those that are emergency and unanticipated, rate their birth experience more positively than any other group, including those who deliver vaginally (Blomquist et al., 2011). There is something to be said for knowing, in advance, when and what is going to happen!

Medications

Some of us were delivered in an era when mothers were routinely drugged into unconsciousness during delivery so that they would not experience any pain, or if they did, they wouldn't remember it. Not surprisingly, concerns have been raised about medications given to mothers during the birth process—analgesics and anesthetics to reduce their pain, sedatives to relax them, and stimulants to induce or intensify uterine contractions. Sedative drugs that act on the entire body cross the placenta and can affect the baby. Babies whose mothers receive large doses of sedative medications during delivery are generally sluggish and irritable, are difficult to feed or cuddle during the first few days of life, and smile infrequently (Elbourne & Wiseman, 2000). In short, they act as though they are drugged. Think about it: Doses of medication large enough to affect mothers can have much greater effects on newborns who weigh only 7 pounds and have immature circulatory and excretory systems that cannot get rid of drugs for days.

Regional analgesics, such as epidurals and spinal blocks, reduce sensation in specific parts of the body. Because they do not cross the placenta, they have fewer ill effects on babies and are preferred by many physicians over sedative drugs that *do* cross the placenta. Use of epidurals has increased from 4% of deliveries in the 1960s to as many as 75% of deliveries to women in the United States (Kjerulff & Zhu, 2014). Mothers rate epidurals as more effective for pain control than other forms of analgesics but despite this advantage, mothers and physicians must weigh disadvantages: Women who have an epidural may obtain some pain relief but in doing so, they tend to lengthen their labor,

and this leads to increased likelihood of needing instrumental assistance—forceps or vacuum extraction (Anim-Soumuah et al., 2011; Hasegawa et al., 2013). Alternative methods for controlling pain, such as systematic relaxation techniques, can be successful, but are not regularly offered and require more time from someone trained in these techniques than administering medication for pain control (Smith et al., 2011).

In sum, taking obstetric medications is not as risky a business today as it once was, but it is still a decision that requires the pros and cons to be weighed carefully. The effects depend on which drug is used, how much is taken, when it is taken, and by which mother.

Possible hazards during birth, then, include anoxia; breech presentation; the need for assisted delivery through forceps, vacuum extraction, or cesarean section; and the use of medications for pain relief or to speed up labor. Fortunately, most deliveries, although unique from the parents' perspective, are routine from a clinical perspective. In the next section, we consider the birth experience from a family perspective.

The Mother's Experience

What is it really like to give birth to a child? For every woman who has given birth, you are likely to hear a unique birth story. Most mothers admit that they experienced pain—some quite significant—and a good deal of anxiety, including feelings of outright panic (Waldenström et al., 1996). Yet most also emerged from the delivery room feeling good about their achievement and their ability to cope ("I did it!"). Overall, 77% felt the experience was positive and only 10% said it was negative. And, despite longer labors and more medication, first-time mothers did not perceive labor and delivery much differently than experienced mothers did.

This woman chose to give birth in water, an experience that has been associated with increased feelings of relaxation and decreased pain. Water births can occur at home or in a birth center and even a hospital. While embraced by some, others express concerns about whether this is as safe as a non-water birth for the baby.

Ross Marks Photography/Alamy Stock Photo

What factors influence a mother's experience of birth? Not surprisingly, women who labor longer report more negative feelings about the birth experience (Ulfsdottir et al., 2014). Psychological factors such as the mother's attitude toward her pregnancy, her knowledge and expectations about the birth process, her sense of control over childbirth, and the social support she receives from her partner or someone else are important determinants of her experience of delivery and of her new baby (Waldenström et al., 1996; Wilcock, Kobayashi, & Murray, 1997). Finally, women report a more negative birth experience when their newborn seems to be struggling immediately after birth, even when the infant quickly rebounds (Ulfsdottir et al., 2014). Regardless of whether women experience their infant's delivery as positive or negative, their feelings about motherhood are largely positive 6 months after the experience (DiPietro et al., 2015).

Cultural Factors

The experience of childbearing is shaped by the cultural context in which it occurs. For example, different cultures have different views of the desirability of having children (■ Figure 4.14). Many Islamic cultures favor large families, believing that children are a gift and blessing. In contrast, starting around 1980, the People's Republic of China promoted a "one-child policy" to discourage multiple childbearing in hopes of slowing population growth and raising the standard of living. As a result of this policy, the average number of children per Chinese family dropped from nearly five children to fewer than two. Along with the overall decrease in number of children, the ratio of boys to girls also changed; many parents wanted their one child to be a boy who could support them in old age and therefore aborted female fetuses identified through ultrasound tests or abandoned their female babies after birth (Fitzpatrick, 2009). Following harsh criticism, China's one-child policy relaxed a bit and has recently transitioned to a two-child policy.

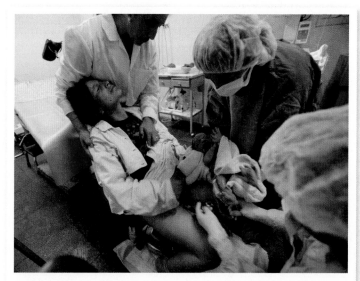

This Peruvian woman gives birth in an upright position, which reduces labor and delivery time by allowing gravity to assist with moving the baby down the birth canal. In societies that have medicalized childbirth, women are more likely to be lying horizontal on a bed, which may sound comfortable but is not the optimal laboring or birthing position.

Mariana Bazo/Reuters/Corbis

Practices surrounding birth also differ widely. Consider three different birth scenarios that reflect different cultural beliefs about pregnancy and delivery. Among the Pokot people of Kenya, there is strong social support of the mother-to-be (O'Dempsey, 1988). The community celebrates the coming birth, and the father-to-be stops hunting lest he be killed by animals. As a result, he is available to support his wife. A midwife, aided by female relatives, delivers the baby. The placenta is buried in the goat enclosure, and the baby is washed in cold water and given a mixture of hot ash and boiled herbs so that it will vomit the amniotic fluid it has

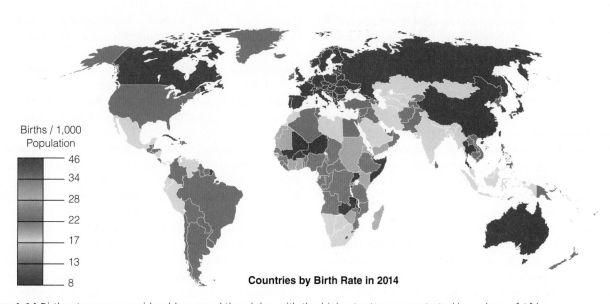

Births / 1,000
Population

46
34
28
22
17
13
8

Countries by Birth Rate in 2014

■ **Figure 4.14** Birth rates vary considerably around the globe, with the highest rates concentrated in regions of Africa.

Childbirth practices vary across cultures. Here, a woman labors at home with assistance from family or village members.

AF archive/Alamy Stock Photo

swallowed. Mothers are given plenty of time to recover. They go into seclusion for 1 month and devote themselves entirely to their babies for 3 months.

A rather different experience of childbirth is found in rural villages of northern India, where a traditional childbirth attendant called a *dai* assists with the delivery. Most women indicate a preference for a home birth over a hospital birth as they believe that their *dai* will be "hands-on," literally using her hands to massage and push on the woman's pregnant belly to help deliver the baby (Iyengar et al., 2008). In contrast, women report that hospital staff are hands-off, preferring to administer "needles and bottles" (injections of drugs and intravenous fluids) and telling mothers-to-be to apply their strength (bear down). Whether at home or in hospital, the pushing can be intense enough to land the newborn on the floor, where it stays until after the placenta is delivered and the umbilical cord has been tied. After 5–15 minutes, the newborn is wrapped and handed to the mother; it many cases, it will be 5–9 days before the baby is washed out of concern that early bathing is associated with death. For the first several days, the baby will be given an herbal concoction rather than milk because it is believed that mother's milk takes about 3 days to come in.

Finally, among the !Kung San of Namibia, women typically labor by themselves (Cassidy, 2006). Giving birth alone is considered to be a strength. When labor begins, the !Kung woman goes off on her own and is expected to labor quietly. To do otherwise is considered a sign of weakness and possibly shows indifference toward the baby.

In contrast to these examples, childbirth in highly industrialized Western societies is highly "medicalized," with women hospitalized, hooked up to monitors, and separated from most friends and family members. Should we return to more traditional ways of birthing that view delivery less like a major medical event and more like a natural life event to be managed at home? There are many who would argue that not all "traditional" practices are in the best interests of parents and babies. Also, Western societies do a far better job than developing countries of preventing mother and infant mortality. In some areas of sub-Saharan Africa, for example, 7–10% of babies die during childbirth or in the first year of life (CIA, 2015). In Western, industrial societies, infant mortality rates have dropped over the past 50 years from 3% (30 infants out of 1,000) to less than 0.5% (4–5 infants out of 1,000) (CIA, 2015). In the United States, infant mortality is more than twice as high for black infants as for white infants, although mortality rates have shown greater improvement over the past 10 years among black infants compared to white infants (Mathews, MacDorman & Thoma, 2015). The secret to a more optimal birth experience may be to blend beneficial traditional practices such as offering emotional support to new mothers with modern medical know-how.

In addition to different cultural influences on childbirth practices, cultural beliefs influence behaviors during the postpartum period. In some cultures, women's activities and interactions with others are restricted for a period of time following childbirth (Eberhard-Gran et al., 2010). Depending on the culture, this practice may be to protect her and her newborn from "evil forces" or from the wind and cold, or it may be associated with fears that childbirth and the new mother are somehow unclean. Many postnatal differences across cultures have shrunk over the past several decade, although they have not entirely disappeared. In Western countries such as the United States and Canada, new mothers and their newborns might get a few days to a week respite from the hustle and bustle of daily living, but probably do not spend 40 days in isolation while other family or community members cover the typical chores needed to run a household (Eberhard-Gran et al., 2010).

Postpartum Depression

Some new mothers suffer from depression following the birth of their baby. Many new mothers report feeling tearful, irritable, moody, anxious, and depressed within the first few days after birth. This condition—the baby blues—is relatively mild, passes quickly, and is probably linked to the steep drops in levels of female hormones that normally occur after delivery and to the stresses associated with delivering a child and taking on the responsibilities of parenthood (not to mention coping with the lack of sleep experienced by many new mothers). Indeed, it may be difficult to find a new mother who does not experience at least some degree of moodiness or baby blues in the week following delivery.

A second, and far more serious, condition is **postpartum depression**—an episode of clinical depression lasting 2 or more weeks (rather than days) in a woman who has just given birth. It affects approximately 15–20% of new mothers (O'Hara & McCabe, 2013). Only rarely does a woman who has never had significant emotional problems become clinically depressed for the first time after giving birth. Most affected women have histories of depression, and many were depressed during pregnancy. Also, women vulnerable to depression are more likely to become depressed if they are experiencing other life stresses on top of the stresses of becoming a mother (Honey, Bennett, & Morgan,

2003). Lack of social support—especially a poor relationship with a partner—also increases the odds (Webster et al., 2011). Fortunately, the risk of developing postpartum depression can be reduced through various interventions including home visits or telephone conversations with at-risk new mothers during the postpartum period (Dennis & Dowswell, 2013).

Postpartum depression has significant implications for the parent–infant relationship. Compared to children of nondepressed mothers, children whose mothers experienced postpartum depression may become less securely attached to their mothers during infancy and less responsive during interactions with their mothers at age 5 (Murray, Fearon, & Cooper, 2015). These negative patterns of interaction are most likely to occur when the mother's depression is prolonged and when there are other risk factors in the home. Children of postpartum depressed mothers are also more likely to have experienced depression by age 16 (Murray et al., 2011).

Mothers who had been postnatally depressed report more behavioral problems in their children. At age 11, children of postnatally depressed mothers show more violent behavior even when researchers control for family characteristics and later episodes of maternal depression (Hay et al., 2003). The violence exhibited by these children is associated with anger management problems, attention problems, and hyperactive behavior. Adolescents whose mothers had been postnatally depressed also show elevated levels of cortisol, which is associated with major depression (Halligan et al., 2004). The implication of these results is that early experiences with a depressed mother, prenatally or postnatally, might predispose these children to later depression.

How exactly might maternal depression in the weeks and months following delivery affect children's behavior and increase their odds of developing depression? Mothers who are depressed tend to be relatively unresponsive to their babies and may even feel hostility toward them. They are tired, distracted, and often lack the energy needed to be fully engaged with their infants. Even though mothers typically recover from postnatal depression, research suggests that their early attitudes about their babies and the resulting pattern of early mother–child interactions set the stage for ongoing interaction problems that affect the child's behavior (Murray et al., 2015; Weinberg et al., 2006). The contribution of genes inherited from their depression-prone mothers, fetal programming from exposure to the prenatal chemistry of their mothers, and poor quality of the postnatal mother–child relationship can combine to precipitate depression or other problems in the child (Field, 2011). Thus, for their own sakes and for the sakes of their infants, mothers experiencing more than a mild case of the baby blues should seek professional help in overcoming their depression.

The Father's Experience

When birthing moved into hospitals, the medical establishment aggressively prohibited fathers from participating in their children's birth on the grounds that they would contaminate the sterile environment needed for a safe birth (Cassidy, 2006). It would take many decades, many lawsuits, and more progressive views about birth support before men were routinely accepted—and

expected—in the delivery room. Today, many men prepare for fatherhood before delivery, attend prenatal classes with their partner, and are present for their child's birth. Fathers report that they want to be involved with their partner's pregnancy, although they don't always know how to make this happen (Draper, 2002).

Like mothers, fathers experience the process of becoming a parent as a significant event in their lives that involves a mix of positive and negative emotions. Also like mothers, fathers tend to be anxious during pregnancy and birth and some even experience some of the same physiological symptoms as their pregnant partner. These symptoms, called couvade (from the French word meaning "to hatch"), include bloating, weight gain, fatigue, insomnia, and nausea (Cassidy, 2006). And before you conclude that these symptoms must be "all in their heads," consider that some research shows hormonal shifts among expectant fathers that are similar to the hormonal shifts experienced by pregnant women (Cassidy, 2006).

As for the labor and delivery period, new fathers report feeling scared, unprepared, helpless, and frustrated (Chandler & Field, 1997; Chapman, 2000; Hallgren et al., 1999). They find labor to be more work than they had expected and sometimes feel excluded as the medical professionals take over. For most men, attending prenatal classes with their partner improves their experience of childbirth, although for a few men the added knowledge that comes with these classes increases their anxiety (Greenhalgh, Slade, & Spiby, 2000). Stress levels among men tend to be highest during their partner's pregnancy and then decrease after the birth of the baby. Despite the stresses, negative emotions usually give way to relief, pride, and joy when the baby finally arrives (Chandler & Field, 1997). Those fathers present for delivery who cut their newborn's umbilical cord are found to have greater emotional connection to their infants at 1 month (Brandão & Figueiredo, 2012). This doesn't mean that all fathers-to-be need to reach for the scissors and cut the umbilical cord, though; there are many other opportunities to develop a strong emotional connection between father and infant.

Checking Mastery

1. What steps occur during the process of childbirth?
2. What risks does the baby potentially face during the birth process?

Making Connections

1. Considering the research on birth and the perinatal environment, arrange the perfect birth experience for you and your baby and justify its features. Where would you be, who would be with you, and what would be done?
2. Some experts worry that cesarean sections are overused. What do you think? Should a woman be able to choose whether she delivers vaginally or by cesarean section? Should hospitals be permitted to force a woman to deliver by cesarean if they believe the fetus is in danger?

4.4

The Neonatal Environment

LEARNING OBJECTIVES

- Compare and contrast breast- and bottle-feeding, offering pros and cons of both practices.
- Explain how we can optimize the development of at-risk newborns.

So now that parents have a baby, what do they do? Here we will look at the **neonatal** environment—the events of the first month and how parents might optimize the development of young infants.

There are marked differences in how parents interact with their newborns. As Meredith Small (1999) characterizes it, "Our ideas about parenting and infant care are as culturally constructed as what we wear, what we eat, or how we dance" (p. 41). For example, in societies where infant mortality is high, babies may not even be named or viewed as people until they seem likely to survive (Nsamenang, 1992). The Beng, who are concentrated in small farming towns along the Ivory Coast, believe that newborns are not entirely in this world but exist in the world the babies will eventually inhabit after death (Gottlieb, 2000). Once their umbilical cord stump falls off on the fourth or fifth day of life, they begin to inhabit this world but still vacillate between the two worlds for another 4–5 years. During this time, the Beng regard their children as vulnerable. Spiritual beliefs influence their child care practices, leading, for example, to twice-daily enemas for infants using a chili pepper solution.

In Central Africa, babies born to forager families are carried upright in slings during the day and sleep in the same bed with their mothers at night. They are touched more than 70% of daytime hours, are breast-fed whenever they want (usually 20–40 times per day), and may not be weaned until the age of 4 (Fouts, Hewlett, & Lamb, 2012). Infants in such societies are indulged considerably, at least until their survival is assured. In contrast, babies born to farming families in Central Africa are touched less often, breast-fed less often, and weaned at an earlier age than the babies in foraging families.

Infant care practices are considerably different in modern, industrialized societies where infant mortality is lower. Infants in industrialized nations like the United States are touched only 12–20% of daytime hours, and they are often trained to breast-feed or bottle-feed on a schedule, usually five to seven times a day (Hewlett, 1996). Babies may sleep in the same bed or room as their parents for just a few weeks before being settled into a crib in their own room, a practice that mothers in many other cultures, who sleep in the same bed with their babies until they are toddlers, find quite bizarre. Parents who do sleep with their babies should be mindful that babies are at increased risk of suffocation when they sleep in adult beds. Adults are obviously much larger and heavier, posing a hazard if they roll onto a baby while sleeping. Adult beds also have more bedding and pillows than an infant crib, and these can suffocate a tiny infant.

Regardless of where they live, new parents are often uncertain about how to relate to their babies and may find the period after birth stressful. Many seek information on what is "normal" behavior from their infant as well as feedback on their own behaviors as parents. To help parents appreciate their baby's competencies and feel competent themselves as parents, the Neonatal Behavioral Assessment Scale (NBAS), intended for practitioners such as pediatricians, and the Newborn Behavioral Observations (NBO) system, geared toward parents, were developed out of the pioneering work of T. Berry Brazelton (see Brazelton & Nugent, 2011; Nugent, et al., 2007). Both instruments are intended to reveal infants' capabilities and readiness for the tasks they will need to navigate to survive and thrive. For instance, the NBO evaluates infants' ability to self-regulate or calm themselves as well as infants' ability to "tune out" lights and sounds so that they can sleep. The NBO is focused on helping parents form relationships with their infants by revealing the individual characteristics of their infant and profiling areas of strength and areas where greater attention might be needed.

Breast or Bottle?

Breast-feeding is the most natural form of nutrition for newborns and until modern times, it was the sole source of

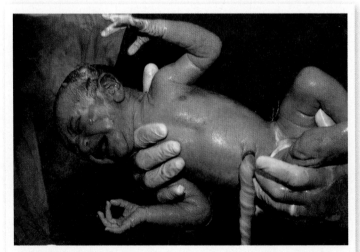

Welcome to the world, little one! Your journey over the past 9 months has been astonishing. At conception, you received all the genetic material necessary to develop into the baby that we now see. You have already taken your first breaths and the umbilical cord that sustained you in the womb will soon be cut. After being cleaned and wrapped up, you will begin to interact with your family and explore the world around you.

MedicImage/Alamy

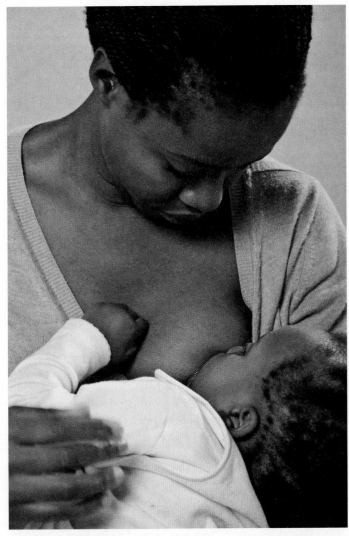

Breast milk provides the perfect balance nutrients for the developing infant.

Grant Difford/Greatstock Photographic Library/Alamy Stock Photo

nourishment until solid foods were introduced. For a variety of reasons, breast-feeding in the United States reached an all-time low in the early 1970s, when only 1 in 4 mothers attempted to nurse their newborn infants. Bottle-feeding with formula had become the norm (Eiger and Olds, 1999). Since then, research has shown numerous advantages of breast milk over formula. Breast milk contains several substances that protect nursing infants from infections, and it has the perfect blend of nutrients for a quickly developing little person. In homes where a caregiver smokes cigarettes, breast-feeding offers some protection against the respiratory infections that frequently plague infants exposed to secondhand (passive) smoke (Yilmaz et al., 2009). Children who breast-feed for at least 4 months have stronger lung function, almost certainly because breast-feeding requires infants to suck stronger and longer to obtain the same amount of milk as when bottle-feeding (Ogbuanu et al., 2008). As well, breast-feeding for the first 4–6 months is associated with a handful of cognitive advances

during infancy, especially among preterm babies (Quigley et al., 2012). For premature babies, breast milk has been referred to as "more of a medicine than a food" because of its positive effects on their immune systems and weight gain (Gross-Loh, 2006, p. 38). And mothers who breast-feed lose the weight gained during pregnancy more quickly than those who do not breast-feed following childbirth.

Campaigns to raise awareness of the health benefits of breast-feeding have significantly increased the percentage of new mothers who start breast-feeding their newborns (Breast-feeding Report Card, 2014). But although 79% of new mothers breast-feed, only 49% are still breast-feeding by age 6 months. Women cite a number of reasons for not continuing with breast-feeding, ranging from their own discomfort to concerns that the infant is not getting adequate nutrition. Young women, those from low socioeconomic backgrounds, and those with less education are less likely to breast-feed than other women (Ryan & Zhou, 2006). Being employed outside the home is also associated with lower breast-feeding rates, presumably because of the logistical problems of breast-feeding while at work (Ryan & Zhou, 2006). Finally, fewer black mothers breast-feed than white mothers (Ip et al., 2007). Interestingly, Hispanic mothers have a fairly high rate of breast-feeding until they immigrate to the United States, and then the rate decreases with the amount of time in the United States (Ahluwalia et al., 2012). This likely reflects U.S. cultural values toward breast-feeding, which are more ambivalent than those in many other countries. To improve breast-feeding rates, ambivalent (and in some cases, downright negative) views of breast-feeding need to be addressed so that women view breast-feeding as *the* option, not just *an* option.

Identifying At-Risk Newborns

A few infants will be considered **at risk** for either short-term or long-term problems because of genetic defects, prenatal hazards, or perinatal damage. It is essential to these infants' survival and well-being that they be identified as early as possible. Newborns are routinely screened using the **Apgar test**, which provides a quick assessment of the newborn's heart rate, respiration, color, muscle tone, and reflexes (●Table 4.7). The test has been used for more than 60 years and, despite its low-tech nature, is still considered a valuable diagnostic tool. The simple test is given immediately and 5 minutes after birth. It yields scores of 0, 1, or 2 for each of the five factors, which are then added to yield a total score that can range from 0 to 10. Infants who score 7 or higher are in good shape. Infants scoring 4 or lower are at risk—their heartbeats are sluggish or nonexistent, their muscles are limp, and their breathing is shallow and irregular, if they are breathing at all. These babies will immediately experience a different postnatal environment than the normal baby experiences because they require medical intervention in intensive care units to survive, as you will see at the end of the chapter.

One particular group of at-risk babies that should be examined more closely are those with **low birth weight (LBW)**. As

Factors	Score		
	0	**1**	**2**
Heart Rate	Absent	Slow (<100 beats per minute)	Moderate (>100 beats per minute)
Respiratory Effort	Absent	Slow or irregular	Good; baby is crying
Muscle Tone	Flaccid; limp	Weak; some flexion	Strong; active motion
Color	Blue or pale	Body pink, extremities blue	Completely pink
Reflex Irritability	No response	Frown, grimace, or weak cry	Vigorous cry

● **Table 4.8** illustrates, the younger (and smaller) babies are at birth, the lower their chances of survival. Approximately 8% of babies born in the United States have an LBW (less than 2,500 grams, or 5½ pounds). Some of these babies are born at term and are called "small for gestational age," but many are born preterm (less than 37 weeks of gestation) and are more at risk as a result. The survival and health of these small infants is a concern, particularly for infants who are very small (less than 1,500 grams or no more than 3.3 pounds).

Although LBW infants account for about 9% of all births, they account for about two-thirds of all infant deaths and nearly 60% of the money spent on pregnancies and deliveries (March of Dimes, 2015; Schmitt, Sneed, & Phibbs, 2006). Very LBW infants are even more costly: They account for less than 1% of all births but 36% of the total hospital costs. Most fragile are the micropreemies—those weighing less than 800 grams or 1.75 pounds at birth. The high emotional and economic costs of LBW have made this an important medical and societal issue, not to mention an intensely personal issue for those families directly affected by a premature delivery. And while aggressive application of medical technology has kept more tiny preemies alive, many experience long-term disabilities (see, e.g., Serenius et al., 2013).

We don't always know what causes LBW, but research has identified a number of factors regularly associated with it, including:

- age of mother (very young or older)
- low socioeconomic status of mother, linked with poor nutrition and inadequate prenatal care
- race: black women are twice as likely as white women to experience premature delivery
- prior premature deliveries, which may indicate underlying and persistent health conditions
- tobacco or alcohol use

- stress
- pregnancies with more than one fetus (twins, triplets, etc.)
- infections
- high blood pressure

Some of these factors can be controlled: A woman can try to eliminate smoking during pregnancy. Other factors such as high blood pressure can be monitored and treated. But some factors may be outside of a woman's direct control and, not surprisingly, the more risk factors experienced during pregnancy, the greater the likelihood of delivering a small baby (Rosenberg, 2001).

The good news is that most LBW babies born since the advent of neonatal intensive care in the 1960s function within the normal range of development and experience significant catch-up growth during their first months and years of life (Chyi et al., 2008; Wilson-Costello et al., 2007). However, compared with normal-birth-weight children, LBW children, especially those with extremely LBW are at greater risk for numerous neurobehavioral problems, including blindness, deafness, cerebral palsy, poor academic achievement, autism, and health problems (Costeloe et al., 2012; Serenius et al., 2013). Respiratory difficulties are likely because premature babies have not yet produced enough **surfactant**, a substance that prevents the air sacs of the lungs from sticking together and therefore aids breathing. Surfactant therapy for LBW infants became common practice around 1990 and seems to improve the survival rate among the sickest infants. However, it has not entirely improved health or long-term achievement scores of LBW babies in general, perhaps because small, earlier-born babies, who have the most complications, are now surviving to be among the school-age population of LBW survivors (Hagen et al., 2006; Paul et al., 2006; see also Bode et al., 2009).

● **Table 4.8** Survival and Health of Premature Babies by Gestational Age

Factors	Results (in Weeks and %)				
Number of completed weeks since last menstruation	22 weeks	23 weeks	24 weeks	25 weeks	26 weeks
Percentage of babies who survived to one year	10%	52%	67%	82%	85%
Percentage of survivors beyond one year with mild or moderate disability	60%	49%	54%	46%	44%
Percentage of survivors beyond one year with a severe disability	40%	21%	13%	10%	7%

Source: Based on data from Serenius et al, 2013.

Although modern technology permits the survival of younger and smaller babies, like this one, many experts believe we have reached the lowest limits of viability around 23 weeks of gestation. What is the long-term prognosis for premature babies?

Steve Lovegrove/Shutterstock.com

In addition to the advances made thanks to the high-tech interventions now available in most neonatal intensive care units (NICUs), research has shown that several low-tech interventions can go far in improving the developmental outcomes of LBW, premature infants. For starters, these vulnerable infants benefit from their mother's breast milk even if they can't effectively nurse when they are hooked up to tubes and machines in the NICU. Mothers can pump their breast milk to provide nutrient-rich nourishment that helps boost their infant's fledgling immune system. Babies with extremely LBW who receive breast milk later score about 5 points higher on the Bayley Scale of Mental Development than similar babies who receive no breast milk (Vohr et al., 2006). And among babies receiving breast milk, there are measurable differences between those who consumed the largest quantities and those who consumed the least.

There is also evidence that skin-to-skin contact is therapeutic for these infants. Sometimes called **kangaroo care**, resting on a parent's chest helps maintain body temperature, heart rate, and oxygen levels in the blood (Conde-Agudelo, Belizán, & Diaz-Rossello, 2011) and the rhythmic sound of the parent's heartbeat calms the infant and may help simulate the environment of the womb. Premature infants who experience kangaroo care settle into more mature patterns of quiet sleep and alert wakefulness than premature infants who do not receive this treatment. And it is not only the infant who benefits: Mothers who participate in kangaroo care of their infants while in neonatal intensive care report positive feelings about the experience as long as they receive adequate education and support of the practice (Blomqvist & Nyqvist, 2010). One of the nice things about kangaroo care is that both mothers and fathers can participate. Doing so improves parents' sensitivity to their infant and makes the dynamics among the trio more positive (Feldman et al., 2003; Tessier, et al., 2009).

In addition to skin-to-skin contact, Tiffany Field and her colleagues (Diego, Field, & Hernandez-Reif, 2005; Field, Diego, & Hernandez-Reif, 2010) have shown that premature infants benefit from massage therapy. For example, in one study, premature babies received either light or moderate massage three times per day for 5 days (Field et al., 2006). Those who received moderate-pressure massage gained significantly more weight on each of the days of the therapy than the premature babies in the light-massage group. Babies receiving moderate massage seemed to be more relaxed and less aroused, which may have facilitated greater weight gain (Field et al., 2006). In addition, the massage increased the efficiency of the digestive system, which is also associated with greater weight gain (Diego, Field, & Hernandez-Reif, 2005).

Although the long-term health prognosis for LBW babies is now good, many children born with an extremely LBW continue to experience neurosensory impairments and academic problems throughout their childhood and teen years (Doyle & Anderson, 2005; Saigal et al., 2007). These cognitive deficits in childhood can be traced to deficits in attention, speed, and memory evident in preterm infants during their first year (Rose et al., 2005). The fate of premature and LBW babies depends

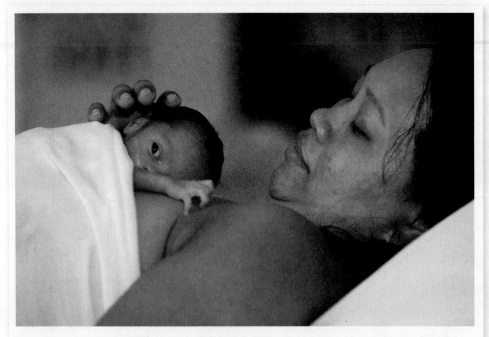

This 2 pound 10 ounce bundle is enjoying skin-to-skin contact with his mother. Such "kangaroo care" helps babies regulate body temperature and maintain a regular heart rate and oxygen levels in the blood.

Paula Bronstein/Staff/Getty Images

considerably on two factors. The first is their biological condition—their health and neurological status in particular. The second is the quality of the postnatal environment they experience. For instance, in a study of more than 8,000 infants, Dennis Hogan and Jennifer Park (2000) found that the disadvantages of LBW were amplified for children of minority status growing up in poverty with a single parent. In contrast, LBW babies who live with two parents and whose mothers are well educated, although they start out with delays, improve and may even catch up to the average child by age 8 (Ment et al., 2003). And children born with very LBW whose mothers are consistently responsive to them throughout infancy and toddlerhood attain higher levels of cognitive achievement than similar children with less responsive mothers (Landry, Smith, & Swank, 2006). In contrast, premature infants whose mothers are "out of synch" with them exhibit less mature outcomes at age 2 (Feldman & Eidelman, 2006). **Exploration 4.1** describes how we might help parents care for their tiny packages.

Studies such as these raise a larger issue about the importance of early experience. Some developmentalists take seriously the concept of critical (or sensitive) periods in early development. Others stress the resilience of human beings, their ability to rebound from early disadvantages and to respond to environmental influences throughout their lives rather than only during so-called critical periods. Which is it?

Risk and Resilience

To what extent does harm done in the prenatal or perinatal period last, and to what extent can postnatal experiences make up for it? You have encountered many examples in this chapter of what can go wrong before or during birth. Some damaging effects are clearly irreversible: The thalidomide baby will never grow normal arms or legs, and the child with FAS will always be intellectually disabled. Yet throughout history, many children turned out fine even though their mothers—unaware of many risk factors—smoked and drank during their pregnancies, received heavy doses of medication during delivery, or experienced serious illness. So, although many factors place a fetus at risk and increase the likelihood of problems after birth, not all at-risk infants end up with problems (Fraser, 2004). Is it also possible that some babies exposed to and clearly affected by risks recover from their deficiencies later in life?

Indeed it is, and researchers now have the results of major longitudinal studies that say so. For 40 years, Emmy Werner and her colleague Ruth Smith studied a group of babies born in 1955 on the island of Kauai in Hawaii (Werner, 1989a, 1989b; Werner & Smith, 1982, 1992, 2001). This was a monumental undertaking. All women of Kauai who were to give birth in 1955 were interviewed in each trimester of pregnancy, and physicians noted any prenatal, perinatal, or postnatal complications. On the basis of this information, each baby was categorized as having been exposed to severe, moderate, mild, or no prenatal or perinatal stress. At ages 1, 2, 10, 18, 32, and 40 years, researchers diligently tracked down their participants and conducted interviews (initially with the mothers and later with the children), administered psychological and cognitive tests, rated the quality of the family environment, and conducted medical examinations. Remarkably, at the 40-year follow-up, 70% (489 of 698) of the original group of babies born in 1955 still participated in the study.

One-third of the children classified as at-risk showed considerable resilience, getting themselves back on a normal course of development. Through this self-righting capacity, they were able to mature into competent, successful adults with no evident learning, social, or vocational problems despite being at risk for poor outcomes. Two major findings emerge from this research:

- The effects of prenatal and perinatal complications decrease over time.
- The outcomes of early risk depend on the quality of the postnatal environment.

The postnatal environments of these successful at-risk children included two types of protective factors, influences that prevent the damaging effects of risk factors or help children overcome disadvantages. These are:

Skills for Parenting Tiny Babies

Research shows that at-risk infants can benefit from programs that teach their parents how to provide responsive care and appropriate intellectual stimulation to them once they are home. Home visits to advise parents, combined with a stimulating day care program for LBW toddlers, can teach mothers how to be better teachers of their young children and stimulate these children's cognitive development. In an ambitious project called the Infant Health and Development Program, premature and LBW infants at eight sites benefited from such early intervention (McCormick et al., 2006). The program involved weekly home visits during the first year of life and then biweekly home visits and attendance by the infant at a special day care center for half a day every day from age 1 to age 3. Mothers were given child care education and support.

The program appeared to help parents provide a more growth-enhancing home environment—for example, to give their babies appropriate toys and learning materials and to interact with them in stimulating ways. The intervention also helped these at-risk babies, especially the heavier ones, achieve more cognitive growth by age 3 than they would otherwise have achieved. An impressive 14-point boost in IQ scores at age 3 for heavier LBW children who received the intervention had dropped to a 4-point advantage over control group children at age 8, but this small advantage was still evident at age 18 (McCarton et al., 1997; McCormick et al., 2006). Children who weighed 2,000 grams (4 pounds 6 ounces) or less at birth did not get much benefit from the program.

Other research indicates that early intervention programs for preterm infants should include psychosocial support for their mothers to help them manage the stress of caring for a preterm infant (Benzies et al., 2013). Psychosocial support can have a positive effect on a mother's anxiety and depression as well as her sense of self-efficacy, or confidence in being able to handle the situation. Mothers who have greater confidence in their ability to care for a preterm infant and who have lower levels of anxiety and depression seem to parent their infants in ways that lead to more positive outcomes.

Researchers have more to learn about what it takes to keep the development of at-risk children on a positive track after the perinatal period comes to a close, but everything we know about life-span environmental forces suggests that supportive parents and programs can do a great deal to optimize every child's development. It seems that premature, LBW babies can achieve normal levels of intellectual functioning during childhood when they live in middle-class homes, when their mothers are relatively educated, and most importantly, when their mothers, rich or poor, are consistently attentive, responsive, and confident when interacting with them (Benzies et al., 2013; Landry et al., 2006).

- *Personal resources.* Possibly because of their genetic makeup, some children have qualities such as intelligence, sociability, and communication skills that help them choose or create more nurturing and stimulating environments and cope with challenges. For example, parents and other observers noted that these children were agreeable, cheerful, and self-confident as infants, which elicited positive caregiving responses. They also believed that they were in control of their own fates—that through their actions, they could bring about positive outcomes.

- *Supportive postnatal environment.* Some at-risk children receive the social support they need within or outside the family. Most importantly, they are able to find at least one person who loves them unconditionally and with whom they feel secure.

- Clearly, hazards during the important prenatal and perinatal periods can leave lasting scars, and yet many children show remarkable resilience. There seem to be some points in the life span, especially early on, in which both positive and negative environmental forces have especially strong effects. Yet *environment matters throughout life*. It would be a mistake to assume that all children who have problems at birth are doomed. In short, early experience by itself can, but rarely does, make or break development; later experience counts, too, sometimes enough to turn around a negative course of development.

┌● Checking Mastery

1. What are two things you can do during your baby's first weeks and months of life to ensure a healthy start to life?
2. What are two factors that allow some babies to show resilience to negative events of the prenatal or perinatal periods?

┌● Making Connections

1. Find out if your mother and grandmothers breast-fed their children, including you, and for how long. What are your thoughts on the breast-versus-bottle choice? What factors might make it more or less likely that you or your partner will breast-feed (or have breast-fed if you are already a parent)?
2. Given the high costs of low birth weight, what programs would you make part of a national effort to reduce the number of LBW babies born each year?

Chapter Summary

4.1 Prenatal Development

- Prenatal development begins with conception and proceeds through the germinal, embryonic, and fetal periods.
- Some couples experience difficulties conceiving and turn to assisted reproduction technologies to assist them with having a baby. These include drugs to stimulate the ovaries to release eggs, artificial insemination to inject sperm into a woman's uterus, and in vitro fertilization to fertilize an egg outside the womb and then insert it into a woman's uterus or fallopian tube.
- The germinal period lasts about 2 weeks. During this time, the single-celled zygote created when a sperm penetrates an egg repeatedly multiplies and travels to the uterus where it implants itself.
- The embryonic period lasts through the eighth week after conception. Every major organ takes shape during this time in a process called organogenesis. The placenta forms and connects the embryo to its mother through the umbilical cord. Major developments occur during this time, including formation and beating of the heart and the start of sexual differentiation.
- The fetal period lasts from the ninth week after conception until the end of pregnancy. The body and brain undergo much growth during this time. Neurons multiply, migrate, and differentiate into what they will finally become. The age of viability is reached at around 23–24 weeks' gestation.
- Growth during the prenatal period is faster than during any other period of the life span.

4.2 The Prenatal Environment and Fetal Programming

- The womb is an environment and can affect the embryo/fetus in positive as well as negative ways.
- Through fetal programming, prenatal conditions can alter the architecture of the fetal brain, setting the stage for later vulnerabilities or for later resilience.
- Teratogens include diseases, drugs, or other environmental agents that can harm the developing fetus. Teratogens are most damaging to an organ during the time when the organ is developing most rapidly. In addition, the longer and stronger the exposure to a teratogen, the more likely that damage will occur to the developing child. The genetic makeup of both mother and unborn baby influence the effect of a teratogen, as does the quality of the prenatal and postnatal environments.
- Numerous drugs—prescription, over-the-counter, and recreational—have been found to have teratogenic effects. One of the most widely used drugs—alcohol—results in a cluster of symptoms that have lifelong effects on the children who are exposed prenatally.
- Diseases such as rubella (German measles), syphilis, and AIDS can adversely affect the developing baby, as can environmental hazards such as radiation and pollution.

- Some aspects of the mother can influence the quality of the prenatal environment, including her age, emotional state, and nutritional status. Women in their 20s have the lowest rates of pregnancy and birth complications. Women who experience prolonged and severe emotional stress during pregnancy may give birth to smaller babies. Good nutrition is important throughout pregnancy and is often supplemented with vitamins and fortified foods.
- Characteristics of the father, such as his age, may also affect the baby.

4.3 The Perinatal Environment

- The perinatal environment includes delivery practices and drugs used to assist with delivery. Many births today take place in the medical setting of a hospital or birthing center.
- Childbirth is a three-stage process that begins with regular contractions of the uterus and dilation of the cervix. The second stage of labor is the actual delivery of the baby out of the woman's body. The third stage is the delivery of the placenta.
- Among the possible birth complications is anoxia, or an oxygen shortage, which may occur for a variety of reasons. Anoxia can lead to brain damage or cerebral palsy if the brain is deprived of oxygen for more than a few minutes.
- Some babies must be assisted through the birth canal with vacuum extraction or forceps. Some women undergo a cesarean section, or surgical removal of the baby. Many women in Western cultures are given medications to assist with delivery. Most common are epidural or spinal blocks to reduce pain and oxytocin to promote contractions.
- The experience of pregnancy and childbirth vary widely, across cultures as well as across women within a culture. Some women experience mild to moderate depression following childbirth. Fathers, too, often need time to adjust to the life changes that accompany becoming a parent, as do older siblings.

4.4 The Neonatal Environment

- The neonatal environment refers to the events of the first month or so after delivery. Caring for a newborn varies across cultures. Nearly all cultures promote breast-feeding as the ideal way to nourish the young infant. For a variety of reasons, some mothers bottle-feed their newborns or switch to bottle-feeding after a trial run with breast-feeding.
- Some infants are considered to be at risk for short-term or long-term problems and must receive extra care during the neonatal period. Babies born prematurely and who have low birth weight are at risk for a number of complications.
- Many at-risk babies show remarkable resilience and outgrow their problems, especially if they have personal resources, such as sociability and intelligence, and grow up in stimulating and supportive postnatal environments where someone loves them.

Key Terms

infertility **91**

endometriosis **91**

artificial insemination **91**

in vitro fertilization (IVF) **91**

embryologist **92**

germinal period **92**

blastocyst **92**

miscarriage **92**

embryonic period **92**

organogenesis **92**

amnion **93**

chorion **93**

placenta **93**

spina bifida **93**

anencephaly **94**

testosterone **94**

fetal period **94**

proliferation **95**

migration **95**

differentiation **95**

age of viability **96**

myelin **96**

fetal programming **98**

teratogen **99**

critical period **99**

thalidomide **99**

sudden infant death syndrome (SIDS) **101**

fetal alcohol syndrome (FAS) **102**

rubella **104**

acquired immunodeficiency syndrome (AIDS) **105**

syphilis **105**

stillbirth **107**

Lamaze method **108**

perinatal environment **111**

perinatologist **112**

oxytocin **112**

anoxia **113**

breech presentation **113**

cerebral palsy **113**

cesarean section **113**

postpartum depression **116**

couvade **117**

neonatal **118**

at risk **119**

Apgar test **119**

low birth weight (LBW) **119**

surfactant **120**

kangaroo care **121**

5 Body, Brain, and Health

Gary Goldfield and his colleagues from the Healthy Active Living & Obesity Research Group in Canada had 30 obese teenagers engage in light to moderate exercise on stationary bikes (Goldfield et al., 2012). After 10 weeks, perhaps the most important finding was not the expected change in weight or fitness levels. Instead, the intriguing outcome was that the teens showed improved psychosocial functioning; in particular, they experienced a boost in body image, social competence, and even perceived academic performance. Interviewed about the research for *Science Daily,* Goldfield noted, "If you can improve your physical activity and fitness even minimally, it can help improve your mental health. By teaching kids to focus on healthy active lifestyle behaviours, they are focusing on something they can control. . . .This new study is proof positive that even a modest dose of exercise is prescriptive for a mental health boost" (Children's Hospital of Eastern Ontario Research Institute, 2012).

This is just one of many examples illustrating the connections among our physical, cognitive, and socioemotional selves. In this chapter, we consider changes across the life span in body and brain and how these changes influence our physical and mental health. We begin with an overview of the major physical systems, most notably the brain and nervous system, underlying human functioning. We also look at the reproductive system as it matures during adolescence and then changes during adulthood. Throughout, we consider factors that can interfere with health as well as those that might optimize health.

5.1

Building Blocks of Growth and Lifelong Health

LEARNING OBJECTIVES

- Associate key processes of the endocrine and nervous systems with important aspects of growth and development.
- Describe and provide an example of each of the three major principles of growth.
- Articulate the main components of the life-span developmental model of health and the value of adopting this sort of approach to understanding health.

Our physical selves—brain, body, and all the behaviors that emerge from these—are fundamental to what we are able to do in life. A 5-year-old child is physically able to experience the world in ways markedly different from those available to a 5-month-old infant. Five-year-old Mariah, for example, can stack blocks with her infant brother, throw a ball with her mom, run with her dog, play hopscotch with her friends, feed and dress herself, and enjoy many of the rides at the amusement park. Changes in her brain have increased her memory abilities and capacity to think, and her language skills are astounding compared with those of the 5-month-old. Yet Mariah and other 5-year-olds are also limited by their physical selves. It will be years before their brains are fully developed, allowing greater concentration and more sophisticated thought processes. Their physical skills will continue to improve, and their bodies will grow taller and heavier and will mature sexually.

Human growth and development is an incredibly complex process, influenced by both genetic and environmental factors. At certain times and for certain developments, genetic influences dominate, whereas at other times, environmental influences are more powerful. But as we have explained in previous chapters, genetic and environmental forces are always working together. Consider height. The average female in the United States is just over 5 feet 4 inches (164 cm) and the average male is about 5 feet 10 inches (178 cm), but there is considerable variability. Until her death in 2012, Yao Defen from China was the tallest woman in the world, her atypical height of 7 feet 8 inches a stark contrast to women with Turner syndrome (see Chapter 3) who are typically 3 feet shorter than this—4 feet 8 inches on average. These are dramatic examples of variability in height, but even among those considered within the average range of height, there is variability. Genes account for some of this: Tall people tend to have tall parents, whereas short people often have "short genes" hanging on their family tree. Heritability studies confirm that, after infancy, there is a strong genetic influence in height (Dubois et al., 2012; Lettre, 2012).

But as noted in Chapter 3, even if you inherit the genetic propensity to be tall (or short), environment can influence the expression of those genes. If you lack adequate nutrition, for example, you may not realize your full growth potential. Especially important to achieving adult height is a childhood diet rich in protein as well as calcium and vitamins A and D (Grasgruber et al., 2014). And consider the case of children with **celiac disease**, an inherited digestive problem in which gluten (the proteins found in all wheat products) triggers an immune response that leads to inflammation and damages the small intestine (see ■ **Figure 5.1**). This leaves affected children unable to absorb

The physical capabilities of this infant have advanced tremendously since birth, but at the ripe old age of 5 years, his sister is able to do many more sophisticated physical tasks.

Emma Tunbridge/Getty Images

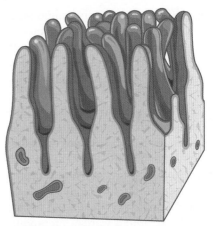

Normal small intestine

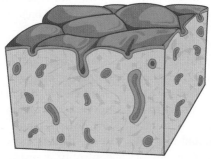

Celiac disease

■ **Figure 5.1** A small intestine damaged by celiac disease makes it difficult to absorb nutrients and can lead to malnutrition. Early diagnosis can permit effective treatment before damage becomes permanent.

Mayo Foundation for Medical Education and Research.

nutrients from food despite adequate consumption. Their disease, if untreated, can lead to malnutrition, which stunts growth and delays puberty. Early diagnosis for the estimated 3 million Americans with celiac disease is key to long-term health. Unfortunately, it often takes 10 years before the vague symptoms of bloating, diarrhea, fatigue, and upset stomach are properly diagnosed. Fortunately, treatment in the form of a gluten-free diet restores absorption of nutrients and can lead to dramatic **catch-up growth**. This catch-up growth after a period of malnutrition or illness reflects the body's struggle to get back on the growth course it is genetically programmed to follow.

To understand more fully how growth can be influenced by genes and environments, we need to consider the workings of the endocrine and nervous systems.

The Endocrine System

The endocrine, or hormonal, system consists of a group of **endocrine glands**, illustrated in ■ **Figure 5.2**, that secrete chemicals called *hormones* directly into the bloodstream. Perhaps the most critical of the endocrine glands is the **pituitary gland**, the so-called master gland located at the base of the brain. Directly controlled by the hypothalamus of the brain, it triggers the release of hormones from all other endocrine glands by sending hormonal messages to those glands. Moreover, the pituitary produces **growth hormone**, which triggers

The endocrine system

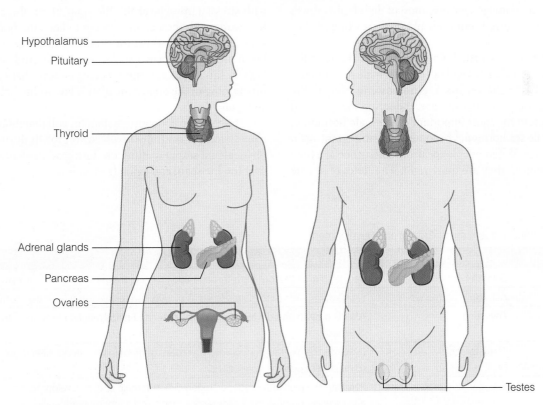

Hypothalamus

Pituitary

Thyroid

Adrenal glands

Pancreas

Ovaries

Testes

■ **Figure 5.2** The glands of the endocrine system secrete their chemicals, called hormones, directly into the bloodstream.

the production of specialized hormones that directly regulate growth. Yao Defen's unusual height of 7 feet 8 inches resulted from unchecked release of growth hormone due to a tumor on her pituitary gland. In contrast, children who lack adequate growth hormone are unlikely to exceed 4 feet (or 130 cm) in height as adults if left untreated. Treatment with synthetic growth hormones can lead to near-expected adult height if administered early—well before the start of puberty (Ross et al., 2015).

Children born small for their gestational age are often shorter as adults. Some of these children may also benefit from growth hormone therapy, but results with this group have been variable and controversial. The physical gains from taking the medication are around 2 inches of height and it is not clear whether these small gains add significantly to quality of life (Sandberg & Gardner, 2015; Sommer et al., 2015). Adults who use human growth hormone in an attempt to enhance their athletic performance are at risk for a variety of health conditions, including cardiac problems and insulin resistance (Holt & Sönksen, 2008). Despite widespread beliefs about its potential performance-enhancing benefits, the actual gains in performance are inconsistent and are accompanied by considerable health risks (Birzniece, 2015).

The thyroid gland also plays a key role in physical growth and development and in the development of the nervous system. Children whose mothers had a thyroid deficiency during pregnancy can experience intellectual problems (LaFranchi, Haddow, & Hollowell, 2005; Moog et al., 2015). Thyroid deficiency during infancy can also lead to intellectual disability and slow growth if unnoticed and untreated (see Zimmerman, 2007). Children who develop a thyroid deficiency later in life will not suffer brain damage, because most of their brain growth will have already occurred, but their physical growth will slow drastically.

In Chapter 4 you learned about another critical role of the endocrine system. A male fetus will not develop male reproductive organs unless (1) a gene on his Y chromosome triggers the development of the testes (which are endocrine glands), and (2) the testes secrete the most important of the male hormones, testosterone. Male sex hormones become highly important again during adolescence. When people speak of adolescence as a time of "raging hormones," they are quite right. The testes of a male

secrete large quantities of testosterone and other male hormones (called **androgens**). These hormones stimulate the production of growth hormone, which in turn triggers the adolescent growth spurt. Androgens are also responsible for the development of the male sex organs and contribute to sexual motivation during adulthood.

Meanwhile, in adolescent girls, the ovaries (also endocrine glands) produce larger quantities of the primary female hormone, **estrogen**, and of progesterone. Estrogen increases dramatically at puberty, stimulating the production of growth hormone and the adolescent growth spurt, much as testosterone does in males. It is also responsible for the development of the breasts, pubic hair, and female sex organs and for the control of menstrual cycles throughout a woman's reproductive years. Progesterone is sometimes called the "pregnancy hormone" because it orchestrates bodily changes that allow conception and then support a pregnancy. Finally, the adrenal glands secrete androgen-like hormones that contribute to the maturation of the bones and muscles in both sexes. The maturation of the adrenal glands during middle childhood results in sexual attraction well before puberty in both boys and girls and relates to sexual orientation in adulthood (Herdt & McClintock, 2000; McClintock & Herdt, 1996). The roles of different endocrine glands in physical growth and development are summarized in ● **Table 5.1**.

In adulthood, endocrine glands continue to secrete hormones, under the direction of the hypothalamus and the pituitary gland, to regulate bodily processes. For example, thyroid hormones help the body's cells metabolize (break down) foods into usable nutrients, and the adrenal glands help the body cope with stress. Throughout the life span, then, the endocrine system works with the nervous system to keep the body on an even keel. Yet changes occur; for example, declines in levels of sex hormones are associated with menopause. And, as you will see later in this chapter, some theorists believe that changes in the functioning of the endocrine glands late in life help bring about aging and death.

In short, the endocrine system, in collaboration with the nervous system, is centrally involved in growth during childhood, physical and sexual maturation during adolescence, functioning over the life span, and aging later in life.

● **Table 5.1** Hormonal Influences on Growth and Development

Endocrine Gland	Hormones Produced	Effects on Growth and Development
Pituitary	Growth hormone	Regulates growth from birth through adolescence; triggers adolescent growth spurt
	Activating hormones	Signal other endocrine glands (such as ovaries and testes) to secrete their hormones
Thyroid	Thyroxine	Affects growth and development of the brain and helps regulate growth of the body during childhood
Testes	Testosterone	Develops the male reproductive system during the prenatal period; directs male sexual development during adolescence
Ovaries	Estrogen and progesterone	Regulate the menstrual cycle; estrogen directs female sexual development during adolescence; progesterone allows conception and supports pregnancy
Adrenal glands	Adrenal androgens	Support the development of muscle and bones; contribute to sexual motivation

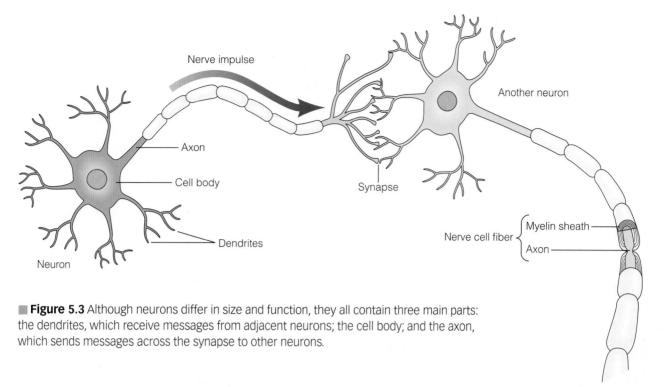

Figure 5.3 Although neurons differ in size and function, they all contain three main parts: the dendrites, which receive messages from adjacent neurons; the cell body; and the axon, which sends messages across the synapse to other neurons.

Labels in figure: Nerve impulse, Axon, Cell body, Dendrites, Neuron, Another neuron, Synapse, Nerve cell fiber, Myelin sheath, Axon

The Brain and Nervous System

None of the physical or mental achievements that we regard as human would be possible without a functioning nervous system. The nervous system consists of the brain and spinal cord (central nervous system) and the neural tissue that extends into all parts of the body (peripheral nervous system). Its basic unit is a **neuron** (■ Figure 5.3). Although neurons come in many shapes and sizes, they have some common features. Branching, bushy dendrites receive signals from other neurons, and the long axon of a neuron transmits electrical signals to other neurons or, in some cases, directly to a muscle cell. The axon of one neuron makes a connection with another neuron at a tiny gap called a **synapse**. By releasing neurotransmitters stored at the ends of its axons, one neuron can either stimulate or inhibit the action of another neuron.

The axons of many neurons become covered by a fatty sheath called *myelin*, which acts like insulation to speed the transmission of neural impulses. The process of **myelination**—neurons becoming encased in this protective substance that speeds transmission—begins prenatally but continues for many years after birth, proceeding from the spinal cord to the hindbrain, midbrain, and forebrain. Myelination has numerous implications for developmental changes observed across the life span. Myelination in the visual cortex is largely complete by age 1, consistent with advances in visual skills over the first year (Deoni et al., 2015). Toddlers experience a vocabulary spurt following a period of rapid myelination of those parts of the brain involved in language development (Su et al., 2008). And teenagers are more likely than children to ask hypothetical "what if" questions and to reason about weighty abstractions, such as truth and justice, owing to myelination within the prefrontal lobes during adolescence. Progressive myelination of the pathways involved in attention and concentration helps explain why infants, toddlers,

school-age children, and even young adolescents have shorter attention spans than do older adolescents and adults. Finally, continued myelination into adulthood may account for adults being better able than teenagers to integrate thoughts and emotions, allowing them to think more clearly in situations where emotions are running high (Arain et al., 2013). We will further explore these changes as we move through the life span in the following sections of this chapter.

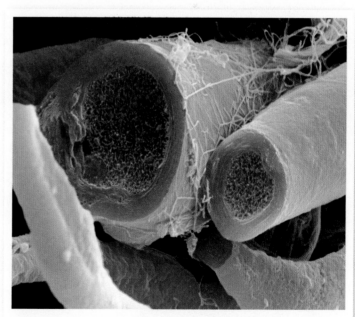

These nerve fibers are covered with myelin, shown here in pink. What role does myelin play in neural activity?

PHOTO QUEST/Getty Images

Principles of Growth

Now that you know something about the endocrine and nervous systems, and how they contribute to growth early in life, is it possible to make general predictions about growth patterns? To do so, researchers often apply three general principles that underlie growth. It is easiest to see these principles in action during infancy when growth is fast. For instance, you have probably noticed that young infants seem to be all head compared with older children and adults. That is because growth follows the **cephalocaudal principle**, according to which growth occurs in a head-to-tail direction. This pattern is clear in ■ **Figure 5.4**: The head is far ahead of the rest of the body during the prenatal period and accounts for about 25% of the newborn's length and 13% of total body weight. But the head accounts for only 12% of an adult's height and 2% of an adult's weight (Zemel, 2002). During the first year after birth, the trunk grows the fastest; in the second year, the legs are the fastest growing part of the body.

While infants are growing from the head downward, they are also growing and developing muscles from the center outward to the extremities. This **proximodistal principle** of growth can be seen during the prenatal period, when the chest and internal organs form before the arms, hands, and fingers. During the first year of life, the trunk is rapidly filling out but the arms remain short and stubby until they undergo their own period of rapid development.

A third important principle of growth and development is the **orthogenetic principle**. This means that development starts globally and undifferentiated and moves toward increasing differentiation and hierarchical integration (Werner, 1957). Consider a human who starts as a single, undifferentiated cell at conception. As growth proceeds, that single cell becomes billions of highly specialized cells (neurons, blood cells, liver cells, and so on). These differentiated cells become organized, or integrated, into functioning systems such as the brain or the digestive system.

Having looked at the building blocks of body and brain, you are ready to examine the development, health, and aging of the physical self. We concentrate on changes in the body and brain that will help us understand the contributions of each to many other areas of development that will be covered in subsequent chapters. We also consider factors that are important to health at different ages. In doing so, we turn once again to a life-span model.

A Life-Span Developmental Model of Health

The life-span developmental perspective introduced in Chapter 1 can be applied to our consideration of health and wellness as follows:

- Health is a lifelong process. It is influenced by personal choices over the life span and is constantly changing in response to these choices. For instance, whether you are 18, 48, or 78 years old when you begin an exercise program or stop smoking, these sorts of changes to your lifestyle can alter the path of your health.
- Health is determined by both genetic and environmental influences. According to the biodevelopmental framework from Harvard's Center on the Developing Child (see Shonkoff,

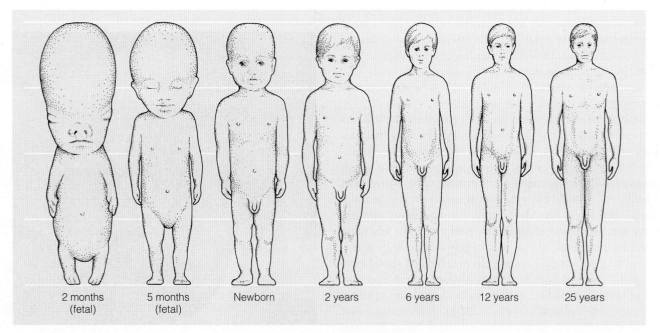

| 2 months (fetal) | 5 months (fetal) | Newborn | 2 years | 6 years | 12 years | 25 years |

■ **Figure 5.4** The cephalocaudal ("head-to-tail") principle of growth is illustrated in our body proportions from the fetal period through adulthood. At 2 months after conception, your head made up half of your total body length, but now, as an adult, your head is a mere 12–13% of your adult height. By contrast, during this same time frame, your legs have gone from being only about 12–13% of your early prenatal length to about half of your adult height.

2010), a person's genetic predispositions interact with their environmental experiences to create adaptive (healthy) outcomes or disruptive (unhealthy) ones. As we learned in Chapter 4, by the time we are old enough to make our own choices, we have already been influenced by choices made by our parents and even our grandparents. As a result of fetal programming, an individual whose mother smoked or drank alcohol during pregnancy, for example, may have different health predispositions than one whose mother did not smoke or drink while pregnant.

- Health—and its study—is multidimensional. As we saw in the chapter opener, physical, mental, and social functioning are intertwined with one another; changes in one area influence other aspects of self.
- Changes in health involve both gains and losses; health both improves and declines over the life span in response to many factors.
- Health occurs in a sociohistorical context and can be enhanced or constrained by the social and historical factors that contribute to it. Especially important is socioeconomic status. Lower socioeconomic status is routinely associated with poorer health and well-being and shorter life expectancy.

Thus, an individual's health is determined by genetic factors, personal choices, and environmental influences working in concert across the life span. The importance of a life-span model of health will be clear as we view health in each of the following sections.

● Checking Mastery

1. How does the endocrine system support development?
2. How does myelination contribute to developmental changes that we can observe?
3. What is one example each of the principles guiding growth: cephalocaudal, proximodistal, and orthogenetic development?

● Making Connections

1. Why is it important to view health from a life-span developmental perspective? Illustrate three aspects or components of this perspective as they apply to you or members of your family.

5.2
The Infant

LEARNING OBJECTIVES

- Discuss typical changes in the brain during infancy.
- Summarize newborn capabilities that promote healthy adaptation to the world outside the womb.

Infancy is characterized by continued brain development, rapid growth, and impressive sensory and reflexive capabilities. Understanding the newborn's capacities and limitations brings a fuller appreciation of the dramatic changes that take place between birth and adulthood.

In Chapter 4 we traced the amazing evolution of the brain during the prenatal period. Here we pick up the story by looking at what goes on in the brain after birth. Although the brain is proportionately the largest and most developed part of the body at birth, much of its development takes place after birth. Postnatally, though, development is not so much about generating new neurons as about connecting existing neurons. Recall our discussion in Chapter 4 of how a new neuron migrates to its home in the nervous system and, like a good neighbor, begins reaching out and communicating with other neurons in the same region. Much of brain development in infancy and childhood consists of forging more and more connections between neurons (Johnson & de Haan, 2015). ■ **Figure 5.5** shows how the complexity of the communication network—the dendrites extending from each neuron—increases over childhood. As we go about our daily business of behaving and thinking, some of the connections among neurons become more numerous. But other connections, seldom used, seem to shrivel up and disappear. In Figure 5.5, the network of connections in the far right panel from a teenager is less dense than the network in the middle panel

from a child. This illustrates the synaptogenesis, or growth of synapses, during childhood as well as the synaptic pruning or removal of unnecessary synapses that is also an important component of brain development.

Synaptic Density

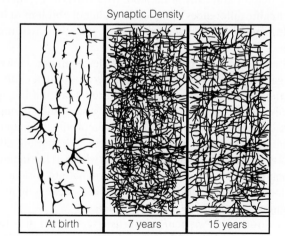

| At birth | 7 years | 15 years |

■ **Figure 5.5** Between birth and 7 years of age, there is a tremendous amount of *synaptogenesis*, or the development of connections between neurons. But between 7 and 15 years of age, there is another process at work: *synaptic pruning* or elimination of unnecessary or unused connections.

The development of the brain early in life is heavily influenced by the unfolding of a genetic program that has evolved over many generations. But genes are not the only influence—an individual's experiences are also crucial to brain development. As Charles Nelson and colleagues (2006) describe it, "The brain's circuitry must rely on experience to customize connections to serve the needs of the individual" (p. 3). Assuming that the infant has normal opportunities to explore and experience the world, the result will be a normal brain and normal development. During the early brain development spurt that begins before birth and continues during infancy, the brain is fine-tuned by experience through the dual processes of synaptogenesis and synaptic pruning.

Thus, the brain, especially early in its formation, has great plasticity; that is, it is responsive to the individual's experiences and can develop in a variety of ways (Kolb, Whishaw, & Teskey, 2016). On the negative side, the developing brain is highly vulnerable to damage if it is exposed to drugs or diseases (recall the description of teratogens in Chapter 4) or if it is deprived of sensory and motor experiences. On the positive side, this highly adaptable brain can often recover successfully from injuries. Neurons that are not yet fully committed to their specialized functions can often take over the functions of damaged neurons. Moreover, the immature brain is especially able to benefit from stimulating experiences. Rodents that grow up in enriched environments with plenty of sensory stimulation develop larger, better-functioning brains with more synapses than rodents that grow up in barren cages (Garthe, Roeder, & Kempermann, 2016; Greenough, Black, & Wallace, 1987). With advances in technology, researchers have now uncovered similar findings with humans: Spending the first few years of life in impoverished families and neighborhoods leads to less "gray matter," the brain tissue believed to be involved in information processing (Hanson et al., 2013). These youngsters start life with the same amount of gray matter as those from wealthier families and neighborhoods, but they experience slower rates of brain growth during infancy and early childhood. By 3 years of age, there are measureable differences in the brain matter of children in high, middle, and low socioeconomic groups. Clearly, environment matters.

Brain plasticity is greatest early in development. However, the organization of synapses within the nervous system continues to change in response to experience throughout the life span. Animals put through their paces in mazes grow bushier dendrites, whereas their brains lose some of their complexity if the animals are then moved to less stimulating quarters (Thompson, 2000). This also holds promise for those children who start life in poverty but then have opportunities to live or learn in more enriched circumstances. We will return to this possibility of catch-up growth in cognitive development in later chapters.

In short, the *critical*, or *sensitive*, *period* for brain development—the time when it proceeds most rapidly—is during the late prenatal period and early infancy. The developing brain is characterized by a good deal of plasticity: Normal genes may provide rough guidelines about how the brain should be configured, but early experience determines the architecture of the brain.

Rapid Growth

Newborns are typically about 20 inches long and weigh 7–7½ pounds. However, weight and length at birth can mislead about eventual weight and height because the growth of some fetuses is stunted by a poor prenatal environment (Özaltin et al., 2010). Size during the first few months of life is related more to prenatal experiences (environment) than to size of parent (genes). This is easy to see in twins and other multiple births, because their prenatal growth is significantly restricted by siblings competing for the limited space in the mother's womb.

In the first few months of life, infants grow rapidly, gaining nearly an ounce of weight a day and an inch in length each month. By age 2, they have already attained about half of their eventual adult height and weigh 27–30 pounds on average. Although we usually think of growth as a slow and steady process, daily measurements of infant length show that babies grow in fits and starts (Lampl & Thompson, 2007). They may go weeks with no growth and then shoot up half an inch in 24 hours! Not surprisingly, these growth spurts are often accompanied by irritability that many parents, unaware of the phenomenal growth taking place, find puzzling. In the end, 90–95% of an infant's days are growth free, but their occasional bursts of physical growth add up to substantial increases in size. Infants whose overall weight gain outpaces gains in length (height) are at risk of childhood obesity, particularly when that weight increase occurs early in infancy (Bjerregaard et al., 2014; Salgin et al., 2015). We'll have more to say about obesity in subsequent sections of this chapter.

Bones and muscles are also developing quickly during infancy. At birth, most bones are soft, pliable, and difficult to break. They are too small and flexible to allow newborns to sit up or balance themselves when pulled to a standing position. The soft cartilage-like tissues of the young infant gradually ossify (harden) into bony material as calcium and other minerals are deposited into them. In addition, more bones develop, and they become more closely interconnected. As for muscles, young infants are relative weaklings. Although they have all the muscle cells they will ever have, their strength will increase only as their muscles grow.

Newborn Capabilities

Newborns used to be viewed as helpless little organisms, ill prepared to cope with the world outside the womb. We now know that they are quite well equipped to begin life. Just what can a newborn do? Among the most important capabilities are reflexes, functioning senses, a capacity to learn, and organized, individualized patterns of waking and sleeping. In this chapter, we'll examine their reflexes and brain development; in subsequent chapters, we address their sensory abilities (Chapter 6) and their potential to learn from experience (Chapters 7 and 8).

Reflexes

One of the newborn's greatest resources is a set of useful reflexes. A reflex is an unlearned and involuntary response to a stimulus, such as when the eye automatically blinks in response to a puff of air. ● Table 5.2 lists some reflexes that can be readily observed in all normal newborns. These seemingly simple reactions are

● **Table 5.2** Major Reflexes of Full-Term Newborns

Survival Reflexes	Developmental Course	Significance
Breathing reflex	Permanent	Provides oxygen; expels carbon dioxide
Eye-blink reflex	Permanent	Protects eyes from bright light or foreign objects
Pupillary reflex: Constriction of pupils to bright light; dilation to dark or dimly lit surroundings	Permanent	Protects against bright light; adapts visual system to low illumination
Rooting reflex: Turning a cheek toward a tactile (touch) stimulus	Weakens by 2 months; disappears by 5 months	Orients child to breast or bottle
Sucking reflex: Sucking on objects placed (or taken) into mouth	Gradually modified by experience over the first few months after birth; disappears by 7 months	Allows child to take in nutrients
Swallowing reflex	Permanent, but modified by experience	Allows child to take in nutrients; protects against choking

Primitive Reflexes	Developmental Course	Significance
Babinski reflex: Fanning then curling toes when bottom of foot is stroked	Disappears by 12–18 months months	Presence at birth and disappearance in first year indicate normal neurological development
Grasping reflex: Curling fingers around objects (such as a finger) that touch the baby's palm	Disappears in first 3–4 months; is replaced by a voluntary grasp	Presence at birth and later disappearance indicate normal neurological development
Moro reflex: Loud noise or sudden change in position of baby's head will cause baby to throw arms outward, arch back, then bring arms toward each other	Disappears by 4 months; however, child continues to react to unexpected noises or a loss of bodily support by showing startle reflex	Presence at birth and later disappearance (or evolution into startle reflex) indicate normal neurological development (which does not disappear)
Swimming reflex: Infant immersed in water will display active movements of arms and legs and will involuntarily hold breath (thus staying afloat for some time)	Disappears in first 4–6 months	Presence at birth and later disappearance indicate normal neurological development
Stepping reflex: Infants held upright so that their feet touch a flat surface will step as if to walk	Disappears in first 8 weeks unless infant has regular opportunities to practice it	Presence at birth and later disappearance indicate normal neurological development

Preterm infants may show little to no evidence of primitive reflexes at birth, and their survival reflexes are likely to be irregular or immature. However, the missing reflexes will typically appear soon after birth and will disappear a little later than they do among full-term infants.

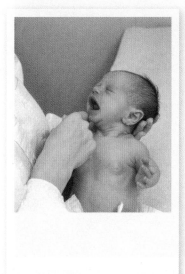

Rooting reflex.

Paul Conklin/PhotoEdit

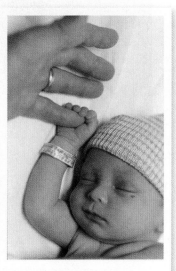

Grasping reflex.

Comstock/Getty Images

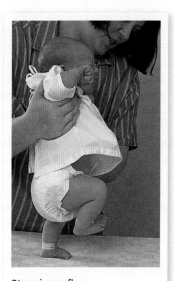

Stepping reflex.

Jennie Woodcock/Reflections Photolibrary/Getty Images

actually quite varied and complex patterns of behavior that provide infants with a way to begin interacting with their world (von Hofsten, 2007; 2013). The presence of these reflexes is important because it lets us know that the infant's nervous system is working.

Some reflexes are called *survival reflexes* because they have clear adaptive value. Examples include the breathing reflex (useful for obvious reasons), the eye-blink reflex (which protects against bright lights or foreign particles), and the sucking reflex (needed to obtain food). Those called *primitive reflexes* are not clearly useful; many are believed to be remnants of evolutionary history that have outlived their purpose (but see Schott & Rossor, 2003, for another perspective). The Babinski reflex is a good example. Why would it be adaptive for infants to fan their toes when the bottoms of their feet are stroked? Frankly, we don't know. Other primitive reflexes may have some adaptive value, at least in some cultures. For example, the grasping reflex may help infants carried in slings or on their mothers' hips to hang on. Finally, some primitive reflexes—for example, the stepping reflex—are forerunners of useful voluntary behaviors that develop later in infancy. The expression of primitive reflexes at age 6 weeks, however, is not related to the expression of later motor behaviors (Bartlett, 1997). Thus, infants who demonstrate a strong primitive grasping reflex at 6 weeks are not necessarily the infants who demonstrate a strong voluntary grasp later in infancy.

Primitive reflexes typically disappear during the early months of infancy. For instance, the grasping reflex becomes weak by 4 months and is replaced by voluntary grasping. These primitive reflexes are controlled by the lower, subcortical areas of the brain and are lost as the higher centers of the cerebral cortex develop and make voluntary motor behaviors possible. Even though many primitive reflexes are not very useful to infants, they have proven to be useful in diagnosing infants' neurological problems. If such reflexes are not present at birth—or if they last too long in infancy—physicians know that something is wrong with a baby's nervous system. The existence of reflexes at birth tells them that infants are ready to respond to stimulation in adaptive ways. The disappearance of certain reflexes tells them that the nervous system is developing normally and that experience is affecting both brain and behavior. Thus, we see that the presence and then the absence of reflexes can serve as a general indicator of neurological health.

Behavioral States

Much to their tired parents' dismay, newborns have no clear sense of night or day and may wake every 1–4 hours. Infants must move from short sleep–wake cycles distributed throughout the day and night to a pattern that includes longer sleep periods at night with longer wake periods during the day. Settling into an organized sleep–wake pattern is an indication that the baby's nervous system is developing as expected and is beginning to integrate a myriad of external signals with internal states. By 3 months, most infants begin to establish a predictable sleep–wake cycle, which becomes fairly stable by 6 months of age for most infants. Much to their relief, about two-thirds of mothers report that their 6-month-old infants are sleeping through the night nearly every night (Weinraub et al., 2012). The other one-third of mothers continue to be awakened by their infants more nights than not and report that this pattern persists until their infants are about 24 months of age.

These early sleep patterns are indicative of other behaviors. For instance, among premature infants, those who transition smoothly from one state to another exhibit more mature neurocognitive outcomes than other premature infants (Weisman et al., 2011). And those infants with poor sleep habits at 12 months of age are reported to have problems with attention regulation as well as behavior problems at 3 to 4 years of age (Sadeh et al., 2015). In contrast, infants who get more sleep at night tend to be more easygoing during the day (Spruyt et al., 2008). Are they more easygoing because they are well rested from a good night's sleep, or do they sleep well at night because they are easygoing? We don't know the answer to this question in infants, but we do know that adults who are normally easygoing can be irritable when deprived of sleep, so perhaps this is true for infants as well.

Newborns spend half of their sleeping hours in active sleep, also called **REM sleep** (for the rapid eye movements that occur during it). Infants older than 6 months spend only 25–30% of their total sleep in REM sleep, which more closely resembles the 20% that adults spend in REM sleep. Why do young infants sleep so much and spend so much more time in REM sleep than adults? Sleep patterns in infancy are associated with brain maturation and plasticity (Tarullo, Balsam, & Fifer, 2011). REM sleep, in particular, may be important for learning and memory processes (Diekelmann, Wilhelm, & Born, 2009). This may help explain why infants, who have so much to learn, spend more time in this sleep. Think about it: Infants are taking in vast amounts of new

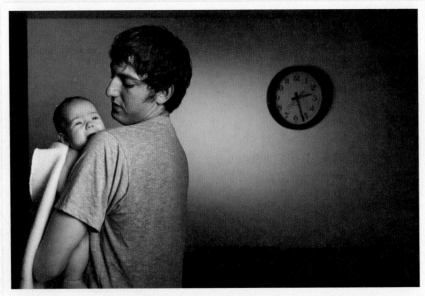

Establishing an organized sleep–wake pattern is an important accomplishment of infancy. It can sometimes take several months before infants sleep through the night.

Andersen Ross/Getty Images

information during the times they are awake. These periods are invariably followed by sleep, which may help their brains learn and remember the new information. If deprived of sleep, infants may become "overloaded" with too much new information that their immature nervous systems cannot fully process. This may explain why infants are notoriously fussy at the end of a busy day—often at dinnertime when parents are tired and hoping for some peace. The infant's nervous system can be overstimulated by the flood of stimulation received during the day. Somehow, the arousal needs to be reduced—perhaps by crying and then sleeping. Adults sometimes marvel at how infants can sleep through the loudest noises and the brightest lights, but being able to do so may serve a valuable function.

Health and Wellness

What health issues must infants—and their parents—navigate? As noted in the previous chapter, modern medicine has made it possible for smaller and smaller babies to survive premature delivery, but sadly, most of the smallest babies—those weighing less than 1 pound 10½ ounces (750 grams)—die within the first year (MacDorman & Mathews, 2008). The health problems associated with premature delivery and low birth weight often continue to challenge infants throughout their first year and beyond, illustrating one of the principles of the life-span model of health: Some events can have lifelong effects on health. Only about 12% of babies in the United States are premature, but complications of premature birth account for 35% of infant deaths. Complications related to labor and delivery account for about one-quarter of deaths, and various types of infections together account for another one-quarter of deaths (Liu et al., 2015). Congenital malformations—defects that are present at birth, either from genetic factors or prenatal events—account for 1 out of 10 deaths during the first year. Such malformations include heart defects, spina bifida, Down syndrome, cleft palates, and more.

Infant health has been dramatically improved in recent decades by administering vaccinations aimed at protecting infants from a variety of diseases (such as diphtheria, pertussis, polio, and measles). The approximately 20% of infants who do not receive the recommended immunizations are more likely than immunized babies to contract illnesses that can compromise their health (CDC, 2013). Socioeconomic status in the United States often determines who has access to health care services that cover immunizations. Yet the parents who deliberately avoid or delay immunization of their infants are more likely to be white and above-average socioeconomic status. They cite concerns about side effects as reasons to delay or not get their little one immunized, and they are less likely to believe that vaccinations are necessary to protect their child's health (Smith et al., 2011). As the life-span model maintains, one's sociohistorical context influences health.

Thus, health during infancy starts well before birth with prenatal care that helps prevent and/or treat potential congenital anomalies and preterm birth. Health after birth is enhanced by well-baby visits to the doctor to ensure that development is proceeding normally and by following recommendations for prevention of illness. Quality and pattern of sleep is an important indicator of nervous system development and is associated with behaviors in childhood.

● Checking Mastery

1. What are the most significant brain changes that occur during infancy?
2. What are two infant reflexes that may help ensure survival in the early months of life?
3. What can an infant's sleep–wake cycle indicate about her development?

● Making Connections

1. In what ways is brain plasticity an advantage and in what ways might it be a disadvantage to the developing human?

5.3
The Child

LEARNING OBJECTIVES

- Discuss the implications of brain lateralization for behavior and functioning.
- Outline the major physical accomplishments and health challenges of childhood.

Slow and steady is probably the best way to describe the growth that occurs throughout much of childhood. From age 2 until puberty, children gain about 2–3 inches and 5–6 pounds every year. This growth is often tracked on a chart that plots an individual's height and weight against normative data. This allows physicians and families to see how a particular child is progressing relative to other children of the same age and gender and to graph the pattern of growth over time. Children who are markedly different—higher, lower, or more erratic in their growth rate—may warrant additional investigation.

During middle childhood (ages 6–11), children may seem to grow little, probably because the gains are small in proportion to the child's size (4–4½ feet and 60–80 pounds on average) and therefore harder to detect. The cephalocaudal and proximodistal principles of growth continue to operate. As the lower parts of the body and the extremities fill out, the child takes on more adultlike body proportions. The bones continue to grow and harden, and the muscles strengthen.

As we'll see in the next section, there are also steady changes going on within the brain. The brain becomes further organized

Brain Lateralization

One important feature of the developing organization of the brain is the lateralization, or asymmetry and specialization of functions, of the two hemispheres of the cerebral cortex. Instead of developing identically, the functions controlled by the two hemispheres diverge (see ■ Figure 5.6). In most people, the left cerebral hemisphere controls the right side of the body and is adept at the *sequential* (that is, step-by-step) processing needed for analytic reasoning and language processing. The right hemisphere generally controls the left side of the body and is skilled at the *simultaneous* processing of information needed for understanding spatial information and processing visual–motor information as well as the emotional content of information (Kensinger & Choi, 2009). Although it is an oversimplification, the left hemisphere is often called the *thinking* side of the brain, whereas the right hemisphere is called the *emotional* brain.

Having two hemispheres of the brain is not the same as having two brains. The hemispheres "communicate" and work together through the corpus callosum, "the super-highway of neurons connecting the halves of the brain" (Gazzaniga, 1998, p. 50). Even though one hemisphere might be more active than the other during certain tasks, they both play a role in all activities. For example, the left hemisphere is considered the seat of language because it controls word content, grammar, and syntax, but the right hemisphere processes melody, pitch, sound intensity, and the affective content of language.

If one hemisphere is damaged, it may be possible for the other hemisphere to "take over" the functions lost. For example, most children who have one hemisphere removed to try to reduce or eliminate severe seizures regain normal language function (Liégeois et al., 2008; Vining et al., 1997). It does not matter whether the remaining hemisphere is the left or the right. Thus, although the left hemisphere processes language in most people (perhaps 92%), the right hemisphere may also be able to fill this function, although it is not yet known how this possibility might be limited—or enhanced—by age or other characteristics of the individual (Gazzaniga, 1998; Knecht et al., 2000).

When does the brain become lateralized? Signs of brain lateralization are clearly evident at birth. Newborns are more likely to turn their heads to the right than to the left and some clearly prefer the right hand in their grasp reflex (Johnson & de Haan, 2015). Newborns may also show more left hemispheric response to speech sounds (Kotilahti et al., 2010), although this response becomes stronger and more reliable in the second half of the first year (Holowka & Petitto, 2002).

Signs of lateralization so early in life suggest that it has a genetic basis. Further support for the role of genes comes from family studies of handedness. Overall, about 9 in 10 people rely on their right hands (or left hemispheres) to write and perform other motor activities with males somewhat more likely to be left-handed than females (Vuoksimaa et al., 2009). In families where both parents are right-handed, the odds of having a left-handed child are only 2 in 100. These odds increase to 17 in 100 when one parent is left-handed and to 46 in 100 when both parents are left-handed (Springer & Deutsch, 2001). Although this suggests a genetic basis to handedness, it could also indicate that children become left-handed because of experiences provided by left-handed parents. However, experience would not account for head-turning preferences in young infants or for the differential activation of the left and right hemispheres observed in newborns when listening to speech sounds.

Overall, then, the brain appears to be structured very early so that the two hemispheres of the cortex will be capable of specialized functioning. As we develop, most of us come to rely more on the left hemisphere to carry out language processing and more on the right hemisphere to do such things as perceive spatial relationships and emotions. We also come to rely more consistently on one hemisphere, usually the left, to control many of our physical activities.

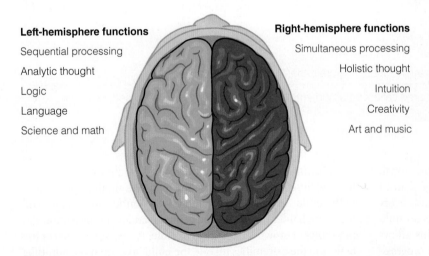

Left-hemisphere functions

Sequential processing

Analytic thought

Logic

Language

Science and math

Right-hemisphere functions

Simultaneous processing

Holistic thought

Intuition

Creativity

Art and music

■ **Figure 5.6** The brain consists of two hemispheres that specialize in different functions. Functions such as logic, analytic reasoning, and language are typically associated with the left hemisphere, whereas such functions as creativity, intuition, and holistic thinking are associated with the right hemisphere.

Physical Behavior

Children's physical behaviors are noticeably advanced compared to those of infants and toddlers. For instance, although toddlers are capable of controlling their movements in relation to a *stationary* world, children master the ability to move capably in a *changing* environment (Haywood & Getchell, 2014). They must learn to modify their movements to adapt to changes in environment as well as changes in their own bodies as they grow bigger (Adolph & Robinson, 2015). These adaptations allow them to bring their hands together at just the right time to catch a ball and to avoid bumping into moving people when walking through a crowded mall. They also refine many motor skills. For example, young children throw a ball only with the arm, but older children learn to step forward as they throw. Their accuracy throwing a ball increases around age 7, as does their speed of throwing (Favilla, 2006). Thus, older children can throw a ball farther than younger ones can, not just because they are bigger and stronger but also because they can integrate multiple body movements—raising their arm, turning their body, stepping forward with one foot, and pushing their body forward with the other foot (Haywood & Getchell, 2014).

As a child, one of your textbook authors was teased by an older brother for apparent lack of skill on the ball field. A regular taunt was "you throw like a girl!" It turns out there is a well-established gender difference in both throwing speed and distance: Girls do, indeed, throw like girls and not like boys (Thomas et al., 2010). A typical 13-year-old girl can throw a ball an average of 38.5 miles per hour, which sounds fast until you learn that the typical 13-year-old boy averages 53.5 miles per hour. Some of this difference seems to be nurture: Boys are given more things to throw, start earlier in sports that involve throwing, and spend more time practicing throwing. But practice and the environment do not explain all of the gender difference in throwing. Boys may also be able to throw faster and farther because of their greater upper body muscle mass and their shoulder width.

We should note that girls are somewhat ahead of boys in hopping and tasks that require manual dexterity (Junaid & Fellowes, 2006; Van Beurden et al., 2002). But again, these differences seem to arise, at least in part, from practice and different expectations for males and females.

Apparently, even Olympic gold medal winner in gymnastics Gabby Douglas "throws like a girl." There are some physical skills where males and females, on average, perform differently from one another.

Jim McIsaac/Getty Images Sport/Getty Images

Health and Wellness

There are many factors that can influence children's health and wellness, but three big areas of concern during this period of life are accidents, nutrition, and physical activity levels. All three factors are influenced by the child's home environment, in particular, the socioeconomic status and education level of parents (Matthews & Gallo, 2011). Children whose parents are less educated are more likely to experience poor or fair health than children with more educated parents. This is particularly true for black children and white children, but less true for Hispanic children and Asian children, whose health outcomes may be buffered by strong social networks that cut across educational and socioeconomic levels (■ Figure 5.7). This is another example of how the sociohistorical context of development plays a role in children's health and well-being.

Accidents

Accidents constitute a major category of negative influences on children's health and well-being. Childhood is unfortunately marked by numerous unintentional injuries, making accidents the leading cause of death throughout the childhood years (National Vital Statistics System, 2015). As ● Table 5.3 shows, drownings top the list of accidental causes of death for 1 to 4 year olds, and crashes involving motor vehicles cause the largest number of fatal injuries throughout the remainder of childhood. Parents can reduce the possibility of accidental drownings by adding fences and coverings to swimming pools and hot tubs and closely monitoring their toddlers around all sources of water, including the bath tub. As well, motor vehicle fatalities may be reduced by properly strapping their infants and young children into car seats, or as they get older, insisting that they sit in the backseat with a shoulder-strap seat belt.

Of course, not all accidents are fatal. Falls and being struck by something cause the largest number of nonfatal injuries during childhood, followed by such things as bee stings, bites, cuts, and overexertion. Most of these injuries are minor and do not constitute a major developmental obstacle. But some injuries for some children can have lasting effects on their physical or mental well-being.

Nutrition

Nutrition continues to be an important contributor to health throughout childhood, as it

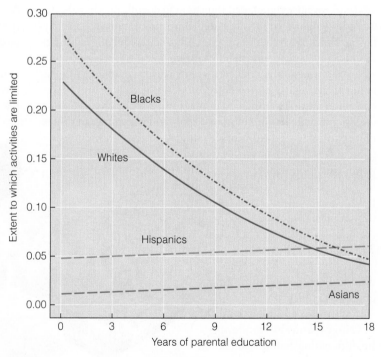

■ **Figure 5.7** Among white families and black families, parents' education levels influence the extent to which children's activities are limited by poor or fair health: Children have more limitations when their parents are less educated. This is not true among Hispanic families and Asian families.

Source: From Chen, E., Martin, A. D., & Matthews, K. A. (2006). Understanding health disparities: The role of race and socioeconomic status in children's health. *American Journal of Public Health, 96, 702–705.* Reprinted by permission of the American Public Health Association.

	Top 3 Accidents Leading to Death			Top 3 Accidents Causing Injury (but not death)		
Rank	**1**	**2**	**3**	**1**	**2**	**3**
Ages 1–4	Drowning	Motor vehicle accident	Suffocation	Falling	Struck by/against something	Other, bite/sting
Ages 5–9	Motor vehicle accident	Drowning	Fire/burns	Falling	Struck by/against something	Unintentional cut/pierce
Ages 10–14	Motor vehicle accident	Suicide, suffocation	Suicide, firearm	Struck by/against something	Falling	Unintentional overexertion
Ages 15–24	Motor vehicle accident	Homicide, firearm	Unintentional poisoning	Struck by/against something	Falling	Unintentional overexertion

Source: National Vital Statistics System from the National Center for Health Statistics (2015), Centers for Disease Control and Prevention; accessed through WISQARS™.

was during infancy. It is probably not surprising to learn that most children do not eat the recommended daily amount of fruits and vegetables (Attorp et al., 2014). Of the total calories consumed by children every day, 27% come from snacks (Kenney et al., 2014). That might be fine if the snacks were healthy, but they tend to be sugary, salty, fatty, and low in nutrients. A determined group of researchers staked out local convenience stores that were located near urban schools (Borradaile et al., 2009). These were small stores within four blocks of the schools that were frequented by children on their way to and from school. For months, the researchers tracked everything the children purchased, briefly surveyed them regarding their purchases, and later analyzed the nutritional content of the food and beverages purchased. The most frequently purchased item was chips, followed by candy, and then sugar-sweetened artificially flavored drinks. In other words, the children were buying fatty, sugary foods and beverages with little nutritional value but high caloric value. Amazingly, these children spent an average of just $1 dollar to ingest an average of 356 empty calories. What a bargain!

Similar findings emerged from a survey of fluid intake across childhood, which found that sodas and artificially flavored drinks made up a large portion of the fluids that children consume (Borradaile et al., 2009; He, Marrero, & MacGregor, 2008). Sodas not only contribute to weight gain and obesity, they are also associated with lower consumption of milk and intake of calcium, an important nutrient for bone health (Keller et al., 2009; Lim et al., 2009). So what can parents do?

Parents can help children to become healthy eaters by regularly offering a variety of healthy foods and beverages and by modeling healthy eating habits. Education level of mothers is a good predictor of whether children adopt healthy eating patterns and consume fewer sugar-laden beverages (Northstone et al., 2013; van Ansem et al., 2014). More education may translate into greater awareness of healthy habits. These parents, for example, may be more aware of the recommendations for healthy eating and steer children away from the sugary sodas and other sugar-sweetened beverages that have become so very popular. Higher education levels may also provide parents with additional strategies for managing their children's behavior, without having to resort to bribing their children with candy and soda to get them to behave (Fisher et al., 2015). Finally, there is also evidence that children may eat more at home and gain more weight if they are living in a stressful home situation, which is often associated with living in poverty. Craig Gundersen and his colleagues (2008) found that young children eat more "comfort foods" when their mothers are stressed, but only if these foods are available to them. These findings illustrate Bronfenbrenner's exosystem (see Chapter 2): A child is influenced by things going on in the mother's life that may relate to her work, finances, and other factors that do not directly involve the child but still affect the child.

Also important is the larger environment—the neighborhood and school—of the child. Neighborhoods with higher levels of poverty and lower education levels are associated with higher rates of obesity (Kimbro & Denney, 2013). And when fast foods and junk foods are available in the neighborhood, in the form of fast-food restaurants and convenience stores, children and their parents are more likely to partake of these often unhealthy eating options (He et al., 2012; Rummo et al., 2015). Children and their families who do not live within easy access of junk food consume less of it. Thus, where you live can influence how you eat. But that's not all.

The schools that children attend are also important influences on children's eating habits and health. Students who attend schools with breakfast programs have healthier weights than students in schools without breakfast programs, as indicated by body mass index (BMI), a marker of

A typical fast-food meal: lots of calories, little nutrition.

Brand X Pictures/Getty Images

The U.S. Department of Agriculture introduced its new recommendations for healthy eating in 2011 with a food plate, replacing the food pyramid that reigned for several decades. According to the new recommendations, fruits and vegetables should make up half of your meal.

USDA

body fat calculated from a person's height and weight (Gleason & Dodd, 2009). Children who participate in their school's meal programs consume more milk, vegetables, and 100% fruit juice than children not participating; it turns out that those lunches packed at home and brought to school are not as healthy as school lunches (Caruso & Cullen, 2015; Johnston et al., 2012).

School lunches, though, are far from perfect nutrition. School lunches tend to have higher levels of fat than recommended by nutrition experts, as well as higher than recommended levels of sodium and lower amounts of fiber (Clark & Fox, 2009; Crepinsek et al., 2009). With the Healthy, Hunger-Free Kids Act of 2010, schools in the United States were put on notice that they would need to roll out healthier lunches by 2012. Has nutrition improved since the new guidelines were adopted? High school students were less impressed than elementary students by the changes to their lunches. And while the presence of a fruit and/or vegetable on the lunch tray has increased, there is also a great deal of waste, with many pounds of fruits and vegetables being wasted every day.

Physical Activity

Health during childhood can be fostered not only by a good diet but also by regular physical activity. Children should do at least 60 minutes of moderate or vigorous physical activity every day. Do they get this much activity? One group of researchers tracked older elementary school children with electronic monitors for a week to determine their activity levels (Trost et al., 2013). The children were

sedentary (think, sitting around), on average, for 63% of the time, somewhat active for 31%, and moderately to vigorously active just 6% of the time. Unfortunately, our contemporary lifestyles may inadvertently promote physical inactivity, which may explain why the fitness levels of children have shown a measurable decline in recent years. Across children of all ages, the average amount of TV viewing is 25 hours per week, and this does not include other screen time from computers and other devices (Statistic Brain Research Institute, 2015). Children who watch more than 5 hours of television a day are about five times more likely to be overweight than children who watch 2 hours a day or less, perhaps because they get little exercise and eat the junk foods that they see advertised on TV (see Shifrin et al., 2015). At the same time, some schools have reduced recess time and physical education requirements. Most kids get chauffeured everywhere they need to go in the family car, further decreasing their opportunities for walking and physical activity.

Children who live in neighborhoods that provide opportunities for safe outdoor activities are less likely to be overweight than their peers who live in settings that offer few such opportunities (Committee on Environmental Health, 2009). Particularly for families in urban neighborhoods, if parents do not believe that it is safe for their children to play outdoors, children tend to replace outdoor activity with sedentary indoor activity such as watching television (Cecil-Karb & Grogan-Kaylor, 2009). But indoor activity does not have to be completely sedentary. Children who play *active* sports or fitness video games—those that require fairly rigorous movement—benefit in comparison to children who play only the traditional, inactive video games, although they do not benefit as much as they would from physically participating in the actual sport (LeBlanc et al., 2013; Sween et al., 2014). Further, children who attend preschools with more portable equipment (for example, balls and bikes) engage in more physical activity over the course of the day than children who attend preschools

Children get more exercise if their playgrounds provide open space and portable equipment such as balls.

AP Images/Alexander Zemlianichenko

with more fixed equipment such as swing sets (Dowda et al., 2009). But even the environments that encourage the most activity cannot turn every couch potato into an athletic powerhouse. Some children are predisposed by temperament to lead more sedentary lifestyles and resist even the most engaging playground equipment and incentives to be physically engaged (Saudino, 2012; Saudino & Zapfe, 2008). Thus, characteristics of the environment in combination with characteristics of the child affect activity levels.

Children who achieve the recommended level of physical activity are, not surprisingly, more physically fit than children who lead a more sedentary lifestyle. What is especially important to consider, though, is that the benefits of exercise go beyond physical fitness: Physical activity enhances cognitive and psychological functioning. One researcher has referred to exercise as "brain food" (Ploughman, 2008). Regular physical activity seems to support effective executive functions, those important cognitive activities involved in planning and executing goal-directed behaviors (Tomporowski et al., 2008). Not surprisingly, then, children engaged in regular physical activity also show higher levels of academic achievement (Michael et al., 2015).

As Charles Basch (2011) phrased it in an introduction to a special issue of *The Journal of School Health*, "healthier students are better learners" (p. 593).

Checking Mastery

1. How are brain functions of the two hemispheres typically organized?
2. What are three major factors that contribute to health during childhood?
3. What are two things that schools or parents can do to influence children's eating behaviors in order to help them maintain or achieve a healthy weight?

Making Connections

1. Design an intervention to increase children's fitness levels and indicate how you will assess the effectiveness of your intervention.

5.4
The Adolescent

LEARNING OBJECTIVES

- Explain how brain changes during adolescence influence teens' behavior.
- Compare and contrast the experience of puberty for males and females, including both physical and psychological correlates of puberty.

Adolescents are intensely focused on their physical self, and rightly so—dramatic physical changes are taking place during this period, both inside and out. Consider your own transformation from child to adult. You rapidly grew taller and took on the body size and proportions of an adult during your growth spurt. Moreover, you experienced puberty—the processes of biological change that result in an individual's attaining sexual maturity and becoming capable of producing a child. And although you could not see them, there were changes taking place in your brain that would contribute to your transition from child to adult. We look at all these processes, starting with the brain.

The Adolescent Brain: What's Going On in There?

The brain undergoes much change during adolescence. Magnetic resonance imaging (MRI) studies show that the brain's "gray matter," made up primarily of cell bodies and dendrites, undergoes change in an inverted-U pattern across adolescence. That is, the volume of gray matter increases, peaks, and then decreases throughout the teen years (Blakemore, Burnett, & Dahl, 2010). This pattern is believed to be associated with increased synaptogenesis just before puberty, followed by a period of heightened pruning of synapses (Johnson & de Haan, 2015). In contrast to this inverted U-pattern, the brain's "white matter," consisting of clusters of axons, increases in linear fashion throughout adolescence, a likely result of the steady progression of myelination of axons (Blakemore et al., 2010).

Adolescents are notorious for taking chances that most adults would not take. Can brain changes explain why adolescents take more risks than adults? They often display poor judgment and decision making when it comes to alcohol, drug, and cigarette use; sexual activities; and driving (see ● **Table 5.4**). These choices have important implications for their health, both in the short term and the long term. Consider the high school students who report occasional heavy or binge drinking. Teens under the influence of alcohol are more likely to make additional risky choices:

1. They are more likely to smoke cigarettes, and the more they smoke, the more likely they are to become addicted to nicotine.
2. They are more likely to engage in risky sexual behaviors, including sex with multiple partners and unprotected sex. In turn, these behaviors are associated with unintended pregnancies and sexually transmitted diseases.
3. They are more likely to get into a car where the driver has been drinking, which greatly increases the risk of an accident.
4. They are more likely to get into physical fights, experience academic problems, and engage in illegal behaviors.

● Table 5.4 Risky Behaviors During Adolescence

Drinking alcohol (45%)
Having sex without a condom (39%)
Getting into a physical fight (35%)
Riding with a driver who has been drinking (29%)
Using alcohol or drugs before sexual intercourse (23%)
Using marijuana (20%)
Smoking cigarettes (reported by 20% of adolescents)
Carrying weapons (18% overall but 30% among males)
Drinking and driving (10%)

Source: Department of Health and Human Services, Youth Risk Behavior Survey, 2009.

These behaviors, or the predisposition to these behaviors, may have been present before the alcohol use, but alcohol use can still exacerbate the problems. By some analyses, making the decision not to drink during adolescence may be one of the teen's most important health decisions.

How might brain changes during adolescence relate to risky behavior? There are two things to consider. One is that the part of the brain involved in regulating self-control has not yet matured (Casey, 2015; Casey & Caudle, 2013). At some point, there may have been evolutionary advantages to this, but at this point, it seems to make teens vulnerable to potentially harmful behaviors (see Casey, 2015). The second thing to consider is that adolescence ushers in a period of increased responsiveness to rewards. Indeed, the reward system of the brain is hyper-responsive: The adolescent brain has greater need for reward, which leads to more reward-seeking behaviors. Adriana Galvan and her colleagues (2007) measured activity in a part of the brain called the *nucleus accumbens* (thought to be associated with reward, pleasure, and addiction) as participants worked on a task with varying rewards for correct answers. They found that adolescents, relative to children and adults, exhibited higher levels of activity—hyper-responsiveness—in the nucleus accumbens in anticipation of both negative and positive consequences of risk taking. In terms of timing, teens experience this higher threshold for reward prior to attaining adult levels of decision making. In particular, the neurons serving the frontal lobes are among the last areas of the brain to become myelinated. The frontal lobes are essential to many higher-order mental activities of thinking, planning, and decision making. Thus, brain changes may leave adolescents in a vulnerable position: Their desire for reward increases before their ability to think through all the consequences of their actions (Geier, 2013). The area of the brain involved in inhibiting risky behavior is not fully developed until around age 25 (Giedd, 2004).

As with all behaviors, there are individual differences. Although adolescents as a group may be more prone to risk-taking behaviors, it is certainly not the case that all adolescents engage in the same level of risk taking. Teens with stronger working memory skills, for instance, are less likely to take risks than their peers with weaker working memory skills (Khurara et al., 2015). In addition, a positive relationship between teens and their parents can help protect them during this period of development (Qu, Fuligni,

Galvan, & Telzer, 2015). On the other hand, teens tend to be more prone to risk taking when hanging out with their peers, again, thanks to what's going on in the brain at this time of development (Somerville, 2013).

The adolescent brain, then, is still a work in progress, and some risk taking by teenagers may be par for the course until further brain developments, such as maturation of the prefrontal cortex, refine their good judgment and decision making. Laurence Steinberg (2015), who has extensively studied adolescent brain development, makes the interesting observation that educational programs aimed at getting teenagers to change their behaviors have been largely ineffective. Instead of trying to change how teenagers think, Steinberg (2015) argues that we should restructure their environments to reduce their exposure to risky situations until their brains have a chance to more fully mature. Their restructured worlds would include, for example, reduced opportunities to obtain alcohol, drugs, and cigarettes, less unstructured time (perhaps by having longer school days), and later start times for their school days to enable them to get adequate sleep, which is important to being mentally sharp throughout the day. **Exploration 5.1** considers another serious threat to brain health during adolescence—concussions.

The Growth Spurt

As noted earlier in the chapter, the adolescent growth spurt is triggered by an increase in the level of growth hormones circulating through the body during adolescence. Boys and girls grow at different rates, as do different body parts. Girls' peak rate of growth for height is just under 12 years; for boys it is 13.4 years (Geithner et al., 1999). The peak rate of growth for weight is 12.5 years for girls and 13.9 years for boys. Thus, boys lag behind girls by 1–2 years. Both sexes return to a slower rate of growth after the peak of their growth spurts. Like infants, adolescents may grow in spurts rather than continuously. Girls achieve their adult height by around 16 years; boys are still growing at 18, 19, or even 20 years (Fryar, Gu, & Ogden, 2012).

Muscles also develop rapidly in both sexes, with boys normally gaining a greater proportion of muscle mass than girls do. Total body weight increases in both sexes, but it is distributed differently: Girls gain extra fat, primarily in the breasts, hips, and buttocks; boys develop broader shoulders.

Sexual Maturation

Long before the physical signs of puberty are evident, the body is changing to prepare for sexual maturity. The adrenal glands increase production of adrenal androgens sometime between the ages of 6 and 8 in both boys and girls. Known as adrenarche, this circulation of adrenal hormones contributes partly to such secondary sex characteristics as pubic and axillary (underarm) hair. But the more obvious signs of sexual maturity emerge with increased production of gonadal hormones (those produced by the testes or ovaries): androgens in males and estrogen and progesterone in females. The gonadal hormones are primarily responsible for the development of secondary sexual characteristics and sexual maturity. This increased hormone production will also trigger sexual thoughts, feelings, and maturation. Yes, teenagers

EXPLORATION 5.1

Sports and Brain Damage

There are many benefits of participating in sports, but for some participants, injuries can leave an unwanted lasting impact. Considerable concern has been raised about head injuries, namely, **concussion**, which is a brief loss of brain function in response to a hit or blow to the head. Most concussions are classified as mild and symptoms resolve within weeks (Daneshvar et al., 2011). It is a fairly common sports injury, with high school football incidents accounting for nearly half of all sports-related concussions, followed by ice hockey and soccer. The number of teens treated in emergency rooms for concussion has dramatically increased over the past decade, likely from increased awareness of the serious consequences of concussion but perhaps also from the increased intensity of competitions.

Immediate symptoms of concussion include headache, sensitivity to light and sound, feeling dizzy or foggy, and slowed reaction time. But perhaps more concerning are the longer-term effects of concussions (see Bramlett & Dietrich, 2015). Researchers at Johns Hopkins University compared nine retired players from the National Football League (NFL) to a group of men who had not played football (Coughlin et al., 2015). The football players ranged in age from mid-50s to mid-70s and self-reported anywhere from zero to forty concussions during their football careers. Participants underwent PET scans and MRIs to uncover possible structural abnormalities as well as the presence of a protein that is linked to damage and repair in the brain. They also completed various memory tests. The findings were fairly dramatic, showing clear evidence of damage in the former football players' brains decades after they had retired from the sport. In particular, there was damage to the parts of the brain associated with memory and regulation of mood.

As a result of sports-related injuries, at least 25% of retired football players are expected to develop **chronic traumatic encephalopathy (CTE)**, a degenerative brain disease with symptoms of memory loss, poor impulse control, depression, and eventually dementia. One such player was Dave Duerson, who played for the Chicago Bears and New York Giants. Duerson

retired from the NFL in 1993 and eventually killed himself in 2011 at the age of 50. In a note to his family, Duerson described "having trouble with spelling, blurred vision, short-term memory problems, issues with putting full concepts and sentences together" (Martin, 2015). Duerson asked that scientists conduct a post-mortem exam of his brain. It showed damage to his frontal and temporal lobes and advanced CTE.

What about "regular" or nonprofessional players? Another group of researchers scanned the brains of 50 patients 4 months after they had experienced a mild concussion and compared these to healthy (nonconcussive) patients (Ling et al., 2013). The brains of those who had experienced a concussion showed abnormalities in the frontal cortex. It's important to note that these patients had experienced mild concussions and outward symptoms of the injury were largely or completely absent at the time of the scans. Still, there was evidence of damage to their brains.

And it's not just male athletes. Female soccer and basketball players are more likely than their male counterparts to experience a concussion in these sports, and they take longer to recover. The reasons for this gender difference are not clear, but it could be that female players report injuries more often than do males. It's also possible that anatomical differences, such as head, spine, and neck muscles, are different and place females at greater risk than males. A review of 21 studies that examined concussion symptoms among males and females, aged 12 to 26 years, found that females had more symptoms, but the researchers were not able to conclude that the male-female difference was truly meaningful

Jonathan Daniel/Getty Images

in terms of the injury (Brown et al., 2015). Women's menstrual cycles may interact with symptoms of concussion, leading to what seems like a gender difference in concussive symptoms.

The American Academy of Neurology (AAN) has issued recommendations aimed at avoiding further damage following an initial traumatic brain injury. In the past, it was common for players to 'tough it out' and continue to play in a game following an injury or to return to practice and play within days of an injury. We now know that insufficient time to recover from a traumatic brain injury can leave the brain more vulnerable to subsequent trauma. Thus, the AAN recommends that players with any symptoms of altered consciousness, regardless of whether they fainted or 'blacked out,' should not be permitted to return to playing until they have been examined and cleared to play by a medical professional trained in head trauma.

Coaches, parents, and medical professionals need to carefully train their players to reduce the sorts of moves and mindsets that increase the risk of head injuries during sports. Doing so will help ensure that athletes get the benefits of sports without the dangers.

Why are boys generally more positive than girls about the physical changes in their bodies during adolescence

Kmiragaya | Dreamstime.com

adult secondary sexual characteristics (● Table 5.5). For girls, the most dramatic event in the sexual maturation process is menarche—the first menstruation—normally between ages 11 and 15, with an average of about 12.5 years. Menstruation is the process of shedding the lining of a uterus prepared to support a fertilized egg. However, some girls begin to menstruate before they have begun to ovulate, so they may not be capable of reproducing for a year or more after menarche (Spear, 2000a). But other girls *do* ovulate—release a mature egg capable of being fertilized—when they begin to menstruate and should know that sexual activity can lead to a pregnancy.

There is a great deal of variability in when secondary sex characteristics (such as breast buds and pubic hair) appear. Sexual maturation also proceeds at different rates in different ethnic groups. Several studies have found that African American and Mexican American girls begin to experience pubertal changes earlier than European American girls (Chumlea et al., 2003; Jean et al., 2011). At age 9, for example, 49% of African American girls have begun to develop breasts compared with only 16% of European American girls and 25% of Mexican American girls (Wu, Mendola, & Buck, 2002). A few girls (1% of European Americans and 3% of African Americans) show signs of breast or pubic hair development at age 3, and a few have not begun to mature even at age 12 (Herman-Giddens et al., 1997).

For the average boy, the sexual maturation process begins around age 11 to age 11½ with an initial enlargement of the testes and scrotum (the saclike structure that encloses the testes). Unpigmented, straight pubic hair appears soon thereafter, and about 6 months later, the penis grows rapidly about the same time that the adolescent growth spurt begins (refer again to Table 5.5). The marker of sexual maturation most like menarche in girls is

think a lot about sex and, as we will discuss in Chapter 12, some (many?) teens begin to act on these thoughts. Here, we focus on the physical changes of puberty and the psychological implications of these changes.

Progression through puberty and attainment of sexual maturity is often measured using the "Tanner Scale," named for the British pediatrician who developed it (see Marshall & Tanner, 1969, 1970). The Tanner Scale includes five stages ranging from prepubertal—no evidence of secondary sexual characteristics—to

● **Table 5.5** Tanner's Stages of Secondary Sexual Characteristics and Annual Growth (in inches) for Boys and Girls

Stage	Boys	Girls
I	Prepubertal AG: 2–2.5 inches	Prepubertal AG: 2–2.5 inches
II Boys: ages 12.5–14.5 Girls: ages 10–12	Testes: a bit larger (first sign in boys) Scrotum: red Penis: still childlike but erections common AG: 2.75–3.25 inches	Breasts: small bud, widened areola AG: 2.8–3.2 inches
III Boys: ages 13–15 Girls: ages 11–13	Testes: larger Scrotum: darker Penis: increases in length AG: 3.25 inches	Breasts: larger and more elevated AG: 3.2 inches
IV Boys: ages 13.5–15.5 Girls: ages 12–14	Testes: more enlargement Scrotum: more darkening Penis: becomes thicker AG: 4 inches	Breasts: secondary mound of areola from body AG: 2.8 inches
V Boys: ages 14–18 Girls: ages 14–18	Testes, scrotum, and penis all adult Final height by 18–19 years	Breasts: adult shape and size Final height by 16 years

AG = annual growth

Source: Adapted from O'Keeffe, Gwenn (2009, December). Puberty resource page. Retrieved (2016, November) from *www.pediatricsnow.com/2009/12/puberty-resource-page/*.

semenarche, or a boy's first ejaculation—the emission of seminal fluid in a "wet dream" or while masturbating. It typically occurs around age 13 (Herman-Giddens et al., 2012). Just as girls often do not ovulate until sometime after menarche, boys often do not produce viable sperm until sometime after their first ejaculation.

Somewhat later, boys begin to sprout facial hair, first at the corners of the upper lip and finally on the chin and jawline. As the voice lowers, many boys have the embarrassing experience of hearing their voices "crack" uncontrollably up and down between a squeaky soprano and a deep baritone, sometimes within a single sentence. Boys may not see the first signs of a hairy chest until their late teens or early 20s, if at all.

What determines an adolescent's rate of development? Genes are part of the answer: Identical twins typically begin and end their growth spurts at very similar times, and early or late maturation tends to run in families (Silventoinen et al., 2008). In both sexes, the changes involved in physical and sexual maturation are triggered when the hypothalamus of the brain stimulates activity in the endocrine system. Boys and girls have similar levels of both male and female sex hormones during childhood. By the time sexual maturation is complete, however, males have larger quantities of male hormones (androgens, including testosterone) circulating in their blood than females do, whereas females have larger quantities of female hormones (estrogen, progesterone, and others).

Physical and sexual maturation, then, are processes set in motion by the genes and executed by hormones. But environment also plays its part in the timing of maturation. This is dramatically illustrated by the secular trend—the historical trend in industrialized societies toward earlier maturation and greater body size. In 1840, for example, the average age of menarche was 16½ years, a full 4 years later than it is today (Rees, 1993).

What explains the secular trend? Better nutrition, advances in medical care, higher rates of obesity, and exposure to a wide array of chemicals that may alter hormone production are the major contributing factors (Gluckman & Hanson, 2006; Herman-Giddens et al., 2012). As ● Table 5.6 shows, the age

of menarche varies across countries and tends to be earlier in countries with good nutrition, long life expectancies, and high literacy rates, reflecting the effect of both biological and environmental factors (Thomas et al., 2001). In industrialized nations, today's children are more likely than their parents or grandparents to reach their genetic potential for maturation and growth because they are better fed and less likely to experience growth-retarding illnesses. Even within the relatively affluent U.S. society, poorly nourished adolescents—both boys and girls—mature later than well-nourished ones do. Girls who are taller and heavier as children tend to mature earlier than other girls (Lee et al., 2007). In particular, being overweight during early childhood (birth to 2 years) is associated with early puberty among girls (Wan, Deng, Archer, & Sun, 2012). By contrast, girls who engage regularly in strenuous physical activity and girls who suffer from anorexia nervosa (the life-threatening eating disorder that involves dieting to the point of starvation, discussed in Chapter 16) may begin menstruating late or stop menstruating after they have begun. These variations seem to be tied not to overall weight but to skeletal development, particularly maturation of the pelvic bones necessary for delivering a baby (Ellison, 2002).

Family situations can also affect the timing of puberty, at least for girls. For instance, girls experience earlier puberty when their family is disrupted by a separation or divorce that removes their biological father from the home at an early age (Culpin et al., 2014). Early absence of the father is associated with adolescent depression as well as with economic disadvantage. These factors, and not the father's absence per se, may be the real reason for early menarche (Culpin et al., 2014; Culpin, Heron, Araya, & Joinson, 2015). The common thread in all this research is stress in the girls' lives, starting at a relatively young age (James, Ellis, Schlomer & Garber, 2012; Simpson et al., 2012). Over time, stress can affect many bodily systems and functions and early menarche may be one by-product of these changes. Truly, then, physical and sexual maturation are the products of an interaction between heredity and environment, with some environments delaying maturation and others hastening it.

● **Table 5.6** Median Age of Menarche and Emergence of Secondary Sexual Characteristics (if available) in Select Countries

	Stage 2 Breast	Stage 2 Pubic Hair	Menarche
Mexico			12.0
China	9.2	10.4	12.3
U.S.	10.0	10.5	12.4
Iran	10.15	10.78	12.65
Canada			12.9
U.K.	10.14	10.92	12.9
Denmark	9.86		13.13
Tanzania			14.3
Bangladesh			15.1
North Korea (refugees)			16

Sources: Aksglaede et al., 2009; Bau et al., 2009; Bosch et al., 2008; Gohlke & Woelfle, 2009; Harris, Prior, & Koehoorn, 2008; Juul et al., 2006; Kashani et al., 2009; Ku et al., 2006; Ma et al., 2009; McDowell, Brody, & Hughes, 2007; Rabbani et al., 2008; Rebacz, 2009; Rubin et al., 2009; Torres-Mejía et al., 2005.

Psychological Implications

As noted previously, there are large individual differences in the timing of physical and sexual maturation. An early-maturing girl may develop breast buds at age 8 and reach menarche at age 10, whereas a late-developing boy may not begin to experience a growth of his penis until age 14½ or a height spurt until age 16. Within a middle school, then, there is a wide assortment of bodies, ranging from entirely childlike to fully adultlike. It is no wonder adolescents are self-conscious about their appearance!

What psychological effects do the many changes associated with puberty have on adolescents? Girls approaching or experiencing puberty tend to become self-conscious about their appearance and worry about how others will respond to them. One adolescent girl may think she is too tall, another that she is too short (Oldehinkel, Verhulst, & Ormel, 2011). One may try to pad her breasts; another may hunch her shoulders to hide hers.

Some girls develop poor body images, possibly because they are bothered by the weight gains that typically accompany menarche (McCabe & Ricciardelli, 2004). These weight gains, though, are not driven solely by pubertal changes. Girls going through puberty report lack of energy and lower levels of activity, perhaps as a result of the hormonal changes but possibly also a result of their increased feelings of self-consciousness (Oldehinkel et al., 2011). Many girls exhibit mood changes, which seem to escalate as they proceed through puberty.

What about boys? Their body images are more positive than those of girls, and they are more likely to welcome their weight gain and voice changes. But they hope to be tall, hairy, and handsome, and they may become preoccupied with their physical and athletic prowess. Boys who experience slow growth and/or short stature can experience a rocky emotional road during adolescence as the smallest kid in the class, the last picked for sports, and the one least likely to be noticed in a romantic way by peers who are more developed. Their smaller size often means that others perceive them as younger and less mature. As they proceed through puberty, though, boys show a decrease in anxiousness and feelings of worthlessness (Oldehinkel et al., 2011).

Whereas menarche is a memorable event for girls, boys are often unaware of some of the physical changes they are experiencing. They notice their first ejaculation, but they rarely tell anyone about it and often were not prepared for it (Stein & Reiser, 1994). Although males express a mix of positive and negative reactions to becoming sexually mature, they generally react more positively to semenarche than girls do to menarche; 62% of boys regard semenarche positively, whereas only 23% of girls view menarche positively (Oldehinkel et al., 2011; Seiffge-Krenke, 1998).

Pubertal changes may prompt changes in family relations. Adolescents physically distance themselves from their parents by engaging in less body contact, especially with fathers, and they go to great lengths to avoid being seen naked by their parents (Schulz, 1991, in Seiffge-Krenke, 1998). Likewise, parents seem to restructure the parent–child relationship, placing greater distance between themselves and their children. Perhaps as a result of the barriers erected between adolescents and their parents, teens become more independent and less close to their parents (Steinberg, 1989). They are also more likely to experience conflicts with their parents, especially with their mothers—mostly about minor issues such as unmade beds, late hours, and loud music rather than about core values. Hormone changes in early adolescence may contribute to this increased conflict with parents and to moodiness, bouts of depression, lower or more variable energy levels, and restlessness (Buchanan, Eccles, & Becker, 1992). However, cultural beliefs about family relations and about the significance of becoming an adult also influence parent–child interactions during adolescence. For example, many Mexican American boys and their parents appear to become closer rather than more distant during the peak of pubertal changes (Molina & Chassin, 1996).

Even when parent–child relationships are disrupted during early adolescence, they become warmer once the pubertal transition is completed. Parents—mothers and fathers alike—can help adolescents adjust successfully to puberty by maintaining close relationships and helping adolescents accept themselves (Swarr & Richards, 1996). Overall, you should not imagine that the physical and hormonal changes of puberty cause direct and straightforward psychological changes in the individual. Instead, biological changes interact with psychological characteristics of the person and with changes in the social environment to influence how adolescence is experienced (Graber, Nichols, & Brooks-Gunn, 2010).

Early versus Late Development

If "timely" maturation has psychological implications, what is it like to be out of synch with your peers—to be an early or late developer? The answer depends on whether we are talking about males or females and also on whether we examine their adjustment during adolescence or later on.

Consider the short-term effects of being an early-developing or late-developing boy. Early-developing boys are judged to be socially competent, attractive, and self-assured, and they enjoy greater social acceptance by their peers (Mendle et al., 2010; Mensah et al., 2013). There are some negative aspects of being an early-maturing boy, namely increased risk of earlier involvement in substance use and other problem behaviors such as bullying, aggression, and delinquency (Kaltiala-Heino et al., 2003; Lynne et al., 2007). By comparison, late maturation in boys has more negative effects. Late-maturing boys tend to be more anxious and less sure of themselves, and they experience more behavior and adjustment problems (Dorn, Susman, & Ponirakis, 2003; Graber et al., 2004). As a group, they even score lower than other students do, at least in early adolescence, on school achievement tests (Dubas, Graber, & Petersen, 1991). However, on the positive side, late-maturing boys are less likely to drink alcohol during adolescence (Bratberg et al., 2005).

Early-maturing girls may find themselves hanging out with older peers and engaging in risky behaviors at an earlier age than their on-time or late-maturing age-mates.

Dean Pictures/Getty Images

Now consider early-maturing and late-maturing girls. Traditionally, physical prowess has not been as important in girls' peer groups as in boys', so an early-developing girl may not gain much status from being larger and more muscled. In addition, because girls develop about two years earlier than boys do, an early-developing girl may be subjected to teasing or bullying for being the only one in her grade who is developed. Perhaps for some of these reasons, early maturation appears to be more of a disadvantage than an advantage for girls. The early-maturing girl expresses higher levels of body dissatisfaction than her prepubertal classmates and may engage in unsafe dieting and exercising as a result of this discomfort. In addition, early maturity seems to alter girls' social environments, thrusting them into socializing with older peers, at least when they are outside of the highly age-organized setting of their classrooms (Allison & Hyde, 2011; Skoog & Stattin, 2014). As a result, they are likely to become involved in dating, smoking, drinking, having sex, and engaging in minor troublemaking at an early age.

Girls who experience puberty earlier than their peers report higher levels of depression at least for the period of time that they are out of synch (Reynolds & Juvonen, 2012). But which comes first: Does being depressed ignite biochemical changes in the body, triggering early puberty and sexual activity? Or does experiencing early puberty and sexual activity lead to being depressed?

Fiona Mensah and her colleagues (2013) used data from approximately 3,500 children in the Longitudinal Study of Australian Children to try to tease apart these two pathways. Multiple measures were collected from children and their parents from age 4–5 through age 10–11. It turns out that both boys and girls who experienced early puberty had also displayed signs of behavior and adjustment problems as early as preschool age. The authors concluded that there are "pre-existing and persistent early childhood differences in mental health-related indicators among children who experience early puberty" (p. 124). Thus, teens are not becoming depressed or engaging in problem behaviors because they have experienced early puberty, but they experienced early puberty because of underlying conditions present long before the first observable signs of puberty.

Late-maturing girls (like late-maturing boys) may experience some anxiety as they wait to mature, but they do not seem to be as disadvantaged as late-maturing boys. Indeed, whereas later-developing boys tend to perform poorly on school achievement tests, later-developing girls outperform other students (Dubas et al., 1991). Perhaps late-developing girls focus on academic skills when other girls have shifted some of their focus to extracurricular activities.

Do differences between early and late developers persist into later adolescence and adulthood? Typically, the effects of being out of synch are greatest during the time when the adolescent is most noticeably different from others. In other words, early-maturing girls experience negative feelings during early adolescence when their early maturation is most noticeable relative to peers. Late-maturing girls are more likely to experience negative feelings in mid- to late-adolescence, again when

their late maturation is most noticeable (Reynolds & Juvonen, 2012). By the end of high school, though, most of the negative effects of being out of synch have disappeared because there are few observable differences by this time. Still, when tracked into adulthood, early-maturing girls have not always attained as much education as girls who were not early maturing (Johansson & Ritzén, 2005). And there may be lasting effects of some of the risky behaviors engaged in by early-maturing girls (such as sex and drinking). Early-maturing girls have a greater likelihood than all other groups of experiencing long-term adjustment problems, including anxiety and depression (Graber, 2013). Some of the advantages of being an early-maturing boy may carry over into adulthood, but early-maturing boys also seem to experience greater anxiety than late-maturing ones, who may learn some lessons about coping in creative ways from their struggles as adolescents (Zehr et al., 2007).

Overall, then, late-maturing boys and early-maturing girls are especially likely to find the adolescent period disruptive. However, psychological differences between early-maturing and late-maturing adolescents become smaller and more mixed in quality by adulthood. It is also important to note that differences between early and late maturers are relatively small and that many factors besides the timing of maturation influence whether this period goes smoothly or not. For example, girls who make the transition from elementary to middle school at the same time they experience puberty exhibit greater adjustment problems than girls who do not experience a school transition and pubertal changes simultaneously (Simmons & Blyth, 1987).

Finally, and perhaps most important, the effects of the timing of puberty depend on the adolescent's perception of whether pubertal events are experienced early, on time, or late (Seiffge-Krenke, 1998). Thus, one girl may believe she is a "late bloomer" when she does not menstruate until age 14; but another girl, who exercises strenuously, may believe that menarche at age 14 is normal because delayed menarche is typical of serious athletes. Peer and family-member reactions to an adolescent's pubertal changes are also instrumental in determining the adolescent's adjustment. This may help explain the difference in adjustment between early-maturing boys and early-maturing girls. Parents may be more concerned and negative about their daughter's emerging sexuality than they are about their son's. These attitudes may be inadvertently conveyed to teens, affecting their experience of puberty and their self-concept.

Health and Wellness

Adolescents should be reaching their peak of physical fitness and health and, indeed, many adolescents are strong, fit, and energetic. Unfortunately, the sedentary lifestyle of modern society may be undermining the health and fitness of an increasing number of teens. Fitness tests of American teenagers show that an alarming number of them have poor physical fitness. Only 25% of teenagers do the recommended 60 minutes of daily physical activity (CDCP, 2015). Barely 15% of students walk or bicycle to school and, once at school, only a small percentage of high schools have *daily* physical activity factored into the school schedule (CDCP, 2015). Girls tend to become less active than boys in adolescence, although this gender gap has certainly narrowed in recent years with federally mandated gender equality in athletics (Yan et al., 2009). Teens may be doing well in school, but they are flunking treadmill tests that measure heart and lung function. Today's teens are showing up with high blood pressure, high cholesterol, and high blood sugar, putting them at risk for heart disease at earlier ages than previous generations.

Weight

As with children, the number of teens who meet the criteria for obesity—being 20% or more above the "ideal" weight for height, age, and sex—is increasing. As ■ Figure 5.8 shows, close to one-third of teenagers are either overweight or obese and these rates have been creeping up over the past 15 years. They are especially higher among certain ethnic minority groups, with, for example, 35% of non-Hispanic blacks meeting the definition for obesity compared to 24% of non-Hispanic whites (Flegal et al., 2012). Some of the same issues that we discussed earlier regarding children's weight also apply to adolescents. Adolescents have more sedentary lifestyles and consume more empty calories than they need, often in the form of beverages. Adolescents who drink more calorie-dense, nutrient-poor beverages not only gain weight, they have higher systolic blood pressure (Nguyen et al., 2009). The weight and the blood pressure put them at risk for later health problems, including heart and kidney disease, diabetes, liver problems, and arthritis. Rates of diabetes—high levels of sugar in the blood leading to various health problems—have significantly increased in recent years among adolescents, with more and more teens now taking antidiabetic drugs (Hsia et al., 2009).

Obesity may also affect brain function through metabolic syndrome (MeTS), which is a combination of risk factors typically associated with obesity and includes high blood pressure, unhealthy cholesterol

levels, and diabetes (Kassi, Pervanidou, Kaltsas, & Chrousos, 2011). Researchers from New York University compared adolescents with MeTS to adolescents without MeTS (Yau et al., 2012). The two groups were matched on multiple factors that might otherwise influence the results: age, gender, ethnicity, and socioeconomic status. The adolescents underwent endocrine testing, were evaluated with MRIs, and were assessed for cognitive and intellectual functioning.

The findings showed that adolescents with MeTS scored slightly lower—4 points—on overall IQ, but nearly 10 points lower on measures of math achievement. They also demonstrated some issues with attention and mental flexibility. While all scores were in the normal or average ranges, it is concerning that adolescents with MeTS are not operating at the same level of cognitive functioning as their non-MeTS peers. And the more MeTS risk factors that these teens had, the lower their cognitive functioning. Further research is needed to better understand how obesity and MeTS relate to brain function. Nonetheless, the cognitive deficits, whether they are permanent or temporary, add to the larger picture of childhood and adolescent obesity, and collectively, the findings indicate this is a serious health concern that cannot be ignored.

Children and adolescents whose parents are overweight have twin risk factors for becoming overweight themselves: the genes that their parents have passed along to them that may predispose them to be overweight, and the environment that

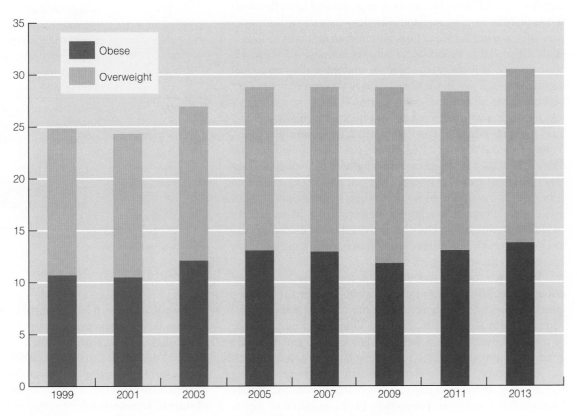

■ **Figure 5.8** Percentage of overweight and obese high school students, 1999–2013.

Source: Centers for Disease Control and Prevention, National Center for Chronic Disease Prevention and Health Promotion, Youth Risk Behavior Surveillance System (YRBSS), various years, 1999–2013.

is created for them by overweight parents (Steffen et al., 2009; Thibault et al., 2010). For instance, overweight parents are less likely to engage their children in vigorous physical activity and they are more likely to model sedentary behaviors, such as watching television. Overweight parents are also more likely to be economically disadvantaged, so they purchase less expensive foods that are often high in calories and low in nutritional value. Adolescents who are overweight tend to gravitate toward other overweight teens (Valente et al., 2009). Being friends with other teens who are overweight may be comfortable in that it reduces the stigma of being overweight. Further, it establishes an unhealthy pattern of behavior—inactivity coupled with poor eating habits—as normative and acceptable. There is little incentive to be different from the peers with whom you spend your time, so if they are sitting around eating junk food and drinking sugary drinks, then it is easy to do the same.

Obesity is usually the product of both nature and nurture: Heredity is certainly important, but poor eating habits, inactivity, and parental behaviors contribute (Steffen et al., 2009). ● **Table 5.7** summarizes some of the environmental factors that contribute to obesity, in particular, the rise in rates of obesity in recent decades.

Sleep

Another health issue that seems to plague many teenagers is insufficient sleep. Puberty ushers in changes in the sleep–wake cycle, melatonin production, and circadian rhythms, which can shift the "natural" time for falling asleep later and later. Research shows that the level of melatonin (a sleep-promoting hormone) rises later at night for teens than for children or adults (Crowley et al., 2015). Teens report later bedtimes from age 12 to age 18, and only 20% of them get the optimal amount of sleep on school nights. Although psychosocial factors may also contribute to later bedtimes than in childhood (for example, doing homework or text messaging with friends late into the night), biological factors—puberty in particular—seem primarily responsible. Teens who go to bed at midnight P.M. should not wake up until around 8 or 9 A.M. if they are to get the recommended 8–9 hours of sleep. However, most teens find themselves getting out of bed around 6:30 A.M. to get to school on time. High schools typically start earlier than elementary schools, often by 7:30 A.M. to accommodate bus schedules. Thus, just when their biological clocks are pushing back sleep times at night, schools are getting teens up earlier in the morning.

What are the consequences for teens who do not get enough sleep? Teens report greater sleepiness during the day, which is associated with decreased motivation, especially for "boring" tasks (Carskadon, 2011b). Tired teens may be able to successfully navigate a favorite class or read a particularly good book, but these same teens may have trouble completing an assignment in their least favorite subject or studying for an exam. Teens who have had their sleep restricted display increased sleepiness in proportion to the number of nights that their sleep is reduced. But surprisingly—at least to many adults—these same teens "perk up" in the evenings and show high levels of energy that discourage them from going to bed early (Carskadon, 2011a).

● **Table 5.7** Environmental Factors Contributing to the Obesity Epidemic

Inactive lifestyles	Among adults, occupations have become more sedentary (think, sitting at computer all day) and, as a result, adults burn 100–150 fewer calories every day. Over a person's work life, this can add nearly 30 pounds of weight.
Portion sizes	In just 20 years, the average soda size has increased from 6.5 to 20 ounces. Burgers at fast food restaurants increased from 4.5 to 8 ounces. The original McDonald's hamburger, in 1955, weighed just 1.6 ounces.
Fat content	In 2000, average fat consumption was 75 pounds per year, up nearly 30 pounds from 1950.
Sugar	In 1822, each person consumed approximately 6 pounds per year; today, each person consumes nearly 108 pounds per year. This figure rises even higher—as much as 150 pounds per year—if all forms of sweeteners are combined. The American Heart Association recommends no more than 9.5 teaspoons per day.
Stress	Prenatal exposure to a mother's stress can craft a neural architecture that is associated with later obesity. And stress in one's own life is associated with accumulation of belly fat. Unhealthy snacking is a common response to stress. Although research has uncovered these connections between stress and obesity, it does not address whether stress has contributed to the rise in obesity.
Poverty	A large proportion of children who live in poverty are obese or overweight relative to children in households not affected by poverty. The number of households meeting the U.S. criteria for poverty has increased in recent years. Among adults, *higher* income tends to be associated with higher obesity rates for men, but with lower obesity rates for women.

Sources: CDC, NCCDPHP, 2012b; CDC, 2012a; Church et al., 2011; Guyenet & Landen, 2012; Molteni et al., 2002; *USDA Factbook*, 2012; Young & Nestle, 2002.

Teens who sleep less at night or who stay up later on the weekends than their peers report higher levels of depression, irritability, and lack of tolerance for frustration (Carskadon, 2011b; Wolfson & Carskadon, 1998). They may also have difficulty controlling their emotional responses, which leads to greater expression of aggression or anger. As with younger children, teens who do not get enough sleep have trouble concentrating in school, experience short-term memory problems, and may doze off in class (National Sleep Foundation, 2015). In an attempt to counterbalance their lack of sleep, many teens begin consuming higher quantities of caffeine, which in turn, can further disrupt their sleep cycles (Carskadon & Tarokh, 2014).

Some teens report that, with their busy schedules, cutting back on sleep is unavoidable. Consider teens who have a big test scheduled for the next day but also have after-school obligations that will push back the start of their study time. Should they stay up late and study or should they go to bed with less study time? If you answered that they should go to bed and get a good night's sleep instead of studying, then you are correct according to research by Cari Gillen-O'Neel, Virginia Huynh, and Andrew Fuligni (2013). The researchers had students keep diaries of their sleep and study times for blocks of time in ninth, tenth, and twelfth grades. They found that the amount of study time throughout the week did not matter if students ended up cutting short their sleep time. Students who got a good night's sleep the night before a test did better than students who sacrificed a good night's sleep to get in more study time. There is an important message here for you: Manage your time so that you get all the study time you need *without sacrificing your sleep time*. Maintaining a consistent sleep–wake cycle with sufficient sleep time is an essential part of optimizing cognitive skills, not to mention physical health.

For all ages, learning more about sleep needs and the effects of sleep deprivation can lead to healthy lifestyle changes. Adhering to a regular bedtime and wake time on the weekends and on school and work days can help

Adolescents seem to be especially likely to doze off during the day as puberty alters their sleep–wake cycles and leaves them short on sleep

F. JIMENEZ MECA/Shutterstock.com

maintain healthy sleep habits. Unfortunately, "sleeping in" on the weekends alters the sleep–wake cycle and makes it more difficult to get up early for work or school Monday morning. So, next time you find yourself dozing off in class or at work, do not jump to the conclusion that the work you are doing is boring. It may be that your sleep–wake cycle is out of sync with the schedule imposed on you by school or work.

Checking Mastery

1. How do the typical brain changes throughout adolescence correlate with teen behavior?
2. Which group of teens is likely to have the "best" experience of puberty and which group is likely to experience more problems with the process of puberty?
3. What factors affect timing of menarche in girls?

Making Connections

1. What are the most significant health concerns during adolescence? If you could get adolescents to change two behaviors to improve their health, what would they be and why?
2. How would you counsel the parents of an early-maturing girl so that they understand the risks she may face and what they can do to help her adjust successfully?

5.5
The Adult

LEARNING OBJECTIVES

- Integrate the findings of both gains and losses in the adult brain.
- Summarize changes in the reproductive system throughout adulthood, with attention to how the physical changes may influence psychological well-being.
- Classify the typical changes of adulthood according to their likely impact on daily functioning.
- Compare the major theories of aging and evaluate their contributions to our understanding of why we age and die.

The body of the young adult is at its prime in many ways. It is strong and fit; its organs are functioning efficiently; it is considered to be in peak health. But it is aging, as it has been all along. Physical aging occurs slowly and steadily over the life span. Physical and health changes begin to have noticeable effects on appearance and functioning in middle age and have an even more significant effect by the time old age is reached, although more so in some people than in others.

But don't equate aging with only loss and decline: There are also gains and increases in some areas. This will be evident when we look at the brain in this chapter and then follow up in greater depth in Chapter 8 with the cognitive abilities of adults. In the next sections, we discuss typical changes that occur as we progress

through middle adulthood and old age. We also look at health issues that can challenge us and consider what it takes to age successfully. You will learn that lifestyle choices play a key role in your overall health and longevity.

The Changing Brain

When does the brain complete its development? In the past, we might have answered that the brain is fully developed by the end of infancy, or even by the end of pregnancy. Today, however, the answer is that *brain development is never truly complete*. The brain is responsive to experience and is capable of **neurogenesis**, the process of generating new neurons, across the life span. Consider first some research with mice. Mice that regularly work out on their treadmills (that is, running wheels) learn more quickly to navigate through a maze than their couch potato counterparts (mice without running wheels) (Pereira et al., 2007). By examining the brain tissue of the active mice, researchers found evidence of neurogenesis—new neurons were being created in response to the mouse's activity. And it turns out that adult songbirds can learn new songs with the help of new neurons (Goldman, 2008).

Neurogenesis in adult humans was once considered impossible, but there is now evidence suggesting it may be possible (Jessberger & Gage, 2014; Kempermann, Song, & Gage, 2015). Consider Terry Wallis who, injured at age 19 in a serious car accident, suffered severe brain damage and existed in a minimally conscious state for nearly 20 years (Hopkins, 2006). Doctors had assumed that recovery was not possible, but one day Terry "woke up" and began to talk. Although he remains disabled from injuries sustained during the accident, he has regained some functions and can communicate. Doctors attribute his miracle awakening to generation of new neurons and connections in the brain. But does what happened with this one individual hold true for other adults?

Fred Gage and his colleagues studied the effects of exercise on brain activity in a small group of adults (Pereira et al., 2007; and see Kempermann, Song, & Gage, 2015). The adults were given a learning task, completed a 3-month aerobic exercise program, and were then given another learning task. Learning improved following the exercise program. The researchers could not examine actual brain tissue after exercise as they do with mice. However, they did study blood volume in the brain and found that it was almost twice as high after the exercise program in the hippocampus, a part of the brain involved in learning and memory. This increased blood volume seems to be associated with production of new neurons. Other researchers have uncovered evidence that certain health conditions such as stroke and epilepsy may increase neurogenesis, whereas other conditions such as depression may decrease it (Balu & Lucki, 2009).

Denise Park and Chih-Mao Huang (2010) reviewed whether culture—growing up surrounded by Eastern Asian versus Western cultural values and experiences—has an effect on the organization of the brain. When asked to view pictures of an individual object, a background, and the object embedded in the background, East Asians and Westerners demonstrated different patterns of brain activity with each type of picture, as illustrated by images of blood flow captured by functional magnetic resonance imaging (fMRI) (see Goh et al., 2007). Over various studies like this one, the findings suggest that different patterns of brain activity are associated with different cultural experiences reflecting the collectivist focus of East Asian and the individualistic focus of Western cultures. In other words, your cultural experiences shape your brain function and possibly also brain structure (Park & Huang, 2010). Your brain continues to be responsive to the environment; it is not "done" or set in stone at birth or even in infancy or childhood.

Thus, the brain displays plasticity early in life and signs of neurogenesis and synaptogenesis throughout life. It can change in response to physical and mental exercise. It may be able to regenerate some functions following injury, which holds great promise for future therapies for patients with a wide range of conditions

such as stroke, epilepsy, and degenerative diseases such as Parkinson's and Alzheimer's (see Ernst & Frisén, 2015). But although the adult brain can generate new neurons, it does so at a much lower rate than the young brain (Lee, Clemenson, & Gage, 2012). What does this mean for the average person? What happens to the typical brain as it ages?

Many people fear that aging means losing brain cells and ultimately becoming "senile." As you will see in Chapter 16, Alzheimer's disease and other conditions that cause serious brain damage and dementia are *not* part of normal aging; they do not affect most older people. Normal aging is associated with gradual and relatively mild degeneration within the nervous system—some loss of neurons, diminished functioning of many remaining neurons, and potentially harmful changes in the tissues surrounding and supporting the neurons, such as the protective myelin covering (Scheibel, 2009). Just as brain weight and volume increase over the childhood years, they decrease over the adult years, especially after age 50 (Bartzokis & Lu, 2009; Taki et al., 2013). As people age, more of their neurons atrophy or shrivel, transmit signals less effectively, and ultimately die (Scheibel, 2009). Elderly adults may end up with 5–30% fewer neurons, depending on the brain site studied, than they had in early adulthood. Neuron loss is greater in the areas of the brain that control sensory and motor activities than in either the association areas of the cortex (involved in thought) or the brain stem and lower brain (involved in basic life functions such as breathing).

Other signs of brain degeneration besides neuron loss include declines in the levels of important neurotransmitters; the formation of "senile plaques," hard areas in the tissue surrounding neurons that may interfere with neuronal functioning and are seen in abundance in people with Alzheimer's disease; and reduced blood flow to the brain, which may starve neurons of the oxygen and nutrients they need to function (Aanerud et al., 2012). One of the main implications of such degeneration, as you will see later, is that older brains typically process information more slowly than younger brains do.

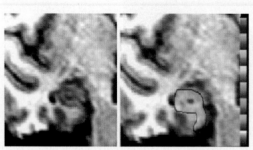

Pre-exercise   Post-exercise

Your brain on exercise. Using magnetic resonance imaging (MRI) technology that maps cerebral blood volume, researchers have found evidence of increased blood volume in a region of the hippocampus after exercise. This suggests the brain is capable of neurogenesis and could pave the way for developing new treatments for various conditions.

Source: Pereira et al. (2007). An in vivo correlate of exercise-induced neurogenesis in the adult dentate gyrus. *Proceedings of the National Academy of Sciences, 104*, 5638–5643.

On the positive side, research shows that middle age brings greater integration of the left and right hemispheres, which may help increase creativity and cognitive functioning. And the brain can remain healthy with exercise—both mental puzzles and physical aerobic workouts. Older adults who engage in high levels of aerobic activity show enhanced mental performance and corresponding increases in activity in certain regions of the brain (Barcelos et al., 2015; Gill et al., 2015). Some intriguing new research suggests that physical aerobic activity may be responsible for the number of new neurons generated in the brain, whereas mental activity influences the number of these new neurons that survive (Curlik & Shors, 2013). And not just any mental activity, but activity that is "new, effortful, and successful" (Shors, 2014, p. 311). Thus, if you want to grow your brain, you are going to have to put in some hard work.

What does it mean for older adults that both degeneration and plasticity—both losses and gains—characterize the aging brain? In some people, degeneration may win and declines in intellectual performance will occur. In other people, plasticity may prevail; their brains may form new and adaptive neural connections faster than they are lost so that performance on some tasks may actually improve with age (at least until very old age). Denise Park and Patricia Reuter-Lorenz (2009; Reuter-Lorenz & Park, 2014) make a compelling case that the aging brain may compensate for losses by increased activity in the prefrontal cortex. In particular, they propose the scaffolding theory of aging and compensation (STAC) to explain how the brain may adapt to losses by revving up in other areas. Thus, where a young adult's brain would use only the area that specializes in a particular kind of task to perform it, an older adult's brain might recruit other brain areas to help out. This kind of compensation may not always be possible due to health issues or genetic predispositions or adverse life experiences, but when it is, older adults may be able to maintain useful cognitive functioning for a longer period of time.

Just as physical activity helps to keep the body healthy, mental activity helps to keep the brain healthy.

Compuinfoto / Dreamstime.com

In a revised version of the STAC model, the researchers acknowledge that life events can have both a negative effect on the brain, depleting neural resources, and a positive effect, conserving and even enriching neural resources (Reuter-Lorenz & Park, 2014). It is important to consider a person's current level of cognitive functioning as well as the *rate* at which cognitive change occurs. Thus, you can reject the view that aging involves nothing but a slow death of neural tissue. Old brains *can* learn new tricks (it may just take some work).

The Changing Reproductive System

During most of adulthood, the sex hormones that prompted puberty and all of its changes continue to be produced, helping to ensure interest in sexual behavior and the ability to have children. These hormones also have psychological implications and effect the experience of aging. In men, testosterone levels fluctuate annually, with peak levels detected in spring and lower levels in fall, and daily, with peak levels in the morning (Moskovic, Eisenberg, & Lipshultz, 2012; van Anders, 2012). Men with high levels of testosterone tend to be more sexually active and aggressive than other men, although this relationship is influenced by other factors (see Trainor & Nelson, 2012). Otherwise, it is not clear that changes in men's hormone levels are tied to changes in their moods and behavior.

By contrast, hormone levels in women shift drastically each month as they progress through their menstrual cycles. For some women, these shifts may be accompanied by symptoms such as bloating, moodiness, breast tenderness, and headaches during the days just before the menstrual flow, symptoms collectively referred to as **premenstrual syndrome (PMS)**. Estimates of how many women experience PMS vary substantially. Roughly half of young women report that they experience PMS and a majority—as high as 90%—report at least some symptoms before menstruation and usually regard these as a normal accompaniment to the menstrual cycle (Delara et al., 2012; Wong, 2011). As many as 10% of women experience symptoms severe enough to interfere with their ability to perform daily activities and a few of these, perhaps 2–3%, may be diagnosed with a severe form of PMS called **premenstrual dysphoric disorder (PDD)**. PDD differs from PMS in that it includes affective symptoms in addition to physical symptoms associated with the menstrual cycle, and it can be disabling—disrupting work and relationships (American Psychiatric Association, 2013). Women with PDD report poorer health-related quality of life than those without PDD (Delara et al., 2012).

In recent decades, there has been some debate about the validity of PMS. In research where women are simply asked to complete mood surveys every day and do not know that their menstrual cycles are being studied, most report little premenstrual mood change. This suggests that expectations and not hormones play a role in at least some cases of PMS. Still, symptoms consistent with PMS are reported across many cultures, including those that generally do not label or acknowledge the syndrome (see Yonkers & Casper, 2012). Changes in estrogen and progesterone levels are the likely causes of the symptoms associated with PMS. Various treatments are available for PMS, depending on the severity and type of symptoms experienced. For instance, some women with severe PMS may find relief when treated with antidepressant drugs such as Prozac (Maharaj & Trevino, 2015). For women with milder forms of PMS, treatment with minerals and vitamins such as calcium, potassium, iron, and vitamin D may alleviate symptoms because the low estrogen levels experienced prior to menstruation can interfere with the absorption of these substances by the body (Chocano-Bedoya et al., 2013; Saeedian Kia, Amani, & Cheraghian, 2015). There is considerable variability in how women experience their menstrual cycles and, as we'll see in the next section, how they navigate through the years when their menstrual cycles end.

Female Menopause

Like other systems of the body, the reproductive system ages. The ending of a woman's menstrual periods in midlife is called menopause. Levels of estrogen and other female hormones decline so that the woman who has been through menopause has a hormone mix that is less "feminine" and more "masculine" than that of the premenopausal woman. When menopause is completed, a woman is no longer ovulating, no longer menstruating, and no longer capable of conceiving a child.

The average woman experiences menopause at age 51, and the usual age range is from 45 to 54 (National Institute on Aging, 2013). The process takes place gradually over 5–10 years as periods become either more or less frequent as well as less regular. Although life expectancy has increased and the age of menarche has decreased over history as part of the secular trend, the age of menopause does not appear to have changed much and is similar from culture to culture (Brody et al., 2000). What has changed is that women are now living long enough to experience a considerable period of postmenopausal life. The age at which a woman reaches menopause is somewhat related to both the age at which she reached menarche and the age at which her mother reached menopause (Varea et al., 2000). Researchers have discovered that menopause can be predicted by a hormone called anti-Müllerian hormone (Mishra & Dobson, 2012; Mishra & Kuh, 2012). Anti-Müllerian hormone peaks around age 16, remains stable until about age 25, and then begins a slow decline (Fong et al., 2012).

Society holds rather stereotypic views of menopausal women. They are regarded as irritable, emotional, depressed, and unstable. How much truth is there to this stereotype? Not much. About two-thirds of women in U.S. society experience hot flashes—sudden experiences of warmth and sweating, usually centered around the face and upper body, that occur at unpredictable times, last for a few seconds or minutes, and are often followed by a cold shiver (Whitbourne & Whitbourne, 2014). Many also experience vaginal dryness and irritation or pain during intercourse. Still other women experience no symptoms.

For years, hormone replacement therapy (HRT) (taking estrogen and progestin to compensate for hormone loss at menopause), was considered an effective cure for the symptoms that some women experience with menopause. For many women, HRT helps relieve physical symptoms of menopause, such as hot flashes and vaginal dryness, and also prevents or slows osteoporosis.

Unfortunately, trust in HRT was shattered in 2002 by a large government study that found that HRT increases women's chances of developing breast cancer and experiencing heart attacks and strokes (Women's Health Initiative, 2004). For most women, these risks outweigh the benefits of HRT, particularly if the hormones estrogen and progestin are taken over a long period. Still, for women with severe menopausal symptoms associated with decreasing production of hormones, short-term HRT (for example, up to 2 years) may be warranted. Lifestyle changes such as exercising and getting adequate sleep may be the best options for menopausal women because they alleviate some complaints and are safe.

What about the psychological symptoms—irritability and depression? Again, researchers have discovered wide variation among menopausal women—and not much truth to the negative stereotypes. In a particularly well-designed study, Karen Matthews and her associates (Matthews, 1992; Matthews et al., 1990) studied 541 initially premenopausal women over a 3-year period, comparing those who subsequently experienced menopause with women of similar ages who did not become menopausal. The typical woman entering menopause initially experienced some physical symptoms such as hot flashes. Some women also reported mild depression and temporary emotional distress, probably in reaction to their physical symptoms, but only about 10% could be said to have become seriously depressed in response to menopause. Typically, menopause had no effect on the women's levels of anxiety, anger, perceived stress, or job dissatisfaction. When women do experience severe psychological problems during the menopausal transition, they often had those problems well before the age of menopause (Greene, 1984).

Why do some women experience more severe menopausal symptoms than others do? Again, part of the answer may lie with biology. Women who have a history of menstrual problems (such as PMS) report more menopausal symptoms, both physical and psychological (Morse et al., 1998). Thus, some women may experience greater biological changes or be more sensitive to them. But psychological and social factors of the sort that influence women's reactions to sexual maturation and to their menstrual cycles also influence the severity of menopausal symptoms. For example, women who expect menopause to be a negative experience are likely to get what they expect (Matthews, 1992). There is also a good deal of variation across cultures in how menopause is experienced. In a recent study, women from the United States, United Kingdom, and Canada reported more symptoms than women from Sweden and Italy (Minkin et al., 2015). Portuguese women report primarily neutral symptoms and feelings about menopause (Pimenta et al., 2011). The effect of menopause is colored by the meaning it has for the woman, as influenced by her society's prevailing views of menopause and by her own personal characteristics.

Women who have been through menopause generally say it had little effect on them or that it even improved their lives; they are usually more positive about it than women who have not been through it yet (Morrison et al., 2014). Of course, this is not true of all women: Some report that the whole thing was worse than expected (Minkin, Reiter, & Maamari, 2015). Perceptions may vary depending on when women are asked and how fresh the experience is for them. In short, despite all the negative stereotypes, menopause seems to be "no big deal" for most women. Indeed, many women find the end of monthly periods to be quite liberating.

Male Andropause

Obviously, men cannot experience menopause because they do not menstruate. They also do not experience the sharp drop in hormones that accompanies menopause in women. But some research has pointed to the possibility that men experience andropause as they age. Andropause, also called *age-associated hypogonadism*, is characterized by slowly decreasing levels of testosterone and a variety of symptoms including low libido, fatigue and lack of energy, erection problems, memory problems, and loss of pubic hair (Samaras, 2015). By age 80, men have between 20% and 50% of the testosterone that they had at age 20. Pharmaceutical companies that manufacture synthetic testosterone would like us to believe that the low testosterone ("Low-T") levels associated with aging represent a disease in need of a treatment (Perls & Handelsman, 2015). This change in hormone levels, though, is a natural part of the aging process.

Some research reports that testosterone levels are markedly lower among men over age 50 with symptoms of andropause than among men without symptoms (Wu, Yu, & Chen, 2000). But other research does not show a clear connection between andropause symptoms and testosterone levels (see, for example, Vermeulen, 2000). In one study, for example, half of 50- to 70-year-old men complained of erectile dysfunction—inability to achieve or sustain an erection for intercourse—despite having sufficient levels of testosterone (Gould, Petty, & Jacobs, 2000). Most cases of erectile dysfunction are caused by medical conditions such as diabetes and not by lower hormone production. Erectile dysfunction among older men is often treatable with *sildenafil*, no doubt more familiar to you by the name Viagra.

In sum, the changes associated with andropause in men are more gradual, more variable, and less complete than those associated with menopause in women. As a result, men experience fewer psychological effects. Frequency of sexual activity does decline as men age. However, this trend cannot be blamed entirely on decreased hormone levels, because sexual activity often declines even when testosterone levels remain high (Gould et al., 2000; see also Chapter 12 on sexuality).

Health and Wellness

There are minor changes in physical appearance during our 20s and 30s and more noticeable signs of aging in our 40s and 50s. Skin becomes wrinkled, dry, and loose, especially among people who have spent more time in the sun. Hair thins and often turns gray from loss of pigment-producing cells. And to most people's dismay, they put on extra weight throughout much of adulthood as their metabolism rate slows but their eating and exercise habits do not adjust accordingly. Only 30% of adults engage in regular physical activity during their leisure time, less than 20% do strength training, and few engage in the level of aerobic exercise needed to maintain, let alone improve, their fitness (Schoenborn & Adams, 2010). Consequently, many middle-aged adults are overweight or even obese.

We discussed many of the health concerns associated with obesity in an earlier section. To impress upon you the magnitude of this issue, consider that obesity is a multi-billion dollar "business," accounting for 20% of the total health care costs in the United States (Cawley & Meyerhoefer, 2012). The U.S. Department of Health and Human Services has identified obesity as one of the most significant health care concerns facing Americans and has issued a number of recommended strategies for combating obesity. Many of these are the same ones recommended for children and adolescents: promoting healthy foods and beverages, discouraging consumption of those foods and beverages that add calories but not nutrition, and increasing physical activity through a variety of community programs. The upward trend in obesity rates must be curbed or future generations will face the unsettling prospect of shorter life spans than their parents or grandparents.

Challenges to Health

By the time people are 65 or older, it is hard to find many who do not have something wrong with their bodies. Acute illnesses such as colds and infections become less frequent from childhood on, but chronic diseases and disorders become more common. National health surveys indicate that many of the 70-and-older age group have at least one chronic impairment—whether a sensory loss, arthritis, hypertension, or a degenerative disease (Federal Interagency Forum, 2012). Arthritis alone affects 43% of elderly men and 54% of elderly women. Osteoarthritis is a common joint problem that results from gradual deterioration of the cartilage that cushions the bones from rubbing against one another. For some older adults, joint disease is deforming and painful and limits their activities. The older person who can no longer fasten buttons, stoop to pick up dropped items, or even get into and out of the bathtub may easily feel incompetent and dependent (Whitbourne & Whitbourne, 2014).

Another common affliction in old age is osteoporosis (meaning "porous bone"), a disease in which a serious loss of minerals leaves the bones fragile and easily fractured. It involves pain and can result in death if the victim falls and fractures a hip. Nearly one-third of elderly adults who fracture a hip die within one year; hip fractures are also a leading cause of nursing home admissions (Whitbourne & Whitbourne, 2014). One fall can change an older person's entire lifestyle, requiring a shift from independent living to assisted living. Not surprisingly, adults who have experienced a fall often begin to restrict their activities out of fear of falling again. Unfortunately, less activity can make them more vulnerable because it can lead to further decreases of muscle and bone mass (Whitbourne & Whitbourne, 2014). Osteoporosis is a special problem for older women, who never had as much bone mass as men and whose bones tend to thin rapidly after menopause. European and Asian women with light frames, those who smoke, and those with a family history of osteoporosis are especially at risk.

What can be done to prevent osteoporosis? For starters, dietary habits can influence a person's risk for osteoporosis. Many individuals do not get enough calcium to develop strong bones when they are young or to maintain bone health as they age (National Osteoporosis Foundation, 2013). Weight-bearing exercises such as walking or jogging can help prevent osteoporosis, as can the HRT that some women take following menopause (but see this chapter's earlier section, "Female Menopause," for a discussion of concerns about HRT). Good bone health starts in childhood and adolescence: Girls and young women who are physically active and eat a healthy diet develop higher bone density that protects them from bone loss in later life (Krucoff, 2000).

Aging also involves a gradual decline in the efficiency of most bodily systems from the 20s on. Most systems increase to a peak sometime between childhood and early adulthood and decline slowly thereafter. No matter what physical function you look at— the capacity of the heart or lungs to meet the demands of exercise, the ability of the body to control its temperature, the ability of the immune system to fight disease, or strength—the gradual effects of aging are evident. For example, we lose nearly 10% of our strength capacity with each passing decade (Katzel & Steinbrenner, 2012). In terms of handgrip strength, both men and women show declines from early to late adulthood, with men's losses fairly evenly distributed over adulthood and women's losses starting out slow but then escalating after age 55 (Samson et al., 2000). Why consider handgrip strength? It turns out that handgrip strength in middle age is a good predictor of disability and ability to function in later life: Those with weaker handgrip in middle age are more likely to report greater difficulty with such everyday activities as housework, walking, dressing, and bathing 25 years later (Rantanen et al., 1999). Those with stronger handgrip at midlife are more likely to beat the odds and live to age 100 (Rantanen et al., 2012). Why would handgrip be associated with health and longevity? Likely because it is an external indication of internal health and wellness. Someone with a strong handgrip is likely more active and healthy than someone with a weak handgrip.

Another fact of physical aging is a decline in the **reserve capacity** of many organ systems—that is, their ability to respond to demands for extraordinary output, such as in emergencies (Goldberg & Hagberg, 1990). For example, old and young people do not differ much in resting heart rates, but older adults, even if they are disease-free, will have lower maximal heart rates (Lakatta, 1990). This means that older adults who do not feel very old as they go about their normal routines may feel very old indeed if they try to run up mountains.

Finally, if you have ever taken a walk with a grandparent or another older adult, you likely found yourself slowing down so as to not leave your older companion behind. Older adults walk more slowly than the average of 4 feet per second clocked by most of their younger counterparts. In many situations, the older adult may simply need to allow additional time for getting places. In other situations, though, their slow speed may pose a safety concern, such as crossing a busy street where stoplights are programmed for the average adult's walking speed and not the average *older* adult's walking speed (Lobjois & Cavallo, 2009). In addition, research has revealed that walking speed can be a useful predictor of survival among older adults. Stephanie Studenski and her colleagues (2011) examined the relationship between the walking speed of more than 34,000 adults over the age of 65 and their 5-year and 10-year survival rates. The findings showed that an older adult's walking speed can effectively predict survival, especially among

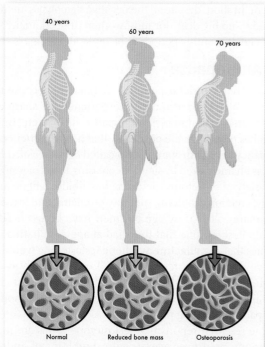

Osteoporosis weakens the bones, leading to the stooped posture displayed by many older adults. It also increases the risk of fractures, which can rob older adults of their independence.

Rob3000/Dreamstime.com

those 75 years and older. Thus, the fast-walking 75-year-old is more likely to be alive 5 and 10 years later than her slow-walking companions. This makes sense when you consider that walking speed, like handgrip strength, gives us a window into the functioning of multiple internal organ systems. When one or more of the organ systems that contribute to walking (for example, lungs, heart, musculature, nervous system, and so on) is damaged or begins to deteriorate, this will be reflected externally in a slower gait.

There is tremendous variability in the health, wellness, and functioning of older adults. Some are limited by health problems, but others enjoy active, healthy lives. A highly fit 75-year-old can outperform a sedentary 40-year-old couch potato. Indeed, some older adults are far more active than younger ones. For instance, Fauja Singh ran a full marathon (26.2 miles) at age 100! Doctors had conducted tests on Singh when he was 94 years old and concluded that his one leg had the bone density of a 35-year-old, while the other leg had the bone density of a 25-year-old. Upon hearing these test results, Singh quipped that he knew his one leg was weak (Morley, 2013). Although Singh is an extreme example, there is little doubt that exercise is an important component of health and wellness.

Exercise: Enhancing Health

Exercise is important mentally and physically across the entire life span. Exercise can improve cardiovascular and respiratory functioning, slow bone loss, and strengthen muscles. In one

A remarkable centenarian and great-great-grandfather, Fauja Singh retired from competing in marathons at age 101. He has attributed his health and longevity to careful food choices, avoidance of smoking and alcohol, and of course, regular exercise.

REUTERS/Bobby Yip

Theories of Aging: Why Do We Age and Die?

No matter what we do to stay fit and healthy and avoid the diseases associated with aging, we all eventually die. There is no simple answer to the question of why we age and die. However, several theories have been proposed, and each of them says something important about the aging process. These theories can be organized into two main categories: **Programmed theories of aging** propose that aging follows a predictable genetic timetable; **damage** or **error theories of aging** call attention to more haphazard processes that cause damage or errors in cells to accumulate and organ systems to deteriorate (Arking, 2006; Campisi & Robert, 2014; Hayflick, 2004). The question, really, is whether aging and death are the result of a biological master plan or of accumulation of random insults to the body while we live.

Programmed Theories

Programmed theories assume that aging will unfold according to a species-specific genetic program. There is no doubt that **maximum life span**—a ceiling on the number of years that anyone lives—varies by species. The fruit fly is lucky to live for 2–3 months, whereas the mighty Galapagos tortoise can reach an astonishing 190 years. Among mammals, humans have the longest maximum life span, estimated at around 125 years (Weon & Je, 2009). To date, the longest documented and verified human life is that of Jeanne Louise Calment, a French woman who died in 1997 at age 122 (Willcox et al., 2009). She lived on her own until age 110 when she could no longer see well enough to safely cook or light her daily cigarette (Cruikshank, 2009). Nearly blind and deaf and confined to a wheelchair, she maintained her sense of humor to the end, attributing her longevity to everything from having a stomach "like an ostrich's" to being forgotten by God (Trueheart, 1997). Calment and others who live almost as long are the basis for setting the maximum human life span around 125 years. Despite the fact that the *average* life expectancy increased 30 plus years during the 20th century and that more and more people today are living to be 100, the *maximum* life span has changed very little (Kinsella, 2005).

Beyond the species-specific maximum life span, an individual's genetic makeup, combined with environmental factors, influences how rapidly he ages and how long he lives compared with other humans. For example, genetic differences among us account for more than 50% of differences in the ability to stay free of major chronic diseases at age 70 or older (Reed & Dick, 2003) and for up to about a third of the variation in longevity (Melzer, Hurst, & Frayling, 2007). Among the oldest of the old, genetic factors may play an even greater role (Sebastiani et al., 2012). Perhaps, then, it is not surprising that a fairly good way to estimate how long you will live is to average the longevity of your parents and grandparents. For more tips on what it might take to live to be 100, check out **Exploration 5.2**.

It is not clear yet exactly how genes influence aging and longevity, though. The most promising programmed aging theory is based on the work of Leonard Hayflick (1976, 1994; 2004; 2007), who discovered that cells from human embryos could divide only

study, older athletes (average age 69 years) were compared with older non-athletes on several physiological measures following exercise. The athletes showed better oxygen uptake capacity and greater cardiovascular stamina than the non-athletes (Jungblut et al., 2000). Our brains need oxygen to function properly, so exercising your body also helps boost your brain power (Ratey, 2013). Exercise can make aging adults feel less stressed and happier, and it can enhance their cognitive functioning (Barnes et al., 2003; Rowe & Kahn, 1998; Yaffe et al., 2001). Physical activity is also associated with a lower incidence of depression among older adults (Lampinen, Heikkinen, & Ruoppila, 2000). Overall, it is estimated that regular exercise by older adults can delay the onset of physical disabilities by up to 7 years (Vita et al., 1998).

Unfortunately, adults decrease their involvement in vigorous physical activity as they get older—females earlier than males (Katzel & Steinbrenner, 2012). Older adults who are socially isolated and lonely reduce their physical activity even more than those who maintain strong social connections (Hawkley, Thisted, & Caciappo, 2009). By late adulthood, older adults may find that they get tired just climbing stairs or carrying groceries; running a marathon is out of the question. The average older person tires more quickly and needs more time to recover after vigorous activity than the average younger person.

Want to Live to Be 100?

An increasing number of people are **centenarians**—people who live to be 100 or older. Dan Buettner (2008) identified five communities around the world with unusually high proportions of centenarians. These so-called "Blue Zones" are located in Ikaria Greece; Loma Linda, California; Sardinia, Italy; Okinawa, Japan; and Nicoya, Costa Rica. By studying these communities and other centenarians, what can we learn about the secrets to a long, and importantly, a healthy life? Consider Don Pellmann, who set five world records in track and field at the 2015 Senior Olympics after reaching the century mark. Although Pellmann had run track as a teenager, he didn't return to the sport until age 70, when a son suggested that he give it a try. Feeling exhausted after that first competition, Pellmann realized he needed to start exercising if he wanted to continue competing. For the next 30 years, Pellmann walked or jogged, threw the shot put and discus, participated in competition after competition, and earned more awards (somewhere in the range of 900) than he could keep in his assisted living apartment (Almond, 2015).

Asked about his secret to a long life, Pellmann provided these pearls of wisdom: "I guess I have pretty good genes" and "I take care of what I got" (Almond, 2015; Crouse, 2015). Genetics does play a role in longevity: If you have long-lived relatives, then you are more likely to live a long life than someone without this family history (Gavrilov & Gavrilova, 2015). Research with a large sample of Danish twins found that genes accounted for about 25% of the differences in longevity (Herskind et al., 1996). The precise nature of this genetic contribution to longevity is still being studied, although several intriguing findings have emerged to date. For instance, there is some indication that a mother's longevity may contribute to longevity of her sons and daughters, whereas a father's longevity may influence only his son's longevity (Deluty et al., 2015). Genes may also influence longevity by offering protection from disease. Those from 'sturdy stock' with no major health conditions may pass along these 'sturdy' genes to their offspring. After all, part of what helps us live a long life is avoiding those diseases and illnesses that can do us in before we reach a ripe old age.

Interestingly, birth month also shows some relation to longevity, with those born in the fall months enjoying better odds of living to be 100 than those born at other times of the year (Gavrilov & Gavrilova, 2011). How could birth month possibly effect longevity? Researchers believe that birth month correlates with a mother's exposure to infections, sunshine and its vitamin D benefits, and nutrition during the prenatal and early postnatal period. These events may exert an epigenetic influence on the developing fetus and newborn, setting the stage for lifelong health (Gavrilov & Gavrilova, 2011).

Genes are important, but they alone are not going to get you to age 100. Gwen Weiss-Numeroff interviewed 30 centenarians for her book, *Extraordinary Centenarians in America: Their Secrets to Living a Long Vibrant Life*, and found that a common thread emerging from these interviews was adaptability. Centenarians had a positive outlook on life and were able to easily adapt to change. In addition, many of the centenarians reported fairly healthy eating habits and avoidance—for the most part—of unhealthy habits such as smoking. This takes us back to Don Pellmann's second piece of wisdom—taking care of what you have. A diet high in fruits, vegetables, nuts, and legumes and low in carbohydrates and fats can reduce the risk of heart disease, diabetes, and various cancers (Davinelli, Willcox, & Scapagnini, 2012).

In their book, *The Longevity Project,* Howard Friedman and Leslie Martin (2011) describe the life outcomes for 1,500 folks who were originally recruited in 1921 by Lewis Terman for a study of giftedness (see Chapter 9). By analyzing the health records and death dates of these Terman study participants, Friedman and Martin found that the trait of conscientiousness in both childhood and adulthood predicted longevity. People who are conscientious likely make decisions that enhance their health rather than detract from it. Conscientious folks are the ones who follow the recommendations for regular checkups and diagnostic tests to detect potential health problems as early as possible. They probably floss their teeth and wear their seatbelts, all of which contributes to a long and healthy life.

So the key to longevity is likely a combination of good genes and a healthy lifestyle. If you would like to calculate how long you can be expected to live based on information about your lifestyle, stress level, eating habits, and health status, try completing "The Living to 100 Life Expectancy Calculator" developed by Dr. Thomas Perls and available at www.livingto100.com. Another interesting tool is the Vitality Compass™ on the bluezones.com website, which will give you an estimate of your biological age and life expectancy as well as information on how your personal habits and life choices might raise or lower your estimated longevity. You do not have to live in one of the "Blue Zones" or have super-centenarian genes to add years to your life.

---

a certain number of times—50 times, plus or minus 10—an estimate referred to as the Hayflick limit. Hayflick also demonstrated that cells taken from human adults divide even fewer times, presumably because they have already used up some of their capacity for reproducing themselves. Moreover, the maximum life span of a species is related to the Hayflick limit for that species: The long-lived Galapagos tortoise's cells can divide 90–125 times whereas the cells of the short-lived fruit fly can divide far less than this.

The mechanism behind the cellular aging clock suggested by Hayflick's limit on cell division has turned out to be telomeres—stretches of DNA that form the tips of chromosomes and that shorten with every cell division (see ■ Figure 5.9). This progressive shortening of telomeres eventually makes cells unable to replicate and causes them to malfunction and die. Thus telomere length is a yardstick of biological aging (see Mather, Jorm, Parslow, & Christensen, 2011).

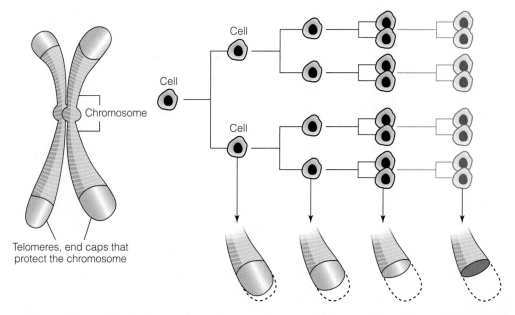

Telomeres, end caps that protect the chromosome

■ **Figure 5.9** As cells divide over time, telomeres shorten until, eventually, cells can no longer divide.

But what determines how fast telomeres shorten? Fascinating research is revealing that chronic stress, such as that involved in caring for an ill child or a parent with dementia, is linked to shorter than normal white-blood-cell telomeres, which in turn are associated with heightened risk for cardiovascular disease and death (Epel, 2009; Epel et al., 2004, 2006). Other research has found shortened telomeres among war veterans suffering from post-traumatic stress disorder (Jergović et al., 2014). Many of us believe that stress ages people; now there is concrete evidence that stress speeds cellular aging. Moreover, lack of exercise, smoking, obesity, and low socioeconomic status—all risk factors for age-related diseases—are also associated with short telomeres (Cherkas et al., 2006, 2008). According to programmed theories of aging, what might we do to extend life? It is possible that researchers might devise ways of manipulating genes to increase longevity or even the maximum life span (Arking, 2006). Life spans of 200–600 years are probably not possible, but some think researchers could raise the average age of death to around 112 years and enable 112-year-olds to function more like 78-year-olds (Miller, 2004). For example, researchers have established that the enzyme telomerase can be used to prevent the telomeres from shortening and thus keep cells replicating and working longer; telomerase treatments could backfire, however, if they also make cancerous cells multiply more rapidly (Wang, 2010; Wright & Shay, 2005).

Damage or Error Theories

In contrast to programmed theories of aging, damage or error theories generally propose that wear and tear—an accumulation of random damage to cells and organs over the years—ultimately causes death (Hayflick, 2004; 2007; Maynard et al., 2015). Like cars, we may have a limited warranty and simply give out after a certain number of years of use and abuse (Olshansky & Carnes, 2004). Early in life, DNA strands and cells replicate themselves faithfully; later in life this fidelity is lost and cells become increasingly damaged. Random error theorists believe that biological aging is about random damage rather than genetically programmed change.

According to one leading error theory, damage to cells that compromises their functioning is done by free radicals, which are toxic and chemically unstable by-products of metabolism, or the everyday chemical reactions in cells such as those involved in the breakdown of food (Maynard et al., 2015; Shringarpure & Davies, 2009). Free radicals are produced when oxygen reacts with certain molecules in the cells. They have an unpaired, or "free," electron and are highly reactive with and damaging to other molecules in the body, including DNA. Over time the genetic code contained in the DNA of more and more cells becomes scrambled, and the body's mechanisms for repairing such genetic damage simply cannot keep up with the chaos. More cells then function improperly or cease to function, and the organism eventually dies.

"Age spots" on the skin of older people are a visible sign of the damage free radicals can cause. Free radicals have also been implicated in some of the major diseases that become more common with age—most notably, cardiovascular diseases, cancer, and Alzheimer's disease (Maynard et al., 2015). Moreover, they are implicated in the aging of the brain (Poon et al., 2004). However, the damage of most concern is damage to DNA, because the result is more defective cells replicating themselves. Unfortunately, we cannot live and breathe without manufacturing free radicals.

Many researchers adopting an error perspective have focused on preventing the damage caused by free radicals. Antioxidants such as vitamins E and C (or foods high in them such as raisins, spinach, and blueberries) can donate one of their electrons to unstable free radicals, thereby neutralizing their damage to your body (see ■ **Figure 5.10**). At least when they are produced by the body or consumed in foods rather than taken in pill form, antioxidants may increase longevity, although not for long, by inhibiting free radical activity and in turn helping prevent

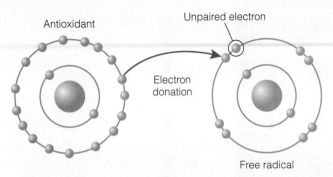

Antioxidant

Unpaired electron

Electron
donation

Free radical

■ **Figure 5.10** Free radicals have an unpaired electron, which can cause damage as these free radicals can indiscriminately absorb or steal electrons from other cells throughout the body. Antioxidants are molecules that can safely donate an electron to free radicals, thereby neutralizing their potential for damage.

age-related diseases (Meydani, 2001). One potential antioxidant receiving a great deal of interest is resveratrol, a natural substance in grapes, red wine, and peanuts (Ferro & DeSouza, 2011; Ungvari et al., 2011). More research is needed to fully understand how resveratrol works and the conditions under which it might be effective in ameliorating age-related damage.

One theory is that resveratrol's effects are similar to those that result from **caloric restriction**—a highly nutritious but severely restricted diet representing a 30–40% or more cut in normal total caloric intake (Anderson & Weindruch, 2012; Omodei & Fontana, 2011). Laboratory studies involving rats and primates suggest that caloric restriction extends both the average longevity and the maximum life span of a species and that it delays or slows the progression of many age-related diseases (Bodkin et al., 2003; Lane et al., 2001). By one estimate, a 40% reduction in daily calories results in a 40% decrease in body weight, a 40% increase in average longevity, and a 49% increase in the maximum life span of diet-restricted rats (Harman, 2001).

How does caloric restriction achieve these results? It clearly reduces the number of free radicals and other toxic products of metabolism. A restricted diet appears to alter gene activity and trigger the release of hormones that slow metabolism and protect cells against oxidative damage (Antebi, 2007; Arking, 2006). These changes help the half-starved organism hang on to life as long as possible. However, we do not know whether caloric restriction works as well for humans as it apparently has for rats, what calorie counts and combinations of nutrients are optimal, or whether humans who have a choice would put up with being half-starved for most of their lives. We do know that exceptionally long-lived people are rarely obese (Willcox et al., 2009).

Nature and Nurture Conspiring

The theories just described are some of the most promising explanations of why we age and die. Programmed theories of aging generally say that aging and dying are as much a part of nature's plan as sprouting teeth or uttering first words and may be the by-products of a genetic makeup that also contributed to early growth, development, and reproduction. Evidence for the genetic control of aging and dying comes from various sources: the maximum life span, the role of individual genetic makeup in longevity, the Hayflick limit on cell replication timed by telomeres, changes in the activity of certain genes as we age, and systematic changes in several bodily systems. By contrast, error theories of aging hold that we eventually succumb to haphazard destructive processes, such as those caused by free radicals—processes that result in increasingly faulty DNA and abnormal cell functioning and ultimately a breakdown in bodily functioning.

Neither of these broad theories of aging has proved to be *the* explanation; instead, many interacting mechanisms involving both aging processes and disease processes are at work (Arking, 2006; Knight, 2000). For example, genes influence the capacity of cells to repair environmentally caused damage, and the random damage caused by free radicals alters genetic material. John Medina (1996) put it this way: "Toxic waste products accumulate because genes shut off. Genes shut off because toxic waste products accumulate" (p. 291). In short, nature and nurture, biological and environmental factors, interact to bring about aging and dying—just as they interact to produce development.

Successful Aging

Aging is inevitable, so how can we do it successfully and what do we even mean by "successful" aging? To some, this may mean living a long life, without necessarily considering the *quality* of life. Others may focus on quality and associate successful aging with being free of diseases that limit physical and mental skills and the ability to actively participate in desired daily activities. In their scaffolding theory of aging and cognition, discussed earlier in this chapter, Reuter-Lorenz & Park (2014) note that successful aging is "simply the absence of age-related pathology" (p. 356). But most older people have at least some chronic disease or impairment, making it hard to know how an elderly person might function if he was disease-free. To explore this, James Birren and his colleagues (1963) conducted extensive medical examinations of men aged 65–91, which allowed them to identify two groups of elderly men: (1) those who were almost perfectly healthy and had no signs of disease and (2) those who had slight traces of some disease in the making but no clinically diagnosable diseases. Several aspects of physical and intellectual functioning were assessed in these men, and the participants were compared with young men.

The most remarkable finding was that the healthier group of older men hardly differed from the younger men. They were equal in their capacity for physical exercise, and they beat the younger men on measures of intelligence that required general information or knowledge of vocabulary words. Their main limitations were the slower brain activity and reaction times that seem to be so basic to the aging process. Overall, aging in the absence of disease had little effect on physical and psychological

Sister Esther, shown here at age 106, enjoys interacting with Nun Study researcher Dr. David Snowdon. What have we learned from the Nun Study?

Steve Liss//Time Life Pictures/Getty Images

as "girls, boys, and sick" that were used by nuns who later developed symptoms of Alzheimer's disease (Snowdon, 2002, p. 107). In particular, idea density, a measure of language-processing ability, measured in early adulthood predicted mental functioning in later adulthood. In addition, nuns whose autobiographies expressed more positive emotions lived longer than nuns whose autobiographies expressed fewer positive emotions.

The message to take away from such research is that both physical and mental activity, along with a positive attitude, can help slow the effects of aging on both the body and brain. Muscles atrophy if they are not used, and the heart functions less well if a person leads a sedentary life (Rosenbloom & Bahns, 2006). The brain also needs "mental exercise" to display plasticity and to continue to function effectively in old age (Black, Isaacs, & Greenough, 1991; Shors, 2014). So while we can't avoid the biological reality of aging, we can make choices across the life span that will increase the odds of living a long life and aging successfully. Clearly, then, our health and well-being are influenced by an interaction of environmental and genetic factors.

functioning. However, the men with slight traces of impending disease were deficient on several measures. Diseases that have progressed to the point of symptoms have even more serious consequences for performance.

In another extraordinary study, David Snowdon (2002) studied 678 nuns ranging in age from 75 to 106 years. Snowdon, an epidemiologist, chose to study the nuns because they were very similar with respect to socioeconomic status, housing, health care, and diet. In this remarkable longitudinal study, participants underwent annual mental and physical testing, provided complete access to a lifetime of health records, and agreed to donate their brains for examination following their deaths.

The first finding to emerge from the so-called Nun Study was that level of education affected longevity and health. Those with a college degree lived longer and were more likely to remain independent. The risk of death among the college-educated nuns was lower at every age. Another major finding was that the nuns who were active, both physically and mentally, lived longer and healthier than nuns who were not as active.

A unique aspect of the Nun Study was that each nun had written an autobiography prior to taking her vows (average age of 22 years) and, decades later, these autobiographies became part of the data analyzed for the study. This analysis revealed that older nuns who were healthy had used more complex vocabulary in their autobiographies decades earlier (on average, 60 years earlier). They used words such as "particularly, privileged, and quarantined" as opposed to simple words such

Checking Mastery

1. What physical changes, including those in the brain, can we expect as we age?
2. What is the major difference between a programmed theory of aging and an error theory of aging?
3. What have we learned about successful aging from the "Nun Study" and other research on centenarians?

Making Connections

1. Many (indeed, most) stereotypes of the physical aging process are negative and depressing. What in this chapter gives you reason to be more optimistic about aging, and why? Cite specific concepts and research findings.
2. Suppose you set as your goal reaching age 100 in superb physical condition. Describe and justify a plan for achieving your goal, then indicate why you might not make it despite your best efforts.

Chapter Summary

5.1 Building Blocks of Growth and Lifelong Health

- Growth is influenced by genes and environments, through the working of the endocrine and nervous systems. The nervous system consists of the brain, the spinal cord, and peripheral neurons. Endocrine glands such as the pituitary, thyroid, testes, and ovaries regulate behavior by secreting hormones directly into the bloodstream. The workings of the endocrine and nervous systems can be hindered or enhanced by environmental forces.
- Physical growth proceeds according to the cephalocaudal (head-to-tail), proximodistal (center outward), and orthogenetic (global and undifferentiated to differentiated and integrated) principles.
- Health is best viewed from a life-span developmental perspective emphasizing genes, personal choice, and environmental factors in interaction.

5.2 The Infant

- The infant's brain undergoes synaptogenesis (growth of synapses) as well as synaptic pruning (loss of unused synapses). It is capable of responding to experiences, both positive and negative.
- Infants come into the world equipped with reflexes and organized states that allow them to adapt to their environments.
- Congenital malformations and complications of preterm birth are the leading causes of infant mortality. Preventative medicine such as well-baby visits to the doctor and vaccinations can improve infant health.

5.3 The Child

- During childhood, neural transmission speeds up and lateralization of various brain functions, although present at birth, becomes more evident in behavior.
- There is steady and marked improvement in all aspects of physical growth over the childhood years.
- Physical activity is an important component of health during childhood. Children's health is also influenced by their parents' socioeconomic status and lifestyle choices.
- Health is enhanced with proper nutrition and regular physical activity. Current lifestyles have decreased physical activity and increased sedentary media time, resulting in increased weight among today's children.

5.4 The Adolescent

- During adolescence, the brain (especially the prefrontal cortex) continues to develop, permitting sustained attention and strategic planning. Brain changes may place adolescents at greater risk for making unsafe decisions.
- The adolescent period is marked by physical growth—the adolescent growth spurt—and attainment of puberty or sexual maturity. Girls experience their growth spurt at a younger age than do boys. The major milestone of sexual maturity for girls is menarche—their first menstruation. For boys, it is the less-noted experience of semenarche, or first ejaculation. A combination of genes, hormones, and environmental factors determine the timing and rate of growth and puberty.
- The physical changes of adolescence are significant and have psychological implications. Girls' experience is often on the negative side, whereas boys tend to report a more positive reaction to growth and puberty. Boys who mature early experience largely positive benefits, whereas late-maturing boys have a more negative experience. In contrast, girls who mature early are sometimes disadvantaged by teasing from their peers and the influence of the older peers with whom they often socialize. Late-maturing girls seem to benefit academically, possibly because they continue to spend more time on schoolwork than their early-maturing peers.
- Adolescents are a relatively healthy bunch, but the fitness level of some teens is poor because of a lack of physical activity and insufficient sleep.

5.5 The Adult

- The adult brain is capable of some degree of neurogenesis, or generating new neurons.
- The aging brain exhibits both degeneration and plasticity. Neurons atrophy and die, and blood flow to the brain decreases; but the aging brain forms new synapses to compensate for neural loss and reorganizes itself in response to learning experiences.
- Changes in health and physical functioning start to become evident during middle adulthood, and declines are noticeable in most older adults. There are large individual differences in physical functioning of older adults.
- For both sexes, changes in the reproductive system are a normal part of aging. Women experience menopause, a cessation of menstruation, and an end of child-bearing years. Men experience andropause, a more gradual change in their reproductive system. The experience of menopause is variable and a variety of treatments are available to alleviate the symptoms.
- Health and well-being during adulthood are influenced by genetic predispositions acting in concert with the environment and lifestyle choices. Exercise can enhance both physical and mental functioning. Common diseases among older adults include osteoporosis, which leads to fragile bones, and osteoarthritis, or joint inflammation.
- Two theories of aging and death include those that emphasize the genetic control of aging—the programmed theories—and those that emphasize haphazard loss—the damage or error theories.
- Physical and mental activity, as well as a positive attitude, improve the odds of successful aging.

Key Terms

6 Sensation, Perception, and Action

When asked to speculate on which of their senses would be most problematic to lose, many students say vision or hearing, as these senses seem to take center stage in so many daily activities. Some believe losing their visual sense would be a devastating loss as they would need to give up such activities as driving, a major source of independence. Others, though, conclude that losing their auditory sense would be most challenging, perhaps because many aspects of social relationships hinge on hearing what others have to say. A survey of adults conducted by www.healthyhearing.com found that most ranked the ability to see as the most valuable sense, followed by the ability to hear. About one in four adults ranked the ability to touch as most valuable, but only one in ten voted for the ability to smell or to taste. Which sense do you believe is the most valuable? After you have read this chapter, consider this question once again because your thoughts might shift after you learn about the remarkable contributions of all the senses to the quality of our lives.

In this chapter, we examine how our senses provide us with the building blocks for understanding the world around us. We discuss the tremendous flood of sensations bombarding the infant and how infants come to "make sense" of this information. We trace major changes in sensation and perception through childhood, adolescence, and early adulthood, and then look at some of the inevitable declines that occur in middle and later adulthood. We also examine how perception is coupled with action in a *synergistic* fashion. As you changed from a largely immobile infant to an on-the-move toddler, for example, you coupled your burgeoning perceptual skills with advances in your nervous system and your body's growing physical capabilities to engage in goal-oriented actions. Finally, we look at the important role that attention plays in our awareness of the world around us and why some information is noticed and other information seems to drop off our "radar screens."

What do we mean by these terms *sensation, perception,* and *action?* Psychologists have long distinguished between sensation and perception. Sensation is the process by which sensory receptor neurons detect information and transmit it to the brain. From birth, infants sense their environment. They detect light, sound, odor-bearing molecules in the air, and other stimuli. But do they *understand* the patterns of stimulation coming in from the various sense organs? This is where perception, or the interpretation of sensory input, comes into play: recognizing what you see, understanding what is said to you, knowing that the odor you have detected is a sizzling steak, and so on. But let's be clear about something: The sense organs are not passive receptacles that detect and merely pass along information to the brain. Your eyes, nose, tongue, ears, and skin actually help shape the brain (see, for example, Schreuder, 2014). Sensation and perception are at the heart of human functioning. *Everything you do—all of your physical and mental actions—depends on your ability to sense and perceive the world around you.* To begin our journey, we consider perspectives on how we perceive the world and gain knowledge of reality, exploring again the nature–nurture issue.

6.1

Perspectives on Perception

LEARNING OBJECTIVES

- Distinguish between the nativist and constructivist positions on perception.

- Summarize Gibson's ecological approach to perception and how it differs from approaches that are primarily constructivist or nativist.

Does the ability to perceive the world around us depend solely on innate biological factors, or is this ability acquired through experience and learning? Constructivists, including Jean Piaget who was introduced in Chapter 2 and will be further discussed in Chapter 7, come down on the side of nurture (Johnson & Hannon, 2015). They argue that perceptions of the world are constructed over time through learning. Yes, we come equipped at birth with functioning sensory systems, but understanding the input coming in through our senses requires interacting with the environment and figuring out what those sensations mean (Johnson & Hannon, 2015). For instance, the retinal image of an object located 50 feet from an observer is different from the retinal image of the same object located just 10 feet from the observer. According to the constructivists, we need experience with viewing objects at various distances to learn how to interpret the different retinal images that they project. With experience, we create an association between the retinal image (for example, small) and its meaning (for example, distant object).

Although the constructivist view of perception has long been very popular, more sophisticated methods of assessing infants' capabilities have yielded new findings about their perceptual abilities. This includes evidence of object understanding at a very early age (see Johnson & Hannon, 2015). As a result, some researchers have shifted toward a more nativist perspective on the origins of some aspects of perception. The nativists argue that perception is *not* created by interpreting external input; instead, innate capabilities and maturational programs are the driving forces in perceptual development. Infants come equipped with basic sensory capabilities, which are further refined according to an innate plan. Nativists would argue that the infant does not need experience to learn how to interpret different retinal images cast by the same object at different distances. The brain automatically understands the meaning of different retinal images created as we move about our world (for example, a small image is automatically "read" by the brain as distant object). Thus, from the nativist perspective, perception is direct—it does not require interpretation based on previous experience (Johnson & Hannon, 2015).

Falling somewhere in the middle of the nurture-based constructivists and the nature-focused nativists is Gibson's ecological theory of perception developed by Eleanor Gibson (2001) and her husband James Gibson (1966, 1979). In Chapter 2, we introduced Bronfenbrenner's ecological (later, bioecological) theory that described how the environment is organized and affects development. Similarly, Gibson's ecological approach also considers the organization of the environment. In particular, Gibson's theory proposes that information important for perception is readily and directly available in the environment: in the to-be-perceived objects. As we move around in our world, our position relative to all other objects in the environment is constantly changing and altering the flow of information and the images projected to our retina. For example, suppose we look at a round object that gradually projects a larger image on our retina; how do we know what this is and how we might interact with it? The constructivists might say that we need to take all the pieces of information coming in from our senses and construct an understanding of what this object is and what it can do. It may take multiple interactions with the object before we put together all the pieces of the puzzle and learn its properties and figure out that a ball is moving toward us. In contrast, the ecological approach argues that we do not

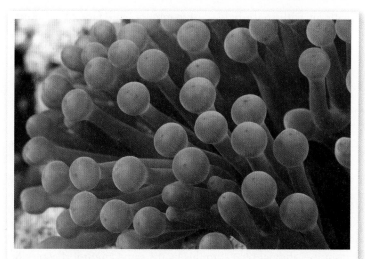

What do you see when you look at this object? According to the constructivist theory of perception, you use past experiences to construct an understanding of what this object might be.

Steve Rosenberg/Getty Images

needed to interpret the current perceptual situation, whereas the Gibson ecologists would say that all the information needed to interpret the current perceptual situation is available in the current situation.

Note that what an object or the environment affords depends on each individual's capabilities, including their genetic predispositions and current goals and motivations (Miller, 2016). A pencil may offer an 8-year-old the possibility of writing something on a piece of paper because the 8-year-old has the capacity to write and therefore perceives this affordance of this object. For a 12-month-old infant who has not yet developed this capability, the pencil may afford something quite different, such as a stick for poking or something else to chew. Thus, Gibson ecologists view nature and nurture as inseparable (Miller, 2016).

In this chapter, we will use the constructivist, nativist, and ecological perspectives to help us gain a better understanding of perception and action across the life span. As we begin our journey in infancy, we will look closely at sensation and perception because most fundamental capacities emerge and quickly develop during the first months of life. Later, you will see how much more "intelligent" perceptual abilities become during childhood and adolescence and will question the image of old age as a time of little more than sensory and perceptual decline.

need to construct how we might interact with this object. Instead, features of the object directly reveal its affordances: what it has to offer us and how it might be used by us. Thus, as the round object moves toward us, the pattern of light reaching our eyes provides all the information we need to know what this object *affords*: the prospect of getting hit in the face if we do not take some action.

In the ecological view, perception drives action. Perception provides us with valuable information about what objects in the environment afford, or can offer us: surfaces to sit on, pots and pans that can serve as musical instruments, sticks that can poke things, and so on. As James Gibson (1979) noted, "we must perceive in order to move, but we must also move in order to perceive" (p. 223). This is an important difference between how the Gibson ecologists and the constructivists view the role of the environment and past experience: The constructivists would argue that past learning experiences are

Checking Mastery

1. How is perception different from sensation?
2. What is the difference between how constructivists and nativists view sensation and perception?
3. In what way is Gibson's ecological theory of perception distinct from the constructivist and the nativist views of perception?

Making Connections

1. How could you demonstrate that perception of an object's distance is innate rather than constructed through experience?

6.2
The Infant

LEARNING OBJECTIVES

- Describe the changes in visual capabilities from birth through the first year, and note the visual preferences exhibited by infants.

- Explain how infants come to "make sense" of the visual world.

- Outline the auditory capabilities of the pre- and early postnatal period, including a description of how researchers evaluate these capabilities.

- Summarize the infant's chemical senses as well as the functioning of their somaesthetic senses.

- Explain the early experiences needed for development of normal perceptual skills and the influence of early experience on the brain.

The pioneering American psychologist William James (1890) claimed that sights, sounds, and other sensory inputs formed a "blooming, buzzing confusion" to the young infant. James was actually noting that impressions from the several senses are fused rather than separable, but his statement has since been quoted to represent the view that the world of the young infant is hopelessly confusing.

Today the accepted view is that young infants have far greater perceptual abilities than anyone suspected. Their senses are functioning even before birth, and in the first few months of life they show many signs that they are perceiving a coherent rather than a chaotic world. Why the change in views? It is not that babies have become smarter. It is that researchers have become smarter. They have developed more sophisticated methods of studying what infants can and cannot do. Infants, after all, cannot tell researchers directly what they perceive, so the trick has been to develop ways to let their behavior speak for them. The main methods used to study infant perception are summarized in ● Table 6.1 and include habituation, preferential looking, evoked potentials, and operant conditioning techniques. These techniques have revealed a good deal about what infants perceive and what they do not, as you will now see.

Vision

As noted in the chapter opener, many of us tend to think of vision as our most indispensable sense. Because vision is indeed important, we examine its early development in some detail before turning to the other major senses.

Basic Capacities

How does something as complicated as vision work? The eye functions by taking in stimulation in the form of light and converting it to electrochemical signals to the brain. Even before birth, the fetus responds to bright lights it detects from the outside world, such as a flashlight directed at the mother's belly (see Johnson & Hannon, 2015). And after birth, the newborn can visually track a slow-moving picture or object. Failure to follow an object when the object is presented within normal viewing range is often an early indicator of a visual problem. Even among sighted newborns, though, visual capabilities are lacking compared with those of a child or an adult. At birth, newborns' visual acuity, or the ability to perceive detail, is 40 times worse than an adult's, but improves across the first month of life to roughly the equivalent of 20/120 vision on the standard eye chart—being able to see only the big E at the top of the chart (Hamer, 2016). Objects are blurry to young infants unless they are within about 12 inches (30 cm) from the face or are bold

patterns with sharp light–dark contrasts—the face of a parent, for example. The young infant's world is also blurred because of limitations in visual accommodation—the ability of the lens of the eye to change shape to bring objects at different distances into focus. It is likely to take 6 months to 1 year before the infant can see as well as an adult (Hofsten et al., 2014).

To some extent, very young infants also see the world in color, not in black and white as some early observers thought (Zemach, Chang, & Teller, 2006). How do researchers know this? Suppose they accustom an infant to a blue disk using the habituation technique described in ● Table 6.1. What will happen if they then present either a blue disk of a different shade or a green disk? Infants 4 months old will show little interest in a disk of a different blue but will be attentive to a green disk—even when the light reflected from these two stimuli differs in wavelength from the original blue stimulus by the same amount (Peeples & Teller, 1975). Thus, 4-month-olds appear to discriminate colors and categorize portions of the continuum of wavelengths of light

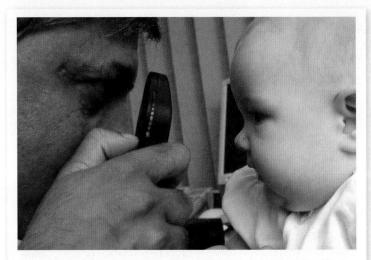

A physician checks a young infant's vision. What is this infant likely to be able to see?

UniversalImagesGroup/Getty Images

● **Table 6.1** Methods for Assessing Infant Perception

Habituation	The same stimulus is repeatedly presented until the infant grows bored with what has become familiar and disengages (e.g., looks away). Researchers can measure how long (e.g., how many trials) until an infant becomes bored. They can also measure how distinct a second, new stimulus needs to be in order to recapture the infant's attention.
Preferential looking	Two stimuli are simultaneously shown to an infant to determine which one they prefer, which is inferred to be the one they look at longer. Adding head-mounted, eye-tracking cameras has allowed researchers to more precisely measure preferential looking.
Evoked potentials	Electrical activity in different parts of the brain is measured while the infant watches, listens to, or is otherwise exposed to stimulation. Electrodes are attached to the surface of the skull and a computer records the pattern of electrical activity corresponding to various stimuli.
Operant conditioning	Infants are conditioned to reliably respond a certain way to a certain stimulus (e.g., they are rewarded for turning their head every time they hear a sound). Once this response is well-established, the researcher can examine the conditions under which the infants will, or will not, continue to produce the behavior. Presumably, continued head turning suggests that infants do not detect a noticeable difference between the original and new stimuli, whereas lack of the conditioned response is evidence that they *do* distinguish between the two stimuli.

into the same basic color categories (red, blue, green, and yellow) that adults do. Color vision is present at birth, but newborns cannot discriminate some color differences well because their receptors are not yet mature. By 3 months, however, color vision seems comparable to that of an adult (Adams, 1987; Zemach et al., 2007). Like adults, 4-month-old infants can detect a colored stimulus on a background that is a different shade of the same color (Franklin, Pilling, & Davies, 2005). However, also like adults, they are *faster* at detecting the stimulus on a background of a different color.

In short, the eyes of the young infant are not working at peak levels, but they are working. As one researcher (Hainline, 1998) summarizes it: Infants are able to see what they need to see, a conclusion consistent with Gibson's ecological approach. Even newborns can perceive light and dark, focus on nearby objects, distinguish colors, and see simple patterns. But does all this visual stimulation make any sense?

Organizing the World of Objects

Alan Slater and his colleagues (2010b) note that, above all else, perception is organized. In what ways do infants organize their perceptions? One of the first challenges for the infant is to separate the visual field into distinct objects, even when parts of objects are hidden behind other objects or are adjacent to one another. In other words, where does one object end and another object begin? From an early age, infants show remarkable abilities to organize and impose order on visual scenes in much the same way that adults do. Research suggests an important breakthrough in **form perception**, or recognition of the patterns that constitute an object, starting around 3 months (Courage, Reynolds, & Richards, 2006). One-month-olds focus on the outer contours of forms such as faces, as if they are finding the boundaries of the object; see ■ **Figure 6.1** (Johnson & de Haan, 2015).

But starting around 2 months, infants no longer focus on some external boundary or contour; instead, they explore the interiors of figures thoroughly (for example, looking at a person's eyes rather than just at the chin, hairline, and top of the head). It is as though they are no longer content to locate where an object starts and where it ends, as 1-month-olds tend to do; they seem to want to know what it is. During this time, infants also become better at shifting their attention or disengaging from a stimulus. Initially, their gaze seems to become "stuck" on the fixated object, and they have difficulty shifting it to another object (Johnson & de Haan, 2015). As you might imagine, this difficulty with shifting gaze limits what young infants can take in from their environment.

How exactly do infants determine where one object ends and another begins? Elizabeth Spelke and her colleagues (Kellman & Spelke, 1983; Spelke, 1990) have concluded that young infants are sensitive to several cues about the wholeness of objects, especially cues available when an object moves. For example, 4-month-olds seem to expect all parts of an object to move in the same direction at the same time, and they therefore use *common motion* as an important cue in determining what is or is not part of the same object (Kellman & Spelke, 1983). It takes infants longer, until about 6 months of age, to determine the boundaries or edges of *stationary* objects (Gibson & Pick, 2000). Thus, babies

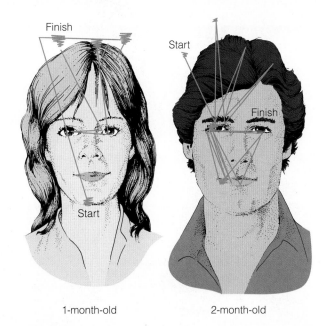

Visual scanning of the human face by 1- and 2-month-old infants

■ **Figure 6.1** Visual scanning by young infants. The 1-month-old spends more time at the edges of the face, as if trying to figure out where it begins and ends. The 2-month-old spends more time exploring the interior features of the face.
Source: Adapted from Salapatek, 1975.

appear to have an innate ability to organize a visual scene into distinct objects, and they are better able to make sense of a world in motion—a world like the one they live in—than to make sense of a stationary world.

It's clear that infants try to impose order on the complex world of objects. In doing so, they demonstrate preferences for certain patterns over others. What are the properties of patterns that capture the young infant's attention?

- Young infants pay attention to patterns that have a large amount of light–dark transition, or **contour**; they are responsive to sharp boundaries between light and dark areas (Banks & Shannon, 1993; Farroni et al., 2005). The soft pastel colors often presented to young infants may not have enough contrast to be detected by them (Brown & Lindsey, 2009).
- Infants are interested in displays that are dynamic (as opposed to static) or contain *movement* (Courage et al., 2006; Kavsek & Yonas, 2006). Newborns can and do track a moving target with their eyes, although their tracking at first is imprecise and likely to falter unless the target is moving slowly (Slater et al., 2010b).
- Young infants seem to be attracted to patterns that are *moderately complex*: not too simple, which would be boring, and not too complex, which would be overwhelming. Thus, they prefer a clear pattern (for example, a bold checkerboard pattern) to either a blank stimulus or an elaborate one such as a page from the *New York Times* (Fantz & Fagan, 1975). As infants mature, they prefer more complex stimuli.

This young infant is attracted to the mobile's well-defined contours (or light–dark contrasts) and bold patterns, which are neither too simple nor too complex.

Ruth Jenkinson/Getty Images

To recap, researchers know that infants younger than 2 months have visual preferences, and they also know something about the physical properties of stimuli that attract infants' attention. Martin Banks and his colleagues have offered a simple explanation for these early visual preferences: *Young infants prefer to look at whatever they can see well* (Banks & Ginsburg, 1985). Because the young infant's eye is small and its neural receptors are immature, it has poor visual acuity and sees a highly complex visual display as a big, dark blob. However, the pattern in a moderately complex display can be seen. Less-than-perfect vision would therefore explain why young infants prefer moderate complexity to high complexity. Indeed, limited vision can account for several of the infant's visual preferences. Young infants seem to actively seek the visual input they can see well—input that will stimulate the development of the visual centers of their brains (Banks & Shannon, 1993; Hainline, 1998).

Face Perception

One special pattern that has garnered much attention from researchers is the human face. Detecting faces from nonfaces and discriminating familiar from nonfamiliar faces are critical skills in successfully navigating the social world. Imagine the possible

consequences, for example, if an infant was unable to detect the difference between a face and a balloon, or was unable to identify his mother's face from among the many faces that appear in his visual field each day.

Soon after birth, young infants prefer to look at schematic drawings of faces rather than other patterned stimuli, and faces elicit more visual tracking by young infants than other targets (Gamé, Carchon, & Vital-Durand, 2003). Newborns can distinguish a human face from a monkey face, although they don't show a preference for the human face (Di Giorgio et al., 2012). They can also distinguish their mother's face from that of a stranger's, at least in static and simplified displays (for example, Bushnell, 2001). Such findings seem to suggest an inborn tendency to discriminate faces from nonfaces. More challenging is being able to discriminate among faces in real settings, where the faces are dynamic (moving) and embedded in an ever-changing environment. Lorraine Bahrick and her colleagues (for example, Bahrick, Gogate, & Ruiz, 2002; Bahrick & Newell, 2008) presented 5-month-olds with displays of women's faces as the women engaged in such tasks as brushing their teeth and blowing bubbles. Weeks later, they tested the infants for recognition of the action as well as the faces. The infants remembered the actions but did not remember or discriminate among the faces until the researchers either increased the infant's exposure time to the faces or removed the action and made the faces static. Bahrick, Lickliter, and Castellanos (2013) conclude that "actions are more salient than faces" (p. 2). Infants do not yet have sufficient attention resources: They can attend to the action or to the face, but not to both, and the action is more salient to their young attentional system.

Much remains to be learned about early perception of faces, including whether this is an innate ability or something that emerges only after having some experience looking at faces. Some scholars believe there is an innate preference for faces. But as we have learned, infants prefer contour, movement, and moderate complexity. Human faces have all of these physical properties. In addition, research shows that newborns have a preference for patterns that have more information in their upper visual field—that is, patterns that are "top heavy" (Cassia, Turati, & Simion, 2004; Cassia et al., 2006; Turati, 2004). Again, faces fit the bill: They are top heavy. Thus, what appears to be a preference for faces may be a preference for the features that happen to be connected with faces.

Nonetheless, we can conclude that infants truly perceive a meaningful face, not merely an appealing pattern, by 2–3 months of age. At this time, infants smile when they see faces as though they recognize them as familiar and appreciate their significance. So it goes with form perception more generally: As infants gain experience with different objects, their attention is drawn to certain objects not only because they have certain physical properties, but also because their forms are recognized as familiar. With experience comes greater expertise. One final note about face perception: Although infants "have" face recognition, there are further refinements in both the accuracy and speed of face recognition throughout childhood (de Heering, Rossion, & Maurer, 2012).

Depth Perception

Another very important aspect of visual perception involves perceiving depth and knowing when objects are near or far. Although it can take years to learn to judge the size of objects in the distance, very

Is face perception innate or does it emerge with experience? This infant is likely attracted to what features of his mother's face?

Ashley Gill/Alamy Stock Photo

young infants have some intriguing abilities to interpret spatial cues involving nearby objects. For example, they react defensively when objects move toward their faces; blinking in response to looming objects first appears around 1 month and becomes more consistent over the next few months (Kayed & van der Meer, 2007; Nanez & Yonas, 1994). By 4 months of age, infants demonstrate understanding of **size constancy**: They recognize that an object is of the same size despite changes in its distance from the eyes, which would project different images on the retina. Carl Granrud (2006) came to this conclusion using the habituation technique. Infants were initially habituated to either a small- or a medium-sized disk presented at different distances. They were then tested to see whether they preferred to look at a disk that was the same physical size but cast a different retinal image or one that was a different (that is, novel) physical size but cast the same retinal image. Keep in mind that once habituated to a stimulus, infants are bored with it and no longer attend to it. To recapture their attention, they need to be presented with a new stimulus that they can recognize as different from the original. Granrud found that the infants responded on the basis of actual object size, not size of the retinal image cast by the object. They preferred to look at the disk that was a novel physical size even though it cast the same retinal image as during the habituation phase. This indicates that infants recognize the size of an object even when the object is presented at different distances and thus produces different images on the retina.

Does this evidence of early spatial perception mean that infants who have begun to crawl know enough about space to avoid crawling off the edges of beds or staircases? The first attempt to examine depth perception in infants was carried out in classic research by Eleanor Gibson and Richard Walk (1960) using an apparatus called the **visual cliff**. This cliff consists of an elevated glass platform divided into two sections by a center board. On the "shallow" side a checkerboard pattern is placed directly under the glass. On the "deep" side the pattern is several feet below the glass, creating the illusion of a drop-off or "cliff." Infants are placed on the center board and coaxed by their mothers to cross both the

shallow and the deep sides. Testing infants 6½ months of age and older, Gibson and Walk found that 27 of 36 infants would cross the shallow side to reach Mom, but only 3 of 36 would cross the deep side. Most infants of crawling age (typically 7 months or older) clearly perceive depth and are afraid of drop-offs.

The testing procedure used by Gibson and Walk depended on the ability of infants to crawl. Would younger infants who cannot yet crawl be able to perceive a drop-off? Joseph Campos and his colleagues (Campos, Langer, & Krowitz, 1970) found that when they slowly lowered babies over the shallow and deep sides of the visual cliff, babies as young as 2 months had a slower heart rate on the deep side than on the shallow side. Why slower? When we are afraid, our hearts beat faster, not slower. A slow heart rate is a sign of interest. So, researchers concluded that 2-month-old infants *perceive a difference* between the deep and the shallow sides of the visual cliff, but they have not yet learned to *fear* drop-offs.

But do infants really avoid drop-offs out of fear? Perhaps not. Karen Adolph and her colleagues (2014) point out several flaws with this conclusion, including the rather circular logic that infants avoid the cliff out of fear and we 'know' they are afraid because they avoid the cliff. Further, Adolph points out that these allegedly fearful infants spend time exploring the edge of the cliff, often with no visible signs of distress such as crying. Rather than being a product of fear, avoidance of drop-offs appears to be learned through crawling—and falling now and then, or at least coming close to it (Campos, Bertenthal, & Kermoian, 1992). Some beginning crawlers will shuffle right off the ends of beds or the tops of stairwells if they are not watched carefully. However, avoidance of drop-offs is stronger in infants who have logged a few weeks of crawling than in infants of the same age who do not yet crawl. Alas, infants who have learned the lesson that crawling over drop-offs is risky do not transfer the lesson to similarly risky situations they encounter once they begin walking. They must again learn what they can and cannot do when faced with, for example, a stair step or an open space in the floor that a foot could fall through (Adolph, Berger, & Leo, 2011; Kretch & Adolph, 2013).

Infants' behavior around drop-offs is consistent with Gibson's theory of affordances, described in the previous section. Features of a cliff provide infants with the necessary information to know how to interact (or not interact) with the cliff. Infants who have some experience with drop-offs, slopes, and the like will have gleaned more information about whether they can safely cross and whether they need to make any adjustments, such as crouching or adjusting their gait, to do so (Adolph, Kretch, & LoBue, 2014).

The Infant as an Intuitive Theorist

The infant's visual perceptual abilities are impressive. But that's not all that is remarkable about the infant's growing perception and knowledge of the world. Researchers have been exploring infants' understandings of the physical laws that govern objects. For example, Elizabeth Spelke and her colleagues have been testing infants to determine what they know of Newtonian physics and the basic laws of object motion (Spelke & Hermer, 1996). Do babies know that a falling object will move downward along a continuous path until it encounters an obstruction? Spelke's studies suggest that infants only 4 months of age seem surprised when a

An infant on the edge of a visual cliff, being encouraged to cross the "deep" side.

Mark Richards/PhotoEdit

ball dropped behind a screen is later revealed below a shelf rather than resting on it. They look longer at this "impossible" event than at the comparison event in which the ball's motion stops when it reaches a barrier. By 6 months, infants also seem surprised when a ball drops behind a screen and then, when the screen is lifted, appears to be suspended in midair rather than lying at the bottom of the display unit (Kim & Spelke, 1992; Spelke et al., 1992). This hints that they know something about the laws of gravity.

Do infants understand any other simple principles of physics? Yes; 4-month-olds watching a moving object disappear behind the left side of a screen seem to expect to see the object reappear from the right side of the screen (Bremner et al., 2005). And 4-month-olds are also surprised when a wide object disappears into a narrow container (Wang, Baillargeon, & Brueckner, 2004).

Such findings have led some developmentalists to conclude that young infants do more than just sense the world—they come equipped with organized systems of knowledge, called intuitive theories, which allow them to make sense of the world (Gelman, 1996; Wellman & Gelman, 1992). From an early age, children distinguish between the domains of knowledge adults know as physics, biology, and psychology. They organize their knowledge in each domain around causal principles and seem to understand that different causal forces operate in different domains (for example, that desires influence the behavior of humans but not of rocks). According to this intuitive theories perspective, young infants have innate knowledge of the world, and they perceive and even reason about it much as adults do. Coming to know the physical world is then a matter of fleshing-out understandings they have had all along rather than constructing entirely new ones as they get older (Spelke, 1994). All in all, it is clear that young infants know a good deal more about the world around them than anyone imagined, although they learn more every year.

Hearing

Hearing is at least as important to us as vision, especially because we depend on it to communicate with others through spoken language. As Anne Fernald (2001) notes, "while vision may be primary in enabling infants to learn about the physical world, audition plays a powerful role in initiating infants into a social world" (p. 37).

The process of hearing begins when moving air molecules enter the ear and vibrate the eardrum. These vibrations are transmitted to the cochlea in the inner ear and are converted to signals that the brain interprets as sounds (see ■ Figure 6.2).

Basic Capacities

Newborns can hear well—better than they can see. They can also localize sounds: They are startled by loud noises and will turn from them, but they will turn toward softer sounds (see Burnham & Mattock, 2010). Even fetuses can hear some of what is going on in the world outside the womb as early as the fourth month of pregnancy. Researchers have detected changes in fetal heart rates that correspond to changes in sounds they are exposed to while in their mother's womb (Fifer, Monk, & Grose-Fifer, 2004; Saffran, Werker, & Werner, 2006).

But, wait, there's even more: Fetuses exposed to music in the womb show behaviors that seem to suggest they are trying to sing and dance along! Researchers in Barcelona, Spain, used ultrasound to observe fetal activity as the fetuses were exposed to music from a 'Babypod,' a device inserted into the mother's vagina (López-Teijón, García-Faura, & Prats-Galino, 2015). When the

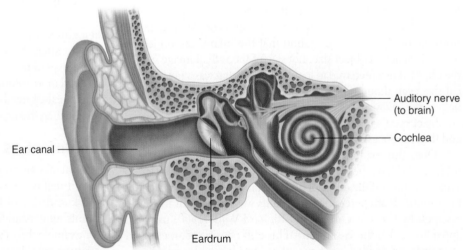

■ **Figure 6.2** Sound waves enter the outer ear and are transmitted through the middle ear to the cochlea in the inner ear.

music was played, fetuses showed increased head and limb movements as well as more mouth and tongue movements. When the music stopped, these movements decreased. Not everyone is impressed with the caliber of the research involving the Babypod (the lead researcher, for example, is also involved in marketing the product for profit), but other research has shown that prenatal exposure to music has a lasting effect on brain activity. Eino Partanen and his colleagues (2013) had mothers-to-be play 'Twinkle, twinkle, little star' repeatedly during the last trimester of their pregnancies. At birth and again at 4 months of age, the infants exposed prenatally to the music, as well as a control group of infants who had not been exposed to the music, were tested to see whether there were any differences in the brain activity of the two groups. Indeed, there were. The infants who had been exposed to the music showed greater response, as measured by the brain's electrical activity, than nonexposed infants, and the responses varied with how often they had been exposed to the tune in the womb. Thus, not only is the auditory system operational prior to birth, but prenatal auditory experiences can shape the neural architecture of the brain.

Under typical conditions, the environment of the womb exposes fetuses to low-frequency sounds, which can be a stark contrast to the high-frequency sounds of the postnatal environment. This may be especially problematic for premature babies whose auditory systems are not as fully developed as those of full-term infants (Graven & Browne, 2008). Researchers are beginning to examine whether this assault on the developing auditory system might place premature infants at risk for later attention, hearing, or language problems (Lahav & Skoe, 2014; McMahon, Wintermark, & Lahav, 2012). Interestingly, preterm infants who are exposed to 'womb-like' sounds (e.g., maternal voice, heartbeat, and intestinal gurgles) in the neonatal intensive care unit (NICU)

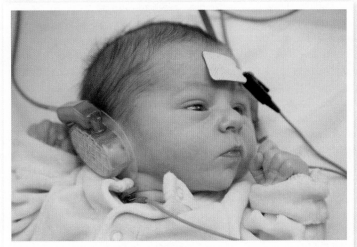

Identifying hearing problems as early as possible allows caregivers to provide early intervention and ensure that development proceeds along a typical path.

BSIP/Getty Images

develop a larger auditory cortex than preterm infants who listen to the standard sounds of the NICU (Webb, Heller, Benson, & Lahav, 2015). This is further evidence that the environment of the womb provides the ideal conditions for development. But what if fetuses or infants have hearing problems? This would place them at risk for later language and communication problems. **Application 6.1** examines the importance of early identification and treatment of hearing problems.

Speech Perception

Young infants seem to be especially responsive to human speech and show a preference for speech over nonspeech sounds (Vouloumanos & Werker, 2007). In many ways, it seems as though the human brain was designed to produce and understand language (Fernald, 2009). We can discriminate basic speech sounds—called phonemes—very early in life. Peter Eimas (1975b, 1985) pioneered research in this area by demonstrating that infants 2–3 months old could discriminate between similar consonant sounds (for example, *ba* and *pa*). And newborns just hours old, recognize vowel sounds from their native language that they were exposed to in the womb. Researchers determined this by measuring how much newborns sucked on a special pacifier when exposed to a variety of vowel sounds from their native language as well as those from a nonnative language that they would not have been exposed to in the womb. The difference in their sucking rates showed that these newborns could discriminate between the native and nonnative sounds. Such results demonstrate that infants are not a blank slate at birth: They have already been learning in their prenatal environments (Moon, Lagercrantz, & Kuhl, 2013).

Infants can actually make some speech sound discriminations better than adults (Kuhl et al., 2014). They begin life biologically prepared to learn any language humans anywhere speak. As they mature, they become especially sensitive to the sound differences significant in their own language and less sensitive to sound differences irrelevant to that language. Patricia Kuhl and her colleagues (2014) demonstrated this with their research measuring brain activity in response to various linguistic sounds. They found that, at 7 months of age, there was no difference in brain activity in response to sounds from infants' native language versus sounds from a nonnative language. By 11–12 months of age, though, the brain response was greater for native language sounds than for nonnative sounds. Again, this is evidence that early auditory experiences can shape the formation of neural connections, or synapses, in the auditory areas of infants' brains so that they are optimally sensitive to the sound contrasts that they have been listening to and that are important in the language they are acquiring (see Chapter 10). In short, experience shapes the brain.

Newborns are especially attentive to female voices (Ecklund-Flores & Turkewitz, 1996), but can they recognize their mother's voice? Indeed they can. Even unborn fetuses can distinguish their mother's voice from a stranger's voice. How do we know this? Canadian researchers measured fetal heart rate in response to a tape recording (played over the mother's stomach) of either

Aiding Infants and Children with Hearing Impairments

Although sensory impairments have the potential to derail normal development, much can be done to help even those individuals who are born totally deaf or blind develop in positive directions and function effectively in everyday life. Here, we examine interventions for infants and children who have hearing impairments; in a later box, we examine interventions for hearing loss at the other end of the age spectrum.

For the 2 to 3 in 1,000 infants born deaf or hearing impaired, early identification and treatment are essential if they are to master spoken language. We know that children who receive no special intervention before age 2 usually have lasting difficulties with speech and language (for example, Vohr et al., 2011). As a result, most states have now mandated that all newborns be screened for hearing loss before they leave the hospital. How do you test the hearing of newborns? By using auditory **evoked potentials** (refer to **Table 6.1**) doctors can determine whether sounds trigger normal activity in the brain. Infants' behaviors also give physicians clues about their hearing. Does she turn her head when spoken to? Does he react to loud noises? Is she soothed by your voice? If the answers to these questions are no, a more thorough examination is warranted.

Once hearing-impaired infants are identified, interventions can be planned. Many programs attempt to capitalize on whatever residual hearing these children have by equipping them with hearing aids and providing them with an enriched language environment. Children whose hearing loss is identified soon after birth and who are raised in an environment that exposes them to a rich array of language opportunities develop better language skills than children raised without as rich a linguistic environment (Vohr et al., 2014).

Today, even profoundly deaf children can be helped to hear through an advanced amplification device called the **cochlear implant** (see the photo in this box). The device is implanted in the inner ear through surgery and connected to a microphone worn outside the ear. It works by bypassing damaged hair cells (sensory receptors located in the inner ear) and directly stimulating the auditory nerve with electrical impulses. The younger children are when they

John Robertson/Barcroft Media/Getty Images

receive the implant, the better the outcome. For example, deaf children who received implants in their first year of life perform better on a variety of vocabulary and speech measures compared to those who received implants in their second or third years (Colletti et al., 2011). In addition, speech production and speech perception are improved in deaf children who have cochlear implants compared with deaf children who have traditional hearing aids, with language development of those with the implants nearly equivalent to that of children with normal hearing (Levine et al., 2016). Children with two cochlear implants—one in each ear—show additional benefits, particularly for localizing sounds (Godar, Grieco, & Litovsky, 2007). For some, cochlear implants have truly opened up new opportunities that were not thought possible before the implant (see, for example, Denworth, 2006; Mishori, 2006).

Close to 80% of congenitally deaf infants and preschoolers now undergo surgery for cochlear implants. But despite their benefits, cochlear implants do not have the full support of the deaf community (see, for example, Humphries et al., 2014; Napoli et al., 2015). Deaf children who use them, some say, will be given the message that they should be ashamed of being deaf. They will be

deprived of participation in the unique culture that has developed in communities of deaf people who share a common language and identity. They may feel that they do not belong to either the deaf or the hearing world, because their hearing will still be far from normal.

The correct amplification device and auditory training have proven effective in improving the ability of hearing-impaired infants and preschoolers to hear speech and learn to speak. Yet for other deaf and severely hearing-impaired children, the most important thing may be early exposure to sign language. Early intervention programs for parents of deaf infants can teach them strategies for getting their infants' attention and involving them in conversations using sign language (Chen, 1996). The earlier in life deaf children acquire some language system, whether spoken or signed, the better their command of language is likely to be later in life (Humphries et al., 2016). Using MRIs, researchers have found that delay in acquiring a language leads to structural changes in the organization of the brain (Pénicaud et al., 2013). Deaf children whose parents are deaf and use sign language with them, as well as deaf children of hearing parents who participate in early intervention programs, generally show normal patterns of development, whereas children who are not exposed to any language system early in life suffer for it (Marschark, 1993).

By talking, singing, and otherwise making sounds during her pregnancy, this mother-to-be is familiarizing her unborn child to the sound of her voice.

Dragon Images/Shutterstock.com

their mother's voice or a stranger's voice (Kisilevsky et al., 2003). Heart rates increased in response to their mother's voice and decreased in response to the stranger's voice, indicating that fetuses detected a difference between the two. Newborns will also learn to suck faster on a special pacifier when it activates a recording of the mother's voice (DeCasper & Fifer, 1980).

Does this early recognition extend to fathers' voices? Not so much. Newborns who had listened to either their father or their mother read a story prior to birth preferred to listen to their mother's voice (Lee & Kisilevsky, 2014). Even by 4 months, infants show no preference for their father's voice over the voice of a strange man (Ward & Cooper, 1999). They can detect differences between various male voices, however, indicating that the lack of preference for the father's voice is not because of a failure to distinguish it.

Why would infants prefer their mother's but not their father's voice? Again, we need to look at what is happening before birth to answer this question. In a now-classic study, Anthony DeCasper and Melanie Spence (1986) had mothers recite a portion of Dr. Seuss's *The Cat in the Hat* many times during the last 6 weeks of their pregnancies. At birth, the infants were tested to see if they would suck more to hear the story they had heard before birth or to hear a different story. Remarkably, they preferred the familiar story. Somehow these infants were able to recognize the distinctive sound pattern of the story they had heard in the womb. Auditory learning before birth could also explain why newborns prefer to hear their mother's voice to those of unfamiliar women but do not show a preference for their father's voice. They are literally bombarded with their mother's voice for months before birth, giving them ample opportunity to learn its auditory qualities. Even when fathers are explicitly asked to read to the fetus prior to birth (e.g., Lee & Kisilevsky, 2014), the exposure to the mother's voice is still likely to be greater. Researcher Eino Partanen (in Kim, 2013) summed this up well: "the voice of the mother is the most salient sound in the womb" (A6). And truth be told, many women might argue that this advantage is well-deserved for all the other issues they may experience over the course of a pregnancy.

So hearing is more developed than vision at birth. Infants can distinguish among speech sounds and recognize familiar sound patterns such as their mother's voice soon after birth. Within the first year, they lose sensitivity to sound contrasts insignificant in the language they are starting to learn, and they further refine their auditory perception skills. Although the speech recognition ability of infants is quite impressive, there will be further refinements during childhood. For instance, when listening to speech that is not clear, children will try to clarify it by using visual cues (e.g., mouth and tongue movements) to augment the auditory information (Jerger, Damain, Tye-Murray, & Abdi, 2014).

The Chemical Senses: Taste and Smell

Can newborns detect different tastes and smells? Both of these senses rely on the detection of chemical molecules; thus, the characterization of them as the "chemical senses." The sensory receptors for taste—taste buds—are located mainly on the tongue. In ways not fully understood, taste buds respond to chemical molecules and produce perceptions of sweet, salty, bitter, or sour tastes. At birth, babies can clearly distinguish sweet, bitter, and sour tastes and show a preference for sweets (Mennella & Bobowski, 2015). Indeed, sugar water—but not plain water—may help calm babies who are experiencing mildly stressful events.

Different taste sensations also produce distinct facial expressions in the newborn (Rotstein et al., 2015). For instance, newborns lick their lips and sometimes smile when they are tasting a sugar solution but purse their lips and even drool to get rid of the foul taste when they are given a bitter solution. Their facial expressions become increasingly pronounced as a solution becomes sweeter or more bitter, suggesting that newborns can discriminate different concentrations of a substance. Even before birth, babies show a preference for sweets when they swallow more amniotic fluid that contains higher concentrations of sugar than amniotic fluid with lower concentrations of sugar (Bakalar, 2012; Fifer, Monk, & Grose-Fifer, 2004).

Although we may have a general—and innate—preference for sweets and avoidance of bitters, flavor preferences are highly responsive to learning. Neuroscientist Gordon Shepherd (2012) studies the sense of smell and its relationship to taste and flavor. He argues that the basic tastes are hardwired and present at birth, whereas more sophisticated perception of flavors is learned. Appreciating the flavor of food comes from having the food in our mouths and not just in front of our noses. Chewing food or swishing fluids around in our mouths releases molecules that are breathed out and travel to the receptors in our nasal passages. From there, the signals are sent to the brain, which processes this information and constructs meaning. In Shepherd's (2012) words, "flavor does not reside in a flavorful food any more than color resides in a colorful object" (p. 5). Like our perception of color, our perception of flavor is highly dependent on how our brains assign meaning to the signals received from our sensory apparatus.

Our early experience with foods may leave us with lasting taste preferences. In one study, for example, infants were fed one of two formulas for 7 months, starting at 2 weeks of age (Mennella, Griffin, & Beauchamp, 2004). One formula was bland, and the other was bitter and tasted sour, at least to most adults. After this period, the babies who had been fed the sour formula continued to consume it, but the other infants refused when it was offered to them. By 4–5 years, children fed the unpleasant-tasting

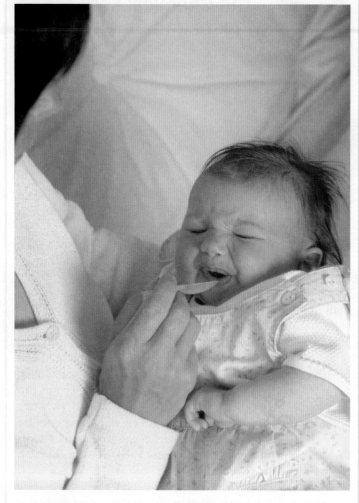

From birth, infants respond to tastes. In response to a sugar solution, newborns part their lips, lick their upper lips, make sucking movements, and sometimes smile. From this infant's expression, we can infer that she is not getting a spoonful of something sweet.

thislife pictures/Alamy Stock Photo

adventuresome eater later on. These early experiences with different flavors also extend to the prenatal period and exposure to different chemicals in the amniotic fluid. The foods eaten by pregnant women flavor the amniotic fluid that fetuses live in for 9 months (Mennella, 2014). Although learning plays a role in taste preferences, we cannot discount genetic predispositions. Discovery of several "taste genes" has shown that genetic differences can account for a lot of the disparity in children and adults' perception of bitterness and some of the variation in children's perception of sweetness (Knaapila etal., 2012; Mennella, Reiter, & Daniels, 2016).

Like taste, the sense of smell, or olfaction, is working well at birth. Even premature babies (born at 28 weeks of gestation) are capable of detecting various odors via sensory receptors located in the nasal passage. Newborns react vigorously to unpleasant smells such as vinegar or ammonia and turn their heads away (Rieser, Yonas, & Wilkner, 1976). Newborns also reliably prefer the scent of their own amniotic fluid over that of other amniotic fluid, suggesting that olfactory cues are detectable prenatally (Schaal, Marlier, & Soussignan, 1998). Exposure to a familiar odor—their own amniotic fluid or their mother's breast milk—can also calm newborns, resulting in less crying when their mothers are absent or when the newborns undergo a painful procedure (Nishitani et al., 2009; Rattaz, Goubet, & Bullinger, 2005). All babies also show a preference for the smell of human milk over formula, even if they have consumed only formula (Delaunay-El Mam, Marlier, & Schaal, 2006; Marlier & Schaal, 2005). Furthermore, babies who are breast-fed can recognize their mothers solely by the smell of their breasts or underarms within 1 or 2 weeks of birth (Cernoch & Porter, 1985; Porter et al., 1992; Vaglio, 2009). Babies who are bottle-fed cannot, probably because they have less contact with their mothers' skin. On the flip side, mothers can identify their newborns by smell, and they are less repulsed by the odor of their own infant's dirty diaper than by one from an unfamiliar infant (Case, Repacholi, & Stevenson, 2006; Porter, 1999). Thus, the sense of smell we often take for granted may help babies and their parents get to know each other.

The Somaesthetic Senses

The somaesthetic senses are your "body" senses, including your sense of touch, temperature, and pain, as well as your *kinesthetic sense* of knowing where your body is in relation to other body parts and to the environment. Whether you realize it or not, you use your kinesthetic sense throughout your waking hours. For example, you know when you are upright as opposed to lying down. And when walking along a crowded sidewalk, you constantly make adjustments to your body to avoid bumping into others. At what point are these somaesthetic senses operational?

The sense of touch seems to be operating nicely before birth and, with the body senses that detect motion, may be among the first senses to develop (Hollins, 2010). You saw in Chapter 5 that newborns respond with reflexes if they are touched in appropriate areas. For example, when touched on the check, a newborn will turn her head and open her mouth. Even in their sleep,

formula were more likely to consume other sour-tasting foods (for example, a sour-flavored apple juice) than children exposed to only bland-tasting formula. Later research uncovered a sensitive period, during the first 4–6 months after birth, when exposure to certain tastes or flavors seems to influence later acceptance of these flavors (Mennella & Castor, 2012). Further, infants need more than a short-term exposure to a flavor. Those fed the rather foul-tasting formula for just 1 month did not later show any greater acceptance of the flavor than those who had not been fed the formula. Only those infants who had been fed the formula for 3 or more months showed later acceptance (Mennella & Castor, 2012).

Such research may be key to helping researchers understand why some people are picky eaters, whereas others are open to a wide variety of tastes. Greater exposure to a variety of flavors during infancy—what a breast-fed baby with a mother who eats many different foods might experience—may lead to a more

newborns will habituate to strokes of the same spot on the skin but respond again if the tactile stimulation is shifted to a new spot—from the ear to the lips, for example (Kisilevsky & Muir, 1984). Sensitivity to tactile stimulation develops in the cephalocaudal (head-to-toe) direction described in Chapter 5, so the face and mouth are more sensitive than lower parts of the body. No wonder babies like to put everything in their mouths—the tactile sensors in and around the mouth allow babies to collect a great deal of information about the world. Most parents quickly recognize the power of touch for soothing a fussy baby. Touch has even greater benefits: Premature babies who are systematically stroked over their entire body gain more weight and exhibit more relaxed behavior and more regular sleep patterns than premature babies who are not massaged (Field, Diego, & Hernandez-Reif, 2010).

Newborns are also sensitive to warmth and cold; they can tell the difference between something cold and something warm placed on their cheeks. Finally, young babies clearly respond to painful stimuli such as needle pricks. For obvious ethical reasons, researchers have not exposed infants to severely painful stimuli. However, analyses of babies' cries and facial movements as they receive injections and have blood drawn leave no doubt that these procedures are painful. Even premature babies show cortical responses to pain (Slater et al., 2006). And pain is responsive to learning. For example, researchers have compared infants born to diabetic mothers, who have their heels pricked every few hours after birth to test their blood sugar levels, with infants born to nondiabetic mothers (Taddio, 2002). Both groups of infants have blood drawn from the back of their hands before they leave the hospital so several routine tests can be conducted. The infants who have already had their heels pricked show a larger response to having blood drawn than the infants who have never experienced presumably painful needle pricks in their feet. Indeed, some infants who had already experienced the heel pricks began to grimace when the nurse prepared their skin for the needle prick, indicating that they had learned from their prior experiences that a painful moment was coming.

Such research challenges the medical wisdom of giving babies who must undergo major surgery little or no anesthesia. It turns out that infants are more likely to survive heart surgery if they receive deep anesthesia that keeps them unconscious during the operation and for a day afterward than if they receive light anesthesia that does not entirely protect them from the stressful experience of pain (Anand & Hickey, 1992). And the American Academy of Pediatrics recommends that local anesthesia be given to newborn males undergoing circumcision (AAP Task Force on Circumcision, 2012). Finally, swaddling and/or breast-feeding during painful events such as getting a vaccination or having blood drawn has been shown to reduce the behavioral signs that infants are experiencing pain (Codipietro, Ceccarelli, & Ponzone, 2008; Ho et al., 2016).

You have now seen that each of the major senses is operating in some form at birth and that perceptual abilities improve dramatically during infancy. Are any special experiences necessary to develop normal perceptual abilities?

Influences on Early Perceptual Development

The perceptual competencies of even very young infants are remarkable, as is the progress made within the first few months of life. All major senses begin working before birth and are clearly functioning at birth; parents would be making a huge mistake to assume that their newborn is not taking in the sensory world. Many perceptual abilities—for example, the ability to perceive depth or to distinguish melodies—emerge within just a few months of birth. Gradually, basic perceptual capacities are fine-tuned, and infants become more able to interpret their sensory experiences—to recognize a pattern of light as a face, for example. By the end of the second year, the most important aspects of perceptual development are complete. The senses and the mind are working to create a meaningful world of recognized objects, sounds, tastes, smells, and bodily sensations.

The fact that perceptual development takes place so quickly can be viewed as support for the "nature" side of the nature–nurture debate. Many basic perceptual capacities appear to be innate or to develop rapidly in all normal infants. What, then, is the role of early sensory experience in perceptual development?

Early Experience and the Brain

Classic studies that would ultimately lead to a Nobel Prize for David Hubel and Torsten Wiesel showed that depriving newborn kittens of normal visual experience by suturing one eye closed for 8 weeks resulted in a lack of normal connections between that eye and the visual cortex—and blindness even after the eye had been reopened (Hubel & Wiesel, 1970). Even as little as 1 week of deprivation during the critical period of the first 8 weeks of life can lead to permanent vision loss in a kitten (Kandel & Jessell, 1991). By contrast, depriving an adult cat's eye of light does not lead to permanent damage.

From other classic research with kittens, we know that kittens need to actively experience their environments to develop normal visual perception (Held & Hein, 1963). In an ingenious study, kittens were able to see their environment but from the vantage point of a passive rider in a cart pulled by another cat (picture a horse pulling a wagon with a passenger in it and then substitute kittens for the horse and passenger). Despite being able to see the world pass by, the passenger kittens did not have the opportunity to learn how their own movement influenced the incoming flow of visual images. They needed to have this active feedback loop between their actions, the visual stimulation, and their perception of this information. For cats, anyway, there seems to be a critical period of time when normal visual experiences are needed in order to develop normal visual perception.

Some clever researchers came up with the idea of using 'sticky mittens' (i.e., mittens with Velcro) to test whether action would similarly benefit human infants who were too young to reach and grasp objects (Libertus & Needham, 2010). Infants in the passive condition could watch as their parents manipulated objects, whereas infants in the active condition could themselves manipulate the objects, which were covered with material that would allow them to stick to their mittens. The Velcro offered an opportunity for young infants to hang on to the objects and manipulate them. Following this experience, infants in the active condition showed more visual searching and more reaching behaviors than infants in the passive condition. The differences between the two groups of infants, though, were not as dramatic as those found by other researchers who studied kittens.

In humans, it is probably more accurate to characterize the effects of early experience on vision in terms of sensitive periods rather than critical periods (Armstrong et al., 2006). A sensitive period is "a window of time during which an individual is *more* affected by experience, and thus has a higher level of plasticity than at other times throughout life" (Armstrong et al., 2006p. 326). Terri Lewis and Daphne Maurer (2005, 2009) provide evidence for multiple sensitive periods during which vision can be influenced by experience. First, there is the period they call visually driven normal development. This is when expected developmental changes in vision will occur with exposure to "normal" visual input; these changes will not occur if visual input is absent. Second, there is a sensitive period for damage; that is, there is a period when abnormal or absent visual input is likely to lead to permanent deficits in some aspect of vision. Third, there is a sensitive period for recovery when the visual system has the potential to recover from damage (Lewis & Maurer, 2005).

Sensory experience is vital in determining the organization of the developing brain. Imagine what visual perception would be like in an infant who was blind at birth but later had surgery to permit vision. This is the scenario for perhaps 3 of every 5,000 infants with congenital cataracts, a clouding of the lens that leaves these infants nearly blind from birth if it is not corrected. In the past, surgery to remove cataracts was often delayed until infants were older. But such delays meant that infants had weeks, months, or even years with little or no visual input. Consequently, some never developed normal vision even after the lens defect was removed.

It turns out that the visual system requires stimulation early in life, including patterned stimulation, to develop normally. Although the visual system has some plasticity throughout childhood, the first 3 months of life are considered critical (Lambert & Drack, 1996). During this time, the brain must receive clear visual information from both eyes. Unfortunately, not all infants with cataracts are identified early enough to benefit from surgery. Identification and removal of cataracts by 10 weeks of age is associated with better long-term outcomes than identification and removal after this age (Chan et al., 2012). Even after surgery restores their sight, these infants have difficulty, at least initially, perceiving their visual world clearly (Maurer, Mondloch, & Lewis, 2007). Although acuity immediately after surgery is what you might find in a newborn without cataracts—in other words, rather poor—it improves significantly during the month following surgery (Maurer et al., 1999).

Years after corrective surgery, individuals who missed out on early visual experience because of congenital cataracts show normal visual abilities in some areas, such as sensitivity to low spatial frequencies (for example, wide stripes) and recognition of faces based on the *shape* of facial features. However, adults who

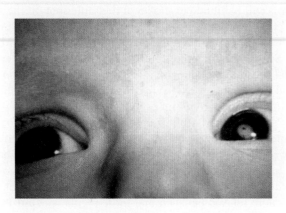

Congenital cataracts can interfere with visual input that is needed to develop normal vision.

Public Health Image Library/Centers for Disease Control and Prevention (CDC)

had cataract surgery as infants are not as adept as other adults at reading emotions from facial expressions (Gao, Maurer, & Nishimura, 2013). In addition, they struggle with certain other visual tasks, including the ability to distinguish between mid- and high-spatial frequencies (for example, medium and narrow stripes) and holistic face processing and recognizing faces based on *spacing* of facial features. What might account for these findings?

Daphne Maurer and her colleagues (2007) argue that the lingering deficits reflect sleeper effects—delayed outcomes—of early visual deficits. Thus, patterned visual input early in life is critical to developing later sensitivity to detail and holistic face processing. Even though these abilities do not normally develop until after early infancy—and after corrective surgery has been done—early visual deprivation likely affects the brain in a way that prevents infants from developing these abilities even when normal visual input is restored (Maurer et al., 2007). Clearly, then, early visual experiences influence later visual perception.

The same message about the importance of early experience applies to the sense of hearing: Exposure to auditory stimulation early in life affects the architecture of the developing brain, which in turn influences auditory perception skills (Finitzo, Gunnarson, & Clark, 1990). Children with hearing impairments who undergo a cochlear implant, which bypasses damaged nerve cells in their inner ear, may struggle to understand the meaning of signals reaching their brain through the implant before they derive benefits. Although the brain is being fed information, it must learn how to interpret these signals. Within 2–4 months after a cochlear implant, infants and young children show brain activity patterns indicating differentiation of long and short vowel sounds, a building block of more advanced language skills (Vavatzanidis et al., 2015; see also **Application 6.1**). The conclusion is clear: Maturation alone is not enough; normal perceptual development also requires normal perceptual experience. The practical implication is also clear: Visual and hearing problems in children should be detected and corrected as early in life as possible.

What Do Infants Need?

Fortunately, parents need not worry about arranging the right sensory environment for their children because young humans actively seek the stimulation they need to develop properly. Infants are active explorers and stimulus seekers; they orchestrate their own perceptual, motor, and cognitive development by exploring their environment and learning what it will *afford*, or allow, them to do (Gibson, 1988; Gibson & Pick, 2000).

According to Eleanor Gibson's (1988) ecological perspective, infants proceed through three phases of exploratory behavior:

1. From birth to 4 months, infants explore their immediate surroundings, especially their caregivers, by looking and listening, and they learn a bit about objects by mouthing them and watching them move.
2. From 5 to 7 months, once the ability to voluntarily grasp objects has developed, babies pay far closer attention to objects, exploring objects with their eyes as well as with their hands.
3. By 8 or 9 months, after most have begun to crawl, infants extend their explorations into the larger environment and carefully examine the objects they encounter on their journeys, learning all about their properties.

By combining perception and action in their exploratory behavior, infants actively create sensory environments that meet their needs and contribute to their own development (Eppler, 1995). As children become more able to attend selectively to the world around them, they become even more able to choose the forms and levels of stimulation that suit them best. Again, we see a coupling of perception and action.

● Checking Mastery

1. Describe two procedures used by researchers to assess perceptual abilities of infants.
2. During their first few months of life, what can infants see best?
3. What sorts of experiences are necessary to develop normal visual perception?

● Making Connections

1. Drawing on your knowledge of the sensory and perceptual capacities of newborns, put yourself in the place of a newborn just emerging from the womb and describe your perceptual experiences. What do you see, feel, hear, and so on? What, if anything, do you make of all this information?
2. How would you design a nursery for an infant to make the best use of his sensory and perceptual abilities?

6.3
The Child

LEARNING OBJECTIVES

- Explain how perception and action work together in the development and refinement of locomotor skills.

- Provide an example of both fine motor and gross motor skills and note the typical order in which these skills develop.

- Discuss the dynamic systems theory of motor development and summarize the research findings supporting this theory.

- Describe and provide two examples of cross-modal perception. Explain how researchers demonstrate that someone has cross-modal perception.

There are some refinements of the sensory systems during childhood. For example, visual acuity improves to adult levels sometime between 4 and 6 years, and sensitivity to visual contrasts develops completely by about 7 years of age (Maurer et al., 2007). Ability to identify odors improves across childhood, although this may reflect improved language skills more than any real change in sensory sensitivity (Bastos et al., 2015). For the most part, sensory and perceptual development is largely complete by the end of infancy. Does anything remain to be accomplished during childhood? Yes, indeed. We will cover two important accomplishments with the transition from infancy to childhood: (1) the coupling of perception and action leading to purposeful movement; and (2) integration of multiple sources of sensory information.

Locomotion: The Coupling of Perception and Action

Locomotion, or movement from one place to another, is a vital aspect of development. One of young children's most impressive accomplishments is getting up off of their bellies, backs, or bottoms and moving with purpose throughout their environment on two legs. This shift from crawling to walking offers toddlers the opportunity to engage differently with their environments. They are no longer restricted to objects that are close by and close to the ground. They can now cross the room to get objects, access higher objects, and use their hands to share and interact with objects in new ways (see Adolph & Robinson, 2014). In Gibson's ecological framework, walking opens up new environments and new affordances, or ways of interacting with objects in the environment. To make this transition, the young child must learn to integrate perception with action (Smitsman & Corbetta, 2010). This coupling occurs gradually and becomes more refined with experience.

The groundwork for walking is laid during infancy. Infants generally acquire **gross motor skills** (skills such as kicking the legs or drawing large circles that involve large muscles and whole-body or limb movements) before mastering **fine motor skills** (skills such as picking Cheerios off the breakfast table or writing letters of the alphabet that involve precise movements of the hands and fingers or feet and toes). If you examine the progression of these motor skills, you will notice the workings of the cephalocaudal and proximodistal principles of development (see Chapter 5). Early motor development follows the *cephalocaudal principle* because the neurons between the brain and the muscles acquire myelin sheaths in a head-to-tail manner. Thus, infants can lift their heads before they can control their trunks enough to sit, and they can sit before they can control their legs to walk. The *proximodistal principle* of development is also evident in early motor development. Activities involving the trunk are mastered before activities involving the arms and legs, and activities involving the arms and legs are mastered before activities involving the hands and fingers or feet and toes. Therefore, infants can roll over before they can walk or bring their arms together to grasp a bottle. As the nerves and muscles mature downward and outward, infants gradually gain control over the lower and the peripheral parts of their bodies. When this happens, infants are ready for the next step, literally.

Although parents must be on their toes when their toddlers begin walking, they take great delight in witnessing this new milestone in motor development, which occurs around age 1. By collecting an enormous number of observations of infants' and toddlers' daily movements, Karen Adolph and her colleagues (2008, 2013) have found that it takes an average of 13 starts and stops over a period of days and sometimes weeks before toddlers show consistent performance of a motor skill. During the transition period of acquiring a new motor skill, they are truly taking "one step forward, two steps backward." They may appear to have started walking, only to revert to crawling, much to the chagrin of their proud parents. From the toddler's perspective, the apparent regression in skills is quite logical. They have mastered crawling and are quite fast at it, whereas walking on two legs is hard work and can slow them down (Adolph & Tamis-LeMonda, 2014). So if they have important things to do, they might find it more efficient to use their reliable crawling skills than to labor at walking. With a little bit of practice, walking will soon become routine. Indeed, by 14 months of age, the average toddler is taking 2,300 steps an hour, which is equivalent to traveling a distance of nearly seven football fields (see Adolph et al., 2012). No wonder parents feel as though they can barely keep up with their toddlers at times. And there's more: Not only are toddlers traveling all over the house, but walking frees up their arms and hands. **Exploration 6.1** considers the remarkable changes taking place with the use of hands and fingers.

Motor Skills as Dynamic Action Systems

How do motor skills emerge? Esther Thelen (1995, 1996) observed infants throughout their first year and discovered that they spent a great deal of time engaged in **rhythmic stereotypies**. That is, they moved their bodies in repetitive ways—rocking, swaying, bouncing, mouthing objects, and banging their arms up and down. Thelen found that infants and toddlers performed these rhythmic stereotypies shortly before a new skill emerged but not after the skill had become established. Thus, infants might rock back and forth while on their hands and knees, but once they were crawling, they no longer rocked.

Esther Thelen's work has culminated in the development of the **dynamic systems theory** to explain such motor developments (Thelen & Smith, 1994; see also Spencer et al., 2006). According to the dynamic systems theory, developments take place over time through a "self-organizing" process in which children use the sensory feedback they receive when they try different movements to modify their motor behavior in adaptive ways (Smith & Thelen, 1993; von Hofsten, 2007). Behaviors that seem to emerge in a moment of time are actually the cumulative effects of motor decisions that the infant makes over a much longer time (Spencer et al., 2006). In this view, motor milestones such as crawling and walking are the learned outcomes of a process of interaction with the environment in which infants do the best they can with what they have in order to achieve their goals (Thelen, 1995). Thus, development is highly individualistic: "[I]nfants must explore a

According to Gibson's ecological theory, this toddler may find that this plank bridge affords, or offers, a sturdy enough surface to walk safely on his own.

INSADCO Photography/Alamy Stock Photo

wide range of behaviors to discover and select their own unique solutions in the context of their intrinsic dynamics and movement history" (Spencer et al., 2006, p. 1528). Neural maturation, physical growth, muscle strength, balance, and other characteristics of the child interact with gravity, floor surfaces, and characteristics of the specific task to influence what children can and cannot learn to do with their bodies. You can probably think of times when you have been through this dynamic self-organizing process: when you were learning to serve a tennis ball, dance a new dance, or drive a car.

Consistent with the dynamic systems approach, Karen Adolph and Anthony Avolio (2000) found that young toddlers could adjust their walking to changes in both their body dimensions and the slope of a walkway. The researchers had toddlers walk on slopes of different degrees while wearing a vest with removable "saddlebags" that could be weighted to simulate changes in their body dimensions (■Figure 6.3). The weights added mass and shifted the toddlers' center of gravity, akin to what happens when toddlers grow. Would toddlers be able to compensate for the changes in their body and their environment? Yes—they adjusted their motor skills to adapt to rapid "growth" of their bodies and to changes in their environment (Adolph & Berger, 2006). Like adults carrying a heavy load on their shoulders, toddlers bent their knees and kept

their upper bodies stiffly upright to maintain their balance with heavier loads. Toddlers with greater walking experience did better than those with less experience (Garciaguirre, Adolph, & Shrout, 2007). Toddlers also seemed to recognize when the walkway was too steep for safe travel—they either avoided it or scooted down on their bottoms or on their hands and knees. Young walkers (16 months) are also clever enough to figure out that they can use handrails to help maintain their balance while walking across bridges (Berger & Adolph, 2003). Further, they quickly discover that a sturdy handrail offers more support than a "wobbly" handrail and they are more adventuresome when they can use a sturdy handrail for support (Berger, Adolph, & Lobo, 2005). If they are not sure how to proceed across a potentially unstable surface, they look to their mothers for advice. With mother's encouragement, 75% of infants will try to navigate a questionable slope; only 25% of infants are brave enough to give it a shot when mothers express discouragement (Karasik et al., 2008; Tamis-LeMonda et al., 2008).

As every parent knows, toddlers do not become proficient walkers without experiencing more than a few falls—as many as 17 per hour and 100 per day by one estimate (Adolph et al., 2012). As it turns out, these tumbles help walkers learn which surfaces are safe and which ones may be problematic (Joh & Adolph, 2006). With age, toddlers become increasingly adept at figuring out how to avoid falls, but they still appear awkward compared with the older child, who takes steps in more fluid and rhythmic strides and is better able to avoid obstacles. And children quickly become able to do more than just walk. By age 3, they can walk or run in a straight line, although they cannot easily turn or stop while running. Kindergarten children can integrate two motor skills hopping on one foot with walking or running—into mature skipping (Loovis & Butterfield, 2000). With each passing year, school-age children can run a little faster, jump a little higher, and throw a ball a little farther.

What does the dynamic systems perspective say about the contribution of nature and nurture to development, then? According to Thelen (1995), toddlers walk not because their genetic code programs them to do so but because they learn that walking works well given their biomechanical properties and the characteristics of the environments they must navigate. In the dynamic systems approach, nature (maturation of the central nervous system) and nurture (sensory and motor experience) are both essential and largely inseparable. Feedback from the senses and from motor actions is integrated with the ever-changing abilities of the infant. Having learned how to adjust one motor skill (such as crawling) to successfully navigate varied environmental conditions, however, does not mean that toddlers will generalize this knowledge to other motor skills (such as walking; see Adolph & Berger, 2006). Different motor skills present different challenges. Crawling toddlers, for instance, must learn to avoid such dangers as bumping their heads on table legs. Walking toddlers face other challenges, such as not toppling over when turning around. To master these challenges, children need opportunities to gather feedback from each motor activity.

Finally, an important contribution of the dynamic systems approach to motor development is its integration of action with thought (von Hofsten, 2007). The motor behaviors we have been describing are not separate and distinct from the child's knowledge.

■ **Figure 6.3** Adolph and Avolio's walkway with adjustable slope. Infants are outfitted with weighted saddlebags to alter their body mass and center of gravity. While an experimenter stays beside infants to ensure safety, parents stand at the end of the walkway and encourage their child to walk toward them.

From Adolph, K. E., & Avolio, A. M. (2000). Walking infants adapt locomotion to changing body dimensions. *Journal of Experimental Psychology: Human Perception and Performance, 26, 1148–1166.* Copyright © 2000 by The American Psychological Association. Reprinted with permission of the American Psychological Association.

Grasping and Reaching

If you look at what children can do with their hands, you will find it progresses from reflexive activity of early infancy to more voluntary, coordinated behavior. By the middle of the first year, infants grasp objects well, although they use a rather clumsy, clamplike grasp in which they press the palm and outer fingers together—the **ulnar grasp**. Initially, they reach for objects using jerky movements and a locked elbow (Berthier & Keen, 2006). Over the next few months, their reaching movements become increasingly smooth and they anticipate how they need to adjust their hand so that it can effectively grasp an approaching object (Barrett & Needham, 2008; von Hofsten, 2007). We can again see the workings of the proximodistal principle of development as we watch infants progress from controlling their arms, then their hands, and finally

their individual fingers enough to use a **pincer grasp**, involving only the thumb and the forefinger (or another finger). The pincer grasp, which is very useful for picking up food and getting it to your mouth, appears as early as 5 months and is reliable by the child's first birthday (Sacrey, Karl, & Whishaw, 2012; Wallace & Whishaw, 2003).

By 16 months, toddlers can scribble with a crayon, and by the end of the second year they can copy a simple horizontal or vertical line and even build towers of five or more blocks. They are rapidly gaining control of specific, *differentiated* movements, then *integrating* those movements into whole, coordinated actions. They use their new loco-motor and manipulation skills to learn about and adapt to the world around them. By cornering bugs and stacking Cheerios, they develop their minds.

This toddler uses the pincer grasp to pick up a crayon.

Mark Wallis/Alamy Stock Photo

Children have to think about how to organize their movements to optimize what they are able to get from their ever-changing environment. Thus, there is far more to motor development than implied by norms indicating when we might expect infants to sit up, stand alone, or walk independently. The emergence of motor skills is complex and is closely connected to perceptual-cognitive developments.

Integrating Sensory Information

Moving around the world opens up the floodgates of sensory information. In most situations, multiple senses provide the brain with different information and, ideally, the brain integrates these pieces of information into a single coherent understanding. Without such integration, our understanding of the world would be fragmented and rather chaotic. At what point are we able to put together information gained from viewing, fingering, sniffing, and otherwise exploring objects?

To some extent, the senses function in an integrated way at birth. For instance, newborns will look in the direction of a sound they hear, suggesting that vision and hearing are linked. They also expect to feel objects that they can see and are frustrated by a visual illusion that looks like a graspable object but proves to be nothing but air when they reach for it (Bower, Broughton, & Moore, 1970).

Thus, vision and touch, as well as vision and hearing, seem to be interrelated early in life. This integration of the senses helps babies perceive and respond appropriately to the objects and people they encounter (Hainline & Abramov, 1992; Walker-Andrews, 1997).

Although present in a rudimentary form in early infancy, fully and meaningfully integrating the senses develops fairly late relative to the development of the individual senses (Burr & Gori, 2012). Thus, it is not enough for each individual sense to be operational for multisensory integration to occur. This more advanced skill requires ongoing "conversation" among the various sensory systems and the brain. As the brain develops, so does the ability to consider multiple pieces of information and draw on memory of past experiences to better understand the meaning of multiple sources of input (Burr & Gori, 2012). With each new encounter of the nearly continuous flow of multisensory information, children refine their understanding of the rich sensory world.

An even more difficult task is to recognize through one sense an object familiar through another, a type of multisensory integration called **cross-modal perception**. This capacity is required in children's games that involve feeling objects hidden in a bag and identifying what they are by touch alone. Although some researchers (for example, Streri, 2003; Streri & Gentaz, 2004)

Intersensory perception. The ability to recognize through one sense (here, touch) what has been learned through another (vision) increases with age during infancy and childhood. Here, the birthday girl must identify prizes in the bag by touch alone.

Mary Kate Denny/PhtoEdit

report that newborns can recognize an object by sight that they had previously touched with their hand, others have had trouble demonstrating cross-modal perception in such young infants (for example, Maurer, Stager, & Mondloch, 1999). Apparently, early cross-modal perception is a fragile ability dependent on various task variables such as which hand is used to manipulate the object (Streri & Gentaz, 2004). Performance on complex cross-modal perception tasks that require matching patterns of sounds with patterns of visual stimuli continues to improve throughout childhood and even adolescence (Bushnell & Baxt, 1999).

Researchers now conclude that impressions from the different senses are "fused" or integrated early in life, making it easier for infants to perceive and use information that comes to them through multiple channels simultaneously (Walker-Andrews, 1997). Then, as the separate senses continue to develop and each becomes a more effective means of exploring objects, toddlers become more skilled at cross-modal perception and are able to coordinate information gained through one sense with information gained through another.

Advances in Attention

We have talked about perception without much focus on an important costar: attention. At least some of the advances in perceptual development across childhood and adolescence reflect the development of attention—the focusing of perception and cognition on something in particular. Youngsters become better

able to use their senses deliberately and strategically to gather the information most relevant to a task at hand.

Infants actively use their senses to explore their environment, and they prefer some sensory stimuli to others. Selective as they are, though, young infants do not deliberately choose to attend to faces and other engaging stimuli. Instead, a novel stimulus attracts their attention and, once their attention is "caught," they sometimes seem unable to turn away (Butcher, Kalverboer, & Geuze, 2000; Ruff & Rothbart, 1996). Thus, there is some truth to the idea that the attention of the infant or very young child is "captured by" something and that of the older child is "directed toward" something. This difference has been described as the difference between having an orienting system, one that reacts to events in the environment, and having a focusing system, one that deliberately seeks out and maintains attention to events (Ruff & Rothbart, 1996). As children get older, three things change: their attention spans become longer, they become more selective in what they attend to, and they are better able to plan and carry out systematic strategies for using their senses to achieve goals.

Longer Attention Span

If you have spent any time in the company of young children, then you are probably aware that they have short attention spans. Researchers know that they should limit their experimental sessions with young children to a few minutes, and nursery-school teachers often switch classroom activities every 15–20 minutes. Even when they are doing things they like, such as watching a television program or playing with a toy, 2- and 3-year-olds spend far less time concentrating on the program or the toy than older children do (Ruff & Capozzoli, 2003; Ruff & Lawson, 1990). In one study of sustained attention, children were asked to put strips of colored paper in appropriately colored boxes (Yendovitskaya, 1971). Children aged 2–3 worked for an average of 18 minutes and were easily distracted, whereas children aged 5–6 often persisted for 1 hour or more. Further improvements in sustained attention occur from ages 5 to 10 as those parts of the brain involved with attention become further myelinated (Betts et al., 2006). Beyond ages 10 to 12 there is not much increase in length of sustained attention, but children do become more accurate on tasks requiring sustained attention over the next few years (Betts et al., 2006; Vakil et al., 2008).

More Selective Attention

Although infants clearly deploy their senses in a selective manner, they are not good at controlling their attention—deliberately concentrating on one thing while ignoring something else, or what is known as selective attention. With age, attention becomes more selective and less susceptible to distraction. As infants approach 2 years, they become able to form plans of action, which then guide what they focus on and what they ignore (Ruff & Rothbart, 1996).

Research suggests that preschool children have an adult-like orienting system but an immature focusing system of attention (Ristic & Kingstone, 2009). Between approximately 3½ and 4 years, there is a significant increase in focused attention. Kathleen Kannass and John Colombo (2007) tested 3½- and 4-year-olds while they worked on a task under one of three conditions: no distraction, constant distraction (a TV program in an unfamiliar language played continuously in the background), or intermittent distraction (the same TV program played in the background but it was frequently turned on and off as the children worked). Among the 3½-year-olds, the two groups working with any distraction had more trouble completing their task than the group working without distraction. Among the 4-year-olds, only the group working with constant distraction had trouble finishing the task. Those working with intermittent distraction were able to stay as focused on the task as children working without distraction. Finally, the researchers found that when a distractor was present, looking away from the task led to worse performance, whereas looking away when there was no distraction did not impair performance. Selective attention continues to improve throughout childhood, with 8- to 11-year-olds better able to ignore irrelevant information and focus on what's important during an auditory task than 4- to 7-year-olds (Jones, Moore, & Amitay, 2015). Similarly, on a visual task, 8- to 10-year-olds show greater selective attention than 6-year-olds (Kovshoff et al., 2015).

These findings should suggest to parents and teachers of young children that performance will be better if distractions in task materials and in the room are kept to a minimum. In particular, the presence of a continuous distractor will lead to trouble completing tasks (Kannass & Colombo, 2007). If distractions cannot be avoided, children can benefit from regular reminders to stay on task (Kannass, Colombo, & Wyss, 2010).

More Systematic Attention

Finally, as they age, children become more able to plan and carry out systematic perceptual searches. You have already seen that older infants are more likely than younger ones to thoroughly explore a pattern. Research with children in the former Soviet Union reveals that visual scanning becomes considerably more detailed and exhaustive over the first 6 years of life (Zaporozhets, 1965). But the most revealing findings come from studies of how children go about a visual search. In general, children search more slowly than adults (Donnelly et al., 2007) but they are also less efficient. Elaine Vurpillot (1968) recorded the eye movements of 4- to 10-year-olds trying to decide whether two houses, each with several windows containing various objects, were identical or different. As ■ Figure 6.4 illustrates, children ages 4 and 5 were not systematic. They often looked at only a few windows and, as a result, came to wrong conclusions.In contrast, most children older than 6 were very systematic; they typically checked each window in one house with the corresponding window in the other house, pair by pair. For most, improvements in visual search continue to be made throughout childhood and into early adulthood (Burack et al., 2000).

5-year-old: "The same"

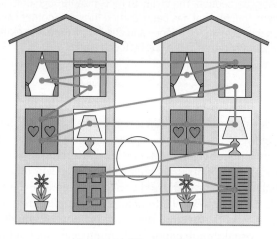

8-year-old: "Not the same"

■ **Figure 6.4** Are the houses in each pair identical or different? As indicated by the lines, 8-year-olds are more likely than 5-year-olds to answer correctly because they systematically scan the visual features of the two pictures.

Adapted from Vurpillot, 1968, The development of scanning strategies and their relation to visual differentiation. Journal of Experimental Child Psychology, 6, 632–650.

Checking Mastery

1. How do children master the important skill of walking and, once they do so, how does this new skill affect their development in general?

2. Why is cross-modal perception important?

3. What are three ways that attention improves during childhood?

Making Connections

1. You have an unlimited budget for redesigning a local child care center that serves children 6 weeks to 6 years old. Given what you know about sensory and perceptual capabilities of infants and young children, what equipment and toys will you purchase, and how will you remodel and redecorate the rooms?

2. You are commissioned by a local pediatrician to write a brochure on "locomotor skills of the infant and young child." Begin this assignment by developing a bulleted list of the skills that support the development of walking and order these by when or in what order they typically emerge.

LEARNING OBJECTIVES

- Document the changes in attention during the adolescent period and discuss the implications of today's multitasking lifestyle of many teens.

- Discuss the challenges to the auditory system during adolescence.

- Outline changes in the chemical senses of adolescents and indicate the likely contributing factors to these changes.

There is little news to report about sensation, attention, and perception during adolescence, except that some developments of childhood are not completed until then. Several issues during this time, though, warrant discussion: refinements in attention, potential insults to hearing from exposure to loud noise, and expanding taste horizons.

Attention

It is fairly clear that adolescents have longer attention spans than children. They can, for example, sit through longer classes, work on papers or study for lengthier periods of time, and take tests that last as long as 3–4 hours (for example, the SAT). This improved ability to sustain attention seems to be tied to increased myelination of those portions of the brain that help regulate attention (Tanner, 1990). As we noted in Chapter 5, a myelin coating on neurons helps insulate them to speed up transmission of neural impulses.

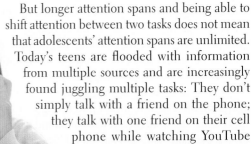

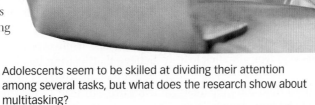

Adolescents seem to be skilled at dividing their attention among several tasks, but what does the research show about multitasking?

Paul Bradbury/OJO Images/Getty Images

In addition, adolescents are better able to switch attention from one task to another (Crone et al., 2006). They become more efficient at ignoring irrelevant information so that they can concentrate on the task at hand. Not only do they learn more than children do about material they are supposed to master, but they also learn *less* about distracting information that could potentially interfere with their performance (Miller & Weiss, 1981). Children have the rudimentary skills to adapt to distractions, but compared with adolescents and adults, they are slowed down and more likely to be thrown off track by distractors.

Similarly, adolescents can divide their attention more systematically between two tasks. For instance, Andrew Schiff and Irwin Knopf (1985) watched the eye movements of 9-year-olds and 13-year-olds during a two-part visual search task. Children were to push a response key when particular symbols appeared at the center of a screen and to remember letters flashed at the corners of the screen. The adolescents developed efficient strategies for switching their eyes from the center to the corners and back at the right times. The 9-year-olds had an unfortunate tendency to look at blank areas of the screen or to focus too much attention on the letters in the corners of the screen, thereby failing to detect the symbols in the center.

But longer attention spans and being able to shift attention between two tasks does not mean that adolescents' attention spans are unlimited. Today's teens are flooded with information from multiple sources and are increasingly found juggling multiple tasks: They don't simply talk with a friend on the phone; they talk with one friend on their cell phone while watching YouTube videos and messaging local friends about what happened at school that day as well as messaging online acquaintances about the latest changes in their shared Internet game world. According to StatisticBrain.com, the vast amount of information available to us 24/7 in the blink of an eye, or the touch of a button, has reduced our attention span to below that of a goldfish! What are the consequences of this constant flow of information and the accompanying **multitasking**, attending to two or more tasks at the same time?

Among college students, about half of their time on the Internet is spent multitasking (Judd, 2013; Moreno et al., 2012). Terry Judd (2013) monitored computer sessions of students in an open computer laboratory and found that only 10% of the sessions were focused on a single task. When students are required to bring a laptop to class, presumably for course-related educational reasons, the majority of students use email and access unrelated material through the browser, and some spend time instant messaging (Kraushaar & Novak, 2010). Students surveyed about their multitasking during class report engaging in a wide range of additional behaviors, including texting (50% of students), working on other course work (18%), eating (26%), posting to Facebook (25%), instant messaging (13%), and listening to music (7%). These percentages are significantly higher when students are asked to report on their multitasking during an online class (Burak, 2012). And we suspect that if students report this much multitasking during class time, they are likely engaged in at least as much multitasking when studying outside of the class.

When college students text during a class lecture, they don't perform as well when tested on the lecture material as students who did not text (Ellis, Daniels, & Jauregui, 2010). The same pattern occurs when students are on a laptop during a class lecture—they do not perform as well when tested on the material (Sana, Weston, & Cepeda, 2013). What's more, students who were close by and could also see their classmate's screen during the lecture also did not do as well on the test.

The relationship here is fairly clear: As multitasking increases, students' grade point averages decrease (Burak, 2012). Students who multitask while reading or studying for a class take longer to complete their assignments. Their perceived study time, therefore, may be longer than their actual study time, deceiving them into thinking they have spent a sufficient amount of time studying. Dividing up our attentional resources can be risky to the learning enterprise. While we may be able to multitask two activities that are familiar and well-learned, our success at multitasking quickly disappears when the tasks are less familiar and relatively new to us (Schumacker et al., 2001). When faced with multiple pieces of information coming in for processing, our brains are forced to make some decisions about what to attend to first and what to "put on the back burner" (Dux et al., 2006).

Many people overestimate their abilities to multitask, believing that they can successfully juggle more than one task at a time. However, those folks who regularly multitask are more distracted by irrelevant information than those who focus on one thing at a time (Ophir, Nass, & Wagner, 2009; Sanbonmatsu et al., 2013). It turns out that the very folks who think they are good at multitasking and engage in this juggling act on a regular basis are less capable of it than are their peers who typically stick to a single task.

Perhaps the lesson here is that the next time you prepare to study for a test, consider whether it would be more beneficial to spend time on this one task rather than allowing yourself to be interrupted and distracted by texting, tweeting, messaging, and more. You may find that focused attention to one task at a time is more efficient than attending to multiple tasks, but not effectively mastering any of them.

Hearing

Adolescence should be a period of optimal acuity of all the senses, but in today's world of concerts, power equipment, and headphones attached to a multitude of sound-producing personal devices, auditory acuity can become compromised in some adolescents (e.g., Jiang et al., 2016). As ● **Table 6.2** shows, loud sounds—those above 75 decibels—may leave the listener with a loss of hearing. Fans of loud music, beware: The noise at rock concerts and nightclubs is often in the 120- to 130-decibel range, well above the level where damage may occur. And if you can hear the music coming from the earbuds or headphones connected to your friend's smartphone, your friend may be damaging her hearing.

The most common outcome of noise exposure is **tinnitus**, or ringing sounds in one or both ears that can last for days, weeks, or indefinitely. Tinnitus is a common complaint among military veterans, and as many as 85% of concert attendees report experiencing tinnitus (Kochkin, Tyler, & Born, 2011; Tunkel et al., 2014). Hearing problems associated with short periods of exposure to loud sounds may be temporary, but damage from regular

● **Table 6.2** Noise Levels

The healthy ear can detect sounds starting at 0 decibels. Damage to hearing can start between 75 and 80 decibels and is more likely with long-term exposure to loud sounds. Using in-ear earphones to listen to music from an iPod at full volume can begin to cause damage after just 5 minutes.

Noise	Number of Decibels
Whisper	30
Normal speech	60
City traffic	80
Lawnmower	90
Rock concerts	110–140
iPod at full volume	110
Jet plane takeoff	120
Jackhammer	130
Firearm discharge	140

Source: The National Institute on Deafness and Other Communication Disorders (NIDCD), 2016b, *It's a Noisy Planet.* www.noisyplanet.nidcd.nih.gov/Pages/Default.aspx

exposure to these same sounds can accumulate over time, leading to moderate or even severe hearing loss by adulthood.

Many teens report that they are aware of the potential for hearing loss from exposure to loud sounds, but they do not believe that hearing loss is a serious health concern for them (Chung et al., 2005). Thus, despite their awareness that noise exposure can lead to hearing loss, and regardless of warnings from parents and health officials that noise can be hazardous, many teens do little to protect their hearing because hearing loss is not perceived as an important issue. Few wear earplugs at concerts or ear protectors when operating power equipment (Bogoch et al., 2005; Chung et al., 2005). Young adults who downplay the risk of hearing loss are less likely to wear protection than those who acknowledge the risk from exposure to loud sounds (Keppler, Dhooge, & Vinck, 2015).

Part of the problem is the perception that ear protection is not "cool." Teens who are more open to behavioral change and those who are less concerned about appearance are more willing to use ear protection (Bogoch et al., 2005). In addition, teens from higher socioeconomic backgrounds tend to rate noise exposure as more negative, and therefore are more open to ear protection, than teens from lower socioeconomic backgrounds (Widén & Erlandsson, 2004; Widén et al., 2009).

Educational programs to improve hearing protection among teens need to focus on several issues to be effective (see, for example, Keppler et al., 2015). They need to help teens recognize that there may be long-term consequences of noise exposure; damage to the auditory system can accumulate over time. Second, they need to address teens' perception that hearing loss is not an important health issue. Until hearing is perceived as a priority, teens and others will have little motivation to protect this sensory system. And finally, education programs need to reduce the stigma associated with wearing hearing protection so teens feel comfortable making the decision to protect their hearing when they are in settings with loud noise.

Another Look at the Chemical Senses

Taste

Earlier, we introduced four basic tastes (sweet, sour, bitter, and salty) and discussed how smell contributes to the taste of foods. Are there any noticeable changes in taste during adolescence? There is a slight decline in preference for sweets and an increased sensitivity to—and liking of—sour tastes (University of Copenhagen, 2008). A preference for sour tastes, or at least a tolerance for sour tastes, is associated with willingness to try new foods and expand food horizons. This slight shift in an adolescent's taste palette leads to another difference between the child and adolescent: Adolescents are more likely to have developed an *acquired taste* for previously disliked or avoided foods. Most children may not enjoy, for example, eating snails (escargot) or fried squid (calamari), but many adolescents and adults have learned that these items can be quite tasty! Teenagers are more likely to enjoy foods with strong or strange tastes because they have had more opportunity to "acquire" these tastes through multiple exposures. Teenagers loosen up on the childhood tendency to reject new foods, and they are more open to experimenting with foods that may have odd textures or odors (Segovia et al., 2002). Of course, there are large individual differences in taste, with some teenagers enjoying very hot, spicy foods and others rejecting anything that has just a tiny amount of spice. Take the test in **Engagement 6.1** to see if you might be a supertaster who is more sensitive to low levels of chemicals hitting your taste receptors.

In addition, it turns out that your sense of taste is mediated by more than smell and taste receptors on the tongue. It is also determined by something called "chemosensory irritation," which is the reaction of your skin—in your mouth and nose—to certain chemical compounds of foods (Beauchamp & Mennella, 2009). When you feel the burn from hot peppers, the cooling sensation from menthol, or the tingle from a carbonated beverage, you are experiencing chemosensory irritation. This irritation of your skin contributes to your experience of a food, with, for example, some people reporting that they love to "feel the burn" of hot peppers and others completely turned off by it.

Taste is also influenced by cognition: You taste what you expect to taste. From past experience, we learn to associate certain features of food with certain tastes. For instance, brightly colored juices are thought to be tastier than pale ones, even when the juices are identical other than the addition of a few drops of artificial coloring to some (Hoegg & Alba, 2007). Thus, we see a bright orange liquid in a cup and we believe that this will be more flavorful than a pale orange liquid.

Smell

Interestingly, gender plays a role in the sense of smell during adolescence and adulthood, with women generally demonstrating greater sensitivity than men to a variety of odors (Doty & Cameron, 2009; Ferdenzi et al., 2013). This may reflect hormonal differences between men and women and the effect of different hormonal levels on detection and interpretation of the chemicals that comprise odors. Among women, hormonal changes influence sensitivity—both discrimination and identification—to different smells (Derntl et al., 2013). Women who are fertile may use odor as part of their criteria for selecting a desirable mate, judging the body odor of some men—those who have symmetrical or balanced physical features—as more desirable than the body odor of other men during the time they are ovulating (Foster, 2008; Yamazaki & Beauchamp, 2007). Symmetry (having balanced features) may be a biological marker of better health.

Men, too, may use differences in women's body odors as a component of mate selection; they rate odor during ovulation as more pleasant than odor at other times of women's menstrual cycles (Havlicek et al., 2006; Singh & Bronstad, 2001). Evolutionary theory would predict that men and women want to select a mate who is healthy and capable of reproduction, and odor may provide some clues in this regard. Both men and women report that odor is an important consideration in choosing romantic partners, even though most cannot clearly articulate what constitutes a "good" or a "bad" smelling person (Sergeant et al., 2005). But be forewarned: Women are more sensitive to body odor than men, and it is more difficult to cover up body odor so that women do not detect it, whereas perfumes and other cover-ups often fool men (Wysocki et al., 2009). We learned earlier that babies and their mothers can recognize one another through smell. Now we see that odor is also important in later relationships, perhaps serving as a filter to allow some people to get close and discourage others.

Cultural Variation

Do people who grow up in different cultural environments encounter different sensory stimulation and perceive the world in different ways? Perceptual preferences obviously differ from culture to culture. In some cultures, people think heavier women are more beautiful than slim ones or relish eating sheep's eyeballs or chicken heads. Are more basic perceptual competencies also affected by socialization?

With their maturing taste buds, adolescents may be more open to trying new foods.

Kablonk! RM/Golden Pixels/Alamy Stock Photo

Are You a Supertaster?

Some folks seem to experience certain tastes with much greater intensity than others. These "supertasters" have more taste buds than the average person and their taste buds are genetically inclined to be more sensitive (Mennella, Pepino, & Reed, 2005; Negri et al., 2012). Although the prevalence of supertasters varies across different regions of the world, on average, about 25% of the adult population has substantially more taste receptors than the other 75%, making them super sensitive to tastes (Bartoshuk, Duffy, & Miller, 1994; Robino et al., 2014). The definitive supertaster test consists of a small paper filter that is infused with a special chemical. When placed on the tongue of a supertaster, it is perceived as incredibly bitter, but tastes bland or mildly bitter to those without the supertaster gene. Your answers to the following questions will give you an estimate of whether you might be a supertaster.

1. Do you enjoy or despise grapefruit juice?
2. Do you like milk chocolate or dark chocolate?
3. Do you hate raw broccoli or Brussels sprouts or think these veggies are okay or even good?
4. As a child, did you eat lots of vegetables?
5. Do you often think that desserts or cookies are too sweet, while others report that the same foods taste just right?

Supertasters are likely to have a strong dislike for the bitter tastes of grapefruit juice, dark chocolate, or raw broccoli/Brussels sprouts. As children, supertasters avoided vegetables because they tasted "too strong." Supertasters are likely to think that too much sweetener has been used in foods and would prefer less sugar. To follow up, you can perform this relatively simple test using a drop of blue food coloring and a small piece of wax paper that you have punched with a single hole-puncher. Place a few drops of the blue food coloring on your tongue. Place the wax paper that has the hole punched in it over the blue patch on your tongue. Now carefully count the little pink circles that are within the circle. If you have a lot (25 or more) of little pink circles, then you have more than the average number of papillae and are a supertaster (each papillae contains 6–15 taste

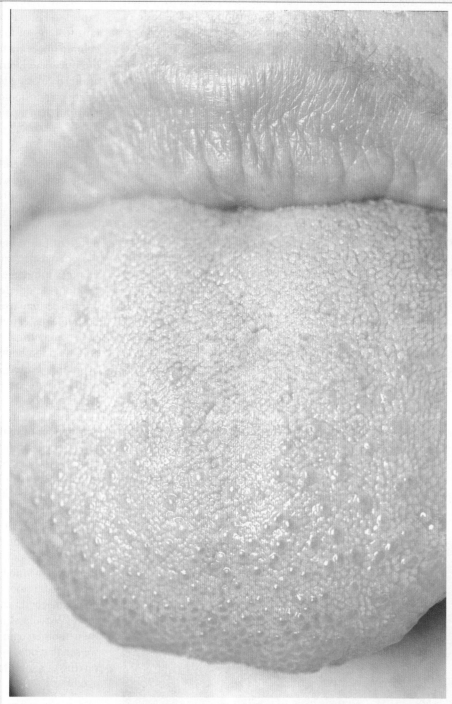

This tongue has an average number of papillae, or bumps containing taste buds. The tongue of a "supertaster" would have as many as twice the papillae seen here.

Koval Image Creation/WorkbookStock/Getty Images

buds). If you have very few pink circles (less than 6), then you are a nontaster and are probably insensitive to bitter and other strong tastes. Anything between these two extremes is where most of us (50%) fall. With our average number of papillae, we enjoy most foods and don't find them too bitter or too sweet, but also don't find them bland.

People from different cultures differ little in basic sensory capacities, such as the ability to discriminate degrees of brightness or loudness (Berry et al., 1992). There is some evidence that the threshold for detecting odors may vary between folks in industrialized settings and those in nonindustrialized locations (Sorokowska et al., 2013). Researchers found that people of the nonindustrialized rainforest could detect lower concentrations of an odor compared with people from an industrialized area of Germany. The difference may reflect compromised olfactory systems due to pollution and chemicals in the industrialized group, or it could be that the nonindustrialized group relies more on the sense of smell, fostering greater sensitivity.

Although there may be some differences in sensory thresholds, the bigger difference seems to be in people's perceptions and interpretations of sensory input. For example, you have already seen that children become insensitive, starting at the end of the first year of life, to speech sound contrasts that they do not hear regularly because they are not important in their primary language. Michael Lynch and his associates (1990) have shown that the same is true for perceptions of music. Infants from the United States, they found, noticed equally notes that violated either Western musical scales or the Javanese pelog scale. This suggests that humans are born with the potential to perceive music from a variety of cultures. However, American adults were less sensitive to bad notes in the unfamiliar Javanese musical system than to mistuned notes in their native Western scale, suggesting that their years of experience with Western music had shaped their perceptual skills.

Another example of cultural influence concerns the ability to translate perceptions of the human form into a drawing. In Papua New Guinea, where there is no cultural tradition of drawing and painting, children aged 10–15 who have had no schooling do not have much luck drawing the human body; they draw scribbles or tadpole-like forms far more often than children in the same society who have attended school and have been exposed many times to drawings of people (Martlew & Connolly, 1996; ■ Figure 6.5). We all have the capacity to create two-dimensional representations, but we apparently develop that capacity more rapidly if our culture provides us with relevant experiences.

Interesting research by Asifa Majid and Niclas Burenhult (2014) suggests that perception of odors is also influenced by culture. Westerners often have a hard time naming an odor, but Majid and Burenhult's research shows that this is not universally true. They studied Jahai, one of the hunter–gatherer subgroups of the Malay Peninsula. It turns out that the Jahai have many more words to describe odors, allowing them to name odors more readily than Westerners whose language does not include such rich descriptors.

Other research compared Japanese and German women's ratings of three groups of odors, including one set of odors that would likely be familiar to Japanese women, a second set likely familiar to German women, and a third set that would likely be familiar to both groups. Consistent with the researcher's hypotheses, Japanese women were better able to describe the 'Japanese smells' and rated these as more pleasant, whereas the German women were better at describing the 'German smells' and thought these were more pleasant (Ayabe-Kanamura et al., 1998).

Cultural factors may not necessarily affect our sensory receptors, but they do play a role throughout infancy, childhood, and adolescence in how we learn to perceive or interpret many of the sensory signals we receive throughout our day.

■ **Figure 6.5** These human figures were drawn by children between the ages of 10 and 15. On the left, the drawings were made by children in Papua New Guinea, who often lack experience with drawing the human form and produce figures much like those done by far younger children (such as 4-year-olds) in the United States. The drawing on the right was made by a 12-year-old child in the United States. The contrast between the drawings on the left and the one on the right illustrates how cultural experience influences the ability to translate visual perceptions into representations on the page.

Source: M. Martlew & K. J. Connolly, (1996), Human figure drawings by schooled and unschooled children in Papua New Guinea. *Child Development*, 6, 2743–2762. Reprinted by permission of John Wiley & Sons, Inc.

Checking Mastery

1. What concerns might we have regarding hearing during the adolescent years?
2. What are two observations regarding the chemical senses during adolescence?

Making Connections

1. You are a tutor and want a 5-year-old and a 15-year-old to systematically compare pairs of maps to determine whether they are similar or different. What can you expect of each child, and what can you do to optimize the performance of the younger child?
2. Design an educational unit for a high school health class that is aimed at reducing the incidence of noise-induced hearing loss.

LEARNING OBJECTIVES

• Describe typical changes in vision and hearing that occur over adulthood and indicate how these changes may affect daily activities.

• Summarize changes of the chemical and somaesthetic sensory systems that occur in the aging individual.

• Provide a balanced summary of the gains and losses that are typical of older adulthood.

What becomes of sensory and perceptual capacities during adulthood? There is good news and bad news, and we might as well dispense with the bad news first: Sensory and perceptual capacities decline gradually with age in the typical person. Whispers become harder to hear, seeing in the dark becomes difficult, food may not taste as good, and so on. Often these declines begin in early adulthood and become noticeable in the 40s, sometimes giving middle-aged people a feeling that they are getting old. Further declines take place in later life, to the point that you would have a hard time finding a person age 65 or older who does not have at least a mild sensory or perceptual impairment. The good news is that these changes are gradual and usually minor. As a result, we can usually compensate for them, making small adjustments such as turning up the volume on the TV set or adding a little extra seasoning to food. Because the losses are usually not severe and because of the process of compensation, only a minority of old people develop serious problems such as blindness and deafness.

The losses we are describing take two general forms. First, sensation is affected, as indicated by raised **sensory thresholds**. The threshold for a sense is the point at which low levels of stimulation can be detected—a dim light can be seen, a faint tone can be heard, a slight odor can be detected, and so on. Stimulation below the

threshold cannot be detected, so the rise of the threshold with age means that sensitivity to very low levels of stimulation is lost. (You saw that the very young infant is also insensitive to some very low levels of stimulation.)

Second, perceptual abilities decline in some aging adults. Even when stimulation is intense enough to be well above the detection threshold, older people sometimes have difficulty processing or interpreting sensory information. As you will see, they may have trouble searching a visual scene, understanding rapid speech in a noisy room, or recognizing the foods they are tasting.

So, sensory and perceptual declines are typical during adulthood, although they are far steeper in some individuals than in others and can often be compensated for. These declines involve both a rise of thresholds for detecting stimulation and a weakening of some perceptual abilities.

Vision

Fortunately, few adults experience complete loss of vision, but many adults face some sort of vision problems as they get older. Why do these changes in the visual system occur, and is there anything you can do to prevent losses? Before we answer these questions, we need to briefly review the basic workings of the visual system.

As ■ **Figure 6.6** shows, light enters the eye through the cornea and passes through the pupil and lens before being projected (upside down) on the retina. From here, images are relayed to the brain by the optic nerve at the back of each eye. The pupil of the eye automatically becomes larger or smaller depending on the lighting conditions, and the lens changes shape, or accommodates, to keep images focused on the retina. In

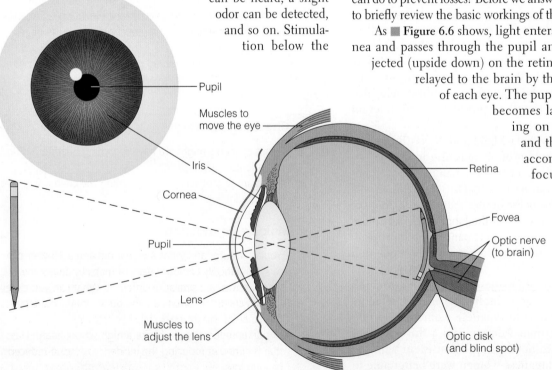

Pupil

Muscles to move the eye

Iris

Cornea

Pupil

Lens

Muscles to adjust the lens

Retina

Fovea

Optic nerve (to brain)

Optic disk (and blind spot)

■ **Figure 6.6** The human eye and retina. Light passes through the cornea, pupil, and lens and falls on the light-sensitive surface of the retina, where images of objects are projected upside down. The information is relayed to the brain by the optic nerve.

● Table 6.3 Age-Related Changes in the Visual System

Part of Eye	Age-Related Changes or Disease	Resulting Limitation(s)
Pupil	Less responsive to changes in lighting conditions and to dim light	Difficulty reading menus in dimly lit restaurants; trouble with night driving; unable to adjust quickly enough to oncoming lights at night or exiting a movie theatre into daylight
Lens	**Cataract:** Cloudiness of the lens **Presbyopia:** Thickening or hardening of the lens	Blurred or distorted vision Decreased ability to see close objects; need for "reading" glasses
Retina	**Age-related macular degeneration (AMD):** Photoreceptors in the middle of the retina, the *macula*, deteriorate **Retinitis pigmentosa (RP):** Deterioration of light-sensitive cells outside the macula	Loss of central vision, an important contributor to reading, driving, watching TV, and other daily activities Loss of peripheral vision
Eyeball	**Glaucoma:** Increased fluid pressure in the eyeball	Loss of peripheral vision and eventual loss of all vision

adolescents and young adults, the visual system is normally at peak performance. Aging brings changes to all components of the visual system. We summarize the most common vision problems in ● **Table 6.3**.

Some of these changes have important implications for everyday functioning. For example, changes in the pupil lead to difficulty with reading in dim lighting conditions, such as those found in many restaurants. Approximately one in three adults over the age of 85 years exhibits a tenfold loss of the ability to read low-contrast words in dim lighting, as in trying to read certain menus in restaurants with 'mood lighting' (Owsley, 2011). But as ▪**Figure 6.7** shows, older adults may continue to read well under ideal conditions of high contrast and bright light. Older adults may also struggle with night driving, as the pupil of the eye requires more time to adapt to the bright lights of oncoming cars and trucks, and then back again to the dark road.

The thickening and increasing rigidity of the lens of the eye make it difficult to focus on close objects. You may notice that many middle-aged and older adults use reading glasses or they may gradually move newspapers and books farther from their eyes to make them clearer—both are methods of compensating for the decline of near vision that is associated with hardening of the eye's lens and is the most noticeable feature of presbyopia, or aging of the eye.

As for distance vision, visual acuity as measured by standard eye charts increases in childhood, peaks in the 20s, remains steady through middle age, and steadily declines in old age. The implications for the average adult are fairly minor. For example, in one major study, three out of four older adults (75 years and older) had good corrected vision (Evans et al., 2002). At worst, most of them could see at 20 feet what a person with standard acuity can see at 25 feet—not a big problem. Among the oldest adults—those in their 90s—only 7% have lost all functional vision (Evans et al., 2002). Several studies show that women experience greater declines in visual acuity than men (see, for example, Zetterberg, 2016). Older women with declining vision are more susceptible to falling and fracturing a bone, which is a serious threat to their independence (Ambrose, Paul, & Hausdorff, 2013; Marks, 2014). Fracturing a hip often triggers a shift from independent to assisted living and can even be fatal. And poor vision that is not correctable can seriously decrease older adults' quality of life. According to one estimate, older adults with poor visual acuity (20/40 or worse) are as impaired as those with a major medical problem such as stroke (Chia et al., 2004).

For those with the serious retinal problem age-related macular degeneration (AMD), vision becomes blurry and begins to fade from the center of the visual field, leading to blank or dark space in the center of the image. Because cataracts are now often successfully corrected with surgery, AMD has become the leading cause of blindness in older adults. The causes of macular degeneration are largely unknown, but some research points to a genetic contribution; other research

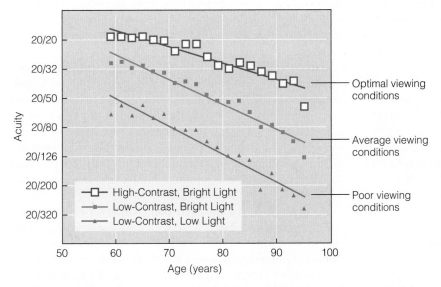

▪**Figure 6.7** Visual acuity of older adults under optimal (high contrast and bright light), average (low contrast and bright light), and poor (low contrast and low light) stimulus conditions.

Adapted from Haegerstrom-Portnoy, G., Schneck, M. E., & Brabyn, J. A. (2000). Seeing into old age: Vision function beyond acuity. *Optometry and Vision Science, 76*, 141–158. Reprinted by permission of Lippincott, Williams, and Wilkins.

As adults age, they often find themselves more bothered by glare from bright lights or sun. What is the likely cause of this increased sensitivity?

iStockphoto.com/Lisay

acceptance rather than wishful thinking adapt more successfully to visual impairment (Reinhardt, Boerner, & Horowitz, 2009). Some older adults will experience serious visual problems, but others will retain good vision and healthy eyes until well into old age, illustrating the wide range of variability in vision among older adults (Dagnelie, 2013).

Attention and Visual Search

As you learned earlier in this chapter, perception is more than just seeing. It is using the senses intelligently and allocating attention efficiently. Francesca Fortenbaugh and her colleagues (2015) cleverly used data from over 10,000 visitors who completed a "continuous concentration" task on the website TestMyBrain.org. Participants ranged in age from 10 to 70 years. Consistent with what we learned in the previous section, sustained attention improved throughout the adolescent years. It was then relatively stable throughout early adulthood, peaked at age 43, and then slowly declined. Most adults are in the prime of their careers at age 43; how is it that their attention peaks 20–25 years before most people retire? Part of the answer is that the researchers measured reaction time, which generally slows across the life span. But by examining the patterns of correct and incorrect responses, as well as response times, the researchers concluded that older adults—wisely—began to use a more cautious strategy than young adults. For example, after a trial with an error, older adults strategically slowed down on the next trial, presumably to increase their accuracy.

Now consider a different type of task, one that requires dividing attention between two tasks (divided attention) or selectively attending to certain stimuli while ignoring others (selective attention; see Juola et al., 2000; Madden & Langley, 2003). The more distractors a task involves, the more the performance of elderly adults falls short of the performance of young adults. In everyday life, this may translate into difficulty carrying on a conversation while driving or problems locating the asparagus amid all the frozen vegetables at the supermarket.

In one test of visual search skills, Charles Scialfa and his colleagues (Scialfa, Esau, & Joffe, 1998) asked young adults and elderly adults to locate a target (for example, a blue horizontal line) in a display where the distractor items were clearly different (for example, red vertical lines) or in a more difficult display where the distractors shared a common feature with the target (for example, blue vertical and red horizontal lines). Older adults were slower and less accurate on the more challenging search task. They were also more distracted by irrelevant information; they were especially slow compared with young adults when the number of distractor items in the display was high.

shows a connection with cigarette smoking (Rasoulinejad et al., 2015). Currently, there is no cure for AMD, but several researchers are working to develop retinal implants that would stimulate the remaining cells of the retina and restore some useful vision (Boston Retinal Implant Project, 2016). In addition, some doctors prescribe vitamin and mineral supplements that have had some success in slowing the progression of AMD, preserving useful vision for as long as possible.

Changes in the retina also lead to decreased visual field, or a loss of peripheral (side) vision. Looking straight ahead, an older adult may see only half of what a young adult sees to the left and the right of center. Can you think of activities that might be hindered by a decreased visual field? Driving a car comes to mind. For example, when approaching an intersection, you need to be able to see what is coming toward you as well as what is coming from the side roads. **Exploration 6.2** describes some other sensory changes that might make driving more hazardous for older people.

To recap, you can expect some changes in vision as you age. (See ■ **Figure 6.8** for a view of how the world looks through aging eyes affected by the conditions discussed here.) Sensory thresholds increase with age so that you need higher levels of stimulation than when you were young. Acuity, or sharpness of vision, decreases, near vision is negatively affected by hardening of the lens (presbyopia), and it takes longer for eyes to adapt to changes. Fortunately, it is possible to correct or compensate for most of these "normal" changes. And older adults who have good family support systems and personal coping mechanisms that focus on

Glaucoma

Cataract

Diabetic Retinopathy

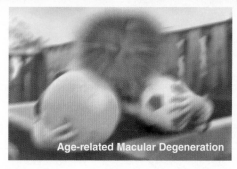
Age-related Macular Degeneration

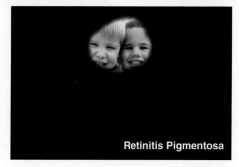
Retinitis Pigmentosa

■ **Figure 6.8** These photos illustrate how a scene might be viewed by someone with various eye conditions: (A) glaucoma; (B) cataracts; (C) diabetic retinopathy; (D) age-related macular degeneration; (E) retinitis pigmentosa.

National Eye Institute, National Institutes of Health

In some situations, elderly people appear to have difficulty inhibiting responses to irrelevant stimuli so that they can focus their attention more squarely on relevant stimuli. Jennifer Weeks and her colleagues (2016) demonstrated that older adults' propensity to encode irrelevant with relevant information could be used to their advantage. In one task, they showed adults a series of faces with names superimposed on the photo of the face and instructed them to pay attention only to the face. Later, they asked the adults to learn a set of faces with names, some of which were the same face-name combinations that had been presented in the earlier task. Older, but not younger, adults had an easier time remembering the names paired with faces in the earlier task, even though they had been told to ignore the names and focus only on the faces in that task.

In short, older adults have their greatest difficulties in processing visual information when the situation is *novel* (when they are not sure exactly what to look for or where to look) and when it is *complex* (when there is a great deal of distracting information to search through or when two tasks must be performed at once). By contrast, they have fewer problems when they have clear expectations about what they are to do and when the task is not overly complicated (Madden, 2007). Thus, an older factory worker who has inspected televisions for years may be just as speedy and accurate as a younger worker at this well-practiced, familiar task, but he might perform relatively poorly if suddenly asked to inspect pocket calculators and look for a much larger number of possible defects—a novel and complex task.

Hearing

There is some truth to the stereotype of the hard-of-hearing older person. Hearing impairment is approximately three times as prevalent as visual impairment among older adults (Davila et al., 2009). About one-third of adults in their 60s have some hearing loss and the majority (80%) of adults 85 years and older have impaired hearing (Walling & Dickson, 2012). According to one estimate, the typical 65-year-old adult can expect to live about 10 years (males) to 13 years (females) with a hearing impairment (Kiely et al., 2015). How might we improve hearing, or maintain good quality of life for those who experience hearing loss? Before we attempt to answer these questions, let's review changes with age in basic hearing capacities.

Basic Capacities

Sources of hearing problems range from excess wax buildup in the ears to infections to a sluggish nervous system. Most age-related hearing problems seem to originate in the inner ear, however (National Institute on Deafness and Other Communication Disorders, 2016a). The cochlear hair cells that serve as auditory receptors, their surrounding structures, and the neurons leading from them to the brain degenerate gradually over the adult years. The most noticeable result is a loss of sensitivity to high-frequency or high-pitched sounds, the most common form of presbycusis, or problems of the aging ear. Thus, an older person may have difficulty hearing a child's high voice, the flutes in an orchestra, and high-frequency consonant sounds such as *s*, *z*, and *ch*

Aging Drivers

Older drivers are perceived by many as more accident prone and slower than other drivers. Perhaps you have had the experience of zipping down the interstate when a slow-moving car driven by an elderly adult pulls into your path, forcing you to brake quickly. Is this experience representative, and is the stereotype of older drivers accurate? This is an important question, because 20% of all drivers will be older than 65 years by 2030 (U.S. Census Bureau, 2014).

It is true that older adults (70 years and older) are involved in more automobile fatalities than middle-aged adults (see the graph in this box). But the most accident-prone group is young drivers between ages 16 and 24 (Insurance Institute for Highway Safety, 2016). When you take into account that young people drive more than elderly people, it turns out that both elderly drivers and young drivers have more accidents per mile driven than middle-aged drivers (Insurance Institute for Highway Safety, 2016).

Why is driving hazardous for elderly adults? Clearly, vision is essential to driving; vision accounts for approximately 90% of the information necessary to operate and navigate a car (National Safety Commission, 2008). Limited visual acuity or clarity is one component of problematic driving, but as noted in the main text, poor acuity is fairly easy to correct and is, therefore, unlikely to account for all the problems older drivers have.

Diminished peripheral vision may be an issue because good drivers must be able to see vehicles and pedestrians approaching from the side. Half the fatal automobile accidents involving older drivers occur at intersections, and older drivers are more than twice as likely as young drivers to have problems making left turns (Cicchino & McGartt, 2015). Why? Poor surveillance is the most common reason. They look, but they do not necessarily see or do not interpret the information in the most effective manner. And, you learned in Chapter 5 that older adults typically have slower response times than younger adults; thus, they need more time to react to the same stimulus.

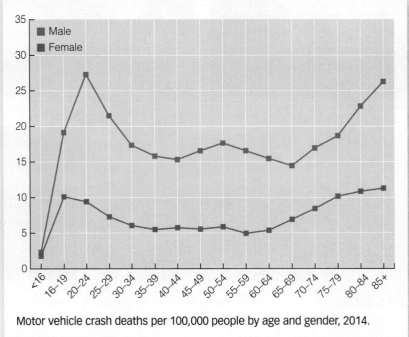

Motor vehicle crash deaths per 100,000 people by age and gender, 2014.

Insurance Institute for Highway Safety. www.iihs.org.

Older adults may also struggle to simultaneously process multiple pieces of information. Thus, older drivers have trouble reading street signs while driving (Dewar, Kline, & Swanson, 1995), and they are less able than younger adults to quickly change their focus from the dashboard to the rearview mirror to the road ahead. When another vehicle is approaching, they must be able to evaluate the speed and trajectory of this vehicle and integrate this information with their own speed and trajectory to determine a course of action. For example, is the car approaching from the left going to hit my car, or will I be through the intersection before it reaches me? Finally, after understanding the dynamics of a potentially dangerous situation, the driver must be able to react quickly to threats (for example, a child chasing a ball into the street).

However, the driving records of older adults are not as bad as might be expected, because many of them compensate for visual and other perceptual difficulties and slower reactions by

driving less frequently, especially in conditions believed to be more hazardous—at night, during rush hour, and when the weather is poor (Messinger-Rapport, 2003). Older adults with visual problems such as cataracts and those with cognitive problems are more likely to limit their driving than older adults without these problems (Messinger-Rapport, 2003). To give up driving is to give up a big chunk of independence, something anyone would be loath to do. Most people want to find ways to drive safely as long as possible.

There is more good news: Today's older drivers are healthier than those of earlier generations. Those who return to the classroom for a refresher course on safe driving and get behind-the-wheel training can improve their driving (Marottoli, 2007). By understanding the strengths and limitations of their sensory-perceptual abilities, older adults will be in a good position to keep driving safely, which is good to remember the next time you are stuck behind a slow driver.

These older adults are unlikely to experience problems locating items at their usual supermarket. But in an unfamiliar context, the same visual search of shelves for items may prove challenging.

LdF/Vetta/Getty images

that most people, men more than women, will experience some loss of sensitivity to high-frequency sounds as part of the basic aging process, but that certain people will experience more severe losses because of their experiences. There are both personal and societal consequences associated with hearing loss as individuals with hearing loss often become more socially isolated, experience lower levels of emotional well-being, and retire earlier than their peers without hearing loss (Contrera et al., 2016; Helvik, Krokstad, & Tambs, 2013).

Speech Perception

Perhaps the most important thing we do with our ears in everyday life is listen to other people during conversations. The ability to hear is one requisite for understanding speech, but this complex auditory perception task also depends on cognitive processes such as attention and memory. How well do aging adults do?

Older adults typically have more difficulty understanding conversation than younger adults do, even under ideal listening conditions. This age difference becomes smaller when differences in hearing are controlled, but it does not entirely disappear. Under poor listening conditions—for example, loud background noise—group differences between older and young adults are larger, even when individual differences in hearing are accounted for (see Wingfield & Lash, 2016). Thus, older adults may recall less information from a conversation that takes place in a crowded, noisy restaurant.

Age-related declines in auditory sensitivity (that is, acuity) are partly responsible, but cognitive declines also seem to contribute to declines in speech perception among older adults (Wingfield & Lash, 2016). Patricia Tun and her colleagues (Tun, McCoy, & Wingfield, 2009) compared two groups of older and younger adults: those with good and poor hearing. Participants listened to words and then recalled as many of these words as possible. On half the trials, they did this while also performing a simple visual tracking task. Older adults with good hearing performed significantly worse than young adults with good hearing, so there is more to the recall of spoken words than having good auditory acuity. Moreover, the additional attentional demands of the second task had no significant effect on the younger adults, regardless of whether they had good or poor hearing, but older adults were disadvantaged by increased attentional demands and recalled few spoken words when they had to divide their attention.

In addition, auditory perception tasks, like visual perception tasks, are more difficult for older people when they are novel and complex. In familiar, everyday situations, older adults are able to use contextual cues to interpret what they hear. In one study, for example, elderly adults were about as able as young adults to recall meaningful sentences they had just heard (Wingfield et al., 1985). However, they had serious difficulty repeating back grammatical sentences that made no sense or random strings of words, especially when these meaningless stimuli were spoken rapidly. So an older person may be able to follow an ordinary conversation but not a technical presentation on an unfamiliar topic—especially if the speaker makes the task harder by talking too fast.

Overall, then, most older adults have only mild hearing losses, especially for high-frequency sounds, and only minor

(Whitbourne & Whitbourne, 2014) but may have less trouble with deep voices, tubas, and sounds such as b. After age 50, lower-frequency sounds also become increasingly difficult to hear (Kline & Scialfa, 1996). Thus, to be heard by the average older adult, a sound—especially a high-pitched sound but ultimately any sound—must be louder than it needs to be to exceed the auditory threshold of a younger adult.

Is this loss of hearing with age the inevitable result of basic aging processes, or is it caused by other factors? Researchers know that the loss is more noticeable among men than among women, that men are more likely to work in noisy industrial jobs, and that those who hold such jobs experience more hearing loss than other men (Masterson et al., 2015). But even when adults who have held relatively quiet jobs are studied, men show detectable hearing losses earlier in life (in their 30s) and lose hearing sensitivity at a faster rate than women do (Pearson et al., 1995). It seems, then,

problems understanding everyday speech, at least under good listening conditions. In addition, they can compensate for their difficulties successfully—for example, by reading lips and relying on contextual cues. Novel and complex speech heard under poor listening conditions is likely to cause more trouble. Returning to the questions we asked at the beginning of this section, **Application 6.2** describes how we might help older people to improve their hearing or compensate for its loss and maintain good quality of life.

Aging of the Chemical Senses

Does the aging of sensory systems also mean that older people become less able to appreciate tastes and aromas? On average, yes: There is a general decline in sensitivity to taste, with older men showing somewhat greater decline than older women (Wehling et al., 2016). But keep in mind that there is great variability: Some older adults will continue to have keen senses of smell and taste, while others experience sharp declines in these chemical senses. Thus, some older adults may report that food tastes bland and use larger amounts of salt, sugar, and other seasonings than they used when they were younger. In addition,

both middle-aged and older adults sometimes have difficulty discriminating among tastes that differ in intensity (Nordin et al., 2003). In one study, older adults were less able than young adults to reliably recognize a food on the basis of smell and taste (see ● **Table 6.4**). Older adults tend to produce less saliva than younger adults, and saliva facilitates distribution of the chemical molecules carrying information about taste around the mouth (Brynie, 2009). Interestingly, though, older adults do not have difficulty distinguishing degrees of sweetness; people apparently do not lose the sweet tooth they are born with!

The ability to perceive odors also typically declines with age. Sensitivity to odors increases from childhood to early adulthood. At peak levels, humans can detect somewhere around a trillion different odors (Bushdid et al., 2014). Declines in olfaction occur during adulthood, more so with increasing age, but differences among age groups are usually small, and many older people retain their sensitivity to odors. The age decline depends on the type of odor: Older adults can identify and remember unpleasant odors just as well as younger adults, although they show some decline in their ability to detect and remember pleasant odors (Larsson, Öberg-Blåvarg, & Jönsson, 2009). Women are more likely than men to maintain their ability to label odors in scratch-and-sniff

● APPLICATION 6.2
Aiding Adults with Hearing Impairments

In **Application 6.1**, we examined ways to help infants and children who have hearing impairments, often from birth. Here we consider the other end of the life span. What can be done to assist hearing-impaired adults, most of whom were born with normal hearing? Unfortunately, many older adults are reluctant to admit that they have a hearing problem and do not seek assistance, or they may not even realize they have hearing loss as it occurs gradually and they have learned to compensate. Among those who acknowledge having a hearing problem, many refuse to wear a hearing aid because they feel it stigmatizes them as old, or they report that hearing aids do not work or do not help them to hear better (Lupsakko, Kautiainen, & Sulkava, 2005).

Those who do not have their hearing corrected may suffer depression, decreased independence, and strained relationships (Appollonio et al., 1996). Imagine how hard social interaction can become if you cannot understand what is being said, misinterpret what is said, or have to keep asking people to repeat what they said. One 89-year-old woman became extremely depressed and isolated: "There is an *awfulness* about silence. . . . I am

days without speaking a word. It is affecting my voice. I fear for my mind. I cannot hear the alarm clock, telephone ring, door bell, radio, television—or the human voice" (Meadows-Orlans & Orlans, 1990, pp. 424–425). In contrast, among those older adults who do use hearing aids, quality of life improves (Vuorialho, Karinen, & Sorri, 2006). We tend to think of vision as our most important sense, but hearing impairments may be more disruptive than visual impairments to cognitive and social functioning.

Hearing aids, although beneficial, cannot restore normal hearing; they tend to distort sounds and to magnify background noise as well as what the wearer is trying to hear. In addition, many older people are ill-served by hearing aids that are of poor quality or that are poorly matched to their specific hearing problems. Because cochlear implants work best for individuals exposed to spoken language before they lost their hearing, elderly people are ideal candidates for them. They tolerate the surgical procedure required for implantation well, and their hearing-test scores increase significantly (Kelsall, Shallop, & Burnelli, 1995). In addition, adults who receive cochlear implants report

that their quality of life improves significantly (Faber & Grontved, 2000). Cochlear implants, however, cannot work overnight miracles; it can take months, even years, to learn how to interpret the messages relayed by the implant to the brain (Colburn, 2000).

Finally, the physical and social environment can be modified to help people of all ages with hearing losses. For example, furniture can be arranged to permit face-to-face contact; lights can be turned on to permit use of visual cues such as gestures and lip movements. Then there are the simple guidelines we can follow to make ourselves understood by hearing-impaired people. One of the most important is to avoid shouting. Shouting not only distorts speech but also raises the pitch of the voice (therefore making it more difficult for elderly people to hear); it also makes it harder for the individual to read lips. It is best to speak at a normal rate, clearly but without overarticulating, with your face fully visible at a distance of about 3–6 feet.

With modern technology, appropriate education, effective coping strategies, and help from those who hear, hearing-impaired and deaf individuals of all ages can thrive.

Elderly adults have more difficulty than young college students in identifying most blended foods by taste and smell alone. Percentages of those recognizing food include reasonable guesses such as "orange" in response to "apple."

Percentage Recognizing Food		
Pureed Food Substance	College Students (ages 18–22)	Elderly People (ages 67–93)
Fruits		
Apple	93	79
Banana	93	59
Pineapple	93	86
Vegetables		
Broccoli	81	62
Carrot	79	55
Cucumber	44	28

Source: Schiffman, (1977), Food recognition by the elderly. *Journal of Gerontology, 32,* 586–592. Reprinted by permission of Oxford University Press.

tests, partly because they are less likely than men to have worked in factories and been exposed to chemicals that could damage the chemical receptors involved in odor perception (Ship & Weiffenbach, 1993). Also, healthy adults of both sexes retain their sense of smell better than do those who have diseases, smoke, or take medications (Wilson et al., 2006). Again, then, perceptual losses in later life are part of the basic aging process but vary from person to person depending on environmental factors.

Are declines in the sense of smell truly significant? Yes. Researchers Johannes Attems, Lauren Walker, and Kurt Jellinger (2015) note that a diminished ability to smell "significantly impairs physical well-being, quality of life, enjoyment of food, everyday safety, and is associated with increased mortality in older adults" (p. 486). If foods do not have much flavor, an older person may lose interest in eating and may not get proper nourishment. Alternatively, an older person may overuse seasonings such as salt or may eat spoiled food, which can threaten health in other ways. Clearly, a diminished sense of smell is more than an inconvenience associated only with minor decreases in flavor perception. As you will learn in Chapter 16, a decreased sense of smell may be a harbinger of serious cognitive impairments (Roberts et al., 2016).

Conclusions about changes in taste and smell must be put in perspective. These sensory and perceptual abilities are highly variable across the entire life span, not just in older adulthood. Taste and smell receptors are replaced throughout the life span and are influenced by such environmental factors as smoke, medications, and extreme temperatures. This means that, under optimal environmental conditions, many older adults will not experience deficits: They can continue to smell the roses and enjoy their food.

Changes in the Somaesthetic Senses

By now you have seen numerous indications that older adults are often less able than younger adults to detect weak sensory stimulation. This holds true for the sense of touch. The detection threshold for touch increases and sensitivity is gradually lost from middle childhood on. It is not clear that minor losses in touch sensitivity have many implications for daily life, however.

Similarly, older people may be less sensitive to changes in temperature than younger adults are (Frank et al., 2000). Some keep their homes too cool because they are unaware of being cold; others may fail to notice that it is too hot. Because older bodies are less able than younger ones to maintain an even temperature, elderly people face an increased risk of death in heat waves or cold spells (Worfolk, 2000).

It seems only fair that older people should also be less sensitive to painful stimulation, but are they? They are indeed less likely than younger adults to report weak levels of stimulation as painful, although the age differences in pain thresholds are not large or consistent (Wickrematchi & Llewelyn, 2006). Yet older people seem to be no less sensitive to stronger pain stimuli. Unfortunately, older adults are more likely to experience chronic pain than younger adults but are less likely to obtain adequate pain relief (Gloth, 2001). Adults with arthritis, osteoporosis, cancer, and other diseases who also experience depression and anxiety are especially likely to perceive pain (Hall, 2016). Treating these secondary conditions and administering effective pain relief can improve the daily functioning and psychological well-being of older adults.

The Adult in Perspective

Of all the changes in sensation and perception during adulthood that we have considered, those involving vision and hearing appear to be the most important and the most universal. Not only do these senses become less keen, but older people also use them less effectively in such complex perceptual tasks as searching a cluttered room for a missing book or following rapid conversation in a noisy room. Declines in the other senses are less serious and do not affect as many people.

Although people compensate for many sensory declines, their effects cannot be entirely eliminated. At some point, aging adults find that changes in sensory abilities affect their activities. As ● **Table 6.5** shows, older adults with one or two sensory impairments are more likely to experience difficulty with basic tasks of living—walking, getting outside, getting in or out of bed or a chair, taking medicines, or preparing meals. Notice, however, that even older adults without sensory impairments report some difficulty with these tasks. People who are limited by sensory impairments usually have physical or intellectual impairments as well, most likely because of general declines in neural functioning that affect both perception and cognition (Baltes & Lindenberger, 1997; Vallet, 2015). Most older adults, even those with sensory impairments, are engaged in a range of activities and are living full lives. Thus, although most adults will experience some declines in sensory abilities with age, these changes do not need to detract from their quality of life.

Activity	With Visual Impairments	With Hearing Impairments	With Both Visual and Hearing Impairments	Without Visual or Hearing Impairments
Difficulty walking	43.3	30.7	48.3	22.2
Difficulty getting outside	28.6	17.3	32.8	11.9
Difficulty getting in or out of a bed or chair	22.1	15.1	25.0	10.4
Difficulty taking medicines	11.8	7.7	13.4	5.0
Difficulty preparing meals	18.7	11.6	20.7	7.8

Source: Adapted from Campbell et al., 1999, Surveillance for sensory impairment, activity limitation, and health-related quality of life among older adults: United States, 1993–1997. *CDC MMWR Surveillance Summaries, 48* (SS08).

● Checking Mastery

1. What are the most common eye problems experienced by older adults?
2. What is the greatest functional difficulty with hearing loss among older adults?
3. Which taste is best perceived across the life span (that is, there is little loss of acuity)?

● Making Connections

1. You have been hired to teach a cooking course to elderly adults. First, analyze the perceptual strengths and weaknesses of your students: What perceptual tasks might be easy for them, and what tasks might be difficult? Second, considering at least three senses, think of five strategies you can use to help your students compensate for the declines in perceptual capacities that some of them may be experiencing.

2. You are the coordinator for social and educational activities at your community center, which means you work with people of all ages, ranging from the youngest infants to the oldest adults. In planning activities, what should you consider in trying to capture and hold the attention of different age groups?

Chapter Summary

6.1 Perspectives on Perception

- Sensation is the detection of sensory stimulation, and perception is the interpretation of what is sensed.
- Constructivists argue that the newborn is a "blank slate" and must acquire an understanding of the world through experience with sensory inputs. Thus, according to the constructivist perspective, nurture drives the development of perception.
- Nativists believe that each person is born with some innate understanding of how to interpret sensory information. Thus, according to the nativists, the origin of perception is largely nature.
- Gibson's ecological theory proposes that everything we need to understand the world around us is available in the environment itself. We are able to directly detect the affordances of objects—what they offer us in terms of how we might interact with them. In the ecological view, nature and nurture are integrally related.

6.2 The Infant

- Methods of studying infant perception include habituation, evoked potentials, preferential looking, and operant conditioning techniques.
- The visual system is fairly well developed at birth. Infants younger than 2 months old discriminate brightness and colors and are attracted to contour, moderate complexity, and movement. Starting at 2 or 3 months, infants more clearly perceive whole patterns such as faces and seem to understand a good deal about objects and their properties, guided by intuitive theories of the physical world.

- Spatial perception develops rapidly, and by about 7 months, after they begin to crawl, infants not only perceive drop-offs but also show fear or concern about them.
- The auditory sense is well developed at birth. Young infants can recognize their mother's voice and distinguish speech sounds that adults cannot discriminate.
- The senses of taste and smell are also well developed at birth. In addition, newborns are sensitive to touch, temperature, and pain.
- The early presence of sensory and perceptual abilities suggests that they are innate, but they are also clearly influenced by early experiences. Certain experiences may be necessary for normal visual perception to develop, suggesting a sensitive period for the visual system.
- Infants actively seek out stimulation by exploring their environments, which typically provides them with the stimulation they need to develop normal sensory and perceptual skills.

6.3 The Child

- Sensory skills undergo little change during childhood, although children learn better how to use the information coming in through their senses.

- Coupling perception with action to develop locomotion skills—the ability to navigate one's body around the environment—is a major accomplishment of childhood made understandable by the dynamic systems theory.
- Cross-modal perception, the ability to recognize through one sense what was learned by a different sense, originates in infancy but becomes more fully developed in childhood.
- Learning to control attention is an important part of perceptual development during childhood. Infants and young children are selectively attentive to the world around them, but they have not fully taken charge of their attentional processes.
- With age, children become more able to concentrate on a task for a long period, to focus on relevant information and ignore distractions, and to use their senses in purposeful and systematic ways to achieve goals.

6.4 The Adolescent

- Basic perceptual and attentional skills are perfected during adolescence. Adolescents are better than children at sustaining their attention and using it selectively and strategically to solve the problem at hand.
- Teens often multitask, which can lead to less efficient learning of new information.
- Exposure to loud noise can cause tinnitus or ringing sounds in the ear that can be temporary or permanent. Damage to the auditory system from exposure to loud noise can accumulate over time, leading eventually to hearing impairment.

- The chemical senses operate at adult levels and may contribute to mate selection.

6.5 The Adult

- During adulthood, sensory and perceptual capacities gradually decline in most individuals, although many changes are minor and can be compensated for. Sensory thresholds—the amount of stimulation required for detection—rise, and perceptual processing of sensory information often declines. Moderate to severe declines that are not corrected can lead to declines in activities and quality of life among older adults.
- Visual changes include cataracts (clouding of the lens), reduced ability of the pupil to change in response to changes in light, thickening of the lens leading to decreased acuity (presbyopia), and retinal changes such as age-related macular degeneration.
- Presbycusis—changes in hearing associated with aging—affects many older adults and most commonly leads to trouble detecting high-pitched sounds. Older adults have more difficulty with speech perception, especially under noisy conditions, than younger adults. Hearing aids can significantly improve older adults' abilities to detect sounds.
- Many older people have difficulty recognizing or enjoying foods, largely because of declines in the sense of smell and memory; touch, temperature, and pain sensitivity also decrease slightly, but intense pain stimuli still hurt.

Key Terms

sensation **166**
perception **166**
constructivist **166**
nativist **166**
affordances **167**
visual acuity **168**
visual accommodation **168**
habituation **168**
form perception **169**
contour **169**
size constancy **171**

visual cliff **171**
intuitive theories **172**
phoneme **173**
evoked potentials **174**
cochlear implant **174**
olfaction **176**
somaesthetic senses **176**
sensitive period **178**
cataract **178**
sleeper effect **178**
locomotion **179**

gross motor skills **180**
fine motor skills **180**
rhythmic stereotypies **180**
dynamic systems theory **180**
ulnar grasp **182**
pincer grasp **182**
cross-modal perception **182**
attention **183**
orienting system **183**
focusing system **183**
selective attention **183**

multitasking **185**
tinnitus **186**
sensory threshold **190**
presbyopia **191**
retinitis pigmentosa (RP) **191**
glaucoma **191**
age-related macular degeneration (AMD) **191**
presbycusis **193**

7 Cognition

"Consider what would happen if children of various ages were given a horseshoe-shaped metal magnet for the first time. Six-month-olds might accommodate to the unfamiliar metallic taste, the peculiar (horseshoe) shape, and the sound of the magnet being dropped. . . . Three-year-olds, if given an assortment of objects, might accommodate to the fact that some of the objects cling to the magnet and might entertain explanations such as 'stickiness' and 'wanting to stay together'. Nine-year-old children might construct the concept that only metal objects are pulled to the magnet and might notice the conditions in which this occurs—through glass, water, and certain distances. Only adolescents could accommodate by formulating an abstract theory of magnetism and simultaneously consider all of the variables involved, such as the size and shape of the magnet and the distance from the object" (Miller, 2016, pp. 59–60).

In this example, four children—an infant, a 3-year-old, a 9-year-old, and an adolescent—interact with the same object, a magnet, but their interactions are influenced by their current level of development and lead to very different understandings. The infant is competent at getting objects into her mouth and so goes the magnet. The 3-year-old is probably amused by how some objects stick to the magnet without having any clue why this occurs. The 9-year-old may do some trial-and-error testing to see which objects stick to the magnet, and from this develops a fairly logical understanding of magnetism. The adolescent may generate hypotheses about magnetism, systematically test these hypotheses, and create an abstract understanding of the properties of magnetism.

At least this is how Piaget's prominent theory of cognitive development would interpret the situation.

According to Piaget's theory, by actively exploring the physical world and seeing how their actions bring about changes, children like these two construct cognitive structures that help them organize and understand their world.

Henglein & Steets/Cultura/Jupiter Images

Psychology was significantly altered by Piaget's curiosity and desire to figure out what children were thinking and why their responses changed with age. The theory dominated the field for many decades and generated a tremendous amount of useful research. Some findings emerging from this research support Piaget's general description of the development of cognition—the activity of knowing and the processes through which knowledge is acquired and problems are solved. Other findings, though, have led to the emergence of alternative theories. Perhaps the most influential of these is Lev Vygotsky's sociocultural perspective on cognitive development. After gaining an understanding of these two theories, we consider a contemporary theory that incorporates some ideas from both Piaget and Vygotsky before turning our attention to changes in cognitive development across the life span.

7.1

Piaget's Constructivist Approach

LEARNING OBJECTIVES

- Describe the processes of developmental change in Piaget's theory and give an example of each process.

- Discuss the strengths of Piaget's theory, noting features that remain fairly well supported by the research in this field.

- Explain the challenges to Piaget's theory that have emerged as scientists have conducted research to test hypotheses generated from the theory.

In their book on theories of development, John Flavell and his colleagues (2001, p. 8) captured the tremendous influence of Jean Piaget with this summation: "[T]heories of cognitive development can be divided into B.P. (Before Piaget), and A.P. (After Piaget)." Our understanding of cognitive development has been forever altered by the theory that emerged from Piaget's careful observations of children. As a young man, Piaget was working at the Alfred Binet laboratories in Paris on the first standardized IQ test. In constructing the IQ test, Binet was interested in estimating an individual's intelligence based on the number of questions they correctly answered. Piaget, though, soon became intrigued by children's *wrong* answers and noticed that children of about the same age gave the same kinds of wrong answers. By questioning them to find out how they were thinking about the problems presented to them, he began to realize that young children do not simply know less than older children; instead, they think differently.

The flexible question-and-answer technique that Piaget used to discover how children think about problems has become known as the clinical method. Consider the following exchange between Piaget and 6-year-old Van (Piaget, 1926, p. 293):

Piaget: Why is it dark at night?
Van: Because we sleep better, and so that it shall be dark in the rooms.
Piaget: Where does the darkness come from?
Van: Because the sky becomes grey.
Piaget: What makes the sky become grey?
Van: The clouds become dark.
Piaget: How is that?
Van: God makes the clouds become dark.

In the clinical method, the initial question may be consistent across children, but subsequent questions to children would vary. Many contemporary researchers consider this method imprecise because it does not involve asking standardized questions of all children tested. But Piaget (1926) believed that the investigator should have the flexibility to pursue an individual child's line of reasoning to fully understand that child's mind. Using his naturalistic observations of his own children and the clinical method to explore how children understand everything from the rules of games to the concepts of space and time, Piaget formulated his view of the development of intelligence.

What Is Intelligence?

Piaget's definition of intelligence reflects his background in biology: *Intelligence is a basic life function that helps an organism adapt to its environment.* You can see adaptation when you watch a toddler attempting to get chunks of food from plate to mouth, a school-age child figuring out how to divide treats among friends, or an adolescent trying to set up a new computer. The newborn enters an unfamiliar world with few means of adapting to it other than working senses and reflexes. But Piaget viewed infants as active agents in their own development, learning about the world of people and things by observing, investigating, and experimenting.

As infants and children explore their world, their brains respond by creating schemes (sometimes called *schema* in the singular and *schemata* in the plural). **Schemes** are cognitive structures—organized patterns of action or thought that people construct to interpret their experiences (Piaget, 1952, 1977). Schemes are like having a set of rules or procedures that can be repeated and generalized across various situations (Miller, 2016). For example, the infant's grasping actions and sucking responses are early behavioral schemes, patterns of action used to adapt to different objects. During their second year, children develop symbolic schemes, or concepts. They use internal mental symbols such as images and words to represent objects and events, such as when a young child sees a funny dance and carries away a mental model of how it was done (Miller, 2016). Older children become able to manipulate symbols in their heads to help them solve problems, such as when they add two numbers together mentally rather than on paper or with the aid of their fingers.

Using Piaget's clinical method, this interviewer might present a simple problem to solve or ask a question and see where the child's answer leads their conversation.

Masterfile

As children develop more sophisticated schemes, or cognitive structures, they become increasingly able to adapt to their environments. Because they gain new schemes as they develop, children of different ages will respond differently to the same objects and events. The infant may get to know a juice box mainly as something to chew, the preschooler may decide to let the juice box symbolize or represent a cell phone and put it to her ear, and the school-age child may read the writing on the box.

How Does Intelligence Develop?

Recall from Chapter 2 that Piaget took an interactionist position on the nature–nurture issue: Children actively create knowledge by building schemes from their experiences (nurture), using two inborn (nature) intellectual functions, which he called organization and adaptation. These processes operate throughout the life span. Through **organization**, children systematically combine existing schemes into new and more complex ones. Thus, their minds are not cluttered with an endless number of independent facts; they contain instead logically ordered and interrelated actions and ideas. For example, the infant who gazes, reaches, and grasps will organize these simple schemes into the complex structure of visually directed reaching. Complex cognitive structures in older children grow out of reorganizations of simpler structures.

Adaptation is the process of adjusting to the demands of environment (Piaget, 1971). It occurs through two complementary processes, assimilation and accommodation. Imagine that you are a 2-year-old, that the world is still new, and that you see your first skunk in the backyard. What will you make of it? You likely will try to relate it to something familiar. **Assimilation** is the process by which we interpret new experiences in terms of existing schemes or cognitive structures. Thus, if you already have a scheme that mentally represents your knowledge of cats, you may label this new beast "kitty." Through assimilation, we deal with our environment in our own terms, sometimes bending the world to squeeze it into our existing categories. Throughout the life span, we rely on our existing cognitive structures to understand new events.

But if you notice that this new "kitty" moves differently than most cats and that it has a bushier tail, a pointier nose and an awful odor, you may be prompted to change your understanding of the world of four-legged animals. **Accommodation** is the process of modifying existing schemes to better fit new experiences. Perhaps you will need to invent a new name for this animal or ask what it is and revise your concept of four-legged animals accordingly.

If we always assimilated new experiences, our understandings would never advance. Piaget believed that all new experiences are greeted with a mix of assimilation and accommodation. Once we have schemes, we apply them to make sense of the world, but we also encounter puzzles that force us to modify our understandings through accommodation. According to Piaget, when new events seriously challenge old schemes, or prove our existing understandings to be inadequate, we experience cognitive conflict. This cognitive conflict, or disequilibrium, then stimulates cognitive growth and the formation of more adequate understandings (Piaget, 1985; ■ **Figure** 7.1). This occurs because mental conflict is not pleasant; we are motivated to reduce conflict through what Piaget called **equilibration**, the process of achieving mental stability where our

Equilibrium

Current understanding of the world (internal data) is consistent with external data.

Small furry animals with fluffy tails are called cats. They meow and smell nice.

Disequilibrium

Along comes a new piece of information that does not fit with current understanding of the world, leading to disequilibrium—an uncomfortable state of mind that the child seeks to resolve.

That's strange—this small furry creature has a fluffy tail but it doesn't meow and it certainly doesn't smell nice!

Assimilation and accommodation

This unbalanced (confused) state can be resolved through the processes of organization and adaptation (assimilation and accommodation).

This can't be a cat. Mommy called it a skunk, which must be a different kind of animal.

Equilibrium

These lead to a new way of understanding the world— a new state of equilibrium.

I'll have to remember that skunks and cats are different types of animals.

■ **Figure 7.1** Process of change in Jean Piaget's theory

internal thoughts are consistent with the evidence we are receiving from the external world (Piaget, 1978).

Intelligence, then, in Piaget's view, develops through the interaction of the individual with the environment. Nature provides the complementary processes of assimilation and accommodation that make adaptation to environments possible. The processes of adaptation and organization are driven by an innate tendency to maintain equilibration. As a result of the interaction of biological maturation and experience, humans progress through four distinct stages of cognitive development:

1. The sensorimotor stage (birth to roughly 2 years)
2. The preoperational stage (roughly 2–7 years)
3. The concrete operations stage (roughly 7–11 years)
4. The formal operations stage (roughly 11 years and beyond)

These stages represent qualitatively different ways of thinking and occur in an invariant sequence—that is, in the same order in all children. However, depending on their experiences, children may progress through the stages at different rates, with some moving more rapidly or more slowly than others. Thus, the age ranges associated with the stages are only guidelines. A child's stage of development is determined by his reasoning processes, not his age. We'll describe each of the stages more fully as we move through this chapter.

Piaget's Contributions

Piaget is a giant in the field of human development. As one scholar quoted by Harry Beilin (1992) put it, "[A]ssessing the impact of Piaget on developmental psychology is like assessing the impact of Shakespeare on English literature or Aristotle on philosophy— impossible" (p. 191). It is hard to imagine that researchers would know even a fraction of what they know about intellectual development without Piaget's groundbreaking work.

One sign of a good theory is that it stimulates research. Piaget asked fundamentally important questions about how humans come to know the world and showed that we can answer them "by paying attention to the small details of the daily lives of our children" (Gopnik, 1996, p. 225). His cognitive developmental perspective has been applied to almost every aspect of human development, and the important questions he raised continue to guide the study of cognitive development. Thus, his theory has undoubtedly stimulated much research in the decades following its creation.

We can credit Piaget with some lasting insights, including ones that have become so deeply entrenched in our way of thinking as to be taken for granted (Flavell, 1996). For example, Piaget showed us that infants and children are active in their own development—that from the start they seek to master problems

Piaget's theory makes the claim that this toddler and his teenage cousin think differently. They have different cognitive structures for guiding their actions and interpreting the world around them.

Septemberlegs/Alamy Stock Photo

and to understand the incomprehensible by using the processes of assimilation and accommodation to resolve their cognitive disequilibrium. And as you will see as you proceed through this chapter, Piaget taught us that young people think differently than older people do—and often in ways we never would have suspected.

In addition, many scholars today agree that Piaget was largely right in his basic *description* of cognitive development. The sequence he proposed—sensorimotor to preoperational to concrete operations to formal operations—seems to describe the general course and content of intellectual development for children and adolescents from the many cultures and subcultures that have been studied (Miller, 2016). Although cultural factors influence the rate of cognitive growth, the direction of development is always from sensorimotor thinking to preoperational thinking to concrete operations to, for many, formal operations (or even postformal operations).

Challenges to Piaget

Partly because Piaget's theory has been so enormously influential, it has had more than its share of criticism: Some of this has been mild—suggesting the need for minor tweaking of the theory—whereas other criticism has been more severe. John Broughton (1984), for example, concluded that Piaget's theory is fundamentally flawed and should be thrown out. We are not ready to throw out what has been a blockbuster theory, but we need to point out four common criticisms (see Lourenco & Machado, 1996; Miller, 2016):

1. **Underestimating young minds.** Piaget seems to have underestimated the cognitive abilities of infants and young children, although he emphasized that he was more interested in understanding the sequences of changes than the specific ages at which they occur (Lourenco & Machado, 1996). When researchers use more familiar problems than Piaget's and simplify the tasks to their essentials, hidden competencies of young children—and of adolescents and adults—are sometimes revealed. What should we make of these earlier competencies when task demands are reduced? It may be that Piaget failed to distinguish between *competence* and *performance*. There is an important difference between understanding a concept (competence) and passing a test designed to measure it (performance). Piaget may have been too quick to assume that children who failed one of his tests lacked competence; they may only have failed to demonstrate their competence in a particular situation. Perhaps more importantly, Piaget may have overemphasized the idea that knowledge is an all-or-nothing concept (Schwitzgebel, 1999). Instead of having or not having a particular competence, children probably gain competence gradually and experience long periods between not understanding and understanding. Indeed, many of the seemingly contradictory results of studies using Piagetian tasks can be accounted for with this idea of gradual change in understanding (Miller, 2016).

2. **Wrongly claiming that broad stages of development exist.** According to Piaget, each new stage of cognitive development is a coherent mode of thinking applied across a range of problems. Piaget emphasized the consistency of thinking *within* a stage and the difference *between* stages. Yet individuals are often inconsistent in their performance on different tasks that presumably measure the abilities defining a given stage. This may occur because cognitive development is domain specific—that is, it is a matter of building skills in particular content areas—and growth in one domain may proceed much faster than growth in another (Fischer, Kenny, & Pipp, 1990). In addition, the transitions between stages are not swift and abrupt, as most of Piaget's writings suggest, but are often lengthy (over several years) and subtle. It is not always clear when a child has made the shift from one set of cognitive structures to a more advanced set of structures. Thus, research findings have cast serious doubts on the idea that stages can adequately describe development (Barrouillet, 2015).

3. **Failing to adequately explain development.** Many critics have noted that Piaget did a better job of describing development than of explaining how it comes about (Bruner, 1997; Miller, 2016). To be sure, Piaget wrote extensively about his interactionist position on the nature–nurture issue and did as much as any developmental theorist to tackle the question of how development comes about. Presumably, humans are always assimilating new experiences in ways that their level of maturation allows, accommodating their thinking to those experiences, and reorganizing their cognitive structures into increasingly complex modes of thought. Yet this explanation is vague. Researchers need to know far more about how specific maturational changes in the brain and specific kinds of experiences contribute to important cognitive advances. A good theory needs to be able to explain and predict the course of cognitive development, something that Piaget's theory struggles to accomplish.

4. **Giving limited attention to social influences on cognitive development.** Some critics say Piaget paid too little attention to how children's minds develop through their social interactions with more competent individuals and how they develop

differently in different cultures (Karpov, 2005). Piaget's child often resembles an isolated scientist exploring the world alone, but children develop their minds through interactions with parents, teachers, peers, and siblings. True, Piaget had interesting ideas about the role of *peers* in helping children adopt other perspectives and reach new conclusions (see Chapter 13 on moral development). But he did not believe that children learned much from their interactions with *adults*. This may seem counterintuitive, but Piaget believed that children see other children, but not adults, as "like themselves." Hearing a different perspective from someone like oneself can trigger internal conflict, but hearing a perspective from someone different from oneself may not be viewed as a challenge to one's current way of thinking because the person—and their views—are simply too different. Thus, in Piaget's model, no notable cognitive disequilibrium, and therefore little cognitive growth, occurs from children interacting with adults. As you will see shortly, the significance of social interaction and culture for cognitive development is the basis of the perspective on cognitive development offered by one of Piaget's early critics, Lev Vygotsky.

A Modern Take on Constructivism

By now, you should know that Piaget adopted a position called *constructivism*, maintaining that children actively create or build their own understandings of the world based on their experiences. Some scholars have attempted to be more precise on the specific mechanisms of *how* development occurs, that is, just how do children construct knowledge? One promising approach to this issue comes from work by Denis Mareschal, Gert Westermann, and Annette Karmiloff-Smith (see, for example, Karmiloff-Smith, 2006, 2009, 2015; Mareschal, 2011; Mareschal et al., 2007; Westermann, Thomas, & Karmiloff-Smith, 2010). They propose a model of cognitive development that builds on this central tenet of Piaget's theory, namely, that we construct increasingly complex mental representations of the world.

According to the neuroconstructivism theory, new knowledge is constructed through changes in the neural structures of the brain in response to experiences (Westermann et al., 2010). Piaget had a

background in biology and certainly believed that biological factors played a role in cognitive development. Consider, though, that Piaget developed his theory in an era devoid of modern tests for measuring electrical activity and blood flow in the brain, before precise reaction time and eye tracking measures, and before genetic analyses could be performed. Thus, theories such as neuroconstructivism are not necessarily an indication that Piaget was incorrect. Instead, they are taking our understanding of cognitive development to a level not possible when Piaget developed his theory. Where Piaget noted that cognitive structures become more sophisticated and others have argued that mental representations become more complex, the neuroconstructivists believe that the neural structures in the brain underlying these cognitive phenomena develop and change in response to experience. As Annette Karmiloff-Smith (2009) states, "human intelligence is a process [that emerges from] dynamic multidirectional interactions between genes, brain, cognition, behavior, and environment" (p. 61). Development of cognition is not static but reflects a complex and ongoing interplay of factors that change across the life span and across different contexts. The manner in which an environmental factor interacts with genetic factors to influence an aspect of cognition may be quite different at different periods of the life span (Karmiloff-Smith, 2006).

Consider some research by Olivier Houdé and colleagues (2011). Children aged 5 to 10 years were given a classic Piagetian cognitive task in which they need to compare two rows of objects and determine whether the rows contain the same number of objects. As they were solving the task, researchers used functional magnetic resonance imaging (fMRI) to monitor brain activity. Children who successfully solved the task showed increased activity in parts of their brains that were not activated in children

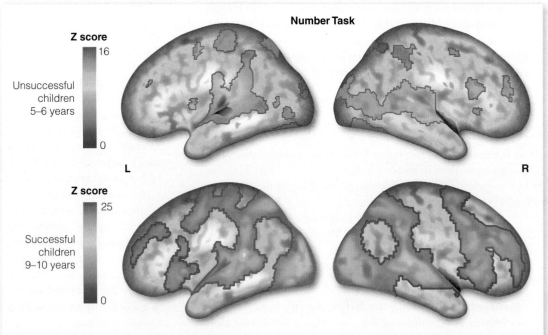

Images from functional magnetic resonance imaging (fMRI) reveal a big difference between children who successfully solve a number conservation task (the bottom images) and children who are not successful (the top images). Successful children employ both the parietal and prefrontal lobes of their brains.

Reed Elsevier

who did not solve the task. Both groups of children, solvers and nonsolvers, showed activity in a part of the brain associated with processing numbers; thus both groups understood the task to be about numbers. Obviously, though, this is not enough for success on the task. Those who were successful also showed activity in an area of their prefrontal lobes associated with working memory control. Thus, the neuroconstructivist theory attempts to modernize Piaget by connecting the patterns of thought he described with patterns of neural activity.

We leave this section by concluding that, although there have been challenges to Piaget's theory, it continues to offer a useful framework for any discussion of cognitive development. Throughout this chapter, we describe advances in cognitive development using research from Piaget and other like-minded scholars in the field. First, though, we consider another influential theorist, Lev Vygotsky, who drew our attention to the role of culture in cognition.

Checking Mastery

1. What is a scheme in Piaget's theory?
2. How do assimilation and accommodation operate to bring about cognitive change?
3. What are two of Piaget's major contributions to our understanding of cognitive development?
4. What are three problems with, or challenges to, Piaget's theory of cognitive development?

Making Connections

1. How might Piaget's theory be updated to accommodate some of the major criticisms and research findings that have emerged since he constructed his theory?
2. Using your own experiences, provide an example of how the inborn processes of organization and adaptation operate.

7.2

Vygotsky's Sociocultural Perspective

LEARNING OBJECTIVES

- Indicate how culture and social interaction affect thought in Vygotsky's theory.
- Explain how tools, especially language, influence thought.

Lev Vygotsky was born in 1896, the same year as Piaget, and was an active scholar in the 1920s and 1930s when Piaget was formulating his theory. For many years, Vygotsky's work was banned for political reasons in his homeland, the former Soviet Union, and North American scholars lacked English translations of his work, which limited consideration of Vygotsky's ideas until recent decades. In addition, Vygotsky died of tuberculosis at age 38, before his theory was fully developed. However, his main theme is clear: Cognitive growth occurs in a sociocultural context and evolves out of the child's social interactions.

Culture and Thought

Culture and society play a pivotal role in Vygotsky's theory. Indeed, intelligence in the Vygotskian model is held by the group, not the individual, and is closely tied to the language system and other tools of thinking the group has developed over time (Case, 1998). Culture and social experiences affect how we think, not just what we think.

Consider some research by Vygotsky's colleague, Alexander Luria (1974/1976), who tested groups of 9- to 12-year-old children growing up in different social environments. Children were given target words and asked to name the first thing that came to mind when they heard each word. Luria found that children growing up in a remote rural village with limited social experiences gave remarkably similar responses, whereas children growing up in a large city gave more distinctly individual answers. Vygotsky and Luria believed that this difference reflected the city children's broader exposure to various aspects of culture. On their own, the

rural children were unable to develop certain types of knowledge. Knowledge, then, depends on social experiences.

Vygotsky would not be surprised to learn that adolescent formal-operational thought is rarely used in some cultures; he expected cognitive development to vary from society to society depending on the mental tools, such as the language, that the

According to Lev Vygotsky's theory, cognitive development is shaped by the culture in which children live and the kinds of problem-solving strategies that adults and other knowledgeable guides pass on to them.

PETE MULLER/National Geographic Creative

culture values and makes available. How do children acquire their society's mental tools? They acquire them by interacting with parents and other more experienced members of the culture and by adopting their language and knowledge (Callaghan & Corbit, 2015).

Social Interaction and Thought

Consider this scenario: Annie, a 4-year-old, receives a jigsaw puzzle, her first, for her birthday. She attempts to work the puzzle but gets nowhere until her father sits down beside her and gives her some tips. He suggests that it would be a good idea to put the corners together first. He points to the pink area at the edge of one corner piece and says, "Let's look for another pink piece." When Annie seems frustrated, he places two interlocking pieces near each other so that she will notice them. And when she succeeds, he offers words of encouragement. As Annie gets the hang of it, he steps back and lets her work more independently. Vygotsky said that this kind of social interaction fosters cognitive growth.

How? First, Annie and her father are operating in what Vygotsky called the zone of proximal development—the gap between what a learner can accomplish independently and what she can accomplish with the guidance and encouragement of a more-skilled partner. Skills within the zone are ripe for development and are the skills at which instruction should be aimed. Skills outside the zone are either well mastered already or still too difficult. In this example, Annie obviously becomes a more competent puzzle-solver with her father's help than without it. More importantly, she will internalize the problem-solving techniques that she discovered in collaboration with her father, working together in her zone of proximal development, and will use them on her own, rising to a new level of independent mastery. What began as a social process involving two people becomes a cognitive process within one.

Support for Vygotsky's idea of the zone of proximal development comes from various sources, including research showing that pairing less-skilled readers with more-skilled ones substantially increases reading fluency when the less-skilled readers are provided with a model of good reading and encouragement (Nes, 2003). Other support for Vygotsky's zone comes from applied research conducted by a group of 7th and 8th grade science teachers (Hui & Mohd Salleh, 2015). The teachers first determined their students' scientific understanding by assessing their abilities to identify patterns in data and use of scientific concepts to explain these patterns. After understanding what students could do on their own, the teachers provided "bite-sized" instruction to introduce students to the knowledge and skills they would need to move forward in their scientific thinking. The teachers found that they sometimes needed to make adjustments in their lessons to keep students "in the zone" so that the concepts were not too difficult but remained within reach of students' abilities. After the instruction, students were again asked to explain scientific principles and they critiqued one another's explanations (i.e., did peer review). This careful approach led to improvement in students' scientific reasoning, supporting Vygotsky's concept of the zone of proximal development.

By working with a more knowledgeable partner, this child is able to accomplish more than would be possible on her own. According to Lev Vygotsky, the difference between what a child can accomplish alone and with a partner is the zone of proximal development.

Brand X Pictures/Getty Images

In many cultures, children do not go to school with other children to learn from teachers, nor do their parents explicitly teach tasks such as weaving and hunting. Instead, they learn through guided participation—by actively participating in culturally relevant activities with the aid and support of their parents and other knowledgeable guides (Rogoff, 1998). Jerome Bruner (1983) had a similar concept in mind when he wrote of the many ways in which parents provide scaffolding for their children's development; that is, the more-skilled person gives structured help to a less-skilled learner but gradually reduces the help as the less-skilled learner becomes more competent. By calling attention to guided participation processes, in the zone of proximal development, Vygotsky was rejecting Piaget's view of children as independent explorers in favor of the view that they learn more sophisticated cognitive strategies through their interactions with more mature thinkers. To Piaget, the child's level of cognitive development determines what he can learn; to Vygotsky, learning in collaboration with more knowledgeable companions drives cognitive development.

Tools of Thought

Vygotsky believed that mental activity, like physical activity, is mediated by tools (Daniels, 2011). If a child wants to start a garden, we wouldn't send her outside empty handed and say, "Go ahead and make a garden." We would, instead, equip her with an array of tools—shovel, rake, gloves, fertilizer, seeds, and so on—that have already been proven useful for accomplishing this task. Further, we would probably show her how to best use these tools to accomplish the desired task. We might show the child how to poke holes in the soil and drop seeds inside, watch while the child attempted this, and perhaps correct her if she pushed the seeds in too deep. As the child practices and masters the use of the tools presented by the adult, the child adopts the tools as her own. The same process is involved in passing along cultural tools for mental activity.

In Vygotsky's view, adults use a variety of tools to pass culturally valued modes of thinking and problem solving to their children. Spoken language is the most important tool, but writing, using numbers, and applying problem-solving and memory strategies also convey information and enable thinking (Vygotsky, 1978). The type of tool used to perform a task influences performance on the task. Consider a study by Dorothy Faulkner and her colleagues (2000) with 9- and 10-year-old children. Children worked in pairs on a science project, originally developed by Inhelder and Piaget (1964), in which they needed to figure out which chemicals to combine to make a colored liquid. Some pairs worked with the actual physical materials and others used a computer simulation of the task. The children who worked with the computerized version talked more, tested more possible chemical combinations, and completed the task more quickly than children who worked with the physical materials. The computer, then, was a tool that changed the nature of the problem-solving activity and influenced performance, as Vygotsky would have predicted.

Look more closely at Vygotsky's notion of how tools—especially language—influence thought. Whereas Piaget maintained that cognitive development influences language development, Vygotsky argued that language shapes thought in important ways and that thought changes fundamentally once we begin to think in words (Bodrova & Leong, 1996). Piaget and Vygotsky both noticed that preschool children often talk to themselves as they go about their daily activities, almost as if they were play-by-play sports announcers. ("I'm putting the big piece in the corner. I need a pink one. Not that one—this one.") Two preschool children playing next to each other sometimes carry on separate monologues rather than conversing. Piaget (1926) regarded such speech as egocentric—further evidence that preoperational thinkers cannot yet take the perspectives of other people (in this case, their conversation partners) and therefore have not mastered the art of social speech. He did not believe that egocentric speech played a useful role in cognitive development.

In contrast, Vygotsky called preschool children's recitations **private speech**—speech to oneself that guides one's thought and behavior. Rather than viewing it as a sign of cognitive immaturity, he saw it as a critical step in the development of mature thought and as the forerunner of the silent thinking-in-words that adults engage in every day. Adults guide children's behavior with speech, a tool that children adopt and initially use externally, just as adults did with them. Gradually, this regulatory speech is internalized.

Talking to oneself or a stuffed animal may help youngsters work through problems and advance their cognitive development.

Susan Northcutt/Alamy Stock Photo

Studies conducted by Vygotsky and other researchers support his claim. For example, in one set of studies, Vygotsky (1934/1962) measured children's private speech first as they worked unhindered on a task, then as they worked to overcome an obstacle placed in their path. Their use of private speech increased dramatically when they confronted an interruption of their work—a problem to solve. Katherine Nelson (2015), who has studied language and its relationship with thought for over 40 years, concurs with Vygotsky when it comes to private speech. In an extensive examination of a toddler's "crib speech," Nelson concluded that this talking out loud to oneself is a way to externally examine and process what is in one's head. Thus, at least some private speech is the external representation of thought and may help young children solve complex problems. Children tend to use more private speech when faced with a new task and use less private speech as the task becomes familiar (Duncan & Pratt, 1997). Even adults sometimes think aloud when they are stumped by a problem (Duncan & Cheyne, 2002).

Both the amount of private speech as well as the nature of what is said are related to performance (Chiu & Alexander, 2000). In particular, children who use private speech to talk themselves through a problem ("No, I need to change this. Try it over here. Yes, that's good.") show greater motivation toward mastery; that is, they are more likely to persist on a task even without adult prodding (Chiu & Alexander, 2000). Thus, private speech not only helps children think their way through challenging problems but also allows them to incorporate into their own thinking the problem-solving strategies they learned during their collaborations with adults. Notice that, as in guided participation, what is at first a social process becomes an individual psychological process. In other words, social speech (for example, the conversation between Annie and her father as they jointly worked a puzzle) gives rise to private speech (Annie talking aloud, much as her father talked to her, as she then tries to work the puzzle on her own), which in turn goes "underground" to become first mutterings and lip movements and then inner speech (Annie's silent verbal thought).

Evaluation of Vygotsky

Although many scholars find Vygotsky's ideas a refreshing addition to Piaget's, some concerns should be noted. Vygotsky died young (age 38), leaving us with many intriguing ideas but without a complete theory of cognitive development. It is, of course, impossible to know how the theory might have evolved had Vygotsky continued to work on it for as long as Piaget worked on his theory. Whereas Piaget has been criticized for placing too much emphasis on the individual and not enough on the social environment, Vygotsky has been criticized for doing the opposite: placing too much emphasis on social interaction (Feldman & Fowler, 1997). Vygotsky seemed to assume that all knowledge and understanding of the world is transmitted through social interaction. But at least some understanding is individually constructed, as Piaget proposed. Vygotsky and Piaget are often presented as opposites on a continuum representing the extent to which cognitive development derives from social experience. However, a careful reading of the two theorists reveals that they are not as dissimilar as they are often presented to be (Lourenço, 2012). Both Piaget and Vygotsky acknowledge the importance of the social context of development. Still, there are differences in their emphasis. ●Table 7.1 summarizes some of the differences between Vygotsky's sociocultural perspective and Piaget's cognitive developmental view. Application 7.1 explains their views on improving cognitive functioning.

● APPLICATION 7.1
Improving Cognitive Functioning

What do the theories of Piaget and Vygotsky have to contribute to the goal of optimizing cognition? Let's start with Piaget. Studies suggest that it is possible to teach many Piagetian concepts to children who are younger than the age at which the concepts would naturally emerge. For instance, 4-year-olds can be trained to recognize the identity of a substance such as a ball of clay before and after its appearance is altered in Piaget's famous conservation task—that is, to understand that although the clay looks different, it is still the same clay and has to be the same amount of clay (Field, 1981). Nearly 75% of the children given this identity training could solve at least three of five conservation problems 2–5 months after training. Despite these sorts of successes, no one has demonstrated that 2-year-olds can be taught formal operations! But at least these studies demonstrate that specific training experiences can somewhat speed a child's progress through Piaget's stages or bring out more advanced capacities in an adult performing at a less advanced level.

In truth, Piaget disapproved of attempts by Americans to speed children's progress through his stages (Piaget, 1970). He believed parents should provide young children with opportunities to explore their world and teachers should use a discovery approach in the classroom that allows children to learn by doing. Given their natural curiosity and normal opportunities to try their hand at solving problems, children would construct ever more complex understandings on their own. Many educators have incorporated Piaget's ideas about discovery-based education into their lesson plans, especially in science classes. Teachers have also taken seriously Piaget's notion that children understand material best if they can assimilate it into their existing understandings. Finding out what the learner already knows or can do and providing instruction matched to the child's level of development are in the spirit of Piaget.

What would Vygotsky recommend to teachers who want to stimulate cognitive growth? As you might guess, Vygotsky's theoretical orientation leads to a different approach to education than Piaget's does—a more social one. Whereas students in Piaget's classroom would most likely be engaged in independent exploration, students in Vygotsky's classroom would be involved in guided participation, with teachers and more knowledgeable peers providing just enough assistance to allow them to solve a new problem (Wass & Golding, 2014). The roles of teachers and other more skillful collaborators would be to organize the learning activity, break it into steps, provide hints and suggestions carefully tailored to the student's abilities, and gradually turn over more of the mental work to the student. According to Vygotsky's sociocultural perspective, the guidance provided by a skilled partner will then be internalized by the learner, first as private speech and eventually as silent inner speech. Education ends up being a matter of providing children with tools of the mind important in their culture, whether hunting strategies or computer skills (Berk & Winsler, 1995; Bodrova & Leong, 1996).

Is there evidence that one of these theoretical approaches might be superior to the other? Consider some research that had 3- to 5-year-old children help a puppet with a sorting task in which they had to decide which furnishings (sofas, beds, bathtubs, stoves, and so on) should be placed in each of six rooms of a dollhouse that the puppet was moving into (Freund, 1990). First the children were tested to determine what they already knew about proper furniture placement. Then each child worked at a similar task, either alone (as might be the case in Piaget's discovery-based education, although here children were provided with corrective feedback by the experimenter) or with his or her mother (Vygotsky's guided learning). Finally, to assess what they had learned, children performed a final, rather complex furniture-sorting task. The results were clear: Children who had sorted furniture with help from their mothers showed dramatic improvements in sorting ability, whereas those who had practiced on their own showed little improvement. Moreover, the children who gained the most from guided participation with their mothers were those whose mothers talked the most about how to tackle the task. So children do not always learn the most when they function as solitary scientists, as Piaget's theory would predict. Instead, consistent with Vygotsky's theory, conceptual growth is more likely to occur when children interact with other people—particularly with competent people who provide an optimal amount of guidance. Perhaps the ideal scenario would be to provide the best of both worlds: opportunities to explore on their own and supportive companions to offer help when needed.

Vygotsky's Sociocultural View	Piaget's Cognitive Developmental View
Processes of animal and human development are fundamentally different.	Processes of animal and human development are fundamentally the same.
Cognitive development is different in different social and historical contexts.	Cognitive development is mostly the same universally.
Appropriate unit of analysis is the social, cultural, and historical context in which the individual develops.	Appropriate unit of analysis is the individual.
Cognitive growth results from social interactions (guided participation in the zone of proximal development).	Cognitive growth results from the child's independent explorations of the world.
Children and their partners co-construct knowledge.	Children construct knowledge on their own.
Social processes become individual psychological ones (e.g., social speech becomes inner speech).	Individual, egocentric processes become more social (e.g., egocentric speech becomes social speech).
Adults are especially important because they know the culture's tools of thinking.	Peers are especially important because the cognitive conflict triggered by different perspectives of other children is not so overwhelming that it cannot be resolved.
Learning precedes development (tools learned with adult help become internalized).	Development precedes learning (children cannot master certain things until they have the requisite cognitive structures).
Training can help mediate development.	Training is largely ineffective in "speeding up" development.

Checking Mastery

1. What theme is stressed in Vygotsky's theory that is largely missing in Piaget's theory?
2. What is the zone of proximal development? Provide an example of this concept.

Making Connections

1. Create descriptions of a Piagetian preschool and a Vygotskian preschool. What are the main differences in how children will be assessed, what they will be taught, and how they will be taught?
2. Piaget and Vygotsky differed in their views of the importance of the individual versus society. Compare their positions on individual versus society in terms of cognitive development.

7.3
Fischer's Dynamic Skill Framework

LEARNING OBJECTIVES

- Describe Fischer's perspective on context and performance.
- Explain what changes or develops in Fischer's dynamic skill framework.
- Compare Fischer's model of cognitive development to Piaget's theory.
- Indicate where Fischer's concepts of developmental change are similar to Vygotsky's concepts.

Kurt Fischer has devoted his professional career to developing, testing, and revising a dynamic skill framework for understanding cognitive development (1980; Fischer & Bidell, 2006; Fischer & Pipp, 1984). According to this perspective, "it is not possible to analyze behavior outside the context in which it occurs. Behavior is not something that a person 'has'; it emerges from interactions between person and context" (Rose & Fischer, 2011, p. 146). Consider the experience of studying for an exam and having your friend test your understanding with questions the day before the exam as you relax in a coffee shop. You answer the questions successfully and go into the exam feeling confident. But now, in the context of the exam room with the palpable stress in the room, you don't seem to "know" nearly as much as you did the day before.

Or perhaps you can relate to the example of the basketball player who can make shots all day long when practicing in the gym, but then "chokes" and misses the hoop in the context of a game. In contrast, maybe you perform well under pressure and need the increased stress that comes with a testing or game situation to really focus and demonstrate your best performance. Fischer believes that such differences in performance across different contexts are perfectly normal. Indeed, when someone consistently performs at the same level over and over, we often say "he's like a machine." Such consistency across different contexts seems more typical of a machine than of a human. Unlike machines, human performance is **dynamic**, that is, it changes in response to changes in context.

Comparison to Piaget and Vygotsky

Fischer's dynamic system view is different from Piaget's view that the cognitive structures underlying each stage are inherent in the person. Piaget, and much of the research sprouting from Piaget's theory, tested children in rather artificial settings with carefully constructed tasks that may not be typical of tasks encountered in everyday life. Fischer and others, including Bronfenbrenner whom we discussed in Chapter 2, firmly believe that developmental psychologists need to put development back into its natural context and not study it in isolation.

Another difference between Piaget and Fischer is their view of *what* develops. According to Piaget, cognitive structures develop, whereas Fischer proposes that skill levels change and develop. A **skill** is a person's ability to perform on a particular task in a specific context (Fischer & Bidell, 2006). Someone who wins spelling bee contests is demonstrating skill to perform this task—spelling words—in the context of a competition. This person may or may not exhibit skill on a related task, such as defining words based on how they are used in sentences. A surgeon who has a 99% success rate of repairing retinal tears on eyeballs has a skill for this type of surgical procedure in the context provided by this type of surgical arena. The same surgeon may not be the one you want to have repairing your damaged heart valve. Thus, a skill is both task-specific and context-specific.

Where Piaget proposed distinct stages in which thinking undergoes fairly dramatic qualitative—abrupt—change from one stage to the next, change in Fischer's model may or may not seem "stage-like." Under conditions with little support, children's development may appear to be gradual and linear as they slowly work themselves through the levels of acquiring a skill. But under conditions of high support, change may occur swiftly and more closely resemble stages, as children master several levels within a short period of time.

Drawing directly from Vygotsky, Fischer uses the concept of *zone of proximal development* to explain how cognition advances from one level to another. The "zone" represents the opportunity for growth that exists between a person's optimal ability and their actual performance on a given task in a particular context, that is, their current skill level. With research and further refinement of dynamic skill theory, Fischer and others have adopted the term **developmental range** to better capture their findings that people's abilities vary with context. With a supportive context, people can perform at an optimal level of skill. Most of the time, though, we perform below our optimal level because the support structure needed to perform optimally is not in place (Rose & Fischer, 1998). Thus, high levels of support can lead to larger jumps in skill acquisition, whereas low levels of support can result in slow linear acquisition of skills.

In sum, the dynamic skill theory that has taken shape over the past 40 years uses some ideas from Piaget and Vygotsky and proposes new concepts to account for the variability observed in actual performance. Piaget was interested in uncovering universal stages of cognitive development. Fischer and other dynamic theorists are especially interested in variability of performance as research has repeatedly shown that people demonstrate inconsistent skills. Once a person "has" a skill, why wouldn't they always demonstrate optimal use of this skill? As we've seen, the dynamic skill theorists believe that skills do not exist in isolation from the task and the context. Seen from this perspective, many seemingly inconsistent performances begin to make much more sense.

We have now examined three major perspectives on cognitive development. In the following sections, we will look at specific aspects of cognitive development in infancy, childhood, adolescence, and adulthood, guided largely by Piaget's theory. We will also see how Vygotsky's and Fischer's perspectives enrich our understanding of cognitive development.

According to the dynamic skill framework, skills depend on both the task and the context. This boy may be able to perform this task in this context with his grandfather but not in a different context.

Blend Images–Kidstock/Getty Images

Checking Mastery

1. Define the terms "dynamic" and "skill" in context of the dynamic skill framework.
2. How is the dynamic skill framework similar to Vygotsky's sociocultural theory?
3. In what ways is the dynamic skill framework different from Piaget's theory of cognitive development?

Making Connections

1. How might a classroom teacher use the concept of Fischer's developmental range to optimize students' performance?
2. If you are preparing a team for a competition, whether this is an athletic, academic, musical, or other type of competition, what features of the dynamic skill theory could you apply to your coaching to enhance your team's performance?

LEARNING OBJECTIVES

- Explain the importance of object permanence and describe the path from lack of object permanence to full understanding of object permanence.

- Note the major cognitive achievements emerging from the period of infancy.

What sort of cognitive activity is possible during infancy? One of the strengths of Piaget's approach to cognitive development is that he provided a rich description of what he observed infants and young children *doing*. From these observations, he drew inferences about what infants were likely *thinking* and how their minds were working. Piaget proposed that the groundwork for cognitive development occurred during the first 2 years of life as infants learn about the world through their senses and their motoric actions (hence, the name *sensorimotor* for this first stage). The dominant cognitive structures of this stage are behavioral schemes—patterns of action that evolve as infants begin to coordinate sensory input (seeing an object) and motor responses (grasping an object). Because infants solve problems through their actions rather than with their minds, their mode of thought is qualitatively different from that of older children.

The six substages of the sensorimotor stage are outlined in ● Table 7.2. At the start of the sensorimotor period, infants may not seem highly intelligent, but they are already active explorers of the world around them. Researchers see increasing signs of intelligent behavior as infants pass through the substages, because they are gradually learning about the world and about cause and effect by observing the effects of their actions. They are transformed from reflexive creatures who adapt to their environment using their innate reflexes to reflective ones who can solve simple problems in their heads. The advances in problem-solving ability captured in the six substages of the sensorimotor period bring many important changes. We can illustrate the impressive advances in thinking across infancy by closely examining the acquisition of one of Piaget's most notable concepts—object permanence.

The Development of Object Permanence

According to Piaget, newborns lack an understanding of **object permanence** (also called *object concept*). This is the fundamental understanding that objects continue to exist—they are permanent—when they are no longer visible or otherwise detectable to the senses. It probably does not occur to you to wonder whether your shoes still exist after you place them in the closet and shut the door. But very young infants, because they rely so heavily on their senses, seem to operate as though objects exist only when they are perceived or acted on. According to Piaget and others, infants must construct the notion that reality exists apart from their experience of it.

Piaget believed that the concept of object permanence develops gradually over the sensorimotor period. Up through roughly 4–8 months, it is "out of sight, out of mind"; infants will not search for a toy if it is covered with a cloth or screen. By the end of the first year (substage 4), they master that trick but still rely on their perceptions and actions to "know" an object (Piaget, 1952). After his 10-month-old daughter, Jacqueline, had repeatedly retrieved a toy parrot from one hiding place, Piaget put it in a new spot while she watched him. Amazingly, she looked in the *original* hiding place. She seemed to assume that her behavior determined where the object would appear; she did not treat the object as if it existed apart from her actions or from its initial location. The surprising

● **Table 7.2** The Substages and Intellectual Accomplishments of the Sensorimotor Period

Substage	Description
1. Reflex activity (birth–1 month)	Active exercise and refinement of inborn reflexes (e.g., change sucking patterns to fit the shapes of different objects).
2. Primary circular reactions (1–4 months)	Repetition of interesting acts centered on the child's own body (e.g., repeatedly suck a thumb, kick legs, or blow bubbles). These typically begin as random acts but are then repeated for pleasure.
3. Secondary circular reactions (4–8 months)	Repetition of interesting acts on objects (e.g., repeatedly shake a rattle to make an interesting noise or bat a mobile to make it wiggle). Thus, circular actions extend beyond one's self (primary) to objects in the environment (secondary to self).
4. Coordination of secondary schemes (8–12 months)	Combination of actions to solve simple problems or achieve goals (e.g., push aside a barrier to grasp an object, using the scheme as a means to an end); first evidence of intentionality.
5. Tertiary circular reactions (12–18 months)	Experimentation to find new ways to solve problems or produce interesting outcomes (e.g., explore bathwater by gently patting it, then hitting it vigorously and watching the results; or stroke, pinch, squeeze, and pat a cat to see how it responds to varied actions).
6. Beginning of thought (18–24 months)	First evidence of insight; able to solve problems mentally and use symbols to stand for objects and actions; visualize how a stick could be used (e.g., move an out-of-reach toy closer).

tendency of 8- to 12-month-olds to search for an object in the place where they last found it (A) rather than in its new hiding place (B) is called the **A-not-B error**. The likelihood of infants making the A-not-B error increases with lengthier delays between hiding and searching and with the number of trials in which the object is found in spot A (Marcovitch & Zelazo, 1999).

As we suggested earlier in this chapter, task demands and physical limitations of infants may influence performance on tasks like the A-not-B task (Lew et al., 2007). This is one of those areas where simplifying the task leads to the conclusion that infants develop at least some understanding of object permanence far earlier than Piaget claimed. For example, Renee Baillargeon and her colleagues have used a method of testing for object concept that does not require reaching for a hidden object, only looking toward where it should be. In one study, infants as young as 2½ months seemed surprised (as demonstrated by looking longer) when a toy that had disappeared behind one screen (left side of ■ Figure 7.2 reappeared from behind a second screen (right side of Figure 7.2) *without* appearing in the open space between the two screens (Aguiar & Baillargeon, 1999).

At this young age, however, understanding of hidden objects is still limited. Consider the scenario shown in ■ **Figure 7.3**. In the high-window condition, a toy is hidden as it moves along a track behind a block that has a window located at its top. There is nothing odd about this condition. In the low-window condition, a toy *should* be visible as it moves along a track behind a block that has a window located at its bottom, but it is not. To someone who understands the properties of object permanence, this should strike them as odd. At 2½ months, infants do not show signs that they detect a difference between objects moving along a track under the high-window and low-window conditions. But just 2 weeks later, 3-month-olds look longer at the low-window event compared with the high-window event, as if surprised (Aguiar & Baillargeon, 2002). Thus, by 3 months, infants have gained an understanding that objects should be visible when nothing is obstructing them (see also Bremner, Slater, & Johnson, 2015).

Until an infant masters the concept of object permanence, objects that are outside of his visual sight are "out of mind."

Doug Goodman/Science Source

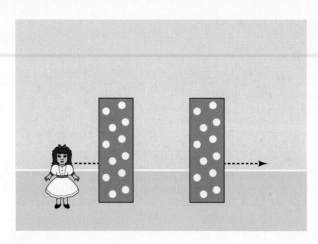

■**Figure 7.2** Test stimuli used by Aguiar and Baillargeon (1999, 2002). The doll moves behind the screen on the left and reappears on the right side of the second screen without appearing in the space between screens.

Source: From Aguiar, A. & Baillargeon, R. (2002). Developments in young infants' reasoning about occluded objects, *Cognitive Psychology, 45,* pp. 267–336, Figure 1. Reprinted by permission of Elsevier.

In general, then, it seems that babies sometimes know a good deal more about object permanence than they reveal through their actions when they are given the kinds of search tasks originally devised by Piaget (Baillargeon, 2002). This illustrates Fischer's notion that skill depends on the task demands and the context. When tested using the task demands specified by Piaget, infants demonstrate less skill. But changing the task demands, by peeling away some of the complexity and providing a supportive context, gives infants the opportunity to demonstrate optimal skill levels (Fischer & Bidell, 1991). In addition to characteristics of the task, characteristics of the infant can influence performance. For instance, researchers at the Uppsala Child and Baby Lab in Sweden have found that infants' activity levels affected their performance on object permanence tasks (Johansson, Forssman, & Bohlin, 2014). Those with lower activity levels performed better, perhaps because their lower activity allowed for greater focus on the cognitive task.

To be fair to Piaget, we should note that he contended that looking behaviors were developmental precursors to the reaching behaviors that he assessed. He did not believe, however, that looking represented complete understanding of object permanence. An analysis of infants' looking behaviors by Carolyn Rovee-Collier (2001) suggests that Piaget was wise to distinguish between infants' looking and reaching. In some situations, looking may developmentally precede reaching for an object, as Piaget suggested. In other situations, however, infants' looking behavior does not predict their subsequent action on an object. Regardless of the specific measure used by researchers, infants gradually become more skilled at acting on their knowledge by searching in the right spot.

By 12–18 months of age (substage 5), the infant has overcome the A-not-B error but may continue to have trouble with invisible displacements—as when you hide a toy in your hand, move your hand under a pillow, and then remove your hand, leaving the toy under the pillow. The infant will search where the object was last seen, seeming confused when it is not in your hand and failing to look under the pillow, where it was deposited. Finally, by the end of the second year (18–24 months), the infant is capable of

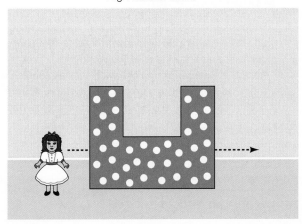

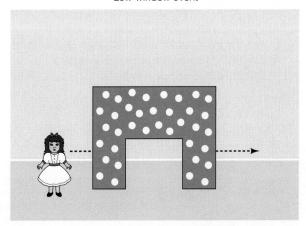

■ **Figure 7.3** There is nothing to be surprised about in the high-window event, but in the low-window event, the doll should (but does not) appear in the middle space as it moves along the track.

Source: From Aguiar, A. & Baillargeon, R. (2002). Developments in young infants' reasoning about occluded objects, *Cognitive Psychology, 45*, pp. 267–336, Figure 2. Reprinted by permission of Elsevier.

mentally representing such invisible moves and conceiving of the object in its final location. According to Piaget, the concept of object permanence is fully mastered at this point.

The Emergence of Symbols

Perhaps the most important cognitive achievement of infancy is the emergence of the symbolic capacity—the ability to use images, words, or gestures to represent or stand for objects and experiences. This allows infants and young children to manipulate ideas mentally, not just motorically, opening the door to more sophisticated thinking based on manipulating ideas in their heads. Consider how the emergence of symbolic capacity changes the quality of infants' play activities. During the first month, young infants react reflexively to internal and external stimulation. In the primary circular reactions substage (1–4 months), they are more interested in their own bodies than in manipulating toys. Moving their tongues or fingers around is entertainment enough at this age. Piaget named this substage **primary circular reactions** because he observed infants repeating (hence, the term *circular*) actions relating to their own bodies (that is, primary to themselves) that had initially happened by chance. Piaget reports the example of his son, Laurent, at just over 1 month accidentally getting his thumb in his mouth. It falls out. This happens again on another day. Indeed, since the first accidental occurrence, Piaget observes it happening over and over again. Increasingly, a finger or thumb successfully makes it into the mouth, which pleases Laurent. He seeks opportunities to repeat this pleasant action involving his body (alas, Laurent was not to be a thumb-sucker for very long—by 2 or 3 months of age, Piaget had bandaged his son's hands to bring this pleasing activity to an end).

By the third substage of secondary circular reactions (4–8 months), infants derive pleasure from repeatedly performing an action on an object, such as sucking or banging a toy. Now the repetitive actions are called **secondary circular reactions** because they involve something in the infant's external environment (that is, secondary to the self). In the fourth substage (8–12 months), called **coordination of secondary schemes**, infants combine (that is,

coordinate) secondary actions to achieve simple goals such as when they *push* an obstacle out of the way in order to *grasp* a desired object.

Later, when they reach the substage of **tertiary circular reactions** (12–18 months), infants experiment in varied ways with toys, exploring them thoroughly and learning all about their properties. In this stage, a true sense of curiosity and interest in novel actions appears. Now it is interesting to the infant to repeat an action with variations, such as the infant who experiments with all the many ways that oatmeal can land on the floor and walls when launched from a highchair in different directions and at different velocities.

With the final substage, the beginning of thought (about 18 months), Piaget believed symbolic capacity became firmly established, allowing one object to be used to represent another. For example, a cooking pot becomes a hat or a shoe becomes a telephone—simple forms of pretend play. It is also in this stage, according to Piaget, that infants can imitate models no longer present, because they can now create and later recall mental representations of what they have seen. Perhaps most importantly, with symbolic capacity, infants and toddlers understand that a word can be used to represent something else, such as an object, which leads to the language explosion associated with toddlerhood, which we will have more to say about in Chapter 10.

As noted earlier, one weakness of Piaget's theory is the underestimation of young children's abilities. Pedro Palacios and Cintia Rodríguez (2015) tracked the emergence of symbol use from 9 to 15 months of age. They found fairly robust use of symbols by 15 months of age, earlier than suggested by Piaget. Yet consistent with Piaget's description of how symbolic capacity unfolds across the substages of the sensorimotor period, Palacios and Rodríguez (2015) did find gradual emergence of symbol use. At 9 months of age, infants could follow an adult's symbolic use of objects. By 12 months of age, infants could make some simple symbolic substitutions, as long as the symbol and object it represented were similar (e.g., talking into a plastic toy phone, representing an actual phone). By 15 months of age, infants could produce larger symbolic substitutions, such as holding a banana to their face and "talking" to it as though holding a phone.

● **Checking Mastery**

1. Why does the name "sensorimotor" stage seem to capture the essence of Piaget's first stage of development?
2. What must infants master or acquire in order to understand object permanence?

● **Making Connections**

1. Suppose an infant fails to develop an understanding of object permanence. How would this deficit influence his behavior and knowledge of the world?
2. Trace the emergence of a behavior, such as opening a cabinet door to get to a box of animal crackers, from the beginning to the end of Piaget's sensorimotor period.

7.5
The Child

LEARNING OBJECTIVES

• Describe the typical preschool-age child's pattern of thinking.

• Outline the characteristics of thought that enable (or inhibit) a child's ability to solve conservation tasks.

• Compare the elementary school child's thinking to that of a preschool child.

As with the period of infancy, our understanding of cognitive development during childhood has benefitted from Piaget's detailed observations of how children solve problems and what aspects of problems challenge their thinking. Here, we discuss how the largely symbolic thinking of preschoolers progresses to the logical thinking of elementary school-aged children.

Preschoolers: Symbolic Thinking

The *symbolic capacity* that emerged at the end of the sensorimotor stage runs wild in the preschool years and is the greatest cognitive strength of the preschooler. Imagine the possibilities: The child can now use words to refer to things, people, and events that are not physically present. Instead of being trapped in the immediate present, the child can refer to past and future. Pretend or fantasy play flourishes at this age: Blocks can stand for houses, cardboard boxes for trains. Some children even invent **imaginary companions**, which can take many forms including humans and animals. Although parents may worry about such flights of fancy, they are normal; their inventors know their companions are not real. Having an imaginary companion may lead to advanced cognitive and social development, as well as higher

levels of creativity and imagery use (Gleason & Kalpidou, 2014). Young children with imaginary companions engage in more private speech than other children (Davis, Meins, & Fernyhough, 2013; 2014), perhaps because they have a "buddy" with them at all times. As noted earlier in this chapter, private speech may help children work through complex problems, which could be the link to the more advanced development sometimes seen among children with these companions.

From his studies of children, Piaget concluded that the young child's mind is limited compared with that of an older child. Piaget called the preschool-age child's thinking *preoperational*, that is, not yet having logical mental operations. Although less so than infants, preschoolers are highly influenced by their immediate perceptions. They often respond as if they have been captured by, or cannot go beyond, the most perceptually salient aspects of a situation. This focus on **perceptual salience**, or the most obvious features of an object or situation, means that preschoolers can be fooled by appearances. They have difficulty with tasks that require them to use logic to arrive at the right answer. Their "logic," if we can indeed refer to it as logic at all, is based on their intuitions. We can best illustrate this reliance on perceptions and lack of logical thought by considering Piaget's classic tests of conservation (also see **Exploration 7.1**)

At the start of the conservation-of-liquid task, children confirm that the two glasses contain equal amounts of liquid.

Marmaduke St. John/Alamy Stock Photo

As the child watches, liquid from one of the original containers is poured into a new container that is a different size.

Now for the test: Does the new glass contain more, less, or the same amount of liquid as the glass next to it?

● EXPLORATION 7.1

Can There Really Be a Santa Claus?

Many young children around the world believe in Santa Claus, St. Nicholas, the Tooth Fairy, or some other magical being. This occurs despite the fact that the existence of these fantasy figures violates numerous principles of logic. How can this be? We know that children whose parents endorse and promote Santa or another mythical being are more likely to believe than children whose parents do not (Shtulman & Yoo, 2015). After all, children normally trust their parents and accept their statements about Santa at face value. Children also tend to accept supporting evidence of Santa (for example, there are gifts under the tree) without questioning whether this evidence is conclusive proof of Santa's existence (Tullos & Woolley, 2009; Wooley & Cornelius, 2013).

At what point, and why, do their beliefs in these figures begin to waver? Research with 5- and 6-year-old children shows that they are already somewhat less confident about the existence of Santa and the Tooth Fairy than they are about two invisible but scientifically proven entities—germs and oxygen (Harris et al., 2006). According to Piaget's theory, children would begin to seriously question the existence of Santa Claus when they acquire concrete-operational thought. With their ability to reason logically, they may begin to ask questions such as, "How can Santa Claus get around to all those houses in one night?"

"How can one sleigh hold all those gifts?" "Why haven't I ever seen a reindeer fly?" and "How does Santa get into houses that don't have chimneys?"

What made sense to the preoperational child no longer adds up to the logical, concrete-operational thinker. With their focus on static endpoints, preschool-age children may not have a problem imagining presents for all the children in the world (or at least those on the "nice" list) sitting at the North Pole waiting to be delivered and then sitting under decorated trees Christmas morning. But once children understand transformations, they are confronted with the problem of how all those presents get from the North Pole to the individual houses in record time. The logical thinker notes that the gifts under the tree are wrapped in the same paper that Mom has in her closet. Indeed, researchers delving into the mystery of Santa Claus have found that disbelief in Santa

Juice Images/Alamy Stock Photo

increases with children's burgeoning logical reasoning abilities (Shtulman & Yoo, 2015).

As adults, we can resolve some of these inconsistencies for children to help perpetuate children's beliefs in Santa Claus. We can, for example, point out that Santa has many helpers and that reindeer native to the North Pole are unlike those ever seen in the wild or in a zoo. Some parents who want to continue the Santa myth get tough and simply tell their children that non-believers will not get any presents. So level of cognitive development as well as the surrounding culture play roles in whether or not children believe in Santa Claus and for how long.

Lack of Conservation

As we noted in Chapter 2, one of the many lessons about the physical world that children must master is the concept of conservation—the idea that certain properties of an object or substance do not change when its appearance is altered in some superficial way. Find a 4- or 5-year-old and try Piaget's conservation-of-liquid-quantity task. Pour equal amounts of water into two identical glasses, and get the child to agree that the two glasses have the same amount of water. Then, as the child watches, pour the water from one glass into a shorter, wider glass. Now ask whether the two containers—the tall, narrow glass and the shorter, broader one—have the same amount of water to drink or whether one has more (or less) water than the other one. Children younger than 6 or 7 will usually say that the taller glass has more water than the shorter one. They lack the understanding that the volume of liquid is conserved despite the change in the shape it takes in different containers.

How can young children be so easily fooled by their perceptions? According to Piaget, the preschooler is limited because they lack certain mental operations, outlined in ● **Table 7.3**. For starters, they are unable to engage in **decentration**—the ability to focus on two or more dimensions of a problem at once. Consider the conservation-of-liquid task: The child must focus on height and width simultaneously and recognize that the increased width of the short, broad container compensates for its lesser height. Preoperational thinkers engage in **centration**—the tendency to center attention on a single aspect of the problem. They focus on height alone and conclude that the taller glass has more liquid; or, alternatively, they focus on width and conclude that the short, wide glass has more. In this and other ways, preschoolers seem to have one-track minds.

A second contributor to success on conservation tasks is **reversibility**—the process of mentally undoing or reversing an action. Older children often display mastery of reversibility by suggesting that the water be poured back into its original container to prove that it is

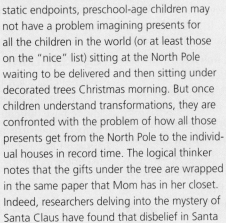

Preoperational Thinkers	Concrete-Operational Thinkers
Fail conservation tasks because they have: • *Irreversible thought*—cannot mentally undo an action • *Centration*—center on a single aspect of a problem rather than two or more dimensions at once • *Static thought*—fail to understand transformations or processes of change from one state to another	Solve conservation tasks because they have: • *Reversibility of thought*—can mentally reverse or undo an action • *Decentration*—can focus on two or more dimensions of a problem at once • *Transformational thought*—can understand the process of change from one state to another
Perceptual salience. Understanding is driven by how things look rather than derived from logical reasoning.	*Logical reasoning*. Children acquire a set of internal operations that can be applied to a variety of problems.
Transductive reasoning. Children combine unrelated facts, often leading them to draw faulty cause–effect conclusions simply because two events occur close together in time or space.	*Inductive reasoning*. Children draw cause–effect conclusions logically, based on factual information presented to them.
Egocentrism. Children have difficulty seeing things from other perspectives and assume that what is in their mind is also what others are thinking.	*Less egocentrism*. Children understand that other people may have thoughts different from their own.
Single classification. Children classify objects by a single dimension at one time.	*Multiple classification*. Children can classify objects by multiple dimensions and can grasp class inclusion.

still the same amount. The young child shows irreversibility of thinking and may insist that the water would overflow the glass if it were poured back. Indeed, one young child tested by a college student shrieked, "Do it again!" as though pouring the water back without causing the glass to overflow were some unparalleled feat of magic.

Finally, preoperational thinkers fail to demonstrate conservation because of limitations in **transformational thought**—the ability to conceptualize transformations, or processes of change from one state to another, as when water is poured from one glass to another. Preoperational thinkers engage in **static thought**, or thought that is fixed on end states rather than the changes that transform one state into another, as when the water is sitting in the two glasses, not being poured or manipulated.

In Piagetian theory, then, preoperational children do not understand the concept of conservation because they engage in centration, irreversible thought, and static thought. The older child, in the stage of concrete operations, has mastered decentration, reversibility, and transformational thought. The correct answer to the conservation task is a matter of logic to the older child; there is no longer a need to rely on perception as a guide. Another interpretation, though, has been offered by the neuroconstructivists, who report that success on logic tasks such as conservation is supported by increased activity in parts of the frontal cortex associated with greater cognitive control that inhibits responding on the basis of perceptual salience (Houdé & Borst, 2014; Simon et al., 2015). Consistent with this interpretation, research shows that being able to think logically requires being able to both activate a correct strategy *and* resist (or inhibit) an incorrect one (Borst et al., 2012; 2013). Preschoolers can be helped to overlook a salient, yet irrelevant, task feature if its irrelevance is pointed out to them before they are asked to solve the problem (Yu & Kushnir, 2016).

Egocentrism

Another characteristic of preschool-age children in Piaget's theory is their tendency to view the world solely from their own perspective and to have difficulty recognizing other points of view, what Piaget termed egocentrism. ■ Figure 7.4 illustrates the task Piaget used to assess children's understanding of perspective. Piaget asked children to choose a drawing that shows what the display of three mountains

■ **Figure 7.4** Piaget's "Three Mountains" task to evaluate egocentrism. When the child is seated on the left and a doll is "seated" on the right, can the child correctly identify how the scene looks from the doll's perspective?

would look like from a particular vantage point. Young children often chose the view that corresponded to their own position (Piaget & Inhelder, 1956). But this is one of those areas where Piaget may have underestimated young children's minds.

By reducing tasks to the bare essentials, several researchers have demonstrated that preschool children are not as egocentric as Piaget claimed. In one study, 3-year-olds were shown a card with a dog on one side and a cat on the other (Flavell et al., 1981). The card was held vertically between the child (who could see the dog) and the experimenter (who could see the cat). When children were asked what the experimenter could see, these 3-year-olds performed flawlessly.

Are there more dogs or more animals in this picture? Children who understand class inclusion would correctly answer that there are more animals than dogs.

Ermolaev Alexander/Shutterstock.com

Difficulty with Classification

The limitations of relying on perceptions and intuitions are also apparent when young children are asked to classify objects and think about classification systems. When 2- or 3-year-old children are asked to sort objects on the basis of similarities, they make interesting designs or change their sorting criteria from moment to moment. Older preoperational children can group objects systematically on the basis of shape, color, function, or some other dimension of similarity (Inhelder & Piaget, 1964). However, even children ages 4–7 have trouble thinking about relations between classes and subclasses or between wholes and parts (Siegler & Svetina, 2006). For instance, given a set of furry animals, most of which are dogs but some of which are cats, preoperational children do fine when they are asked whether all the animals are furry and whether there are more dogs than cats. That is, they can conceive of the whole class (furry animals) or of the two subclasses (dogs and cats). However, when the question is, "Which group would have more—the dogs or the animals?" many 5-year-olds say, "Dogs." They cannot simultaneously relate the whole class to its parts; they lack the concept of **class inclusion**—the logical understanding that the parts are included within the whole. Notice that the child centers on the most striking perceptual feature of the problem—dogs are more numerous than cats—and is again fooled by appearances.

Once again, though, other researchers have found that preschool children seem to know more about classification systems than Piaget believed. Sandra Waxman and Thomas Hatch (1992) asked 3- and 4-year-olds to teach a puppet all the different names they could think of for certain animals, plants, articles of clothing, and pieces of furniture. The goal was to see whether children knew terms associated with familiar classification hierarchies—for example, if they knew that a rose is a type of flower and is a member of the larger category of plants. Children performed well, largely because a clever method of prompting responses was used. Depending on which term or terms the children forgot to mention (rose, flower, or plant), they were asked about the rose: "Is this a dandelion?" "Is this a tree?" "Is this an animal?" Often, children came up with the correct terms in response (for example, "No, silly, [it's not an animal] it's a plant!"). Even though young children typically fail the tests of class inclusion that Piaget devised, then, they appear to have a fairly good grasp of familiar classification hierarchies.

Research such as this also raises an important question about individual differences in cognitive development. Aubrey Alvarez and Amy Booth (2016) have found variability in causal understanding among 3- to 4-year olds, and the observed variability among preschoolers is relatively consistent over time. That is, those youngsters with higher levels of causal understanding at age 3 tend to continue to demonstrate high levels of causal thinking. Interestingly, preschoolers' understanding of causal information is related to how much their mothers talk to them about causal relations. This suggests that interactions with a knowledgeable adult can strengthen young children's thinking, which you should now recognize as being consistent with Vygotsky's theory.

Elementary-Aged Children: Logical Thinking

About the time children start elementary school, their minds undergo another transformation. According to Piaget, this transformation corresponds to the concrete-operational stage of development, extending from roughly 7 to 11 years of age. The concrete operations stage involves mastering the logical operations missing in the preoperational stage—becoming able to perform systematic mental actions on objects, such as adding and subtracting Halloween candies, classifying dinosaurs, or arranging objects from largest to smallest. This allows school-age children to think effectively about the objects and events they experience in everyday life. For every limitation of the preoperational child, there is a corresponding strength of the concrete-operational child. These contrasts are summarized in Table 7.3.

Conservation

Given the conservation-of-liquid task, the preoperational child centers on either the height or the width of the glasses, ignoring the other dimension. The concrete-operational child can decenter and juggle two dimensions at once. Reversibility allows the child to mentally reverse the pouring process and imagine the water in its original container. Transformational thought allows the child to better understand the process of change involved in pouring the water. Overall, armed with logical operations, the child now knows that there must be the same amount of water after it is poured into a different container; the child has logic, not just appearance, as a guide.

First-grade children who demonstrate success on Piaget's conservation-of-liquid task are also more likely to demonstrate success on math problems relative to their peers who do not correctly solve the conservation task (Wubbena, 2013). The logical operations that allow children to understand conservation also allow them to solve addition and subtraction problems, skills that are important to success in school.

Seriation and Transitivity

To appreciate the nature and power of logical operations, consider the child's ability to think about relative size. A preoperational child given a set of sticks of different lengths and asked to arrange them from biggest to smallest is likely to struggle, awkwardly comparing one pair of sticks at a time. Concrete-operational children are capable of the logical operation of seriation, which enables them to arrange items mentally along a quantifiable dimension such as length or weight. Thus, they perform this seriating task quickly and correctly.

Concrete-operational thinkers also master the related concept of transitivity, which describes the necessary relations among elements in a series. If, for example, John is taller than Mark, and Mark is taller than Sam, who is taller—John or Sam? It follows logically that John must be taller than Sam, and the concrete operator grasps the transitivity of these size relationships. Lacking the concept of transitivity, the preoperational child will need to rely on perceptions to answer the question; she may insist that John and Sam stand next to each other to determine who is taller. Preoperational children probably have a better understanding of such transitive relations than Piaget gave them credit for (Gelman, 1978; Trabasso, 1975), but they still have difficulty grasping the logical necessity of transitivity (Chapman & Lindenberger, 1988).

Other Advances

The school-age child overcomes much of the egocentrism of the preschool-age child, becoming increasingly better at recognizing other people's perspectives. Classification abilities improve as the child comes to grasp the concept of class inclusion and can bear in mind that subclasses (brown beads and white beads) are included in a whole class (wooden beads). Mastery of mathematical operations improves the child's ability to solve arithmetic problems and results in an interest in measuring and counting things precisely (and sometimes in fury if companions do not keep accurate score in games). Overall, school-age children appear more logical than preschoolers because they possess a powerful arsenal of "actions in the head." In addition, the school-aged child can inhibit the earlier incorrect or inefficient strategies of the preoperational stage (Lubin et al., 2015).

But surely, if Piaget proposed a fourth stage of cognitive development, there must be some limitations to concrete operations. Indeed, there are. This mode of thought is applied to objects, situations, and events that are real or readily imaginable (thus the term *concrete operations*). As you will see in the next section, concrete operators have difficulty thinking about abstract ideas and unrealistic hypothetical propositions.

● Checking Mastery

1. Name three ways that preoperational thought is limited relative to concrete-operational thought.
2. What is the defining feature of concrete-operational thought?

● Making Connections

1. As a substitute teacher, you sometimes find yourself teaching young children who are mostly preoperational thinkers, while at other times you are teaching children who are concrete-operational thinkers. How would you adjust your lesson plan for a science class to best address these different levels of thought?

7.6
The Adolescent

LEARNING OBJECTIVES
* Explain how adolescent thinking differs from the child's typical pattern of thinking.
* Describe the sorts of tasks that adolescents might be able to solve with their newly emerged reasoning skills.
* Assess Piaget's description of the adolescent as a formal-operational thinker who systematically considers hypothetical and abstract concepts.

Although tremendous advances in cognition occur from infancy to the end of childhood, other transformations of the mind are in store for the adolescent. If teenagers become introspective, question their parents' authority, dream of perfect worlds, and contemplate their futures, cognitive development may help explain why.

Emergence of Abstract Thought

Piaget set the beginning of the formal operations stage of cognitive development around age 11 or 12 and possibly later. If concrete operations are mental actions on objects (tangible things and events), formal operations are mental actions on ideas. Thus, the adolescent who acquires formal operations can mentally juggle and think logically about ideas, which cannot be seen, heard, tasted, smelled, or touched. In other words, formal-operational thought is more hypothetical and abstract than concrete-operational thought; it also involves adopting a more systematic and scientific approach to problem solving (Inhelder & Piaget, 1964).

Hypothetical and Abstract Thinking

If you could have a third eye and put it anywhere on your body, where would you put it, and why? That question was posed to

Tanya's response   John's response

■ **Figure 7.5** Where would you put a third eye? Tanya (age 9) did not show much inventiveness in drawing her "third eye." But John (age 11) wanted a third eye in the palm of his hand: "I could see around corners and see what kind of cookie I'd get out of the cookie jar." John shows early signs of formal-operational thought.

9-year-olds—likely to be in the concrete-operational stage—and to 11- to 12-year-olds—the age when the first signs of formal operations often appear (Piaget, 1970). In their drawings, all the 9-year-olds placed the third eye on their foreheads between their existing eyes; many thought the exercise was stupid (as reported in Shaffer & Kipp, 2014). The 11- and 12-year-olds were not as bound by the realities of eye location. They could invent ideas contrary to fact (for example, the idea of an eye in the palm of a hand) and think logically about the implications of such ideas (■ Figure 7.5). Thus, concrete operators deal with realities, whereas formal operators can deal with possibilities, including those that contradict known reality.

Formal-operational thought is also more abstract than concrete-operational thought. The school-age child may define the justice system in terms of police and judges; the adolescent may define it more abstractly as a branch of government concerned with balancing the rights of different interests in society. Also, the school-age child may be able to think logically about concrete and factually true statements, as in this syllogism: If you drink poison, you will die. Fred drank poison. Therefore, Fred will die. The adolescent can do this but also engage in such if–then thinking about contrary-to-fact statements ("If you drink milk, you will die") or symbols (If P, then Q. P, therefore Q).

Scientific Reasoning

Formal operations also permit systematic and scientific thinking about problems. One of Piaget's famous tests for formal-operational thinking is the pendulum task (■ Figure 7.6). The child is given several weights that can be tied to a string to make a pendulum and is told that he may vary the length of the string, the amount of weight attached to it, and the height

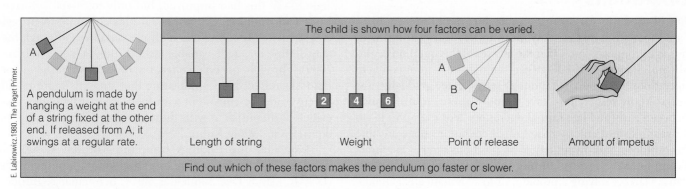

■ **Figure 7.6** The pendulum problem.

from which the weight is released to find out which of these factors, alone or in combination, determines how quickly the pendulum makes its arc. How would you go about solving this problem?

The concrete operator is likely to jump right in without much advanced planning, using a trial-and-error approach. That is, the child may try a variety of things but fail to test different hypotheses systematically—for example, the hypothesis that the shorter the string is, the faster the pendulum swings, all other factors remaining constant. Concrete operators are therefore unlikely to solve the problem. They can draw proper conclusions from their observations—for example, from watching as someone else demonstrates what happens if a pendulum with a short string is released, compared with a pendulum with a long string.

What will the formal-operational individual do? In all likelihood, the teenager will first sit and think, planning an overall strategy for solving the problem. All the possible hypotheses should be generated; after all, the one overlooked may be the right one. Then it must be determined how each hypothesis can be tested. This is a matter of **hypothetical-deductive reasoning**, or reasoning from general ideas or rules to their specific implications. In the pendulum problem, it means starting with a hypothesis and tracing the specific implications of this idea in an if–then fashion: "If the length of the string matters, then I should see a difference when I compare a long string with a short string while holding other factors constant." The trick in hypothesis testing is to vary each factor (for example, the length of the string) while holding all others constant (the weight, the height from which the weight is dropped, and so on). (It is, by the way, the length of the string that matters; the shorter the string, the faster the swing.)

In sum, formal-operational thought involves being able to think systematically about hypothetical ideas and abstract concepts. It also involves mastering the hypothetical-deductive approach that scientists use—forming many hypotheses and systematically testing them through an experimental method. Before continuing, take a few minutes to assess your understanding of Piaget's stages of cognitive development with the questions in **Engagement 7.1.**

Adolescents are more likely than children to benefit from some types of science instruction because formal-operational thought opens the door for reasoning about abstract and hypothetical material.

Jon Feingersh/Getty Images

Progress Toward Mastery of Formal Operations

Are 11- and 12-year-olds really capable of all these sophisticated mental activities? Anyone who has had dealings with this age group will know that the answer to this question is usually not. Piaget (1970) described the transition from concrete operations to formal operations as taking place gradually over years. Many researchers have found it useful to distinguish between early and late formal operations. For example, 11- to 13-year-olds just entering the formal operations stage are able to consider simple hypothetical propositions such as the three-eye problem. But most are not yet able to devise an overall game plan for solving a problem or to systematically generate and test hypotheses. On a battery of Piagetian tasks designed to evaluate scientific reasoning, 11- to 14-year-old girls correctly solved only 20–30% of the problems (Martorano, 1977). By ages 16–17 this had improved, but only to 50–60% correct. Even with training, 11- to 12-year-olds continue to struggle to systematically coordinate multiple variables, although they may do fine on single-variable tasks (Kuhn, Pease, & Wirkala, 2009). Throughout adolescence, responses to scientific reasoning tasks reflect biases indicating that students more readily accept evidence consistent with their preexisting beliefs than evidence inconsistent with these beliefs (Klaczynski & Gordon, 1996a, 1996b; Kuhn, 1993).

Consider the findings from the Munich Longitudinal Study on the Ontogenesis of Individual Competencies (LOGIC) study (see Schneider, 2014; Schneider & Bullock,

How Well Do You Understand Piaget's Stages of Cognitive Development?

Choose the appropriate answer for each of the following questions. Answers are printed upside down at the bottom of this box.

1. Baby Joel seems to be fascinated with the dog's tail: He repeatedly kicks at it with his foot, which makes the dog wag his big tail. Joel finds this highly amusing. This suggests that Joel is in which sub-stage of the sensorimotor period?
   a. Primary circular reactions
   b. Secondary circular reactions
   c. Coordination of secondary schemes
   d. Tertiary circular reactions

2. Brian is playing with his infant daughter, Carrie, showing her a stuffed bear and then dropping it behind the sofa. Carrie seems interested in the toy when it is in front of her, but as soon as Brian drops it behind the sofa, she stops "playing" the game and looks at other things. This illustrates that Carrie:
   a. Has not yet developed object permanence
   b. Is not really interested in the toy
   c. Is mentally trying to figure out where the toy has gone after it is dropped
   d. Is still operating with secondary circular reactions but has not yet learned to combine them to solve the problem

3. Which of the following statements is TRUE regarding Piaget's first stage of cognitive development?
   a. Piaget may have overestimated infants' abilities by allowing them multiple attempts to solve problems.
   b. Infants progress through the substages in an individualized order that does not permit researchers to make any generalizations about developments of this stage.
   c. Piaget underestimated infants' abilities because he placed many task demands on them in assessing their knowledge.
   d. Piaget was right on the mark with his description of the ages when infants typically acquire symbolic logic.

4. Jeremy used to just bang his shoe on the coffee table, but now he has started to run it along the floor as if it were a car. Jeremy has acquired:
   a. Decentration
   b. Transformational thought
   c. Symbolic capacity
   d. Object permanence

5. Mira emphatically tells her older brother that "there *is* a Santa Claus because I see lots of gifts under the tree!" Mira's thinking reflects:
   a. The "A-not-B error"
   b. Conservation
   c. Transformational thought
   d. The influence of perceptual salience

6. When Mom presents the kids with some cookies, big brother Derek immediately grabs for the unbroken cookie, saying he doesn't want the broken one. Little sister Sal happily takes the cookie broken in half, saying, "Ha-ha! I got more than you!" Sal seems to lack an understanding of:
   a. Egocentrism
   b. Conservation
   c. Class inclusion
   d. Object permanence

7. Ramon understands that if A is bigger than B, and B is bigger than C, then A must also be bigger than C. This shows that he has mastered:
   a. Transitivity
   b. Conservation
   c. Seriation
   d. Reversibility of thought

8. Kira is furious that her father won't let her go out with a friend on a school night. She screams, "You have no idea what I'm feeling! You just want me to be miserable." Kira's response indicates that she:
   a. Has not yet acquired conservation of thought
   b. Is spoiled or has unreasonable parents
   c. Shows centration of thought
   d. Shows adolescent egocentrism

9. An important distinction between concrete-operational thought and preoperational thought is:
   a. The acquisition of logical reasoning skills in the concrete stage
   b. The acquisition of symbolic logic in the concrete stage
   c. The acquisition of hypothetical thinking in the concrete stage
   d. The use of deductive reasoning in the concrete stage

10. The defining difference between concrete-operational thought and formal-operational thought is:
    a. The use of logical reasoning
    b. The ability to reason about abstract and hypothetical problems
    c. The ability to imagine performing before an audience
    d. The ability to use relativistic thinking

Answers: 1.b 2.a 3.c 4.c 5.d 6.b 7.a 8.d 9.a 10.b

2009). LOGIC began in the 1980s with 200 school-aged children who were observed and tested on multiple dimensions over a 20-year period. One of the areas of study was scientific reasoning, and in particular, whether participants understood a crucial component of scientific reasoning—control of variables. Did they understand that scientific testing requires identifying and holding constant all relevant variables while systematically testing the effects of varying the variable of interest?

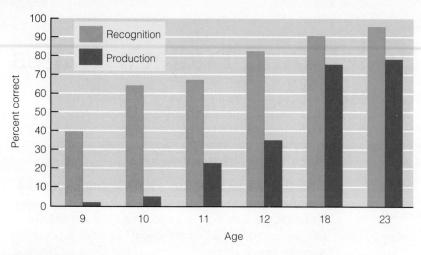

Figure 7.7 Performance on control of variables strategy (CVS) use for recognition and production tasks (percent correct)

Source: From Bullock, M., Sodian, B., & Koerber, S. (2009). Doing experiments and understanding science: Development of scientific reasoning from childhood to adulthood. In Schneider, W. & Bullock, M. (Eds.) (2009). *Human development from early childhood to early adulthood: Findings from a 20-year longitudinal study*, pp. 173–197. Reprinted by permission of Taylor & Francis Group.

The LOGIC participants were given a group of experiments to evaluate; each experiment contained a design error, such as not keeping all variables but one constant or not having a comparison group for an intervention study. In addition to evaluating experimental designs, participants were also tested to determine if they could produce their own experiments.

As ■ Figure 7.7 shows, most participants, even those as young as 10, showed an understanding of this important principle of scientific thinking. However, there was a marked difference between their ability to recognize good scientific reasoning and their ability to produce it. For example, among 12-year-olds, more than 80% could recognize good and bad examples of experiments, but only 35% could create a good experiment themselves. By age 18, though, the ability to create a good experiment was catching up to the ability to recognize a good experiment (91% versus 85%). Thus, adolescents show an awareness of scientific reasoning ("I know it when I see it"), but they may not be able to produce logical scientific reasoning until they are older (and see Kail, 2013).

Piaget claimed that the perceptual reasoning of young children is *replaced* by scientific reasoning as children age, but it turns out that the two forms of reasoning—intuitive and scientific—*coexist* in older thinkers (Klaczynski, 2013). Being able to shift between intuitive and scientific reasoning provides flexibility in problem-solving situations as long as the thinker can effectively select the appropriate strategy. However, like children (and adults), adolescents often seem to adopt an intuitive strategy, perhaps because it is generally easier than applying scientific reasoning. In cases where the conclusion from the intuitive approach is clearly incorrect, adolescents more readily shift to using scientific judgment (Klaczynski, 2013). In addition, adolescents are increasingly able to decontextualize, or separate prior knowledge and beliefs from the demands of the task at hand (Kuhn &

Franklin, 2006; Stanovich, 2011). For example, someone who believes that males are better at math than females may find it difficult to accept new evidence that girls attain higher classroom math grades than boys if intuitions based on their prior experiences do not allow them to scientifically process the new information. Decontextualizing increases the likelihood of using reasoning to analyze a problem logically rather than relying on intuition or faulty existing knowledge.

There is some evidence that recent cohorts of teens (ages 13–15) are better able than earlier cohorts to solve formal-operational tasks. For example, 66% of teens tested in 1996 showed formal-operational thought on a probability test, whereas only 49% of teens tested in 1967 showed such skills (Flieller, 1999). Why might formal-operational skills improve over time? Changes in school curricula are the likely explanation. Notably, science curricula were revised in the 1960s and have increasingly incorporated more hands-on discovery learning activities, perhaps reflecting adoption of Piaget's concept of active learning. The achievement of formal-operational thinking depends on opportunities to learn scientific reasoning, as through exposure to math and science education (Babai & Levit-Dori, 2009; Karpov, 2005). The more hands-on the learning, the greater the benefit to performance on hands-on, formal-operational tasks.

Progress toward the mastery of formal operations is slow, at least as measured by Piaget's scientific tasks. These findings have major implications for secondary-school teachers, who are often trying to teach abstract material to students who have a range of thinking patterns. Teachers may need to give concrete thinkers extra assistance by using specific examples and demonstrations to help clarify general principles.

Implications of Formal Thought

Formal-operational thought contributes to other changes in adolescence—some good, some not so good. First, the good news: As you will see in upcoming chapters, formal-operational thought may prepare the individual to gain a sense of identity, think in more complex ways about moral issues, and understand other people better. Advances in cognitive development help lay the groundwork for advances in many other areas of development, including the appreciation of humor.

Now, the bad news: Hypothetical thinking may also be related to some of the more painful aspects of the adolescent experience. Children tend to accept the world as it is and to heed the words of authority figures. The adolescent armed with hypothetical and scientific reasoning abilities can think more independently, imagine alternatives to present realities, and raise questions about everything from why parents set certain rules to why there is injustice in the world. Questioning can lead to confusion and sometimes to rebellion against ideas

A teenage girl may feel that everyone is as preoccupied with her appearance as she is, a form of adolescent egocentrism known as the imaginary audience phenomenon.

Image Source/Getty Images

own and others' thoughts. Elkind identified two types of adolescent egocentrism: the imaginary audience and the personal fable.

The **imaginary audience** phenomenon involves confusing your own thoughts with those of a hypothesized audience for your behavior. Thus, the teenage girl who ends up with pizza sauce on the front of her shirt at a party may feel extremely self-conscious: "They're all thinking what a slob I am! I wish I could crawl into a hole." She assumes that everyone in the room is as preoccupied with the blunder as she is. Or a teenage boy may spend hours in front of the mirror getting ready for a date, then may be so concerned with how he imagines his date is reacting to him that he hardly notices her: "Why did I say that? She looks bored. Did she notice my pimple?" (She, of course, is equally preoccupied with how she is playing to her audience. No wonder teenagers are often awkward and painfully aware of their every slip on first dates.)

The second form of adolescent egocentrism is the **personal fable**—a tendency to think that you and your thoughts and feelings are unique (Elkind, 1967). If the imaginary audience is a product of the inability to differentiate between self and other, the personal fable is a product of differentiating too much. Thus, the adolescent in love for the first time imagines that no one in the history of the human race has ever felt such heights of emotion. When the relationship breaks up, no one—least of all a parent—could possibly understand the crushing agony. The personal fable may also lead adolescents to feel that rules that apply to others do not apply to them. Thus, they will not be hurt if they speed down the highway without wearing a seat belt or drive under the influence of alcohol. And they will not become pregnant if they engage in sex without contraception, so they do not need to bother with contraception. As it turns out, high scores on measures of adolescent egocentrism are associated with behaving in risky ways (Greene et al., 1996; Holmbeck et al., 1994).

Although the idea of adolescent egocentrism has some intuitive appeal, as many parents can attest to having to put up with bouts of "it's all about me" from their teens, there has not been a great deal of research support for Elkind's idea of adolescent egocentrism. In particular, researchers have been unable to link the onset of the formal operations stage to the rise of adolescent egocentrism (Galanaki, 2012). Indeed, Evangelia Galanaki (2012) tested various aspects of adolescent egocentrism and found only that preoccupation with one's self increased during the transition from adolescence to young adulthood. In other research, Joanna Bell and Rachel Bromnick (2003) suggest that adolescents are preoccupied with how they present themselves in public not because of an imaginary audience but because of a *real audience*. That is, the research indicates that adolescents are aware that there are real consequences to how they present themselves. Their popularity and peer approval, as well as their self-confidence and self-esteem, are often influenced by how others (the real audience) perceive them. Adults, too, are aware that their actions and appearance are often judged by others, but although these adult concerns are usually assumed to be realistic, similar concerns by adolescents are sometimes viewed, perhaps unfairly, as trivial (Bell & Bromnick, 2003).

that do not seem logical enough. Some adolescents become idealists, inventing perfect worlds and envisioning logical solutions to problems they detect in the imperfect world around them, sometimes losing sight of practical considerations and real barriers to social change. Just as infants flaunt the new schemes they develop, adolescents may go overboard with their new cognitive skills, irritate their parents, and become frustrated when the world does not respond to their flawless logic.

Many years ago, David Elkind (1967) proposed that formal-operational thought also leads to **adolescent egocentrism**—difficulty differentiating one's own thoughts and feelings from those of other people. The young child's egocentrism is rooted in ignorance that different people have different perspectives, but the adolescent's reflects an enhanced ability to reflect about one's

1. What change in thinking marks the shift from concrete to formal-operational thinking?
2. What is the hypothetical-deductive approach to problem solving?

1. Consider one or more assignments or tests that you recently completed for one (or more) of your courses. Conduct an analysis to determine whether your responses reflect primarily a concrete or a formal level of thinking. If they were primarily concrete, was this appropriate to the task demands? What distinguished the assignments that elicited concrete-operational answers from those that elicited formal-operational answers?
2. Design an educational plan or program that you think would help foster formal-operational thought in students who have not yet mastered it.

7.7

The Adult

LEARNING OBJECTIVES

- Outline the characteristic features of adult cognition.

- Discuss ways that adult thought is the most advanced level of thinking and ways that adult thought is limited.

- Evaluate whether a stage beyond Piaget's formal operations is warranted and outline what this stage might look like.

- Describe changes to cognitive skills in later adulthood.

Do adults think differently than adolescents do? Does cognition change over the adult years? Until fairly recently, developmentalists have not asked such questions. Piaget indicated that the highest stage of cognitive development, formal operations, was fully mastered by most people between age 15 and age 18. Why bother studying cognitive development in adulthood? As it turns out, it has been worth the effort. Research has revealed limitations in adult performance that must be explained, and it suggests that at least some adults progress beyond formal operations to more advanced forms of thought (Jacobs & Klaczynski, 2002).

Limitations in Adult Cognitive Performance

If many high school students are shaky in their command of formal operations, do most of them gain fuller mastery after the high school years? Gains are indeed made between adolescence and adulthood (Blackburn & Papalia, 1992). However, only about half of all college students show firm and consistent mastery of formal operations on Piaget's scientific reasoning tasks (Neimark, 1975). Those college students who have attained formal-operational thought perform better, as evidenced by higher GPAs, than those who are still functioning at the concrete-operational level (Fowler & Watford, 2000). Similarly, sizable percentages of American adults do not solve scientific problems at the formal level, and there are some societies in which no adults solve formal-operational problems (Neimark, 1975).

Why do more adults not do well on Piagetian tasks? An average level of performance on standardized intelligence tests seems to be necessary for a person to achieve formal-operational thought (Inhelder, 1966). What seems more important than basic intelligence, however, is formal education (Neimark, 1979). In cultures in which virtually no one solves Piaget's problems, people do not receive advanced schooling. If achieving formal-operational thought requires education or specific experiences, Piaget's theory may be culturally biased, and his stages may not be as universal as he believed.

But neither lack of intelligence nor lack of formal education is a problem for most college students. Instead, they have difficulty with tests of formal operations when they lack expertise in a domain of knowledge. Piaget (1972) suggested that adults are likely to use formal operations in a field of expertise but to use concrete operations in less familiar areas. This is precisely what seems to happen. For example, Richard De Lisi and Joanne Staudt (1980) gave three kinds of formal-operational tasks—the pendulum problem, a political problem, and a literary criticism problem—to college students majoring in physics, political science, and English. As ■ Figure 7.8 illustrates, each group of students did well on the problem relevant to that group's field of expertise. On problems outside their fields, however, about half the students failed. Consistent with these results, other research shows that task relevancy affects performance on reasoning tasks (Sebby & Papini, 1994). Possibly, then, many adolescents and adults fail to use formal reasoning on Piaget's scientific problems simply because these problems are unfamiliar to them and they lack relevant expertise.

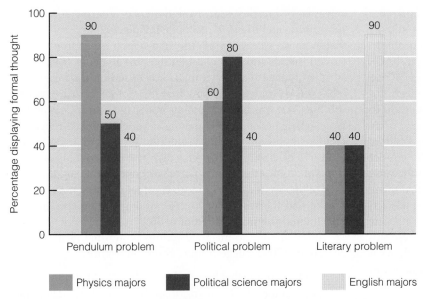

Figure 7.8 Expertise and formal operations. College students show the greatest command of formal-operational thought in the subject area most related to their major.

Source: De Lisi, R., & Staudt, J. (1980). Individual differences in college students' performance on formal operations tasks. *Journal of Applied Psychology, 1,* 163–174.

As noted earlier, Fischer maintains that each person has an optimal level of cognitive performance that will show itself in familiar and well-trained content domains (Fischer, 1980; Fischer, Kenny, & Pipp, 1990). However, performance is likely to be highly inconsistent across content areas unless the person has had a chance to build knowledge and skills in all these domains. More often, adults may use and strengthen formal modes of thinking only in their areas of expertise. By adopting a contextual perspective on cognitive development, you can appreciate that the individual's experience and the nature of the tasks she is asked to perform influence cognitive performance across the life span (Salthouse, 1990).

Growth Beyond Formal Operations?

While some researchers have been asking why adults sometimes perform so poorly on cognitive tasks, others have been asking why they sometimes perform so well. Take Piaget. Was his ability to generate a complex theory of development no more than the application of formal-operational thought? This seems unlikely and, indeed, Fernando Vidal (1994) uses Piaget's own writings as a teen and young man to show how his thinking shifted over time from largely formal operational to something beyond formal operations. Others have argued that formal operations involves applying logic to a *closed* set of ideas and not to the *open* sets of ideas that characterize most adult issues (Broughton, 1984; Ricco, 1990). To illustrate this concept, consider again the pendulum problem. A defined or closed set of variables is associated with this problem; solving the problem is possible by systematically applying logic to this closed set of variables. You do not need to go beyond the problem set. But how do adults make decisions about complex dilemmas and problems that have no well-defined set of variables or that have variables that are constantly changing rather than static?

Several intriguing ideas have been proposed about stages of cognitive development that may lie beyond formal operations—that is, about **postformal thought,** or ways of thinking that are more complex than those of the formal-operational stage (see Commons & Richards, 2003; Commons & Ross, 2008; Gurba, 2005). How might thought be qualitatively different in adulthood than it is in adolescence? Several theorists have taken a shot at exploring postformal thinking, and here we consider two of the possibilities: relativistic thinking and dialectical thinking.

As noted earlier, adolescents who have attained formal operations sometimes get carried away with their new powers of logical thinking. They insist that there is a logically correct answer for every question—that if you simply apply logic, you will arrive at the right answer, at some absolute truth. In contrast, adults often think flexibly and recognize that there is not a single right or wrong answer; there are shades of gray to many problems and flexible or creative thinking may be required to successfully navigate many of the complex issues of the adult world. Thus, adults are more likely to engage in relativistic thinking, or understanding that knowledge depends on its context and the subjective perspective of the knower (Marchand, 2002; Sinnott, 1984, 1996). Whereas an absolutist assumes that truth lies in the nature of reality and that there is only one truth, a relativist assumes that his starting assumptions influence the "truth" discovered and that a problem can be viewed in multiple ways.

Consider this logic problem: "Subject A grows 1 cm per month. Subject B grows 2 cm per month. Who is taller?" (Yan & Arlin, 1995, p. 230). The absolutist might say, "Subject B," based on the information given, but the relativist would be more likely to say, "It depends." It depends on how tall A and B were to begin with and on how much time passes before their heights are measured. The relativistic thinker will recognize that the problem is ill defined and that further information is needed, and he will be able to think flexibly about what the answer would be if he made certain assumptions rather than others.

Or consider this problem, given to preadolescents, adolescents, and adults by Gisela Labouvie-Vief and her colleagues (1983, p. 5):

> John is known to be a heavy drinker, especially when he goes to parties. Mary, John's wife, warns him that if he gets drunk one more time she will leave him and take the children. Tonight John is out late at an office party. John comes home drunk.

Does Mary leave John? Most preadolescents and many adolescents quickly and confidently said, "Yes." They did not question the assumption that Mary would stand by her word; they simply applied logic to the information they were given. Adults were more likely to realize that different starting assumptions were possible and that the answer depended on which assumptions were chosen. One woman, for example, noted that if Mary had stayed with

John for years, she would be unlikely to leave him now. This same woman said, "There was no right or wrong answer. You could get logically to both answers" (p. 12). Postformal thinkers seem able to devise more than one logical solution to a problem (Sinnott, 1996).

In a fascinating study of cognitive growth over the college years, William Perry (1970) found that beginning college students often assumed that there were absolute, objective truths to be found by consulting their textbooks or their professors. They looked to what they believed were authoritative sources for *the* answer to a question, as if all problems have a single, correct answer. As their college careers progressed, they often became frustrated in their search for absolute truths. They saw that many questions seemed to have several answers, depending on the perspective of the respondent. Taking the extremely relativistic view that any opinion was as good as any other, several of these students said they were not sure how they could ever decide what to believe. Eventually, many understood that some opinions can be better supported than others; they were then able to commit themselves to specific positions, fully aware that they were choosing among relative perspectives.

Between adolescence and adulthood, then, many people start as absolutists, become relativists, and finally make commitments to positions despite their more sophisticated awareness of the nature and limits of knowledge (Sinnott, 1996). Not surprisingly, students at the absolute level of thinking use fewer thinking styles; they stick mainly with traditional or conventional modes of thinking (Zhang, 2002). Students who are relativistic thinkers use a greater variety of thinking styles, including ones that promote creativity and greater cognitive complexity (see Wu & Chiou, 2008). Some refer to this as "thinking outside the box," or thinking unconventionally. Try the 9-dot problem in ■ **Figure 7.9** to see if you can think outside the box. (You can find the answer online.)

Another possibility for advanced thought beyond formal operations is **dialectical thinking**, or detecting paradoxes and inconsistencies among ideas and trying to reconcile them (Basseches, 1984, 2005; Kramer, 1989; Riegel, 1973). For example, you engage in dialectical thinking when you recognize that the problem facing you is multifaceted and will be difficult to

solve; you "wrestle" with it mentally, considering the various possibilities and trying to reconcile the pieces that do not immediately make sense to you. You may solicit input from several trusted friends and then consider the pros and cons of each possible solution. Finally, you make a decision on the best way to address the problem, knowing that it is not necessarily a perfect solution, but it is the best option under the current conditions. By engaging in dialectical thinking, advanced thinkers repeatedly challenge and change their understanding of what constitutes "truth." For example, they may arrive at one conclusion, then think of an idea that contradicts their conclusion, and then synthesize the two ideas into a more complete understanding. They realize that the search for truth is an ongoing process and can take them down many different paths.

In an attempt to integrate various postformal ideas, Helena Marchand (2002) suggests these common features:

1. Understanding that knowledge is relative, not absolute; there are far more shades of gray than there are clear dichotomies of knowledge.
2. Accepting that the world (physical and mental) is filled with contradictions: inconsistent information can exist side by side.
3. Attempting to integrate the contradictions into some larger understanding.

Environments that expose us to a wider range of ideas, roles, and experiences seem to foster this higher level of thinking. College students who have greater diversity among their friends tend to exhibit more of these postformal characteristics than those whose friends are very similar (Galupo, Cartwright, & Savage, 2009). Among high school and college students, females report greater gender role conflict than males and also a more relativistic perspective on relationships (Kramer & Melchior, 1990).

It is not yet clear whether relativistic, dialectical, or other forms of advanced thinking might qualify as a new, postformal stage of cognitive development. Marchand (2002) concludes that a fifth stage of postformal thought may not be warranted. Adult thought may indeed be different or more advanced than the formal-operational thought of adolescence, though. Much research confirms that cognitive growth does not end in adolescence. Yet growth during adulthood may not reflect a new Piagetian stage—a qualitatively different, structural change in thinking that is universal and irreversible (Lerner, 2006).

Aging and Cognitive Skills

What becomes of cognitive capacities in later adulthood? Some mental abilities decline as the average person ages, and it appears that older adults often have trouble solving Piagetian tests of formal-operational thinking (Blackburn & Papalia, 1992). Indeed, elderly adults sometimes perform poorly relative to young and middle-aged adults even on concrete-operational tasks assessing conservation and classification skills.

This does not mean that elderly adults regress to immature modes of thought. For one thing, these studies have involved cross-sectional comparisons of different age groups. The poorer

■ **Figure 7.9** Your task is to connect all nine dots using four straight lines or less, without lifting your pen or pencil from the paper. Hint: To be successful, you need to think outside the box! For the solution, try typing "Solution for Nine Dot Problem" into an Internet search engine.

performance of older groups does not necessarily mean that cognitive abilities are lost as people age. It could be caused by a cohort effect, because the average older adult today has had less formal schooling than the average younger adult has had. Older adults attending college tend to perform as well as younger college students on tests of formal operations (Blackburn, 1984; Hooper, Hooper, & Colbert, 1985). Moreover, brief training can quickly improve the performance of older adults long out of school, which suggests that the necessary cognitive abilities are there but merely need to be reactivated (Blackburn & Papalia, 1992).

Questions have also been raised about the relevance of the skills assessed in Piagetian tasks to the lives of older adults (Labouvie-Vief, 1985). Not only are these problems unfamiliar to many older adults, but they also resemble the intellectual challenges that children confront in school, not those that most adults encounter in everyday contexts. Thus, older people may not be motivated to solve them. Also, older adults may rely on modes of cognition that have proved useful to them in daily life but that make them look cognitively deficient in the laboratory (Salthouse, 1990).

Consider this example: Kathy Pearce and Nancy Denney (1984) found that elderly adults, like young children but unlike other age groups, often group two objects on the basis of some functional relationship between them (for example, putting a pipe and matches together because matches are used to light pipes) rather than on the basis of similarity (for example, putting a pipe and a cigar together because they are both ways of smoking tobacco). In school and in some job situations, Pearce and Denney suggest, people are asked to group objects on the basis of similarity, but in everyday life it may make more sense to associate objects commonly used together.

Such findings suggest that what appear to be deficits in older people may merely be differences in style. Similar stylistic differences in classification skills have been observed cross-culturally and can, if researchers are not careful, lead to the incorrect conclusion that uneducated adults from non-Western cultures lack basic cognitive skills. A case in point: Kpelle adults in Africa, when asked to sort foods, clothing, tools, and cooking utensils into groups, sorted them into pairs based on functional relationships. "When an exasperated experimenter finally asked, 'How would a fool do it?' he was given sorts of the type that were initially expected—four neat piles with foods in one, tools in another, and so on" (Glick, 1975, p. 636).

So today's older adults appear not to perform concrete-operational and formal-operational tasks as well as their younger contemporaries do. Planners of adult education for senior citizens might bear in mind that some (although by no means all) of their students may benefit from more concrete forms of instruction. However, these differences may be related to factors other than age, such as education and motivation; an age-related decline in operational abilities has not been firmly established. Most importantly, older adults who perform poorly on unfamiliar problems in laboratory situations often perform far more capably on the sorts of problems that they encounter in everyday contexts (Cornelius & Caspi, 1987; Salthouse, 1990). This is precisely the message from Fischer's skill theory: Abilities vary with context. By providing older adults with a supportive context, we can optimize their level of performance.

Checking Mastery

1. When, or under what conditions, is an adult most likely to use formal-operational thinking?
2. What is relativistic thinking?

Making Connections

1. How important is it to achieve formal-operational thought? What limitations would you experience at work and school if you operated at a concrete-operational level all the time and never progressed to formal-operational thought?
2. What sorts of questions or answers do you contribute to class discussions? Do they reflect primarily concrete operational, formal operational, or something beyond formal-operational thinking such as relativistic or dialectical thinking?

Chapter Summary

7.1 Piaget's Constructivist Approach

- Jean Piaget developed a theory of how children come to know their world by constructing their own schemes or cognitive structures through active exploration.
- Studying children using the clinical method, a flexible question-and-answer technique, Piaget formulated four stages of cognitive development in which children construct increasingly complex schemes through an interaction of maturation and experience.
- Intelligence is a basic life function that allows organisms (including humans) to adapt to the demands of their environment.
- Children adapt to the world through the processes of organization and adaptation (assimilating new experiences to existing understandings and accommodating existing understandings to new experiences).

- Piaget's theory has stimulated much research over the years, which has added considerably to our understanding of cognitive development. Piaget showed us that infants are active, not passive, in their own development. He argued that children think differently during different phases of their development, as reflected in his four qualitatively different stages.
- Piaget has been criticized for underestimating the capacities of infants and young children, not considering factors besides competence that influence performance, failing to demonstrate that his stages have coherence, offering vague explanations of development, and underestimating the role of language and social interaction in cognitive development.
- Modern constructivist theories such as neuroconstructivism propose that observed differences in cognitive skills result from experience-induced changes in the underlying neural structures supporting these skills.

7.2 Vygotsky's Sociocultural Perspective

- Lev Vygotsky's sociocultural perspective emphasizes cultural and social influences on cognitive development more than Piaget's theory does.
- Through guided participation in culturally important activities, children learn problem-solving techniques from knowledgeable partners sensitive to their zone of proximal development.
- Language is the most important tool that adults use to pass culturally valued thinking and problem solving to their children. Language shapes their thought and moves from social speech to private speech and later to inner speech.

7.3 Fischer's Dynamic Skill Framework

- Development results from changes in skill levels. Skills reflect what a person can do on a particular task in a specific context.
- People operate within a developmental range, with higher levels of performance demonstrated within a supportive context and after more experience with a task.

7.4 The Infant

- Infants progress through six substages of the sensorimotor period by perceiving and acting on the world; they progress from using their reflexes to adapt to their environment to using symbolic or representational thought to solve problems in their heads.
- Major accomplishments of the sensorimotor stage include the development of object permanence, or the realization that objects continue to exist even when they are not directly experienced, and the symbolic capacity, or the ability to allow one thing to represent something else. The emergence of the symbolic capacity paves the way for language and pretend play.

7.5 The Child

- Preschool-age children are in Piaget's preoperational stage and do not yet reason logically; instead they rely on perceptually salient features of a task or object. Their prelogical set of cognitive structures leads them to have trouble with conservation and classification tasks. In particular, preoperational children lack the abilities to decenter, reverse thought, and understand transformations. In addition, they tend to be egocentric—viewing the world from their own perspective and not recognizing others' points of view.
- School-age children are in Piaget's concrete-operational stage and can reason logically about concrete information, which allows them to solve conservation and classification tasks. Concrete-operational children have acquired the abilities of decentration, reversibility of thought, and transformational thought. They can think about relations, grasping seriation and transitivity, and they understand the concept of class inclusion.

7.6 The Adolescent

- Adolescents may advance to Piaget's last stage of cognitive development—formal-operational thought, in which they can think about abstract concepts and apply their logical reasoning to hypothetical problems. Formal-operational thinkers can simultaneously consider multiple task components.
- Formal-operational thought may give rise to special forms of egocentrism, namely, the imaginary audience and personal fable.

7.7 The Adult

- Many adults seem to function at the concrete-operational level, rather than at Piaget's highest level of formal-operational thought. Formal-operational thought appears to be highly dependent on formal education. It is also influenced by culture and area of expertise.
- Some adults may acquire advanced levels of thought not considered by Piaget, such as relativistic thinking, or understanding that knowledge is dependent on the knower's subjective perspective, and dialectical thinking, or detecting and reconciling contradictory ideas.

Key Terms

8 Memory and Information Processing

Think about everything you have learned and experienced up to this point in your life. Like most people, you probably have a rich and varied set of memories relating to your family, friends, school, work, and life. You rely on these memories every day: They provide you with a solid grounding in who you are, where you have been, and where you hope to go. Now imagine that every one of these memories is gone. It's hard to imagine, but this is what happened to Su Meck at the age of 22. One minute, she was making macaroni and cheese in the kitchen and lifting her young son up in the air, and in the next minute, the ceiling fan had dislodged and struck Su in the head (De Vise, 2011). She awoke a week later with no memories of her past. None. She did not know herself, let alone her husband and two young children. She had to start over. According to her husband, "She was Su 2.0. She had rebooted. . . . It was literally like she had died. Her personality was gone" (McGrory, 2013).

Su Meck started over at the age of 22 when a freak accident wiped out every memory up to that point. Su 2.0, as her husband dubbed her, completed a college degree 23 years after her brain "rebooted."

Matt McClain/The Washington Post/Getty Images

Over the next 30 years, Su would need to relearn everything and begin to form new memories. As her children were learning new things in school, Su would often be learning the same things alongside them. She eventually went to college (for the second time, as she had been in college prior to her freak accident) and earned a degree in music. To date, she has not recovered any memories from the first 22 years of her life.

This is an astonishing case of true **retrograde amnesia**, or loss of memory for information and events occurring prior to the incident that caused the amnesia. Such cases illustrate just how vital memory is to who we are and what we do; it allows us to learn from the past, function in the present, and plan for the future. It would be nearly impossible to overemphasize the importance of our memory system.

In this chapter, we consider how **memory**, our ability to store and later retrieve information about past events, develops and changes over the life span. We begin our journey down memory lane by examining the components of memory and the models that attempt to organize some of the findings that have emerged in the field of memory.

8.1
Conceptualizing Memory

LEARNING OBJECTIVES

- Explain the workings of the memory system, from first exposure to information or an event, to eventual retrieval of this information from memory.

- List and define the different forms of memory.

- Describe the neural underpinnings of memory.

- Discuss how stored information is processed to solve problems.

Modern models of memory originated about 60 years ago when Donald Broadbent (1958) speculated on how humans process information. At about this same time, the modern computer, with its capacity to systematically convert input to output, was emerging and garnering much interest. The computer seemed to provide a good analogy to the human mind, and indeed, efforts to program computers to play chess and solve other problems as efficiently as human experts helped scientists understand a great deal about the strengths and limitations of human cognition (Newell & Simon, 1961; Simon, 1995). The computer, then, was the model for the **information-processing approach** to human cognition, which emphasizes the basic mental processes involved in attention, perception, memory, and decision making. And just as today's more highly developed computers have far greater capacity than those of the past, maturation of the nervous system plus experience presumably enable adults to remember more than young children can and to perform more complex cognitive feats with greater accuracy.

Richard Atkinson and Richard Shiffrin (1968) proposed a simple information-processing framework with three memory components, organized primarily by their duration:

- **Sensory register**, which ever-so-briefly (less than a second) holds the abundant sensory information—sights, sounds, smells, and more—that swirls around us
- **Short-term memory**, which holds a limited amount of information, perhaps only four chunks, for a short period of time

- **Long-term memory**, believed to be a relatively permanent and seemingly unlimited store of information

To illustrate the memory stores, imagine you are listening to a history lecture and among the many facts presented, your professor notes that the U.S. Constitution was ratified in 1789. This statement is an environmental stimulus "hitting" your sensory register. Assuming that you are not lost in a daydream, your sensory register will log it, holding it for a fraction of a second as a kind of afterimage (or, in this example, a kind of echo). Much that strikes the sensory register quickly disappears without further processing. Attentional processes (see Chapter 6) play a large role in what information enters the sensory register and may be processed further. If you think you may need to remember 1789, it will be moved into short-term memory, but to be remembered for any length of time, it will need to be moved into long-term memory, which represents what most people mean by memory. More than likely, you will hold the professor's statement in short-term memory just long enough to record it in your notes. Later, as you study your notes, you will rehearse the information to move it into long-term memory so that you can retrieve it the next day or week when you are taking the test.

This simplified model shows what you must do to learn and remember something. The first step is to **encode** the information: get it into the system. If it never gets in, it cannot be remembered. Second, information undergoes **consolidation**, processes that stabilize and organize the information to facilitate long-term storage.

These processes include *synaptic consolidation*, which occurs in the minutes or hours after initial learning, and *system consolidation*, which takes place over a longer period of time (Dudai, 2004).

The processes of consolidation are facilitated by sleep (Barham et al., 2016; Marshall & Born, 2007; Rasch & Born, 2013) and disrupted by stress (McGaugh & Roozendaal, 2002). Consolidation is also assisted when we can relate new material with prior knowledge, a process reflected in patterns of brain activity measured during sleep (Hennies et al., 2016). In particular, when sleep spindles—those spikes of neural activity observed during REM sleep—are denser, there seems to be greater retention of new learning that is associated with prior knowledge (Hennies et al., 2016).

In the absence of consolidation, the information would not make the leap from the first step of encoding to the third step of storage. **Storage**, of course, refers to holding information in a long-term memory store. Memories fade over time unless they are appropriately stored in long-term memory. Research has also made it clear that storing memories is a constructive process and not a static recording of what was encoded. As Mary Courage and Nelson Cowan (2009) describe it, "human memory does not record experience as a video camera would, but rather as an historian would: as a dynamic and inferential process with reconstructions that depend on a variety of sources of information" (p. 2).

Finally, for the memory process to be complete, there must be **retrieval**—the process of getting information out when it is needed. People say they have successfully remembered something when they can retrieve it from long-term memory. Retrieval can be accomplished in several ways. If you are asked a multiple-choice question about when the Constitution was ratified, you need not actively retrieve the correct date; you merely need to recognize it among the options. This is an example of **recognition memory**. If, instead, you are asked, "When was the Constitution ratified?" this is a test of **recall memory**; it requires active retrieval without the aid of cues. Between recognition and recall memory is **cued recall memory**, in which you would be given a hint or cue to facilitate retrieval (for example, "When was the Constitution ratified? It is the year the French Revolution began and rhymes with *wine*."). Most people find questions requiring recognition memory easier to answer than those requiring cued recall, and those requiring cued recall easier than those requiring pure recall. This holds true across the life span, which suggests that many things people have apparently encoded or learned are "in there someplace" even though they may be difficult to retrieve without cues. Breakdowns in remembering may involve difficulties in initial encoding, storage, or retrieval.

Useful as this model has been, modifications and alternative models have been proposed as research has uncovered more and more about memory processes. A more comprehensive model is illustrated in ■ **Figure 8.1**. It shows, for example, that short-term memory is more complex than originally conceived. For one,

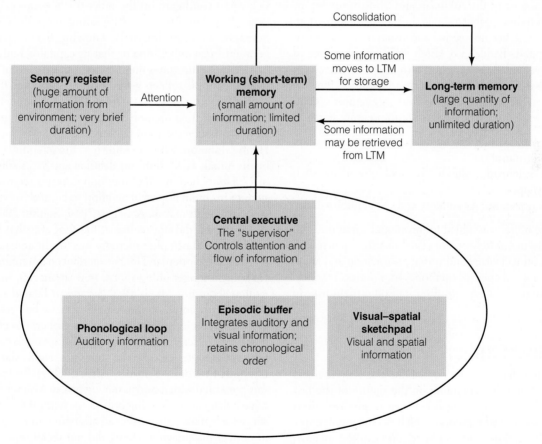

■ **Figure 8.1** A comprehensive model of memory. The central executive manages the important business of the short-term memory store. The bottom three boxes show the three types of short-term memory: phonological, visual-spatial, and the episodic buffer, which integrates the other two types of short-term memory.

most cognitive researchers distinguish between passive and active forms of short-term memory and use the term **working memory** to refer to short-term memory being used to achieve a goal. Working memory is akin to a mental "scratch pad" that temporarily stores information while actively operating on it (Baddeley, 2012). It is what is being manipulated in one's mind at any moment. As you know, people can juggle only so much information at once without some of it slipping away or "falling out" of working memory. To illustrate working memory, look at the following seven numbers. Then look away and add the numbers in your head while trying to remember them:

7 2 5 6 1 4 7

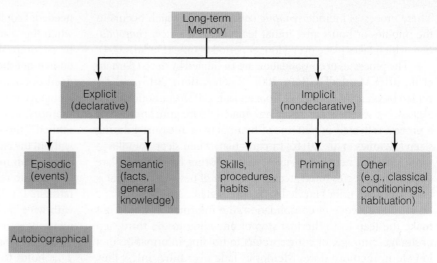

Figure 8.2 Types of long-term memory.

Most likely, having to actively manipulate the numbers in working memory to add them disrupted your ability to rehearse them to remember them. People who are fast at adding numbers would have better luck than most people, because they would have more working-memory space left for remembering the items (Byrnes, 1996).

Alan Baddeley (1986, 2001, 2012) has proposed a four-component model of working memory to try to address the limitations in this area in the Atkinson and Shiffrin model. In particular, research showed that a single short-term memory store just was not sufficient, because verbal and visual memories seem to be stored separately (Baddeley & Hitch, 1974). As illustrated in Figure 8.1, this expanded view of short-term memory consists of a **central executive**, which directs attention and controls the flow of information; it is the supervisor of the working-memory system. In addition, there are three types of short-term memory storage:

- Phonological loop, which briefly holds auditory information such as words or music
- Visual-spatial sketchpad, which holds visual information such as colors and shapes
- Episodic buffer, which links auditory and visual information

The episodic buffer was added to this model when research showed that some memories are not visual or verbal per se, but instead serve to connect visual and verbal information and facilitate long-term storage of episodic memories (memories of events). In the next section, we'll explore these episodic memories in greater detail.

Implicit and Explicit Memory

Memory researchers have concluded that the long-term memory store responds differently depending on the nature of the task (Schneider, 2015). They distinguish between **implicit memory** (also called nondeclarative memory), which occurs unintentionally, automatically, and without awareness, and **explicit memory** (also called declarative memory), which involves deliberate, effortful recollection of events (see ■ **Figure 8.2**). Explicit memory is tested through traditional recognition and recall tests (such as a course's final exam with multiple-choice and essay questions) and

can be further divided into **semantic memory** for general facts and **episodic memory** for specific experiences. Most memory experts agree that explicit memories, whether they are semantic general knowledge or the specific personal memories that make up episodic memories, are deeply entwined with language. To further clarify the two types of explicit memory, an example of episodic memory might be remembering that you were home sick when you heard on the news that a major earthquake had struck Nepal on April 25, 2015, killing more than 8,000 people. Semantic memory might be knowing that Nepal is situated between India and China or that its capital is Kathmandu. The first example illustrates memory for a specific event, whereas the second example reflects general knowledge about the world.

Implicit memory is a different beast. Learners are typically unaware that their memory is being assessed with implicit "tests." Consider one of the most famous case studies of memory, that of Henry Molaison, who was known in the scientific literature only by his initials H.M. until his death at age 82 in 2008. At the age of 27, Henry had much of the hippocampus removed from both sides of his brain as part of an effort to control his severe seizures (see Shah, Pattanayak, & Sagar, 2014; Squire, 2009). What his neurosurgeon did not realize at the time was that Henry would suffer from catastrophic memory loss for the remaining 55 years of his life. In particular, Henry experienced **anterograde amnesia**: He was no longer able to form new memories; indeed, a book written about this case is titled *Permanent Present Tense* (Corkin, 2013). Henry could not remember what he had eaten for dinner or watched on television just minutes earlier, nor could he learn new words or remember new people. Despite this devastating loss of ability to form new episodic memories, Henry showed evidence of implicit memory (Lloyd & Miller, 2014). To test this, Henry was presented with a mirror tracing task in which he was asked to trace a diagram by looking only at his hand reflected in the mirror, which makes this rather challenging and requires practice to perfect the drawing. Henry did not recall repeatedly practicing this task, yet his performance improved over the course of three days, indicating some retention of this procedural task (see ■ **Figure 8.3**). He had acquired memory for the procedure without any awareness of doing so. Many forms of amnesia, like the one

(a) The mirror tracing task.

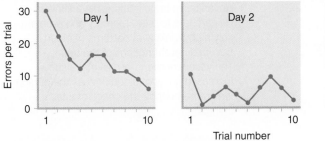

(b) Performance of H.M. on mirror-tracing task

■ **Figure 8.3** H.M.'s performance on the mirror tracing task.

experienced by Henry, destroy explicit memory but leave implicit memory undamaged (Schacter, 1996). As Patricia Bauer (2007) describes it, explicit memory is fallible—subject to forgetting—whereas implicit memory is largely infallible—it remains intact.

Neural Bases of Memory

Until fairly recently, the neural underpinnings of memory were largely a mystery, with only small glimpses into the inner workings of the brain afforded by occasional case studies of patients who had sustained brain damage and with this, specific memory problems. Su Meck, described in this chapter's opening, and Henry Molaison, are fascinating examples of what we can learn from case studies.

Henry's unfortunate case provided the first solid evidence that memory has a neural basis. Up to that point, it was assumed that memories were somehow spread throughout the brain. Henry's surgeon reported that he had removed a specific region of the medial temporal lobe—the **hippocampus**—in order to treat Henry's seizures. Given the devastating loss of memory resulting from this removal, scientists concluded that the hippocampus was instrumental in creating new episodic memories, such as recalling that you went to the dentist on Monday morning.

Some 40 years after his surgery, technological advances in imaging allowed researchers to use functional magnetic resonance imaging (fMRI) to get a closer look at Henry's brain. To their surprise, they found that the surgery had not removed all of the hippocampus, as his surgeon had believed. Yet, even with the remaining portion of the hippocampus, Henry had no memory for new information, indicating that there must be more to memory than this one structure. Not until after Henry's death would researchers be able to create a 3-dimensional model of his brain and find that a part of the temporal lobe, called the *entorhinal cortex*, had been removed (Annese et al., 2014). This structure plays a critical role in connecting the hippocampus to other parts of the brain. Annese and colleagues concluded that Henry's memory problems were likely a result of the loss of the entorhinal cortex, which effectively cut off the hippocampus from the rest of the brain.

Positron emission tomography (PET) scans of the brain have allowed researchers to make inferences about memory processes by observing brain activity taking place as subjects perform various types of memory tasks. From such studies, we have learned that different parts of the brain are involved in different forms of memory (see ■**Figure** 8.4). Procedural memory (such as memory of how to ride a bike), which is a type of implicit memory, is mediated by an area of the forebrain called the striatum. Explicit memory is largely localized in the medial temporal lobe of the brain (*medial* refers to the middle of the brain and the temporal lobe is located at the base of the brain). In particular, the medial temporal structures are thought to be crucial to consolidating information into a memory trace for long-term storage. As noted earlier, sleep facilitates the consolidation of memories. This process seems especially swift during childhood. Charline Urbain and her colleagues (2016) demonstrated that a 90-minute nap after a learning task helps integrate the new learning with existing knowledge and assists with retention of the new material among children.

The actual storage and retrieval of new information take place in whichever area of the cortex originally encoded or was activated by the information. For example, vocabulary seems to be stored in the limbic-temporal cortex, as evidenced by the vocabulary impairment experienced by individuals with damage to this part of the brain (Bauer, 2009). Thus, sensory information initially activates one of the cortical association areas distributed throughout the brain. This information then passes to the medial temporal lobe for consolidation. If and when this consolidation occurs, the resulting memory trace is stored in the cortical association area of the brain that first registered the information, and it is from this area that the information must be retrieved.

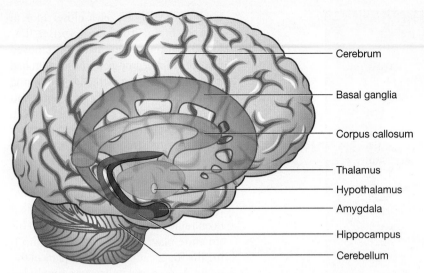

Cerebrum

Basal ganglia

Corpus callosum

Thalamus

Hypothalamus

Amygdala

Hippocampus

Cerebellum

■ **Figure 8.4** The hippocampus is part of the limbic system, located in the medial ("middle") temporal lobe of the brain. Scientists believe that the hippocampus is responsible for consolidation and formation of explicit memories. Just next to the hippocampus is the amygdala, which is involved in forming emotionally charged memories. Other parts of the brain, namely the basal ganglia and cerebullum, are important in the formation of procedural memories.

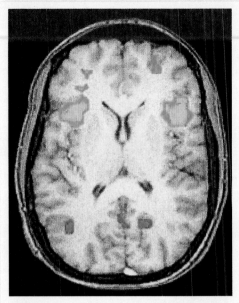

Advances in brain imaging have allowed researchers to "see" memory and problem solving by looking at patterns of blood flow in different regions of the brain. The yellow portions in this image show increased areas of blood flow as the person was remembering the image of a face.

NIMH Laboratory of Brain and Cognition

Research suggests that implicit memory develops earlier in infancy than explicit memory (Lloyd & Miller, 2014; Schneider, 2015). Explicit memory improves as the hippocampus becomes more mature during the second half of the first year (Nelson, Thomas, & de Haan, 2006). Further, the two types of memory follow different developmental paths. Explicit memory capacity increases from infancy to adulthood, then declines in later adulthood. By contrast, implicit memory capacity changes little; young children often do no worse than older children and elderly adults often do no worse than younger adults on tests of implicit memory (Schneider, 2015; Schneider & Bjorklund, 1998). Research on implicit memory shows that young and old alike learn and retain a tremendous amount of information from their everyday experiences without any effort.

Problem Solving

Think back to our example of the history professor who seems to want you to remember when the U.S. Constitution was ratified (1789, in case this did not get into your long-term memory store). Now imagine that you are asked how many years passed between this event and the signing of the Declaration of Independence (1776, remember?). This is a simple example of **problem solving**, or use of the information-processing system to achieve a goal or arrive at a decision (in this case, to answer the question). Here, too, the information-processing model describes what happens between stimulus and response. The question will move through the memory system. You will need to draw on your long-term memory to understand the question, then you will have to search long-term memory for the two relevant dates. Moreover, you will need to locate your stored knowledge of the mathematical operation of subtraction. You will then transfer this stored information to working memory so that you can use your subtraction "program" (1789 minus 1776) to derive the correct answer.

Notice that processing information successfully requires both knowing what you are doing and making decisions. This is why researchers have added **executive control processes** to the memory model. These control processes run the show, guiding the selection, organization, manipulation, and interpretation of information throughout. Stored knowledge about the world and about information processing guides what is done with new information.

Cognitive psychologists now recognize that information processing is more complex than this model or similar models suggest (Bjorklund, 1997). For example, they appreciate that people, like computers, engage in **parallel processing**, carrying out multiple cognitive activities simultaneously (for example, listening to a lecture and taking notes at the same time) rather than performing operations in a sequence (such as solving a math problem by carrying out a series of ordered steps). They also appreciate that different processing approaches are used in different domains of knowledge. Still, the information-processing approach to cognition has the advantage of focusing attention on *how* people remember things or solve problems, not just on what they recall or what answer they give. A young child's performance on a problem could break down in any number of ways: The child might not be paying attention to the relevant aspects of the problem, might be unable to hold all the relevant pieces of information in working memory long enough to do anything with them, might lack the strategies for transferring new information into long-term memory or retrieving information from long-term memory as needed, might simply not have enough stored knowledge to understand the problem, or might not have the executive control processes needed to manage the steps in solving a problem. If researchers can identify how information processes in the younger individual differ from those in the older person, they will gain much insight into cognitive development.

Many processes involved in memory and problem solving improve between infancy and adulthood and then decline somewhat in old age, although this pattern is not uniform for all processes or all people. Our task in this chapter is to describe these age trends and, of greater interest, to try to determine why they occur.

Checking Mastery

1. What steps are required in order to learn, remember, and recall material?
2. What is the difference between implicit and explicit memory?
3. Why are recognition tasks generally easier than recall tasks?

Making Connections

1. Consider your own memory profile. On what types of memory tasks and under what conditions is your memory good, and conversely, which types of tasks and conditions challenge your memory?
2. In creating a memory assessment, how would you tap into someone's implicit memories as opposed to their explicit memories?

8.2
The Infant

LEARNING OBJECTIVES

- Explain how researchers are able to assess the memory capabilities of infants.
- Outline the characteristics of infant memory.
- Describe the types of information that infants are likely to remember.

You have already seen that infants explore the world thoroughly through their senses. But are they remembering anything of their experiences?

Uncovering Evidence of Memory

Assessing infant memory requires some ingenuity because infants cannot tell researchers what they remember. Several methods have been used to uncover infants' memory capabilities. Here we consider habituation, operant conditioning, object search, and imitation techniques before examining infants' abilities to recall previously presented information.

Habituation

One method to assess memory uses habituation, a simple and often overlooked form of learning introduced in Chapter 6. Habituation—learning *not* to respond to a repeated stimulus—might be thought of as learning to be bored by the familiar (for example, eventually not hearing the continual ticking of a clock or the drip of a leaky faucet) and is evidence that a stimulus is recognized as familiar. From birth, humans habituate to repeatedly presented lights, sounds, and smells; such stimuli are recognized as "old hat" (Rovee-Collier & Barr, 2010). Indeed, as we noted in Chapter 5, fetuses demonstrate through habituation that they can learn and remember prior to birth (see Leader, 2016). It is clear that newborns are capable of recognition memory and prefer a new sight to something they have seen many times. As they age, infants need less "study time" before a stimulus becomes old hat,

and they can retain what they have learned for days or even weeks (Rovee-Collier & Cuevas, 2009b).

Operant Conditioning

To test long-term memory of young infants, Carolyn Rovee-Collier and her colleagues devised a clever task that relies on the operant conditioning techniques introduced in Chapter 2 (see Rovee-Collier & Cuevas, 2009b). When a ribbon is tied to a baby's ankle and connected to an attractive mobile, the infant will shake a leg now and then and learn very quickly (in minutes) that leg kicking brings about a positively reinforcing consequence: the jiggling of the mobile.

To test infant memory, the mobile is presented at a later time to see whether the infant will kick again. To succeed at this task, the infant must not only recognize the mobile but also recall that the thing to do is to kick. Before we review the research findings, what type of memory do you believe this task assesses? Consider whether infants are deliberately and effortfully remembering something or are unintentionally and automatically learning and remembering a connection between their kicking and the movement of the mobile. This task is tapping into implicit or procedural memory. When given two 9-minute training sessions, 2-month-olds remember how to make the mobile move for up to 2 days, 3-month-olds for about 1 week, and 6-month-olds for about 2 weeks (Rovee-Collier & Cuevas, 2009b). Using a modification of this task for older infants, Rovee-Collier and her colleagues (see Hartshorn et al., 1998) have shown that by 18 months, infants can remember for at least 3 months—rather impressive! Further, the researchers could enhance young infants' memory by giving them three 6-minute learning sessions rather than two 9-minute sessions. Although the total training time was the same in the two conditions, the distributed, or spread out, training was more effective. As it turns out, distributed practice is beneficial across the life span—a good thing to keep in mind when you are studying for tests (Litman & Davachi, 2008).

What if stronger cues to aid recall are provided? Three-month-old infants who were reminded of their previous learning, by seeing the mobile move 2–4 weeks after their original learning experience, kicked up a storm as soon as the ribbon was attached to their ankles, whereas infants who were not reminded showed no sign of remembering to kick (Rovee-Collier & Barr, 2004). It seems, then, that cued recall (in this case, memory cued by the presence of the mobile or, better yet, its rotation by the experimenter) emerges during the first couple of months of life

When ribbons are tied to their ankles, young infants soon learn to make a mobile move by kicking their legs. Carolyn Rovee-Collier has made use of this operant conditioning paradigm to find out how long infants will remember the trick for making the mobile move.

Michael Newman/PhotoEdit

and that infants remember best when they are reminded of what they have learned. Other research shows that verbal reminders are also effective with 15-month-olds and can help them remember an event after a month as well as they did after a week (Hayne & Simcock, 2009).

However, this research also suggests that young infants have difficulty recalling what they have learned if cues are insufficient or different. They have trouble remembering when the mobile (for example, the specific animals hanging from it) or the context in which they encountered it (for example, the design on the playpen liner) is even slightly different from the context in which they learned. In short, early memories are *cue-dependent and context-specific.*

Object Search

In Chapter 7, we noted that Piaget used an object search task, the A-not-B task, to help understand cognitive changes during infancy. Performance on this task can also contribute to our understanding of memory capabilities. For this task, an infant or toddler is seated at a table that contains two identical cloths, under which a small toy can be hidden (see ■ Figure 8.5). As the youngster watches, the toy is placed under one of the cloths (A). The infant who reaches for the correct location of A is demonstrating memory. After several successful trials of watching and retrieving the toy from location A, the researcher switches things up and hides the toy under the other cloth (location B). This stumps many infants, as demonstrated by their continued searching in the original location (hence the name of the task, A-not-B). By 8 months of age, though, more than half of infants correctly reach for the toy in location B (Bell & Morasch, 2007). But when researchers examine the *looking* behavior of infants, presumably less demanding than reaching, then infants as young as 5–6 months show memory for the correct location based on their looking behavior.

Imitation

Researchers can learn something about memory by noting whether or not infants can imitate an action performed by a model. Some studies suggest that young infants, even newborns, can imitate certain actions, such as sticking out the tongue or opening the mouth (see Meltzoff, 2004). These findings are exciting because they challenge Piaget's claim that infants cannot imitate actions until about 1 year, when they have some ability to represent mentally what they have seen.

Such findings have been viewed with skepticism by some, who believe that early tongue protrusions do not demonstrate true imitation but instead reflect reflexive responses to specific stimuli or attempts to "explore" interesting sights (see, for example, Bjorklund, 1995; Jones, 1996). However, observations of infants sticking out their tongues and moving their mouths in ways consistent with a model have now been replicated with different populations (Marshall & Meltzoff, 2014; Meltzoff & Moore, 1997). More importantly, though, infants as young as 6 months display **deferred imitation**, the ability to imitate a novel act after a delay, which clearly requires memory ability and represents an early form of explicit or declarative memory (Jones & Herbert, 2006; Sundqvist et al., 2016). Infants' deferred imitation

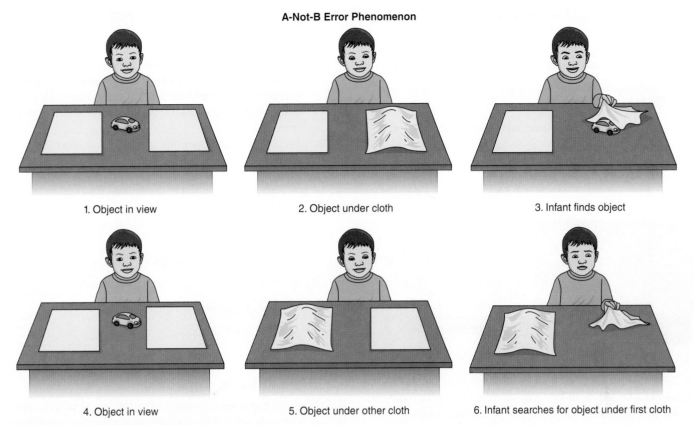

1. Object in view

2. Object under cloth

3. Infant finds object

4. Object in view

5. Object under other cloth

6. Infant searches for object under first cloth

■ **Figure 8.5** An illustration of Piaget's 'A-not-B' task.

of actions at age 9 months predicts their productive language skills at 16 months, showing a connection between performance on an early memory task and performance on a more complex memory task, in this case, words produced or remembered at 16 months (Sundqvist et al., 2016).

As infants age, they demonstrate recall or deferred imitation over longer periods. By 6 months, infants can defer their imitation of an action over a longer delay and can recall the order of a simple sequence of events (Bauer, 2007). By age 2, events can be recalled for months, and recall is more flexible—less bound by the specific cues present at the time of learning (see Lukowski & Bauer, 2014).

Patricia Bauer (1996; Bauer et al., 2000) and her colleagues have shown sequences of actions to infants of different ages and then asked them to imitate what they saw—for example, putting a teddy bear in bed, covering him with a blanket, and reading him a story. Infants as young as 13 months can reconstruct a sequence of actions for as long as 3 months afterward. Older infants (16 and 20 months) can store and retrieve events for 12 months after exposure (Bauer et al., 2000, 2011). Much like children and adults, infants remember best when they have repeated exposures to what they are to remember, when they are given plenty of cues to help them remember, and when the events they must remember occur in a meaningful or logical order.

By age 2, infants have become verbal and can use words to reconstruct events that happened months earlier. In one study, for example, researchers interviewed young children about emergency room visits for accidents the children had between about 1 and 3 years of age (Peterson & Rideout, 1998). Interviews were conducted soon after the ER visits and 6, 12, 18, or 24 months

later. Children who were 18 months or younger at the time of their ER visit were unable to verbally recall aspects of their visits after a 6-month delay, but children 20 months or older were able to do so. Children who were at least 26 months old at the time of their ER visit could retain information and answer verbal questions about their experiences for at least 2 years following the event. In addition, children as young as 2 years can benefit from simple verbal reminders about previously experienced events (Imuta, Scarf, & Hayne, 2013). It's clear that language helps memory performance.

Problem Solving

Infants, like children and adults, face problem-solving tasks every day. For example, they may want to obtain an object beyond their reach or to make a toy repeat the interesting sound it produced earlier. Can infants overcome obstacles to achieve desired goals? It appears they can. In one study, infants were presented with an object out of their reach; however, by pulling on a cloth with one hand, they could drag the object to within reach (Willats, 1990). Although 6-month-olds did not retrieve the object, 9-month-olds solved this problem. Even the younger infants were successful when given hints about how they might retrieve the object (Kolstad & Aguiar, 1995). In situations where solving the problem requires coordination of both hands, success does not occur until later in childhood (Birtles et al., 2011). By 14 months of age, infants have figured out that adults are often useful sources of information in problem-solving situations (Csibra & Gergely, 2009; Kovács et al., 2014). As they get older, infants increasingly pay attention to the cues provided by adults and they increasingly solicit help by pointing, reaching, or otherwise letting the adult know that assistance is needed. Simple problem-solving behaviors improve considerably over the first 2 years of life and then, as you will see shortly, flourish during childhood.

● Checking Mastery

1. How can researchers assess memory abilities of preverbal infants?
2. At what age do infants begin to show reliable recall for events?

● Making Connections

1. Uncle Jed says there is no way a baby can learn or remember anything. His position is that babies just eat, sleep, cry, and poop. What three key pieces of evidence might you use to convince Uncle Jed that there is something going on inside the infant's head in terms of learning and memory?
2. Would you characterize infants' memory as robust or fragile? What factors influence the robustness of infants' memory?

8.3

The Child

LEARNING OBJECTIVES

- Discuss and evaluate the four major reasons why memory improves over childhood.
- Describe autobiographical memory, provide an example, and list contributing factors.
- Use evidence to evaluate the accuracy of children's eyewitness memory.
- Explain changes in problem-solving ability throughout childhood.

The 2-year-old is already a highly capable information processor, as evidenced by the rapid language learning that takes place at this age. But dramatic improvements in learning, memory, and problem solving occur throughout the childhood years as children learn everything from how to flush toilets to how to work advanced math problems.

Memory Development

In countless situations, older children learn faster and remember more than younger children do. For example, 2-year-olds can repeat back about two digits immediately after hearing them, 5-year-olds about four digits, and 10-year-olds about six digits. And second-graders not only are faster learners than kindergartners but also retain information longer. Why is this? Here are four major hypotheses about why learning and memory improve (see Schneider, 2011):

1. **Changes in basic capacities.** Older children have higher-powered "hardware" than younger children do; neural advances in their brains have contributed to more working-memory space for manipulating information and an ability to process information faster.
2. **Changes in memory strategies.** Older children have better "software"; they have learned and consistently use effective methods for putting information into long-term memory and retrieving it when they need it.
3. **Increased knowledge of memory.** Older children know more about memory (for example, how long they must study to learn things thoroughly, which kinds of memory tasks take more effort, and which strategies best fit each task).
4. **Increased knowledge of the world.** Older children know more than younger children about the world in general. This knowledge, or expertise, makes material to be learned more familiar, and familiar material is easier to learn and remember than unfamiliar material.

Changes in Basic Capacities?

Because the nervous system continues to develop in the years after birth, it seems plausible that older children remember more than younger children do because they have a better "computer"—a larger or more efficient information-processing system. We can rule out the idea that the storage capacity of long-term memory impairs memory performance in infants and young children. There is no consistent evidence that capacity changes much across the life span and, indeed, young and old alike probably have more room for storage than they could ever use (Cunningham, Yassa, & Egeth, 2015). If long-term storage capacity does not contribute to developmental differences in memory, then what about the encoding and consolidation processes needed to move information into long-term storage?

Encoding begins with the sensory registration of stimuli from the environment. As we learned in Chapter 6, the sensory systems are working fairly well from a very early age and undergo only slight improvements during the first year. But although the senses themselves are functioning well, there is evidence that the *encoding* of this information improves over the first several years of life as the prefrontal cortex and medial temporal lobes mature (see Ghetti & Lee, 2014). It is also clear that the memory consolidation process undergoes developmental change. Of course, information that is not encoded in the first place is not going to be consolidated and stored. But separate from the changes in encoding, consolidation and storage of memories show improvement over infancy and childhood that seem to correspond to maturation of the hippocampus within the medial temporal lobes as well as other parts of the brain believed to be centrally involved in consolidation of memories. We also know that the *speed* of mental processes improves with age, as neurons become myelinated, and this allows older children and adults to simultaneously perform more mental operations in working memory than young children can (Cowan, 2016; Ghetti & Lee, 2014). As basic mental processes become automatic, they can also be performed with little mental effort. This, in turn, frees space in working memory for other purposes, such as storing the information needed to solve a problem.

The degree of improvement in short-term memory capacity that is evident as children age may depend on what is tested or how it is tested. That is, short-term memory capacity is domain-specific—it varies with background knowledge and type of task (see Schneider, 2015). Greater knowledge in a domain or area of study increases the speed with which new, related information can be processed. In other words, the more you know about a subject, the faster you can process information related to this subject.

In sum, the basic capacities of the sensory register and long-term memory do not change much with age. There are, however, improvements with age in operating speed and efficiency of working memory, which includes improvements in the encoding and consolidation processes through which memories are processed for long-term storage. These changes correspond to maturational changes in the brain. During infancy, brain activity during working-memory tasks is scattered and general (Bell & Wolfe, 2007). By age 4 or 5, working memory has found its "home" in the frontal lobes of the brain. Maturation of the frontal lobes continues throughout childhood and adolescence, bringing further improvements in working memory and consolidation of memories.

Changes in Memory Strategies?

If shown the 12 items in ■ **Figure** 8.6, 4-year-olds might recall only 2–4 of them, 8-year-olds would recall 7–9 items, and adults might recall 10–11 of the items after a delay of several minutes. Are there specific memory strategies that evolve during childhood to permit this dramatic improvement in performance?

Strategies to aid memory can be applied at the time information is presented for learning (encoding strategies) or they can be applied at the time when retrieval of the information is sought (retrieval strategies). Strategies can employ mental activities such as silent rehearsal of the names of items to be remembered, or can employ behavioral activities such as placing your book bag by the door as a cue to remember to take it to school. The

■ **Figure 8.6** A memory task. Imagine that you have 120 seconds to learn the 12 objects pictured here. What tricks or strategies might you devise to make your task easier?

likelihood of using a strategy to aid memory seems to be greater when the goal is personally relevant. For instance, children as young as 2 years can deliberately remember to do such "important" things as reminding Mom to buy candy at the grocery store. They are more likely to use external or behavioral memory aids (for example, pointing at or holding a toy pig when asked to remember where it was hidden) if they are instructed to remember than if they are not (Fletcher & Bray, 1996; 1997). However, children younger than 4 show little flexibility in switching from an ineffective strategy to an effective one, and they typically do not generate new strategies even as they gain experience with a task (Chen, 2007). In contrast, many 4- and 5-year-olds will flexibly switch strategies and generate new strategies, making them do better on memory tasks than younger children. Four-year-olds can also selectively focus on relevant information and ignore irrelevant information, although this ability is evident only on very simple tasks and will become more robust with age and experience (Schneider, 2015). Younger children have a tendency to make **perseveration errors**: they continue to use the same strategy that was successful in the *past* despite the strategy's *current* lack of success. Thus, if they previously found their favorite toy under the sofa, they search this location on future occasions when the toy is lost (Chen, 2007). They seem to be unable to get the old strategy—ineffective in the new situation—out of their mind and move on to a different strategy that could be successful, similar to the infant and the "A-not-B error." By age 4, we see a decline in these perseveration errors.

Yet even 4-year-olds have not mastered many of the effective strategies for moving information into long-term memory. For example, when instructed to remember toys they have been shown, 3- and 4-year-olds will look carefully at the objects and will often label them once, but they only rarely use the memory strategy called **rehearsal**—the repeating of items they are trying to learn and remember (Baker-Ward, Ornstein, & Holden, 1984). To rehearse the objects in Figure 8.6, you might simply say, "apple, truck, grapes . . ." repeatedly. John Flavell and his associates found that only 10% of 5-year-olds repeated the names of pictures they were asked to recall, but more than half of 7-year-olds and 85% of 10-year-olds used this strategy (Flavell, Beach, & Chinsky, 1966). This repetition is believed to help form memories by activating the hippocampus with each repetition.

Another important memory strategy is **organization**, or classifying items into meaningful groups. You might cluster the apple, the grapes, and the hamburger in Figure 8.6 into a category of foods and form other categories for animals, vehicles, and baseball equipment. You would then rehearse each category and recall it as a cluster. Another organizational strategy, *chunking*, could be used to break a long number (6065551843) into manageable subunits (606-555-1843, a phone number) or a series of letters (e.g., F R H O X T O X O L G S M) into meaningful chunks (FOX SOX HTML ORG). Organization is mastered later in childhood than rehearsal. Although 10-year-olds who use chunking recall more than 6-year-olds, the younger children still demonstrate effective use of chunking (Mathy et al., 2016). Under conditions where chunking could be used, 6-year-olds showed as much improvement in recall as 10-year-olds: Both groups recalled more than without chunking.

Finally, the strategy of **elaboration** involves actively creating meaningful links between items to be remembered. Elaboration is achieved by adding something to the items, in the form of either words or images. Creating and using a sentence such as "the apple fell on the horse's nose" could help you remember two of the items in Figure 8.6. Elaboration is especially helpful in learning foreign languages. For example, you might link the Spanish word *pato* (pronounced pot-o) to the English equivalent *duck* by imagining a duck with a pot on its head. Children who can elaborate on the relationship between two items (for example, generating similar and different features of the items) have improved retention of these items (Howe, 2006).

Memory or encoding strategies develop in a fairly predictable order, with rehearsal emerging first, followed by organization, and then by elaboration. Children do not suddenly start using strategies, however, and even once they have demonstrated knowledge of a strategy, they do not consistently apply it in all situations. Initially, children have a **mediation deficiency**, which means they cannot spontaneously use or benefit from strategies, even if they are taught how to use them. Children with mediation deficiencies seem unable to grasp the concept of the strategy. This type of strategy deficiency is not common (Schneider, 2015). More typical is a **production deficiency**, in which children can use strategies they are taught but do not produce them on their own. A third problem is a **utilization deficiency**, in which children spontaneously produce a strategy but their task performance does not yet benefit from using the strategy. Why would children who use a strategy fail to benefit from it? One possibility is that using a new strategy is mentally taxing and leaves no free cognitive resources for other aspects of the task (Pressley & Hilden, 2006). Once using the strategy becomes routine, then other components of the task can be addressed simultaneously. Whatever the reason for utilization deficiencies, they reflect a child–task interaction; that is, it is not task difficulty per se, but how difficult a task is for a particular child that matters (Bjorklund et al., 2009).

Using effective encoding strategies such as rehearsal, organization, and elaboration to learn material is only half the battle;

This young girl is searching for a toy that she put away months ago when asked to clean up her room. What strategies might she use to help her recall the toy's location?

Sappington Todd/Getty Images

retrieval strategies can also influence how much is recalled. Indeed, retrieving something from memory can often be a complex adventure when solving problems, such as when you try to remember when you went on a trip by searching for cues that might trigger your memory ("Well, I still had long hair then, but it was after Muffy's wedding, and . . ."). In general, young children rely more on external cues or behavioral actions for both encoding and retrieving information than do older children (Schneider & Pressley, 1997). Thus, young children may need to put their toothbrushes next to their pajamas so that they have a physical reminder to brush their teeth before they go to bed. With repetition, older children can remember to brush their teeth as part of their evening routine, in the absence of having a physical reminder. In many ways, command of memory strategies increases over the childhood years, but the path to effective strategy use is characterized more by noticeable jumps than by steady increases (Schneider, 2015).

Increased Knowledge of Memory?

The term **metamemory** refers to knowledge of memory and to monitoring and regulating memory processes. It is knowing, for example, what your memory limits are, which memory strategies are more or less effective for you, and which memory tasks are more or less difficult for you. It is also noting that your efforts to remember something are not working and that you need to try something different. Sounds like this could be useful knowledge for a student to possess! More broadly, metamemory is one aspect of **metacognition**, or knowledge of the human mind and of the range of cognitive processes. Your store of metacognitive knowledge might include an understanding that you are better at learning a new language than at learning algebra, that it is harder to pay attention to a task when there is distracting noise in the background than when it is quiet, and that it is wise to check a proposed solution to a problem before concluding that it is correct.

When do children first show evidence of metacognition? If instructed to remember where the *Sesame Street* character Big Bird has been hidden so that they can later wake him up, even 2- and 3-year-olds will go stand near the hiding spot, or at least look or point at that spot; they do not do these things as often if Big Bird is visible and they do not need to remember where he is (DeLoache, Cassidy, & Brown, 1985). By age 2, then, children understand that to remember something, you have to work at it. Researchers have found that 3-year-olds understand the difference between thinking about an object in their heads and experiencing it in reality and that 4-year-olds realize behavior is guided by beliefs (Flavell, 1999). These findings indicate that metacognitive awareness is present at least in a rudimentary form at a young age but there continue to be significant improvements throughout childhood.

Are increases in metamemory a major contributor to improved memory performance over the childhood years? Children with greater metamemory awareness demonstrate better memory ability, but several factors influence the strength of this relationship (Geurten, Catale, & Meulemans, 2015; Schneider, 2015). Researchers are most likely to see a connection between metamemory and memory performance among older children and among children who have been specifically asked to remember something (DeMarie & Ferron, 2003; Schneider & Bjorklund, 1998). Not only is task experience important, but the nature of the task is also relevant. Awareness of memory processes benefits even young children on tasks that are simple and familiar and where connections between metamemory knowledge and memory performance are fairly obvious (Schneider & Sodian, 1988). Yet children who know what to do may not always do it, so good metamemory is no guarantee of good recall (Geurten et al., 2015). It seems that children not only must know that a strategy is useful but also must know why it is useful in order to be motivated to use it and to benefit from its use. Metamemory is also influenced by children's language skills and by their general knowledge about mental states and their roles in behavior—what is known as theory of mind (Lockl & Schneider, 2007; and see Chapter 13 for definition and discussion). The links between metamemory and memory performance, although not perfect, are strong enough to suggest the merits of teaching children more about how memory works and how they can make it work more effectively for them.

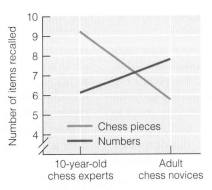

■ **Figure 8.7** Effects of expertise on memory. Michelene Chi found that child chess experts outperformed adult chess novices on a test of recall for the location of chess pieces (although, in keeping with the usual developmental trend, these children could not recall strings of numbers as well as adults could).

Increased Knowledge of the World?

As we have seen, 10-year-olds remember more than 2-year-olds do, but then 10-year-olds *know* more than 2-year-olds do. An individual's knowledge of a content area to be learned, or **knowledge base**, as it is called, clearly affects learning and memory performance. Think about the difference between reading about a topic that you already know well and reading about a new topic. In the first case, you can read quickly because you are able to link the information to the knowledge you have already stored. All you really need to do is check for any new information or information that contradicts what you already know. Learning about a highly unfamiliar topic is more difficult ("It's Greek to me").

Perhaps the most dramatic illustration of the powerful influence of knowledge base on memory was provided by Michelene Chi (1978). She demonstrated that even though adults typically outperform children on tests of memory, this age difference could be reversed if children have more expertise than adults. Chi recruited children who were expert chess players and compared their memory skills with those of adults who were familiar with the game but lacked expertise. On a test of memory for sequences of digits, the children recalled fewer than the adults did, demonstrating their usual deficiencies. But on a test of memory for the locations of chess pieces, the children clearly beat the adults (■ Figure 8.7). Because they were experts, these children were able to form more and larger mental chunks, or meaningful groups, of chess pieces, which allowed them to remember more. When child experts were compared with adult experts, there were no differences in performance (Schneider et al., 1993). Knowledge in a content area probably allows you to make better use of the limited capacity of working memory.

Consider, though, some research by Nelson Cowan and his colleagues (2015). They tested college students as well as 7-, 9-, and 12-year-olds with two sets of materials, one consisting of familiar English language letters and another consisting of symbols from a language unfamiliar to the participants. Older children and the young adults performed better than younger children with both the familiar letters and the unfamiliar symbols, suggesting that memory improvements over this age span are not solely attributable to greater knowledge base. Thus, the older children performed better even when they were tested under conditions that eliminated any advantage they might have from increased knowledge of the world. What should we conclude, then, about changes in memory across childhood?

Revisiting the Explanations

We can draw four conclusions about the development of learning and memory:

1. Older children are faster information processors and can juggle more information in working memory. Maturation of the nervous system leads to improvements in consolidation of memories. Older and younger children, however, do not differ in terms of sensory register or long-term memory capacity.
2. Older children use more effective memory strategies in encoding and retrieving information. Acquisition of memory strategies reflects qualitative rather than quantitative changes.
3. Older children know more about memory, and good metamemory may help children choose more appropriate strategies and control and monitor their learning more effectively.
4. Older children generally know more, and their larger knowledge base may provide some boost to their ability to learn and remember. A richer knowledge base allows faster and more efficient processing of information related to the domain of knowledge.

Is one of these explanations of memory development better than the others? Darlene DeMarie and John Ferron (2003) tested whether a model that includes three of these factors—basic capacities, strategies, and metamemory—could explain recall memory better than a single factor. For both younger (5–8 years) and older (8–11 years) children, the three-factor model predicted memory performance better than a single-factor model. Use of memory strategies was an especially strong predictor of recall. Importantly, there were also correlations among factors. Having good basic capacities, for example, was related to advanced metamemory and to command of strategies and had its own influence on recall as well. So all these phenomena may contribute something to the dramatic improvements in learning and memory that occur over the childhood years. We return to these four hypotheses when we consider changes in learning and memory in adulthood.

Autobiographical Memory

Children effortlessly remember all sorts of things: a birthday party last week, where they left their favorite toy, what to do when they go to a fast-food restaurant, and much more. Much of what children remember and talk about consists of personal experiences or events that have happened to them at a particular time and place. These autobiographical memories, episodic memories of personal events, are essential ingredients of present and future experiences as well as our understanding of who we are (see Berntsen & Rubin, 2012). Su Meck, introduced at the beginning of this chapter, lost all autobiographical memories from before her accident and with them, she lost herself, or at least the self she had been. Here we look at how autobiographical memories are stored and organized and at factors that influence their accuracy.

When Do Autobiographical Memories Begin?

You learned earlier in this chapter that infants and toddlers are able to store memories. You also know that children and adults have many specific autobiographical events stored in long-term memory. Yet research shows that older children and adults exhibit childhood (or infantile) amnesia; that is, they have few autobiographical memories of events that occurred during the first few years of life. As Patricia Bauer (2014) describes it, it's as though our lives don't really begin until we are at least 3 to 4 years of age (p. 519).

To determine how old we have to be when we experience significant life events to remember them, researchers typically ask adults to answer questions about early life experiences such as the birth of a younger sibling, a hospitalization, the death of a family member, or a family move early in life. In one study using this method, college students were able to recall some information from events that happened as early as age 2 (Usher & Neisser, 1993). But age 2 seems to be the lowest age limit for recall of early life events as an adult. Other research shows that most adults do not remember much until they were 4 or 5 years old (Davis, Gross, & Hayne, 2008; Jack & Hayne, 2007). For example, Nicola Davis and her colleagues (2008) asked college students who had experienced the birth of a younger sibling by the age of 5 to recall as much as they could about this early event. As ■ Figure 8.8 shows, college students who had been 1, 2, or 3 years old at the time recalled very little of the event, but those who were 4 or 5 when their sibling was born recalled significantly more. Why do we remember little about our early years? As you have seen, infants

and toddlers are certainly capable of encoding their experiences and young preschool children seem able to remember a good deal about events that occurred when they were infants. In one study, children between 4 and 13 years of age were interviewed twice, with a gap of about 2 years between the two interviews. On both occasions, children were asked to recall their earliest memories (Peterson, Warren, & Short, 2011). All of the children were able to describe events they had experienced at a young age, demonstrating solid autobiographical memory. But among children who were 4–7 years of age when first interviewed, most did not recall the same events two years later, suggesting these early autobiographical memories are prone to being forgotten.

Let's consider several reasons for this loss of early memories.

1. **Space in working memory.** One explanation of childhood amnesia is that infants and toddlers may not have enough space in working memory to hold the multiple pieces of information about actor, action, and setting needed to encode and consolidate a coherent memory of an event. As you learned earlier in this chapter, functional working-memory capacity increases with age as the brain, particularly the frontal lobe, matures. But this explanation is unsatisfactory because, as we have just noted, toddlers can remember these events, indicating that they were encoded to some degree.

2. **Lack of language.** Perhaps infants' lack of language is the answer. Because autobiographical memory seems to rely heavily on language skills, we would expect such memories to increase with increased language skills. Gabrielle Simcock and Harlene Hayne (Hayne & Simcock, 2009; Simcock & Hayne, 2002, 2003) assessed the verbal skills of young children (27, 33, and 39 months old) who participated in a unique event involving a "magic shrinking machine" that seemingly made items smaller in a matter of seconds. After a 6- or 12-month delay, children were tested for both verbal

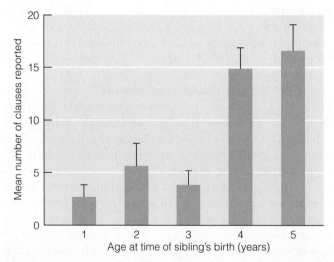

■ **Figure 8.8** College students' recall of the birth of a younger sibling increases as a function of how old they were at the time of the event. Those who were at least 4 years of age when their sibling was born recall much more than those who were younger than 4.

Source: Davis, N., Gross, J., & Hayne, H. (2008). Defining the boundary of childhood amnesia, *Memory, 16(5)*, 465–474, Figure 2. Reprinted by permission of Taylor & Francis Group.

recall (answers to open-ended questions) and nonverbal recall (identification of photos of the items used in the activity) of the unique event. Their nonverbal recall improved across the age groups but was good at all ages. Verbal recall was poor and largely dependent on the simpler verbal skills present at the time of encoding rather than the more developed verbal skills present at the time of recall. Although a relative lack of verbal skills during the first few years of life may limit what we are able to recall from this period, other research suggests that it does not completely block us from later attaching verbal labels to our preverbal memories (Bauer et al., 1998).

3. **Level of sociocultural support.** Although toddlers may have limited verbal skills, their parents presumably do not. There are large individual differences in toddler–parent "conversations" about past events (see Fivush, 2014). An examination of mother–toddler conversations about past events shows that some mothers provide rich elaborations of these events, whereas others do not, in the course of conversing with their toddlers (Fivush, 2014). Years later, adolescents whose mothers had been more elaborative during their early mother–toddler conversations have stronger autobiographical memories than adolescents whose mothers were less elaborative (Jack et al., 2009). It may be that regular rehearsal, in this case in the form of a parent repeating the story, is the sociocultural context needed to ensure long-term recall of an early event. Consider again the children who participated in the "magic shrinking machine" study. They were asked about the event 6 years later (Jack, Simcock, & Hayne, 2012). Only those whose parents had talked with them about the experience sustained any long-term recall of the event.

4. **Sense of self.** We need to consider that infants and toddlers lack a strong sense of self and as a result may not have the necessary 'pages' on which they can write memories of personally experienced events (Howe, 2014; Reese, 2014). Without a sense of self, it is difficult to organize events as "things that happened to *me*." Indeed, young children's ability to recognize themselves in a mirror is a good predictor of children's ability to talk about their past (see Howe, 2014).

5. **Verbatim versus gist storage.** Some researchers have tried to explain childhood amnesia in terms of **fuzzy-trace theory** (Brainerd & Reyna, 2014; 2015). According to this explanation, children store verbatim and general accounts of an event separately. Verbatim information (such as word-for-word recall of a biology class lecture) is unstable and likely to be lost over long periods (Leichtman & Ceci, 1993); it is easier to remember the gist of an event (for example, recall of the general points covered in a biology lecture) than the details (Brainerd & Reyna, 2014; 2015). With age, we are increasingly likely to rely on gist or fuzzy memory traces, which are less likely to be forgotten and are more efficient than verbatim memory traces in the sense that they take less space in memory (Brainerd & Gordon, 1994; Klaczynski, 2001). Children pass through a transition period from storing largely verbatim memories to storing more gist memories, and the earlier verbatim memories are unlikely to be retained over time (Howe, 2000).

6. **Neurogenesis.** Finally, some intriguing research with mice suggests that neurogenesis, the birth of new cells, in the hippocampus early in life 'refreshes' our memory store (Akers et al., 2014; Frankland & Josselyn, 2016). That is, new cells and new memories displace older cells and older memories. After birth, the period with the highest rate of neurogenesis is infancy, so perhaps this is why memories from infancy are largely nonexistent. More research is needed before we conclude that this is a legitimate cause of childhood amnesia.

Whether it is neurogenesis, insufficient working memory to encode events, language skills, a sense of self, or encoding only the verbatim details of what happened rather than a "fuzzy trace," the events of our early childhood do not seem to undergo the *consolidation* needed to store robust memories of this time (Bauer et al., 2007).

Scripts

As children engage in routine daily activities such as getting ready for bed or eating at a fast-food restaurant, they construct **scripts** or **general event representations (GERs)** of these activities (Nelson, 1986; 2014). Scripts or GERs represent the typical sequence of actions related to an event and guide future behaviors in similar settings. For instance, children who have been to a fast-food restaurant might have a script like this: You wait in line, tell the person behind the counter what you want, pay for the food, carry the tray of food to a table, open the packages and eat the food, gather the trash, and throw it away before leaving. With this script in mind, children can act effectively in similar settings. Children as young as 3 years use scripts when reporting familiar events (Hudson & Mayhew, 2009; Nelson, 1997). When asked about their visit to a fast-food restaurant the day before, children usually report what happens *in general* when they go to the restaurant rather than what specifically happened during yesterday's visit (Kuebli & Fivush, 1994). As children age, their scripts become more detailed. Perhaps more important than age, however, is experience: Children with greater experience of an event develop richer scripts than children with less experience (DeMarie, Norman, & Abshier, 2000).

Children develop scripts in memory for routine activities, such as visiting a fast-food restaurant, that guide their behavior in these situations.

Directphoto.org/Alamy Stock Photo

Children's scripts affect how they form memories of new experiences as well as how they recall past events. For example, when presented with information inconsistent with their scripts, preschoolers may misremember the information so that it better fits their script (Nelson & Hudson, 1988). Four-year-old Damian may have a script for birthdays that includes blowing out candles, eating cake, and opening presents. Although his brother is sick on his birthday and eats applesauce instead of cake, Damian later recalls that they all ate cake before opening presents. This demonstrates that memory is a reconstruction, not an exact replication (Hudson & Mayhew, 2009). This, in turn, has significant implications for eyewitness memory (or testimony), or the reporting of events witnessed or experienced—for example, a child's reporting that she saw her little brother snitch some candy before dinner. Children are increasingly asked to report events that have happened in the context of abuse cases or custody hearings. **Application 8.1** explores the accuracy of children's memory in these sorts of situations.

Problem Solving

Memories are vital to problem-solving skills. To solve any problem, a person must process information about the task, as well as use stored information, to achieve a goal. Thus, working memory is a critical component of problem solving. How do problem-solving capacities change during childhood? Piaget provided one answer

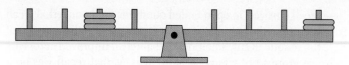

Figure 8.9 The balance beam apparatus used by Robert Siegler to study children's problem-solving abilities. Which way will the balance beam tip?

Source: Siegler, R. S. (1981). Developmental sequences within and between concepts, *Monographs of the Society for Research in Child Development, 46,* (2, Serial No. 189). Copyright © 1981. Reprinted with permission of John Wiley & Sons, Inc.

to this question by proposing that children progress through broad stages of cognitive growth, but information-processing theorists were not satisfied with this explanation. They sought to pinpoint more specific reasons why problem-solving prowess improves so dramatically as children age.

Consider the problem of predicting what will happen to the balance beam in ■ **Figure 8.9** when weights are put on each side of the fulcrum, or balancing point. The goal is to decide which way the balance beam will tip when it is released. To judge correctly, you must take into account both the number of weights and their distances from the fulcrum. Piaget believed that concrete-operational thinkers can appreciate the significance of either the amount of weight or its distance from the center but will not grasp the inverse relationship between the two factors. Only when they reach the stage of formal

• APPLICATION 8.1
Children's Memory as Eyewitnesses

Children may be asked to provide information in situations with high stakes outcomes, such as custody hearings, sexual abuse cases, and a variety of criminal investigations (see Howe & Knott, 2015). To what extent can we "trust" a child's memory for events related to these situations? When asked generally about events ("Tell me what happened at Uncle Joe's house"), preschoolers recall less information than older children, but the recall of both groups is accurate (Goodman et al., 2014). Those children with stronger vocabulary skills are able to provide more information about an event than their peers with weaker vocabulary skills (Chae et al., 2014; 2016). The use of general prompts (such as "What happened next?" or "Tell me more about that . . .") can elicit additional recall of information. Specific questions ("Was Uncle Joe wearing a red shirt?") can also elicit more information, but accuracy of recall begins to slip, especially as the questions become more directed or leading ("Uncle Joe touched you here, didn't he?").

Preschool-age children, more so than older children and adults, are suggestible; they can be influenced by information implied in direct questioning and by relevant information introduced after the event (Schaaf, Alexander, & Goodman, 2008).

Perhaps it is unfortunate, then, that preschoolers, because they initially offer less information in response to open-ended questions, may be asked a larger number of directed questions than older children. They are also frequently subjected to repeated questioning, which increases errors in reporting among children (Bjorklund, Brown, & Bjorklund, 2002). Although repeated questioning with general, open-ended questions can increase accuracy, repeated questioning with directed or closed questions can decrease accuracy. For example, in a study with 5- and 6-year-olds, researchers "cross-examined" children about events that occurred on a field trip to a police station during which the children saw a jail cell and police car and were fingerprinted and photographed

(Zajac & Hayne, 2003). After a delay of 8 months, children's memories were probed using irrelevant, leading, and ambiguous questions like those you might hear in a courtroom. Many children "cracked" under the pressure as evidenced by backing down and changing their answers in response to the questioning. Fully one out of three children changed *all* their answers, and most changed at least one answer. So although children can demonstrate accurate recall when asked clear and unbiased questions, this study shows that young children's memory for past events can quickly become muddied when the questioning becomes tough.

Fortunately, protocols for interviewing young children have evolved to incorporate greater understanding of how memory develops and how it functions (see Goodman et al., 2014). These retrieval protocols may improve the collection of eyewitness testimony, but memory remains highly dependent on characteristics of the individual as well as the context of the event.

operations will new cognitive structures allow them to understand that balance can be maintained by decreasing a weight *and* moving it farther from the fulcrum or by increasing a weight *and* moving it closer to the fulcrum (Piaget & Inhelder, 1969).

Robert Siegler (1981, 2000) proposed that the information-processing perspective could provide a fuller analysis. His **rule assessment approach** determines what information about a problem children take in and what rules they then formulate to account for this information. This approach assumes that children's problem-solving attempts are not hit or miss but are governed by rules; it also assumes that children fail to solve problems because they fail to encode all the critical aspects of the problem and are guided by faulty rules.

Siegler (1981) administered balance beam problems to individuals ages 3–20. He detected clear age differences in the extent to which both weight and distance from the fulcrum were taken into account in the rules that guided decisions about which end of the balance beam would drop. Few 3-year-olds used a rule; they guessed. By contrast, 4- and 5-year-olds were governed by rules. More than 80% of these children used a simple rule that said the side of the balance beam with greater weight would drop; they ignored distance from the fulcrum. By age 8, most children had begun to consider distance from the fulcrum and weight under some conditions: When the weight on the two sides was equal, they appreciated that the side of the balance beam with the weights farthest from the fulcrum would drop. By age 12, most children considered both weight and distance on a range of problems, although they still became confused on complex problems in which one side had more weights but the other had its weights farther from the fulcrum. Finally, 30% of 20-year-olds discovered the correct rule—that the pull on each arm is a function of weight times distance. For example, if there are three weights on the second peg to the left and two weights on the fourth peg to the right, the left torque is $3 \times 2 = 6$ and the right torque is $2 \times 4 = 8$, so the right arm will drop.

The increased accuracy of young adults comes with a price—increased time to solve the problem (van der Maas & Jansen, 2003). Although, in general, information-processing time gets faster with age, the complex rules needed to successfully solve all the variations of the balance beam problem demand more time. So on some problems, adults are slower than children because they are using a more sophisticated strategy.

In most important areas of problem solving, Siegler (1996) concluded, children do not simply progress from one way of thinking to another as they age, as his balance beam research suggested (see also Hofman et al., 2015). Instead, in working problems in arithmetic, spelling, science, and other school subjects, most children in any age group use multiple rules or problem-solving strategies rather than just one. In working a subtraction problem such as $12 - 3 = 9$, for example, children sometimes count down from 12 until they have counted off 3 and arrive at 9 but other times count from 3 until they reach 12. In one study of second- and fourth-graders, more than 90% of the children used three or more strategies in working subtraction problems (Siegler, 1989). Similarly, Michael Cohen (1996) found that most preschoolers used all possible strategies when attempting to solve a practical mathematical problem in the context of playing store. He also found that children's selection and use of strategies became more efficient over multiple task trials; that is, they increasingly selected strategies that would allow them to solve the task in fewer steps.

Success on memory and problem-solving tasks improves over time as we increasingly test out strategies, keeping those that lead to greater success and dropping the ones that are duds. Rather than picturing development as a series of stages resembling stair steps, Siegler argues, we should picture it as overlapping waves, as shown in ■ **Figure 8.10**. According to Siegler's (2006) **overlapping waves theory**, the development of problem-solving skills is a matter of knowing a variety of strategies, becoming increasingly selective with experience about which strategy to use, changing strategies as needed, and getting better at using known strategies (Fazio, DeWolf, & Siegler, 2016). At each age, children have multiple problem-solving strategies available to them. As children gain more experience, which typically occurs as they age, they decrease their use of less-adaptive strategies and increase their use of more-adaptive strategies; occasionally, new strategies may appear. Strategies evolve from their initial acquisition in a particular context to their generalization to other contexts, which helps strengthen the fledgling strategies.

Gradually, children not only learn to choose the most useful strategy for a problem but also become increasingly effective at executing new strategies. Familiarity with a task and with strategies frees processing space, allowing children to engage in more meta-cognitive analysis of the strategies at their disposal. Throughout, there is significant variability—both between children and within the same child across time and tasks. Research with students of varying mathematical abilities suggests that one of the problems for the low-performing students is their regular choice of a 'questionable' strategy (Fazio et al., 2016). Training on selecting an effective strategy from among the options is a start, but it must be paired with training on effective *use or application* of the strategy.

Imagine how effective teachers might be if they, like Siegler, could accurately diagnose the information-processing strategies of their learners to know what each child is noticing (or failing to notice) about a problem and what rules or strategies each child is

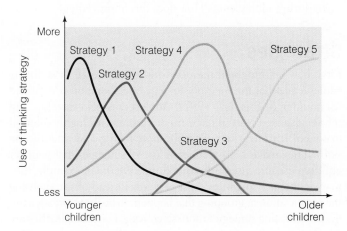

■ **Figure 8.10** Cognitive development may resemble overlapping waves more than a staircase leading from one stage to another. Children of a particular age typically use multiple thinking strategies rather than just one.

Source: Siegler, R. S. (1996). *Emerging minds: The process of change in children's thinking.* Copyright © 1996 by Oxford University Press, Inc. Used by permission of Oxford University Press, Inc.

using, and when. Like a good car mechanic, the teacher would be able to pinpoint the problem and encourage less use of faulty strategies and rules and more use of adaptive ones. Much remains to be learned about how problem-solving strategies evolve as children age, and why. However, the rule-assessment approach and overlapping waves theory give a fairly specific idea of what children are doing (or doing wrong) as they attack problems and illustrate how the information-processing approach to cognitive development provides a different view of development than Piaget's account does.

Checking Mastery

1. What are two reasons why older children have improved memories relative to younger children?
2. How do scripts or GERs relate to memory?
3. What is the "take-home" message of the overlapping waves theory of problem solving?

Making Connections

1. You are a first-grade teacher, and one of the first things you notice is that some of your students remember a good deal more than others about the stories you read to them. Based on what you have read in this chapter, what are your main hypotheses about why some children have better memories than other children the same age?
2. You have been called in to interview a young child who may have witnessed a shooting. Given the research on children's memory, how will you gather information from your young witness?
3. If you are typical, then you probably have few, if any, memories from the period of your infancy and even toddlerhood. Why can't we remember the early events of our lives?

8.4
The Adolescent

LEARNING OBJECTIVES

- Compare the typical adolescent's memory capabilities to those of the typical child.
- Explain why adolescents demonstrate stronger memory abilities than children.

Although parents in the midst of reminding their adolescent sons and daughters to do household chores or homework may wonder whether teenagers process any information at all, learning, memory, and problem solving continue to improve considerably during the adolescent years. Research on episodic memory shows that the performance of young teens (11–12 years) is quite similar to that of children, and both groups do markedly worse than young adults (Brehmer et al., 2007). Clearly, then, there is room for improvement during adolescence. How does this improvement occur?

Strategies

First, new learning and memory strategies emerge. It is during adolescence that the memory strategy of elaboration is mastered (Schneider & Pressley, 1997). Adolescents also develop and refine advanced learning and memory strategies highly relevant to school learning—for example, note-taking and underlining skills. They make more deliberate use of strategies that younger children use unconsciously (Bjorklund, 1985). For example, they may deliberately organize a list of words instead of simply using the organization or grouping that happens to be there already. And they use existing strategies more selectively. For example, they are adept at using their strategies to memorize the material on which they know they will be tested and at letting go of irrelevant information. To illustrate, Patricia Miller and Michael Weiss (1981) asked children and adolescents to remember the locations of animals that had been hidden behind small doors and to ignore the

household objects hidden behind other doors. As ■ Figure 8.11 shows, 13-year-olds recalled more than 7- and 10-year-olds about where the animals had been hidden, but they remembered less about task-irrelevant information (the locations of the household

Adolescents are more aware than children that they need to use strategies such as note-taking to help with encoding and retrieval of information to be remembered.

Joanne Harris/Dreamstime.com

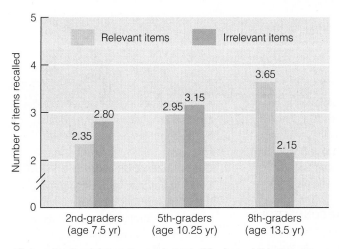

Figure 8.11 Adolescents are better able than children to concentrate on learning relevant material and to ignore irrelevant material.

Source: Miller, P. H. & Weiss, M. G. (1981). Children's attention allocation, understanding of attention and performance on the incidental learning task, *Child Development, 52,* 1183–1190. Reprinted with permission of John Wiley & Sons, Inc.

objects). Apparently, they are better able to push irrelevant information out of working memory so that it does not interfere with task performance (Lorsbach & Reimer, 1997). So, during elementary school, children get better at distinguishing between what is relevant and what is irrelevant, but during adolescence they advance further by selectively using their memory strategies only on the relevant material. If it is not going to be on the test, forget it!

Basic Capacities

In addition to these changes in memory strategies, basic capacities continue to increase during adolescence. As discussed earlier in this chapter, adolescents have greater functional use of their working memory because maturational changes in the brain allow them to process information more quickly and to simultaneously process more chunks of information. Younger teens (13 years) with greater working memory perform better on a variety of academic subjects (Alloway, Banner, & Smith, 2010), perhaps because greater working memory is associated with better reading skills (Alexander & Fox, 2011; Titz & Karbach, 2014). Interestingly, weaker working memory is associated with impulsivity and adolescent alcohol use (Khurana et al., 2013). Improving working memory may help strengthen academic skills as well as nonacademic decision-making. Fortunately, there is evidence that training programs can improve working memory among teenagers, including those born with extremely low birth weight (Lohaugen et al., 2011).

Metamemory and Knowledge Base

There is little to say about knowledge base other than that it continues to expand during adolescence. Therefore, adolescents may do better than children on some tasks simply because they know more about the topic.

Metamemory and metacognition also improve. In general, adolescents are more skilled than children at adjusting their learning strategies to different purposes (e.g. studying versus skimming) and better able to judge when a task is likely to be 'easy' versus 'hard' (Paulus et al., 2014; Weil et al., 2013). About 80% of twelvth-graders report that they monitor their memory and learning strategies. But only 50–60% report that they think in advance to develop an effective plan for a difficult task or think back after completing a task to evaluate what worked or did not work (Leutwyler, 2009). Teenagers who have received explicit training on metacognitive skills from their teachers show improvements in learning outcomes (Williams et al., 2002). This suggests that it may be important to teach not only content but also how to monitor one's understanding of content acquisition (Farrington et al., 2012).

Successful metacognition can be seen in adolescents who choose the strategy of elaboration over rote repetition when they realize that the former is more effective (Pressley, Levin, & Ghatala, 1984). Adolescents are also fairly accurate at monitoring whether or not they have allocated adequate study time to learn new material, and they allocate more study time to information judged to be difficult. This regulation of study time shows awareness of the task demands as well as their own strengths in light of the task's difficulty (Lai, 2011).

Interestingly, when pressed for time, college students devote more study time to easy items (Dunlosky & Ariel, 2011; Metcalfe, 2009). Apparently, they decide it is futile to work on the difficult material when they do not have adequate time, so they spend their time on what seems most likely to pay off. Hopefully, you can see the implication of this for your own studying: Set aside enough time to study all the material; otherwise, you may end up in a time crunch reviewing only the easy material. When time is available, students proceed from the material they judge to be easy to the more difficult material. For more tips on how to improve your memory, which may help you perform better on your next test, visit **Engagement 8.1**.

Before leaving this section, it is interesting to note that use of metacognition during cognitive tasks varies by gender and socioeconomic background (Leutwyler, 2009). Adolescent girls consistently report using more metacognitive strategies than adolescent boys. This may help explain why girls earn higher grades in school than boys, a finding that we will explore in greater detail in Chapter 10. And students from higher socioeconomic backgrounds report more use of metacognitive strategies than their lower socioeconomic peers. Families with higher socioeconomic status may have more resources, such as books in the home, and may talk more explicitly about effective learning strategies.

Growth in strategies, basic capacities, knowledge base, and metacognition probably also helps explain the growth in everyday problem-solving ability that occurs during the adolescent years. Teenagers perfect several information-processing skills and become able to apply them deliberately and spontaneously across a variety of tasks.

Improve Your Memory!

What are some practical steps you can use to improve your memory? First, keep in mind that your brain, which is absolutely essential for memory, does not operate in isolation from the rest of you. Your brain, and therefore your memory, is affected by such factors as the amount of sleep you get, your nutrition, and your physical activity.

Consider sleep. The process of consolidation of memories is critical to moving them into long-term storage and is improved with sleep. Try reviewing to-be-remembered information right before you go to sleep at night and then get the recommended hours of sleep for your age (see Chapter 5). Studying in the afternoon and then taking a nap has also been shown to help consolidate memories. And before you start to study, plan to do some aerobic exercise. This increases oxygen to your brain and also helps you stay alert and focused once you settle down to study. As for nutrition, a growing body of research suggests that omega-3 fatty acids contribute to brain function, as do B vitamins and antioxidants. A good meal for your brain might be salmon, spinach salad, and a strawberry-blueberry smoothie.

So you have adopted healthy eating, exercise, and sleep habits. What can you do to improve your memory when actually studying course material for that upcoming test? We'll focus on a few things that will assist with encoding and consolidation of memories, as well as some helpful hints for retrieval.

1. **PAY ATTENTION!** If you are daydreaming in class or thinking of something else or multitasking while reading, you will not encode the information to be learned. If you don't encode it, you will be out of luck when it comes time to retrieve the memory—it simply won't be there. To increase your attention, reduce the distractions that may be present in your environment.

2. **ORGANIZE AND MAKE CONNECTIONS** to existing knowledge. Organizing to-be-learned material into logical groups can aid in consolidation and storage of the information. What is logical depends on each individual and each task. The organizational scheme must make sense to the learner in the context that it needs to be learned. Consolidation is also more likely to occur when the new material can be related to existing knowledge. Think of how you might use familiar ideas to help you remember new ideas.

3. **USE STRATEGIES THAT ENRICH AND ELABORATE** the new material. Repeating items over and over is a simplistic strategy that helps store fairly simple facts. You need to dig deeper into your toolbox of strategies and choose those that will create richer connections to existing material or will allow you to elaborate the new material. Examples of these strategies might be to associate each new word to an existing concept; this could be taken a step further—elaborated—by thinking of the similarities and differences between the new and old material. Or think of an acronym using the first letter of each to-be-learned word. You could create a story that ties together a new set of concepts that you want to recall later; by retelling the story, you recall the concepts.

4. **CUSTOMIZE YOUR LEARNING STRATEGIES** to optimize your learning style. Some research suggests that students who use the strategy of verbal elaboration (that is, creating sentences about the material) have better recall than students who use mental imagery or another visual strategy (Kirchhoff & Buckner, 2006). But this same research also showed that individuals choose different strategies to learn the same material. Some learners tend to be more visual, whereas others excel with more verbal material and strategies.

5. **OVERLEARN** new material. If you study new material just enough to recognize or recall it for a short period, chances are good you will forget a considerable amount of this material. To prevent this from happening, you need to overlearn the material. Don't stop studying when you reach that point where you think you might be able to remember the material if you take the test very soon. Keep studying until retrieval of the information becomes quick and effortless. There is evidence that overlearning strengthens the neural connections involved in storing information and makes it more likely that you will be able to retrace these neural paths when it comes time to retrieve it.

● Checking Mastery

1. What are the differences in basic memory capacities of children and adolescents?

2. What memory improvements are we likely to notice when a child becomes an adolescent?

● Making Connections

1. Using the information-processing model presented earlier in the chapter (see Figure 8.1), explain why 17-year-old Nathaniel outperforms his 7-year-old sibling when asked to recall a TV program on the Civil War both watched last week.

2. Abigail has a big exam coming up—the results could determine whether or not she earns a scholarship for college. How should she prepare for the exam and what characteristics of the test itself or the testing conditions might affect her performance?

LEARNING OBJECTIVES

- Distinguish characteristics of someone with expertise in a field relative to someone who is a novice.

- Describe the characteristics of adult autobiographical memory.

- Discuss age-related changes in memory across adulthood, noting factors that enhance and factors that impede memory.

- Explain how older adults may compensate for declines in memory and problem-solving ability.

For many years, researchers have used emerging adult college students as the standard of effective information processing, against which all other age groups are compared. This occurs because information processing is thought to be most efficient—at its peak—in emerging and young adults. Still, improvements in cognitive performance continue during the adult years before aging begins to take its toll on some memory and problem-solving capacities.

Developing Expertise

Comparing people new to their chosen fields of study with those more experienced tells researchers that experience pays off in more effective memory and problem-solving skills. In Chapter 7, you saw that people in Piaget's highest stage of cognitive development, formal operations, often perform better in their areas of specialization than in unfamiliar areas. Similarly, information-processing research shows that adults often function best cognitively in domains in which they have achieved expertise (Ericsson, 1996; Glaser & Chi, 1988). It has been estimated that it takes about 10 years of training and experience to become a true expert in a field and to build a rich and well-organized knowledge base (Ericsson, 1996). But once this base is achieved, the expert not only knows and remembers more but also thinks more effectively than individuals who lack expertise.

Consider first the effects of semantic memory, or knowledge base, on performance. Adults who have considerable interest in and knowledge of cars—experts in the domain of cars—are more successful on recognition and recollection tasks about cars than the typical adult who is a car novice (Herzmann & Curran, 2011). Similar knowledge base effects are found for other areas of expertise, including American football (Van Overschelde et al., 2005), chess (Gong, Ericsson, & Moxley, 2015), maps (Ooms, De Maeyer, & Fack, 2015), and taxi drivers' knowledge of street names (Kalakoski & Saariluoma, 2001). Expertise provides an advantage because, in part, it allows experts to hold and manipulate more information in short-term memory than nonexperts (see Tashman, 2013). Chess experts, for example, might look at a chess board with 20 pieces and "see" 3 or 4 clusters of chess pieces in play, whereas the novice chess player looks at the same board and sees 20 different chess pieces that seem to have little logic to their placement. Creating meaningful chunks out of the pieces on the chess board also shows that long-term memory plays a role in expertise. What expert players have previously learned allows them to quickly identify meaningful patterns when shown a new chess board with pieces in play.

In addition, experts are able to use their elaborately organized and complete knowledge bases to solve problems effectively and efficiently (Bilalić et al., 2012; Sheridan & Reingold, 2014). They are able to size up a situation quickly, see what the problem really is, and recognize how a new problem is similar to and different from problems encountered in the past (Glaser & Chi, 1988). They can quickly, surely, and almost automatically call up the right information from their extensive knowledge base to devise effective solutions to problems and to carry them out efficiently.

Are the benefits of expertise content-specific, or does gaining expertise in one domain carry over into other domains and make a person a more generally effective learner or problem solver? This is an interesting and important question. One research team (Ericsson, Chase, & Faloon, 1980) put an average college student to work improving the number of digits he could recall. He practiced for about 1 hour a day, 3–5 days a week, for more than 1½ years—more than 200 hours in all. His improvement? He went from a memory span of 7 digits to one of 79 digits! His method involved forming meaningful associations between strings of digits and, of all things, running times because of his keen interest in running. For example, he would convert the numbers 3492 to "3 minutes and 49 point 2 seconds, near world-record mile time" (p. 1181). It also involved chunking numbers into groups of three or four, then organizing the chunks into large units.

Did all this work pay off in a better memory for information other than numbers? Not really. When he was given letters of the alphabet to recall, this young man's memory span was unexceptional (about six letters). Clearly the memory ability he developed was based on strategies of use only in the subject matter he was trying to remember. Similarly, Bob Petrella, a man with an exceptional memory for anything and everything related to sports, turns out to have ordinary prospective memory, or remembering things that need to be done in the future (ABC News, 2010). Each expert apparently relies on domain-specific knowledge and domain-specific information-processing strategies to achieve cognitive feats (Ericsson & Kintsch, 1995; Schunn & Anderson, 1999).

Overall, experts know more than novices do, their knowledge base is more organized, and they are able to use their

Adults who have gained proficiency in their chosen fields can draw from their well-organized knowledge bases to find just the right information to fit the problem at hand. Solving problems is automatic and effortless for experts.

Robert Gerhardt/Dreamstime.com

knowledge and the specialized strategies they have devised to learn, remember, and solve problems efficiently in their areas of expertise—but not in other domains. In effect, experts do not need to think much; they are like experienced drivers who can put themselves on "autopilot" and carry out well-learned routines quickly and accurately (Callan & Naito, 2014). By gaining expertise over the years, adults can often compensate to some extent for age-related losses in information-processing capacities (Badham et al., 2016; Jastrzembski, Charness, & Vasyukova, 2006).

Autobiographical Memory

Earlier in this chapter, we examined the emergence of autobiographical memories and you learned that most adults do not remember much about their first few years of life. Yet we also noted that the long-term memory store seems limitless in terms of space and longevity. Is everything we have ever experienced "in there" somewhere? Likely not, as most adults report difficulties recalling past events. So what determines whether an event is likely to be recalled at a later point in time? We will consider four factors identified by Patricia Bauer (2007) that may influence autobiographical memories: personal significance, distinctiveness, emotional intensity, and life phase of the event.

1. Most people believe that the *personal significance* of an event affects our memory for the event—that events of great importance to the self will be remembered better than less important events. As it turns out, the personal significance of an event, as rated at the time the event occurs, has little effect on one's ability to later recall the event. It may be that what was once considered important becomes less so with the passage of time and with the broader perspective gained over

the years. For example, imagine that at age 19, you break up with your boyfriend or girlfriend of 2 years. This is traumatic and of great importance to you as a 19-year-old. You expect you'll never get over it and that the details of the event will be forever etched into your memory. But over the next 10, 20, 30 years, or more, so many other events occur that the importance of this youthful breakup fades as you date others, marry, work, raise children, and so on. Thus, personal significance of events may influence memory for these events as long as they remain important to us (Bauer, Hättenschwiler, & Larkina, 2016). But as some events become less important and others become more important over time, there is an associated shift in memory for these events.

2. The *distinctiveness* or *uniqueness* of an event has been consistently associated with better recall (Bauer, 2007). The more unique an event is, the more likely it is to be recalled later on, and to be recalled as a distinct event with relevant details. Common events and experiences are often recalled, if at all, as multiple events lumped together as one (Burt, Kemp, & Conway, 2003). Thus, if you attended the same camp every summer throughout your childhood, you may retain fond memories of your experiences at the camp. But the chances are good that you have integrated in your memory many of the common and similar camp experiences: You remember singing songs around the campfire, but because you did this every year of the camp, you don't recall the experience of one year as separate from your experience of all the other years. On the other hand, consider the rather unique event of experiencing a tornado. Teenagers who had been young children at the time of the event, as well as adults, had good recall of this distinctive event 9 years after its occurrence (Bauer et al., 2016).

3. The *affective* or *emotional intensity* of an event also influences later recall (Bauer, 2007). Events associated with either highly negative or highly positive emotions are recalled better than events that were experienced in the context of more neutral emotions. This enhanced memory for emotion-arousing events occurs even though the emotion associated with the event tends to dissipate with time, especially if it is a negative emotion (Paz-Alonso et al., 2009). It is likely that strong emotions activate the body's arousal system and the neural components associated with arousal enhance encoding and consolidation of events. This can be seen with fMRI scans of the brain as participants are cued to retrieve an autobiographical memory. The brain scans show activation of the amygdala, an area of the brain associated with emotions, when participants retrieve an emotionally charged memory but not when they retrieve a neutral memory (see Rubin, 2012; St. Jacques, 2012). And if you are an angry person, you tend to recall more negative, angry autobiographical memories (Hung & Bryant, 2016). Similar findings have emerged for other personal characteristics, which may provide valuable insight into the variability of memory across individuals.

4. Finally, research on autobiographical memory has revealed that people recall more information from the *life phase* of

their teens and 20s than from any other time except the near present (Fitzgerald, 1999; Rubin, 2002). ■ **Figure 8.12** shows the number of memories recalled by 70-year-old adults. Not surprisingly, they recalled a lot from their recent past (for example, age 65). But the number of memories recalled from about ages 15–25 was higher than the number recalled from other points of the life span, especially for positive life events (Zaragoza et al., 2015). This memory or **reminiscence bump** (Koppel & Berntsen, 2016; Koppel & Rubin, 2016) may occur because memories from adolescence and early adulthood are more easily accessible than memories from other periods of the life span. They are more accessible because of their distinctiveness and the effort applied by adolescents and young adults to understanding the meaning of the events. Notably, this time of life typically coincides with the major life events of leaving home, acquiring education or training for a job or career, forming romantic relationships, starting a family, and having other experiences signifying adulthood (Bohn & Berntsen, 2014). These events form one's cultural **life script**, those stories of our lives that we tell over and over again (see Chapter 11 on narrative identities). These life scripts are biased toward positive, life-affirming events. A typical life script might go something like this: "After high school, I traveled half-way across the country to go to college, where I met my future spouse. Upon graduation from college, we both managed to get jobs in the same large city, close to his family but far from where I had grown up. We ended up staying there for

5 years, establishing our careers while helping out his ailing parents. Once they passed away, though, we saw an opportunity to move to a more ideal setting and settle down to have a family." Such life scripts are repeated over time and contexts, becoming further consolidated with each retelling, ensuring that these major life events are solidly secured in our memory system. Research shows that there may be other "bumps" in memory across the life span that are influenced by what particular cultures prescribe as important life events (Berntsen & Rubin, 2004; Fitzgerald & Broadbridge, 2012).

Memory and Aging

No less an expert on learning than B. F. Skinner complained about memory problems: "One of the more disheartening experiences of old age is discovering that a point you have just made—so significant, so beautifully expressed—was made by you in something you published a long time ago" (Skinner, 1983, p. 242). Most elderly adults report that they have at least minor difficulties remembering things (Reid & Maclullich, 2006; Vestergren & Nilsson, 2011). They are especially likely to have trouble recalling names and items they will need later; they are also more upset than young adults by memory lapses, perhaps because they view them as signs of aging. **Exploration 8.1** describes when forgetfulness is normal and when it is indicative of a more serious problem.

Areas of Strength and Weakness

Much research indicates that, on average, older adults do not fare as well as younger adults under a variety of conditions that require memory. However, as we discuss areas of concern with memory of older adults, keep in mind the following qualifications:

- Most of the research is based on cross-sectional studies that compare age groups, which suggests that the age differences detected could be related to factors other than age. (If needed, you can refresh your memory of the strengths and weaknesses of cross-sectional designs by referring back to Chapter 1.)
- Declines, when observed, typically do not become noticeable until we hit our 70s.
- Difficulties in remembering affect elderly people more noticeably as they continue to age and are most severe among the oldest elderly people.
- Not all older people experience these difficulties.
- Not all kinds of memory tasks cause older people difficulty.

Studies of memory skills in adulthood suggest that the aspects of learning and memory in which older adults look most deficient in comparison with young and middle-aged adults are some of the same areas in which young children compare unfavorably with older children (see Bauer, 2007). Older adults often struggle to perform well on memory tasks that are timed, i.e., where completing the task quickly is more advantageous than completing the task at a slower pace. In contrast, on tasks where timing is not an issue and respondents have as much time as they want,

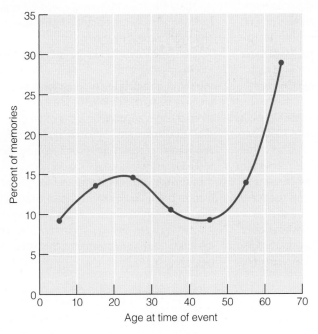

■ **Figure 8.12** Seventy-year-olds recall the times of their lives: What does this graph illustrate about the recall of autobiographical memories by older adults?

Source: Rubin, D.C, Wetzler, S. E., & Nebes, R. D. (1986). Autobiographical memory across the adult lifespan. In D. C. Rubin (ed.), *Autobiographical memory across the lifespan.* Cambridge University Press. Reprinted with permission.

Forgetting: What Is Normal and What Is Not?

As we age, or watch parents and grandparents age, how can we distinguish between normal forgetfulness and abnormal memory changes? Many older adults worry that forgetting an appointment or where they put their reading glasses is a precursor to the devastating memory loss associated with Alzheimer's disease (AD) (see Chapter 16). Fortunately, most of us will not develop AD and the atypical memory changes that accompany it. Most will, however, exhibit some changes in memory and information-processing skills. So how can we discriminate between normal memory changes and those associated with disease?

Cynthia Green (2001) suggests three criteria that can be used to alert us to atypical memory problems:

- Has memory gotten noticeably worse over the past 6 months?
- Do memory problems interfere with everyday activities at home or work?
- Are family and friends concerned about an individual's memory problems?

Answering "yes" to these questions may indicate unusual memory loss that should be evaluated by a professional.

In practical terms, it is normal to forget where you put something but abnormal to forget how to use it (Cherry & Smith, 1998). Thus, do not worry when Grandpa cannot find his car keys, but be alert if he cannot remember how to use them when they are in his hand. Similarly, it is normal to forget a new phone number you recently looked up in the phone book but abnormal to forget phone numbers you have known and used for years.

Researchers who study memory have identified a step between normal memory loss with age and severe, disease-related loss

(Brandt et al., 2009; Petersen et al., 1997, 2001). Individuals with **mild cognitive impairment** experience significant memory problems—forgetting important appointments, having trouble learning new names, and repeating themselves to the same person—but otherwise do not appear to be suffering from dementia. At least not yet. Some research suggests that a majority of those with mild cognitive impairment will eventually develop forms of dementia such as AD (Lopez, 2013). Research also suggests that patients with mild cognitive impairment display deficits on other cognitive tasks as well, which could mean their problem is more general than memory impairment (Ribeiro, de Mendonca, & Guerreiro, 2006). This is a serious concern because 22% of older adults may have mild cognitive impairment and will require increased assistance as they continue to age (Plassman et al., 2008).

The good news is that age-related memory loss may be preventable, and some losses may be reversible. Reducing stress, for example, is one way to improve memory performance (Bremner & Narayan, 1998). Chronic stress elevates levels of cortisol in the brain, which impedes memory. Studies by the Mayo Clinic and the MacArthur Foundation found that three things predicted good memory over time: physical fitness and activity, mental activity, and a sense of control over life events (Geda et al., 2012; Rowe & Kahn, 1998). Mental activity—working crossword puzzles, reading, using a computer—increases connections among neurons. Physical activity increases blood flow to the brain and seems to release chemicals that protect neurons involved in cognitive function. Older adults who engage in moderate to high levels of physical activity are less likely to develop cognitive impairment

Fuse/Corbis/Getty Images

than those who are not active (Etgen et al., 2010). Thus, remaining physically and mentally active can help protect against memory loss associated with aging. Having a sense of control over memory can boost both confidence and memory performance.

In sum, significant memory loss is not likely among healthy older adults. It is true that, relative to young adults, older adults exhibit poorer memory performance in some situations. But these changes are minor and can often be avoided or minimized by remaining physically and mentally active. Families and professionals should be on the lookout for older adults who show marked declines in their memory performance. They may be experiencing mild cognitive impairment and may eventually develop AD and impaired memory. The earlier they are identified and receive treatment, the better (see Chapter 16).

older adults may not show significant memory deficits, at least not until very old age. As well, older adults fare poorly compared with younger adults when the material to be learned is unfamiliar or unimportant to them. Lars Bäckman (1991) tested young and old adults for facial recognition of two groups of people: those who had been famous in the 1930s and 1940s when the older adults were young and those who were famous 50–60 years later when the research was conducted. Findings supported the researcher's predictions that the older adults would perform better with the faces familiar to them from long ago, whereas the young adults would perform better with the contemporary faces that were presumably familiar to them. Researchers often do not take into consideration that stimuli familiar to one group of participants may not be especially familiar to another group of participants. Yet as this study and others have shown, familiarity with the information-to-be-remembered contributes to success (Badham et al., 2016).

Like their younger counterparts, older adults are likely to be more deficient on tasks requiring recall memory than on tasks requiring only recognition of what was learned. In a classic study of memory for high school classmates (Bahrick, Bahrick, & Wittlinger, 1975), even adults who were almost 35 years past graduation showed remarkable recognition memory: They could recognize which of five names matched a picture in their yearbook about 90% of the time. However, the ability to actively *recall* names of classmates when given only their photos as cues dropped considerably as the age of the rememberer increased. A large gap between recognition and recall shows that older people have encoded and stored the information but cannot retrieve it without the help of cues. Sometimes older adults fail to retrieve information because they never thoroughly encoded or learned it, but at other times they simply cannot retrieve information that is "in there."

Finally, older adults seem to have more trouble with explicit memory tasks that require mental effort than with implicit memory tasks that are largely automatic (Nyberg et al., 2012). Older adults, then, have little trouble with skills and procedures that have been routinized over the years—established as habits—although there might be some slight decline, often in the form of slower response times (Ward, Berry, & Shanks, 2013). And with explicit memory, where there tends to be a larger decline, the magnitude of the decline varies with the type of explicit memory. Older adults retain fairly good semantic memory (general factual knowledge accumulated over time) but show steady declines in episodic memory (recall of specific events that are tied to a specific time and place) (Nyberg et al., 2012).

Overall, these findings suggest that older adults, like young children, have difficulty with tasks that are cognitively demanding—that require speed, the learning of unfamiliar material, the use of unexercised abilities, recall rather than recognition, or explicit and effortful rather than implicit and automatic memory. Yet older adults and young children have difficulty for different reasons, as you will now see.

Explaining Declines in Old Age

In asking why some older adults struggle with some learning and memory tasks, we will first return to the hypotheses used to explain childhood improvements in performance: knowledge base, metamemory, strategy use, and basic processing capacities. Then we will consider some additional possibilities.

Knowledge Base. If you start with the hypothesis that differences in knowledge base explain memory differences between older and younger adults, you immediately encounter a problem: Young children may lack knowledge, but elderly adults do not. Indeed, older adults are generally at least as knowledgeable

as young adults: Semantic memory for vocabulary *increases* until about age 65 (Rönnlund et al., 2005; Salthouse, 2016). Verbal knowledge shows no decrease throughout mid- and older adulthood and may not decline until we are pushing 90 (Park et al., 2002)! Older adults also know more than younger adults about real-world categories of information such as U.S. presidents, countries, international cities, and bodies of water (Foos & Sarno, 1998; Rendell, Castel, & Craik, 2005). In an important study, Harry Bahrick (1984) tested adults of various ages on their retention of Spanish vocabulary from high school or college classes. Amazingly, as much as 50% of the vocabulary learned was retained nearly 50 *years* later! And it may be worth your time and effort to learn as much as you can in your classes now: Bahrick also found that the more classes taken in a subject and the higher the grades in those courses, the better the retention of this material in the years to come. Adults who took several Spanish classes and earned "A" grades remembered more Spanish vocabulary 50 years later than adults who took one Spanish class and earned "C" grades remembered after a delay of just 1 year. Information that undergoes meaningful consolidation can clearly be retained in long-term memory for many years to come. So deficiencies in knowledge base are probably not the source of most memory problems that many older adults display. On the contrary, gains in knowledge probably help older adults compensate for losses in information-processing efficiency (Salthouse, 2015).

Metamemory. Could elderly adults, like young children, be deficient in the specific knowledge called metamemory? Is their knowledge of some of the strategies that prove useful in school learning—and in laboratory memory tasks—rusty? This theory sounds plausible, but research shows that older adults seem to know as much as younger adults about such things as which memory strategies are best and which memory tasks

Dorothy Emmrich, 100, uses a memory program to exercise her information-processing skills. Research suggests that both physical and mental workouts can aid memory across the life span.

are hardest (Castel, McGillivray, & Friedman, 2012). They can also monitor their memory to assist their learning (Hines, Touron, & Hertzog, 2009). Still, older adults are more likely than younger ones to misjudge the accuracy of some aspects of their memory, such as the source of the memories (Dodson, Bawa, & Krueger, 2007).

So whereas metamemory seems largely intact across the life span, there may be some isolated areas of weakness. Moreover, although older adults know a lot about memory, they express more negative beliefs about their memory skills than do younger adults (Cavanaugh, 1996). Memory loss may contribute to a drop in confidence in memory skills, but negative beliefs about one's memory skills also appear to hurt memory performance (Barber & Mather, 2014; Hess & Hinson, 2006). Therefore, it's not clear whether declines in actual memory performance lead to the development of negative beliefs about memory or whether negative beliefs—either one's own or those of the surrounding culture—undermine memory performance.

Becca Levy (1996) has shed light on this issue by showing that activating negative stereotypes in the minds of elderly adults (through rapid, subliminal presentation of words such as *Alzheimer's* and *senile* on a computer screen) causes them to perform worse on memory tests and to express less confidence in their memory skills than when positive stereotypes of old age are planted in their minds (through words such as *wise* and *sage*). In another study, Levy and her colleagues (2012) assessed beliefs about aging among adults aged 22 to 77 years. Over the next 38 years, the researchers found that these beliefs predicted memory performance. In particular, those who had more negative beliefs about old people experienced a 30% decline in memory compared to other adults the same age who had less negative beliefs. Findings such as these clearly call into question the idea of a universal decline in memory skills in later life and point to the influence of culture and its views of aging on performance (see also Castel et al., 2012; Nelson, 2016).

Memory Strategies. What about the hypothesis that failure to use effective memory strategies accounts for deficits in old age? Many older adults do not spontaneously use strategies, even those as simple as writing notes to help remember a phone message (Schryer & Ross, 2013). At least some older adults show improved memory performance when they are prompted to use a strategy (Frankenmolen et al., 2016). Whether or not memory improves seems to depend on a person's level of intelligence: Those with higher intelligence benefit from strategy use whereas those with lower intelligence do not benefit, possibly because they do not correctly implement the strategy (Frankenmolen et al., 2016).

Other research shows that older adults can be trained to use cognitive strategies. George Rebok, Sherry Willis, and their colleagues (see Rebok et al., 2014) in the Advanced Cognitive Training for Independent and Vital Elderly (ACTIVE) Group followed four groups of older adults (average age of 74 years at the start of the study) over a period of 10 years. The groups differed in the type of cognitive training they received at the beginning of the study:

- Memory training—participants were taught strategies of organization, visualization, and association to remember verbal material.
- Reasoning training—participants were taught strategies for detecting a pattern in a series of letters or words.
- Speed training—participants learned to complete visual search tasks in increasingly less time, and they were trained to divide their attention between two tasks.
- No training—these participants served as a control group.

How did the groups fare across the 10 years? Compared with the control group, the adults who received memory training did better on memory tasks for the first 5 years, but this advantage was washed out by 10 years. Those who received reasoning training performed better on reasoning tasks and those who received speed training were much faster, and both of these findings held true across the entire 10-year period of the study. Importantly, the benefits of training were evident not just on laboratory tasks but on activities important to daily living, such as driving or understanding the interactions and side-effects of prescription drugs.

This study and others (e.g., Karbach & Verhaeghen, 2014; Zinke et al., 2014) show that older adults can profit from mental exercise that increasingly challenges them. Just as physical exercise contributes to overall physical well-being, mental exercise contributes to overall mental well-being. And just as your physical workouts need to increasingly challenge you (if you start out walking a half-mile at a slow pace, you need to increase your distance and/or your pace to reap the most benefits), your mental workouts must become more rigorous. If you start out solving easy Sudoku puzzles, you need to push yourself to move on to more difficult ones.

Basic Processing Capacities. Changes in basic processing capacities that occur with age are perhaps the biggest issue with memory. For starters, declines in sensory abilities may tax available processing resources, leading to memory deficits (Baltes & Lindenberger, 1997). In addition, working-memory capacity diminishes with age. Research indicates that working-memory capacity increases during childhood and adolescence, peaks around age 45, then begins to decline (Swanson, 1999). Moreover, working-memory capacity predicts how well adults will perform on a range of cognitive tasks (Hoyer & Verhaeghen, 2006). Older adults do fine on short-term memory tasks that require them to juggle just a few pieces of information in working memory. However, when the amount of information that they are to "operate on" increases, they begin to show deficits. Older adults may have more trouble than younger ones ignoring irrelevant task information. For instance, trying to memorize a list of words while walking is more problematic for older adults than for middle-aged or younger adults (Li et al., 2001; Lindenberger, Marsiske, & Baltes, 2000). Brain research confirms that older adults show a pattern of neural activity consistent with increased monitoring of their environment when working under conditions with more distractions and task-irrelevant information (Stevens et al., 2008). Thus, their working-memory space may become cluttered with unnecessary information, limiting the space available for the task at hand (Hoyer & Verhaeghen, 2006).

Limitations in working-memory capacity are most likely rooted in slower functioning of the nervous system both early and late in life (see Hartley, 2006; also see Chapter 5). Much research shows that speed of processing increases during childhood and adolescence, peaks in early adulthood, then declines slowly over the adult years (Baudouin et al., 2009). Age differences in performance on cognitive tasks often shrink when age differences in speed of information processing are taken into account and controlled. Experience in a domain of learning can certainly enhance performance, but if children and older adults generally have sluggish "computers," they simply may not be able to keep up with the processing demands of complex learning and memory tasks (Hartley, 2006).

Using brain imaging techniques, researchers have also identified different patterns of activity during memory tasks in the prefrontal cortex of younger and older adults (see, for example, Galdo-Alvarez, Lindin, & Diaz, 2009; Rypma et al., 2001). Although some studies show underactivity in older adults' brains, others show overactivity. Underactivity in the older brain is assumed to result from a deficiency of either the hardware of the brain or of the software it uses, such as the strategies that could be employed on a task (Reuter-Lorenz & Cappell, 2008). Overactivity, on the other hand, may indicate that the older brain is trying to compensate for age-related losses. By compensating, or working harder and drawing on more brain areas, the older brain may be able to perform as well as a younger brain, at least until this overactivity can no longer overcome steeper age-related declines (Meulenbroek et al., 2010).

Some promising research with mice points to the role of a protein (called B2M) that accumulates with age and inhibits the formation of new brain cells and results in an associated loss of memory (Villeda et al., 2014). Injecting this "old age" protein into young mice led to impaired memory but once the protein had dispersed from their bodies, their memories rebounded to normal levels. And consistent with our discussion in Chapter 5 about the importance of a good night's sleep, sleep deprivation, at least in mice, interferes with the synthesis of hippocampal protein, leading to memory deficits (Tudor et al., 2016). Future research needs to determine whether the same connection between this protein and memory exists for humans and, if so, what—if anything—can be done to circumvent this potential problem.

Slow neural transmission as well as too much or too little of certain proteins, then, may be behind limitations in working memory in old age. Limitations in working memory, in turn, may contribute not only to limitations in long-term memory but also to difficulties performing a range of cognitive tasks, including problem-solving tasks and tests of intelligence, even those that have no time limits (Salthouse, 2015).

To this point, then, you might conclude that many older adults, although they have a vast knowledge base and a good deal of knowledge about learning and memory, experience declines

in basic processing capacity that make it difficult for them to carry out memory strategies that will drain their limited working-memory capacity. But the basic processing capacity hypothesis cannot explain everything about age differences in memory. We need to dig deeper and consider several contextual factors.

Contextual Contributors. Many researchers have adopted a contextual perspective on learning and memory, emphasizing both biological and genetic factors along with environmental and situational factors (Hess & Emery, 2012). They emphasize that performance on learning and memory tasks is the product of an interaction among (1) characteristics of the learner, such as goals, motivations, abilities, and health; (2) characteristics of the task or situation; and (3) characteristics of the broader environment, including the cultural context in which a task is performed. They are not convinced that there is a universal biological decline in basic learning and memory capacities, because older individuals often perform capably in certain contexts.

First, cohort differences in education and IQ can explain age differences in some learning and memory skills. Elderly people today are less educated, on average, than younger adults are, and they are further removed from their school days. When education level is controlled for, age differences shrink, although they do not disappear (Nilsson et al., 2002; Rönnlund et al., 2005). Thus, to some extent, education can compensate for aging. Older adults who are highly educated or who have high levels of intellectual ability often perform as well as younger adults (Cherry & LeCompte, 1999; Haught et al., 2000). Similarly, health and lifestyle differences between cohorts may contribute to age differences in learning and memory. Older adults are more likely than younger adults to have chronic or degenerative diseases, and even mild diseases can impair memory performance (Houx, Vreeling, & Jolles, 1991; Hultsch, Hammer, & Small, 1993). Older adults also lead less active lifestyles and perform fewer cognitively demanding activities than younger adults do, on average. These age group differences in lifestyle also contribute to age differences in cognitive performance. Older adults who engage in fitness training show enhanced cognitive ability, possibly because physical activity increases blood flow to the brain (Colcombe et al., 2004; Etgen et al., 2010). Increased blood flow to the hippocampus is associated with improved memory performance (Heo et al., 2010). Similarly, older adults who remain *mentally* active or take on challenging mental activities outperform other older adults on working memory and other cognitive tasks (Stine-Morrow et al., 2008).

Notice that if we compare older adults with lower education levels to younger adults with higher education levels, or compare older adults with health challenges to younger, healthy adults, then in both cases, we are conducting cross-sectional research (see Chapter 1). Cross-sectional research on memory performance often paints a more negative picture of aging than longitudinal research (Nyberg et al., 2012). ■ **Figure 8.13** illustrates the typical pattern of a fairly steep drop in both semantic and episodic memory found with cross-sectional studies (top half of figure) compared to the pattern found with longitudinal studies

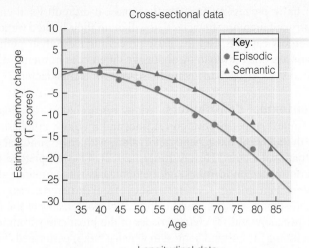

Cross-sectional data

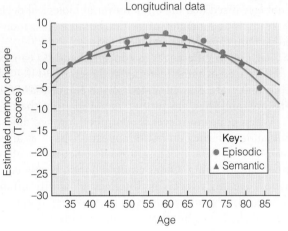

Longitudinal data

Figure 8.13 Episodic and semantic memory changes typically found with cross-sectional research (top half) and longitudinal research (bottom half). The rather sharp decline in memory suggested by cross-cultural studies may reflect cohort differences rather than effects of aging per se.

Source: Adapted from Figure 1, Lars Nyberg, Martin Lövdén, Katrine Riklund, Ulman Lindenberger, & Lars Bäckman, (2012). Memory aging and brain maintenance, *Trends in Cognitive Sciences*, Volume 16, Issue 5, 292–305.

where memory performance actual improves across much of the life span with only a small dip after the age of about 75 (bottom half of figure).

The implications of such research are clear: Declines in information-processing skills are not inevitable or universal. Nature may place some boundaries on the information-processing system, but nurture plays a significant role in sustaining memory and problem-solving skills. Older adults may be able to maintain their memory skills if they are relatively well educated, stay healthy, and exercise their bodies and minds. Still, factors such as education and health cannot account completely for age differences in cognitive performance.

Perhaps the truth lies somewhere between the basic processing capacity view, which emphasizes nature by pointing to a universal decline in cognitive resources, such as speed and working memory, that affect performance on many cognitive tasks, and the contextual view, which emphasizes nurture. Contextual theorists stress variability from person to person and situation to situation based on cohort differences, motivational factors, and task demands. Most adults, at least if they live to an advanced old age, may experience some loss of basic processing resources. However, they may also have developed specialized knowledge and strategies that allow them to compensate for these losses as they carry out the everyday cognitive activities most important to them.

Problem Solving and Aging

You know that problem-solving skills improve steadily from early childhood through adolescence, but what becomes of them in adulthood? On the one hand, you might expect to see a decline in problem-solving prowess paralleling declines in learning and memory performance. On the other hand, if adults increase their knowledge bases and develop expertise as they age, might not older adults outwit younger novices on many problem-solving tasks?

Familiar versus Unfamiliar Tasks

When given traditional problem-solving tasks to perform in the laboratory, young adults typically perform better than middle-aged adults, who in turn outperform older adults (Denney, 1989). However, consider research using the Twenty Questions task in which participants are shown an array of items and asked to find out, using as few questions as possible, which item the experimenter has in mind. The best problem-solving strategy is to ask **constraint-seeking questions**—ones that rule out more than one item (for example, "Is it an animal?"). Young children and older adults tend to pursue specific hypotheses instead ("Is it a pig?" "Is it a pencil?"). Consequently, they must ask more questions to identify the right object. However, if the task is altered to make it more familiar (for example, through the use of playing cards as stimuli), then older adults do far better. The familiarity of the material allows them to draw on their knowledge base to solve the problem. Thus, older adults are capable of using effective problem-solving strategies but do not use them in some contexts, especially when given unfamiliar tasks in a laboratory.

What if adults are asked to deal with real-life problems such as leaky water pipes, family squabbles, or refrigerators that break down in the middle of the night? Nancy Denney and Kathy Pearce (1989) asked elderly adults to help them devise everyday problems that would be meaningful and familiar to older individuals. One problem was to generate ideas about how a 65-year-old recently widowed woman could improve her social life; another was to advise an elderly couple living on Social Security what to do when they were unable to pay their heating bill one winter. On these everyday problems, performance increased from early adulthood to middle age and declined in old age.

Other findings echo this one: When given everyday problems to which they can apply the expertise they have gained through experience, middle-aged adults often outperform young adults. Elderly adults sometimes equal and sometimes do worse than young and middle-aged adults; either way, they show smaller deficits on the everyday problems than they do on unfamiliar problems in the laboratory (Berg & Klaczynski, 1996; Marsiske & Willis, 1995). Ultimately, declines in basic capacities may limit the problem-solving skills of many elderly adults, not only in the laboratory but also in real life (Denney, 1989; Kasworm & Medina, 1990). You should bear in mind, however, the contextual view that cognitive competence among older adults varies widely because of differences in health, education, experience, and so on.

Selection, Optimization, and Compensation

Some cognitive researchers believe that older adults may approach problem solving differently than younger adults. It's true that younger adults generate more possible solutions to a problem than do older adults. But the solutions generated by older adults tend to be more goal-focused and selective, emphasizing quality over quantity (Marsiske & Margrett, 2006). When faced with a broken water pipe in the middle of the night, an older couple may generate one solution—call their grown son who lives down the street. Although this may not seem like an ideal solution to the son, the older adults may realize that this is the easiest and fastest solution.

In addition, researchers have proposed a framework called *selective optimization with compensation* (SOC), to understand how older adults may cope with and compensate for their diminishing cognitive resources (Baltes & Baltes, 1990; Baltes & Rudolph, 2013; Riediger, Li, & Lindenberger, 2006; and see Chapter 11). Three processes are involved: *selection* (focus on a limited set of goals and the skills most needed to achieve them), *optimization* (practice those skills to keep them sharp), and *compensation* (develop ways around the need for other skills). If cognitive resources are limited or unstable, then you can't take on everything; you need to be selective. Choose those tasks that are most important or have to be done. For example, prepare dinner (after all, you have to eat), but don't worry about getting every surface of the house dusted. Focus on what you do well—optimize your strengths and minimize weaknesses. If you still have the skills to balance a checkbook and this is something your partner struggles with, then you should take over managing the checkbook. If your vision is so bad that you cannot tell that your "clean" dishes have chunks of food remaining on them, then offload this task to a dishwasher or partner.

Research suggests that both middle-aged and older adults take advantage of SOC, although older adults less so than middle-aged ones (Robinson, Rickenbauch, & Lachman, 2016). Both groups are more likely to use SOC on days when they experience greater stress. In addition, SOC has been used to try to help older adults overcome weaknesses in explicit memory by taking advantage of their relative strength of implicit memory. For instance, Cameron Camp and his colleagues (Camp et al., 1996; Camp & McKitrick, 1992) have worked with patients who have dementia caused by Alzheimer's disease (AD). They have taught patients with AD to remember the names of staff members by having the patients name photos of staff members repeatedly and at ever longer intervals between trials. People who could not retain names for more than a minute were able to recall the names weeks later after training. The technique appears to work because it uses implicit memory processes that are often retained even when explicit memory ability is lost; adults learn effortlessly when they repeatedly encounter the material to be learned. By selecting and optimizing, older adults can often compensate for their diminishing explicit memory, allowing them to maintain independence for a longer period of time (Riediger et al., 2006).

Checking Mastery

1. On what types of tasks are older adults most likely to experience memory problems?
2. How can adults minimize the effects of aging on memory and problem-solving tasks?

Making Connections

1. As a teacher in an Elderhostel program for older adults, you want to base your teaching methods on knowledge of the information-processing capacities of elderly adults. What practical recommendations would you derive from (a) the view that there is a universal decline with age in basic processing capacities and (b) the contextual perspective on cognitive aging?
2. Revisit Figure 8.12 showing the distribution of autobiographical memories over the life span. What factors might account for the rise and fall of autobiographical memories at different phases of the life span?
3. Every time your mother and grandmother forget something, they express concerns about "losing it" and "getting senile." Knowing that you have taken a course in life-span human development, they seek you out for reassurance. What can you tell them about memory and aging that might alleviate their concerns?

Chapter Summary

8.1 Conceptualizing Memory

- The information-processing approach uses a computer analogy to illustrate how the mind processes information. The human "computer" takes in information through the sensory registers, which hold the information for a very brief period. Information attended to may be further processed in short-term, or working, memory.

- Eventually, information may be stored in long-term memory, which seems to be unlimited in terms of size and permanency. In order for something to move into the long-term memory store, it must undergo a process of consolidation in which a memory trace of the event is created.

- Encoding and retrieval strategies influence memory performance. Types of retrieval include recognition, recall, and cued recall.

- Explicit memory is deliberate and effortful and changes over the life span, whereas implicit memory is automatic and relatively stable over the life span. Explicit and implicit memories are separate components of long-term memory and are localized in different parts of the brain.

- Memory has neurological underpinnings that influence memory effectiveness and contribute to developmental changes across the life span.

- Stored memories are instrumental to success at problem solving; stored information is used to achieve a goal. Executive control processes select, organize, manipulate, and interpret what is going on in the context of problem solving.

8.2 The Infant

- Using imitation, habituation, and operant conditioning techniques, researchers have gone from believing that infants have no memory beyond a few seconds to appreciating that even young 1-year-olds can recall experiences for weeks and even months under certain conditions.

- Infants clearly show recognition memory for familiar stimuli at birth and cued recall memory by about 2 months. More explicit memory, which requires actively retrieving an image of an object or event no longer present, appears to emerge toward the end of the first year. By age 2, it is even clearer that infants can recall events that happened long ago, for they, like adults, use language to represent and describe what happened.

- Simple problem solving improves throughout infancy, and infants realize that they can get adults to help them solve problems.

8.3 The Child

- Basic information-processing capacity increases as the brain matures and fundamental processes are automated to free working-memory space.

- Memory strategies such as rehearsal, organization, and elaboration improve. Metamemory improves and the general knowledge base grows. All these changes improve the processing of new information in areas of expertise.

- According to Robert Siegler, even young children use systematic rules to solve problems, but their problem-solving skills improve as they replace faulty rules with ones that incorporate all the relevant aspects of the problem. Multiple strategies are used at any age so that development proceeds through a natural selection process and resembles overlapping waves more than a set of stairsteps leading from one way of thinking to the next.

- Memory improves during childhood with increased efficiency of basic information-processing capacities, greater use of memory strategies, improvement in metamemory, and growth of general knowledge base.

- By age 3, children store routine daily events as scripts that they can draw on in similar situations. Our scripts influence what we remember about an event, which is also influenced by information related to but coming after the event.

- Much of what we remember is autobiographical. Even though infants and toddlers show evidence of memory, older children and adults often experience childhood amnesia, or lack of memory for events that happened during infancy and early childhood.

8.4 The Adolescent

- Adolescents master advanced learning strategies such as elaboration, note-taking, and underlining, and they use their strategies more deliberately and selectively.

- Adolescents have larger knowledge bases, and their metamemory skills also improve and contribute to increased memory performance and problem-solving ability.

8.5 The Adult

- As adults gain expertise in a domain, they develop large and organized knowledge bases and highly effective, specialized, and automated ways of retrieving and using their knowledge.

- Many older adults perform less well than young adults on memory tasks that require speed, the learning of unfamiliar or meaningless material, the use of unexercised abilities, recall rather than recognition memory, and explicit rather than implicit memory.

- Declines in basic processing capacity and difficulty using strategies, plus contextual factors such as cohort differences and the irrelevance of many laboratory tasks to everyday life, contribute to age differences in memory.

- On average, older adults also perform less well than younger adults on laboratory problem-solving tasks, but everyday problem-solving skills are likely to improve from early adulthood to middle adulthood and to be maintained in old age.

Key Terms

9 Intelligence and Creativity

Do you know someone who is very intelligent but still manages to do things that seem stupid or foolish? If you don't personally know someone like this, then perhaps you are familiar with the fictional character Sheldon Cooper on television's *The Big Bang Theory*. Sheldon is super smart, with an alleged IQ of 187. He graduated from college at age 14, obtained multiple advanced degrees, and works as a theoretical physicist. Despite his high level of intelligence, there are times when Sheldon shows evidence of irrational thought and lack of social understanding. This sort of incongruity raises many questions. Is intelligence a general ability that should somehow be available and applied in all situations? Are there different types of intelligence and, depending on our particular profiles of ability, might we be intelligent in one situation but not so intelligent in others? If we have gaps in intelligence, can these be filled in with training? And if people like Sheldon can have high scores on intelligence tests but show less than intelligent behavior in 'real-world' settings, can these tests really be measuring intelligence? Finally, how does intelligence relate to creativity? In many cultures and many workplaces, creativity is highly valued, both in terms of the products that result from it, such as artistic masterpieces, and in terms of the process behind it, such as when a creative approach to a problem leads to a brilliant solution that may not otherwise have been considered.

Is being intelligent the same as being smart?

Collection Christophel/Alamy Stock Photo

In this chapter, we tackle these sorts of fascinating questions. In doing so, we examine how performance on intelligence tests typically changes and stays the same over the life span, what IQ tests reveal about a person, and why people's IQ scores differ. We also look at both gifted and intellectually disabled individuals from a life-span perspective. We consider what might be missed by intelligence tests, including creativity and 'street smarts,' or what some scientists call rational thought (Stanovich, 2009). Before going further, take the quiz in **Engagement 9.1** to see if you have any misconceptions about intelligence and intelligence tests; this chapter will clarify why the correct answers are correct.

9.1
Defining Intelligence and Creativity

LEARNING OBJECTIVES

- State how intelligence and creativity are typically defined.

- Analyze the accuracy and usefulness of traditional IQ tests.

- Explain the most prominent theories of intelligence.

- Evaluate the strengths and weaknesses of the theories of intelligence.

Let's begin by trying to understand intelligence as defined by some of the most prominent scholars in this field. As noted in Chapter 7, Piaget defined intelligence as thinking or behavior that is adaptive to the demands of your situation or environment. Other experts have offered different definitions, many of them centering on the ability to think abstractly or to solve problems effectively (for example, Sternberg, 2010a, 2010b). Early definitions of intelligence tended to reflect the assumption that intelligence is an innate ability—that it is genetically determined and fixed at conception. But it has become clear that intelligence is not fixed; it is changeable and subject to environmental influence (see Nisbett et al., 2012). As a result, an individual's intelligence test scores sometimes vary considerably over a lifetime. Bear in mind that understanding of this complex human quality has changed since the first intelligence tests were created at the turn of the last century—and that there is still no single, universally accepted definition of intelligence.

The Psychometric Approach

The research tradition that spawned the development of standardized tests of intelligence is the **psychometric approach**. According to psychometric theorists, intelligence is a trait or a set of traits that characterizes some people to a greater extent than others. The goals, then, are to identify these traits precisely and to measure them so that differences among individuals can

be described. But from the start, experts could not agree on whether intelligence is one general cognitive ability or many specific abilities.

Early on, Charles Spearman (1927) proposed a two-factor theory of intelligence involving, first, a general mental ability (called g) that contributes to performance on many different kinds of tasks. This g factor is what accounts for Spearman's observation that people were often consistent across a range of tasks. For example, general intelligence has been found to correlate with performance on exams in 25 different academic subjects (Deary et al., 2007). However, Spearman also noticed that a student who excelled at most tasks might score low on a particular measure (for example, memory for words). So he proposed a second aspect of intelligence: s, or special abilities, each of which is specific to a particular kind of task. Some research suggests that g may play a greater role in IQ test performance during childhood than it does during adolescence (Kane & Brand, 2006). By adolescence, many effortful processes that underlie the expression of g have become automated, freeing up cognitive resources to sharpen certain specific abilities.

Raymond Cattell and John Horn have greatly influenced current thinking concerning intelligence by distinguishing between two broad dimensions of intellect: fluid intelligence and crystallized intelligence (Cattell, 1963; Horn & Cattell, 1967; Horn & Noll, 1997). **Fluid intelligence** is the ability to use your mind actively to solve novel problems such as recognizing relationships

What Do You Know about Intelligence and Creativity?

Answer each question true or false:

1. On the leading tests of intelligence, a score of 100 is average.
2. Scholars now conclude that there is no such thing as general intelligence; there are only separate mental abilities.
3. Individuals who are intellectually gifted are typically gifted in all mental abilities.
4. Intellectually gifted children do well in school but are more likely than most children to have social and emotional problems.
5. IQ predicts both a person's occupational status and his success compared with others in the same occupation.

6. On average, performance on IQ tests declines for people in their 70s and 80s.
7. Qualities associated with wisdom are as common among young and middle-aged adults as among elderly adults.
8. It has been established that children's IQs are far more influenced by their environments than by their genes.
9. How well a child does on a test of creativity cannot be predicted well from her IQ score.
10. Creative achievers (great musicians, mathematicians, writers, and so on) typically do all their great works before about age 40 or 45 and produce only lesser works from then on.

Answers: 1-T, 2-F, 3-F, 4-F, 5-T, 6-T, 7-F, 8-F, 9-T, 10-F

among geometric figures (■ **Figure 9.1**). The skills involved—reasoning, seeing relationships among stimuli, and drawing inferences—are usually not taught and are believed to represent a person's "raw information processing power" (Gottfredson & Saklofske, 2009). **Crystallized intelligence**, in contrast, is the use

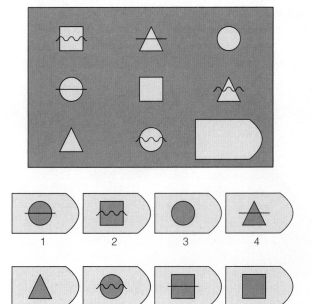

■ **Figure 9.1** An example of a problem used to assess fluid intelligence. Which of the 8 numbered pieces would you select to complete the design shown in the large box? If you chose #7, you are correct.

of knowledge acquired through schooling and other life experiences. Tests of general information (At what temperature does water boil?) and word comprehension (What is the meaning of *duplicate?*) are measures of crystallized intelligence. Thus, fluid intelligence involves using your mind in new and flexible ways, whereas crystallized intelligence involves using what you have already learned through experience.

Obviously, there is no single answer to the question *What is intelligence?* Nonetheless, some consensus has emerged from the vast amount of research conducted over the years on this construct. Intelligence is most often viewed as a hierarchy that includes (1) a general ability factor at the top that influences how well people do on a range of cognitive tasks; (2) a few broad dimensions of ability that are distinguishable in a **factor analysis**, a statistical technique in which test items are correlated to identify groups of items that correlate highly with each other but not with other groups of items (for example, fluid intelligence, crystallized intelligence, memory capacity, and processing speed); and (3) at the bottom, many specific abilities such as numerical reasoning, spatial discrimination, and word comprehension that also influence how well a person performs cognitive tasks that tap these specific abilities (Carroll, 1993; Horn & Noll, 1997).

One of the most significant contributions to the psychometric approach to intelligence occurred in 1904 when Alfred Binet and Theodore Simon were commissioned by the French government to devise a test that would identify "dull" children who might need special instruction. Binet and Simon devised a set of tasks measuring the skills believed to be necessary for classroom learning: attention, perception, memory, reasoning, verbal comprehension, and so on. Items that discriminated between typically developing children and those described by their teachers as slow were kept in the final test.

This forerunner of the modern IQ test was soon revised so that the items were age-graded. For example, a set of "6-year-old" items could be passed by most 6-year-olds but by few 5-year-olds; "12-year-old" items could be handled by most 12-year-olds but not by younger children. This approach permitted the testers to describe a child's **mental age (MA)**—the level of age-graded problems that the child is able to solve. Thus, a child who passes all items at the 5-year-old level but does poorly on more advanced items—regardless of the child's actual age—is said to have a MA of 5.

Binet's test became known as the **Stanford–Binet Intelligence Scale** after Lewis Terman of Stanford University translated and published a revised version of the test for use with American children. Terman developed a procedure for comparing a child's MA with his chronological age (CA) by calculating an **intelligence quotient (IQ)**, which consisted of MA divided by CA and then multiplied by 100 ($IQ = MA/CA \times 100$). An IQ score of 100 indicates average intelligence, regardless of a child's age: The average child passes just the items that age-mates typically pass; MA increases each year, but so does CA, so that typically IQ remains about the same. The child of 8 with a MA of 10 has experienced rapid intellectual growth and has a high IQ (specifically, 125); if she suffered brain damage and still had a MA of 10 at 15, she would have an IQ of only 67 and would clearly be below average compared with children of the same age.

The Stanford–Binet has been revised numerous times over the years and is still in use. Its **test norms**—standards of normal performance expressed as average scores and the range of scores around the average—are based on the performance of a large, representative sample of people (2-year-olds through adults) from many socioeconomic and racial backgrounds. The concept of MA is no longer used to calculate IQ; instead, individuals receive scores that reflect how well or how poorly they do compared with others of the same age. An IQ of 100 is still average, and the higher the IQ score an individual attains, the better the performance is in comparison with that of age-mates.

David Wechsler constructed a set of intelligence tests, collectively referred to as the **Wechsler Scales**, also in wide use. The Wechsler Preschool and Primary Scale of Intelligence (WPPSI-IV) is for children between ages 3 and 8 (Wechsler, 2012). The Wechsler Intelligence Scale for Children (WISC-V) is appropriate for schoolchildren ages 6–16 (Wechsler, 2014), and the Wechsler Adult Intelligence Scale (WAIS-IV) is used with adults (Wechsler, 2008). The Wechsler tests yield a verbal IQ score based on items measuring vocabulary, general knowledge, arithmetic reasoning, and the like, and a performance IQ score based on such nonverbal skills as the ability to assemble puzzles, solve mazes, reproduce geometric designs with colored blocks, and rearrange pictures to tell a meaningful story. As with the Stanford–Binet, a score of 100 is defined

Individually administered intelligence tests such as the Stanford–Binet and the Wechsler Scales assess a wide range of intellectual abilities that comprise intelligence.

LAURENT/AUBOURG/BSIP SA/Alamy Stock Photo

as average performance for the person's age. A person's full-scale IQ is a combination of the verbal and performance scores.

Scores on both the Stanford–Binet and Wechsler Scales form a **normal distribution**, or a symmetrical, bell-shaped spread around the average score of 100 (■ **Figure 9.2**). Scores around the average

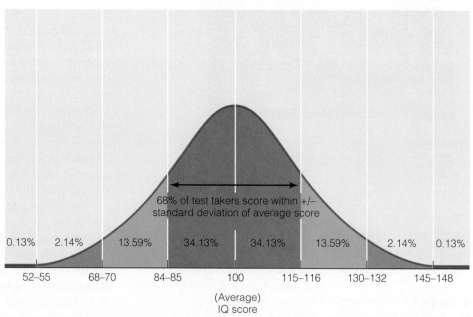

68% of test takers score within +/– standard deviation of average score

| 0.13% | 2.14% | 13.59% | 34.13% | 34.13% | 13.59% | 2.14% | 0.13% |

| 52–55 | 68–70 | 84–85 | 100 | 115–116 | 130–132 | 145–148 |

(Average)
IQ score

■ **Figure 9.2** A normal distribution curve showing traditional intelligence test scores in the classic bell shape around the average score of 100.

are common; very high and very low scores are rare. We also know that the standard deviation is 16 points for the Stanford–Binet and 15 points for the Wechsler Scales. The **standard deviation** is a measure of how tightly the scores are clustered around the mean score. As Figure 9.2 shows, about two-thirds of people taking the Wechsler test have scores between 85 and 115 (one standard deviation unit above and below the mean) and nearly 95% have scores between 70 and 130 (two standard deviation units above and below the mean). Fewer than 3% have scores of 130 or above, a score often used as one criterion of giftedness. Similarly, fewer than 3% have IQs below 70, a cutoff commonly used to define intellectual disability.

In the end, the intelligence tests guided by psychometric theories have emphasized general intellectual ability by summarizing performance in a single IQ score, and they have assessed only some of the specialized abilities humans possess. Critics believe traditional psychometric tests have not fully described what it means to be an intelligent person, and some have offered alternative ways of thinking about intelligence that represent challenges to the traditional view. Reading about these approaches in the following sections will help you capture the nature of intelligence and appreciate the limitations of the tests used to measure it.

Gardner's Theory of Multiple Intelligences

As noted, not everyone agrees that the psychometric approach that led to the development of IQ tests is the best way to understand intelligence. Howard Gardner (1999/2000) rejects the idea that a single IQ score is a meaningful measure of human intelligence. He argues that there are many intelligences, most of which have been ignored by the developers of standardized intelligence tests. Instead of asking, "How smart are you?" researchers should be asking, "How are you smart?" and identifying people's strengths and weaknesses across the full range of human mental faculties (Chen & Gardner, 1997). Gardner (1999/2000) argues that there are eight or nine distinct intellectual abilities, which are shown in ■ **Figure 9.3**.

Traditional IQ tests emphasize two of Gardner's multiple intelligences: linguistic and logical–mathematical intelligence, and to some extent they test a third intelligence, spatial intelligence, perhaps because those are the forms of intelligence Western societies value most highly and work the hardest to nurture in school. But IQ tests can be faulted for ignoring most of the other forms of intelligence. Although Gardner does not claim that his is the definitive list of intelligences, he presents evidence suggesting that each of the abilities is distinct. For example, it is clear that a person can be exceptional in one ability but poor in others—witness **savant syndrome**, the phenomenon in which extraordinary talent in a particular area is displayed by a person otherwise intellectually challenged (Treffert, 2010; 2014). Leslie Lemke, one such individual, is affected by cerebral palsy, blindness, and intellectual

disability, and could not talk until he was an adult (Treffert, 2010). Yet he can hear a musical piece once and play it flawlessly on the piano or imitate songs in perfect German or Italian even though his own speech is primitive. He clearly has a high level of musical intelligence despite a traditional IQ score of 58 (Treffert, 2014). Other savants, despite IQs below 70, can draw well enough to gain admittance to art school or can calculate on the spot what day of the week it was January 19, 1909 (Kennedy & Squire, 2007). Some scholars think that the skills shown by savants are so specific and depend so much on memory that they do not qualify as separate "intelligences." Analyses of **prodigies**, those endowed with one or more extraordinary abilities, similarly suggest that their skills are related to their exceptional working memory abilities as well as their elevated attention to detail, and not to exceptional intelligence, either *g* or *s* (Ruthsatz, Ruthsatz-Stephens, & Ruthsatz, 2014; Ruthsatz & Urbach, 2012).

Gardner has amassed evidence to show that each type of intelligence has its own distinctive developmental course. Many great musical composers and athletes, for example, revealed their genius in childhood, whereas exceptional logical–mathematical intelligence typically shows up later, after the individual has gained the capacity for abstract thought and has mastered an area of science. Gardner also links his distinct intelligences to distinct structures in the brain, arguing that the multiple intelligences are neurologically distinct.

Gardner's theory has been adopted by educators to help understand differences in how students learn and how instruction might be modified to better resonate with students who have different styles (Baum, Viens, & Slatin, 2005). In many cases, schools use a simplified version of Gardner's multiple intelligences by

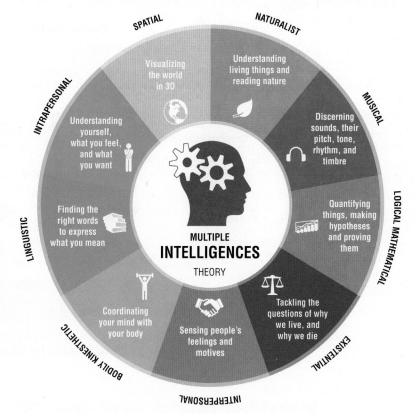

■ **Figure 9.3** Gardner's theory of multiple intelligences.

focusing on three of them: visual, auditory, and kinesthetic. These educators believe that some students learn by *seeing* (e.g., looking at PowerPoint slides, textbooks), others by *hearing* (e.g., listening to lectures, participating in discussions), and still others by *doing* (e.g., conducting experiments, acting out scenes from a novel).

Sternberg's Triarchic Theory and Successful Intelligence

Agreeing with Gardner that the traditional psychometric approach does not capture all that it means to be an intelligent person, Robert Sternberg (1985, 1988a, 2003, 2009b, 2011) has proposed a **triarchic theory of intelligence** that emphasizes three components that jointly contribute to intelligent behavior: practical, creative, and analytic intelligences (■ Figure 9.4).

The Practical Component

First, according to the **practical component**, what is defined as intelligent behavior varies from one sociocultural context to another. What might be intelligent in one context may be quite illogical in another. People who are high in this practical component of intelligence can adapt to the environment that they find themselves in, and they can shape the environment to optimize their strengths and minimize their weaknesses. These people have "street smarts," or common sense.

Just as intelligent behavior varies from one context to another, it also changes over time. Numerical abilities may not play as

important a role in intelligent behavior now that calculators and computers are widely used, for example, whereas analytical skills may be more important than ever in a complex, urban world. And certainly the infant learning how to master new toys shows a different kind of intelligence than the adult mastering a college curriculum. Thus, the definition of intelligence in the context of infancy must differ from the definition of intelligence in the context of adulthood.

The practical component of Sternberg's triarchic theory, then, defines intelligent behavior differently depending on the context in which it is displayed. Intelligent people adapt to the environment they are in (for example, a job setting), shape that environment to make it suit them better, or find a better environment. They can walk into a new situation, quickly evaluate it, and adapt their behavior to be successful in this new context. Although recognized by many people as an important form of intelligence, this real-world adaptability is not assessed by traditional intelligence tests.

The Creative Component

According to the **creative component** of the triarchic theory, what is intelligent when a person first encounters a new task is not the same as what is intelligent after extensive experience with that task. The first kind of intelligence, *response to novelty*, requires active and conscious information processing. Sternberg believes that relatively novel tasks provide the best measures of intelligence because they tap the individual's ability to come up with creative ideas or fresh insights.

In daily life, however, people also perform more or less intelligently on familiar and repetitive tasks (driving a car, for example).

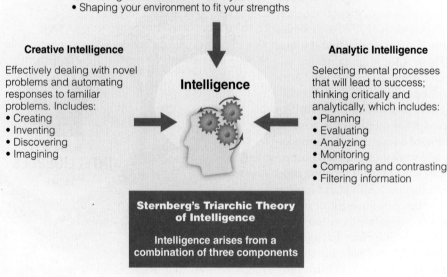

■ **Figure 9.4** Sternberg's triarchic theory of intelligence includes three components: practical, creative, and analytic intelligences.

This second kind of intelligence reflects **automatization**, or an increased efficiency of information processing with practice. It is intelligent to develop little "programs in the mind" for performing common, everyday activities efficiently and unthinkingly. Thus, according to Sternberg, it is crucial to know how familiar a task is to a person before assessing that person's behavior. For example, giving people of two different cultural groups an intelligence test whose items are familiar to one group and novel to the other introduces **culture bias** into the testing process, making it difficult to obtain a fair assessment of the groups' relative abilities.

The Analytic Component

The third aspect of the triarchic theory, the **analytic component**, focuses on the information-processing skills that produce answers to questions in traditional intelligence tests. These include thinking critically and analytically. Specifically, people who are high on this component can plan what to do, monitor progress, filter out irrelevant information and focus on the relevant, compare new information to existing knowledge, and evaluate outcomes.

As an information-processing theorist, Sternberg believes that the theories of intelligence underlying the development of traditional IQ tests ignore *how* people produce intelligent answers. He argues that a full picture of intelligence includes not only the number of answers people get right but also the processes they use to arrive at their answers and the efficiency with which they use those processes. So, to fully assess how intelligent people are, researchers must consider the *practical context* in which they perform (their age, culture, and historical period), their ability to respond *creatively* to new tasks, and their *analytic* strategies. Individuals who are intelligent, according to this triarchic model, are able to carry out logical thought processes efficiently and effectively to solve both novel and familiar problems and to adapt to their environment. Before moving on, review Sternberg's three components of intelligence with the examples provided in ● **Table 9.1**.

Successful Intelligence

Sternberg (1999b, 2003, 2011) expanded his triarchic theory to include what he calls the theory of **successful intelligence**. According to the most recent version of this theory, successful intelligence consists of being able to:

Robert Sternberg has advanced our thinking about intelligence by proposing a triarchic theory. What are the three components of this theory?

AP Images/Michelle McLoughlin

- establish and achieve reasonable goals consistent with your skills and circumstances,
- optimize your strengths and minimize weaknesses,
- adapt to the environment through a combination of selecting a good environment and making modifications to yourself or the environment to increase the fit,
- use all three components of intelligence—analytic, creative, and practical.

The path to successful intelligence, then, is figuring out a reasonable goal given your skills and circumstances, and positioning yourself to allow your strengths to blossom and weaknesses to fade. It also means that when circumstances or skills change, you can adapt or alter the environment or move on to something that is a better fit. Consider Bob's story. After struggling with academics throughout middle and high school, Bob decided that college was not his best option. Instead, he found himself "in the right place at the right time" as his grandfather was getter older and looking for some help with his landscaping business. Bob had always loved working outdoors and had an eye for how to arrange plantings to their best advantage, something for which his grandfather never

● **Table 9.1** Sternberg's Triarchic Theory of Intelligence: Examples of Three Hypothetical Students, Each Excelling at One of the Three Components

Component	Description of Hypothetical Student
Practical	Practical Patty is not terribly creative, nor does she get the best grades in the classroom. However, if you want to get something done, enlist Patty's help; she can figure out a way to get a job done or get from point A to point B efficiently.
Analytic	Many people rate Analytic Alice as a gifted student, and teachers love having her in their classrooms. Although not very imaginative, she is able to analyze a collection of ideas and provide a logical critique of them.
Creative	Creative Cathy does not get as "deep" into understanding the material as her classmate Alice. But she generates lots of new ideas and can be counted on to offer a different perspective in class discussions.

Source: Adapted from Sternberg, R. J. (1985). *Beyond IQ: A triarchic theory of human intelligence*. Cambridge, MA: Cambridge University Press.

had much patience. After a few years, when his grandfather was ready to retire, Bob knew he had most of the skills needed to take over the business. He realized, though, that the business had not really been modernized and that he himself lacked the bookkeeping skills that would be needed to maintain and grow the business. He took a few courses at the local college and talked to some of the customers about their needs. From this, he developed a marketing and growth plan for the business. The business thrived, but after a few years, Bob recognized that his customers increasingly asked about water gardens, something he had not previously offered. After considering the pros and cons of branching out, Bob decided he could handle it. After all, he didn't want to lose customers to his competitors just because water gardens had not been "his thing" in the past. He figured he knew enough to incorporate this alternative type of garden into the business.

Bob does not necessarily exhibit the type of intelligence that many people may think of when they consider the meaning of intelligence, that is, intelligence for academic tasks. However, Bob illustrates successful intelligence: establishing a goal that made sense for him given his situation, being aware of his strengths and weaknesses, and adapting to changes over time. Take a few minutes to consider your own goals, your circumstances, and your pattern of strengths and weaknesses. What path might be an intelligent option for you?

Creativity

According to Sternberg, creativity is one of the three main components of intelligence. Most scholars define creativity as the ability to produce novel responses appropriate in context and valued by others—products both original and meaningful (e.g., Runco & Jaeger, 2012). Thus, someone who comes up with a novel and useful idea is considered creative, whereas someone who comes up with a novel idea that has no apparent value may not be considered creative. Some researchers who study creativity, however, have concerns about limiting the definition of creativity to include only those ideas that are deemed useful (Simonton, 2012). After all, who decides what is useful, and who is to say whether something will be valued by someone at some time? Consequently, some researchers examine all novel outputs and not just those that are deemed useful or valuable.

Research shows some correlation between creativity and intelligence, although not a particularly strong one (see Kaufman & Plucker, 2011). It turns out that IQ scores and creativity scores do not correlate very well because they measure two different types of thinking. IQ tests measure convergent thinking, which involves "converging" on the best answer to a problem. If we could typecast someone as a *convergent thinker*, it would be the person who wants to know *the* correct answer to a problem. In contrast, creativity involves divergent thinking, or coming up with a variety of ideas or solutions to a problem when there is no single correct answer. Responses on divergent thinking tasks can be analyzed along three dimensions: the originality or uniqueness of the generated ideas, the flexibility of thinking or how many different categories are expressed by the ideas, and the fluency of the ideas (Runco, 2014). This last one—ideational fluency, or the sheer number of different (including novel) ideas that a person

can generate—is most often used to assess creativity because it is easy to score. Quick—list all the uses you can think of for a pencil. An uncreative person might say you could write letters, notes, postcards, and so forth; by contrast, one creative person envisioned a pencil as "a backscratcher, a potting stake, kindling for a fire, a rolling pin for baking, a toy for a woodpecker, or a small boat for a cricket" (Richards, 1996, p. 73).

This use of divergent thinking tasks to assess creativity reflects a psychometric approach. That is, it assumes that creativity is a trait that is held to a greater or lesser degree by individuals and can be measured. While the psychometric approach can be useful, it may not consider the multitude of factors that constitute creativity. This is where Sternberg's investment theory of creativity is valuable (Sternberg, 2012). According to studies of creative achievement, creativity emerges from a *confluence*, or coming together, of these six factors:

- intellectual skills that include the trio of abilities comprising Sternberg's triarchic theory of intelligence discussed earlier,
- enough knowledge of a field to have an understanding of the current state and what might be missing or needed in the field,
- a thinking style that "enjoys" mentally toying with ideas,
- a personality style that is open to some risk and is comfortable stepping outside the norm,
- motivation to stay focused on the task and not give up when faced with obstacles,
- an environment that supports and rewards creative output.

Thus, according to the investment theory, creativity is a confluence of many factors, each added in appropriate concentrations at the proper time. We might think of creativity as analogous to making a good soufflé: It requires certain ingredients—including intelligence—in specific amounts, sometimes combined in a particular order, baked at the proper temperature, and for the right amount of time. All these things must come together or your soufflé will be a flop. And so it is with creativity.

As you can see, although the two constructs are related, intelligence, with its focus on convergent thinking, and creativity, with its focus on divergent thinking, are distinct, although there may be tasks best solved through application of both types of thinking. In subsequent sections, as we discuss the intellectual profiles of children, adolescents, and adults, we will also consider the development of their creative selves. Note, however, that the infant is not included in our discussion of creativity because, to date, researchers have not developed a method for uncovering signs of creativity at this young age.

Checking Mastery

1. What is the difference between fluid and crystallized intelligence?
2. What is the main point of Gardner's theory of intelligence?
3. What three factors contribute to intelligence according to Sternberg?
4. How does creativity compare to intelligence and how is it typically measured?

• Making Connections

1. Imagine that you are chosen to head a presidential commission on intelligence testing whose task it is to devise an IQ test for use in the schools that is better than any that currently exists. Sketch out the features of your model IQ test. What would be included and excluded from your definition of intelligence? How would you measure intelligence? In what ways would your test improve upon the tests that are currently used?

2. Traditional IQ tests assess convergent thinking. Should they also assess divergent thinking? Why or why not?

9.2
The Infant

LEARNING OBJECTIVES

• Name and describe methods of assessing infant intelligence.

• Indicate the infant behaviors that are best connected to later intelligent behaviors and explain the reason for this connection.

As you saw in Chapters 7 and 8, the mind develops rapidly in infancy. But how can an infant's intellectual growth be measured? Is it possible to identify infants who are more or less intelligent than their age-mates? And how well does high (or low) intelligence in infancy predict high (or low) intelligence in childhood and adulthood?

Bayley Scales

None of the standard intelligence tests can be used with children much younger than 3, because the test items require verbal skills and attention spans that infants and toddlers do not have. Some developmentalists have tried to measure infant intelligence by assessing the rate at which infants achieve important developmental milestones. Perhaps the best known and most widely used infant test is the **Bayley Scales of Infant Development (BSID)** now in its third edition (Bayley, 2006). This test, designed for infants and toddlers ages 1 month to 42 months, collects information on social-emotional skills and adaptive behavior from parents and has three parts administered to the child:

• The *motor scale* measures the infant's ability to do such things as grasp a cube and throw a ball.
• The *cognitive scale* assesses how the young child thinks and reacts to various typical events such as reaching for a desirable object, searching for a hidden toy, and following directions.
• The *language scale* rates the child's preverbal communication and budding vocabulary skills.

On the basis of responses on the various scales, the infant is assigned scores for cognitive, language, motor, and social-emotional development, and all of these contribute to a **General Adaptive Composite (GAC)**. The Bayley GAC summarizes how well or how poorly the infant performs in comparison with a large norm group of infants and toddlers the same age.

Infant Intelligence as a Predictor of Later Intelligence

As they age, infants progress through many developmental milestones of the kind assessed by the Bayley scales, so such scales are useful in charting infants' developmental progress. They can provide valuable

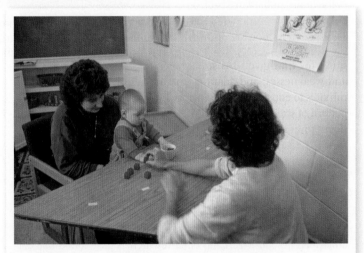

The Bayley Scales of Infant Development allow practitioners to evaluate an infant's performance relative to their peers on important developmental milestones.

Cliff Moore/Science Source

information to assist with diagnosing neurological problems and intellectual disability—even when these conditions are mild and difficult to detect through standard pediatric or neurological examinations (Honzik, 1983; 1986). But developmentalists have also been interested in the larger issue of continuity versus discontinuity in intellectual development: Is it possible to predict which infants are likely to be gifted, average, or intellectually disabled during the school years?

Not from their Bayley scores, at least not from the earlier versions of the Bayley (see, for example, Bode et al. 2014 for predictive validity of the most recent Bayley Scales). For the most part, correlations between infant Bayley scores and child IQ scores have been low, demonstrating that the infant who does well on the Bayley scales or other infant tests may or may not obtain a high IQ score later in life (Hack et al., 2005). True, the infant who scores markedly low on an infant test often turns out to be intellectually challenged, but otherwise there seems to be a great deal of discontinuity between early and later scores—at least until an infant is one year or older.

What might explain the poor connection between scores on infant development scales and children's later IQs? The main reason seems to be that infant tests and IQ tests tap qualitatively different kinds of abilities (Columbo, 1993). Piaget would likely support this argument; after all, the infant scales focus heavily on the sensory and motor skills that Piaget believed are so important in infancy. In contrast, IQ tests such as the Stanford–Binet and WISC-V emphasize more abstract abilities, such as verbal reasoning, concept formation, and problem solving.

Another explanation is that the growth of intelligence during infancy is highly influenced by powerful and universal maturational processes (McCall, 1981; 1983). Maturational forces (such as genetically influenced changes in the brain) pull infants back on course if environmental influences (such as growing up in an impoverished home and neighborhood) cause them to stray. For this reason, higher or lower infant test scores may be nothing more than temporary deviations from a universal developmental path. As the child nears age 2, maturational forces become less strong, so individual differences become larger and more stable over time. Consistent differences, related to both individual genetic makeup and environment, begin to emerge.

Rather than sticking with the traditional infant development scales focused on motor milestones, some researchers looked to the information-processing approach discussed in Chapter 8 to give new life to the idea that there is continuity in intelligence from infancy to childhood. Joseph Fagan and other researchers have found that certain measures of infant attention predict later IQ better than do the rather misnamed infant intelligence tests (Fagan, 2011). For example, speed of habituation (how fast the infant loses interest in a repeatedly presented stimulus) and preference for novelty (the degree to which an infant prefers a novel stimulus to a familiar one), assessed in the first year of life, have an average correlation of about 0.45 with IQ in childhood,

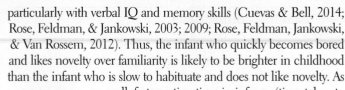

Infants who are able to quickly process new information and move on to the next 'new' thing may grow up to be more intelligent than their peers who needed more time to process new information.

Paul Baldesare/Alamy Stock Photo

particularly with verbal IQ and memory skills (Cuevas & Bell, 2014; Rose, Feldman, & Jankowski, 2003; 2009; Rose, Feldman, Jankowski, & Van Rossem, 2012). Thus, the infant who quickly becomes bored and likes novelty over familiarity is likely to be brighter in childhood than the infant who is slow to habituate and does not like novelty. As well, fast reaction time in infancy (time taken to look in the direction of a visual stimulus as soon as it appears) predicts later IQ about as well as speed of habituation and novelty preferences scores. From this information, we can characterize the "smart" infant as the speedy information processor—the infant who quickly becomes bored by the same old thing, seeks novel experiences, and soaks up information rapidly. There seems to be some continuity between infant intelligence and childhood intelligence after all (Fagan, 2011; Rose et al., 2012). Such Bayley scale accomplishments as throwing a ball are unlikely to carry over into vocabulary-learning or problem-solving skills in childhood. However, the extent to which the young infant processes information quickly can predict the extent to which he will learn quickly and solve problems efficiently later in childhood.

Checking Mastery

1. What do the Bayley Scales of Infant Development assess?
2. What characteristics or behaviors of infants are associated with later intelligence?

Making Connections

1. Are there specific activities that parents should be doing with their infants to ensure that they develop to their intellectual potential? What might some of these activities be?

9.3
The Child

LEARNING OBJECTIVES

- Summarize the research on stability of IQ scores over the course of childhood and indicate reasons why IQ scores might change or remain the same.
- Discuss the effects of poverty on children's intellectual abilities.
- Chart the path of creative abilities across childhood.

Over the childhood years, children generally become able to answer more questions, and more difficult questions, on IQ tests. That is, their mental ages increase. But what happens to the IQ scores of individual children, which reflect how they compare with peers?

The Stability of IQ Scores during Childhood

It was once assumed that a person's IQ reflected her genetically determined intellectual capacity and therefore would remain stable over

time. In other words, a child with an IQ of 120 at age 5 was expected to obtain a similar IQ at age 10, 15, or 20. Is this idea supported by research? As you have seen, infant Bayley scores do not do a very good job of predicting later IQ scores. However, starting around age 4 there is a fairly strong relationship between early and later IQ, and the relationship grows even stronger by middle childhood. We know this from such studies as the Munich Longitudinal Study on the Ontogenesis of Individual Competencies (LOGIC), which tracked various cognitive measures over a period of 20 years (see Schneider & Bullock, 2009; Schneider, Niklas, & Schmiedeler, 2014). The

	Correlation of IQ Scores			
Age at First (Earlier) Testing	Retested at Age 9	Retested at Age 12	Retested at Age 17	Retested at Age 23
5	0.66	0.60	0.54	0.48
7	0.78	0.75	0.64	0.58
9	–	0.84	0.72	0.66
12	–	–	0.89	0.88
17	–	–	–	0.95

Source: Schneider, W., Niklas, F., & Schmiedeler, S. (2014). Intellectual development from early childhood to early adulthood: The impact of early IQ differences on stability and change over time. *Learning and Individual Differences, 32,* 156–162.

correlations of intelligence scores at different points of time over the course of this study are summarized in ● **Table 9.2**. We can see that correlations are higher when the interval between two testings is shorter. Even when several years have passed, however, IQ seems to be a stable attribute. For instance, the scores children obtain at age 12 are clearly related to those they obtain 11 years later, at age 23.

These correlations do not reveal everything, however. They are based on a large group of children, and they do not necessarily mean that the IQs of individual children will remain stable over the years. As it turns out, many children show sizable ups and downs in their IQ scores over the course of childhood. Patterns of change differ considerably from child to child, as though each were on a private developmental trajectory (Gottfried et al., 1994). For instance, in one study, stability of scores was examined over a 2- to 3-year period (Watkins & Smith, 2013). For most of these children —three out of four—scores from one time to the next were relatively stable, with variations of just a few points. Indeed, the average difference in scores for the entire group of children was less than one-quarter of one point, indicating remarkable stability for the group as a whole. However, for the remaining one out of four children, the test–retest scores varied by 10 or more points. One child's score changed by a whopping 28 points (Watkins & Smith, 2013).

How do researchers reconcile the conclusion that IQ is relatively stable with this clear evidence of instability, at least for some children? They can still conclude that, *within* a group, children's rankings (high or low) in comparison with peers stay stable from one point to another during the childhood years (Sternberg, Grigorenko, & Bundy, 2001). But many individual children experience drops or gains in IQ scores over the years. Remember, however, that this relates to performance on IQ tests rather than underlying intellectual competence. IQ scores are influenced not only by people's intelligence but also by their motivation, testing procedures and conditions, and many other factors that we will discuss in this chapter. As a result, IQ may be more changeable over the years than intellectual ability.

Causes of Gain and Loss

Some wandering of IQ scores upward or downward over time is just random fluctuation—a good day at one testing, a bad day at the next. Yet there are patterns. Children whose scores fluctuate the most tend to live in unstable home environments; their life experiences fluctuate between periods of happiness and turmoil.

In addition, some children gain IQ points over childhood and others lose them. Who are the gainers, and who are the losers? Gainers seem to have parents who converse more with them, exposing them to a wide vocabulary, and offer more encouragement relative to the inevitable reprimands (Hart & Risley, 1995). Noticeable drops in IQ with age often occur among children who live in poverty. Poverty is often defined by low family income, but **child poverty** involves more than low parent income: It also involves low levels of meeting children's basic needs (see Lipina & Colombo, 2009). Thus, children who live in poverty often have inadequate health and dental care and nutrition; they live in overcrowded and unsafe neighborhoods; their families experience chronic stress; their relationships with parents are often not as affectionate or supportive; and they lack opportunities for cognitive stimulation that are commonplace in other homes. Numerous studies with animals demonstrate that being raised in an impoverished environment has a direct impact on brain development (see, for example, Markham & Greenough, 2004; Rosenzweig & Bennett, 1996). For example, rats raised in a large cage with a few other rats for company, wheels for exercising, and blocks to play with develop more neurons, more connections between neurons, and more glial cells supporting neurons than rats raised in isolation (Greenough, Black, & Wallace, 1987; Mohammed et al., 2002). The message is clear: The brain is influenced by the environment. Later in this chapter, we will consider more directly what happens when children are raised in impoverished environments.

The Emergence of Creativity

We often hear young children's play activities and artwork described as "creative." When does creativity emerge, and what is the child who scores high on tests of creativity like? To answer the first question, researchers have measured divergent thinking at different ages throughout childhood. Early on, it became apparent that preschool-aged children display fairly high levels of divergent thought—generating many original ideas. As ■**Figure 9.5** shows, creativity scores, as measured by *ideational fluency*, how many different ideas can be produced, increase until about third grade, level off during fourth and fifth grade, and then begin to decline rather significantly (Kim, 2011). Another measure of creativity, *originality*, the ability to produce original ideas, shows a sharp drop-off starting in sixth grade (see again Figure 9.5). Such declines may reflect pressures in middle school to conform to the group rather than be a "free spirit." Traditional classrooms tend to emphasize and reinforce convergent thinking, with tests constructed to assess whether students know *the* answer to a problem.

To address the second question, what the creative child is like, one group of researchers compared children who had high creativity scores but normal-range IQ scores with children who scored high in IQ but not in creativity (Getzels & Jackson, 1962). Personality measures suggested that the creative children showed more freedom, originality, humor, aggression, and playfulness than the high-IQ children. Perhaps as a result, the high-IQ children were

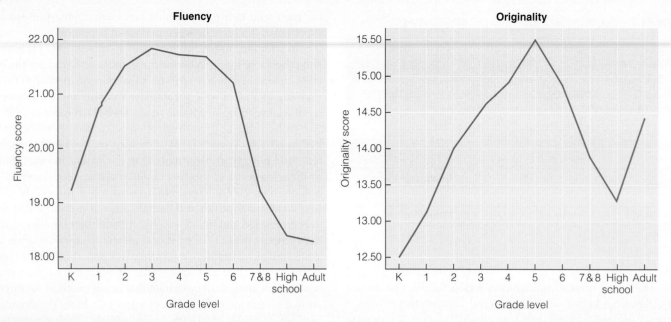

Fluency

Fluency score

Originality

Originality score

Grade level

Grade level

■ **Figure 9.5** Two measures of creativity. On the left, fluency scores increase from kindergarten to third grade, but then plateau and begin a marked decline from fifth grade on. On the right, originality scores peak in fifth grade, drop dramatically, and then increase from high school to adulthood. What factors might explain these patterns of creativity?

Adapted from Figure 1 (p. 288) of Kim, K. H. (2011). The creativity crisis: The decrease in creative thinking scores on the Torrance Tests of Creative Thinking. *Creativity Research Journal, 23,* 285–295.

more success oriented and received more approval from teachers. The unconventional responses of highly creative children are not always appreciated in the conventional classroom (Runco, 2014). Compared with their less creative peers, creative children also engage in more fantasy or pretend play, often inventing new uses for familiar objects and new roles for themselves (Kogan, 1983). They have active imaginations, and their parents are often tolerant of their sometimes unconventional ideas (Runco, 2014). Finally, creative children are more likely to be open to new experiences and ideas, as are their parents (Simonton, 1999).

As you will see later in this chapter, average IQ scores differ across racial and socioeconomic groups, but scores on creativity tests usually do not, nor do self-perceptions of one's creativity (Kaufman, 2006; Kogan, 1983). Moreover, genetic influences (a source of individual differences in IQ) have little to do with performance on tests of creativity; twins are similar in the degree of creativity they display, but identical twins are typically no more similar than fraternal twins (Plomin, 1990; Reznikoff et al., 1973). This suggests that certain qualities of the home environment tend to make brothers and sisters alike in their degree of creativity. What qualities? Although there is little research to go on, parents of creative children and adolescents tend to value nonconformity and independence, accept their children as they are, encourage their curiosity and playfulness, and grant them a good deal of freedom to explore new possibilities on their own (Harrington, Block, & Block, 1987). In some cases, the parent–child relationship is even distant; a surprising number of eminent creators seem to have experienced rather lonely, insecure, and unhappy childhoods (Ochse, 1990; Simonton, 1999). Out of their adversity may have come an active imagination and a strong desire to develop their talents. Although this may

be true for some creative individuals, it is certainly not true for all of them. Overall, though, creative abilities are influenced by factors distinct from those that influence the cognitive abilities measured on IQ tests.

Creativity takes many different forms.

Micheko Productions, Michele Vitucci/Alamy Stock Photo

1. Once children reach elementary school, how stable are their IQ scores as a group?
2. What is one reason for an individual's IQ score to increase and what is one reason for an individual's IQ score to decrease during childhood?

1. Would you want to know your IQ or your child's IQ? How might this knowledge affect you? Would you think or act any differently if you learned that you (or your child) had an IQ of 105 versus an IQ of 135? You might also consider whether teachers should know their students' IQ scores. What are some potential pros and cons of teachers having access to this information?
2. Would you rather have a child who has average intelligence but is highly creative or one who has high intelligence but average creativity? What are the pros and cons of each?

9.4
The Adolescent

LEARNING OBJECTIVES

- Describe the Flynn effect and what factors might account for this finding.
- Explain how IQ scores relate to school achievement.
- Discuss how schools and parents can foster creativity during adolescence.

Intellectual growth continues its rapid pace in early adolescence, then slows and levels off in later adolescence (Thorndike, 1997). As noted in Chapter 5, a spurt in brain development occurs around age 11 or age 12, when children are believed to enter Piaget's formal operational stage. Brain development may give children the information-processing speed and working-memory capacity they need to perform at adultlike levels on IQ tests (Kail & Salthouse, 1994). Thus, basic changes in the brain in early adolescence may underlie a variety of cognitive advances—the achievement of formal operations, improved memory and information-processing skills, and better performance on tests of intelligence.

Although adolescence is a time of impressive mental growth, it is also a time of increased stability of individual differences in intellectual performance. During the teen years, IQ scores become even more stable than they were in childhood and strongly predict IQ in middle age (Deary et al., 2004). Even while adolescents as a group are experiencing cognitive growth, then, each individual is establishing a characteristic level of intellectual performance that will most likely be carried into adult life unless the individual's environment changes dramatically.

Flynn Effect

Some evidence suggests that today's teens are smarter than their parents and grandparents were as teenagers. Indeed, over the 20th century, average IQ scores have increased in all countries studied, a phenomenon called the **Flynn effect** after James Flynn (1987, 1998, 1999, 2007, 2011), who focused our attention on this phenomenon. In the United States, the increase has amounted to about 3 IQ points per decade. So a group of adults born in, say, 1980, scores on average 3 points higher than a similar group of adults born in 1970 and 6–8

points higher than those born in 1960 (Trahan et al., 2014). ■ Figure 9.6 illustrates the gains in intelligence over a period of more than 50 years. Full-scale IQ scores have increased 18 points over this time, with scores on some subscales increasing as much as 24 points (for example, similarities and Raven's progressive matrices), others increasing 10 points (such as comprehension), and some increasing a slight 2–3 points (for example, information, arithmetic, and vocabulary). Further, Flynn (2007) presents data that suggest these trends extend

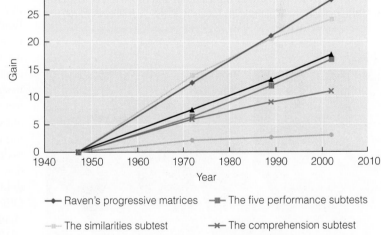

Key:
- ◆ Raven's progressive matrices
- ■ The five performance subtests
- □ The similarities subtest
- ✕ The comprehension subtest
- ▲ Full scale IQ
- ● Information and arithmetic and vocabulary

■ **Figure 9.6** Over a 50-year period, test scores on several measures of intelligence have risen substantially, illustrating the "Flynn effect." Are people really getting smarter? What factors might explain such a rise in intelligence test scores?

Source: Flynn, J. R. (2007). *What is intelligence? Beyond the Flynn effect*, Figure 1, p. 8. Reprinted by permission of Cambridge University Press.

back more than 100 years, leading him to ask, "How can our recent ancestors have been so unintelligent compared to ourselves?" (p. 9). How indeed?

Many researchers argue that increases of this size cannot be caused by genetic evolution and therefore must have environmental causes. For one thing, children today are better educated than earlier generations; 85% today complete high school, compared with just 5% in 1895 (Greve, 2006). But Flynn and others have suggested that improved economic conditions have brought improved nutrition and living conditions over the course of the 20th century, and this has contributed to the rise in intellectual functioning (Pietschnig & Voracek, 2015).

Researchers have examined average IQ scores by country and found that they are associated with the country's incidence and prevalence of infectious disease (Eppig, Fincher, & Thornhill, 2010). People in countries where rates of infectious diseases are high have, on average, lower IQ scores than those in countries where rates of infectious diseases are low. The researchers believe that infectious diseases, especially parasitic diseases that cause diarrhea in infants and children, divert energy from the brain and rob the brain of needed nutrients. As developing countries reduce airborne and water-borne diseases through vaccinations, clean water, and sewers, we can expect to see a rise in the average IQ scores of their citizens.

IQ and School Achievement

The original purpose of IQ tests was to estimate how well children would do in school, and they do this fairly well. Correlations between children's and adolescents' IQ scores and their grades range from 0.50 to 0.86, making general intellectual ability one of the best predictors of school achievement available (Deary et al., 2007; Neisser et al., 1996). Adolescents with high IQs are also less likely to drop out of high school and more likely to go on to college than their peers with lower IQs; the correlation between

IQ and years of education obtained averages 0.55 (Neisser et al., 1996). However, IQ scores do not predict college grades as well as they predict high school grades (Brody & Brody, 1976). Most college students probably have at least the average intellectual ability needed to succeed in college; success is therefore more influenced by personal qualities such as motivation. Overall, an IQ score is a good predictor of academic achievement, but it does not reveal everything about a student. Factors such as work habits, interests, and motivation to succeed also affect academic achievement.

Fostering Creativity

We noted earlier that there is a drop in creativity as children enter middle school. What happens during adolescence? In general, creativity, as measured by traditional divergent tasks or ideational fluency, remains rather depressed throughout adolescence, yet some evidence shows continuity between childhood scores on creativity tasks and later creative output during adulthood (Cramond et al., 2005). This suggests that adolescents may be putting their creativity temporarily "on hold," perhaps to focus on other pressing issues of this important developmental period, but their creativity is not lost. There is at least one measure of creativity—the ability to elaborate on ideas—that continues to increase across adolescence and does not begin to drop until adulthood (Kim, 2011). Elaborating on ideas is one form of creative thinking that may continue to be emphasized and rewarded in the classroom. Overall, the developmental course of creativity may vary depending on when children are pressured to conform and whether unusual answers are rewarded in school.

Is it possible to foster creativity? Training studies indicate that people can learn techniques to improve their creativeness (Ma, 2006; Scott et al., 2004). But training may only be effective if the person's environment supports and rewards creativity. Researchers have looked at individuals who demonstrate creativity in a particular field to try to identify the factors that contribute to their accomplishments. David Feldman (1982, 1986), for example, has studied children and adolescents who are prodigies in such areas as chess, music, and mathematics. These individuals were generally similar to their peers in areas outside their fields of expertise. What contributed to their special achievements? On the nature side, they had *talent* as well as a powerful *motivation* to develop their special talents—a real passion for what they were doing. Olympic gymnast Olga Korbut put it well: "If gymnastics did not exist, I would have invented it" (Feldman, 1982, p. 35). Other research confirms that internal motivation and a thirst for challenge are crucial elements of creative productivity (Sternberg, 2010a; 2010b; Yeh & Wu, 2006). Individuals with a positive outlook also seem more likely to display creativity, perhaps because they are more open to challenges and derive more pleasure from challenges (see Yeh & Wu, 2006). Creative thinkers have other personal qualities as well—they display a willingness to take risks and are able to put up with some ambiguity without becoming frustrated (Heilman, 2016; Sternberg, 2010a; 2010b).

On the nurture side, creative individuals seem to be blessed with *environments* that recognize, value, and nurture

Intelligence 'flows' into nearly all we do, but certainly the classroom offers unique opportunities to exercise our intelligence.

Cultura Creative (RF)/Alamy Stock Photo

their creative endeavors (Sternberg, 2010a; 2010b). Their environments allow them a certain degree of independence to explore different fields and acquire knowledge of their chosen field. According to Feldman (1982), the child with creative potential in a specific field must become intimately familiar with the state of the field if he is to advance or transform it, as the groundbreaking artist or musician does. Thus, building a knowledge base is a necessary, although not sufficient, component of creativity (Sternberg, 2006b). So parents can help foster creativity by giving their children freedom to explore and opportunities to experiment with ideas and activities. Likewise, schools can assist by encouraging idea generation, multiple correct answers, or multiple pathways to arrive at an answer, and elaboration of ideas.

Checking Mastery

1. Is creativity or intelligence more stable during adolescence?
2. What might might explain the rise in IQ scores over the past century?
3. What is one environmental factor that could help enhance creativity?

Making Connections

1. To what extent have your schools fostered creativity? Is this something that *can* be fostered in schools and *should* it be fostered in schools?
2. IQ scores stabilize in adolescence and are highly correlated with adult IQ scores. Given this stability, should greater use be made of IQ scores? If so, what would be one or two meaningful uses of IQ scores during adolescence?

9.5
The Adult

LEARNING OBJECTIVES

- Evaluate whether IQ scores are a useful predictor of occupational status and health status of adults.

- Explain how intelligence might be expected to change over adulthood.

- Analyze the connection between wisdom and intelligence and determine who might be most likely to develop wisdom.

- Summarize the research on creative endeavors during adulthood.

We turn our attention now to intelligence during adulthood. Do IQ scores predict achievement and success after people have left school? Does performance on IQ tests change during the adult years? And do IQ scores decline in old age, as performance on Piagetian cognitive tasks and some memory tasks does?

IQ and Occupational Success

What is the relationship between IQ and occupational status? Professional and technical workers (such as scientists and engineers) score higher on IQ tests than white-collar workers (such as bank managers), who in turn score higher than blue-collar, or manual, workers (such as construction workers) (Nyborg & Jensen, 2001; Schmidt & Hunter, 2004). The connections between intelligence and income and occupational prestige are striking when we look at findings from a longitudinal study of a large U.S. sample (Judge, Klinger, & Simon, 2010). ■ Figure 9.7 shows that over the nearly 30-year period of the study, general intelligence was significantly related to both income and occupational prestige. Further, the gap between those with higher intelligence and those with lower intelligence widened considerably over time. Those with higher intelligence started with a slight advantage for income and occupational prestige but quickly began rising at a faster rate than those with lower intelligence. Also, income did not plateau and occupational prestige did not drop among those with higher intelligence as they did for those with lower intelligence.

The reason for the relationship between IQ and occupational success is clear: It undoubtedly takes more intellectual ability to complete law school and become a lawyer, a high-status and higher-paying occupation, than it does to be a farmhand, a low-status and lower-paying occupation. However, the prestige or status of the occupation is not as important as the complexity of the work (Gottfredson, 1997; Kuncel, Hezlett, & Ones, 2004). Greater intelligence is required to handle more complex or cognitively challenging work. Those with higher intelligence obtain more education and training and they use this knowledge to tackle more demanding jobs, which leads to a faster and steeper rise to the top of the occupational ladder (Judge et al., 2010). Still, IQs vary considerably in every occupational group, so many people in low-status jobs have high IQs.

Now a second question: Are bright lawyers, electricians, or farmhands more successful or productive than their less intelligent colleagues? The answer seems to be yes, as correlations between scores on tests of intellectual ability and such measures of job performance as supervisor ratings average 0.30 to 0.50 (Drasgow, 2012; Neisser et al., 1996). Before we go further, though, we should note that not all scholars are convinced that there is a solid correlation between IQ and job performance (Richardson & Norgate, 2015). Instead, the correlation might reflect the role of other factors such as socioeconomic status, motivation, education, and opportunity. Those individuals raised in higher socioeconomic families typically live in better neighborhoods, go to better schools, and have better connections when it comes to landing internships and jobs. Whether it is intelligence per se, or other factors that correlate with intelligence, it does seem that more intellectually capable

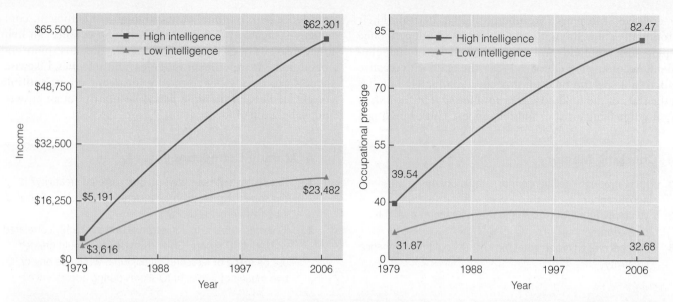

■ **Figure 9.7** The two graphs show income (*left*) and occupational prestige (*right*) of participants over nearly 30 years in relation to their intelligence test performance: Those with high intelligence start with a slight advantage over their less intelligent peers but quickly leave them behind. Why don't those with lower intelligence keep rising at the same rate over the years?

Source: Judge, T. A., Klinger, R. L, & Simon, L. S. (2010). Time is on my side: Time, general mental ability, human capital, and extrinsic career success. *Journal of Applied Psychology, 95*(1): 92–107. Figure 2. Copyright © 2010 American Psychological Association.

adults are better able to learn what they need to know about their occupations and to solve the problems that arise. This literally pays off (see again Figure 9.7): Individuals with greater cognitive ability earn more money than those with lower cognitive ability (Judge et al., 2010). However, as **Exploration 9.1** notes, intelligent people are by no means infallible.

IQ and Health

People who score higher on measures of intelligence tend to be healthier and live longer than those who score lower on these tests (see, for example, Gottfredson, 2004; and Leon et al., 2009). This connection between intelligence and health and longevity has now been confirmed by research in multiple countries. For instance, researchers in Scotland tracked nearly everyone born in that country in 1921 and 1936 who had taken an intelligence test during childhood (Deary, Whalley, & Starr, 2009). Following up on health and death records of these individuals decades later, researchers found that those who scored one standard deviation (15 points) below the average were less likely to be alive at age 76 and more likely to have experienced stomach or lung cancers and cardiovascular or coronary heart disease. Indeed, those children who scored in the top 25% on intelligence at age 11 were 2–3 times more likely to be alive 65 years later than those scoring in the bottom 25% (Deary et al., 2009). Similar results are emerging from a study in the United States that has tracked participants from adolescence to age 40 (Der, Batty, & Deary, 2009). Consistent with the Scotland research, higher intelligence in early adolescence is associated with fewer health problems at age 40.

A common explanation for this connection between IQ and health is socioeconomic status: Smart people may have better jobs, giving them the resources to obtain better health care. But when living conditions are statistically controlled (that is, held constant), there is still a connection between intelligence and health (Gottfredson & Deary, 2004). Similarly, providing equal access to health care reduces but does not eliminate social-class differences in health (Steenland, Henley, & Thun, 2002).

Research shows a connection between intelligence and health, perhaps because more-intelligent folks are knowledgeable of the value of preventive measures, such as applying sunscreen.

Blend Images/Superstock

● EXPLORATION 9.1

Intelligent AND Dumb?

If done properly, thinking can be hard work!

Wavebreak Media/Alamy Stock Photo

Are intelligent people always smart or are there conditions that might lead even the most intelligent among us to do dumb things or make poor decisions? Alas, yes. Keith Stanovich (2009; 2016) has even coined a term for this paradox: **dysrationalia**, which he defines as the inability to think and behave rationally despite having adequate intelligence" (Stanovich, 2009, p. 7). Stanovich argues that standard intelligence tests measure some aspects of what is considered to be intelligent, but miss a very important aspect, namely thinking rationally. Questions on intelligence tests have been carefully framed and worded to assess how test takers handle the information provided to them. But, as Stanovich notes in his book, *What Intelligence Tests Miss*, IQ tests do not assess whether a person can frame a logical question, collect relevant and unbiased data, and then critically assess this information and arrive at a decision based on rational thought. Outside of classrooms and intelligence tests, many of life's problems are unscripted and messy. We must determine the root of the problem, identify possible solutions, and then select the best option. So if we are intelligent, why don't we always solve problems

in the most logical or rational manner?

It turns out that, when it comes to thinking (and most other human behaviors), we are inclined to go with the easiest or most obvious solution first. And why wouldn't we? If there is a quick and easy way to get an answer, it can certainly be efficient to go in this direction rather than embarking on a long and difficult process. The key may be knowing when it is OK to stick with the quick and easy versus knowing when the long and difficult is needed.

Scholars have referred to this as the dual process approach to cognition, with two systems or two types of thinking (Kahneman, 2011; Toplak, West, & Stanovich, 2014). The operation of System 1 is automatic: An event occurs or a situation is presented to us and we respond quickly and almost automatically, *without thinking*. An advantage of System 1 is that an answer or response is arrived at in a very short amount time with very little effort, that is, it's easy. Unfortunately, this leads to the disadvantage of System 1 thinking, which is that the answer is not always correct. In contrast, the operation of System 2 thinking is slow and deliberate, and many times leads to a correct answer, an advantage, yet it does so by expending a great deal of our time and energy. Susan Fiske and Shelley Taylor (1984) first used the term "cognitive miser" to label our inclination to default to System 1, but the origins of this idea go back to Nobel prize-winning work on heuristics, or mental shortcuts, by Amos Tversky and Daniel Kahneman (Tversky and Kahneman, 1971, 1973; Kahneman & Tversky, 1973). People use mental shortcuts all the time to make decisions quickly and efficiently.

There are many different heuristics, but let's consider just one—the availability heuristic—as an example. To test this, Tversky and Kahneman (1973) gave participants this mental puzzle to ponder: "If a random word is taken from an English text, is it more likely that the word starts with a K, or that K is the third letter?" If you are like many folks, you immediately start thinking of words that begin with the letter K, and you also manage to think of some words that have K as the third letter. In the end, though, you probably came up with more words that begin with K than words with K as the third letter, making words that begin with K more available to you. Being able to think of more words that begin with K, the tendency is to conclude that it is more likely that a random word taken from an English text begins with K. If this was your answer, then you are incorrect. There are three times as many words with K as the third letter, but because these are harder to think of, this information is not readily available to us.

People along the full continuum of intelligence use heuristics or mental shortcuts to lighten their cognitive load. This helps explain how intelligent people can make some not-so-intelligent decisions. Ideally, what we should do is go ahead and 'allow' our minds to use a mental shortcut or apply System 1 thinking; after all, we will probably form an automatic response without even consciously deciding to do so. But, we should then stop and consider whether we need to apply more effortful cognitive processes, which will take more time and energy, but may help us avoid making an irrational and possibly costly decision. Finally, we need to keep reminding ourselves that we are just as fallible as the next person. We might be intelligent, but we can be just as likely to engage in some lazy cognitive processing as the next person.

So what else could be going on? Linda Gottfredson (2004) argues that good health takes more than access to material resources. It requires some of the abilities measured by intelligence tests, such as efficient learning and problem solving. In other words, successfully monitoring one's health and properly applying treatment protocols require a certain amount of intelligence. Consider the chronic illness diabetes. Successful management requires acquiring knowledge of the disease symptoms and course, identifying signs of inappropriate blood sugar levels, and making judgments about how to respond to blood sugar fluctuations. A patient's IQ predicts how much knowledge of diabetes she acquires during the year following diagnosis (Taylor

9.5 I The Adult   **281**

et al., 2003). Other research shows that many people with diabetes who have limited literacy, which correlates with intelligence, do not know the signs of high or low blood sugar and do not know how to correct unhealthy levels (Williams et al., 1998).

A study of nearly 10,000 adults examined the relationship between their IQ scores at age 11 and markers of health collected from blood samples at age 45 (Calvin et al., 2011). Blood samples were examined for two inflammatory markers associated with cardiovascular disease. Higher IQ scores at age 11 were associated with lower levels of these cardiovascular disease markers in adulthood. The connection was partly explained by differences in parental socioeconomic status between higher and lower IQ adults. Research on relationships between IQ and health is still relatively new, but it suggests that IQ influences socioeconomic status, which in turn influences health, and that IQ also influences health directly to the extent that smarter people are able to apply their intellectual skills to understanding and managing their health.

Changes in IQ with Age

Perhaps no question about adult development has been studied as thoroughly as that of how intellectual abilities change with age. We know that an individual's IQ score remains relatively stable from preadolescence (age 11) until well into older adulthood (Deary, Pattie, & Starr, 2013; Tucker-Drob & Briley, 2014). Ian Deary and his colleagues (2013) have examined stability of intelligence over a lifetime by following up with individuals born in 1921 who had completed an intelligence test at age 11 and were tested again at age 90.

In general, the findings of this remarkable longitudinal study show a high level of stability over many decades of life. The strongest predictor of intelligence in old age was intelligence at age 11. Such factors as education and socioeconomic status contributed only slightly to changes in IQ scores. Thus, where a person's IQ score falls within the spread of scores in a group is a good predictor of where this person's score will fall if retested with the same group later in life: High scorers tend to remain high scorers and low scorers tend to remain low scorers. Other longitudinal research confirms this conclusion of very stable intelligence over adulthood (Rönnlund, Sundström, & Nilsson, 2015; Schalke et al., 2013).

As we learned earlier from the research on IQ scores in childhood, even when there is high group stability, there are still bound to be some changes in individuals' IQs. This is true for adults as well. What might account for changes in IQ scores in adulthood? A comprehensive sequential study directed by K. Warner Schaie (2012) provides some evidence regarding the pattern of changes in IQ. Schaie's study began in 1956 with a sample of members of a health maintenance organization ranging in age from 22 to 70. They were given a revised test of primary mental abilities that yielded scores for five separate mental abilities: verbal meaning, spatial ability, reasoning, numerical ability, and word

fluency. Seven years later, as many of them as could be found were retested. In addition, a new sample of adults ranging from their 20s to their 70s was tested. This design made it possible to determine how the performance of the same individuals changed over 7 years and to compare the performance of people who were 20 years old in 1956 with that of people who were 20 years old in 1963. This same strategy was repeated at regular intervals, giving the researchers a wealth of information about different cohorts, including longitudinal data on some people over a 45-year period.

Several findings have emerged from this important study. First, it seems that *when a person was born* has at least as much influence on intellectual functioning as age does. In other words, there are cohort or generational differences in performance. This evidence confirms the suspicion that cross-sectional comparisons of different age groups have usually yielded too grim a picture of declines in intellectual abilities during adulthood. Specifically, recently born cohorts (the youngest people in the study were born in 1973) tended to outperform earlier generations (the oldest were born in 1889) on most tests. Yet on the test of numerical ability, people born between 1903 and 1924 performed better than both earlier and later generations. Inductive reasoning scores have increased with every cohort tested since 1889. Scores on verbal meanings increased until 1952 but dropped off in the three most recently born cohorts (Schaie & Zanjani, 2006). So different generations may have a special edge in different areas of intellectual performance. Overall, though, judging from Schaie's findings, young and middle-aged adults today can look forward to better intellectual functioning in old age than their grandparents experienced—more evidence of the Flynn effect.

Another important message of Schaie's study, and of other research, is that patterns of aging differ for different abilities (■ **Figure** 9.8). Fluid intelligence (those abilities requiring active

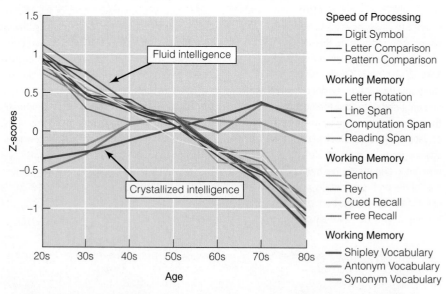

■ **Figure 9.8** The lines on this chart show that scores on measures of crystallized intelligence remain high throughout life. In contrast, scores on various measures of fluid intelligence are on a downward trajectory through all of adulthood, apparently starting as soon as most people complete their education.

Source: Park & Bischof (2013). The aging mind: neuroplasticity in response to cognitive training. *Dialogues Clin Neurosci, 15*(1): 109–119.

thinking and reasoning applied to novel problems, as measured by tests such as the primary mental abilities tests of reasoning and space) usually declines earlier and more steeply than crystallized intelligence (those abilities involving the use of knowledge acquired through experience, such as in answering the verbal meaning test used by Schaie). Consistently, adults lose some of their ability to grapple with new problems starting in middle age, but their crystallized general knowledge and vocabulary stay steady throughout middle and older adulthood.

Why is this? Tests of performance and fluid IQ are often timed, and, as noted in Chapter 8, performance on timed tests declines more in old age than performance on untimed tests does. This may be linked to the slowing of central nervous system functioning that most people experience as they age. When researchers control for processing speed, declines are not as steep (Scheiber et al., 2016). We have seen that speed of information processing is related to intellectual functioning across the life span. Not only is rapid information processing in infancy associated with high IQ scores in childhood, but young adults with quick reaction times also outperform their more sluggish age-mates on IQ tests, and adults who lose information-processing speed in later life lose some of their ability to think through complex and novel problems (Jensen, 1993). It is not just that older adults cannot finish tests that have time limits; declines in performance intelligence occur in later life even on untimed tests (Kaufman & Kaufman, 1997). The problem is that the slower information processor cannot keep in mind (that is, in working memory) and process simultaneously all relevant aspects of a complex problem.

You now have an overall picture of intellectual functioning in adulthood. Age group differences in performance suggest that older adults today are at a disadvantage on many tests compared with younger adults, partly because of deficiencies in the amount and quality of education they received early in life. But actual declines in intellectual abilities associated with aging are generally minor until people reach their late 60s or 70s. Even in old age, declines in fluid intelligence, performance intelligence, and performance on timed tests are more apparent than declines in crystallized intelligence, verbal intelligence, and performance on untimed tests. As you will soon see, declines in fluid intelligence can be reduced when adults remain cognitively stimulated through work or other activities (Weinert & Hany, 2003).

One last message of this research is worth special emphasis: Declines in intellectual abilities are not universal. Even among the 81-year-olds in Schaie's study, only about 30%–40% had experienced a significant decline in intellectual ability in the previous 7 years (Schaie, 2012). Moreover, although few 81-year-olds maintained all five mental abilities, almost all retained at least one ability from testing to testing and about half retained four out of five (Schaie & Zanjani, 2006). The range of differences in intellectual functioning in a group of older adults is extremely large, which means that anyone who stereotypes all elderly adults as intellectually limited is likely to be wrong most of the time.

Predictors of Decline

What is most likely to affect whether or not a person experiences declines in intellectual performance in old age? *Poor health*, not surprisingly, is one risk factor. People who have cardiovascular

diseases or other chronic illnesses show steeper declines in mental abilities than their healthier peers (Schaie, 2012). Diseases (and most likely the drugs used to treat them) also contribute to a rapid decline in intellectual abilities within a few years of death (Johansson, Zarit, & Berg, 1992; Singer et al., 2003). This phenomenon has been given the depressing label **terminal drop**. Perhaps there is something, then, to the saying "Sound body, sound mind."

A second factor in decline of intellectual performance is an *unstimulating lifestyle*. K. Warner Schaie and his colleagues found that the biggest intellectual declines were shown by elderly widows who had low social status, engaged in few activities, and were dissatisfied with their lives (Schaie, 2012). These women lived alone and seemed disengaged from life. Individuals who maintain their performance or even show gains tend to have above-average socioeconomic status, advanced education, intact marriages, intellectually capable spouses, and physically and mentally active lifestyles. Interestingly, married adults are affected by the intellectual environment they provide for each other. Their IQ test scores become more similar over the years, largely because the lower-functioning partner's scores rise closer to those of the higher-functioning partner (Gruber-Baldini, Schaie, & Willis, 1995; Weinert & Hany, 2003).

The moral is "Use it or lose it." This rule, applicable to muscular strength and sexual functioning, also pertains to intellectual functioning in later life. The plasticity of the nervous system throughout the life span enables elderly individuals to benefit from intellectual stimulation and training, to maintain the intellectual skills most relevant to their activities, and to compensate for the loss of less-exercised abilities (Dixon, 2003; Weinert & Hany, 2003; see also **Application 9.1**). There is still much to learn about how health, lifestyle, and other factors shape the individual's intellectual growth and decline. What is certain is that most people can look forward to

People tend to believe that age brings wisdom, which may help explain why U.S. Supreme Court justices such as Ruth Bader Ginsberg, pictured here, are often not appointed until middle adulthood and serve well into 'old age.'

ZUMA Press/Alamy Stock Photo

Intelligence Training for Aging Adults

Can you teach old dogs new tricks? And can you reteach old dogs who have suffered declines in mental abilities the old tricks they have lost? K. Warner Schaie, Sherry Willis, and their colleagues (1986; 2010; 2013; Willis & Schaie, 1986) have sought an answer to these questions by training elderly adults in spatial ability and reasoning, two of the fluid mental abilities most likely to decline in old age. Within a group of older people ranging in age from 64 to 95 who participated in Schaie's longitudinal study of intelligence, they first identified individuals whose scores on one of the two abilities had declined over a 21-year period and individuals who had remained stable over the same period. The goal with the decliners would be to restore lost ability; the goal with those who had maintained their ability would be to improve it. Participants took pretests measuring both abilities, received 5 hours of training in either spatial ability or reasoning, and then were given posttests on both abilities. The spatial training involved learning how to rotate objects in space, at first physically and then mentally. Training in reasoning involved learning how to detect a recurring pattern in a series of stimuli (for example, musical notes) and to identify what the next stimulus in the sequence should be.

The training worked. Both those who had suffered ability declines and those who had maintained their abilities before the study improved, although decliners showed significantly more improvement in spatial ability than non-decliners did. Schaie and Willis found that about 40% of the decliners gained enough through training to bring them back to the level of performance they had achieved when originally tested, before decline set in. What is more, effects of the training among those who had experienced declines in performance were still evident from one testing

to the next. And, as noted in Chapter 8, the benefits of cognitive training with older adults extends beyond improving their performance on laboratory-type tests; their daily functioning improved as well (Willis et al., 2006).

Other research shows similar evidence of *neuroplasticity*, or restructuring of the brain in response to training or experience, among older adults. Michelle Carlson and her colleagues (2009) conducted a pilot study with older women who were either trained for and then served as volunteers in the Experience Corps program or were on a waitlist for future participation and served as the control group. Experience Corps volunteers spend 15 hours per week for 6 months in classrooms assisting kindergarten through third-graders with their learning. Their activities draw upon memory, literacy, and problem-solving skills. The researchers took a look inside their brains using functional magnetic resonance imaging (fMRI). The results, seen in the figure in this box, are striking: Women

who volunteered in the classroom as part of the Experience Corps program showed significant gains in brain activity relative to the women who had not yet volunteered. Their activity changed the workings of their brains. Similar findings are emerging from other programs, such as the "Synapse" project (see Park & Bischof, 2013).

The larger messages? You can teach old dogs new tricks—and reteach them old tricks—in a short amount of time. This research does not mean that cognitive abilities can be restored in elderly people who have Alzheimer's disease or other brain disorders and have experienced significant neural loss. Instead, it suggests that many intellectual skills decline in later life because they are not used—and that these skills can be revived with a little coaching and practice. This research, combined with research on children, provides convincing evidence of the neuroplasticity of cognitive abilities over the entire life span (see Hertzog et al., 2009).

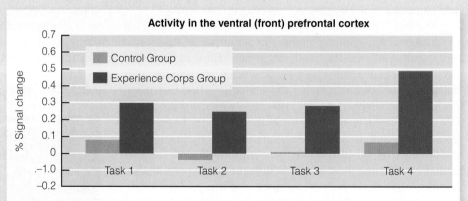

Activity in the prefrontal cortex was greater for older adults who engaged in 'mental calisthenics.'

Carlson, M. C., et al. (2009). Evidence for neurocognitive plasticity in at-risk older adults: The Experience Corps Program. *Journal of Gerontology A: Biological Sciences and Medical Sciences, 64*(12): 1275–1282. Figure 3. Reprinted by permission of Oxford University Press.

many years of optimal intellectual functioning before some of them experience losses of some mental abilities in later life.

Potential for Wisdom

Many people believe—incorrectly, as you have seen—that intellectual decline is an inevitable part of aging. Yet many people also believe that old people are wise. Indeed, this belief has been expressed in many cultures throughout history. It is also featured in Erik Erikson's influential theory of life-span development. Erikson says that older adults often gain wisdom as they face

the prospect of death and attempt to find meaning in their lives (see Chapter 11). Notice, too, that the word *wise* is rarely used to describe children, adolescents, or even young adults (unless perhaps it is to call one of them a *wise guy*).

What does it mean to be a wise person? Wisdom is not the same as high intelligence: There are many highly intelligent people who are not wise. Paul Baltes and his colleagues define **wisdom** as a constellation of rich factual knowledge about life combined with procedural knowledge such as strategies for giving advice and handling conflicts (Pasupathi, Staudinger, & Baltes, 2001). Similarly, Robert Sternberg (2003) defines a wise person as someone who can combine successful intelligence with creativity to solve problems that require balancing multiple interests or perspectives. Katherine Bangen and her colleagues (2013) searched through the literature for definitions of wisdom and found many variations, but most had certain features in common: "knowledge of life, prosocial values, self-understanding, acknowledgment of uncertainty, emotional homeostasis [balance], tolerance, openness, spirituality, and sense of humor" (p. 1254). The relative contribution of these factors to wisdom remains largely unknown.

Some older adults are blessed with wisdom, but the old wise person is by no means universal. Where we do see wisdom, does is arise from increasing age or from life experiences? Ursula Staudinger, Jacqui Smith, and Paul Baltes (1992) attempted to find out by interviewing young (ages 25–35) and elderly (ages 65–82) women who were clinical psychologists or similarly well-educated professionals in other fields. The goal was to assess the relative contributions of age and specialized experience to wisdom, based on the assumption that clinical psychologists gain special sensitivity to human problems from their professional training and practice.

These women were interviewed about a person named Martha, who had chosen to have a family but no career and who met an old friend who had chosen to have a career but no family. The women were asked to talk about how Martha might review and evaluate her life after this encounter. Answers were scored for qualities judged to be indicators of wisdom.

What was found? First, wisdom proved to be rare; it seems that only about 5% of the answers given by adults to problems such as these qualify as wise (Smith & Baltes, 1990). Second, expertise proved to be more relevant than age to the development of wisdom. That is, clinical psychologists, whether young or old, displayed more signs of wisdom than other women did. Older women were generally no wiser—or less wise—than younger women.

Age, then, does not predict wisdom well. Yet the knowledge base that contributes to wisdom, like other crystallized intellectual abilities, holds up well later in life (Baltes et al., 1995). Older adults, like younger adults, are more likely to display wisdom if they have life experiences (such as work as a clinical psychologist) that sharpen their insights into the human condition. The immediate social context also influences the degree to which wisdom is expressed; wiser solutions to problems are generated when adults have an opportunity to discuss problems with someone whose judgment they value and when they are encouraged to reflect after such discussions (Staudinger & Baltes, 1996). Thus, consulting with your fellow students and work colleagues and thinking about their advice may be the beginning of wisdom.

Finally, wisdom seems to reflect a particular combination of intelligence, personality, and cognitive style (Baltes & Staudinger, 2000). For example, individuals who have a cognitive style of comparing and evaluating relevant issues and who show tolerance of ambiguity are more likely to demonstrate wisdom than individuals without these characteristics. In addition, external factors influence the development of wisdom. Monika Ardelt (2000) found that a supportive social environment (loving family, good friends) during early adulthood was positively associated with wisdom 40 years later.

Our understanding of wisdom continues to evolve as new research emerges to help clarify what it is, how it develops, and how it is related to other mental abilities. It is safe to say that research on wisdom provides further evidence that different mental faculties develop and age differently over the adult years.

Creative Endeavors

Many studies of creativity during the adult years have focused on a small number of so-called eminent creators in such fields as art, music, science, and philosophy. A major question of interest has been this: When in adulthood are such individuals most productive and most likely to create their best works? Is it early in adulthood, when they can benefit from youth's enthusiasm and freshness of approach? Or is it later in adulthood, when they have fully mastered their field and have the experience and knowledge necessary to make a breakthrough in it? And what becomes of the careers of eminent creators in old age?

Early studies by Harvey Lehman (1953) and Wayne Dennis (1966) provided a fairly clear picture of how creative careers unfold (see also Runco, 2014, and Sternberg, 1999a). In most fields, creative production increases steeply from the 20s to the late 30s and early 40s, then gradually declines thereafter, although not to the same low levels that characterized early adulthood. Of course, there are notable exceptions. Michelangelo, for instance, was in his 70s and 80s when he worked on St. Peter's Cathedral, and Frank Lloyd Wright was 91 when he finished the blueprint for the Guggenheim Museum in New York City. Peak times of creative achievement also vary from field to field (Csikszentmihalyi & Nakamura, 2006). For instance, productivity of scholars in the humanities (for example, historians and philosophers) continues well into old age and peaks in the 60s, possibly because creative work in these fields often involves integrating knowledge that has crystallized over years. By contrast, productivity in the arts (for example, music or drama) peaks in the 30s and 40s and declines steeply thereafter, perhaps because artistic creativity depends on a more fluid or innovative kind of thinking.

How can researchers account for changes in creative production over the adult years? One explanation, proposed long ago (Beard, 1874, in Simonton, 1984), is that creative achievement requires both enthusiasm and experience. In early adulthood, the enthusiasm is there, but the experience is not; in later adulthood, the experience is there, but the enthusiasm or vigor has fallen off. People in their 30s and 40s have it all.

Dean Simonton (1999) has offered another theory: Each creator may have a certain potential to create that is realized over the adult years; as the potential is realized, less is left to express. According to Simonton, creative activity involves two processes: ideation (generating creative ideas) and elaboration (executing ideas to produce poems, paintings, or scientific publications). After a career is launched, some time elapses before any ideas are generated or any works are completed. This would explain the rise in creative achievement between the 20s and 30s. Also, some kinds of work take longer to formulate or complete than others, which helps explain why a poet (who can generate and carry out ideas quickly) might reach a creative peak earlier in life than, say, a historian (who may need to devote years to the research and writing necessary to complete a book once the idea for it is hatched).

Why does creative production begin to taper off? Simonton (1999) suggests that older creators may simply have used up much of their stock of potential ideas. They never exhaust their creative potential, but they have less of it left to realize. Simonton argues, then, that changes in creative production over the adult years have more to do with the nature of the creative process than with a loss of mental ability in later life. Creators who start their careers late are likely to experience the same rise and fall of creative output that others do, only later in life. And those lucky creators with immense creative potential to realize will not burn out; they will keep producing great works until they die.

What about mere mortals? Here, researchers have fallen back on tests designed to measure creativity. In one study, scores on a test of divergent thinking abilities decreased at least modestly after about age 40 and decreased more steeply starting around 70 (McCrae, Arenberg, & Costa, 1987). It seems that elderly adults do not differ much from younger adults in the originality of their ideas; the main difference is that they generate fewer of them (Jaquish & Ripple, 1981). Generally, then, these studies agree with the studies of eminent achievers: Creative behavior becomes less frequent in later life, but it remains possible throughout the adult years.

Checking Mastery

1. What do IQ scores predict during adulthood?
2. What are two factors that contribute to a decline in IQ scores among older adults?
3. How is wisdom different from intelligence?

Making Connections

1. As the administrator of a large health maintenance organization, would it be useful to collect information on intelligence from your clients? Why or why not?
2. In what ways are you smarter than your parents and grandparents, and in what ways are these two older generations smarter or wiser than you? What are some factors that contribute to generational differences in intelligence and age differences in wisdom?

9.6

Factors that Influence IQ Scores over the Life Span

LEARNING OBJECTIVES

• Analyze the research on genetic and environmental contributions to intelligence and formulate a conclusion about how these factors contribute to our intellectual abilities.

• Critique the research on race and intelligence to reach a balanced conclusion about whether these two constructs are connected in meaningful ways.

Now that we have surveyed changes in intellectual functioning over the life span, we will address a different question: Why do children or adults who are the same age differ in IQ? Part of the answer is that they differ in the kinds of motivational and situational factors that can affect performance on a given day. Yet there are real differences in underlying intellectual ability that need to be explained. As usual, the best explanation is that genetic and environmental factors interact to make us what we are.

Genes and Environments

The pioneers of the IQ testing movement believed that individual differences in IQ exist because some people inherit "better" genes at conception than others do. This position is still held by hereditarians who draw upon twin studies and other family research to demonstrate a genetic contribution to intelligence. As you saw in Chapter 3, identical twins obtain more similar IQ scores than fraternal twins do even when they have been raised apart. Moreover, the IQs of adopted children, once they reach adolescence, are more strongly correlated with those of their biological parents than with those of their adoptive parents. Overall, most researchers find that about half of the variation in IQ scores within a group of individuals is associated with genetic differences among them. But the influence of genes on intelligence varies across the lifespan. In infancy, genes account for somewhere around 20% of the observed differences in intelligence. This figure rises to about 40% in childhood, 50% in adolescence, and roughly 60% by adulthood. By old age, it may be as high as 80%, meaning that the observed differences in intelligence among elderly adults can be largely explained by the genetic differences between them (Plomin & Deary, 2015).

What exactly does it mean to conclude that there is a genetic influence on intelligence? First, we must make clear what it does *not* mean: Genetic influence, even if it is strong, does not mean that a trait, in this case intelligence, is "set in stone" or unresponsive to the environment (see Nisbett et al., 2012). Genes need environments for expression. In studies using U.S. samples, high socioeconomic status during childhood amplifies genetic influence on intelligence during adulthood (Tucker-Drob & Bates, 2016). That is, we see greater genetic influence on intelligence among samples from more enriched socioeconomic backgrounds and less genetic influence among those from impoverished backgrounds. This relationship among SES, genes, and intelligence is not evident in samples from Western Europe and Australia, possibly because of differences in social policies that allow for greater differences in education and health care in the United States than in other Western societies. Poverty, it seems, dampens the influence of genes on intelligence. In the United States, higher socioeconomic status during childhood is associated with better education and health care, and these factors boost intelligence as well as provide the opportunity for genetic influences to be more fully expressed (Bates, Lewis, & Weiss, 2013). In countries where healthcare and social-welfare programs are available to all citizens regardless of socioeconomic status, genetic influences are evident across all socioeconomic levels (Bates et al., 2013).

How does the environment influence intelligence? Research by Arnold Sameroff and his colleagues (1993) provides a broad overview of some of the environmental factors that put children at risk for having low IQ scores—and, by implication, some of the factors associated with higher IQs. These researchers assessed the 10 risk factors shown in ●Table 9.3 at age 4 and again at age 13. Every factor was related to IQ at age 4, and most predicted IQ at age 13. In addition, the greater the number of these risk factors affecting a child, the lower his IQ, a finding confirmed by other research (Lipina & Colombo, 2009). Which risk factors children experienced was less important than how many risks were experienced. Clearly, it is not good for intellectual development to grow up in a disadvantaged home with an adult unable to provide much intellectual nurturance.

In what ways do parents and the home influence children's intellectual development? Several of the risk factors in Table 9.3 relate to the socioeconomic status of the family environment (e.g., head of household is unemployed, mother did not complete high school, four or more children in the family). Sophie von Stumm and Robert Plomin (2015) looked at the relationship between socioeconomic status and IQ scores across childhood, from age 2 to 16. Socioeconomic status included parents' highest level of education, their occupational status, and family income. Over the nearly 15 years of the study, socioeconomic status was fairly stable.

■ Figure 9.9 shows what the researchers found for males and females when they clustered families into high, medium, and low socioeconomic status. Children who experience persistent (long-term) poverty average some 10–20 points below their middle-class age-mates on IQ tests. Socioeconomic status affects IQ scores as well as children's rate of intellectual growth (von Stumm & Plomin, 2015). Thus, the cognitive development of low-SES children is slower and their endpoint is lower—on average, they end up a full standard deviation below their age peers. Otto Klineberg (1963) proposed a **cumulative-deficit hypothesis** to describe how impoverished environments inhibit intellectual growth and these negative effects accumulate over time. What if socioeconomic conditions were to improve?

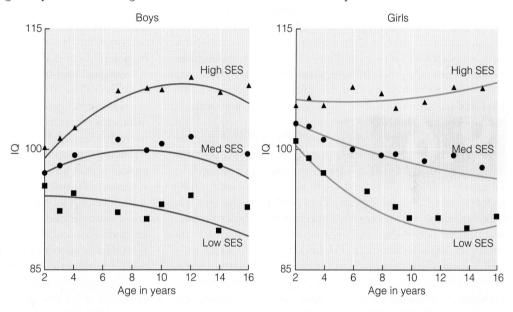

■ **Figure 9.9** Changes in IQ growth across childhood for boys and girls, according to SES background.

Source: Sophie von Stumm and Robert Plomin. (2015). Socioeconomic status and the growth of intelligence from infancy through adolescence. *Intelligence, 48,* 30–36.

● **Table 9.3** How 10 Environmental Risk Factors Affect IQ of Children at Age 4

Risk Factor	Average IQ for Children Who *Experienced* Risk Factor	Average IQ for Children Who *Did Not Experience* Risk Factor	Difference in Average IQ Depending on Whether Children Experienced or Did Not Experience Risk Factor
Child is member of minority group	90	110	20
Head of household is unemployed or low-skilled worker	90	108	18
Mother did not complete high school	92	109	17
Family has four or more children	94	105	11
Father is absent from family	95	106	11
Family experienced many stressful life events	97	105	8
Parents have rigid child-rearing values	92	107	15
Mother is highly anxious or distressed	97	105	8
Mother has poor mental health or diagnosed disorder	99	107	8
Mother shows little positive affect toward child	88	107	19

Source: Adapted from Sameroff, A. J., Seifer, R., Baldwin, A., & Baldwin, C. (1993). Stability of intelligence from preschool to adolescence: The influence of social and family risk factors. *Child Development, 64,* 80–97. Blackwell Publishing. Reprinted with permission.

The brain is responsive to environmental change—it has *neuroplasticity*. So improving the economic conditions of children's homes can improve their IQs (Duncan, Magnuson, & Votruba-Drzal, 2015). For example, Sandra Scarr and Richard Weinberg charted the intellectual growth of children adopted before their first birthday (Scarr & Weinberg, 1983; Weinberg, Scarr, & Waldman, 1992). Many of these children came from disadvantaged family backgrounds and had biological parents who were poorly educated and somewhat below average in IQ. They were placed in middle-class homes with adoptive parents who were highly educated and above average in intelligence. Throughout childhood and adolescence, these adoptees had average or above-average scores on standardized IQ tests—higher scores than they would have obtained if they had stayed in the disadvantaged environments offered by their natural parents. Similarly, research with French children who were adopted later than infancy—around age 5—indicates that increases in IQ are much larger among children adopted into affluent homes with highly educated parents than among those adopted into disadvantaged homes (Duyme, Dumaret, & Tomkiewicz, 1999).

Andrew Dickerson and Gurleen Popli (2016) distinguish between persistent poverty and episodic, or occasional, poverty. The researchers obtained measures of cognitive development for nearly 19,000 children in the UK Millennium Cohort Study tested at ages 3, 5, and 7 years of age. For those children who experienced persistent poverty, Dickerson and Popli's research confirms the fairly substantial negative impact of poverty on children's cognitive development. Further, even children who experienced episodic poverty early in life continued to show some ill effects of this at age 7. The effects were not as large as for those children experiencing persistent poverty, but the early disadvantage conferred by poverty may not be completely alleviated by an improvement in economic status.

Is it possible to identify characteristics of the home environment that are more (or less) important to cognitive development? A widely used assessment of the intellectual stimulation of the home environment is the **Home Observation for Measurement of the Environment (HOME) inventory** (Bradley et al., 2001). Sample items from the preschool version of a HOME inventory include:

- Parent responds verbally to child's vocalization or verbalizations.
- Parent does not scold, criticize, or spank child.
- Child's play environment is safe.
- Parent provides toys or other items appropriate to facilitate learning.
- Parent talks to child while doing household chores.

It turns out that scores on the HOME can predict the IQs of African American and European American children at age 3, with correlations of about 0.50 (Bradley et al., 1989; Cleveland et al., 2000). HOME scores continue to predict IQ scores between ages 3 and 6 (Espy, Molfese, & DiLalla, 2001). Gains in intellectual performance from age 1 to age 3, as measured by habituation and speed of processing, are likely to occur among children from stimulating homes, whereas children from families with low HOME scores often experience drops in performance over the same period. These findings are consistent across numerous countries and racial/ethnic groups, with a few exceptions (Farah et al., 2008; Lipina & Colombo, 2009).

What aspects of the home environment best predict high IQs? Studies using the HOME inventory indicate that the most important factors are parental involvement with the child and opportunities for stimulation (Gottfried et al., 1994). However, the amount of stimulation parents provide to their young children may not be as important as whether that stimulation is responsive to the child's behavior (a smile in return for a smile) and matched to the child's competencies so that it is neither too simple nor too challenging (Miller, 1986; Smith, Landry, & Swank, 2000). In short, an intellectually stimulating home is one in which parents are eager to be involved with their children and are responsive to their developmental needs and behavior. This may help explain why some research on intelligence finds a connection to family size and birth order, with firstborns and children from small families scoring just slightly higher (about two points) on IQ tests than later-borns and children from large families (see, for example, Zajonc, 2001a, 2001b; see also Sulloway, 2007).

Do differences in stimulation in the home really cause individual differences in IQ? Parents with greater intelligence are more likely than less intelligent parents to provide intellectually stimulating home environments for their children and to pass on to their children genes that contribute to high intelligence; that is, there is evidence of the gene–environment correlations described in Chapter 3. Maternal IQ, for example, is correlated with a child's IQ at 3 years and is also correlated with family income and the quality of the home environment (Bacharach & Baumeister, 1998). Although a mother's IQ is reliably associated with her children's IQ, a father's IQ is a less reliable predictor of his children's IQ.

So bright children are bright, not because of the genes they inherited *or* because of the home environment their bright parents provided. Instead, they are bright because genes and environments get combined in ways that allow children with particular genetic makeups to display high intelligence under favorable environmental conditions. Overall, intellectual development

Home environments can foster intellectual development when they provide appropriate play materials, a variety of daily activities, and have parents who are responsive to children's needs.

Hero Images/Alamy Stock Photo

seems to go best when a motivated, intellectually capable child, begging for intellectual nourishment, is fortunate enough to get it from involved and responsive adults.

Race and Ethnicity

Many studies, using samples from numerous countries, find racial and ethnic differences in IQ scores, which has sparked much controversy (see Daley & Onwuegbuzie, 2011). In the United States, for example, Asian American and European American children tend to score higher, on average, on IQ tests than African American, Native American, and Hispanic American children (Lynn, 2008b). Although some research suggests that racial differences on IQ tests have been shrinking in recent decades, other research shows little narrowing of the gap between, for example, black and white children on IQ tests (Dickens & Flynn, 2006; Murray, 2006; Yeung & Pfeiffer, 2009). Different subcultural groups sometimes show distinctive profiles of mental abilities; for example, black children often do well on verbal tasks, whereas Hispanic children, perhaps because of language differences, tend to excel on nonverbal items (Lynn, 2009; Taylor & Richards, 1991). It is essential to keep in mind that we are talking about *group averages*. Like the IQ scores of white children, those of minority children run the range from intellectually disabled to gifted. Researchers certainly cannot predict an individual's IQ merely on the basis of racial or ethnic identity. Indeed, lumping people together based on some notion of a common racial background makes little sense to many scientists who find that the variability within groups and the overlap between groups renders the group concept meaningless (Daley & Onwuegbuzie, 2011). Having said that, why do these average group differences exist? Consider the following hypotheses: bias in the tests, motivational factors, genetic differences among groups, and environmental differences among groups.

Biased Tests?

Racial differences in IQ tests may be attributable to culture bias in testing; that is, IQ tests may be more appropriate for children from white middle-class backgrounds than for those from other subcultural groups. Low-income African American children who speak a dialect of English (such as Ebonics or Black English) different from that spoken by middle-class European American children, as well as Hispanic children who hear Spanish rather than English at home, may not understand some test instructions or items. What is more, their experiences may not allow them to become familiar with some of the information called for on the tests (for example, What is a 747? Who wrote *Hamlet*?).

Minority-group children often do not have as much exposure to the culture reflected in the tests as nonminority children do. If IQ tests assess "proficiency in European American culture," minority children are bound to look deficient (Helms, 1992). Using IQ tests designed to be fair to all ethnic groups and introducing procedures to help minority children feel more comfortable and motivated can cut the usual IQ gap between African American and European American children in half (Kaufman, Kamphaus, & Kaufman, 1985). But even though standardized IQ test items sometimes have a white middle-class flavor, group differences in IQ probably cannot

be traced solely to test bias. Culture-fair IQ tests include items that should be equally unfamiliar (or familiar) to people from all ethnic groups and social classes—for example, items that require completing a geometric design with a piece that matches the rest of the design. Still, racial and ethnic differences emerge on such tests. In addition, IQ tests predict future school achievement as well for African Americans and other minorities as they do for European Americans (Neisser et al., 1996).

Motivational Differences?

Another possibility is that minority individuals are not motivated to do their best in testing situations because they are anxious or resist being judged by an examiner who is often of a different racial/ethnic background (Huang, 2009; Ogbu, 1994; Steele, 1997). Disadvantaged children score some 7–10 points higher when they are given time to get to know a friendly examiner or are given a mix of easy and hard items so that they do not become discouraged by a long string of difficult items (Zigler et al., 1982). Even though most children do better with a friendly examiner, it seems that African American children, even those from middle-class homes, are often less comfortable in testing situations than white middle-class children are (Moore, 1986). Minority children may be less likely to see value to themselves for performing well on a test (Okagaki, 2001). And their peers may accuse (or tease) them of "acting white" if they place too much emphasis on academic success and strong test scores, values that they may associate with white culture.

Claude Steele and his colleagues have argued that the performance of African Americans is especially likely to suffer whenever negative stereotypes of their group come into play (Steele, 1997, 1999; Steele & Aronson, 1995; see also Sackett, Hardison, & Cullen, 2004). In one study, female students at Stanford University were given difficult test items. Some students were told that they were taking a test of verbal abilities and would get feedback about their strengths and weaknesses; others were told that they were going to do some verbal problems but that their ability would not be evaluated. As ■ Figure 9.10 shows, African American students performed poorly when they were led to believe that the test

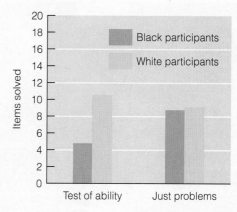

■ **Figure 9.10** African American students perform poorly on tests of mental abilities when they think they are taking a test that may result in their being stereotyped as unintelligent.

Source: Steele, C. M., & Aronson, J. (1995). Stereotype threat and the intellectual test performance of African Americans. *Journal of Personality and Social Psychology, 69,* 797–811. © American Psychological Association. Reprinted by permission.

would reveal their level of intellectual ability, but performed more like European American students when they did not think their ability would be judged. Even being asked to identify their race in a personal information section at the start of a test of intellectual ability can undermine the performance of African American college students (Steele & Aronson, 1995).

Why? Steele concluded that African Americans perform poorly on IQ tests partly because of stereotype threat—fear that they will be judged to have the qualities associated with negative stereotypes of African Americans (see also Aronson et al., 1999). It is not that African Americans have internalized stereotypes and believe they are intellectually inferior, according to Steele. Instead, they become anxious and unable to perform well in testing situations that arouse concerns about being negatively stereotyped.

Gregory Walton and Steven Spencer (2009) conducted two meta-analyses of the effects of stereotype threat on test performance of thousands of students. They found substantial effects on SAT scores, the standardized test taken by many college-bound high school students. Stereotype threat seems to account for 40 points of the score gap between majority (white) and nonmajority (black and Hispanic) students. Thus, minority student performance is underestimated as a result of pervasive negative stereotypes.

On the positive side, other research has demonstrated that positive stereotypes about a group can increase the performance of members of that group. Margaret Shih and her colleagues (Shih, Pittinsky, & Ambady, 1999) gave Asian American women a math test under one of three conditions. In one, their identity as women was made noticeable; in another, their Asian American identity was made evident; and in a third condition, no identity was emphasized. Consistent with stereotypes, these women performed worse when their gender was emphasized and better when their ethnic background was emphasized, relative to the group that was not primed to think about either identity. So stereotypes can either hinder or enhance performance, depending on whether a person identifies with a group that is viewed negatively or positively on the dimension measured.

How does stereotype threat operate to potentially affect the test performance of this young African American woman?

© Superstudio/Getty Images

The effects of stereotype threat can be reduced by providing students with a mentor. Catherine Good, Joshua Aronson, and Michael Inzlicht (2003) had college students serve as mentors to seventh-graders who were likely to experience stereotype threat as a result of being female, impoverished, and a member of a minority group. The mentors encouraged students to interpret their academic troubles as a result of the transition to a new school for seventh grade. In addition, they talked about intelligence being flexible and responsive to new learning. Following such mentoring, the students performed better on standardized tests than students who did not receive mentoring. These findings provide a practical means for eliminating or reducing the negative influence of stereotype threat. Of course, eliminating the negative stereotypes that create the threat should also be a goal.

Genetic Factors?

We discussed the overall influence of genetic factors on intelligence, but is there any evidence that genetic differences *between* racial or ethnic groups account for different levels of performance? This is perhaps one of the most controversial ideas in psychology, and it has sparked much heated debate. Scholars such as Arthur Jensen (1969) and Herrnstein and Murray (1994) have suggested that IQ differences between European Americans and African Americans may be because of genetic differences between the races, and they have written books to present their positions.

However, most psychologists do not think the evidence that heredity contributes to *within-group* differences says much about the reasons for *between-group* differences. Consider this analogy from Richard Lewontin (1976): Suppose that corn seeds with different genetic makeups are randomly drawn from a bag and planted in two fields—one that has terrible soil with no nutrients and one that has rich, fertile soil. Because all the plants *within* each field were grown in the same soil, their differences in height would have to be because of differences in genetic makeup. A genetic explanation of differences would fit. But if the plants in the fertile field are generally taller than those in the nonfertile field, this *between-field* variation must be entirely because of environment. Similarly, even though genes partially explain individual differences in IQ *within* African American and European American groups, the average difference *between* the racial groups may still reflect nothing more than differences in the environments they typically experience. There is no direct evidence that differences in genetic makeup between the races account for average group differences in IQ (Neisser et al., 1996).

Environmental Influences?

It is time, then, to return to an environmental hypothesis about racial and ethnic differences in IQ. Many of the intellectual and academic differences attributed to race or ethnicity probably reflect racial and ethnic differences in socioeconomic status instead (Patterson, Kupersmidt, & Vaden, 1990). As noted earlier, placement in more advantaged homes has allowed lower-income African American children to equal or exceed the average IQ in the general population and to exceed the IQs of comparable African American children raised in more disadvantaged environments by 20 points (Moore, 1986; Scarr & Weinberg, 1983; Weinberg et al., 1992). This could not have happened if African American children were genetically deficient.

The major message of this research is that children, whatever their racial background, perform better on IQ tests when they grow up in intellectually stimulating environments with involved, responsive parents and are exposed to the "culture of the tests and the schools" (Scarr & Weinberg, 1983, p. 261). How much of the racial gap in IQ can be explained by racial differences in neighborhood and family socioeconomic conditions, mother's education, and qualities of the home environment? Jeanne Brooks-Gunn, Pamela Klebanov, and Greg Duncan (1996) used statistical procedures to correct for these environmental differences between African American and European American children so that they could estimate what the IQ difference would be if the two racial groups had been raised in similar environments. Without any controls for environmental differences, there was an IQ gap of 18 points. The gap narrowed to 8 points when family and neighborhood income levels were controlled and was reduced to 3 points, a trivial difference, when racial differences in the provision of a stimulating home environment (HOME scores) were also controlled. In short, the fact that more African American than European American children live in poverty and have limited learning opportunities at home has a lot to do with racial difference in average IQ scores. Reducing poverty and offering more early developmental programs to offset the costs of impoverished home environments would go a long way toward eliminating racial differences in intellectual performance.

● Checking Mastery

1. How does home environment, as measured with the HOME inventory, influence IQ scores?
2. What are two hypotheses about why IQ tests yield racial/ethnic differences in scores?

● Making Connections

1. The Maori are a socioeconomically disadvantaged group in New Zealand, a country colonized by the British long ago. Maori children typically score lower on IQ tests than children of British background. Knowing what you know about minorities in the United States, what are your top two hypotheses about why Maori children perform relatively poorly, and how might you test these hypotheses?
2. What are two or three things that society—schools, local governments, and parents—can do to ensure that children born into poverty are not intellectually disadvantaged by this circumstance?
3. Considering material from this chapter as well as material from Chapter 3 on genetic influences, evaluate the relative contributions of nature and nurture to intelligence. Does one or the other have a greater contribution to intelligence? How do their effects combine? What evidence supports your position?

9.7
The Extremes of Intelligence

LEARNING OBJECTIVES

- Distinguish among different levels of intellectual disability.
- Summarize the likely causes of intellectual disability and what efforts might help reduce rates of intellectual disability.
- Explain the criteria used to identify someone as gifted.
- Trace the likely developmental path of a gifted individual through the life span.
- Compare and contrast, integrating where possible, the various theoretical perspectives on cognitive development covered in Chapters 7, 8, and now 9.

Although we have identified some of the factors that contribute to individual differences in intellectual performance, you cannot fully appreciate the magnitude of these differences without considering people at the extremes of the IQ continuum: gifted at one end and intellectually disabled at the other end.

Intellectual Disability

Intellectual disability, or mental retardation as it was called for many decades, is defined as significantly below-average intellectual functioning with limitations in areas of adaptive behavior such as self-care and social skills, originating before age 18 (see American Association on Intellectual and Developmental Disabilities., 2016; Schalock et al., 2010). An IQ score of 70–75 or lower suggests a limitation in intellectual functioning. This, along with difficulties meeting age-appropriate expectations in important areas of everyday functioning, is indicative of intellectually disability. Thus, intellectual disability is not merely a deficiency within the person; rather, it is the product of the interaction between person and environment, strongly influenced by the type and level of supportive help the individual receives. If this sounds familiar to you, perhaps you are thinking of Fischer's dynamic skill theory, discussed in Chapter 8, which proposed that skills can be optimized with a high level of support. A person with an IQ score of 65 in a supportive environment that is structured in ways that allow the individual to fit in and flourish may not be considered disabled in this environment. However, in an environment with different expectations and support, this same individual may be viewed as disabled.

Individuals with intellectual disability differ greatly in their levels of functioning (● Table 9.4). An adult with an IQ in the range of about 52–70 is likely to have a mental age comparable

● Table 9.4 Levels and Characteristics of Intellectual Disability

	Level			
	Mild	**Moderate**	**Severe**	**Profound**
Approximate Range of IQ Scores	52–70	35–51	20–34	Below 19
Degree of Independence	Usually independent	Some independence; needs some supervision	May be semi-independent with close supervision	Dependent; needs constant supervision
Educational Achievement	Can do some academic work—usually to sixth-grade level; focus is on career	Focus is on daily living skills rather than academics; some career training	Focus is on self-care (toileting, dressing, eating) and communication skills	Focus is on self-care, mobility, and basic communication education

Source: Adapted from Carr, A. & O'Reilly, G. (2016). Diagnosis, classification, and epidemiology. In A. Carr, C. Linehan, G. O'Reilly, P. N. Walsh, & J. McEvoy (Eds.), *The Handbook of Intellectual Disability and Clinical Psychology Practice*, 2nd ed. New York, NY: Routledge.

to that of an 8- to 12-year-old child. Individuals with mild intellectual disability can learn both academic and practical skills in school, and they can potentially work and live independently as adults. Many of these individuals are integrated into regular classrooms, where they excel academically and socially relative to comparable individuals who are segregated into special classrooms (Freeman, 2000). At the other end of the continuum, individuals with IQs below 20–25 and mental ages below 3 years ("profoundly disabled") show major delays in all areas of development and require basic care, sometimes in institutional settings. However, they, too, can benefit considerably from training.

Intellectual disability has many causes. Those who are severely and profoundly disabled are often affected by "organic" conditions, meaning that their disability is because of some identifiable biological cause associated with hereditary factors, diseases, or injuries. Down syndrome, the condition associated with an extra 21st chromosome, and phenylketonuria (PKU) are familiar examples of conditions causing intellectual disability that are associated with genetic factors (Gilissen et al., 2014; Roizen, 2013). Less common is the genetic condition that leads to Williams Syndrome, associated with IQ scores in the range of mild intellectual disability (Hodapp et al., 2011). Other forms of organic disability are associated with prenatal risk factors—an alcoholic mother, exposure to rubella, and so on (Paulson, 2013; see also Chapter 4). Because many such children are seriously delayed or have physical defects, they can often be identified at birth or during infancy and come from all socioeconomic levels. However, most cases of intellectual disability have no identifiable organic cause; they are characterized by milder symptoms and appear to result from some combination of genetic endowment and environmental factors (Batshaw, Gropman, & Lanpher, 2013). Not surprisingly, then, these children often come from poor areas, have neglectful or abusive families, and frequently have a parent or sibling who is also disabled (Batshaw et al., 2013; Zigler, 1995).

Historically, about 3% of school-age children have been classified with intellectual disability, although this rate has decreased as fewer children today are diagnosed with mild disability (Patton, 2000). Oftentimes, these children have associated impairments, such as cerebral palsy, behavioral problems, physical impairments,

or sensory disorders. As for children not diagnosed at birth, those with milder disabilities are typically diagnosed when, as toddlers, they fail to meet developmental milestones at a typical age. Once children are diagnosed, their parents experience complex reactions to their child and the disability itself (Boström, Broberg, & Hwang, 2010). Parents—mothers more so than fathers—of intellectually disabled children report higher levels of stress than parents of nondisabled children, but this stress is reduced where there are higher levels of marital and parenting satisfaction (Gerstein et al., 2009; Hill & Rose, 2009).

What becomes of these children as they grow up? Generally, they proceed along the same paths and through the same sequences of developmental milestones as other children do, although often at a slower rate (Hodapp et al., 2011). Their IQs remain low because they do not achieve the same level of growth that others do. Like nondisabled people, they show signs of intellectual aging in later life, especially on tests that require speed (Devenny et al., 1996). Individuals with Down syndrome may experience even greater intellectual deterioration later in life because they are at risk for premature Alzheimer's disease (Roizen, 2013).

As for their outcomes in life, consider a series of follow-up studies with a group of individuals with intellectual disabilities known as the "Camberwell Cohort" for the region of England from where they were originally recruited (Beadle-Brown, Murphy, & DiTerlizzi, 2009; Beadle-Brown, Murphy, & Wing, 2005, 2006). In their 40s, about 50% lived in community group homes, 25% lived with their family, 20% lived in a larger residential facility, and the remainder had some other type of living arrangement. Social skills, important to daily interactions with others, remained largely unchanged over the 25-year period of study. But for those who, as children, started out more socially impaired than others in the sample, social impairments tended to worsen with age, possibly because social demands increased in adulthood or because support in social situations was diminished. The combination of intellectual disability and social impairment led to a poor or fair overall outcome for most of the individuals in the cohort. Not surprisingly, those who were not as intellectually disabled and did not have associated impairments had more favorable outcomes.

The results from the Camberwell Cohort suggest that overall quality of life is lower for adults diagnosed with intellectual disability early in life. However, outcomes varied and were related to severity of the disability. Other research shows a relationship between life span and intellectual disability, with shorter life-spans among those with greater intellectual disabilities (Arvio, Salokivi, & Bjelogrlic-Laakso, 2016). Despite the relatively lackluster outcomes for these individuals, there are some promising findings. Fewer folks with intellectual disabilities are living in what might be considered an institutional setting; most live in the community, either in small group homes or with their family, and participate in typical community activities. This is a marked improvement from previous decades, when nearly everyone with any level of disability lived segregated from the mainstream of society, but there is room for greater improvement in the future (Beadle-Brown et al., 2016).

Giftedness

The gifted child used to be identified solely by an IQ score—one that was at least 130. Programs for gifted children still focus mainly on those with very high IQs, but there is increased recognition that some children are gifted because they have special abilities—think again of Gardner's multiple intelligences discussed at the beginning of this chapter—rather than because they have high general intelligence. Today's definitions emphasize that **giftedness** involves having a high IQ or showing special abilities in areas valued in society, such as mathematics, the performing and visual arts, or even leadership. Even high-IQ children are usually not equally talented in all areas. Like their average peers, high-IQ children typically have a varied profile of abilities: all may be above average, but some are higher than others (Makel et al., 2016). As they get older, they tend to pursue those areas of study and work where they have the greatest talents as well as the highest interest to them personally (Makel et al., 2016).

Joseph Renzulli (1998; Reis & Renzulli, 2011; Renzulli & Delcourt, 2013) has long argued that giftedness emerges from a combination of above-average ability, creativity, and task commitment. According to this view, someone might have a high IQ and even creative ability, but Renzulli questions whether they are truly gifted if they are not motivated to use this intelligence. Here we focus on individuals with exceptional IQs.

How early can intellectually gifted children be identified? Giftedness is usually apparent by toddlerhood, according to the Fullerton Longitudinal Study by Allen Gottfried and his colleagues (1994). They tracked a large sample of children from age 1–8, determined which children had IQs of 130 or above at age 8, and then looked for differences between these gifted children and other children earlier in life. The gifted children turned out to be identifiable as early as 18 months, primarily by their advanced language skills. Other recent research confirms that early language ability is a good, although not perfect, clue to later intellectual giftedness (Colombo et al., 2009). Gifted children were also highly curious and motivated to learn; they even enjoyed the challenge of taking IQ tests more than most children.

Linda Silverman and her colleagues at the Gifted Development Center have used the Characteristics of Giftedness Scale to

Gifted children have either high IQ scores or special abilities. This young girl is performing with the Pacific Symphony of Orange County, California.

Tony Freeman/PhotoEdit

identify gifted children (see Gifted Development Center, 2016). They have found that gifted children can be distinguished from average children by the following attributes:

- Rapid learning
- Extensive vocabulary
- Good memory
- Long attention span
- Perfectionism
- Preference for older companions
- Excellent sense of humor
- Early interest in reading
- Strong ability with puzzles and mazes
- Maturity
- Perseverance on tasks

The early emergence of giftedness is consistent with research showing a strong genetic influence on high intellect (see Brant et al., 2009; and Haworth et al., 2009). Still, prediction of giftedness is not perfect, although the prediction of nongiftedness is nearly so (Colombo et al., 2009). That is, experts are nearly always correct when they identify a child as not gifted; but among children identified early as gifted, some of these children drift out of this category as they get older (Colombo et al., 2009).

We get a richer understanding of the development of high-IQ children from a major longitudinal study launched in 1921 by Lewis Terman, developer of the Stanford–Binet test (Holahan & Sears, 1995; Oden, 1968; Terman, 1954). The participants were more than 1,500 California schoolchildren who were nominated by their teachers as gifted and who had IQs of 140 or higher. It soon became apparent that these high-IQ children (who came to be called *Termites*) were exceptional in many other ways. For example, they had weighed more at birth and had learned to walk and talk sooner than most toddlers. They reached puberty somewhat earlier than average and had better-than-average health. Their teachers rated them as better adjusted and more morally mature than their less intelligent peers. And, although they were no more popular than their classmates, they were quick to take on leadership responsibilities. Taken together, these findings destroy the stereotype that most gifted children are frail, sickly youngsters who are socially inadequate and emotionally immature.

Another demonstration of the personal and social maturity of most gifted children comes from a study of high-IQ children who skipped high school and entered the University of Washington as part of a special program to accelerate their education (see Robinson Center, 2016). Contrary to the common wisdom that gifted children will suffer socially and emotionally if they skip grades and are forced to fit in with much older students, these youngsters showed no signs of maladjustment (see Noble & Childers, 2009). On several measures of psychological and social maturity and adjustment, they equaled their much older college classmates and similarly gifted students who attended high school. Many of them thrived in college, for the first time finding friends like themselves—friends who were like-minded rather than like-aged (Noble, Childers, & Vaughan, 2008). Other research similarly shows that acceleration through school is associated with higher academic achievement and more positive social-emotional outcomes for gifted children than lack of acceleration (Steenbergen-Hu & Moon, 2011).

What happens as gifted children move into adulthood? Most of Terman's gifted children remained as remarkable in adulthood as they had been in childhood. Fewer than 5% were rated as seriously maladjusted. Their rates of such problems as ill health, mental illness, alcoholism, and delinquent behavior were but a fraction of those observed in the general population (Terman, 1954), although they were no less likely to divorce (Holahan & Sears, 1995).

The occupational achievements of the men in the sample were impressive. In middle age, 88% were employed in professional or high-level business jobs, compared with 20% of men in the general population (Oden, 1968). As a group, they had taken out more than 200 patents and written some 2,000 scientific reports, 100 books, 375 plays or short stories, and more than 300 essays, sketches, magazine articles, and critiques. These findings of notable accomplishment are echoed in recent follow-ups of other adults identified as gifted by age 13 (see Park, Lubinski, & Benbow, 2007). What about the gifted women in Terman's study? Because of the influence of gender-role expectations during the period covered by the study, gifted women achieved less than gifted men vocationally, often interrupting their careers or sacrificing their career goals to raise families. Still, they were more likely to have careers, and distinguished ones, than most women of their generation.

Finally, the Termites aged well. In their 60s and 70s, most of the men and women in the Terman study were highly active, involved, healthy, and happy people (Holahan & Sears, 1995). The men kept working longer than most men do and stayed involved in work even after they retired. The women, too, led exceptionally active lives. Contrary to the stereotype that gifted individuals burn out early, the Termites continued to burn bright throughout their lives.

Yet just as it is wrong to view intellectually gifted children as emotionally disturbed misfits, it is inaccurate to conclude that intellectually gifted children are models of good adjustment, perfect in every way. Some research suggests that children with IQs closer to 180 than 130 are often unhappy and socially isolated, perhaps because they are so out of step with their peers, and sometimes even have serious problems (Winner, 1996). Not all research on the profoundly gifted, as those with IQs of 180 and higher are often called, finds an unusual level of social maladjustment, however (Lubinski et al., 2001). Even within this elite group, the quality of the individual's home environment was important. The most well-adjusted and successful adults had highly educated parents who offered them both love and intellectual stimulation (Tomlinson-Keasey & Little, 1990).

Integrating Cognitive Perspectives

Our account of cognitive development over the life span is now complete. We hope you appreciate that each of the major approaches to the mind that we have considered—the Piagetian cognitive-developmental approach, Fischer's dynamic skill theory, and Vygotsky's sociocultural theory described in Chapter 7; the information-processing approach explained in Chapter 8; and the psychometric, or testing, approach, and Sternberg's triarchic model covered here—offers something of value. ●Table 9.5 lists how these approaches compare on their views of intelligence.

We can summarize the different approaches to cognitive development this way: Piaget has shown that comparing the thought of a preschooler with the thought of an adult is like comparing a caterpillar with a butterfly. Modes of thought change qualitatively with age. Fischer emphasized the concept of a developmental range of skills that might result depending on level of support provided. Vygotsky has highlighted the importance of culturally transmitted modes of thinking and interactions with others. The information-processing approach has helped researchers understand thinking processes and explain why the young child cannot remember as much information or solve problems as effectively as the adult can. The psychometric approach has told researchers that, if they look at the range of tasks to which the mind can be applied, they can recognize distinct mental abilities that each person consistently displays in greater or lesser amounts. Finally, Sternberg has pushed us to look beyond traditional psychometric tests of intelligence that emphasize analytic skills valued in the classroom to consider creative and practical intelligence alongside the analytical. You need not choose one approach and reject the others. Your understanding of the mind is likely to be richer if all six approaches continue to thrive. There are truly many intelligences, and it is foolish to think that a single IQ score can describe the complexities of human cognitive development.

	Piagetian Cognitive-Developmental Theory	Fischer's Dynamic Skill Theory	Vygotskian Sociocultural Theory	Information-Processing Approach	Psychometric Approach	Sternberg's Triarchic Model
What Is Intelligence?	Cognitive structures that help people adapt	Refining skills to optimize performance given the task and context	Tools of culture	Attention, memory, and other mental processes	Mental abilities and scores on IQ tests	Components that allow people to succeed in their lives
What Changes with Age?	Stage of cognitive development	Skill levels change	Ability to solve problems without assistance of others and with use of inner speech	Hardware (speed) and software (strategies) of the mind	Mental age (difficulty of problems solved)	Ability to respond to novel problems and automate familiar ones, adapt to current environmental demands, and select appropriate "mental tools" for solving problems
What Is of Most Interest?	Universal changes	Variability in performance	Culturally influenced changes and processes	Universal processes	Individual differences	Adapting behavior to environmental challenges

Checking Mastery

1. How is intellectual disability defined?
2. What characterizes the typical gifted person?
3. How does the definition of intelligence vary across the various approaches presented in Chapters 7, 8, and 9?

Making Connections

1. Should gifted, "regular," and intellectually disabled children be educated in the same classroom? What are some of the pros and cons of such integrated education for each of the three groups of children?
2. Putting together material from Chapters 7, 8, and 9, how would you describe the cognitive functioning of a typical 70-year-old person? What are the greatest cognitive strengths of older adults, what are their greatest limitations, and how much can an individual do to optimize her functioning?

Chapter Summary

9.1 Defining Intelligence and Creativity

- The psychometric, or testing, approach to cognition defines intelligence as a set of traits that allows some people to think and solve problems more effectively than others. It can be viewed as a hierarchy consisting of a general factor (*g*), broad abilities such as fluid and crystallized intelligence, and many specific abilities. The Stanford–Binet and Wechsler Scales are the most common intelligence tests and compare an individual's performance on a variety of cognitive tasks with the average performance of age-mates.

- Gardner's theory of multiple intelligences, with its focus on eight distinct forms of intelligence, offers an alternative view.

His theory includes these types of intelligence: linguistic, logical-mathematical, musical, spatial, bodily kinesthetic, interpersonal, intrapersonal, and naturalist.

- Sternberg's triarchic theory of intelligence proposes three components to intelligence. The practical component predicts that intelligent behavior will vary across different sociocultural contexts. According to the creative component, intelligent responses will vary depending on whether problems are novel or routine (automated). Finally, the analytical aspect of intelligence includes the thinking skills that a person brings to a problem-solving situation. This theory has been extended to the theory of successful intelligence, which identifies the additional factors needed to maximize your intelligence.

- Creativity is the ability to produce novel and socially valuable work. It involves divergent rather than convergent thinking and is often measured in terms of ideational fluency, the sheer number of different (including novel) ideas that a person can generate.

9.2 The Infant

- The Bayley scales include motor, mental, and behavior ratings to assess infant development. Although traditionally used as a measure of infant intelligence, they do not correlate well with later IQ scores.
- Infant measures that capture speed of information processing and preference for novelty are better at predicting later intelligence. Infants who can quickly process information are able to take in more information than those who are slower.

9.3 The Child

- During childhood, IQ scores become more stable so that scores at one point in time are generally consistent with scores obtained at a second point.
- Despite group stability, many individuals show wide variations in their IQ scores over time. Those who gain IQ points often have favorable home environments, whereas disadvantaged children often show a cumulative deficit.
- Creativity increases throughout early childhood but dips during later elementary school, possibly in response to societal expectations to conform. Creativity is associated with playfulness, openness to new experiences, and originality.

9.4 The Adolescent

- The Flynn effect describes a global increase in IQ scores over the past century that is likely the result of better nutrition, living conditions, and education.
- During adolescence, IQ scores are relatively stable and intellectual performance reaches near-adult level. IQ scores are useful for predicting the academic achievement of adolescents.
- Levels of creativity vary considerably from one individual to another. Some adolescents conform to societal norms and express little creativity, while others show a great deal of innovation.
- Adolescents with exceptional talents or creativity have both talent and motivation on the nature side and environments that foster their talents and value independence on the nurture side.

9.5 The Adult

- IQ scores are correlated with occupational status as well as health in adulthood.
- Both cross-sectional studies and longitudinal studies tend to show age-related decreases in IQ. Schaie's sequential study suggests that (1) date of birth (cohort) influences test performance, (2) no major declines in mental abilities occur until the late 60s or 70s, (3) some abilities (especially fluid ones) decline more than others (especially crystallized ones), and (4) not all people's abilities decline.
- A few adults display wisdom, or exceptional insight into complex life problems, which requires a rich knowledge base along with particular personality traits and cognitive styles and is influenced more by experience than age.
- Creative output increases sharply from early to middle adulthood, and although it then drops somewhat, it remains above the level where it started in young adulthood. The peak period of creativity varies from one field to another. Creative output may drop-off in older adulthood because people have already generated and expressed their creative potential.

9.6 Factors That Influence IQ Scores over the Life Span

- Individual differences in IQ at a given age are linked to genetic factors and to differences in intellectually stimulating qualities of the home environment such as parental involvement and responsive stimulation.
- Social class impacts IQ scores, raising the issue of middle-class testing bias. Children who are moved from low to higher socioeconomic status homes show an increase in IQ scores.
- Racial and ethnic differences in IQ also exist, with African American and Hispanic children typically scoring, on average, lower than European American children. Motivational differences, stereotype threat, genetic factors, and environment have all been considered as contributors.

9.7 The Extremes of Intelligence

- The extremes of intelligence are represented by intellectual disability at one end of the continuum and giftedness at the other end.
- Intellectual disability is defined by deficits in adaptive behavior combined with low IQ scores. Functioning varies by level of disability and is worse when accompanied by other conditions. Most intellectually disabled adults live in the community, either in group homes or with their families.
- Giftedness has most often been defined by high IQ scores, although more recent definitions recognize special talents not measured by traditional IQ tests. Life outcomes for gifted people are generally above average.
- Six major approaches to cognitive development have been presented in Chapters 7, 8, and 9. These include Piaget's focus on qualitatively different stages of thought, Fischer's dynamic skills, and Vygotsky's emphasis on culturally transmitted modes of thought. The information-processing approach reveals how memory and problem solving are influenced by characteristics of the person such as age, and task factors such as complexity. The psychometric approach defines cognitive abilities in measurable ways, illustrating that people have more or less of distinct mental abilities. Sternberg's triarchic theory adds creative and practical intelligence to the more traditional analytic intelligence.

Key Terms

psychometric approach **266**

fluid intelligence **266**

crystallized intelligence **267**

factor analysis **267**

mental age (MA) **268**

Stanford–Binet Intelligence Scale **268**

intelligence quotient (IQ) **268**

test norms **268**

Wechsler Scales **268**

normal distribution **268**

standard deviation **269**

savant syndrome **269**

prodigies **269**

triarchic theory of intelligence **270**

practical component **270**

creative component **270**

automatization **271**

culture bias **271**

analytic component **271**

successful intelligence **271**

creativity **272**

convergent thinking **272**

divergent thinking **272**

ideational fluency **272**

investment theory **272**

General Adaptive Composite (GAC) **273**

Bayley Scales of Infant Development (BSID) **273**

child poverty **275**

Flynn effect **277**

dysrationalia **281**

terminal drop **283**

wisdom **284**

cumulative-deficit hypothesis **287**

Home Observation for Measurement of the Environment (HOME) inventory **288**

stereotype threat **290**

intellectual disability **291**

giftedness **293**

10 Language and Education

In her autobiography, Helen Keller, who was blind and deaf from a very young age, described the moment when she realized that everything could be named. This insight opened up the door to language, learning, and communication. "As the cool stream gushed over one hand, she [Annie] spelled into the other the word water, first slowly, then rapidly. I stood still, my whole attention fixed upon the motions of her fingers. Suddenly I felt a misty consciousness as of something forgotten—a thrill of returning thought; and somehow the mystery of language was revealed to me. I knew then that W-A-T-E-R meant the wonderful cool something that was flowing over my hand. . . . I left the well-house eager to learn. Everything had a name, and each name gave birth to a new thought. As we returned to the house every object which I touched seemed to quiver with life"(Keller, 1954, p. 36).

One of the most important milestones in development is mastering some type of language. Language, whether it is spoken or signed, allows communication with people around us. As you learned in Chapter 7, psychologist Lev Vygotsky argued that language is the primary vehicle through which adults pass culturally valued modes of thinking and problem solving to their children. He also believed that language is our most important tool of thinking.

In this chapter, we examine language skills, which become established largely through an informal education system consisting of parents, other grownups, peers, and even the media. We also consider formal education, which uses basic language skills to cultivate the reading, writing, thinking, and problem-solving skills that allow individuals to become fully functioning members of society. However, getting the most out of education requires more than acquiring language and literacy skills. As Terrel Bell, former secretary of education, asserted: "There are three things to remember about education. The first one is motivation. The second one is motivation. The third one is motivation"(quoted in Maehr & Meyer, 1997, p. 372). Thus, we also examine achievement motivation and its relationship to education and educational outcomes.

10.1 The System of Language

LEARNING OBJECTIVES

- Describe the function of each component of a spoken language system.
- Articulate how the brain is organized to support language.
- Explain the major theoretical approaches to understanding how language develops.

Although language is one of the most intricate forms of knowledge we will ever acquire, all typically developing children master a language early in life. Indeed, many infants are talking before they can walk. Can language be complex, then? It certainly can be. Linguists (scholars who study language) define **language** as a communication system in which a limited number of signals—sounds or letters (or gestures, in the case of the sign language used by deaf people)—can be combined according to agreed-upon rules to produce an infinite number of messages. Linguists have yet to fully describe the rules of the 6,000 or so languages that exist throughout the world. To master a spoken language such as English, a child must learn basic sounds, how sounds are combined to form words, how words are combined to form meaningful statements, what words and sentences mean, and how to use language effectively in social interactions. How is this accomplished? To address this, we are guided, once again, by consideration of both nature and nurture. But first, we need to understand the basic components of language.

Basic Components

Every human language must have words (symbols) that represent the objects, people, ideas, and so on that are relevant to the community. In addition, there must be a system of rules to organize how the words are used and combined to facilitate communication among members of the community. Perhaps the most fundamental system involves **phonemes**, which are the basic units of *sound* that can change the meaning of a word. Substituting the phoneme /p/ for /b/ in the word *bit* changes the meaning of the word. Although there are 26 letters in the English alphabet, there are more phonemes than this because letters can be pronounced different ways. Trying to identify the precise number of phonemes in a language, though, is like trying to identify the exact number of colors that exist in a rainbow; there are numerous subtleties and interpretations. In addition to individual phonemes, languages also specify how phonemes can be combined. In English, for example, we can combine /b/ and /r/ to say "brat"but we cannot combine /b/ with /m/ to produce "bmat."

Languages also have a system for organizing the **morphemes**, the basic units of *meaning* that exist in a word. Some words consist of just one morpheme: *view*. But we can add another morpheme, *re*, and the meaning of the word changes (*review*). Add a different morpheme, *pre*, and the meaning changes again (*preview*). Morphemes are not the same as syllables: A word with multiple syllables, such as the two-syllable *apple*, consists of one morpheme because it cannot be further broken down into smaller meaningful units. To convey the meaning of what we intend when we say "apple," we have to include both syllables.

Language allows us to generate an infinite number of new sentences to communicate with others.

WORDS AND MEANINGS/MARK SYKES/Alamy Stock Photo

An important step in language acquisition is mastering its syntax, the systematic rules for forming sentences. Consider these three sentences: (1) Fang Fred bit. (2) Fang bit Fred. (3) Fred bit Fang. The first violates the rules of English sentence structure or syntax, although this word order would be acceptable in German. The second and third are both grammatical English sentences, but their different word orders—determined by rules of syntax—convey different meanings. Understanding the meanings of sentences also requires knowing the semantics of language. To understand the sentence "Sherry was green with jealousy," we must move beyond the literal meaning of each word, which would suggest that Sherry was the color green, to the meaning that is created when we combine these words into this particular sentence.

Finally, we must understand something of the pragmatics of language—rules for specifying how language is used appropriately in different social contexts. That is, children (and adults) have to learn when to say what to whom. They must learn to communicate effectively by taking into account who the listener is, what the listener already knows, and what the listener needs or wants to hear. "Give me that cookie!" may be grammatically correct English, but the child is far more likely to win Grandma's heart (not to mention a cookie) with a polite "May I please have one of your yummy cookies, Grandma?"

In addition to these features of language, producing meaningful speech also involves prosody, or *how* the sounds are produced. Prosody has been called the "melody" of speech because it includes pitch or intonation, the stress or accentuation of certain syllables in a word or certain words in a sentence, and the duration or timing of speech. A child may say "dog" with little change in pitch, perhaps to make a statement meaning, *"There is a dog."* By raising his voice at the end of the word, though, the meaning is changed to a question, "Dog?" A parent may produce a loud, short, "NO!" to stop a child from running into the street, but produce a long "nooo" to perhaps sarcastically make a point with a teenager. Even young infants are sensitive to the prosody of speech and can distinguish between two languages based on their rhythms (Gervain & Werker, 2013).

Thus, mastering a language includes knowing the phonemes and morphemes and how these can be combined, the syntax for turning words into sentences, the semantics for understanding the meaning of words and sentences, the pragmatics for how to best use language to suit the context and our conversational partner, and the prosody or sound features of speech.

We have now covered the basic components of language. How, though, do infants pull all of these parts together into a coherent language system? To answer this, we need to first have some understanding of how the brain processes language and then we need to consider the theoretical explanations for language.

Biology

The basics of language are supported by a brain that is uniquely structured for language. Until recently, our understanding of the brain's role in language came from observations of individuals who had the misfortune to sustain brain damage and an associated loss of some aspect of language. From this, scientists concluded that

This infant may not understand the words her mother is speaking, but she probably gathers information from the prosody, or melody, of how the words are spoken.

Ali Russell/Alamy Stock Photo

language was largely a product of left hemisphere activity, with a region called Broca's area associated with speech production and another region called Wernicke's area associated with comprehension of language (see ■ **Figure 10.1**). Thanks to improved methodologies such as functional magnetic resonance imaging (fMRI) and event-related potentials (ERPs), we are beginning to craft a more precise picture of how neural activity relates to and supports language.

We have learned that human brains show remarkably consistent organization for language across the life span, with the left hemisphere showing increased activity when listening to speech and the right hemisphere showing more activity when processing the melody or rhythm of speech (Gervain & Mehler, 2010). Adults attempting to learn new words show different patterns of brain activity depending on whether they are successful or not: Those who are successful show more connectivity between the left

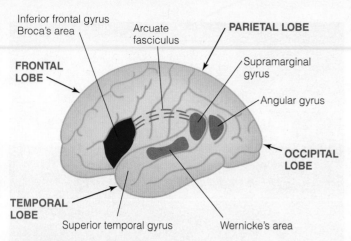

■ **Figure 10.1** Brain regions associated with language.

and right supramarginal gyrus (refer again to **Figure 10.1**), located in the parietal lobe, one of four main brain regions (Veroude et al., 2010). Studies using fMRI show that areas in both the left and right hemispheres are active in women's brains when processing language, whereas activity in men's brains is more typically localized in the left hemisphere (Shaywitz et al., 1995). We have also learned that Wernicke's area and Broca's area are connected with a band of fibers called the arcuate fasciculus. Typically, incoming language is processed—comprehended—in Wernicke's area and then sent to Broca's area via the connecting fibers to be turned into speech. Damage to this band of fibers can cause a type of aphasia, or language disorder, in which the person might hear and understand linguistic input but be unable to vocally repeat the information. Some research suggests that neurons in Broca's area are activated not only when a person produces speech but also when a person sees or hears another person speaking (Fogassi & Ferrari, 2007). This may facilitate language learning and suggests the presence of a mirror neuron system, which we discuss in more detail in Chapter 13.

Finally, there is evidence that the capacity for acquiring language has a genetic basis. Some of our linguistic competencies, including the ability to combine symbols to form short sentences, are shared with chimpanzees and other primates, suggesting that they arose during the course of evolution and are part of our genetic endowment as humans (Greenfield & Savage-Rumbaugh, 1993; Pinker, 1994). Many genes are implicated in language abilities, one of which, *FOXP2*, is associated with the motor skills necessary for speech (Hickok &

Small, 2016). Individuals whose *FOXP2* gene is damaged are unable to speak, although they may have no other limitations. Some intriguing research suggests that girls, who demonstrate advanced language skills relative to boys, have higher concentrations of *FOXP2* protein, but further research is needed to fully understand this link between sex or gender and *FOXP2* (Bowers et al., 2013).

Theories: Nature and Nurture

To understand how children manage to master the remarkable skills of language, we revisit the nature—nurture issue to frame the theoretical explanations of language development.

Nature: Innate Predispositions

On the nature side, the nativists minimize the role of the language environment and focus instead on the role of the child's biologically programmed capacities to acquire language. Noted linguist Noam Chomsky (2000) proposed that humans have a unique genetic capacity to learn language. According to this view, humans are equipped with knowledge of a universal grammar, a system of common rules and properties for learning any of the world's languages. Universal grammar offers a limited number of possibilities for forming language. As many as 75% of the world's languages have the basic word order of subject-verb-object (SVO; English, for example) or subject-object-verb (SOV; Japanese, for example). Another 15% have a word order that begins with a verb, whereas word order that begins with an object is quite unusual (Goodluck, 2009). Thus, most of the world's languages are based on a grammatical system that starts with a subject, followed by a verb and then an object or by an object and then a verb.

Universal grammar provides the framework for acquiring a language, but it is not language specific. Exposure to language activates the areas of the brain collectively called the language acquisition device (LAD). Although LAD is not a specific structure in the brain, it is theorized to be an innate brain function that sifts through language, applies the universal rules, and begins tailoring the system to the specifics of the language spoken in the young child's environment (■ **Figure 10.2**). Infants listening to English determine that SVO is the typical grammatical sequence, whereas infants listening to Japanese detect that SOV is typical.

What evidence supports a nativist perspective on language development? First, there is what Chomsky and others have

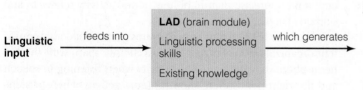
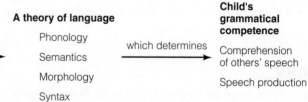

■ **Figure 10.2** The language acquisition device (LAD).

Source: Chomsky, 1965

called the poverty of the stimulus (POTS): children could not possibly acquire such an incredibly complex communication system with the limited linguistic input they receive (Berwick et al., 2011; Clark & Lappin, 2011). That is, the environmental stimulus of language input is just too impoverished to support the linguistic output that we see emerge. For example, 18-month-olds show an understanding of syntax that they could not have acquired solely from information provided to them by others; they must have inferred rules of syntax on their own (Lidz, Waxman, & Freedman, 2003). Second, children all progress through the same sequences at roughly similar ages, and they even make the same kinds of errors, which suggests that language development is guided by a species-wide maturational plan. Third, these universal aspects of early language development occur despite cultural differences in the styles of speech that adults use in talking to young children.

Other evidence for the nativist position comes from studies of second-language learning. Much research shows that young children learn their native language with ease but often struggle later to learn a second language to the same level of proficiency. Does this mean that there is a critical period for language acquisition and that the brain becomes less responsive to language learning? As noted in Chapter 6, by the time infants begin to speak at around age one, they have already become largely insensitive to sounds that are not made in their native language (see, for example, Werker, Yeung & Yoshida, 2012). This may make it more difficult to hear the nuances of speech needed to fully develop native-like mastery of another language. Consider also research with deaf children, some of whom (especially those with hearing parents) do not have an opportunity to learn any language, oral or signed, in their early years. Rachel Mayberry (2010) studied language mastery in deaf college students exposed to American Sign Language (ASL) at different ages and found that the rule "the earlier, the better" applies. Mastery of the syntax and semantics of sign language was greatest among students exposed to it in infancy or early childhood. Those who learned ASL later in their development (ages 9–16) mastered it better if they had some exposure to English early in life than if they had not been exposed to any language system before they encountered sign language. **Exploration 10.1** provides more details on what we can learn about language in general by studying language acquisition among deaf children. And in a later section of this chapter, we will consider lessons from studying individuals who acquire more than one language, either as infants or when older.

It is possible that the language-processing areas of the brain are shaped for a lifetime by early experience with language in ways that limit later learning of other languages. But it seems unlikely that there is a hard-and-fast critical period for language acquisition. Janet Werker and Richard Tees (2005) suggest that it is more accurate to say there is an "optimal period" during which languages are most easily and flawlessly acquired. And studies of brain architecture confirm that it is more appropriate to conclude that there may be a *sensitive*

period for language acquisition (Fox, Levitt, & Nelson, 2010). Perhaps the main message is that young children are supremely capable of learning languages and advancing their cognitive development in the process.

Nurture: Environment and Learning

How does the environment influence language development? It is no accident that children learn the language their parents speak, down to the regional accent. Children learn the words they hear spoken by others—even when the words are not spoken directly to them (Floor & Akhtar, 2006). For example, 18-month-olds can learn object labels and verbs by "eavesdropping" on a conversation between two adults (so be careful about what you say within earshot of toddlers). But passive exposure to language can only go so far. Young children are more likely to start using new words if they are reinforced for doing so than if they are not (Whitehurst & Idez-Menchaca, 1988). Children whose caregivers frequently encourage them to converse by asking questions, making requests, and the like are more advanced in early language development than those whose parents are less conversational (Bohannon & Bonvillian, 2017).

Learning theorists, with their focus on environment, have had an easier time explaining the development of phonology and semantics than accounting for how rules of syntax are acquired. For example, after analyzing conversations between mothers and young children, Roger Brown, Courtney Cazden,

How would learning theorists describe language acquisition that occurs through interactions such as this one, as a young boy listens to his father?

Niamh Baldock/Alamy Stock Photo

Language Acquisition among Deaf Children

Many deaf children gain their first exposure to language by learning a sign language such as American Sign Language (ASL). These are true languages: The signs are arbitrary symbols, not attempts to mimic objects and events, and they are used according to a system of grammatical rules that determines their ordering. We should be able to learn some interesting lessons about language acquisition in general, then, by studying language acquisition among deaf children.

On average, deaf children growing up in homes where sign is the native language (that is, one or both parents use sign as their primary means of communication) acquire sign language in much the same sequence and at much the same rate as hearing children acquire their native spoken language (Lederberg, Schick, & Spencer, 2013). Interestingly, deaf infants whose parents are deaf "babble" in sign language. They experiment with gestures in much

the same way that hearing infants experiment with sounds in preparation for their first meaningful communications. They sign their first meaningful single words around 12 months, use their first syntax (combinations of two signs) between 18 and 24 months, and master many rules of language, such as past tense formation, between 2 and 3 years (Mayberry & Squires, 2006). Just as hearing children have difficulty with the pronunciation of certain words and overgeneralize certain rules, deaf children make predictable errors in their signing.

The language environment experienced by deaf infants is also far more similar to that of hearing infants than you would imagine. For example, deaf mothers communicate using "child-directed signs." They present signs at a slower pace, repeat signs more, and exaggerate their signing motions more when they talk to their infants than when they talk to their deaf friends (Holzrichter & Meier, 2000). Moreover, just as hearing babies prefer the exaggerated intonations of child-directed speech, deaf infants pay more attention and give more emotional response when they are shown videos of infant-directed signing than tapes of adult-directed signing.

Finally, it turns out that language areas of the brain

develop much the same in deaf children exposed to sign as in hearing children exposed to speech (Newman et al., 2002). In particular, reliance on areas of the left hemisphere of the cortex to process sentences is as evident among deaf children who acquired ASL early in life (that is, native signers) as among hearing individuals who acquired English early in life (native speakers). Aaron Newman and his colleagues (2002) examined brain activity during the processing of English and ASL sentences by native signers and those who acquired sign later, as a second language. Parts of the left hemisphere were activated in both groups when viewing the English sentences. A part of the right hemisphere was activated in both groups when viewing the ASL sentences. But only the native signers showed activation in a part of the right hemisphere called the angular gyrus when viewing the ASL sentences. The authors believe these findings may be evidence of a sensitive period for learning sign, similar to the sensitive period for learning a native spoken language. Early exposure to sign changes the way the brain responds when later exposed to sign language (see also Campbell, MacSweeney, & Water, 2008; Mayberry, 2010).

As you have seen, language development is sometimes delayed among deaf children of hearing parents if they cannot hear well enough to understand spoken language but are not exposed to sign language (Mayberry, 2010). Overall, then, studies of language acquisition among deaf children suggest that young humans are biologically prepared to master language and will do so if given the opportunity, whether that language is signed or spoken and whether it involves visual–spatial skills or auditory ones (see Goldin-Meadow, 2009).

This mother signs with her infant, which supports language development in much the same way as a spoken language contributes to language development among hearing infants.

Disability Images/Alamy Stock Photo

and Ursula Bellugi (1969) discovered that a mother's approval or disapproval depended on the truth value or semantics of what was said, not on the grammatical correctness of the statement. Thus, when a child looking at a cow says, "Her cow"(accurate but grammatically incorrect), Mom is likely to provide reinforcement ("That's right, darling", whereas if

the child were to say, "There's a dog, Mommy" (grammatically correct but inaccurate), Mom would probably correct the child ("No, sweetie—that's a cow"). Similarly, parents seem just as likely to reward a grammatically primitive request ("Want milk") as a well-formed version of the same idea (Brown & Hanlon, 1970). Such evidence casts doubt on the idea that the major mechanism behind syntactic development is reinforcement.

Could imitation of adults account for the acquisition of syntax? The problem here is that young children produce many sentences they are unlikely to have heard adults using ("All gone cookie," "It swimmed," and so on). These kinds of sentences are not imitations. Also, an adult is likely to get nowhere in teaching syntax by saying, "Repeat after me,"unless the child already has at least some knowledge of the grammatical form to be learned (Baron, 1992; McNeill, 1970). Young children frequently imitate other people's speech, and this may help them get to the point of producing new structures. But it is hard to see how imitation and reinforcement alone can account for the learning of grammatical rules.

Nature and Nurture Working Together

It's now time to merge the two sides of the nature–nurture issue and construct an interactionist account of language development. Consider what Steven Pinker (1995) concludes about the importance of considering both the nature and nurture of language acquisition:

> All humans talk but no house pets or house plants do, no matter how pampered, so heredity must be involved in language. But a child growing up in Japan speaks Japanese whereas the same child brought up in California would speak English, so the environment is also crucial. Thus, there is no question about whether heredity or environment is involved in language, or even whether one or the other is "more important."Instead, language acquisition might be our best hope of finding out how heredity and environment interact. (p. 136)

Interactionists believe that both learning theorists (nurture) and nativists (nature) are correct: Children's biologically based competencies and their language environment interact to shape the course of language development (Bloom, 1998; Bohannon & Bonvillian, 2017). They emphasize that acquisition of language skills depends on and is related to the acquisition of many other capacities: perceptual, cognitive, motor, social, and emotional. They point out that the capacity for acquiring language is not unique, as nativists who speak of universal grammar and the LAD claim (Bates, O'Connell, & Shore, 1987). It is, instead, interrelated to other developments that are taking place concurrently with language acquisition. For example, young children first begin to use words as meaningful symbols when they begin to display nonlinguistic symbolic capacities, such as the ability to use gestures (waving bye-bye), and begin to engage in pretend play (treating a bowl as if it were a hat). The interactionists' position is not unlike that taken by Piaget (1970). He believed that

milestones in cognitive development pave the way for progress in language development and that maturation and environment interact to guide both cognitive development and language development. Like Piaget (but unlike learning theorists), many interactionists argue that language development depends on the maturation of cognitive abilities such as the capacity for symbolic thought. However, the interactionist position also emphasizes—as Vygotsky did but Piaget did not—ways in which social interactions with adults contribute to cognitive and linguistic development. Language is primarily a means of communicating—one that develops in the context of social interactions as children and their companions strive to get their messages across (Tomasello, 2009).

Long before infants use words, Jerome Bruner (1983) says, their caregivers show them how to take turns in conversations—even if the most these young infants can contribute when their turn comes is a laugh or a bit of babbling. As adults converse with young children, they create a supportive learning environment—a *scaffold*, in Bruner's terms, a *zone of proximal development* in Vygotsky's—that helps the children grasp the regularities of language. For example, parents may go through their children's favorite picture books at bedtime and ask "What's this?" and "What's that?" These interactions give their children repeated opportunities to learn that conversing involves taking turns, that things have names, and that there are proper ways to pose questions and give answers. When toddlers use a familiar word or phrase ("that plane"), mothers often respond with an expansion—a more grammatically complete expression of what the toddler stated ("Yes, that's a loud airplane"). Adults use conversational techniques such as expansions mainly to improve communication, not to teach grammar (Penner, 1987).

When speaking to their infants, adults adjust their style of communication in ways that may facilitate acquisition of new language skills. Language researchers use the term child-directed speech to describe the speech adults use with infants and young children: short, simple sentences spoken slowly, in a high-pitched voice, often with much repetition, and with exaggerated emphasis on key words (Hills, 2013). For example, the mother trying to get her son to eat his peas might say, "Eat your *peas* now. Not the cracker. See those *peas*? Yes, eat the *peas*. Oh, such a good boy for eating your *peas*." From the earliest days of life, infants seem to pay more attention to the high-pitched sounds and varied intonational patterns of child-directed speech than to the speech adults use when communicating with one another (Ma et al., 2011). This is not to say that "background speech" occurring among adults in the infant's presence has no effect. As many a parent has learned, toddlers often pick up some of the colorful vocabulary that adults toss around thinking that sweet Suzy will not notice. She did, and it will slip out at some inopportune

Adults are not the only ones who use child-directed speech. Children also adjust their speech to their listener. How could this girl alter her speech to make it appealing and appropriate for her baby sister?

tomborro/Alamy Stock Photo

moment. Importantly, caregivers' child-directed speech occurs within a dynamic social context that helps infants and toddlers understand not only how language is used, but why it is used: to share ideas and communicate within one's social group (Golinkoff, Can, Soderstrom, & Hirsh-Pasek, 2015).

Developing language competence may be our earliest and greatest learning challenge, but it is only the beginning. There is much more to be mastered during the school years and beyond. Language lays the foundation for acquiring reading, writing, and countless other skills. But unlike language, which seems to develop effortlessly in the absence of formal education, these other skills typically require directed education. In the following sections, we look not only at language development but at education across the life span, examining changes in motivation for learning and changes in educational environments as learners get older.

● **Checking Mastery**

1. What are the basic components of language that children must master in order to communicate effectively?
2. How is the brain structured to support language skills?
3. What are the main features of the nativist and learning theories of language acquisition?

● **Making Connections**

1. How should adults interact and talk with infants to ensure they have the best opportunities to develop a strong start with their language development?
2. What is the most compelling evidence that language is influenced by nature? And what evidence shows that it is not nature alone that determines language acquisition?

10.2

The Infant

LEARNING OBJECTIVES

- Describe the typical path of language acquisition during the first 2 years.
- Identify factors that facilitate language development.
- Explain the course of early mastery motivation.
- Evaluate the components of a quality early education program.

Infants have a great deal to learn in the informal educational system of their family and neighborhoods before they enter the formal education system. In particular, they must master a language system, and most do so quickly and with little deliberate effort. Indeed, the speed with which most infants and children master language is astonishing. We trace the path to mastering language skills and then turn our attention to how infants take on mastering their environments.

Mastering Language

As you learned in Chapter 6, newborns seem to tune in to human speech immediately and show a preference for speech over nonspeech sounds and for their native language, which they listened to in the womb, over other languages (Gervain & Mehler, 2010; Moon, Lagercrantz, & Kuhl, 2013). Very young infants can distinguish between phonemes such as /b/ and /p/ or /d/ and /t/ (Eimas, 1975a). Before they ever speak a word, infants are also becoming sensitive to the fact that pauses in speech fall between clauses, phrases, and words rather than in the middle of these important language units. By 7½ months, infants demonstrate word **segmentation** ability when they detect a target word in a stream of speech (see Jusczyk, Houston, & Newsome, 1999). Thus, when they hear the sentence "The cat chased the mouse," they understand that this is not one long word but a string of five words. Word segmentation is a formidable task, but infants seem to be sensitive to a number of cues marking the boundaries between words, and this skill improves throughout the first 2 years of life (Saffran et al., 2006). One thing that helps infants with this task is the repetition of many common words throughout the days, weeks, and months leading to language acquisition. By repeatedly hearing "cat" embedded in many different sentences, infants come to understand that "cat" must represent a unit that is separate from other spoken units. They are also sensitive to the stress placed on certain syllables (see Hollich, 2010). In English, for example, the first syllable of nouns is typically stressed, and infants exposed to English language learn that when they hear a stressed syllable, it probably signals the start of a word.

What about producing sounds? From birth, infants produce sounds—cries, burps, grunts, and sneezes. These sounds help exercise the vocal cords and give infants an opportunity to learn how airflow and different mouth and tongue positions affect sounds. By 5 months, infants realize that their sounds have an effect on their caregivers' behavior (Goldstein, Schwade, & Bornstein, 2009). Parents respond to as many as 50% of prelinguistic sounds as if they were genuine efforts to communicate (Goldstein et al., 2009; McCune et al., 1996). For instance, in response to her infant's hiccup sound, a mother replies, "My goodness! What's going on in there? Huh? Tell Mommy." The mother draws her infant into a sort of dialogue. Such prelinguistic sounds, and the feedback infants receive, eventually pave the way for meaningful speech sounds (Hoff, 2014).

The next milestone in vocalization, around 6–8 weeks of age, is **cooing**—repeating vowel-like sounds such as "ooooh" and "aaaaah." Babies coo when they are content and often in response to being spoken to in a happy voice. Do infants this age understand the words spoken to them? Not likely—they primarily respond to the intonation or "melody" of speech (Hirsh-Pasek, Golinkoff, & Hollich, 1999). Parents can say some rather nasty things to their young infants ("You're driving me nuts today!") as long as they say them with a happy voice, illustrating the importance of prosody.

Around 3–4 months, infants expand their vocal range considerably as they begin to produce consonant sounds. They enter a period of babbling between about 4 and 6 months, repeating consonant–vowel combinations such as "baba" or "dadadada," in what Jean Piaget would call a primary circular reaction—the repeating of an interesting noise for the pleasure of making it.

Up to about 6 months, infants all over the world, even deaf ones, sound pretty much alike, but the effects of experience soon become apparent. Without auditory feedback, deaf infants fall behind hearing infants in their ability to produce well-formed syllables (Oller & Eilers, 1988). By the time infants are about 8 months old, they babble with something of an accent; adults can often tell which language infants have been listening to from the sound of their babbling (Poulin-Dubois & Goodz, 2001). These advanced babblers increasingly restrict their sounds to phonemes in the language they are hearing, and they pick up the intonation patterns of that language (Hoff, 2014; Snow, 2006). Once these intonation patterns are added to an infant's babbles, the utterances sound a great deal like real speech until you listen closely and realize you have no idea what the infant is saying! (Hollich, 2010). We shouldn't assume, though, that infants are as clueless as we are: What they are "saying" may make complete sense to them. As they attempt to master the semantics of language, infants come to understand many words before they can produce them. That is, *comprehension* (or reception) is ahead of *production* (or expression) in language development. Ten-month-olds can comprehend, on average, about 50 words but do not yet produce any of these (Golinkoff & Hirsh-Pasek, 2006). This gap between comprehension and production persists and may reflect the relative importance of understanding speech over producing speech (Bornstein & Hendricks, 2012). Research shows that early understanding of words is related to academic achievement in elementary school: The 10-month-olds who understand more words are later the children who get better grades (Hohm et al., 2007).

Shortly before speaking their first true words, as they approach 1 year, infants really seem to understand familiar words. How do they figure out what words mean? When Mom points to a small, four-legged furry animal and says, "There's Furrball," how do infants learn that "Furrball" refers to this particular cat and not to its movement or to its tail or to a general category of furry animals? It turns out that infants and toddlers use a variety of cues in learning to connect words with their referents—the objects, people, or ideas represented by a name. At first, 10-month-old infants rely on attentional cues such as how important an object seems to be from their perspective (Pruden et al., 2006). Thus, if their attention is captured by the ball in front of them, they may

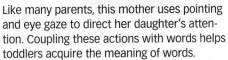

Like many parents, this mother uses pointing and eye gaze to direct her daughter's attention. Coupling these actions with words helps toddlers acquire the meaning of words.

Gabriel Blaj/Alamy Stock Photo

assume that mom's verbalizations refer to this ball. By 12 months of age, though, their reliance on personal relevance is decreasing and infants begin to use social and linguistic cues to learn words.

One important social cue is joint attention, or social eye gaze—two people looking at the same thing. Infants listen to parents repeatedly labeling and pointing at objects, directing their gaze, and otherwise making clear the connection between words and their referents (Hollich, Hirsh-Pasek, & Golinkoff, 2000). If Mom says "cat" when both she and her child are looking at the furry animal, then this likely is the referent for the label. Importantly, early development of joint attention skills seems to pave the way for early vocabulary development (Beuker et al., 2013).

Finally, children use the process of syntactic bootstrapping when they use the syntax of a sentence—that is, where a word is placed in a sentence—to help determine the meaning of the word (Naigles & Swensen, 2007). In the earlier example, if mom had said, "There's *a* furball" or "The cat is hacking up a furball" instead of the original "There's Furrball," the syntactic placement—how *furball* was used in the sentence—would have changed the meaning of the word.

The First Words

An infant's first meaningful word, spoken around 1 year, is a special event for parents. First words have been called holophrases because a single word often conveys an entire sentence's worth of meaning. These single-word "sentences" can serve different communication functions depending on the way they are said and the context in which they are said (Tomasello, 2009). For example, 17-month-old Shelley used the word *ghetti* (spaghetti) in three different ways over a 5-minute period. First, she pointed to the pan on the stove and seemed to be asking, "Is that spaghetti?" Later, the function of her holophrase was to name the spaghetti when shown the contents of the pan, as in "It's spaghetti." Finally, there was little question that she was requesting spaghetti when she tugged at her companion's sleeve as he was eating and used the word in a whining tone.

Although there are limits to the meaning that can be packed into a single word and its accompanying intonation pattern and gestures, 1-year-olds in the holophrastic stage of language development seem to have mastered such basic language functions as naming, questioning, requesting, and demanding. When they begin to use words as symbols, they also begin to use nonverbal symbols—gestures such as pointing, raising their arms to signal "up," or panting heavily to say "dog" (Goldin-Meadow, 2009).

What do 1-year-olds talk about? They talk mainly about familiar objects and actions—those things that they encounter every day

Table 10.1 Examples of Words Used by Children Younger than 20 Months

Category	Words
Sound effects	baa baa, meow, moo, ouch, uh-oh, woof, yum-yum
Food and drink	apple, banana, cookie, cheese, cracker, juice, milk, water
Animals	bear, bird, bunny, dog, cat, cow, duck, fish, kitty, horse, pig, puppy
Body parts and clothing	diaper, ear, eye, foot, hair, hand, hat, mouth, nose, toe, tooth, shoe
House and outdoors	blanket, chair, cup, door, flower, keys, outside, spoon, tree, TV
People	baby, daddy, gramma, grampa, mommy, [child's own name]
Toys and vehicles	ball, balloon, bike, boat, book, bubbles, plane, truck, toy
Actions	down, eat, go, sit, up
Games and routines	bath, bye, hi, night-night, no, peek-a-boo, please, shhh, thank you, yes
Adjectives and descriptors	all gone, cold, dirty, hot

Source: Jean Berko Gleason, *The development of language*, 6th ed., Table 4.1, p. 122. Copyright © 2005. Reprinted by permission of Pearson Education, Inc.

and are important to them (● Table 10.1). Most research shows that the first 50 words typically consist of common nouns representing objects and people (Waxman et al., 2013). It may be easier for young children to decipher nouns and their referents in the language around them, and adults tend to use more nouns in their conversations with children (Uccelli & Pan, 2013). Another possibility, though, is that it is easy to create an image of the things represented by nouns and images to give us something tangible to remember (McDonough et al., 2011). Verbs, though, pose more of a challenge because it can be difficult to create an image for an action.

Initial language acquisition proceeds literally at one word at a time. Three or four months may pass before the child has a vocabulary of 10 words, slowly acquired one by one. There is a great deal of variability in early language acquisition: While one child may be speaking her fiftieth word as she celebrates her first birthday, another child may be reaching this milestone around the time of his second birthday (Newman & Sachs, 2012).

Then, in what is called the **vocabulary spurt**, around 18 months of age, when the child has mastered about 30–50 words, the pace of word learning quickens dramatically (Bloom, 1998; Carroll, 2008). Steven Pinker (1995), an experimental psychologist who has studied and written extensively on all aspects of language development, estimates that a new word is acquired every 2 hours during this time! At 20 months, children are producing an average of 150 words, and just 4 months later, this has doubled to 300 words (Camaioni, 2004). What makes this possible? Something called **fast mapping**, which allows children to use sentence context to help them make an educated guess about word meaning. This is a quick and efficient method of

learning new words. Although infants as young as 6 months demonstrate rudimentary fast mapping, the ability becomes much more refined between 20 and 24 months (Borgström, Torkildsen, & Lindgren, 2015). Of course, this is a simplification of what is, undoubtedly, a very complex process. Contributing to fast mapping is the greater memory capabilities of the toddler as well as the growing ability to use a word's context to decipher its meaning. Like Helen Keller with her "aha" realization that the letters being tapped on her one hand were related to the object (water) in her other hand, toddlers seem to arrive at the critical realization that everything has a name and that, by learning the names of things, they can share what they are thinking with someone else and vice versa (Bloom & Tinker, 2001). Toddlers who acquire more vocabulary during this time may be quicker information processors and this may serve them well as they move into formal schooling: Those who demonstrate larger vocabularies at age 2 enter kindergarten with higher levels of reading and math achievement than their peers with less vocabulary (Morgan et al., 2015).

With such a rapidly increasing vocabulary, it should come as no surprise that children sometimes make mistakes. Although they rarely get the meaning entirely wrong, they often use a word too broadly or too narrowly (Uccelli & Pan, 2013). One error is **overextension**, or using a word to refer to too wide a range of objects or events, as when a 2-year-old calls all furry, four-legged animals "doggie." The second, and opposite, error is **underextension**, as when a child initially uses the word *doggie* to refer only to basset hounds like the family pet. Notice that both overextension and underextension are examples of Piaget's concept of assimilation, using existing concepts to interpret new experiences. Getting semantics right seems to be mainly a matter of discriminating similarities and differences—for example, categorizing animals on the basis of size, shape, the sounds they make, and other perceptual features (Clark & Clark, 1977). By 2½–3 years of age, these sorts of semantic errors begin to disappear from children's conversations.

But might children know more about the world than their semantic errors suggest? Yes. Two-year-olds who say "doggie" when they see a cow will point to the cow rather than the dog when asked to find the cow (Naigles & Gelman, 1995; Thompson & Chapman, 1977). Children may overextend the meaning of certain words such as *doggie* not because they misunderstand word meanings but because they want to communicate, have only a small vocabulary with which to do so, and have not yet learned to call something a "whatchamacallit" when they cannot come up with the word for it (Naigles & Gelman, 1995).

We need to be careful about applying these generalizations about early language acquisition to all children because they mask large individual differences in language development. As ■ Figure 10.3 shows, one 24-month-old may have a vocabulary of approximately 50 words, and another may be able to produce more than 500 words (Fenson et al., 1994). What might account for these large differences in language expression? A large factor seems to be socioeconomic status of the family. A classic study by Betty Hart and Todd Risley (1995) examined how parents talked with their infants and toddlers. They found that among the poorest families in their sample, children heard about 620 words per

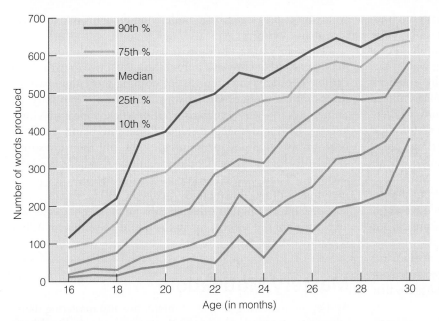

Figure 10.3 The range of individual differences in vocabulary size from 16 to 30 months. Each line on this figure represents the words produced by an individual child, from 16 to 30 months of age.

Source: Fenson, L., et al. (1994). Variability in early communicative development. *Monographs of the Society for Research in Child Development, 59* (Serial No. 242). Copyright © 1994. Reprinted with permission of John Wiley & Sons, Inc.

hour, whereas children in the wealthiest families heard more than 3 times this number of words. The researchers surmised that by the age of 4, this hourly difference would add up to a gap of approximately 30 million words. Further, they found that children who heard more words as they were growing up were the children who entered school with bigger vocabularies and higher IQ scores. In the roughly 25 years since these findings were published, much attention has been given to this gap of 30 million words between wealthy and poor families. Various programs have been developed to encourage parents in lower-income families to talk more with their infants and toddlers (see Suskind, Suskind, & Lewinter-Suskind, 2015).

Other research has disputed the size of the word gap across the range of socioeconomic statuses, but has nonetheless found some truth to the premise that parents' talk can have a powerful influence on their children's development. To try to clarify the issue, several researchers took advantage of a relatively new piece of technology that is like an exercise tracker but for language (Ramirez-Esparza, Garcia-Sierra, & Kuhl, 2014). Infants who were about 1 year old wore the small language tracker on multiple days, racking up a total of 32 hours of language for analysis. The language tracker analysis was able to distinguish who was speaking (infant or an adult), type of speech (child-directed or standard), and context (one or multiple adults). The researchers also collected a measure of word production from the infants when they were about 2 years of age.

What did the researchers find? It turns out that the sheer *quantity* of speech infants are exposed to did not significantly affect their later language, but that the amount of quality speech they heard was important (see also Hirsh-Pasek et al., 2015). In particular, those infants who heard more child-directed speech

from one adult at a time later produced more words than other infants. Although there were fewer lower-income parents who engaged with their infants in what the researchers defined as high-quality speech, there were certainly some who did so. The important variable did not seem to be socioeconomic status per se, but the values and beliefs that parents held regarding how to interact with their youngsters. More of the lower-income parents were unaware of the value of early stimulation for brain development and did not realize that they could make a difference in their children's lives by simply talking with them. But it takes more than awareness; it also requires time and energy, which are often less available in families where parents are working multiple jobs and worrying about safety issues. As Annette Laureau, a sociologist, has described it, middle- and upper-class families use a childrearing style of constantly cultivating their children for adulthood—in other words, very 'hands-on' with much negotiating and explaining going on between parent and child (McKenna, 2012). In contrast, lower-class families tend to use a style of 'hands-off' parenting with little negotiating and explaining. There are pros and cons of both styles, but in terms of language development, one con of the hands-off style is exposure to less child-directed speech from adults, with longer-term effects on academic achievement (see Hoff, 2013).

Telegraphic Speech

The next step in language development, normally occurring at 18–24 months of age, is combining two words into a simple sentence. Toddlers all over the world use two-word sentences to express the same basic ideas (●Table 10.2). Early combinations of two, three, or more words are sometimes called **telegraphic speech** because, like telegrams of the past where costs were minimized by eliminating unnecessary words, these sentences contain critical content words and omit frills such as articles, prepositions, and auxiliary verbs.

It is ungrammatical in adult English to say "No want" or "Where ball." However, these two-word sentences are not just random word combinations or mistakes; they reflect children's

●**Table 10.2** Two-Word Sentences Serve Similar Functions in Different Languages

	Language	
Function of Sentence	**English**	**German**
To locate or name	*There book*	*Buch da (book there)*
To demand	*More milk*	*Mehr Milch (more milk)*
To negate	*No wet*	*Nicht blasen*
To indicate possession	*My shoe*	*Mein Ball (my ball)*
To modify or qualify	*Pretty dress*	*Armer Wauwau (poor doggie)*
To question	*Where ball*	*Wo Ball (where ball)*

Source: Adapted from Slobin, 1979

developing understanding of syntax. Psycholinguists such as Lois Bloom (1998) believe it is appropriate to describe children's early sentences in terms of a **functional grammar**—one that emphasizes the semantic relationships among words, the meanings being expressed, and the functions served by sentences (such as naming, questioning, or commanding). For example, young children often use the same word order to convey different meanings. "Mommy nose" might mean "That's Mommy's nose" in one context, but for one 22-month-old girl one afternoon it meant "Mommy, I've just wiped my runny nose the length of the living room couch." Word order sometimes does matter: "Billy hit" and "Hit Billy" may mean different things. Body language and tone of voice also communicate meanings, such as when a child points and whines to request ice cream, not merely to note its existence.

Between ages 2 and 5, children experience a dramatic increase in the number and type of sentences they produce. Consider 3-year-old Kyle's reply to his mother after she suggests that he release a bug:

> After I hold him, then I'll take the bug back to his friends. Mommy, where did the bug go? Mommy, I didn't know where the bug go. Find it. Maybe Winston's on it [the family dog], Winston, get off the bug! [Kyle spots the bug and picks it up. His mother again asks him to "let the bug go back to his friends."] He does not want to go to his friends. [Kyle drops the bug and squashes it, much to his mother's horror.] I stepped on it and it will not go to his friends.

Compared with a child in the telegraphic stage, Kyle's sentences are much longer and more grammatically complex, although not free of errors, and he is better able to participate in the give-and-take of conversation. Kyle has also begun to add the little function words such as articles and prepositions that are often missing in the earlier telegraphic sentences (Hoff, 2014). How do people know when children are mastering new rules? Oddly enough, their progress sometimes reveals itself in new "mistakes." A child who has been saying "feet" and "went" may suddenly start to say "foots" and "goed." Does this represent a step backward? Not at all. The child was probably using the correct irregular forms at first by imitating adult speech without understanding the meaning of plurality or verb tense. The use of "foots" and "goed" is a breakthrough: The child has inferred the morphological rules of adding -s to pluralize nouns and adding -ed to signal past tense. At first, however, the youngster engages in **overregularization**: overapplying the rules to cases in which the proper form is irregular. When the child masters exceptions to the rules, she will say "feet" and "went" once more.

Children must also master rules for creating variations of the basic declarative sentence; that is, they must learn the syntactic rules for converting a basic idea such as "I am eating pizza" into such forms as questions ("Am I eating pizza?"), negative sentences ("I am not eating pizza"), and imperatives ("Eat the pizza!"). The prominent linguist Noam Chomsky (1968, 1975) drew attention to the child's learning of these rules by proposing that language be described in terms of a **transformational grammar**, or rules of syntax for transforming basic underlying thoughts into a variety of sentence forms.

How do young children learn to phrase the questions that they so frequently ask to fuel their cognitive growth? The earliest questions often consist of nothing more than two- or three-word sentences with rising intonation ("See kitty?"). Sometimes *wh-* words such as *what* or *where* appear ("Where kitty?"). During the second stage of question asking, children begin to use auxiliary, or helping, verbs, but their questions are of this form: "What Daddy is eating?" "Where the kitty is going?" Their understanding of transformation rules is still incomplete (Tager-Flusberg & Zukowski, 2013). Finally, they learn the transformation rule that calls for moving the auxiliary verb ahead of the subject (as in the adultlike sentence "What is Daddy eating?").

Mastery Motivation

As they are mastering language, infants are also mastering many other important tasks to prepare them for success in life. Much evidence supports the claim that infants are curious, active explorers constantly striving to understand and to exert control over the world around them. This, you should recall, was one of Piaget's major themes. **Mastery motivation**, a striving for mastery or competence, appears to be inborn and universal and will display itself in the behavior of all typical infants without prompting from parents. We can clearly see this desire for mastery when infants struggle to open kitchen cabinets, take their first steps, or figure out how new toys work—and derive great pleasure from their efforts (Jennings & Dietz, 2003; Masten & Reed, 2002). Even so, some infants appear to be more mastery oriented than others. Given a new push toy, one baby may simply look at it, but another may mouth it, bang it, and push it across the floor (Jennings & Dietz, 2003). Why might some infants have a stronger mastery motive than others?

One possibility is that the goal itself may hold greater value to some infants: If that red ball looks highly appealing to Joanie, she may expend more time and energy to retrieve it than Naomi, who just doesn't judge it worthy of her attention (Kenward et al., 2009). Mastery motivation also seems higher when parents frequently provide sensory stimulation designed to arouse and amuse their babies—tickling them, bouncing them, playing games of pat-a-cake, giving them stimulating toys, and so on (Busch-Rossnagel, 1997). Mastery motivation flourishes when infants grow up in a responsive environment that provides plenty of opportunities to see for themselves that they can control their environments and experience successes (Maddux, 2002; Masten & Reed, 2002). Consider the toddler who, faced with the challenge of retrieving a cookie from the kitchen counter, struggles to maneuver a chair across the room and to climb up without tipping the chair or falling off. When Mom offers to help him, he shrieks, "Me do it!" And when he does it, he feels a sense of accomplishment that increases the likelihood he will tackle future challenges. Parents who return smiles and coos or respond promptly to cries show infants they can affect people around them.

Unfortunately, infants of parents who are depressed show less interest in and persistence on challenging tasks, perhaps because

Every day, infants and young children display their innate mastery motive.

Image Source Plus/Alamy Stock Photo

also Christakis, 2008) studied infants who watched *Baby Einstein* or *Brainy Baby* videos. They found, rather alarmingly, that for each hour spent watching videos, babies understood 6–8 fewer words than babies who did not watch videos. The research did not follow infants into childhood to determine if the video-watching babies later caught up to the other babies, but the findings do raise a red flag, at least with respect to early language abilities. Other research on the effects of these programs shows a similarly dismal outcome. Infants who spent 6 weeks watching *Baby Wordsmith* videos, which focus on vocabulary, demonstrated absolutely no differences in vocabulary knowledge or language development from infants who did not view this program (Richert et al., 2010; and see Chapter 1's discussion of baby videos and language development). If educational videos are not valuable, and may even be detrimental, what about educational infant and preschool programs?

In one study, 4-year-olds in preschools with strong academic thrusts gained an initial advantage in basic academic skills such as knowledge of letters and numbers but lost it by the end of kindergarten (Hyson, Hirsh-Pasek, & Rescorla, 1991). What is more, they proved to be less creative, more anxious in testing situations, and more negative toward school than children who attended preschool programs with a social rather than academic emphasis. Similarly, Deborah Stipek and her colleagues (1995) have found that highly academic preschool programs raise children's academic achievement test scores but decrease their expectancies of success and pride in accomplishment. So it may be possible to undermine achievement motivation by overemphasizing academics in the preschool years.

However, preschool programs that offer a healthy mix of play and academic activities in the form of guided play can be beneficial to young children (Weisberg, Hirsh-Pasek, & Golinkoff, 2013). This sort of academic skill-building may be especially helpful to disadvantaged children. This was the premise for the federally funded Head Start program, started in 1965 as part of the "War on Poverty." The idea behind Head Start was to provide a variety of social

their parents are not responsive to them (Sparks et al., 2012). As well, children who are raised by parents who constantly stifle their initiatives ("you will *not* move the chair across the room!") may be less likely to take on new tasks.

An infant's level of mastery motivation affects her later achievement behavior. Babies who actively attempt to master challenges at 6 and 12 months score higher on tests of mental development at 2 and 3 years than their less mastery-oriented peers (Jennings & Dietz, 2003; Messer et al., 1986). In sum, infants are intrinsically motivated to master challenges, but parents may help strengthen this inborn motive by stimulating their infants appropriately and responding to their actions. What about infants and toddlers who spend considerable amounts of time away from their parents? Is their motivation influenced by time spent in preschool?

Early Education

As you have seen in previous chapters, babies learn a great deal in the first few years of life. But do infants and toddlers need specific educational experiences? Despite the popular appeal of products such as *Baby Einstein* and *Baby Mozart*, many experts dispute the idea that typically developing children, raised in typical family environments, need direct instruction during their first 3 years (for example, Carlsson-Paige, 2008). And some, such as David Elkind (1987), author of *Miseducation: Preschoolers at Risk*, fear that the push for earlier education may be going too far and that young children today are not given enough time simply to be children — to play and socialize as they choose. Elkind even worries that children may lose their self-initiative and intrinsic motivation to learn when their lives are orchestrated by parents who pressure them to achieve at early ages. Is there anything to these concerns?

Some research seems to confirm Elkind's fears. Frederick Zimmerman, Dimitri Christakis, and Andrew Meltzoff (2007; see

How would you balance structure and free play to optimize young children's learning?

David Grossman/Alamy Stock Photo

and intellectual experiences that might better prepare disadvantaged children for school and "break the cycle of poverty." High-quality Head Start programs provide the nutrition, health care, parent training, and intellectual stimulation that can get these children off to a good start. At first, Head Start and similar programs seemed to be a big success; children in the programs showed average gains of about 10 points on IQ tests. Unfortunately, these early gains were completely wiped out by the time children reached second or third grade (Gray, Ramsey, & Klaus, 1982; Puma et al., 2012).

But the results are not all discouraging. With more than 50 years' worth of study, we know that the benefits of programs such as Head Start are often indirect and may not show up until much later. Consider the Abecedarian Project, a full-time educational program from infancy (starting around 4–5 months) to age 5 for children from low-income families (Campbell et al., 2001). Compared with children who did not participate, Abecedarian children showed impressive cognitive gains during and immediately after the program (■ Figure 10.4). But are the effects of good early educational programs truly life changing? To find out, the researchers followed-up on the Abecedarian participants at age 30 (Campbell et al., 2012). Remarkably, they were able to examine outcomes for a majority of the original participants. Those who had participated in the Abecedarian program had completed more years of education than those in the comparison group. In particular, 23% of the children who had been in the program had earned a college degree compared to only 6% in the comparison group. About 75% of the Abecedarian adults worked full-time compared to 50% of the nonparticipant adults. Despite these advantages of a high-quality preschool program, such early intervention did not "fix" everything. There were no differences, for example, between the two groups in criminal activity at age 30: In both the Abecedarian and the comparison adults, just over 25% had been convicted of a crime. Other research, though, suggests that early education programs can help reduce the number of arrests logged by age 40 (Schweinhart et al., 2005).

An alternative type of program focuses on educating parents about the importance of the early environment and the types of experiences that can be beneficial to their children. It turns out that parent training pays off. In one such program, *Born to Learn*, children displayed higher levels of mastery motivation than nonparticipants by 36 months of age, or even earlier — 24 months — if they were from disadvantaged families (Drotar et al., 2008). In another program, the *Milwaukee Project* (Garber, 1988), full-time child care was provided for youngsters along with job and academic training for mothers. Following-up on these participants in the eighth grade showed that they remained intellectually ahead of their peers who had not participated.

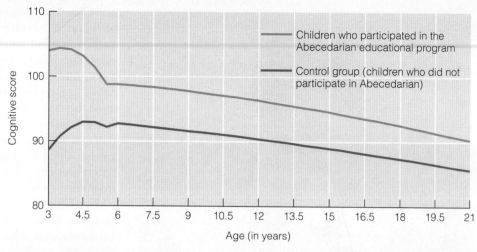

■ Figure 10.4 Cognitive growth curves as a function of preschool treatment, showing a bigger initial gain as well as a sustained advantage in cognitive growth for children in the Abecedarian program.

Source: Campbell, F. A., et al. (2001). The development of cognitive and academic abilities: Growth curves from an early childhood educational experiment. *Developmental Psychology, 37*, 231–242. Copyright © 2001, American Psychological Association.

The programs that experience greater success are those that find ways to address underlying issues, one of which is poverty. In Chapter 9, we discussed how children who grow up in poverty are likely to have lower IQ scores, on average, than their peers who did not experience poverty. It should be no surprise, then, to learn that poverty can also affect educational attainment. Early education programs may not be able to directly combat poverty, but they can address some associated factors that adversely affect academic achievement. These would include strengthening the language environment of the home, as discussed earlier in the chapter, and helping parents to understand the importance of the early environment for children's development.

Checking Mastery

1. Through what stages does early language acquisition progress?
2. Give an example of an overregularization of language.
3. What is mastery motivation?
4. What is one advantage and one potential disadvantage of early education programs for infants and toddlers?

Making Connections

1. What should parents and early childhood educators look for (or listen for) to confirm that infants and toddlers are progressing typically with regard to their language acquisition at ages 1, 2, and 3?
2. Should preschool education be mandatory? At what age should formal education begin? Provide some evidence to support your answer.
3. How can parents and early childhood teachers foster mastery motivation in their children?

LEARNING OBJECTIVES

- Indicate the changes in language development that occur in childhood.
- Demonstrate understanding of different types of motivational styles by describing and giving an example of each.
- Analyze the outcomes typically associated with each motivational style.

With infancy behind them, children begin to expand their language skills and show true achievement motivation. As you'll now see, formal education uses these building blocks to develop lifelong skills and knowledge.

Expanding Language Skills

School-age children improve their pronunciation skills, produce longer and more complex sentences, and continue to expand their vocabularies. The average first-grader starts school with a vocabulary of about 10,000 words and adds somewhere between 5 and 13 new words a day throughout the elementary-school years (Hoff, 2014). School-age children also begin to think about and manipulate language in ways previously impossible (Melzi & Schick, 2013). They can, for example, interpret passive sentences such as "Goofy was liked by Donald" and conditional sentences such as "If Goofy had come, Donald would have been delighted" (Boloh & Champaud, 1993; Sudhalter & Braine, 1985).

Throughout childhood, advances in cognitive development are accompanied by advances in language and communication skills. For example, as children become less cognitively egocentric, they are more able to take the perspective of their listeners (Hoff, 2014). Middle childhood also brings increased **metalinguistic awareness**, or knowledge of language as a system (Melzi & Schick, 2013). Children with metalinguistic awareness understand the concept of words and can define words (semantics). Development of metalinguistic awareness also means that children can distinguish between grammatically correct and grammatically incorrect sentences (syntax) and can understand how language can be altered to fit the needs of the specific social context in which it is used (pragmatics). Children who are **bilingual**, knowing two or more languages, have better metalinguistic skills than non-bilingual (that is, monolingual) children (Schwartz et al., 2008). Are there other benefits to being bilingual?

For starters, ongoing exposure to multiple languages alters the neural connections in the brain (Petitto et al., 2012). As monolingual infants begin to lose some sensitivity to sounds produced in other languages, bilingual and multilingual infants retain sensitivity to the wider range of sounds used in the languages they hear. This may help explain why infants and young children who are regularly exposed to multiple languages seem to acquire the multiple languages with just about as much ease as those learning a single language. There may be times when children learning two languages struggle to find the correct vocabulary word or may take slightly longer on some linguistic tasks. But, for the most part, children who are bilingual end up with more advantages than disadvantages (Bialystok, Craik, & Luk, 2012).

We have also learned that when folks who are bilingual use one of their languages, it activates the other language at the same time (Marian & Shook, 2012). Although they may not realize that both languages are active, studies of eye movements and neuroimages of the brain indicate that both are indeed activated. Perhaps as a result of this activity, bilingual children and adults demonstrate enhanced abilities to switch back and forth between different tasks (Barac & Bialystok, 2012). Their working memory is more robust than that of monolinguals and they are also more skilled at ignoring irrelevant information and focusing on the relevant features of a task (Morales, Calvo, & Bialystok, 2013; Rubio-Fernández & Glucksberg, 2012).

Such evidence tells us that the constant juggling of two languages that bilinguals must perform strengthens the higher level executive control components of the cognitive system. Just as physical exercise affects your body's structure as well as its functioning, the early and regular mental exercise required to become bilingual affects the brain's neural wiring as well as the brain's functioning (Grady, Luk, Craik, & Bialystok, 2015; Marian et al., 2014; Wong, Yin, & O'Brien, 2016).

What's more, bilingualism seems to bolster a person's cognitive reserve (Bialystok et al., 2012). As we get older, cognitive reserve may allow us to retain our mental capabilities longer by increasing our mental processing efficiency. In one study, bilingual adults developed symptoms and were diagnosed with Alzheimer's disease 4–5 years later than monolingual adults (Alladi et al., 2013).

What if we acquire a second language later in life? The outcomes are not the same for later second language learners as for those who are exposed to a second language from birth and acquire the two languages simultaneously. For one thing, early versus later learning of a second language results in different changes in brain architecture, indicating that second language learning may follow different paths depending on the age it occurs (Jasińska & Petitto, 2013; Klein, Mok, Chen, & Watkins, 2014).

Research with native speakers of Korean or Chinese, who had come to the United States between age 3 and age 39, examined their mastery of English grammar and found that those who learned it earliest—prior to puberty—knew it best (Johnson & Newport, 1989). Among those who arrived in the United States after puberty, performance was generally poor regardless of age of arrival or number of years using English. Such findings have been used to argue that there is a sensitive period for language acquisition that ends around puberty, but other research shows that it is more one's age at the time of arrival in the United States that is related to proficiency in English as a second language (Birdsong, 1999, 2005). Although adults are generally less likely than children to attain native-like proficiency in a second language—suggesting a sensitive period—some adults do achieve such proficiency, usually through massive effort and exposure to the second language (Birdsong, 1999).

So it seems as though it is easier to learn a second language when learning a first language during infancy, that is, to be bilingual rather than to acquire a second language later. Bilingualism also imposes some benefits that do not seem to come with later second language learning. In particular, bilinguals experience enhanced executive control and cognitive reserve. Given the benefits of bilingualism, perhaps more parents should be encouraged to brush up on their multilanguage skills in order to raise their children bilingual. When their children are old, they might appreciate having that extra cognitive reserve.

Achievement Motivation

Researchers who study achievement motivation strive to understand and explain people's behaviors in achievement situations such as those found in the classroom. Understanding what motivates students to perform (or not) can set the stage for creating conditions to foster higher levels of motivation. The importance of this should not be underestimated: Children's beliefs about their competence for various tasks predicts their performance on those tasks (Denissen, Zarratt, & Eccles, 2007).

All children occasionally experience failure in their efforts to master challenges and meet achievement standards. Why do some children persist and triumph in the face of failure, whereas others give up when they experience failure? Carol Dweck and her colleagues (for example, Dweck, 2006; Yeager, Paunesku, Walton, & Dweck, 2013; Blackwell, Trzesniewski, & Dweck, 2007) have spent over 30 years searching for answers. From this research, Dweck has concluded that it is not so much what you have—your ability, talent, or intelligence—as *how you think about* what you have (Dweck, 2006). In particular, those who have a **fixed mindset** tend to believe that "what they have" is fixed or static. Thus, they either "have" a talent or do not; they either "are" intelligent or they are not. With this sort of mindset, there is little reason to put forth great effort on a task because it cannot change a fixed trait. Students with a fixed mindset, even those who are highly talented, typically select tasks that they know will showcase their talents with little effort. They tend to avoid challenging tasks as they do not believe they can be successful on these.

In contrast, those who have a **growth mindset** believe that abilities and talent are not fixed but are malleable: They can be fostered through hard work and effort. With this sort of mindset, students are motivated to put forth effort as this will lead to learning and advancement. A growth mindset can be fostered by praising students' efforts, not just the end products of their work (Dweck, 2007; 2015). For instance, a teacher or parent might say, "That was a really hard assignment, but you kept working on it, trying different strategies, until you finished it. Way to go!" In contrast, praising students for their intelligence ("You did well on that test because you are so smart") may lead students to think that their performance is driven by (their fixed amount of) intelligence alone and is not related to effort. What about the inevitable feedback about mistakes? Students with a fixed mindset interpret such feedback as an indication that they lack ability. Thus, when they receive low grades or a paper filled with lots of comments from

their teacher, students with a fixed mindset are more likely to feel defeated by their sense of lack of ability rather than energized to work harder and improve. Students with a growth mindset are more likely to interpret feedback about mistakes as useful information that can be used to improve for the future (Moser et al., 2011). How do some children end up with growth rather than fixed mindsets? Characteristics of children, parents, and schools all contribute to motivation style and level.

Child Contributions

Several characteristics of the child contribute to achievement levels and their motivation or mindset to succeed. First is the child's age or developmental level. By age 3, children are beginning to react differently to their successes and failures, yet they remain unrealistically optimistic about their abilities until age 7–8 (Wigfield et al., 2015). With age, children's perceptions of their academic abilities become more accurate, likely because they become better at understanding feedback—from parents, teachers, and peers—about their performance (Wigfield et al., 2015). Young children may also give up if their failures are clear-cut and they conclude they have been bad, as they equate success and failure with being a good or bad person (Burhans & Dweck, 1995; Heyman, Dweck, & Cain, 1992).

Young children are protected from damaging self-perceptions partly because they believe that ability is a changeable quality and that they can become smarter and improve their ability if they work hard. That is, they start out with a growth mindset. This view of ability encourages them to adopt **mastery goals** (also called learning goals) in achievement situations, aiming to learn new things so that they can improve their abilities (Brophy, 2010). A focus on mastery goals tends to dominate throughout the lower elementary grades (Bong, 2009).

As children age, in our society at least, they begin to see ability as a fixed trait that does not change much with effort. As a result, by late elementary and middle school, more of them have a fixed

What factors will determine whether this student remains motivated and focused on mastery goals or shifts to performance goals and possibly becomes disinterested with school?

Tom & Dee Ann McCarthy/Corbis/Getty Images

Mastery Goals	Performance Goals
Ability as a changeable trait	Ability as a fixed trait
Focus on increasing competence or knowledge ("I understand this material better than I did before")	Focus on increasing status relative to others ("I did better on this than the other students did")
Self-regulated learning; ability to monitor understanding of material and adjust behavior (for example, effort) accordingly	Other-regulated learning; ability to monitor performance relative to peers and increase effort (approach) to outperform them or decrease effort (avoidance) to save face (to say that failures are because of a lack of effort, not incompetence)
Deep-level processing of material (for example, learning to understand)	Superficial-level processing of material (for example, memorizing for a test)
Feelings of pride and satisfaction associated with success, with failures indicating a need for more effort or different learning strategies	Feelings of anxiety and shame associated with failure; boastful feelings associated with success

Source: Adapted from Covington, 2000; Elliot & Church, 1997.

mindset and adopt **performance goals** in school; they aim to *prove* their ability rather than to *improve* it and seek to be judged smart rather than dumb (Bong, 2009; Dweck & Leggett, 1988; Erdley et al., 1997; and see ● **Table 10.3**). These changes in the understanding of ability are probably caused both by cognitive development—especially an increased ability to analyze the causes of successes and failures and to infer enduring traits from behavior—and by an accumulation of feedback in school (Stipek, 1984).

Importantly, children with growth mindsets who continue to focus on mastery or learning goals tend to do better in school than those who adopt fixed mindsets and switch to performance goals (Yeager et al., 2013). Children who focus on mastery goals do not become as disheartened by a low grade if they have nonetheless progressed in their understanding of the material. For these children, the *process* of learning is enjoyable; it helps quench their curiosity (Fisher, Marshall, & Nanayakkara, 2009). Their ability to enjoy the learning process may help explain why these children exhibit higher levels of achievement (von Stumm, Hell, & Chamorro-Premuzic, 2011). In contrast, children who focus on performance goals are more discouraged because, for them, the *outcome*—the grade—is the goal, not the process of learning. These children are more likely to report anxiety and boredom, factors that are negatively associated with achievement (Daniels et al., 2009; Pekrun, Elliot, & Maier, 2009). The two groups of children—those with mastery or learning goals and those with performance goals—even display different patterns of neurological activity in response to their performance outcomes, further evidence that these two groups are truly experiencing their successes and failures differently (Fisher et al., 2009). Importantly, the two types of goals are not mutually exclusive; that is, it is possible to be motivated by both mastery goals and performance goals (Darnon et al., 2010). What is important, though, is the predominant focus that students hold as they work to achieve their goals. As Table 10.3 illustrates, when students believe that ability is primarily a fixed entity that they either have or do not have and conclude that they lack it, they set performance goals rather than learning goals; figuring that hard work will not payoff, they run the risk of giving up in the classroom (Dweck & Leggett, 1988). Even gifted students can fall into this trap (Ablard & Mills, 1996). Evaluate your own motivation style with the exercise in **Engagement 10.1**.

In addition to their age, children's level of intelligence, not surprisingly, contributes to their success in academics (Spinath et al., 2006). But clearly level of intelligence is just one piece of the puzzle because some students with above average intelligence do not do particularly well in school and others exceed expectations based solely on their IQ scores. It turns out that both motivation and achievement levels are higher when children value a subject—they believe it is important and they are interested in a subject (Spinath et al., 2006). Think of this in relation to your own learning and motivation and you will likely recognize that you try harder and perform better when something is important and interesting to you.

Parent Contributions

Parents can foster their children's achievement motivation by stressing and reinforcing the *process* of learning rather than emphasizing the product (Dweck, 2015). They can also emphasize the learning opportunities provided by making mistakes. Consider research by Kyla Haimovitz and Carol Dweck (2016). Over several studies, they demonstrated that parents tend to hold mindsets about *failure* as either debilitating or enhancing. Children pick up on these parental mindsets about failure and these help shape children's own mindsets about intelligence. In particular, parents who view failures as debilitating tend to have children with fixed mindsets about their intelligence. As we have already learned, fixed mindsets are not as productive as growth mindsets. Instead, individuals who believe intelligence is influenced by effort—how hard they work—are more likely to show improvement following mistakes than individuals who believe that intelligence is a fixed trait.

In their review of research on achievement motivation, Allan Wigfield, Jacquelynne Eccles, and their colleagues (2015) concluded that three aspects of parenting style can influence children's motivation:

1. Providing an appropriate balance of structure for daily activities, without being controlling, overly prescriptive, or holding unrealistic expectations;
2. Offering consistent and supportive responses to children's activities and behaviors;
3. Presenting opportunities for children to observe healthy responses to life's challenges from the adults in their lives.

What's Your Motivation Style?

Indicate whether you agree (A) or disagree (D) with each of the following statements, as they pertain to your typical approach or thoughts about learning and coursework.

___ 1. I read the chapter because the material was interesting to me.

___ 2. I read the chapter because the instructor said there would be a quiz on the material.

___ 3. I often look up some additional information related to the course material so that I can better understand what is discussed in class or presented in the textbook.

___ 4. I feel good when I am able to convey my understanding of the material on the exam.

___ 5. I need to earn a B+ or higher in this class to maintain my scholarship.

___ 6. I want to get an A on this test to show the professor that I'm good.

___ 7. I want to get an A on all the quizzes this semester because then I will be exempt from taking the final exam.

___ 8. As long as I pass this class, I'll be happy because I know I've learned something new from a really challenging professor.

___ 9. I like to see how others in the class score on the assignments so I can get an idea of how well I'm doing.

___ 10. I don't really care how other people in the class score because their performance is unrelated to my learning.

___ 11. I get bored and frustrated when the instructor spends time on easy material and quizzes us on stuff that seems obvious.

___ 12. I get frustrated when the instructor goes over difficult material that is going to be hard to study to earn a good grade.

___ 13. There is nothing I like more than a good challenging homework assignment that makes me think harder or differently.

___ 14. I like getting a homework assignment that is easy and fairly mindless to complete. I know I can get it done and the instructor will be happy with my answers.

___ 15. I usually find that I can master a task or material by working really hard on it.

___ 16. If I cannot solve a task right away, I usually stop working on it because I'm not going to be able to solve it.

Scoring: Count the number of "Agree" answers to these questions: 1, 3, 4, 8, 10, 11, 13, 15. Count the number of "Agree" answers to these questions: 2, 5, 6, 7, 9, 12, 14, 16. If the number of "Agree" answers to the first set (1, 3, 4, 8, 10, 11, 13, 15) is higher than the number of "Agree" answers to the second set (2, 5, 6, 7, 9, 12, 14, 16), then you focus more on learning or mastery goals. You are more interested in mastering material for the sake of learning than for the sake of grades. If, on the other hand, the number of your "Agree" answers to the second set of questions is higher than the number of "Agree" answers to the first set, then you focus more on performance goals. You are motivated to perform well and earn good grades. According to the text, which of these motivation styles—mastery versus performance—ultimately leads to a deeper and richer understanding of material? What could you do to shift from one style to the other?

Thus, parents should provide a safe, structured environment that encourages children to challenge themselves with new tasks or set higher goals for those tasks already familiar to them. Children who are encouraged and supported in a positive manner are likely to enjoy new challenges and feel confident about mastering them.

School Contributions

How do schools affect achievement? Nearly every school asserts that the major goal of classroom instruction is improvement of children's learning. Many of these same schools, however, are structured in ways that focus on the external rewards that students can earn (such as grades or stickers). As a result, they may encourage children, either deliberately or inadvertently, to set performance goals rather than mastery or learning goals. Many classrooms are competitive places where students try to outdo each other to earn the best grades and gain teacher recognition. Students receive a grade (good or bad), indicating their performance on a test or project, and that is the end of it. If they did not fully learn the material, they are given no opportunity to do so: They learn that the grade, not learning, is the goal.

What if schools downplayed the competitive race for the best grades in class? Consider some research by Elaine Elliott and Carol Dweck (1988). They asked fifth-graders to perform a novel task. The students were led to believe that they had either low or high ability and were warned that they would soon be performing similar tasks that would prove difficult. Half the children worked under a performance goal (not unlike the goals emphasized in many classrooms): They were told that their performance would be compared with that of other children and evaluated by an expert. The remaining children were induced to adopt a learning or mastery goal: Although they would make some mistakes, they were told, working at the tasks would "sharpen the mind" and help them at school.

As expected, the only children who became frustrated and gave up were those who believed they had low ability and were pursuing a performance goal. For them, continuing to work on the difficult task meant demonstrating again that they were stupid. By contrast, even "low ability" students who pursued a mastery goal persisted despite their failures and showed remarkably little frustration, probably because they believed they could grow from their experience. Perhaps, then, teachers undermine achievement motivation by distributing gold stars and grades and frequently calling attention to how students compare with one another (Brophy, 2010). Children might be better off if teachers nurtured their intrinsic motivation to master challenges and structured their classrooms to emphasize mastery rather than performance goals (Murayama & Elliot, 2009). Then, slower learners could view their mistakes as a sign that they should change strategies to improve their competencies rather than as further proof that they lack ability.

In a fascinating study, Harvard economist Roland Fryer, Jr. (2011) spent millions of dollars to learn whether students could be bribed into earning higher standardized test scores. He enlisted school districts in three major cities and used a different set of incentives in each location. In Chicago, ninth-graders could earn up to $2,000 per year by getting paid $50 for each A test grade, $35 for each B grade, and $20 for each C grade. Students in New York City were paid for completing assignments throughout the term. In Dallas, second-graders were paid $2 every time they read a book and completed a quiz on their reading.

The results may surprise you. The program was a bust in Chicago and New York City: Students earned lots of money for getting good grades on tests throughout the year but showed no improvement on standardized tests given at the end of the school year. The program that proved to have the biggest bang for the bucks was the one in Dallas that paid the least and targeted, not grades, but a behavior that all children could already perform and could control—their reading. Young students who were paid for reading books and answering quiz questions significantly improved their standardized reading comprehension scores. We still need to see how students in the various groups perform over time—and ensure that rewarding activities such as reading books does not eventually undermine intrinsic motivation for reading. But the results suggest that rewarding children not for the final products of their work (that is, the grades) but for the steps that contribute to the final product can have a positive effect on their performance. Fryer and others involved in the study found that students who had the opportunity to earn the most money for high test scores were very excited by this prospect but did not know how to go about achieving it. Instead of bribing students for the grades they earn, it might be better to encourage students to involve themselves in behaviors they can control that contribute to greater engagement with the course material. Ultimately, this is what will lead to greater achievement gains.

Finally, schools can help students develop growth mindsets through fairly simple interventions. In one program, researchers developed a workshop on mindset and study skills for minority and low-income students. Over the course of eight sessions, "students learned to think of their brains as muscles that get stronger as you exercise them. Students visualized new neuronal connections growing as they completed hard math problems" (Yeager et al., 2013, p. 8). Another group of students participated in a workshop on study skills, but without the focus on mindset. Math scores before and after the intervention were tracked for both groups and the results were quite remarkable (Blackwell, Trzesniewski, & Dweck, 2007). Math scores of both groups were nearly identical prior to the intervention, but deviated significantly after the training. Those with the mindset training showed upward progress, whereas those without the mindset training showed declining progress, despite receiving study skills training.

To recap what you have learned so far, children approach achievement tasks with either a fixed or growth mindset, based on how they view their abilities: unchangeable or malleable. As they age, children are more likely to believe that ability is a stable trait and shift from focusing on mastery goals to focusing on performance goals. These changes, brought about by both cognitive development and feedback in school, may make them more vulnerable to "failure syndrome," a tendency to give up at the first obstacle they encounter (Brophy, 2010). Yet some children remain far more motivated to succeed in school than others, and parents and schools have a lot to do with that.

Learning to Read

Perhaps children's most important achievement in school is acquiring the ability to read. Mastery of reading paves the way for mastering other academic skills. Skilled readers consume more printed material than unskilled readers, giving them an advantage in other academic areas that increasingly rely on reading skills over the school years (Sparks, Patton, & Murdoch, 2013;

Students who are given external rewards for good performance in the classroom or on tests may end up losing their intrinsic motivation for learning.

Marmaduke St. John/Alamy Stock Photo

Stanovich, 1986). Unlike language acquisition, a natural learning task that typically requires no formal education, reading acquisition usually requires direct instruction. Fortunately, the brain seems to be structured to support the acquisition of reading skills (Dehaene, 2009). How, though, do children master this complex and important skill?

Mastering the Alphabetic Principle

Before children can read, they must understand the **alphabetic principle**—the idea that the letters in printed words represent the sounds in spoken words in a systematic way (Lonigan, 2015). According to Linnea Ehri (1999), this is a four-step process, as follows:

- *Prealphabetic phase:* Children memorize selected visual cues to remember words. They can "read" text that they have memorized during previous readings. A picture on a page in a favorite book, for instance, triggers a child to recall the words she has often heard her mother read when they turned to this page.
- *Partial alphabetic phase:* Children learn the shapes and sounds of letters. They begin to connect at least one letter in a word—usually the first—to its corresponding sound. For example, they recognize the curved shape of the letter C and begin to associate this with a particular sound. Not surprisingly, children typically recognize the initial letter of their first name before other letters (Treiman & Broderick, 1998).
- *Full alphabetic phase:* Children know all the letters and make complete connections between written letters and their corresponding sounds. To do this, they rely on **phonological awareness**—the sensitivity to the sound system of language that enables them to segment spoken words into sounds or phonemes (Carroll et al., 2003). Children who have phonological awareness can recognize that *cat* and *trouble* both have the phoneme /t/ in them, can tell you how many distinct sounds there are in the word *dark*, and can tell you what will be left if you take the /f/ sound out of *fat*. Children can decode words never before seen by applying their knowledge of phonetics. • Table 10.4 shows what happened when a third-grade boy with poor phonological awareness tried to read the sentence, "A boy said, 'Run, little girl.'" He ended up with an incorrect interpretation ("A baby is running little go") and lost the intended meaning of the sentence, illustrating the importance of phonological awareness.
- *Consolidated alphabetic phase:* Children are able to group letters that regularly occur together into a unit. For instance, the letter sequence *ing*, which frequently appears at the end of

Repeatedly reading the same story fosters vocabulary and deepens children's understanding of the story content

imageBROKER/Alamy Stock Photo

verbs, is perceived as a single unit rather than as three separate letters. This grouping speeds the processing of the multisyllabic words that older children are increasingly exposed to in their books.

Thus, the basic components of literacy include mastering a language system, understanding connections between sounds and their printed symbols (the alphabetic principle), and discriminating phonemes that make up words (phonological awareness). How does the child pull all this together into reading?

Emergent Literacy

Several factors influence **emergent literacy**—the developmental precursors of reading skills in young children (Whitehurst & Lonigan, 1998). Emergent literacy includes knowledge, skills, and attitudes that will facilitate the acquisition of reading ability. Children with greater working memory and attention control demonstrate a higher degree of reading readiness than other children, suggesting that activities strengthening these skills can help foster reading achievement (Welsh et al., 2010). One way to do this is through reading storybooks to preschoolers (Evans & Shaw, 2008). Repetitious storybook reading enhances children's vocabulary and

• **Table 10.4** One Boy's Misreading of the Sentence "A Boy Said, 'Run, Little Girl.'"

Words in Target Sentence	Strategies Employed by Reader	Words "Read"
A	Sight word known to reader	A
boy	Unknown; uses beginning *b* to guess *baby*	baby
said, "Run,	*Said* unknown; jumps to the next word (*run*), which he recognizes, then uses the *s* in *said* and his knowledge of syntax to generate *is running*	is running
little	Sight word known to reader	little
girl	Unknown; uses beginning *g* to guess *go*	go

Source: Adapted from Ely, 2001

allows them to see the connection between printed and spoken words. Importantly, parents should read *with* their child rather than to their child, meaning they should actively involve their child in the activity rather than having the child remain the passive recipient (Phillips, Norris, & Anderson, 2008). With each successive reading, parents who ask increasingly complex questions about the text can move their child from a superficial to a deeper understanding (van Kleeck et al., 1997). Even older children benefit from reading the same book on multiple occasions (Faust & Glenzer, 2000) and from shared reading with a parent (Clarke-Stewart, 1998). Parents, with their greater mastery of reading, can help their fledgling readers develop an understanding of printed words. If you think of this in Vygotsky's framework, it is an example of parent and child operating in the zone of proximal development.

Rhyming stories and games can help foster phonological awareness. For this reason, listening to books with a rhyming structure (for example, Dr. Seuss's *The Cat in the Hat*) can benefit children. Young children's sensitivity to rhyme (for example, *cat-sat*) helps predict their later reading success (Bryant, 1998; Goswami, 1999).

By assessing preschool children's emergent literacy skills, parents and early childhood educators can develop a fairly accurate idea of what children's later reading skills will be. In particular, differences among children in knowledge of letters (for example, knowing the alphabet), phonological awareness, and word segmentation skills predict later differences in their reading ability (Carroll et al., 2003; Kendeou et al., 2009). In addition, semantic knowledge as reflected in children's ability to retrieve words, provide word definitions, and assign meaning to the printed symbols that represent words predicts later reading ability (Kendeou et al., 2009; Roth, Speece, & Cooper, 2002). This suggests that parents can help children get a head start on reading by encouraging activities such as rhyming, repeating the ABCs, and defining words.

Skilled and Unskilled Readers

After children have received reading instruction, why are some children quick, advanced readers but others struggle to master the most basic reading material? For starters, skilled readers have a solid understanding of the alphabetic principle—the notion that letters must be associated with phonemes. Thus, when they see the letter *b*, they know the sound that it represents. A large body of research also confirms that reading ability is influenced by a child's level of phonological awareness (see Lonigan, 2015). Children with higher levels of phonological awareness usually become better readers than children with lower levels of phonological awareness.

But there is more to being a skilled reader than connecting letters with sounds. Analyses of eye movement patterns show that unskilled readers skip words or parts of words, whereas skilled readers' eyes hit all the words (Perfetti, 1999). Skilled readers spend less time looking at the printed words than less-skilled readers, and their eyes are also less likely to skip back to a previous word in the sentence (Valle et al., 2013). In other words, their eye movements suggest that they are faster information processors. Speed of information processing influences performance on a variety of tasks and is important from infancy through old age.

Some children have serious difficulties learning to read, even though they have normal intellectual ability and no sensory impairments or emotional difficulties that could account for their problems. These children have dyslexia, or a reading disability. A minority have the kind of visual perception problem that used to be seen as the heart of dyslexia; they cannot distinguish between letters with similar appearances, or they read words backward (*top* might become *pot*). However, it is now clear that the difficulties of most dyslexic children involve auditory perception more than visual perception (see, for example, Temple et al., 2000).

Specifically, children who become dyslexic readers often show deficiencies in phonological awareness well before they enter school (Bruck, 1992; Melby-Lervåg, Lyster, & Hulme, 2012). There is even evidence that the brains of dyslexic children respond differently than those of other children to speech sounds soon after birth; functional imaging of the brain shows that this distinctive pattern of neural activity is still evident when the children are later diagnosed as having dyslexia (see, for example, Caylak, 2009; Shaywitz et al., 2001). This suggests that a perceptual deficit may develop during the prenatal period of brain development. Because dyslexic children have difficulty analyzing the sounds in speech, they also have trouble detecting sound–letter correspondences, which in turn impairs their ability to recognize printed words automatically and effortlessly (Bruck, 1990). They must then devote so much effort to decoding the words on the page that they have little attention to spare for interpreting and remembering what they have read. Dyslexic children continue to perform poorly on tests of phonological awareness and tests of word recognition as adolescents and adults, even if they have become decent readers (Bruck, 1990, 1992; Shaywitz et al., 1999). It is now clear that dyslexia is a lifelong disability, not just a developmental delay that is eventually overcome.

Let's broaden our attention now from effective reading instruction to effective education. How well are schools doing at educating children? What factors contribute to effective schools, and in doing so, presumably contribute to more effective learning by children?

Effective Schools, Effective Learning

Some schools seem to do a better job than others—they graduate a higher percentage of students or have a higher percentage of students at or above the proficient level in one or more subjects. Why? To understand why some schools seem more effective than others, we must consider characteristics of the students, characteristics of the teachers and school settings, as well as the interaction between student and environment.

Student Characteristics

Over the years, some scholars have argued that a school's effectiveness is only as good as what it has to work with—the students it takes in. We know there are genetic differences among children and these differences contribute to differences in aptitude among them. As you learned in Chapters 3 and 9, IQ scores have a genetic component, and children with higher

IQs attain higher grades throughout their 12 years of school. Schools cannot eliminate these genetic differences among children, but they can influence (that is, raise) overall levels of academic achievement. In addition, academic achievement, on average, tends to be higher in schools with a preponderance of economically advantaged students; children are better able to make academic progress in school when they come from homes that are stocked with computers, books, and intellectually stimulating toys (Portes & MacLeod, 1996). However, this does not mean that schools are only as good as the students they serve. Many schools that serve disadvantaged populations are highly effective at motivating students and preparing them for jobs or further education. To really determine a school's effectiveness, researchers need to look at how students change from before to after they receive instruction (Zvoch & Stevens, 2006).

This was, in large part, the goal of the federally mandated *No Child Left Behind* (NCLB) in the United States—to ensure that children, regardless of how high or low they score at the start, improve their performance after each year of instruction. After nearly 20 years, though, studies examining the influence of the controversial NCLB law have found mixed results. According to a Brookings Institution report, math performance of disadvantaged children improved in elementary school, although not by as much as had been hoped (Dee & Jacob, 2010). Reading performance remained fairly stable from before to after implementation of NCLB.

Studies of effective learning environments provide another illustration of the interaction of nature and nurture. High-achieving parents pass their genes to their children, providing genetic potential for high achievement to their children (Rutter & Maughan, 2002). These same high-achieving parents are likely to select schools with strong academic reputations, often by choosing to live in a neighborhood served by a "good" school district. This is an example of a passive gene–environment correlation, described in Chapter 3, in which children are influenced by their parent's genes directly through genetic transmission and indirectly through the environments their parents create for them.

Teacher and School Characteristics

Andrew Wayne and Peter Youngs (2003) reviewed research on the relationship between teacher characteristics and student achievement. They found that student achievement scores rose with increases in the quality of their teachers' undergraduate institutions and their teachers' licensure examination scores. Other research similarly finds that higher cognitive skills of teachers in their content area translates into better student performance (Hanushek, Piopiunik, & Wiederhold, 2014; Kunter et al., 2013; Sadler et al., 2013). Perhaps the most intriguing findings about teacher effectiveness come from statistical analyses conducted by William Sanders, who found that students who are lucky enough to get the best teachers 3 years in a row achieve as much as 50 points higher on standardized tests than students who are unfortunate enough to get the worst teachers 3 years in a row (Sanders & Horn, 1995; Sanders & Rivers, 1996). What is an effective teacher? According to Sanders, effectiveness can be defined by how far teachers can advance their students each year. Eric Hanushek reached a similar conclusion after finding that students with the best teachers advance 1.5 years in 1 school year, whereas students with the worst teachers advance only half a year over the course of the school year (see Hanushek, Rivkin, & Kain, 2005). These effects are cumulative and long-lasting: A student with the best teachers 2 years in a row progresses the equivalent of 3 years, whereas the student with the worst teachers 2 years in a row progresses just 1 year and will be 2 years behind the other student in achievement level. Ultimately, a person's earnings over their lifetime may be impacted by whether they had teachers who were highly effective, average, or below average (see ■ Figure 10.5).

What might be going on in the classrooms of the students who show the most progress each year? The collection of research shows that in effective classrooms, teachers:

- Strongly emphasize academics. They demand a lot from their students, expect them to succeed, regularly assign homework, and work hard to achieve their objectives in the classroom (Hoy, 2012).
- Create a task-oriented but comfortable atmosphere. For example, they waste little time starting activities or dealing with distracting discipline problems, provide clear instructions and feedback, and encourage and reward good work.
- Manage discipline problems effectively. For instance, they enforce the rules on the spot rather than send offenders to the principal's office, and they avoid the use of physical punishment.

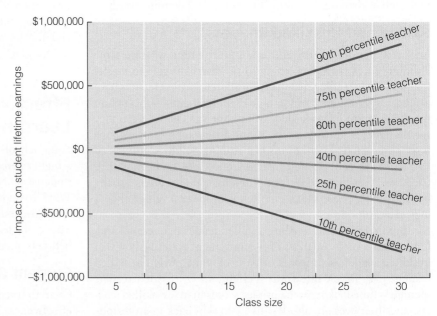

■ **Figure 10.5** As this striking analysis by economist Eric Hanushek shows, having a more effective teacher can make a big difference, especially in larger classes.

Source: Hanushek, E. A. (2011). The economic value of higher teacher quality. *Economics of Education Review, 30,* 466–479.

- Foster an atmosphere of social cohesion in the classroom so that everyone—students, teachers, and aides—feel as though they have a stake in the group and its success (Hoy, 2012).

Student-Environment Interaction

Finally, characteristics of the student and characteristics of the learning environment often interact to affect student outcome. This is an example of the concept of goodness of fit—an appropriate match between the person's characteristics and her environment (see Chapter 11). Many educational institutions seem to be based on the assumption that one teaching method, organizational system, or philosophy of education will prove superior for all students, regardless of their ability levels, learning styles, personalities, and cultural backgrounds. This assumption is often wrong. Instead, many educational practices are highly effective with some kinds of students but ineffective with other students. The secret is to find an appropriate match between the learner and the teaching method.

In a good illustration of goodness of fit between learners and environments, highly achievement-oriented students adapt well to unstructured classrooms in which they have a good deal of choice, whereas students who are less achievement oriented often do better with more structure (Peterson, 1977). Sometimes an alternative teaching method works as well as a traditional one for highly capable students but only one of these methods suits less capable students. In one study, for example, highly distractible students got more from computer-assisted instruction than from a teacher's presentation of the same material, whereas more

attentive students benefited equally from both methods (Orth & Martin, 1994). Finally, students tend to have more positive outcomes when they and their teacher share similar backgrounds and students feel as though they are understood and valued by their teacher (Wigfield et al., 2015). Evidence of the importance of the fit between student and classroom environment implies that educational programs are likely to be most effective when they are highly individualized—tailored to suit each student's developmental competencies and needs.

Checking Mastery

1. What is the difference between a mastery (or learning) goal and a performance goal?
2. What is one characteristic that differentiates a skilled reader from a less-skilled reader?
3. What are three factors that characterize an effective learning environment?

Making Connections

1. Using the material on effective learning environments, evaluate your high school and indicate ways it could improve to become a highly effective learning environment.
2. Unlike most of his peers, Johnny, age 7, is not yet reading despite having the usual classroom instruction. What might account for Johnny's trouble with reading?

10.4
The Adolescent

LEARNING OBJECTIVES

- Explain why levels of academic achievement decline in adolescence and provide two methods to stop this decline.
- Describe the main findings of cross-cultural research on math performance and delineate steps to improve math scores in countries near or below average relative to other countries.
- Analyze the pros and cons of employment during high school.
- Indicate conditions that contribute to a smooth transition for teens completing high school and moving on to college or work.

Adolescents make critical decisions about such matters as how much time to devote to studying, whether to work part-time after school, whether to go to college, and what to be when they grow up. They become more capable of making these educational and vocational choices as their cognitive and social skills expand; in turn, the choices they make shape their development. But many of them lose interest in school when they leave elementary school.

Declining Levels of Achievement

You might think that adolescents would become more dedicated to academic success once they begin to realize that they need a good education to succeed in life. But consider what Deborah Stipek (1984) concluded after reviewing studies on the development of achievement motivation from early childhood to adolescence:

On the average, children value academic achievement more as they progress through school, but their expectations for success and self-perceptions of competence decline, and their affect toward school becomes more negative. Children also become increasingly concerned about achievement outcomes and reinforcement (for example, high grades) associated with positive outcomes and less concerned about intrinsic satisfaction in achieving greater competence. (p. 153)

Many of the negative trends Stipek describes become especially apparent as young adolescents make the transition from elementary school to middle school (typically grades 6–8) or junior high school (grades 7–9). At this critical juncture, achievement motivation, self-esteem, and grades may all

By adolescence, some students have little motivation to achieve in the classroom. How can this be prevented?

Gabe Palmer/Alamy Stock Photo

decline. ■ **Figure 10.6** shows the academic trajectories for four groups of students studied by Leslie Gutman and his colleagues: those with high and low IQ scores who had either many or few risk factors (Gutman, Sameroff, & Cole, 2003). Risk factors included minority group status, low maternal education and mental health, stressful life events, large family size, and father absence. Students with more risk factors showed a steady decline in academic achievement throughout their schooling, regardless of whether they began with high or low IQ scores. Students with few risk factors showed a slight increase in achievement until around grade 6 or 7, at which time achievement began to drop slowly. Boys show greater declines in motivation and school interest than girls (Dotterer, McHale, & Crouter, 2009).

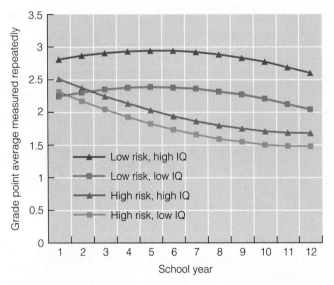

■ **Figure 10.6** Grade point average from 1st grade to 12th grade for students with high and low risk and IQ.

Source: Gutman, L. M., Sameroff, A. J., & Cole, R. (2003). Academic growth curve trajectories from 1st grade to 12th grade: Effects of multiple social risk factors and preschool child factors. *Developmental Psychology, 39,* 777–790. Copyright © 2003 by the American Psychological Association.

What might explain these discouraging trends? To answer this question, we'll first examine what is going on at the individual level, and then consider family and peer influences before ending with a look at the wider context of school and society.

At the individual level, children become increasingly capable of analyzing the causes of events, interpreting feedback from teachers, and inferring enduring traits such as high or low ability from their behavior (Stipek & Mac Iver, 1989). The result is that they view their strengths and weaknesses more realistically—and lose some of their high academic self-esteem and high expectancies of success (Stipek & Mac Iver, 1989; Wigfield et al., 1997). Those who manage to maintain an emphasis on mastery or learning goals attain higher grades in high school than those who do not (Gutman, 2006). Students who believe that success is a matter of luck have lower grades than students without this attributional style (House, 2006).

Fortunately, higher levels of academic achievement can be promoted by continuing to emphasize a growth mindset throughout adolescence (e.g., Wiersema et al., 2015). Parents can help their teens to appreciate learning for learning's sake and not over-emphasize the importance of grades. Middle-school students who are encouraged to assume responsibility for their learning and decision-making are more likely to complete high school and continue their education than their classmates who place greater value on grades than on learning (Tenenbaum et al., 2007). Adolescents' achievement motivation is also affected by the increasing importance of the peer group, which at times seems to undermine parents' and teachers' efforts to encourage school achievement. Peer pressures that undermine achievement motivation tend to be especially strong for many lower-income males and for minority students (Véronneau et al., 2008). In particular, African American and Hispanic peer cultures in many low-income areas actively discourage academic achievement, whereas European American and especially Asian American peer groups tend to value and encourage it (Steinberg, Dornbusch, & Brown, 1992). High-achieving African American students in some inner-city schools risk being rejected by their African American peers if their academic accomplishments cause them to be perceived as "acting white" (Fordham & Ogbu, 1986). They may feel that they have to abandon their cultural group and racial identity to succeed in school, and this takes a psychological toll (Arroyo & Zigler, 1995; Ogbu, 2003). Some students may disengage from academics to preserve their cultural identity with a group that has historically not always been treated fairly by the educational system (Ogbu, 2003). Although African American parents are as likely as European American parents to value education and to provide the kind of authoritative parenting that encourages school achievement, their positive influences are sometimes canceled out by negative peer influences (Steinberg et al., 1992).

For those African American teens who belong to a supportive peer group, academic achievement is strengthened (Gutman et al., 2002). In addition, African American teens who strongly value their ethnic group membership and have positive beliefs about how society views African Americans tend to have more positive beliefs about education (Chavous et al., 2003). But even a strong ethnic identity may not be able to overcome the subtle and negative effects of the discrimination still experienced by many minority students in the classroom that erodes their self-confidence and lowers their motivation (Thomas et al., 2009).

It is also possible that some of the decline in the achievement motivation of adolescents may reflect a poor fit between person and environment. Adopting a goodness-of-fit explanation, Jacquelynne Eccles and her colleagues (Eccles, Lord, & Midgley, 1991; Eccles et al., 1993) argue that the transition to middle school or junior high school is likely to be especially difficult because young adolescents are often experiencing major physical and psychological changes at the time they are switching schools. For example, girls who were reaching puberty when they were moving from sixth grade in an elementary school to seventh grade in a junior high school were more likely to experience drops in self-esteem and other negative changes than girls who remained in a K–8 school during this vulnerable period (Simmons & Blyth, 1987).

Could it be that more adolescents would remain interested in school if they did not have to change schools when they are experiencing pubertal changes? This idea became an important part of the rationale for shifting from junior high schools, in which students transitioned between the sixth and seventh grades, to middle schools where the transition occurs between the fifth and sixth grades. Research conducted in Germany, where the transition to a new school happens even earlier—after fourth grade, prior to pubertal changes for most students—helps answer this question (Arens et al., 2013). Students, both boys and girls, experienced lowered self-perceptions, including perceptions of their academic competence, following the school transition. This suggests that the school transition itself can be challenging, apart from whether pubertal changes are occurring at the same time.

The transition to middle or junior high school often involves going from a small school with close student–teacher relationships, a good deal of choice regarding learning activities, and reasonable discipline to a larger, more bureaucratized environment in which student–teacher relationships are impersonal, good grades are more emphasized but harder to come by, opportunities for choice are limited, assignments are not as intellectually stimulating, and discipline is rigid—all when adolescents are seeking more rather than less autonomy and are becoming more rather than less intellectually capable (Eccles et al., 1993; Hill & Tyson, 2009). Giving students a sense of ownership and some degree of control in their learning helps maintain their interest and motivation (Tsai et al., 2008; Valiente et al., 2008).

Other research shows the importance of having the right balance between challenge and support. David Shernoff and his colleagues (2016) looked at engagement of high school students in relation to what they called the complexity of the learning environment. Complexity is to the extent to which a class challenges students but also provides support to meet those challenges. In those classrooms where teachers require higher level thinking, students rise to the challenge if teachers also provide the environment needed for concentration and a means for capturing students' interest and enjoyment in the subject matter. Thus, the material may be hard to understand at first, but the teacher is able to make it interesting to students. When we are interested in something, we can be highly motivated to learn it even when the process of learning is hard. Those students fortunate enough to have teachers who are able to lead them through this interesting challenge *enjoy* learning. They will be more likely to take on challenges in the future.

The message? Declines in academic motivation and performance are not inevitable during early adolescence. Students may indeed form more realistic expectancies of success as their growing cognitive abilities allow them to use the increasingly informative feedback they receive from teachers. Experiencing pubertal changes at the same time as other stressful changes and needing to downplay academics to gain popularity may also hurt school achievement. However, educators can help keep adolescents engaged in school by creating school environments that provide a better fit to the developmental needs and interests of adolescents. Whether they are called middle schools or junior high schools, such schools should provide warm, supportive relationships with teachers, intellectual challenges, and increased opportunities for self-direction (Eccles et al., 1993). Parents can also help by remaining supportive and involved in their child's education throughout the middle-school years rather than pulling back (Hill & Tyson, 2009).

Cross-Cultural Differences

Mathematics, reading, and writing are considered basic skills important for success in many industrialized nations. By looking at cross-national educational outcomes, we may be able to learn how to optimize achievement. Every 4 years, the Trends in Mathematics and Science Study (TIMSS) is conducted with fourth- and eighth-graders from around the world (TIMSS, 2016). ■ Figure 10.7 shows average mathematics achievement scores of eighth-grade students in various countries. Students in the United States score above the international average but significantly below achievement levels in nations such as Singapore, Japan, and Korea. When researchers looked at the best students—those in the top 10% of all eighth-graders surveyed in the 48 nations—only 7% of U.S. students met the criteria in math compared to nearly half of eighth-graders in Chinese Taipei, Singapore, and the Republic of Korea. What might account for these international differences in achievement? Are students in some nations simply more intelligent than students in other nations?

Consider some research by Amy Hsin and Yu Xie (2014). They were interested in whether the observed gap between Asian American and white students, shown in ■ Figure 10.8, was attributable to socioeconomic factors, cognitive ability, or greater work ethic and motivation. They discovered that socioeconomic status of the family could not entirely account for the gap as there was a mix of SES backgrounds sprinkled across the range of low to high academic achievers (see Lee & Zhou, 2014a). There also did not seem to be significant differences in cognitive ability that could explain the widening gap in academic achievement over the years. Instead, Hsin and Xie's (2014) research pointed to a difference in work ethic and motivation as the likely explanation for the gap. They had access to data collected from children in kindergarten through twelfth grade. As ■ Figure 10.9 shows, they found a difference in academic effort between Asian and white

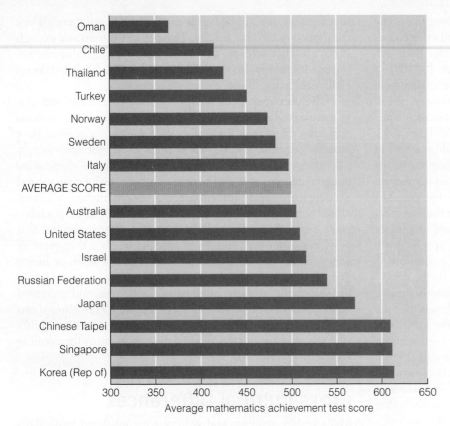

■ Figure 10.7 International comparison of eighth-grade mathematics performance.

Source: Adapted from Table 4 (p. 11) of Kastberg, D., Ferraro, D., Lemanski, N., Roey, S., & Jenkins, F. (2012). *Highlights from TIMSS 2011: Mathematics and science achievement of U.S. fourth- and eighth-grade students in an international context.* National Center for Education Statistics.

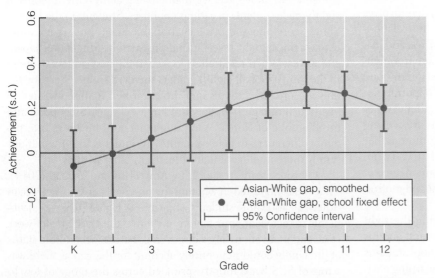

■ Figure 10.8 Gap in academic achievement between Asian American and white children, showing no difference at the start of formal schooling and an increasing difference over time, peaking around tenth grade.

Source: Hsin, A., & Xie, Y. (2014). Explaining Asian Americans' academic advantage over whites. *Proceedings of the National Academy of Sciences, 111,* 8416–8421.

students, as assessed by teacher ratings, but no gap in cognitive ability. Thus, Asian Americans do not do better than white students because they are smarter but because they work harder. Why? Hsin and Xie (2014) found that Asian Americans are less likely to believe ability is fixed or inborn and more likely to hold a growth mindset. Asian Americans also reported feeling greater pressure from their parents to succeed academically.

From this and other research, we can draw the following conclusions about cross-cultural differences in academic achievement:

• Asian parents are strongly committed to the educational process and communicate their high expectations to their students. In addition to parental expectations, societal stereotypes of the smart, high-achieving Asian student also serve to motivate Asian American students to work hard to live up to these expectations, which Jennifer Lee and Min Zhou (2014b) refer to as "stereotype promise."

• Asian parents, teachers, and students all share a strong belief that hard work or effort will pay off in better academic performance (that is, they have a growth mindset and set what Dweck calls learning goals), whereas Americans tend to put more emphasis on ability as a cause of good or poor performance. The result may be that Americans give up too quickly on a child who appears to have low intellectual ability. In doing so, they may help create a case of learned helplessness.

• Asian students spend more time being educated. They attend school more days of the year and their school day is often longer than that of American students (Stevenson, Lee, & Stigler, 1986). When they are in school, Asian students spend more time on-task: They spend about 95% of their time engaged in activities such as listening to the teacher and completing assignments, whereas American students spend only about 80% of their time on-task. This additional time on academics extends outside the classroom and regular school hours as well. Asian students, especially Japanese students, are assigned and complete considerably more homework than American students (Verma & Larson, 2003).

This cross-cultural research and comparison of Asian American and European American students carries an important message: The secret of effective learning is to get teachers, students, and parents working together, to set high achievement goals, and to invest the day-by-day effort required to attain those goals. Many states and local school

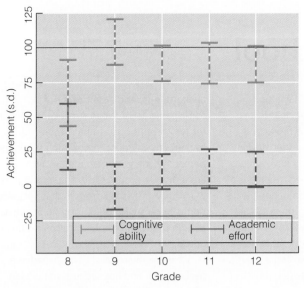

■Figure 10.9 On this chart, the blue bars show the influence of cognitive ability on the Asian-White gap in academic achievement, and the red bars show the influence of academic effort. Clearly, academic effort has a larger impact on this gap than does cognitive ability.

Source: Hsin, A., & Xie, Y. (2014). Explaining Asian Americans' academic advantage over whites. *Proceedings of the National Academy of Sciences, 111,* 8416–8421.

districts have begun to respond to evidence that American schools are being outclassed by schools in other countries by strengthening curricula, tightening standards for teacher certification, and raising standards for graduation and promotion from grade to grade.

Pathways to Adulthood

In the United States, approximately 4 out of 5 students graduate from high school "on time," or in four years (National Center for Education Statistics, 2013). But if we look closer, we see some disparities across racial/ethnic groups with Black, Hispanic, and American Indians/Alaskan Native students less likely to complete high school that white or Asian students. To some extent, the educational paths and attainments of adolescents are set long before they enter high school. Because many individuals' IQ test scores remain stable from childhood on, some children enter adolescence with more aptitude for schoolwork than others do (see Chapter 9). Moreover, some students have more achievement motivation than others. Clearly, a bright and achievement-oriented student is more likely to obtain good grades and go on to college and is less likely to drop out of school than a student with less ability and less desire to achieve. By early elementary school, and sometimes even before they enter school, future dropouts are often identifiable by such warning signs as low IQ and achievement test scores, poor grades, aggressive behavior, low socioeconomic status, and troubled homes (Bierman et al., 2013; Ensminger & Slusarcick, 1992). Among middle-school students, those who regularly smoke cigarettes, drink alcohol, and engage in sexual activity are more likely to drop out of high school than their peers who do not engage in such problem behaviors (Hawkins, Jaccard, & Needle, 2013). Perhaps not surprisingly, students who are victims of bullying also have higher dropout rates (Cornell et al., 2013). Employment during high school may also affect success, which is considered in **Exploration 10.2**. But it is often

not just a single factor that leads students to drop out or fail out of school. Instead, there is often a combination of two or more factors that place students at risk for failure (Lucio, Hunt & Bornovalova, 2012).

Those who graduate from high school stand a chance of being among the nearly 40% of Americans who complete 4 years of college or more (National Center for Education Statistics, 2013). These youth, in turn, are likely to have higher career aspirations and to end up in higher status occupations than their peers who do not attend college or do not even finish high school (McCaul et al., 1992). If their grades are good, they are likely to perform well in those jobs and advance far in their careers (Roth et al., 1996). In a real sense, then, individuals are steered along "high success" or "low success" routes starting in childhood. Depending on their own decisions and family, peer, and school influences, adolescents are more distinctly "sorted" in ways that will affect their adult lifestyles, income levels, and adjustment. Meanwhile, high school dropouts not only have less successful careers but also miss out on the beneficial effects that every year of schooling has on intellectual functioning (Ceci & Williams, 1997). In addition, they experience more psychological problems than those who stay in school (Kaplan, Damphousse, & Kaplan, 1994).

Graduation from high school is an important milestone for most teens and helps set the stage for a successful transition to adulthood.

Hill Street Studios/Sarah Golonka/Blend Images/Alamy Stock Photo

Combining Work and School

High school students who work long hours in rather mindless jobs may also be disengaged from their school work.

RosalreneBetancourt 1/Alamy Stock Photo

Laurence Steinberg and his associates have conducted numerous studies to understand how students who work during high school might be advantaged or disadvantaged relative to their nonworking classmates (Greenberger & Steinberg, 1986; Steinberg & Dornbusch, 1991; Steinberg, Fegley, & Dornbusch, 1993). On the positive side, working students seem to gain knowledge about work, consumer issues, and financial management and sometimes about greater self-reliance. However, high school students who worked 20 or more hours a week had lower grade-point averages than students who did not work or who worked only 10 or fewer hours per week (Steinberg & Dornbusch, 1991). Working students were also more likely than nonworkers to be disengaged from school—bored and uninvolved in class, and prone to cut class and spend little time on homework. In addition, the more adolescents worked, the more independent they were of parental control, the more likely they were to be experiencing psychological distress (anxiety, depression, and physical symptoms such as headaches), and the more frequently they used alcohol and drugs and engaged in delinquent acts.

What is not clear from this research is whether students may have already been disengaged from school, leading them to seek employment and work more hours (Mortimer, 2010). As well, those students more invested in their classes may be less likely to pursue employment. This is indeed what Jerald Bachman and his colleagues (2003, 2011) have found: Not-yet-employed students who want to work long hours tend to be disenchanted with school, have low grades, and are more likely to use alcohol and cigarettes. Once they start working, the disenchantment and problem behaviors are exacerbated (Bachman et al., 2003, 2011). Similarly, longitudinal research on adolescents and work confirms that academically struggling students are the ones likely to work more hours (Warren, LePore, & Mare, 2000).

But the negative outcomes associated with working in high school are not entirely attributable to preexisting characteristics of these teens. Bachman and his colleagues (2011) found some negatives of work even when they attempted to control for a variety of preexisting problem behaviors among the teens who worked the most hours during high school. Notably, teens who worked the most were less likely to have completed college when the researchers followed up with them when they were 29–30 years of age.

Somewhat surprisingly, the teens who were most disadvantaged by working long hours during high school were whites, especially whites from high socioeconomic backgrounds, and Asian Americans, relative to Hispanic and African Americans. The latter two groups tend to have more trouble finding employment during high school, so perhaps those who managed to find work are a unique group, for example, more hard working. And whites from higher socioeconomic homes who work long hours while in high school are probably also an unusual group.

When all the research is examined as a package, the findings suggest that working while attending high school is often more detrimental than beneficial. Much depends on the nature of the work adolescents do (Taylor et al., 2012). For those lucky teenagers who land a part-time job that offers them an opportunity for self-direction or decision making, and draws on academic skills such as reading and mathematics, they may be building valuable skills that will serve them in their future full-time jobs (Greenberger & Steinberg, 1986). Unfortunately, part-time jobs held by teenagers are generally lower-level, unskilled positions that can erode mastery motivation (Call, Mortimer, & Shanahan, 1995; Shanahan et al., 1991).

Over the past 10–15 years, the percentage of teens working during high school has declined (Baum & Ruhm, 2014; Staff et al., 2014). Many of the "teen jobs" such as flipping burgers at fast-food restaurants have increasingly gone to adults, including older adults returning to the work force to make ends meet following the 2008–2009 recession. Following the recession, more teens are working informally as babysitters and grass mowers, and they are less likely to be working long—20 plus—hours. In sum, there is no clear answer on whether part-time work during high school will prove to be an opportunity for growth or a tedious distraction from schoolwork, so parents should help teens consider all the pros and cons and discuss how they might gain value even if they end up in a job that is not especially challenging.

Checking Mastery

1. What are two reasons why achievement motivation may decline during adolescence?
2. Why might students in Asian schools outperform many other students in science and math?
3. What is one advantage and one disadvantage of working while in high school?

Making Connections

1. Research shows that achievement motivation and grades often drop as students move through middle school and high school. Develop a program to combat this trend, keeping in mind that students of different backgrounds may lose motivation for different reasons.
2. After finishing up ninth grade, your teenager says he wants to work for the next 3 years while in high school. What advice will you give him?

10.5
The Adult

LEARNING OBJECTIVES

- Describe language changes in adulthood.
- Explore the achievement motivations of adults.
- Explain the challenges for adults who struggle with literacy.
- Outline pros and cons of continuing education for adults.

The lives of adults are dominated by work—paid or unpaid, outside the home or within the home. We consider, first, how language and achievement motivation change during this period of life. We also examine the educational options available to adults and the benefits of lifelong education.

Language

What happens to language skills during adulthood? Adults simply hold onto the knowledge of phonology they gained as children, although elders can have difficulty distinguishing speech sounds (such as /b/ from /p/) if they have hearing impairments or deficits in the cognitive abilities required to make out what they hear (Thornton & Light, 2006). Adults also retain their knowledge of grammar or syntax. Older adults tend to use less complex sentences than younger adults do, however. Also, those with memory difficulties may have trouble understanding sentences that are highly complex syntactically (for example, "The children warned about road hazards refused to fix the bicycle of the boy who crashed"); they may not be able to remember the beginning of the sentence by the time they get to the end (Kemtes & Kemper, 1997; Stine, Soederberg, & Morrow, 1996).

Meanwhile, knowledge of the semantics of language, of word meanings, often expands during adulthood, at least until people are in their 70s or 80s (Obler, 2013; Schaie, 1996). After all, adults gain experience with the world from year to year, so it is not surprising that their vocabularies continue to grow and that they enrich their understandings of the meanings of words. However, older adults more often have the "tip-of-the-tongue" experience of not being able to recall the name of an object (or especially a person's name) when they need it (Thornton & Light, 2006). This problem is a matter of not being able to retrieve information stored in memory rather than a matter of no longer knowing the words. In order to maintain fluency in the face of these retrieval problems, older adults speak a little more slowly and plan their choice of words further in advance than when they were younger (Spieler & Griffin, 2006).

Adults also refine their pragmatic use of language—adjusting it to different social and professional contexts (Obler, 2013). Physicians, for example, must develop a communication style that is effective with their patients. Partners who have been together for years often develop a unique way of communicating with one another that is distinctly different from how they communicate with others. Overall, command of language holds up well in later life unless the individual experiences major declines in cognitive functioning (Kemper & Mitzner, 2001; Stine et al., 1996).

Achievement Motivation

The level of achievement motivation that we acquire in childhood and adolescence carries into adulthood to influence our decisions and life outcomes (Wlodkowski, 1999). For instance, women who have a strong need to achieve are more likely than less achievement-oriented women to work outside the home (Krogh, 1985). Adults with strong achievement needs are also likely to be more competent workers than adults who are less interested in mastering challenges (Helmreich, Sawin, & Carsrud, 1986; Spence, 1985).

What happens to achievement motivation in later life? Adults, at least those who are in "learner mode" and are taking classes, often score higher than adolescents and young adults on mastery or learning goals (Eppler & Harju, 1997). As we learned earlier in this chapter, those pursuing mastery goals may be more motivated to learn than those who adopt performance goals. In related research, adult learners rated their class experiences as more enjoyable than their younger counterparts (Remedios & Richardson, 2013). Those who enjoy their classroom experience are likely paying more attention and gaining more from their experience than those who do not find the experience especially enjoyable. Despite the sharp rise in adult learners in recent years, there is very little research on this group of learners, so we don't have a deep understanding of what motivates them or how to best foster a continued love of learning.

What about motivation in the main sphere of many adults' lives—the workplace? Motivation levels do seem to decline, but certainly this is not universal (Ackerman & Kanfer, 2004). This may reflect a "top of the ladder" effect, as many older adults may be in one of the highest positions in their workplace or may believe they are as high as they are going to get (or want to get). Other research suggests that this is not so much a decline in motivation but a *shift* in motivation from extrinsic to intrinsic (Inceoglu, Segers, & Bartram, 2012). Early in our careers, we may be more strongly motivated by external factors such as new titles and increased pay. At the other end of our careers, we may care more about doing work that is personally satisfying.

There is evidence that women's achievement motivation declines fairly steeply with age (see Mellinger & Erdwins, 1985). However, this age trend pertained mainly to career-related motivation and an interest in striving for success in competitive situations. Women's motivation in other areas remained high. Many women have traditionally set aside career-achievement goals after they have children and make nurturing those children their priority (Krogh, 1985). However, highly educated women often regain a strong motive to achieve outside the home once their children are older and they can invest more energy in outside work. Thus, women are especially likely to be motivated to achieve career success when they have the educational background that would allow them to pursue attractive career goals and when they are not pursuing family-related goals.

Overall, adults' achievement-related motives are far more affected by changes in work and family contexts than by the aging process (Filipp, 1996). Adults of different ages are often more alike than they are different, and different people tend to retain their characteristic levels of achievement motivation over the years, much as they retain many personality traits (Stevens & Truss, 1985). There is little evidence that elderly adults inevitably lose their motivation to pursue important goals. Moreover, those elders who have a strong sense of purpose and direction and feel they are achieving their goals enjoy greater physical and psychological well-being than those who do not (Hooker & Siegler, 1993; Rapkin & Fischer, 1992; Reker, Peacock, & Wong, 1987). Throughout the life span, then, setting and achieving goals are important.

Literacy

Literacy is the ability to use printed information to function in society, achieve goals, and develop one's potential. Few adults are completely illiterate, but many adults do not have functional literacy skills despite years of formal education. According to the National Institute of Literacy, 14% of adults in the United States are below a basic literacy rate, which is roughly equivalent to a third-grade or lower reading ability (U.S. Department of Education, 2015). Such an adult could probably find an expiration date on a driver's license and sign a form but would have trouble filling out an application or reading a simple book to a child. Although one-quarter of this group consists of immigrants learning English as a second language, most individuals in this group are U.S.-born citizens and nearly two-thirds did not finish high school.

Another 29% of adults have just rudimentary, or basic, literacy skills, allowing them to perform simple literacy tasks such as using a television guide or comparing prices on two receipts, but limiting their abilities to consult reference information online or in texts. Approximately half of the adults demonstrated proficient, or higher, levels of literacy. Literacy contributes to economic security through occupational advancement. Nearly half of the adults with the lowest literacy scores live in poverty, whereas few adults with the highest literacy scores do (Bowen, 1999). Improving the literacy skills of impoverished adults, however, does not automatically raise them out of poverty. For many low-income and functionally illiterate adults, other obstacles must be overcome, including addiction, discrimination, and disabilities (Bowen, 1999).

Programs to raise the literacy level of adults are rarely successful. Several factors limit the success of such programs. For one thing, despite having limited literacy skills, many of these adults (75%) reported that they could read or write "well" or "very well"—attitudes that must make it difficult to motivate them to improve their literacy skills. Second, adults do not stay in literacy programs long enough to make improvements (Amstutz & Sheared, 2000). The dropout rate is as high as 70%–80%, and many leave in the first weeks of the program (Quigley & Uhland, 2000). Adults who do not persist report that the programs are boring and do not meet their needs (Imel, 1996; Kerka, 1995; Quigley, 1997). Materials, for example, are often geared toward children, not adults who have families, jobs, and different interests than children do.

Continuing Education

As noted earlier, an increasing number of adults are seeking education beyond basic literacy skills. In 2011, 33% of all college students were 25 years or older, and a full 50% of students attending college part-time were over the age of 25 (National Center for Education Statistics, 2013). The number of "older" adults attending college is expected to increase as the overall population ages. Whether we call them adult learners, nontraditionals, returning students, mature students, or lifelong learners, these adults represent a diverse group. They bring different work and life experiences to the classroom, and they report a variety of reasons for enrolling in postsecondary education (Ross-Gordon, 2011).

Many "traditional" students (17- to 24-year-olds) are motivated to attend college by external expectations, but older students are often motivated by internal factors (Ross-Gordon, 2011). Women are more likely to return to the classroom for personal enrichment or interest, whereas men are more likely to take classes required or recommended for their work (Sargant et al., 1997). Both men and women today sometimes find that they need further education in order to become employable as the job market changes. The internal motivation of adult students often leads to deeper levels of processing information (Harper & Kember, 1986). In other words, returning students may put forth greater effort to truly understand material because they want to learn and want (or need) to use the material. Traditional students who do not have

Many older adults remain motivated to learn and seek challenging experiences.

De Visu/Alamy Stock Photo

the benefit of experience may learn the material necessary to do well on an examination but may not process the material in ways that will lead to long-term retention.

Although it is tempting to conclude that there are only positive outcomes associated with continued education, there are a few drawbacks. Mainly, it is often difficult for adults already busy with jobs and family to find the time to take classes, at least those offered in traditional classrooms. Successful continuing education programs are those that have met the needs of adult learners by scheduling classes at convenient times and being flexible to accommodate the lifestyles of their adult learners. Yet the benefits of lifelong education typically outweigh drawbacks. For instance, continued education allows adults to remain knowledgeable and competitive in fields that change rapidly. Adults who return to school for bachelor's or master's degrees can also advance their careers, particularly if their education and work are closely related (Senter & Senter, 1997). Finally, you learned in Chapter 5 that higher education is associated with maintaining or improving physical and mental health.

In this and previous chapters, you have examined a great deal of material on thinking and learning across the life span. How can principles of cognitive development be used to improve education for all ages? Before closing this chapter, we summarize, in **Application 10.1**, what theorists Piaget and Vygotsky contribute to education and what research on information processing, intelligence, and perception suggests about optimal learning environments.

• APPLICATION 10.1

What Can Theory and Research Contribute to Education?

To help you appreciate the practical implications for school reform and school achievement of the material in Chapters 6 through 9, we provide the following recommendations based on the research and theories discussed in these chapters:

Piaget

- Provide opportunities for independent, hands-on interaction with the physical environment, especially for younger children.
- With the child's current level of understanding in mind, create some disequilibrium by presenting new information slightly above the child's current level. Children who experience disequilibrium— cognitive discomfort with their understanding (or lack of understanding)—will work to resolve it, achieving a higher level of mastery of the material.
- Encourage interaction with peers, which will expose children to other perspectives and give them an opportunity to reevaluate and revise their own view.

Vygotsky

- Provide opportunities for children to interact with others who have greater mastery of the material—an older peer, teacher, or parent. These more advanced thinkers can help "pull" children to a level of understanding they would be unable to achieve on their own.
- Encourage students, especially young ones, to talk to themselves as they work on difficult tasks. Such private speech can guide behavior and facilitate thought.
- Present challenging tasks, but do not expect students to complete such tasks successfully without guidance. With support, students can accomplish more difficult tasks than those they would be able to achieve independently.

Research on Information Processing

- Provide opportunities for rehearsal and other memory strategies to move information into long-term memory. Realize that young children do not spontaneously use

memory strategies but often can use them when prompted.
- Structure assignments so that retrieval cues are consistent with cues present at acquisition to facilitate retrieval of information from long-term memory.
- Enable learners to develop a knowledge base and expertise in domains of study. When beginning a new lesson, start with and build on what students already know.
- Assess the knowledge and strategies required to solve assigned problems; then determine which aspects of a task pose difficulties for learners and target these for further instruction.
- Be aware that well-learned and frequently repeated tasks become automatized over time, freeing information-processing capacity for other tasks.

Research on Intelligence

- Realize that individual differences in intelligence have implications for the classroom. Students at both ends of the continuum

(continued)

What Can Theory and Research Contribute to Education? (continued)

may need special educational services to optimize their learning.

- Recognize that although IQ scores do a reasonably good job of predicting achievement in the classroom, such tests have weaknesses that limit their usefulness, especially in assessing members of minority groups.

Research on Sensory and Perceptual Abilities

- Test all children early and regularly for sensory and perceptual problems that might limit their ability to benefit from regular classroom instruction.
- Be aware of developmental differences in attention span. Clearly, a young child will

not be able to attend to a task for as long as a teenager.

- Minimize distractions in the learning environment. Younger students have trouble "tuning out" background noise and focusing on the task at hand.

● **Checking Mastery**

1. How might men's and women's achievement motivation change during adulthood?
2. Why is literacy important to adults and are literacy programs successful?

● **Making Connections**

1. If you find that one of your parents (or spouse) is going through a midlife "career slump," what might you do to foster a higher level of achievement motivation during this stage of his or her life?
2. Based on what you have learned in this and previous chapters about memory, thinking, problem solving, and language skills, how would you teach older adult students versus students of traditional high school or college age?

Chapter Summary

10.1 The System of Language

- The complex process of language acquisition appears to occur effortlessly through an interaction of inborn readiness and a normal language environment.
- To acquire language, children must master phonology (sound), semantics (meaning), and syntax (sentence structure). They must also learn how to use language appropriately (pragmatics) and how to understand prosody.
- Theories of language development include learning theories, nativist theories, and interactionist theories. The interactionist view emphasizes the child's biologically based capacities and experience conversing with adults who use child-directed speech and strategies such as expansion that simplify the language-learning task.

10.2 The Infant

- Infants are able to discriminate speech sounds and progress from crying, cooing, and babbling to one-word holophrases (at 12 months) and then to telegraphic speech (at 18 months).

- During the preschool years, language abilities improve dramatically, as illustrated by overregularizations and new transformation rules.
- Precursors of achievement motivation can be seen among infants who strive to master their environments. Mastery motivation is fostered by a responsive environment that provides plenty of opportunities for infants to learn that they can control their environments and experience successes.
- Early education can help prepare disadvantaged children for formal schooling, but an overemphasis on academics at the expense of exploration and play may hinder young children's development.

10.3 The Child

- School-age children and adolescents refine their language skills and become less egocentric communicators.
- During childhood, some children develop higher levels of achievement motivation than others; they tend to have a growth mindset rather than a fixed mindset regarding abilities, and they set learning goals rather than performance goals in the classroom.
- To read, children must master the alphabetic principle and

develop phonological awareness so that they can grasp letter–sound correspondence rules. Emergent literacy activities such as listening to storybooks facilitate later reading. Compared with unskilled readers, skilled readers have better understanding of the alphabetic principle and greater phonological awareness.

- Learning is influenced by characteristics of students and their teachers. Students perform best when (1) they are intellectually capable and motivated; (2) their teachers create a motivating, comfortable, and task-oriented setting and involve parents in their children's schooling; and (3) there is a good fit between children's characteristics and the kind of instruction they receive.

10.4 The Adolescent

- Achievement motivation and grades tend to drop during adolescence for a variety of reasons, including cognitive growth, family characteristics, peer pressure, and a poor fit between the student and the school.
- Middle school and high school include a greater focus on mathematics education. U.S. students score close to the international average but below several other countries in math. Cross-cultural research suggests that the success of Asian schools is rooted in more class time spent on academics, more homework, more parent involvement, more peer support, and a stronger belief that hard work pays off.

10.5 The Adult

- Language skills remain fairly stable throughout adulthood, unless there are substantial sensory impairments or cognitive declines.
- Level of achievement carries over from adolescence into adulthood. There may be some decline in achievement motivation among women who set aside career goals to raise children, but career goals reemerge as their children age, especially among women with higher levels of education.
- Some adults, despite years of education, have not acquired the skills of functional literacy. Literacy programs have had minimal success in improving literacy rates.
- Adults increasingly are seeking continued educational opportunities for both personal and work-related reasons.

Key Terms

language **300**
phoneme **300**
morphemes **300**
syntax **301**
semantics **301**
pragmatics **301**
prosody **301**
aphasia **302**
universal grammar **302**
language acquisition device
   (LAD) **302**

poverty of the stimulus
   (POTS) **303**
expansion **305**
child-directed speech **305**
word segmentation **306**
cooing **306**
babbling **307**
joint attention **307**
syntactic bootstrapping **307**
holophrase **307**
vocabulary spurt **308**

fast mapping **308**
overextension **308**
underextension **308**
telegraphic speech **309**
functional grammar **310**
overregularization **310**
transformational grammar **310**
mastery motivation **310**
metalinguistic awareness **313**
bilingual **313**
fixed mindset **314**

growth mindset **314**
mastery (learning) goal **314**
performance goal **315**
alphabetic principle **318**
phonological awareness **318**
emergent literacy **318**
dyslexia **319**
literacy **328**

11 Self and Personality

In her memoir *My Beloved World* (2013), Supreme Court Justice Sonia Sotomayor describes her humble beginnings: growing up in a poor, Puerto Rican section of New York City as a child with diabetes, an alcoholic father who died when she was only 9, and an overworked and emotionally distant mother (see Barnes, 2013). Not being sure she could count on her parents and fearing that she would die young, she learned to give herself insulin injections at age 7 and developed a strong independent streak and a drive to succeed that contributed to her later success in law. She had doubts about whether she was as capable as her classmates at Princeton but concluded that some of her deficiencies in knowledge were the product of her background and that she could overcome them through hard work. She also says this about herself: "I think my life approach is never to look at the negative of what I'm experiencing but also always trying to see its positive" (Barnes, 2013, p. C3).

Sonia Sotomayor, by writing her autobiography, created a life story that defines her as a unique person who overcame challenges and self-doubts and rose to a position of prominence. How would you tell your life story? Who are you and what is unique about you?

This chapter is about the self and the personality and the ways in which personalities, and our perceptions of those personalities, change—and remain the same—over the life span. It is, in other words, about the issue of continuity (consistency or stability) and discontinuity (change) in human development (see Chapter 2). It is also about influences on and implications of our self-concepts and personalities. We begin our inquiry by clarifying some terms used in describing the personality and the self and then briefly compare theoretical perspectives on the self and personality.

Sonia Sotomayor's life story involved turning experiences of poverty, childhood diabetes, and an alcoholic father into an independence and drive that propelled her to the Supreme Court of the United States.

iStockphoto.com/EdStock

11.1
Conceptualizing the Self and Personality

LEARNING OBJECTIVES

- Define and give examples of the aspects of personality called dispositional traits, characteristic adaptations, and narrative identity.

- Distinguish among self-concept, self-esteem, and identity.

- Compare how psychoanalytic, trait, and social learning theorists view personality and its development.

Basic Concepts

Personality is often defined as an organized combination of attributes, motives, values, and behaviors unique to each individual. Pause for a moment: How would you describe your own personality? One way we describe our own and other people's personalities is in terms of relatively enduring dispositional traits such as extraversion or introversion, independence or dependence, and the like. We invite you to complete the brief personality scale in **Engagement 11.1** to get a feel for describing your own personality in terms of dispositional traits.

As Dan McAdams and Jennifer Pals (2006; and see McAdams, 2013) argue, though, at least two other aspects of personality besides traits deserve attention. People also differ in characteristic adaptations, more situation-specific and changeable ways in which people adapt to their roles and environments. Characteristic adaptations include motives, goals, plans, schemas, self-conceptions, developmental issues and concerns, and coping mechanisms. Did any of these characteristic adaptations come to mind when you thought about your own personality?

A third aspect of personality is narrative identities, unique and integrative life stories that we construct about our pasts and futures to give ourselves an identity and our lives meaning (as Sonia Sotomayor has done in her memoir). In a study of narrative identity, you might be asked to picture your life as a book, outline the major scenes and turning points that have defined who you

are, and lay out your dreams and fears for the future (McAdams, 2008, 2011). McAdams and Pals believe that both biological factors, including a "human nature" shared by fellow humans and individual genetic makeup, and cultural and situational influences help shape all three aspects of personality: dispositional traits, characteristic adaptations, and narrative identities.

When you describe yourself, you may not be describing your personality so much as revealing your self-concept—your perceptions, positive or negative, of your unique attributes and traits as a person. We all know people who seem to have unrealistic self-conceptions—the fellow who thinks he knows it all (but doesn't) or the woman who believes she is a dull plodder (but is actually brilliant). A closely related aspect of self-perception is self-esteem—your overall evaluation of your worth as a person, high or low, based on all the positive and negative self-perceptions that make up your self-concept. Self-concept is about "what I am," whereas self-esteem concerns "how good I am" (Harter, 1999, 2012). We will examine both, as well as how adolescents pull together their various self-perceptions to form an identity—an overall sense of who they are, where they are heading, and where they fit into society.

Theories of Personality

We can gain a sense of issues in understanding the development of the self and personality by contrasting the very different views offered by psychoanalytic theory, trait theory, and social learning theory.

A Brief Personality Scale

Here are several personality traits that may or may not apply to you. Write a number from 1 to 7 next to each statement to indicate the extent to which you agree or disagree with that statement. You should rate the extent to which the pair of traits applies to you, even if one characteristic applies more strongly than the other.

1 = Disagree strongly   5 = Agree a little
2 = Disagree moderately   6 = Agree moderately
3 = Disagree a little   7 = Agree strongly
4 = Neither agree nor disagree

I see myself as:

1. _____Extraverted, enthusiastic
2. _____Critical, quarrelsome
3. _____Dependable, self-disciplined
4. _____Anxious, easily upset
5. _____Open to new experiences, complex
6. _____Reserved, quiet
7. _____Sympathetic, warm
8. _____Disorganized, careless
9. _____Calm, emotionally stable
10. _____Conventional, uncreative

To score yourself, reverse the scoring of items marked below with R so that a score of 1 becomes 7, 2 becomes 6, 3 becomes 5, 4 stays 4, 5 becomes 3, 6 becomes 2, and 7 becomes 1. Then add the pair of scores listed here for each of the Big Five personality dimensions:

Extraversion   Item 1 + item 6R = _____
Agreeableness   Item 2R + item 7 = _____
Conscientiousness   Item 3 + item 8R = _____
Low neuroticism (high   Item 4R + item 9 = _____
emotional stability)
Openness to experience   Item 5 + item 10R = _____

To help you see roughly where you stand on the Big Five personality dimensions, the average sums for each pair of two items for a sample of 1813 college students tested by Samuel Gosling and colleagues (2003) were 8.88 for extraversion, 10.46 for agreeableness, 10.80 for conscientiousness, 9.66 for low neuroticism (high emotional stability), and 10.76 for openness to experience.

Bear in mind that this scale is much shorter than standard measures of the Big Five personality dimensions. It may not provide an accurate reading of your personality, but it will acquaint you with the trait approach to studying personality and with the Big Five personality dimensions as well.

Source: Reprinted from Gosling, S. D., Rentfrow, P. J., & Swann, W. B. (2003). A very brief personality scale. *Journal of Research in Personality, 37,* 525, with permission from Elsevier, © 2003.

Psychoanalytic Theory

Psychoanalytic theorists generally use in-depth interviews and similar techniques to get below the surface of the person and her behavior and understand the inner dynamics of personality. As you will recall from Chapter 2, Sigmund Freud believed that children progress through universal stages of psychosexual development, ending with the genital stage of adolescence. Freud did not see psychosexual growth continuing during adulthood. Indeed he believed that the personality was formed during the first 5 years of life and showed considerable continuity thereafter. Anxieties arising from harsh parenting or other unfavorable early experiences in the family, he said, would leave a permanent mark on the personality and reveal themselves in adult personality traits.

The psychosocial theory of personality development formulated by neo-Freudian Erik Erikson, also introduced in Chapter 2, will be highlighted in this chapter. Like Freud, Erikson concerned himself with the inner dynamics of personality and proposed that people undergo similar personality changes at similar ages as they confront the challenges associated with different stages of development (Erikson, 1963, 1968, 1982). However, Erikson placed more emphasis on social influences beyond parents such as peers, teachers, and cultures; the rational ego and its adaptive powers; and possibilities for overcoming the effects of harmful early experiences. Most importantly, he saw the potential for personal growth and change throughout the life span.

Trait Theory

The approach to personality that has most strongly influenced efforts to study it is trait theory, based on the *psychometric approach* that guided the development of intelligence tests (see Chapter 9). According to trait theorists, personality is a set of dispositional trait dimensions along which people can differ. To identify distinct trait dimensions, researchers administer personality scales to people and use the statistical technique of factor analysis to identify groupings of personality scale items that are correlated with each other but not with other groupings of items. Trait theorists assume that personality traits are quite consistent across situations and relatively enduring. Like psychoanalytic theorists, then, they expect to see carryover in personality over the years; unlike psychoanalytic theorists, however, they do not believe that the personality unfolds in a series of stages.

How many personality trait dimensions are there? Many scholars now agree that human personalities can best be described in terms of a five-factor model—with five major dimensions of personality that have come to be known as the **Big Five** (Digman, 1990; McCrae & Costa, 2003, 2008). The Big Five personality dimensions—openness to experience, conscientiousness, extraversion, agreeableness, and neuroticism—are described in ● **Table 11.1.** If you took and scored the short personality scale in Engagement 11.1, you got a rough sense of where you fall on these Big Five trait dimensions.

Dimension	Basic Definition	Key Characteristics
Openness to experience	Curiosity and interest in variety vs. preference for sameness	Openness to fantasy, esthetics, feelings, actions, ideas, values
Conscientiousness	Discipline and organization vs. lack of seriousness	Competence, order, dutifulness, striving for achievement, self-discipline, deliberation
Extraversion	Sociability and outgoingness vs. introversion	Warmth, gregariousness, assertiveness, activity, excitement seeking, positive emotions
Agreeableness	Compliance and cooperativeness vs. suspiciousness	Trust, straightforwardness, altruism, compliance, modesty, tender-mindedness
Neuroticism	Emotional instability vs. stability	Anxiety, hostility, depression, self-consciousness, impulsiveness, vulnerability

As a mnemonic device, notice that the first letters of the five dimensions spell *ocean*.

Source: Adapted from Costa & McCrae, 1992.

The Big Five appear to be both genetically and environmentally influenced and emerge in childhood (McCrae & Costa, 2008). The Big Five also seem to be universal; they capture the ways in which people all over the world describe themselves and other people (Heine & Buchtel, 2009; McCrae, 2004). This is true even though levels of Big Five traits differ from culture to culture (for example, Europeans appear to be more extroverted on average than Asians or Africans) and even though traits may be expressed differently in different cultures (as when a Chinese extravert smiles warmly at seeing an old friend but an American extravert grins and gives the friend a big bear hug). You will soon learn more about the development of these dispositional trait dimensions.

Social Learning Theory

Finally, social learning (or social cognitive) theorists such as Albert Bandura (1986; and see Chapter 2) and Walter Mischel (1973; Mischel & Shoda, 2008) not only reject the notion of universal stages of personality development but also question the existence of enduring personality traits that show themselves across a variety of situations and over long stretches of the life span. Instead, they emphasize that people's behavior is influenced by the situations they are in and changes if their environments change and different behaviors are modeled and reinforced.

From the social learning perspective, personality boils down to a set of behavioral tendencies shaped by interactions with other people in specific social situations. Because social context is so powerful, consistency in personality over time is most likely if the person's social environment remains the same. Thus, if Rick the rancher continues to run the same ranch in the same small town for a lifetime, he might stay the "same old Rick." However, most of us experience new social environments as we grow older. Just as we behave differently when we are in a library than when we are in a bar, we become "different people" as we take on new roles, develop new relationships, or move to new locations. Different situation, different personality.

Armed with basic concepts and a sense of the strikingly different perspectives that psychoanalytic, trait, and social learning theorists take on personality (see ● **Table 11.2** for a summary), we will now explore continuity and discontinuity in self-conceptions and personality traits across the life span.

● **Table 11.2** Perspectives on Personality

Perspective	Theorists	Themes
Psychoanalytic theory	Sigmund Freud and Erik Erikson	Personality as inner qualities that develop in a stagelike manner. Freud believed the personality was formed in first 5 years of life, whereas Erikson saw growth and change continuing through adulthood.
Trait theory	Paul Costa and Robert McCrae	Personality as a set of dispositional traits (the Big Five) that are enduring over time and consistent across situations.
Social learning theory	Albert Bandura and Walter Mischel	Personality as behavior that is influenced by situational factors and changes if the environment changes. We should not expect universal stages of personality development or enduring traits.

● Checking Mastery

1. What is the difference between a dispositional trait and a characteristic adaptation? Give an example of each.

2. What is the difference between self-esteem and self-concept?

3. Why do social learning theorists think trait theorists are wrong about personality?

1. Using the concepts of dispositional traits, characteristic adaptations, and narrative identities, the three aspects of personality highlighted by McAdams and Pals, do an analysis of the main features of your own personality. What are your prominent dispositional traits and characteristic adaptations, and what is the plot of your narrative identity or life story?

2. Think about two people you know well and list for each of them five traits that you believe capture their personalities well. Now look at the Big Five trait dimensions in Table 11.1 and see if you can match the traits you see in these individuals to the Big Five personality dimensions. Based on this analysis, do you agree that the Big Five dimensions capture the main ways in which humans differ—or do you believe that something is missing from the Big Five? Why?

LEARNING OBJECTIVES

- Explain how we come to know ourselves in the first 2 years of life.
- Summarize two approaches to describing infants' temperaments and the role of goodness of fit in the development of temperament.

When do infants display a sense of themselves as distinct individuals? Do they have unique personalities?

The Emerging Self

Infants may be born without a sense of self, but they quickly develop an implicit, if not conscious, sense of self. It is based in their perceptions of their bodies and actions and grows out of their interactions with caregivers (Rochat, 2010; Rochat & Striano, 2000; Trevarthen, 2011). The capacity to differentiate self from world becomes more apparent by around 2 or 3 months of age, when infants display a sense of agency—a sense that they can cause things to happen in the world. For example, 2-month-old infants whose arms are connected by strings to audiovisual equipment delight in producing the sight of a smiling infant's face and the theme from *Sesame Street* by pulling the strings (Lewis, Alessandri, & Sullivan, 1990). When the strings are disconnected and the infants can no longer produce such effects, they pull harder and become frustrated and angry. Over the first 6 months of life, then, infants discover properties of their physical selves, distinguish between themselves and the rest of the world, and discover that they can act upon other people and objects.

In the second half of their first year, infants realize that they and their companions are separate beings who have different perspectives and on occasion can share perspectives (Goodvin, Thompson, & Winer, 2015). Thus a 9-month-old infant may point to a toy and look toward her companion to focus his attention on the same toy. You may recall from Chapter 7 that this breakthrough is called *joint attention*, or the sharing of perceptual experiences by infants and their caregivers from about 9 months of age on.

Around 18 months, infants experience an even more amazing breakthrough in the development of the self when they recognize themselves visually as distinct individuals. How do we know this? Michael Lewis and Jeanne Brooks-Gunn (1979) used an ingenious technique first used with chimpanzees to study self-recognition—the ability to recognize oneself in a mirror or

photograph. Mother daubs a spot of rouge or lipstick on an infant's nose and then places the infant in front of a mirror. If the infant has some mental image of his own face and recognizes his mirror image as himself, he should soon notice the red spot and reach for or wipe his own nose or turn to a companion and point to his own nose rather than touch the nose of the mirror image or look behind the mirror to find this interesting new playmate.

When infants 9–24 months old were given this mirror test, the youngest infants showed no self-recognition: They seemed to treat the image in the mirror as if it were "some other baby" and sometimes touched the mirror. Some 15-month-olds recognized themselves, but only starting at 18 months of age did most infants pass the test, showing clear evidence of self-recognition.

As babies get to know themselves better, they also form a **categorical self**; that is, they classify themselves into social categories based on age, sex, and other visible characteristics, figuring out what is "like me" and what is "not like me" and recognizing that they are babies, not adults, and boys or girls. By 18–24 months, then, most infants have an awareness of who they are—at least as a physical self with a unique appearance and as a categorical self. They now begin to use their emerging language skills to talk about themselves by name and to construct stories about events in their lives (Goodvin et al., 2015).

Cognitive, Social, and Cultural Influences

What contributes to self-awareness in infancy? First, self-recognition depends on *cognitive development* and requires the maturation of certain areas of the brain (Bertenthal & Fischer, 1978; Lewis & Carmody, 2008). For example, intellectually disabled children are slow to recognize themselves in a mirror but can do so once they have attained a mental age of around 18 months (Hill & Tomlin, 1981).

Second, self-awareness depends on *social interaction*. Chimpanzees who have been raised without contact with other chimps fail to recognize themselves in a mirror as normal chimps do (Gallup, 1979). Human children's early responsiveness to other people is linked to their later self-recognition (Kristen-Antonow

Does this boy know that he is the fascinating tot in the mirror? Probably not. Most infants do not master self-recognition until they are 18 months old.

Joseph Pobereskin/Getty Images

et al., 2015). And human toddlers who have formed secure attachments to their parents are better able to recognize themselves in a mirror and know more about their names and genders than do toddlers whose relationships are less secure (Pipp, Easterbrooks, & Harmon, 1992). Throughout life, we forge our self-concepts from the information and feedback we receive from interacting with other people (Harter, 2012).

Third, the *cultural context* may influence the emergence of self-awareness. In studying cultural influences on mirror self-recognition, researchers have focused primarily on how much a culture emphasizes individuality. Joscha Kärtner and his colleagues (2012) expected that self-awareness might develop more rapidly in individualistic cultures—cultures that emphasize autonomy and encourage children to pursue their own goals as individuals—than in collectivist cultures—cultures that emphasize relatedness to others and subordinating individual goals to the goals of the group (see Triandis, 1989, 1995). Parents in individualistic cultures would be likely to help children get to know themselves and their preferences and assert themselves, whereas parents in collectivist cultures would not call attention to the

child as an individual and would instead socialize their children to be sensitive to others and respectful of their elders.

The researchers compared the development of mirror self-recognition in two individualistic cultures (urban Germany and urban India) and two collectivist ones (rural India and the Nso culture in rural Cameroon, Africa). Sure enough, almost all toddlers in the individualistic/urban cultures recognized themselves in a mirror by 18 or 19 months (for example, touched the mark that had been placed on their face), whereas only a minority of those in the collectivist/rural cultures did. In earlier work (Keller et al., 2005), these researchers had discovered that urban German mothers engaged in more face-to-face interaction with and were more responsive to their 3-month-old babies' actions than rural Nso mothers. Moreover, this maternal responsiveness to the infant as an individual was correlated with later self-recognition.

Yet other researchers are not so sure the mirror self-recognition task is equally valid in all cultures. Tanya Broesch and her colleagues (2011), testing children in several different cultures, found that only 2 of 82 Kenyan children ranging in age from 18 to 72 months touched the mark that had been put on their face during the mirror self-recognition task; instead, they froze and stared at the mirror. The researchers were convinced that most of these children knew who they were but simply did not know how to react in this unusual situation or did not think they had permission to touch or remove the mark. So, we cannot be certain yet how to explain earlier emergence of mirror self-recognition skills in individualistic cultures than in collectivist cultures. Nonetheless, we can conclude that cognitive development, social interaction, and cultural context all influence the development of self-awareness.

Implications of Self-Recognition

Achieving conscious self-awareness is an exciting breakthrough that paves the way for other critical social and emotional developments. Toddlers who recognize themselves in the mirror are more able than those who do not to:

- Talk about themselves and to assert their wills (DesRosiers et al., 1999)
- Experience self-conscious emotions such as pride upon mastering a new toy or embarrassment if asked to show off by dancing or singing for strangers (Lewis et al., 1989; and see Chapter 14)
- Understand other people—for example, empathize with peers in distress (Eisenberg, Spinrad, & Sadovsky, 2006; Taumoepeau & Reese, 2014)
- Coordinate their own perspectives with those of other individuals—for example, cooperate with peers to achieve common goals such as retrieving toys from containers (Brownell & Carriger, 1990).

Temperament

Although it takes infants some time to become aware of themselves as individuals, they have distinctive personalities from the first weeks of life. The study of infant personality has centered on temperament—early, genetically based but also environmentally influenced tendencies to respond in predictable ways to events that serve as the basis for later personality (see Chen & Schmidt, 2015; Rothbart, 2011; Shiner et al., 2012). Learning theorists have tended to view babies as "blank slates" who can be shaped in any number of directions by their experiences. However, it is now clear that babies are not blank slates—that they differ from the start in basic response tendencies.

Easy, Difficult, and Slow-to-Warm-Up Temperaments

One of the first attempts to characterize infant temperaments was the influential work of Alexander Thomas, Stella Chess, and their colleagues (Chess & Thomas, 1999; Thomas & Chess, 1977, 1986). These researchers gathered information about nine dimensions of infant behavior, including typical mood, regularity or predictability of biological functions such as feeding and sleeping habits, tendency to approach or withdraw from new stimuli, intensity of emotional reactions, and adaptability to new experiences and changes in routine. Based on the overall patterning of these temperamental qualities, most infants could be placed into one of three categories:

- Easy temperament. Easy infants are even tempered, typically content or happy, and open and adaptable to new experiences such as the approach of a stranger or their first taste of strained plums. They have regular feeding and sleeping habits, and they tolerate frustrations and discomforts.
- Difficult temperament. Difficult infants are active, irritable, and irregular in their habits. They often react negatively (and vigorously) to changes in routine and are slow to adapt to new people or situations. They cry frequently and loudly and often have tantrums when they are frustrated by such events as being restrained or having to live with a dirty diaper.
- Slow-to-warm-up temperament. Slow-to-warm-up infants are relatively inactive, somewhat moody, and only moderately regular in their daily schedules. Like difficult infants, they are slow to adapt to new people and situations, but they typically

Because temperament is genetically based, identical twins often react similarly to new experiences.

leungchopan/Shutterstock.com

respond in mildly, rather than intensely, negative ways. For example, they may resist cuddling by looking away from the cuddler rather than by kicking or screaming. They eventually adjust, showing a quiet interest in new foods, people, or places.

Of the infants in Thomas and Chess's longitudinal study of temperament, 40% were easy infants, 10% were difficult infants, and 15% were slow-to-warm-up infants. The remaining third could not be placed in only one category because they shared qualities of two or more categories.

Thomas and Chess went on to conduct a longitudinal study of continuity and discontinuity in temperament from infancy to early adulthood (Chess & Thomas, 1984; Thomas & Chess, 1986). Difficult infants who had fussed when they could not have more milk often became children who fell apart when they could not work mathematics problems correctly. By adulthood, however, an individual's adjustment had little to do with her temperament during infancy, suggesting a good deal of discontinuity over this long time span (Guerin et al., 2003).

Surgency/Extraversion, Negative Affect, and Effortful Control

Mary Rothbart and her colleagues (Putnam, Gartstein, & Rothbart, 2006; Rothbart, 2007, 2011; Rothbart, Ahadi, & Evans, 2000; Rothbart & Derryberry, 2002) have gone in a different direction and have defined infant temperament in terms of dimensions rather than types such as easy or difficult babies. They have also considered not only infants' reactivity to experiences, as Thomas and Chess did, but also their capacity for self-regulation. That is, they have focused on how easily infants become emotionally aroused and how able they are to control or regulate their arousal. Rothbart became interested in temperament in part because her two sons were so different. For example, the first liked to be rocked or handed a pacifier when he was distressed, but the second son found these tactics upsetting; he preferred low levels of stimulation and wanted to lie quietly by himself to calm himself down (Rothbart, 2011).

Rothbart and her colleagues have identified at least three major dimensions of temperament, each made up of more specific dimensions. The first two are evident from infancy on; the third, effortful control, emerges more clearly in toddlerhood and early childhood and continues to develop into adulthood:

- Surgency/extraversion—the tendency to actively, confidently, and energetically approach new experiences in an emotionally positive way (rather than to be inhibited and withdrawn). Surgent/extraverted babies are eagerly and actively engaged in life; they enjoy interacting with people and smile and laugh a lot.
- Negative affectivity—the tendency to be sad, fearful, easily frustrated, irritable, and difficult to soothe (as opposed to laid back and adaptable).
- Effortful control—the ability to focus and shift attention when desired, inhibit responses, and appreciate low-intensity activities such as sitting on a parent's lap. Perhaps you remember the children's game, "Simon Says." Effortful control is

illustrated by being able to inhibit hand clapping when the command is "Clap your hands" rather than "*Simon says* clap your hands." At age 3, only 22% can inhibit forbidden actions like this; by age 4, 90% can (Rothbart, 2011). This rapid development of self-control at around age 3 is followed by more rapid growth in adolescence (Eisenberg et al., 2014).

A number of frameworks have been devised to characterize and measure infant temperament (see Chen & Schmidt, 2015). Thomas and Chess pioneered the study of temperament with their easy, difficult, and slow-to-warm-up temperament types. Today, Rothbart's dimensions of temperament have become especially influential because they have been well-researched and because they share similarities with the Big Five dimensions used to describe adult personality (Rothbart, 2011). Perhaps you have noticed yourself that surgency/extraversion matches up well with the Big Five's extraversion dimension, negative affectivity with neuroticism, and effortful control with conscientiousness (Rothbart, 2011).

Goodness of Fit

Differences in temperament are rooted in part in genetically based differences in levels of certain neurotransmitters in the brain (Chen & Schmidt, 2015; Saudino & Wang, 2012). However, prenatal influences such as maternal stress and substance use also help shape it (Huizink, 2012; see Chapter 4). And the postnatal environment then helps determine how adaptive particular temperamental qualities are and whether they persist or change (Bates, Schermerhorn, & Petersen, 2012; Rothbart, 2011). In short, genes and environment interact to influence the development of temperament (Saudino & Micalizzi, 2015).

Thomas and Chess must have appreciated this when they called attention to the **goodness of fit** between child and environment—the extent to which the child's temperament is compatible with the demands and expectations of the social world to which she must adapt (Thomas & Chess, 1977). Consider Carl, one of the children studied by Thomas and Chess. Early in life, Carl was clearly a difficult child: "Whether it was the first bath or the first solid foods in infancy, the beginning of nursery and elementary school, or the first birthday parties or shopping trips, each experience evoked stormy responses, with loud crying and struggling to get away" (Chess & Thomas, 1984, p. 188). Carl's mother became convinced that she was a bad parent, but his father accepted and even delighted in Carl's "lusty" behavior. He

Temperamentally difficult children may remain so if there is a "bad fit" between them and an impatient parent.
LoisjoyThurstun/BubblesPhotolibrary/Alamy Stock Photo

patiently and supportively waited for Carl to adapt to new situations. As a result, Carl did not develop serious behavioral problems as a child and became a well-adjusted adult after weathering some difficulties when he started college.

If the fit between Carl's difficult temperament and his parents' demands and expectations had been poor—for example, if his parents had been impatient, angry, and overly demanding instead of sensitive—Carl might have been headed for serious problems (Guerin et al., 2003; Leerkes, Blankson, & O'Brien, 2009). Similarly, shy, inhibited children are likely to remain inhibited if their parents are either overprotective or angry and impatient, but can overcome their inhibition if their parents create a "good fit" by preparing them for potentially upsetting experiences and making firm but reasonable demands that they cope (Kagan, 1994).

The moral for parents is clear: Get to know your baby as a person, and allow for his personality quirks. Training parents of irritable, difficult babies in how to interpret their infants' cues and respond sensitively and appropriately to them can produce calmer infants who cry less and become less irritable preschoolers (van den Boom, 1995; Crockenberg & Leerkes, 2003). Infants' temperaments and their parents' parenting reciprocally influence one another, of course (Bates et al., 2012; Chen & Schmidt, 2015). Sensitive parenting can make a difficult baby less difficult, but a difficult baby can also make a sensitive parent less sensitive.

● Checking Mastery

1. What important breakthrough in the development of the self occurs at around 18 months of age, and what influences when it happens?

2. How might Mary Rothbart describe Serena, a child whom Thomas and Chess would classify as an easy baby?

● Making Connections

1. The mirror test has become the main way of assessing self-awareness in infants. What do you see as the strengths and limitations of this approach? Can you think of other ways to assess infant self-awareness?

2. Gracie the toddler throws fits when her routines are changed, a stranger comes to visit, or she is asked to try something new and unfamiliar. Using the two different systems for analyzing temperament, help her parents understand her temperament and, more importantly, what they can do to help her become as well adjusted as possible.

11.3
The Child

LEARNING OBJECTIVES
- Summarize how children's self-concepts typically change as they get older.
- Explain the multidimensional nature of self-esteem and the factors that contribute to its being high or low.
- Assess the implications of personality in early childhood for later personality and adjustment.

Children's personalities continue to form, and children acquire much richer understandings of themselves as individuals, as they continue to experience cognitive growth and interact with other people during the preschool and school years.

Elaborating on a Sense of Self

Once toddlers begin to talk, they can and do tell us about their emerging self-concepts. Parent–child conversations that focus on children's experiences and the emotions associated with them help young children pull together what they know of themselves into a self-concept (Goodvin et al., 2015). The preschool child's emerging self-concept is concrete and physical (Damon & Hart, 1988; Harter, 2012). Asked to describe themselves, preschoolers note their physical characteristics, possessions, physical activities and accomplishments, and preferences. One exuberant 3-year-old described herself this way:

> I'm 3 years old and I live in a big house with my mother and father and my brother, Jason, and my sister, Lisa. I have blue eyes and a kitty that is orange and a television in my own room. I know all of my ABC's, listen: A B, C, D, E, F, G, H, J, L, K, O, M, P, Q, X, Z. I can run real fast. I like pizza and I have a nice teacher at preschool. I can count up to 100, want to hear me? I love my dog Skipper. (Harter, 2012, p. 29)

Few young children mention their psychological traits or inner qualities. At most, young children use global terms such as *nice* or *mean* and *good* or *bad* to describe themselves and others (Livesley & Bromley, 1973). Children note their psychological and social qualities more by around age 8, thanks in part to cognitive growth (Harter, 2012). First, they describe their enduring qualities using personality trait terms such as *funny* and *smart* and *honest* (Harter, 2012; Livesley & Bromley, 1973). Second, children form social identities, defining themselves in terms of their identifications with social groups ("I'm a Kimball, a second-grader at Brookside School, a Brownie Scout"; Damon & Hart, 1988). Third, they become more capable of **social comparison**—of using information about how they compare with others to characterize and evaluate themselves (Frey & Ruble, 1985; Pomerantz et al., 1995). The preschooler who said she could hit a baseball becomes the elementary school child who says she is a better batter than her teammates.

Preschool children typically think they are quite wonderful, even in the face of compelling evidence that they have been outclassed by other kids (Butler, 1990; Diehl et al., 2011). By first grade, children are not only very interested in social comparisons

but also more aware of their implications. They glance at each other's papers, ask "How many did you miss?" and say things like "I got more right than you did" (Frey & Ruble, 1985; Pomerantz et al., 1995). As they get older, children learn to be more diplomatic about what they say when they outperform others, but they increasingly use social comparisons to get a more accurate sense of their strengths and weaknesses (Diehl et al., 2011).

Self-Esteem

As children amass a range of perceptions of themselves and engage in social comparisons, they begin to evaluate their worth.

Changes in Self-Esteem

Susan Harter (2003, 2012) has developed self-perception scales for use with different age groups and has found that self-esteem becomes more differentiated or *multidimensional* with age. Preschool children distinguish only two broad aspects of self-esteem: their competence (both physical and cognitive) and their personal and social adequacy (for example, their social acceptance). By mid–elementary school, children differentiate among five aspects of self-worth:

- scholastic competence (feeling smart or doing well in school)
- social acceptance (being popular or feeling liked)
- behavioral conduct (staying out of trouble)
- athletic competence (being good at sports)
- physical appearance (feeling good-looking)

When Harter's scale was given to third- through ninth-graders, even third-graders showed that they had well-defined senses of where they stood, high or low, in each of these five areas. As children get older, they also integrate their self-perceptions in these distinct domains to form an overall sense of self-worth (Harter, 2012; Marsh & Ayotte, 2003). Meanwhile the accuracy of their self-evaluations increases steadily (Harter, 2012; Marsh, Craven, & Debus, 1999). For example, those with high scholastic self-esteem are more likely than those with low scholastic self-esteem to be rated as intellectually competent by their teachers, and those with high athletic self-esteem are frequently chosen by peers to be on sports teams (Harter, 2012).

At the same time, children are forming an ever grander sense of what they "should" be like—an **ideal self**. With age, the gap between the real self and the ideal self increases; older children therefore run a greater risk than younger children do of thinking that they fall short of what they should be (Glick & Zigler, 1985; Oosterwegel & Oppenheimer, 1993). Social comparisons that do not always come out well, a widening gap between the real self and the ideal self, and a tendency for parents and teachers to "raise the bar" and give older children more critical feedback than they give younger children all contribute to a decrease in average self-esteem from early to middle childhood (Harter, 2012).

Influences on Self-Esteem

Why do some children develop higher self-esteem than others? Three influences stand out (Harter, 2012). First, *genetic makeup* is part of the answer; surprising as it may seem, level of self-esteem is a heritable characteristic, influenced by genes as well as by unique or nonshared experiences (Kamakura, Ando, & Ono, 2007; Svedberg et al., 2014). Second, some children display more *competence* than others; they experience more success and come out better in social comparisons as a result. Thus, putting the basketball in the basket more often than the other kids do tells you that you are good at basketball, and doing well in school has a positive effect on academic self-concept (Guay, Marsh, & Boivin, 2003; Marsh & Craven, 2006).

Third, even when two children are equally competent and do equally well in social comparisons, *social feedback* from parents, teachers, and peers can make a big difference in their self-perceptions. Parents are especially important. Children with high self-esteem tend to be securely attached to parents who are warm and democratic (Arbona & Power, 2003; Coopersmith, 1967). These parents frequently communicate approval and acceptance rather than saying, through words, looks, or actions, "Why can't you be better?" (Doyle et al., 2000). The parents' democratic approach also gives their children a sense that their opinions matter. The relationship between high self-esteem and warm, democratic parenting holds up in a variety of ethnic groups and cultures (Scott, Scott, & McCabe, 1991; Steinberg, Dornbusch, & Brown, 1992). High self-esteem, in turn, is positively correlated with good adjustment in childhood (Coopersmith, 1967; Harter, 2012).

Self-esteem is based in part on demonstrating competence and coming out well in social comparisons.

Alistair Berg/Stone+/Getty Images

Should we do all we can to boost children's self-esteem, then? Some observers believe that American parents and educators go overboard in trying to make all children feel good about themselves by handing out stickers, stars, and shouts of "Good job!" at every turn (Damon, 1994; Harter, 2012). Self-esteem means little, they argue, unless it grows out of a child's real achievements. Indeed, giving children an inflated and unrealistic sense of their worth is likely to do more harm than good. One team of researchers, for example, found that if children who are low in self-esteem are given exaggerated praise ("You made an incredibly beautiful drawing!"), it causes them to shy away from challenges, possibly because they believe they will be judged by impossibly high standards (Brummelman et al., 2014). So, it will probably not work in the long run to tell children that they are the greatest when they can see for themselves that they are not. However, helping children succeed at important tasks can boost their self-esteem, and higher self-esteem can then help fuel future achievements (Marsh & Craven, 2006).

The Developing Personality

The early response tendencies called temperament are elaborated into a predictable personality during childhood, which then predicts later personality and adjustment (Shiner & Caspi, 2012). As noted earlier, some of the dimensions of early temperament studied by Mary Rothbart are related to Big Five personality traits (Hagekull & Bohlin, 1998; Rothbart, 2011; Shiner & Caspi, 2012). Consider self-control or self-regulation in childhood. It is an outgrowth of Rothbart's effortful-control dimension of temperament, is linked to the Big Five dimension of conscientiousness later in life, and is associated with a range of good developmental outcomes (Eisenberg et al., 2014; Rueda, 2012). Self-controlled children do well in school, are socially and morally mature, and have fewer adjustment problems than their less self-controlled peers. They even go on to become adults who are healthier, more successful in their careers, more financially stable, and less likely to get into trouble with substance use and crime (Daly et al., 2015; Moffitt et al., 2011; and see Chapter 13). These highly self-regulated, conscientious individuals are able to focus on their long-term goals, act responsibly to pursue them, and resist temptations (such as that party down the hall) that might distract them.

Despite such evidence of continuity between early temperament and later personality, however, we must reject Freud's view that the personality is mostly formed by age 5. Personalities change in response to parenting, cultural pressures, and life events, and the aspects of personality that best characterize young children are sometimes different than the Big Five dimensions that fit adolescents and adults so well (Soto & Tackett, 2015). As a result, correlations between early childhood traits and adult traits are usually quite small. Some dimensions of personality do not fully "gel" until the elementary school years, when children's traits begin to predict their adolescent and adult personality and adjustment much better (McAdams & Olson, 2010; Tackett et al., 2008). Other aspects of personality do not seem to stabilize until adolescence or even adulthood, as we will see later. So the roots of adult personality can be found in childhood, but it takes many years for a personality to fully form.

● **Checking Mastery**

1. What are three major ways in which the self-description of 9-year-old Alonzo might differ from that of his brother, 4-year-old Jamal?
2. What are three main reasons that Lisa may have higher self-esteem than Lula?

● **Making Connections**

1. Some educators believe that nurturing high self-esteem in all children is critical; they favor giving all children lots of positive feedback and sparing them from failure experiences so that they will feel competent. What are the pros and cons of doing this, and what does research say about it?
2. Revisit the Big Five personality dimensions in Table 11.1 If you wanted to determine whether these trait dimensions are evident at age 2 or 3, how would you go about doing so?

11.4
The Adolescent

LEARNING OBJECTIVES

- Discuss how self-descriptions and self-esteem typically change between childhood and adolescence.

- Explain how identity formation in adolescence has been studied and what has been learned about progress in such key areas as ethnic identity and vocational identity.

- Identify and illustrate the major influences on the achievement of identity.

Perhaps no period of the life span is more important to the development of the self than adolescence. Adolescence is truly a time for "finding oneself," as research on adolescent self-conceptions, self-esteem, and identity formation illustrates.

Self-Concept

Some years ago, Raymond Montemayor and Marvin Eisen (1977) learned a great deal about the self-concepts of children and adolescents in grades 4–12 by asking students to write 20 different answers to the question "Who am I?" How would you answer that question? And, looking at **Engagement 11.2**, how would you describe the developmental trends evident there in the answers given by a 9-year-old, an 11½-year-old, and a 17-year-old?

Self-descriptions change considerably between childhood and adolescence (Damon & Hart, 1988; Harter, 2012). Self-conceptions become:

- *less physical and more psychological* (contrast "I have brown eyes" with "I am lonely" in Engagement 11.2).
- *less concrete and more abstract*, thanks to cognitive development (contrast "I love! sports" with "I am a truthful person" or the even more abstract "I am a pseudoliberal").
- *more differentiated*; for example, the child's "social self," which reflects perceived acceptance by others, splits into three distinct aspects in adolescence: acceptance by the larger peer group, acceptance by close friends, and acceptance by romantic partners (Harter, 2012); adolescents also appreciate that they are different "selves" in different social contexts (Diehl et al., 2011; Harter & Monsour, 1992).
- *more integrated and coherent*; thus, adolescents can notice and integrate discrepant self-perceptions, perhaps explaining that they are happy in some situations and grumpy in others because they are moody or because they are happier around people who accept them than around people who are critical of them (Harter & Monsour, 1992).

● **ENGAGEMENT 11.2**

How Do Self-Conceptions Change with Age?

What do these three answers to the question, "Who am I?" say about how self-conceptions change with age? Come to your own conclusions and then compare them to those in Section 11.4.

9-year-old: My name is Bruce C. I have brown eyes. I have brown hair . . . I have great! eye sight. I have lots! of friends. I live at . . . I have an uncle who is almost 7 feet tall. My teacher is Mrs. V. I play hockey! I'm almost the smartest boy in the class. I love! food ... I love! school.

11½-year-old: My name is A. I'm a human being . . . a girl . . . a truthful person. I'm not pretty. I do so-so in my studies. I'm a very good cellist. I'm a little tall for my age. I like several boys . . . I'm old fashioned. I am a very good swimmer . . . I try to be helpful . . . Mostly I'm good, but I lose my temper.

17-year-old: I am a human being . . . a girl . . . an individual . . . I am a Pisces. I am a moody person . . . an indecisive person . . . an ambitious person. I am a big curious person . . . I am lonely. I am an American (God help me). I am a Democrat. I am a liberal person. I am a radical. I am conservative. I am a pseudoliberal. I am an Atheist. I am not a classifiable person (i.e., I don't want to be). (Montemayor & Eisen, 1977, pp. 317–318)

- *more reflected upon*; adolescents become more self-aware, think more about the self, and sometimes become painfully self-conscious (Harter, 2012); for example, adolescents are more likely than either children or adults to show signs of self-consciousness such as embarrassment, along with heightened activity in social and emotional processing centers of the brain, when they are told they are being observed (Somerville et al., 2013).

In sum, from childhood to adolescence and over the course of adolescence, self-understandings become more psychological, abstract, differentiated, integrated, and reflected upon. Many adolescents even become sophisticated personality theorists who reflect for hours upon the workings of their own personalities and those of their companions.

Self-Esteem

Self-esteem tends to decrease from childhood to early adolescence (Robins et al., 2002). This may happen because adolescents are learning more about their strengths and weaknesses, and also because their bodies are changing, they typically change schools, and they face many social pressures. This early adolescent dip in self-esteem affects only some teens, though. It seems to be most common among white females, especially those facing multiple stressors at once—for example, entering middle school, coping with pubertal changes, beginning to date, and so on (Gray-Little & Hafdahl, 2000; Simmons et al., 1987).

In the end, though, adolescence is not as hazardous to self-esteem as most people believe. Although some adolescents do experience dips in self-esteem in early adolescence, most maintain moderate or high levels of self-esteem over the adolescent years or emerge from this developmental period with higher self-esteem than they had at the start (Erol & Orth, 2011; Morin et al., 2013). It matters: As adults, adolescents with high self-esteem tend to have better physical and mental health, better career and financial prospects, and less involvement in criminal behavior than adolescents with low self-esteem (Trzesniewski et al., 2006).

Forging an Identity

Erik Erikson (1968) characterized adolescence as a critical period in the lifelong process of forming an identity as a person—a time for the psychosocial conflict of **identity versus role confusion**. The concept of *identity*, as noted at the start of the chapter, refers to a definition of who you are, where you are going, and where you fit into society. To achieve a sense of identity, adolescents

Adolescents sometimes experiment with a variety of looks in their search for a sense of identity.

XiXinXing/Shutterstock.com

must integrate their self-perceptions into a coherent sense of self. The search for identity involves grappling with many important questions: What kind of career do I want? What religious, moral, and political values can I really call my own? Who am I as a man or woman and as a sexual being? Where do I fit in?

If you have struggled with such issues, you can appreciate the uncomfortable feelings that adolescents may experience when they cannot seem to work out a clear sense of who they are. Erikson believed that many young people experience a full-blown and painful "identity crisis." After all, adolescents' bodies are changing and they must therefore revise their body images and come to think of themselves as sexual beings; their new cognitive abilities allow them to think systematically about hypothetical possibilities, including ideal selves and possible future selves; and society pressures them to "grow up—to decide what they want to do in life and to get on with it. According to Erikson (1968), our society supports youths by allowing them a **moratorium period**—a time during the high school and college years when they are relatively free of responsibilities and can experiment with different possibilities to find themselves. But complex societies like ours also make establishing an identity hard by giving youths a huge number of options and encouraging them to believe they can be anything they want to be.

Developmental Trends

James Marcia (1966) expanded on Erikson's theory and stimulated much research on identity formation by developing an interview procedure to assess where an adolescent is in the process of identity formation. Adolescents are classified into one of four identity statuses (*statuses*, not stages) based on their progress toward an identity in each of several domains (for example, occupational, religious, and political–ideological). The key questions are whether an individual has experienced a *crisis* (or has seriously grappled with identity issues and explored alternatives) and whether he has achieved a *commitment* (that is, resolved the questions raised and settled on an identity). On the basis of crisis and commitment, the individual is classified into one of the four identity statuses shown in ■ **Figure 11.1**.

When do we achieve a sense of identity? Philip Meilman's (1979) study of college-bound boys between 12 and 18, 21-year-old college males, and 24-year-old young men gives us some answers (■ **Figure 11.2**). Most of the 12- and 15-year-olds were in either the identity diffusion status or the identity foreclosure status. At these ages, many adolescents simply have not yet thought

	No Commitment Made	Commitment Made
No Crisis Experienced	**Diffusion Status** The individual has not yet thought about or resolved identity issues and has failed to chart directions in life. Example: "I haven't really thought much about religion, and I guess I don't know what I believe exactly."	**Foreclosure Status** The individual seems to know who he or she is but has latched onto an identity prematurely with little thought. Example: "My parents are Baptists, and I'm a Baptist; it's just the way I grew up."
Crisis Experienced	**Moratorium Status** The individual is experiencing an identity crisis, actively raising questions, and seeking answers. Example: "I'm in the middle of evaluating my beliefs and hope that I'll be able to figure out what's right for me. I've become skeptical about some of what I have been taught and am looking into other faiths for answers."	**Identity Achievement Status** The individual has resolved his/her identity crisis and made commitments to particular goals, beliefs, and values. Example: "I really did some soul-searching about my religion and other religions, too, and finally know what I believe and what I don't."

Crisis? (vertical label at left)

■ **Figure 11.1** The four identity statuses as they apply to religious identity.

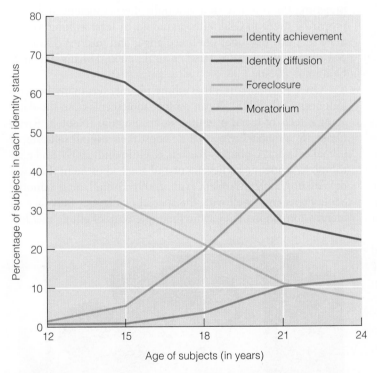

■ **Figure 11.2** Percentage of subjects in each of James Marcia's four identity statuses as a function of age. Note that only 4% of the 15-year-olds and 20% of the 18-year-olds had achieved a firm identity.

Source: From Meilman, P.W. (1979). Cross-sectional age changes in ego identity status during adolescence. *Developmental Psychology*, 15, 230–231.

they have never thought through on their own what suits them best or investigated alternatives; they have simply accepted identities suggested to them by their parents or other people (the **foreclosure status**, involving a commitment without a crisis).

As Figure 11.2 indicates, progress toward identity achievement becomes more evident starting at age 18. More individuals begin to fall into the **moratorium status**. Now they are experiencing a crisis or actively exploring identity issues; now they may be questioning their religious upbringing, experimenting with drugs, changing majors or relationships, or putting outrageous postings on Facebook, all to find themselves. If they can not only raise questions but answer them, they will move to the **identity achievement status**. About 20% of the 18-year-olds, 40% of the college students, and slightly more than half of the 24-year-olds in Meilman's study had achieved a firm identity based on a careful weighing of alternatives. Females progress toward achieving a sense of identity at about the same rate as males do (Kroger, 2007).

Judging from such research, identity formation *takes a long time*. Many young men and women do not raise identity questions or reach the identity achievement status until their late teens or early 20s, during the period of emerging adulthood. Some adults continue in a moratorium status for years; others reopen the question of who they are and recycle through the identity statuses after thinking they had all the answers earlier in life (Anthis & LaVoie, 2006; Kroger, 2007). Even in late adulthood, some adults are reworking and strengthening their identities (Zucker, Ostrove, & Stewart, 2002).

Identity formation not only takes a long time but *occurs at different rates in different domains of identity*. For example, Sally Archer (1982) assessed the identity statuses of 6th- to 12th-graders

about who they are (the **diffusion status**, with no crisis and no commitment). Other adolescents have made commitments, may say things like "I'm going to be a doctor like my dad," and appear to have their acts together. However, it becomes apparent that

in four domains: occupational choice, gender-role attitudes, religious beliefs, and political ideologies. Only 5% of the adolescents were in the same identity status in all four areas. In short, identity formation takes a long time, can be revisited after adolescence, and occurs at different rates in different domains.

Constructing Narrative Identities

Some researchers have taken a different approach to studying identity formation and examined adolescents' *narrative identities,* or life stories (McAdams, 2008, 2011; McAdams & McLean, 2013). A life story, much like an identity in Erikson's sense, tells "who I am, how I came to be, and where my life is going in the future" (McAdams, 2005, p. 241). The process of constructing a meaningful life story begins in childhood but becomes very important during late adolescence and emerging adulthood.

Developing a life story is correlated with making progress through Marcia's identity statuses toward identity achievement (McLean & Pratt, 2006). Life stories then become an important element of our adult personalities and are revised over the years and reflected upon in old age (Birren & Schroots, 2006; McAdams & McLean, 2013). People whose life stories feature overcoming adversity and achieving redemption—for example, people who gain a powerful sense of the meaning of life after almost dying of a drug overdose or after working their way out of poverty to become a Supreme Court justice—tend to have high well-being and good adjustment (McAdams & McLean, 2013).

Developing a Positive Ethnic Identity

An important aspect of identity development is forging an ethnic identity—a sense of personal identification with an ethnic group and its values and cultural traditions (Phinney, 2006; Spencer, Swanson, & Harpalani, 2015; Santos & Umaña-Taylor, 2015). Although everyone has an ethnic and racial background, members of minority groups tend to put more thought than majority group adolescents into defining who they are ethnically or racially. Multiracial or multiethnic youth may have even more reason to think about their ethnic identity; they may be pressed to identify with only one group (for example, to identify as Black rather than Asian when they have both a Black and an Asian parent) and may need to learn how to shift from one identity to another, depending on who they are with (Gaither, 2015). By contrast, white adolescents in the United States often do not even think of themselves as having a race or ethnicity (Bracey, Bamaca, & Umaña-Taylor, 2004).

The process of forming an ethnic identity begins in infancy as babies notice visible differences among people. Three-month-old Caucasian infants already prefer to look at other Caucasian babies rather than at babies from other ethnic backgrounds (Kelly et al., 2005). African babies show a similar preference for African faces, though not if they grow up among Caucasians, suggesting that babies form these preferences based on the faces they see most often (Bar-Haim et al., 2006).

During the preschool years, children learn about different racial and ethnic categories and gradually become able to classify themselves correctly (Spencer & Markstrom-Adams, 1990).

For example, Mexican American preschool children may learn behaviors associated with their culture, such as how to give a Chicano handshake; by about age 8, they may know what ethnic labels apply to them and understand that their ethnicity will last a lifetime (Bernal & Knight, 1997). During elementary school, children learn a lot more about their ethnic group and can talk about it in terms of qualities such as language, physical appearance, heritage, and status in society (Rogers et al., 2012).

In forming a positive ethnic identity, adolescents seem to work through the same identity statuses as they do in forming a vocational or religious identity (Douglass & Umaña-Taylor, 2015; Seaton, Scottham, & Sellers, 2006). School-age children and young adolescents say either that they identify with their racial or ethnic group because their parents and others in their ethnic group influenced them to do so (foreclosure status) or that they have not given it much thought (diffusion status). In their mid- to late teens or early 20s, more minority youths move into the moratorium and achievement statuses (Phinney, 2006; Seaton et al., 2006).

What helps adolescents form a positive ethnic identity? It helps when their parents socialize them regarding their race or ethnicity by teaching them about their group's cultural traditions, preparing them to live in a culturally diverse society, and even preparing them to deal with prejudice, at least as long as it is done in a way that does not breed anger and mistrust (Douglass & Umaña-Taylor, 2015; Hughes et al., 2006; Umaña-Taylor & Guimond, 2010).

Once formed, a positive ethnic identity has many benefits (Spencer et al., 2015). It can protect adolescents from the damaging effects of racial or ethnic discrimination (Neblett, Rivas-Drake, & Umaña-Taylor, 2012), boost their overall self-esteem (Umaña-Taylor, Gonzales-Backen, & Guimond, 2009), and contribute to academic achievement and good adjustment (Laursen & Williams, 2002; Mandara et al., 2009). Overall, most minority adolescents cope well with the special challenges they face in identity formation. They settle their questions of ethnic identity,

Establishing a positive ethnic identity is more central for minority adolescents than for white ones.

Monkey Business Images/Shutterstock.com

resolve other identity issues around the same ages that European American youth do (Markstrom-Adams & Adams, 1995), and wind up feeling at least as good about themselves (Gray-Little & Hafdahl, 2000).

Vocational Identity and Choice

> I wanted to be a firefighter, then I touched a spark. I'm too afraid. I wanted to be a teacher, then I babysat for a 4-year-old. I'm too impatient. I wanted to be a model, then I looked in the mirror. I'm too short.
>
> I know, I know—I can be anything I want when I am all grown up. But I am rapidly approaching all grown up and I see less of what I can be and more of what I cannot be. (Kelly Witte, *The Washington Post*, April 2, 2006, p. D1)

Vocational identity is another important aspect of identity, one with implications for adult career development. How do we choose career paths? Children younger than about age 10 actively explore vocational possibilities but their choices often reflect fantasy rather than reality; they may want to be zookeepers, professional basketball players, firefighters, rock stars, or whatever else strikes them as glamorous and exciting (Ginzberg, 1972, 1984; Hartung, Porfeli, & Vondracek, 2005). Children make important progress, though, by narrowing their ideas about future careers to those consistent with their emerging self-concepts—as humans rather than as lions or ninja turtles, as males or females, and so on (Gottfredson, 1996; Luke & Redekop, 2014). From an early age, for instance, boys choose traditionally masculine occupations, and girls choose traditionally female occupations, setting themselves on paths to traditional gender-stereotyped careers (Hartung et al., 2005; Schuette, Ponton, & Charlton, 2012; Weisgram, Bigler, & Liben, 2010). Elementary school children also learn about the prestige or social status associated with different careers; they may begin to prefer the idea of being a surgeon to the idea of being a car mechanic (Gottfredson, 1996).

Like teenager Kelly Witte, quoted in the beginning of this section, adolescents become more realistic, begin to weigh factors other than their wishes, and make preliminary vocational choices. According to theorist Eli Ginzberg (1972, 1984), they consider their *interests* ("Would I enjoy counseling people?"), their *capacities* ("Am I skilled at relating to people?"), and their *values* ("Is it really important to me to help people, or do I value power or money more?").

As they get still older, adolescents also begin to take into account the realities of the job market and the physical and intellectual requirements for different occupations, and they begin serious preparation for chosen occupations (Ginzberg, 1984; Hirschi & Vondracek, 2009; Walls, 2000). By late adolescence or emerging adulthood, they may consider the availability of job openings in a field such as school counseling, the years of education required, the work conditions, and other relevant factors.

The main developmental trend evident in vocational choice, then, is *increasing realism with age*—a shift from the child's fantasies to informed choice based on knowledge of both the self and the world of work. As adolescents narrow career choices in terms of both personal factors (their own interests, capacities, and values) and environmental factors (the realities of the job market), they seek the vocation that best suits them.

According to influential vocational theorist John Holland (1985, 1996), vocational choice is just this: a search for an optimal fit between one's personality and an occupation (see also Wilson & Hutchison, 2014). Holland's pioneering work led many who study vocational development and adjustment to emphasize the importance of person-environment fit, a concept much like the *goodness of fit* concept discussed earlier that concerns the match between personality and environment, in this case work environment (Su, Murdock, & Rounds, 2015).

You may well have taken a vocational interest inventory guided by Holland's theory of vocational development (if not, and if you would like to do so, go to the U.S. Department of Labor's Interest Profiler website at www.mynextmove.org/explore/ip). Holland identified six personality types, each suited to a different cluster of occupations:

- *investigative* types who enjoy learning, solving problems, and working creatively with ideas (for example, scientists)
- *social* types who like interacting with and helping other people (for example, teachers and counselors)
- *realistic* types who favor practical work with concrete objects (for example, car mechanics, construction workers)
- *artistic* types who are nonconforming and want to express themselves creatively (for example, artists, musicians)
- *conventional* types who prefer order, structure, and predictability (for example, librarians, accountants)
- *enterprising* types who seek to influence others and attain status (for example, sales people, entrepreneurs, leaders of organizations)

Unfortunately, youth from lower-income families, especially minority group families, may face limited vocational opportunities and discrimination. They may aim high at first but, as they become more aware of constraints on their success, lower their career aspirations and aim toward the jobs they think they can get rather than the jobs that interest them most or fit best with their personalities (Armstrong & Crombie, 2000; Hartung et al., 2005; Phillips & Pittman, 2003).

Similarly, the vocational choices of females have been and continue to be constrained by traditional gender norms (Weisgram et al., 2010). Young women who have adopted traditional gender-role attitudes and expect to marry and start families early in adulthood sometimes set their educational and vocational sights low, choosing careers they think will make it easier for them to combine work and family (Bleske-Rechek et al., 2011; Mahaffy & Ward, 2002). More young women today than ever, though, aspire toward high-status and male-dominated occupations.

Those adolescents who do as Erik Erikson and vocational theorist John Holland advise—explore a range of possible occupations, then make informed choices—are more likely than those who do not to choose careers that fit their personalities (Grotevant &

Cooper, 1986). In turn, a good person-environment fit between personality and vocation predicts greater job satisfaction, better performance, and a higher likelihood of staying in the job, in support of Holland's theory of vocational development (Nye, Su, Rounds, & Drasgow, 2012; Spokane, Meir, & Catalano, 2000). The saving grace is that those who do not explore thoroughly enough as adolescents have plenty of time to change their minds as adults.

Influences on Identity Formation

Taking everything into consideration, an adolescent's progress toward achieving identity in various domains is a product of at least five factors:

- **Cognitive development.** Adolescents who have achieved solid mastery of formal-operational thought, who think in complex and abstract ways, and who actively seek relevant information when they face decisions are more likely than other adolescents to raise and resolve identity issues (Berzonsky & Kuk, 2000; Waterman, 1992).
- **Personality.** Adolescents who explore and achieve identity tend to score low in neuroticism and high in openness to experience and conscientiousness (Ozer & Benet-Martinez, 2006). That is, they are emotionally stable, curious, and responsible.
- **Quality of relationship with parents.** Youths who get stuck in the diffusion status of identity formation and drift for years are sometimes neglected or rejected by their parents and emotionally distant from them. Adolescents in the foreclosure status are often extremely close to parents who are loving but overly protective and controlling; these adolescents have few opportunities to make decisions and may never question their parents' ideas about what they should be. Adolescents in the moratorium and identity achievement statuses generally have warm and democratic parents, the same kind of parents who foster high self-esteem (Grotevant & Cooper, 1986; Emmanuelle, 2009; Kroger, 2007).

In traditional societies, teens do not explore a variety of careers in order to choose the best fit. Instead, they simply learn to do whatever adults in their society do.

sutiporn/Shutterstock.com

- **Opportunities for exploration.** Adolescents who attend college are exposed to diverse ideas and are encouraged to think through issues independently and explore different possibilities. College provides the kind of moratorium period with freedom to explore that Erikson felt was essential to identity formation (Kroger, 2007).
- **Cultural context.** The cultural and historical context influences identity formation. Think about some of the difficulties faced by gay adolescents living in Western societies today in forming their sexual identities. Now think about how much harder it was a few decades ago in Western societies when being gay was more stigmatized—or how hard it must be today in a number of Middle Eastern and African societies where homosexuality is viewed as a sickness, a sin, or a crime—sometimes a crime punishable by death. Consider too that the very idea that adolescents should forge a personal identity after carefully exploring options may well be most relevant in modern, industrialized Western societies (Côté & Levine, 2016; Flum & Blustein, 2000). Teens in more traditional societies centered around farming, fishing, or herding may simply adopt the adult roles most adults in their culture adopt, without much soul-searching or experimentation; that is, identity foreclosure may be the most adaptive path to adulthood in such cultures (Côté & Levine, 2016).

Overall, in Western industrialized societies anyway, the adolescent who is able to raise serious questions about identity and answer them is likely to be better off for it. Identity achievement is associated with psychological well-being and high self-esteem, complex thinking about moral and social issues, a willingness to accept and cooperate with other people, better mental health, and a variety of other psychological strengths (Waterman, 1992; Waterman et al., 2013).

Checking Mastery

1. How are 17-year-old Tom's self-descriptions likely to differ from those of his 9-year-old brother Ben?
2. College student Kwan is in the foreclosure status with respect to vocational identity, whereas his roommate Min is in the diffusion status. What does each status mean, and what kind of parenting might give rise to it?
3. What besides warm, democratic parenting is likely to foster identity achievement?

Making Connections

1. Write three brief descriptions of yourself to show how you might have answered the question "Who am I?" at age 4, age 8, and age 18. What developmental changes in self-conceptions do your self-descriptions illustrate?
2. Analyze your own, current identity statuses in the areas of vocational, ethnic, and religious identity and what you perceive to be the major influences on these aspects of identity.

11.5

The Adult

LEARNING OBJECTIVES

- Discuss age and gender differences in self-esteem across the life span and strategies that aging adults use to maintain self-esteem, as well as how self-conceptions differ in individualistic and collectivist cultures.

- Referring to the two different senses of continuity or discontinuity in personality, summarize what we know about continuity and discontinuity in the Big Five trait dimensions over the adult years.

- Analyze the extent to which research supports Erikson's stages of adult development and Levinson's concept of midlife crisis.

- Summarize the typical course of career development and the factors that would enable older workers to adjust well to retirement and have a successful aging experience.

We enter adulthood having gained a great deal of understanding of what we are like as individuals—but we are far from done developing. Both self-conceptions and personalities change, and both can affect and be affected by the careers that adults establish and end.

Self-Concepts and Self-Esteem

Adults differ greatly in their self-perceptions and levels of self-esteem. To what extent do age, gender, and cultural context contribute to this variation?

Age and Gender Differences

It is commonly believed that adults gain self-esteem as they cope successfully with the challenges of adult life but then lose it as aging, disease, and losses of roles and relationships take their toll in later life. Is there truth to this view? A large Internet survey of more than 300,000 people ages 9–90 conducted by Richard Robins and his colleagues (2002) suggests there is. On average, self-esteem tends to be relatively high in childhood, to drop in adolescence, to rise gradually through the adult years until the 50s and 60s, and then to drop in late old age, as shown in ■ **Figure 11.3**. The same pattern is seen in longitudinal studies (Orth, Robins, & Widaman, 2012; Orth, Trzesniewski, & Robins, 2010). Longitudinal studies also tell us that adults' rankings within a group in level of self-esteem remain quite stable over the years (Orth & Robins, 2014).

As Figure 11.3 also shows, males often display higher self-esteem than females in early adulthood but gender differences fade in old age. We know less about racial and ethnic differences. Black and white adults generally have similar levels of self-esteem but blacks tend to show more of an increase in early adulthood and more of a decline in late adulthood, possibly because they experience steeper declines in financial well-being and health (Orth & Robins, 2014).

Do these age and gender differences apply across cultures? Both the rise in self-esteem from adolescence to middle age and the finding that males have higher self-esteem than females were indeed evident across cultures when Wiebke Bleidorn and his colleagues (2016) examined the responses of almost one million

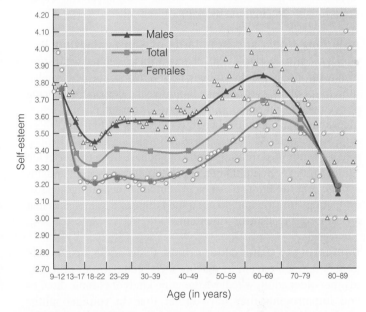

■ **Figure 11.3** Self-esteem dips in early adolescence and rises during the adult years until it declines in very old age. Males have higher scores than females except in childhood and late old age. The lines graph mean, or average, self-esteem for the various age groups shown; the triangles (for males) and circles (for females) plot mean self-esteem at particular ages in the various studies summarized in this meta-analysis.

Source: From Robins, R. W., et al. (2002). Global self-esteem across the life span, *Psychology and Aging, 17*, 423–434.

respondents in 48 nations to an online self-esteem scale. So, we know that these trends are not peculiar to the United States. They may reflect biological universals such as hormonal changes or cultural universals such as the entry of adults worldwide into roles as workers and parents during early adulthood or cross-cultural similarities in gender roles (Bleidorn et al., 2016). There were differences across societies in the size of age and gender differences, however.

In adulthood, as in childhood and adolescence, self-esteem matters: It is associated with relationship and job satisfaction, health, and happiness. Moreover, it appears to be more the cause of these good life outcomes than the consequence of them (Orth & Robins, 2014). How, then, can older adults maintain positive self-images as long as possible, even as they experience some of the difficulties and losses that may come with aging? Reducing the gap between the ideal and real self, changing one's goals and standards of self-evaluation, making social comparisons to other old people, and avoiding negative self-stereotyping can all help.

Reducing the Gap between Ideal and Real Self Comparing young, middle-aged, and elderly adults, Carol Ryff (1991) found that self-ratings of the present self changed little across the adult years, but that older adults scaled down their visions of what they could ideally be. As a result, their ideal and present selves converged. Notice, then, that the gap between the ideal self and the real self that opens up during childhood, widens during adolescence, and gives us a sense of falling short, apparently closes again in later life, helping us maintain self-esteem.

Adjusting Goals and Standards of Self-Evaluation People's goals and standards often change with age so that what seem like losses or setbacks to a younger person may not be perceived as such by an older adult. A 40-year-old may be devastated at being passed over for a promotion, whereas a 60-year-old nearing retirement may not be bothered at all (Carstensen & Freund, 1994). And, for the older adult with a disability, walking a mile may be as much a triumph as running a mile might have been earlier in life (Rothermund & Brandtstädter, 2003b). As our goals and standards change over the life span, we apply different measuring sticks in evaluating ourselves and do not mind failing to achieve goals that are no longer realistic or important.

Comparing to Other Older Adults Older adults are also able to maintain self-esteem by making social comparisons primarily to other older adults who have the same kinds of chronic diseases and impairments they have rather than to younger adults (Brandtstädter & Greve, 1994; Helgeson & Mickelson, 2000). Indeed, if they really want to feel good about themselves, they can strategically select worse-off peers to judge themselves against, making what are called downward social comparisons, as in, "My mind's a lot sharper than poor Bessie's is" (Bauer, Wrosch, & Jobin, 2008; Frieswijk et al., 2004).

Not Internalizing Ageist Stereotypes Finally, older adults are likely to maintain self-esteem better if they can resist applying negative stereotypes of aging people to themselves. Negative stereotypes breed the prejudice and discrimination against older people we call ageism. Ageism shows up in everything from patronizing an elderly customer in a restaurant ("How are we doing, dear?") to discriminating against older adults in hiring.

Becca Levy (2003, 2009) argues that stereotypes of old people, which we learn in childhood, can result in self-stereotyping when we reach old age. Although we hold a few positive stereotypes of older people (they are wise, agreeable, and kindly), negative stereotypes of older adults (they are sick, fragile, forgetful, incompetent, and so on) far outnumber positive ones and show

up in a variety of cultures (see Chan et al., 2012; Miche, 2015). These negative stereotypes are reinforced over the years and are available to be applied to the self once people begin to think of themselves as "old." This may be why so many aging adults go to great lengths to deny that they are old! If they can avoid identifying with their age group, they are likely to feel younger than they actually are, perceive more time ahead of them, and enjoy higher self-esteem (Weiss & Lang, 2012; Weiss & Freund, 2012; Westerhof, Whitbourne, & Freeman, 2012).

But eventually, when aging adults can deny their years no longer, they apply the "old" label to themselves and run the risk of negatively stereotyping themselves and suffering as a result (Levy, 2009; Rothermund & Brandtstädter, 2003a). In one demonstration of how negative self-stereotyping can hurt the performance of elderly adults (Hausdorff, Levy, & Wei, 1999), words reflecting either negative or positive stereotypes of aging were flashed rapidly on a computer screen to elderly adults so that the words were perceived but below the level of awareness. After this priming experience, these adults were asked to walk down a hall wearing measuring devices on their feet that registered how rapidly and sprightly (how long they kept their feet off the ground) they walked. Older adults primed with positive stereotypes of aging clocked faster speeds and more foot-off-the-floor time than older adults who were exposed to negative stereotypes and shuffled along like "old" people. As Chapter 8 revealed, Levy (1996) has also found that priming older adults with words such as *senile* results in poorer memory performance than priming them with words such as *wise*.

By contrast, resisting taking negative stereotypes of aging to heart—for example, disagreeing with statements such as "Things keep getting worse as I get older"—is positively associated with good health and longevity (Levy, Slade, and Kasl, 2002; Levy et al., 2009), fewer signs of psychological disorder (Levy, Pilver, & Pietrzak, 2014), and even fewer signs of the brain changes associated with Alzheimer's disease at autopsy (Levy et al., 2016). These studies and others suggest that ageist stereotypes can do real damage to those older adults who identify themselves as "old" and then apply old-age stereotypes to themselves and that older adults are better off if they can resist this self-stereotyping (Hess, 2006; Hummert, 2015; Kotter-Grühn, 2015). **Application 11.1** asks what else can be done to combat ageist stereotypes.

In sum, self-esteem appears to rise in early and middle adulthood and to drop off in old age. Older adults can maintain self-esteem, however, by bringing their ideal selves into line with their real selves, adjusting their goals and standards of self-evaluation, making social comparisons with other older people, and not applying negative stereotypes of old people to themselves.

Cultural Differences

Self-conceptions in adulthood show the imprint not only of age and gender but also of culture. Recall that in an *individualistic culture*, individuals are socialized to put their own goals ahead of their social group's goals, whereas in a *collectivist culture*, people give group goals and relationships higher priority than personal goals. North American and Western European societies typically

Combating Negative Stereotypes of Aging

Frail, forgetful, lonely? What other negative stereotypes pop into your head when you think about "old people." As you have seen, negative stereotypes of older adults can damage their self-perceptions, functioning, and longevity if they are internalized and applied to the self through self-stereotyping. So how might we as a society combat these ageist stereotypes and the harm they do?

Intervention might need to begin in childhood, as that is when we first learn ageist stereotypes (Kotter-Grühn, 2015). For example, intergenerational programs in which retired adults work with children in the schools not only help children learn but also improve their attitudes toward older people (Cummings, Williams, & Ellis, 2003).

Efforts to combat ageism need to be aimed at seniors too, though. If it's all in their heads, it makes sense to change their negative views of aging (Kotter-Grühn, 2015). For example, activating positive stereotypes of aging before older people perform tasks can boost their cognitive performance (Levy, 2003) and physical functioning (Levy et al., 2014), at least temporarily. Moreover, telling older adults who just had their handgrip strength measured that they did much better than most people their age makes them feel younger and even makes them do better on a second test of handgrip strength (Stephan et al., 2013). Moreover, the activity levels and rated health of nursing home residents can be boosted by convincing them that the difficulties in

physical functioning they are experiencing are due to the nursing home environment (slippery tile floors, for example) rather than to aging (Rodin & Langer, 1980).

Other studies suggest that older adults may feel younger and even live longer if they minimize cues to their own aging—for example, by dying their hair or socializing or even living with people younger than themselves (Hsu, Chung, & Langer, 2010). Our society's overvaluing of youthfulness may be part of what needs changing, however. Interventions like this could backfire if they only end up reinforcing negative views of aging (Kotter-Grühn, 2015).

Ultimately, broader societal change is needed. People in some countries (China and Japan, for example) have more positive views of old age and grant elders more respect than people the United States do (Levy & Langer, 1994). Possibly more positive views of aging can be promoted through social policies, media campaigns, and education and training programs (Braithwaite, 2002; Ferrario et al., 2008). While they are waiting for broad social change, older adults may be best off if they simply become more aware of the incorrectness of many negative stereotypes of old people and

What stereotypes do you have of elderly people—and to what extent do they believe the stereotypes apply to them?

Golden Pixels/Alamy Stock Photo

their potentially damaging effects, resist taking them personally, and avoid blaming every memory lapse or stumble on the ravages of old age.

have an individualistic orientation, whereas many societies in Latin America, Africa, and East Asia are primarily collectivist.

Hazel Markus and her colleagues have carefully studied the meanings of self in the United States and Japan (Cross, 2000; Markus, 2004; Markus, Mullally, & Kitayama, 1997; and see Heine & Buchtel, 2009). They have found that being a person in the United States (an individualistic culture) means being independent and different from other people, whereas being a person in Japan (a collectivist culture) means being interdependent with others. Thus, when asked to describe themselves, American adults talk about their unique personal qualities but Japanese adults more often refer to their social roles and social identities and mention other people (for example, "I try to make my parents happy").

In addition, Americans describe their generalizable personality traits—traits they believe they display in most situations and relationships. By contrast, Japanese adults describe their behavior in specific contexts such as home, school, or work and often describe themselves differently depending on the social situation or context they are talking about. Interestingly, the Japanese language has no word to refer to *I* apart from social context (Cross, 2000). In short, Americans think like trait theorists and feel they have an inner self that is consistent across situations and over time, whereas Japanese people seem to adopt a social learning theory perspective on personality and see situational influences on behavior as powerful (Heine & Buchtel, 2009; Tafarodi et al., 2004).

Finally, Americans are more obsessed with self-esteem and show more self-enhancing biases when they evaluate themselves, believing they are above average (Harter, 2012). Japanese and other East Asian adults are more modest and self-effacing. They readily note their inadequacies and a desire to overcome them, seem reluctant to call attention to ways in which they are better than other people or even to make social comparisons, and are not as concerned with bolstering their self-esteem (Harter, 2012; Heine & Buchtel, 2009; also see ● Table 11.3 for a summary of these differences).

Differences in self-descriptions between individuals in individualistic and collectivist cultures can be detected as early as age 3 or 4 (Wang, 2004, 2006). American children talk about their preferences, characteristics, and feelings, whereas Chinese children describe themselves in terms of social roles and social routines such as family dinners. They are a good deal more modest, too, saying things like "I sometimes forget my manners." Parents probably help create these cultural differences through everyday conversations. For example, American mothers tell stories in which their children are the stars, whereas Chinese mothers talk about the experiences of the family as a group (Wang, 2004). Perhaps as a result, as American children become adolescents, they put less emphasis on their relationships with their parents in their self-definitions, whereas Chinese students continue to see their relationships with their parents as an integral part of who they are (Pomerantz, Qin, Wang, & Chen, 2009).

Cross-cultural studies of individualistic and collectivist cultures challenge the Western assumption that a person must individuate himself from others. In much of the world, it's about "self-in-relation-to-others," not about being a unique self distinct from others (Shweder et al., 2006). These studies even suggest that commonly used methods for studying the self and personality—asking people who they are, having them respond to global self-esteem scales, and giving them personality scales about how they *generally* behave across social contexts—may be culturally biased. It is wise to remind ourselves, then, that the self is culturally defined.

Continuity and Discontinuity in Personality

As we now turn to personality development during adulthood, we must ask two questions:

- Do *individual* adults retain their rankings on trait dimensions compared with others in a group over the years?
- Do *average* scores on personality trait measures increase, decrease, or remain the same as age increases?

Do People Retain Their Rankings?

Paul Costa, Robert McCrae, and their colleagues have closely studied personality change and continuity by giving adults from their 20s to their 90s Big Five personality tests and administering these tests repeatedly over the years (McCrae & Costa, 2003, 2008). They have found a good deal of *consistency in rankings within a group*, as indicated by high correlations between scores on the same trait dimensions at different ages. In other words, the person who tends to be extraverted as a young adult is likely to be extraverted as an elderly adult, and the introvert is likely to remain introverted over the years. Similarly, the adult who shows high or low levels of neuroticism, conscientiousness, agreeableness, or openness to new experiences is likely to retain that ranking when compared with peers years later. Correlations between personality trait scores on two occasions 20–30 years apart average about 0.60 across Big Five personality dimensions, suggesting consistency in personality over time but also room for change (McCrae & Costa, 2003; Morizot & Le Blanc, 2003).

The tendency to be consistent increases with age. Analyzing many studies, Brent Roberts and Wendy DelVecchio (2000) found that the average correlation between scores at two testings increased quite steadily from infancy and early childhood to late adulthood, as shown in ■ Figure 11.4. Personalities are still forming in childhood and even adolescence and young adulthood; after around age 50, they are quite consistent (Lodi-Smith, Turiano, & Mroczek, 2011; Roberts & DelVecchio, 2000).

Do Mean Personality Scores Change?

But do most people change in similar ways over the years? You may be consistently more extraverted than your best friend over the years, and yet both of you could, along with others, become less extraverted from age 20 to age 70. This second major type of continuity in personality, *stability in the mean level of a trait*, is relevant when we ask whether there is growth in personality after adolescence or whether there is truth to stereotypes of older adults.

McCrae, Costa, and their colleagues (2000) have examined age-group differences in scores on the Big Five personality dimensions in countries as diverse as Turkey, the Czech Republic, and

● **Table 11.3** Views of the Self in Individualistic and Collectivist Cultures

Individualistic (e.g., United States)	Collectivist (e.g., Japan)
Separate	Connected
Independent	Interdependent
Emphasis on uniqueness	Emphasis on group memberships and similarities to others
Traitlike (personal qualities transcend specific situations and relationships)	Flexible (different in different social contexts)
Self-enhancing: Need for self-esteem results in seeing self as above average	Self-effacing: Self-critical, aware of inadequacies

Source: Adapted from Markus, H. R., Mullally, P. R., & Kitayama, S. Self-ways: Diversity in modes of cultural participation. In U. Neisser & D. A. Jopling (Eds.), *The conceptual self in context: Culture, experience, self-understanding.* Copyright © 1997 Cambridge University Press. Reprinted with permission.

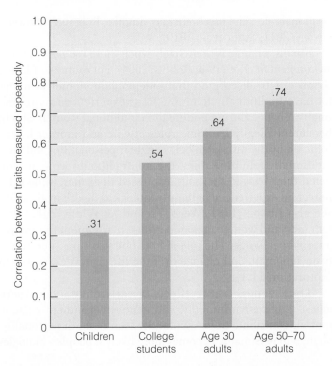

Figure 11.4 Rank-order consistency of personality trait measures at different ages. Consistency, as indicated by strong correlations between scores obtained 6–7 years apart, increases with age.

Source: Data from Roberts, B. W., & DelVecchio, W. F. (2000). The rank-order consistency of personality traits from childhood to old age: A quantitative review of longitudinal studies. *Psychological Bulletin, 126,* 3–25.

Japan. They and other researchers have discovered a shift toward maturity in which people become more emotionally stable (less neurotic), more cooperative and easy to get along with, and more disciplined and responsible from adolescence to middle adulthood (see also Lodi-Smith et al., 2011; Roberts, Walton, & Viechtbauer, 2006; Roberts, Donnellan, & Hill, 2013). This shift toward greater emotional stability, agreeableness, and conscientiousness with age has come to be called the **maturity principle**.

Because this personality maturation shows up across cultures, Robert McCrae and Paul Costa (2008) concluded that it was probably built into the human species by evolution. Others believe that the maturity principle depends on more experience, especially entering roles that require responsible behavior—for example starting work, marrying, becoming a parent. If so, there should be differences across societies in the ages at which maturational changes in personality occur that can be linked to the ages at which adolescents and young adults enter key adult roles (Bleidorn, 2015).

To sort out this nature-nurture issue, Wiebke Bleidorn and his colleagues (2013) analyzed data from an online Big Five personality inventory completed by almost 900,000 young people ranging in age from 16 to 40 in 62 countries. The shift toward greater emotional stability, agreeableness, and conscientiousness was evident across cultures, suggesting that there could well be something universal and possibly biologically based about it. Yet the size of the shift was larger in some cultures than in others,

and it occurred earlier in cultures where the transition to work occurred early than in cultures where the work transition occurred later. The ages of typical transitions to marriage and parenthood in a culture did not make as much difference. Overall, then, this research and other studies like it suggest that both nature and nurture may be behind the maturation principle of personality development (Bleidorn, 2015).

What personality changes can people expect later—from middle age to old age? Not as many. So much for the accuracy of many stereotypes of older people. Activity level—the tendency to be energetic and action oriented, an aspect of extraversion—begins to decline in people's 50s and continues declining through the 80s and 90s (McCrae & Costa, 2003). Otherwise, few consistent changes in personality in later life have been detected. Either we will remain much the same or we will change in response to life experiences but in our own ways and at our own times (Helson, Jones, & Kwan, 2002; but see Kandler et al., 2015).

Overall, most evidence points to (1) a good deal of cross-age consistency, more with age, in people's rankings compared with other people on Big Five personality trait dimensions, as indicated by correlations; (2) personality growth from adolescence to middle adulthood in the form of the maturity principle (greater average emotional stability, conscientiousness, and agreeableness); and (3) little systematic personality change from middle adulthood to later adulthood except for a decreased activity level.

Why Do People Change or Remain the Same?

What makes personalities remain stable over the years? Here are a few ideas (see Roberts, Wood, & Caspi, 2008). First, *genetic makeup* contributes to continuity (Borkenau et al., 2001; Krueger & Johnson, 2008). Second, *lasting effects of childhood experiences*

Research on changes in personality during adulthood suggests that both the father and grandfather in this family may be more mature (emotionally stable, agreeable, and conscientious) than their son/grandson.

Ariel Skelley/Blend Images/Getty Images

may contribute. Third, traits tend to remain stable when people's *environments remain stable*; playing consistent social roles like mother or engineer may breed consistency in personality (Roberts, Wood, & Caspi, 2008). Fourth, *gene–environment correlations* can promote continuity. That is, genetic endowment may influence the kinds of experiences we have, and those experiences, in turn, may strengthen our genetically based predispositions through a kind of snowball effect (Caspi, 1998; Roberts & Caspi, 2003; also see Chapter 3). Thus, an extrovert's early sociability will elicit friendly responses from others, cause her to seek out social activities, and in the process strengthen her initial tendency to be extroverted—while the introvert seeks and experiences an environment that reinforces introversion.

What, then, might cause the significant changes in personality that some adults experience? *Biological factors* such as disease and dementia can certainly contribute. The nervous system deterioration associated with Huntington's disease or Alzheimer's disease, for example, can cause affected individuals to become moody, irritable, and irresponsible (McCrae & Costa, 2003). Adult personalities also change in response to *changes in the environment*, including major life events, changes in social and vocational roles, and psychotherapy (Lüdtke, Roberts, Trautwein, & Nagy, 2011; Sutin et al., 2010).

Finally, change is more likely when there is *a poor person–environment fit* (Roberts & Robins, 2004). For example, Florine Livson (1976) discovered that independent women who did not have traditionally feminine traits experienced more personality change during midlife than traditional women who fit the stereotypically feminine roles of wife and mother better. Bothered by the mismatch between their personalities and their traditionally feminine roles, the nontraditional women redirected their lives in their 40s, expressed their masculine sides more, and experienced better psychological health by their 50s (see also Livson, 1981; Weiss, Freund, & Wiese, 2012). For both men and women, a poor person–environment fit prompts personality change. The role of fit to one's culture in personality development and change over the life span is examined in **Exploration 11.1**.

Thus, genes, lasting effects of early childhood experiences, stable environments, and gene–environment correlations all contribute to the continuity seen in adult personality. Change in personality becomes more likely if people's biologies

• EXPLORATION 11.1

Personality and Culture: The Importance of Fit

The goodness of fit concept developed by Thomas and Chess to understand infant temperament and the person–environment fit concept used by John Holland and others to understand vocational development also help us think about personality development in its cultural context. Adults in some cultures, for example, value emotional expressiveness and assertiveness in children, whereas adults in other cultures want their children to be quiet, respectful, and self-controlled (Chen & Schmidt, 2015). These sorts of differences in cultural values translate into differences in personality development as children try to meet adults' expectations. They can also spell trouble for the child whose biologically based temperament is a poor fit to her cultural setting. So, for example, a difficult temperament tends to be maladaptive in many cultural environments (Thomas & Chess, 1977). Yet a difficult temperament proved very adaptive for Masai babies in East Africa during a famine: Their lusty crying got them more attention from caregivers (DeVries, 1984).

Another wonderful illustration of the importance of person–environment fit comes from research by Xinyin Chen and his colleagues on the implications of shyness for children in Eastern and Western cultures (see Chen, Cen, Li, & He, 2005; Chen, Wang, & Wang, 2009; Chen, Yang, & Fu, 2012). In North America's individualistic culture, where autonomy and initiative are highly valued, shyness can be a disadvantage. It is sometimes linked to poor functioning at school and in social relationships, low self-esteem, and even depression. In China's collectivist culture, by contrast, the personality of the shy child has traditionally been prized and predicts good adjustment. Shy children are appropriately humble, do not call attention to themselves, and try to fit in rather than stand out. Interestingly, although shyness continues to be an asset in rural China today, it has become correlated with poor rather than good adjustment in urban areas of China. Why the change? Western capitalism has rapidly taken hold in China's cities and a more forceful, outgoing, and enterprising personality is now valued.

Finally, consider an intriguing study of adult personality and culture. Derya Güngör and colleagues (2013) gave personality scales to three groups of young mothers: Japanese women living in Japan, European-American women living in the United States, and Japanese-American immigrants who had lived in the United States for an average of 5–6 years. The Japanese-American immigrants had a Big Five personality profile somewhere between that of the Japanese women and the European-American women, suggesting that their personalities may have changed to fit in better with their new American cultural setting. Their personalities were especially likely to be more American and less Japanese to the extent that they became highly acculturated to the United States and took on more American habits, friends, language usage, and so on.

We see, then, that an individual's historical and cultural environment, by influencing which personality traits are most valued, influences which traits are reinforced and strengthened and which prove most adaptive over the life span (Chen & Schmidt, 2015; Rothbart, 2011). We also learn that personality is not set in stone by genetic makeup; rather, it is malleable and can change shapes to achieve a better fit to its cultural environment (Güngör et al., 2013).

or environments change or if there is a poor fit between their personalities and lifestyles. All things considered, the forces for continuity are often stronger than the forces for change, perhaps in part because we want to retain our identities as individuals and because we keep building the same niches for ourselves even when we move, change jobs, or make other life changes (Roberts et al., 2008).

Personality and Adjustment

When all is said and done, personality has a tremendous impact on life-span development. Personal strengths such as emotional stability and conscientiousness are correlated with good physical and mental health (Kern & Friedman, 2010; Hampson & Friedman, 2008; Lucas & Diener, 2008). Moreover, personality affects how we react to and cope with life events. For example, highly agreeable people are able to adjust better than most people to becoming disabled (Boyce & Wood, 2011), and people high in emotional stability (low in neuroticism) handle the deaths of loved ones better (Robinson & Marwit, 2006). Personality—not only self-rated personality but personality as judged by friends—even predicts longevity (Jackson et al., 2015). In these and other ways, personality plays a critical role in adjustment throughout the life span.

Eriksonian Psychosocial Growth

The trait approach to studying personality focuses on enduring dispositional traits and probably reveals the most stable aspects of personality. We get a sense of much more growth and change from research inspired by Erikson's psychoanalytic theory of psychosocial development through the life span. Erikson's stages of psychosocial development are outlined in ● **Table 11.4** (see also Chapter 2). Both maturational forces and social demands, Erikson believed, push humans everywhere through these eight psychosocial crises. Later conflicts may prove difficult to resolve if early conflicts were not resolved successfully. For development to proceed optimally, a healthy balance between the terms of each conflict must be struck; if this happens, the individual gains a particular "virtue," or psychosocial strength. Consider briefly how the self and personality unfold prior to adulthood according to Erikson before examining his adult stages.

The Path to Adulthood

During Erikson's first psychosocial conflict trust versus mistrust, infants learn to trust other people if their caregivers are responsive to their needs; otherwise, the balance of trust versus mistrust will tip in the direction of mistrust. Erikson believed that infants come to recognize that they are separate from their caregivers. Indeed, as you saw earlier in this chapter, infants begin to distinguish self from other as early as the first 2 or 3 months of life.

Toddlers acquire an even clearer sense of themselves as individuals as they struggle with the psychosocial conflict of **autonomy versus shame and doubt**. According to Erikson, they assert that they have wills of their own. Consistent with this view, toddlers recognize themselves in a mirror and lace their speech with "me" around 18–24 months of age. Some "terrible twos" also make "no" their favorite word—a clear signal that they are now in charge.

Four- and five-year-olds who have achieved a sense of autonomy then enter Erikson's stage of **initiative versus guilt**. They develop a sense of purpose by devising bold plans and taking great pride in accomplishing the goals they set ("I did it!"). As you have seen, preschoolers define themselves in terms of their physical activities and accomplishments. A sense of initiative, Erikson believed, paves the way for success when elementary school children face the conflict of industry versus inferiority and focus on mastering important cognitive and social skills. As you have seen, elementary school children engage in more social comparison than younger children and are likely to acquire a sense of industry rather than inferiority if those comparisons turn out favorably.

According to Erikson, children who successfully master each of these childhood psychosocial conflicts gain new ego strengths. Moreover, they learn a good deal about themselves and position themselves to resolve the adolescent crisis of *identity versus role confusion*, Erikson's fifth stage, which was discussed in some detail earlier in this chapter.

What happens to adolescents with newfound identities during the adult years? Erikson thought that stagelike changes in personality—and exciting possibilities for personal growth— continue during adulthood through psychosocial crises focused on intimacy versus isolation, generativity versus stagnation, and

● **Table 11.4** The Eight Stages of Erikson's Psychosocial Theory

Stage	Age Range	Central Issue	Virtue or Strength
1. Trust vs. mistrust	Birth–1 year	Can I trust others?	Hope
2. Autonomy vs. shame and doubt	1–3 years	Can I act on my own?	Will
3. Initiative vs. guilt	3–6 years	Can I carry out my plans successfully?	Purpose
4. Industry vs. inferiority	6–12 years	Am I competent compared with others?	Competence
5. Identity vs. role confusion	12–20 years	Who am I and where am I going?	Fidelity
6. Intimacy vs. isolation	20–40 years	Am I ready for a committed relationship?	Love
7. Generativity vs. stagnation	40–65 years	Have I given something to future generations?	Care
8. Integrity vs. despair	65 years and older	Has my life been meaningful?	Wisdom

integrity versus despair. In a longitudinal study of college students from their college years to their 40s and 50s, Susan Whitbourne and her colleagues (Whitbourne, Sneed, & Sayer, 2009) assessed progress in resolving all eight of Erikson's issues. They found steady growth even in qualities like trust and autonomy that are associated with the childhood stages, along with especially rapid growth in qualities related to the adult conflicts centering on intimacy, generativity, and integrity. So, as Erikson maintained, there is most certainly psychosocial growth throughout the life span.

Early Adult Intimacy

As Erikson saw it, early adulthood is a time for dealing with the psychosocial conflict of intimacy versus isolation. A person must achieve a sense of individual identity before becoming able to commit himself to a shared identity with another person. The young adult who has no clear identity may be threatened by the idea of entering a committed, long-term relationship and being "tied down," or he may become overdependent on a romantic partner as a source of identity.

Does identity indeed pave the way for genuine intimacy? To find out, Susan Whitbourne and Stephanie Tesch (1985) measured identity statuses and intimacy statuses among college seniors and 24- to 27-year-old alumni from the same university. College graduates had progressed farther than college seniors in resolving intimacy issues. In addition, the college graduates who had achieved a sense of identity were more likely than those who had not to be capable of genuine and lasting intimacy. Specifically, they were more often in relationships in which they and their partners had close involvement in each other's lives, open communication about their feelings, and a long-term commitment to one another.

As Erikson theorized, then, we must know ourselves before we can truly love another person. Yet Erikson believed that women resolve identity questions when they choose a mate and fashion an identity around their roles as wife and mother-to-be. Is this old-fashioned view correct? Only for some women, especially those who develop in a sociocultural context with traditional gender-role expectations (Dyk & Adams, 1990; George, Helson, & John, 2011; Kroger, 2007). Other women, also influenced by traditional gender-role expectations, resolve intimacy issues before identity issues: They marry and have children and, only after the children are older, ask who they

Early adulthood is the time, according to Erik Erikson, for deciding whether to commit to a shared identity with another person—for resolving the conflict of intimacy versus isolation.

Cassy Muronaka/PhotoEdit

are as individuals and pursue careers that suit their personalities (George et al., 2011). Still other women, especially those with less traditional gender-role orientations, follow the identity-before-intimacy route that characterizes most men, settling on a career first, thinking about a serious relationship later (Dyk & Adams, 1990). Today, more and more women are following this identity-before-intimacy path (Beyers & Seiffge-Krenke, 2010), further evidence that development is shaped by its historical and cultural context.

Midlife Generativity

What does psychosocial development look like in middle age? George Vaillant (1977), a psychoanalytic theorist, conducted an in-depth longitudinal study of mentally healthy Harvard men from college to middle age and a similar longitudinal study of blue-collar workers (Vaillant, 1983, 2012; Vaillant & Milofsky, 1980). Vaillant found support for Erikson's view that the 20s are a time for intimacy issues. He found that in their 30s, men shifted their energies to advancing or consolidating their careers and were seldom reflective or concerned about others. In their 40s, though, many men became concerned with Erikson's issue of generativity versus stagnation. This psychosocial conflict involves gaining the capacity to generate or produce something that outlives you and to care about the welfare of future generations. It is realized through such activities as parenting, teaching, mentoring, and leading (de St. Aubin, McAdams, & Kim, 2004; Slater, 2003).

Vaillant's 40-something men expressed more interest in passing on something of value to their own children, to younger people at work, or to their communities. They were growing as individuals, often becoming more caring and self-aware as they entered their 50s. One of these men expressed the developmental progression Vaillant detected perfectly: "At 20 to 30, I think I learned how to get along with my wife. From 30 to 40, I learned how to be a success in my job. And at 40 to 50, I worried less about myself and more about the children" (1977, p. 195).

Middle-aged men and women are more likely than young adults to have achieved a sense of generativity (de St. Aubin et al., 2004; McAdams, Hart, & Maruna, 1998). Moreover, those adults who have attained identity and intimacy are more likely than other adults to achieve generativity as well, as Erikson would predict (Christiansen & Palkovitz, 1998). The middle-age conflict of generativity versus stagnation may

Reminiscence and life review can help older adults achieve a sense of integrity.

Masterfile

play out differently in different cultural contexts; for example, for Mexican-American parents with a collectivist orientation it may center on relationships with children, whereas for Anglo-Americans it may more often center on individual contributions such as book writing or community service (de St. Aubin & Bach, 2015). Either way, research supports Erikson's view that both women and men are capable of impressive psychosocial growth during middle adulthood.

Old-Age Integrity

Elderly adults, according to Erikson, confront the psychosocial issue of **integrity versus despair**. They search for a sense of meaning in their lives that will help them face the inevitability of death. If they constructed a life story or narrative identity during their early adult years, they may work on accepting it in old age as the only life they could have led (McAdams, 2011; McAdams & Adler, 2006). Those older adults who achieve integrity tend to be well-adjusted people who think in mature and complex ways and have a sense of great well-being (Hearn et al., 2012; James & Zarrett, 2005; Torges, Stewart, & Duncan, 2008).

Noted gerontologist Robert Butler (1963) proposed that older adults engage in a process called **life review**, in which they reflect on unresolved conflicts of the past to come to terms with themselves, find new meaning and coherence in their lives, and prepare for death (see also Haber, 2006; Webster & Haight, 2002). Elders who engage in life review display a stronger sense of integrity and better overall adjustment and well-being than those who do not reminisce much or who mainly stew about unresolved regrets (Bohlmeijer et al., 2007; Wong & Watt, 1991). Finding that life review can be beneficial, Butler and other gerontologists have turned it into a therapy approach in which elderly adults reconstruct and reflect on their life stories, sometimes with the

help of photo albums and other memorabilia (Haight & Haight, 2007; Kunz & Soltys, 2007).

On balance, Erikson's view that humans experience psychosocial growth throughout the life span is well supported by research. Erikson's childhood stages capture important milestones in the development of the self, and there is support for his idea that achieving a sense of identity in adolescence paves the way for forming a truly intimate relationship in early adulthood, gaining a sense of generativity in middle adulthood, and resolving the issue of integrity versus despair through life review in later adulthood.

Midlife Crisis?

> Midlife is when you reach the top of the ladder and find that it was against the wrong wall. (Joseph Campbell, cited in S. Weiss, 2008)

This quotation captures the essence of midlife crisis. But where in all the evidence of stability and change in personality traits over the adult years and of psychosocial growth through Erikson's stages is the midlife crisis that many people believe is a standard feature of personality development in middle age? Although Erikson, and Vaillant after him, saw few signs of a midlife crisis, another psychoanalytic theorist, Daniel Levinson (1986, 1996; Levinson et al., 1978) did. He proposed a stage theory of adult development based on intensive interviews with 40 men and later reported that it applied to a sample of women he interviewed as well (Levinson, 1996).

Levinson claimed that adults worldwide go through a repeated process of first building a "life structure," or overall pattern of living, and then questioning and altering it during a transition period every 7 years or so. He believed that the transition period from age 40 to age 45 is an especially significant transition, a time of **midlife crisis** in which a person questions his life structure and raises unsettling issues about where he has been and where he is heading. Most middle-aged adults Levinson interviewed did not seek divorces, quit their jobs, buy red sports cars, or behave like lovesick adolescents, as popular images of the midlife crisis would have it. However, most did seem to experience a significant psychological crisis in their early 40s.

In support of Levinson, many researchers agree that middle age is often a time when people confront important issues like aging, evaluate their lives, and revise their goals (Freund & Ritter, 2009; Hermans & Oles, 1999; McAdams & Adler, 2006). There is even intriguing evidence that life satisfaction shows a U-shaped pattern over the adult years, decreasing from early adulthood to a low in middle adulthood and then increasing from middle adulthood to old age (Cheng, Powdhavee, & Oswald, 2016). In addition, some middle-aged adults change in response to life events. So it was for K., a woman who was thrown off balance in her 40s by her father's death, her mother's stroke, her husband's leaving her, and a layoff from work and who told herself that "at least she had so many troubles that she couldn't dwell on all of them at once" (Rauch, 2014, p. 92).

In the end, though, there is not much support for Levinson's claim that adults universally experience a genuine psychic crisis in the narrow age range of 40 to 45 (Freund & Ritter, 2009; Hedlund & Ebersole, 1983; Vaillant, 1977). It seems sounder to call what many middle-aged adults experience *midlife questioning*, to recognize that it can occur in response to life events at a variety of ages, and to appreciate that it is usually not a true psychological crisis. The cultural context also must be considered: Midlife may be viewed more positively in a culture like Japan where people believe that we become wiser and more capable as we age than in a youth-oriented culture like the United States where middle age may be viewed as the beginning of decline (Menon, 2015).

Vocational Development and Adjustment

Although Levinson's concept of midlife crisis is not well supported, he was right to emphasize that adults revise important life decisions as they develop. To illustrate, consider adult vocational development, an outgrowth and expression of an individual's self-concept and personality (George et al., 2011; Judge & Bono, 2001). After much experimenting in early adulthood, people settle into chosen occupations in their 30s and strive for success. Ultimately, they prepare for the end of their careers, make the transition into retirement, and attempt to establish a satisfying lifestyle during their "golden years."

Establishing a Career

Early adulthood is a time for exploring vocational possibilities, launching careers, making tentative commitments, revising them if necessary, seeking advancement, and establishing yourself firmly in what you hope is a suitable occupation. This often takes time and involves lots of false starts and job changes.

To illustrate, Susan Phillips (1982), using data from a longitudinal study of males tracked from adolescence to age 36, examined whether men's decisions about jobs at different ages were tentative and exploratory (for example, "to see if I really liked that kind of work") or more final (for example, "to get started in a field I wanted [to enter]"). The proportions of decisions that were predominantly exploratory were 80% at age 21, 50% at age 25, and 37% at age 36. From age 21 to age 36, then, young adults progressed from wide-open exploration of different career possibilities to tentative or trial commitments to a stabilization of their choices. Even in their mid-30s, however, about a third of adults were still exploring what they wanted to be when they grew up! A recent longitudinal study of Americans born from 1957 to 1964 confirms this, showing that the average worker held almost 12 jobs from age 18 to age 48 (Bureau of Labor Statistics, 2015). Nearly half of these were held from age 18 to 24; job change declined with age but was still happening in people's 40s. This picture of frequent job change was very similar for men and women.

After their relatively unsettled 20s and decision-making 30s, adults often reach the peaks of their careers in their 40s (Simonton, 1990). They often have major responsibilities and define themselves in terms of their work. Personality is an important influence on how successful a person becomes. Vocational success is consistently correlated with Big Five qualities such as conscientiousness, agreeableness, extraversion, and emotional stability (Ozer & Benet-Martinez, 2006; Sackett & Walmsley, 2014). Person–environment fit can be critical too: People tend to perform poorly and become open to leaving their jobs when the fit between their personality and aptitudes and the demands of their job or workplace is poor (Hoffman & Woehr, 2006; Nye et al., 2012).

Gender is another significant influence on vocational choice and development. Although women are entering a much wider range of fields today and aiming higher than they were a few decades ago, most administrative assistants, teachers, and nurses are still women, and overall working women still earn less than men. Although gender discrimination is a contributor, gender differences in vocational success and earnings also arise because traditional gender-role norms have led many women to subordinate career goals to family goals. Women are more likely than men to interrupt their careers, drop down to part-time work, take less demanding jobs, and turn down promotions that would require transferring to a new location so that they can have and raise children (Biemann, Zacher, & Feldman, 2012; Kirchmeyer, 2006; Moen, 1992). In the process, women have ended up with lower odds of rising to higher paid, more responsible positions.

Since the recession of 2008, many adults have experienced the stress that accompanies unemployment.

Frances Roberts/Alamy Stock Photo

So, although we make preliminary vocational choices as adolescents, we remain open to making new choices as young and even middle-aged adults and take some time to settle on careers that fit our personalities and gender roles. Meanwhile, our vocational experiences affect our personalities (Wille, Beyers, & De Fruyt, 2012). For instance, people whose work is complex and intellectually challenging become able to handle intellectual problems more adeptly and self-confidently (Kohn & Schooler, 1982; Schooler, Mulatu, & Oates, 1999). Mentally challenging work even appears to help people maintain good cognitive functioning when they reach old age (Then et al., 2015). Attaining a responsible position at work can also make people more conscientious and emotionally stable (Roberts et al., 2008). In the end, person–environment fit and the dynamic, reciprocal influences of personality on career and of career on personality shape adult vocational development (Hesketh, Griffin, & Loh, 2011; Wille et al., 2012).

Job Loss and Unemployment

How are adults affected when they suddenly lose their jobs? As we continue to live with the effects of the global economic recession that began in 2008, this is an especially important question to ask. Because work is such a central part of adulthood, job loss and unemployment can threaten adults' identities, disrupt their goals, and lower their self-esteem (Brand, 2015; Price, Friedland, & Vinokur, 1998). Moreover, job loss is likely to be accompanied by a cascade of other stressors such as the need to apply for unemployment benefits, alter routines, move to cheaper housing, or borrow money. It can, as a result, have negative effects on both physical and mental health (Brand, 2015; Feldman & Ng, 2013;

Howe et al., 2012). In the long run, one instance of unemployment may not have much lasting effect. However, after they have retired, adults who had repeated periods of unemployment experience more depression and anxiety symptoms and have lower life satisfaction than those who managed to stay employed during their adult years (Zenger, Brähler, Berth, & Stöbel-Richter, 2011).

Unemployment also affects the individual's whole family (Brand, 2015). Not only may job losers become angry and depressed, but their partners may too, and the quality of the couple's relationship may suffer (Howe, Levy, & Caplan, 2004). When economic hardship causes parents to be depressed and to fight with one another, parenting often deteriorates. As a result, children's behavior problems tend to increase while their performance in school and their well-being suffer (Brand, 2015; Conger et al., 1992; and see Chapter 15). In sum, the whole family may need help coping with job loss.

The Aging Worker

Many people believe that adults become less able or less motivated to perform well on the job as they approach retirement. As it turns out, the job performance of workers in their 50s and 60s is largely similar overall to that of younger workers (Rhodes, 1983). Judging from a meta-analysis of multiple studies (Ng & Feldman, 2008), age is largely unrelated to quality of task performance and creativity on the job. Older workers actually outperform younger workers in areas such as good citizenship and safety and have fewer problems with counterproductive behavior such as aggression, substance use, tardiness, and absenteeism. Most negative stereotypes of older workers are baseless (Ng & Feldman, 2012).

Why is the performance of older workers not hurt by some of the age-related physical and cognitive declines described earlier in this book? First, these declines typically do not become significant until people are in their 70s and 80s, long after they have retired, and even then they do not affect everyone. The "older" workers in most studies are mainly middle-aged adults in their 40s, 50s, and 60s. Second, older workers have often accumulated a good deal of on-the-job expertise that helps them continue to perform well (Hansson et al., 1997).

Third and finally, the answer may lie in the strategies that aging adults use to cope with aging. Gerontologists Paul and Margaret Baltes (1990) theorized that older people can best cope with aging through the strategy of *selective optimization with compensation (SOC)* (Baltes & Baltes, 1990; Lang, Rohr, & Williger, 2011; and see Chapter 8). Using SOC, an overworked 60-year-old lawyer might, for example, avoid spreading herself too thin by focusing on her strongest specialty area and delegating other types of assignments to younger workers (selection); put a lot of time into staying up-to-date in her main area of specialization (optimization); and make up for her failing memory by taking more notes at meetings (compensation). For pianist Arthur Rubenstein,

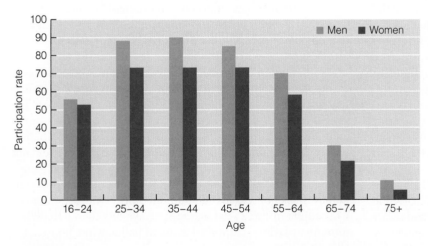

■ **Figure 11.5** Male and female labor force participation by age group in the United States in 2014. Labor force participation increases in people's 20s, peaks in their late 20s through 40s, and declines steeply starting at age 55. Most adults are out of the labor force by age 65–69. Men's participation is higher than women's, especially during the child-rearing years, but the gender gap is much narrower than it used to be.

Source: U.S. Department of Labor, U.S. Bureau of Labor Statistics; Table 3.3, Civilian labor force participation rates by age, sex, race, and ethnicity. www.bls.gov/emp/ep_table_303.htm.

maintaining excellence in old age meant playing fewer different pieces (selection), practicing them more (optimization), and compensating for loss of speed by increasing the contrast between the slower and faster parts of a piece to make the faster parts sound faster (Baltes, Lindenberger, & Staudinger, 2006).

The federal government may have recognized that older workers are generally effective workers when it raised or eliminated mandatory retirement ages, increased the age of eligibility for receiving Social Security, and, through the Age Discrimination in Employment Act, protected workers age 40 and older from age discrimination in hiring and retention (Hansson et al., 1997). But job applicants in their 60s, especially women, are still discriminated against by employers, even when they have the same credentials as younger applicants (Neumark, Burn, & Button, 2015), and older workers still have more difficulty than younger ones getting rehired after losing a job (Wanberg et al., 2016). So, much remains to be done to combat ageism in the workplace and to meet the needs of those who have the desire and ability to continue working well into old age (see Hedge, Borman, & Lammlein, 2006).

Retirement

A century ago in North America, most working adults continued working as long as they were able, as people in many traditional societies today do. The introduction of Social Security in 1934, affluence, and the increased availability of private pension plans changed that, making it financially possible for more men and women to retire and to do so earlier. And they have! As shown in ■ Figure 11.5, the labor force participation of men and women increases in early adulthood, plateaus, and then starts decreasing steeply in people's late 50s. As of 2014, around half of adults were out of the labor force by age 62–64, over two-thirds were out by age 65–69, and over 90% were out by age 75 and older. From the 1960s to the 1990s, the average age of retirement dropped from over 67 to 62. However, it has been inching up again since the mid-1990s. In 1991, only about 1 in 10 workers intended to keep working beyond age 65; now almost 4 in 10 do (Reid, 2015). Why the recent rise in the retirement age? Today's older workers are healthier and want to keep contributing, mandatory retirement policies are gone, economic uncertainty and rising health care costs make people feel they need or want to continue working for financial reasons, and the age of eligibility for full Social Security benefits has increased (Song & Manchester, 2009; Toossi, 2012).

Retirement is not a single event; it is a process that often plays out over a number of years. While some workers do retire "cold turkey" all at once, many others retire gradually, cutting back their work hours, becoming self-employed, taking part-time "bridge" jobs between full-time work and retirement, and sometimes cycling in and out of retirement multiple times before they settle into full retirement (Calvo, Haverstick, & Sass, 2009; Zissimopoulos & Karoly, 2009).

How do people adjust to the final chapter of the work life cycle? They face two main challenges: adjusting to the loss of their work role and developing a satisfying and meaningful lifestyle in retirement (van Solinge & Henkens, 2008). Robert Atchley (1976) proposed that adults progress through phases as they make the transition from worker to retiree. The process of adjustment begins with a *preretirement phase* in which workers nearing

retirement gather information and plan for the future (Ekerdt, Kosloski, & DeViney, 2000). Discussing retirement with one's spouse and working out a financial plan during the preretirement phase are likely to pay off in greater well-being after retirement (Noone, Stephens, & Alpass, 2009).

Just after they retire, according to Atchley, workers often experience a *honeymoon phase* in which they relish their newfound freedom; they head for the beach, golf course, or camp grounds and do all the projects they never had time to do while they worked. Then, according to Atchley, many enter a *disenchantment phase* as the novelty wears off; they feel aimless and sometimes unhappy. Finally, they move to a *reorientation phase* in which they begin to put together a realistic and satisfying lifestyle.

Consider Don, a businessman who retired early at age 58. In the first weeks, he took trips and renovated his house: "That was great—I loved it." But after some months of this fun and of taking on more volunteer consulting jobs than he intended, he was reassessing how he wanted to spend his time and worrying that his money might not last: "Here I am over a year down the road and I don't like where I am. I don't think I've got my life coursed out correctly." After a few more months, he felt he'd worked out a lifestyle that suited him.

Research offers some support for Atchley's view of the adjustment process. For example, David Ekerdt and his colleagues (Ekerdt, Bossé, & Levkoff, 1985) found that (1) men who had been retired only a few months were in a honeymoon period, highly satisfied with life and optimistic about the future, (2) men who had been retired 13–18 months were rather disenchanted, and (3) men who had been retired for longer periods were relatively satisfied. Yet not everyone fits this pattern; for example, almost half of retirees in one study adjusted easily and within a month to retirement, whereas one in five found it took much longer and was challenging (van Solinge & Henkens, 2008).

After retirees have adjusted to retirement, are they better or worse off than they were before they retired? Negative images of the retired person abound; the retiree supposedly ends up feeling old, useless, bored, sickly, and dissatisfied. Yet research shows that retirement has surprisingly few effects on adults (Hansson et al., 1997; Palmore et al., 1985). Retirement's most consistent effect is to reduce the individual's income (Palmore et al., 1985). This is a problem in that many people, especially women and minorities, have very little saved up for retirement, whether because their earnings were low when they worked, they did not save enough, they were not eligible for pensions, or other reasons (Copeland, 2014; Rhee, 2013a, 2013b). For example, three out of four Black households and four out of five Latino households with adults in the 25–64 age range have less than $10,000 in retirement savings, compared to about half of white households (Rhee, 2013a).

However, apart from experiencing a drop in income, retired people fare well. They generally do not experience a decline in health simply because they retire. Poor health more often causes retirement than retirement causes poor health. Similarly, retirement does not typically diminish cognitive functioning (Coe et al., 2012), or cause a deterioration of people's social networks and social interactions, lower people's life satisfaction, or undermine their mental health (Palmore et al., 1985).

In sum, retirees are likely to experience an initial adjustment process, sometimes involving preretirement and then honeymoon, disenchantment, and reorientation phases. They then usually adapt successfully to retirement and to the drop in income that it typically involves. Yet there are huge differences in how it goes. What makes for a good adjustment? According to research (Bender, 2012; Palmore et al., 1985; Wang, Henkens, & van Solinge, 2011; Wong & Earl, 2009), good long-term adjustment to retirement is most likely among adults who:

- retire voluntarily rather than involuntarily and feel in control of their retirement decision
- enjoy good physical and mental health
- have positive personality traits such as agreeableness and emotional stability
- have the financial resources to live comfortably
- are married or otherwise have strong social support

Personality and Successful Aging

What lifestyle decisions make not only for a successful transition to retirement but also for a happy and fulfilling old age? Several theories have been offered about the best path to a satisfying old age (Stowe & Cooney, 2015). Some have emphasized the value of staying highly active (Havighurst, Neugarten, & Tobin, 1968). Others have argued that our needs change in later life and we want to disengage from society—retire from work, drop out of some activities, build a more relaxed lifestyle (Cumming & Henry, 1961). After reading this chapter, we hope you can appreciate that there is no one path to successful aging that fits all.

We must take the role of personality into consideration. A good fit between the individual's lifestyle and the individual's needs, preferences, and personality seems to be the real secret to successful aging (Fry, 1992; Seleen, 1982). Energetic and outgoing Linda may want to maintain her active lifestyle in old age by being highly involved in church activities and family affairs, whereas Albert, who always found work to be stressful and annoying, may like nothing better than to disengage by fishing the day away. Linda might be delighted but Albert might be miserable if made to participate in a retirement community's sing-alongs and skits. In sum, the key to successful aging can be found in the person–environment fit concept that helps explain adjustment throughout the life span.

Some seniors believe that the key to successful aging is a highly active lifestyle, but what suits one type of person may not suit others.

pgaborphotos/Shutterstock.com

Checking Mastery

1. Identify two different senses in which there could be continuity in the Big Five dimension of conscientiousness from age 40 to age 50.
2. According to Erikson, when and how might an adult gain a sense of generativity?
3. Who theorizes that adults experience a true midlife crisis in their early 40s, and what does research say about that?
4. What are three factors likely to make retirement a negative experience?

Making Connections

1. After reading this chapter, what makes you optimistic that you may well be a better person at age 50 than you are now? Cite specific findings.
2. If you were counseling adults in their 50s about retirement, what would you say?

Chapter Summary

11.1 Conceptualizing the Self and Personality

- Personality is an organized combination of attributes unique to the individual. McAdams and Pals describe personality in terms of three aspects: dispositional traits, characteristic adaptations, and narrative identities. Self-concept is an individual's perceptions of those attributes; self-esteem is one's overall evaluation of self-worth; and identity is a coherent self-definition.
- Psychoanalytic theorists such as Erikson maintain that we all experience stagelike personality changes at similar ages; trait theorists believe that aspects of personality such as the Big Five trait dimensions are expressed across situations and are enduring, and social learning theorists maintain that people can change in any number of directions at any time if their social environments change.

11.2 The Infant

- Early in their first year, infants sense that they are separate from the world around them and develop a sense of agency; at around 18 months, possibly later in collectivist cultures, they display mirror self-recognition and form a categorical self based on age and gender.
- Infants differ in temperament: in easy, difficult, or slow-to-warm-up temperament (Thomas and Chess), and in surgency/extraversion, negative affectivity, and effortful control (Rothbart). Temperament is influenced by genes and goodness of fit with the environment, and some dimensions of temperament match up with Big Five personality dimensions.

11.3 The Child

- Whereas the self-concepts of preschool children are focused on physical characteristics and activities, 8-year-olds describe their inner psychological traits and social ties and evaluate their competencies through social comparison.
- Children are most likely have high self-esteem when they have the genes for it, are competent, receive positive feedback in social comparisons, and have warm, democratic parents.
- Links between temperament in early childhood and later personality and adjustment are evident, but some personality traits do not gel until middle childhood or even later.

11.4 The Adolescent

- During adolescence, self-concepts become more psychological, abstract, differentiated, integrated, and reflected upon; self-esteem dips for some but mainly holds steady or increases over adolescence.
- In resolving Erikson's conflict of identity versus role confusion, many college-age youths progress from the diffusion or foreclosure to the moratorium and identity achievement statuses, at different rates in different domains. Analyzing life stories, or narrative identities, is another approach to studying identity.
- Developing a positive ethnic identity is more central to minority than to majority group adolescents and has many benefits.
- Vocational choices become increasingly realistic from childhood through adolescence; the choices made by low-income youth and females are sometimes constrained, but as John Holland theorized, a good person–environment fit between personality and vocation predicts good vocational outcomes.
- Cognitive development, personality, parenting, opportunities for exploration, and culture all influence identity development.

11.5 The Adult

- Although self-esteem typically rises through middle age and declines in late old age, older adults can maintain self-esteem by converging their ideal and real selves, changing their standards of self-evaluation, comparing themselves with other aging adults, and resisting ageist self-stereotyping. Self-conceptions differ in individualistic cultures and collectivist cultures.
- Individuals' rankings on the Big Five dimensions of personality, as indicated by correlations, become more stable with age; at the same time, a shift called the maturity principle from adolescence to middle age, evident across cultures, brings higher levels of emotional stability, conscientiousness, and agreeableness. In later adulthood few changes other than a decline in activity level are consistently observed.
- Stability of personality may be caused by genes, early experience, stable environments, and gene–environment correlations; personality change may result from biological or environmental changes or a poor person–environment fit, including a poor fit to one's culture.
- Consistent with Erikson's psychosocial theory, resolution of early conflicts paves the way for achieving intimacy in early adulthood, generativity in middle age, and integrity through life review in old age.
- Daniel Levinson's theory that adults experience a midlife crisis in their early 40s is not well supported, but young adults do engage in much career exploration and questioning before they settle down in their 30s and achieve peak success in their 40s. Older workers are generally as effective as younger workers, in part because they use selective optimization with compensation (SOC) to cope with aging.
- Retiring workers may experience preretirement, honeymoon, disenchantment, and reorientation phases, and a drop in income, but little change in health, social involvement, or psychological well-being. However, several factors influence adjustment to retirement.
- When explaining successful aging in general, it is useful to consider person–environment fit.

Key Terms

12 Gender Roles and Sexuality

Many of us have grown up taking our sex and gender for granted and living comfortably in our assigned category: male–female, boy–girl, man–woman. But are sex and gender really so simple that they can be captured with two distinct categories? Consider Kathryn who, at age 2, told her parents that she was a boy (see Dvorak, 2012). She was so determined that she was a boy and so unhappy about being viewed as a girl that her parents took her to a psychologist for advice. After much thought, they allowed their child to begin living as a boy, changed his name, shopped for "boy" clothes and toys, and referred to their child with masculine pronouns. The family's decision to allow their child to make this change was influenced, in part, by another family whose son, "Will," struggled throughout childhood with his male sex and gender, firmly believing that he was a girl (Dvorak, 2012). He threatened suicide at age 6 and was taken to therapists who concluded that the child "was probably just gay." It wasn't until their child was a teenager that the family finally capitulated and allowed "him" to live as "her," but then felt great remorse for forcing the male gender on their child for so long, leading to a childhood of misery.

Test Your Understanding of Sex and Gender

Which of the following are "real" sex differences or accurate characterizations of gender? Mark each statement true or false. Answers are printed upside down; they will be clarified in the main text.

1. _____Males are more aggressive than females.
2. _____Gender identity is determined by whether a person is born with male or female genitals.
3. _____Sexual orientation can be changed with counseling.
4. _____Females have stronger verbal abilities than males.
5. _____Androgynous people have a mix of both feminine and masculine traits.
6. _____Gender identity is determined by parenting styles.
7. _____Gender stereotypes represent the roles associated with men and women in society.
8. _____Men typically score higher than women on standardized tests of mathematical ability.

Answers: 1-T, 2-F, 3-F, 4-T, 5-T, 6-F, 7-T, 8-T.

As illustrated by these two examples of transgender children—individuals who identify with a gender other than their biological one—sex and gender may not be as simple as we try to make them. These are not new issues. Among many Native American cultures, there has long been a third gender category ("two spirits") for those individuals who do not neatly fit into the male or the female category (Bonvillain, 2012). Similarly, in India, the term *hijras* is used to describe third-sex individuals, often individuals with biologically male or ambiguous genitalia who dress in ways that appear feminine but do not view themselves as either male or female. And in Sulawesi, an island in Indonesia, as many as five gender categories are recognized to capture the diversity of this characteristic (Davies, 2007). Clearly, there is much more complexity than the dichotomy of male-female, man-woman, suggests.

Gender matters. It used to be that the first question asked following a birth was whether the baby was a boy or girl. With today's technology, this question is often posed as soon as a pregnancy is announced and the answer to this question begins to influence how we think of the developing child. In most cases, as children develop, girls discover that they are girls and many acquire a taste for wearing pink clothes and playing with dolls, while boys discover that they are boys and often wrestle each other on the lawn. As an adult, you may define yourself partly in terms of roles or activities that highlight gender, such as mother, boyfriend, husband, wife, and so on. In short, being female or male is a highly

Indian *hijras*, "neither women nor men," challenge the concept that gender can be fully characterized by two distinct categories of women and men.

PawelBienkowskiphotos/Alamy Stock Photo

important aspect of the self throughout the life span. Before you read any further, try the quiz in **Engagement 12.1** to see if you know which of the many beliefs we hold about males and females have some truth to them.

12.1
Sex and Gender

LEARNING OBJECTIVES

- Distinguish between the concepts of sex and gender.

- Explore the emergence of gender stereotypes and explain the two main gender roles.

- Evaluate whether it makes more sense to talk about gender differences or gender similarities.

Chances are good that sex and gender have influenced several characteristics that make you the unique person that you are, from your physical characteristics and abilities, to some of the roles you play in society, to some of your psychological characteristics. When we talk about your biological sex, we mean those physical

characteristics that define male and female, whereas gender incorporates all those features that a society associates with or considers appropriate for men and women. For example, females menstruate as a result of their hormonal and physiologic makeup, making this a component of their biological sex. Males typically have larger bones and muscle mass than females, another biological sex difference. Consider, though, that women as a group earn less money than men. This is not a sex difference but a gender difference because it arises from societal forces that have created different expectations and outcomes for males and females in the workforce. To understand how sex and gender might influence your life, let us consider some of the obvious physical differences before examining the psychological correlates of gender.

The physical differences between most males and most females are undeniable. A zygote that receives an X chromosome from each parent is a genetic (XX) female, whereas a zygote that receives a Y chromosome from the father is a genetic (XY) male. In rare cases of sex chromosome abnormalities (see Chapter 3), this is not the case; a girl may have only one X chromosome or a boy may have three sex chromosomes (XYY or XXY). Chromosomal differences result in different prenatal hormone balances in males and females, and hormone balances before and after birth are responsible for the fact that males and females have different genitalia. Males typically grow to be taller, heavier, and more muscular than females, although females may be the hardier sex in that they live longer and are less susceptible to many physical disorders (but see Van Oyen et al., 2013 for a discussion of how longer life span may come at the cost of living with greater infirmities). As you will see later in the chapter, some theorists argue that biological differences between males and females are responsible for psychological and social differences.

There is, however, much more to being a man or woman than the biological features that define one's sex. Virtually all societies expect the two sexes to take on different gender roles—the patterns of behavior that females and males should adopt in a particular society (for example, the roles of wife, mother, and woman for females and of husband, father, and man for males). Characteristics and behaviors viewed as desirable for males or females are specified in *gender-role norms*—society's expectations or standards concerning what males and females *should be* like. Each society's norms generate gender stereotypes, overgeneralized and largely inaccurate beliefs about the characteristics of all males and all females (Halim & Ruble, 2010). For example, when trying to decide who should drive to a friend's house in an unfamiliar location, John may say to his new girlfriend, "I'll drive because you women always get lost," to which she replies, "Well, unlike you guys, at least women stop to ask for directions." They have both applied stereotypes about a group to an individual member of the group. The reality is that this particular woman may be a superb navigator and John may be highly likely to stop and ask for directions. Where did such gender stereotypes come from and is there any truth behind them?

Gender Roles and Stereotypes

Many stereotypes originate with a grain of truth, and in the case of gender stereotypes, the grain may be the physical makeup of males and females. One clear physical difference between the sexes is women's ability to bear and nurse children. As a result, women have adopted the role of childbearer and nurturer and this role has shaped the gender-role norms that prevail in many societies, including our own. At the heart of the nurturer gender role is

communality (or communion), an orientation that emphasizes connectedness to others and includes traits of emotionality and sensitivity to others (Abele & Wojciszke, 2014; Best & Williams, 1993). Girls who adopt communal traits will presumably be prepared to play the roles of wife and mother—to keep the family functioning and to raise children successfully. By contrast, the central aspect of the masculine gender role is agency, an orientation toward individual action and achievement that emphasizes traits of dominance, independence, assertiveness, and competitiveness. Boys have been encouraged to adopt agentic traits to fulfill the traditionally defined roles of husband and father, which involve providing for the family and protecting it from harm. Taking this one step further, Baron-Cohen (2003) claims that men's focus on work, achievement, and independence stems from the male brain's tendency to systemize, or analyze and explore how things work. Communion and agency have long been viewed as two fundamental psychological dimensions of human nature that are widespread across a variety of cultures (Abele & Wojciszke, 2014).

With gender-role norms in many cultures mandating that females play a communal role and males play an agentic role, stereotypes have arisen saying that females possess communal traits and males possess agentic traits (Williams & Best, 1990). If you are thinking that these stereotypes have disappeared as attention to women's rights has increased and as more women have entered the labor force, think again. Although some changes have occurred, children, adolescents, and adults still endorse many traditional stereotypes about men and women (see Sczesny et al., 2008). Boys are more likely than girls to endorse traditional stereotypes, perhaps because stereotypes about males (such as "independent") tend to be more positive than the stereotypes about females (for example, "dependent") (Rowley et al., 2007).

Moreover, males and females continued to describe themselves differently after gender roles changed dramatically during the 20th century. When Jean Twenge (1997) analyzed studies conducted from 1970 to 1995 in which standard scales assessing gender-relevant traits had been administered, she found that men and women in the mid-1990s described themselves more similarly than men and women did 20 years previously, largely because modern women saw themselves as having more agentic traits. In the 20 years since this analysis, women have continued to identify about the same as before with masculine traits, but their identification with feminine traits has declined (Donnelly & Twenge, 2016). Traditional feminine gender roles just do not seem to resonate with most of today's young women. Most millennials, male and female, embrace egalitarian views about the roles for men and women (Donnelly & Twenge, 2016).

Gender Differences or Similarities?

Much research has attempted to answer the question of whether there are meaningful behavioral or psychological differences based on one's sex or gender. Although differences in some areas have been identified, other areas show no gender differences. Early research on gender seemed focused on trying to reveal differences of any size or value, and psychological differences between men and women were emphasized (see, for example,

Tannen, 1991). More recently, Janet Hyde (2005, 2007, 2014) and others have proposed that it is more appropriate to focus on gender similarities. They advance a **gender similarities hypothesis**, which states that "males and females are similar on most, but not all, psychological variables. That is, men and women, as well as boys and girls, are more alike than they are different" (Hyde, 2005, p. 581). As you review the following research on gender, try to evaluate for yourself whether there are more gender similarities or differences, and where there are differences, decide whether they are large and meaningful or negligible and unimportant. Also keep in mind that these are *group differences*, and even when research shows that women score higher (or lower) than men on average, there will be individual women who score lower (or higher) than individual men. With this in mind, here is what the research shows:

- There are fairly large differences in how most men and most women perceive themselves in terms of gender identity. In particular, *most men hold a masculine gender identity, whereas most women have a feminine gender identity* (Hines, 2015).
- *Boys and girls engage in different play activities.* These differences seem to arise from a combination of hormone-driven preferences and a society that promotes the "genderization" of children throughout their development (Berenbaum & Meyer-Bahlburg, 2015; Hines, 2015).
- *Females sometimes display greater verbal abilities than males, but on most verbal tasks the difference is small.* One verbal task where females consistently outperform males is reading (Organisation for Economic Co-operation and Development [OECD], 2012). This difference is observed in many different countries, and the size of the difference is often quite large.
- *Males outperform females on many tests of spatial ability*, especially three-dimensional mental rotations, starting in childhood and persisting across the life span. Training in the form of

Suppose you are asked to imagine how this fruit bowl would appear from a different perspective. How quickly and accurately can you mentally rotate the image in your mind and determine the appearance of the fruit from another viewpoint? Historically, males have demonstrated greater mental rotation skills than females.

Alexey Stiop/Alamy Stock Photo

playing action video games can reduce or eliminate the gender difference on most spatial tasks (Feng, Spence, & Pratt, 2007). It may also be the case that it is having a masculine gender identity, something males have more than females, that leads to the apparent gender difference on mental rotation tasks (Reilly & Neumann, 2013).

- Historically, males outperformed females on standardized tests of mathematical ability, but this male advantage has been shrinking in the United States and many other countries: *Females and males perform similarly on most but not all standardized math tests, and females obtain slightly higher math grades in the classroom than males* (Else-Quest, Hyde, & Linn, 2010; Lachance & Mazzocco, 2006). In some countries (such as Austria, Chile, Germany, and Japan), there is a male advantage in math, perhaps reflecting different educational opportunities for males and females in these countries (OECD, 2012). In a handful of countries, females score higher than males (for example, Qatar and Jordan). Thus, in most cases there are not significant gender differences in math performance, but in those cases where there is a difference, it typically is in favor of males. Interestingly, males express more positive attitudes about math than females do, and this more positive outlook may create more opportunities for males to gain experience and comfort with math; for example, they may be more likely to sign up for higher level math classes than females do (Else-Quest et al., 2010). A notable exception to the disappearing gender differences in this area is the College Board SAT Mathematics test, on which males continue to score approximately 30 points higher than females (College Board, 2012). Among the top scorers on the SAT-Math test, males outnumber females by a ratio of 2 to 1.

Boys and girls often display traditional gender roles in their pretend play.

Angela Waye/Alamy Stock Photo

- *Girls display greater memory ability than boys.* Some studies show that this is a general or overall advantage (Johnson & Bouchard, 2007), whereas other research suggests that female's memory advantage is in specific areas such as remembering object locations. Other research shows that females excel at recalling verbal information, as well as faces, particularly female faces (see Herlitz & Lovén, 2013). Finally, listen to your female friends if they tell you something smells bad, because women also show an advantage over men when it comes to recognizing familiar odors (Herlitz & Rehnman, 2008).
- *Males engage in more physical and verbal aggression than females, starting as early as 17 months* (Baillargeon et al., 2007; Burton, Hafetz, & Henninger, 2007; Buss & Perry, 1992). Across 21 diverse countries, teachers in nearly all the countries report that boys are more aggressive than girls (Rescorla et al., 2007; but see Kim, Kim, & Kamphaus, 2010). Sex differences are more obvious for physical aggression than for other forms of aggression. For example, at 17 months, for every one girl who is physically aggressive there are five boys who display frequent physical aggression (Baillargeon et al., 2007). Males also commit more serious and more physically violent crimes (Barash, 2002). Some research shows that females tend to specialize in subtle, indirect, and relational forms of aggression, such as gossiping about and excluding others (Crick & Bigbee, 1998; Murray-Close, et al., 2016).
- Even before birth and throughout childhood, *boys are more physically active* than girls (Almli, Ball, & Wheeler, 2001); they fidget and squirm more as infants and run around more as children. In 19 out of 21 countries studied by Leslie Rescorla and colleagues (2007), teachers report that boys are more hyperactive than girls.
- *Both males and females report that females are more nurturant and empathic.* Sex differences in behaviors are small but show females empathizing more than males (Baron-Cohen, 2003; Van der Graaff et al., 2014).
- *Females are more prone to develop anxiety disorders, depression, and eating disorders* (American Psychiatric Association [APA], 2013). In contrast, *males are more likely to display antisocial behaviors and drug and alcohol abuse and are more frequently diagnosed with autism* (APA, 2013).
- *Males use computers more than females do and express greater confidence in their computer abilities* (Li & Kirkup, 2007; Misa, 2010). These findings do not tell us, though, whether there are gender differences in computer ability.

What have you concluded from this collection of research on gender? Are males and females different in meaningful ways or are differences trivial, as would be predicted by the gender similarities hypothesis? To help answer this, consider that if we ordered people based on degree of aggressiveness from most aggressive to the least aggressive person in a group, only 5% of the observed differences could be attributed to whether a person is male or female (Hyde, 1984). It is worth repeating the point we made earlier: *Average* levels of a behavior such as aggression may be noticeably different for males and females, but within each sex there are both extremely aggressive and extremely nonaggressive

individuals. Therefore it is impossible to predict accurately how aggressive a person is simply by knowing that person's biological sex. Gender differences in most other abilities and personality traits are similarly small.

If, as we have just seen, females and males are more psychologically similar than different, then why do unfounded stereotypes persist? Partly because we, as the holders of male—female stereotypes, are biased in our perceptions. We are more likely to notice and remember behaviors that confirm our beliefs than to notice and remember exceptions, such as independent behavior in a woman or emotional sensitivity in a man (Martin & Halverson, 1981).

In addition, Alice Eagly's (2012) **social-role theory** suggests that differences in the roles that women and men play in society do a lot to create and maintain gender stereotypes. For example, men have traditionally occupied powerful roles in business and industry that require them to be dominant and forceful. Women have more often filled the role of homemaker and therefore have been called upon to be nurturant and sensitive to their children's needs. As a result, we begin to see men as dominant or agentic by nature and women as nurturant or communal by nature. We lose sight of the fact that the differences in the social roles they play cause men and women to behave differently; it is not all "by nature." Individuals even perceive themselves differently depending on which of their roles they are considering: more agentic when thinking of their work role and more communal when thinking of their family role (Uchronski, 2008). Might gender differences in behavior be minimized or reversed if women ran companies and men raised children?

According to Alice Eagly's social-role theory, this man would be perceived as nurturant, warm, and caring because he has assumed the role of caregiver.

Olesia Bilkei/Shutterstock.com

Some research suggests that this may be the case. Both men and women rate male and female homemakers as equally communal (Bosak, Sczesny, & Eagly, 2008). Thus, men who are in the role of homemaker are perceived as being just as caring and affectionate as women in this role. Still, women presented in employee roles are not always judged as equally agentic as men in employee roles. This may be a result of continued gender segregation of the workforce, with far more women in such occupations as nurse and teacher and far more men in occupations such as plumber, corporate executive, and construction worker. Thus, conjuring up the role of employee for men and women may lead not to a single image of what this role involves but to multiple images based on existing gender differences in types of work (Bosak et al., 2008).

Although psychological gender differences are often small, it still makes a difference in society whether a person is male or female. First, gender norms and stereotypes, even when they are unfounded, affect how we perceive ourselves and other people. As long as people expect females to be less competent in math than males, for example, females may lack confidence in their abilities and perform less competently (Eccles, Jacobs, & Harold, 1990). This was the conclusion reached by Zachary Estes and Sydney Felker (2012) in their research on mental rotation ability: Gender differences on this task were eliminated when males and females had the same confidence levels.

In addition, even though males and females are similar psychologically, they are steered toward different roles in society. In childhood, girls and boys conform to their gender roles by segregating themselves by biological sex and developing different interests and play activities (Maccoby, 1998). As adolescents and adults, males and females pursue different vocations and lifestyles. Although more women are entering male-dominated fields today than in the past, they are underrepresented in many traditionally male-dominated fields, and men rarely enter female-dominated fields (Bureau of Labor Statistics, U.S. Department of Labor, 2016). Occupations therefore remain highly gender segregated.

For instance, the top five occupations held by U.S. women continue to be secretary, nurse, teacher, cashier, and nursing or health aide. More men are sharing child-rearing and household responsibilities with their partners, but many couples still divide the labor along traditional lines, so that the woman is primarily responsible for child care and housework and the man is primarily responsible for income and money management (Austin Institute, 2014). When we think about who asks whom out on a date, who stays home from work when a child has an ear infection, or who does the laundry, we must conclude that, despite significant social change, traditional gender roles are alive and well.

Checking Mastery

1. What is the central feature of agency and of communion?
2. What are four differences between males and females, two that favor females and two that favor males, and how large or meaningful are these differences?
3. How does Eagly's social-role theory explain gender differences?

Making Connections

1. What roles do you play as a result of your biological sex? For example, are you a son or a daughter? How do these roles influence your behavior? Would you, for instance, behave any differently if you were a son rather than a daughter (or vice versa)?
2. Your grandmother strongly believes that boys and girls (and men and women) are quite different. Sometimes, she is even bothered by some of your behaviors because she doesn't believe you are behaving like a "proper" young woman or man. How did her thinking about gender become so entrenched, and what could be done to soften her views?

12.2
The Infant

LEARNING OBJECTIVES

- Describe how infants may be treated differently based on their biological sex and indicate how this may lead to gender differences.

- Explain what infants know about gender as a social category.

At birth there are few differences, other than the obvious anatomical ones, between males and females. Male newborns tend to be somewhat more irritable than females, and female newborns are more alert than males (Boatella-Costa et al., 2007). But overall, differences between males and females at birth are small and inconsistent. Nonetheless, it does not take long after newborns are labeled as girls or boys for gender stereotypes to affect how they are perceived and treated—and for infants to notice that males and females are different.

Differential Treatment

When the baby is still in the hospital delivery room or nursery, parents tend to use masculine terms when talking to or about their infant son (such as "big guy" or "tiger") and to comment on the strength of his cries, kicks, and grasps. Female infants are more likely to be labeled "sugar" or "sweetie" and to be described as soft, cuddly, and adorable (see Leaper, 2013; 2015). Even when objective examinations reveal no such differences between boys and girls at birth, adults perceive boys as strong, large featured, and coordinated and view girls as weaker, finer featured, and more awkward (Rubin, Provenzano, & Luria, 1974). Soon boys and girls are decked out in either blue or pink and provided with "sex-appropriate" hairstyles, toys, and room furnishings (Pomerleau et al., 1990).

In an early study of the effects of gender stereotyping, college students watched a videotape of a 9-month-old infant who was introduced as either "Dana," a girl, or as "David," a boy (Condry

Take a look at this baby boy and write down a few adjectives describing what you think he might have been feeling or thinking at the time this photo was taken. Now suppose you learn that this "boy" is actually a girl. Do the adjectives still seem to fit? Do any of them reflect gender stereotyping?

Pavel Galkevich/Alamy Stock Photo

stereotypes (such as a man mowing the grass; Hill & Flom, 2007). Their response shows that they recognize something incongruent or odd about males and females engaged in activities inconsistent with gender stereotypes.

As they begin to categorize other people as males and females, they also figure out which of these two significant social categories they belong to. By 18 months, most toddlers seem to have an emerging understanding that they are either like other males or like other females, even if they cannot verbalize it (Martin, Ruble, & Szkrybalo, 2002). Girls as young as 24 months understand which activities are associated with males and which ones are more typical of females (Poulin-Dubois et al., 2002; see also Serbin, Poulin-Dubois, & Eichstedt, 2002). Boys, however, do not show the same understanding until at least 6 months later. Almost all children give verbal proof that they have acquired a basic sense of **gender identity**, or an awareness that they are either a boy or a girl, by age 2½ to age 3 (see Leaper, 2015).

As they acquire their gender identities, boys and girls also begin to behave differently. At an early age, boys usually prefer trucks and cars to other playthings, whereas girls of this age would rather play with dolls and soft toys (Berenbaum et al., 2008). Many 18- to 24-month-old toddlers are not interested in playing with toys regarded as appropriate for the opposite sex—even when there are no other toys to play with (Caldera, Huston, & O'Brien, 1989). As they approach age 2, then, infants are already beginning to behave in ways considered gender appropriate in our society.

& Condry, 1976). Students who saw "David" interpreted his strong reaction to a jack-in-the-box as anger, whereas students who watched "Dana" concluded that the same behavior was fear. A similar study found that college students rated babies introduced as males as stronger and more "masculine" than babies introduced as females (Burnham & Harris, 1992). Although stereotyping of boys and girls from birth could be partly the effect of differences between the sexes, it may also be a cause of such differences. This was the conclusion from a longitudinal study of young children's aggressive behavior: Those children whose fathers held strong gender stereotypes were more often subjected to physical control by their parents, which later led to higher levels of aggression from the children (Endendijk et al., 2017).

Early Learning

Yet infants are not merely the passive targets of other people's reactions to them; they are actively trying to get to know themselves and the social world around them. Several studies have examined visual tracking of objects by infants at various ages. It turns out that throughout much of infancy, males spend more time looking at a truck whereas females spend more time looking at a doll (Alexander, Wilcox, & Woods, 2009; Jadva, Hines, & Golombok, 2010). This suggests a rudimentary recognition of gender-stereotypic information. At around 3–4 months of age, infants can distinguish between male and female faces (Quinn et al., 2002). By the end of the first year, babies look longer at a male (or female) face when they hear a male (or female) voice than when they hear a voice that does not match the gender of the face, demonstrating cross-modal association of gender-related information (Fagot & Leinbach, 1993; Poulin-Dubois & Serbin, 2006). By 24 months, they look longer at males and females performing gender-inconsistent activities (such as a man putting on makeup) than those performing activities consistent with gender

The Beginnings of a Sexual Self

Sigmund Freud (see Chapter 2) made the seemingly outrageous claim that humans are sexual beings from birth onward. We are born, he said, with a reserve of sexual energy redirected toward different parts of the body as we develop. Freud may have been wrong about some things, but he was right that infants are sexual beings.

Young children tend to be comfortable with their bodies and are curious about how they work and how they compare to other bodies. Most societies, though, impose restrictions on nakedness and discourage children from expressing too much curiosity about bodies, which adults interpret as sexual expressions.

Andrew Holt/Alamy Stock Photo

Babies are biologically equipped at birth with male or female chromosomes, hormones, and genitals. Moreover, young infants in Freud's oral stage of development appear to derive pleasure from sucking, mouthing, biting, and other oral activities. But the clincher is this: Both male babies and female babies have been observed to touch and manipulate their genital areas, to experience physical arousal, and to undergo what appear to be orgasms (see Galenson, 2015).

What should you make of these infant behaviors? Infants feel body sensations, but they are hardly aware that their behavior is "sexual" (Crooks & Baur, 2017). Infants are sexual beings primarily in the sense that their genitals are sensitive and their nervous systems allow sexual responses. They are also as curious about their bodies as they are about the rest of the world (Schuhrke, 2000). They enjoy touching all parts of their body, especially those that produce pleasurable sensations, and are likely to continue touching themselves unless reprimands from parents or other grownups

discourage this behavior, at least in public (Thigpen, 2009). From these early experiences, children begin to learn what human sexuality is about and how the members of their society regard it.

● **Checking Mastery**

1. What is gender identity, and what evidence shows understanding of this concept during infancy?

● **Making Connections**

1. Think of someone who recently became a new parent. In what ways has this person's thinking, and the thinking of his or her surrounding social network, already been shaped by knowing the biological sex of the baby? What is the baby's world like—can you tell by looking at its room or clothes whether it is a boy or girl?

12.3

The Child

LEARNING OBJECTIVES

- Analyze how children acquire gender stereotypes and how they are influenced by these stereotypes.

- Explain how children acquire a solid understanding of gender identity.

- Describe typical gendered behaviors that we can expect to see throughout childhood.

- Summarize and evaluate the usefulness of each theory of gender-role development.

- Outline children's understanding of sex and reproduction.

Much of the action in gender-role development takes place during the toddler and preschool years. Having already come to understand their basic gender identity, young children rapidly acquire gender stereotypes, or beliefs about what groups of males and females are supposedly like, and gender-typed behavioral patterns, or tendencies to favor "gender-appropriate" activities and behaviors over those typically associated with the other sex. Through the process of **gender typing**, children not only become aware that they are biological males or females but also acquire the motives, values, and patterns of behavior that their culture considers appropriate for members of their biological sex. Through the gender-typing process, for example, Susie may learn a gender-role norm stating that women should strive to be good mothers and gender-role stereotypes indicating that women are more skilled at nurturing children than men are. As an adult, Susan may then adopt the traditional communal role by switching from full-time to part-time work when her first child is born and devoting herself to the task of mothering.

It would be a mistake, then, to attribute any differences that we observe between girls and boys (or women and men) solely to biological causes. They could just as easily be caused by differences in the ways males and females are perceived and raised.

Acquiring Gender Stereotypes

As early as 2–3 years of age, children seem to understand society's gender stereotypes and act in gendered ways. Judith Blakemore

(2003) showed pictures of toys to 3- to 11-year-olds and asked them whether boys or girls would usually play with each toy. Toys included masculine-stereotyped ones (for example, GI Joe dolls) and feminine-stereotyped ones (for example, Barbie dolls). Even the youngest children (3 years) knew that girls, but not boys, play with Barbie dolls and vice versa for GI Joes. They also recognized that boys and girls differ in clothes and hairstyles. By age 5–6, girls show a preference for feminine toys and boys show a preference for masculine toys (Li & Wong, 2016). In addition, boys seem to hold more gender-stereotypical toy preferences than girls (Cherney, Harper, & Winter, 2006).

Over the next several years, children acquire considerably more "knowledge" about the toys and activities considered appropriate for girls or boys (Blakemore, 2003; Serbin, Powlishta, & Gulko, 1993). In one study, for instance, researchers (Levy, Sadovsky, & Troseth, 2000) asked 4- and 6-year-olds whether men or women would be better in two masculine-stereotyped occupations (car mechanic and airplane pilot) and two feminine-stereotyped occupations (clothes designer and secretary). Children believed that men would be more competent than women as mechanics and pilots, whereas women would make better designers and secretaries. Boys and girls also expressed positive emotions at the thought of growing up and holding gender-stereotypic occupations. They reacted negatively, however, when asked to consider holding gender-counterstereotypic occupations.

How seriously do children take the gender-role norms and stereotypes that they are rapidly learning? It depends on how old they are. Robin Banerjee and Vicki Lintern (2000) tested the rigidity of 4- to 9-year-olds' gender-stereotypic beliefs with four brief stories in which characters had either gender-stereotypic interests (for example, a boy named Tom who was best friends with another boy and liked playing with airplanes) or gender-counterstereotypic interests (for example, a boy named John who was best friends with a girl and liked playing with doll carriages). Children were then asked whether the target child would like to play with dolls, play football, skip, or play with toy guns.

Younger children (4- and 6-year-olds) were considerably more rigid in their beliefs than older children; they did not believe boys would want to play with dolls or skip (stereotypic girl activities) or girls would want to play with footballs or toy guns (stereotypic boy activities). Some children seem particularly offended when peers step outside of traditional gender-stereotypic behaviors and will act as "enforcers" of gender-stereotyped behaviors, telling boys, "You shouldn't be playing with that doll" or telling girls, "That game is for boys" (see Martin & Ruble, 2010). Rigidity about gender stereotypes is especially high during the preschool years (around ages 4–7), but then decreases over the elementary school years (Conry-Murray, Kim, & Turiel, 2015; Ruble et al., 2007). Using fMRI scans, Eva Telzer and her colleagues (2015) were able to demonstrate different patterns of brain activity in the amygdala as children of various ages viewed same- or opposite-sex faces. The amygdala of young children (4–7 years) seemed to register differences between viewing same-sex and opposite-sex faces, whereas 10- to 12-year-old children did not show this same reaction. The researchers believe that the pattern of findings reflects the "cootie effect," the dislike that young boys and girls often seem to harbor toward members of the "other" sex.

Research with children of different ethnic backgrounds also shows strong adherence to gender-typed behavior in the preschool-age group (Halim et al., 2013). Similar findings also emerged from a longitudinal study of gender stereotypes. Hanns Trautner and his colleagues (2005) followed the same group of children from age 5 through age 10 to see if children who held rigid beliefs about gender stereotypes at age 5 remained unshakable in these beliefs over the next 5 years. As ■ Figure 12.1 shows, peak levels of rigidity occurred between ages 5 and 7, followed by significant relaxation of beliefs from age 7 to 10.

Why? The younger children are in the process of acquiring a clear understanding that their biological sex will remain constant, making them intolerant of anyone who violates traditional gender-role standards. These norms now have the force of absolute moral laws and must be obeyed: Boys must not play with dolls. Eleanor Maccoby (1998) suggests that young children may exaggerate gender roles to cognitively clarify these roles. However, once their gender identities are more firmly established, children can afford to be more flexible in their thinking about what is "for boys" and what is "for girls." They still know the stereotypes but no longer believe the stereotypes are "written in stone" (Martin et al., 2002). Other research suggests that children's rigidity about gender-role violations depends on how essential a behavior is to children's understanding of gender identity (Blakemore, 2003). Thus, children believe it would be bad for boys to wear dresses because dresses are strongly associated with the feminine gender role. But if boys wanted to play with a toy kitchen, this would not

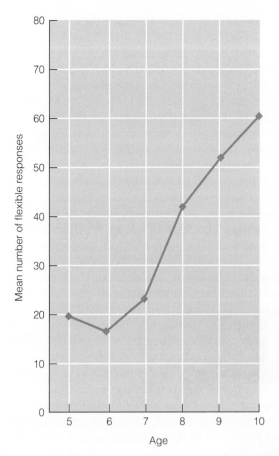

■ **Figure 12.1** Once gender identities are clearly established, usually by age 7, children become much more open about gender behaviors, as illustrated by the sharp increase in number of flexible responses to questions about what is "acceptable" behavior for boys and girls.

Source: From Trautner, H. M., et al. (2005). Rigidity and flexibility of gender stereotypes in childhood: Developmental or differential? *Infant and Child Development, 14,* 370. Copyright © 2005. Reprinted with permission of John Wiley & Sons, Inc.

be too bad because, although the toy kitchen may be associated with the feminine gender role, it is not considered an essential aspect of the feminine gender role (Blakemore, 2003).

Gender-Typed Behavior

Finally, children rapidly come to behave in "gender-appropriate" ways. As you have seen, preferences for gender-appropriate toys are detectable in infancy. Apparently, babies establish preferences for "boys' toys" (such as action figures and building toys) or "girls' toys" (such as dolls and stuffed animals) even before they have established clear identities as males or females or can correctly label toys as "boy things" or "girl things" (Cherney & London, 2006; Fagot, Leinbach, & Hagan, 1986). In childhood, preference for gender-congruent toys and activities is still evident, although occasionally both boys and girls choose "boys' toys" more than "girls' toys" (Cherney, 2005; Martin & Dinella, 2012). Their leisure activities also differ, with boys spending more time playing sports and video/computer games than girls (Cherney & London, 2006). And it turns out that gender-typed behavior in childhood—as early as age 3—is consistent with later gender-typed behavior (Golombok et al., 2012). Thus, boys and girls who display feminine or masculine behaviors at age 3 continue to have feminine or masculine preferences in adolescence.

Children begin to favor same-sex playmates as early as 30–36 months of age (see, for example, Howes, 1988; Martin, Fabes, & Hanish, 2014). During the elementary school years, boys and girls develop even stronger preferences for peers of their own sex and show increased **gender segregation**, separating themselves into boys' and girls' peer groups and interacting far more often with their own sex than with the other sex (Halim & Ruble, 2010). Gender segregation occurs in a variety of cultures, including Botswana, Kenya, India, and the Philippines, and it increases with age (Bock, 2005; Leaper, 1994; Whiting & Edwards, 1988). At age 4½, children in the United States spend three times more time with same-sex peers than with peers of the other sex; by age 6½, they spend 11 times more time (■ Figure 12.2; Maccoby & Jacklin, 1987). This is partly because of incompatibilities between boys' and girls' play styles. Boys are too rowdy, domineering, and unresponsive to suit the tastes of many girls, so girls gravitate toward other girls and develop a style of interacting among themselves different from the rather timid style they adopt in the company of boys (Maccoby, 1998; Pellegrini et al., 2007).

But there is more to gender segregation than different activity levels of boys and girls (Martin et al., 2013). Preschool girls who are just as active as boys often start the school year playing with boys but end up in gender-segregated groups as they progress through the year in preschool (Pellegrini et al., 2007). Socialization pressures seem to encourage these active girls to drift away from the boys and create their own playgroup, separate from the active boys and the less-active girls. In an analysis of gender segregation, Carol Martin and her colleagues (2013) found that the

What percentage of boys versus girls are likely to receive boxing gloves to play with? Chances are good that most of these purchases are made for boys and not girls. What traits are likely to be encouraged by such play, and what message is conveyed to children by such gendered gifts?

Nachaphon/Shutterstock.com

gender of potential playmates, and not the activity of the playmates, is the primary criterion for selecting playmates.

Some research suggests that children who insist most strongly on clear boundaries between the sexes and avoid consorting with the opposite sex tend to be socially competent and popular, whereas children who violate gender segregation rules tend to be less well-adjusted and run the risk of being rejected by their peers (Rieger & Savin-Williams, 2012). But other research challenges these findings (Martin et al., 2012). Nonconforming children do seem to have fewer peer interactions, which means they have fewer socialization opportunities. Importantly, though, their more limited socialization does not seem to lead to problem behavior as earlier research suggested (Martin et al., 2012).

Boys face stronger pressures to adhere to gender-role expectations than girls do, which may help explain why they develop stronger gender-typed preferences at earlier ages (Banerjee & Lintern, 2000; O'Brien et al., 2000). Just ask your female classmates if they were tomboys when they were young; you are likely to find that somewhere between one-third and one-half readily acknowledge that they were "tomboys" or had masculine interests (Bailey, Bechtold, & Berenbaum, 2002; Martin & Dinella, 2012). But we challenge you to find many male classmates who willingly admit they were "sissies" or had feminine interests in their youth. Even when the label is changed (for example, to "mama's boy"), and the traits associated with the label are positive (for example, "well-mannered"), people still believe that it is not desirable for boys to behave in gender nonconforming ways (Coyle, Fulcher, & Trübutschek, 2016).

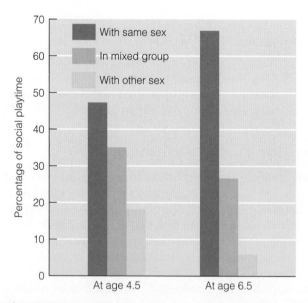

■ **Figure 12.2** Do children prefer playmates of their own sex? Apparently so. Both boys and girls spend more time playing with same-sex peers, especially at age 6.

Source: Reprinted from Maccoby, E. E., & Jacklin, C. N. (1987). Gender segregation in childhood. In H. W. Reese (Ed.), *Advances in child development and behavior* (Vol. 20). Copyright © 1987 with permission from Elsevier.

We have now surveyed some major milestones in gender-role development. Now comes the most intriguing question about gender-role development in childhood and adolescence: How can it be explained?

Explaining Gender-Role Development

There are numerous theories about the development of gender roles. We will once again use the framework of the nature–nurture issue to organize these theories into those that emphasize biological factors, those that emphasize the environment and socialization, and then those that attempt to integrate these factors.

Influence of Nature

On the nature side, how might genetic and hormonal factors influence one's gender-role development? To start, most of us receive either the standard male pattern of sex chromosomes (XY) or the female pattern of sex chromosomes (XX). These set the stage for various other events to unfold:

1. If certain genes on the Y chromosome are present, a previously undifferentiated tissue develops into testes as the embryo develops; otherwise, it develops into ovaries.
2. The testes of a male embryo normally secrete more of the male hormone testosterone, which stimulates the development of a male internal reproductive system, and another hormone that inhibits the development of female organs. Without these hormones, the internal reproductive system of a female will develop from the same tissues.

3. Three to four months after conception, secretion of additional testosterone by the testes normally leads to the growth of a penis and scrotum. If testosterone is absent (as in typically developing females), or if a male fetus's cells are insensitive to the male sex hormones he produces, female external genitalia (labia and clitoris) will form.
4. The relative amount of testosterone alters the development of the brain and nervous system. For example, it signals the male brain to stop secreting hormones in a cyclical pattern so that males do not experience menstrual cycles at puberty.

According to the **biosocial theory** of gender-role development, proposed by John Money and Anke Ehrhardt (1972), these early biological developments influence how people react to a child, and these social reactions have much to do with children's assuming gender roles. Parents and other people label and begin to react to children on the basis of the appearance of their genitalia. If children's genitals are atypical and they are mislabeled as members of the other sex, this incorrect label will affect their future development. For example, the biosocial theory predicts that if a biological male were consistently labeled and treated as a girl, he would, by about age 3, acquire the gender identity of a girl. Finally, biological factors reenter the scene at puberty when large quantities of hormones are released, stimulating the growth of the reproductive system and the appearance of secondary sex characteristics. These events, combined with a person's earlier self-concept as a male or female, provide the basis for adult gender identity and role behavior. The complex series of critical points in biological maturation and social reactions to biological changes that Money and Ehrhardt (1972) propose is diagrammed in ■ **Figure 12.3**. But how much is nature, and how much is nurture?

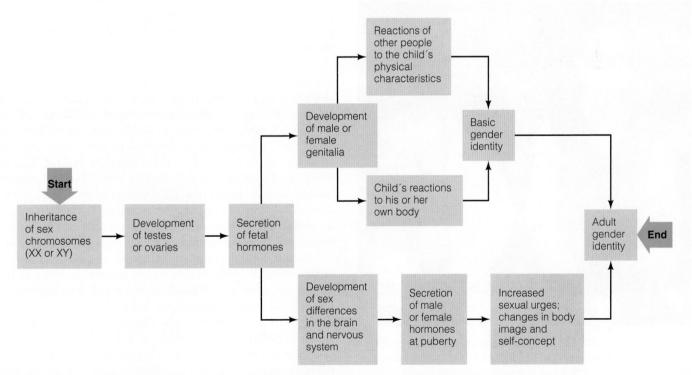

■ **Figure 12.3** Critical events in John Money and Anke Ehrhardt's biosocial theory of gender typing.

Source: From Money, J., & Ehrhardt, A. (1972). *Man and woman, boy and girl.* Baltimore, MD: Johns Hopkins University Press. Reprinted by permission.

Biological influences on development are evident in studies of children exposed to the "wrong" hormones prenatally. For instance, consider the consequences to offspring of mothers who, in past decades, were given drugs containing progestins to help prevent miscarriages (Brunskill, 1992). The drugs were converted by the mother's body into the male hormone testosterone and, depending on the dose and timing, ended up masculinizing female fetuses so that, despite their XX genetic endowment and female internal organs, they were born with external organs that resembled those of a boy (for example, a large clitoris that looked like a penis and fused labia that resembled a scrotum). Several of these androgenized females—girls prenatally exposed to excess androgens—were recognized as genetic females, underwent surgery to alter their genitals, and were then raised as girls. When compared with their sisters and other girls, it became apparent that many more androgenized girls were tomboys and preferred boys' toys and vigorous activities to traditionally feminine pursuits (Money & Ehrhardt, 1972; see also Meyer-Bahlburg et al., 2006). As adolescents, they began dating somewhat later than other girls and felt that marriage should be delayed until they had established their careers. A relatively high proportion (37%) described themselves as homosexual or bisexual (Money, 1985; see also Dittman, Kappes, & Kappes, 1992). Androgenized females also tend to perform better than most other females on tests of spatial ability, further evidence that early exposure to male hormones has "masculinizing" effects on a female fetus (Hines, Constantinescu & Spencer, 2015).

In addition, male exposure to testosterone and other male hormones may be part of the reason males are more likely than females to commit violent acts (Rubinow & Schmidt, 1996).

Brothers, yet very different personalities, as reflected here in how they are dressed. According to the biosocial theory, what factors influence children's acquisition of gender-typed behaviors?

Maria Teijeiro/Getty Images

Evidence from experiments conducted with animals is quite convincing. For example, female rhesus monkeys exposed prenatally to the male hormone testosterone often threaten other monkeys, engage in rough-and-tumble play, and try to "mount" a partner as males do at the beginning of a sexual encounter (Young, Goy, & Phoenix, 1964; Wallen, 1996). Men with high testosterone levels tend to have high rates of delinquency, drug abuse, abusiveness, and violence, although nature interacts with nurture so that these links between testosterone and antisocial behavior are not nearly as evident among men high in socioeconomic status as among men low in socioeconomic status (Dabbs & Morris, 1990). Note, however, that these are correlational studies showing an association between testosterone and aggression; they do not show us the direction of the relationship. Indeed, being in an aggressive situation may raise testosterone levels (Batrinos, 2012; Sapolsky, 1998). Because testosterone levels rise as a result of aggressive and competitive activities, it has been difficult to establish unambiguously that high concentrations of male hormones cause aggressive behavior in humans (Archer, 1991). Still, much evidence suggests that prenatal exposure to male or female hormones has lasting effects on the organization of the brain and, in turn, on sexual behavior, aggression, cognitive skills such as spatial abilities, and other aspects of development (Auyeung et al., 2012; Rubinow & Schmidt, 1996). Yet biology does not dictate gender-role development. Instead, gender-role development evolves from the complex interaction of biology, social experience, and the individual's behavior.

Influence of Nurture

The environment and socialization may influence gender roles in a variety of ways. Here, we consider ways in which the social environment of the child may push him or her into certain roles as well as ways in which children may socialize themselves to assume certain gender roles. We look first at social learning theories and then consider cognitive theories.

Social Learning Theory. Social learning theorists argue that children learn masculine or feminine identities, preferences, and behaviors through two processes introduced in Chapter 2. First, through *differential reinforcement*, children are rewarded for sex-appropriate behaviors and are punished for behaviors considered more appropriate for members of the other sex. Second, through *observational learning*, children adopt the attitudes and behaviors of same-sex models. In this view, children's gender-role development depends on which of their behaviors people reinforce or punish and on what sorts of social models are available. Change the social environment and you change the course of gender-role development.

Parents use differential reinforcement to teach boys how to be boys and girls how to be girls (Lytton & Romney, 1991). By the second year of life, parents are already encouraging sex-appropriate play and discouraging cross-sex play, before children have acquired solid gender identities or display clear preferences for male or female activities (Fagot & Leinbach, 1989). By 20–24 months, daughters are reinforced for dancing, dressing up (as women), following their parents around, asking for help, and playing with dolls; they are discouraged from manipulating objects, running, jumping, and climbing. By contrast, sons are not encouraged to pursue such "feminine" behavior as playing with dolls or seeking help and they receive more positive responses from their parents when they play with "masculine" toys such as blocks, trucks, and push-and-pull toys (Blakemore, 2003; Fagot, 1978; Fagot, Leinbach, & O'Boyle, 1992). Mothers and fathers may also discipline their sons and daughters differently, with fathers more likely to use physical forms of discipline (such as spanking) than mothers and mothers more likely to use reasoning to explain rules and consequences (Conrade & Ho, 2001; Russell et al., 1998). In addition, boys end up on the receiving end of a spanking more often than girls do (Day & Peterson, 1998). Some of this differential treatment is influenced by multiple factors, including children's birth order and gender composition of siblings (Crouter, Whiteman, & Osgood, 2007). For instance, being the youngest daughter with only brothers as siblings leads to a different set of experiences in the family than being the youngest brother with only sisters as siblings.

In research by Barbara Morrongiello and Kerri Hogg (2004), mothers were asked to imagine how they would react if their 6- to 10-year-old son or daughter misbehaved in some way that might be dangerous (for example, bicycling fast down a hill they had been told to avoid). Mothers reported that they would be angry with their sons but disappointed and concerned with their daughters for misbehaving and putting themselves in harm's way. Boys will be boys, they reasoned, but girls should know better. To prevent future risky behaviors, mothers said they would be more rule-bound with their daughters but would not do anything different with their sons. After all, they reasoned, there is no point in trying to prevent these risky behaviors in boys because it is "in their nature." Girls' behavior, on the other hand, can be influenced, so mothers may believe that it is worth enforcing an existing rule or instituting a new one. It's not just mothers: Other research shows that fathers are more protective of their preschool-aged daughters than their preschool-aged sons (Hagan & Kuebli, 2007).

Does the "gender curriculum" in the home influence children? It certainly does. Parents who show the clearest patterns of differential reinforcement have children who are relatively quick to label themselves as girls or boys and to develop strongly sex-typed toy and activity preferences (Fagot & Leinbach, 1989; Fagot et al., 1992). Fathers play a central role in gender socialization; they are more likely than mothers to reward children's gender-appropriate behavior and to discourage behavior considered more appropriate for the other sex (Leve & Fagot, 1997; Lytton & Romney, 1991). This may reflect fathers' use of more explicit—directly stated—gender stereotypes about how boys and girls should act, whereas mothers are less likely to explicitly express gender stereotypes (Endendijk et al., 2013). Thus, fathers may overtly state their gender stereotypes (for example, "guys shouldn't wear jewelry"), whereas mothers may be unconsciously influenced by implicit stereotypes without directly stating these stereotypes (for example, throwing away a brochure for a math camp, assuming a daughter will not be interested in this). Fathers, then, may be an especially important influence on the gender-role development of both sons and daughters.

Could differential treatment of boys and girls by parents also contribute to gender differences in ability? Possibly so. Jacquelynne Eccles and her colleagues (1990) have conducted several studies to determine why girls tend to shy away from math and science courses and are underrepresented in occupations that involve math and science (see also Benbow & Arjmand, 1990). They suggest that parental expectations about gender differences in mathematical ability become self-fulfilling prophecies. The plot goes something like this:

- Parents, influenced by societal stereotypes about gender differences in ability, expect their sons to outperform their daughters in math and expect their sons will be more interested in math and science than their daughters (Tenenbaum & Leaper, 2003).
- Parents attribute their sons' successes in math to ability but credit their daughters' successes to hard work. Perhaps as a result of this, fathers talk differently to their sons and daughters when discussing science with them (Tenenbaum & Leaper, 2003). With their sons, they use more scientific terms, provide more detailed explanations, and ask more abstract questions than with their daughters. These differences reinforce the belief that girls lack mathematical talent and turn in respectable performances only through plodding effort.
- Children begin to internalize their parents' views, so girls come to believe that they are "no good" in math. Girls report that they are less competent and more anxious about their performance than boys (Pomerantz, Altermatt, & Saxon, 2002).
- Thinking they lack ability, girls become less interested in math, are less likely to take math courses, and are less likely to pursue career possibilities that involve math after high school.

In short, parents who expect their daughters to have trouble with numbers may get what they expect. The negative effects of low parental expectations on girls' self-perceptions are evident regardless of their performance. Indeed, girls feel less competent than do boys about math and science even when they outperform the boys (Pomerantz et al., 2002). Girls whose parents are nontraditional in their gender-role attitudes and behaviors do not show the declines in math and science achievement in early adolescence that girls from more traditional families display, so apparently the chain of events Eccles describes can be broken (Updegraff, McHale, & Crouter, 1996).

Social learning theorists also emphasize that *observational* learning contributes in important ways to gender typing. Children see which toys and activities are "for girls" and which are "for boys" and imitate individuals of their own sex. Around age 6 or 7, children begin to pay much closer attention to same-sex models than to other-sex models; for example, they will choose toys that members of their own sex prefer even if it means passing up more attractive toys (Frey & Ruble, 1992). Children who see their mothers perform agentic tasks and their fathers perform household and child care tasks tend to be less aware of gender stereotypes and less gender typed than children exposed to traditional gender-role models at home (Sabattini & Leaper, 2004; Turner & Gervai, 1995). Similarly, boys with sisters and girls with brothers have less gender-typed activity preferences than children who grow up with same-sex siblings perhaps, as you learned earlier, because socialization within the family is affected by both the gender composition and the ages of siblings (Colley et al., 1996; Endendijk et al., 2013; Rust et al., 2000).

Not only do children learn by watching the children and adults with whom they interact, but they also learn from the media—radio, television, movies, video games—and even from their picture books and elementary school texts. Although sexism in children's books has decreased over the past 50 years, male characters are still more likely than female characters to engage in active, independent activities such as climbing, riding bikes, and making things, whereas female characters are more often depicted as passive, dependent, and helpless, spending their time picking flowers, playing quietly indoors, and "creating problems that require masculine solutions" (Crabb & Marciano, 2011; Diekman & Murnen, 2004). Several analyses of children's books show continued gender-stereotypic representations of men and women in these books (Adams, Walker, & O'Connell, 2011; Anderson & Hamilton, 2007; DeWitt, Cready, & Seward, 2013). Although discouraging, the reality is that these gender-stereotypic portrayals in children's books largely mirror the continued gender-stereotypic roles in real life.

In recent decades, blatant gender stereotyping of television characters has decreased but not disappeared. Male characters still dominate on many children's programs, prime-time programs, and advertisements (Matthes, Prieler, & Adam, 2016; Ganahl, Prinsen, & Netzley, 2003; Glascock, 2001; Smith et al., 2010). Similarly, among the top 100 films of 2014, 75% of the main characters were male, 13% were comprised of a group with both males and females, and only 12% were females (Lauzen, 2015). Children who watch a large amount of television are more likely to choose gender-appropriate toys and to hold stereotyped views of males and females than their classmates who watch little television (Signorielli & Lears, 1992).

Perhaps the strongest traditional gender stereotypes are found in video games, which males play at a much higher rate than females (Ogletree & Drake, 2007). College students, both male and female, report that female video game characters are portrayed as helpless and sexually provocative, in contrast to male characters who are portrayed as strong and aggressive (Ogletree & Drake, 2007). Men do not find these stereotypes as offensive as women do, perhaps because men already hold more traditional gender stereotypes than women (Brenick et al., 2007).

To recap, there is much evidence that both differential reinforcement and observational learning contribute to gender-role development. However, social learning theorists often portray children as the passive recipients of external influences: Parents, peers, television and video game characters, and others show them what to do and reinforce them for doing it. Perhaps this perspective does not put enough emphasis on what children contribute to their own gender socialization. Youngsters do not receive gender-stereotyped birthday presents simply because their parents choose these toys for them. Instead, parents tend to select gender-neutral and often educational toys for their children, but their boys ask for trucks and their girls request tea sets (Alexander, 2003; Robinson & Morris, 1986; Servin, Bohlin, & Berlin, 1999).

Cognitive Theories. Cognitive theories offer a different perspective on gender-role socialization, placing greater emphasis on children's active involvement in acquiring gender roles.

To begin, Kohlberg (1966a) proposed a cognitive theory of gender typing with two major themes:

- Gender-role development depends on stage-like changes in cognitive development; children must acquire certain

Children may learn societal gender-typed behavior by watching and imitating role models.
Blend Images/Alamy Stock Photo

understandings about gender before they will be influenced by their social experiences.
- Children engage in self-socialization; instead of being the passive targets of social influence, they actively socialize themselves.

Kohlberg suggests that children *first* understand that they are girls or boys and *then* actively seek same-sex models and a range of information about how to act like a girl or a boy. To Kohlberg, it is not "I'm treated like a boy; therefore, I must be a boy." It is more like "I'm a boy, so now I'll do everything I can to find out how to behave like one." Or, as May Ling Halim and Diane Ruble (2010) explain, the theory "views children as internally, self-initiated 'gender detectives'—agents who actively construct the meaning of gender categories, rather than as passive recipients of external gender socialization agents" (p. 495).

What understandings are necessary before children will teach themselves to behave like boys or girls? Kohlberg believes that children everywhere progress through the following three steps as they acquire **gender constancy**, or understanding that our genders remain the same throughout our lives and despite superficial changes in appearance.

1. Basic gender identity is established by age 2 or 2½, when children can recognize and label themselves as males or females (Campbell, Shirley, & Caygill, 2002; Zosuls et al., 2009).
2. Somewhat later—around age 3—children acquire **gender stability**—that is, they come to understand that gender identity is stable over time. They know that boys invariably become men and girls grow up to be women.
3. The gender concept is complete, somewhere between age 5 and age 7, when children achieve **gender consistency** and realize that their sex is also stable across situations. Now children know that their sex cannot be altered by superficial changes such as dressing up as a member of the other sex or engaging in cross-sex activities.

Research shows that toddlers often do lack the concepts of gender stability and gender consistency; they often say that a boy could become a mommy if he really wanted to or that a girl could become a boy if she cut her hair and wore a football uniform (Warin, 2000). But as they acquire gender stability, they often become rather rigid in their gender behaviors (Halim, 2016; Halim et al., 2014). It is at this point that many girls succumb to "pink frilly dress" or "PFD syndrome," the strong desire to wear pink frilly dresses and embrace all that is pink (see Halim and Ruble, 2010; Halim et al., 2014). Doing so may help these young 'gender detectives' solidify their new understanding of themselves as girls. Boys seem to go through a similar stage where they adhere to all things boy-like (for example, clothing with action figures or camouflage) and, just as importantly for boys, avoid all things girl-like such as pink frilly dresses (Halim et al., 2014).

As children enter Piaget's concrete-operational stage of cognitive development and come to grasp concepts such as conservation of liquids, they also realize that gender is conserved—remains constant—despite changes in appearance. Gender constancy is demonstrated by very few 3- to 5-year-olds, about half of 6- to 7-year-olds, and a majority of 8- to 9-year-olds (Trautner, Gervai, & Nemeth, 2003). In support of Kohlberg's theory, Jo Warin (2000)

The "PFD" (pink frilly dress) phase.

Andrea Jones Images/Alamy Stock Photo

found that children who have achieved the third level of understanding display more gender-stereotypic play preferences than children who have not yet grasped gender consistency.

Not all research supports this view of gender-role development. In one study, children who had acquired only the first step in the process—applying gender labels to themselves—began to engage in more gender-typed play, which, according to Kohlberg's model, shouldn't occur until after the third step (Zosuls et al., 2009). Other research similarly shows that children need not reach the concrete operations stage to understand gender stability and consistency if they have sufficient knowledge of male and female anatomy to realize that people's genitals make them male or female (Bem, 1989). Children who have younger siblings often arrive at this understanding earlier than children with only older siblings or those without siblings (Karniol, 2009). The most controversial aspect of Kohlberg's cognitive-developmental theory, however, has been his claim that only when children fully grasp that their biological sex is unchangeable, around age 5 to age 7, do they actively seek same-sex models and attempt to acquire values, interests, and behaviors consistent with their cognitive judgments about themselves. Although some evidence supports some aspects of Kohlberg's version of cognitive-developmental theory, this chapter shows that children learn many gender-role stereotypes and develop clear preferences for same-sex activities and playmates long before they master the concepts of gender stability and gender consistency and then, according to Kohlberg, attend more selectively to same-sex models (Halim & Ruble, 2010). It seems that only a rudimentary understanding of gender is required before children learn gender stereotypes and preferences.

Martin and Halverson (1981, 1987) have proposed a somewhat different cognitive theory, an information-processing one that overcomes the key weakness of Kohlberg's theory. Like Kohlberg, they believe that children are intrinsically motivated to acquire values, interests, and behaviors consistent with their cognitive judgments about the self. However, Martin and Halverson argue that self-socialization begins as soon as children acquire a basic gender identity, around age 2 or age 3. According to their schematic-processing model, children acquire **gender schemata** (plural of schema)—organized sets of beliefs and expectations about males and females that influence the kinds of information they will attend to and remember.

First, children acquire a simple in-group–out-group schema that allows them to classify some objects, behaviors, and roles as appropriate for males and others as appropriate for females (cars are for boys, girls can cry but boys should not, and so on). Then they seek more elaborate information about the role of their own sex, constructing an own-sex schema. Thus, a young girl who knows her basic gender identity might first learn that sewing is for girls and building model airplanes is for boys. Then, because she is a girl and wants to act consistently with her own self-concept, she gathers a great deal of information about sewing to add to her own-sex schema, largely ignoring any information that comes her way about how to build model airplanes (■ **Figure 12.4**).

Consistent with this schema-processing theory, children appear to be especially interested in learning about objects or activities that fit their own-sex schemata. For instance, in one study, elementary-school-aged children who perceived themselves as gender typical

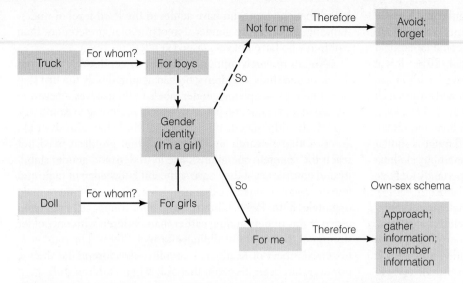

Figure 12.4 Gender schema theory in action. A young girl classifies new information according to an in-group–out-group schema as either "for boys" or "for girls." Information about boys' toys and activities is ignored, but information about toys and activities for girls is relevant to the self and is added to an even larger own-sex schema.

Source: Adapted from Martin & Halverson, 1987.

showed greater interest in gender-typical activities than in gender atypical ones (Patterson, 2012). In another study, 4- to 9-year-olds were given boxes of gender-neutral objects (hole punches, burglar alarms, and so on) and were told that some objects were "girl" items and some were "boy" items (Bradbard et al., 1986). Boys explored boy items more than girls did, and girls explored girl items more than boys did. A week later, the children easily recalled which items were for boys and which were for girls; they had apparently sorted the objects according to their in-group–out-group schemata. In addition, boys recalled more in-depth information about boy items than did girls, whereas girls recalled more than boys about these same objects if they had been labeled girl items. If children's

information-gathering efforts are guided by their own-sex schemata in this way, you can easily see how boys and girls might acquire different stores of knowledge as they develop.

Once gender schemata are in place, children will distort new information in memory so that it is consistent with their schemata (Liben & Signorella, 1993; Martin & Halverson, 1983). For example, Martin and Halverson (1983) showed 5- and 6-year-olds pictures of children performing gender-consistent activities (for example, a boy playing with a truck) and pictures of children performing gender-inconsistent activities (for example, a girl sawing wood). A week later, the children easily recalled the sex of the actor performing gender-consistent activities; when an actor expressed gender-inconsistent behavior, however, children often distorted the scene to reveal gender-consistent behavior (for example, by saying that it was a boy, not a girl, who had sawed wood). This research gives some insight into why inaccurate gender stereotypes persist. The child who believes that women cannot be doctors may be introduced to a female doctor but may remember meeting a nurse instead and continue to state that women cannot be doctors. Even adults have trouble suppressing gender stereotypes and are influenced by their gender stereotypes when reading and interpreting text (Oakhill, Garnham, & Reynolds, 2005). To learn whether researchers have had any success in changing gender-role attitudes and behavior, check out the material in

Nature and Nurture Working Together

The biosocial, social learning, and cognitive perspectives all contribute to our understanding of sex differences and gender-role development (● **Table 12.1**). The biosocial model offered by Money and Ehrhardt notes the importance of biological

● **Table 12.1** An Integrative Overview of the Gender-Typing Process

Developmental Period	Events and Outcomes	Pertinent Theory or Theories
Prenatal period	The fetus develops male or female genitalia, which others will react to once the child is born.	Biosocial
Birth to 3 years	Parents and other companions label the child as a boy or a girl; they begin to encourage gender-consistent behavior and discourage cross-sex activities. As a result of these social experiences and the development of basic classification skills, the young child acquires some gender-typed behavioral preferences and the knowledge that he or she is a boy or a girl (basic gender identity).	Social learning
3–6 years	Once children acquire a basic gender identity, they begin to seek information about sex differences, form gender schemata, and actively try to behave in ways viewed as appropriate for their own sex.	Gender schema
7 to puberty	Children finally acquire the concepts of gender stability and consistency, recognizing that they will be males or females all their lives and in all situations. They begin to look closely at the behavior of same-sex models to acquire attributes consistent with their firm self-categorization as male or female.	Cognitive developmental
Puberty and beyond	The biological changes of adolescence, with social pressures, intensify gender differences and stimulate formation of an adult gender identity.	Biosocial, Social learning, Gender schema, Cognitive developmental

developments that influence how people label and treat a child. Yet socialization agents are teaching children how to be girls or boys well before they understand that they are girls or boys. Differences in social learning experiences may also help explain why, even though virtually all children form gender concepts and schemata, some children are far more gender typed than others in their preferences and activities (Serbin et al., 1993).

How children are labeled and treated by society can affect their gender development. For instance, some androgenized females were labeled as boys at birth and raised as such until their underlying condition was detected. Money and Ehrhardt (1972) report that the discovery and correction of this condition (by surgery and relabeling as a girl) caused few adjustment problems if the change took place before 18 months. After age 3, though, sexual reassignment was exceedingly difficult because these genetic females had experienced prolonged masculine gender typing and had already labeled themselves as boys. These findings led Money and Ehrhardt to conclude that there is a critical period between 18 months and 3 years for the establishment of gender identity when the label society attaches to the child is likely to stick.

Some research seems to support Money and Ehrhardt's emphasis on the importance of societal reactions to biological sex in shaping gender identity. A review of research in which infants were presented to some people as boys but to others as girls showed that, to some extent adults, and to a large extent children, interacted differently with the infants based on whether they believed the infants were male or female (Stern & Karraker, 1989). One implication of these findings is that older siblings may be especially important in communicating gender messages to infants. In other research, mothers were asked to estimate how their 11-month-old infants would perform on several crawling tasks (Mondschein, Adolph, & Tamis-LeMonda, 2000). Mothers over-estimated their infant sons' abilities and under-estimated their infant daughters' abilities. The researchers proceeded to test crawling ability of the infants and found no differences between males and females, showing that mothers had preconceived ideas of motor skills of baby boys and girls.

Other research, though, calls into question whether early socialization in reaction to biological sex is as powerful as Money and Ehrhardt proposed. Consider an unusual study of a group of 18 biological males in the Dominican Republic who had a genetic condition that made their cells insensitive to the effects of male hormones (Imperato-McGinley et al., 1979; see also Herdt & Davidson, 1988). They had begun life with ambiguous genitals,

● APPLICATION 12.1
Changing Gender-Role Attitudes and Behavior

Some people believe that the world would be a better place if boys and girls were no longer socialized to adopt traditional masculine or feminine roles, interests, and behaviors. Children of both sexes would then have the freedom to be androgynous; women would no longer suffer from a lack of assertiveness in the world of work, and men would no longer be forced to suppress their emotions. Just how successful are efforts to encourage more flexible gender roles?

In several projects designed to change gender-role behavior, children have been exposed to nonsexist films, encouraged to imitate models of cross-sex behavior, reinforced by teachers for trying cross-sex activities, and provided with nonsexist educational materials (Katz, 1986; Katz & Walsh, 1991). For example, Rebecca Bigler and Lynn Liben (1990) reasoned that if they could alter children's gender stereotypes, they could head off the biased information processing that stereotypes promote. They exposed 6- to 11-year-olds to a series of problem-solving discussions emphasizing that (1) the most important considerations in deciding who could perform well in such traditionally masculine or feminine occupations as construction worker and beautician

are the person's interests and willingness to learn and (2) the person's gender is irrelevant. Compared with children who received no such training, program participants showed a clear decline in occupational stereotyping, especially if they had entered the study with firm ideas about which jobs are for women and which are for men. Moreover, this reduction in stereotyping brought about the predicted decrease in biased information processing: Participants were more likely than nonparticipants to remember counterstereotypic information presented to them in stories (for example, recalling that the garbage collector in a story was a woman).

Yet many efforts at change that work in the short run fail to have lasting effects (see Vogel & Wänke, 2016). Children who are encouraged to interact in mixed-sex groups revert to their preference for same-sex friends as soon as the program ends (Lockheed, 1986; Serbin, Tonick, & Sternglanz, 1977). Why is it so difficult to change children's thinking? Perhaps because children are groomed for their traditional gender roles from birth and are bombarded with traditional gender-role messages every day. A short-term intervention project may have little chance of succeeding in this larger context.

Other research shows that it is often difficult to change the gender schemata we have constructed. Farah Hughes and Catherine Seta (2003) gave fifth-graders descriptions of men and women behaving in ways inconsistent with traditional gender stereotypes. The children were then asked to rate the likelihood that another man or woman would behave in gender-inconsistent ways. Despite being exposed to a model of gender-stereotype inconsistent behavior, children believed that the other man (although not the other woman) would behave in a gender-consistent manner. The authors interpret this in terms of gender schema theory and children's desire to maintain their stereotypic gender schemata by countering an inconsistent piece of information with a highly consistent one. It also illustrates that simply exposing children to models of people who defy gender stereotypes is not going to miraculously lead to changes in the way children think about gender-stereotypic behavior: Men should still behave in masculine ways, women in feminine ways, although, consistent with other research presented in this chapter, Hughes and Seta found that women were given more flexibility than men to express both their feminine and masculine sides.

were mistaken for girls, and so were labeled and raised as girls. However, under the influence of male hormones produced at puberty, they sprouted beards and became entirely masculine in appearance. How, in light of Money and Ehrhardt's critical-period hypothesis, could a person possibly adjust to becoming a man after leading an entire childhood as a girl?

Amazingly, 16 of these 18 individuals seemed able to accept their late conversion from female to male and to adopt masculine lifestyles, including the establishment of heterosexual relationships. One retained a female identity and gender role, and the remaining individual switched to a male gender identity but still dressed as a female. This study also casts doubt on the notion that socialization during the first 3 years is critical to later gender-role development. Instead, it suggests that hormonal influences may be more important than social influences. It is possible, however, that Dominican adults, knowing that this genetic disorder was common in their society, treated these girls-turned-boys differently from other girls when they were young or that these youngsters recognized on their own that their genitals were not normal (Ehrhardt, 1985). As a result, these "girls" may never have fully committed themselves to being girls.

What studies such as these of individuals with genital abnormalities appear to teach us is this: We are predisposed by our biology to develop as males or females; the first 3 years of life are a sensitive period perhaps, but not a critical period, for gender-role development; and both biology and social labeling contribute to gender-role development. Thus, we must respect the role of genes and hormones in gender-role development but also view this process from a contextual perspective and appreciate that the patterns of male and female development that we observe in society today are not inevitable. In another era, in another culture, the process of gender-role socialization could produce different kinds of boys and girls.

Childhood Sexuality

Although boys and girls spend much of their time in gender-segregated groups, most are nonetheless preparing for the day they will participate in sexual relationships with the other sex. They learn a great deal about sexuality and reproduction, continue to be curious about their bodies, and begin to interact with the other sex in ways that will prepare them for dating in adolescence.

Understanding Sex and Reproduction

With age, children learn that sexual anatomy is the key differentiator between males and females, and they acquire a more correct and explicit vocabulary for discussing sexual organs (Gordon, Schroeder, & Abrams, 1990). Children's understandings of where babies come from proceeds through a sequence consistent with Piaget's cognitive-developmental stages (Bernstein & Cowan, 1975; see Chapter 7). Accordingly, young children with their preoperational reasoning seem to assume either that babies are just there all along or that they are somehow manufactured, much as toys might be. According to Jane, age 3½, "You find [the baby] at a store that makes it . . . . Well, they get it and then they put it in the tummy and then it goes quickly out" (p. 81). Another preschooler, interpreting what he could of an explanation about reproduction from his mom, created this scenario (author's files):

The woman has a seed in her tummy that is fertilized by something in the man's penis. *(How does this happen?)* The fertilizer has to travel down through the man's body into the ground. Then it goes underground to get to the woman's body. It's like in our garden. *(Does the fertilizer come out of his penis?)* Oh no. Only pee-pee comes out of the penis. It's not big enough for fertilizer.

As these examples illustrate, young children construct their own understandings of reproduction well before they are told the "facts of life." Consistent with Piaget's theory of cognitive development, children construct their understanding of sex by assimilating and accommodating information into their existing cognitive structures. Some children as young as age 6 know that sexual intercourse plays a role in the making of babies, but their understanding of just how this works is limited (Caron & Ahlgrim, 2012). By age 12, most children have integrated information about sexual intercourse with information about the biological union of egg and sperm and can provide an accurate description of intercourse and its possible outcomes. Thus, as children mature cognitively and as they gain access to information, they are able to construct ever more accurate understandings of sexuality and reproduction.

Sexual Behavior

According to Freudian theory, preschoolers in the phallic stage of psychosexual development are actively interested in their genitals and seek bodily pleasure through masturbation, but school-age children enter a latency period during which they repress their sexuality and turn their attention instead to schoolwork and friendships with same-sex peers. It turns out that Freud was half right and half wrong.

Freud was correct that preschoolers are highly curious about their bodies, masturbate, and engage in both same-sex and cross-sex sexual play (see Kellogg, 2009). Between ages 2 and 5, interest increases and at least half of all children engage in sexual play (playing doctor or house), and sexual exploration such as looking at and touching genitals—their own, a peer's, or a younger sibling's (Kellogg, 2009; Larsson & Svedin, 2002). Freud was wrong, though, to believe that such activities occur infrequently among school-age children. Elementary school age children in Freud's latency period may be more discreet about their sexual experimentation than preschoolers, but they have by no means lost their sexual curiosity. Surveys show, for example, that about two-thirds of boys and half of girls have masturbated by age 13 (Janus & Janus, 1993; Larsson & Svedin, 2002) and are beginning to engage in "light" sexual activities (holding hands, kissing) with other young teens (Williams, Connolly, & Cribbie, 2008).

Gilbert Herdt and Martha McClintock (2000) have gathered evidence that age 10 is an important point in sexual development, a time when many boys and girls experience their first sexual attraction (often to a member of the other sex if they later become heterosexual or to a member of their own sex if they later become gay or lesbian). This milestone in development appears to be influenced by the maturation of the adrenal glands (which produce male androgens). It comes well before the maturation of the sex organs during puberty and therefore challenges the view of Freud (and many of the rest of us) that puberty is the critical time in sexual development. As Herdt and McClintock note, our society does little to encourage fourth-graders to have sexual thoughts, especially about members of their own sex, so perhaps a hormonal explanation of early sexual attraction makes more sense than an environmental one (see also Halpern, 2006).

Sexual Abuse

Children's sexual activity with their peers is typically absent or, at most, exploratory ("I'll show you mine if you show me yours."). Some children, unfortunately, are victims of sexual abuse by, in most cases, someone older than themselves. By the end of childhood, 27% of females and 5% of males have experienced sexual assault or sexual abuse (Finkelhor et al., 2014). Clearly, sexual abuse is a serious and widespread social problem. Sadly, only one out of every four abused children tells someone about the abuse within the first 24 hours and one in four remains silent, never telling anyone about their painful experience (Kogan, 2004).

What is the effect of sexual abuse on the survivor? Kathleen Kendall-Tackett, Linda Williams, and David Finkelhor (1993) offer a useful account, based on their review of 45 studies. No single distinctive "syndrome" of psychological problems characterizes abuse survivors. Instead, they may experience any number of problems commonly seen in emotionally disturbed individuals, including anxiety, depression, low self-esteem, aggression, acting out, withdrawal, and school learning problems. Roughly 20%–30% experience each of these problems, and boys seem to experience the same types and degrees of disturbance as girls do.

Many of these aftereffects boil down to lack of self-worth and difficulty trusting others (Freyd et al., 2005; Putnam, 2003). A college student who had been abused repeatedly by her father and other relatives wrote this about her experience (author's files):

> It was very painful, emotionally, physically, and psychologically. I wanted to die to escape it. I wanted to escape from my body . . . . I developed a "good" self and a "bad" self. This was the only way I could cope with the experiences . . . . I discovered people I trusted caused me harm . . . . It is difficult for me to accept the fact that people can care for me and expect nothing in return . . . . I dislike closeness and despise people touching me.

Two problems seem to be especially linked to being sexually abused. First, about a third of survivors engage in sexualized behavior, acting out sexually by putting objects in their vaginas, masturbating in public, behaving seductively, or if they are older, behaving promiscuously (Kendall-Tackett et al., 1993). One theory is that this sexualized behavior helps survivors master or control the traumatic events they experienced (Tharinger, 1990). Second, about a third of survivors display the symptoms of **posttraumatic stress disorder**. This clinical disorder, involving nightmares, flashbacks to the traumatizing events, and feelings of helplessness and anxiety in the face of danger, affects some soldiers who have experienced combat and other survivors of extreme trauma (Kendall-Tackett et al., 1993).

In a few children, sexual abuse may contribute to severe psychological disorders, yet about a third of children seem to experience no psychological symptoms (Kendall-Tackett et al., 1993;

Putnam, 2003). Some of these symptomless children may experience problems in later years. Nevertheless, some children are less severely damaged and more able to cope than others are.

Which children have the most difficulty? The effects of abuse are likely to be most severe when the abuse involved penetration and force and occurred frequently over a long period, when the perpetrator was a close relative such as the father, and when the child's mother did not serve as a reliable source of emotional support (Beitchman et al., 1991; Kendall-Tackett et al., 1993; Trickett & Putnam, 1993). Children are likely to recover better if they have high-quality relationships with their mother and friends (Adams & Bukowski, 2007; Aspelmeier, Elliott, & Smith, 2007). Psychotherapy aimed at treating the anxiety and depression many survivors experience and teaching them coping and problem-solving skills so that they will not be revictimized can also contribute to the healing process (Cuevas et al., 2010; Finkelhor & Berliner, 1995).

Finally, not all sex abuse offenders fit the stereotype of an adult who is an obvious pervert. Some offenders are themselves juveniles taking advantage of peers or somewhat younger children (Finkelhor, 2009). With appropriate and timely intervention and education, they can learn acceptable behaviors that reduce the likelihood of continued offending. Education can also prepare children to respond to inappropriate advances in ways that derail the possibility of an offense occurring. This three-pronged approach—working with the survivors, the offenders, and all children on prevention of sexual abuse—may be behind a recent decline in reports of childhood abuse (Finkelhor et al., 2010).

Checking Mastery

1. At what age are children likely to be most concerned about adhering to traditional gender-role behaviors? Why?
2. What are two factors that contribute to gender segregation during childhood?
3. What are gender schemas, and what role do they play in gender typing?
4. What are some of the long-term effects of childhood sexual abuse?

Making Connections

1. Jen and Ben are fraternal twins whose parents are determined that they should grow up having no gender-stereotypic attitudes or behaviors. Nonetheless, when the twins are only 4, Jen wants frilly dresses and loves to play with her Barbie doll, and Ben wants a machine gun and loves to pretend he's a football player and tackle people. Each seems headed for a traditional gender role. Which of the theories in this chapter do you think explains this best, which has the most difficulty explaining it, and why did you reach these conclusions?
2. Boys and girls have sometimes been characterized as living in two different worlds. Thinking about your own childhood, how was your world similar to or different from that of your other-sexed siblings (if any) and friends?
3. After reviewing the theories of gender-role development, where do you stand on the relative contributions of biology and environment to one's gender-role identity?

LEARNING OBJECTIVES

- Describe the typical path of gender-role development in adolescence.

- Discuss the emergence of sexual identity and indicate where paths may diverge for those with heterosexual, homosexual, transgender, and/or bisexual identities.

- Analyze the evolution of sexual morality that has led to the current perspectives on sexual morality among adolescents.

- Outline the typical pattern of adolescent sexual behaviors and note factors that influence sexual behaviors of males and females.

After going their separate ways in childhood, boys and girls come together in the most intimate ways during adolescence. How do they prepare for the gender roles that will likely characterize their adulthood?

Adhering to Gender Roles

As you learned in the prior section, young elementary school children are highly rigid in their thinking about gender roles, whereas older children think more flexibly, recognizing that gender norms are not absolute, inviolable laws. Curiously, adolescents again seem to become highly intolerant of certain role violations and stereotyped in their thinking about the proper roles of males and females in adolescence. They are more likely than somewhat younger children to make negative judgments about peers who violate expectations by engaging in cross-sex behavior or expressing cross-sex interests (Alfieri, Ruble, & Higgins, 1996; Sigelman, Carr, & Begley, 1986).

Consider what Trish Stoddart and Elliot Turiel (1985) found when they asked children ages 5–13 questions about boys who wear a barrette in their hair or put on nail polish and about girls who sport a crew haircut or wear a boy's suit. Both the kindergartners and the adolescents judged these behaviors to be wrong, whereas third-graders and fifth-graders viewed them far more tolerantly. Like the elementary school children, eighth-graders clearly understood that gender-role expectations are just social conventions that can easily be changed and do not necessarily apply in all societies. However, these adolescents had also begun to conceptualize gender-role violations as a sign of psychological abnormality and could not tolerate them.

Increased intolerance of deviance from gender-role expectations is tied to a larger process of **gender intensification**, in which gender differences may be magnified by hormonal changes associated with puberty and increased pressure to conform to gender roles (Boldizar, 1991; Galambos, Almeida, & Petersen, 1990). According to this process, boys begin to see themselves as more masculine and girls emphasize their feminine side. There is some support for this, at least in terms of higher levels of "femininity" reported by teen girls than by boys (Priess, Lindberg, & Hyde, 2009). When it comes to "masculinity," though, teen boys and girls report roughly the same levels.

When gender intensification does occur, it is largely related to peer influence and the growing importance of dating. Adolescents increasingly find that they must conform to traditional gender norms to appeal to the other sex. A girl who was a tomboy and thought nothing of it may find that, as a teenager, she must dress and behave in more "feminine" ways to attract boys and must give up her tomboyish ways (Burn, O'Neil, & Nederend, 1996; Carr, 2007). A boy may find that he is more popular if he projects a more sharply "masculine" image. Social pressures on adolescents to conform to traditional roles may even help explain why sex differences in cognitive abilities sometimes become more noticeable as children enter adolescence (Hill & Lynch, 1983; Roberts et al., 1990). It should be noted that the social pressure to conform to gender stereotypes does not need to be real—adolescents' *perceptions* of their peers' thoughts and expectations can affect their behaviors and lead to gender intensification (Pettitt, 2004). Later in adolescence, teenagers again become more comfortable with their identities as men and women and more flexible in their thinking.

Not Adhering to Gender Roles: Transgender Youth

Navigating the many changes of adolescence can be challenging for all youth, but they can be especially difficult for those who are transgender or are exploring their gender identity. We introduced two transgender children in this chapter's opener and gave a general definition of transgender. It is important to keep in mind that the concept of transgender is multifaceted and means different things to different people. It could mean an individual who was assigned as a male at birth who later perceives herself as a girl. Growing into adulthood, this individual may present as a woman who may be sexually attracted to women or to men or to others regardless of the others' gender identity. Clearly, there are many variations within the transgender label (Levitt & Ippolito, 2014).

A solid majority (2 out of every 3) transgender youth report bullying, harassment, and verbal abuse by not only their peers, but in some cases by their own parents (Grossman, D'Augelli, & Frank, 2011). Those who have support from family and/or peers benefit from this, but it does not eliminate the harmful effects of bullying and other abuse directed towards them (Mustanski, Newcomb, & Garofalo, 2011). Heidi Levitt and Maria Ippolito (2014) analyzed interviews with transgender people and concluded that transgender identity development was a balancing act. That is, in acknowledging their transgender identity, people considered how to balance their internal feelings about their gender with what they believed would be the external consequences

The transgender symbol is intended to be inclusive of all gender identities, not just the traditional identities of men and women.

Peter Hermes Furian/Alamy Stock Photo

of their life as a transgendered person. Importantly, there is no single path or outcome that is right for everyone; it is very much a personal journey that depends on the resources and characteristics of each individual. Still, there have been attempts to characterize the process of adopting a transgender identity. Here, we consider a five-stage process articulated by Walter Bockting and Eli Coleman (2016). Their five stages are:

1. Pre-coming out
2. Coming out
3. Exploration
4. Intimacy
5. Identity integration

We have learned that society sends powerful messages about how boys and girls should act to fit into the binary categories of boy–girl and man–woman to which most societies adhere. During the pre-coming out stage, children begin to feel confused as they realize they do not fit nicely into the two big gender categories that everyone else seems to embrace and expect of them. Depending on their age and developmental stage, children may not understand what they are feeling and may not be able to verbalize their feelings. In a world where they are presented with limited options—act like a boy if assigned as a male at birth or act like a girl if assigned as a female at birth—children who have transgender feelings may feel quite baffled. They are often bullied for being different or not conforming to societal norms.

During the second stage, coming out, individuals begin to acknowledge to selves and others that they do not fit the standard gender identities and are, instead, transgender. This realization can occur at any time across the life span, although most

transgender adults acknowledge feeling different from others from a young age (Grossman et al., 2005).

With the realization of one's transgender identity comes a phase of exploration, or learning as much as possible and, in a sense, testing the boundaries of what this new identity means. During this stage, most individuals conduct a great deal of research and give considerable thought to how to best live as transgender, trying to answer questions about name, clothing, surgery, hormones, and even which bathroom to use.

Following exploration of "how to be" transgender, the next stage is to navigate intimacy in one's new identity. Bockting and Coleman (2016) note that transgender men seem to have an easier time with this stage than transgender women. Whether male or female, the ease of developing positive intimate relationships is influenced by one's sexual orientation. Those whose sexual orientation is heterosexual have a smoother path than those with a homosexual orientation, as is the case with non-transgender youth.

Finally, there is identity integration, which Bockting and Coleman (2016) describe as a union of one's public and private selves. This integration promotes living comfortably as one's true self, whatever that means to the individual. Among children who have transitioned from a traditional gender identity to transgender, research indicates that their gender perceptions of self are much like those of non-transgendered children of their expressed gender (Olson, Key, & Eaton, 2015). In other words, a transgender girl (a child assigned as male at birth but now living as a girl) thinks of herself very much like girls who were assigned female at birth and whose gender identity is consistent with this sex assignment.

Just as transgender children need time, resources, and support to navigate to the identity that best suits them, so do their parents and friends. Even the most supportive parents can often feel overwhelmed with trying to understand the changes in their child and answer the inevitable questions from other family members, school officials, and others who knew their child prior to transitioning. Parents identify accurate medical information and professional support among their top needs as they try to support their child and make informed decisions (Riley et al., 2011). At school, transgender youth should be protected from discrimination by the federal law known as Title IX (see U.S. Department of Education, Office for Civil Rights, 2016). Many schools have had to scramble to make accommodations for male-to-female and female-to-male transgender students who want to be educated in a safe and welcoming environment, regardless of their gender status.

Attaining Sexual Maturity

Although infants and children are sexual beings, sexuality assumes far greater importance once sexual maturity is achieved. Adolescents must incorporate into their identities as males or females concepts of themselves as sexual males or females. Moreover, they must figure out how to express their sexuality in relationships. As part of their search for identity, teenagers raise questions about their sexual attractiveness, their sexual values, and their goals in close relationships. They also experiment with sexual behavior—sometimes with good outcomes, sometimes with bad ones. And what do the teens' parents think of this burgeoning sexuality? As

Sinikka Elliott (2012) describes in her book, *Not My Kid*, parents believe that other teenagers are sexual beings and may be trying to lure their innocent child into sexual exploits, but their child is not yet sexual or is far too young for such matters. As you will see, however, it is not the case that only *other* adolescents are interested in sexual activity!

Sexual Orientation

Part of establishing a sexual identity, part of an individual's larger task of resolving Erikson's conflict of identity versus role confusion, is becoming aware of one's sexual orientation—that is, preference for sexual partners of the same or other sex, or both. Sexual orientation exists on a continuum, with many experts now recognizing five classifications of sexual identity: heterosexual, mostly heterosexual, mostly homosexual, homosexual, or bisexual (Vrangalova & Savin-Williams, 2012). Most adolescents establish a heterosexual sexual orientation without much soul-searching, what Elizabeth Morgan (2012) refers to as "commitment with passive exploration." For youths attracted to members of their own sex, however, the process of accepting that they have a homosexual, mostly homosexual, or bisexual orientation and establishing a positive identity in the face of societal attitudes that may be negative or ambivalent can be difficult. Many have an initial awareness of their sexual preference before reaching puberty but do not accept being gay or lesbian, or gather the courage to "come out," until their mid-20s (Savin-Williams, 2001). Among 17- to 25-year-olds with same-sex attractions in one study, fewer than half had told both their parents and about one-third had not told either parent about their sexual orientation (Savin-Williams & Ream, 2003). Those who had disclosed to one or both parents did so around age 19. By this age, most are out of high school and have achieved some independence from their parents, which may give them the confidence to share this information. In recent years, coming out as gay or lesbian has become, if not easy, then perhaps easier than it was for previous generations (Savin-Williams & Cohen 2015). Teens who have disclosed their same-sex orientation to someone report higher levels of self-esteem and overall well-being than other teens who have not done so (Kosciw, Palmer, & Kull, 2015). Those who come out may feel more comfortable with their identity and have the personal resources to manage the stresses that accompany coming out.

Experimentation with homosexual activity is fairly common during adolescence, but few adolescents become part of the estimated 5–6% of adults who establish an enduring homosexual or bisexual sexual orientation (Savin-Williams & Ream, 2007). Contrary to societal stereotypes of gay men as effeminate and lesbian women as masculine, gay and lesbian individuals have the same range of psychological and social attributes that heterosexual adults do. Knowing that someone prefers same-sex romantic partners reveals no more about his or her personality than knowing that someone is heterosexual.

For the most part, sexual orientation is stable across the life span, at least for those individuals who identify themselves as 100% heterosexual or 100% homosexual (Mock & Eibach, 2012; Savin-Williams, Joyner, & Rieger, 2012). For individuals who identify as bisexual, there is less stability over time, with only one in four remaining in this category over time. Ritch Savin-Williams and colleagues (2012) report that females who initially

According to a 2013 Gallup poll, 3.5% of the U.S. population self-identifies as lesbian, gay, bisexual, or transgender.
Jari Hindstroem/Shutterstock.com

identified as bisexual are most likely to later identify as "mostly heterosexual," whereas males who initially identify as bisexual are much more variable in their identity at later points in time. In longitudinal research with women, Lisa Diamond (2008) found that orientation as lesbian or bisexual was relatively enduring over a 10-year period, although women often defied attempts to be defined exclusively by a single sexual orientation. Many preferred to be unlabeled, perhaps reflecting an openness to changes in sexual orientation or an attraction to the person without regard to that person's biological sex (see Diamond, 2008).

What influences the development of sexual orientation? Part of the answer lies in the genetic code. Twin studies have established that identical twins are more alike in sexual orientation than fraternal twins (see Ngun & Vilain, 2014; Pillard & Bailey, 1998). As ● **Table 12.2** reveals, however, in as many as two-thirds of identical twin pairs, one twin is homosexual or bisexual but the other is heterosexual. Thus, although more identical twins than fraternal twins are concordant (alike) for sexual orientation, the majority of identical twins are still not concordant—they are dissimilar—for sexual orientation. This means that environment contributes at least as much as genes to the development of sexual orientation (Bailey, Dunne, & Martin, 2000; Kendler et al., 2000).

Looking at childhood behaviors, research shows that many gay men and lesbian women expressed strong cross-sex

● **Table 12.2** Percentage of Twins Who Are Concordant (Alike) for Nonheterosexual Sexual Orientation

Identical twins	32%
Same-sex fraternal twins	13%
All fraternal twins (same and other sex)	8%

Source: Adapted from Kendler, K. S., Thornton, L. M., Gilman, S. E., & Kessler, R. C. (2000). Sexual orientation in a U.S. national sample of twin and nontwin sibling pairs. *American Journal of Psychiatry, 157,* 1843–1846, Figure 2.

Note: Nonheterosexual is any sexual orientation other than heterosexual (that is, includes homosexual and bisexual). Higher rates of similarity for identical twin pairs than for fraternal twin pairs provide evidence of genetic influence on nonheterosexuality.

interests when they were young, despite being subjected to the usual pressures to adopt a traditional gender role (Bailey et al., 2000; Golombok et al., 2012; Lippa, 2008). For example, as ■ Figure 12.5 shows, Richard Lippa (2008) found that homosexual adults—both male and female—were significantly more likely than heterosexual adults to recall **childhood gender nonconformity (CGN)**. CGN, or not adhering to the typical gender-role norms expected for members of one's assigned gender group, is also more common for females than males.

Still, it is important to note that sexual orientation is every bit as heritable among gay men who were typically masculine boys and lesbian women who were typically feminine girls as among those who showed early gender nonconformity (Bailey & Pillard, 1991; Bailey et al., 1993). Although it might be tempting to infer sexual orientation from early childhood behaviors, all we really know is that *some* gay and lesbian adults knew from an early age that traditional gender-role expectations did not suit them, but others did not.

What environmental factors may help determine whether a genetic predisposition toward homosexuality is actualized? We do not know yet, although we can reject the old psychoanalytic view that male homosexuality stems from having a domineering mother and a weak father (LeVay, 1996). Growing up with a gay or lesbian parent also seems to have little effect on later sexual orientation (Patterson, 2004). We can also rule out the shared family environment: In a fairly large analysis of the same-sex behavior of nearly 4,000 pairs of identical and fraternal twins, researchers concluded that the shared environment contributed next to nothing to the concordance of twins' sexual orientation (Långström et al., 2010). Instead, genetics played a role and was stronger for males than females.

A more promising hypothesis is that hormonal influences during the prenatal period influence sexual orientation (Ellis et al., 1988; Meyer-Bahlburg et al., 1995). For example, androgenized females are more likely than other women to adopt a lesbian or bisexual orientation, suggesting that high prenatal doses of male hormones may predispose at least some females to homosexuality (Dittman et al., 1992; Money, 1988). Later-born males with older brothers may be more prone to a homosexual orientation because, according to one theory, their mother produces anti-male antibodies that accumulate over the course of each pregnancy with a male (see Blanchard & Lippa, 2007). However, this does not explain why some firstborn males or males without older brothers develop a homosexual orientation (see Gooren, 2006). Another possibility is that nature and nurture interact: Biological factors may predispose an individual to have certain traits, which in turn influence the kinds of social experiences the person has, which in turn shape her sexual orientation (Byne, 1994). However, even the experts cannot yet clearly define which factors in the prenatal or postnatal environment contribute, with genes, to a homosexual orientation.

Beliefs about Sexuality

Whatever their sexual orientation, adolescents establish beliefs about what is and is not appropriate sexual behavior. The sexual beliefs of adolescents changed dramatically during the 20th century, especially during the 1960s and 1970s, yet at least some of the old values have endured (Caron & Moskey, 2002). Several generalizations emerge from the research on sexual beliefs.

First, many adolescents—approximately three out of four—have come to believe that sex with affection in the context of a committed relationship is acceptable (Caron & Moskey, 2002). They no longer buy the traditional view that premarital intercourse is always morally wrong (● Table 12.3). Brooke Wells and Jean Twenge (2005) analyzed 530 studies of sexual behavior and attitudes, spanning a period of over 50 years. They found that the percentage of men who approved of premarital sex jumped from 40% to 79%, but the change in women's attitudes was even more dramatic, going from 12% to 73% who approved of premarital sex. However, adolescents do not all go so far as to approve of casual or "nonromantic" sex, although males have somewhat more permissive attitudes about this than females (see Olmstead et al., 2013). Consistent with this, most adolescents believe that partners should be in a long-term romantic relationship or feel a close emotional involvement with each other (Caron & Moskey, 2002). Most adolescents—both male and female—report that their first sexual relationship was with someone with whom they were romantically, not casually, involved (Ryan, Manlove, & Franzetta, 2003; Williams & Russell, 2013). On average, teens wait about 5 months before having sex with a romantic partner. Even adolescents who have sex with a nonromantic partner report that there were emotional and social components to the relationship (Williams & Russell, 2013). Thus, casual sex is not the norm among young teenagers.

Teens who go off to college may find casual sexual encounters somewhat more normative in this context. The typical **hookup** is a casual, often brief, sexual encounter between two people who have often just met at a party and have little expectation of forming a romantic relationship. Males and females are similar in their descriptions of what transpires during a typical hookup, but women express a wider range of mostly negative emotional reactions to hooking up (Lyons et al., 2014; Uecker, Pearce, & Andercheck, 2015). Women with higher rates of casual

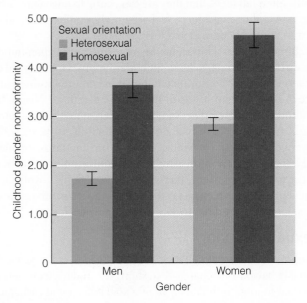

■ **Figure 12.5** Childhood gender nonconformity as a function of gender and sexual orientation (bars represent 95% confidence intervals).

	1950	1975	2000
Having sex as a teenager would go against my beliefs, even if in a serious relationship.	65%	27%	20%
I believe it is OK to have sex as a teenager.	24%	60%	70%
If I had sex as a teenager, it would have been OK with my parents.	6%	8%	33%
If I had sex as a teenager, it would have been OK with my friends.	15%	75%	81%
If I had sex with boyfriend/girlfriend, it would have made our relationship stronger.	14%	21%	37%
Based on Your Beliefs While in High School, When Was It Acceptable to Have Sex?			
Within the first month of dating	8%	18%	15%
After the relationship became serious	19%	72%	76%
Only after becoming married	73%	10%	9%
Respondents Who Had Sex in High School			
	24%	65%	69%
Of Those Respondents Who Had Sex by the End of High School, Their Age at First Sex			
12–14 years	21%	15%	22%
15 years old	32%	10%	9%
16 years old	32%	30%	45%
17 years or older	15%	45%	24%

Source: Adapted from Caron, S. L., & Moskey, E. G. (2002). Changes over time in teenage sexual relationships: Comparing the high school class of 1950, 1975, and 2000. *Adolescence, 37*, 515–526, Tables 1 and 4.

sex—hookups—are more likely to experience depression relative to those having no or little casual sex (Welsh, Grello & Harper, 2006). In contrast, men with higher rates of casual sex have some of the lowest levels of depression. Women are also more likely than men to experience guilt and remorse following casual sex (Fielder & Carey, 2010; Owen et al., 2010). These differences may be explained, at least in part, by the next finding.

A second generalization is that the **double standard** has declined but not disappeared over the years (Kreager & Staff, 2009; Peterson & Hyde, 2010). According to the double standard, sexual behavior that is viewed as appropriate, and even good, for males is considered inappropriate or bad for females; there is one standard for males, another for females. In the "old days," a young man was expected to obtain some sexual experience, and gained respect from peers for his sexual exploits ("he's a stud"). In contrast, a young woman was expected to remain a virgin until she married and was viewed negatively for engaging in sexual behaviors ("she's a slut"). Teens and young adults still tend to believe that a woman who has many sexual partners is more immoral than an equally promiscuous man (Boislard, van de Bongardt, & Blais, 2016). In part, the double standard for male–female sexuality may persist because it fits entrenched societal expectations, even though actual sexual behaviors of males and females are more similar than different. Males are more likely than females to retain the double standard, although both males and females believe women should be more careful with casual sexual encounters out of fear that women may experience social stigma or be subjected to various rape myths (Conley, Ziegler, & Moors, 2013; Rudman, Fetterolf, & Sanchez, 2013). The persistence of the double standard may help explain why males report primarily positive feelings from casual hookups, whereas females report mostly negative feelings from these encounters.

A third generalization that emerges from research on sexual beliefs is that adolescents are confused about sexual norms. Adolescents continually receive mixed messages about sexuality (Ponton, 2001). They are encouraged to be popular and attractive to the other sex, and they watch countless television programs and movies that glamorize sexual behavior. The more sexualized content they watch, the more likely they are to be sexually active themselves (Chandra et al., 2008). Yet many adolescents are told to value virginity and to fear and avoid pregnancy, bad reputations, and AIDS and other sexually transmitted infections (STIs). Adults often tell teens that they are too young to engage in sexual activity, yet they make teens feel ashamed or embarrassed about masturbating (Halpern et al., 2000; Ponton, 2001).

Finally, today's adolescents are more tolerant or open-minded of a variety of sexual behaviors and orientations. Homosexual orientation may not be normative, but it is certainly more widely accepted today than it was in previous generations. Nearly half of adults today agree that "same-sex sexual activity is not wrong at all," compared to only about 12% of adults 40 years earlier (Twenge, Sherman, & Wells, 2016). The standards for males and females are now more similar, and adolescents tend to agree that sexual intercourse in the context of emotional involvement is acceptable; but teenagers still must forge their own codes of behavior, and they differ widely in what they decide.

Sexual Behavior

If beliefs about sexual behavior have changed over the years, has sexual behavior itself changed? In short, yes. Today's teenagers are involved in more intimate forms of sexual behavior at earlier ages than adolescents of the past were. Rates of sexual activity climbed in the 1960s and continued to climb through the 1980s before leveling off and then declining somewhat from the mid-1990s on

(Martinez & Abma, 2015). For instance, the percentage of 15–19 year old males who have ever had sex declined from 60% in 1988 to 42% in 2008 (Martinez & Abma, 2015). Over this same 20-year period, the percentage of females who ever had sexual intercourse dipped from 51% to 43%, nearly identical to the male rate. By age 20, 75% of young adults report having had sexual intercourse, and by age 24, 85% report having had sexual intercourse (Chandra, Mosher, Copen, & Sionean, 2011; Meschke et al., 2000).

Rates of sexual activity depend greatly on how sexual activity is defined. What constitutes "having sex"? Virtually all college students—both male and female—agree that penile–vaginal intercourse is having sex, but in a 2007 survey only 20% of college students agreed that they had "had sex" when they engaged in oral–genital stimulation (Hans, Gillen, & Akande, 2010). Perhaps this is why there are higher rates of oral sex than intercourse among today's high school students (Prinstein, Meade, & Cohen, 2003). If their cognitive schema of having sex does not include oral sex (or anal sex for some teens), they can engage in oral sex without feeling they are really having sex. Consequently, as many as 40% of college students who label themselves virgins report giving or receiving oral sex, and some of these have had three or more oral sex partners (Chambers, 2007).

Interestingly, today's teens rate oral sex as less intimate than intercourse, the opposite of what many from their parents' generation believe (Chambers, 2007). This may help explain the rise in oral sex among teenagers. Another reason is teens' inaccurate perception that oral sex is safer than vaginal penetration. Although oral sex without intercourse may sharply reduce pregnancy rates, it does not prevent transmission of STIs unless partners consistently use protection. Unfortunately, many teens lack knowledge about how to protect themselves during oral sex (Brady & Halpern-Fisher, 2007; Chambers, 2007). In addition to possible health consequences, there may be emotional consequences for teens who engage in oral sex. Teens who engage only in oral sex (without intercourse) report less positive feelings about themselves and their relationship than other sexually active teens (Brady & Halpern-Fisher, 2007).

Becoming sexually active is a normal part of development, but parents and society often express concerns about teens becoming sexually active when they are too young, because early sexual activity is associated with risky behaviors that can lead to unwanted pregnancies and STIs. Just a year or two can make a big difference in whether or not teens take precautions to reduce risks: Among teens who start having intercourse at age 17 or younger, 82% of males and 77% of females report using contraception when they became sexually active (Martinez & Abma, 2015). But among those teens who start having intercourse at ages 18–19, they are significantly more likely (99% males and 93% females) to report using contraception when they have sex.

Jessica Siebenbruner and her colleagues (2007) studied the antecedents of early sexual behavior among three groups of 16-year-olds who had previously been evaluated on a variety of measures at ages 6, 9, 12, and 13. The researchers distinguished among three groups on the basis of self-reported sexual behaviors at age 16: sexual abstainers who had not yet had sexual intercourse, low risk-takers who reported having five or fewer sexual partners and always using contraception, and high risk-takers who reported having six or more sexual partners and inconsistently using contraception. The researchers wanted to know whether they could predict which of these three groups a teen would end up in at age 16 based on information collected at the earlier ages.

Several findings emerged from this research. High-risk sexual behavior at age 16 seemed to be part of a general pattern of problem behavior that started at birth with a mother who was unmarried (Siebenbruner et al., 2007). Unwed mothers tend to be younger, less educated, and more likely to experience economic hardships. High-risk teens grew up in homes that were characterized as less emotionally responsive, and they were rated by teachers as engaging in more externalizing behaviors at ages 9 and 12. In these respects, the high-risk teens were different from both the low-risk teens and the abstainers throughout childhood.

By contrast, the low-risk teens and the abstainers were similar throughout childhood, yet began to diverge in early adolescence. At age 13, low-risk teens *looked* more mature than abstainers and were more involved in romantic relationships. They were also somewhat more likely to drink alcohol at age 16 than the abstainers. Their mature appearance may have led others to respond to them differently, leading them to romantic relationships, sexual involvement, and alcohol use at an earlier age than their peers who appeared less mature. These findings suggest that parents who are concerned about early involvement in sex should be on the alert for problem behaviors during childhood, provide an emotionally responsive home environment, and talk to their teens about how their appearance may influence how others perceive and treat them.

Some teens seem headed for engaging in riskier sexual behaviors than other teens. M. Lynne Cooper (2010) evaluated the sexual behaviors of nearly 2,000 young adults and found that numerous factors, including within-person factors, situational factors, and interactions of the two, contribute to the chances of engaging in risky sex. Within-person factors associated with more risky sexual behaviors included low levels of impulse control and communality, high levels of being adventurous, and a tendency towards negative emotionality (a tendency to feel anxious and depressed and react poorly to stressful situations). Situations involving sex with a new partner were associated with drinking more alcohol and choosing a riskier partner but also with a greater likelihood of using a condom. Research consistently shows that alcohol use is associated with riskier sexual behaviors. Compared with adults, teens and young adults from minority groups, especially males, are more likely to engage in risky sex practices, with potentially life-altering consequences (see Espinosa-Hernandez & Lefkowitz, 2009; Lee & Hahm, 2010). **Exploration 12.1** examines the concerning issue of sexual assault on college campuses, which is often accompanied by alcohol or drug use by one or both parties.

Although most adolescents seem to adjust successfully to becoming sexually active, there have also been some casualties among those who are psychologically unprepared for sex or who end up with an unintended pregnancy or an STI. Sexually active adolescent couples often fail to use contraception, partly because they are cognitively immature and do not take seriously the possibility that their behavior could have unwanted long-term consequences (Loewenstein & Furstenberg, 1991). Although condom use has increased over past decades, it is still lower than health-care professionals would like to see. In addition, adolescent

Sexual Assaults on College Campuses

One in five, or 20%: That's how many women in college report that they have been sexually assaulted (Krebs et al., 2007). **Sexual assault** refers to unwanted and nonconsensual sexual contact or behavior (Krebs et al., 2016). It includes rape and attempted rape, as well as unwanted fondling, touching, kissing, and other nonconsensual contact with your body. The figure in this box tells an important story: Women are most likely to experience a sexual assault during the first month or two of their first year in college (Krebs et al., 2016).

According to this same survey (Krebs et al., 2016), a majority of women tell a friend, roommate, or family member, but do not report the incident to a school official or to law enforcement. Reasons for not making an official report include not wanting to make a "big deal" out of it and concern that others will blame them for what happened.

Women report a variety of problems in the aftermath of a sexual assault, including trouble with friends and roommates, withdrawal from classes, and even thoughts about dropping out or transferring schools (Jordan, Combs, & Smith, 2014; Krebs et al., 2016).

What factors contribute to the incidence of sexual assaults on college campuses? Alcohol consumption, especially excessive episodic consumption (binge drinking), is common by both parties involved in the sexual assault (Fedina, Holmes, & Backes, 2016; White & Hingson, 2014). A culture of "hooking up" can also contribute to the likelihood of perpetrating a sexual assault or experiencing one (Sutton & Simons, 2015). Fraternity and athletic subcultures on college campuses may also encourage attitudes and behaviors that promote sexual misconduct.

There are actions that individuals can take to reduce personal risk, and there are programs that schools can implement to decrease the sexual assaults on their campuses and to promote healthy behaviors. For one, intervention programs that teach students how they can intervene when one of their friends appears at-risk for inappropriate behavior have been effective (Coker et al., 2015). These "bystander intervention" programs are designed to empower peers to take action if they witness risky behavior. Other programs focus on fostering clearer communication about issues of consent. One such promising program is *RealConsent*, which consists of six 30-minute online, interactive modules on various aspects of sexual relationships. In one study, researchers were able to randomly assign male college students to complete either the *RealConsent* program or a different web program on general health promotion (Salazar et al., 2014). Six months after completing the webinars, the *RealConsent* students showed more positive behaviors (for example, intervening when someone else was at risk) and fewer negative behaviors (for example, less often being involved in sexual violence) than students in the control group. In addition, the *RealConsent* students reported greater knowledge of effective consent and healthier attitudes about women and relationships (for example, less hostility toward women and more empathy toward victims).

Comprehensive reviews of dozens of studies of sexual assault prevention identify several important features needed for program success (White House Task Force to Protect Students from Sexual Assault, 2014). These features focus on four important elements: characteristics of the individuals involved, their relationships with others, their physical environments, and the broader social and cultural contexts in which they function (DeGue, 2014; DeGue et al., 2012). Short, one-time programs are largely ineffective in making measurable and lasting changes to behavior. Working effectively with potential perpetrators of sexual violence requires programming that gets at some of the underlying risk factors, such as the individual's beliefs about women and the messages they receive from the culture around them about acceptable behaviors. Although the number of sexual assaults on college campuses is high, there are many promising signs that individuals and institutions are no longer willing to stand by silently and permit this problem to continue. With increasing numbers of institutions implementing aggressive prevention programs, the payoff is likely to be fewer and fewer college students who experience sexual assaults.

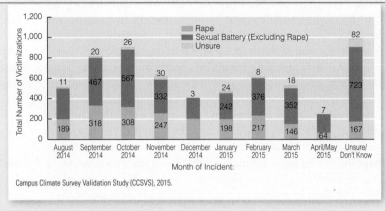

Campus Climate Survey Validation Study (CCSVS), 2015.

---

couples who are in long-term, monogamous relationships often stop using condoms because they no longer fear transmission of human immunodeficiency virus (HIV) or other STIs.

Sexual behaviors are also shaped by the social and cultural contexts in which children develop. For example, research shows that teens are less likely to use condoms if their friends report engaging in sex without condoms (Henry et al., 2007). Conversely, teens are more likely to use condoms if they believe their friends are using condoms. Examining the larger cultural context, Eric Widmer and his colleagues (Widmer, Treas, & Newcomb, 1998) found wide variations in sexual beliefs across the 24 countries that they studied. These prevailing cultural beliefs, whether conservative, permissive, or somewhere in the middle, influence how teens construct their individual sexual identities. Teens growing up in cultures with more permissive attitudes about sexuality are likely to interpret their own behaviors differently than teens growing up in cultures with largely

Becoming sexually active is a normal part of development, occurring during adolescence for some and adulthood for others.

Daniel Vrabec/Alamy Stock Photo

conservative beliefs. Thus, sexual behavior is not driven simply by the surge in hormones that accompanies puberty; it is mediated by social context and by the personal beliefs that are constructed in response to physical changes and cultural beliefs.

For the adolescent who gives birth, the consequences of teenage sexuality can include an interrupted education, a low income, and a difficult start for both her and her child (see Hoffman & Maynard, 2008). This young mother's life situation and her child's developmental status are likely to improve later, especially if she goes back to school and limits her family size, but she is likely to remain economically disadvantaged compared with her peers who postpone parenthood until their 20s or later (Hoffman & Maynard, 2008). Fortunately, after increasing for many years, rates of teenage pregnancy have begun to decline in recent years (Kost, Henshaw, & Carlin, 2010).

In addition to unplanned pregnancy, poorly planned sexual activity can have health consequences, namely STIs. ● Table 12.4 provides an overview of STIs that can result from inconsistent or

● **Table 12.4** Sexually Transmitted Infections (STIs) with Their Cause, Symptoms, and Treatment

STI	Cause and Treatment	Symptoms and Side Effects
Chlamydia: Highest rates among 15- to 19-year-olds, followed by 20- to 24-year-olds	Caused by bacteria; can be treated and cured with antibiotics	Few or no symptoms; when present, symptoms include slight discharge from vagina or penis, burning with urination, and lower abdominal pain. If left untreated, it can result in pelvic inflammatory disease, which is associated with infertility.
Trichomoniasis: Highest rates among women aged 30 and older	Caused by a parasite; can be treated and cured with antibiotics	Few or no symptoms; when present, symptoms include irritation or itching of the genital area, painful urination and intercourse, and possibly lower abdominal pain.
Gonorrhea: Highest rates among adolescents and young adults	Caused by bacteria; can be treated and usually cured with antibiotics, although some strains have become resistant	Few or no symptoms; when present, symptoms include genital discharge and painful urination. Gonorrheal infections can also invade the mouth and throat through oral sex with an infected partner, or the anus and rectum through anal sex with an infected partner. Can lead to infertility if untreated.
Genital Herpes: Incidence increases across age groups, peaking in middle adulthood	Caused by herpes simplex virus; can be treated but not cured	Symptoms include genital discharge, itching or burning, and painful blisters in the genital and anal regions. Although blisters may disappear in 2–3 weeks, the underlying virus that causes genital herpes remains and can cause symptom recurrence at any time. On average, infected persons have four occurrences per year.
Genital *Warts*: Highest rates among those in their early 20s	Caused by human papillomavirus (HPV); can be treated with surgery or cauterization of warts but may recur if immune system does not completely eliminate virus	Symptoms include small painless bumps on the vagina, cervix, or vulva (females) and penis (males); the anus and mouth may also be affected. If left untreated, the growths can grow into a larger clump of warts resembling cauliflower. Some strains of HPV are associated with cervical cancer, and a vaccine has been developed to prevent HPV.
Syphilis: Highest rates among 20-somethings	Caused by *Treponema pallidum* bacteria, which is highly contagious; can be treated in early stages with antibiotics	Symptoms emerge in stages: The first symptom is typically one or more ulcerlike sores around the genitals, although these sores, called chancres, can also appear in the mouth or anal area depending on point of contact with an infected person. This is followed by a body rash and flulike symptoms, which may last for several weeks. The underlying bacteria can remain dormant for years, or it can resurface in the lungs, heart, or brain. Can cause brain disease, dementia, or blindness if left untreated.

Sources: Adapted from Centers for Disease Control and Prevention (CDCP). (2012d, December). *Sexually transmitted disease surveillance*, 2011. Atlanta: U.S. Department of Health and Human Services; Dunne, E. F., Unger, E. R., Sternberg, M., McQuillan, G., Swan, D. C, Patel, S. S., & Markowitz, L. E. (2007). Prevalence of HPV infection among females in the United States. *JAMA, 297*, 813–819; Guttmacher Institute. (2016). *HIV and STIs*. Available at: www.guttmacher.org/united-states/hiv-stis. Accessed September 10, 2016.

inadequate safe-sex practices. Sadly, few adolescents are doing what they would need to do to protect themselves from STIs: abstaining from sex or using a condom *every* time. No wonder many educators are calling for stronger programs of sex education and distribution of free condoms at school. There is little chance of preventing the unwanted consequences of teenage sexuality unless more adolescents either postpone sex or practice safer sex.

One encouraging finding is that teens who feel close to their parents, especially their mothers, and who report having closer parental supervision are more likely to delay initiating sexual activity (L'Engle & Jackson, 2008). Parents who have clear household routines, monitor their teens, and establish strong relationships with their sons and daughters tend to have adolescents who delay sex or avoid casual sex (Manlove et al., 2012). Parent–teen communication about sexuality can also delay the age of first intercourse, particularly when mothers (rather than fathers) have the conversation and point out the negative consequences of having sex at an early age (Widman et al., 2016). Unfortunately, many parents do not communicate clearly or regularly with their teens about matters of sexuality (Guilamo-Ramos et al., 2008). In a survey of mothers of at-risk urban middle-school students, those who thought that a conversation about sex would embarrass their teen or felt unsure of what to say or how to initiate such a conversation tended not to talk to their teen about sex. In contrast, mothers who thought that talking about sex would encourage their teen to think more maturely, believed it wouldn't be too embarrassing, thought they would be able to answer their teen's questions, and felt comfortable with themselves and with the idea of talking about sex were more likely to have such conversations (Guilamo-Ramos et

al., 2008; Pluhar, Dilorio, & McCarty, 2008). This suggests that successful sex education programs need to reach out to parents and help educate parents as well as their teens.

Another encouraging finding is that educational programs that emphasize abstinence can be effective (Jemmott, Jemmott, & Fong, 2010). Such programs can encourage young adolescents to delay sexual intercourse. Importantly, when teens who participate in abstinence-only programs have intercourse, they are just as likely to use a condom as teens who participate in alternative educational programs focusing on safe sex (Jemmott et al., 2010). This is good news for those who worry that focusing on abstinence may not provide teens with sufficient knowledge about safe sex.

● Checking Mastery

1. What do we know about the sexual beliefs of many of today's teens?
2. Are there differences in sexual behavior of males and females?
3. What factors likely contribute to one's sexual orientation?

● Making Connections

1. What factors are likely to influence the age at which young people today become sexually active?
2. If you wanted to delay the age of first intercourse, what would be two ways to do this?

12.5
The Adult

LEARNING OBJECTIVES

- Explore changes in gender roles across adulthood.
- Evaluate the pros and cons of androgyny.
- Indicate how women and men have managed to integrate the various roles of adulthood: career, relationships, and parenting.
- Discuss changes in sexual behaviors and sexuality throughout adulthood.

You might think that once children and adolescents have learned their gender roles, they simply play them out during adulthood. Instead, as people face the challenges of adult life and enter new social contexts, their gender roles and their concepts of themselves as men and women change. So, too, do their sexual behaviors and their perceptions of their own sexuality.

Changes in Gender Roles

Although males and females fill their agentic or communal roles throughout their lives, the specific content of those roles changes considerably over the life span. The young boy may act out his agentic role by playing with trucks or wrestling with his buddies; the grown man may play his role by holding down a job. Moreover, the degree of difference between male and female roles also changes. Children and adolescents adopt behaviors consistent

with their "boy" or "girl" roles, but the two sexes otherwise adopt similar roles in society—namely, those of children and students. Even as they enter adulthood, male and female roles differ little because members of both sexes are often single and in school or working.

However, the roles of men and women become more distinct when they marry or settle into a stable romantic relationship and especially when (and if) they become parents. Anthropologist David Gutmann (1987, 1997) has offered the intriguing hypothesis that gender roles and gender-related traits in adulthood are shaped by what he calls the **parental imperative**—the requirement that mothers and fathers adopt different roles to raise children successfully. Drawing on his own cross-cultural research and that of others, he suggests that in many cultures, young and middle-aged men must emphasize their "masculine" qualities to feed and protect their families, whereas young and middle-aged women must express their "feminine" qualities to nurture the young and meet the emotional needs of their families.

The birth of a child tends to make even egalitarian couples divide their labors in more traditional ways than they did before the birth and migrate toward more traditional gender-role attitudes: Mothers become primarily responsible for child care and household tasks and fathers tend to emphasize their role as breadwinner for the family. Consistent with this, Andrea Abele (2014) found that women's work hours dropped significantly after becoming mothers, but men's work hours were virtually unchanged after becoming fathers. The American Time Use Survey shows that, for most heterosexual couples with children, the mother typically does about 18 hours of housework and 14 hours of childcare, whereas the father does about 10 hours of housework and 7 hours of childcare (Pew Research Center, 2013). In contrast, fathers spend more hours working outside the home (37 hours per week) compared to mothers (21 hours). Thus, there may be something to the concept of the parental imperative, although perhaps not to the extent suggested by Gutmann.

Women have less leisure time than men, perhaps as a result of their desire to "have it all." Michelle Hoffnung (2004; Hoffnung and Williams, 2013) interviewed women in their senior year of college and found that these young women wanted marriage, career, and motherhood. Following graduation, the women planned to focus first on establishing their careers. When Hoffnung (2004) checked up on the women 7 years after graduation, she found that some of the women were now married, but marital status was not related to educational attainment or career status. In contrast, motherhood was related to both educational attainment and career status: Those women who had children had not gone as far with their education or career as those women without children. Thus, as they neared the age of 30, women seemed to be able to have marriage and a career, or marriage and a baby, but having all three led to some compromises, namely less progress in their careers.

Sixteen years after college graduation, when they were in their mid- to late-30s, Hoffnung and Williams (2013) again interviewed the women. At this point, about 90% had married and about 75% had children. Only 57% of those with children were employed full time. Most women indicated that they still "wanted to have it all," but not necessarily all at the same time. Women with children who were not employed full time indicated that they looked forward to working full time sometime in the future. And some child-free working women indicated that they had not ruled out becoming mothers. Thus, women may have it all by juggling the various roles and adjusting their expectations to the realities of fitting all the pieces together.

What happens after the children are grown? Based on his cross-cultural studies, Gutmann suggests that, freed from the demands of the parental imperative, men become less active and more passive, take less interest in community affairs, and focus more on religious contemplation and family relationships. They also become more sensitive and emotionally expressive. Women, meanwhile, are changing in the opposite direction. After being relatively passive and nurturing in their younger years, they become more active, domineering, and assertive in later life. In many cultures, they take charge of the household after being the

What traits might we associate with this woman based on her agentic role in the workplace?

Rainer Elstermann/DigitalVision/Getty Images

underlings of their mothers-in-law and become stronger forces in their communities. In short, then, the roles of men and women are fairly similar before marriage, maximally different during the child-rearing years, and similar again later (Gutmann, 1997).

Androgyny?

Do the shifts in the roles played by men and women during adulthood affect them psychologically? For years, psychologists assumed that "being masculine" or having agentic traits and "being feminine" or having communal traits were at opposite ends of a single continuum and mutually exclusive. If a person possessed agentic traits, then that person must be noncommunal, whereas being highly communal implied being nonagentic. This bipolar view was challenged with evidence that at least some individuals can be characterized by psychological androgyny—that is, by a balancing or blending of both agentic traits and communal traits (Spence, Helmreich, & Stapp, 1973). According to this perspective, then, agency and communion are two separate dimensions of personality. A male or female who has many agentic traits and few communal ones is considered to have a stereotypic "masculine" gender type. A person who has many communal traits and few agentic traits is said to have a "feminine" gender type. The androgynous person possesses both agentic and communal traits, whereas the undifferentiated individual lacks both kinds of attributes.

Most college students—both males and females—believe that the ideal person is androgynous (Slavkin & Stright, 2000). However, being well-adjusted psychologically is generally associated with gender-congruent personality traits (that is, males displaying agentic traits and females expressing communal traits), agentic traits in general, and having flexible attitudes about gender (Didonato & Berenbaum, 2010). In addition, you may need to distinguish between the androgynous individual who possesses *positive* agentic and communal traits and the one who possesses *negative* agentic and communal traits (Woodhill & Samuels, 2003, 2004). People with positive androgyny score higher on measures of mental health and well-being than those with negative androgyny (Woodhill & Samuels, 2003). It may be premature, then, to conclude that it is better in all respects to be androgynous rather than either agentic or communal in orientation. Still, you can at least conclude that it is unlikely to be damaging for men to become a little more communal or for women to become a little more agentic than they have traditionally been.

Changes in Sexuality

Adults' sexual lifestyles are as varied as their personalities and intellects. Some adults remain single—some of them actively seeking a range of partners, others having one partner at a time, and still others leading celibate lives. Almost 9 of 10 Americans marry, and most adults are married at any given time. Men have more sexual partners and report more sexual activity than women during their adult lives, but most members of both sexes have just one sexual partner at a time (Chandra, Mosher, Copen, & Sionean, 2011; Copen, Chandra, & Febo-Vazquez, 2016).

Among married couples, there is a small decline in the quality of sex over the course of marriage, as well as a drop in the quantity of sex (Liu, 2003). There are also some gender differences, with married women reporting somewhat less satisfaction with their sex lives than married men (Liu, 2003). Middle-aged women report more positive moods and lower stress levels on days following sexual behavior with a partner (Burleson, Trevathan, & Todd, 2007). This benefit may be due to sexual activity alone or in combination with the affection that many women report with the sexual activity. Tim Wadsworth (2013) analyzed survey results on frequency of sex and happiness levels of over 15,000 men and women. He found that as one went up, so did the other: Adults are happier when they are having more frequent sex. What's more, adults who believe they are having sex more frequently than their peers are even happier (Wadsworth, 2013).

What becomes of people's sex lives as they age? Just as parents may be uncomfortable thinking of their teens as sexual beings, many young people struggle to conceive of their parents or—heaven forbid—their grandparents as sexual beings. We tend to stereotype older adults as sexless or asexual. But we are wrong: People continue to be sexual beings throughout the life span. For example, on surveys of adults ranging in age from 25 to 85, most adults reported being interested in sex and being sexually active (Lindau & Gavrilova, 2010; Thomas et al., 2014). As ■ Figure 12.6 shows, most sexual activity among adults consists of vaginal intercourse or oral sex with an opposite-sex partner.

Gender differences were small among younger adults but became larger with age, leading to relatively large differences among the oldest adults: 75- to 85-year-old men were twice as likely to be sexually active and four times as likely to express interest in sex as women the same age. Other research shows a decline in sexual desire with age, although as ■ Figure 12.7 illustrates, desire can remain moderate or high well into old age.

With longer and healthier life spans and greater recognition and acceptance of middle and older adults' sexual activity, there have been some unexpected consequences. Perhaps most alarming has been the doubling of STIs among those 45 and older (Bodley-Tickell et al., 2008). Many postmenopausal women assume that there is no need to practice "safe sex" because the threat of an unintended pregnancy is no longer present. They may be uninformed about STIs and too embarrassed to ask for information. Even more disturbing, many older adults do not get tested for STIs, including HIV, and may not get the treatment to save their life or improve the quality of their life (Jacobs & Kane, 2010). Consider Jane Fowler's story (Evans & Goldman, 2010): Divorced at age 47 after 23 years of marriage and monogamous sex, Jane dated a few men whom she knew from her larger circle of friends. She didn't worry about using condoms because she knew pregnancy wouldn't be an issue and, after all, she *knew* these men; they weren't strangers. But a routine blood test for

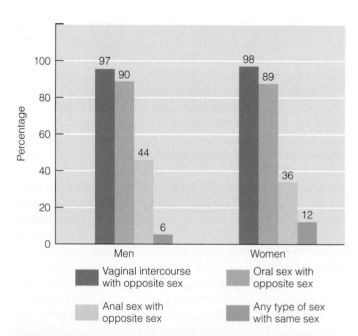

■ **Figure 12.6** Percentages of adults aged 25–44 ever having different types of sex. Most sex consists of intercourse or oral sex with a partner of the opposite sex.

Source: From Chandra, A., Mosher, W. D., Copen, C. & Sionean, C. (2011, March 3). Sexual behavior, sexual attraction, and sexual identity in the United States: Data from the 2006-2008 National Survey of Family Growth. *National Health Statistics Reports, 36*, Figure 1 (p. 9).

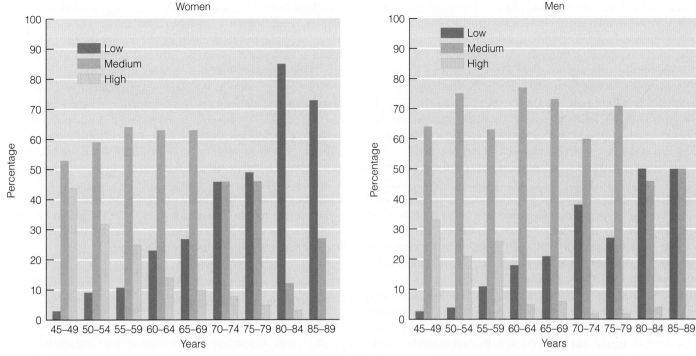

Figure 12.7 Percentage of women (*left*) and men (*right*), by age, reporting low, moderate, and high levels of sexual desire.

Source: From DeLamater, J. D., & Sill, M. (2005). Sexual desire in later life. *Journal of Sex Research, 42,* 138–149.

an insurance company revealed that Jane was infected with HIV. In the aftermath of her shocking diagnosis, Jane withdrew from many activities and retired from her career as a journalist. Fortunately, she eventually overcame her embarrassment and fears over contracting an STI in midlife and founded an organization, *HIV Wisdom for Older Women,* to educate other women on the importance of safe-sex practices at all ages (Evans & Goldman, 2010). Such cases illustrate that we need to do much more to improve sex education across the entire life span.

For older adults who experience declines in sexual interest and activity, what might explain this change? Consider first the physiological changes in sexual capacity that occur with age, as revealed by the pioneering research of William Masters and Virginia Johnson (1966, 1970). Males are at their peak of sexual responsiveness in their late teens and early 20s and gradually become less responsive thereafter. A young man is easily and quickly aroused; his orgasm is intense; and he may have a refractory, or recovery, period of only minutes before he is capable of sexual activity again. The older man is likely to be slower—slower to arouse, slower to ejaculate after being aroused, and slower to recover afterward. In addition, levels of male sex hormones decline gradually with age in many men. This may contribute to diminished sexual functioning among older men (Schiavi et al., 1991), although most researchers do not believe that hormonal factors fully explain the changes in sexual behavior that most men experience (Kaye, 1993).

Physiological changes in women are less dramatic. Females reach their peak of sexual responsiveness later than men do, often not until their mid-30s. Women are capable of more orgasms in a given time span than men are because they have little or no refractory period after orgasm, and this capacity is retained into old age.

As noted in Chapter 5, menopause does not seem to reduce sexual activity or interest for most women. However, like older men, older women typically are slower to become sexually excited. Moreover, some experience discomfort associated with decreased lubrication that occurs as estrogen levels drop with menopause.

The physiological changes that men and women experience do not explain why many of them become less sexually active in

Most adults continue to be interested in sex and engage in sexual behaviors on a regular basis. For those older adults who experience a decline in sexual desire or behavior, what factors might be behind the change?

Rappholdt/Shutterstock.com

middle and old age. Masters and Johnson (1966) concluded that both men and women are physiologically capable of sexual behavior well into old age. Women retain this physiological capacity even longer than men, yet they are less sexually active in old age.

Apparently, we must turn to factors other than biological aging to explain changes in sexual behavior. In summarizing these factors, Pauline Robinson (1983) quotes Alex Comfort (1974): "In our experience, old folks stop having sex for the same reason they stop riding a bicycle—general infirmity, thinking it looks ridiculous, and no bicycle" (p. 440; and see DeLamater, 2012).

Under the category of infirmity, diseases and disabilities, as well as the drugs prescribed for them, can limit sexual functioning (DeLamater & Sill, 2005). Older adults in good or excellent health not only report engaging in more frequent sex than their peers in poor or fair health, they also report more interest in sex and greater satisfaction with their sexual activity (Lindau & Gavrilova, 2010). Poor health may be especially problematic for men, who may become impotent if they have high blood pressure, coronary disease, diabetes, or other health problems. Mental health problems are also important: Many cases of impotence among middle-aged and elderly men are attributable to psychological causes such as stress at work and depression rather than to physiological causes (Persson & Svanborg, 1992).

The second source of problems is social attitudes that view sexual activity in old age as ridiculous, or at least inappropriate. Old people are stereotyped as sexually unappealing and sexless (or as "dirty old men") and are discouraged from expressing sexual interests. These negative attitudes may be internalized by elderly people, causing them to suppress their sexual desires (Kaye, 1993; Purifoy, Grodsky, & Giambra, 1992). Older females may be even further inhibited by the double standard of aging, which regards aging in women more negatively than aging in men (Arber & Ginn, 1991).

Third, there is the "no bicycle" part of Comfort's analogy—the lack of a partner, or at least of a willing and desirable partner. Most older women are widowed, divorced, or single and face the reality that there just are not enough older men to go around. Lack of a partner, then, is the major problem for elderly women, many of whom continue to be interested in sex, physiologically capable of sexual behavior, and desirous of love and affection (DeLamater & Sill, 2005; Karraker, DeLamater, & Schwartz, 2011).

Perhaps we should add one more element to Comfort's bicycle analogy: lack of cycling experience. Masters and Johnson (1966, 1970) proposed a "use it or lose it" principle of sexual behavior to reflect two findings. First, an individual's level of sexual activity early in adulthood predicts his level of sexual activity in later life. The relationship is not necessarily causal, by the way; it could simply be that some people are more sexually motivated than others throughout adulthood. A second aspect of the use it or lose it rule may be causal, however: Middle-aged and elderly adults who experience a long period of sexual abstinence often have difficulty regaining their sexual capacity.

Checking Mastery

1. How do gender roles shift during adulthood?
2. What is androgyny? Is it beneficial to be androgynous?
3. How do sexual behaviors change across adulthood?

Making Connections

1. The extent to which males and females differ changes from infancy to old age. When are gender differences in psychological characteristics and roles played in society most evident, and when are they least evident? How would you account for this pattern?
2. Fewer women than men become architects. Drawing on the material in this chapter, explain the extent to which nature and nurture may be responsible for this, citing evidence.

Chapter Summary

12.1 Sex and Gender

- Differences between males and females can be detected in the physical, psychological, and social realms; gender differences arise from an interaction of biological influences and socialization into gender roles (including the learning of gender-role norms and stereotypes).
- Research comparing males and females indicates that the two sexes are far more similar than different psychologically. The average male is more aggressive and better at spatial tasks and some mathematical problem-solving tasks, but less adept at verbal tasks, than the average female. Males also tend to be more active and assertive than females, who tend to be more nurturant and anxious. Children tend to play in highly gendered

ways and most men and women have gender identities that are quite distinct. Most gender differences are small, however, and some are becoming smaller.

12.2 The Infant

- During infancy, boys and girls are similar but adults treat them differently.
- Because their sex is important to those around them, and because they see that males and females differ, infants begin to form categories of "male" and "female."
- By age 2, infants have often gained knowledge of their basic gender identity and display "gender-appropriate" play preferences.

12.3 The Child

- Gender-role development proceeds with remarkable speed. By the time they enter school, children have long been aware of their basic gender identities, have acquired many stereotypes about how the sexes differ, and have come to prefer gender-appropriate activities and same-sex playmates.
- During middle childhood, their knowledge continues to expand as they learn more about gender-stereotyped psychological traits, but they also become more flexible in their thinking about gender roles. Their behavior, especially if they are boys, becomes even more gender typed, and they segregate themselves even more from the other sex.
- Theories of gender-role development consider biological and socialization factors. These include prenatal biological developments (as illustrated by the biosocial theory), the differential reinforcement and observational learning highlighted by social learning theorists, and developing cognitive understanding of gender concepts and the formation of gender schemas.
- School-age children engage in sex play and appear to experience their first sexual attractions around age 10.
- Some children experience sexual abuse, which can have significant and long-lasting effects on their development.

12.4 The Adolescent

- Adolescents become intolerant in their thinking about gender-role deviations and, through gender intensification, show increased concern with conforming to gender norms.

- In adolescence, forming a positive sexual identity is an important task, one that can be difficult for those with a gay or lesbian sexual orientation.
- Some adolescents wrestle with the identity they were assigned at birth and may transition to transgender.
- During the past century, we have witnessed increased endorsement of the view that sex with affection is acceptable, a weakening of the double standard, and increased confusion about sexual norms.
- An increasing number of college women report being sexually assaulted on campus.

12.5 The Adult

- Gender roles become more distinct when adults marry and have children, as men and women fulfill their roles as husband/wife and father/mother. Once children are grown, however, older adults often display greater flexibility in their behavior.
- Some adults display androgyny, a combination of both masculine-stereotypic and feminine-stereotypic traits. Some evidence suggests that androgyny is beneficial, but not at all ages or in all situations.
- Many older adults continue having sexual intercourse, and many of those who cease having it or have it less frequently continue to be sexually motivated. Elderly people can continue to enjoy an active sex life if they retain their physical and mental health, do not allow negative attitudes surrounding sexuality in later life to stand in their way, have a willing and able partner, and continue to "use" their capacity for sex.

Key Terms

transgender **366**
biological sex **366**
gender **366**
gender role **367**
gender stereotypes **367**
communality **367**
agency **367**
systemize **367**

gender similarities hypothesis **368**
social-role theory **369**
gender identity **371**
gender typing **372**
gender segregation **374**
biosocial theory **375**
androgenized female **376**
gender constancy **378**

gender stability **378**
gender consistency **378**
gender schema (schemata) **379**
posttraumatic stress disorder **383**
gender intensification **384**
sexual orientation **386**
childhood gender nonconformity (CGN) **387**

hookup **387**
double standard **388**
oral sex **389**
sexual assault **390**
parental imperative **392**
androgyny **393**

13 Social Cognition and Moral Development

Certain campers one summer repeatedly pulled a prank on Edward. Edward was a small, uneven-legged, mildly retarded adult who was the basic maintenance staffer for the camp. He was kind, conscientious in his duties, and proud that he was earning his way in life. There was just one thing: At a point of frustration or moment of embarrassment, Ed would invariably unleash a torrent of profanities that was surprising and, to some campers, entertaining. Several campers had devised a way to set off this "entertainment." Ed worked hard mowing and doing other chores on the camp grounds and would sometimes take a nap during the day. . . . Seeing Ed asleep, the plotters would move in. They would gently sink one of Ed's hands into a pail of water. Ed would wet his pants in bed and awaken, swearing madly and running frantically after the hysterically laughing campers (Gibbs, 2010, p. 1).

John Gibbs, author of the book *Moral Development and Reality*, attended the camp just described, watched the torment of Edward play out again and again, and feels guilty to this day that he did nothing to stop it, fearful of his fellow campers' reactions if he did. Many of you, we wager, can recall episodes like this when you and/or your peers did something hurtful to a nerdy, overweight, or otherwise different individual who did not deserve it, when you failed to take the perspective of and empathize with an innocent victim. What might have stopped you from mistreating someone like Edward or prompted you to intervene to save him from abuse by others? What does it take to optimize the helpful and cooperative tendencies of human beings and reduce the antisocial ones?

In this chapter, we continue our examination of the development of the self by exploring how we come to understand the social world and make decisions about issues of right and wrong like those raised by the campers' treatment of Edward. We begin with a look at the development of thinking about people and their behavior, which includes learning to take the perspectives of other people, including victims like Edward. We then look closely at moral development and positive and negative social behavior. We ask how humans acquire moral standards, how they decide what to do when faced with moral dilemmas, how empathy, guilt, and other emotions influence what they do, and why some individuals behave more morally than others.

13.1 Social Cognition

LEARNING OBJECTIVES

- Define social cognition and explain the meaning and significance of having a theory of mind.

- Summarize key steps in the development of a theory of mind and the contributions of nature and nurture to this development.

- Describe developments in trait perception and perspective taking and explain whether or not social cognitive skills hold up well in later life.

Social cognition is thinking about the perceptions, thoughts, emotions, motives, and behaviors of self, other people, groups, and even whole social systems (Flavell, 1985). We have touched already on some important aspects of social cognitive development, seeing, for example, that older children think differently than younger children about what they are like as individuals and about how males and females differ. Here, we focus on developmental changes in the ability to understand human psychology, describe other people, and adopt other people's perspectives.

Developing a Theory of Mind

Imagine that you are a young child, are brought to the laboratory, and are led through the research scenario portrayed in ▪ **Figure 13.1**. A girl named Sally, you are told, puts her marble in her basket and leaves the room. While she is gone, Anne moves the marble to her box. Sally returns to the room. Where will Sally look for her marble?

This task, called a **false belief task**, assesses the understanding that people can hold incorrect beliefs and that these beliefs, even though incorrect, can influence their behavior. The task was used in a pioneering study by Simon Baron-Cohen, Alan Leslie, and Uta Frith (1985) to determine whether young children, children with Down syndrome, and children with autism have a theory of mind. A **theory of mind** is the understanding that (a) people have mental states such as desires, beliefs, and intentions and that (b) these mental states guide (and help explain) their behavior. We all rely on a theory of mind, also called mind-reading skills, to predict and explain human behavior. We refer to mental states every day, saying, for example, that people did what they did because they wanted to, intended to, or believed that doing so would have a desired effect.

Children who pass the false belief task in **Figure 13.1**, and therefore show evidence of having a theory of mind to explain human behavior, say that Sally will look for her marble in the basket (where she falsely believes it to be) rather than in the box (where it

was moved without her knowledge). Children who have a theory of mind believe that Sally's behavior will be guided by her false belief about the marble's location. They are able to set aside their own knowledge of where the marble ended up after Anne moved it.

Sally places her marble in a basket.

Sally leaves the room.

The child being tested watches as Anne transfers Sally's marble to the box.

Sally returns.

The child being tested is asked the critical question: Where will Sally look for her marble?

▪ **Figure 13.1** The false belief task involving Sally and Anne. The child who has developed a theory of mind should say that Sally will look in the basket based on her false belief that the marble is there. The child who has not yet developed a theory of mind fails this false belief task, saying that Sally will look in the box (where the child knows the marble has been moved).

Source: From Baron-Cohen, S., Leslie, A. M., & Frith, U. (1985). Does the autistic child have a "Theory of Mind"? *Cognition, 21,* 37–46 Copyright © 1985. Reprinted with permission from Elsevier.

In the study by Baron-Cohen and his colleagues, about 85% of 4-year-olds of average intelligence and older children with Down syndrome passed the false belief task about Sally and her marble. Yet despite mental ages greater than those of the children with Down syndrome, 80% of the children with autism failed.

This study aroused much excitement because it suggested that children with autism display the social deficits they display because they lack a theory of mind and suffer from a kind of "mindblindness" (Baron-Cohen, 1995; and see Chapter 16). Imagine trying to understand and interact with people if you were unable to appreciate such fundamentals of human psychology as that people look for objects where they believe the objects are located, choose things that they want and reject things that they dislike, and sometimes attempt to plant false beliefs in others (that is, lie).

Temple Grandin, a now-famous woman with autism who is intelligent enough to be a professor of animal sciences, describes what it is like to lack a theory of mind: She must create a memory bank of how people behave and what emotions they express in various situations and then "compute" how people might be expected to behave in similar situations (Sacks, 1993). Although she can grasp simple emotions like happiness, she confesses that she could never quite get what *Romeo and Juliet* was all about. She feels awkward trying to carry on everyday conversations with people but relates well to animals and has used that talent to develop more humane ways of handling livestock. Just as we cannot understand falling objects without employing the concept of gravity, we cannot understand humans without invoking the concept of mental states and our theory of mind.

First Steps in Infancy

Although children normally do not pass the false belief task in Figure 13.1 until about age 4, a theory of mind begins to form in infancy. Indeed, infants have far more sophisticated social cognitive skills than we ever suspected. Consider these early steps in developing a theory of mind; most of these skills are deficient in children with autism (see, for example, Charman, 2000; and Doherty, 2009):

- **Joint attention.** Starting around 9 months, infants and their caregivers engage in joint attention, both looking at the same object at the same time. At this age, infants sometimes point to toys and then look toward their companions, encouraging others to look at what they are looking at. By doing so, infants show awareness that other people have different perceptual experiences than they do—and that two people can share a perceptual experience.
- **Understanding intentions.** In their first months of life, infants seem to understand that other people have *intentions*, set goals, and act to achieve them (Woodward, 2009). For example, by 6 months of age, if not earlier, infants much prefer a "helper" puppet who helps an actor achieve a goal to a "hinderer" who blocks goal achievement, showing that they understand good and bad intentions when they see them (Hamlin & Wynn, 2011; Hamlin, Wynn, & Bloom, 2007).
- **Pretend play.** When infants engage in their first simple *pretend play*, between 1 and 2 years, they show that they distinguish between pretense (a kind of false belief) and reality (see Chapter 14). They show that they know the difference between a pretend tea party and a real one, for example, when they make exaggerated lip-smacking noises and laugh as they drink from a cup at a pretend tea party.

Temple Grandin, who has autism, is an animal sciences professor, author, and subject of films. Yet understanding people is a daily challenge for her because of limitations in her theory-of-mind skills.

Frank Trapper/Corbis Entertainment/ Getty Images

- **Imitation.** Imitation of other people in the first year of life reveals an ability to mentally represent others' actions—and very likely the goals or intentions behind them.
- **Emotional understanding.** In the second year of life, teasing a sibling or comforting a playmate who is crying reflects an understanding that other people have emotions and that these emotions can be influenced for bad or good (Flavell, 1999; and see Section 13.3).

Some researchers even claim that infants as young as 15 months understand that people can hold false beliefs. By simplifying the false belief task, Kristine Onishi and Renée Baillargeon (2005) found that infants this age are surprised (as indicated by looking longer) when an actor does not look for a toy where she should believe it was hidden (and see Scott & Baillargeon, 2009). This intuitive surprise is probably not the same as the more explicit, conscious understanding of how false beliefs can lead people astray that children normally achieve by age 4 (Hughes & Devine, 2015; Sodian, 2011). However, it certainly adds to our picture of an infant who is very ready to understand and participate in the social world.

Desire and Belief–Desire Psychologies

Henry Wellman (1990) has theorized that children's theories of mind unfold in two main phases. Around age 2, children develop a **desire psychology**. Toddlers talk about what they want and explain their own behavior and that of others in terms of wants or desires. Thus Ross (at 2 years, 7 months), asked why he kept asking why, replied, "I want to say 'why,'" explaining his behavior in terms of his desire (Wellman & Bartsch, 1994, p. 345). This early desire psychology was observed among 18-month-olds in a clever study by Betty Repacholi and Alison Gopnik (1997). An experimenter tried two foods—Goldfish crackers and broccoli florets—and

Even 1-year-olds show awareness that other people can have mental states (perceptions) different from their own when they point at objects so that they and their companions can jointly attend to the same object.

wonderlandstock/Alamy Stock Photo

expressed delight in response to one but disgust in response to the other. Because the toddlers almost universally preferred the crackers to the broccoli, the acid test was a scenario in which toddlers saw the experimenter express her liking for broccoli but her disgust at the crackers ("Eww! Crackers! I tasted crackers! Eww!"). When confronted with the two bowls of food and asked to give the experimenter some, would these toddlers give her broccoli or crackers? The 14-month-olds in the study either did not comply with the request or gave the experimenter crackers, despite her distaste for them. However, the 18-month-olds gave her broccoli (undoubtedly against their better judgment!), showing that they were able to infer and honor her desire based on her previous emotional reactions to the two foods.

By age 3 or 4, children normally progress to a **belief–desire psychology**. They appreciate that people do what they do because they *desire* certain things and because they *believe* that certain actions will help them fulfill their desires. They now pass false belief tasks like the one about Sally and her marble, understanding that beliefs, true or false, guide people's behavior just as desires do (Wellman, Cross, & Watson, 2001; Wellman & Liu, 2004). So, Adam (at 3 years, 3 months), commenting on a bus, said "I thought it was a taxi," showing awareness that he held a false belief about the bus (Wellman & Bartsch, 1994, p. 345).

Notice that the 4-year-olds described by theory-of-mind researchers are more sophisticated students of psychology than the egocentric preschoolers described by Jean Piaget (see Chapter 7). However, it is better to think of a theory of mind as a set of understandings that children begin to develop in infancy and continue to refine into adolescence than to view it as something children "have" at age 4 (Miller, 2012; Wellman & Liu, 2004). Even much older children can be challenged when they are asked to understand sarcasm, where the intended meaning of a statement is different from the literal meaning, as in the theory-of-mind task in **Engagement 13.1** (Peterson, Wellman, & Slaughter, 2012). In late elementary school, children are also still mastering

● ENGAGEMENT 13.1
Do You Have a Theory of Mind?

Try this example of a higher-level theory-of-mind problem suitable for elementary school-aged children (from Peterson et al., 2012, pp. 474 and 485; based on Happé, 1994):

The girl and boy [shown in a picture] are going on a picnic. It is the boy's idea. He says it will be a lovely sunny day.

But when they get the food out, big storm clouds come. It rains and the food gets all wet. The girl says: "It's a lovely day for a picnic."

1. Is it true, what the girl said?
2. Why did the girl say "it's a lovely day for a picnic"?
3. Was the girl happy about the rain?

In the Peterson et al. (2012) study, only 4% of children ages 3 to 5 passed the key item, question 2, compared to 41% of children 7½ to 11½. Thus even the older children tested found this theory-of-mind task challenging. How did you do? (See the scoring guide, upside down.)

This task assesses a child's ability to recognize sarcasm. The critical test question is the second question, "Why did the girl say 'it's a lovely day for a picnic'?"

Passing Answers:
(reflecting understanding that the girl's intended meaning is different from the literal meaning of what she said):
She's being sarcastic/using sarcasm; she doesn't mean it; because it's an idiom; she tricked him; it's her way of telling him she is upset; just to make up a little joke; she is saying politely that she is not happy; because she is a smart aleck; because she is meaning "Why tell me it was nice?"

Failing Answers:
Because it is sunny [raining]; it's lovely outside; she likes rain [picnics/we need rain; she wants to play in the puddles; because she [the cake] got wet; because he lied to her; she thought it was sunny/did not see clouds; she's cross; to tell him off; because it's not sunny, so he doesn't feel bad; because he said it first; because her Dad likes the rain but she doesn't.

complex second-order belief statements such as, "Mary thinks that Jeff thinks that she hates him," in which people have beliefs about other people's beliefs (Miller, 2012). Indeed, theory-of-mind skills continue to improve from adolescence to adulthood (Dumontheil, Apperly, & Blakemore, 2010; Hughes & Devine, 2015).

Nature and Nurture

How do nature and nurture contribute to the development of theory-of-mind skills? We seem to need both the brain for it and the right kinds of social experience.

An Evolved Brain On the nature side of the nature–nurture issue, evolutionary theorists argue that having a theory of mind proved adaptive to our ancestors and became part of our biological endowment as a species through natural selection (Buss, 2012; Tomasello & Herrmann, 2010). Figuring out other people's intentions would be useful in deciding whether to trust them or be wary of them. Social behaviors such as bargaining, conflict resolution, cooperation, and competition all depend on understanding other people and predicting their behavior accurately. Although chimpanzees, like humans, can be deceptive at times, human children have more advanced theory-of-mind skills than chimps and distinguish themselves by being more able to cooperate with others to achieve a goal (Tomasello & Herrmann, 2010).

In further support of the nature side of the nature–nurture issue, developing a theory of mind requires neurological and cognitive maturation. This may be why children everywhere develop a theory of mind and progress from a desire psychology to a belief–desire psychology in the same manner at about the same age (Wellman et al., 2001). Meanwhile, atypical brain development in children with autism seems to be behind their great difficulty passing theory-of-mind tasks (Hughes & Devine, 2015).

Neuropsychologists have identified areas in the prefrontal cortex and the temporoparietal junction of the brain that are highly active when we are thinking about people's beliefs (Saxe, Carey, & Kanwisher, 2004; Spunt & Adolphs, 2015). Using *functional magnetic resonance imaging (fMRI)* to determine which areas of the brain are active while a person completes a task, for example, Rebecca Saxe and Nancy Kanwisher (2003) found that the areas of adults' brains that respond strongly during false belief tasks do not respond as strongly to similar tasks that do not involve thinking about mental states. Moreover, 4- to 6-year-old children who pass false belief tasks rely on the same brain areas to think about others' beliefs as adults do, whereas children who fail these tasks have not yet come to rely on these brain areas (Liu, Meltzoff, & Wellman, 2009; Gweon et al., 2012; and Saxe et al., 2009).

Neuropsychologists also believe social cognition involves **mirror neurons**, neurons that are activated both when we perform an action and when we observe someone else perform the same action (Iacoboni, 2009; Oberman & Ramachandran, 2007; Pineda, 2009; Rizzolatti & Sinigaglia, 2008). Thus, observing someone grasp a ball activates the same neurons that fire when we grasp a ball ourselves. Mirror neuron systems may therefore facilitate observational learning and imitation of what we see and hear. These neurons, found in many areas of the brain, may also be critical in allowing us to quickly infer another person's mental state based on

our own experiences of the same actions and facial expressions and of corresponding internal states. For example, watching a person reach for a Coke on a hot day, we readily infer that she's thirsty and wants a drink, and when she takes a sip, we readily infer from her facial expression that she's happy. Thanks to mirror neurons, we are likely to unconsciously and subtly imitate her happy face (as we cringe a bit in response to the face of someone cringing in pain).

Mirror neuron systems appear to be involved in imitation, theory-of-mind understandings, language, and empathy, although their exact roles are still not certain (Iacoboni & Dapretto, 2006; Lamm & Majdandžic, 2015). Meanwhile, mirror neuron deficits may help explain the difficulties individuals with autism have in these areas of development (Gallese, Rochat, & Berchio, 2013; Glenberg, 2011). For example, the mirror neurons of individuals with autism are not as active as those of typically developing individuals when they are asked to observe others' facial expressions or imitate their actions (Dapretto et al., 2006; McIntosh et al., 2006; Williams et al., 2006). In sum, our human genetic endowment makes for brains that are exquisitely designed for social cognition.

Talk of Mental States On the nurture side of the nature–nurture issue is evidence that acquiring a theory of mind and other social cognitive skills, much like acquiring language, requires not only a normal human brain but also experience interacting with other humans—participating in a "community of minds" (Nelson et al., 2003). Children do not construct their theories of mind on their own; instead, they construct them jointly with others during conversations about mental states.

The evidence? Here is a sampling (and see Hughes & Devine, 2015):

- **Language experience.** Deaf children of deaf parents, who can communicate with their companions using sign language, develop theory-of-mind skills right on schedule. However, deaf children of hearing parents, who usually do not have an opportunity to converse in sign language from an early age, achieve milestones in social cognitive development slowly, sometimes struggling with false belief tasks even at ages 8–10 (Peterson & Siegal, 1999; Peterson & Wellman, 2009; Peterson et al., 2012).
- **Mind-minded parents.** Parents who form secure attachments with their children and are sensitive to their needs and perspectives (Symons & Clark, 2000; Thompson, 2012), and parents who show **mind-mindedness** and talk with their children in elaborated ways about mental states ("You were probably sad because you thought Grandma would stay with us longer") tend to have children with advanced theory-of-mind skills (Meins et al., 2002; Peterson & Slaughter, 2003).
- **Interactions with siblings and peers.** Conversations with siblings and peers also contribute to mind-reading skills (Hughes & Devine, 2015). Children with siblings seem to grasp the elements of a theory of mind earlier than children without siblings (McAlister & Peterson, 2006, 2007). And children have plenty of opportunities to think and talk about mental states in bouts of pretend play ("Pretend the robber stole your money") and in conflicts with siblings and peers ("I thought you were done with your ice cream," "I didn't mean to step on your head").

This mother signs "You" to her deaf son on his fifth birthday. Deaf children who can communicate with their companions through sign language develop theory-of-mind skills on schedule, but deaf children of hearing parents who have limited early language experience often develop such skills more slowly.

Huntstock/Getty Images

- **Cultural differences.** Although most children worldwide master theory-of-mind skills in much the same order and at much the same rate, children are slow to develop theory-of-mind skills in cultures where there is not much talk about mental states (Hughes & Devine, 2015). In Samoa, for example, others' minds are considered unknowable so mental states are not discussed much. Perhaps as a result, it was not until age 8 that a majority of Samoan children in one study passed false belief tasks (Mayer & Trauble, 2013; and see Vinden & Astington, 2000).

In sum, acquiring a theory of mind—the foundation for all later social cognitive development—begins in infancy and toddlerhood with first steps such as joint attention, understanding of intentions, pretend play, imitation, and emotional understanding. It advances from a desire psychology to a belief–desire psychology and beyond universally (see ● **Table 13.1** for a timetable). It is the product of both nature and nurture. It is an evolved and genetically influenced set of skills that relies on specialized areas of the brain and mirror neurons and that will not emerge without normal neurological and cognitive growth. But its development also requires social experiences that involve learning and using a language to communicate and frequently talking about mental states with parents, siblings, peers, and other companions.

Implications

It is essential to master theory-of-mind skills if we want to participate in the social world. Children who have mastered these skills well generally can think more maturely about moral issues and other social problems, and they tend to have more advanced social skills and better social adjustment than those who have not (Doherty, 2009; Miller, 2012; Repacholi et al., 2003). However, theory-of-mind skills can be used for good or bad ends. Bullies and liars often prove to be very adept at "mind reading" too (Repacholi et al., 2003; Talwar & Lee, 2008). And training 3-year-olds

● **Table 13.1** Milestones in the Development of Theory of Mind

Age	Achievements
Birth to 2	Joint attention, understanding of intentions, pretend play, imitation, emotional understanding
Age 2	Desire psychology
Age 4	Belief–desire psychology
Age 5 and beyond	Understanding of second-order beliefs, sarcasm, different views of reality

in theory-of-mind skills actually makes them more likely than untrained children to lie when they are given the opportunity to deceive someone (Ding et al., 2015). So, developing a theory of mind is an important ingredient of social competence, but there is no guarantee that good "mind readers" will be socially well-adjusted or will behave in moral ways.

Trait Perception

Although research on theory of mind shows that even infants and preschool children are budding psychologists, they still have a way to go to understand people in terms of their enduring personality traits and to predict how others will react and behave. Consider how children of different ages describe people they know—parents, friends, disliked classmates, and so on.

As you discovered in Chapter 11, children younger than 7 or 8 describe themselves primarily in physical rather than psychological terms. They describe other people that way, too (Livesley & Bromley, 1973; Yuill, 1993). Thus, 4-year-old Evan says of his father, "He has one nose, one Mom, two eyes, brown hair." And 5-year-old Keisha says, "My daddy is big. He has hairy legs and eats mustard. Yuck! My daddy likes dogs—do you?" Not much of a personality profile there.

Young children perceive others primarily in terms of their physical appearance, possessions, and activities. When they use psychological terms, the terms are often global, evaluative ones such as "nice" or "mean," "good" or "bad," rather than specific personality-trait labels (Ruble & Dweck, 1995). Moreover, preschool children do not yet seem to understand traits as enduring qualities that predict how a person will behave in the future and explain why a person behaves as he does. The 5-year-old who describes a friend as "dumb" may be using this trait label only to describe that friend's recent "dumb" behavior; she may expect "smart" behavior tomorrow and may not view "dumbness" as the cause of the recent dumb behavior. Preschool children have difficulty inferring a trait from past behavior *and* using it to predict future behavior (Liu, Gelman, & Wellman, 2007).

Around age 7 or 8, children's descriptions of people show that they think about others in terms of their enduring psychological traits. Thus, 10-year-old Juanita describes her friend Tonya: "She's funny and friendly to everyone, and she's in the gifted program because she's smart, but sometimes she's very bossy." As children reach age 11 or 12, they also make more use of psychological traits to explain why people behave as they do, saying, for instance, that Mike pulled the dog's tail *because* he is cruel (Gnepp &

Chilamkurti, 1988). Clearly, then, children become more psychologically minded as their emerging social cognitive abilities permit them to make inferences about enduring inner qualities from people's behavior.

When asked to describe people they know, adolescents offer personality profiles that are even more psychological than those provided by children (Livesley & Bromley, 1973). They see people as unique individuals with distinctive personality traits, interests, values, and feelings. Moreover, they are able to create more integrated personality profiles, analyzing how an individual's often inconsistent traits fit together and make sense as a whole personality—for example, how a friend's insecurity could lead her to brag at times but seem very unsure of herself at other times. Some adolescents spend hours "psychoanalyzing" people, trying to figure out what makes them tick.

In sum, characterizations of other people progress from (1) physical descriptions and global evaluations during the preschool years to (2) more differentiated descriptions that refer to inner and enduring personality traits starting at age 7 or 8 and, finally, to (3) more integrated personality profiles during adolescence that show how even seemingly inconsistent traits fit together.

Perspective Taking

Another important aspect of social cognitive development involves outgrowing the egocentrism of early childhood and developing **perspective-taking skills**, also called role-taking skills: the ability to adopt another person's perspective and understand her thoughts and feelings. Perspective-taking skills are critical in thinking about moral issues from different points of view, predicting the consequences of a person's actions for others, and empathizing with others (Gibbs, 2010). If the campers at the start of the chapter had taken Edward's perspective, perhaps they would have laid off him.

Robert Selman (1976, 1980; Yeates & Selman, 1989) contributed greatly to our understanding of role-taking abilities by asking children questions about interpersonal dilemmas like this one (Selman, 1976, p. 302):

> Holly is an 8-year-old girl who likes to climb trees. She is the best tree climber in the neighborhood. One day while climbing down from a tall tree, she falls . . . but does not hurt herself. Her father sees her fall. He is upset and asks her to promise not to climb trees anymore. Holly promises.
>
> Later that day, Holly and her friends meet Shawn. Shawn's kitten is caught in a tree and can't get down. Something has to be done right away or the kitten may fall. Holly is the only one who climbs trees well enough to reach the kitten and get it down but she remembers her promise to her father.

Selman asked children questions to assess how well they understand the perspectives of Holly, her father, and Shawn. He concluded that perspective-taking abilities develop in a stagelike manner as children progress through Piaget's stages of cognitive development. Here are highlights of this progression:

- Children 3–6 years old tend to respond egocentrically, assuming that others share their point of view. If young children like

Adolescents who have limited role-taking, or social perspective-taking, skills are less able than those who have advanced skills to resolve conflicts with their parents (Selman et al., 1986). They may not adopt the perspectives of their parents (and parents in general) in order to identify mutually acceptable solutions.

Gpointstudio/Dreamstime.com

kittens, for example, they assume that Holly's father does, too, and therefore will be delighted if Holly saves the kitten.

- By age 8–10, children appreciate that two people can have different points of view even when they have access to the same information. Children are able to think about their own thoughts and about the thoughts of another person. Thus, they can appreciate that Holly may think about her father's concern for her safety but also believe that he will understand her reasons for climbing the tree.

- At around age 12, adolescents become capable of mentally juggling multiple perspectives—their own, that of another person, and even that of the "generalized other," or a broader social group such as children or fathers. Thus, an adolescent might consider how fathers in general react when children disobey them and consider whether Holly's father is similar to or different from the typical father.

Children and adolescents with advanced perspective-taking skills are likely to be sociable and popular and enjoy good relationships with peers (Kurdek & Krile, 1982; LeMare & Rubin, 1987). They are also better able than children with less advanced skills to resolve conflicts with parents and peers (Selman et al., 1986).

Social Cognition in Adulthood

As you saw in earlier chapters, nonsocial cognitive abilities, such as those used in solving scientific problems, tend to improve during early and middle adulthood and decline in later life. Do social cognitive skills also increase to a peak in middle age and decline later?

Overall, social cognitive skills seem to hold up better during adulthood than nonsocial cognitive skills (Blanchard-Fields, 1996; Hess, 1999). For example, Fredda Blanchard-Fields (1986)

Close social relationships and frequent social interactions keep social cognitive skills sharp in later life.

CREATISTA/Shutterstock.com

presented adolescents, young adults, and middle-aged adults with dilemmas that required them to engage in perspective taking and to integrate discrepant perspectives—for example, between a teenage boy and his parents regarding whether he must visit his grandparents with the family. Adults, especially middle-aged ones, were better able than adolescents to see both sides of the issues and to integrate the perspectives of both parties into a workable solution. Here, then, is evidence that social cognitive skills continue to improve after adolescence.

Do older adults continue to display the sophisticated social cognitive skills that middle-aged adults display or do their skills decline? Igor Grossmann and his colleagues (2010) asked young, middle-aged, and older American adults from diverse socioeconomic backgrounds to reason about conflicts between individuals that appeared in letters to advice columns and conflicts between ethnic or national groups as described in newspaper articles. Social cognitive performance improved across the three age groups, as indicated by such criteria as taking multiple perspectives and seeing possibilities for compromise. This improvement in social cognition with age occurred despite a decline in fluid intelligence with age. Growth with age was not evident in a sample of Japanese adults (Grossmann et al., 2012), but that was because Japanese young and middle-aged adults outperformed their American counterparts and achieved about the same level of performance as both Japanese and American elders. Possibly in Japan's collectivist society, then, people learn earlier in adulthood sophisticated ways of resolving social conflicts.

Yet other studies sometimes find that older adults perform less well than middle-aged and young adults on social cognitive tasks. For example, they sometimes have a harder time understanding sarcasm and passing adult versions of theory-of-mind tasks (Henry et al., 2013; Phillips et al., 2015). This is especially likely if tasks overload their basic cognitive capacities by requiring fast information processing or high levels of executive control (Charlton et al., 2009; Moran, 2013; Sullivan & Ruffman, 2004).

So, declines in basic cognitive capacities such as processing speed sometimes take a toll on social cognitive performance, but social cognitive skills hold up fairly well—better than nonsocial cognitive abilities—in later life. This may be because people use their social cognitive abilities every day and accumulate expertise about the world of people over the years (Charlton et al., 2009; Hess & Queen, 2014). Those seniors who have the sharpest social cognitive skills tend to be socially active and involved in meaningful social roles such as spouse, grandparent, church member, and worker (Dolen & Bearison, 1982; Hess et al., 2005). Moreover, a few hours of training can also help older adults brush up on their social cognitive skills (Rosi et al., 2016).

In sum, social cognition takes shape in infancy through precursors of a theory of mind such as joint attention and pretend play; a desire psychology at age 2; and then a belief–desire psychology at age 4, thanks to both nature and nurture. Children's descriptions of other people progress from a focus on physical appearance and activities to a focus on inner psychological traits to the integration of trait descriptions, and perspective-taking skills improve with age. Social cognitive skills then often improve during early and middle adulthood and hold up well in old age if tasks are not too cognitively demanding and adults remain socially engaged.

Having examined some important and dramatic changes in social cognition over the life span, we are well positioned to focus on an important area of development in which social cognitive skills play a crucial role: moral development. Along the way, we will see how theory-of-mind and perspective-taking skills help shape thinking about right and wrong.

Checking Mastery

1. Sharon wonders if Baby Ben, age 18 months, is on his way to developing a theory of mind. What three developments in infancy can you point to as early signs of a developing theory of mind?

2. If you were trying to make sure a deaf child, Luis, develops a theory of mind, what kinds of experiences would you try to provide him?

3. What breakthrough in perspective-taking skills is achieved at about age 8–10 according to Robert Selman?

Making Connections

1. Eavesdrop on a conversation in which your friends gossip or talk about other people, and write down any statements in which they refer to beliefs, desires, intentions, emotions, and the like in attempting to account for someone's behavior. What evidence do you see that your friends have and use a theory of mind?

2. For whatever reasons, Alice has very poor theory-of-mind, trait-perception, and perspective-taking skills. How would each of these limitations affect her social relationships?

13.2

Perspectives on Moral Development

LEARNING OBJECTIVES

- Define and illustrate the three main components of morality.

- Compare and contrast the main messages about moral development of psychoanalytic, cognitive-developmental, social learning, and evolutionary theorists.

- Distinguish between Kohlberg's preconventional, conventional, and postconventional levels of moral reasoning.

Although we could debate endlessly what **morality** is, most of us might agree that it involves the ability to distinguish right from wrong, to act on this distinction, and to experience emotions such as pride when we do the right things and guilt or shame when we do not. Accordingly, three basic components of morality have been of interest to developmental scientists (see Gibbs, 2014; Vozzola, 2014):

1. The *emotional* component consists of the feelings (guilt, concern for others' feelings, and so on) that surround right or wrong actions and that motivate moral thoughts and actions.
2. The *cognitive* component centers on how we think about right and wrong and make decisions about how to behave, drawing on social cognitive skills such as perspective taking.
3. The *behavioral* component is about how we behave when, for example, we experience the temptation to cheat or are called upon to help a person in need.

Major theoretical perspectives on moral development focus on different aspects of morality. So in this section we look at what psychoanalytic theory says about moral emotions, what cognitive-developmental theory says about moral cognition or reasoning, and what social learning (or social cognitive) theory reveals about moral behavior. Then we view all three components of morality from a broad, evolutionary perspective.

Moral Emotion: Psychoanalytic Theory and Beyond

What kind of moral emotions do you experience if you contemplate cheating or lying? Chances are you experience such negative feelings as shame, guilt, anxiety, and fear of being detected—feelings that keep you from doing what you know is wrong. You may also experience disgust or righteous anger when witnessing harmful acts and injustices (Tangney, Stuewig, & Mashek, 2007). Positive emotions, such as pride and self-satisfaction when you have done the right thing and admiration or gratitude when you witness moral acts, are also important moral emotions (Turiel, 2006). We are generally motivated to avoid negative moral emotions and to experience positive ones by acting in moral ways.

Sigmund Freud's (1960) psychoanalytic theory called attention to the role of emotions in the development of morality (see Chapter 2). As you will recall, Freud believed that the *superego*, or conscience, has the important task of ensuring that any plans formed by the rational ego to gratify the id's selfish urges are morally acceptable. The superego is formed during the phallic stage of psychosexual development (ages 3–6). According to Freud, children experience an emotional conflict over their love for the other-sex parent and resolve it by identifying with the same-sex parent, taking on the parent's moral standards as their own. Having a superego, then, is like having a parent inside your head—there, even when your parent is not, to tell you what is right or wrong and to arouse emotions such as shame and guilt if you so much as think about doing wrong.

Although the particulars of Freud's theory of moral development lack support (Hoffman, 2000; Silverman, 2003), his main themes are taken very seriously today. Research has shown that: (1) moral emotions are an important part of morality, motivating moral behavior, (2) early relationships with parents contribute in important ways to moral development, and (3) children must internalize moral standards if they are to behave morally even when no authority figure is present to detect and punish their misbehavior (Kochanska & Aksan, 2006).

Empathy is the vicarious experiencing of another person's feelings. Although it is not a specific emotion, it is an emotional process believed to be especially important in moral development by modern theorists such as Martin Hoffman (2000, 2008), whom we will encounter later. Empathizing with individuals who are suffering—not only taking their perspective but feeling their pain—can motivate **prosocial behavior**—positive social acts, such as helping or sharing, that reflect

Young children learn to experience moral emotions such as guilt and shame when they violate rules.

iStockphoto.com/Kali9

concern for the welfare of others. Empathy can also keep us from engaging in **antisocial behavior**—behavior that violates social norms, rules, or laws and often involves harming other people or society (for example, lying, stealing, behaving aggressively). If the campers in the chapter opener had really empathized with Edward's distress, they might have refrained from picking on him. As we will see later, modern theorists such as Martin Hoffman (2000) and Grazyna Kochanska (1993, 2002), like Freud, place a great deal of emphasis on the motivating role of emotional processes such as empathy and guilt in moral development.

Moral Reasoning: Cognitive-Developmental Theory

Cognitive-developmental theorists focus on the development of **moral reasoning**—the thinking process involved in deciding whether an act is right or wrong. These theorists assume that moral development depends on social cognitive development, particularly perspective-taking skills that allow us to picture how our victims might react to our misdeeds or how people in distress must feel. Moral reasoning is said to progress through universal stages, each of which represents a consistent way of thinking about moral issues. To cognitive-developmental theorists, what is of interest is *how* we decide what to do, not what we decide or what we actually do. A young child and an adult may both decide not to steal a pen, but the reasons they give for their decision may be entirely different.

Jean Piaget paved the way for the influential cognitive-developmental theory of moral development put forth by Lawrence Kohlberg. Piaget (1965) studied children's concepts of rules by asking Swiss children about their games of marbles and explored children's concepts of right and wrong by presenting them with moral dilemmas to ponder. He concluded that preschool children do not truly understand rules and are best thought of as "premoral." Children ages 6–10, he observed, emphasize consequences more than intentions in judging the wrongness of acts (for example, they judge a boy who accidentally broke 15 cups while obeying his mother naughtier than a boy who broke only one cup while trying to sneak jam from the kitchen). They also tend to believe that rules are handed down by parents and other authorities and are unalterable. At age 10 or 11, Piaget found, children weigh more heavily whether a person's intentions were good or bad in judging his actions. They also begin to appreciate that rules are agreements among individuals—agreements that can be changed through a consensus of those individuals.

Inspired by Piaget's pioneering work, Lawrence Kohlberg (1963, 1981, 1984; Colby & Kohlberg, 1987) formulated his own, highly influential cognitive-developmental theory of moral development by asking 10-, 13-, and 16-year-old boys questions about various moral dilemmas to assess how they thought about these issues. Kohlberg concluded that moral growth progresses through a universal and invariant sequence of three broad moral levels, each of which is composed of two distinct stages. Each stage represents a more complex way of thinking about moral issues.

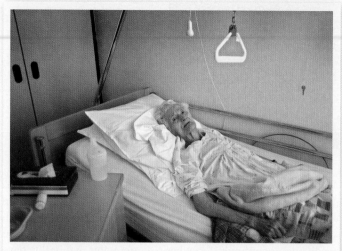

Moral dilemma: Do you think a doctor should give a pain-ridden and terminal patient a drug that would hasten her death if she asks for it? Amelie Van Esbeen, pictured in her bed in a home for the elderly in Belgium, thought so. The 93-year-old went on a hunger strike when her request for mercy killing was denied. She had already tried to commit suicide.

AFP/Stringer/Getty Images

Kohlberg's Stages of Moral Reasoning

Think about how you would respond to the following moral dilemma posed by Kohlberg and his colleagues (Colby et al., 1983, p. 79):

> There was a woman who had very bad cancer, and there was no treatment known to medicine that would save her. Her doctor, Dr. Jefferson, knew that she had only about 6 months to live. She was in terrible pain, but she was so weak that a good dose of a pain killer like ether or morphine would make her die sooner. She was delirious and almost crazy with pain, and in her calm periods she would ask Dr. Jefferson to give her enough ether to kill her. She said she couldn't stand the pain and she was going to die in a few months anyway. Although he knows that mercy killing is against the law, the doctor thinks about granting her request.

Should Dr. Jefferson give her the drug that would make her die? Why or why not? Should the woman have the right to make the final decision? Why or why not? These are among the questions that people are asked after hearing the dilemma. You may want to answer them for yourself before reading further so that you can then analyze your own moral thinking.

Remember, Kohlberg's goal is to understand the complexity of a person's reasoning, not whether he or she is for or against providing the woman with the drug. Individuals at each stage of moral reasoning might endorse either of the alternative courses of action, but for different reasons. Following are Kohlberg's three levels of moral reasoning, and the two stages within each level.

Level 1: Preconventional Morality At the level of **preconventional morality**, rules are external to the self rather than internalized. The child conforms to rules imposed by authority figures to avoid punishment or to obtain personal rewards. The perspective of the self dominates: What is right is what one can get away with or what is personally satisfying.

- **Stage 1: Punishment-and-Obedience Orientation.** The goodness or badness of an act depends on its consequences. The child will obey authorities to avoid punishment but may not consider an act wrong if it will not be punished. The greater the harm done or the more severe the punishment, the more "bad" the act is.
- **Stage 2: Instrumental Hedonism.** A person at the second stage of moral development conforms to rules to gain rewards or satisfy personal needs. There is some concern for the perspectives of others, but it is motivated by the hope of benefit in return. "You scratch my back and I'll scratch yours" and "an eye for an eye" are the guiding philosophies.

Level 2: Conventional Morality At the level of conventional morality, the individual has internalized many moral values. He shows respect for the rules set by others (parents, peers, the government), at first to win their approval, later to maintain social order. The perspectives of other people are clearly recognized and given serious consideration.

- **Stage 3: "Good Boy" or "Good Girl" Morality.** What is right is now what pleases, helps, or is approved by others. People are often judged by their intentions; "meaning well" is valued, and being "nice" is important. Other people's feelings, not just one's own, should be considered. At its best, Stage 3 thinking involves reciprocity, or mutual give-and-take in relationships, leading to a simple Golden Rule morality of doing unto someone else what you would want done unto you.
- **Stage 4: Authority and Social Order–Maintaining Morality.** Now what is right is what conforms to the rules of legitimate authorities and is good for society as a whole. The reason for conforming is not so much a fear of punishment as a belief that rules and laws maintain a social order worth preserving. Doing one's duty and respecting law and order are valued.

Level 3: Postconventional Morality At the final level of moral reasoning, postconventional morality, the individual defines what is right in terms of broad principles of justice that have validity apart from the views of particular authority figures. The individual may distinguish between what is morally right and what is legal, recognizing that some laws—for example, the racial segregation laws that Dr. Martin Luther King, Jr., challenged—violate basic moral principles or human rights. Thus, the person transcends the perspective of a particular social group or authority and begins to take the perspective of *all* individuals.

- **Stage 5: Morality of Contract, Individual Rights, and Democratically Accepted Law.** At this "social contract" stage, there is an understanding of the underlying purposes served by laws and a concern that rules should be arrived at through a democratic consensus so that they express the will of the majority and maximize social welfare. Whereas the person at Stage 4 is unlikely to challenge an established law, the moral reasoner at Stage 5 might call for democratic change in a law that compromises basic rights.

- **Stage 6: Morality of Individual Principles of Conscience.** At this "highest" stage of moral reasoning, the individual defines right and wrong on the basis of self-generated principles that are broad and universal in application. The Stage 6 thinker does not just make up whatever principles she chooses. She discovers, through reflection, abstract principles of respect for all individuals and their rights—principles that all religious and moral authorities would view as moral. Kohlberg (1981) described Stage 6 thinking as a kind of "moral musical chairs" in which the person facing a moral dilemma is able to take the "chair," or perspective, of each person and group and social system, present or future, that could potentially be affected by a decision and to arrive at a solution that would be regarded as just from every chair. Stage 6 is Kohlberg's vision of ideal moral reasoning, but it is so rarely observed that Kohlberg stopped attempting to measure its existence.

In ● Table 13.2, we present examples of how people at the preconventional, conventional, and postconventional levels might reason about the mercy-killing dilemma. As you can see, progress through Kohlberg's stages of moral reasoning is linked to the development of perspective-taking abilities. Specifically, as individuals become more able to consider perspectives other than their own, moral reasoning progresses from an egocentric focus on personal welfare at the preconventional level, to a concern with the perspectives of other people (parents, friends, and other members of society) at the conventional level, and to an ability to coordinate multiple perspectives and determine what is right from the perspective of all people at the postconventional level (Carpendale, 2000).

Influences on Moral Thinking

Whereas Freud emphasized the role of parents in moral development, Kohlberg, like Piaget before him, believed that the two main influences on moral development are cognitive growth and social interactions with peers. Regarding cognitive growth, reaching the conventional level of moral reasoning and becoming concerned about living up to the moral standards of parents and society requires perspective-taking skills, and gaining the capacity for postconventional moral reasoning requires still more cognitive growth—namely, a solid command of formal-operational thinking (Tomlinson-Keasey & Keasey, 1974; Walker, 1980).

The social interactions that count involve taking the perspectives of others and experiencing growth-promoting cognitive disequilibrium when one's own ideas conflict with those of other people. Piaget and Kohlberg both maintained that interactions with peers or equals, in which we must work out differences between our own and others' perspectives through negotiation, contribute more to moral growth than one-sided interactions with adult authority figures in which we are expected to bow to the adult's power. So, moral growth is facilitated by:

- discussions of moral issues with peers, especially when peers challenge our ideas;
- advanced schooling; going to college both contributes to cognitive growth and exposes students to diverse perspectives (Pratt et al., 1991); and
- participating in a complex, diverse, democratic society where people weigh various opinions and appreciate that laws reflect a consensus of the citizens.

Give the Drug	Do Not Give the Drug
Preconventional Morality	**Preconventional Morality**
Stage 1: The doctor should give the terminally ill woman a drug that will kill her because there is little chance that he will be found out and punished.	**Stage 1:** The doctor runs a big risk of losing his license and being thrown in prison if he gives her the drug.
Stage 2: He should give her the drug; he might benefit from the gratitude of her family if he does what she wants. He should think of it as the right thing to do if it serves his purposes to be for mercy killing.	**Stage 2:** He has little to gain by taking such a big chance. If the woman wants to kill herself, that is her business, but why should he help her if he stands to gain little in return?
Conventional Morality	**Conventional Morality**
Stage 3: Most people would understand that the doctor was motivated by concern for the woman's welfare rather than by self-interest. They would be able to forgive him for what was essentially an act of kindness.	**Stage 3:** Most people are likely to disapprove of mercy killing. The doctor would clearly lose the respect of his colleagues if he administered the drug. A good person simply would not do this.
Stage 4: The doctor should give the woman the drug because of the Hippocratic oath, which spells out a doctor's duty to relieve suffering. This oath is binding and should be taken seriously by all doctors.	**Stage 4:** Mercy killing with this drug is against the laws that doctors are obligated to uphold. The Bible is another compelling authority, and it says, "Thou shalt not kill." The doctor simply cannot take the law into his own hands; rather, he has a duty to uphold the law.
Postconventional Morality	**Postconventional Morality**
Stage 5: Although most of our laws have a sound basis in moral principle, laws against mercy killing do not. The doctor's act is morally justified because it relieves the suffering of an agonized human without harming other people. Yet if he breaks the law in the service of a greater good, he should still be willing to be held legally accountable; society would be damaged if everyone simply ignored laws they do not agree with.	**Stage 5:** The laws against mercy killing protect citizens from harm at the hands of unscrupulous doctors and selfish relatives and should be upheld because they serve a positive function for society. If the laws were to be changed through the democratic process, that might be another thing, but right now the doctor can do the most good for society by adhering to them.
Stage 6: We must consider the effects of this act on everyone concerned—the doctor, the dying woman, other terminally ill people, and all people everywhere. Basic moral principle dictates that all people have a right to dignity and self-determination as long as others are not harmed by their decisions. Assuming that no one else will be hurt, then, the dying woman has a right to live and die as she chooses. The doctor may be doing right if he respects her integrity as a person and saves her, her family, and all of society from needless suffering.	**Stage 6:** If we truly adhere to the principle that human life should be valued above all else and all lives should be valued equally, it is morally wrong to "play God" and decide that some lives are worth living and others are not. Before long, we would have a world in which no life has value.

So, Kohlberg maintained that progress from preconventional to conventional to postconventional moral reasoning is most likely to occur if the individual has acquired the necessary cognitive skills (perspective-taking skills and, later, formal-operational thinking) and has growth-inducing social interactions, especially discussions with peers, advanced education, and participation in democratic governance.

Moral Behavior: Social Learning Theory

Social learning theorists such as Albert Bandura (1991, 2002, 2015), whose social cognitive theory was introduced in Chapter 2, have been primarily interested in the behavioral component of morality—in what we actually do when faced with temptation or with an opportunity to behave prosocially. These theorists say that moral behavior is learned in the same way that other social behaviors are learned: through observational learning and reinforcement and punishment principles. They also emphasize situational influences on moral behavior—for example, how closely a professor watches exam takers, whether jewelry items are on the counter or behind glass in a department store. Due to situational influences, what we do is not always consistent with our moral values and standards.

Applying his social cognitive perspective, Bandura went on to emphasize that moral cognition is linked to moral action through *self-regulatory mechanisms* that involve monitoring and evaluating our own actions (or anticipated actions), disapproving of ourselves when we contemplate doing wrong, and approving of ourselves when we behave responsibly or humanely. By applying consequences to ourselves in this way, we become able to exert self-control, inhibit urges to misbehave, and keep our behavior in line with internalized standards of moral behavior.

Sometimes this system of moral self-regulation can triumph over strong situational influences pushing us to do wrong.

Did you ever cheat on a test in high school? In one survey of high school students across the United States, 64% admitted to cheating in the past year, more than in earlier surveys; yet 93% said that they were satisfied with their "personal ethics and character" (Crary, 2008). Most college students also admit to cheating, sometimes justifying it by saying that "anything goes" in the pursuit of achievement goals (Pulfrey & Butera, 2013). Why do you think cheating is so rampant today? Is it pressure to succeed? Peer influence? Albert Bandura's concept of moral disengagement?

Yellow Dog Productions/The Image Bank/Getty Images

However, according to Bandura we have also devised mechanisms of **moral disengagement** that allow us to avoid condemning ourselves when we engage in immoral behavior, even though we know the difference between right and wrong (Bandura, 2015). For example, a store clerk who feels underpaid and mistreated by his employer may convince himself that he is justified in pilfering items from the store, or citizens may disengage morally from the use of military force by their country by dehumanizing their foes as "animals" or by calling the civilians who are accidentally killed during bombing raids "collateral damage." Most of us learn moral standards, but some people hold themselves strictly to those standards while others find ways to disengage morally and slither out from under guilt. Those of us who have perfected techniques of moral disengagement engage in more antisocial and unethical

behavior than other people (Detert, Treviño, & Sweitzer, 2008; Gini, Pozzoli, & Bussey, 2015; Paciello et al., 2008).

Foundations of Morality: Evolutionary Theory

Finally, evolutionary theorists such as Dennis Krebs, Michael Tomasello, and others argue that all three aspects of morality (moral emotion, thought, and behavior) have become part of our human nature because they helped humans adapt to their environments over the course of evolution (see Buss, 2012; Jensen & Silk, 2014; Krebs, 2008, 2011; Tomasello, 2009; Tomasello & Vaish, 2013). Just as having a theory of mind helps humans get along with others and adapt to living in groups, prosocial behaviors such as cooperation and altruism may have evolved because our ancestors were better able to obtain food and protect themselves from harm if they worked together than if they went it alone and pursued their selfish interests (Krebs, 2011). Mechanisms for controlling and inhibiting selfish, antisocial behavior such as rules and laws against theft and assault may also have proved adaptive. To evolutionary theorists, then, morality and prosocial behavior are rooted in human nature. Unfortunately, so are immorality and antisocial behavior (Krebs, 2011).

How could humans have evolved to have altruistic tendencies when altruists, who sacrifice their lives for others, die rather than pass on their genes? Evolutionary theorists have argued that it can be in our genetic self-interest to act altruistically toward kin because they will pass on the family's genes if we help them survive (Verbeek, 2006). Even helping nonrelatives may be adaptive if we have reason to believe that the help we give will be reciprocated. Similarly, cooperating with other people to obtain resources that the individual could not obtain alone, abiding by society's rules in order to avoid punishment, and punishing people who *do* violate society's rules all make good genetic sense (Krebs, 2008). So, whereas Freud emphasized the dark, selfish, and aggressive side of human nature, and social learning theorists have seen us as blank slates who can be molded in a variety of directions, evolutionary theorists argue that humans have an evolved genetic makeup that predisposes them not only to behave antisocially at times but also to behave prosocially and morally in many situations.

Indeed, humans may be a uniquely prosocial species. Michael Tomasello has concluded that what makes us different from chimpanzees and other great apes is our ability to collaborate and cooperate with others (Tomasello, 2009; Tomasello & Herrmann, 2010; Tomasello & Vaish, 2013). Primates are quite good at figuring out others' goals and intentions but their social cognitive skills likely evolved in competitive situations where they could get food, mates, and other resources by outwitting their rivals. To not only understand others' intentions but to be able to *share* intentions with others in order to pursue common goals—that's what Tomasello believes distinguishes the human species.

To highlight differences among the four theoretical perspectives on moral development we have discussed, ● **Table 13.3** compares them and shows how different theorists might try to predict whether a college student (call him Bart) will cheat on his upcoming math test.

We are now ready to trace the development of morality, and aspects of prosocial and antisocial behavior, from infancy to old age, considering moral emotion, cognition, and behavior as we go.

Perspective/ Theorists	Focus	Message	Predicting Behavior (Will Bart cheat on his math test?)
Psychoanalytic theory (Freud)	Moral emotion	Early parenting and emotional conflicts forge the superego and guilt.	Did Bart develop a strong superego (conscience) and sense of guilt in his preschool years?
Cognitive-developmental theory (Piaget, Kohlberg)	Moral reasoning	Cognitive maturation and interaction with peers bring stagelike changes in thinking about moral issues.	At what stage is Bart's reasoning about moral dilemmas?
Social learning theory (Bandura)	Moral behavior	Observational learning, reinforcement, self-regulation processes, moral disengagement, and situational influences affect what we do.	Did Bart's parents model and reinforce moral behavior and punish misbehavior? Do well-developed self-regulatory mechanisms cause Bart to take responsibility for his actions rather than disengage morally? Do situational forces in the class discourage or encourage cheating?
Evolutionary theory (Krebs, Tomasello)	Moral emotion, reasoning, and behavior	Humans have evolved not only to be aggressive on occasion but to have moral and prosocial tendencies that equip them to live cooperatively in groups.	Does cheating, or refraining from cheating, serve adaptive functions for Bart and his social group? Might he cheat in the interest of cooperating with friends? Does the classroom environment encourage or discourage cheating?

● Checking Mastery

1. What are the three major components of morality, and what is one theory of moral development that emphasizes each?
2. What is the main difference between conventional and pre-conventional moral reasoning about why stealing is wrong?
3. How do evolutionary theorists differ from Freud in their view of human nature?

● Making Connections

1. A preconventional thinker, a conventional thinker, and a postconventional thinker all face a moral dilemma the night before the final exam: A friend has offered them a key to the test. Should they use it? Provide examples of the reasoning you might expect at each of Kohlberg's three main levels of moral development—one argument in favor of cheating and one against it at each level. Are any of these arguments especially easy or difficult to make? Why?
2. Jamal decides to become a kidney donor and live the rest of his life with only one kidney so that his brother Malcolm can live. How do you think Freud, Kohlberg, Bandura, and Krebs would explain his altruistic action?

13.3 The Infant

LEARNING OBJECTIVES

*   Summarize evidence that infants are capable of empathy and prosocial behavior.
*   Describe antisocial behavior in infancy and how it differs from that of older children.
*   Explain how parents can help their infants develop a conscience.

Do infants have a sense of right or wrong? If an infant bashes another child on the head with a sippy cup, would you insist that the infant be put on trial for assault? Of course not. We tend to view infants as amoral—lacking any sense of morality. We do not believe that infants are capable of evaluating their behavior in relation to moral standards, and so we do not hold them responsible for wrongs they commit (although we certainly attempt to prevent them from harming others). Nor do we expect them to be "good" when we are not around to watch them. Yet we learn a lot about human nature from infant behavior. It is now clear that infants are not as amoral as we thought. Nor are they as selfish and in need of proper socialization as Freud and others have claimed. Although infants do indeed have a capacity for selfishness and aggression, they are at the same time predisposed to be empathic, prosocial beings (Bloom, 2013; Hamlin, 2013). They also learn many important moral lessons during their first 2 years of life and develop a conscience.

Empathy, Prosocial Behavior, and Morality

Infants are not as selfish, egocentric, and unconcerned about other people as Freud, Piaget, Kohlberg, and many other theorists have assumed. Rather, some of their behavior supports the view of evolutionary theorists such as Michael Tomasello that empathy and prosocial behavior are part of our evolutionary heritage.

Start at birth: Even newborns display a primitive form of empathy, becoming distressed by the cries of other newborns (Eisenberg, Spinrad, & Knafo-Noam, 2015; Hastings, Zahn-Waxler, & McShane, 2006). It is unclear whether these very young infants are experiencing empathy for another or are simply distressed by crying sounds, however. From age 1 to age 2, according to Martin Hoffman (2000, 2008), infants become capable of a truer form of empathy that motivates helping and other forms of moral behavior. Toddlers begin to understand that someone else's distress is different from their own, and they try to comfort the person in distress. So, for example, a 10-month-old watching a peer cry looked sad and buried her head in her mother's lap, as she often did when she herself was distressed. A 2-year-old, though, brought his own teddy bear to comfort a distressed friend and, when that failed, offered the friend's teddy instead, showing an ability to take the perspective of the friend (Hoffman, 2000). As children get older, according to Hoffman, empathy becomes more sophisticated as cognitive processes, including the child's developing perspective-taking skills, shape empathy into a variety of moral emotions such as guilt, sympathy, and eventually a sense of injustice (see also Eisenberg et al., 2015; Gibbs, 2014).

How prosocial are infants and toddlers? Some years ago, Carolyn Zahn-Waxler and her colleagues (1992) reported that more than half of the 13- to 15-month-old infants they observed engaged in at least one act of prosocial behavior—helping, sharing, expressing concern, comforting, and so on. These behaviors became increasingly common from age 1 to age 2, when all but one child in the study acted prosocially. More recently, Michael Tomasello and other researchers have been documenting just how prosocial and morally sophisticated infants and toddlers are:

- **Helping.** As early as 14 months, infants will spontaneously—without being asked—help an adult who drops a clothes pin on the floor while trying to hang items on a clothesline, who is carrying an armful of papers and cannot open a cabinet door, or who otherwise needs help to achieve a goal (Warneken & Tomasello, 2007). This early spontaneous helping has been observed in cultures as diverse as Canada, India, and Peru (Callaghan et al., 2011).
- **Cooperation.** As early as 14 months, infants can also participate in simple cooperative games and will even try to get their adult partner reengaged if she stops playing, suggesting that they understand that they and their partner had a shared goal while they were cooperating (Warneken & Tomasello, 2007).
- **Altruistic rather than selfish motivations.** Before they are 2, children show greater happiness when they give treats like Goldfish crackers to an appreciative puppet than when they receive them, especially when they altruistically give up their own treats (Aknin, Hamlin, & Dunn, 2012). They find prosocial behavior intrinsically rewarding (Hepach, Vaish, & Tomasello, 2012).

Before they are age 2, toddlers show evidence of a moral sense when they attempt to comfort distressed peers.

altrendo images/Altrendo /Getty Images

- **A sense of fairness.** At 15 months of age, infants are more surprised (look longer) when they see one actor given three crackers and another given one than when the actors get two apiece, suggesting that they recognize fairness and unfairness when they see it (Schmidt & Sommerville, 2011; and see ■ Figure 13.2). Yet despite their preference for dividing rewards equally if two actors both clean up their toys, infants are surprised and look longer when a hard worker and a loafer are rewarded equally than when the hard worker gets more (Sloane, Baillargeon, & Premack, 2012).
- **Moral judgments.** As noted earlier, infants much prefer to interact with a "helper" puppet who aids another puppet in achieving a goal than with a "hinderer" puppet who blocks another puppet from achieving a goal (see Hamlin, 2013). And despite their positive view of helping, they seem to think it is quite appropriate to punish a "hinderer" by taking things away from him (Hamlin et al., 2011). In short, babies distinguish between and have quite different feelings about good guys and bad guys!

Antisocial Behavior

If prosocial tendencies are so evident by a year or two of age, when do antisocial tendencies first show themselves? Physical aggression, behavior that harms another person physically, comes naturally to humans, starting as soon as babies are able to hit, bite, push, or otherwise harm others (Tremblay, 2011). And verbal aggression begins almost as soon as infants utter their first words. Antisocial behavior therefore seems to be as much a part of human nature as empathy and prosocial behavior are. Infants are less likely than older children to intend to cause harm, however.

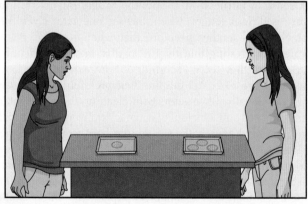

■ **Figure 13.2** When 15-month-olds are shown two girls asking for crackers and then see a screen lifted to reveal either a fair, equal distribution (two crackers to each) or an unfair distribution (one cracker to one girl, three to the other), which do they look at longer? The unfair distribution surprises them, suggesting that they already have an intuitive sense of fairness.

Source: Adapted from Schmidt, M. F. H., & Sommerville, J. A. (2011). Fairness expectations and altruistic sharing in 15-month-old human infants. *PloS ONE, 6, e23223.* Figure 1.

Most often their goal is to get a toy they want or to defend a toy they had played with and put down (Hay, Hurst, et al., 2011; Tremblay, 2011). As they develop better self-control, they will become more able to delay gratification and wait for the toy.

As early as 1½ years of age, some toddlers engage in more physical aggression than others, though (Tremblay, 2011). Their high rates of aggressive behavior can be traced to both their genetic

makeup and environmental factors such as harsh, coercive parenting or a depressed, emotionally unavailable parent (Dionne et al., 2003; Hay, Mundy, et al., 2011; Tremblay, 2011). Their peers, meanwhile, are learning to control their aggressive urges better. The frequency of aggression normally rises from infancy to a peak around age 3 and then decreases with age as verbal skills, social skills, and self-control skills improve (Eisner & Malti, 2015; Tremblay, 2011).

Early Moral Training

Part of the reason for increased prosocial and decreased antisocial tendencies as infants become children is moral socialization. Drawing on learning principles, parents and others reinforce toddlers for helpful actions such as putting toys away and chastise or otherwise punish them for wrongdoings. Through such learning experiences, infants and toddlers come to understand and internalize simple moral rules and standards such as "Don't hit," "Don't steal," and "Share." They see that their actions have consequences, some good, some bad. Parents can help foster early moral development by discussing their toddlers' behavior and its good or bad effects on the toddler and other people (Dunn, 2014; Thompson, Meyer, & McGinley, 2006; Thompson, 2012).

Grazyna Kochanska has studied the development of a conscience in toddlerhood and believes it involves mastering: (1) moral emotions—learning to associate negative emotions like guilt with violating rules, and learning to empathize with people who are in distress, and (2) self-control—becoming able to inhibit one's impulses when tempted to violate internalized rules (Kochanska, 1993, 2002).

By 18–24 months, children are already beginning to show visible signs of distress when they break things, spill their drinks, or otherwise violate standards of behavior (Cole, Barrett, & Zahn-Waxler, 1992; Kagan, 1981). Made to think that they have caused a doll's head to fall off, some toddlers even show signs of guilt, as opposed to mere distress, making frantic attempts to repair the doll or otherwise make amends (Kochanska, Casey, & Fukumoto, 1995). Self-control also becomes more evident by age 2, as when toddlers comply with a parent's request not to play with certain toys even after the parent leaves the room (Aksan & Kochanska, 2005). In **Exploration 13.1**, we see just how important **self-control**—the ability to regulate one's desires, impulses, and behavior—is in many aspects of life-span development.

How can parents help children develop moral emotions, self-control, and thus a strong conscience? Kochanska and her colleagues have found that forming a secure parent–infant attachment is the best way to get moral socialization off to a good start (Kochanska, Barry, Stellern, & O'Bleness, 2009). Then it is important for caregiver and child to establish a **mutually responsive orientation**—a close, emotionally positive, and cooperative relationship in which child and caregiver care about each other and are sensitive to each other's needs (Kochanska & Aksan, 2006). Parents who are responsive to their infants are likely to raise children who are responsive to them. A mutually responsive orientation makes children trust their caregivers and want to comply with their rules and adopt their

Marshmallows and the Life-Span Significance of Self-Control

imageBROKER/Alamy Stock Photo

Whether you call it the aspect of temperament called effortful control, the dimension of personality called conscientiousness, self-control, executive control, or even willpower, it is a good thing to have. Nowhere is this better illustrated than in the famous marshmallow study conducted by social learning theorist Walter Mischel in the 1960s (Mischel, Shoda, & Peake, 1988; Mischel, 2014). The experimenter gave 4- to 5-year-olds a choice: Eat the marshmallow I am giving you now, or get a second marshmallow if you wait until I return (in 15–20 minutes). How many children do you think waited?

Apparently marshmallows are irresistible to 4-year-olds: Only about 30% of the children passed this **delay of gratification** task and were able to wait for the more desirable two-marshmallow reward later. Most children gave in to their desire to eat the marshmallow in less than 3 minutes. (Search for "marshmallow test" on the Internet and you'll find entertaining film clips from this famous study.)

But the most fascinating finding of the research was revealed when the children were followed up as adolescents and then as adults. As adolescents, the children who delayed gratification were judged by their parents to be more academically and socially competent, more responsible, and more able to cope with stress; they even scored significantly higher on the SAT exam than their peers who gave in to temptation (Mischel et al., 1988; Shoda, Mischel, & Peake, 1990). As adults, these more self-controlled individuals also had fewer drug problems and lower body mass indexes (Casey et al., 2011; Mischel et al., 2011). Measuring children's self-control, not with tempting marshmallows but through behavioral observations and parent-, teacher-, and child-reports of behavior, Terri Moffitt and her colleagues (2011) obtained similar results: Childhood self-control predicted becoming an adolescent who stayed in school and avoided delinquent behavior—and later a 30-year-old with good physical health and financial stability who avoided substance dependence and criminal activity. So, whether self-control shows itself in

being able to wait for that second yummy marshmallow, keeping at your studies while your friends party, staying on your diet, saving money, or resisting the temptation to do wrong, it is a very important life skill.

Yet you should not conclude that self-control is a genetically based trait that we either have or do not have for life. Mischel and others have shown that children can be taught strategies of self-control—for example, distracting themselves by singing songs or covering their eyes. And in an interesting demonstration of how environmental influences may affect self-control, Kidd, Palmeri, and Aslin (2013) told 4-year-olds that if they waited, the experimenter would bring them better art supplies than the lousy ones they had been given. The catch was that in the "reliable" condition, she delivered the new supplies, whereas in the "unreliable" condition she confessed that she did not have any better art supplies after all. When they were then given the marshmallow test, the children in the reliable condition waited an average of 12 minutes for two marshmallows, but the children in the unreliable condition waited only 3 minutes. Moreover, Melissa Sturge-Apple and her colleagues (2016) have shown that a physiological indicator of self-control that is associated with longer delay of gratification among high SES children predicts *shorter* delay of gratification among poor children. Perhaps, then, regardless of their temperamental traits, children living in poverty learn through experience an adaptive strategy: Gobble any marshmallows that come your way right away rather than wait for bigger rewards that may or may not come tomorrow.

values and standards. These children then learn moral emotions such as guilt and empathy and develop the self-control needed to resist temptation even when no one is around to catch them.

In sum, moral development builds on a base of empathy and prosocial behavior that strengthens with age as physical aggression

is brought under better control. By establishing a secure attachment and a mutually responsive orientation and by discussing the emotional consequences of the child's behavior, parents help infants and toddlers develop a conscience (Emde et al., 1991; Thompson et al., 2006).

1. According to Martin Hoffman, when is empathy first evident in infancy and how does it change thereafter?
2. When one infant pushes another, what is usually the motive?
3. What is Grazyna Kochanska's main message to parents who want their infants to develop a conscience?

1. Philosopher John Locke and learning theorists like B. F. Skinner have viewed human beings as "blank slates" (tabulae rasae) who have no biologically based predispositions to be either antisocial or prosocial. Thinking about evolutionary theory and research on infant social behavior, what arguments can you give for and against the blank slate position?
2. Given what you have learned about moral socialization in infancy, do you think it is possible to raise a moral child without ever using physical punishment? Why or why not?

13.4
The Child

LEARNING OBJECTIVES
- Discuss key ways in which children are more morally sophisticated than Piaget and Kohlberg believed.
- Summarize an optimal approach to socializing morality in childhood.

Research on moral development during childhood has explored how children of different ages think about moral issues and how parents can raise moral children. This research shows that children's moral thinking is far more sophisticated than Piaget and Kohlberg believed and that parents can have a much bigger impact on their children's moral development than these two theorists believed.

Moral Understandings

The hypothetical moral dilemmas that Lawrence Kohlberg devised to assess stages of moral reasoning (for example, the mercy-killing dilemma presented in Section 13.2) were intended primarily for adolescents and adults; the youngest individuals Kohlberg studied were age 10. As a result, Kohlberg did not have much to say about children except that they are mostly preconventional moral reasoners. They take an egocentric perspective on morality and define as right those acts that are rewarded and as wrong those acts that are punished (Colby et al., 1983). At best, older school-age children are beginning to make the transition to conventional moral reasoning by internalizing authorities' rules and displaying a Stage 3 concern with being a good boy or a good girl who takes others' perspectives and is concerned with others' approval. However, both Piaget and Kohlberg seriously underestimated children. Having already seen that infants are well on their way to being moral beings, you will not be surprised to learn that children engage in some very sophisticated thinking about right and wrong.

Weighing Intentions

Both Piaget and Kohlberg believed that young children (indeed, children under 10) were primarily focused on the consequences of acts rather than the intentions behind them. However, it turns out that even 3-year-olds can take both intentions and consequences into account if presented with simple stories portrayed in drawings (Nelson, 1980). They judge a ball thrower less favorably when he hits his playmate in the head than when the playmate catches the ball, but they also judge a well-intentioned boy who had wanted to play ball more favorably than a boy who intended to hurt his friend—even when the friend caught the ball and was not harmed. Apparently, then, even young children can base their moral judgments on both a person's intentions and the consequences of his act. Sensitivity to good or bad intentions does increase as children get older, however (Lapsley, 2006).

Intentions are mental states, of course, and are therefore part of what children come to understand better as they develop a theory of mind. Indeed, children's moral thinking becomes more sophisticated once they have the basics of a theory of mind down at about age 4 (Killen et al., 2011; Lane et al., 2010). Children who have mastered theory-of-mind skills not only try to evade punishment by crying, "I didn't mean it!" but they are also:

- more forgiving than children lacking theory-of-mind skills of wrongs committed accidentally than of wrongs committed intentionally (Chandler, Sokol, & Wainryb, 2000; Fu et al., 2014; Killen et al., 2011);
- better able to distinguish between lying (deliberately promoting a false belief) and simply having one's facts wrong or exaggerating for the sake of a good story (Peterson & Siegal, 2002); and
- more attuned to other people's feelings and welfare when they think about the morality of snatching a friend's toy or calling a friend a bad name (Dunn, Cutting, & Demetriou, 2000).

In short, mastering the basics of a theory of mind at age 4 and refining theory-of-mind skills later put children in better position to interpret the motives behind and the consequences of people's actions. The development of moral judgment and theory of mind develop hand in hand and influence one another (Smetana, Jambon, et al., 2012).

Distinguishing among Rules

Piaget claimed that 6- to 10-year-old children view *all* rules as sacred prescriptions laid down by authority figures that cannot be questioned or changed. However, Elliot Turiel (1978, 1983, 2006), Judith Smetana (Smetana, Jambon, & Ball, 2014), and others have discovered that children distinguish between different kinds of rules. Most importantly, they distinguish between **moral rules**, or standards that focus on the welfare and basic rights of others, and **social–conventional rules**, standards determined by social consensus that tell us what is appropriate in particular social settings. Moral rules include rules against hitting, stealing, lying, and otherwise harming others or violating their rights. Social-conventional rules are more like rules of social etiquette; they include the rules of games, school rules that forbid eating snacks in class or going to the restroom without permission, and parent rules that require saying "Please" and "Thank you."

From their preschool years, children understand that moral rules are more compelling and unalterable than social-conventional rules (Smetana, 2006; Turiel, 2006). Judith Smetana (1981; Smetana, Rote, et al., 2012), for example, has discovered that children as young as age 3 regard moral transgressions such as hitting, stealing, or refusing to share as more serious and deserving of punishment than social-conventional violations. Young children also appreciate that hitting is wrong even if the teacher did not see it; even if the rules say hitting is okay; and whether it is done at home, at school, or in a faraway land with different laws. They feel very differently about social-conventional rules; it might be okay for another country to declare that girls should wear pants and boys should wear skirts.

Being Fair

As you have seen already, even infants seem to have a sense of fairness, as shown when they expect goods to be shared equally between two people. Indeed, children's first concept of fairness is an equality rule: Everyone should get the same—or else "It's not fair!". It was long believed that children younger than 5 or 6 did not understand or use another important rule of justice: an equity rule that takes merit into account and gives more to whoever did the most to earn the rewards to be distributed (Damon, 1977).

Yet we now know that even 3- and 4-year-olds are able to take merit into account if you can get them past their strong preference to give equal rewards to all. Thus, if children are given three cookies to distribute to two workers, they very often give each worker one cookie and set aside the third cookie. However, if prompted to give the third cookie to someone, they will give it to the more meritorious of the two workers (Baumard, Mascaro, & Chevallier, 2012).

As children progress through elementary school, their ideas of fairness and justice become more elaborated and they show more understanding of which rule is fairest in which situation. Thus, 5-year-olds often use an equality rule regardless of the context, but 9- and 13-year-olds use an equality rule when distributing voting ballots to campers who will vote to select a new game for the camp, an equity rule when rewarding workers according to the number of pots they made for sale by the camp, and a need-based rule in giving more of the funds donated to the camp to a poor camper than to campers who are not as needy (Sigelman & Waitzman, 1991). Cross-cultural research tells us that children in different societies may develop different ideas of fairness; thus, among the Akhoe Hai of Namibia, African foragers who value equal relationships and share food often, children much prefer to reward workers using an equality rule rather than the merit-based equity rule that Western children prefer in such situations (Schafer, Haun, & Tomasello, 2015).

Children are not above giving themselves more than they give others, of course. However, they clearly have a basic sense of fairness. At first, they favor an equality rule but soon they apply rules of equality, equity or merit, and need appropriately depending on the situation and their cultural context (see also Killen & Smetana, 2015).

Overall, then, both Piaget and Kohlberg seriously underestimated how sensitive even toddlers are to moral issues and how much moral growth takes place during infancy and early childhood. We now know that even young children judge acts as right or wrong according to whether the actor's intentions were good or bad, using their theories of mind; distinguish between moral rules and social-conventional rules and view only moral rules as absolute, sacred, and unchangeable; and appreciate and apply rules of fairness.

Moral Socialization

How can parents best raise a child who can be counted on to behave morally? You have already seen that a secure attachment and a mutually responsive orientation between parent and child starting in infancy help. Social learning theorists like Bandura would also advise parents to reinforce moral behavior, punish immoral behavior (but mildly and with caution, as discussed in Chapter 2), and serve as models of moral rather than immoral behavior.

The important work of Martin Hoffman (2000) has provided additional insights into how to foster moral development. As you saw earlier, Hoffman (2000) believes that empathy is a key motivator of moral behavior and that a key task in moral socialization, therefore, is to foster empathy. Hoffman (1970) compared the pros and cons of three major approaches to disciplining children:

1. **Love withdrawal.** Withholding attention, affection, or approval after a child misbehaves—in other words, creating anxiety by threatening a loss of reinforcement from parents.
2. **Power assertion.** Using power to threaten, chastise, administer spankings, take away privileges, and so on—in other words, using punishment.
3. **Induction.** Explaining to a child why the behavior is wrong and should be changed by emphasizing how it affects other people.

Suppose that little Angel has just put the beloved family cat through a cycle in the clothes dryer. Using love withdrawal, a parent might say, "How could you do something like that? I can't stand to look at you!" Using power assertion, a parent might say, "Go to your room this minute; you're going to get it." Using induction, a parent might say, "Angel, look how scared Fluffball is. You could have killed her, and you know how sad we'd be if she died." Induction, then, is a matter of providing rationales or explanations that focus attention on the consequences of wrongdoing for other people (or cats).

Martin Hoffman's formula for raising a moral child involves lots of induction and affection and only occasional power assertion.

Pavel L Photo and Video/Shutterstock.com

Which approach best fosters moral development? Induction wins hands down over love withdrawal and power assertion, and power assertion has proven to be the least effective approach (Brody & Shaffer, 1982). In Hoffman's (2000) view, induction works well because it breeds empathy. Anticipating empathic distress if we contemplate harming someone keeps us from doing harm; empathizing with individuals in distress motivates us to help them.

Although expressing disappointment in a child's behavior can be effective on occasion, making a child worry that their parents' love can be snatched away at any time usually is not effective (Patrick & Gibbs, 2007). Frequent use of power assertion is more often associated with moral immaturity than with moral maturity. Power assertion does not foster empathy, the internalization of moral rules, or the development of self-control, and physical punishment in particular can produce unwanted consequences such as anxiety and aggression (see Chapter 2).

Despite this evidence, Hoffman (2000) concludes that mild power assertion tactics such as a forceful "No," a reprimand, or the taking away of privileges can be useful occasionally if they arouse some but not too much fear and motivate a child to pay close attention to the inductions that follow. Such careful uses of power assertion work best in the context of a loving and mutually responsive parent–child relationship. All in all, Hoffman's work provides a fairly clear roadmap for parents: The winning formula is "a blend of frequent inductions, occasional power assertions, and a lot of affection" (Hoffman, 2000, p. 23).

Let's add that effective parents also use **proactive parenting strategies**, tactics designed to prevent misbehavior and therefore reduce the need for any of Hoffman's types of discipline. Proactive parenting techniques include distracting young children from temptations and explicitly teaching children values such as the importance of telling the truth, sharing, and being kind (Thompson et al., 2006).

Yet parents do not settle on one best approach and use it all the time. Both the moral socialization technique chosen in a situation and its effectiveness depend on a host of factors such as the particular misdeed, child, parent, situation, and cultural context (Grusec, 2006). For example, a child's temperament is an important influence on how morally trainable she is and what motivates her to comply with parents' rules and requests (Thompson et al., 2006). Grazyna Kochanska and her colleagues have found that children are likely to be easiest to socialize if they are by temperament (1) fearful or inhibited and therefore are likely to experience guilt when they do wrong, become appropriately distressed when they are disciplined, and want to avoid such distress in the future; and (2) capable of self-control and therefore are able to inhibit their urges to engage in wrongdoing (Kochanska, Barry, Jimenez, et al., 2009).

Children with different temperaments may require different socialization approaches. Fearful, inhibited children can be socialized through a gentle approach that capitalizes on their anxiety but does not terrorize them (Fowles & Kochanska, 2000). Children who are fearless or uninhibited do not respond to this gentle approach—but they do not respond to being treated harshly, either. These fearless children are most likely to learn to comply with rules and requests when there is a mutually responsive orientation between parent and child, and the child is therefore motivated to please the parent and maintain a good relationship (Fowles & Kochanska, 2000; and see Kochanska, Aksan, & Joy, 2007). Here, then, is another example of the importance of the goodness of fit between a child's temperament and her social environment. Socialized in a way that suits their temperament, most children will internalize rules of conduct, experience appropriate moral emotions, learn to regulate their behavior, and behave more prosocially than antisocially.

Checking Mastery

1. How is a moral rule different from a social-conventional rule and at what age can children tell the difference?
2. What are two capacities shown by preschool children that contradict Piaget's and Kohlberg's views that they are limited moral thinkers?
3. Create an example of induction and explain why Martin Hoffman concludes that it is the best approach to discipline.

Making Connections

1. Teddy, age 6, lies and steals frequently, bullies other children, and rarely complies with rules at home or at school. Using what you have learned about moral socialization and referring to appropriate concepts and research, describe how ineffective parenting might have contributed to the development of this apparently immoral child.
2. What approaches to moral socialization did your parents use with you? Did they make their moral values clear? Did they explain their rules? Did they threaten you with punishment or make you feel you would lose their love if you broke their rules? Finally, do your parents' strategies seem sound in view of research on moral socialization?

LEARNING OBJECTIVES

- Describe how moral reasoning changes during adolescence and the significance of developing a moral identity.

- Compare how Kenneth Dodge and Gerald Patterson account for the behavior of aggressive youth.

- Explain the roles of nature and nurture in aggression and what has been learned about preventing and treating it.

As adolescents gain the capacity to think about abstract and hypothetical ideas, and as they begin to chart their future identities, many of them reflect on their values and moral standards and some make morality a central part of their identities. At the other extreme are the adolescents who end up engaging in serious antisocial behavior.

Moral Identity

Some teens come to view being a moral person who is caring, fair, and honest as a central part of who they are—that is, they develop a moral identity (Krettenauer & Hertz, 2015). Adolescents who have a sense of moral identity tend to be more capable than other adolescents of advanced moral reasoning (Hart, 2005). Especially if something in the situation reminds them of their moral values, they are also more likely to act morally than adolescents who do not define themselves in moral terms (Aquino & Reed, 2002; Aquino et al., 2009). Thus developing a moral identity may be critical when it comes to translating moral values into moral action (Hardy & Carlo, 2011). If you have a strong moral identity, you cannot live with yourself if you do wrong.

A moral identity starts to take shape as children develop a sense of being a good boy or good girl who tries to follow rules, avoids misbehaving, and cares about other people (Kochanska et al., 2010). The development of a moral identity in adolescence

can be fostered by parents who use induction and on occasion express disappointment in their teen's behavior rather than relying on power assertion and love withdrawal (Patrick & Gibbs, 2012). It can also be fostered through involvement in community service and other prosocial activities (Hardy & Carlo, 2011; Pratt et al., 2003). In adulthood, a strong moral identity is more predictive than a person's stage of moral reasoning of ethical and prosocial behavior in the workplace (Cohen et al., 2014).

Changes in Moral Reasoning

Adolescence is a period of significant growth in moral reasoning. Consider the results of Lawrence Kohlberg's 20-year longitudinal study that involved repeatedly asking the 10-, 13-, and 16-year-old boys he originally studied to respond to moral dilemmas (Colby et al., 1983). ■ Figure 13.3 shows the percentage of judgments offered at each age that reflected each of Kohlberg's stages.

A moral identity can be built stronger through community service.

KidStock/Blend Images/Getty Images

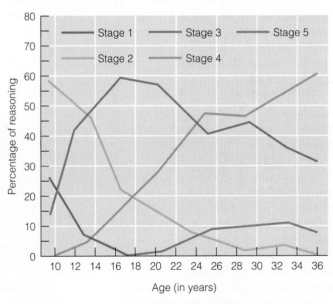

■ **Figure 13.3** Average percentage of moral reasoning at each of Lawrence Kohlberg's stages for males from age 10 to age 36. You can see the decline of preconventional thinking and the rise of conventional thinking with age—and very little postconventional thinking.

Source: From Colby, A., Kohlberg, L, Gibbs, J., & Lieberman, M. A. (1983). A longitudinal study of moral judgment. *Monographs of the Society for Research in Child Development, 48* (1–2, Serial No. 200). Copyright © 1983 Blackwell Publishing. Reprinted with permission.

Notice that the preconventional reasoning (Stage 1 and 2 thinking) that dominates among 10-year-olds decreases considerably during the teen years. During adolescence, conventional reasoning (Stages 3 and 4) becomes the dominant mode of moral thinking. So, among 13- to 14-year-olds, most moral judgments reflect either a Stage 2 (instrumental hedonism) approach—"You scratch my back and I'll scratch yours"—or a Stage 3 (good boy or good girl) concern with being nice and earning approval. More than half the judgments offered by 16- to 18-year-olds embody Stage 3 reasoning, and about a fifth were scored as Stage 4 (authority and social order–maintaining morality) arguments. These older adolescents were beginning to take a broad societal perspective on justice and to ask whether actions would help maintain or undermine the social system.

In short, the main developmental trend in moral reasoning during adolescence is a shift from preconventional to conventional reasoning. During this period, most individuals begin to express a genuine concern with living up to the moral standards that parents and other authorities have taught them and ensuring that laws designed to make human relations just and fair are taken seriously and maintained. Postconventional reasoning does not emerge until adulthood—stay tuned.

Antisocial Behavior

Although most adolescents internalize society's moral standards and behave morally, a few youths engage in serious antisocial conduct—muggings, rapes, armed robberies, knifings, drive-by shootings. School shootings by adolescent and young adult males—from Columbine to Virginia Tech to Newtown and beyond—have heightened concern about what causes serious antisocial behavior and how to prevent it. Is it weak gun laws, violent video games, mental illness, a violent culture, or what?

The quality of antisocial behavior changes from childhood to adolescence; physical aggression decreases, while non-aggressive rule-breaking behavior such as vandalism and theft increases (Burt, 2015). The consequences of teens' early misbehavior cumulate, and they engage in **juvenile delinquency**, lawbreaking by a minor. They may then find themselves leaving school early, participating in troubled and sometimes abusive relationships, having difficulty keeping jobs, and engaging in lawbreaking as adults (Huesmann, Dubow, & Boxer, 2009; Maughan & Rutter, 2001). The most seriously disturbed of these individuals may qualify as youth for psychiatric diagnoses such as **conduct disorder**—a persistent pattern of violating the rights of others or age-appropriate societal norms through such behaviors as fighting, bullying, and cruelty; as adults, they may be recognized as "psychopaths" and qualify for a

diagnosis of antisocial personality disorder (see Dodge, Coie, & Lynam, 2006). Some also end up in the 5% or so of the population who are identified as career criminals and account for most of the violent crimes committed in the United States (DeLisi, 2016).

Yet most adolescents who engage in aggressive behavior and other antisocial acts do not grow up to be antisocial adults. There seem to be two subgroups of antisocial youths, then (Moffitt & Caspi, 2001; Monahan, Steinberg, & Cauffman, 2009; Odgers et al., 2008):

1. a small, early onset, seriously disturbed group that is recognizable in childhood and is persistently antisocial across the life span; and
2. a larger, late onset, less seriously antisocial group that begins to behave antisocially during adolescence, partly in response to peer influences, and outgrows this behavior in early adulthood.

The decline of antisocial behavior after adolescence in the second group may reflect increased autonomy and increased ability to resist peer pressures as well as the taking on of adult responsibilities. It may also reflect brain development—the maturation of the prefrontal cortex that continues into the mid-20s and results in better self-control and a greater ability to think through the consequences of behavior (Giedd et al., 2013). Crime rates rise to peak during adolescence and emerging adulthood and then fall in most societies, especially for "hell-raising" crimes such as vandalism (Agnew, 2003; Tremblay, 2010). This developmental trend is reflected in the official statistics on arrests for violent crime in the United States shown in ■ **Figure 13.4**. The graph also shows that males are far more involved in violent crime than females (see Chapter 12 on gender differences in aggression).

What causes some youths to become menaces to society? Might adolescents who engage repeatedly in antisocial acts be

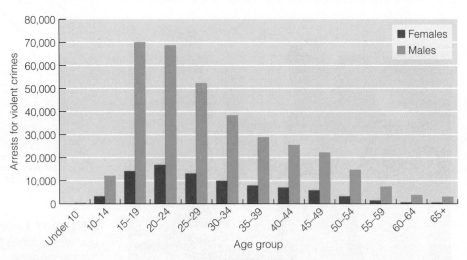

■ **Figure 13.4** Arrests for violent crimes by males and females of different ages in the United States, 2010. Violent crimes include murder, manslaughter, rape, robbery, and aggravated assault.

Source: U.S. Department of Justice, Federal Bureau of Investigation, Crime in the United States 2010. Figures retrieved and calculated from Tables 39 and 40, www.fbi.gov/about-us/cjis/ucr/crime-in-the-u.s/2010/crime-in-the-u.s.-2010/persons-arrested

cases of arrested moral development who have not internalized conventional moral values? Juvenile delinquents are indeed more likely than nondelinquents to rely on preconventional moral reasoning (Spenser, Betts, & Das Gupta, 2015; Stams et al., 2006). They also do more poorly on tests of theory-of-mind skills (Spenser et al., 2015). Yet many delinquents have good social cognitive skills and can engage in conventional moral reasoning but commit illegal acts anyway. So to understand the origins of antisocial conduct, we must consider more than social cognitive skills and stage of moral reasoning (see Gibbs, 2014; Quinsey et al., 2004).

What about moral emotions? The highly aggressive, antisocial adolescents destined to become career criminals are less likely than other adolescents to show empathy and concern for others in distress or to feel guilty after they do wrong (Gibbs, 2014; Lovett & Sheffield, 2007). They are described as having "callous-unemotional traits" (Fontaine et al., 2011; Marsee & Frick, 2010). And indeed, their brain's amygdala, center of emotional experience, does not respond as much as those of other youths to photographs of painful injuries suffered by other people that should arouse empathy (Marsh et al., 2013). So lack of appropriate moral emotions is important, but as will now become clear, highly antisocial adolescents also process social information differently than other adolescents do and have often grown up in family environments that breed aggression.

Dodge's Social Information-Processing Model

Kenneth Dodge and his colleagues have advanced our understanding by offering a social information-processing model of aggressive behavior (Crick & Dodge, 1994; Dodge, 1986). Imagine that you are walking down the aisle in a classroom, trip over a classmate's leg, and end up in a heap on the floor. As you fall, you are not sure what happened. Dodge believes that our reactions to frustration, anger, or provocation depend on the ways in which we process and interpret cues in situations like this. An individual who is provoked (as by being tripped) progresses through the six steps in information processing shown in ● **Table 13.4**, according to Dodge.

Highly aggressive youths, including adolescents incarcerated for violent crimes, show deficient or biased information processing at every step (Dodge, 1993; Slaby & Guerra, 1988), as illustrated in Table 13.4. Many aggressive youths act impulsively, "without thinking"; they respond automatically based on their past experiences. These youths have often developed a **hostile attribution bias**; they tend to see the world as a hostile place and quickly assume that any harm to them was deliberate rather than accidental. Severely violent youths have often experienced abandonment, neglect, abuse, bullying, and other insults that may have given them some cause to view the world as a hostile place and to feel justified in retaliating against individuals they believe are "out to get them" (Gibbs, 2014; Lansford et al., 2007). Of course the responses that pop to mind when they are provoked are mostly aggressive ones.

Dodge's social information-processing model is helpful in understanding why certain children and adolescents might behave aggressively when provoked. However, it leaves somewhat unclear the extent to which the underlying problem is *how one thinks* (how skilled the individual is at processing social information), *what one thinks* (for example, whether the individual has a hostile attribution bias), or *whether one thinks* (how impulsively the person acts). Moreover, we have to look elsewhere to understand why only some children develop the social information-processing styles associated with aggressive behavior.

Patterson's Coercive Family Environments

Gerald Patterson and his colleagues have found that highly antisocial children and adolescents often grow up in **coercive family environments** in which family members are locked in power struggles, each trying to control the others through negative, coercive tactics (Patterson, 2008; Patterson, DeBaryshe, & Ramsey, 1989). Parents learn (through B. F. Skinner's principle of negative reinforcement) that they can stop their children's misbehavior, temporarily at least, by threatening, yelling, and hitting. Meanwhile, children learn (also through negative reinforcement) that they can get their parents to lay off them by ignoring requests, whining, throwing full-blown temper

● **Table 13.4** The Six Steps in Dodge's Social Information-Processing Model and Sample Responses of Aggressive Youth

Step	Behavior	Likely Response of Aggressive Youth
1. Encoding of cues	Search for, attend to, and register cues in the situation	Focus on cues suggesting hostile intent; ignore other relevant information
2. Interpretation of cues	Interpret situation; infer other's motive	Show hostile attribution bias, assuming other person meant to do harm
3. Clarification of goals	Formulate goal in situation	Make goal to retaliate rather than smooth relations
4. Response search	Generate possible responses	Generate few options, most of them aggressive
5. Response decision	Assess likely consequences of responses generated; choose the best	See advantages in responding aggressively rather than nonaggressively (or fail to evaluate consequences)
6. Behavioral enactment	Carry out chosen response	Behave aggressively

Based on material in Dodge (1993) and Crick & Dodge (1994).

Social information processors use a database of information about past social experiences, social rules, and social behavior at each step of the process and may skip or repeat steps.

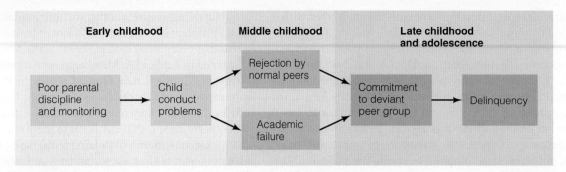

Figure 13.5 Gerald Patterson's model of the development of antisocial behavior shows how poor discipline and coercive family influence lead to involvement in a deviant peer group and delinquency.

Source: Adapted from Patterson, G. R., DeBaryshe, B. D., & Ramsey, E. (1989). A developmental perspective on antisocial behavior. *American Psychologist, 44*, 329–335.

tantrums, and otherwise being difficult. As both parents and children learn to rely on coercive tactics to avoid or escape unpleasant encounters, parents increasingly lose control over their children's behavior until even the loudest lectures and hardest spankings have little effect and the child's conduct problems spiral out of control. It is easy to see how a child who has grown up in a coercive family environment might attribute hostile intent to other people and rely on aggressive tactics to resolve disputes.

Growing up in a coercive family environment sets in motion the next steps in the making of an antisocial adolescent, according to Patterson and his colleagues (see ■ Figure 13.5): The child, already aggressive and unpleasant to be around, performs poorly in school and is rejected by other children. Having no better options, he becomes involved in a peer group made up of other low-achieving, antisocial, and unpopular youths, who positively reinforce one another's delinquency. There is much support for Patterson's view that ineffective parenting in childhood contributes to behavior problems, poor academic performance, peer rejection, involvement with antisocial peers, and, in turn, antisocial behavior in adolescence (Dodge et al., 2008; Lansford et al., 2014).

Nature and Nurture

However, neither Kenneth Dodge's social-information processing model nor Gerald Patterson's coercive family environments model considers the role of genetic endowment in aggression. Some individuals are more genetically predisposed than others to develop difficult, irritable temperaments, impulsive tendencies, psychological disorders, and other response tendencies and personality traits that contribute to aggressive, delinquent, and criminal behavior (Niv & Baker, 2013; Rhee & Waldman, 2002). Genetic differences among us are estimated to account for about 40% of individual differences in antisocial behavior and environmental influences for the remaining 60% of the variation (Rhee & Waldman, 2002). A number of specific genes that affect neurotransmitters and hormones have been identified as contributors to antisocial behavior. Researchers are also discovering *epigenetic effects* of harsh parenting and other stressful early experiences on the expression of certain

genes that play a role in aggressive behavior (Niv & Baker, 2013; Tremblay, 2010).

Genes and environment conspire to produce antisocial youth. Through the mechanism of *gene–environment interaction*, children with certain genetic predispositions are especially likely to become antisocial if they receive poor parenting or, worse, are physically abused (DeLisi, 2016; Dodge, 2009; Kuny-Slock & Hudziak, 2013). For example, the monoamine oxidase A (MAO-A) gene, a gene on the X chromosome that affects our ability to control our tempers, has been linked to aggression (Dodge, 2009; Tiihonen et al., 2015). If children have a variant of this gene that results in low MAO-A activity *and* if they are abused or mistreated, they readily attribute hostile intentions to others if provoked, cannot control their anger, lash out impulsively, and show higher levels of antisocial behavior as adults (Caspi et al., 2002; DeLisi, 2016). By contrast, children with this high-risk gene are far less likely to become aggressive if they live in a stable, two-parent home or have nondelinquent friends (Guo, 2011).

Through the mechanism of *gene–environment correlation*, children who have a genetically based predisposition to become aggressive may actually evoke the coercive parenting that Patterson and his colleagues find breeds aggression. This *evocative gene–environment correlation* effect is evident when aggression-prone children who grow up with adoptive parents rather than with their biological parents bring out negativity in their adoptive parents (Fearon et al., 2015). In the end, child antisocial behavior and negative parenting influence one another reciprocally over time: Aggressive children evoke negative, coercive parenting, and negative, coercive parenting further strengthens children's aggressive tendencies (Larsson et al., 2008; O'Connor et al., 1998).

Many other environmental risk and protective factors can help determine whether or not a child develops a pattern of antisocial behavior (Eisner & Malti, 2015; Guerra & Williams, 2006). Rates of aggression and violent crime are two to three times higher in lower socioeconomic neighborhoods and communities, especially transient and unstable ones, than in middle-class ones (Elliott & Ageton, 1980; Maughan, 2001). Similarly, certain schools have higher rates of delinquency and aggression than others, even when socioeconomic factors are controlled (Barboza et al., 2009; Maughan, 2001).

Finally, some cultural contexts are more likely to breed aggression than others (Eisner & Malti, 2015; Lansford et al., 2012). In Japan, a collectivist culture in which children are taught early to value social harmony, children are less angered by interpersonal conflicts and less likely to react to them aggressively than American children are (Zahn-Waxler et al., 1996). Homicides by youth also occur much less frequently in Asian countries like Japan and in European countries than in North and South America (Eisner & Malti, 2015). Cultural values can make a difference even within a society; for example, Hispanic American youths who have been brought up with traditional Hispanic cultural values such as the importance of family are less likely than those who are more acculturated into American society to engage in antisocial behavior (Cota-Robles, 2003; Soriano et al., 2004). This should not be surprising, as the United States is a relatively violent country: Guns are numerous, homicide rates are high, corporal punishment of children is common, and violence pervades the media (Anderson et al., 2010; Lansford & Dodge, 2008; Lim, Bond, & Bond, 2005).

In sum, we must recognize the contributions of biology and genetic predisposition, psychological factors such as information-processing styles and personality traits, and sociocultural and contextual factors to aggression. Genes, in combination with environmental influences such as harsh parenting and interaction with antisocial peers, can lead to chronic and serious violence in adolescence and adulthood (Dodge et al., 2008). Unfortunately the antisocial adult who emerges from this developmental process stands a good chance of becoming the kind of harsh, coercive parent who helps raise another generation of aggressive children, who then use the same coercive style with their own children (Conger et al., 2003; Margolin et al., 2016).

Prevention and Treatment

Prevention and treatment of antisocial behavior should clearly be a national priority, but how do we go about it? Many approaches have been tried. **Application 13.1** focuses on the widespread problem of **bullying**, repeatedly inflicting harm through words or actions on a targeted peer, and a prevention program that has been used in many schools to combat it. Other researchers, drawing on Kohlberg's theory of moral development, have involved youth, including juvenile offenders, in discussion of moral dilemmas and democratic decision making in the schools in order to improve their moral reasoning (Gibbs, 2014; Nucci, 2006; Power & Higgins-D'Alessandro, 2008). Dodge's model has been applied to improve the social information-processing skills of juvenile delinquents (Guerra & Slaby, 1990). Others have focused on training to improve self-control and reduce impulsivity (DeLisi, 2016). And Patterson's coercive cycles model has been used to train parents of at-risk youth in positive behavior management techniques (Bank et al., 1991; Patterson, 2005; Reed et al., 2013). All these approaches have had some success, but none has been able to completely prevent antisocial behavior or turn around the lives of serious juvenile offenders.

Many experts believe that prevention is the key and that it should start early in childhood (Dodge, Coie, & Lynam, 2006; Tremblay, 2010). Since risk factors like harsh parenting and disruptive child behavior reciprocally influence each other, it also makes sense to try to change both the child and the environment (Jaffee, Strait, & Odgers, 2012). For instance, the Fast Track Program, designed by Kenneth Dodge and a large team of researchers (Conduct Problems Prevention Research Group, 2002; Sorensen et al., 2016), began in first grade, extended over 10 years, and used a multipronged approach involving the teaching of social information processing and social skills, efforts to improve academic skills, and behavior management training for parents. It has proven effective in reducing antisocial behavior, including arrests, and preventing diagnoses of conduct disorder and related psychiatric disorders in adolescence and early adulthood (Sorensen, Dodge, & Conduct Problems Prevention Research group, 2016). The program achieves its results, in part, by improving participants' social information-processing and self-regulation skills (Dodge et al., 2013; Sorensen et al., 2016). Even in their 20s, high-risk participants in Fast Track respond more calmly to provocations in the lab such as having items stolen from them; they show lower rises in the male hormone testosterone and, in turn, less aggressive behavior than control adults (Carré et al., 2014).

Finally, still other researchers believe there has been too much emphasis on reducing adolescent problem behavior and too little on helping youth develop in positive directions. **Positive youth development (PYD)** is an approach that emphasizes developing the strengths of youth. In one formulation (Lerner et al., 2005; Lerner, Phelps, Forman, & Bowers, 2009), "five Cs" serve as the goals:

1. Competence (academic, vocational, and so on)
2. Confidence (self-esteem and self-efficacy)
3. Character (moral development, respect for rules)
4. Connection (bonds to family, friends, and institutions like schools and churches)
5. Caring (empathy, prosocial behavior)

PYD programs help youths develop more positive identities, build "five C" strengths, increase their positive contributions to their communities—and yes, reduce their problem behaviors (Jelicic et al., 2007; Lerner et al., 2005; Mueller et al., 2011). For racial and ethnic minority youth, who too often have been viewed more in terms of their vulnerabilities to problems than in terms of their strengths, this "emphasize the positive" approach may be especially welcomed. Indeed, the strengths of particular racial and ethnic groups—racial pride, family values, spirituality—are being incorporated in PYD programs (Evans et al., 2012; Kenyon & Hanson, 2012; Knight & Carlo, 2012). In short, to prevent antisocial behavior we would do well to begin early, use a multipronged approach, and nurture the positive potentials of youth.

Stopping the Bullies

Phoebe Prince, a 15-year-old in Massachusetts who was believed to be moving in on other girls' boyfriends, was taunted mercilessly—jokes about an "Irish slut" on Facebook (she had recently moved to the United States from Ireland), a humiliating accusation in the school cafeteria, kids cruising up next to her in a car as she walked home, throwing an empty soda can at her, and calling her "whore" (Bennett, 2010). Phoebe killed herself.

Bullying, repeatedly inflicting harm through words or actions on a targeted peer, was once written off as just a normal part of growing up but is now a major societal concern (Hwang, Kim, & Leventhal, 2013; Olweus, 1993; Salmivalli & Peets, 2009). The victims can be almost anyone, but recent immigrants, gay and lesbian youth, and youth with disabilities or emotional problems get more than their fair share of bullying (Blake et al., 2012; Burton et al., 2013). Bullying takes many forms, from physical aggression to more indirect or covert forms of aggression such as excluding or gossiping about someone. It includes cyberbullying, which enables bullies to spread rumors, insults, embarrassing photographs, and threats quickly and widely via digital devices (Hinduja & Patchin, 2013; Smith et al., 2008).

We can divide the world of youth into bullies, victims, bully-victims, and neither (Hwang et al., 2013; Zych, Ortega-Ruiz, & Del Ray, 2015). A survey in 40 Western countries revealed that, overall, about 26% of 11- to 15-year-olds report repeatedly bullying and/or being bullied by peers at least two to three times a month (Craig et al., 2009). Rates vary considerably, though, from under 10% in Scandinavian countries like Sweden to around 40% in Baltic countries like Lithuania, with the United States in the middle. Bullying is also a life-span phenomenon; for example, adult bullying in the workplace is also a matter of societal concern (Samnani & Singh, 2012).

The effects of bullying are serious. Being hounded by bullies can lead to becoming a bully and to aggression and delinquency, as well as to depression, health problems such as stress-related headaches and pains, and self-harmful behavior, including suicide (Barker et al., 2008; Espinoza, Gonzales, & Fuligni, 2012; Hwang et al., 2013; Wolke et al., 2013). Academic performance suffers as well (Cornell et al., 2012; Strøm et al., 2013).

Being bullied as a child may even have long-term implications for adult development. William Copeland and his colleagues (2014) discovered that a marker in the blood indicating inflammation—a sign of an overactive immune system that is associated with a number of chronic illnesses—was at higher levels during childhood and continuing into early adulthood in individuals who had experienced the stress of being bullied during childhood than in those who were not bullied. The more chronic the bullying, the greater the evidence of inflammation. Meanwhile, childhood bullies showed lower levels of inflammation than children who had neither been bullies nor victims, possibly because they achieved status in the peer group through their bullying. This research team also found that bullied children and bully/victims have poorer health, lower incomes, more risky and illegal behavior, and poorer social relationships as young adults than nonbullied individuals—even controlling for family socioeconomic status and child psychiatric problems (Wolke et al., 2013).

So what is being done to stop the bullying? Antibullying laws mandate antibullying programs in the schools and sometimes establish criminal penalties for bullying (Bennett, 2010). Schools now take active steps to combat bullying and to encourage students to report or intervene in bullying incidents rather than reinforcing the bullies (Saarento & Salmivalli, 2015; Beane, 2009). One of the most widely used and well-known interventions is the Olweus Bullying Prevention Program (Olweus, 1993; Olweus & Limber, 2010). Launched in Norway in the wake of three teen suicides attributed to bullying, it is

a comprehensive program with several components. It focuses on the school as a whole (for example, through a school coordinating group with staff and student representatives and teacher training), the class (for example, through posting of rules against bullying and regular class discussions of bullying), the individual (through talks with bullies, victims, and their parents and development of individual action plans for those involved in bullying), and the broader community (through school-community partnerships).

So far, this multifaceted program has had some success reducing bullying and changing attitudes toward it. However, it has proven more effective in Norway and other relatively homogeneous societies than in the more diverse context of the United States (Evans, Fraser, & Cotter, 2014; Olweus & Limber, 2010; Schroeder et al., 2012). If we analyze bullying using Bronfenbrenner's bioecological model (Hong & Espelage, 2012; Chapter 2), we quickly appreciate that a host of problems within the person, family, peer group, school, community, and broader culture must be addressed to stop the bullies once and for all.

STOP BULLYING. SERIOUSLY, JUST STOP.
stopbullying.gov

istockphoto.com/Gina Neal

1. What is the main change in the level of moral reasoning during adolescence?
2. What are the main contributions of (1) Kenneth Dodge and (2) Gerald Patterson to understanding why some adolescents are highly aggressive?
3. What is an example of the contribution of a gene–environment interaction to the development of aggression?

● Making Connections

1. To demonstrate to yourself that Dodge's social information-processing model can be applied not only to antisocial behavior but to prosocial behavior, picture a situation in which you are one of the campers in the story at the beginning of this chapter and witness two other campers put the hand of Edward, the camp employee, in a bucket of water while he naps. Show how considerations at each of the six steps of Dodge's model (see Table 13.4) might contribute to your intervening to help Edward—and then how they might keep you from helping.

2. You hear that still another teenage boy has gone on a shooting rampage at his school. Drawing on material in this section, what main hypotheses would you have about why he might have done what he did?

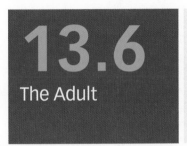

13.6
The Adult

LEARNING OBJECTIVES

- Summarize changes in moral reasoning over the adult years.
- Analyze the limitations of Kohlberg's theory of moral development with reference to cultural differences in moral thinking and dual-process models of moral decision making.
- Distinguish between religiousness and spirituality and discuss their development and relationships to adjustment.

How does moral thinking change during adulthood, and how is it related to moral emotion and moral behavior? And how does moral development intersect with religiousness and spirituality in adults' lives?

Changes in Moral Reasoning

Much research on moral development in adulthood has been guided by Kohlberg's theory. As you have discovered (reexamine Figure 13.3), Kohlberg's postconventional moral reasoning appears to emerge only during the adult years—if it emerges. In Kohlberg's 20-year longitudinal study (Colby et al., 1983), most adults in their 30s still reasoned at the conventional level, although many of them had shifted from Stage 3 to Stage 4. A minority of individuals—one out of six at most—had begun to use Stage 5 postconventional reasoning, showing a deeper understanding of the basis for laws and distinguishing between just and unjust laws. Clearly there is opportunity for continued moral growth in early adulthood.

Do these growth trends continue into later adulthood? Most studies find no major age differences in complexity of moral reasoning, at least when the age groups compared have similar amounts of education (Pratt & Norris, 1999; Pratt et al., 1991, 1996). Older adults are also more likely than younger adults to feel that they have learned important lessons from moral dilemmas they have faced during their lives (Pratt & Norris, 1999). This, then, is further evidence that social cognitive skills hold up relatively well across the life span.

Overall, research based on Kohlberg's influential theory of moral development shows that children think about hypothetical moral dilemmas primarily in a preconventional manner, that adolescents adopt a conventional mode of moral reasoning, and that a minority of adults shift to a postconventional perspective. Moreover, longitudinal studies of moral growth in several countries show that at least the first three or four of Kohlberg's six stages form an invariant and universal developmental sequence (Colby & Kohlberg, 1987; Gibbs, 2014; Rest et al., 1999).

However, despite Kohlberg's major contributions to the study of moral development, his theory has its limitations. You have already seen that young children are more sophisticated moral thinkers than either Piaget or Kohlberg appreciated. Let us now consider concerns about whether Kohlberg's focus on reasoning about rights and justice adequately captures the nature of moral thinking in non-Western cultures, whether it neglects a much more intuitive or emotional way of responding to moral issues, and whether Kohlberg said enough about influences on how people actually behave when they face moral dilemmas.

Culture and Morality

Are basic aspects of morality universal or are they culture specific? Although support for the early stages of Kohlberg's theory has been obtained in many countries, critics charge that Kohlberg's highest stages reflect a Western ideal of justice centered on individual rights and the rule of law—and that there's more to morality than that. Kohlberg, they argue, did not adequately appreciate that people in non-Western societies often emphasize different moral concepts (Jensen, 2015; Miller & Bland, 2014; Shweder, Mahapatra, & Miller, 1990). Indeed, cross-cultural research suggests that postconventional moral reasoning emerges primarily in Western democracies (Snarey,

1985). Meanwhile, people in *collectivist cultures*, which emphasize social harmony and place the good of the group ahead of the good of the individual, often look like Stage 3 conventional moral thinkers in Kohlberg's system. Yet many have sophisticated concepts of justice that focus on the individual's duty to the group or community and responsibility for others' welfare (Snarey, 1985; Tietjen & Walker, 1985). In **Exploration 13.2**, we look at moral development in India, where moral reasoning based on religious and spiritual concepts can lead to quite different conclusions about what is right or wrong than in Western countries like the United States.

Cross-cultural findings challenge the cognitive-developmental position that moral development proceeds through universal stages. Instead, they support a social learning perspective on moral development, suggesting that our moral judgments are shaped by the social context in which we develop. Possibly the resolution is this: Individuals all over the world think in more complex ways about moral issues as they get older, as Kohlberg claimed, but they also adopt different notions about right and wrong depending on their culture's teachings (Jensen, 2015; Miller, 2006).

Moral Intuition and Emotion

(Before you read this section, we invite you to read and respond to **Engagement 13.2**.) Developmentalists today are trying to correct for Kohlberg's overemphasis on moral reasoning by exploring the

---

● **EXPLORATION 13.2**

Moral Thinking in India

Some time ago, Richard Shweder et al. (1990) studied the moral judgments of children and adults in India and the United States and identified some striking cultural differences in thinking about right and wrong. For example, Hindu children and adults rated a son's getting a haircut and eating chicken the day after his father's death as one of the most morally offensive of the 39 acts they were asked to rate, whereas Americans dismissed it as only a matter of breaking what seemed to them an arbitrary social-conventional rule about appropriate mourning behavior. Meanwhile, Americans viewed a husband's beating of his "disobedient" wife for going to the movies without his permission as a serious moral violation, whereas Hindus viewed it as appropriate behavior. To orthodox Hindus, not showing proper respect for the dead violates a moral rule required by divine law, not an arbitrary social-conventional rule, and it is morally necessary for a man to beat his disobedient wife to uphold his obligations as head of the family. In India, religious and spiritual concepts were integral to moral thinking; yet they had been ignored in Kohlberg's theory of moral development (Shweder et al., 1990).

Based on such cross-cultural studies, Shweder and his colleagues (1997) suggested that three different ethics inform moral thinking around the world and that the balance of them differs from culture to culture:

- an ethic of autonomy (as in Kohlberg's theory, a concern about individual rights and fairness or justice);
- an ethic of community (as in many collectivist cultures, an emphasis on duty,

loyalty, and concern for the welfare of the group); and
- an ethic of divinity (an emphasis on divine law and a quest for spiritual purity).

Niyati Pandya and Rachana Bhangaokar (2015) gave 8- and 11-year-old Indian children moral dilemmas to ponder and found that they often thought about moral issues in religious or spiritual terms. They considered individual rights about as often and the good of the community too, but less often. These children were concerned about what behavior will please or displease God. Talking about why telling a lie would be wrong, for example, an 11-year-old girl said, "We will feel guilty, and our soul will be restless. That means that we are not doing right, we cannot steal or lie while we also worship God or pray for his blessings. . ." (Pandya & Bhangaokar, 2015, p. 33). Studying Indian adolescents and adults, Kapadia and Bhangaokar (2015) found emphasis on individual autonomy and rights to be greater among adolescents than among adults, but

emphasis on community and divinity themes to be greater among adults.

Lene Arnett Jensen (2015) has used Shweder's three ethics as the basis for a cultural-developmental perspective on morality—a perspective that guided these studies of Indian children and adults. She maintains that individuals in different cultural and subcultural contexts follow different developmental trajectories that involve different mixes of the ethics of autonomy, community, and divinity at different ages. Much remains to be learned about these trajectories, but cross-cultural research has already made an important point: There are more ways to think about moral issues than Kohlberg's rights and justice model suggests.

IndiaPicture/Alamy Stock Photo

Runaway Trolleys

We invite you to read and respond to these two moral dilemmas (Greene et al., 2001, p. 2105) and then return to the section Moral Intuition and Emotion.

1. **Switch Dilemma.** A runaway trolley is headed for five people who will be killed if it proceeds on its present course. The only way to save them is to hit a switch that will turn the trolley onto an alternate set of tracks where it will kill one person instead of five. Ought you to turn the trolley in order to save five people at the expense of one?

2. **Footbridge Dilemma.** As before, a trolley threatens to kill five people. You are standing next to a large stranger on a footbridge that spans the tracks, in between the oncoming trolley and the five people. . . . The only way to save the five people is to push this stranger off the bridge, onto the tracks below. He will die if you do this, but his body will stop the trolley from reaching the others. Ought you to save the five others by pushing this stranger to his death?

emotional component of morality more fully. As you have seen already, Martin Hoffman, Grazyna Kochanska, and others have long highlighted the importance of emotions like empathy and guilt in motivating moral action. Now a number of scholars are converging on the idea that gut emotional reactions and intuitions play a critical role in moral decision making (Gibbs, 2014; Greene, 2008, 2013; Haidt, 2008).

Think about whether you would eat your fellow passengers after a plane crash in the mountains if there were nothing else to eat. Most of us say, "Ewww," finding the idea morally repugnant. We immediately know in our gut, without a need for contemplation, that cannibalism is wrong. Jonathan Haidt (2001, 2008, 2012) argues that we have evolved as a species to have many such quick moral intuitions, often rooted in emotions like disgust. He believes that these intuitions are more important than deliberative reasoning in shaping moral decisions. If deliberate thought of the sort emphasized by Kohlberg plays a role at all, Haidt suggests, it is mainly to rationalize after the fact what we have already decided intuitively. Often, we cannot even come up with logical reasons for our gut reactions.

Like Haidt, Joshua Greene has proposed a **dual-process model of morality** in which deliberate thought and intuition/emotion play distinct roles in morality (see ● **Table 13.5**; and Gibbs, 2014). Greene maintains that both reason and intuition/emotion are important and has tried to figure out why we sometimes make judgments based on quick, emotion-based intuitions and other times make judgments using more deliberative

cognitive processes and what parts of the brain are involved in each. Look again at Engagement 13.2. Despite the similarities between the two trolley car scenarios there, most people would hit the switch in the switch scenario but would not push the stranger off the bridge in the footbridge scenario. Was that your response? Why do you think you reacted that way?

Greene and his colleagues (2001) have proposed that it is because the footbridge dilemma evokes a strong emotional response that the first scenario does not: we are appalled at the idea of directly killing a person with our own hands, possibly because we have evolved to feel such revulsion. Using the fMRI imaging techniques of cognitive neuroscience, Greene and his colleagues have demonstrated that areas of the brain associated with emotion are more active when people think about killing the large man in the footbridge scenario, whereas areas of the brain associated with rational cognition are more active when people weigh the idea of sacrificing the one for the many in the switch problem. Thus the findings were consistent with Greene's (2008) concept of a dual-process model of morality involving: (1) an emotion-based intuitive process that prompts us, quickly and without awareness, to focus on (and abhor) the harm that would be done if we violated moral principle (as by pushing a stranger to his death); and (2) a more deliberative, cognitive approach in which we weigh the costs and benefits of an action in a cool and calculating manner (and conclude that it is more rational to sacrifice one life than to lose five).

Other evidence supports Greene's dual-process model and the idea that we use different parts of the brain to make intuitive and deliberative moral decisions (Greene, 2009, 2013; Greene et al., 2008; Moore, Lee, Clark, & Conway, 2011). Much remains to be learned, though. When do we go with our gut reactions and when do we rely on conscious deliberation? How do we integrate signals from the amygdala of the brain (emotion) and the prefrontal cortex (reasoning), especially when they are pulling us in different directions (Shenhav & Greene, 2014)? We do not yet know much about the development of the intuitive and deliberative systems. So far, brain imaging studies suggest that empathic responses may decrease from childhood to adulthood while cognitive appraisal increases. With age, the emotional responses of

● **Table 13.5** Dual-Process Models of Morality

Moral Cognition/ Reasoning (Emphasized by Kohlberg)	Moral Emotion/Intuition (Emphasized by Haidt, Greene)
Rational thought	Intuition
Cold logic	Hot emotion
Controlled processes	Automatic processes
Impartiality	Empathy
Careful deliberation	Quick gut reaction

the amygdala and the cognitive responses of the prefrontal cortex also become better integrated (Decety & Howard, 2014; Decety, Michalska, & Kinzler, 2012). In sum, the dual-processing perspective raises new and interesting questions about the distinct roles of quick, emotion-based intuition and deliberate reasoning in morality—and about how we come to integrate them to guide our behavior.

Predicting Moral Action

Kohlberg focused primarily on moral reasoning rather than moral behavior. But does how one reasons predict how one behaves? Although a person may decide to uphold or to break a law at any of Kohlberg's stages of moral reasoning, Kohlberg argued that more advanced moral reasoners are more likely to behave morally than less advanced moral reasoners are. For example, where the preconventional thinker might readily decide to cheat if the chances of being detected were small and the potential rewards were large, the postconventional thinker would be more likely to appreciate that cheating is wrong in principle, regardless of the chances of punishment or reward, because it infringes on the rights of others and undermines social order.

What does research tell us? Individuals determined to be at higher stages of moral reasoning are indeed more likely than individuals at lower stages to behave prosocially and ethically and less likely to behave immorally (Gibbs, 2014; Villegas & Vargas-Trujillo, 2015; Walker, 2004; Wu & Liu, 2014). Yet relationships between stage of moral reasoning and moral behavior are usually fairly weak (Cohen et al., 2014; Wu & Liu, 2014). This is likely because a variety of other factors influence behavior—the situational factors social learning theorists like Bandura emphasize, the gut emotional reactions Haidt and Greene call attention to, the moral ethics and norms that dominate in a given culture, and so on.

In sum, Kohlberg's stage theory has a good deal of support, but it

- underestimates children's moral sophistication;
- fails to appreciate cultural differences in thinking about morality;
- neglects intuition/emotion, as pointed out by dual-process theorists such as Haidt and Greene; and
- says too little about the many influences besides moral reasoning on moral behavior.

In the end, we do best recognizing that the moral reasoning of interest to Piaget and Kohlberg, the moral emotions and intuitions of interest to Freud and Hoffman and more recently Haidt and Greene, and the self-regulatory and moral disengagement processes highlighted by Albert Bandura—together with many other personal and situational factors—all help predict whether a person will behave morally or immorally when faced with an important moral choice.

Religion and Spirituality

Lawrence Kohlberg viewed moral development and religious development as distinct, but they are closely interrelated for the many people around the world whose religious or spiritual values and beliefs guide their moral thinking and behavior (Cohen, 2015; Nelson, 2009). Indeed, James Fowler (1981; Fowler & Dell, 2006) proposed stages in the development of religious faith from infancy to adulthood that parallel quite closely Kohlberg's stages of moral development. Fowler's stages lead from concrete images of God in childhood, to internalization of conventional religious beliefs during adolescence, to soul searching in emerging or early adulthood, and, for a few, progression to a more abstract, universal perspective on faith in middle age and beyond. This idea of universal stages of religious development, like Kohlberg's stages of moral development, has come into question. However, researchers are more interested than ever in the roles religion and spirituality play in life-span development (Ai, Wink, & Ardelt, 2010; King & Boyatzis, 2015; Nelson, 2009; Pargament, Exline, & Jones, 2013). Not only do religious and spiritual beliefs inform people's moral judgments and behavior but they shape their self-perceptions and relationships with other people and groups and affect their adjustment (Cohen, 2015; King & Boyatzis, 2015).

Religiousness has generally been defined as sharing the beliefs and participating in the practices of an organized religion. **Spirituality** is harder to define but involves a quest for ultimate meaning and for a connection with something greater than oneself, whether God, love, nature, or some other cosmic force (see King & Boyatzis, 2015; Nelson, 2009). Spiritual seeking may be carried out within the context of a religion (some people are both religious and spiritual) or outside it (some people say they are spiritual but not religious).

Children often adopt the beliefs of their parents, especially if their parents are religious and are warm and supportive (Power & McKinney, 2013). Children also think on their own about religious and spiritual matters, though, and do so in increasingly complex ways as they get older (Boyatzis, 2013). Adolescence or emerging adulthood is a particularly important time for raising religious and spiritual questions as part of identity formation (Alisat & Pratt, 2012; Good & Willoughby, 2008; Nelson, 2009). For most, the result is staying in the religious tradition in which they were raised but sometimes with a deeper and more personalized understanding. For others, questioning results in rejecting the religious beliefs one was taught as a child, undergoing a spiritual conversion, or developing one's own belief system, whether religious or not. Religious commitment, if it translates into a strong moral identity, can encourage empathy for others and work against antisocial tendencies (Hardy, Walker, Rackham, & Olsen, 2012; King & Boyatzis, 2015).

Is old age also a time for religious and spiritual growth? Most studies suggest that while formal participation in religious activities may decline in late adulthood owing to illness and disability, the importance attached to religion and involvement in more personal forms of participation like prayer remain steady or even increase (Ai et al., 2010). Michelle Dillon and Paul Wink traced changes over the years in both religiousness and spirituality in a sample of adults (Dillon & Wink, 2007; Wink & Dillon, 2002, 2003). The average level of religiousness was high in adolescence; decreased somewhat in middle age, possibly because people had many responsibilities and little time; and

The church is at the center of the African American community and can have both health and mental health benefits for those elderly people who are highly involved in it.

Blend Images/Dream Pictures/Getty Images

and spirituality are positively associated with health, mental health, and well-being (Ai et al., 2010; Greenfield, Vaillant, & Marks, 2009; Spilman et al., 2013; Wink & Dillon, 2008). Why might this be? Perhaps because religiousness and spirituality foster a sense of meaning and purpose in life and provide social support (Ai et al., 2010; Krause, 2013; Nelson, 2009).

Religion and spirituality may be especially important for certain racial and ethnic groups (King & Boyatzis, 2015; Krause, 2013; Mattis & Grayman-Simpson, 2013). For example, both African American and Caribbean Blacks age 55 and older report more religious participation of various types, more use of prayer to cope with stress, and more spirituality than Whites do (Taylor, Chatters, & Jackson, 2007). And compared to older White adults in the United States, older Black adults derive more meaning from their religion, and this sense of meaning is more strongly related for them than for Whites to life satisfaction, self-esteem, and optimism (Krause, 2003). Being highly religious and spiritual also serves to protect African American adults from depression (Cheadle et al., 2015; Ellison & Flannelly, 2009).

In sum, religiousness and spirituality are distinct, and spirituality especially may increase in later life. Moreover, both can contribute positively to a sense of meaning or purpose in life and to social support and, in turn, to good physical and mental health and a sense of well-being.

We have now completed our series of chapters on the development of the person as an individual, having examined the development of self-conceptions and personality (Chapter 11), identities as males or females (Chapter 12), and now social cognition and morality. Our task in upcoming chapters will be to put the individual even more squarely in social and cultural context. It should become clear that throughout our lives we are both independent and interdependent—separate from and connected to other developing persons.

rose again in people's late 60s and 70s. Meanwhile, spirituality also increased from middle age to later adulthood (Dillon & Wink, 2007). This was especially true among women, who are generally more religious and more spiritual than men (see also Brown et al., 2012). These findings confirm Erik Erikson's view of old age as centered on the issue of integrity versus despair—as a time for reflecting and finding meaning in life (Atchley, 2009; Nelson, 2009).

Does it benefit people to be highly religious or spiritual? Correlation is not necessarily causation, but both religiousness

Checking Mastery

1. How does moral reasoning typically change over the adult years?
2. What are the two distinct processes in dual-process models of morality?
3. What is the main difference between being highly religious and being highly spiritual?

Making Connections

1. Thinking about all the material on moral development, what do you view as the main strengths and weaknesses of Lawrence Kohlberg's theory of morality and moral development?
2. To what extent do religious or spiritual beliefs enter into your own thinking about moral choices? You might start with your thinking about controversial matters of life and death—abortion, mercy killing, and capital punishment.

Chapter Summary

13.1 Social Cognition

- Social cognition (thinking about self and others) is involved in all social behavior, including moral behavior. Starting in infancy with milestones such as joint attention, understanding of intentions, and pretend play, children develop a theory of mind—a desire psychology at age 2 and a belief–desire psychology at age 4 as evidenced by passing false belief tasks. Developing a theory of mind requires a normal brain and experience communicating about mental states.

- In characterizing other people, preschool children focus on physical features and activities, children 8 years and older on inner psychological traits, and adolescents on integrating trait descriptions to create personality profiles. With age, children also become more adept at perspective taking. Social cognitive skills often improve during adulthood and hold up well but may decline late in life if basic cognitive abilities are taxed or a person becomes socially isolated.

13.2 Perspectives on Moral Development

- Morality has emotional, cognitive, and behavioral components. Sigmund Freud's psychoanalytic theory emphasized the superego and moral emotions, and Martin Hoffman has emphasized empathy as a motivator of moral behavior.

- Building on the work of cognitive-developmental theorist Jean Piaget, Lawrence Kohlberg proposed three levels of moral reasoning—preconventional, conventional, and postconventional— each with two stages.

- Social cognitive theorist Albert Bandura focused on how moral behavior is influenced by learning, situational forces, self-regulatory processes, and moral disengagement.

- Evolutionary theorists (Krebs, Tomasello) consider emotion, cognition, and behavior and maintain that humans have evolved to have moral and prosocial tendencies.

13.3 The Infant

- Although infants are amoral in some respects, they begin learning about right and wrong through early disciplinary encounters, internalize rules, and display impressive empathy and prosocial behavior early in life, just as they show antisocial behavior on occasion. Their moral growth is facilitated by a secure attachment and what Kochanska calls a mutually responsive orientation between parent and child.

13.4 The Child

- Kohlberg and Piaget underestimated the moral sophistication of young children (for example, their ability to consider intentions, to distinguish between moral and social-conventional rules, and to seek fairness); still, most children display preconventional moral reasoning.

- Reinforcement, modeling, Hoffman's disciplinary approach of induction, and proactive parenting strategies can foster moral growth, and a child's temperament interacts with the approach to moral training parents adopt to influence outcomes.

13.5 The Adolescent

- During adolescence, a shift from preconventional to conventional moral reasoning is evident, and some adolescents forge a moral identity.

- Adolescent antisocial behavior, both early and late onset, can be understood in terms of Kenneth Dodge's social information-processing model and Gerald Patterson's coercive family environments and the negative peer influences they set in motion. Genetic predisposition interacts with a variety of social–environmental influences. Attempts to prevent or reduce antisocial behavior, including bullying, are varied, including the Fast Track program and the positive youth development movement.

13.6 The Adult

- A minority of adults progress from the conventional to the postconventional level of moral reasoning; elderly adults typically reason as complexly as younger adults.

- Kohlberg's early stages of moral reasoning form an invariant sequence, but he underestimated children, failed to appreciate cultural differences in bases for moral judgment, and slighted moral emotion and the many other influences on moral behavior.

- Researchers like Haidt and Greene have proposed dual-process models of morality that include both deliberative reasoning and emotion-based intuitions.

- Religiousness and spirituality become stronger in later life and are associated with good physical and mental health and well-being for many people.

Key Terms

social cognition **400**

false belief task **400**

theory of mind **400**

desire psychology **401**

belief–desire psychology **402**

mirror neurons **403**

mind-mindedness **403**

perspective-taking skills **405**

morality **407**

empathy **407**

prosocial behavior **407**

antisocial behavior **408**

moral reasoning **408**

preconventional morality **408**

conventional morality **409**

reciprocity **409**

postconventional morality **409**

moral disengagement **411**

amoral **412**

self-control **414**

mutually responsive orientation **414**

delay of gratification **415**

moral rules **417**

social–conventional rules **417**

love withdrawal **417**

power assertion **417**

induction **417**

proactive parenting strategies **418**

moral identity **419**

juvenile delinquency **420**

conduct disorder **420**

hostile attribution bias **421**

coercive family environment **421**

bullying **423**

positive youth development (PYD) **423**

dual-process model of morality **427**

religiousness **428**

spirituality **428**

14 Emotions, Attachment, and Social Relationships

Mike Pohle was about to graduate and wanted to find a job close to his fiancee, Marcy Crevonis (Jones, 2007). He slept every night in a Phillies jersey she gave him and had already named the five children they hoped to have. They were soul mates. As Marcy put it, "We were the same person. We shared the same thoughts. We finished each other's sentences" (Jones, 2007, p. C1).

Mike Pohle was one of the 32 victims of the mass murders at Virginia Tech University, April 16, 2007. Marcy had walked him part of the way to his German class that morning and raced to find him when his class was to end but was blocked by the police. Told of Mike's death, she went back to his apartment, put on the Phillies jersey, and wept.

The shooter, Seung Hui Cho, had no soul mates. He was an unusually quiet child who did not respond to greetings; one high school classmate recalled the jokes about him: "We would just say, 'Did you see Seung say nothing again today?'" (Cho & Gardner, 2007, p. A8). Cho spent his lonely days writing stories of violence and death. He had been diagnosed and treated for social anxiety disorder and selective mutism as a child, but he never made this known to Virginia Tech, and deteriorated in college (Schulte & Craig, 2007). As a result, he was almost completely isolated from the human community.

How did their developmental experiences prepare Mike and Marcy to fall in love? What kept Seung from developing close human relationships, and what made him so angry at his fellow humans? Think about Mike Pohle and Seung Hui Cho as you read this chapter. It concerns our emotional lives and closest social relationships and their interrelationships across the life span. We explore how we develop the emotional security and social competence it takes to interact positively with other people and to enter into intimate relationships with them. We also examine the developmental implications of being deprived of close relationships. We begin by examining the emotions that are so much a part of our close relationships.

LEARNING OBJECTIVES

- Distinguish between primary and secondary or self-conscious emotions, giving examples and indicating when they emerge.

- Discuss age-related changes in mastery of emotion regulation skills, the concept of mixed emotions, and display rules for emotion.

- Using socioemotional selectivity theory, explain why older adults typically have greater emotional well-being than adolescents.

What is an emotion? It is a complex phenomenon that involves a subjective feeling ("I'm mad," "I feel hot"), physiological changes (a pounding heart), behavior (an enraged face, a door slammed), and often a cognitive appraisal as well ("No wonder I'm mad—He embarrassed me in front of everyone.") (see Goodvin, Thompson, & Winer, 2015; Gross, 2014). Emotions are detectable in the first days of life, but their character changes as we develop cognitively and as we learn to express and regulate or control them. Parent–child relationships involve strong emotions, and caregivers are critical in shaping the course of emotional development.

First Emotions and Emotion Regulation

Carroll Izard (1982; Izard & Ackerman, 2000) and his colleagues maintain that basic emotions are biologically based, develop early in life, and play critical roles in motivating and organizing behavior. By videotaping infants' responses to such events as having a toy taken away or seeing their mothers return after a separation, analyzing specific facial movements (such as the raising of the brows and the wrinkling of the nose), and asking raters to judge what emotion a baby's face reveals, Izard has established that very young infants express distinct emotions in response to different experiences and that adults can interpret which emotions they are expressing (see also Saarni et al., 2006). The work of Izard and others allows us to piece together an account of the early development of a number of so-called primary emotions, distinct basic emotions that emerge within the first 6 months of life (Lewis, 2008, 2015; and see ■ Figure 14.1).

At birth, babies show contentment (by smiling), interest (by staring intently at objects), and distress (grimaces in response to pain or discomfort). Within the first 6 months, six specific primary emotions evolve from these three. By 3 months of age or so, contentment becomes joy—pleasure at the sight of something

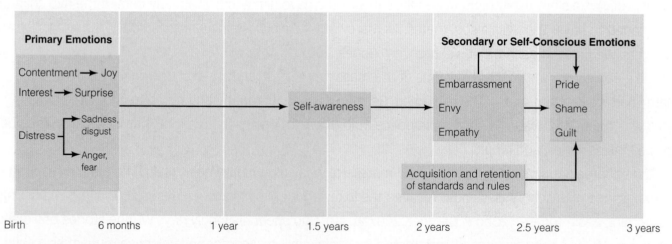

■ **Figure 14.1** The emergence of different emotions. Primary emotions (joy, surprise, fear, anger, sadness, and disgust) emerge in the first 6 months of life and evolve from there. Once self-awareness or mirror self-recognition is achieved, the first of the secondary or self-conscious emotions (embarrassment, for instance) emerge starting at about 18 months of age. Later in the second year, self-conscious emotions that require evaluating the self against standards (pride, for example) emerge.

Source: From Lewis, M. (2008). The emergence of human emotions. In M. Lewis, J. M. Haviland-Jones, & L. Feldman Barrett (Eds.), *Handbook of Emotions* (3rd ed.). © 2008. Reprinted with permission of Guilford Publications, Inc.

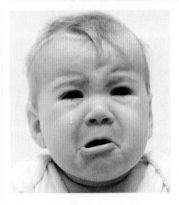

(a)   **(b)**

What emotions do you see in Baby A and Baby B? Your choices are the six primary emotions: anger, disgust, fear, surprise, joy, and sadness. (a) sadness; (b) anger

MitarArt/Shutterstock.com/Yasin Emir Akbas/iStock/Getty Images

familiar such as a big smile in response to Mom's face. Interest becomes surprise, such as when expectations are violated in games of peekaboo. Distress soon evolves into four familiar negative emotions, starting with disgust (in response to foul-tasting foods) and sadness. Angry expressions appear as early as 4 months—about the time infants acquire enough control of their limbs to push unpleasant stimuli away. Now instead of just being distressed when they are physically restrained, they look angrily at the person who is restraining them. Finally, fear is the last to appear.

Next, as Figure 14.1 also shows, come the so-called secondary or **self-conscious emotions** (Lewis, 2015). These emotions require self-awareness and begin to emerge at about 18 months of age, the age when infants become able to recognize themselves in a mirror and may start using words like "I" and "me" (see Chapter 11 on self-recognition). Once they achieve self-awareness, infants may show embarrassment when they are asked to dance or sing for guests. Then, later in the second year, when toddlers become able to judge their behavior against standards of performance, they may display the self-conscious emotions that involve evaluating the self: pride, shame, and guilt (Lewis, 2008). They can feel proud if they catch a ball because they know that's what you're supposed to do when a ball is tossed your way—or guilty if they spill their milk because they know you are not supposed to make messes. Michael Lewis (2015) has gone on to argue that the primary emotions are only action patterns rather than true emotions until children develop self-consciousness and can have thoughts such as, "I'm scared of that dog," or "I'm mad at that kid!"

Nature, Nurture, and Emotions

Primary or basic emotions such as interest and fear seem to be biologically programmed. They emerge in all normal infants at roughly the same ages and are displayed and interpreted similarly across cultures (Izard, 1982; Malatesta et al., 1989). As Charles Darwin recognized long ago, basic emotions probably evolved in humans because they helped our ancestors appraise and respond

appropriately in certain situations (Cole, Martin, & Dennis, 2004). These emotions also play a central role in the formation of attachments between infants and their caregivers. As John Bowlby, a theorist you will soon meet, emphasized, infants' emotional signals—whether expressions of joy or distress—prompt their caregivers to respond to them and have adaptive value for that reason as well (Kopp & Neufield, 2003).

Whether an infant tends to be predominantly happy and eager to approach new stimuli or irritable and easily upset depends in part on his genetically influenced temperament (Goldsmith, 2003; Rothbart, 2011). However, caregivers also help shape infants' predominant patterns of emotional expression (Fitness, 2013). Observational studies of face-to-face interactions between mothers and infants suggest that young infants display a range of positive and negative emotions, changing their expressions with lightning speed (once every 7 seconds) while their mothers do the same (Malatesta et al., 1986, 1989). Mothers mainly display interest, surprise, and joy, thus serving as models of positive emotions and eliciting positive emotions from their babies. Mothers also respond selectively to their babies' expressions; over the early months, they become increasingly responsive to their babies' expressions of happiness, interest, and surprise and less responsive to their negative emotions. Through basic learning processes, then, infants are trained to show happy faces more often than grumpy or sad ones—and they do just that over time. This early emotion socialization takes different shapes in different cultures (Friedlmeier, Corapci, & Benga, 2015).

At around 9 months of age, infants also begin to monitor their companions' emotional reactions to stimuli and use this information to decide how they should feel and behave—a phenomenon called **social referencing** (Feinman, 1992). If their mothers are wary when a stranger approaches, they too may be wary and back away. However, if their mothers smile at the stranger, they may approach the stranger eagerly. It is not just that 1-year-olds are imitating their parents' emotions, then; they are using their parents' emotional reactions to decide how to behave in new situations (Kim & Kwak, 2011). Unfortunately, this means that social referencing may be one way in which parents who are socially anxious train their babies to be socially anxious too (Murray et al., 2008).

Parents also socialize their infants' and young children's emotions by talking about emotions in daily life (Fitness, 2013; Thompson, 2014), for example, by saying things like, "What a happy baby you are now!" and "You're mad that you can't have more, aren't you?" Sensitive parents also help children express their feelings so that the parents can respond to their emotional needs. Gradually, in the context of a secure parent–child relationship in which there is plenty of emotional communication, infants and young children learn to understand emotions and express them appropriately (Thompson, 2014).

Emotion Regulation

To conform to their culture's and caregivers' rules about when and how different emotions should be expressed, and, perhaps most importantly, to keep themselves from being overwhelmed by their emotions, infants must develop strategies for **emotion regulation**—the processes involved in initiating, maintaining, and altering emotional responses (see Calkins & Mackler, 2011;

Gross, 2014; Schulz & Lazarus, 2011). Emotion regulation can be accomplished through such tactics as not putting oneself in, or thinking about, situations likely to arouse unwanted emotions (by avoiding monster movies and thoughts of monsters), reappraising or reinterpreting events or one's reactions to them (saying it wasn't really a monster or I wasn't really afraid—I was just surprised), or altering one's emotional responses to events (putting on a brave face to replace a scared face). Emotion regulation often involves suppressing or otherwise controlling negative emotions like anger and fear, but it also includes trying to heighten or prolong positive emotional experiences.

Infants are active from the start in regulating their emotions, but at first they have only a few simple emotion regulation strategies. Very young infants are able to reduce their negative arousal by turning away from unpleasant stimuli or by sucking vigorously on a pacifier (Mangelsdorf, Shapiro, & Marzolf, 1995). By the end of the first year, infants can move away from upsetting events or rock themselves. They also actively seek comfort from their caregivers when they are upset.

By 18–24 months, toddlers will try to control whatever is upsetting them—for example, by pushing a bothersome peer or a noisy mechanical toy away (Mangelsdorf et al., 1995). They may be able to cope with the frustration of waiting for snacks and gifts by playing with toys and otherwise distracting themselves (Grolnick, Bridges, & Connell, 1996), and they may knit their brows or compress their lips in an attempt to suppress their anger or sadness (Malatesta et al., 1989). Finally, as children gain the capacity for symbolic thought and language, they become able to regulate their distress cognitively—for example, by repeating the words, "Mommy home soon, Mommy home soon," after Mom goes out the door (Thompson, 1994).

The development of emotion regulation skills is influenced by both an infant's temperament and a caregiver's behavior (Grolnick, McMenamy, & Kurowski, 2006). Recall from Chapter 11 that babies differ temperamentally in both how emotionally reactive they are to events and how able they are to exert effortful control over their reactions (Rothbart, 2011). These aspects of temperament matter, but so does parenting. Very young infants who have few emotion regulation strategies of their own rely heavily on caregivers to help them—for example, by stroking them gently or rocking them when they are distressed, by calming them down after a joyful bout of play (Calkins & Hill, 2007; Cole, Michel, & Teti, 1994). As infants age, they gain control of emotion regulation strategies first learned in the context of the parent–child relationship and can regulate their emotions on their own (for example, by rocking themselves rather than looking to be rocked). By being sensitive and responsive caregivers, parents can help keep fear, anger, and other negative emotions to a minimum (Pauli-Pott, Mertesacker, & Beckmann, 2004). Much improvement in emotion regulation occurs at around age 3 to 4 as the prefrontal cortex develops and effortful control improves (Diaz & Eisenberg, 2015). Children who are not able to get a grip on their negative emotions, either because of their temperamental characteristics or because their caregivers do not help them master emotion regulation, tend to experience stormy relationships with both caregivers and peers and are at risk to develop behavior problems (Rothbart, 2011; Saarni et al., 2006).

Emotional Learning in Childhood

Preschool and school-aged children gain still more emotional competence; that is, they develop characteristic patterns of emotional expression, greater understanding of emotion, and better emotion regulation skills (Denham, Bassett, & Wyatt, 2007; Denham et al., 2003; Goodvin et al., 2015). Children who express emotions appropriate to the situation and have a good balance of positive to negative emotions, who understand their own and others' feelings and what situations trigger them, and who manage their emotions well make enjoyable companions. Perhaps that is why early emotional competence is a good predictor of social competence as reflected in peer acceptance and teachers' ratings of social adjustment (Denham et al., 2003).

One important advance in understanding emotions is recognizing that people can have mixed emotions about something—for example, that a child can both love and hate her mother. Susan Harter and Bonnie Buddin (1987) showed children aged 4–12 photographs of two different facial expressions of emotion at a time and asked them to explain how someone could have both emotions at once. Preschool children could not think of how to put two emotions together. As one put it, "It's hard to think of two feelings at the same time because you only have one mind" (Harter & Buddin, 1987). At age 8–9, children were better able to explain how two positive or two negative emotions could co-occur—for example, how you could be both sad and mad when a toy breaks. Only by age 11–12, though, were most children able to explain how you could have both a positive and a negative emotion about something simultaneously— for example, how you could be happy you made it to the finals but afraid you would do poorly. As children get older, then, they learn more about different emotions and the situations that arouse them and become more able to integrate different emotions into the same emotional experience (see also Larsen, To, & Fireman, 2007).

As children get older, they also learn about emotional display rules—cultural rules specifying what emotions should and should not be expressed under what circumstances (Saarni, 1984; Thompson et al., 2011). Rules such as "Don't laugh when someone falls down," "Look sad at a funeral," and "Act pleased when you receive a lousy gift" are examples. As children learn display rules, the gap between what they are experiencing inside and what they express to the world widens (a nice way of saying that they become better liars). They also become more aware of this gap between inner emotions and expressed emotions in themselves and others.

Carolyn Saarni (1984) conducted an interesting study of display-rule learning. Children aged 7, 9, and 11 were rewarded for their labors in a first research session with a nice gift, but after a second research session they received a boring baby toy. Here, then, was a situation (not unlike that faced by children who are given weird gifts from distant relatives for their birthdays) in which our culture's display rule is, "Look pleased about a gift, even if it's a disappointing one."

Children's reactions were coded as positive (an enthusiastic "thank you," a big smile), negative (an "ugh," shrug, wrinkled nose, and so on), and transitional (a lame attempt to follow the display rule such as a mumbled "thank you" or distressed smile). The 7-year-olds in the study, especially the boys, were not skilled at all at masking their disappointment; they said "ugh" a lot. Older children, especially girls, were more able to conform to the display rule by pretending to be delighted. In order to follow the display rule and regulate their emotions appropriately when given a lousy gift, children must develop (a) the understanding of emotions and emotional display rules needed to know what to do, and (b) the self-control skills needed to hide their negative reactions (Hudson & Jacques, 2014). It may not seem good that children become increasingly able to hide and alter their true feelings as they grow older, but life might be unbearable if adults were as open about their feelings as most young children are!

Display rules and how parents react to and socialize their children's emotions differ from culture to culture (see Friedlmeier et al., 2015; Mesquita, De Leersnyder, & Albert, 2014). For example, parents in individualistic cultures like the United States are more likely than parents in collectivist cultures like China to encourage the open expression of emotion; they want their children to assert themselves and feel proud when they do well and even to express negative emotions like anger when appropriate. Chinese, Japanese, and other East Asian parents are likely to view such self-centered emotional displays as disruptive to smooth social relationships and to want their children to suppress self-focused emotions like anger. They encourage the expression of other-focused emotions—for example, empathy for someone in distress or shame after letting people down—and point out the negative effects of emotions like anger on others. **Exploration 14.1** examines more closely how parents' beliefs about emotional expression can affect their children's development.

● EXPLORATION 14.1

Emotion Coaching or Emotion Dismissing?

Good emotion coaching starts with noticing that a child is having an emotional experience.

Lisa Spindler Photography Inc/The Image Bank/Getty Images

How emotionally expressive were your parents when you were growing up, and how did they react to your emotional outbursts? Parents differ a good deal in their beliefs about emotions, and these emotional philosophies guide how they express and regulate their own emotions, react to their children's emotions, and teach their children about emotions (Bariola, Gullone, & Hughes, 2011; Halberstadt, 1991; Katz, Maliken, & Stettler, 2012). Moreover, the emotional training they provide their children can be changed through interventions (Gus, Rose, & Gilbert, 2015).

John Gottman and his colleagues (Gottman, Katz, & Hooven, 1996) identified two quite different approaches parents take to emotions.

Emotion coaching involves:

- being aware of even low-intensity emotions;
- viewing children's expressions of emotion, including negative ones, as opportunities for closeness and teaching;
- accepting and empathizing with children's emotional experiences;
- helping children understand and express their feelings; and
- helping children deal with whatever triggered their emotions.

The following example of a mother comforting her 5-year-old son after a frustrating game-playing session with other boys captures the spirit of emotion coaching:

You didn't like that he was bouncing your guy off the game, and that made you really mad. It's hard when you feel so angry. You're going "AAAH, he's bouncing my guy off there!" right? It makes you sad thinking about it, doesn't it? You know, after you stopped the game, the other guys said, "You know, Joey wasn't really doing so bad." You thought you were losing, but you weren't (Thompson et al., 2011, p. 238).

Emotion dismissing, by contrast, involves ignoring, denying, or even criticizing or punishing negative emotions or trying to convert them as quickly as possible into positive emotions. Consider a child who is not allowed to express sadness or frustration and anger by well-meaning parents who want nothing but happiness for their child and try to cheer her out of her bad moods or convince her that she is not really upset. This child misses opportunities to learn about anger and how to deal with it and does not get the sense that someone understands and empathizes with her and will help her cope with whatever prompted her emotional reaction.

In studies comparing emotion coaching and emotion dismissing, the emotion coaching approach wins hands down. It is associated with healthy emotional development and fewer emotional and behavioral problems (Katz et al., 2012). An intervention called Tuning in to Kids teaches emotion coaching skills to parents of preschool children and appears to be effective in increasing children's emotional knowledge and reducing their behavior problems (Havighurst et al., 2009, 2010, 2015). "Tuning in to Teens," a similar emotion coaching program for adolescents, has proven successful in improving emotion socialization by parents and, in turn, reducing family conflict and teen acting-out behavior (Havighurst, Kehoe, & Harley, 2015; and see Shortt et al., 2010). Research on emotion coaching provides still more evidence of the power of parents to foster healthy emotional development.

Adolescents' Emotional Lives

Ever since the founder of developmental psychology, G. Stanley Hall, characterized adolescence as a time of *storm and stress*, adolescents have been viewed as moody and emotionally volatile. Although most adolescents do not experience extreme emotional storm and stress, adolescents do seem to experience more negative and mixed emotions and more emotional ups and downs than either children or adults (Larson & Lampman-Petraitis, 1989; Riediger & Klipker, 2014). Why might this be?

One reason is that adolescents experience more negative life events than children do and so may simply have more to be depressed, anxious, angry, or moody about (Larson & Ham, 1993; Schulz & Lazarus, 2011). Because they are experiencing more emotional arousal at a time when the executive control centers of their brains have not fully developed, they can also have more difficulty than adults regulating their emotions (Lougheed & Hollenstein, 2012; Riediger & Klipker, 2014; Silvers et al., 2012).

But there's another interesting possibility: Teens may have different emotion regulation goals than other age groups. Michaela Riediger and her colleagues (Riediger, Schmiedek, Wagner, & Lindenberger, 2009) called participants ranging in age from 14 to 86 at random times on mobile phones and had them report their emotional experience—specifically, whether they were currently experiencing joyful, contented, interested, angry, nervous, and downhearted feelings. Participants were also asked about their emotion regulation goals at that moment—specifically, whether they were trying to enhance, maintain, or dampen their positive or negative emotions.

As ■ Figure 14.2 shows, teens showed more "contra-hedonic" motives than adults: Rather than seeking to optimize their

good moods, they often wanted to maintain or enhance their bad moods or dampen their good ones. At the other extreme, elderly adults were the most "prohedonic" of all age groups, often reporting that they were trying to maintain positive affect and dampen negative affect. As a result, the adolescents had the most mixed emotional lives, and emotional well-being—the difference between positive and negative affect—was lower in adolescence than in old age.

Why did the teens seem to want to go with their negative emotions? A closer look revealed that they often reported positive and negative emotions simultaneously and seemed to crave being able to combine the two, as in being afraid at a horror movie while enjoying the scary experience with friends, or being furious at a classmate but enjoying plotting revenge. Teens may have somewhat more negative emotional lives than children or adults, then, because they lead stressful lives, because they have difficulty regulating their emotions at times, and because they sometimes actively choose to savor negative and mixed emotions (see also Riediger, Wrzus, & Wagner, 2014).

Emotions and Aging

As you have just seen, older adults seem to live more positive emotional lives than other age groups. This is quite surprising to the many people who believe—wrongly—that there is a blunting of emotional experience in old age or that old people are generally miserable because of the losses and health problems that come with aging.

As it turns out, the emotional experiences of younger and older adults are far more similar than different and, when they differ, older adults seem to live more positive emotional lives. For example, the faces of older adults are equally expressive when they are asked to recall events that had made them feel various emotions (Malatesta & Kalnok, 1984; and see Levenson et al., 1991). Older adults are also skilled at emotion regulation, especially at achieving their main emotion regulation goal: maximizing positive emotions and minimizing negative ones (Charles & Carstensen, 2014; Labouvie-Vief et al., 2007; Magai et al., 2006; Mroczek, 2004). The main exception to the rule is this: On occasion, older adults may become emotionally overwhelmed by stressful life events that overtax their resources (Charles & Carstensen, 2014; Wrzus, Müller, et al., 2013).

In an especially revealing study, Laura Carstensen and her colleagues (2000, 2011) sampled the emotional experiences of African American and European American adults between age 18 and age 94 by paging them at random times over a 1-week period as they went about their lives and asking them to report their emotional states. They reassessed these people's daily emotional experiences 5 and 10 years later. In this longitudinal study, frequency of positive emotions did not change much over the years, but negative emotions became less frequent with age. As a result,

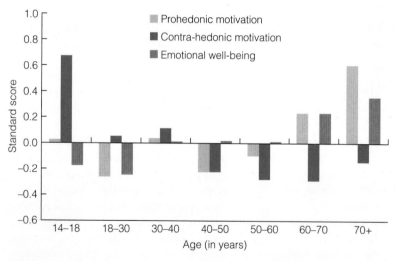

■ **Figure 14.2** Age differences in use of emotion regulation strategies aimed at optimizing positive emotions and minimizing negative ones (prohedonic motivation) versus optimizing negative emotions and minimizing positive ones (contra-hedonic motivation). Also shown is everyday emotional well-being (the balance of positive to negative emotions). Adolescents seem to seek—and experience—lots of negative and mixed emotions, whereas elderly adults have the strongest prohedonic motivation and experience greater emotional well-being than any other age group.

Source: Riediger, M., Schmiedek, F., Wagner, G. G., & Lindenberger, U. (2009). Seeking pleasure and seeking pain. Differences in prohedonic and contra-hedonic motivation from adolescence to old age, *Psychological Science*, 20, 1529–1535, Figure 1, p. 1531.

overall emotional well-being—the balance of positive to negative emotions—increased with age, until leveling off in very old age.

Older adults also experienced longer-lasting positive emotions and more fleeting negative ones and fewer emotional ups and downs in a day, suggesting that they are more able than younger adults to savor happy emotions while cutting short the sad and angry ones (see also Kliegel, Jager, & Phillips, 2007). As Carstensen et al. (2011), concluded, "Contrary to the popular view that youth is the 'best time in life,' . . . the peak of emotional life may not occur until well into the 7th decade (p. 29)." Finally, this study revealed that everyday emotional experience may matter: A positive ratio of positive to negative emotional experiences predicted survival over a 13-year period.

Based on her research, Carstensen (1992) has put forth **socioemotional selectivity theory** to help explain both the positive emotional lives and the changing social relationships of aging adults (see also Charles & Carstensen, 2010; Lang & Carstensen, 2002). According to this view, the perception that one has little time left to live prompts aging adults to put less emphasis on the goal of acquiring information for future use and more emphasis on the goal of fulfilling current emotional needs. As a result, older adults narrow their range of social partners to those who bring them emotional pleasure, usually family members and close friends, and let other social relationships fall by the wayside. By contrast, younger adults, seeing all kinds of time ahead of them, want the social stimulation and new information that strangers and acquaintances provide—and are even willing to sacrifice some emotional well-being to deal with these sometimes unpleasant people.

Carstensen has discovered that older adults achieve their goal of emotional fulfillment in part through what she calls a **positivity effect**: a tendency for older adults to pay more attention to, better remember, and place more priority on positive information than on negative information (Charles & Carstensen, 2014; Reed & Carstensen, 2012). This helps them optimize positive emotions and maintain well-being despite some of the challenges associated with aging. Interestingly, neuroscientists find that two key brain centers involved in emotions—the amygdala and the ventromedial area of the prefrontal cortex—degenerate less with age than the main brain areas involved in cognition (Mather, 2016).

In sum, older adults lead rich and rewarding emotional lives. They are able to experience and express emotions fully but also regulate them effectively to optimize positive feelings and minimize negative ones. Other factors are undoubtedly involved, but Carstensen's socioemotional selectivity theory and the positivity effect suggest that an emphasis on emotional fulfillment goals and a bias toward positive information contribute. So does continued good functioning by the emotion processing centers of the brain. Indeed, we learn from research on emotions and emotion regulation that, across the life span, humans actively shape their emotional experiences to suit their goals (Riediger & Luong, 2016). We now turn to the social relationships that have so much to do with our emotional lives.

Contrary to stereotype, elderly adults lead rich and generally positive emotional lives, possibly because they see little time left to them and seek emotional gratification in close relationships.

iStockphoto.com/annedehaas

Checking Mastery

1. What milestone in development must be achieved before an infant will show embarrassment, and what kind of emotion is embarrassment?
2. What is an example of an emotional display rule?
3. According to Carstensen's socioemotional selectivity theory, why do older adults typically have good emotional well-being?

Making Connections

1. Describe a couple of instances in your own life when you have displayed the "contra-hedonic motivation" that Michaela Riediger and her colleagues have found to be more common during adolescence than during late adulthood. Explain why you might have sought to enhance a negative emotion or dampen a positive one.
2. Much research suggests that good emotion regulation in childhood is associated with good developmental outcomes. Argue that a child could show too much of this good thing called emotion regulation and suggest some negative effects this could have.

14.2

Perspectives on Relationships

LEARNING OBJECTIVES

- Outline the main argument of Bowlby and Ainsworth's attachment theory, with emphasis on the role of nature and nurture in attachment and the mechanism through which early attachments have lasting effects on development.

- Discuss two theorists who claim that peers are more important than parents in development.

Developmental theorists agree that social relationships are critical in human development, but they have disagreed about which relationships are most critical. Many noted theorists have argued that no social relationship is more important than the first: the one between parent and child. Sigmund Freud (1930) left no doubt: A warm and stable mother–child relationship is essential for normal personality development. His follower Erik Erikson tended to agree, emphasizing the importance of responsive parenting to the development of trust in the parent–infant relationship. These theorists, in turn, influenced the architects of today's most influential theory of close human relationships, attachment theory, to focus on the lasting significance of early parent–child relationships.

Attachment Theory

Attachment theory was formulated by British psychiatrist John Bowlby (1969, 1973, 1980, 1988), and it was elaborated on by his colleague Mary Ainsworth, an American developmental psychologist (1989; Ainsworth et al., 1978; and see Cassidy & Shaver, 2016). The theory was based primarily on **ethology**, the study of the behavior of various species in their natural environments and the evolution of that behavior (Archer, 1992). Attachment theory therefore asked how attachment might have helped our ancestors adapt to their environment. Bowlby also drew on concepts from psychoanalytic theory (he was a psychoanalytic therapist who studied the contribution of mother–child relationships to later psychopathology) and cognitive theory (he was interested in expectations about self and other, as you will see).

According to Bowlby (1969), an **attachment** is a strong affectional tie that binds a person to an intimate companion. It is also a behavioral system through which humans regulate their emotional distress when under threat and achieve security by seeking proximity to another person. For most of us, the first attachment we form, around 6 or 7 months of age, is to a parent.

How do we know when a baby becomes attached to his mother? He will try to maintain proximity to her—crying, clinging, approaching, following, doing whatever it takes to maintain the desired closeness to her and expressing his displeasure when he cannot. He will prefer her to other people, reserving his biggest smiles for her and seeking her when he is upset, discomforted, or afraid; she is irreplaceable in his eyes. He will also be confident about exploring his environment as long as he knows that his mother is there to provide the security he needs.

Notice that an infant attached to a parent is rather like an adult "in love" (like Mike or Marcy at the start of the chapter). True, close emotional ties are expressed in different ways, and

serve different functions, at different points in the life span. Adults, for example, do not usually feel compelled to follow their mates around the house, and they look to their loved ones for more than comforting hugs and smiles. Nonetheless, there are basic similarities among the infant attached to a caregiver, the child attached to a best friend, and the adolescent or adult attached to a romantic partner. Throughout the life span, the objects of our attachments are special, irreplaceable people to whom we want to be close and from whom we derive a sense of security (Ainsworth, 1989).

Nature, Nurture, and Attachment

Drawing on ethological theory and research, Bowlby argued that both infants and parents are biologically predisposed to form attachments because they contribute to survival. It makes sense to think, for example, that young birds tended to survive if they stayed close to their mothers so that they could be fed and protected from predators—but that they starved or were gobbled up, and therefore failed to pass their genes to future generations, if they strayed. Thus, chicks, ducks, and goslings may have evolved to engage in **imprinting**, an innate form of learning in which the young will follow and become attached to a moving object (usually the mother) during a critical period early in life.

Noted ethologist Konrad Lorenz (1937) observed imprinting in young goslings and found that it is automatic and unlearned,

Ethologist Konrad Lorenz demonstrated that goslings would become imprinted to him rather than to their mother if he was the first moving object they encountered during their critical period for imprinting. Human attachment is more complex but is also biologically based.

Nina Leen/Time & Life Pictures/Getty Images

that it occurs only within a critical period shortly after the bird has hatched, and that it is irreversible—once the gosling begins to follow a particular object, whether its mother or Lorenz, it will remain attached to that object. The imprinting response is considered a prime example of a species-specific and largely innate behavior that has evolved because it has survival value. Subsequent research has shown that it is not quite as automatic and different from other learning as originally claimed, that the "critical" period is more like a "sensitive" period, and that imprinting can be reversed (Spencer et al., 2009).

What about human infants? Babies may not become imprinted to their mothers, but they certainly form attachments in infancy and follow their love objects around. Bowlby argued that they come equipped with several other behaviors besides proximity-seeking that help ensure adults will love them, stay with them, and meet their needs. Among these behaviors are sucking and clinging, smiling and vocalizing (crying, cooing, and babbling), and expressions of negative emotion (fretting and crying).

Moreover, Bowlby argued, just as infants are programmed to respond to their caregivers, adults are biologically programmed to respond to an infant's signals. Just see if you can ignore a baby's cry or fail to smile when a baby grins at you. Adults are even hormonally prepared for caregiving. Oxytocin is a hormone produced primarily in the hypothalamus that plays roles in facilitating caregiving and parent–infant attachment in animals and humans (Feldman, 2016). It affects the muscles that facilitate contractions during labor and the release of milk during breastfeeding. Moreover, mothers with high levels of oxytocin before birth engage in higher levels of positive attachment behavior after the birth, think more about their relationships with their infants, and check more often on their infants than mothers with lower levels of the hormone (Feldman et al., 2007). Oxytocin seems to prime parents (fathers too) to form attachments to their babies, then. Administered by nasal spray, it also seems to increase interpersonal trust among adult partners, although only for some people in some contexts (Bartz, 2016; Schneiderman, Zagoory-Sharon, Leckman, & Feldman, 2012).

Just as the imprinting of goslings occurs during a critical period, human attachments form during what Bowlby viewed as a sensitive period for attachment, the first 3 years of life. But attachments do not form automatically. According to Bowlby, a responsive social environment is critical: An infant's preprogrammed signals to other people may eventually wane if caregivers are unresponsive to them. Ultimately, the security of an attachment relationship depends on both nature and nurture—on the interaction over time between a biologically prepared infant and a biologically prepared caregiver and on the sensitivity of each partner to the other's signals.

Attachment and Later Development

Bowlby maintained that the quality of the early parent–infant attachment has lasting impacts on development, especially on later relationships. He proposed that, based on their interactions with caregivers, infants construct expectations about relationships called internal working models—cognitive representations of themselves and other people that guide their processing of social information and their behavior in relationships (Bowlby, 1973;

see also Bretherton, 1996). Securely attached infants who have received responsive care will form internal working models suggesting that they are lovable and that other people can be trusted to care for them. By contrast, insecurely attached infants subjected to insensitive, neglectful, or abusive care may conclude that they are difficult to love, that other people are unreliable, or both. Because of their internal working models, insecure infants would be expected to avoid or to be anxious in close relationships later in life. They may, for example, be wary of getting too close to anyone or become jealous and overly dependent if they do.

In sum, attachment theory, as developed by John Bowlby and elaborated with Mary Ainsworth, claims the following:

- The capacity to form attachments is part of our evolutionary heritage.
- Attachments unfold through an interaction of biological and environmental forces during a sensitive period early in life.
- The quality of the attachment between infant and caregiver shapes later development and the quality of later relationships.
- Internal working models of self and others are the mechanism through which early experience affects later development.

Peers: The Second World of Childhood

But what about other kids: Aren't they also critical to a child's development? A peer is a social equal, someone who functions at a similar level of behavioral complexity—often someone of similar age (Lewis & Rosenblum, 1975). Although the parent–child relationship is undoubtedly important in development, some theorists argue that relationships with peers are at least as significant. In effect, they argue, there are "two social worlds of childhood"—one involving adult–child relationships, the other involving peer relationships—and these two worlds contribute differently to development (Rubin et al., 2015; Youniss, 1980).

From an evolutionary perspective, it makes sense to think that humans evolved to live as members of groups, just as they evolved to form close one-on-one attachments to their parents. And as you saw in Chapter 13, Jean Piaget believed that because peers are equals rather than powerful authority figures, they help children learn that relationships are reciprocal, force them to hone their perspective-taking skills, and contribute to their social cognitive and moral development in ways that parents cannot. Peer relationships are more equal, more voluntary, and less lasting than parent–child relationships, so we simply must learn to get along with peers (Rubin et al., 2015).

Another theorist who believed in the power of peer relationships, especially friendships, was neo-Freudian theorist Harry Stack Sullivan (1953; see also Buhrmester & Furman, 1986). Sullivan stressed that social needs change as we get older and are gratified through different kinds of social relationships at different ages. The parent–child relationship is central up to about age 6 in providing tender care and nurturance, but then peers become increasingly important. At first children need playmates; then they need acceptance by the peer group; and then around age 9 to age 12 they most need intimacy in the form of a close friendship. Sullivan stressed the developmental significance of these chumships, or close childhood friendships.

Having a close friend or chum not only teaches children to take others' perspectives but validates and supports children and can protect them from the otherwise harmful effects of a poor parent–child relationship or rejection by the larger peer group. Chumships also teach children how to participate in emotionally intimate relationships and therefore pave the way for romantic relationships during adolescence. Research bears Sullivan out (Bukowski, Motzoi, & Mayer, 2009), as we will see as we now examine the roles of both parents and peers in our changing social worlds.

Checking Mastery

1. How do ethological theorists explain why imprinting occurs in young goslings?

2. According to attachment theory, what is the mechanism through which early experience affects later social development?
3. Which two theorists believed that peers are at least as important as parents as contributors to development?

Making Connections

1. Ethological theory and psychoanalytic theory both influenced John Bowlby as he formulated attachment theory. Analyze how each contributed.
2. To whom do you believe you are "attached" right now, and what evidence would you cite that each such relationship is a true attachment?

14.3
The Infant

LEARNING OBJECTIVES

- Discuss how both the caregiver's attachment and the infant's attachment grow during the first year of life.

- Distinguish among the four types of parent-infant attachments and explain how a parent's behavior, an infant's temperament, and the cultural context can influence which type of attachment develops.

- Summarize the main lessons learned about attachment and later development from studies of infants in deprived institutions, infants separated from parents, infants attending day care, and infants with secure versus insecure attachments.

- Characterize the ability of infants to participate in relationships with peers.

Human infants are social beings from the start, but their social relationships change dramatically once they form close attachments to caregivers and develop the social skills that allow them to coordinate their own activities with those of other infants.

An Attachment Forms

Like any relationship, the parent–infant attachment is reciprocal. Parents become attached to their infants, and infants become attached to their parents.

The Caregiver's Attachment to the Infant

Parents often begin to form emotional attachments to their babies even before they are born. Moreover, parents who have an opportunity for skin-to-skin contact with their babies during the first few hours after birth often feel a special bond forming, although such bonding at birth is neither crucial nor sufficient for the development of strong parent–infant attachments (Goldberg, 1983). Not only are newborns cute, but their early reflexive behaviors, such as sucking, rooting, and grasping, help endear them to their parents (Bowlby, 1969). Smiling is an especially important social signal. Although it is initially a reflexive response to almost any stimulus, it is triggered by voices at 3 weeks of age and by faces at 5 or 6 weeks (Bowlby, 1969: Wolff, 1963).

Over the weeks and months, caregivers and infants develop synchronized routines much like dances, in which the partners

Smiling is one of the biologically based behaviors that help ensure adults will fall in love with babies.

zulufoto/Shutterstock.com

take turns responding to each other's leads (Stern, 1977; Tronick, 1989). Watch the synchrony as this mother plays peekaboo with her infant (Tronick, 1989, p. 112):

The infant abruptly turns away from his mother as the game reaches its "peak" of intensity and begins to suck on his thumb and stare into space with a dull facial expression. The mother stops playing and sits back watching. . . . After a few seconds the infant turns back to her with an inviting expression. The mother moves closer, smiles, and says in a high-pitched, exaggerated voice, "Oh, now you're back!"

Synchronized routines are likely to develop when caregivers are sensitive, providing social stimulation when a baby is alert and receptive but not pushing their luck when the infant's message is "Cool it—I need a break." When good parent–infant synchrony is achieved, it contributes to a secure attachment relationship (Jaffe et al., 2001) as well as to the development of emotion regulation skills (Feldman, 2007).

The Infant's Attachment to the Caregiver

Infants progress through four phases in forming attachments (Ainsworth, 1973; Bowlby, 1969):

1. **Undiscriminating social responsiveness** (birth to 2 or 3 months). Very young infants are responsive to voices, faces, and other social stimuli, but any human interests them.
2. **Discriminating social responsiveness** (2 or 3 months to 6 or 7 months). Infants begin to show preferences for familiar companions. They direct their biggest grins and most enthusiastic babbles toward those companions, although they are still friendly toward strangers.
3. **Active proximity seeking or true attachment** (6 or 7 months to about 3 years). Around 6 or 7 months, infants form their first clear attachments. Now an infant will follow her mother, protest when her mother leaves, and greet her mother warmly when she returns. Soon most infants become attached to other people as well—fathers, siblings, grandparents, regular babysitters (Schaffer & Emerson, 1964).
4. **Goal-corrected partnership** (3 years and older). By about age 3, partly because they have more advanced social cognitive abilities, children can participate in a **goal-corrected partnership**, taking a parent's goals and plans into consideration and adjusting their behavior accordingly. Thus, a 1-year-old cries and tries to follow when Dad leaves the house to talk to a neighbor, whereas a 4-year-old can understand where Dad is going and wait for his return. This final, goal-corrected partnership phase lasts a lifetime.

Attachment-Related Fears

Infants no sooner experience the pleasures of love than they discover the agonies of fear. One form of fear is **separation anxiety**: Once attached to a parent, a baby often becomes wary or fretful when separated from that parent. Separation anxiety normally appears after the first attachment forms, peaks between 14 and 18 months, and gradually becomes less frequent and less intense (Weinraub & Lewis, 1977). Still, even children and adolescents may become homesick and distressed when separated from their parents for a long time (Thurber, 1995).

A second fearful response that often emerges shortly after an infant becomes attached to someone is **stranger anxiety**—a wary or fretful reaction to the approach of an unfamiliar person that can vary in strength from staring and whimpering to screaming in terror (Schaffer & Emerson, 1964). Anxious reactions to strangers—often mixed with signs of interest—become common late in the first year and then decline (Sroufe, 1996).

How might babysitters, child care workers, and health professionals prevent stranger anxiety? Stranger anxiety is less likely to occur if an attachment figure is nearby (Morgan & Ricciuti, 1969), especially if the attachment figure reacts positively to the stranger and affects the baby's reactions positively through social referencing. It helps if the setting is a familiar one, but an unfamiliar environment like a doctor's office can become familiar if infants are given a few minutes to get used to it (Sroufe, Waters, & Matas, 1974). It also helps if the stranger approaches slowly while smiling, talking, and offering a familiar toy or suggesting a familiar activity and if he takes his cues from the infant rather than being pushy (Bretherton, Stolberg, & Kreye, 1981; Mangelsdorf, 1992; Sroufe, 1977). Finally, the stranger should not look any stranger than need be: Infants are most likely to fear strangers who violate their mental schemas or expectations (Kagan, 1972), as by wearing spiked green hair or a surgical mask and stethoscope.

Exploratory Behavior

The formation of a strong attachment to a caregiver also has the positive effect of facilitating exploratory behavior. Ainsworth and her colleagues (1978) emphasized that an attachment figure serves as a **secure base** for exploration—a point of safety from which an infant can feel free to venture—as well as a **safe haven** to which the infant can return for comfort if frightened. Thus Isabelle, a securely attached infant visiting a neighbor's home with Mom, may be comfortable cruising the living room as long as she can check occasionally to see that Mom is still on the sofa but may freeze and fret and stop exploring if Mom disappears into the bathroom. Isabelle may also beat a hasty retreat to the safe haven Mom provides if stressed by the doorbell, the entry of the neighbor's German shepherd, or some other unexpected event. Secure attachments allow us to explore the world but they also protect us from it when it becomes too scary.

Stranger anxiety is common at about a year of age but it can be prevented.

ERproductions Ltd/Blend Images/Getty Images

Quality of Attachment

Ainsworth's most important contribution to attachment theory was to devise a way to assess differences in the quality of parent–infant attachments. She and her associates created the **Strange Situation**, a now-famous procedure for measuring the quality of an attachment (Ainsworth et al., 1978). It consists of eight episodes that gradually escalate the amount of stress infants experience as they react to the approach of an adult stranger and two departures and returns of their caregiver. On the basis of an infant's pattern of behavior across the episodes, the quality of his attachment to a parent can be characterized as one of four types, one secure and three insecure (resistant, avoidant, and disorganized–disoriented).

1. **Secure attachment.** About 60% of 1-year-olds in the many societies that have been studied are securely attached to their mothers or primary caregivers (Colin, 1996; Howe, 2011). The securely attached infant actively explores the room when alone with his mother because she serves as a secure base. The infant is upset by separation but greets his mother warmly and is quickly comforted by her presence when she returns. The securely attached child is outgoing with a stranger when his mother is present. In the Bowlby–Ainsworth view, the securely attached infant "stays close and continuously monitors [the caregiver's] whereabouts (*proximity maintenance*), retreats to her for comfort if needed (*safe haven*), resists and is distressed by separations from her (*separation distress*), and explores happily as long as she is present and attentive (*secure base*)" (Hazan, Campa, & Gur-Yaish, 2006, p. 190).

2. **Resistant attachment.** About 10% of 1-year-olds show a resistant attachment, an insecure attachment characterized by anxious, ambivalent reactions (and also called anxious/ambivalent attachment). The resistant infant does not dare venture off to play even when her mother is present; her mother does not seem to serve as a secure base for exploration. Yet this infant becomes distressed when her mother departs, often showing stronger separation anxiety than the securely attached infant. When her mother returns, the infant is ambivalent: she may try to remain near her but is not comforted and does not calm down; she seems to resent the mother for having left, may resist if she tries to make physical contact, and may even hit and kick her in anger (Ainsworth et al., 1978). Resistant infants are also wary of strangers, even when their mothers are present. It seems, then, that resistant or ambivalent infants do all they can to get affection and comfort but never quite succeed.

3. **Avoidant attachment.** Infants with avoidant attachments (up to 15% of 1-year-olds) may play alone but are not very adventuresome, show little apparent distress when separated from their mothers, and avoid contact or seem indifferent when their mothers return. These insecurely attached infants are not particularly wary of strangers but sometimes avoid or ignore them, much as these babies avoid or ignore their mothers. In contrast to resistant infants, avoidant infants seem to have shut down their emotions and distanced themselves from their parents, as if they were denying their need for affection or had learned not to express their emotional needs.

4. **Disorganized–disoriented attachment.** Ainsworth's work initially focused on secure, resistant, and avoidant attachment styles, but some infants do not develop any of these consistent attachment styles. They seem confused. Up to 15% of infants—more in high-risk families—display what is now recognized as a fourth attachment classification, one that is associated with later emotional problems (Main & Solomon, 1990; van IJzendoorn, Schuengel, & Bakermans-Kranenburg, 1999).

Reunited with their mothers after a separation, these infants may act dazed and freeze or lie on the floor immobilized—or they may seek contact but then abruptly move away as their mothers approach them, only to seek contact again. Infants with a disorganized–disoriented attachment have not been able to devise a consistent strategy for regulating their negative emotions; they seem frightened of their parent and stuck between approaching and avoiding this frightening figure (Hesse & Main, 2006). She is clearly not a source of comfort for them.

● **Table 14.1** summarizes the features of these four patterns of attachment. What determines which of these attachment patterns will characterize a parent–infant relationship? The caregiver, the infant, and the cultural and social context all contribute.

The Caregiver's Contributions

According to Freud, infants in the oral stage of psychosexual development become attached to the individual who provides

The wire and cloth surrogate "mothers" used in Harlow's classic research. This infant monkey has formed an attachment to the cloth mother that provides "contact comfort," even though it must stretch to the wire mother in order to feed.

Science Source

● **Table 14.1** Child Behaviors in the Strange Situation Associated with Attachment Types and Related Parenting Styles

Behavior	Type of Attachment			
	Secure	**Resistant**	**Avoidant**	**Disorganized–Disoriented**
Child explores when caregiver is present to provide a secure base for exploration?	Yes, actively	No, clings	Yes, but play is not as constructive as that of secure infant	No
Child responds positively to stranger?	Yes, comfortable if caregiver is present	No, fearful even when caregiver is present	No, often indifferent, as with caregiver	No, confused responses
Child protests when separated from caregiver?	Yes, at least mildly distressed	Yes, extremely upset	No, seemingly unfazed	Sometimes; unpredictable
Child responds positively to caregiver at reunion?	Yes, happy to be reunited, quickly calmed	Yes and no, seeks contact, but resents being left; ambivalent, sometimes angry	No, ignores or avoids caregiver	Confused; may approach or avoid caregiver or do both
Parenting style	Sensitive, responsive	Inconsistent, often unresponsive (e.g., depressed)	Rejecting–unresponsive or intrusive–overly stimulating	Frightened (e.g., overwhelmed) and frightening (e.g., abusive)

them with oral pleasure, and the attachment bond will be most secure if a mother is relaxed and generous in her feeding practices. In a classic study conducted by Harry Harlow and Robert Zimmerman (1959), Freud's psychoanalytic view was put to the test—and failed. Monkeys were reared with two surrogate mothers: a wire "mother" and a cloth "mother" wrapped in foam rubber and covered with terrycloth. Half the infants were fed by the cloth mother, and the remaining infants were fed by the wire mother. To which mother did these infants become attached? There was no contest: Infants strongly preferred the cuddly cloth mother, *regardless of which mother had fed them*. They spent most of their time clinging to her, ran to her when they were upset or afraid, and showed every sign of being attached to her.

Harlow's research demonstrated that **contact comfort**, the pleasurable tactile sensations provided by a soft and cuddly "parent," is a more powerful contributor to attachment in monkeys than feeding. Contact comfort also promotes human attachments (Anisfeld et al., 1990). Moreover, many infants become attached to someone other than the adult who feeds them (Schaffer & Emerson, 1964).

In the end, it is the parent's behavior that most influences the quality of attachment, as shown in Table 14.1. Infants who enjoy *secure* attachments to their parents have parents who are sensitive and responsive to their needs and emotional signals, just as Bowlby and Ainsworth proposed (Ainsworth et al., 1978; De Wolff & van IJzendoorn, 1997). The importance of sensitive, responsive parenting in creating a secure attachment is one of the most established findings in developmental science.

Babies who show a *resistant* pattern of attachment often have parents who are inconsistent in their caregiving; they react enthusiastically or indifferently, depending on their moods, and are frequently unresponsive (Isabella, 1993; Isabella & Belsky, 1991). Mothers who are depressed, for example, often have difficulty responding

sensitively to their babies' signals and do not provide the comforting that helps babies regulate their negative emotions (Dawson & Ashman, 2000). The resistant infant may learn to cope with such unreliable caregiving by trying desperately—through clinging, crying, and other attachment behaviors—to obtain emotional support and comfort, and then becomes sad and resentful when these efforts fail.

The parents of infants with an *avoidant* attachment sometimes deserve to be avoided. Some are rejecting; they are impatient, unresponsive, and resentful when the infant interferes with their plans (Ainsworth, 1979; Isabella, 1993). Others have been called "intrusive"; often meaning well, they provide high levels of stimulation even when their babies become uncomfortably aroused and need a break so that they can regain control of their emotions (Isabella & Belsky, 1991). Infants with an avoidant attachment style may learn to avoid and make few emotional demands on adults who either seem to dislike their company or bombard them with stimulation they cannot handle.

Finally, a *disorganized–disoriented* style of attachment is evident in as many as 80% of infants who have been physically abused or maltreated (Carlson et al., 1989; and see Baer & Martinez, 2006) and is also common among infants whose mothers are severely depressed or abuse alcohol and drugs (Beckwith, Rozga, & Sigman, 2002). The parents of infants with a disorganized attachment pattern have been described as frightening and frightened—as fearful adults who are not up to the challenge of caring for an infant and create an unpredictable, scary environment for their babies (Hesse & Main, 2006). Infants with a disorganized attachment are understandably confused about whether to approach or avoid a parent who can be loving one minute but angry and abusive or indifferent the next. You can see each of the four types of attachment, then, as a quite reasonable way of coping with a particular brand of parenting.

The Infant's Temperament

An infant's temperament can also influence the quality of an attachment. Attachments tend to be insecure when infants are by temperament fearful, irritable, or unresponsive (Beckwith et al., 2002). The caregiver's style of parenting and the infant's temperament can also interact to determine the outcome. To illustrate, ■ Figure 14.3 shows the percentages of 12-month-olds who tested as securely attached as a function of whether they were difficult-to-read infants born prematurely and whether their mothers were depressed (Poehlmann & Fiese, 2001). When a difficult-to-read, premature infant was paired with a depressed mother, the odds of a secure attachment were especially low (see Leerkes, Blankson, & O'Brien, 2009).

So who affects the quality of parent–infant attachment more, the parent or the infant? The parent is clearly more influential. We know the infant's temperament is not the main influence on security of attachment because:

- Relationships between infant temperament and quality of attachment are often quite weak (Roisman & Groh, 2011).
- Many infants are securely attached to one parent but insecurely attached to the other (Kochanska & Kim, 2013; van IJzendoorn & De Wolff, 1997).
- An infant's genetic makeup, although it influences the infant's temperament, has little influence on quality of attachment (Fearon et al., 2006; Raby et al., 2012; Roisman & Fraley, 2008).
- Caregivers who are responsive and adjust to their baby's temperamental quirks are able to establish secure relationships even with temperamentally difficult babies (Leerkes et al., 2009; Mangelsdorf et al., 1990).

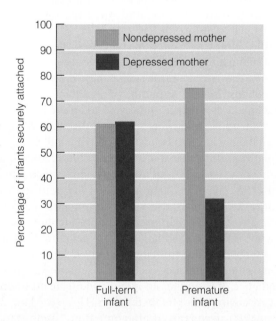

■ **Figure 14.3** The combination of a depressed mother and a premature infant means low odds that a secure attachment will form.

Source: Data from Poehlmann, J. & Fiese, B. H. The interaction of maternal and infant vulnerabilities on developing attachment relationships, *Development and Psychopathology, 13,* 1–11. © 2001 Guilford. Reprinted by permission from Cambridge University Press.

Compared with American babies, Japanese infants become more anxious in the Strange Situation because they are rarely separated from their mothers.

kdshutterman/Shutterstock.com

Cultural and Social Context

Finally, the broader social context surrounding caregiver and infant can affect how they react to each other. For example, the stresses associated with living in poverty or experiencing marital conflict may make it difficult for parents to provide sensitive care and may contribute to insecure attachments (Roisman & Booth-LaForce, 2014).

The cultural context in which caregiver and baby interact also colors their relationship. For instance, in Germany, an individualistic culture, parents strongly encourage independence and discourage clingy behavior, fearing that if they are too responsive to cries they will spoil their infants. This may explain why many German infants make few emotional demands on their parents and are often classified as avoidantly attached (Grossmann, Grossmann, & Keppler, 2005). By contrast, babies in the collectivist culture of Japan are rarely separated from their mothers early in life and are encouraged to be dependent on their mothers. They become highly distressed by separations such as those they must endure in the Strange Situation. As a result, they are more likely than American babies to be classified as resistantly attached (Takahashi, 1990; van IJzendoorn & Sagi, 1999).

Could findings like this mean that research on infant attachment is culturally biased? Might those Japanese babies who freak out in the Strange Situation actually be securely attached? Very possibly. In addition, we must appreciate that in many cultures infants do not have a single primary caregiver but instead are passed from caregiver to caregiver during the day. Among the Efe of the Democratic Republic of Congo, for example, infants were observed to be in contact with an average of 9 to 14 different people during a two-hour observation period (Morelli, 2015).

A number of researchers conclude that secure attachment may mean somewhat different things in different societies (Miller, Goyal, & Wice, 2015; Rothbaum & Morelli, 2005). At the same time, many of the key signs of a secure attachment are consistent across cultures (Posada et al., 2013). And the main predictions of attachment theory—especially the critical importance of parent sensitivity and responsiveness in fostering a secure attachment—are well supported across cultures (see Morelli, 2015; van IJzendoorn & Sagi-Schwartz, 2008). Overall, then, sensitivity and responsiveness of the caregiver (or in many cultures, the caregivers) is the primary influence on the quality of caregiver–infant attachment, but characteristics of both the baby's temperament and the surrounding cultural and social environment also affect it.

Implications of Early Attachment

From Freud on, psychologists have assumed that a secure parent–child relationship is critical in human development. Just how important is it? Several lines of research offer answers: studies of socially deprived infants; studies of infants who experience separations from their caregivers; and studies comparing the later development of securely and insecurely attached infants.

Social Deprivation

What happens to infants who never have an opportunity to form an attachment? It is better to have loved and lost than never to have loved at all, say studies of infants who grow up in deprived institutional settings where they are unable to form attachments (Leiden Conference, 2012; MacLean, 2003). In the 1990s, children from deprived institutions in Romania were adopted into homes in the United States, the United Kingdom, and Canada after the fall of the Romanian government (Gunnar, Bruce, & Grotevant, 2000). These adoptees reportedly spent their infancies in orphanages with 20–30 children in a room and only one caregiver for every 10–20 children; they spent most of their time rocking in their cribs with little human contact, much less hugs and synchronous routines (Fisher et al., 1997). How did they turn out?

Infants who spent their first several months or more in deprived orphanages displayed a host of problems—poor growth, medical problems, brain abnormalities, and delays in physical, cognitive, and social-emotional development (Leiden Conference, 2012; MacLean, 2003; McCall & Groark, 2015). What of their attachments after they were adopted? The good news is that about 90% had clearly become attached to their adoptive parents 9 months after adoption (Carlson et al., 2014). However, high proportions showed disorganized attachment behavior, as though they saw their parents as both comforting and threatening (see also Bakermans-Kranenburg et al., 2011; Zeanah, Berlin, & Boris, 2011). Many institutionalized children continue to show insecure and atypical attachment behavior as adolescents (Palacios et al., 2014).

A meta-analysis of many studies of institutionalized and otherwise maltreated and neglected children concluded that those who are adopted before 1 year of age have a good chance of becoming as securely attached to their caregivers as other children (van den Dries et al., 2009). However, high rates of insecure and disturbed attachment are observed among children adopted after their first birthday, and the problem is not lack of a single "mother figure." In adequately staffed institutions and communes, infants cared for by a few responsive caregivers turn out fine (Groark et al., 2005; St. Petersburg-USA Orphanage Research Team, 2008).

Apparently, then, normal development requires sustained interactions with sensitive and responsive caregivers—whether one or a few. Apparently too, children are resilient if they are given a reasonable chance to find someone to love. However, as Bowlby claimed, early social deprivation can leave lasting marks on development.

Separations

Now consider babies who form an attachment but are separated from their caregivers as a result of illness, war, death, divorce, or other circumstances. Bowlby (1960, 1980) discovered that these infants go through a grieving process in which they first protest and search frantically for their loved one, then become sad and listless once they give up, and sometimes then ignore or avoid their caregiver if she returns, only gradually warming up to her again.

Long-term separation of young children from a parent is an issue for military families when a family member is deployed. This can be a Strange Situation-like stress test not only for infants and children but for their parents, whose attachments to their partners are disrupted. Although most families cope well, some infants and children develop emotional and behavioral problems (Maholmes, 2012; Riggs & Riggs, 2011). The most important influence on whether children adapt well is whether the at-home parent or substitute caregiver provides sensitive and responsive care (Posada, Longoria, Cocker, & Lu, 2011). Programs specially designed for military families can help reduce the negative effects of deployment on infants and children (Lester et al., 2012).

Similarly, infants who are permanently separated from an attachment figure caregiver due to death, divorce, or another reason often have adjustment difficulties but normally recover if they have the security of an existing attachment or can form a new one (Bowlby, 1960, 1980; van IJzendoorn & Juffer, 2006). We should worry more about children who experience a series of permanent separations from caregivers, as happens to some infants and children who are

For military families, deployment arouses separation anxiety in all concerned.

AP Images/Heribert Proepper

repeatedly moved from one foster care placement to another. They may have long-lasting attachment problems and psychological disorders as a result of their repeated experiences of loving and losing (Tarren-Sweeney, 2013; Ward, Munro, & Dearden, 2006).

Day Care

What of the daily separations from their parents that infants experience when they are placed in day care centers or in family care homes (in which caregivers take children into their homes)? A major national longitudinal study of child care supported by the National Institute of Child Health and Human Development tracked infants through adolescence (NICHD, 2006; NICHD Early Child Care Research Network [ECCRN], 1997, 2006; Vandell et al., 2010). Overall, infants who experienced routine care by someone other than their mothers were not much different than infants cared for almost exclusively by their mothers in the many aspects of development studied. Most importantly, infants who received alternative care were no less securely attached to their mothers overall than infants who were tended by their mothers (Friedman & Boyle, 2008; Phillips, 2015; NICHD ECCRN, 1997).

Quality of parenting was a much stronger influence on these infants' attachments and later development than whether they had day care experience. Quality of day care also had impacts, though; infants fared poorest if their mothers were insensitive and unresponsive *and* they were subjected to poor-quality day care on top of it (NICHD ECCRN, 1997, 2006; Vandell et al., 2010). In sum, infants and young children who spend time in day care are not less securely attached to their parents than infants and young children cared for at home, on average. However, they are most likely to thrive if they receive both good quality parenting and good quality child care. From a policy perspective, it makes sense to make affordable and high-quality child care available to more families (Phillips, 2015).

Later Development of Securely and Insecurely Attached Infants

Finally, we can assess the importance of early attachment experiences by asking the following question: How much difference does having a secure rather than insecure attachment in infancy make later in life? Three main qualities distinguish children who were securely attached infants from those who were insecurely attached:

- **Intellectual competence**. Children who were securely attached as infants are described by teachers as more curious, self-directed, and eager to learn than insecurely attached children (Waters, Wippman, & Sroufe, 1979) and they are more engaged in classroom activities (Drake, Belsky, & Pasco Fearon, 2014). They have benefitted from having a secure base for exploration.
- **Social competence**. Children who had been securely attached as infants are more able to initiate play activities, are more sensitive to the needs and feelings of other children, and are more popular and socially competent (Booth-LaForce & Kerns, 2009; Waters et al.,

1979). Their positive interactions with caregivers have allowed them to develop good social skills and positive internal working models of self and others.

- **Emotion regulation**. Secure attachment in infancy is also linked to good emotion regulation and coping skills (Gunnar, 1998; Kochanska, 2001). The comforting and help with emotion regulation securely attached babies receive from their sensitive parents make them less reactive to stress than children who had insecure attachments (Diamond & Fagundes, 2010). Good emotion regulation, as you saw earlier, is in turn associated with fewer emotional and behavioral problems in childhood.

In late childhood, adolescence, and even adulthood, children who have enjoyed secure relationships with their parents early in life often continue to be well adjusted and to enjoy good relationships later in life (Elicker, Englund, & Sroufe, 1992; Simpson et al., 2007). In a revealing longitudinal study spanning the years from infancy to the early 20s, Jeffrey Simpson and his colleagues (2007) found that secure attachment in the Strange Situation at 12 months of age was linked to the quality of a child's peer relations in elementary school, which in turn predicted quality of friendships in adolescence, which in turn predicted the emotional quality of romantic relationships in early adulthood. Although quality of attachment during infancy and quality of romantic relationship in adulthood were not significantly correlated, they were indirectly associated through a chain of influence in which the quality of relationships in each developmental period affects the quality of relationships in the next period (see ■ Figure 14.4); see also Cassidy & Shaver, 2016; Fraley et al., 2013).

In sum, children are unlikely to develop normally if they never have the opportunity to form an attachment or if their relationships with adults are repeatedly severed. By contrast, a secure attachment during infancy and early childhood has positive implications for later intellectual, social, and emotional development and for the quality of later relationships. Yet you must avoid concluding that infants who are securely attached to their caregivers are forever blessed—or that infants who are insecurely attached to their caregivers are doomed. Early attachments may have few long-term consequences if they change later—and they quite often do. Factors such as a decline in a mother's sensitivity, the departure of a father from the home, and negative life events in the family can change a secure attachment into an insecure one—just as improvements in a mother's sensitivity or a family's circumstances can convert an insecure attachment into a secure one (Roisman & Booth-LaForce, 2014; and see Beijersbergen

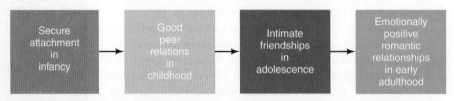

■ **Figure 14.4** Simpson et al. (2007) found that relationship quality at each step in development affects relationship quality at the next step.

Source: From Simpson, J. A., Collins, W. A., Tran, S., & Haydon, K. C. (2007). Attachment and the experience and expression of emotions in romantic relationships: A developmental perspective. *Journal of Personality and Social Psychology, 92*, 355–367. © 2007 American Psychological Association. Reprinted with permission.

et al., 2012). As Bowlby appreciated, then, internal working models are just that: *working* models, subject to revision in response to later social experiences (Sroufe et al., 2005).

All things considered, the Bowlby–Ainsworth attachment theory is well supported. Studies of the long-term consequences of early attachment support Bowlby's claim that internal working models formed early in life shape later relationships and development. Still, many of us learn new social skills and different attitudes toward relationships in our later interactions not only with parents but also with peers, friends, lovers, and spouses. It is time, then, to supplement this description of parent–child relations in infancy with a look at the "second world of childhood"—the world of peer relations.

First Peer Relations

Evolution seems to have equipped human infants not only with a capacity for forming attachments to caregivers but also with a capacity for establishing social relationships with peers (Hay, Caplan, & Nash, 2009; Rubin, Bukowski, & Parker, 2006). Infants show an interest in other babies from an early age and show capacities for sharing, cooperation, and empathy as early as their first and second years (see Chapter 13).

Although interested in other babies from start, infants begin to interact with peers in earnest in about the middle of the first year. By then, infants will often smile or babble at their tiny companions, vocalize, offer toys, and gesture to one another, although many of their friendly gestures go unnoticed and unreciprocated (Hay, Nash, & Pedersen, 1983; Vandell, Wilson, & Buchanan, 1980). During their first year, they may share toys nicely one moment but fight over them the next (Hay et al., 2009).

By about 18 months, infants are able to engage in simple forms of reciprocal play with peers (Brownell, Ramani, & Zerwas, 2006; Mueller & Lucas, 1975; Howes & Matheson, 1992). They imitate one another, and they adopt and reverse roles in their play. Thus, the toddler who receives a toy may immediately offer a toy in return, or the one who has been the chaser will become the chasee. Toward the end of the second year, infants have become quite proficient at this kind of turn-taking and reciprocal exchange, especially those who learned turn-taking through secure attachments to their parents (Fagot, 1997). Some infants even form special relationships with certain preferred playmates—friendships (Hay et al., 2009; Rubin et al., 2006).

And we now also know that mere 2-year-olds are ready to participate in peer groups, learn group norms, and conform to their peers. In a clever study (Haun, Rekers, & Tomasello, 2014), 2-year-olds, chimpanzees, and orangutans each played a simple game in which they learned to drop balls through a hole in one of three boxes to earn a treat. Then they were shown three peers who, in turn, played the game but dropped balls in a different hole. What did they do when they had a chance to play again? The apes stuck with their own successful strategy, but most of the 2-year-old children switched to the strategy they saw three other 2-year-olds use. Peer influence and conformity clearly begin much earlier than adolescence! By conforming to peers, young children are socialized quickly into the social norms, rules, and behaviors of those around them. Clearly the caregiver–infant relationship is not the only important social relationship that develops during infancy; peer relations are well under way, too.

Even at a year of age, infants seem ready to engage in social interactions.

Myrleen Pearson/PhotoEdit

Checking Mastery

1. What are two important types of fear that develop soon after infants form their first attachments?
2. Compare how infants with a resistant attachment and infants with an avoidant attachment react to separations from their caregivers and the reunions that follow.
3. What does research on infants from deprived institutions suggest infants most need in order to develop normally?

Making Connections

1. Some years ago, a 2-year-old named Baby Jessica made news because she was taken suddenly from the parents who thought they had adopted her and awarded by the court to her biological parents because her biological father had not consented to the adoption. What would attachment theory and research on attachment predict about Jessica's reactions and later development? Once you answer, speculate about why Jessica reportedly turned into a happy, well-adjusted child instead (Ingrassia & Springen, 1994).
2. Explain how infants with resistant attachments, avoidant attachments, and disorganized attachments are each trying to regulate their emotions as best they can, given the parenting they receive.

LEARNING OBJECTIVES

- Describe how parent–child attachments and peer networks change during childhood.

- Explain how play becomes more social, more imaginative, and more rule-governed over the childhood years and what we can conclude about its contributions to development.

- Describe what we learn from sociometric studies of peer acceptance about children who are popular, rejected, or neglected.

- Explain the unique contributions of friendships to child development.

Relationships with parents and peers change from infancy to childhood as children become more involved in play activities and seek acceptance by their peers. These social relationships contribute to development in a variety of ways.

Parent–Child Attachments

Starting at about age 3, according to Bowlby (1969), the parent–child attachment becomes a *goal-corrected partnership* in which parent and child accommodate to each other's needs. Children become more sensitive partners and grow more independent of their parents. They continue to seek attention and approval from their parents, and it is important that they continue to perceive their parents as psychologically available to them, even when they are not physically present. However, children also look to peers for social and emotional support now and rely on their parents less and their peers more as they get older (Furman & Buhrmester, 1992; Kerns, Tomich, & Kim, 2006).

Peer Networks

From age 2 to age 12, children spend more time with peers and less time with adults; about 10% of social interactions in toddlerhood but 30% of those in middle childhood are with peers (Ellis, Rogoff, & Cromer, 1981; Rubin et al., 2006). American children spend much of their time in day care, preschool, and school classes in which they are segregated by age. Cross-cultural research tells us that children elsewhere consort more with different-age children and adults. As shown in ■ **Figure 14.5**, for instance, Barbara Rogoff and her colleagues found that 2- and 3-year-old Efe children in the Democratic Republic of the Congo and Mayan children in Guatemala spend more time with older children and less with age-mates than children in two U.S. cities do (Rogoff, Morelli, & Chavajay, 2010). Children in traditional cultures are often involved in the day-to-day activities of the community and mingle with people of all ages. The implications are not entirely clear, but American children may miss out on some opportunities to learn from older and wiser children and adults because they grow up in a relatively age-segregated world.

In the United States and in most cultures, children also live in a gender-segregated world (Ellis, Rogoff, & Cromer, 1981; Munroe & Romney, 2006). This gender segregation becomes increasingly strong with age (Martin et al., 2013; and see Chapter 12). Once in their sex-segregated worlds, boys and girls experience different kinds of social relationships, activities, and interactions

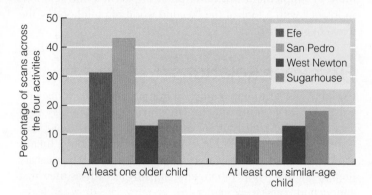

■ **Figure 14.5** Involvement of 2- and 3-year-old children with older children versus similar-age children in four cultural settings: Efe children in a nomadic community of foragers in the Democratic Republic of the Congo; Mayan children in San Pedro, Guatemala; and middle-class American children in West Newton, Massachusetts, and Sugarhouse, Utah. Children were observed in naturally occurring activities (lessons, work, play, and conversations). Young children interacted less with older children and more with similar-age children in the United States than in the other two cultures, suggesting that American children live in a relatively age-segregated social world.

Source: Rogoff, B., Morelli, G. A., & Chavajay, P. (2010). Children's integration in communities and segregation from people of differing ages. *Perspectives on Psychological Science, 5*, 431–440, Figure 1, p. 435.

that affect their development. Overall, then, children spend an increasing amount of time with peers as they get older, most often peers of the same gender.

Play

Children spend a lot of time playing and play in a variety of ways (Pellegrini, 2009): through locomotor play (as in games of tag or ball), object play (stacking blocks, making crafts), social play (as in mutual imitation or playing board games), and pretend play (enacting roles). So important is play in the life of the child from age 2 to age 5 that these years are sometimes called *the play years*. This is when children hop about the room shrieking with delight, don capes and go off on dragon hunts, and whip up cakes and cookies made of clay, sand, or air. We can detect two major changes in play between infancy and age 5: it becomes more social, and it becomes more imaginative. After age 5 or so, the exuberant and fanciful play of the preschool years gives way to somewhat more serious, rule-governed and skill-building play (Smith, 2005).

Play Becomes More Social

Years ago, Mildred Parten (1932) classified the types of play engaged in by preschool children of different ages. Her main categories of activity (besides being unoccupied or being an onlooker) are arranged from least to most social, as follows:

1. **Solitary play.** Children play alone, typically with objects, and appear to be highly involved in what they are doing.
2. **Parallel play.** Children play next to one another, doing much the same thing, but they interact little (for example, two girls might sit near each other, both drawing pictures, without talking to each other much).
3. **Associative play.** Children interact by swapping materials, conversing, or following each other's lead, but they are not united by the same goal (for example, the two girls may swap crayons and comment on each other's drawings as they draw).
4. **Cooperative play.** Children join forces to achieve a common goal; they act as a pair or group, dividing their labor and coordinating their activities in a meaningful way (for example, the two girls collaborate to draw a big mural).

The major message of Parten's study (and of others like it) is that play becomes increasingly social and socially skilled from age 2 to age 5 (Barnes, 1971). As shown in ■ **Figure 14.6**, solitary and parallel play become less frequent with age, while associative and cooperative play, the most social and complex of the types of play, become more frequent with age. Solitary and parallel play continue to serve useful functions for older children at times, however (Coplan & Abreau, 2009; Rubin et al., 2011).

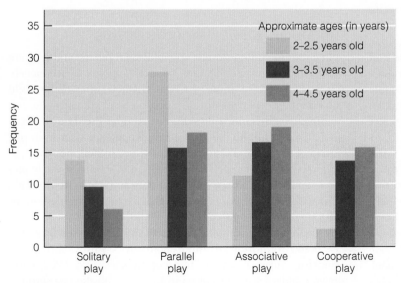

■ **Figure 14.6** Frequency of play activities engaged in by preschool children of different ages. With age, solitary and parallel play occur less frequently, whereas associative and cooperative play occur more frequently.

Source: Adapted from Barnes, 1971.

Play Becomes More Imaginative

The first **pretend play**—play in which one actor, object, or action symbolizes or stands for another—occurs around age 1, when an infant may raise an empty cup, or perhaps a forbidden treat, to her lips, smile, give a parent a knowing glance, and make loud lip-smacking sounds (Nicolich, 1977). The earliest pretend play is just like this: The infant performs actions that symbolize familiar activities such as eating, sleeping, and washing. By age 2, toddlers readily join in pretense; if you hand them a towel and suggest that they wipe up the imaginary tea you just spilled at your pretend tea party, they will (Harris & Kavanaugh, 1993)! These toddlers can use their new symbolic capacity to construct a mental representation of a pretend event and act according to this representation.

Pretend play blossoms from age 2 to age 5, increasing in both frequency and sophistication (Howes & Matheson, 1992; Rubin et al., 2006). Most important, children combine their capacity for increasingly social play and their capacity for pretense to create **social pretend play**, play in which children cooperate with others to enact sometimes very sophisticated dramas (Howes & Matheson, 1992). Watch as a 5-year-old (M) tries to convince her partner (E), playing the role of a mother, to leave her babies and come to M's house. The two girls negotiate what will happen next, managing to stay in role and keep in mind the other's role as they do so (Garvey, 1990, p. 137):

M: You come here. The babies are sleeping now and ... (interrupted).
E: No, they'll cry when I leave 'cause they'll hear the car.
M: Nooo. The car's broken. I have the car.
E: All right, but one baby will have to take care of these little babies.

Although social pretend play is universal, the quality and content of preschoolers' play are culturally influenced (Haight et al., 1999). For example, U.S. children like to play superheroes and act out themes of danger and fantasy, whereas Korean children take on family roles and enact everyday activities (Farver & Lee-Shin, 1997). American children also talk a lot about their own actions, reject other children's ideas, and boss others around, whereas Korean children are more prone to focus on their partners' activities, make polite requests, and agree with one another. Through their play, then, children in the United States (an individualistic culture) learn to assert their identities as individuals, whereas children in Korea (a collectivist culture) learn how to keep their egos and emotions under control to achieve group harmony.

Play Becomes More Rule-Governed

After they enter school, children engage less frequently in pretend play. They become members of peer groups in their neighborhoods or schools—groups that hang out together, have their own norms of behavior, and are often organized into hierarchies or pecking orders with leaders and followers (Rubin et al., 2015). Now children spend more of their time playing organized games with rules—board and computer games, games of tag or hide-and-seek, organized sports, and so on (Smith,

Pretend play during the preschool years contributes to intellectual, social, and emotional development.

Donald Iain Smith/Moment Select/Getty Images

2005). They also develop individual hobbies, such as building model cars, collecting coins, or making scrapbooks, activities that require learning rules and help them acquire skills and knowledge. Partly because of cognitive advances, then, the play of the school-age child is more organized and rule-governed—and less fanciful—than that of the preschool child.

What Good Is Play?

Parents who program their children's days in hopes of molding little Einsteins, like preschool teachers who emphasize learning one's ABCs over playing, may have lost sight of the importance of play in child development (Bartlett, 2011; Hirsh-Pasek et al., 2009; Singer, Golinkoff, & Hirsh-Pasek, 2006). The fact that playful activity occurs among the young of so many species strongly suggests that play is an evolved behavior that helps the young adapt during childhood and prepare for adulthood (Coplan & Abreau, 2009; Pellegrini, 2009). It is easy to see how girls playing house with dolls might be grooming themselves for traditional roles as mothers or how the rough-and-tumble play of boys, like the playful fighting observed in young males of many species, prepares them to compete with other males later in life.

Play allows children to develop and practice many skills. Play is, in fact, associated with development in many domains: motor, cognitive, language, social, and emotional (Pellegrini, 2009; Smith, 2005). For example, physical or locomotor play, from the leg kicking of infants to the soccer playing of children, is associated with neural maturation and the refinement of motor skills. Both Jean Piaget and Lev Vygotsky (see Chapter 7) highlighted the significance of pretend play in cognitive development. Indeed, engaging in lots of pretend play has been linked to better performance on tests of cognitive development, language skills, executive function, and creativity (Lillard et al., 2013). Meanwhile, social pretend play is linked to children's understanding of others' perspectives, social skills, and popularity (Connolly

& Doyle, 1984; Lillard et al., 2013). Finally, play contributes to healthy emotional development by providing opportunities to act out or express bothersome feelings, regulate emotions, and resolve emotional conflicts (Coplan & Abreau, 2009). So it was that Jackie, an abused 5-year-old, coped with his abuse by having an alligator puppet swallow a small child doll and then smashing the alligator with a mallet and burying it in the sandbox (Landreth & Homeyer, 1998).

So, although children play because it is fun, not because it sharpens their skills, they contribute to their own development by playing. Experts agree that young children often learn best when they can do so in self-chosen, hands-on, and playful ways (Hirsh-Pasek et al., 2009; Lillard et al., 2013).

Peer Acceptance

Being accepted by peers means having the opportunity to play and interact with other children and in the process develop normally. Researchers study peer-group acceptance through **sociometric techniques**—methods for determining who is liked and who is disliked in a group (Cillessen, 2009; Cillessen, Schwartz, & Mayeux, 2011). In a sociometric survey, children in a classroom may be asked to nominate several classmates whom they like and several whom they dislike or to rate all their classmates in terms of their desirability or undesirability as companions. It is important to find out both who is liked and who is disliked; this allows children to be classified into the following distinct social categories (Coie, Dodge, & Coppotelli, 1982):

1. **Popular.** Well liked by most and rarely disliked.
2. **Rejected.** Rarely liked and often disliked.
3. **Neglected.** Neither liked nor disliked; these children seem to be invisible to their classmates.
4. **Controversial.** Liked by many but also disliked by many.
5. **Average.** In the middle on both the liked and disliked scales.

Influences on Sociometric Status

Why are some children more popular than others, and why are other children rejected by their peers? Popularity or peer acceptance is affected by some personal characteristics that a child can do little to change—for instance, physical attractiveness and intelligence (Bellanti, Bierman, & Conduct Problems Prevention Research Group, 2000). Social competence—for example, initiating social interactions skillfully, responding positively to peers, resolving interpersonal conflicts, and so on—strongly predicts popularity (Coie, Dodge, & Kupersmidt, 1990; Rubin et al., 2015). Well-liked children are also able to regulate their emotions well (Graziano, Keane, & Calkins, 2007).

What does it take to be rejected or highly disliked by peers? "Rejected" children are often aggressive—pushy, disruptive, annoying, mean. A smaller number are socially isolated, withdrawn children who do not seem to fit in with the peer group's norms (Parkhurst & Asher, 1992; Rubin et al., 2015). Children who fall into the neglected category of sociometric status often have reasonably good social skills but they tend to be shy and unassertive; they may hover around the fringes of a play group or prefer to play alone, so no one really notices them (Coie et al., 1990; Coplan, Ooi, & Nocita, 2015). Controversial children are interesting: They often have good social skills and leadership qualities, like popular children, but they are also viewed as aggressive bullies, like many rejected children (DeRosier & Thomas, 2003; Miller-Johnson et al., 2003).

In sum, popularity or peer acceptance is affected by many factors. It helps to have an attractive face and a high IQ, but it is probably more important to behave in socially competent ways and to be able to regulate one's emotions. As you have learned, children who have enjoyed secure relationships with their parents tend to become popular children because they have learned social and emotion regulation skills that make for positive relationships with peers.

Implications of Peer Acceptance

Do the outcomes of childhood popularity polls matter? Very much so, especially for the 10%–15% of children who are rejected by their peers (Rubin et al., 2006). Children who are neglected by peers often gain greater acceptance later, maybe because they often have reasonably good social skills (Bierman, 2004; Cillessen et al., 1992). Poorer outcomes would be expected for extremely socially withdrawn children—children whose social anxiety keeps them from interacting with peers and exposes them to victimization (Rubin, Coplan, & Bowker, 2009).

Children who are rejected because of their aggressive behavior are at risk. They are likely to maintain their rejected status from grade to grade (Bierman, 2004; Cillessen et al., 1992). What's more, they may become even more poorly adjusted as a result of the experience of being rejected. Their self-esteem suffers, they lose opportunities to learn social skills, they develop negative attitudes toward others, they are negatively influenced by the other antisocial children they end up hanging out with by default, and their academic performance suffers (Coie, 2004; Prinstein et al., 2009). There is even evidence that the stress of being rejected by peers is associated with inflammatory processes in the body that can contribute to health problems later in life (Murphy, Slavich, Rohleder, & Miller, 2012). Yet social skills training and coaching programs that aim to improve children's interaction skills can improve their acceptance by peers (Bierman & Powers, 2009).

Friendships

Being accepted by the wider peer group and having close friends are distinct and serve different functions for children. Popular children are more likely than unpopular children to have friends, but many unpopular children have at least one reciprocated friendship in which there is mutual affection and many popular children do not (Gest, Graham-Bermann, & Hartup, 2001).

Having at least one friend increases the odds that a child will be happy and socially competent and reduces the odds that a child will be lonely and depressed (Bukowski, Motzoi, & Meyer, 2009; Rubin et al., 2015). This is especially true if

Chumships in late elementary school, said Harry Stack Sullivan, are a training ground for later intimate relationships.

Elena Elisseeva/Shutterstock.com

the friend is well adjusted and supportive (Rubin et al., 2015; Vaughn et al., 2000). As you learned in Section 14.2, psychoanalytic theorist Harry Stack Sullivan (1953) theorized that having a close friend or chum has many developmental benefits, and research bears him out (Bukowski et al., 2009). Chumships teach us how to be emotionally intimate with someone and, as we will see shortly, pave the way for romantic relationships in adolescence. We become attached to friends, who then serve as secure bases and safe havens for us. Friends can provide critical social support and comfort that help children weather stressful events, such as the first day of kindergarten, torment by a bully, or the turmoil of a divorce (Bukowski et al., 2009; Ladd, 1999; Rubin et al., 2015).

Checking Mastery

1. Which two of Parten's types of play are the most socially complex?
2. What are the two main trends in the development of play over the preschool years?
3. What are three important influences on popularity or sociometric status in childhood?

Making Connections

1. Addi's parents would like to help advance her physical, cognitive, and social development through play activities, but they do not know how to go about it. Give them some ideas of what they can do with a 1-, 4-, and 8-year-old to provide age-appropriate play experiences.
2. Darren's sociometric status is neglected, whereas Alonzo's is rejected. What training program might you design for each boy to help him become more popular and why?

14.5

The Adolescent

LEARNING OBJECTIVES

- Describe the significance of attachments to parents and friendships in adolescence.

- Distinguish between cliques and crowds and describe their evolution and functions during adolescence.

- Describe four phases in the development of adolescent romantic relationships and the typical effects of dating on adolescent development.

Compared to children, adolescents spend even more time with peers and less time with parents. The quality of a teen's attachment to parents continues to be highly important throughout adolescence, but peers, including both same- and other-sex friends and romantic partners, begin to rival or surpass parents as sources of intimacy and support (Furman & Buhrmester, 1992). As they age, adolescents are constructing and reconstructing internal working models not only for their attachments to their parents but for their attachments to close friends and their attachments to romantic partners. These mental representations differ from one another, each depending most on the quality of interactions within each type of relationship (Furman, Stephenson, & Rhoades, 2014).

Attachments to Parents

Just as infants must have a secure base if they are to explore, adolescents need the security, as well as the encouragement to explore, provided by supportive parents in order to become independent and autonomous individuals (Markiewicz et al., 2006). A balance of exploration and attachment is the key to successful development at this age (Allen, 2008). Adolescents who enjoy secure attachment relationships with their parents generally have a stronger sense of identity, higher self-esteem, greater social competence, better emotional adjustment, and fewer behavioral problems than their less securely attached peers (Allen, 2008; Arbona & Power, 2003; Kenny & Rice, 1995). They are likely to form higher quality attachment to friends—and later to romantic partners—than adolescents with insecure attachments to their parents (Furman & Rose, 2015). They also show better adjustment during the potentially difficult transition to college than students who are insecurely attached (Larose, Bernier, & Tarabulsy, 2005; Mayseless, Danieli, & Sharabany, 1996).

Friendships

Friendships change qualitatively with age. They are based largely on (1) enjoyment of common activities in early childhood, (2) mutual loyalty and caring in late childhood, and (3) intimacy and self-disclosure in adolescence (Collins & Madsen, 2006). Like children, teenagers form friendships with peers who are similar to themselves in physical characteristics (age, gender, and race/ethnicity, for example), as well as in behavior (for example, academic motivation, hobbies). However, adolescents increasingly choose friends whose *psychological* qualities—interests, attitudes, values, and personalities—match their own. In adolescence—and this applies to both males and females and across racial and ethnic

Going to college is a "Strange Situation" that activates attachment behaviors, such as hugging, phoning, Skyping, and texting, designed to maintain contact with attachment figures. Some separation anxiety is normal and usually decreases over the first semester (Berman & Sperling, 1991).

David Burch/Media Bakery

groups—friends become like-minded individuals who understand you and whom you can tell anything, people you can trust with your secrets and count on to be there when you need them (Way & Silverman, 2011).

Although same-sex friendships remain important throughout adolescence, teenagers increasingly form close cross-sex friendships too. Ruth Sharabany and her colleagues (Sharabany, Gershoni, & Hofman, 1981) found that same-sex friendships were emotionally intimate throughout adolescence but that cross-sex friendships did not attain a high level of emotional intimacy until 11th grade. These findings and others support Harry Stack Sullivan's view that children learn lessons about intimate attachments in their chumships or friendships that they later apply in their romantic relationships (Buhrmester & Furman, 1986; Furman & Rose, 2015).

Sociometric Popularity and Perceived Popularity

In childhood, popular kids have many likable characteristics, but, starting in late childhood and adolescence, it is important to distinguish between sociometric popularity, or being liked by many peers, and perceived popularity, or being viewed as someone who has status, power, and visibility in the peer group (Mayeux, Houser, & Dyches, 2011; Parkhurst & Hopmeyer, 1998). If you conjure up an image of the "popular" kids in high school, you quickly realize that they had lots of power but that not all were well liked.

Teens with high perceived popularity have good social and leadership skills and are often attractive and well dressed. Some are even very likeable (that is, sociometrically popular). But others seek control and status and sometimes do a lot of damage by snubbing, excluding, bullying, and otherwise being mean to others kids. They often excel at relational aggression—subtle and indirect aggression that involves gossiping about and ignoring or excluding others (see Voulgaridou & Kokkinos, 2015).

Just think of Regina George and her clique, the Plastics, in the film *Mean Girls* and you have the idea. Insults, vicious rumors, and betrayals permeated this society of "mean girls." Apparently relational aggression works: It enhances girls' perceived popularity and makes boys like them more as dating partners (Houser, Mayeux, & Cross, 2015; Rose, Swenson, & Waller, 2004; Smith, Rose, & Schwartz-Mette, 2010). Indeed, adolescents of both sexes may find that aggression, both physical and relational, helps them climb the social status ladder and maintain their position there—at the expense of their victims (Juvonen, Wang, & Espinoza, 2013).

Although being stabbed in the back by someone you thought was your friend is no fun and adolescence can be agonizing as a result, relational aggression seems to serve the positive function of encouraging conformity to group norms and strengthening the peer culture (Killen, Rutland, & Jampol, 2009). Teens with high perceived popularity also blaze the trail toward dating relationships, as you will now see.

Changing Social Networks

Most elementary school children take interest in members of the other sex, talk at length about who likes whom, develop crushes, and in the process prepare themselves for heterosexual relationships (Thorne, 1993). Still, how do boys and girls who live in their own gender-segregated worlds and often seem to hate each other eventually come to date each other?

Some time ago, Dexter Dunphy (1963) offered a plausible account of how peer-group structures change during adolescence to pave the way for dating relationships. His five steps are still helpful today in understanding how peer relations lay the foundation for romantic attachments (see also Brown, 2011; Collins & Madsen, 2006; Furman & Rose, 2015; and Rubin et al., 2015):

1. In late childhood, boys and girls typically become members of same-sex cliques, or small friendship groups, and have little to do with the other sex.
2. Boy cliques and girl cliques then begin to interact. Just as parents provide a secure base for peer relationships, same-sex cliques provide a secure base for romantic relationships. For an adolescent boy, talking to a girl at the mall with his friends and her friends there is far less threatening than doing so on his own.
3. In early adolescence, the most popular boys and girls lead the way and form a heterosexual clique.
4. As less popular teens also form mixed-sex cliques of their own, a new peer-group structure, the crowd, completes its evolution during the high school years. The crowd, a loose collection of heterosexual cliques with similar characteristics, provides a vehicle for socializing with the other sex through organized social gatherings such as parties. In larger schools, there are likely to be multiple crowds, each with its own distinctive identity and lifestyle. Those adolescents who become members of a mixed-sex clique and a crowd (not all do) have many opportunities to get to know members of the other sex as both friends and romantic partners.
5. More and more couples form and the crowd disintegrates in late high school, having served its purpose of bringing boys and girls together.

Crowds and Their Implications

High school crowds not only bring boys and girls together but give adolescents a social identity and a place in the social order. The names may vary, but most schools have their crowds of, for example, elites ("populars"), academics ("brains"), athletes ("jocks"), and deviants ("druggies," "goths," "emos," and so on), each consisting of adolescents who are similar in some way (Brown & Dietz, 2009; Brown, Mory, & Kinney, 1994). Everyone in high school seems to recognize these differences: "[The brains] all wear glasses and 'kiss up' to teachers and after school they all tromp uptown to the library" (Brown et al., 1994, p. 128), "The partiers goof off a lot more than the jocks do, but they don't come to school stoned like the burnouts do" (p. 133). In large, diverse high schools, racial or ethnic groups may function as crowds for minority teens (Brown et al., 2008).

An interesting study of high school social networks by Daniel McFarland and his colleagues (2014) shows that characteristics of a school's ecology, such as its size and racial/ethnic composition, strongly influence who hangs out with whom. In a large, diverse school with lots of options, a defined crowd structure with a hierarchy, a pecking order with popular students and groups at the top, is likely to take shape. Students tend to be cliquish, choosing friends similar to themselves in age, gender, race, and social class. In a small school, this hierarchical social structure and sorting by similarity are less likely. Students in smaller schools are likely to form friendships based on group classwork or school activities, such as sports and music, perhaps because there are fewer students to choose among as friends and because being excluded would carry a huge cost. As a result, they mix more with students from a variety of social backgrounds and racial segregation is less pronounced. Thus the ecology of a high school can make a big difference in where an adolescent fits in the peer culture.

Which crowd or crowds an adolescent belongs to has important implications for her social identity and self-esteem; it is easier to feel good about yourself if you are a "popular" or a "jock" than if you are a "dweeb," a "burnout," or a social isolate who does not belong to any crowd (Brown & Lohr, 1987). Indeed, self-perceived crowd membership in high school predicts adjustment in adulthood. In one study, "brains" tended to graduate from college and have high self-esteem at age 24; "basket cases" were more likely than their peers to have seen a psychologist and attempted suicide; "jocks" achieved financial success but shared with "criminals" a tendency to drink too much; and "criminals" were the least well adjusted (Barber, Eccles, & Stone, 2001; see also Doornwaard et al., 2012).

Do crowds really shape adolescents' future characteristics or does crowd membership merely reflect an adolescent's existing characteristics? This question concerns the **peer selection versus peer socialization issue**. Crowd membership does partly reflect personality traits, abilities, and values that existed before the adolescent ever got involved with a particular crowd; teens often select or are selected into the crowds that suit them. However, experiences in a crowd then socialize behavior and shape development (Burk, van der Vorst, Kerr, & Stattin, 2012; Giordano, 2003). That is, both selection and socialization contribute to similarity among members of the same crowd. Thus, for example, adolescents who drink often select drinkers rather than teetotalers as friends, but friends then develop even more similar drinking patterns—heavy

The self-esteem and social identity of adolescents often hinge on which cliques and crowds they belong to. In any era and any group, conformity in dress and behavior helps adolescents fit in and avoid being excluded.

Peter Turnley/Corbis Historical/Getty Images

or otherwise—as a result of socializing with each other (Burk et al., 2012). Later in adolescence, as adolescents forge their own identities and become more resistant to peer influences, crowds and the group identities they provide become less important (Brown, 2011; Monahan, Steinberg, & Cauffman, 2009).

Peer Influence

A common misconception in our society is that peers are a bad influence on adolescents. As it turns out, peers typically do more to foster important social learning and positive behavior than to encourage antisocial behavior (Rubin et al., 2015). True, at around age 14 or 15, adolescents are more dependent on their peers and more susceptible to peer influence than before or after; they may "go along with the crowd" and take risks that they would not take when alone (Steinberg, 2015). The nature of peer pressure depends on the crowd to which an adolescent belongs, however: "brains" discourage drug use, for example, while "druggies" encourage it (Sussman et al., 2007).

Parents have considerable influence on whether peer influences are good or bad. Getting in trouble by conforming to peers is much less likely among adolescents who have secure attachments to warm and authoritative parents who are neither too lax nor too strict (Brown et al., 1993; Goldstein, Davis-Kean, & Eccles, 2005). These parents are likely to ask where and with whom their kids are going; they do not let their kids run wild, nor do they forbid them from seeing certain friends—a technique that may backfire and increase involvement with deviant peers and delinquent behavior (Keijsers et al., 2012). In sum, the influences of peers and friends on development are usually healthy but can be destructive, depending on what cliques and crowds adolescents belong to, how good their relationships with their parents are, and how much they need the security of peer acceptance.

Dating

As you have seen, the transition to dating takes place in the context of the larger peer group (Collins & Laursen, 2004; Furman & Rose, 2015). Dating relationships in early adolescence are more superficial and short lived than dating relationships in later adolescence and emerging adulthood (Brown, Feiring, & Furman, 1999; Connolly & McIsaac, 2011). In B. Bradford Brown's (1999) view, adolescent romantic relationships evolve through the following four phases:

1. **Initiation phase**. In early adolescence, the focus is on coming to see oneself as a person capable of a romantic relationship. This is a time of crushes, posturing, and awkward beginnings.
2. **Status phase**. In mid-adolescence, peer approval is what counts; having a romantic relationship, and having it with the "right kind" of partner, is important for the status it brings in the larger peer group.
3. **Affection phase**. In late adolescence, the focus is finally on the relationship rather than on self-concept or peer status. Romantic relationships become more personal and caring.
4. **Bonding phase**. In the transition to emerging adulthood, the emotional intimacy achieved in the affection phase may be coupled with a long-term commitment to create a lasting attachment.

Searching for Love as an LGBT Youth

How does the development of romantic relationships play out for sexual minority youth—lesbian, gay, bisexual, and transgender teens, as well as teens who are not yet sure of their sexual orientation or are open to different possibilities? These teens often try out a variety of types of relationships: sexual experimentation with both same-sex and other-sex partners, including the hookups common among heterosexual youth; passionate friendships that are about emotional intimacy rather than about sex; and dating relationships (Diamond, Savin-Williams, & Dubé, 1999; Shulman & Connolly, 2016).

Sexual minority youth, like straight ones, ultimately seek intimate romantic relationships. However, they face a number of obstacles to finding them. For one thing, they cannot rely on support from within the larger, heterosexually oriented peer culture to serve as a "secure base for exploration" of relationships. They may be stigmatized and often face higher than average risks of being the victims of peer bullying, sexual harassment, and dating violence (Burton et al., 2013; Reuter, Sharp & Temple, 2015; Williams, Connolly, Pepler, & Craig, 2003). Their parents, especially if they have traditional values, may also react negatively to them when they come out, adding to their challenges (Baiocco et al., 2015).

Yet most sexual minority youth succeed in forming healthy romantic attachments despite such barriers. Moreover, attachment theory applies to LGBT youth just as well as it applies to heterosexual youth and can help us understand how their early experiences in relationships affect their romantic relationships. This was clear in a longitudinal study of LGBT youth aged 16–20 in the Chicago area who were followed over 3.5 years (Starks, Newcomb, & Mustanski, 2015). Just as for heterosexual youths, both secure attachments with parents and secure attachments with friends were linked to better mental health and closer, more satisfying romantic relationships later on.

Brown's phases were quite evident in an 8-year longitudinal study of German adolescents who were age 13 at the start of the study (Seiffge-Krenke, 2003). The 13-year-olds had romantic relationships that, although emotionally intense, lasted an average of only about 3 months. With age, relationships lasted longer (an average of 21 months by age 21) and became more emotionally intimate and supportive. Supportive relationships with parents proved to be at least as important as supportive relationships with peers in predicting involvement in a love relationship in early adulthood (see also Connolly & McIsaac, 2011; Furman & Rose, 2015; Shulman & Connolly, 2016). **Exploration 14.2** looks at some special challenges faced by sexual minority youth in their search for love.

How does dating affect development and adjustment overall? Dating at an early age seems to have more negative than positive implications for social and emotional adjustment, either because troubled adolescents start dating early or because early daters get hurt or become involved in problem behavior such as sex, drinking, and drug use before their time (Furman & Collibee, 2014; Mendle et al., 2013). By late adolescence or emerging adulthood, having a romantic partner becomes a plus; it is associated with less substance use and fewer emotional and behavioral problems, possibly because finding a romantic partner has become an appropriate developmental task by this age (Furman & Collibee, 2014). In the end, involvement in a steady relationship is good for self-esteem and well-being (although breakups certainly hurt), and adolescents who date tend to be better adjusted than those who do not (Connolly & McIsaac, 2011; Furman & Rose, 2015).

Adolescence is clearly a tremendously important time of change in attachment relationships. As adolescents get older, they look more to peers, both friends and romantic partners, to fulfill some of the attachment needs that parents fulfilled when they were younger—needs for closeness, a secure base for exploration, and a safe haven in times of trouble (Markiewicz et al., 2006). Secure attachments to friends, like secure attachments to parents, can help adolescents cope with stress, and a lack of such attachments is linked to anxiety and depression (Gorrese, 2016). Even so, parents, especially mothers, remain a critical source of security and support throughout the adolescent years. Moreover, the quality of parent–adolescent relationships and parents' parenting styles have a lot to do with the quality of an adolescent's relationships with peers and romantic partners (Brown & Bakken, 2011; Gorrese & Ruggieri, 2012; Oudekerk et al., 2015).

Checking Mastery

1. What is the difference between a clique and a crowd?
2. Before they are capable of truly caring romantic relationships, what two things do young teens seek from dating relationships, according to B. Bradford Brown's four phases of dating?

Making Connections

1. Analyze the clique and crowd structure in your high school, where you fit in it, and how you might have been affected by your experience.
2. How well does Brown's account of four phases in adolescent dating relationships fit you? Where does your dating history differ, and why might that be?

14.6
The Adult

LEARNING OBJECTIVES

- Explain how social networks change over the adult years and how socioemotional selectivity theory accounts for this change.

- Characterize romantic relationships in terms of the primary basis for partner choice, the triangular theory of love, and the four adult attachment styles.

- Describe the positive effects on adult development of a secure adult attachment style and of having at least one close friend or confidant and the negative effects of social isolation and loneliness.

Relationships with family and friends are no less important during adulthood than they are earlier in life, but they take on different qualities. How do people's social networks change over the adult years and why, and what is the character of their romantic relationships and friendships?

Social Networks

With whom do adults of different ages interact and what are the implications? Young adults are busily forming romantic relationships and friendships and work contacts. The trend toward greater intimacy in cross-gender relationships that began in adolescence continues (Reis et al., 1993). Young women also continue to form closer friendship ties than men do (Antonucci, Birditt, & Akiyama, 2009). Because of all their social network building, young adults typically have more friends than middle-aged and older adults do.

As adults have children, take on increasing job responsibilities, and age, their social networks of not-so-close friends and acquaintances shrink, but their numbers of close relationships with family and friends stay about the same (Antonucci et al., 2009; English & Carstensen, 2014; Wrzus, Hänel, et al., 2013). The trend toward smaller social networks with age after early adulthood can be seen in many ethnic groups, but ethnic group differences are also evident. For example, from early adulthood on, African American adults' networks tend to be smaller, to be more dominated by kin, and to involve more frequent contact than those of European Americans (Ajrouch, Antonucci, & Janevic, 2001). Cultural differences are evident too; for example, although their family networks are similar in size, adults in individualistic cultures often have larger networks of friends and acquaintances than adults in collectivist cultures do (Wrzus, Hänel, et al., 2013).

Shrinking social networks in late adulthood may be forced in part by chronic illness and disability. Life events and changes in roles also affect network size; for example, getting married or starting a new job increases social network size, and the death of a spouse decreases it (Wrzus, Hänel, et al., 2013). But as you saw in Section 14.1, Laura Carstensen's *socioemotional selectivity theory* states that older adults actively choose to shrink their social networks to better meet their emotional needs as they realize that little time is left to them. Consistent with this theory, older adults narrow their social networks to close family and friends to whom they feel very emotionally close and end up with social networks that give them more positive and fewer negative emotional experiences than young adults obtain from their

relationships (Carstensen, 1992; English & Carstensen, 2014; Lang & Carstensen, 1994).

Socioemotional selectivity, loss of roles, and failing health may all lead to shrinking social networks with age, then. However, older adults typically find their relationships satisfying and emotionally fulfilling.

Romantic Relationships

An important developmental task for young adults is to resolve Erikson's issue of intimacy versus isolation by finding a romantic partner and entering into a committed relationship. How do we choose partners, what does love involve, and how do the internal working models of self and others that we form starting in infancy affect our romantic attachments?

Partner Choice

Many models and schemes have been developed to answer the question of how people choose romantic partners (see Regan, 2008; Strong, DeVault, & Cohen, 2011). Filter theories of mate selection or partner choice have envisioned it as a process in which we progress through a series of filters leading us from all possible partners to one partner in particular (see Regan, 2008; Strong et al., 2011). Assuming two people have an opportunity to meet, similarities in physical appearance, race or ethnicity, education, socioeconomic status, religion, and the like serve as the first filters and provide a basis for dating. Then partners may disclose more about themselves and look for similarity in inner qualities such as values, attitudes, beliefs, and personality traits. If they continue to find themselves compatible, their relationship may survive; if not, it may end. There is little agreement, though, on how many such filters there might be. More importantly, mate selection does not appear to unfold in a neat, steplike manner as filter theories imply (Regan, 2008).

Researchers do agree on one thing: The greatest influence on mate selection is similarity, or homogamy (Finkel et al., 2012; Strong et al., 2011). Once homogamy is assured, people may also look for complementarity—for partners who are different from them but who have strengths that compensate for their own weaknesses or otherwise complement their own characteristics. However, the saying "birds of a feather flock together" has far more validity than the saying "opposites attract" when it comes to mate selection. Partner choice works much the same in gay and lesbian relationships as in heterosexual relationships (Diamond & Butterworth, 2009).

According to filter theories, we choose romantic partners mainly on the basis of homogamy or similarity—at first surface similarities such as belonging to the same ethnic group may attract us to someone, but we look for psychological similarities as well.

Hero Images/Brand X Pictures/Getty Images

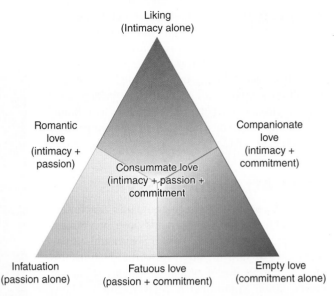

■ **Figure 14.7** The three components of love in Sternberg's triangular theory of love. Think about each component being high or low and what the resulting quality of a relationship would be. For example, companionate love has high intimacy and commitment but low passion; infatuation has high passion but low intimacy and commitment.

Source: Adapted from Sternberg, R. J. (1988b). Triangulating love. In R. J. Sternberg & M. L. Barnes (Eds.), *The psychology of love*. New Haven, CT: Yale University Press, p. 122.

Some online dating sites use algorithms to match partners for similarity and sometimes complementarity as well based on responses to questionnaires. However, research to date suggests that this kind of mechanical matching can go only so far. Why? It ignores the important fact that relationships grow out of partners' interactions over time, that aspects of personality like emotional stability and agreeableness influence the success of relationships, and that in the end it is very hard to predict which relationships will turn into lasting "true love" (Finkel et al., 2012).

Love

Philosophers and poets have struggled for centuries to define love, but it is an elusive concept and there are many kinds of it (Berscheid, 2010; Reis et al., 2013). The concept of romantic love is not just a Western phenomenon or a modern phenomenon, as some people incorrectly believe; it has been documented throughout history and in virtually all of the world's cultures (Hatfield, Mo, & Rapson, 2015; Jankowiak & Fischer, 1992). It is even associated with similar patterns of brain activity across cultures (Acevedo & Aron, 2014). This suggests it is part of our evolutionary heritage that plays a role in committing us to a particular partner and then investing in the rearing of children with that partner (Fletcher et al., 2015). We can think about romantic relationships as a merger of sexual attraction and emotional attachment (Birnbaum, 2015).

Robert Sternberg (1988b, 2006a) puts some of these ideas together in his **triangular theory of love**, which identifies different types of love based on the strength of three components of love. As shown in ■ **Figure 14.7**, the three components are passion, intimacy, and commitment:

- *Passion* involves sexual attraction, romantic feelings, and excitement. A 24-year-old woman in love expressed it well: "I get so excited when I know that I'm going to see him, and then when I do see him, I can't breathe I'm so full of want" (Regan, 2008, p. 142).
- *Intimacy* involves feelings of warmth, caring, closeness, trust, and respect in the relationship. It is about emotional togetherness, attachment, and communication.
- *Commitment* involves first deciding that one loves the other person and then committing to a long-term relationship.

Sternberg identified seven types of love that can result depending on whether each of the three dimensions of love is high or low, making the point that love can take a variety of forms. In our culture, couples often experience passion early in a dating relationship and then move on to greater intimacy and finally to commitment as their relationship evolves. In cultures with arranged marriages, commitment may come first, with the parents who arranged the marriage hoping that passion and intimacy will bloom later (Regan, 2008).

If couples are lucky, they will enjoy high levels of passion, intimacy, and commitment—or what is called **consummate love**—all of their days. Adolescents score lower on scales measuring these three aspects of love than young adults do (Sumter, Valkenburg, & Peter, 2013), reinforcing Erikson's idea that early adulthood is the time to establish intimate relationships. Passion, that intense feeling of "being in love," may have evolved because it lures partners into relationships that will lead to mating and childbearing (Reis & Aron, 2008). However, passion often wanes with time in a relationship, whereas commitment often grows or at least holds steady over the adult years (Ahmetoglu, Swami, & Chamorro-Premuzic, 2010; Sumter et al., 2013). Thus romantic relationships involving lots of passion in their early stages sometimes evolve into relationships characterized by **companionate love**, friendshiplike, affectionate love defined by high intimacy and commitment but not much passion (Reis & Aron, 2008). Some lucky couples, though, are able to keep all three aspects of love, including passion, alive for many years. Indeed, the reward areas of their brains still "light up" when they look at photos of their partners (Acevedo et al., 2012).

		MODEL OF SELF	
		POSITIVE	NEGATIVE
MODEL OF OTHER	POSITIVE	**SECURE** *Secure attachment history* Healthy balance of attachment and autonomy; freedom to explore Low anxiety, low avoidance	**PREOCCUPIED** *Resistant attachment history* Desperate for love to feel worthy as a person; worry about abandonment; express anxiety and anger openly High anxiety, low avoidance
	NEGATIVE	**DISMISSING** *Avoidant attachment history* Shut out emotions; defend against hurt by avoiding intimacy, dismissing the importance of relationships, and being "compulsively self-reliant" Low anxiety, high avoidance	**FEARFUL** *Disorganized–disoriented attachment history* Need relationships but doubt own worth and fear intimacy; lack a coherent strategy for meeting attachment needs High anxiety, high avoidance

■ **Figure 14.8** Adult attachment styles based on internal working models of self and other people arising from early experiences in relationships. These four types of attachment also differ in terms of attachment anxiety (fear of abandonment) and avoidance (discomfort being intimate and dependent) dimensions.

Source: Adapted with permission from Bartholomew, K., & Horowitz, L. M. (1991). Attachment styles among young adults: A test of a four-category model. *Journal of Personality and Social Psychology, 61,* 226–244. © 1991 American Psychological Association.

Adult Attachment Styles

Intrigued by parallels between an infant's attachment to a parent figure and a young adult's love for a romantic partner, researchers like Phillip Shaver and his colleagues began studying adult romantic relationships from the perspective of attachment theory (Fraley & Shaver, 2008; Mikulincer & Shaver, 2007). Many, though not all, love relationships qualify as attachment relationships; the intimacy component of Sternberg's triangular theory of love suggests a caring attachment between romantic partners. And signs of attachment anxiety early in a dating relationship are at least as important as passion or sexual desire in predicting whether a serious relationship will evolve (Eastwick & Finkel, 2008). Like the infant who is attached to a parent, the adult who is in love experiences a strong emotional bond to her partner, wants to be close, takes comfort from the bond, is upset by separations, and finds the partner irreplaceable, as illustrated by the story of star-crossed lovers Mike and Marcy at the start of the chapter. Adults often have other attachments, of course: to their children, their parents, and sometimes their best friends.

■ **Figure 14.8** shows how the internal working models that Bowlby theorized we start to construct early in life may affect the quality of our romantic relationships (Bartholomew & Horowitz, 1991; Crowell, Fraley, & Shaver, 1999). It describes the four adult attachment styles that result when view of the self is either positive or negative and view of other people is either positive or negative. These four adult attachment styles can also be described in terms of two dimensions of attachment (Roisman, 2009): anxiety (extent of concern about whether partners will be emotionally available and responsive) and avoidance (extent of discomfort being intimate with and depending on a partner).

Adults with a *secure* working model and adult attachment style feel good about both themselves and others; they are not afraid of entering intimate relationships or of being abandoned once they do. People with a *preoccupied* internal working model have a positive view of other people but feel unlovable. Resembling resistantly attached infants, they crave closeness to others as a means of validating their self-worth, tend to become overly dependent on their partners, and are highly fearful of abandonment; thus, they are high in attachment anxiety but low in avoidance.

Adults with a *dismissing* style of attachment often have a positive view of self but do not trust other people and dismiss the importance of close relationships. Like avoidantly attached infants, they defend themselves against hurt by not expressing their need for love. They downplay the importance of relationships, find it hard to trust or depend upon partners, feel that others want them to be more intimate than they wish to be, and keep partners at a distance. That is, they are low in attachment anxiety but high in avoidance. Bowlby (1973) described dismissing or avoidant individuals as "compulsively self-reliant." Finally, adults with a *fearful* internal working model show both high anxiety and high avoidance, resembling infants with disorganized attachments. They take a dim view of both themselves and other people and display a confusing, unpredictable mix of neediness and fear of closeness. You may wish to see if you can identify the adult attachment styles expressed by the statements in **Engagement 14.1**.

In a pioneering study, Cindy Hazan and Phillip Shaver (1987) demonstrated that adults' styles of attachment are related to the quality of their romantic relationships (see also Creasey & Jarvis, 2009). For example, adults with a secure attachment style experience a good deal of trust and many positive emotions in their current love relationships, and their relationships tend to last longer than those of adults with insecure attachment styles. Avoidant lovers fear intimacy, whereas resistant individuals tend to be obsessed with their partners and jealous. When engaged

Internal Working Models of Attachment

Which of the internal working models of attachment or attachment styles in Figure 14.8—secure, dismissing, preoccupied, or fearful—is expressed in each of the following statements? And which working model best describes you (Bartholomew & Horowitz, 1991, p. 244; adapted from Hazan & Shaver, 1987)?

—1. "I want to be completely emotionally intimate with others, but I often find that others are reluctant to get as close as I would like. I am uncomfortable being without close relationships, but I sometimes worry that others don't value me as much as I value them."

—2. "I am somewhat uncomfortable getting close to others. I want emotionally close relationships, but I find it difficult to trust others completely or to depend on them. I sometimes worry that I will be hurt if I allow myself to become too close to others."

—3. "It is relatively easy for me to become emotionally close to others. I am comfortable depending on others and having others depend on me. I don't worry about being alone or having others not accept me."

—4. "I am comfortable without close emotional relationships. It is very important to me to feel independent and self-sufficient, and I prefer not to depend on others or have others depend on me."

Answers: 1. Preoccupied 2. Fearful 3. Secure 4. Dismissing

---

and married partners discuss problems in their relationships, those with a secure attachment style calmly share their feelings and thoughts; avoidant-style adults show physiological signs of shutting down or inhibiting their true feelings; and resistant-style adults become highly emotionally aroused (Roisman, 2007).

The quality of the parent–child relationship that an adult experienced earlier in life predicts both adult attachment style and romantic relationship quality (Fraley et al., 2013; Grossmann et al., 2002a; Howe, 2011; Raby et al., 2015). Attachments to friends in childhood and adolescence help account for the link between the quality of early parent–child attachments and later romantic attachments—and they contribute something extra of their own, too (Fraley & Roisman, 2015). Sensitive partners can make a difference too—for example, turning an avoidant/dismissing partner into a more trusting and cooperative one by expressing confidence in him and appreciating his efforts (Farrell et al., 2016; Simpson & Overall, 2014). So, as Bowlby theorized, internal working models of self and others formed on the basis of parent–child interactions—but modified by later experiences—color the quality of later relationships. **Application 14.1** illustrates how attachment theory is being applied to improve both parent–child and couple relationships.

Adults' attachment styles predict a lot more about adults than the quality of their romantic relationships, though (see Cassidy & Shaver, 2016). A secure internal working model provides a secure base for exploration, predicting the extent to which adults have the confidence and curiosity to explore and master their environments (Elliot & Reis, 2003; Luke, Sedikides, & Carnelley, 2012). Securely attached adults enjoy their work and are good employees in a variety of ways, preoccupied (resistantly attached) adults may need a lot of emotional support and grumble about not being valued enough, and dismissing (avoidantly attached) adults may bury themselves in work and do little socializing with coworkers (Hazan & Shaver, 1990; and see Paetzold, 2015).

Internal working models and attachment styles are also related to an adult's capacity for caregiving—most importantly, to being a sensitive and responsive parent. Mothers and fathers who had secure relations with their parents tend to interact more sensitively with their children and form more secure attachments with them than parents whose early attachments were insecure (Roisman & Groh, 2011; Shlafer et al., 2015). Attachment styles also predict the quality of caregiving adults provide to their aging parents (Morse et al., 2011).

Finally, attachment styles are related to well-being and both physical and mental health in later life (Howe, 2011; Waldinger et al., 2015). In a study of 60- to 99-year-olds, Victor Cicirelli (2010) concluded that 50% of the older adults studied could be categorized as secure, most of the rest (38%) dismissing-avoidant, and only 12% preoccupied or fearful. As it turns out, older adults who have either a secure or dismissing-avoidant attachment style tend to be happier with their lives than those with either a preoccupied or fearful attachment style (Magai et al., 2001; Bodner & Cohen-Fridel, 2010). Indeed, across cultures middle-aged and older adults appear to be less anxious than young adults about relationships but more avoidant or dismissing (Chopik & Edelstein, 2014). Whether to cope with the loss of a spouse, cope with an imperfect marriage, or optimize independence and minimize dependency on others, then, many older adults seem to become quite self-reliant in their old age and are happy that way.

We can conclude that a secure attachment style is most likely to be associated with good functioning and high well-being throughout the life span (Van Assche et al., 2013; Waldinger et al., 2015). Secure, preoccupied, dismissing, and fearful adult attachment styles have significant implications for adult development—for quality of romantic relationships, exploratory and mastery behavior at work, parenting and caregiving, and adjustment in later life.

Adult Relationships and Adult Development

As you are learning, adults are better off in many ways when they enjoy close social relationships. Research tells us this: The quality rather than the quantity of an individual's social relationships is most closely related to that person's sense of well-being and life

Building Secure Attachments

Attachment theory is increasingly being applied to help parents and children as well as adults develop closer and more developmentally beneficial relationships. For example, programs that teach parents how to be more sensitive and responsive to their infants have contributed to better parenting and better infant and child development in families with stressed, low-income mothers coping with irritable babies (van den Boom, 1995) as well as depressed mothers (Berlin, Zeanah, & Lieberman, 2008; Van Doesum et al., 2008; Velderman et al., 2006). A program aimed at mothers at high risk for maltreating their infants provided 10 sessions that emphasized "providing nurturing care when children are distressed, following children's lead and expressing delight when children are not distressed, and not behaving in frightening ways," as abusive

parents often do (Bernard et al., 2012, p. 623). Compared to children whose parents received a control treatment, children in the special program had significantly higher rates of secure attachment (52% vs. 33%) and lower rates of disorganized attachments (32% vs. 57%).

Attachment-based therapy is also being used to treat adolescents and young adults with problems (Diamond et al., 2016; Kobak & Kerig, 2015). For example, attachment-based family therapy—family therapy guided by attachment theory—has proven effective in helping parents provide depressed and potentially suicidal adolescents with a more secure base of support during crises (Ewing, Diamond, & Levy, 2015). It has also helped young adults overcome unresolved anger that they may have toward one of their parents (Diamond et al., 2016).

Finally, attachment theory provides a basis for treating couples with relationship problems (Berry & Danquah, 2016). The emotionally focused therapy developed by Susan Johnson (2004, 2008; Johnson & Wittenborn, 2012), for example, helps partners understand their attachment-related emotions (to appreciate that it is okay to need one another or to be fearful of separation); to communicate their emotions, including painful ones about experiences of betrayal or unresponsiveness; and to collaborate to better meet one another's emotional needs and heal old wounds. Apparently, then, insecure and troubled relationships can be converted into more secure ones that serve as secure bases for exploration, safe havens in times of stress, and foundations for healthy development across the life span.

---

satisfaction (Litwin & Shiovitz-Ezra, 2011; Pinquart & Sorensen, 2000). Similarly, perceived social support is more important than the social support actually received (Uchino, 2009). Just as people can feel lonely despite being surrounded by other people, or deprived of social support even though they receive a lot of it, they can have small social networks and receive little social support yet be quite satisfied.

The size of an adult's social network is not nearly as important as whether it includes at least one confidant—a spouse, relative, or friend to whom the individual feels especially attached and with whom thoughts and feelings can be shared (de Jong-Gierveld, 1986; Levitt, 1991). For most married adults, spouses are the most important confidants, and the quality of an adult's marriage is one of the strongest influences on overall satisfaction with life (Fleeson, 2004). Men are particularly dependent on their spouses; women rely more than men on friends, siblings, and children for emotional support (Gurung, Taylor, & Seeman, 2003). Even in very old age, most adults have at least one close friend and are in frequent contact with them (Ueno & Adams, 2006).

Adults benefit not only from having at least one confidant but also from having interactions that are rewarding rather than stressful (Krause, 1995). Probably because of their personality traits and attachment styles, people who have positive (or

Most older adults have at least one close friend or confidant—and it is good they do.

Gaby Gerster/laif/Redux

negative) interactions in one relationship tend to have similar experiences in other relationships, creating a constellation of supportive (or stressful) relationships (Krause & Rook, 2003). Relationships with spouses, children, or other significant companions can undermine rather than bolster physical and mental health if they involve mostly conflict and irritation (Newsom et al., 2003; Rook, 2015).

So a small number of close, harmonious, and supportive relationships can improve the quality of an adult's life, whereas negative relationships (or a lack of relationships) can make life miserable, as discussed in **Exploration 14.3** on the widespread problem of loneliness. It's a matter of life and death: Social support, especially that provided by close family attachments, has positive effects on the cardiovascular, endocrine, and immune systems; improves the body's ability to cope with stress; and contributes to better physical and cognitive functioning and even to a longer life (J. Cacioppo et al., 2015; Pietromonaco, DeBuse, & Powers, 2013; Uchino, 2009). Whatever our ages, our well-being and development hinge considerably on the quality of our ties to our fellow humans—particularly on having a close and gratifying emotional bond with at least one person.

● **EXPLORATION 14.3**

Lonely Hearts

All the lonely people—Where do they all come from?

—The Beatles, "Eleanor Rigby"

Almost all of us have experienced loneliness at some time in our life, but for some individuals it is a chronic and very painful state. It is a life-span concept that may be caused by being excluded from peer groups, lacking a friend as a child, or being abandoned by friends and lovers as an adolescent or adult (Qualter et al., 2015). Loneliness is reported at all ages but the percentages of people saying they "sometimes" or "often" feel lonely hover around 40–50% and appear to be especially high in adolescence and in old age (Qualter et al., 2015). Lonely people can be almost anyone, even people who are popular and have high status, or people who are surrounded by other people (S. Cacioppo et al., 2015).

It is becoming clear that loneliness takes a significant toll on health and mental health and should be viewed as a major public health problem (Gerst-Emerson & Jayawardhana, 2015). John Cacioppo and his colleagues conclude that humans have evolved to be with other people and that isolation and loneliness stress and wear down the body, affecting genes, stress hormones and responses to stress, and brain functioning. These physical impacts speed the aging process and contribute to such problems as cardiovascular disease, poor immune system functioning, cognitive decline, and depression (J. Cacioppo et al., 2015; Cacioppo & Patrick, 2008; Luo et al., 2012). It does not seem to matter much whether social isolation is real or perceived; measures of social isolation, loneliness, and living alone are all associated with decreased longevity (Holt-Lunstad et al., 2015). But loneliness and social isolation are distinct, and loneliness can have negative effects on health and mental health independent of the effects of objective social isolation, especially when it is caused by the loss of important attachment figures (J. Cacioppo et al., 2015).

What can be done to help lonely people? A meta-analysis of different approaches to treating loneliness indicates that it may be more effective to change the maladaptive cognitions behind loneliness (for example, "No one cares about me") than to give people more opportunities for social interaction, increase their social support (for example, through buddy programs), or teach them social skills (S. Cacioppo et al., 2015; Masi et al., 2011). This makes perfect sense if loneliness is mainly a matter of how we perceive our social relationships. With more adults living alone today than ever before, addressing the problem of loneliness is more urgent than ever.

⌐● **Checking Mastery**

1. What qualities does a companionate love relationship have, according to Sternberg's triangular theory of love?
2. How would you characterize people with a preoccupied internal working model in terms of their (1) views of self and others and (2) position on the dimensions of attachment anxiety and avoidance?
3. What kinds of relationships contribute most to adult well-being?

⌐● **Making Connections**

1. Laura Carstensen's socioemotional selectivity theory suggests that adults narrow their social networks with age to better meet their emotional needs. Develop some alternative hypotheses about why elderly adults have smaller social networks than young adults.
2. Analyze the internal working models that seem to guide you and your partner in your current (or if you are not in a current relationship, most recent) romantic relationship. What are (were) the implications? To help, you may wish to take the Attachment Styles and Close Relationships surveys at www.web-research-design.net/cgi-bin/crq/crq.pl.

Chapter Summary

14.1 Emotional Development

- Biologically based primary emotions such as anger and fear appear in the first 6 months of life, and secondary or self-conscious emotions at around 18 months of age after self-awareness is achieved. Attachment figures socialize emotions and help infants regulate their emotions until they can develop better emotion regulation strategies of their own.
- Children gain emotional competence (emotional expression, understanding, and regulation) with age; they come to understand that it is possible to have mixed emotions and they learn to follow emotional display rules.
- Adolescents have more negative moods than children or adults, sometimes because they seek them.
- Carstensen's socioemotional selectivity theory and the positivity effect suggest that older adults, realizing that time is short, achieve high emotional well-being by emphasizing emotional fulfillment rather than information seeking and by focusing on positive rather than negative information.

14.2 Perspectives on Relationships

- The developmental significance of early parent–child relationships is emphasized in the Bowlby-Ainsworth attachment theory, which argues that attachments are built into the human species, develop through an interaction of nature and nurture during a sensitive period, and affect later development by shaping internal working models of self and others.
- The second world of childhood, the peer world, was believed to be especially important by Jean Piaget, who emphasized the reciprocal nature of relations with equals, and by Harry Stack Sullivan, who emphasized chumships as a source of social support and a training ground for later intimate relationships.

14.3 The Infant

- Parents typically become attached to infants before or shortly after birth, and parent and child quickly establish synchronized routines. Infants progress through phases of undiscriminating social responsiveness, discriminating social responsiveness, active proximity seeking, and goal-corrected partnership. The formation of a first attachment around 6 or 7 months is accompanied by separation anxiety and stranger anxiety, as well as by exploration from a secure base and retreat to the safe haven the caregiver provides.
- Research using Mary Ainsworth's Strange Situation classifies the quality of parent–infant attachment as secure, resistant, avoidant, or disorganized–disoriented. Harry Harlow demonstrated that contact comfort is more important than feeding in attachment; secure attachment is most closely associated with sensitive, responsive parenting but infant temperament and cultural factors also contribute.
- Repeated long-term separations and social deprivation can make it difficult for an infant to form secure attachments, although recovery is evident. Attending day care normally does not disrupt parent–child attachments, although quality of care matters.

Secure attachments contribute to later cognitive, social, and emotional competence, but attachment quality often changes over time, and insecurely attached infants are not doomed to a lifetime of poor relationships.
- Infants are interested in peers and become increasingly able to coordinate their own activity with that of their small companions; by 18 months, they participate in reciprocal complementary play and may form friendships.

14.4 The Child

- From ages 2 to 12, children participate in goal-corrected partnerships with their parents and spend increasing amounts of time with peers, especially same-sex ones, engaging in increasingly social and imaginative play, including social pretend play, and later in rule-governed games and hobbies.
- Physical attractiveness, intellectual ability, social competence, and emotion regulation skills contribute to popular—rather than rejected, neglected, or controversial—sociometric status. Children who are rejected by their peers and children who have no friends are especially at risk for future problems.

14.5 The Adolescent

- During adolescence, same-sex, and later cross-sex, friendships increasingly involve emotional intimacy and self-disclosure, and a transition is made, led by teens with high perceived popularity, from same-sex cliques, to mixed-sex cliques and larger crowds, and finally to dating relationships, which at first meet self-esteem and status needs and later become more truly affectionate and committed.
- Although susceptibility to negative peer pressure peaks around age 14 or 15, peers are more often a positive than a negative force in development, unless poor relationships with parents lead to association with the wrong crowd.

14.6 The Adult

- Adult social networks, except for family networks, shrink with age, in part because of increased socioemotional selectivity.
- Various filters may be involved in partner choice or mate selection and choices are based mainly on homogamy, with complementarity a lesser consideration. According to Sternberg's triangular theory, love involves passion, intimacy, and commitment and different types of love differ in the amounts of each component.
- Adults have secure, preoccupied, dismissing, or fearful internal working models and adult attachment styles that appear to be rooted in their early attachment experiences and that affect their romantic relationships, approaches to work, caregiving skills, and adjustment in old age.
- At least one close confidant and supportive rather than stressful relationships benefit life satisfaction, physical health, cognitive functioning, and even longevity in adulthood.

Key Terms

15 The Family

Listen to the words of Susan Klebold, mother of one of two students, Eric Harris and Dylan Klebold, who, in 1999, killed 12 students and a teacher and injured 24 more students before taking their own lives in a now-infamous massacre at Columbine High School in Colorado (Klebold, 2009, p. 5):

"I was widely viewed as a perpetrator or at least an accomplice since I was the person who had raised a 'monster.' In one newspaper survey, 83 percent of respondents said that the parents' failure to teach Dylan and Eric proper values played a major part in the Columbine killings. If I turned on the radio, I heard angry voices condemning us for Dylan's actions. Our elected officials stated publicly that bad parenting was the cause of the massacre. . . I tried to identify a pivotal event in his upbringing that could account for his anger. Had I been too strict? Not strict enough? Had I pushed too hard, or not hard enough?"

Susan Klebold has lived every mother's nightmare. By her telling, "Tom and I were loving, attentive, and engaged parents, and Dylan was an enthusiastic, affectionate child," in his early years at least (Klebold, 2016, p. xx). In adolescence, he lost interest in school and became quiet and a little resistant when asked to help around the house, and he and Eric Harris were arrested after they broke into a van, but he was not that different from other teens, was looking into where to attend college, and certainly did not seem deranged. His mother had no idea that Dylan was severely depressed and suicidal and certainly had no idea that he was capable of murder.

Undoubtedly the parents of other mass murderers have experienced anguish similar to Susan Klebold's; we *do* tend to blame parents when their children do horrible things. But are we justified in doing so? One of the big issues we address in this chapter concerns parenting and the extent to which parents influence how children turn out. You will learn that it's more complex than "blame the parent" thinking would suggest.

The Klebold family's story also illustrates the important concept, put forward by Glen Elder and his colleagues (Elder & Johnson, 2003; Elder & Shanahan, 2006), that we lead linked lives—that our lives and development are intertwined with those of other members of our families. Susan Klebold's life, and that of her husband and other son, were changed forever the day of the Columbine massacre. Despite hours of therapy, she is still in anguish over not seeing her son's problem coming so that she could have helped him and prevented the tragedy of Columbine. Just as parents influence their children, then, children influence their parents—for good or bad.

This chapter examines the family and its central roles in human development throughout the life span. How should

Susan Klebold, mother of Columbine High School shooter Dylan Klebold. Does she look like the producer of a mass murderer?

AP Images/David Zalubowski

we think about families and how have they changed in recent decades? How do infants, children, and adolescents experience family life, and how are they affected by their relationships with parents and siblings and the parenting they receive? How is adult development affected by such family transitions as marrying, becoming a parent, watching children leave the nest, and becoming a grandparent? Finally, what are the implications of the immense diversity that characterizes today's families—and of such decisions as remaining childless or divorcing?

15.1
Understanding the Family

LEARNING OBJECTIVES

- Discuss the concept of the family as a changing system within a changing world, using the concepts of family systems theory, Bronfenbrenner's bioecological model, and the family life cycle to do so.

- Describe some of the major changes in the family since the 1950s and evaluate which are most positive and most negative.

The family is a system—and a system within other systems. It is also a changing system—and a changing system in a changing world. We invite you to see how much you know about American family life today by completing **Engagement 15.1** before reading on.

The Family as a System within Systems

Despite a Supreme Court ruling on the matter, debate continues to rage in the United States today about whether marriage, the basis for most families, must be between a husband and wife or can be between two men or two women. This controversy illustrates that it may not be possible to define *family* in a way that applies across all cultures and eras of history; many forms of family life have worked and continue to work for humans (Coontz, 2000; Leeder, 2004). However we define family, proponents of family systems theory conceptualize the family as

a system. This means that the family, like the human body, is truly a whole consisting of interrelated parts, each of which affects and is affected by every other part, and each of which contributes to the functioning of the whole (Bornstein & Sawyer, 2006; Bowen, 1978; Thoburn & Sexton, 2016). Moreover, the family is a dynamic system—a self-organizing system that adapts itself to changes in its members and to changes in its environment.

The traditional nuclear family consists of father, mother, and at least one child. Some scholars think it makes more sense to talk of the "immediate family" consisting of children and whoever cares for them to embrace single-parent families, gay and lesbian families, and so on (McGoldrick, Garcia Preto, & Carter, 2016). In any case, even a simple man, woman, and infant "family system" is complex. An infant interacting with her mother is already involved in a process of reciprocal influence: The baby's smile is greeted by a smile from Mom, and Mom's smile is reciprocated by the infant's grin. However, the presence

Do You Know Today's American Family?

Do you have a good feel for characteristics of American family life today? Fill in the blanks below with a number you would guess is close to the correct percentage and then compare your answers with the statistics in the section "A Changing System in a Changing World" on pages 470–471. Read that section a bit more closely if your guesses are wildly different from the real percentages.

_____ 1. What percentage of adults can be expected to marry at some point in their lives?

_____ 2. What percentage of births are now to unmarried rather than married women?

_____ 3. What percentage of women with children younger than age 6 work outside the home?

_____ 4. What percentage of newly married couples can expect to divorce?

_____ 5. What percentage of children live with two parents (whether biological, adoptive, or stepparents)?

_____ 6. What percentage of women age 65 and older live alone?

of both parents means that we must consider husband–wife, mother–infant, and father–infant relationships (Belsky, 1981). Every individual and every relationship within the family affects every other individual and relationship through reciprocal influence.

Now think about how complex the family system becomes if we add another child (or two or six) to it. We must then understand the husband–wife or couple relationship, the relationship between each parent and each of their children, and the relationship between each pair of siblings. The family now becomes a system with subsystems—specifically, the couple, parent–child, and sibling subsystems (Parke & Buriel, 2006). And let's add a fourth subsystem identified by family researchers, coparenting, or the ways in which two parents coordinate their parenting and function well (or poorly) as a team in raising their children (Feinberg & Kan, 2016; McHale & Lindahl, 2011; McHale et al., 2002). Do they talk to each other about the children and agree on the basics of child-rearing? Have they worked out a division of responsibility for parenting? Are they consistent in their rules and enforcement of rules? And do they back one another up—or do they undermine each other's parenting, contradict one another, and compete for their children's affection? Mutually supportive coparenting can make a big difference in child development, beyond the impact of a close marital or couple relationship (Lamb & Lewis, 2015).

Now consider the complexity of an extended family household, in which parents and their children live with other kin—some combination of grandparents, siblings, aunts, uncles, nieces, and nephews. Extended family households are common in many cultures (Ruggles, 1994). Indeed, it has been suggested that humans evolved to involve the whole "village," or at least many members of the extended family along with a mother and father, in raising children (Hrdy, 2005). In the United States, African Americans, Hispanic Americans, and other ethnic minorities tend to place more emphasis on extended family bonds than European Americans do (Parke & Buriel, 2006). For example, African American single mothers often obtain needed help with child care and social support by living with their mothers (Burton, 1990; Oberlander, Black,

& Starr, 2007). Even when members of the extended family live in their own households, they often interact frequently and share responsibility for raising children, often to the benefit of the children.

The family is also a _system within other systems_; whether it is of the nuclear or the extended type, it does not exist in a vacuum. Urie Bronfenbrenner's _bioecological model_, a systems theory introduced in Chapter 2, emphasizes nicely that the family is a system (a microsystem, if you recall) that is embedded in and interacts with larger social systems such as a neighborhood, a community, a subculture, and a broader culture (Bronfenbrenner & Morris, 2006). The family experience in our culture is different from that in cultures where new brides become underlings in the households of their mothers-in-law or where men can have several wives (Strong & Cohen, 2017). There is an almost infinite variety of family forms and family contexts in the world and so a wide range of developmental experiences within the family.

The Family as a Changing System

It would be difficult enough to study the family as a system if it kept the same members and continued to perform the same activities for as long as it existed. However, family membership changes as new children are born, grown children leave the nest, and parents depart or die. Moreover, each family member is a developing individual, and the relationships between husband and wife, parent and child, and sibling and sibling change in systematic ways over the years. Changes in family membership and changes in any person or relationship within the family affect the dynamics of the whole system.

The earliest theories of family development featured the concept of a family life cycle—a sequence of changes in family composition, roles, relationships, and developmental tasks from the time people marry until they die (Duvall, 1977; Hill & Rodgers, 1964). Family theorist Evelyn Duvall (1977), for example, outlined eight stages of the family life cycle, from the married couple without children through the family with children to the aging family, as shown in ● **Table 15.1**. Each stage has a particular set

Stage	Available Roles
1. Married couple without children	Wife Husband
2. Childbearing family (oldest child from birth to 30 months)	Wife–mother Husband–father Infant daughter or son
3. Family with preschool children (oldest child from 30 months to 6 years)	Wife–mother Husband–father Daughter–sister Son–brother
4. Family with school-age children (oldest child up to 12 years)	Wife–mother Husband–father Daughter–sister Son–brother
5. Family with teenagers (oldest child from 13 to 20 years)	Wife–mother Husband–father Daughter–sister Son–brother
6. Family launching young adults (First child gone to last child gone)	Wife–mother–grandmother Husband–father–grandfather Daughter–sister–aunt Son–brother–uncle
7. Family without children (empty nest to retirement)	Wife–mother–grandmother Husband–father–grandfather
8. Aging family (retirement to death)	Wife–mother–grandmother Husband–father–grandfather Widow or widower

Source: Adapted from Duvall, 1977.

of family members, each with distinctive roles (for example, wife, brother) and distinctive developmental tasks—for example, establishing a satisfying relationship in the newlywed phase, adjusting to the demands of new parenthood in the childbearing phase, and adapting to the departure of children in the "launching" phase.

In this chapter, we look at some of these common family transitions, but you will see that an increasing number of people do not experience this traditional family life cycle. Many adults enter into romantic relationships but remain single or childless, marry multiple times, or otherwise follow a different path than the one in which a man and woman form a nuclear family, raise children, and grow old together (Cherlin, 2009; McGoldrick et al., 2016). As a result, many family researchers today find fault with early models of the family life cycle like Duvall's. They have embraced Duvall's concept that family systems develop and change. However, they are expanding on the traditional family life cycle concept to describe the tremendous variety in family life cycle experiences today.

A Changing System in a Changing World

Not only is the family a system embedded within systems, and not only is it a developing system, but the world in which it is embedded is ever changing. Since the 1950s, several dramatic social changes have altered the family experience. Here are some of the trends that have changed family life in the United States (see Cherlin, 2009; Federal Interagency Forum on Child and Family Statistics, 2015; Silverstein & Giarrusso, 2010; Wilmoth & Longino, 2006):

1. **More single adults.** More adults today than in the past are living as singles (never-married, divorced, and widowed adults). About 20% of adults age 25 and older are in the "never married" category, compared to 9% in 1960, and it is projected that more of today's young singles will still be in the "never married" group when they reach middle age (Wang & Parker, 2014).

2. **More postponed marriages.** Do not conclude that marriage is out of style, though; almost 90% of adults can still be expected to marry at some time in their lives (Cherlin, 2009). It is mainly that marriage is being postponed—a worldwide trend. In 1960, the average age at first marriage was 20 for women and 23 for men; more recently, it is 27 for women and 29 for men (Wang & Parker, 2014).

3. **More unmarried parents.** With marriage being postponed, more and more females, especially less educated ones, are not married when they give birth. About 18% of births in 1980 but a whopping 41% of births by 2013 were to unmarried women, often parenting single-handedly (Federal Interagency Forum on Child and Family Statistics, 2015).

4. **Fewer children.** Today's adults are also having fewer children than women in the mid-20th century did and therefore spend fewer years of their lives raising children. Increasing numbers of young women are also remaining childless: The percentage has climbed from 10% in the 1970s to almost 20% (Livingston & Cohn, 2010).

5. **More working mothers.** In 1950, 12% of married women with children younger than 6 years worked outside the home; by 2015 the figure had climbed to about 64%, a truly remarkable social change (Bureau of Labor Statistics, 2016). Almost 75% of mothers of children aged 6 to 17 are in the labor force.

6. **More divorce.** The divorce rate increased over the 20th century. More than 40% of newly married couples can expect to divorce (Cherlin, 2010), and up to half of children can expect to experience a divorce at some point in their development (Lansford, 2009).

7. **More single-parent families.** Because of more births to unmarried women and more divorce, more children live in single-parent families. In 1960, only 9% of children lived with one parent, usually a widowed one (Whitehead & Popenoe, 2003). In 2015, although 68% of children younger than 18 years lived with two parents, 24% lived with their mothers only, 4% with their fathers only, and 4% with grandparents or other nonparents (Federal Interagency Forum on Child and Family Statistics, 2015; and see ■ Figure 15.1).

8. **More remarriages.** As more married couples have divorced, more adults have remarried. Often they form new,

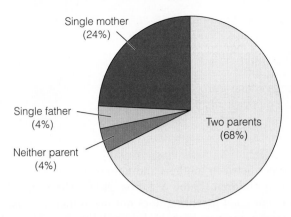

Figure 15.1 Percentage of children from birth to age 17 in various living arrangements. In all, 68% of children live with two parents (64% with married parents, 4% with unmarried parents). The rest (32%) do not: 24% live with their mother only, 4% with their father only, and 4% with someone else, most often grandparents.

Source: Data from Federal Interagency Forum on Child and Family Statistics. (2015). *America's children: Key national indicators of well-being, 2015.* Washington, DC: U.S. Government Printing Office. Available at childstats.gov.

reconstituted families, also called blended families, that include at least a parent, a stepparent, and one child.

9. **More years without children.** Because modern couples are having fewer children, because some divorced adults do not remarry, and mainly because people are living longer, adults today spend more of their later years as couples— or, especially if they are women, as single adults—without children in their homes. Older women are more likely than older men to live alone rather than with a spouse (32% vs. 18%), mainly because more women are widowed (Stepler, 2016).

10. **More multigenerational families.** As a result of these same trends, three- and even four-generation families became more common over the 20th century. More children today than in the past know their grandparents and even their great-grandparents, parent–child and grandparent–child relationships are lasting longer, and multigenerational bonds are becoming more important (Bengtson, 2001).

11. **Fewer caregivers for aging adults.** Yet owing to smaller families and increased longevity, more and more aging adults need care from relatives but have fewer children to provide it, some of whom (stepchildren?) may not feel much obligation to provide it (Roberto & Blieszner, 2015; Silverstein & Giarrusso, 2010).

Do you view all these changes in the family as good news or bad news? Some observers view these changes as evidence of a "decline of the family." They emphasize the often negative effects on children of increased births to unmarried parents, divorce, and single-parent families, and the problem of more elderly adults having fewer children to support them. Some observers also worry because most Americans now view marriage as an institution whose purpose is more to meet the

emotional needs of adults than to nurture children (Cohn et al., 2011; Whitehead & Popenoe, 2003). Family scholar Andrew Cherlin (2009) adds that American children today are being harmed by a dizzying "merry-go-round" of family instability in which their parents switch from one partner to another and from singlehood to cohabitation or marriage and back in their quest for emotional fulfillment. It means that more children are not living with both of their parents, that more parents are not living with their children, and that "the family" is harder to find these days because it is not all living under one roof anymore (Cherlin, 2010).

Can you see any positives in our list of trends in family life? Some scholars can (Connidis, 2010; White & Rogers, 2000). For example, postponing marriage improves its chances of success because partners are more mature and financially stable, men's and women's roles in the family are more equal than they used to be now that more women work, and families are better off financially with two wage earners than with only one. Moreover, more children have relationships with their grandparents and great-grandparents. From this perspective, the family is not dying; it is just changing. It can even be characterized as a highly "adaptable institution" in that it has survived despite many social changes that could have done it in (Amato et al., 2003).

Whether it is in decline or not, the American family is more diverse than ever before. Our stereotyped image of the family—the nuclear family with a married couple consisting of a breadwinner–husband/father, a full-time housewife/mother, plus children—has become just that: a stereotype. Clearly, we must broaden our image of the family to include the many dual-career, single-parent, reconstituted, childless, and other types of families that exist today. We must also avoid assuming that families that do not fit the stereotypical family pattern are deficient.

● Checking Mastery

1. What does Urie Bronfenbrenner's bioecological theory add to our understanding of the family?
2. What are four subsystems in a family with a mother, father, and three children?
3. What are three changes over the 20th century that have resulted in fewer children living their childhoods in a stereotypical nuclear family with a married breadwinner father and homemaker mother?

● Making Connections

1. What does it really mean to be a family? Bearing in mind the diversity of families today, offer a definition of "family" and justify it.
2. In what ways are your family's experiences traditional and in what ways are they modern and reflective of the trends in family life over the past few decades?

15.2

The Infant

LEARNING OBJECTIVES

- Compare and contrast the traditional roles of mothers and fathers in childrearing and describe how these roles have been changing.

- Define and give an example of good coparenting and of a positive indirect effect of one parent on the other parent's interaction with their infant.

We begin this look at family development by exploring relationships between parenting and the child's development in the family from infancy to adolescence. Later, we will adopt the perspective of this child's parents and see how the family life cycle looks to them. The family is changed when a child is born, becoming a system consisting of mother, father, and infant. The main caregiving role for parents of infants is to nurture them and form secure attachments with them (see Chapter 14).

Mothers and Fathers

Once developmentalists took seriously the idea that the family is a system, they discovered the existence of fathers and began to look more carefully at how both mothers and fathers interact with and influence their children. Gender stereotypes would suggest that fathers are not cut out to care for infants and young children, but the evidence says they are (Lamb, 2013; Lamb & Lewis, 2015). For example, fathers prove to be no less able than mothers to feed their babies effectively (Parke & Sawin, 1976). And fathers, like mothers, provide sensitive parenting, form attachments with their babies, and serve as secure bases for exploration (Cox et al., 1992; Schoppe-Sullivan et al., 2006). We have no basis for thinking that mothers are uniquely qualified to parent or that men are hopelessly inept around babies. Throughout childhood, in fact, there are surprisingly few

differences between mothers and fathers in how they interact with their children (Lamb & Lewis, 2015). However, fathers' capacity for good parenting does not mean that they play the same roles as mothers in their children's lives.

Fathers today are more involved with their children than ever (Bianchi, 2011; Pleck & Masciadrelli, 2004). ■Figure 15.2 shows just how much the daily lives of mothers and fathers have changed from 1965 to 2011. As women have increased their involvement in paid work, they have decreased their involvement in housework and somehow managed (by not sleeping?) to spend more time caring for their children than mothers in 1965 did. Fathers have helped make this possible by increasing their involvement in child care from 2.5 to 7 hours a week and their housework time from 4 to 10 hours a week. Some fathers are even sharing responsibility for child care equally with their spouses rather than just "helping," especially if they hold egalitarian views about gender roles (Bulanda, 2004; Deutsch, 2001). As a result, the roles of

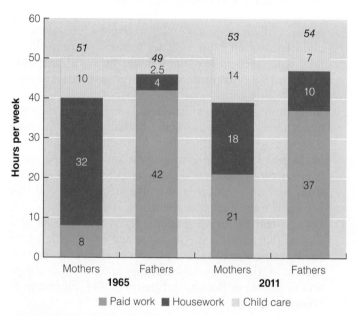

■ **Figure 15.2** Changes in time use of mothers and fathers between 1965 and 2011. Roles are converging.

Source: Parker, K. & Wang, W. (2013). *Modern parenthood: Roles of Moms and Dads converge as they balance work and family*. Pew Research Center Social and Demographic Trends. Retrieved from www.pewsocialtrends.org/2013/03/14/modern-parenthood-roles-of-moms-and-dads-converge-as-they-balance-work-and-family/. Data for 1965 from Bianchi, Robinson, and Milkie, 2006; data for 2011 from Pew Research analysis of the American Time Use Survey.

Fathers are just as capable as mothers of sensitive, responsive parenting.

Romona Robbins Photography/Image Source/Getty Images

mothers and fathers are converging. Yet mothers still spend more overall time with children, and more time directly caring for them and interacting with them, than fathers do (Bianchi, 2011). This gender difference in involvement in child care is common across cultures, causing some to argue that it has a biological basis.

Mothers and fathers also differ somewhat in their styles of interacting with young children. When mothers interact with their babies, a large proportion of their time is devoted to caregiving: offering food, changing diapers, wiping noses, and so on. Fathers spend much of their time with children playing (Lamb, 2013). They specialize in tickling, poking, bouncing, and surprising infants, whereas mothers hold, talk to, and play quietly with them (Laflamme, Pomerleau, & Malcuit, 2002; Neville & Parke, 1997). Yet fathers adopt a "motherlike" caregiver role if they have primary responsibility for their children, so their playful parenting may be more about being in the role of the "backup" parent than about being male rather than female (Phares, 1999). The rowdy play style shown by many fathers in our culture does not show up in all cultures, either (Lamb, 2013). It seems, then, that both nature (evolution) and nurture (societal gender-role norms) contribute to mother–father differences in parental involvement and styles of interacting with young children.

In the end, fathers contribute best to development when they, like mothers, are sensitive and responsive caregivers and form secure attachments with their infants. Children fare better cognitively, socially, and emotionally if they have a supportive father in their lives than if they do not (Holden, 2010; Lamb, 2013). However, much the same can be said for any second parent figure, male or female (Biblarz & Stacey, 2010). So fathers are important, but their contribution may not be as unique as once thought (Lamb, 2013).

Although more American fathers are involved in child care than ever before, more fathers also live apart from their children than ever before. As Livingston and Parker (2011) put it, we have "a tale of two fathers," the engaged kind and the absent kind. What does the fact that 41% of babies are now born to unmarried mothers mean for father involvement? Unmarried fathers who do not live with their child's mother are usually not very involved parents. However, they can be under some conditions. Studies of low-income, urban fathers over the first 3 years of their child's life suggest that much hinges on the quality of the relationship between mother and father and on how effectively they coparent even though they do not live together (Cabrera, Fagan, & Farrie, 2008; Fagan & Palkovitz, 2011; Fagan et al., 2009; Palkovitz, Fagan, & Hull, 2013). If mother and father have a good relationship, even if it is no longer a romantic one, and if the father feels supported as a coparent, he is likely to be more involved with his child.

Unmarried mothers and their children clearly benefit when nonresident fathers become involved fathers and develop positive relationships with their children (Adamsons & Johnson, 2013). Meanwhile, becoming an involved father seems to help some young men mature and make positive changes in their lives

(Fagan et al., 2009). Interventions emphasizing the importance of fathers, good parenting, and supportive coparenting can positively affect the child's development (Cowan et al., 2009; Marczak et al., 2015).

Mothers, Fathers, and Infants: The System at Work

Now let's view the new family as a three-person system. The mother–child relationship cannot be understood without considering the father; nor can the father–child relationship be understood without taking the mother into account. This is because parents have **indirect effects** on their children by influencing the behavior of their partners. Family members (or subsystems of the family) can have either direct or indirect effects on one another. Direct effects within the family include, for example, a mother's or a father's effects on an infant's development. Indirect effects are instances in which the relationship or interaction between two individuals in the family is modified by the behavior or attitudes of a third family member.

Fathers indirectly influence the mother–infant relationship in many ways. For example, mothers who have close, supportive relationships with their husbands tend to interact more patiently and sensitively with their babies than do mothers who are experiencing marital problems or feel that they are raising their children largely without help (Cox et al., 1992; Lamb & Tamis-Lemonda, 2004). Similarly, mothers indirectly affect the father–infant relationship. For example, fathers who have just had pleasant conversations with their wives are more supportive and engaged when they interact with their children than fathers who have just had arguments with their wives (Kitzmann, 2000). And when the mother of an infant is depressed, the father tends to devote more time to caregiving (Planalp & Braungart-Rieker, 2016). Of course, babies have indirect effects too: A screaming baby can negatively affect a couple's relationship by causing a stressed father to blow up at his wife.

As you can imagine, infant development goes best when parents get along well. A strong relationship between partners helps both parents engage with their infant (Carlson et al., 2011). When the relationship is good, couples are also likely to coparent effectively (Parke & Buriel, 2006). When parents compete rather than cooperate, their infants may show signs of insecure attachment or may become securely attached to one parent but be blocked from enjoying close relationships with both parents (Caldera & Lindsey, 2006).

It is in the nature of systems to settle into certain patterns of functioning and to resist change, so once an unhealthy pattern of interaction such as fighting between parents becomes established, it can be difficult to change. However, family systems also show a capacity to change in response to changes both within and outside the family, so there is hope for turning maladaptive patterns of interaction into more adaptive ones (Thoburn & Sexton, 2016).

1. In terms of their parenting roles, what is one way in which fathers are similar to mothers and one way in which they are different?
2. Give an example of a negative indirect effect of a father on the mother–infant relationship.

1. Because of his wife's death during childbirth, Alex suddenly finds himself the sole parent of his infant son, Aaron. Given the material in this section, how do you think this will affect Aaron's welfare and development compared with what would have happened if Alex had been the one who died and his wife had to raise Aaron on her own?

15.3

The Child

LEARNING OBJECTIVES

- Compare and contrast the authoritarian, authoritative, permissive, and neglectful parenting styles in terms of where they fall on the acceptance–responsiveness and demandingness–control dimensions of parenting and how they are likely to affect development.

- Discuss three explanations of why high- and low-SES parents use different parenting styles.

- Define and illustrate with examples the parent effects, child effects, interactional, and transactional models of family influence.

- Summarize the nature of the sibling relationship and its contributions to development.

As children reach age 2 or age 3, parents continue to be caregivers and playmates, but they also become socialization agents. They teach their offspring how (and how not) to behave and how to become contributing members of society using child rearing and discipline techniques, teaching, and other means (Grusec & Davidov, 2010). Siblings also serve as socialization agents and become an important part of the child's developmental experience.

Parenting Styles

How can I be a good parent? Certainly this question is uppermost in most parents' minds. You can go far in understanding which parenting styles are effective by considering just two dimensions of parenting: acceptance–responsiveness and demandingness–control (Baumrind, 2013; Bornstein, 2015; Darling & Steinberg, 1993; Holden, 2010; Maccoby & Martin, 1983; Schaefer, 1959).

Parental **acceptance–responsiveness** refers to the extent to which parents are warm, supportive, sensitive to their children's needs, and willing to provide affection and praise when their children meet their expectations. Accepting, responsive parents are affectionate and often smile at, praise, and encourage their children; they consider their children's perspectives, although they also let children know when they misbehave. Less accepting and responsive parents are often quick to criticize, belittle, punish, or ignore their children and rarely communicate to children that they are loved and valued.

Demandingness–control (sometimes called *permissiveness–restrictiveness*) refers to how much control over decisions lies with the parent as opposed to with the child. Controlling and demanding parents set rules, expect their children to follow them, and monitor their children closely to ensure that the rules are followed. Less controlling and demanding parents make fewer demands and allow their children a great deal of autonomy in exploring the environment, expressing their opinions and emotions, and making decisions about their activities.

By crossing the acceptance and demandingness dimensions, we have four basic patterns of child rearing to consider, as shown in ■ **Figure 15.3**:

1. **Authoritarian parenting.** This is a restrictive parenting style combining high demandingness–control and low acceptance–responsiveness. Parents impose many rules, expect strict obedience, rarely explain why the child should comply with rules, and often rely on power-assertion tactics such as physical punishment to gain compliance.

2. **Authoritative parenting.** Authoritative parents are more flexible; they are quite demanding and exert control, but they are also sensitive to their children. They set clear rules and consistently enforce them, but they have rationales for their rules and explain them, are responsive to their children's needs and points of view, and involve their children in family decision making. They are reasonable and democratic in their approach; although it is clear that they are in charge, they communicate respect for their children.

3. **Permissive parenting** (sometimes called *indulgent parenting*). This style is high in acceptance–responsiveness but low in demandingness–control. Permissive parents are child-centered; they have relatively few rules and make relatively few demands, encourage children to express their feelings and impulses, and rarely exert control over their behavior.

4. **Neglectful parenting** (sometimes called *disengaged* or *uninvolved parenting*). Finally, parents who combine low demandingness–control and low acceptance–responsiveness are relatively uninvolved in their children's upbringing. They seem not to care much about their children. They may be hostile and rejecting or indifferent—or they may be so overwhelmed by their own problems that they cannot devote sufficient energy to expressing love and setting and enforcing rules (Maccoby & Martin, 1983).

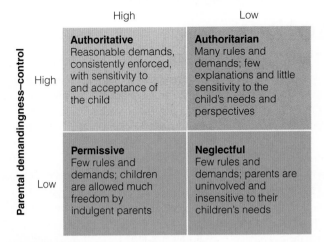

Parental acceptance–responsiveness

	High	Low
High (Parental demandingness–control)	**Authoritative** Reasonable demands, consistently enforced, with sensitivity to and acceptance of the child	**Authoritarian** Many rules and demands; few explanations and little sensitivity to the child's needs and perspectives
Low	**Permissive** Few rules and demands; children are allowed much freedom by indulgent parents	**Neglectful** Few rules and demands; parents are uninvolved and insensitive to their children's needs

■ **Figure 15.3** The acceptance–responsiveness and demandingness–control dimensions of parenting. Which combination best describes your parents' approach?

Source: From Maccoby, E. E., & Martin, J. A. (1983). Socialization in the context of the family: Parent–child interaction. In E. M. Hetherington (Vol. Ed.), P. H. Mussen (Ed.-in-Chief), *Handbook of child psychology: Vol. 4, Socialization, personality, and social development* (4th ed.). Copyright © 1983 by Wiley. Reprinted with permission.

We assume that you have no difficulty deciding that parental acceptance and responsiveness are preferable to parental rejection, hostility, neglect, or insensitivity. As you have seen in this book, warm, responsive parenting is associated with secure attachments to parents, academic competence, high self-esteem, good social skills, peer acceptance, a strong sense of morality, good mental health, and many other virtues. The benefits of perceived parent acceptance are clear across the life span (Holden, 2010; Khaleque & Rohner, 2012).

The degree of demandingness and control shown by parents is also important. The authoritarian, authoritative, and permissive parenting styles were originally identified and defined by Diana Baumrind (1967, 1977, 1991, 2013). In a pioneering longitudinal study, Baumrind found that children raised by authoritative parents were the best adjusted: They were cheerful, socially responsible, self-reliant, achievement oriented, and cooperative with adults and peers. Children of permissive parents were often impulsive, aggressive, self-centered, rebellious, aimless, and low in independence and achievement. Given little guidance, they did not learn self-control and self-direction. Children of authoritarian parents tended to be moody and unhappy, relatively aimless, and unpleasant to be around. They had little opportunity to learn self-reliance and lacked confidence in their own decision-making skills.

Subsequent research has shown that the worst developmental outcomes are associated with the neglectful, uninvolved style of parenting. Children of neglectful parents display behavioral problems such as aggression and frequent temper tantrums and tend to become hostile and antisocial adolescents who abuse alcohol and drugs and get in trouble (Lamborn et al., 1991; Miller et al., 1993; Weiss & Schwarz, 1996). Parents who provide little guidance and communicate that they do not care breed children who are resentful and prone to strike back at their uncaring parents and other authority figures.

In short, children develop best when they have both love and limits. The link between authoritative parenting and positive developmental outcomes is evident in most ethnic groups and socioeconomic groups in the United States (Sorkhabi & Mandara, 2013; Steinberg, 2001) and in a variety of other cultures (Sorkhabi & Mandara, 2013; Vazsonyi, Hibbert, & Snider, 2003). Nonetheless, the effectiveness of different parenting approaches can differ depending on the cultural or subcultural context in which they are used. Much seems to hinge on how common a parenting style is in a culture or subculture and whether children view it as normal and acceptable (see Grolnick & Pomerantz, 2009; Lansford et al., 2005; Sorkhabi & Mandara, 2013). Case in point: African American parents living in high-crime poverty areas in the United States sometimes rely on authoritarian and even harsh parenting in an effort to protect their children from harm. Their children tend to view this as a sign that their parents care rather than as a sign of hostility and rejection. As a result, this authoritarian parenting style does not have as many negative effects as it has in middle-class communities (Deater-Deckard, Dodge, & Sorbring, 2005; Laird et al., 2009; McElhaney & Allen, 2012). We further explore the importance of cultural context in influencing the effectiveness of parenting styles in **Exploration 15.1**.

Social Class, Economic Hardship, and Parenting

Over the past few decades, economic inequality has increased in our society as a result of technological advances, globalization, and other major societal changes. Wealthy families have accumulated still more wealth while other families have seen little improvement in their finances and, in many cases, have lost what they had as a result of unemployment, housing foreclosures, and evictions (Amato, Booth, & McHale, 2015; Duncan, Magnuson, & Votruba-Drzal, 2015). As sociologist Robert Putnam (2015) demonstrates vividly in his book *Our Kids*, growing economic inequality translates into a growing gap between rich and poor kids in their developmental experiences and life outcomes. How exactly does a family's economic fortunes affect development?

Start with the fact that parents of different socioeconomic (SES) levels rely on different parenting styles in raising children—with some important implications. Compared with middle-class and upper-class parents, lower-class and working-class parents tend to place more emphasis on obedience and respect for authority. They are often more restrictive and authoritarian, reason with their children less frequently, and show less warmth and affection (Conger & Dogan, 2007; McLoyd, 1990). Parents dealing with poverty and economic hardship tend to be especially harsh and inconsistent, sometimes to the point of being abusive and/ or neglectful (Brooks-Gunn, Britto, & Brady, 1999; Seccombe, 2000). You will find a range of parenting styles in any social group, of course. However, these average social-class differences in parenting help explain social-class differences in developmental outcomes such as school achievement, adjustment, and life success (Conger & Dogan, 2007).

Culture and the Tiger Mother

Sophia and Lulu could never attend sleepovers or have playdates, watch television or play computer games, get a grade less than A, or choose their own extracurricular activities or musical instruments. Their mother rejected the birthday cards they made for her one year because they were poorly done. Their mother once called Sophia "garbage" for disrespecting her. And poor 7-year-old Lulu: After she tore her musical score for "Little White Donkey" to bits during a long battle over playing the difficult piano piece, her mother put her doll-house in the car and said she'd donate it to the Salvation Army, threatened no dinner and no birthday parties for years, and called her lazy and pathetic.

Not exactly our image of the perfect parent. Amy Chua, a law professor at Yale, caused a firestorm with her book, *Battle Hymn of the Tiger Mother* (Chua, 2011a, 2011b). This "Tiger Mother" described raising her daughters, Sophia and Lulu, in what struck most American parents as an almost abusively demanding, controlling, and unresponsive manner: Authoritarian parenting to the max. Chua, meanwhile, accused American parents (including her husband) of being too child-centered and spineless. They worry too much about their children's self-esteem, she charged, and protect their children from struggling with difficult challenges and facing criticism. They don't view children as obligated to obey their parents and make them proud, as Chinese parents do, and they bow to their children's desires rather than relying on their own judgment about what is best for children.

Lulu did finally play the piano piece correctly after hours more work on it, beamed at her hard-won accomplishment, and celebrated with her mother. As far as we can tell, both Sophia and Lulu have turned out pretty well: Both went to Harvard and both not only appreciated their Tiger Mother but planned to become Tiger Mothers themselves, pushing their children to be the best they can be (Carey, 2016). Is this really the model parents

should follow if they want high-achieving children?

Perhaps not. Chua admits that she went too far at times; she moved toward a more moderate parenting style, partly in response to Lulu's rebellion. What this Tiger Mother did is also not representative of what most Chinese parents do, although they do tend to be more strict and controlling than most European American parents (Ng, Pomerantz, & Deng, 2014). How do we square the generally positive outcomes of a traditional Chinese upbringing with mounds of research suggesting that the warmer and more reasonable authoritative parenting style is the best way to raise children? Why aren't Chinese children stressed, moody, and incapable of making their own decisions rather than achievement oriented and accomplished?

Plenty of studies say that the authoritative parenting style works well, not only for European Americans but for children from a variety of cultural and ethnic backgrounds, including Chinese-American children like Tiger Mother's daughters (Kim et al., 2013; Sorkhabi & Mandara, 2013). Su Yeong Kim and her colleagues (2013) did an interesting study of 444 Chinese-American youth over the 8 years from early adolescence to emerging adulthood. She looked at both positive aspects of parenting (warmth, reasoning, monitoring, and democratic approach) and negative aspects (hostility, control, shaming, and punitiveness). The goal was to identify different parenting profiles. It turned out that almost half the parents fit a "supportive" profile, much like the authoritative style, in which they showed high warmth and reasonable control. Another 28% were "tiger parents" (defined as high on both positive and negative scales), 20% were easy going (low across scales), and only 7% were harsh (low warmth, high control).

As in most studies, children with supportive, authoritative parents fared best overall, academically and otherwise. By comparison, tiger parents' children had lower grade

point averages, felt more academic pressure, experienced more depressive symptoms, and felt more alienated. At least in these Chinese-American families and with adolescents, then, tiger parenting was neither the most common approach nor the best approach. Moreover, there seems to be more acceptance and warmth to the typical Chinese parenting approach than Tiger Mother let on.

Ruth Chao (1994, 2000) concluded from her research that we must look more closely at what Chinese parenting involves and understand it in its cultural context. She maintains that Chinese parents are not really authoritarian in our Western sense of the term. In Chinese culture, training children entails parent involvement and self-sacrifice, along with an emphasis on hard work, discipline, and doing well to uphold the family's honor. Parents are indeed demanding; they offer clear and specific guidelines for behavior, believing that this is the best way to express their love and train their children properly. Children understand that their parent's strictness is an expression of love and that their responsibility as a child is to obey, work hard, and meet their parents' high expectations. Parents may not explain their rules or involve their children in decision making—but children do not expect them to. Although the Chinese style seems overly controlling to European American eyes, Chinese parents and children view it as warm and caring—and thus more like authoritative parenting than like the colder, more arbitrary authoritarian style). Children respond well to it as a result.

Parents in many cultures around the world adopt a more traditional, controlling approach to parenting and get good results with it. The real moral of the Tiger Mother story is that we must always interpret parenting in its cultural and subcultural context and understand that styles that do not look acceptable to us may be acceptable and effective in other sociocultural settings.

Why do these socioeconomic differences in parenting styles and child outcomes exist? Three major explanations, all with some truth to them, center on SES differences in financial stress, resources invested in children, and cultural values and socialization goals (see Conger & Dogan, 2007; Duncan et al., 2015).

Financial Stress

One well-established explanation, developed by Glen Elder, Rand Conger, and their colleagues and called the **family stress model**, centers on the negative effects of financial stresses on parent mental health, parenting, and, in turn, child development (Conger & Dogan, 2007; Donnellan, Martin, Conger, & Conger, 2013). As shown in ■ **Figure 15.4**, Conger and his associates (1992, 2002; Conger, Patterson, & Ge, 1995) have found that parents who experience financial problems feel economic pressure, which tends to make them depressed, which increases conflict between the couple, which disrupts each partner's ability to be an effective parent. Financially stressed parents tend to be less warm and nurturant, more authoritarian, and less consistent. This breakdown in parenting then contributes to negative child outcomes such as low self-esteem, poor school performance, poor peer relations, and adjustment problems such as aggression and depression. The family stress model seems to have good support and applies across ethnic groups and cultures (Neppl, Senia, & Donnellan, 2016; Donnellan et al., 2013). It is also useful in explaining the effects of a variety of stressors on low-income parents and, in turn, children—for example, the effects of living in a dangerous neighborhood or being immigrant parents who do not speak English or understand the culture well (Duncan et al., 2015; White et al., 2009).

Now consider the even worse effects of poverty on development. About 20% of children in the United States—one in five—live in poverty today, more than in other Western nations (Federal Interagency Forum on Child and Family Statistics, 2015). Those affected are disproportionately children under 6, children in female-headed homes (where 46% are poor), and

minority children (39% of Black, non-Hispanic children and 30% of Hispanic children, compared to 11% of White, non-Hispanic children). Stresses are magnified for families living in poverty or moving in and out of poverty as a result of job loss and other economic crises. Both parents and children experience stress as they cope with a physical environment characterized by pollution, noise, and crowded, unsafe living conditions and a social environment characterized by family instability and violence (Duncan et al., 2015; Evans, 2004).

As noted previously, parents coping with poverty tend to be harsh, punitive, and inconsistent. Partly owing to its effects on parenting, poverty is associated with child health problems, emotional and behavioral problems, and academic failure (Bradley & Corwyn, 2002; Evans, 2004; Evans & Kim, 2013). We also know that the many chronic stressors associated with poverty can alter children's stress response systems in ways that pave the way for health and mental health problems later in life and can disrupt the development of regions of the brain that are involved in attention and self-regulation and that are therefore important in coping with challenges (Duncan et al., 2015; Evans & Kim, 2013). The negative effects of poverty on development are most severe when poverty is experienced early in life and over many years (Duncan et al., 2015; Wagmiller, 2015).

Resource Investment

A second explanation of social-class differences in parenting and child outcomes is that low-SES parents have fewer resources to invest in their children's development than high-SES parents do (Conger & Dogan, 2007; Donnellan et al., 2013; Duncan et al., 2015). Wealthier parents can invest more money and time in getting their children a good education; providing books, computers, and other learning materials in the home; taking their children to educational events; and devoting time to interacting with their children and stimulating their minds. They can also spend more on good nutrition, child care, and health care.

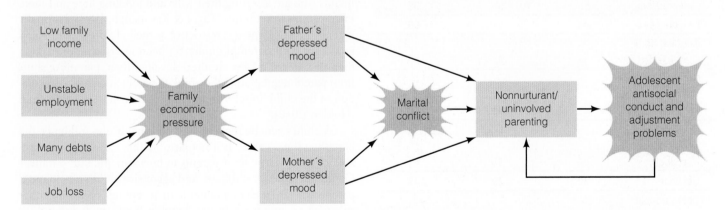

■ **Figure 15.4** A model of the relationship among family economic stress, patterns of parenting, and adolescent adjustment.

Source: Adapted from Conger, R. D., Conger, K. J., Elder, G. H., Jr., Lorenz, F. O., Simons, R. L, & Whitbeck, L. B. (1992). A family process model of economic hardship and adjustment of early adolescent boys. *Child Development, 63*, 526–541.

Cultural Values and Socialization Goals

Third and finally, high- and low-SES parents may have different values and socialization goals in socializing their children (Conger & Dogan, 2007; Duncan et al., 2015). As ● **Table 15.2** shows, for example, poor parents have more worries about their children's welfare than wealthier parents do, especially when it comes to the possibility that their children could be the victims of violence, become teen parents, or get in trouble with the law. These concerns may contribute to their more authoritarian, controlling style of parenting.

High- and low-SES parents may also parent in ways that prepare their children for the kinds of jobs the parents hold. Wealthier parents may reason more with their children and foster initiative and creativity because these are the attributes that count for business executives, professionals, and other white-collar workers. Parents from lower socioeconomic groups may be authoritarian and emphasize obedience to authority figures in part because that is what is required in jobs like their own (Kohn, 1969).

In sum, low family SES and economic hardship may be associated with poor developmental outcomes because of (1) economic stresses that result in less warm and nurturant, more authoritarian, and less consistent parenting; (2) limited investment of resources, mainly money and time, in children's development; and (3) socialization goals centered more on keeping children

● **Table 15.2** Comparison of Parents' Concerns for Their Children Based on Family Income Levels

Concern that your child(ren) might:	Family Income		
	$75,000+	$30,000–$74,999	$30,000
Be bullied	61%	62%	60%
Struggle with anxiety or depression	55	55	55
Be kidnapped	44	51	59
Get beat up or attacked	38	44	55
Get pregnant/Get a girl pregnant as a teenager	43	40	50
Have problems with drugs or alcohol	44	36	41
Get shot	22	29	47
Get in trouble with the law	21	25	40

Source: Parker, K., Horowitz, J. M., & Rohal, M. (2015, December 17). *Parenting in America. Outlooks, worries, aspirations are strongly linked to financial situation.* Pew Research Center, p. 49. Retrieved from www.pewsocialtrends.org/files/2015/12/2015-12-17_parenting-in-america_FINAL.pdf.

out of trouble and preparing them to obey a boss rather than be the boss. These are important things to know in the wake of the economic recession of 2008 and its continuing negative effects on parents and children (Adrian & Coontz, 2010; Donnellan et al., 2013). Experimental programs designed to boost the incomes of families living in poverty can change these negative influences, putting children on a path to better achievement in school and better life outcomes (Duncan et al., 2015).

Models of Influence in the Family

So far, you have seen that parents, through their parenting, affect their children's development. But there are other ways of thinking about influence in the family and they give us a more sophisticated understanding. Consider four different models of influence in the family: the parent effects, child effects, interactional, and transactional models.

Parent Effects Model

The study of human development has been guided through most of its history by a simple **parent effects model** of family influence (Holden, 2010; Maccoby, 2007). This model assumes that influences run one way, from parent—particularly mother—to child. This is the "blame the parents" model that Susan Klebold encountered after her son became a mass murderer. You have just reviewed research demonstrating positive and negative effects of different parenting styles on child development. But what if you turn things around: Could it be that a child's behavior influences the style of parenting his parents adopt and that what appear to be parent effects are instead child effects?

Child Effects Model

A **child effects model** of family influence highlights the influences of children on their parents (Crouter & Booth, 2003; Sanson, Hemphill, & Smart, 2004). One good example of a child effect is the influence of a child's age and competence on the style of parenting used with that child. For example, infants in their first year of life require and elicit sensitive care, whereas older infants who are asserting their wills and toddling here and there force parents to set limits (Fagot & Kavanaugh, 1993). Normally parents then become less restrictive as their children mature and gradually, with parental guidance, become capable of making their own decisions. As children develop, then, parenting shifts from parent regulation of the child, to parent and child coregulation of the child, to self-regulation by a now more capable child (Holden, 2010).

A child's genetic makeup and personality also influence the parenting she receives. Is it not possible that easygoing, manageable children cause their parents to be warm and authoritative? Could not difficult, stubborn, and aggressive children help mold parents who are rejecting rather than accepting—and who either rule with an authoritarian iron hand or throw up their hands in defeat and become neglectful? The *gene–environment correlations* discussed in Chapter 3, especially evocative ones in which children evoke certain reactions from other people, are examples of child effects. Indeed, evidence is accumulating that children's genetically influenced characteristics can influence not only parenting styles but marital relationships and the behavior of siblings—the whole family system (Reiss & Neiderhiser, 2011).

In a clever experiment to detect child effects, Barbara Keller and Richard Bell (1979) had female college students attempt to convince 9-year-old girls to behave altruistically (for example, to spend more time sewing a pillow for a handicapped child than sewing a pillow for themselves). The girls had been coached to respond either attentively or inattentively. As expected, college students confronted with an attentive child used what Chapter 13 called induction, explaining how other children might feel if the child behaved selfishly. By contrast, college students who interacted with an inattentive child relied on power-assertion techniques such as promising rewards for altruism and threatening penalties for selfishness.

Interactional Model

The interactional model improves on the parent effects and child effects models by recognizing that parent and child characteristics may combine in certain ways to influence development. The concept of *gene–environment interaction* (see Chapter 3) illustrates the interactional model; for example, aggressive behavior is most likely to develop if a child has a variant of the MAO-A gene associated with temper control problems *and* is raised by an abusive parent (Caspi et al., 2002; Dodge, 2009). It takes the combination of an at-risk child and an abusive environment. There appear to be many examples of such interactions between child characteristics and characteristics of the child-rearing environment (Dodge & Rutter, 2011). They tell us that the effect of a particular parenting approach depends on the child with whom it is used, and that the effect of a particular child characteristic depends on how a child with that characteristic is parented.

Transactional Model

The interactional model is a step forward, but it focuses on what characteristics child and parent bring to their interactions—not how they change each other as they interact. In the transactional model of family influence, both parent effects and child effects are at work as parent and child influence one another reciprocally over time (Sameroff, 1975, 2009). Child problems may develop when *the relationship* between parent and child somehow goes bad as the two interact. We could imagine a pretty average child and a pretty average parent somehow getting off on the wrong foot and developing a toxic relationship that has increasingly negative effects on the child's development. By the same token, healthy child development could result when, whatever characteristics parent and child bring to the relationship, the transactions between them evolve in a more positive direction over time.

As Chapter 13 revealed, antisocial behavior can result when a child who behaves aggressively elicits negative, coercive parenting and when that parenting contributes further to the child's aggression—that is, when an escalating *coercive cycle* of influence develops (Ge et al., 1996; O'Connor et al., 1998; Williams & Steinberg, 2011). When such a destructive family process evolves, it becomes difficult to say who is more influential, parent or child. It also becomes clear that changing the child's problem behavior requires focusing on both parent and child.

Demonstrations of child effects, interactional effects, and transactional effects within the family are tremendously important. They mean that parents are not solely responsible for whether their children turn out "good" or "bad." True, parents probably have more influence overall than children do on how the parent–child relationship unfolds (Holden, 2010; Kuczynski & Parkin, 2007). Yet the transactional model captures best the concept that the family is a system in which family members lead linked lives and influence one another. ● Table 15.3 compares the models of family influence discussed in this section.

Sibling Relationships

A family system consisting of mother, father, and child is changed by the arrival of a new baby and becomes a new—and considerably more complex—family system. How do children adapt to a new baby in the house, how does the sibling relationship change as children age, and what do brothers and sisters contribute to each other's development in the final analysis?

A New Baby Arrives

When Judy Dunn and Carol Kendrick (1982; see also Dunn, 1993, 2007) carefully studied young children's reactions to a new sibling, they found that mothers typically pay less attention to their firstborns after the new baby arrives than before its birth. Why shouldn't firstborns find being "dethroned" an unpleasant experience? They sometimes become more difficult and demanding, or more dependent and clingy, and they may develop problems with their sleeping, eating, and toileting routines. Most of their battles are with their mothers, but a few firstborns are not above hitting, poking, and pinching their younger brothers or sisters. Secure attachments can even become insecure (Teti et al., 1996). Although positive effects such as an increased insistence on doing things independently and helping out are also evident, it is clear that some firstborns resent losing their parents' attention.

● **Table 15.3** Models of Family Influence

Model	Pattern of Influence
Parent effects model	Parent influences child
Child effects model	Child influences parent
Interactional model	The combination of a particular kind of child with a particular kind of parent determines developmental outcomes
Transactional model	The reciprocal influence of parent and child on one another over time determines how the parent–child relationship and the child's development unfold

Just how common are jealous responses? Brenda Volling and her colleagues (2014) observed how 2- to 3-year-old firstborns reacted when their mothers, and separately their fathers, interacted positively with their 1-month-old siblings. The researchers expected that this stress test would arouse the attachment systems of firstborns, causing them to reduce their exploratory behavior and seek proximity to their parent. Most firstborns (60%) coped well: They watched closely and sometimes approached but often just sat quietly. Another 31% clearly found the experience threatening: They watched very intently and seemed unable to play by themselves constructively or to approach their parent for comfort. Only 3% were disruptive, actively protesting and being aggressive. Another small number (6%) were very anxious and clingy. Reactions were quite similar whether mother or father interacted with the baby. The 30% of firstborns who were clearly threatened and the 3% who were disruptive showed the most behavior problems a few months later. Overall, then, this study and others suggest that entry of a new family member perturbs the family system, but that most firstborns take interest in and adapt well to a new sibling while a minority have difficulty coping temporarily (Volling, 2012).

How can adjustment problems be minimized? It helps if both parents have good mental health and a sense of self-efficacy as parents and if they have good social support to help them cope with the challenges of parenting (Volling, 2012). Adjustment to a new sibling is also easier if the marital relationship is good and remains good after the birth and if the firstborn had secure relationships with both parents before the younger sibling arrived—and continues to enjoy close relationships with them afterward (Dunn, 2007; Teti et al., 1996). If parents continue to provide love and attention to their firstborn and maintain the child's routines as much as possible—a cause helped greatly if the father increases his involvement in child care and the two parents coparent effectively—things are likely to go well (Song & Volling, 2015; Volling, 2005).

Ambivalence in Sibling Relationships

Although most older siblings adjust well and fairly quickly to the arrival of a new brother or sister, sibling rivalry—the spirit of competition, jealousy, and resentment between brothers and sisters—is a normal part of sibling relationships. It may be rooted in an evolutionary fact: Although siblings are genetically related, they compete with one another for their parents' time and resources to ensure their own survival and welfare (Bjorklund & Pellegrini, 2002). Siblings may also be at odds because they live in close proximity but lack the mature social skills needed to resolve conflicts and because they often feel they are treated differently by their parents (Holden, 2010). For all these reasons, perhaps, sibling relationships typically involve both closeness and conflict and are therefore best described as ambivalent.

The number of skirmishes between very young siblings can be as high as 56 per hour (Dunn, 1993). Jealousies, bouts of teasing, shouting matches, and occasional kicks and punches continue to be part of the sibling relationship throughout childhood; squabbles are most often over possessions (McGuire et al., 2000). Thankfully, levels of conflict normally decrease after early adolescence as teenagers spend more time away from home (Furman & Buhrmester, 1992; Larson et al., 1996).

Most firstborns adjust well to the arrival of a new sibling, but sibling relationships are ambivalent—both close and rivalrous.

O M/Shutterstock.com

Sibling relationships are friendlier and less conflicted if mothers and fathers get along well as a couple and if they respond warmly and sensitively to all their children rather than unfairly favoring one over another (Dunn, 2007). Children are wise enough to accept that differences in treatment can be fair if they are based on differences in age and competencies, but they resent seemingly unfair differences in treatment (Kowal et al., 2002).

Sibling Influences on Development

Despite its element of sibling rivalry, the sibling relationship is generally close, interactions with siblings are mostly positive, and siblings play mostly positive roles in one another's development (McHale, Updegraff, & Whiteman, 2012). Four important functions of siblings stand out:

- **Emotional support**. Brothers and sisters confide in one another, often more than they confide in their parents (Howe et al., 2000). They protect and comfort one another in rough times. Even preschoolers jump in to comfort their infant siblings when their mothers leave or when strangers approach (Stewart & Marvin, 1984).
- **Caregiving.** Siblings babysit and tend young children. Indeed, in a study of 186 societies, older children were the principal caregivers for infants and toddlers in 57% of the cultures studied (Weisner & Gallimore, 1977; and see Rogoff, 2003).
- **Teaching.** Although older brothers and sisters are not always as skilled at teaching as parents are (Perez-Granados & Callanan, 1997), they clearly feel a special responsibility to teach, and younger siblings actively seek their guidance.
- **Social experience.** Having at least one sibling to interact with can have positive effects on a child's social cognitive skills and social competence (Dunn, 2007; McHale, Kim, & Whiteman, 2006; and see Chapter 13). In their interactions with siblings, especially all those skirmishes, children learn how to take others' perspectives, read others' minds, express feelings, negotiate, and resolve conflicts.

In many societies, older siblings are major caregivers for young children. This girl in Laos looks after her brother every day.

iStockphoto.com/pressdigital

So siblings provide emotional support, caregiving, teaching, and social experience. However, siblings also hold the power to affect one another negatively—as when they develop a hostile relationship or, as teens, influence one another to use drugs or engage in delinquent acts (Sisler & Ittel, 2015). And siblings can affect each other not only directly but also through the indirect effects they have on their parents—for good or ill. In an excellent illustration, Gene Brody (2003, 2004) discovered that if an older sibling is competent, this contributes positively to his mother's psychological functioning, which makes her more likely to provide supportive parenting to a younger sibling, which in turn increases the odds that the younger sibling will also be competent. By contrast, an incompetent older sibling can set in motion a negative chain of influence in the family system leading to less supportive parenting and less positive outcomes for the younger sibling. Interventions aimed at improving the parenting of siblings and the quality of sibling relationships can benefit the whole family (Updegraff et al., 2016).

Checking Mastery

1. Referring to the dimensions of acceptance–responsiveness and demandingness–control, how would you characterize an authoritative parenting style?
2. What are two reasons that low-SES parents might use a more authoritarian and less warm and nurturing parenting style than high-SES parents do?
3. How would you distinguish between the interactional model and the transactional model of family influence?
4. How would you characterize the most common response of a firstborn to a new sibling?

Making Connections

1. Alison, a 16-year-old teenager who was drunk at the time, plowed the family car into a Dairy Queen and is being held at the police station for driving under the influence. Her father must pick her up. What would you expect an authoritarian, authoritative, permissive, and neglectful father to say and do in this situation? What implications might these contrasting approaches to parenting have for this young woman's development?
2. If only the child effects model of family influence were at work, what behavior by children do you think would be most likely to push parents to use each of the four main parenting styles: authoritarian, authoritative, permissive, and neglectful?

15.4
The Adolescent

LEARNING OBJECTIVES
- Describe how the parent–child relationship both changes and remains the same in early adolescence.
- Discuss how parents can best foster autonomy and how the process may differ in individualistic versus collectivist cultures.

When you picture the typical relationship between a teenager and her parents, do you envision a teenager who is out all the time with friends, resents every rule and restriction, and rolls her eyes or talks back at every opportunity? Do you imagine parents wringing their hands in despair and wondering if they will survive their children's adolescent years? Many people believe that the period of the family life cycle during which parents have adolescents in the house is a particularly stressful time, with close parent–child relationships deteriorating into bitter tugs-of-war. How much truth is there to these characterizations?

Ripples in the Parent–Child Relationship

Contrary to belief, most parent–adolescent relationships are close, and most retain whatever quality they had in childhood (Collins & Laursen, 2006). It is rare for a parent–child relationship to suddenly turn bad at adolescence; more likely, a troubled parent–adolescent relationship has grown out of a troubled parent–child relationship and has been shaped by both the parent's parenting and the child's personality and behavior (Eisenberg et al., 2008).

Parent–child conflict escalates in early adolescence, but it is generally about minor issues.

Corbis/SuperStock

Yet the parent–child relationship does change during adolescence. Time spent together decreases as adolescents become more involved with peers. This can make adolescents feel less involved with and supported by their parents (Collins & Laursen, 2006; De Goede, Branje, & Meeus, 2009). Parent–child conflict also increases temporarily in early adolescence, around the onset of puberty (McGue et al., 2005; Shanahan et al., 2004). Young adolescents assert themselves, and they and their parents squabble more. The bickering is mainly about minor matters such as disobedience, homework, household chores, and privileges (Collins & Laursen, 2006). These skirmishes in early adolescence alter the parent–child relationship—not so much its closeness as the balance of power between parents and adolescents, as we will now see.

Achieving Autonomy

A key developmental task of adolescence is achieving autonomy, or the capacity to make decisions independently and manage life tasks without being overly dependent on other people. If adolescents are to "make it" as adults, they cannot be rushing home for reassuring hugs after every little setback or depending on parents to get them to work on time or manage their checkbooks. Achieving autonomy is about establishing an identity separate from one's parents and preparing to leave the nest and fly on one's own.

As children reach puberty and become more physically and cognitively mature and more capable of acting autonomously, they assert themselves more. As they do so, their parents give up some of their power, adolescents assume more control of their lives, and the parent–child relationship becomes more equal (De Goede et al., 2009; Steinberg, 2011). It is usually best for the development of autonomy if adolescents maintain close attachments with their parents and

parents maintain authoritative control but also gradually grant teens more responsibility for decision making (Lamborn & Steinberg, 1993; Longmore, Manning, & Giordano, 2013). Gaining some separation from parents is healthy; becoming detached from them is not (Beyers et al., 2003). A blend of autonomy and attachment, or independence and interdependence, is the goal.

From this point of view, it is healthy for teens to argue some with their parents. True, fighting can be damaging if it goes too far and results in mutual hostility and Patterson's coercive cycles (see Chapter 13). However, in most families parent–adolescent conflict fosters autonomy by helping teens formulate their own values and beliefs and learn how to negotiate and resolve conflicts (Noller & Atkin, 2014).

How much autonomy adolescents want and how much parents grant differ from culture to culture. In individualistic cultures like ours, autonomy is clearly prized, whereas in collectivist cultures maintaining respect for parents and family harmony are valued more (McElhaney & Allen, 2012; Pomerantz et al., 2011). Studying different ethnic groups in the United States, Andrew Fuligni (1998) discovered that Filipino and Mexican American adolescents are more likely than European American adolescents to believe that they should not disagree with their parents, and Chinese American adolescents are less likely to expect the freedom to go to parties and to date at a young age. In collectivist Asian cultures like China, parents continue to be in command, the balance of power does not shift as much, and the quest for autonomy is less evident, at least during early and middle adolescence, than in the United States. Yet most adolescents in both individualistic and collectivist cultures strive for—and will eventually achieve—more autonomy than they displayed as children.

Across cultures, adolescents are most likely to become autonomous, achievement oriented, and well-adjusted if their parents consistently enforce a reasonable set of rules, involve their teenagers in decision making, recognize their need for greater autonomy, monitor their comings and goings, gradually loosen the reins, and continue to be warm, supportive, and involved throughout adolescence (Holden, 2010; Lamborn et al., 1991; Longmore et al., 2013). In short, the winning approach is usually authoritative parenting.

When parents are extremely strict and controlling and stifle autonomy, or when they are extremely lax and fail to guide and monitor their adolescents, teens are likely to become psychologically distressed, rebel, socialize with the wrong crowds, and get into trouble (Goldstein, Davis-Kean, & Eccles, 2005; Lamborn et al., 1991; Van Petegem, 2015). Keep in mind, though, that in some cultural and subcultural contexts a more authoritarian style or a more permissive style may also produce good outcomes (Garcia & Gracia, 2009; McElhaney & Allen, 2012; Steinberg, Dornbusch, & Brown, 1992). In **Exploration 15.2**, we ask an interesting question: Does the helicopter parenting favored by some American parents today interfere with the development of autonomy among their college-aged children?

Helicopter Parents and the Quest for Autonomy

Are your parents helicopter parents? The term **helicopter parenting** refers to developmentally inappropriate levels of control and assistance to late adolescents and emerging adults—also called overparenting (Segrin et al., 2013, 2015). Helicopter parents try to micromanage their children's lives during the college years, and often beyond, through such tactics as closely monitoring their children's activities through frequent texting and calling, looking into job opportunities and arranging dentist appointments and activities for them, calling their professors about unfair grades, trying to settle disputes with their roommates, and generally removing obstacles in their paths and orchestrating their success. Some helicopter parents may fit the authoritarian parenting profile, but most seem to be loving and mostly authoritative parents who try too hard to be good parents. By hovering over their children and solving problems for them, do they help their children succeed or do they inhibit the development of autonomy and self-reliance?

Parent involvement in children's lives is generally a good thing, but overinvolvement may not be. College students who report on scales that their parents engage in helicopter parenting tactics also report negative self-perceptions and low self-efficacy (Bradley-Geist & Olson-Buchanan, 2014; LeMoyne & Buchanan, 2011; van Ingen et al., 2015). They are prone to use medication for anxiety and depression (LeMoyne & Buchanan, 2011), and they are not very engaged in school (Padilla-Walker & Nelson, 2012). They tend to show high levels of narcissism (an inflated sense of self and sense of entitlement) and poor coping skills (Segrin et al., 2013). Importantly, they have low levels of self-perceived autonomy and competence, which, in turn, are linked to more depression symptoms and lower life satisfaction (Schiffrin et al., 2014).

So helicopter parents may do more harm than good. They may inhibit the growth of autonomy in their adolescent and emerging adult children and might do better encouraging their children to rely on themselves rather than on their parents. Without longitudinal research, however, we cannot rule out the possibility that child effects are operating. That is, students who are struggling to cope with life may prompt their parents to hover over them.

● Checking Mastery

1. What do the parent–adolescent conflicts of early adolescence generally concern?
2. What parenting style is most likely to foster autonomy, and why?

● Making Connections

1. At age 13, Miki moved from Japan to the United States with her family and now finds her relationship with her parents strained. Drawing on the material in this section, how would you analyze what is going on?
2. Analyze how your parents (or those of one of your high school friends) handled (or mishandled) the parenting challenge of maintaining a close relationship with their teen, maintaining reasonable authoritative control, and allowing for greater autonomy. Use specific examples to illustrate your points.

15.5 The Adult

LEARNING OBJECTIVES

- Characterize the major effects on couples of the first year of marriage, new parenthood, raising two or more children, entering the empty nest phase of family life, and grandparenting.

- Summarize how marital, sibling, and parent–child relationships are likely to change during adulthood.

So far we have offered a child's-eye view of family life. How does it look to adults? We will follow a couple through the establishment, new-parenthood, child-rearing, empty nest, and grandparenthood phases of the family life cycle.

Establishing a Marriage

In U.S. society, almost 90% of adults choose to marry at some point in their lives (Cherlin, 2009). Although love and marriage go together in most modern societies today, in many traditional societies marriages are not formed on the basis of love. They are arranged by leaders of kin groups who are concerned with acquiring property, allies, and the rights to any children the marriage produces (Ingoldsby & Smith, 1995; Regan, 2008). So in reading what follows, remember that the modern, Western way of establishing families is not the only way.

Marriage is a significant life transition for most adults: it involves taking on a new role (as husband or wife) and adjusting to life as a couple. We rejoice at weddings and view newlyweds as supremely happy beings. Indeed, they feel on top of the world,

The honeymoon is great, but for many couples marital satisfaction declines somewhat during the first year of marriage.

Elyse Lewin/Photographer's Choice/Getty Images

their self-esteem and sense of mastery rise, and their emotional distress level drops (Chen, Enright, & Tung, 2016; Mernitz & Kamp Dush, 2016).

However, Ted Huston and his colleagues have found that the honeymoon is often short (Huston, 2009; Huston, McHale, & Crouter, 1986; Huston & Melz, 2004; Huston et al., 2001). In their longitudinal study of newlywed couples, perceptions of the marital relationship became less favorable and marital satisfaction declined during the first year after the wedding. Behavior changed as well: "One year into marriage, the average spouse says, 'I love you,' hugs and kisses their partner, makes their partner laugh, and has sexual intercourse about half as often as when they were newly wed" (Huston & Melz, 2004, p. 951). Although partners spend only slightly less time together, more of that time is devoted to getting tasks done and less to having fun or just talking.

Most couples are far more satisfied than dissatisfied with their relationships after the "honeymoon" is over. Moreover, high marital satisfaction holds steady for some couples while it is declining for others (Lavner & Bradbury, 2010; Lorber et al., 2015). Still, adapting to marriage clearly involves some strains. Blissfully happy relationships often evolve into still happy but more realistic ones. Whether this happens because couples begin to see "warts" that they did not notice before the marriage when they were "blinded by love," stop trying to be on their best behavior, have run-ins as an inevitable part of living together and coping with life's problems, or start taking each other for granted, it is normal.

Does the quality of a couple's relationship early in their marriage have implications for their later marital adjustment? Newlyweds believe their blissful feelings will endure or even increase, even though these feelings will, in fact, decline on average (Lavner, Karney, & Bradbury, 2013). However, Huston and his colleagues found that, compared with couples who were happily married after 13 years, couples who remained married but were unhappy had had relatively poor quality relationships all along (Huston et al., 2001; Huston, 2009). Even as newlyweds these couples acted more negatively toward each other than couples

who stayed married and remained happy in their marriages. Couples who divorced early were even more negative toward each other early in their relationship.

So the establishment phase of the family life cycle involves a modest loss of enthusiasm on average, although not for all. Couples seem most likely to survive when they can maintain a high level of positive and supportive interaction to help them weather the conflicts that inevitably arise in any relationship (Fincham, 2003; Gottman, 2011).

New Parenthood

By age 40, 85% of women have given birth to a child and 76% of men have fathered one (Martinez, Daniels, & Chandra, 2012). How does the arrival of a new baby affect a mother, a father, and their relationship? (Gay and lesbian families are discussed in Section 15.6.) Some people believe that having children draws a couple closer together; others believe that children strain a relationship. Which is it?

On average, new parenthood is best described as a stressful life transition that involves both positive and negative changes (Cowan & Cowan, 2000; Nomaguchi & Milkie, 2003). On the positive side, parents claim that having a child brings them joy and fulfillment and contributes to their own growth as individuals (Emery & Tuer, 1993; Palkovitz, 2002). But couples have added new roles (as mothers and fathers) to their existing roles (as spouses, workers, and so on), and new parents often find juggling work and family responsibilities challenging. They not only have a lot of new work to do as caregivers, but they also lose sleep, worry about their baby, find that they have less time to themselves, and sometimes face financial difficulties. All of this adds up to stress.

In addition, couples often adopt more traditional gender-role attitudes and divide their labors along more traditional lines—a phenomenon called the *parental imperative* (see Chapter 12). She specializes in the "feminine" role by becoming the primary caregiver and housekeeper, often reducing her involvement in work outside the home and increasing her hours of labor inside the home, while he emphasizes his "masculine" role as provider and works harder in his job (Cowan & Cowan, 2000; Katz-Wise, Priess, & Hyde, 2010; McClain & Brown, 2016). As Figure 15.2 suggested, mothers' and fathers' roles are converging. Yet time-use diaries suggest that, even among highly educated and dual-career couples that equally share tasks before the birth, new mothers take on more than 2 hours of added work a day, compared to 40 minutes more for new fathers (Yavorsky, Kamp Dush, & Schoppe-Sullivan, 2015).

What are the effects of increased stress and of sharper gender-role differentiation? Marital satisfaction typically declines somewhat in the first year after a baby is born and continues to decline thereafter (Doss et al., 2009; Gottman & Notarius, 2000; Mitnick, Heyman, & Smith Slep, 2009). This decline is often steeper for women than for men, mainly because they usually do the lion's share of child care (Levy-Shiff, 1994; Noller, 2006), and it's steeper when couples do adopt more traditional gender roles (McClain & Brown, 2016). Especially for mothers, self-esteem and sense of mastery, which rise when adults marry, fall when they become parents (Chen et al., 2016). Yet some new parents experience the transition as a bowl of cherries, others as the pits—as a

New parenthood brings joy, but it is also a stressful transition involving new challenges.

Cultura Creative (RF)/Alamy Stock Photo

full-blown crisis in their lives. What might make this life event easier or harder to manage? Characteristics of the baby, the parent, and the social context all count.

A baby who is difficult (for example, cries endlessly because of colic) creates more stresses and anxieties for parents than an infant who is quiet, sociable, responsive, and otherwise easy to love (Levy-Shiff, 1994; Russell & Lincoln, 2016). Parent characteristics matter too. Parents who have good problem-solving and communication skills, are in good mental health, and find adaptive ways to restructure their lives to accommodate a new baby adjust well (Cox et al., 1999; Levy-Shiff, 1994). Similarly, parents who have realistic expectations about parenthood and about infants and children tend to adjust more easily than those who have an unrealistically rosy view (Kalmuss, Davidson, & Cushman, 1992). It also helps to have a sense of self-efficacy as a parent, something women are more likely to have than men (Fillo et al., 2015; Gross & Marcussen, 2016).

Finally, the social context can make a big difference to the new parent. Most important is social support, possibly from friends and relatives but especially from a partner. Things go better for a new mother when she has a good relationship with her partner and when he does his fair share of child care and housework than when she has no partner or an unsupportive one (Demo & Cox, 2000; Levy-Shiff, 1994). When a mother feels that she has less

quality time with her partner and thinks that the division of labor is unfair, her marital satisfaction drops (Dew & Wilcox, 2011). Well aware that new parenthood is a stressful transition for many couples, developmental scientists have developed preventive interventions to help expecting mothers and fathers prepare realistically for the challenges ahead and support each other as they deal with these challenges (Schulz, Cowan, & Cowan, 2006). Strengthening supportive coparenting—helping couples work as a team—can improve the couple's relationship, their relationships with the new child, and their child's development (Feinberg & Kan, 2016; McClain & Brown, 2016).

In sum, parents who have an easy baby to contend with; who possess positive personal qualities and coping skills; and who receive support from their partners and other people are in the best position to cope adaptively with new parenthood, a transition that is normally both satisfying and stressful and that can undermine marital satisfaction.

The Child-Rearing Family

Having a second child is more likely when the experience of having the first child is positive (Margolis & Myrskylä, 2015). What can parents look forward to during their child-rearing years if they do have additional children? A heavier workload! The stresses and strains of caring for a toddler are greater than those of caring for an infant, and the arrival of a second child means added stress (O'Brien, 1996). Parents complain of the hassles of cleaning up food and toys, constantly keeping an eye on their children, and dealing with their perfectly normal but irritating demands for attention, failures to comply with requests, and bouts of whining. A mother who is raising multiple children as a single parent or a mother whose partner is not very involved may find herself without a moment's rest as she tries to keep up with two or more active, curious, mobile, and dependent youngsters.

Because the workload increases when a second child is born, fathers often become more involved in child care (Dunn, 2007). Indeed, now that most mothers work outside the home, half or more of both moms and dads in dual-career families say they find it difficult to balance work and family; it's no longer just a woman's problem (Parker & Wang, 2013). Work-family conflict is especially common when children are young (Erickson, Martinengo, & Hill, 2010). Working parents are also subject to spillover effects—positive or negative effects of events at work on family life and effects of events at home on work (Barnett, 1994; Crouter, 2006). After parents have a stressful day at work, for example, they tend to be withdrawn from their spouse and children and angry and irritable if provoked (Repetti, Wang, & Saxbe, 2009). By contrast, a rewarding, stimulating job can have positive effects on a parent's interactions within the family (Greenberger, O'Neil, & Nagel, 1994).

Additional challenges sometimes arise for parents when their children enter adolescence. As you saw earlier, parent–child conflicts escalate for a while in early adolescence. Moreover, parents' conflicts with each other over how to raise their adolescent children can stress their marriage (Cui & Donnellan, 2009). When the firstborn child in the family reaches puberty, marital love and satisfaction often decline further (Whiteman, McHale, &

Crouter, 2007). Mothers of middle school students have a lower sense of well-being than either mothers of infants or mothers of adult children (Luthar & Ciciolla, 2016).

Middle-aged parents are also affected by how well adjusted their children are. They may have difficulty maintaining a sense of well-being if their children are experiencing problems or are having trouble launching themselves successfully into adulthood (Greenfield & Marks, 2006). The negative effects on parents' mental health of a child's problems as a teenager can still be detected in old age (Milkie, Norris, & Bierman, 2011). Here, then, is another example of child effects within the family system. But it works the other way, too: When parents are unhappy or are experiencing marital problems, parenting and parent–child relationships can deteriorate, placing teens at greater risk for problems such as delinquency, alcohol and drug use, anxiety, depression, and emotional distress (Chung, Flook, & Fuligni, 2009; Cui, Conger, & Lorenz, 2005).

Children clearly complicate their parents' lives by demanding everything from fresh diapers and close monitoring to college tuition. By claiming time and energy that might otherwise go into nourishing the marital relationship and by adding stress to their parents' lives, children seem to have a negative—although typically only slightly negative—effect on marital satisfaction through the child-rearing years (Gorchoff, John, & Helson, 2008; Kurdek, 1999; Rollins & Feldman, 1970). Yet when parents are interviewed about parenthood, they emphasize the positives, saying that parenthood has contributed a great deal to their personal development and made them more responsible and caring people (Palkovitz, 2002).

The Empty Nest

As children reach maturity, the family becomes a "launching pad" that fires adolescents and young adults into the world to work and start their own families. The term empty nest describes the family after the departure of the last child. It can bring moments of deep sadness:

> Pamela automatically started to toss Doritos and yucky dip into her cart—and then remembered. "I almost burst into tears," she recalls. "I wanted to stop some complete stranger and say, 'My son's gone away to college.' I had such a sense of loss." (Span, 2000, p. 15)

But it brings moments of celebration to other parents:

> We can find the TV remote. The only dirty dishes are in the dishwasher. No doors slam at 2 a.m. The floors are clothes-free zones. We always know where the car keys are. Grocery bills are mere double-digits. (Kelly, 2013, p. B2)

On balance, parents react more positively than negatively to the emptying of the nest. Whereas the entry of children into the family causes modest decreases in marital satisfaction, the departure of the last child seems to be associated with increases, especially for women (Bouchard, 2014; Gorchoff et al., 2008; White & Edwards, 1990). After the nest empties, women often feel that their marriages are more equitable and that their spouses are more accommodating to their needs (Mackey & O'Brien, 1995; Suitor, 1991). Only a minority of parents find this transition disturbing or depressing and suffer from what has been called "empty nest syndrome."

Why are parents generally not upset by the empty nest? First, they have fewer roles and responsibilities and therefore experience less stress and strain. Second, they have more opportunity to focus on their relationship; for women, increased enjoyment of time with their partners is a key reason for increased marital satisfaction (Gorchoff et al., 2008). Third, parents are likely to view the emptying of the nest as evidence that they have done their job of raising children well and have earned what Erik Erikson called a sense of generativity (Mitchell & Lovegreen, 2009). One 44-year-old mother put it well: "I have five terrific daughters who didn't just happen. It took lots of time to mold, correct, love, and challenge them. It's nice to see such rewarding results." Finally, most parents continue to enjoy a good deal of contact with their children after the nest empties, so it is not as if they are really losing the parent–child relationship (White & Edwards, 1990).

What if the children don't leave or come flying back? In recent years, an increasing number of adult children have been remaining in the nest, or leaving and then refilling it in a kind of "boomerang effect." In fact, for the first time in modern times, living with parents has become the most common living arrangement for 18-to-34-year olds in the United States (Fry, 2016). In 1960, only about 20% of Americans aged 18 to 34 lived with parents, whereas 62% lived with a spouse or partner (Fry, 2016). Now 32.1% live with parents, 31.6% with a spouse or partner. More years in school, lack of financial means to live independently, and postponement of marriage have all played a role in this change. Over 40% of Canadians and Europeans in this age range live with their parents, so the United States may only be catching up to the rest of the Western world (Rampell, 2016).

Boomerang children who return home are often unemployed, have limited finances, are divorced or separated, or have experienced other difficulties or delays getting their adult lives off the ground (Bouchard, 2014; Ward & Spitze, 1992; White & Rogers, 1997). Most empty nest parents adapt well to their children's return, especially if they are responsible young adults who are attending school, working, or otherwise making progress toward flying on their own (Aquilino, 2006; Parker, 2012; Ward & Spitze, 2004).

Grandparenthood

Although we tend to stereotype grandparents as white-haired, jovial elders who knit mittens and bake cookies, most adults become grandparents when they are middle-aged, not elderly (Conner, 2000; Connidis, 2010). Becoming a first-time grandparent can be a wonderful milestone in an adult's life; Leslie Stahl (2016), reporter on the program 60 Minutes, said this: "I nearly swooned, staring at her like a lover. . . Aha! There it was. We grandmas literally, actually, fall in love" (p. 63).

Grandparenting styles are diverse, as illustrated by the results of a national survey of grandparents of teenagers that identified three major styles of grandparenting (Cherlin & Furstenberg, 1986):

1. **Remote**. Remote grandparents (29% of the sample) were symbolic figures seen only occasionally by their grandchildren. Primarily because they were geographically distant, they were emotionally distant as well.

2. **Companionate**. This was the most common style of grandparenting (55% of the sample). Companionate grandparents saw their grandchildren frequently and enjoyed doing things with them. They only rarely played a parental role and liked it that way. As one companionate grandparent put it, "I'm happy to see them when they come and I'm happy to see them go" (Bates & Taylor, 2013, p. 59).

3. **Involved**. Finally, 16% of the grandparents took on a parent-like role. Like companionate grandparents, they saw their grandchildren frequently and were playful with them, but unlike companionate grandparents, they often helped with child care, gave advice, and played other practical roles in their grandchildren's lives. Indeed, some involved grandparents lived with and served as substitute parents for their grandchildren because their daughters or sons could not care for the children themselves. More and more grandparents today, especially in African American and Hispanic families, are the primary parent figures for their grandchildren (Hayslip, 2009).

You can see, then, that grandparenting takes many forms but that most grandparents see at least some of their grandchildren frequently and prefer a companionate role that is high in enjoyment and affection but low in responsibility. Most grandparents find the role gratifying, especially if they *do* see their grandchildren frequently (Connidis, 2010; Hayslip et al., 2015). Although being a grandparent does not in itself boost life satisfaction, contact with grandchildren does, for grandmothers at least (Bouchard & McNair, 2016). Yet parents control grandparents' access to their grandchildren, and grandparents may suffer if they suddenly lose all contact with their grandchildren because their child loses a custody battle or they fall out of favor with a son- or daughter-in-law (Bates & Taylor, 2013; Hayslip et al., 2015).

Grandparents have been called "the family national guard" because they must be ever ready to come to the rescue when there is a crisis in the family and they never know when they will be called (Hagestad, 1985). Grandmothers often help their daughters adjust to new parenthood and aid with child care when their grandchildren are very young—or step in to raise grandchildren when an unmarried teenage daughter gives birth or a son or daughter divorces, cannot make it in a bad economy, develops a drug problem, or dies (Dunn, Fergusson, & Maughan, 2006; Seltzer & Yahirun, 2013).

Grandparents who do get "called to duty" often contribute greatly to their grandchildren's development. Indeed, maternal grandmothers have probably been the most important helpers of mothers throughout history and continue to be important today (Coall & Hertwig, 2011). A grandmother who mentors a young single mother and coparents with her can help her gain confidence and competence as a parent and optimize her grandchildren's development (Dunifon, 2013; S. E. Oberlander et al., 2007). A close grandparent–grandchild relationship can also protect the child of a depressed mother from becoming depressed (Silverstein & Ruiz, 2006). And although teenagers raised by single mothers tend to have low educational attainment and high rates of problem behavior on average, they resemble children raised by two parents if they are raised by a single mother and a grandparent (DeLeire & Kalil, 2002; Dunifon, 2013).

Involved grandparenting can take a toll on grandparents, however. These grandparents are often poor or have health problems and sometimes suffer from stress, depression, and deteriorating health when grandchildren move in with them and they must become the primary parents (Hayslip et al., 2015; Musil et al., 2011).

Changing Family Relationships

What becomes of relationships between spouses, siblings, and parents and children over the adult years? All family relationships develop and change with time.

Marital Relationships

As you have seen, marital satisfaction dips somewhat after the honeymoon period is over, dips still lower in the new-parenthood phase, continues to drop during the child-rearing years, and may recover only when the children leave the nest, especially for women. This U-shaped curve in marital satisfaction over the phases of the family life cycle does not affect all but does suggest that parenthood takes something away from a couple's relationship.

The character of marital relationships also changes over the years. Frequency of sexual intercourse often decreases (see Chapter 12), and the love relationship often changes from one that is passionate to one that is companionate, more like a best-friends relationship (Bierhoff & Schmohr, 2003; Reis & Aron, 2008). With age, couples become more affectionate and experience fewer negative emotions (Carstensen, Levenson, & Gottman, 1995; Smith et al., 2009).

Overall, though, knowing what stage of the family life cycle an adult is in does not tell us much about how satisfied that person is with his marriage. Personality is far more important. Happily married people have more agreeable personalities than unhappily

Most grandparents prefer and adopt a companionate style of grandparenting in which the idea is to have fun.

Blend Images - KidStock/Brand X Pictures/Getty Images

married people; for example, they are more emotionally stable and vent negative feelings less often (Robins, Caspi, & Moffitt, 2000). Moreover, in happy marriages, the partners' personalities are similar and are likely to remain so or become even more similar over the years, as each partner reinforces in the other the traits that brought them together in the first place (Caspi, Herbener, & Ozer, 1992; Gonzaga, Campos, & Bradbury, 2007).

Over the years, romantic partners affect each other's development. For example, having a conscientious spouse is related to occupational success for both men and women—apart from the effects of their own conscientiousness (Solomon & Jackson, 2014). This may be because a conscientious partner contributes to a satisfying life at home. Meanwhile, Denis Gerstorf and his colleagues (2009) studied older married couples averaging 75 years of age over a 10-year period. If a husband had good memory skills, his wife was less likely to suffer a decline in memory performance over the next 2 years. If a wife was depressed, her husband was likely to experience increased symptoms of depression and decreased memory performance. These and other studies show that we really do lead linked lives and that, consistent with the transactional model of family influence, we influence and are influenced by our partners in close relationships.

By the time they reach age 65 or older, about 72% of men are married and live with their wives but only 42% of women are married and live with their husbands (Federal Interagency Forum on Aging Related Statistics, 2012). Marriages face new challenges when one of the partners becomes seriously ill or impaired and needs care. As our upcoming discussion of caregiver burden will suggest, wives may develop physical and mental health problems and become socially isolated when they must care for a dying husband. However, they typically manage to cope with their spouse's death and rebuild their lives (Connidis, 2010; and see Chapter 17). The family life cycle ends with widowhood.

Without question, the marital relationship is centrally important in the lives and development of most adults (Finkel et al., 2015). Overall, married adults tend to be "happier, healthier, and better off financially" than unmarried adults and are likely to remain so if they can weather bad times in their marriages (Waite & Gallagher, 2000). Married adults even live longer (Robles et al., 2014).

Sibling Relationships

The sibling relationship is typically the longest-lasting relationship we have, linking us to individuals who share many of our genes and experiences throughout our lives (Cicirelli, 1991; Connidis, 2010; Greif & Woolley, 2016). Today, of course, sibling relationships involve not only biological siblings but often half siblings, stepsiblings, and adoptive siblings. These relationships too can be close, conflicted, or, for most of us, ambivalent.

Relationships between siblings often change for the better once they no longer live together in the same home. In a recent study asking 261 adults age 40 and older about their sibling relationships (Greif & Woolley, 2016), it was clear that conflict and rivalry had decreased and feelings of warmth and equality had increased since childhood. Whereas 46% reported fighting and arguing with their sibs as children, only 12% reported conflict in their current relationships. Moreover, these adults generally trusted their siblings, viewed them as supportive, and appreciated their importance.

Some of the ambivalence that characterizes sibling relationships during childhood carries over into adulthood, however (Cicirelli, 1995; Connidis, 2010). Siblings may compete with one another as they build their lives. And whereas siblings who enjoyed a close relationship during childhood are likely to be drawn closer after significant life events such as a parent's illness or death, siblings who had poor relationships during childhood may clash in response to the same life events—for example, bickering about who is doing more to help an ailing parent or how a deceased parent's estate should be divided (Lerner et al., 1991; Ross & Milgram, 1982). Adult siblings who perceive that their parents played favorites when they were children or play favorites now do not get along as well as those who believe their parents have treated them equitably—evidence that parents have an indirect effect on the quality of sibling relationships (Greif & Woolley, 2016; Suitor et al., 2009).

Parent–Child Relationships

Parent and child generations in most families are in close contact and enjoy affectionate give-and-take relationships throughout the adult years. When aging parents eventually need support, children are there to help.

Evolving Relationships. Even after emerging adults have left the nest, there are likely to be some tensions along with the love in most parent–child relationships (Birditt & Fingerman, 2013). Parents can become stressed when their adult children have problems or when they are asked to help solve those problems; children can become irritated when their parents try to meddle in their lives or demand more of them than they want to give (Birditt et al., 2009; Blieszner, 2006; Connidis, 2010). Because parents and children are at different points in the life cycle, parents are often more invested in the parent–child relationship than children who are busy building their own families are. As a result, the well-being of parents is often positively affected when their children marry or become parents, but negatively affected when their children experience divorce or other negative events (Kalmijn & De Graaf, 2012).

Adult children have an opportunity to negotiate a new phase of their relationship with their parents in which they move beyond playing out roles as child and parent, see their parents as "real people" with flaws, understand them better, get past any strains in their relationship during adolescence, and become more like friends (Birditt & Fingerman, 2013; Birditt et al., 2008; Tasi, Telzer, & Fuligni, 2013). A more mutual, friendlike relationship is especially likely to evolve if parents were supportive, authoritative parents earlier in the child's life (Belsky et al., 2001). Young adults whose parents are highly supportive of them tend to be better adjusted than those who lack continued parent support (Fingerman et al., 2012).

When children are middle-aged and their parents are elderly, the two generations typically continue to care about, socialize with, and help each other (Umberson & Slaten, 2000). Aging mothers enjoy closer relations and more contact with their children, especially their daughters, than aging fathers do (Umberson & Slaten, 2000). And Hispanic American, African American, and other minority group elders often enjoy more supportive relationships

Many Hispanic American families benefit from close relationships and lots of mutual support across generations.

Tim Mantoani/Masterfile

with their families than European Americans typically do, especially when it comes to living together or near one another and providing mutual help (Bengtson, Rosenthal, & Burton, 1996; Sarkisian, Gerena, & Gerstel, 2007).

Typically, relationships between the generations are not only close but equitable: Each generation gives something, and each generation gets something in return (Conner, 2000; Markides, Boldt, & Ray, 1986). If anything, aging parents give more (E. Brody, 2004; Fingerman & Birditt, 2011). Aging families do *not* typically experience what has been called **role reversal**, in which the parent becomes the child and the child becomes the caregiver. Only when parents reach advanced ages and develop serious physical or mental problems does the parent–child relationship sometimes become lopsided like this and usually it is only for a short time (Connidis, 2010; Fingerman & Birditt, 2011).

Caring for Aging Parents. Elaine Brody (1985, 2004) uses the term **middle generation squeeze** (others call it the *sandwich generation* phenomenon) to describe the situation of middle-aged adults pressured by demands from both the younger and the older generations simultaneously (see also Grundy & Henretta, 2006; Zarit & Talley, 2013). Imagine a 55-year-old woman caring for her daughter's children (and maybe even her granddaughter's children) as well as for her own ailing parents (and possibly her grandparents). That's middle generation squeeze!

Adults with children who still depend on them increasingly find themselves caring for their aging parents too; about one-third of women ages 55–69 report helping members of both the older and younger generations (Grundy & Henretta, 2006). As a result of the global economic recession of 2008, more middle-aged parents in many countries are being called upon to provide more financial support for longer to their young adult children while also helping their aging parents (Parker & Patten, 2013).

Spouses or partners are the first in line to care for frail elders. The burden of caregiving can be especially heavy for aging and sometimes frail husbands and wives (Zarit & Heid, 2015). One 84-year-old woman who had been caring for her 86-year-old husband was driven to suicide and explained her suicide attempt this way:

> As he got worse, it got very, very bad, . . . mentally, for me to cope . . . But I didn't ever say anything because that's just what I had to do. . . I could not stand another 24 hours. . . . I asked my husband more than once, wouldn't he like some of those people to come in and help him? At least bathe and things like that. . . . He said no. (Adelman et al., 2014, p. 1052, 1054)

If spouses are not available or up to the challenge, caregiving responsibility falls on adult children (Silverstein & Giarrusso, 2010). Daughters spend more time than sons providing emotional support to aging parents and in-laws and carry more of the burden overall, although sons are about as involved as daughters in providing help with practical tasks and financial assistance (Chesley & Poppie, 2009). Traditional gender-role norms call for women to be the **kinkeepers** of the family—the ones who keep family members in touch with each other and handle family problems when they arise (Brody, 2004).

In our society, most aging parents strongly resist having to live with and be dependent on their children. They prefer to live close to but not with their children; they enjoy their independence and do not want to burden their children when their health fails (Connidis, 2010; Brody, 2004). However, families remain the major providers of care for the frail elderly today. We see little support for the view that today's families have abandoned or failed to meet their responsibilities to their oldest members. However, concerns are now being expressed about whether children whose parents divorced or stepchildren will be as supportive of older adults, especially fathers and stepfathers, in future years (Silverstein & Giarrusso, 2010; Stein, 2009). **Exploration 15.3** looks at how the Chinese government's one-child policy and rapid industrialization have affected care of elders in China.

Middle-aged adults who must foster their children's development while tending to their own development and caring for aging parents sometimes find their situation overwhelming. They may experience **caregiver burden**—psychological distress associated with the demands of providing care for someone with physical or cognitive impairments (Adelman et al., 2014; Knight & Losada, 2011; Zarit & Talley, 2013). Caring for an ailing loved one can be rewarding and can even have beneficial effects on health and well-being (Brown et al., 2009). Yet many adult children providing such care experience emotional, physical, and financial strains and suffer for it (Pinquart & Sorensen, 2006). A woman who is almost wholly responsible for a dependent elder may feel angry and resentful because she has no time for herself. She may experience role conflict between her caregiver role and her roles as wife, mother, and employee (Stephens et al., 2001, 2009). This can undermine her sense of well-being and put her at risk for depression.

Caregiver burden is likely to be heavier if:

- the recipient of care has Alzheimer's disease or another form of dementia rather than physical health problems and engages in the disruptive and socially inappropriate behavior that often accompanies dementia (Chiao, Wu, & Hsiao, 2015; Pinquart & Sorensen, 2003);

Caring for Aging Parents in China

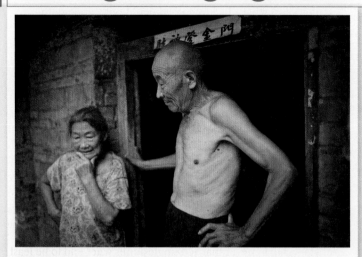

Qilai Shen/Getty Images

In the collectivist society of China, daughters-in-law have traditionally been the first choice as caregivers for aging parents. Aging parents have often been taken in by a son, usually the oldest, and cared for by his wife (Youn et al., 1999). But this tradition is changing. The Chinese government's long-running policy of allowing only one child per family has limited the number of potential caregivers available to aging parents. Meanwhile, rapid industrialization has meant that many of these children, especially in rural areas, have left to find work in the cities (Raymo et al., 2015; Zhang, 2009). For many Chinese elders, then, the emptying of the nest, which is happening more often now than in the past, is not the positive milestone it is for many American parents. Instead, it tends to be associated with a sense of abandonment and with loneliness, depression, low life satisfaction, and low income (Bouchard, 2014; Gao et al., 2014; Zhai et al., 2015).

Chinese elders in urban areas are faring better. Although they do not as often live with their children as they used to, they have better pensions, medical care, and housing than rural elders. And more and more are living together and providing one another with support. Yet with about a third of the Chinese population expected to be older than 60 by 2050, a crisis looms: One child may need to support two parents and up to four grandparents without sufficient help from the government (Beech, 2013). This may be one reason the Chinese government has now relaxed its one-child-per-family policy. Yet as more countries' aging populations balloon, more societies will face challenges like China's.

- the caregiver lacks personal resources such as a secure attachment style (Karantzas, Evans, & Foddy, 2010; Morse et al., 2011);
- the caregiver lacks social support—especially in the form of a supportive marriage (Brody et al., 1992; Scharlach, Li, & Dalvi, 2006; Stephens et al., 2009);
- cultural and contextual factors do not support caregiving; for example, white caregiver devote fewer hours to care but feel more burdened by it than African American caregivers do, possibly because of differences in cultural norms regarding family responsibility for elder care (Kosberg et al., 2007).

In short, the caregivers most likely to experience caregiver burden are those who must care for parents or spouses with dementia and associated behavioral problems, who lack personal resources such as a secure attachment style, and who lack social and cultural support for caregiving.

What can be done for burdened caregivers? Behavior management training, anger management training, and cognitive behavioral therapy can help caregivers sharpen their caregiving skills, teach their aging parents self-care skills, learn to react less negatively to the difficult behavior often shown by elderly adults with dementia, and cope with the stress associated with their role and the conflicts that may arise between it and their other roles (Zarit, 2009; Zarit & Talley, 2013). Respite services that give caregivers a break now and then can also be tremendously important. Mainly, family caregivers need to be recognized as the most important sources of care for aging adults and integrated into long-term care service systems for aging adults (Qualls, 2016).

● Checking Mastery

1. Compare how new parenthood and the empty nest affect marital satisfaction.
2. What are three factors that can make new parenthood a stressful transition?
3. Which of the three main grandparental roles do grandparents prefer, and what does it involve?
4. What are two factors that might increase the caregiver burden on a middle-aged woman caring for her ailing mother?

● Making Connections

1. Martha has just married George and wonders how her experience of the events in the traditional family life cycle is likely to differ from his. Can you enlighten her?
2. You may want to ask your mother, but to what extent does the research on changes in the marital relationship and in parent–child relationships (relationships with both parents and children) apply to your mother? If there are differences, why do you think they arose?

LEARNING OBJECTIVES

• Describe the "typical" implications of never marrying, cohabiting with a partner, remaining childless, living in a dual-career family, and living in a gay or lesbian family.

• Discuss the "typical" effects of divorce on parents and children and what factors are likely to make for good adjustment.

Useful as it is, the traditional family life cycle concept does not capture the tremendous diversity of family experiences today. Some adults never marry, and some of those live alone, whereas others cohabit with a romantic partner, heterosexual or homosexual, sometimes raising children together, sometimes not. Some, married or not, never have children. And an increasing number of adults change their family circumstances—for example, marrying, divorcing, and then cohabiting or remarrying. Let us examine some of these variations in family life.

Singles

It is nearly impossible to describe the "typical" single adult. This category obviously includes young adults who have not yet married. Because adults have been postponing marriage, the number of young, single adults has grown considerably (Cohn et al., 2011). Singles also include middle-aged and elderly people who never married or who experienced divorce or the death of a spouse. Overall, as ■ Figure 15.5 shows, the percentage of adults

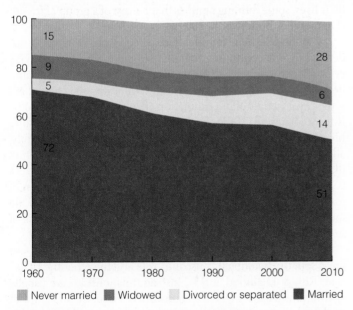

■ **Figure 15.5** The percentage of U.S. adults who are married fell between 1960 and 2010, while the percentages of never married and divorced or separated adults rose. Postponement of marriage accounts for much, but not all, of the drop in the percentage of adults who are married.

Source: Cohn, D., Passel, J. S., Wang, W., & Livingston, G. (2011). *Barely half of U.S. adults are married—A record low.* Washington, DC: Pew Research Center Social & Demographic Trends. Retrieved from www.pewsocialtrends.org.

who are married has dropped considerably since 1960, whereas the percentages of never-married and divorced or separated adults have grown.

What do we know about the 10% or so of adults who never marry? Stereotypes suggest that they are miserably lonely and maladjusted. However, single adults often make up for their lack of spouse and children by forming close bonds with siblings, friends, or younger adults who become like sons or daughters to them (Connidis, 2010; Rubinstein et al., 1991). It is divorced or widowed rather than never-married single adults who tend to be least happy with their singlehood in old age (Pudrovska, Schieman, & Carr, 2006).

Many single adults enter into romantic relationships that may or may not lead to marriage. Cohabitation, living with a romantic partner without being married, is on the rise, to the point that most marriages are now preceded by cohabitation (Cohan, 2013). Unmarried people live together for a variety of reasons (Cohan, 2013; Connidis, 2010):

• **Convenience**: They are in a romantic relationship and want an affordable living arrangement or get tired of commuting to be together.

• **Trial marriage**: They live together to find out whether they are compatible enough to marry.

• **Alternative to marriage**: They have no intention to marry. Some reject the concept of marriage. Some are older adults who want companionship but do not want to jeopardize their financial situation or upset their children by remarrying (Brown, Bulanda, & Lee, 2012; Connidis, 2010). Some of these older adults decide instead to "live apart together," maintaining their own households but staying at each other's places with some frequency (Benson & Coleman, 2016).

It makes sense to think that couples who live together before marrying would have more opportunity than those who do not to determine whether they are truly compatible before they tie the knot. Yet couples who live together and then marry are, on average, more dissatisfied with their marriages and more likely to divorce than couples who do not live together before marrying (Cohan, 2013). How can this be?

One explanation is that cohabiters are different from people who marry without cohabiting; for example, they tend to be younger and lower in income and they may have less conventional family attitudes and less commitment to marriage as an institution (Booth & Johnson, 1988; Cohan, 2013). This is less likely to be the reason, though, as more and more couples cohabit. Indeed, in European countries where cohabitation is widespread and well-accepted and gender attitudes are more egalitarian, cohabiting women are no less happy than married women (Lee & Ono, 2012).

A second explanation is that many adults who cohabitate do not go into it with an intention to marry but end up marrying anyway, largely out of inertia (Stanley et al., 2010). That is, some couples whose relationship is not very strong may slide into more nights in the same bed without a commitment to each other and marry only because their lives and assets have become entangled and it has become difficult to leave (Cohan, 2013; Stanley et al., 2010).

If partners are engaged before they decide to live together, if they have not cohabited with other partners before, and if they do not have a child before they marry, their odds of marital success improve (Cohan, 2013; Tach & Halpern-Meekin, 2009). But if couples who live together have characteristics that make them poor bets for marital success or if they marry out of inertia rather than true love, their marriages are more likely to fail.

Many cohabiting couples have children. Even when biological parents cohabit, they are more likely than a married couple to break up and to have limited income. As a result, their children tend to perform more poorly in school and have more mental health and behavior problems on average than children of married parents (Ganong, Coleman, & Russell, 2015).

This lesbian couple has twins, thanks to a sperm donation. Research tells us that the children of gay and lesbian parents generally turn out much like children of heterosexual couples on average. The secret to success in any family is good parenting.

67 Photo/Alamy Stock Photo

Childless Married Couples

Many married couples who remain childless want children but cannot have them. However, a growing number of adults voluntarily decide to delay having children or to be "child free" (Abma & Martinez, 2006; Allen & Wiles, 2013; Keizer, Dykstra, & Jansen, 2008).

Trying and failing to conceive a child is a difficult and demoralizing experience (Schwerdtfeger & Shreffler, 2009). Yet childlessness generally does not diminish the well-being of adults and sometimes boosts it (Umberson, Pudrovska, & Reczek, 2010). Indeed, the marital satisfaction of childless couples tends to be higher than that of couples with children during the child-rearing years (Hansen, 2012; Kurdek, 1999). And middle-aged and elderly childless couples are no less satisfied with their lives than parents whose children have left the nest (Rempel, 1985; Bures, Koropeckyj-Cox, & Loree, 2009). Children apparently do not guarantee happiness; nor does not having children doom people to an unhappy adulthood (Connidis, 2010).

Gay and Lesbian Families

What are the family experiences of gay men, lesbian women, and other sexual minority adults like? They are most notable for their diversity (Goldberg, 2009; Peplau & Fingerhut, 2007; Rith & Diamond, 2013). Generally, gay and lesbian relationships evolve through the same stages of development, are satisfying or dissatisfying for the same reasons, and are typically as rewarding as those of married or cohabiting heterosexuals (Kurdek, 1995, 2006; Peplau & Fingerhut, 2007). Sexual minority couples end their relationships more than married heterosexual couples do but at about the same rate as cohabiting heterosexual couples (Rith & Diamond, 2013). We know very little about the relationships of LGBT adults in later life (Kimmel, Hinrichs, & Fisher, 2015).

In the United States, several million gay men and lesbian women are parents, most through previous heterosexual relationships, others through adoption, artificial insemination, or surrogate parents. Some no longer live with their children, but others raise them as single parents and still others raise them in families that have two mothers or two fathers. Other gay men and lesbian women live as singles or as couples without children throughout their lives, some forming families that consist of a group of friends (Diamond & Butterworth, 2009).

Gay and lesbian families face special challenges, as evidenced by our continuing national struggles over gay marriage even after the Supreme Court ruling legalizing it. These families are often not fully recognized as families by society and are sometimes victims of discrimination (Peplau & Fingerhut, 2007; Rith & Diamond, 2013). For example, a gay or lesbian person's life partner may not be embraced as a full member of the family, allowed to make life-and-death decisions if their partner becomes ill, or given custody of the partner's children if the partner dies (Connidis, 2010). In one study, the well-being of the children of sexual minority individuals was linked to the extent to which the social climate of the area in which they lived was supportive of sexual minorities (Lick et al., 2012).

Contrary to myth, gay and lesbian couples usually do not have one adopt the traditional "husband" role and the other the "wife" role (Rith & Diamond, 2013). Instead, relationships are usually egalitarian; partners share responsibilities equally and tend to work out a division of labor based on who is especially talented at or does not mind doing certain tasks (Huston & Schwartz, 1995). After they become parents, most couples report that their child has two very involved parents, although the biological parent usually takes the lead role (Goldberg & Perry-Jenkins, 2007; Rith & Diamond, 2013).

What are the implications for children of being raised by gay or lesbian parents? Comparing lesbian mothers with heterosexual mothers in two-parent and single-parent homes, Susan Golombok and her colleagues (2003) discovered that lesbian mothers tend to hit children less and to engage in imaginative and domestic play more but are otherwise similar to heterosexual mothers. Moreover, children who lived with two parents of the same sex had better developmental outcomes than children living with a single mother, and they were no different than children living with two heterosexual parents. Lesbian couples are more likely than either gay couples or heterosexual couples to engage in supportive coparenting—a factor associated with good child adjustment (Farr & Patterson, 2013). These studies and others suggest that gay and lesbian adults who raise children are at least as likely as heterosexual parents to parent effectively and to produce competent and well-adjusted children (Farr, Forssell, & Patterson, 2010; Ganong et al., 2015; Goldberg, 2009; Rith & Diamond, 2013). Moreover, their children are typically no more likely than the children of heterosexual parents to develop a homosexual or bisexual orientation, although they may become more flexible in their thinking about sexual identity issues (Ganong et al., 2015).

Divorcing Families

Progress through the family life cycle is disrupted when a married couple divorces. Divorce is not just one life event. Rather, divorce—and the same can be said of the separation of a cohabiting couple—is a series of stressful experiences for the entire family that begins with difficulties before the divorce or separation and includes a complex series of life changes as the relationship unravels and family members reorganize their lives (Amato, 2000, 2010; Demo & Fine, 2010; Hetherington & Kelly, 2002). Why do couples divorce (or separate)? What effects does divorce typically have on family members? And how can we explain why some adults and children thrive after a divorce whereas others experience persisting problems?

Before the Divorce

Scholars have pieced together a profile of the couples at highest risk for divorce (Amato, 2010; Demo & Fine, 2010; Kitson, 1992; Teachman, 2002). Generally they are young adults, in their 20s and 30s, who have been married for an average of only about 7 years (hence the term "seven year itch"?) and who often have young children. Couples are especially likely to divorce if they married as teenagers, had a short courtship, conceived a child before marrying, and are of low SES—all factors that might suggest an unreadiness for marriage and unusually high financial and psychological stress accompanying new parenthood. Difficult personalities and alcohol or drug abuse often play a role as well.

Couples typically divorce because they feel their marriages lack communication, emotional fulfillment, or compatibility. Wives tend to have longer lists of complaints than their husbands do and often have more to do with initiating the breakup (Hewitt, Western, & Baxter, 2006; Thompson & Amato, 1999). Whereas, historically, divorce was considered a drastic step taken only when adultery, desertion, abuse, or a similar crisis was involved, starting in the late 20th century it came to be viewed as an action to be taken when people do not feel fulfilled in their relationship (Cherlin, 2009). Most divorcing couples experience a few years

of marital distress and often try separations before they make the final decision to divorce (Demo & Fine, 2010; Kitson, 1992).

After the Divorce

Most families going through a divorce experience it as a genuine crisis—a period of considerable disruption that often lasts at least 1–2 years (Amato, 2000; Demo & Fine, 2010; Hetherington, 2006). The wife, who usually ends up as the primary caregiver for any children, is likely to be distressed, although she is often relieved as well. The husband is also likely to be distressed, particularly if he did not want the divorce and feels shut off from his children. Both individuals must revise their identities and their relationship. Both may feel isolated from former friends and unsure of themselves in new romantic relationships. Divorced women with children are likely to face the added problem of getting by with considerably less money (Amato, 2000). Because of these stressors, divorced (or separated) adults are at higher risk than married adults for depression and other forms of psychological distress, physical health problems, and even death (Amato, 2000; Kamp Dush, 2011, 2013; Sbarra, Law, & Portley, 2011).

As you might suspect, psychologically distressed adults do not make the best parents. Moreover, children going through a divorce do not make the best children because they too are suffering. They are often angry, fearful, depressed, and guilty, especially if they believe that they were somehow responsible for their parents' breakup (Buehler, Lange, & Franck, 2007; Hetherington, 1981). They may be whiny, dependent, disobedient, and disrespectful.

Mavis Hetherington and her associates (Hetherington, Cox, & Cox, 1982; Hetherington & Kelly, 2002) have found that stressed custodial mothers often become impatient and insensitive to their children's needs. In terms of parenting styles, they tend to become less authoritative and less consistent; they occasionally try to seize control of their children with a heavy-handed, authoritarian approach, but more often they fail to carry through in enforcing rules and make few demands that their children behave maturely (see also Demo & Buehler, 2013). Noncustodial fathers, meanwhile, are likely to be overly permissive, indulging their children during visitations (Amato & Sobolewski, 2004). Good coparenting becomes a challenge.

This is not the formula for producing well-adjusted, competent children. A vicious circle of the sort described by the transactional model of family influence can result: Children's behavioral problems make effective parenting more difficult, and deterioration in parenting aggravates children's behavioral problems. When this breakdown in family functioning occurs, children are likely to display academic problems and adjustment difficulties at school, behavior problems ranging from aggression to depression, and strained relations with peers (Ehrenberg et al., 2014; Hetherington, 2006).

Families typically begin to pull themselves back together about 2 years after the divorce, and by the 6-year mark most differences between children of divorce and children of intact families have disappeared (Hetherington & Kelly, 2002). Yet even after the crisis phase has passed, divorce can leave a residue of negative effects on as many as 25% of children into adulthood (Amato, 2006; Hetherington & Kelly, 2002). For example, as adolescents, children of divorce are less likely than other youth to perceive their relationships with their parents, especially their fathers, as close and caring (Amato, 2010; Woodward, Fergusson, & Belsky, 2000). Adults whose parents divorced are also less likely than adults from intact families to marry and more likely to experience relationship problems and divorce or separation if they do (Afifi & Denes, 2013; Amato, 2006).

However, some of the problems observed in children of divorce are evident before the divorce and are actually the result of marital conflict rather than divorce (Demo & Buehler, 2013; Lansford, 2009). Mark Cummings and his colleagues have shown that couples who fight all the time become irritable parents, which in turn causes their children to become emotionally upset and poorly adjusted (Cummings & Davies, 2010).

Moreover, not all families experience divorce as a major crisis with negative effects; some even grow as a result of their experience (Demo & Fine, 2010; Hetherington & Kelly, 2002). Some adults feel better about themselves and their lives after extracting themselves from a bad marriage. And children may benefit when they escape a conflict-ridden two-parent family, which is more detrimental to a child's development than a cohesive single-parent family (Afifi & Denes, 2013; Amato, 2006). In short, the impacts of divorce vary widely; it is not always best to "stay together for the good of the children."

Influences on Adjustment

Several factors can help facilitate a positive adjustment to divorce and prevent lasting damage (Demo & Fine, 2010; Ehrenberg et al., 2014; Ganong et al., 2015):

1. **Adequate financial support.** Families fare better after a divorce if the noncustodial parent, usually the father, pays child support and the family has adequate finances (Amato & Sobolewski, 2004; Marsiglio et al., 2000).
2. **Good parenting by the custodial parent.** If the custodial parent can manage to remain authoritative and consistent, children are far less likely to experience problems (Hetherington, 2006; Weaver & Schofield, 2015).
3. **Good parenting by the noncustodial parent.** Children may suffer when they lose contact with their noncustodial parent over time, as a quarter or so of children living with their mothers do (Cheadle, Amato, & King, 2010; Demo & Cox, 2000). Continued father involvement is generally a plus so long as the father is not a harsh, hostile person (Coley, Carrano, & Lewin-Bizan, 2011; Elam et al., 2016).
4. **Minimal conflict between parents.** Children should be protected from continuing marital conflict and efforts by parents to undermine each other in their children's eyes after the divorce (Elam et al., 2016; Ganong et al., 2015; Lansford, 2009). When parents can agree on joint custody, both parents' and

children's adjustment tends to be better (Bauserman, 2002, 2012). When the mother has custody, supportive coparenting in which parents coordinate and cooperate can help keep fathers close to and involved with their children and reduce behavior problems (Amato, Kane, & James, 2011; Sobolewski & King, 2005).

5. **Additional social support.** Divorcing adults are less depressed if they have close confidants than if they do not (Menaghan & Lieberman, 1986). Children also benefit from support from close friends (Lustig, Wolchik, & Braver, 1992).
6. **Minimal other changes.** Generally families do best if additional changes are kept to a minimum—for example, if parents do not have to move, get new jobs, and so on (Buehler et al., 1985–1986). It is easier to deal with a couple of stressors than a mountain of them.
7. **Personal resources.** Finally, personal resources such as intelligence, emotional stability, and good coping skills often put some individuals—even some members of the same family—on a more positive trajectory than others after a divorce (Demo & Fine, 2010; Lansford, 2009).

Interventions for divorced parents can improve their parenting skills and, in turn, their children's adjustment (Forgatch & DeGarmo, 1999; Sandler et al., 2015). Children can benefit from school-based programs in which they and other children of divorce can share their feelings and learn positive coping skills (Grych & Fincham, 1992; Pelleboer-Gunnink et al., 2015). As Paul Amato (1993) concludes, adjustment to divorce will depend on the "total configuration" of stressors the individual faces and on the resources he has available to aid in coping, including both personal strengths and social supports.

Reconstituted Families

Within 3–5 years of a divorce, about 75% of single-parent families experience yet another major transition when a parent remarries and the children acquire a stepparent—and sometimes new siblings (Hetherington & Stanley-Hagan, 2000; and see McGoldrick et al., 2016; Teachman & Tedrow, 2008). Because about 60% of remarried couples divorce, an increasing number of adults and children today find themselves on a merry-go-round of cohabitation or marriage, conflict, separation or divorce, and remarriage or cohabitation (Cherlin, 2009).

How do children fare when their custodial parent remarries? The first few years are a time of disruption as a new family system takes shape and new family roles and relationships are ironed out (Hetherington & Stanley-Hagan, 2000). The difficulties are likely to be worse if both parents bring children to the family than if only one parent does (Hetherington, 2006). Girls sometimes have more trouble adjusting

Most children adjust to being part of a reconstituted family, but it can be challenging for a while, especially when both partners bring children to remarriage.

Catchlight Visual Services/Alamy Stock Photo

than boys: They are often so closely allied with their mothers that they may resent either a stepfather competing for their mother's attention or a stepmother attempting to play a substitute-mother role. Most adapt with time, but on average adolescents in reconstituted or blended families with children from more than one marriage, like children in single-parent families after a divorce, are less well-adjusted than adolescents in intact two-parent families (Hetherington, 2006). Stepparents too may suffer (Pace & Shafer, 2015).

There is hope, though. Outcomes are better when children whose mothers remarry maintain good relationships with both their mother and stepfather (Amato, King, & Thorsen, 2016; King, Amato, & Lindstrom, 2015). And training for parents in newly reconstituted families can improve parenting skills, strengthen coparenting, and reduce child behavior problems at school, as well as enhance the couple's relationship (Bullard et al., 2010).

What should we conclude overall about the implications of today's diverse families for child development? It's quite simple. As Mavis Hetherington (2006) concludes, "It is family process rather than family structure that is critical to the well-being of children" (p. 232). That is, children and adolescents can thrive in any type of family as long as they receive good parenting.

● Checking Mastery

1. What are two main reasons that cohabitation before marriage is associated with later marital problems?
2. What kind of parenting should divorcing parents provide if they want to prevent adjustment problems in their children?
3. After a divorce, how does a custodial parent's remarriage typically affect the children?

● Making Connections

1. Three months after her divorce from Alex, Blanca has become depressed and increasingly withdrawn. Her son Carlos, age 7, has become a terror around the house and a discipline problem at school. How might (a) the parent effects model, (b) the child effects model, (c) the interactional model, and (d) the transactional model of family influence explain what is going on in this single-parent family?
2. Suppose you are a counseling psychologist and Blanca comes to you for advice on how she and her family can deal most effectively with their divorce. What would you tell her based on research on factors affecting adjustment to divorce?

15.7
The Problem of Family Violence

LEARNING OBJECTIVES
- Describe the various forms that family violence can take.
- Illustrate how characteristics of the abuser, child, and social context can all contribute to child abuse.
- Summarize the effects of child abuse on victims and two approaches to preventing abuse.

As this chapter makes clear, family relationships are as basic to human development through the life span as food and water. At the same time, families can be the cause of much anguish and of development gone astray. Nowhere is this more obvious than in cases of family violence:

> From a young age, I have had to grow up fast. I see families that are loving and fathers who care for their children, and I find myself hating them. . . . I have nightmares pertaining to my father. I get angry and frustrated when family is around. (St. George, 2001, p. A20)

These sobering words were written by Sonyé Herrera, an abused adolescent who for years had been hit, threatened with guns, choked, and otherwise victimized—and had witnessed her mother abused—by an alcoholic father. The abuse continued even after the couple divorced. At age 15, unable to stand any more, Herrera had her father charged with assault, but he returned one afternoon, hit her, and shot and killed both her and her mother before turning his gun on himself (St. George, 2001).

Child abuse, mistreating or harming a child physically, emotionally, or sexually, is perhaps the most visible form of family violence. Every day, infants, children, and adolescents are burned, bruised, beaten, starved, suffocated, sexually abused, or otherwise mistreated by their caretakers (Del Vecchio, Eckardt Erlanger, & Smith Slep, 2013; Miller & Knudsen, 2007). Accurate statistics are hard to come by because much abuse goes unreported, but official statistics for the United States suggest that, in 2013, 1 of every 100 children under age 18 was the victim of substantiated **child maltreatment**, a broad term that includes both child abuse and neglect of the child's basic needs (Federal Interagency Forum on Child and Family Statistics, 2015). Of all maltreated children, 76% overall are neglected, 17% physically abused, 8% sexually abused, 8% emotionally or psychologically abused, and 9% experience other types of maltreatment. Many children experience more than one of these types of maltreatment, which is why the percentages add up to more than 100%. Rates of maltreatment decrease with the age of the child.

Child abuse commands a good deal of attention and tugs at our heartstrings, but the potential for abuse exists in all possible relationships within the family system (Tolan, Gorman-Smith, & Henry, 2006). Children and adolescents batter, and in rare cases kill, their parents (Agnew & Huguley, 1989). Siblings, especially brothers, abuse one another in countless ways, especially if there is violence elsewhere in the family (Hoffman, Kiecolt, &

Child abuse occurs in all ethnic and racial groups, often when a vulnerable parent is overwhelmed by stress.

iStockphoto/Sturti

Edwards, 2005). And spousal or intimate partner abuse appears to be the most common form of family violence worldwide. Globally it has been estimated that about one-third of women are beaten, coerced into sex, or emotionally abused by their partners (Murphy, 2003). In the United States, surveys suggest that about 15% of couples experience physical violence in a year, ranging from pushing to use of weapons (Heyman, Foran, & Wilkinson, 2013; Straus & Gelles, 1990). This means that millions of children witness domestic violence and are harmed by what they see (Grych, Oxtoby, & Lynn, 2013; McDonald et al., 2006).

Elderly adults are targets of family violence too. Frail or impaired older people are physically or psychologically mistreated, neglected, financially exploited, and stripped of their rights—most often by stressed adult children or spouses serving as their caregivers (Jayawardena & Liao, 2006; Nerenberg, 2008). Around 5% of elderly adults are probably neglected or abused in various ways (Tolan, Gorman-Smith, & Henry, 2006).

Family violence is not a pretty picture. Here is a social problem of major dimensions that causes untold suffering and harms the development of family members of all ages. What can be done to prevent it, or to stop it once it has started? To answer this question, we must understand why family violence occurs.

Why Does Child Abuse Occur?

Various forms of family violence have many similarities, and the contributors are often similar (Tolan et al., 2006). Because child abuse, especially physical abuse, has been studied the longest, we will look at what has been learned about how characteristics of the abuser, the abused, and the social context contribute to it.

The Abuser

The abusive parent is most often a young mother who is likely to have many children, to live in poverty, to be unemployed, and to have no partner to share her load (U.S. Department of Health and Human Services, 2007; Wolfner & Gelles, 1993). Yet child abusers come from all races, ethnic groups, and social classes. Many of them appear to be fairly typical, loving parents—except for their tendency to become extremely irritated with their children and to do things they will later regret.

A few reliable differences between parents who abuse their children and those who do not have been identified. First, *child abusers tend to have been abused as children*. Although most maltreated children do not abuse their own children when they become parents, a relatively high percentage, about 30%, do (Institute of Medicine & National Research Council, 2014). Adults who have been abused and neglected as children are also more prone than those who were not maltreated to engage in other forms of violence—partner violence and violent crime (Milaniak & Widom, 2015).

This "cycle of violence" is an example of a broader phenomenon, the **intergenerational transmission of parenting**, or the passing down from generation to generation of parenting styles, whether abusive or positive (Conger, Belsky & Capaldi, 2009). What is behind the intergenerational transmission of abusive parenting? One possibility, suggested by Albert Bandura's social cognitive theory, is observational learning—for example, of a harsh style of parenting and the use of force. Genetics (for example, genes associated with an explosive temper and aggression passed from parent to child) may also contribute. And epigenetic effects cannot be ruled out; the stress of being abused could alter the expression of genes that affect parenting and make for an overreactive stress response system later in life (McGowan et al., 2009; Moore, 2015; and see Chapter 3 on epigenetic effects).

Notice that the intergenerational transmission of abusive parenting does *not* occur for about 70% of abuse victims, though. Some harshly treated children are protected from becoming abusive by their temperament (Scaramella & Conger, 2003). Others have supportive partners who keep them from becoming overly harsh parents (Conger, Schofield, & Neppl, 2012). Still others seek psychotherapy and are helped by it (Maxwell et al., 2016).

Second, *abusive mothers are often battered by their partners* (Coohey & Braun, 1997; McCloskey, Figueredo, & Koss, 1995). Many abusive mothers may have learned through their experiences both as children and as romantic partners that violence is the way to solve problems, or they may take out some of their frustrations about being abused on their children.

Third, *abusers often have mental health problems*. Only about 1 in 10 has a severe psychological disorder (Jaffee, 2013; Kempe & Kempe, 1978). However, many are insecure individuals with low self-esteem, and many struggle with depression and substance abuse (IOM & NRC, 2014). These adults see themselves as victims, feel powerless as parents, and find the normal challenges of parenting stressful and threatening (Bugental, 2009; Bugental & Beaulieu, 2003).

Fourth, *abusive parents often have distorted perceptions of the normal behavior of infants and young children* (Haskett, Johnson, & Miller, 1994). For example, when infants cry to communicate needs such as hunger, abusive mothers may infer that the baby is somehow criticizing or rejecting them (Egeland, 1979; Egeland, Sroufe, & Erickson, 1983). One mother interpreted her 3-month-old's babbling as "talking back" (Bugental, 2009). (See why the study of human development is useful?)

In short, abusive parents tend to have been exposed to harsh parenting as children and to abusive romantic relationships, suffer from mental health problems and low self-esteem, and misinterpret normal child behavior as ego threatening. Still, it has been difficult to identify a particular kind of person who is highly likely to turn into a child abuser. Could some children bring out the worst in parents?

The Abused

An abusive parent sometimes singles out only one child in the family as a target; this offers a hint that child characteristics might matter (Gil, 1970). No one is suggesting that children are to blame for being abused, but some children appear to be more at risk than others. For example, children who have medical problems or who have difficult temperaments are more likely to be treated harshly or abused than quiet, healthy, and responsive infants who are easier to care for (Bugental & Beaulieu, 2003; Ganiban et al., 2011). Yet many difficult children are not mistreated, and many seemingly cheerful and easygoing children are.

Just as characteristics of the caregiver cannot fully explain why abuse occurs, then, neither can characteristics of children. But could parent and child characteristics interact? In support of an interactional model of family influence, we now know that the combination of a high-risk parent and a challenging child can spell trouble. For example, a mother who feels powerless to deal with children, and who must raise a child who has a disability or illness or is otherwise challenging, is prone to overreact emotionally when the child cannot be controlled and use harsh discipline (Bugental, 2009; Martorell & Bugental, 2006). Such powerless parents experience higher levels of stress than most parents, as indicated by high cortisol levels and fast heart rates, when interacting with children who are unresponsive. Consistent with the transactional model of family influence, their uneasiness can make such children even less responsive, provoking even more use of power tactics by the parent. So, even the match between child and caregiver may not be enough to explain abuse; as the transactional model suggests, relationships between parents and children sometimes evolve in bad directions over time as each influences the other.

The Context

We must also consider the ecological context of abuse (Cicchetti & Toth, 2015). Abuse is most likely to occur when a parent is under great stress and has little social support (Cano & Vivian, 2003; Egeland et al., 1983). Life changes such as the loss of a job or a move can disrupt family functioning and contribute to abuse or neglect (Berger et al., 2011; Wolfner & Gelles, 1993). Abuse rates are also highest in deteriorating neighborhoods where families are poor, transient, socially isolated, and lacking in community services and informal social support (Korbin, 2001).

Finally, the larger macroenvironment is important. Ours is a violent society in which the use of physical punishment is common and the line between physical punishment and child abuse can be difficult to draw (Crouch & Behl, 2001; Lansford & Dodge, 2008). Child abuse is less common in societies that discourage or outlaw physical punishment of children (Holden, Vittrup, & Rosen, 2011; Levinson, 1989).

As you can see, child abuse is a complex phenomenon with many causes and contributing factors. It is not easy to predict who will become a child abuser and who will not, but abuse seems most likely when a vulnerable individual faces overwhelming stress with insufficient social support. Much the same is true of intimate partner abuse, elder abuse, and other forms of family violence.

What Are the Impacts of Child Abuse?

Physically abused and otherwise maltreated children tend to have problems in virtually every area of development: physical injuries, health problems, atypical brain development, cognitive deficits, social, emotional, and behavioral problems, and psychological disorders (Cicchetti & Toth, 2015; Del Vecchio et al., 2013; IOM & NRC, 2014). Our information on the effects of abuse comes from correlational rather than experimental studies, of course, so it is difficult to firmly establish cause-effect relationships between abuse and development.

Maltreatment can have damaging effects on the developing brain, the stress response system, and other biological systems that affect psychological functioning (IOM & NRC, 2014). Intellectual deficits and academic difficulties are common among mistreated children (Cicchetti & Toth, 2015; Malinosky-Rummell & Hansen, 1993; Shonk & Cicchetti, 2001). Social, emotional, and behavioral problems are also common (Cicchetti & Toth, 2015; Flores, Cicchetti, & Rogosch, 2005). Maltreated children tend to have poor understanding of emotions, experience many negative emotions, and have difficulty regulating their emotions (Cicchetti & Toth, 2015). Some are explosively aggressive youngsters, rejected by their peers for that reason (Bolger & Patterson, 2001); others are anxious, depressed, and withdrawn. Some also fail to display empathy in response to the distress of others. Whereas toddlers typically show concern and offer comfort when a peer cries, abused toddlers are likely to become angry and attack the crying child, reacting to the distress of peers much as their abusive parents react to their distress (Main & George, 1985).

As we saw in Chapter 14, abused children form attachments to their abusive parents but the attachments are often of the disorganized type, suggesting that these children need but also fear their caregivers and are unsure whether to approach or avoid these scary people. They tend to have negative views of both their parents and themselves (Cicchetti & Toth, 2015). Even as adults, individuals who were abused as children tend to have higher-than-average rates of depression, anxiety, and other psychological problems (Nemeroff & Binder, 2014). They still show deficits in the processing of emotion (Young & Widom, 2014). Their marriages are more negative and less satisfying and their relationships with their families are less emotionally close (Nguyen, Karney, & Bradbury, 2016; Savla et al., 2013).

Remarkably, though, some maltreated children—between 10% and 25%—are resilient and get back on an adaptive developmental path (Cicchetti & Toth, 2015). Some appear to have genes that protect them—that make them stress resistant, confident, and able to cope effectively (Caspi et al., 2002; Cicchetti & Toth,

2015; Kim-Cohen & Gold, 2009). Environment matters too: An attachment to at least one nonabusive adult may be especially important (Houshyar, Gold, & DeVries, 2013).

Clearly family life can make us or break us. **Application 15.1** explores approaches to preventing and treating child maltreatment.

Meanwhile, we hope this examination of diverse family experiences has convinced you that we do indeed live linked lives throughout the life span and that the family is centrally important in human development. Our next chapter looks more closely at some of the many ways in which development can go awry.

● APPLICATION 15.1
How Do We Stop the Violence?

Knowing what we know about child abuse, what can be done to prevent it, stop it, and undo the damage? What would you propose?

Home visitation programs to help new parents cope with their babies and their lives can prevent maltreatment (IOM & NRC, 2014). For example, Daphne Bugental and her colleagues (Bugental, 2009; Bugental & Beaulieu, 2003; Bugental et al., 2002) developed a program to empower stressed, low-income parents who are at high-risk to become abusive because they feel helpless in the face of the challenge of raising a child who is unresponsive and difficult. Home visitors taught mothers to analyze the causes of caregiving problems without blaming either themselves or their children and to devise, try out, and evaluate the effectiveness of solutions to these caregiving problems.

After the intervention period, mothers who received empowerment training had a greater sense of power than mothers in control groups did. Most importantly, their rate of physical abuse, including spanking and

slapping, was only 4%, compared with 23% in a home visitation group that was given no empowerment training and 26% in a group that was referred to the usual community services. Moreover, the children in the empowerment group were in better health and were better able to manage stress (see also Bugental, Corpuz, & Schwartz, 2012; Bugental & Schwartz, 2009).

Another effective approach to prevention and treatment is to teach parents positive parenting skills—for example, through behavior management programs that apply principles of positive reinforcement to prevent or weaken coercive cycles in the family (Chen & Chan, 2016; Forgatch, Patterson, & Gewirtz, 2013; Knerr, Gardner, & Cluver, 2013). Psychotherapy can help too: A trauma-focused form of cognitive behavior therapy helps both abusive parents and their abused children deal with their memories of abuse and overcome maladaptive beliefs about themselves (IOM & NRC, 2014).

Ultimately, a comprehensive, ecological approach designed to convert a pathological family system into a healthy one is likely to be most effective. Abusive parents need emotional support and the opportunity to learn more effective parenting, problem-solving, and coping skills. Victims of abuse need day care programs, developmental training, and psychotherapy to help them overcome the many negative effects of abuse (Leenarts et al., 2013; Malley-Morrison & Hines, 2004). Change is also needed in families' neighborhoods and communities to ensure that families have the services and supports they need (Dodge & Coleman, 2009). Interventions guided by a "Communities That Care" approach, for example, mobilize community leaders and whole communities to decrease risk factors and increase protective factors affecting the community's children and to change the whole ecology surrounding abuse (Salazar et al., 2016). Stopping the violence requires determination and funding, but there is hope.

● Checking Mastery

1. Identify one characteristic of the parent, one characteristic of the child, and one contextual factor that could contribute to child abuse.

2. What are two explanations of the intergenerational transmission of abusive parenting?

● Making Connections

1. Given what you now know about the roles of the abuser, the abused, and the context in child abuse, how do you think these three sets of factors enter into intimate partner violence?

2. Given the societal problems that stem from abuse and neglect of children, what do you think about the idea of licensing parents, much as we license drivers, to ensure that they have the appropriate knowledge and skills and possibly even temperament? Licensing could involve pledging to support children financially and to refrain from maltreating them; it could even involve being of a certain age or passing a parenting skills course (see Holden, 2010). What do you see as the pros and cons of such a policy?

Chapter Summary

15.1 Understanding the Family

- The family, whether nuclear or extended, is best viewed, as suggested by Bronfenbrenner's bioecological perspective, the family life cycle concept, and family systems theory, as a changing social system embedded in larger social systems that are also changing. Social changes in the past half century or more have resulted in more single adults, later marriage, more unmarried parents, fewer children, more women working, more divorce, more single-parent families, more reconstituted families, more empty nest years, more multigenerational families, and fewer caregivers for aging adults.

15.2 The Infant

- Infants affect and are affected by their parents. Fathers are capable parents but have been less involved in caregiving than mothers, although the roles of mothers and fathers have been converging.
- Developmental outcomes are likely to be positive when parents engage in supportive coparenting and have positive indirect effects on child development through their positive influences on each other.

15.3 The Child

- Parenting styles can be described in terms of the dimensions of acceptance–responsiveness and demandingness–control; children are generally most competent when their parents adopt an authoritative style rather than an authoritarian, permissive, or neglectful style. Socioeconomic status and economic hardship, as illustrated by the family stress model, as well as culture and subculture, affect parenting styles.
- Research on four models of family influence—the parent effects, child effects, interactional, and transactional models—tells us that children's problem behaviors are not always solely caused by ineffective parenting.
- When a second child enters the family system, firstborns may find the experience stressful but usually adapt; sibling relationships are characterized by ambivalence, and siblings play important roles as providers of emotional support, caregiving, teaching, and social experience and can have indirect effects on the parenting their siblings receive.

15.4 The Adolescent

- Parent–child relationships typically remain close in adolescence but involve increased conflict around puberty.
- Parent–child relationships are renegotiated to become more equal as adolescents strive for autonomy; the goal of autonomy is best supported by authoritative parenting.

15.5 The Adult

- Marital satisfaction declines somewhat, on average, as newlyweds adjust to each other and undergo the positive but stressful transition to new parenthood and raise children, whereas the empty nest transition often increases marital satisfaction. A companionate style of grandparenting is generally a positive experience but involved grandparents can find raising grandchildren burdensome.
- In adulthood, siblings have less contact but often continue to feel both emotionally close and at least somewhat rivalrous.
- Young adults often establish more mutual relationships with their parents, and most middle-aged adults continue to experience mutually supportive relationships with their elderly parents until some experience middle generation squeeze, caregiver burden, and possibly a short period of role reversal.

15.6 Diverse Family Experiences

- Inadequately described by the traditional family life cycle concept are single adults (some of whom cohabit with partners for a variety of reasons), childless married couples, and gay and lesbian families.
- Divorce creates a crisis in the family for 1 or 2 years; most adjust, but some children of divorce living in single-parent and reconstituted families experience not only short-term but longer-term adjustment problems, although many factors can make the experience better.

15.7 The Problem of Family Violence

- Parent characteristics such as having been abused, child characteristics such as a difficult temperament, and contextual factors such as lack of social support all contribute to child maltreatment. Child abuse has serious and often long-lasting effects on development, but some victims show considerable resilience.

Key Terms

16 Developmental Psychopathology

Peggy, a 17-year-old female, was referred by her pediatrician to a child psychiatry clinic for evaluation of an eating disorder. She had lost 10 pounds in 2 months and her mother was concerned. . . . At the clinic she stated that she was not trying to lose weight, had begun to sleep poorly about 2 months ago unless she had several beers, and that she and friends "got trashed" on weekends. Her relationship with her parents was poor; she had attempted suicide a year previously with aspirin and was briefly hospitalized. The day before this evaluation she had taken a razor to school to try to cut her wrists, but it was taken away by a friend. She admitted being depressed and wanting to commit suicide and finally told of discovering that she was pregnant 4 months earlier. Her boyfriend wanted her to abort, she was ambivalent, and then she miscarried spontaneously about 2 months after her discovery. After that, "It didn't really matter how I felt about anything" (Committee on Adolescence, 1996, pp. 71–72).

Does Peggy have any diagnosable psychological disorders? It would seem from this description that she may have diagnosable problems with substance abuse and depression and possibly even an eating disorder. However, her pregnancy and miscarriage may have provoked her symptoms: How do we differentiate between psychological disorders and normal responses to negative life events? How did Peggy's problems unfold and where might they lead?

We do not all have as many problems as Peggy, but it is the rare person who makes it through the life span without having at least some difficulty adapting to the challenges of living. Each phase of life poses unique challenges, and some of us inevitably run into trouble mastering them. This chapter is about psychological disorder—about some of the ways in which human development can go awry. It is about how development influences psychopathology and how psychopathology influences development. By applying a life-span development perspective to the study of psychological disorders, we understand them better. And by learning more about divergent patterns of development, we gain new perspectives on the forces that guide and channel—or block and distort—human development more generally.

16.1 What Makes Development Abnormal?

LEARNING OBJECTIVES

- Describe three broad criteria of abnormal behavior and the approach taken by DSM-5 in diagnosing disorders such as major depressive disorder.

- Define developmental psychopathology and contrast the developmental psychopathology perspective to a medical or disease perspective.

- Explain and illustrate the diathesis–stress model of psychopathology.

Clinical psychologists, psychiatrists, and other mental health professionals struggle to define the line between normal and abnormal behavior and diagnose psychological disorders, often guided by three broad criteria in doing so:

- **Statistical deviance.** Does the person's behavior fall outside the normal range of behavior? By this criterion, a mild case of the "blahs" or "blues" would not be diagnosed as clinical depression because it is so statistically common, but a more enduring, severe, and persistent case might be.
- **Maladaptiveness.** Does the person's behavior interfere with adaptation or pose a danger to self or others? Psychological disorders disrupt functioning and create problems for the individual, other people, or both.
- **Personal distress.** Does the behavior cause personal anguish or discomfort? Many psychological disorders involve personal suffering and are of concern for that reason alone.

Although these general guidelines provide a start at defining atypical behavior, they are vague. We must identify specific forms of statistical deviation, maladaptiveness, and personal distress.

DSM Diagnostic Criteria

Professionals who diagnose and treat psychological disorders use the more specific diagnostic criteria in the *Diagnostic and Statistical Manual of Mental Disorders*. The newest version, DSM-5, was published in 2013 (American Psychiatric Association, 2013). It spells out defining features and symptoms for numerous psychological disorders. Some hope that advances in genetics, brain imaging, blood testing, and other diagnostic approaches will allow better identification of the biological state or disease underlying a disorder's symptoms, much as doctors can test for the HIV virus when someone appears to have symptoms of AIDS. That goal will be difficult to achieve, though (Addington & Rapoport, 2012). As you'll learn, rather than having one clear biological cause, most psychological disorders in DSM-5 have many variations and many contributors, both biological and environmental.

Because depression is so common across the life span, we will highlight it in this chapter and use it here as an example of how DSM-5 defines disorders. Depression is a family of several affective or mood disorders, some relatively mild and some severe. One of the most important is major depressive disorder, defined in DSM-5 as at least one episode of feeling profoundly depressed, sad, and hopeless, and/or losing interest in and the ability to derive pleasure from almost all activities, for at least 2 weeks (American Psychiatric Association, 2013). To qualify as having a major depressive episode, the individual must experience at least five of the following types of symptoms, including one of the first two, persistently during a 2-week period:

- Depressed mood (or irritable mood in children and adolescents) nearly every day
- Greatly decreased interest or pleasure in activities most of the day
- Significant weight loss when not dieting or weight gain (or for children, failure to achieve expected weight gains)
- Insomnia or sleeping too much
- Agitation or restlessness, or sluggishness and slowing, of behavior
- Fatigue and loss of energy
- Feelings of worthlessness or extreme guilt
- Decreased ability to think or concentrate or indecisiveness
- Recurring thoughts of death, recurring suicidal ideas, or a suicide attempt or plan to commit suicide

By DSM-5 criteria, a man suffering from major depression might feel extremely discouraged, no longer seem to care about his job or even about sexual relations with his wife, lose weight or have difficulty sleeping, speak and move slowly as though lacking the energy to perform even the simplest actions, have trouble getting his work done, dwell on how guilty he feels about his many failings, and begin

As the story of Peggy illustrates, major depressive disorder involves statistical deviance, maladaptiveness, and personal distress.

Amazingmikael/Shutterstock.com

to think he would be better off dead. A woman with major depressive disorder described it this way: "Like living behind glass. You can see life, but you can't hear it or feel it" (Rowan, 2015, p. E4). Major depressive disorder would not be diagnosed if an individual is merely a little "down"; many more people experience depressive symptoms than qualify as having a clinically defined depressive disorder.

DSM-5 notes that both cultural and developmental considerations should be taken into account in diagnosing major depressive disorder. For example, some studies find that Asians who are depressed are likely to complain of somatic symptoms (body symptoms such as tiredness and aches) more than psychological symptoms such as guilt and may be underdiagnosed if this cultural difference is not taken into account (Sue et al., 2012). And although DSM-5 takes the position that depression in a child is fundamentally similar to depression in an adult, it points out that some depressed children express their depression by being irritable rather than sad. An interesting question we'll ask in this chapter is how the flavor of depression changes over the life span.

Developmental Psychopathology

Psychologists and psychiatrists have long brought major theories of human development to bear in attempting to understand and treat psychological disorders. Freudian psychoanalytic theory once guided most thinking about psychopathology and clinical practice; behavioral theorists have applied learning principles to understand and treat behavioral problems; and cognitive psychologists have called attention to how individuals interpret their experiences and perceive themselves. More recently, evolutionary psychologists have been asking whether psychological disorders may have evolved because they sometimes served adaptive functions for our ancestors. For example, might depression be an adaptive response to loss? After all, it allows us to conserve energy, avoid additional stressors, and analyze what went wrong (Mealey, 2005; Rottenberg, 2014).

There is now an entire field devoted to the study of abnormal behavior from a developmental perspective—developmental

psychopathology (Cicchetti & Toth, 2009; Cummings & Valentino, 2015; Lewis & Rudolph, 2014; Sroufe, 2009, 2013). As defined by pioneers L. Alan Sroufe and Michael Rutter (1984), developmental psychopathology is the study of the origins and course of maladaptive behavior. Developmental psychopathologists appreciate the need to evaluate atypical development in relation to typical development and to study the two in tandem. They want to know how disorders arise and how their expression changes as the individual develops, and they search for causal pathways and mechanisms involving genes, the nervous system, the person, and the social environment that lead to normal or abnormal adjustment. In doing so, they bring life span, interdisciplinary, and systems perspectives to the study of psychopathology, looking at the interplay among biological, psychological, and social factors over the course of development.

Psychopathology as Development, Not Disease

Some developmental psychopathologists fault DSM-5 and similar diagnostic systems for being rooted in a medical or disease model of psychopathology that views psychological problems as disease-like entities that people either have or do not have. Alan Sroufe (2009) puts it this way:

> Psychopathology is not a condition that some individuals simply have or are born to have; rather, it is the outcome of a developmental process. It derives from the successive adaptations of individuals in their environment across time, each adaptation providing a foundation for the next. (p. 181)

■ **Figure 16.1** illustrates the concept of psychopathology as development. It portrays progressive branchings that lead development on either an optimal or a less-than-optimal course. Start with the assumption that typical human genes and typical human environments push development along an adaptive course and pull it back on course if it strays (Grossman et al., 2003). Some individuals—even some whose genes or experiences put them at risk to develop a disorder—manage to stay on a route to competence and good adjustment. Some start out poorly but get back on a more adaptive course later; others start off well but deviate later. Still others start on a maladaptive course due to genes and early experience and deviate further from developmental norms as they age because their early problems make it harder and harder for them to master later developmental tasks and challenges (Kendler, Gardner, & Prescott, 2002).

Now picture Figure 16.1 with many more roadways. In this developmental pathways model, change is possible at many points, and the lines between typical and atypical development are blurred. A number of different pathways can lead to the same disorder, and the same risk factors can lead to a variety of different outcomes (Cicchetti & Toth, 2009). A model of this sort may seem complex, but it fits the facts of development.

More is being learned every day about relationships among genes, neural circuits and neurotransmitters, and behaviors associated with psychological disorder. As a result, many experts view psychological disorders as life-span *neurodevelopmental* disorders (Davis, 2012; Hyde, 2015). This neurodevelopmental perspective requires looking at typical and atypical pathways of brain development and their implications for functioning. It involves using genetic and brain imaging techniques in diagnosing disorders in hopes of intervening early with individuals who are at risk for various disorders to put them on a healthier developmental trajectory.

Social Norms and Age Norms

Developmental psychopathologists appreciate that behaviors are abnormal or normal only within the social and cultural contexts that help shape them (Causadias, 2013; Chen, Fu, & Leng, 2014). **Social norms** are expectations about how to behave in particular social contexts—whether a culture, a subculture, or an everyday setting like a church. What is normal in one social context may be abnormal in another. For example, John Weisz and his colleagues (1997) discovered that Thai children are more likely than American children to report (or to be reported by their parents to have) symptoms of inner distress such as anxiety and depression and are less likely to engage in aggression and other forms of "acting out." One reason for the difference may be that the Thai culture places high value on emotional control and socializes children to control rather than vent their negative emotions (see also Chen et al., 2014; Weiss et al., 2009).

Another example of the need to consider cultural norms concerns one of the behaviors used in diagnosing autism (see later section): lack of normal eye contact. But what is normal eye contact? In China and certain other East Asian cultures, it is viewed as rude to look directly into someone's eyes; looking at the nose area is more culturally appropriate (Norbury & Sparks, 2013). If an evaluator is not attentive to such cultural differences, an incorrect diagnosis could be made. As such examples hint, the definitions, meanings, symptoms, rates, and developmental courses and correlates of psychological disorders are likely to vary from culture to culture, from subculture to subculture, and from historical period to historical period (Norbury & Sparks, 2013; Serafica & Vargas, 2006).

In addition, developmental psychopathologists are very aware that atypical behavior must be defined in relation to *age norms*—societal expectations about what behavior is appropriate or normal at various ages. The 4-year-old boy who frequently cries, acts impulsively, wets his bed, is afraid of the dark, and talks to his imaginary friend may be perceived as—and may be—normal. The 40-year-old who does the same things needs help! You simply cannot define atypical behavior and development without having a solid grasp of typical behavior and development.

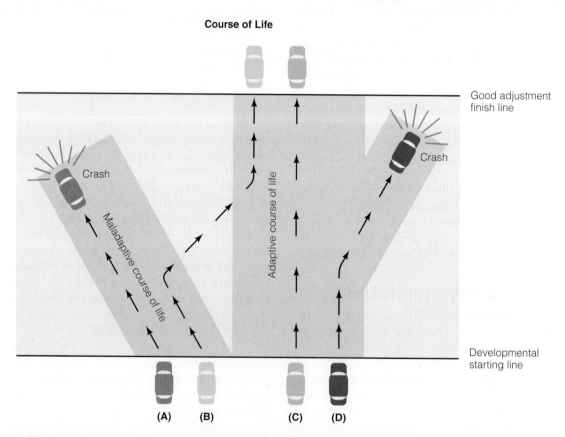

Course of Life

■ **Figure 16.1** Developmental pathways leading to typical and atypical developmental outcomes. Some individuals start on a maladaptive course and deviate further from developmental norms as they age (route A); some start poorly but return to a more adaptive course later (route B); others stay on a route to competence and good adjustment all along (route C); and still others start off well but deviate later in life (route D). Now imagine many more roads and on and off ramps.

Source: Patterned after Sroufe, L.A. (1997). Psychopathology as an outcome of development. *Development and Psychopathology, 9,* 251–268. © Cambridge University Press. Reprinted with permission.

In Thailand, boys like this one are socialized to restrain their expressions of emotion rather than act them out. As a result, children there are more prone to depression and anxiety but less aggressive than children in the United States.

Martin Puddy/Getty Images

Developmental Issues

As they attempt to trace developmental pathways to adaptive or maladaptive functioning, developmental psychopathologists grapple with the same developmental issues that have concerned us throughout this book—most notably, the nature–nurture issue and the issue of continuity and discontinuity in development (see Chapter 2). Addressing the nature–nurture issue involves asking important questions such as these:

- How do biological, psychological, and social factors interact over time to give rise to psychological disorders?
- What are the important risk factors for psychological disorders—and what are the protective factors that keep some individuals who are at risk from developing disorders?

Addressing the continuity–discontinuity issue means asking these sorts of questions:

- Are most childhood problems passing phases that have no bearing on adjustment in adulthood, or does poor functioning in childhood predict poor functioning later in life?
- How do expressions of psychopathology change as the developmental status of the individual changes?

The Diathesis–Stress Model

In their efforts to understand how nature and nurture contribute to psychopathology, developmental psychopathologists have long found a **diathesis–stress model** of psychopathology useful (Coyne & Whiffen, 1995; Ingram & Price, 2001). This model proposes that psychopathology results from the interaction over time of a vulnerability to psychological disorder (called a *diathesis*, which can involve a predisposing genetic makeup, physiology, set of cognitions, personality, or a combination of these) and the experience of stressful events. The diathesis–stress concept should remind you of the concept of gene–environment interaction.

Consider depression. We know that certain people are genetically predisposed to become depressed. Genetic factors account for about 40%–60% of the variation in a group of people in symptoms of major depressive disorder (Garber, 2010). A genetic vulnerability to depression manifests itself as imbalances in serotonin, dopamine, and other key neurotransmitters that affect mood and in such characteristics as high emotional reactivity to stress, including high production of the stress hormone cortisol, and self-defeating patterns of thinking in the face of negative events (Beck & Bredemeier, 2016; Gotlib et al., 2006).

According to the diathesis–stress model, however, individuals predisposed to become depressed are not likely to do so unless they experience significant losses or other stressful events, as illustrated in ■ Figure 16.2. One stressful life event is usually not enough to trigger major depression, but when negative events pile up or become chronic, a vulnerable person may succumb. Meanwhile, individuals who do not have a diathesis—a vulnerability to depression—may be able to withstand high levels of stress without becoming depressed.

Researchers can now pinpoint many specific diathesis–stress interactions. For example, inheriting a particular variant of a gene involved in controlling levels of the neurotransmitter serotonin and experiencing multiple stressful events results in an especially high probability of major depression (Caspi, Sugden, Moffitt, et al., 2003; and see Petersen et al., 2012). Among people with one or two of the

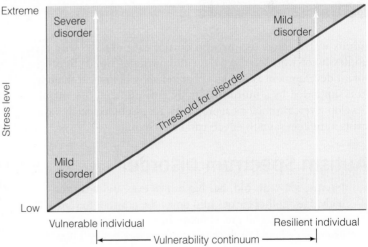

■ **Figure 16.2** The diathesis–stress model. For a vulnerable individual, even mild stress can result in disorder. For an individual who does not have a vulnerability or diathesis to disorder, it would take extremely high levels of stress to cause disorder; even then, the disorder might be only mild and temporary.

Source: Adapted from Ingram & Price, 2001.

high-risk genes, about 10% became depressed if they experienced no negative life events between ages 21 and 26, but 33% became depressed if they experienced four or more such events. By comparison, even when exposed to many stressful events, only 17% of individuals with two low-risk versions of the gene became depressed.

Depressive disorders (and many other psychological disorders) often evolve from an interaction of diathesis and stress—or, to use familiar developmental terms, from an interaction between genes and environment. It is messier than Figure 16.2 implies, though. For example, genes not only predispose some people to depression but also influence the extent to which they experience stressful life events (Rice, Harold, & Thapar, 2003). Moreover, the relationship between stress and disorder is reciprocal: Life stress aggravates disorder, but disorder also makes life more stressful (Garber, 2010; Grant et al., 2004). Finally, in a person genetically predisposed to depression, a depressive episode early in life in response to intense stress may bring about changes in gene activity and in the neurobiology of the stress-response system (the hypothalamic–pituitary–adrenal [HPA] axis). These changes may lower the threshold for a future depressive episode (the diagonal line in Figure 16.2) so that later in life depression may reoccur even in response to less stressful experiences (Grossman et al., 2003; Monroe & Reid, 2009).

This chapter will now illustrate the concepts of developmental psychopathology in action by examining a few developmental problems associated with different phases of the life span—for example, autism to illustrate disorders arising in infancy; ADHD to illustrate childhood disorders; anorexia nervosa and substance abuse to illustrate disorders arising in adolescence; and Alzheimer's disease to illustrate disorders of old age. In addition, we look at depression in every developmental period to see how its symptoms and significance change over the life span.

16.2
The Infant

LEARNING OBJECTIVES

• Describe the two defining features and main characteristics, including brain functioning, of autism spectrum disorder.

• Explain why rates of autism spectrum disorder are increasing, how nature and nurture may contribute to it, and what can be done to treat it.

• Explain why there is controversy about whether infants can have true depressive disorders and what factors contribute to depression symptoms in infancy.

Adults worry about infants who do not eat properly, who cry endlessly, or who seem overly withdrawn and timid. Because infant development is strongly channeled by biological maturation supported by a nurturing family environment, few infants develop severe psychological problems. Yet psychological disorder exists in infancy, and its effects can be profound.

Autism Spectrum Disorder

Jeremy, 3½ years old, has big brown eyes and a sturdy body. His mother carries him down the corridor toward the examiner, who greets them. Jeremy glances at the examiner's face but does not smile or say hello. They walk together into a playroom. Jeremy's mother puts him down, and he sits on the carpet in front of some toys. He picks up two blocks, bangs them together, and begins to stack the blocks, one on top of the other, not stopping until he has used the entire set. Jeremy does not look at the examiner or his mother while he works, nor when he finishes. And he does not make a sound. The examiner asks him to give her a red block. He does not respond. On their way out, Jeremy and his mother stop to look at a poster of a waterfall surrounded by redwood trees. "Yosemite Valley," Jeremy reads out—the name beneath the picture. His voice sounds automated, almost robotic. (Sigman & Capps, 1997, p. 1)

Autism was first identified and described by Leo Kanner in 1943. Now diagnosed as **autism spectrum disorder (ASD)**, it usually begins in infancy and is characterized by abnormal social and communication development and restricted interests and repetitive behavior. Picture the typical infant that we have described in this book: a social being who responds to others and forms close attachments starting at 6 or 7 months of age, a linguistic being who babbles and later uses one- and two-word sentences to converse with companions, and a curious explorer who is fascinated by new objects and experiences. Now consider the two defining features of autism highlighted in DSM-5 (and see Waterhouse, 2013):

• **Social and communication deficits.** Autistic children have difficulty responding appropriately to social cues, sharing experiences with other people, and participating in social interactions. Some autistic children are mute and quite asocial; others acquire language skills with varying degrees of success but are socially awkward and have difficulty carrying on true, back-and-forth conversations (Tager-Flusberg, 2014; Waterhouse, 2013).

- **Restricted and repetitive interests and behavior.** Autistic children seek sameness and repetition. They may become obsessed with particular objects and interests—bug collecting, for example—and may repeat phrases over and over. They may engage in stereotyped behaviors such as rocking, flapping their hands in front of their faces, or spinning toys. If they are more intellectually able, they may carry out elaborate rituals and routines such as a particular sequence of getting-dressed activities. They resist change and can become highly distressed when their physical environment is even slightly altered.

Children with autism spectrum disorder benefit from special training to help them do what typically developing children do naturally: take part in the give-and-take of social relationships.

Sergey Novikov/Shutterstock.com

The social impairments associated with ASD strike us most. Like Jeremy, some children with ASD seem to live in a world of their own. They are far less likely than other infants to make eye contact, jointly attend to something with a social partner, seek other people for comfort, snuggle when held, and make friends. They also have great difficulty reading other people's minds and emotions, responding with empathy when others are distressed, and demonstrating self-awareness and self-conscious emotions such as embarrassment and guilt. Although over half of autistic children form secure attachments to their parents (Rutgers et al., 2004), a higher than average number develop what Chapter 14 described as disorganized–disoriented attachments (Sigman & Capps, 1997).

It is critical to recognize that individuals with ASD vary tremendously in the degree and nature, as well as the causes, of their deficits. As a result, some experts talk of "autisms" rather than autism, believing that ASD is actually a number of different underlying disorders (Hu, 2013; Jones & Klin, 2009). Others conclude that even the "autisms" perspective is flawed because the symptoms, brain deficits, and causes of ASD are so unique to the individual (Waterhouse, 2013). There's a saying in the autism community, attributed to Dr. Stephen Shore: "If you've met one person with autism, you've met one person with autism."

The concept of ASD was devised to reflect this diversity. In DSM-5, previously distinct disorders are all diagnosed as ASD, which can vary from mild to severe. As a result, ASD is now the diagnosis given to individuals who show classic autism as well as those who used to be diagnosed as having **Asperger syndrome**, a mild form of ASD. The child with Asperger's syndrome has normal or above-average intelligence, good verbal skills, and a clear desire to establish social relationships but has deficient social cognitive and social-communication skills. Affected children are sometimes called "little professors" because they talk rather stiffly and formally, and sometimes at mind-numbing length, about the particular subjects that obsess them. Their strength is that they see the trees very clearly; their weakness is that they often miss the forest (Grandin & Panek, 2013; Pellicano, 2010). Many have been largely invisible until recently; rather than being diagnosed with a disorder, they were simply viewed as odd and socially awkward.

Is There an Epidemic?

Rates of autism are rising. DSM-III-R, published in 1987, indicated that autism affected about 4 or 5 of every 10,000 children (American Psychiatric Association, 1987). The rate has been climbing dramatically since, to 1 in 68 children age 8 (about 1.5%) in the latest survey of community sources in the United States that diagnose and educate or treat children with the condition (Autism and Developmental Disabilities Monitoring Network, 2014). An even higher rate was discovered in a survey of parents in the United States in 2014 about whether a doctor or health professional had ever told them that a target child in the family had ASD: Here, the estimated rate of ASD was 1 in 45, or over 2.2% (Zablotsky et al., 2015). There are four or five affected boys for every girl, and white children are more likely to be diagnosed than Hispanic or African-American children.

Why have rates of autism been rising so steeply over the past few decades? If you have heard that the vaccine infants receive for measles, mumps, and rubella is the culprit, forget what you have heard. There is no support for this claim, which unfortunately has made some parents fear having their children immunized and has bumped up rates of childhood diseases (Waterhouse, 2013). The main research study linking vaccinations to autism was found to be fraudulent and incorrect (Editors of *The Lancet*, 2010). Still, because some celebrities have spread this myth, and perhaps because the vaccination is normally given to infants at about 15 months of age when symptoms of autism are often first being recognized, the dangerous vaccine myth has persisted.

Why are rates of ASD increasing, then? Most researchers believe that increased rates are mainly a result of increased awareness of the condition, a broader definition that includes the entire autistic spectrum (including more mild cases), increased diagnosis of children who were previously diagnosed with language impairments or learning disabilities or simply considered to be odd children, and policy changes in the 1990s that made children with ASD eligible for educational and medical services (Benaron, 2009; Waterhouse, 2013).

In sum, the recent rise in the prevalence of ASD seems to be more about detection of cases that were there all along than about new cases and causes. Variations in diagnostic practices probably contribute not only to increased rates of ASD in recent years but also to large differences in rates of ASD across cultures—from as low as 1 or 2 per 10,000 in Oman to as high as 260 in 10,000 in South Korea (Norbury & Sparks, 2013). Although ASD is not often diagnosed in China, for example, the rate zooms higher when the same diagnostic methods used in Western countries are applied to Chinese children (Sun et al., 2015). Still, no one can quite rule out the possibility that there has been a true increase in the prevalence of ASD associated with some as yet unidentified cause (Autism and Developmental Disabilities Monitoring Network, 2014; Waterhouse, 2013).

Characteristics

Most children with ASD are probably autistic from birth. However, because they often seem to be typically developing babies in their first year, and because physicians are slow to make the diagnosis even when parents express concerns about their child's development, many autistic children are not diagnosed until they are 4 or older, even though they could be diagnosed at 2 or possibly even at 1 (Autism and Developmental Disabilities Monitoring Network, 2014; Benaron, 2009; Klin et al., 2004). Researchers are working feverishly to improve early diagnosis because the earlier these children receive treatment, the more likely it is that they can be steered onto a more typical developmental pathway.

By age 1, autistic infants may be given away by their lack of normal interest in and responsiveness to social stimuli—for example, by failure to display normal infant behaviors such as orienting to someone calling their name, preference for human over nonhuman stimuli, eye contact, visual focus on faces in a scene (autistic babies tend to focus on objects in the background), joint attention (a key precursor of theory-of-mind skills), imitation, and turn taking, as in mutual smiling and peekaboo games (Ingersoll, 2011; Klin et al., 2004; Zwaigenbaum et al., 2005). Checklists of such abilities can be used to screen 1-year-olds for ASD (Pierce et al., 2011; Tager-Flusberg, 2014). Still others are using brain imaging techniques to try to identity these babies (Wolff et al., 2012) and are looking for diagnostically useful biomarkers in the blood (Glatt et al., 2012).

Complicating efforts to understand ASD is the fact that it is often **comorbid** with—that is, co-occurs with—other disorders such as intellectual disability, language disorders, ADHD,

epilepsy, anxiety disorders, and more (Waterhouse, 2013). Consider intellectual functioning. Almost half of children with ASD have average or above-average IQs, but the rest have below average IQs, some low enough to qualify for a diagnosis of intellectual disability (Autism and Developmental Disabilities Monitoring Network, 2014; Ingersoll, 2011). Meanwhile, a minority of autistic individuals, whether their IQs are high or low, show *savant abilities*—that is, special talents such as the ability to quickly calculate days of the week corresponding to dates on the calendar or to memorize whole train schedules (see Heaton & Wallace, 2004; and the description of *savant syndrome* in Chapter 9). Consider Ezra, age 15. Obsessed with animated films (he memorized the release dates of hundreds of them), animals, and breakfast cereals, he would greet people he knew with unusual conversation openers like, "Hi, Bonnie! You had Post Honeycombs in your kitchen in August of 2004!" (Fields-Meyer, 2011). Yet he could not seem to remember the names of the seven children in his classroom at school.

Autism used to be viewed as a prime example of development that is qualitatively different from typical development. No more. Because we know more about the milder end of the autism spectrum, autism is now located at the extreme end of a continuum of social responsiveness, quantitatively rather than qualitatively different from typical social behavior (Baron-Cohen, 2010; Robinson et al., 2011). In other words, many of us have some of the traits associated with autism to some degree.

Brain Functioning

Many autistic children display neurological abnormalities (Volkmar et al., 2004; Waterhouse, 2013). However, the neurological abnormalities are varied, and it is not yet clear which, if any, best explains the characteristics of individuals with ASD. We'll highlight here (a) *early brain overgrowth*, and (b) *later underconnectivity* between areas of the brain involved in social cognition.

As you may recall from Chapter 5, neurons typically proliferate during the prenatal period and early infancy. In at least some infants who later develop ASD, neurons in the frontal cortex and certain other areas of the brain proliferate wildly during this early sensitive period for brain development (Courchesne, Carper, & Akshoomoff, 2003; Schumann et al., 2009). Analyses of the brains of young infants with ASD show a higher than usual volume of neurons and number of connections among them. Moreover, areas of the cortex have disorganized patches of neurons within them (Stoner et al., 2014).

Neural growth then seems to slow and the usual pruning process does not go as it should. By early childhood and beyond, connections among key brain regions involved in social information processing are noticeably underdeveloped (Solso et al., 2016; Wolff et al., 2012). Many brain areas are called into action and must communicate well with others in key neural networks for us to interact smoothly with other people. Thus underconnectivity among brain areas helps explain the social and communication impairments associated with ASD (Pelphrey et al., 2011). It has been suggested that the brains of individuals with ASD take a "second hit" during adolescence that makes teens with ASD struggle with the peer and romantic relationships so important in adolescence as well as with the development of self-control and autonomy (Picci & Scherf, 2015). Important regions of their brains are experiencing neural loss in adolescence at a time when other adolescents' brains are undergoing a growth spurt and reorganizing.

Like most hypotheses, though, the early brain overgrowth and later underconnectivity hypothesis does not fit all children with ASD (Waterhouse, 2013). Moreover, although abnormalities in early brain development may cause later social information-processing deficits, we cannot rule out that the possibility that a shortage of early social experience contributes to atypical brain development (Pelphrey et al., 2011). We can at least agree that atypical patterns of brain development are evident in individuals with ASD and that they affect a number of important areas of development.

Suspected Causes

Early theorists suggested that rigid and cold parenting by "refrigerator moms" caused autism, but this harmful myth has long been put to rest (Achenbach, 1982). It is now understood that interacting with an autistic child can easily cause parents to be tense and frustrated. Moreover, the parents of autistic children, because ASD is genetically influenced, sometimes have mild autistic spectrum traits themselves. Bad parenting is not responsible for autism.

Genes do contribute strongly to autism (Curran & Bolton, 2009; Yoo, 2015). Almost 19% of 3-year-olds who have an older sibling with ASD have it too; 32% have it if more than one older sibling has it (Ozonoff et al., 2011). In twin studies, if one identical twin is autistic, the other is autistic in 60–70% of the cases, whereas fraternal twins are hardly alike at all (Yoo, 2015). But since one identical twin can have ASD when the other does not, nonshared environmental factors must also be at work (Ronald & Hoekstra, 2011). And in one twin study (Hallmayer et al., 2011), shared environmental influences were also evident—possibly prenatal or postnatal experiences that could make even fraternal twins similar.

Hundreds of genes on several chromosomes, each with small effects, have been implicated (Waterhouse, 2013). Most likely, individuals with autism inherit from their parents, or acquire through new mutations, several genes that interact with each other and with environmental influences to put them at risk (Yoo, 2015). In some cases too, segments of DNA that affect neural communication appear to have been copied too many or too few times during cell division (Yoo, 2015). Autism occurs more often when parents, especially fathers, are older; this is because as we age, genetic mutations and copy number variations become more common, especially in the formation of sperm (Hultman et al., 2011; O'Roak et al., 2012). When these genetic errors occur, the processes through which genes and experience guide the development of the brain and its neural connections can be disrupted.

Early environmental influences also contribute to ASD (Mandy & Lai, 2016; Tordjman et al., 2014; Waterhouse, 2013). An environmental trigger such as a virus or chemicals in the environment can interact with a genetic predisposition to cause autism. For example, the combination of genetic copy number variants associated with ASD and a maternal infection during pregnancy is associated with more severe ASD symptoms (Mazina et al., 2015). Prenatal exposure to teratogens such as rubella, alcohol, and thalidomide are known to contribute to ASD. Autism also occurs more frequently when there is maternal bleeding or other complications during pregnancy (Gardener, Spiegelman, & Buka, 2009). *Epigenetic effects* are probably at work too: Early environmental influences can alter the expression of genes that guide brain development (Hall & Kelley, 2014; Tordjman et al., 2014). In short, there are about as many possible environmental contributors to ASD as genetic ones.

Developmental Outcomes and Treatment

What becomes of children with autism as they get older? A small minority outgrow their autism and function like typically developing children (Fein et al., 2013). However, although most individuals with ASD improve in functioning with age, they are usually autistic to some extent for life. Fewer than half are totally independent as adults in the sense of living away from their parents and having a job; few marry and many have physical and mental health problems. Positive outcomes are most likely among those who have IQ scores above 70 and reasonably good communication skills by age 5. We know almost nothing about what happens to adults with ASD in old age (Howlin & Moss, 2012).

Can treatment help? Absolutely! Researchers continue to search for drugs that will correct the brain dysfunctions of individuals with ASD, but there is probably no "magic pill." The most effective approach to treating ASD is intensive and highly structured behavioral and educational programming, beginning as early as possible, continuing throughout childhood, and involving the family (Schreibman et al., 2015). The goal is to make the most of the plasticity of the young brain during its sensitive period for development.

O. Ivar Lovaas and his colleagues pioneered the use of **applied behavior analysis (ABA)**, the application of reinforcement principles to teach skills and change behavior, to shape social and language skills in children with autism (Lovaas & Smith, 2003). In an early study, Lovaas (1987) trained student therapists to use reinforcement principles to reduce these children's aggressive and self-stimulatory behavior and to teach them developmentally appropriate skills such as how to imitate others, play with toys and with peers, and use language. Parents were taught to use the same behavioral techniques at home. Lovaas reported astounding results for a 40-hours-a-week intervention—for example, IQ scores were about 30 points higher in the treatment group than in the comparison group that received much less of this training.

Subsequent research suggests that early behavioral interventions usually do not convert children with ASD into typically functioning children. Nonetheless, many children with autism, especially those who are young and do not have severe intellectual disabilities, make impressive gains if they receive intensive cognitive and behavioral training and comprehensive family services starting early in life (Dawson et al., 2010; Reichow & Wolery, 2009). Newer early intervention programs that build on both applied behavior analysis and developmental science focus on training foundational social communication skills such as pointing, joint attention, and imitation and use more natural reinforcers to do so (Hardan et al., 2015; Schreibman et al., 2015). Thus, where Lovaas and his colleagues might have given a child a cereal bit for saying "car," a therapist would now give the child a car to play with. The therapist would also try to develop a relationship with the child in which the child learns to initiate and participate in give-and-take interactions. Typically family members become trainers too, so that the training becomes embedded in the child's everyday life.

In an especially well-conducted study with random assignment of children to treatment and control groups, one of these more modern ABA programs, called the Early Start Denver Model, was evaluated (Dawson et al., 2012). It not only increased IQ scores, language, and social skills but also changed brain functioning, making ASD children's neural responses to faces like those of typically developing children. And its positive effects were still evident when 18- to 30-month-olds, who were trained for two years, were reassessed at age 6 (Estes et al., 2015). We know that the young brain is very plastic, so there is a good chance that such early intervention programs, by increasing a child's social interaction, change the course of brain development. But ASD remains a lifelong disorder for many and a growing number of adults with autism need training and services too (Turcotte et al., 2016).

Depression

Does it seem possible to you that an infant could experience major depressive disorder as defined in DSM-5? Infants are not capable of the negative cognitions common among depressed adults—the low self-esteem, guilt, worthlessness, hopelessness, and so on. After all, until late infancy, they have not yet acquired the capacity for symbolic thought or self-awareness that would allow them to reflect on their experience. Yet infants *can* exhibit some of depression's behavioral symptoms (such as loss of interest in activities or psychomotor slowing) and somatic, or physical, symptoms such as weight loss (Garber, 2010; Luby & Belden, 2012).

DSM-5 allows diagnosis of major depressive disorder in childhood but is silent about infancy. While psychologists and psychiatrists are debating whether true depression can occur in infancy, a small number of babies are clearly experiencing serious depressive states and symptoms (Garber, 2010; Luby, 2009). Moreover, young children who receive diagnoses of major depressive disorder are often said by their parents to have shown symptoms such as tearfulness, irritability, and a lack of joy even as infants (Luby & Belden, 2012). Indeed, babies can experience a whole range of mental health problems—problems involving feeding, sleeping, anxiety, attachment, and more (Keren et al., 2010; Zeanah, 2009). As a result, a special DSM-like diagnostic system has been developed by the Zero to Three Project to help infant mental health specialists better identify psychological disorders in infants so that they can be treated (Northcutt & McCarroll, 2014; Zero to Three, 2005). The developers of this system believe that major depressive disorder can indeed occur in infancy, contrary to what the authors of DSM-5 suggest. The developers also know that diagnosing infants and young children is challenging.

Why would a baby become depressed? Depressive symptoms are most likely to be observed in infants who are abused or neglected, have an all-important attachment severed, or have a depressed caregiver (Boris & Zeanah, 1999). Infants who display a disorganized pattern of attachment, in which they do not seem to know whether to approach or avoid their caregiver (see Chapter 14)—an attachment style common among abused children—are especially likely to show symptoms of depression (Egeland & Carlson, 2004). And infants who are permanently separated from their mothers between 6 and 12 months of age have long been known to be at risk to become sad, weepy, listless, unresponsive, and withdrawn and to show delays in virtually all aspects of development (Spitz, 1946).

Infants whose mothers—or fathers—are depressed are also at risk (Gotlib et al., 2006). These babies adopt an interaction style that resembles that of their depressed caregivers; they vocalize little and look sad, even when interacting with women other than their mothers, and they show developmental delays (Field, 1995). They are at increased risk of becoming clinically depressed themselves later in life and of developing other psychological disorders. This may be because of a combination of genes and stressful experiences with their unpredictable caregivers (that is, because of diathesis–stress). Stress early in life, we now know, can produce children with an overactive stress-response system who are easily distressed, cannot regulate their negative emotions, are more reactive to stress later in life, and are more likely to develop psychological disorders (Bruce et al., 2013; Gunnar & Quevedo, 2007).

In sum, mental health problems in infants can often be traced to a family environment in which parent–infant attachment and interaction are maladaptive (Keren et al., 2010). Intervening to change the family system—for example, to treat a depressed mother so that she can parent more effectively—helps both her and her child (Cuijpers et al., 2015).

What are the implications for this baby of growing up with a depressed mother? Infants whose mothers are depressed may show heightened reactivity to stress and develop depression symptoms of their own.

SpeedKingz/Shutterstock.com

Checking Mastery

1. What two major groups of symptoms would you expect to see in a child with autism spectrum disorder?
2. How does brain development in children with ASD appear to differ from that in typically developing children?
3. What are two early experiences that could contribute to depressive symptoms in an infant?

Making Connections

1. What are two myths about autism that have been discredited, and how might they have arisen or have seemed believable?
2. If you were trying to judge whether Baby Baboo is depressed, what would you look for? Refer to the DSM-5 definition of major depressive disorder in Section 16.1.

16.3
The Child

LEARNING OBJECTIVES

- Distinguish between externalizing and internalizing problems and discuss nature/nurture and continuity/discontinuity issues pertaining to childhood problems.

- Characterize ADHD in terms of its symptoms, developmental course, suspected causes, and treatment.

- Discuss the importance and challenges of recognizing depression in children.

Many children experience developmental problems—fears, recurring stomachaches, temper tantrums, and so on. A smaller proportion qualify as having a psychological disorder and a smaller proportion still are diagnosed as having a psychological disorder and treated for it.

Externalizing and Internalizing Problems

Many developmental problems of childhood can be placed in one of two broad categories that reflect whether the child's behavior is out of control or overly controlled (Achenbach & Edelbrock, 1978). When children have **externalizing problems**, they lack self-control and act out in ways that disturb other people and violate social expectations. They may be aggressive, disobedient, difficult to control, or disruptive. We discussed conduct disorder and aggressive behavior in Chapter 13 and will discuss ADHD here as an example. In **internalizing problems**, negative emotions are internalized, or bottled up, rather than externalized, or expressed. Internalizing problems include anxiety disorders (such as persistent worrying about separation from loved ones), phobias, severe shyness and withdrawal, and depression.

Externalizing behaviors decrease from age 4 to age 18, whereas internalizing difficulties increase (Bongers et al., 2003). Externalizing problems are typically more common among boys, whereas internalizing problems are more prevalent among girls—a gender difference evident across cultures (Crijnen, Achenbach, & Verhulst, 1997). Yet cultural differences in values and parenting behavior make for cultural differences in how children's problems are expressed. For example, children in collectivist Asian cultures tend to show more depression, anxiety, and other internalizing symptoms than children in individualistic Western countries like the United States and Canada, whereas rates of externalizing problems such as aggression and disruptive behavior are higher in Western societies (Chen et al., 2014). Finally children from low socioeconomic status (SES) families show more externalizing and internalizing problems than children from higher SES families, partly because their environments are more stressful (Amone-P'Olak et al., 2009).

How do externalizing and internalizing problems arise, and to what extent do such problems in childhood spell trouble later in life? These questions concern the issues of nature–nurture and continuity–discontinuity in development.

Nature and Nurture

Most of us have a strong belief in the power of the social environment, particularly the family, to shape child development. This belief in a *parent effects model* of family influence (see Chapter 15) often leads us to blame parents—especially mothers—if their children are sad and withdrawn, uncontrollable and "bratty," or otherwise different from most children. Parents whose children develop problems often draw the same conclusion, feeling guilty because they assume they are at fault. If instead we view developmental disorders from a family systems perspective and apply a *transactional model* of family influence, we appreciate how emerging problems both affect and are affected by family interactions. We understand that parents are important but that they both influence and are influenced by their children (Cowan & Cowan, 2006; Cummings & Valentino, 2015).

It is true that youngsters with depression, conduct disorder, and many other psychological disorders tend to come from families in which there is a history of psychological disorder, marital conflict, child maltreatment, or other problems (Connell & Goodman, 2002; Cummings & Valentino, 2015). However, a child in such a family may have a genetically based predisposition to disorder that would be expressed even if the child were adopted into another home early in life (Plomin et al., 2013). Moreover, "bad parenting" is sometimes the effect of a child's disorder rather than its cause (Cowan & Cowan, 2006).

Unquestionably, stress on a family and the ineffective or even abusive parenting that sometimes results from it contribute to and aggravate many childhood problems. In addition, children who are at genetic risk for psychological disorders may or may not develop disorders depending on whether they are parented effectively (Johnson et al., 2001; Sentse et al., 2009). As the diathesis–stress model suggests, then, disorders often arise from the toxic interaction of a genetically based vulnerability and stressful experiences. Atypical development, like typical development, is the product of the interplay of nature and nurture.

Continuity and Discontinuity

The parents of children who develop psychological problems often most want to know this: Will my child outgrow these problems or will they persist? These parents are understandably concerned with the issue of continuity versus discontinuity in development. You have already seen that ASD persists beyond childhood in most individuals, but what about the broader range of childhood problems?

Consider some of the findings of a remarkable project called the Great Smoky Mountains Study (Costello, Copeland, & Angold, 2016). This study involved conducting psychiatric diagnostic interviews nine times by questioning a sample of children and their parents in the southeastern United States between the ages of 9 and 21 (Copeland et al., 2011). By age 21, 61% of participants had met the criteria for a psychological disorder at some point in their young lives. Another 21% at some point had shown evidence of what DSM calls disorders "not otherwise specified," or mixed pictures of symptoms, bringing the grand total of individuals who had experienced at least one psychological disorder in childhood and adolescence to a whopping 82%. Although the percentage of youth with a disorder at any particular point in time is much lower, apparently abnormal behavior is very normal. Most of us clearly move back and forth between "normal" and "abnormal" developmental pathways over our lives.

The Great Smoky Mountains researchers have also examined connections between having a disorder at one age and having the same disorder, or possibly a different one, at a later age (Copeland et al., 2013). Overall, having a disorder early was associated with at least three times the risk of having it at a later time. Continuity was especially strong for externalizing problems such as ADHD, less strong for internalizing problems such as depression and anxiety. Quite often, an early disorder was also linked to a different kind of problem in adolescence or adulthood; for example, conduct disorder in childhood predicted a later substance use disorder, and anxiety in adolescence predicted depression in adulthood. This may have to do with the fact that comorbidity among psychiatric disorders is very common, especially in childhood. Overall, there was a good deal of continuity of psychological disorders from childhood to early adulthood—sometimes continuity of a particular disorder over time, other times continuity of a pattern of maladaptation that expressed itself differently in different life periods.

Finally, this project shed light on the implications of problems in childhood for adult adjustment by assessing adverse outcomes in early adulthood: psychiatric and health problems, legal problems such as incarceration, financial problems such as losing jobs, and social problems such as lack of social support (Costello et al., 2016; Copeland et al., 2015). About 60% of participants with one or more childhood psychiatric disorder had at least one adverse outcome in adulthood, compared to only about 20% of those without any childhood diagnoses.

There is room for discontinuity along with the continuity in development, however: Some children outgrow their problems.

For example, in another study of children and adolescents with behavioral and emotional problems, about 40% still had significant problems in adulthood, but most did not (Hofstra, Van der Ende, & Verhulst, 2000). So, having psychological problems as a child is a risk factor for later problems but it does not doom an individual to a life of maladjustment. If children have mild rather than severe problems and if they receive help, their difficulties are more likely to be overcome (Essex et al., 2009).

Indeed, some children show remarkable **resilience**, functioning well despite exposure to risk factors for disorder or overcoming even severe early problems to become well adjusted (Garmezy, 1994; Masten & Tellegen, 2012). Resilient children appear to benefit from protective factors such as their own competencies (especially intellectual ability and social skills) and strong social support (especially a stable family situation with at least one caring and effective parent figure). Overall, research on continuity and discontinuity in psychopathology brings home the importance of identifying and treating children with psychological problems early so that their developmental trajectories can be altered.

With the nature–nurture and continuity–discontinuity issues in mind, let us now focus on two illustrative childhood problems: attention deficit hyperactivity disorder, an externalizing disorder, and depression, an internalizing disorder.

Attention Deficit Hyperactivity Disorder

Upon entering high school I was determined to make high honor roll every quarter. It didn't quite work out that way though. . . . I was completely lost. I couldn't focus on work, I couldn't pay attention in class, and I couldn't concentrate on homework, rarely completing it as a result. . . . I was completely frustrated because I didn't understand why I was having such trouble. . . . My teachers knew I had the potential to do well, but they just figured I was lazy and not motivated. My parents were angry with me because my teachers told them I never did my homework. . . . I would try to sit down and write a paper, but there were too many thoughts in my head and too many things going on around me to even get a paragraph down. I would sit in the front row of my math class, with my notebook open and ready to take notes, but then something would catch my eye out the window and I'd miss the whole lesson. (Stone, 2009)

In this story, Rachel Stone describes her struggles with sustaining and focusing her attention, illustrating a key feature of **attention deficit hyperactivity disorder (ADHD)**. ADHD is diagnosed if either one of the following two sets of symptoms, or a combination of the two, is present (American Psychiatric Association, 2013 [DSM-5]; see also Hinshaw & Ellison, 2016; Selikowitz, 2009; Weyandt, 2007):

1. **Inattention**. The individual does not seem to listen, is easily distracted, makes careless errors, has trouble following instructions, misses details, is distractible, does not stick to activities and finish tasks, and tends to be forgetful and unorganized.

2. **Hyperactivity and Impulsivity**. The individual is restless, perpetually fidgeting, finger tapping, or chattering, and

Most children with attention deficit hyperactivity disorder show inattention but not hyperactivity; they often seem "spaced out" in the classroom.

Wolfgang Flamisch/Getty Images

the grade-school years, overactive behavior is less of a problem, but children with ADHD are fidgety, restless, and inattentive to schoolwork (American Psychiatric Association, 2013).

What becomes of hyperactive children later in life? It used to be thought that they outgrew their problems. Most children with ADHD do outgrow their overactive behavior. However, as illustrated by Rachel's story, adolescents with ADHD continue to be restless, to have difficulty concentrating on their academic work, and to behave impulsively; on average, they perform poorly in school and are prone to car accidents, substance abuse, and reckless delinquent acts (Hinshaw & Ellison, 2016). Those able to go on to college may need extra help to make the transition successfully (Weyandt & DuPaul, 2013).

The picture is somewhat more positive by early adulthood. Yet many individuals with ADHD get in trouble because of disorganization, lapses of concentration, impulsive decisions, and procrastination (Schmidt & Petermann, 2009; Volkow & Swanson, 2013). In one study following ADHD and control children from about age 7 to age 21, the adults who had been identified as ADHD in childhood had lower educational attainment and achievement, had become involved in sexual activity and parenthood earlier, had been fired more and received lower performance ratings from their employers, and had fewer close friends and more problems in social relations (Barkley et al., 2006; and see Schmidt & Petermann, 2009).

In a national study, about half of children diagnosed with ADHD continued to meet the diagnostic criteria for ADHD as adults; inattention problems persisted more than hyperactivity/impulsivity problems (Kessler, Green et al., 2010). This evidence of continuity in ADHD across the life span is consistent with findings that over 4% of adults in the United States have diagnosable ADHD (Kessler et al., 2006). ADHD is evident even in old age (Brod et al., 2012); it is clearly not "kid stuff." If you complete the short assessment in **Engagement 16.1**, you can see whether you show some of the behaviors characteristic of adult ADHD.

has trouble remaining seated; he or she acts impulsively before thinking, cannot wait to have a turn in an activity, and may talk too much, blurt things out, and interrupt others.

ADHD is common—and like autism spectrum disorder, it is becoming more common now that it is better known and makes an affected child eligible for educational and medical services. Based on parent reports, 11% of children aged 4 to 17 in 2011 had been diagnosed as ADHD at some point in their lives, compared to 7.8% in 2003 (Visser et al., 2014). At least two boys for every girl have the disorder, although girls have often been underdiagnosed because they often show inattention rather than the more easily observable and often exasperating hyperactive behavior that boys more often show (Hinshaw & Ellison, 2016). The primarily inattentive form of ADHD is roughly twice as common as the primarily hyperactive-impulsive form (Froehlich et al., 2007). Most children with ADHD also have other comorbid conditions ranging from conduct disorder to anxiety and depression.

Developmental Course

ADHD expresses itself differently at different ages. When the predominant symptom is hyperactivity/impulsivity, the condition may reveal itself in infancy, though it cannot be diagnosed until about age 4. As infants, children with ADHD are typically very active, have difficult temperaments, and show irregular feeding and sleeping patterns (Teeter, 1998). As preschool children, they are in perpetual motion, quickly moving from one activity to another. Because most young children are energetic and have short attention spans, behavior must be judged in relation to developmental norms; otherwise, we might mistake most average 3- and 4-year-olds for hyperactive children. Finally, by

Suspected Causes

What causes this disorder? Russell Barkley (1997, 2015) has put forth the view that the frontal lobes of individuals with ADHD do not function as they do in typically developing children; this results in difficulties in **executive functions**–higher level control functions based in the prefrontal cortex of the brain that are critical in self-control—most importantly, difficulty inhibiting responses and organizing and regulating one's emotions and behavior. Low levels or inefficient use of the neurotransmitters dopamine and

Could You Have ADHD?

Check the box that best describes how you have felt and conducted yourself over the past 6 months.

	Never	Rarely	Sometimes	Often	Very Often
1. How often do you have trouble wrapping up the final details of a project once the challenging parts have been done?					
2. How often do you have difficulty getting things in order when you have to do a task that requires organization?					
3. How often do you have problems remembering appointments or obligations?					
4. When you have a task that requires a lot of thought, how often do you avoid or delay getting started?					
5. How often do you fidget or squirm with your hands or feet when you have to sit down for a long time?					
6. How often do you feel overly active and compelled to do things, like you were driven by a motor?					

Add up the number of check marks in the shaded boxes. If you have four or more checks in the shaded boxes, then you may want to talk to a professional about your behaviors and feelings to determine if you might have ADHD. Remember that this self-assessment is not a definitive diagnosis and needs follow-up if your answers are suggestive of ADHD.

Source: Adapted from the World Health Organization's 18-question Adult ADHD Self-Report Scale, Version 1.1 (Adult ASRS-V1.1), Symptom Checklist. ASRS-V1.1 Screener © 2003 World Health Organization (WHO). Reprinted by permission. Retrieved from: add.org/wp-content/uploads/2015/03/adhd-questionnaire-ASRS111.pdf.

norepinephrine, which are involved in communication among neurons in the frontal lobes, seem to be at the root of the inattention, executive function impairments, and other differences in cognitive functioning that individuals with ADHD show (Hinshaw & Ellison, 2016). The frontal cortexes of children with ADHD may also be slower to mature than those of other children and may or may not catch up by adulthood (Shaw et al., 2012).

Genes predispose some individuals to develop ADHD and probably underlie the differences in brain functioning associated with it. Genes account for as much as 60–90% of the variation among individuals in whether they have ADHD (Scerif & Baker, 2015; Waldman & Gizer, 2006). First-degree relatives of someone with ADHD have 4 to 5 times the usual risk (Thapar, 2003). There is not one ADHD gene, however. There may be 100 or more gene variants common in individuals with ADHD that influence levels of dopamine and other relevant neurotransmitters in their brains.

Environmental influences are also important, as they help determine whether a genetic risk turns into a reality and whether the individual adapts well or poorly as she develops (Hinshaw & Ellison, 2016). The myth that ADHD is due to consuming sugar has long been put to rest (Weyandt, 2007). There is still some uncertainty about whether food colorings or dyes contribute. It seems clear that food dyes are not a major cause of ADHD, but they may have small negative effects on some children (Arnold, Lofthouse, & Hurt, 2012; Kleinman et al., 2011). Low birth weight and teratogens such as maternal smoking and alcohol use and exposure to lead, air pollution, and other toxic chemicals during pregnancy appear to contribute to some cases of ADHD (Banerjee, Middleton, & Faraone, 2007; Hinshaw & Ellison, 2016). And

genes and environment interact: Individuals who inherit genes that lower dopamine levels in the brain and who also experience family adversity show more ADHD symptoms than children who do not have both genes and environment working against them (Laucht et al., 2007). Meanwhile, parents who are able to remain authoritative parents in the face of the challenges of raising a child with ADHD are likely to end up with a more manageable child than parents who respond negatively and harshly to their children's behavior (Hinshaw & Ellison, 2016).

Treatment

Most children with ADHD are prescribed stimulant drugs (often Ritalin or Adderall), and most are helped by these drugs. Although it may seem odd to give overactive children stimulants, the brains of individuals with ADHD are actually underaroused. These drugs increase levels of dopamine and other neurotransmitters to normal levels and, by doing so, allow these children to concentrate (Hinshaw & Ellison, 2016). Listen to Rachel Stone again:

I was put on the medication Adderall one month before sophomore year concluded. I was able to pull up all my grades. . . . Things only got better with junior year. . . . With the Adderall, I was able to focus in class and remember how much I liked math! I ended up with the highest average in the pre-calculus classes. . . (Stone, 2009)

Yet controversy surrounds the use of stimulants with ADHD children. Some critics argue that these drugs are prescribed to too many children, including many who do not actually have ADHD (Mayes, Bagwell, & Erkulwater, 2009). Other critics are concerned that stimulant drugs have undesirable side effects such as loss of appetite and headaches and may do longer-term damage that we do not yet know about (Mayes et al., 2009). What's more, stimulant drugs do not cure ADHD; they improve functioning only until their effects wear off.

Behavioral treatment is also used to treat ADHD. The Multimodal Treatment Study of Attention Deficit Hyperactivity Disorder (MTA), a carefully conducted national study of 579 children with ADHD ranging in age from 7 to 9, pitted medication and behavioral treatment against each other (Jensen et al., 2001; Molina et al., 2009). The study randomly assigned children to receive optimally delivered medication, state-of-the-art behavioral treatment (a combination of parent training, child training through a summer program, and school intervention), a combination of the two approaches, or routine care in the community over 14 months. The findings were clear: Medication alone was more effective than behavioral treatment alone or routine care in reducing ADHD symptoms such as inattention (see also Scheffler et al., 2009). However, a combination of medication and behavioral treatment was superior to medication alone when the goal was defined as not only reducing ADHD symptoms but also improving academic performance, social adjustment, and parent–child relations. A multipronged approach is generally recommended now (Chronis, Jones, & Raggi, 2006; Hinshaw & Ellison, 2016):

- medication;
- behavioral programming designed to teach children with ADHD to stay focused on tasks, control their impulsiveness, and interact socially;
- parent training designed to help parents understand and manage the behavior of these often-difficult youngsters; and
- interventions at school to make the learning environment more structured and increase motivation.

A caveat, though: An 8-year follow-up of children in the Multimodal Treatment Study revealed that differences among the treatment groups had faded by the time these children were adolescents and that, regardless of which treatment they received, children with ADHD had more academic and social problems than comparison children who did not have ADHD (Molina et al., 2009). Most children who had received medication during the study had since stopped using it but were doing as well as those who continued their medication. Overall, then, the study suggests that, while medication and behavior treatment can significantly improve functioning in the short term, achieving long-term improvement is more challenging. This means that some individuals with ADHD may need to continue taking medication or receiving psychotherapy during adulthood (Volkow & Swanson, 2013).

Depression

As you saw earlier, the depressive symptoms displayed by some infants may or may not qualify as major depressive disorder. When, then, can children experience true clinical depression? For years many psychologists and psychiatrists, especially those influenced by psychoanalytic theory, argued that young children simply could not be depressed. Feelings of worthlessness, hopelessness, and self-blame were not believed to be possible until the child was older (Garber, 1984). Besides, childhood is supposedly a happy, carefree time, right?

It is now clear that children as young as 3 can meet the same DSM criteria for major depressive disorder used in diagnosing adults (Garber, 2010). Depression in children is rarer than depression in adolescents and adults, but an estimated 2% of children have diagnosable depressive disorders (Gotlib & Hammen, 1992). Their depression is often comorbid with other disorders, especially anxiety disorders, but also conduct disorder, oppositional defiant disorder, and ADHD (Garber, 2010; Whalen et al., 2015). Such comorbidity, so common in childhood, not only makes it difficult to diagnose psychological problems but raises larger questions about how distinct different DSM disorders really are.

Depression expresses itself differently in a young child than in an adult. Like depressed infants, depressed preschool children are more likely to display the behavioral and somatic symptoms of depression (losing interest in activities, eating poorly, and so on) than to talk about feeling depressed or hopeless (Kaslow et al., 2000). Yet as early as age 3 some children who are depressed express excessive shame or guilt—claiming, for example, that they are bad (Luby et al., 2009). In diagnosing depression, the main characteristics to look for are either sadness or irritability (children may express their depression either way) along with the lack of interest in usually enjoyable activities that depressed adults display (Garber, 2010; Luby et al., 2006).

Suicide Attempts?

Some young children—about one in ten 3- to 7-year-olds in one study—also have suicidal thoughts or act out themes of death and suicide in their play (Whalen et al., 2015). What may not have occurred to you is that children as young as 3 are also capable of

Even young children can experience a major depressive episode.

Jeges-Varga Ferenc/Shutterstock.com

not only thinking about suicide but attempting it (Rosenthal & Rosenthal, 1984; Shaffer & Pfeffer, 2001):

- At age 3, Jeffrey repeatedly hurled himself down a flight of stairs and banged his head on the floor; upset by the arrival of a new brother, he was heard to say, "Jeff is bad, and bad boys have to die" (Cytryn & McKnew, 1996, p. 72).
- An 8-year-old, after writing her will, approached her father with a large rock and asked in all seriousness, "Daddy, would you crush my head, please?" (Cytryn & McKnew, 1996, pp. 69–70).
- Other children have jumped from high places, run into traffic, and stabbed themselves, often in response to abuse, rejection, or neglect.

Moreover, children who attempt suicide once often try again (Shaffer & Pfeffer, 2001). Very few children actually commit suicide (Westefeld et al., 2010), but the moral is clear: Parents, teachers, and human service professionals need to appreciate that childhood is not always a happy, carefree time and that children can develop serious depressive disorders and suicidal tendencies. Children's claims that they want to die should be taken dead seriously.

Carryover of Depression

Do depressed children tend to have recurring bouts of depression, becoming depressed adolescents and adults? Most children make it through mild episodes of sadness, and carryover of depression problems from childhood to adulthood is not as strong as carryover from adolescence to adulthood. However, there is indeed carryover of depression from the preschool years to the school years and from the school years to adolescence (Luby et al., 2014). It is estimated that half of children and adolescents diagnosed as having major depressive disorder have recurrences in adulthood (Kessler, Avenevoli, & Merikangas, 2001).

Is it possible to identify in early childhood individuals who may not be diagnosable as depressed yet but who are at risk to become depressed in adolescence or adulthood? Major depression in a parent and traumatic early experiences such as being abused are clear warning signs, but neuropsychologists are also looking for biological signs of a predisposition to depression. To illustrate, one group of researchers (Luking et al., 2016b) is focusing on the brain's response to reward. People who are depressed do not seem to derive pleasure from their experiences. Brain imaging studies show that the reward centers of their brains show a blunted response to rewards such as candy, a happy face image, or acceptance of an invitation to chat by a peer. This blunted response to reward can also be observed in adolescents who have not been diagnosed with depression but who are at risk for it because a parent has experienced major depression.

Katherine Luking and her colleagues (2016a) used fMRI to look for a blunted response to reward in the brains of children aged 7–10 as they played a game in which they guessed whether the number on a card was more or less than 5 and got candy if they were correct but lost candy if they were wrong. Children whose mothers had had major depression showed the same blunted response to reward that adolescents of depressed mothers had shown. Interestingly, they also showed a heightened sensitivity to losing, suggesting that neural responses to the loss of rewards may be even more important than responses to reward in identifying children who are at risk for depression. Think about

the implications: If researchers can identify, through brain imaging or other methods, children who show biological signs of risk for depression, it may become possible to intervene early to prevent depression as well as to prevent the further changes in brain development that result from depression (Luby et al., 2016).

Treatment

Most depressed children—and children with other psychological disorders too—respond well to psychotherapy (Carr, 2009; Kazdin, 2003). Cognitive behavioral therapy, a well-established psychotherapy approach that identifies and changes distorted thinking and the maladaptive emotions and behavior that stem from it, has proved especially effective (Brent & Maalouf, 2009; Weisz, McCarty, & Valeri, 2006). But since preschool children have limited cognitive and linguistic skills, might there be a more developmentally appropriate way to treat them? This question is explored in **Application 16.1.**

Depressed children have also been treated with antidepressant drugs called selective serotonin reuptake inhibitors, such as Prozac (fluoxetine), that correct for low levels of the neurotransmitter serotonin in their brains. These drugs can help correct for biased information processing that emphasizes negative emotional material and for overreactivity to stress (Gotlib, Joormann, & Foland-Ross, 2014). However, antidepressant drugs do not appear to be as effective with children as with adults, and a warning that they may increase suicidality in children and adolescents who take them was issued by the U.S. Food and Drug Administration in 2004 (Vitiello, Zuvekas, & Norquist, 2006). Antidepressants are still prescribed in some cases for seriously depressed youth who are likely to be at even greater risk of suicide if they are not treated with medication, but antidepressant drugs are now prescribed less often and with more careful monitoring of the child's reactions (Nemeroff et al., 2007). In sum, both ADHD and major depression can significantly alter the course of development in childhood and beyond, so detecting and treating these problems early is important.

● Checking Mastery

1. How would you describe the main difference between an externalizing and an internalizing disorder in childhood?
2. What two major sets of symptoms characterize ADHD?
3. What is the agreed-upon best way to treat ADHD and in what way is it limited?
4. How is major depression in a preschool child similar to and different from major depression in an adult?

● Making Connections

1. Focusing on depression in childhood and citing evidence, what do you conclude about the nature/nurture and continuity/discontinuity issues as they pertain to depression?
2. Some experts believe that ADHD is overdiagnosed and overtreated with medications. Others, however, believe that not enough cases of ADHD are being treated with medications. What is your position on diagnosis and treatment of ADHD and how does the material in this chapter support—and fail to support—your view?

How Do You Treat a Depressed 3-Year-Old?

So, children as young as 3 years can be diagnosed with major depressive disorder, but how in the world do you treat a depressed preschool child? Antidepressant drugs are generally not advisable at this age, and many forms of "talking" therapy designed for adults are simply not usable with children because of their limited verbal and cognitive skills. We do not know much yet about the effectiveness of treatments for depression and anxiety disorders in the preschool years (Luby, 2013). However, Joan Luby and her colleagues have developed one promising approach that illustrates how psychotherapy can be adapted to the developmental characteristics of young children.

Luby and her associates started with a child therapy approach called **Parent–Child Interaction Therapy (PCIT)** that was originally developed by Sylvia Eyberg and her colleagues (see Eyberg & Bussing, 2010) to treat children with disruptive behavior. The PCIT approach centers on modifying the parent–child relationship and building more effective parenting skills. Parents first learn to let their children take the lead in play while giving them positive attention and reinforcement; in a second phase, they learn to lead the child's activity

using effective discipline techniques (for example, getting them to comply with requests). Through parent training, especially coaching by the therapist through a wireless system while parent and child interact, the parent becomes the vehicle for changing the quality of parent–child interactions and the child's behavior.

Luby, Lenze, and Tillman (2012) adapted PCIT to treat depression in young children, creating what they called Parent–Child Interaction Therapy—Emotional Development (PCIT-ED). They added to the usual PCIT components a component focused on enhancing the child's emotional development and emotion regulation skills. Because depression involves too much negative affect and too little positive affect, parents are taught to help their children recognize, express, and regulate negative and positive emotions—for example, to minimize sad feelings and intensify happy feelings. In other words, parents learn to be good emotion coaches (see Chapter 14).

Children aged 3 to 7 who had been diagnosed with major depression were randomly assigned to either the PCIT-ED treatment or to a control intervention in which small groups of parents learned about child development. After

some families dropped out, especially from the control group, the researchers were left with only 19 children in the PCIT-ED group and 10 in the control group, groups too small to provide a definitive test. However, compared to the control children, the children treated with PCIT-ED showed better emotion recognition skills and executive functioning and fewer symptoms of depression. Meanwhile, their parents scored lower on a measure of parenting stress as well as on a measure of their own depression symptoms, a finding that might be significant for future parent–child interactions given what we know about the negative effects of parent depression on parent–child interactions and child development.

Because depression in the preschool years predicts major depressive disorder later in childhood (Luby et al., 2014), it makes great sense to be on the lookout for depressed children and get them the treatment they need before their condition becomes more firmly rooted. It also makes sense to mobilize their parents as therapists. The PCIT approach is also being applied successfully to treat preschool children with conduct problems (Niec et al., 2016) as well as those with anxiety disorders (Carpenter et al., 2014).

16.4
The Adolescent

LEARNING OBJECTIVES

- Evaluate the "storm and stress" view of adolescence and discuss the factors that contribute to a peaking of risky problem behaviors in adolescence.

- Summarize the nature, causes, and preferred treatment of anorexia nervosa.

- Describe substance use in adolescence and how the cascade model accounts for the development of substance use problems.

- Explain why depression rates climb in adolescence, especially among females.

- Describe gender differences in adolescent suicidal behavior and explain why some adolescents attempt or commit suicide.

If any age group has a reputation for having problems, it is adolescents. This is supposedly the time when angelic children are transformed into emotionally unstable, uncontrollable delinquents. The view that adolescence is a time of emotional storm and stress was set forth by the founder of developmental psychology, G. Stanley Hall (1904). It has been with us ever since.

Storm and Stress?

Are adolescents really more likely than either children or adults to experience psychological problems? On one hand, adolescents have a worse reputation than they deserve. Most adolescents are not emotionally disturbed and do not engage in serious problem behaviors such as drug abuse and chronic delinquency. Instead, significant mental health problems—real signs of storm and stress in the form of diagnosable disorders—characterize a minority of adolescents, adolescents like Peggy, described at the beginning of the chapter (Merikangas et al., 2010). Moreover, many of these adolescents were maladjusted before they reached puberty and continue to be maladjusted during adulthood (Reinherz et al., 1999).

Yet there is some truth to the storm-and-stress view. Adolescence is a period of risk taking, of problem behaviors such as substance abuse and delinquency, and of heightened vulnerability to certain forms of psychological disorder (Cicchetti & Rogosch, 2002; Steinberg, 2011). The Centers for Disease Control and Prevention (2013) estimates that 13% to 20% of children aged 3 to 17 experience a psychological disorder in a given year and that rates of disorder climb with age from childhood to adolescence. It is estimated that about 25% of adults are affected by a disorder in a given year (Kessler & Wang, 2008).

Teenagers face greater stress than children; they must cope with physical maturation, changing brains and cognitive abilities, tribulations of dating, changes in family dynamics, moves to new and more complex school settings, societal demands to become more responsible and to assume adult roles, and more (Cicchetti & Rogosch, 2002). Most adolescents cope with these challenges remarkably well, maintain the level of adjustment they had when they entered adolescence, and undergo impressive psychological growth. Many feel depressed, anxious, and irritable occasionally, though, and as many as one in five experiences a diagnosable psychological disorder. These adolescents' problems should not be dismissed as a "phase" they are going through.

Adolescent Problem Behaviors

Many adolescents get themselves into trouble by binge drinking and using drugs, having risky sex, engaging in vandalism and other law-breaking behavior, and displaying other so-called adolescent problem behaviors. Adolescents are more likely than either children or adults to engage in some of these risky behaviors (Defoe et al., 2015). Adolescent problem behaviors usually do not reach the level of seriousness to qualify as psychological disorders, but they are of concern nonetheless (Boles, Biglan, & Smolkowski, 2006; Jessor, 1998).

Why do problem behaviors increase in adolescence? First, these behaviors often grow out of normal developmental tasks of adolescence: establishing an identity, establishing autonomy and independence from parents, and gaining acceptance by peers and romantic partners. Teens experiment with lots of new behavior to find out who they are, challenge their parents' authority, and impress other kids. Second, puberty and the hormonal changes that come with it appear to contribute to increases in both internalizing and externalizing problems (Mendle, 2014). And third, the timetable for brain development makes risk taking especially likely in adolescence. As you learned in Chapter 5, adolescents' brains combine strong sensation- and reward-seeking tendencies with immature prefrontal cortexes and therefore limited capacities for self-regulation (Albert, Chein, & Steinberg, 2013; Shulman et al., 2016; and see Chapter 5). The result is sometimes impulsive risk taking in pursuit of excitement and enjoyment without much self-control or thought of the likely consequences. Such risky behavior is most likely when

adolescents are with friends and when their emotions are aroused. Children, whose prefrontal cortexes are also underdeveloped, often show as much risk taking as adolescents do in laboratory settings. However, in the real world adolescents have much more opportunity than children to take risks because they are more often around temptations and out of the sight of adults (Defoe et al., 2015). Advice to parents: Recognize that your teens have immature brains and do what you can to minimize their opportunities to take risks that can hurt themselves or others (Steinberg, 2015).

In sum, adolescence is a challenging period of the life span; problem behaviors such as substance use and delinquency increase—the result of risk taking fueled by needs for identity, autonomy, and peer acceptance, the hormonal changes of puberty, and incomplete brain development. Partly for these same reasons, certain diagnosable disorders also become more prevalent in adolescence. Having discussed adolescent externalizing problems like aggression and conduct disorder in Chapter 13, let us look here at eating disorders such as anorexia nervosa that can make the adolescent period treacherous and even fatal; experimentation with alcohol and drugs that can turn into substance abuse; and depression, whose rate increases dramatically from childhood to adolescence. These problems interfere with adolescent development; yet they become far more understandable when viewed in the context of adolescence.

Eating Disorders

Perhaps no psychological disorders are more closely associated with adolescence than the eating disorders that disproportionately strike adolescent females, especially during the transition from childhood to adolescence at around age 14 and again during the transition from adolescence to emerging adulthood at around age 18 (Bryant-Waugh, 2007; Eddy, Keel, & Leon, 2010). Eating disorders—anorexia nervosa, bulimia nervosa, binge eating disorder (a new distinct disorder starting in DSM-5), and related conditions—have become more common in industrialized countries in recent decades (Eddy et al., 2010; Milos et al., 2004). They are serious—indeed, potentially fatal—conditions that are difficult to cure.

Anorexia nervosa, which literally means "nervous loss of appetite," is characterized by:

- body weight that is less than minimally normal for the person's gender, height, and age;
- a strong fear of becoming overweight or behavior that interferes with gaining weight; and
- a tendency to feel fat despite being emaciated, to be overly influenced by weight or shape in evaluating the self, and to fail to appreciate the seriousness of one's low body weight (American Psychiatric Association, 2013).

Bulimia nervosa, the so-called binge–purge syndrome, involves recurrent episodes of consuming huge quantities of food followed by purging activities such as self-induced vomiting, use of laxatives, rigid dieting and fasting, or obsessive exercising (Pinhas et al., 2007). **Binge eating disorder** involves binge eating without the purging.

A study of adolescent females involving annual diagnostic interviews administered from age 13 to age 21 revealed that by age 20 over

5% of these young women had experienced at least one of these three disorders (Stice, Marti, & Rohde, 2012). A total of 13% had experienced either one of these eating disorders or a less clearcut, "subthreshold" form of eating disorder. We will focus here on anorexia, the least common but most life threatening of the three disorders.

The typical individual with anorexia may begin dieting soon after reaching puberty and simply continue, insisting, even when she weighs only 60 or 70 pounds, that she needs to lose a few more pounds (Hsu, 1990). Praised at first for losing weight, she becomes increasingly obsessed with dieting and exercising and may gain a sense of control by resisting the urgings of parents and friends to eat more (Levenkron, 2000).

There are about 11 affected females for every 1 affected male (van Hoeken, Seidell, & Hoek, 2003), a huge gender difference. It is a myth that anorexia nervosa is restricted to European American females from upper-middle-class backgrounds. It occurs at all socioeconomic levels and in all racial and ethnic groups. African American females are less affected, however, probably because they are more satisfied with their bodies and less concerned than European American and Asian American females with dieting and being thin (Franko & George, 2009).

Suspected Causes

Nature and nurture contribute in complex ways to eating disorders. On the nurture side, sociocultural factors are significant. Rates of eating disorders vary widely around the world, being highest in Western or Westernized countries and in urban areas within

Anorexia can be life threatening.

Angela Hampton Picture Library/Alamy Stock Photo

countries (Anderson-Fye, 2009; Culbert, Racine, & Klump, 2015). We live in a society obsessed with thinness as the ideal of physical attractiveness—a society that makes it hard for young women to feel good about their bodies (Eddy et al., 2010; Keel & Klump, 2003). As the Western thinness ideal has spread to other countries, rates of eating disorders in those countries have risen. Interestingly, exposure to television on the island of Fiji converted girls raised to view plump bodies as a status symbol associated with the generous sharing of food into girls who feel too fat and try to lose weight (Becker et al., 2002).

Well before they reach puberty, starting as early as preschool, girls in our society begin to associate being thin with being attractive, fear becoming fat, and wish they were thinner (Hill, 2007; Ricciardelli & McCabe, 2001). They play with ultrathin Barbie dolls and see ultrathin models and celebrities on television and in magazines (Dittmar, Halliwell, & Ive, 2006; Dohnt & Tiggemann, 2006). These kinds of cultural messages about the **thin ideal** help explain why about a fourth of second-grade girls in one study said they dieted (Thelen et al., 1992; and see Hill, 2007).

Genes, though we are not sure which ones, serve as a diathesis, predisposing certain individuals to develop eating disorders (Eddy et al., 2010; Keel & Klump, 2003). Twin and adoption studies suggest that around half of the variation in risk for eating disorders is attributable to genes; the remainder is mostly tied to nonshared or individual experiences rather than to experiences shared with siblings (Culbert, Racine, & Klump, 2015).

Biochemical abnormalities have been detected in individuals with anorexia that may underlie their symptoms. For example, low levels of the neurotransmitter serotonin, which is involved in both appetite and mood and has been linked to both eating disorders and mood disorders, may be involved (Klump & Culbert, 2007). The neurotransmitter dopamine, important in the brain's reward system, has also been implicated; eating disorders, like alcohol and drug addiction, may involve compulsive behavior that becomes reinforcing (Halmi, 2009; and see Klump & Culbert, 2007). Genes also contribute, along with environment, to a personality profile that puts certain individuals at risk; females with anorexia tend to be obsessive perfectionists and score high on measures of negative emotionality or neuroticism (Culbert, Racine, & Klump, 2015).

Why is adolescence the prime time for the emergence of eating disorders in females? Here, too, we must consider both social and biological factors. As girls steeped in the thinness ideal experience normal pubertal changes, they naturally gain fat and become, in their minds, less attractive just when the pressure is on to be more attractive (Murnen & Smolak, 1997). Genetic and hormonal influences also help explain why some girls are so susceptible to eating disorders when they reach puberty. Kelly Klump and her colleagues have discovered in twin studies that, among prepubertal girls, genes have little to do with eating attitudes and behaviors; but among girls who have reached puberty, genes explain over 50% of the variation in eating attitudes and behaviors (Klump, McGue, & Iacono, 2003; Klump et al., 2012). In boys, by contrast, genetic influences on eating attitudes and behaviors are evident before puberty, during puberty, and after puberty (Klump et al., 2012). Possibly, then, increases in female hormones during puberty activate a genetically based risk for eating disorders in certain girls (Culbert et al., 2015; Klump et al., 2010, 2012).

Yet anorexia still may not emerge unless a genetically predisposed adolescent girl living in a weight-conscious culture also experiences an environment that fosters eating problems and a buildup of stressful events (Eddy et al., 2010). Girls who are overly concerned about their weight sometimes come from families that are preoccupied with weight, where mothers may model and reinforce disordered eating or even have eating disorders themselves (Eddy et al., 2010; Micali et al., 2015; Sim et al., 2009). Some experience pressure and criticism at home; family environment may then interact with genetic makeup to increase the risk of an eating disorder (Culbert et al., 2015). It often takes stressors or traumatic events of some kind to push a vulnerable young woman over the edge (Reyes-Rodríguez et al., 2011).

In anorexia nervosa, then, we have another clear example of the diathesis–stress model at work. A young woman who is at risk for it partly because of her genetic makeup and the hormonal changes associated with puberty may not develop anorexia unless she also grows up in an environment that overvalues thinness and faces overwhelming stress.

Prevention and Treatment

Can eating disorders be prevented before they start? Eric Stice and his colleagues have been testing the effectiveness of what they call the Body Project, a preventive program that can be administered either on the Internet or in groups (Stice & Presnell, 2007; Stice et al., 2009). The program attempts to get adolescent girls and college women who have body image concerns to stop buying into the thin ideal by having them critique it in essays, role plays, and other exercises. The cognitive dissonance created by coming out against the thin ideal is expected to motivate these young women to stop pursuing thinness as their goal.

In an intervention study with 306 adolescent girls who had body image concerns, the researchers compared a school-based version of their cognitive dissonance program with an educational brochure on eating disorders. The program proved effective in reducing internalization of the thin ideal and, in turn, reducing body dissatisfaction, dieting efforts, and eating disorder symptoms. An Internet-based version of the program and group sessions led by peer leaders have also proven effective with both high school and college students (Stice et al., 2012; Stice, Becker, & Yokum, 2013). The program even results in neural responses assessed through fMRI that suggest less valuing of thin models as compared to average-weight models (Stice, Yokum, & Waters, 2015). Here, then, an ounce of prevention may be worth at least a pound of cure.

What can be done for individuals who develop eating disorders? Effective treatment of individuals who have anorexia typically starts with behavior modification designed to bring their eating behavior under control, help them gain weight, and deal with any medical problems they may have, in a hospital or treatment facility if necessary (Patel, Pratt, & Greydanus, 2003). Then it is possible to move on to such options as psychotherapy designed to help them understand and gain control of their problem and medication for depression and related psychological problems (see Grilo & Mitchell, 2010).

Family therapy approaches appear to be more effective in the long run than individual treatment (Couturier, Kimber, & Szatmari, 2013). In the well-regarded Maudsley Hospital approach developed in London, the goal is to involve parents and other family members as part of the treatment team, help them respond more constructively to the patient's eating behavior in order to facilitate weight gain, and once weight is under control, help them focus on broader family or individual issues such as the adolescent's need for more autonomy (Blessitt, Voulgari, & Eisler, 2015; Hurst, Read, & Wallis, 2012).

Substance Use Disorders

She lost count of the vodka shots. It was New Year's Eve . . ., and for this high school freshman, it was time to party. She figured she'd be able to sleep it off—she'd done it before. But by the time she got home the next day, her head was still pounding, her mouth was dry, and she couldn't focus. This time, the symptoms were obvious even to her parents. After that night, she realized the weekend buzzes had gone from being a maybe to a must. (Aratani, 2008, p. C1)

One of the ways in which some adolescents explore their identities, strive for peer acceptance, and reach toward adulthood is by experimenting with smoking, drinking, and drug use. For some, like this high school freshman (and Peggy at the start of the chapter), substance use moves beyond experimentation to abuse. In DSM-5 language, **substance use disorders** occur when a person continues to use a substance, whether alcohol, marijuana, or something else, despite adverse consequences such as putting the individual in physically dangerous situations, interfering with performance in school or at work, or contributing to interpersonal problems. People with substance use disorders may crave a substance or substances, be unable to control their use of substances or quit, develop an increased tolerance for a substance, and experience withdrawal symptoms if use is terminated.

The tolls of substance use disorders on development can be heavy. As noted in Chapter 5, for example, teens under the influence of alcohol are likely to make additional risky choices that can have negative consequences for themselves or others: smoking, having risky sex, driving under the influence, getting into fights, and engaging in illegal behavior, for example. Concerns also include effects of drinking, especially binge drinking, on the nervous system during a period of important brain development when the brain is vulnerable to being rewired in ways that make negative effects on cognitive abilities and future addiction more likely (Conrod & Nikolaou, 2016; Lisdahl et al., 2013; Spear, 2015). Similar evidence of negative effects of marijuana on brain development, cognitive functioning, and motivation in adolescence is emerging (Volkow et al., 2016). Indeed, both heavy alcohol use and heavy marijuana use in adolescence have negative impacts on occupational and financial success and the quality of interpersonal relationships in adulthood (Cerdá et al., 2016; Chassin et al., 2010; Volkow et al., 2016).

Substance Use Rates

Just how widespread is substance use in adolescence? For years, the Monitoring the Future study has tracked rates (Johnston et al.,

2016). The percentages of adolescents at various grade levels who reported in 2015 that they had used different substances are shown in ■ **Figure 16.3**. These percentages are not as high as those reported in the 1970s and early 1980s, but they indicate that some experimentation with alcohol and marijuana is quite common and increases with age.

Alcohol has long been the most widely used substance. By 12th grade (age 17 or 18), about two thirds of teens have had a drink, and 17% report binge drinking in the past 2 weeks—drinking five or more drinks on one occasion (Johnston et al., 2016). Binge drinking is an even more serious problem among college students; about 35% reported binge drinking in the two weeks before they were surveyed (Johnston et al., 2015). The risk of brain damage and even death from this kind of drinking to get drunk, especially for teens, is real. One emergency room physician put it this way: "We're seeing kids coming in with blood alcohol levels in the mid-.3s, even .4, which is four to five times the legal limit for driving. That's the level at which 50% of people die" (Listfield, 2011, p. 7).

Males have traditionally had higher rates of substance use and abuse than females, but the gap has narrowed over the years (Johnston et al., 2016). Ethnic differences in substance use are also evident: Native American youth have high rates of use, Hispanic white and non-Hispanic white youth have medium rates, and Asian American and African American youth have the lowest rates (Johnston et al., 2016; Woo & Keatinge, 2008).

Binge drinking is common among both high school and college students; for some, it leads to substance use disorder.

Image Source/Getty Images

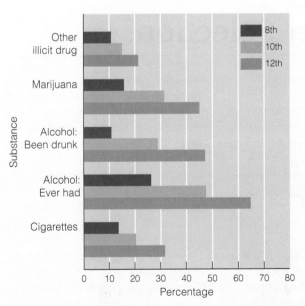

■ **Figure 16.3** Percentages of adolescents in grades 8, 10, and 12 who report ever using various substances. Alcohol use and marijuana use are common and increase with age. The other illicit drugs besides marijuana that were studied, such as cocaine, heroin, and amphetamines, have each been tried by under 10% of the adolescents.

Source: Johnston, L.D., O'Malley, P. M., Miech, R. A., Bachman, J. G., & Schulenberg, J. E. (2016). *Monitoring the Future national survey results on drug use 1975–2015: Overview, key findings on adolescent drug use.* Ann Arbor: Institute for Social Research, The University of Michigan; data are from Table 5, pp. 58–63. Retrieved from: www.monitoringthefuture.org/pubs/monographs/mtf-overview2015.pdf.

A Cascade of Contributors

It is now evident that the developmental pathway to adolescent substance use and abuse begins in childhood. A major study by Kenneth Dodge and others (2009) attempted to integrate what is known about contributors to the use of illicit drugs in adolescence in a cascade model of substance use. Similar cascade models have been formulated to help account for the development of a variety of problems (Dodge et al., 2008; Masten et al., 2005; and see Chapter 13 on aggression). A cascade model is a transactional, multifactor model that envisions development as a flow of water over a series of waterfalls, gaining momentum as it goes, as each influence along the way helps realize the previous factors and contributes to the next influence in the chain of influence. Dodge's cascade of substance use begins with:

1. a child who is at risk due to a difficult temperament, born into
2. an adverse family environment characterized by such problems as poverty, stress, and substance use, who is
3. exposed to harsh parenting and family conflict, and therefore develops
4. behavior problems, especially aggression and conduct problems, and therefore is
5. rejected by peers and gets into more trouble at school, so that
6. parents give up trying to monitor and supervise their now difficult-to-control adolescent, which contributes to
7. involvement in a deviant peer group, where the adolescent is exposed to and reinforced for drug taking and other deviant behavior.

The cascade model was tested in a longitudinal study that entailed annual assessments of 585 children from prekindergarten through 12th grade. Substance use was measured in grade 7 to grade 12 as any use of marijuana, inhalants, cocaine, heroin, or another illicit drug. Use clearly increased with age, from 5% in grade 7 to 22% in grade 10 to 51% in grade 12. The seven groups of factors in the cascade model each predicted both the next step in the cascade and involvement in substance use. All in all, the model captures well the developmental concept that adolescent problem behaviors and psychological disorders do not spring out of nowhere. Instead, they grow out of the accumulating effects of transactions between an individual and parents, peers, and other aspects of the social environment over many years. The model points to the possible value of substance abuse prevention programs targeting at-risk children long before adolescence. Although it becomes harder to stop the cascade toward substance use as the years go by, there are new opportunities to intervene at each step. We know that preventive interventions to delay drinking and drug use in adolescence can head off problematic substance use in adulthood (Spoth et al., 2009; and see Sloboda, 2009).

How can this cascade model be improved? Many explanations of substance use and abuse put more emphasis on genetics. Because of their genes, some individuals are more vulnerable to substance abuse as well as to the effects of environmental influences described in the cascade model (Dick, Prescott, & McGue, 2009; Sartor et al., 2010). Moreover, what we often assume are peer socialization effects on substance use (effects of friends on an adolescent's substance use) need to be studied more closely, as they could instead be peer selection effects (effects of an adolescent's substance use tendencies, possibly genetically based, on whether she chooses drinking or nondrinking friends). As **Exploration 16.1** illustrates, this peer socialization/peer selection issue is important in gauging whether peers truly influence us. In the end, alcohol and drug abuse are the developmental outcomes of interactions among many genes and a cascade of many environmental factors.

Depression and Suicidal Behavior

Before puberty, boys and girls have similarly low rates of depression; after puberty, rates climb, and the rate of depression for females becomes twice that of males in adolescence and adulthood—in our society and in others (Garber, 2010). In one study of female adolescents, the rate of major depressive disorder at some time in the individual's life was 1% among girls younger than age 12 but 17% among young women age 19 and older (Glowinski et al., 2003). Adolescent depression looks more like adult depression, with cognitive symptoms such as hopelessness (Garber, 2010; Mendle, 2014). However, depressed adolescents sometimes act out and look more like delinquents than like

● EXPLORATION 16.1

Peer Socialization or Peer Selection?

If we don't blame adolescent problem behaviors on bad parenting, we tend to blame them on negative peer influences. We say, for example, that someone got into trouble with alcohol and drugs because she got in with the "wrong crowd." But are similarities between adolescents and their friends in, say, alcohol use the result of peer socialization (peer influence on adolescents) or peer selection (the tendency of adolescents to choose friends who are like themselves, whether they are heavy drinkers or teetotalers). Much tells us that peer selection is a real phenomenon—that birds of a feather flock together. And often both socialization and selection are at work in adolescent substance use (Cruz, Emery, & Turkheimer, 2012; Hill et al., 2008; Simons-Morton & Farhat, 2010).

Using the twin study approach, for example, Jennifer Cruz and her colleagues (2012) established that the level of alcohol use in an adolescent's peer network predicted changes over time in the adolescent's

drinking, even with genetic factors controlled. In fact, when identical twins differed in their drinking habits, the twin whose peer group drank a lot drank more than the twin whose peer group drank less—solid evidence of a true peer socialization effect. At the same time, there was evidence that certain teens, due to a genetic predisposition to drink, chose drinking friends more often than other teens did—support for the selection hypothesis.

Here, then, is another illustration of the need to take genes into account before jumping to conclusions about environmental (whether parent or peer) influence on development. It appears that an adolescent's substance use can indeed be influenced by friends' use of substances—but that to establish that we have to rule out the fact that an adolescent's genetic makeup influences who that adolescent selects as friends.

The same peer socialization/peer selection issue arises in studying peer influence on

other psychological disorders. For example, studies suggest that hanging out with weight-conscious friends leads to disordered eating attitudes and behavior. But does it? Recent studies of adolescent female twins suggest that girls select friends with levels of weight consciousness similar to their own and that much of what looked like peer socialization influence in previous studies may reflect peer selection at least as much as peer socialization (O'Connor et al., 2016; VanHuysse et al., 2016). Similarly, researchers find that yes, adolescents who affiliate with antisocial peers develop externalizing problems but that having externalizing problems also results in selecting antisocial friends (Samek et al., 2016). In short, to fully understand peer influences on psychopathology and development more generally, we must grapple repeatedly with the peer socialization/peer selection issue. Both processes often seem to be at work: We select friends who are like us and then become even more like them due to their influence on us.

victims of depression. They also may show more "vegetative" symptoms such as lacking energy and sleeping all the time.

Factors in Depression

Why is adolescence a depressing period for some? For one thing, genetic influences on depression seem to become more powerful after puberty than they were in childhood (Conley & Rudolph, 2009; Ge et al., 2003; Scourfield et al., 2003). For example, in one study, a gene–environment interaction—a combination of risky variants of the *5-HTTLPR* gene associated with difficulty handling stress and interpersonal stress such as a lack of friends plus conflict-ridden relationships—pushed adolescents, but not children, to depression (Hankin et al., 2015).

As it turns out, girls are more likely than boys to experience an accumulation of stressful events in early adolescence (Ge et al., 1994; Mezulis et al., 2011). Experiencing such events—especially interpersonal ones such as relationship break-ups and fights with family or friends—predicts increases in depressive symptoms (Ge, Natsuaki, & Conger, 2006; Hamilton et al., 2015). The greater interpersonal stress experienced by girls also contributes to their being more likely than boys to engage in **ruminative coping**, dwelling unproductively on their problems, often by co-ruminating about their woes with their friends (Hamilton et al., 2015; ; Nolen-Hoeksema, 1990; Rose, Carlson & Waller, 2007). Compared to coping tactics favored by boys, such as distraction and active problem solving, ruminative coping and co-rumination can make depression and anxiety worse. Indeed, heavy reliance on ruminative coping is now viewed as a risk factor not only for depression but for anxiety, substance use, and eating disorders (Nolen-Hoeksema & Watkins, 2011; Nolen-Hoeksema et al., 2007).

Suicidal Behavior

As depression becomes more common from childhood to adolescence, so do suicidal thoughts, suicide attempts, and actual suicides. Individuals with major depression are more likely to make suicide attempts during adolescence than before or after (Rohde et al., 2013). Indeed, suicide is the second leading cause of death for 15- to 24-year-olds, behind accidental injuries and ahead of assaults or homicides (Heron, 2016). For every adolescent suicide, there are many unsuccessful attempts. Suicidal thoughts are even more common (Shaffer & Pfeffer, 2001). Almost 12% of male and 19% of female high school students in the United States seriously considered suicide in the past year; 6% of males and almost 10% of females attempted it (Eaton et al., 2012).

Before you conclude that adolescence is the peak time for suicidal behavior, however, consider the suicide rates for different age groups shown in ■ **Figure 16.4**. It is clear that adults are more likely to commit suicide than adolescents are. The suicide rate for non-Hispanic white women peaks in middle age, and the

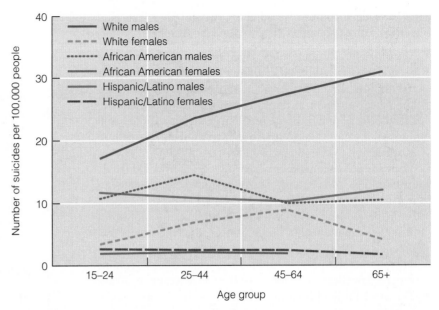

■ **Figure 16.4** Number of suicides per 100,000 people by age and sex among European Americans, African Americans, and Hispanic Americans in the United States.

Source: National Center for Health Statistics (2016). *Health, United States, 2015. With special feature on racial and ethnic health disparities*. Hyattsville, MD: U.S. Department of Health and Human Services, Centers for Disease Control and Prevention, National Center for Health Statistics. Retrieved from www.cdc.gov/nchs/hus.htm.

suicide rate for non-Hispanic white men peaks in old age and is considerably higher than that of other groups. Rates for minority group members, especially minority females, are very low by comparison.

Overall, males are more likely to commit suicide than females, by a ratio of at least three to one—a difference that holds up across most cultures studied (Girard, 1993; Shaffer & Pfeffer, 2001). When we look at suicide attempts, this ratio is reversed, with females leading males by a ratio of about three to one. Apparently, then, females attempt suicide more often than males do, but males more often commit suicide when they try. This is mainly because men use more lethal techniques (especially guns).

Suicide rates are very much influenced by their sociohistorical context. In the United States, they decreased from 1986 to 1999 but have increased since then (Curtin, Warner, & Hedegaard, 2016). The recent increases have been especially steep among middle-aged women and men, possibly because the 2008 economic recession hit them hard.

If suicide rates are higher in adulthood than in adolescence, why do we hear so much about teenage suicide? Probably because adolescents attempt suicide more frequently than adults do. The typical adolescent suicide attempt has been characterized as a "cry for help"—a desperate effort to get others to notice and help resolve problems that have become unbearable (Berman & Jobes, 1991; Lester, 1994). The adolescent who attempts suicide often wants a better life rather than death. This by no means suggests that adolescent suicide attempts should be taken lightly. Their message is clear: "I've got serious problems; wake up and help me!"

Suicidal behavior in adolescence is the product of diathesis–stress. Four key risk factors are youth psychological disorder, family pathology and psychopathology, stressful life events, and access to firearms (Gould et al., 2003; and see Beautrais, 2003):

- More than 90% of adolescent suicide victims, partly because of genetic predisposition, suffered from depression, a substance-use disorder, an anxiety disorder, or another diagnosable psychological problem at the time of their deaths (Shaffer & Pfeffer, 2001). And the more problem behaviors an adolescent displays, the more likely she is to go from thinking suicidally to taking action (Miller & Taylor, 2005).
- Many suicide attempters also have histories of troubled family relationships, and often psychopathology and even suicide run in the family.
- In the period leading up to a suicide attempt, the adolescent has often experienced a buildup of stressful life events that breeds a sense of helplessness—deteriorating relationships with parents and peers, academic and social failures, run-ins with the law (Berman & Jobes, 1991; Woo & Keatinge, 2008).
- The availability of firearms makes it easy to act on suicidal impulses.

Engagement 16.2 shows some of the behavioral warning signs that can help you recognize that someone you know may be planning to commit suicide and needs help. The adolescent who attempts suicide once may try again if he receives little help (Rotheram-Borus et al., 2000). Although, as we have seen, adolescence is not a time of "storm and stress" for most, it is a period in which biological, psychological, and social influences can conspire to make several mental health problems more likely.

Checking Mastery

1. What does the fact that 20% or so of adolescents have diagnosable psychological disorders say for and against the notion that adolescence is a period of storm and stress?
2. How does the sociocultural environment contribute to anorexia nervosa?
3. Judging from the cascade model of substance use, what are three factors you might look for if you want to identify children who are at risk for illicit drug use when they become adolescents?
4. How do males and females differ with respect to (a) suicide attempts and (b) completed suicides?

Making Connections

1. How would you characterize your own mental health during adolescence? Consider whether the concept of "storm and stress," as well as adolescent problem behaviors and specific diagnoses we have discussed in this section, apply to you.
2. Peggy, the young woman described at the beginning of the chapter, attempted suicide. Using the material on suicide in this section, develop a theory of why she might have done so, showing how both diathesis and stress may have contributed.

● ENGAGEMENT 16.2

Is Anyone You Know Suicidal? Know the Warning Signs

Do you have any friends, relatives, or acquaintances who you think might be suicidal? If so, see if they show the following warning signs of suicidality in young people, compiled by a committee of suicide experts (Rudd et al., 2006) and disseminated by the U.S. government's Substance Abuse and Mental Health Services Administration (SAMHSA, 2012):

Call 9-1-1 or seek immediate help from a mental health provider when you hear, say, or see any one of these behaviors:

- Someone threatening to hurt or kill themselves

- Someone looking for ways to kill themselves: seeking access to pills, weapons, or other means
- Someone talking or writing about death, dying, or suicide

Seek help by contacting a mental health professional or calling 1-800-273-TALK for a referral should you witness, hear, or see anyone exhibiting any one or more of these behaviors:

- Hopelessness
- Rage, anger, seeking revenge
- Acting reckless or engaging in risky activities, seemingly without thinking

- Feeling trapped—like there's no way out
- Increasing alcohol or drug use
- Withdrawing from friends, family, or society
- Anxiety, agitation, unable to sleep, or sleeping all the time
- Dramatic changes in mood
- No reason for living; no sense of purpose in life

Source: Rudd, M. D., Berman, A. L, Joiner, T. E. Jr., Nock, M. K., Silverman, M. M., Mandrusiak, M., . . . Witte, T. (2006). Warning signs for suicide: Theory, research, and clinical applications. *Suicide and Life-Threatening Behavior*, 36 (3), Table 2, p. 259.

As you have seen, by the time we reach adulthood, most of us have already had at least one diagnosable psychological disorder, whether it was recognized and treated or not (Copeland et al., 2011). Most adult psychological disorders originate in childhood or adolescence, but rates and forms of disorder change over the adult years.

Stress and Disorder

Many psychological problems in adulthood emerge when a vulnerable individual faces overwhelming stress. When do adults typically experience the greatest number of life strains and stressors? No question about it: in early adulthood (Almeida et al., 2011; McLanahan & Sorensen, 1985; Pearlin, 1980). Life strains decrease from early to middle adulthood, perhaps as many adults settle into more stable lifestyles and stop changing residences, jobs, and relationships so much. Meanwhile, despite their increased health problems, elderly adults report fewer hassles and strains overall than middle-aged adults do (Almeida & Horn, 2004; Martin, Grunendahl, & Martin, 2001). This may be because they have fewer roles and responsibilities to juggle or because they have learned to take many problems in stride.

Age differences in stressful experiences help explain age differences in rates of psychological disorder. Diagnostic interviews with adults age 18 or older in the United States reveal that rates of affective disorders (major depression and related mood disorders), alcohol abuse and dependence, schizophrenia, anxiety disorders, and antisocial personality all decrease from early adulthood to late adulthood (Myers et al., 1984; Robins & Regier, 1991). The only category of disorder that increases with age is cognitive impairment, as increasing numbers of older adults develop Alzheimer's disease and other forms of dementia (to be described shortly). Overall, about 25% of American adults are judged in clinical interviews to have experienced a psychological disorder in the past year (Kessler & Wang, 2008).

With that as background, we can look more closely at one of the disorders to which young adults are especially susceptible, depression, and then turn to an examination of Alzheimer's disease and related cognitive impairments in later life.

Depression

Major depression and other affective disorders are among the most common psychological problems experienced by adults. Who gets depressed, and what does this reveal?

Age, Gender, and Ethnic Differences

The average age of onset of major depression is in the early 20s (Woo & Keatinge, 2008). Contrary to stereotypes of older adults, they tend to be less vulnerable to major depression and other severe affective disorders than young or middle-aged adults are (Hybels, Blazer, & Hays, 2009, Kessler et al., 2010). Still, there are good reasons to be concerned about depression in old age. First, depressed elderly adults are more likely than depressed adolescents to take their own lives. Second, reports of depression symptoms, though not diagnosable disorders, increase when people reach their 70s and beyond (Nguyen & Zonderman, 2006; Teachman, 2006). Although only about 1%–2% of elderly adults have major depressive disorder at a given time, somewhere between 15% and 25% experience symptoms of depression (Hybels et al., 2009; Knight et al., 2006). These individuals are most likely to be very old women who are physically ill, poor, and socially isolated, and many could benefit from treatment (Blazer, 1993; Falcon & Tucker, 2000).

Might some of these mildly depressed and demoralized elders have a more serious but undiagnosed depressive disorder? It's quite possible. Depression can be difficult to diagnose in later life (Charney et al., 2003; Edelstein et al., 2015). Think about it: Symptoms of depression include fatigue and lack of energy, sleeping difficulties, weight loss, cognitive deficits, and somatic (body) complaints. What if an 80-year-old woman and/or her doctor interpret these symptoms as nothing more than aging, as the result of the chronic illnesses so common in old age or medications for them, or as signs of dementia? A case of depression could be missed. To complicate diagnosis, elderly adults sometimes deny that they are sad, guilty, or suicidal and may instead report the very somatic symptoms that can easily be misinterpreted as signs of physical illness if the individual's physical health status is not carefully reviewed (Edelstein et al., 2015; Nguyen & Zonderman, 2006). So clinicians working with older adults need to be sensitive to the lines between normal aging, physical disease, and psychopathology.

As noted already, women are twice as likely as men to be diagnosed with depression. This gender difference probably stems from a variety of factors (Kuehner, 2003; Nolen-Hoeksema, 2002): female hormones and biological reactions to stress; levels of stress (including more interpersonal stress among women); ways of expressing distress (women being more likely to express classic depression symptoms, men being more likely to become angry

Although few elderly adults have diagnosed depression, a sizable minority experiences at least some symptoms of depression.

Mark Richards/PhotoEdit

or overindulge in alcohol and drugs); and styles of coping with distress (especially the tendency for women to engage in counterproductive ruminative coping).

Ethnic differences in depression are also evident. In a national study of adults age 55 and older (Woodward et al., 2012), the percentages of adults who had been affected by mood disorders, including major depressive disorder, during their lifetime were quite high for Latinos (13.9%) and non-Hispanic Whites (13.8%), and much lower for African Americans (5.4%) and Asian Americans (6.4%). Possibly elderly Latino adults who are recent immigrants to the United States feel socially isolated and stressed as younger members of their families become acculturated (Jimenez et al., 2010). Older African Americans who are religious may be protected from depression by their religious faith and the social support they receive through their churches (Jimenez et al., 2010). African Americans are also more likely than other groups to go undiagnosed and untreated when they are depressed (Akincigil et al., 2012). Older Asian Americans may also be underdiagnosed; for example, they tend to view mental illness in terms of somatic symptoms and may be hesitant to admit that they have psychological problems or seek help for them (Jimenez et al., 2010; Sue et al., 2012). Whatever the reasons, we can expect rates of depression to be highest among young adults, females, and both Hispanic and non-Hispanic whites.

Treatment

One of the biggest challenges in treating adults with major depression and other psychological disorders is getting them to seek treatment; many eventually do but often after going years without help (Wang et al., 2005). Older adults are especially likely to go undiagnosed and untreated, particularly if they are minority group members (Karel, Gatz, & Smyer, 2012; Neighbors et al., 2007). Meanwhile, few psychologists and psychiatrists are specially trained to treat a growing global population of older adults.

Despite these barriers, depressed elderly adults who seek psychotherapy or begin taking antidepressant medications benefit (Edelstein et al., 2015). For older and younger depressed adults alike, the most effective approach is often a combination of drug treatment and psychotherapy, especially cognitive behavioral therapy aimed at addressing carefully identified problems.

Aging and Dementia

Perhaps nothing scares us more about aging than the thought that we will become "senile." Dementia is a progressive deterioration of neural functioning associated with cognitive decline—for example, memory impairment, declines in tested intellectual ability, poor judgment, difficulty thinking abstractly, and often personality changes as well (see La Rue, 2015; Lyketsos, 2009). The term dementia has been dropped from DSM-5 in favor of the term "neurocognitive disorder," although we will continue to refer to dementia here. Different causes of neurocognitive disorder such as Alzheimer's disease are distinguished as subtypes, and each has "major" and "minor," or more and less severe, forms (American Psychiatric Association, 2013; Bajenaru et al., 2012).

Developing dementia is not part of typical aging. Yet rates of dementia increase steadily with age, making old age the biggest risk factor for dementia. Overall, dementia affects up to 10% of adults age 65 and older (Karel et al., 2012). Rates climb steeply with age, as shown in ■ Figure 16.5—from less than 2% at age 65–69 to over 35% at age 90 and older.

Dementia is not a single disorder. Much damage can be done by labeling any older person with cognitive impairments senile—or even as having Alzheimer's disease—and then assuming that he is a lost cause. Many different conditions can produce symptoms we associate with senility, and some of them are curable or reversible. Let us look at the leading cause of dementia, Alzheimer's disease, and then at related conditions.

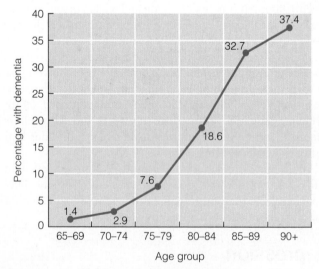

■ **Figure 16.5** Percentage of older adults with dementia by age group.

Source: Data compiled by Karel, M. J., Gatz, M., & Smyer, M. A. (2012). Aging and mental health in the decade ahead: What psychologists need to know. *American Psychologist, 67*, 184–198, Table 1, p. 186.

Alzheimer's Disease

With Alzheimer's disease, you just know you're going to forget things, and it's impossible to put things where you can't forget them because people like me can always find a place to lose things and we have to flurry all over the house to figure where in the heck I left whatever it was. . . . It's usually my glasses. . . . You've got to have a sense of humor in this kind of business, and I think it's interesting how many places I can find to lose things. . . . [People with Alzheimer's] want things like they used to be. And we just hate the fact that we cannot be what we used to be. It hurts like hell. (Cary Henderson, age 64, former history professor diagnosed with Alzheimer's disease at age 55; Rovner, 1994, pp. 12–13)

Alzheimer's disease is the most common subtype of dementia, or major neurocognitive disorder, accounting for over half the cases, including those of former president Ronald Reagan and, more recently, famed women's basketball coach Pat Summitt, who died of it in 2016 (Castro & Smith, 2015; Geldmacher, 2009; Qui & Fratiglioni, 2009). The disease can strike in middle age but becomes increasingly likely with advancing age, and it affects about twice as many women as men, partly because they live longer. Because more people are living into advanced old age, more will end up with Alzheimer's disease unless ways of preventing it or slowing its progression are found.

Alzheimer's disease leaves two telltale signs in the brain: *senile plaques* (masses of dying neural material outside neurons with a toxic protein called beta-amyloid at their core), and *neurofibrillary tangles* (twisted strands made of neural fibers and the protein tau within the bodies of neural cells). The effects of these physical changes—loss of connections between neurons, deterioration and death of neurons, increasingly impaired mental functioning, and personality changes—are progressive and irreversible or incurable. The disease typically begins to affect the brain in middle adulthood, maybe earlier, long before cognitive functioning is affected and even longer before the disease is diagnosed. The first noticeable symptoms of Alzheimer's, detectable 2–3 years before dementia can be diagnosed, are usually difficulties remembering recently encountered material such as new acquaintances' names or yesterday's lunch menu (Geldmacher, 2009).

The individual on a path to Alzheimer's may be recognized as having *mild cognitive impairment (MCI)*, discussed in Chapter 8. MCI is often—though not always—an early warning that dementia will follow (Castro & Smith, 2015). Similar to what is now called minor neurocognitive disorder in DSM-5, it is more serious than the slower cognitive functioning and minor memory problems common among typically aging adults. If all it took to warrant a diagnosis of MCI or dementia were occasional episodes of misplacing keys or being unable to remember someone's name, many young and middle-aged adults, not to mention textbook writers, would qualify!

In the early stages of Alzheimer's disease, warning signs include getting lost, having trouble managing money and paying bills, telling and retelling the same stories to the same people or repeatedly asking the same questions, and losing items but not being able to retrace one's steps to find them. As the disorder progresses, people

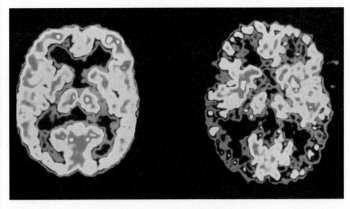

Positron emission tomography (PET scanning) shows metabolic activity in the brain and reveals areas of high brain activity (in red and yellow) and low brain activity (in blue or black). Here we see more activity in a normally functioning brain (*left*) than in the brain of a person with Alzheimer's disease (*right*).

Dr. Robert Friedland/Science Source

with Alzheimer's may have trouble remembering not only recently acquired but old information, have more trouble coming up with the words they want during conversations, and forget what to do next midway through making a sandwich or getting ready for bed. If tested, they may be unable to answer simple questions about where they are, what the date is, and who the president of the United States is. Eventually they become incapable of caring for themselves; no longer recognize loved ones; lose all verbal abilities; and die some years after they are diagnosed.

Not only do patients with Alzheimer's disease become increasingly unable to function, but they also often test the patience of caregivers by forgetting they have left something cooking on the stove, wandering away and getting lost, accusing people of stealing the items they have misplaced, or taking off their clothes in public. Some become highly agitated and uncontrollable; large numbers suffer from depression and become apathetic; and some experience psychotic symptoms such as hallucinations (Geldmacher, 2009).

Causes and Contributors. What causes Alzheimer's disease? It has a genetic basis, but there is no single "Alzheimer's gene" (Gatz, 2007). Alzheimer's disease strikes repeatedly and early in some families, and researchers have identified genetic mutations on three chromosomes that cause early-onset Alzheimer's disease (before age 60). Anyone who inherits just one of these dominant genes will develop the disease. However, these genes account for less than 5% of all cases of Alzheimer's disease (Gatz, 2007).

Genetic contributors to late-onset Alzheimer's disease, which is by far more common than the early-onset variety, are not as clear-cut. Rather than making Alzheimer's disease inevitable, a large number of genes increase a person's risk slightly (Gatz, 2007; National Institute on Aging, 2015). *APOE e4* is the most famous of these susceptibility genes; having two of the risk-inducing *APOE e4* variants of the *APOE* gene means having up to 15 times the normal risk of Alzheimer's disease (Lyketsos, 2009). It is believed that the *APOE e4* gene is linked to an increased buildup of beta-amyloid—the damaging substance in senile plaques—and speeds the progression of Alzheimer's disease (National Institute on Aging, 2015). Yet not everyone with the *APOE e4* gene, or even a pair of them, develops Alzheimer's disease, and many people with Alzheimer's disease lack this risky gene variant.

Overall, genes account for about 60% of the variation in Alzheimer's, which means that environmental factors are also involved (Qui & Fratiglioni, 2009). It has not been easy to pinpoint environmental contributors, however (Gatz, 2007). Epigenetic effects—environmental influences on the expression of genes involved in beta-amyloid production, for example—are now believed to be important (Chouliaras et al., 2010; National Institute on Aging, 2015). Traumatic brain injuries, such as those suffered by some boxers and football and soccer players, increase the risk of Alzheimer's disease, especially in combination with risky genes such as *APOE e4* (Delano-Wood et al., 2015). Other risk factors include unhealthy lifestyle factors such as a poor diet, smoking, and inactivity—and conditions linked with them such as obesity, diabetes, high blood pressure, and cardiovascular disease (La Rue, 2015).

Researchers are also becoming more aware of the importance of **cognitive reserve**—extra brain power or cognitive capacity that some people can fall back on as aging and disease begin to take a toll on brain functioning (Delano-Wood et al., 2015; Sharp & Gatz, 2011). People who have advanced education and high intelligence and have been mentally, physically, and socially active over the years have more cognitive reserve than less active people. As a result, if they do develop Alzheimer's disease, their more elaborate neural connections may allow them to continue functioning well even as the disease begins to damage their brains.

Prevention and Treatment. What can be done to prevent, or at least slow the progression of, and treat Alzheimer's disease? Since the same lifestyle factors that contribute to cardiovascular disease and to metabolic disorders such as diabetes and obesity contribute to dementia as well, the same healthy lifestyle recommendations are appropriate in staving off Alzheimer's disease: eat a healthy diet, control smoking, exercise regularly (La Rue, 2015). Physical exercise—and cognitive exercise as well—can delay cognitive decline in later life and slow the progression of dementia (Hertzog et al., 2009; La Rue, 2015). Researchers are searching frantically for more precise methods of diagnosing Alzheimer's disease earlier, through brain imaging and biomarkers in the blood or cerebrospinal fluid, in hopes of intervening to slow or even halt the disease's progression before much damage is done (National Institute on Aging, 2015). While we wait, the best advice is to take good care of your health throughout the life span.

Drugs are regularly prescribed for individuals who have Alzheimer's disease (for example, Aricept [donepezil] to alter neurotransmitter levels and Namenda [memantine]) to combat amyloid plaques. Drugs can modestly improve cognitive functioning, reduce behavioral problems, and slow the progression of the disease in some patients (Castro & Smith, 2015; La Rue, 2015). However, they are not very effective and are certainly not a cure. The search for more effective drugs continues (National Institute on Aging, 2015).

However, even though deterioration leading to death must be expected in today's Alzheimer's patients, a great deal can be done to make the disease more bearable for them and their caregivers.

This woman with Alzheimer's disease is visited by her grandson.

Ocskaymark/Getty Images

Memory training and memory aids (for example, reminder notes around the house), the use of behavioral management techniques and medications to deal with behavioral problems, and educational programs and psychological interventions for both patients and their caregivers to help them understand and cope with dementia and function better can all contribute (La Rue, 2015).

Other Causes of Cognitive Impairment

Many other conditions can result in cognitive impairment in aging adults. Another common type of neurocognitive disorder, often occurring in combination with Alzheimer's disease, is **vascular dementia** (Nyenhuis, 2015; Szoeke et al., 2009). Also called multi-infarct dementia, most cases are caused by a series of minor strokes that cut off the blood supply to areas of the brain. Whereas Alzheimer's disease usually progresses slowly and steadily, vascular dementia often progresses in a steplike manner, with further deterioration after each small stroke. And whereas Alzheimer's disease is more strongly influenced by genes, vascular dementia is more closely associated with lifestyle risk factors for cerebrovascular diseases that affect blood flow in the brain.

Rivaling vascular dementia as the second or third most common type of neurocognitive disorder behind Alzheimer's disease is **Lewy body dementia**, which involves fluctuations in cognitive functioning, visual hallucinations, and often motor and balance problems (Sperling, Geneser, & Manning, 2015). It is caused by protein deposits in neurons called Lewy bodies, which are also involved in Parkinson's disease. Some other causes of neurocognitive disorder are described in ● **Table 16.1**. Patients may have more than one of these diagnoses.

Careful diagnosis is critical because certain treatable conditions can be mistaken for irreversible dementia. First, some individuals—as many as 10%—have **reversible dementias**, cases of significant cognitive decline that can be treated and cured (La Rue, 2015; Lipton & Weiner, 2003). Reversible dementias can be caused by alcoholism, toxic reactions to medication, infections,

Comedian and actor Robin Williams, who committed suicide in 2014 at the age of 63, had recently been diagnosed with Parkinson's disease and may have been in the early stage of dementia—either Parkinson's disease dementia or dementia with Lewy bodies (Porcher, 2014). Both are associated with the presence of protein deposits called Lewy bodies in the brain (Porcher, 2014). Williams was experiencing depression, anxiety, and paranoia at the time of his death—symptoms that often accompany both types of dementia.

Vera Anderson/WireImage/Getty Images

● **Table 16.1** Some Common Forms and Causes of Dementia, or Neurocognitive Disorder, Besides Alzheimer's Disease

Name	Description
Vascular dementia	Also called multi-infarct dementia. Caused by minor strokes that cut off blood supply to areas of the brain; results in steplike deterioration after each stroke; functioning depends on location and extent of brain damage.
Lewy body dementia	May be as common as vascular dementia. Caused by protein deposits called Lewy bodies in neurons. Motor problems, as in Parkinson's disease; visual hallucinations, attention and alertness problems, unpredictable cognitive functioning.
Frontotemporal dementia	Early-onset dementia associated with shrinking of the frontal and temporal lobes. Executive function problems (e.g., impulsive behavior) and poor judgment are more common than memory problems. The best known type is Pick's disease.
Parkinson's disease dementia	Lewy bodies in subcortical areas of the brain contribute to motor problems (tremors, slowing/freezing while walking); treatment of Parkinson's disease with the drug L-dopa to make up for dopamine deficiency is effective, but some patients go on to develop what is called Parkinson's disease dementia in the later stages.
Huntington's disease	Caused by a single dominant gene (see Chapter 3). Subcortical brain damage results in involuntary flicking movement of the arms and legs; hallucinations, paranoia, depression, personality changes.
Alcohol-related dementia	Caused by alcohol abuse; memory problems are the primary symptom in what is called Wernicke–Korsakoff's syndrome.
AIDS dementia complex or ADC	Caused by HIV virus infection. Encephalitis, behavioral changes, decline in cognitive function, progressive slowing of motor functions.

Note: The first two conditions in the table are the most common causes of dementia besides Alzheimer's disease; the rest are rarer.

Sources: La Rue (2015); www.alz.org/dementia/types-of-dementia.asp; www.dementiacarecentral.com/node/576; www.ninds.nih.gov/disorders/dementias/detail_dementia.htm#2300219213.

metabolic disorders, vitamin deficiencies, and malnutrition. If these problems are corrected—for example, if the individual is taken off a recently prescribed medicine or is placed on a nutritious diet—a once "senile" person can be restored to normal mental functioning. By contrast, if that same person is written off as a hopeless case of Alzheimer's disease, a potentially curable condition may become a progressively worse and irreversible one.

Second, some elderly adults are mistakenly diagnosed as suffering from dementia when they are actually experiencing delirium. This treatable neurocognitive disorder, which emerges more rapidly than dementia and comes and goes over the course of the day, is a disturbance of consciousness characterized by periods of disorientation, wandering attention, confusion, and

hallucinations (American Psychiatric Association, 2013; Na & Manning, 2015; Weiner et al., 2009). One 66-year-old woman with a history of seizures, for example, called 911 repeatedly because she believed burglars were in her home; in her agitated state, she even threatened her housemate with a knife (Weiner et al., 2009). After she was taken to the hospital, she continued to be highly agitated, moving and talking constantly, not trusting the staff. Her episode of delirium appeared to be the result of a urinary infection combined with early Alzheimer's disease, and she was able to return home after 5 days in the hospital.

Hospital patients of any age—but especially elderly ones—experience delirium in reaction to any number of stressors—illness, surgery, drug overdoses, interactions of drugs, and malnutrition (Na & Manning, 2015). It is critical to watch for signs of delirium, identify possible causes, and intervene to change them quickly. Unfortunately the condition often goes undetected or misdiagnosed. When elderly patients experience delirium but are not identified and are sent home from the hospital without treatment for it, they are at high risk to show worsening dementia or to die (Kakuma et al., 2003; Na & Manning, 2015).

Third, elderly adults who are depressed are sometimes misdiagnosed as suffering from dementia (Edelstein et al., 2015; Butters et al., 2004). After all, depression's symptoms include cognitive impairments such as being forgetful and mentally slow. Treatment of depression with antidepressant drugs and psychotherapy can significantly improve the functioning of such individuals. However, if their depression goes undetected and they are written off as senile, they may deteriorate further.

Fourth, relatives who do not understand dementia may mistake the cognitive declines that many people experience as part of typical aging for incurable dementia. The moral is clear: It is critical to distinguish among irreversible dementias (most notably, Alzheimer's, vascular dementia, and Lewy body dementia), reversible dementias, delirium, depression, and other conditions that may be mistaken for irreversible dementias—including aging itself. This requires a thorough assessment, including a medical history, physical and neurological examinations, and assessments of cognitive functioning (La Rue, 2015). Only after all other causes, especially potentially treatable ones, have been ruled out should a diagnosis of Alzheimer's disease be made.

So ends our tour of psychopathology across the life span. It can be discouraging to read about the countless ways in which genes and environment can conspire to make human development go awry and about the high odds that most of us will experience a psychological disorder sometime during our lives. Yet research provides an increasingly solid basis for intervening to prevent developmental psychopathology through a two-pronged

strategy of eliminating risk factors (such as abusive parenting and stress) and strengthening protective factors (such as effective parenting and social support). If prevention proves impossible, most psychological disorders and developmental problems can be treated successfully, enabling the individual to move onto a healthier developmental pathway.

● Checking Mastery

1. In which adult age group, gender, and ethnic groups would you expect the highest rates of major depressive disorder?

2. How does Alzheimer's disease progress with regard to the timing of plaques and tangles in the brain, cognitive deficits, diagnosable dementia, and death?

3. What are two approaches used to treat Alzheimer's disease?

4. What are two key differences between delirium and dementia?

● Making Connections

1. So now that you have read this whole chapter, what do you think of the DSM-5's position that major depressive disorder is basically the same from early childhood to old age? Argue for the DSM-5 position and then argue against it.

2. Grandpa Fred is starting to display memory problems: Sometimes he asks questions that he just asked, leaves water boiling on the stove, and cannot come up with the names of visiting grandchildren. Fred's son Will is convinced that his father has Alzheimer's disease and is a lost cause. What possibilities would you like to rule out before accepting that conclusion—and why?

Chapter Summary

16.1 What Makes Development Abnormal?

- To diagnose psychological disorders, clinicians may consider broad criteria such as statistical deviance, maladaptiveness, and personal distress and apply DSM-5 criteria to diagnose specific disorders based on their symptoms.

- Developmental psychopathology is concerned with the origins and course of maladaptive behavior and contrasts with a medical or disease model.

- A diathesis–stress model has proved useful in understanding how nature and nurture contribute to many psychological disorders

16.2 The Infant

- Autism spectrum disorder is characterized by social and communication impairments and by restricted and repetitive interests and behavior. It is genetically influenced, involves atypical early

brain growth and connectivity, and responds well to early and intensive behavioral training.

- Infants who have been maltreated, separated from their attachment figures, or raised by a depressed caregiver may display symptoms of depression.

16.3 The Child

- Many childhood disorders can be categorized as externalizing (acting out) or internalizing (bottling up) problems; they are often a product of diathesis–stress, they are common, and externalizing problems especially often predict problems in adolescence and adulthood.

- Attention deficit hyperactivity disorder (ADHD) involves inattention and/or hyperactivity/impulsivity, often continues into adulthood, and can be treated most effectively through a combination of stimulant drugs and behavioral intervention.

- Major depressive disorder and suicidal behavior can occur during early childhood; depression manifests itself somewhat differently in childhood and tends to recur but can be treated.

16.4 The Adolescent

- Adolescents are more vulnerable than children but no more vulnerable than adults to psychological disorders; 20% or so at any given time experience the "storm and stress" of a psychological disorder and many more engage in risky problem behaviors as they seek to complete developmental tasks of adolescence with raging hormones and immature brains.
- Anorexia nervosa arises when a genetically predisposed female who lives in a society that values the thin ideal experiences stressful events.
- Substance use disorders can grow out of adolescent experimentation with substances; according to the cascade model, the developmental pathway toward illicit drug use begins in childhood.
- The risks of depression rise during adolescence, especially among females. Adolescents, in a cry for help, are more likely to

attempt but less likely to commit suicide than adults, older white men being the group most likely to commit suicide.

16.5 The Adult

- Young adults experience both more stressful life events and more psychological disorders, including depression, than older adults.
- Diagnosing depression among older adults can be tricky if their symptoms are attributed to aging, chronic disease, or dementia; older adults have low rates of diagnosable depression but 15%–25% suffer some symptoms of depression.
- Dementia, now called major neurocognitive disorder, is a progressive deterioration in neural functioning associated with significant cognitive decline that increases with age. Alzheimer's disease, the most common cause of dementia, and vascular dementia and Lewy body dementia, other irreversible dementias, must be carefully distinguished from correctible conditions such as reversible dementia, delirium, and depression.

Key Terms

DSM-5 **502**

major depressive disorder **502**

somatic symptoms **503**

developmental psychopathology **503**

social norm **504**

diathesis–stress model **505**

autism spectrum disorder (ASD) **506**

Asperger syndrome **507**

comorbid **508**

applied behavior analysis (ABA) **509**

externalizing problem **511**

internalizing problem **511**

resilience **512**

attention deficit hyperactivity disorder (ADHD) **512**

executive functions **513**

cognitive behavioral therapy **516**

Parent–Child Interaction Therapy (PCIT) **517**

anorexia nervosa **518**

bulimia nervosa **518**

binge eating disorder **518**

thin ideal **519**

substance use disorders **520**

cascade model of substance use **521**

peer socialization/peer selection issue **522**

ruminative coping **523**

dementia **526**

Alzheimer's disease **527**

beta-amyloid **527**

tau **527**

cognitive reserve **528**

vascular dementia **528**

Lewy body dementia **528**

reversible dementia **528**

delirium **529**

17 The Final Challenge: Death and Dying

On Sunday, June 12, 2016, at the Pulse nightclub in Orlando, Florida, friends and relatives desperately sought news of their loved ones in the wake of the deadliest mass shooting in U.S. history. When it was over, 49 people had been murdered and 53 injured, most of them Latino and gay. Eddie Meltzer, the son of a German father and Costa Rican mother, witnessed much confusion in the waiting area set up for loved ones after the shooting:

> "There was a woman who came in, she didn't speak English, and they were reading some names, and she was like, 'Oh, thank God, my son is alive!'" said Meltzer, who had left Pulse five minutes before the shooting began. "And I had to say, 'I'm sorry, ma'am, but that is the list of people who didn't make it.'"

> The woman wailed and began to hit him. "You're lying!" she screamed in Spanish.

> Instead of pushing her away, he wrapped his arms around her, holding on as the rage transformed to grief (Santich & Salazar, 2016).

Images of 9/11, Virginia Tech, Aurora, Sandy Hook, the Boston Marathon bombing, Charleston, San Bernardino, Orlando, and other tragedies in the United States—along with massacres in Brussels, Paris, Nice, Istanbul, Baghdad, and elsewhere around the world—have come to symbolize for many of us the horror of death. Whether we are 4, 24, or 84 when death strikes a loved one, death hurts. By adulthood, most of us have experienced a significant loss, even if it was "only" the death of a beloved pet. Even when death is not striking so closely, it is there, lurking somewhere in the background as we go about the tasks of living—in the newspaper, on television or the Internet, fleeting through our minds. Some psychologists argue that much of human behavior and human culture is an effort to defend against the terror of death (Park & Pyszczynski, 2016; Pyszczynski, Solomon, & Greenberg, 2003). Yet sooner or later we all face the ultimate developmental task: the task of dying.

This chapter explores death and its place in life-span human development, starting with a discussion of the meanings and causes of death. You will discover that death is part of the human experience throughout the life span, but that each person's experience of it depends on his level of development, personality, life circumstances, and sociocultural context.

Friends and family release doves and balloons at the funeral for Franky Jimmy De Jesus Velazquez in his hometown of Caguas, Puerto Rico, June 21, 2016. He was one of the 49 victims of the Pulse nightclub shooting on June 12, 2016, near Orlando, Florida.

Alvin Baez/REUTERS/Alamy Stock Photo

17.1

Matters of Life and Death

LEARNING OBJECTIVES

- Discuss the biological definition of death and the issues it raises.

- Distinguish between active euthanasia, passive euthanasia, and physician-assisted suicide and attitudes toward them.

- Illustrate how social reactions to death differ in different cultures and racial/ethnic groups.

- Analyze trends in the likelihood of death and causes of death across the life span.

What is death, biologically and socially? When are we most vulnerable to it, and what kills us?

What Is Death?

There is a good deal of confusion and controversy in our society today about when life begins and when it ends. Proponents and opponents of legalized abortion argue vehemently about when life really begins. And we hear similarly heated debates about whether a person in an irreversible coma is truly alive and whether a terminally ill patient who is in agonizing pain should be able to choose to die. Definitions of death as a biological phenomenon change; so do the social meanings attached to death.

Biological Death

Biological death is hard to define because it is not a single event but a complex process. Different systems of the body die at different rates, and some individuals who have stopped breathing or who lack a heartbeat or pulse, and who would have been declared dead in earlier times, can now be revived before their brains cease to function. Moreover, basic body processes such as respiration and blood circulation can be maintained by life-support machines in patients who have fallen into a coma and whose brains have ceased to function.

In 1993, the Uniform Determination of Death Act in the United States defined biological death in terms of brain functioning. The Act insisted that, in cases where there is uncertainty, death cannot be said to have occurred until there is total brain death, defined as an irreversible loss of functioning in the entire brain, both the higher centers of the cerebral cortex that are involved in conscious awareness and thought and the centers in the brain stem that control basic life processes such as breathing.

As further elaborated by the American Academy of Neurology, determining brain death requires extensive testing following specific guidelines (Wijdicks et al., 2010; but see Greer et al., 2016, on wide variations in application of the guidelines across the country). A person in a coma must be observed to be totally unresponsive to stimuli, show no movement in response to noxious stimuli, and have no reflexes such as a constriction of the eye's pupils in response to light. An electroencephalogram (EEG) or other measures should indicate an absence of electrical activity in the cortex of the brain. Because a coma is sometimes reversible if the cause is a drug overdose or an abnormally low body temperature, these and certain other conditions must be ruled out before a person in a coma is pronounced dead. This definition means that a coma patient whose heart and lungs are kept going only through artificial means such as a mechanical ventilator but who has no sign of functioning in the brain stem is dead.

Since the definition of brain death was settled upon, there has been continued debate about people in comas. In the mid-2000s, one young woman in a coma, Terri Schiavo, spurred a ferocious national debate (Cerminara, 2006; Foley, 2011). In 1990 Ms. Schiavo had suffered a cardiac arrest that caused irreversible and massive brain damage. She was unconscious but her brain stem allowed her to breathe, swallow, and undergo sleep–wake cycles. After losing hope of a recovery as the years passed, her husband wanted to remove her feeding tube as he believed she would have wanted. However, her parents believed that she retained some awareness of her environment and wanted to keep her alive. After receiving medical testimony, a Florida court ruled that her feeding tube should be withdrawn. Finally, after the issue was debated at length in legislative bodies (including Congress), courts (including the Supreme Court), and the media, the tube was removed when appeals of the court's decision failed. Ms. Schiavo died at the age of 41 in 2005.

Famous right-to-die cases like the Terri Schiavo case highlight the different positions people can take on the issue of when a person is dead. The definition of death as total brain death is quite conservative. By this definition, Ms. Schiavo was not dead, even though she was in an irreversible coma, because her brain stem was still functioning enough to support breathing and other basic body functions. Shouldn't we keep such seemingly hopeless patients alive in case we discover ways to revive them? A more liberal position is that a person should be declared dead when the cerebral cortex is irreversibly dead, even if some body functions are still maintained by the more primitive portions of the brain. After all, is a person really a person if she lacks any awareness and if there is no hope that conscious mental activity will be restored?

Do you believe Terri Schiavo, who could breathe on her own but suffered massive brain damage, should or should not have been taken off her feeding tube? Her husband Michael thought she should be taken off it, but her parents fought him.

But are we sure there is no awareness? Defining the line between life and death has become more complicated since Adrian Owen and his colleagues (2006) demonstrated that at least some people who are in "vegetative states" may have more awareness than suspected. Unlike coma patients, who lack both awareness and wakefulness, people in vegetative states (a dehumanizing term if there ever was one) lack awareness but experience sleep–wake cycles, may open their eyes, and move now and then. Owen asked a young woman who had been in a vegetative state for 5 months as a result of a car accident to imagine playing tennis or visiting the rooms of her house. Brain imaging with fMRI techniques showed that her brain responded exactly as healthy adults' brains respond to these tasks, suggesting that this woman could understand and respond intentionally to instructions and implying that she had some degree of consciousness. Subsequent studies have confirmed that a small proportion of people in vegetative states are most likely treated as if they were dead when they are mentally alive (Cruse et al., 2011, 2013; Graham et al., 2015; Monti et al., 2010).

Life and Death Choices

Cases such as these raise issues concerning euthanasia—a term meaning "happy" or "good" death that usually refers to hastening the death of someone suffering from an incurable illness or injury. *Active euthanasia*, or "mercy killing," is deliberately and directly causing a person's death—for example, by administering a lethal dose of drugs to a pain-racked patient in the late stages of cancer or smothering a spouse who has advanced Alzheimer's disease. *Passive euthanasia*, by contrast, means allowing a terminally ill person to die of natural causes—for example, by withholding extraordinary life-saving treatments (as happened when Terri Schiavo's feeding tube was removed). Between active euthanasia and passive euthanasia is assisted suicide—not directly killing someone, as in active euthanasia, but making available to a person who wishes to die the means by which she may do so. This includes physician-assisted suicide—for example, a doctor's writing a prescription for sleeping pills at the request of a terminally ill patient who has expressed his desire to die (Foley, 2011).

How do we as a society view these options? We invite you to explore your own views in **Engagement 17.1**. There is overwhelming support among medical personnel and members of the general public for passive euthanasia (Shannon, 2006; Stillion & McDowell, 1996). And 68% of adults in the Unites States support physician-assisted suicide when a disease cannot be cured and the patient is in severe pain and requests help in committing suicide—a figure that has risen recently, especially among young adults (Dugan, 2015). African Americans and other minority group members are often less accepting of actions to hasten death than European Americans, possibly because they do not trust the medical establishment or possibly for religious or philosophical reasons (Kwak & Haley, 2005; Werth et al., 2002).

What does the law say about end-of-life interventions? Although active euthanasia is still treated as murder in the United States and most countries, it is legal in most states to withhold extraordinary life-extending treatments from terminally ill patients and to "pull the plug" on life-support equipment when that is the wish of the dying person or when the

Life and Death Attitudes

Imagine that you have terminal cancer and are told that there is no more that can be done for you and no hope of recovery. What would be your answers to the following questions? There are no right or wrong answers.

1. Who would you want with you and what would you want to do with your last days or weeks?

2. Would you want to spend your last days or weeks in a hospital, in a hospice facility for terminally ill people, or at home?

3. Would you want the doctors to do all that is possible to keep you alive as long as possible, in case a new treatment is discovered?

4. Would you choose to take large doses of pain medicine even though it might limit your ability to think clearly and interact with people?

5. Would you want the following applied to you to keep you alive: (a) resuscitation if your heart stops, (b) a respirator to keep you breathing if you stop breathing on your own, (c) a feeding tube inserted in your nose or abdomen to provide nourishment if you can no longer take food through your mouth?

6. Would you want to be able to ask your doctor for and receive a drug with which you could end your own life if you desired?

immediate family can show that the individual expressed, when she was able to do so, a desire to reject life-support measures (Cantor, 2001). A living will, a type of advance directive in which people express their wishes after death, allows people to state that they do not want extraordinary medical procedures applied to them if they become hopelessly ill. (You can download state-specific advance directives at Caring Connections, www.caringinfo.org.)

In 1997, Oregon became the first state to legalize physician-assisted suicide. Following strict guidelines, terminally ill adults in Oregon who have 6 or fewer months to live can request lethal medication from a physician, as patients in European countries such as the Netherlands, Belgium, and Luxembourg can do. The few people in Oregon who have taken this option—70 some a year—have usually had terminal cancer and believed that they faced only hopeless pain and suffering and a loss of dignity with no chance of recovery (Angell, 2014). Washington State, Vermont, Montana (with court approval), and California have since moved to allow assisted suicide under certain conditions (Gostin & Roberts, 2016; Medina, 2016), but a number of other states have enacted laws *against* assisted suicide (Glascock, 2009). As a result, there is a big gap between supportive public attitudes and the laws of most states (Allen et al., 2006; Cohen et al., 2013). There is also a big gap between public attitudes and the views of doctors, most of whom oppose physician-assisted suicide (Angell, 2014). Brittany Maynard, a 29-year-old with incurable brain cancer, brought considerable attention to the issue in 2014 by moving from California to Oregon to obtain a prescription to hasten her death (Angell, 2014). In part in reaction, California enacted a physician-assisted suicide law (Gostin & Roberts, 2016).

On such life-or-death issues, right-to-die advocates, who maintain that terminally ill people should have a say in how and when they die, fight right-to-life advocates, who say that everything possible should be done to maintain life and that nothing should be done to cut it short. It makes sense to think through these issues now in case you must someday decide whether you or a loved one should live or die (see Shannon, 2006).

Brittany Maynard focused attention on the right-to-die issue by deciding at age 29 that she did not want to suffer any longer from the seizures and pain caused by her terminal brain cancer. She moved from California to Oregon to seek legal physician-assisted suicide and died as planned in November 2014. "I did this," she said, "because I want to see a world where everyone has access to death with dignity, as I have had" (Bever, 2014). Here, her husband tells of their experience.

Rich Pedroncelli/ASSOCIATED PRESS

Social Meanings of Death

Death is not only a biological process but also a psychological and social one. The social meanings attached to death vary widely from historical era to historical era and from culture to culture (Parkes, Laungani, & Young, 2015; Rosenblatt, 2015b). True, people everywhere die, and people everywhere grieve deaths. Moreover, all societies have evolved some manner of reacting to this universal experience—of interpreting its meaning, disposing of corpses, and expressing grief. Beyond these universals, however, the similarities end.

Historical Change. As Philippe Ariès (1981) has shown, the social meanings of death have changed over the course of history. In Europe during the Middle Ages, people were expected to recognize that their deaths were approaching so that they could bid their farewells and die with dignity surrounded by loved ones. Since the late 19th century, Ariès argues, Western societies have engaged in a "denial of death." We have taken death out of the home and put it in the hospital and funeral parlor to be managed by physicians and funeral directors; as a result, we have less direct experience with it than our ancestors did (Röcke & Cherry, 2002; Taylor, 2003).

Right-to-die and death-with-dignity advocates have been arguing that we should return to the old ways, bringing death into the open, allowing it to occur more naturally, and making it again a normal life experience to be shared with family rather than a medical failure. As you will see later, this is just what the hospice movement has aimed to achieve.

Cultural Variation. The experience of dying also differs from culture to culture. Societies take different stands, for example, on whether to support frail elders or speed their deaths. Anthony Glascock (2009) found that in 21 of 41 cultures he examined, practices that hastened the death of frail elderly people existed—practices such as depriving ailing elders of food, driving them from their homes, or stabbing them upon their request. Only 12 of the societies were entirely supportive of frail elders and had no death-hastening practices.

If we look at how people in other cultures grieve and mourn a death, we quickly realize that there are many alternatives to our Western ways and no single, biologically mandated grieving process (Klass, 2001; Park & Pyszczynski, 2016; Rosenblatt, 2008, 2015b). Yes, sadness is a common response, but there are no universal emotional responses to death. Depending on the society, "funerals are the occasion for avoiding people or holding parties, for fighting or having sexual orgies, for weeping or laughing, in a thousand different combinations" (Metcalf & Huntington, 1991, p. 24). In most societies, there is some concept of spiritual immortality. Yet here, too, there is much variety, from concepts of heaven and hell to the idea of reincarnation to a belief in ancestral ghosts who meddle in the lives of the living (Rosenblatt, 1993).

We need not look beyond North America to find considerable variation in the social meanings of death. Different ethnic and racial groups clearly have different rules for expressing grief. For example, it is customary among Puerto Ricans, especially women, to display intense emotions after a death (Cook & Dworkin, 1992), and Mexican American mourners do more viewing, touching, and kissing of the deceased than European Americans (Bonanno, 2009). Japanese Americans, by contrast, are socialized to restrain their grief—to smile so as not to burden others with their pain and to avoid the shame associated with losing self-control (Cook & Dworkin, 1992).

Different ethnic and racial groups also have different mourning practices. Irish Americans have traditionally believed that the dead deserve a good send-off, a wake with food, drink, and jokes—the kind of party the deceased might have enjoyed (McGoldrick et al., 1991). African Americans tend to regard the funeral not as a time for rowdy celebration but as a forum for expressing grief, in some congregations by wailing and singing spirituals (McGoldrick et al., 1991; Perry, 1993). Jewish families are even more restrained; they quietly withdraw from normal activities for a week of mourning, called *shivah*, then honor the dead again at the 1-month and 1-year marks (Cytron, 1993).

In short, the experiences of dying individuals and of their survivors are shaped by the historical and cultural contexts in which death occurs. Death may be universal, and the human tendency to mourn a loss may be too (Parkes, 2000). Otherwise, death is truly what we humans make of it; there is no one "right" way to die or to grieve a death.

What Kills Us and When?

As Chapter 5's discussion of basic theories of aging and death revealed, genes and environment conspire to ensure that all

The dama funeral ceremony practiced by the Dogon people of Mali in western Africa involves a masquerade that leads the souls of the deceased to their final resting places in the next world. Mourning rituals differ considerably from culture to culture.

David Sutherland/Getty Images

humans not only develop but age and die. How long are we likely to live, and what is likely to kill us?

Life Expectancy

In the United States the life expectancy at birth—the average number of years a newborn can be expected to live—is almost 79 years (Miniño & Murphy, 2012). This average life expectancy disguises important differences between males and females, among racial and ethnic groups, and among social classes. As shown in ■ **Figure 17.1**, the life expectancy for males is generally lower than that for females: 76 years versus 81 years overall. Female hormones seem to protect women from high blood pressure and heart problems, and they are less exposed than men to violent deaths and accidents and to health hazards such as smoking and drinking (Kajantie, 2008; Kaplan & Erickson, 2000). Ethnic differences are evident as well: Life expectancy is highest for Hispanics, medium for non-Hispanic whites, and lowest for African Americans, more of whom experience the stressors and health hazards associated with poverty. Across racial and ethnic groups, life expectancies are lower in poor areas than in affluent areas (Malmstrom et al., 1999).

Despite historical improvements in longevity in all regions of the world, however, life expectancies in some parts of the world lag far behind life expectancies in others. In some less developed countries plagued by malaria, famine, AIDS, and other such killers, many of them in Africa, the life expectancy is barely above 50 (Central Intelligence Agency, 2015). Among these countries are Chad, Somalia, Swaziland, and Afghanistan. By contrast, the life expectancy at birth is over 80 now in about 40 highly developed and affluent countries such as Japan, Hong Kong, and Singapore in Asia and Iceland, Italy, Sweden, and Switzerland in Europe (Central Intelligence Agency, 2015).

Death across the Life Span

Death rates change over the life span, as illustrated by the "Total Deaths" statistics for different age groups in ● **Table 17.1**. Infants are relatively vulnerable; infant mortality in the United States has dropped considerably in recent years, however, and

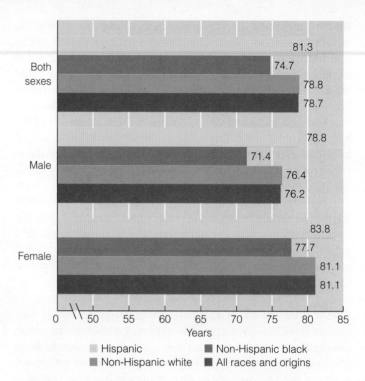

■ **Figure 17.1** Life expectancy at birth for males and females of different racial and ethnic groups in the United States in 2010. Females outlive males; Hispanics have the longest, African Americans the shortest life expectancy.

Source: Miniño, A. M., & Murphy, S. L. (2012, July). *Death in the United States, 2010.* NCHS Data Brief, No. 99. U.S. Department of Health and Human Services, Centers for Disease Control and Prevention, National Center for Health Statistics. Retrieved from: www.cdc.gov/nchs/data/databriefs/db99.htm

now stands at a bit over 6 out of 1,000 live births (Miniño & Murphy, 2012). Assuming that we survive infancy, we have a relatively small chance of dying during childhood or adolescence. Death rates then climb steeply and steadily throughout adulthood.

What kills us? The leading causes of death change dramatically over the life span, as also shown in **Table 17.1** (Heron, 2016).

● **Table 17.1** Leading Causes of Death for Different Age Groups in the United States

Age Group	Total Deaths, 2013	No. 1 Cause	No. 2 Cause	No. 3 Cause
Younger than 1 year	23,440	Congenital abnormalities	Short gestation, low birth weight	Maternal complications of pregnancy
1–4 years	4,068	Accidents (unintentional injuries)	Congenital abnormalities	Assault (homicide)
5–9 years	2,427	Accidents	Cancers	Assault (homicide)
10–14 years	2,913	Accidents	Cancers	Suicide (self-harm)
15–19 years	9,480	Accidents	Suicide	Assault (homicide)
20-24 years	19,006	Accidents	Suicide	Assault (homicide)
25–44 years	115,036	Accidents	Cancers	Heart diseases
45–64 years	515,851	Cancers	Heart diseases	Unintentional injuries
65 years and older	1,904,640	Heart diseases	Cancers	Chronic respiratory diseases

Source: Heron, M. (2016, February 16). Deaths: Leading causes for 2013. *National Vital Statistics Reports, 65*(2). Retrieved from: www.cdc.gov/nchs/data/nvsr/nvsr65/nvsr65_02.pdf

Infant deaths are mainly associated with congenital abnormalities that infants bring with them to life, low birth weight or short gestation, and complications of pregnancy. The leading cause of death among preschool and school-age children is unintentional injuries or accidents (especially car accidents but also poisonings, falls, fires, drownings, and so on). Adolescence and early adulthood are generally periods of good health. Accidents (especially car accidents), suicides, and homicides are the leading killers of adolescents and emerging adults, making this a time for sudden and traumatic death.

Accidents and cancers kill young adults, and heart diseases also begin to take a toll. In the 45–64 age group, cancers have become the leading cause of death, followed by heart diseases. These and other chronic illnesses brought on by some combination of genetic risk and environmental factors become more likely causes of death as age increases. Among adults 65 and older, heart diseases lead the list by far, followed by cancers and chronic respiratory diseases, with strokes close behind.

In sum, life expectancies are higher than ever. After we make it through the vulnerable period of infancy, we are at low risk of death through adolescence and are most likely to die suddenly in an accident if we do die. As we age, we become more vulnerable to chronic diseases—and the often slower and more expected deaths associated with them.

● Checking Mastery

1. Why was Terry Schiavo not dead according to the total brain death definition of death?
2. What would be most likely to kill a 10-year-old? A 70-year-old?

● Making Connections

1. What would you have decided about whether Terri Schiavo should have been taken off her feeding tube and why—and what does your answer imply about how you think death should be defined?
2. An 85-year-old British man and his 74-year-old wife, who was dying of terminal liver and pancreatic cancer, paid an organization in Switzerland to help them achieve an assisted suicide in which they both drank poison and lay down to die together (Gibbs, 2009). The husband had weak vision and hearing but no major health problems; he mainly did not want to go on living without his beloved wife. Do you believe that (1) the wife and (2) the husband should be able to choose death in circumstances like these? Why or why not?

17.2
The Experience of Death

LEARNING OBJECTIVES

- Assess Elisabeth Kübler-Ross's stages of dying and the limitations of her view of the dying person's experience.
- Assess the Parkes/Bowlby attachment model of bereavement and compare how it is similar to and different from Kübler-Ross's model.
- Compare the dual-process model of bereavement to the Parkes/Bowlby model.

People who develop life-threatening illnesses face the challenge of coping with the knowledge that they are seriously ill and are likely to die. What is it like to be dying, and how does the experience compare to the experience of losing a loved one to death?

Perspectives on Dying

Perhaps no one has done more to focus attention on the emotional needs and reactions of dying patients than psychiatrist Elisabeth Kübler-Ross, whose "stages of dying" are widely known and whose 1969 book *On Death and Dying* revolutionized the care of dying people. In interviews with terminally ill patients, Kübler-Ross (1969, 1974) detected a common set of emotional responses to the knowledge that one has a serious, and probably fatal, illness. She believed that similar reactions might occur in response to any major loss, so bear in mind that the family and friends of the dying person may experience similar emotional reactions during the loved one's illness and after the death.

Kübler Ross's Stages of Dying

Kübler-Ross's five "stages of dying" are as follows:

1. **Denial**. A common first response to dreadful news is to say, "No! It can't be!" Denial is a defense mechanism in which anxiety-provoking thoughts are kept out of conscious awareness. A woman who has just been diagnosed as having lung cancer may insist that the diagnosis is wrong—or accept that she is ill but be convinced that she will beat the odds and recover. Denial can be a marvelous coping device: It can get us through a time of acute crisis until we are ready to cope more constructively. Yet even after dying patients face the facts and become ready to talk about dying, care providers and family members often engage in their own denial.

2. **Anger**. As the bad news begins to register, the dying person asks, "Why me?" Feelings of rage or resentment may be directed at anyone who is handy—doctors, nurses, or family members. Kübler-Ross advises those close to the dying person to be sensitive to this reaction so that they will not avoid this irritable person or become angry in return.

Psychiatrist Elisabeth Kübler-Ross called on physicians to emphasize caring rather than curing.

Duane Howell/Denver Post/Getty Images

3. **Bargaining**. When the dying person bargains, he says, "Okay, me, but please. . . ." The bargainer begs for some concession from God, the medical staff, or family members—if not for a cure, perhaps for a little more time, a little less pain, or provision for his children.

4. **Depression**. As the dying person becomes even more aware of the reality of the situation, depression, despair, and a sense of hopelessness become the predominant emotional responses. Grief focuses on the losses that have already occurred (for example, the loss of functional abilities) and the losses to come (separation from loved ones, inability to achieve dreams, and so on).

5. **Acceptance**. If the dying person is able to work through the emotional reactions of the preceding stages, she may accept the inevitability of death in a calm and peaceful manner. Kübler-Ross (1969) described the acceptance stage this way: "It is almost void of feelings. It is as if the pain had gone, the struggle is over, and there comes a time for 'the final rest before the long journey,' as one patient phrased it" (p. 100).

In addition to these five stages of dying, Kübler-Ross emphasized a sixth response that runs throughout the stages: *hope*. She believed that it is essential for terminally ill patients to retain some sense of hope, even if it is only the hope that they can die with dignity. Sadly, Kübler-Ross spent her own dying days mostly alone, a prisoner in her armchair with the television for company (O'Rourke, 2010).

Problems with Kübler-Ross's Stages

Kübler-Ross deserves immense credit for sensitizing our society to the emotional needs of dying people. She convinced medical professionals to emphasize caring rather than curing in working with terminally ill people. At the same time, there are flaws in her account of the dying person's experience (Kastenbaum, 2012; Walter & McCoyd, 2009). Among the points

critics make are these: Emotional responses to dying are not stagelike; the nature and course of an illness affects reactions to it; individuals differ widely in their responses; and dying people focus on living, not just dying.

The first and most important problem with Kübler-Ross's stages is that *the dying process is simply not stagelike*. Although many dying patients display symptoms of depression as death nears, the other emotional reactions Kübler-Ross describes seem to affect only minorities of dying people (Schulz & Aderman, 1974). Moreover, when these responses occur, they do not unfold in a standard order. It might have been better if Kübler-Ross had, from the start, described her stages simply as emotional reactions to dying. Unfortunately, some overzealous medical professionals have tried to push dying patients through the "stages" in order, believing incorrectly that their patients would never accept death unless they experienced the "right" emotions at the "right" times (Kastenbaum, 2012).

Edwin Shneidman (1973, 1980) offered an alternate view, arguing that dying patients experience a complex and ever-changing interplay of emotions, alternating between denial and acceptance of death. One day a patient may seem to understand that death is near; the next day she may talk of getting better and going home. Along the way many reactions—disbelief, hope, terror, bewilderment, rage, apathy, calm, anxiety, and others—come and go and are even experienced simultaneously. According to Shneidman, then, dying people experience many unpredictable emotional swings rather than distinct stages. Research tends to support him (Chochinov & Schwartz, 2002).

Second, Kübler-Ross's theory *does not take into account the disease a person has and its course or trajectory* (Glaser & Strauss, 1968; Kastenbaum, 2012). When a patient is slowly and gradually worsening over time, the patient, family members, and staff can all become accustomed to the death that lies ahead, whereas when the path toward death is more erratic, perhaps involving remissions and relapses and surgeries along the way, emotional ups or downs are likely each time the patient's condition takes a turn for better or worse.

Third, Kübler-Ross's approach *overlooks the influence of personality on how a person experiences dying*. People cope with dying much as they have coped with life (Schulz & Schlarb, 1987–1988). For example, cancer patients who previously faced life's problems directly and effectively, were satisfied with their lives, and maintained good interpersonal relationships before they became ill display less anger and are less depressed and withdrawn during their illnesses than patients who were not so well adjusted before their illnesses (Hinton, 1975). Depending on their predominant personality traits and coping styles, some dying people may deny until the bitter end, some may "rage against the dying of the light," some may quickly be crushed by despair, and still others may display incredible strength.

Fourth and finally, Kübler-Ross focused on emotional responses to the news that one is dying but *gave little attention to how dying people approach living*. An interesting study by Rinat Nissim and colleagues (2012) identified themes in interviews with Canadian patients who had advanced cancer and less than 2 years to live. An important discovery was that these patients continued to set and work toward goals. Their goals centered on:

- *controlling dying* (primarily by focusing on their chemotherapy and other treatments but also, for some, by holding in the back of their mind the possibility of suicide if necessary)
- *valuing life in the present* (getting the most out of their remaining time, even if they could no longer make long-range plans)
- *creating a living legacy* (for example, getting their affairs in order, creating good memories in their children, touching others' lives)

In short, these patients were not just coping with difficult emotions and they were certainly not just lying back waiting to die. As the researchers put it, they were "striving to grow in the land of the living/dying" (Nissim et al., 2012, p. 368). In sum, Kübler-Ross highlighted five relevant emotional responses to dying, but we should not think of them as stages, or as applicable to all diseases or all personalities, or as all that is going on in people who are not only coping with dying but trying to live.

Perspectives on Bereavement

Most of us are more familiar with the process of grieving a death than the process of dying. To describe responses to the death of a loved one, we must distinguish among three terms: **Bereavement** is a state of loss, **grief** is an emotional response to loss, and **mourning** is a culturally prescribed way of displaying reactions to death. Thus, we can describe a bereaved person who grieves by experiencing such emotions as sadness, anger, and guilt and who mourns by attending the funeral and laying flowers on the grave each year.

Unless a death is sudden, relatives and friends, like the dying person, will experience many painful and changing emotions before the death, from the initial diagnosis through the last breath (Grbich, Parker, & Maddocks, 2001). They, too, may alternate between acceptance and denial. They also may experience what has been termed **anticipatory grief**—grieving before death occurs for what is happening and for what lies ahead (Rando, 1986). Anticipatory grief occurs but it typically does not reduce grieving after the death (Nielsen et al., 2016). How, then, do we grieve?

The Parkes/Bowlby Attachment Model

Pioneering research on the grieving process was conducted by Colin Murray Parkes and his colleagues in Great Britain (Parkes, 1991, 2006; Parkes & Prigerson, 2010; Parkes & Weiss, 1983). John Bowlby (1980), whose influential theory of attachment was outlined in Chapter 14, and Parkes conceptualized grieving in the context of attachment theory as a reaction to separation from a loved one. As Parkes (2006) notes, "love and loss are two sides of the same coin. We cannot have one without risking the other" (p. 1). The grieving adult is very much like the infant who experiences separation anxiety when her mother disappears from view. As humans, we have evolved not only to form attachments but also to protest their loss.

A family systems perspective is needed to understand the impacts of death on the bereaved—here, the wife and children of a slain police officer.

Peter Casolino/Alamy Stock Photo

The Parkes/Bowlby attachment model of bereavement describes four predominant reactions. They overlap considerably and therefore should be viewed as phases, not as sequential stages. These reactions are numbness, yearning, disorganization and despair, and reorganization (see also Jacobs et al., 1987–1988, and see ● Table 17.2 to view this phase model of bereavement side by side with Kübler-Ross's stages of dying):

1. **Numbness**. In the first few hours or days after the death, the bereaved person is often in a daze—gripped by a sense of unreality and disbelief and almost empty of feelings. Underneath this state of numbness and shock is a sense of being on the verge of bursting, and, occasionally, painful emotions break through. The bereaved person is struggling to defend himself against the full weight of the loss; the bad news has not fully registered.
2. **Yearning**. As the numbing sense of shock and disbelief diminishes, the bereaved person experiences more agony. This is the time of acute separation anxiety and efforts to reunite with the lost loved one. Grief comes in pangs or waves that typically are most severe from 5 to 14 days after the death. The grieving person has feelings of panic, bouts of uncontrollable

● **Table 17.2** Models of Dying and Bereavement

Kübler-Ross's Stages of Dying	The Parkes/Bowlby Attachment Model of Bereavement
1. Denial	1. Numbness
2. Anger	2. Yearning (including anger and guilt)
3. Bargaining	
4. Depression	3. Disorganization and despair
5. Acceptance	4. Reorganization

weeping, and physical aches and pains. She is likely to be extremely restless, unable to concentrate or to sleep, and preoccupied with thoughts of the loved one and of the events leading to the death. Most importantly, the bereaved person pines and yearns and searches for the loved one, longing to be reunited.

According to Parkes and Bowlby, it is these signs of separation anxiety—the distress of being parted from the object of attachment—that most clearly make grieving different from other kinds of emotional distress. A widow may think she heard her husband's voice or saw him in a crowd; she may sense his presence in the house and draw comfort from it; she may be drawn to his favorite chair—or may try to recover him by smelling his bathrobe. Ultimately the quest to be reunited, driven by separation anxiety, fails.

Both anger and guilt are common during these early weeks and months of bereavement. Frustrated in their quest for reunion, bereaved people often feel irritable and sometimes experience intense rage—at the loved one for dying, at the doctors for not doing a better job, at anyone handy. They seem to need to pin blame somewhere. Unfortunately, they often find reason to blame themselves—to feel guilty. A father may moan that he should have spent more time teaching his son gun safety; the friend of a young man who dies of AIDS may feel that he was not a good enough friend. One of the London widows studied by Parkes felt guilty because she never made her husband bread pudding.

3. **Disorganization and despair**. As time passes, pangs of intense grief and yearning become less frequent, although they still occur. As it sinks in that a reunion with the loved one is impossible, depression, despair, and apathy increasingly predominate. During most of the first year after the death, and longer in many cases, bereaved individuals often feel apathetic and may have difficulty managing and taking interest in their lives.

4. **Reorganization**. Gradually, bereaved people begin to pull themselves together again as their pangs of grief and periods of apathy become less frequent. They invest less emotional energy in their attachment to the deceased and more in their attachments to the living. If they have lost a spouse, they begin to make the transition from being a wife or husband to being a widow or widower, revising their identities. They begin to feel readier for new activities and possibly for new relationships or attachments.

In ■Figure 17.2, you can see the changing mix of overlapping reactions predicted by this attachment model of grief (Jacobs et al., 1987–1988). To test the Parkes/Bowlby model, Paul Maciejewski and his colleagues (2007) assessed disbelief, yearning, anger, depression, and acceptance in 233 bereaved individuals from 1 to 24 months after their loss of a loved one to death from natural causes. The different emotional reactions peaked in the predicted order (disbelief, yearning, anger, and despair/depression), while acceptance steadily gained strength over time. Although the worst of the grieving process for widows and widowers is during the first 6 months after the loss, the process typically takes a year or more and can take much longer (Parkes & Prigerson, 2010).

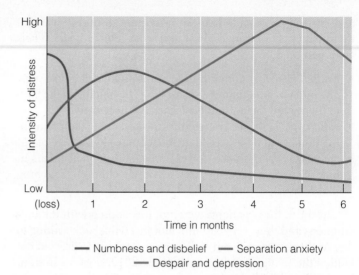

■ **Figure 17.2** The overlapping phases of grief in the Parkes/Bowlby attachment model of bereavement. Numbness and disbelief quickly give way to yearning and pining (signs of separation anxiety) and then to despair or depression (and, although not shown here, growing acceptance and reorganization).

Source: Jacobs, S. C., et al. (1987–1988). Attachment theory and multiple dimensions of grief. *Omega: Journal of Death and Dying, 18*, 41–52, Figure 1. Reprinted by permission of Baywood Publishing Co., Inc.

The Dual-Process Model of Bereavement

Like responses to dying, responses to bereavement have proven to be messy—messier than the Parkes/Bowlby attachment model suggests (Röcke & Cherry, 2002). Margaret Stroebe and Henk Schut have put forth a dual-process model of bereavement in which the bereaved oscillate, often unpredictably, between coping with the emotional blow of the loss and coping with the practical challenges of living, as illustrated in ■Figure 17.3 (Stroebe & Schut, 1999; and see Hansson & Stroebe, 2007; Stroebe & Schut, 2010). Loss-oriented coping involves dealing with one's emotions and reconciling oneself to the loss, whereas restoration-oriented coping is focused on managing daily living, rethinking one's life, and mastering new roles and challenges that come in the wake of the loss. The bereaved need to grieve, but they also need to figure out their finances, take over household tasks that the loved one used to do, get reinvolved in life, revise their identities, and manage other challenges.

Both loss- and restoration-oriented issues need to be confronted, but they also need to be avoided at times or they would exhaust us. We therefore have to strike a balance between confrontation and avoidance of coping challenges and between loss-oriented and restoration-oriented coping. So, for example, working on practical tasks like preparing taxes—or just watching a movie—may give a widow relief from dealing with painful emotions so that she can reenergize for a while before shifting back to a focus on her loss. Bereaved people ideally oscillate

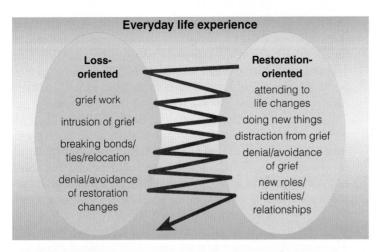

Everyday life experience

Loss-
oriented

grief work

intrusion of grief

breaking bonds/
ties/relocation

denial/avoidance
of restoration
changes

Restoration-
oriented

attending to
life changes

doing new things

distraction from grief

denial/avoidance
of grief

new roles/
identities/
relationships

■ **Figure 17.3** The dual-process model of coping with bereavement. The bereaved oscillate between loss-oriented and restoration-oriented coping, both of which involve both positive and negative emotions and thoughts.

Source: From Stroebe, M. S., & Schut, H. A. W. (1999). The dual process model of coping with bereavement: Rationale and description. *Death Studies, 23,* 197–224, Figure 1. Reprinted by permission of Taylor & Francis Group.

flexibly between the two types of coping rather than focusing on only one; otherwise, they would either fail to deal with their loss or fail to take steps toward recovery. Over time, emphasis shifts from loss-oriented to restoration-oriented coping and from more negative to more positive thoughts and emotions.

More recently, Stroebe and Schut (2015) have extended their model to consider how the family as a whole deals with its loss. Family dynamics affect how individual family members cope, and individual family members affect overall family coping as well. For example, after a child's death, a father may try to avoid talking about the loss or expressing grief to protect his wife from pain. As it turns out, this strategy may backfire, leading both he and his wife to experience more intense grief later on (Stroebe et al., 2013). At the family level too, there is oscillation between loss-oriented coping (for example, shared mourning activities) and restoration-oriented coping (for example, reconfiguring family roles). In the end, some families prove to be more resilient than others (Bonanno, Romero, & Klein, 2015).

Most researchers agree that bereavement is a complex and not-very-stagelike process that involves many ever-shifting emotions (like Shneidman's description of the emotional responses of dying people), varies greatly from person to person, and can take a long time. Meanwhile, the rest of us are sympathetic toward the bereaved immediately after a death— eager to help in any way we can—but we quickly grow weary of someone who is depressed, irritable, or preoccupied. We begin to think, sometimes after only a few days or weeks, that it is time for the bereaved person to cheer up and get on with life. We are wrong. To be of help to bereaved people, we must understand that their reactions of numbness and disbelief, yearning, and despair, and their needs to engage in both loss-oriented and restoration-oriented coping, may last a long time.

We have now considered some major perspectives on how people experience dying and bereavement. However, these perspectives have been based primarily on the responses of adults. How do infants, children, and adolescents respond to death? What does death even mean to infants and young children? A life-span perspective on death and dying is needed.

Checking Mastery

1. What are three of the four main criticisms of Kübler-Ross's stage theory of dying?

2. How does attachment theory inform the Parkes/Bowlby model of bereavement?

3. What oscillates in the dual-process model of bereavement?

Making Connections

1. Look carefully at the five stages of dying that Elisabeth Kübler-Ross believes terminally ill patients experience and at the four phases of adjustment bereaved people experience according to Colin Murray Parkes and John Bowlby (see Table 17.2). What common themes do you see? How do these models differ?

2. If you worked in a hospital wing with terminally ill adults, how might you use Kübler-Ross's perspective to improve care? And how might you avoid misusing it?

17.3
The Infant

LEARNING OBJECTIVES

• Explain how infants might first come to understand death.

• Describe how John Bowlby characterized infants' responses to separation from an attachment figure and how these responses resemble grief.

Looking at bereavement from an attachment theory perspective makes us wonder how infants understand and cope with the death of an attachment figure. Infants surely do not comprehend death as the cessation of life, but they do gain an understanding of concepts that pave the way for an understanding of death (Corr, 2010).

Infants may, for example, come to grasp the concepts of being and nonbeing, here and "all gone," from such experiences as watching objects and people appear and disappear, playing peekaboo, and even going to sleep and "coming alive" again in the morning (Maurer, 1961). Possibly, infants first form a global category of

Games of peekaboo help infants understand the concept of "all gone" and pave the way for an understanding of death.

Tony Freeman/PhotoEdit

Bowlby (1980) observed that infants separated from their attachment figures first engage in vigorous *protest*—yearning and searching for the loved one and expressing outrage when they fail. One 17-month-old girl said only, "Mum, Mum, Mum" for 3 days after her mother died. She was willing to sit on a nurse's lap but would turn her back, as if she did not want to see that the nurse was not "Mum" (Freud & Burlingham, cited in Bowlby, 1980).

If, after some hours or days of protest, an infant has not succeeded in finding the loved one, he begins to *despair*, displaying depression-like symptoms. The baby loses hope, ends the search, and becomes apathetic and sad. Grief may be reflected in a poor appetite, a change in sleeping patterns, excessive clinginess, or regression to less mature behavior (Furman, 1984; Walter & McCoyd, 2009; and see the description of depressed infants in Chapter 16). After some days—longer in some cases—the bereaved infant may enter a *detachment* phase, in which he takes renewed interest in toys and companions. Infants will recover from their protest, despair, and detachment most completely if they can rely on an existing attachment figure (for example, the surviving parent) or can attach themselves to someone else who will be sensitive and responsive to them (Walter & McCoyd, 2009). Notice the similarities between these reactions and the yearning, disorganization and despair, and reorganization phases of the Parkes/Bowlby attachment model of adult bereavement.

things that are "all gone" and later divide it into subcategories, one of which is "dead" (Kastenbaum, 2000). Infants lack the concept of death as permanent separation and loss, however. And, although they may notice changes in the emotional climate in their home when their companions are grieving or may miss a no longer present caregiver (Corr, 2010), they lack the cognitive capacity to interpret what has happened when someone in the family dies.

The experience most directly relevant to the infant's emerging concept of death is separation from a loved one, and it is here that Bowlby's theory of attachment and research are helpful. Only after infants form their first attachments around 6 or 7 months do they begin to display separation anxiety when their beloved caregivers leave them. According to Bowlby, they are biologically programmed to protest separations by crying, searching for their loved one, and attempting to follow, thereby increasing the chances that they will be reunited with the caregiver and protected from harm.

Checking Mastery

1. What kinds of experiences in infancy may pave the way for an understanding of the concept of death?

2. When in infancy would you expect an infant to show grief reactions if a parent were to die?

Making Connections

1. Baby Seth was a year old when his mother died in a car accident. How would you expect him to react, and how would his reactions compare to those of a bereaved adult, as described by the Parkes/Bowlby attachment model of bereavement?

17.4
The Child

LEARNING OBJECTIVES

• Summarize the four key components of an understanding of biological death and when they develop in childhood.

• Characterize the reactions of terminally ill children to their situation.

• Describe children's common reactions to bereavement and what is most critical in helping them to adjust.

Much as parents would like to shelter their children from unpleasant life experiences, children encounter death in their early years, whether only of bugs and birds or, in the case of Sandy Hook Elementary School students, of their siblings, classmates, and teachers. How do they come to understand and cope with their experiences of death?

Grasping the Concept of Death

Contrary to what many adults assume, young children are highly curious about death, think about it with some frequency, build it into their play, and talk about it (Kastenbaum, 2012). Yet their beliefs about death often differ considerably from those of adults. In Western societies, a "mature" understanding of death has several components (Brent et al., 1996; Hoffman & Strauss, 1985; Slaughter, Jaakkola, & Carey, 1999). We see death as characterized by the following:

- **Finality**. It is the cessation of life and of all life processes, such as movement, sensation, and thought.
- **Irreversibility**. It cannot be undone.
- **Universality**. It is inevitable and happens to all living beings.
- **Biological causality**. It is the result of natural processes internal to the organism, even if external causes set off these internal changes.

Researchers have studied children's conceptions of death by asking them the sorts of questions contained in ● **Table 17.3**. Children between age 3 and age 5 have some understanding of death, especially of its universality (Brent et al., 1996). Rather than viewing death as a final cessation of life functions, however, many of them picture the dead as living under altered circumstances and retaining at least some of their capacities (Slaughter et al., 1999). According to these preschoolers, the dead may have hunger pangs, wishes, and beliefs and may continue to love their moms (Bering & Bjorklund, 2004).

Some preschool-age children also view death as reversible rather than irreversible. They may liken it to sleep (from which a person can awaken) or to a trip (from which a person can return). With the right medical care, the right chicken soup, or a bit of magic, a dead person might be brought back to life (Speece & Brent, 1984). Finally, young children think death is caused by one external agent or another; one may say that people die because they eat aluminum foil; another may say the cause is eating a dirty bug or a Styrofoam cup (Koocher, 1974). They do not grasp the ultimate biological cause of death.

Children ages 5–7 (the age range of the classmates of the children slain at Sandy Hook Elementary School) make considerable progress in acquiring a mature concept of death. Most children this age understand that death is characterized by finality (cessation of life functions), irreversibility, and

Even preschool children understand some aspects of death.
Bernhard Classen/Alamy Stock Photo

universality (Rosengren, Gutiérrez, & Schein, 2014; Speece & Brent, 1992). Understanding the biological causality of death is the hardest concept of death for children to master, although 6-year-olds show some basic understandings (Rosengren et al., 2014). Paula, age 12, had clearly mastered the concept that all deaths are ultimately caused by a failure of internal biological processes: "When the heart stops, blood stops circulating, you stop breathing and that's it. . . . there's lots of ways it can get started, but that's what really happens" (Koocher, 1974, pp. 407–408).

Children's understandings of death are influenced in part by their level of cognitive development. Major breakthroughs in the understanding of death occur in the 5–7 age range—when, according to Piaget's theory, children progress from the preoperational stage of cognitive development to the concrete-operational stage. However, Piaget's theory underestimates how much even 3- and 4-year-olds grasp (Rosengren et al., 2014).

In addition, children's concepts of death are influenced by the cultural context in which they live and the cultural and religious beliefs to which they are exposed (Sagara-Rosemeyer & Davies, 2007; Stambrook & Parker, 1987). For example, Jewish and Christian children in Israel, who are taught our Western concept of death, provide more "mature" answers to questions about death than Druze children, who are taught to believe in reincarnation (Florian & Kravetz, 1985). Understandably, a child who is taught that dead people are reincarnated may not view death as an irreversible cessation of life processes.

Another good example of the influence of cultural beliefs comes from a comparison of European American and Mexican American immigrant children in a Midwestern city (Gutiérrez, Rosengren, & Miller, 2014). European American parents typically believed that they should protect their children from death, whereas Mexican American parents believed that they had a responsibility to educate their children about it and included them in the community's yearly *Dia de los Muertos*, or Day of the Dead, ceremonies. Among the differences detected between

● **Table 17.3** Western Children's Concepts of Death and Questions Pertaining to Them

Concept	Questions
Finality/Cessation of functions	Can a dead person move? Get hungry? Speak? Think? Dream? Do dead people know that they are dead?
Irreversibility	Can a dead person become a live person again? Is there anything that could make a dead animal come back to life?
Universality	Does everyone die at some time? Will your parents die someday? Your friends? Will you die?
Biological causality	What makes a person die? Why do animals die?

Sources: Adapted from Hoffman & Strauss, 1985; Florian & Kravetz, 1985; and other sources.

children in the two groups were these: Mexican American children asked more questions about death and dying, were better able to answer a question about what parents should say to a child after the child's relative died, and more often saw the dead as continuing to function biologically and psychologically after death, probably because they had been taught that the dead come back to the world of the living on *Dia de los Muertos* to eat their favorite foods.

Finally, within any society or cultural group, children's unique life experiences also affect their understanding of death. Children who have had personal experience with a death in their immediate or extended family often have more mature understandings of death than similar children who have not yet experienced the loss of a family member (Bonoti, Leondari, & Mastora, 2013). How children's parents communicate with them about death can also make a difference. How is a young child to overcome the belief that death is temporary, for example, if parents and other adults claim that relatives who have died are "asleep"? And if a child is told that "Grandma has gone away," is it not logical to ask why she cannot hop a bus and return?

Experts on death insist that adults only make death more confusing and frightening to young children when they use such euphemisms. They point out that children often understand more than we think, as illustrated by some of the research described above—and by the 3-year-old who, after her father explained that her deceased grandfather had "gone to live on a star in the sky," looked at him quizzically and said, "You mean he is dead?" (Silverman, 2000, pp. 2–3). Experts recommend that parents give children simple but honest answers to the many questions they naturally ask about death and capitalize on events such as the death of a pet to teach children about death and help them understand and express their emotions (Kastenbaum, 2012; Silverman, 2000). In sum, through a combination of cognitive development, cultural learning, and individual experiences, children typically master the concept of death as final, irreversible, universal, and biologically caused.

The Dying Child

Parents and doctors often assume that terminally ill children are unaware that they will die and are better off remaining so. Yet research shows that dying children are far more aware of what is happening to them than adults realize (Essa & Murray, 1994; Stevens et al., 2010). Consider what Myra Bluebond-Langner (1977) found when she observed children ranging in age from 2 to 14 who had leukemia. Even many preschool children arrived, over time, at an understanding that they were going to die and that death is irreversible. Despite the secretiveness of adults, these children noticed changes in their treatments and subtle changes in the way adults interacted with them, and they paid close attention to what happened to other children who had the same disease and were receiving the same treatments. Over time, many of these ill children stopped talking about

the long-term future and wanted to celebrate holidays such as Christmas early. A doctor trying to get one boy to cooperate with a procedure said, "I thought you would understand, Sandy. You told me once you wanted to be a doctor." Sandy threw an empty syringe at the doctor and screamed, "I'm not going to be anything!" (p. 59). Some dying children even start thinking about giving away their toys or planning their funerals (Jalmsell et al., 2015).

How do terminally ill children cope with the knowledge that they are dying? They experience many of the emotions that dying adults experience (Waechter, 1984). Preschool children may not talk about dying, but they may reveal their anxiety by throwing temper tantrums or portraying violent acts in their pretend play. School-age children understand more about their situation and can talk about their feelings if given an opportunity to do so. They want to participate in normal school and sports activities so that they will not feel inadequate compared with their peers, and they want to maintain a sense of control or mastery, even if the best they can do is take charge of deciding which finger should be pricked for a blood sample.

Children with terminal illnesses need the love and support of parents, siblings, and other significant individuals in their lives. Most of all they need a strong sense that their parents are there to care for them (Worchel, Copeland, & Barker, 1987). In one study of Swedish families (Kreicbergs et al., 2004), about a third of parents of terminally ill children talked to their children about dying, and none regretted it. By comparison, about a fourth of the parents who did not talk with their children regretted not having done so, especially if they sensed their child was aware of dying (as over half the parents did). A study of Dutch parents found that the two-thirds of parents who did not discuss death with their terminally ill children offered a variety of good reasons for their decision, mainly centered on their desire to protect their

Lilly Williams paints with Marie the Penguin at the children's hospital where she is being treated for cancer.

Kayte Deioma/Alamy Stock Photo

child (van der Geest et al., 2015). In short, this is a difficult call for parents; their best path is often to follow the child's lead, enabling children to talk about their feelings if they wish and answering their questions simply and directly (Faulkner, 1997; Jalmsell et al., 2015).

The Bereaved Child

Children's coping capacities are also tested when a parent, sibling, pet, or other loved one dies. Four major messages have emerged from studies of bereaved children: Children grieve, they express their grief differently than adults do, they lack some of the coping resources that adults command, and some are vulnerable to long-term negative effects of bereavement (Lieberman et al., 2003; Osterweis, Solomon, & Green, 1984; Silverman, 2000).

Consider first some of the reactions that have been observed in young children whose parents have died (Christ, 2010; Lewis & Lippman, 2004; Lieberman et al., 2003; Silverman, 2000). These children often misbehave or strike out in rage at their surviving parent; they can become unglued when favorite routines are not honored (Lieberman et al., 2003). They ask endless questions: Where is Daddy? When is he coming back? Will I get a new Daddy? Anxiety about attachment and separation is common; many bereaved children report being scared that other family members might die (Sanchez et al., 1994). Yet at other times bereaved children go about their activities as if nothing had happened, denying the loss or distracting themselves from it by immersing themselves in play. You can see how caregivers might be disturbed by some of these behaviors. As you may also have noticed, they are not unlike the emotional swings and oscillations that bereaved adults experience.

Because they lack the cognitive abilities and coping skills that older individuals command, young children may have trouble grasping what has happened and attempt to deny and avoid emotions too overwhelming to face. Young children also have mainly behavioral or action coping strategies at their disposal (Skinner & Zimmer-Gembeck, 2007). So, for example, 2-year-old Reed found comfort by taking out a picture of his mother and putting it on his pillow at night, then returning it carefully to the photo album in the morning (Lieberman et al., 2003). Older children are able to use cognitive coping strategies such as conjuring up mental representations of their lost parents (Compas et al., 2001; Skinner & Zimmer-Gembeck, 2007). It is very important to children to have their grief recognized and to be included in the family's mourning rituals (Søfting, Dyregrov, & Dyregrov, 2016).

Grief reactions differ greatly from child to child, but the preschooler's grief is likely to manifest itself in problems with sleeping, eating, toileting, and other daily routines (Oltjenbruns, 2001; Osterweis et al., 1984). Negative moods, dependency, and temper tantrums are also common. Older children express their sadness, anger, and fear more directly, although somatic symptoms such as headaches and other physical ailments are also common (Worden & Silverman, 1996).

Well beyond the first months after the death, some bereaved children continue to display problems such as unhappiness, low self-esteem, social withdrawal, difficulty in school, and problem behavior (Osterweis et al., 1984; Rostila et al., 2016; Worden & Silverman, 1996). In a longitudinal study of school-age children, one in five children who had lost a parent had serious adjustment problems 2 years after the death (Worden & Silverman, 1996; see also Dowdney, 2000). A minority of children develop psychological problems that carry into adulthood—for example, overreactivity to stress, stress-related health problems, depression and other psychological disorders, and insecurity in later attachment relationships (Harris & Bifulco, 1991; Luecken, 2008; Mireault, Bearor, & Thomas, 2001–2002).

However, most bereaved children are resilient and adapt quite well. By 2 to 5 years after their loss, children who have experienced the death of a parent typically look much like similar nonbereaved children in both socioemotional and academic functioning (Williams & Aber, 2016). A child is especially likely to fare well if her caregiver maintains her own mental health, has a secure relationship with the child, and provides good parenting (Little et al., 2011).

Supportive friends can also help a child who has lost a parent adjust (Dopp & Cain, 2012; LaFreniere & Cain, 2015). Yet relationships with peers can become strained if the child develops behavior problems or withdraws socially. Peers can also do damage through insensitive remarks. Some bereaved children are told by other kids that they are making up the death (Dopp & Cain, 2012). Others are taunted by peers (Cain & LaFreniere, 2015). One 7-year-old girl was distraught when told, "You can't go to the father-daughter dance because your daddy is dead," and was calmed only when her mother assured her that her uncles very much wanted to take her (Christ, 2010, p. 172).

● Checking Mastery

1. What are two factors that might lead Jared to develop a fuller understanding of death concepts than Jeremy at age 5?

2. What three concepts of death are children likely to master by ages 5–7 and what concept might still be incomplete?

3. What reactions on the part of bereaved children might irritate their caregivers?

● Making Connections

1. How might you as a parent help or hinder your child's development of a mature concept of death?

2. If your child had untreatable cancer, would you talk to her about dying? Why or why not? Would the child's age affect your decision? How?

LEARNING OBJECTIVES

• Explain how understandings of death change in adolescence.

• Analyze how features of the adolescent period are reflected in the dying and bereavement experiences of adolescents.

Adolescents expand their understandings of death and show some of the characteristics we associate with the adolescent period when they encounter death.

Advanced Understandings of Death

Adolescents typically understand death as the irreversible cessation of biological processes. They also are able to think in more abstract ways about death, consistent with the shift from Piaget's concrete-operational stage to his formal-operational stage (Corr, 1995; Koocher, 1973). They use their new cognitive capacities to ponder the meaning of death (Balk, 2014; McCarthy, 2009). Yet many adolescents (and adults too) share with young children a belief that psychological functions such as knowing, believing, and feeling continue even after bodily functions have ceased (Bering & Bjorklund, 2004; Bonoti et al., 2013). Do they regress to childish beliefs?

Not really. By adolescence, children have often acquired a belief in an afterlife—a belief that is common across cultures (Bering & Bjorklund, 2004; Park & Pyszczynski, 2016). Many people end up, then, with both a biological concept of death and a supernatural or religious view of it. Developing a belief that the soul or spirit lives on after death does not mean giving up a biological understanding of death as a cessation of bodily functions, nor does learning about biology undo beliefs about the supernatural based on cultural and religious teachings. Rather, the two sets of beliefs live side by side in adolescents' thinking and can be called upon as needed, depending on the situation and what they are trying to explain (Legare et al., 2012).

Experiences with Death

Themes of the adolescent period are reflected in how adolescents deal with having a terminal illness, losing a parent, and losing a friend.

Dying

Just as children's reactions to death and dying reflect their developmental capacities and needs, adolescents' reactions to becoming terminally ill reflect the themes of adolescence (Balk & Corr, 2009; Knapp et al., 2010). Concerned about their body images as they experience physical and sexual maturation, adolescents may be acutely disturbed if their illness brings hair loss, weight gain, amputation, loss of sexual attractiveness and responsiveness, or other such physical changes. Wanting to be accepted by peers, they may feel like "freaks" or become upset when friends who do not know what to say or do avoid them. Eager to become more autonomous, they may be distressed by having to depend on parents and medical personnel and may struggle to assert their will and maintain a sense of control. Wanting to establish their own

identities and chart future goals, adolescents may be angry and bitter at having their dreams snatched from them.

Losing a Parent

"When my mother died I thought my heart would break," recalled Geoffrey, age 14. "Yet I couldn't cry. It was locked inside. It was private and tender and sensitive like the way I loved her. They said to me, 'You're cool man, real cool, the way you've taken it,' but I wasn't cool at all. I was hot—hot and raging. All my anger, all my sadness was building up inside me. But I just didn't know any way to let it out." (Raphael, 1983, p. 176)

The reactions of adolescents to the deaths of family members also reflect the themes of the adolescent period (Balk, 2014; Tyson-Rawson, 1996). As in Geoffrey's case, adolescents are sometimes reluctant to express their grief for fear of seeming abnormal, losing control, or seeming overdependent; they may express their anguish instead through delinquent behavior and somatic ailments (Osterweis et al., 1984; Walter & McCoyd, 2009). Still being dependent on their parents for emotional support and guidance, adolescents who lose a parent to death may carry on an internal dialogue with the dead parent for years (Silverman & Worden, 1993). They may weave the death of the parent into their emerging identity and life story (Christ, 2010).

As is true of children, some adolescents experience mental health problems and have difficulty functioning after a loss. Children's and adolescents' responses to the sudden loss of a parent through suicide, accident, or sudden natural causes like heart attacks were studied by David Brent and his colleagues (Brent et al., 2009, 2012; Dietz et al., 2013; Melhem et al., 2011). Participants ranged from age 7 to age 18 at the time of the death and were assessed periodically until 5 years after the death. Among the important findings were these:

- About 30% experienced significant grief reactions in the first year that then gradually diminished, while another 10% continued to experience significant grief reactions even 3 years later (Melhem et al., 2011). The remainder (almost 60%) had milder grief reactions.
- Bereaved youth were more likely than nonbereaved comparison youth to suffer from major depression, alcohol and substance abuse, and, in the first year, posttraumatic stress disorder, or PTSD (Brent et al., 2009).
- Cortisol measurements suggested that the stress response systems of bereaved youth were affected; their cortisol levels were higher than those of nonbereaved youth and showed a different pattern of response to a social stress task (Dietz et al., 2013).

- Bereavement also disrupted the completion of key developmental tasks of adolescence. Compared to nonbereaved youth, bereaved youth had less close attachments to peers, more difficulties at work, lower educational aspirations, and less well-developed career plans (Brent et al., 2012).
- Overall, outcomes were poorest for those who lost their mothers, blamed others for the death, had low self-esteem, used negative coping strategies, had earlier bouts of depression, and had a surviving parent or caregiver who was suffering from severe grief reactions or depression (Brent et al., 2009; Melhem et al., 2011).

Losing a Friend

Given the importance of peers in adolescence, it is not surprising that some adolescents also experience psychological problems after a close friend dies (Balk, 2014; Servaty-Seib, 2009). As **Table 17.1** revealed, the leading causes of death in adolescence are unintentional injuries (especially car accidents), suicides, and homicides, so a friend's death is often sudden, violent, and potentially traumatic. A national survey of adolescents revealed that one in five adolescents ages 12–17 experienced the death of a close friend in the past year (Rheingold et al., 2004). Moreover, experiencing such a death was associated with higher rates of substance abuse. In another study, 32% of teenagers who lost a friend to suicide experienced clinical levels of depression after the suicide (Bridge et al., 2003).

The death of a friend can be a deeply affecting and transformational experience for adolescents.

Mike Brown/ZUMA Press/Alamy Stock Photo

So, the death of a friend can have serious implications for the mental health of some teens. Yet grief over the loss of a friend is often not taken as seriously as grief over the loss of a family member. Parents, teachers, and friends may not appreciate how much the bereaved adolescent is hurting and provide needed support (Balk, 2014).

Checking Mastery

1. Why might someone conclude that adolescents "regress" to a less mature concept of death, and why would this be incorrect?
2. In David Brent's study of bereavement after a parent's death, what were two differences between bereaved and nonbereaved youth?
3. Why might some bereaved adolescents have difficulty expressing their grief?

Making Connections

1. Miki (age 3), Rosario (age 9), and Jasmine (age 16) have all been diagnosed with cancer. They have been given chemotherapy and radiation treatments for several months but seem to be getting worse rather than better. Write a short monologue for each child conveying how she understands death.
2. Think about Miki (3), Rosario (9), and Jasmine (16) again but this time write about each girl's major concerns and wishes based on what you have learned about typical development at each age.

17.6
The Adult

LEARNING OBJECTIVES

- Summarize what research tells us about the effects of widowhood on adults, including the different trajectories of grief uncovered by George Bonanno and others.
- Compare the impacts of the death of a child and the death of a parent.
- Outline and critique the grief work perspective on bereavement, citing relevant evidence.
- Analyze key factors that can contribute to complicated or prolonged grief after a death—or to posttraumatic growth.

For adults, dealing with the loss of a spouse or partner and accepting their own mortality can be considered normal developmental tasks (Röcke & Cherry, 2002). We have already introduced models describing adults' experiences of dying and bereavement.

Here we will elaborate by examining bereavement from a family systems perspective, trying to define the line between normal and abnormal grief reactions, and identifying factors that make coping easier or harder.

Death in the Family Context

To better understand bereavement, it is useful to adopt a family systems perspective and examine how a death alters relationships, roles, and patterns of interaction within the family, as well as interactions between the family and its social environment (Kissane et al., 2013; Silverman, 2000; Walsh & McGoldrick, 2013). Recall the concept of "linked lives" from Chapter 15 and you can appreciate how the death of a family member affects other family members and alters the relationships among them. The death of a child, for example, changes parents, siblings, grandparents, and other relatives and their interactions with one another and the rest of the world. Adjustment can depend on where the family is in the family life cycle (Is it a young couple or an elderly couple?) and on the sociocultural context, so we need to blend developmental, family systems, and contextual perspectives to fully appreciate the ripple effects of a death (Walsh & McGoldrick, 2013). Consider the challenges associated with three kinds of death in the family: the loss of a spouse or partner, the loss of a child, and the loss of a parent.

Loss of a Spouse or Partner

> How odd to smile during Richard's funeral. He was dead and I was smiling to myself. Grief does that. Laughter lies close in with despair, numbness nearby acuity, and memory with forgetfulness. I would have to get used to it, but I didn't know this at the time. All I knew, as I sat in Thomas Jefferson's church next to Richard's coffin, was that memory had given pleasure first, and then cracking pain. (Jamison, 2009, pp. 126–127)

Most of what we know about bereavement is based on studies of widows and widowers. Experiencing the death of a spouse or partner becomes increasingly likely as we age. In heterosexual relationships, it is something most women can expect to endure because women tend both to live longer than men and to marry men who are older than they are. The marital relationship is a central one for most adults, and the loss of a spouse or other romantic partner can mean the loss of a great deal. Moreover, the death of a partner often precipitates a cascade of other stressors—the need to move, enter the labor force or change jobs, assume responsibilities that the partner formerly performed, parent single-handedly, cope with less money, and so on. Finally, bereaved partners must often redefine their identities and assumptions about life in fundamental ways (Lopata, 1996; Parkes & Prigerson, 2010). Consider Rachel after her husband died of a heart attack: "I was Frank's wife, that was it mostly. He's gone. And I am basically, I am, now—I am nobody" (Bonanno, 2009, p. 97).

Colin Murray Parkes, co-developer of the *Parkes/Bowlby attachment model of bereavement*, concluded based on his extensive studies of widows and widowers younger than age 45 that bereaved adults progress through overlapping phases of numbness, yearning, disorganization and despair, and reorganization. What tolls does this grieving process take on physical, emotional, and cognitive functioning? Parkes (2006) found that widows and widowers are at risk for illness and physical symptoms such as loss of appetite and sleep disruption, and they tend to overindulge in

alcohol, tranquilizers, and cigarettes. Cognitive functions such as memory and decision making are often impaired, and emotional problems such as loneliness and anxiety are common. Most bereaved partners do not become clinically depressed, but many feel lonely and experience symptoms of depression in the year after the death (Fried et al., 2015; Wilcox et al., 2003). Widows and widowers as a group even have a higher-than-average risk of death (Shah et al., 2013). For those who served as caregivers for their loved ones, a deterioration in health appears to begin before the death (Vable et al., 2015).

Modest disruptions in physical, cognitive, emotional, and social functioning are common, usually lasting for a year; less severe, recurring grief reactions may then continue for several years (Bonanno & Kaltman, 2000). Although not captured in the Parkes/Bowlby attachment model, positive thoughts about the deceased, expressions of love, and feelings of gaining from the loss are also part of the typical picture, as in the quote at the beginning of this section.

Importantly, though, George Bonanno and his colleagues have found much diversity in patterns of response to loss by looking for subgroups of bereaved adults rather than just describing the average response (Boerner, Mancini, & Bonanno, 2013; Bonanno, Boerner, & Wortman, 2008). Bonanno studied adults who lost a partner from an average of 3 years before the death to 6 and 18 months afterward (Boerner, Wortman, & Bonanno, 2005; Bonanno, Wortman, & Nesse, 2004; Bonanno et al., 2002; and see Galatzer-Levy & Bonanno, 2012). The sample was assessed again 4 years after their loss to examine the long-term implications of different patterns of grieving.

■ **Figure 17.4** shows the average depression symptom scores over time associated with five distinct patterns of adjustment shown by widows and widowers:

- A resilient pattern in which distress is at low levels all along
- Common grief, a recovery pattern with heightened and then diminishing distress after the loss
- Chronic grief in which loss brings distress and the distress lingers
- Chronic depression in which individuals were depressed before the loss and remained so after it
- A depressed–improved pattern in which individuals who were depressed before the loss become less depressed after the death

Resilience. The biggest surprise in this study was that the resilient pattern of adjustment involving low levels of distress all along turned out to be the most common pattern of response, characterizing almost half the sample. The resilient grievers were not just cold, unfeeling people who did not really love their partners. Rather, before the death they seemed to be well-adjusted and happily married people with good coping resources (Bonanno et al., 2002). They experienced emotional pangs in the first months after the death, but they were more comforted than most by positive thoughts of their partners and simply coped effectively with their loss.

Patterns of Depression. This study also helps us understand that some bereaved people who display symptoms of depression after a loss were depressed even before the death, whereas others become depressed in response to their loss. Those who become

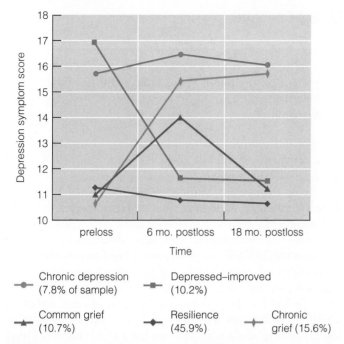

Figure 17.4 Depression symptom scores of five subgroups of elderly widows and widowers an average of 3 years before, 6 months after, and 18 months after the death of their spouse. In parentheses are the percentages of the sample showing each pattern. Notice that resilience—a low level of depression all along—is the most common response, characterizing almost half. This result runs counter to our belief that all bereaved people must go through a period of significant distress.

Source: From Bonanno, G. A., Wortman, C. B., & Neese, R. M. (2004). Prospective patterns of resilience and maladjustment during widowhood. *Psychology and Aging,* *19,* 260–271. Copyright © 2004 American Psychological Association. Reprinted with permission.

depressed in response to the loss often recover from their depression within a year or so; they show the "common grief" or recovery pattern of adjustment (Boerner et al., 2005; Bonanno et al., 2004). Yet this group was small in Bonanno's study (see also Maccallum, Galatzer-Levy, & Bonanno, 2015). Another 15%, the chronic grief group, become depressed after the loss and stay depressed for a year or two before they show signs of recovery.

Some of the ones who were depressed before the loss were chronically depressed and remained so even 4 years later (Galatzer-Levy & Bonanno, 2012). The "depressed–improved" individuals who were depressed before the death but recovered quickly afterward are intriguing. Most likely many were experiencing caregiver burden (see Chapter 15) before the death and were relieved of stress after it. It is common among those who bear the burden of caring for a family member with Alzheimer's disease or another form of dementia to experience more depression before their partner's death than after (Schulz et al., 2003). More than 70% admit that the death came as a relief to both themselves and their loved one.

But What Is Resilience? Could Bonanno's study have overestimated the percentage of widows and widowers who are resilient? Bonanno focused only on depression symptoms in defining resilience. What if other indicators were examined? Frank Infurna and Suniya Luthar (2016) studied 421 Australian adults who had lost a spouse. The participants completed five measures of adjustment from as many as 5 years before to as many as 5 years after their loss: life satisfaction, negative affect, positive affect, self-perceived health, and physical functioning (ability to carry out activities of daily living).

Only 8% of the participants were resilient in the sense of showing good adjustment over the years on all five measures of adjustment. The percentage of people judged to be resilient varied considerably depending on which indicator was used, as shown in ■ **Figure 17.5**. For example, 66% were judged to be resilient in the sense of maintaining high life satisfaction before, during, and after their loss but only 19% consistently registered low scores on a measure of negative emotions. Many adults in the study showed a recovery pattern in which their adjustment suffered after their loss but rebounded; another 20% showed consistently poor adjustment across the five measures.

Overall, then, it is difficult to pin down what percentage of bereaved adults show resilience: It depends on what measures of adjustment and methods of analysis the researchers use. On this much bereavement researchers can agree, though: *There is no one standard response to bereavement; different people follow different grief trajectories.* Some adults who lose spouses or partners are resilient, showing low levels of distress and disruption all along; others experience a decline in well-being and functioning for somewhere between about 6 months and 2 years and then recover, and others show still other trajectories.

Complicated Grief. For a minority of bereaved individuals, up to about 15%, significant grieving and psychological distress continue for many months or even years (Bonanno, 2009; Neimeyer & Holland, 2015). In such cases psychologists speak of **complicated grief** to refer to grief that is unusually prolonged or intense and that impairs functioning. People who have difficulty coping with loss are sometimes diagnosed as having a

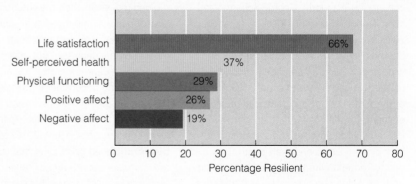

Figure 17.5 Percentages of Australian widows and widowers judged to be "resilient" on five measures. Resilient adults were able to maintain their pre-loss level of adjustment steady for up to 5 years after their spouse's death. The proportion of adults judged to be resilient varied widely across measures.

Source: Created from data in: Infurna, F. J., & Luthar, S. S. (2016). The multidimensional nature of resilience to spousal loss. *Journal of Personality and Social Psychology.* Advance online publication, dx.doi.org/10.1037/pspp0000095.

depressive disorder or, if the death was traumatic, PTSD. However, some experts have concluded that complicated grief, also called prolonged grief disorder, has unique symptoms, is distinct from these other conditions, and should be considered a distinct psychological disorder (Boelen & Prigerson, 2013; Prigerson, Vanderwerker, & Maciejewski, 2008). Complicated grief persists for 6 months or longer and involves intense distress over separation from the deceased, as well as a sense of meaninglessness, bitterness over the loss, difficulty getting past the loss, and difficulty functioning.

The 2013 *Diagnostic and Statistical Manual of Mental Disorders*, DSM-5, recognizes complicated grief (which it calls "persistent complex bereavement-related disorder") as worthy of further study as a distinct disorder (American Psychiatric Association, 2013). Meanwhile, critics warn that what is viewed as complicated grief will vary from society to society (Rosenblatt, 2013) or question the whole idea of treating certain responses to the normal human experience of bereavement as psychological disorders (Wakefield, 2013).

In sum, the loss of a spouse or partner is a painful and sometimes damaging experience that carries risks of developing physical or mental health problems or even dying. Yet possibly as many as half of those who lose spouses or romantic partners, depending on how one counts, show resilience and manage to cope without becoming highly distressed or incapacitated. **Exploration 17.1** looks more closely at some of the challenges faced by the partners and spouses of adults with HIV/AIDS.

Loss of a Child

My child has died! My heart is torn to shreds. My body is screaming. My mind is crazed. The question is always present on my mind. Why? How could this possibly have happened? The anger is ever so deep, so strong, so frightening.

Bertman, 1991, p. 323

As the parents whose children were killed in the Sandy Hook school shooting know too well, no loss seems more difficult for an adult than the death of a child (Murphy, 2008; Parkes, 2006). Even when there is forewarning, the loss of a child seems unexpected, untimely, and unfair and can make parents feel guilty even when they bear no blame—reactions that can complicate their recovery (Duncan & Cacciatore, 2015). In one study, only 12% of parents whose adolescent or young adult child died of an accident, suicide, or homicide said they had found meaning in the death 1 year later, and only 57% had found it 5 years later (Murphy, Johnson, & Lohan, 2003b). Even 10 years after their loss, bereaved parents tend to be less happy than adults who have not lost a child (Moor & Graaf, 2016). Yet researchers find the same diversity of grief trajectories among parents who have lost children as among adults who have lost spouses—for example, many who show resilience, a minority who show prolonged or complicated grief (Maccallum et al., 2015).

The age of the child who dies has little relation to the severity of the grief. True, in some societies with high infant mortality,

● EXPLORATION 17.1

Bereavement among the Partners of Gay Men with HIV/AIDS

The AIDS epidemic continues to take a heavy toll on the gay community in the United States and around the world. George Bonanno and his colleagues (Bonanno, Moskowitz, et al., 2005) wondered whether the resilience he had observed in many heterosexual widows and widowers would also be evident among the partners of gay men who die of AIDS. Many of these men not only experienced the burden of caring for their dying partners but were also HIV infected themselves and therefore stressed by their own illness and likely death. They also had to contend with the stigma surrounding both AIDS and homosexuality. As it turned out, about half of the HIV-positive caregiver partners of gay men who died of AIDS studied by Bonanno showed resilience when compared to nonbereaved, HIV-positive individuals—the same proportion as when heterosexual widows

and widowers were compared to nonbereaved married people. A lower percentage, 27%, showed resilience when the criterion was a low level of depression symptoms all along, from before to after their partner's death. Many others became depressed but returned to their low levels of depression after a year or two.

The finding of considerable resilience in this group is all the more surprising because gay and lesbian partners often experience what Kenneth Doka (1989, 2016) calls **disenfranchised grief**, grief that is not fully recognized or appreciated by other people and therefore may not receive much sympathy and support. Losses of ex-spouses, extramarital lovers, foster children, pets, and fetuses can also result in disenfranchised grief, which is likely to be harder to cope with than socially supported grief.

Gay widowers report that they are indeed disenfranchised before and after their losses (Piatczanyn, Bennett, & Soulsby, 2016). James, for example, watched his partner's brother and sister move in with him and his dying partner, apparently not trusting him to be the caregiver. Adrian, whose partner's mother took over making funeral arrangements, said this: "We were in a partnership that wasn't recognized by anyone else" (Piatczanyn et al., 2016, p. 176). And Steve, in love for three years with a co-worker who had not come out of the closet, had little choice but to grieve alone after his loved one died because his co-workers knew nothing of the relationship (Doka, 2016). Given disenfranchised grief, stigma, and other challenges, gay partners of victims of HIV/AIDS cope surprisingly well with their losses.

parents may not mourn the loss of fetuses or very young infants (Papadatou, 2015). Yet in many societies, including our own, parents, especially mothers, can experience severe grief reactions after a miscarriage, the loss of a premature baby, or the loss of a young infant to sudden infant death syndrome (Buchi et al., 2007; Kulathilaka, Hanwella, & de Silva, 2016). And parents grieve for an adult child as much as for a younger child or adolescent (Walter & McCoyd, 2009).

The death of a child rattles the whole family system, affecting the marital relationship, parenting, and the well-being of surviving siblings, grandparents, and other relatives. The marital relationship is likely to be strained because each partner is grieving and is not always able to provide emotional support for the other. Listen to this father: "When my wife talks about the day our daughter died, I know she is only trying to make sense out of it. But it literally makes me nauseated and I have to leave the room" (Barlé et al., 2015, p. xxx). This powerful life event pushes some couples on a path toward marital distress and even divorce but strengthens the relationship of other couples (Albuquerque, Pereira, & Narciso, 2016). Outcomes are likely to be poor if the marriage was shaky before the death, better if the relationship was close.

Meanwhile, the brothers and sisters of a child who dies have their own challenges. While their sibling is dying, they often feel shut out; they want information about what is going on and what to expect and they want a meaningful role in their sibling's care but they don't always get either (Lövgren et al., 2016). After the death, some feel guilty about some of the unsavory feelings of rivalry they have had or feel pressure to be perfect or to replace the lost child in their parents' eyes (Koehler, 2010). In the year or so after the death, they are often deeply affected and may develop mental health problems (Rosenberg et al., 2015). However, their grief is often not fully appreciated, and their distraught parents are not always able to support them effectively (Koehler, 2010; Lohan & Murphy, 2001–2002). One 12-year-old boy whose brother died described his experience this way: "My dad can't talk about it, and my mom cries a lot. It's really hard on them. I pretend I'm O.K. I usually just stay in my room" (Wass, 1991, p. 29). How well brothers and sisters adjust to a sibling's death often hinges on whether their parents can maintain their mental health and continue to be supportive parents (Morris et al., 2016).

Finally, grandparents also grieve after the death of a child, both for their grandchild and for their child, the bereaved parent. As one grandparent said, "It's like a double whammy!" (DeFrain, Jakub, & Mendoza, 1991–1992, p. 178). The grandmother of a boy killed in the Sandy Hook mass shooting put it this way:

> It's hard to cope with your own pain when your child is so shattered. My daughter is my flesh and blood, but there is nothing I can say that can help her feel better . . . I don't think any of us will get over this. When my daughter visits us now, I hear only three car doors open instead of four. When they leave, I have a good hard cry (Goodwin, 2013–2014, p. 48).

So grandparents may feel quite helpless (Fry, 1997). They may also experience disenfranchised grief, ignored while everyone focuses their support on the parents (Hayslip & White, 2008). Clearly the whole family suffers when a child dies.

The death of a child can be devastating for parents.
Oleg Popov OP/DL/REUTERS

Loss of a Parent

Even if we escape the death of a child or spouse, the death of a parent is a normative life transition that most of us will experience. As noted already, some children experience long-lasting problems after the death of a parent. Fortunately, most of us do not have to face this event until we are in middle age. We are typically less dependent on our parents by then. Moreover, we expect that our parents will die someday and have prepared ourselves, at least to some degree.

Perhaps for these reasons, adjusting to the death of a parent is usually not as difficult as adjusting to the death of a romantic partner or child (Parkes, 2006). Yet it can be a turning point in an adult's life, with effects on his identity and his relationships with his partner, children (who are grieving the loss of their grandparent), surviving parent, and siblings (Umberson, 2003). Adult children may feel vulnerable and alone in the world when their parents no longer stand between them and death (Walter & McCoyd, 2009). Guilt about not doing enough for the deceased parent is also common (Moss et al., 1993). Daughters who lose their mothers tend to show the largest decreases in life satisfaction, especially if the death is off-time and they are young adults when it happens (Leopold & Lechner, 2015; Hayslip, Pruett, & Caballero, 2015).

The Grief Work Perspective and Challenges to It

It's time to step back and reflect. The view that has guided much research on bereavement has come to be called the **grief work perspective**—the view that to cope adaptively with death, bereaved people must:

- confront their loss
- experience painful emotions and work through those emotions
- detach psychologically from the deceased

In Mexico, the Day of the Dead (*Dia de los Muertos*) on November 2 is a time to remember deceased loved ones and to encourage their souls to visit (Bonanno, 2009). Costumes are worn, skulls and skeletons are everywhere, and the festivities are lighthearted, making this yearly event somewhat like American's Halloween. Altars in the home with sugar skulls, marigolds, and the deceased's favorite foods are assembled, and gifts are taken to the grave. "Grief work" takes different forms in different cultures.

Judy Bellah/Alamy Stock Photo

This view, which grew out of Freudian psychoanalytic theory, is widely held in our society, not only among therapists but among the general public, and it influences what we view as an "abnormal" reaction to death (Stroebe, 2001; Wortman & Silver, 2001). From the grief work perspective, either complicated, prolonged grief that lasts longer and is more intense than usual, or an absence, inhibition, or delay of grief, in which the bereaved never seems to confront and express painful feelings, is viewed as pathological.

This grief work perspective has come under attack, however. Questions have been raised about its assumptions that there is a right way to grieve, that bereaved people must experience and work through intense grief to recover, and that they must sever their bonds with the deceased to move on with their lives (Bonanno, 2004; Doka, 2016; Wortman & Boerner, 2007). Let us look at some of the misconceptions built into the grief work perspective.

One Right Way?

Cross-cultural studies reveal that there are many ways to grieve and suggest that the grief work model of bereavement may be culturally biased (Rosenblatt, 2013). An Egyptian mother may be conforming to her culture's norms of mourning if she sits alone, withdrawn and mute, for months or even years after a child's death. Likewise, a Balinese mother is following the rules of her culture if she is calm, composed, and even seemingly cheerful soon after a child's death; by her culture's rules, she would be vulnerable to illness and sorcery if she expressed her emotional pain (Wikan, 1988, 1991). We would be wrong to conclude, based on our own society's norms, that the Egyptian mother is suffering from prolonged grief or the Balinese mother from absent or inhibited grief. As you have also seen, different individuals in our society or any other society experience different trajectories of grief.

Working Through Grief?

There is also surprisingly little support for the grief work perspective's assumption that bereaved individuals must confront their loss and experience painful emotions to cope successfully (Boerner et al., 2013; Wortman & Silver, 2001). The many bereaved individuals who are resilient and do not show much emotional distress during the early months after the loss do not seem to pay for their lack of grief with delayed grief later, as the grief work model says they should. Delayed grief is extremely rare, and the individuals who adjust best to bereavement are those resilient individuals who display little severe distress at any point in their bereavement, experience many positive emotions and thoughts, and manage to carry on with life despite their loss (Boerner et al., 2013). In fact, there is growing evidence that too much "grief work," like ruminative coping that involves overanalyzing one's problems, may backfire and *prolong* psychological distress rather than relieve it (Bonanno et al., 2005).

Breaking Bonds?

Finally, the grief work view that we must break our attachment bonds to the deceased to overcome our grief is flawed. Freud believed that bereaved people had to let go in order to invest their psychic energy elsewhere. However, John Bowlby (1980) noticed that many bereaved individuals revise their internal working models of self and others and continue their relationships with their deceased loved ones on new terms (Bonanno & Kaltman, 1999). Recent research supports Bowlby, suggesting

This Vietnamese woman maintains a continuing bond with her deceased relatives through ancestor worship. Such practices are common in East Asian countries.

robertharding/Alamy Stock Photo

that many bereaved individuals maintain their attachments to the deceased indefinitely through continuing bonds (Klass, 2001; Neimeyer & Holland, 2015). They reminisce and share memories of the deceased, derive comfort from the deceased's possessions, consult with the deceased and feel his or her presence, seek to make the deceased proud of them, and so on. Bereavement rituals in some cultures (in Japan, China, and other East Asian societies, for instance) are actually designed to ensure a continued bond between the living and the dead (Klass, 2001).

Individuals who continue their bonds rather than severing them sometimes suffer from doing so but sometimes benefit (Field et al., 1999; Hayes & Leudar, 2016; Neimeyer & Holland, 2015; Stroebe, Schut, & Boerner, 2010). Nigel Field and his colleagues (1999) tried to determine why this is by investigating whether a continuing attachment to a deceased spouse was positively or negatively related to grief symptoms among widows and widowers at 6 months, 14 months, and 25 months after their loss. Those who expressed their continuing attachment by having and sharing fond memories of the deceased and by sensing that their loved one was watching over and guiding them experienced relatively low levels of distress. By contrast, those who used their spouse's possessions to comfort themselves at the 6-month mark showed high levels of distress and little decrease in grief over the coming months. Researchers have concluded that internal approaches to continuing the bond, such as carrying a mental image of the loved one that provides comfort, tend to aid adjustment, but that externalized approaches, such seeking comfort from the loved one's possessions or visiting the grave every day, may reflect continued efforts to reunite and difficulty coping (Field, 2008; Field & Filanosky, 2010; Scholtes & Browne, 2015).

Cultural context can also make a difference in whether continuing bonds are adaptive. In a study comparing bereaved adults in China and the United States (Lalande & Bonanno, 2006), maintaining continuing bonds was associated with distress soon after the death among bereaved adults in both societies. By 18 months after the death, though, it was related to better adjustment in China but to poorer adjustment in the United States. Why? Most likely because continuing a relationship with the deceased is viewed as more appropriate in Chinese culture. In sum, maintaining continuing bonds is adaptive for some people, especially those who do so through an internal approach in a culture that encourages continuing bonds, but can be a sign of continued yearning and prolonged or complicated grief for others.

Overall, then, research does not support the traditional grief work model that many people assume is correct:

- Ways of expressing grief vary widely across cultures and across individuals, so there is no one "right" way to grieve.
- There is little evidence that bereaved people must do intense "grief work" to adapt or that those who do not do it will pay later with a delayed grief reaction.
- People do not need to sever their attachment to the deceased to adjust to a loss; indeed, they can benefit from internal continuing bonds.

Who Copes and Who Succumbs?

What risk and protective factors distinguish people who cope well with loss from people who cope poorly? Coping with bereavement is influenced by the individual's personal resources, the nature of the loss, and the surrounding context of support and stressors (Burke & Neimeyer, 2013; Dyregrov & Dyregrov, 2013; Piper et al., 2011).

Personal Resources

Just as some individuals are better able to cope with their own dying than others are, some are better equipped to handle the stresses of bereavement due to their *personal resources*. Start with *personality and coping style*. For example, individuals who are emotionally stable cope well, whereas those who have difficulty coping tend to score high on the Big Five personality dimension of neuroticism (Robinson & Marwit, 2006; Wijngaards-de-Meij et al., 2007). Some who have difficulty coping have also had chronic psychological problems such as depression before they were bereaved (Bonanno et al., 2004; Piper et al., 2011). Many also rely on ineffective coping strategies such as denial or avoidance, escape through alcohol and drugs, or unproductive rumination about their loss rather than active coping strategies (Morina, 2011; Murphy, Johnson, & Lohan, 2003a; Riley et al., 2007). By contrast, people who are optimistic, look for and find positive ways of interpreting their loss, and use active coping strategies experience less intense grief reactions and are more likely to report personal growth after their losses than other bereaved adults.

Attachment style is another important resource (or liability). Bowlby's attachment theory emphasizes that early experiences in attachment relationships, along with later experiences, shape the internal working models we have of self and others. If infants and young children receive loving and responsive care, they form internal working models of self and others that tell them that they are lovable and that other people can be trusted, and they develop a secure attachment style (see Chapter 14). Otherwise, they may develop one of the insecure attachment styles.

Attachment styles are systematically related to reactions to death (Beverung & Jacobvitz, 2016; Fraley et al., 2006; Kho et al., 2015; Mikulincer & Shaver, 2013; Parkes, 2006):

- A secure attachment style is associated with coping relatively well with the death of a loved one.
- A resistant (or preoccupied) style of attachment, which involves being highly anxious about being abandoned, is linked to being overly dependent and displaying extreme and prolonged grief and anxiety after a loss, ruminating about the death, and clinging to the lost loved one.
- An avoidant (or dismissing) attachment style is associated with difficulty expressing emotions or seeking comfort; such individuals may do little visible grieving, may minimize how much they miss their loved one, and may disengage from or even devalue this person.
- A disorganized (or fearful) attachment style, which is rooted in unpredictable and anxiety-arousing parenting, is associated

with being especially unequipped to cope with loss; these individuals may turn inward, harm themselves, or abuse alcohol or drugs.

In the language of the dual-process model of bereavement, anxious or resistant/preoccupied individuals focus on their loss and dwell on their negative thoughts and emotions, whereas avoidant/dismissing individuals focus on restoration and avoid dealing with their emotions (Delespaux et al., 2013; Stroebe et al., 2010). By contrast, securely attached individuals are able to oscillate flexibly between loss-oriented and restoration-oriented coping and tend to emphasize positive memories of the deceased.

Nature of the Loss

Bereavement outcomes are also influenced by the nature of the loss. The closeness of the person's relationship to the deceased is a key factor. For example, we grieve more for members of our immediate family than for distant relatives (Armstrong & Shakespeare-Finch, 2011), and spouses grieve especially hard if their relationship to the deceased was very close and if they were highly dependent on their partners (Mancini, Sinan, & Bonanno, 2015; Piper et al., 2011).

The cause of death can also matter in bereavement outcomes. Surprisingly, sudden deaths are not necessarily harder to cope with in the long run than expected deaths from illnesses, although the initial grief reaction may be more intense (Piper et al., 2011). Any advantages of being forewarned of death may be offset by the strains of caregiver burden during a long illness (Schulz, Boerner, & Hebert, 2008). However, sudden deaths that are violent or traumatic, such as suicides, homicides, car crashes, and terrorist attacks appear to be especially difficult to bear (Barlé, Wortman, & Latack, 2015; Boelen et al., 2016; Piper et al., 2011). In a study of African American parents whose children had been murdered, for example, around 40% showed the signs of complicated grief—and many of them symptoms of PTSD and depression as well—even more than 2 years after the murder (McDevitt-Murphy et al., 2012). Traumatic deaths may be especially difficult to bear because they require coping with both bereavement and trauma (Barlé et al., 2015).

Supports and Stressors

Finally, grief reactions are influenced positively by the presence of social support and negatively by additional life stressors (Hansson & Stroebe, 2007; Parkes, 2006). Social support is crucial at all ages. It is especially important for the child or adolescent whose parent dies to have good parenting (Haine et al., 2006). Brothers and sisters can help each other cope (Hurd, 2002). Adult children can ease the adjustment of their widowed parents (Ha, 2010). Indeed, family members of all ages recover best when the family is cohesive and family members can share their feelings and support one another (Walsh & McGoldrick, 2013).

Many of us are clueless about what to say or do that will be helpful. This can make us avoid the bereaved or say pretty

Sensitive social support can make all the difference to the bereaved.

Monkey Business Images/Shutterstock.com

unhelpful things—for example, trying to talk people out of their grief with cheery messages, claiming to know how they feel, offering advice on how to grieve. Yet there are also simple things we can do to be supportive. Bereaved individuals report that they are helped most by family and friends who say they are sorry to hear of the loss, make themselves available to serve as confidants, ask how things are going, and allow bereaved individuals to express painful feelings freely if and when they choose rather than trying to cheer them up and talk them out of their grief (Dyregrov, 2003–2004; Lehman, Ellard, & Wortman, 1986).

Just as social support helps the bereaved, additional stressors hurt. For example, outcomes tend to be poor for widows and widowers who must cope with financial problems after bereavement, manage household tasks they are not used to managing, single-handedly raise young children, find new jobs, or move (Lopata, 1996; Parkes, 1996; Worden & Silverman, 1993). In some cultures, a widow may be tossed out of her home and thrown into poverty, whereas in others she may find herself with more resources and freedom than she had before her husband died (Rosenblatt, 2015a).

By taking into account the person who has experienced a death, the nature of the death, and the context of supports and stressors surrounding it, we can put together a profile of the individuals who are most likely to have long-term problems after bereavement. These individuals have had an unfortunate history of interpersonal relationships, perhaps suffering the death of a parent when they were young or experiencing insecurity in their early attachments. They have had previous psychological problems and generally have difficulty coping effectively with adversity. The person who died is someone whom they loved deeply and on whom they depended greatly, and the death was untimely and traumatic. Finally, these high-risk individuals lack the kinds of social support that can aid them in overcoming their loss, and they are burdened by multiple stressors.

Posttraumatic Growth

The grief work perspective on bereavement put the focus on the negative side of bereavement, but psychologists have come to appreciate that bereavement and other life crises also have positive consequences and sometimes foster personal growth (Joseph, 2012; Tedeschi & Calhoun, 2004). Granted, it can be a painful way to grow, and we could hardly recommend it as a plan for optimizing human development. Still, the literature on death and dying is filled with testimonials about the lessons that can be learned. We invite you to consider the statements in **Engagement 17.2** and whether they apply to you.

Posttraumatic growth refers to positive psychological change resulting from highly challenging experiences such as being diagnosed with a life-threatening illness or losing a loved one (Tedeschi & Calhoun, 1995). Posttraumatic stress and posttraumatic growth seem to go hand in hand. Growth is unlikely where there is little psychological distress and it is unlikely where the distress is overwhelming. Instead, growth seems most likely when distress is significant but not crushing (Armstrong & Shakespeare-Finch, 2011; Currier, Holland, & Neimeyer, 2012; Joseph, 2012).

Many bereaved individuals, young and old, believe that they have become stronger, wiser, more loving, or more spiritual people with a greater appreciation of life (Kilmer et al., 2014; Tedeschi & Calhoun, 2004). Many widows master new skills, become more independent, and emerge with new identities and higher self-esteem (Carr, 2004; Lopata, 1996). A

mother whose infant died said it all: "Now I can survive anything" (DeFrain, Taylor, & Ernst, 1982, p. 57). So perhaps by encountering tragedy we learn to cope with tragedy, and perhaps by struggling to find meaning in death we come to find meaning in life.

● Checking Mastery

1. What appears to be the most common pattern of adjustment observed in studies of widows and widowers?
2. What are two elements of the grief work perspective that are not well supported by evidence?
3. How would individuals with a resistant (preoccupied) attachment style or orientation and those with an avoidant (or dismissing) style be expected to differ in their grief reactions?

● Making Connections

1. Using the section "Who Copes and Who Succumbs," analyze your capacity to cope with death. If you have experienced a significant loss, analyze your actual success in coping and the factors that may have influenced it; if you have not experienced a significant loss, predict how you will respond to your first significant loss and why you think so.
2. Many people have misconceptions about what is normal or abnormal when it comes to grieving, as this chapter has illustrated. Identify two such misconceptions and, using relevant research, show why they are just that—misconceptions.

● ENGAGEMENT 17.2

The Bright Side of Bereavement: Posttraumatic Growth

Think about your greatest loss, crisis, or trauma, whether a death or another difficult experience. Now respond to the following items on a scale from 0 to 5, where 0 means "I did not experience this change as a result of my crisis," and 5 means, "I experienced this change to a very great degree as a result of my crisis."

_____1. I changed my priorities about what is important in life.
_____2. I have a greater appreciation for the value of my own life.
_____3. I am able to do better things with my life.
_____4. I have a better understanding of spiritual matters.
_____5. I have a greater sense of closeness with others.

_____ 6. I established a new path for my life.
_____ 7. I know better that I can handle difficulties.
_____ 8. I have a stronger religious faith.
_____ 9. I discovered that I'm stronger than I thought I was.
_____10. I learned a great deal about how wonderful people are.

To the extent that you agreed with these statements, you show signs of posttraumatic growth.

Source: Cann, A., Calhoun, L. G., Tedeschi, R. G., Taku, K., Vishnevsky, T., Triplett, K. N., & Danhauer, S. C. (2010). A short form of the Posttraumatic Growth Inventory. *Anxiety, Stress & Coping, 23*(2), 127–137, Table 1, p. 130.

LEARNING OBJECTIVES

• Assess how the hospice/palliative care approach differs from the standard medical approach to dying patients and how it affects patients and their families.

• Illustrate how individual therapy, family interventions, and mutual support groups can benefit bereaved individuals.

What can be done to help children and adults who are dying or who are bereaved grapple with death and their feelings about it? Here is a sampling of strategies.

For the Dying

Dramatic changes in the care of dying people have occurred in the past few decades, thanks in part to the efforts of Elisabeth Kübler-Ross and others. The hospice movement is a prime example. A hospice is a program that supports dying people and their families through a philosophy of "caring" rather than "curing" (Connor, 2000; Knee, 2010; Saunders, 2002). The hospice concept spread quickly from St. Christopher's Hospice in London, where it originated, to North America, leading to the establishment of hospice facilities in many communities to serve individuals with cancer, AIDS, and other life-threatening diseases. Participants typically must be judged to be within 6 months of death. In many hospice programs today, however, dying patients stay at home and are visited by hospice workers. Hospice care is part of a larger movement to provide palliative care, care aimed at bringing comfort to and meeting the physical, psychological, and spiritual needs of people with serious illnesses even if their illnesses are still being treated (Shannon, 2006; Van den Block et al., 2015).

What makes hospice care different from hospital care? Whether hospice care is provided in a facility or at home, it entails these key features (Connor, 2000; Corr & Corr, 1992; Siebold, 1992):

• The dying person and his family—not the "experts"—decide what support they need and want.
• Attempts to cure the patient or prolong his life are deemphasized (but death is not hastened either).
• Pain control is emphasized.
• The setting for care is as normal as possible (preferably the patient's own home or a homelike facility that does not have the sterile atmosphere of many hospital wards).
• Bereavement counseling is provided to the family before and after the death.

Do dying patients and their families fare better when they receive hospice care? They seem to. Patients have less interest in physician-assisted suicide because their pain is better controlled (Foley & Hendin, 2002); they feel more emotionally supported (Teno et al., 2004); and they spend more of their last days without pain, undergoing fewer medical interventions and operations (Seale, 1991). Meanwhile, the relatives of dying people rate the quality of the death experience more positively (Hales et al., 2014) and display fewer symptoms of grief and have a greater sense of

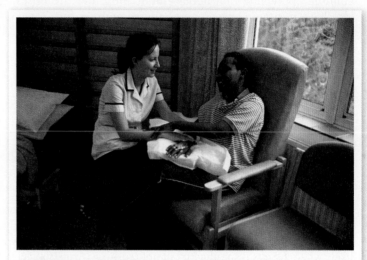

St. Christopher's Hospice in London started what is now a worldwide hospice movement.

BH Generic Stock Images/Alamy Stock Photo

well-being 1 to 2 years after the death than similar family members who did not receive hospice care (Ragow-O'Brien, Hayslip, & Guarnaccia, 2000).

In sum, the hospice and palliative care approach can mean an opportunity to die with dignity, free of pain and surrounded by loved ones. The next challenge may be to extend this philosophy of caring rather than curing to more children (Davies et al., 2007; Orloff & Huff, 2010). Many children who die of cancer and other terminal illnesses die in hospitals, rather than at home with palliative care, possibly because their doctors and parents cannot accept that the child is dying. Parents of dying children who do participate in palliative care are highly satisfied with it (Sheetz & Bowman, 2013).

In some cultures, uneasiness in talking about death—even with adult patients—may be a barrier to the development of hospice and palliative care. In China, for example, it has been taboo for health professionals to talk to dying patients about cancer, because cancer is viewed as a death sentence, and it is believed that open talk about death may undermine hope and bring bad luck or an earlier death (Dong et al., 2016). Family members, wanting to protect their loved one, also avoid talk of death. In this cultural context, it has taken a while for the hospice concept to take root. Meanwhile, in our own society, some ethnic groups (African Americans and Asian Americans) have been more reluctant than others (European and Hispanic Americans) to embrace hospice services (LoPresti, Dement, & Gold, 2016).

For the Bereaved

Most bereaved individuals deal with this normal life transition on their own, with support from family and friends (Mancini, Griffin, & Bonanno, 2012). What is available for bereaved children, adolescents, and adults who are experiencing or are likely to experience complicated grief? Bereaved individuals at risk for complicated grief can benefit from individual psychotherapy aimed at preventing or treating debilitating grief (Boelen, van den Hout, & van den Bout, 2013; Neimeyer & Currier, 2009; Rosner, Kruse, & Hagl, 2010). Because death takes place in a family context, family therapy often makes even better sense (Kissane et al., 2013). Interventions designed for the whole family can help bereaved parents and children communicate more openly and support one another. Family interventions can also help parents deal with their own emotional issues so that they can provide the warm and supportive parenting that can be so critical to their children's adjustment. This is well illustrated by research on the Family Bereavement Program, described in **Application 17.1**.

Mutual support or self-help groups are another option (Lieberman & Videka-Sherman, 1986; Murphy et al., 2003a). These days, of course, bereavement self-help groups are available online (Hartig & Viola, 2016; Wagner, 2013). Examples of well-established self-help organizations with local chapters around the country are: The Compassionate Friends for parents whose children have died; the Widowed Persons Service for widows and widowers; and the National Alliance for Grieving Children. Support groups offer everything from practical advice to emotional support and friendship. Sometimes other bereaved people are in the best position to understand what a bereaved person is going through and to offer effective social support. One widow summed it up this way: "What's helpful? Why, people who are in the 'same boat'" (Bankoff, 1983, p. 230).

Taking Our Leave

We have reached the end not only of the life span but of this book and want to leave you with a few parting words. Notice that the book's inside back cover provides a chart summarizing key developments in different periods of the life span; it will help you put the "whole person" back together again and see relationships among the domains of physical, cognitive, personal, and social development. Also notice the Appendix on Careers in Human Development—a resource for those of you who think you may want to make a life of studying development or intervening to optimize it.

Finally, we leave you with a reminder of some of the themes echoed throughout this book, many of them part of the life-span perspective on development formulated by Paul Baltes (1987; see Chapter 1). We hope you can now think of many illustrations of each:

1. **Nature and Nurture Truly Interact in Development:** It's clear that both biology and environment, reciprocally influencing each other all the way, steer development.

2. **We Are Whole People throughout the Life Span:** Advances in one area of development have implications for other areas of development (for example, motor development advances cognitive development through exploration); we must understand interrelationships among domains of development to understand whole human beings.

● APPLICATION 17.1

The Family Bereavement Program

The Family Bereavement Program is a successful intervention for families in which a parent has died (Ayers et al., 2014; Sandler et al., 2003; Sandler, Ayers, et al., 2010; Sandler, Ma, et al., 2010; Schoenfelder et al., 2015). Children and adolescents who were ages 8 to 16 and had lost a parent, along with the surviving parent or caregiver in the family, were randomly assigned to either the program or a control condition that involved self-study of books about grief. Program participants, 244 in all, met for 14 sessions. The aims of the sessions for children and adolescents included helping them interpret stressful events, use positive coping strategies, and find adaptive ways to express their grief. The aims for surviving parents were to help them deal with their mental health problems and maintain close parent–child relationships and

effective discipline at home. A behavioral approach involving modeling and role-playing of target skills and homework assignments to apply skills was used. The developers of the program based it on research on bereavement and on evidence that the parenting bereaved children receive after their loss is critical in their adjustment.

Outcomes were assessed immediately after, 11 months after, and 6 years after the program ended. Were there lasting effects? Six years after the program ended, child participants showed fewer problematic grief symptoms than control youth did (Sandler, Ma, et al., 2010). Some subgroups of children and adolescents in the program also showed fewer internalizing problems (depression, anxiety) and externalizing problems (acting out, aggression) and improved self-esteem

(Sandler, Ayers, et al., 2010). The program even had positive effects on students' stress response systems, as measured by their cortisol levels (Luecken et al., 2013). And, for some students, participating in the program was associated with higher academic expectations and grade point averages (Schoenfelder et al., 2015).

The Family Bereavement Program was effective, in part, because it focused on the whole family. It reduced surviving parents' depression symptoms (Sandler, Ayers, et al., 2010). Moreover, it increased their warmth toward their children and use of effective discipline techniques (Hagan et al., 2012). Overall, then, the program enabled surviving parents to do a better job of helping their children cope with their loss while strengthening the ability of children and adolescents to help themselves.

3. **Development Proceeds in Multiple Directions:** We experience gains and losses, along with changes that simply make us different than we were, at every age. We must reject the view that childhood is only gain—and old age only loss.

4. **There Is Both Continuity and Discontinuity in Development:** Each of us is at once "the same old person" and a new person, qualitatively different from the person who came before; development is also both gradual and stagelike.

5. **There Is Much Plasticity in Development:** We can change in response to experience at any age, getting off one developmental pathway and onto another. Plasticity, both neural and behavioral, is greatest among infants and young children, but it continues through life.

6. **We Are Individuals, Becoming Even More Diverse with Age:** Developing humans are diverse from the start—and become even more diverse with age.

7. **We Develop in a Cultural and Historical Context:** Human development takes different forms in different times and cultures, in different socioeconomic and racial/ethnic groups, and in different social niches.

8. **We Are Active in Our Own Development:** We help create our environments, influence those around us, and, by doing so, help shape our own development.

9. **Development Is a Lifelong Process:** We never stop developing, and our development during any one phase of life is best understood in relation to what came before and what is to come.

10. **Development Is Best Viewed from Multiple Perspectives:** Many disciplines have something to contribute to a comprehensive understanding of human development—and we need them all.

We hope that you are intrigued enough by the mysteries of life-span human development to observe more closely your own development and that of those around you—or even to seek further course work and practical experience in the field. And we sincerely hope that you will use what you learn to steer your own and others' development in positive directions.

● Checking Mastery

1. What are three of the key features of hospice care?
2. What are two approaches used to help bereaved individuals cope?

● Making Connections

1. If you were in charge of developing policies and programs to help families deal with death and dying, what would you propose and why?
2. Which of the life-span development themes illustrated throughout this book can you detect in this chapter on death and dying?

Chapter Summary

17.1 Matters of Life and Death

- In defining death as a biological process, the definition of total brain death has been influential. Many controversies surround issues of active and passive euthanasia and assisted suicide, complicated by findings of higher brain functioning in some people who are supposedly in "vegetative states"; meanwhile, the social meanings of death vary widely.

- The average life expectancy for a newborn in the United States has risen to almost 79 years; life expectancy varies across nations from the 50s to the 80s; it also differs by gender, race/ethnicity, and socioeconomic status. Death rates decline after infancy but rise in adulthood as accidents give way to chronic diseases as the primary causes of death.

17.2 The Experience of Death

- Elisabeth Kübler-Ross stimulated much concern for dying patients by describing five stages of dying, but, as Edwin Shneidman emphasized, dying people experience ever-changing emotions; their reactions also depend on the course of their disease and on their personality, and they include setting goals for living rather than just coping with dying.

- Bereavement precipitates grief and mourning; grief is expressed, according to the Parkes/Bowlby attachment model, in overlapping phases of numbness, yearning, disorganization and despair, and reorganization.

- The dual-process model describes oscillation between loss-oriented coping and restoration-oriented coping.

17.3 The Infant

- Infants may not comprehend death except as a form of "all gone," but, as John Bowlby noticed, they clearly grieve—protesting, despairing, and detaching after separations from attachment figures.

17.4 The Child

- Children are curious about death and usually understand by age 5 to 7 or even earlier that it is a final cessation of life functions that is irreversible and universal, later realizing that it is ultimately caused by internal biological changes.

- Terminally ill children often become very aware of their plight, and bereaved children may experience somatic symptoms, academic difficulties, and behavioral problems, especially if they lack a secure attachment and good parenting.

17.5 The Adolescent

- Adolescents understand death more abstractly than children do and typically develop a supernatural view of death that includes an afterlife but do not abandon their understanding of death's biological finality.
- They cope with dying and bereavement in ways that reflect the developmental themes of adolescence, and some display adjustment difficulties and even psychological disorders after a significant loss.

17.6 The Adult

- Widows and widowers experience diverse trajectories of grief, many showing great resilience; yet on average widows and widowers experience physical, emotional, and cognitive symptoms for a year or more and are at increased risk of dying.
- The death of a child is often especially difficult for an adult to bear, whereas the death of a parent may be easier because it is more expected.
- The grief work perspective has been challenged. What is normal depends on the cultural context and individual; many people display resilience, never doing "grief work" or paying with delayed grief because they did not; and many people benefit from continuing rather than severing their attachment bonds.
- Complicated grief is especially likely among individuals who have neurotic personalities, ineffective coping skills, and insecure attachment styles; who had close and dependent relationships with individuals who died traumatically; and who lack social support or face additional stressors.
- When grief is significant but not crushing, bereaved individuals often report posttraumatic growth.

17.7 Taking the Sting Out of Death

- Successful efforts to take the sting out of death have included hospices and other forms of palliative care for dying patients and their families and individual therapy, family therapy, and mutual support groups for the bereaved.
- Themes of this book include many that are part of the life-span perspective on development formulated by Paul Baltes and introduced in Chapter 1.

Key Terms

total brain death **534**
euthanasia **535**
assisted suicide **535**
living will **536**
denial **539**
bereavement **541**
grief **541**

mourning **541**
anticipatory grief **541**
Parkes/Bowlby attachment model of bereavement **541**
dual-process model of bereavement **542**
loss-oriented coping **542**

restoration-oriented coping **542**
complicated grief **551**
disenfranchised grief **552**
grief work perspective **553**
continuing bond **555**
posttraumatic growth **557**

hospice **558**
palliative care **558**

Appendix: Careers in Human Development

What career possibilities lie ahead for students interested in understanding or optimizing human development? We would argue that anyone who works with people can benefit from an understanding of life-span human development. We are not alone in our belief: Preparation for many "people" professions—teaching, counseling, and nursing and other allied health professions—includes coursework in human development. Indeed, some of you are taking this course because it is required for your chosen career.

If you think you are interested in a career in human development, you might first ask yourself some basic questions:

- What *level of education* do you seek—bachelor's, master's, or doctoral?
- Are you interested in a particular *age* group—infants, children, adolescents, adults, elderly people?
- Are you interested in a particular *aspect of development*—physical, cognitive, or social development, typical or atypical development?
- Are you most interested in *research*, *teaching*, or *practice* (work as a helping professional of some kind)?

We will sketch out some career possibilities within the broad areas of research, teaching, and professional practice, illustrating as we go how the level of education you seek and the age groups and aspects of development of interest to you come into play. Some of this information is drawn from the U.S. Bureau of Labor Statistics's *Occupational Outlook Handbook* (see Resources list at end of this appendix), available online; you may want to consult it to learn more about the employment outlook and average salaries in some of the professions discussed.

Research

Depending on what level of authority and responsibility you seek, you can conduct research on human development with a bachelor's degree, master's degree (typically 2 years of coursework and either a comprehensive examination or completion of a thesis), or doctoral degree (typically 5–7 years of work, including courses, a qualifying or comprehensive exam, and completion of a doctoral dissertation research project). Research on human development and aging and influences on them is conducted in a variety of settings:

- colleges and universities
- medical schools, hospitals, and other healthcare facilities
- government institutes and agencies (for example, the National Institutes of Health, including the National Institute of Child Health and Human Development and the National Institute on Aging, and state and local health and human services agencies)
- social research organizations (some of the larger ones that conduct research on children, families, aging, and social policy are Abt Associates, SRI International, Mathematica, MDRC, RAND, and Westat)
- other for-profit and nonprofit organizations

How can you get a start on a career in human development research now? Ask your professors or advisor about graduate programs and job opportunities in areas of development that interest you. Seek as much research experience as you can get, too:

- Ask your professors whether they need help with their research and be on the lookout for notices about research projects that need student assistants on either a voluntary or paid basis.
- Sign up for an independent study course that would allow you to conduct a literature review or do a research project with guidance from a professor.
- Seek undergraduate research fellowships that might allow you to do a research project with financial support, possibly a summer living stipend; some colleges and universities offer such research fellowships not only to their own students but also to students from other universities (for example, through the National Science Foundation's Research Experiences for Undergraduates program).
- Do a senior thesis or capstone research project if it is an option in your major.
- Take extra research methods, statistics, and laboratory courses if possible.
- If you are seeking an internship or job, look for ones that involve research, program evaluation, or policy analysis; even if the research is not directly related to human development, you may learn useful research skills.
- Attend lectures and professional conferences to gain exposure to researchers in your area of interest and hear about the latest research they are conducting.
- Use PsycInfo and other online databases to find out who is doing good research of interest to you and at what universities.

These sorts of activities will help you find out whether or not you like research and what aspects of it you prefer. They will also help you acquire research skills, get to know professors who can write reference letters for you and otherwise help you pursue your career plans, and demonstrate to graduate programs or employers that you are interested in research and have research experience. Increasingly, admission to doctoral programs requires experience assisting with research, presenting papers at professional conferences, or even publishing articles with professors.

With a bachelor's degree, you could be hired as a research assistant, interviewer, or other member of a research team and might work on research tasks such as reviewing literature,

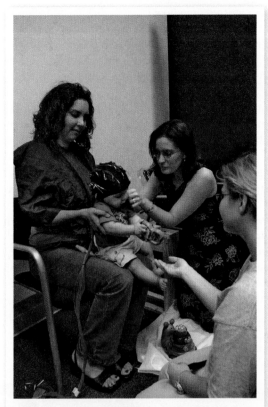

Getting research experience as an undergraduate student is great preparation for graduate school.

Bob Daemmrich/PhotoEdit

conducting telephone surveys, testing children, observing and coding behavior, analyzing physiological data, and compiling tables and graphs. With additional work experience—or with a master's degree in a relevant field such as developmental psychology, including coursework in research methods and statistics—you would become eligible for positions of greater responsibility. For example, you might be hired as the project coordinator for an investigator's study, responsible for implementing the data collection plan and supervising the work of research assistants, or you might become a specialist in testing infants, administering tasks to elderly adults, or analyzing data.

Some students seek paid research staff positions after completing their bachelor's degree, do well, and work their way up to more responsible positions or decide to go on for an advanced degree so that they can move up the career ladder. Some enter a master's program after graduation, possibly gaining hands-on experience by serving as research assistants for professors while they are taking courses and then drawing on this apprenticeship experience in designing and conducting a master's thesis.

Still others, certain they want a research career, apply directly to doctoral programs as college seniors. With a doctor of philosophy (PhD) degree in developmental psychology, clinical psychology, or a related field, you would qualify to be a principal investigator and head a research team—to be the one who designs research projects, submits research proposals to the federal government or foundations to obtain funding, guides implementation of

the study, supervises the research staff, analyzes data, writes up findings, and submits papers for publication in professional journals (publications that are then cited in textbooks like this one). Career options as a PhD include becoming a college or university professor who combines teaching and research or working as a research scientist at a university, hospital, government agency, or research organization. The topics you can study are as wide ranging as those in this book.

If you are considering applying to doctoral programs, we strongly recommend that you do the hard work required to identify programs that are a good fit to your interests and qualifications. Doctoral-level training in human development can be found in a bewildering array of departments, schools, centers, and institutes within universities. The American Psychological Association's yearly publication *Graduate Study in Psychology* is a good resource for students seeking a graduate program in developmental psychology (typically located in a psychology department), human development (typically an interdisciplinary program located in its own department or even its own school), family studies (also interdisciplinary, sometimes part of a larger "human development and family studies" or "family and consumer sciences" program), educational psychology (in either schools of education or psychology departments), or gerontology (also often interdisciplinary and sometimes based in a center or institute).

Most doctoral-level researchers who conduct research on human development or aging did their doctoral work in either psychology or education, but some departments of sociology and anthropology around the country also have strength in the study of families or aging. Moreover, graduate programs in biology often have faculty who specialize in developmental biology, and neuroscience and cognitive neuroscience programs often have specialists in developmental neuroscience, developmental disabilities, dementia, and other topics relevant to development and aging. The more you know about your own research interests, the better; you will then be able to seek programs that are a good fit to your interests and that have scholars whose work excites you. Doctoral programs are highly competitive, but if you're selected, you may have your studies supported by fellowships and teaching and research assistantships.

Teaching

Teachers clearly need to understand the developmental characteristics and learning capacities of their students to teach effectively and make a difference in their students' lives. As a result, coursework in human development is a required part of teacher training at the bachelor's and master's levels. Colleges of education offer teacher preparation programs in preschool or early childhood, kindergarten, elementary school, middle school, secondary school, and adult education; in the teaching of specific subjects such as English or science; and in special education (the teaching of students with developmental disabilities, behavior disorders, and other special learning needs). Teachers normally need to complete a teacher education program leading to a bachelor's or master's degree and then obtain certification from the state in which they will teach by demonstrating that they have taken the required coursework and have passed a standardized teacher exam (see teach.com).

Teachers need to understand their children's cognitive, emotional, and social competencies.

Blend Images/Alamy Stock Photo

To teach at the college or university level, a doctor of philosophy (PhD) degree is normally required. In schools of education, either a PhD or an EdD (doctor of education) is acceptable. The PsyD degree, discussed later, prepares people to be practicing psychologists and is not the best choice for those interested primarily in research and teaching positions in higher education.

Much of what we said earlier about doctoral education for researchers applies to doctoral education for professors. Most PhD programs are highly research-oriented and involve learning the field (through coursework) and how to contribute to the field (through research and scholarship). Teaching responsibilities are heavy and research responsibilities are light at a community college, whereas research may be the first and foremost responsibility of a professor at a large research university.

Professional Practice

By *professional practice* we mean the use of knowledge of human development to optimize development and functioning. Opportunities for professional practice are even more varied than those for research and teaching.

Pre-Bachelor's- or Bachelor's-Level Positions

If you decide you want to enter one of the many helping professions, it makes sense to seek applied experience while you are completing your bachelor's degree or afterward—for example, through unpaid or paid internships or jobs in counseling centers, hospitals, human services agencies, treatment facilities for children or adolescents, or senior centers or nursing homes, depending on your interests (Landrum, 2009). This is a great way to gauge your interests and abilities and develop skills. Jobs available to individuals with a bachelor's degree or less include:

- **Child care worker** The pay is not good, but individuals who love working with children can, with a bachelor's degree or less, work in day care and preschool facilities, before- and after-school programs, camps and recreation programs, and residential programs for disturbed children (U.S. Bureau of Labor Statistics, 2015).
- **Social and human service assistant** Countless entry-level positions in human services, mental health, and health care are available, carrying diverse titles such as case management aide, community outreach worker, residential counselor, life skills counselor, and gerontology aide. Social and human service assistants assist psychologists, nurses, social workers, and other professionals in hospitals, mental health centers and facilities, and government agencies, performing such tasks as assessing client needs, conducting intake interviews, keeping case records, processing paperwork, teaching life skills, supervising clients in residential facilities, and leading group or family sessions.
- **Social and community service manager** A bachelor's degree, especially if combined with work experience, may qualify an individual to manage a social service program or community outreach organization, setting policies and practices, overseeing the budget, supervising staff, and so on (U.S. Bureau of Labor Statistics, 2015). Fundraising is often part of the job description in nonprofit organizations that depend on grants and donations for their survival.

Some human service workers organize and lead activities at senior day care centers and residential facilities for elderly adults. Here an aide helps an elderly woman at the On Lok Senior Health Service in San Francisco.

Ronnie Kaufman/Getty Images

Most of the following career options require graduate training in areas such as assessment and treatment approaches; supervised practicum and internship experiences in which learning is put to practice; and the passing of an examination after completion of studies in order to be licensed or certified by a state to practice.

Applied Developmental Psychologist

If you want to be squarely in the field of human development and have a positive impact on development but do not want to become a therapist or a counselor, you might look into master's or doctoral programs in applied developmental psychology. Although many graduate programs in developmental psychology, human development, and family studies engage in real-world, policy-relevant research, applied developmental psychology programs make a point of it. Applied developmental psychologists may be trained to conduct research on practical problems such as improving early childhood education, supporting at-risk families, or reducing childhood injuries; assess the developmental status of infants and children; design, implement, and evaluate interventions aimed at preventing or treating problems such as alcohol and drug abuse, aggression, or abusive parenting; and consult or serve as expert witnesses in juvenile court proceedings, custody hearings, and the like. After earning a doctorate, applied developmental psychologists may seek a license to practice psychology as a scientist-practitioner; they must obtain the required supervised field experience and pass a licensure examination (Kuther & Morgan, 2013).

Counselor, Psychologist, or Therapist

Now consider some options if you want to provide counseling or psychotherapy to individuals or families as a state-licensed or certified psychologist. Wearing the title "psychologist" generally requires doctoral-level training in the United States. Individuals with master's degrees in fields such as clinical or counseling psychology are needed in mental health centers and facilities, but they are hired as "psychological assistants" or "psychological associates" and must be supervised by doctoral-level psychologists or psychiatrists (see U.S. Bureau of Labor Statistics, 2015). There are three main types of doctoral-level, practicing psychologists.

Clinical Psychologist

Clinical psychologists are trained to diagnose and treat individuals with psychological disorders. Child clinical psychologists focus their practice and research on infants, children, and adolescents. Pediatric psychologists, who may obtain their degree in clinical psychology, health psychology, or pediatric psychology programs, focus their practice and research on child and adolescent illnesses and health care, often working in medical schools, hospitals, and other pediatric care settings. Clinical geropsychologists specialize in treatment of elderly adults.

Becoming a clinical psychologist normally requires earning either a PhD or a PsyD (the doctor of psychology degree, a more practice-oriented and less research-oriented degree than the PhD). You should decide whether you want to be primarily a scientist, primarily a practitioner, or a scientist-practitioner who integrates the two roles and then look closely at the extent to which a program of interest is practice-oriented versus research-oriented. You should also understand that clinical psychology programs are extremely selective, requiring high grades, high scores on the Graduate Record Examinations (GREs), relevant experience, and excellent recommendations.

Counseling Psychologist

Counseling psychologists may earn a PhD, EdD, or PsyD. Like clinical psychologists they qualify to be licensed as psychologists. Compared with clinical psychologists, though, they tend to emphasize optimizing mental health and more often work with everyday problems of adjustment (for example, as a counselor in a college or university, company, or community mental health center).

School Psychologist

After completing either an education specialist (EdS) degree (which requires about 3 years of study and a yearlong internship) or a PhD, EdD, or PsyD in school psychology, a school psychologist is prepared to use IQ tests and other assessment instruments to evaluate students believed to have learning disabilities or other special educational needs, consult with teachers and parents on how best to educate them, and provide other supportive psychological services in schools.

Psychiatrist

Becoming a psychiatrist involves earning a doctor of medicine (MD) degree and choosing psychiatry as one's specialty; job descriptions and employment opportunities are much like those of clinical psychologists, but psychiatrists can prescribe medications for psychological disorders.

Now consider some additional possibilities for careers in the helping professions, some of which do not require doctoral-level education.

Counselor

A wide range of counseling programs exist in psychology departments, schools of education, and human development and family studies programs. Many provide opportunities for independent practice after earning a master's degree and passing a state licensing examination. Subareas of counseling include school counseling (which may involve helping students who have academic or personal problems or, at the secondary school level, helping high school students plan their futures), career counseling, rehabilitation counseling (work in the vocational rehabilitation field helping adults with disabilities adapt to their disabilities and find appropriate jobs), substance abuse or addiction counseling, mental health or community counseling, marriage and family therapy, genetic counseling, gerontological counseling, and more (see U.S. Bureau of Labor Statistics, 2015, on Counselors).

Family therapy may be provided by clinical or counseling psychologists or by clinical social workers.

Lisa F. Young/Alamy Stock Photo

Social Worker

Careers in social work normally require at least a master's degree in social work (MSW). Specialties include child, family, and school social work; medical and public health social work; and mental health or clinical social work (U.S. Bureau of Labor Statistics, 2015). Some social workers are employed by human services agencies as caseworkers who work with families on welfare, neglected or abused children and their families, or aging adults and their families; medical social workers are based in healthcare facilities and support patients and their families. Clinical social workers are trained in diagnosing personal and family problems and in providing counseling and therapy. Clinical social workers with an MSW can practice independently, whereas psychologists must have a doctoral degree to do so.

Given the steady growth of the aging population, career opportunities for psychologists, counselors, and social workers with training in gerontology are likely to expand. A number of universities offer certificates or minors in gerontology that students can combine with any number of academic majors to position themselves to work with elderly people; other universities offer bachelor's, master's, and even doctoral programs in gerontology (see Association for Gerontology in Higher Education under Resources). Services for older adults are varied and are expanding, providing plenty of opportunities for individuals with bachelor's and master's degrees. Our society clearly needs more individuals in a variety of disciplines and professions who care about and have expertise in aging.

Health and Allied Health Professionals

Let's briefly note that a wide range of careers in medicine and allied health professions offer opportunities to apply knowledge of human development and aging to practice. Physicians can focus their careers on newborns, children, adolescents, or elderly adults, as they choose, selecting specialties such as pediatrics or geriatrics in medical school and seeking positions that allow them to work with the age groups and health problems of greatest interest to them. Similarly, nurses can become hospice or palliative care nurses who work with terminally ill patients, developmental disabilities nurses, or psychiatric nurses—or can specialize in the care of a particular age group. Schools of public health offer opportunities for training for roles studying the epidemiology of health problems, providing health education, and delivering community health services to various populations. Other allied health professions such as speech therapy, physical therapy, and occupational therapy also allow for specialization in particular age groups and type of problems.

Other Options

Finally, we need an "Other" category to say that individuals with training in developmental psychology and other human development fields land in surprising places. Many people who enter the occupations we have discussed here advance to become administrators; for example, a teacher may become a principal; a psychologist, counselor, or social worker may become the director of a treatment facility or human service agency. Some of these helping professionals seek further education relevant to their administrative roles (for example, a master's degree in business administration, public administration, or heath care management); others simply take on higher administrative roles and learn on the job.

Many people with training in human development also find their way into business and industry. One may become a book editor in a company that publishes books on psychology; another may test toys or other products for children or conduct market research on them; another may design computer products for older adults; still another may advise a company's employees on retirement issues. Many also work as self-employed consultants, offering help to agencies, organizations, and businesses in areas in which they have expertise. ● **Table A.1** summarizes some of the career options we have discussed.

We hope this is enough to get you thinking and dreaming— and, better yet, taking concrete steps now to gain the knowledge, skills, and experience that will help you formulate and realize your dream. We are confident that the need for individuals who understand the complexities and marvels of life-span human development and can steer it in healthy directions will remain strong as long as humans develop and age.

Resources

American Psychological Association The APA website, www.apa.org/careers/index.aspx, has information and publications about careers in psychology. Find a short overview of the different types of jobs psychologists hold at: www.apa .org/careers/resources/guides/careers.aspx

● Table A.1 Some Career Options in Human Development

Degree Required	Research	Teaching	Professional Practice
Bachelor's or master's degree	Research assistant Research staff member Project coordinator	Teacher's aide Teacher in preschool, elementary, secondary, or adult education	Child care worker Social and human services worker Psychological assistant or associate Social worker* School psychologist*
Doctoral degree	Professor or research professor Principal investigator in university, hospital, health or mental health facility, research organization	Professor (e.g., of developmental psychology, human development, family studies, clinical or counseling psychology, or social work)	Applied developmental psychologist Clinical psychologist Counseling psychologist Psychiatrist Counselor Health professional (medicine, allied health)

* Master's degree required.

American Psychological Association. (2016). *Graduate study in psychology: 2017 Edition.* **Washington, DC: American Psychological Association** This invaluable guide for students looking for appropriate graduate programs profiles more than 600 graduate programs in the United States and Canada, noting program emphases, admission standards, information about the employment of graduates, and the like. Your library may have it.

Association for Gerontology in Higher Education This organization's website, www.aghe.org, lists member universities and provides other resources on educational programs and job opportunities in gerontology and geriatrics. It offers an *Online Directory of Educational Programs in Gerontology and Geriatrics* at www.aghe.org/resources/online-directory.

Careers in Aging The website, Exploring Careers in Aging, lists different types of career opportunities in gerontology and geriatrics. Go to businessandaging.blogs.com/ecg/101_careers_in_aging/.

GradSchools.com This website allows you to search for graduate programs at the master's and doctoral levels in various fields, and contains links to the web pages of those programs.

Kuther, T. L. (2016). *The psychology major's handbook* **(4th ed.). Boston, MA: Cengage Learning** A good general guide to succeeding as a psychology major and preparing for graduate school and careers available with a bachelor's, master's, or doctoral degree.

Kuther, T. L., & Morgan, R. D. (2013). *Careers in psychology: Opportunities in a changing world* **(4th ed.). Belmont,**

CA: Cengage Learning A survey of opportunities in the various subfields of psychology, including developmental psychology, along with advice on applying to graduate school and seeking jobs.

Landrum, R. R. (2009). *Finding jobs with a psychology bachelor's degree: Expert advice for launching your career.* **Washington, DC: American Psychological Association** Professionals in a wide range of careers describe their jobs, how a bachelor's degree in psychology helped them in their careers, and how to search for jobs.

Teach.com A wealth of information about why and how to become a teacher, including information about education and licensing criteria and needs for teachers in each of the 50 states, opportunities for teaching abroad.

U.S. Bureau of Labor Statistics. (2015). *Occupational outlook handbook* A huge but wonderful government resource describing, for all major occupational fields, the nature of the work involved, working conditions, training and other qualifications, employment data, job prospects, and average earnings. It includes sections on psychologists and counselors, is updated yearly, and is available free at: www.bls.gov/ooh.

Wegenek, A. R., & Buskist, W. (2010). *The insider's guide to the psychology major: Everything you need to know about the degree and profession.* **Washington, DC: American Psychological Association** This guide aims to help psychology majors get the most out of their education and position themselves for careers in psychology.

Glossary

A-not-B error The tendency of 8- to 12-month-old infants to search for a hidden object in the place they last found it (A) rather than in its new hiding place (B).

acceptance–responsiveness A dimension of parenting capturing the extent to which parents are supportive, sensitive to their children's needs, and willing to provide affection and praise when their children meet their expectations.

accommodation In Piaget's cognitive developmental theory, the process of modifying existing schemes to incorporate or adapt to new experiences. Contrast with *assimilation*. In vision, a change in the shape of the eye's lens to bring objects at differing distances into focus.

acquired immunodeficiency syndrome (AIDS) The life-threatening disease in which the human immunodeficiency virus (HIV) destroys the immune system and makes victims susceptible to rare, so-called opportunistic, infections that eventually kill them. AIDS is transmitted through sexual activity, drug needle sharing, and from mother to child before or during birth.

active gene–environment correlation Phenomenon in which children's genotypes influence the kinds of environments they seek out and therefore experience. Contrast with *evocative gene–environment correlation and passive gene–environment correlation*.

activity–passivity issue The issue in developmental theory centering on whether humans are active contributors to their own development or are passively shaped by forces beyond their control.

adaptation In Piaget's cognitive developmental theory, a person's inborn tendency to adjust to the demands of the environment, consisting of the complementary processes of *assimilation* and *accommodation*.

adolescence The transitional period between childhood and adulthood that begins with puberty and ends when the individual has acquired adult competencies and responsibilities; roughly ages 10 to 18 or later.

adolescent egocentrism A characteristic of adolescent thought that involves difficulty differentiating between the person's own thoughts and feelings and those of other people; evident in the *personal fable* and *imaginary audience* phenomena.

adolescent growth spurt The rapid increase in physical growth that occurs during adolescence.

adoption study Method of studying genetic and environmental influence that involves determining whether adopted children are more similar to their biological parents (whose genes they share) or adoptive parents (who shaped their environment).

adrenarche A period of increased production of adrenal hormones, starting around 6–8 years of age, that normally precedes increased production of gonadal hormones associated with puberty.

affordances In Eleanor and James Gibson's ecological theory of perception, characteristics of an object that reveal what it has to offer humans and how it might be used by them.

age effects In developmental research, the effects of getting older or of developing. Contrast with *cohort effects* and *time of measurement effects*.

age grades Socially defined age groups or strata, each with different statuses, roles, privileges, and responsibilities in society.

age norms Expectations about what people should be doing or how they should behave at different points in the life span.

age of viability A point (around the 24th prenatal week) when a fetus may survive outside the uterus if the brain and respiratory system are well enough developed and if excellent medical care is available.

ageism Prejudice and discrimination against elderly people.

agency An orientation toward individual action and achievement that emphasizes traits of dominance, independence, assertiveness, and competitiveness; considered masculine.

age-related macular degeneration (AMD) Damage to cells in the retina responsible for central vision.

aging To most developmentalists, positive, negative, and neutral changes in the mature organism; different from *biological aging*.

alphabetic principle The idea that the letters in printed words represent the sounds in spoken words.

Alzheimer's disease A pathological condition of the nervous system that results in an irreversible loss of cognitive capacities; the leading cause of dementia, or neurocognitive disorder, in later life.

amniocentesis A method of extracting amniotic fluid from a pregnant woman so that fetal body cells within the fluid can be tested for chromosomal abnormalities and other genetic defects.

amnion A watertight membrane that surrounds the developing embryo, regulating its temperature and cushioning it against injuries.

amoral Lacking any sense of morality; without standards of right and wrong.

analytic component In Sternberg's triarchic theory of intelligence, the information-processing skills such as thinking critically and analytically.

androgenized female A genetic female who was exposed to male sex hormones during the prenatal period and therefore developed malelike external genitals and some masculine behaviors.

androgens Male hormones that help trigger the adolescent growth spurt and the development of the male sex organs, secondary sex characteristics, and sexual motivation.

androgyny A gender-role orientation in which the person blends both positive masculine-stereotyped and positive feminine-stereotyped personality traits.

androgyny shift A psychological change that begins in midlife, when parenting responsibilities are over, in which both men and women retain their gender-typed qualities but add to them qualities traditionally associated with the other sex, thus becoming more androgynous.

andropause The slower and less-dramatic male counterpart of *menopause*, characterized by decreasing levels of testosterone and symptoms that include low libido, fatigue and lack of energy, erection problems, memory problems, and loss of pubic hair.

anencephaly Condition in which the top of the neural tube fails to close and the main portion of the brain above the brain stem fails to develop properly.

anorexia nervosa A life-threatening eating disorder characterized by failure to maintain a normal weight, a strong fear of weight gain, and a distorted body image; literally, "nervous lack of appetite."

anoxia A lack of sufficient oxygen to the brain that may result in neurological damage or death.

anterograde amnesia The inability to form new memories of recent experiences. Contrast with *retrograde amnesia*.

anticipatory grief Grieving before death for what is happening and for what lies ahead.

antioxidant Vitamins C, E, and similar substances that may increase longevity, although not for long, by inhibiting the free radical activity associated with oxidation and in turn preventing age-related diseases.

antisocial behavior Behavior that violates social norms, rules, or laws and harms others or society (for example, lying, stealing, behaving aggressively).

Apgar test A test routinely used to assess a newborn's heart rate, respiration, color, muscle tone, and reflexes immediately after birth and 5 minutes later; used to identify high-risk babies.

aphasia A language disorder.

applied behavior analysis (ABA) The application of reinforcement principles to teach skills and change behavior, for example to shape social and language skills in children with autism.

artificial insemination A method of conception that involves injecting sperm from a woman's partner or from a donor into the uterus.

Asperger syndrome A form of autistic spectrum disorder in which the individual has normal or above-average intelligence, has good verbal skills, and wants to establish social relationships but has seriously deficient mindreading and social skills. No longer a separate diagnosis in DSM-5.

assimilation Piaget's term for the process by which children interpret new experiences in terms of their existing schemata. Contrast with *accommodation*.

assisted suicide Making available to individuals who wish to commit suicide the means by which they may do so, such as when a physician provides a terminally ill patient who wants to die with enough medication to overdose.

at risk Children who have a higher than normal chance of either short-term or long-term problems because of genetic defects, prenatal hazards, or perinatal damage.

attachment A strong affectional tie that binds a person to an intimate companion and is characterized by affection and a desire to maintain proximity.

attachment theory The theory of close relationships developed by Bowlby and Ainsworth and grounded in ethological theory (with psychoanalytic theory and cognitive theory); it says that close emotional bonds such as parent-child attachments are biologically based and contribute to species survival.

attention Focusing perception and cognition on something in particular.

attention deficit hyperactivity disorder (ADHD) A disorder characterized by attentional difficulties, or overactive and impulsive behavior, or both.

authoritarian parenting A restrictive style of parenting combining high demandingness–control and low acceptance–responsiveness in which adults impose many rules, expect strict obedience, and often rely on power tactics rather than explanations to elicit compliance.

authoritative parenting A flexible style of parenting combining high demandingness–control and high acceptance–responsiveness in which adults lay down clear rules but also take their children's views into account and explain the rationale for their restrictions.

autism See *autism spectrum disorder*.

autism spectrum disorder (ASD) A category of pervasive developmental disorders that includes what was previously called autism, Asperger syndrome, and related conditions and that involves (1) social and communication problems and (2) restricted interests and repetitive behavior.

autobiographical memory Memory of everyday events that the individual has experienced.

automatization The process by which information processing becomes effortless and highly efficient as a result of continued practice or increased expertise.

autonomy The capacity to make decisions independently, serve as one's own source of emotional strength, and otherwise manage life tasks without being overdependent on other people; an important developmental task of adolescence.

autonomy versus shame and doubt The psychosocial conflict in which toddlers attempt to demonstrate their independence from and control over other people; second of Erikson's stages.

avoidant attachment An insecure infant caregiver bond or other intimate relationship characterized by little separation anxiety and

a tendency to avoid or ignore the attachment object upon reunion.

babbling An early form of vocalization that appears between 4 and 6 months of age and involves repeating consonant–vowel combinations such as "baba" or "dadada."

baby biographies Carefully recorded observations of the growth and development of children by their parents over a period; the first scientific investigations of development.

baby boom generation The huge generation of people born between 1946 (the close of World War II) and 1964.

Bayley Scales of Infant Development (BSID) Standardized test to measure the mental, motor, and behavioral progress of infants and young children.

behavioral genetics The scientific study of the extent to which genetic and environmental differences among individuals are responsible for differences among them in traits such as intelligence and personality.

behavioral inhibition A temperamental characteristic reflecting a person's tendency to withdraw from unfamiliar people and situations.

behaviorism A school of thinking in psychology that holds that conclusions about human development should be based on controlled observations of overt behavior rather than on speculation about unconscious motives or other unobservable phenomena; the philosophical underpinning of early theories of learning.

belief–desire psychology The theory of mind reflecting an understanding that people's desires and beliefs guide their behavior and that their beliefs are not always an accurate reflection of reality; evident by age 4. Contrast with *desire psychology*.

bereavement A state of loss that provides the occasion for grief and mourning.

beta-amyloid A toxic protein that injures neurons and is located in the senile plaques outside neural cells that are associated with Alzheimer's disease.

Big Five The five major dimensions used to characterize people's personalities: neuroticism, extraversion, openness to experience, agreeableness, and conscientiousness.

bilingual Knowing two or more languages.

binge eating disorder Eating disorder that, like bulimia, involves binge eating but, unlike bulimia, does not involve purging.

bioecological model Bronfenbrenner's model of development that emphasizes the roles of both nature and nurture as the developing person interacts with a series of environmental systems (microsystem, mesosystem, exosystem, and macrosystem) over time (chronosystem).

biological aging The deterioration of organisms that leads inevitably to their death.

biological sex The physical characteristics that define male and female.

biosocial theory Money and Ehrhardt's theory of gender-role development that focuses on how biological events influence the development of boys and girls and how early biological developments influence how society reacts to children.

blastocyst A hollow sphere of about 100 to 150 cells that the zygote forms by rapid cell division as it moves through the fallopian tube.

body mass index (BMI) An indicator of body fat calculated from a person's height and weight.

bonding As distinguished from attachment, a more biologically-based process in which parent and infant form a connection through contact in the first hours after birth when both are highly alert.

breech presentation A delivery in which the fetus emerges feet first or buttocks first rather than head first.

bulimia nervosa A life-threatening eating disorder characterized by recurrent eating binges followed by purging activities such as vomiting.

bullying Repeatedly inflicting harm through words or actions on weaker peers who cannot or do not defend themselves.

caloric restriction A technique demonstrated to extend the life span of laboratory animals involving a highly nutritious but severely calorie-restricted diet.

caregiver burden The psychological distress associated with providing care for someone with physical, cognitive, or both types of impairment.

carrier In genetics, individuals who possesses a recessive gene associated with a disease and who, although they do not have the disease, can transmit the gene for it to offspring.

cascade model of substance use Transactional, multifactor model of substance use that envisions a chain of influences starting with a child with a difficult temperament born into troubled family and ending with involvement in a deviant adolescent peer group.

case study An in-depth examination of an individual (or a small number of individuals), typically carried out by compiling and analyzing information from a variety of sources such as observing, testing, and interviewing the person or people who know the individual.

cataract A pathologic condition of the eye involving opacification (clouding) of the lens that can impair vision or cause blindness.

catch-up growth A phenomenon in which children who have experienced growth deficits will grow rapidly and catch up to the growth trajectory they are genetically programmed to follow.

categorical self A person's classification of the self along socially significant dimensions such as age and sex.

celiac disease An inherited digestive problem in which gluten (the proteins found in all wheat products) triggers an immune response that damages a person's small intestine.

centenarian An individual who lives to be 100 years of age.

central executive Mechanism that directs attention and controls the flow of information in the working memory system.

centration In Piaget's theory, the tendency to focus on only one aspect of a problem when two or more aspects are relevant.

cephalocaudal principle The principle that growth proceeds from the head (cephalic region) to the tail (caudal region).

cerebral palsy A neurological disability caused by anoxia that is associated with difficulty controlling muscle movements.

cesarean section A surgical procedure in which an incision is made in the mother's abdomen and uterus so that the baby can be removed through the abdomen.

characteristic adaptations Compared to traits, more situation-specific and changeable aspects of personality; ways in which people adapt to their roles and environments, including motives, goals, plans, schemas, self-conceptions, stage-specific concerns, and coping mechanisms.

child abuse Mistreating or harming a child physically, emotionally, or sexually, as distinguished from another form of child maltreatment, neglect of the child's basic needs.

child effects model A model of family influence in which children are believed to influence their parents rather than vice versa.

child maltreatment A broad term for inadequate care or harmful treatment of a child; encompasses both child abuse and child neglect.

child poverty A household climate that includes low income along with low levels of response to children's basic needs.

child-directed speech Speech used by adults speaking with young children; it involves short, simple sentences spoken slowly and in a high-pitched voice, often with much repetition and with exaggerated emphasis on key words.

childhood amnesia A lack of memory for the early years of a person's life.

childhood gender nonconformity (CGN) Lack of adherence as a child to the typical gender-role norms for members of one's assigned gender group.

chorion A membrane that surrounds the amnion and becomes attached to the uterine lining to gather nourishment for the embryo.

chorionic villus sampling (CVS) An alternative to amniocentesis in which a catheter is inserted through the cervix to withdraw fetal cells from the chorion for prenatal testing to detect genetic defects.

chromosome A threadlike structure made up of genes; in humans, there are 46 chromosomes in the nucleus of each cell.

chromosome abnormalities Conditions in which a child has too few, too many, or incomplete chromosomes because of errors in the formation of sperm or ova.

chronic traumatic encephalopathy (CTE) A degenerative brain disease with symptoms of memory loss, poor impulse control, depression, and eventually dementia; a risk for football players and participants in other contact sports.

chronosystem In Bronfenbrenner's bioecological approach, the system that captures the way changes in environmental systems, such as social trends and life events, are patterned over a person's lifetime.

chumship According to neo-Freudian Harry Stack Sullivan, a close friendship in childhood that provides emotional support and teaches children how to participate in intimate relationships.

class inclusion The logical understanding that parts or subclasses are included in the whole class and that the whole is therefore greater than any of its parts.

classical conditioning A type of learning in which a stimulus that initially had no effect on the individual comes to elicit a response because of its association with a stimulus that already elicits the response.

clinical method An unstandardized interviewing procedure used by Piaget in which a child's response to each successive question (or problem) determines what the investigator will ask next.

clique A small friendship group that interacts frequently. See *crowd*.

cochlear implant A surgically implanted amplification device that stimulates the auditory nerve to provide the sensation of hearing to a deaf individual.

coercive family environment A home in which family members are locked in power struggles, each trying to control the other through aggressive tactics such as threatening, yelling, and hitting.

cognition The activity of knowing and the processes through which knowledge is acquired (for example, attending, perceiving, remembering, and thinking).

cognitive behavioral therapy Well-established psychotherapy approach that involves identifying and changing distorted thinking and maladaptive emotions and behavior associated with it.

cognitive reserve The extra brain power or cognitive capacity that some people can fall back on as aging and diseases such as Alzheimer's begin to take a toll on brain functioning.

cohabitation The living together of two single adults as an unmarried couple.

cohort A group of people born at the same time; a particular generation of people.

cohort effects In cross-sectional research, the effects on findings that the different age groups (cohorts) being compared were born at different times and had different formative experiences. Contrast with *age effects* and *time-of-measurement effects*.

collectivist culture A culture in which people define themselves in terms of group memberships, give group goals higher priority than personal goals, and socialize children to seek group harmony. Contrast with *individualistic culture*.

communality An orientation that emphasizes the well-being of others and includes traits of emotionality and sensitivity to others; considered feminine.

comorbid Co-occurring, as when two or more psychiatric conditions affect the same individual.

companionate love In Sternberg's triangular theory of love, affectionate love characterized by high intimacy and commitment but low passion.

complementarity Basis for mate selection in which people choose partners who are different from them but have strengths that compensate for their weaknesses or otherwise complement their own characteristics. Contrast with *homogamy*.

complicated grief An emotional response to a death that is unusually prolonged or intense and that impairs functioning; pathological grief.

conception The moment of fertilization, when a sperm penetrates an ovum, forming a zygote.

concordance rate The percentage of cases in which a particular attribute is present for both members of a pair of people (for example, twins) if it is present for one member.

concrete operations stage Piaget's third stage of cognitive development, lasting from about age 7 to age 11, when children are acquiring logical operations and can reason effectively about real objects and experiences.

concussion A brain injury involving a brief loss of brain function in response to a hit or blow to the head; immediate symptoms include headache, sensitivity to light and sound, feeling dizzy or foggy, and slowed reaction time.

conduct disorder A persistent pattern of behavior in which a child or adolescent violates the rights of others or age-appropriate societal norms, as through fighting, bullying, and cruelty.

confidant A spouse, relative, or friend to whom a person feels emotionally close and with whom that person can share thoughts and feelings.

congenital malformations Defects that are present at birth and are caused by genetic factors, prenatal events, or both.

conservation The recognition that certain properties of an object or substance do not change when its appearance is altered in some superficial way.

consolidation In information processing, the processing and organizing of information into a form suitable for long-term storage.

constraint-seeking questions In the Twenty Questions task and similar hypothesis-testing tasks, questions that rule out more than one answer to narrow the field of possible choices rather than asking about only one hypothesis at a time.

constructivist A proponent of constructivism, the position taken by Piaget and others that humans actively create their own understandings of the world from their experiences, as opposed to being born with innate ideas or being programmed by the environment.

consummate love In Sternberg's triangular theory of love, love with high levels of all three components of love: passion, intimacy, and decision/commitment.

contact comfort The pleasurable tactile sensations provided by a parent or a soft, terry cloth mother substitute; believed to foster attachments in infant monkeys and possibly humans.

continuing bond Maintenance of attachment to a loved one after the person's death through reminiscence, use of the person's possessions, consultation with the deceased, and the like.

continuity–discontinuity issue The debate among theorists about whether human development is best characterized as gradual and continuous or abrupt and stagelike.

contour The amount of light-dark transition or boundary area in a visual stimulus.

conventional morality Kohlberg's term for the third and fourth stages of moral reasoning in which societal values are internalized and judgments are based on a desire to gain approval or uphold law and social order.

convergent thinking Thinking that involves "converging" on the one best answer to a problem; what IQ tests measure. Contrast with *divergent thinking*.

cooing An early form of vocalization that involves repeating vowel-like sounds.

coordination of secondary schemes During Piaget's sensorimotor period, the infant's combining of actions to solve problems, using one scheme as a means to an end, as in batting aside a barrier in order to grasp a toy.

coparenting The extent and manner in which the two parents coordinate their parenting and function as a team in relation to their children.

copy number variations Instances in which a person receives too many or too few copies of a stretch of DNA; like gene mutations, they can either be inherited from a parent or arise spontaneously and can contribute to diseases and disorders.

correlation coefficient A measure, ranging from +1.00 to –1.00, of the extent to which two variables or attributes are systematically related to each other in either a positive or a negative way.

correlational method A research technique that involves determining whether two or more variables are related. It cannot indicate that one thing caused another, but it can suggest that a causal relationship exists or allow us to predict one characteristic from our knowledge of another.

co-rumination Excessive discussion and analysis of personal problems with a close friend.

couvade Sympathetic pregnancy, or the experiencing by fathers of some of the same physiological symptoms their pregnant partners experience (for example, bloating, weight gain, fatigue, insomnia, and nausea).

creative component In Sternberg's triarchic theory of intelligence, the aspect of intelligence that varies with experience on a task.

creativity The ability to produce novel responses or works; see also *divergent thinking*.

critical period A defined period in the development of an organism when it is particularly sensitive to certain environmental influences; outside this period, the same influences will have far less effect.

crossing over A process in which genetic material is exchanged between pairs of chromosomes during meiosis.

cross-modal perception The ability to use one sensory modality to identify a stimulus or a pattern of stimuli already familiar through another modality.

cross-sectional design A developmental research design in which different age groups are studied at the same point in time and compared.

crowd A network of heterosexual cliques that forms during adolescence and facilitates mixed-sex social activities. See *clique*.

crystallized intelligence Those aspects of intellectual functioning that involve using knowledge acquired through experience. Contrast with *fluid intelligence*.

cued recall memory Recollecting objects, events, or experiences in response to a hint or cue. Contrast with pure *recall memory* and *recognition memory*.

cultural evolution Change in a species achieved not through biological evolution but through learning and passing on from one generation to the next new ways of adapting to the environment.

culture A system of meanings shared by a population of people and transmitted from one generation to the next.

culture bias The situation that arises in testing when one cultural or subcultural group is more familiar with test items than another group and therefore has an unfair advantage.

cumulative-deficit hypothesis The notion that impoverished environments inhibit intellectual growth and that these inhibiting effects accumulate over time.

decentration The ability to focus on two or more dimensions of a problem at one time.

decontextualize To separate the demands of a task at hand from prior beliefs and knowledge.

defense mechanisms Mechanisms used by the ego to defend itself against anxiety caused by conflict between the id's impulses and social demands.

deferred imitation The ability to imitate a novel act after a delay.

delay of gratification The willingness to give up a reward now for a more desirable reward later; related to *self-control*.

delirium A clouding of consciousness characterized by alternating periods of disorientation and coherence.

demandingness–control A dimension of parenting reflecting the extent to which parents as opposed to children exert control over decisions and set and enforce rules; also called permissiveness–restrictiveness.

dementia A progressive loss of cognitive capacities such as memory and judgment that affects some aging individuals and that has a variety of causes; now called neurocognitive disorder.

denial A defense mechanism in which anxiety-provoking thoughts are kept out of, or isolated from, conscious awareness.

dependent variable The aspect of behavior measured in an experiment and assumed to be under the control of, or dependent on, the *independent variable*.

depression See *major depressive disorder*.

desire psychology The earliest theory of mind: An understanding that desires guide behavior (for example, that people seek things they like and avoid things they hate). Contrast with *belief–desire psychology*.

development Systematic changes in the individual occurring between conception and death; such changes can be positive, negative, or neutral.

developmental norm The age at which half of a large group of infants or children master a skill or display a behavior; the average age for achieving a milestone in development.

developmental psychopathology A field of study concerned with the origins and course of maladaptive or psychopathological behavior.

developmental quotient (DQ) A numerical measure of an infant's performance on a developmental test relative to the performance of other infants the same age.

developmental range In Fischer's dynamic skill framework, the concept that people's abilities vary depending on the context, from optimal levels in highly supportive contexts to lower levels in unsupportive situations.

developmental stage A distinct phase within a larger sequence of development; a period characterized by a particular set of abilities, motives, behaviors, or emotions that occur together and form a coherent pattern.

diabetes A metabolic disorder characterized by high levels of glucose or sugar in the blood leading to symptoms of thirst, excessive urination, fatigue, and problems involving eyes, kidneys, and other organs.

dialectical thinking An advanced form of thought that involves detecting paradoxes and inconsistencies among ideas and trying to reconcile them.

diathesis–stress model The view that psychopathology results from the interaction of a person's predisposition to psychological problems and the experience of stressful events.

differential susceptibility hypothesis The concept that some people's genetic makeup makes them more reactive than other people to both good and bad environmental influences.

differentiation In brain development, the progressive diversification of cells that results in their taking on different characteristics and functions.

difficult temperament Characteristic mode of response in which the individual is irregular in habits and adapts slowly, often with vigorous protest, to changes in routine or new experiences. Contrast with *easy temperament* and *slow-to-warm-up temperament*.

diffusion status Identity status characterizing individuals who have not questioned who they are and have not committed themselves to an identity.

directionality problem The problem in correlational studies of determining whether a presumed causal variable is the cause or the effect. See also *third variable problem*.

disenfranchised grief Grief that is not fully recognized or appreciated by other people and therefore may not receive much sympathy and support, as in the loss of a gay partner.

disorganized–disoriented attachment An insecure infant–caregiver bond, common among abused children, that combines features of the resistant and avoidant attachment styles and is characterized by the infant's dazed response to reunion and confusion about whether to approach or avoid the caregiver.

dispositional traits Relatively enduring dimensions or qualities of personality along which people differ (for example, extraversion, aloofness).

divergent thinking Thinking that requires coming up with a variety of ideas or solutions to a problem when there is no one right answer. Contrast with *convergent thinking*.

DNA Deoxyribonucleic acid, the double helix molecule whose chemical code makes up chromosomes and serves as our genetic endowment; it is made up of sequences of the chemicals A (adenine), C (cytosine), G (guanine), and T (thymine).

dominant gene A relatively powerful gene that is expressed phenotypically and masks the effect of a less-powerful *recessive gene*.

double standard The view that sexual behavior appropriate for members of one gender is inappropriate for members of the other.

Down syndrome A chromosomal abnormality in which the child has inherited an extra 21st chromosome and is, as a result, intellectually disabled; also called trisomy 21.

DSM-5 The fifth edition of the *Diagnostic and Statistical Manual of Mental Disorders* published by the American Psychiatric Association, which spells out defining features and symptoms for the range of psychological disorders.

dual-process model of bereavement A theory of coping with bereavement in which the bereaved oscillate between loss-oriented coping in which they deal with their emotions, restoration-oriented coping in which they try to manage practical tasks and reorganize their lives, and periods of respite from coping.

dual-process model of morality The view that *both* deliberate thought and more automatic emotion-based intuitions can inform decisions about moral issues and motivate behavior.

dynamic In Fischer's dynamic skill framework, the idea that human performance changes in response to changes in context.

dynamic systems theory A perspective on development which, when applied to motor development, proposes that more sophisticated patterns of motor behavior emerge over time through a "self-organizing" process in which children modify their motor behavior in adaptive ways on the basis of the sensory feedback they receive when they try different movements.

dyslexia Serious difficulties learning to read in children who have normal intellectual ability and no sensory impairments or emotional difficulties that could account for their learning problems.

dysrationalia A term coined by Keith Stanovich for a quite common inability to think and behave rationally despite having adequate intelligence.

easy temperament Characteristic mode of response in which the individual is even-tempered, content, and open and adaptable to new experiences. Contrast with *difficult temperament* and *slow-to-warm-up temperament*.

eclectic In the context of science, an individual who recognizes that no single theory can explain everything but that each has something to contribute to our understanding.

effortful control Dimension of temperament pertaining to being able to sustain attention, control one's behavior, and regulate one's emotions (as opposed to unable to regulate one's arousal and stay calm and focused). See also *negative affectivity* and *surgency/extraversion*.

ego Psychoanalytic term for the rational component of the personality.

egocentrism The tendency to view the world from the person's own perspective and fail to recognize that others may have different points of view.

elaboration A strategy for remembering that involves adding something to or creating meaningful links between the bits of information the person is trying to retain.

Electra complex Female version of the *Oedipus complex*, in which a 4- to 6-year-old girl is said to envy her father for possessing a penis and would choose him as a sex object in the hope of sharing this valuable organ that she lacks.

embryologist Scientist who studies early growth and development during the prenatal period.

embryonic period Second phase of prenatal development, lasting from the third through the eighth prenatal week, during which the major organs and anatomical structures begin to develop.

emergent literacy The developmental precursors of reading skills in young children, including knowledge, skills, and attributes that will facilitate the acquisition of reading competence.

emerging adulthood Newly identified period of the life span extending from about age 18 to age 25 or even later, when young people are neither adolescents nor adults and are exploring their identities, careers, and relationships.

emotion regulation The processes involved in initiating, maintaining, and altering emotional responses.

emotional competence Mastery of emotions in terms of appropriate expression of emotions, understanding of emotions and what triggers them, and ability to regulate emotions.

emotional display rules Cultural rules specifying what emotions should and should not be expressed under what circumstances (for example, "look pleased when you receive a lousy gift").

empathy The vicarious experiencing of another person's feelings.

emotionally focused therapy Psychotherapy approach based on attachment theory that helps partners understand their attachment-related emotions, communicate their emotions, and collaborate to better meet one another's emotional needs.

empty nest The term used to describe the family after the last child departs the household.

encoding The first step in learning and remembering something, it is the process of getting information into the information-processing system, or learning it.

endocrine gland A type of gland that secretes chemicals called hormones directly into the bloodstream. Endocrine glands play critical roles in stimulating growth and regulating bodily functions.

endometriosis A condition arising when bits of tissue lining the uterus grow outside the uterus; a cause of infertility.

environment Events or conditions outside the person that are presumed to influence and be influenced by the individual.

epigenesis The process through which nature and nurture, genes and environment, jointly bring forth development in ways that are difficult to predict at the outset.

epigenetic effects Ways in which environmental influences alter the expression of genes (whether genes are turned on or off) and therefore the influence of genes on traits.

episodic memory A type of explicit memory consisting of specific episodes that one has experienced.

equilibration In Piaget's theory, the process of seeking a state of mental stability in which our thoughts (schemes) are consistent with the information we receive from the external world.

erectile dysfunction A man's inability to achieve or sustain an erection for intercourse, despite having sufficient levels of testosterone.

error (damage) theories of aging Theories of aging that call attention to haphazard processes that cause damage or errors in cells to accumulate and organ systems to deteriorate. Contrast with *programmed theories of aging*.

estrogen The female hormone responsible for the development of the breasts, the female sex organs, and secondary sex characteristics and for the beginning of menstrual cycles.

ethnic identity A sense of personal identification with the individual's ethnic group and its values and cultural traditions.

ethnicity A person's classification in or affiliation with a group based on common heritage or traditions.

ethnocentrism The belief that one's own cultural or ethnic group is superior to others.

ethology A discipline and theoretical perspective that focuses on the evolved behavior of different species in their natural environments.

euthanasia Literally, "good death"; specifically, hastening, either actively or passively, the death of someone suffering from an incurable illness or injury.

evidence-based practice Grounding what professionals do in research and ensuring that the curricula and treatments provided to students or clients have been demonstrated to be effective.

evocative gene–environment correlation Phenomenon in which children's genotypes *evoke* certain kinds of reactions from other people so that their genetic makeup and experiences are correlated. Contrast with *active gene–environment correlation* and *passive gene–environment correlation*.

evoked potentials Electrical activity in the brain, as measured through electrodes attached to the surface of the skull, in response to various stimuli; used to study infant perception.

evolutionary psychology The application of evolutionary theory and its concept of natural selection to understanding why humans think and behave as they do.

executive control processes Processes that direct and monitor the selection, organization, manipulation, and interpretation of information in the information-processing system, including executive functions.

executive functions The planning, organizational, and inhibitory functions carried out in the prefrontal cortex of the brain.

exosystem In Bronfenbrenner's bioecological approach, settings not experienced directly by individuals that still influence their development (for example, effects of events at a parent's workplace on children's development).

expansion A conversational tactic used by adults in speaking to young children in which they respond to a child's utterance with a more grammatically complete expression of the same thought.

experiment A research strategy in which the investigator manipulates or alters some aspect of a person's environment to measure its effect on the individual's behavior or development.

experimental control The holding of all other factors besides the independent variable in an experiment constant so that any changes in the dependent variable can be said to be caused by the manipulation of the independent variable.

explicit memory Memory that involves consciously recollecting the past. Contrast with *implicit memory*.

extended family household A family unit composed of parents and children living with other kin such as grandparents, aunts and uncles, cousins, or a combination of these. Compare with *nuclear family*.

externalizing problem Childhood behavioral problem that involves "undercontrolled" behavior such as aggression or acting out difficulties that disturb other people. Contrast with *internalizing problem*.

extinction The gradual weakening and disappearance of a learned response when it is no longer reinforced.

eyewitness memory Remembering and reporting events the person has witnessed or experienced.

factor analysis Statistical technique to identify meaningful groupings of personality scale or intelligence test items that are correlated with each other but not with other groupings of items.

false belief task A research paradigm used to assess an important aspect of a theory of mind, mainly the understanding that people can hold incorrect beliefs and be influenced by them.

family life cycle The sequence of changes in family composition, roles, and relationships that occurs from the time people marry until they die.

family stress model Model of the effects of economic hardship in families that centers on the negative effects of financial stresses on parent mental health, parenting, and, in turn, child development.

family study Method of studying genetic and environmental influence that examines similarities in traits between pairs of siblings who have different degrees of genetic similarity—for example, identical twins, full biological siblings, half siblings, and unrelated stepsiblings who live together in stepfamilies.

family systems theory The conceptualization of the family as a whole consisting of interrelated parts, each of which affects and is affected by every other part, and each of which contributes to the functioning of the whole.

fast mapping The capacity of young language learners to readily determine the object or other referent of a word and then remember this for future encounters with the word.

fetal alcohol syndrome (FAS) A group of symptoms commonly observed in the offspring of mothers who use alcohol heavily during pregnancy, including a small head, widely spaced eyes, and mental retardation.

fetal period The third phase of prenatal development, lasting from the ninth prenatal week until birth; during this period, the major organ systems begin to function effectively and the fetus grows rapidly.

fetal programming Processes through which the prenatal environment affects the genetic unfolding of the embryo/fetus and its physiologic functions in ways that can influence health and mental health much later in life.

fine motor skills Skills that involve precise movements of the hands and fingers or feet and toes. Contrast with *gross motor skills*.

fixation In psychoanalytic theory, a defense mechanism in which development is arrested and part of the libido remains tied to an early stage of development.

fixed mindset The belief that intelligence and other traits are fixed or static; associated with the tendency to want to prove rather than improve one's ability. Contrast with *growth mindset*.

fluid intelligence Aspects of intelligence that involve actively thinking and reasoning to solve novel problems. Contrast with *crystallized intelligence*.

Flynn effect The rise in average IQ scores over the 20th century.

focusing system Attentional system that deliberately seeks out and maintains attention to events. Contrast with *orienting system*, which is captured by stimuli.

foreclosure status An identity status characterizing individuals who appear to have committed themselves to a life direction but who have adopted an identity prematurely, without much thought.

form perception In visual perception, recognition of the patterns that constitute an object.

formal operations stage Piaget's fourth and final stage of cognitive development (from age 11 or 12), when the individual begins to think more rationally and systematically about abstract concepts and hypothetical ideas.

fragile X syndrome A chromosome abnormality in which one arm of the X chromosome is only barely connected to the rest of the chromosome; the most common hereditary cause of mental retardation.

fraternal twins Twins who are not identical and who result when a mother releases two ova at roughly the same time and each is fertilized by a different sperm.

free radicals Chemically unstable byproducts of metabolism that have an unpaired electron and react with other molecules to produce toxic substances that damage cells and contribute to aging.

functional grammar An analysis of the semantic relations (meanings such as naming and locating) that children express in their earliest sentences.

functional magnetic resonance imaging (fMRI) A brain-scanning technique that uses magnetic forces to measure the increase in blood flow to an area of the brain that occurs when that brain area is active. By having children and adults perform cognitive tasks while lying very still in an fMRI scanner, researchers can determine which parts of the brain are involved in particular cognitive activities.

fuzzy-trace theory The view that verbatim and general or gistlike accounts of an event are stored separately in memory.

gender A combination of all those features that a society associates with or considers appropriate for being a man and woman.

gender consistency The stage of gender typing in which children realize that their sex is stable across situations or despite changes in activities or appearance.

gender constancy A solid understanding of oneself as male–female, man–woman, over time and across situations.

gender identity Individuals' basic awareness that they are either a male or a female.

gender intensification A magnification of differences between males and females during adolescence associated with increased pressure to conform to traditional gender roles.

gender role A pattern of behaviors and traits that defines how to act the part of a female or a male in a particular society.

gender schema (plural: **schemata**) Organized sets of beliefs and expectations about males and females that guide information processing.

gender segregation The formation of separate boys' and girls' peer groups during childhood.

gender similarities hypothesis The hypothesis that males and females are similar on most, but not all, psychological variables.

gender stability The stage of gender typing in which children realize that their sex remains the same over time.

gender stereotypes Overgeneralized and largely inaccurate beliefs about what males and females are like.

gender typing The process by which children become aware of their gender and acquire the motives, values, and behaviors considered appropriate for members of their biological sex.

gene A functional unit of heredity made up of DNA and transmitted from generation to generation.

gene expression The activation of particular genes in particular cells of the body at particular times in life.

gene therapy Interventions that involve substituting normal genes for the genes associated with a disease or disorder; otherwise altering a person's genetic makeup.

gene–environment correlation A systematic interrelationship between an individual's genes and that individual's environment; ways in which genes influence the kind of home environment provided by parents (*passive gene–environment correlation*), the social reactions to the individual (*evocative gene–environment correlation*), and the types of experiences the individual seeks (*active gene–environment correlation*).

gene–environment interaction The phenomenon in which the effects of people's genes depend on the kind of environment they experience and in which the effects of the environment depend on their genetic endowment.

General Adaptive Composite (GAC) An overall score on the *Bayley Scales of Infant Development* reflecting the cognitive, language, motor, and social–emotional development of an infant in comparison with a large norm group of infants or toddlers the same age.

general event representation (GER) Representations that people create over time of the typical sequence of actions related to an event; also called "scripts."

generativity versus stagnation The psychosocial conflict in which middle-aged adults must gain the sense that they have produced something that will outlive them and genuinely care for younger generations to avoid self-preoccupation; seventh of Erikson's stages.

genetic counseling A service designed to inform people about genetic conditions they or their unborn children are at risk of inheriting.

genetically informed study A study designed to determine whether there are genetic explanations for apparent environmental effects and establish more firmly whether environment matters (for example, by seeing whether the influence of a parenting behavior is as powerful for adopted children as for biological children).

genotype The genetic endowment that an individual inherits. Contrast with *phenotype*.

germinal period First phase of prenatal development, lasting about 2 weeks from conception until the developing organism becomes attached to the wall of the uterus.

gerontology The study of aging and old age.

giftedness The possession of unusually high general intellectual potential or of special abilities in such areas as creativity, mathematics, or the arts.

glaucoma A condition in which increased fluid pressure in the eye damages the optic nerve and causes progressive loss of peripheral vision and ultimately blindness.

goal-corrected partnership In Bowlby's attachment theory, the most mature phase of attachment in which parent and child accommodate to each other's needs and the child becomes more independent.

goodness of fit The extent to which the child's temperament and the demands of the child's social environment are compatible or mesh, according to Thomas and Chess; more generally, a good match between person and environment.

grief The emotional response to loss. Contrast with *mourning*.

grief work perspective The view commonly held, but now challenged, that to cope adaptively with death bereaved people must confront their loss, experience painful emotions, work through these emotions, and move toward a detachment from the deceased.

gross motor skills Skills that involve large muscles and whole body or limb movements (for example, kicking the legs or drawing large circles). Contrast with *fine motor skills*.

growth The physical changes that occur from conception to maturity.

growth hormone Hormone produced by the pituitary gland that stimulates childhood physical growth and the adolescent growth spurt.

growth mindset The belief that intelligence is not fixed but malleable and can therefore be improved through hard work and effort. Contrast with *fixed mindset*.

guided participation A process in which children learn by actively participating in culturally relevant activities with the aid and support of their parents and other knowledgeable individuals.

habituation A simple form of learning that involves learning not to respond to a repeated stimulus; learning to be bored by the familiar.

Hayflick limit The estimate that human cells can double only 50 times, plus or minus 10, and then will die.

helicopter parenting Also called overparenting, parenting characterized by developmentally inappropriate levels of control of and assistance to late adolescent and emerging adult children.

hemophilia A deficiency in the blood's ability to clot. It is more common among males than females because it is associated with a sex-linked gene on the X chromosome.

heritability The amount of variability in a population on some trait dimension that is attributable to genetic differences among those individuals.

hippocampus Structure in the medial temporal lobe of the brain centrally involved in the formation of memories.

holophrase A single-word utterance used by an infant that represents an entire sentence's worth of meaning.

Home Observation for Measurement of the Environment (HOME) inventory A widely used instrument that allows an observer to determine how intellectually stimulating or impoverished a home environment is.

homogamy Basis for mate selection centered on similarity between partners in demographic and personal characteristics. Contrast with *complementarity*.

hookup A sexual encounter between two people who have often just met and have little expectation of forming a romantic relationship.

hormone replacement therapy (HRT) Taking estrogen and progestin to compensate for hormone loss because of menopause in women.

hospice A program that supports dying persons and their families through a philosophy of caring rather than curing, either in a facility or at home.

hostile attribution bias The tendency of aggressive individuals to attribute hostile intentions to others, assuming that any harm to them was deliberate rather than accidental.

hot flash A sudden experience of warmth and sweating, often followed by a cold shiver, that occurs in a menopausal woman.

Human Genome Project The massive, government-sponsored effort to decipher the human genetic code.

Huntington's disease A genetic disease caused by a single, dominant gene that strikes in middle age to produce a deterioration of physical and mental abilities and premature death.

hyperactivity See *attention deficit hyperactivity disorder (ADHD)*.

hypothesis A theory-based prediction about what will hold true if we observe a phenomenon.

hypothetical–deductive reasoning A form of problem solving in which a person starts with general or abstract ideas and deduces or traces their specific implications; "if–then" thinking.

id A psychoanalytic term for the inborn component of the personality that is driven by the instincts or selfish urges.

ideal self Idealized expectations of what one's attributes and personality should be like.

ideational fluency The sheer number of different (including novel) ideas that a person can generate; a measure of *creativity* or *divergent thinking*.

identical twins Monozygotic twins who develop from a single zygote that later divides to form two genetically identical individuals.

identification Freud's term for the individual's tendency to emulate, or adopt the attitudes and behaviors of, another person, particularly the same-sex parent.

identity A self-definition or sense of who one is, where one is going, and how one fits into society.

identity achievement status An identity status characterizing individuals who have carefully thought through identity issues and made commitments or resolved their identity issues.

identity versus role confusion The psychosocial conflict in which adolescents must form a coherent self-definition or remain confused about their life directions; fifth of Erikson's stages.

imaginary audience A form of adolescent egocentrism that involves confusing one's own thoughts with the thoughts of a hypothesized audience for behavior and concluding that others share these preoccupations.

imaginary companion A play companion invented by a child in the preoperational stage who has developed the capacity for symbolic thought.

implicit memory Memory that occurs unintentionally and without consciousness or awareness. Contrast with *explicit memory*.

imprinting An innate form of learning in which the young of certain species will follow and become attached to moving objects (usually their mothers) during a critical period early in life.

independent variable The aspect of the environment that a researcher deliberately changes or manipulates in an experiment to see its effect on behavior; a causal variable. Contrast with *dependent variable*.

indirect effect The instance in which the relationship between two individuals in a family is modified by the behavior or attitudes of a third family member.

individualistic culture A culture in which individuals define themselves as individuals and put their own goals ahead of their group's goals and in which children are socialized to be independent and self-reliant. Contrast with *collectivist culture*.

induction A form of discipline that involves explaining why a child's behavior is wrong and should be changed by emphasizing its effects on other people.

industry versus inferiority The psychosocial conflict in which school-aged children must master important cognitive and social skills or feel incompetent; fourth of Erikson's stages.

infertility A couple's inability to get pregnant after a year of trying to do so.

information-processing approach An approach to cognition that emphasizes the fundamental mental processes involved in attention, perception, memory, and decision making.

initiative versus guilt The psychosocial conflict in which preschool children must learn to initiate new activities and pursue bold plans or become self-critical; third of Erikson's stages.

instinct An inborn biological force assumed to motivate a particular response or class of responses.

integrity versus despair The psychosocial conflict in which elderly adults attempt to find a sense of meaning in their lives and to accept the inevitability of death; eighth of Erikson's stages.

intellectual disability Significantly below-average intellectual functioning with limitations in areas of adaptive behavior such as self-care and social skills, originating before age 18 (previously known as *mental retardation*).

intelligence quotient (IQ) A numerical measure of a person's performance on an intelligence test relative to the performance of other examinees of the same age, typically with a score of 100 defined as average.

interactional model A model of family influence in which it is the combination of a particular kind of child with a particular kind of parent that determines developmental outcomes.

intergenerational transmission of parenting The passing down from generation to generation of parenting styles, abusive or otherwise.

internal working model In attachment theory, cognitive representation of self and other that children construct from their interactions with caregivers and that shape their expectations about relationships.

internalizing problem Childhood behavioral problem that represents an "overcontrolled" pattern of coping with difficulties and is expressed in anxiety, depression, and other forms of inner distress. Contrast with *externalizing problem.*

intimacy versus isolation The psychosocial conflict in which young adults must commit themselves to a shared identity with another person or remain aloof and unconnected to others; sixth of Erikson's stages.

intuitive theories Organized systems of knowledge, believed to be innate, that allow children to make sense of the world in areas such as physics and psychology.

investment theory Sternberg's view that creativity emerges from a confluence, or coming together, of several ingredients, each in the right amounts and at the right times: intellectual abilities, knowledge, cognitive style, personality, motivation, and a supportive environment.

in vitro fertilization (IVF) Procedure in which several eggs are removed from a woman's ovary, fertilized by sperm in a petri dish in the laboratory, then transferred to the woman's uterus in hopes that one will implant on the wall of the uterus.

joint attention The act of looking at the same object at the same time with someone else; a way in which infants share perceptual experiences with their caregivers.

juvenile delinquency Lawbreaking by a minor.

kangaroo care Holding a young infant skin-to-skin on a parent's chest; often used with premature babies to help maintain body temperature, heart rate, and oxygen levels in the blood.

karyotype A chromosomal portrait created by staining chromosomes, photographing them under a high-power microscope, and arranging them into a predetermined pattern.

kinkeeper An individual, typically a woman, who keeps family members in touch with each other and handles family problems when they arise.

knowledge base A person's existing information about a content area, significant for its influence on how well that individual can learn and remember.

Lamaze method Prepared childbirth in which parents attend classes and learn mental exercises and relaxation techniques to ease delivery.

language A symbolic system in which a limited number of signals can be combined according to rules to produce an infinite number of messages.

language acquisition device (LAD) A set of linguistic processing skills that nativists believe to be innate; presumably the LAD enables a child to infer the rules governing others' speech and then use these rules to produce language.

latent learning Learning occurs but is not evident in behavior; children can learn from observation even though they do not imitate (perform) the learned responses.

lateralization The specialization of the two hemispheres of the cerebral cortex of the brain.

learning A relatively permanent change in behavior (or behavioral potential) that results from a person's experiences or practice.

learning goal A goal adopted by learners in which they seek to learn new things so that they can improve their abilities. Contrast with *performance goal.*

Lewy body dementia Considered the second or third most common neurocognitive disorder after Alzheimer's disease, a condition associated with protein deposits in neurons called Lewy bodies that cause changes in cognitive functioning, visual hallucinations, and often motor and balance problems.

libido Freud's term for the biological energy of the sex instinct.

life expectancy The average number of years a newborn baby can be expected to live; now about 78 years in the United States.

life review Process in which elderly adults reflect on unresolved conflicts of the past and evaluate their lives; it may contribute to a sense of integrity and readiness for death.

life script The story a person constructs about his or her life story and tells over and over again.

life-span perspective A perspective that views development as a lifelong, multidirectional process that involves gain and loss, is characterized by considerable plasticity, is shaped by its historical–cultural context, has many causes, and is best viewed from a multidisciplinary perspective.

linked lives The concept that the development of the individual is intertwined with the development of other family members.

literacy The ability to use printed information to function in society, achieve goals, and develop potential.

living will A document, also called an advance directive, in which people state

in advance that they do not wish to have extraordinary medical procedures applied if they are hopelessly ill.

locomotion The process of moving from one location to another.

longitudinal design A developmental research design in which one group of subjects is studied repeatedly over months or years.

long-term memory Memory store in which information that has been examined and interpreted is stored relatively permanently.

loss-oriented coping In the dual-process model of bereavement, coping focused on dealing with one's emotions and reconciling oneself to the loss. Contrast with *restoration-oriented coping.*

love withdrawal A form of discipline that involves withholding attention, affection, or approval after a child misbehaves.

low birth weight (LBW) A weight at birth of less than 2500 grams, or 5½ pounds, associated with increased risk of developmental problems.

macrosystem In Bronfenbrenner's bioecological approach, the larger cultural or subcultural context of development.

major depressive disorder An affective or mood disorder characterized by at least one episode of feeling profoundly sad and hopeless, losing interest in almost all activities, or both.

mastery (learning) goal In achievement situations, aiming to learn new things in order to learn or improve ability; contrast with *performance goal.*

mastery motivation An intrinsic motive to master and control the environment evident early in infancy.

maternal blood sampling A noninvasive method of prenatal diagnosis involving testing for substances in maternal blood; more recently, analysis of fetal cells that have slipped through the placenta into the mother's blood.

maturation Developmental changes that are biologically programmed by genes rather than caused primarily by learning, injury, illness, or some other life experience.

maturity principle A shift toward greater emotional stability, agreeableness, and conscientiousness in personality from adolescence to middle adulthood.

maximum life span A ceiling on the number of years that any member of a species lives; 120 years for humans.

mediation deficiency The initial stage of mastery of memory strategies in which children cannot spontaneously use or benefit from strategies even if they are taught to use them.

meiosis The process in which a germ cell divides, producing sperm or ova, each containing half of the parent cell's original complement of chromosomes; in humans, the products of meiosis normally contain 23 chromosomes.

memory The ability to store and later retrieve information about past events.

menarche A female's first menstrual period.

menopause The ending of a woman's menstrual periods and reproductive capacity around age 51.

mental age (MA) A measure of intellectual development that reflects the level of age-graded problems that a child is able to solve; the age at which a child functions intellectually.

mental retardation See *intellectual disability*.

mesosystem In Bronfenbrenner's bioecological approach, interrelationships between microsystems or immediate environments (for example, ways in which events in the family affect a child's interactions at a day care center).

meta-analysis A research method in which the results of multiple studies addressing the same question are synthesized to produce overall conclusions.

metabolic syndrome (MeTS) A combination of risk factors that can lead to heart disease; notably obesity, high blood pressure, unhealthy cholesterol levels, and insulin resistance (which can lead to diabetes).

metacognition Knowledge of the human mind and of the range of cognitive processes, including thinking about personal thought processes.

metalinguistic awareness Knowledge of language as a system.

metamemory A person's knowledge about memory and about monitoring and regulating memory processes.

microsystem In Bronfenbrenner's bioecological approach, the immediate settings in which the person functions (for example, the family).

middle generation squeeze The phenomenon in which middle-aged adults sometimes experience heavy responsibilities for both the younger and the older generations in the family.

midlife crisis A period of major questioning, inner struggle, and re-evaluation hypothesized to occur in an adult's early 40s.

migration Process in early brain development in which neurons move from their place of origin in the center of the brain to particular locations throughout the brain where they will become part of specialized functioning units.

mild cognitive impairment A level of memory loss between normal loss with age and pathological loss from disease.

millennials Also called Generation Y or the "baby boomlet" generation, the American generation born from 1982 to 2004.

mind-mindedness The tendency to think and talk in elaborated ways about mental states; parents' mind-mindedness contributes to the development of children's theory-of-mind and other social cognitive skills.

mirror neurons Neural cells in several brain areas that are activated not only when we perform an action but also when we observe someone else performing it. Implicated in imitation, theory of mind skills, empathy, and language.

miscarriage Loss of a pregnancy before survival of the baby outside the womb is possible.

mitosis The process in which a cell duplicates its chromosomes and then divides into two genetically identical daughter cells.

molecular genetics The analysis of particular genes and their effects, including the identification of specific genes that influence particular traits and the comparison of animals or humans who have these specific genes and those who do not.

moral disengagement According to Bandura, the ability to avoid self-condemnation when engaged in immoral behavior by justifying, minimizing, or blaming others for one's actions.

moral identity Viewing being caring, fair, honest, and otherwise moral as a central aspect of who you are.

moral reasoning The cognitive component of morality; the thinking that occurs when people decide whether acts are right or wrong.

moral rules Standards of conduct that focus on the basic rights and privileges of individuals. Contrast with *social-conventional rules*.

morality The ability to distinguish right from wrong, to act on this distinction, and to experience pride when doing something right and to experience guilt or shame when doing something wrong. Morality has emotional, cognitive, and behavioral components.

moratorium period A period of time in high school or college when young adults are relatively free of responsibilities and can experiment with different roles to find their identities.

moratorium status Identity status characterizing individuals who are experiencing an identity crisis or actively exploring identity issues but who have not yet achieved an identity.

morphemes The basic units of meaning that exist in a word.

mourning Culturally prescribed ways of displaying reactions to a loss. Contrast with *grief*.

multitasking Attending to and performing two or more tasks at the same time.

mutation A change in the structure or arrangement of one or more genes that produces a new phenotype.

mutually responsive orientation A close, affectively positive, and cooperative relationship in which child and parent are attached to each other and are sensitive to each other's needs; a contributor to moral development.

myelin A fatty sheath that insulates neural axons and thereby speeds the transmission of neural impulses.

myelination The depositing of a fatty sheath around neural axons that insulates them and thereby speeds the transmission of neural impulses.

narrative identities Unique and integrative "life stories" that we construct about our pasts and futures to give ourselves an identity and our lives meaning; an aspect of personality.

nativist An individual whose approach to human development emphasizes the contribution of genetic factors; specifically, a person who believes that infants enter the world equipped with knowledge that allows them to perceive a meaningful world from the start.

natural selection The evolutionary principle that individuals who have characteristics advantageous for survival in a particular environment are most likely to survive and reproduce. Over many generations, this process of "survival of the fittest" will lead to changes in a species and the development of new species.

naturalistic observation A research method in which the scientist observes people as they engage in common everyday activities in their natural habitats. Contrast with *structured observation*.

nature–nurture issue The debate over the relative roles of biological predispositions (nature) and environmental influences (nurture) as determinants of human development.

negative affectivity Dimension of temperament that concerns the tendency to be sad, fearful, easily frustrated, and irritable (as opposed to laid back and adaptable). See also *effortful control* and *surgency/extraversion*.

negative punishment The process in operant conditioning in which a response is weakened or made less probable when its consequence is the removal of a pleasant stimulus from the situation.

negative reinforcement The process in operant conditioning in which a response is strengthened or made more probable when its consequence is the removal of an unpleasant stimulus from the situation.

neglectful parenting A parenting style low in demandingness–control and low in acceptance–responsiveness; uninvolved parenting.

neonatal Pertaining to events or developments in the first month after birth.

neuro-constructivism theory Approach that explains the construction of new knowledge by the child in terms of changes in neural structures in response to experience.

neurogenesis The process of generating new neurons across the life span.

neuron The basic unit of the nervous system; a nerve cell.

neuroplasticity The brain's remarkable ability to change in response to experience throughout the life span, as when it recovers from injury or benefits from stimulating learning experiences.

nonshared environmental influences Experiences unique to the individual that are not shared by other members of the family and that tend to make members of the same family different. Contrast with *shared environmental influences*.

normal distribution A symmetrical (bell-shaped) curve that describes the variability of a characteristic within a population. Most people fall at or near the average score; there are relatively few high or low scores.

nuclear family A family unit consisting of husband–father, wife–mother, and at least one child. Compare with *extended family household*.

obesity Condition of being overweight; specifically, being 20% or more above the "ideal" weight for one's height, age, and sex.

object permanence The understanding that objects continue to exist when they are no longer visible or otherwise detectable to the senses; fully mastered by the end of infancy.

observational learning Learning that results from observing the behavior of other people; emphasized in Bandura's social cognitive theory.

Oedipus complex Freud's term for the conflict that 4- to 6-year-old boys experience when they develop an incestuous desire for their mothers and a jealous and hostile rivalry with their fathers.

olfaction The sense of smell, made possible by sensory receptors in the nasal passage that react to chemical molecules in the air.

operant conditioning Also called instrumental conditioning, a form of learning in which freely emitted acts (or operants) become more or less probable depending on the consequences they produce.

oral sex Sexual activity involving contact between the mouth and genitals.

organization In Piaget's cognitive developmental theory, a person's inborn tendency to combine and integrate available schemes into more coherent and complex systems or bodies of knowledge; as a memory strategy, a technique that involves grouping or classifying stimuli into meaningful clusters.

organogenesis The process, occurring during the period of the embryo, in which major organs take shape.

orienting system An attentional system that reacts to events in the environment; contrast with a *focusing system* that deliberately seeks out and maintains attention to events.

orthogenetic principle Werner's principle that development proceeds from global and undifferentiated states toward more differentiated and integrated patterns of response.

osteoarthritis A joint problem among older adults resulting from a gradual deterioration of the cartilage that cushions the bones and keeps them from rubbing together.

osteoporosis A disease affecting older adults in which bone tissue is lost, leaving bones fragile and easily fractured.

overextension The young child's tendency to use a word to refer to a wider set of objects, actions, or events than adults do (for example, using the word *car* to refer to all motor vehicles). Contrast with *underextension*.

overimitation An adaptive and apparently universal tendency of children to imitate every detail of what they see a model do, even actions that are not directly useful in achieving a goal.

overlapping waves theory Siegler's view that the development of problem-solving skills is not a matter of moving from one problem-solving approach to a better one with age but of knowing and using a variety of strategies at each age, becoming increasingly selective with experience about which strategies to use in particular situations, and adding new strategies to one's collection.

overregularization The overgeneralization of observed grammatical rules to irregular cases to which the rules do not apply (for example, saying *mouses* rather than *mice*).

oxytocin A hormone that plays important roles in facilitating parent-infant attachment as well as reducing anxiety and encouraging affiliation in other social relationships.

palliative care Care aimed not at curing but at meeting the physical, psychological, and spiritual needs of dying patients.

parallel processing Carrying out multiple cognitive operations simultaneously rather than in a sequence.

parent–child interaction therapy (PCIT) A therapy approach to treat young children with behavioral or psychological problems that centers on modifying the parent–child relationship and building more effective parenting skills.

parent effects model A model of family influence in which parents are believed to influence their children rather than vice versa.

parental imperative The notion that the demands of parenthood cause men and women to adopt distinct roles and psychological traits.

Parkes/Bowlby attachment model of bereavement Model of grieving describing four predominant reactions to loss of an attachment figure: numbness, yearning, disorganization and despair, and reorganization.

passive gene–environment correlation Phenomenon in which, because parents provide children with both their genes and a home environment compatible with those genes, the home environments to which children are exposed are correlated with (and typically reinforce) their genotypes. Contrast with *active gene–environment correlation* and *evocative gene–environment correlation*.

peer A social equal; a person who functions at a level of behavioral complexity similar to that of the self, often someone of similar age.

peer selection/socialization issue Issue in the study of peer influence asking whether adolescents resemble their peers because they select similar others as friends or because their friends socialize them in certain directions.

perception The interpretation of sensory input.

perceptual salience Phenomenon in which the most obvious features of an object or situation have disproportionate influence on the perceptions and thoughts of young children.

perceived popularity Perceived status, power, and visibility in the peer group, as distinct from likeability. Contrast with *sociometric popularity*.

performance goal A goal adopted by learners in which they attempt to prove their ability rather than to improve it. Contrast with *learning* (or *mastery*) goal.

perinatal environment The environment surrounding birth.

perinatologist A maternal-fetal specialist who focuses on high-risk pregnancies.

permissive parenting A lax style of parenting combining low demandingness–control and high acceptance–responsiveness in which adults love their children but make few demands on them and rarely attempt to control their behavior.

perseveration error Mistake made when an information processor continues to use the same strategy that was successful in the past over and over despite the strategy's lack of success in the current situation.

person–environment fit The match between the individual's personality and environment (for example, work environment); similar to *goodness of fit* between temperament and environment.

personal fable A form of adolescent egocentrism that involves thinking that oneself and one's thoughts and feelings are unique or special.

personality The organized combination of attributes, motives, values, and behaviors that is unique to each individual.

perspective-taking skills The ability to assume other people's perspectives and understand their thoughts, feelings, and behaviors; role-taking skills.

phenotype The way in which a person's genotype is expressed in observable or measurable characteristics.

phenylketonuria (PKU) A genetic disease in which the child is unable to metabolize phenylalanine; if left untreated, it soon causes hyperactivity and mental retardation.

phoneme One of the basic units of sound used in a particular spoken language.

phonological awareness The understanding that spoken words can be decomposed into some number of basic sound units, or phonemes; an important skill in learning to read.

pincer grasp A grasp in which the thumb is used in opposition to the fingers, enabling an infant to become more dexterous at lifting and manipulating objects.

pituitary gland The "master gland" located at the base of the brain that regulates the other endocrine glands and produces growth hormone.

placenta An organ, formed from the chorion and the lining of the uterus, that provides for the nourishment of the unborn child and the elimination of its metabolic wastes.

plasticity An openness of brain cells or of the organism as a whole to positive and negative environmental influence; a capacity to change in response to experience.

polygenic inheritance Mechanism of inheritance in which multiple gene pairs interact with environmental factors to influence a trait.

polygenic trait A characteristic influenced by the action of many gene pairs rather than a single pair.

population A well-defined group that a researcher who studies a sample of individuals is interested in drawing conclusions about.

positive punishment The process in operant conditioning whereby a response is weakened when its consequence is an unpleasant event.

positive reinforcement The process in operant conditioning whereby a response is strengthened when its consequence is a pleasant event.

positive youth development (PYD) An approach that emphasizes developing the strengths of youth rather than reducing their problem behaviors.

positivity effect The tendency of older adults to pay more attention to, better remember, and put more priority on positive information than on negative information; see also *socioemotional selectivity theory*.

postconventional morality Kohlberg's term for the fifth and sixth stages of moral reasoning, in which moral judgments are based on a more abstract understanding of democratic social contracts or on universal principles of justice that have validity apart from the views of particular authority figures.

postformal thought Proposed stages of cognitive development that lie beyond formal operations.

postpartum depression An episode of severe, clinical depression lasting for months in a woman who has just given birth; to be contrasted with milder cases of the "baby blues," in which a new mother is tearful and moody in the first days after birth.

posttraumatic growth Positive psychological change resulting from highly challenging experiences such as being diagnosed with a life-threatening illness or losing a loved one.

posttraumatic stress disorder A psychological disorder involving flashbacks to traumatizing events, nightmares, and feelings of helplessness and anxiety in the face of danger experienced by victims of extreme trauma such as soldiers in combat and sexually abused children.

poverty of the stimulus (POTS) Term for the notion that the language input to young children is so impoverished or limited that they could not possibly acquire language (without a powerful, innate *language acquisition device*).

power assertion A form of discipline that involves the use of superior power to administer spankings, withhold privileges, and so on.

PPCT model In Bronfenbrenner's bioecological theory, a call for doing more than comparing children who live at different social addresses by examining development as a function of four factors: process, person, context, and time.

practical component In Sternberg's triarchic theory of intelligence, the aspect of intelligence that varies from one sociocultural context to another.

pragmatics Rules specifying how language is to be used appropriately in different social contexts to achieve goals.

preconventional morality Kohlberg's term for the first two stages of moral reasoning, in which society's rules are not yet internalized and judgments are based on the punishing or rewarding consequences of an act.

preimplantation genetic diagnosis Prenatal diagnostic procedure in which a mother's eggs are fertilized in the laboratory using in vitro fertilization techniques, DNA tests are conducted on the first cells that result from mitosis of each fertilized egg, and only eggs that do not have chromosome abnormalities or genes associated with disorders are implanted in the uterus.

premenstrual dysphoric disorder (PDD) Severe form of premenstrual syndrome that includes affective symptoms in addition to physical symptoms associated with the menstrual cycle and that can be disabling or disruptive to work and relationships.

premenstrual syndrome (PMS) Several symptoms experienced shortly before each menstrual period that include having tender breasts, feeling bloated, and being irritable and moody.

prenatal environment The physical environment of the womb during the 9 months of pregnancy.

preoperational stage Piaget's second stage of cognitive development, lasting from about age

2 to age 7, when children think at a symbolic level but have not yet mastered logical operations.

presbycusis Problems of the aging ear, which commonly involve loss of sensitivity to high-frequency or high-pitched sounds.

presbyopia Problems of the aging eye, especially loss of near vision related to a decreased ability of the lens to accommodate to objects close to the eye.

pretend play Symbolic play in which one actor, object, or action symbolizes or stands for another.

primary circular reaction During Piaget's sensorimotor period, the infant's repetition of interacting acts centered on his or her own body (for example, repeatedly kicking).

primary emotion One of the distinct basic emotions that emerges within the first six months of life universally (joy, surprise, sadness, disgust, anger, fear).

private speech Nonsocial speech, or speech for the self, commonly used by preschoolers to guide their activities and believed by Vygotsky to be the forerunner of inner speech, or silent thinking in words.

proactive parenting strategies Parenting tactics that prevent misbehavior and therefore reduce the need for discipline (for example, teaching values, removing temptations).

problem solving The use of the information-processing system to achieve a goal or arrive at a decision.

prodigies Individuals, especially children, endowed with one or more extraordinary ability.

production deficiency A phase in the mastery of memory strategies in which children can use strategies they are taught but cannot produce them on their own.

programmed theories of aging Theories that emphasize the systematic genetic control of aging processes. Contrast with *random error theories of aging*.

proliferation Process in early brain development in which neurons multiply at a staggering rate throughout the prenatal period

prosocial behavior Positive actions toward other people such as helping and cooperating.

prosody The melody or sound pattern of speech, including intonation, stress, and timing with which something is said.

protective factors Influences that prevent the damaging effects of risk factors or help children overcome disadvantages.

proximal processes In Bronfenbrenner's bioecological theory, the important recurring,

reciprocal interactions between the individual and other people, objects, or symbols that move development forward (for example, parent and child reading bedtime stories together nightly).

proximodistal principle In development, the principle that growth proceeds from the center of the body (or the proximal region) to the extremities (or the distal regions).

psychoanalytic theory The theoretical perspective associated with Freud and his followers that emphasizes unconscious motivations for behavior, conflicts within the personality, and stages of psychosexual development.

psychometric approach The research tradition that spawned standardized tests of intelligence and that views intelligence (or personality) as a set of traits that can be measured and that varies from person to person.

psychosexual stages Freud's five stages of development, associated with biological maturation and shifts in the libido: oral, anal, phallic, latency, and genital.

psychosocial stages Erikson's eight stages of development (trust, autonomy, initiative, industry, identity, intimacy, generativity, and integrity), emphasizing social influences more and biological urges less than Freud's psychosexual stages.

puberty The processes of biological change that result in an individual's attaining sexual maturity and becoming capable of producing a child.

random assignment A technique in which research participants are placed in experimental conditions in an unbiased or random way so that the resulting groups are not systematically different.

random sample A sample formed by identifying all members of the larger population of interest and then selecting a portion of them in an unbiased or random way to participate in the study; a technique to ensure that the sample studied is representative or typical of the larger population of interest.

reaction time The interval between the presentation of a stimulus and a response to it.

recall memory Recollecting or actively retrieving objects, events, and experiences when examples or cues are not provided. Contrast with *cued recall memory* and *recognition memory*.

recessive gene A less powerful gene that is not expressed phenotypically when paired with a *dominant gene*.

reciprocal determinism The notion in social cognitive theory that the flow of influence between people and their environments is a

two-way street; the environment may affect the person, but the person's characteristics and behavior will also influence the environment.

reciprocity The mutual give and take by both parties in a human relationship that forms an important basis for morality.

recognition memory Identifying an object or event as one that has been experienced before, such as when a person must select the correct answer from several options. Contrast with *cued recall memory* and *recall memory*.

reconstituted family A new family that forms after the remarriage of a single parent, sometimes involving the blending of two families into a new one.

reflex An unlearned and automatic response to a stimulus.

regression A defense mechanism that involves retreating to an earlier, less traumatic stage of development.

rehearsal A strategy for remembering that involves repeating the items the person is trying to retain.

relational aggression Subtle and indirect aggression that involves gossiping about and ignoring or excluding others.

relativistic thinking A form of postformal operational thought in which it is understood that there are multiple ways of viewing a problem and that the solutions people arrive at will depend on their starting assumptions and perspective.

religiousness Sharing the beliefs and participating in the practices of an organized religion. Contrast with *spirituality*.

REM sleep A state of active, irregular sleep associated with dreaming; named for the rapid eye movements associated with it.

repression Removing unacceptable thoughts or traumatic memories from consciousness, as when a young woman who was raped has no memory at all of having been raped (or less drastically, engages in denial, knowing deep down that she was raped but not accepting the reality of it).

research ethics Standards of conduct that investigators are ethically bound to honor to protect their research participants from physical or psychological harm.

reserve capacity The ability of many organ systems to respond to demands for extraordinary output, such as when the heart and lungs work at maximal capacity.

resilience The ability to function well despite exposure to risk factors for maladaptive development or to overcome early developmental problems to become well adjusted.

resistant attachment An insecure infant–caregiver bond or other intimate relationship characterized by strong separation anxiety and a tendency to show ambivalent reactions to the attachment object upon reunion, seeking and yet resisting contact and not being comforted.

restoration-oriented coping In the dual-process model of bereavement, coping focused on managing daily living, rethinking one's life, and mastering new roles and challenges. Contrast with *loss-oriented coping*.

retinitis pigmentosa (RP) A group of hereditary disorders that involve gradual deterioration of the light-sensitive cells of the retina.

retrieval The process of retrieving information from long-term memory when it is needed.

retrograde amnesia Loss of memory for information and events occurring prior to the incident that caused the amnesia. Contrast with *anterograde amnesia*.

reversibility In Piaget's theory, the ability to reverse or negate an action by mentally performing the opposite action.

reversible dementia Significant cognitive decline that, unlike most dementia, can be cured or reversed; causes include alcoholism, toxic reactions to medication, infections, metabolic disorders, vitamin deficiencies, and malnutrition.

rhythmic stereotypies Repetitive movements observed in infants shortly before a new motor skill emerges.

rite of passage A ritual that marks a person's "passage" from one status to another, usually in reference to rituals marking the transition from childhood to adulthood.

role reversal Phenomenon in which the aging parent becomes the child and the child becomes the caregiver, not typical of most aging parent–child relationships.

role-taking skills The ability to assume other people's perspectives and understand their thoughts, feelings, and behaviors. See *perspective-taking skills*.

rubella A disease that has little effect on a pregnant woman but may cause several serious birth defects, such as blindness, deafness, and mental retardation, in unborn children exposed in the first 3 to 4 months of gestation; German measles.

rule assessment approach Siegler's approach to studying the development of problem solving that determines what information about a problem children take in and what rules they then formulate to account for this information.

ruminative coping Way of managing stress that involves dwelling on problems and attempting to analyze them; may help explain higher rates of depression in females than in males.

safe haven A point of safety, represented by an infant's attachment figure, to which the infant can return for comfort if frightened.

sample The group of individuals chosen to be the subjects of a study.

savant syndrome The phenomenon in which extraordinary talent in a particular area is displayed by a person who is otherwise mentally retarded.

scaffolding Jerome Bruner's term for providing structure to a less skilled learner to encourage advancement.

scheme (or **schema**; plural: **schemes** or **schemata**) A cognitive structure or organized pattern of action or thought used to deal with experiences.

schizophrenia A serious form of mental illness characterized by disturbances in logical thinking, emotional expression, and interpersonal behavior.

scientific method An attitude or value about the pursuit of knowledge that dictates that investigators must be objective and must allow their data to decide the merits of their theorizing.

script A mental representation of a typical sequence of actions related to an event that is created in memory and that then guides future behaviors in similar settings.

secondary circular reaction During Piaget's sensorimotor period, the infant's repetition of interesting actions on objects (for example, repeatedly shaking a rattle to make a noise).

secular trend A trend in industrialized societies toward earlier maturation and greater body size.

secure attachment An infant–caregiver bond or intimate relationship in which the individual welcomes close contact, uses the attachment object as a source of comfort, and dislikes but can manage separations.

secure base A point of safety, represented by an infant's attachment figure, that permits exploration of the environment.

selective attention Deliberately concentrating on one thing and ignoring something else.

selective optimization with compensation (SOC) The concept that older people cope with aging through a strategy that involves focusing on the skills most needed, practicing those skills, and developing ways to avoid the need for declining skills.

self-concept People's perceptions of their unique attributes or traits.

self-conscious emotion A "secondary emotion" such as embarrassment or pride that requires an awareness of self; unlikely to emerge until about 18 months of age.

self-control The ability to control or regulate one's desires, impulses, and behavior.

self-efficacy The belief that one can effectively produce desired outcomes in a particular area of life.

self-esteem People's overall evaluation of their worth as based on an assessment of the qualities that make up the self-concept.

self-recognition The ability to recognize oneself in a mirror or photograph, which occurs in most infants by 18 to 24 months of age.

self-stereotyping Applying stereotypes of one's group (for example, negative stereotypes of older adults) to oneself.

semantic memory A type of explicit memory consisting of general facts.

semantics The aspect of language centering on meanings.

semenarche A boy's first ejaculation.

sensation The process by which information is detected by the sensory receptors and transmitted to the brain; the starting point in perception.

sensitive period As compared to a critical period, a period of life during which the developing individual is especially susceptible to the effects of experience or has an especially high level of plasticity.

sensorimotor stage Piaget's first stage of cognitive development, spanning the first 2 years of life, in which infants rely on their senses and motor behaviors in adapting to the world around them.

sensory register The first memory store in information processing in which stimuli are noticed and are briefly available for further processing.

sensory threshold The point at which low levels of stimulation can be detected.

separation anxiety A wary or fretful reaction that infants display when separated from their attachment objects.

sequential design A developmental research design that combines the cross-sectional approach and the longitudinal approach in a single study to compensate for the weaknesses of each.

seriation A logical operation that allows a person to mentally order a set of stimuli along a quantifiable dimension such as height or weight.

sex chromosome abnormality A chromosome abnormality in which a child receives too many or too few sex chromosomes (X or Y).

sex-linked characteristic An attribute determined by a gene that appears on one of the two types of sex chromosomes, usually the X chromosome.

sex-linked inheritance Mechanism of inheritance in which a characteristic is influenced by single genes located on the sex chromosomes (usually the X chromosome).

sexual assault Unwanted and nonconsensual sexual contact or behavior ranging from unwanted touching to rape.

sexual orientation A person's preference for sexual partners of the same or other sex, often characterized as primarily heterosexual, homosexual, or bisexual.

shared environmental influences Experiences that individuals living in the same home environment share and that work to make them similar. Contrast with *nonshared environmental influences*.

short-term memory The memory store in which limited amounts of information are temporarily held; called *working memory* when its active quality is being emphasized.

sibling rivalry A spirit of competition, jealousy, or resentment that may arise between two or more brothers or sisters.

sickle-cell disease A genetic blood disease in which red blood cells assume an unusual sickle shape and become inefficient at distributing oxygen throughout the body.

single gene-pair inheritance The genetic mechanism through which a characteristic is influenced by only one pair of genes, one gene from the mother and its partner from the father.

size constancy The tendency to perceive an object as the same size despite changes in its distance from the eyes.

skill In Fischer's dynamic skill framework, a person's ability to perform a particular task in a specific context.

sleeper effect The delayed effect of an earlier experience, for example, the effect of early deprivation of visual stimulation.

slow-to-warm-up temperament A characteristic mode of response in which the individual is relatively inactive and moody and displays mild resistance to new routines and experiences but gradually adapts. Contrast with *easy temperament* and *difficult temperament*.

social clock A personal sense of when things should be done in life and when the individual is ahead of or behind the schedule dictated by age norms.

social cognition Thinking about the thoughts, feelings, motives, and behavior of the self and other people.

social cognitive theory Bandura's social learning theory, which holds that children and adults can learn novel responses merely by observing the behavior of a model, making mental notes on what they have seen, and then using these mental representations to reproduce the model's behavior; more broadly, a theory emphasizing the importance of cognitive processing of social experiences.

social comparison The process of defining and evaluating the self through comparisons with other people.

social learning theory See *social cognitive theory*.

social norm A socially defined expectation about how people should behave in particular social contexts.

social pretend play A form of play that involves both cooperation with playmates and pretend or symbolic activity.

social referencing Infants' monitoring of companions' emotional reactions in ambiguous situations and use of this information to decide how they should feel and behave.

social–conventional rules Standards of conduct determined by social consensus that indicate what is appropriate within a particular social setting. Contrast with *moral rules*.

social-role theory Eagly's view that gender-role stereotypes are created and maintained by differences in the roles that men and women play in society rather than being inherent in males and females.

sociocultural perspective Vygotsky's theory of development, which maintains that cognitive development is shaped by the sociocultural context in which it occurs and grows out of children's social interactions with members of their culture.

socioeconomic status (SES) The position people hold in society based on such factors as income, education, occupational status, and the prestige of their neighborhoods.

socioemotional selectivity theory Carstensen's notion that our needs change as we grow older and that we actively choose to narrow our range of social partners to those who can best meet our emotional needs.

sociometric popularity Being liked by many peers and disliked by few. Contrast with *perceived popularity*.

sociometric techniques Methods for determining who is well liked and popular and who is disliked or neglected in a group.

somaesthetic senses Body senses, including the senses of touch, temperature, and pain, as well as the *kinesthetic sense* of where one's body parts are in relation to other body parts and to the environment.

somatic symptoms Physical or bodily signs of emotional distress such as loss of appetite or disruption of normal sleep patterns.

species heredity The genetic endowment that members of a particular species have in common; a contributor to universal species traits and patterns of maturation.

spillover effects Instances in which events at work affect home life, and events at home carry over into the work place.

spina bifida Condition in which the bottom of the neural tube fails to fully close during prenatal development and part of the spinal cord is not fully encased in the protective covering of the spinal column.

spirituality A search for ultimate meaning in life that may or may not be carried out in the context of religion. Contrast with *religiousness*.

standard deviation A measure of the dispersion or spread around the mean of a distribution of scores; in the case of IQ tests with a mean score of 100, the standard deviation is 15, meaning that about two-thirds of people taking the test have scores between 85 and 115.

Stanford–Binet Intelligence Scale One of the most widely used, individually administered intelligence tests, which yields an IQ score.

static thought In Piaget's theory, the thought characteristic of the preoperational period that is fixed on end states rather than on the changes that transform one state into another. Contrast with *transformational thought*.

stem cell Undifferentiated, primitive cells that have the ability both to multiply and to differentiate into a variety of specific cells.

stereotype threat An individual's fear of being judged to have the qualities associated with negative stereotypes of his or her social group.

Sternberg's Triarchic Abilities Tests (STAT) An intelligence test based on Sternberg's triarchic theory that uses a variety of question formats to assess practical, creative, and analytical components of intelligence.

stillbirth Fetal death that occurs late in pregnancy when survival outside womb would normally have been possible.

storage In information processing, the holding of information in the long-term memory store.

storm and stress G. Stanley Hall's term for the emotional ups and downs and rapid changes that he believed characterize adolescence.

Strange Situation A series of mildly stressful experiences involving the departure of the parent and exposure to a stranger to which infants are exposed to determine the quality of their attachments; developed by Ainsworth.

stranger anxiety A wary or fretful reaction that infants often display when approached by an unfamiliar person.

structured observation A research method in which scientists create special conditions designed to elicit the behavior of interest to achieve greater control over the conditions under which they gather behavioral data. Contrast with *naturalistic observation*.

substance use disorders Diagnostic term for continued use of alcohol or psychoactive drugs despite adverse consequences for health, performance, and/or interpersonal relations.

successful intelligence Sternberg's concept that people are intelligent to the extent that they are able to succeed in life in their sociocultural context.

sudden infant death syndrome (SIDS) The death of a sleeping baby because of a failure of the respiratory system; linked to maternal smoking.

superego The psychoanalytic term for the component of the personality that consists of the individual's internalized moral standards.

surfactant A substance that aids breathing by preventing the air sacs of the lungs from sticking together.

surgency/extraversion Dimension of temperament that involves the tendency to actively and energetically approach new experiences in an emotionally positive way (rather than to be inhibited and withdrawn). See *negative affectivity* and *effortful control*.

symbolic capacity The capacity to use symbols such as words, images, or actions to represent or stand for objects and experiences; representational thought.

synapse The point at which the axon or dendrite of one neuron makes a connection with another neuron.

synaptic pruning The removal of unnecessary synapses between neurons in response to experience.

synaptogenesis The growth of synapses, or connections between neurons.

synchronized routine Harmonious, dancelike interaction between infant and caregiver in which each adjusts behavior in response to that of the other.

syntactic bootstrapping Using the syntax of a sentence—that is, where a word is placed in a sentence—to determine the meaning of the word.

syntax Rules specifying how words can be combined to form meaningful sentences in a language.

syphilis A common sexually transmitted disease that may cross the placental barrier in the middle and later stages of pregnancy, causing miscarriage or serious birth defects.

systemize To analyze things and explore how they work; male brains (and the brains of autistic individuals) are hypothesized by Baron-Cohen to excel at systemizing, whereas females excel at empathizing.

systems theories Theories of development holding that changes over the life span arise from the ongoing interrelationships between a changing organism and a changing environment, both of which are part of a larger, dynamic system.

tabula rasa The idea that the mind of an infant is a "blank slate" and that all knowledge, abilities, behaviors, and motives are acquired through experience.

tau Protein in the neurofibrillary tangles in the bodies of neural cells of individuals with Alzheimer's disease.

telegraphic speech Early sentences that consist primarily of content words and omit the less meaningful parts of speech such as articles, prepositions, pronouns, and auxiliary verbs.

telomere A stretch of DNA that forms the tip of a chromosome and that shortens after each cell division, serving as an aging clock and timing the death of cells.

temperament A genetically based pattern of tendencies to respond in predictable ways; building blocks of personality.

teratogen Any disease, drug, or other environmental agent that can harm a developing fetus.

terminal drop A rapid decline in intellectual abilities that people within a few years of dying often experience.

tertiary circular reaction During Piaget's sensorimotor period, the infant's experimenting with actions to find new ways to solve problems or produce interesting effects.

test norms Standards of normal performance on psychometric instruments based on the average scores and range of scores obtained by a large, representative sample of test takers.

testosterone The most important of the male hormones, or androgens; essential for normal sexual development during the prenatal period and at puberty.

thalidomide A mild tranquilizer that, taken early in pregnancy, can produce a variety of malformations of the limbs, eyes, ears, and heart.

theory A set of concepts and propositions designed to organize, describe, and explain a set of observations.

theory of mind The understanding that people have mental states (feelings, desires, beliefs, intentions) and that these states underlie and help explain their behavior.

thin ideal The cultural message that associates being thin with being attractive and teaches young girls to fear being fat, wish to be thinner, and diet at young ages.

third variable problem In correlation studies, the problem posed by the fact that the association between the two variables of interest may be caused by some third variable; see also *directionality problem*.

time-of-measurement effects In developmental research, the effects on findings of historical events occurring when the data for a study are being collected (for example, psychological changes brought about by an economic depression rather than as a function of aging). Contrast with *age effects* and *cohort effects*.

tinnitus Condition caused by exposure to high noise levels that involves ringing sounds in one or both ears and that can last for days, weeks, or indefinitely.

total brain death An irreversible loss of functioning in the entire brain, both the higher centers of the cerebral cortex that are involved in thought and the lower centers of the brain that control basic life processes such as breathing.

transactional model A model of family influence in which parent and child are believed to influence each other reciprocally over time, and development is influenced by how their relationship evolves.

transformational grammar Rules of syntax that allow a person to transform statements into questions, negatives, imperatives, and other kinds of sentences.

transformational thought In Piaget's theory, the ability to conceptualize transformations, or processes of change from one state to another, which appears in the stage of concrete operations. Contrast with *static thought*.

transgender Pertaining to individuals who identify with a gender other than their biological one.

transitivity The ability to recognize the necessary or logical relations among elements in a serial order (for example, that if A is taller than B, and B is taller than C, then A must be taller than C).

triangular theory of love Robert Sternberg's model describing types of love in terms of three components: passion, intimacy, and commitment.

triarchic theory of intelligence Sternberg's information-processing theory of intelligence that emphasizes three aspects of intelligent behavior: a practical component emphasizing the effect of context on what is intelligent; a creative component centering on coping with both novel and familiar problems; and an analytic component focused on the cognitive processes used to solve a problem.

trust versus mistrust The psychosocial conflict of infancy in which infants must learn to trust others to meet their needs in order to trust themselves; first stage in Erikson's theory.

twin study Method of studying genetic and environmental influence in which the similarity of identical twins is compared to that of (less genetically similar) fraternal twins, often in studies involving both twins reared together and twins reared apart.

ulnar grasp Holding objects by clamping them between the palm of hand and the fingers.

ultrasound Method of examining physical organs by scanning them with sound waves— for example, scanning the womb and thereby producing a visual outline of the fetus to detect gross abnormalities.

unconscious motivation Freud's term for feelings, experiences, and conflicts that influence a person's thinking and behavior even though they cannot be recalled.

underextension The young child's tendency to use general words to refer to a smaller set of objects, actions, or events than adults do (for example, using *candy* to refer only to mints). Contrast with *overextension*.

universal grammar A system of common rules and properties of language that may allow infants to grow up learning any of the world's languages.

universality–context specificity issue The debate over the extent to which developmental changes are common to everyone (universal, as in most stage theories) or different from person to person (particularistic).

utilization deficiency The third phase in mastery of memory strategies in which children fail to benefit from a memory strategy they are able to produce.

vascular dementia The deterioration of functioning and cognitive capacities caused by a series of minor strokes that cut off the blood supply to areas of the brain; also called multi-infarct dementia, it is one of the leading causes of neurocognitive disorder.

vicarious reinforcement In observational learning, the consequences experienced by models, because of their behavior, that affect the learner's likelihood of imitating the behavior.

video deficit The difficulty infants have learning from video presentations as compared with live interactions with social partners.

visual accommodation The ability of the lens of the eye to change shape to bring objects at different distances into focus.

visual acuity The ability to perceive detail in a visual stimulus.

visual cliff An elevated glass platform that creates an illusion of depth and is used to test the depth perception of infants.

vocabulary spurt A phenomenon occurring around 18 months of age when the pace of word learning quickens dramatically.

Wechsler Scales A set of widely used, individually administered intelligence tests that yield verbal, performance, and overall IQ scores.

WEIRD people An acronym referring to people living in societies that are Western, Educated, Industrialized, Rich, and Democratic. The field of psychology has been characterized as the study of WEIRD people (for example, American college students).

wisdom A combination of rich factual knowledge about life and procedural knowledge such as strategies for giving advice and handling conflicts.

word segmentation In language development, the ability to break the stream of speech sounds into distinct words.

working memory A memory store, often referred to as a mental "scratch pad," that temporarily holds information when it is being actively operated upon or in one's consciousness.

X chromosome The longer of the two sex chromosomes; normal females have two X chromosomes, whereas normal males have only one.

Y chromosome The shorter of the two sex chromosomes; normal males have one Y chromosome, whereas females have none.

zone of proximal development Vygotsky's term for the difference between what a learner can accomplish independently and what a learner can accomplish with the guidance and encouragement of a more skilled partner.

zygote A single cell formed at conception from the union of a sperm and an ovum.

References

Aanerud, J., Borghammer, P., Chakravarty, M. M., Vang, K., Rodell, A. B., Jonsdottir, K. Y., & Gjedde, A. (2012). Brain energy metabolism and blood flow differences in healthy aging. *Journal of Cerebral Blood Flow and Metabolism, 32,* 1177–1187.

Aarons, S. J., & Jenkins, R. R. (2002). Sex, pregnancy, and contraception-related motivators and barriers among Latino and African-American youth in Washington, DC. *Sex Education, 2,* 5–30.

ABC News. (2010). *He never forgets: Meet the super-memory man.* Retrieved from www.abcnews.go.com/Nightline/story?id=7075443&page=3.

Abele, A. E. (2003). The dynamics of masculine-agentic and feminine-communal traits: Findings from a prospective study. *Journal of Personality and Social Psychology, 85,* 768–776.

Abele, A. E. (2014). How gender influences objective career success and subjective career satisfaction: The impact of self-concept and of parenthood. In I. Schoon & J. S. Eccles (Eds.), *Gender differences in aspirations and attainment: A life course perspective* (pp. 412–426). Cambridge, Eng: Cambridge University Press.

Abele, A. E., Uchronski, M., Suitner, C., & Wojciszke, B. (2008). Towards an operationalization of the fundamental dimensions of agency and communion: Trait content ratings in five countries considering valence and frequency of word occurrence. *European Journal of Social Psychology, 38,* 1202–1217.

Abele, A. E., & Wojciszke, B. (2014). Communal and agentic content in social cognition: A dual perspective model. In J. M. Olson & M. P. Zanna (Eds.), *Advances in experimental social psychology: Vol. 50.* (pp. 195–255). Waltham, MA: Academic Press.

Aber, L., Morris, P., & Raver, C. (2012). Children, families and poverty. Definitions, trends, emerging science and implications for policy. *SRCD Social Policy Report, 26,* 1–19.

Ablard, K. E., & Mills, C. J. (1996). Implicit theories of intelligence and self-perceptions of academically talented adolescents and children. *Journal of Youth and Adolescence, 25,* 137–148.

Abma, J. C., & Martinez, G. M. (2006). Childlessness among older women in the United States: Trends and profiles. *Journal of Marriage and Family, 68,* 1045–1056.

Abma, J. C., Martinez, G. M., & Copen, C. E. (2010). *Teenagers in the United States: Sexual activity, contraceptive use, and childbearing, National Survey of Family Growth 2006–2008* (Series 23, Number 31). Hyattsville, MD: National Center for Health Statistics, Vital Health Statistics.

Acevedo, B. P., & Aron, A. P. (2014). Romantic love, pair-bonding, and the dopaminergic reward system. In M. Mikulincer & P. R. Shaver (Eds.), *Mechanisms of social connection: From brain to group* (pp. 55–69). Washington, DC: American Psychological Association.

Acevedo, B. P., Aron, A., Fisher, H. E., & Brown, L. (2012). Neural correlates of long-term intense romantic love. *Social and Cognitive Neuroscience, 7,* 145–159.

Achenbach, J. (2015, December 2). Faster, cheaper way to alter DNA points up ethics issues. *The Washington Post,* p. A7.

Achenbach, T. M. (1982). *Developmental psychopathology* (2nd ed.). New York, NY: Wiley.

Achenbach, T. M., & Edelbrock, C. S. (1978). The classification of child psychopathology: A review and analysis of empirical efforts. *Psychological Bulletin, 85,* 1275–1301.

Achter, J. A., Benbow, C. P., & Lubinski, D. (1997). Rethinking multipotentiality among the intellectually gifted: A critical review and recommendations. *Gifted Child Quarterly, 41,* 5–15.

Ackerman, P. L., & Kanfer, R. (2004). Cognitive, affective, and conative aspects of adult intellect within a typical and maximal performance framework. In D. Y. Dai & R. J. Sternberg (Eds.), *Motivation, emotion, and cognition: Integrative perspectives on intellectual functioning and development* (pp. 119–141). New York, NY: Routledge.

Ackerman, S. J. (2007). The adolescent brain. In F. Bloom, M. F. Beal, & D. J. Kupfer (Eds.), *The DANA guide to brain health: A practical family reference from medical experts. Journal of Neurology Neurosurgery and Psychiatry, 78,* 779.

Adams, C. (1991). Qualitative age differences in memory for text: A life-span developmental perspective. *Psychology and Aging, 6,* 323–336.

Adams, M. J., Treiman, R., & Pressley, M. (1998). Reading, writing, and literacy. In I. E. Sigel & K. A. Renninger (Vol. Eds.), W. Damon (Editor-in-Chief), *Handbook of child psychology: Vol. 4. Child psychology in practice* (5th ed., pp. 275–355). New York, NY: Wiley.

Adams, M., Walker, C., & O'Connell, P. (2011). A content analysis of representations of parenting in young children's picture books in the UK. *Sex Roles, 65,* 259–270.

Adams, R. E., & Bukowski, W. M. (2007). Relationships with mothers and peers moderate the association between childhood sexual abuse and anxiety disorders. *Child Abuse and Neglect, 31,* 645–656.

Adams, R. J. (1987). An evaluation of color preference in early infancy. *Infant Behavior and Development, 10,* 143–150.

Adamsons, K., & Johnson, S. K. (2013). An updated and expanded meta-analysis of nonresident fathering and child well-being. *Journal of Family Psychology, 27,* 589–599.

Addington, A. M., & Rapoport, J. L. (2012). Annual research review: Impact of advances in genetics in understanding developmental psychopathology. *Journal of Child Psychology and Psychiatry, 53,* 510–518.

Adelman, R. D., Tmanova, L. L., Delgado, D., Dion, S., & Lachs, M. S. (2014). Caregiver burden: A clinical review. *JAMA: Journal of the American Medical Association, 311,* 1052–1059.

Adey, P. S., & Shayer, M. (1992). Accelerating the development of formal thinking in middle and high school students: II. Postproject effects on science achievement. *Journal of Research in Science Teaching, 29,* 81–92.

Adler, J. (2005, November 14). The Boomer Files: Hitting 60. *Newsweek,* 50–58.

Adolph, K. E. (2008). Learning to move. *Current directions in psychological science, 17,* 213–218.

Adolph, K. E., & Avolio, A. M. (2000). Walking infants adapt locomotion to changing body dimensions. *Journal of Experimental Psychology: Human Perception and Performance, 26,* 1148–1166.

Adolph, K. E., & Berger, S. E. (2006). Motor development. In D. Kuhn & R. Siegler (Vol. Eds.), *Handbook of child psychology: Cognition, perception, and language* (6th ed.). Hoboken, NJ: Wiley and Sons.

Adolph, K. E., Berger, S. E., & Leo, A. J. (2011). Developmental continuity? Crawling, cruising, and walking. *Developmental Psychology, 14,* 306–318.

Adolph, K. E., Cole, W. G., Komati, M., Garciaguirre, J. S., Badaly, D., Lingeman, J. M., Chan, G. L. Y., & Sotsky, R. B. (2012). How do you learn to walk? Thousands of steps and dozens of falls per day. *Psychological Science, 23,* 1387–1394.

Adolph, K. E., Kretch, K. S., & LoBue, V. (2014). Fear of heights in infants? Current *Directions in Psychological Science, 23,* 60–66.

Adolph, K. E., & Robinson, S. R. (2013). The road to walking: What learning to walk tells us about development. In P. Zelazo (Ed.), *Oxford handbook of developmental psychology: Vol. 1.* (pp. 403–443). New York, NY: Oxford University Press.

Adolph, K. E., & Robinson, S. R. (2015). Motor development. In R. M. Lerner, L. S. Liben, & U. Müller (Eds.), *Handbook of child psychology and developmental science: Vol. 2. Cognitive processes* (7th ed., pp. 113–157). Wiley.

Adolph, K. E., Robinson, S. R., Young, J. W., & Gill-Alvarez, F. (2008). What is the shape of developmental change? *Psychological Review, 115,* 527–543.

Adolph, K. E., & Tamis-LeMonda, C. S. (2014). The costs and benefits of development: The transition from crawling to walking. *Child Development Perspectives, 8,* 187–192.

Adrian, V., & Coontz, S. (2010). *The long-range impact of the recession on families.* A report for the 13th Annual Conference on Contemporary Families, Augustana College, April 16–17, 2010. Retrieved from www.contemporaryfamilies.org/economic-issues/the-long-range-impact-of-the-recession-on-families.html.

Afifi, T. D., & Denes, A. (2013). Divorced and single-parent families. Risk, resiliency, and the role of communication. In A. L. Vangelisti (Ed.), *Routledge handbook of family communication.* New York, NY: Routledge.

Agnew, R. (2003). An integrated theory of the adolescent peak in offending. *Youth & Society, 34,* 263–299.

Agnew, R., & Huguley, S. (1989). Adolescent violence toward parents. *Journal of Marriage and the Family, 51,* 699–711.

Aguiar, A., & Baillargeon, R. (1999). 2.5-month-old infants' reasoning about when objects should and should not be occluded. *Cognitive Psychology, 39,* 116–157.

Aguiar, A., & Baillargeon, R. (2002). Developments in young infants' reasoning about occluded objects. *Cognitive Psychology, 45,* 267–336.

Ahluwalia, I. B., D'Angelo, D., Morrow, B., & McDonald, J. A. (2012). Association between acculturation and breastfeeding among Hispanic women: Data from the pregnancy risk assessment and monitoring system. *Journal of Human Lactation, 28,* 167–173.

Ahmetoglu, G., Swami, V., & Chamorro-Premuzic, T. (2010). The relationship between dimensions of love, personality, and relationship length. *Archives of Sexual Behavior, 39,* 1181–1190.

Ai, A. L., Wink, P., & Ardelt, M. (2010). Spirituality and aging: A journey. In J. C. Cavanaugh & C. K. Cavanaugh (Eds.), *Aging in america: Vol. 3. Societal issues.* Santa Barbara, CA: Praeger/ABC-CLIO.

AIDS Education and Research Trust (2015). HIV Transmission & prevention. Last modified 11/25/2015. www.avert.org/hiv-transmission-prevention.

Ainsworth, M. D. S. (1973). The development of infant–mother attachment. In B. M. Caldwell & H. N. Ricciuti (Eds.), *Review of child development research: Vol. 3.* Chicago, IL: University of Chicago Press.

Ainsworth, M. D. S. (1979). Attachment as related to mother–infant interaction. In J. G. Rosenblatt, R. A. Hinde, C. Beer, & M. Busnel (Eds.), *Advances in the study of behavior: Vol. 9.* New York, NY: Academic Press.

Ainsworth, M. D. S. (1989). Attachments beyond infancy. *American Psychologist, 44,* 709–716.

Ainsworth, M. D. S., Blehar, M., Waters, E., & Wall, S. (1978). *Patterns of attachment.* Hillsdale, NJ: Erlbaum.

Ajrouch, K. J., Antonucci, T. C., & Janevic, M. R. (2001). Social networks among blacks and whites: The interaction between race and age. *Journals of Gerontology: Psychological Sciences and Social Sciences, 56,* S112–S118.

Akers, K. G., Martinez-Canabal, A., Restivo, L., Yiu, A. P., De Cristofaro, A., Hsiang, H. L., & Frankland, P. W. (2014). Hippocampal neurogenesis regulates forgetting during adulthood and infancy. *Science, 344,* 598–602.

Akhtar, N., & Gernsbacher, M. A. (2007). Joint attention and vocabulary development: A critical look. *Language and linguistics compass, 1,* 195–207.

Akincigil, A., Olfson, M., Siegel, M., Zurlo, K. A., Walkup, J. T., & Crystal, S. (2012). Racial and ethnic disparities in depression care in community-dwelling elderly in the United States. *American Journal of Public Health, 102,* 319–328.

Aknin, L. B., Hamlin, J. K., & Dunn, E. W. (2012). Giving leads to happiness in young children. *PLoS ONE, 7,* e39211.

Aksan, N., & Kochanska, G. (2005). Conscience in childhood: Old questions, new answers. *Developmental Psychology, 41,* 506–516.

Aksglaede, L., Sørensen, K., Petersen, J. H., Skakkebaek, N. E., & Juul, A. (2009). Recent decline in age at breast development: The Copenhagen Puberty Study. *Pediatrics, 123,* e932–939.

Albert, D., Chein, J., & Steinberg, L. (2013). The teenage brain: Peer influences on adolescent decision making. *Current Directions in Psychological Science, 22,* 114–120.

Albuquerque, S., Pereira, M., & Narciso, I. (2016). Couple's relationship after the death of a child: A systematic review. *Journal of Child and Family Studies, 25,* 30–53.

Aldwin, C. M., Spiro, A., & Park, C. L. (2006). Health, behavior, and optimal aging. In J. E. Birren & K. W. Schaie (Eds.), *Handbook of the psychology of aging.* Boston, MA: Elsevier Academic Press.

Alegría, M., Chatterji, P., Wells, K., Cao, Z., Chen, C., Takeuchi, D., . . . Meng, X. (2008). Disparity in depression treatment among racial and ethnic minority populations in the United States. *Psychiatric Services, 59,* 1264–1272.

Alexander, G. M. (2003). An evolutionary perspective of sex-typed toy preferences: Pink, blue, and the brain. *Archives of Sexual Behavior, 32,* 7–14.

Alexander, G. M., Wilcox, T., & Woods, R. (2009). Sex differences in infants' visual interest in toys. *Archives of Sexual Behavior, 38,* 427–433.

Alexander, P. A., & Fox, E. (2011). Adolescents as readers. In P. D. Pearson, R. Barr, & M. L. Kamil (Eds.), *Handbook of reading research: Vol. 4.* (pp. 157–176). New York, NY: Routledge.

Alfieri, T., Ruble, D. N., & Higgins, E. T. (1996). Gender stereotypes during adolescence: Developmental changes and the transition to junior high school. *Developmental Psychology, 32,* 1129–1137.

Alio, A. P., Salihu, H. M., McIntosh, C., August, E. M., Weldeselasse, H., Sanchez, E., & Mbah, A. K. (2012). The effect of paternal age on fetal birth outcomes. *American Journal of Men's Health, 6,* 427–435.

Alisat, S., & Pratt, M. W. (2012). Characteristics of young adults' personal religious narratives and their relation with the identity status model: A longitudinal, mixed methods study. *Identity: An International Journal of Theory and Research, 12,* 29–52.

Alladi, S., Bak, T. H., Duggirala, V., Surampudi, B., Shailaja, M., Shukla, A. K., Chaudhuri, J. R., & Kaul, S. (2013). Bilingualism delays age at onset of dementia, independent of education and immigration status. *Neurology, 18,* 1938–1944.

Allen, J. P. (2008). The attachment system in adolescence. In J. Cassidy & P. R. Shaver (Eds.), *Handbook of attachment theory: Research, and clinical applications* (2nd ed.). New York, NY: Guilford.

Allen, J. P., Seitz, V., & Apfel, N. H. (2007). The sexually mature teen as a whole person: New directions in prevention and intervention for teen pregnancy and parenthood. In J. L. Aber, S. J. Bishop-Josef, S. M. Jones, K. T. McLearn, & D. A. Phillips (Eds.), *Child development and social policy: Knowledge for action.* Washington, DC: American Psychological Association.

Allen, J., Chavez, S., DeSimone, S., Howard, D., Johnson, K., LaPierre, L., et al. (2006). Americans' attitudes toward euthanasia and physician-assisted suicide, 1936–2002. *Journal of Sociology and Social Welfare, 33,* 5–23.

Allen, M. C., & Capute, A. J. (1986). Assessment of early auditory and visual abilities of extremely premature infants. *Developmental medicine and child neurology, 28,* 458–466.

Allen, R. E. S., & Wiles, J. L. (2013). How older people position their late-life childlessness: A qualitative study. *Journal of Marriage and Family, 75,* 206–220.

Allison, C. M., & Hyde, J. S. (2011). Early menarche: Confluence of biological and contextual factors. *Sex Roles, 68,* 55–64.

Alloway, T. P., Banner, G. E., & Smith, P. (2010). Working memory and cognitive styles in adolescents' attainment. *British Journal of Educational Psychology, 80,* 567–581.

Allum, J. H., Greisiger, R., Straubhaar, S., & Carpenter, M. G. (2000). Auditory perception and speech identification in children with cochlear implants tested with the EARS protocol. *British Journal of Audiology, 34,* 293–303.

Almeida, D. M., & Horn, M. C. (2004). Is daily life more stressful during middle adulthood? In O. G. Brim, C. D. Ryff, & R. C. Kessler (Eds.), *How healthy are we? A national study of well-being at midlife.* Chicago: University of Chicago Press.

Almeida, D. M., Piazza, J. R., Stawski, R. S., & Klein, L. C. (2011). The speedometer of life: Stress, health and aging. In K. W. Schaie & S. L. Willis (Eds.), B. G. Knight, B. Levy, & D. C. Park (Assoc. Eds.), *Handbook of the psychology of aging.* Burlington, MA: Academic Press/Elsevier.

Almli, C. R., Ball, R. H., & Wheeler, M. E. (2001). Human fetal and neonatal movement patterns: Gender differences and fetal-to-neonatal continuity. *Developmental Psychobiology, 38,* 252–273.

Almond, D., Edlund, L., & Palme, M. (2009). Chernobyl's subclinical legacy: Prenatal exposure to radioactive fallout and school outcomes in Sweden. *Quarterly Journal of Economics 124,* 1729–1772.

Almond, E. (2015, October 8). 100-year-old track star's secret: 'I take care of what I got'. *San Jose Mercury News.* Retrieved from www.mercurynews.com/sports/ci_28941967/100-year-old-track-stars-secret-i-take.

Alvarez, A., & Booth, A. E. (2016). Exploring individual differences in preschoolers' causal stance. *Developmental Psychology, 52,* 411–422.

Alwin, D. F. (2009). History, cohorts, and patterns of cognitive aging. In H. B. Bosworth & C. Hertzog (Eds.), *Aging and cognition: Research methodologies and empirical advances.* Washington, DC: American Psychological Association.

Amato, P. R. (1993). Children's adjustment to divorce: Theories, hypotheses, and empirical support. *Journal of Marriage and the Family, 55,* 23–38.

Amato, P. R. (2000). The consequences of divorce for adults and children. *Journal of Marriage and the Family, 62,* 1269–1287.

Amato, P. R. (2006). Marital discord, divorce, and children's well-being: Results from a 20-year longitudinal study of two generations. In A. Clarke-Stewart & J. Dunn (Eds.), *Families count: Effects on child and adolescent development.* New York, NY: Cambridge University Press.

Amato, P. R. (2010). Research on divorce: Continuing trends and new developments. *Journal of Marriage and Family, 72,* 650–666.

Amato, P. R., Booth, A., McHale, S. M., & Van Hook, J. (Eds.) (2015). *Families in an era of inequality: Diverging destinies.* Cham, Switzerland: Springer International Publishing.

Amato, P. R., & Cheadle, J. E. (2008). Parental divorce, marital conflict and children's behavior problems: A comparison of adopted and biological children. *Social Forces, 86,* 1139–1161.

Amato, P. R., Johnson, D. R., Booth, A., & Rogers, S. J. (2003). Continuity and change in marital quality between 1980 and 2000. *Journal of Marriage and the Family, 65,* 1–22.

Amato, P. R., Kane, J. B., & James, S. (2011). Reconsidering the "good divorce." *Family Relations, 60,* 511–524.

Amato, P. R., King, V., & Thorsen, M. L. (2016). Parent–child relationships in stepfather families and adolescent adjustment: A latent class analysis. *Journal of Marriage and Family, 78,* 482–497.

Amato, P. R., & Sobolewski, J. M. (2004). The effects of divorce on fathers and children: Nonresidential fathers and stepfathers. In M. E. Lamb (Ed.), *The role of the father in child development* (4th ed.). Hoboken, NJ: John Wiley & Sons.

Ambrose, A. F., Paul, G., & Hausdorff, J. M. (2013). Risk factors for falls among older adults: A review of the literature. *Maturitas, 75,* 51–61.

American Academy of Pediatrics (2010). Policy statement—Media education. *Pediatrics, 126,* 1012–1017.

American Academy of Pediatrics Task Force on Circumcision. (2012). Male circumcision. *Pediatrics, 130,* 585.

American Academy of Pediatrics. (2000). Prevention and management of pain and stress in the neonate (RE9945). *Pediatrics, 105,* 454–461.

American Association on Intellectual and Developmental Disabilities. (2010). *Definition of intellectual disability.* Retrieved from www.aaidd.org.

American Association on Intellectual and Developmental Disabilities. (2016). Frequently asked questions on intellectual disability. Retrieved 7/1/2016 from www.aaidd.org/.

American Psychiatric Association. (2000). *Diagnostic and statistical manual of mental disorders DSM–IV–TR* (4th ed., text revision). Arlington, VA: American Psychiatric Association.

American Psychiatric Association. (2013). *Diagnostic and statistical manual of mental disorders* (5th ed.). Washington, DC: American Psychiatric Association.

Amone-P'Olak, K., Ormel, J., Huisman, M., Verhulst, F. C., Oldehinkel, A. J., & Burger, H. (2009). Life stressors as mediators of the relation between socioeconomic position and mental health problems in early adolescence: The TRAILS study. *Journal of the American Academy of Child & Adolescent Psychiatry, 48,* 1031–1038.

Amsel, E., Klaczynski, P. A., Johnston, A., Bench, S., Close, J., Sadler, E., et al. (2008). A dual-process account of the development of scientific reasoning: The nature and development of metacognitive intercession skills. *Cognitive Development, 23,* 452–471.

Amstutz, D. D., & Sheared, V. (2000). The crisis in adult basic education. *Education and Urban Society, 32,* 155–166.

Anand, K. J., & Hickey, P. R. (1992). Halothane-morphine compared with high-dose sufentanil for anesthesia and postoperative analgesia in neonatal cardiac surgery. *New England Journal of Medicine, 326,* 1–9.

Anastasi, A. (1958). Heredity, environment, and the question, "how?" *Psychological Review, 65,* 197–208.

Anderson, A. N., Roncaroli, F., Hodges, A., Deprez, M., & Turkheimer, F. E. (2008). Chromosomal profiles of gene expression in Huntington's disease. *Brain, 131,* 381–388.

Anderson, C. A., Shibuya, A., Ihori, N., Swing, E. L., Bushman, B. J., Sakamoto, A., et al. (2010). Violent video game effects on aggression, empathy, and prosocial behavior in Eastern and Western countries: A meta-analytic review. *Psychological Bulletin, 136,* 151–173.

Anderson, D. A., & Hamilton, M. (2007). Gender role stereotyping of parents in children's picture books: The invisible father. *Sex Roles, 52,* 145–151.

Anderson, D. R., & Pempek, T. A. (2005). Television and very young children. *American Behavioral Scientist, 48,* 505–522.

Anderson, R. M., & Weindruch, R. (2012). The caloric restriction paradigm: Implications for healthy human aging. *American Journal of Human Biology, 24,* 101–106.

Anderson-Fye, E. (2009). Cross-cultural issues in body image among children and adolescents. In L. Smolak & J. K. Thompson (Eds.), *Body image, eating disorders, and obesity in youth.* Washington, DC: American Psychological Association.

Andrade, J. Q., Bunduki, V., Curti, S. P., Figueiredo, C. A., de Oliveira, M. I., Zugaib, M. (2006). Rubella in pregnancy: Intrauterine transmission and perinatal outcome during a Brazilian epidemic. *Journal of Clinical Virology 35,* 285–291.

Angell, M. (2014, November 2). From 'assisted suicide' to 'death with dignity'. *The Washington Post,* p. B3.

Anim-Soumuah, M., Smyth, R. M., & Jones, L. (2011, December 7). Epidural versus non-epidural or no analgesia in labour. *Cochrane Database of Systematic Reviews.* doi:10.1002/14651858.CD000331.pub3

Anisfeld, E., Casper, V., Nozyce, M., & Cunningham, N. (1990). Does infant carrying promote attachment? An experimental study of the effects of increased physical contact on the development of attachment. *Child Development, 61,* 1617–1627.

Annese, J., Schenker-Ahmed, N. M., Bartsch, H., Maechler, P., Sheh, C., Thomas, N., & Corkin, S. (2014). Postmortem examination of patient H.M.'s brain based on histological sectioning and digital 3D reconstruction. *Nature Communications, 5,* article 3122.

Anstey, K. J., Hofer, S. M., & Luszcz, M. A. (2003). A latent growth curve analysis of late-life sensory and cognitive function over 8 years: Evidence for specific and common factors underlying change. *Psychology and Aging, 18,* 714–726.

Antebi, A. (2007). Ageing: When loss is more. *Nature, 447,* 536–537.

Anthis, K., & LaVoie, J. C. (2006). Readiness to change: A longitudinal study of changes in adult identity. *Journal of Research in Personality, 40,* 209–219.

Antonucci, T. C., Birditt, K. S., & Akiyama, H. (2009). Convoys of social relations: An interdisciplinary approach. In V. L. Bengtson, M. Silverstein, N. M. Putney, & D. Gans (Eds.), *Handbook of theories of aging* (2nd ed.). New York, NY: Springer.

Apgar, V., & Beck, J. (1974). *Is my baby all right?* New York, NY: Pocket Books.

Applebome, P., & Maker, E. (2013, January 20). Private pain and public debate take toll on Newtown parents. *The New York Times*. Retrieved from www.nytimes.com/2013/01/21/nyregion/ newtown-families-negotiate-private-pain-amid-public-debate.html?_r=0.

Appollonio, I., Carabellese, C., Frattola, L., & Trabucchi, M. (1996). Effects of sensory aids on the quality of life and mortality of elderly people: A multivariate analysis. *Age and Ageing, 25,* 89–96.

Aquilino, W. S. (2006). Family relationships and support systems in emerging adulthood. In J. J. Arnett & J. L. Tanner (Eds.), *Coming of age in the 21st century*. Washington, DC: American Psychological Association.

Aquino, K., & Reed, A. (2002). The self-importance of moral identity. *Journal of Personality & Social Psychology, 83,* 1423–1440.

Aquino, K., Freeman, D., Reed, A., II, Felps, W., & Lim, V. K. G. (2009). Testing a social-cognitive model of moral behavior: The interactive influence of situations and moral identity centrality. *Journal of Personality and Social Psychology, 97,* 123–141.

Arain, M., Haque, M., Johal, L., Mathur, P., Nel, W., Rais, A., & Sharma, S. (2013). Maturation of the adolescent brain. *Neuropsychiatric Disease and Treatment, 9,* 449–461.

Aratani, L. (2008, February 10). Catching up to the boys, in the good and the bad. *The Washington Post*, pp. C1, C14.

Arbeit, M. R. (2014). What does healthy sex look like among youth? Towards a skills-based model for promoting adolescent sexuality development. *Human Development, 57,* 259–286.

Arber, S., & Ginn, J. (1991). *Gender and later life: A sociological analysis of resources and constraints*. London, UK: Sage.

Arbona, C., & Power, T. G. (2003). Parental attachment, self-esteem, and antisocial behaviors among African American, European American, and Mexican American adolescents. *Journal of Counseling Psychology, 50,* 40–51.

Archer, J. (1991). The influence of testosterone on human aggression. *British Journal of Psychology, 82,* 1–28.

Archer, J. (1992). *Ethology and human development*. Hertfordshire, UK: Harvester Wheatsheaf.

Archer, J. (1996). Sex differences in social behavior: Are the social role and evolutionary explanations compatible? *American Psychologist, 51,* 909–917.

Archer, S. L. (1982). The lower age boundaries of identity development. *Child Development, 53,* 1551–1556.

Ardelt, M. (2000). Antecedents and effects of wisdom in old age. *Research on Aging, 22,* 360–394.

Arens, A. K., Yeung, A. S., Craven, R. G., Watermann, R., & Hasselhorn, M. (2013). Does timing of transition matter? Comparison of German students' self-perceptions before and after transition to secondary school. *International Journal of Educational Research, 57,* 1–11.

Ariès, P. (1962). *Centuries of childhood*. New York, NY: Knopf.

Ariès, P. (1981). *The hour of our death* (H. Weaver, Trans.). New York, NY: Knopf. (Original work published 1977).

Arim, R., Tramonte, L., Shapka, J. D., Dahinten, V. S., & Willms, J. D. (2011). The family antecedents and the subsequent outcomes of early puberty. *Journal of Youth & Adolescence, 40,* 1423–1435.

Arking, R. (2006). *The biology of aging: Observations and principles* (3rd ed.). New York, NY: Oxford University Press.

Armstrong, D., & Shakespeare-Finch, J. (2011). Relationship to the bereaved and perceptions of severity of trauma differentiate elements of posttraumatic growth. *Omega: Journal of Death and Dying, 63,* 125–140.

Armstrong, P. I., & Crombie, G. (2000). Compromises in adolescents' occupational aspirations and expectations from grades 8 to 10. *Journal of Vocational Behavior, 56,* 82–98.

Armstrong, V. L., Brunet, P. M., He, C., Nishimura, M., Poole, H. L., & Spector, F. (2006). What is so critical? A commentary on the reexamination of critical periods. *Developmental Psychobiology, 48,* 326–331.

Arnett, J. J. (2000). Emerging adulthood: A theory of development from the late teens through the twenties. *American Psychologist, 55,* 469–480.

Arnett, J. J. (2004). *Emerging adulthood: The winding road from the late teens through the twenties*. New York, NY: Oxford University Press.

Arnett, J. J. (2008). The neglected 95%. Why American psychology needs to become less American. *American Psychologist, 63,* 602–614.

Arnett, J. J. (2011). Emerging adulthoods(s): The cultural psychology of a new life stage. In L. A. Jensen (Ed.), *Bridging cultural and developmental approaches to psychology: New syntheses in theory, research, and policy* (pp. 255–275). New York, NY: Oxford University Press.

Arnett, J. J. (2015). The cultural psychology of emerging adulthood. In L. A. Jensen (Ed.), *The Oxford handbook of human development and culture: An interdisciplinary perspective* (pp. 487–501). New York, NY: Oxford University Press.

Arnold, J., Graesch, A., & Ochs, E. (2012). *Life at home in the twenty-first century: 32 families open their doors*. Los Angeles, CA: Cotsen Institute of Archaeology Press.

Arnold, L. E., Lofthouse, N., & Hurt, E. (2012). Artificial food colors and attention-deficit/hyperactivity symptoms: Conclusions to dye for *Neurotherapeutics, 9,* 599–609.

Aronson, J., Lustina, M. J., Good, C., Keough, K., Steele, C. M., & Brown, J. (1999). When white men can't do math: Necessary and sufficient factors in stereotype threat. *Journal of Experimental Social Psychology, 35,* 29–46.

Arroyo, C. G., & Zigler, E. (1995). Racial identity, academic achievement, and the psychological well-being of economically disadvantaged adolescents. *Journal of Personality and Social Psychology, 69,* 903–914.

Arvio, M., Salokivi, T., & Bjelogrlic-Laakso, N. (2016, July 1). Age at death in individuals with intellectual disabilities. *Journal of Applied Research in Intellectual Disabilities, 29.*

Aspelmeier, J. E., Elliott, A. N., & Smith, C. H. (2007). Childhood sexual abuse, attachment, and trauma symptoms in college females: The moderating role of attachment. *Child Abuse and Neglect, 31,* 549–566.

Atchley, R. C. (1976). *The sociology of retirement*. Cambridge, MA: Schenkman.

Atchley, R. C. (2009). *Spirituality and aging*. Baltimore: Johns Hopkins University Press.

Athey, I. (1984). Contributions of play to development. In T. D. Yawkey & A. D. Pellegrini (Eds.), *Child's play: Developmental and applied*. Hillsdale, NJ: Erlbaum.

Atkinson, R. C., & Shiffrin, R. M. (1968). Human memory: A proposed system and its control processes. In K. W. Spence & J. T. Spence (Eds.), *The psychology of learning and motivation: Vol. 2. Advances in research and theory*. New York, NY: Academic Press.

Attems, J., Walker, L., & Jellinger, K. A. (2015). Olfaction and aging: A mini-review. *Gerontology, 61,* 485–90.

Attorp, A., Scott, J. E., Yew, A. C., Rhodes, R. E., Barr, S. I., & Naylor, P.-J. (2014). Associations between socioeconomic, parental and home environment factors and fruit and vegetable consumption of children in grades five and six in British Columbia, Canada. *BMC Public Health, 14*(1), 150.

Austin Institute. (2014). *Family: Division of labor, perception and reality*. Retrieved 8/19/2016 from www.austin-institute.org/research/modern-family-division-of-labor-perception-and-reality/.

Autism and Developmental Disabilities Monitoring Network Surveillance Year 2010 Principal Investigators (2014, March 28). *Prevalence of autism spectrum disorder among children aged 8 years—Autism and developmental disabilities monitoring network, 11 sites, United States, 2010. MMWR,* 63(SS02), 1–21. Retrieved from www.cdc.gov/mmwr/preview/mmwrhtml/ss6302a1.htm.

Auyeung, B., Knickneyer, R., Ashwin, E., Taylor, K., Hackett, G., & Baron-Cohen, S. (2012). Effects of fetal testosterone on visuospatial ability. *Archives of Sexual Behavior, 41,* 571–581.

Avert. (2016). *Preventing mother-to-child transmission of HIV (PMTCT)*. Retrieved from www.avert.org/motherchild.htm.

Ayabe-Kanamura, S., Schicker, I., Laska, M., Hudson, R., Distel, H., Kobayakawa, T., & Saito, S. (1998). Differences in perception of everyday odors: A Japanese-German cross-cultural study. *Chemical Senses, 23,* 31–38.

Ayers, T. S., Wolchik, S. A., Sandler, I. N., Twohey, J. L., Weyer, J. L., Padgett-Jones, S., . . . Kriege, G. (2014). The family bereavement program: Description of a theory-based prevention program for parentally-bereaved children and adolescents. *Omega: Journal of Death and Dying, 68,* 293–314.

Azmitia, M. (1992). Expertise, private speech, and the development of self-regulation. In R. M. Diaz & L. E. Berk (Eds.), *Private speech: From social interaction to self-regulation*. Hillsdale, NJ: Erlbaum.

Baart, M., Bortfeld, H., & Vroomen, J. (2015). Phonetic matching of auditory and visual speech develops during childhood: Evidence from sine-wave speech. *Journal of Experimental Child Psychology, 129,* 157–164.

Babai, R., & Levit-Dori, T. (2009). Several CASE lessons can improve students' control of variables reasoning scheme ability. *Journal of Science Education and Technology, 18,* 429–446.

Bacharach, V. R., & Baumeister, A. A. (1998). Direct and indirect effects of maternal intelligence, maternal age, income, and home environment on intelligence of preterm, low-birth-weight children. *Journal of Applied Developmental Psychology, 19,* 361–375.

Bachman, J. G., Safron, D. J., Sy, S. R., & Schulenberg, J. E. (2003). Wishing to work: New perspectives on how adolescents' part-time work intensity is linked to educational disengagement, substance use, and other problem behaviors. *International Journal of Behavioral Development, 27,* 301–315.

Bachman, J. G., Staff, J., O'Malley, P. M., & Freedman-Doan, P. (2013). Adolescent work intensity, school performance, and substance use: Links vary by race/ethnicity and socioeconomic status. *Developmental Psychology, 49,* 2125–2134.

Bachman, J. G., Staff, J., O'Malley, P. M., Schulenberg, J. E., & Freedman-Doan, P. (2011). Twelfth-grade student work intensity linked to later educational attainment and substance use: New longitudinal evidence. *Developmental Psychology, 47,* 344–363.

Bäckman, L. (1991). Recognition memory across the adult life span: The role of prior knowledge. *Memory & Cognition, 19,* 63–71.

Bada, H. S., Das, A., Bauer, C. R., Shankaran, S., Lester, B. M., Gard, C. C., Wright, L. L., Lagasse, L. L., & Higgins, R. (2005). Low birth weight and preterm births: Etiologic fraction attributable to prenatal drug exposure. *Journal of Perinatology: Official Journal of the California Perinatal Association, 25,* 631–637.

Baddeley, A. (1986). *Working memory*. Oxford: Oxford University Press.

Baddeley, A. (1992). Working memory. *Science, 255,* 556–559.

Baddeley, A. (2000). The episodic buffer: a new component of working memory? *Trends in Cognitive Science, 4,* 417–423.

Baddeley, A. (2001). Is working memory still working? *American Psychologist, 56,* 851–864.

Baddeley, A. (2012). Working memory: Theories, models, and controversies. *Annual Review of Psychology, 63,* 1–29.

Baddeley, A., & Hitch, G. J. (1974). Working memory. In G. Bower (Ed.), *The psychology of learning and motivation: Vol. 8. Advances in research and theory* (pp. 47–89). New York, NY: Academic Press.

Badham, S. P., Hay, M., Foxon, N., Kaur, K., & Maylor, E. A. (2016). When does prior knowledge disproportionately benefit older adults' memory? *Neuropsychology, Development, and Cognition. Section B, Aging, Neuropsychology and Cognition, 23,* 338–365.

Baer, J. C., & Martinez, C. D. (2006). Child maltreatment and insecure attachment: A meta-analysis. *Journal of Reproductive and Infant Psychology, 24,* 187–197.

Bahrick, H. P. (1984). Semantic memory content in permastore: Fifty years of memory for Spanish learned in school. *Journal of Experimental Psychology: General, 113,* 1–29.

Bahrick, H. P., Bahrick, P. O., & Wittlinger, R. P. (1975). Fifty years of memory for names and faces: A cross-sectional approach. *Journal of Experimental Psychology: General, 104,* 54–75.

Bahrick, L. E. (2010). Intermodal perception and selective attention to intersensory redundancy: Implications for typical social development and autism. In J. G. Bremner & T. D. Wachs (Eds.), *The Wiley-Blackwell handbook of infant development* (2nd ed., *Vol 1*: Basic research, pp. 120–166). Malden, MA: John Wiley & Sons.

Bahrick, L. E., & Newell, L. (2008). Infant discrimination of faces in naturalistic events: Actions are more salient than faces. *Developmental Psychology, 44*, 983–996.
Bahrick, L. E., Gogate, L. J., & Ruiz, I. (2002). Attention and memory for faces and actions in infancy: The salience of actions over faces in dynamic events. *Child Development, 73*, 1629–1643.
Bahrick, L. E., Lickliter, R., & Castellanos, I. (2013). The development of face perception in infancy: Intersensory interference and unimodal visual facilitation. *Developmental Psychology, 49*, 1919–1930.
Bailey, H., Dunlosky, J., & Hertzog, C. (2009). Does differential strategy use account for age-related deficits in working-memory performance? *Psychology and Aging, 24*, 82–92.
Bailey, J. M., & Pillard, R. C. (1991). A genetic study of male sexual orientation. *Archives of General Psychiatry, 48*, 1089–1096.
Bailey, J. M., Bechtold, K. T., & Berenbaum, S. A. (2002). Who are tomboys and why should we study them? *Archives of Sexual Behavior, 31*, 333–341.
Bailey, J. M., Dunne, M. P., & Martin, N. G. (2000). Genetic and environmental influences on sexual orientation and its correlates in an Australian twin sample. *Journal of Personality and Social Psychology, 78*, 524–536.
Bailey, J. M., Pillard, R. C., Neale, M. C., & Agyei, Y. (1993). Heritable factors influence sexual orientation in women. *Archives of General Psychiatry, 50*, 217–223.
Bailey, R. N., Indian, R. W., Zhang, X., Geiss, L. S., Duenas, M. R., & Saaddine, J. B. (2006). Visual impairment and eye care among older adults—five states. *Morbidity and Mortality Weekly Report, 55*, 1321–1325.
Baillargeon, R. (2002). The acquisition of physical knowledge in infancy: A summary in eight lessons. In U. Goswami (Ed.), *Blackwell handbook of child cognitive development* (pp. 47–83). Oxford: Blackwell.
Baillargeon, R. H., Zoccolillo, M., Keenan, K., Côté, S., Pérusse, D., Wu, H., Boivin, M., & Tremblay, R. E. (2007). Gender differences in physical aggression: A prospective population-based survey of children before and after 2 years of age. *Developmental Psychology, 43*, 13–26.
Baiocco, R., Fontanesi, L., Santamaria, F., Ioverno, S., Marasco, B., Baumgartner, E., . . . Laghi, F. (2015). Negative parental responses to coming out and family functioning in a sample of lesbian and gay young adults. *Journal of Child and Family Studies, 24*, 1490–1500.
Bajenaru, O., Tiu, C., Antochi, F., & Roceanu, A. (2012). Neurocognitive disorders in DSM 5 project—Personal comments. *Journal of the Neurological Sciences, 322*, 17–19.
Bajpai, A., Kabra, M., Gupta, A. K., & Menon, P. S. (2006). Growth pattern and skeletal maturation following growth hormone therapy in growth hormone deficiency: Factors influencing outcome. *Indian Pediatrics, 43*, 593–599.
Bakalar, N. (2012). Sensory science: Partners in flavour. *Nature, 486*, S4–5.
Bakan, D. (1966). *The duality of human existence: Isolation and communion in Western man*. Boston: Beacon Press.
Baker, L., & Brown, A. L. (1984). Metacognitive skills and reading. In P. D. Pearson (Ed.), *A handbook of reading research*. New York, NY: Longman.
Baker, T. B., McFall, R. M., & Shoham, V. (2009). Current status and future prospects of clinical psychology. Toward a scientifically principled approach to mental and behavioral health care. *Psychological Science in the Public Interest, 9*, 67–103.
Bakermans-Kranenburg, M. J., Sonuga-Barke, E. J. S., Bos, K. B., Kelley, M., Dobrova-Krol, N. A., Engle, P. L., et al (2011). Children without permanent parents: Research, practice, and policy. *Monographs of the Society for Research in Child Development, 76*(4, Serial No. 291).
Baker-Ward, L., Gordon, B. N., Ornstein, P. A., Larus, D. M., & Clubb, P. A. (1993). Young children's long-term retention of a pediatric examination. *Child Development, 64*, 1519–1533.
Baker-Ward, L., Ornstein, P. A., & Holden, D. J. (1984). The expression of memorization in early childhood. *Journal of Experimental Child Psychology, 37*, 555–575.
Balassone, M. L. (1991). A social learning model of adolescent contraceptive behavior. *Journal of Youth and Adolescence, 20*, 593–616.
Balk, D. E. (2014). *Dealing with dying, death, and grief during adolescence*. New York, NY: Routledge.
Balk, D. E., & Corr, C. A. (Eds.) (2009). *Adolescent encounters with death, bereavement, and coping*. New York, NY: Springer.
Baltes, P. B. (1987). Theoretical propositions of life-span developmental psychology: On the dynamics between growth and decline. *Developmental Psychology, 23*, 611–626.
Baltes, P. B., & Baltes, M. M. (1990). Psychological perspectives on successful aging: The model of selective optimization with compensation. In P. B. Baltes & M. M. Baltes (Eds.), *Successful aging: Perspectives from the behavioral sciences*. New York, NY: Cambridge University Press.
Baltes, P. B., & Carstensen, L. L. (2003). The process of successful aging: Selection, optimization and compensation. In U. M. Staudinger & U. Lindenberger (Eds.), *Understanding human development: Dialogues with life-span psychology*. Dordecht, Netherlands: Kluwer Academic Press.
Baltes, P. B., & Lindenberger, U. (1997). Emergence of a powerful connection between sensory and cognitive functions across the adult life span: A new window to the study of cognitive aging? *Psychology and Aging, 12*, 12–21.
Baltes, P. B., & Rudolph, C. W. (2013). The theory of selection, optimization, and compensation. In M. Wang (Ed.), *The Oxford handbook of retirement* (pp. 88–101). New York, NY: Oxford University Press.
Baltes, P. B., & Staudinger, U. M. (2000). Wisdom: A metaheuristic (pragmatic) to orchestrate mind and virtue toward excellence. *American Psychologist, 55*, 122–136.
Baltes, P. B., Lindenberger, U., & Staudinger, U. M. (2006). Life span theory in developmental psychology. In W. Damon & R. M. Lerner (Eds. in Chief) & R. M. Lerner (Vol. Ed.), *Handbook of child psychology: Vol. 1. Theoretical models of human development* (6th ed.). Hoboken, NJ: Wiley.
Baltes, P. B., Smith, J., & Staudinger, U. M. (1992). Wisdom and successful aging. In T. B. Sonderegger (Ed.), *Nebraska symposium on motivation: Vol. 39. Psychology and aging*. Lincoln: University of Nebraska Press.
Baltes, P. B., Staudinger, U. M., Maercker, A., & Smith, J. (1995). People nominated as wise: A comparative study of wisdom-related knowledge. *Psychology and Aging, 10*, 155–166.
Balu, D. T., & Lucki, I. (2009). Adult hippocampal neurogenesis: Regulation, functional implications, and contribution to disease pathology. *Neuroscience and Biobehavioral Reviews, 33*(3), 232–252.
Banai, K., Ortiz, J. A., Oppenheimer, J. D., & Wright, B. A. (2010). Learning two things at once: Differential constraints on the acquisition and consolidation of perceptual learning. *Neuroscience, 165*, 436–444.
Bandstra, E. S., Morrow, C. E., Mansoor, E., & Accornero, V. H. (2010). Prenatal drug exposure: Infant and toddler outcomes. *Journal of Addictive Disorders, 29*, 245–258.
Bandura, A. (1977). *Social learning theory*. Englewood Cliffs, NJ: Prentice-Hall.
Bandura, A. (1986). *Social foundations of thought and action: A social cognitive theory*. Englewood Cliffs, NJ: Prentice Hall.
Bandura, A. (1989). Social cognitive theory. In R. Vasta (Ed.), *Annals of child development: Vol. 6. theories of child development: Revised formulations and current issues*. Greenwich, CT: JAI Press.
Bandura, A. (1991). Social cognitive theory of moral thought and action. In W. M. Kurtines & J. L. Gewirtz (Eds.), *Handbook of moral behavior and development: Vol. 1. Theory*. Hillsdale, NJ: Erlbaum.
Bandura, A. (2000). Social cognitive theory: An agentic perspective. *Annual Review of Psychology, 52*, 1–26.
Bandura, A. (2002). Selective moral disengagement in the exercise of moral agency. *Journal of Moral Education, 31*, 101–119.
Bandura, A. (2006). Toward a psychology of human agency. *Perspectives on Psychological Science, 1*, 164–180.
Bandura, A. (2015). *Moral disengagement: How good people can do harm and feel good about themselves*. New York, NY: Worth.
Banerjee, R., & Lintern, V. (2000). Boys will be boys: The effect of social evaluation concerns on gender-typing. *Social Development, 9*, 397–408.
Banerjee, T. D., Middleton, F., & Faraone, S. V. (2007). Environmental risk factors for attention-deficit hyperactivity disorder. *Acta paediatrica, 96*, 1269–1274.
Bangen, K. J., Meeks, T. W., & Jeste, D. V. (2013). Defining and assessing wisdom: A review of the literature. *American Journal of Geriatric Psychiatry, 21*, 1254–1266.
Bank, L., Marlowe, J., Reid, J., Patterson, G., & Weinrott, M. (1991). A comparative evaluation of parent-training interventions for families of chronic delinquents. *Journal of Abnormal Child Psychology, 19*, 15–33.
Bankoff, E. A. (1983). Aged parents and their widowed daughters: A support relationship. *Journal of Gerontology, 38*, 226–230.
Banks, M. S., & Ginsburg, A. P. (1985). Infant visual preferences: A review and new theoretical treatment. In H. W. Reese (Ed.), *Advances in child development and behavior: Vol. 19*. Orlando, FL: Academic Press.
Banks, M. S., & Shannon, E. (1993). Spatial and chromatic visual efficiency in human neonates. In C. E. Granrud (Ed.), *Visual perception and cognition in infancy*. Hillsdale, NJ: Erlbaum.
Banti, S., Mauri, M., Oppo, A., Borri, C., Rambelli, C., Ramacciotti, D., et al. (2011). From the third month of pregnancy to 1 year postpartum. Prevalence, incidence, recurrence, and new onset of depression. Results from the perinatal depression-research & screening unit study. *Comprehensive Psychiatry, 52*, 343–351.
Barac, R., & Bialystok, E. (2012). Bilingual effects on cognitive and linguistic development: Role of language, cultural background, and education. *Child Development, 83*, 413–422.
Barash, D. P. (2002, May 24). Evolution, males, and violence. *The Chronicle of Higher Education*, B7–B9.
Barber, B. L., Eccles, J. S., & Stone, M. R. (2001). Whatever happened to the jock, the brain, and the princess? Young adult pathways linked to adolescent activity involvement and social identity. *Journal of Adolescent Research, 16*, 429–455.
Barber, S., & Mather, M. (2014). Stereotype threat in older adults: When and why does it occur and who is most affected? In P. Verhaeghen & C. Hertzog (Eds.), *The Oxford handbook of emotion, social cognition, and problem solving in adulthood* (pp. 302–320). Oxford University Press.
Barboza, G. E., Schiamberg, L. B., Oehmke, J., Korzeniewski, S. J., Post, L. A., & Heraux, C. G. (2009). Individual characteristics and the multiple contexts of adolescent bullying: An ecological perspective. *Journal of Youth and Adolescence, 38*, 101–121.
Barcelos, N., Shah, N., Cohen, K., Hogan, M. J., Mulkerrin, E., Arciero, P. J., & Anderson-Hanley, C. (2015). Aerobic and cognitive exercise (ACE) pilot study for older adults: Executive function improves with cognitive challenge while exergaming. *Journal of the International Neuropsychological Society: JINS, 21*(10), 768–779.
Bargh, J. A., & Morsella, E. (2008). The unconscious mind. *Perspectives on Psychological Science, 3*, 73–79.
Bar-Haim, Y., Ziv, T., Lamy, D., & Hodes, R. M. (2006). Nature and nurture in own-race face processing. *Psychological Science, 17*, 159–163.
Barham, M. P., Enticott, P. G., Conduit, R., & Lum, J. A. (2016). Transcranial electrical stimulation during sleep enhances declarative (but not procedural) memory consolidation: Evidence from a meta-analysis. *Neuroscience & Biobehavioral Reviews, 63*, 65–77.
Bariola, E., Gullone, E., & Hughes, E. K. (2011). Child and adolescent emotion regulation: The role of parental emotion regulation and expression. *Clinical Child and Family Psychology Review, 14*, 198–212.
Barker, E. D., Arseneault, L., Brendgen, M., Fontaine, N., & Maughan, B. (2008). Joint development of bullying and victimization in adolescence: Relations to delinquency and self-harm. *Journal of the American Academy of Child & Adolescent Psychiatry, 47*, 1030–1038.
Barkley, R. A. (1997). Behavioral inhibition, sustained attention, and executive functions: Constructing a unifying theory of ADHD. *Psychological Bulletin, 121*, 65–94.
Barkley, R. A. (2015). Emotional dysregulation is a core component of ADHD. In R. A. Barkley (Ed.), *Attention-deficit hyperactivity disorder: A handbook for diagnosis and treatment* (4th ed., pp. 81–115). New York, NY: Guilford Press.
Barkley, R. A., Fischer, M., Smallish, L., & Fletcher, K. (2006). Young adult outcome of hyperactive children: Adaptive functioning in major life activities. *Journal of the American Academy of Child & Adolescent Psychiatry, 45*, 192–202.

Barlé, N., Wortman, C. B., & Latack, J. A. (2015). Traumatic bereavement: Basic research and clinical implications. *Journal of Psychotherapy Integration*. dx.doi.org/10.1037/int0000013.

Barnes, D. E., Yaffe, K., Satariano, W. A., & Tager, I. B. (2003). A longitudinal study of cardiorespiratory fitness and cognitive function in healthy older adults. *Journal of the American Geriatrics Society, 51*, 459–465.

Barnes, K. E. (1971). Preschool play norms: A replication. *Developmental Psychology, 5*, 99–103.

Barnes, R. (2013, January 14). In memoir, Sotomayor lays bare a tough life. *The Washington Post*, pp. C1, C3.

Barnett, R. C. (1994). Home-to-work spillover revisited: A study of full-time employed women in dual-earner couples. *Journal of Marriage and the Family, 56*, 647–656.

Barnett, W. S., Brown, K. C., Finn-Stevenson, M., & Henrich, C. (2007). From visions to systems of universal prekindergarten. In J. L. Aber, S. J. Bishop-Josef, S. M. Jones, K. T. McLearn, & D. A. Phillips (Eds.), *Child development and social policy: Knowledge for action*. Washington, DC: American Psychology Association.

Baron, N. S. (1992). *Growing up with language: How children learn to talk*. Reading, MA: Addison-Wesley.

Baron-Cohen, S. (1995). *Mindblindness: An essay on autism and theory of mind*. Cambridge, MA: MIT Press.

Baron-Cohen, S. (2003). *The essential difference: The truth about the male and female brain*. New York, NY: Basic Books.

Baron-Cohen, S. (2010). Autism and the empathizing-systemizing (E-S) theory. In P. D. Zelazo, M. Chandler, & E. Crone (Eds.), *Developmental social cognitive neuroscience*. New York, NY: Psychology Press.

Baron-Cohen, S., Leslie, A. M., & Frith, U. (1985). Does the autistic child have a "Theory of Mind"? *Cognition, 21*, 37–46.

Barouki, R., Gluckman, P. D., Grandjean, P., Hanson, M., & Heindel, J. J. (2012). Developmental origins of non-communicable disease: Implications for research and public health. *Environmental Health, 11*, 3–9. Retrieved from www.ehjournal.net/content/11/1/42.

Barr, R., Dowden, A., & Hayne, H. (1996). Developmental changes in deferred imitation by 6- to 24-month-old infants. *Infant Behavior & Development, 19*, 159–170.

Barrett, T. M., & Needham, A. (2008). Developmental differences in infants' use of an object's shape to grasp it securely. *Developmental Psychobiology, 50*, 97–106.

Barrett, T. R., & Wright, M. (1981). Age-related facilitation in recall following semantic processing. *Journal of Gerontology, 36*, 194–199.

Barrouillet, P. (2015). Theories of cognitive development: From Piaget to today. *Developmental Review, 38*, 1–12.

Barrouillet, P., & Gauffroy, C. (2013). Introduction—from Piaget to dual-process theories: The complexities of thinking and reasoning development. In P. Barrouillet & C. Gauffroy (Eds.), *The development of thinking and reasoning* (pp. 1–10). Taylor & Francis.

Bartholomew, K., & Horowitz, L. M. (1991). Attachment styles among young adults: A test of a four-category model. *Journal of Personality and Social Psychology, 61*, 226–244.

Bartlett, D. (1997). Primitive reflexes and early motor development. *Journal of Developmental and Behavioral Pediatrics, 18*, 151–157.

Bartlett, T. (2011, February 25). The case for play. How a handful of researchers are trying to save childhood. *Chronicle of Higher Education*, pp. B6–B10.

Bartoshuk, L. M., Duffy, V. B., & Miller, I. J. (1994). PTC/PROP tasting: Anatomy, psychophysics, and sex effects. *Physiology & Behavior, 56*, 1165–1171.

Bartz, J. A. (2016). Oxytocin and the pharmacological dissection of affiliation. *Current Directions in Psychological Science, 25*, 104–110.

Bartzokis, G., & Lu, P. H. (2009). Brain volume: Age-related changes. In P. R. Hof & C. V. Mobbs (Eds.), *Handbook of the neuroscience of aging* (pp. 27–38). London, UK: Academic Press.

Basch, C. E. (2011). Healthier students are better learners: A missing link in school reforms to close the achievement gap. *The Journal of School Health, 81*(10), 593–598.

Basseches, M. (1984). *Dialectical thinking and adult development*. Norwood, NJ: Ablex.

Basseches, M. (2005). The development of dialectical thinking as an approach to integration. *Integral Review, 1*, 47–63.

Bastos, L. O. D., Guerreiro, M. M., Lees, A. J., Warner, T. T., & Silveira-Moriyama, L. (2015). Effects of age and cognition on a cross-cultural paediatric adaptation of the Sniffin' Sticks Identification Test. *PLoS ONE, 10(8)*, e0131641.

Bates, E., O'Connell, B., & Shore, C. (1987). Language and communication in infancy. In J. D. Osofsky (Ed.), *Handbook of infant development* (2nd ed.). New York, NY: Wiley.

Bates, J. E., Schermerhorn, A. C., & Petersen, I. T. (2012). Temperament and parenting in developmental perspective. In M. Z. Zentner & R. L. Shiner (Eds.), *Handbook of temperament*. New York, NY: Guilford.

Bates, J. S., & Taylor, A. C. (2013). Taking stock of theory in grandparent studies. In M. A. Fine & F D. Fincham (Eds.), *Handbook of family theories. A context-based approach*. New York, NY: Routledge.

Bates, T. C., Lewis, G. J., & Weiss, A. (2013). Childhood socioeconomic status amplifies genetic effects on adult intelligence. *Psychological Science, 24*, 2111–2116.

Batrinos, M. L. (2012). Testosterone and aggressive behavior in man. *International Journal of Endocrinology & Metabolism, 10*, 563–568.

Batshaw, M. L., Gropman, A., & Lanpher, B. (2013). Genetics and developmental disabilities. In M. L. Batshaw, N. J. Roizen, & G. R. Lotrecchiano (Eds.), *Children with disabilities* (7th ed., pp. 3–24). Baltimore: Paul H. Brookes.

Bau, A. M., Ernert, A., Schenk, L., Wiegand, S., Martus, P., Grüters, A., et al. (2009). Is there a further acceleration in the age at onset of menarche? A cross-sectional study in 1840 school children focusing on age and bodyweight at the onset of menarche. *European Journal of Endocrinology, 160*, 107–113.

Baudouin, A., Clarys, D., Vanneste, S., & Isingrini, M. (2009). Executive functioning and processing speed in age-related differences in memory: Contribution of a coding task. *Brain and Cognition, 71*, 240–245.

Bauer, I., Wrosch, C., & Jobin, J. (2008). I'm better off than most other people: The role of social comparisons for coping with regret in young adulthood and old age. *Psychology and Aging, 23*, 800–811.

Bauer, P. J. (1996). What do infants recall of their lives? Memory for specific events by one- to two-year-olds. *American Psychologist, 51*, 29–41.

Bauer, P. J. (2007). *Remembering the times of our lives: Memory in infancy and beyond*. Mahwah, NJ: Lawrence Erlbaum.

Bauer, P. J. (2008). Toward a neuro-developmental account of the development of declarative memory. *Developmental Psychobiology, 50*, 19–31.

Bauer, P. J. (2009). The cognitive neuroscience of the development of memory. In M. L. Courage & N. Cowan (Eds.), *The development of memory in infancy and childhood* (pp. 115–144). New York, NY: Psychology Press.

Bauer, P. J. (2014). The development of forgetting: Childhood amnesia. In P. Bauer & R. Fivush (Eds.), *The Wiley handbook on the development of children's memory* (pp. 519–544). Malden, MA: Wiley Blackwell.

Bauer, P. J., Burch, M. M., Scholin, S. E., & Güler, O. E. (2007). Using cue words to investigate the distribution of autobiographical memories in childhood. *Psychological Science, 18*, 910–916.

Bauer, P. J., & Fivush, R. (Eds.). (2014). *The Wiley handbook on the development of children's memory*. Malden, MA: Wiley Blackwell.

Bauer, P. J., Hättenschwiler, N., & Larkina, M. (2016). "Owning" the personal past: Adolescents' and adults' autobiographical narratives and ratings of memories of recent and distant events. *Memory (Hove, England), 24*, 165–183.

Bauer, P. J., Kroupina, M. G., Schwade, J. A., Dropik, P. L., & Wewerka, S. S. (1998). If memory serves, will language? Later verbal accessibility of early memories. *Development and Psychopathology, 10*, 655–679.

Bauer, P. J., Larkina, M., & Deocampo, J. (2011). Early memory development. In U. Goswami (Ed.), *The Wiley-Blackwell handbook of childhood cognitive development* (2nd ed., pp. 153–179). Malden, MA: John Wiley & Sons.

Bauer, P. J., Stark, E. N., Ackil, J. K., Larkina, M., Merrill, N., & Fivush, R. (2016, May 14). The recollective qualities of adolescents' and adults' narratives about a long-ago tornado. *Memory*, 1–13 [Epub ahead of print].

Bauer, P. J., Wenner, J. A., Dropik, P. L., & Wewerka, S. S. (2000). Parameters of remembering and forgetting in the transition from infancy to early childhood. *Monographs of the Society for Research in Child Development, 65*(Serial No. 263).

Baum, C., & Ruhm, C. J. (2014). *The changing benefits of early work experience*. National Bureau of Economic Research, Working Paper No. 20413.

Baum, S., Viens, J., & Slatin, B. (2005). *Multiple intelligences in the elementary classroom: A teacher's toolkit*. New York, NY: Teachers College Press.

Baumard, N., Mascaro, O., & Chevallier, C. (2012). Preschoolers are able to take merit into account when distributing goods. *Developmental Psychology, 48*, 492–498.

Baumrind, D. (1967). Child care practices anteceding three patterns of preschool behavior. *Genetic Psychology Monographs, 75*, 43–88.

Baumrind, D. (1977, March). *Socialization determinants of personal agency*. Paper presented at the biennial meeting of the Society for Research in Child Development, New Orleans.

Baumrind, D. (1991). Effective parenting during the early adolescent transition. In P. A. Cowan & M. Hetherington (Eds.), *Family transitions*. Hillsdale, NJ: Erlbaum.

Baumrind, D. (2013). Authoritative parenting revisited: History and current status. In R. E. Larzelere, A. S. Sheffield, & A. W. Harrist (Eds.), *Authoritative parenting. Synthesizing nurturance and discipline for optimal child development*. Washington, DC: American Psychological Association.

Bauserman, R. (2002). Child adjustment in joint-custody versus sole-custody arrangements: A meta-analytic review. *Journal of Family Psychology, 16*, 91–102.

Bauserman, R. (2012). A meta-analysis of parental satisfaction, adjustment, and conflict in joint custody and sole custody following divorce. *Journal of Divorce & Remarriage, 53*, 464–488.

Bayley, N. (2006). *Bayley scales of infant and toddler development*, (3rd ed.). New York, NY: Pearson.

Beadle-Brown, J., Leigh, J., Whelton, B., Richardson, L., Beecham, J., Baumker, T., & Bradshaw, J. (2016). Quality of life and quality of support for people with severe intellectual disability and complex needs. *Journal of Applied Research in Intellectual Disabilities, 29*, 409–421.

Beadle-Brown, J., Murphy, G., & DiTerlizzi, M. (2009). Quality of life for the Camberwell Cohort. *Journal of Applied Research in Intellectual Disabilities, 22* (4), 380–390.

Beadle-Brown, J., Murphy, G., & Wing, L. (2005). Long-term outcome for people with severe intellectual disabilities: Impact of social impairment. *American Journal on Mental Retardation, 110*, 1–12.

Beadle-Brown, J., Murphy, G., & Wing, L. (2006). The Camberwell Cohort 25 years on: Characteristics and changes in skills over time. *Journal of Applied Research in Intellectual Disabilities, 19*, 317–329.

Beane, A. L. (2009). *Bullying prevention for schools: A step-by-step guide to implementing a successful anti-bullying program*. San Francisco, CA: Jossey-Bass.

Beauchamp, G. K., & Mennella, J. A. (2009). Early flavor learning and its impact on later feeding behavior. *Journal of Pediatric Gastroenterology and Nutrition, 48*, S25–S30.

Beauchamp, G. K., & Mennella, J. A. (2011). Flavor perception in human infants: Development and functional significance. *Digestion, 83*, 1–6.

Beautrais, A. L. (2003). Life course factors associated with suicidal behaviors in young people. *American Behavioral Scientist, 46*, 1137–1156.

Beck, A. T., & Bredemeier, K. (2016). A unified model of depression: Integrated clinical, cognitive, biological, and evolutionary perspectives. *Clinical Psychological Science, 4*, 596–619.

Becker, A. E., Burwell, R. A., Herzog, D. B., Hamburg, P., & Gilman, S. E. (2002). Eating behaviours and attitudes following prolonged exposure to television among ethnic Fijian adolescent girls. *British Journal of Psychiatry, 180*, 509–514.

Beckwith, L., Rozga, A., & Sigman, M. (2002). Maternal sensitivity and attachment in atypical groups. In R. V. Kail (Ed.), *Advances in child development and behavior: Vol. 30*. San Diego, CA: Academic Press.

Becquet, R., Marston, M., Dabis, F., Moulton, L. H., Gray, G., Coovadia, H. M., et al. (2012). Children who acquire HIV infection perinatally are at higher risk of early death than those acquiring infection through breastmilk: A meta-analysis. *PLoS ONE, 7*, e28510.

Beech, H. (2013, December 2). Why China needs more children. *Time*, pp. 36–39.

Beemsterboer, S. N., Homburg, R., Gorter, N. A., Schats, R., Hompes, P. G., & Lambalk, C. B. (2006). The paradox of declining fertility but increasing twinning rates with advancing maternal age. *Human reproduction, 21*, 1531–1532.

Behnke, M., Smith, V. C., Committee on Substance Abuse, and Committee of Fetus and Newborn (2013). Prenatal substance abuse: Short- and long-term effects on the exposed fetus. *Pediatrics, 131*, e1009–e1024.

Behrend, D. A., Rosengren, K., & Perlmutter, M. (1989). A new look at children's private speech: The effects of age, task difficulty, and parent presence. *International Journal of Behavioral Development, 12*, 305–320.

Beijersbergen, M. D., Juffer, F., Bakermans-Kranenburg, M., & van IJzendoorn, M. H. (2012). Remaining or becoming secure: Parental sensitive support predicts attachment continuity from infancy to adolescence in a longitudinal adoption study. *Developmental Psychology, 48*, 1277–1282.

Beilin, H. (1992). Piaget's enduring contribution to developmental psychology. *Developmental Psychology, 28*, 191–204.

Beitchman, J. H., Zucker, K. J., Hood, J. E., daCosta, G. A., & Akman, D. (1991). A review of the short-term effects of child sexual abuse. *Child Abuse & Neglect, 15*, 537–556.

Bell, E., & Kandler, C. (2015). The origins of party identification and its relationship to political orientations. *Personality and Individual Differences, 83*, 136–141.

Bell, J. H., & Bromnick, R. D. (2003). The social reality of the imaginary audience: A grounded theory approach. *Adolescence, 38*, 205–219.

Bell, M. A., & Morasch, K. C. (2007). The development of working memory in the first 2 years of life. In L. M. Oakes & P. J. Bauer (Eds.), *Short and long-term memory in infancy and early childhood* (pp. 27–50). New York, NY: Oxford University Press.

Bell, M. A., & Wolfe, C. D. (2007). Changes in brain functioning from infancy to early childhood: Evidence from EEG power and coherence working memory tasks. *Developmental Neuropsychology, 31*, 21–38.

Bellanti, C. J., Bierman, K. L., & Conduct Problems Prevention Research Group. (2000). Disentangling the impact of low cognitive ability and inattention on social behavior and peer relationships. *Journal of Clinical Child Psychology, 29*, 66–75.

Belloc, S., Cohen-Bacrie, P., Benkhalifa, M., Cohen-Bacrie, M., DeMouzon, J., Hazout, A., & Ménéza, Y. (2008). Effect of maternal and paternal age on pregnancy and miscarriage rates after intrauterine insemination. *Reproductive BioMedicine Online, 17*, 392–397. Available at www.rbmonline.com/Article/3526.

Bellugi, U. (1988). The acquisition of a spatial language. In F. S. Kessel (Ed.), *The development of language and language researchers: Essays in honor of Roger Brown*. Hillsdale, NJ: Erlbaum.

Belsky, J. (1981). Early human experience: A family perspective. *Developmental Psychology, 17*, 3–23.

Belsky, J., & Beaver, K. M. (2011). Cumulative-genetic plasticity, parenting and adolescent self-regulation. *Journal of Child Psychology and Psychiatry, 52*, 619–626.

Belsky, J., Burchinal, M., McCartney, K., Vandell, D. L., Clarke-Stewart, K. A., Owen, M. T., et al. (2007). Are there long-term effects of early child care? *Child Development, 78*, 681–701.

Belsky, J., Jaffee, S., Hsieh, K., & Silva, P. A. (2001). Child-rearing antecedents of intergenerational relations in young adulthood: A prospective study. *Developmental Psychology, 37*, 801–813.

Bem, S. L. (1989). Genital knowledge and gender constancy in preschool children. *Child Development, 60*, 649–662.

Bemporad, J. R. (1979). Adult recollections of a formerly autistic child. *Journal of Autism and Developmental Disorders, 9*, 179–197.

Benaron, L. D. (2009). *Autism*. Westport, CT: Greenwood Press.

Benbow, C. P., & Arjmand, O. (1990). Predictors of high academic achievement in mathematics and science by mathematically talented students: A longitudinal study. *Journal of Educational Psychology, 82*, 430–441.

Bender, K. A. (2012). An analysis of well-being in retirement: The roles of pensions, health, and

'voluntariness' of retirement. *The Journal of Socio-Economics, 41*, 424–433.

Benenson, J. F., Philippoussis, M., & Leeb, R. (1999). Sex differences in neonates' cuddliness. *Journal of Genetic Psychology, 160*, 332–342.

Benes, F. M. (1998). Human brain growth spans decades. *American Journal of Psychiatry, 155*, 1489.

Bengtson, V. L. (2001). Beyond the nuclear family: The increasing importance of multigenerational bonds. *Journal of Marriage and Family, 63*, 1–16.

Bengtson, V., Rosenthal, C., & Burton, L. (1996). Paradoxes of families and aging. In R. H. Binstock, L. K. George, V. W. Marshall, G. C. Myers, & J. H. Schulz (Eds.), *Handbook of aging and the social sciences* (4th ed.). San Diego: Academic Press.

Benjet, C., & Kazdin, A. E. (2003). Spanking children: The controversies, findings, and new directions. *Clinical Psychology Review, 23*, 197–224.

Benn, P. A., & Chapman, A. R. (2009). Practical and ethical considerations of noninvasive prenatal diagnosis. *JAMA, 301*, 2154–2156.

Bennett, D. A., Wilson, R. S., Arvanitakis, Z., Boyle, P. A., de Toledo-Morrell, L., & Schneider, J. A. (2013). Selected findings from the Religious Orders Study and Rush Memory and Aging Project. *Journal of Alzheimer's Disease, 33* (Suppl. 1), S397–403.

Bennett, J. (2010, October 11). From lockers to lockup. *Newsweek*, pp. 38–41.

Benson, J. E., & Elder, G. H., Jr. (2011). Young adult identities and their pathways: A developmental and life course model. *Developmental Psychology, 47*, 1646–1657.

Benson, J. J., & Coleman, M. (2016). Older adults developing a preference for living apart together. *Journal of Marriage and Family, 78*, 797–812.

Benzies, K. M., Magill-Evans, J. E., Hayden, K. A., & Ballantyne, M. (2013). Key components of early intervention programs for preterm infants and their parents: A systematic review and meta-analysis. *BioMed Central Pregnancy and Childbirth 13*, S10.

Berenbaum, S. A., & Meyer-Bahlburg, H. F. L. (2015). Gender development and sexuality in disorders of sex development. *Hormone and Metabolic Research, 47*, 361–366.

Berenbaum, S. A., Martin, C. L., Hanish, L. D., Briggs, P. T., & Fabes, R. A. (2008). Sex differences in children's play. In J. B. Becker, K. J. Berkley, N. Geary, E. Hampson, J. Herman, & E. Young (Eds.), *Sex differences in the brain: From genes to behavior* (pp. 275–290). New York, NY: Oxford University Press.

Berg, C. A., & Klaczynski, P. A. (1996). Practical intelligence and problem solving: Searching for perspectives. In F. Blanchard-Fields & T. M. Hess (Eds.), *Perspectives on cognitive change in adulthood and aging*. New York, NY: McGraw-Hill.

Bergen, D. (2008). *Human development. Traditional and contemporary theories*. Upper Saddle River, NJ: Pearson.

Berger, R. P., Fromkin, J. B., Stutz, H., Makoroff, K., Scribano, P. V., Feldman, K., et al. (2011). Abusive head trauma during a time of increased unemployment: A multicenter analysis. *Pediatrics, 128*, 637–643.

Berger, S. E., & Adolph, K. E. (2003). Infants use handrails as tools in locomotor task. *Developmental Psychology, 39*, 594–605.

Berger, S. E., Adolph, K. E., & Lobo, S. A. (2005). Out of the toolbox: Toddlers differentiate wobbly and wooden handrails. *Child Development, 76*, 1294–1307.

Berger, T. M., Steurer, M. A., Woerner, A., Meyer-Schiffer, P., & Adams, M. (2012). Trends and centre-to-centre variability in survival rates of very preterm infants (<32 weeks) over a 10-year-period in Switzerland. *Archives of Disease in Childhood-Fetal and Neonatal Edition, 97*, F323–F328.

Bergman, K., Sarkar, P., O'Connor, T. G., Modi, N., & Glover, V. (2007). Maternal stress during pregnancy predicts cognitive ability and fearfulness in infancy. *Journal of the American Academy of Child Psychiatry, 46*, 1454–1463.

Bering, J. M., & Bjorklund, D. F. (2004). The natural emergence of reasoning about the afterlife as a developmental regularity. *Developmental Psychology, 40*, 217–233.

Berk, L. E. (1992). Children's private speech: An overview of theory and the status of research. In R. M. Diaz &

L. E. Berk (Eds.), *Private speech: From social interaction to self-regulation*. Hillsdale, NJ: Erlbaum.

Berk, L. E., & Landau, S. (1993). Private speech of learning disabled and normally achieving children in classroom academic and laboratory contexts. *Child Development, 64*, 556–571.

Berk, L. E., & Winsler, A. (1995). *Scaffolding children's learning: Vygotsky and early childhood education*. Washington, DC: National Association for the Education of Young Children.

Berlin, L. J., Ispa, J. M., Fine, M. A., Malone, P. S., Brooks-Gunn, J., Brady-Smith, C., Ayoub, C., & Bai, Y. (2009). Correlates and consequences of spanking and verbal punishment for low-income White, African American, and Mexican American toddlers. *Child Development, 80*, 1403–1420.

Berlin, L. J., Zeanah, C. H., & Lieberman, A. F. (2008). Prevention and intervention programs for supporting early attachment security. In J. Cassidy & P. R. Shaver (Eds.), *Handbook of attachment: Theory, research, and clinical applications* (2nd ed.). New York, NY: Guilford.

Berman, A. L., & Jobes, D. A. (1991). *Adolescent suicide: Assessment and intervention*. Washington, DC: American Psychological Association.

Berman, W. H., & Sperling, M. B. (1991). Parental attachment and emotional distress in the transition to college. *Journal of Youth and Adolescence, 20*, 427–440.

Bernal, M. E., & Knight, G. P. (1997). Ethnic identity of Latino children. In J. G. Garcia & M. C. Zea (Eds.), *Psychological interventions and research with Latino populations*. Boston, MA: Allyn & Bacon.

Bernard, K., Dozier, M., Bick, J., Lewis-Morrarty, E., Lindhiem, O., & Carlson, E. (2012). Enhancing attachment organization among maltreated children: Results of a randomized clinical trial. *Child Development, 83*, 623–636.

Berney, T. (2009). Ageing in Down syndrome. In G. O'Brien, L. Rosenbloom, G. O'Brien, & L. Rosenbloom (Eds.), *Developmental disability and ageing*. London, UK: Mac Keith Press.

Bernstein, A. C., & Cowan, P. A. (1975). Children's concepts of how people get babies. *Child Development, 46*, 77–91.

Berntsen, D., & Rubin, D. C. (2002). Emotionally charged autobiographical memories across the lifespan: The recall of happy, sad, traumatic, and involuntary memories. *Psychology and Aging, 17*, 636–652.

Berntsen, D., & Rubin, D. C. (2004). Cultural life scripts structure recall from autobiographical memory. *Memory & Cognition, 32*, 427–442.

Berntsen, D., & Rubin, D. C. (Eds.). (2012). *Understanding autobiographical memory: Theories and approaches*. New York, NY: Cambridge University Press.

Berry, J. W., Poortinga, Y. H., Segall, M., & Dasen, P. R. (1992). *Cross-cultural psychology: Research and applications*. Cambridge, UK: Cambridge University Press.

Berry, K., & Danquah, A. (2016). Attachment-informed therapy for adults: Towards a unifying perspective on practice. *Psychology and Psychotherapy: Theory, Research, and Practice, 89*, 15–32.

Berscheid, E. (2010). Love in the fourth dimension. *Annual Review of Psychology, 61*, 1–25.

Bertenthal, B. I., & Fischer, K. W. (1978). Development of self-recognition in the infant. *Developmental Psychology, 14*, 44–50.

Berthier, N. E., & Keen, R. (2006). Development of reaching in infancy. *Experimental Brain Research, 169*, 507–518.

Bertman, S. L. (1991). Children and death: Insights, hindsights, and illuminations. In D. Papadatou & C. Papadatos (Eds.), *Children and death*. New York, NY: Hemisphere.

Berwick, R. C., Pietroski, P., Yankama, B., & Chomsky, N. (2011). Poverty of the stimulus revisited. *Cognitive Science, 35*, 1207–1242.

Berzoff, J. (2008). Psychosocial ego development: The theory of Erik Erikson. In J. Berzoff, L. M. Flanagan, L. Melano, & P. Hertz (Eds.), *Inside out and outside in: Psychodynamic clinical theory and psychopathology in contemporary multicultural contexts* (2nd ed.). Lanham, MD: Jason Aronson.

Berzonsky, M. D., & Kuk, L. S. (2000). Identity status, identity processing style, and the transition to university. *Journal of Adolescent Research, 15*, 81–98.

Best, D. L., & Williams, J. E. (1993). A cross-cultural viewpoint. In A. E. Beall & R. J. Sternberg (Eds.), *The psychology of gender* (pp. 215–248). New York, NY: Guilford Press.

Betts, J., McKay, J., Maruff, P., & Anderson, V. (2006). The development of sustained attention in children: The effect of age and task load. *Child Neuropsychology, 12*, 205–221.

Beuker, K. T., Rommelse, N. N. J., Donders, R., & Buitelaar, J. K. (2013). The development of early communication skills in the first two years of life. *Infant Behavior & Development, 36*, 71–83.

Bever, L. (2014, November 2). Brittany Maynard, as promised, ends her life at 29. *The Washington Post*. Retrieved from www.washingtonpost.com.

Beverung, L. M., & Jacobvitz, D. (2016). Women's retrospective experiences of bereavement: Predicting unresolved attachment. *Omega: Journal of Death and Dying, 73*, 126–140.

Beyers, J. M., Bates, J. E., Pettit, G. S., & Dodge, K. A. (2003). Neighborhood structure, parenting processes, and the development of youths' externalizing behaviors: A multilevel analysis. *American Journal of Community Psychology, 31*, 35–53.

Beyers, W., & Seiffge-Krenke, I. (2010). Does identity precede intimacy? Testing Erikson's theory on romantic development in emerging adults of the 21st century. *Journal of Adolescent Research, 25*, 387–415.

Bhatara, V., Loudenberg, R., & Ellis, R. (2006). Association of attention deficit hyperactivity disorder and gestational alcohol exposure: An exploratory study. *Journal of Attention Disorders, 9*, 515–522.

Bialystok, E., & Feng, X. (2011). Language proficiency and its implications for monolingual and bilingual children. In A. Y. Durgunoglu & C. Goldenberg (Eds.), *Language and literacy development in bilingual settings* (pp. 121–139). Guilford Press.

Bialystok, E., Craik, F. I. M., & Luk, G. (2012). Bilingualism: Consequences for mind and brain. *Trends in Cognitive Sciences, 16*, 240–250.

Bialystok, E., Craik, F. I., Binns, M. A., Ossher, L., & Freedman, M. (2014). Effects of bilingualism on the age of onset and progression of MCI and AD: Evidence from executive function tests. *Neuropsychology, 28*, 290–304.

Bianchi, S. M. (2011). Family change and time allocation in American families. *Annals of the American Academy of Political and Social Science, 638*, 21–44.

Bianchi, S. M., Robinson, J. P., & Milkie, M. A. (2006). *Changing rhythms of American family life*. New York, NY: Russell Sage.

Biblarz, T. J., & Stacey, J. (2010). How does the gender of parents matter? *Journal of Marriage and Family, 72*, 3–22.

Biemann, T., Zacher, H., & Feldman, D. C. (2012). Career patterns: A twenty-year panel study. *Journal of Vocational Behavior, 81*, 159–170.

Bierhoff, H., & Schmohr, M. (2003). Romantic and marital relationships. In F. R. Lang & K. L. Fingerman (Eds.), *Growing together. Personal relationships across the life span*. Cambridge, UK: Cambridge University Press.

Bierman, K. L. (2004). *Peer rejection: Developmental processes and intervention strategies*. New York, NY: Guilford.

Bierman, K. L., & Powers, C. J. (2009). Social skills training to improve peer relations. In K. H. Rubin, W. M. Bukowski, & B. Laursen (Eds.), *Handbook of peer interactions, relationships, and groups*. New York, NY: Guilford.

Bierman, K. L., Coie, J., Dodge, K., Greenberg, M., Lochman, J., McMohan, R., et al. (2013). School outcomes of aggressive-disruptive children: Prediction from kindergarten risk factors and impact of the Fast Track Prevention Program. *Aggressive Behavior, 39*, 114–130.

Bigler, R. S., & Liben, L. S. (1990). The role of attitudes and interventions in gender-schematic processing. *Child Development, 61*, 1440–1452.

Bihaqi, S. W., Schumacher, A., Maloney, B., Lahiri, D. K., & Zawia, N. H. (2012). Do epigenetic pathways initiate late onset Alzheimer disease (LOAD): Towards a new paradigm. *Current Alzheimer Research, 9*, 574–588.

Bilalić, M., Turella, L., Campitelli, G., Erb, M., & Grodd, W. (2012). Expertise modulates the neural basis of context dependent recognition of objects and their relations. *Human Brain Mapping, 33*, 2728–2740.

Birditt, K. S., & Fingerman, K. L. (2013). Parent-child and intergenerational relationships in adulthood. In M. A. Fine & F. D. Fincham (Eds.), *Handbook of family theories. A context-based approach*. New York, NY: Routledge.

Birditt, K. S., Fingerman, K. L., Lefkowitz, E. S., & Kamp Dush, C. M. (2008). Parents perceived as peers: Filial maturity in adulthood. *Journal of Adult Development, 15*, 1–12.

Birditt, K. S., Miller, L. M., Fingerman, K. L., & Lefkowitz, E. S. (2009). Tensions in the parent and adult child relationship: Links to solidarity and ambivalence. *Psychology and Aging, 24*, 287–295.

Birdsong, D. (1999). Introduction: Whys and why nots of the critical period hypothesis for second language acquisition. In D. Birdsong (Ed.), *Second language acquisition and the critical period hypothesis*. Mahwah, NJ: Erlbaum.

Birdsong, D. (2005). Interpreting age effects in second language acquisition. In J. Kroll & A. de Groot (Eds.), *Handbook of bilingualism: Psycholinguistic approaches*. New York, NY: Oxford University Press.

Birnbaum, G. E. (2007). Attachment orientations, sexual functioning, and relationship satisfaction in a community sample of women. *Journal of Social and Personal Relationships, 24*, 21–35.

Birnbaum, G. E. (2015). On the convergence of sexual urges and emotional bonds: The interplay of the sexual and attachment systems during relationship development. In J. A Simpson & W. S. Rholes (Eds.), *Attachment theory and research: New directions and emerging themes* (pp. 170–194). New York, NY: Guilford.

Birren, J. E., & Schroots, J. J. F. (2006). Autobiographical memory and the narrative self over the life span. In J. E. Birren & K. W. Schaie (Eds.), *Handbook of the psychology of aging* (6th ed.). Burlington, MA: Elsevier Academic Press.

Birren, J. E., Butler, R. N., Greenhouse, S. W., Sokoloff, L., & Yarrow, M. R. (Eds.). (1963). *Human aging: A biological and behavioral study*. Washington, DC: U.S. Government Printing Office.

Birtles, D., Anker, S., Atkinson, J., Shellens, R., Briscoe, A., Mahoney, M., & Braddick, O. (2011). Bimanual strategies for object retrieval in infants and young children. *Experimental brain research, 211*, 207–218.

Birzniece, V. (2015). Doping in sport: Effects, harm and misconceptions. *Internal Medicine Journal, 45*(3), 239–248.

Bishop, J. A., & Cooke, L. M. (1975). Moths, melanism and clean air. *Scientific American, 232*, 90–99.

Bishop, J. E., & Waldholz, M. (1990). *Genome. The story of the most astonishing scientific adventure of our time: The attempt to map all the genes in the human body*. New York, NY: Simon & Schuster.

Bivens, J. A., & Berk, L. E. (1990). A longitudinal study of the development of elementary school children's private speech. *Merrill-Palmer Quarterly, 36*, 443–463.

Bjerregaard, L. G., Rasmussen, K. M., Michaelsen, K. F., Skytthe, A., Mortensen, E. L., Baker, J. L., & Sorensen, T. I. A. (2014). Effects of body size and change in body size from infancy through childhood on body mass index in adulthood. *International Journal of Obesity, 38*, 1305–1311.

Bjork, J. M., Knutson, B., Fong, G. W., Caggiano, D. M., Bennett, S. M., Hommer, D. W. (2004). Incentive-elicited brain activation in adolescents: similarities and differences from young adults. *Journal of Neuroscience, 24*, 1793–1802.

Bjork, R. A., & Bjork, E. L. (Eds.). (1998). *Memory*. New York, NY: Academic Press.

Bjorklund, D. F. (1985). The role of conceptual knowledge in the development of organization in children's memory. In C. J. Brainerd & M. Pressley (Eds.), *Basic processes in memory development: Progress in cognitive development research*. New York, NY: Springer-Verlag.

Bjorklund, D. F. (1995). *Children's thinking: Developmental function and individual differences*. Pacific Grove, CA: Brooks/Cole.

Bjorklund, D. F. (1997). In search of a metatheory for cognitive development (or, Piaget is dead and I don't feel so good myself). *Child Development, 68*, 144–148.

Bjorklund, D. F., & Pellegrini, A. D. (2002). *The origins of human nature*. Washington, DC: American Psychological Association.

Bjorklund, D. F., Brown, R. D., & Bjorklund, B. R. (2002). Children's eyewitness memory: Changing reports and changing representations. In P. Graf & N. Ohta (Eds.), *Life-span development of human memory* (pp. 101–126). Cambridge, MA: Massachusetts Institute of Technology.

Bjorklund, D. F., Dukes, C., & Brown, R. D. (2009). The development of memory strategies. In M. L. Courage & N. Cowan (Eds.), *The development of memory in infancy and childhood* (pp. 145–176). New York, NY: Psychology Press.

Black, J. E., Isaacs, K. R., & Greenough, W. T. (1991). Usual vs. successful aging: Some notes on experiential factors. *Neurobiology of Aging, 12*, 325–328.

Black, S. E., Bütikofer, A., Devereux, P. J., & Salvanes, K. G. (2014, July). This is only a test? Long-run and intergenerational impacts of prenatal exposure to radioactive fallout. Available at www.utexas.app.box.com/s/lm94cxxwvcpsslgcze4k.

Blackburn, J. A. (1984). The influence of personality, curriculum, and memory correlates on formal reasoning in young adults and elderly persons. *Journal of Gerontology, 39*, 207–209.

Blackburn, J. A., & Papalia, D. E. (1992). The study of adult cognition from a Piagetian perspective. In R. J. Sternberg & C. A. Berg (Eds.), *Intellectual development*. New York, NY: Cambridge University Press.

Blackwell, L. S., Trzesniewski, K. H., & Dweck, C. S. (2007). Implicit theories of intelligence predict achievement across an adolescent transition: A longitudinal study and an intervention. *Child Development, 78*, 246–263.

Blair, C., & Raver, C. C. (2012). Child development in the context of adversity: Experiential canalization of brain and behavior. *American Psychologist, 6*, 309–318.

Blake, J. J., Lund, E. M., Zhou, Q., Kwok, O., & Benz, M. R. (2012). National prevalence rates of bully victimization among students with disabilities in the United States. *School Psychology Quarterly, 27*, 210–222.

Blakemore, J. E. O. (2003). Children's beliefs about violating gender norms: Boys shouldn't look like girls, and girls shouldn't act like boys. *Sex Roles, 49*, 411–420.

Blakemore, S., & Robbins, T. W. (2012). Decision-making in the adolescent brain. *Nature Neuroscience, 15*, 1184–1191.

Blakemore, S. J., Burnett, S., & Dahl, R. E. (2010). The role of puberty in the developing adolescent brain. *Human Brain Mapping, 31*, 926–933.

Blanchard, R., & Lippa, R. A. (2007). Birth order, sibling sex ratio, handedness, and sexual orientation of male and female participants in a BBC Internet research project. *Archives of Sexual Behavior, 36*, 163–176.

Blanchard-Fields, F. (1986). Reasoning on social dilemmas varying in emotional saliency: An adult developmental perspective. *Psychology and Aging, 1*, 325–333.

Blanchard-Fields, F. (1996). Social cognitive development in adulthood and aging. In F. Blanchard-Fields & T. M. Hess (Eds.), *Perspectives on cognitive change in adulthood and aging*. New York, NY: McGraw-Hill.

Blanchard-Fields, F., Chen, Y., & Norris, L. (1997). Everyday problem solving across the adult life span: Influence of domain specificity and cognitive appraisal. *Psychology and Aging, 12*, 684–693.

Blanchette, H. (2011). The rising cesarean delivery rate in America: What are the consequences? *Obstetrics and Gynecology, 118*, 687–690.

Blazer, D. G. (1993). *Depression in late life*. St. Louis, MO: Mosby.

Bleakley, A., Hennessy, M., Fishbein, M., & Jordan, A. (2011). Using the integrative model to explain how exposure to sexual media content influences adolescent sexual behavior. *Health Education & Behavior, 38*, 530–540.

Bleidorn, W. (2015). What accounts for personality maturation in early adulthood? *Current Directions in Psychological Science, 24*, 245–252.

Bleidorn, W., Arslan, R., Denissen, J., Rentfrow, P., Gebauer, J., & Potter, J. (2016). Age and gender differences in self-esteem—A cross-cultural window. *Journal of Personality and Social Psychology, 111*, 396–410.

Bleidorn, W., Klimstra, T. A., Denissen, J. J. A., Rentfrow, P. J., Potter, J., & Gosling, S. D. (2013). Personality maturation around the world: A cross-cultural examination of social-investment theory. *Psychological Science, 24*, 2530–2540.

Blencowe, H., Cousens, S., Kamb, M., Berman, S., & Lawn, J. E. (2011). Lives Saved Tool supplement detection and treatment of syphilis in pregnancy to reduce syphilis related stillbirths and neonatal mortality. *BMC Public Health, 11*(Suppl. 3), S9.

Bleske-Rechek, A., Fuerstenberg, E. A., Harris, H. D., & Ryan, D. E. (2011). Men and women, work and family: A test of competing perspectives. *Journal of Social, Evolutionary, and Cultural Psychology, 5*, 275–292.

Blessitt, E., Voulgari, S., & Eisler, I. (2015). Family therapy for adolescent anorexia nervosa. *Current Opinion in Psychiatry, 28*, 455–460.

Blieszner, R. (2006). A lifetime of caring: Dimensions and dynamics in late-life close relationships. *Personal Relationships, 13*, 1–18.

Blomquist, J. L., Quiroz, L. H., MacMillan, D., Mccullough, A., & Handa, V. L. (2011). Mothers' satisfaction with planned vaginal and planned cesarean birth. *American Journal of Perinatology, 28*, 383–388.

Blomqvist, Y. T., & Nyqvist, K. H. (2010). Swedish mothers' experience of continuous Kangaroo mother care. *Journal of Clinical Nursing, 20*, 1472–1480.

Bloom, L. (1998). Language acquisition in its developmental context. In D. Kuhn & R. S. Siegler (Vol. Eds.), W. Damon (Editor-in-Chief), *Handbook of child psychology: Vol. 2. Cognition, perception, and language* (5th ed., pp. 309–370). New York, NY: Wiley.

Bloom, L., & Tinker, E. (2001). The intentionality model and language acquisition: Engagement, effort, and the essential tension. *Monographs of the Society for Research in Child Development, 66* (Serial No. 267).

Bloom, P. (2013). *Just babies. The origins of good and evil.* New York, NY: Crown Publishers.

Bluebond-Langner, M. (1977). Meanings of death to children. In H. Feifel (Ed.), *New meanings of death.* New York, NY: McGraw-Hill.

Blumberg, E. S. (2003). The lives and voices of highly sexual women. *The Journal of Sex Research, 40*, 146–157.

Boatella-Costa, E., Costas-Moragas, C., Botet-Mussons, F., Fornieles-Deu, A., & De Cáceres-Zurita, M. L. (2007). Behavioral gender differences in the neonatal period according to the Brazelton scale. *Early Human Development, 83*, 91–97.

Bock, J. (2005). Farming, foraging, and children's play in the Okavango Delta, Botswana. In A. D. Pellegrini & P. K. Smith (Eds.), *The nature of play: Great apes and humans.* New York, NY: Guilford Press.

Bockting, W., & Coleman, E. (2016). Developmental stages of the transgender coming-out process: Toward an integrated identity. In R. Ettner, S. Monstrey, & E. Coleman (Eds.), *Principles of transgender medicine and surgery* (pp. 137–158). New York, NY: Routledge.

Bode, M. M., D'Eugenio, D. B., Forsyth, N., Coleman, J., Gross, C. R, & Gross, S. J. (2009). Outcome of extreme prematurity: A prospective comparison of 2 regional cohorts born 20 years apart. *Pediatrics, 124*, 866–874.

Bode, M. M., D'Eugenio, D. B., Mettelman, B. B., & Gross, S. J. (2014). Predictive validity of the Bayley, Third Edition at 2 years for intelligence quotient at 4 years in preterm infants. *Journal of Developmental and Behavioral Pediatrics, 35*, 570–575.

Bodkin, N. L., Alexander, T. M., Ortmeyer, H. K., Johnson, E., & Hansen, B. C. (2003). Morbidity and mortality in laboratory-maintained rhesus monkeys and effects of long-term dietary restriction. *Journal of Gerontology Series A: Biological Sciences, 58A*, 212–219.

Bodley-Tickell, A. T., Olowokure, B., Bhaduri, S., White, D. J., Ward, D., Ross, J. D., et al. (2008). Trends in sexually transmitted infections (other than HIV) in older people: Analysis of data from an enhanced surveillance system. *Sexually Transmitted Infections, 84*, 312–317.

Bodner, E., & Cohen-Fridel, S. (2010). Relations between attachment styles, ageism and quality of life in late life. *International Psychogeriatrics, 22*, 1353–1361.

Bodrova, E., & Leong, D. J. (1996). *Tools of the mind: The Vygotskian approach to early childhood education.* Englewood Cliffs, NJ: Prentice Hall.

Boelen, P. A., & Prigerson, H. G. (2013). Prolonged grief disorder as a new diagnostic category in DSM-5. In M. Stroebe, H. Schut & J. van den Bout (Eds.), *Complicated grief: Scientific foundations for health care professionals.* New York, NY: Routledge/Taylor & Francis.

Boelen, P. A., Reijntjes, A., Djelantik, A. A. A. M., & Smid, G. E. (2016). Prolonged grief and depression after unnatural loss: Latent class analyses and cognitive correlates. *Psychiatry Research, 240*, 358–363.

Boelen, P. A., van den Hout, M., & van den Bout, J. (2013). Prolonged grief disorder: Cognitive-behavioral theory and therapy. In M. Stroebe, H. Schut & J. van den Bout (Eds.), *Complicated grief: Scientific foundations for health care professionals.* New York, NY: Routledge/ Taylor & Francis.

Boerner, K., Mancini, A. D., & Bonanno, G. (2013). On the nature and prevalence of uncomplicated and complicated patterns of grief. In M. Stroebe, H. Schut & J. van den Bout (Eds.), *Complicated grief: Scientific foundations for health care professionals.* New York, NY: Routledge/Taylor & Francis.

Boerner, K., Wortman, C. B., & Bonanno, G. A. (2005). Resilient or at risk? A 4-year study of older adults who initially showed high or low distress following conjugal loss. *Journal of Gerontology: Psychological Sciences, 60B*, P67–P73.

Bogoch, I. I., House, R. A., & Kudla, I. (2005). Perceptions about hearing protection and noise-induced hearing loss of attendees of rock concerts. *Canadian Journal of Public Health, 96*, 69–72.

Bohannon, J. N., & Bonvillian, J. D. (2013). Theoretical approaches to language acquisition. In J. Berko Gleason & N. B. Ratner (Eds.), *The development of language* (7th ed.). Boston, MA: Allyn & Bacon.

Bohannon, J. N., & Bonvillian, J. D. (2017). Theoretical approaches to language acquisition. In Gleason, J. B. & Ratner, N. B. (Eds.), *The development of language* (9th ed., pp. 158–195). Boston, MA: Pearson.

Bohlmeijer, E., Roemer, M., Cuijpers, P., & Smit, F. (2007). The effects of reminiscence on psychological well-being in order adults: A meta-analysis. *Aging & Mental Health, 11*, 291–300.

Bohn, A., & Berntsen, D. (2014). Cultural life scripts and the development of personal memories. In P. Bauer & R. Fivush (Eds.), *The Wiley handbook on the development of children's memory* (pp. 626–644). Malden, MA: Wiley Blackwell.

Boislard, M. A., van de Bongardt, D., & Blais, M. (2016). Sexuality (and lack thereof) in adolescence and early adulthood: A review of the literature. *Behavioral Sciences, 6*, 1–24.

Boldizar, J. P. (1991). Assessing sex-typing and androgyny in children: The children's sex-role inventory. *Developmental Psychology, 27*, 505–515.

Boles, S., Biglan, A., & Smolkowski, K. (2006). Relationships among negative and positive behaviours in adolescence. *Journal of Adolescence, 29*, 33–52.

Bolger, K. E., & Patterson, C. J. (2001). Developmental pathways from child maltreatment to peer rejection. *Child Development, 72*, 549–568.

Boloh, Y., & Champaud, C. (1993). The past conditional verb form in French children: The role of semantics in late grammatical development. *Journal of Child Language, 20*, 169–189.

Bombard, Y., Veenstra, G., Friedman, J. M., Creighton, S., Currie, L., Paulsen, J. S., Bottorff, J. L., & Hayden, M. R. (2009). Perceptions of genetic discrimination among people at risk for Huntington's disease: A cross sectional survey. *BMJ: British Medical Journal, 338* (7708).

Bonanno, G. A. (2001). Introduction. New direction in bereavement research and theory. *American Behavioral Scientist, 44*, 718–725.

Bonanno, G. A. (2004). Loss, trauma, and human resilience: Have we underestimated the human capacity to thrive after extremely aversive events? *American Psychologist, 59*, 20–28.

Bonanno, G. A. (2009). *The other side of sadness. What the new science of bereavement tells us about life after loss.* New York, NY: Basic Books.

Bonanno, G. A., & Kaltman, S. (1999). Toward an integrative perspective on bereavement. *Psychological Bulletin, 125*, 760–776.

Bonanno, G. A., & Kaltman, S. (2000). The varieties of grief experience. *Clinical Psychology Review, 21*, 705–734.

Bonanno, G. A., Boerner, K., & Wortman, C. B. (2008). Trajectories of grieving. In M. S. Stroebe, R. O. Hansson, H. Schut, & W. Stroebe (Eds.), *Handbook of bereavement research and practice. Advances in theory and intervention.* Washington, DC: American Psychological Association.

Bonanno, G. A., Moskowitz, J. T., Papa, A., & Folkman, S. (2005). Resilience to loss in bereaved spouses, bereaved parents, and bereaved gay men. *Journal of Personality and Social Psychology, 88*, 827–843.

Bonanno, G. A., Papa, A., Lalande, K., Zhang, N., & Noll, J. G. (2005). Grief processing and deliberate grief avoidance: A prospective comparison of bereaved spouses and parents in the United States and the People's Republic of China. *Journal of Consulting and Clinical Psychology, 73*, 86–98.

Bonanno, G. A., Romero, S. A., & Klein, S. I. (2015). The temporal elements of psychological resilience: An integrative framework for the study of individuals, families, and communities. *Psychological Inquiry, 26*, 139–169.

Bonanno, G. A., Wortman, C. B., & Nesse, R. M. (2004). Prospective patterns of resilience and maladjustment during widowhood. *Psychology and Aging, 19*, 260–271.

Bonanno, G. A., Wortman, C. B., Lehman, D. R., Tweed, R. G., Haring, M., Sonnega, J., et al. (2002). Resilience to loss and chronic grief: A prospective study from preloss to 18 months postloss. *Journal of Personality and Social Psychology, 83*, 1150–1164.

Bong, M. (2009). Age-related differences in achievement goal differentiation. *Journal of Educational Psychology, 101*, 879–896.

Bongers, I. L., Koot, H. M., van der Ende, J., & Verhulst, F. C. (2003). The normative development of child and adolescent problem behavior. *Journal of Abnormal Psychology, 112*, 179–192.

Bonoti, F., Leondari, A., & Mastora, A. (2013). Exploring children's understanding of death: Through drawings and the death concept questionnaire. *Death Studies, 37*, 47–60.

Bonvillain, N. (2010). *Cultural anthropology* (2nd ed.). New Jersey, NJ: Pearson.

Bonvillain, N. (2012). *Cultural anthropology* (3rd ed.). New York, NY: Pearson.

Booij, L., Tremblay, R. E., Szyf, M., & Benkelfat, C. (2015). Genetic and early environmental influences on the serotonin system: Consequences for brain development and risk for psychopathology. *Journal of Psychiatry & Neuroscience, 40*, 5–18.

Booth, A., & Johnson, D. (1988). Premarital cohabitation and marital success. *Journal of Family Issues, 9*, 255–272.

Booth-LaForce, C., & Kerns, K. A. (2009). Child-parent attachment relationships, peer relationships, and peer-group functioning. In K. H. Rubin, W. M. Bukowski, & B. Laursen (Eds.), *Handbook of peer interactions, relationships, and groups.* New York, NY: Guilford.

Borgström, K., Torkildsen, J. v. K., & Lindgren, M. (2015). Substantial gains in word learning ability between 20 and 24 months: A longitudinal ERP study. *Brain and Language, 149*, 33–45.

Boris, N. W., & Zeanah, C. H. (1999). Disturbances and disorders of attachment in infancy: An overview. *Infant Mental Health Journal, 20*, 1–9.

Borkenau, P., Riemann, R., Angleitner, A., & Spinath, F. M. (2001). Genetic and environmental influences on observed personality: Evidence from the German Observational Study of Adult Twins. *Journal of Personality and Social Psychology, 80*, 655–668.

Bornstein, M. H. (2015). Children's parents. In M. H. Bornstein & T. Leventhal (Vol. Eds.) & R. M. Lerner (General Ed.), *Handbook of child psychology and developmental science: Vol. 4. Ecological settings and processes* (pp. 55–132). Hoboken, NJ: Wiley.

Bornstein, M. H., & Bradley, R. H. (2003). *Socioeconomic status, parenting, and child development.* Mahwah, NJ: Erlbaum.

Bornstein, M. H., & Hendricks, C. (2012). Basic language comprehension and production in >100,000 young children from sixteen developing nations. *Journal of Child Language, 39*, 899–918.

Bornstein, M. H., & Putnick, D. L. (2012). Stability of language in childhood: A multiage, multidomain, multimeasure, and multisource study. *Developmental Psychology, 48*, 477–491.

Bornstein, M. H., & Sawyer, J. (2006). Family systems. In K. McCartney & D. Phillips (Eds.), *Blackwell handbook of early childhood development.* Malden, MA: Blackwell.

Borradaile, K. E., Sherman, S., Vander Veur, S., McCoy, T., Sandoval, B., Nachmani, J., et al. (2009). Snacking in children: The role of urban corner stores. *Pediatrics, 124*, 1292–1297.

Borst, G., Poirel, N., Pineau, A., Cassotti, M., & Houdé, O. (2013). Inhibitory control efficiency in a Piaget-like class-inclusion task in school-age children and adults: A developmental negative priming study. *Developmental Psychology, 49*, 1366–1374.

Borst, G., Poirel, N., Pineau, A., Cassotti, M., & Houdé, O. (2012). Inhibitory control in number-conservation and class-inclusion tasks: A neo-Piagetian inter-task priming study. *Cognitive Development, 27*, 283–298.

Bosak, J., Sczesny, S., & Eagly, A. H. (2008). Communion and agency judgments of women and men as a function of role information and response format. *European Journal of Social Psychology, 38*, 1148–1155.

Bosch, A. M., Willekens, F. J., Baqui, A. H., Van Ginneken, J. K., & Hutter, I. (2008). Association between age at menarche and early-life nutritional status in rural Bangladesh. *Journal of Biosocial Science, 40*, 223–237.

Boston Retinal Implant Project. (2013). Retrieved from www.bostonretinalimplant.org/ index.php/blindness-and-disease/.

Boström, P. K., Broberg, M., & Hwang, P. (2010). Parents' descriptions and experiences of young children recently diagnosed with intellectual disability. *Child: Care, Health and Development, 36*, 93–100.

Bouchard, G. (2014). How do parents react when their children leave home? An integrative review. *Journal of Adult Development, 21*, 69–79.

Bouchard, G., & McNair, J. L. (2016). Dyadic examination of the influence of family relationships on life satisfaction at the empty-nest stage. *Journal of Adult Development, 23*, 174–182.

Bouchard, T. J., Jr. (1984). Twins reared together and apart: What they tell us about human diversity. In S. W. Fox (Ed.), *Individuality and determinism: Chemical and biological bases*. New York, NY: Plenum.

Bouchard, T. J., Jr., & McGue, M. (1981). Family studies of intelligence: A review. *Science, 212*, 1055–1059.

Bouchard, T. J., Jr., Lykken, D. T., McGue, M., Segal, N. L., & Tellegen, A. (1990). Sources of human psychological differences: The Minnesota Study of Twins Reared Apart. *Science, 250*, 223–228.

Bouldin, P. (2006). An investigation of fantasy predisposition and fantasy style of children with imaginary companions. *The Journal of Genetic Psychology, 167*, 17–29.

Bowen, B. A. (1999). Four puzzles in adult literacy: Reflections on the National Adult Literacy Survey. *Journal of Adolescent & Adult Literacy, 42*, 314–323.

Bowen, M. (1978). *Family therapy in clinical practice*. New York, NY: Aronson.

Bowen, M. W., & Firestone, M. H. (2011). Pathological use of electronic media: Case studies and commentary. *Psychiatric Quarterly, 82*, 229–238.

Bower, T. G. R., Broughton, J. M., & Moore, M. K. (1970). The coordination of vision and tactile input in infancy. *Perception and Psychophysics, 8*, 51–53.

Bowers, M., Perez-Pouchoulen, M., Edwards, N. S., & Mccarthy, M. M. (2013, February 20). Foxp2 mediates sex differences in ultrasonic vocalization by rat pups and directs order of maternal. *The Journal of Neuroscience, 33*(8), 3276-3283.

Bowker, J. C., Spencer, S. V., Thomas, K. K., & Gyoerkoe, E. A. (2012). Having and being an other-sex crush during early adolescence. *Journal of Experimental Child Psychology, 111*, 629–643.

Bowlby, J. (1960). Separation anxiety. *International Journal of Psychoanalysis, 41*, 89–113.

Bowlby, J. (1969). *Attachment and loss: Vol. 1. Attachment*. New York, NY: Basic Books.

Bowlby, J. (1973). *Attachment and loss: Vol. 2. Separation*. New York, NY: Basic Books.

Bowlby, J. (1980). *Attachment and loss: Vol. 3. Loss, sadness and depression*. New York, NY: Basic Books.

Bowlby, J. (1988). *A secure base: Parent-child attachment and healthy human development*. New York, NY: Basic Books.

Boyatzis, C. J. (2013). The nature and functions of religion and spirituality in children. In K. I. Pargament, J. J. Exline, & J. W. Jones (Eds.), *APA handbook of psychology, religion, and spirituality: Vol. 1. Context, theory, and research*. Washington, DC: American Psychological Association.

Boyce, C. J., & Wood, A. M. (2011). Personality prior to disability determines adaptation: Agreeable individuals recover lost life satisfaction faster and more completely. *Psychological Science, 22*, 1397–1402.

Boyce, W. T., & Ellis, B. J. (2005). Biological sensitivity to context: I. An evolutionary–developmental theory of the origins and functions of stress reactivity. *Development and Psychopathology, 17*, 271–301.

Boyce, W. T., & Kobor, M. S. (2015). Development and the epigenome: The 'synapse" of gene-environment interplay. *Developmental Science, 18*, 1–23.

Bracey, J. R., Bamaca, M. Y., & Umaña-Taylor, A. J. (2004). Examining ethnic identity and self-esteem among biracial and monoracial adolescents. *Journal of Youth and Adolescence, 33*, 123–132.

Bradbard, M. R., Martin, C. L., Endsley, R. C., & Halverson, C. F. (1986). Influence of sex stereotypes on children's exploration and memory: A competence versus performance distinction. *Developmental Psychology, 22*, 481–486.

Bradley, R. H., & Corwyn, R. F. (2002). Socioeconomic status and child development. *Annual Review of Psychology, 53*, 371–399.

Bradley, R. H., Caldwell, B. M., Rock, S. L., Ramey, C. T., Barnard, K. E., Gray, C., et al. (1989). Home environment and cognitive development in the first 3 years of life: A collaborative study involving six sites and three ethnic groups in North America. *Developmental Psychology, 25*, 217–235.

Bradley, R. H., Convyn, R. F., Burchinal, M., McAdoo, H. P., & Coll, C. G. (2001). The home environments of children in the United States, part II: Relations with behavioral development through age thirteen. *Child Development, 72*, 1868–1886.

Bradley-Geist, J., & Olson-Buchanan, J. (2014). Helicopter parents: An examination of the correlates of over-parenting of college students. *Education & Training, 56*, 314–328.

Bradshaw, C. P., Zmuda, J. K., Kellam, S. G., & Ialongo, N. S. (2009). Longitudinal impact of two universal preventive interventions in first grade on educational outcomes in high school. *Journal of Educational Psychology, 101*, 926–937.

Brady, S. S., & Halpern-Fisher, B. L. (2007). Adolescents' reported consequences of having oral sex versus vaginal sex. *Pediatrics, 119*, 229–236.

Brainerd, C. J. & Reyna, V. F. (2014). Dual processes in memory development: Fuzzy-trace theory. In P. Bauer & R. Fivush (Eds.), *The Wiley handbook on the development of children's memory* (pp. 480–512). Malden, MA: Wiley Blackwell.

Brainerd, C. J., & Gordon, L. L. (1994). Development of verbatim and gist memory for numbers. *Developmental Psychology, 30*, 163–177.

Brainerd, C. J., & Reyna, V. F. (1993). Domains of fuzzy trace theory. In M. L. Howe & R. Pasnak (Eds.), *Emerging themes in cognitive development: Vol. 1. Foundations*. New York, NY: Springer-Verlag.

Brainerd, C. J., & Reyna, V. F. (2015). Fuzzy-trace theory and lifespan cognitive development. *Developmental Review: DR, 38*, 89–121.

Braithwaite, V. (2002). Reducing ageism. In T. D. Nelson (Ed.), *Ageism: Stereotyping and prejudice against older persons*. Cambridge, MA: The MIT Press.

Bramlett, H. M., & Dietrich, W. D. (2015). Long-term consequences of traumatic brain injury: Current status of potential mechanisms of injury and neurological outcomes. *Journal of Neurotrauma, 32*, 1834–1848.

Brand, J. E. (2015). The far-reaching impact of job loss and unemployment. *Annual Review of Sociology, 41*, 359–375.

Brandão, S., & Figueiredo, B. (2012). Fathers' emotional involvement with the neonate: Impact of the umbilical cord cutting experience. *Journal of Advanced Nursing, 68*, 2730–2739.

Brandt, J., Aretouli, E., Neijstrom, E., Samek, J., Manning, K., Albert, M. S., et al. (2009). Selectivity of executive function deficits in mild cognitive deficit. *Neuropsychology, 23*, 607–618.

Brandtstädter, J., & Greve, W. (1994). The aging self: Stabilizing and protective processes. *Developmental Review, 14*, 52–80.

Brant, A. M., Haberstick, B. C., Corley, R. P., Wadsworth, S. J., DeFries, J. C., & Hewitt, J. K. (2009). The developmental etiology of high IQ. *Behavior Genetics, 39*, 393–405.

Bratberg, G. H., Nilsen, T. I., Holmen, T. L., & Vatten, L. J. (2005). Sexual maturation in early adolescence and alcohol drinking and cigarette smoking in late adolescence: A prospective study of 2,129 Norwegian girls and boys. *European Journal of Pediatrics, 164*, 621–625.

Braungart-Rieker, J., Hill-Soderlund, A., & Karrass, J. (2010). Fear and anger reactivity trajectories from 4 to 16 months: The roles of temperament, regulation, and maternal sensitivity. *Developmental Psychology, 46*, 791–804.

Braver, E. R., & Trempel, R. E. (2004). Are older drivers actually at higher risk of involvement in collisions resulting in deaths or non-fatal injuries among their passengers and other road users? *Injury Prevention, 10*, 27–32.

Bray, N. W., Hersh, R. E., & Turner, L. A. (1985). Selective remembering during adolescence. *Developmental Psychology, 21*, 290–294.

Brazelton, T. B., & Nugent, J. K. (2011). *Neonatal behavioral assessment scale* (4th ed.). London, UK: Mac Keith Press.

Breedlove, S. M. (1994). Sexual differentiation of the human nervous system. *Annual Review of Psychology, 45*, 389–418.

Brehmer, Y., Li, S. C., Muller, V., von Oertzen, T., & Lindenberger, U. (2007). Memory plasticity across the life span: Uncovering children's latent potential. *Developmental Psychology, 43*, 465–478.

Bremner, J. D., & Narayan, M. (1998). The effects of stress on memory and the hippocampus throughout the life cycle: Implications for childhood development and aging. *Development and Psychopathology, 10*, 871–886.

Bremner, J. G., Johnson, S. P., Slater, A., Mason, U., Foster, K., Cheshire, A., et al. (2005). Conditions for young infants' perception of object trajectories. *Child Development, 76*, 1029–1043.

Bremner, J. G., Slater, A. M., & Johnson, S. P. (2015). Perception of object persistence: The origins of object permanence in infancy. *Child Development Perspectives, 9*, 7–13.

Brendgen, M., Vitaro, F., & Girard, A. (2012). Evaluating gene-environment interplay. In B. Laursen, T. D. Little, & N. A. Card (Eds.), *Handbook of developmental research methods* (pp. 687–705). New York, NY: Guilford.

Brenick, A., Henning, A., Killen, M., O'Connor, A., & Collins, M. (2007). Social evaluations of stereotypic images in video games: Unfair, legitimate, or 'just entertainment'? *Youth & Society, 38*, 395–419.

Brent, D. A., & Maalouf, F. T. (2009). Pediatric depression: Is there evidence to improve evidence-based treatments? *Journal of Child Psychology and Psychiatry, 50*, 143–152.

Brent, D., Melhem, N., Donohoe, M. B., & Walker, M. (2009). The incidence and course of depression in bereaved youth 21 months after the loss of a parent to suicide, accident, or sudden natural death. *American Journal of Psychiatry, 166*, 786–794.

Brent, D., Melhem, N., Masten, A., Porta, G., & Payne, M. (2012). Longitudinal effects of parental bereavement on adolescent developmental competence. *Journal of Clinical Child and Adolescent Psychology, 41*, 778–791.

Brent, S. B., Speece, M. W., Lin, C. G., Dong, Q., & Yang, C. M. (1996). The development of the concept of death among Chinese and U.S. children 3–17 years of age: From binary to "fuzzy" concepts? *Omega: Journal of Death and Dying, 33*, 67–83.

Bretherton, I. (1996). Internal working models of attachment relationships as related to resilient coping. In G. G. Noam, & K. W. Fischer (Eds.), *Development and vulnerability in close relationships*. Mahwah, NJ: Erlbaum.

Bretherton, I., & Beeghly, M. (1982). Talking about internal states: The acquisition of an explicit theory of mind. *Developmental Psychology, 18*, 906–921.

Bretherton, I., Stolberg, U., & Kreye, M. (1981). Engaging strangers in proximal interaction: Infants' social initiative. *Developmental Psychology, 17*, 746–755.

Bridge, J. A., Day, N. L., Day, R., Richardson, G. A., Birmaher, B., & Brent, D. A. (2003). Major depressive disorder in adolescents exposed to a friend's suicide. *Journal of the American Academy of Child & Adolescent Psychiatry, 42*, 1294–1300.

Briefel, R. R., Crepinsek, M. K., Cabili, C., Wilson, A., & Gleason, P. M. (2009). School food environments and practices affect dietary behaviors of U.S. public school children. *Journal of the American Dietetic Association, 109*, S91–107.

Broadbent, D. (1958). *Perception and communication*. London: Pergamon Press.

Brod, M., Schmitt, E., Goodwin, M., Hodgkins, P., & Niebler, G. (2012). ADHD burden of illness in older adults: A life course perspective. *Quality of Life Research, 21*, 795–799.

Brody, E. B., & Brody, N. (1976). *Intelligence: Nature, determinants, and consequences.* New York, NY: Academic Press.

Brody, E. M. (2004). *Women in the middle: Their parent care years* (2nd ed.). New York, NY: Springer.

Brody, E. M., Litvin, S. J., Hoffman, C., & Kleban, M. H. (1992). Differential effects of daughters' marital status on their parent care experiences. *Gerontologist, 32*, 58–67.

Brody, G. H. (2003). Parental monitoring: Action and reaction. In A. C. Crouter, & A. Booth (Eds.), *Children's influence on family dynamics: The neglected side of family relationships.* Mahwah, NJ: Erlbaum.

Brody, G. H. (2004). Siblings' direct and indirect contributions to child development. *Current Directions in Psychological Science, 13*, 124–126.

Brody, G. H., Beach, S. R. H., Philibert, R. A., Chen, Y., & Murry, V. M. (2009). Prevention effects moderate the association of 5-HTTLPR and youth risk behavior initiation: Gene x environment hypotheses tested via a randomized prevention design. *Child Development, 80*, 645–661.

Brody, G. H., & Shaffer, D. R. (1982). Contributions of parents and peers to children's moral socialization. *Developmental Review, 2*, 31–75.

Brody, G. H., Yu, T., & Beach, S. R. H. (2015). A differential susceptibility analysis reveals the 'who and how' about adolescents' responses to preventive interventions: Tests of first- and second-generation gene × intervention hypotheses. *Development and Psychopathology, 27*, 37–49.

Brody, J. A., Grant, M. D., Frateschi, L. J., Miller, S. C., & Zhang, H. (2000). Reproductive longevity and increased life expectancy. *Age and Ageing, 29*, 75–78.

Broesch, T., Callaghan, T., Henrich, J., Murphy, C., & Rochat, P. (2011). Cultural variations in children's mirror self-recognition. *Journal of Cross-Cultural Psychology, 42*, 1018–1029.

Bronfenbrenner, U. (1977). Toward an experimental ecology of human development. *American Psychologist, 32*, 513–531.

Bronfenbrenner, U. (1979). *The ecology of human development: Experiments by nature and design.* Cambridge, MA: Harvard University Press.

Bronfenbrenner, U. (1989). Ecological systems theory. In R. Vasta (Ed.), *Annals of child development: Vol. 6. Theories of child development: Revised formulations and current issues.* Greenwich, CT: JAI Press.

Bronfenbrenner, U., & Ceci, S. J. (1994). Nature–nurture reconceptualized: A bioecological model. *Psychological Review, 101*, 568–586.

Bronfenbrenner, U., & Morris, P. A. (2006). The bioecological model of human development. In W. Damon & R. M. Lerner (Eds. in Chief) & R. M. Lerner (Vol. Ed.), *Handbook of child psychology: Vol. 1. Theoretical models of human development* (6th ed.). Hoboken, NJ: Wiley.

Brooks-Gunn, J., Britto, P. R., & Brady, C. (1999). Struggling to make ends meet: Poverty and child development. In M. E. Lamb (Ed.), *Parenting and child development in "nontraditional" families.* Mahwah, NJ: Erlbaum.

Brooks-Gunn, J., Klebanov, P. K., & Duncan, G. J. (1996). Ethnic differences in children's intelligence test scores: Role of economic deprivation, home environment, and maternal characteristics. *Child Development, 67*, 396–408.

Brophy, J. (2010). *Motivating students to learn* (3rd ed.). New York, NY: Routledge.

Broughton, J. M. (1984). Not beyond formal operations, but beyond Piaget. In M. L. Commons, F. A. Richards, & C. Armon (Eds.), *Beyond formal operations: Late adolescent and adult cognitive development* (pp. 395–411). New York, NY: Praeger.

Brown, A. L., & Smiley, S. S. (1978). The development of strategies for studying text. *Child Development, 49*, 1076–1088.

Brown, A. M., & Lindsey, D. T. (2009). Contrast insensitivity: The critical immaturity in infant visual performance. *Optometry and Vision Science, 86*, 572–576.

Brown, A., & Avery, A. (2012). Healthy weight management during pregnancy: What advice and information is being provided. *Journal of Human Nutrition & Diet, 25*, 378–388.

Brown, B. B. (1999). "You're going out with who?" Peer group influences on adolescent romantic relationships. In W. Furman, B. B. Brown, & C. Feiring (Eds.), *The development of romantic relationships in adolescence.* Cambridge, UK: Cambridge University Press.

Brown, B. B. (2011). Popularity in peer group perspective. The role of status in adolescent peer systems. In A. H. N. Cillessen, D. Schwartz, & L. Mayeux (Eds.), *Popularity in the peer system.* New York, NY: Guilford.

Brown, B. B., & Bakken, J. P. (2011). Parenting and peer relationships: Reinvigorating research on family–peer linkages in adolescence. *Journal of Research on Adolescence, 21*, 153–165.

Brown, B. B., & Dietz, E. L. (2009). Informal peer groups in middle childhood and adolescence. In K. H. Rubin, W. M. Bukowski, & B. Laursen (Eds.), *Handbook of peer interactions, relationships, and groups.* New York, NY: Guilford.

Brown, B. B., & Lohr, M. J. (1987). Peer-group affiliation and adolescent self-esteem: An integration of ego–identity and symbolic-interaction theories. *Journal of Personality and Social Psychology, 52*, 47–55.

Brown, B. B., Feiring, C., & Furman, W. (1999). Missing the love boat. Why researchers have shied away from adolescent romance. In W. Furman, B. B. Brown, & C. Feiring (Eds.), *The development of romantic relationships in adolescence.* Cambridge, UK: Cambridge University Press.

Brown, B. B., Herman, M., Hamm, J. V., & Heck, D. J. (2008). Ethnicity and image: Correlates of crowd affiliation among ethnic minority youth. *Child Development, 79*, 529–546.

Brown, B. B., Mory, M. S., & Kinney, D. (1994). Casting adolescent crowds in a relational perspective: Caricature, channel, and context. In R. Montemayor, G. R. Adams, & T. P. Gulotta (Eds.), *Personal relationships during adolescence.* Thousand Oaks, CA: Sage.

Brown, B. B., Mounts, N., Lamborn, S. D., & Steinberg, L. (1993). Parenting practices and peer group affiliation in adolescence. *Child Development, 64*, 467–482.

Brown, D. A., Elsass, J. A., Miller, A. J., Reed, L. E., & Reneker, J. C. (2015). Differences in symptom reporting between males and females at baseline and after a sports-related concussion: A systematic review and meta-analysis. *Sports Medicine, 45*, 1027–1040.

Brown, D., & Boytchev, H. (2012, September 6). Our 'junk DNA' not so useless after all. *The Washington Post*, pp. A1, A20.

Brown, H. & Graves, C. (2013). Smoking and marijuana use in pregnancy. *Clinical Obstetrics & Gynecology 56*, 107–113.

Brown, I. T., Chen, T., Gehlert, N. C., & Piedmont, R. L. (2012). Age and gender effects on the Assessment of Spirituality and Religious Sentiments (ASPIRES) Scale: A cross-sectional analysis. *Psychology of Religion and Spirituality*, No Pagination Specified. doi: 10.1037/a0030137

Brown, J. D., L'Engle, K. D., Pardun, C. J., Guang, G., Kenneavy, K., & Jackson, C. (2006). Sexy media matter: Exposure to sexual content in music, movies, television, and magazines predicts black and white adolescents' sexual behavior. *Pediatrics, 117*, 1018–1027.

Brown, R., & Hanlon, C. (1970). Derivational complexity and order of acquisition. In J. R. Hayes (Ed.), *Cognition and the development of language.* New York, NY: Wiley.

Brown, R., Cazden, C., & Bellugi, U. (1969). The child's grammar from I to III. In J. P. Hill (Ed.), *Minnesota Symposia on child psychology: Vol. 2.* Minneapolis, MN: University of Minnesota Press.

Brown, S. L., Bulanda, J. R., & Lee, G. R. (2012). Transitions into and out of cohabitation in later life. *Journal of Marriage and Family, 74*, 774–793.

Brown, S. L., Smith, D. M., Schulz, R., Kabeto, M. U., Ubel, P. A., Poulin, M., Yi, J., Kim, C., & Langa, K. M. (2009). Caregiving behavior is associated with decreased mortality risk. *Psychological Science, 20*, 488–494.

Brownell, C. A., & Carriger, M. S. (1990). Changes in cooperation and self/other differentiation during the second year. *Child Development, 61*, 1164–1174.

Brownell, C. A., Ramani, G. B., & Zerwas, S. (2006). Becoming a social partner with peers: Cooperation and social understanding in one- and two-year-olds. *Child Development, 77*, 803–821.

Bruce, J., Gunnar, M. R., Pears, K. C., & Fisher, P. A. (2013). Early adverse care, stress neurobiology, and prevention science: Lessons learned. *Prevention Science.* doi: 10.1007/s11121–012–0354–6

Bruck, M. (1990). Word recognition skills of adults with childhood diagnoses of dyslexia. *Developmental Psychology, 26*, 439–454.

Bruck, M. (1992). Persistence of dyslexics' phonological awareness deficits. *Developmental Psychology, 28*, 874–886.

Brummelman, E., Thomaes, S., Orobio de Castro, B., Overbeek, G., & Bushman, B. J. (2014). "That's not just beautiful—that's incredibly beautiful!": The adverse impact of inflated praise on children with low self-esteem. *Psychological Science, 25*, 728–735.

Brundin, P., Winkler, J., & Masliah, E. (2008). Adult neurogenesis in neurodegenerative diseases. In F. H. Gage, G. Kempermann, & H. Song (Eds.), *Adult neurogenesis* (pp. 503–533). New York, NY: Cold Spring Harbor Laboratory Press.

Bruner, J. S. (1983). *Child's talk: Learning to use language.* New York, NY: Norton.

Bruner, J. S. (1997). Celebrating divergence: Piaget and Vygotsky. *Human Development, 40*, 63–73.

Brunskill, P. J. (1992). The effects of fetal exposure to danazol. *British Journal of Obstetrics & Gynaecology, 99*, 212–215.

Brütt, A. L., Sandberg, D. E., Chaplin, J., Wollmann, H., Noeker, M., Kołtowska-Häggström, M., & Bullinger, M. (2009). Assessment of health-related quality of life and patient satisfaction in children and adolescents with growth hormone deficiency or idiopathic short stature - part 1: A critical evaluation of available tools. *Hormone Research, 72*, 65–73.

Bryant, P. (1998). Sensitivity to onset and rhyme does predict young children's reading: A comment on Muter, Hulme, Snowling, and Taylor (1997). *Journal of Experimental Child Psychology, 71*, 39–44.

Bryant-Waugh, R. (2007). Anorexia nervosa in children and adolescents. In T. Jaffa & B. McDermott (Eds.), *Eating disorders in children and adolescents.* Cambridge, UK: Cambridge University Press.

Brynie, F. H. (2009). *Brain sense: The science of the senses and how we process the world around us.* New York, NY: AMACOM.

Buchanan, C. M., Eccles, J. S., & Becker, J. B. (1992). Are adolescents the victims of raging hormones? Evidence for activational effects of hormones on moods and behavior at adolescence. *Psychological Bulletin, 111*, 62–107.

Buchanan, D., Fisher, C. B., & Gable, L. (Eds.). (2009). *Research with high-risk populations: Balancing science, ethics, and law.* Washington, DC: American Psychological Association.

Buchi, S., Morgeli, H., Schnyder, U., Jenewein, J., Hepp, U., Jina, E., Neuhaus, R., Fauchere, J., Bucher, H. U., & Sensky, T. (2007). Grief and post-traumatic growth in parents 2–6 years after the death of their extremely premature baby. *Psychotherapy and Psychosomatics, 76*, 106–114.

Bucur, B., Madden, D. J., Spaniol, J., Provenzale, J. M., Cabeza, R., White, L. E., et al. (2008). Age-related slowing of memory retrieval: Contributions of perceptual speed and cerebral white matter integrity. *Neurobiological Aging, 29*, 1070–1079.

Buehler, C. A., Hogan, M. J., Robinson, B. E., & Levy, R. J. (1985–1986). The parental divorce transition: Divorce-related stressors and well-being. *Journal of Divorce, 9*, 61–81.

Buehler, C., Lange, G., & Franck, K. L. (2007). Adolescents' cognitive and emotional responses to marital hostility. *Child Development, 78*, 775–789.

Buerger, M. (2011, June 23). Two brothers make a splash: 'Age of Champions' highlights athletes in Senior Games [Local Living section]. *The Washington Post*, pp. 18–19.

Buettner, D. (2008). *The blue zones: Lessons for living longer from the people who've lived the longest.* Washington, DC: National Geographic Society.

Bugental, D. (2009). Predicting and preventing child maltreatment: A biocognitive transactional approach. In A. Sameroff (Ed.), *The transactional model of development. How children and contexts shape each other.* Washington, DC: American Psychological Association.

Bugental, D. B., & Beaulieu, D. A. (2003). A bio-social-cognitive approach to understanding and promoting the outcomes of children with medical and physical disorders. In R. V. Kail (Ed.), *Advances in child development and behavior: Vol. 31.* San Diego, CA: Academic Press.

Bugental, D. B., & Schwartz, A. (2009). A cognitive approach to child mistreatment prevention among medically at-risk infants. *Developmental Psychology, 45,* 284–288.

Bugental, D. B., Beaulieu, D. A., & Silbert-Geiger, A. (2010). Increases in parental investment and child health as a result of an early intervention. *Journal of Experimental Child Psychology, 106,* 30–40.

Bugental, D. B., Corpuz, R., & Schwartz, A. (2012). Preventing children's aggression: Outcomes of an early intervention. *Developmental Psychology, 48,* 1443–1449.

Bugental, D. B., Ellerson, P. C., Lin, E. K., Rainey, B., Kokotovic, A., & O'Hara, N. (2002). A cognitive approach to child abuse prevention. *Journal of Family Psychology, 16,* 243–258.

Bugg, J. M., & Head, D. (2011). Exercise moderates age-related atrophy of the medial temporal lobe. *Neurobiology of Aging, 32,* 506–514.

Buhrmester, D., & Furman, W. (1986). The changing functions of friends in childhood: A neo-Sullivanian perspective. In V. J. Derlega & B. A. Winstead (Eds.), *Friendship and social interaction.* New York, NY: Springer-Verlag.

Buil, J. M., Koot, H. M., Olthof, T., Nelson, K. A., & van Lier, Pol A. C. (2015). DRD4 genotype and the developmental link of peer social preference with conduct problems and prosocial behavior across ages 9–12 years. *Journal of Youth and Adolescence, 44,* 1360–1378.

Bukowski, W. M., Buhrmester, D., & Underwood, M. K. (2011). Peer relations as a developmental context. In M. K. Underwood & L. H. Rosen (Eds.), *Social development. Relationships in infancy, childhood, and adolescence.* New York, NY: Guilford.

Bukowski, W. M., Motzoi, C., & Meyer, F. (2009). Friendship as process, function, and outcome. In K. H. Rubin, W. M. Bukowski, & B. Laursen (Eds.), *Handbook of peer interactions, relationships, and groups.* New York, NY: Guilford.

Bulanda, R. E. (2004). Paternal involvement with children: The influence of gender ideologies. *Journal of Marriage and Family, 66,* 40–45.

Bulik, C. M., Sullivan, P. F., Tozzi, F., Furberg, H., Lichtenstein, P., & Pedersen, N. L. (2006). Prevalence, heritability, and prospective risk factors for anorexia nervosa. *Archives of General Psychiatry, 63,* 305–312.

Bullard, L., Wachlarowicz, M., DeLeeuw, J., Snyder, J., Low, S., Forgatch, M., & DeGarmo, D. (2010). Effects of the Oregon model of parent management training (PMTO) on marital adjustment in new stepfamilies: A randomized trial. *Journal of Family Psychology, 24,* 485–496.

Bullock, M., Sodian, B., & Koerber, S. (2009). Doing experiments and understanding science: Development of scientific reasoning from childhood to adulthood. In W. Schneider & M. Bullock (Eds.), *Human development from early childhood to early adulthood: Findings from a 20-year longitudinal study* (pp. 173–197). New York, NY: Psychology Press.

Burack, J. A. (2012). *The Oxford handbook of intellectual disability and development* (2nd ed.). New York, NY: Oxford University Press.

Burack, J. A., Enns, J. T., Iarocci, G., & Randolph, B. (2000). Age differences in visual search for compound patterns: Long-versus short-range grouping. *Developmental Psychology, 36,* 731–740.

Burack, J. A., Hodapp, R. M., & Zigler, E. (Eds.). (1998). *Handbook of development and mental retardation.* New York, NY: Cambridge University Press.

Burak, L. (2012). Multitasking in the university classroom. *International Journal for the Scholarship of Teaching and Learning, 6,* 1–12.

Bureau of Labor Statistics (2015, March 31). *Number of jobs held, labor market activity, and earnings growth among the youngest baby boomers: Results from a longitudinal study.* Available at www.bls.gov/news.release/nlsoy.nr0. htm.

Bureau of Labor Statistics, U.S. Department of Labor. (2016). *Labor Force Statistics from the Current Population Survey.* Retrieved 8/19/2016 from www.bls. gov/cps/cpsaat11.htm.

Bureau of Labor Statistics. (2012). *Employment characteristics of families summary.* Retrieved from www. bls.gov/news.release/famee.toc.htm.

Bureau of Labor Statistics. (2016). *Employment characteristics of families—2015.* Retrieved from www. bls.gov/news.release/pdf/famee.pdf.

Bures, R. M., Koropeckyj-Cox, T., & Loree, M. (2009). Childlessness, parenthood, and depressive symptoms among middle-aged and older adults. *Journal of Family Issues, 30,* 670–687.

Burgard, S. A., Brand, J. E., & House, J. S. (2007). Toward a better estimation of the effect of job loss on health. *Journal of Health and Social Behavior, 48,* 369–384.

Burhans, K. K., & Dweck, C. S. (1995). Helplessness in early childhood: The role of contingent worth. *Child Development, 66,* 1719–1738.

Burk, W. J., van der Vorst, H., Kerr, M., & Stattin, H. (2012). Alcohol use and friendship dynamics: Selection and socialization in early-, middle-, and late-adolescent peer networks. *Journal of Studies on Alcohol and Drugs, 73,* 89–98.

Burke, L. A., & Neimeyer, R. A. (2013). Prospective risk factors for complicated grief: A review of the empirical literature. In M. Stroebe, H. Schut & J. van den Bout (Eds.), *Complicated grief: Scientific foundations for health care professionals.* New York, NY: Routledge/ Taylor & Francis.

Burke, S. M., & Bakker, J. (2015). *The role of pubertal hormones in the development of gender identity: fMRI studies.* In J-P. Bourguignon, J-C. Carel, & Y. Christen (Eds.), *Brain crosstalk in puberty and adolescence* (pp. 29–43). Switzerland: Springer International Publishing.

Burleson, M. H., Trevathan, W. R., & Todd, M. (2007). In the mood for love or vice versa? Exploring the relations among sexual activity, physical affection, affect, and stress in the daily lives of mid-aged women. *Archives of Sexual Behavior, 36,* 357–368.

Burn, S., O'Neil, A. K., & Nederend, S. (1996). Childhood tomboyishness and adult androgyny. *Sex Roles, 34,* 419–428.

Burnham, D. K., & Harris, M. B. (1992). Effects of real gender and labeled gender on adults' perceptions of infants. *Journal of Genetic Psychology, 153,* 165–183.

Burnham, D., & Mattock, K. (2010). Auditory development. In J. G. Bremner & T. D. Wachs (Eds.), *The Wiley-Blackwell handbook of infant development: Vol 1: Basic research* (2nd ed., pp. 81–119). Malden, MA: John Wiley & Sons.

Burns, G. W., & Bottino, P. J. (1989). *The science of genetics* (6th ed.). New York, NY: Macmillan.

Burr, D., & Gori, M. (2012). Multisensory integration develops late in humans. In M. M. Murray & M. T. Wallace (Eds.), *The neural bases of multisensory processes.* Boca Raton, FL: CRC Press.

Burr, D., & Gori, M. (2012). Multisensory integration develops late in humans. In M. M. Murray & M. T. Wallace (Eds.), *Frontiers in neuroscience. The neural bases of multisensory processes.* Boca Raton: CRC Press.

Burstyn, I. I., Kuhle, S. S., Allen, A. C., & Veugelers, P. P. (2012). The role of maternal smoking in effect of fetal growth restriction on poor scholastic achievement in elementary school. *International Journal of Environmental Research on Public Health, 9,* 408–420.

Burt, C. D. B., Kemp, S., & Conway, M. A. (2003). Themes, events, and episodes in autobiographical memory. *Memory & Cognition, 31,* 317–325.

Burt, S. A. (2015). Evidence that the gene-environment interactions underlying youth conduct problems vary across development. *Child Development Perspectives, 9,* 217–221.

Burton, C. M., Marshal, M. P., Chisolm, D. J., Sucato, G. S., & Friedman, M. S. (2013). Sexual minority-related victimization as a mediator of mental health disparities in sexual minority youth: A longitudinal analysis. *Journal of Youth and Adolescence, 42,* 394–402.

Burton, L. A., Hafetz, J., & Henninger, D. (2007). Gender differences in relational and physical aggression. *Social Behavior and Personality, 35,* 41–50.

Burton, L. M. (1990). Teenage childrearing as an alternative life-course strategy in multigenerational black families. *Human Nature, 1,* 123–143.

Burton, L. M. (1996). Age norms, the timing of family role transitions, and intergenerational caregiving among aging African American women. *Gerontologist, 36,* 199–208.

Burton, R. V. (1984). A paradox in theories and research in moral development. In W. M. Kurtines & J. L. Gewirtz (Eds.), *Morality, moral behavior, and moral development.* New York, NY: Wiley.

Bus, A. G., & van IJzendoorn, M. H. (1999). Phonological awareness and early reading: A meta-analysis of experimental training studies. *Journal of Educational Psychology, 91,* 403–414.

Busch-Rossnagel, N. A. (1997). Mastery motivation in toddlers. *Infants and Young Children, 9,* 1–11.

Bushdid, C., Magnasco, M. O., Vosshall, L. B., & Keller, A. (2014). Humans can discriminate more than 1 trillion olfactory stimuli. *Science, 343,* 1370–1372.

Bushnell, E. W., & Baxt, C. (1999). Children's haptic and cross-modal recognition with familiar and unfamiliar objects. *Journal of Experimental Psychology: Human Perception and Performance, 25,* 1867–1881.

Bushnell, I. (2001). Mother's face recognition in newborn infants: Learning and memory. *Infant and Child Development, 10,* 67–74.

Buss, A. H., & Perry, M. (1992). The aggression question. *Journal of Personality and Social Psychology, 63,* 452–459.

Buss, A. H., & Plomin, R. (1984). *Temperament: Early developing personality traits.* Hillsdale, NJ: Erlbaum.

Buss, D. M. (1995). Psychological sex differences: Origins through sexual selection. *American Psychologist, 50,* 164–168.

Buss, D. M. (2012). *Evolutionary psychology: The new science of the mind* (4th ed.). Boston: Allyn & Bacon.

Bussières, E. L., Tarabulsy, G. M., Pearson, J., Tessier, R., Forest, C., & Giguere, Y. (2015). Maternal prenatal stress and infant birth weight and gestational age: A meta-analysis of prospective studies. *Developmental Review 36,* 179–199.

Butcher, L. M., & Plomin, R. (2008). The nature of nurture: A genomewide association scan for family chaos. *Behavior Genetics, 38,* 361–371.

Butcher, L. M., Davis, O. S. P., Craig, I. W., & Plomin, R. (2008). Genome-wide quantitative trait locus association scan of general cognitive ability using pooled DNA and 500K single nucleotide polymorphism microarrays. *Genes, Brain & Behavior, 7,* 435–446.

Butcher, P. R., Kalverboer, A. F., & Geuze, R. H. (2000). Infants' shifts of gaze from a central to a peripheral stimulus: A longitudinal study of development between 6 and 26 weeks. *Infant Behavior & Development, 23,* 3–21.

Butler, R. (1990). The effects of mastery and competitive conditions on self-assessment at different ages. *Child Development, 61,* 201–210.

Butler, R. (1999). Information seeking and achievement motivation in middle childhood and adolescence: The role of conceptions of ability. *Developmental Psychology, 35,* 146–163.

Butler, R. N. (1963). The life review: An interpretation of reminiscence in the aged. *Psychiatry, 26,* 65–76.

Butters, M. A., Whyte, E. M., Nebes, R. D., Begley, A. E., Dew, M. A., Mulsant, B. H., et al. (2004). The nature and determinants of neuropsychological functioning in late-life depression. *Archives of General Psychiatry, 61,* 587–595.

Bybee, R. W. (1995). Science curriculum reform in the United States. In R. W. Bybee & J. D. McInerney (Eds.), *Redesigning the science curriculum.* Colorado Springs, CO: Biological Sciences Curriculum Study.

Byne, W. (1994). The biological evidence challenged. *Scientific American, 270,* 50–55.

Byrnes, J. P. (1996). *Cognitive development and learning in instructional contexts.* Boston, MA: Allyn & Bacon.

Cabrera, N. J., Fagan, J., & Farrie, D. (2008). Explaining the long reach of fathers? Prenatal involvement on later paternal engagement. *Journal of Marriage and Family, 70,* 1094–1107.

Cacioppo, J. T., & Cacioppo, S. (2014). Social relationships and health: The toxic effects of perceived social isolation. *Social and Personality Psychology Compass*, 8, 58–72.

Cacioppo, J. T., & Patrick, B. (2008). *Loneliness: Human nature and the need for social connection.* New York, NY: W. W. Norton.

Cacioppo, J. T., Cacioppo, S., Capitanio, J. P., & Cole, S. W. (2015). The neuroendocrinology of social isolation. *Annual Review of Psychology*, 66, 733–767.

Cacioppo, S., Grippo, A. J., London, S., Goossens, L., & Cacioppo, J. T. (2015). Loneliness: Clinical import and interventions. *Perspectives on Psychological Science*, 10, 238–249.

Cain, A. C., & LaFreniere, L. S. (2015). The taunting of parentally bereaved children: An exploratory study. *Death Studies*, 39, 219–225.

Cairns, R. B., & Cairns, B. (2006). The making of developmental psychology. In W. Damon & R. M. Lerner (Eds. in Chief) & R. M. Lerner (Vol. Ed.), *Handbook of child psychology: Vol. 1. Theoretical models of human development* (6th ed.). Hoboken, NJ: Wiley.

Caldera, Y. M., & Lindsey, E. W. (2006). Coparenting, mother–infant interaction, and infant–parent attachment relationships in two-parent families. *Journal of Family Psychology*, 20, 275–283.

Caldera, Y. M., Huston, A. C., & O'Brien, M. (1989). Social interactions and play patterns of parents and toddlers with feminine, masculine, and neutral toys. *Child Development*, 60, 70–76.

Caldwell, B. M., & Bradley, R. H. (1984). *Manual for the home observation for measurement of the environment.* Little Rock, AR: University of Arkansas.

Calkins, S. D., & Hill, A. (2007). Caregiver influences on emerging emotion regulation: Biological and environmental transactions in early development. In J. J. Gross (Ed.), *Handbook of emotion regulation.* New York, NY: Guilford.

Calkins, S. D., & Mackler, J. S. (2011). Temperament, emotion regulation, and social development. In M. K. Underwood & L. H. Rosen (Eds.), *Social development. Relationships in infancy, childhood, and adolescence.* New York, NY: Guilford.

Call, K. T., Mortimer, J. T., & Shanahan, M. (1995). Helpfulness and the development of competence in adolescence. *Child Development*, 66, 129–138.

Callaghan, T., & Corbit, J. (2015). The development of symbolic representation. In R. M. Lerner (Ed.), *Handbook of child psychology and developmental science* (pp. 250–295). Hoboken, NJ: Wiley.

Callaghan, T., Moll, H., Rakoczy, H., Warneken, F., Liszkowski, U., Behne, T., & Tomasello, M. (2011). Early social cognition in three cultural contexts. *Monographs of the Society for Research in Child Development*, 76 (2, Serial No. 299).

Callan, D. E., & Naito, E. (2014). Neural processes distinguishing elite from expert and novice athletes. *Cognitive and Behavioral Neurology*, 27, 183–188.

Calvert, S. L. (2015). Children and digital media. In M. H. Bornstein (Vol. Ed.), T. Leventhal (Vol. Ed.), & R. M. Lerner (Ed.) *Handbook of child psychology and developmental science: Vol. 4. Ecological settings and processes* (pp. 375–415). Hoboken, NJ: Wiley.

Calvin, C. M., Batty, G. D., Lowe, G. D. O., & Deary, I. J. (2011). Childhood intelligence and midlife inflammatory and hemostatic biomarkers: The National Child Development Study (1958) cohort. *Health Psychology*, 30, 710–718.

Calvo, E., Haverstick, K., & Sass, S. A. (2009). Gradual retirement, sense of control, and retirees' happiness. *Research on Aging*, 31, 112–135.

Camaioni, L. (2004). Early language. In G. Bremner & A. Fogel (Eds.), *Blackwell handbook of infant development* (pp. 404–426). Malden, MA: Blackwell Publishing.

Cameron, C. E., Brock, L. L., Murrah, W. M., Bell, L. H., Worzalla, S. L., Grissmer, D., & Morrison, F. J. (2012). Fine motor skills and executive function both contribute to kindergarten achievement. *Child Development*, 83, 1229–1244.

Camp, C. J., & McKitrick, L. A. (1992). Memory interventions in Alzheimer's-type dementia populations: Methodological and theoretical issues. In R. L. West & J. D. Sinnott (Eds.), *Everyday memory and aging: Current research and methodology* (pp. 155–172). New York, NY: Springer-Verlag.

Camp, C. J., Foss, J. W., O'Hanlon, A. M., & Stevens, A. B. (1996). Memory interventions for persons with dementia. *Applied Cognitive Psychology*, 10, 193–210.

Campbell, A., Shirley, L., & Caygill, L. (2002). Sex-typed preferences in three domains: Do two-year-olds need cognitive variables? *British Journal of Psychology*, 93, 203–217.

Campbell, F. A., & Ramey, C. T. (1995). Cognitive and school outcomes for high-risk African-American students at middle adolescence: Positive effects of early intervention. *American Educational Research Journal*, 32, 743–772.

Campbell, F. A., Pungello, E. P., Burchinal, M., Kainz, K., Pan, Y., Wasik, B. H., Barbarin, O. A., Sparling, J. J., & Ramey, C. T. (2012). Adult outcomes as a function of an early childhood educational program: An Abecedarian Project follow-up. *Developmental Psychology*, 48, 1033–1043.

Campbell, F. A., Pungello, E. P., Miller-Johnson, S., Burchinal, M., & Ramey, C. T. (2001). The development of cognitive and academic abilities: Growth curves from an early childhood educational experiment. *Developmental Psychology*, 37, 231–242.

Campbell, L., & Fletcher, G. J. O. (2015). Romantic relationships, ideal standards, and mate selection. *Current Opinion in Psychology*, 1, 97–100.

Campbell, R., MacSweeney, M., & Water, D. (2008). Sign language and the brain: A review. *Journal of Deaf Studies and Deaf Education*, 13.

Campbell, V. A., Crews, J. E., Moriarty, D. G., Zack, M. M., & Blackman, D. K. (1999). Surveillance for sensory impairment, activity limitation, and health-related quality of life among older adults: United States, 1993–1997. *CDC MMWR Surveillance Summaries*, 48(SS08), 131–156.

Campisi, J., & Robert, L. (2014). Cell senescence: Role in aging and age-related diseases. *Interdisciplinary Topics in Gerontology*, 39, 45–61.

Campos, J. J., Bertenthal, B. I., & Kermoian, R. (1992). Early experience and emotional development: The emergence of wariness of heights. *Psychological Science*, 3, 61–64.

Campos, J. J., Langer, A., & Krowitz, A. (1970). Cardiac responses on the visual cliff in prelocomotor human infants. *Science*, 170, 196–197.

Canfield, R. L., Henderson, C. R., Cory-Slechta, D. A., Cox, C., Jusko, T. A., & Lanphaer, B. P. (2003). Intellectual impairment in children with blood lead concentrations below 10 microg per deciliter. *New England Journal of Medicine*, 348, 1517–1526.

Cann, A., Calhoun, L. G., Tedeschi, R. G., Taku, K., Vishnevsky, T., Triplett, K. N., & Danhauer, S. C. (2010). A short form of the Posttraumatic Growth Inventory. *Anxiety, Stress & Coping*, 23, 127–137.

Cano, A., & Vivian, D. (2003). Are life stressors associated with marital violence? *Journal of Family Psychology*, 17, 302–314.

Cantor, N. L. (2001). Twenty-five years after Quinlan: A review of the jurisprudence of death and dying. *Journal of Law, Medicine, and Ethics*, 29, 182–196.

Caplan, L. J., & Schooler, C. (2001). Age effects on analogy-based memory for text. *Experimental Aging Research*, 27, 151–165.

Cardno, A. G., & Pepper, E. (2014). Schizophrenia and bipolar disorder. In S. H. Rhee & A. Ronald (Eds.), *Behavior genetics of psychopathology* (pp. 153–184). New York, NY: Springer.

Carey, S., Zaitchik, D., & Bascandziev, I. (2015). Theories of development: In dialog with Jean Piaget. *Developmental Review*, 38, 36–54.

Carey, T. (2016, January 17). Whatever happened to the original tiger mum's children? *The Telegraph*. Retrieved from www.telegraph.co.uk/women/life/whatever-happened-to-the-original-tiger-mums-children/.

Carlson, D. L., McNulty, T. L., Bellair, P. E., & Watts, S. (2014). Neighborhoods and racial/ethnic disparities in adolescent sexual risk behavior. *Journal of Youth and Adolescence*, 43, 1536–1549.

Carlson, E. A., Hostinar, C. E., Mliner, S. B., & Gunnar, M. R. (2014). The emergence of attachment following social deprivation. *Development and Psychopathology*, 26, 479–489.

Carlson, M. C., Erickson, K. I., Kramer, A. F., Voss, M. W., Bolea, N., Mielke, M., et al. (2009). Evidence for neurocognitive plasticity in at-risk older adults: The

Experience Corps Program. *Journals of Gerontology A: Biological Sciences and Medical Sciences*, 64, 1275–1282.

Carlson, M. J., Pilkauskas, N. V., McLanahan, S. S., & Brooks-Gunn, J. (2011). Couples as partners and parents over children's early years. *Journal of Marriage and Family*, 73, 317–334.

Carlson, V., Cicchetti, D., Barnett, D., & Braunwald, K. (1989). Disorganized/disoriented attachment relationships in maltreated infants. *Developmental Psychology*, 25, 525–531.

Carlsson-Paige, N. (2008). *Taking back childhood.* London, Penguin.

Carmichael, S. L., Shaw, G. M., Schaffer, D. M, Laurent, C., & Selvin, S. (2003). Dieting behaviors and risk of neural tube defects. *American Journal of Epidemiology*, 158, 1127–1131.

Caron, S. L., & Moskey, E. G. (2002). Changes over time in teenage sexual relationships: Comparing the high school class of 1950, 1975, and 2000. *Adolescence*, 37, 515–526.

Caron, S., & Ahlgrim, C. J. (2012). Children's understanding and knowledge of conception and birth: Comparing children from England, the Netherlands, Sweden, and the United States. *American Journal of Sexuality Education*, 7, 16–36.

Carpendale, J. I. M. (2000). Kohlberg and Piaget on stages and moral reasoning. *Developmental Review*, 20, 181–205.

Carpenter, A. L., Puliafico, A. C., Kurtz, S. M. S., Pincus, D. B., & Comer, J. S. (2014). Extending parent–child interaction therapy for early childhood internalizing problems: New advances for an overlooked population. *Clinical Child and Family Psychology Review*, 17, 340–356.

Carpenter, M., Nagell, K., & Tomasello, M. (1998). Social cognition, joint attention, and communicative competence from 9 to 15 months of age. *Monographs of the Society for Research in Child Development*, 63(Serial No. 255).

Carr, A. (2009). *What works with children, adolescents and adults? A review of research on the effectiveness of psychotherapy.* New York, NY: Routledge/Taylor & Francis Group.

Carr, A., & O'Reilly, G. (2016). Diagnosis, classification, and epidemiology. In A. Carr, C. Linehan, G. O'Reilly, P. N. Walsh, & J. McEvoy (Eds.), *The handbook of intellectual disability and clinical psychology practice* (2nd ed.). New York: Routledge.

Carr, C. L. (2007). Where have all the tomboys gone? Women's accounts of gender in adolescence. *Sex Roles*, 56, 439–448.

Carr, D. (2004). Gender, preloss marital dependence, and older adults' adjustment to widowhood. *Journal of Marriage and Family*, 66, 220–235.

Carré, J. M., Iselin, A. R., Welker, K. M., Hariri, A. R., & Dodge, K. A. (2014). Testosterone reactivity to provocation mediates the effect of early intervention on aggressive behavior. *Psychological Science*, 25, 1140–1146.

Carrera, M., Kaye, J. W., Philliber, S., & West, E. (2000). Knowledge about reproduction, contraception, and sexually transmitted infections among young adolescents in American cities. *Social Policy*, 30, 41–50.

Carroll, D. W. (2008). *Psychology of language* (5th ed.). Belmont, CA: Wadsworth.

Carroll, J. B. (1993). *Human cognitive abilities: A survey of factor-analytic studies.* Cambridge, UK: Cambridge University Press.

Carroll, J. M., Snowling, M. J., Hulme, C., & Stevenson, J. (2003). The development of phonological awareness in preschool children. *Developmental Psychology*, 39, 913–925.

Carroll-Scott, A., Gilstad-Hayden, K., Rosenthal, L., Peters, S. M., McCaslin, C., Joyce, R., & Ickovics, J. R. (2013). Disentangling neighborhood contextual associations with child body mass index, diet, and physical activity: The role of built, socioeconomic, and social environments. *Social Science & Medicine*, 95, 106–114.

Carskadon, M. A. (2011a). Sleep in adolescents: The perfect storm. *Pediatric Clinics of North America*, 58, 637–647.

Carskadon, M. A. (2011b). Sleep's effects on cognition and learning in adolescence. *Progress in Brain Research*, 190, 137–143.

Carskadon, M. A., & Tarokh, L. (2014). Developmental changes in sleep biology and potential effects on adolescent behavior and caffeine use. *Nutrition Reviews, 72* (Suppl. 1), 60–64.

Carstensen, L. L. (1992). Social and emotional patterns in adulthood: Support for socio-emotional selectivity theory. *Psychology and Aging, 7,* 331–338.

Carstensen, L. L., & Freund, A. M. (1994). Commentary: The resilience of the aging self. *Developmental Review, 14,* 81–92.

Carstensen, L. L., Levenson, R. W., & Gottman, J. M. (1995). Emotional behavior in long-term marriages. *Psychology and Aging, 10,* 140–149.

Carstensen, L. L., Pasupathi, M., Mayr, U., & Nesselroade, J. R. (2000). Emotional experience in everyday life across the adult life span. *Journal of Personality and Social Psychology, 79,* 644–655.

Carstensen, L. L., Turan, B., Scheibe, S., Ram, N., Ersner-Hershfield, H., Samanez-Larkin, G., et al. (2011). Emotional experience improves with age: Evidence based on over 10 years of experience sampling. *Psychology and Aging, 26,* 21–33.

Caruso M. L, & Cullen K. W. (2015). Quality and cost of student lunches brought from home. *JAMA Pediatrics, 169*(1), 86–90.

Case, R. (1985). *Intellectual development: Birth to adulthood.* Orlando, FL: Academic Press.

Case, R. (1998). The development of conceptual structures. In D. Kuhn & R. S. Siegler (Vol. Eds.), W. Damon (Editor-in-Chief), *Handbook of child psychology: Vol. 2. Cognition, perception, and language* (5th ed., pp. 745–800). New York, NY: Wiley.

Case, T. I., Repacholi, B. M., & Stevenson, R. J. (2006). My baby doesn't smell as bad as yours: The plasticity of disgust. *Evolution and Human Behavior, 27,* 357–365.

Casey, B. J. (2015). Beyond simple models of self-control to circuit-based accounts of adolescent behavior. *Annual Review of Psychology, 66,* 295–319.

Casey, B. J., Somerville, L. H., Gotlib, I. H., Ayduk, O., Franklin, N. T., Askren, M. K., & Shoda, Y. (2011). Behavioral and neural correlates of delay of gratification 40 years later. *Proceedings of the National Academy of Sciences of the United States of America, 108,* 14998–15003.

Casey, B., & Caudle, K. (2013). The teenage brain: Self control. *Current Directions in Psychological Science, 22,* 82–87.

Caspi, A. (1998). Personality development across the life course. In R. M. Lerner (Vol. Ed.), W. Damon (Editor-in-Chief), *Handbook of child psychology: Vol. 1. Theoretical models of human development* (5th ed.). New York, NY: Wiley.

Caspi, A., Hariri, A. R., Holmes, A., Uher, R., & Moffitt, T. E. (2011). Genetic sensitivity to the environment: The case of the serotonin transporter gene and its implications for studying complex diseases and traits. In K. A. Dodge & M. Rutter (Eds.), *Gene-environment interactions in developmental psychopathology* (pp. 18–58). New York, NY: Guilford.

Caspi, A., Harrington, H., Milne, B., Amell, J. W., Theodore, R. F., & Moffitt, T. E. (2003). Children's behavioral styles at age 3 are linked to their adult personality traits at age 26. *Journal of Personality, 71,* 495–513.

Caspi, A., Herbener, E. S., & Ozer, D. J. (1992). Shared experiences and the similarity of personalities: A longitudinal study of married couples. *Journal of Personality and Social Psychology, 62,* 281–291.

Caspi, A., McClay, J., Moffitt, T., Mill, J., Martin, J., Craig, I. W., Taylor, A., & Poulton, R. (2002). Role of genotype in the cycle of violence in maltreated children. *Science, 297,* 851–854.

Caspi, A., Sugden, K., Moffitt, T. E., Taylor, A., Craig, I. W., Harrington, H., McClay, J., Mill, J., Martin, J., Braithwaite, A., & Poulton, R. (2003, July 18). Influence of life stress on depression: Moderation by a polymorphism in the 5-HTT gene. *Science, 301,* 386–389.

Cassia, V. M., Kuefner, D., Westerlund, A., & Nelson, C. A. (2006). A behavioural and ERP investigation of 3-month-olds' face preferences. *Neuropsychologia, 44,* 2113–2125.

Cassia, V. M., Turati, C., & Simion, F. (2004). Can a nonspecific bias toward top-heavy patterns explain newborns' face preference? *Psychological Science, 15,* 379–383.

Cassidy, J., & Shaver, P. R. (Eds.) (2016). *Handbook of attachment. Theory, research, and clinical applications* (3rd ed.). New York, NY: Guilford.

Cassidy, T. (2006). *Birth: The surprising history of how we are born.* New York, NY: Atlantic Monthly Press.

Cassina, M., Salviati, L., Di Gianantonio, E., & Clementi, M. (2012). Genetic susceptibility to teratogens: State of the art. *Reproductive Toxicology, 34,* 186–191.

Castel, A. D., McGillivray, S., & Friedman, M. C. (2012). Metamemory and memory efficiency in older adults: Learning about the benefits of priority processing and value-directed remembering. In M. Naveh-Benjamin & N. Ohta (Eds.), *Memory and aging: Current issues and future directions* (pp. 245–270). New York, NY: Psychology Press.

Castro, M., & Smith, G. E. (2015). Mild cognitive impairment and Alzheimer's disease. In P. A. Lichtenberg & B. T. Mast (Eds. in Chief), B. D. Carpenter & J. L. Wetherell, (Assoc. Eds.), *APA handbook of clinical geropsychology: Vol. 2. Assessment, treatment, and issues of later life* (pp. 173–207). Washington, DC: American Psychological Association.

Catalano, P. M., McIntyre, H. D., Cruickshank, J. K., McCance, D. R., Dyer, A. R., Metzger, B. E., et al. (2012). The hyperglycemia and adverse pregnancy outcome study: Associations of GDM and obesity with pregnancy outcomes. *Diabetes Care, 35,* 780–786.

Cattell, R. B. (1963). Theory of fluid and crystallized intelligence: A critical experiment. *Journal of Educational Psychology, 54,* 1–22.

Cattell, R. B. (1987). *Intelligence: Its structure, growth, and action* (p. 206). New York, NY: Elsevier Science.

Causadias, J. M. (2013). A roadmap for the integration of culture into developmental psychopathology. *Development and Psychopathology, 25,* 1375–1398.

Cavanaugh, J. C. (1996). Memory self-efficacy as a moderation of memory change. In F. Blanchard-Fields & T. M. Hess (Eds.), *Perspectives on cognitive change in adulthood and aging.* New York, NY: McGraw-Hill.

Cavanaugh, J. C., Grady, J. G., & Perlmutter, M. (1983). Forgetting and use of memory aids in 20 to 70 year olds' everyday life. *International Journal of Aging and Human Development, 17,* 113–122.

Cawley, J., & Meyerhoefer, C. (2012). The medical care costs of obesity: An instrumental variables approach. *Journal of Health Economics, 31,* 219.

Caylak, E. (2009). Neurobiological approaches on brains of children with dyslexia: Review. *Academic Radiology, 16,* 1003–1024.

Ceci, S. J., & Williams, W. M. (1997). Schooling, intelligence, and income. *American Psychologist, 52,* 1051–, 1058.

Cecil-Karb, R., & Grogan-Kaylor, A. (2009). Childhood body mass index in community context: Neighborhood safety, television viewing, and growth trajectories of BMI. *Health & Social Work, 34,* 169–177.

Celgene Corporation. (2012). *System for thalidomide education and prescribing safety.* Retrieved from www. thalomid.com.

Celgene Corporation. (2016). *Welcome to the Celgene REMS Program.* Accessed 6/2016. www. celgeneriskmanagement.com/REMSPortal/rems/portal/ REMSPortal.portal.

Center on the Developing Child at Harvard University (2011). *Building the brain's "air traffic control" system: How early experiences shape the development of executive function: Working paper No. 11.* Retrieved from www. developingchild.harvard.edu.

Centers for Disease Control and Prevention. (2010). *Adverse childhood experiences study.* Retrieved from www.cdc. gov/nccdphp/ace/ prevalence.htm.

Centers for Disease Control and Prevention (2011). School health guidelines to promote healthy eating and physical activity. *MMWR, 60* (5), 3–14.

Centers for Disease Control and Prevention. (2012a). *Assisted reproductive technology.* Retrieved from www. cdc.gov/art/.

Centers for Disease Control and Prevention. (2012b). *Radiation and pregnancy: A fact sheet for the public.* Retrieved from www.bt.cdc.gov/radiation/prenatal.asp.

Centers for Disease Control and Prevention. (2012c). *Sexually transmitted diseases.* Retrieved from www.cdc. gov/std/pregnancy/STDFact-Pregnancy.htm.

Centers for Disease Control and Prevention. (2012d). *Sexually transmitted disease surveillance, 2011.* Atlanta: U.S. Department of Health and Human Services. Retrieved from www.cdc.gov/std/stats11/default.htm.

Centers for Disease Control and Prevention. (2012e). *Youth risk behavior surveillance—United States,* 2011. Morbidity and Mortality Weekly Report, 61, 1–268.

Centers for Disease Control and Prevention. (2013). Mental health surveillance among children—United States, 2005–2011. *MMWR, 62* (Suppl. 2), 1–35. Retrieved from www.cdc.gov/media/dpk/2013/docs/ Child_menatal_health/su6202.pdf.

Centers for Disease Control and Prevention. (2013). What would happen if we stopped vaccinations? Retrieved from www.cdc. gov/vaccines/vac-gen/whatifstop.htm.

Centers for Disease Control and Prevention. (2015). Physical activity facts. Retrieved from www.cdc.gov/ healthyschools/physicalactivity/facts.htm.

Centers for Disease Control and Prevention. (2015). Reproductive health: Tobacco use and pregnancy. Last modified 9/9/2015. www.cdc.gov/reproductivehealth/ maternalinfanthealth/tobaccousepregnancy/index.htm.

Centers for Disease Control and Prevention. (2016). "Fetal Deaths." Last modified 2/23/2016. www.cdc.gov/nchs/ nvss/fetal_death.htm.

Central Intelligence Agency (2015). *Infant mortality rate.* www.cia.gov/library/publications/the-world-factbook/ rankorder/2091rank.html.

Central Intelligence Agency (2015). *The world factbook.* Country comparison: Life expectancy at birth. Retrieved from www.cia.gov/library/publications/the-world-factbook/rankorder/2102rank.html.

Cerdá, M., Moffitt, T., Meier, M., Harrington, H., Houts, R., Ramrakha, S., Hogan, S., Poulton, R., & Caspi, A. (2016). Persistent cannabis dependence and alcohol dependence represent risks for midlife economic and social problems: A longitudinal cohort study. *Clinical Psychological Science, 4,* 1028–1046.

Cerminara, K. L. (2006). Theresa Marie Schiavo's long road to peace. *Death Studies, 30,* 101–112.

Cernoch, J. M., & Porter, R. H. (1985). Recognition of maternal axillary odors by infants. *Child Development, 56,* 1593–1598.

Cervera, T. C., Soler, M. J., Dasi, C., & Ruiz, J. C. (2009). Speech recognition and working memory capacity in young-elderly listeners: Effects of hearing sensitivity. *Canadian Journal of Experimental Psychology, 63,* 216–226.

Chabris, C. F., Hebert, B. M., Benjamin, D. J., Beauchamp, J., Cesarini, D., van der Loos, M., et al. (2012). Most reported genetic associations with general intelligence are probably false positives. *Psychological Science, 23,* 1314–1323.

Chae, Y., Kulkofsky, S., Debaran, F., Wang, Q., & Hart, S. L. (2014). Low-SES children's eyewitness memory: The effects of verbal labels and vocabulary skills. *Behavioral Sciences & the Law, 32,* 732–745.

Chae, Y., Kulkofsky, S., Debaran, F., Wang, Q., & Hart, S. L. (2016). Low-SES preschool children's eyewitness memory: The role of narrative skill. *Behavioral Sciences & the Law, 34,* 55–73.

Chambers, W. C. (2007). Oral sex: Varied behaviors and perceptions in a college population. *Journal of Sex Research, 44,* 28–42.

Champagne, F. A. (2010). Epigenetic influence of social experiences across the lifespan. *Developmental Psychobiology, 52,* 299–311.

Champagne, F. A. (2013). Epigenetics and developmental plasticity across species. *Developmental Psychobiology, 55,* 33–41.

Chan, M. Y., Haber, S., Drew, L. M., & Park, D. C. (2016). Training older adults to use tablet computers: Does it enhance cognitive function? *The Gerontologist, 56,* 475–484.

Chan, W. H., Biswas, S., Ashworth, J. L., & Lloyd, I. C. (2012). Congenital and infantile cataract: Aetiology and management. *European Journal of Pediatrics, 171,* 625–630.

Chan, W., McCrae, R. R., Fruyt, F. D., Jussim, L., Lockenhoff, C. E., De Bolle, M., Costa, P. T., Jr. (2012). Stereotypes of age differences in personality traits: Universal and accurate? *Journal of Personality and Social Psychology, 103,* 1050–1066.

Chandler, M. J., Sokol, B. W., & Wainryb, C. (2000). Beliefs about truth and beliefs about rightness. *Child Development, 71,* 91–97.

Chandler, M., Fritz, A. S., & Hala, S. (1989). Small-scale deceit: Deception as a marker of two-, three-, and four-year-olds' early theories of mind. *Child Development, 60,* 1263–1277.

Chandler, S., & Field, P. A. (1997). Becoming a father: First-time fathers' experience of labor and delivery. *Journal of Nurse-Midwifery, 42* 17–24.

Chandra, A., Martino, S. C., Collins, R. L., Elliott, M. N., Berry, S. H., Kanouse, D. E., & Miu, A. (2008). Does watching sex on television predict teen pregnancy? Findings from a national longitudinal survey of youth. *Pediatrics, 122,* 1047–1054.

Chandra, A., Mosher, W. D., Copen, C., & Sionean, C. (2011). Sexual behavior, sexual attraction, and sexual identity in the United States: Data from the 2006–2008 National Survey of Family Growth. *National Health Statistics Reports, 36,* 1–36.

Chao, R. K. (1994). Beyond parental control and authoritarian parenting style: Understanding Chinese parenting through the cultural notion of training. *Child Development, 65,* 1111–1119.

Chao, R. K. (2000). Cultural explanations for the role of parenting in the school success of Asian American children. In R. D. Taylor & M. C. Wang (Eds.), *Resilience across contexts: Family, work, culture, and community.* Mahwah, NJ: Erlbaum.

Chapman, L. L. (2000). Expectant fathers and labor epidurals. *American Journal of Maternity and Child Nursing, 25,* 133–138.

Chapman, M., & Lindenberger, U. (1988). Functions, operations, and décalage in the development of transitivity. *Developmental Psychology, 24,* 542–551.

Charles, S. T., & Carstensen, L. L. (2007). Emotion regulation and aging. In J. J. Gross, J. J. (Ed.), *Handbook of emotion regulation.* New York, NY: Guilford.

Charles, S. T., & Carstensen, L. L. (2010). Social and emotional aging. *Annual Review of Psychology, 61,* 383–409.

Charles, S. T., & Carstensen, L. L. (2014). Emotion regulation and aging. In J. J. Gross (Ed.), *Handbook of emotion regulation* (2nd ed.) (pp. 203–218). New York, NY: Guilford.

Charles, S. T., Mather, M., & Carstensen, L. L. (2003). Aging and emotional memory: The forgettable nature of negative images for older adults. *Journal of Experimental Psychology: General, 132,* 310–324.

Charlton, R. A., Barrick, T. R., Markus, H. S., & Morris, R. G. (2009). Theory of mind associations with other cognitive functions and brain imaging in normal aging. *Psychology and Aging, 24,* 338–348.

Charman, T. (2000). Theory of mind and the early diagnosis of autism. In S. Baron-Cohen, H. Tager-Flusberg, & D. J. Cohen (Eds.), *Understanding other minds: Perspectives from developmental cognitive neuroscience* (2nd ed.). Oxford, UK: Oxford University Press.

Charney, D. S., Reynolds, C. F., Lewis, L., Lebowitz, B. D., Sunderland, T., Alexopoulos, G. S. et al. (2003). Depression and Bipolar Support Alliance consensus statement on the unmet needs in diagnosis and treatment of mood disorders in late life. *Archives of General Psychiatry, 60,* 664–672.

Chassin, L., Beltran, I., Lee, M., Haller, M., & Villalta, I. (2010). Vulnerability to substance use disorders in childhood and adolescence. In R. E. Ingram & J. M. Price (Eds.), *Vulnerability to psychopathology: Risk across the lifespan* (2nd ed.). New York, NY: Guilford.

Chauhan, N. B. (2014). Chronic neurodegenerative consequences of traumatic brain injury. *Restorative Neurology and Neuroscience, 32,* 337–365.

Chavous, T. M., Bernat, D. H., Schmeelk-Cone, K., Caldwell, C. H., Kohn-Wood, L., & Zimmerman, M. A. (2003). Racial identity and academic attainment among African American adolescents. *Child Development, 74,* 1076–1090.

Cheadle, A. C. D., Schetter, C. D., Lanzi, R. G., Vance, M. R., Sahadeo, L. S., Shalowitz, M. U., & the Community Child Health Network. (2015). Spiritual and religious resources in African American women: Protection from depressive symptoms after childbirth. *Clinical Psychological Science, 3,* 283–291.

Cheadle, J. E., Amato, P. R., & King, V. (2010). Patterns of nonresident father contact. *Demography, 47,* 205–225.

Chen, A. (2007). Learning to map: Strategy discovery and strategy change in young children. *Developmental Psychology, 43,* 386–403.

Chen, C. K., Waters, H. S., Hartman, M., Zimmerman, S., Miklowitz, D. J., & Waters, E. (2013). The secure base script and the task of caring for elderly parents: Implications for attachment theory and clinical practice. *Attachment & Human Development, 15,* 332–348.

Chen, C., & Stevenson, H. W. (1995). Motivation and mathematics achievement: A comparative study of Asian-American, Caucasian-American, and East Asian high school students. *Child Development, 66,* 1214–1234.

Chen, D. (1996). Parent-infant communication: Early intervention for very young children with visual impairment or hearing loss. *Infants and Young Children, 9,* 1–12.

Chen, E. Y., Enright, R. D., & Tung, E. Y. (2016). The influence of family unions and parenthood transitions on self-development. *Journal of Family Psychology, 30,* 341–352.

Chen, E., Martin, A. D., & Matthews, K. A. (2006). Understanding health disparities: The role of face and socioeconomic status in children's health. *American Journal of Public Health, 96,* 702–708.

Chen, J. Q., & Gardner, H. (1997). Alternative assessment from a multiple intelligences theoretical perspective. In D. P. Flanagan, J. Genshaft, & P. L. Harrison (Eds.), *Contemporary intellectual assessment: Theories, tests, and issues.* New York, NY: Guilford.

Chen, M., & Chan, K. L. (2016). Effects of parenting programs on child maltreatment prevention: A meta-analysis. *Trauma, Violence, & Abuse, 17,* 88–104.

Chen, X., & Schmidt, L. A. (2015). Temperament and personality. In M. E. Lamb (Vol. Ed.) & R. M. Lerner (Ed.) *Handbook of child psychology and developmental science, Vol. 3: Socioemotional processes* (pp. 152–200). Hoboken, NJ: Wiley.

Chen, X., Cen, G., Li, D., & He, Y (2005). Social functioning and adjustment in Chinese children: The imprint of historical time. *Child Development, 76,* 182–195.

Chen, X., Fu, R., & Leng, L. (2014). Culture and developmental psychopathology. In M. Lewis & K. D. Rudolph (Eds.), *Handbook of developmental psychopathology* (3rd ed., pp. 225–241). New York, NY: Springer.

Chen, X., Wang, L., & Wang, Z. (2009). Shyness-sensitivity and social, school, and psychological adjustment in rural migrant and urban children in China. *Child Development, 80,* 1499–1513.

Chen, X., Yang, F., & Fu, R. (2012). Culture and temperament. In M. Z. Zentner & R. L. Shiner (Eds.), *Handbook of temperament.* New York, NY: Guilford.

Cheng, A. K., Rubin, H. R., Powe, N. R., Mellon, M. K., Francis, H. W., & Niparko, J. K. (2000). Cost-utility analysis of the cochlear implant in children. *Journal of the American Medical Association, 284,* 850–856.

Cheng, T. C., Powdhavee, N., & Oswald, A. J. (2016). Longitudinal evidence for a midlife nadir in human well-being: Results from four data sets. *The Economic Journal.* Advance online publication.

Cherkas, L. F., Aviv, A., Valdes, A. M., Hunkin, J. L., Gardner, J. P., Surdulescu, G. L., et al. (2006). The effects of social status on biological aging as measured by white-blood-cell telomere length. *Aging Cell, 5,* 361–365.

Cherkas, L. F., Hunkin, J. L., Kato, B. S., Richards, J. B., Gardner, J. P., Surdulescu, G. L., et al. (2008). The association between physical activity in leisure time and leukocyte telomere length. *Archives of Internal Medicine, 168,* 154–158.

Cherlin, A. J. (2009). *The marriage-go-round. The state of marriage and the family in America today.* New York, NY: Knopf Doubleday Publishing Group.

Cherlin, A. J. (2010). Demographic trends in the United States: A review of research in the 2000s. *Journal of Marriage and Family, 72,* 403–419.

Cherlin, A. J., & Furstenberg, F. F., Jr. (1986). *The new American grandparent: A place in the family, a life apart.* New York, NY: Basic Books.

Cherney, I. D. (2005). Children's and adults' recall of sex-stereotyped toy pictures: Effects of presentation and memory task. *Infant and Child Development, 14,* 11–27.

Cherney, I. D., Harper, H. J., & Winter, J. A. (2006). Nouveaux jouets: Ce que les enfants identifient comme 'jouets de garçons' et 'jouets de filles.' *Enfance, 58,* 266–282.

Cherney, I. S., & London, K. (2006). Gender-linked differences in the toys, television shows, computer games, and outdoor activities of 5- to 13-year-old children. *Sex Roles, 54,* 717–726.

Cherry, K. E., & LeCompte, D. C. (1999). Age and individual differences influence prospective memory. *Psychology and Aging, 14,* 60–76.

Cherry, K. E., & Smith, A. D. (1998). Normal memory aging. In M. Hersen & V. B. Van Hasselt (Eds.), *Handbook of clinical geropsychology* (pp. 87–110). New York, NY: Plenum.

Chesley, N., & Poppie, K. (2009). Assisting parents and in-laws: Gender, type of assistance, and couples' employment. *Journal of Marriage and Family, 71,* 247–262.

Chess, S., & Thomas, A. (1984). *Origins and evolution of behavior disorders: From infancy to early adult life.* New York, NY: Brunner/Mazel.

Chess, S., & Thomas, A. (1999). *Goodness of fit: Clinical applications from infancy through adult life.* Ann Arbor, MI: Edwards Brothers.

Chi, M. T. H. (1978). Knowledge structures and memory development. In R. Siegler (Ed.), *Children's thinking: What develops?* Hillsdale, NJ: Erlbaum.

Chia, E. M., Wang, J. J., Rochtchina, E., Smith, W., Cumming, R. R., & Mitchell, P. (2004). Impact of bilateral visual impairment on health-related quality of life: The Blue Mountains Eye Study. *Investigations in Ophthalmology & Visual Science, 45,* 71–76.

Chiao, C., Wu, H., & Hsiao, C. (2015). Caregiver burden for informal caregivers of patients with dementia: A systematic review. *International Nursing Review, 62,* 340–350.

Childbirth Connection. (2015). *Cesarean section.* Retrieved from www.childbirthconnection.org/giving-birth/c-section/.

Children's Defense Fund (2014). *The state of America's children 2014.* Retrieved from www.childrensdefense.org/library/state-of-americas-children/2014-soac.pdf?utm_source=2014-SOAC-PDF&utm_medium=link&utm_campaign=2014-SOAC.

Children's Hospital of Eastern Ontario Research Institute (2012, October 1). Overweight teens get mental health boost from even small amounts of exercise. *ScienceDaily.* Retrieved from www.sciencedaily.com.

Chin, H. B., Sipe, T. A., Elder, R. W., Mercer, S. L., Chattopadhyay, S. K., Jacob, V., . . . Community Preventive Services Task Force (2012). The effectiveness of group-based comprehensive risk-reduction and abstinence education interventions to prevent or reduce the risk of adolescent pregnancy, Human Immunodeficiency Virus, and sexually transmitted infections: Two systematic reviews for the Guide to Community Preventive Services. *American Journal of Preventive Medicine, 42,* 272–294.

China one-child policy: Government think tank urges country's leaders to start phasing out policy immediately (2012, October 31). Retrieved from www.huffingtonpost.com/2012/10/31/china-one-child-policy-think-tank-phase-out_n_2050149.html.

Chiu, S., & Alexander, P. A. (2000). The motivational function of preschoolers' private speech. *Discourse Processes, 30,* 133–152.

Cho, D., & Gardner, A. (2007, April 21). Virginia Tech killer: An isolated boy in a world of strangers. *The Washington Post,* A1, A8.

Chocano-Bedoya, P. O., Manson, J. E., Hankinson, S. E., Johnson, S. R., Chasan-Taber, L., Ronnenberg, A. G., & Bertone-Johnson, E. R. (2013). Intake of selected minerals and risk of premenstrual syndrome. *American Journal of Epidemiology, 177,* 1118–1127.

Chochinov, H. M., & Schwartz, L. (2002). Depression and the will to live in the psychological landscape of terminally ill patients. In K. Foley, & H. Hendin (Eds.), *The case against assisted suicide: For the right to end-of-life care.* Baltimore, MA: The Johns Hopkins Press.

Choi, J., & Silverman, I. (2003). Processes underlying sex differences in route-learning strategies in children and adolescents. *Personality and Individual Differences, 34,* 1153–1166.

Chomsky, N. (1965). *Aspects of the theory of syntax.* Cambridge, MA: MIT Press.

Chomsky, N. (1968). *Language and mind.* New York, NY: Harcourt Brace & World.

Chomsky, N. (1975). *Reflections on language.* New York, NY: Pantheon Books.

Chomsky, N. (2000). *New horizons in the study of language and mind.* Cambridge, UK: Cambridge University Press.

Chopik, W. J., & Edelstein, R. S. (2014). Age differences in romantic attachment around the world. *Social Psychological and Personality Science, 5,* 892–900.

Chopik, W. J., Edelstein, R. S., & Fraley, R. C. (2013). From the cradle to the grave: Age differences in

attachment from early adulthood to old age. *Journal of Personality, 81*, 171–183.
Chouliaras, L., Rutten, B. P. F., Kenis, G., Peerbooms, O., Visser, P. J., Verhey, F., et al. (2010). Epigenetic regulation in the pathophysiology of Alzheimer's disease. *Progress in Neurobiology, 90*, 498–510.
Christ, G. H. (2010). Children bereaved by the death of a parent. In C. A. Corr & D. E. Balk (Eds.), *Children's encounters with death, bereavement, and coping*. New York, NY: Springer.
Christakis, D. (2008). The effects of infant media usage: What do we know and what should we learn? *Acta Paediatrica, 98*, 8–16.
Christiansen, S. L., & Palkovitz, R. (1998). Exploring Erikson's psychosocial theory of development: Generativity and its relationship to parental identity, intimacy, and involvement with others. *Journal of Men's Studies, 7*, 133–156.
Christianson, A., Howson, C. P., & Modell, B. (2006). *March of Dimes Global report on birth defects: The hidden toll of dying and disabled children*. White Plains, NY: March of Dimes Birth Defects Foundation.
Chronis, A. M., Jones, H. A., & Raggi, V. L. (2006). Evidence-based psychosocial treatments for children and adolescents with attention-deficit/hyperactivity disorder. *Clinical Psychology Review, 26*, 486–502.
Chua, A. (2011a). *Battle hymn of the Tiger Mother*. New York, NY: Penguin.
Chua, A. (2011b, January 8). Why Chinese mothers are superior. Can a regimen of no playdates, no TV, no computer games and hours of music practice create happy kids? And what happens when they fight back? *Wall Street Journal* (Online). Retrieved from online.wsj.com/article/SB10001424052748704111504576059713528698754.html.
Chumlea, W. C., Schubert, C. M., Roche, A. F., Kulin, H. E., Lee, P. A., Himes, J. H., et al. (2003). Age at menarche and racial comparisons in US girls. *Pediatrics, 111*, 110–113.
Chung, G. H., Flook, L., & Fuligni, A. J. (2009). Daily family conflict and emotional distress among adolescents from Latin American, Asian, and European backgrounds. *Developmental Psychology, 45*, 1406–1415.
Chung, J. H., Des Roches, C. M., Meunier, J., & Eavey, R. D. (2005). Evaluation of noise-induced hearing loss in young people using a web-based survey technique. *Pediatrics, 115*, 861–867.
Church, T. S., Thomas, D. M., Tudor-Locke, C., Katzmarzyk, P. T., & Earnest, C. P., et al. (2011). Trends over 5 decades in U.S. occupation-related physical activity and their associations with obesity. *PLoS ONE, 6*(5), e19657.
Chyi, L. J., Lee, H. C., Hintz, S. R., Gould, J. B., Sutcliffe, T. (2008). School outcomes of late preterm infants: Special needs and challenges for infants born at 32 to 36 weeks gestation. *Journal of Pediatrics, 153*, 25–31.
CIA (2012). *World fact book*. Retrieved from www.cia.gov/library/publications/the-world-factbook/rankorder/2091rank.html.
Cicchetti, D. (Ed.). (2016). *Developmental psychopathology* (3rd ed). Hoboken, NJ: Wiley.
Cicchetti, D., & Rogosch, F. A. (2002). A developmental psychopathology perspective on adolescence. *Journal of Consulting and Clinical Psychology, 70*, 6–20.
Cicchetti, D., & Toth, S. L. (2009). The past achievements and future promises of developmental psychopathology: The coming of age of a discipline. *Journal of Child Psychology and Psychiatry, 50*, 16–25.
Cicchetti, D., & Toth, S. L. (2015). Child maltreatment. In M. E. Lamb (Vol. Ed.) & R. M. Lerner (General Ed.), *Handbook of child psychology and developmental science: Vol. 3. Socioeomotional processes* (pp. 513–563). Hoboken, NJ: Wiley.
Cicchino, J. B., & McCartt, A. T. (2015). Critical older driver errors in a national sample of serious U.S. crashes. *Accident; Analysis and Prevention, 80*, 211–219.
Cicirelli, V. G. (1991). Sibling relationships in adulthood. *Marriage and Family Review, 16*, 291–310.
Cicirelli, V. G. (1995). *Sibling relationships across the life span*. New York, NY: Plenum.
Cicirelli, V. G. (2010). Attachment relationships in old age. *Journal of Social and Personal Relationships, 27*, 191–199.
Cillessen, A. H. N. (2009). Sociometric methods. In K. H. Rubin, W. M. Bukowski, & B. Laursen (Eds.), *Handbook of peer interactions, relationships, and groups*. New York, NY: Guilford.
Cillessen, A. H. N., Schwartz, D., & Mayeux, L. (Eds.) (2011). *Popularity in the peer system*. New York, NY: Guilford.
Cillessen, A. H., Van IJzendoorn, H. W., Van Lieshout, C. F., & Hartup, W. W. (1992). Heterogeneity among peer-rejected boys: Subtypes and stabilities. *Child Development, 63*, 893–905.
Clark, A., & Lappin, S. (2011). *Linguistic nativism and the poverty of the stimulus*. Hoboken, NJ: Wiley-Blackwell.
Clark, D. O., & Maddox, G. L. (1992). Racial and social correlates of age-related changes in functioning. *Journal of Gerontology Series B: Social Sciences, 47*, S222–S232.
Clark, H. H., & Clark, E. V. (1977). *Psychology and language: An introduction to psycholinguistics*. New York, NY: Harcourt Brace Jovanovich.
Clark, M. A., & Fox, M. K. (2009). National quality of the diets of U.S. public school children and the role of the school meal programs. *Journal of the American Dietetic Association, 109*, S44–56.
Clarke-Stewart, K. A. (1998). Reading with children. *Journal of Applied Developmental Psychology, 19*, 1–14.
Class, Q. A., Khashan, A. S., Lichtenstein, P., Långström, N., & D'Onofrio, B. M. (2013) Maternal stress and infant mortality: The importance of the preconception period. *Psychological Science, 24*, 1309–1316.
Claxton, A. F., Pannells, T. C., & Rhoads, P. A. (2005). Developmental trends in the creativity of school-age children. *Creativity Research Journal, 17*, 327–335.
Cleveland, E. S., & Reese, E. (2008). Children remember early childhood: Long-term recall across the offset of childhood amnesia. *Applied Cognitive Psychology, 22*, 127–142.
Cleveland, H. H., Jacobson, K. C., Lipinski, J. J., & Rowe, D. C. (2000). Genetic and shared environmental contributions to the relationship between the home environment and child and adolescent achievement. *Intelligence, 28*, 69–86.
Coall, D. A., & Hertwig, R. (2011). Grandparental investment: A relic of the past or a resource for the future? *Current Directions in Psychological Science, 20*, 93–98.
Cobb, R. W., & Coughlin, J. F. (1998). Are elderly drivers a road hazard? Problem definition and political impact. *Journal of Aging Studies, 12*, 411–420.
Codipietro, L., Ceccarelli, M., & Ponzone, A. (2008). Breastfeeding or oral sucrose solution in term neonates receiving heel lance: A randomized, controlled trial. *Pediatrics, 122*, 716–721.
Coe, N. B., von Gaudecker, H., Lindeboom, M., & Maurer, J. (2012). The effect of retirement on cognitive functioning. *Health Economics, 21*, 913–927.
Cohan, C. L. (2013). The cohabitation conundrum. In M. A. Fine & F. D. Fincham (Eds.), *Handbook of family theories. A context-based approach*. New York, NY: Routledge.
Cohen, A. B. (2015). Religion's profound influences on psychology: Morality, intergroup relations, self-construal, and enculturation. *Current Directions in Psychological Science, 24*, 77–82.
Cohen, J. F. W., Richardson, S., Austin, S. B., Economos, C. D., & Rimm, E. B. (2013). School lunch waste among middle school students: Nutrients consumed and costs. *American Journal of Preventive Medicine, 44*, 114–121.
Cohen, J., Van Landeghem, P., Carpentier, N., & Deliens, L. (2013). Public acceptance of euthanasia in Europe: A survey study in 47 countries. *International Journal of Public Health*.
Cohen, M. (1996). Preschoolers' practical thinking and problem solving: The acquisition of an optimal solution strategy. *Cognitive Development, 11*, 357–373.
Cohen, S., & Janicki-Deverts, D. (2009). Can we improve our physical health by altering our social networks? *Perspectives on Psychological Science, 4*, 375–378.
Cohen, T. R., Panter, A. T., Turan, N., Morse, L., & Kim, Y. (2014). Moral character in the workplace. *Journal of Personality and Social Psychology, 107*, 943–963.
Cohn, A., & Richters, J. (2013). 'My vagina makes funny noises': Analyzing online forums to assess the real sexual health concerns of young people. *International Journal of Sexual Health, 25*, 93–103.
Cohn, D., Passel, J. S., Wang, W., & Livingston, G. (2011). *Barely half of U.S. adults are married—A record low*. Washington, DC: Pew Research Center Social & Demographic Trends. Retrieved from www.pewsocialtrends.org/2011/12/14/barely-half-of-u-s-adults-are-married-a-record-low/.
Coie, J. D. (2004). The impact of negative social experiences on the development of antisocial behavior. In J. B. Kupersmidt & K. A. Dodge (Eds.), *Children's peer relations: From development to intervention*. Washington, DC: American Psychological Association.
Coie, J. D., Dodge, K. A., & Coppotelli, H. (1982). Dimensions and types of social status: A cross-age perspective. *Developmental Psychology, 18*, 557–570.
Coie, J. D., Dodge, K. A., & Kupersmidt, J. B. (1990). Peer group behavior and social status. In S. R. Asher & J. D. Coie (Eds.), *Peer rejection in childhood*. Cambridge, UK: Cambridge University Press.
Coker, A. L., Fisher, B. S., Bush, H. M., Swan, S. C., Williams, C. M., Clear, E. R., & DeGue, S. (2015). Evaluation of the Green Dot bystander intervention to reduce interpersonal violence among college students across three campuses. *Violence Against Women, 21*, 1507–1527.
Colapinto J. (2004, June 3). *What were the real reasons behind David Reimer's suicide?* Retrieved from www.slate.com/id/2101678.
Colapinto, J. (1997, December 11). The true story of John Joan. *Rolling Stone*, pp. 54–97.
Colapinto, J. (2000). *As nature made him: The boy who was raised as a girl*. New York, NY: Harper Collins.
Colburn, D. (2000, October 3). Wired for sound. *The Washington Post—Health*, pp. 13–18.
Colby, A., & Kohlberg, L. (1987). *The measurement of moral judgment: Vol. 1. Theoretical foundations and research validation*. Cambridge, UK: Cambridge University Press.
Colby, A., Kohlberg, L., Gibbs, J., & Lieberman, M. (1983). A longitudinal study of moral judgment. *Monographs of the Society for Research in Child Development, 48* (1–2, Serial No. 200).
Colcombe, S. J., Kramer, A. F., Erickson, K. I., Scalf, P., McAuley, E., Cohen, N. J., et al. (2004). Cardiovascular fitness, cortical plasticity, and aging. *Proceedings of the National Academy of Sciences, 101*, 3316–3321.
Cole, J. (1995). *Pride and a daily marathon*. Cambridge, MA: MIT Press.
Cole, M., & Packer, M. (2011). Culture in development. In M. E. Lamb & M. H. Bornstein (Eds.), *Social and personality development: An advanced textbook* (pp. 67–123). New York, NY: Psychology Press.
Cole, P. M., Barrett, K. C., & Zahn-Waxler, C. (1992). Emotion displays in two-year-olds during mishaps. *Child Development, 63*, 314–324.
Cole, P. M., Martin, S. E., & Dennis, T. A. (2004). Emotion regulation as a scientific construct: Methodological challenges and directions for child development research. *Child Development, 75*, 317–333.
Cole, P. M., Michel, M. K., & Teti, L. O. (1994). The development of emotion regulation and dysregulation: A clinical perspective. In N. Fox (Ed.), *The development of emotion regulation: Biological and behavioral considerations. Monographs of the Society for Research in Child Development, 59* (Nos. 2–3, Serial No. 240).
Cole, P. M., Tamang, B. L., & Shrestha, S. (2006). Cultural variations in the socialization of young children's anger and shame. *Child Development, 77*, 1237–1251.
Coleman, J. (1961). *The adolescent society*. New York, NY: Free Press.
Coley, R. L., Carrano, J., & Lewin-Bizan, S. (2011). Unpacking links between fathers' antisocial behaviors and children's behavior problems: Direct, indirect, and interactive effects. *Journal of Abnormal Child Psychology, 39*, 791–804.
Colin, V. (1996). *Human attachment*. New York, NY: McGraw-Hill.
College Board. (2012). *Total group profile report*. Retrieved from media.collegeboard.com/digitalServices/pdf/research/TotalGroup-2012.pdf.
Colletti, L., Mandalà, M., Zoccante, L., Shannon, R. V., & Colletti, V. (2011). Infants versus older children fitted with cochlear implants: Performance over 10 years. *International Journal of Pediatric Otorhinolaryngology, 75*, 504–509.
Colley, A., Griffiths, D., Hugh, M., Landers, K., & Jaggli, N. (1996). Childhood play and adolescent leisure preferences: Associations with gender typing and the presence of siblings. *Sex Roles, 35*, 233–245.
Collins, N. L., & Feeney, B. C. (2013). Attachment and caregiving in adult close relationships: Normative

processes and individual differences. *Attachment & Human Development*, 15, 241–245.
Collins, W. A., & Laursen, B. (2004). Changing relationships, changing youth: Interpersonal contexts of adolescent development. *Journal of Early Adolescence*, 24, 55–62.
Collins, W. A., & Laursen, B. (2006). Parent-adolescent relationships. In P. Noller, & J. A. Feeney (Eds.), *Close relationships: Functions, forms and processes*. Hove, England: Psychology Press/Taylor & Francis.
Collins, W. A., & Madsen, S. D. (2006). Personal relationships in adolescence and early adulthood. In A. L. Vangelisti & D. Perlman (Eds.), *The Cambridge handbook of personal relationships*. New York, NY: Cambridge University Press.
Colombo, J. (2001). The development of visual attention in infancy. *Annual Review of Psychology*, 52, 337–367.
Colombo, J., Shaddy, D. J., Blaga, O. M., Anderson, C. J., & Kannass, K. N. (2009). High cognitive ability in infancy and early childhood. In F. D. Horowitz, R. F. Subotnik, & D. J. Matthews (Eds.), *The development of giftedness and talent across the life span*. Washington, DC: American Psychological Association.
Columbo, J. (1993). *Infant cognition: Predicting later intellectual functioning*. Newbury Park, CA: Sage.
Comfort, A. (1974). Sexuality in old age. *Journal of the American Geriatrics Society*, 22, 440–442.
Committee on Adolescence. (1996). *Adolescent suicide* (Group for the Advancement of Psychiatry, Report No. 140). Washington, DC: American Psychiatric Press.
Committee on Environmental Health. (2009). The built environment: Designing communities to promote physical activity in children. *Pediatrics*, *123*(6), 1591–1598.
Commons, M. L., & Richards, F. A. (2003). Four postformal stages. In J. Demick & C. Andreoletti (Eds.), *Handbook of adult development* (pp. 199–220). New York, NY: Plenum.
Commons, M. L., & Ross, S. N. (2008). What postformal thought is, and why it matters. *World Futures*, *64*, 321–329.
Compas, B. E., Connor-Smith, J. K., Saltzman, H., Thomsen, A. H., & Wadsworth, M. E. (2001). Coping with stress during childhood and adolescence: Problems, progress, and potential in theory and research.*Psychological Bulletin*, *127*, 87–127.
Conde-Agudelo, A., Belizán, J. M., & Diaz-Rossello, J. (2011). Kangaroo mother care to reduce morbidity and mortality in low birthweight infants. *Cochrane Database of Systematic Reviews*, Issue 3. Art. No.: CD002771. doi:10.1002/14651858.CD002771.pub2
Condon, E. M., Crepinsek, M. K., & Fox, M. K. (2009). School meals: Types of foods offered to and consumed by children at lunch and breakfast. *Journal of the American Dietetic Association*, *109*, S67–78.
Condry, J., & Condry, S. (1976). Sex differences: A study in the eye of the beholder. *Child Development*, *47*, 812–819.
Conduct Problems Prevention Research Group. (2002). Evaluation of the first 3 years of the Fast Track prevention trial with children at high risk for adolescent conduct problems. *Journal of Abnormal Child Psychology*, 30, 19–35.
Conduct Problems Prevention Research Group. (2007). Fast Track randomized controlled trial to prevent externalizing psychiatric disorders: Findings from grades 3 to 9. *Journal of the American Academy of Child & Adolescent Psychiatry*, *46*, 1250–1262.
Conger, K. J., Rueter, M. A., & Conger, R. D. (2000). The role of economic pressure in the lives of parents and their adolescents: The family stress model. In L. J. Crockett, & R. K. Silbereisen (Eds.), *Negotiating adolescence in times of social change*. New York, NY: Cambridge University Press.
Conger, R. D., & Dogan, S. J. (2007). Social class and socialization in families. In J. E. Grusec & P. D. Hastings (Eds.), *Handbook of socialization theory and research*. New York, NY: Guilford.
Conger, R. D., & Donnellan, M. B. (2007). An interactionist perspective on the socioeconomic context of human development. *Annual Review of Psychology*, 58, 175–199.
Conger, R. D., Belsky, J., & Capaldi, D. M. (2009). The intergenerational transmission of parenting: Closing comments for the special section. *Developmental Psychology*, 45, 1276–1283.
Conger, R. D., Conger, K. J., Elder, G. H., Jr., Lorenz, F. O., Simons, R. L., & Whitbeck, L. B. (1992). A family process model of economic hardship and adjustment of early adolescent boys. *Child Development*, 63, 526–541.
Conger, R. D., Neppl, T., Kim, K. J., & Scaramella, L. (2003). Angry and aggressive behavior across three generations: A prospective, longitudinal study of parents and children. *Journal of Abnormal Child Psychology*, 31, 143–160.
Conger, R. D., Patterson, G. R., & Ge, X. (1995). It takes two to replicate: A mediational model for the impact of parents' stress on adolescent adjustment. *Child Development*, *66*, 80–97.
Conger, R. D., Schofield, T. J., & Neppl, T. K. (2012). Intergenerational continuity and discontinuity in harsh parenting. *Parenting: Science and Practice*, *12*, 222–231.
Conger, R. D., Wallace, L. E., Sun, Y., Simons, R. L., McLoyd, V. C., & Brody, G. H. (2002). Economic pressure in African American families: A replication and extension of the family stress model. *Developmental Psychology*, 38, 179–193.
Conklin, H. M., Luciana, M., Hooper, C. J., & Yarger, R. S. (2007). Working memory performance in typically developing children and adolescents: Behavioral evidence of protracted frontal lobe development. *Developmental Neuropsychology*, 31, 103–128.
Conley, C. S., & Rudolph, K. D. (2009). The emerging sex difference in adolescent depression: Interacting contributions of puberty and peer stress. *Development and Psychopathology*, *21*, 593–620.
Conley, T. D., Ziegler, A., & Moors, A. C. (2013). Backlash from the bedroom: Stigma mediates gender differences in acceptance of casual sex offers. *Psychology of Women Quarterly*, 37, 392–407.
Connell, A. M., & Goodman, S. H. (2002). The association between psychopathology in fathers versus mothers and children's internalizing and externalizing behavior problems: A meta-analysis. *Psychological Bulletin*, *128*, 746–773.
Conner, K. A. (2000). *Continuing to care. Older Americans and their families*. New York, NY: Falmer Press.
Connidis, I. A. (2010). *Family ties and aging* (2nd ed.). Thousand Oaks, CA: Pine Forge Press.
Connolly, J. A., & Doyle, A. B. (1984). Relation of social fantasy play to social competence in preschoolers. *Developmental Psychology*, 20, 797–806.
Connolly, J., &McIsaac, C. (2011). Romantic relationships in adolescence. In M. K. Underwood & L. H. Rosen (Eds.), *Social development. Relationships in infancy, childhood, and adolescence*. New York, NY: Guilford.
Connolly, J., McIsaac, C., Shulman, S., Wincentak, K., Joly, L., Heifetz, M., & Bravo, V. (2014). Development of romantic relationships in adolescence and emerging adulthood: Implications for community mental health. *Canadian Journal of Community Mental Health*, 33, 7–19.
Connolly, M. P., Hoorens, S., & Chambers, G. M. (2010, June 8). The costs and consequences of assisted reproductive technology: An economic perspective. *Human Reproduction Update*, *16*, 603–613.
Connor, S. R. (2000). Hospice care and the older person. In A. Tomer (Ed.), *Death attitudes and the older adult: Theories, concepts, and applications*. Philadelphia, PA: Brunner-Routledge.
Conrade, G., & Ho, R. (2001). Differential parenting styles for fathers and mothers: Differential treatment for sons and daughters. *Australian Journal of Psychology*, 53, 29–35.
Conrod, P. J., & Nikolaou, K. (2016). Annual research review: On the developmental neuropsychology of substance use disorders. *Journal of Child Psychology and Psychiatry*, 57, 371–394.
Conry-Murray, C., Kim, J. M., & Turiel, E. (2015). Judgments of gender norm violations in children from the United States and Korea. *Cognitive Development*, 35, 122–136.
Contrera, K. J., Betz, J., Deal, J. A., Choi, J. S., Ayonayon, H. N., Harris, T., & Lin, F. R. (2016). Association of hearing impairment and emotional vitality in older adults. *The Journals of Gerontology. Series B, Psychological Sciences and Social Sciences*. [Epub ahead of print]
Conway, M. A. (2005). Memory and the self. *Journal of Memory and Language*, 53, 594–628.
Conway, M. A., Cohen, G., & Stanhope, N. (2006). Very long-term memory for knowledge acquired at school and university. *Applied Cognitive Psychology*, *6*, 467–482.
Coohey, C., & Braun, N. (1997). Toward an integrated framework for understanding child physical abuse. *Child Abuse and Neglect*, *21*, 1081–1094.
Cook, A. S., & Dworkin, D. S. (1992). *Helping the bereaved. Therapeutic interventions for children, adolescents, and adults*. New York, NY: Basic Books.
Coontz, S. (2000). Historical perspectives on family diversity. In D. H. Demo, K. R. Allen, & M. A. Fine (Eds.), *Handbook of family diversity*. New York, NY: Oxford University Press.
Cooper, M. L. (2002). Alcohol use and risky sexual behavior among college students and youth: Evaluating the evidence. *Journal of Studies on Alcohol*, *14*(Suppl.), 101–117.
Cooper, M. L. (2010). Toward a person x situation model of sexual risk-taking behaviors: Illuminating the conditional effects of traits across sexual situations and relationship contexts. *Journal of Personality and Social Psychology*, 98, 319–341.
Coopersmith, S. (1967). *The antecedents of self-esteem*. San Francisco, CA: W. H. Freeman.
Copeland, C. (2014, May). *Individual retirement account balances, contributions, and rollovers, 2012; With longitudinal results 2010–2012: The EBRI IRA Database*. Employee Benefit Research Institute, Issue Brief No. 399. Available at www.ebri.org/pdf/EBRI_IB_399_May14.IRAs.pdf.
Copeland, W. E., Adair, C. E., Smetanin, P., Stiff, D., Briante, C., Colman, I., . . . Angold, A. (2013). Diagnostic transitions from childhood to adolescence to early adulthood. *Journal of Child Psychology and Psychiatry*, *54*, 791–799.
Copeland, W. E., Wolke, D., Lereya, S. T., Shanahan, L., Worthman, C., & Costello, E. J. (2014). Childhood bullying involvement predicts low-grade systemic inflammation into adulthood. *PNAS Proceedings of the National Academy of Sciences of the United States of America*, *111*, 7570–7575.
Copeland, W. E., Wolke, D., Shanahan, L., & Costello, E. J. (2015). Adult functional outcomes of common childhood psychiatric problems: A prospective, longitudinal study. *JAMA Psychiatry*, 72, 892–899.
Copeland, W., Shanahan, L., Costello, E. J., & Angold, A. (2011). Cumulative prevalence of psychiatric disorders by young adulthood: A prospective cohort analysis from the Great Smoky Mountains Study. *Journal of the American Academy of Child & Adolescent Psychiatry*, 50, 252–261.
Copen, C. E., Chandra, A., & Febo-Vazquez, I. (2016). Sexual behavior, sexual attraction, and sexual orientation among adults aged 18–44 in the United States: Data from the 2011–2013 National Survey of Family Growth. *National Health Statistics Reports*, 88, 1–14.
Coplan, R. J., & Abreau, K. A. (2009). Peer interactions and play in early childhood. In K. H. Rubin, W. M. Bukowski, & B. Laursen (Eds.), *Handbook of peer interactions, relationships, and groups*. New York, NY: Guilford.
Coplan, R. J., Ooi, L. L., & Nocita, G. (2015). When one is company and two is a crowd: Why some children prefer solitude. *Child Development Perspectives*, 9, 133–137.
Corkin, S. (2013). *Permanent present tense: The unforgettable life of the amnesic patient, H.M.* Allen Lane.
Cornelius, S. W., & Caspi, A. (1987). Everyday problem solving in adulthood and old age. *Psychology and Aging*, 2, 144–153.
Cornell, D., Gregory, A., Huang, F., & Fan, X. (2013). Perceived prevalence of teasing and bullying predicts high school dropout rates. *Journal of Educational Psychology*, *105*, 138–149.
Corr, C. A. (1995). Entering into adolescent understanding of death. In E. A. Grollman (Ed.), *Bereaved children and teens*. Boston, MA: Beacon Press.
Corr, C. A. (2010). Children's emerging awareness and understandings of loss and death. In C. A. Corr & D. E. Balk (Eds.), *Children's encounters with death, bereavement, and coping*. New York, NY: Springer.
Corr, C. A., & Corr, D. M. (1992). Children's hospice care. *Death Studies*, *16*, 431–449.
Corwin, J., Loury, M., & Gilbert, A. N. (1995). Workplace, age, and sex as mediators of olfactory function: Data

from the National Geographic Smell Survey. *Journals of Gerontology Series B: Psychological Sciences and Social Sciences, 50,* 179–186.

Costa, P. T., Jr., & McCrae, R. R. (1992). Trait psychology comes of age. In T. B. Sonderegger (Ed.), *Nebraska symposium on motivation: Vol. 39. Psychology and aging.* Lincoln, NE: University of Nebraska Press.

Costello, E. J., Copeland, W., & Angold, A. (2016). The Great Smoky Mountains Study: Developmental epidemiology in the southeastern United States. *Social Psychiatry and Psychiatric Epidemiology, 51,* 639–646.

Costeloe, K. L., Hennessy, E. M., Haider, S., Stacey, F., Marlow, N., & Draper, E. S. (2012). Short term outcomes after extreme preterm birth in England: Comparison of two birth cohorts in 1995 and 2006 (the EPICure studies). *British Medical Journal, 345,* e7976.

Cota-Robles, S. (2003, April). *Traditional Mexican cultural values and the reduced risk for delinquency: Acculturation, familism and parent–adolescent process.* Poster presented at the biennial meeting of the Society for Research in Child Development, Tampa, FL.

Côté, J. E., & Levine, C. G. (2016). *Identity formation, youth, and development. A simplified approach.* New York, NY: Psychology Press.

Cotten, S. R., McCullough, B. M., & Adams, R. G. (2011). Technological influences on social ties. In K. L. Fingerman, C. A. Berg, J. Smith, & T. C. Antonucci (Eds.), *Handbook of lifespan development* (pp. 649–674). New York, NY: Springer.

Coughlin, J. M., Wang, Y., Munro, C. A., Ma, S., Yue, C., Chen, S., & Pomper, M. G. (2015). Neuroinflammation and brain atrophy in former NFL players: An in vivo multimodal imaging pilot study. *Neurobiology of Disease, 74,* 58–65.

Council on Communications and Media. (2011). Children, adolescents, obesity, and the media. *Pediatrics, 128,* 201–209.

Courage, M. L., & Cowan, N. (Eds.). (2009). *The development of memory in infancy and childhood.* New York, NY: Psychology Press.

Courage, M. L., Reynolds, G. D., & Richards, J. E. (2006). Infants' attention to patterned stimuli: Developmental change from 3 to 12 months of age. *Child Development, 77,* 680–695.

Courchesne, E., Carper, R., & Akshoomoff, N. (2003). Evidence of brain overgrowth in the first year of life in autism. *Journal of the American Medical Association, 290,* 337–344.

Courchesne, E., Chisum, H. J., Townsend, J., Cowles, A., Covington, J., Egaas, B., et al. (2000). Normal brain development and aging: Quantitative analysis at in vivo MR imaging in healthy volunteers. *Radiology, 216,* 672–682.

Couturier, J., Kimber, M., & Szatmari, P. (2013). Efficacy of family-based treatment for adolescents with eating disorders: A systematic review and meta-analysis. *International Journal of Eating Disorders, 46,* 3–11.

Covington, M. V. (1998). *The will to learn.* New York, NY: Cambridge University Press.

Covington, M. V. (2000). Goal theory, motivation, and school achievement: An integrative review. *Annual Review of Psychology, 51,* 171–200.

Cowan, B. W. (2011). Forward-thinking teens: The effects of college costs on adolescent risky behavior. *Economics of Education Review, 30,* 813–825.

Cowan, C. P., & Cowan, P. A. (2000). *When partners become parents: The big life change for couples.* Mahwah, NJ: Erlbaum.

Cowan, N. (2016). Working memory maturation: Can we get at the essence of cognitive growth? *Perspectives on Psychological Science, 11,* 239–264.

Cowan, N., Morey, C. C., AuBuchon, A. M., Zwilling, C. E., & Gilchrist, A. L. (2010). Seven-year-olds allocate attention like adults unless working memory is overloaded. *Developmental Science, 13,* 120–133.

Cowan, N., Ricker, T. J., Clark, K. M., Hinrichs, G. A., & Glass, B. A. (2015). Knowledge cannot explain the developmental growth of working memory capacity. *Developmental Science, 18,* 132–145.

Cowan, P. A., & Cowan, C. P. (2006). Developmental psychopathology from family systems and family risk factors perspectives: Implications for family research, practice, and policy. In D. Cicchetti & D. J. Cohen (Eds.), *Developmental psychopathology: Vol. 1. Theory and method* (2nd ed.). Hoboken, NJ: Wiley.

Cowan, P. A., Cowan, C. P., Pruett, M. K., Pruett, K., & Wong, J. J. (2009). Promoting fathers' engagement with children: Preventive interventions for low-income families. *Journal of Marriage and Family, 71,* 663–679.

Cox, M. J., Owen, M. T., Henderson, V. K., & Margand, N. A. (1992). Prediction of infant-father and infant-mother attachment. *Developmental Psychology, 28,* 474–483.

Cox, M. J., Paley, B., Burchinal, M., & Payne, C. C. (1999). Marital perceptions and interactions across the transition to parenthood. *Journal of Marriage and the Family, 61,* 611–625.

Coyle, E. F., Fulcher, M., & Trübutschek, D. (2016). Sissies, mama's boys, and tomboys: Is children's gender nonconformity more acceptable when nonconforming traits are positive? *Archives of Sexual Behavior, 45,* 1827–1838.

Coyne, J. C., & Whiffen, V. E. (1995). Issues in personality as diathesis for depression: The case of sociotropy dependency and autonomy self-criticism. *Psychological Bulletin, 118,* 358–378.

Crabb, P. B., & Marciano, D. L. (2011). Representations of material culture and gender in award-winning children's books: A 20-year follow-up. *Journal of Research in Childhood Education, 25,* 390–398.

Crago, M. B., Allen, S. E., & Hough-Eyamir, W. P. (1997). Exploring innateness through cultural and linguistic variation. In M. Gopnik (Ed.), *The inheritance and innateness of grammars* (pp. 70–90). New York, NY: Oxford University Press.

Craig, W., Harel-Fisch, Y., Fogel-Grinvald, H., Dostaler, S., Hetland, J., Simons-Morton, B., . . . Pickett, W. (2009). A cross-national profile of bullying and victimization among adolescents in 40 countries. *International Journal of Public Health, 54* (Suppl. 2), 216–224.

Craik, F. I., Bialystok, E., & Freedman, M. (2010). Delaying the onset of Alzheimer disease: bilingualism as a form of cognitive reserve. *Neurology, 75,* 1726–9.

Cramond, B., Matthews-Morgan, J., Bandalos, D., & Zuo, L. (2005). A report on the 40-year follow-up of the Torrance Tests of Creative Thinking: Alive and well in the new millennium. *Gifted Child Quarterly, 49,* 283–291.

Crary, D. (2008, December 1). Survey finds growing deceit among teens. *The Washington Post,* A6.

Crawford, M., & Popp, D. (2003). Sexual double standards: A review and methodological critique of two decades of research. *The Journal of Sex Research, 40,* 13–26.

Creanga, A. A., Bateman, B. T., Kuklina, E. V., et al. (2014). Racial and ethnic disparities in severe maternal morbidity: A multistate analysis, 2008–2010. *American Journal of Obstetrics & Gynecology, 210,* e1–8.

Creasey, G., & Jarvis, P. (2009). Attachment and marriage. In M. C. Smith (Ed.) & N. DeFrates-Densch (Asst. Ed.), *Handbook of research on adult learning and development.* New York, NY: Routledge.

Creasy, R., Resnik, R., & Iams, J. (2009). *Creasy and Resnik's maternal-fetal medicine: principles and practice* (6th ed.). Philadelphia, PA: Elsevier Health Sciences.

Creasy, R., Resnik, R., & Iams, J. (2013). *Creasy and Resnik's maternal-fetal medicine: Principles and practice* (7th ed.). Philadelphia, PA: Elsevier Saunders.

Crepinsek, M. K., Gordon, A. R., McKinney, P. M., Condon, E. M., & Wilson, A. (2009). Meals offered and served in U.S. public schools: Do they meet nutrient standards? *Journal of the American Dietetic Association, 109,* S31–43.

Crews, F. (1996). The verdict on Freud (Review of Freud evaluated: The completed arc). *Psychological Science, 7,* 63–68.

Crick, N. R., & Bigbee, M. (1998). Relational and overt forms of peer victimization: A multiinformant approach. *Journal of Consulting and Clinical Psychology, 66,* 337–347.

Crick, N. R., & Dodge, K. A. (1994). A review and reformulation of social information-processing mechanisms in children's social adjustment. *Psychological Bulletin, 115,* 74–101.

Crijnen, A. A. M., Achenbach, T. M., & Verhulst, F. C. (1997). Comparisons of problems reported by parents of children in 12 cultures: Total problems, externalizing, and internalizing. *Journal of the American Academy of Child & Adolescent Psychiatry, 36,* 1269–1277.

Crockenberg, S., & Leerkes, E. (2003). Infant negative emotionality, caregiving, and family relationships. In A. C. Crouter & A. Booth (Eds.), *Children's influence on family dynamics. The neglected side of family relationships.* Mahwah, NJ: Erlbaum.

Crone, E. A., Bunge, S. A., van der Molen, M. W., & Ridderinkhof, K. R. (2006). Switching between tasks and responses: A developmental study. *Developmental Science, 9,* 278–287.

Crooks, R. L., & Baur, K. (2014). *Our sexuality* (12th ed.). Belmont, CA: Wadsworth Cengage Learning.

Crooks, R., & Baur, K. (2017). *Our sexuality* (13th ed). Boston, MA: Cengage Learning.

Cross, S. E. (2000). What does it mean to "know thyself" in the United States and Japan? The cultural construction of the self. In T. J. Owens (Ed.), *Self and identity through the life course in cross-cultural perspective.* Stamford, CT: JAI Press.

Crouch, J. L., & Behl, L. E. (2001). Relationships among parental beliefs in corporal punishment, reported stress, and physical child abuse potential. *Child Abuse and Neglect, 25,* 413–419.

Crouse, K. (2015, September 21). 100 years old. 5 world records. *The New York Times.* Retrieved from www.nytimes.com/2015/09/22/sports/a-bolt-from-the-past-don-pellmann-at-100-is-still-breaking-records.html.

Crouter, A. C. (2006). Mothers and fathers at work: Implications for families and children. In A. Clarke-Stewart & J. Dunn (Eds.), *Families count: Effects on child and adolescent development.* New York, NY: Cambridge University Press.

Crouter, A. C., & Booth, A. (Eds.) (2003). *Children's influence on family dynamics. The neglected side of family relationships.* Mahwah, NJ: Erlbaum.

Crouter, A. C., Whiteman, S. D., McHale, S. M., & Osgood, D. W. (2007). Development of gender attitude traditionality across middle childhood and adolescence. *Child Development, 78,* 911–926.

Crouter, A. C., Whiteman, S., & Osgood, D. W. (2007). Development of gender attitude traditionality across middle childhood and adolescence. *Child Development, 78,* 911–926.

Crowell, J. A., Fraley, R. C., & Shaver, P. R. (1999). Measurement of individual differences in adolescent and adult attachment. In J. Cassidy & P. R. Shaver (Eds.), *Handbook of attachment: Theory, research, and clinical applications.* New York: Guilford.

Crowley, S. J., Cain, S. W., Burns, A. C., Acebo, C., & Carskadon, M. A. (2015). Increased sensitivity of the circadian system to light in early/mid-puberty. *The Journal of Clinical Endocrinology and Metabolism, 100,* 4067–4073.

Cruickshanks, K. J., Nondahl, D. M., Tweed, T. S., Wiley, T. L., Klein, B. E., Klein, R., et al. (2010). Education, occupation, noise exposure history and the 10-yr cumulative incidence of hearing impairment in older adults. *Hearing Research, 264,* 3–9.

Cruikshank, M. (2009). *Learning to be old: Gender, culture, and aging* (2nd ed.). Lanham, MD: Rowman & Littlefield.

Cruse, D., Chennu, S., Chatelle, C., Bekinschtein, T. A., Fernández-Espejo, D., Pickard, J. D., & Owen, A. M. (2011). Bedside detection of awareness in the vegetative state: A cohort study. *Lancet, 378*(9809), 2088–2094.

Cruse, D., Chennu, S., Chatelle, C., Bekinschtein, T. A., Fernández-Espejo, D., Pickard, J. D., & Owen, A. M. (2013). Reanalysis of "Bedside detection of awareness in the vegetative state: A cohort study" - authors' reply. *Lancet, 381*(9863), 291–292.

Cruz, J. E., Emery, R. E., & Turkheimer, E. (2012). Peer network drinking predicts increased alcohol use from adolescence to early adulthood after controlling for genetic and shared environmental selection. *Developmental Psychology, 48,* 1390–1402.

Crystal, S., Kleinhaus, K., Perrin, M., & Malaspina, D. (2011). Advancing paternal age and the risk for schizophrenia. In A. S. Brown & P. H. Patterson (Eds.), *The origins of schizophrenia* (pp. 140–155). New York, NY: Columbia University Press.

Csibra, G., & Gergely, G. (2009). Natural pedagogy. *Trends in Cognitive Sciences, 13,* 148–153.

Csikszentmihalyi, M., & Nakamura, J. (2006). Creativity through the life span from an evolutionary systems perspective. In C. Hoare (Ed.), *Handbook of adult development and learning.* New York, NY: Oxford University Press.

Cuevas, C. A., Finkelhor, D., Clifford, C., Ormrod, R. K., & Turner, H. A. (2010). Psychological distress as a risk factor for re-victimization in children. *Child Abuse & Neglect, 34*, 235–243.

Cuevas, K., & Bell, M. A. (2014). Infant attention and early childhood executive function. *Child Development, 85*, 397–404.

Cui, M., & Donnellan, M. B. (2009). Trajectories of conflict over raising adolescent children and marital satisfaction. *Journal of Marriage and Family, 71*, 478–494.

Cui, M., Conger, R. D., & Lorenz, F. O. (2005). Predicting change in adolescent adjustment from change in marital problems. *Developmental Psychology, 41*, 812–823.

Cuijpers, P., Weitz, E., Karyotaki, E., Garber, J., & Andersson, G. (2015). The effects of psychological treatment of maternal depression on children and parental functioning: A meta-analysis. *European Child & Adolescent Psychiatry, 24*, 237–245.

Culbert, K. M., Racine, S. E., & Klump, K. L. (2015). Research review: What we have learned about the causes of eating disorders—A synthesis of sociocultural, psychological, and biological research. *Journal of Child Psychology and Psychiatry, 56*, 1141–1164.

Culpin, I., Heron, J., Araya, R., & Joinson, C. (2015). Early childhood father absence and depressive symptoms in adolescent girls from a UK cohort: The mediating role of early menarche. *Journal of Abnormal Child Psychology, 43*, 921–931.

Culpin, I., Heron, J., Araya, R., Melotti, R., Lewis, G., & Joinson, C. (2014). Father absence and timing of menarche in adolescent girls from a UK cohort: The mediating role of maternal depression and major financial problems. *Journal of Adolescence, 37*, 291–301.

Cumming, E., & Henry, W. E. (1961). *Growing old, the process of disengagement.* New York, NY: Basic Books.

Cummings, E. M., & Davies, P. (2010). *Marital conflict and children: An emotional security perspective.* New York, NY: Guilford.

Cummings, E. M., & Valentino, K. (2015). Developmental psychopathology. In W. F. Overton (Vol. Ed.), P. C. M. Molenaar (Vol. Ed.), & R. M. Lerner (Ed.), *Handbook of child psychology and developmental science: Vol. 1. Theory and method* (pp. 369–406). Hoboken, NJ: Wiley.

Cummings, S. M., Williams, M. M., & Ellis, R. A. (2003). Impact of an intergenerational program on 4th graders' attitudes toward elders and school behaviors. *Journal of Human Behavior in the Social Environment, 6*, 91–107.

Cunha, D. (2015, October 13). Giving birth at home is still no simple decision. *The Washington Post*, E5.

Cunningham, C. A., Yassa, M. A., & Egeth, H. E. (2015). Massive memory revisited: Limitations on storage capacity for object details in visual long-term memory. *Learning & Memory (Cold Spring Harbor, NY), 22*, 563–566.

Curley, J. P., Mashoodh, R., & Champagne, F. A. (2011). Epigenetics and the origins of paternal effects, *Hormones and Behavior, 59*, 306–314.

Curlik, D. M., & Shors, T. J. (2013). Training your brain: Do mental and physical (MAP) training enhance cognition through the process of neurogenesis in the hippocampus? *Neuropharmacology, 64*, 506–514.

Curran, S., & Bolton, P. (2009). Genetics of autism. In Y. Kim (Ed.), *Handbook of behavior genetics.* New York, NY: Springer.

Currier, J. M., Holland, J. M., & Neimeyer, R. A. (2012). Prolonged grief symptoms and growth in the first 2 years of bereavement: Evidence for a nonlinear association. *Traumatology, 18*, 65–71.

Curtin S. C., Warner, M., & Hedegaard, H. (2016, April). Increase in suicide in the United States, 1999–2014. *NCHS Data Brief, no. 241*, National Center for Health Statistics. Retrieved from www.cdc.gov/nchs/products/databriefs/db241.htm.

Cytron, B. D. (1993). To honor the dead and comfort the mourners: Traditions in Judaism. In D. P. Irish, K. F. Lundquist, & V. J. Nelson (Eds.), *Ethnic variations in dying, death, and grief: Diversity in universality.* Washington, DC: Taylor & Francis.

Cytryn, L., & McKnew, D. H., Jr. (1996). *Growing up sad: Childhood depression and its treatment.* New York, NY: W. W. Norton.

Dabbs, J. M., & Morris, R. (1990). Testosterone, social class, and antisocial behavior in a sample of 4462 men. *Psychological Science, 1*, 209–211.

Dagnelie, G. (2013). Age-related psychophysical changes and low vision. *Investigative Ophthalmology & Visual Science, 54*, ORSF88–93.

Daley, C. E., & Onwuegbuzie, A. J. (2011). Race and intelligence. In R. Sternberg & S. B. Kaufman (Eds.), *The Cambridge handbook of intelligence* (pp. 293–306). New York, NY: Cambridge University Press.

Dalton, D. S., Cruickshanks, K. J., Klein, B. E., Klein, R., Wiley, T. L., & Nonhdahl, D. M. (2003) The impact of hearing loss on quality of life in older adults. *Gerontologist 43*, 661–668.

Daly, M., Delaney, L., Egan, M., & Baumeister, R. F. (2015). Childhood self-control and unemployment throughout the life span: Evidence from two British cohort studies. *Psychological Science, 26*, 709–723.

Damon, W. (1977). *The social world of the child.* San Francisco, CA: Jossey-Bass.

Damon, W. (1994). *Greater expectations: Overcoming the culture of indulgence in America's homes and schools.* New York, NY: Free Press.

Damon, W., & Hart, D. (1988). *Self-understanding in childhood and adolescence.* New York, NY: Cambridge University Press.

Damon, W., & Lerner, R. M. (Eds.). (2006). *Handbook of child psychology* (6th ed.). Hoboken, NJ: John Wiley & Sons.

Daneshvar, D. H., Riley, D. O., Nowinski, C. J., McKee, A. C., Stern, R. A., & Cantu, R. C. (2011). Long-term consequences: Effects on normal development profile after concussion. *Physical Medicine and Rehabilitation Clinics of North America, 22*, 683–700, ix.

Daniels, H. (2011). Vygotsky and psychology. In U. Goswami, (Ed.), *The Wiley-Blackwell handbook of childhood cognitive development*, (2nd ed., pp. 673–696). Malden, MA: John Wiley.

Daniels, L. M., Stupnisky, R. H., Pekrun, R., Haynes, T. L., Perry, R. P., & Newall, N. E. (2009). A longitudinal analysis of achievement goals: From affective antecedents to emotional effects and achievement outcomes. *Journal of Educational Psychology, 101*, 948–963.

Dapretto, M., Davies, M. S., Pfeifer, J. H., Scott, A. A., Sigman, M., Bookheimer, S. Y., & Iacoboni, M. (2006). Understanding emotions in others: Mirror neuron dysfunction in children with autism spectrum disorders. *Nature Neuroscience, 9*, 28–30.

Darling, N., & Steinberg, L. (1993). Parenting style as context: An integrative model. *Psychological Bulletin, 113*, 487–496.

Darnon, C., Dompnier, B., Gilliéorn, O., & Butera, F. (2010). The interplay of mastery and performance goals in social comparison: A multiple-goal perspective. *Journal of Educational Psychology, 102*, 212–222.

Darwin, C. (1859). *The origin of species.* New York, NY: Modern Library.

Darwin, C. A. (1877). A biographical sketch of an infant. *Mind, 2*, 285–294.

Datan, N., Greene, A. L., & Reese, H. W. (Eds.). (1986). *Life-span developmental psychology: Intergenerational relations.* New York, NY: Lawrence Erlbaum Associates.

Daugherty, A. M., & Ofen, N. (2015). That's a good one! Belief in efficacy of mnemonic strategies contributes to age-related increase in associative memory. *Journal of Experimental Child Psychology, 136*, 17–29.

Davies, B., Collins, J., Steele, R., Cook, K., Distler, V., & Brenner, A. (2007). Parents' and children's perspectives of a children's hospice bereavement program. *Journal of Palliative Care, 23*, 14–23.

Davies, S. G. (2006). Thinking of gender in a holistic sense: Understandings of gender in Sulawesi, Indonesia. In D. Vasilikie & M. T. Segal (Eds.), *Gender and the local-global nexus: Vol. 10. Theory, research, and action* (pp. 1–24). Emerald Group Publishing Limited.

Davies, S. G. (2007). *Challenging gender norms: Five genders among Bugis in Indonesia. Case studies in cultural anthropology.* Belmont, CA: Thomson Wadsworth.

Davies, S. L., DiClemente, R. J., Wingood, G. M., Harrington, K. F., Crosby, R. A., & Sionean, C. (2003). Pregnancy desire among disadvantaged African American adolescent females. *American Journal of Health Behavior, 27*, 55–62.

Davila, E. P., Caban-Martinez, A. J., Muennig, P., Lee, D. J., Fleming, L. E., Ferraro, K. F., et al. (2009). Sensory impairment among older US workers. *American Journal of Public Health, 99*, 1378–1385.

Davinelli, S., Willcox, D. C., & Scapagnini, G. (2012). Extending healthy ageing: Nutrient sensitive pathway and centenarian population. *Immunity & Ageing: I & A, 9*, 9.

Davis, A. S. (Ed.). (2012). *Psychopathology of childhood and adolescence. A neuropsychological approach.* New York, NY: Springer.

Davis, D. W., Finkel, D., Turkheimer, E., & Dickens, W. (2015). Genetic and environmental contributions to behavioral stability and change in children 6–36 months of age using Louisville Twin Study data. *Behavior Genetics, 45*, 610–621.

Davis, E. P., Glynn, L. M., Waffram, F., & Sandman, C. A. (2011). Prenatal maternal stress programs infant stress regulation. *Journal of Child Psychology and Psychiatry, 52*, 119–129.

Davis, K., Christodoulou, J., Seider, S., & Gardner, H. (2011). The theory of multiple intelligence. In R. J. Sternberg & S. B. Kaufman (Eds.), *The Cambridge handbook of intelligence* (pp. 485–503). New York, NY: Cambridge University Press.

Davis, N., Gross, J., & Hayne, H. (2008). Defining the boundary of childhood amnesia. *Memory, 16*, 465–474.

Davis, O. S. P., Butcher, L. M., Docherty, S. J., Meaburn, E. L., Curtis, C. J. C., Simpson, M. A., et al. (2010). A three-stage genome-wide association study of general cognitive ability: Hunting the small effects. *Behavior Genetics, 40*, 759–767.

Davis, O., Haworth, C., & Plomin, R. (2009). Dramatic increase in heritability of cognitive development from early to middle childhood: An 8-year longitudinal study of 8,700 pairs of twins. *Psychological Science, 20*, 1301–1308.

Davis, P. E., Meins, E., & Fernyhough, C. (2013). Individual differences in children's private speech: The role of imaginary companions. *Journal of Experimental Child Psychology, 116*, 561–571.

Davis, P. E., Meins, E., & Fernyhough, C. (2014). Children with imaginary companions focus on mental characteristics when describing their real-life friends. *Infant and Child Development, 23*, 622–633.

Dawood, K., Bailey, J. M., & Martin, N. G. (2009). Genetic and environmental influences on sexual orientation. In Y. Kim (Ed.), *Handbook of behavior genetics.* New York, NY: Springer.

Dawson, G., & Ashman, S. B. (2000). On the origins of a vulnerability to depression: The influence of the early social environment on the development of psychobiological systems related to risk for affective disorder. In C. A. Nelson (Ed.), *Minnesota Symposium on Child Psychology: Vol. 31. The effects of early adversity on neurobehavioral development.* Mahwah, NJ: Erlbaum.

Dawson, G., Jones, E. J. H., Merkle, K., Venema, K., Lowy, R., Faja, S., et al. (2012). Early behavioral intervention is associated with normalized brain activity in young children with autism. *Journal of the American Academy of Child & Adolescent Psychiatry, 51*, 1150–1159.

Dawson, G., Rogers, S., Munson, J., Smith, M., Winter, J., Greenson, J., et al. (2010). Randomized, controlled trial of an intervention for toddlers with autism: The Early Start Denver Model. *Pediatrics, 125*, e17–e23.

Day, N. L., Goldschmidt, L., & Thomas, C. A. (2006). Prenatal marijuana exposure contributes to the prediction of marijuana use at age 14. *Addiction, 101*, 1313–1322.

Day, R. D., & Peterson, G. W. (1998). Predicting spanking of younger and older children by mothers and fathers. *Journal of Marriage & the Family, 60*, 79–92.

Daysal, N. M., Trandafir, M., & van Ewijk, R. (2015). Saving lives at birth: The impact of home births on infant outcomes. *American Economic Journal: Applied Economics, 7*, 28–50.

de Heering, A., Rossion, B., & Maurer, D. (2012). Developmental changes in face recognition during childhood: Evidence from upright and inverted faces. *Cognitive Development, 27*, 17–27.

De Goede, I. H. A., Branje, S. J. T., & Meeus, W. H. J. (2009). Developmental changes in adolescents' perceptions of relationships with their parents. *Journal of Youth and Adolescence, 38*, 75–88.

De Graaf, H., Vanwesenbeeck, I., & Meijer, S. (2015). Educational differences in adolescents' sexual health: A pervasive phenomenon in a national Dutch sample. *Journal of Sex Research, 52*, 747–757.

de Jong-Gierveld, J. (1986). Loneliness and the degree of intimacy in interpersonal relationships. In R. Gilmour & S. Duck (Eds.), *The emerging field of personal relationships.* Hillsdale, NJ: Erlbaum.

De Lisi, R., & Staudt, J. (1980). Individual differences in college students' performance on formal operations tasks. *Journal of Applied Psychology, 1*, 163–174.

de St. Aubin, E., & Bach, M. (2015). Explorations in generativity and culture. In L. A. Jensen (Ed.), *The Oxford handbook of human development and culture: An interdisciplinary perspective* (pp. 653–665). New York, NY: Oxford University Press.

de St. Aubin, E., McAdams, D. P., & Kim, T. (2004). The generative society: An introduction. In E. de St. Aubin, D. P. McAdams, & T. Kim (Eds.), *The generative society: Caring for future generations.* Washington, DC: American Psychological Association.

De Vise, D. (2011, May 21). Gaithersburg woman earns college degree two decades after complete memory loss. *The Washington Post, Education Section.* Retrieved from articles.washingtonpost.com/2011-05-21/local/35265255_1_amnesia-memory-husband.

de Weerth, C., van Hees, Y. H., & Buitelaar, J. K. (2003). Prenatal maternal cortisol levels and infant behavior during the first 5 months. *Early Human Development, 74*, 139–151.

De Wolff, M. S., & van IJzendoorn, M. H. (1997). Sensitivity and attachment: A meta-analysis on parental antecedents of infant attachment. *Child Development, 68*, 571–591.

Deary, I. J., & Ritchie, S. J. (2016). Processing speed differences between 70- and 83-year-olds matched on childhood IQ. *Intelligence, 55*, 28–33.

Deary, I. J., Pattie, A., & Starr, J. M. (2013). The stability of intelligence from age 11 to age 90 years: The Lothian birth cohort of 1921. *Psychological Science, 24*, 2361–2368.

Deary, I. J., Strand, S., Smith, P., & Fernandes, C. (2007). Intelligence and educational achievement. *Intelligence, 35*, 13–21.

Deary, I. J., Whalley, L. J., & Starr, J. M. (2009). *A lifetime of intelligence: Follow-up studies of the Scottish mental surveys of 1932 and 1947.* Washington, DC: American Psychological Association.

Deary, I. J., Whiteman, M. C., Starr, J. M., Whalley, L. J., & Fox, H. C. (2004). The impact of childhood intelligence on later life: Following up the Scottish Mental Surveys of 1932 and 1947. *Journal of Personality and Social Psychology, 86*, 130–147.

Deater-Deckard, K., Dodge, K. A., & Sorbring, E. (2005). Cultural differences in the effects of physical punishment. In M. Rutter & M. Tienda (Eds.), *Ethnicity and causal mechanisms.* New York, NY: Cambridge University Press.

Debnath, M., Venkatasubramanian, G., & Berk, M. (2015). Fetal programming of schizophrenia: Select mechanisms. *Neuroscience and Biobehavioral Reviews, 49*, 90–104.

DeCasper, A. J., & Fifer, W. P. (1980). Of human bonding: Newborns prefer their mothers' voices. *Science, 208*, 1174–1176.

DeCasper, A. J., & Spence, M. J. (1986). Prenatal maternal speech influences newborns' perception of speech sounds. *Infant Behavior and Development, 9*, 133–150.

Decety, J., & Howard. L. H. (2014). A neurodevelopmental perspective on morality. In M. Killen & J. G. Smetana (Eds.), *Handbook of moral development* (2nd ed., pp. 454–474). New York, NY: Psychology Press.

Decety, J., Michalska, K. J., & Kinzler, C. D. (2012). The contribution of emotion and cognition to moral sensitivity: A neurodevelopmental study. *Cerebral Cortex, 22*, 209–220.

Declercq, E. (2012). Trends in midwife-attended births in the United States, 1989–2009. *Journal of Midwifery & Women's Health, 57*, 321–326.

Dee, T., & Jacob, B. A. (2010). The impact of No Child Left Behind on students, teachers, and schools. *Brookings Papers on Economic Activity, 149*–207.

Defoe, I. N., Dubas, J. S., Figner, B., & van Aken, M. A. G. (2015). A meta-analysis on age differences in risky decision making: Adolescents versus children and adults. *Psychological Bulletin, 141*, 48–84.

DeFrain, J. D., Jakub, D. K., & Mendoza, B. L. (1991–1992). The psychological effects of sudden infant death on grandmothers and grandfathers. *Omega: Journal of Death and Dying, 24*, 165–182.

DeFrain, J., Taylor, J., & Ernst, L. (1982). *Coping with sudden infant death.* Lexington, MA: Lexington Books.

DeFranco, E., Hall, E., Hossain, M., Chen, A., Haynes, E. N., Jones, D., et al. (2015). Air pollution and stillbirth risk: Exposure to airborne particulate matter during pregnancy is associated with fetal death. *PLoS ONE 10*(3): e0120594.

DeGue, S. (2014). *Preventing sexual violence on college campuses: Lessons from research and practice.* Retrieved 8/19/2016 from www.notalone.gov/assets/evidence-based-strategies-for-the-prevention-of-sv-perpetration.pdf.

DeGue, S., Holt, M. K., Massetti, G. M., Matjasko, J. L., Tharp, A. T., & Valle, L. A. (2012). Looking ahead toward community-level strategies to prevent sexual violence. *Journal of Women's Health, 21*, 1–3.

Dehaene, S. (2009). *Reading in the brain: The science and evolution of a human invention.* New York, NY: Viking.

Dekker, T. M., & Karmiloff-Smith, A. (2011). The dynamics of ontogeny. In O. J. Braddick, J. Atkinson, & G. M. Innocenti (Eds.), *Progress in brain research, 0079–6123: Vol. 189. Gene expression to neurobiology and behavior: Vol. 189. Human brain development and developmental disorders* (pp. 23–33). Amsterdam, Oxford, UK: Elsevier.

Del Giudice, M. (2009). Sex, attachment, and the development of reproductive strategies. *Behavioral Brain Science, 32*, 1–67.

Del Vecchio, T., Eckardt Erlanger, A. C., & Smith Slep, A. M. (2013). Theories of child abuse. In M. A. Fine & F. D. Fincham (Eds.), *Handbook of family theories. A context-based approach.* New York, NY: Routledge.

DeLamater, J. (2012). Sexual expression in later life: A review and synthesis. *Journal of Sex Research, 49*, 125–141.

DeLamater, J. D., & Sill, M. (2005). Sexual desire in later life. *Journal of Sex Research, 42*, 138–149.

Delano-Wood, L., Bigler, E. D., Nation, D. A., Clark, A., Au, R., & Bondi, M. W. (2015). Clinico-behavioral and neuropathological sequelae of traumatic brain injury in the aging brain. In P. A. Lichtenberg & B. T. Mast (Eds. in Chief), B. D. Carpenter & J. L. Wetherell, (Assoc. Eds.), *APA handbook of clinical geropsychology: Vol. 2. Assessment, treatment, and issues of later life* (pp. 247–270). Washington, DC: American Psychological Association.

Delara, M., Ghofranipour, F., Azadfallah, P. Tavafian, S. S., Kazemnejad, A., & Montazeri, A. (2012). Health related quality of life among adolescent with premenstrual disorders: A cross sectional study. *Health and Quality of Life Outcomes, 10*, 1–5.

Delaunay-El Allam, M., Marlier, L., & Schaal, B. (2006). Learning at the breast: Preference formation for an artificial scent and its attraction against the odor of material milk. *Infant Behavioral Development, 29*, 308–321.

DeLeire, T. C., & Kalil A. (2002). Good things come in threes: Single-parent multigenerational family structure and adolescent adjustment. *Demography, 39*, 393–413.

Delespaux, E., Ryckebosch-Dayez, A., Heeren, A., & Zech, E. (2013). Attachment and severity of grief: The mediating role of negative appraisal and inflexible coping. *Omega: Journal of Death and Dying, 67*, 269–289.

DeLisi, M. (2016). Career criminals and the antisocial life course. *Child Development Perspectives, 10*, 53–58.

DeLoache, J. S., Cassidy, D. J., & Brown, A. L. (1985). Precursors of mnemonic strategies in very young children's memory. *Child Development, 56*, 125–137.

DeLoache, J. S., Chiong, C. S., Sherman, K., Islam, N., Vanderborght, M., Troseth, G. L., et al. (2010). Do babies learn from baby media? *Psychological Science, 21*, 1570–1574.

DeLoache, J. S., Miller, K. F., & Pierroutsakos, S. L. (1998). Reasoning and problem solving. In D. Kuhn & R. Siegler (Vol. Eds.), W. Damon (Editor-in-Chief), *Handbook of child psychology: Vol. 2. Cognition, perception, and language* (5th ed., pp. 801–850). New York, NY: Wiley.

Deluty, J. A., Atzmon, G., Crandall, J., Barzilai, N., & Milman, S. (2015). The influence of gender on inheritance of exceptional longevity. *Aging, 7*, 412–418.

DeMarie, D., & Ferron, J. (2003). Capacity, strategies, and metamemory: Tests of a three-factor model of memory development. *Journal of Experimental Child Psychology, 84*, 167–193.

DeMarie, D., Norman, A., & Abshier, D. W. (2000). Age and experience influence different verbal and nonverbal measures of children's scripts for the zoo. *Cognitive Development, 15*, 241–262.

Demo, D. H., & Buehler, C. (2013). Theoretical approaches to studying divorce. In M. A. Fine & F. D. Fincham (Eds.), *Handbook of family theories. A context-based approach.* New York, NY: Routledge.

Demo, D. H., & Cox, M. J. (2000). Families with young children: A review of research in the 1990s. *Journal of Marriage and the Family, 62*, 876–895.

Demo, D. H., & Fine, M. A. (2010). *Beyond the average divorce.* Los Angeles, CA: Sage.

Denham, S. A., Bassett, H. H., & Wyatt, T. (2007). The socialization of emotional competence. In J. E. Grusec, & P. D. Hastings (Eds.), *Handbook of socialization: Theory and research.* New York, NY: Guilford Press.

Denham, S. A., Blair, K. A., DeMulder, E., Levitas, J., Sawyer, K., Auerbach-Major, S., & Queenan, P. (2003). Preschool emotional competence: Pathway to social competence? *Child Development, 74*, 238–256.

Denissen, J. J., Zarratt, N. R., & Eccles, J. S. (2007). I like to do it, I'm able, and I know I am: Longitudinal couplings between domain-specific achievement, self-concept, and interest. *Child Development, 78*, 430–447.

Denney, N. W. (1989). Everyday problem solving: Methodological issues, research findings, and a model. In L. W. Poon, D. C. Rubin, & B. A. Wilson (Eds.), *Everyday cognition in adulthood and late life.* Cambridge, UK: Cambridge University Press.

Denney, N. W., & Pearce, K. A. (1989). A developmental study of practical problem solving in adults. *Psychology and Aging, 4*, 438–442.

Dennis, C. L., & Dowswell, T. (2013). Psychosocial and psychological interventions for preventing postpartum depression (Review). *Cochrane Database Systematic Review, 2.*

Dennis, W. (1966). Creative productivity between the ages of 20 and 80 years. *Journal of Gerontology, 21*, 1–8.

Denworth, L. (2006, April 10). The sun has finally come out for Alex. *Newsweek*, p. 26.

Deoni, S. C. L., Dean, D. C., III, Remer, J., Dirks, H., & O'Muircheartaigh, J. (2015). Cortical maturation and myelination in healthy toddlers and young children. *NeuroImage, 115*, 147–161.

Der, G., Batty, G. D., & Deary, I. J. (2009). The association between IQ in adolescence and a range of health outcomes at 40 in the 1979 US National Longitudinal Study of Youth. *Intelligence, 37*, 573–580.

deRegnier, R., & Desai, S. (2010). Fetal development. In J. Gavin Bremner & T. D. Wachs (Eds.), *The Wiley-Blackwell handbook of infant development: Vol. 2. Applied and Policy Issues* (2nd ed., pp. 9–32). West Sussex, UK: Blackwell Publishing.

Derntl, B., Schöpf, V., Kollndorfer, K., & Lanzenberger, R. (2013). Menstrual cycle phase and duration of oral contraception intake affect olfactory perception. *Chemical Senses, 38*, 67–75.

DeRosier, M. E., & Thomas, J. M. (2003). Strengthening sociometric prediction: Scientific advances in the assessment of children's peer relations. *Child Development, 74*, 1379–1392.

DES Action. (2010). *DES daughters.* Retrieved from www.desaction.org/desdaughters.htm.

DESAction. (2015). www.desaction.org/.

Desrochers, S. (2008). From Piaget to specific Genevan developmental models. *Child Development Perspectives, 2*, 7–12.

DesRosiers, F., Vrsalovic, W. T., Knauf, D. E., Vargas, M., & Busch-Rossnagel, N. A. (1999). Assessing the multiple dimensions of the self-concept of young children: A focus on Latinos. *Merrill-Palmer Quarterly, 45*, 543–566.

Detert, J. R., Treviño, L. K., & Sweitzer, V. L. (2008). Moral disengagement in ethical decision making: A study of antecedents and outcome. *Journal of Applied Psychology, 93*, 374–391.

Deutsch, F. M. (1999). *Having it all: How equally shared parenting works.* Cambridge, MA: Harvard University Press.

Deutsch, F. M. (2001). Equally shared parenting. *Current Directions in Psychological Science, 10*, 25–28.

Devenny, D. A., Silverman, W. P., Hill, A. L., Jenkins, E., Sersen, E. A., & Wisniewski, K. E. (1996). Normal ageing in adults with Down's syndrome: A longitudinal study. *Journal of Intellectual Disability Research, 40*, 208–221.

DeVries, M. W. (1984). Temperament and infant mortality among the Masai of East Africa. *American Journal of Psychiatry, 141*, 1189–1194.
DeVries, R. (2000). Vygotsky, Piaget, and education: A reciprocal assimilation of theories and educational practices. *New Ideas in Psychology, 18*, 187–213.
Dew, J., & Wilcox, W. B. (2011). If momma ain't happy: Explaining declines in marital satisfaction among new mothers. *Journal of Marriage and Family*, 73, 1–12.
Dewar, R. E., Kline, D. W., & Swanson, H. A. (1995). Age differences in the comprehension of traffic sign symbols. *Transportation Research Record, 1456*, 1–10.
DeWitt, A. L., Cready, C. M., & Seward, R. R. (2013). Parental role portrayals in twentieth century children's picture books: More egalitarian or ongoing stereotyping? *Sex Roles, 69*, 89–106.
Dewsbury, D. A. (2009). Charles Darwin and psychology at the bicentennial and sesquicentennial: An Introduction. *American Psychologist, 64*, 67–74.
Di Giorgio, E., Leo, I., Pascalis, O., & Simion, F. (2012). Is the face-perception system human-specific at birth? *Developmental Psychology*, 48, 1083–1090.
Diamond, G. M., Shahar, B., Sabo, D., & Tsvieli, N. (2016). Attachment-based family therapy and emotion-focused therapy for unresolved anger: The role of productive emotional processing. *Psychotherapy*, 53, 34–44.
Diamond, L. (2008). Female bisexuality from adolescence to adulthood: Results from a 10-year longitudinal study. *Developmental Psychology, 44*, 5–14.
Diamond, L. M., & Butterworth, M. (2009). The close relationships of sexual minorities. Partners, friends, and family. In M. C. Smith (Ed.) & N. DeFrates-Densch (Asst. Ed.), *Handbook of research on adult learning and development*. New York, NY: Routledge.
Diamond, L. M., & Fagundes, C. P. (2010). Psychobiological research on attachment. *Journal of Social and Personal Relationships, 27*, 218–225.
Diamond, L. M., Pardo, S. T., & Butterworth, M. R. (2011). Transgender experience and identity. In J. S. Schwartz, K. Luyckx, & L. V. Vignoles, (Eds.), *Handbook of identity theory and research* (pp. 629–647). New York, NY: Springer.
Diamond, L. M., Savin-Williams, R., & Dubé, E. M. (1999). Sex, dating, passionate friendships, and romance: Intimate peer relations among lesbian, gay, and bisexual adolescents. In W. Furman, B. B. Brown & C. Feiring (Eds.), *The Development of Romantic Relationships in Adolescents* (pp. 175–210). New York, NY: Cambridge University Press.
Diamond, M., & Sigmundson, H. K. (1997). Sex reassignment at birth: Long-term review and clinical implications. *Archives of Pediatric and Adolescent Medicine, 151*, 298–304.
Diaz, A., & Eisenberg, N. (2015). The process of emotion regulation is different from individual differences in emotion regulation: Conceptual arguments and a focus on individual differences. *Psychological Inquiry, 26*, 37–47.
Dick, D. M., Meyers, J. L., Latendresse, S. J., Creemers, H. E., Lansford, J. E., Pettit, G. S., et al. (2011). CHRM2, parental monitoring, and adolescent externalizing behavior: Evidence for gene-environment interaction. *Psychological Science, 22*, 481–899.
Dick, D. M., Prescott, C., & McGue, M. (2009). The genetics of substance use and substance use disorders. In Y. Kim (Ed.), *Handbook of behavior genetics*. New York, NY: Springer.
Dickens, W. T., & Flynn, J. R. (2006). Black Americans reduce the racial IQ gap: Evidence from standardization samples. *Psychological Science, 17*, 913–920.
Dickerson, A., & Popli, G. K. (2016). Persistent poverty and children's cognitive development: Evidence from the UK Millennium Cohort Study. *Journal of the Royal Statistical Society: Series A, 179*, 535–558.
Didonato, M. D., & Berenbaum, S. A. (2010, April 3). The benefits and drawbacks of gender typing: How different dimensions are related to psychological adjustment. *Archives of Sexual Behavior, 40*, 457–463.
Diego, M. A., Field, T., & Hernandez-Reif, M. (2005). Vagal activity, gastric motility, and weight gain in massaged preterm neonates. *The Journal of Pediatrics, 147*, 50–55.
Diehl, M., Youngblade, L. M., Hay, E. L., & Chui, H. (2011). The development of self-representations across the life span. In K. L. Fingerman, C. A. Berg, J. Smith, & T. C. Antonucci (Eds.). *Handbook of life-span development*. New York, NY: Springer.
Diekelmann, S., & Born, J. (2010). The memory function of sleep. *Nature Reviews, 11*, 114–126.
Diekelmann, S., Wilhelm, I., & Born, J. (2009). The whats and whens of sleep-dependent memory consolidation. *Sleep Medicine Reviews, 13*(5), 309–321.
Diekman, A. B., & Murnen, S. K. (2004). Learning to be little women and little men: The inequitable gender equality of nonsexist children's literature. *Sex Roles, 50*, 373–385.
Dietz, L. J., Stoyak, S., Melhem, N., Porta, G., Matthews, K. A., Walker Payne, M., & Brent, D. A. (2013). Cortisol response to social stress in parentally bereaved youth. *Biological Psychiatry*, 73, 379–387.
Digman, J. M. (1990). Personality structure: Emergence of the 5-factor model. *Annual Review of Psychology, 41*, 417–440.
DiLalla, L. F., Bersted, K., & John, S. G. (2015). Peer victimization and DRD4 genotype influence problem behaviors in young children. *Journal of Youth and Adolescence, 44*, 1478–1493.
Dillon, M., & Wink, P. (2007). *In the course of a lifetime: Tracing religious belief, practice, and change*. Ewing, NJ: University of California Press.
Dimmock, P. W., Wyatt, K. M., Jones, P. W., & O'Brien, P. M. S. (2000). Efficacy of selective serotonin-reuptake inhibitors in premenstrual syndrome: A systematic review. *Lancet*, 356, 1131–1136.
Ding, X. P., Wellman, H. M., Wang, Y., Fu, G., & Lee, K. (2015). Theory-of-mind training causes honest young children to lie. *Psychological Science, 26*, 1–10.
Dionne, G., Tremblay, R., Boivin, M., Laplante, D., & Perusse, D. (2003). Physical aggression and expressive vocabulary in 19-month-old twins. *Developmental Psychology*, 39, 261–273.
DiPietro, J. A., Bornsetin, M. H., Hahn, C., Costigan, K., & Achy-Brou, A. (2007). Fetal heart rate and variability: Stability and prediction to developmental outcomes in early childhood. *Child Development*, 78, 1788–1798.
DiPietro, J. A., Goldshore, M. A., Kivlighan, K. T., Pater, H. A., & Costigan, K. A. (2015). The ups and downs of early mothering. *Journal of Psychosomatic Obstetrics & Gynecology*, 36, 94–102.
DiPietro, J. A., Hodgson, D. M., Costigan, K. A., Hilton, S. C., & Johnson, T. R. B. (1996a). Fetal antecedents of infant temperament. *Child Development*, 67, 2568–2583.
DiPietro, J. A., Hodgson, D. M., Costigan, K. A., Hilton, S. C., & Johnson, T. R. B. (1996b). Fetal neurobehavioral development. *Child Development, 67*, 2553–2567.
DiPietro, J. A., Novak, M. F. S. X., Costigan, K. A., Atella, L. D., & Reusing, S. P. (2006). Maternal psychological distress during pregnancy in relation to child development at age two. *Child Development*, 77, 573–587.
Dirix, C. E. H., Nijhuis, J. G., Jongsma, H. W., & Hornstra, G. (2009). Aspects of fetal learning and memory. *Child Development*, 80, 1251–1258.
Dittman, R. W., Kappes, M. E., & Kappes, M. H. (1992). Sexual behavior in adolescent and adult females with congenital adrenal hyperplasia. *Psychoneuroendocrinology*, 17, 153–170.
Dittmar, H., Halliwell, E., & Ive, S. (2006). Does Barbie make girls want to be thin? The effect of experimental exposure to images of dolls on the body image of 5- to 8-year-old girls. *Developmental Psychology*, 42, 283–292.
Dixon, R. A. (1992). Contextual approaches to adult intellectual development. In R. J. Sternberg & C. A. Berg (Eds.), *Intellectual development*. New York, NY: Cambridge University Press.
Dixon, R. A. (2003). Themes in the aging of intelligence: Robust decline with intriguing possibilities. In R. J. Sternberg, J. Lautrey, & T. I. Lubart (Eds.), *Models of intelligence: International perspectives* (pp. 151–167). Washington, DC: American Psychological Association.
Dobbie, W., & Fryer, R. G. (2013). Getting beneath the veil of effective schools: Evidence from New York City. *American Economic Journal: Applied Economics*, 5, 28–60.
Dodge, K. A. (1986). A social information processing model of social competence in children. In M. Perlmutter (Ed.), *Minnesota Symposia on Child Psychology: Vol. 18*. Hillsdale, NJ: Erlbaum.
Dodge, K. A. (1993). Social-cognitive mechanisms in the development of conduct disorder and depression. *Annual Review of Psychology*, 44, 559–584.
Dodge, K. A. (2009). Mechanisms of gene-environment interaction effects in the development of conduct disorder. *Perspectives on Psychological Science, 4*, 408–414.
Dodge, K. A., & Coleman, D. L. (Eds.) (2009). *Preventing child maltreatment. Community approaches*. New York, NY: Guilford.
Dodge, K. A., & Rutter, M. (Eds.). (2011). *Gene-environment interactions in developmental psychopathology*. New York, NY: Guilford.
Dodge, K. A., Coie, J. D., & Lynam, D. (2006). Aggression and antisocial behavior in youth. In N. Eisenberg (Vol. Ed.), & W. Damon & R. M. Lerner (Eds. in Chief), *Handbook of child psychology: Vol. 3. Social, emotional, and personality development* (6th ed.). Hoboken, NJ: Wiley.
Dodge, K. A., Godwin, J., & the Conduct Problems Prevention Research Group. (2013). Social-information-processing patterns mediate the impact of preventive intervention on adolescent antisocial behavior. *Psychological Science*, 24, 456–465.
Dodge, K. A., Greenberg, M. T., Malone, P. S., & Conduct Problems Prevention Research Group. (2008). Testing an idealized dynamic cascade model of the development of serious violence in adolescence. *Child Development*, 79, 1907–1927.
Dodge, K. A., Malone, P. S., Lansford, J. E., Miller, S., Pettit, G. S., & Bates, J. E. (2009). A dynamic cascade model of the development of substance-use onset. *Monographs of the Society for Research in Child Development*, 74(3, Serial No. 294).
Dodson, C. S., Bawa, S., & Krueger, L. E. (2007). Aging, metamemory, and high-confidence errors: A misrecollection account. *Psychological Aging, 22*, 122–133.
Doherty, M. J. (2009). *Theory of mind. How children understand others' thoughts and feelings*. New York, NY: Psychology Presss.
Dohnt, H., & Tiggemann, M. (2006). The contribution of peer and media influences to the development of body satisfaction and self-esteem in young girls: A prospective study. *Developmental Psychology*, 42, 929–936.
Doka, K. J. (1989). *Disenfranchised grief: Recognizing hidden sorrow*. Lexington, MA: Lexington Books.
Doka, K. J. (2008). Disenfranchised grief in historical and cultural perspective. In M. S. Stroebe, R. O. Hansson, H. Schut, & W. Stroebe (Eds.), *Handbook of bereavement research and practice. Advances in theory and intervention*. Washington, DC: American Psychological Association.
Doka, K. J. (2016). *Grief is a journey. Finding your path through loss*. New York, NY: Atria Books.
Dolen, L. S., & Bearison, D. J. (1982). Social interaction and social cognition in aging. *Human Development*, 25, 430–442.
Domjan, M. J. (1993). *Principles of learning and behavior* (3rd ed.). Pacific Grove, CA: Brooks/Cole.
Donat, D. J. (2006). Reading their way: A balanced approach that increases achievement. *Reading and Writing Quarterly*, 22, 305–323.
Dong, F., Zheng, R., Chen, X., Wang, Y., Zhou, H., & Sun, R. (2016). Caring for dying cancer patients in the Chinese cultural context: A qualitative study from the perspectives of physicians and nurses. *European Journal of Oncology Nursing, 21*, 189–196.
Donkin, I., Versteyhe, S. Ingerslev, L. R., Qian, K., Mechta, M., Nordkap, L., ...& Barrès, R. (2016). Obesity and bariatric surgery drive epigenetic variation of spermatozoa in humans. *Cell Metabolism*, 23, 1–10.
Donnellan, M. B., Martin, M. J., Conger, K. J., & Conger, R. D. (2013). Economic distress and poverty in families. In M. A. Fine & F. D. Fincham (Eds.), *Handbook of family theories. A context-based approach*. New York, NY: Routledge.
Donnelly, K., & Twenge, J. M. (2016). Masculine and feminine traits on the Bem Sex-Role Inventory, 1993–2012: A cross-temporal meta-analysis. *Sex Roles*, 39, 1–10.
Donnelly, K., Twenge, J. M., Clark, M. A., Shaikh, S. K., Beiler-May, A., & Carter, N. T. (2016). Attitudes toward women's work and family roles in the United States, 1976–2013. *Psychology of Women Quarterly*, 40, 41–54.
Donnelly, N., Cave, K., Greenway, R., Hadwin, J. A., Stevenson, J., & Sonuga-Barke, E. (2007). Visual search in children and adults: Top-down and bottom-

up mechanisms. *Quarterly Journal of Experimental Psychology, 60*, 120–136.
Doornwaard, S. M., Branje, S., Meeus, W. H. J., & ter Bogt, T. F. M. (2012). Development of adolescents' peer crowd identification in relation to changes in problem behaviors. *Developmental Psychology, 48*, 1366–1380.
Dopp, A. R., & Cain, A. C. (2012). The role of peer relationships in parental bereavement during childhood and adolescence. *Death Studies, 36*, 41–60.
Dorn, L. D., Susman, E. J., & Ponirakis, A. (2003). Pubertal timing and adolescent adjustment and behavior: Conclusions vary by rater. *Journal of Youth and Adolescence*, 32, 157–167.
Doss, B. D., Rhoades, G. K., Stanley, S. M., & Markman, H. J. (2009). The effect of the transition to parenthood on relationship quality: An eight-year prospective study. *Journal of Personality and Social Psychology, 96*, 601–619.
Dotterer, A. M., McHale, S. J., & Crouter, A. C. (2009). The development and correlates of academic interests from childhood through adolescence. *Journal of Educational Psychology, 101*, 509–519.
Doty, R. L., & Cameron, E. L. (2009). Sex differences and reproductive hormone influences on human odor perception. *Physiological Behavior*, 97, 213–228.
Dougherty, T. M., & Haith, M. M. (1997). Infant expectations and reaction time as predictors of childhood speed of processing and IQ. *Developmental Psychology*, 33, 146–155.
Douglass, S., & Umaña-Taylor, A. J. (2015). Development of ethnic–racial identity among Latino adolescents and the role of family. *Journal of Applied Developmental Psychology, 41*, 90–98.
Dowda, M., Brown, W. H., McIver, K. L., Pfeiffer, K. A., O'Neill, J. R., Addy, C. L., & Pate, R. R. (2009). Policies and characteristics of the preschool environment and physical activity of young children. *Pediatrics, 123*, e261–e266.
Dowdney, L. (2000). Annotation: Childhood bereavement following parental death. *Journal of Child Psychology and Psychiatry and Allied Disciplines, 41*, 819–830.
Dowling, G. J., Weiss, S. R., & Condon, T. P. (2008). Drugs of abuse and the aging brain. *Neuropsychopharmacology*, 33, 209–218.
Down syndrome prevalence at birth—United States, 1983–1990 (1994, August 26). *Mortality and Morbidity Weekly Reports, 43*, 617–622.
Downey, J., Elkin, E. J., Ehrhardt, A. A., Meyer-Bahlburg, H. F., Bell, J. J., & Morishima, A. (1991). Cognitive ability and everyday functioning in women with Turner syndrome. *Journal of Learning Disabilities, 24*, 32–39.
Doyle, A. B., Markiewicz, D., Brendgen, M., Lieberman, M., & Voss, K. (2000). Child attachment security and self-concept: Associations with mother and father attachment style and marital quality. *Merrill-Palmer Quarterly, 46*, 514–539.
Doyle, L. W., & Anderson, P. J. (2005). Improved neurosensory outcome at 8 years of age of extremely low birthweight children born in Victoria over three distinct years. *Archives of Disease in Childhood–Fetal and Neonantal Edition, 90*, 484–488.
Drake, K., Belsky, J., & Pasco Fearon, R. M. (2014). From early attachment to engagement with learning in school: The role of self-regulation and persistence. *Developmental Psychology, 50*, 1350–1361.
Draper, J. (2002). It's the first scientific evidence: A man's experience of pregnancy confirmation. *Journal of Advanced Nursing*, 39, 563–570.
Drasgow F. (2012). Intelligence and the workplace. In I. B. Weiner, N. W. Schmitt, & S. Highouse (Eds.), *Handbook of psychology, industrial and organizational psychology* (pp. 184–210). London, England: Wileys.
Drotar, D. (2008). Ethics of treatment and intervention research with children and adolescents with behavioral and mental disorders: Recommendations for a future research agenda. *Ethics & Behavior*, 18(2–3), 307–313. doi:10.1080/10508420802067450
Drotar, D., Robinson, J., Jeavons, L., & Kirchner, H. L. (2008). A randomized, controlled evaluation of early intervention: The Born to Learn curriculum. *Child: Care, Health, and Development*, 35, 643–649.
du Plessis, A. (2013). Fetal Development. In M. L. Batshaw, N. J. Roizen, & G. R. Lotrecchiano (Eds.), *Children with disabilities* (7th ed., pp. 25–36). Baltimore, MD: Paul H. Brookes.
Dubas, J. S., Graber, J. A., & Petersen, A. C. (1991). The effects of pubertal development on achievement during adolescence. *American Journal of Education*, 99, 444–460.
Dubois, L., Farmer, A., Girard, M., & Peterson, K. (2007). Regular sugar-sweetened beverage consumption between meals increases risk of overweight among preschool-aged children. *Journal of the American Dietetic Association, 107*, 924–934.
Dubois, L., Ohm Kyvik, K., Girard, M., Tatone-Tokuda, F., Perusse, D., et al. (2012) Genetic and Environmental Contributions to Weight, Height, and BMI from Birth to 19 Years of Age: An International Study of Over 12,000 Twin Pairs. *PLoS ONE* 7(2): e30153.
Dudai, Y. (2004). The neurobiology of consolidations, or, how stable is the engram? *Annual Review of Psychology*, 55, 51–86.
Dugan, A. (2015, May 27). In U. S., support up for doctor-assisted suicide. Gallup poll retrieved from www.gallup.com/poll/183425/support-doctor-assisted-suicide.aspx.
Duijts, L., Jaddoe, V. W., van der Valk, R. J. P., Henderson, J. A., Hofman, A., Raat, H., et al. (2012). Fetal exposure to maternal and paternal smoking and the risks of wheezing in preschool children: The Generation R study. *Chest, 141*, 876–885.
Dumontheil, I., Apperly, I. A., & Blakemore, S. (2010). Online usage of theory of mind continues to develop in late adolescence. *Developmental Science, 13*, 331–338.
Duncan, C., & Cacciatore, J. (2015). A systematic review of the peer-reviewed literature on self-blame, guilt, and shame. *Omega: Journal of Death and Dying, 71*, 312–42.
Duncan, G. J., Magnuson, K., & Votruba-Drzal, E. (2015). Children and socioeconomic status. In M. H. Bornstein & T. Leventhal (Vol. Eds.) & R. M. Lerner (General Ed.), *Handbook of child psychology and developmental science: Vol. 4. Ecological settings and processes* (pp. 534–573). Hoboken, NJ: Wiley.
Duncan, R. M., & Cheyne, J. A. (2002). Private speech in young adults: Task difficulty, self-regulation, and psychological predication. *Cognitive Development, 16*, 889–906.
Duncan, R. M., & Pratt, M. W. (1997). Microgenetic change in the quantity and quality of preschoolers' private speech. *International Journal of Behavioral Development, 20*, 367.
Dunifon, R. (2013). The influence of grandparents on the lives of children and adolescents. *Child Development Perspectives*, 7, 55–60.
Dunlosky, J., & Ariel, R. (2011). Self-regulated learning and the allocation of study time. *Psychology of Learning and Motivation-Advances in Research and Theory, 54*, 103.
Dunn, J. (1993). *Young children's close relationships. Beyond attachment.* Newbury Park, CA: Sage.
Dunn, J. (2007). Siblings and socialization. In J. E. Grusec & P. D. Hastings (Eds.), *Handbook of socialization: Theory and research*. New York, NY: Guilford.
Dunn, J. (2014). Moral development in early childhood and social interaction in the family. In M. Killen & J. G. Smetana (Eds.), *Handbook of moral development* (2nd ed., pp. 135–159). New York, NY: Psychology Press.
Dunn, J., & Kendrick, C. (1982). *Siblings: Love, envy, and understanding*. Cambridge, MA: Harvard University Press.
Dunn, J., Cutting, A. L., & Demetriou, H. (2000). Moral sensibility, understanding others, and children's friendship interactions in the preschool period. *British Journal of Developmental Psychology, 18*, 159–177.
Dunn, J., Fergusson, E., & Maughan, B. (2006). Grandparents, grandchildren, and family change in contemporary Britain. In A. Clarke-Stewart & J. Dunn (Eds.), *Families count: Effects on child and adolescent development*. New York, NY: Cambridge University Press.
Dunn, L. B., & Misra, S. (2009). Research ethics issues in geriatric psychiatry. *Psychiatric Clinics of North America*, 32(2), 395–411.
Dunne, E. F., Unger, E. R., Sternberg, M., McQuillan, G., Swan, D. C., Patel, S. S., & Markowitz, L. E. (2007). Prevalence of HPV infection among females in the United States. *Journal of the American Medical Association*, 297, 813–819.
Dunphy, D. C. (1963). The social structure of urban adolescent peer groups. *Sociometry, 26*, 230–246.
Dunstan, D. W., Barr, E.L.M., Healy, G. N., Salmon, J., Shaw, J. E., Balkau, B., Magliano, D. J., Cameron, A.J., Zimmet, P. Z., & Owen, N. (2010). Television viewing time and mortality: The Australian Diabetes, Obesity and Lifestyle Study (AusDiab). *Circulation, 121*, 384–391.
Durik, A. M., Hyde, J. S., & Clark, R. (2000). Sequelae of cesarean and vaginal deliveries: Psychosocial outcomes for mothers and infants. *Developmental Psychology, 36*, 251–260.
Durrant, J., & Ensom, R. (2012). Physical punishment of children: Lessons from 20 years of research. *Canadian Medical Association Journal, 184*, 1373–1377.
Duvall, E. M. (1977). *Marriage and family development* (5th ed.). Philadelphia: J. B. Lippincott.
Dux, P. E., Ivanoff, J. G., Asplund, C. L., & Marois, R. (2006). Isolation of a central bottleneck of information processing with time-resolved FMRI. *Neuron, 52*, 1109–1120.
Duyme, M., Dumaret, A., & Tomkiewicz, S. (1999). How can we boost IQs of "dull children"? A late adoption study. *Proceedings of the National Academy of Sciences of the United States of America, 96*, 8790–8794.
Dvorak, P. (2012, May 20). Transgender at five. *The Washington Post*, pp. A1, A14–15.
Dweck, C. S. (2006). *Mindset: The new psychology of success*. New York, NY: Ballantine Books.
Dweck, C. S. (2007). The perils and promise of praise. *Educational Leadership, 65*, 34–39.
Dweck, C. S. (2015, January 1). The secret to raising smart kids. *Scientific American*. Retrieved from www.scientificamerican.com/article/the-secret-to-raising-smart-kids1/.
Dweck, C. S., & Elliott, E. S. (1983). Achievement motivation. In P. H. Mussen (Gen. Ed.), E. M. Hetherington (Vol Ed.), *Handbook of child psychology: Vol. IV. Social and personality development* (pp. 643–691). New York, NY: Wiley.
Dweck, C. S., & Leggett, E. L. (1988). A social-cognitive approach to motivation and personality. *Psychological Review*, 95, 256–273.
Dyk, P. H., & Adams, G. R. (1990). Identity and intimacy: An initial investigation of three theoretical models using cross-lag panel correlations. *Journal of Youth and Adolescence, 19*, 91–110.
Dyregrov, A., & Dyregrov, K. (2013). Complicated grief in children. In M. Stroebe, H. Schut & J. van den Bout (Eds.), *Complicated grief: Scientific foundations for health care professionals*. New York, NY: Routledge/Taylor & Francis.
Dyregrov, K. (2003–2004). Micro-sociological analysis of social support following traumatic bereavement: Unhelpful and avoidant responses from the community. *Omega: Journal of Death and Dying, 48*, 23–44.
Eagly, A. H. (2012). Social role theory. In P. A. M. Van Lange, A. W. Kruglanski, & E. T. Higgins (Eds.), *Handbook of theory of social psychology: Vol. 2*. (pp. 458–476). Thousand Oaks, CA: Sage Publications.
Eastwick, P. W., & Finkel, E. J. (2008). The attachment system in fledgling relationships: An activating role for attachment anxiety. *Journal of Personality and Social Psychology*, 95, 628–647.
Eaton, D. K., Kann, L., Kinchen, S., Ross, J., Hawkins, J., Harris, W. A., et al. (2006, June 9). Youth risk behavior surveillance—United States, 2005. *Mortality Weekly Report*, 55, 1–108.
Eaton, D. K., Kann, L., Kinchen, S., Shanklin, S., Flint, K. H., Hawkins, J., et al. (2012, June 8).Youth Risk Behavior Surveillance—United States, 2011. *Morbidity and Mortality Weekly Reports, 61*. Retrieved from www.cdc.gov/mmwr/pdf/ss/ss6104.pdf.
Ebbeck, M. (1996). Parents' expectations and child rearing practices in Hong Kong. *Early Child Development and Care, 119*, 15–25.
Eberhard-Gran, M., Garthus-Niegel, S., Garthus-Niegel, K., & Eskild, A. (2010). Postnatal care: A cross-cultural and historical perspective. *Archives of Women's Mental Health, 13*, 459–466.
Eberhart, E. K. & Harris, R. A. (2013). Understanding variability in ethanol teratogenicity. *Proceedings of the National Academy of Sciences of the United States, 110*, 5285–5286.
Eccles, J. S., Jacobs, J. E., & Harold, R. D. (1990). Gender role stereotypes, expectancy effects, and parents' socialization of gender differences. *Journal of Social Issues, 46*, 183–201.
Eccles, J. S., Lord, S., & Midgley, C. (1991). What are we doing to early adolescents? The impact of educational

contexts on early adolescents. *American Journal of Education*, 99, 521–542.
Eccles, J. S., Midgley, C., Wigfield, A., Buchanan, C. M., Reuman, D., Flanagan, C., et al. (1993). Development during adolescence: The impact of stage-environment fit on young adolescents' experiences in schools and in families. *American Psychologist*, 48, 90–101.
Echemendia, R., Iverson, G. L., Brand, J. G., Rossetti, H. R., & Broshek, D. K. (Eds.). (2015). The Oxford handbook of sports-related concussion. New York, NY: Oxford University Press.
Ecklund-Flores, L., & Turkewitz, G. (1996). Asymmetric headturning to speech and nonspeech in human newborns. *Developmental Psychobiology*, 29, 205–217.
Eddy, K. T., Keel, P. K., & Leon, G. R. (2010). Vulnerability to eating disorders in childhood and adolescence. In R. E. Ingram & J. M. Price (Eds.).*Vulnerability to psychopathology: Risk across the lifespan* (2nd ed.). New York, NY: Guilford.
Edelstein, B. A., Bamonti, P. M., Gregg, J. J., & Gerolimatos, L. A. (2015). Depression in later life. In P. A. Lichtenberg & B. T. Mast (Eds. in Chief), B. D. Carpenter & J. L. Wetherell, (Assoc. Eds.), APA handbook of clinical geropsychology: *Vol. 2. Assessment, treatment, and issues of later life* (pp. 3–47). Washington, DC: American Psychological Association.
Editors of *The Lancet*. (2010, February 2). Retraction—Ileal-lymphoid-nodular hyperplasia, non-specific colitis, and pervasive developmental disorder in children. Retrieved from www.thelancet.com.
Egeland, B. (1979). Preliminary results of a prospective study of the antecedents of child abuse. *International Journal of Child Abuse and Neglect*, 3, 269–278.
Egeland, B., & Carlson, E. A. (2004). Attachment and psychopathology. In L. Atkinson & S. Goldberg (Eds.), *Attachment issues in psychopathology and intervention*. Mahwah, NJ: Erlbaum.
Egeland, B., Jacobvitz, D., & Sroufe, L. A. (1988). Breaking the cycle of abuse. *Child Development*, 59, 1080–1088.
Egeland, B., Sroufe, L. A., & Erickson, M. (1983). The developmental consequences of different patterns of maltreatment. *International Journal of Child Abuse and Neglect*, 7, 459–469.
Ehrenberg, M., Regev, R., Lazinski, M., Behrman, L. J., & Zimmerman, J. (2014). Adjustment to divorce for children. In L. Grossman & S. Walfish (Eds.), *Translating psychological research into practice* (pp. 1–7). New York, NY: Springer.
Ehrhardt, A. A. (1985). The psychobiology of gender. In A. S. Rossi (Ed.), *Gender and the life course*. New York, NY: Aldine.
Ehri, L. C. (1999). Phases of development in learning to read words. In J. Oakhill & R. Beard (Eds.), *Reading development and the teaching of reading* (pp. 79–108). Oxford, UK: Blackwell.
Eichas, K., Albrecht, R. E., Garcia, A. J., Ritchie, R. A., Varela, A., Garcia, A., et al. (2010). Mediators of positive youth development intervention change: Promoting change in positive and problem outcomes? *Child & Youth Care Forum*, 39, 211–237.
Eiger, M. S., & Olds, S. W. (1999). *The complete book of breastfeeding* (3rd ed.). New York, NY: Workman Publishing & Bantam Books.
Eimas, P. D. (1975a). Auditory and phonetic cues for speech: Discrimination of the (r-l) distinction by young infants. *Perception and Psychophysics*, 18, 341–347.
Eimas, P. D. (1975b). Speech perception in early infancy. In L. B. Cohen & P. Salapatek (Eds.), *Infant perception: From sensation to cognition*. New York, NY: Academic Press.
Eimas, P. D. (1985). The perception of speech in early infancy. *Scientific American*, 252, 46–52.
Eisenberg, M., Neumark-Sztainer, D., & Story, M. (2003). Associations of weight-based teasing and emotional well-being among adolescents. *Archives of Pediatric Medicine*, 157, 733–738.
Eisenberg, N., Duckworth, A. L., Spinrad, T. L., & Valiente, C. (2014). Conscientiousness: Origins in childhood? *Developmental Psychology*, 50, 1331–1349.
Eisenberg, N., Hofer, C., Spinrad, T. L., Gershoff, E. T., Valiente, C., Losoya, S., Zhou, Q., Cumberland, A., Liew, J., Reiser, M., & Maxon, E. (2008). Understanding mother-adolescent conflict discussions: Concurrent and across-time prediction from youths' dispositions and parenting. *Monographs of the Society for Research in Child Development*, 73 (2, Serial No. 290).
Eisenberg, N., Smith, C. L., & Spinrad, T. L. (2011). Effortful control: Relations with emotion regulation, adjustment, and socialization in childhood. In K. D. Vohs, & R. F. Baumeister (Eds.), *Handbook of self-regulation: Research, theory, and applications* (2nd ed.). New York, NY: Guilford Press.
Eisenberg, N., Spinrad, T. L., & Knafo-Noam, A. (2015). Prosocial development. In M. E. Lamb (Vol. Ed.) & R. M. Lerner (Ed.), *Handbook of child psychology and developmental science: Vol. 3. Socioemotional processes* (pp. 610–656). Hoboken, NJ: Wiley.
Eisner, M. P., & Malti, T. (2015). Aggressive and violent behavior. In M. E. Lamb (Vol. Ed.) & R. M. Lerner (Ed.), *Handbook of child psychology and developmental science: Vol. 3. Socioemotional processes* (pp. 794–841). Hoboken, NJ: Wiley.
Ekerdt, D. J., Bossé, R., & Levkoff, S. (1985). Empirical test for phases of retirement: Findings from the Normative Aging Study. *Journal of Gerontology*, 40, 95–101.
Ekerdt, D. J., Kosloski, K., & DeViney, S. (2000). The normative anticipation of retirement by older adults. *Research on Aging*, 22, 3–22.
Elam, K. K., Sandler, I., Wolchik, S., & Tein, J. (2016). Non-residential father–child involvement, interparental conflict and mental health of children following divorce: A person-focused approach. *Journal of Youth and Adolescence*, 45, 581–593.
Elbourne, D., & Wiseman, R. A. (2000). Types of intra-muscular opioids for maternal pain relief in labor. *Cochrane Database Systems Review* 2000 (CD001237).
Elder, G. H., Jr. (1998). The life course as developmental theory. *Child Development*, 69, 1–12.
Elder, G. H., Jr., & Shanahan, M. J. (2006). The life course and human development. In W. Damon & R. M. Lerner (Eds. in Chief) & R. M. Lerner (Vol. Ed.), *Handbook of child psychology: Vol. 1. Theoretical models of human development* (6th ed.). Hoboken, NJ: Wiley.
Elder, G. H., Jr., Liker, J. K., & Cross, C. E. (1984). Parent–child behavior in the Great Depression: Life course and intergenerational influences. In P. B. Baltes & O. G. Brim, Jr. (Eds.), *Life-span development and behavior: Vol. 6*. Orlando, FL: Academic Press.
Elder, G. H., Jr., Shanahan, M. J., & Jennings, J. A. (2015). Human development in time and place. In M. H. Bornstein (Vol. Ed.), T. Leventhal (Vol. Ed.), & R. M. Lerner (Ed.), *Handbook of child psychology and developmental science: Vol. 4. Ecological settings and processes* (pp. 6–54). Hoboken, NJ: Wiley.
Elder, G., Jr., & Johnson, M. K. (2003). The life course and aging: Challenges, lessons and new directions. In R. Settersten, Jr. (Ed.), *Invitation to the life course: Toward new understandings of later life*. Amityville, NY: Baywood.
Elicker, J., Englund, M., & Sroufe, L. A. (1992). Predicting peer competence and peer relationships in childhood from early parent–child relationships. In R. D. Parke & G. W. Ladd (Eds.), *Family-peer relationships: Modes of linkage*. Hillsdale, NJ: Erlbaum.
Eliot, L. (2009). *Pink brain, blue brain: How small differences grow into troublesome gaps—and what we can do about it*. Boston, MA: Houghton Mifflin Harcourt.
Elkind, D. (1967). Egocentrism in adolescence. *Child Development*, 38, 1025–1034.
Elkind, D. (1987). *Miseducation: Preschoolers at risk*. New York, NY: Knopf.
Elkind, D., & Bowen, R. (1979). Imaginary audience behavior in children and adolescents. *Developmental Psychology*, 15, 38–44.
Elliot, A. J., & Church, M. A. (1997). A hierarchical model of approach and avoidance achievement motivation. *Journal of Personality and Social Psychology*, 72, 218–232.
Elliot, A. J., & Reis, H. T. (2003). Attachment and exploration in adulthood. *Journal of Personality & Social Psychology*, 85, 317–331.
Elliott, D. S., & Ageton, S. S. (1980). Reconciling race and class differences in self-reported and official estimates of delinquency. *American Sociological Review*, 45, 95–110.
Elliott, E. S., & Dweck, C. S. (1988). Goals: An approach to motivation and achievement. *Journal of Personality and Social Psychology*, 54, 5–12.
Elliott, S. (2012). *Not my kid: What parents believe about the sex lives of their teenagers*. New York, NY: New York University Press.
Ellis, B. J., & Garber, J. (2000). Psychosocial antecedents of variation in girls' pubertal timing: Maternal depression, stepfather presence, and marital and family stress. *Child Development*, 71, 485–501.
Ellis, B. J., Boyce, W. T., Belsky, J., Bakermans-Kranenburg, M. J., & van IJzendoorn, M. H. (2011). Differential susceptibility to the environment: An evolutionary-neurodevelopmental theory. *Development and Psychopathology*, 23, 7–28.
Ellis, L., Ames, M. A., Peckham, W., & Burke, D. M. (1988). Sexual orientation in human offspring may be altered by severe emotional distress during pregnancy. *Journal of Sex Research*, 25, 152–157.
Ellis, S., Rogoff, B., & Cromer, C. C. (1981). Age segregation in children's social interactions. *Developmental Psychology*, 17, 399–407.
Ellis, Y., Daniels, W., & Jauregui, A. (2010). The effect of multitasking on the grade performance of business students. *Research in Higher Education Journal*, 8, 1–11.
Ellison, C. G., & Flannelly, K. J. (2009). Religious involvement and risk of major depression in a prospective nationwide study of African American adults. *Journal of Nervous and Mental Disease*, 197, 568–573.
Ellison, P. T. (2002). Puberty. In N. Cameron (Ed.), *Human growth and development* (pp. 65–84). New York , NY: Academic Press.
Else-Quest, N. M., Hyde, J. S., & Linn, M. C. (2010). Cross-national patterns of gender differences in mathematics: A meta-analysis. *Psychological Bulletin*, 136, 103–127.
Ely, R. (2001). Language and literacy in the school years. In J. B. Gleason (Ed.), *The development of language* (5th ed.). Boston, MA: Allyn & Bacon.
Emde, R. N., Biringen, Z., Clyman, R. B., & Oppenheim, D. (1991). The moral self of infancy: Affective core and procedural knowledge. *Developmental Review*, 11, 251–270.
Emery, R. E., & Tuer, M. (1993). Parenting and the marital relationship. In T. Luster & L. Okagaki (Eds.), *Parenting. An ecological perspective*. Hillsdale, NJ: Erlbaum.
Emmanuelle, V. (2009). Inter-relationships among attachment to mother and father, self-esteem, and career indecision. *Journal of Vocational Behavior*, 75, 91–99.
Endendijk, J. J., Groeneveld, M. G., van Berkel, S. R., Hallers-Haalboom, E. T., Mesman, J., & Bakermans-Kranenburg, M. J. (2013). Gender stereotypes in the family context: Mothers, fathers, and siblings. *Sex Roles*, 68, 577–590.
Endendijk, J. J., Groeneveld, M. G., van der Pol, L. D., van Berkel, S. R., Hallers-Haalboom, E. T., Bakermans-Kranenburg, M. J., & Mesman, J. (2017). Gender differences in child aggression: Relations with gender-differentiated parenting and parents' gender-role stereotypes. *Child Development*, 88, 299–316.
English, T., & Carstensen, L. L. (2014). Selective narrowing of social networks across adulthood is associated with improved emotional experience in daily life. *International Journal of Behavioral Development*, 38, 195–202.
Enright, R., Lapsley, D., & Shukla, D. (1979). Adolescent egocentrism in early and late adolescence. *Adolescence*, 14, 687–695.
Ensminger, M. E., & Slusarcick, A. L. (1992). Paths to high school graduation or dropout: A longitudinal study of a first-grade cohort. *Sociology of Education*, 65, 95–113.
Epel, E. S. (2009). Telomeres in a life-span perspective: A new "psychobiomarker"? *Current Direction in Psychological Science*, 18, 6–10.
Epel, E. S., Blackburn, E. H., Lin, J., Dhabhar, F. S., Adler, N. E., Morrow, J. D., & Cawthon, R. M. (2004). Accelerated telomere shortening in response to life stress. *Proceedings of the National Academy of Sciences*, 101, 17312–17315.
Epel, E. S., Lin, J., Wilhelm, F. H., Wolkowitz, O. M., Cawthon, R., Adler, N. E., Dolbier, C., Mendes, W. B., & Blackburn, E. H. (2006). Cell aging in relation to stress arousal and cardiovascular disease risk factors. *Psychoneuroendrocrinology*, 31, 277–287.
Eppig, C., Fincher, C. L., & Thornhill, R. (2010). Parasite prevalence and the worldwide distribution of cognitive ability. *Proceedings of the Royal Society*, 277, 3801–3808.
Eppler, M. A. (1995). Development of manipulatory skills and the deployment of attention. *Infant Behavior & Development*, 18, 391–405.
Eppler, M. A., & Harju, B. J. (1997). Achievement motivation goals in relation to academic performance in traditional and non-traditional college students. *Research in Higher Education*, 38, 557–573.

Epstein, R. (2013, January/February). Yet another stage of life? *Scientific American Mind*, pp. 18–19.

Erdley, C. A., Loomis, C. C., Cain, K. M., & Dumas-Hines, F. (1997). Relations among children's social goals, implicit personality theories, and responses to social failure. *Developmental Psychology, 33*, 263–272.

Erickson, J. J., Martinengo, G., & Hill, E. J. (2010). Putting work and family experiences in context: Differences by family life stage. *Human Relations, 63*, 955–979.

Ericsson, K. A. (1996). The acquisition of expert performance: An introduction to some of the issues. In K. A. Ericsson (Ed.), *The road to excellence: The acquisition of expert performance in the arts and sciences, sports, and games.* Mahwah, NJ: Erlbaum.

Ericsson, K. A., & Kintsch, W. (1995). Long-term working memory. *Psychological Review, 102*, 211–245.

Ericsson, K. A., & Polson, P. G. (1988). An experimental analysis of the mechanisms of a memory skill. *Journal of Experimental Psychology: Learning, Memory, and Cognition, 14*, 305.

Ericsson, K. A., Chase, W. G., & Faloon, S. (1980). Acquisition of a memory skill. *Science, 208*, 1181–1182.

Eriksen, W., Sundet, J. M., & Tambs, K. (2009). Register data suggest lower intelligence in men born the year after flu pandemic. *Annals of Neurology, 66*, 284–9.

Erikson, E. H. (1963). *Childhood and society* (2nd ed.). New York, NY: Norton.

Erikson, E. H. (1968). *Identity: Youth and crisis.* New York, NY: Norton.

Erikson, E. H. (1982). *The life cycle completed: A review.* New York, NY: Norton.

Ernst, A., & Frisén, J. (2015). Adult neurogenesis in humans: Common and unique traits in mammals. *PLoS Biology, 13*(1), e1002045.

Erol, R. Y., & Orth, U. (2011). Self-esteem development from age 14 to 30 years: A longitudinal study. *Journal of Personality and Social Psychology, 101*, 607–619.

Escalona, S. (1968). *The roots of individuality: Normal patterns of individuality.* Chicago, IL: Aldine.

Eskritt, M., & Lee, K. (2002). "Remember where you last saw that card": Children's production of external symbols as a memory aid. *Developmental Psychology, 38*, 254–266.

Espinosa-Hernandez, G., & Lefkowitz, E. S. (2009). Sexual behaviors and attitudes and ethnic identity during college. *Journal of Sex Research, 46*, 471–482.

Espinoza, G., Gonzales, N. A., & Fuligni, A. J. (2012). Daily school peer victimization experiences among Mexican American adolescents: Associations with psychosocial, physical and school adjustment. *Journal of Youth and Adolescence, 42*, 1775–1788.

Espy, K. A., Molfese, V. J., & DiLalla, L. F. (2001). Effects of environmental measures on intelligence in young children: Growth curve modeling of longitudinal data. *Merrill-Palmer Quarterly, 47*, 42–73.

Essa, E. L., & Murray, C. I. (1994). Young children's understanding and experience with death. *Young Children, 49*, 74–81.

Essex, M. J., Kraemer, H. C., Slattery, M., Burk, L. R., Boyce, W. T., Woodward, H. R., & Kupfer, D. J. (2009). Screening for childhood mental health problems: Outcomes and early identification. *Journal of Child Psychology and Psychiatry, 50*, 562–570.

Estes, A., Munson, J., Rogers, S. J., Greenson, J., Winter, J., & Dawson, G. (2015). Long-term outcomes of early intervention in 6-year-old children with autism spectrum disorder. *Journal of the American Academy of Child & Adolescent Psychiatry, 54*, 580–587.

Estes, Z., & Felker, S. (2012). Confidence mediates the sex difference in mental rotation performance. *Archives of Sexual Behavior, 41*, 557–590.

Etgen, T., Sander, D., Huntgeburth, U., Poppert, H., Förstl, H., & Bickel, H. (2010). Physical activity and incident cognitive impairment in elderly persons. *Archives of Internal Medicine, 170*, 186–193.

Ettner, R., Monstrey, S., & Coleman, E. (Eds.). (2016). *Principles of transgender medicine and surgery* (2nd ed.). New York, NY: Routledge.

European Centre for Disease Prevention and Control (2015). Measles and rubella monthly monitoring reports. ecdc.europa.eu/en/publications/surveillance_reports/vpd/Pages/emmo.aspx.

Evans, A. B., Banerjee, M., Meyer, R., Aldana, A., Foust, M., & Rowley, S. (2012). Racial socialization as a mechanism for positive development among African American youth. *Child Development Perspectives, 6*, 251–257.

Evans, C. B. R., Fraser, M. W., & Cotter, K. L. (2014). The effectiveness of school-based bullying prevention programs: A systematic review. *Aggression and Violent Behavior, 19*, 532–544.

Evans, D., & Goldman, B. (2010). First person: Jane Fowler. *The Body: The Complete HIV/AIDS Resource, HIV/AIDS Resource Center for Women.* Retrieved from www.thebody.com/content/art45791.html.

Evans, G. W. (2004). The environment of childhood poverty. *American Psychologist, 59*, 77–92.

Evans, G. W. (2006). Child development and the physical environment. *Annual Review of Psychology, 57*, 423–451.

Evans, G. W., & Kim, P. (2012). Childhood poverty and young adults' allostatic load: The mediating role of childhood cumulative risk exposure. *Psychological Science, 23*, 979–983.

Evans, G. W., & Kim, P. (2013). Childhood poverty, chronic stress, self-regulation, and coping. *Child Development Perspectives, 7*, 43–48.

Evans, J. R. (2001). Risk factors for age-related macular degeneration. *Progress in Retinal and Eye Research, 20*, 227.

Evans, J. R., Fletcher, A. E., Wormald, R. P., Ng, E. S., Stirling, S., Smeeth, L., et al. (2002). Prevalence of visual impairment in people aged 75 years and older in Britain: Results from the MRC Trial of assessment and management of older people in the community. *Ophthalmology*, 795–800.

Evans, J. St. B. T., & Stanovich, K. E. (2013). Dual-process theories of higher cognition: Advancing the debate. *Perspectives on Psychological Science, 8*, 223–241.

Evans, M. A., & Shaw, D. (2008). Home grown for reading: Parental contributions to young children's emergent literacy and word recognition. *Canadian Psychology, 49*, 89–95.

Ewing, E. K., Diamond, G., & Levy, S. (2015). Attachment-based family therapy for depressed and suicidal adolescents: Theory, clinical model and empirical support. *Attachment & Human Development, 17*, 136–156.

Eyberg, S. M., & Bussing, R. (2010). Parent-child interaction therapy for preschool children with conduct problems. In R. C. Murrihy, A. D. Kidman, & T. H. Ollendick (Eds.), *Clinical handbook of assessing and treating conduct problems in youth* (pp. 139–162). New York, NY: Springer Science + Business Media.

Faber, C. E., & Grontved, A. M. (2000). Cochlear implantation and change in quality of life. *Acta Otolaryngology Supplement, 543*, 151–153.

Fagan, J. F. (2011). Intelligence in infancy. In R. J. Sternberg & S. B. Kaufman (Eds.), *The Cambridge handbook of intelligence* (pp. 130–143). New York, NY: Cambridge University Press.

Fagan, J., & Palkovitz, R. (2011). Coparenting and relationship quality effects on father engagement: Variations by residence, romance. *Journal of Marriage and Family, 73*, 637–653.

Fagan, J., Palkovitz, R., Roy, K., & Farrie, D. (2009). Pathways to paternal engagement: Longitudinal effects of risk and resilience on nonresident fathers. *Developmental Psychology, 45*, 1389–1405.

Fagot, B. I. (1978). The influence of sex of child on parental reactions to toddler children. *Child Development, 49*, 459–465.

Fagot, B. I. (1997). Attachment, parenting, and peer interactions of toddler children. *Developmental Psychology, 33*, 489–499.

Fagot, B. I., & Kavanaugh, K. (1993). Parenting during the second year: Effects of children's age, sex, and attachment classification. *Child Development, 64*, 258–271.

Fagot, B. I., & Leinbach, M. D. (1989). The young child's gender schema: Environmental input, internal organization. *Child Development, 60*, 663–672.

Fagot, B. I., & Leinbach, M. D. (1993). Gender-role development in young children: From discrimination to labeling. *Developmental Review, 13*, 205–224.

Fagot, B. I., Leinbach, M. D., & Hagan, R. (1986). Gender labeling and the adoption of sex-typed behaviors. *Developmental Psychology, 22*, 440–443.

Fagot, B. I., Leinbach, M. D., & O'Boyle, C. (1992). Gender labeling, gender stereotyping, and parenting behaviors. *Developmental Psychology, 28*, 225–230.

Falcon, L. M., & Tucker, K. L. (2000). Prevalence and correlates of depressive symptoms among Hispanic elders in Massachusetts. *Journal of Gerontology: Social Sciences, 55*, S108–S116.

Fallone, M. D., LaGasse, L. L., Lester, B. M., Shankaran, S., Bada, H. S., & Bauer, C. R. (2014). Reactivity and regulation of motor responses in cocaine-exposed infants, *Neurotoxicology and Teratology, 43*, 25–32.

Fan, H. C., Gu, W., Wang, J., Blumenfeld, Y. J., El-Sayed, Y. Y., & Quake, S. R. (2012). Noninvasive prenatal measurement of the fetal genome. *Nature, 48*(7407), 320–326.

Fantz, R. L., & Fagan, J. F. (1975). Visual attention to size and number of pattern details by term and preterm infants during the first six months. *Child Development, 46*, 3–18.

Farah, M. J., Betancourt, L., Shera, D. M., Savage, J. H., Giannetta, J. M., Brodsky, N. L., et al. (2008). Environmental stimulation, parental nurturance and cognitive development in humans. *Developmental Science, 11*, 793–801.

Farr, R. H., & Patterson, C. J. (2013). Coparenting among lesbian, gay, and heterosexual couples: Associations with adopted children's outcomes. *Child Development, 84*, 1226–1240.

Farr, R. H., Forssell, S. L., & Patterson, C. J. (2010). Parenting and child development in adoptive families: Does parental sexual orientation matter? *Applied Developmental Science, 14*, 164–178.

Farrell, A. K., Simpson, J. A., Overall, N. C., & Shallcross, S. L. (2016). Buffering the responses of avoidantly attached romantic partners in strain test situations. *Journal of Family Psychology.* Advance online publication.

Farrington, C.A., Roderick, M., Allensworth, E., Nagaoka, J., Keyes, T.S., Johnson, D.W., & Beechum, N.O. (2012). *Teaching adolescents to become learners. The role of noncognitive factors in shaping school performance: A critical literature review.* Chicago, IL: University of Chicago Consortium on Chicago School Research.

Farroni, T., Johnson, M. H., Menon, E., Zulian, L., Faraguna, D., & Csibra, G. (2005). Newborns' preference for face-relevant stimuli: Effects of contrast polarity. *Proceedings of the National Academy of Sciences, 102*, 17245–17250.

Farver, J. A. M., & Lee-Shin, Y. (1997). Social pretend play in Korean and Anglo American preschoolers. *Child Development, 68*, 544–556.

Faulkner, D., Joiner, R., Littleton, K., Miell, D., & Thompson, L. (2000). The mediating effect of task presentation on collaboration and children's acquisition of scientific reasoning. *European Journal of Psychology of Education, 15*, 417–430.

Faulkner, K. W. (1997). Talking about death with a dying child. *American Journal of Nursing, 97*, 64, 66, 68–69.

Faust, M. A., & Glenzer, N. (2000). "I could read those parts over and over": Eighth graders rereading to enhance enjoyment and learning with literature. *Journal of Adolescent and Adult Literacy, 44*, 234–239.

Favilla, M. (2006). Reaching movements in children: Accuracy and reaction time development. *Journal of Experimental Brain Research, 169*, 122–125.

Fazio, L. K., DeWolf, M., & Siegler, R. S. (2016). Strategy use and strategy choice in fraction magnitude comparison. *Journal of Experimental Psychology: Learning, Memory, and Cognition, 42*, 1–16.

Fearon, R. M., Reiss, D., Leve, L. D., Shaw, D. S., Scaramella, L. V., Ganiban, J. M., & Neiderhiser, J. M. (2015). Child-evoked maternal negativity from 9 to 27 months: Evidence of gene–environment correlation and its moderation by marital distress. *Development and Psychopathology, 27*, 1251–1265.

Fearon, R. M., van IJzendoorn, M. H., Fonagy, P., Bakermans-Kranenburg, M. J., Schuengel, C., & Bokhorst, C. L. (2006). In search of shared and nonshared environmental factors in security of attachment: A behavior-genetic study of the association between sensitivity and attachment security. *Developmental Psychology, 42*, 1026–1040.

Federal Interagency Forum on Aging Related Statistics. (2012). *Older Americans 2012. Key indicators of well-being.* Washington, DC: U.S. Government Printing Office. Retrieved from www.agingstats.gov.

Federal Interagency Forum on Child and Family Statistics. (2012). *America's children in brief: Key national indicators of well-being,* 2012. Washington, DC: U.S. Government Printing Office. Retrieved from www.childstats.gov/americaschildren.

Federal Interagency Forum on Child and Family Statistics. (2015). *America's children: Key national indicators of well-being,* 2015. Washington, DC: U.S. Government Printing Office. Retrieved from www.childstats.gov/.

Fedina, L., Holmes, J. L., & Backes, B. L. (2016). Campus sexual assault: A systematic review of prevalence research from 2000 to 2015. *Trauma, Violence, & Abuse*. Feb. 22. Epub.

Fehlings, D., Hunt, C., & Rosenbaum, P. (2007). Cerebral palsy, 279–286. In I. Brown & M. Percy (Eds.), *A comprehensive guide to intellectual & developmental disabilities*. Baltimore, MD: Paul H. Brookes.

Fein, D., Barton, M., Eigsti, I., Kelley, E., Naigles, L., Schultz, R. T., et al. (2013). Optimal outcome in individuals with a history of autism. *Journal of Child Psychology and Psychiatry*, *54*, 195–205.

Feinberg, M. E., & Kan, M. L. (2016). Family Foundations. In M. J. Van Ryzin, K. L. Kumpfer, G. M. Fosco, & M. T. Greenberg. (Eds.), *Family-based prevention programs for children and adolescents. Theory, research, and large-scale dissemination* (pp. 23–41). New York & London: Psychology Press.

Feingold, A. (1994). Gender differences in personality: A meta-analysis. *Psychological Bulletin*, *116*, 429–456.

Feinman, S. (1992). *Social referencing and the social construction of reality in infancy*. New York, NY: Plenum.

Feldman, D. C., & Ng, T. W. H. (2013). Theoretical approaches to the study of job transitions. In N. W. Schmitt, S. Highhouse, & I. B. Weiner (Eds.), *Handbook of psychology: Vol. 12. Industrial and organizational psychology*. Hoboken, NJ: Wiley.

Feldman, D. H. (Ed.). (1982). Developmental approaches to giftedness and creativity. *New Directions for Child & Adolescent Development: Vol. 1*. San Francisco, CA: Jossey-Bass.

Feldman, D. H. (1986). *Nature's gambit: Child prodigies and the development of human potential*. New York, NY: Basic Books.

Feldman, D. H., & Fowler, R. C. (1997). The nature(s) of developmental change: Piaget, Vygotsky, and the transition process. *New Ideas in Psychology*, *3*, 195–210.

Feldman, H., Jones, K., Lindsay, S., Slymen, D., Klonoff-Cohen, H., Kao, K., et al. (2012). Feldman, R. (2007). Parent-infant synchrony. Biological foundations and developmental outcomes. *Current Directions in Psychological Science*, *16*, 340–345.

Feldman, R. (2016). The neurobiology of mammalian parenting and the biosocial context of human caregiving. *Hormones and Behavior*, *77*, 3–17.

Feldman, R. D. (1982). *Whatever happened to the quiz kids? Perils and profits of growing up gifted*. Chicago, IL: Chicago Review Press.

Feldman, R., & Eidelman, A. I. (2006). Neonatal state organization, neuromaturation, mother–infant interaction, and cognitive development in small-for-gestational-age premature infants. *Pediatrics*, *118*, 869–879.

Feldman, R., Weller, A., Sirota, L., & Eidelman, A. (2003). Testing a family intervention hypothesis: The contribution of mother–infant skin-to-skin contact (kangaroo care) to family interaction, proximity, and touch. *Journal of Family Psychology*, *17*, 94–107.

Feldman, R., Weller, A., Zagoory-Sharon, O., & Levine, A. (2007). Evidence for a neuroendocrinological foundation of human affiliation. *Psychological Science*, *18*, 965–970.

Feng, J., Spence, I., & Pratt, J. (2007). Playing an action video game reduces gender differences in spatial cognition. *Psychological Science*, *18*, 850–855.

Fenson, L., Dale, P. S., Reznick, J. S., Bates, E., Thal, D. J., & Pethick, S. J. (1994). Variability in early communicative development. *Monographs of the Society for Research in Child Development*, *59* (Serial No. 242).

Ferdenzi, C., Roberts, S. C., Schirmer, A., Delplanque, S., Cekic, S., Porcherot, C., et al. (2013). Variability of affective responses to odors: Culture, gender, and olfactory knowledge. *Chemical Senses*, *38*, 175–186.

Ferguson, C. J. (2013). Violent video games and the Supreme Court. Lessons for the scientific community in the wake of Brown v. Entertainment Merchants Association. *American Psychologist*, *68*, 57–74.

Ferguson, C. J., & Donnellan, M. B. (2014). Is the association between children's baby video viewing and poor language development robust? A reanalysis of Zimmerman, Christakis, and Meltzoff (2007). *Developmental Psychology*, *50*, 129–137.

Fernald, A. (2009). Hearing, listening, and understanding: Auditory development in infancy. In J. G. Bremner & A. Fogel (Eds.), *Blackwell handbook of infant development* (pp. 35–70). Malden, MA: Blackwell Publishing.

Ferrario, C. G., Freeman, F. J., Nellett, G., & Scheel, J. (2008). Changing nursing students' attitudes about aging: An argument for the successful aging paradigm. *Educational Gerontology*, *34*, 51–66.

Ferro, M., & DeSouza, R. R. (2011). The importance of resveratrol in tissue aging: A review. *Journal of Morphological Science*, *28*, 77–80.

Fetal alcohol syndrome: Dashed hopes, damaged lives. (2011). *Bulletin World Health Organization* [online], *89*, 398–399. Retrieved from www.scielosp.org/scielo php?script=sci_arttext&pid=S0042.

Field, D. (1981). Can preschool children really learn to conserve? *Child Development*, *52*, 326–334.

Field, D., & Gueldner, S. H. (2001). The oldest-old: How do they differ from the old-old? *Journal of Gerontological Nursing*, *27*, 20–27.

Field, N. P. (2008). Whether to relinquish or maintain a bond with the deceased. In M. S. Stroebe, R. O. Hansson, H. Schut, & W. Stroebe (Eds.), *Handbook of bereavement research and practice. Advances in theory and intervention*. Washington, DC: American Psychological Association.

Field, N. P., & Filanosky, C. (2010). Continuing bonds, risk factors for complicated grief, and adjustment to bereavement. *Death Studies*, *34*, 1–29.

Field, N. P., Nichols, C., Holen, A., & Horowitz, M. J. (1999). The relation of continuing attachment to adjustment in conjugal bereavement. *Journal of Consulting & Clinical Psychology*, *67*, 212–218.

Field, T. (2011). Prenatal depression effects on early development: A review. *Infant Behavior and Development*, *34*, 1–14.

Field, T. M. (1995). Infants of depressed mothers. *Infant Behavior and Development*, *18*, 1–13.

Field, T., Diego, M. A., Hernandez-Reif, M., Deeds, O., & Figuereido, B. (2006). Moderate versus light pressure massage therapy leads to greater weight gain in preterm infants. *Infant Behavior and Development*, 574–578.

Field, T., Diego, M., & Hernandez-Reif, M. (2010). Preterm infant massage therapy research: A review. *Infant Behavior & Development*, 33, 115–124.

Fielder, R. L., & Carey, M. P. (2010). Predictors and consequences of sexual "hookups" among college students: A short-term prospective study. *Archives of Sexual Behavior*, *39*, 1105–1119.

Fields-Meyer, T. (2011, December 13). Trivia is hardly trivial for my son. *The Washington Post*, pp. E1, E6.

Fifer, W. P., Monk, C. E., & Grose-Fifer, J. (2004). Prenatal development and risk. In G. Bremner & A. Fogel (Eds.), *Blackwell handbook of infant development* (pp. 505–542). Malden, MA: Blackwell Publishing.

Filipp, S. H. (1996). Motivation and emotion. In J. E. Birren, K. W. Schaie, R. P. Abeles, M. Gatz, & T. A. Salthouse (Eds.), *Handbook of the psychology of the aging* (4th ed.). San Diego, CA: Academic Press.

Fillo, J., Simpson, J. A., Rholes, W. S., & Kohn, J. L. (2015). Dads doing diapers: Individual and relational outcomes associated with the division of childcare across the transition to parenthood. *Journal of Personality and Social Psychology*, *108*, 298–316.

Fincham, F. D. (2003). Marital conflict: Correlates, structure, and context. *Current Directions in Psychological Science*, *12*, 23–27.

Fingerman, K. L., & Birditt, K. S. (2011). Relationships between adults and their aging parents. In K. W. Schaie & S. L. Willis (Eds.) B. G. Knight, B. Levy, & D. C. Park (Assoc. Eds.), *Handbook of the psychology of aging*, MA: Academic Press/Elsevier.

Fingerman, K. L., Cheng, Y., Wesselmann, E. D., Zarit, S., Furstenberg, F., & Birditt, K. S. (2012). Helicopter parents and landing pad kids: Intense parental support of grown children. *Journal of Marriage and Family*, *74*, 880–896.

Finitzo, T., Gunnarson, A. D., & Clark, J. L. (1990). Auditory deprivation and early conductive hearing loss from otitis media. *Topics in Language Disorders*, *11*, 29–42.

Finkel, D., & Reynolds, C. A. (2010). Cognitive and physical aging pathways: Contributions from behavioral genetics. In J. C. Cavanaugh & C. K. Cavanaugh (Eds.), *Aging in America: Vol. 2. Physical and mental health* (pp. 26–56). Santa Barbara, CA: ABC-CLIO.

Finkel, D., Gerritsen, L., Reynolds, C. A., Dahl, A. K., & Pedersen, N. L. (2014). Etiology of individual differences in human health and longevity. *Annual Review of Gerontology & Geriatrics*, *34*, 189–227.

Finkel, E. J., Cheung, E. O., Emery, L. F., Carswell, K. L., & Larson, G. M. (2015). Why marriage in America is becoming an all-or-nothing institution. *Current Directions in Psychological Science*, *24*, 238–244.

Finkel, E. J., Eastwick, P. W., Karney, B. R., Reis, H. T., & Sprecher, S. (2012). Online dating: A critical analysis from the perspective of psychological science. *Psychological Science in the Public Interest*, *13*, 1–66.

Finkelhor, D. (2009). The prevention of childhood sexual abuse. *Future Children*, *19*, 169–194.

Finkelhor, D., & Berliner, L. (1995). Research on the treatment of sexually abused children: A review and recommendations. *Journal of the American Academy of Child & Adolescent Psychiatry*, *34*, 1408–1423.

Finkelhor, D., Shattuck, A., Turner, H. A., & Hamby, S. L. (2014). The lifetime prevalence of child sexual abuse and sexual assault assessed in late adolescence. *Journal of Adolescent Health*, *55*, 329–333.

Finkelhor, D., Turner, H., Ormrod, R., & Hamby, S. L. (2010). Trends in childhood violence and abuse exposure: Evidence from two national surveys. *Archives of Pediatric & Adolescent Medicine*, *164*, 238–242.

Finkelstein, J. A., & Schiffman, S. S. (1999). Workshop on taste and smell in the elderly: An overview. *Physiological Behavior*, *66*, 173–176.

Finnerty-Myers, K. (2011). Understanding the dynamics behind the relationship between exposure to negative consequences of risky sex on entertainment television and emerging adults' safe-sex attitudes and intentions. *Mass Communication & Society*, *14*, 743–764.

Fisch, H., Hyun, G., Golder, R., Hensle, T. W., Olsson, C. A., & Liberson, G. L. (2003). The influence of paternal age on Down syndrome. *Journal of Urology*, *169*, 2275–2278.

Fischer, K. W. (1980). A theory of cognitive development: The control and construction of hierarchies of skills. *Psychological Review*, *87*, 477–531.

Fischer, K. W., & Bidell, T. (1991). Constraining nativist inferences about cognitive capacities. In S. Carey & Gelman (Eds.), *The epigenesis of mind: Essays on biology and cognition*. Hillsdale, NJ: Erlbaum.

Fischer, K. W., & Bidell, T. R. (1998). Dynamic development of psychological structures in action and thought. In R. M. Lerner (Ed.), *Handbook of child psychology. Vol 1: Theoretical models of human development* (5th ed., pp. 467–561). New York, NY: Wiley.

Fischer, K. W., & Bidell, T. R. (2006). Dynamic development of action and thought. In W. Damon & R. M. Lerner (Eds.), *Handbook of child psychology* (6th ed.). Hoboken, NJ: John Wiley & Sons.

Fischer, K. W., & Pipp, S. L. (1984). Processes of cognitive development: Optimal level and skill acquisition. In R. J. Steinberg (Ed.), *Mechanisms of cognitive development* (pp. 45–80). San Francisco: Freeman.

Fischer, K. W., & Yan, Z. (2002). The Development of Dynamic Skill Theory. In R. Lickliter & D. Lewkowicz (Eds.), *Conceptions of development: Lessons from the laboratory*. Hove, UK: Psychology Press.

Fischer, K. W., Kenny, S. L., & Pipp, S. L. (1990). How cognitive processes and environmental conditions organize discontinuities in the development of abstractions. In C. N. Alexander & E. J. Langer (Eds.), *Higher stages of human development: Perspectives on adult growth*. New York, NY: Oxford University Press.

Fisher, C., Gertner, Y., Scott, R. M., & Yuan, S. (2010). Syntactic bootstrapping. *Cognitive Science*, *1*, 143–149.

Fisher, E. P. (1992). The impact of play on development: A meta-analysis. *Play and Culture*, *5*, 159–181.

Fisher, J. O., Wright, G., Herman, A. N., Malhotra, K., Serrano, E. L., Foster, G. D., & Whitaker, R. C. (2015). "Snacks are not food": Low-income, urban mothers' perceptions of feeding snacks to their preschool-aged children. *Appetite*, *84*, 61–67.

Fisher, K. R., Marshall, P. J., & Nanayakkara, A. R. (2009). Motivational orientation, error monitoring, and academic performance in middle childhood: A behavioral and electrophysiological investigation. *Mind, Brain, and Education*, 3, 56–62.

Fisher, L., Ames, E. W., Chisholm, K., & Savoie, L. (1997). Problems reported by parents of Romanian orphans adopted to British Columbia. *International Journal of Behavioral Development*, 20, 67–82.

Fisher, P. A., Van Ryzin, M. J., & Gunnar, M. R. (2011). Mitigating HPA axis dysregulation associated with placement changes in foster care. *Psychoneuroendocrinology, 36,* 531–539.

Fisher, S., & Greenberg, R. P. (1977). *The scientific credibility of Freud's theories and therapy.* New York, NY: Basic Books.

Fitness, J. (2013). The communication of emotion in families. In A. L. Vangelisti (Ed.), *The Routledge handbook of family communication.* New York, NY: Routledge.

Fitzgerald, J. M. (1999). Autobiographical memory and social cognition: Development of the remembered self in adulthood. In T. M. Hess & F. Blanchard-Fields (Eds.), *Social cognition and aging* (pp. 143–171). San Diego, CA: Academic Press.

Fitzgerald, J. M., & Broadbridge, C. L. (2012). Theory and research in autobiographical memory: A life-span developmental perspective. In D. Berntsen & D. C. Rubin (Eds.), *Understanding autobiographical memory* (pp. 246–266). Cambridge, UK: Cambridge University Press.

Fitzpatrick, J. P., Latimer, J., Carter, M., Oscar, J., Ferreira, M. L., Carmichael Olson, H., Lucas, B. R., Doney, R., Salter, C., Try, J., Hawkes, G., Fitzpatrick, E., Hand, M., Watkins, R. E., Martiniuk, A. L., Bower, C., Boulton, J. & Elliott, E. J. (2015). Prevalence of fetal alcohol syndrome in a population-based sample of children living in remote Australia: The Lililwan Project. *Journal of Paediatrics and Child Health, 51,* 450–457.

Fitzpatrick, L. (2009, July 27). Brief history of China's One-Child Policy. *Time World.* www.time.com/time/world/article/0,8599,1912861,00.html

Fivush, R. (2009). Sociocultural perspectives on autobiographical memory. In M. L. Courage & N. Cowan (Eds.), *The development of memory in infancy and childhood* (pp. 283–302). New York, NY: Psychology Press.

Fivush, R. (2014). Maternal reminiscing style: The sociocultural construction of autobiographical memory across childhood and adolescence. In P. Bauer & R. Fivush (Eds.), *The Wiley handbook on the development of children's memory* (pp. 568–585). Malden, MA: Wiley Blackwell.

Fivush, R., Gray, J. T., & Fromhoff, F. A. (1987). Two-year-olds talk about the past. *Cognitive Development, 2,* 393–409.

Flavell, J. H. (1963). *The developmental psychology of Jean Piaget.* New York, NY: Van Nostrand Reinhold.

Flavell, J. H. (1985). *Cognitive development* (2nd ed.). Englewood Cliffs, NJ: Prentice Hall.

Flavell, J. H. (1996). Piaget's legacy. *Psychological Science, 7,* 200–203.

Flavell, J. H. (1999). Cognitive development: Children's knowledge about the mind. *Annual Review of Psychology, 50,* 21–45.

Flavell, J. H., Beach, D. R., & Chinsky, J. M. (1966). Spontaneous verbal rehearsal in a memory task as a function of age. *Child Development, 37,* 283–299.

Flavell, J. H., Everett, B. H., Croft, K., & Flavell, E. R. (1981). Young children's knowledge about visual perception: Further evidence for the level 1– level 2 distinction. *Developmental Psychology, 17,* 99–103.

Flavell, J. H., Miller, P. H., & Miller, S. A. (2001). *Cognitive development* (4th ed.). Englewood Cliffs, NJ: Prentice Hall.

Fleeson, W. (2004). The quality of American life at the end of the century. In O. G. Brim, C. D. Ryff, & R. C. Kessler (Eds.), *How healthy are we? A national study of well-being at midlife.* Chicago, IL: University of Chicago Press.

Flegal, K. M., Carroll, M. D., Kit, B. K., & Ogden, C. L. (2012). Prevalence of obesity and trends in the distribution of body mass index among US adults, 1999–2010. *Journal of the American Medical Association, 307,* 491–497.

Fletcher, G. J. O., Simpson, J. A., Campbell, L., & Overall, N. C. (2015). Pair-bonding, romantic love, and evolution: The curious case of Homo sapiens. *Perspectives on Psychological Science, 10,* 20–36.

Fletcher, K. L., & Bray, N. W. (1996). External memory strategy use in preschool children. *Merrill-Palmer Quarterly, 42,* 379–396.

Fletcher, K. L., & Bray, N. W. (1997). Instructional and contextual effects on eternal memory strategy use

in young children. *Journal of Experimental Child Psychology, 67,* 204–222.

Flieller, A. (1999). Comparison of the development of formal thought in adolescent cohorts aged 10 to 15 years (1967–1996 and 1972–1993). *Developmental Psychology, 35,* 1048–1058.

Flook, L. (2011). Gender differences in adolescents' daily interpersonal events and well-being. *Child Development, 82,* 454–461.

Flook, L., & Fuligni, A. J. (2008). Family and school spillover in adolescents' daily lives. *Child Development, 79,* 776–787.

Floor, P., & Akhtar, N. (2006). Can 18-month-old infants learn words by listening in on conversations? *Infancy, 9,* 327–339.

Flores, E., Cicchetti, D., & Rogosch, F. A. (2005). Predictors of resilience in maltreated and nonmaltreated Latino children. *Developmental Psychology, 41,* 338–351.

Florian, V., & Kravetz, S. (1985). Children's concepts of death. A cross-cultural comparison among Muslims, Druze, Christians, and Jews in Israel. *Journal of Cross-Cultural Psychology, 16,* 174–189.

Flum, H., & Blustein, D. L. (2000). Reinvigorating the study of vocational research. *Journal of Vocational Behavior, 56,* 380–404.

Flynn, E., & Whiten, A. (2010). Studying children's social learning experimentally 'in the wild'. *Learning & Behavior, 38,* 284–296.

Flynn, J. R. (1987). Massive IQ gains in 14 nations: What IQ tests really measure. *Psychological Bulletin, 101,* 171–191.

Flynn, J. R. (1998). IQ gains over time: Toward finding the causes. In U. Neisser (Ed.), *The rising curve: Long-term gains in IQ and related measures.* Washington, DC: American Psychological Association.

Flynn, J. R. (1999). Search for justice: The discovery of IQ gains over time. *American Psychologist, 54,* 5–20.

Flynn, J. R. (2007). *What is intelligence? Beyond the Flynn effect.* New York, NY: Cambridge University Press.

Flynn, J. R. (2011). Secular changes in intelligence. In R. J. Sternberg & S. B. Kaufman (Eds.), *The Cambridge handbook of intelligence* (pp. 647–665). New York, NY: Cambridge University Press.

Flyvbjerg, B. (2011). Case study. In N. K. Denzin & Y. S. Lincoln (Eds.), *The Sage handbook of qualitative research* (4th ed., pp. 301–316). Thousand Oaks, CA: Sage.

Fogassi, L., & Ferrari, P. F. (2007). Mirror neurons and the evolution of embodied language. *Current Directions in Psychological Science, 17,* 136–141.

Foley, E. P. (2011). *The law of life and death.* Cambridge, MA: Harvard University Press.

Foley, K., & Hendin, H. (2002). Conclusion: Changing the culture. In K. Foley, & H. Hendin (Eds.), *The case against assisted suicide: For the right to end-of-life care.* Baltimore, MD: The Johns Hopkins Press.

Fonagy, P., & Target, M. (2000). The place of psychodynamic theory in developmental psychopathology. *Development and Psychopathology, 12,* 407–425.

Fong, L.S., Visser, J. A., Welt, C. K., de Rijke, Y. B., Eijkemans, M. J. C., Broekmans, F. J., Roes, E. M., Peters, W. H. M., Hokken-Koelega, A. C. S., Fauser, B. C. J. M., Themmen, A. P. N., de Jong, F. H., Schipper, I., Laven, J. S. E. (2012). Serum anti-Müllerian hormone levels in healthy females: A nomogram ranging from infancy to adulthood. *Journal of Clinical Endocrinology & Metabolism, 97,* 4650–4655.

Fontaine, N. M. G., McCrory, E. J. P., Boivin, M., Moffitt, T. E., & Viding, E. (2011). Predictors and outcomes of joint trajectories of callous-unemotional traits and conduct problems in childhood. *Journal of Abnormal Psychology, 120,* 730–742.

Foorman, B. R. (1995). Research on "The Great Debate": Code-oriented versus whole language approaches to reading instruction. *School Psychology Review, 24,* 376–392.

Foorman, B. R., Francis, D. J., Fletcher, J. M., Schatschneider, C., & Mehta, P. (1998). The role of instruction in learning to read: Preventing reading failure in at-risk children. *Journal of Educational Psychology, 90,* 37–55.

Foos, P. W., & Sarno, S. J. (1998). Adult age differences in semantic and episodic memory. *Journal of Genetic Psychology, 159,* 297–312.

Ford, E. S., Kohl, H. W., Mokdad, A. H., & Ajani, U. A. (2005). Sedentary behavior, physical activity, and the metabolic syndrome among U.S. adults. *Obesity Research, 13,* 608–614.

Fordham, S., & Ogbu, J. U. (1986). Black students' school success: Coping with the "burden of 'acting white.'" *Urban Review, 18,* 176–206.

Forgatch, M. S., & DeGarmo, D. S. (1999). Parenting through change: An effective prevention program for single mothers. *Journal of Consulting and Clinical Psychology, 67,* 711–724.

Forgatch, M. S., Patterson, G. R., & Gewirtz, A. H. (2013). Looking forward: The promise of widespread implementation of parent training programs. *Perspectives on Psychological Science, 8,* 682–694.

Forhan, S. E., Gottlieb, S. L., Sternberg, M. R., Xu, F., Datta, S. D., McQuillan, G. M., . . . Markowitz, L. E. (2009). Prevalence of sexually transmitted infections among female adolescents aged 14 to 19 in the United States. *Pediatrics, 124,* 1505–1512.

Fortenbaugh, F. C., DeGutis, J., Germine, L., Wilmer, J. B., Grosso, M., Russo, K., & Esterman, M. (2015). Sustained attention across the life span in a sample of 10,000: Dissociating ability and strategy. *Psychological Science, 26,* 1497–1510.

Foster, J. D. (2008). Beauty is mostly in the eye of the beholder: Olfactory versus visual cues of attractiveness. *Journal of Social Psychology, 148,* 765–773.

Fouquereau, E., Fernandez, A., Fonseca, A. M., Paul, M. C., & Uotinen, V. (2005). Perceptions of and satisfaction with retirement: A comparison of six European Union countries. *Psychology and Aging, 20,* 524–528.

Fouquet, M., Besson, F. L., Gonneaud, J., La Joie, R., & Chételat, G. (2014). Imaging brain effects of APOE4 in cognitively normal individuals across the lifespan. *Neuropsychology Review, 24,* 290–299.

Fouts, H. N., Hewlett, B. S., & Lamb, M. E. (2012). A biocultural approach to breastfeeding interactions in Central Africa. *American Anthropologist, 114,* 123–136.

Fowler, J. W. (1981). *Stages of faith: The psychology of human development and the quest for meaning.* San Francisco, CA: Harper & Row.

Fowler, J., & Dell, M. (2006). Stages of faith from infancy through adolescence: Reflections on three decades of faith development theory. In E. Roehlkepartain, P. King, L. Wagener, & P. Benson (Eds.), *The handbook of spiritual development in childhood and adolescence.* Thousand Oaks, CA: Sage.

Fowler, L. M., & Watford, L. J. (2000). Formal reasoning and academic performance in college mathematics and psychology courses. *Educational Research Quarterly, 24,* 43.

Fowles, D. C., & Kochanska, G. (2000). Temperament as a moderator of pathways to conscience in children: The contribution of electrodermal activity. *Psychophysiology, 37,* 788–795.

Fox, M. K., Dodd, A. H., Wilson, A., & Gleason, P. M. (2009). Association between school food environment and practices and body mass index of U.S. public school children. *Journal of the American Dietetic Association, 109,* S108–117.

Fox, S. E., Levitt, P., & Nelson, C. A. (2010). How the timing and quality of early experiences influence the development of brain architecture. *Child Development, 81,* 28–40.

Fozard, J. L., & Gordon-Salant, T. (2001). Changes in vision and hearing with aging. In J. E. Birren & K. W. Schaie (Eds.), *Handbook of the psychology of aging* (5th ed., pp. 241–266). San Diego, CA: Academic Press.

Fraga, M. F., Ballestar, E., Paz, M. F., Ropero, S., Setien, F., Ballestar, M. L., Heine-Suner, D., Cigudosa, J. C., Urioste, M., Benitez, J., Boix-Chornet, M., Sanchez-Aguilera, A., Ling, C., Carlsson, E., Poulsen, P., Vaag, A., Stephan, Z., Spector, T. D., Wu, Y-Z., Plass, C., & Esteller, M. (2005). Epigenetic differences arise during the lifetime of monozygotic twins. *Proceedings of the National Academy of Sciences, 102,* 10604–10609.

Fragouli, E., Spath, K., Alfarawati, S., Kaper, F., Craig, A., Michel, C. E., et al. (2015) Altered levels of mitochondrial DNA are associated with female age, aneuploidy, and provide an independent measure of embryonic implantation potential. *PLoS Genetics* 11(6): e1005241.

Fraley, R. C., & Roisman, G. I. (2015). Early attachment experiences and romantic functioning: Developmental pathways, emerging issues, and future directions. In J. A Simpson & W. S. Rholes (Eds.), *Attachment theory and research: New directions and emerging themes* (pp. 9–38). New York, NY: Guilford.

Fraley, R. C., & Shaver, P. R. (2008). Attachment theory and its place in contemporary personality theory. In O. P. John, R. W. Robins, & L. A. Pervin (Eds.), *Handbook of personality theory and research* (3rd ed.). New York, NY: Guilford.

Fraley, R. C., Fazzari, D. A., Bonanno, G. A., & Dekel, S. (2006). Attachment and psychological adaptation in high exposure survivors of the September 11th attack on the World Trade Center. *Personality and Social Psychology Bulletin, 32*, 538–551.

Fraley, R. C., Roisman, G. I., Booth-LaForce, C., Owen, M. T., & Holland, A. S. (2013). Interpersonal and genetic origins of adult attachment styles: A longitudinal study from infancy to early adulthood. *Journal of Personality and Social Psychology, 104*, 817–838.

Franchak, J. M., Kretch, K. S., Soska, K. C., & Adolph, K. E. (2011). Head-mounted eye tracking: A new method to describe infant looking. *Child Development, 82*, 1738–1750.

Francis, D., Diorio, J., Liu, D., & Meaney, M. J. (1999). Nongenomic transmission across generations of maternal behavior and stress responses in the rat. *Science, 286* (5442), 1155–1158.

Francis, E. (2012, June 4). M.D. at 21, Sho Yano is real-life 'Doogie Howser.' *ABCNews*. Retrieved from abcnews. go.com/blogs/ headlines/2012/06/m-d-at-21-sho-yano-is-real-life-doogie-howser/.

Frank, S. M., Raja, S. N., Bulcao, C., & Goldstein, D. S. (2000). Age-related thermoregulatory differences during core cooling in humans. *American Journal of Physiological Regulation, Integration, and Comparative Physiology, 279*, R349–354.

Frankenmolen, N. L., Altgassen, M., Kessels, R., de Waal, M. M., Hindriksen, J. A., Verhoeven, B., & Oosterman, J. M. (2016). Intelligence moderates the benefits of strategy instructions on memory performance: An adult-lifespan examination. *Neuropsychology, Development, and Cognition. Section B, Aging, Neuropsychology and Cognition*, 1–17.

Frankland, P. W., & Josselyn, S. A. (2016). Hippocampal neurogenesis and memory clearance. *Neuropsychopharmacology, 41*, 382–383.

Franklin, C., & Corcoran, J. (2000). Preventing adolescent pregnancy: A review of programs and practices. *Social Work, 45*, 40–52.

Franklin, Z., Pilling, M., & Davies, I. (2005). The nature of infant color categorization: Evidence from eye movements on a target detection task. *Journal of Experimental Child Psychology, 91*, 227–248.

Franko, D. L., & George, J. B. E. (2009). Overweight, eating behaviors, and body image in ethnically diverse youth. In L. Smolak & J. K. Thompson (Eds.), *Body image, eating disorders, and obesity in youth*. Washington, DC: American Psychological Association.

Frans, E. M., McGrath, J. J., Sandin, S., Lichtenstein, P., Reichenberg, A., Långström, N., et al. (2011). Advanced paternal and grandpaternal age and schizophrenia: A three-generation perspective. *Schizophrenia Research, 133*, 120–124.

Fraser, M. W. (2004). The ecology of childhood: A multisystems perspective. In M. W. Fraser (Ed.), *Risk and resilience in childhood: An ecological perspective* (2nd ed., 1–9). Washington, D. C. NASW Press.

Fraser, S. L., Muckle, G., Abdous, B. B., Jacobson, J. L., & Jacobson, S. W. (2012). Effects of binge drinking on infant growth and development in an Inuit sample. *Alcohol, 46*, 277–283.

Frattarelli, J. L., Miller, K. A., Miller, B. T., Elkind-Hirsch, K., & Scott, R. T. (2008). Male age negatively impacts embryo development and reproductive outcome in donor oocyte assisted reproductive technology cycles. *Fertility and Sterility, 90*, 97–103.

Frawley, W. (1997). *Vygotsky and cognitive science: Language and the unification of the social and computational mind*. Cambridge, MA: Harvard University Press.

Frederick, D. A., Peplau, L. A., & Lever, J. (2006). The swimsuit issue: Correlates of body image in a sample of 52,677 heterosexual adults. *Body Image, 3*, 413–419.

Frederick, S. (2005). Cognitive reflection and decision making. *Journal of Economic Perspectives, 19*, 25–42.

Freedman, D. H. (2012, June). The perfected self. *The Atlantic, 309*, 42–52.

Freeman, S. F. N. (2000). Academic and social attainments of children with mental retardation in general education and special education settings. *Remedial and Special Education, 21*, 3–19.

Freud, S. (1930). *Three contributions to the theory of sex*. New York, NY: Nervous and Mental Disease Publishing Company. (Original work published 1905).

Freud, S. (1933). *New introductory lectures in psychoanalysis*. New York, NY: Norton.

Freud, S. (1960). *A general introduction to psychoanalysis*. New York, NY: Washington Square Press. (Original work published 1935).

Freud, S. (1964). An outline of psychoanalysis. In J. Strachey (Ed.), *The standard edition of the complete psychological works of Sigmund Freud: Vol. 23*. London: Hogarth Press. (Original work published 1940).

Freund, A. M., & Ritter, J. O. (2009). Midlife crisis: A debate. *Gerontology, 55*, 582–591.

Freund, L. S. (1990). Maternal regulation of children's problem solving behavior and its impact on children's performance. *Child Development, 61*, 113–126.

Frey, K. S., & Ruble, D. N. (1985). What children say when the teacher is not around: Conflicting goals in social comparison and performance assessment in the classroom. *Journal of Personality and Social Psychology, 48*, 550–562.

Frey, K. S., & Ruble, D. N. (1992). Gender constancy and the cost of sex-typed behavior: A test of the conflict hypothesis. *Developmental Psychology, 28*, 714–721.

Freyd, J. J., Putnam, F. W., Lyon, T. D., Becker-Blease, K. A., Cheit, R. E., Siegel, N. B., et al. (2005). The science of child sexual abuse. *Science, 308*, 501.

Fried, E. I., Bockting, C., Arjadi, R., Borsboom, D., Amshoff, M., Cramer, A. O. J., . . . Stroebe, M. (2015). From loss to loneliness: The relationship between bereavement and depressive symptoms. *Journal of Abnormal Psychology, 124*, 256–265.

Friedlmeier, W., Corapci, F., & Benga, O. (2015). Early emotional development in cultural perspective. In L. A. Jensen (Ed.), *Oxford handbook of human development and culture* (pp. 127–148). New York, NY: Oxford University Press.

Friedman, H., & Martin, L. (2011). *The longevity project: Surprising discoveries for health and long life from the landmark eight-decade study*. New York, NY: Penguin Group.

Friedman, J. M., & Polifka, J. E. (2000). *Teratogenic effects of drugs: A resource for clinicians (TERIS)*. Baltimore, MD: Johns Hopkins University Press.

Friedman, L. J. (1999). *Identity's architect: A biography of Erik H. Erikson*. New York, NY: Scribner.

Friedman, S. L., & Boyle, D. E. (2008). Attachment in US children experiencing nonmaternal care in the early 1990s. *Attachment and Human Development, 10*, 225–261.

Frieswijk, N., Buunk, B. P., Steverink, N., & Slaets, J. P. J. (2004). The effect of social comparison information on the life satisfaction of frail older persons. *Psychology and Aging, 19*, 183–190.

Froehlich, T. E., Lanphear, B. P., Epstein, J. N., Barbaresi, W. J., Katusic, S. K., & Kahn, R. S. (2007). Prevalence, recognition, and treatment of attention-deficit/hyperactivity disorder in a national sample of US children. *Archives of Pediatric & Adolescent Medicine, 161*, 857–864.

Fry, C. L. (1985). Culture, behavior, and aging in the comparative perspective. In J. E. Birren & K. W. Schaie (Eds.), *Handbook of the psychology of aging* (2nd ed.). New York, NY: Van Nostrand Reinhold.

Fry, C. L. (2009). Out of the armchair and off the veranda: Anthropological theories and the experiences of aging. In V. L. Bengtson, M. Silverstein, N. M. Putney, & D. Gans (Eds.), *Handbook of theories of aging* (2nd ed.). New York, NY: Springer.

Fry, P. S. (1992). Major social theories of aging and their implications for counseling concepts and practice: A critical review. *Counseling Psychologist, 20*, 246–329.

Fry, P. S. (1997). Grandparents' reactions to the death of a grandchild: An exploratory factor analytic study. *Omega: Journal of Death and Dying, 35*,119–140.

Fry, R. (2016, May 24). *For first time in modern era, living with parents edges out other living arrangements for 18- to 34-year-olds*. Pew Research Center. Retrieved from www.pewsocialtrends.org/2016/05/24/for-first-time-in-modern-era-living-with-parents-edges-out-other-living-arrangements-for-18-to-34-year-olds/.

Fryar, C. D., Gu, Q., & Ogden, C. L. (2012). Anthropometric reference data for children and adults: United States, 2007–2010. National Center for Health Statistics. Vital Health Statistics, *11*(252).

Fryer, R. G. (2011). Financial incentives and student achievement: Evidence from randomized trials. *The Quarterly Journal of Economics, 126*, 1755–1798.

Fu, G., Xiao, W. S., Killen, M., & Lee, K. (2014). Moral judgment and its relation to second-order theory of mind. *Developmental Psychology, 50*, 2085–2092.

Fuglenes, D., Aas, E., Botten, G., Øian, P., & Kristiansen, I. S. (2012). Maternal preference for cesarean delivery: Do women get what they want? *Obstetrics and Gynecology, 120*, 252–260.

Fuligni, A. J. (1998). Authority, autonomy, and parent–adolescent conflict and cohesion: A study of adolescents from Mexican, Chinese, Filipino, and European backgrounds. *Developmental Psychology, 34*, 782–792.

Furman, E. (1984). Children's patterns in mourning the death of a loved one. In H. Wass & C. A. Corr (Eds.), *Childhood and death*. Washington, DC: Hemisphere.

Furman, W., & Buhrmester, D. (1992). Age and sex differences in perceptions of networks of personal relationships. *Child Development, 63*, 103–115.

Furman, W., & Collibee, C. (2014). A matter of timing: Developmental theories of romantic involvement and psychosocial adjustment. *Developmental Psychopathology, 26*, 1149–1160.

Furman, W., & Collins, W. A. (2009). Adolescent romantic relationships and experiences. In K. H. Rubin, W. M. Bukowski, & B. Laursen (Eds.), *Handbook of peer interactions, relationships, and groups*. New York, NY: Guilford.

Furman, W., & Rose, A. J. (2015). Friendships, romantic relationships, and peer relationships. In M. E. Lamb (Vol. Ed.) & R. M. Lerner (Ed.), *Handbook of child psychology and developmental science: Vol. 3. Socioemotional processes* (7th ed., pp. 932–974). Hoboken, NJ: Wiley.

Furman, W., Stephenson, J. C., & Rhoades, G. K. (2014). Positive interactions and avoidant and anxious representations in relationships with parents, friends, and romantic partners. *Journal of Research on Adolescence, 24*, 615–629.

Furstenberg, F. F., Jr. (2000). The sociology of adolescence and youth in the 1990s: A critical commentary. *Journal of Marriage and the Family, 62*, 896–910.

Furstenberg, F. F., Jr., Kennedy, S., McLoyd, V. C., Rumbaut, R. G., & Settersten, R. A., Jr. (2004). Growing up is harder to do. *Contexts, 3*(3), 33–41.

Gage, F. H., Song, H., & Kempermann, G. (2008). Adult neurogenesis: A prologue. In F. H. Gage, G. Kempermann, & H. Song (Eds.), *Adult neurogenesis* (pp. 1–6). New York: Cold Spring Harbor Laboratory Press.

Gaither, S. E. (2015). "Mixed" results: Multiracial research and identity explorations. *Current Directions in Psychological Science, 24*, 114–119.

Galambos, N. L., Almeida, D. M., & Petersen, A. C. (1990). Masculinity, femininity, and sex role attitudes in early adolescence: Exploring gender intensification. *Child Development, 61*, 1905–1914.

Galanaki, E. (2012). The imaginary audience and the personal fable: A test of Elkind's theory of adolescent egocentrism. *Psychology, 03*, 457–466.

Galatzer-Levy, I., & Bonanno, G. A. (2012). Beyond normality in the study of bereavement: Heterogeneity in depression outcomes following loss in older adults. *Social Science & Medicine, 74*, 1987–1994.

Galdo-Alvarez, S., Lindin, M., & Diaz, F. (2009). Age-related prefrontal over-recruitment in semantic memory retrieval: Evidence from successful face naming and the tip-of-the-tongue state. *Biological Psychology, 82*, 89–96.

Galenson, E. (2015). Observation of early infantile sexual and erotic development. In N. L. Thompson (Ed.), *Play, gender, therapy: Selected papers of Eleanor Galenson* (pp. 129–142). London, UK: Karnac Books.

Gallese, V., Rochat, M. J., & Berchio, C. (2013). The mirror mechanism and its potential role in autism spectrum disorder. *Developmental Medicine & Child Neurology, 55*, 15–22.

Gallup, G. G., Jr. (1979). Self-recognition in chimpanzees and man: A developmental and comparative perspective.

In M. Lewis & L. A. Rosenblum (Eds.), *Genesis of behavior: Vol. 2. The child and its family*. New York, NY: Plenum.

Galupo, M. P., Cartwright, K. B., & Savage, L. S. (2009, December 16). Cross-category friendships and postformal thought among college students. *Journal of Adult Development*. Springer Netherlands: Published online.

Galvan, A. (2010). Adolescent development of the reward system. *Frontiers of Human Neuroscience, 4*, 6.

Galvan, A., Hare, T., Voss, H., Gover, G., & Casey, B. J. (2007). Risk-taking and the adolescent brain: Who is at risk? *Developmental Science, 10*, F8–F14.

Gamé, F., Carchon, I., & Vital-Durand, F. (2003). The effect of stimulus attractiveness on visual tracking in 2- to 6-month-old infants. *Infant Behavior & Development, 26*, 135–150.

Gameiro, S., van den Belt-Dusebout, A. W., Bleiker, E., Braat, D., van Leeuwen, F. E. & Verhaak, C. M. (2014). Do children make you happier? Sustained child-wish and mental health in women 11–17 years after fertility treatment. *Human Reproduction, 29*, 2238–2246.

Ganahl, D. J., Prinsen, T. J., & Netzley, S. B. (2003). A content analysis of prime time commercials: A contextual framework of gender representation. *Sex Roles, 49*, 545–551.

Ganiban, J. M., Ulbricht, J., Saudino, K. J., Reiss, D., & Neiderhiser, J. M. (2011). Understanding child-based effects on parenting: Temperament as a moderator of genetic and environmental contributions to parenting. *Developmental Psychology, 47*, 676–692.

Gannon, L., & Ekstrom, B. (1993). Attitudes toward menopause: The influence of sociocultural paradigms. *Psychology of Women Quarterly, 17*, 275–288.

Ganong, L., Coleman, M., & Russell, L. T. (2015). Children in diverse families. In M. H. Bornstein & T. Leventhal (Vol. Eds.) & R. M. Lerner (General Ed.), *Handbook of child psychology and developmental science: Vol. 4 Ecological settings and processes* (pp. 133–174). Hoboken, NJ: Wiley.

Gao, X., Maurer, D., & Nishimura, M. (2013). Altered representation of facial expressions after early visual deprivation. *Frontiers in Psychology, 4*, 878.

Gao, Y., Wei, Y., Shen, Y., Tang, Y., & Yang, J. (2014). China's empty nest elderly need better care. *Journal of the American Geriatrics Society, 62*, 1821–1822.

Garber, H. L. (1988). *The Milwaukee Project: Preventing mental retardation in children at risk*. Washington, DC: American Association on Mental Retardation.

Garber, J. (1984). The developmental progression of depression in female children. In D. Cicchetti & K. Schneider-Rosen (Eds.), *Childhood depression* (New Directions for Child Development, No. 26). San Francisco, CA: Jossey-Bass.

Garber, J. (2010). Vulnerability to depression in childhood and adolescence. In R. E. Ingram & J. M. Price (2010). *Vulnerability to psychopathology: Risk across the lifespan* (2nd ed.). New York, NY: Guilford.

Garces, E., Thomas, D., & Currie, J. (2002). Longer term effects of Head Start. *American Economic Review, 92*, 999–1102.

Garcia, F., & Gracia, E. (2009). Is always authoritative the optimum parenting style? Evidence from Spanish families. *Adolescence, 44*, 101–131.

Garcia, J. R., Reiber, C., Massey, S. G., & Merriwether, A. M. (2012). Sexual hookup culture: A review. *Review of General Psychology, 16*, 161–176.

Garciaguirre, J. S., Adolph, K. E., & Shrout, P. E. (2007). Baby carriage: Infants walking with loads. *Child Development, 78*, 664–680.

Gardener, H., Spiegelman, D., & Buka, S. L. (2009). Prenatal risk factors for autism: Comprehensive meta-analysis. *British Journal of Psychiatry, 195*, 7–14.

Gardner, H. (1993a). *Creating minds: An anatomy of creativity as seen through the lives of Freud, Einstein, Picasso, Stravinsky, Eliot, Graham, and Gandhi*. New York, NY: Basic Books.

Gardner, H. (1993b). *Frames of mind: The theory of multiple intelligences* (Tenth anniversary ed.). New York: Basic Books.

Gardner, H. (1999/2000). *Intelligence reframed: Multiple intelligences for the 21st century*. New York: Basic Books.

Gardner, H. (2006). *Multiple intelligences: New horizons in theory and practice* (Rev. and updated ed.). New York, NY: Basic Books.

Gardner, M., & Steinberg, L. (2005). Peer influence on risk taking, risk preference, and risky decision making in adolescence and adulthood: An experimental study. *Developmental Psychology, 41*, 625–635.

Gardner, P., Katagiri, K., Parsons, J., Lee, J., & Thevannoor, R. (2012). "Not for the fainthearted": Engaging in cross-national comparative research. *Journal of Aging Studies, 26*, 253–261.

Gardner, R. J. M., Sutherland, G. R., & Shaffer, L. G. (Eds.). (2012). *Chromosome abnormalities and genetic counseling* (4th ed.). New York, NY: Oxford University Press.

Garmezy, N. (1994). Reflections and commentary on risk, resilience, and development. In R. J. Haggerty, L. R. Sherrod, N. Garmezy, & M. Rutter (Eds.), *Stress, risk and resilience in children and adolescents: Processes, mechanisms, and interventions*. Cambridge, UK: Cambridge University Press.

Garthe, A., Roeder, I., & Kempermann, G. (2016). Mice in an enriched environment learn more flexibly because of adult hippocampal neurogenesis. *Hippocampus, 26*, 261–271.

Garvey, C. (1990). *Play* (enlarged ed.). Cambridge, MA: Harvard University Press.

Gatz, M. (2007). Genetics, dementia, and the elderly. *Current Directions in Psychological Science, 16*, 123–127.

Gatz, M., Reynolds, C. A., Fratiglioni, L., Johansson, B., Mortimer, J. A., Berg, S., Fiske, A., & Pedersen, N. L. (2006). Role of genes and environments for explaining Alzheimer disease. *Archives of General Psychiatry, 63*, 168–174.

Gauvain, M., & Perez, S. (2015). Cognitive development and culture. In R. M. Lerner (Ed.), *Handbook of child psychology and developmental science* (pp. 854–896). Hoboken, NJ: Wiley.

Gauvain, M., & Rogoff, B. (1989). Collaborative problem-solving and children's planning skills. *Developmental Psychology, 25*, 139–151.

Gavin, N., Gaynes, B., Lohr, K., Meltzer-Brody, S., Gartlehner, G., & Swinson, T. (2005). Perinatal depression: A systematic review of prevalence and incidence. *Obstetrics and Gynecology, 106*, 1071–1083.

Gavrilov, L. A., & Gavrilova, N. S. (2011). Season of birth and exceptional longevity: Comparative study of American centenarians, their siblings, and spouses. *Journal of Aging Research: Vol. 2011*, 104616.

Gavrilov, L. A., & Gavrilova, N. S. (2015). Predictors of exceptional longevity: Effects of early-life and midlife conditions, and familial longevity. *North American Actuarial Journal, 19*, 174–186.

Gazzaniga, M. S. (1998). The split brain revisited. *Scientific American, 279*, 50–55.

Ge, X., Best, K. M., Conger, R. D., & Simons, R. L. (1996). Parenting behaviors and the occurrence and co-occurrence of adolescent depressive symptoms and conduct problems. *Developmental Psychology, 32*, 717–731.

Ge, X., Kim, I. J., Brody, G. H., Conger, R. D., Simons, R. L., Gibbons, F. X., & Cutrona, C. E. (2003). It's about timing and change: Pubertal transition effects on symptoms of major depression among African American youths. *Developmental Psychology, 39*, 430–439.

Ge, X., Lorenz, F. O., Conger, R. D., Elder, G. H., Jr., & Simons, R. L. (1994). Trajectories of stressful life events and depressive symptoms during adolescence. *Developmental Psychology, 30*, 467–483.

Ge, X., Natsuaki, M. N., & Conger, R. D. (2006). Trajectories of depressive symptoms and stressful life events among male and female adolescents in divorced and nondivorced families. *Development and Psychopathology, 18*, 253–273.

Geda, Y. E., Silber, T. C., Roberts, R. O., Knopman, D. S., Christianson, T. J. H., Pankratz, V. S., et al. (2012). Computer activities, physical exercise, aging, and mild cognitive impairment: A population-based study. *Mayo Clinic Proceedings, 87*, 437–442.

Geddes, L. (2013, August 27). Are designer babies coming in the future? *The Washington Post*, p. E6.

Geier, C. F. (2013). Adolescent cognitive control and reward processing: Implications for risk taking and substance use. *Hormones and Behavior, 64*, 333–342.

Geithner, C. A., Satake, T., Woynarowska, B., & Malina, R. M. (1999). Adolescent spurts in body dimensions: Average and modal sequences. *American Journal of Human Biology, 11*, 287–295.

Geldmacher, D. S. (2009). Alzheimer disease. In M. F. Weiner & A. M. Lipton (Eds.), *The American Psychiatric Publishing textbook of Alzheimer disease and other dementias*. Washington, DC: American Psychiatric Publishing.

Gelman, R. (1978). Cognitive development. *Annual Review of Psychology, 29*, 297–332.

Gelman, R. S. (1972). Logical capacity of very young children: Number invariance rules. *Child Development, 43*, 75–90.

Gelman, S. A. (1996). Concepts and theories. In R. Gelman & T. K. Au (Eds.), *Perceptual and cognitive development*. San Diego, CA: Academic Press.

George, L. G., Helson, R., & John, O. P. (2011). The "CEO" of women's work lives: How Big Five conscientiousness, extraversion, and openness predict 50 years of work experiences in a changing sociocultural context. *Journal of Personality and Social Psychology, 101*, 812–830.

Gershoff, E. T. (2002). Corporal punishment by parents and associated child behaviors and experiences: A meta-analytic and theoretical review. *Psychological Bulletin, 128*, 539–579.

Gershoff, E. T. (2008). *Report on physical punishment in the United States: What research tells us about its effects on children*. Columbus, OH: Center for Effective Discipline. Retrieved from The Center for Effective Discipline website: www.phoenixchildrens.com/ community/injury-prevention-center/effective-discipline.html.

Gershoff, E. T. (2013). Spanking and child development: We know enough now to stop hitting our children. *Child Development Perspectives, 7*, 133–137.

Gershon, E. S., & Alliey-Rodriguez, N. (2013). New ethical issues for genetic counseling in common mental disorders. *American Journal of Psychiatry, 170*, 968–976.

Gerstein, E. D., Crnic, K. A., Blacher, J., & Baker, B. L. (2009). Resilience and the course of daily parenting stress in families of young children with intellectual disabilities. *Journal of Intellectual Disability Research, 53*, 981–997.

Gerst-Emerson, K., & Jayawardhana, J. (2015). Loneliness as a public health issue: The impact of loneliness on health care utilization among older adults. *American Journal of Public Health, 105*, 1013–1019.

Gerstorf, D., Hoppmann, C. A., Kadlec, K. M., & McArdle, J. J. (2009). Memory and depressive symptoms are dynamically linked among married couples: Longitudinal evidence from the AHEAD study. *Developmental Psychology, 45*, 1595–1610.

Gervain, J., & Mehler, J. (2010). Speech perception and language acquisition in the first year of life. *Annual Review of Psychology, 61*, 191–218.

Gervain, J., & Werker, J. F. (2013). Prosody cues word order in 7-month-old bilingual infants. *Nature Communications, 4*, 1490.

Gest, S. D., Graham-Bermann, S. A., & Hartup, W. W. (2001). Peer experience: Common and unique features of number of friendships, social network centrality, and sociometric status. *Social Development, 10*, 23–40.

Getzels, J. W., & Jackson, P. W. (1962). *Creativity and intelligence: Explorations with gifted children*. New York, NY: Wiley.

Geurten, M., Catale, C., & Meulemans, T. (2015). When children's knowledge of memory improves children's performance in memory. *Applied Cognitive Psychology, 29*, 244–252.

Ghetti, S., & Lee, J. K. (2014). Implicit memory. In P. Bauer & R. Fivush (Eds.), *The Wiley handbook on the development of children's memory* (pp. 336–360). Malden, MA: Wiley Blackwell.

Ghetti, S., Lyons, K. E., & Cornoldi, C. (2008). The development of metamemory monitoring during retrieval: The case of memory strength and memory absence. *Journal of Experimental Child Psychology, 99*, 157–181.

Giarrusso, R., Feng, D., Silverstein, M., & Bengtson, V. L. (2000). Self in the context of the family. In K. W. Schaie & J. Hendrick (Eds.), *The evolution of the aging self. The societal impact on the aging process*. New York, NY: Springer.

Gibbs, J. C. (2010). *Moral development and reality. Beyond the theories of Kohlberg and Hoffman* (2nd ed.). Boston, MA: Allyn & Bacon.

Gibbs, J. C. (2014). *Moral development and reality. Beyond the theories of Kohlberg, Hoffman, and Haidt* (3rd ed.). New York, NY: Oxford University Press.

Gibbs, J. C., Basinger, K. S., Grime, R. L., & Snarey, J. R. (2007). Moral judgment development across cultures:

Revisiting Kohlberg's universality claims. *Developmental Review, 27*, 443–500.
Gibbs, N. (2009, August 3). Dying together. An elderly British couple's suicide pact is a beautifully romantic act—and a troubling one. *Time, 64*.
Gibson, E. J. (1988). Exploratory behavior in the development of perceiving, acting, and the acquiring of knowledge. *Annual Review of Psychology, 39*, 1–41.
Gibson, E. J. (2001). *Perceiving the affordances: A portrait of two psychologists*. Mahwah, NJ: Lawrence Erlbaum Associates.
Gibson, E. J., & Pick, A. D. (2000). *An ecological approach to perceptual learning and development*. New York, NY: Oxford University Press.
Gibson, E. J., & Walk, R. D. (1960). The "visual cliff." *Scientific American, 202*, 67–71.
Gibson, J. J. (1966). *The senses considered as perceptual systems*. Boston, MA: Houghton Mifflin.
Gibson, J. J. (1979). *The ecological approach to visual perception*. Hillsdale: Lawrence Erlbaum Associates.
Giedd, J. N. (2004). Structural magnetic resonance imaging of the adolescent brain. *Annals of the New York Academic of Sciences, 1021*, 77–85.
Giedd, J. N., Adeyemi, E., Stockman, M., Alexander-Block, A., Lee, N. R., Raznahan, A., Lenroot, R. K., & Kruesi, M. J. P. (2013). Neuroanatomic maturation and aggression during adolescence. In C. R. Thomas & K. Pope (Eds.), *The origins of antisocial behavior: A developmental perspective*. New York, NY: Oxford University Press.
Gifted Development Center. (2016). *Characteristics of Giftedness Scale*. Retrieved from www.gifteddevelopment.com/sites/default/files/Characteristics%20of%20Giftedness%20Scale%202014.pdf.
Gil, D. G. (1970). *Violence against children*. Cambridge, MA: Harvard University Press.
Gilissen, C., Hehir-Kwa, J. Y., Thung, D. T., van de Vorst, M., van Bon, B. W., Willemsen, M. H., . . . Veltman, J. A. (2014). Genome sequencing identifies major causes of severe intellectual disability. *Nature, 511*, 344–347.
Gill, S. J., Friedenreich, C. M., Sajobi, T. T., Longman, R. S., Drogos, L. L., Davenport, M. H., & Poulin, M. J. (2015). Association between lifetime physical activity and cognitive functioning in middle-aged and older community dwelling adults: Results from the Brain in Motion Study. *Journal of the International Neuropsychological Society, 21*, 816–830.
Gillen-O'Neel, C., Huynh, V. W., & Fuligni, A. J. (2013). To study or to sleep? The academic costs of extra studying at the expense of sleep. *Child Development, 84*, 133–142.
Gini, G., Pozzoli, T., & Bussey, K. (2015). Moral disengagement moderates the link between psychopathic traits and aggressive behavior among early adolescents. *Merrill-Palmer Quarterly, 61*, 51–67.
Ginsburg, G. S., & Bronstein, P. (1993). Family factors related to children's intrinsic/extrinsic motivational orientation and academic performance. *Child Development, 64*, 1461–1474.
Ginzberg, E. (1972). Toward a theory of occupational choice: A restatement. *Vocational Guidance Quarterly, 20*, 169–176.
Ginzberg, E. (1984). Career development. In D. Brown, L. Brooks, & Associates (Eds.), *Career choice and development*. San Francisco, CA: Jossey-Bass.
Giordano, P. C. (2003). Relationships in adolescence. *Annual Review of Sociology, 29*, 257–281.
Girard, C. (1993). Age, gender, and suicide: A cross-national analysis. *American Sociological Review, 58*, 553–574.
Givertz, M., & Segrin, C. (2014). The association between overinvolved parenting and young adults' self-efficacy, psychological entitlement, and family communication. *Communication Research, 41*, 1111–1136.
Glascock, A. (2009). Is killing necessarily murder? Moral questions surrounding assisted suicide and death. In J. Sokolovsky (Ed.), *The cultural context of aging* (3rd ed.). Westport, CT: Praeger.
Glascock, J. (2001). Gender roles on prime-time network television: Demographics and behaviors. *Journal of Broadcasting & Electronic Media, 45*, 656–669.
Glaser, B. G., & Strauss, A. L. (1968). *Time for dying*. Chicago: Aldine.
Glaser, R., & Chi, M. T. H. (1988). Overview. In M. T. H. Chi, R. Glaser, & M. Farr (Eds.), *The nature of expertise*. Hillsdale, NJ: Erlbaum.
Glasgow, K. L., Dornbusch, S. M., Troyer, L., Steinberg, L., & Ritter, P. L. (1997). Parenting styles, adolescents' attributions, and educational outcomes in nine heterogeneous high schools. *Child Development, 68*, 507–529.
Glass, G. V., McGaw, B., & Smith, M. L. (1981). *Meta-analysis in social research*. Beverly Hills, CA: Sage.
Glatt, S. J., Tsuang, M. T., Winn, M., Chandler, S. D., Collins, M., Lopez, L., et al. (2012). Blood-based gene expression signatures of infants and toddlers with autism. *Journal of the American Academy of Child and Adolescent Psychiatry, 51*, 934–944.
Gleason, J. B. (2005). *The development of language* (6th ed). Upper Saddle River, NJ: Pearson Education.
Gleason, J. B., & Ratner, N. B., Eds. (2017). *The development of language* (9th ed.). Boston, MA: Pearson.
Gleason, P. M., & Dodd, A. H. (2009). School breakfast program but not school lunch program participation is associated with lower body mass index. *Journal of the American Dietetic Association, 109*, S118–S128.
Gleason, T. R., & Kalpidou, M. (2014). Imaginary companions and young children's coping and competence. *Social Development, 23*, 820–839.
Glenberg, A. M. (2011). Positions in the mirror are closer than they appear. *Perspectives on Psychological Science, 6*, 408–410.
Glick, J. C. (1975). Cognitive development in cross-cultural perspective. In F. Horowitz (Ed.), *Review of child development research: Vol. 1*. Chicago, IL: University of Chicago Press.
Glick, M., & Zigler, E. (1985). Self-image: A cognitive developmental approach. In R. L. Leahy (Ed.), *The development of the self*. Orlando, FL: Academic Press.
Gloth, F. M. (2000). Geriatric pain: Factors that limit pain relief and increase complications. *Geriatrics, 55*, 51–54.
Gloth F. M. (2001). Pain management in older adults: Prevention and treatment. *Journal of the American Geriatric Society, 49*, 188–199.
Glowinski, A. L., Madden, P. A. F., Bucholz, K. K., Lynskey, M. T., & Heath, A. C. (2003). Genetic epidemiology of self-reported lifetime DSM-IV major depressive disorder in a population-based twin sample of female adolescents. *Journal of Child Psychology and Psychiatry and Allied Disciplines, 44*, 988–996.
Gluckman, P. D., & Hanson, M. A. (2006). Evolution, development and timing of puberty. *Trends in Endocrinology and Metabolism, 17*, 7–12.
Gnepp, J., & Chilamkurti, C. (1988). Children's use of personality attributions to predict other people's emotional and behavioral reactions. *Child Development, 59*, 743–754.
Godar, S. P., Grieco, T. M., & Litovsky, R. Y. (2007, April). *Emergence of bilateral abilities in children who transition from using one to two cochlear implants*. Presented at the 11th International Cochlear Implant Conference, Charlotte, NC.
Goh, J. O., & Park, D. C. (2009). Neuroplasticity and cognitive aging: The scaffolding theory of aging and cognition. *Restorative Neurology and Neuroscience, 27*, 391–403.
Goh, J. O., Chee, M. W., Tan, J. C., Venkatraman, V., Hebrank, A., Leshikar, E. D., et al. (2007). Age and culture modulate object processing and object-scene binding in the ventral visual area. *Cognitive, Affective, & Behavioral Neuroscience, 7*, 44–52.
Gohlke, B., & Woelfle, J. (2009). Growth and puberty in German children: Is there still a positive secular trend? *Deutsches Ärzteblatt International, 106*, 377–382.
Goldberg, A. E. (2009). *Lesbian and gay parents and their children: Research on the family life cycle*. Washington, DC: American Psychological Association.
Goldberg, A. E., & Perry-Jenkins, M. (2007). The division of labor and perceptions of parental roles: Lesbian couples across the transition to parenthood. *Journal of Social and Personal Relationships, 24*, 297–318.
Goldberg, A. P., & Hagberg, J. M. (1990). Physical exercise in the elderly. In E. L. Schneider & J. W. Rowe (Eds.), *Handbook of the biology of aging* (3rd ed.). San Diego, CA: Academic Press.
Goldberg, S. (1983). Parent-infant bonding: Another look. *Child Development, 54*, 1355–1382.
Goldfield, G. S., Adamo, K. B., Rutherford, J., & Murray, M. (2012). The effects of aerobic exerciese on psychosocial functioning of adolescents who are overweight or obese. *Journal of Pediatric Psychology, 37*, 1136–1147.
Goldhaber, D. (2012). *The nature-nurture debates: Bridging the gap*. New York, NY: Cambridge University Press.
Goldhaber, D. E. (2000). *Theories of human development. Integrative perspectives*. Mountain View, CA: Mayfield.
Goldin-Meadow, S. (2009). From gesture to word. In E. L. Bavin (Ed.), *The Cambridge handbook of child language* (pp. 145–160). New York, NY: Cambridge University Press.
Goldman, S. (2008). Neurogenesis in the adult songbird: A model for inducible striatal neuronal addition. In F. H. Gage, G. Kempermann, & H. Song (Eds.), *Adult neurogenesis* (pp. 593–617). New York, NY: Cold Spring Harbor Laboratory Press.
Goldschmidt, L., Richardson, G. A., Cornelius, M. D., & Day, N. L. (2004). Prenatal marijuana and alcohol exposure and academic achievement at age 10. *Neurotoxicology& Teratology, 26*, 521–532.
Goldsmith, H. H. (2003). Genetics of emotional development. In R. J. Davidson, K. R. Scherer, & H. H. Goldsmith (Eds.), *Handbook of affective sciences*. New York, NY: Oxford University Press.
Goldstein, E. B. (2007). *Sensation and perception* (7th ed.). Belmont, CA: Wadsworth.
Goldstein, M. H., Schwade, J. A., & Bornstein, M. H. (2009). The value of vocalizing: Five-month-old infants associate their own noncry vocalizations with responses from caregivers. *Child Development, 80*, 636–644.
Goldstein, S. E., Davis-Kean, P. E., & Eccles, J. S. (2005). Parents, peers, and problem behavior: A longitudinal investigation of the impact of relationship perceptions and characteristics on the development of adolescent problem behavior. *Developmental Psychology, 41*, 401–413.
Goldstein, S., & Reynolds, C. R. (Eds.). (2011). *Handbook of neurodevelopmental and genetic disorders in children* (2nd ed.). New York, NY: Guilford.
Goldwater, O. D., & Nutt, R. L. (1999). Teachers' and students' work-culture variables associated with positive school outcome. *Adolescence, 34*, 653–664.
Golinkoff, R. M., & Hirsh-Pasek, K. (2006). Baby wordsmith: From associationist to social sophisticate. *Current Directions in Psychological Science, 15*, 30–33.
Golinkoff, R. M., Can, D. D., Soderstrom, M., & Hirsh-Pasek, K. (2015). (Baby) talk to me: The social context of infant-directed speech and its effects on early language acquisition. *Current Directions in Psychological Science, 24*, 339–344.
Golombok, S., Perry, B., Burston, A., Murray, C., Mooney-Somers, J., Stevens, M., & Golding, J. (2003). Children with lesbian parents: A community study. *Developmental Psychology, 39*, 20–33.
Golombok, S., Rust, J., Zervoulis, K., Golding, J., & Hines, M. (2012). Continuity in sex-typed behavior from preschool to adolescence: A longitudinal population study of boys and girls aged 3–13 years. *Archives of Sexual Behavior, 41*, 591–597.
Gong, Y., Ericsson, K. A., & Moxley, J. H. (2015). Recall of briefly presented chess positions and its relation to chess skill. *PLoS ONE, 10*, e0118756.
Gonzaga, G. C., Campos, B., & Bradbury, T. (2007). Similarity, convergence, and relationship satisfaction in dating and married couples. *Journal of Personality and Social Psychology, 93*, 34–48.
Good, C., Aronson, J., & Inzlicht, M. (2003). Improving adolescents' standardized test performance: An intervention to reduce the effects of stereotype threat. *Journal of Applied Developmental Psychology, 24*, 645–662.
Good, M., & Willoughby, T. (2008). Adolescence as a sensitive period for spiritual development. *Child Development Perspectives, 2*, 32–37.
Goodlett, C. R., & Horn, K. H. (2001). Mechanisms of alcohol-induced damage to the developing nervous system. *Alcohol Research & Health, 25*, 175–184.
Goodluck, H. (2009). Formal and computational constraints on language development. In E. Hoff & M. Shatz (Eds.), *Blackwell handbook of language development* (pp. 46–67). Malden, MA: Wiley-Blackwell.
Goodman, G. S., Ogle, C. M., McWilliams, K., Narr, R. K., & Paz-Alonso, P. M. (2014). Memory development in forensic context. In P. Bauer & R. Fivush (Eds.), *The Wiley handbook on the development of children's memory* (pp. 920–942). Malden, MA: Wiley Blackwell.
Goodvin, R., Thompson, R. A., & Winer, A. C. (2015). The individual child: Temperament, emotion, self, and personality. In M. H. Bornstein & M. E. Lamb (Eds.),

Developmental science: An advanced textbook (7th ed., pp. 491–533). New York, NY: Psychology Press.

Goodwin, J. (December 2013–January 2014). A grief like no other. AARP The Magazine, pp. 44–50, 63–64.

Gooren, L. (2006). The biology of human psychosexual differentiation. Hormonal Behavior, 50, 589–601.

Gopnik, A. (1996). The post-Piaget era. Psychological Science, 7, 221–225.

Gopnik, A., & Choi, S. (1995). Names, relational words, and cognitive development in English and Korean speakers: Nouns are not always learned before verbs. In M. Tomasello & W. E. Merriman (Eds.), Beyond names for things: Young children's acquisition of verbs (pp. 83–90). Hillsdale, NJ: Erlbaum.

Gopnik, A., Griffiths, T. L., & Lucas, C. G. (2015). When younger learners can be better (or at least more open-minded) than older ones. Psychological Science, 24, 87–92.

Gorchoff, S. M., John, O. P., & Helson, R. (2008). Contextualizing change in marital satisfaction during middle age. Psychological Science, 19, 1194–1200.

Gordon, B. N., Schroeder, C. S., & Abrams, J. M. (1990). Children's knowledge of sexuality: A comparison of sexually abused and nonabused children. American Journal of Orthopsychiatry, 60, 250–257.

Gordon-Salant, S., Fitzgibbons, P. J., & Yeni-Komshian, G. H. (2011). Auditory temporal processing and aging: Implications for speech understanding of older people. Audiology Research, 1, e4.

Gorrese, A. (2016). Peer attachment and youth internalizing problems: A meta-analysis. Child & Youth Care Forum, 45, 177–204.

Gorrese, A., & Ruggieri, R. (2012). Peer attachment: A meta-analytic review of gender and age differences and associations with parent attachment. Journal of Youth and Adolescence, 41, 650–672.

Gosling, S. D., Rentfrow, P. J., & Swann, W. B. (2003). A very brief measure of the Big-Five personality domains. Journal of Research in Personality, 37, 504–528.

Gostin, L. O., & Roberts, A. E. (2016). Physician-assisted dying: A turning point? JAMA: Journal of the American Medical Association, 315, 249–250.

Goswami, U. (1999). Causal connections in beginning reading: The importance of rhyme. Journal of Research in Reading, 22, 217–241.

Gotlib, I. H., & Hammen, C. L. (1992). Psychological aspects of depression. Toward a cognitive-interpersonal integration. Chichester, UK: John Wiley & Sons.

Gotlib, I. H., & Hammen, C. L. (2002). Introduction. In I. H. Gotlib & C. L. Hammen (Eds.), Handbook of depression. New York, NY: Guilford.

Gotlib, I. H., Joormann, J., & Foland-Ross, L. (2014). Understanding familial risk for depression: A 25-year perspective. Perspectives on Psychological Science, 9, 94–108.

Gotlib, I. H., Joormann, J., Minor, K. L., & Cooney, R. E. (2006). Cognitive and biological functioning in children at risk for depression. In T. Canli (Ed.), Biology of personality and individual differences. New York, NY: Guilford.

Gottesman, I. I. (1991). Schizophrenia genesis: The origins of madness. New York, NY: W. H. Freeman.

Gottesman, I. I., & Hanson, D. R. (2005). Human development: Biological and genetic processes. Annual Review of Psychology, 56, 263–286.

Gottfredson, L. S. (1996). Gottfredson's theory of circumscription and compromise. In D. Brown, L. Brooks, & Associates (Eds.), Career choice and development (3rd ed.). San Francisco, CA: Jossey-Bass.

Gottfredson, L. S. (1997). Why g matters: The complexity of everyday life. Intelligence, 24, 79–132.

Gottfredson, L. S. (2002). g: Highly general and highly practical. In R. J. Sternberg & E. L. Grigorenko (Eds.), The general factor in intelligence: How general is it? Mahwah, NJ: Erlbaum.

Gottfredson, L. S. (2004). Intelligence: Is it the epidemiologists' elusive "fundamental cause" of social class inequalities in health? Journal of Personality and Social Psychology, 86, 174–199.

Gottfredson, L. S., & Deary, I. (2004). Intelligence predicts health and longevity, but why? Current Directions in Psychological Science, 13, 1–4.

Gottfredson, L., & Saklofske, D. H. (2009). Intelligence: Foundations and issues in assessment. Canadian Psychology, 50, 183–195.

Gottfried, A. E., Fleming, J. S., & Gottfried, A. W. (1998). Role of cognitively stimulating home environment in children's academic intrinsic motivation: A longitudinal study. Child Development, 69, 1448–1460.

Gottfried, A. E., Marcoulides, G. A., Gottfried, A. W., & Oliver, P. H. (2009). A latent curve model of parental motivational practices and developmental decline in math and science academic intrinsic motivation. Journal of Educational Psychology, 101, 729–739.

Gottfried, A. W., Gottfried, A. E., Bathurst, K., & Guerin, D. W. (1994). Gifted IQ: Early developmental aspects: The Fullerton Longitudinal Study. New York, NY: Plenum.

Gottlieb, G. (2000). Environmental and behavioral influences on gene activity. Current Directions in Psychological Science, 9, 93–97.

Gottlieb, G., & Halpern, C. T. (2008). Individual development as a system of coactions: implications for research and policy. In A. Fogel, B. J. King, & S. G. Shanker (2008). Human development in the twenty-first century. Visionary ideas from systems scientists. New York, NY: Cambridge University Press.

Gottman, J. M. (2011). The science of trust. Emotional attunement for couples. New York: W. W. Norton.

Gottman, J. M., & Notarius, C. I. (2000). Decade review: Observing marital interaction. Journal of Marriage and the Family, 62, 927–947.

Gottman, J. M., Katz, L., & Hooven, C. (1996). Parental meta-emotion philosophy and the emotional life of families: Theoretical models and preliminary data. Journal of Family Psychology, 10, 243–268.

Goubet, N., Rochat, P., Maire-Leblond, C., & Poss, S. (2006). Learning from others in 9–18-month-old infants. Infant and Child Development, 15, 161–177.

Gouin, K., Murphy, K., Shah, P. S., et al. (2011). Effects of cocaine use during pregnancy on low birthweight and preterm birth: systematic review and meta-analyses. American Journal Obstetrics & Gynecology, 204, 340.e1–12.

Gould, D. C., Petty, R., & Jacobs, H. S. (2000). The male menopause—does it exist? British Medical Journal, 320, 858–861.

Gould, M. S., Greenberg, T., Velting, D. M., & Shaffer, D. (2003). Youth suicide risk and preventive interventions: A review of the past 10 years. Journal of the American Academy of Child & Adolescent Psychiatry, 42, 386–405.

Gourounti, K., Anagnostopoulos, F., Potamianos, G., Lykeridou, K., Schmidt, L., & Vaslamatzis, G. (2012). Perception of control, coping and psychological stress of infertile women undergoing IVF. Reproductive BioMedicine Online, 24, 670–679.

Govarts, E., Nieuwenhuijsen, M., Schoeters, G., Ballester, F., Bloemen, K., de Boer, M., et al. (2012). Birth weight and prenatal exposure to polychlorinated biphenyls (PCBs) and dichlorodiphenyldichloroethylene (DDE): A meta-analysis within 12 European birth cohorts. Environmental Health Perspectives, 120, 162–170.

Gow, A. J., Johnson, W., Pattie, A., Brett, C. E., Roberts, B., Starr, J. M., et al. (2011). Stability and change in intelligence from age 11 to ages 70, 79, and 87: The Lothian birth cohorts of 1921 and 1936. Psychology and Aging, 26, 232–240.

Grabe, S., & Shibley Hyde, J. (2006). Ethnicity and body dissatisfaction among women in the United States: A meta-analysis. Psychological Bulletin, 132, 622–640.

Graber, J. A. (2013). Pubertal timing and the development of psychopathology in adolescence and beyond. Hormones and Behavior, 64, 262–269.

Graber, J. A., Lewinsohn, P. M., Seeley, J. R., & Brooks-Gunn, J. (1997). Is psychopathology associated with the timing of pubertal development? Journal of the American Academy of Child and Adolescent Psychiatry, 36, 1768–1776.

Graber, J. A., Nichols, T. R., & Brooks-Gunn, J. (2010). Putting pubertal timing in developmental context: Implications for prevention. Developmental Psychobiology, 52, 254–262.

Graber, J. A., Seeley, J. R., Brooks-Gunn, J., & Lewinsohn, P. M. (2004). Is pubertal timing associated with psychopathology in young adulthood? Journal of the American Academy of Child and Adolescent Psychiatry, 43, 718–726.

Grady, C. L., Luk, G., Craik, F. I., & Bialystok, E. (2015). Brain network activity in monolingual and bilingual older adults. Neuropsychologia, 66, 170–181.

Graf, P., Squire, L. R., & Mandler, G. (1984). The information that amnesic patients do not forget. Journal of Experimental Psychology: Learning, Memory, and Cognition, 10, 164–178.

Graham, M., Weijer, C., Peterson, A., Naci, L., Cruse, D., Fernández-Espejo, D., . . . Owen, A. M. (2015). Acknowledging awareness: Informing families of individual research results for patients in the vegetative state. Journal of Medical Ethics, 41, 534–538.

Grandin, T., & Panek, R. (2013, October 7). What's right with the autistic mind. Time, pp. 56–59.

Grandjean, P. (2008). Late insights into early origins of disease. Basic Clinical Pharmacological Toxicology, 102, 94–99.

Grandjean, P., & Landrigan, P. J. (2006). Developmental neurotoxicity of industrial chemicals. The Lancet, 368, 2167–2178.

Granrud, C. E. (2006). Size constancy in infants: 4-month-olds' responses to physical versus retinal image size. Journal of Experimental Psychology: Human Perception and Performance, 32, 1398–1404.

Grant, K. E., Compas, B. E., Thurm, A. E., McMahon, S. D., & Gipson, P. Y. (2004). Stressors and child and adolescent psychopathology: Measurement issues and prospective effects. Journal of Clinical Child and Adolescent Psychology, 33, 412–425.

Grasgruber, P., Cacek, J., Kalina, T., & Sebera, M. (2014). The role of nutrition and genetics as key determinants of the positive height trend. Economics and Human Biology, 15, 81–100.

Graven, S. N., & Browne, J. V. (2008). Auditory development in the fetus and infant. Newborn and Infant Nursing Reviews, 8, 187–193.

Gray, S. W., Ramsey, B. K., & Klaus, R. A. (1982). From 3 to 20: The early training project. Baltimore, MD: University Park Press.

Gray, W. M., & Hudson, L. M. (1984). Formal operations and the imaginary audience. Developmental Psychology, 20, 619–627.

Gray-Little, B., & Hafdahl, A. R. (2000). Factors influencing racial comparisons of self-esteem: A quantitative review. Psychological Bulletin, 126, 26–54.

Graziano, P. A., Keane, S. P., & Calkins, S. D. (2007). Cardiac vagal regulation and early peer status. Child Development, 78, 264–278.

Grbich, C., Parker, D., & Maddocks, I. (2001). The emotions and coping strategies of caregivers of family members with a terminal cancer. Journal of Palliative Care, 17, 30–36.

Green, C. R. (2001). Total memory workout: 8 easy steps to maximum memory fitness. New York, NY: Bantam Doubleday.

Greenberger, E., & Steinberg, L. (1986). When teenagers work: The psychological and social costs of adolescent employment. New York, NY: Basic Books.

Greenberger, E., O'Neil, R., & Nagel, S. K. (1994). Linking workplace and homeplace: Relations between the nature of adults' work and their parenting behaviors. Developmental Psychology, 30, 990–1002.

Greene, J. (2013). Moral tribes: Emotion, reason, and the gap between us and them. New York, NY: Penguin Press.

Greene, J. D. (2008). The secret joke of Kant's soul. In W. Sinnott-Armstrong (Ed.), Moral psychology: The neuroscience of morality: Emotion, brain disorders, and development. Cambridge, MA: MIT Press.

Greene, J. D. (2009). Dual-process morality and the personal/impersonal distinction: A reply to McGuire, Langdon, Coltheart, and MacKenzie. Journal of Experimental Social Psychology, 45, 581–584.

Greene, J. D., Morelli, S. A., Lowenberg, K., Nystrom, L. E., & Cohen, J. D. (2008). Cognitive load selectively interferes with utilitarian moral judgment. Cognition, 107, 1144–1154.

Greene, J. D., Sommerville, R. B., Nystrom, L. E., Darley, J. M., & Cohen, J. D. (2001). An fMRI investigation of emotional engagement in moral judgment. Science, 293, 2105–2108.

Greene, J. G. (1984). The social and psychological origins of the climacteric syndrome. Hants, England & Brookfield, VT: Gower.

Greene, K., Rubin, D. L., Hale, J. L., & Walters, L. H. (1996). The utility of understanding adolescent egocentrism in designing health promotion messages. Health Communication, 8, 131–152.

Greenfield, E. A., & Marks, N. F. (2006). Linked lives: Adult children's problems and their parents' psychological and relational well-being. *Journal of Marriage and Family, 68,* 442–454.

Greenfield, E. A., Vaillant, G. E., & Marks, N. E. (2009). Do formal religious participation and spiritual perceptions have independent linkages with diverse dimensions of psychological well-being? *Journal of Health and Social Behavior, 50,* 196–212.

Greenfield, P. M., & Savage-Rumbaugh, E. S. (1993). Comparing communicative competence in child and chimp: The pragmatics of repetition. *Journal of Child Language, 20,* 1–26.

Greenfield, R. A. (2012). *Pediatric HIV infection.* Retrieved from emedicine.medscape.com/article/965086-overview.

Greenhalgh, R., Slade, P., & Spiby, H. (2000). Fathers' coping style, antenatal preparation, and experiences of labor and the postpartum. *Birth, 27,* 177–184.

Greenough, W. T., Black, J. E., & Wallace, C. S. (1987). Experience and brain development. *Child Development, 58,* 539–559.

Greer, D. M., Wang, H. H., Robinson, J. D., Varelas, P. N., Henderson, G. V., & Wijdicks, E. F. M. (2016). Variability of brain death policies in the United States. *JAMA Neurology, 73,* 213–218.

Greif, G. L., & Woolley, M. E. (2016). *Adult sibling relationships.* New York, NY: Columbia University Press.

Greiff, S., Wustenberg, S., Goetz, T., Vainikainen, M. P., Hautamaki, J., & Bornstein, M. H. (2015). A longitudinal study of higher-order thinking skills: Working memory and fluid reasoning in childhood enhance complex problem solving in adolescence. *Frontiers in Psychology, 6,* 1060.

Greve, F. (2006, February 3). Rise in average IQ scores makes kids today exceptional by earlier standards. *Knight Ridder Washington Bureau.*

Grigoriadis, S., VonderPorten, E. H., Mamisashvili, L., Tomlinson, G., Dennis, C. L., Koren, G., Steiner, M., Mousmanis, P., Cheung, A., Radford, K., Martinovic, J., & Ross, L. E. (2013). The impact of maternal depression during pregnancy on perinatal outcomes: A systematic review and meta-analysis. *Journal of Clinical Psychiatry, 74,* e321–341.

Grilo, C. M., & Mitchell, J. E. (Eds.). (2010). *The treatment of eating disorders: A clinical handbook.* New York, NY: Guilford.

Grilo, C. M., & Pogue-Geile, M. F. (1991). The nature of environmental influences on weight and obesity: A behavior genetic analysis. *Psychological Bulletin, 110,* 520–537.

Groark, C. J., Muhamedrahimov, R. J., Palmov, O. I., Nikiforova, N. V., & McCall, R. B. (2005). Improvements in early care in Russian orphanages and their relationship to observed behaviors. *Infant Mental Health Journal, 26,* 96–109.

Grolnick, W. S., & Pomerantz, E. M. (2009). Issues and challenges in studying parental control: Toward a new conceptualization. *Child Development Perspectives, 3,* 165–170.

Grolnick, W. S., Bridges, L. J., & Connell, J. P. (1996). Emotion regulation in two-year-olds: Strategies and emotional expression in four contexts. *Child Development, 67,* 928–941.

Grolnick, W. S., McMenamy, J. M., & Kurowski, C. O. (2006). Emotional self-regulation in infancy and toddlerhood. In L. Balter & C. S. Tamis-LeMonda (Eds.), *Child psychology: A handbook of contemporary issues* (2nd ed.). New York, NY: Psychology Press.

Grosjean, F. (2010). *Bilingual: Life and reality.* Cambridge, MA: Harvard University Press.

Gros-Louis, J., West, M. J., Goldstein, M. H., & King, A. P. (2006). Mothers provide differential feedback to infants' prelinguistic sounds. *International Journal of Behavioral Development, 30,* 509–516.

Gross, C. L., & Marcussen, K. (2016). Postpartum depression in mothers and fathers: The role of parenting efficacy expectations during the transition to parenthood. *Sex Roles.* doi.org/10.1007/s11199-016-0629-7.

Gross, J. J. (2014). Emotion regulation: Conceptual and empirical foundations. In J. J. Gross (Ed.), *Handbook of emotion regulation* (2nd ed., pp. 3–20). New York, NY: Guilford.

Gross, J. J. (Ed.) (2007). *Handbook of emotion regulation.* New York, NY: Guilford.

Gross, J., Gardiner, B., & Hayne, H. (2016). Developmental reversals in recognition memory in children and adults. *Developmental Psychobiology, 58,* 52–59.

Gross-Loh, C. (2006). Caring for your premature baby: Find out why breastfeeding and skin-to-skin contact are key components in making sure your premature infant thrives. *Mothering, 135,* 38–47.

Grossman, A. H., D'Augelli, A. R., & Frank, J. A. (2011). Aspects of psychological resilience among transgender youth. *Journal of LGBT Youth, 8,* 103–115.

Grossman, A. H., D'Augelli, A. R., Howell, T. J., & Hubbard, S. (2005). Parents' reactions to transgender youths' gender nonconforming expression and identity. *Journal of Gay & Lesbian Social Services, 18,* 3–16.

Grossman, A. W., Churchill, J. D., McKinney, B. C., Kodish, I. M., Otte, S. L., & Greenough, W. T. (2003). Experience effects on brain development: Possible contributions to psychopathology. *Journal of Child Psychology and Psychiatry and Allied Disciplines, 44,* 33–63.

Grossmann, I., Karasawa, M., Izumi, S., Na, J. Varnum, M. E. W., Kitayama, S., Nisbett, R. E. (2012). Aging and wisdom: Culture matters. *Psychological Science, 23,* 1059–1066.

Grossmann, I., Na, J., Varnum, M. E. W., Park, D. C, Kitayama, S., & Nisbett, R. E. (2010). Reasoning about social conflicts improves into old age. *Proceedings of the National Academy of Sciences—PNAS, 107,* 7246–7250.

Grossmann, K. E., Grossmann, K., & Keppler, A. (2005). Universal and culture-specific aspects of human behavior: The case of attachment. In W. Friedlmeier, P. Chakkarath, & B. Schwarz (Eds.), *Culture and human development. The importance of cross-cultural research for the social sciences.* New York, NY: Psychology Press.

Grossmann, K. E., Grossmann, K., Winter, M., & Zimmermann, P. (2002a). Attachment relationships and appraisal of partnership: From early experience of sensitive support to later relationship representation. In L. Pulkkinen & A. Caspi (Eds.), *Paths to successful development: Personality in the life course.* Cambridge, UK: Cambridge University Press.

Grotevant, H. D., & Cooper, C. R. (1986). Individuation in family relations. A perspective on individual differences in the development of identity and role-taking skills in adolescence. *Human Development, 29,* 82–100.

Gruber-Baldini, A. L., Schaie, K. W., & Willis, S. L. (1995). Similarity in married couples: A longitudinal study of mental abilities and rigidity-flexibility. *Journal of Personality and Social Psychology, 69,* 191–203.

Grundy, E., & Henretta, J. C. (2006). Between elderly parents and adult children: A new look at the intergenerational care provided by the 'sandwich generation.' *Ageing and Society, 26,* 707–722.

Grusec, J. E. (2006). The development of moral behavior and conscience from a socialization perspective. In M. Killen & J. G. Smetana (Eds.), *Handbook of moral development.* Mahwah, NJ: Erlbaum.

Grusec, J. E., & Davidov, M. (2010). Integrating different perspectives on socialization theory and research: A domain-specific approach. *Child Development, 81,* 687–709.

Grusec, J. E., Goodnow, J. J., & Kuczynski, L. (2000). New directions in analyses of parenting contributions to children's acquisition of values. *Child Development, 71,* 205–211.

Grych, J. H., & Fincham, F. D. (1992). Interventions for children of divorce: Toward greater integration of research and action. *Psychological Bulletin, 111,* 434–454.

Grych, J., Oxtoby, C., & Lynn, M. (2013). The effects of interparental conflict on children. In M. A. Fine & F. D. Fincham (Eds.), *Handbook of family theories. A context-based approach.* New York, NY: Routledge.

Guay, F., Marsh, H. W., & Boivin, M. (2003). Academic self-concept and academic achievement: Developmental perspectives on their causal ordering. *Journal of Educational Psychology, 95,* 124–136.

Gudsnuk, K. M. A., & Champagne, F. A. (2011). Epigenetic effects of early developmental experiences. *Clinical Perinatology, 38,* 703–717.

Guerin, D. W., Gottfried, A. W., Oliver, P. H., & Thomas, C. W. (2003). *Temperament: Infancy through adolescence: The Fullerton Longitudinal Study.* New York, NY: Kluwer Academic/Plenum Publishers.

Guerra, N. G. (2012). Can we make violent behavior less adaptive for youth? *Human Development, 55,* 105–106.

Guerra, N. G., & Slaby, R. G. (1990). Cognitive mediators of aggression in adolescent offenders: 2. Intervention. *Developmental Psychology, 26,* 269–277.

Guerra, N. G., & Williams, K. R. (2006). Ethnicity, youth violence, and the ecology of development. In N. G. Guerra, & E. P. Smith (Eds.), *Preventing youth violence in a multicultural society.* Washington, DC: American Psychological Association.

Guilamo-Ramos, V., Jaccard, J., Dittus, P., & Collins, S. (2008). Parent-adolescent communication about sexual intercourse: An analysis of maternal reluctance to communicate. *Health Psychology, 27,* 760–769.

Gundersen, C., Lohman, B. J., Garasky, S., Stewart, S., & Eisenmann, J. (2008). Food security, maternal stressors, and overweight among low-income US children: Results from the National Health and Nutrition Examination Survey (1999–2002). *Pediatrics, 122,* e529–e540.

Güngör, D., Bornstein, M. H., De Leersnyder, J., Cote, L., Ceulemans, E., & Mesquita, B. (2013). Acculturation of personality: A three-culture study of Japanese, Japanese Americans, and European Americans. *Journal of Cross-Cultural Psychology, 44,* 701–718.

Gunnar, M. R. (1998). Quality of early care and buffering of neuroendocrine stress reactions: Potential effects on the developing human brain. *Preventive Medicine, 27,* 208–211.

Gunnar, M. R., Bruce, J., & Grotevant, H. D. (2000). International adoption of institutionally reared children: Research and policy. *Development and Psychopathology, 12,* 677–693.

Gunnar, M., & Quevedo, K. (2007). The neurobiology of stress and development. *Annual Review of Psychology, 58,* 145–153.

Guo, G. (2011). Gene-environment interactions for delinquency: Promises and difficulties. In K. A. Dodge & M. Rutter (Eds.). *Gene-environment interactions in developmental psychopathology.* New York: Guilford.

Gurba, E. (2005). On the specific character of adult thought: Controversies over post-formal operations. *Polish Psychological Bulletin, 36,* 175–185.

Gurung, R. A. R., Taylor, S. E., & Seeman, T. E. (2003). Accounting for changes in social support among married older adults: Insights from the MacArthur Studies of Successful Aging. *Psychology and Aging, 18,* 487–496.

Gus, L., Rose, J., & Gilbert, L. (2015). Emotion coaching: A universal strategy for supporting and promoting sustainable emotional and behavioural well-being. *Educational and Child Psychology, 32,* 31–41.

Gutiérrez, I. T., Rosengren, K. S., & Miller, P. J. (2014). Children's understanding of death: Toward a contextualized and integrated account: VI. Mexican American immigrants in the Centerville region: Teachers, children, and parents. *Monographs of the Society for Research in Child Development, 79,* 97–112.

Gutman, L. (2006). How student and parent goal orientations and classroom goal structures influence the math achievement of African Americans during the high school transition. *Contemporary Educational Psychology, 31,* 44–63.

Gutman, L. M., Sameroff, A. J., & Cole, R. (2003). Academic growth curve trajectories from 1st grade to 12th grade: Effects of multiple social risk factors and preschool child factors. *Developmental Psychology, 39,* 777–790.

Gutman, L. M., Sameroff, A. J., & Eccles, J. S. (2002). The academic achievement of African American students during early adolescence: An examination of multiple risk, promotive, and protective factors. *American Journal of Community Psychology, 39,* 367–399.

Gutmann, D. (1987). *Reclaimed powers: Toward a new psychology of men and women in later life.* New York, NY: Basic Books.

Gutmann, D. (1997). *The human elder in nature, culture, and society.* Boulder, CO: Westview.

Guttmacher Institute. (2006). *Facts on American teens' sexual and reproductive health.* Retrieved from www.guttmacher.org/pubs/fb_ATSRH.html.

Guttmacher Institute. (2016). *HIV and STIs.* Available at www.guttmacher.org/united-states/hiv-stis.

Guxens, M., Garcia-Esteban, R., Giorgis-Allemand, L., Forns, J., Badaloni, C., & Ballester, F. (2014). Air pollution during pregnancy and childhood cognitive and psychomotor development: Six European birth cohorts. *Epidemiology, 25,* 636–647.

Guyenet, S., & Landen, J. (2012, Feb 19). American per-capita sugar consumption hits 100 pounds per year. *Whole health source.* Retrieved from www.articles.businessinsider.com/2012-02-19/news/31076374_1_chart-capita-american#ixzz2As44BTCt.

Gweon, H., Dodell-Feder, D., Bedny, M., & Saxe, R. (2012). Theory of mind performance in children correlates with functional specialization of a brain region for thinking about thoughts. *Child Development, 83,* 1853–1868.

Ha, J. (2010). The effects of positive and negative support from children on widowed older adults' psychological adjustment: A longitudinal analysis. *The Gerontologist, 50,* 471–481.

Haber, D. (2006). Life review: Implementation, theory, research, and therapy. *International Journal of Aging & Human Development, 63,* 153–171.

Hack, M., Taylor, H. G., Drotar, D., Schluchter, M., Cartar, L., Wilson-Costello, D., & Morrow, M. (2005). Poor predictive validity of the Bayley Scales of Infant Development for cognitive function of extremely low birth weight children at school age. *Pediatrics, 116,* 333–341.

Haegerstrom-Portnoy, G., Schneck, M. E., & Brabyn, J. A. (2000). Seeing into old age: Vision function beyond acuity. *Optometry and Vision Science, 76,* 141–158.

Hagan, L. K., & Kuebli, J. (2007). Mothers' and fathers' socialization of preschoolers' physical risk taking. *Journal of Applied Developmental Psychology, 28,* 2–14.

Hagan, M. J., Tein, J., Sandler, I. N., Wolchik, S. A., Ayers, T. S., & Luecken, L. J. (2012). Strengthening effective parenting practices over the long term: Effects of a preventive intervention for parentally bereaved families. *Journal of Clinical Child and Adolescent Psychology, 41,* 177–188.

Hagekull, B., & Bohlin, G. (1998). Preschool temperament and environmental factors related to the five-factor model of personality in middle childhood. *Merrill-Palmer Quarterly, 44,* 194–215.

Hagen, E. W., Palta, M., Albanese, A., & Sadek-Badawi, M. (2006). School achievement in a regional cohort of children born very low birthweight. *Developmental & Behavioral Pediatrics, 27,* 112–119.

Hagestad, G. O. (1985). Continuity and connectedness. In V. L. Bengtson & J. F. Robertson (Eds.), *Grandparenthood.* Beverly Hills, CA: Sage.

Haidt, J. (2001). The emotional dog and its rational tail: A social intuitionist approach to moral judgment. *Psychological Review, 108,* 814–834.

Haidt, J. (2008). Morality. *Perspectives on Psychological Science, 3,* 65–72.

Haidt, J. (2012). *The righteous mind: Why good people are divided by politics and religion.* New York, NY: Pantheon Books.

Haight, B. K., & Haight, B. S. (2007). *The handbook of structured life review.* Baltimore, MD: Health Professions Press.

Haight, W. L., Wong, X., Fung, H. H., Williams, K., & Mintz, J. (1999). Universal, developmental, and variable aspects of young children's play: A cross-cultural comparison of pretending at home. *Child Development, 70,* 1477–1488.

Haimovitz, K., & Dweck, C. S. (2016). What predicts children's fixed and growth intelligence mind-sets? Not their parents' views of intelligence but their parents' views of failure. *Psychological Science, 27,* 859–869.

Haine, R. A., Wolchik, S. A., Sandler, I. N., & Milsap, R. E. (2006). Positive parenting as a protective resource for parentally bereaved children. *Death Studies, 30,* 1–28.

Hainline, L. (1998). The development of basic visual abilities. In A. Slater (Ed.), *Perceptual development: Visual, auditory and speech perception in infancy* (pp. 37–44). Hove, East Sussex, UK: Psychology Press.

Hainline, L., & Abramov, I. (1992). Assessing visual development: Is infant vision good enough? *Advances in Infancy Research, 7,* 39–102.

Halberstadt, A. G. (1991). Toward an ecology of expressiveness: Family socialization in particular and a model in general. In R. S. Feldman & B. Rime (Eds.), *Fundamentals of nonverbal behavior.* New York, NY: Cambridge University Press.

Hales, S., Chiu, A., Husain, A., Braun, M., Rydall, A., Gagliese, L., . . . Rodin, G. (2014). The quality of dying and death in cancer and its relationship to palliative care and place of death. *Journal of Pain and Symptom Management, 48,* 839–851.

Halim, M. L. D. (2016). Princesses and superheroes: Social-cognitive influences on early gender rigidity. *Child Development Perspectives, 10,* 155–160.

Halim, M. L., & Ruble, D. (2010). Gender identity and stereotyping in early and middle childhood. In J. C. Chrisler & D. R. McCreary (Eds.), *Handbook of gender research in psychology* (pp. 495–525). New York, NY: Springer Science+Business Media.

Halim, M. L., Ruble, D. N., Tamis-LeMonda, C. S., Zosuls, K. M., Lurye, L. E., & Greulich, F. K. (2014). Pink frilly dresses and the avoidance of all things "girly": Children's appearance rigidity and cognitive theories of gender development. *Developmental Psychology, 50,* 1091–1101.

Halim, M. L., Ruble, D., Tamis-LeMonda, C., & Shrout, P. E. (2013). Rigidity in gender-typed behaviors in early childhood: A longitudinal study of ethnic minority children. *Child Development, 84,* 1269–1284.

Hall, C. S. (1954). *A primer of Freudian psychology.* New York, NY: New American Library.

Hall, G. S. (1891). The contents of children's minds on entering school. *Pedagogical Seminary, 1,* 139–173.

Hall, G. S. (1904). *Adolescence* (2 vols.). New York, NY: Appleton.

Hall, J., Trent, S., Thomas, K. L., O'Donovan, M. C., & Owen, M. J. (2015). Genetic risk for schizophrenia: Convergence on synaptic pathways involved in plasticity. *Biological Psychiatry, 77,* 52–58.

Hall, L., & Kelley, E. (2014). The contribution of epigenetics to understanding genetic factors in autism. *Autism, 18,* 872–881.

Hall, T. (2016). Management of persistent pain in older people. *Journal of Pharmacy Practice and Research, 46,* 60–67.

Hallgren, A., Kihlgren, M., Forslin, L., & Norberg, A. (1999). Swedish fathers' involvement in and experiences of childbirth preparation and childbirth. *Midwifery, 15,* 6–15.

Halligan, S. L., Herbert, J., Goodyer, I. M., & Murray, L. (2004). Exposure to postnatal depression predicts elevated cortisol in adolescent offspring. *Biological Psychiatry, 55,* 376–381.

Hallmayer, J., Cleveland, S., Torres, A., Phillips, J., Cohen, B., Torigoe, T., et al. (2011). Genetic heritability and shared environmental factors among twin pairs with autism. *Archives of General Psychiatry, 68,* 1095–1102.

Halmi, K. A. (2009). Perplexities and provocations of eating disorders. *Journal of Child Psychology and Psychiatry, 50,* 163–169.

Halpern, C. J. T., Udry, J. R., Suchindran, C., & Campbell, B. (2000). Adolescent males' willingness to report masturbation [Special issue]. *Journal of Sex Research, 37,* 327–332.

Halpern, C. T. (2006). Integrating hormones and other biological factors into a developmental systems model of adolescent female sexuality. *New Directions for Child and Adolescent Development, 112,* 9–22.

Hamann, K., Warneken, F., & Tomasello, M. (2012). Children's developing commitments to joint goals. *Child Development, 83,* 137–145.

Hambleton, L. (2014, March 4). The inheritance. Passed down by parents, sickle cell disease was once a dire diagnosis. But treatment has improved, and research offers additional hope. *The Washington Post,* pp. E1, E5.

Hamer, R. D. (2016). What can my baby see? Retrieved from www.legacy.ski.org/Vision/babyvision.pdf.

Hamilton, B. E., Martin, J. A., & Ventura, S. J. (2011). Births: Preliminary data for 2010. *National Vital Statistics Report, 60,* 1–25. Retrieved from www.cdc.gov/nchs/data/nvsr/nvsr60/nvsr60_02.pdf.

Hamilton, J. L., Stange, J. P., Abramson, L. Y., & Alloy, L. B. (2015). Stress and the development of cognitive vulnerabilities to depression explain sex differences in depressive symptoms during adolescence. *Clinical Psychological Science, 3,* 702–714.

Hamilton, M. T., Healy, G. N., Dunstan, D. W., Zderic, T. W., & Owen, N. (2008). Too little exercise and too much sitting: Inactivity physiology and the need for new recommendations on sedentary behavior. *Current Cardiovascular Risk Reports, 2,* 292–298.

Hamlin, J. K. (2013). Moral judgment and action in preverbal infants and toddlers: Evidence for an innate moral core. *Current Directions in Psychological Science, 22,* 186–193.

Hamlin, J. K., & Wynn, K. (2011). Young infants prefer prosocial to antisocial others. *Cognitive Development, 26,* 30–39.

Hamlin, J. K., Wynn, K., & Bloom, P. (2007). Social evaluation by preverbal infants. *Nature, 450,* 557–560.

Hamlin, J. K., Wynn, K., Bloom, P., & Mahajan, N. (2011). How infants and toddlers react to antisocial others. *PNAS Proceedings of the National Academy of Sciences of the United States of America, 108,* 19931–19936.

Hamm, M. P., Newton, A. S., Chisholm, A., Shulhan, J., Milne, A., Sundar, P., . . . Hartling, L. (2015). Prevalence and effect of cyberbullying on children and young people: A scoping review of social media studies. *JAMA Pediatrics, 169,* 770–777.

Hampson, S. E., & Friedman, H. S. (2008). Personality and health. A lifespan perspective. In O. P. John, R. W. Robins, & L. A. Pervin (Eds.), *Handbook of personality theory and research* (3rd ed.). New York, NY: Guilford.

Hankin, B. L., Young, J. F., Abela, J. R. Z., Smolen, A., Jenness, J. L., Gulley, L. D., . . . Oppenheimer, C. W. (2015). Depression from childhood into late adolescence: Influence of gender, development, genetic susceptibility, and peer stress. *Journal of Abnormal Psychology, 124,* 803–816.

Hans, J. D., Gillen, M., & Akande, K. (2010, June). Sex redefined: The reclassification of oral-genital contact. *Perspectives on Sexual and Reproductive Health, 42,* 74–78.

Hansen, T. (2012). Parenthood and happiness: A review of folk theories versus empirical evidence. *Social Indicators Research, 108,* 29–64.

Hanson, J. L., Hair, N., Shen, D. G., Shi, F., Gilmore, J. H., Wolfe, B. L., & Pollak, S. D. (2013). Family poverty affects the rate of human infant brain growth. *PLoS ONE, 8*(12), e80954.

Hansson, R. O., DeKoekkoek, P. D., Neece, W. M., & Patterson, D. W. (1997). Successful aging at work: Annual review, 1992–1996: The older worker and transitions to retirement. *Journal of Vocational Behavior, 51,* 202–233.

Hansson, R. O., & Stroebe, M. S. (2007). *Bereavement in late life: Coping, adaptation, and developmental influences.* Washington, DC: American Psychological Association.

Hanushek, E. A. (2011). The economic value of higher teacher quality. *Economics of Education Review, 30,* 466–479.

Hanushek, E. A., Piopiunik, M., & Wiederhold, S. (2014). *The value of smarter teachers: International evidence on teacher cognitive skills and student performance.* National Bureau of Economic Research, Working Paper No. 20727.

Hanushek, E., Rivkin, S., & Kain, J. (2005). Teachers, schools and academic achievement. *Econometrica, 73,* 417–458.

Happé, F. (1994). An advanced test of theory of mind. *Journal of Autism & Developmental Disorders, 24,* 129–154.

Hardan, A. Y., Gengoux, G. W., Berquist, K. L., Libove, R. A., Ardel, C. M., Phillips, J., . . . Minjarez, M. B. (2015). A randomized controlled trial of pivotal response treatment group for parents of children with autism. *Journal of Child Psychology and Psychiatry, 56,* 884–892.

Harden, K. P., & Mann, F. D. (2015). Biological risk for the development of problem behavior in adolescence: Integrating insights from behavioral genetics and neuroscience. *Child Development, 9,* 211–216.

Harden, K. P., Turkheimer, E., & Loehlin, J. C. (2007). Genotype by environment interaction in adolescents' cognitive aptitude. *Behavior Genetics, 37,* 273–283.

Hardy, S. A., & Carlo, G. (2011). Moral identity: What is it, how does it develop, and is it linked to moral action? *Child Development Perspectives, 5,* 212–218.

Hardy, S. A., Walker, L. J., Rackham, D. D., & Olsen, J. A. (2012). Religiosity and adolescent empathy and aggression: The mediating role of moral identity. *Psychology of Religion and Spirituality, 4,* 237–248.

Harlow, H. F., & Zimmerman, R. R. (1959). Affectional responses in the infant monkey. *Science, 130,* 421–432.

Harper, G., & Kember, D. (1986). Approaches to study of distance education students. *British Journal of Educational Technology, 17,* 211–212.

Harper, L. M., Caughey, A. B., Obibo, A. O., Roehl, K. A., Zhao, Q., & Cahill, A. G. (2012). Normal progress of induced labor. *Obstetrics & Gynecology, 119,* 1113–1118.

Harrington, D. M., Block, J. H., & Block, J. (1987). Testing aspects of Carl Rogers's theory of creative environments: Child-rearing antecedents of creative potential in young adolescents. *Journal of Personality and Social Psychology*, 52, 851–856.

Harris, J. R. (2000). Context-specific learning, personality, and birth order. *Current Directions in Psychological Science*, 9, 174–177.

Harris, J. R., Pedersen, N. L., McClearn, G. E., Plomin, R., & Nesselroade, J. R. (1992). Age differences in genetic and environmental influences for health from the Swedish Adoption/Twin Study of Aging. *Journal of Gerontology Series B: Psychological Sciences*, 47, 213–220.

Harris, M. (1992). *Language experience and early language development: From input to uptake*. Hove, UK: Erlbaum.

Harris, M. (2011). Adolescent sexuality. In M. H. Williams (Ed.), *Adolescence: Talks and papers by Donald Meltzer and Martha Harris* (pp. 75–80). London, England: Karnac Books.

Harris, M. A., Prior, J. C., & Koehoorn, M. (2008). Age at menarche in the Canadian population: Secular trends and relationship to adulthood BMI. *Journal of Adolescent Health*, 43, 548–554.

Harris, P. L. (1989). *Children and emotion: The development of psychological understanding*. Oxford, UK: Basil Blackwell.

Harris, P. L., & Kavanaugh, R. D. (1993). Young children's understanding of pretense. *Monographs of the Society for Research in Child Development*, 58 (1, Serial No. 181).

Harris, P. L., Pasquini, E. S., Duke, S., Asscher, J. J., & Pons, F. (2006). Germs and angels: The role of testimony in young children's ontology. *Developmental Science*, 9, 76–96.

Harris, T., & Bifulco, A. (1991). Loss of parent in childhood, attachment style, and depression in adulthood. In C. M. Parkes, J. Stevenson-Hinde, & P. Marris (Eds.), *Attachment across the life cycle*. London, UK: Tavistock/Routledge.

Harrison, R. V., Gordon, K. A., & Mount, R. J. (2005). Is there a critical period for cochlear implantation in congenitally deaf children? Analyses of hearing and speech perception performance after implantation. *Developmental Psychobiology*, 46, 252–261.

Hart, B., & Risley, T. R. (1995). *Meaningful differences in the everyday experience of young American children*. Baltimore, MD, London: P. H. Brookes.

Hart, B., & Risley, T. (1995). *Meaningful differences in the everyday experience of young American children*. Baltimore: Paul H. Brookes Publishing.

Hart, D. (2005). The development of moral identity. *Nebraska Symposium on Motivation*, 51, 165–196.

Hart, M. A., & Foster, S. N. (1997). Couples' attitudes toward childbirth participation: Relationship to evaluation of labor and delivery. *Journal of Perinatal & Neonatal Nursing*, 11, 10–20.

Hart, S. A., Logan, J. A. R., Soden-Hensler, B., Kershaw, S., Talor, J., & Schatschneider, C. (2013). Exploring how nature and nurture affect the development of reading: An analysis of the Florida Twin Project on reading. *Developmental Psychology*, 49, 1971–1981.

Harter, S. (1999). *The construction of the self. A developmental perspective*. New York, NY: Guilford.

Harter, S. (2003). The development of self-representations during childhood and adolescence. In M. R. Leary & J. P. Tangney (Eds.), *Handbook of self and identity*. New York, NY: Guilford.

Harter, S. (2012). *The construction of the self: Developmental and sociocultural foundations* (2nd ed.). New York: Guilford.

Harter, S., & Buddin, B. J. (1987). Children's understanding of the simultaneity of two emotions: A five stage developmental acquisition sequence. *Developmental Psychology*, 23, 388–399.

Harter, S., & Monsour, A. (1992). Development analysis of conflict caused by opposing attributes in the adolescent self-portrait. *Developmental Psychology*, 28, 251–260.

Hartig, J., & Viola, J. (2016). Online grief support communities: Therapeutic benefits of membership. *Omega: Journal of Death and Dying*, 73, 29–41.

Hartley, A. (2006). Changing role of the speed of processing construct in the cognitive psychology of human aging. In J. E. Birren & K. W. Schaie (Eds.), *Handbook of the psychology of aging*. Boston, MA: Elsevier Academic Press.

Hartshorn, K., Rovee-Collier, C., Gerhardstein, P., Bhatt, R. S., Wondoloski, T. L., Klein, P., et al. (1998). The ontogeny of long-term memory over the first year and a half of life. *Developmental Psychobiology*, 32, 69–89.

Hartshorne, J. K., & Germine, L. T. (2015). When does cognitive functioning peak? The asynchronous rise and fall of different cognitive abilities across the life span. *Psychological Science*, 26, 433–443.

Hartung, P. J., Porfeli, E. J., & Vondracek, F. W. (2005). Child vocational development: A review and reconsideration. *Journal of Vocational Behavior*, 66, 385–419.

Hartup, W. W. (2006). Relationships in early and middle childhood. In A. L. Vangelisti & D. Perlman (Eds.), *The Cambridge handbook of personal relationships*. New York, NY: Cambridge University Press.

Hasegawa, J., Farina, A., Turchi, G., Hasegawa, Y., Zanello, M., & Baroncini, S. (2013). Effects of epidural analgesia on labor length, instrumental delivery, and neonatal short-term outcome. *Journal of Anesthesia*, 27, 43–47.

Haskett, M. E., Johnson, C. A., & Miller, J. W. (1994). Individual differences in risk of child abuse by adolescent mothers: Assessment in the perinatal period. *Journal of Child Psychology and Psychiatry and Allied Disciplines*, 35, 461–476.

Hastings, P. D., Zahn-Waxler, C., & McShane, K. (2006). Empathy, emotions, and aggression: Biological bases of concern for others. Mahwah, NJ: Erlbaum.

Hatfield, E., Mo, Y., & Rapson, R. L. (2015). Love, sex, and marriage across cultures. In L. A. Jensen (Ed.), *Oxford handbook of human development and culture* (pp. 570–585). New York, NY: Oxford University Press.

Hattie, J., Biggs, J., & Purdie, N. (1996). Effects of learning skills interventions on student learning: A meta-analysis. *Review of Educational Research*, 66, 99–136.

Haught, P. A., Hill, L. A., Nardi, A. H., & Walls, R. T. (2000). Perceived ability and level of education as predictors of traditional and practical adult problem solving. *Experimental Aging Research*, 26, 89–101.

Haun, D. B. M., Rekers, Y., & Tomasello, M. (2014). Children conform to the behavior of peers; other great apes stick with what they know. *Psychological Science*, 25, 2160–2167.

Hausdorff, J. M., Levy, B. R., & Wei, J. Y. (1999). The power of ageism on physical function of older persons: Reversibility of age-related gait changes. *Journal of the American Geriatrics Society*, 47, 1346–1349.

Havighurst, R. J., Neugarten, B. L., & Tobin, S. S. (1968). Disengagement and patterns of aging. In B. L. Neugarten (Ed.), *Middle age and aging*. Chicago, IL: University of Chicago Press.

Havighurst, S. S., Duncombe, M., Frankling, E., Holland, K., Kehoe, C., & Stargatt, R. (2015). An emotion-focused early intervention for children with emerging conduct problems. *Journal of Abnormal Child Psychology*, 43, 749–760.

Havighurst, S. S., Kehoe, C. E., & Harley, A. E. (2015). Tuning in to Teens: Improving parental responses to anger and reducing youth externalizing behavior problems. *Journal of Adolescence*, 42, 148–158.

Havighurst, S. S., Wilson, K. R., Harley, A. E., & Prior, M. R. (2009). Tuning in to Kids: An emotion-focused parenting program—Initial findings from a community trial. *Journal of Community Psychology*, 37, 1008–1023.

Havighurst, S. S., Wilson, K. R., Harley, A. E., Prior, M. R., &Kehoe, C. (2010).Tuning in to Kids: Improving emotion socialization practices in parents of preschool children – findings from a community trial. *Journal of Child Psychology and Psychiatry*, 51, 1342–1350.

Havlicek, J., Dvorakova, R., Bartos, L., & Flegr, J. (2006). Non-advertized does not mean concealed: Body odour changes across the human menstrual cycle. *Ethology*, 112, 81–90.

Hawkins, R. L., Jaccard, J., & Needle, E. (2013). Nonacademic factors associated with dropping out of high school: Adolescent problem behaviors. *Journal of the Society for Social Work and Research*, 4, 58–75.

Hawkley, L. C., Thisted, R. A., & Caciappo, J. T. (2009). Loneliness predicts reduced physical activity: Cross-sectional & longitudinal analyses. *Health Psychology*, 28, 354–363.

Haworth, C. M. A., Wright, M. J., Martin, N. W., Martin, N. G., Boomsma, D. I., Bartels, M., et al. (2009). A twin study of the genetics of high cognitive ability selected from 11,000 twin pairs in six studies from four countries. *Behavior Genetics*, 39, 359–370.

Hay, D. F. (2009). The roots and branches of human altruism. *British Journal of Psychology*, 100, 473–479.

Hay, D. F., Caplan, M., & Nash, A. (2009). The beginnings of peer relations. In K. H. Rubin, W. M. Bukowski, & B. Laursen (Eds.), *Handbook of peer interactions, relationships, and groups*. New York, NY: Guilford.

Hay, D. F., Hurst, S., Waters, C. S., & Chadwick, A. (2011). Infants' use of force to defend toys: The origins of instrumental aggression. *Infancy*, 16, 471–489.

Hay, D. F., Mundy, L., Roberts, S., Carta, R., Waters, C. S., Perra, O., et al. (2011). Known risk factors for violence predict 12-month-old infants' aggressiveness with peers. *Psychological Science*, 22, 1205–1211.

Hay, D. F., Nash, A., & Pedersen, J. (1983). Interaction between six-month-old peers. *Child Development*, 54, 557–562.

Hay, D. F., Pawlby, S., Angold, A., Harold, G. T., & Sharp, D. (2003). Pathways to violence in the children of mothers who were depressed postpartum. *Developmental Psychology*, 39, 1083–1094.

Hayes, J., & Leudar, I. (2016). Experiences of continued presence: On the practical consequences of 'hallucinations' in bereavement. *Psychology and Psychotherapy: Theory, Research and Practice*, 89, 194–210.

Hayflick, L. (1976). The cell biology of human aging. *New England Journal of Medicine*, 295, 1302–1308.

Hayflick, L. (1994). *How and why we age*. New York, NY: Ballantine.

Hayflick, L. (2004). "Anti-aging" is an oxymoron. *Journal of Gerontology Series A: Biological Sciences*, 59A, 573–578.

Hayflick, L. (2007). Biological aging is no longer an unsolved problem. *Annals of the New York Academy of Sciences*, 1100, 1–13.

Hayne, H., & Simcock, G. (2009). Memory development in toddlers. In M. L. Courage & N. Cowan (Eds.), *The development of memory in infancy and childhood* (pp. 43–68). New York, NY: Psychology Press.

Hayslip, B., Jr. (2009). Ethnic and cross-cultural perspectives on custodial grandparenting. In J. Sokolovsky (Ed.), *The cultural context of aging* (3rd ed.). Westport, CT: Praeger.

Hayslip, B., Jr., Maiden, R. J., Page, K. S., & Dolbin-MacNab, M. (2015). Grandparenting. In P. A. Lichtenberg & B. T. Mast (Eds. in Chief) & B. D. Carpenter & J. L. Wetherell (Vol. Eds.), *APA handbook of clinical geropsychology: Vol. 1. History and status of the field and perspectives on aging* (pp. 497–511). Washington, DC: American Psychological Association.

Hayslip, B., Jr., Pruett, J. H., & Caballero, D. M. (2015). The 'how' and 'when' of parental loss in adulthood: Effects on grief and adjustment. *Omega: Journal of Death and Dying*, 71, 3–18.

Hayslip, B., Jr., & White, D. L. (2008). The grief of grandparents. In M. S. Stroebe, R. O. Hansson, H. Schut, & W. Stroebe (Eds.), *Handbook of bereavement research and practice. Advances in theory and intervention*. Washington, DC: American Psychological Association.

Haywood, K., & Getchell, N. (2014). *Life span motor development* (6th ed.). Champaign, IL: Human Kinetics.

Hazan, C., & Shaver, P. (1987). Romantic love conceptualized as an attachment process. *Journal of Personality and Social Psychology*, 52, 511–524.

Hazan, C., & Shaver, P. (1990). Love and work: An attachment-theoretical perspective. *Journal of Personality and Social Psychology*, 59, 270–280.

Hazan, C., Campa, M., & Gur-Yaish, N. (2006). Attachment across the lifespan. In P. Noller & J. A. Feeney (Eds.), *Close relationships: Functions, forms, and processes*. New York, NY: Psychology Press.

Hazlett, H. C., De Alba, M. G., & Hooper, S. R. (2011). Klinefelter syndrome. In S. Goldstein & C. R. Reynolds (Eds.), *Handbook of neurodevelopmental and genetic disorders in children* (2nd ed., pp. 382–424). New York, NY: Guilford.

Hazlett, H. C., Hammer, J., Hooper, S. R., & Kamphaus, R. W. (2011). Down syndrome. In S. Goldstein & C. R. Reynolds (Eds.), *Handbook of neurodevelopmental and genetic disorders in children* (2nd ed., pp. 362–381). New York, NY: Guilford.

He, F. J., Marrero, N. M., & MacGregor, G. A. (2008). Salt intake is related to soft drink consumption in children

and adolescents: A link to obesity? *Hypertension, 51*, 629–634.
He, M., Tucker, P., Gilliland, J., Irwin, J. D., Larsen, K., & Hess, P. (2012). The influence of local food environments on adolescents' food purchasing behaviors. *International Journal of Environmental Research and Public Health*, 9, 1458–1471.
Hearn, S., Saulnier, G., Strayer, J., Glenham, M., Koopman, R., & Marcia, J. E. (2012). Between integrity and despair: Toward construct validation of Erikson's eight stage. *Journal of Adult Development, 19*, 1–20.
Heaton, P., & Wallace, G. L. (2004). Annotation: The savant syndrome. *Journal of Child Psychology and Psychiatry, 45*, 899–911.
Hedge, J. W., Borman, W. C., & Lammlein, S. E. (Eds.) (2006). *The aging workforce: Realities, myths, and implications for organizations.* Washington, DC: American Psychological Association.
Hedlund, B., & Ebersole, P. (1983). A test of Levinson's midlife reevaluation. *Journal of Genetic Psychology, 143*, 189–192.
Heilman, K. M. (2016). Possible brain mechanisms of creativity. *Archives of Clinical Neuropsychology, 31*, 285–296.
Heine, S. J., & Buchtel, E. E. (2009). Personality: The universal and the culturally specific. *Annual Review of Psychology, 60*, 369–394.
Held, R. and Hein A. (1963). Movement-produced stimulation in the development of visually guided behavior. *Journal of Comparative and Physiological Psychology, 56*, 872–876.
Helderman, R. S. (2003, June 13). Inseparable sisters say a first goodbye. *The Washington Post*, B5.
Helgeson, V. S., & Mickelson, K. (2000). Coping with chronic illness among the elderly: Maintaining self-esteem. In S. B. Manuck, R. Jennings, B. S. Rabin, & A. Baum (Eds.), *Behavior, health, and aging.* Mahwah, NJ: Erlbaum.
Helmreich, R. L., Sawin, L. L., & Carsrud, A. L. (1986). The honeymoon effect in job performance: Temporal increases in the predictive power of achievement motivation. *Journal of Applied Psychology, 71*, 185–188.
Helms, J. E. (1992). Why is there no study of cultural equivalence in standardized cognitive-ability testing? *American Psychologist, 47*, 1083–1101.
Helms, J. E. (1997). The triple quandary of race, culture, and social class in standardized cognitive ability testing. In D. P. Flanagan, J. Genshaft, & P. L. Harrison (Eds.), *Contemporary intellectual assessment: Theories, tests, and issues.* New York, NY: Guilford.
Helms, J. E., Jernigan, M., & Mascher, J. (2005). The meaning of race in psychology and how to change it. *American Psychologist, 60*, 27–36.
Helson, R., Jones, C., & Kwan, V. S. Y. (2002). Personality change over 40 years of adulthood: Hierarchical linear modeling analyses of two longitudinal samples. *Journal of Personality and Social Psychology, 83*, 752–766.
Helvik, A.-S., Krokstad, S., & Tambs, K. (2013). Hearing loss and risk of early retirement. The HUNT study. *The European Journal of Public Health, 23*, 617–622.
Henig, R. M. (2000). The monk in the garden: The lost and found genius of Gregor Mendel, the father of genetics. Boston, MA: Houghton Mifflin.
Henker, B., & Whalen, C. K. (1989). Hyperactivity and attention deficits. *American Psychologist, 44*, 216–223.
Hennies, N., Ralph, M. A. L., Kempkes, M., Cousins, J. N., & Lewis, P. A. (2016). Sleep spindle density predicts the effect of prior knowledge on memory consolidation. *The Journal of Neuroscience, 36*, 3799–3810.
Henrich, C. C., Brookmeyer, K. A., Shrier, L. A., & Shahar, G. (2006). Supportive relationships and sexual risk behavior in adolescence: An ecological–transactional approach. *Journal of Pediatric Psychology, 31*, 286–297.
Henrich, J., Heine, S.J., & Norenzayan, A. (2010). The weirdest people in the world? *Behavioral and Brain Sciences, 33*, 61–135.
Henry, D. B., Schoeny, M. E., Deptula, D. P., & Slavick, J. T. (2007). Peer selection and socialization effects on adolescent intercourse without a condom and attitudes about the costs of sex. *Child Development, 78*, 825–838.
Henry, J. D., MacLeod, M. S., Phillips, L. H., & Crawford, J. R. (2004). A meta-analytic review of prospective memory and aging. *Psychology and Aging, 19*, 27–39.
Henry, J. D., Phillips, L. H., Ruffman, T., & Bailey, P. E. (2013). A meta-analytic review of age differences in theory of mind. *Psychology and Aging, 28*, 826–839.
Heo, S., Prakash, R. S., Voss, M. W., Erickson, K. L., Ouyang, C., Sutton, B. P., et al. (2010). Resting hippocampal blood flow, spatial memory and aging. *Brain Research, 1315*, 119–127.
Hepach, R., Vaish, A., & Tomasello, M. (2012). Young children sympathize less in response to unjustified emotional distress. *Developmental Psychology, 49*, 1132–1138.
Herdt, G., & Davidson, J. (1988). The Sambia "turnim-man": Sociocultural and clinical aspects of gender formation in male pseudohermaphrodites with 5-alpha-reductase deficiency in Papua New Guinea. *Archives of Sexual Behavior, 17*, 33–56.
Herdt, G., & McClintock, M. (2000). The magical age of 10. *Archives of Sexual Behavior, 29*, 587–606.
Herlitz, A., & Lovén, J. (2013). Sex differences and the own-gender bias in face recognition: A meta-analytic review. *Visual Cognition, 21*, 1306–1336.
Herlitz, A., & Rehnman, J. (2008). Sex differences in episodic memory. *Current Directions in Psychological Science, 17*, 52–56.
Herman-Giddens, M. E., Slora, E. J., Wasserman, R. C., Bourdony, C. J., Bhapkar, M. V., Koch, G. G., et al. (1997). Secondary sexual characteristics and menses in young girls seen in office practice: A study from the Pediatric Research in Office Settings Network. *Pediatrics, 99*, 505–512.
Herman-Giddens, M. E., Steffes, J., Harris, D., Slora, E., Hussey, M., Dowshen, S. A., & Reiter, E. O. (2012). Secondary sexual characteristics in boys: Data from the Pediatric Research in Office Settings Network. *Pediatrics, 130*, e1058–68.
Hermans, H. J., & Oles, P. K. (1999). Midlife crisis in men: Affective organization of personal meanings. *Human Relations, 52*, 1403–1426.
Hermelin, B. (with foreword by M. Rutter). (2001). *Bright splinters of the mind: A personal story of research with autistic savants.* London, UK: Jessica Kingsley Publishers, Ltd.
Hernandez, R. K., Werler, M. M., Romitti, P., Sun, L., & Anderka, M. (2012). Nonsteroidal anti-inflammatory drug use among women and the risk of birth defects. *American Journal of Obstetrics & Gynecology, 206*, e1–8.
Heron, M. (2016, February 16). Deaths: Leading causes for 2013. *National Vital Statistics Reports, 65*(2). Retrieved from www.cdc.gov/nchs/data/nvsr/nvsr65/nvsr65_02.pdf.
Herrnstein, R. J., & Murray, C. (1994). *The bell curve: Intelligence and class structure in American life.* New York, NY: Free Press.
Herskind, A. M., McGue, M., Holm, N. V., Sorensen, T. I., Harvald, B., & Vaupel, J. W. (1996). The heritability of human longevity: A population-based study of 2872 Danish twin pairs born 1870–1900. *Human Genetics, 97*, 319–323.
Hertzog, C., Kramer, A. F., Wilson, R. S., & Lindenberger, U. (2009). Enrichment effects on adult cognitive development: Can the functional capacity of older adults be preserved and enhanced? *Psychological Science in the Public Interest, 9*, 1–65.
Herzmann, G., & Curran, T. (2011). Experts' memory: An ERP study of perceptual expertise effects on encoding and recognition. *Memory & Cognition, 39*, 412–432.
Hesketh, B., Griffin, B., & Loh, V. (2011). A future-oriented retirement transition adjustment framework. *Journal of Vocational Behavior, 79*, 303–314.
Hess, T. M. (1999). Cognitive and knowledge-based influences on social representations. In T. M. Hess & F. Blanchard-Fields (Eds.), *Social cognition and aging.* San Diego, CA: Academic Press.
Hess, T. M. (2006). Attitudes toward aging and their effects on behavior. In J. E. Birren & K. W. Schaie (Eds.), *Handbook of the psychology of aging* (6th ed.). Burlington, MA: Elsevier Academic Press.
Hess, T. M., & Emery, L. (2012). Memory in context: The impact of age-related goals on performance. In M. Naveh-Benjamin & N. Ohta (Eds.), *Memory and aging: Current issues and future directions* (pp. 183–214). New York, NY: Psychology Press.
Hess, T. M., & Hinson, J. T. (2006). Age-related variation in the influences of aging stereotypes on memory in adulthood. *Psychology and aging, 21*, 621–625.
Hess, T. M., Hinson, J. T., & Hodges, E. A. (2009). Moderators of and mechanisms underlying stereotype threat effects on older adults' memory performance. *Experimental Aging Research, 35*, 153–177.
Hess, T. M., Osowski, N. L., & Leclerc, C. M. (2005). Age and experience influences on the complexity of social inferences. *Psychology and Aging, 20*, 447–459.
Hess, T. M., & Queen, T. L. (2014). Aging influences on judgment and decision processes: Interactions between ability and experience. In P. Verhaeghen & C. Hertzog (Eds.), *The Oxford handbook of emotion, social cognition, and problem solving in adulthood* (pp. 238–255). New York, NY: Oxford University Press.
Hesse, E., & Main, M. (2006). Frightened, threatening, and dissociative parental behavior in low-risk samples: Description, discussion, and interpretations. *Development and Psychopathology, 18*, 309–343
Heston, L. L. (1970). The genetics of schizophrenia and schizoid disease. *Science, 167*, 249–256.
Hetherington, E. M. (1981). Children and divorce. In R. W. Henderson (Ed.), *Parent–child interaction: Theory, research and prospects.* New York, NY: Academic Press.
Hetherington, E. M. (2006). The influence of conflict, marital problem solving and parenting on children's adjustment in nondivorced, divorced and remarried families. In A. Clarke-Stewart & J. Dunn (Eds.), *Families count: Effects on child and adolescent development.* New York, NY: Cambridge University Press.
Hetherington, E. M., & Kelly, J. (2002). *For better or for worse: Divorce reconsidered.* New York: Norton.
Hetherington, E. M., & Stanley-Hagen, M. (2000). Diversity among stepfamilies. In D. H. Demo, K. R. Allen, & M. A. Fine (Eds.), *Handbook of family diversity.* New York, NY: Oxford University Press.
Hetherington, E. M., Cox, M., & Cox, R. (1982). Effects of divorce on parents and children. In M. E. Lamb (Ed.), *Nontraditional families.* Hillsdale, NJ: Erlbaum.
Hewitt, B., Western, M., & Baxter, J. (2006). Who decides? The social characteristics of who initiates marital separation. *Journal of Marriage and Family, 68*, 1165–1177.
Hewlett, B. S. (1996). Diverse contexts of human infancy. In C. Ember & M. Ember (Eds.), *Cross-cultural research for social science* (pp. 287–297). Englewood Cliffs, NJ: Prentice Hall.
Heyman, G. D., Dweck, C. S., & Cain, K. M. (1992). Young children's vulnerability to self-blame and helplessness: Relationship to beliefs about goodness. *Child Development, 63*, 401–415.
Heyman, R. E., Foran, H. M., & Wilkinson, J. L. (2013). Theories of intimate partner violence. In M. A. Fine & F. D. Fincham (Eds.), *Handbook of family theories. A context-based approach.* New York, NY: Routledge.
Hickok, G., & Small, S. L. (2016). *Neurobiology of language.* London, UK: Elsevier.
Hicks, B. M., Blonigen, D. M., Kramer, M. D., Krueger, R. F., Patrick, C. J., Iacono, W. G., et al. (2007). Gender differences and developmental change in externalizing disorders from late adolescence to early adulthood: A longitudinal twin study. *Journal of Abnormal Psychology, 116*, 433–447.
Hilgard, E. R., & Loftus, E. F. (1979). Effective interrogation of the eyewitness. *International Journal of Clinical and Experimental Psychology, 27*, 342–357.
Hill, A. J. (2007). The development of children's shape and weight concerns. In T. Jaffa & B. McDermott (Eds.), *Eating disorders in children and adolescents.* Cambridge, UK: Cambridge University Press.
Hill, C., & Rose, J. (2009). Parenting stress in mothers of adults with an intellectual disability: Parental cognitions in relation to child characteristics and family support. *Journal of Intellectual Disability Research, 53*, 969–980.
Hill, J. P., & Lynch, M. E. (1983). The intensification of gender-related role expectations during early adolescence. In J. Brooks-Gunn & A. C. Petersen (Eds.), *Girls at puberty: Biological and psychosocial perspectives.* New York, NY: Plenum.
Hill, J., Emery, R. E., Harden, K. P., Mendle, J., & Turkheimer, E. (2008). Alcohol use in adolescent twins and affiliation with substance using peers. *Journal of Abnormal Child Psychology, 36*, 81–94.
Hill, N. E., & Tyson, D. F. (2009). Parental involvement in middle school: A meta-analytic assessment of the strategies that promote achievement. *Developmental Psychology, 45*, 740–763.
Hill, R., & Rodgers, R. H. (1964). The developmental approach. In H. Christensen (Ed.), *Handbook of marriage and the family.* Chicago, IL: Rand-McNally.
Hill, S. D., & Tomlin, C. (1981). Self-recognition in retarded children. *Child Development, 52*, 145–150.
Hill, S. E., & Flom, R. (2007). 18- and 24-month-olds' discrimination of gender-consistent and inconsistent activities. *Infant Behavior & Development, 30*, 168–173.

Hills, T. (2013). The company that words keep: Comparing the statistical structure of child-versus adult-directed language. *Journal of Child Language, 40*, 586–604.

Hinduja, S., & Patchin, J. W. (2013). Social influences on cyberbullying behaviors among middle and high school students. *Journal of Youth and Adolescence, 42*, 711–722.

Hines, J. C., Touron, D. R., & Hertzog, C. (2009). Metacognitive influences on study time allocation in an associative recognition task: An analysis of adult age differences. *Psychology and Aging, 24*, 462–475.

Hines, M. (2015). Gendered development. In M. E. Lamb (Ed.), *Handbook of child psychology and developmental science: Vol 3. Socioemotional processes* (7th ed., pp. 842–887). Hoboken, NJ: Wiley.

Hines, M., Constantinescu, M., & Spencer, D. (2015). Early androgen exposure and human gender development. *Biology of Sex Differences, 6*, 3. Available at www.researchgate.net/publication/273146299_Early_androgen_exposure_and_human_gender_development.

Hinshaw, S. P., & Ellison, K. (2016). *ADHD. What everyone needs to know.* New York, NY: Oxford University Press.

Hinton, J. (1975). The influence of previous personality on reactions to having terminal cancer. *Omega: Journal of Death and Dying, 6*, 95–111.

Hirschi, A., & Vondracek, F. W. (2009). Adaptation of career goals to self and opportunities in early adolescence. *Journal of Vocational Behavior, 75*,120–128.

Hirsh-Pasek, K., Adamson, L. B., Bakeman, R., Owen, M. T., Golinkoff, R. M., Pace, A., Yust, P. K., & Suma, K. (2015). The contribution of early communication quality to low-income children's language success. *Psychological Science, 26*, 1071–1083.

Hirsh-Pasek, K., Golinkoff, R. M, Berk, L. E., & Singer, D. G. (2009). *A mandate for playful learning in preschool: Presenting the evidence.* New York, NY: Oxford University Press.

Hirsh-Pasek, K., Golinkoff, R. M., & Hollich, G. (1999). Trends and transitions in language development: Looking for the missing piece. *Developmental Neuropsychology, 16*, 139–162.

Ho, L. P., Ho, S. S., Leung, D. Y., So, W. K., & Chan, C. W. (2016). A feasibility and efficacy randomised controlled trial of swaddling for controlling procedural pain in preterm infants. *Journal of Clinical Nursing, 25*, 472–482.

Hoare, C. (2009). Models of adult development in Bronfenbrenner's bioecological theory and Erikson's biopsychosocial life stage theory: Moving to a more complete three-model view. In M. C. Smith & N. DeFrates-Densch (Eds.), *Handbook of research on adult learning and development* (pp. 68–102). New York, NY: Routledge.

Hobbs, F. B. (with B. L. Damon). (1996). *65 in the United States.* Washington, DC: U.S. Bureau of the Census.

Hodapp, R. M., Griffin, M. M., Burke, M. M., & Fisher, M. H. (2011). Intellectual disabilities. In R. J. Sternberg & S. B. Kaufman (Eds.), *The Cambridge handbook of intelligence* (pp. 193–209). New York, NY: Cambridge University Press.

Hodnett, E. D., Gates, S., Hofmeyr, G. J., Sakala, C., & Weston, J. (2013). Continuous support for women during childbirth. *Cochrane Database Systematic Review, 7*(7), CD003766.

Hodnett, E. D., Simon, G., Hofmeyr, G. J., & Sakala, C. (2012). Continuous support for women during childbirth. *Cochrane Database of Systematic Reviews,* Issue 10. Art. No.: CD003766. doi:10.1002/14651858.CD003766. pub4

Hoegg, J., & Alba, J. W. (2007, March). Taste perception: More than meets the tongue. *Journal of Consumer Research, 33*, 490–498.

Hof, P., & Mobbs, C. (2001). *Functional neurobiology of aging.* San Diego, CA: Academic Press.

Hof, P. R., & Mobbs, C. V. (Eds.). (2009). *Handbook of the neuroscience of aging.* London, UK: Academic Press.

Hofer, S. M., Christensen, H., MacKinnon, A. J., Korten, A. E., Jorm, A. F., Henderson, A. S., & Easteal, S. (2002). Change in cognitive functioning associated with ApoE genotype in a community sample of older adults. *Psychology and Aging, 17*, 194–208.

Hoff, E. (2013). Interpreting the early language trajectories of children from low-SES and language minority homes: Implications for closing achievement gaps. *Developmental Psychology, 49*, 4–14.

Hoff, E. (2014). *Language development* (5th ed.). Belmont, CA: Wadsworth.

Hoff, E. V. (2005a). A friend living inside me—The forms and functions of imaginary companions. *Imagination, Cognition, and Personality, 24*, 151–189.

Hoff, E. V. (2005b). Imaginary companions, creativity, and self-image in middle childhood. *Creativity Research Journal, 17*, 167–180.

Hoffman, B. J., & Woehr, D. J. (2006). A quantitative review of the relationship between person-organization fit and behavioral outcomes. *Journal of Vocational Behavior, 68*, 389–399.

Hoffman, K. L., Kiecolt, K. J., & Edwards, J. N. (2005). Physical violence between siblings: A theoretical and empirical analysis. *Journal of Family Issues, 26*, 1103–1130.

Hoffman, M. L. (1970). Moral development. In P. H. Mussen (Ed.), *Carmichael's manual of child psychology: Vol. 2.* New York, NY: Wiley.

Hoffman, M. L. (2000). *Empathy and moral development: Implications for caring and justice.* Cambridge, UK: Cambridge University Press.

Hoffman, M. L. (2008). Empathy and prosocial behavior. In M. Lewis, J. M. Haviland-Jones, & L. F. Barrett (Eds.), *Handbook of emotions* (3rd ed.). New York, NY: Guilford.

Hoffman, S. I., & Strauss, S. (1985). The development of children's concepts of death. *Death Studies, 9*, 469–482.

Hoffman, S., & Maynard, R. A. (2008). *Kids having kids: Economic costs and social consequences of teen pregnancy.* Washington, DC: The Urban Institute Press.

Hoffnung, M. (2004). Wanting it all: Career, marriage, and motherhood during college-educated women's 20s. *Sex Roles, 50*, 711–723.

Hoffnung, M., & Williams, M. A. (2013). Balancing act: Career and family during college-educated women's 30s. *Sex Roles, 68*, 321–334.

Hofman, A. D., Visser, I., Jansen, B. R., & van der Maas, H. L. (2015). The balance-scale task revisited: A comparison of statistical models for rule-based and information-integration theories of proportional reasoning. *PLoS ONE, 10*, e0136449.

Hofsten, O. von, Hofsten, C. von, Sulutvedt, U., Laeng, B., Brennen, T., & Magnussen, S. (2014). Simulating newborn face perception. *Journal of Vision, 14*, 16.

Hofstra, M. B., Van der Ende, J., & Verhulst, F. C. (2000). Continuity and change of psychopathology from childhood into adulthood. *Journal of the American Academy of Child & Adolescent Psychiatry, 39*, 850–858.

Hogan, D. P., & Park, J. M. (2000). Family factors and social support in the developmental outcomes of very low-birth weight children. *Clinical Perinatology, 27*, 433–459.

Hogström, L., Johansson, M., Janson, P. O., Berg, M., Francis, J., Sogn, J., et al. (2012). Quality of life after adopting compared with childbirth with or without assisted reproduction. *Actaobstetricia Et Gynecologicascandinavica, 91*, 1077–1085.

Hohm, E., Jennen-Steinmetz, C., Schmidt, M. H., & Laucht, M. (2007). Language development at ten months: Predictive of language outcome and school achievement ten years later? *European Child & Adolescent Psychiatry, 16*, 149–156.

Hohmann, S., Adamo, N., Lahey, B. B., Faraone, S. V., & Banaschewski, T. (2015). Genetics in child and adolescent psychiatry: Methodological advances and conceptual issues. *European Child & Adolescent Psychiatry, 24*, 619–634.

Holahan, C., & Sears, R. (1995). *The gifted group in later maturity.* Stanford, CA: Stanford University Press.

Holden, G. W. (2010). *Parenting. A dynamic perspective.* Thousand Oaks, CA: Sage.

Holden, G. W., Vittrup, B., & Rosen, L. H. (2011). Families, parenting, and discipline. In M. K. Underwood & L. H. Rosen (Eds), *Social development: Relationships in infancy, childhood and adolescence.* New York: Guilford.

Holland, J. L. (1985). *Making vocational choices: A theory of vocational personalities and work environments* (2nd ed.). Englewood Cliffs, NJ: Prentice-Hall.

Holland, J. L. (1996). Exploring careers with a typology: What we have learned and some new directions. *American Psychologist, 51*, 397–406.

Hollich, G. (2010). Early language. In J. G. Bremner & T. D. Wachs (Eds.), *The Wiley-Blackwell handbook of infant development: Vol. 1. Basic research* (2nd ed., pp. 426–449). Malden, MA: Blackwell.

Hollich, G. J., Hirsh-Pasek, K., & Golinkoff, R. M. (2000). Breaking the language barrier: An emergentist coalition model for the origins of word learning. *Monographs of the Society for Research in Child Development, 65* (No. 262).

Hollins, M. (2010). Somesthetic senses. *Annual Review of Psychology, 61*, 243–271.

Holmbeck, G. N., Crossman, R. E., Wandrei, M. L., & Gasiewski, E. (1994). Cognitive development, egocentrism, self-esteem, and adolescent contraceptive knowledge, attitudes, and behavior. *Journal of Youth and Adolescence, 23*, 169–193.

Holowka, S., & Petitto, L. A. (2002). Left hemisphere cerebral specialization for babies while babbling. *Science, 297*, 1515.

Holt, R. I., & Sönksen, P. H. (2008). Growth hormone, IGF-I and insulin and their abuse in sport. *British Journal of Pharmacology, 154*, 542–556.

Holt-Lunstad, J., Smith, T. B., Baker, M., Harris, T., & Stephenson, D. (2015). Loneliness and social isolation as risk factors for mortality: A meta-analytic review. *Perspectives on Psychological Science, 10*, 227–237.

Holzrichter, A. S., & Meier, R. P. (2000). Child-directed signing in American sign language. In C. Chamberlain, J. P. Morford, & R. Mayberry (Eds.), *Language acquisition by eye.* Mahwah, NJ: Lawrence Erlbaum.

Honey, K. L., Bennett, P., & Morgan, M. (2003). Predicting postnatal depression. *Journal of Affective Disorders, 76*, 201–210.

Hong, J. S., & Espelage, D. L. (2012). A review of research on bullying and peer victimization in school: An ecological system analysis. *Aggression and Violent Behavior, 17*, 311–322.

Honzik, M. P. (1983). Measuring mental abilities in infancy: The value and limitations. In M. Lewis (Ed.), *Origins of intelligence: Infancy and early childhood* (2nd ed.). New York, NY: Plenum.

Honzik, M. P. (1986). The role of the family in the development of mental abilities: A 50-year study. In N. Datan, A. L. Greene, H. W. Reese (Ed.), *Life-span developmental psychology: Intergenerational relations* (pp. 185–210). New York, NY: Lawrence Erlbaum.

Hooker, K., & Siegler, I. C. (1993). Life goals, satisfaction, and self-rated health: Preliminary findings. *Experimental Aging Research, 19*, 97–110.

Hooper, F. H., Hooper, J. O., & Colbert, K. K. (1985). Personality and memory correlates of intellectual functioning in adulthood: Piagetian and psychometric assessments. *Human Development, 28*, 101–107.

Hopkins, M. (2006, July 3). 'Miracle recovery' shows brain's resilience. Retrieved from www.bioedonline.org/news/news.cfm?art=2630.

Horn, J. L., & Cattell, R. B. (1967). Age differences in fluid and crystallized intelligence. *Acta Psychologica, 26*, 107–129.

Horn, J. L., & Noll, J. (1997). Human cognitive capabilities: Gf-Gc theory. In D. P. Flanagan, J. Genshaft, & P. L. Harrison (Eds.), *Contemporary intellectual assessment: Theories, tests, and issues.* New York, NY: Guilford.

Horner, V., & Whiten, A. (2005). Causal knowledge and imitation/emulation switching in chimpanzees (Pan troglodytes) and children (Homo sapiens). *Animal Cognition, 8*, 164–181.

Horswill, M. S., Marrington, S. A., McCullough, C. M., Wood, J., Pachana, N. A., McWilliam, J., et al. (2008). The hazard perception ability of older drivers. *Journals of Gerontology, Series B: Psychological Sciences and Social Sciences, 63*, P212–P218.

Houdé, O., Pineau, A., Leroux, G., Poirel, N., Perchey, G., Lanoë, C., et al. (2011). Functional magnetic resonance imaging study of Piaget's conservation-of-number task in preschool and school-age children: A neo-Piagetian approach. *Journal of Experimental Child Psychology.*

Houdé, O., Rossi, S., Lubin, A., & Joliot, M. (2010). Mapping numerical processing, reading, and executive functions in the developing brain: An fMRI meta-analysis on 52 studies including 842 children. *Developmental Science, 13*, 876–885.

Houdé, O., & Borst, G. (2014). Measuring inhibitory control in children and adults: Brain imaging and mental chronometry. *Frontiers in Psychology, 5*, 695.

House, J. D. (2006). Mathematics beliefs, instructional strategies, and algebra achievement of adolescent students in Japan: Results from the TIMSS 1999 assessment. *International Journal of Instructional Media, 33*, 443–462.

Houser, J. J., Mayeux, L., & Cross, C. (2015). Peer status and aggression as predictors of dating popularity in adolescence. *Journal of Youth and Adolescence, 44*, 683–695.

Houshyar, S., Gold, A., & DeVries, M. (2013). Resiliency in maltreated children. In S. Goldstein, & R. B. Brooks (Eds.), *Handbook of resilience in children* (2nd ed.). New York, NY: Springer Science+Business Media.

Houston, D. M., Pisoni, D. B., Kirk, K. I., Ying, E. A., & Miyamoto, R. T. (2005). Speech perception skills of deaf infants following cochlear implantation: A first report. *International Journal of Pediatric Otorhinolaryngology*, 67, 1479–495.

Houx, P. J., Vreeling, F. W., & Jolles, J. (1991). Rigorous health screening reduces age effect on memory scanning task. *Brain and Cognition, 15*, 246–260.

Howe, D. (2011). *Attachment across the lifecourse. A brief introduction.* New York, NY: Palgrave Macmillan.

Howe, G. W., Hornberger, A. P., Weihs, K., Moreno, F., & Neiderhiser, J. M. (2012). Higher-order structure in the trajectories of depression and anxiety following sudden involuntary unemployment. *Journal of Abnormal Psychology, 121*, 325–338.

Howe, G. W., Levy, M. L., & Caplan, R. D. (2004). Job loss and depressive symptoms in couples: Common stressors, stress transmission, or relationship disruption? *Journal of Family Psychology, 18*, 639–650.

Howe, M. L. (2000). *The fate of early memories: Developmental science and the retention of childhood experiences.* Washington, DC: American Psychological Association.

Howe, M. L. (2006). Developmental invariance in distinctiveness effects in memory. *Developmental Psychology*, 42, 1193–1205.

Howe, M. L. (2014). The co-emergence of the self and autobiographical memory. In P. Bauer & R. Fivush (Eds.), *The Wiley handbook on the development of children's memory* (pp. 545–567). Malden, MA: Wiley Blackwell.

Howe, M. L., & Knott, L. M. (2015). The fallibility of memory in judicial processes: Lessons from the past and their modern consequences. *Memory, 23*, 633–656.

Howe, M. L., Courage, M. L., & Rooksby, M. (2009). In M. L. Courage & N. Cowan (Eds.), *The development of memory in infancy and childhood* (pp. 177–196). New York, NY: Psychology Press.

Howe, N., Aquan-Assee, J., Bukowski, W. M., Rinaldi, C. M., & Lehoux, P. M. (2000). Sibling self-disclosure in early adolescence. *Merrill-Palmer Quarterly, 46*, 653–671.

Howes, C. (1988). Same- and cross-sex friends: Implications for interaction and social skills. *Early Childhood Research Quarterly*, 3, 21–37.

Howes, C., & Matheson, C. C. (1992). Sequences in the development of competent play with peers: Social and social pretend play. *Developmental Psychology*, 28, 961–974.

Howieson, D. B., Dame, A., Camicioli, R., Sexton, G., Payami, H., & Kaye, J. A. (1997). Cognitive markers preceding Alzheimer's dementia in the healthy oldest old. *Journal of the American Geriatrics Society*,45, 584–589.

Howlin, P., & Moss, P. (2012). Adults with autism spectrum disorders. *Canadian Journal of Psychiatry*, 57, 275–283.

Hoy, W. (2012). School characteristics that make a difference for the achievement of all students. *Journal of Educational Administration*, 50, 76–97.

Hoyer, W. J., & Verhaeghen, P. (2006). Memory aging. In J. E. Birren & K. W. Schaie (Eds.), *Handbook of the psychology of aging*. Boston: Elsevier Academic Press.

Hrdy, S. B. (2005). On why it takes a village. Cooperative breeders, infant needs, and the future. In R. L. Burgess & K. MacDonald (Eds.), *Evolutionary perspectives on human development*. Thousand Oaks, CA: Sage.

Hsia, Y., Neubert, A. C., Rani, F., Viner, R. M., Hindmarsh, P. C., & Wong, I. C. (2009). An increase in the prevalence of type 1 and 2 diabetes in children and adolescents: Results from prescription data from a UK general practice database. *British Journal of Clinical Pharmacology*, 67, 242–249.

Hsin, A., & Xie, Y. (2014). Explaining Asian Americans' academic advantage over whites. *Proceedings of the National Academy of Sciences, 111*, 8416–8421.

Hsu, L. K. G. (1990). *Eating disorders*. New York, NY: Guilford Press.

Hsu, L. M., Chung, J., & Langer, E. J. (2010). The influence of age-related cues on health and longevity. *Perspectives on Psychological Science, 5*, 632–648.

Hu, V. W. (2013). From genes to environment: Using integrative genomics to build a "systems-level" understanding of autism spectrum disorders. *Child Development, 84*, 89–103.

Huang, M. (2009). Race of the interviewer and the black-white test score gap. *Social Science Research*, 38, 29–38.

Hubbard, J. A., Smithmyer, C. M., Ramsden, S. R., Parker, E. H., Flanagan, K. D., Dearing, K. F., Relyea, N., & Simons, R. F. (2002). Observational, physiological, and self-report measures of children's anger: Relations to reactive versus proactive aggression. *Child Development*, 73, 1101–1118.

Hubel, D. H., & Wiesel, T. N. (1970). The period of susceptibility to the physiological effects of unilateral eye-closure in kittens. *Journal of Physiology, 206*, 419–436.

Hudson, A., & Jacques, S. (2014). Put on a happy face! Inhibitory control and socioemotional knowledge predict emotion regulation in 5- to 7-year-olds. *Journal of Experimental Child Psychology, 123*, 36–52.

Hudson, J. A., & Mayhew, E. M. Y. (2009). The development of memory for recurring events. In M. L. Courage & N. Cowan (Eds.), *The development of memory in infancy and childhood* (pp. 69–92). New York, NY: Psychology Press.

Huesmann, L. R., Dubow, E. F., & Boxer, P. (2009). Continuity of aggression from childhood to early adulthood as a predictor of life outcomes: Implications for the adolescent-limited and life-course-persistent models. *Aggressive Behavior, 35*, 136–149.

Hughes, C., & Devine, R. T. (2015). A social perspective on theory of mind. In M. E. Lamb (Vol. Ed.) & R. M. Lerner (Ed.), *Handbook of child psychology and developmental science: Vol. 3. Socioemotional processes* (pp. 564–609). Hoboken, NJ: Wiley.

Hughes, D., Rodriguez, J., Smith, E. P., Johnson, D. J., Stevenson, H. C., & Spicer, P. (2006). Parents' ethnic socialization practices: A review of research and directions for future study. *Developmental Psychology*, 42, 747–770.

Hughes, F. M., & Seta, C. E. (2003). Gender stereotypes: Children's perceptions of future compensatory behavior following violations of gender roles. *Sex Roles, 49*, 685–691.

Hui, D., & Mohd Salleh, S. B. (2015). A scaffolding strategy for helping lower secondary science students construct scientific explanations for experimental based questions in science. *ALAR: Action Learning and Action Research Journal, 21*, 36–91.

Huizink, A. C. (2012). Prenatal factors in temperament: The role of prenatal stress and substance use exposure. In M. Z. Zentner & R. L. Shiner (Eds.), *Handbook of temperament*. New York, NY: Guilford.

Hultman, C. M., Sandin, S., Levine, S. Z., Lichtenstein, P., & Reichenberg, A. (2011). Advancing paternal age and risk of autism: New evidence from a population-based study and a meta-analysis of epidemiological studies. *Molecular Psychiatry, 16*, 1203–1212.

Hultsch, D. F., Hammer, M., & Small, B. J. (1993). Age differences in cognitive performance in later life: Relationships to self-reported health and activity life style. *Journal of Gerontology Series B: Psychological Sciences*, 48, 1–11.

Hummert, M. L. (2015). Experimental research on age stereotypes: Insights for subjective aging. In M. Diehl & H. Wahl, (Eds.), *Annual review of gerontology and geriatrics: Vol. 35*. (pp. 79–97). New York, NY: Springer.

Humphries, T., Kushalnagar, P., Mathur, G., Napoli, D. J., Padden, C., Rathmann, C., & Smith, S. (2014). Bilingualism: A pearl to overcome certain perils of cochlear implants. *Journal of Medical Speech-Language Pathology, 21*, 107–125.

Humphries, T., Kushalnagar, P., Mathur, G., Napoli, D. J., Padden, C., Rathmann, C., & Smith, S. (2016). Language choices for deaf infants: Advice for parents regarding sign languages. *Clinical Pediatrics*, 55, 513–517.

Hung, L., & Bryant, R. A. (2016). Autobiographical memory in the angry self. *PLoS ONE, 11* (3), e0151349.

Hurd, L. C. (1999). "We're not old!" Older women's negotiation of aging and oldness. *Journal of Aging Studies, 13*, 419–439.

Hurd, R. C. (2002). Sibling support systems in childhood after a parent dies. *Omega: Journal of Death and Dying, 45*, 299–320.

Hure, A. J., Powers, J. R., Mishra, G. D., Herbert, D. L., Byles, J. E., & Loxton, D. (2012). Miscarriage, preterm delivery, and stillbirth: Large variations in rates within a cohort of Australian women. *PLoS ONE*, 7(5), e37109.

Hurst, K., Read, S., & Wallis, A. (2012). Anorexia nervosa in adolescence and Maudsley family-based treatment. *Journal of Counseling & Development, 90*, 339–345.

Huston, A. C., & Bentley, A. C. (2010). Human development in societal context. *Annual Review of Psychology, 61*, 411–437.

Huston, M., & Schwartz, P. (1995). The relationships of lesbians and gay men. In J. T Wood & S. Duck (Eds.), *Under-studied relationships: Off the beaten track*. Thousand Oaks, CA: Sage.

Huston, T. L. (2009). What's love got to do with it? Why some marriages succeed and others fail. *Personal Relationships, 16*, 301–327.

Huston, T. L., Caughlin, J. P., Houts, R. M., Smith, S. E., & George, L. J. (2001). The connubial crucible: Newlywed years as predictors of marital delight, distress, and divorce. *Journal of Personality and Social Psychology, 80*, 237–252.

Huston, T. L., & Melz, H. (2004). The case for (promoting) marriage: The devil is in the details. *Journal of Marriage and Family, 66*, 943–958.

Huston, T. L., McHale, S. M., & Crouter, A. C. (1986). When the honeymoon's over: Changes in the marriage relationship over the first year. In R. Gilmour & S. Duck (Eds.), *The emerging field of personal relationships*. Hillsdale, NJ: Erlbaum.

Hwang, S., Kim, Y. S., & Leventhal, B. (2013). Bullying and the development of antisocial behavior. In C. R. Thomas & K. Pope (Eds.), *The origins of antisocial behavior. A developmental perspective*. New York, NY: Oxford University Press.

Hybels, C. F., Blazer, D. G., & Hays, J. C. (2009). Demography and epidemiology of psychiatric disorders in late life. In D. G. Blazer & D. C. Steffens (Eds.), *The American Psychiatric Publishing textbook of geriatric psychiatry* (4th ed.). Washington, DC: American Psychiatric Publishing.

Hyde, J. S. (1984). How large are gender differences in aggression? A developmental meta-analysis. *Developmental Psychology, 20*, 722–736.

Hyde, J. S. (2005). The gender similarities hypothesis. *American Psychologist, 60*, 581–592.

Hyde, J. S. (2007). New directions in the study of gender similarities and differences. *Current Directions in Psychological Science, 16*, 259–263.

Hyde, J. S. (2014). Gender similarities and differences. *Annual Review of Psychology, 65*, 373–398.

Hyde, J. S., & DeLamater, J. D. (2014). *Human sexuality* (12th ed.). McGraw-Hill.

Hyde, L. W. (2015). Developmental psychopathology in an era of molecular genetics and neuroimaging: A developmental neurogenetics approach. *Development and Psychopathology, 27*, 587–613.

Hyson, M. C., Hirsh-Pasek, K., & Rescorla, L. (1991). *Academic instruction in early childhood: Challenge or pressure?* San Francisco, CA: Jossey-Bass.

Iacoboni, M. (2009). Imitation, empathy, and mirror neurons. *Annual Review of Psychology, 60*, 653–670.

Iacoboni, M., & Dapretto, M. (2006). The mirror neuron system and the consequences of its dysfunction. *Nature Reviews Neuroscience*, 7, 942–951.

Iervolino, A. C., Hines, M., Golombok, S. E., Rust, J., & Plomin, R. (2005). Genetic and environmental influences on sex-typed behavior during the preschool years. *Child Development, 76*, 826–840.

Imel, S. (1996). *Adult literacy education: Emerging directions in program development. ERIC Digest No. 179.* Columbus, OH: ERIC Clearinghouse on Adult, Career and Vocational Education, Ohio State University.

Imperato-McGinley, J., Miller, M., Wilson, J. D., Peterson, R. E. Shackleton, C., Gajdusek, D. C. (1991. A cluster of male pseudohermaphrodites with 5a-reductase deficiency in Papua, New Guinea. *Clinical Embryology*, 34, 293–298.

Imperato-McGinley, J., Peterson, R. E., Gautier, T, & Sturla, E. (1979). Androgens and the evolution of male gender identity among male pseudohermaphrodites with 5a-reductase deficiency. *New England Journal of Medicine, 300*, 1233–1237.

Imuta, K., Scarf, D., & Hayne, H. (2013). The effect of verbal reminders on memory reactivation in 2-, 3-, and 4-year-old children. *Developmental Psychology, 49*, 1058–1065.

Inceoglu, I., Segers, J., & Bartram, D. (2012). Age-related differences in work motivation. *Journal of Occupational and Organizational Psychology, 85*, 300–329.

Infurna, F. J., & Luthar, S. S. (2016). The multidimensional nature of resilience to spousal loss. *Journal of Personality and Social Psychology*, July 11. [Epub ahead of print].

Ingersoll, B. (2011). Recent advances in early identification and treatment of autism. *Current Directions in Psychological Science, 20*, 335–338.

Ingoldsby, B. B., & Smith, S. (1995). *Families in multicultural perspective*. New York, NY: Guilford.

Ingram, R. E., & Price, J. M. (2001). The role of vulnerability in understanding psychopathology. In R. E. Ingram & J. M. Price (Eds.), *Vulnerability to psychopathology. Risk across the lifespan*. New York, NY: Guilford.

Ingrassia, M., & Springen, K. (1994, March 21). She's not baby Jessica anymore. *Newsweek, 123*, 60–66.

Inhelder, B. (1966). Cognitive development and its contribution to the diagnosis of some phenomena of mental deficiency. *Merrill-Palmer Quarterly, 12*, 299–319.

Inhelder, B., & Piaget, J. (1958). *The growth of logical thinking from childhood to adolescence: An essay on the construction of formal operational structures* (A. Parsons & S. Milgram, Trans.). New York, NY: Basic Books.

Inhelder, B., & Piaget, J. (1964). *Early growth of logic in the child: Classification and seriation*. New York, NY: Harper & Row.

Institute of Medicine (IOM), & National Research Council (NRC). (2014). *New directions in child abuse and neglect research*. Washington, DC: The National Academies Press. Retrieved from www.nap.edu/read/18331/chapter/1.

Insurance Institute for Highway Safety (2016). Retrieved from www.iihs.org/iihs/topics/t/older-drivers/topicoverview.

International Human Genome Sequencing Consortium (2004, October 21). Finishing the euchromatic sequence of the human genome. *Nature, 431*, 931–945.

International Labor Organization (2014). *Maternity and paternity at work: Law and practice across the world*. Geneva, Switzerland: Addati, Laura; Cassirer, Naomi; Gilchrist, Katherine. Retrieved from www.fortunedotcom.files.wordpress.com/2014/05/wcms_242615.pdf.

Ip, S., Chung, M., Raman, G., Chen, P., Magula, N., DeVine, D., Trikalinos, T., & Lau, J. (2007). Breastfeeding and maternal and infant health outcomes in developed countries. Rockville, MD: US Department of Health and Human Services. Available at www.ahrq.gov/downloads/pub/evidence/pdf/brfout/brfout.pdf.

Isabella, R. A. (1993). Origins of attachment: Maternal interactive behavior across the first year. *Child Development, 64*, 605–621.

Isabella, R. A., & Belsky, J. (1991). Interactional synchrony and the origins of infant-mother attachment: A replication study. *Child Development, 62*, 373–384.

Iyengar, S. D., Iyengar, K., Martines, J. C., Dashora, K., & Deora, K. K. (2008). Childbirth practices in rural Rajasthan, India: Implications for neonatal health and survival. *Journal of Perinatology: Official Journal of the California Perinatal Association, 28*, S23–30.

Izard, C. E. (1982). *Measuring emotions in infants and children*. New York, NY: Cambridge University Press.

Izard, C. E., & Ackerman, B. P. (2000). Motivational, organizational, and regulatory functions of discrete emotions. In M. Lewis & J. M. Haviland-Jones (Eds.), *Handbook of emotions* (2nd ed.). New York: Guilford.

Jack, F., & Hayne, H. (2007). Eliciting adults' earliest memories: Does it matter how we ask the question? *Memory, 15*, 647–663.

Jack, F., Simcock, G., & Hayne H. (2012). Magic memories: Young children's verbal recall after a 6-year delay. *Child Development, 83*, 159–172.

Jack, F., MacDonald, S., Reese, E., & Hayne, H. (2009). Maternal reminiscing style during early childhood predicts the age of adolescents' earliest memories. *Child Development, 80*, 496–505.

Jacklin, C. N. (1989). Male and female: Issues of gender. *American Psychologist, 44*, 127–133.

Jackson, J. J., Connolly, J. J., Garrison, S. M., Leveille, M. M., & Connolly, S. L. (2015). Your friends know how long you will live: a 75-year study of peer-rated personality traits. *Psychological Science, 26*, 335–340.

Jacobs, J. E., & Klaczynski, P. A. (2002). The development of judgment and decision making during childhood and adolescence. *Current Directions in Psychological Science, 11*, 145–149.

Jacobs, R. J., & Kane, M. N. (2010). HIV-related stigma in midlife and older women. *Social Work Health Care, 49*, 68–89.

Jacobs, S. C., Kosten, T. R., Kasl, S. V., Ostfeld, A. M., Berkman, L., & Charpentier, P. (1987–1988). Attachment theory and multiple dimensions of grief. *Omega: Journal of Death and Dying, 18*, 41–52.

Jacobson, J. L., & Jacobson, S. W. (1999). Drinking moderately and pregnancy: Effects on child development. *Alcohol Research and Health, 25*, 25–30.

Jacobson, J. L., Jacobson, S. W., Sokol, R. J., Martier, S. S., Ager, J. W., & Kaplan-Estrin, M. G. (1993). Teratogenic effects of alcohol on infant development. *Alcoholism: Clinical and Experimental Research, 17*, 174–183.

Jadva, V., Hines, M., & Golombok, S. (2010). Infants' preferences for toys, colors, and shapes: Sex differences and similarities. *Archives of Sexual Behavior, 39*, 1261–1273.

Jaffe, J., Beebe, B., Feldstein, S., Crown, C. L., & Jasnow, M. D. (2001). Rhythms of dialogue in infancy: Coordinated timing in development. *Monographs of the Society for Research in Child Development, 66* (2, Serial No. 265).

Jaffee, S. R. (2013). Family violence and parent psychopathology: Implications for children's socioemotional development and resilience. In S. Goldstein, & R. B. Brooks (Eds.), *Handbook of resilience in children* (2nd ed.). New York, NY: Springer Science+Business Media.

Jaffee, S. R., Strait, L. B., & Odgers, C. L. (2012). From correlates to causes: Can quasi-experimental studies and statistical innovations bring us closer to identifying the causes of antisocial behavior? *Psychological Bulletin, 138*, 272–295.

Jalmsell, L., Kontio, T., Stein, M., Henter, J., & Kreicbergs, U. (2015). On the child's own initiative: Parents communicate with their dying child about death. *Death Studies, 39*, 111–117.

James, J. B., & Zarrett, N. (2005). Ego integrity in the lives of older women: A follow-up of mothers from the Sears, Maccoby, and Levin (1951) Patterns of Child Rearing Study. *Journal of Adult Development, 12*, 155–167.

James, J., Ellis, B. J., Schlomer, G. L., & Garber, J. (2012). Sex-specific pathways to early puberty, sexual debut, and sexual risk taking: Tests of an integrated evolutionary-developmental model. *Developmental Psychology, 48*, 687–702.

James, W. (1890). *The principles of psychology*. London, UK: Henry Holt & Co.

Jamison, K. R. (2009). *Nothing was the same*. New York, NY: Alfred A. Knopf.

Janisse, J. J., Bailey, B. A., Ager, J., & Sokol, R. J. (2014). Alcohol, tobacco, cocaine, and marijuana use: Relative contributions to preterm delivery and fetal growth restriction. *Substance Abuse, 35*, 60–67.

Jankowiak, W. R., & Fischer, E. F. (1992). A cross-cultural perspective on romantic love. *Ethnology, 31*, 149–155.

Janus, J. S., & Janus, C. L. (1993). *The Janus report on sexual behavior*. New York, NY: Wiley.

Jaquish, G. A., & Ripple, R. E. (1981). Cognitive creative abilities and self-esteem across the adult life-span. *Human Development, 24*, 110–119.

Jasińska, K. K., & Petitto, L. A. (2013). How age of bilingual exposure can change the neural systems for language in the developing brain: A functional near infrared spectroscopy investigation of syntactic processing in monolingual and bilingual children. *Developmental Cognitive Neuroscience, 6*, 87–101.

Jastrzembski, T. S., Charness, N., & Vasyukova, C. (2006). Expertise and age effects on knowledge activation in chess. *Psychology and Aging, 21*, 401–405.

Jayawardena, K. M., & Liao, S. (2006). Elder abuse at the end of life. *Journal of Palliative Medicine, 9*, 127–136.

Jean, R. T., Wilkinson, A. V., Spitz, M. R., Prokhorov, A., Bondy, M., & Forman, M. R. (2011). Psychosocial risk and correlates of early menarche in Mexican-American girls. *American Journal of Epidemiology, 173*, 1203–1210.

Jedrychowski, W., Perera, F. P., Jankowski, J., Mrozek-Budzyn, D., Mroz, E., Flak, E., Edwards, S., Skarupa, A., & Lisowska-Miszczyk, I. (2009). Very low prenatal exposure to lead and mental development of children in infancy and early childhood: Krakow Perspective Cohort Study. *Neuroepidemiology, 32*, 270–278.

Jelicic, H., Bobek, D. L., Phelps, E., Lerner, R. M., & Lerner, J. V. (2007). Using positive youth development to predict contribution and risk behaviors in early adolescence: Findings from the first two waves of the 4-H study of positive youth development. *International Journal of Behavioral Development, 31*, 263–273.

Jemmott, J. B., III, Jemmott, L. S., & Fong, G. T. (2010). Efficacy of a theory-based abstinence-only intervention over 24 months: A randomized controlled trial with young adolescents. *Archives of Pediatric & Adolescent Medicine, 164*, 152–159.

Jennings, K. D., & Dietz, L. J. (2003). Mastery motivation and goal persistence in young children. In M. H. Bornstein & L. Davidson (Eds.), *Well-being: Positive development across the life course* (pp. 295–309). Mahwah, NJ: Lawrence Erlbaum.

Jennings, K. D., Yarrow, L. J., & Martin, P. D. (1984). Mastery motivation and cognitive development: A longitudinal study from infancy to 3 and 1/2 years of age. *International Journal of Behavioral Development, 7*, 441–461.

Jensen, A. R. (1969). How much can we boost IQ and scholastic achievement? *Harvard Educational Review, 39*, 1–123.

Jensen, A. R. (1977). Cumulative deficit in the IQ of blacks in the rural South. *Developmental Psychology, 13*, 184–191.

Jensen, A. R. (1980). *Bias in mental testing:*. New York: Free Press.

Jensen, A. R. (1993). Why is reaction time correlated with psychometric g? *Current Directions in Psychological Science, 2*, 53–56.

Jensen, A. R. (1998). *The g factor: The science of mental ability*. Westport, CN: Praeger.

Jensen, K., & Silk, J. B. (2014). Searching for the evolutionary roots of human morality. In M. Killen & J. G. Smetana (Eds.), *Handbook of moral development* (2nd ed., pp. 475–494). New York, NY: Psychology Press.

Jensen, L. A. (2015). Moral reasoning: Developmental emergence and life course pathways among cultures. In L. A. Jensen (Ed.), *The Oxford handbook of human development and culture: An interdisciplinary perspective* (pp. 230–254). New York: Oxford University Press.

Jensen, P. S., Hinshaw, S. P., Swanson, J. M., Greenhill, L. L., Conners, C. K., Arnold, L. E., Abikoff, H. B., Elliott, G., Hechtman, L., Hoza, B., March, J. S., Newcorn, J. H., Severe, J. B., Vitiello, B., Wells, K., & Wigal, T. (2001). Findings from the NIMH Multimodal Treatment Study of ADHD (MTA): Implications and applications for primary care providers. *Journal of Developmental and Behavioral Pediatrics, 22*, 60–73.

Jerger, S., Damian, M. F., Tye-Murray, N., & Abdi, H. (2014). Children use visual speech to compensate for non-intact auditory speech. *Journal of Experimental Child Psychology, 126*, 295–312.

Jergović, M., Tomičević, M., Vidović, A., Bendelja, K., Savić, A., Vojvoda, V., & Sabioncello, A. (2014). Telomere shortening and immune activity in war veterans with posttraumatic stress disorder. *Progress in Neuro-Psychopharmacology & Biological Psychiatry, 54*, 275–283.

Jessberger, S., & Gage, F. H. (2014). Adult neurogenesis: Bridging the gap between mice and humans. *Trends in Cell Biology, 24*, 558–563.

Jessberger, S., & Parent, J. M. (2008). Epilepsy and adult neurogenesis. In F. H. Gage, G. Kempermann, & H. Song (Eds.), *Adult neurogenesis* (pp. 535–547). New York, NY: Cold Spring Harbor Laboratory Press.

Jessor, R. (Ed.) (1998). *New perspectives on adolescent risk behavior*. Cambridge, UK: Cambridge University Press.

Jetha, M. K., & Segalowitz, S. (2012). *Adolescent brain development: Implications for behavior*. Waltham, MA: Academic Press.

Jiang, F., Stecker, G. C., Boynton, G. M., & Fine, I. (2016). Early blindness results in developmental plasticity for auditory motion processing within auditory and occipital cortex. *Frontiers in Human Neuroscience, 10*, 324.

Jimenez, D. E., Alegría, M., Chen, C., Chan, D., & Laderman, M. (2010). Prevalence of psychiatric illnesses in older ethnic minority adults. *Journal of the American Geriatrics Society, 58,* 256–264.

Joh, A. S., & Adolph, K. E. (2006). Learning from falling. *Child Development, 77,* 89–102.

Johansson, B., Zarit, S. H., & Berg, S. (1992). Changes in cognitive functioning of the oldest old. *Journal of Gerontology Series B: Psychological Sciences, 47,* P75–P80.

Johansson, M., Forssman, L., & Bohlin, G. (2014). Individual differences in 10-month-olds' performance on the A-not-B task. *Scandinavian Journal of Psychology, 55,* 130–135.

Johansson, T., & Ritzén, E. M. (2005). Very long-term follow-up of girls with early and late menarche. *Endocrine Development, 8,* 126–136.

Johnson, J. G., Cohen, P., Kasen, S., Smailes, E., & Brook, J. (2001). Association of maladaptive parental behavior with psychiatric disorder among parents and their offspring. *Archives of General Psychology, 58,* 453–460.

Johnson, J., & Newport, E. (1989). Critical period effects in second language learning: The influence of maturational state on the acquisition of English as a second language. *Cognitive Psychology, 21,* 60–99.

Johnson, M. H. (1997). *Developmental cognitive neuroscience.* Cambridge, MA: Blackwell.

Johnson, M. H., & de Haan, M. (2015). *Developmental cognitive neuroscience* (4th ed.). Hoboken, NJ: Wiley-Blackwell.

Johnson, M. H., & de Haan, M. D. (2001). Developing cortical specialization for visual-cognitive function: The case of face recognition. In J. L. McClelland & R. S. Siegler (Eds.), *Mechanisms of cognitive development: Behavioral and neural perspectives* (pp. 253–270). Mahwah, NJ: Lawrence Erlbaum.

Johnson, S. M. (2004). *The practice of emotionally focused couple therapy: Creating connection.* New York: Brunner/Routledge.

Johnson, S. M. (2008). Couple and family therapy. An attachment perspective. In J. Cassidy & P. R. Shaver (Eds.), *Handbook of attachment: Theory, research, and clinical applications* (2nd ed.). New York, NY: Guilford.

Johnson, S. M., & Wittenborn, A. K. (2012). New research findings on emotionally focused therapy: Introduction to special section. *Journal of Marital and Family Therapy, 38,* 18–22.

Johnson, S. P., & Hannon, E. E. (2015). Perceptual development. In R. M. Lerner, L. S. Liben, & U. Mueller (Eds.), *Handbook of child psychology and developmental science: Cognitive processes* (pp. 63–112). New York: Wiley.

Johnson, W., & Bouchard, T. J. (2007). Sex differences in mental abilities: g masks the dimensions on which they lie. *Intelligence, 35,* 23–39.

Johnson, W., Turkheimer, E., Gottesman, I. I., & Bouchard, T. J., Jr. (2009). Beyond heritability. Twin studies in behavioral research. *Current Directions in Psychological Science, 18,* 217–220.

John-Steiner, V. (1992). Private speech among adults. In R. M. Diaz & L. E. Berk (Eds.), *Private speech: From social interaction to self-regulation* (pp. 285–296). Hillsdale, NJ: Erlbaum.

Johnston, C. A., Moreno, J. P., El-Mubasher, A., & Woehler, D. (2012). School lunches and lunches brought from home: A comparative analysis: Childhood obesity. *Childhood Obesity, 8,* 364–368.

Johnston, L. D., O'Malley, P. M., Bachman, J. G., & Schulenberg, J. E. (2009). *Monitoring the future. National results on adolescent drug use. Overview of key findings, 2008.* Bethesda, MD: National Institute on Drug Abuse, U.S. Department of Health and Human Services. Retrieved from www.monitoringthefuture.org/pubs/monographs/overview2008.pdf.

Johnston, L. D., O'Malley, P. M., Bachman, J. G., Schulenberg, J. E. & Miech, R. A. (2015). *Monitoring the Future national survey results on drug use, 1975–2014: Volume 2, College students and adults ages 19–55.* Ann Arbor, MI: Institute for Social Research, The University of Michigan. Retrieved from www.monitoringthefuture.org/pubs/monographs/mtf-vol2_2014.pdf.

Johnston, L. D., O'Malley, P. M., Miech, R. A., Bachman, J. G., & Schulenberg, J. E. (2016). *Monitoring the Future national survey results on drug use 1975–2015: Overview, key findings on adolescent drug use.* Ann Arbor,

MI: Institute for Social Research, The University of Michigan. Retrieved from www.monitoringthefuture.org/pubs/monographs/mtf-overview2015.pdf.

Joint Committee on Infant Hearing. (2000). Year 2000 position statement: Principles and guidelines for early hearing detection and intervention programs. *Pediatrics, 106,* 798–817.

Jones, E. J. H., & Herbert, J. S. (2006). Exploring memory in infancy: Deferred imitation and the development of declarative memory. *Infant and Child Development, 15,* 195–205.

Jones, H., Karuri, S., Cronin, C., Ohlsson, A., Peliowski, A., Synnes, A., et al. (2005). Actuarial survival of a large Canadian cohort of preterm infants. *BMC Pediatrics, 5,* 1–13.

Jones, J. R., Kogan, M. D., Singh, G. K., Dee, D. L., & Grummer-Strawn, L. M. (2011). Factors associated with exclusive breastfeeding in the United States. *Pediatrics, 128,* 1117–1125.

Jones, L. M., Mitchell, K. J., & Finkelhor, D. (2013). Online harassment in context: Trends from three youth internet safety surveys (2000, 2005, 2010). *Psychology of Violence, 3,* 53–69.

Jones, M. C. (1924). A laboratory study of fear: The case of Peter. *Pedagogical Seminary, 31,* 308–315.

Jones, P. R., Moore, D. R., & Amitay, S. (2015). Development of auditory selective attention: Why children struggle to hear in noisy environments. *Developmental Psychology, 51,* 353–369.

Jones, S. S. (1996). Imitation or exploration? Young infants' matching of adults' oral gestures. *Child Development, 67,* 1952–1969.

Jones, T. (2007, April 18). A tragedy beyond the imagination. *The Washington Post,* pp. C1, C4.

Jones, W., & Klin, A. (2009). Heterogeneity and homogeneity across the autism spectrum: The role of development. *Journal of the American Academy of Child & Adolescent Psychiatry, 48,* 471–473.

Jordahl, T., & Lohman, B. J. (2009). A bioecological analysis of risk and protective factors associated with early sexual intercourse of young adolescents. *Children and Youth Services Review, 31,* 1272–1282.

Jordan, C. E., Combs, J. L., & Smith, G. T. (2014). An exploration of sexual victimization and academic performance among college women. *Trauma Violence & Abuse, 15,* 191–200.

Joseph, S. (2012). What doesn't kill us . . . . *The Psychologist, 25,* 816–819.

Juárez, F., & Gayer, C. (2014). Transitions to adulthood in developing countries. *Annual Review of Sociology, 40,* 521–538.

Judd, T. (2013). Making sense of multitasking: Key behaviours. *Computers & Education, 63,* 358–367.

Judge, T. A., & Bono, J. E. (2001). Relationship of core self-evaluation traits—self-esteem, generalized self-efficacy, locus of control, and emotional stability—with job satisfaction and job performance: A meta-analysis. *Journal of Applied Psychology, 86,* 80–92.

Judge, T. A., Klinger, R. L., & Simon, L. S. (2010). Time is on my side: Time, general mental ability, human capital, and extrinsic career success. *Journal of Applied Psychology, 95,* 92–107.

Junaid, K. A., & Fellowes, S. (2006). Gender differences in the attainment of motor skills on the Movement Assessment Battery for Children. *Physical and Occupational Therapy in Pediatrics, 26,* 5–11.

Jungblut, P. R., Ostorne, J. A., Quigg, R. J., McNeal, M. A., Clauser, J., Muster, A. J., et al. (2000). Echocardiographic Doppler evaluation of left ventricular diastolic filling in older, highly trained male endurance athletes. *Echocardiography, 17,* 7–16.

Juola, J. F., Koshino, H., Warner, C. B., McMickell, M., & Peterson, M. (2000). Automatic and voluntary control of attention in young and older adults. *American Journal of Psychology, 113,* 159–178.

Jusczyk, P. W., Houston, D. M., & Newsome, M. (1999). The beginnings of word segmentation in English-learning infants. *Cognitive Psychology, 39,* 159–207.

Justice, E. M., Bakerward, L., Gupta, S., & Jannings, L. R. (1997). Means to the goal of remembering: Developmental changes in awareness of strategy use-performance relations. *Journal of Experimental Child Psychology, 65,* 293–314.

Juul, A., Teilmann, G., Scheike, T., Hertel, N. T., Holm, K., Laursen, E. M., et al. (2006). Pubertal development

in Danish children: Comparison of recent European and US data. *International Journal of Andrology, 29,* 247–255.

Juvonen, J., Wang, Y., & Espinoza, G. (2013). Physical aggression, spreading of rumors, and social prominence in early adolescence: Reciprocal effects supporting gender similarities? *Journal of Youth and Adolescence, 42,* 1801–1810.

Kabir, A. A., Pridjian, G., Steinmann, W. C., Herrera, E. A., & Khan, M. M. (2005). Racial differences in cesareans: An analysis of U.S. 2001 national inpatient sample data. *Obstetrics & Gynecology, 105,* 710–718.

Kaffman, A., & Meaney, M. J. (2007). Neurodevelopmental sequelae of postnatal maternal care in rodents: Clinical and research implications of molecular insights. *Journal of Child Psychology and Psychiatry, 48,* 224–244.

Kagan, J. (1972). Do infants think? *Scientific American, 226,* 74–82.

Kagan, J. (1981). *The second year: The emergence of self-awareness.* Cambridge, MA: Harvard University Press.

Kagan, J. (1994). *Galen's prophecy: Temperament in human nature.* New York, NY: Basic Books.

Kahneman, D. (2011). *Thinking, fast and slow* (1st ed.). New York: Farrar, Straus and Giroux.

Kahneman, D., & Tversky, A. (1973). On the psychology of prediction. *Psychological Review, 80,* 237–251.

Kail, R. (1991). Developmental change in speed of processing during childhood and adolescence. *Psychological Bulletin, 109,* 490–501.

Kail, R. V. (2013). Influences of credibility of testimony and strength of statistical evidence on children's and adolescents' reasoning. *Journal of Experimental Child Psychology, 116,* 747–754.

Kail, R., & Bisanz, J. (1992). The information-processing perspective on cognitive development in childhood and adolescence. In R. J. Sternberg & C. A. Berg (Eds.), *Intellectual development.* New York, NY: Cambridge University Press.

Kail, R., & Salthouse, T. A. (1994). Processing speed as a mental capacity. *Acta Psychologica, 86,* 199–225.

Kajantie, E. (2008). Physiological stress response, estrogen, and the male-female mortality gap. *Current Directions in Psychological Science, 17,* 348–352.

Kakuma, R., duFort, G. G., Arsenault, L., Perrault, A., Platt, R. W., Monette, J., Moride, Y., & Wolfson, C. (2003). Delirium in older emergency department patients discharged home: Effect on survival. *Journal of the American Geriatrics Society, 51,* 443–450.

Kalakoski, V., & Saariluoma, P. (2001). Taxi drivers' exceptional memory of street names. *Memory & Cognition, 29,* 634–638.

Kalmijn, M., & De Graaf, P. M. (2012). Life course changes of children and well being of parents. *Journal of Marriage and Family, 74,* 269–280.

Kalmuss, D., Davidson, A., & Cushman, L. (1992). Parenting expectancies, experiences, and adjustment to parenthood: A test of the violated expectations framework. *Journal of Marriage and the Family, 54,* 516–526.

Kaltiala-Heino, R., Marttunen, M., Rantanen, P., & Rimpela, M. (2003). Early puberty is associated with mental health problems in middle adolescence. *Social Science Medicine, 57,* 1055–1064.

Kamakura, T., Ando, J., & Ono, Y. (2007). Genetic and environmental effects on stability and change in self-esteem during adolescence. *Personality and Individual Differences, 42,* 181–190.

Kamp Dush, C. M. (2011). Relationship-specific investments, family chaos, and cohabitation dissolution following a nonmarital birth. *Family Relations, 60,* 586–601.

Kamp Dush, C. M. (2013). Marital and cohabitation dissolution and parental depressive symptoms in fragile families. *Journal of Marriage and Family, 75,* 91–109.

Kandel, E. R., & Jessell, T. (1991). Early experience and the fine tuning of synaptic connections. In E. R. Kandel, J. H. Schwartz, & T. Jessell (Eds.), *Principles of neural science* (3rd ed., pp. 945–958). Norwalk, CT: Appleton & Lange.

Kandler, C., Kornadt, A. E., Hagemeyer, B., & Neyer, F. J. (2015). Patterns and sources of personality development in old age. *Journal of Personality and Social Psychology, 109,* 175–191.

Kane, H. D., & Brand, C. R. (2006). The variable importance of general intelligence (g) in the cognitive abilities of children and adolescents. *Educational Psychology, 26,* 751–767.

Kann, L., Kinchen, S., Shanklin, S. L., Flint, K. H., Hawkins, J., Harris, W. A., ... Zaza, S. (2014). Youth risk behavior surveillance—United States, 2013. MMWR, 63, 1–168.

Kannass, K. N., & Colombo, J. (2007). The effects of continuous and intermittent distractors on cognitive performance and attention in preschoolers. *Journal of Cognition and Development, 8,* 63–77.

Kannass, K. N., Colombo, J., & Wyss, N. (2010). Now, pay attention! The effects of instruction on children's attention. *Journal of Cognition and Development: Official Journal of the Cognitive Development Society, 11,* 509–532.

Kanner, L. (1943). Autistic disturbances of affective contact. *Nervous Child, 2,* 217–250.

Kapadia, S., & Bhangaokar, R. (2015). An Indian moral worldview: Developmental patterns in adolescents and adults. In L. A. Jensen (Ed.), *Moral development in a global world: Research from a cultural-developmental perspective.* (pp. 69–91). New York, NY: Cambridge University Press.

Kaplan, D. S., Damphousse, K. R., & Kaplan, H. B. (1994). Mental health implications of not graduating from high school. *Journal of Experimental Education, 62,* 105–123.

Kaplan, J. S. (2012). The effects of shared environment on adult intelligence: A critical review of adoption, twin, and MZA studies. *Developmental Psychology, 48,* 1292–1298.

Kaplan, R. M., & Erickson, J. (2000). Quality adjusted life expectancy for men and women in the United States. In S. B. Manuck, R. Jennings, B. S. Rabin, & A. Baum (Eds.), *Behavior, health, and aging.* Mahwah, NJ: Erlbaum.

Karantzas, G. C., Evans, L., & Foddy, M. (2010). The role of attachment in current and future parent caregiving. *Journals of Gerontology: Series B: Psychological Sciences and Social Sciences, 65B,* 573–580.

Karasik, L. B., Tamis-LeMonda, C. S., & Adolph, K. E. (2011). Transition from crawling to walking and infants' actions with objects and people. *Child Development, 82,* 1199–1209.

Karasik, L. B., Tamis-LeMonda, C. S., Adolph, K. E., & Dimitropoulou, K. A. (2008). How mothers encourage and discourage infants' motor actions. *Infancy, 13,* 366–392.

Karbach, J., & Verhaeghen, P. (2014). Making working memory work: A meta-analysis of executive-control and working memory training in older adults. *Psychological Science, 25,* 2027–2037.

Karel, M. J., Gatz, M., & Smyer, M. A. (2012). Aging and mental health in the decade ahead: What psychologists need to know. *American Psychologist, 67,* 184–198.

Karg, K., Burmeister, M., Shedden, K., & Sen, S. (2011). The serotonin transporter promoter variant (5-HTTLPR), stress, and depression meta-analysis revisited: Evidence of genetic moderation. *Archives of General Psychiatry, 68,* 444–454.

Karlawish, J., Rubright, J., Casarett, D., Cary, M., Ten Have, T., & Sankar, P. (2009). Older adults' attitudes toward enrollment of noncompetent subjects participating in Alzheimer's research. *American Journal of Psychiatry, 166,* 182–188.

Karmiloff-Smith, A. (1992). *Beyond modularity: A developmental perspective on cognitive science.* Cambridge, MA: MIT Press.

Karmiloff-Smith, A. (2006). The tortuous route from genes to behavior: A neuroconstructivist approach. *Cognitive, Affective, & Behavioral Neuroscience, 6,* 9–17.

Karmiloff-Smith, A. (2009). Nativism versus neuroconstructivism: Rethinking the study of developmental disorders. *Developmental Psychology, 45,* 56–63.

Karmiloff-Smith, A. (2015). An alternative to domain-general or domain-specific frameworks for theorizing about human evolution and ontogenesis. *AIMS Neuroscience, 2,* 91–104.

Karniol, R. (2009). Israeli kindergarten children's gender constancy for others' counter-stereotypic toy play and appearance: The role of sibling gender and relative age. *Infant and Child Development, 18,* 73–94.

Karpov, Y. V. (2005). *The neo-Vygotskian approach to child development.* New York, NY: Cambridge University Press.

Karraker, A., DeLamater, J., & Schwartz, C. R. (2011). Sexual frequency decline from midlife to later life. *Journals of Gerontology, Series B: Psychological Sciences and Social Sciences, 66,* 502–512.

Kart, C. S., Metress, E. K., & Metress, S. P. (1992). *Human aging and chronic disease.* Boston: Jones and Bartlett.

Kärtner, J., Keller, H., Chaudhary, N., & Yovsi, R. D. (2012). The development of mirror self-recognition in different sociocultural contexts. *Monographs of the Society for Research in Child Development, 77*(4), 4–101.

Kashani, H. H., Kavosh, M. S., Keshteli, A. H., Montaze, M., Rostampour, N., Kelishadi, R., et al. (2009). Age of puberty in a representative sample of Iranian girls. *World Journal of Pediatrics, 5,* 132–135.

Kaslow, N., Mintzer, M. B., Meadows, L. A., & Grabill, C. M. (2000). A family perspective on assessing and treating childhood depression. In C. E. Bailey (Ed.), *Children in therapy. Using the family as a resource.* New York, NY: W. W. Norton.

Kassi, E., Pervanidou, P., Kaltsas, G., & Chrousos, G. (2011). Metabolic syndrome: definitions and controversies. *BMC Medicine,9*(48), 1–13.

Kastberg, D., Ferraro, D., Lemanski, N., Roey, S., & Jenkins, F. (2012). *Highlights from TIMSS 2011: Mathematics and science achievement of U.S. fourth- and eighth-grade students in an international context.* Washington, DC: National Center for Education Statistics.

Kastenbaum, R. (2000). *The psychology of death.* New York, NY: Springer.

Kastenbaum, R. J. (2012). *Death, society, and human experience* (11th ed.). Boston, MA: Pearson.

Kastorini, C., Milionis, H. J., Esposito, K., Giugliano, D., Goudevenos, J. A., & Panagiotakos, D. B. (2011). The effect of Mediterranean diet on metabolic syndrome and its components: A meta-analysis of 50 studies and 534,906 individuals. *Journal of the American College of Cardiology, 57,* 1299.

Kasworm, C. E., & Medina, R. A. (1990). Adult competence in everyday tasks: A cross-sectional secondary analysis. *Educational Gerontology, 16,* 27–48.

Katz, L. F., Maliken, A. C., & Stettler, N. M. (2012). Parental meta-emotion philosophy: A review of research and theoretical framework. *Child Development Perspectives, 6,* 417–422.

Katz, P. A. (1986). Modification of children's gender-stereotyped behavior: General issues and research considerations. *Sex Roles, 14,* 591–602.

Katz, P. A., & Walsh, P. V. (1991). Modification of children's gender-stereotyped behavior. *Child Development, 62,* 338–351.

Katzel, L. I., & Steinbrenner, G. M. (2012). Physical exercise and health. In S. K. Whitbourne & M. J. Sliwinski (Eds.) *The Wiley-Blackwell handbook of adulthood and aging* (pp. 97–117). Malden, MA: Wiley-Blackwell.

Katz-Wise, S., Priess, H. A., & Hyde, J. S. (2010). Gender-role attitudes and behavior across the transition to parenthood. *Developmental Psychology, 46,* 18–28.

Kaufman, A. S., & Kaufman, N. L. (1997). The Kaufman Adolescent and Adult Intelligence Test. In D. P. Flanagan, J. L. Genshaft, & P. L. Harrison (Eds.), *Contemporary intellectual assessment: Theories, tests, and issues.* New York, NY: Guilford.

Kaufman, A. S., & Kaufman, N. L. (2003). *Kaufman Assessment Battery for Children* (2nd ed.). San Antonio, TX: Pearson.

Kaufman, A. S., Kamphaus, R. W., & Kaufman, N. L. (1985). New directions in intelligence testing: The Kaufman Assessment Battery for Children (K-ABC). In B. B. Wolman (Ed.), *Handbook of intelligence.* New York, NY: Wiley.

Kaufman, J. C. (2006). Self-reported differences in creativity by ethnicity and gender. *Applied Cognitive Psychology, 20,* 1065–1082.

Kaufman, J. C., & Plucker, J. A. (2011). Intelligence and creativity. In R. J. Sternberg & S. B. Kaufman (Eds.), *The Cambridge handbook of intelligence* (pp. 771–783). New York, NY: Cambridge University Press.

Kaufman, S. B. (2007). Sex differences in mental rotation and spatial visualization ability: Can they be accounted for by differences in working memory capacity? *Intelligence, 35,* 211–223.

Kavsek, M., & Yonas, A. (2006). The perception of moving subjective contours by 4-month-old infants. *Perception, 35,* 215–227.

Kaye, R. A. (1993). Sexuality in the later years. *Aging and Society, 13,* 415–426.

Kayed, N. S., & van der Meer, A. L. (2007). Infants' timing strategies to optical collisions: A longitudinal study. *Infant Behavior and Development, 30,* 50–59.

Kazdin, A. E. (2003). Psychotherapy for children and adolescents. *Annual Review of Psychology, 54,* 253–276.

Kazdin, A. E., & Rotella, C. (2013). *The everyday parenting toolkit: The Kazdin Method for easy, step-by-step lasting change for you and your child.* Boston, MA: Houghton Mifflin Harcourt.

Keel, P. K., & Klump, K. L. (2003). Are eating disorders culture-bound syndromes? Implications for conceptualizing their etiology. *Psychological Bulletin, 129,* 747–769.

Keijsers, L., Branje, S., Hawk, S. T., Schwartz, S. J., Frijns, T., Koot, H. M., . . . Meeus, W. (2012). Forbidden friends as forbidden fruit: Parental supervision of friendships, contact with deviant peers, and adolescent delinquency. *Child Development, 83,* 651–666.

Keither, J. (1985). Age in anthropological research. In R. H. Binstock & E. Shanas (Eds.), *Handbook of aging and the social sciences* (2nd ed.). New York, NY: Van Nostrand Reinhold.

Keizer, R., Dykstra, P. A., & Jansen, M. D. (2008). Pathways into childlessness: Evidence of gendered life course dynamics. *Journal of Biosocial Science, 40,* 863–878.

Kelemen, W. L. (2000). Metamemory cues and monitoring accuracy: Judging what you know and what you will know. *Journal of Educational Psychology, 92,* 800–810.

Keller, B. B., & Bell, R. Q. (1979). Child effects on adult's method of eliciting altruistic behavior. *Child Development, 50,* 1004–1009.

Keller, H. (1954). *The story of my life.* New York: Doubleday.

Keller, H., Kärtner, J., Borke, J., Yovsi, R., & Kleis, A. (2005). Parenting styles and the development of the categorical self: A longitudinal study on mirror self-recognition in Cameroonian Nso and German families. *International Journal of Behavioral Development, 29,* 496–504.

Keller, K. L., Kirzner, J., Pietrobelli, A., St-Onge, M. P., & Faith, M. S. (2009). Increased sweetened beverage intake is associated with reduced milk and calcium intake in 3- to 7-year-old children at multi-item laboratory lunches. *Journal of the American Dietetic Association, 109,* 497–501.

Kellman, P. J., & Arterberry, M. E. (2006). Infant visual perception. In D. Kuhn & R. Siegler (Vol. Eds.), *Handbook of child psychology: Cognition, perception, and language.* Hoboken, NJ: Wiley.

Kellman, P. J., & Spelke, E. S. (1983). Perception of partly occluded objects in infancy. *Cognitive Psychology, 15,* 483–524.

Kellogg, N. D. (2009). Clinical report—The evaluation of sexual behaviors in children. *Pediatrics, 124,* 992–998.

Kelly, D. J., Quinn, P. C., Slater, A. M., Lee, K., Gibson, A., Smith, M., Ge, L. Z., & Pascalis, O. (2005). Three-month-olds, but not newborns, prefer own-race faces. *Developmental Science, 8,* F31–F36.

Kelly, J. (2013, March 20). An empty-nester sampler: What some parents do when the children have flown. *Washington Post,* p. B2.

Kelsall, D. C., Shallop, J. K., & Burnelli, T. (1995). Cochlear implantation in the elderly. *American Journal of Otology, 16,* 609–615.

Kempe, R. S., & Kempe, C. H. (1978). *Child abuse.* Cambridge, MA: Harvard University Press.

Kempen, G. I. J. M., Jelicic, M., & Ormel, J. (1997). Personality, chronic medical morbidity, and health-related quality of life among older persons. *Health Psychology, 16,* 539–546.

Kemper, S., & Mitzner, T. L. (2001). Production and comprehension. In J. E. Birren & K. W. Schaie (Eds.), *Handbook of the psychology of aging* (5th ed.). San Diego, CA: Academic Press.

Kempermann, G., Song, H., & Gage, F. H. (2015). Neurogenesis in the adult hippocampus. *Cold Spring Harbor Perspectives in Medicine, 5*(7), a018812.

Kemtes, K. A., & Kemper, S. (1997). Younger and older adults' on-line processing of syntactically ambiguous sentences. *Psychology and Aging, 12,* 362–371.

Kendall-Tackett, K. A., Williams, L. M., & Finkelhor, D. (1993). Impact of sexual abuse on children: A review and synthesis of recent empirical studies. *Psychological Bulletin, 113,* 164–180.

Kendeou, P., van den Broek, P., White, M. J., & Lynch, J. S. (2009). Predicting reading comprehension in early elementary school: The independent contributions of oral language and decoding skills. *Journal of Educational Psychology, 101*, 765–778.

Kendler, K. S., Gardner, C. O., & Prescott, C. A. (2002). Toward a comprehensive developmental model for major depression in women. *American Journal of Psychiatry, 159*, 1133–1145.

Kendler, K. S., Neale, M., Kessler, R., Heath, A., & Eaves, L. (1993). A twin study of recent life events and difficulties. *Archives of General Psychiatry, 50*, 789–796.

Kendler, K. S., Thornton, L. M., Gilman, S. E., & Kessler, R. C. (2000). Sexual orientation in a U.S. national sample of twin and nontwin sibling pairs. *American Journal of Psychiatry, 157*, 1843–1846.

Keniston, K. (1970). Youth: A "new" stage of life. *American Scholar, 39*, 631–654.

Kennedy, D. P., & Squire, L. R. (2007). An analysis of calendar performance in two autistic calendar savants. *Learning & Memory, 14*, 533–538.

Kennedy, S., & Bumpass, L. (2008). Cohabitation and children's living arrangements: New estimates from the United States. *Demographic Research, 19*, 1663–1692.

Kenney, E. L., Austin, S. B., Cradock, A. L., Giles, C. M., Lee, R. M., Davison, K. K., & Gortmaker, S. L. (2014). Identifying sources of children's consumption of junk food in Boston after-school programs, April–May 2011. *Preventing Chronic Disease, 11*, E205. Available at www.cdc.gov/pcd/issues/2014/14_0301.htm.

Kenny, L. C., Lavender, T., McNamee, R., O'Neill, S. M., Mills, T., & Khashan, A. S. (2013). Advanced maternal age and adverse pregnancy outcome: Evidence from a large contemporary cohort. *PLoS ONE, 8*(2), e56583.

Kenny, M. E., & Rice, K. G. (1995). Attachment to parents and adjustment in late adolescent college students: Current status, applications, and future considerations. *The Counseling Psychologist, 23*, 433–456.

Kensinger, E. A., & Choi, E. S. (2009). When side matters: Hemispheric processing and the visual specificity of emotional memories. *Journal of Experimental Psychology: Learning, Memory, and Cognition, 35*, 247–253.

Kenward, B., Folke, S., Holmberg, J., Johansson, A., & Gredebäck, G. (2009). Goal directedness and decision making in infants. *Developmental Psychology, 45*, 809–819.

Kenyon, D. B., & Hanson, J. D. (2012). Incorporating traditional culture into positive youth development programs with American Indian/Alaska native youth. *Child Development Perspectives, 6*, 272–279.

Keppler, H., Dhooge, I., & Vinck, B. (2015). Hearing in young adults. Part I: The effects of attitudes and beliefs toward noise, hearing loss, and hearing protector devices. *Noise & Health, 17*, 237–244.

Keppler, H., Ingeborg, D., Sofie, D., & Bart, V. (2015). The effects of a hearing education program on recreational noise exposure, attitudes and beliefs toward noise, hearing loss, and hearing protector devices in young adults. *Noise & Health, 17*, 253–262.

Keren, M., Dollberg, D., Koster, T., Danino, K., & Feldman, R. (2010). Family functioning and interactive patterns in the context of infant psychopathology. *Journal of Family Psychology, 24*, 597–604.

Kerka, S. (1995). *Adult learner retention revisited. ERIC Digest No. 166.* Columbus, OH: ERIC Clearinghouse on Adult, Career, and Vocational Education.

Kern, M. L., & Friedman, H. S. (2010). Why do some people thrive while others succumb to disease and stagnation? Personality, social relations, and resilience. In P. S. Fry & C. L. M. Keyes (Eds.), *New frontiers in resilient aging. Life-strengths and well-being in late life.* New York, NY: Cambridge University Press.

Kerns, K. A., Tomich, P. L., & Kim, P. (2006). Normative trends in children's perceptions of availability and utilization of attachment figures in middle childhood. *Social Development, 15*, 1–22.

Kessler, R. C., & Wang, P. S. (2008). The descriptive epidemiology of commonly occurring mental disorders in the United States. *Annual Review of Public Health, 29*, 115–129.

Kessler, R. C., Avenevoli, S., & Merikangas, K. R. (2001). Mood disorders in children and adolescents: An epidemiologic perspective. *Biological Psychiatry, 49*, 1002–1014.

Kessler, R. C., Birnbaum, H. G., Shahly, V., Bromet, E., Hwang, I., McLaughlin, K. A., et al. (2010). Age

differences in the prevalence and co-morbidity of DSM-IV major depressive episodes: Results from the WHO world mental health survey initiative. *Depression and Anxiety, 27*, 351–364.

Kessler, R. C., Chiu, W. T., Demler, O., & Walters, E. E. (2005). Prevalence, severity, and comorbidity of 12-month DSM–IV disorders in the National Comorbidity Survey Replication. *Archives of General Psychiatry, 62*, 617–627.

Kessler, R. C., Galea, S., Jones, R., & Parker, H. (2006). Mental illness and suicidality after Hurricane Katrina. *Bulletin of the World Health Organization, 84*, 930–939.

Kessler, R. C., Green, J. G., Adler, L. A., Barkley, R. A., Chatterji, S., Faraone, S. V., et al. (2010). Structure and diagnosis of adult attention-deficit/hyperactivity disorder: Analysis of expanded symptom criteria from the adult ADHD clinical diagnostic scale. *Archives of General Psychiatry, 67*, 1168–1178.

Kett, J. F. (1977). *Rites of passage: Adolescence in America 1790 to the present.* New York, NY: Basic Books.

Kettlewell, H. B. D. (1959). Darwin's missing evidence. *Scientific American, 200*(3), 48–53.

Khaleque, A., & Rohner, R. P. (2012). Pancultural associations between perceived parental acceptance and psychological adjustment of children and adults: A meta-analytic review of worldwide research. *Journal of Cross-Cultural Psychology, 43*, 784–800.

Khalil, A., Syngelaki, A., Maiz, N., Zinevich, Y., Nicolaides, K. H. (2013). Maternal age and adverse pregnancy outcome: A cohort study. *Ultrasound in Obstetrics & Gynecology, 42*, 634–643.

Khan, J. C., Thurlby, D. A., Shahid, H., Yates, J. R. W., Bradley, M., Moore, A. T., & Bird, A. C. (2006). Smoking and age related macular degeneration: The number of pack years of cigarette smoking is a major determinant of risk for both geographic atrophy and choroidal neovascularization. *British Journal of Ophthalmology, 90*, 75–80.

Kho, Y., Kane, R. T., Priddis, L., & Hudson, J. (2015). The nature of attachment relationships and grief responses in older adults: An attachment path model of grief. *PLoS ONE, 10*(10), e0133703.

Khoury, J. C., Dolan, L. M., VanDyke, R., Rosenn, B., Feghali, M., & Miodovnik, M. (2012). Fetal development in women with diabetes: Imprinting for a life-time? *Journal of Maternal-Fetal & Neonatal Medicine, 25*, 11–14.

Khurana, A., Romer, D., Betancourt, L. M., Brodsky, N. L., Giannetta, J. M., & Hurt, H. (2013). Working memory ability predicts trajectories of early alcohol use in adolescents: The mediational role of impulsivity. *Addiction, 108*, 506–515.

Khurana, A., Romer, D., Betancourt, L. M., Brodsky, N. L., Giannetta, J. M., & Hurt, H. (2015). Stronger working memory reduces sexual risk taking in adolescents, even after controlling for parental influences. *Child Development, 86*, 1125–1141.

Kidd, C., Palmeri, H., & Aslin, R. N. (2013). Rational snacking: Young children's decision-making on the marshmallow task is moderated by beliefs about environmental reliability. *Cognition, 126*, 109–114.

Kiely, K. M., Mitchell, P., Gopinath, B., Luszcz, M. A., Jagger, C., & Anstey, K. J. (2015). Estimating the years lived with and without age-related sensory impairment. *Journals of Gerontology. Series A, Biological Sciences and Medical Sciences, 71*, 637–642.

Kiesner, J., Dishion, T. J., & Poulin, F. (2001). A reinforcement model of conduct problems in children and adolescents: Advances in theory and intervention. In J. Hill & B. Maughan (Eds.), *Conduct disorders in childhood and adolescence.* New York, NY: Cambridge University Press.

Killen, M., & Smetana, J. (2008). Moral judgment and moral neuroscience: Intersections, definitions, and issues. *Child Development Perspectives, 2*, 1–6.

Killen, M., & Smetana, J. G. (2015). Origins and development of morality. In M. E. Lamb (Vol. Ed.) & R. M. Lerner (Ed.), *Handbook of child psychology and developmental science: Vol. 3. Socioemotional processes* (pp. 701–749). Hoboken, NJ: Wiley.

Killen, M., Mulvey, K. L., Richardson, C., Jampol, N., & Woodward, A. (2011). The accidental transgressor: Morally-relevant theory of mind. *Cognition, 119*, 197–215.

Killen, M., Rutland, A., & Jampol, N. S. (2009). Social exclusion in childhood and adolescence. In K. H. Rubin, W. M. Bukowski, & B. Laursen (Eds.), *Handbook of peer interactions, relationships, and groups.* New York, NY: Guilford Press.

Kilmer, R. P., Gil-Rivas, V., Griese, B., Hardy, S. J., Hafstad, G. S., & Alisic, E. (2014). Posttraumatic growth in children and youth: Clinical implications of an emerging research literature. *American Journal of Orthopsychiatry, 84*, 506–518.

Kim, G., & Kwak, K. (2011). Uncertainty matters: Impact of stimulus ambiguity on infant social referencing. *Infant and Child Development, 20*, 449–463.

Kim, K. H. (2011). The creativity crisis: The decrease in creative thinking scores on the Torrance Tests of Creative Thinking. *Creativity Research Journal, 23*, 285–295.

Kim, K. H., Cramond, B., & VanTassel-Baska, J. (2010). The relationship between creativity and intelligence. In J. C. Kaufman & R. J. Sternberg (Eds.), *The Cambridge Handbook of Creativity: Vol. 2.* (pp. 395–412). New York, NY: Cambridge University Press.

Kim, K., & Spelke, E. J. (1992). Infants' sensitivity to effects of gravity on visible object motion. *Journal of Experimental Psychology: Human Perception and Performance, 18*, 385–393.

Kim, M. (2013, November 3). Newborn babies in study recognized songs played to them while in the womb. *The Washington Post*, p. A6.

Kim, S. Y., Wang, Y., Orozco-Lapray, D., Shen, Y., & Murtuza, M. (2013). Does 'tiger parenting' exist? Parenting profiles of Chinese Americans and adolescent developmental outcomes. *Asian American Journal of Psychology, 4*, 7–18.

Kim, S., Kim, S., & Kamphaus, R. W. (2010). Is aggression the same for boys and girls? Assessing measurement invariance with confirmatory factor analysis and item response theory. *School Psychology Quarterly, 25*, 45–61.

Kim, Y. (2007). Folic acid fortification and supplementation–good for some but not so good for others. *Nutrition Review, 65*, 504–511.

Kimbro, R. T., & Denney, J. T. (2013). Neighborhood context and racial/ethnic differences in young children's obesity: Structural barriers to interventions. *Social Science and Medicine, 95*, 97–105.

Kim-Cohen, J., & Gold, A. L. (2009). Measured gene—environment interactions and mechanisms promoting resilient development. *Current Directions in Psychological Science, 18*, 138–142.

Kimmel, D. C., Hinrichs, K. L. M., & Fisher, L. D. (2015). Understanding lesbian, gay, bisexual, and transgender older adults. In P. A. Lichtenberg & B. T. Mast (Eds. in Chief) & B. D. Carpenter & J. L. Wetherell (Vol. Eds.), *APA handbook of clinical geropsychology: Vol. 1. History and status of the field and perspectives on aging* (pp. 459–472). Washington, DC: American Psychological Association.

Kimura, D. (1992). Sex differences in the brain. *Scientific American, 267*, 119–125.

King, A. C., Castro, C., Wilcox, S., Eyler, A. A., Sallis, J. F., & Brownson, R. C. (2000). Personal and environmental factors associated with physical inactivity among different racial-ethnic groups of U.S. middle-aged and older-aged women. *Health Psychology, 19*, 354–364.

King, P. E., & Boyatzis, C. J. (2015). Religious and spiritual development. In M. E. Lamb (Vol. Ed.) & R. M. Lerner (Ed.), *Handbook of child psychology and developmental science: Vol. 3. Socioemotional processes* (pp. 975–1021). Hoboken, NJ: Wiley.

King, S., St. Hilaire, A., & Heidkamp, D. (2010). Prenatal factors in schizophrenia. *Current Directions in Psychological Science, 19*, 209–213.

King, V., Amato, P. R., & Lindstrom, R. (2015). Stepfather–adolescent relationship quality during the first year of transitioning to a stepfamily. *Journal of Marriage and Family, 77*, 1179–1189.

Kingston, H. M. (2008). *ABC of clinical genetics* (3rd ed.). Hoboken, NJ: Blackwell.

Kinsella, K. G. (2005). Future longevity—Demographic concerns and consequences. *Journal of the American Geriatrics Society, 53*, S299–S303.

Kirby, D., & Laris, B. A. (2009). Effective curriculum-based sex and STD/HIV education programs for adolescents. *Child Development Perspectives, 3*, 21–29.

Kirchhoff, B. A., & Buckner, R. L. (2006). Functional-anatomic correlates of individual differences in memory. *Neuron, 51*, 263–274.
Kirchmeyer, C. (2006). The different effects of family on objective career success across gender: A test of alternative explanations. *Journal of Vocational Behavior, 68*, 323–346.
Kirkbride, J. B., Susser, E., Kundakovic, M., Kresovich, J. K., Smith, G. D., & Relton, C. L. (2012). Prenatal nutrition, epigenetics and schizophrenia risk: Can we test causal effects? *Epigenomics, 4*, 303–315.
Kirsch, I. S., Jungeblut, A., Jenkins, L., & Kolstad, A. (2002). *Adult literacy in America: A first look at the findings on the National Adult Literacy Survey* (3rd ed.). Washington, DC: National Center for Education Statistics.
Kisilevsky, B. S., & Muir, D. W. (1984). Neonatal habituation and dishabituation to tactile stimulation during sleep. *Developmental Psychology, 20*, 367–373.
Kisilevsky, B. S., Hains, S. M., Lee, K., Xie, X., Huang, H., Ye, H. H., et al. (2003). Effects of experience on fetal voice recognition. *Psychological Science, 14*, 220–224.
Kissane, D. W., Zaider, T. I., Li, Y., & Del Gaudio, F. (2013). Family therapy for complicated grief. In M. Stroebe, H. Schut & J. van den Bout (Eds.), *Complicated grief: Scientific foundations for health care professionals*. New York, NY: Routledge/Taylor & Francis.
Kitamura, C., & Burnham, D. (2003). Pitch and communicative intent in mother's speech: Adjustments for age and sex in the first year. *Infancy, 4*, 85–110.
Kitson, G. C. (1992). *Portrait of divorce: Adjustment to marital breakdown.* New York, NY: Guilford.
Kitzmann, K. M. (2000). Effects of marital conflict on subsequent triadic family interactions and parenting. *Developmental Psychology, 36*, 3–13.
Kjerulff, K., & Zhu, J. (2014, November 15). *Epidural analgesia use during labor and adverse maternal and neonatal outcomes: A large-scale observational study*. Presented at 142nd APHA Annual Meeting and Exposition, New Orleans, LA.
Klaczynski, P. (2013). Culture and developments in heuristics and biases from preschool through adolescence. In P. Barrouillet & C. Gauffroy (Eds.), *The development of thinking and reasoning* (pp. 150–192). Taylor & Francis.
Klaczynski, P. A. (2000). Motivated scientific reasoning biases, epistemological beliefs, and theory polarization: A two-process approach to adolescent cognition. *Child Development, 71*, 1347–1366.
Klaczynski, P. A. (2001). Analytic and heuristic processing influences on adolescent reasoning and decision-making. *Child Development, 72*, 844–861.
Klaczynski, P. A. (2009). Cognitive and social cognitive development: Dual-process research and theory. In J. S. B. T. Evans & K. Frankish (Eds.), *In two minds: Dual processes and beyond* (pp. 265–292). New York, NY: Oxford University Press.
Klaczynski, P. A., & Gordon, D. H. (1996a). Everyday statistical reasoning during adolescence and young adulthood: Motivational, general ability, and developmental influences. *Child Development, 67*, 2873–2892.
Klaczynski, P. A., & Gordon, D. H. (1996b). Self-serving influences on adolescents' evaluations of belief-relevant evidence. *Journal of Experimental Child Psychology, 62*, 317–339.
Klass, D. (2001). Continuing bonds in the resolution of grief in Japan and North America. *American Behavioral Scientist, 44*, 742–763.
Klausli, J. F., & Owen, M. T. (2011). Exploring actor and partner effects in associations between marriage and parenting for mothers and fathers. *Parenting: Science and Practice, 11*, 264–279.
Klebold, S. (2009, November). I will never know why. *O Magazine*. Retrieved from www.oprah.com/world/Susan-Klebolds-O-Magazine-Essay-I-Will-Never-Know-Why.
Klebold, S. (2016). *A mother's reckoning: Living in the aftermath of tragedy*. New York, NY: Crown.
Klein, D., Mok, K., Chen, J. K., & Watkins, K. E. (2014). Age of language learning shapes brain structure: A cortical thickness study of bilingual and monolingual individuals. *Brain and Language, 131*, 20–24.
Klein, P. J., & Meltzoff, A. N. (1999). Long-term memory, forgetting, and deferred imitation in 12-month-old infants. *Developmental Science, 2*, 102–113.
Klein, R., Klein, B. E., Lee, K. E., Cruickshanks, K. J., & Chappell, R. J. (2001). Changes in visual acuity in a population over a 10-year period: The Beaver Dam Eye Study. *Ophthalmology, 108*, 1757–1766.
Kleinman, R. E., Brown, R. T., Cutter, G. R., DuPaul, G. J., & Clydesdale, F. M. (2011). A research model for investigating the effects of artificial food colorings on children with ADHD. *Pediatrics, 127*, e1575–e1584.
Kliegel, M., Jager, T., & Phillips, L. H. (2007). Emotional development across adulthood: Differential age-related emotional reactivity and emotion regulation in a negative mood induction procedure. *International Journal of Aging and Human Development, 64*, 217–244.
Klin, A., Chawarska, K., Rubin, E., & Volkmar F. (2004). Clinical assessment of young children at risk for autism. In R. DelCarmen-Wiggins & A. Carter (Eds.), *Handbook of infant, toddler, and preschool mental health assessment.* New York, NY: Oxford University Press.
Kline, D. W., & Scialfa, C. T. (1996). Visual and auditory aging. In J. E. Birren & K. W. Schaie (Eds.), *Handbook of the psychology of aging* (4th ed.). San Diego, CA: Academic Press.
Klineberg, O. (1963). Negro-white differences in intelligence test performance: A new look at an old problem. *American Psychologist, 18*, 198–203.
Klump, K. L., & Culbert, K. M. (2007). Molecular genetic studies of eating disorders. Current status and future directions. *Current Directions in Psychological Science, 16*, 37–41.
Klump, K. L., Culbert, K. M., Slane, J. D., Burt, S. A., Sisk, C. L., & Nigg, J. T. (2012). The effects of puberty on genetic risk for disordered eating: Evidence for a sex difference. *Psychological Medicine, 42*, 627–637.
Klump, K. L., Keel, P. K., Sisk, C., & Burt, S. A. (2010). Preliminary evidence that estradiol moderates genetic influences on disordered eating attitudes and behaviors during puberty. *Psychological Medicine, 40*, 1745–1753.
Klump, K. L., McGue, M., & Iacono, W. G. (2003). Differential heritability of eating attitudes and behaviors in prepubertal versus pubertal twins. *International Journal of Eating Disorders, 33*, 287–292.
Knaapila, A., Hwang, L., Lysenko, A., Duke, F. F., Fesi, B., Khoshnevisan, A., et al. (2012). Genetic analysis of chemosensory traits in human twins. *Chemical Senses, 37*, 869–881.
Knafo, A., Zahn-Waxler, C., Van Hulle, C., Robinson, J. L., & Rhee, S. H. (2008). The developmental origins of a disposition toward empathy: Genetic and environmental contributions. *Emotion, 8*, 737–752.
Knapp, C., Quinn, G. P., Murphy, D., Brown, R., & Madden, V. (2010). Adolescents with life-threatening illnesses. *American Journal of Hospice and Palliative Care, 27*, 139–144.
Knecht, S., Deppe, M., Drager, B., Bobe, L., Lohmann, H., Ringelstein, E., et al. (2000). Language lateralization in healthy righthanders. *Brain, 123*, 74–81.
Knee, D. O. (2010). Hospice care for the aging population in the United States. In J. C. Cavanaugh & C. K. Cavanaugh (Eds.), *Aging in America: Vol. 3. Societal issues*. Santa Barbara, CA: Praeger/ABC-CLIO.
Knerr, W., Gardner, F., & Cluver, L. (2013). Improving positive parenting skills and reducing harsh and abusive parenting in low-and middle-income countries: A systematic review. *Prevention Science, 14*, 352–362.
Knight, B. G., & Losada, A. (2011). Family caregiving for cognitively or physically frail older adults: Theory, research, and practice. In K. W. Schaie & S. L. Willis (Eds.), B. G. Knight, B. Levy, & D. C. Park (Assoc. Eds.), *Handbook of the psychology of aging*. MA: Academic Press/Elsevier.
Knight, B. G., Kaskie, B., Shurgot, G. R., & Dave, J. (2006). Improving the mental health of older adults. In J. E. Birren & K. W. Schaie (Eds.), *Handbook of the psychology of aging* (6th ed.). Burlington, MA: Elsevier Academic Press.
Knight, G. P., & Carlo, G. (2012). Prosocial development among Mexican American youth. *Child Development Perspectives, 6*, 258–263.
Knight, J. A. (2000). The biochemistry of aging. *Advances in Clinical Chemistry, 35*, 1–62.
Knopik, V. S., Jacob, T., Haber, J. R., Swenson, L. P., & Howell, D. N. (2009). Paternal alcoholism and offspring ADHD problems: A children of twins design. *Twin Research & Human Genetics, 12*, 53–62.
Kobak, R. R., & Kerig, P. K. (2015). Introduction to the special issue: Attachment-based treatments for adolescents. *Attachment & Human Development, 17*, 111–118.
Kochanska, G. (1993). Toward a synthesis of parental socialization and child temperament in early development of conscience. *Child Development, 64*, 325–347.
Kochanska, G. (2001). Emotional development in children with different attachment histories: The first three years. *Child Development, 72*, 474–490.
Kochanska, G. (2002). Mutually responsive orientation between mothers and their young children: A context for the early development of conscience. *Current Directions in Psychological Science, 11*(6), 191–195.
Kochanska, G., & Aksan, N. (2006). Children's conscience and self-regulation. *Journal of Personality, 74*, 1587–1617.
Kochanska, G., & Kim, S. (2013). Early attachment organization with both parents and future behavior problems: From infancy to middle childhood. *Child Development, 84*, 283–296.
Kochanska, G., Aksan, N., & Joy, M. E. (2007). Children's fearfulness as a moderator of parenting in early socialization: Two longitudinal studies. *Developmental Psychology, 43*, 222–237.
Kochanska, G., Barry, R. A., Jimenez, N. B., Hollatz, A. L., & Woodard, J. (2009). Guilt and effortful control: Two mechanisms that prevent disruptive developmental trajectories. *Journal of Personality and Social Psychology, 97*, 322–333.
Kochanska, G., Barry, R. A., Stellern, S. A., & O'Bleness, J. J. (2009). Early attachment organization moderates the parent—child mutually coercive pathway to children's antisocial conduct. *Child Development, 80*, 1288–1300.
Kochanska, G., Casey, R. J., & Fukumoto, A. (1995). Toddlers' sensitivity to standard violations. *Child Development, 66*, 643–656.
Kochanska, G., Koenig, J. L., Barry, R. A., Kim, S., & Yoon, J. E. (2010). Children's conscience during toddler and preschool years, moral self, and a competent, adaptive developmental trajectory. *Developmental Psychology, 46*, 1320–1332.
Kochkin, S., Tyler, R., & Born, J. (2011). MarkeTrak VIII: The prevalence of tinnitus in the United States and the self-reported efficacy of various treatments. *Hearing Review*. Retrieved from www.hearingreview.com/2011/11/marketrak-viii-the-prevalence-of-tinnitus-in-the-united-states-and-the-self-reported-efficacy-of-various-treatments/.
Kodama, K., Mabuchi, K., & Shigematsu, I. (1996). A long-term cohort study of the atomic-bomb survivors. *Journal of Epidemiology, 6*, S95–S105.
Kodish, E. (2005). Ethics and research with children: An introduction. In E. Kodish (Ed.), *Ethics and research with children: A case-based approach.* Cary, NC: Oxford University Press.
Koehler, K. (2010). Sibling bereavement in childhood. In C. A. Corr & D. E. Balk (Eds.), *Children's encounters with death, bereavement, and coping.* New York, NY: Springer.
Kogan, N. (1983). Stylistic variation in childhood and adolescence: Creativity, metaphor, and cognitive styles. In J. H. Flavell & E. H. Markman (Eds.), *Handbook of child psychology: Vol. 3. Cognitive development* (4th ed.). New York, NY: Wiley.
Kogan, S. M. (2004). Disclosing unwanted sexual experiences: Results from a national sample of adolescent women. *Child Abuse & Neglect, 28*, 147–165.
Kohlberg, L. (1963). The development of children's orientations toward a moral order: I. Sequence in the development of moral thought. *Vita Humana, 6*, 11–33.
Kohlberg, L. (1966a). A cognitive-developmental analysis of children's sex-role concepts and attitudes. In E. E. Maccoby (Ed.), *The development of sex differences.* Stanford, CA: Stanford University Press.
Kohlberg, L. (1966b). Cognitive stages and preschool education. *Human Development, 9*, 5–17.
Kohlberg, L. (1981). *Essays on moral development: Vol. 1. The philosophy of moral development.* San Francisco, CA: Harper & Row.
Kohlberg, L. (1984). *Essays on moral development: Vol. 2. The psychology of moral development.* San Francisco, CA: Harper & Row.
Kohn, M. L. (1969). *Class and conformity: A study of values.* Homewood, IL: Dorsey Press.
Kohn, M. L., & Schooler, C. (1982). Job conditions and personality: A longitudinal assessment of their reciprocal effects. *American Journal of Sociology, 87*, 1257–1286.

Kojima, H. (2003). The history of children and youth in Japan. In W. Koops & M. Zuckerman (Eds.), *Beyond the century of the child. Cultural history and developmental psychology*. Philadelphia, PA: University of Pennsylvania Press.

Kolb, B., Whishaw, I. Q., & Teskey, G. C. (2016). *An introduction to brain and behavior* (5th ed). New York, NY: Worth Publishers.

Kolstad, V., & Aguiar, A. (1995, March). *Means–end sequences in young infants*. Paper presented at the biennial meeting of the Society for Research in Child Development, Indianapolis.

Kong, A., Frigge, M. L., Masson, G., Besenbacher, S., Sulem, P., Magnusson, G., et al. (2012). Rate of de novo mutations and the importance of father's age to disease risk. *Nature*, *488*(7412), 471–475.

Koocher, G. P. (1973). Childhood, death, and cognitive development. *Developmental Psychology*, *9*, 369–375.

Koocher, G. P. (1974). Talking with children about death. *American Journal of Orthopsychiatry*, *44*, 404–411.

Kopasz, M., Loessi, H. M., Riemann, D., Nissen, C., Piosczyk, H., & Voderholzer, U. (2010). Sleep and memory in healthy children and adolescents—A critical review. *Sleep Medicine Reviews*, *14*, 167–177.

Kopp, C. B., & Krakow, J. B. (1982). *The child: Development in a social context*. Reading, MA: Addison-Wesley.

Kopp, C. B., & Neufield, S. J. (2003). Emotional development during infancy. In R. J. Davidson, K. R. Scherer, & H. H. Goldsmith (Eds.), *Handbook of affective sciences*. New York, NY: Oxford University Press.

Koppel, J., & Berntsen, D. (2016). The reminiscence bump in autobiographical memory and for public events: A comparison across different cueing methods. *Memory*, *24*, 44–62.

Koppel, J., & Rubin, D. C. (2016). Recent advances in understanding the reminiscence bump: The importance of cues in guiding recall from autobiographical memory. *Current Directions in Psychological Science*, *25*, 135–140.

Korbin, J. E. (2001). Context and meaning in neighborhood studies of children and families. In A. Booth, & A. C. Crouter (Eds.), *Does it take a village? Community effects on children, adolescents, and families*. Mahwah, NJ: Erlbaum.

Koriat, A., Goldsmith, M., & Pansky, A. (2000). Toward a psychology of memory accuracy. *Annual Review of Psychology*, *51*, 481–538.

Kosberg, J. I., Kaufman, A. V., Burgio, L. D., Leeper, J. D., & Sun, F. (2007). Family caregiving to those with dementia in rural Alabama: Racial similarities and differences. *Journal of Aging and Health*, *19*, 3–21.

Kosciw, J. G., Palmer, N. A., & Kull, R. M. (2015). Reflecting resiliency: Openness about sexual orientation and/or gender identity and its relationship to well-being and educational outcomes for LGBT students. *American Journal of Community Psychology*, *55*, 167–178.

Kost, K., Henshaw, S., & Carlin, L. (2010). *U.S. teenage pregnancies, births and abortions: National and state trends and trends by race and ethnicity*. Retrieved from www.guttmacher.org/pubs/USTPtrends.pdf.

Kotilahti, K., Nissilä, I., Näsi, T., Lipiäinen, L., Noponen, T., Meriläinen, P., et al. (2010). Hemodynamic responses to speech and music in newborn infants. *Human Brain Mapping*, *31*, 595–603.

Kottak, C. P. (2009). *Cultural anthropology* (13th ed.). New York, NY: McGraw Hill.

Kotter-Grühn, D. (2015). Changing negative views of aging: Implications for intervention and translational research. In M. Diehl & H. Wahl, (Eds.), *Annual review of gerontology and geriatrics*: *Vol*. 35. (pp. 167–186). New York, NY: Springer.

Koutstaal, W., Schacter, D. L., Johnson, M. K., Angell, K. E., & Gross, M. S. (1998). Post-event review in older and younger adults: Improving memory accessibility of complex everyday events. *Psychology and Aging*, *13*, 277–296.

Kovács, Á. M., Tauzin, T., Téglás, E., Gergely, G., & Csibra, G. (2014). Pointing as epistemic request: 12-month-olds point to receive new information. *Infancy*, *19*, 543–557.

Kovshoff, H., Iarocci, G., Shore, D. I., & Burack, J. A. (2015). Developmental trajectories of form perception: A story of attention. *Developmental Psychology*, *51*, 1544.

Kowal, A., Kramer, L., Krull, J. L., & Crick, N. R. (2002). Children's perceptions of the fairness of parental preferential treatment and their socioemotional well-being. *Journal of Family Psychology*, *16*, 297–306.

Kowalski, R. M., Giumetti, G. W., Schroeder, A. N., & Lattanner, M. R. (2014). Bullying in the digital age: A critical review and meta-analysis of cyberbullying research among youth. *Psychological Bulletin*, *140*, 1073–1137.

Krafft, K. C., & Berk, L. E. (1998). Private speech in two preschools: Significance of open-ended activities and make-believe play for verbal self- regulation. *Early Childhood Research Quarterly*, *13*, 637–658.

Kramer, D. A. (1989). A developmental framework for understanding conflict resolution processes. In J. D. Sinnott (Ed.), *Everyday problem solving in adulthood* (pp. 133–152). New York, NY: Praeger.

Kramer, D. A., & Melchior, J. (1990). Gender, role conflict, and the development of relativistic and dialectical thinking. *Sex Roles*, *23*, 553–575.

Krampe, R. T., Schaefer, S., Lindenberger, U., & Baltes, P. B. (2011). Lifespan changes in multi-tasking: Concurrent walking and memory search in children, young, and older adults. *Gait & Posture*, 33, 401–405.

Krause, N. (1995). Negative interaction and satisfaction with social support among older adults. *Journal of Gerontology: Psychological Sciences*, *50*B, 59–73.

Krause, N. (2003). Religious meaning and subjective well-being in late life. *Journals of Gerontology*, *58*, S160–S170.

Krause, N. (2013). Religious involvement in the later years of life. In K. I. Pargament, J. J. Exline, & J. W. Jones (Eds.), *APA handbook of psychology, religion, and spirituality: Vol. 1. Context, theory, and research*. Washington, DC: American Psychological Association.

Krause, N., & Rook, K. S. (2003). Negative interaction in late life: Issues in the stability and generalizability of conflict across relationships. *Journals of Gerontology: Psychological Sciences and Social Sciences*, *58*, 88–99.

Kraushaar, J. M., & Novak, D. C. (2010). Examining the effect of student multitasking with laptops during lecture. *Journal of Information Systems Education*, *21*, 241–251.

Kreager, D. A., & Staff, J. (2009). The sexual double standard and adolescent peer acceptance. *Social Psychology Quarterly*, *72*, 143–164.

Krebs, C. P., Lindquist, C. H., Warner, T. D., Fisher, B. S., & Martin, S. L. (2007). *The Campus Sexual Assault (CSA) Study: Final report*. Washington, DC: National Institute of Justice, U.S. Department of Justice.

Krebs, C. P., Lindquist, C. H., Berzofsky, M., Shook-Sa, B. E., Peterson, K., Planty, M. G., Langton, L., & Stroop, J. (2016). Campus climate survey validation study final technical report. *Bureau of Justice Statistics*. Available at www.bjs.gov/index.cfm?ty=pbdetail&iid=5540.

Krebs, D. L. (2008). Morality. An evolutionary account. *Perspectives on Psychological Science*, 3, 149–172.

Krebs, D. L. (2011). *The origins of morality. An evolutionary account*. New York, NY: Oxford University Press.

Kreicbergs, U., Valdimarsdottir, U., Onelov, E., Henter, J., & Steineck, G. (2004). Talking about death with children who have severe malignant disease. *New England Journal of Medicine*, *351*, 1175–1186.

Kretch, K. S., & Adolph, K. E. (2013). Cliff or step? Posture-specific learning at the edge of a dropoff. *Child Development*, *84*, 226–240.

Krettenauer, T., & Hertz, S. (2015). What develops in moral identities? A critical review. *Human Development*, *58*, 137–153.

Kristen-Antonow, S., Sodian, B., Perst, H., & Licata, M. (2015, June). A longitudinal study of the emerging self from 9 months to the age of 4 years. *Frontiers in Psychology*, *6*, article 789.

Kroger, J. (2007). *Identity development. Adolescence through adulthood* (2nd ed.). Thousand Oaks, CA: Sage.

Krogh, K. M. (1985). Women's motives to achieve and to nurture in different life stages. *Sex Roles*, *12*, 75–90.

Krucoff, C. (2000, May 16). Good to the bone. *The Washington Post—Health*, p. 8.

Krueger, R. F., & Johnson, W. (2008). Behavioral genetics and personality. A new look at the integration of nature and nurture. In O. P. John, R. W. Robins, & L. A. Pervin (Eds.), *Handbook of personality theory and research* (3rd ed.). New York, NY: Guilford.

Krueger, R. F., Markon, K. E., & Bouchard, T. J., Jr. (2003). The extended genotype: The heritability of personality accounts for the heritability of recalled family environments in twins reared apart. *Journal of Personality*,*71*, 809–833.

Ku, S. Y., Kang, J. W., Kim, H., Kim, Y. D., Jee, B. C., Suh, C. S., et al. (2006). Age at menarche and its influencing factors in North Korean female refugees. *Human Reproduction*, *21*, 833–836.

Kübler-Ross, E. (1969). *On death and dying*. New York, NY: Macmillan.

Kübler-Ross, E. (1974). *Questions and answers on death and dying*. New York, NY: Macmillan.

Kuczynski, L., & Parkin, C. M. (2007). Agency and bidirectionality in socialization. Interactions, transactions, and relational dialectics. In J. E. Grusec & P. D. Hastings (Eds.), *Handbook of socialization: Theory and research*. New York, NY: Guilford.

Kuebli, J., & Fivush, R. (1994). Children's representation and recall of event alternatives. *Journal of Experimental Child Psychology*, *58*, 25–45.

Kuehner, C. (2003). Gender differences in unipolar depression: An update of epidemiological findings and possible explanations. *Acta Psychiatrica Scandinavia*, *108*, 163–174.

Kuhl, P. K., Ramírez, R. R., Bosseler, A., Lin, J. F., & Imada, T. (2014). Infants' brain responses to speech suggest analysis by synthesis. *Proceedings of the National Academy of Sciences of the United States of America*, *111*, 11238–11245.

Kuhl, P. K., Stevens, E., Hayashi, A., Deguchi, T., Kiritani, S., & Iverson, P. (2006). Infants show a facilitation effect for native language phonetic perception between 6 and 12 months. *Developmental Science*, *9*, F13–F21.

Kuhn, D. (1993). Connecting scientific and informal reasoning. *Merrill-Palmer Quarterly*, *39*, 74–103.

Kuhn, D., & Franklin, S. (2006). The second decade: What develops (and how)? In D. Kuhn & R. Siegler (Eds.), *Handbook of child psychology: Vol. 2. Cognitive, perception, and language* (6th ed., pp. 953–994). New York, NY: Wiley.

Kuhn, D., Pease, M., & Wirkala, C. (2009). Coordinating the effects of multiple variables: A skill fundamental to scientific thinking. *Journal of Experimental Child Psychology*, *103*, 268–284.

Kulathilaka, S., Hanwella, R., & de Silva, V. A. (2016). Depressive disorder and grief following spontaneous abortion. *BMC Psychiatry*, *16*, 100.

Kumar, P., Khare, M., Harrison, R. M., Bloss, W. J., & Lewis, A. C. (2015). New directions: Air pollution challenges for developing megacities like Delhi. *Atmospheric Environment*, *122*, 657–661.

Kuncel, N. R., Hezlett, S. A., & Ones, D. S. (2004). Academic performance, career potential, creativity, and job performance: Can one construct predict them all? *Journal of Personality and Social Psychology*, *86*, 148–161.

Kunter, M., Klusmann, U., Baumert, J., Richter, D., Voss, T., & Hachfeld, A. (2013). Professional competence of teachers: Effects on instructional quality and student development. *Journal of Educational Psychology*, *105*, 805–820.

Kuny-Slock, A. V., & Hudziak, J. J. (2013). Genetic and environmental influences on aggression and deviant behavior. In C. R. Thomas & K. Pope (Eds.), *The origins of antisocial behavior. A developmental perspective*. New York, NY: Oxford University Press.

Kunz, J. A., & Soltys, F. G. (Eds.). (2007). *Transformational reminiscence: Life story work*. New York, NY: Springer.

Kurdek, L. A. (1995). Lesbian and gay couples. In A. R. Augelli & C. J. Patterson (Eds.), *Lesbian and gay identities over the life span: Psychological perspectives on personal, relational, and community processes*. New York, NY: Oxford University Press.

Kurdek, L. A. (1999). The nature and predictors of the trajectory of change in marital quality for husbands and wives over the first 10 years of marriage. *Developmental Psychology*, 35, 1283–1296.

Kurdek, L. A. (2006). Differences between partners from heterosexual, gay, and lesbian cohabiting couples. *Journal of Marriage and Family*, *68*, 509–528.

Kurdek, L. A., & Krile, D. (1982). A developmental analysis of the relation between peer acceptance and both interpersonal understanding and perceived social self-competence. *Child Development*, *53*, 1485–1491.

Kvitvær, B. G., Miller, J., & Newell, D. (2012). Improving our understanding of the colicky infant: A prospective observational study. *Journal of Clinical Nursing*, *21*, 63–69.

Kwak, J., & Haley, W. E. (2005). Current research findings on end-of-life decision making among racially and ethnically diverse groups. *Gerontologist*, *45*, 634–641.

L'Engle, K. L., & Jackson, C. (2008). Socialization influences on early adolescents' cognitive susceptibility and transition to sexual intercourse. *Journal of Research on Adolescence, 18*, 353–378.

La Rue, A. (2015). Dementia: A health care team perspective. In P. A. Lichtenberg & B. T. Mast (Eds. in Chief), B. D. Carpenter & J. L. Wetherell, (Assoc. Eds.), *APA handbook of clinical geropsychology: Vol.1. History and status of the field and perspective on aging* (pp. 515–547). Washington, DC: American Psychological Association.

Labinowicz, E. (1980). *The Piaget Primer: Thinking, Learning, Teaching*. Menlo Park, CA: *Addison-Wesley Longman, 83*.

Labouvie-Vief, G. (1985). Intelligence and cognition. In J. E. Birren & K. W. Schaie (Eds.), *Handbook of the psychology of aging* (2nd ed.). New York, NY: Van Nostrand Reinhold.

Labouvie-Vief, G., Diehl, M., Jain, E., & Zhang, F. (2007). Six-year change in affect optimization and affect complexity across the adult life span: A further examination. *Psychology and Aging, 22*, 738–751.

Lachance, J. A., & Mazzocco, M. M. (2006). A longitudinal analysis of sex differences in math and spatial skills in primary school age children. *Learning and Individual Differences, 16*, 195–216.

Ladd, G. W. (1999). Peer relationships and social competence during early and middle childhood. *Annual Review of Psychology, 50*, 333–359.

Laflamme, D., Pomerleau, A., & Malcuit, G. (2002). A comparison of fathers' and mothers' involvement in childcare and stimulation behaviors during free-play with their infants at 9 and 15 months. *Sex Roles, 47*, 507–518.

LaFranchi, S. H., Haddow, J. E., & Hollowell, J. G. (2005). Is thyroid inadequacy during gestation a risk factor for adverse pregnancy and developmental outcomes? *Thyroid, 15*, 60–71.

LaFreniere, L., & Cain, A. (2015). Parentally bereaved children and adolescents: The question of peer support. *Omega: Journal of Death and Dying, 71*, 245–271.

Lahav, A., & Skoe, E. (2014). An acoustic gap between the NICU and womb: A potential risk for compromised neuroplasticity of the auditory system in preterm infants. *Frontiers in Neuroscience, 8*, 381.

Lai, E. R. (2011). Metacognition: A literature review. Retrieved from www.pearsonassessments.com/images/tmrs/Metacognition_Literature_Review_Final.pdf on July, 17, 2015.

Laird, R. D., Criss, M. M., Pettit, G. S., Bates, J. E., & Dodge, K. A. (2009). Developmental trajectories and antecedents of distal parental supervision. *Journal of Early Adolescence, 29*, 258–284.

Lakatta, E. G. (1990). Heart and circulation. In E. L. Schneider & J. W. Rowe (Eds.), *Handbook of the biology of aging* (3rd ed.). San Diego, CA: Academic Press.

Lalande, K. L., & Bonanno, G. A. (2006). Culture and continuing bonds: A prospective comparison of bereavement in the United States and the People's Republic of China. *Death Studies, 30*, 303–324.

Lamb, M. E. (2013). The changing faces of fatherhood and father-child relationships. From fatherhood as status to father as Dad. In M. A. Fine & F. D. Fincham (Eds.), *Handbook of family theories. A context-based approach*. New York, NY: Routledge.

Lamb, M. E., & Lewis, C. (2015). The role of parent-child relationships in child development. In M. H. Bornstein & M. E. Lamb (Eds.), *Developmental science. An advanced textbook* (7th ed., pp. 535–586). New York, NY: Psychology Press.

Lamb, M. E., & Tamis-Lemonda, C. S. (2004). The role of the father: An introduction. In M. E. Lamb (Ed.), *The role of the father in child development* (4th ed.). Hoboken, NJ: John Wiley & Sons.

Lambert, S. R., & Drack, A. V. (1996). Infantile cataracts. *Survey of Ophthalmology, 40*, 427–458.

Lambert, S. R., Lynn, M. J., Reeves, R., Plager, D. A., Buckley, E. G., & Wilson, M. E. (2006). Is there a latent period for the surgical treatment of children with dense bilateral congenital cataracts? *Journal of the American Association for Pediatric Ophthalmology and Strabismus, 10*, 30–36.

Lamborn, S. D., & Steinberg, L. (1993). Emotional autonomy redux: Revisiting Ryan and Lynch. *Child Development, 64*, 483–499.

Lamborn, S. D., Mounts, N. S., Steinberg, L., & Dornbusch, S. M. (1991). Patterns of competence and adjustment among adolescents from authoritative, authoritarian, indulgent, and neglectful families. *Child Development, 62*, 1049–1065.

Lamm, C., & Majdandžić, J. (2015). The role of shared neural activations, mirror neurons, and morality in empathy—A critical comment. *Neuroscience Research, 90*, 15–24.

Lampinen, P., Heikkinen, R., & Ruoppila, I. (2000). Changes in intensity of physical exercise as predictors of depressive symptoms among older adults: An eight-year follow-up. *Preventive Medicine, 30*, 371–380.

Lampl, M., & Thompson, A. L. (2007). Growth chart curves do not describe individual growth biology. *American Journal of Human Biology, 19*, 643–653.

Lancaster, S. M., Schick, U. M., Osman, M. M., & Enquobahrie, D. A. (2012). Risk factors associated with epidural use. *Journal of Clinical Medicine Research, 4*, 119–126.

Landreth, G., & Homeyer, L. (1998). Play as the language of children's feelings. In D. P. Fromberg & D. Bergen (Eds.), *Play from birth to twelve and beyond*. New York, NY: Garland.

Landry, S. H., Smith, K. E., & Swank, P. R. (2006). Responsive parenting: Establishing early foundations for social, communication, and independent problem-solving skills. *Developmental Psychology, 42*, 627–642.

Lane, J. D., Wellman, H. M., Olson, S. L., LaBounty, J., & Kerr, D. C. R. (2010). Theory of mind and emotion understanding predict moral development in early childhood. *British Journal of Developmental Psychology, 28*, 871–889.

Lane, M. A., Black, A., Handy, A., Tilmont, E. M., Ingram, D. K., & Roth, G. S. (2001). Caloric restriction in primates. In S. C. Park, E. S. Hwang, H. Kim, & W. Park (Eds.), *Annals of the New York Academy of Sciences: Vol. 928. Molecular and cellular interactions in senescence*. New York, NY: The New York Academy of Sciences.

Lang, F. R., & Carstensen, L. L. (1994). Close emotional relationships in late life: Further support for proactive aging in the social domain. *Psychology and Aging, 9*, 315–324.

Lang, F. R., & Carstensen, L. L. (2002). Time counts: Future time perspective, goals, and social relationships. *Psychology and Aging, 17*, 125–139.

Lang, F. R., Rohr, M. K., & Williger, B. (2011). Modeling success in life-span psychology: The principles of selection, optimization, and compensation. In K. L. Fingerman, C. A. Berg, J. Smith, & T. C. Antonucci (Eds.), *Handbook of life-span development*. New York, NY: Springer.

Lange, G., & Pierce, S. H. (1992). Memory-strategy learning and maintenance in preschool children. *Developmental Psychology, 28*, 453–462.

Langley, K., Heron, J., Smith, G. D., & Thapar, A. (2012). Maternal and paternal smoking during pregnancy and risk of ADHD symptoms in offspring: Testing for intrauterine effects. *American Journal of Epidemiology, 176*, 261–268.

Langley-Evans, A. J., & Langley-Evans, S. C. (2003). Relationship between maternal nutrient intakes in early and late pregnancy and infants' weight and proportions at birth: Prospective cohort study. *Journal of Research in Social Health, 123*, 210–216.

Långström, N., Rahman, Q., Carlström, E., & Lichtenstein, P. (2010). Genetic and environmental effects on same-sex sexual behavior: A population study of twins in Sweden. *Archives of Sexual Behavior, 39*, 75–80.

Lansford, J. E. (2009). Parental divorce and children's adjustment. *Perspectives on Psychological Science, 4*, 140–152.

Lansford, J. E., & Dodge, K. A. (2008). Cultural norms for adult corporal punishment of children and societal rates of endorsement and use of violence. *Parenting: Science and Practice, 8*, 257–270.

Lansford, J. E., Chang, L., Dodge, K. A., Malone, P. S., Oburu, P., Palmerus, K., Bacchini, D., Pastorelli, C., Bombi, A. S., Zelli, A., Tapanya, S., Chaudhary, N., Deater-Deckard, K., Manke, B., & Quinn, N. (2005). Physical discipline and children's adjustment: Cultural normativeness as a moderator. *Child Development, 76*, 1234–1246.

Lansford, J. E., Dodge, K. A., Fontaine, R. G., Bates, J. E., & Pettit, G. S. (2014). Peer rejection, affiliation with deviant peers, delinquency, and risky sexual behavior. *Journal of Youth and Adolescence, 43*, 1742–1751.

Lansford, J. E., Miller-Johnson, S., Berlin, L. J., Dodge, K. A., Bates, J. E., & Pettit, G. S. (2007). Early physical abuse and later violent delinquency: A prospective longitudinal study. *Child Maltreatment, 12*, 233–245.

Lansford, J. E., Skinner, A. T., Sorbring, E., Di Giunta, L. D., Deater-Deckard, K., Dodge, K. A., et al. (2012). Boys' and girls' relational and physical aggression in nine countries. *Aggressive Behavior, 38*, 298–308.

Lansford, J. E., Yu, T., Erath, S. A., Pettit, G. S., Bates, J. E., & Dodge, K. A. (2010). Developmental precursors of number of sexual partners from ages 16 to 22. *Journal of Research on Adolescence, 20*, 651–677.

Laopaiboon, M., Lumbiganon, P., Intarut, N., Mori, R., Ganchimeg, T., Vogel, J. P., Souza, J. P., & Gülmezoglu, A. M. on behalf of the WHO Multicountry Survey on Maternal Newborn Health Research Network. (2014). Advanced maternal age and pregnancy outcomes: A multicountry assessment. *BJOG: An International Journal of Obstetrics & Gynaecology, 21*, Issue Supplement s1, 49–56.

Laplante, D. P., Brunet, A., Schmitz, N., Ciampi, A., & King, S. (2008). Project ice storm: Prenatal maternal stress affects cognitive and linguistic functioning in 5 1/2-year-old children. *Journal of the American Academy of Child & Adolescent Psychiatry, 47*, 1063–1072.

Lapsley, D. K. (2006). Moral stage theory. In M. Killen & J. G. Smetana (Eds.), *Handbook of moral development*. Mahwah, NJ: Erlbaum.

Lapsley, D. K., Milstead, M., Quintana, S. M., Flannery, D., & Buss, R. R. (1986). Adolescent egocentrism and formal operations: Tests of a theoretical assumption. *Developmental Psychology, 22*, 800–807.

Lapsley, H., Pattie, A., Starr, J. M., & Deary, I. J. (2016). Life review in advanced age: Qualitative research on the 'start in life' of 90-year-olds in the Lothian Birth Cohort 1921. *BMC Geriatrics, 16*, 74.

Larose, S., Bernier, A., & Tarabulsy, G. M. (2005). Attachment state of mind, learning dispositions, and academic performance during the college transition. *Developmental Psychology, 41*, 281–289.

Larsen, J. T., To, Y. M., & Fireman, G. (2007). Children's understanding and experience of mixed emotions. *Psychological Science, 18*, 186–191.

Larson, R. W., Richards, M. H., Moneta, G., Holmbeck, G., & Duckett, E. (1996). Changes in adolescents' daily interactions with their families from ages 10 to 18: Disengagement and transformation. *Developmental Psychology, 32*, 744–753.

Larson, R., & Ham, M. (1993). Stress and "storm and stress" in early adolescence: The relationship of negative events with dysphoric affect. *Developmental Psychology, 29*, 130–140.

Larson, R., & Lampman-Petraitis, C. (1989). Daily emotional states as reported by children and adolescents. *Child Development, 60*, 1250–1260.

Larsson, H., Viding, E., Rijsdijk, F. V., & Plomin, R. (2008). Relationships between parental negativity and childhood antisocial behavior over time: A bidirectional effects model in a longitudinal genetically informative design. *Journal of Abnormal Child Psychology, 36*, 633–645.

Larsson, I., & Svedin, C. (2002). Sexual experiences in childhood: Young adults' recollections. *Archives of Sexual Behavior, 31*, 263–273.

Larsson, M., Öberg-Blåvarg, C., & Jönsson, F. U. (2009). Bad odors stick better than good ones: Olfactory qualities and odor recognition. *Experimental Psychology, 56*, 375–380.

Laucht, M., Skowronek, M. H., Becker, K., Schmidt M. H., Esser, G., Schulze, T. G., & Rietschel, M. (2007). Interacting effects of the dopamine transporter gene and psychosocial adversity on attention-deficit/hyperactivity disorder symptoms among 15-year-olds from a high-risk community sample. *Archives of General Psychiatry, 64*, 585–590.

Laughon, S. K., Branch, D. W., Beaver, J., & Zhang, J. (2012). Changes in labor patterns over 50 years. *American Journal of Obstetrics & Gynecology, 419*, e1–e9.

Laumann, E. O., Paik, A., & Rosen, R. C. (1999). Sexual dysfunction in the United States: Prevalence and predictors. *Journal of the American Medical Association, 281*, 537–544.

Laurens, K. R., Luo, L., Matheson, S. L., Carr, V. J., Raudino, A., Harris, F., & Green, M. J. (2015). Common or distinct pathways to psychosis? A systematic review of evidence from prospective studies for developmental risk factors and antecedents of the schizophrenia spectrum disorders and affective psychoses. *BMC Psychiatry*, *15*(205), 1–20.

Laursen, B., & Williams, V. (2002). The role of ethnic identity in personality development. In L. Pulkkinen & A. Caspi (Eds.), *Paths to successful development. Personality in the life course.* Cambridge, UK: Cambridge University Press.

Lauzen, M. M. (2015). It's a man's (celluloid) world: On-screen representations of female characteristics in the top 100 films of 2014. Retrieved from www.womenintvfilm.sdsu.edu/files/2014_Its_a_Mans_World_Report.pdf.

Lavner, J. A., & Bradbury, T. N. (2010). Patterns of change in marital satisfaction over the newlywed years. *Journal of Marriage and Family*, *72*, 1171–1187.

Lavner, J. A., Karney, B. R., & Bradbury, T. N. (2013). Newlyweds' optimistic forecasts of their marriage: For better or for worse? *Journal of Family Psychology*, *27*, 531–540.

Lawton, M. P., Moss, M. S., Winter, L., & Hoffman, C. (2002). Motivation in later life: Personal projects and well-being. *Psychology and Aging*, *17*, 539–547.

Leader, L. R. (2016). The potential value of habituation in the fetus. In N. Reissland & B. S. Kisilevsky (Eds.), *Fetal development. Research on brain and behavior, environmental influences, and emerging technologies* (1st ed., pp. 189–209). Cham, Switzerland: Springer.

Leaper, C. (1994). *Childhood gender segregation: Causes and consequences (New directions for child development:* Vol. 65. San Francisco, CA: Jossey-Bass.

Leaper, C. (2013). Parents' socialization of gender in children. *Gender: Early socialization, Encyclopedia on early childhood development.* Available at www.child-encyclopedia.com/sites/default/files/textes-experts/en/2492/parents-socialization-of-gender-in-children.pdf.

Leaper, C. (2015). Gender and social-cognitive development. In R. M. Lerner (Series Ed.), L. S. Liben, & U. Müller (Vol. Eds.), *Handbook of child psychology and developmental science: Vol. 2. Cognitive processes* (7th ed., pp. 806–853). New York, NY: Wiley.

LeBlanc, A. G., Chaput, J. P., McFarlane, A., Colley, R. C., Thivel, D., Biddle, S. J. H., & Tremblay, M. S. (2013). Active video games and health indicators in children and youth: A systematic review. *PloS ONE* 8(6), e65351.

Lederberg, A. R., Schick, B., & Spencer, P. E. (2013). Language and literacy development of deaf and hard-of-hearing children: Successes and challenges. *Developmental Psychology*, *49*, 15–30.

Lederman, S. A., Rauh, V., Weiss, L., Stein, J. L., Hoepner, L. A., Becker, M., Perera, F. P. (2004). The effects of the World Trade Center event on birth outcomes among term deliveries at three lower Manhattan hospitals. *Environmental Health Perspectives*, *112*, 1772–1778.

Lee, C. (2012). Deafness and cochlear implants: A deaf scholar's perspective. *Journal of Child Neurology*, *27*, 821–823.

Lee, G. Y., & Kisilevsky, B. S. (2014). Fetuses respond to father's voice but prefer mother's voice after birth. *Developmental Psychobiology*, *56*, 1–11.

Lee, J. M., Appugliese, D., Kaciroti, N., Corwyn, R. F., Bradley, R. H., & Lumeng, J. C. (2007). Weight status in young girls and the onset of puberty. *Pediatrics*, *119*, E624–E630.

Lee, J., & Hahm, H. C. (2010). Acculturation and sexual risk behaviors among Latina adolescents transitioning to young adulthood. *Journal of Youth and Adolescence*, *39*, 414–427.

Lee, J., & Zhou, M. (2014a). From unassimilable to exceptional: The rise of Asian Americans and "Stereotype Promise." *New Diversities*, *16*, 7–22.

Lee, J., & Zhou, M. (2014b). The success frame and achievement paradox: The costs and consequences for Asian Americans. *Race and Social Problems*, *6*, 38–55.

Lee, K. S., & Ono, H. (2012). Marriage, cohabitation, and happiness: A cross national analysis of 27 countries. *Journal of Marriage and Family*, *74*, 953–972.

Lee, K., Ng, E. L., & Ng, S. F. (2009). The contributions of working memory and executive functioning to problem representation and solution generation in algebraic word problems. *Journal of Educational Psychology*, *101*, 373–387.

Lee, R., Zhai, F., Brooks-Gunn, J., Han, W., & Waldfogel, J. (2014, March 25). Head Start participation and school readiness: Evidence from the Early Childhood Longitudinal Study–Birth Cohort. *Developmental Psychology*, *50*, 202–215.

Lee, S. J., Altschul, I., & Gershoff, E. T. (2015). Wait until your father gets home? Mother's and fathers' spanking and development of child aggression. *Children and Youth Services Review*, *52*, 158–166.

Lee, S. W., Clemenson, G. D., Gage, F. H. (2012). New neurons in an aged brain. *Behavioural Brain Research*, *227*, 497–507.

Leeder, E. J. (2004). *The family in global perspective. A gendered journey.* Thousand Oaks, CA: Sage.

Leenarts, L. E. W., Diehle, J., Doreleijers, T. A. H., Jansma, E. P., & Lindauer, R. J. L. (2013). Evidence-based treatments for children with trauma-related psychopathology as a result of childhood maltreatment: A systematic review. *European Child & Adolescent Psychiatry*, *22*, 269–283.

Leerkes, E. M., Blankson, A. N., & O'Brien, M. (2009). Differential effects of maternal sensitivity to infant distress and nondistress on social-emotional functioning. *Child Development*, *80*, 762–775.

Legare, C. H., Evans, E. M., Rosengren, K. S., & Harris, P. L. (2012). The coexistence of natural and supernatural explanations across cultures and development. *Child Development*, *83*, 779–793.

Lehman, D. R., Ellard, J. H., & Wortman, C. B. (1986). Social support for the bereaved: Recipients' and providers' perspectives on what is helpful. *Journal of Consulting and Clinical Psychology*, *54*, 438–446.

Lehman, H. C. (1953). *Age and achievement.* Princeton, NJ: Princeton University Press.

Leichtman, M. D., & Ceci, S. J. (1993). The problem of infantile amnesia: Lessons from fuzzy-trace theory. In M. L. Howe & R. Pasnak (Eds.), *Emerging themes in cognitive development: Vol. 1. Foundations.* New York, NY: Springer-Verlag.

Leiden Conference on the Development and Care of Children without Permanent Parents. (2012). The development and care of institutionally reared children. *Child Development Perspectives*, *6*, 174–180.

Lejarraga, H. (2002). Growth in infancy and childhood: A pediatric approach. In N. Cameron (Ed.), *Human growth and development* (pp. 21–44). New York, NY: Academic Press.

LeMare, L. J., & Rubin, K. H. (1987). Perspective taking and peer interaction: Structural and developmental analyses. *Child Development*, *58*, 306–315.

LeMoyne, T., and Buchanan, T. (2011). Does "hovering" matter? Helicopter parenting and its effect on well-being. *Sociological Spectrum*, *31*, 399–418.

Lenhart, A., Smith, A., Anderson, M., Duggan, M., Perrin, A. (2015) *Teens, technology and friendships.* Pew Research Center. Retrieved from www.pewinternet.org/2015/08/06/teens-technology-and-friendships/.

Lenroot, R. K., & Giedd, J. N. (2011). Developmental considerations of gene by environment interactions. *Journal of Child Psychology and Psychiatry and Allied Disciplines*, *52*, 429–441.

Leon, D. A., Lawlor, D. A., Clark, H., Batty, G. D., & Macintyre, S. (2009). The association of childhood intelligence with mortality risk from adolescence to middle age: Findings from the Aberdeen children of the 1950s cohort study. *Intelligence*, *37*, 520–528.

Leonard, K. E., & Das Eiden, R. (2002). Cognitive functioning among infants of alcoholic fathers. *Drug and Alcohol Dependence*, *67*, 139–147.

Leopold, T., & Lechner, C. M. (2015). Parents' death and adult well-being: Gender, age, and adaptation to filial bereavement. *Journal of Marriage and Family*, *77*, 747–760.

Lepore, J. (2011, March). Twilight: Growing old and even older. *The New Yorker*, pp. 30–35.

Lerner, J. V., Phelps, E., Forman, Y., & Bowers, E. P. (2009). Positive youth development. In R. M. Lerner, & L. Steinberg (Eds.), *Handbook of adolescent psychology: Vol. 1. Individual bases of adolescent development* (pp. 524–558). Hoboken, NJ: Wiley.

Lerner, M. J., Somers, D. G., Reid, D., Chiriboga, D., & Tierney, M. (1991). Adult children as caregivers: Egocentric biases in judgments of sibling contributions. *Gerontologist*, *31*, 746–755.

Lerner, R. M. (2006). Developmental science, developmental systems, and contemporary theories of human development. In W. Damon & R. M. Lerner (Editor-in-Chief), R. M. Lerner (Vol. Ed.), *Handbook of child psychology: Vol. 1. Theoretical models of human development* (6th ed.). Hoboken, NJ: Wiley.

Lerner, R. M., & Kauffman, M. B. (1985). The concept of development in contextualism. *Developmental Review*, *5*, 309–333.

Lerner, R. M., Hershberg, R. M., Hilliard, L. J., & Johnson, S. K. (2015). Concepts and theories of human development. In M. H. Bornstein & M. E. Lamb (Eds.), *Developmental science: An advanced textbook* (7th ed., pp. 3–41). New York, NY: Psychology Press.

Lerner, R. M., Lerner, J. V., Almerigi, J. B., Theokas, C., Phelps, E., Gestsdottir, S., et al. (2005). Positive youth development, participation in community youth development programs, and community contributions of fifth-grade adolescents: Findings from the first wave of the 4-H study of positive youth development. *Journal of Early Adolescence*, *25*, 17–71.

Lerner, R. M., Liben, L. S., & Mueller, U. (Eds.). (2015). *Handbook of child psychology and developmental science: Vol. 2. Cognitive processes.* Hoboken, NJ: Wiley.

Lester, D. (1994). Are there unique features of suicide in adults of different ages and developmental stages. *Omega: Journal of Death and Dying*, *29*, 337–348.

Lester, P., Saltzman, W. R., Woodward, K., Glover, D., Leskin, G. A., Bursch, B., et al. (2012). Evaluation of a family-centered prevention intervention for military children and families facing wartime deployments. *American Journal of Public Health*, *102*, S48–S54.

Lettre, G. (2012). Using height association studies to gain insights into human idiopathic short and syndromic stature phenotypes. *Pediatric Nephrology*, 1–6.

Leung, A. K. C., & Robson, W. L. M. (1993). Childhood masturbation. *Clinical Pediatrics*, *32*, 238–241.

Leutwyler, B. (2009). Metacognitive learning strategies: Differential development patterns in high school. *Metacognition Learning*, *4*, 111–123.

LeVay, S. (1996). *Queer science: The use and abuse of research into homosexuality.* Cambridge, MA: MIT Press.

Leve, L. D., & Fagot, B. I. (1997). Gender-role socialization and discipline processes in one- and two-parent families. *Sex Roles*, *36*, 1–21.

Levenkron, S. (2000). *Anatomy of anorexia.* New York, NY: W. W. Norton.

Levenson, R. W., Carstensen, L. L., Friesen, W. V., & Ekman, P. (1991). Emotion, physiology, and expression in old age. *Psychology and Aging*, *6*, 28–35.

Levine, D., Strother-Garcia, K., Golinkoff, R. M., & Hirsh-Pasek, K. (2016). Language development in the first year of life: What deaf children might be missing before cochlear implantation. *Otology & Neurotology*, *37*, e56–e62.

Levinson, D. (1989). *Family violence in cross-cultural perspective.* Newbury Park, CA: Sage.

Levinson, D. J. (1986). A conception of adult development. *American Psychologist*, *41*, 3–13.

Levinson, D. J. (in collaboration with J. D. Levinson) (1996). *The seasons of a woman's life.* New York, NY: Alfred A. Knopf.

Levinson, D. J., Darrow, C. N., Klein, E. B., Levinson, M. H., & McKee, B. (1978). *The seasons of a man's life.* New York, NY: Ballantine Books.

Levitt, H. M., & Ippolito, M. R. (2014). Being transgender: The experience of transgender identity development. *Journal of Homosexuality*, *61*, 1727–1758.

Levitt, M. J. (1991). Attachment and close relationships: A life-span perspective. In J. L. Gewirtz & W. M. Kurtines (Eds.), *Intersections with attachment.* Hillsdale, NJ: Erlbaum.

Levy, B. (1996). Improving memory in old age through implicit self-stereotyping. *Journal of Personality and Social Psychology*, *71*, 1092–1107.

Levy, B. (2009). Stereotype embodiment. A psychosocial approach to aging. *Current Directions in Psychological Science*, *18*, 332–336.

Levy, B. R. (2003). Mind matters: Cognitive and physical effects of aging self-stereotypes. *Journals of Gerontology: Psychological Sciences & Social Sciences*, *58*, 203–211.

Levy, B. R., Ferrucci, L., Zonderman, A. B., Slade, M. D., Troncoso, J., & Resnick, S. M. (2016). A culture–brain link: Negative age stereotypes predict Alzheimer's disease biomarkers. *Psychology and Aging*, *31*, 82–88.

Levy, B. R., Pilver, C. E., & Pietrzak, R. H. (2014). Lower prevalence of psychiatric conditions when negative age stereotypes are resisted. *Social Science & Medicine*, *119*, 170–174.

Levy, B. R., Pilver, C., Chung, P. H., & Slade, M. D. (2014). Subliminal strengthening: Improving older individuals' physical function over time with an implicit-age-stereotype intervention. *Psychological Science, 25,* 2127–2135.

Levy, B. R., Slade, M. D., & Kasl, S. V. (2002). Longitudinal benefit of positive self-perceptions of aging on functional health. *Journals of Gerontology: Psychological Sciences and Social Sciences, 57,* 409–417.

Levy, B. R., Zonderman, A. B., Slade, M. D., & Ferrucci, L. (2009). Age stereotypes held earlier in life predict cardiovascular events in later life. *Psychological Science, 20,* 296–298.

Levy, B. R., Zonderman, A. B., Slade, M. D., & Ferrucci, L. (2012). Memory shaped by age stereotypes over time. *The Journals of Gerontology, Series B: Psychological Sciences and Social Sciences, 67,* 432–436.

Levy, B., & Langer, E. (1994). Aging free from negative stereotypes: Successful memory in China and among the American deaf. *Journal of Personality and Social Psychology, 66,* 989–997.

Levy, G. D., Sadovsky, A. L., & Troseth, G. L. (2000). Aspects of young children's perceptions of gender-typed occupations. *Sex Roles, 42,* 993–1006.

Levy-Shiff, R. (1994). Individual and contextual correlates of marital change across the transition to parenthood. *Developmental Psychology, 30,* 591–601.

Lew, A. R., Hopkins, B., Owen, L. H., & Green, M. (2007, March 1). Postural change effects on infants' AB task performance: Visual, postural, or spatial? *Journal of Experimental Psychology, 97,* 1–13.

Lewis, B. A., Minnes, S., Short, E. J., Weishampel, P., Satayathum, S., Min, M. O., et al. (2011). The effects of prenatal cocaine on language development at 10 years of age. *Neurotoxicology and Teratology, 33,* 17–24.

Lewis, D. A., Sesack, S. R., Levey, A. I., & Rosenberg, D. R. (1998). Dopamine axons in primate prefrontal cortex: Specificity of distribution, synaptic targets, and development. *Advances in Pharmacology, 42,* 703–706.

Lewis, L. E., & Conway, J. M. (2010). Self-other awareness and peer relationship in toddlers: Gender comparisons. *Infant and Child Dvelopment, 19,* 455–464.

Lewis, M. (2008). The emergence of human emotions. In M. Lewis, J. M. Haviland-Jones, & L. Feldman Barrett (Eds.), *Handbook of emotions* (3rd ed.). New York, NY: Guilford.

Lewis, M. (2015). Emotional development and consciousness. In W. F. Overton & P. C. M. Molenaar (Vol. Eds.) & R. M. Lerner (Ed.), *Handbook of child psychology and developmental science: Vol 1. Theory and method* (pp. 407–451). Hoboken, NJ: Wiley.

Lewis, M., & Brooks-Gunn, J. (1979). *Social cognition and the acquisition of self.* New York, NY: Plenum.

Lewis, M., & Carmody, D. P. (2008). Self-representation and brain development. *Developmental Psychology, 44,* 1329–1334.

Lewis, M., & Rosenblum, M. A. (1975). *Friendship and peer relations.* New York, NY: Wiley.

Lewis, M., & Rudolph, K. D. (Eds.) (2014). *Handbook of developmental psychopathology* (3rd ed.). New York, NY: Springer.

Lewis, M., Alessandri, S. M., & Sullivan, M. W. (1990). Violation of expectancy, loss of control, and anger expressions in young infants. *Developmental Psychology, 26,* 745–751.

Lewis, M., Sullivan, M. W., Stanger, C., & Weiss, M. (1989). Self-development and self-conscious emotions. *Child Development, 60,* 146–156.

Lewis, P. G., & Lippman, J. G. (2004). *Helping children cope with the death of a parent. A guide for the first year.* Westport, CT: Praeger.

Lewis, R. (2012). *Forever fix: Gene therapy and the boy who saved it.* New York, NY: St. Martin's.

Lewis, R. (2015). *Human genetics: Concepts and applications* (11th ed.). New York, NY: McGraw-Hill.

Lewis, T. L., & Maurer, D. (2005). Multiple sensitive periods in human visual development: Evidence from visually deprived children. *Developmental Psychobiology, 46,* 163–183.

Lewis, T. L., & Maurer, D. (2009). Effects of early pattern deprivation on visual development. *Optometry and Vision Science, 86,* 640–646.

Lewontin, R. C. (1976). Race and intelligence. In N. J. Block & G. Dworkin (Eds.), *The IQ controversy.* New York, NY: Pantheon.

Li, D. K., Liu, L., & Odouli, R. (2003). Exposure to non-steroidal anti-inflammatory drugs during pregnancy and risk of miscarriage: population based cohort study. *British Medical Journal, 327,* 368.

Li, K. Z. H., Lindenberger, U., Freund, A. M., & Baltes, P. B. (2001). Walking while memorizing: Age-related differences in compensatory behavior. *Psychological Science, 12,* 230–237.

Li, N., & Kirkup, G. (2007). Gender and cultural differences in Internet use: A study of China and the UK. *Computers & Education, 48,* 301–317.

Li, R. Y. H., & Wong, W. I. (2016). Gender-typed play and social abilities in boys and girls: Are they related? *Sex Roles, 74,* 399–410.

Liben, L. S., & Muller, U. (Eds.). (2015). *Handbook of child psychology and developmental science: Vol 2. Cognitive processes* (7th ed.). Hoboken, NJ: Wiley.

Liben, L. S., & Signorella, M. L. (1993). Gender-schematic processing in children: The role of initial interpretations of stimuli. *Developmental Psychology, 29,* 141–149.

Libertus, K., & Needham, A. (2010). Teach to reach: The effects of active vs. passive reaching experiences on action and perception. *Vision Research, 50,* 2750–2757.

Lick, D. J., Tornello, S. L., Riskind, R. G., Schmidt, K. M., & Patterson, C. J. (2012). Social climate for sexual minorities predicts well-being among heterosexual offspring of lesbian and gay parents. *Sexuality Research & Social Policy: A Journal of the NSRC, 9,* 99–112.

Lickliter, R., & Honeycutt, H. (2015). Biology, development, and human systems. In W. F. Overton (Vol. Ed.), P. C. M. Molenaar (Vol. Ed.), & R. M. Lerner (Ed.), *Handbook of child psychology and developmental science: Vol. 1. Theory and method* (pp. 162–207). Hoboken, NJ: Wiley.

Lidz, J., Waxman, S., & Freedman, J. (2003). What infants know about syntax but couldn't have learned: Experimental evidence for syntactic structure at 18 months. *Cognition, 89,* B65–B73.

Lie, E., & Newcombe, N. S. (1999). Elementary school children's explicit and implicit memory for faces of preschool classmates. *Developmental Psychology, 35,* 102–112.

Lieberman, A. F., Compton, N. C., Van Horn, P., & Ippen, C. G. (2003). *Losing a parent to death in the early years. Guidelines for the treatment of traumatic bereavement in infancy and early childhood.* Washington, DC: Zero to Three Press.

Lieberman, M. A., & Videka-Sherman, L. (1986). The impact of self-help groups on the mental health of widows and widowers. *American Journal of Orthopsychiatry, 56,* 435–449.

Liégeois, F., Cross, J. H., Polkey, C., Harkness, W., & Vargha-Khadem, F. (2008). Language after hemispherectomy in childhood: Contributions from memory and intelligence. *Neuropsychologia, 46,* 3101–3107.

Light, L. L. (1991). Memory and aging: Four hypotheses in search of data. *Annual Review of Psychology, 42,* 333–376.

Lillard, A. S., Lerner, M. D., Hopkins, E. J., Dore, R. A., Smith, E. D., & Palmquist, C. M. (2013). The impact of pretend play on children's development: A review of the evidence. *Psychological Bulletin, 139,* 1–34.

Lim, F., Bond, M. H., & Bond, M. K. (2005). Linking societal and psychological factors to homicide rates across nations. *Journal of Cross-Cultural Psychology, 36,* 515–536.

Lim, S., Zoellner, J. M., Lee, J. M., Burt, B. A., Sandretto, A. M., Sohn, W., et al. (2009). Obesity and sugar-sweetened beverages in African-American preschool children: A longitudinal study. *Obesity, 17,* 1262–1268.

Lindau, S. T., & Gavrilova, N. (2010). Sex, health, and years of sexually active life gained due to good health: Evidence from two US population based cross sectional surveys of ageing. *British Medical Journal, 340,* C810. Retrieved from www.bmj.com/cgi/content/full/340/mar09_2/c810.

Lindenberger, U., Marsiske, M., & Baltes, P. B. (2000). Memorizing while walking: Increase in dual-task costs from young adulthood to old age. *Psychology and Aging, 15,* 417–436.

Lindvall, O., & Kokaia, Z. (2008). Neurogenesis following stroke affecting the adult brain. In F. H. Gage, G. Kempermann, & H. Song (Eds.), *Adult neurogenesis* (pp. 549–570). New York, NY: Cold Spring Harbor Laboratory Press.

Ling, J. M., Klimaj, S., Toulouse, T., & Mayer, A. R. (2013). A prospective study of gray matter abnormalities in mild traumatic brain injury. *Neurology, 81,* 2121–2127.

Lipina, S. J., & Colombo, J. A. (2009). *Poverty and brain development during childhood: An approach from cognitive psychology and neuroscience.* Washington, DC: American Psychological Association.

Lippa, R. A. (2008). The relation between childhood gender nonconformity and adult masculinity-femininity and anxiety in heterosexual and homosexual men and women. *Sex Roles, 59,* 684–693.

Liptak, G. S. (2013). Neural tube defects. In M. L. Batshaw, N. J. Roizen, & G. R. Lotrecchiano (Eds.), *Children with disabilities* (7th ed., pp. 451–472). Baltimore, MA: Paul H. Brookes.

Lipton, A. M., & Weiner, M. F. (2003). Differential diagnosis. In M. F. Weiner & A. M. Lipton (Eds.), *The dementias. Diagnosis, treatment, and research.* Washington, DC: American Psychiatric Publishing.

Lisdahl, K. M., Gilbart, E. R., Wright, N. E., & Shollenbarger, S. (2013). Dare to delay? The impacts of adolescent alcohol and marijuana use onset on cognition, brain structure, and function. *Frontiers in Psychiatry, 4,* 53.

Listfield, E. (2011, June 12). The underage drinking epidemic. *Parade Magazine,* pp. 6–8, 12.

Litman, L., & Davachi, L. (2008). Distributed learning enhances relational memory consolidation. *Learning & Memory* (Cold Spring Harbor, NY), *15,* 711–716.

Little, M., Sandler, I. N., Schoenfelder, E., & Wolchik, S. A. (2011). A contextual model of gender differences in the development of depression after the death of a parent. In T. J. Strauman, P. R. Costanzo, & J. Garber (Eds.), *Depression in adolescent girls. Science and prevention.* New York, NY: Guilford.

Litwin, H., & Shiovitz-Ezra, S. (2011). Social network type and subjective well-being in a national sample of older Americans. *The Gerontologist, 51,* 379–388.

Liu, C. (2003). Does quality of marital sex decline with duration? *Archives of Sexual Behavior, 32,* 55–60.

Liu, D., Gelman, S. A., & Wellman, H. M. (2007). Components of young children's trait understanding: Behavior-to-trait inferences and trait-to-behavior predictions. *Child Development, 78,* 1543–1558.

Liu, D., Meltzoff, A., & Wellman, H. M. (2009). Neural correlates of belief- and desire-reasoning. *Child Development, 80,* 1163–1171.

Liu, L., Oza, S., Hogan, D., Perin, J., Rudan, I., Lawn, J. E., Cousens, S., & Mathers, C. (2015). Global, regional, and national causes of child mortality in 2000–13, with projections to inform post-2015 priorities: An updated systematic analysis. *The Lancet, 385,* 430–440.

Livesley, W. J., & Bromley, D. B. (1973). *Person perception in childhood and adolescence.* London, UK: Wiley.

Livingston, G., & Cohn, D. (2010). *Childlessness up among all women; down among women with advanced degrees.* Pew Research Center Social and Demographic Trends. Retrieved from www.pewsocialtrends.org/2010/06/25/childlessness-up-among-all-women-down-among-women-with-advanced-degrees/.

Livingston, G., & Parker, K. (2011). *A tale of two fathers. More are active, but more are absent.* Pew ResearchCenter Social and Demographic Trends. Retrieved from www.pewsocialtrendsorg/2011/06/15/a-tale-of-two-fathers/.

Livson, F. B. (1976). Patterns of personality in middle-aged women: A longitudinal study. *International Journal of Aging and Human Development, 7,* 107–115.

Livson, F. B. (1981). Paths to psychological health in the middle years: Sex differences. In D. H. Eichorn, J. A. Clausen, N. Haan, M. P. Honzik, & P. H. Mussen (Eds.), *Present and past in middle life.* New York, NY: Academic Press.

Lloyd, M. E., & Miller, J. K. (2014). Implicit memory. In P. Bauer & R. Fivush (Eds.), *The Wiley handbook on the development of children's memory* (pp. 336–360). Malden, MA: Wiley Blackwell.

Lobjois R, & Cavallo V. (2009). The effects of aging on street-crossing behavior: From estimation to actual crossing. *Accident Analysis and Prevention, 41,* 259–267.

Lock, A., & Zukow-Goldring, P. (2010). Preverbal communcation. In J. G. Bremner & T. D. Wachs (Eds.), *The*

Wiley-Blackwell handbook of infant development: Vol. 1. Basic research (2nd ed., pp. 394–425). Malden, MA: Blackwell.

Locke, J. L. (1997). A theory of neurolinguistic development. Brain and Language, 58, 265–326.

Lockheed, M. E. (1986). Reshaping the social order: The case of gender segregation. Sex Roles, 14, 617–628.

Lockl, K., & Schneider, W. (2007). Knowledge about the mind: Links between theory of mind and later metamemory. Child Development, 78, 148–167.

Lodi-Smith, J., Turiano, N., & Mroczek, D. (2011). Personality trait development across the life span. In K. L. Fingerman, C. A. Berg, J. Smith, & T. C. Antonucci (Eds.), Handbook of life-span development. New York, NY: Springer.

Loehlin, J. C. (1985). Fitting heredity-environment models jointly to twin and adoption data from the California Psychological Inventory. Behavior Genetics, 15, 199–221.

Loehlin, J. C. (1992). Genes and environment in personality development (Individual differences and development series: Vol. 2. Newbury Park, CA: Sage.

Loewenstein, G., & Furstenberg, F. (1991). Is teenage sexual behavior rational? Journal of Applied Social Psychology, 21, 957–986.

Lohan, J. A., & Murphy, S. A. (2001–2002). Parents' perceptions of adolescent sibling grief responses after an adolescent or young adult child's sudden, violent death. Omega: Journal of Death and Dying, 44, 77–95.

Lohaugen, G. C., Antonsen, I., Haberg, A., Gramstad, A., Vik, T., Brubakk, A. M., & Skranes, J. (2011). Computerized working memory training improves function in adolescents born at extremely low birth weight. The Journal of Pediatrics, 158, 555–561.

Longmore, M. A., Manning, W. D., & Giordano, P. (2013). Parent-child relationships in adolescence. In M. A. Fine & F. D. Fincham (Eds.), Handbook of family theories. A context-based approach. New York, NY: Routledge.

Lonigan, C. J. (2015). Literacy development. In L. S. Liben & U. Müller (Eds.), Handbook of child psychology and developmental science: Vol 2 (pp. 763–805). Hoboken, NJ: Wiley.

Loomans, E. M., Hofland, L., van der Stelt, O., van der Wal, M. F., Koot, H. M., Van den Bergh, B. R. H., et al. (2012). Caffeine intake during pregnancy and risk of problem behavior in 5- to 6-year-old children. Pediatrics, 130, e305–e313.

Loovis, E. M., & Butterfield, S. A. (2000). Influence of age, sex, and balance on mature skipping by children in grades K-8. Perceptual and Motor Skills, 90, 974–978.

Lopata, H. Z. (1996). Current widowhood: Myths and realities. Thousand Oaks, CA: Sage.

Lopez, E. C. (1997). The cognitive assessment of limited English proficient and bilingual children. In D. P. Flanagan, J. Genshaft, & P. L. Harrison (Eds.), Contemporary intellectual assessment: Theories, tests, and issues. New York, NY: Guilford.

Lopez, O. L. (2013). Mild cognitive impairment. CONTINUUM: Lifelong Learning in Neurology, 19, 411–424.

López-Teijón, M., García-Faura, Á., & Prats-Galino, A. (2015). Fetal facial expression in response to intravaginal music emission. Ultrasound, 23, 216–223.

LoPresti, M. A., Dement, F., & Gold, H. T. (2016). End-of-life care for people with cancer from ethnic minority groups: A systematic review. American Journal of Hospice & Palliative Medicine, 33, 291–305.

Lorber, M. F., Erlanger, A. C. E., Heyman, R. E., & O'Leary, K. D. (2015). The honeymoon effect: Does it exist and can it be predicted? Prevention Science, 16, 550–559.

Lorenz, K. Z. (1937). The companion in the bird's world. Auk, 54, 245–273.

Lorsbach, T. C., & Reimer, J. F. (1997). Developmental changes in the inhibition of previously relevant information. Journal of Experimental Child Psychology, 64, 317–342.

Lougheed, J. P., &Hollenstein, T. (2012). A limited repertoire of emotion regulation strategies is associated with internalizing problems in adolescence. Social Development, 21, 704–721.

Lourenço, O., & Machado, A. (1996). In defense of Piaget's theory: A reply to 10 common criticisms. Psychological Review, 103, 143–164.

Lourenço, O. (2012). Piaget and Vygotsky: Many resemblances, and a crucial difference. New Ideas in Psychology, 30, 281–295.

Lovaas, O. I. (1987). Behavioral treatment and normal educational and intellectual functioning in young autistic children. Journal of Consulting and Clinical Psychology, 55, 3–9.

Lovaas, O. I., & Smith, T. (2003). Early and intensive behavioral intervention in autism. In A. E. Kazdin & J. R. Weisz (Eds.), Evidence-based psychotherapies for children and adolescents. New York, NY: Guilford.

Lovett, B. J., & Sheffield, R. A. (2007). Affective empathy in aggressive children and adolescents: A critical review. Clinical Psychology Review, 27, 1–13.

Lövgren, M., Bylund-Grenklo, T., Jalmsell, L., Wallin, A. E., & Kreicbergs, U. (2016). Bereaved siblings' advice to health care professionals working with children with cancer and their families. Journal of Pediatric Oncology Nursing, 33, 297–305.

Lowry, K. A., Vallejo, A. N., Studenski, S. A. (2012). Successful aging as a continuum of functional independence: Lessons from physical disability models of aging. Aging and Disease, 3, 5–15.

Lubin, A., Simon, G., Houdé, O., & Neys, W. D. (2015). Inhibition, conflict detection, and number conservation. ZDM, 47, 793–800.

Lubinski, D., Webb, R. M., Morelock, M. J., & Benbow, C. P. (2001). Top 1 in 10,000: A 10-year follow-up of the profoundly gifted. Journal of Applied Psychology, 86, 718–729.

Luby, J. L. (2004). Affective disorders. In R. DelCarmen-Wiggins & A. Carter (Eds.), Handbook of infant, toddler, and preschool mental health assessment. New York, NY: Oxford University Press.

Luby, J. L. (2009). Depression. In C. H. Zeanah (Ed.), Handbook of infant mental health (3rd ed.). New York, NY: Guilford.

Luby, J. L. (2013). Treatment of anxiety and depression in the preschool period. Journal of the American Academy of Child & Adolescent Psychiatry, 52, 346–358.

Luby, J. L., Belden, A. C., Jackson, J. J., Lessov-Schlaggar, C., Harms, M. P., Tillman, R., . . . Barch, D. M. (2016). Early childhood depression and alterations in the trajectory of gray matter maturation in middle childhood and early adolescence. JAMA Psychiatry, 73, 31–38.

Luby, J. L., Gaffrey, M. S., Tillman, R., April, L. M., & Belden, A. C. (2014). Trajectories of preschool disorders to full DSM depression at school age and early adolescence: Continuity of preschool depression. American Journal of Psychiatry, 171, 768–776.

Luby, J. L., Sullivan, J., Belden, A., Stalets, M., Blankenship, S., & Spitznagel, E. (2006). An observational analysis of behavior in depressed preschoolers: Further validation of early-onset depression. Journal of the American Academy of Child & Adolescent Psychiatry, 45, 203–212.

Luby, J., & Belden, A. (2012). Depressive symptom onset during toddlerhood in a sample of depressed preschoolers: Implications for future investigations of major depressive disorder in toddlers. Infant Mental Health Journal, 33, 139–147.

Luby, J., Belden, A., Sullivan, J., Hayen, R., McCadney, A., & Spitznagel, E. (2009). Shame and guilt in preschool depression: Evidence for elevations in self-conscious emotions in depression as early as age 3. Journal of Child Psychology and Psychiatry, 50, 1156–1166.

Luby, J., Lenze, S., & Tillman, R. (2012). A novel early intervention for preschool depression: Findings from a pilot randomized controlled trial. Journal of Child Psychology and Psychiatry, 53, 313–322.

Lucas, R. E., & Diener, E. (2008). Personality and subjective well-being. In O. P. John, R. W. Robins, & L. A. Pervin (Eds.), Handbook of personality theory and research (3rd ed.). New York, NY: Guilford.

Luciana, M., Conklin, H. M., Hooper, C. J., & Yarger, R. S. (2005). The development of nonverbal working memory and executive control processes in adolescents. Child Development, 76, 697–712.

Lucio, R., Hunt, E., & Bornovalova, M. (2012). Identifying the necessary and sufficient number of risk factors for predicting academic failure. Developmental Psychology, 48, 422–428.

Lüdtke, O., Roberts, B. W., Trautwein, U., & Nagy, G. (2011). A random walk down university avenue: Life paths, life events, and personality trait change at the transition to university life. Journal of Personality and Social Psychology, 101, 620–637.

Ludwig, J., & Phillips, D. A. (2008). Long-term effects of Head Start on low-income children. Annals of the New York Academy of Science, 1136, 257–268.

Luecken, L. J. (2008). Long-term consequences of parental death in childhood: Psychological and physiological manifestations. In M. S. Stroebe, R. O. Hansson, H. Schut, & W. Stroebe (Eds.), Handbook of bereavement research and practice: Advances in theory and intervention. Washington, DC: American Psychological Association.

Luecken, L. J., Hagan, M. J., Sandler, I. N., Tein, J., Ayers, T. S., & Wolchik, S. A. (2013). Longitudinal mediators of a randomized prevention program effect on cortisol for youth from parentally bereaved families. Prevention Science.

Luke, C., & Redekop, F. (2014). Gottfredson's theory of career circumscription and compromise. In G. Eliason, T. Eliason, J. Samide, & J. Patrick (Eds.), Career development across the lifespan: Counseling for community, schools, higher education, and beyond (pp. 65–84). Charlotte, NC: Information Age Publishing.

Luke, M. A., Sedikides, C., & Carnelley, K. (2012). Your love lifts me higher! The energizing quality of secure relationships. Personality and Social Psychology Bulletin, 38, 721–733.

Luking, K. R., Pagliaccio, D., Luby, J. L., & Barch, D. M. (2016a). Depression risk predicts blunted neural responses to gains and enhanced responses to losses in healthy children. Journal of the American Academy of Child & Adolescent Psychiatry, 55, 328–337.

Luking, K. R., Pagliaccio, D., Luby, J. L., & Barch, D. M. (2016b). Reward processing and risk for depression across development. Trends in Cognitive Sciences, 20, 456–468.

Lukowski, A. F., & Bauer, P. J. (2014). Long-term memory in infancy and early childhood. In P. Bauer & R. Fivush (Eds.), The Wiley handbook on the development of children's memory (pp. 230–254). Malden, MA: Wiley Blackwell.

Luo, S., & Klohnen, E. C. (2005). Assortative mating and marital quality in newlyweds. Journal of Personality and Social Psychology, 88, 304–326.

Luo, Y. L., Haworth, C. M., & Plomin, R. (2010). A novel approach to genetic and environmental analysis of cross-lagged associations over time: The cross-lagged relationship between self-perceived abilities and school achievement is mediated by genes as well as the environment. Twin Research and Human Genetics, 13, 426–436.

Luo, Y., & Johnson, S. C. (2009). Recognizing the role of perception in action at 6 months. Developmental Science, 12, 142–149.

Luo, Y., Hawkley, L. C., Waite, L. J., &Cacioppo, J. T. (2012). Loneliness, health, and mortality in old age: A national longitudinal study. Social Science & Medicine, 74, 907–914.

Luong, G., Wrzus, C., Wagner, G. G., & Riediger, M. (2016). When bad moods may not be so bad: Valuing negative affect is associated with weakened affect-health links. Emotion, 16, 387–401.

Lupsakko, T. A., Kautiainen, H. J., & Sulkava, R. (2005). The non-use of hearing aids in people aged 75 years and over in the city of Kuopio in Finland. European Archives of Oto-Rhino-Laryngology, 262, 165–169.

Luria, A. R. (1974/1976). Cognitive development: Its cultural and social foundations. Cambridge, MA: Harvard University Press.

Lustig, J. L., Wolchik, S. A., & Braver, S. L. (1992). Social support in chumships and adjustment in children of divorce. American Journal of Community Psychology, 20, 393–399.

Luthar, S. S., & Ciciolla, L. (2016). What it feels like to be a mother: Variations by children's developmental stages. Developmental Psychology, 52, 143–154.

Lyketsos, C. G. (2009). Dementia and milder cognitive syndromes. In D. G. Blazer & D. C. Steffens (Eds.), The American Psychiatric Publishing textbook of geriatric psychiatry (4th ed.). Washington, DC: American Psychiatric Publishing.

Lykken, D. T., Tellegen, A., & Iacono, W. G. (1982). EEG spectra in twins: Evidence for a neglected mechanism of genetic determination. Physiological Psychology, 10, 60–65.

Lyman, S., Ferguson, S. A., Braver, E. R., & Williams, A. F. (2002). Older driver involvements in police reported crashes and fatal crashes: Trends and projections. *Injury Prevention, 8*, 116–120.

Lynch, M. P., Eilers, R. E., Oller, D. K., & Urbano, R. C. (1990). Innateness, experience, and music perception. *Psychological Science, 1*, 272–276.

Lynn, R. (2008b). *The global bell curve: Race, IQ, and inequality worldwide.* Augusta, GA: Washington Summit Publishers.

Lynn, R. (2009). Fluid intelligence but not vocabulary has increased in Britain, 1979–2008. *Intelligence, 37*, 249–255.

Lynne, S. D., Graber, J. A., Nichols, T. R., Brooks-Gunn, J., & Botvin, G. J. (2007). Links between pubertal timing, peer influences, and externalizing behaviors among urban students followed through middle school. *Journal of Adolescent Health, 40*, 181.e7–181.e13.

Lyons, H. A., Manning, W. D., Longmore, M. A., & Giordano, P. C. (2014). Young adult casual sexual behavior: Life-course-specific motivations and consequences. *Sociological Perspectives, 57*, 79–101.

Lytton, H., & Romney, D. M. (1991). Parents' differential socialization of boys and girls: A meta-analysis. *Psychological Bulletin, 109*, 267–296.

Ma, H. H. (2006). A synthetic analysis of the effectiveness of single components and packages in creativity training programs. *Creativity Research Journal, 18*, 435–446.

Ma, H. M., Du, M. L., Luo, X. P., Chen, S. K., Liu, L., Chen, R. M., et al. (2009). Onset of breast and pubic hair development and menses in urban Chinese girls. *Pediatrics, 124*, e269–77.

Ma, W., Golinkoff, R. M., Houston, D. M., & Hirsh-Pasek, K. (2011). Word learning in infant- and adult-directed speech. *Language Learning and Development, 7*, 185–201.

Mac Iver, D. J., & Reuman, D. A. (1988, April). *Decision-making in the classroom and early adolescents' valuing of mathematics.* Paper presented at the annual meeting of the American Educational Research Association, New Orleans.

Mac Iver, D. J., Reuman, D. A., and Main, S. R. (1995). Social structuring of school: Studying what is, illuminating what could be. *Annual Review of Psychology, 46*, 375–400.

Maccallum, F., Galatzer-Levy, I., & Bonanno, G. A. (2015). Trajectories of depression following spousal and child bereavement: A comparison of the heterogeneity in outcomes. *Journal of Psychiatric Research, 69*, 72–79.

Maccoby, E. E. (1998). *The two sexes: Growing up apart, coming together.* Cambridge, MA: Harvard University Press.

Maccoby, E. E. (2007). Historical overview of socialization research and theory. In J. E. Grusec & P. D. Hastings (Eds.), *Handbook of socialization theory and research.* New York, NY: Guilford.

Maccoby, E. E., & Jacklin, C. N. (1987). Gender segregation in childhood. In H. W. Reese (Ed.), *Advances in child development and behavior: Vol. 20.* Orlando, FL: Academic Press.

Maccoby, E. E., & Martin, J. A. (1983). Socialization in the context of the family: Parent–child interaction. In E. M. Hetherington (Vol. Ed.), P. H. Mussen (Editor-in-Chief), *Handbook of child psychology: Vol. 4. Socialization, personality, and social development* (4th ed.). New York, NY: Wiley.

MacDorman, M. F. & Gregory, E. C. (2015). National vital statistics reports from the Centers for Disease Control and Prevention. *National Center for Health Statistics, National Vital Statistics System, 64*, 1–24.

MacDorman, M. F., & Mathews, T. J. (2008, October). *Recent trends in infant mortality in the United States* (NCHS Data Brief No. 9). Hyattsville, MD: National Center for Health Statistics.

MacDorman, M. F., Kirmeyer, S. E., & Wilson, E. C. (2012). Fetal and perinatal mortality, United States, 2006. *National Vital Statistics Reports, 60* (8).

MacDorman, M. F., Mathews, T. J., & Declercq, E. (2012). Home births in the United States, 1990–2009. *NCHS Data Brief 84*, 1–8.

MacDorman, M. F., Mathews, T. J., & Declercq, E. (2014). Trends in out-of-hospital births in the United States, 1990–2012. NCHS Data Brief, no 144. Hyattsville, MD: National Center for Health Statistics.

MacDorman, M., & Kirmeyer, S. (2009). *The challenge of fetal mortality* (NCHS Data Brief, no 16). Hyattsville, MD: National Center for Health Statistics.

Maciejewski, P. K., Zhang, B., Block, S. D., & Prigerson, H. G. (2007). An empirical examination of the stage theory of grief. *JAMA, 297*, 716–723.

Mackey, A. P., Finn, A. S., Leonard, J. A., Jacoby-Senghor, D. S., West, M. R., Gabrieli, C. F. O., & Gabrieli, J. D. E. (2015). Neuroanatomical correlates of the income-achievement gap. *Psychological Science, 26*, 925–933.

Mackey, R. A., & O'Brien, B. A. (1995). *Lasting marriages: Men and women growing together.* Westport, CT: Praeger.

Mackinlay, R. J., Kliegel, M., Mäntylä, T., & Kliegel, M. (2009). Predictors of time-based prospective memory in children. *Journal of Experimental Child Psychology, 102*, 251–264.

MacLean, K. (2003). The impact of institutionalization on child development. *Development and Psychopathology, 15*, 853–884.

Madden, D. J. (2007). Aging and visual attention. *Current Directions in Psychological Science, 16*, 70–74.

Madden, D. J., & Langley, L. K. (2003). Age-related changes in selective attention and perceptual load during visual search. *Psychology and Aging, 18*, 54–67.

Madden, D. J., Gottlob, L. R., & Allen, P. A. (1999). Adult age differences in visual search accuracy: Attentional guidance and target detectability. *Psychology and Aging, 14*, 683–694.

Maddux, J. E. (2002). Self-efficacy: The power of believing you can. In C. R. Snyder & S. J. Lopez (Eds.), *Handbook of positive psychology* (pp. 277–287). New York, NY: Oxford University Press.

Madey, S. F., & Rodgers, L. (2009). The effect of attachment and Sternberg's triangular theory of love on relationship satisfaction. *Individual Differences Research, 7*, 76–84.

Madsen, S. D., & Collins, W. A. (2011). The salience of adolescent romantic experiences for romantic relationship qualities in young adulthood. *Journal of Research on Adolescence, 21*, 789–801.

Maehr, M., & Meyer, H. (1997). Understanding motivation and schooling: Where we've been, where we are, and where we need to go. *Educational Psychology Review, 9*, 371–409.

Maestripieri, D., Lindell, S. G., & Higley, J. D. (2007). Intergenerational transmission of maternal behavior in rhesus macaques and its underlying mechanisms. *Developmental Psychobiology, 49*, 165–171.

Magai, C., Cohen, C., Milburn, N., Thorpe, B., McPherson, R., & Peralta, D. (2001). Attachment styles in older European American and African American adults. *Journals of Gerontology: Psychological Sciences and Social Sciences, 56*, S28–S35.

Magai, C., Consedine, N. S., Krivoshekova, Y. S., Kudadjie-Gyamfi, E., & McPherson, R. (2006). Emotion experience and expression across the adult life span: Insights from a multimodal assessment study. *Psychology and Aging, 21*, 303–317.

Maguire-Jack, K., Gromoske, A. N., & Berger, L. M. (2012). Spanking and child development during the first 5 years of life. *Child Development, 83*, 1960–1977.

Mahaffy, K. A., & Ward, S. K. (2002). The gendering of adolescents' childbearing and educational plans: Reciprocal effects and the influence of social context. *Sex Roles, 46*, 403–417.

Maharaj, S., & Trevino, K. (2015). A comprehensive review of treatment options for premenstrual syndrome and premenstrual dysphoric disorder. *Journal of Psychiatric Practice, 21*, 334–350.

Maholmes, V. (2012). Adjustment of children and youth in military families: Toward developmental understandings. *Child Development Perspectives, 6*, 430–435.

Main, M., & George, C. (1985). Responses of abused and disadvantaged toddlers to distress in agemates: A study in the day-care setting. *Developmental Psychology, 21*, 407–412.

Main, M., & Solomon, J. (1990). Procedures for identifying infants as disorganized/disoriented during the Ainsworth Strange Situation. In M. T. Greenberg, D. Cicchetti, & E. M. Cummings (Eds.), *Attachment in the preschool years: Theory, research, and intervention.* Chicago, IL: University of Chicago Press.

Majid, A., & Burenhult, N. (2014). Odors are expressible in language, as long as you speak the right language. *Cognition, 130*, 266–270.

Makel, M. C., Kell, H. J., Lubinski, D., Putallaz, M., & Benbow, C. P. (2016). When lightning strikes twice: Profoundly gifted, profoundly accomplished. *Psychological Science, 27*, 1004–1018.

Malatesta, C. Z., & Kalnok, M. (1984). Emotional experience in younger and older adults. *Journal of Gerontology, 39*, 301–308.

Malatesta, C. Z., Culver, C., Tesman, J. R., & Shepard, B. (1989). The development of emotion expression during the first two years of life. *Monographs of the Society for Research in Child Development, 54* (1–2, Serial No. 219).

Malatesta, C. Z., Grigoryev, P., Lamb, C., Albin, M., & Culver, C. (1986). Emotional socialization and expressive development in preterm and full-term infants. *Child Development, 57*, 316–330.

Malinosky-Rummell, R., & Hansen, D. J. (1993). Long-term consequences of childhood physical abuse. *Psychological Bulletin, 114*, 68–79.

Malley-Morrison, K., & Hines, D. A. (2004). *Family violence in a cultural perspective. Defining, understanding, and combating abuse.* Thousand Oaks, CA: Sage.

Malmstrom, M., Sundquist, J., Bajekal, M., & Johansson, S. E. (1999). Ten-year trends in all-cause mortality and coronary heart disease mortality in socioeconomically diverse neighbourhoods. *Public Health,113*, 279–284.

Maloney, E. A., Converse, B. A., Gibbs, C. R., Levine, S. C., & Beilock, S. L. (2015). Jump-starting early childhood education at home: Early learning, parent motivation, and public policy. *Perspectives on Psychological Science, 10*, 727–732.

Malouf, M. A., Migeon, C. J., Carson, K. A., Petrucci, L., & Wisniewski, A. B. (2006). Cognitive outcome in adult women affected by congenital adrenal hyperplasia due to 21-hydroxylase deficiency. *Hormone Research, 65*, 142–150.

Manago, A. M., Taylor, T., & Greenfield, P. M. (2012). Me and my 400 friends: The anatomy of college students' Facebook networks, their communication patterns, and well-being. *Developmental Psychology, 48*, 369–380.

Mancini, A. D., Griffin, P., & Bonanno, G. A. (2012). Recent trends in the treatment of prolonged grief. *Current Opinion in Psychiatry, 25*, 46–51.

Mancini, A. D., Sinan, B., & Bonanno, G. A. (2015). Predictors of prolonged grief, resilience, and recovery among bereaved spouses. *Journal of Clinical Psychology, 71*, 1245–1258.

Mandal, B., Ayyagari, P., & Gallo, W. T. (2011). Job loss and depression: The role of subjective expectations. *Social Science and Medicine, 72*, 576–583.

Mandara, J., Gaylord-Harden, N. K., Richards, M. H., & Ragsdale, B. L. (2009). The effects of changes in racial identity and self-esteem on changes in African-American adolescents' mental health. *Child Development, 80*, 1660–1675.

Mandoki, M. W., Sumner, G. S., Hoffman, R. P., & Riconda, D. L. (1991). A review of Klinefelter's syndrome in children and adolescents. *Journal of the American Academy of Child & Adolescent Psychiatry, 30*, 167–172.

Mandy, W., & Lai, M. (2016). Annual research review: The role of the environment in the developmental psychopathology of autism spectrum condition. *Journal of Child Psychology and Psychiatry, 57*, 271–292.

Mangelsdorf, S. C. (1992). Developmental changes in infant-stranger interaction. *Infant Behavior and Development, 15*, 191–208.

Mangelsdorf, S. C., Gunnar, M., Kestenbaum, R., Lang, S., & Andreas, D. (1990). Infant proneness-to-distress temperament, maternal personality, and mother–infant attachment: Associations and goodness of fit. *Child Development, 61*, 820–831.

Mangelsdorf, S. C., Shapiro, J. R., & Marzolf, D. (1995). Developmental and temperamental differences in emotion regulation in infancy. *Child Development, 66*, 1817–1828.

Manlove, J., Wildsmith, E., Ikramullah, E., Terry-Humen, E, & Schelar, E. (2012). Family environments and the relationship context of first adolescent sex: Correlates of first sex in a casual versus steady relationship. *Social Science Research, 41*, 861–875.

Mansoor, E., Morrow, C. E., Accornero, V. H., Xue, L., Johnson, A. L., Anthony, J. C., et al. (2012). Longitudinal effects of prenatal cocaine use on mother-child interactions at ages 3 and 5 years. *Journal of Developmental & Behavioral Pediatrics, 33*, 32–41.

Marceau, J. R., Murray, H., & Nanan, R. K. (2009). Efficacy of oral sucrose in infants of methadone-maintained mothers. *Neonatology, 97*, 67–70.

Marceau, K., Neiderhiser, J. M., Lichtenstein, P., & Reiss, D. (2012). Genetic and environmental influences on the association between pubertal maturation and internalizing symptoms. *Journal of Youth and Adolescence, 41,* 1111–1126.

March of Dimes (2015). The impact of premature birth on society. www.marchofdimes.org/mission/the-economic-and-societal-costs.aspx.

March of Dimes (2015). What are the effects of maternal cocaine use? www.drugabuse.gov/publications/research-reports/cocaine/what-are-effects-maternal-cocaine-use.

March, J. S. (2009). The future of psychotherapy for mentally ill children and adolescents. *Journal of Child Psychology and Psychiatry, 50,* 170–179.

Marchand, H. (2002). Some reflections on postformal thought. *The Genetic Epistemologist, 29,* 2–9.

Marcia, J. E. (1966). Development and validation of ego identity status. *Journal of Personality and Social Psychology, 3,* 551–558.

Marcovitch, S., & Zelazo, D. (1999). The A-not-B error: Results from a logistic meta-analysis. *Child development, 70,* 1297–1313.

Marczak, M. S., Becher, E. H., Hardman, A. M., Galos, D. L., & Ruhland, E. (2015). Strengthening the role of unmarried fathers: Findings from the Co-Parent Court Project. *Family Process, 54,* 630–638.

Mareschal, D. (2011). From NEOconstructivism to NEUROconstructivism. *Child Development Perspectives, 5,* 169–170.

Mareschal, D., Johnson, M. H., Sirois, S., Spratling, M., Thomas, M. S. C., & Westermann, G. (2007). *Neuroconstructivism: How the brain constructs cognition.* Cambridge University Press.

Margolin, G., Ramos, M. C., Timmons, A. C., Miller, K. F., & Han, S. C. (2016). Intergenerational transmission of aggression: Physiological regulatory processes. *Child Development Perspectives, 10,* 15–21.

Margolis, R., & Myrskylä, M. (2015). Parental well-being surrounding first birth as a determinant of further parity progression. *Demography, 52,* 1147–1166.

Marian, V., Chabal, S., Bartolotti, J., Bradley, K., & Hernandez, A. E. (2014). Differential recruitment of executive control regions during phonological competition in monolinguals and bilinguals. *Brain and Language, 139,* 108–117.

Marian, V., & Shook, A. (2012, October 12). *The cognitive benefits of being bilingual.* The Dana Foundation. Retrieved from www.dana.org/news/cerebrum/detail.aspx?id=39638.

Marini, Z., & Case, R. (1994). The development of abstract reasoning about the physical and social world. *Child Development, 65,* 147–159.

Markham, J. A., & Greenough, W. T. (2004). Experience-driven brain plasticity: Beyond the synapse. *Neuron and Glia Biology, 1,* 351–363.

Markides, K. S., Boldt, J. S., & Ray, L. A. (1986). Sources of helping and intergenerational solidarity: A three-generations study of Mexican Americans. *Journal of Gerontology, 41,* 506–511.

Markiewicz, D., Lawford, H., Doyle, A. B., & Haggart, N. (2006). Developmental differences in adolescents' and young adults' use of mothers, fathers, best friends, and romantic partners to fulfill attachment needs. *Journal of Youth and Adolescence, 35,* 127–140.

Marks, R. (2014). Falls among the elderly and vision: A narrative review. *Open Medicine Journal, 1,* 54–65.

Markstrom-Adams, C., & Adams, G. R. (1995). Gender, ethnic group, and grade differences in psychosocial functioning during middle adolescence. *Journal of Youth and Adolescence, 24,* 397–417.

Markus, H. R. (2004). Culture and personality: Brief for an arranged marriage. *Journal of Research in Personality, 38,* 75–83.

Markus, H. R., Mullally, P. R., & Kitayama, S. (1997). Self-ways: Diversity in modes of cultural participation. In U. Neisser & D. A. Jopling (Eds.), *The conceptual self in context. Culture, experience, self-understanding.* Cambridge, UK: Cambridge University Press.

Marlier, L., & Schaal, B. (2005). Human newborns prefer human milk: Conspecific milk odor is attractive without postnatal exposure. *Child Development, 76,* 155–168.

Marottoli, R. A. (2007). *Enhancement of driving performance among older drivers.* Washington, DC: AAA Foundation for Traffic Safety. Retrieved from www.aaafoundation.org/pdf/EnhancingSeniorDrivingPerfReport.pdf.

Marples, D. R. (1996). *Belarus: From Soviet rule to nuclear catastrophe.* Hampshire: MacMillan Press.

Marschark, M. (1993). *Psychological development of deaf children.* New York, NY: Oxford University Press.

Marsee, M. A., & Frick, P. J. (2010). Callous-unemotional traits and aggression in youth. In W. F. Arsenio & E. A. Lemerise (Eds.), *Emotions, aggression, and morality in children. Bridging development and psychopathology.* Washington, DC: American Psychological Association.

Marsh, A. A., Finger, E. C., Fowler, K. A., Adalio, C. J., Jurkowitz, I. T. N., Schechter, J. C., . . . Blair, R. J. R. (2013). Empathic responsiveness in amygdala and anterior cingulate cortex in youths with psychopathic traits. *Journal of Child Psychology and Psychiatry, 54,* 900–910.

Marsh, H. W., & Ayotte, V. (2003). Do multiple dimensions of self-control become more differentiated with age? The differential distinctiveness hypothesis. *Journal of Educational Psychology, 95,* 687–706.

Marsh, H. W., & Craven, R. G. (2006). Reciprocal effects of self-concept and performance from a multidimensional perspective: Beyond seductive pleasure and unidimensional perspectives. *Perspectives on Psychological Science, 1,* 133–163.

Marsh, H. W., Craven, R., & Debus, R. (1999). Separation of competency and affect components of multiple dimensions of academic self-concept: A developmental perspective. *Merrill-Palmer Quarterly, 45,* 567–701.

Marshall, L., & Born, J. (2007). The contribution of sleep to hippocampus-dependent memory consolidation. *Trends in Cognitive Sciences, 11,* 442–450.

Marshall, P. J., & Meltzoff, A. N. (2014). Neural mirroring mechanisms and imitation in human infants. *Philosophical Transactions of the Royal Society: Biological Sciences, 369,* 20130620.

Marshall, W. A., & Tanner, J. M. (1969). Variations in the pattern of pubertal changes in girls. *Archives of Disease in Childhood, 44,* 291–303.

Marshall, W. A., & Tanner, J. M. (1970). Variations in the pattern of pubertal changes in boys. *Archives of Disease in Childhood, 45,* 13–23.

Marsiglio, W., Amato, P., Day, R. D., & Lamb, M. E. (2000). Scholarship on fatherhood in the 1990s and beyond. *Journal of Marriage and the Family, 62,* 1173–1191.

Marsiske, M., & Margrett, J. A. (2006). Everyday problem solving and decision making. In J. E. Birren & K. W. Schaie (Eds.), *Handbook of the psychology of aging.* Boston, MA: Elsevier Academic Press.

Marsiske, M., & Willis, S. L. (1995). Dimensionality of everyday problem solving in older adults. *Psychology and Aging, 10,* 269–283.

Martin, A. (2008). Enhancing student motivation and engagement: The effects of a multidimensional intervention. *Contemporary Educational Psychology, 33,* 239–269.

Martin, C. L, Ruble, D. N., & Szkrybalo, J. (2002). Cognitive theories of early gender development. *Psychological Bulletin, 128,* 903–933.

Martin, C. L., & Dinella, L. M. (2012). Congruence between gender stereotypes and activity preference in self-identified tomboys and non-tomboys. *Archives of Sexual Behavior, 41,* 599–610.

Martin, C. L., & Fabes, R. A. (2001). The stability and consequences of young children's same-sex peer interactions. *Developmental Psychology, 37,* 431–446.

Martin, C. L., & Halverson, C. F., Jr. (1981). A schematic processing model of sex typing and stereotyping in children. *Child Development, 52,* 1119–1134.

Martin, C. L., & Halverson, C. F., Jr. (1983). The effects of sex-typing schemas on young children's memory. *Child Development, 54,* 563–574.

Martin, C. L., & Halverson, C. F., Jr. (1987). The roles of cognition in sex-roles and sex-typing. In D. B. Carter (Ed.), *Current conceptions of sex roles and sex-typing: Theory and research.* New York, NY: Praeger.

Martin, C. L., & Ruble, D. N. (2004). Children's search for gender cues: Cognitive perspectives on gender development. *Current Directions in Psychological Science, 13,* 67–70.

Martin, C. L., & Ruble, D. N. (2010). Patterns of gender development. *Annual Review of Psychology, 61,* 353–381.

Martin, C. L., DiDonato, M. D., Clary, L., Fabes, R. A., Kreiger, T., Palermo, F., & Hanish, L. et al. (2012).

Preschool children with gender normative and gender non-normative peer preferences: Psychosocial and environmental correlates. *Archives of Sexual Behavior, 41,* 831–847.

Martin, C. L., Fabes, R. A., & Hanish, L. D. (2014). Gendered-peer relationships in educational contexts. *Advances in Child Development and Behavior, 47,* 151–187.

Martin, C. L., Kornienko, O., Schaefer, D. R., Hanish, L. D., Fabes, R. A., & Goble, P. (2013). The role of sex of peers and gender-typed activities in young children's peer affiliative networks: A longitudinal analysis of selection and influence. *Child Development, 84,* 921–937.

Martin, F. N., & Clark, J. G. (2002). *Introduction to audiology* (8th ed.). New York, NY: Allyn & Bacon.

Martin, M., & Lantos, J. (2005). Bioethics meets the barrio: Community-based research involving children. In E. Kodish (Ed.), *Ethics and research with children: A case-based approach.* Cary, NC: Oxford University Press.

Martin, M., Grunendahl, M., & Martin, P. (2001). Age differences in stress, social resources, and well-being in middle and old age. *Journal of Gerontology: Psychological Sciences, 56,* 214–222.

Martin, P., Hagberg, B., & Poon, L. W. (2012). Models for studying centenarians and healthy ageing. *Asian Journal of Gerontology & Geriatrics, 7,* 14–18.

Martin, R. (2015, August 9). Is football worth the brain-injury risk? For some, the answer is no [Television broadcast]. NPR. Retrieved from www.npr.org/2016/01/03/461770760/brain-scans-and-big-screens-dangers-of-concussions-on-and-off-the-field.

Martinez, G. M., & Abma, J. C. (2015). *Sexual activity, contraceptive use, and childbearing of teenagers aged 15–19 in the United States.* Hyattsville, MD: National Center for Health Statistics. Retrieved from www.cdc.gov/nchs/products/databriefs/db209.htm.

Martinez, G., Daniels, K., & Chandra, A. (2012, April 12). Fertility of men and women aged 15–44 years in the United States: National survey of family growth, 2006–2010. *National Health Statistics Reports,* No. 51.

Martinez-Frias, M. L. (2012). The thalidomide experience: Review of its effects 50 years later. *MedicinaClinca, 139,* 25–32.

Martlew, M., & Connolly, K. J. (1996). Human figure drawings by schooled and unschooled children in Papua New Guinea. *Child Development, 67,* 2743–2762.

Martorano, S. C. (1977). A developmental analysis of performance on Piaget's formal operations tasks. *Developmental Psychology, 13,* 666–672.

Martorell, G. A., & Bugental, D. B. (2006). Maternal variations in stress reactivity: Implications for harsh parenting practices with very young children. *Journal of Family Psychology, 20,* 641–647.

Masataka, N. (2000). The role of modality and input in the earliest stage of language acquisition: Studies of Japanese sign language. In C. Chamberlain, J. Morford, & R. I. Mayberry (Eds.), *Language acquisition by eye* (pp. 3–24). Mahwah, NJ: Lawrence Erlbaum.

Mascolo, M. F., & Fischer, K. W. (2015). Dynamic development of thinking, feeling, and acting. In R. M. Lerner (Ed.), *Handbook of child psychology and developmental science: Vol. 1. Theory and method* (pp. 113–161). Hoboken, NJ: Wiley.

Masi, C. M., Chen, H., Hawkley, L. C., & Cacioppo, J. T. (2011). A meta-analysis of interventions to reduce loneliness. *Personality and Social Psychology Review, 15,* 219–266.

Masten, A. S., & Reed, M. J. (2002). Resilience in development. In C. R. Snyder & S. J. Lopez (Eds.), *Handbook of positive psychology* (pp. 74–88). New York, NY: Oxford University Press.

Masten, A. S., & Tellegen, A. (2012). Resilience in developmental psychopathology: Contributions of the Project Competence Longitudinal Study. *Development and Psychopathology, 24,* 345–361.

Masten, A. S., Roisman, G. I., Long, J. D., Burt, K. B., Obradovic, J., Riley, J. R., Boelcke-Stennes, K., & Tellegen, A. (2005). Developmental cascades: Linking academic achievement and externalizing and internalizing symptoms over 20 years. *Developmental Psychology, 41,* 733–746.

Masters, W. H., & Johnson, V. E. (1966). *Human sexual response.* Boston, MA: Little, Brown.

Masters, W. H., & Johnson, V. E. (1970). *Human sexual inadequacy*. Boston, MA: Little, Brown.
Masterson, E. A., Deddens, J. A., Themann, C. L., Bertke, S., & Calvert, G. M. (2015). Trends in worker hearing loss by industry sector, 1981–2010. *American Journal of Industrial Medicine, 58*, 392–401.
Matchar, E. (2012, August 19). Why your office needs more bratty millennials. *The Washington Post*, pp. B1, B4.
Mather, K. A., Jorm, A. F., Parslow, R. A., & Christensen, H. (2011). Is telomere length a biomarker of aging? A review. *Journals of Gerontology. Series A, Biological Sciences and Medical Sciences, 66*, 202–213.
Mather, K. A., Kwok, J. B., Armstrong, N., & Sachdev, P. S. (2014). The role of epigenetics in cognitive ageing. *International Journal of Geriatric Psychiatry, 29*, 1162–1171.
Mather, M. (2016). The affective neuroscience of aging. *Annual Review of Psychology, 67*, 213–238.
Mathews, F., Youngman, L, & Neil, A. (2004). Maternal circulating nutrient concentrations in pregnancy: Implications for birth and placental weights of term infants. *American Journal of Clinical Nutrition, 79*, 103–110.
Mathews, J. (2003, October 1). Not quite piling on the homework. *The Washington Post*, pp. A1, A4.
Mathews, T. J., MacDorman, M. F., & Thoma, M. E. (2015). Infant mortality statistics from the 2013 period linked birth/infant death data set. *National Vital Statistics Reports, 64* (no. 9).
Mathy, F., Fartoukh, M., Gauvrit, N., & Guida, A. (2016). Developmental abilities to form chunks in immediate memory and its non-relationship to span development. *Frontiers in Psychology, 7*, 201.
Matthes, J., Prieler, M., & Adam, K. (2016). Gender-role portrayals in television advertising across the globe. *Sex Roles, 75*, 314–327.
Matthews, K. A. (1992). Myths and realities of the menopause. *Psychosomatic Medicine, 54*, 1–9.
Matthews, K. A., & Gallo, L. C. (2011). Psychological perspectives on pathways linking socioeconomic status and physical health. *Annual Review of Psychology, 62*, 501–530.
Matthews, K. A., Wing, R. R., Kuller, L. H., Meilahn, E. N., Kelsey, S. F., Costello, E. J., & Caggiula, A. W. (1990). Influences of natural menopause on psychological characteristics and symptoms of middle-aged healthy women. *Journal of Consulting and Clinical Psychology, 58*, 345–351.
Matthews, M., & Fair, D. A. (2015). Functional brain connectivity and child psychopathology: Overview and methodological considerations for investigators new to the field. *Journal of Child Psychology and Psychiatry, 56*, 400–414.
Mattis, J. S., & Grayman-Simpson, N. (2013). Faith and the sacred in African American life. In K. I. Pargament, J. J. Exline, & J. W. Jones (Eds.), *APA handbook of psychology, religion, and spirituality: Vol. 1. Context, theory, and research* (pp. 547–564). Washington, DC: American Psychological Association.
Maughan, B. (2001). Conduct disorder in context. In J. Hill & B. Maughan (Eds.), *Conduct disorders in childhood and adolescence*. New York, NY: Cambridge University Press.
Maughan, B., & Rutter, M. (2001). Antisocial children grown up. In J. Hill & B. Maughan (Eds.), *Conduct disorders in childhood and adolescence*. New York, NY: Cambridge University Press.
Maurer, A. (1961). The child's knowledge of nonexistence. *Journal of Existential Psychiatry, 2*, 193–212.
Maurer, D., Lewis, T. L., Brent, H. P., & Levin, A. V. (1999). Rapid improvement in the acuity of infants after visual input. *Science, 286*, 108–110.
Maurer, D., Mondloch, C. J., & Lewis, T. L. (2007). Sleeper effects. *Developmental Science, 10*, 40–47.
Maurer, D., Stager, C. L., & Mondloch, C. J. (1999). Cross-modal transfer of shape is difficult to demonstrate in one-month-olds. *Child Development, 70*, 1047–1057.
Maxwell, K., Callahan, J. L., Ruggero, C. J., & Janis, B. (2016). Breaking the cycle: Association of attending therapy following childhood abuse and subsequent perpetration of violence. *Journal of Family Violence, 31*, 251–258.
May, P. A., Fiorentino, D., Coriale, G., Kalberg, W. O., Hoyme, H. E., & Aragon, A. S. (2011). Prevalence of children with severe fetal alcohol spectrum disorders in communities near Rome, Italy: New estimated rates are higher than previous estimates. *International Journal of Environmental Research and Public Health, 8*, 2331–2351.
Mayberry, R. I. (2010). Early language acquisition and adult language ability: What sign language reveals about the critical period for language. In M. Marschark & P. Spencer (Eds.), *Oxford handbook of deaf studies, language, and education, 2*, 281–291.
Mayberry, R. I., & Squires, B. (2006). Sign language: Acquisition. In K. Brown (Ed.), *Encyclopedia of language and linguistics: Vol. 11* (2nd ed., pp. 739–743). Oxford, UK: Elsevier.
Mayer, A., & Träuble, B. E. (2013). Synchrony in the onset of mental state understanding across cultures? A study among children in Samoa. *International Journal of Behavioral Development, 37*, 21–28.
Mayer, C. (2011, April). Amortality: Why acting your age is a thing of the past. *Time*, pp. 44–51.
Mayes, R., Bagwell, C., & Erkulwater, J. (2009). *Medicating children: ADHD and pediatric mental health*. Cambridge, MA: Harvard University Press.
Mayeux, L., Houser, J. J., & Dyches, K. D. (2011). Social acceptance and popularity: Two distinct forms of peer status. In A. H. N. Cillessen, D. Schwartz, & L. Mayeux (Eds.), *Popularity in the peer system*. New York, NY: Guilford.
Mayeux, L., Sandstrom, M. J., & Cillessen, A. H. N. (2008). Is being popular a risky proposition? *Journal of Research on Adolescence, 18*, 49–74.
Maynard, S., Fang, E. F., Scheibye-Knudsen, M., Croteau, D. L., & Bohr, V. A. (2015). DNA damage, DNA repair, aging, and neurodegeneration. *Cold Spring Harbor Perspectives in Medicine, 5*(10).
Mayseless, O., Danieli, R., & Sharabany, R. (1996). Adults' attachment patterns: Coping with separations. *Journal of Youth and Adolescence, 25*, 667–690.
McAdams, D. P. (2005). Studying lives in time: A narrative approach. In R. Levy, P. Ghisletta, J. Le Goff, D. Spini, & E. Widmer (Eds.), *Advances in life course research: Vol. 10. Towards an interdisciplinary perspective on the life course*. Amsterdam: Elsevier.
McAdams, D. P. (2008). Personal narratives and the life story. In O. P. John, R. W. Robins, & L. A. Pervin (Eds.), *Handbook of personality theory and research* (3rd ed.). New York, NY: Guilford.
McAdams, D. P. (2011). Life narratives. In K. L. Fingerman, C. A. Berg, J. Smith, & T. C. Antonucci (Eds.), *Handbook of life-span development*. New York, NY: Springer.
McAdams, D. P. (2013). The psychological self as actor, agent, and author. *Psychological Science, 8*, 272–295.
McAdams, D. P., & Adler, J. M. (2006). How does personality develop? In D. K. Mroczek & T. D. Little (Eds.), *Handbook of personality development*. Mahwah, NJ: Erlbaum.
McAdams, D. P., & McLean, K. C. (2013). Narrative identity. *Current Directions in Psychological Science, 22*, 233–238.
McAdams, D. P., & Olson, B. D. (2010). Personality development: Continuity and change over the life course. *Annual Review of Psychology, 61*, 517–542.
McAdams, D. P., & Pals, J. L. (2006). A new Big Five: Fundamental principles for an integrative science of personality. *American Psychologist, 61*, 204–217.
McAdams, D. P., Hart, H. M., & Maruna, S. (1998). The anatomy of generativity. In D. P. McAdams & E. de St. Aubin (Eds.), *Generativity and adult development: How and why we care for the next generation*. Washington, DC: American Psychological Association.
McAdams, P. P., de St. Aubin, E., & Logan, R. L. (1993). Generativity among young, middle, and older adults. *Psychology and Aging, 8*, 221–230.
McAlister, A., & Peterson, C. C. (2006). Mental playmates: Siblings, executive functioning and theory of mind. *British Journal of Developmental Psychology, 24*, 733–751.
McAlister, A., Peterson, C. (2007). A longitudinal study of child siblings and theory of mind development. *Cognitive Development, 22*, 258–270.
McCabe, L. L., & McCabe, E. R. B. (2008). *DNA: Promise and peril*. Berkeley, CA: University of California Press.
McCabe, M. P., & Ricciardelli, L. A. (2004). A longitudinal study of pubertal timing and extreme body change behaviors among adolescent boys and girls. *Adolescence, 39*, 145–66.
McCall, R. B. (1977). Challenges to a science of developmental psychology. *Child Development, 48*, 333–344.
McCall, R. B. (1981). Nature-nurture and the two realms of development: A proposed integration with respect to mental development. *Child Development, 52*, 1–12.
McCall, R. B. (1983). A conceptual approach to early mental development. In M. Lewis (Ed.), *Origins of intelligence: Infancy and early childhood* (2nd ed.). New York, NY: Plenum.
McCall, R. B., & Carriger, M. S. (1993). A meta-analysis of infant habituation and recognition memory performance as predictors of later IQ. *Child Development, 64*, 57–79.
McCall, R. B., & Groark, C. J. (2015). Research on institutionalized children: Implications for international child welfare practitioners and policymakers. *International Perspectives in Psychology: Research, Practice, Consultation, 4*, 142–159.
McCarthy, J. R. (2009). Young people making meaning in response to death and bereavement. In D. E. Balk & C. A. Corr (Eds.), *Adolescent encounters with death, bereavement, and coping*. New York, NY: Springer.
McCartney, K., Harris, M. J., & Bernieri, F. (1990). Growing up and growing apart: A developmental meta-analysis of twin studies. *Psychological Bulletin, 107*, 226–237.
McCarton, C. M., Brooks-Gunn, J., Wallace, I. F., Bauer, C. R., Bennett, F. C., Bernbaum, J. C., Broyles, S., Casey, P. H., McCormick, M. C., Scott, D. T., Tyson, J., Tonascia, J., & Meinert, C. L. (1997). Results at age 8 years of early intervention for low-birth-weight premature infants. *Journal of the American Medical Association, 277*, 126–132.
McCaul, E. J., Donaldson, G. A., Coladarci, T., & Davis, W. E. (1992). Consequences of dropping out of school: Findings from high school and beyond. *Journal of Educational Research, 85*, 198–207.
McClain, L., & Brown, S. L. (2016). The roles of fathers' involvement and coparenting in relationship quality among cohabiting and married parents. *Sex Roles*. March 28 [Epub ahead of print].
McClintock, M. K., & Herdt, G. (1996). Rethinking puberty: The development of sexual attraction. *Current Directions in Psychological Science, 5*, 178–183.
McCloskey, L. A., Figueredo, A. J., & Koss, M. P. (1995). The effects of systematic family violence on children's mental health. *Child Development, 66*, 1239–1261.
McCormick, M. C., Brooks-Gunn, J., Buka, S. L., Goldman, J., Yu, J., Salganik, M., Scott, D. T., Bennett, F. C., Kay, L. L., Bernbaum, J. C., Bauer, C. R., Martin, C., Woods, E. R., Martin, A., & Casey, P. (2006). Early intervention in low birth weight premature infants: Results at 18 years of age for the Infant Health and Development Program. *Journal of Pediatrics, 117*, 771–780.
McCrae, R. R. (2004). Human nature and culture: A trait perspective. *Journal of Research in Personality* 38, 3–14.
McCrae, R. R., & Costa, P. T., Jr. (2003). *Personality in adulthood: A five-factor theory perspective* (2nd ed.). New York, NY: Guilford Press.
McCrae, R. R., & Costa, P. T., Jr. (2008). *The five-factor theory of personality*. In O. P. John, R. W. Robins, & L. A. Pervin (Eds.), *Handbook of personality theory and research* (3rd ed.). New York, NY: Guilford.
McCrae, R. R., Arenberg, D., & Costa, P. T., Jr. (1987). Declines in divergent thinking with age: Cross-sectional, longitudinal, and cross-sequential analyses. *Psychology and Aging, 2*, 130–137.
McCrae, R. R., Costa, P. T., Jr., Ostendorf, F., Angleitner, A., Hrebickova, M., Avia, M. D., Sanz, J., Sanchez-Bernardos, M. L., Kusdil, M. E., Woodfield, R., Saunders, P. R., & Smith, P. B. (2000). Nature over nurture: Temperament, personality, and life span development. *Journal of Personalty and Social Psychology, 78*, 173–186.
McCune, L., Vihman, M. M., Roug-Hellichius, L., Delery, D. B., & Gogate, L. L. (1996). Grunt communication in human infants (Homo sapiens). *Journal of Comparative Psychology, 110*, 27–27.
McDevitt-Murphy, M., Neimeyer, R. A., Burke, L. A., Williams, J. L., & Lawson, K. (2012). The toll of traumatic loss in African Americans bereaved by homicide. *Psychological Trauma: Theory, Research, Practice, and Policy, 4*, 303–311.

McDonald, A. (2007). Prenatal development—the Dana guide. In F. E. Bloom, M. F. Beal, & D. J. Kupfer (Eds.), *The Dana Gguide to brain health* (pp. 61–82). New York, NY: The Dana Foundation.

McDonald, R., Jouriles, E. N., Ramisetty-Mikler, S., Caetano, R., & Green, C. E. (2006). Estimating the number of American children living in partner-violent families. *Journal of Family Psychology*, *20*, 137–142.

McDonough, C., Song, L., Hirsh-Pasek, K., Golinkoff, R. M., & Lannon, R. (2011). An image is worth a thousand words: Why nouns tend to dominate verbs in early word learning. *Developmental Science*, *14*, 181–189.

McDowell, M. A., Brody, D. J., & Hughes, J. P. (2007). Has age at menarche changed? Results from the National Health and Nutrition Examination Survey (NHANES) 1999–2004. *Journal of Adolescent Health*, *40*, 227–231.

McElhaney, K. B., & Allen, J. P. (2012). Sociocultural perspectives on adolescent autonomy. In P. K. Kerig, M. S. Schulz, & S. T. Hauser (Eds.), *Adolescence and beyond. Family processes and development*. New York, NY: Oxford University Press.

McFarland, D. A., Moody, J., Diehl, D., Smith, J. A., & Thomas, R. J. (2014). Network ecology and adolescent social structure. *American Sociological Review*, *79*, 1088–1121.

McGaugh, J. L., & Roozendaal, B. (2002). Role of adrenal stress hormones in forming lasting memories in the brain. *Current Opinion in Neurobiology*, *12*, 205–210.

McGoldrick, M., & Carter, B. (2011). Families transformed by the divorce cycle: Reconstituted, multinuclear, recoupled, and remarried families. In M. McGoldrick, B. Carter, & N. Garcia Preto, *The expanded family life cycle: Individual, family, and social perspectives* (4th ed.). Boston, MA: Allyn & Bacon.

McGoldrick, M., Almeida, R., Hines, P. M., Garcia-Preto, N., Rosen, E., & Lee, E. (1991). Mourning in different cultures. In F. Walsh & M. McGoldrick (Eds.), *Living beyond loss: Death in the family*. New York, NY: W. W. Norton.

McGoldrick, M., Garcia-Preto, N., & Carter, B. (2016). *The expanded family life cycle: Individual, family, and social perspectives* (5th ed.). Boston, MA: Allyn & Bacon.

McGowan, P. O. (2013). Epigenomic mechanisms of early adversity and HPA dysfunction: Considerations for PTSD research. *Frontiers of Psychiatry*, *4*, Article 110.

McGowan, P. O., Meaney, M. J., & Szyf, M. (2008). Diet and the epigenetic (re)programming of phenotypic differences in behavior. *Brain Research*, *1237*, 12–24.

McGowan, P. O., Sasaki, A., D'Alessio, A.C., Dymov, S., Labonté, B., Szyf, M., Turecki, G., & Meaney, M. J. (2009). Epigenetic regulation of the glucocorticoid receptor in human brain associates with childhood abuse. *Nature Neuroscience*, *12*, 342–348.

McGrath, E. P., & Repetti, R. L. (2000). Mothers' and fathers' attitudes toward their children's academic performance and children's perceptions of their academic competence. *Journal of Youth and Adolescence*, *29*, 713–723.

McGrory, C. (2013). *Reboot and rebirth*. Retrieved from www.realitysandwich.com/ reboot_and_rebirth.

McGue, M., Elkins, I., Walden, B., & Iacono, W. G. (2005). Perceptions of the parent-adolescent relationship: A longitudinal investigation. *Developmental Psychology*, *41*, 971–984.

McGuire, S., Manke, B., Eftekhari, A., & Dunn, J. (2000). Children's perceptions of sibling conflict during middle childhood: Issues and sibling (dis)similarity. *Social Development*, *9*, 173–190.

McHale, J. P., & Lindahl, K. M. (Eds.). (2011). *Coparenting. A conceptual and clinical examination of family systems*. Washington, DC: American Psychological Association.

McHale, J., Khazan, I., Erera, P., Rotman, T., DeCourcey, W., & McConnell, M. (2002). Coparenting in diverse family systems. In M. H. Bornstein (Ed.), *Handbook of parenting: Vol. 3*. Being and becoming a parent (2nd ed.). Mahwah, NJ: Erlbaum.

McHale, S. M., Kim, J., & Whiteman, S. D. (2006). Sibling relationships in childhood and adolescence. In P. Noller & J. A. Feeney (Eds.), *Close relationships: Functions, forms, and processes*. New York, NY: Psychology Press.

McHale, S. M., Updegraff, K. A., & Whiteman, S. D. (2012). Sibling relationships and influences in childhood and adolescence. *Journal of Marriage and Family*, *74*, 913–930.

McKenna, L. (2012, Feb 16). Explaining Annette Lareau, or, why parenting style ensures inequality. *The Atlantic*.

McKusick, V. A. (1990). *Mendelian inheritance in man* (9th ed.) Baltimore, MD: Johns Hopkins Press.

McLanahan, S. S., & Sorensen, A. B. (1985). Life events and psychological well-being over the life course. In G. H. Elder, Jr. (Ed.), *Life course dynamics: Trajectories and transitions, 1968–1980*. Ithaca, NY: Cornell University Press.

McLean, K. C., & Pratt, M. W. (2006). Life's little (and big) lessons: Identity statuses and meaning-making in the turning point narratives of emerging adults. *Developmental Psychology*, *42*, 714–722.

McLoyd, V. C. (1990). The impact of economic hardship on black families and children: Psychological distress, parenting, and socio-emotional development. *Child Development*, *61*, 311–346.

McMahon, E., Wintermark, P., & Lahav, A. (2012). Auditory brain development in premature infants: The importance of early experience. *Annals of the New York Academy of Sciences*, *1252*, 17–24.

McMullen, S., Langley-Evans, S. C., Gambling, L., Lang, C., Swali, A., & McArdle, H. J. (2012). A common cause for a common phenotype: The gatekeeper hypothesis in fetal programming. *Medical Hypotheses*, *78*, 88–94.

McNeill, D. (1970). *The acquisition of language*. New York, NY: Harper & Row.

Meadows, S. (2006). *The child as thinker: The development and acquisition of cognition in childhood* (2nd ed.). New York, NY: Routledge.

Meadows-Orlans, K. P., & Orlans, H. (1990). Responses to loss of hearing in later life. In D. F. Moores & K. P. Meadows-Orlans (Eds.), *Educational and developmental aspects of deafness*. Washington, DC: Gallaudet University Press.

Mealey, L. (2005). Evolutionary psychopathology and abnormal development. In R. L. Burgess & K. MacDonald (Eds.), *Evolutionary perspectives on human development*. Thousand Oaks, CA: Sage.

Meaney, M. (2010). Epigenetics and the biological definition of gene x environment interactions. *Child Development*, *81*, 41–79.

Measles and rubella monitoring (2012, June). *Surveillance Report #12*. Stockholm: European Centre for Disease Prevention and Control.

Medina, J. (2016, June 9). Who may die? California patients and doctors wrestle with assisted suicide. *The New York Times*. Retrieved from www.nytimes.com.

Medina, J. J. (1996). *The clock of ages: Why we age—how we age—Winding back the clock*. Cambridge, UK: Cambridge University Press.

Meier, R. P. (1991). Language acquisition by deaf children. *American Scientist*, *79*, 69–70.

Meier, T. B., Bergamino, M., Bellgowan, P. S. F., Teague, T. K., Ling, J. M., Jeromin, A., & Mayer, A. R. (2016). Longitudinal assessment of white matter abnormalities following sports-related concussion. *Human Brain Mapping*, *37*, 833–845.

Meijer, J., & Elshout, J. J. (2001). The predictive and discriminant validity of the zone of proximal development. *British Journal of Educational Psychology*, *71*, 93–113.

Meilman, P. W. (1979). Cross-sectional age changes in ego identity status during adolescence. *Developmental Psychology*, *15*, 230–231.

Meins, E., Fernyhough, C., Wainwright, R., Gupta, M., Fradley, E., & Tuckey, M. (2002). Maternal mind-mindedness and attachment security as predictors of theory of mind understanding. *Child Development*, *73*, 1715–1726.

Melby-Lervåg, M., Lyster, S. A., & Hulme, C. (2012). Phonological skills and their role in learning to read: A meta-analytic review. *Psychological Bulletin*, *138*, 322–352.

Melhem, N. M., Porta, G., Shamseddeen, W., Payne, M. W., & Brent, D. A. (2011). Grief in children and adolescents bereaved by sudden parental death. *Archives of General Psychiatry*, *68*, 911–919.

Mellinger, J. C., & Erdwins, C. J. (1985). Personality correlates of age and life roles in adult women. *Psychology of Women Quarterly*, *9*, 503–514.

Meltzoff, A. N. (2004). Imitation as a mechanism of social cognition: Origins of empathy, theory of mind, and the representation of action. In U. Goswami (Ed.), *Blackwell handbook of childhood cognitive development* (pp. 6–25). Malden, MA: Blackwell Publishing.

Meltzoff, A. N., & Moore, M. K. (1997). Explaining facial imitation: Theoretical model. *Early Development and Parenting*, *6*, 179–192.

Melzer, D., Hurst, A. J., & Frayling, T. (2007). Genetic variation and human aging: Progress and prospects. *Journal of Gerontology Series A: Medical Sciences*, *62A*, 301–307.

Melzi, G., & Schick, A. (2013). Language and literacy in the school years. In J. Berko Gleason & N. B. Ratner (Eds.), *The development of language* (7th ed.). Boston, MA: Allyn & Bacon.

Memon, A., & Vartoukian, R. (1996). The effects of repeated questioning on young children's eyewitness testimony. *British Journal of Psychology*, *87*, 403–415.

Menacker, F., MacDorman, M. F., & Declercq, E. (2010). Neonatal mortality risk for repeat cesarean compared to vaginal birth after cesarean (VBAC) deliveries in the United States, 1998–2002 birth cohorts. *Maternal and Child Health Journal*, *14*, 147–154.

Menaghan, E. G., & Lieberman, M. A. (1986). Changes in depression following divorce: A panel study. *Journal of Marriage and the Family*, *48*, 319–328.

Mendle, J. (2014). Why puberty matters for psychopathology. *Child Development Perspectives*, *8*, 218–222.

Mendle, J., Ferrero, J., Moore, S. R., & Harden, K. P. (2013). Depression and adolescent sexual activity in romantic and nonromantic relational contexts: A genetically-informative sibling comparison. *Journal of Abnormal Psychology*, *122*, 51–63.

Mendle, J., Harden, K.P., Brooks-Gunn, J., & Graber, J.A. (2010). Development's tortoise and hare: Pubertal timing, pubertal tempo, and depressive symptoms in boys and girls. *Developmental Psychology*, *46*, 1341–1353

Mennella, J. A. (2014). Ontogeny of taste preferences: Basic biology and implications for health. *The American Journal of Clinical Nutrition*, *99*, 704S–711S.

Mennella, J. A., and Beauchamp, G. K. (2002). Flavor experiences during formula feeding are related to preferences during childhood. *Early Human Development*, *68*, 71–82.

Mennella, J. A., & Bobowski, N. K. (2015). The sweetness and bitterness of childhood: Insights from basic research on taste preferences. *Physiology & Behavior*, *152*, 502–507.

Mennella, J. A., & Castor, S. M. (2012). Sensitive period in flavor learning: Effects of duration of exposure to formula flavors on food likes during infancy. *Clinical Nutrition*, *31*, 1022–1025.

Mennella, J. A., Forestell, C. A., Morgan, L. K., & Beauchamp, G. K. (2009). Early milk feeding influences taste acceptance and liking during infancy. *American Journal of Clinical Nutrition*, *90*, 780S–788S.

Mennella, J. A., Griffin, C. E., & Beauchamp, G. K. (2004). Flavor programming during infancy. *Pediatrics*, *113*, 840–845.

Mennella, J. A., Jagnow, C. P., & Beauchamp, G. K. (2001). Prenatal and postnatal flavor learning by human infants. *Pediatrics*, *107*, e88.

Mennella, J. A., Pepino, M. Y., & Reed, D. R. (2005). Genetic and environmental determinants of bitter perception and sweet preferences. *Pediatrics*, *115*, e216–e222.

Mennella, J. A., Reiter, A. R., & Daniels, L. M. (2016). Vegetable and fruit acceptance during infancy: Impact of ontogeny, genetics, and early experiences. *Advances in Nutrition*, *7*, 211S–219.

Menon, U. (2015). Midlife narratives across cultures: Decline or pinnacle? In L. A. Jensen (Ed.), *The Oxford handbook of human development and culture: An interdisciplinary perspective* (pp. 637–652). New York, NY: Oxford University Press.

Mensah, F. K., Bayer, J. K., Wake, M., Carlin, J. B., Allen, N. B., & Patton, G. C. (2013). Early puberty and childhood social and behavioral adjustment. *Journal of Adolescent Health*, *53*, 118–124.

Ment, L. R., Vohr, B., Allan, W., Katz, K. H., Schneider, K. C., Westerveld, M., Duncan, C. C., & Makuch, R. W. (2003). Change in cognitive function over time in very low-birth-weight infants. *Journal of the American Medical Association*, *289*, 705–711.

Mercer, J. (2006). *Understanding attachment: Parenting, child care, and emotional development*. Westport, CT: Praeger.

Merikangas, K. R., He, J., Burstein, M., Swanson, S. A., Avenevoli, S., Cui, L., et al. (2010). Lifetime prevalence of mental disorders in U.S. adolescents: Results from the National Comorbidity Survey Replication-Adolescent Supplement (NCS-A). *Journal of the American Academy of Child & Adolescent Psychiatry, 49*, 980–989.

Mernitz, S. E., & Kamp Dush, C. M. (2016). Emotional health across the transition to first and second unions among emerging adults. *Journal of Family Psychology, 30*, 233–244.

Merzenich, M. M., Jenkins, W. M., Johnston, P., Schreiner, C., Miller, S. L., & Tallal, P. (1996). Temporal processing deficits of language-learning impaired children ameliorated by training. *Science, 271*, 77–81.

Meschke, L. L., Zweig, J. M., Barber, B. L., & Eccles, J. S. (2000). Demographic, biological, psychological, and social predictors of the timing of first intercourse. *Journal of Research on Adolescence, 10*, 315–338.

Mesquita, B., De Leersnyder, J., & Albert, D. (2014). The cultural regulation of emotions. In J. J. Gross (Ed.), *Handbook of emotion regulation* (2nd ed.) (pp. 284–301). New York, NY: Guilford.

Messer, D. J., McCarthy, M. E., McQuiston, S., MacTurk, R. H., Yarrow, L. J., & Vietze, P. M. (1986). Relation between mastery behavior in infancy and competence in early childhood. *Developmental Psychology, 22*, 366–372.

Messinger-Rapport, B. J. (2003). Assessment and counseling of older drivers: A guide for primary care physicians. *Geriatrics, 58*, 16.

Metcalf, P., & Huntington, R. (1991). *Celebrations of death. The anthropology of mortuary ritual* (2nd ed.). Cambridge, UK: Cambridge University Press.

Metcalfe, J. (2009). Metacognitive judgments and control of study. *Current Directions in Psychological Science, 18*, 159–163.

Metcalfe, J., Casal-Roscum, L., Radin, A., & Friedman, D. (2015). On teaching old dogs new tricks. *Psychological Science, 26*, 1833–1842.

Meulenbroek, O., Kessels, R. P. C., de Rover, M., Petersson, M., Rikkert, M. G., Rijpkema, M., et al. (2010). Age-effects on associative object-location memory. *Brain Research, 22*, 100–110.

Meydani, M. (2001). Nutrition interventions in aging and age-associated disease. In S. C. Park, E. S. Hwang, H. Kim, & W. Park (Eds.), *Annals of the New York Academy of Sciences: Vol. 928. Molecular and cellular interactions in senescence*. New York, NY: The New York Academy of Sciences.

Meyer, S., Raikes, H. A., Virmani, E. A., Waters, S. F., & Thompson, R. A. (2014). Parent emotion representations and the socialization of emotion regulation in the family. *International Journal of Behavioral Development, 38*, 164–173.

Meyer-Bahlburg, H. F. L., Ehrhardt, A. A., Rosen, L. R., & Gruen, R. S. (1995). Prenatal estrogens and the development of homosexual orientation. *Developmental Psychology, 31*, 12–21.

Meyer-Bahlburg, H. F., Dolezal, C., Baker, S. W., Ehrhardt, A. A., & New, M. I. (2006). Gender development in women with congenital adrenal hyperplasia as a function of disorder severity. *Archives of Sexual Behavior, 35*, 667–684.

Mezulis, A. H., Hyde, J. S., Simonson, J., & Charbonneau, A. M. (2011). Integrating affective, biological, and cognitive vulnerability models to explain the gender difference in depression. The ABC model and its implications for intervention. In T. J. Strauman, P. R. Costanzo, & J. Garber (Eds.), *Depression in adolescent girls. Science and prevention*. New York, NY: Guilford.

Micali, N., De Stavola, B., Ploubidis, G., Simonoff, E., Treasure, J., & Field, A. E. (2015). Adolescent eating disorder behaviours and cognitions: Gender-specific effects of child, maternal and family risk factors. *British Journal of Psychiatry, 207*, 320–327.

Michael, S. L., Merlo, C. L., Basch, C. E., Wentzel, K. R., & Wechsler, H. (2015). Critical connections: Health and academics. *Journal of School Health, 85*, 740–758.

Michaelson, D. M. (2014). APOE ε4: The most prevalent yet understudied risk factor for Alzheimer's disease. *Alzheimer's & Dementia: The Journal of the Alzheimer's Association, 10*, 861–868.

Miche, M., Brothers, A., Diehl, M., & Wahl, H. (2015). The role of subjective aging within the changing ecologies of aging: Perspectives for research and practice. In M. Diehl & H. Wahl (Eds.), *Annual review of gerontology and geriatrics: Vol. 35.* (pp. 211–245). New York, NY: Springer.

Midgley, C., Feldlaufer, H., & Eccles, J. S. (1989). Student/teacher relations and attitudes toward mathematics before and after the transition to junior high school. *Child Development, 60*, 981–992.

Mikulincer, M., & Shaver, P. R. (2007). *Attachment in adulthood. Structure, dynamics, and change.* New York, NY: Guilford.

Mikulincer, M., & Shaver, P. R. (2013). Attachment insecurities and disordered patterns of grief. In M. Stroebe, H. Schut & J. van den Bout (Eds.), *Complicated grief: Scientific foundations for health care professionals.* New York, NY: Routledge/Taylor & Francis.

Milaniak, I., & Widom, C. S. (2015). Does child abuse and neglect increase risk for perpetration of violence inside and outside the home? *Psychology of Violence, 5*, 246–255.

Milkie, M. A., Norris, D. R., & Bierman, A. (2011). The long arm of offspring: adult children's troubles as teenagers and elderly parents' mental health. *Research and Aging, 33*, 327.

Miller, A. (1985). A developmental study of the cognitive basis of performance impairment after failure. *Journal of Personality and Social Psychology, 49*, 529–538.

Miller, G. E., Chen, E., Fok, A. K., Walker, H., Lim, A., Nicholls, E. F., et al. (2009). Low early-life social class leaves a biological residue manifested by decreased glucocorticoid and increased proinflammatory signaling. *Proceedings of the National Academy of Sciences of the United States of America, 106*, 14716–14721.

Miller, J. G. (2006). Insight into moral development from cultural psychology. In M. Killen & J. G. Smetana (Eds.), *Handbook of moral development*. Mahwah, NJ: Erlbaum.

Miller, J. G., & Bland, C. G. (2014). A cultural psychology perspective on moral development. In M. Killen & J. G. Smetana (Eds.), *Handbook of moral development* (2nd ed., pp. 299–314). New York, NY: Psychology Press.

Miller, J. G., Goyal, N., & Wice, M (2015). Ethical considerations in research on human development and culture. In L. A. Jensen (Ed.), *The Oxford handbook of human development and culture: An interdisciplinary perspective* (pp. 14–27). New York, NY: Oxford University Press.

Miller, J., & Knudsen, D. D. (2007). *Family abuse and violence: A social problems perspective.* Lanham, MD: AltaMira Press.

Miller, N. B., Cowan, P. A., Cowan, C. P., Hetherington, E. M., & Clingempeel, W. G. (1993). Externalizing in preschoolers and early adolescents: A cross-study replication of a family model. *Developmental Psychology, 29*, 3–18.

Miller, P. H. (1990). The development of strategies of selective attention. In D. F. Bjorklund (Ed.), *Children's strategies: Contemporary views of cognitive development.* Hillsdale, NJ: Erlbaum.

Miller, P. H. (1994). Individual differences in children's strategic behavior: Utilization deficiencies. *Learning and Individual Differences, 6*, 285–307.

Miller, P. H. (2002). *Theories of developmental psychology* (4th ed.). New York, NY: Worth.

Miller, P. H. (2011). Piaget's theory: past, present, and future. In U. Goswami, (Ed.), *The Wiley-Blackwell handbook of childhood cognitive development,* (2nd ed., pp. 650–672). Malden, MA: John Wiley.

Miller, P. H. (2016). *Theories of developmental psychology.* New York, NY: Worth Publishers.

Miller, P. H., & Seier, W. S. (1994). Strategy utilization deficiencies in children: When, where and why. In H. W. Reese (Ed.), *Advances in child development and behavior: Vol. 25.* (pp. 107–156). New York, NY: Academic Press.

Miller, P. H., & Weiss, M. G. (1981). Children's attention allocation, understanding of attention, and performance on the incidental learning task. *Child Development, 52*, 1183–1190.

Miller, R. A. (2004). Extending life: Scientific prospects and political obstacles. In S. G. Post & R. H. Binstock (Eds.), *The Fountain of Youth: Cultural, scientific, and ethical perspectives on a biomedical goal.* New York, NY: Oxford University Press.

Miller, S. A. (1986). Parents' beliefs about their children's cognitive abilities. *Developmental Psychology, 22*, 276–284.

Miller, S. A. (2013). *Developmental research methods* (4th ed.). Thousand Oaks, CA: Sage.

Miller, T. R., & Taylor, D. M. (2005). Adolescent suicidality: Who will ideate, who will act? *Suicide and Life-Threatening Behavior, 35*, 425–435.

Miller. S. A. (2012). *Theory of mind. Beyond the preschool years.* New York, NY: Psychology Press/Taylor and Francis.

Miller-Johnson, S., Costanzo, P. R., Coie, J. D., Rose, M. R., Browne, D. C., & Johnson, C. (2003). Peer social structure and risk-taking behaviors among African American early adolescents. *Journal of Youth and Adolescence, 32*, 375–384.

Millheiser, L. S., Helmer, A. E., Quintero, R. B., Westphal, L. M., Milki, A. A., & Lathi, R. B. (2010). Is infertility a risk factor for female sexual dysfunction? A case-control study. *Fertility and Sterility, 94*, 2022–2025.

Milos, G., Spindler, A., Schnyder, U., Martz, J., Hoek, H. W., & Willi, J. (2004). Incidence of severe anorexia nervosa in Switzerland: 40 years of development. *International Journal of Eating Disorders, 35*, 250–258.

Mineka, S., & Zinbarg, R. (2006). A contemporary learning theory perspective on the etiology of anxiety disorders. *American Psychology, 61*, 10–26.

Mingroni, M. A. (2004). The secular rise in IQ: Giving heterosis a closer look. *Intelligence, 32*, 65–83.

Miniño, A. M., & Murphy, S. L. (2012, July). Death in the United States, 2010. NCHS Data Brief, No. 99. U.S. Department of Health and Human Services, Centers for Disease Control and Prevention, National Center for Health Statistics. Retrieved from http//www.cdc.gov/nchs/data/databriefs/db99.htm.

Minkin, M. J., Reiter, S., & Maamari, R. (2015). Prevalence of postmenopausal symptoms in North America and Europe. *Menopause, 22*(11), 1231–1238.

Minnes, S., Singer, L. T., Arendt, R., & Satayathum, S. (2005). Effects of prenatal cocaine/polydrug use on maternal–infant feeding interactions during the first year of life. *Journal of Developmental and Behavioral Pediatrics, 26*, 194–200.

Mireault, G., Bearor, K., & Thomas, T. (2001–2002). Adult romantic attachment among women who experienced childhood maternal loss. *Omega: Journal of Death and Dying, 44*, 97–104.

Misa, T. J. (Ed.). (2010). *Gender codes: Why women are leaving computing.* Hoboken, NJ: John Wiley & Sons.

Mischel, W. (1973). Toward a cognitive social learning reconceptualization of personality. *Psychological Review, 80*, 252–283.

Mischel, W. (2014). *The marshmallow test. Why self-control is the engine of success.* New York, NY: Little, Brown.

Mischel, W., & Shoda, Y. (2008). Toward a unified theory of personality: Integrating dispositions and processing dynamics within the cognitive–affective processing system. In O. P. John, R. W. Robins & L. A. Pervin (Eds.), *Handbook of personality theory and research* (3rd ed.). New York, NY: Guilford.

Mischel, W., Ayduk, O., Berman, M. G., Casey, B. J., Gotlib, I. H., Jonides, J., et al. (2011). 'Willpower' over the life span: Decomposing self-regulation. *Social Cognitive and Affective Neuroscience, 6*, 252–256.

Mischel, W., Shoda, Y., & Peake, P. K. (1988). The nature of adolescent competencies predicted by preschool delay of gratification. *Journal of Personality and Social Psychology, 54*, 687–696.

Mishori, R. (2006, January 10). Increasingly, wired for sound. *The Washington Post*, pp. F1, F5.

Mishra, G. D., & Dobson, A. (2012). Using longitudinal profiles to characterize women's symptoms through midlife: Results from a large prospective study. *Menopause, 19*, 549–555.

Mishra, G. D., & Kuh, D. (2012). Health symptoms during midlife in relation to menopausal transition: British prospective cohort study. *British Medical Journal, 344*, e402.

Mistry, J., & Dutta, R. (2015). Human development and culture. In W. F. Overton (Vol. Ed.), & P. C. M. Molenaar (Vol. Ed.), & R. M. Lerner (Ed.), *Handbook of child psychology and developmental science: Vol. 1. Theory and method* (pp. 369–406). Hoboken, NJ: Wiley.

Mitchell, A. A., Gilboa, S. M., Werler, M. M., Kelley, K. E., Louik, C., Hernandez-Diaz, S., et al. (2011). Medication use during pregnancy, with particular focus on prescription drugs: 1976–2008. *American Journal of Obstetrics & Gynecology, 205*, e1–e8.

Mitchell, B. A., & Lovegreen, L. D. (2009). The empty nest syndrome in midlife families: A multimethod exploration of parental gender differences and cultural dynamics. *Journal of Family Issues, 30*, 1651–1670.

Mitchell, M. B., Cimino, C. R., Benitez, A., Brown, C. L., Gibbons, L. E., Kennison, R. F., ... Piccinin, A. M. (2012).

Cognitively stimulating activities: Effects on cognition across four studies with up to 21 years of longitudinal data. *Journal of Aging Research, 6,* 111–121.

Mitnick, D. M., Heyman, R. E., & Smith Slep, A. M. (2009). Changes in relationship satisfaction across the transition to parenthood: A meta-analysis. *Journal of Family Psychology, 23,* 848–852.

Miyawaki, K., Strange, W., Verbrugge, R., Liberman, A. M., Jenkins, J. J., & Fujimura, D. (1975). An effect of linguistic experience: The discrimination of [r] and [l] by native speakers of Japanese and English. *Perception and Psychophysics, 18,* 331–340.

Mock, S. E., & Eibach, R. P. (2012). Stability and change in sexual orientation identity over a 10-year period in adulthood. *Archives of Sexual Behavior, 41,* 641–648.

Moen, P. (1992). *Women's two roles: A contemporary dilemma.* New York, NY: Auburn House.

Moen, P., & Wethington, E. (1999). Midlife development in a life course context. In S. L. Willis & J. D. Reid (Eds.), *Life in the middle. Psychological and social development in middle age.* San Diego, CA: Academic Press.

Moffitt, T. E., & Caspi, A. (2001). Childhood predictors differentiate life-course persistent and adolescence-limited antisocial pathways among males and females. *Development and Psychopathology, 13,* 355–375.

Moffitt, T. E., Arseneault, L., Belsky, D., Dickson, N., Hancox, R. J., Harrington, H., Houts, R., Poulton, R., Roberts, B. W., Ross, S., Sears, M. R., Thomson, W. M., & Caspi, A. (2011). A gradient of childhood self-control predicts health, wealth, and public safety. *Proceedings of the National Academy of Sciences, 108,* 2693–2698.

Mohammed, A. H., Zhu, S. W., Darmopil, S., Hjerling-Leffler, J., Ernfors, P., Winblad, B., et al. (2002). Environmental enrichment and the brain. *Progress in Brain Research, 138,* 109–133.

Molina, B. S. G., & Chassin, L. (1996). The parent-adolescent relationship at puberty: Hispanic ethnicity and parent alcoholism as moderators. *Developmental Psychology, 32,* 675–686.

Molina, B. S. G., Hinshaw, S. P., Swanson, J. M., Arnold, L. E., Vitiello, B., Jensen, P. S., et al. (2009). The MTA at 8 years: Prospective follow-up of children treated for combined-type ADHD in a multisite study. *Journal of the American Academy of Child & Adolescent Psychiatry, 48,* 484–500.

Mollborn, S. (2009). Norms about nonmarital pregnancy and willingness to provide resources to unwed parents. *Journal of Marriage and Family, 71,* 122–134.

Molteni, R., Barnard, R.J., Zing, Z., Roberts, C.K., & Gómez-Pinilla, F. (2002). A high-fat, refined sugar diet reduces hippocampal brain-derived neurotrophic factor, neuronal plasticity, and learning. *Neuroscience, 112,* 803–814.

Monahan, K. C., Steinberg, L., & Cauffman, E. (2009). Affiliation with antisocial peers, susceptibility to peer influence, and antisocial behavior during the transition to adulthood. *Developmental Psychology, 45,* 1520–1530.

Mondschein, E. R., Adolph, K. E., & Tamis-LeMonda, C. S. (2000). Gender bias in mothers' expectations about infant crawling. *Journal of Experimental Child Psychology, 77,* 304–316.

Money, J. (1985). Pediatric sexology and hermaphroditism. *Journal of Sex and Marital Therapy, 11,* 139–156.

Money, J. (1988). *Gay, straight, and in-between: The sexology of erotic orientation.* New York, NY: Oxford University Press.

Money, J., & Ehrhardt, A. (1972). *Man and woman, boy and girl.* Baltimore, MD: Johns Hopkins University Press.

Money, J., & Tucker, P. (1975). *Sexual signatures: On being a man or a woman.* Boston, MA: Little, Brown.

Monroe, S. M., & Reid, M. W. (2009). Life stress and major depression. *Current Directions in Psychological Science, 18,* 68–72.

Montemayor, R., & Eisen, M. (1977). The development of self-conceptions from childhood to adolescence. *Developmental Psychology, 13,* 314–319.

Monti, M. M., Vanhaudenhuyse, A., Coleman, M. R., Boly, M., Pickard, J. D., Tshibanda, L., Owen, A. M., & Laureys, S. (2010). Willful modulation of brain activity in disorders of consciousness. *New England Journal of Medicine, 362,* 579–589.

Montoya, E. R., Terburg, D., Bos, P. A., & van Honk, J. (2012). Testosterone, cortisol, and serotonin as key regulators of social aggression: A review and theoretical perspective. *Motivation and Emotion, 36,* 65–73.

Moog, N. K., Entringer, S., Heim, C., Wadhwa, P. D., Kathmann, N., & Buss, C. (2015, Oct 3). Influence of maternal thyroid hormones during gestation on fetal brain development. *Neuroscience,* pii: S0306–4522(15)00897–0 [Epub ahead of print].

Moon, C., Lagercrantz, H., & Kuhl, P. (2013). Language experienced in utero affects vowel perception after birth: A two-country study. *Acta Paediatrica, 102,* 156–160.

Moor, N., & Graaf, P. M. (2016). Temporary and long-term consequences of bereavement on happiness. *Journal of Happiness Studies, 17,* 913–936.

Moore, A. B., Lee, N. Y. L., Clark, B. A. M., & Conway, A. R. A. (2011). In defense of the personal/impersonal distinction in moral psychology research: Cross-cultural validation of the dual process model of moral judgment. *Judgment and Decision Making, 6,* 186–195.

Moore, D. S. (2015). *The developing genome. An introduction to behavioral epigenetics.* New York, NY: Oxford University Press.

Moore, E. G. J. (1986). Family socialization and the IQ test performance of traditionally and transracially adopted black children. *Developmental Psychology, 22,* 317–326.

Moore, K. L., Persaud, T. V. N., & Torchia, M. G. (2013). *The developing human: Clinically oriented embryology* (9th ed.). Philadelphia, PA: Saunders.

Moore, M. K., & Meltzoff, A. N. (2008). Factors affecting infants' manual search for occluded objects and the genesis of object permanence. *Infant Behavior and Development, 31,* 168–180.

Morales, J., Calvo, A., & Bialystok, E. (2013). Working memory development in monolingual and bilingual children. *Journal of Experimental Child Psychology, 114,* 187–202.

Moran, J. M. (2013). Lifespan development: The effects of typical aging on theory of mind. *Behavioural Brain Research, 237,* 32–40.

Morelli, G. (2015). The evolution of attachment theory and cultures of human attachment in infancy and early childhood. In L. A. Jensen (Ed.), *Oxford handbook of human development and culture* (pp. 149–164). New York, NY: Oxford University Press.

Morello, C. (2013, January 2). Conflict in Syria takes emotional toll on children. *The Washington Post,* pp. A1, A9.

Moreno, M. A., Jelenchick, L., Koff, R., Eikoff, J., Diermyer, C., & Christakis, D. A. (2012). Internet use and multitasking among older adolescents: An experience sampling approach. *Computers in Human Behavior, 28,* 1097–1102.

Morgan, E. M. (2012). Not always a straight path: College students' narratives of heterosexual identity development. *Sex Roles, 66,* 79–93.

Morgan, G. A., & Ricciuti, H. N. (1969). Infants' responses to strangers during the first year. In B. M. Foss (Ed.), *Determinants of infant behavior: Vol. 4.* London, UK: Methuen.

Morgan, P. L., Farkas, G., Hillemeier, M. M., Hammer, C. S., & Maczuga, S. (2015). 24-month-old children with larger oral vocabularies display greater academic and behavioral functioning at kindergarten entry. *Child Development, 86,* 1351–1370.

Morin, A. J. S., Maiano, C., Marsh, H. W., Nagengast, B., & Janosz, M. (2013). School life and adolescents' self-esteem trajectories. *Child Development, 84,* 1967–1988.

Morin, R. (2003, January 9). Words matter. *The Washington Post,* B5.

Morina, N. (2011). Rumination and avoidance as predictors of prolonged grief, depression, and posttraumatic stress in female widowed survivors of war. *Journal of Nervous and Mental Disease, 199,* 921–927.

Morizot, J., & Le Blanc, M. (2003). Continuity and change in personality traits from adolescence to midlife: A 25-year longitudinal study comparing representative and adjudicated men. *Journal of Personality, 71,* 705–755.

Morley, G. (2013). World's oldest marathon man, 102, can't imagine life without running shoes. *CNN.* Retrieved from www.sikhphilosophy.net/threads/fauja-singh-cant-imagine-life-without-running-shoes.40728/.

Morrell, R. W., Park, D. C., & Poon, L. W. (1989). Quality of instructions on prescription drug labels: Effects on memory and comprehension in young and old adults. *Gerontologist, 29,* 345–354.

Morris, A. T., Gabert-Quillen, C., Friebert, S., Carst, N., & Delahanty, D. L. (2016). The indirect effect of positive parenting on the relationship between parent and sibling bereavement outcomes after the death of a child. *Journal of Pain and Symptom Management, 51,* 60–70.

Morrison, L. A., Brown, D. E., Sievert, L. L., Reza, A., Rahberg, N., Mills, P., & Goodloe, A. (2014). Voices from the Hilo Women's Health Study: Talking story about menopause. *Health Care for Women International, 35*(5), 529–548.

Morrongiello, B. A., & Hogg, K. (2004). Mothers' reactions to children misbehaving in ways that can lead to injury: Implications for gender differences in children's risk taking and injuries. *Sex Roles, 50,* 1003–1118.

Morrow, D., Leirer, V., Altieri, P., & Fitzsimmons, C. (1994). When expertise reduces age differences in performance. *Psychology and Aging, 9,* 134–148.

Morse, C. A., Dudley, E., Guthrie, J., & Dennerstein, L. (1998). Relationships between premenstrual complaints and perimenopausal experiences. *Journal of Psychosomatic Obstetrics and Gynecology, 19,* 182–191.

Morse, J. Q., Shaffer, D. R., Williamson, G. M., Dooley, W. K., & Schulz, R. (2011). Models of self and others and their relation to positive and negative caregiving responses. *Psychology and Aging, 27,* 211–218.

Mortimer, J. (2010). The benefits and risks of adolescent employment. *The Prevention Researcher, 17,* 8–11.

Moser, J. S., Schroder, H. S., Heeter, C., Moran, T. P., & Lee, Y. (2011). Mind your errors: Evidence for a neural mechanism linking growth mind-set to adaptive post-error adjustments. *Psychological Science, 22,* 1484–1489.

Moskovic, D. J., Eisenberg, M. L., Lipshultz, L. I. (2012). Seasonal fluctuations in testosterone-estrogen ratio in men from the Southwest United States. *Journal of Andrology, 33,* 1298–1304.

Moss, M. S., Moss, S. Z., Rubinstein, R., & Resch, N. (1993). Impact of elderly mother's death on middle age daughters. *International Journal of Aging and Human Development, 37,* 1–22.

Mroczek, D. K. (2004). Positive and negative affect at midlife. In O. G. Brim, C. D. Ryff, & R. C. Kessler (Eds.), *How healthy are we? A national study of well-being at midlife.* Chicago, IL: University of Chicago Press.

Mueller, E., & Lucas, T. (1975). A developmental analysis of peer interactions among toddlers. In M. Lewis & L. Rosenblum (Eds.), *Friendship and peer relations.* New York, NY: Wiley.

Mueller, M. K., Phelps, E., Bowers, E. P., Agans, J. P., Urban, J. B., & Lerner, R. M. (2011). Youth development program participation and intentional self-regulation skills: Contextual and individual bases of pathways to positive youth development. *Journal of Adolescence, 34,* 1115–1125.

Munroe, R. L., & Romney, A. K. (2006). Gender and age differences in same-sex aggregation and social behavior: A four-culture study. *Journal of Cross-Cultural Psychology, 37,* 3–19.

Murayama, K., & Elliot, A. J. (2009). The joint influence of personal achievement goals and classroom goal structures on achievement-relevant outcomes. *Journal of Educational Psychology, 101,* 432–447.

Murnen, S. K., & Smolak, L. (1997). Femininity, masculinity and disordered eating: A meta-analytic review. *International Journal of Eating Disorders, 22,* 231–242.

Murphy, C. (1985). Cognitive and chemosensory influences on age-related changes in the ability to identify blended foods. *Journal of Gerontology, 40,* 47–52.

Murphy, C., Nordin, S., & Acosta, L. (1997). Odor learning, recall, and recognition memory in young and elderly adults. *Neuropsychology, 11,* 126–137.

Murphy, D. R., Craik, F. I. M., Li, K. Z. H., & Schneider, B. A. (2000). Comparing the effects of aging and background noise on short-term memory performance. *Psychology and Aging, 15,* 323–334.

Murphy, D. R., Daneman, M., & Schneider, B. A. (2006). Why do older adults have difficulty following conversations? *Psychology and Aging, 21,* 49–61.

Murphy, E. M. (2003). Being born female is dangerous for your health. *American Psychologist, 58,* 205–210.

Murphy, M. L. M., Slavich, G. M., Rohleder, N., & Miller, G. E. (2012). Targeted rejection triggers differential pro- and anti-inflammatory gene expression in adolescents as a function of social status. *Clinical Psychological Science, 1,* 30–40.

Murphy, S. A. (2008). The loss of a child: Sudden death and extended illness perspectives. In M. S. Stroebe, R. O. Hansson, H. Schut, & W. Stroebe (Eds.), *Handbook of bereavement research and practice. Advances in theory and intervention*. Washington, DC: American Psychological Association.

Murphy, S. A., Johnson, C., & Lohan, J. (2003a). The effectiveness of coping resources and strategies used by bereaved parents 1 and 5 years after the violent deaths of their children. *Omega: Journal of Death and Dying, 47*, 25–44.

Murphy, S. A., Johnson, C., & Lohan, J. (2003b). Finding meaning in a child's violent death: A five-year prospective analysis of parents' personal narratives and empirical data. *Death Studies, 27*, 381–404.

Murray, C. (2006). Changes over time in the black-white difference on mental tests: Evidence from the children of the 1979 cohort of the National Longitudinal Survey of Youth. *Intelligence*, 34, 527–540.

Murray, L., Arteche, A., Fearon, P., Halligan, S., Goodyer, I., & Cooper, P. (2011). Maternal postnatal depression and the development of depression in offspring up to 16 years of age. *Journal of the American Academy of Child & Adolescent Psychiatry*, 50(5), 460–470.

Murray, L., de Rosnay, M., Pearson, J., Bergeron, C., Schofield, E., Royal-Lawson, M., & Cooper, P. J. (2008). Intergenerational transmission of social anxiety: The role of social referencing processes in infancy. *Child Development, 79*, 1049–1064.

Murray, L., Fearon, P., & Cooper, P. (2015). Postnatal depression, mother-infant interactions, and child development: Prospects for screening and treatment (pp. 139–159). In J. Milgrom & A. W. Gemmill (Eds.), *Identifying perinatal depression and anxiety: Evidence-based practice in screening, psychosocial assessment, and management*. Malden, MA: Wiley.

Murray, L., Halligan, S., & Cooper, P. (2010). Effects of postnatal depression on mother-infant interactions, and child development. In T. Wachs & G. Bremner (Eds.), *Blackwell handbook of infant development* (pp. 192–220). New York, NY: Wiley.

Murray, M. M., & Wallace, M. T. (Eds.). (2012). *Frontiers in neuroscience. The neural bases of multisensory processes*. Boca Raton, FL: CRC Press.

Murray-Close, D., Nelson, D. A., Ostrov, J. M., Casas, J. F., & Crick, N. R. (2016). Relational aggression: A developmental psychopathology perspective. In D. Cicchetti (Ed.) *Developmental psychopathology: Vol. 4. Risk, resilience, and intervention* (pp. 1–63). Hoboken, NJ: Wiley.

Murray-Close, D., Ostrov, J. M., & Crick, N. R. (2007). A short-term longitudinal study of growth of relational aggression during middle childhood: Associations with gender, friendship intimacy, and internalizing problems. *Development and Psychopathology, 19*, 187–203.

Musil, C. M., Gordon, N. L., Warner, C. B., Zauszniewski, J. A., & Standing, T., & Wykle, M. (2011). Grandmothers and caregiving to grandchildren: Continuity, change, and outcomes over 24 months. *The Gerontologist, 51*, 86–100.

Mustanski, B., Newcomb, M. E., & Garofalo, R. (2011). Mental health of lesbian, gay, and bisexual youths: A developmental resiliency perspective. *Journal of Gay & Lesbian Social Services, 23*, 204–225.

Mwamwenda, T. S. (1999). Undergraduate and graduate students' combinatorial reasoning and formal operations. *Journal of Genetic Psychology, 160*, 503–506.

Mwamwenda, T. S., & Mwamwenda, B. A. (1989). Formal operational thought among African and Canadian college students. *Psychological Reports, 64*, 43–46.

Myers, J. K., Weissman, M. M., Tischler, G. L., Holzer, C. E., III, Leaf, P. J., & Orvaschel, H. (1984). Six-month prevalence of psychiatric disorders in three communities. *Archives of General Psychiatry, 41*, 959–967.

Na, H. R., & Manning, C. A. (2015). Delirium in clinical geropsychology. In P. A. Lichtenberg & B. T. Mast (Eds. in Chief), B. D. Carpenter & J. L. Wetherell, (Assoc. Eds.), *APA handbook of clinical geropsychology: Vol. 1. History and status of the field and perspective on aging* (pp. 549–562). Washington, DC: American Psychological Association.

Naigles, L. G., & Gelman, S. A. (1995). Overextensions in comprehension and production revisited: Preferential-looking in a study of dog, cat, and cow. *Journal of Child Language, 22*, 19–46.

Naigles, L. R., & Swensen, L. D. (2007). Syntactic supports for word learning. In E. Hoff & M. Shatz (Eds.), *Blackwell handbook of language development* (pp. 212–231). Malden, MA: Blackwell Publishing.

Nanez, J. E., & Yonas, A. (1994). Effects of luminance and texture motion on infant defensive reactions to optical collision. *Infant Behavior and Development, 17*, 165–174.

Napoli, D. J., Mellon, N. K., Niparko, J. K., Rathmann, C., Mathur, G., Humphries, T., . . . Lantos, J. D. (2015). Should all deaf children learn sign language? *Pediatrics, 136*, 170–176.

National Center for Chronic Disease Prevention and Health Promotion (2014). *Breastfeeding Report Card: United States 2014*. Accessed 7/1/2016 at www.cdc.gov/breastfeeding/pdf/2014breastfeedingreportcard.pdf.

National Center for Education Statistics (1998). National Household Education Survey (NHES), "Adult Education Interview," 1991, 1995, 1999. *Projections of Education Statistics to 2008* (NCES 98–016).

National Center for Education Statistics (2013). *The condition of education*. Table A-48–1. Percentage of 25- to 29-year-olds who attained the selected levels of education, by race/ethnicity and sex: Selected years, 1980–2011. Retrieved from www.nces.ed.gov/programs/coe/tables/table-eda-1.asp.

National Center for Health Statistics (2010). *Health, United States, 2009*. Hyattsville, MD: U.S. Department of Health and Human Services, Centers for Disease Control and Prevention, National Center for Health Statistics. Retrieved from www.cdc.gov.nchs/ hus.htm.

National Center for Health Statistics (2011). *Health, United States, 2010: With special feature on death and dying* (DHHS Publication No. 2011–1232). Hyattsville, MD: Department of Health and Human Services.

National Center for Health Statistics (2015). *Health, United States, 2014: With special feature on adults aged 55–64*. Hyattesville, MD: Author, p. 28. Retrieved from www .cdc.gov/nchs/data/hus/hus14.pdf.

National Human Genome Research Institute (2015). Specific genetic disorders. Available at www.genome .gov/10001204.

National Institute on Aging (2015). *2014–2015 Alzheimer's disease progress report: Advancing research toward a cure*. Retrieved from www.nia.nih.gov/alzheimers/publication/2014–2015-alzheimers-disease-progress-report/introduction.

National Institute on Aging of the National Institutes of Health. (2013). *AgePage*. Retrieved from www.nia.nih .gov/health/publication/menopause.

National Institute on Deafness and Other Communication Disorders (NIDCD). (2016a). Age-related hearing loss. Retrieved from www.nidcd.nih.gov/health/hearing/Pages/Age-Related-Hearing-Loss.aspx#3.

National Institute on Deafness and Other Communication Disorders (NIDCD) (2016b). It's a noisy planet. Retrieved from www.noisyplanet.nidcd.nih.gov/Pages/Default.aspx.

National Organization on Fetal Alcohol Syndrome (2015). *Light Drinking During Pregnancy*. www.nofas.org/light-drinking/.

National Osteoporosis Foundation (2013). Calcium and Vitamin D: What you need to know. Retrieved from www.nof.org/articles/10.

National Partnership for Women & Families (2016). Facility labor and birth charges by site and mode of birth, United States, 2009–2011. *Transforming Maternity Care*. Accessed 6/2016. www.transform.childbirthconnection .org/resources/datacenter/chargeschart.

National Reading Panel (1999). *Teaching children to read: An evidence-based assessment of the scientific literature on reading and its implications for reading instruction*. Washington, DC: National Institute of Child Health & Human Development.

National Safety Commission (2008). Shedding light on driving in the dark. Retrieved from www.alerts. nationalsafetycommission.com/2008/09/shedding-light-on-driving-in-dark.php.

National Scientific Council on the Developing Child. (2007). *The timing and quality of early experiences combine to shape brain architecture: Working paper #5*. www.developingchild.net.

National Sleep Foundation (2015). *Teens and sleep*. Retrieved from www.sleepfoundation.org/sleep-topics/teens-and-sleep.

National Vital Statistics System, National Center for Health Statistics, Centers for Disease Control and Prevention(2015). 10 leading causes of death by age group, United States, 2013. Retrieved from www.cdc.gov/injury/wisqars/LeadingCauses.html.

Neale, M. C., & Martin, N. G. (1989). The effects of age, sex, and genotype on self-report drunkenness following a challenge dose of alcohol. *Behavior Genetics, 19*, 63–78.

Neblett, E. W. J., Rivas-Drake, D., & Umaña-Taylor, A. J. (2012). The promise of racial and ethnic protective factors in promoting ethnic minority youth development. *Child Development Perspectives, 6*, 295–303.

Negri, R., Di Feola, M., Di Domenico, S., Scala, M. G., Artesi, G., Valente, S., . . . Greco, L. (2012). Taste perception and food choices. *Journal of Pediatric Gastroenterology and Nutrition, 54*, 624–629.

Neighbors, H. W., Caldwell, C., Williams, D. R., Nesse, R., Taylor, R. J., Bullard, K. M., Torres, M., & Jackson, J. S. (2007). Race, ethnicity, and the use of services for mental disorders: Results from the National Survey of American Life. *Archives of General Psychiatry, 64*, 485–494.

Neimark, E. D. (1975). Longitudinal development of formal operations thought. *Genetic Psychology Monographs, 91*, 171–225.

Neimark, E. D. (1979). Current status of formal operations research. *Human Development, 22*, 60–67.

Neimeyer, R. A., & Currier, J. M. (2009). Grief therapy. Evidence of efficacy and emerging directions. *Current Directions in Psychological Science, 18*, 352–356.

Neimeyer, R. A., & Holland, J. M. (2015). Bereavement in later life: Theory, assessment, and intervention. In P. A. Lichtenberg & B. T. Mast (Eds. in Chief), B. D. Carpenter & J. L. Wetherell (Assoc. Eds.), *APA handbook of clinical geropsychology: Vol. 2. Assessment, treatment, and issues of later life* (pp. 645–666). Washington, DC: American Psychological Association.

Neisser, U., Boodoo, G., Bouchard, T. J., Jr., Boykin, A. W., Brody, N., Ceci, S. J., et al. (1996). Intelligence: Knowns and unknowns. *American Psychologist, 51*, 77–101.

Nelson, C. A., Thomas, K. M., & de Haan, M. (2006). Neural bases of cognitive development. In D. Kuhn & R. Siegler (Vol. Eds.), *Handbook of child psychology: Vol. 2. Theoretical models of human development* (6th ed.). Hoboken, NJ: Wiley.

Nelson, G., Westhues, A., & MacLeod, J. (2003). A meta-analysis of longitudinal research on preschool prevention programs for children. *Prevention & Treatment*, 6. Retrieved from www.journals.apa.org/prevention/volume6/toc-dec18–03.html.

Nelson, J. M. (2009). *Psychology, religion, and spirituality*. New York, NY: Springer Science+Business Media.

Nelson, K. (1986). *Event knowledge: Structure and function in development*. Hillsdale, NJ: Erlbaum.

Nelson, K. (1997). Event representations then, now, and next. In P. W. van den Broek & P. J. Bauer (Eds.), *Developmental spans in event comprehension and representation: Bridging fictional and actual* events (pp. 1–26). Mahwah, NJ: Erlbaum.

Nelson, K. (2007). *Young minds in social worlds: Experience, meaning, and memory*. Cambridge, MA: Harvard University Press.

Nelson, K. (2014). Sociocultural theories of memory development. In P. Bauer & R. Fivush (Eds.), *The Wiley handbook on the development of children's memory* (pp. 87–108). Malden, MA: Wiley Blackwell.

Nelson, K. (2015). Making sense with private speech. *Cognitive Development*, 36, 171–179.

Nelson, K., & Hudson, J. (1988). Scripts and memory: Functional relationship in development. In F. E. Weinert & M. Perlmutter (Eds.), *Memory development: Universal changes and individual differences*. Hillsdale, NJ: Erlbaum.

Nelson, K., Skwerer, D. P., Goldman, S., Henseler, S., Presler, N., & Walkenfeld, F. F. (2003). Entering a community of minds: An experiential approach to "theory of mind." *Human Development, 46*, 24–46.

Nelson, S. A. (1980). Factors influencing young children's use of motives and outcomes as moral criteria. *Child Development, 51*, 823–829.

Nelson, T. D. (2016). Promoting healthy aging by confronting ageism. *The American Psychologist, 71*, 276–282.

Nemeroff, C. B., & Binder, E. (2014). The preeminent role of childhood abuse and neglect in vulnerability to major psychiatric disorders: Toward elucidating the underlying

neurobiological mechanisms. *Journal of the American Academy of Child & Adolescent Psychiatry, 53*, 395–397.
Nemeroff, C. B., Kalai, A., Keller, M. B., Charney, D. S. Lenderts, S. E., Cascade, E. F., Stephenson, H., & Schatzberg, A. F. (2007). Impact of publicity concerning pediatric suicidality data on physician practice patterns in the United States. *Archives of General Psychiatry, 64*, 466–472.
Neppl, T. K., Senia, J. M., & Donnellan, M. B. (2016). Effects of economic hardship: Testing the family stress model over time. *Journal of Family Psychology, 30*, 12–21.
Nerenberg, L. (2008). *Elder abuse prevention. Emerging trends and promising strategies*. New York, NY: Springer.
Nes, S. L. (2003). Using paired reading to enhance the fluency skills of less-skilled readers. *Reading Improvement, 40*, 179–193.
Nettelbeck, T., & Young, R. (1996). Intelligence and savant syndrome: Is the whole greater than the sum of the fragments? *Intelligence, 22*, 49–68.
Neugarten, B. L. (1968). Adult personality: Toward a psychology of the life cycle. In B. L. Neugarten (Ed.), *Middle age and aging: A reader in social psychology*. Chicago, IL: University of Chicago Press.
Neugarten, B. L., Moore, J. W., & Lowe, J. C. (1965). Age norms, age constraints, and adult socialization. *American Journal of Sociology, 70*, 710–717.
Neuman, S. B., Kaefer, T., Pinkham, A., & Strouse, G. (2014). Can babies learn to read? A randomized trial of baby media. *Journal of Educational Psychology, 106*, 815–830.
Neumark, D., Burn, I., & Button, P. (2015). Is it harder for older workers to find jobs? New and improved evidence from a field experiment. National Bureau of Economic Research, Working Paper 21669. Available at www.nber.org/papers/w21669.
Neville, B., & Parke, R. D. (1997). Waiting for paternity: Interpersonal and contextual implications of the timing of fatherhood. *Sex Roles, 37*, 45–59.
Neville, H., Stevens, C., Pakulak, E., & Bell, T. A. (2013). Commentary: Neurocognitive consequences of socioeconomic disparities. *Developmental Science, 16*, 708–712.
Newbold, R. R., Padilla-Banks, E., Jefferson, W. N., & Heindel, J. J. (2009) Environmental estrogens and obesity. *Molecular and Cellular Endocrinology, 304*, 84–89.
Newell, A., & Simon, H. A. (1961). Computer simulation of human thinking. *Science, 134*, 2011–2017.
Newman, A. J., Bavelier, D., Corina, D., Jezzard, P., & Neville, H. J. (2002). A critical period for right hemisphere recruitment in American Sign Language processing. *Nature Neuroscience, 5*, 76–80.
Newman, B. M., & Newman, P. R. (2016). *Theories of human development* (2nd ed.). New York, NY: Psychology Press.
Newman, C. (2013). Fruit and vegetable consumption by school lunch participants: Implications for the success of new nutrition standards. ERR-154, U.S. Department of Agriculture, Economic Research Service.
Newman, R., & Sachs, J. (2012). Communication development in infancy. In J. Berko Gleason & N. B. Ratner (Eds.), *The development of language* (8th ed.). Boston, MA: Allyn & Bacon.
Newport, E. L. (1991). Contrasting conceptions of the critical period for language. In S. Carey & R. Gelman (Eds.), *The epigenesis of mind: Essays on biology and cognition*. Hillsdale, NJ: Erlbaum.
Newsom, J. T., Nishishiba, M., Morgan, D. L., & Rook, K. S. (2003). The relative importance of three domains of positive and negative social exchanges: A longitudinal model with comparable measures. *Psychology and Aging, 18*, 746–754.
Ng, F. F., Pomerantz, E. M., & Deng, C. (2014). Why are Chinese mothers more controlling than American mothers? 'My child is my report card'. *Child Development, 85*, 355–369.
Ng, S. F., Yin, R. C. Y., Laybutt, R., Barres, R., Owens, J. A., & Morris, M. J. (2010). Chronic high-fat diet in fathers programs beta-cell dysfunction in female rat offspring. *Nature, 467*, 963–967.
Ng, T. W. H., & Feldman, D. C. (2008). The relationship of age to ten dimensions of job performance. *Journal of Applied Psychology, 93*, 392–423.
Ng, T. W. H., & Feldman, D. C. (2012). Evaluating six common stereotypes about older workers with meta-analytical data. *Personnel Psychology, 65*, 821–858.
Ngun, T. C., & Vilain, E. (2014). The biological basis of human sexual orientation: Is there a role for epigenetics? *Advances in Genetics, 86*, 167–184.
Nguyen, H. T., & Zonderman, A. B. (2006). Relationship between age and aspects of depression: Consistency and reliability across two longitudinal studies. *Psychology and Aging, 21*, 119–126.
Nguyen, S., Choi, H. K., Lustig, R. H., & Hsu, C. Y. (2009). Sugar-sweetened beverages, serum uric acid, and blood pressure in adolescents. *Journal of Pediatrics, 154*, 807–813.
Nguyen, T. P., Karney, B. R., & Bradbury, T. N. (2016). Childhood abuse and later marital outcomes: Do partner characteristics moderate the association? *Journal of Family Psychology*. www.ncbi.nlm.nih.gov/pmc/articles/PMC5064817/.
NICHD Early Child Care Research Network (1997). The effects of infant child care on infant-mother attachment security: Results of the NICHD Study of Early Child Care. *Child Development, 68*, 860–879.
NICHD Early Child Care Research Network. (2006). Child-care effect sizes for the NICHD Study of Early Child Care and Youth Development. *American Psychologist, 61*, 99–116.
NICHD (2006). *The NICHD Study of Early Child Care and Youth Development: Findings for children up to age 4 ½ years*. Retrieved from www.nichd.nih.gov/publications/pubs.cfm.
Nickerson, R. S. (2011). Developing intelligence through instruction. In R. J. Sternberg & S. B. Kaufman (Eds.), *The Cambridge handbook of intelligence* (pp. 107–129). New York, NY: Cambridge University Press.
Nicolich, L. M. (1977). Beyond sensorimotor intelligence: Assessment of symbolic maturity through analysis of pretend play. *Merrill-Palmer Quarterly, 23*, 89–99.
Niec, L. N., Barnett, M. L., Prewett, M. S., & Shanley Chatham, J. R. (2016). Group parent–child interaction therapy: A randomized control trial for the treatment of conduct problems in young children. *Journal of Consulting and Clinical Psychology, 84*, 682–698.
Nielsen, M. K., Neergaard, M. A., Jensen, A. B., Bro, F., & Guldin, M. (2016). Do we need to change our understanding of anticipatory grief in caregivers? A systematic review of caregiver studies during end-of-life caregiving and bereavement. *Clinical Psychology Review, 44*, 75–93.
Nielsen, M., & Tomaselli, K. (2010). Overimitation in Kalahari Bushman children and the origins of human cultural cognition. *Psychological Science, 21*, 729–736.
Nielsen, M., Mushin, I., Tomaselli, K., & Whiten, A. (2014). Where culture takes hold: "Overimitation" and its flexible deployment in Western, aboriginal, and bushmen children. *Child Development, 85*, 2169–2184.
Nilsson, L., Adolfsson, R., Bäckman, L., Cruts, M., Edvardsson, H., Nyberg, L., et al. (2002). Memory development in adulthood and old age: The Betula prospective-cohort study. In P. Graf & N. Ohta (Eds.), *Lifespan development of human memory* (pp. 185–204). Cambridge, MA: Massachusetts Institute of Technology.
Nilsson, M., Perfilieva, E., Johansson, U., Orwar, O., & Eriksson, P. S. (1999). Enriched environment increases neurogenesis in the adult rat dentate gyrus and improves spatial memory. *Journal of Neurobiology, 39*, 569–578.
Nisbett, R. E., Aronson, J., Blair, C., Dickens, W., Flynn, J., Halpern, D. F., & Turkheimer, E. (2012). Intelligence: New findings and theoretical developments. *American Psychologist, 67*, 130–159.
Nishitani, S., Miyamura, T., Tagawa, M., Sumi, M., Takase, R., Doi, H., et al. (2009). The calming effect of a maternal breast milk odor on the human newborn infant. *Neuroscience Research, 63*, 66–71.
Nissim, R., Rennie, D., Fleming, S., Hales, S., Gagliese, L., & Rodin, G. (2012). Goals set in the land of the living/dying: A longitudinal study of patients living with advanced cancer. *Death Studies, 36*, 360–390.
Niv, S., & Baker, L A. (2013). Genetic markers for antisocial behavior. In C. R. Thomas & K. Pope (Eds.), *The origins of antisocial behavior. A developmental perspective*. New York, NY: Oxford University Press.
Noble, K. D., & Childers, S. A. (2009). Swimming in deep waters: 20 years of research about early university entrance at the University of Washington. In L. V. Shavinina (Ed.), *The international handbook on giftedness* (pp. 1345–1364). New York, NY: Springer Science+Business Media.
Noble, K. D., Childers, S. A., & Vaughan, R. C. (2008). A place to be celebrated and understood: The impact of early university entrance from parents' points of view. *Gifted Child Quarterly, 52*, 256–268.
Nolen-Hoeksema, S. (1990). *Sex differences in depression*. Stanford, CA: Stanford University Press.
Nolen-Hoeksema, S. (2002). Gender differences in depression. In I. H. Gotlib & C. L. Hammen (Eds.), *Handbook of depression*. New York, NY: Guilford.
Nolen-Hoeksema, S., & Watkins, E. R. (2011). A heuristic for developing transdiagnostic models of psychopathology: Explaining multifinality and divergent trajectories. *Perspectives on Psychological Science, 6*, 589–609.
Nolen-Hoeksema, S., Stice, E., Wade, E., & Bohon, C. (2007). Reciprocal relations between rumination and bulimic, substance abuse, and depressive symptoms in female adolescents. *Journal of Abnormal Psychology, 116*, 198–207.
Noller, P. (2006). Marital relationships. In P. Noller & J. A. Feeney (Eds.), *Close relationships: Functions, forms, and processes*. New York, NY: Psychology Press.
Noller, P., & Atkin, S. (2014). *Family life in adolescence*. Berlin: De Gruyter Open.
Nomaguchi, K. M., & Milkie, M. A. (2003). Costs and rewards of children: The effects of becoming a parent on adults' lives. *Journal of Marriage and the Family, 65*, 356–374.
Noone, J. H., Stephens, C., & Alpass, F. M. (2009). Preretirement planning and well-being in later life. A prospective study. *Research on Aging, 31*, 295–317.
Norbury, C. F., & Sparks, A. (2013). Difference or disorder? Cultural issues in understanding neurodevelopmental disorders. *Developmental Psychology, 49*, 45–58.
Nordin, S., Razani, L. J., Markison, S., & Murphy, C. (2003). Age-associated increases in intensity discrimination for taste. *Experimental Aging Research, 29*, 371–381.
North, M. S., & Fiske, S. T. (2012). An inconvenienced youth? Ageism and its potential intergenerational roots. *Psychological Bulletin, 138*, 982–997.
Northcutt, C., & McCarroll, B. (2014). DC:0–3R. A diagnostic schema for infants and young children and their families. In K. Brandt, B. D. Perry, S. Seligman, & E. Tronick (Eds.), *Infant and early childhood mental health. Core concepts and clinical practice* (pp. 175–193). Washington DC: American Psychiatric Publishing.
Northstone, K., Smith, A. D., Newby, P.K., Emmett, P. M. (2013). Longitudinal comparisons of dietary patterns derived by cluster analysis in 7- to 13-year-old children. *British Journal of Nutrition, 109*, 2050–2058.
Nsamenang, A. B. (1992). *Human development in cultural context: A third world perspective*. Newbury Park, CA: Sage.
Nucci, L. (2006). Education for moral development. In M. Killen & J. G. Smetana (Eds.), *Handbook of moral development*. Mahwah, NJ: Erlbaum.
Nugent, J. K., Keefer, C. H., Minear, S., Johnson, L. C., & Blanchard, Y. (2007). *Understanding newborn behaviors and early relationships: The Newborn Behavioral Observation (NBO) system handbook*. Baltimore, MD: Brookes Publishing.
Nulman, I., Ickowicz, A., Koren, G., & Knittel-Keren, D. (2007). Fetal alcohol spectrum disorder. In I. Brown & M. Percy (Eds.), *A comprehensive guide to intellectual & developmental disabilities*. Baltimore, MD: Paul H. Brookes.
Nussbaum, R. L., McInnes, R. R., & Willard, H. F. (2016). *Thompson & Thompson genetics in medicine* (8th ed.). New York, NY: Elsevier/Saunders.
Nutt, A. E. (2015, January 13). Study links BPA alternative to hyperactivity. *The Washington Post*, A3.
Nyberg, L., Lövdén, M., Riklund, K., Lindenberger, U., & Bäckman, L. (2012). Memory aging and brain maintenance. *Trends in Cognitive Sciences, 16*, 292–305.
Nyborg, H., & Jensen, A. R. (2001). Occupation and income related to psychometric g. *Intelligence, 29*, 45–55.
Nye, C. D., Su, R., Rounds, J., & Drasgow, F. (2012). Vocational interests and performance: A quantitative summary of over 60 years of research. *Perspectives on Psychological Science, 7*, 384–403.
Nyenhuis, D. (2015). Vascular cognitive impairment. In P. A. Lichtenberg & B. T. Mast (Eds. in Chief), B. D. Carpenter & J. L. Wetherell, (Assoc. Eds.), *APA*

handbook of clinical geropsychology: Vol. 2. Assessment, treatment, and issues of later life (pp. 209–226). Washington, DC: American Psychological Association.

O'Brien, M. (1996). Child-rearing difficulties reported by parents of infants and toddlers. Journal of Pediatric Psychology, 21, 433–446.

O'Brien, M., Peyton, V., Mistry, R., Hruda, L., Jacobs, A., Caldera, Y., et al. (2000). Gender-role cognition in three-year-old boys and girls. Sex Roles, 42, 1007–1025.

O'Connor, B. P., & Nikolic, J. (1990). Identity development and formal operations as sources of adolescent egocentrism. Journal of Youth and Adolescence, 19, 149–158.

O'Connor, R. E. (2011). Phoneme awareness and the alphabetic principle. In R. E. O'Connor & P. F. Vadasy (Eds.), Handbook of reading interventions (pp. 9–26). New York, NY: The Guilford Press.

O'Connor, S. M., Burt, S. A., VanHuysse, J. L., & Klump, K. L. (2016). What drives the association between weight-conscious peer groups and disordered eating? Disentangling genetic and environmental selection from pure socialization effects. Journal of Abnormal Psychology, 125, 356–368.

O'Connor, T. G., Deater-Deckard, K., Fulker, D., Rutter, M., & Plomin, R. (1998). Genotype-environment correlations in late childhood and early adolescence: Antisocial behavioral problems and coercive parenting. Developmental Psychology, 34, 970–981.

O'Dempsey, T. J. D. (1988). Traditional belief and practice among the Pokot people of Kenya with particular reference to mother and child health: 2. Mother and child health. Annals of Tropical Pediatrics, 8, 125.

O'Hara, R. E., Gibbons, F. X., Gerrard, M., Li, Z., & Sargent, J. D. (2012). Greater exposure to sexual content in popular movies predicts earlier sexual debut and increased sexual risk taking. Psychological Science, 23, 984–993.

O'Leary, C. M., & Bower, C. (2012). Guidelines for pregnancy: What's an acceptable risk, and how is the evidence (finally) shaping up? Drug & Alcohol Review, 31, 170–183.

O'Mara, A. J., Marsh, H. W., Craven, R. G., & Debus, R. L. (2006). Do self-concept interventions make a difference? A synergistic blend of construct validation and meta-analysis. Educational Psychologist, 41, 181–206.

O'Mathúna, D. P. (2006). Human growth hormone for improved strength and increased muscle mass in athletes. Alternative Medicine Alert, 8, 97–101.

O'Roak, B. J., Vives, L., Girirajan, S., Karakoc, E., Krumm, N., Coe, B. P., et al. (2012). Sporadic autism exomes reveal a highly interconnected protein network of de novo mutations. Nature, 485, 246–250.

O'Rourke, M. (2010, February 1). Good grief. Is there a better way to be bereaved? The New Yorker, 66–72.

Oakhill, J., Garnham, A., & Reynolds, D. (2005). Immediate activation of stereotypical gender information. Memory and Cognition, 33, 972–983.

Oberlander, S. E., Black, M. M., & Starr, R. H., Jr. (2007). African American adolescent mothers and grandmothers: A multigenerational approach to parenting. American Journal of Community Psychology, 39, 37–46.

Oberlander, T. F., Reebye, P., Misri, S., Papsdorf, M., Kim, J., & Grunau, R. E. (2007). Externalizing and attentional behaviors in children of depressed mothers treated with a selective serotonin reuptake inhibitor antidepressant during pregnancy. Archives of Pediatric & Adolescent Medicine, 161, 22–29.

Oberlander, T. F., Warburton, W., Misri, S., Aghajanian, J., Hertzman, C. (2006). Neonatal outcomes after prenatal exposure to selective serotonin reuptake inhibitor antidepressants and maternal depression using population-based linked health data. Journal of the American Medical Association, 63, 898–906.

Oberman, L. M., & Ramachandran, V. S. (2007). The simulated social mind: The role of the mirror neuron system and simulation in the social and communicative deficits of autism spectrum disorders. Psychological Bulletin, 133, 310–327.

Obler, L. K. (2013). Developments in the adult years. In J. Berko Gleason & N. B. Ratner (Eds.), The development of language (7th ed.). Boston, MA: Allyn & Bacon.

Ochs, E. (1982). Talking to children in Western Samoa. Language in Society, 11, 77–104.

Ochs, E., & Izquierdo, C. (2009). Responsibility in childhood: Three developmental trajectories. Ethos, 37, 391–413.

Ochse, R. (1990). Before the gates of excellence: The determinants of creative genius. Cambridge, UK: Cambridge University Press.

Oden, M. H. (1968). The fulfillment of promise: 40-year follow-up of the Terman gifted group. Genetic Psychology Monographs, 77, 3–93.

Odendaal, H. J., Steyn, D. W., Elliott, A., & Burd, L. (2009). Combined effects of cigarette smoking and alcohol consumption on perinatal outcome. Gynecologic and Obstetric Investigation, 67, 1–8.

Odgers, C. L., Moffitt, T. E., Broadbent, J. M., Dickson, N., Hancox, R. J., Harrington, H., Poulton, R., Sears, M. R., Thomson, W. M., & Caspi, A. (2008). Female and male antisocial trajectories: From childhood origins to adult outcomes. Development and Psychopathology, 20, 673–716.

Ogbu, J. U. (1981). Origins of human competence: A cultural–ethological perspective. Child Development, 52, 413–429.

Ogbu, J. U. (1994). From cultural differences to differences in cultural frames of reference. In P. M. Greenfield & R. R. Cocking (Eds.), Cross-cultural roots of minority child development. Hillsdale, NJ: Erlbaum.

Ogbu, J. U. (2003). Black American students in an affluent suburb: A study of academic disengagement. Lawrence Erlbaum.

Ogbuanu, I., U., Karmaus, W., Arshad, S. H., Kurukulaaratchy, R. J., & Ewart, S. (2008). Effect of breastfeeding duration on lung function at age 10 years: A prospective birth cohort study, Thorax, 64, 62–66.

Ogletree, S. M., & Drake, R. (2007). College students' video game participation and perceptions: Gender differences and implications. Sex Roles, 56, 537–542.

Ogletree, S. M., Martinez, C. N., Turner, T. R., & Mason, B. (2004). Pokemon: Exploring the role of gender. Sex Roles, 50, 851–859.

O'Hara, M. W. & McCabe, J. E. (2013). Postpartum depression: Current status and future directions. Annual Review of Clinical Psychology, 9, 379–407.

Ohman, A., & Mineka, S. (2003). The malicious serpent: Snakes as a prototypical stimulus for an evolved module of fear. Current Directions in Psychological Science, 12, 5–9.

Okagaki, L. (2001). Triarchic model of minority children's school achievement. Educational psychologist, 36, 9–20.

Oldehinkel, A. J., Verhulst, F. C., & Ormel, J. (2011). Mental health problems during puberty: Tanner stage-related differences in specific symptoms: The TRAILS study. Journal of Adolescence, 34, 73–85.

Oliveira-Pinto, A. V., Santos, R. M., Coutinho, R. A., Oliveira, L. M., Santos, G. B., Alho, A. T. L., . . . Lent, R. (2014). Sexual dimorphism in the human olfactory bulb: Females have more neurons and glial cells than males. PLoS ONE, 9, e111733.

Oller, D. K., & Eilers, R. E. (1988). The role of audition in infant babbling. Child Development, 59, 441–449.

Olmstead, S. B., Billen, R. M., Conrad, K. A., Pasley, K., & Fincham, F. D. (2013). Sex, commitment, and casual sex relationships among college men: A mixed-methods analysis. Archives of Sexual Behavior, 42, 561–571.

Olshansky, S. J., & Carnes, B. A. (2004). In search of the holy grail of senescence. In S. G. Post & R. H. Binstock (Eds.), The fountain of youth: Cultural, scientific, and ethical perspectives on a biomedical goal. New York, NY: Oxford University Press.

Olshansky, S. J., Antonucci, T., Berkman, L., Binstock, R. H., Boersch-Supan, A., Cacioppo, J. T., et al. (2012). Differences in life expectancy due to race and educational differences are widening, and many may not catch up. Health Affairs, 31, 1803–1813.

Olson, J. M., & Zanna, M. P. (Eds.). (2014). Advances in experimental social psychology, Vol. 50 (1st ed.). Waltham, MA: Academic Press.

Olson, J., & Masur, E. F. (2012). Mothers respond differently to infants' familiar versus non-familiar verbal imitations. Journal of Child Language, 39, 731–752.

Olson, K. R., Key, A. C., & Eaton, N. R. (2015). Gender cognition in transgender children. Psychological Science, 26, 467–474.

Oltjenbruns, K. A. (2001). Developmental context of childhood: Grief and regrief phenomena. In M. S. Stroebe, R. O. Hansson, W. Stroebe, & H. Schut (Eds.), Handbook of bereavement research. Consequences, coping, and care. Washington, DC: American Psychological Association.

Olweus, D. (1993). Bullying at school. Oxford, UK: Blackwell.

Olweus, D., & Limber, S. P. (2010). Bullying in school: Evaluation and dissemination of the Olweus Bullying Prevention Program. American Journal of Orthopsychiatry, 80, 124–134.

Omodei, D., & Fontana, L. (2011). Calorie restriction and prevention of age-associated chronic disease. Federation of European Biochemical Societies, 585, 1537–1542.

Onishi, K. H., & Baillargeon, R. (2005). Do 15-month-old infants understand false beliefs? Science, 308, 255–258.

Ono, K. E., Burns, T. G., Bearden, D. J., McManus, S. M., King, H., & Reisner, A. (2016). Sex-based differences as a predictor of recovery trajectories in young athletes after a sports-related concussion. American Journal of Sports Medicine, 44, 748–52.

Ooms, K., De Maeyer, P., & Fack, V. (2015). Listen to the map user: Cognition, memory, and expertise. Cartographic Journal, 52, 3–19.

Oosterwegel, A., & Oppenheimer, L. (1993). The self-system: Developmental changes between and within self-concepts. Hillsdale, NJ: Erlbaum.

Open Science Collaboration (2015). Estimating the reproducibility of psychological science. Science, 349(6251), aac4716-1-aac4716-8.

Ophir, E., Nass, C., & Wagner, A. D. (2009). Cognitive control in media multitaskers. Proceedings of the National Academy of Sciences of the United States of America, 106, 15583–15587.

Organisation for Economic Co-operation and Development (OECD). (2012). Factbook 2012, mean scores by gender in PISA. OECD Publishing.

Orloff, S. F., & Huff, S. M. (2010). Pediatric palliative and hospice care. In C. A. Corr & D. E. Balk (Eds.), Children's encounters with death, bereavement, and coping. New York, NY: Springer.

Orth, L. C., & Martin, R. P. (1994). Interactive effects of student temperament and instruction method on classroom behavior and achievement. Journal of School Psychology, 32, 149–166.

Orth, U., & Robins, R. W. (2014). The development of self-esteem. Current Directions in Psychological Science, 23, 381–387.

Orth, U., Robins, R. W., & Widaman, K. F. (2012). Life-span development of self-esteem and its effects on important life outcomes. Journal of Personality and Social Psychology, 102, 1271–1288.

Orth, U., Trzesniewski, K. H., & Robins, R. W. (2010). Self-esteem development from young adulthood to old age: A cohort-sequential longitudinal study. Journal of Personality and Social Psychology, 98, 645–658.

Ortman, J. M., Velkoff, V. A., & Hogan, H. (2014). An aging nation: The older population in the United States. Population estimates and projections. Current Population Reports, P25–1140, 1028. Retrieved from www.census .gov/prod/2014pubs/p25–1140.pdf.

Osilla, K. C., Miles, J. N. V., Hunter, S. B., & D'Amico, E. J. (2015). The longitudinal relationship between employment and substance use among at-risk adolescents. Journal of Child and Adolescent Behavior, 3, 202.

Österman, K., Björkqvist, K., & Wahlbeck, K. (2014). Twenty-eight years after the complete ban on the physical punishment of children in Finland: Trends and psychosocial concomitants. Aggressive Behavior, 40, 568–581.

Osterman, M. J. K., Martin, J. A., Mathews, T. J., & Hamilton, B. E. (2011). Expanded data from the new birth certificate, 2008. National Vital Statistics Reports; vol 59, no 7. Hyattsville, MD: National Center for Health Statistics.

Osterman, M. J., & Martin, J. A. (2011, April 6). Epidural and spinal anesthesia use during labor: 27-state reporting area, 2008. National Vital Statistics Reports: From the Centers for Disease Control and Prevention, National Center for Health Statistics, 59, 1–13, 16.

Osterweis, M., Solomon, F., & Green, M. (Eds.). (1984). Bereavement: Reactions, consequences, and care. Washington, DC: National Academy Press.

Ostrov, J. M., & Godleski, S. A. (2010). Toward an integrated gender-linked model of aggression subtypes in early and middle childhood. Psychological Review, 117, 233–242.

Oudekerk, B. A., Allen, J. P., Hessel, E. T., & Molloy, L. E. (2015). The cascading development of autonomy and relatedness from adolescence to adulthood. *Child Development, 86,* 472–485.

Ouellet-Morin, I., Danese, A., Bowes, L., Shakoor, S., Ambler, A., Pariante, C. M., et al. (2011). A discordant monozygotic twin design shows blunted cortisol reactivity among bullied children. *Journal of the American Academy of Child & Adolescent Psychiatry, 50,* 574–582.

Overton, W. F. (2010). Life-span development: Concepts and issues. In W. F. Overton (Vol. ed.) & R. M. Lerner (Editor-in-Chief), *Handbook of life-span development: Vol. 1. Cognition, biology, and methods across the lifespan* (pp. 1–29). Hoboken, NJ: Wiley.

Owen, A. M., Coleman, M. R., Boly, M., Davis, M. H., Laureys, S., & Pickard, J. D. (2006). Detecting awareness in the vegetative state. *Science, 313*(5792), 1402.

Owen, J. J., Rhoades, G. K., Stanley, S. M., & Fincham, F. D. (2010). "Hooking up" among college students: Demographic and psychosocial correlates. *Archives of Sexual Behavior, 39,* 653–663.

Owen, M. J., & O'Donovan, M. C. (2003). Schizophrenia and genetics. In R. Plomin, J. C. DeFries, I. W. Craig, & P. McGuffin (Eds.), *Behavioral genetics in the postgenomic era.* Washington, DC: American Psychological Association.

Owsley, C. (2011). Aging and vision. *Vision Research, 51,* 1610–1622.

Özaltin, E., Hill, K., & Subramanian, S. V. (2010). Association of maternal stature with offspring mortality, underweight, and stunting in low- to middle-income countries. *JAMA, 303*(15), 1507–1516.

Ozer, D. J., & Benet-Martinez, V. (2006). Personality and the prediction of consequential outcomes. *Annual Review of Psychology, 57,* 401–421.

Ozonoff, S. (2012). DSM-5 and autism spectrum disorders—two decades of perspectives from the JCPP. *Journal of Child Psychology and Psychiatry and Allied Disciplines, 53,* e4–e6.

Ozonoff, S., Young, G.S., Carter, A, Messinger, D., Yirmiya, N., Zwaigenbaum, L., et al. (2011). Recurrence risk for autism spectrum disorders: A Baby Siblings Research Consortium study. *Pediatrics, 128,* 488–495.

Pace, G. T., & Shafer, K. (2015). Parenting and depression: Differences across parental roles. *Journal of Family Issues, 36,* 1001–1021.

Paciello, M., Fida, R., Tramontano, C., Lupinetti, C., & Caprara, G. V. (2008). Stability and change of moral disengagement and its impact on aggression and violence in late adolescence. *Child Development, 79,* 1288–1309.

Packer, M., & Cole, M. (2015). Culture in development. In M. H. Bornstein & M. E. Lamb (Eds.), *Developmental science: An advanced textbook* (7th ed., pp. 43–111). New York, NY: Psychology Press.

Padilla-Walker, L., & Nelson, L. J. (2012). Black hawk down? Establishing helicopter parenting as a distinct construct from other forms of parental control during emerging adulthood. *Journal of Adolescence, 35,* 1177–1190.

Paetzold, R. L. (2015). Attachment theory in organizational settings. In J. A Simpson & W. S. Rholes (Eds.), *Attachment theory and research: New directions and emerging themes* (pp. 261–286). New York, NY: Guilford.

Pakistani eunuchs to have distinct gender (2009, December 23). *BBC News.* Retrieved from www.news.bbc.co.uk/2/hi/south_asia/8428819.stm.

Palacios, J., Román, M., Moreno, C., León, E., &, Peñarrubia, M. (2014). Differential plasticity in the recovery of adopted children after early adversity. *Child Development Perspectives, 8,* 169–174.

Palacios, P., & Rodríguez, C. (2015). The development of symbolic uses of objects in infants in a triadic context: A pragmatic and semiotic perspective. *Infant and Child Development, 24,* 23–43.

Palkovitz, R. (2002). *Involved fathering and men's adult development: Provisional balances.* Mahwah, NJ: Erlbaum.

Palkovitz, R., Fagan, J., & Hull, J. (2013). Coparenting and children's well-being. In N. J. Cabrera & C. S. Tamis-LeMonda (Eds.), *Handbook of father involvement. Multidisciplinary perspectives* (2nd ed., pp. 202–219). New York, NY: Taylor & Francis.

Palmore, E. B., Burchett, B. M., Fillenbaum, G. G., George, L. K., & Wallman, L. M. (1985). *Retirement. Causes and consequences.* New York, NY: Springer.

Palmsten, K., Hernández-Díaz, S., Chambers, C., Mogun, H., Lai, S., Gilmer, T., & Huybrechts, K. (2015). The most commonly dispensed prescription medications among pregnant women enrolled in the U.S. Medicaid program. *Obstetrics & Gynecology, 126,* 465–473.

Pandya, N., & Bhangaokar, R. (2015). Divinity in children's moral development: An Indian perspective. In L. A Jensen (Ed.), *Moral development in a global world: Research from a cultural-developmental perspective.* (pp. 20–45). New York, NY: Cambridge University Press.

Papadatou, D. (2015). Childhood death and bereavement across cultures. In C. M. Parkes, P. Laungani, & B. Young (Eds.), *Death and bereavement across cultures* (pp. 151–165). New York, NY: Routledge.

Pargament, K. I., Exline, J. J., & Jones, J. W. (Eds.) (2013), *APA handbook of psychology, religion, and spirituality: Vol. 1. Context, theory, and research.* Washington, DC: American Psychological Association.

Park, D. C., & Bischof, G. N. (2013). The aging mind: Neuroplasticity in response to cognitive training. *Dialogues in Clinical Neuroscience, 15,* 109–119.

Park, D. C., & Huang, C. M. (2010). Culture wires the brain: A cognitive neuroscience perspective. *Perspectives on Psychological Science, 5,* 391–400.

Park, D. C., & Reuter-Lorenz, P. (2009). The adaptive brain: Aging and neurocognitive scaffolding. *Annual Review of Psychology, 60,* 173–196.

Park, D. C., Lautenschlager, G., Hedden, T., Davidson, N. S., Smith, A. D., & Smith, P. K. (2002). Models of visuospatial and verbal memory across the adult life span. *Psychological Aging, 17,* 299–320.

Park, D. C., Lodi-Smith, J., Drew, L., Haber, S., Hebrank, A., Bischof, G. N., & Aamodt, W. (2014). The impact of sustained engagement on cognitive function in older adults: The Synapse Project. *Psychological Science, 25,* 103–112.

Park, D. C., Morrell, R. W., Frieske, D., & Kincaid, D. (1992). Medication adherence behaviors in older adults: Effects of external cognitive supports. *Psychology and Aging, 7,* 252–256.

Park, G., Lubinski, D., & Benbow, C. P. (2007). Contrasting intellectual patterns predict creativity in the arts and sciences. *Psychological Science, 18,* 948–952.

Park, Y. C., & Pyszczynski, T. (2016). Cultural universals and differences in dealing with death. In L. A. Harvell & G. S. Nisbett (Eds.), *Denying death. An interdisciplinary approach to terror management theory* (pp. 193–213). New York, NY: Routledge.

Parke, R. D., & Buriel, R. (2006). Socialization in the family: Ethnic and ecological perspectives. In N. Eisenberg (Ed.), W. Damon & R. M. Learner (Eds. in Chief), *Handbook of child psychology: Vol. 3. Social, emotional, and personality development.* Hoboken, NJ: Wiley.

Parke, R. D., & Sawin, D. B. (1976). The father's role in infancy: A reevaluation. *Family Coordinator, 25,* 365–371.

Parke, R. D., Ornstein, P. A., Rieser, J. J., & Zahn-Waxler, C. (1994). The past as prologue: An overview of a century of developmental psychology. In R. D. Parke, P. A. Ornstein, J. J. Rieser, & C. Zahn-Waxler (Eds.), *A century of developmental psychology.* Washington, DC: American Psychological Association.

Parker, K. (2012). *The boomerang generation. Feeling OK about living with Mom and Dad.* Pew Research Center Social and Demographic Trends. Retrieved from www.pewsocialtrends.org/2012/03/15/the-boomerang-generation/.

Parker, K., & Patten, E. (2013). *The sandwich generation. Rising financial burdens for middle-aged Americans.* Pew Research Center Social and Demographic Trends. Retrieved from www.pewsocialtrends.org/2013/01/30/the-sandwich-generation/.

Parker, K., & Wang, W. (2013). *Modern parenthood. Roles of Moms and Dads converge as they balance work and family.* Pew Research Center Social and Demographic Trends. Retrieved from www.pewsocialtrends.org/2013/03/14/modern-parenthood-roles-of-moms-and-dads-converge-as-they-balance-work-and-family/

Parker, K., Horowitz, J. M., & Rohal, M. (2015, December 17). *Parenting in America. Outlooks, worries, aspirations are strongly linked to financial situation.* Retrieved from www.pewsocialtrends.org/files/2015/12/2015–12–17_parenting-in-america_FINAL.pdf.

Parkes, C. M. (1991). Attachment, bonding, and psychiatric problems after bereavement in adult life. In C. M. Parkes, J. Stevenson-Hinde, & P. Marris (Eds.), *Attachment across the life cycle.* London, UK: Tavistock/Routledge.

Parkes, C. M. (1996). *Bereavement: Studies of grief in adult life* (3rd ed.). London, UK: Routledge.

Parkes, C. M. (2000). Comments on Dennis Klass' article "Developing a cross-cultural model of grief." *Omega: Journal of Death and Dying, 41,* 323–326.

Parkes, C. M. (2006). *Love and loss. The roots of grief and its complications.* London, UK: Routledge.

Parkes, C. M., Laungani, P., & Young, B. (Eds.). (2015). *Death and bereavement across cultures* (2nd ed.). New York, NY: Routledge.

Parkes, C. M., & Prigerson, H. G. (2010). *Bereavement. Studies of grief in adult life* (4th ed.). New York, NY: Routledge.

Parkes, C. M., & Weiss, R. S. (1983). *Recovery from bereavement.* New York, NY: Basic Books.

Parkhurst, J. T., & Asher, S. R. (1992). Peer rejection in middle school: Subgroup differences in behavior, loneliness, and interpersonal concerns. *Developmental Psychology, 28,* 231–241.

Parkhurst, J. T., & Hopmeyer, A. (1998). Sociometric popularity and peer-perceived popularity: Two distinct dimensions of peer status. *Journal of Early Adolescence, 18,* 125–144.

Parnham, J. (2001). Lifelong learning: A model for increasing the participation of non-traditional adult learners. *Journal of Further and Higher Education, 25,* 57–65.

Partanen, E., Kujala, T., Tervaniemi, M., & Huotilainen, M. (2013). Prenatal music exposure induces long-term neural effects. *PLoS ONE, 8*(10), e78946.

Parten, M. B. (1932). Social participation among preschool children. *Journal of Abnormal and Social Psychology, 27,* 243–269.

Pascalis, O., de Schonen, S., Morton, J., Deruelle, C., & Fabre-Grenet, M. (1995). Mother's face recognition by neonates: A replication and an extension. *Infant Behavior and Development, 16,* 79–85.

Pasupathi, M., Staudinger, U. M., & Baltes, P. B. (2001). Seeds of wisdom: Adolescents' knowledge and judgment about difficult life problems. *Developmental Psychology, 37,* 351–361.

Patel, D. R., Pratt, H. D., & Greydanus, D. E. (2003). Treatment of adolescents with anorexia nervosa. *Journal of Adolescent Research, 18,* 244–260.

Patel, R., & Brayton, J. T. (2009). Identifying prosodic contrasts in utterances produced by 4-, 7-, and 11-year-old children. *Journal of Speech, Language, and Hearing Research, 52,* 790–801.

Patrick, R. B., & Gibbs, J. C. (2007). Parental expression of disappointment: Should it be a factor in Hoffman's model of parental discipline? *Journal of Genetic Psychology, 168,* 131–145.

Patrick, R. B., & Gibbs, J. C. (2012). Inductive discipline, parental expression of disappointed expectations, and moral identity in adolescence. *Journal of Youth and Adolescence, 41,* 973–983.

Patrick, S. W., Schumacher, R. E., Benneyworth, B. D., Krans, E. E., McAllister, J. M., & Davis, M. M. (2012). Neonatal Abstinence Syndrome and associated health care expenditures: United States, 2000–2009. *Journal of the American Medical Association, 307,* 1934–1940.

Patterson, C. J. (2004). Gay fathers. In M. E. Lamb (Ed.), *The role of the father in child development* (4th ed.). Hoboken, NJ: John Wiley & Sons.

Patterson, C. J., Kupersmidt, J. B., & Vaden, N. A. (1990). Income level, gender, ethnicity, and household composition as predictors of children's school-based competence. *Child Development, 61,* 485–494.

Patterson, G. R. (2005). The next generation of PMTO models. *The Behavior Therapist, 28,* 27–33.

Patterson, G. R. (2008). A comparison of models for interstate wars and for individual violence. *Perspectives on Psychological Science, 3,* 203–223.

Patterson, G. R., DeBaryshe, B. D., & Ramsey, E. (1989). A developmental perspective on antisocial behavior. *American Psychologist, 44,* 329–335.

Patterson, G. R., Forgatch, M. S., & DeGarmo, D. S. (2010). Cascading effects following intervention. *Development and Psychopathology, 22,* 949–970.

Patterson, M. M. (2012). Self-perceived gender typicality, gender-typed attributes, and gender stereotype endorsement in elementary-school-aged children. *Sex Roles, 67,* 422–434.

Patton, J. R. (2000). Educating students with mild mental retardation. *Focus on Autism and Other Developmental Disabilities, 15,* 80–89.

Paul, A. M. (2010). *Origins: How the nine months before birth shape the rest of our lives.* New York, NY: Free Press.

Paul, D. A., Lee, K. H., Locke, R. G., Bartoshesky, L., Walrath, J., & Stefano, J. L. (2006). Increasing illness severity in very low birth weight infants over a 9-year period. *BMC Pediatrics, 6,* Retrieved from biomedcentral.com/1471-2431/6/2.

Paul, E. L., & Hayes, A. (2002). The casualties of 'casual' sex: A qualitative exploration of the phenomenology of college students' hookups. *Journal of Social and Personal Relationships, 19,* 639–661.

Paul, E. L., McManus, B., & Hayes, A. (2000). "Hookups": Characteristics and correlates of college students' spontaneous and anonymous sexual experiences. *Journal of Sex Research, 37,* 76–88.

Pauli-Pott, U., Mertesacker, B., & Beckmann, D. (2004). Predicting the development of infant emotionality from maternal characteristics. *Development and Psychopathology, 16,* 19–42.

Paulson, J. (2013). Environmental toxicants and neurocognitive development. In M. L. Batshaw, N. J. Roizen, & G. R. Lotrecchiano (Eds.), *Children with disabilities* (7th ed., pp. 37–46). Baltimore, MD: Paul H. Brookes.

Paulus, M., Tsalas, N., Proust, J., & Sodian, B. (2014). Metacognitive monitoring of oneself and others: Developmental changes during childhood and adolescence. *Journal of Experimental Child Psychology, 122,* 153–165.

Paz-Alonso, P. E., Larson, R. P., Castelli, P., Alley, D., & Goodman, G. (2009). In M. L. Courage & N. Cowan (Eds.), *The development of memory in infancy and childhood* (pp. 197–240). New York, NY: Psychology Press.

Pea, R., Nass, C., Meheula, L., Rance, M., Kumar, A., Bamford, H., et al. (2012). Media use, face-to-face communication, media multitasking, and social well-being among 8- to 12-year-olds. *Developmental Psychology, 48,* 327–336.

Pearce, K. A., & Denney, N. W. (1984). A lifespan study of classification preference. *Journal of Gerontology, 39,* 458–464.

Pearlin, L. I. (1980). Life strains and psychological distress among adults. In N. J. Smelser & E. H. Erikson (Eds.), *Themes of work and love in adulthood.* Cambridge, MA: Harvard University Press.

Pears, K. C., & Moses, L. J. (2003). Demographics, parenting, and theory of mind in preschool children. *Social Development, 12,* 1–19.

Pearson, J. D., Morell, C. H., Gordon-Salant, S., Brant, L. J., Metter, E. J., Klein, L., et al. (1995). Gender differences in a longitudinal study of age-associated hearing loss. *Journal of the Acoustical Society of America, 97,* 1196–1205.

Pearson, P. D., Barr, R., & Kamil, M. L. (Eds.). (2011). *Handbook of reading research: Vol. 4.* New York, NY: Routledge.

Pedersen, N. L., McClearn, G. E., Plomin, R., & Friberg, L. (1985). Separated fraternal twins: Resemblance for cognitive abilities. *Behavior Genetics, 15,* 407–419.

Pediatrics Now (2016). *Puberty resource page.* Available at www.pediatricsnow.com/2009/12/puberty-resource-page.

Pedula, K. L., Coleman, A. L., Hillier, T. A., Ensrud, K. E., Nevitt, M. C., Hochberg, M. C., et al. (2006). Visual acuity, contract sensitivity, and mortality in older women: Study of osteoporotic fractures. *Journal of American Geriatric Society, 54,* 1871–1877.

Peeples, D. R., & Teller, D. Y. (1975). Color vision and brightness discrimination in two-month-old human infants. *Science, 189,* 1102–1103.

Pekrun, R., Elliot, A. J., & Maier, M. A. (2009). Achievement goals and achievement emotions: Testing a model of their joint relations with academic performance. *Journal of Educational Psychology, 101,* 115–135.

Pelleboer-Gunnink, H. A., Van der Valk, I. E., Branje, S. J. T., Van Doorn, M. D., & Dekovic, M. (2015). Effectiveness and moderators of the preventive intervention kids in divorce situations: A randomized controlled trial. *Journal of Family Psychology, 29,* 799–805.

Pellegrini, A. D. (1996). *Observing children in their natural worlds: A methodological primer.* Mahwah, NJ: Erlbaum.

Pellegrini, A. D., Long, J. D., Roseth, C. J., Bohn, C. M., & Van Ryzin, M. (2007). A short-term longitudinal study of preschoolers' (*Homo sapiens*) sex segregation: The role of physical activity, sex, and time. *Journal of Comparative Psychology, 121,* 282–289.

Pellegrini, A. D. (2009). Research and policy on children's play. *Child Development Perspectives, 3,* 131–136.

Pellicano, E. (2010). Individual differences in executive function and central coherence predict developmental changes in theory of mind in autism. *Developmental Psychology, 46,* 530–544.

Pelphrey, K. A., Shultz, S., Hudac, C. M., & Vander Wyk, B. C. (2011). Research review: Constraining heterogeneity: The social brain and its development in autism spectrum disorder. *Journal of Child Psychology and Psychiatry, 52,* 631–644.

Pénicaud, S., Klein, D., Zatorre, R. J., Chen, J., Witcher, P., Hyde, K., et al. (2013). Structural brain changes linked to delayed first language acquisition in congenitally deaf individuals. *NeuroImage, 66,* 42–49.

Penner, S. G. (1987). Parental responses to grammatical and ungrammatical child utterances. *Child Development, 58,* 376–384.

Peplau, L. A., & Fingerhut, A. W. (2007). The close relationships of lesbians and gay men. *Annual Review of Psychology, 58,* 405–424.

Pepper, S. C. (1942). *World hypotheses: A study in evidence.* Berkeley, CA: University of California Press.

Pereira, A. C., Huddleston, D. E., Brickman, A. M., Sosunov, A. A., Hen, R., McKhann, G. M., et al. (2007). An in vivo correlate of exercise-induced neurogenesis in the adult dentate gyrus. *Proceedings of the National Academy of Sciences, 104,* 5638–5643.

Perera, F. P., Tang, D., Rauh, V., Tu, Y. H., Tsai, W. Y., Becker, M., & Lederman, S. A. (2007). Relationship between polycyclic aromatic hydrocarbon-DNA adducts, environmental tobacco smoke, and child development in the World Trade Center cohort. *Environmental Health Perspectives, 115,* 1497–1502.

Perera, F., & Herbstman, J. (2011). Prenatal environmental exposures, epigenetics, and disease. *Reproductive Toxicology, 31,* 363–373.

Perez-Granados, D. R., & Callanan, M. A. (1997). Conversations with mothers and siblings: Young children's semantic and conceptual development. *Developmental Psychology, 33,* 120–134.

Perfetti, C. A. (1999). Cognitive research and the misconceptions of reading education. In J. Oakhill & R. Beard (Eds.), *Reading development and the teaching of reading* (pp. 42–58). Malden, MA: Blackwell.

Perkins, H. W., & DeMeis, D. K. (1996). Gender and family effects on the "second-shift" domestic activity of college educated young adults. *Gender & Society, 10,* 78–93.

Perlmutter, M. (1986). A life-span view of memory. In P. B. Baltes, D. L. Featherman, & R. M. Lerner (Eds.), *Life-span development and behavior: Vol. 7.* Hillsdale, NJ: Erlbaum.

Perls, T., & Handelsman, D. J. (2015). Disease mongering of age-associated declines in testosterone and growth hormone levels. *Journal of the American Geriatrics Society, 63,* 809–811.

Perry, H. L. (1993). Mourning and funeral customs of African Americans. In D. P. Irish, K. F. Lundquist, & V. J. Nelson (Eds.), *Ethnic variations in dying, death, and grief: Diversity in universality.* Washington, DC: Taylor and Francis.

Perry, W. G., Jr. (1970). *Forms of intellectual and ethical development in the college years: A scheme.* New York, NY: Holt, Rinehart & Winston.

Persson, G., & Svanborg, A. (1992). Marital coital activity in men at the age of 75: Relation to somatic, psychiatric, and social factors at the age of 70. *Journal of the American Geriatrics Society, 40,* 439–444.

Peters, A. (2002). The effects of normal aging on myelin and nerve fibers: A review. *Journal of Neurocytology, 31,* 581–593.

Petersen, I. T., Bates, J. E., Goodnight, J. A., Dodge, K. A., Lansford, J. E., Pettit, G. S., et al. (2012). Interaction between serotonin transporter polymorphism (5-HTTLPR) and stressful life events in adolescents' trajectories of anxious/depressed symptoms. *Developmental Psychology, 48,* 1463–1475.

Petersen, R. C., Smith, G. E., Waring, S. C., & Ivnik, R. J. (1997). Aging, memory, and mild cognitive impairment. *International Psycho-Geriatrics, 65*(Supplement).

Petersen, R. C., Stevens, J. C., Ganguli, M., Tangalos, E. G., Cummings, J. L., & DeKosky, S. T. (2001). Early detection of dementia: Mild cognitive impairment. *Neurology, 56,* 1133–1142.

Peterson, C. C., & Rideout, R. (1998). Memory for medical emergencies experienced by 1 and 2-year-olds. *Developmental Psychology, 34,* 1059–1072.

Peterson, C. C., & Siegal, M. (1999). Representing inner worlds: Theory of mind in autistic, deaf, and normal hearing children. *Psychological Science, 10,* 126–129.

Peterson, C. C., & Siegal, M. (2002). Mind reading and moral awareness in popular and rejected preschoolers. *British Journal of Developmental Psychology, 20,* 205–224.

Peterson, C. C., & Slaughter, V. (2003). Opening windows into the mind: Mothers' preferences for mental state explanations and children's theory of mind. *Cognitive Development, 18,* 399–429.

Peterson, C. C., & Wellman, H. M. (2009). From fancy to reason: Scaling deaf and hearing children's understanding of theory of mind and pretense. *British Journal of Developmental Psychology, 27,* 297–310.

Peterson, C. C., Wellman, H. M., & Slaughter, V. (2012). The mind behind the message: Advancing theory-of-mind scales for typically developing children, and those with deafness, autism, or Asperger syndrome. *Child Development, 83,* 469–485.

Peterson, C., Warren, K. L., & Short, M. M. (2011). Infantile amnesia across the years: A 2-year follow-up of children's earliest memories. *Child Development, 82,* 1092–1105.

Peterson, J. L., & Hyde, J. S. (2010). A meta-analytic review of research on gender differences in sexuality, 1993–2007. *Psychological Bulletin, 136,* 21–38.

Peterson, P. L. (1977). Interactive effects of student anxiety, achievement orientation, and teacher behavior on student achievement and attitude. *Journal of Educational Psychology, 69,* 779–792.

Petitto, L. A., & Marentette, P. F. (1991). Babbling in the manual mode: Evidence for the ontogeny of language. *Science, 251,* 1493–1496.

Petitto, L. A., Berens, M. S., Kovelman, I., Dubins, M. H., Jasinska, K., & Shalinsky, M. (2012). The "Perceptual Wedge Hypothesis" as the basis for bilingual babies' phonetic processing advantage: New insights from fNIRS brain imaging. *Brain and Language, 121,* 130–143.

Pettitt, L. M. (2004). Gender intensification of peer socialization during puberty. *New Directions for Child and Adolescent Development, 106,* 23–34.

Pew Research Center (2014, April). *Older adults and technology use.* Retrieved from www.pewinternet.org/2014/04/03/older-adults-and-technology-use/.

Pew Research Center (2014, March). *Millennials in adulthood: Detached from institutions, networked with friends.* Retrieved from www.pewsocialtrends.org/files/2014/03/2014-03-07_generations-report-version-for-web.pdf.

Pew Research Center. (2013, March 14). *Modern parenthood: Roles of moms and dads converge as they balance work and family.* Retrieved from www.pewsocialtrends.org/files/2013/03/FINAL_modern_parenthood_03-2013.pdf.

Phares, V. (1999). *"Poppa" psychology. The role of fathers in children's mental well-being.* Westport, CT: Praeger.

Phelan, S., Phipps, M. G., Abrams, B., Darroch, F., Schaffner, A., & Wing, R. R. (2011). Practitioner advice and gestational weight gain. *Journal of Women's Health, 20,* 585–591.

Phillips, D. A. (2015). 'Facts, fantasies, and the future of child care' revisited. *Observer, 28,* 15–17.

Phillips, L. H., Allen, R., Bull, R., Hering, A., Kliegel, M., & Channon, S. (2015). Older adults have difficulty in decoding sarcasm. *Developmental Psychology, 51,* 1840–1852.

Phillips, L. M., Norris, S. P., & Anderson, J. (2008). Unlocking the door: Is parents' reading to children the key to early literacy development? *Canadian Psychology, 49,* 82–88.

Phillips, M. (1997). What makes schools effective? A comparison of the relationships of communitarian climate and academic climate to mathematics achievement and attendance during middle school. *American Educational Research Journal, 34,* 633–662.

Phillips, S. D. (1982). Career exploration in adulthood. *Journal of Vocational Behavior, 20,* 129–140.

Phillips, T. M., & Pittman, J. F. (2003). Identity processes in poor adolescents: Exploring the linkages between economic disadvantage and the primary task of adolescence. *Identity, 3*, 115–129.
Phinney, J. S. (1993). A three-stage model of ethnic identity development in adolescence. In M. E. Bernal, & G. P. Knight (Eds.), *Ethnic identity: Formation and transmission among Hispanics and other minorities*. Albany, NY: State University of New York Press.
Phinney, J. S. (2006). Ethnic identity exploration in emerging adulthood. In J. J. Arnett, & J. L. Tanner (Eds.), *Emerging adults in America: Coming of age in the 21st century*. Washington, DC: American Psychological Association.
Piaget, J. (1926). *The child's conception of the world*. New York, NY: Harcourt, Brace & World.
Piaget, J. (1950). *The psychology of intelligence*. New York, NY: Harcourt, Brace & World.
Piaget, J. (1952). *The origins of intelligence in children*. New York, NY: International Universities Press.
Piaget, J. (1965). *The moral judgment of the child*. New York, NY: Free Press. (Original work published 1932).
Piaget, J. (1970). Piaget's theory. In P. H. Mussen (Ed.), *Carmichael's manual of child psychology: Vol. 1*. New York, NY: Wiley.
Piaget, J. (1971). *Biology and knowledge*. Edinburgh, UK: Edinburgh University Press.
Piaget, J. (1972). Intellectual evolution from adolescence to adulthood. *Human Development, 15*, 1–12.
Piaget, J. (1977). The role of action in the development of thinking. In W. F. Overton & J. M. Gallagher (Eds.), *Knowledge and development: Vol. 1*. New York, NY: Plenum.
Piaget, J. (1978). *The development of thought: Equilibration of cognitive structures*. Oxford, UK: Blackwell.
Piaget, J. (1985). *The equilibration of cognitive structures: The central problem of intellectual development* (T. Brown & K. J. Thampy, Trans.). Chicago, IL: University of Chicago Press.
Piaget, J., & Inhelder, B. (1956). *The child's conception of space*. New York, NY: Norton.
Piaget, J., & Inhelder, B. (1969). In H. Weaver (Ed.), *The psychology of the child* (H. Weaver, Trans.). New York, NY: Basic Books. (Original work published 1966).
Piatczanyn, S. A., Bennett, K. M., & Soulsby, L. K. (2016). 'We were in a partnership that wasn't recognized by anyone else': Examining the effects of male gay partner bereavement, masculinity, and identity. *Men and Masculinities, 19*, 167–191.
Pierce, K., Carter, C., Weinfeld, M., Desmond, J., Hazin, R., Bjork, R., & Gallagher, N. (2011). Detecting, studying, and treating autism early: The one-year well-baby check-up approach. *Journal of Pediatrics, 159*, 458–465.
Pietromonaco, P. R., DeBuse, C. J., & Powers, S. I. (2013). Does attachment get under the skin? Adult romantic attachment and cortisol responses to stress. *Current Directions in Psychological Science, 22*, 63–68.
Pietschnig, J., & Voracek, M. (2015). One century of global IQ gains: A formal meta-analysis of the Flynn effect (1909–2013). *Perspectives on Psychological Science, 10*, 282–306.
Pigott, T. A. (2002). Anxiety disorders. In S. G. Kornstein & A. H. Clayton (Eds.), *Women's mental health: A comprehensive textbook* (pp. 195–221). New York, NY: The Guilford Press.
Pilgrim, N. A., & Blum, R. W. (2012). Protective and risk factors associated with adolescent sexual and reproductive health in the English-speaking Caribbean: A literature review. *Journal of Adolescent Health, 50*, 5–23.
Pillard, R. C., & Bailey, J. M. (1998). Human sexual orientation has a heritable component. *Human Biology, 70*, 347–365.
Pimenta, F., Leal, I., Maroco, J., & Ramos, C. (2011). Representations and perceived consequences of menopause by peri- and post-menopausal Portuguese women: A qualitative research. *Health Care for Women International, 32*, 1111–1125.
Pimple, K. D. (Ed.). (2008). *Research ethics*. Burlington, VT: Ashgate.
Pineda, J. A. (Ed.). (2009). *Mirror neuron systems: The role of mirroring processes in social cognition*. Totowa, NJ: Humana Press.
Pinhas, L., Katzman, D. K., Dimitropoulos, G., & Woodside, D. B. (2007). Bingeing and bulimia nervosa in children and adolescents. In T. Jaffa & B. McDermott (Eds.), *Eating disorders in children and adolescents*. Cambridge, UK: Cambridge University Press.
Pinker, S. (1994). *The language instinct*. New York, NY: Harper Collins.
Pinker, S. (1995). Language acquisition. In L. R. Gleitman, M. Liberman, & D. N. Osherson (Eds.), *An invitation to cognitive science: Vol. 1. Language* (2nd ed., pp. 135–182). Cambridge, MA: MIT Press.
Pinquart, M., & Sorenson, S. (2000). Influences of socioeconomic status, social network, competence, or subjective competence in later life: A meta-analysis. *Psychology and Aging, 15*, 187–224.
Pinquart, M., & Sorensen, S. (2003). Associations of stressors and uplifts of caregiving with caregiver burden and depressive mood: A meta-analysis. *Journal of Gerontology: Psychological Sciences*, 58B, 112–128.
Pinquart, M., & Sorensen, S. (2006). Gender differences in caregiver stressors, social resources, and health: An updated meta-analysis. *Journals of Gerontology: Psychological Sciences, 61*B, P33–P45.
Pinto, J. M., Wroblewski, K. E., Kern, D. W., Schumm, L. P., & McClintock, M. K. (2014). Olfactory dysfunction predicts 5-year mortality in older adults. *PLoS ONE, 9*, e107541.
Piontelli, A. (2015). *Development of normal fetal movements*. Milano: Springer Milan.
Pipe, M. E., Thierry, K., & Lamb, M.-E. (2007). The development of event memory: Implications for child witness testimony. In M. P. Toglia, J. D. Read, D. F. Ross, & R. C. L. Lindsay (Eds.), *Handbook of eyewitness psychology. Volume 1: Memory for events*. Mahwah, NJ: Lawrence Erlbaum.
Pipe, M., & Salmon, K. (2009). Memory development in the forensic context. In M. L. Courage & N. Cowan (Eds.), *The development of memory in infancy and childhood* (pp. 241–282). New York, NY: Psychology Press.
Piper, W. E., Ogrodniczuk, J. S., Joyce, A. S., & Weideman, R. (2011). *Short-term group therapies for complicated grief. Two research-based models*. Washington, DC: American Psychological Association.
Pipp, S., Easterbrooks, M. A., & Harmon, R. J. (1992). The relation between attachment and knowledge of self and mother in one-year-old infants to three-year-old infants. *Child Development, 63*, 738–750.
Planalp, E. M., & Braungart-Rieker, J. (2016). Determinants of father involvement with young children: Evidence from the Early Childhood Longitudinal Study–birth cohort. *Journal of Family Psychology, 30*, 135–146.
Plassman, B. L., Langa, K. M., Fisher, G. G., Heeringa, S. G., Weir, D. R., Ofstedal, M. B., et al. (2008). Prevalence of cognitive impairment without dementia in the United States. *Annals of Internal Medicine, 148*, 427–434.
Pleck, J. H., & Masciadrelli, B. P. (2004). Paternal involvement by U.S. residential fathers: Levels, sources, and consequences. In M. E. Lamb (Ed.), *The role of the father in child development* (4th ed.). Hoboken, NJ: John Wiley & Sons.
Plomin, R. (1990). *Nature and nurture. An introduction to human behavioral genetics*. Pacific Grove, CA: Brooks/Cole.
Plomin, R. (2013). Child development and molecular genetics: 14 years later. *Child Development, 84*, 104–120.
Plomin, R., & Bergeman, C. S. (1991). The nature of nurture: Genetic influence on environmental measures. *Behavioral and Brain Sciences, 14*, 373–385.
Plomin, R., & Davis, O. S. P. (2009). The future of genetics in psychology and psychiatry: Microarrrays, genome-wide association, and non-coding RNA. *Journal of Child Psychology and Psychiatry, 50*, 63–71.
Plomin, R., & Deary, I. J. (2015). Genetics and intelligence differences: Five special findings. *Molecular Psychiatry, 20*, 98–108.
Plomin, R., Corley, R., DeFries, J. C., & Fulker, D. W. (1990). Individual differences in television viewing in early childhood: Nature as well as nurture. *Psychological Science, 1*, 371–377.
Plomin, R., DeFries, J. C., & Loehlin, J. C. (1977). Genotype–environment interaction and correlation in the analysis of human behavior. *Psychological Bulletin, 84*, 309–322.
Plomin, R., DeFries, J. C., Knopik, V. S., & Neiderhiser, J. M. (2013). *Behavioral genetics* (6th ed.). New York, NY: Worth.
Plomin, R., DeFries, J. C., McClearn, G. E., & McGuffin, P. (2008). *Behavioral genetics* (5th ed.). New York, NY: Worth.
Plomin, R., Pedersen, N. L., McClearn, G. E., Nesselroade, J. R., & Bergeman, C. S. (1988). EAS temperaments during the last half of the life span: Twins reared apart and twins reared together. *Psychology and Aging, 3*, 43–50.
Ploughman, M. (2008). Exercise is brain food: The effects of physical activity on cognitive function. *Developmental Neurorehabilitation, 11*, 236–240.
Pluhar, E. I., DiIorio, C. K., & McCarty, F. (2008). Correlates of sexuality communication among mothers and 6- to 12-year-old children. *Child: Care, Health and Development, 34*, 283–290.
Poehlmann, J., & Fiese, B. H. (2001). The interaction of maternal and infant vulnerabilities on developing attachment relationships. *Development and Psychopathology, 13*, 1–11.
Polakowski, L. L., Akinbami, L. J., & Mendola, P. (2009). Prenatal smoking cessation and the risk of delivering preterm and small-for-gestational-age newborns. *Obstetrics & Gynecology, 114*, 318–325.
Polderman, T. J. C., Benyamin, B., de Leeuw, C. A., Sullivan, P. F., van Bochoven, A., Visscher, P. M., & Posthuma, D. (2015). Meta-analysis of the heritability of human traits based on fifty years of twin studies. *Nature Genetics, 47*, 702–709.
Pomerantz, E. M., Altermatt, E. R., & Saxon, J. L. (2002). Making the grade but feeling distressed: Gender differences in academic performance and internal distress. *Journal of Educational Psychology, 94*, 396–404.
Pomerantz, E. M., Qin, L., Wang, Q., & Chen, H. (2009). American and Chinese early adolescents' inclusion of their relationships with their parents in their self-construals. *Child Development, 80*, 792–807.
Pomerantz, E. M., Qin, L., Wang, Q., & Chen, H. (2011). Changes in early adolescents' sense of responsibility to their parents in the United States and China: Implications for academic functioning. *Child Development, 82*, 1136–1151.
Pomerantz, E. M., Ruble, D. N., Frey, K. S., & Grenlich, F. (1995). Meeting goals and confronting conflict: Children's changing perceptions of social comparison. *Child Development, 66*, 723–738.
Pomerleau, A., Bolduc, D., Malcuit, G., & Cossette, L. (1990). Pink or blue: Environmental gender stereotypes in the first two years of life. *Sex Roles, 22*, 359–367.
Ponton, L. (2001). *The sex lives of teenagers: Revealing the secret world of adolescent boys and girls*. New York, NY: Plume.
Poon, H. F., Calabrese, V., Scapagnini, G., & Butterfield, D. A. (2004). Free radicals: Key to brain aging and heme oxygenase as a cellular response to oxidative stress. *Journal of Gerontology Series A: Medical Science, 59A*, 478–493.
Poortman, A., & Van Der Lippe, T. (2009). Attitudes toward housework and child care and the gendered division of labor. *Journal of Marriage & Family, 71*, 526–541.
Porcher, N. (2014, November 10). LBDA clarifies autopsy report on comedian, Robin Williams. Retrieved from www.lbda.org/content/lbda-clarifies-autopsy-report-comedian-robin-williams, pp. 566–606.
Porfeli, E. J., & Vondracek, F. W. (2009). Career development, work, and occupational success. In M. C. Smith (Ed.) & N. DeFrates-Densch (Asst. Ed.), *Handbook of research on adult learning and development*. New York, NY: Routledge.
Porter, R. H. (1999). Olfaction and human kin recognition. *Genetica, 104*, 259–263.
Porter, R. H., Makin, J. W., Davis, L. B., & Christensen, K. M. (1992). Breast-fed infants respond to olfactory clues from their own mother and unfamiliar lactating females. *Infant Behavior and Development, 15*, 85–93.
Portes, A., & MacLeod, D. (1996). Educational progress of children of immigrants: The roles of class, ethnicity, and school context. *Sociology of Education, 69*, 255–275.
Portion Distortion. (2012). Retrieved from www.nhlbi .nih.gov/health/educational/wecan/portion/
Posada, G., Longoria, N., Cocker, C., & Lu, T. (2011). Attachment ties in military families: Mothers' perception of interactions with their children, stress, and social competence. In S. M. Wadsworth, & D. Riggs (Eds.), *Risk and resilience in U.S. military families*. New York, NY: Springer Science+Business Media.
Posada, G., Lu, T., Trumbell, J., Kaloustian, G., Trudel, M., Plata, S. J., . . . Lay, K. L. (2013). Is the secure base phenomenon evident here, there, and anywhere?

A cross-cultural study of child behavior and experts' definitions. *Child Development, 84*, 1896–1905.
Potti, S., Jain, N. J., Mastrogiannis, D. S., & Dandolu, V. (2012). Obstetric outcomes in pregnant women with diabetes versus hypertensive disorders versus both. *Journal of Maternal-Fetal and Neonatal Medicine, 25*, 385–388.
Poulin-Dubois, D., & Goodz, N. (2001). Language differentiation in bilingual infants: Evidence from babbling. In J. Cenoz & F. Genesee (Eds.) *Trends in bilingual acquisition* (pp. 95–106). Amsterdam: Netherlandsing Company.
Poulin-Dubois, D., & Serbin, L. A. (2006). Infants' knowledge about gender stereotypes and categories. *Enfance, 58*, 283–310.
Poulin-Dubois, D., Serbin, L. A., Eichstedt, J. A., Sen, M. G., & Beissel, C. F. (2002). Men don't put on make-up: Toddlers' knowledge of the gender stereotyping of household activities. *Social Development, 11*, 166–181.
Powell, M. P., & Schulte, T. (2011). Turner syndrome. In S. Goldstein & C. R. Reynolds (Eds.), *Handbook of neurodevelopmental and genetic disorders in children* (2nd ed., pp. 261–275). New York, NY: Guilford.
Power, F. C., & Higgins-D'Alessandro, A. (2008). The Just Community approach to moral education and the moral atmosphere of the school. In L. P. Nucci & D. Narvaez (Eds.), *Handbook of moral and character education*. New York, NY: Routledge.
Power, L., & McKinney, C. (2013). Emerging adult perceptions of parental religiosity and parenting practices: Relationships with emerging adult religiosity and psychological adjustment. *Psychology of Religion and Spirituality, 5*, 99–109.
Powers, H. J. (2007). Folic acid under scrutiny. *British Journal of Nutrition, 98*, 665–666.
Pratt, M. W., & Norris, J. E. (1999). Moral development in maturity. Life-span perspectives on the processes of successful aging. In T. M. Hess & F. Blanchard-Fields (Eds.), *Social cognition and aging*. San Diego, CA: Academic Press.
Pratt, M. W., Diessner, R., Hunsberger, B., Pancer, S. M., & Savoy, K. (1991). Four pathways in the analysis of adult development and aging: Comparing analyses of reasoning about personal-life dilemmas. *Psychology and Aging, 4*, 666–675.
Pratt, M. W., Diessner, R., Pratt, A., Hunsberger, B., & Pancer, S. M. (1996). Moral and social reasoning and perspective taking in later life: A longitudinal study. *Psychology and Aging, 11*, 66–73.
Pratt, M. W., Hunsberger, B., Pancer, S. M., & Alisat, S. (2003). A longitudinal analysis of personal values socialization: Correlates of a moral self-ideal in late adolescence. *Social Development, 12*, 563–585.
Prenatal alcohol exposure patterns and alcohol-related birth defects and growth deficiencies: A prospective study. *Alcoholism: Clinical and Experimental Research*, 36(4), 670–676.
Pressley, M., & Hilden, K. (2006). Cognitive strategies. In D. Kuhn & R. Siegler (Vol. Eds.), *Handbook of child psychology: Vol. 2. Cognition, perception, and language*. Hoboken, NJ: Wiley and Sons.
Pressley, M., Levin, J. R., & Ghatala, E. S. (1984). Memory strategy monitoring in adults and children. *Journal of Verbal Learning and Verbal Behavior, 23*, 270–288.
Pribis, P., Burtnack, C. A., McKenzie, S. O., & Thayer, J. (2010). Trends in body fat, body mass index and physical fitness among male and female college students. *Nutrients, 2*, 1075–1085.
Price, D. W. W., & Goodman, G. S. (1990). Visiting the wizard: Children's memory for a recurring event. *Child Development, 61*, 664–680.
Price, R. H., Friedland, D. S., & Vinokur, A. D. (1998). Job loss: Hard times and eroded identity. In J. H. Harvey (Ed.), *Perspectives on loss: A sourcebook*. Philadelphia, PA: Brunner/ Mazel.
Priess, H. A., Lindberg, S. M., & Hyde, J. S. (2009). Adolescent gender-role identity and mental health: Gender intensification revisited. *Child Development, 80*, 1531–1544.
Prigerson, H. G., Vanderwerker, L. C., & Maciejewski, P. K. (2008). A case for inclusion of Prolonged Grief Disorder in DSM-V. In M. Stroebe, R. Hansson, H. Schut, & W. Stroebe (Eds.), *Handbook of bereavement research and practice: Advances in theory and intervention*. Washington, DC: American Psychological Association.
Prinstein, M. J., Meade, C. S., & Cohen, G. L. (2003). Adolescent oral sex, peer popularity, and perceptions of best friends' sexual behavior. *Journal of Pediatric Psychology, 28*, 243–249.
Prinstein, M. J., Rancourt, D., Guerry, J. D., & Browne, C. R. (2009). Peer reputations and psychological adjustment. In K. H. Rubin, W. M. Bukowski, & B. Laursen (Eds.), *Handbook of peer interactions, relationships, and groups*. New York, NY: Guilford.
Prinz, W., Beisert, M., & Herwig, A. (Eds.). (2013). Action science: Foundations of an emerging discipline. In W. Prinz, M. Beisert, & A. Herwig (Eds.), *Action science. Foundations of an emerging discipline*. Cambridge, MA: MIT Press.
Prior, A., & MacWhinney, B. (2010). A bilingual advantage in task switching. *Bilingualism: Language and Cognitive, 13*, 253–262.
Prior, E., Santhakumaran, S., Gale, C., Phillipps, L. H., Modi, N., & Hyde, M. J. (2012). Breastfeeding after cesarean delivery: A systematic review and meta-analysis of world literature. *American Journal of Clinical Nutrition, 95*, 1113–1135.
Pritchard, D. J., & Korf, B. R. (2008). *Medical genetics at a glance* (2nd ed.). Malden, MA: Blackwell.
Proctor, R. M. J., & Burnett, P. C. (2004). Measuring cognitive and dispositional characteristics of creativity in elementary students. *Creativity Research Journal, 16*, 421–429.
Proffitt, J. B., Coley, J. D., & Medin, D. L. (2000). Expertise and category-based induction. *Journal of Experimental Psychology: Learning, Memory, and Cognition, 26*, 811–828.
Protzko, J., Aronson, J., & Blair, C. (2013). How to make a young child smarter: Evidence from the Database of Raising Intelligence. *Perspectives on Psychological Science, 8*, 25–40.
Pruden, S. M., Hirsh-Pasek, K., Golinkoff, R. M., & Hennon, E. A. (2006). The birth of words: Ten-month-olds learn words through perceptual salience. *Child Development, 77*, 266–280.
Pudrovska, T., Schieman, S., & Carr, D. (2006). Strains of singlehood in later life: Do race and gender matter? *Journals of Gerontology: Social Sciences, 61*B, S315–S322.
Pujol, J., Soriano-Mas, C., Ortiz, H., Sebastián-Gallés, N., Losilla, J. M., & Deus, J. (2006). Myelination of language-related areas in the developing brain. *Neurology, 66*, 339–343.
Pulfrey, C., & Butera, F. (2013). Why neoliberal values of self-enhancement lead to cheating in higher education: A motivational account. *Psychological Science, 24*, 2153–2162.
Pulkkinen, L., & Kokko, K. (2012). Foundational issues in longitudinal data collection. In B. Laursen, T. D. Little, & N. A. Card (Eds.), *Handbook of developmental research methods* (pp. 129–147). New York, NY: Guilford.
Puma, M., Bell, S., Cook, R., Heid, C., Broene, P., Jenkins, F., et al. (2012). *Third grade follow-up to the Head Start impact study final report, executive summary* (OPRE Report # 2012–45b). Washington, DC: Office of Planning, Research and Evaluation, Administration for Children and Families, U.S. Department of Health and Human Services.
Punnoose, A. R., Lynm, C., & Golub, R. M. (2012). Adult hearing loss. *Journal of the American Medical Association, 307*, 1215.
Purifoy, F. E., Grodsky, A., & Giambra, L. M. (1992). The relationship of sexual daydreaming to sexual activity, sexual drive, and sexual attitudes for women across the life-span. *Archives of Sexual Behavior, 21*, 369–385.
Putnam, F. W. (2003). Ten-year research update review: Child sexual abuse. *Journal of the American Academy of Child & Adolescent Psychiatry, 42*, 269–278.
Putnam, R. D. (2015). *Our kids. The American Dream in crisis*. New York, NY: Simon & Schuster.
Putnam, S. P., Gartstein, M. A., & Rothbart, M. K. (2006). Measurement of fine-grained aspects of toddler temperament: The Early Childhood Behavior Questionnaire. *Infant Behavior and Development, 29*, 386–401.
Pyszczynski, T., Solomon, S., & Greenberg, J. (2003). *In the wake of 9/11: The psychology of terror*. Washington, DC: American Psychological Association.
Qin, J., Yang, T., Xiao, S., Tan, H., Feng, T., Fu, H. (2014). Reported estimates of adverse pregnancy outcomes among women with and without syphilis: A systematic review and meta-analysis. *PLoS ONE* 9(7), e102203.
Qu, Y., Fuligni, A. J., Galvan, A., & Telzer, E. H. (2015). Buffering effect of positive parent-child relationships on adolescent risk taking: A longitudinal neuroimaging investigation. *Developmental Cognitive Neuroscience, 15*, 26–34.
Qualls, S. H. (2016). Caregiving families within the long-term services and support system for older adults. *American Psychologist, 71*, 283–293.
Qualter, P., Vanhalst, J., Harris, R., Van Roekel, E., Lodder, G., Bangee, M., . . . Verhagen, M. (2015). Loneliness across the life span. *Perspectives on Psychological Science, 10*, 250–264.
Qui, C., & Fratiglioni, L. (2009). Epidemiology of Alzheimer's disease. In G. Waldemar & A. Burns (Eds.), *Alzheimer's disease*. Oxford: Oxford University Press.
Quigley, B. A. (1997). *Rethinking literacy education: The critical need for practice-based change*. San Francisco, CA: Jossey-Bass.
Quigley, B. A., & Uhland, R. L. (2000). Retaining adult learners in the first three critical weeks: A quasi-experimental model for use in ABE programs. *Adult Basic Education, 10*, 55–68.
Quigley, M. A., Hockley, C., Carson, C., Kelly, Y., Renfrew, M. J., & Sacker, A. (2012). Breastfeeding is associated with improved child cognitive development: A population-based cohort study. *The Journal of Pediatrics, 160*, 25–32.
Quinn, P. C., Yahr, J., Kuhn, A., Slater, A. M., & Pascalis, O. (2002). Representation of the gender of human faces by infants: A preference for female. *Perception, 31*, 1109–1121.
Quinsey, V. L. Skilling, T. A., Lalumiere, M. L., & Craig, W. M. (2004). *Juvenile delinquency. Understanding the origins of individual differences*. Washington, DC: American Psychological Association.
Rabbani, A., Khodal, S., Mohammad, K., Sotoudeh, A., Karbakhsh, M., Nouri, K., et al. (2008). Pubertal development in a random sample of 4.020 urban Iranian girls. *Journal of Pediatric Endocrinology & Metabolism, 21*, 681–687.
Rabbitt, P., Chetwynd, A., & McInnes, L. (2003). Do clever brains age more slowly? Further exploration of a nun result. *British Journal of Psychology, 94*, 63–71.
Raby, K. L., Cicchetti, D., Carlson, E. A., Cutuli, J. J., Englund, M. M., & Egeland, B. (2012). Genetic and caregiving-based contributions to infant attachment: Unique associations with distress reactivity and attachment security. *Psychological Science, 23*, 1016–1023.
Raby, K. L., Roisman, G. I., Simpson, J. A., Collins, W. A., & Steele, R. D. (2015). Greater maternal insensitivity in childhood predicts greater electrodermal reactivity during conflict discussions with romantic partners in adulthood. *Psychological Science, 26*, 348–353.
Ragow-O'Brien, D., Hayslip, B., & Guarnaccia, C. A. (2000). The impact of hospice on attitudes toward funerals and subsequent bereavement adjustment. *Omega: Journal of Death and Dying, 41*, 291–305.
Ramey, C. T., & Ramey, S. L. (1992). Effective early intervention. *Mental Retardation, 30*, 337–345.
Ramirez-Esparza, N., Garcia-Sierra, A., & Kuhl, P. K. (2014). Look who's talking: Speech style and social context in language input to infants are linked to concurrent and future speech development. *Developmental Science, 17*, 880–891.
Rampell, C. (2016, May 27). Mom and dad's basement is looking pretty good right now. *The Washington Post*, p. A19.
Ramvi, E., & Tangerud, M. (2011). Experiences of women who have a vaginal birth after requesting a cesarean section due to fear of birth: A biographical, narrative, interpretative study. *Nursing and Health Sciences, 13*, 269–274.
Rando, T. A. (1986). A comprehensive analysis of anticipatory grief: Perspectives, processes, promises, and problems. In T. A. Rando (Ed.), *Loss and anticipatory grief*. Lexington, MA: Lexington Books.
Rangmar, J., Hjern, A., Vinnerljung, B., Strömland, K., Aronson, M., & Fahlke, C. (2015). Psychosocial outcomes of fetal alcohol syndrome in adulthood. *Pediatrics, 135*, e52–58.
Rantanen, T., Guralnik, J. M., Foley, D., Masaki, K., Leveille, S., Curb, J. D., et al. (1999). Midlife hand grip

strength as a predictor of old age disability. *Journal of the American Medical Association*, *281*, 558–560.
Rantanen, T., Masaki, K., He, Q., Ross, G. W., Willcox, B. J., & White, L. (2012). Midlife muscle strength and human longevity up to age 100 years: A 44-year prospective study among a decedent cohort. *Age*, *34*, 563–70.
Raphael, B. (1983). *The anatomy of bereavement*. New York, NY: Basic Books.
Rapkin, B. D., & Fischer, K. (1992). Personal goals of older adults: Issues in assessment and prediction. *Psychology and Aging*, *7*, 127–137.
Rasch, B., & Born, J. (2013). About sleep's role in memory. *Physiological Reviews*, *93*, 681–766.
Rasoulinejad, S. A., Zarghami, A., Hosseini, S. R., Rajaee, N., Rasoulinejad, S. E., & Mikaniki, E. (2015). Prevalence of age-related macular degeneration among the elderly. *Caspian Journal of Internal Medicine*, *6*, 141–147.
Ratey, J. J. (2013). *Spark: The revolutionary new science of exercise and the brain*. New York, NY: Little, Brown and Company.
Rattan, A., Good, C., & Dweck, C. S. (2012). "It's ok—Not everyone can be good at math": Instructors with an entity theory comfort (and demotivate) students. *Journal of Experimental Social Psychology*, *48*, 731–737.
Rattan, A., Savani, K., Chugh, D., & Dweck, C. S. (2015). Leveraging mindsets to promote academic achievement: Policy recommendations. *Perspectives on Psychological Science*, *10*, 721–726.
Rattaz, C., Goubet, N., & Bullinger, A. (2005). The calming effect of a familiar odor on full-term newborns. *Journal of Developmental and Behavioral Pediatrics*, *26*, 86–92.
Rauch, J. (2014, December). The real roots of midlife crisis. *The Atlantic*, pp. 88–95.
Rawal, S., Hoffman, H. J., Bainbridge, K. E., Huedo-Medina, T. B., & Duffy, V. B. (2016). Prevalence and risk factors of self-reported smell and taste alterations: Results from the 2011–2012 U.S. National Health and Nutrition Examination Survey (NHANES). *Chemical Senses*, *41*, 69–76.
Raymo, J. M., Park, H., Xie, Y., & Yeung, W. J. (2015). Marriage and family in East Asia: Continuity and change. *Annual Review of Sociology*, *41*, 471–492.
Raz, S., Goldstein, R., Hopkins, T. L., Lauterbach, M. D., Shah, F., Porter, C. L., et al. (1994). Sex differences in early vulnerability to cerebral injury and their neurodevelopmental implications. *Psychobiology*, *22*, 244–253.
Re, L., & Birkhoff, J. M. (2015). The 47, XYY syndrome, 50 years of certainties and doubts: A systematic review. *Aggression and Violent Behavior*, *22*, 9–17.
Rebacz, E. (2009). Age at menarche in schoolgirls from Tanzania in light of socioeconomic and sociodemographic conditioning. *Collegium Antropologicum*, *33*, 23–29.
Rebok, G. W., Ball, K., Guey, L. T., Jones, R. N., Kim, H. Y., King, J. W., & Willis, S. L. (2014). Ten-year effects of the advanced cognitive training for independent and vital elderly cognitive training trial on cognition and everyday functioning in older adults. *Journal of the American Geriatrics Society*, *62*, 16–24.
Redding, R. E., Harmon, R. J., & Morgan, G. A. (1990). Maternal depression and infants' mastery behaviors. *Infant Behavior and Development*, *13*, 391–395.
Reder, L. M., Wible, C., & Martin, J. (1986). Differential memory changes with age: Exact retrieval versus plausible inference. *Journal of Experimental Psychology: Learning, Memory, and Cognition*, *12*, 72–81.
Reed, A. E., & Carstensen, L. L. (2012). The theory behind the age-related positivity effect. *Frontiers in Psychology*, 3, Article 339. Published online September 27 2012, doi:10.3389/fpsyg.2012.00339
Reed, A., Snyder, J., Staats, S., Forgatch, M. S., DeGarmo, D. S., Patterson, G. R., . . . Schmidt, N. (2013). Duration and mutual entrainment of changes in parenting practices engendered by behavioral parent training targeting recently separated mothers. *Journal of Family Psychology*, *27*, 343–354.
Reed, T., & Dick, D. M. (2003). Heritability and validity of healthy physical aging (wellness) in elderly male twins. *Twin Research*, *6*, 227–234.
Rees, M. (1993). Menarche when and why? *Lancet*, *342*, 1375–1376.
Reese, E. (2014). Taking the long way: Longitudinal approaches to autobiographical memory development. In P. Bauer & R. Fivush (Eds.), *The Wiley handbook on the development of children's memory* (pp. 972–995). Malden, MA: Wiley Blackwell.
Reese, E., Hayne, H., & MacDonald, S. (2008). Looking back to the future: Māori and Pakeha mother-child birth stories. *Child Development*, *79*, 114–125.
Reese, H. W., & Overton, W. F. (1970). Models of development and theories of development. In L. R. Goulet & P. B. Baltes (Eds.), *Life-span developmental psychology: Research and theory*. New York, NY: Academic Press.
Reeves, R. V., & Cuddy, E. (2014, November 6). *Hitting kids: American parenting and physical punishment*. Retrieved from www.brookings.edu/blogs/social-mobility-memos/posts/2014/11/06-parenting-hitting-mobility-reeves.
Regan, P. C. (2008). *The mating game* (2nd ed.). Thousand Oaks, CA: Sage.
Reich, S. M., Subrahmanyam, K., & Espinoza, G. (2012). Friending, IMing, and hanging out face-to-face: Overlap in adolescents' online and offline social networks. *Developmental Psychology*, *48*, 356–368.
Reichow, B., & Wolery, M. (2009). Comprehensive synthesis of early intensive behavioral interventions for young children with autism based on the UCLA Young Autism Project model. *Journal of Autism and Developmental Disorders*, *39*, 23–41.
Reid, L. M., & Maclullich, A. M. (2006). Subjective memory complaints and cognitive impairment in older people. *Dementia and Geriatric Cognitive Disorders*, *22*, 471–485.
Reid, T. R. (1993, January 16). 2 million accept duty of being 20. *The Washington Post*, A14, A24.
Reid, T. R. (2015, September). The value of older workers. *AARP Bulletin/Real Possibilities*, pp. 21–24.
Reilly, D., & Neumann, D. (2013). Gender-role differences in spatial ability: A meta-analytic review. *Sex Roles*, *68*, 521–535.
Reinhardt, J. P., Boerner, K., & Horowitz, A. (2009). Personal and social resources and adaptation to chronic vision impairment over time. *Aging & Mental Health*, *13*, 367–375.
Reinherz, H. Z., Giaconia, R. M., Hauf, A. M. C., Wasserman, M. S., & Silverman, A. B. (1999). Major depression in the transition to adulthood: Risks and impairments. *Journal of Abnormal Psychology*, *108*, 500–510.
Reis, H. T., & Aron, A. (2008). Love: What is it, why does it matter, and how does it operate? *Perspectives on Psychological Science*, 3, 80–86.
Reis, H. T., Aron, A., Clark, M. S., & Finkel, E. J. (2013). Ellen Berscheid, Elaine Hatfield, and the emergence of relationship science. *Perspectives on Psychological Science*, *8*, 558–572.
Reis, H. T., Lin, Y., Bennett, M. E., & Nezlek, J. B. (1993). Change and consistency in social participation during early adulthood. *Developmental Psychology*, *29*, 633–645.
Reis, S. M., & Renzulli, J. S. (2011). Intellectual giftedness. In R. J. Sternberg & S. B. Kaufman (Eds.), *The Cambridge handbook of intelligence* (pp. 235–252). New York, NY: Cambridge University Press.
Reiss, D., & Neiderhiser, J. M. (2011). Marital dynamics and child proaction. Genetics takes a second look at developmental theory. In K. A. Dodge & M. Rutter (Eds.), *Gene-environment interactions in developmental psychopathology*. New York, NY: Guilford.
Reiss, D., Neiderhiser, J. M., Hetherington, E. M., & Plomin, R. (2000). *The relationship code: Deciphering genetic and social influences on adolescent development*. Cambridge, MA: Harvard University Press.
Reissland, N., & Kisilevsky, B. S. (Eds.). (2016). *Fetal development: Research on brain and behavior, environmental influences, and emerging technologies* (1st ed.). Cham, Switzerland: Springer.
Reiter, E. O., Price, D. A., Wilton, P., Albertsson-Wikland, K., & Ranke, M. B. (2006). Effect of growth hormone (GH) treatment on the near-final height of 1258 patients with idiopathic GH deficiency: Analysis of a large international database. *The Journal of Clinical Endocrinology and Metabolism*, *91*, 2147–2054.
Reker, G. T, Peacock, E. J., & Wong, P. T P. (1987). Meaning and purpose in life and well-being: A lifespan perspective. *Journal of Gerontology*, *42*, 44–49.
Remedios, R., & Richardson, J. T. E. (2013). Achievement goals in adult learners: Evidence from distance education. *The British Journal of Educational Psychology*, *83*, 664–685.
Rempel, J. (1985). Childless elderly: What are they missing? *Journal of Marriage and the Family*, *47*, 343–348.
Rendell, P. G., Castel, A. D., & Craik, F. I. (2005). Memory for proper names in old age: A disproportionate impairment? *The Quarterly Journal of Experimental Psychology. Section A, Human Experimental Psychology*, *58*, 54–71.
Renzulli, J. S. (1998). The three-ring conception of giftedness. In S. M. Baum, S. M. Reis, & L. R. Maxfield (Eds.), *Nurturing the gifts and talents of primary grade students*. Mansfield Center, CT: Creative Learning Press.
Renzulli, J., & Delcourt, M. A. B. (2013). Gifted behaviors versus gifted individuals. In C. Callahan & H. H. Davis (Eds.), *Fundamentals of gifted education: Considering multiple perspectives* (pp. 36–48). New York, NY: Taylor & Francis.
Repacholi, B. M., & Gopnik, A. (1997). Early reasoning about desires: Evidence from 14- and 18-month-olds. *Developmental Psychology*, *33*, 12–21.
Repacholi, B., Slaughter, V., Pritchard, M., & Gibbs, V. (2003). Theory of mind, Machiavellianism, and social functioning in childhood. In B. Repacholi & V. Slaughter (Eds.). *Individual differences in theory of mind: Implications for typical and atypical development*. New York, NY: Psychology Press.
Repetti, R., Wang, S., & Saxbe, D. (2009). Bringing it all back home. How outside stressors shape families' everyday lives. *Current Directions in Psychological Science*, *18*, 106–111.
Reproductive Health (2015). www.cdc.gov/reproductivehealth/maternalinfanthealth/pregcomplications.htm.
Rescorla, L. A., Achenbach, T. M., Ginzburg, S., Ivanova, M., Dumenci, L., Almqvist, F., et al. (2007). Consistency of teacher-reported problems for students in 21 countries. *School Psychology Review*, *36*, 91–110.
Resnick, S. M. (2000). One-year age changes in MRI brain volumes in older adults. *Cerebral Cortex*, *10*, 464–472.
Resnick, S. M., Berenbaum, S. A., Gottesman, I. I., & Bouchard, T. J., Jr. (1986). Early hormonal influences on cognitive functioning in congenital adrenal hyperplasia. *Developmental Psychology*, *22*, 191–198.
Rest, J., Narvaez, D., Bebeau, M. J., & Thoma, S. J. (1999). *Postconventional moral thinking. A neo-Kohlbergian approach*. Mahwah, NJ: Erlbaum.
Reuben, D. B., Walsh, K., Moore, A. A., Damesyn, M., & Greendale, G. A. (1998). Hearing loss in community-dwelling older persons: National prevalence data and identification using simple questions. *Journal of the American Geriatric Society*, *46*, 1008–1011.
Reuter, T. R., Sharp, C., & Temple, J. R. (2015). An exploratory study of teen dating violence in sexual minority youth. *Partner Abuse*, *6*, 8–28.
Reuter-Lorenz, P. A., & Cappell, K. A. (2008). Neurocognitive aging and the compensation hypothesis. *Current Directions in Psychological Science*, *17*, 177–182.
Reuter-Lorenz, P. A., & Park, D. C. (2014). How does it STAC up? Revisiting the scaffolding theory of aging and cognition. *Neuropsychology Review*, *24*(3), 355–370.
Reyes-Rodríguez, M. L., Von Holle, A., Ulman, T. F., Thornton, L. M., Klump, K. L., Brandt, H., et al. (2011). Posttraumatic stress disorder in anorexia nervosa. *Psychosomatic Medicine*, *73*, 491–497.
Reyna, V. F., & Brainerd, C. J. (1995). Fuzzy-trace theory: An interim synthesis. *Learning and Individual Differences*, *7*, 1–75.
Reynolds, B. M., & Juvonen, J. (2012). Pubertal timing fluctuations across middle school: Implications for girls' psychological health. *Journal of Youth & Adolescence*, *41*, 677–690.
Reznikoff, M., Domino, G., Bridges, C., & Honeyman, M. (1973). Creative abilities in identical and fraternal twins. *Behavior Genetics*, *3*, 365–377.
Rhee, N. (2013a). *Race and retirement insecurity in the United States*. Washington, DC: National Institute on Retirement Security. Available at www.nirsonline.org/storage/nirs/documents/Race%20and%20Retirement%20Insecurity/race_and_retirement_insecurity_final.pdf.
Rhee, N. (2013b). *The retirement savings crisis: Is it worse than we think?* Washington, DC: National Institute on Retirement Security. Available at www.nirsonline.org/index.php?option=content&task=view&id=768.

Rhee, S. H., & Waldman, I. D. (2002). Genetic and environmental influences on antisocial behavior: A meta-analysis of twin and adoption studies. *Psychological Bulletin, 128*, 490–529.

Rheingold, A. A., Smith, D. W., Ruggiero, K. J., Saunders, B. E., Kilpatrick, D. G., & Resnick, H. S. (2004). Loss, trauma exposure, and mental health in a representative sample of 12–17-year-old youth: Data from the national survey of adolescents. *Journal of Loss and Trauma, 9*, 1–19.

Rhodes, S. R. (1983). Age-related differences in work attitudes and behavior: A review and conceptual analysis. *Psychological Bulletin, 93*, 328–367.

Ribeiro, F., de Mendonca, A., & Guerreiro, M. (2006). Mild cognitive impairment: Deficits in cognitive domains other than memory. *Dementia and Geriatric Cognitive Disorders, 21*, 284–290.

Ricciardelli, L. A., & McCabe, M. P. (2001). Children's body image concerns and eating disturbance: A review of the literature. *Clinical Psychology Review, 21*, 325–344.

Ricco, R. B. (1990). Necessity and the logic of entailment. In W. Overton (Ed.), *Reasoning, necessity, and logic: Developmental perspectives* (pp. 45–66). Hillsdale, NJ: Lawrence Earlbaum.

Rice, F., Harold, G. T., & Thapar, A. (2003). Negative life events as an account of age-related differences in the genetic aetiology of depression in childhood and adolescence. *Journal of Child Psychology and Psychiatry and Allied Disciplines, 44*, 977–987.

Rice, F., Harold, G. T., Boivin, J., van den Bree, M., Hay, D. F., & Thapar, A. (2010). The links between prenatal stress and offspring development and psychopathology: Disentangling environmental and inherited influences. *Psychological Medicine, 40*, 335–345.

Richard, J. F., Normandeau, J., Brun, V., & Maillet, M. (2004). Attracting and maintaining infant attention during habituation: Further evidence of the importance of stimulus complexity. *Infant and Child Development, 13*, 277–286.

Richards, R. (1996). Beyond Piaget: Accepting divergent, chaotic, and creative thought. In M. A. Runco (Ed.), *Creativity from childhood through adulthood: The developmental issues*. San Francisco, CA: Jossey-Bass.

Richardson, G. A., Goldschmidt, L., Larkby, C., & Day, N. L. (2015). Effects of prenatal cocaine exposure on adolescent development. *Neurotoxicology and Teratology, 49*, 41–48.

Richardson, K., & Norgate, S. H. (2015). Does IQ really predict job performance? *Applied Developmental Science, 19*, 153–169.

Richert, R. A., Robb, M. B., Fender, J. G., & Wartella, E. (2010). Word learning from baby videos. *Archives of Pediatric and Adolescent Medicine, 164*, 432–437.

Rideout, V. J., Foehr, U. G., & Roberts, D. F. (2010). *Generation M2. Media in the lives of 8- to 18-year-olds. A Kaiser Family Foundation Study*. Menlo Park, CA: Kaiser Foundation. Retrieved from www .kaiserfamilyfoundation.files.wordpress.com/2013/04/ 8010.pdf.

Riediger, M., & Klipker, K. (2014). Emotion regulation in adolescence. In J. J. Gross (Ed.), *Handbook of emotion regulation* (2nd ed., pp. 187–202). New York, NY: Guilford.

Riediger, M., & Luong, G. (2016). Happy to be unhappy? Pro- and contrahedonic motivations from adolescence to old age. In A. D. Ong & C. E. Löckenhoff (Eds.), *Emotion, aging, and health* (pp. 97–118). Washington, DC: American Psychological Association.

Riediger, M., Li, S., & Lindenberger, U. (2006). Selection, optimization, and compensation as developmental mechanisms of adaptive resource allocation: Review and preview. In J. E. Birren & K. W. Schaie (Eds.), *Handbook of the psychology of aging*. Boston, MA: Elsevier Academic Press.

Riediger, M., Schmiedek, F., Wagner, G. G., & Lindenberger, U. (2009). Seeking pleasure and seeking pain. Differences in prohedonic and contra-hedonic motivation from adolescence to old age. *Psychological Science, 20*, 1529–1535.

Riediger, M., Wrzus, C., & Wagner, G. G. (2014). Happiness is pleasant, or is it? Implicit representations of affect valence are associated with contrahedonic motivation and mixed affect in daily life. *Emotion, 14*, 950–961.

Riegel, K. F. (1973). Dialectic operations: The final period of cognitive development. *Human Development, 16*, 346–370.

Rieger, G., & Savin-Williams, R. C. (2012). Gender nonconformity, sexual orientation, and psychological well-being. *Archives of Sexual Behavior, 41*, 611–621.

Rieser, J., Yonas, A., & Wilkner, K. (1976). Radial localization of odors by human newborns. *Child Development, 47*, 856–859.

Rigby, K. (2012). Bullying in schools: Addressing desires, not only behaviours. *Educational Psychology Review, 24*, 339–348.

Riggs, S. A., & Riggs, D. S. (2011). Risk and resilience in military families experiencing deployment: The role of the family attachment network. *Journal of Family Psychology, 25*, 675–687.

Riley, E. A., Sitharthan, G., Clemson, L., & Diamond, M. (2011). The needs of gender-variant children and their parents: A parent survey. *International Journal of Sexual Health, 23*, 181–195.

Riley, L. P., LaMontagne, L. L., Hepworth, J. T., & Murphy, B. A. (2007). Parental grief responses and personal growth following the death of a child. *Death Studies, 31*, 277–299.

Rilling, M. (2000). John Watson's paradoxical struggle to explain Freud. *American Psychologist, 55*, 301–312.

Ripley, A. (2010, April 8). Should kids be bribed to do well in school? *Time*. Retrieved from www.time.com/time/ printout/0,8816,1978589,00.html.

Ristic, J., & Kingstone, A. (2009). Rethinking attentional development: Reflexive and volitional orienting in children and adults. *Developmental Science, 12*, 289–296.

Rith, K. A., & Diamond, L. M. (2013). Same-sex relationships. In M. A. Fine & F. D. Fincham (Eds.), *Handbook of family theories. A context-based approach*. New York, NY: Routledge.

Ritz, B., Wilhelm, M., & Zhao, Y. (2006). Air pollution and infant death in Southern California, 1989–2000. *Pediatrics, 118*, 493–502.

Rizzolatti, G., & Sinigaglia, C. (2008). *Mirrors in the brain: How our minds share actions, emotions* (F. Anderson, Trans.). Oxford, NY: Oxford University Press. (Original work published 2006).

Roberto, K. A., & Blieszner, R. (2015). Diverse family structures and the care of older persons. *Canadian Journal on Aging, 34*, 305–320.

Roberts, B. W., & Caspi, A. (2003). The cumulative continuity model of personality development: Striking a balance between continuity and change in personality traits across the life course. In U. M. Staudinger & U. Lindenberger (Eds.), *Understanding human development: Dialogues with life-span psychology*. Dordrecht, Netherlands: Kluwer Academic.

Roberts, B. W., & DelVecchio, W. F. (2000). The rank-order consistency of personality traits from childhood to old age: A quantitative review of longitudinal studies. *Psychological Bulletin, 126*, 3–25.

Roberts, B. W., Donnellan, M. B., & Hill, P. L. (2013). Personality trait development in adulthood. In H. Tennen, J. Suls & I. B Weiner (Eds.), *Handbook of psychology: Vol. 5. Personality and social psychology* (2nd ed.). Hoboken, NJ: John Wiley & Sons Inc.

Roberts, B. W., Edmonds, G., & Grijalva, E. (2010). It is developmental me, not generation me: Developmental changes are more important than generational changes in narcissism—Commentary on Trzesniewski & Donnellan (2010). *Perspectives on Psychological Science, 5*, 97–102.

Roberts, B. W., & Robins, R. W. (2004). Person–environment fit and its implications for personality development: A longitudinal study. *Journal of Personality, 72*, 89–110.

Roberts, B. W., Walton, K. E., & Viechtbauer, W. (2006). Patterns of mean-level change in personality traits across the life course: A meta-analysis of longitudinal studies. *Psychological Bulletin, 132*, 1–25.

Roberts, B. W., Wood, D., & Caspi, A. (2008). The development of personality traits in adulthood. In O. P. John, R. W. Robins, & L. A. Pervin (Eds.), *Handbook of personality theory and research* (3rd ed.). New York, NY: Guilford.

Roberts, L. R., Sarigiani, P. A., Petersen, A. C., & Newman, J. L. (1990). Gender differences in the relationship between achievement and self image during early adolescence. *Journal of Early Adolescence, 10*, 159–175.

Roberts, R. O., Christianson, T. J. H., Kremers, W. K., Mielke, M. M., Machulda, M. M., Vassilaki, M., . . .

Petersen, R. C. (2016). Association between olfactory dysfunction and amnestic mild cognitive impairment and Alzheimer disease dementia. *JAMA Neurology, 73*, 93–101.

Roberts, S. E., Wotton, C. J., Williams, J. G., Griffith, M., & Goldacre, M. J. (2011). Perinatal and early life risk factors for inflammatory bowel disease. *World Journal of Gastroenterology, 17*, 743–749.

Robino, A., Mezzavilla, M., Pirastu, N., Dognini, M., Tepper, B. J., & Gasparini, P. (2014). A population-based approach to study the impact of PROP perception on food liking in populations along the Silk Road. *PLoS ONE, 9*, e91716.

Robins, L. N., & Regier, D. A. (Eds.). (1991). *Psychiatric disorders in America. The Epidemiologic Catchment Area Study*. New York, NY: The Free Press.

Robins, R. W., Caspi, A., & Moffitt, T. E. (2000). Two personalities, one relationship: Both partners' personality traits shape the quality of their relationship. *Journal of Personality and Social Psychology, 79*, 251–259.

Robins, R. W., Trzesniewski, K. H., Tracy, J. L., Gosling, S. D., & Potter, J. (2002). Global self-esteem across the life span. *Psychology and Aging, 17*, 423–434.

Robinson Center. (2016). *Early Entrance Program*. Retrieved from www.robinsoncenter.uw.edu.

Robinson, C. C., & Morris, J. T. (1986). The gender-stereotyped nature of Christmas toys received by 36-, 48-, and 60-month-old children: A comparison between nonrequested vs. requested toys. *Sex Roles, 15*, 21–32.

Robinson, E. B., Koenen, K. C., McCormick, M. C., Munir, K., Hallett, V., Happé, F., et al. (2011). Evidence that autistic traits show the same etiology in the general population and at the quantitative extremes (5%, 2.5%, and 1%). *Archives of General Psychiatry, 68*, 1113–1121.

Robinson, P. K. (1983). The sociological perspective. In R. B. Weg (Ed.), *Sexuality in the later years: Roles and behavior*. New York, NY: Academic Press.

Robinson, S. A., Rickenbach, E. H., & Lachman, M. E. (2016). Self-regulatory strategies in daily life: Selection, optimization, and compensation and everyday memory problems. *International Journal of Behavioral Development*, doi: 10.1177/0165025415592187.

Robinson, T., & Marwit, S. J. (2006). An investigation of the relationship of personality, coping, and grief intensity among bereaved mothers. *Death Studies, 30*, 677–696.

Robles, T. F., Slatcher, R. B., Trombello, J. M., & McGinn, M. M. (2014). Marital quality and health: A meta-analytic review. *Psychological Bulletin, 140*, 140–187.

Robles-De-La-Torre, G. (2006, July–September). The importance of the sense of touch in virtual and real environment. *IEEE MultiMedia*, 24–30.

Roccella, M., & Testa, D. (2003). Fetal alcohol syndrome in developmental age: Neuropsychiatric aspects. *Minerva Pediatrics, 55*, 63–69.

Rochat, P. (2010). The innate sense of the body develops to become a public affair by 2–3 years. *Neuropsychologia, 48*, 738–745.

Rochat, P., & Striano, T. (2000). Perceived self in infancy. *Infant Behavior and Development, 23*, 513–530.

Rochat, P., Broesch, T., & Jayne, K. (2012). Social awareness and early self-recognition. *Consciousness and Cognition: An International Journal, 21*, 1491–1497.

Rochman, B. (2012, February 27). Early decision: Will new advances in prenatal testing shrink the ranks of babies with Down syndrome? *Time*, pp. 35–40.

Röcke, C., & Cherry, K. E. (2002). Death at the end of the 20th century: Individual processes and developmental tasks in old age. *International Journal of Aging and Human Development, 54*, 315–333.

Rodin, J., & Langer, E. (1980). Aging labels: The decline of control and the fall of self-esteem. *Journal of Social Issues, 36*, 12–29.

Rodriguez, A., Olsen, J., Kotimaa, A. J., Kaakinen, M., Moilanen, I., Henriksen, T. B., Linnet, K. M., Miettunen, J., Obel, C., Taanila, A., Ebeling, H., & Järvelin, M. R. (2009). Is prenatal alcohol exposure related to inattention and hyperactivity symptoms in children? Disentangling the effects of social adversity. *Journal of Child Psychology and Psychiatry, 50*, 1073–1083.

Rogers, L. O., Zosuls, K. M., Halim, M. L., Ruble, D., Hughes, D., & Fuligni, A. (2012). Meaning making in middle childhood: An exploration of the meaning of ethnic identity. *Cultural Diversity and Ethnic Minority Psychology, 18*, 99–108.

Rogler, L. H. (2002). The case of the Great Depression and World War II. *American Psychologist, 57,* 1013–1023.
Rogoff, B. (1998). Cognition as a collaborative process. In D. Kuhn & R. S. Siegler (Vol. Eds.), W. Damon (Editor-in-Chief), *Handbook of child psychology: Cognition, perception, and language* (5th ed.). New York, NY: Wiley.
Rogoff, B. (2003). *The cultural nature of human development.* New York, NY: Oxford University Press.
Rogoff, B., Morelli, G. A., & Chavajay, P. (2010). Children's integration in communities and segregation from people of differing ages. *Perspectives on Psychological Science, 5,* 431–440.
Rohde, P., Lewinsohn, P. M., Klein, D. N., Seeley, J. R., & Gau, J. M. (2013). Key characteristics of major depressive disorder occurring in childhood, adolescence, emerging adulthood, and adulthood. *Clinical Psychological Science, 1,* 41–53.
Roid, G. (2003). *Stanford-Binet Intelligence Scales* (5th ed.). Itasca, IL: Riverside Publishing.
Roisman, G. I. (2007). The psychopathology of adult attachment relationships: Autonomic reactivity in marital and premarital interactions. *Developmental Psychology, 43,* 39–53.
Roisman, G. I. (2009). Adult attachment. Toward a rapprochement of methodological cultures. *Current Directions in Psychological Science, 18,* 122–126.
Roisman, G. I., & Booth-LaForce, C. (2014). The Adult Attachment Interview: Psychometrics, stability and change from infancy, and developmental origins: VIII. General discussion. *Monographs of the Society for Research in Child Development, 79* (3), 126–137.
Roisman, G. I., & Fraley, R. C. (2008). A behavior-genetic study of parenting quality, infant attachment security, and their covariation in a nationally representative sample. *Developmental Psychology, 44,* 831–839.
Roisman, G. I., & Groh, A. M. (2011). Attachment theory and research in developmental psychology: An overview and appreciative critique. In M. K. Underwood & L. H. Rosen (Eds.), *Social development. Relationships in infancy, childhood, and adolescence.* New York, NY: Guilford.
Roizen, N. J. (2013). Down syndrome (Trisomy 21). In M. L. Batshaw, N. J. Roizen, & G. R. Lotrecchiano (Eds.), *Children with disabilities* (7th ed., pp. 307–318). Baltimore, MD: Paul H. Brookes.
Roizen, N. J., & Patterson, D. (2003). Down's syndrome. *Lancet, 361,* 1281–1289.
Rollins, B. C., & Feldman, H. (1970). Marital satisfaction over the family life cycle. *Journal of Marriage and the Family, 32,* 20–28.
Rolls, B. J. (1999). Do chemosensory changes influence food intake in the elderly? *Physiological Behavior, 66,* 193–197.
Ronald, A., & Hoekstra, R. A. (2011). Autism spectrum disorders and autistic traits: A decade of new twin studies. *American Journal of Medical Genetics, Part B, Neuropsychiatric Genetics, 156B,* 255–274.
Rönnlund, M., Nyberg, L., Bäckman, L., & Nillson, L.-G. (2005). Stability, growth, and decline in adult life span development of declarative memory: Cross-sectional and longitudinal data from a population-based study. *Psychology and Aging, 20,* 3–18.
Rönnlund, M., Sundström, A., & Nilsson, L.-G. (2015). Interindividual differences in general cognitive ability from age 18 to age 65 years are extremely stable and strongly associated with working memory capacity. *Intelligence, 53,* 59–64.
Rook, K. S. (2015). Social networks in later life: Weighing positive and negative effects on health and well-being. *Current Directions in Psychological Science, 24,* 45–51.
Rönnlund, M., Nyberg, L., Backman, L., & Nilsson, L. G. (2005). Stability, growth, and decline in adult life span development of declarative memory: Cross-sectional and longitudinal data from a population-based study. *Psychology and Aging, 20,* 3–18.
Rosa, E. M., & Tudge, J. (2013). Urie Bronfenbrenner's theory of human development: Its evolution from ecology to bioecology. *Journal of Family Theory & Review, 5,* 243–258.
Rose, A. J., Carlson, W., & Waller, E. M. (2007). Prospective associations of co-rumination with friendship and emotional adjustment: Considering the socioemotional trade-offs of co-rumination. *Developmental Psychology, 43,* 1019–1031.
Rose, A. J., Schwartz-Mette, R. A., Smith, R. L., Asher, S. R., Swenson, L. P., Carlson, W., & Waller, E. M. (2012). How girls and boys expect disclosure about problems will make them feel: Implications for friendships. *Child Development, 83,* 844–863.
Rose, A. J., Swenson, L. P., & Waller, E. M. (2004). Overt and relational aggression and perceived popularity: Developmental differences in concurrent and prospective relations. *Developmental Psychology, 40,* 378–387.
Rose, L. T., & Fischer, K. W. (2007). Dynamics systems theory. In R. A. Shweder (Ed.), *Chicago companion to the child.* Chicago, IL: University of Chicago Press
Rose, L. T., & Fischer, K. W. (2011). Intelligence in childhood. In R. Sternberg & S. B. Kaufman (Eds.), *The Cambridge handbook of intelligence* (pp. 144–173). New York, NY: Cambridge University Press.
Rose, S. A., & Feldman, J. F. (1997). Memory and speed: Their role in the relation of infant information processing to later IQ. *Child Development, 68,* 630–641.
Rose, S. A., Feldman, J. F., & Jankowski, J. J. (2003). Infant visual recognition memory: Independent contributions of speed and attention. *Developmental Psychology, 39,* 563–571.
Rose, S. A., Feldman, J. F., & Jankowski, J. J. (2009). Information processing in toddlers: Continuity from infancy and persistence of preterm deficits. *Intelligence, 37,* 311–320.
Rose, S. A., Feldman, J. F., Jankowski, J. J., & Van Rossem, R. (2005). Pathways from prematurity and infant abilities to later cognition. *Child Development, 76,* 1172–1184.
Rose, S. A., Feldman, J. F., Jankowski, J. J., & Van Rossem, R. (2012). Information processing from infancy to 11 years: Continuities and prediction of IQ. *Intelligence, 40,* 445–457.
Rose, S. A., Feldman, J. F., Wallace, I. F., & McCarton, C. (1989). Infant visual attention: Relation to birth status and developmental outcome during the first 5 years. *Developmental Psychology, 25,* 560–576.
Rose, S. P., & Fischer, K. W. (1998). Models and rulers in dynamical development. *British Journal of Developmental Psychology, 16,* 123–131.
Roseberry, S., Hirsh-Pasek, K., & Golinkoff, R. M. (2014). Skype me: Socially contingent interactions help toddlers learn language. *Child Development, 85,* 956–970.
Rosenberg, A. R., Postier, A., Osenga, K., Kreicbergs, U., Neville, B., Dussel, V., & Wolfe, J. (2015). Long-term psychosocial outcomes among bereaved siblings of children with cancer. *Journal of Pain and Symptom Management, 49,* 55–65.
Rosenberg, H. G. (2009). Complaint discourse, aging, and caregiving among the Ju/'hoansi of Botswana. In J. Sokolovsky (Ed.), *The cultural context of aging* (3rd ed.). Westport, CT: Praeger.
Rosenberg, J. (2001). Exposure to multiple risk factors linked to delivery of underweight infants. *Family Planning Perspectives, 33,* 238.
Rosenblatt, P. C. (1993). Cross-cultural variation in the experience, expression, and understanding of grief. In D. P. Irish, K. F. Lundquist, & V. J. Nelson (Eds.), *Ethnic variations in dying, death, and grief: Diversity in universality.* Washington, DC: Taylor and Francis.
Rosenblatt, P. C. (2008). Grief across cultures: A review and research agenda. In M. S. Stroebe, R. O. Hansson, H. Schut, & W. Stroebe (Eds.), *Handbook of bereavement research and practice.* Advances in theory and intervention. Washington, DC: American Psychological Association.
Rosenblatt, P. C. (2013). The concept of complicated grief: Lessons from other cultures. In M. Stroebe, H. Schut & J. van den Bout (Eds.), *Complicated grief: Scientific foundations for health care professionals.* New York, NY: Routledge/Taylor & Francis.
Rosenblatt, P. C. (2015a). Death and bereavement in later adulthood: Cultural beliefs, behaviors, and emotions. In L. A. Jensen (Ed.), *The Oxford handbook of human development and culture. An interdisciplinary perspective* (pp. 697–709). New York, NY: Oxford University Press.
Rosenblatt, P. C. (2015b). Grief in small scale societies. In C. M. Parkes, P. Laungani, & B. Young (Eds.), *Death and bereavement across cultures* (pp. 25–41). New York, NY: Routledge.
Rosenbloom, C., & Bahns, M. (2006). What can we learn about diet and physical activity from master athletes? *Holistic Nursing Practice, 20,* 161–167.
Rosengren, K. S., Gutiérrez, I. T., & Schein, S. S. (2014). Children's understanding of death: Toward a contextualized and integrated account: IV. Cognitive dimensions of death in context. *Monographs of the Society for Research in Child Development, 79,* 62–82.
Rosenkrantz, P., Vogel, S., Bee, H., Broverman, I., & Broverman, D. M. (1968). Sex-role stereotypes and self-concepts in college students. *Journal of Consulting and Clinical Psychology, 32,* 287–295.
Rosenthal, P. A., & Rosenthal, S. (1984). Suicidal behavior by preschool children. *American Journal of Psychiatry, 141,* 520–525.
Rosenzweig, M. R., & Bennett, E. L. (1996). Psychobiology of plasticity: Effects of training and experience on brain and behavior. *Behavioral Brain Research, 78,* 57–65.
Rosi, A., Cavallini, E., Bottiroli, S., Bianco, F., & Lecce, S. (2016). Promoting theory of mind in older adults: Does age play a role? *Aging & Mental Health, 20,* 22–28.
Rosner, R., Kruse, J., & Hagl, M. (2010). A meta-analysis of interventions for bereaved children and adolescents. *Death Studies, 34,* 99–136.
Ross, H. G., & Milgram, J. I. (1982). Important variables in adult sibling relationships: A qualitative study. In M. E. Lamb & B. Sutton-Smith (Eds.), *Sibling relationships: Their nature and significance across the lifespan.* Hillsdale, NJ: Erlbaum.
Ross, J. L., Lee, P. A., Gut, R., & Germak, J. (2015). Increased height standard deviation scores in response to growth hormone therapy to near-adult height in older children with delayed skeletal maturation: Results from the ANSWER Program. *International Journal of Pediatric Endocrinology, 2015,* 1.
Ross-Gordon, J. M. (2011, Winter). Research on adult learners: Supporting the needs of a student population that is no longer nontraditional. *Peer Review, 13*(1). Retrieved from www.aacu.org/peerreview/pr-wi11/prwi11_rossgordon.cfm.
Rostila, M., Berg, L., Arat, A., Vinnerljung, B., & Hjern, A. (2016). Parental death in childhood and self-inflicted injuries in young adults—A national cohort study from Sweden. *European Child & Adolescent Psychiatry, 25,* 1103.
Roth, F. P., Speece, D. L., & Cooper, D. H. (2002). A longitudinal analysis of the connection between oral language and early reading. *Journal of Educational Research, 95,* 259–272.
Roth, P. L., Bevier, C. A., Switzer, F. S., & Schippmann, J. S. (1996). Meta-analyzing the relationship between grades and job performance. *Journal of Applied Psychology, 81,* 548–556.
Rothbart, M. K. (2007). Temperament, development, and personality. *Current Directions in Psychological Science, 16,* 207–212.
Rothbart, M. K. (2011). *Becoming who we are: Temperament and personality development.* New York, NY: Guilford.
Rothbart, M. K., Ahadi, S. A., & Evans, D. E. (2000). Temperament and personality: Origins and outcomes. *Journal of Personality and Social Psychology, 78,* 122–135.
Rothbart, M. K., & Bates, J. E. (2006). Temperament. In N. Eisenberg (Vol. Ed.) & W. Damon & R. M. Lerner (Eds. in Chief), *Handbook of child psychology: Vol. 3. Social, emotional, and personality development* (6th ed.). Hoboken, NJ: Wiley.
Rothbart, M. K., & Derryberry, D. (2002). Temperament in children. In C. von Hofsten & L. Backman (Eds.), *Psychology at the turn of the millennium: Vol. 2. Social, developmental, and clinical perspectives.* New York, NY: Taylor & Francis.
Rothbaum, F., & Morelli, G. (2005). Attachment and culture: Bridging relativism and universalism. In W. Friedlmeier, P. Chakkarath, & B. Schwarz (Eds.), *Culture and human development: The importance of cross-cultural research for the social sciences.* New York, NY: Psychology Press.
Rotheram-Borus, M. J., Piacentini, J., Cantwell, C., Belin, T. R., & Song, J. W. (2000). The 18-month impact of an emergency room-intervention for adolescent female suicide-attempters. *Journal of Consulting and Clinical Psychology, 68,* 1081–1093.
Rothermund, K., & Brandtstädter, J. (2003a). Age stereotypes and self-views in later life: Evaluating rival assumptions. *International Journal of Behavioral Development, 27,* 549–554.
Rothermund, K., & Brandtstädter, J. (2003b). Coping with deficits and losses in later life: From compensatory action to accommodation. *Psychology and Aging, 18,* 896–905.

Rotstein, M., Stolar, O., Uliel, S., Mandel, D., Mani, A., Dollberg, S., . . . Leitner, Y. (2015). Facial expression in response to smell and taste stimuli in small and appropriate for gestational age newborns. *Journal of Child Neurology, 30,* 1466–1471.

Rottenberg, J. (2014, January 31). An evolved view of depression. *The Chronicle Review,* pp. B10–B12.

Rovee-Collier, C. (2001). Information pick-up by infants: What is it, and how can we tell? *Journal of Experimental Child Psychology, 78,* 35–49.

Rovee-Collier, C., & Barr, R. (2004). Infant learning and memory. In G. Bremner & A. Fogel (Eds.), *Blackwell handbook of infant development* (pp. 139–168). Malden, MA: Blackwell Publishing.

Rovee-Collier, C., & Barr, R. (2010). Infant learning and memory. In J. G. Bremner & T. D. Wachs (Eds.), *The handbook of infant development: Vol. 1* (2nd ed., pp. 271–294). Malden, MA: John Wiley & Sons.

Rovee-Collier, C., & Cuevas, K. (2009a). Multiple memory systems are unnecessary to account for infant memory development: An ecological model. *Developmental Psychology, 45,* 160–174.

Rovee-Collier, C., & Cuevas, K. (2009b). The development of infant memory. In M. L. Courage & N. Cowan (Eds.), *The development of memory in infancy and childhood* (pp. 11–42). New York, NY: Psychology Press.

Rovner, S. (1994, March 29). An Alzheimer's journal. *The Washington Post—Health,* pp. 12–15.

Rowan, A. (2015, December 8). A mom's depression, a daughter's worry. *The Washington Post,* pp. E1, E4.

Rowe, D. C. (1994). *The limits of family influence: Genes, experience, and behavior.* New York, NY: Guilford.

Rowe, J. W., & Kahn, R. L. (1998). *Successful aging.* New York, NY: Pantheon.

Rowley, S. J., Jurtz-Costes, B., Mistry, R., & Feagans, L. (2007). Social status as a predictor of race and gender stereotypes in late childhood and early adolescence. *Social Development, 16,* 150–156.

Rubin, C., Maisonet, M., Kieszak, S., Monteilh, C., Holmes, A., Flanders, D., et al. (2009). Timing of maturation and predictors of menarche in girls enrolled in a contemporary British cohort. *Paediatric and Perinatal Epidemiology,* 23, 492–504.

Rubin, D. C. (2002). Autobiographical memory across the lifespan. In P. Graf & N. Ohta (Eds.), *Lifespan development of human memory* (pp. 159–184). Cambridge, MA: Massachusetts Institute of Technology.

Rubin, D. C. (2012). The basic systems model of autobiographical memory. In D. Berntsen & D. C. Rubin (Eds.), *Understanding autobiographical memory: Theories and approaches* (pp. 11–32). New York, NY: Cambridge University Press.

Rubin, D. C., Wetzler, S. E., & Nebes, R. D. (1986). Autobiographical memory across the adult lifespan. In D. C. Rubin (Ed.), *Autobiographical memory across the lifespan.* Cambridge University Press.

Rubin, J. Z., Provenzano, F. J., & Luria, Z. (1974). The eye of the beholder: Parents' views on sex of newborns. *American Journal of Orthopsychiatry, 44,* 512–519.

Rubin, K. H., Bukowski, W. M., & Parker, J. G. (2006). Peer interactions, relationships, and groups. In N. Eisenberg (Vol. Ed.), & W. Damon & R. M. Lerner (Eds. in Chief), *Handbook of child psychology: Vol. 3. Social, emotional, and personality development* (6th ed.). Hoboken, NJ: Wiley.

Rubin, K. H., Coplan, R. J., & Bowker, J. C. (2009). Social withdrawal in childhood. *Annual Review of Psychology, 60,* 141–171.

Rubin, K. H., Coplan, R., Chen, X., Bowker, J., & McDonald, K. L. (2011). Peer relationships in childhood. In M. E. Lamb & M. H. Bornstein (Eds.), *Social and personality development. An advanced textbook* (6th ed.). New York, NY: Psychology Press.

Rubin, K. H., Coplan, R. J., Chen, X., Bowker, J. C., McDonald, K. L., & Heverly-Fitt, S. (2015). Peer relationships. In M. H. Bornstein & M. E. Lamb (Eds.), *Developmental science. An advanced textbook* (7th ed., pp. 587–644). New York, NY: Psychology Press.

Rubin, R. (2012, November 27). New fetal test creates dilemma for some women. *The Washington Post,* pp. E1, E6.

Rubinow, D. R., & Schmidt, P. J. (1996). Androgens, brain, and behavior. *American Journal of Psychiatry, 153,* 974–984.

Rubinstein, R. L., Alexander, R. B., Goodman, M., & Luborsky, M. (1991). Key relationships of never married, childless older women: A cultural analysis. *Journal of Gerontology: Social Sciences, 46,* S270–S277.

Rubio-Fernández, P., & Glucksberg, S. (2012). Reasoning about other people's beliefs: Bilinguals have an advantage. *Journal of Experimental Psychology: Learning, Memory, and Cognition, 38,* 211–217.

Ruble, D. N., & Dweck, C. S. (1995). Self-conceptions, person conceptions, and their development. In N. Eisenberg (Ed.), *Social development.* Thousand Oaks, CA: Sage.

Ruble, D. N., Eisenberg, R., & Higgins, E. T. (1994). Developmental changes in achievement evaluation: Motivational implications of self-other differences. *Child Development, 65,* 1095–1110.

Ruble, D. N., Lurye, L. E., & Zosuls, K. M. (2007). *Pink frilly dresses (PFD) and early gender identity: Vol. 2. Princeton Report on Knowledge.* Retrieved from www.princeton.edu/prok/issues/2-2/pink_frilly.xml.

Ruble, D. N., Taylor, L. J., Cypers, L., Greulich, F. K., Lurye, L. E., & Shrout, P. E. (2007). The role of gender constancy in early gender development. *Child Development, 78,* 1121–1136.

Rucker, J. H., & McGuffin, P. (2012). Genomic structural variation in psychiatric disorders. *Development and Psychopathology, 24,* 1335–1344.

Rudd, M. D., Berman, A. L., Joiner, T. E. Jr., Nock, M. K., Silverman, M. M., Mandrusiak, M., et al. (2006). Warning signs for suicide: Theory, research, and clinical applications. *Suicide and Life-Threatening Behavior, 36,* 255–262.

Rudman, L. A., Fetterolf, J. C., & Sanchez, D. T. (2013). What motivates the sexual double standard? More support for male versus female control theory. *Social Psychology Bulletin,* 39, 250–263.

Rudolph, K. D., & Flynn, M. (2007). Childhood adversity and youth depression: Influence of gender and pubertal status. *Development and Psychopathology, 19,* 497–521.

Rueda, M. R. (2012). Effortful control. In M. Z. Zentner & R. L. Shiner (Eds.), *Handbook of temperament.* New York, NY: Guilford.

Ruff, H. A., & Capozzoli, M. C. (2003). Development of attention and distractibility in the first 4 years of life. *Developmental Psychology,* 39, 877–890.

Ruff, H. A., & Lawson, K. R. (1990). Development of sustained, focused attention in young children during free play. *Developmental Psychology, 26,* 85–93.

Ruff, H. A., & Rothbart, M. K. (1996). *Attention in early development: Themes and variations.* New York, NY: Oxford University Press.

Ruffman, T. K., & Olson, D. R. (1989). Children's ascriptions of knowledge to others. *Developmental Psychology, 25,* 601–606.

Ruffman, T., Slade, L., & Redman, J. (2005). Young infants' expectations about hidden objects. *Cognition, 97,* 835–843.

Ruffman, T., Slade, L., Sandino, J. C., & Fletcher, A. (2005). Are A-Not-B errors caused by a belief about object location? *Child Development, 76,* 122–136.

Ruggles, S. (1994). The origins of African-American family structure. *American Sociological Review, 59,* 136–151.

Rummo, P. E., Meyer, K. A., Boone-Heinonen, J., Jacobs, D. R., Jr., Kiefe, C. I., Lewis, C. E., & Gordon-Larsen, P. (2015). Neighborhood availability of convenience stores and diet quality: Findings from 20 years of follow-up in the Coronary Artery Risk Development in Young Adults Study. *American Journal of Public Health, 105,* e65–73.

Runco, M. A. (2007). *Creativity—Theories and themes: Research, development, and practice.* Burlington, MA: Elsevier Academic Press.

Runco, M. A. (2010). Divergent thinking, creativity, and ideation. In J. C. Kaufman & R. J. Sternberg (Eds.), *The Cambridge handbook of creativity: Vol. 2.* (pp. 413–446). New York, NY: Cambridge University Press.

Runco, M. A. (2014). *Creativity: Theories and themes: Research, development, and practice* (2nd ed.). Burlington, MA: Elsevier Science.

Runco, M. A., & Jaeger, G. J. (2012). The standard definition of creativity. *Creativity Research Journal, 24,* 92–96.

Russell, A., Aloa, V., Feder, T., Glover, A., Miller, H., & Palmer, G. (1998). Sex-based differences in parenting styles in a sample with preschool children. *Australian Journal of Psychology, 50,* 89–99.

Russell, B. S., & Lincoln, C. R. (2016). Distress tolerance and emotion regulation: Promoting maternal well-being across the transition to parenthood. *Parenting: Science and Practice, 16,* 22–35.

Rust, J., Golombok, S., Hines, M., Johnston, K., & Golding, J. (2000). The role of brothers and sisters in the gender development of preschool children. *Journal of Experimental Child Psychology, 77,* 292–303.

Rutgers, A. H., Bakermans-Kranenburg, M., van IJzendoorn, M. H., & van Berckelaer-Onnes, I. A. (2004). Autism and attachment: A meta-analytic review. *Journal of Child Psychology and Psychiatry, 45,* 1123–1134.

Rutherford, A. (2009). *Beyond the box: B. F. Skinner's technology of behavior from laboratory to life, 1950s–1970s.* Toronto, ON: University of Toronto Press.

Ruthsatz, J., & Urbach, J. B. (2012). Child prodigy: A novel cognitive profile places elevated general intelligence, exceptional working memory and attention to detail at the root of prodigiousness. *Intelligence, 40,* 419–426.

Ruthsatz, J., Ruthsatz-Stephens, K., & Ruthsatz, K. (2014). The cognitive bases of exceptional abilities in child prodigies by domain: Similarities and differences. *Intelligence, 44,* 11–14.

Rutledge, P. C., Park, A., & Sher, K. J. (2008). 21st birthday drinking: Extremely extreme. *Journal of Consulting and Clinical Psychology, 76,* 511–516.

Rutter, M. (1983). School effects on pupil progress: Research findings and policy implications. *Child Development, 54,* 1–29.

Rutter, M. (2006). *Genes and behavior. Nature-nurture interplay explained.* Malden, MA: Blackwell.

Rutter, M., & Maughan, B. (2002). School effectiveness findings 1979–2002. *Journal of School Psychology, 50,* 451–475.

Rutter, M., Kim-Cohen, J., & Maughan, B. (2006). Continuities and discontinuities in psychopathology between childhood and adult life. *Journal of Child Psychology and Psychiatry, 47,* 276–295.

Rutter, M., Moffitt, T. E., & Caspi, A. (2006). Gene-environment interplay and psychopathology: Multiple varieties but real effects. *Journal of Child Psychology and Psychiatry, 47,* 226–261.

Ryan, A. S., & Zhou, W. (2006). Lower breastfeeding rates persist among the special supplemental nutrition program for women, infants, and children participants, 1978–2003. *Pediatrics, 117,* 1136–1146.

Ryan, R. M., & Kuczkowski, R. (1994). The imaginary audience, self-consciousness, and public individuation in adolescence. *Journal of Personality, 62,* 219–238.

Ryan, S., Manlove, J., & Franzetta, K. (2003). *The first time: Characteristics of teens' first sexual relationships* (Pub. no. 2003-16). Washington, DC: Child Trends.

Ryff, C. D. (1991). Possible selves in adulthood and old age: A tale of shifting horizons. *Psychology and Aging, 6,* 286–295.

Rypma, B., Prabhakaran, V., Desmond, J. E., & Gabrieli, J. D. E. (2001). Age differences in prefrontal cortical activity in working memory. *Psychology and Aging, 16,* 371–384.

Saarento, S., & Salmivalli, C. (2015). The role of classroom peer ecology and bystanders' responses in bullying. *Child Development Perspectives, 9,* 201–205.

Saarni, C. (1984). An observational study of children's attempts to monitor their expressive behavior. *Child Development, 55,* 1504–1513.

Saarni, C., Campos, J. J., Camras, L. A., & Withington, D. (2006). Emotional development: Action, communication, and understanding. In N. Eisenberg (Vol. Ed.), & W. Damon & R. M. Lerner (Eds. in Chief), *Handbook of child psychology: Vol. 3. Social, emotional, and personality development* (6th ed.). Hoboken, NJ: Wiley.

Sabattini, L., & Leaper, C. (2004). The relation between mothers' and fathers' parenting styles and their division of labor in the home: Young adults' retrospective reports. *Sex Roles, 50,* 217–225.

Sachdev, P. S., Lee, T., Wen, W., Ames, D., Batouli, A. H., Bowden, J., ... Wright, M. J. (2013). The contribution of twins to the study of cognitive ageing and dementia: The Older Australian Twins Study. *International Review of Psychiatry, 25,* 738–747.

Sackett, P. R., & Walmsley, P. T. (2014). Which personality attributes are most important in the workplace? *Perspectives on Psychological Science, 9,* 538–551.

Sackett, P. R., Hardison, C. M., & Cullen, M. J. (2004). On interpreting stereotype threat as accounting for African

American-White differences on cognitive tests. *American Psychologist, 59,* 7–13.

Sacks, O. (1993, December 27). A neurologist's notebook: An anthropologist on Mars. *The New Yorker,* 106–125.

Sacrey, L. -A. R., Karl, J. M., & Whishaw, I. Q. (2012). Development of rotational movements, hand shaping, and accuracy in advance and withdrawal for the reach-to-eat movement in human infants aged 6–12 months. *Infant Behavior & Development, 35,* 543–560.

Sadeh, A. (1994). Assessment of intervention for infant night waking: Parental reports and activity-based home monitoring. *Journal of Consulting and Clinical Psychology, 62,* 63–68.

Sadeh, A. (1996). Evaluating night wakings in sleep-disturbed infants: A methodological study of parental reports and actigraphy. *Sleep, 19,* 757–762.

Sadeh, A., De Marcas, G., Guri, Y., Berger, A., Tikotzky, L., & Bar-Haim, Y. (2015). Infant sleep predicts attention regulation and behavior problems at 3–4 years of age. *Developmental Neuropsychology, 40,* 122–137.

Sadler, P. M., Sonnert, G., Coyle, H. P., Cook-Smith, N., & Miller, J. L. (2013). The influence of teachers' knowledge on student learning in middle school physical science classrooms. *American Educational Research Journal, 50,* 1020–1049.

Sadler, T. W. (2015). *Langman's medical embryology* (13th ed.) Philadelphia: Wolters Kluwer.

Saeedian Kia, A., Amani, R., & Cheraghian, B. (2015). The association between the risk of premenstrual syndrome and vitamin D, calcium, and magnesium status among university students: A case control study. *Health Promotion Perspectives, 5*(3), 225–230.

Saffran, J. R., Werker, J. F., & Werner, L. A. (2006). The infant's auditory world: Hearing, speech, and the beginnings of language. In D. Kuhn & R. Siegler (Vol. Eds.), *Handbook of child psychology: Cognition, perception, and language: Vol. 2.* (6th ed.). Hoboken, NJ: Wiley.

Sagara-Rosemeyer, M., & Davies, B. (2007). The integration of religious traditions in Japanese children's view of death and afterlife. *Death Studies, 31,* 223–247.

Şahin, M. (2012). An investigation into the efficiency of empathy training program on preventing bullying in primary schools. *Children and Youth Services Review, 34,* 1325–1330.

Saigal, S., Stoskopf, B., Boyle, M., Paneth, N., Pinelli, J., Streiner, D., & Godderis, J. (2007). Comparison of current health, functional limitations, and health care use of young adults who were born with extremely low birth weight and normal birth weight. *Pediatrics, 119,* e562–e573.

Sakalidis, V. S., Williams, T. M., Hepworth, A. R., Garbin, C. P., Hartmann, P. E., Paech, M. J., Al-Tamimi, Y., & Geddes, D. T. (2013). A comparison of early sucking dynamics during breastfeeding after Cesarean section and vaginal birth. *Breastfeeding Medicine, 8,* 79–85.

Salapatek, P. (1975). Pattern perception in early infancy. In L. B. Cohen & P. Salapatek (Eds.), *Infant perception: From sensation to cognition, Vol. 1.* New York, NY: Academic Press.

Salazar, A. M., Haggerty, K. P., de Haan, B., Catalano, R. F., Vann, T., Vinson, J., & Lansing, M. (2016). Using Communities that Care for community child maltreatment prevention. *American Journal of Orthopsychiatry, 86,* 144–155.

Salazar, L. F., Vivolo-Kantor, A., Hardin, J., & Berkowitz, A. (2014). A web-based sexual violence bystander intervention for male college students: Randomized controlled trial. *Journal of Medical Internet Research, 16,* e203.

Salgin, B., Norris, S. A., Prentice, P., Pettifor, J. M., Richter, L. M., Ong, K. K., & Dunger, D. B. (2015). Even transient rapid infancy weight gain is associated with higher BMI in young adults and earlier menarche. *International Journal of Obesity, 39*(6), 939–944.

Salmivalli, C., & Peets, K. (2009). Bullies, victims, and bully-victim relationships in middle childhood and early adolescence. In K. H. Rubin, W. M. Bukowski, & B. Laursen (Eds.), *Handbook of peer interactions, relationships, and groups.* New York, NY: Guilford.

Salthouse, T. (2012). Consequences of age-related cognitive declines. *Annual Review of Psychology, 63,* 201–226.

Salthouse, T. A. (1990). Cognitive competence and expertise in aging. In J. E. Birren & K. W. Schaie (Eds.),

The handbook of the psychology of aging (3rd ed.). San Diego, CA: Academic Press.

Salthouse, T. A. (1993). Speed and knowledge as determinants of adult age differences in verbal tasks. *Journal of Gerontology Series B: Psychological Sciences, 48,* 29–36.

Salthouse, T. A. (1996). General and specific speed mediation of adult age differences in memory. *Journals of Gerontology B: Psychological Sciences and Social Sciences, 51B,* 30–42.

Salthouse, T. A. (2000). Aging and measures of processing speed. *Biological Psychology, 54,* 35–54.

Salthouse, T. A. (2015). Individual differences in working memory and aging. In R. H. Logie & R. G. Morris (Eds.), *Working memory and aging* (pp. 1–20). New York, NY: Psychology Press.

Salthouse, T. A. (2016). Aging cognition unconfounded by prior test experience. *The Journals of Gerontology. Series B, Psychological Sciences and Social Sciences, 71,* 49–58.

Salthouse, T. A., Hancock, H. E., Meinz, E. J., & Hambrick, D. Z. (1996). Interrelations of age, visual acuity, and cognitive functioning. *Journals of Gerontology: Psychological Sciences and Social Sciences, 51,* 317–330.

Samaras, N. (2015). Diagnosing andropause. *Maturitas, 81*(1), 117.

Samek, D. R., Goodman, R. J., Erath, S. A., McGue, M., & Iacono, W. G. (2016). Antisocial peer affiliation and externalizing disorders in the transition from adolescence to young adulthood: Selection versus socialization effects. *Developmental Psychology, 52,* 813–823.

Sameroff, A. (1975). Early influences on development: Fact or fancy? *Merrill-Palmer Quarterly, 21,* 263–294.

Sameroff, A. (2009). The transactional model. In A. Sameroff (Ed.), *The transactional model of development. How children and contexts shape each other.* Washington, DC: American Psychological Association.

Sameroff, A. J., Seifer, R., Baldwin, A., & Baldwin, C. (1993). Stability of intelligence from preschool to adolescence: The influence of social and family risk factors. *Child Development, 64,* 80–97.

Samnani, A., & Singh, P. (2012). 20 years of workplace bullying research: A review of the antecedents and consequences of bullying in the workplace. *Aggression and Violent Behavior, 17,* 581–589.

Samson, M. M., Meeuwsen, I. B. A. E., Crowe, A., Dessens, J. A. G., Duursma, S. A., & Verhaar, H. J. J. (2000). Relationships between physical performance measures, age, height and body weight in healthy adults. *Age and Ageing, 29,* 235–242.

Sana, F., Weston, T., & Cepeda, N. J. (2013). Laptop multitasking hinders classroom learning for both users and nearby peers. *Computers & Education, 62,* 24–31.

Sanbonmatsu, D. M., Strayer, D. L., Medeiros-Ward, N., & Watson, J. M. (2013). Who multi-tasks and why? Multi-tasking ability, perceived multi-tasking ability, impulsivity, and sensation seeking. *PLoS ONE, 8,* e54402.

Sanchez, L., Fristad, M., Weller, R. A., Weller, E. B., & Moye, J. (1994). Anxiety in acutely bereaved prepubertal children. *Annals of Clinical Psychiatry, 6,* 39–43.

Sandberg, D. E., & Gardner, M. (2015). Short stature: Is it a psychosocial problem and does changing height matter? *Pediatric Clinics of North America, 62,* 963–982.

Sandberg, D. E., Bukowski, W. M., Fung, C. M., Noll, R. B. (2004). Height and social adjustment: are extremes a cause for concern and action? *Pediatrics, 114,* 744–50.

Sanders, W. (1999, September 1). Teachers, teachers, teachers! *DLC: Blueprint Magazine.* Retrieved from www.dlc.org/ndol_ci.cfm?contentid=1199&kaid=110&subid=135.

Sanders, W. L., & Horn, S. P. (1995). The Tennessee Value-Added Assessment System: (TVAAS): Mixed model methodology in educational assessment. In A. J. Shrinkfield & D. Stufflebeam (Eds.), *Teacher evaluation: Guide to effective practice* (pp. 337–350). Boston, MA: Kluwer.

Sanders, W. L., & Rivers, J. C. (1996, November). *Cumulative and residual effects of teachers on future student academic achievement* (Research Progress Report). Knoxville, TN: University of Tennessee Value-Added Research and Assessment Center.

Sandler, I., Ayers, T. S., Tein, J., Wolchik, S., Millsap, R., Khoo, S. T., et al. (2010). Six-year follow-up of a preventive intervention for parentally bereaved youths.

Archives of Pediatric and Adolescent Medicine, 164, 907–914.

Sandler, I. N., Ayers, T. S., Wolchik, S. A., Tein, J., Kwok, O., Haine, R. A., Twohey-Jacobs, J., Suter, J., Lin, K., Padgett-Jones, S., Weyer, J. L., Cole, E., Kriege, G., & Griffin, W. A. (2003). The Family Bereavement Program: Efficacy evaluation of a theory-based prevention program for parentally-bereaved children and adolescents. *Journal of Consulting and Clinical Psychology, 71,* 587–600.

Sandler, I., Ingram, A., Wolchik, S., Tein, J., & Winslow, E. (2015). Long-term effects of parenting-focused preventive interventions to promote resilience of children and adolescents. *Child Development Perspectives, 9,* 164–171.

Sandler, I. N., Ma, Y., Tein, J., Ayers, T. S., Wolchik, S., Kennedy, C., & Millsap, R. (2010). Long-term effects of the Family Bereavement Program on multiple indicators of grief in parentally bereaved children and adolescents. *Journal of Consulting and Clinical Psychology, 78,* 131–143.

Sandman, C. A., Davis, E. P., & Glynn, L. M. (2012). Prescient human fetuses thrive. *Psychological Science, 23,* 93–100.

Sanson, A., Hemphill, S. A., & Smart, D. (2004). Connections between temperament and social development: A review. *Social Development, 13,* 142–170.

Santich, K., & Salazar, C. (2016, June 18). For Latino community, nightclub shooting left gaping loss. *Orlando Sentinel.* Retrieved from www.orlandosentinel.com.

Santos, C. E., & Umaña-Taylor, A. J. (Eds.). (2015). *Studying ethnic identity: Methodological and conceptual approaches across disciplines.* Washington, DC: American Psychological Association.

Sapolsky, R. (1998). *The trouble with testosterone and other essays on the biology of the human predicament.* New York, NY: Scribner.

Sargant, N., Field, J., Francis, H., Schuller, T., & Tuckett, A. (1997). *The learning divide.* Brighton, UK: National Organisation for Adult Learning.

Sarkisian, N., Gerena, M., & Gerstel, N. (2007). Extended family integration among Euro and Mexican Americans: Ethnicity, gender, and class. *Journal of Marriage and Family, 69,* 40–54.

Sartor, C. E., Grant, J. D., Bucholz, K. K., Madden, P. A. F., Heath, A. C., Agrawal, A., Whitfield, J. B., Statham, D. J., Martin, N. G., & Lynskey, M. T. (2010). Common genetic contributions to alcohol and cannabis use and dependence symptomatology. *Alcoholism: Clinical and Experimental Research, 34,* 545–554.

Saucier, D., & Ehresman, C. (2010). The physiology of sex differences. In J. C. Chrisler & D. R. McCreary (Eds.), *Handbook of gender research in psychology* (pp. 215–233). New York, NY: Spring Science+Business Media.

Saudino, K. J. (2012). Sources of continuity and change in activity level in early childhood. *Child Development, 83,* 266–281.

Saudino, K. J., & Micalizzi, L. (2015). Emerging trends in behavioral genetic studies of child temperament. *Child Development Perspectives, 9,* 144–148.

Saudino, K. J., & Wang, M. (2012). Quantitative and molecular genetic studies of temperament. In M. Z. Zentner & R. L. Shiner (Eds.), *Handbook of temperament.* New York, NY: Guilford.

Saudino, K. J., & Zapfe, J. A. (2008). Genetic influences on activity level in early childhood: Do situations matter? *Child Development, 79,* 930–943.

Saunders, C. (2002). A hospice perspective. In K. Foley, & H. Hendin (Eds.), *The case against assisted suicide: For the right to end-of-life care.* Baltimore, MD: The Johns Hopkins Press.

Saunders, C. J., Miller, N. A., Soden, S. E., Dinwiddie, D. L., Noll, A., Alnadi, N. A., et al. (2012). Rapid whole-genome sequencing for genetic disease diagnosis in neonatal intensive care units. *Science Translational Medicine, 4*(154), 154ra135.

Savin-Williams, R. C. (2001). *Mom, Dad. I'm gay. How families negotiate coming out.* Washington DC: American Psychological Association.

Savin-Williams, R. C., & Cohen, K. M. (2015). Developmental trajectories and milestones of lesbian, gay, and bisexual young people. *International Review of Psychiatry, 27,* 357–366.

Savin-Williams, R. C., Joyner, K., & Rieger, G. (2012). Prevalence and stability of self-reported sexual orientation identity during young adulthood. *Archives of Sex Behavior, 41,* 103–110.

Savin-Williams, R. C., & Ream, G. L. (2003). Sex variations in the disclosure to parents of same-sex attractions. *Journal of Family Psychology, 17,* 429–438.

Savin-Williams, R. C., & Ream, G. L. (2007). Prevalence and stability of sexual orientation components during adolescence and young adulthood. *Archives of Sexual Behavior, 36,* 385–394.

Savla, J. T., Roberto, K. A., Jaramillo-Sierra, A., Gambrel, L. E., Karimi, H., & Butner, L. M. (2013). Childhood abuse affects emotional closeness with family in mid- and later life. *Child Abuse & Neglect, 37,* 388–399.

Saxe, R. R., Whitfield-Gabrieli, S., Scholz, J., & Pephrey, K. A. (2009). Brain regions for perceiving and reasoning about other people in school-aged children. *Child Development, 80,* 1197–1209.

Saxe, R., & Kanwisher, N. (2003). People thinking about thinking people: The role of the temporo-parietal junction in "theory of mind." *NeuroImage, 19,* 1835–1842.

Saxe, R., Carey, S., & Kanwisher, N. (2004). Understanding other minds: Linking developmental psychology and functional neuroimaging. *Annual Review of Psychology, 55,* 87–124.

Sayal, K., Heron, J., Golding, J., & Emond, A. (2007). Prenatal alcohol exposure and gender differences in childhood mental health problems: A longitudinal population-based study. *Pediatrics, 119,* e426–e434.

Sayer, L. C. (2005). Gender, time and inequality: Trends in women's and men's paid work, unpaid work and free time. *Social Forces, 84,* 285–303.

Sayre, N. E., & Gallagher, J. D. (2001). *The young child and the environment.* Boston, MA: Allyn & Bacon.

Sbarra, D. A., Law, R. W., & Portley, R. M. (2011). Divorce and death: A meta-analysis and research agenda for clinical, social, and health psychology. *Perspectives on Psychological Science, 6,* 454–474.

Scafidi, F. A., Field, T., & Schanberg, S. M. (1993). Factors that predict which preterm infants benefit most from massage therapy. *Journal of Developmental and Behavioral Pediatrics, 14,* 176–180.

Scaramella, L. V., & Conger, R. D. (2003). Intergenerational continuity of hostile parenting and its consequences: The moderating influence of children's negative emotional reactivity. *Social Development, 12,* 420–439.

Scarr, S., & McCartney, K. (1983). How people make their own environments: A theory of genotype → environment effects. *Child Development, 54,* 424–435.

Scarr, S., & Weinberg, R. A. (1978). The influence of family background on intellectual attainment. *American Sociological Review, 43,* 674–692.

Scarr, S., & Weinberg, R. A. (1983). The Minnesota adoption studies: Genetic differences and malleability. *Child Development, 54,* 260–267.

Scerif, G., & Baker, K. (2015). Annual research review: Rare genotypes and childhood psychopathology—Uncovering diverse developmental mechanisms of ADHD risk. *Journal of Child Psychology and Psychiatry, 56,* 251–273.

Schaaf, J. M., Alexander, K. W., & Goodman, G. S. (2008). Children's false memory and true disclosure in the face of repeated questions. *Journal of Experimental Child Psychology, 100,* 157–185.

Schaal, B., Marlier, L., & Soussignan, R. (1998). Olfactory function in the human fetus: Evidence from selective neonatal responsiveness to the odor of amniotic fluid. *Behavioral Neuroscience, 112,* 1438–1449.

Schacter, D. L. (1996). *Searching for memory: The brain, the mind, and the past.* New York, NY: Basic Books.

Schaefer, E. S. (1959). A circumplex model for maternal behavior. *Journal of Abnormal and Social Psychology, 59,* 226–235.

Schafer, M., Haun, D. B. M., & Tomasello, M. (2015). Fair is not fair everywhere. *Psychological Science, 26,* 1252–1260.

Schaffer, H. R., & Emerson, P. E. (1964). The development of social attachments in infancy. *Monographs of the Society for Research in Child Development, 29* (3, Serial No. 94).

Schaie, K. W. & Willis, S. L. (Ed.). (2016). *Handbook of the psychology of aging* (8th ed.) San Diego, CA: Elsevier.

Schaie, K. W. (1994). Developmental designs revisited. In S. H. Cohen & H. W. Reese (Eds.), *Life-span developmental psychology: Methodological contributions.* Hillsdale, NJ: Erlbaum.

Schaie, K. W. (1996). *Intellectual development in adulthood: The Seattle Longitudinal Study.* Cambridge, UK: Cambridge University Press.

Schaie, K. W. (2000). The impact of longitudinal studies on understanding development from young adulthood to old age. *International Journal of Behavioral Development, 24,* 257–266.

Schaie, K. W. (2011). Historical influences on aging and behavior. In K. W. Schaie & S. L. Willis (Eds.), B. G. Knight, B. Levy, & D. C. Park (Assoc. Eds.), *Handbook of the psychology of aging* (pp. 41–55). Burlington, MA: Academic Press/Elsevier.

Schaie, K. W. (2012). *Developmental influences on adult intelligence: The Seattle longitudinal study* (2nd ed.). Oxford University Press.

Schaie, K. W. (2013). *Developmental influences on adult intelligence: The Seattle Longitudinal Study* (2nd ed.). New York, NY: Oxford University Press.

Schaie, K. W., & Caskie, G. I. L. (2005). Methodological issues in aging research. In D. M. Teti (Ed.), *Handbook of research methods in developmental science.* Malden, MA: Blackwell Publishing.

Schaie, K. W., & Willis, S. L. (1986). Can decline in adult intellectual functioning be reversed? *Developmental Psychology, 22,* 223–232.

Schaie, K. W., & Willis, S. L. (2010). The Seattle Longitudinal Study of adult cognitive development. *ISSBD Bulletin, 57,* 24–29.

Schaie, K. W., & Zanjani, F. A. K. (2006). Intellectual development across adulthood. In C. Hoare (Ed.), *Handbook of adult development and learning.* New York, NY: Oxford University Press.

Schalke, D., Brunner, M., Geiser, C., Preckel, F., Keller, U., Spengler, M., & Martin, R. (2013). Stability and change in intelligence from age 12 to age 52: Results from the Luxembourg MAGRIP study. *Developmental Psychology, 49,* 1529–1543.

Schalock, R. L., Borthwick-Duffy, S. A., Bradley, V. J., Buntinx, W. H. E., Coulter, D. L., Craig, E. M., et al. (2010). *Intellectual disability: Definition, classification, and systems of supports* (11th ed.). Washington, DC: American Association on Intellectual and Developmental Disabilities.

Schank, R. C., & Abelson, R. P. (1977). *Scripts, plans, goals, and understanding.* Hillsdale, NJ: Erlbaum.

Scharlach, A., Li, W., & Dalvi, T. B. (2006). Family conflict as a mediator of caregiver strain. *Family Relations, 55,* 625–635.

Scheffler, R. M., Brown, T. T., Fulton, B. D., Hinshaw, S. P., Levine, P., Stone, S. (2009, May). Positive association between attention deficit/hyperactivity disorder medication use and academic achievement during elementary school. *Pediatrics, 123,* 1273–1279.

Scheibel, A. B. (2009). Aging of the brain. In P. R. Hof & C. V. Mobbs (Eds.), *Handbook of the neuroscience of aging* (pp. 5–10). London, UK: Academic Press.

Scheiber, C., Chen, H., Kaufman, A. S., & Weiss, L. G. (2016, April 14). How much does WAIS-IV perceptual reasoning decline across the 20 to 90-year lifespan when processing speed is controlled? *Applied Neuropsychology: Adult,* 1–16 [epub ahead of publication].

Schery, T. K., & Peters, M. L. (2003). Developing auditory learning in children with cochlear implants. *Topics in Language Disorders, 23,* 4–15.

Schiavi, R. C., Schreiner-Engel, P., White, D., & Mandeli, J. (1991). The relationship between pituitary-gonadal function and sexual behavior in healthy aging men. *Psychosomatic Medicine, 53,* 363–374.

Schieffelin, B. B. (1986). *How Kaluli children learn what to say, what to do, and how to feel.* New York, NY: Cambridge University Press.

Schiepers, O. J. G., Harris, S. E., Gow, A. J., Pattie, A., Brett, C. E., Starr, J. M., et al. (2012). APOE E4 status predicts age-related cognitive decline in the ninth decade: Longitudinal follow-up of the Lothian birth cohort 1921. *Molecular Psychiatry, 17,* 315–324.

Schiff, A. R., & Knopf, I. J. (1985). The effect of task demands on attention allocation in children of different ages. *Child Development, 56,* 621–630.

Schiffman, H. R. (2000). *Sensation and perception* (5th ed.). New York, NY: Wiley.

Schiffman, S. S. (1977). Food recognition by the elderly. *Journal of Gerontology, 32,* 586–592.

Schiffman, S. S. (2009). Effects of aging on the human taste system. *Annals of the New York Academy of Sciences, 1170,* 725–729.

Schiffman, S. S., & Warwick, Z. S. (1993). Effect of flavor enhancement of foods for the elderly on nutritional status: Food intake, biochemical indices, and anthropometric measures. *Physiological Behavior, 53,* 395–402.

Schiffrin, H. H., Liss, M., Miles-McLean, H., Geary, K. A., Erchull, M. J., & Tashner, T. (2014). Helping or hovering? The effects of helicopter parenting on college students' well-being. *Journal of Child and Family Studies, 23,* 548–557.

Schiraldi, V. & Western, B. (2015, October 4). Time to raise the juvenile age limit. *The Washington Post,* A21.

Schlegel, A., & Barry, H., III. (2015). Leaving childhood: The nature and meaning of adolescent transition rituals. In L. A. Jensen (Ed.), *The Oxford handbook of human development and culture: An interdisciplinary perspective* (pp. 327–340). New York, NY: Oxford University Press.

Schleppenbach, M., Perry, M., Miller, K. F., Sims, L., & Fang, G. (2007). The answer is only the beginning: Extended discourse in Chinese and U.S. mathematics classrooms. *Journal of Educational Psychology, 99,* 380–396.

Schmidt, F. L., & Hunter, J. E. (1998). The validity and utility of selection methods in personnel psychology: Practical and theoretical implications of 85 years of research findings. *Psychological Bulletin, 124,* 262–274.

Schmidt, F. L., & Hunter, J. E. (2004). General mental ability in the world of work: Occupational attainment and job performance. *Journal of Personality and Social Psychology, 86,* 162–173.

Schmidt, M. F. H., & Sommerville, J. A. (2011). Fairness expectations and altruistic sharing in 15-month-old human infants. *PloS ONE, 6,* e23223.

Schmidt, S., & Petermann, F. (2009). Developmental psychopathology: Attention deficit hyperactivity disorder (ADHD). *BMC Psychiatry, 9,* 58.

Schmitt, S. K., Sneed, L., & Phibbs, C. S. (2006). Costs of newborn care in California: A population-based study. *Pediatrics, 117,* 154–160.

Schneider, W. (2011). Memory development in childhood. In U. Goswami (Ed.), *The Wiley-Blackwell handbook of childhood cognitive development* (2nd ed., pp. 347–376). Malden, MA: John Wiley & Sons.

Schneider, W. (2014). Individual differences in memory development and educational implications: Cross-sectional and longitudinal evidence. In P. J. Bauer & R. Fivush (Eds.), *The Wiley handbook on the development of children's memory* (pp. 947–971). Malden, MA: Wiley Blackwell.

Schneider, W. (2015). *Memory development from early childhood through emerging adulthood.* London, UK: Springer.

Schneider, W., & Bjorklund, D. F. (1998). Memory. In D. Kuhn & R. S. Siegler (Vol. Eds.), W. Damon (Editor-in-Chief), *Handbook of child psychology: Vol. 2. Cognition, perception, and language* (5th ed., pp. 467–522). New York, NY: Wiley.

Schneider, W., Bjorklund, D. F., & Maier-Bruckner, W. (1996). The effects of expertise and IQ on children's memory: When knowledge is, and when it is not enough. *International Journal of Behavioral Development, 19,* 773–796.

Schneider, W., & Bullock, M. (Eds.). (2009). *Human development from early childhood to early adulthood.* New York, NY: Psychology Press.

Schneider, W., & Ornstein, P. A. (2015). The development of children's memory. *Child Development Perspectives, 9,* 190–195.

Schneider, W., & Pressley, M. (1997). *Memory development between two and 20* (2nd ed.). Mahwah, NJ: Erlbaum.

Schneider, W., & Sodian, B. (1988). Metamemory-memory behavior relationships in young children: Evidence from a memory-for-location task. *Journal of Experimental Child Psychology, 45,* 209–233.

Schneider, W., Gruber, H., Gold, A., & Opwis, K. (1993). Chess expertise and memory for chess positions in children and adults. *Journal of Experimental Child Psychology, 56,* 328–349.

Schneider, W., Kron-Sperl, V., & Hünnerkopf, M. (2009). The development of young children's memory strategies: Evidence from the Wurzburg Longitudinal Memory

Study. *European Journal of Developmental Psychology*, 6, 70–99.

Schneider, W., Niklas, F., & Schmiedeler, S. (2014). Intellectual development from early childhood to early adulthood: The impact of early IQ differences on stability and change over time. *Learning and Individual Differences*, 32, 156–162.

Schneider, W., Roth, E., & Ennemoser, M. (2000). Training phonological skills and letter knowledge in children at risk for dyslexia: A comparison of three kindergarten intervention programs. *Journal of Educational Psychology*, 92, 284–295.

Schneiderman, I., Zagoory-Sharon, O., Leckman, J. F., & Feldman, R. (2012). Oxytocin during the initial stages of romantic attachment: Relations to couples' interactive reciprocity. *Psychoneuroendocrinology*, 37, 1277–1285.

Schoenborn, C. A., & Adams, P. F. (2010). Health behaviors of adults: United States, 2005–2007. National Center for Health Statistics. *Vital Health Statistics*, 10(245).

Schoenfelder, E. N., Tein, J., Wolchik, S., & Sandler, I. N. (2015). Effects of the family bereavement program on academic outcomes, educational expectations and job aspirations 6 years later: The mediating role of parenting and youth mental health problems. *Journal of Abnormal Child Psychology*, 43, 229–241.

Schofield, H. T., Bierman, K. L., & Heinrichs, B. (2008). Predicting early sexual activity with behavior problems exhibited at school entry and in early adolescence. *Journal of Abnormal Child Psychology*, 36, 1175–1188.

Scholtes, D., & Browne, M. (2015). Internalized and externalized continuing bonds in bereaved parents: Their relationship with grief intensity and personal growth. *Death Studies*, 39, 75–83.

Schooler, C., Mulatu, M. S., & Oates, G. (1999). The continuing effects of substantively complex work on the intellectual functioning of older workers. *Psychology and Aging*, 14, 483–506.

Schoppe-Sullivan, S. J., Diener, M. L., Mangelsdorf, S. C., Brown, G. L., & McHale, J. L. (2006). Attachment and sensitivity in family context: The roles of parent and infant gender. *Infant and Child Development*, 15, 367–385.

Schot, M. J. C., Halbertsma, F. J. J., Katgert, T., & Bok, L. A. (2013). Development of children with symptomatic intracranial hemorrhage born after vacuum extraction. *Journal of Child Neurology*, 28, 520–523.

Schott, J. M., & Rossor, M. N. (2003). The grasp and other primitive reflexes. *Journal of Neurology and Neurosurgical Psychiatry*, 74, 558–560.

Schreibman, L., Dawson, G., Stahmer, A. C., Landa, R., Rogers, S. J., McGee, G. G., . . . Halladay, A. (2015). Naturalistic developmental behavioral interventions: Empirically validated treatments for autism spectrum disorder. *Journal of Autism and Developmental Disorders*, 45, 2411–2428.

Schreuder, D. A. (2014). *Vision and visual perception*. Bloomington, IN: Archway Publishing.

Schroeder, B. A., Messina, A., Schroeder, D., Good, K., Barto, S., Saylor, J., & Masiello, M. (2012). The implementation of a statewide bullying prevention program: Preliminary findings from the field and the importance of coalitions. *Health Promotion Practice*, 13, 489–495.

Schryer, E., & Ross, M. (2013). The use and benefits of external memory aids in older and younger adults. *Applied Cognitive Psychology*, 27, 663–671.

Schubert, C. R., Cruickshanks, K. J., Fischer, M. E., Huang, G., Klein, B. E. K., Klein, R., et al. (2012). Olfactory impairment in an adult population: The Beaver Dam Offspring Study. *Chemical Senses*, 37, 325–334.

Schuette, C. T., Ponton, M. K., & Charlton, M. L. (2012). Middle school children's career aspirations: Relationship to adult occupations and gender. *Career Development Quarterly*, 60, 35–46.

Schuhrke, B. (2000). Young children's curiosity about other people's genitals. *Journal of Psychology & Human Sexuality*, 12, 27–48.

Schulte, B. (2014, June 23) The U.S. ranks last in every measure when it comes to family policy, in 10 charts. *The Washington Post*. Retrieved from www.washingtonpost.com/blogs/she-the-people/wp/2014/06/23/global-view-how-u-s-policies-to-help-working-families-rank-in-the-world/.

Schulte, B., & Craig, T. (2007, August 27). Unknown to Va. Tech, Cho had a disorder. Fairfax helped student cope with anxiety. *The Washington Post*, pp. A1, A8.

Schulz, J. H., & Binstock, R. H. (2006). *Aging nation. The economics and politics of growing older in America*. Baltimore, MD: Johns Hopkins University Press.

Schulz, M. S., & Lazarus, R. S. (2011). Regulating emotion in adolescence: A cognitive-mediational conceptualization. In P. K. Kerig, M. S. Schulz, & S. T. Hauser (Eds.), *Adolescence and beyond. Family processes and development*. New York, NY: Oxford University Press.

Schulz, M. S., Cowan, C. P., & Cowan, P. A. (2006). Promoting healthy beginnings: A randomized controlled trial of a preventive intervention to preserve marital quality during the transition to parenthood. *Journal of Consulting and Clinical Psychology*, 74, 20–31.

Schulz, R., & Aderman, D. (1974). Clinical research and the stages of dying. *Omega: Journal of Death and Dying*, 5, 137–143.

Schulz, R., & Schlarb, J. (1987–1988). Two decades of research on dying: What do we know about the patient? *Omega: Journal of Death and Dying*, 18, 299–317.

Schulz, R., Belle, S. H., Czaja, S. J., Gitlin, L. N., Wisniewski, S. R., & Ory, M. G. (2003). Introduction to the special section on Resources for Enhancing Alzheimer's Caregiver Health (REACH). *Psychology and Aging*, 18, 357–360.

Schulz, R., Boerner, K., & Hebert, R. S. (2008). Caregiving and bereavement. In M. S. Stroebe, R. O. Hansson, H. Schut, & W. Stroebe (Eds.), *Handbook of bereavement research and practice. Advances in theory and intervention*. Washington, DC: American Psychological Association.

Schumacker, E. H., Seymour, T. L., Glass, J.M., Fencsik, D. E., Lauber, E. J., Kieras, D. E., & Meyer, D. E. (2001). Virtually perfect time sharing in dual-task performance: Uncorking the central cognitive bottleneck. *Psychological Science*, 12, 101–108.

Schumann, C. M., Barnes, C. C., Lord, C., & Courchesne, E. (2009). Amygdala enlargement in toddlers with autism related to severity of social and communication impairments. *Biological Psychiatry*, 66, 942–949.

Schunn, C. D., & Anderson, J. R. (1999). The generality/specificity of expertise in scientific reasoning. *Cognitive Science*, 23, 337–370.

Schwartz, M., Share, D. L., Leikin, M., & Kozminsky, E. (2008). On the benefits of bi-literacy: Just a head start in reading or specific orthographic insights? *Reading and Writing*, 21, 905–927.

Schwartz, S. J., Luyckx, K., & Vignoles, L. V. (Eds.). (2011). *Handbook of identity theory and research*. New York, NY: Springer.

Schwartz-Mette, R., & Rose, A. J. (2012). Co-rumination mediates contagion of internalizing symptoms within youths' friendships. *Developmental Psychology*, 48, 1355–1365.

Schweinhart, L. J., Montie, J., Xiang, Z., Barnett, W. S., Belfield, C. R., & Nores, M. (2005). *Lifetime effects: The High Scope Perry Preschool Study through age 40*. Ypsilanti, MI: High Scope Educational Research Foundation.

Schwenck, C., Bjorklund, D. F., & Schneider, W. (2007). Factors influencing the incidence of utilization deficiencies and other patterns of recall/strategy-use relations in a strategic memory task. *Child Development*, 78, 1771–1787.

Schwenck, C., Bjorklund, D. F., & Schneider, W. (2009). Developmental and individual differences in young children's use and maintenance of a selective memory strategy. *Developmental Psychology*, 45, 1034–1050.

Schwerdtfeger, K. L., & Shreffler, K. M. (2009). Trauma of pregnancy loss and infertility among mothers and involuntarily childless women in the United States. *Journal of Loss and Trauma*, 14, 211–227.

Schwitzgebel, E. (1999). Gradual belief change in children. *Human Development*, 42, 283–296.

Scialfa, C. T., Esau, S. P., & Joffe, K. M. (1998). Age, target-distracter similarity, and visual search. *Experimental Aging Research*, 24, 337–358.

Scott, G. D., Karns, C. M., Dow, M. W., Stevens, C., & Neville, H. J. (2014). Enhanced peripheral visual processing in congenitally deaf humans is supported by multiple brain regions, including primary auditory cortex. *Frontiers in Human Neuroscience*, 8, 177.

Scott, G., Leritz, L. E., & Mumford, M.D. (2004). The effectiveness of creativity training: A quantitative review. *Creativity Research Journal*, 16, 361–388.

Scott, R. M., & Baillargeon, R. (2009). Which penguin is this? Attributing false beliefs about object identity at 18 months. *Child Development*, 80, 1172–1196.

Scott, W. A., Scott, R., & McCabe, M. (1991). Family relationships and children's personality: A cross-cultural, cross-source comparison. *British Journal of Social Psychology*, 30, 1–20.

Scourfield, J., Rice, F., Thapar, A., Harold, G. T., Martin, N., & McGuffin, P. (2003). Depressive symptoms in children and adolescents: Changing etiological influences with development. *Journal of Child Psychology and Psychiatry and Allied Disciplines*, 44, 968–976.

Sczesny, S., Bosak, J., Diekman, A. B., & Twenge, J. M. (2008). Dynamics of sex-role stereotypes. In Y. Kashima, K. Fiedler, & P. Freytag (Eds.), *Stereotype dynamics: Language-based approaches to the formation, maintenance, and transformation of stereotypes* (pp. 135–163). New York, NY: Taylor & Francis.

Seale, C. (1991). A comparison of hospice and conventional care. *Social Science and Medicine*, 32, 147–152.

Seaton, E. K., Scottham, K. M., & Sellers, R. M. (2006). The status model of racial identity development in African American adolescents: Evidence of structure, trajectories, and well-being. *Child Development*, 77, 1416–1426.

Sebastiani, P., Solovieff, N., DeWan, A. T., Walsh, K. M., Puca, A., et al. (2012). Genetic signatures of exceptional longevity in humans. *PLoS ONE* 7(1), e29848.

Sebby, R., & Papini, D. (1994). Postformal reasoning during adolescence and young adulthood: The influence of problem relevancy. *Adolescence*, 29, 389–400.

Seccombe, K. (2000). Families in poverty in the 1990s: Trends, causes, consequences, and lessons learned. *Journal of Marriage and the Family*, 62, 1094–1113.

Sedgh, G., Finer, L. B., Bankole, A., Eilers, M. A., & Singh, S. (2015). Adolescent pregnancy, birth, and abortion rates across countries. *Journal of Adolescent Health*, 56, 223–230.

Segal, N. L. (2000). Virtual twins: New findings on within-family environmental influences on intelligence. *Journal of Educational Psychology*, 92, 442–448.

Segal, N. L. (2005). Evolutionary studies of cooperation, competition, and altruism. A twin-based approach. In R. L. Burgess & K. MacDonald (Eds.), *Evolutionary perspectives on human development*. Thousand Oaks, CA: Sage.

Segal, N. L. (2012). *Born together—reared apart. The landmark Minnesota Twin Study*. Cambridge, MA: Harvard University Press.

Segal, N. L., & Johnson, W. (2009). Twin studies of general mental ability. In Y. Kim (Ed.), *Handbook of behavior genetics*. New York, NY: Springer.

Segovia, C., Hutchinson, I., Laing, D. G., & Jinks, A. L. (2002). A quantitative study of fungiform papillae and taste pore density in adults and children. *Developmental Brain Research*, 138, 135–146.

Segrin, C., Givertz, M., Swaitkowski, P., & Montgomery, N. (2015). Overparenting is associated with child problems and a critical family environment. *Journal of Child and Family Studies*, 24, 470–479.

Segrin, C., Woszidlo, A., Givertz, M., & Montgomery, N. (2013). Parent and child traits associated with overparenting. *Journal of Social and Clinical Psychology*, 32, 569–595.

Seiffge-Krenke, I. (1998). *Adolescents' health: A developmental perspective*. Mahwah, NJ: Erlbaum.

Seiffge-Krenke, I. (2003). Testing theories of romantic development from adolescence to young adulthood: Evidence of a developmental sequence. *International Journal of Behavioral Development*, 27, 519–531.

Seleen, D. R. (1982). The congruence between actual and desired use of time by older adults: A predictor of life satisfaction. *Gerontologist*, 22, 95–99.

Selikowitz, M. (2009). *ADHD: The facts* (2nd ed.). New York, NY: Oxford.

Selman, R. L. (1976). Social cognitive understanding: A guide to educational and clinical experience. In T. Lickona (Ed.), *Moral development and behavior: Theory, research and social issues*. New York, NY: Holt, Rinehart & Winston.

Selman, R. L. (1980). *The growth of interpersonal understanding*. New York, NY: Academic Press.

Selman, R. L., Beardslee, W., Schultz, L. H., Krupa, M., & Podorefsky, D. (1986). Assessing adolescent interpersonal negotiation strategies: Toward the integration of structural and functional models. *Developmental Psychology, 22,* 450–459.

Seltzer, J. A., & Yahirun, J. J. (2013, November 6). *Diversity in old age: The elderly in changing economic and family contexts. US2010.* Retrieved from www.s4.brown.edu/us2010/Data/Report/report11062013.pdf.

Seltzer, M. M., & Li, L. W. (2000). The dynamics of caregiving: Transitions during a three-year prospective study, *Gerontologist, 40,* 165–178.

Senter, M. S., & Senter, R. (1997). Student outcomes and the adult learner. *Continuing Higher Education Review, 61,* 75–87.

Sentse, M., Veenstra, R., Lindenberg, S., Verhulst, F. C., & Ormel, J. (2009). Buffers and risks in temperament and family for early adolescent psychopathology: Generic, conditional, or domain-specific effects? The Trails Study. *Developmental Psychology, 45,* 419–435.

Serafica, F. C., & Vargas, L. A. (2006). Cultural diversity in the development of child psychopathology. In D. Cicchetti & D. J. Cohen (Eds.), *Developmental psychopathology: Vol. 1. Theory and method* (2nd ed.). Hoboken, NJ: Wiley.

Serbin, L. A., Poulin-Dubois, D., & Eichstedt, J. A. (2002). Infants' response to gender-inconsistent events. *Infancy, 3,* 531–542.

Serbin, L. A., Powlishta, K. K., & Gulko, J. (1993). The development of sex typing in middle childhood. *Monographs of the Society for Research in Child Development, 58*(2, Serial No. 232).

Serbin, L. A., Tonick, I. J., & Sternglanz, S. H. (1977). Shaping cooperative cross-sex play. *Child Development, 48,* 924–929.

Serenius, F., Källén, K., Blennow, M., Ewald, U., Fellman, V., Holmström, G., Lindberg, E., Lundqvist, P., Maršál, K., Norman, M., Olhager, E., Stigson, L., Stjernqvist, K., Vollmer, B., & Strömberg, B. for the EXPRESS Group (2013). Neurodevelopmental outcome in extremely preterm infants at 2.5 years after active perinatal care in Sweden. *Journal of the American Medical Association, 309,* 1810–1820.

Sergeant, M. J. T., Davies, M. N. O., Dickins, T. E., & Griffiths, M. D. (2005). The self-reported importance of olfaction during human mate choice. *Sexualities, Evolution, and Gender, 7,* 199–213.

Serjeant, G. R. (2010). One hundred years of sickle cell disease. *British Journal of Haematology, 151,* 425–429.

Servaty-Seib, H. L. (2009). Death of a friend during adolescence. In D. E. Balk & C. A. Corr (Eds.), *Adolescent encounters with death, bereavement, and coping.* New York, NY: Springer.

Servin, A., Bohlin, G., & Berlin, L. (1999). Sex differences in 1-, 3-, and 5-year-olds' toy-choice in a structured play-session. *Scandinavian Journal of Psychology, 40,* 43–48.

Settersten, R. A., Jr. (1998). A time to leave home and a time never to return? Age constraints on the living arrangements of young adults. *Social Forces, 76,* 1373–1400.

Settersten, R. A., Jr. (2005). Linking the two ends of life: What gerontology can learn from childhood studies. *Journals of Gerontology: Social Sciences, 60*B, S173–S180.

Shafer, V. L., & Garrido-Nag, K. (2009). The neurodevelopmental bases of language. In E. Hoff & M. Shatz (Eds.), *Blackwell handbook of language development* (pp. 21–45). Malden, MA: Wiley-Blackwell.

Shaffer, D. R., & Kipp, K. (2014). *Developmental psychology: Childhood and adolescence* (9th ed.). Belmont, CA: Cengage Learning.

Shaffer, D., & Pfeffer, C. R. (2001). Practice parameters for the assessment and treatment of children and adolescents with suicidal behavior. *Journal of the American Academy of Child & Adolescent Psychiatry, 40,* 24S–51S.

Shah, B., Pattanayak, R. D., & Sagar, R. (2014). The study of patient Henry Molaison and what it taught us over past 50 years: Contributions to neuroscience. *Journal of Mental Health and Human Behaviour, 19,* 91.

Shah, P. S. (2010). Paternal factors and low birthweight, preterm, and small for gestational age births: A systematic review. *American Journal of Obstetrics & Gynecology, 202,* 103–123.

Shah, S. M., Carey, I. M., Harris, T., Dewilde, S., Victor, C. R., & Cook, D. G. (2013). The effect of unexpected bereavement on mortality in older couples. *American Journal of Public Health, 103,* 1140–1145.

Shanahan, L., McHale, S. M., Osgood, D. W., & Crouter, A. C. (2004). Conflict frequency with mothers and fathers from middle childhood to late adolescence: Within- and between-families comparisons. *Developmental Psychology, 43,* 539–550.

Shanahan, M. J. (2000). Pathways to adulthood in changing societies: Variability and mechanisms in life course perspective. *Annual Review of Sociology, 26,* 667–692.

Shanahan, M. J., Finch, M. D., Mortimer, J. T., & Ryu, S. (1991). Adolescent work experience and depressive affect. *Social Psychology Quarterly, 54,* 299–317.

Shannon, J. B. (2006). *Death and dying sourcebook* (2nd ed.). Detroit, MI: Omnigraphics.

Sharabany, R., Gershoni, R., & Hofman, J. E. (1981). Girlfriend, boyfriend: Age and sex differences in intimate friendship. *Developmental Psychology, 17,* 800–808.

Sharp, E. S., & Gatz, M. (2011). Relationship between education and dementia: An updated systematic review. *Alzheimer Disease and Associated Disorders, 25,* 289–304.

Sharpe, P. A., Jackson, K. L., White, C., Vaca, V. L., Hickey, T., Gu, J., et al. (1997). Effects of a one-year physical activity intervention for older adults at congregate nutrition sites. *Gerontologist, 37,* 208–215.

Shaver, P. R., & Fraley, R. C. (2008). Attachment, loss, and grief: Bowlby's views and current controversies. In J. Cassidy & P. R. Shaver (Eds.), *Handbook of attachment: Theory, research, and clinical applications* (2nd ed.). New York, NY: Guilford.

Shaw, P., Malek, M., Watson, B., Sharp, W., Evans, A., & Greenstein, D. (2012). Development of cortical surface area and gyrification in attention-deficit/hyperactivity disorder. *Biological Psychiatry, 72,* 191–197.

Shaywitz, B. A., Shaywitz, S. E., Pugh, K. R., Constable, R. T., Skudlarski, P., & Fulbright, R. K. (1995). Sex differences in the functional organization of the brain for language. *Nature, 373,* 607–609.

Shaywitz, B. A., Shaywitz, S. E., Pugh, K. R., Fulbright, R. K., Mencl, E., Bonstable, R. T., et al. (2001). The neurobiology of dyslexia. *Clinical Neuroscience, 1,* 291–299.

Shaywitz, S. E., Fletcher, J. M., Holahan, J. M., Shneider, A. E., Marchione, K. E., Stuebing, K. K., et al. (1999). Persistence of dyslexia: The Connecticut Longitudinal Study at Adolescence. *Pediatrics, 104,* 1351–1359.

Sheetz, M. J., & Bowman, M. S. (2013). Parents' perceptions of a pediatric palliative program. *American Journal of Hospice & Palliative Care, 30,* 291–296.

Shekhar, S., Rana, N., & Jaswal, R. (2013). A prospective randomized study comparing maternal and fetal effects of forceps delivery and vacuum extraction. *The Journal of Obstetrics and Gynecology of India, 2013, 63,* 116–119.

Shenhav, A., & Greene, J. D. (2014). Integrative moral judgment: Dissociating the roles of the amygdala and ventromedial prefrontal cortex. *Journal of Neuroscience, 34,* 4741–4749.

Shepard, R. J. (1997). Curricular physical activity and academic performance. *Pediatric Exercise Science, 9,* 113–126.

Shepard, T. H., & Lemire, R. J. (2010). *Catalog of teratogenic agents* (13th ed.). Baltimore, MD: Johns Hopkins University Press.

Shepherd, G. M. (2012). *Neurogastronomy: How the brain creates flavor and why it matters.* New York, NY: Columbia University Press.

Sheridan, H., & Reingold, E. M. (2014). Expert vs. novice differences in the detection of relevant information during a chess game: Evidence from eye movements. *Frontiers in Psychology, 5,* 941.

Shernoff, D. J., Kelly, S., Tonks, S. M., Anderson, B., Cavanagh, R. F., Sinha, S., & Abdi, B. (2016). Student engagement as a function of environmental complexity in high school classrooms. *Learning and Instruction, 43,* 52–60.

Shifrin, D., Brown, A., Hill, D., Jana, L., & Flinn, S. K. (2015, October 1). Growing up digital: Media Research Symposium. Retrieved from www.aap.org/en-us/documents/digital_media_symposium_proceedings.pdf.

Shih, M., Pittinsky, T. L., & Ambady, N. (1999). Stereotype susceptibility: Identity salience and shifts in quantitative performance. *Psychological Science, 10,* 80–83.

Shiner, R. L., & Caspi, A. (2012). Temperament and the development of personality traits, adaptation, and narratives. In M. Z. Zentner & R. L. Shiner (Eds.), *Handbook of temperament.* New York, NY: Guilford.

Shiner, R. L., Buss, K. A., McClowry, S. G., Putnam, S. P., Saudino, K. J., & Zentner, M. (2012). What is temperament now? Assessing progress in temperament research on the twenty-fifth anniversary of Goldsmith et al. (1987). *Child Development, 6,* 436–444.

Ship, J. A., Pearson, J. D., Cruise, L. J., Brant, L. J., & Metter, E. J. (1996). Longitudinal changes in smell identification. *Journals of Gerontology: Biological Sciences and Medical Sciences, 51,* M86–M91.

Ship, J. A., & Weiffenbach, J. M. (1993). Age, gender, medical treatment, and medication effects on smell identification. *Journal of Gerontology, 48,* M26–M32.

Shlafer, R. J., Raby, K. L., Lawler, J. M., Hesemeyer, P. S., & Roisman, G. I. (2015). Longitudinal associations between adult attachment states of mind and parenting quality. *Attachment & Human Development, 17,* 83–95.

Shneidman, E. S. (1973). *Deaths of man.* New York, NY: Quadrangle.

Shneidman, E. S. (1980). *Voices of death.* New York, NY: Harper & Row.

Shneidman, L. A., & Goldin-Meason, S. (2012). Language input and acquisition in a Mayan village: How important is directed speech? *Developmental Science, 15,* 659–673.

Shoda, Y., Mischel, W., & Peake, P. K. (1990). Predicting adolescent cognitive and self-regulatory competencies from preschool delay of gratification: Identifying diagnostic conditions. *Developmental Psychology, 26,* 978–986.

Shonk, S. M., & Cicchetti, D. (2001). Maltreatment, competency deficits, and risk for academic and behavioral maladjustment. *Developmental Psychology, 37,* 3–17.

Shonkoff, J. P. (2010). Building a new biodevelopmental framework to guide the future of early childhood policy. *Child Development, 81,* 357–367.

Shors, T. J. (2014). The adult brain makes new neurons, and effortful learning keeps them alive. *Current Directions in Psychological Science, 23,* 311–318.

Shors, T. J., Olson, R. L., Bates, M. E., Selby, E. A., & Alderman, B. L. (2014). Mental and physical (MAP) training: A neurogenesis-inspired intervention that enhances health in humans. *Neurobiology of Learning and Memory, 115,* 3–9.

Shortt, J. W., Stoolmiller, M., Smith-Shine, J., Mark Eddy, J., & Sheeber, L. (2010). Maternal emotion coaching, adolescent anger regulation, and siblings externalizing symptoms. *Journal of Child Psychology and Psychiatry, 51,* 799–808.

Shringarpure, R., & Davies, K. J. A. (2009). Free radicals and oxidative stress in aging. In V. L. Bengtson, M. Silverstein, N. M. Putney, & D. Gans (Eds.), *Handbook of theories of aging* (2nd ed.). New York, NY: Springer.

Shrivastava, A., Murrin, C., O'Brien, J., Viljoen, K., Heavey, P., Grant, T., et al. (2012). Grandparental morbidity and mortality patterns are associated with infant birth weight in the Lifeways Cross-Generation Cohort Study 2001–2010. *Journal of Developmental Origins of Health and Disease, 3,* 458–468.

Shtulman, A., & Yoo, R. I. (2015). Children's understanding of physical possibility constrains their belief in Santa Claus. *Cognitive Development, 34,* 51–62.

Shulman, E. P., Smith, A. R., Silva, K., Icenogle, G., Duell, N., Chein, J., & Steinberg, L. (2016). The dual systems model: Review, reappraisal, and reaffirmation. *Developmental Cognitive Neuroscience, 17,* 103–117.

Shulman, S., & Connolly, J. (2016). The challenge of romantic relationships in emerging adulthood. In J. J. Arnett (Ed.), *The Oxford handbook of emerging adulthood* (pp. 230–244). New York, NY: Oxford University Press.

Shweder, R. A., Goodnow, J. J., Hatano, G., LeVine, R. A., Markus, H. R., & Miller, P. J. (2006). The cultural psychology of development: One mind, many mentalities. In W. Damon & R. M. Lerner (Eds. in Chief) & R. M. Lerner (Vol. Ed.), *Handbook of child psychology: Vol. 1. Theoretical models of human development* (6th ed.). Hoboken, NJ: Wiley.

Shweder, R. A., Mahapatra, M., & Miller, J. G. (1990). Culture and moral development. In J. W. Stigler, R. A. Shweder, & G. Herdt (Eds.), *Cultural psychology. Essays on comparative human development.* Cambridge, UK: Cambridge University Press.

Shweder, R. A., Much, N. C., Mahapatra, M., & Park, L. (1997). The "big three" of morality (autonomy, community, divinity) and the "big three" explanations of suffering. In A. Brandt & P. Rozin (Eds.), *Morality and health* (pp. 119–159). New York, NY: Routledge.

Siebenbruner, J., Zimmer-Gembeck, M. J., & Egeland, B. (2007). Sexual partners and contraceptive use: A 16-year prospective study predicting abstinence and risk behavior. *Journal of Research on Adolescence, 17,* 179–206.

Siebold, C. (1992). *The hospice movement. Easing death's pains.* New York, NY: Twayne Publishers.

Siegler, R. S. (1981). Developmental sequences within and between concepts. *Monographs of the Society for Research in Child Development, 46*(2, Serial No. 189).

Siegler, R. S. (1989). Hazards of mental chronometry: An example from children's subtraction. *Journal of Educational Psychology, 81,* 497–506.

Siegler, R. S. (1996). *Emerging minds: The process of change in children's thinking.* New York, NY: Oxford University Press.

Siegler, R. S. (2000). The rebirth of children's learning. *Child Development, 71,* 26–35.

Siegler, R. S. (2006). Microgenetic analysis of learning. In D. Kuhn & R. Siegler (Vol. Eds.), *Handbook of child psychology: Vol. 2. Cognition, perception, and language* (pp. 464–510). Hoboken, NJ: Wiley and Sons.

Siegler, R. S., & Svetina, M. (2006). What leads children to adopt new strategies? A microgenetic/cross sectional study of class inclusion. *Child Development, 77,* 997–1015.

Sigelman, C. K., Carr, M. B., & Begley, N. L. (1986). Developmental changes in the influence of sex-role stereotypes on person perception. *Child Study Journal, 16,* 191–205.

Sigelman, C. K., & Waitzman, K. A. (1991). The development of distributive justice orientations: Contextual influences on children's resource allocations. *Child Development, 62,* 1367–1378.

Sigman, M., & Capps, L. (1997). *Children with autism. A developmental perspective.* Cambridge, MA: Harvard University Press.

Signorielli, N., & Kahlenberg, S. (2001). Television's world of work in the nineties. *Journal of Broadcasting and Electronic Media, 45,* 4–22.

Signorielli, N., & Lears, M. (1992). Children, television, and conceptions about chores: Attitudes and behaviors. *Sex Roles, 27,* 157–170.

Silventoinen, K., Haukka, J., Dunkel, L., Tynelius, P., & Rasmussen, F. (2008). Genetics of pubertal timing and its associations with relative weight in childhood and adult height: The Swedish young male twins study. *Pediatrics, 121,* e885–e891.

Silverman, I. W. (2003). Gender differences in resistance to temptation: Theories and evidence. *Developmental Review, 23,* 219–259.

Silverman, P. R. (2000). *Never too young to know. Death in children's lives.* New York, NY: Oxford University Press.

Silverman, P. R., & Worden, J. W. (1993). Children's reactions to the death of a parent. In M. S. Stroebe, W. Stroebe, & R. O. Hansson (Eds.), *Handbook of bereavement. Theory, research, and intervention.* Cambridge, UK: Cambridge University Press.

Silvers, J. A., McRae, K., Gabrieli, J. D. E., Gross, J. J., Remy, K. A., & Ochsner, K. N. (2012). Age-related differences in emotional reactivity, regulation, and rejection sensitivity in adolescence. *Emotion, 12,* 1235–1247.

Silverstein, M., & Giarrusso, R. (2010). Aging and family life: A decade review. *Journal of Marriage and Family, 72,* 1039–1058.

Silverstein, M., & Ruiz, S. (2006). Breaking the chain: How grandparents moderate the transmission of maternal depression to their grandchildren. *Family Relations, 55,* 601–612.

Sim, L. A., Homme, J. H., Lteif, A. N., Vande Voort, J. L., Schak, K. M., & Ellingson, J. (2009). Family functioning and maternal distress in adolescent girls with anorexia nervosa. *International Journal of Eating Disorders, 42,* 531–539.

Simcock, G., & Hayne, H. (2002). Breaking the barrier? Children fail to translate their preverbal memories into language. *Psychological Science, 13,* 225–231.

Simcock, G., & Hayne, H. (2003). Age-related changes in verbal and nonverbal memory during early childhood. *Developmental Psychology, 39,* 805–814.

Simmons, R. G., & Blyth, D. A. (1987). *Moving into adolescence: The impact of pubertal change and school context.* New York, NY: Hawthorne, Aldine de Gruyter.

Simmons, R. G., Burgeson, R., Carlton-Ford, S., & Blyth, D. A. (1987). The impact of cumulative change in early adolescence. *Child Development, 58,* 1220–1234.

Simon, G., Lubin, A., Houdé, O., & Neys, W. D. (2015). Anterior cingulate cortex and intuitive bias detection during number conservation. *Cognitive Neuroscience, 6,* 158–168.

Simon, H. A. (1995). The information-processing theory of mind. *American Psychologist, 50,* 507–508.

Simon, H. A. (2001). Creativity in the arts and sciences. *The Canyon Review and Stand, 23,* 203–220.

Simons-Morton, B. G., & Farhat, T. (2010). Recent findings on peer group influences on adolescent smoking. *Journal of Primary Prevention, 31,* 191–208.

Simonton, D. K. (1984). *Genius, creativity, and leadership: Historiometric inquiries.* Cambridge, MA: Harvard University Press.

Simonton, D. K. (1990). Creativity in the later years: Optimistic prospects for achievement. *Gerontologist, 30,* 626–631.

Simonton, D. K. (1999). Creativity from a historiometric perspective. In R. J. Sternberg (Ed.), *Handbook of creativity.* New York, NY: Cambridge University Press.

Simonton, D. K. (2012). Quantifying creativity: Can measures span the spectrum? *Dialogues in Clinical Neuroscience, 14,* 100–104.

Simpson, J. A., & Overall, N. C. (2014). Partner buffering of attachment insecurity. *Current Directions in Psychological Science, 23,* 54–59.

Simpson, J. A., Collins, W. A., Tran, S., & Haydon, K. C. (2007). Attachment and the experience and expression of emotions in romantic relationships: A developmental perspective. *Journal of Personality and Social Psychology, 92,* 355–367.

Simpson, J. A., Griskevicius, V., Kuo, S. I. Sung, S., & Collins, W. A. (2012). Evolution, stress, and sensitive periods: The influence of unpredictability in early versus late childhood on sex and risky behavior. *Developmental Psychology, 48,* 674–686.

Singer, D. G., Golinkoff, R. M., & Hirsh-Pasek, K. (Eds.) (2006). *Play = learning: How play motivates and enhances children's cognitive and social-emotional growth.* New York, NY: Oxford University Press.

Singer, T., Verhaeghen, P., Ghisletta, P., Lindenberger, U., & Baltes, P. B. (2003). The fate of cognition in very old age: Six-year longitudinal findings in the Berlin Aging Study (BASE). *Psychology and Aging, 18,* 318–331.

Singh, D., & Bronstad, P. M. (2001). Female body odour is a potential cue to ovulation. *Proceedings of Biological Science, 268,* 797–801.

Sinnott, J. (1996). The developmental approach: Postformal thought as adaptive intelligence. In F. Blanchard-Fields & T. M. Hess (Eds.), *Perspectives on cognitive change in adulthood and aging.* New York, NY: McGraw-Hill.

Sinnott, J. D. (1984). Postformal reasoning: The relativistic stage. In M. L. Commons, F. A. Richards, & C. Armon (Eds.), *Beyond formal operations* (pp. 298–325). New York, NY: Praeger.

Sirois, S., Spratling, M. W., Thomas, M. S. C., Westermann, G., Mareschal, D., & Johnson, M. H. (2008). Précis of neuroconstructivism: How the brain constructs cognition. *Behavioral and Brain Sciences, 31,* 321–331.

Sisler, A., & Ittel, A. (2015). *Siblings in adolescence. Emerging individuals, lasting bonds.* London & New York, NY: Psychology Press.

Skinner, B. F. (1953). *Science and human behavior.* New York, NY: Macmillan.

Skinner, B. F. (1983). Intellectual self-management in old age. *American Psychologist, 38,* 239–244.

Skinner, E. A., & Zimmer-Gembeck, M. J. (2007). The development of coping. *Annual Review of Psychology, 58,* 119–144.

Skoe, E., & Kraus, N. (2014). Auditory reserve and the legacy of auditory experience. *Brain Sciences, 4,* 575–593.

Skoog, T., & Stattin, H. (2014). Why and under what contextual conditions do early-maturing girls develop problem behaviors? *Child Development Perspectives, 8,* 158–162.

Slaby, R. G., & Guerra, N. G. (1988). Cognitive mediators of aggression in adolescent offenders: 1. Assessment. *Developmental Psychology, 24,* 580–588.

Slater, A., Morison, V., Town, C., Rose, D. (1985). Movement perception and identity constancy in the newborn baby. *British Journal of Developmental Psychology, 3,* 211–220.

Slater, A., Quinn, P. C., Kelly, D. J., Longmore, C. A., McDonald, P. R., & Pascalis, O. (2010). The shaping of face space in early infancy: Becoming a native face processor. *Child Development Perspective, 4,* 205–211.

Slater, A., Riddell, P., Quinn, P. C., Pascalis, O., Lee, K., & Kelly, D. J. (2010). Visual perception. In J. G. Bremner & T. D. Wachs (Eds.), *The Wiley-Blackwell handbook of infant development, 2nd ed., Vol 1: Basic research* (pp. 40–80). Malden, MA: John Wiley & Sons.

Slater, C. L. (2003). Generativity versus stagnation: An elaboration of Erikson's adult stage of human development. *Journal of Adult Development, 10,* 53–65.

Slater, R., Cantarella, A., Gallella, S., Worley, A., Boyd, S., Meek, J., et al. (2006). Cortical pain responses in human infants. *The Journal of Neuroscience, 26,* 3662–3666.

Slaughter, V., Jaakkola, R., & Carey, S. (1999). Constructing a coherent theory: Children's biological understanding of life and death. In M. Siegal & C. C. Peterson (Eds.), *Children's understanding of biology and health.* Cambridge, UK: Cambridge University Press.

Slavkin, M., & Stright, A. D. (2000). Gender role differences in college students from one- and two-parent families. *Sex Roles, 42,* 23–37.

Sliwinski, M., & Buschke, H. (1999). Cross-sectional and longitudinal relationships among age, cognition, and processing speed. *Psychology and Aging, 14,* 18–33.

Sloane, S., Baillargeon, R., & Premack, D. (2012). Do infants have a sense of fairness? *Psychological Science, 23,* 196–204.

Slobin, D. I. (1979). *Psycholinguistics* (2nd ed.). Glenview, IL: Scott, Foresman.

Sloboda, Z. (2009). School prevention. In C. G. Leukefeld, T. P. Gullotta, & M. Staton-Tindall (Eds.), *Adolescent substance abuse. Evidence-based approaches to prevention and treatment.* New York, NY: Springer.

Slotkin, T. A. (1998). Fetal nicotine or cocaine exposure: Which one is worse? *Journal of Pharmacology and Experimental Therapy, 285,* 931–945.

Slykerman, R. F., Thompson, J., Waldie, K., Murphy, R., Wall, C. & Mitchell, E. A. (2015). Maternal stress during pregnancy is associated with moderate to severe depression in 11-year-old children. *Acta Paediatrica, 104,* 68–74.

Smagorinsky, P. (1995). The social construction of data: Methodological problems of investigating learning in the zone of proximal development. *Review of Educational Research, 65,* 191–212.

Small, M. (1999). *Our babies, ourselves: How biology and culture shape the way we parent.* New York, NY: Anchor Publishing.

Small, S., & Memmo, M. (2004). Contemporary models of youth development and problem prevention: Toward an integration of terms, concepts, and models. *Family Relations, 53,* 3–11.

Smetana, J. G. (1981). Preschool children's conceptions of moral and social rules. *Child Development, 52,* 1333–1336.

Smetana, J. G. (2006). Social-cognitive domain theory: Consistencies and variations in children's moral and social judgments. In M. Killen & J. G. Smetana (Eds.), *Handbook of moral development.* Mahwah, NJ: Erlbaum.

Smetana, J. G., Jambon, M., & Ball, C. (2014). The social domain approach to children's moral and social judgments. In M. Killen & J. G. Smetana (Eds.), *Handbook of moral development* (2nd ed., pp. 23–45). New York, NY: Psychology Press.

Smetana, J. G., Jambon, M., Conry-Murray, C., & Sturge-Apple, M. (2012). Reciprocal associations between young children's developing moral judgments and theory of mind. *Developmental Psychology, 48,* 1144–1155.

Smetana, J. G., Rote, W. M., Jambon, M., Tasopoulos-Chan, M., Villalobos, M., & Comer, J. (2012). Developmental changes and individual differences in young children's moral judgments. *Child Development, 83,* 683–696.

Smith, A. D., & Earles, J. L. K. (1996). Memory changes in normal aging. In F. Blanchard-Fields & T. M. Hess (Eds.), *Perspectives on cognitive change in adulthood and aging.* New York, NY: McGraw-Hill.

Smith, A. K., Mick, E., & Raraone, S. V. (2009). Advances in genetic studies of attention-deficit/ hyperactivity disorder. *Current Psychiatry Reports, 11,* 143–148.

Smith, C. A., Levett, K. M., Collins, C. T., & Crowther, C. A. (2011, December 7). Relaxation techniques for pain management in labour. *Cochrane Database of Systematic Reviews,* CD009514.

Smith, G. E., Petersen, R. C., Ivnik, R. J., Malec, J. F., & Tangalos, E. G. (1996). Subjective memory complaints, psychological distress, and longitudinal change in objective memory performance. *Psychology and Aging, 11*, 272–279.

Smith, G. J. W. (2005). How should creativity be defined? *Creativity Research Journal, 17*, 293–295.

Smith, J. T., & Baker, D. A. (2011). Sickle cell disease. In S. Goldstein & C. R. Reynolds (Eds.), *Handbook of neurodevelopmental and genetic disorders in children* (2nd ed., pp. 338–361). New York, NY: Guilford.

Smith, J., & Baltes, P. B. (1990). Wisdom-related knowledge: Age/cohort differences in response to life-planning problems. *Developmental Psychology, 26*, 494–505.

Smith, K. E., Landry, S. H., & Swank, P. R. (2000). Does the content of mothers' verbal stimulation explain differences in children's development of verbal and nonverbal cognitive skills? *Journal of School Psychology, 38*, 27–49.

Smith, L. B., & Thelen, E. (1993). *A dynamic systems approach to development: Applications.* Cambridge, MA: MIT Press.

Smith, P. J., Humiston, S. G., Marcuse, E. K., Zhao, Z., Dorell, C. G., Howes, C., & Hibbs, B. (2011). Parental delay or refusal of vaccine doses, childhood vaccination coverage at 24 months of age, and the health belief model. *Public Health Reports, 126* (Suppl. 2), 135–146.

Smith, P. K. (2005). Types and functions of play in human development. In B. J. Ellis & D. F. Bjorklund (Eds.), *Origins of the social mind.* New York, NY: Guilford Press.

Smith, P. K., Mahdavi, J., Carvalho, M., Fisher, S., Russell, S., & Tippett, N. (2008). Cyberbullying: Its nature and impact in secondary school pupils. *Journal of Child Psychology and Psychiatry, 49*, 376–385.

Smith, R. L., Rose, A. J., & Schwartz-Mette, R. A. (2010). Relational and overt aggression in childhood and adolescence: Clarifying mean-level gender differences and associations with peer acceptance. *Social Development, 19*, 243–269.

Smith, S. L., Pieper, K. M., Granados, A., & Choueiti, M. (2010). Assessing gender-related portrayals in top-grossing G-rated films. *Sex Roles, 62*, 774–786.

Smith, T. W., Berg, C. A., Florsheim, P., Uchino, B. N., Pearce, G., Hawkins, M., Henry, N. J. M., Beveridge, R. M., Skinner, M. A., & Olsen-Cerny, C. (2009). Conflict and collaboration in middle-aged and older couples: I. Age differences in agency and communion during marital interaction. *Psychology and Aging, 24*, 259–273.

Smitsman, A. W., & Corbetta, D. (2010). Action in infancy—Perceptives, concepts, and challenges. In J. G. Bremner & T. D. Wachs (Eds.), *The Wiley-Blackwell handbook of infant development: Vol. 1. Basic research* (2nd ed., pp. 167–203). Malden, MA: John Wiley & Sons.

Snarey, J. R. (1985). Cross-cultural universality of social–moral development: A critical review of Kohlbergian research. *Psychological Bulletin, 97*, 202–232.

Snarey, J., & Samuelson, P. (2008). Moral education in the cognitive developmental tradition: Lawrence Kohlberg's revolutionary ideas. In L. P. Nucci & D. Narvaez (Eds.), *Handbook of moral and character education.* New York, NY: Routledge.

Snow, C. E., Arlman-Rupp, A., Hassing, Y., Jobse, J., Joosken, J., & Vorster, J. (1976). Mother's speech in three social classes. *Journal of Psycholinguistic Research, 5*, 1–20.

Snow, D. (2006). Regression and reorganization of intonation between 6 and 23 months. *Child Development, 77*, 281–296.

Snowdon, D. (2002). *Aging with grace: What the Nun Study teaches us about leading longer, healthier, and more meaningful lives.* New York, NY: Bantam Books.

Sobolewski, J. M., & King, V. (2005). The importance of the coparental relationship for nonresident fathers' ties to children. *Journal of Marriage and Family, 67*, 1196–1212.

Sodian, B. (2011). Theory of mind in infancy. *Child Development Perspectives, 5*, 39–43.

Søfting, G. H., Dyregrov, A., & Dyregrov, K. (2016). Because I'm also part of the family. Children's participation in rituals after the loss of a parent or sibling: A qualitative study from the children's perspective. *Omega: Journal of Death and Dying, 73*, 141–158.

Sohrabvand, F., Jafari, M., Shariat, M., Haghollahi, F., & Lotfi, M. (2015). Frequency and epidemiologic aspects of male infertility. *Acta Medica Iranica, 53*, 231–235.

Solomon, B. C., & Jackson, J. J. (2014). The long reach of one's spouse: Spouses' personality influences occupational success. *Psychological Science, 25*, 2189–2198.

Solso, S., Xu, R., Proudfoot, J., Hagler, D. J. J., Campbell, K., Venkatraman, V., . . . Courchesne, E. (2016). Diffusion tensor imaging provides evidence of possible axonal overconnectivity in frontal lobes in autism spectrum disorder toddlers. *Biological Psychiatry, 79*, 676–684.

Somerville, L. H. (2013). Special issue on the teenage brain: Sensitivity to social evaluation. *Current Directions in Psychological Science, 22*, 121–127.

Somerville, L. H., Jones, R. M., Ruberry, E. J., Dyke, J. P., Glover, G., & Casey, B. J. (2013). The medial prefrontal cortex and the emergence of self-conscious emotion in adolescence. *Psychological Science, 24*, 1554–1562.

Sommer, G., Gianinazzi, M. E., Kuonen, R., Bohlius, J., l'Allemand, D., Hauschild, M., & Swiss Society for Paediatric Endocrinology and Diabetology. (2015). Health-related quality of life of young adults treated with recombinant human growth hormone during childhood. *PLoS ONE, 10*(10), e0140944.

Son, L. K. (2004). Spacing one's study: Evidence for a metacognitive control strategy. *Journal of Experimental Psychology: Learning, Memory, and Cognition, 30*, 601–604.

Son, L. K., & Metcalfe, J. (2000). Metacognitive and control strategies in study-time allocation. *Journal of Experimental Psychology: Learning, Memory, and Cognition, 26*, 204–221.

Song, J., & Manchester, J. (2009). Revisiting the 1983 Social Security reforms, 25 years later. *Research on Aging, 31*, 233–260.

Song, J., & Volling, B. L. (2015). Coparenting and children's temperament predict firstborns' cooperation in the care of an infant sibling. *Journal of Family Psychology, 29*, 130–135.

Sookoian, S., Gianotti, T. F., Burgueno, A. L., & Pirola, C. J. (2013). Fetal metabolic programming and epigenetic modifications: A systems biology approach. *Pediatric Research, 73*, 531–542.

Sorensen, L. C., Dodge, K. A., & the Conduct Problems Prevention Research Group (2016). How does the Fast Track intervention prevent adverse outcomes in young adulthood? *Child Development, 87*, 429–445.

Soriano, F. I., Rivera, L. M., Williams, K. J., Daley, S. P., & Reznik, V. M. (2004). Navigating between cultures: The role of culture in youth violence. *Journal of Adolescent Health, 34*, 169–176.

Sorkhabi, N., & Mandara, J. (2013). Are the effects of Baumrind's parenting styles culturally specific or culturally equivalent? In R. E. Larzelere, A. S. Sheffield, & A. W. Harrist (Eds.), *Authoritative parenting. Synthesizing nurturance and discipline for optimal child development.* Washington, DC: American Psychological Association.

Sorokowska, A., Sorokowski, P., Hummel, T., & Huanca, T. (2013). Olfaction and environment: Tsimane' of Bolivian rainforest have lower threshold of odor detection than industrialized German people. *PLoS ONE, 8*, e69203.

Sostek, A. M., Vietze, P., Zaslow, M., Kreiss, L., van der Waals, F., & Rubinstein, D. (1981). Social context in caregiver-infant interaction: A film study of Fais and the United States. In T. M. Field, A. M. Sostek, P. Vietze, & P. H. Liederman (Eds.), *Culture and early interactions.* Hillsdale, NJ: Erlbaum.

Soto, C. J., & Tackett, J. L. (2015). Personality traits in childhood and adolescence: Structure, development, and outcomes. *Psychological Science, 24*, 358–362.

Sotomayor, S. (2013). *My beloved world.* New York, NY: Knopf.

Sotomi, O., Ryan, C. A., O'Connor, G., & Murphy, B. P. (2007). Have we stopped looking for a red reflex in newborn screening? *Irish Medical Journal, 100*, 398–400.

Soubry, A., Hoyo, C., Jirtle, R. L., & Murphy, S. K. (2014). A paternal environmental legacy: Evidence for epigenetic inheritance through the male germ line. *BioEssays, 36*, 359–371.

Span, P. (2000, August 27). Home alone. *The Washington Post Magazine*, pp. 12–15, 24–25.

Spaniol, J., Madden, D. J., & Voss, A. (2006). A diffusion model analysis of adult age differences in episodic and semantic long-term memory retrieval. *Journal of Experimental Psychology: Learning, Memory, and Cognition, 32*, 101–117.

Sparks, R. L., Patton, J., & Murdoch, A. (2014). Early reading success and its relationship to reading achievement and reading volume: Replication of '10 years later.' *Reading and Writing, 27*, 189–211.

Sparks, T. A., Hunter, S. K., Backman, T. L., Morgan, G. A., & Ross, R. G. (2012). Maternal parenting stress and mothers' reports of their infants' mastery motivation. *Infant Behavior & Development, 35*, 167–173.

Sparrow, R. (2010). Implants and ethnocide: Learning from the cochlear implant controversy. *Disability and Society, 25*, 455–466.

Sparrow, S. S., & Davis, S. M. (2000). Recent advances in the assessment of intelligence and cognition. *Journal of Child Psychology and Psychiatry, 41*, 117–131.

Spear, L. P. (2000a). The adolescent brain and age-related behavioral manifestations. *Neuroscience and Biobehavioral Reviews, 24*, 417–463.

Spear, L. P. (2015). Adolescent alcohol exposure: Are there separable vulnerable periods within adolescence? *Physiology & Behavior, 148*, 122–130.

Spearman, C. (1927). *The abilities of man.* New York, NY: Macmillan.

Speece, M. W., & Brent, S. B. (1984). Children's understanding of death: A review of three components of a death concept. *Child Development, 55*, 1671–1686.

Speece, M. W., & Brent, S. B. (1992). The acquisition of a mature understanding of three components of the concept of death. *Death Studies, 16*, 211–229.

Spelke, E. S. (1990). Principles of object perception. *Cognitive Science, 14*, 29–56.

Spelke, E. S. (1994). Initial knowledge: Six suggestions. *Cognition, 50*, 431–445.

Spelke, E. S., & Hermer, L. (1996). Early cognitive development: Objects and space. In R. Gelman & T. Fong (Eds.), *Handbook of perception and cognition* (2nd ed.). New York, NY: Academic Press.

Spelke, E. S., Breinlinger, K., Macomber, J., & Jacobson, K. (1992). Origins of knowledge. *Psychological Review, 99*, 605–632.

Spence, J. T. (1985). Achievement American style: The rewards and costs of individualism. *American Psychologist, 40*, 1285–1295.

Spence, J. T., Helmreich, R. L., & Stapp, J. (1973). The Personal Attributes Questionnaire: A measure of sex-role stereotypes and masculinity-femininity. *JSAS Catalog of Selected Documents in Psychology, 4*, 43–44 (Ms. 617).

Spencer, J. P., Blumberg, M. S., McMurray, B., Robinson, S. R., Samuelson, L. K., & Tomblin, J. B. (2009). Short arms and talking eggs: Why we should no longer abide the nativist-empiricist debate. *Child Development Perspectives, 3*, 79–87.

Spencer, J. P., Corbetta, D., Buchanan, P., Clearfield, M., Ulrich, B., & Schoner, G. (2006). Moving toward a grand theory of development: In memory of Esther Thelen. *Child Development, 77*, 1521–1538.

Spencer, M. B. (2006). Phenomenology and ecological systems theory: Development of diverse groups. In W. Damon & R. M. Lerner (Eds. in Chief) & R. M. Lerner (Vol. Ed.), *Handbook of child psychology: Vol. 1. Theoretical models of human development* (6th ed.). Hoboken, NJ: Wiley.

Spencer, M. B., & Markstrom-Adams, C. (1990). Identity processes among racial and ethnic minority children in America. *Child Development, 61*, 290–310.

Spencer, M. B., Swanson, D. P., & Harpalani, V. (2015). Development of the self. In M. E. Lamb & R. M. Lerner (Eds.), *Handbook of child psychology and developmental science: Vol. 3. Socioemotional processes* (7th ed., pp. 750–793). Hoboken, NJ: Wiley.

Spencer, P. E. (1996). The association between language and symbolic play at two years: Evidence from deaf toddlers. *Child Development, 67*, 867–876.

Spengler, M., Gottschling, J., & Spinath, F. M. (2012). Personality in childhood. A longitudinal behavior genetic approach. *Personality and Individual Differences, 53*, 411–416.

Spenser, K. A., Betts, L. R., & Das Gupta, M. (2015). Deficits in theory of mind, empathic understanding and moral reasoning: A comparison between young offenders and non-offenders. *Psychology, Crime & Law, 21*, 632–647.

Spera, C. (2006). Adolescents' perceptions of parental goals, practices, and styles in relation to the motivation and achievement. *Journal of Early Adolescence, 26*, 456–490.

Sperling, S. A., Geneser, A., & Manning, C. A. (2015). Parkinson's disease dementia and dementia with Lewy bodies. In P. A. Lichtenberg & B. T. Mast (Eds. in Chief), B. D. Carpenter & J. L. Wetherell, (Assoc. Eds.), *APA handbook of clinical geropsychology: Vol. 2. Assessment, treatment, and issues of later life* (pp. 227–246). Washington, DC: American Psychological Association.

Spiegel, C., & Halberda, J. (2011). Rapid fast-mapping abilities in 2-year-olds. *Journal of Experimental Psychology, 109*, 132–140.

Spieler, D. H., & Griffin, Z. M. (2006). The influence of age on the time course of word preparation in multiword utterances. *Language and Cognitive Processes, 21*, 291–321.

Spilich, G. J., Vesonder, G. T., Chiesi, H. L., & Voss, J. F. (1979). Text processing of domain-related information for individuals with high and low domain knowledge. *Journal of Verbal Learning and Verbal Behavior, 18*, 275–290.

Spilman, S. K., Neppl, T. K., Donnellan, M. B., Schofield, T. J., & Conger, R. D. (2013). Incorporating religiosity into a developmental model of positive family functioning across generations. *Developmental Psychology, 49*, 762–774.

Spinath, B., Spinath, F. M., Harlaar, N., & Plomin, R. (2006). Predicting school achievement from general cognitive ability, self-perceived ability, and intrinsic value. *Intelligence, 34*, 363–374.

Spittle, A., Orton, J., Anderson, P. J., Boyd, R., & Doyle, L. W. (2015). Early developmental intervention programmes provided post hospital discharge to prevent motor and cognitive impairment in preterm infants. *The Cochrane Database of Systematic Reviews*, CD005495.

Spitz, R. A. (1946). Anaclitic depression: An inquiry into the genesis of psychiatric conditions in early childhood, II. *Psychoanalytic Study of the Child, 2*, 313–342.

Spokane, A. R., Meir, E. I., & Catalano, M. (2000). Person-environment congruence and Holland's theory: A review and reconsideration. *Journal of Vocational Behavior, 57*, 137–187.

Spoth, R., Trudeau, L., Guyll, M., Shin, C., & Redmond, C. (2009). Universal intervention effects on substance use among young adults mediated by delayed adolescent substance initiation. *Journal of Consulting and Clinical Psychology, 77*, 620–632.

Springer, S., & Deutsch, G. (2001). *Left brain, right brain: Perspectives from cognitive neuroscience* (5th ed.). New York, NY: W. H. Freeman.

Spruyt, K., Aitken, R., So, K., Charlton, M., Adamson, T., & Horne, R. (2008). Relationship between sleep/wake patterns, temperament and overall development in term infants over the first year of life. *Early Human Development, 84*(5), 289–296.

Spunt, R. P., & Adolphs, R. (2015). Folk explanations of behavior: A specialized use of a domain-general mechanism. *Psychological Science, 26*, 724–736.

Squire, L. R. (2009). The legacy of patient H.M. for neuroscience. *Neuron, 61*, 6–9.

Sroufe, L. A. (1977). Wariness of strangers and the study of infant development. *Child Development, 48*, 1184–1199.

Sroufe, L. A. (1996). *Emotional development: The organization of emotional life in the early years.* Cambridge, UK: University of Cambridge Press.

Sroufe, L. A. (1997). Psychopathology as an outcome of development. *Development and Psychopathology, 9*, 251–268.

Sroufe, L. A. (2009). The concept of development in developmental psychopathology. *Child Development Perspectives, 3*, 178–183.

Sroufe, L. A. (2013). The promise of developmental psychopathology: Past and present. *Development and Psychopathology, 25*, 1215–1224.

Sroufe, L. A., Egeland, B., Carlson, E., & Collins, W. A. (2005). Placing early attachment experiences in developmental context: The Minnesota Longitudinal Study. In K. E. Grossmann, K. Grossmann, & E. Waters (Eds.), *Attachment from infancy to adulthood: The major longitudinal studies.* New York, NY: Guilford Press.

Sroufe, L. A., & Rutter, M. (1984). The domain of developmental psychopathology. *Child Development, 55*, 17–29.

Sroufe, L. A., Waters, E., & Matas, L. (1974). Contextual determinants of infant affectional response. In M. Lewis & L. A. Rosenblum (Eds.), *The origins of fear.* New York, NY: Wiley.

St. George, D. (2001, June 8). A child's unheeded cry for help. *The Washington Post*, pp. A1, A20–A21.

St. George, D. (2010, March 18). Households with little room for a generation gap. *The Washington Post*, p. B6.

St. Jacques, P. L. (2012). Functional neuroimaging of autobiographical memory. In D. Berntsen & D. C. Rubin (Eds.), *Understanding autobiographical memory: Theories and approaches* (pp. 114–138). New York, NY: Cambridge University Press.

St. Petersburg–USA Orphanage Research Team. (2008). The effects of early social-emotional and relationship experience on the development of young orphanage children. *Monographs of the Society for Research in Child Development, 73* (3, Serial No. 291).

Staff, J., Johnson, M. K., Patrick, M. E., & Schulenberg, J. E. (2014). The great recession and recent employment trends among secondary students in the United States. *Longitudinal and Life Course Studies, 5*, 173–188.

Stahl, L. (2016, February/March). On becoming a grandmother. *AARP The Magazine/Real Possibilities*, pp. 62–63.

Stambrook, M., & Parker, K. C. H. (1987). The development of the concept of death in childhood: A review of the literature. *Merrill-Palmer Quarterly, 33*, 133–157.

Stams, G. J., Brugman, D., Dekovic, M., van Rosmalen, L., van der Laan, P., & Gibbs, J. C. (2006). The moral judgment of juvenile delinquents: A meta-analysis. *Journal of Abnormal Child Psychology, 34*, 692–708.

Stanley, S. M., Rhoades, G. K., Amato, P. R., Markman, H. J., & Johnson, C. A. (2010). The timing of cohabitation and engagement: Impact on first and second marriages. *Journal of Marriage and Family, 72*, 906–918.

Stanovich, K. E. (1986). Matthew effects in reading: Some consequences of individual differences in the acquisition of literacy. *Reading Research Quarterly, 21*, 360–407.

Stanovich, K. E. (2009). *What intelligence tests miss: The psychology of rational thought.* New Haven, CT: Yale University Press.

Stanovich, K. E. (2011). *Rationality and the reflective mind.* New York, NY: Oxford University Press.

Stanovich, K. E. (2016). The comprehensive assessment of rational thinking. *Educational Psychologist, 51*, 23–34.

Stanovich, K. E., & West, R. F. (1997). Reasoning independently of prior belief and individual differences in actively open-minded thinking. *Journal of Educational Psychology, 89*, 342–357.

Starks, T. J., Newcomb, M. E., & Mustanski, B. (2015). A longitudinal study of interpersonal relationships among lesbian, gay, and bisexual adolescents and young adults: Mediational pathways from attachment to romantic relationship quality. *Archives of Sexual Behavior, 44*, 1821–1831.

Statistic Brain Research Institute. (2015). *Television watching statistics.* Retrieved from www.statisticbrain.com/television-watching-statistics/.

Staudinger, U. M., & Baltes, P. B. (1996). Interactive minds: A facilitative setting for wisdom-related performance? *Journal of Personality and Social Psychology, 71*, 746–762.

Staudinger, U. M., & Glück, J. (2011). Intelligence and wisdom. In R. J. Sternberg & S. B. Kaufman (Eds.), *The Cambridge Handbook of Intelligence* (pp. 827–846). New York, NY: Cambridge University Press.

Staudinger, U. M., Smith, J., & Baltes, P. B. (1992). Wisdom-related knowledge in a life review task: Age differences and the role of professional specialization. *Psychology and Aging, 7*, 271–281.

Stearns, P. N. (2015). Children in history. In M. H. Bornstein (Vol. Ed.), T. Leventhal (Vol. Ed.), & R. M. Lerner (Ed.), *Handbook of child psychology and developmental science: Vol. 4. Ecological settings and processes* (pp. 787–810). Hoboken, NJ: Wiley.

Steele, C. M. (1997). A threat in the air: How stereotypes shape intellectual identity and performance. *American Psychologist, 52*, 613–629.

Steele, C. M. (1999). Thin ice: "Stereotype threat" and black college students. *Atlantic, 284*, 44–54.

Steele, C. M., & Aronson, J. (1995). Stereotype threat and the intellectual test performance of African Americans. *Journal of Personality and Social Psychology, 69*, 797–811.

Steenbergen-Hu, S., & Moon, S. (2011). The effects of acceleration on high-ability learners: A meta-analysis. *Gifted Child Quarterly, 55*, 39–53.

Steenland, K., Henley, J., & Thun, M. (2002). All-cause and cause-specific death rates by educational status for two million people in two American Cancer Society cohorts, 1959–1999. *American Journal of Epidemiology, 156*, 11–21.

Steffen, L. M., Dai, S., Fulton, J. E., & Labarthe, D. R. (2009). Overweight in children and adolescents associated with TV viewing and parental weight: Project HeartBeat! *American Journal of Preventive Medicine, 37*(Suppl. 1), S50–S55.

Stein, C. H. (2009). "I owe it to them": Understanding felt obligation toward parents in adulthood. In K. Shifren (Ed.), *How caregiving affects development. Psychological implications for child, adolescent, and adult caregivers.* Washington, DC: American Psychological Association.

Stein, J. H., & Reiser, L. W. (1994). A study of white middle-class adolescent boys' responses to "semenarche" (the first ejaculation). *Journal of Youth and Adolescence, 23*, 373–384.

Steinberg, L. (1989). Pubertal maturation and parent-adolescent distance: An evolutionary perspective. In G. R. Adams, R. Montemayor, & T. P. Gullotta (Eds.), *Advances in adolescent behavior and development* (pp. 71–97). Newbury Park, CA: Sage.

Steinberg, L. (2001). We know some things: Parent-adolescent relationships in retrospect and prospect. *Journal of Research on Adolescence, 11*, 1–19.

Steinberg, L. (2007). Risk taking in adolescence: New perspectives from brain and behavioural science. *Current Directions in Psychological Sciences, 16*, 55–59.

Steinberg, L. (2010). A dual systems model of adolescent risk-taking. *Developmental Psychobiology, 52*, 216–224.

Steinberg, L. (2011). *Adolescence* (9th ed.). New York, NY: McGraw-Hill.

Steinberg, L. (2015). How to improve the health of American adolescents. *Perspectives on Psychological Science, 10*, 711–715.

Steinberg, L. (2015). The neural underpinnings of adolescent risk-taking: The roles of reward-seeking, impulse control, and peers. In G. Oettingen & P. M. Gollwitzer (Eds.), *Self-regulation in adolescence* (pp. 173–192). New York, NY: Cambridge University Press.

Steinberg, L., & Dornbusch, S. M. (1991). Negative correlates of part-time employment during adolescence: Replication and elaboration. *Developmental Psychology, 27*, 304–313.

Steinberg, L., Dornbusch, S. M., & Brown, B. B. (1992). Ethnic differences in adolescent achievement: An ecological perspective. *American Psychologist, 47*, 723–729.

Steinberg, L., Fegley, S., & Dornbusch, S. M. (1993). Negative impact of part-time work on adolescent adjustment: Evidence from a longitudinal study. *Developmental Psychology, 29*, 171–180.

Steiner, J. E. (1979). Human facial expressions in response to taste and smell stimulation. In H. W. Reese & L. P. Lipsitt (Eds.), *Advances in child development and behavior: Vol. 13.* New York, NY: Academic Press.

Stemler, S. E., Grigorenko, E. L., Jarvin, L., & Sternberg, R. J. (2006). Using the theory of successful intelligence as a basis for augmenting AP exams in psychology and statistics. *Contemporary Educational Psychology, 31*, 344–376.

Stephan, Y., Chalabaev, A., Kotter-Grühn, D., & Jaconelli, A. (2013). "Feeling younger, being stronger": An experimental study of subjective age and physical functioning among older adults. *Journals of Gerontology. Series B, Psychological Sciences and Social Sciences, 68*, 1–7.

Stephens, M. A. P., Franks, M. M., Martire, L. M., Norton, T. R., & Atienza, A. A. (2009). Women at midlife: Stress and rewards of balancing parent care with employment and other family roles. In K. Shifren (Ed.), *How caregiving affects development. Psychological implications for child, adolescent, and adult caregivers.* Washington, DC: American Psychological Association.

Stephens, M. A., Townsend, A. L., Martire, L. M., & Druley, J. A. (2001). Balancing parent care with other roles: Interrole conflict of adult daughter caregivers. *Journal of Gerontology: Psychological Sciences, 56B*, P24–34.

Stepler, R. (2016, February 18). *Smaller share of women ages 65 and older are living alone. More are living with spouse or children.* Pew Research Center. Retrieved from www.pewsocialtrends.org/2016/02/18/smaller-share-of-women-ages-65-and-older-are-living-alone/.

Stern, D. (1977). *The first relationship: Infant and mother.* Cambridge, MA: Harvard University Press.
Stern, M., & Karraker, K. H. (1989). Sex stereotyping of infants: A review of gender labeling studies. *Sex Roles, 20,* 501–522.
Stern, Y. (2002). What is cognitive reserve? Theory and research application of the reserve concept. *Journal of the International Neuropsychological Society, 8,* 448–460.
Sternberg, R. J. (1985). *Beyond IQ: A triarchic theory of human intelligence.* Cambridge, MA: Cambridge University Press.
Sternberg, R. J. (1988a). *The triarchic mind: A new theory of human intelligence.* New York, NY: Viking.
Sternberg, R. J. (1988b). Triangulating love. In R. J. Sternberg and M. L. Barnes (Eds.), *The psychology of love.* New Haven, CT: Yale University Press.
Sternberg, R. J. (Ed.). (1999a). *Handbook of creativity.* New York, NY: Cambridge University Press.
Sternberg, R. J. (1999b). The theory of successful intelligence. *Review of General Psychology, 3,* 292–316.
Sternberg, R. J. (2003). *Wisdom, intelligence, and creativity synthesized.* Cambridge, UK: Cambridge University Press.
Sternberg, R. J. (2006a). A duplex theory of love. In R. J. Sternberg & K. Weis (Eds.), *The new psychology of love.* New Haven, CT: Yale University Press.
Sternberg, R. J. (2006b). The nature of creativity. *Creativity Research Journal, 18,* 87–98.
Sternberg, R. J. (2010a). Academic intelligence is not enough! WICS: An expanded model for effective practice in school and later life. In D. D. Preiss & R. J. Sternberg (Eds.), *Innovations in educational psychology: Perspectives on learning, teaching, and human development* (pp. 403–440). New York, NY: Springer.
Sternberg, R. J. (2010b). WICS: A new model for cognitive education. *Journal of Cognitive Education and Psychology, 9,* 34–46.
Sternberg, R. J. (2011). The theory of successful intelligence. In R. J. Sternberg & S. B. Kaufman (Eds.), *The Cambridge handbook of intelligence* (pp. 504–527). New York, NY: Cambridge University Press.
Sternberg, R. J. (2012). The assessment of creativity: An investment-based approach. *Creativity Research Journal, 24,* 3–12.
Sternberg, R. J., Grigorenko, E. L., & Bundy, D. A. (2001). The predictive value of IQ. *Merrill-Palmer Quarterly, 47,* 1–41.
Sternberg, R. J., Kaufman, J. C., & Grigorenko, E. L. (2008). Why intelligent people fail (too often). In R. J. Sternberg, J. C. Kaufman, & E. L. Grigorenko (Eds.), *Applied intelligence* (pp. 384–392). New York, NY: Cambridge University Press.
Sternberg, R. J., Kaufman, J. C., & Grigorenko, E. L. (Eds.). (2008). *Applied intelligence.* New York, NY: Cambridge University Press.
Stevens, D. P., & Truss, C. V. (1985). Stability and change in adult personality over 12 and 20 years. *Developmental Psychology, 21,* 568–584.
Stevens, G. (1999). Age at immigration and second language proficiency among foreign-born adults. *Language in Society, 28,* 555–578.
Stevens, M. M., Rytmeister, R. J., Proctor, M., & Bolster, P. (2010). Children living with life-threatening or life-limiting illnesses: A dispatch from the front lines. In C. A. Corr & D. E. Balk (Eds.), *Children's encounters with death, bereavement, and coping.* New York, NY: Springer.
Stevens, W. D., Hasher, L., Chiew, K. S., & Grady, C. L. (2008). A neural mechanism underlying memory failure in older adults. *Journal of Neuroscience, 28,* 12820–12824.
Stevenson, H. W., Chen, C., & Lee, S. (1993). Mathematics achievement of Chinese, Japanese, and American children: Ten years later. *Science, 259,* 53–58.
Stevenson, H. W., & Lee, S. Y. (1990). Contexts of achievement: A study of American, Chinese, and Japanese children. *Monographs of the Society for Research in Child Development, 55*(1–2, Serial No. 221).
Stevenson, H. W., Lee, S. Y., & Stigler, J. W. (1986). Mathematics achievement of Chinese, Japanese, and American children. *Science, 231,* 693–699.
Stevenson, H. W., & Stigler, J. (1992). *Learning gap: Why our schools are failing and what we can learn from Japanese and Chinese education.* New York, NY: Simon & Schuster.
Stevenson, H. W., Stigler, J. W., Lee, S., Lucker, G. W., Kitamura, S., & Hsu, C. (1985). Cognitive performance and academic achievement of Japanese, Chinese, and American children. *Child Development, 56,* 718–734.
Stevenson, R. J., Mahmut, M., & Sundqvist, N. (2007). Age related changes in odor discrimination. *Developmental Psychology, 43,* 253–260.
Stewart, P. W., Lonky, E., Reihman, J., Pagano, J., Gump, B. B., & Darvill, T. (2008). The relationship between prenatal PCB exposure and intelligence (IQ) in 9-year-old children. *Environmental Health Perspectives, 116,* 1416–1422.
Stewart, R. B., & Marvin, R. S. (1984). Sibling relations: The role of conceptual perspective-taking in the ontogeny of sibling caregiving. *Child Development, 55,* 1322–1332.
Stice, E., Becker, C. B., & Yokum, S. (2013). Eating disorder prevention: Current evidence-base and future directions. *International Journal of Eating Disorders, 46,* 478–485.
Stice, E., Marti, C. N., & Rohde, P. (2012). Prevalence, incidence, impairment, and course of the proposed DSM-5 eating disorder diagnoses in an 8-year prospective community study of young women. *Journal of Abnormal Psychology, 122,* 445–457.
Stice, E., & Presnell, K. (2007). *The Body Project: Promoting body acceptance and preventing eating disorders: Facilitator guide.* New York, NY: Oxford University Press.
Stice, E., Rohde, P., Gau, J., & Shaw, H. (2009). An effectiveness trial of a dissonance-based eating disorder prevention program for high-risk adolescent girls. *Journal of Consulting and Clinical Psychology, 77,* 825–834.
Stice, E., Rohde, P., Shaw, H., & Marti, C. N. (2013). Efficacy trial of a selective prevention program targeting both eating disorders and obesity among female college students: 1- and 2-year follow-up effects. *Journal of Consulting and Clinical Psychology, 81,* 183–189.
Stice, E., Yokum, S., & Waters, A. (2015). Dissonance-based eating disorder prevention program reduces reward region response to thin models; how actions shape valuation. *PLoS ONE, 10,* e0144530.
Stillion, J. M., & McDowell, E. E. (1996). *Suicide across the life span: Premature exits* (2nd ed.). Washington, DC: Taylor & Francis.
Stine, E. A. L., Soederberg, L. M., & Morrow, D. G. (1996). Language and discourse processing through adulthood. In F. Blanchard-Fields & T. M. Hess (Eds.), *Perspectives on cognitive change in adulthood and aging.* New York, NY: McGraw-Hill.
Stine-Morrow, E. A. L., Loveless, M. K., & Soederberg, L. M. (1996). Resource allocation in online reading by younger and older adults. *Psychology and Aging, 11,* 475–486.
Stine-Morrow, E. A. L., Parisi, J. M., Morrow, D. G., Greene, J., & Park, D. C. (2007). An engagement model of cognitive optimization through adulthood. *Journals of Gerontology B: Psychological and Social Sciences, 62,* 62–69.
Stine-Morrow, E. A. L., Parisi, M. M., Morrow, D. G., & Park, D. C. (2008). The effects of an engaged lifestyle on cognitive vitality: A field experiment. *Psychology and Aging, 23,* 778–786.
Stipek, D. J. (1984). The development of achievement motivation. In R. Ames & C. Ames (Eds.), *Research on motivation in education: Vol. 1.* Orlando, FL: Academic Press.
Stipek, D. J., Feiler, R., Daniels, D., & Milburn, S. (1995). Effects of different instructional approaches on young children's achievement and motivation. *Child Development, 66,* 209–223.
Stipek, D. J., & Gralinski, J. H. (1996). Children's beliefs about intelligence and school performance. *Journal of Educational Psychology, 88,* 397–407.
Stipek, D., & Hakuta, K. (2007). Strategies to ensure that no child starts from behind. In J. L. Aber, S. J. Bishop-Josef, S. M. Jones, K. T. McLearn, & D. A. Phillips (Eds.), *Child development and social policy: Knowledge for action.* Washington, DC: American Psychology Association.
Stipek, D. J., & Mac Iver, D. J. (1989). Developmental change in children's assessment of intellectual competence. *Child Development, 60,* 521–538.
Stoddart, T., & Turiel, E. (1985). Children's concepts of cross-gender activities. *Child Development, 56,* 1241–1252.
Stone, R. (2009). *A teenager talks about growing up with ADHD.* NYU Child Study Center. Retrieved from www.aboutoutkids.org.
Stoner, R., Chow, M. L., Boyle, M. P., Sunkin, S. M., Mouton, P. R., Roy, S., . . . Courchesne, E. (2014). Patches of disorganization in the neocortex of children with autism. *New England Journal of Medicine, 370,* 1209–1219.
Stones, M. J., & Kozma, A. (1985). Physical performance. In N. Charness (Ed.), *Aging and human performance.* Chichester, UK & NY: Wiley.
Story, M., Nanney, M. S., & Schwartz, M. B. (2009). Schools and obesity prevention: Creating school environments and policies to promote healthy eating and physical activity. *Milbank Quarterly, 87,* 71–100.
Stowe, J. D., & Cooney, T. M. (2015). Examining Rowe & Kahn's concept of successful aging: Importance of taking a life course perspective. *The Gerontologist, 55,* 43–50.
Strauch, B. (2010). *The secret life of the grown-up brain.* New York, NY: Penguin.
Straus, M. A., & Gelles, R. J. (Edited with C. Smith) (1990). *Physical violence in American families. Risk factors and adaptations to violence in 8145 families.* New Brunswick, NJ: Transaction Publishers.
Streissguth, A. P., Barr, H. M., Bookstein, F. L., Sampson, P. D., & Olson, H. C. (1999). The long-term neurocognitive consequences of prenatal alcohol exposure: A 14-year study. *Psychological Science, 10,* 186–190.
Streissguth, A. P., & Dehaene, P. (1993). Fetal alcohol syndrome in twins of alcoholic mothers: Concordance of diagnosis and IQ. *American Journal of Medical Genetics, 47,* 857–861.
Streri, A. (2003). Cross-modal recognition of shape from hand to eyes in human newborns. *Somatosensory Motor Research, 20,* 13–18.
Streri, A., & Gentaz, E. (2004). Cross-modal recognition of shape from hand to eyes and handedness in human newborns. *Neuropsychologia, 42,* 1365–1369.
Stringer, J. S., Sinkala, M., Goldenberg, R. L., Kumwenda, R., Acosta, E. P., Aldrovandi, G. M., Stout, J. P., & Vermund, S. H. (2004). Universal nevirapine upon presentation in labor to prevent mother-to-child HIV transmission in high prevalence settings. *AIDS, 18,* 939–943.
Stroebe, M. (2001). Bereavement research and theory: Retrospective and prospective. *American Behavioral Scientist, 44,* 854–865.
Stroebe, M., Finkenauer, C., Wijngaards-de Meij, L., Schut, H., van den Bout, J., & Stroebe, W. (2013). Partner-oriented self-regulation among bereaved parents: The costs of holding in grief for the partner's sake. *Psychological Science, 24,* 395–402.
Stroebe, M. S., & Schut, H. A. W. (1999). The dual process model of coping with bereavement: Rationale and description. *Death Studies, 23,* 197–224.
Stroebe, M., & Schut, H. (2010). The dual process model of coping with bereavement: A decade on. *Omega: Journal of Death and Dying, 61,* 273–289.
Stroebe, M., & Schut, H. (2015). Family matters in bereavement: Toward an integrative intra-interpersonal coping model. *Perspectives on Psychological Science, 10,* 873–879.
Stroebe, M., Schut, H., & Boerner, K. (2010). Continuing bonds in adaptation to bereavement: Toward theoretical integration. *Clinical Psychology Review, 30,* 259–268.
Strøm, I. F., Thoresen, S., Wentzel-Larsen, T., & Dyb, G. (2013). Violence, bullying and academic achievement: A study of 15-year-old adolescents and their school environment. *Child Abuse & Neglect, 37,* 243–251.
Strong, B., & Cohen, T. F. (2017). *The marriage and family experience: Intimate relationships in a changing society* (12th ed.). Stamford, CT: Cengage.
Strouse, G. A. & Troseth, G. L. (2014). Supporting toddlers' transfer of word learning from video. *Cognitive Development, 30,* 47–64.
Studenski, S., Perera, S., Patel, K., Rosano, C., Faulkner, K., Inzitari, M., Brach, J., Chandler, J., Cawthon, P., Connor, E. B., Nevitt, M., Visser, M., Kritchevsky, S., Badinelli, S., Harris, T., Newman, A. B., Cauley, J., Ferrucci, L., & Guralnik, J. (2011). Gait speed and survival in older adults. *Journal of the American Medical Association, 305,* 50–8.
Sturge-Apple, M., Suor, J. H., Davies, P. T., Cicchetti, D., Skibo, M. A., & Rogosch, F. A. (2016). Vagal tone and children's delay of gratification: Differential sensitivity in resource-poor and resource-rich environments. *Psychological Science, 27,* 885–893.

Su, P., Kuan, C.-C., Kaga, K., Sano, M., & Mima, K. (2008). Myelination progression in language-correlated regions in brain of normal children determined by quantitative MRI assessment. *International Journal of Pediatric Otorhinolaryngology*, *72*, 1751–1763.

Su, R., Murdock, C., & Rounds, J. (2015). Person-environment fit. In P. J. Hartung, M. L. Savickas, & W. B. Walsh (Eds.), *APA handbook of career intervention: Vol. 1. Foundations* (pp. 81–98). Washington, DC: American Psychological Association.

Substance Abuse and Mental Health Services Administration (2011). *Results from the 2010 National Survey on Drug Use and Health: Summary of national findings*, NSDUH Series H-41, HHSPublication No. (SMA) 11-4658. Rockville, MD: Substance Abuse and Mental Health Services Administration, 2011.

Substance Abuse and Mental Health Services Administration (2012). *Preventing suicide: A toolkit for high schools*. HHS Publication No. (SMA) 12-4669. Rockville, MD: Center for Mental Health Services, Substance Abuse and Mental Health Services Administration.

Substance Abuse and Mental Health Services Administration. (2012). *Results from the 2011 National Survey on Drug Use and Health: Summary of National Findings* NSDUH Series H-44, HHS Publication No. (SMA) 12-4713). Rockville, MD: Author.

Substance Abuse and Mental Health Services Administration (2014). *Results from the 2013 National Survey on Drug Use and Health: Summary of National Findings* NSDUH Series H-48, HHS Publication No. (SMA) 14-4863. Rockville, MD: Substance Abuse and Mental Health Services Administration.

Sudhalter, V., & Braine, M. D. S. (1985). How does comprehension of passives develop? A comparison of actional and experiential verbs. *Journal of Child Language*, *12*, 455–470.

Sue, S., Cheng, J. K. Y., Saad, C. S., & Chu, J. P. (2012). Asian American mental health. A call to action. *American Psychologist*, *67*, 532–544.

Sugden, K., Arseneault, L., Harrington, H., Moffitt, T. E., Williams, B., & Caspi, A. (2010). Serotonin transporter gene moderates the development of emotional problems among children following bullying victimization. *Journal of the American Academy of Child & Adolescent Psychiatry*, *49*, 830–840.

Suitor, J. J. (1991). Marital quality and satisfaction with the division of household labor across the family life cycle. *Journal of Marriage and the Family*, *53*, 221–230.

Suitor, J. J., Sechrist, J., Plikuhn, M., Pardo, S. T., Gilligan, M., & Pillemer, K. (2009). The role of perceived maternal favoritism in sibling relations in midlife. *Journal of Marriage and Family*, *71*, 1026–1038.

Sullivan, H. S. (1953). *The interpersonal theory of psychiatry*. New York, NY: Norton.

Sullivan, S., & Ruffman, T. (2004). Social understanding: How does it fare with advancing years? *British Journal of Psychology*, *95*, 1–18.

Sulloway, F. J. (2007). Birth order and intelligence. *Science*, *316*, 1711–1717.

Sumner, J. A., McLaughlin, K. A., Walsh, K., Sheridan, M. A., & Koenen, K. C. (2015). Caregiving and 5-HTTLPR genotype predict adolescent physiological stress reactivity: Confirmatory tests of gene × environment interactions. *Child Development*, *86*, 985–994.

Sumter, S. R., Valkenburg, P. M., & Peter, J. (2013). Perceptions of love across the lifespan: Differences in passion, intimacy, and commitment. *International Journal of Behavioral Development*, *37*, 417–427.

Sun, X., Allison, C., Auyeung, B., Zhang, Z., Matthews, F. E., Baron-Cohen, S., & Brayne, C. (2015). Validation of existing diagnosis of autism in mainland China using standardised diagnostic instruments. *Autism*, *19*, 1010–1017.

Sundqvist, A., Nordqvist, E., Koch, F. S., & Heimann, M. (2016). Early declarative memory predicts productive language: A longitudinal study of deferred imitation and communication at 9 and 16 months. *Journal of Experimental Child Psychology*, *151*, 109–119.

Suri, R., Lin, A. S., Cohen, L. S., & Altshuler, L. L. (2014). Acute and long-term behavioral outcome of infants and children exposed in utero to either maternal depression or antidepressants: A review of the literature. *Journal of Clinical Psychiatry*, *75*, e1142–1152.

Suskind, D., Suskind, B., & Lewinter-Suskind, L. (2015). *Thirty million words: Building a child's brain: Tune in, talk more, take turns*. New York, NY: Dutton.

Susser, E., St. Clair, D., & He, L. (2008). Latent effects of prenatal malnutrition on adult health: The example of schizophrenia. *Annual New York Academy of Sciences*, *1136*, 185–192.

Sussman, S., Pokhrel, P., Ashmore, R. D., & Brown, B. B. (2007). Adolescent peer group identification and characteristics: A review of the literature. *Addictive Behaviors*, 32, 1602–1627.

Sutin, A. R., Costa, P. T., Jr., Wethington, E., & Eaton, W. (2010). Turning points and lessons learned: Stressful life events and personality trait development across middle adulthood. *Psychology and Aging*, *25*, 524–533.

Sutter, C., Zöllig, J., Allemand, M., & Martin, M. (2012). Sleep quality and cognitive function in healthy old age: The moderating role of subclinical depression. *Neuropsychology*, *26*, 768–775.

Sutton, T. E., & Simons, L. G. (2015). Sexual assault among college students: Family of origin hostility, attachment, and the hook-up culture as risk factors. *Journal of Child and Family Studies*, *24*, 2827–2840.

Sutton-Brown, M., & Suchowersky, O. (2003). Clinical and research advances in Huntington's disease. *Canadian Journal of Neurological Sciences*, *30* (Suppl. 1), S45.

Svedberg, P., Blom, V., Narusyte, J., Bodin, L., Bergström, G., & Hallsten, L. (2014). Genetic and environmental influences on performance-based self-esteem in a population-based cohort of Swedish twins. *Self and Identity*, *13*, 243–256.

Swaminathan, S., Shen, L., Kim, S., Inlow, M., West, J. D., Faber, K. M., . . . Saykin, A. J. (2012). Analysis of copy number variation in Alzheimer's disease: The NIALOAD/NCRAD family study. *Current Alzheimer Research*, *9*, 801–814.

Swamy, R., Mohapatra, S., Bythell, M., & Embleton, N. D. (2010). Survival in infants live born at less than 24 weeks' gestation: The hidden morbidity of non-survivors. *Archives of Disease in Childhood-Fetal and Neonatal Edition*, 95, 293–294.

Swanson, H. L. (1999). What develops in working memory? A life span perspective. *Developmental Psychology*, *35*, 986–1000.

Swarr, A. E., & Richards, M. H. (1996). Longitudinal effects of adolescent girls' pubertal development, perceptions of pubertal timing, and parental relations on eating problems. *Developmental Psychology*, 32, 636–646.

Sween, J., Wallington, S. F., Sheppard, V., Taylor, T., Llanos, A. A., & Adams-Campbell, L. L. (2014). The role of exergaming in improving physical activity: A review. *Journal of Physical Activity & Health*, *11*, 864–870.

Symons, D. K., & Clark, S. E. (2000). A longitudinal study of mother–child relationships and theory of mind in the preschool period. *Social Development*, *9*, 3–23.

Szoeke, C. E. I., Campbell, S., Chiu, E., & Ames, D. (2009). Vascular cognitive disorder. In M. F. Weiner & A. M. Lipton (Eds.), *The American Psychiatric Publishing Textbook of Alzheimer disease and other dementias*. Washington, DC: American Psychiatric Publishing.

Tach, L., & Halpern-Meekin, S. (2009). How does premarital cohabitation affect trajectories of marital quality? *Journal of Marriage and Family*, *71*, 298–317.

Tackett, J. L., Krueger, R. F., Iacono, W. G., & McGue, M. (2008). Personality in middle childhood: A hierarchical structure and longitudinal connections with personality in late adolescence. *Journal of Research in Personality*, *42*, 1456–1462.

Taddio, A. (2002). Conditioning and hyperalgesia in newborns exposed to repeated heel lances. *Journal of the American Medical Association*, 288, 857–861.

Tafarodi, R. W., Lo, C., Yamaguchi, S., Lee, W. W., & Katsura, H. (2004). The inner self in three countries. *Journal of Cross-Cultural Psychology*, *35*, 97–117.

Tager-Flusberg, H. (2014). Autism spectrum disorder: Developmental approaches from infancy through childhood. In M. Lewis & K. D. Rudolph (Eds.), *Handbook of developmental psychopathology* (3rd ed., pp. 651–664). New York, NY: Springer.

Tager-Flusberg, H., & Zukowski, A. (2013). Putting words together: Morphology and syntax in the preschool years. In J. B. Gleason & N. B. Ratner (Eds.), *The development of language* (7th ed.). Boston, MA: Allyn & Bacon.

Takahashi, K. (1990). Are the key assumptions of the "Strange Situation" procedure universal? A view from Japanese research. *Human Development*, 33, 23–30.

Taki, Y., Thyreau, B., Kinomura, S., Sato, K., Goto, R., Wu, K., & Fukuda, H. (2013). A longitudinal study of age- and gender-related annual rate of volume changes in regional gray matter in healthy adults. *Human Brain Mapping*, *34*, 2292–2301.

Tallal, P., Miller, S. L., Bedi, G., Byma, G., Wang, X., Nagarajan, S. S., et al. (1996). Language comprehension in language-learning impaired children improved with acoustically modified speech. *Science*, *271*, 81–84.

Talwar, V., & Lee, K. (2008). Social and cognitive correlates of children's lying behavior. *Child Development*, *79*, 866–881.

Tamis-LeMonda, C. S., Adolph, K. E., Lobo, S. A., Karasik, L. B., Ishak, S., & Dimitropoulou, K. A. (2008). When infants take mothers' advice: 18-month-olds integrate perceptual and social information to guide motor action. *Developmental Psychology*, *44*, 734–746.

Tan, R. S., & Pu, S. J. (2004). Is it andropause? Recognizing androgen deficiency in aging men. *Postgraduate Medicine*, *115*, 62–66.

Tan, U., & Tan, M. (1999). Incidences of asymmetries for the palmar grasp reflex in neonates and hand preference in adults. *Neuroreport: For Rapid Communication of Neuroscience Research*, *10*, 3254–3256.

Tangney, J. P., Stuewig, J., & Mashek, D. J. (2007). Moral emotions and moral behavior. *Annual Review of Psychology*, *58*, 345–372.

Tannen, D. (1991). *You just don't understand: Women and men in conversation*. New York, NY: Ballantine.

Tanner, A. E., Jelenewicz, S. M., Ma, A., Rodgers, C. R. R., Houston, A. M., & Paluzzi, P. (2013). Ambivalent messages: Adolescents' perspectives on pregnancy and birth. *Journal of Adolescent Health*, *53*, 105–111.

Tanner, J. M. (1990). *Foetus into man: Physical growth from conception to maturity* (2nd ed.). Cambridge, MA: Harvard University Press.

Tanner Stapleton, L., & Bradbury, T. N. (2012). Marital interaction prior to parenthood predicts parent-child interaction 9 years later. *Journal of Family Psychology*, 26, 479–487.

Tarren-Sweeney, M. (2013). An investigation of complex attachment- and trauma-related symptomatology among children in foster and kinship care. *Child Psychiatry and Human Development*, 2013, *44*, 727–741.

Tarullo, A. R., Balsam, P. D. and Fifer, W. P. (2011), Sleep and infant learning. *Infant and Child Development*, *20*, 35–46.

Tashman, L. S. (2013). The development of expertise in performance: The role of memory, knowledge, learning, and practice. *Journal of Multidisciplinary Research*, *5*, 33.

Tasi, K. M., Telzer, E. H., Fuligni, A. J. (2013). Continuity and discontinuity in perceptions of family relationships from adolescence to young adulthood. *Child Development*, *84*, 471–484.

Taste science (2010). The Taste Science Laboratory. Retrieved from www.tastescience.com.

Taumoepeau, M., & Reese, E. (2014). Understanding the self through siblings: Self-awareness mediates the sibling effect on social understanding. *Social Development*, *23*, 1–18.

Taveras, E. M., Rifas-Shiman, S. L., Belfort, M. B., Kleinman, K. P., Oken, E., & Gillman, M. W. (2009). Weight status in the first 6 months of life and obesity at 3 years of age. *Pediatrics*, *123*, 1177–1183.

Tavernise, S. (July 17, 2012). F.D.A. makes it official: BPA can't be used in baby bottles and cups. *The New York Times*.

Taylor, C. A., Manganello, J. A., Lee, S. J., & Rice, J. C. (2010). Mothers' spanking of 3-year-old children and subsequent risk of children's aggressive behavior. *Pediatrics*, *125*, 1057–1065.

Taylor, C., Schloss, K., Palmer, S. E., & Franklin, A. (2013). Color preferences in infants and adults are different. *Psychonomic Bulletin & Review*, *20*, 916–922.

Taylor, G., Lekes, N., Gagnon, H., Kwan, L., & Koestner, R. (2012). Need satisfaction, work–school interference and school dropout: An application of self-determination theory. *British Journal of Educational Psychology*, 82, 622–646.

Taylor, M. (Ed.). (2013). *The Oxford handbook of the development of imagination*. Oxford University Press.

Taylor, M. D., Frier, B. M., Gold, A. E., & Deary, I. J. (2003). Psychosocial factors and diabetes-related outcomes following diagnosis of Type 1 diabetes. *Diabetic Medicine*, *20*, 135–146.

Taylor, M. R. (2003). Dealing with death: Western philosophical strategies. In C. D. Bryant (Ed.), *Handbook of death and dying*. Thousand Oaks, CA: Sage.

Taylor, M., Carlson, S. M., Maring, B. L., Gerow, L., & Charley, C. M. (2004). The characteristics and correlates of fantasy in school-age children: Imaginary companions, impersonation, and social understanding. *Developmental Psychology, 40*, 1173–1187.

Taylor, R. E., & Richards, S. B. (1991). Patterns of intellectual differences of black, Hispanic, and white children. *Psychology in the Schools, 28*, 5–9.

Taylor, R. J., Chatters, L. M., & Jackson, J. S. (2007). Religious and spiritual involvement among older African Americans, Caribbean black, and non-Hispanic whites: Findings from the National Survey of American Life. *Journal of Gerontology: Social Sciences, 62B*, S238–S250.

Teachman, B. A. (2006). Aging and negative affect: The rise and fall and rise of anxiety and depression symptoms. *Psychology and Aging, 21*, 201–207.

Teachman, J. D. (2002). Stability across cohorts in divorce risk factors. *Demography, 39*, 331–351.

Teachman, J., & Tedrow, L. (2008). The demography of stepfamilies in the United States. In J. Pryor (Ed.), *The international handbook of stepfamilies: Policy and practice in legal, research, and clinical environments.* Hoboken, NJ: Wiley.

Tedeschi, R. G., & Calhoun, L. G. (1995). *Trauma and transformation: Growing in the aftermath of suffering.* Thousand Oaks, CA: Sage.

Tedeschi, R. G., & Calhoun, L. G. (2004). Posttraumatic growth: Conceptual foundations and empirical evidence. *Psychological Inquiry, 15*, 1–18.

Teeter, P. A. (1998). *Interventions for ADHD. Treatment in developmental context.* New York, NY: Guilford.

Telzer, E. H., Flannery, J., Humphreys, K. L., Goff, B., Gabard-Durman, L., Gee, D. G., & Tottenham, N. (2015). "The cooties effect": Amygdala reactivity to opposite-versus same-sex faces declines from childhood to adolescence. *Journal of Cognitive Neuroscience, 27*, 1685–1696.

Temple, E., Poldrack, R. A., Protopapas, A., Nagarajan, S., Salz, T., Tallal, P., et al. (2000). Disruption of the neural response to rapid acoustic stimuli in dyslexia: Evidence from functional MRI. *Proceedings of the National Academy of Science, 97*, 13907–13912.

Tenenbaum, H. R., & Leaper, C. (2003). Parent-child conversations about science: The socialization of gender inequities. *Developmental Psychology, 39*, 34–47.

Tenenbaum, H. R., Poe, M. V., Snow, C. E., Tabors, P., & Ross, S. (2007). Maternal and child predictors of low-income children's educational attainment. *Journal of Applied Development Psychology, 28*, 227–238.

Teno, J. M., Clarridge, B. R., Casey, V., Welch, L. C., Wetle, T., Shield, R., & Mor, V. (2004). Family perspectives on end-of-life care at the last place of care. *Journal of the American Medical Association, 291*, 88–93.

Terman, L. M. (1954). The discovery and encouragement of exceptional talent. *American Psychologist, 9*, 221–238.

Tessier, R., Charpak, N., Giron, M., Cristo, M., de Calume, Z. F., & Ruiz-Peláez, J. G. (2009). Kangaroo mother care, home environment and father involvement in the first year of life: A randomized controlled study. *Acta Paediatrica, 98*, 1444–1450.

Testa, M., Hoffman, J. H., & Livingston, J. A. (2010). Alcohol and sexual risk behaviors as mediators of the sexual victimization-revictimization relationship. *Journal of Consulting and Clinical Psychology, 78*, 249–259.

Teti, D. M., Sakin, J. W., Kucera, E., & Corns, K. M. (1996). And baby makes four: Predictors of attachment security among preschool-age firstborns during the transition to siblinghood. *Child Development, 67*, 579–596.

Thapar, A. (2003). Attention deficit hyperactivity disorder: New genetic findings, new directions. In R. Plomin, J. C. DeFries, I. W. Craig, & P. McGuffin (Eds.), *Behavioral genetics in the postgenomic era.* Washington, DC: American Psychological Association.

Thapar, A., Harold, G., Rice, F., Ge, X., Boivin, J., Hay, D., van den Bree, M., & Lewis, A. (2007). Do intrauterine or genetic influences explain the foetal origins of chronic disease? A novel experimental method for disentangling effects. *BMC Medical Research Methodology, 7*, 25.

Tharinger, D. (1990). Impact of child sexual abuse on developing sexuality. *Professional Psychology: Research & Practice, 21*, 331–337.

The National Safety Commission. (2008). Shedding light on driving in the dark. Retrieved from www.alerts.nationalsafetycommission.com/2008/09/shedding-light-on-driving-in-dark.php.

Thelen, E. (1995). Motor development: A new synthesis. *American Psychologist, 50*, 79–95.

Thelen, E. (1996). The improvising infant: Learning about learning to move. In M. R. Merrens & G. G. Brannigan (Eds.), *The developmental psychologists: Research adventures across the life span* (pp. 21–35). New York, NY: McGraw-Hill.

Thelen, E., & Smith, L. B. (1994). *A dynamic systems approach to the development of cognition and action.* Cambridge, MA: MIT Press.

Thelen, M. H., Powell, A. L., Lawrence, C., & Kuhnert, M. E. (1992). Eating and body image concerns among children. *Journal of Clinical Child Psychology, 21*, 41–46.

Then, F. S., Luck, T., Luppa, M., König, H., Angemeyer, M. C., & Riedel-Heller, S. G. (2015). Differential effects of enriched environment at work on cognitive decline in old age. *Neurology, 84*, 2169–2176.

Thibault, H., Contrand, B., Saubusse, E., Baine, M., & Maurice-Tison, S. (2010). Risk factors for overweight and obesity in French adolescents: Physical activity, sedentary behavior and parental characteristics. *Nutrition, 26*, 192–2000.

Thiede, K. W., & Dunlosky, J. (1999). Toward a general model of self-regulated study: An analysis of selection of items for study and self-paced study time. *Journal of Experimental Psychology: Learning, Memory, and Cognition, 25*, 1024–1037.

Thigpen, J. W. (2009). Early sexual behavior in a sample of low-income, African American children. *Journal of Sex Research, 46*, 67–79.

Thoburn, J. W., & Sexton, T. L. (2016). *Family psychology. Theory, research, and practice.* Santa Barbara, CA: Praeger/ABC-Clio.

Thomas, A. K., & Bulevich, J. B. (2006). Effective cue utilization reduces memory errors in older adults. *Psychological Aging, 21*, 379–389.

Thomas, A., & Chess, S. (1977). *Temperament and development.* Oxford, England: Brunner/Mazel.

Thomas, A., & Chess, S. (1986). The New York Longitudinal Study: From infancy to early adult life. In R. Plomin & J. Dunn (Eds.), *The study of temperament: Changes, continuities, and challenges.* Hillsdale, NJ: Erlbaum.

Thomas, F., Renaud, F., Benefice, E., de Meeus, T., & Guegan, J. (2001). International variability of ages at menarche and menopause: Patterns and main determinants. *Human Biology, 73*, 271.

Thomas, H. N., Chang, C. H., Dillon, S., & Hess, R. (2014). Sexual activity in midlife women: Importance of sex matters. *JAMA Internal Medicine, 174*, 631–633.

Thomas, J. R., Alderson, J. A., Thomas, K. T., Campbell, A. C., & Elliott, B. C. (2010). Developmental gender differences for overhand throwing in Aboriginal Australian children. *Research Quarterly in Exercise Sport, 81*, 432–441.

Thomas, O. N., Caldwell, C. H., Faison, N., & Jackson, J. S. (2009). Promoting academic achievement: The role of racial identity in buffering perceptions of teacher discrimination on academic achievement among African American and Caribbean Black adolescents. *Journal of Educational Psychology, 101*, 420–431.

Thompson, A. M., & Smart, J. L. (1993). A prospective study of the development of laterality: Neonatal laterality in relation to perinatal factors and maternal behavior. *Cortex, 29*, 649–659.

Thompson, D. (2009). A brief history of research and theory on adult learning and cognition. In M. C. Smith (Ed.) & N. DeFrates-Densch (Asst. Ed.), *Handbook of research on adult learning and development.* New York, NY: Routledge.

Thompson, J. R., & Chapman, R. S. (1977). Who is "Daddy" revisited? The status of two-year-olds' overextended words in use and comprehension. *Journal of Child Language, 4*, 359–375.

Thompson, K. M., Simons, E. A., Badizadegan, K., Reef, S. E. & Cooper, L. Z. (2016). Characterization of the risks of adverse outcomes following rubella infection in pregnancy. *Risk Analysis, 36*, 1315–1331.

Thompson, R. A. (1994). Emotion regulation: A theme in search of definition. In N. A. Fox (Ed.), The development of emotion regulation: Biological and behavioral considerations. *Monographs of the Society for Research in Child Development, 59* (Nos. 2–3, Serial No. 240).

Thompson, R. A. (2006). Conversation and developing understanding: Introduction to the special issue. *Merrill-Palmer Quarterly, 52*, 1–16.

Thompson, R. A. (2012). Whither the preconventional child? Toward a life-span moral development theory. *Child Development Perspectives, 6*, 423–429.

Thompson, R. A. (2014). Socialization of emotion and emotion regulation in the family. In J. J. Gross (Ed.), *Handbook of emotion regulation* (2nd ed., pp. 187–202). New York, NY: Guilford.

Thompson, R. A., & Amato, P. R. (1999). The post divorce family. An introduction to the issues. In R. A. Thompson & P. R. Amato (Eds.), *The post divorce family. Children, parenting, & society.* Thousand Oaks, CA: Sage.

Thompson, R. A., Meyer, S., & McGinley, M. (2006). Understanding values in relationships: The development of conscience. In M. Killen & J. G. Smetana (Eds.), *Handbook of moral development.* Mahwah, NJ: Erlbaum.

Thompson, R. A., Winer, A. C., & Goodvin, R. (2011). The individual child: Temperament, emotion, self, and personality. In M. E. Lamb & M. H. Bornstein (Eds.), *Social and personality development. An advanced textbook.* New York, NY: Psychology Press.

Thompson, R. F. (2000). *The brain: An introduction to neuroscience* (3rd ed.). New York, NY: Worth.

Thorndike, R. L. (1997). The early history of intelligence testing. In D. P. Flanagan, J. L. Genshaft, & P. L. Harrison (Eds.), *Contemporary intellectual assessment: Theories, tests, and issues.* New York, NY: Guilford.

Thorne, B. (1993). *Gender play: Girls and boys in school.* New Brunswick, NJ: Rutgers University Press.

Thornton, R., & Light, L. L. (2006). Language comprehension and production in normal aging. In J. E. Birren & K. W. Schaie (Eds.), *Handbook of the psychology of aging.* Boston, MA: Elsevier Academic Press.

Thurber, C. A. (1995). The experience and expression of homesickness in preadolescent and adolescent boys. *Child Development, 66*, 1162–1178.

Thys-Jacobs, S. (2000). Micronutrients and the premenstrual syndrome: The case for calcium. *Journal of the American College of Nutrition, 19*, 220–227.

Tietjen, A. M., & Walker, L. J. (1985). Moral reasoning and leadership among men in a Papua New Guinea society. *Developmental Psychology, 21*, 982–992.

Tiggemann, M., & Lacey, C. (2009). Shopping for clothes: Body satisfaction, appearance investment, and functions of clothing among female shoppers. *Body Image, 6*, 285–291.

Tiihonen, J., Rautiainen, M., Ollila, H. M., Repo-Tiihonen, E., Virkkunen, M., Palotie, A., . . . Paunio, T. (2015). Genetic background of extreme violent behavior. *Molecular Psychiatry, 20*, 786–792.

Tilly, J. L. & Sinclair, D. A. (2013). Germline energetics, aging, and female infertility. *Cell Metabolism, 17*, 838–850.

TIMSS. (2016). *Trends in international mathematics and science study.* Available at www.nces.ed.gov/timss/timss15.asp.

Tita, A. T., Landon, M. B., Spong, C. Y., Lai, Y., Leveno, K. J., Varner, M. W., Moawad, A. H., Caritis, S. N., Meis, P. J., Wapner, R. J., Sorokin, Y., Miodovnik, M., Carpenter, M., Peaceman, A. M., O'Sullivan, M. J., Sibai, B. M., Langer, O., Thorp, J. M., Ramin, S. M., Mercer, B. M., & the Eunice Kennedy Shriver NICHD Maternal–Fetal Medicine Units Network (2009). Timing of elective repeat cesarean delivery at term and neonatal outcomes. *New England Journal of Medicine, 360*, 111–120.

Tither, J. M., & Ellis, B. J. (2008). Impact of fathers on daughters' age at menarche: A genetically and environmentally controlled sibling study. *Developmental Psychology, 44*, 1409–1420.

Titz, C., & Karbach, J. (2014). Working memory and executive functions: Effects of training on academic achievement. *Psychological Research, 78*, 852–868.

Tolan, P., Gorman-Smith, D., & Henry, D. (2006). Family violence. *Annual Review of Psychology, 57*, 557–583.

Tomasello, M. (2003). *Constructing a language: A usage-based theory of language acquisition.* Cambridge, MA: Harvard University Press.

Tomasello, M. (2006). Acquiring linguistic constructions. In D. Kuhn & R. Siegler (Vol. Eds.), *Handbook of child psychology: Cognition, perception, and language: Vol. 2.* (6th ed.). Hoboken, NJ: Wiley and Sons.

Tomasello, M. (2009). The usage-based theory of language acquisition. In E. L. Bavin (Ed.), *The Cambridge*

handbook of child language (pp. 69–87). New York, NY: Cambridge University Press.
Tomasello, M. (with C. Dweck, J. Silk, B. Skryms, & E. Spelke) (2009). *Why we cooperate*. Cambridge, MA: MIT Press.
Tomasello, M., & Herrmann, E. (2010). Ape and human cognition: What's the difference? *Current Directions in Psychological Science, 19*, 3–8.
Tomasello, M., & Vaish, A. (2013). Origins of human cooperation and morality. *Annual Review of Psychology, 64*, 231–255.
Tomblin, J. B. (2009). Children with specific language impairment. In E. L. Bavin (Ed.), *The Cambridge handbook of child language* (pp. 418–431). New York, NY: Cambridge University Press.
Tomlinson-Keasey, C., & Keasey, C. B. (1974). The mediating role of cognitive development in moral judgment. *Child Development, 45*, 291–298.
Tomlinson-Keasey, C., & Little, T. D. (1990). Predicting educational attainment, occupational achievement, intellectual skill, and personal adjustment among gifted men and women. *Journal of Educational Psychology, 82*, 442–455.
Tomporowski, P. D., Davis, C. L., Miller, P. H., & Naglieri, J. A. (2008). Exercise and children's intelligence, cognition, and academic achievement. *Educational Psychology Review, 20*, 111–131.
Toossi, M. (2012). Labor force projections to 2020: A more slowly growing workforce. *Monthly Labor Review, 135*, 43–64.
Topal, J., Gergely, G., Miklosi, A., Erdohegyi, A., & Csibra, G. (2008). Infants' perseverative search errors are induced by pragmatic misinterpretation. *Science, 321*, 1831–1834.
Toplak, M. E., West, R. F., & Stanovich, K. E. (2014). Assessing miserly information processing: An expansion of the Cognitive Reflection Test. *Thinking & Reasoning, 20*, 147–168.
Tordjman, S., Somogyi, E., Coulon, N., Kermarrec, S., Cohen, D., Bronsard, G., . . . Xavier, J. (2014). Gene × environment interactions in autism spectrum disorders: Role of epigenetic mechanisms. *Frontiers in Psychiatry, 5*, 53.
Torges, C. M., Stewart, A. J., & Duncan, L. E. (2008). Achieving ego integrity: Personality development in late midlife. *Journal of Research in Personality, 42*, 1004–1019.
Torres-Mejía, G., Cupul-Uicab, L. A., Allen, B., Galal, O., Salazar-Martínez, E., & Lazcano-Ponce, E. C. (2005). Comparative study of correlates of early age at menarche among Mexican and Egyptian adolescents. *American Journal of Human Biology, 17*, 654–658.
Trabasso, T. (1975). Representation, memory, and reasoning: How do we make transitive inferences? In A. D. Pick (Ed.), *Minnesota Symposia on Child Psychology: Vol. 9*. Minneapolis, MN: University of Minnesota.
Trahan, L. H., Stuebing, K. K., Fletcher, J. M., & Hiscock, M. (2014). The Flynn effect: A meta-analysis. *Psychological Bulletin, 140*, 1332.
Trainor, B.C., Nelson, R. J. (2012). Neuroendocrinology of Aggression. In G. Fink, D. W. Pfaff, & J. E. Levine (Eds.) *Handbook of Neuroendocrinology* (pp. 509–520). San Diego, CA: Academic Press.
Trautner, H. M., Gervai, J., & Nemeth, R. (2003). Appearance-reality distinction and development of gender constancy understanding in children. *International Journal of Behavioral Development, 27*, 275–281.
Trautner, H. M., Ruble, D. N., Cyphers, L., Kirsten, B., Behrendt, R., & Hartmann, P. (2005). Rigidity and flexibility of gender stereotypes in childhood: Developmental or differential? *Infant and Child Development, 14*, 365–381.
Treas, J. & Hill, T. (2009). Social trends and public policy in an aging society. In M. C. Smith (Ed.) & N. DeFrates-Densch (Asst. Ed.), *Handbook of research on adult learning and development*. New York, NY: Routledge.
Treffert, D. (2010). *Islands of genius: The bountiful mind of the autistic, acquired, and sudden savant*. Philadelphia, PA: Jessica Kingsley Publishers.
Treffert, D. (2014). Whatever happened to Leslie Lemke? *Scientific American*. Retrieved from www.blogs.scientificamerican.com/guest-blog/whatever-happened-to-leslie-lemke/.
Treffert, D. A. (2000). *Extraordinary people: Understanding savant syndrome*. Lincoln, Nebraska: iUniverse.com.
Treiman, R., & Broderick, V. (1998). What's in a name? Children's knowledge about the letters in their own names. *Journal of Experimental Child Psychology, 70*, 97–116.
Tremblay, M. S., Inman, J. W., & Willms, J. D. (2000). The relationship between physical activity, self-esteem, and academic achievement in 12-year-old children. *Pediatric Exercise Science, 12*, 312–323.
Tremblay, R. E. (2010). Developmental origins of disruptive behaviour problems: The original sin hypothesis, epigenetics and their consequences for prevention. *Journal of Child Psychology and Psychiatry, 51*, 341–367.
Tremblay, R. E. (2011). Origins, development, and prevention of aggressive behavior. In D. P. Keating (Ed.), *Nature and nurture in early child development*. New York, NY: Cambridge University Press.
Trevarthen, C. (2011). What is it like to be a person who knows nothing? Defining the active intersubjective mind of a newborn human being. *Infant and Child Development, 20*, 119–135.
Triandis, H. C. (1989). Self and social behavior in differing cultural contexts. *Psychological Review, 96*, 269–289.
Triandis, H. C. (1995). *Individualism and collectivism*. Boulder, CO: Westview Press.
Trickett, P. K., & Putnam, F. W. (1993). Impact of child sexual abuse on females: Toward a developmental, psychobiological integration. *Psychological Science, 4*, 81–87.
Tronick, E. Z. (1989). Emotions and emotional communication in infants. *American Psychologist, 44*, 112–119.
Troseth, G. L., Saylor, M. M., & Archer, A. H. (2006). Young children's use of video as socially relevant information. *Child Development, 77*, 786–799.
Trost, S. G., McCoy, T. A., Vander Veur, S. S., Mallya, G., Duffy, M. L., & Foster, G. D. (2013). Physical activity patterns of inner-city elementary school children. *Medicine & Science in Sports and Exercise, 45*, 470–474.
Trueheart, C. (1997, August 5). Champion of longevity ends her reign at 122. *The Washington Post*, pp. A1, A12.
Trzesniewski, K. H., Donnellan, M. B., Moffitt, T. E., Robins, R. W., Poulton, R., & Caspi, A. (2006). Low self-esteem during adolescence predicts poor health, criminal behavior, and limited economic prospects during adulthood. *Developmental Psychology, 42*, 381–390.
Tsai, Y.-M., Kunter, M., Ludtke, O., Trautwein, U., & Ryan, R. M. (2008). What makes lessons interesting? The role of situational and individual factors in three school subjects. *Journal of Educational Psychology, 100*, 460–472.
Tucker-Drob, E. M., & Bates, T. C. (2016). Large cross-national differences in gene × socioeconomic status interaction on intelligence. *Psychological Science, 27*, 138–149.
Tucker-Drob, E. M., & Briley, D. A. (2014). Continuity of genetic and environmental influences on cognition across the life span: A meta-analysis of longitudinal twin and adoption studies. *Psychological Bulletin, 140*, 949–979.
Tucker-Drob, E. M., Briley, D. A., & Harden, K. P. (2013). Genetic and environmental influences on cognition across development and context. *Current Directions in Psychological Science, 22*, 349–355.
Tucker-Drob, E. M., & Harden, K. P. (2012). Intellectual interest mediates gene x socioeconomic status interaction on adolescent academic achievement. *Child Development, 83*, 743–757.
Tucker-Drob, E. M., Rhemtulla, M., Harden, K. P., Turkheimer, E., & Fask, D. (2011). Emergence of a gene x socioeconomic status interaction on infant mental ability between 10 months and 2 years. *Psychological Science, 22*, 125–133.
Tudor, J. C., Davis, E. J., Peixoto, L., Wimmer, M. E., van Tilborg, E., Park, A. J., & Huang, J. (2016). Sleep deprivation impairs memory by attenuating mTORC1-dependent protein synthesis. *Science Signaling, 9*, ra41–ra41.
Tulandi, T. (2015). Patient information: Miscarriage (Beyond the Basics). www.uptodate.com/contents/miscarriage-beyond-the-basics.
Tulandi, T., & Al-Fozan, H. M. (2011). Spontaneous abortion: Risk factors, etiology, clinical manifestations, and diagnostic evaluation. *Up to Date*, Wolters Kluwer. Retrieved from www.uptodate.com/ contents/spontaneous-abortion-risk-factors-etiology-clinical-manifestations-and-diagnostic-evaluation.
Tullos, A., & Woolley, J. D. (2009). The development of children's ability to use evidence to infer reality status. *Child Development, 80*, 101–114.
Tummeltshammer, K. S., Mareschal, D., & Kirkham, N. Z. (2014). Infants' selective attention to reliable visual cues in the presence of salient distractors. *Child Development, 85*, 1981–1994.
Tun, P. A., & Lachman, M. E. (2010). The association between computer use and cognition across adulthood: Use it so you won't lose it? *Psychology and Aging, 25*, 560–568.
Tun, P. A., McCoy, S., & Wingfield, A. (2009). Aging, hearing acuity, and the attentional costs of effortful listening. *Psychology and Aging, 24*, 761–766.
Tunkel, D. E., Bauer, C. A., Sun, G. H., Rosenfeld, R. M., Chandrasekhar, S. S., Cunningham, E. R. & Whamond, E. J. (2014). Clinical practice guideline: Tinnitus. *Otolaryngology—Head and Neck Surgery, 151*, S1–S40.
Turati, C. (2004). Why faces are not special to newborns: An alternative account of the face preference. *Current Directions in Psychological Science, 13*, 5–8.
Turcotte, P., Mathew, M., Shea, L. L., Brusilovskiy, E., & Nonnemacher, S. L. (2016). Service needs across the lifespan for individuals with autism. *Journal of Autism and Developmental Disorders, 46*, 2480–2489.
Turiel, E. (1978). The development of concepts of social structure: Social convention. In J. Glick & A. Clarke-Stewart (Eds.), *The development of social understanding*. New York, NY: Gardner Press.
Turiel, E. (1983). *The development of social knowledge. Morality and convention*. Cambridge, UK: Cambridge University Press.
Turiel, E. (2006). The development of morality. In N. Eisenberg (Vol. Ed.), & W. Damon & R. M. Lerner (Eds. in Chief), *Handbook of child psychology: Vol. 3. Social, emotional, and personality development* (6th ed.). Hoboken, NJ: Wiley.
Turkheimer, E., Haley, A., Waldron, M., D'Onofrio, B., & Gottesman, I. I. (2003). Socioeconomic status modifies heritability of IQ in young children. *Psychological Science, 14*, 623–628.
Turner, P. J., & Gervai, J. (1995). A multidimensional study of gender typing in preschool children and their parents: Personality, attitudes, preferences, behavior, and cultural differences. *Developmental Psychology, 31*, 759–772.
Turnpenny, P. D., & Ellard, S. (2012). *Emery's elements of medical genetics* (14th ed.). London, UK: Elsevier.
Tversky, A., & Kahneman, D. (1971). Belief in the law of small numbers. *Psychological Bulletin, 76*, 105–110.
Tversky, A., & Kahneman, D. (1973). Availability: A heuristic for judging frequency and probability. *Cognitive Psychology, 5*, 207–232.
Twenge, J. M. (1997). Changes in masculine and feminine traits over time: A meta-analysis. *Sex Roles, 36*, 305–325.
Twenge, J. M. (2006). *Generation me. Why today's young Americans are more confident, assertive, entitled—and more miserable than ever before*. New York, NY: Free Press.
Twenge, J. M., & Foster, J. D. (2010). Birth cohort increases in narcissistic personality traits among American college students, 1982–2009. *Social Psychological and Personality Science, 1*, 99–106.
Twenge, J. M., Konrath, S., Foster, J. D., Campbell, W. K., & Bushman, B. J. (2008). Egos inflating over time: A cross-temporal meta-analysis of the Narcissistic Personality Inventory. *Journal of Personality, 76*, 875–902.
Twenge, J. M., Sherman, R. A., & Wells, B. E. (2016). Changes in American adults' reported same-sex sexual experiences and attitudes, 1973–2014. *Archives of Sexual Behavior, 45*, 1713–1730
Tyson-Rawson, K. J. (1996). Adolescent responses to the death of a parent. In C. A. Corr & D. E. Balk (Eds.), *Handbook of adolescent death and bereavement*. New York, NY: Springer.
U.S. Department of Health and Human Services, Administration on Children, Youth, and Families. (2007). *Child maltreatment 2005*. Washington, DC: U. S. Government Printing Office. Retrieved from www.acf.hhs.gov/programs/cb/pubs/cm05/index.htm.
U.S. Census Bureau, Population Division. (2012, December). Table 2. Projections of the population by selected age groups and sex for the United States: 2015 to 2060 (NP2012-T2).
U.S. Census Bureau. (2014). Projections of the population by age and sex for the United States: 2015 to 2060 (Table NP2014-T9). Retrieved from

www.census.gov/population/projections/data/national/2014/summarytables.html.

U.S. Department of Education. (2015). *National assessment of adult literacy*. Available at www.nces.ed.gov/naal/kf_demographics.asp.

U.S. Department of Education, Office for Civil Rights. (2016). Dear colleague letter on transgender students. Retrieved from www2.ed.gov/about/offices/list/ocr/letters/colleague-201605-title-ix-transgender.pdf.

U.S. Department of Labor, Bureau of Labor Statistics. (2013). *Women as a percent of total employed in selected occupations, 2011*. Retrieved from www.bls.gov/opub/ted/2012/ted_20120501.htm.

U.S.D.A. Factbook. (2012). *Profiling food consumption in America*. Retrieved from www.usda.gov/factbook/chapter2.pdf. Accessed 10/28/2012.

Uccelli, P., & Pan, B. A. (2013). Semantic development: Learning the meanings of words. In J. B. Gleason & N. B. Ratner (Eds.), *The development of language* (7th ed.). Boston, MA: Allyn & Bacon.

Uchida, N., Fujita, K., & Katayama, T. (1999). Detection of vehicles on the other crossing path at an intersection: Visual search performance of elderly drivers. *Japanese Society of Automotive Engineers Review, 20*, 381.

Uchino, B. N. (2009). Understanding the links between social support and physical health. A life-span perspective with emphasis on the separation of perceived and received support. *Perspectives on Psychological Science, 4*, 236–255.

Uchronski, M. (2008). Agency and communion in spontaneous self-descriptions: Occurrence and situational malleability. *European Journal of Social Psychology, 38*, 1093–1102.

Uecker, J. E., Pearce, L. D., & Andercheck, B. (2015). The four U's: Latent classes of hookup motivations among college students. *Social Currents, 2*, 163–181.

Ueno, K., & Adams, R. G. (2006). Adult friendship: A decade review. In P. Noller & J. A. Feeney (Eds.), *Close relationships: Functions, forms, and processes*. New York, NY: Psychology Press.

Ulfsdottir, H., Nissen, E., Ryding, E. L., Lund-Egloff, D., & Wiberg-Itzel, E. (2014). The association between labour variables and primiparous women's experience of childbirth: A prospective cohort study. *BioMed Central Pregnancy Childbirth, 14*, 208.

Umaña-Taylor, A. J. (2015). Ethnic identity research: How far have we come? In C. E. Santos & A. J. Umaña-Taylor (Eds.), *Studying ethnic identity: Methodological and conceptual approaches across disciplines* (pp. 11–26). Washington, DC: American Psychological Association.

Umaña-Taylor, A. J., Gonzales-Backen, M. A., & Guimond, A. B. (2009). Latino adolescents' ethnic identity: Is there a developmental progression and does growth in ethnic identity predict growth in self-esteem? *Child Development, 80*, 391–405.

Umaña-Taylor, A. J., & Guimond, A. B. (2010). A longitudinal examination of parenting behaviors and perceived discrimination predicting Latino adolescents' ethnic identity. *Developmental Psychology, 46*, 636–650.

Umanath, S., & Marsh, E. J. (2014). Understanding how prior knowledge influences memory in older adults. *Perspectives on Psychological Science, 9*, 408–426.

Umberson, D. (2003). *Death of a parent: Transition to a new adult identity*. Cambridge, UK: Cambridge University Press.

Umberson, D., Pudrovska, T., & Reczek, C. (2010). Parenthood, childlessness, and well-being: A life course perspective. *Journal of Marriage and Family, 72*, 612–629.

Umberson, D., & Slaten, E. (2000). Gender and intergenerational relationships. In D. H. Demo, K. R. Allen, & M. A. Fine (Eds.), *Handbook of family diversity*. New York, NY: Oxford University Press.

Unger, J. B., Molina, G. B., & Teran, L. (2000). Perceived consequences of teenage childbearing among adolescent girls in an urban sample. *Journal of Adolescent Health, 26*, 205–212.

Ungvari, Z., Sonntag, W. E., de Cabo, R., Baur J. A., & Csiszar, A. (2011). Mitochondrial protection by resveratrol. *Exercise and Sports Science Review, 39*, 128–132.

University of Copenhagen (2008, December 18). Girls have superior sense of taste to boys. *Sciencedaily*. Retrieved from www.sciencedaily.com/releases/2008/12/081216104035.htm.

Unternaehrer, E., Luers, P., Mill, J., Dempster, E., Meyer, A. H., Staehli, S., . . . Meinlschmidt, G. (2012). Dynamic changes in DNA methylation of stress-associated genes (OXTR, BDNF) after acute psychosocial stress. *Translational Psychiatry, 2*, e150–e150.

Updegraff, K. A., Umaña-Taylor, A. J., Rodríguez, D. J., McHale, S. M., Feinberg, M. F., & Kuo, S. I. (2016). Family-focused prevention with Latinos: What about sisters and brothers? *Journal of Family Psychology, 30*, 633–640.

Updegraff, K., McHale, S. M., & Crouter, A. C. (1996). Gender roles in marriage: What do they mean for girls' and boys' school achievement? *Journal of Youth and Adolescence, 25*, 73–88.

Urbain, C. M., De Tiège, X., Op de Beeck, M., Bourguignon, M., Wens, V., Verheulpen, D., & Peigneux, P. (2016). Sleep in children triggers rapid reorganization of memory-related brain processes. *NeuroImage, 134*, 213–222.

Urbina, S. (2011). Tests of intelligence. In R. J. Sternberg & S. B. Kaufman (Eds.), *The Cambridge handbook of intelligence* (pp. 20–38). New York, NY: Cambridge University Press.

Urdan, T., & Mestas, M. (2006). The goals behind performance goals. *Journal of Educational Psychology, 98*, 354–365.

Usher, J. A., & Neisser, U. (1993). Childhood amnesia and the beginnings of memory for four early life events. *Journal of Experimental Psychology: General, 122*, 155–165.

Usher-Seriki, K. K., Bynum, M. S., & Callands, T. A. (2008). Mother-daughter communication about sex and sexual intercourse among middle- to upper-class African American girls. *Journal of Family Issues, 29*, 901–917.

Vable, A. M., Subramanian, S. V., Rist, P. M., & Glymour, M. M. (2015). Does the 'widowhood effect' precede spousal bereavement? Results from a nationally representative sample of older adults. *American Journal of Geriatric Psychiatry, 23*, 283–292.

Vaglio, S. (2009). Chemical communication and mother-infant recognition. *Communicative and Integrative Biology, 2*, 279–281.

Vaillant, G. E. (1977). *Adaptation to life*. Boston, MA: Little, Brown.

Vaillant, G. E. (1983). Childhood environment and maturity of defense mechanisms. In D. Magnusson & V. L. Allen (Eds.), *Human development. An interactional perspective*. New York, NY: Academic Press.

Vaillant, G. E. (2012). *Triumphs of experience. The men of the Harvard Grant Study*. Cambridge, MA: Belknap Press of Harvard University Press.

Vaillant, G. E., & Milofsky, E. (1980). Natural history of male psychological health. IX: Empirical evidence for Erikson's model of the life cycle. *American Journal of Psychiatry, 137*, 1348–1359.

Vakil, E., Blachstein, H., Sheinman, M., & Greenstein, Y. (2008). Developmental changes in attention tests norms: Implications for the structure of attention. *Child Neuropsychology, 15*, 21–39.

Valente, T. W., Fujimoto, K., Chou, C. P., & Spruijt-Metz, D. (2009). Adolescent affiliations and adiposity: A social network analysis of friendships and obesity. *Journal of Adolescent Health, 45*, 202–204.

Valiente, C., Lemery-Chalfant, K., Swanson, J., & Reiser, M. (2008). Prediction of children's academic competence from their effortful control, relationships, and classroom participation. *Journal of Educational Psychology, 100*, 67–77.

Valkenburg, P. M., & Peter, J. (2009). Social consequences of the internet for adolescents. *Current Directions in Psychological Sciences, 18*, 1–5.

Valle, A., Binder, K. S., Walsh, C. B., Nemier, C., & Bangs, K. E. (2013). Eye movements, prosody, and word frequency among average- and high-skilled second-grade readers. *School Psychology Review, 42*, 171–190.

Vallet, G. T. (2015). Embodied cognition of aging. *Frontiers in Psychology, 6*, 643.

van Anders, S. (2012). Testosterone and sexual desire in healthy women and men. *Archives of Sexual Behavior, 41*, 1471–1484.

van Ansem, W. J. C., van Lenthe, F. J., Schrijvers, C. T. M., Rodenburg, G., & van de Mheen, D. (2014). Socio-economic inequalities in children's snack consumption and sugar-sweetened beverage consumption: The contribution of home environmental factors. *British Journal of Nutrition, 112*, 467–476.

Van Assche, L., Luyten, P., Bruffaerts, R., Persoons, P., van de Ven, L., & Vandenbulcke, M. (2013). Attachment in old age: Theoretical assumptions, empirical findings and implications for clinical practice. *Clinical Psychology Review, 33*, 67–81.

Van Beurden, E., Zask, A., Barnett, L. M., & Dietrich, U. C. (2002). Fundamental movement skills—How do primary school children perform? The "Move it, Groove it" program in rural Australia. *Journal of Science and Medicine on Sport, 5*, 244–252.

Van den Block, L., Albers, G., Pereira, S. M., Onwuteaka-Philipsen, B., Pasman, R., & Deliens, L. (Eds.). (2015). *Palliative care for older people: A public health perspective*. New York, NY: Oxford University Press.

van den Boom, D. C. (1995). Do first-year intervention effects endure? Follow-up during toddlerhood of a sample of Dutch irritable infants. *Child Development, 66*, 1798–1816.

van den Dries, L., Juffer, F., van IJzendoorn, M. H., & Bakermans-Kranenburg, M. J. (2009). Fostering security? A meta-analysis of attachment in adopted children. *Children and Youth Services Review, 31*, 410–421.

van den Hooven, E. H., Pierik, F. H., de Kluizenaar, Y., Willemsen, S. P., Hofman, A., van Ratingen, S. W., et al. (2012). Air pollution exposure during pregnancy, ultrasound measures of fetal growth, and adverse birth outcomes: A prospective cohort study. *Environmental Health Perspectives, 120*, 150–156.

van der Geest, I. M. M., van den Heuvel-Eibrink, M. M., van Vliet, L. M., Pluijm, S. M. F., Streng, I. C., Michiels, E. M. C., Pieters, R., & Darlington, A. E. (2015). Talking about death with children with incurable cancer: Perspectives from parents. *Journal of Pediatrics, 167*, 1320–1326.

Van der Graaff, J., Branje, S., De Wied, M., Hawk, S., Van Lier, P., & Meeus, W. (2014). Perspective taking and empathic concern in adolescence: Gender differences in developmental changes. *Developmental Psychology, 50*, 881–888.

van der Maas, H., & Jansen, B. R. J. (2003). What response times tell of children's behavior on the balance scale task. *Journal of Experimental Child Psychology, 85*, 141–177.

van den Dries, L., Juffer, F., van IJzendoorn, M. H., Bakermans-Kranenburg, M., & Alink, L. R. A. (2012). Infants' responsiveness, attachment, and indiscriminate friendliness after international adoption from institutions or foster care in China: Application of emotional availability scales to adoptive families. *Development and Psychopathology, 24*, 49–64.

van Solinge, H., & Henkens, K. (2008). Adjustment to and satisfaction with retirement: Two of a kind? *Psychology and Aging, 23*, 422–434.

Van Doesum, K. T. M., Riksen-Walraven, J. M., Hosman, C. M. H., & Hoefnagels, C. (2008). A randomized controlled trial of a home-visiting intervention aimed at preventing relationship problems in depressed mothers and their infants. *Child Development, 79*, 547–561.

Van Hecke, A. V., Mundy, P. C., Acra, C. F., Block, J. J., Delgado, C. E. F., Parlade, M. V., Meyer, J. A., Neal, A. R., & Pomares, Y. B. (2007). Infant joint attention, temperament, and social competence in preschool children. *Child Development, 78*, 53–69.

van Hoeken, D., Seidell, J., & Hoek, H. (2003). Epidemiology. In J. Treasure, U. Schmidt, & E. Van Furth (Eds.), *Handbook of eating disorders* (2nd ed.). Chichester, UK: Wiley.

van IJzendoorn, M. H., Bakermans-Kranenburg, M. J., & Alink, L. R. A. (2012). Meta-analysis in developmental science. In B. Laursen, T D. Little, & N. A. Card (Eds.), *Handbook of developmental research methods* (pp. 667–686). New York, NY: Guilford.

van IJzendoorn, M. H., & DeWolff, M. S. (1997). In search of the absent father: Meta-analyses of infant-father attachment: A rejoinder to our discussants. *Child Development, 68*, 604–609.

van IJzendoorn, M. H., & Juffer, F. (2005). *Adoption is a successful natural intervention enhancing adopted children's IQ and school performance. Current Directions in Psychological Science, 14*, 326–330.

van IJzendoorn, M. H., & Juffer, F. (2006). The Emanuel Miller Memorial Lecture 2006: Adoption as intervention: Meta-analytic evidence for massive catch-up and plasticity in physical, socio-emotional, and cognitive development. *Journal of Child Psychology and Psychiatry, 47*, 1228–1245.

van IJzendoorn, M. H., & Sagi, A. (1999). Cross-cultural patterns of attachment: Universal and contextual dimensions. In J. Cassidy & P. R. Shaver (Eds.), *Handbook of attachment*. New York, NY: Guilford.

van IJzendoorn, M. H., & Sagi-Schwartz, A. (2008). Cross-cultural patterns of attachment. Universal and contextual dimensions. In J. Cassidy & P. R. Shaver (Eds.), *Handbook of attachment: Theory, research, and clinical applications* (2nd ed.). New York, NY: Guilford.

van IJzendoorn, M. H., Schuengel, C., & Bakermans-Kranenburg, M. J. (1999). Disorganized attachment in early childhood: Meta-analysis of precursors, concomitants, and sequelae. *Development and Psychopathology, 11*, 225–249.

van Ingen, D. J., Freiheit, S. R., Steinfeldt, J. A., Moore, L. L., Wimer, D. J., Knutt, A. D., . . . Roberts, A. (2015). Helicopter parenting: The effect of an overbearing caregiving style on peer attachment and self-efficacy. *Journal of College Counseling, 18*, 7–20.

van Kleeck, A., Gillam, R. B., Hamilton, L., & McGrath, C. (1997). The relationship between middle-class parents' book-sharing discussion and their preschooler's abstract language development. *Journal of Speech, Language, and Hearing Research, 40*, 1261–1271.

Van Leeuwen, M., Van den Berg, S. M., & Boomsma, D. I. (2008). A twin-family study of general IQ. *Learning and Individual Differences, 18*, 76–88.

Van Overschelde, J. P., Rawson, K. A., Dunlosky, J., & Hunt, R. R. (2005). Distinctive processing underlies skilled memory. *Psychological Science, 16*, 358–361.

Van Oyen, H., Nusselder, W., Jagger, C., Kolip, P., Cambois, E., & Robine, J. (2013). Gender differences in healthy life years within the EU: An exploration of the "health-survival" paradox. *International Journal of Public Health, 58*, 143–155.

Van Petegem, S. (2015). Rebels with a cause? Adolescent defiance from the perspective of reactance theory and self-determination theory. *Child Development, 86*, 903–918.

Vandell, D. L., Belsky, J., Burchinal, M., Steinberg, L., Vandergrift, N., & NICHD Early Child Care Research Network. (2010). Do effects of early child care extend to age 15 years? Results from the NICHD Study of Early Child Care and Youth Development. *Child Development, 81*, 737–756.

Vandell, D. L., Wilson, K. S., & Buchanan, N. R. (1980). Peer interaction in the first year of life: An examination of its structure, content, and sensitivity to toys. *Child Development, 51*, 481–488.

VanHuysse, J. L., Burt, S. A., O'Connor, S. M., Thompson, J. K., & Klump, K. L. (2016). Socialization and selection effects in the association between weight conscious peer groups and thin-ideal internalization: A co-twin control study. *Body Image, 17*, 1–9.

VanKim, N. A., Laska, M. N., Ehlinger, E., Lust, K., & Story, M. (2010). Understanding young adult physical activity, alcohol and tobacco use in community colleges and 4-year post-secondary institutions: A cross-sectional analysis of epidemiological surveillance data. *British Medical Journal, 10*, 208.

Varea, C., Bernis, C., Montero, P., Arias, S., Barroso, A., & Gonzalez, B. (2000). Secular trend and intrapopulational variation in age of menopause in Spanish women. *Journal of Biosocial Science, 32*, 383–393.

Vargha-Khadem, F., Gadian, D. G., Watkins, K. E., Connelly, A., Van Paesschen, W., & Mishkin, M. (1997). Differential effects of early hippocampal pathology on episodic and semantic memory. *Science, 277*, 376–380.

Vargha-Khadem, F., Watkins, K., Alcock, K., Fletcher, P., & Passingham, R. (1995). Praxic and nonverbal cognitive deficits in a large family with a genetically transmitted speech and language disorder. *Proceedings of the National Academy of Sciences of the United States of America, 92*, 930–933.

Vartanian, L. R., & Powlishta, K. K. (1996). A longitudinal examination of the social-cognitive foundations of adolescent egocentrism. *Journal of Early Adolescence, 16*, 157–178.

Vaughn, B. E., Azria, M. R., Krzysik, L., Caya, L. R., Bost, K. K., Newell, W., & Kazura, K. L. (2000). Friendship and social competence in a sample of preschool children attending Head Start. *Developmental Psychology, 36*, 326–338.

Vavatzanidis, N. K., Murbe, D., Friederici, A., & Hahne, A. (2015). The basis for language acquisition: Congenitally deaf infants discriminate vowel length in the first months after cochlear implantation. *Journal of Cognitive Neuroscience, 27*, 2427–2441.

Vazsonyi, A. T., Hibbert, J. R., & Snider, J. B. (2003). Exotic enterprise no more? Adolescent reports of family and parenting processes from youth in four countries. *Journal of Research on Adolescence, 13*, 129–160.

Velderman, M.K., Bakermans-Kranenburg, M. J., Juffer, F., & van IJzendoorn, M. H. (2006). Effects of attachment-based interventions on maternal sensitivity and infant attachment: Differential susceptibility of highly reactive infants. *Journal of Family Psychology, 20*, 266–274.

Vellutino, F. R., Scanlon, D. M., Sipay, E. R., & Small, S. G. (1996). Cognitive profiles of difficult-to-remediate and readily remediated poor readers: Early intervention as a vehicle for distinguishing between cognitive and experiential deficits as basic causes of specific reading disability. *Journal of Educational Psychology, 88*, 601–638.

Ventura, S. J., & Hamilton, B. E. (2011). *U. S. teenage birth rate resumes decline* (NCHS Data Brief No. 58). Hyattsville, MD: National Center for Health Statistics.

Verbeek, P. (2006). Everyone's monkey: Primate moral roots. In M. Killen & J. G. Smetana (Eds.), *Handbook of moral development*. Mahwah, NJ: Erlbaum.

Verhaeghen, P., & Hertzog, C. (Eds.). (2016). *The Oxford handbook of emotion, social cognition, and problem solving in adulthood*. New York, NY: Oxford University Press.

Verhage, M. L., Oosterman, M., & Schuengel, C. (2015). The linkage between infant negative temperament and parenting self-efficacy: The role of resilience against negative performance feedback. *British Journal of Developmental Psychology, 33*, 506–518.

Verloigne, M., van Lippevelde, W., Maes, L., Yıldırım, M., Chinapaw, M., Manios, Y., & de Bourdeaudhuij, I. (2012). Levels of physical activity and sedentary time among 10- to 12-year-old boys and girls across 5 European countries using accelerometers: An observational study within the ENERGY-project. *The International Journal of Behavioral Nutrition and Physical Activity, 9*, 34.

Verma, S., & Larson, R. (Eds.). (2003). *Examining adolescent leisure time across cultures: New directions for child and adolescent development*, No. 99. San Francisco, CA: Jossey-Bass.

Vermeulen, A. (2000). Andropause. *Maturitas, 15*, 5–15.

Veroff, J., Reuman, D., & Feld, S. (1984). Motives in American men and women across the adult life span. *Developmental Psychology, 20*, 1142–1158.

Véronneau, M-H., Vitaro, F., Pedersen, S., & Tremblay, R. E. (2008). Do peers contribute to the likelihood of secondary school graduation among disadvantaged boys? *Journal of Educational Psychology, 100*, 429–442.

Veroudea, K., Norrisa, D. G., Shumskayaa, E., Gullberg, M., & Indefrey, P. (2010). Functional connectivity between brain regions involved in learning words of a new language. *Brain and Language, 113*, 21–27.

Verrillo, R. T., & Verrillo, V. (1985). Sensory and perceptual performance. In N. Charness (Ed.), *Aging and human performance*. Chichester, UK: Wiley.

Verweij, E. J., van den Oever, J. M., de Boer, M. A., Boon, E. M., & Oepkes, D. (2012). Diagnostic accuracy of noninvasive detection of fetal trisomy 21 in maternal blood: A systematic review. *Fetal Diagnosis and Therapy, 31*, 81–86.

Vestergren, P., & Nilsson, L.-G. (2011). Perceived causes of everyday memory problems in a population-based sample aged 39–99. *Applied Cognitive Psychology, 25*, 641–646.

Vidal, F. (1994). *Piaget before Piaget*. MA: Harvard University Press.

Viding, E., Fontaine, N. M. G., Oliver, B. R., & Plomin, R. (2009). Negative parental discipline, conduct problems and callous-unemotional traits: Monozygotic twin differences study. *British Journal of Psychiatry, 195*, 414–419.

Vikström, J., Josefsson, A., Bladh, M., & Sydsjö, G. (2015). Mental health in women 20–23 years after IVF treatment: A Swedish cross-sectional study. *British Medical Journal Open, 5*, e009426.

Villeda, S. A., Plambeck, K. E., Middeldorp, J., Castellano, J. M., Mosher, K. I., Luo, J., & Wyss-Coray, T. (2014). Young blood reverses age-related impairments in cognitive function and synaptic plasticity in mice. *Nature Medicine, 20*, 659–663.

Villegas de Posada, C., & Vargas-Trujillo, E. (2015). Moral reasoning and personal behavior: A meta-analytical review. *Review of General Psychology, 19*, 408–424.

Vinden, P. G., & Astington, J. W. (2000). Culture and understanding other minds. In S. Baron-Cohen, H. Tager-Flusberg, & D. J. Cohen (Eds.), *Understanding other minds. Perspectives from developmental cognitive neuroscience* (2nd ed.). Oxford: Oxford University Press.

Vining, E. P. G., Freeman, J. M., Pillas, D. J., Uematsu, S., Carson, B. S., Brandt, J., et al. (1997). Why would you remove half a brain? The outcome of 58 children after hemispherectomy—The Johns Hopkins experience: 1968 to 1996. *Pediatrics, 100*, 163–171.

Visser, S. N., Danielson, M. L., Bitsko, R. H., Holbrook, J. R., Kogan, M. D., Ghandour, R. M., . . . Blumberg, S. J. (2014). Trends in the parent-report of health care provider-diagnosed and medicated attention-deficit/hyperactivity disorder: United States, 2003–2011. *Journal of the American Academy of Child & Adolescent Psychiatry, 53*, 34–46.

Vita, A. J., Terry, R. B., Hubert, H. B., & Fries, J. F. (1998). Aging, health risks, and cumulative disability. *New England Journal of Medicine, 338*, 1035–1041.

Vitario, F., Boivin, M., & Bukowski, W. M. (2009). The role of friendship in child and adolescent psychosocial development. In K. H. Rubin, W. M. Bukowski, & B. Laursen (Eds.), *Handbook of peer interactions, relationships, and groups*. New York, NY: Guilford.

Vitiello, B., Zuvekas, S. H., & Norquist, G. S. (2006). National estimates of antidepressant medication use among U.S. children. *Journal of the American Academy of Child & Adolescent Psychiatry, 45*, 271–279.

Vogel, S., Horwitz, S., & Fahrenthold, D. A. (2012, December 16). Wrenching details but few answers. *The Washington Post*, pp. A1, A12, 14–15.

Vogel, T., & Wänke, M. (2016). *Attitudes and attitude change* (2nd ed.). New York, NY: Routledge.

Vohr, B. R., Poindexter, B. B., Dusick, A. M., McKinely, L. T., Wright, L. L., Langer, J.C., & Poole, W. K. (2006). Beneficial effects of breast milk in the neonatal intensive care unit on the developmental outcome of extremely low birth weight infants at 18 months of age. *Pediatrics, 118*, 115–123.

Vohr, B. R., Topol, D., Watson, V., St Pierre, L., & Tucker, R. (2014). The importance of language in the home for school-age children with permanent hearing loss. *Acta Paediatrica, 103*, 62–69.

Vohr, B., Jodoin-Krauzyk, J., Tucker, R., Topol, D., Johnson, M. J., Ahlgren, M., et al. (2011). Expressive vocabulary of children with hearing loss in the first 2 years of life: Impact of early intervention. *Journal of Perinatology, 31*, 274–280.

Voight, B. F., Kudaravalli, S., Wen, X., & Pritchard, J. K. (2006). A map of recent positive selection in the human genome. *PLoS Biology, 4*, 0446–0458.

Volkmar, F. R., Lord, C., Bailey, A., Schultz, R. T., & Klin, A. (2004). Autism and pervasive developmental disorders. *Journal of Child Psychology and Psychiatry and Allied Disciplines, 45*, 135–170.

Volkow, N. D., & Swanson, J. M. (2013). Adult attention deficit–hyperactivity disorder. *New England Journal of Medicine, 369*, 1935–1944.

Volkow, N. D., Swanson, J. M., Evins, A. E., DeLisi, L. E., Meier, M. H., Gonzalez, R., . . . Baler, R. (2016). Effects of cannabis use on human behavior, including cognition, motivation, and psychosis: A review. *JAMA Psychiatry, 73*, 292–297.

Volling, B. L. (2005). The transition to siblinghood: A developmental ecological systems perspective and directions for future research. *Journal of Family Psychology, 19*, 542–549.

Volling, B. L. (2012). Family transitions following the birth of a sibling: An empirical review of changes in the firstborn's adjustment. *Psychological Bulletin, 138*, 497–528.

Volling, B. L., Yu, T., Gonzalez, R., Kennedy, D. E., Rosenberg, L., & Oh, W. (2014). Children's responses to mother–infant and father–infant interaction with a baby sibling: Jealousy or joy? *Journal of Family Psychology, 28*, 634–644.

von Hofsten, C. (2007). Action in development. *Developmental Science, 10*, 54–60.

von Hofsten, C. (2013). Action in infancy: A foundation for cognitive development. In W. Prinz, M. Beisert, & A. Herwig (Eds.), *Action science. Foundations of an emerging discipline* (pp. 255–280). Cambridge, MA: MIT Press.

von Stumm, S., Hell, B., & Chamorro-Premuzic, T. (2011). The hungry mind: Intellectual curiosity as third pillar of academic performance. *Perspectives on Psychological Science, 6,* 574–588.

von Stumm, S., & Plomin, R. (2015). Socioeconomic status and the growth of intelligence from infancy through adolescence. *Intelligence, 48,* 30–36.

Voss M. W., Nagamatsu, L. S., Liu-Ambrose, T., Kramer, A. F. (2011). Exercise, brain, and cognition across the life span. *Journal of Applied Physiology, 111,* 1505–1513.

Voulgaridou, I., & Kokkinos, C. M. (2015). Relational aggression in adolescents: A review of theoretical and empirical research. *Aggression and Violent Behavior, 23,* 87–97.

Vouloumanos, A., & Werker, J. F. (2007). Listening to language at birth: Evidence for a bias for speech in neonates. *Developmental Science, 10,* 159–171.

Voyer, D., Postma, A., Brake, B., & Imperato-McGinley, J. (2007). Gender differences in object location memory: A meta-analysis. *Psychonomic Bulletin and Review, 14,* 23–38.

Vozzola, E. C. (2014). *Moral development: Theory and applications.* New York, NY: Routledge.

Vrangalova, Z., & Savin-Williams, R. C. (2012). Mostly heterosexual and mostly gay/lesbian: Evidence for new sexual orientation identities. *Archives of Sex Behavior, 41,* 85–101.

Vukasović, T., & Bratko, D. (2015). Heritability of personality: A meta-analysis of behavior genetic studies. *Psychological Bulletin, 141,* 769–785.

Vuoksimaa, E., Koskenvuo, M., Rose, R. J., & Kaprio, J. (2009). Origins of handedness: A nationwide study of 30,161 adults. *Neuropsychologia, 47,* 1294–1301.

Vuorialho, A., Karinen, P., & Sorri, M. (2006). Effect of hearing aids on hearing disability and quality of life in the elderly. *International Journal of Audiology, 45,* 400–405.

Vurpillot, E. (1968). The development of scanning strategies and their relation to visual differentiation. *Journal of Experimental Child Psychology, 6,* 632–650.

Vygotsky, L. S. (1962). *Thought and language* (E. Hanfmann & G. Vakar, Eds.). Cambridge, MA: MIT Press.

Vygotsky, L. S. (1978). *Mind in society: The development of higher mental processes* (M. Cole, V. John-Steiner, S. Scribner, & E. Souberman, Eds.). Cambridge, MA: Harvard University Press. (Original work published 1930, 1933, 1935).

Wachs, T. D. (2015). Assessing bioecological influences. In M. H. Bornstein (Vol. Ed.), T. Leventhal (Vol. Ed.), & R. M. Lerner (Ed.), *Handbook of child psychology and developmental science: Vol. 4. Ecological settings and processes* (7th ed., pp. 811–846). Hoboken, NJ: Wiley.

Wadhwa, P. D., Buss, C., Entringer, S., & Swanson, J. M. (2009). Developmental origins of health and disease: Brief history of the approach and current focus on epigenetic mechanisms. *Seminars in Reproductive Medicine, 27,* 358–368.

Wadsworth, T. (2014). Sex and the pursuit of happiness: How other people's sex lives are related to our sense of well-being. *Social Indicators Research, 116,* 115–135.

Waechter, E. H. (1984). Dying children. Patterns of coping. In H. Wass & C. A. Corr (Eds.), *Childhood and death.* Washington, DC: Hemisphere.

Wagmiller, R. L., Jr. (2015). The temporal dynamics of childhood economic deprivation and children's achievement. *Child Development Perspectives, 9,* 158–163.

Wagner, B. (2013). Internet-based bereavement interventions and support: An overview. In M. Stroebe, H. Schut & J. van den Bout (Eds.), *Complicated grief: Scientific foundations for health care professionals.* New York, NY: Routledge/Taylor & Francis.

Wainstock, T., Shoham-Vardia, I., Glasserb, S., Antebyc, E., & Lerner-Gevabd, L. (2015). Fetal sex modifies effects of prenatal stress exposure and adverse birth outcomes. *Stress: The International Journal on the Biology of Stress, 18,* 49–56.

Waisbren, S. E. (2011). Phenylketonuria. In S. Goldstein & C. R. Reynolds (Eds.), *Handbook of neurodevelopmental and genetic disorders in children* (2nd ed., pp. 398–424). New York, NY: Guilford.

Waite, L. J., & Gallagher, M. (2000). *The case for marriage. Why married people are happier, healthier, and better off financially.* New York, NY: Doubleday.

Wakefield, J. C. (2013). Is complicated/prolonged grief a disorder? Why the proposal to add a category of complicated grief disorder to the DSM-5 is conceptually and empirically unsound. In M. Stroebe, H. Schut & J. van den Bout (Eds.), *Complicated grief: Scientific foundations for health care professionals.* New York, NY: Routledge/Taylor & Francis.

Waldenström, U., Borg, I., Olsson, B., Sköld, M., & Wall, S. (1996). The childbirth experience: A study of 295 new mothers. *Birth, 23,* 144–153.

Waldinger, R. J., Cohen, S., Schulz, M. S., & Crowell, J. A. (2015). Security of attachment to spouses in late life: Concurrent and prospective links with cognitive and emotional well-being. *Clinical Psychological Science, 3,* 516–529.

Waldman, I. D., & Gizer, I. R. (2006). The genetics of attention deficit hyperactivity disorder. *Clinical Psychology Review, 26,* 396–432.

Waldorf, K. M. A. & McAdams, R. M. (2013). Influence of infection during pregnancy on fetal development. *Reproduction, 146,* 151–162.

Walker, L. J. (1980). Cognitive and perspective-taking prerequisites of moral development. *Child Development, 51,* 131–139.

Walker, L. J. (2004). Gus in the gap: Bridging the judgment-action gap in moral reasoning. In D. K. Lapsley & D. Narvaez (Eds.), *Moral development, self, and identity.* Mahwah, NJ: Erlbaum.

Walker, L. J., & Frimer, J. A. (2011). The science of moral development. In M. K. Underwood, & L. H. Rosen (Eds.), *Social development: Relationships in infancy, childhood, and adolescence* (pp. 235–262). New York, NY: Guilford Press.

Walker-Andrews, A. S. (1997). Infants' perception of expressive behaviors: Differentiation of multimodal information. *Psychological Bulletin, 121,* 437–456.

Wallace, P. S., & Whishaw, I. Q. (2003). Independent digit movements and precision grip patterns in 1–5-month-old human infants: Hand-babbling, including vacuous then self-directed hand and digit movements, precedes targeted reaching. *Neuropsychologia, 41,* 1912–1918.

Wallander, J. L., Taylor, W. C., Grunbaum, J. A., Franklin, F.A., Harrison, G. G., Kelder, S. H., & Schuster, M. A. (2009). Weight status, quality of life, and self-concept in African American, Hispanic, and white fifth-grade children. *Obesity, 17,* 1363–1368.

Wallen, K. (1996). Nature needs nurture: The interaction of hormonal and social influences on the development of behavioral sex differences in rhesus monkeys. *Hormones and Behavior, 30,* 364–378.

Walling, A. D., & Dickson, G. M. (2012). Hearing loss in older adults. *American Family Physician, 85,* 1150–1156.

Walls, R. T. (2000). Vocational cognition: Accuracy of 3rd-, 6th-, 9th-, and 12th-grade students. *Journal of Vocational Behavior, 56,* 137–144.

Walsh, F., & McGoldrick, M. (2013). Bereavement: A family life cycle perspective. *Family Science, 4,* 20–27.

Walter, C. A., & McCoyd, J. L. M. (2009). *Grief and loss across the lifespan. A biopsychosocial perspective.* New York, NY: Springer.

Walton, G., & Spencer, S. (2009). Latent ability: Grades and test scores systematically underestimate the intellectual ability of negatively stereotyped students. *Psychological Science, 20,* 1132–1139.

Wan, W., Deng, X., Archer, K. J., & Sun, S. S. (2012). Pubertal pathways and the relationship to anthropometric changes in childhood: The Fels longitudinal study. *Open Journal of Pediatrics, 2,* 1128–126.

Wanberg, C. R., Kanfer, R., Hamann, D. J., & Zhang, Z. (2016). Age and reemployment success after job loss: An integrative model and meta-analysis. *Psychological Bulletin, 142,* 400–426.

Wang, A. H., Walters, A. M., & Thum, Y. M. (2013). Identifying highly effective urban schools: Comparing two measures of school success. *International Journal of Educational Management, 27,* 517–540.

Wang, M., Henkens, K., & van Solinge, H. (2011). Retirement adjustment: A review of theoretical and empirical advancements. *American Psychologist, 66,* 204–213.

Wang, P. S., Berglund, P., Olfson, M., Pincus, H. A., Wells, K. B., & Kessler, R. C. (2005). Failure and delay in initial treatment contact after first onset of mental disorders in the National Comorbidity Survey Replication. *Archives of General Psychiatry, 62,* 603–613.

Wang, Q. (2004). Cultural self-constructions: Autobiographical memory and self-description in European American and Chinese children. *Developmental Psychology, 40,* 3–15.

Wang, Q. (2006). Culture and the development of self-knowledge. *Current Directions in Psychological Science, 15,* 182–187.

Wang, S. H., Baillargeon, R., & Brueckner, L. (2004). Young infants' reasoning about hidden objects: Evidence from violation-of-expectation tasks with test trials only. *Cognition, 93,* 167–198.

Wang, S. S. (2010, March 30). Making cells live forever in quest for cures. *The Wall Street Journal,* p. D3.

Wang, W., & Parker, K. (2014, September 24). *Record share of Americans have never married.* Pew Research Center. Retrieved from www.pewsocialtrends. org/2014/09/24/record-share-of-americans-have-never-married/.

Ward, C. D., & Cooper, R. P. (1999). A lack of evidence in 4-month-old human infants for paternal voice preference. *Developmental Psychobiology, 35,* 49–59.

Ward, E. V., Berry, C. J., & Shanks, D. R. (2013). Age effects on explicit and implicit memory. *Frontiers in Psychology, 4,* 639.

Ward, H., Munro, E. R., & Dearden, C. (2006). *Babies and young children in care: Life pathways, decision-making and practice.* London, UK: Jessica Kingsley.

Ward, R., & Spitze, G. (1992). Consequences of parent–adult child coresidence. *Journal of Family Issues, 13,* 533–572.

Ward, R., & Spitze, G. (2004). Marital implications of parent–adult child coresidence: A longitudinal view. *Journal of Gerontology: Social Sciences, 59B,* S2–S8.

Warin, J. (2000). The attainment of self-consistency through gender in young children. *Sex Roles, 42,* 209–231.

Warneken, F., & Tomasello, M. (2007). Helping and cooperation at 14 months of age. *Infancy, 11,* 271–294.

Warren, J. R., LePore, P. C., & Mare, R. D. (2000). Employment during high school: Consequences for students' grades in academic courses. *American Educational Research Journal, 37,* 943–970.

Washburn, L., Dillard, R., Goldstein, D., Klinepeter, K., deRegnier, R., & O'Shea, T. (2007). Survival and major neurodevelopmental impairment in extremely low gestational age newborns born 1990–2000: A retrospective cohort study. *BMC Pediatrics, 7,* 1–9.

Wass, H. (1991). Helping children cope with death. In D. Papadatou & C. Papadatos (Eds.), *Children and death.* New York, NY: Hemisphere.

Wass, R., & Golding, C. (2014). Sharpening a tool for teaching: The zone of proximal development. *Teaching in Higher Education, 19,* 671–684.

Waterhouse, L. (2013). *Rethinking autism. Variation and complexity.* Waltham, MA: Academic Press.

Waterman, A. S. (1982). Identity development from adolescence to adulthood: An extension of theory and a review of research. *Developmental Psychology, 18,* 341–358.

Waterman, A. S. (1992). Identity as an aspect of optimal psychological functioning. In G. R. Adams, T. P. Gullotta, & R. Montemayor (Eds.), *Adolescent identity formation: Vol. 4.* (Advances in Adolescent Development). Newbury Park, CA: Sage.

Waterman, A. S., Schwartz, S. J., Hardy, S. A., Kim, S. Y., Lee, R. M., Armenta, B. E., … Agocha, V. B. (2013). Good choices, poor choices: Relationship between the quality of identity commitments and psychosocial functioning. *Emerging Adulthood, 1,* 163–174.

Waters, E., Wippman, J., & Sroufe, L. A. (1979). Attachment, positive affect, and competence in the peer group: Two studies in construct validation. *Child Development, 50,* 821–829.

Watkins, M. W., & Smith, L. G. (2013). Long-term stability of the Wechsler Intelligence Scale for Children—(4th ed.). *Psychological Assessment, 25,* 477–483.

Watson, J. B. (1913). Psychology as the behaviorist views it. *Psychological Review, 20,* 158–177.

Watson, J. B. (1925). *Behaviorism.* New York, NY: Norton.

Watson, J. B., & Raynor, R. (1920). Conditioned emotional reactions. *Journal of Experimental Psychology, 3,* 1–14.

Waxman, S. R., & Hatch, T. (1992). Beyond the basics: Preschool children label objects flexibly at multiple hierarchical levels. *Journal of Child Language, 19,* 153–166.

Waxman, S. R., & Lidz, J. (2006). Early word learning. In D. Kuhn & R. Siegler (Eds.), *Handbook of child psychology, Vol. 2* (6th ed., pp. 299–335). Hoboken NJ: Wiley.

Waxman, S., Fu, X., Arunachalam, S., Leddon, E., Geraghty, K., & Song, H. (2013). Are nouns learned before verbs? Infants provide insight into a long-standing debate. *Child Development Perspectives, 7*, 155–159.

Way, N., & Silverman, L. R. (2011). The quality of friendships during adolescence: Patterns across context, culture, and age. In P. K. Kerig, M. S. Schulz, & S. T. Hauser (Eds.), *Adolescence and beyond. Family processes and development*. New York, NY: Oxford University Press.

Wayne, A. J., & Youngs, P. (2003). Teacher characteristics and student achievement gains: A review. *Review of Educational Research, 73*, 89–122.

Weaver, J. M., & Schofield, T. J. (2015). Mediation and moderation of divorce effects on children's behavior problems. *Journal of Family Psychology, 29*, 39–48.

Webb, A. R., Heller, H. T., Benson, C. B., & Lahav, A. (2015). Mother's voice and heartbeat sounds elicit auditory plasticity in the human brain before full gestation. *Proceedings of the National Academy of Sciences of the United States of America, 112*, 3152–3157.

Webster, J. D., & Haight, B. K. (Eds.) (2002). *Critical advances in reminiscence work: From theory to application*. New York, NY: Springer.

Webster, J., Nicholas, C., Velacott, C., Cridland, N., & Fawcett, L. (2011). Quality of life and depression following childbirth: Impact of social support. *Midwifery, 27*, 745–749.

Wechsler, D. (2002). *Wechsler preschool and primary scale of intelligence* (3rd ed.). The Psychological Corporation.

Wechsler, D. (2003). *Wechsler intelligence scale for children* (4th ed.). San Antonio, TX: The Psychological Corporation.

Wechsler, D. (2008). *Wechsler adult intelligence scale* (4th ed.). Toronto, ON: Pearson.

Wechsler, D. (2012). *Wechsler preschool and primary scale of intelligence* (4th ed.). San Antonio, TX: The Psychological Corporation.

Wechsler, D. (2014). *Wechsler intelligence scale for children* (5th ed.). Bloomington, MN: Pearson.

Weeks, J. C., Biss, R. K., Murphy, K. J., & Hasher, L. (2016). Face-name learning in older adults: A benefit of hyper-binding. *Psychonomic Bulletin & Review, 23*:1559.

Wehling, E. I., Lundervold, A. J., Nordin, S., & Wollschlaeger, D. (2016). Longitudinal changes in familiarity, free and cued odor identification, and edibility judgments for odors in aging individuals. *Chemical Senses, 41*, 155–161.

Weiffenbach, J. M., Cowart, B. J., & Baum, B. J. (1986). Taste intensity perception in aging. *Journal of Gerontology, 41*, 460–468.

Weil, L. G., Fleming, S. M., Dumontheil, I., Kilford, E. J., Weil, R. S., Rees, G., … Blakemore, S.-J. (2013). The development of metacognitive ability in adolescence. *Consciousness and Cognition, 22*, 264–271.

Weinberg, K. M., Olson, K. L., Beeghly, M., & Tronick, E. Z. (2006). Making up is hard to do, especially for mothers with high levels of depressive symptoms and their infant sons. *Journal of Child Psychology and Psychiatry and Allied Disciplines, 47*, 670–683.

Weinberg, R. A., Scarr, S., & Waldman, I. D. (1992). The Minnesota transracial adoption study: A follow-up of IQ test performance at adolescence. *Intelligence, 16*, 117–135.

Weiner, M. F., Garrett, R., & Bret, M. E. (2009). Neuropsychiatric assessment and diagnosis. In M. F. Weiner & A. M. Lipton (Eds.), *The American Psychiatric Publishing textbook of Alzheimer disease and other dementias*. Washington, DC: American Psychiatric Publishing.

Weinert, F. E., & Hany, E. A. (2003). The stability of individual differences in intellectual development: Empirical evidence, theoretical problems, and new research questions. In R. J. Sternberg, J. Lautrey, & T. I. Lubart (Eds.), *Models of intelligence: International perspectives* (pp. 169–181). Washington, DC: American Psychological Association.

Weinert, F. E., & Schneider, W. (1999). *Individual development from 3 to 12: Findings from the Munich Longitudinal Study*. Cambridge, UK: Cambridge University Press.

Weingarten, G. (2011, July). Touchy subject: Warning— This may rub you the wrong way. *The Washington Post Magazine*, p. 29.

Weinraub, M., & Lewis, M. (1977). The determinants of children's responses to separation. *Monographs of the Society for Research in Child Development, (4*, Serial No. 172).

Weinraub, M., Bender, R. H., Friedman, S. L., Susman, E. J., Knoke, B., Bradley, R., & Williams, J. (2012). Patterns of developmental change in infants' nighttime sleep awakenings from 6 through 36 months of age. *Developmental Psychology, 48*, 1511–1528.

Weisberg, D. S., Hirsh-Pasek, K., & Golinkoff, R. M. (2013). Guided play: Where curricular goals meet a playful pedagogy. *Mind, Brain, and Education, 7*, 104–112.

Weisberg, P. (1963). Social and nonsocial conditioning of infant vocalization. *Child Development, 34*, 377–388.

Weisgram, E. S., Bigler, R. S., & Liben, L. S. (2010). Gender, values, and occupational interests among children, adolescents, and adults. *Child Development, 81*, 778–796.

Weisman, O., Magori-Cohen, R., Louzoun, Y., Eidelman, A. I., & Feldman, R. (2011). Sleep-wake transitions in premature neonates predict early development. *Pediatrics, 128*, 706 –714.

Weisner, T. S., & Gallimore, R. (1977). My brother's keeper: Child and sibling caretaking. *Current Anthropology, 18*, 169–190.

Weiss, B., Tram, J. M., Weisz, J. R., Rescorla, L., & Achenbach, T. M. (2009). Differential symptom expression and somatization in Thai versus U. S. children. *Journal of Consulting and Clinical Psychology, 77*, 987–992.

Weiss, D., & Freund, A. M. (2012). Still young at heart: Negative age-related information motivates distancing from same-aged people. *Psychology and Aging, 27*, 173–180.

Weiss, D., Freund, A. M., & Wiese, B. S. (2012). Mastering developmental transitions in young and middle adulthood: The interplay of openness to experience and traditional gender ideology on women's self-efficacy and subjective well-being. *Developmental Psychology, 48*, 1774–1784.

Weiss, D., & Lang, F. R. (2012). "They" are old but "I" feel younger: Age-group dissociation as a self-protective strategy in old age. *Psychology and Aging, 27*, 153–163.

Weiss, L. H., & Schwarz, J. C. (1996). The relationship between parenting types and older adolescents' personality, academic achievement, adjustment, and substance use. *Child Development, 67*, 2101–2114.

Weiss, R. (2003a, February 28). Dream unmet 50 years after DNA milestone. *The Washington Post*, A1, A10.

Weiss, R. (2003b, April 15). Genome Project completed. *The Washington Post*, A6.

Weiss, S. (2008, April 1). Midlife. What crisis? *The Washington Post*, pp. F1, F5.

Weiss-Numeroff, G. (2013). *Extraordinary centenarians in America: Their secrets to living a long vibrant life*. Victoria, Canada: Agio Publishing House.

Weisz, J. R., McCarty, C. A., & Valeri, S. M. (2006). Effects of psychotherapy for depression in children and adolescents: A meta-analysis. *Psychological Bulletin, 132*, 132–149.

Weisz, J. R., McCarty, C. A., Eastman, K. L., Chaiyasit, W., & Suwanlert, S. (1997). Developmental psychopathology and culture: Ten lessons from Thailand. In S. S. Luthar, J. A. Burack, D. Cicchetti, & J. R. Weisz (Eds.). *Developmental psychopathology: Perspectives on adjustment, risk and disorder*. Cambridge, UK: Cambridge University Press.

Weizman, A. O., & Snow, C. E. (2001). Lexical input as related to children's vocabulary acquisition: Effects of sophisticated exposure and support for meaning. *Developmental Psychology, 37*, 265–279.

Wellman, H. M. (1990). *The child's theory of mind*. Cambridge, MA: MIT Press.

Wellman, H. M., & Bartsch, K. (1994). Before belief: Children's early psychological theory. In C. Lewis & P. Mitchell (Eds.), *Children's early understanding of mind: Origins and development*. Hove, UK: Erlbaum.

Wellman, H. M., Cross, D., & Watson, J. (2001). Meta-analysis of theory-of-mind development: The truth about false-belief. *Child Development, 72*, 655–684.

Wellman, H. M., & Gelman, S. A. (1992). Cognitive development: Foundational theories of core domains. *Annual Review of Psychology, 43*, 337–375.

Wellman, H. M., & Liu, D. (2004). Scaling of theory-of-mind-tasks. *Child Development, 75*, 523–541.

Wells, B. E., & Twenge, J. M. (2005). Changes in young people's sexual behavior and attitudes, 1943–1999: A cross-temporal meta-analysis. *Review of General Psychology, 9*, 249–261.

Welsh, D. P., Grello, C. M., & Harper, M. S. (2006). No strings attached: The nature of casual sex in college students. *Journal of Sex Research, 43*, 255–267.

Welsh, J. A., Nix, R. L., Blair, C., Bierman, K. L., & Nelson, K. E. (2010). The development of cognitive skills and gains in academic school readiness for children from low-income families. *Journal of Educational Psychology, 102*, 43–53.

Weon, B. M., & Je, J. H. (2009). Theoretical estimation of maximum human lifespan. *Biogerontology, 10*, 65–71.

Werker, J. F., & Hensch, T. K. (2015). Critical periods in speech perception: new directions. *Annual Review of Psychology, 66*, 173–196.

Werker, J. F., & Tees, R. C. (1999). Influences on infant speech processing: Toward a new synthesis. *Annual Review of Psychology, 50*, 509–535.

Werker, J. F., & Tees, R. C. (2005). Speech perception as a window for understanding plasticity and commitment in language systems of the brain. *Developmental Psychobiology, 46*, 233–234.

Werker, J. F., Yeung, H. H., & Yoshida, K. A. (2012). How do infants become experts at native-speech perception? *Current Issues in Psychological Science, 21*, 221–226.

Werner, E. A., Myers, M. M., Fifer, W. P., Cheng, B., Fang, Y., Allen, R., & Monk, C. (2007). Prenatal predictors of infant temperament. *Developmental Psychobiology, 49*, 474–484.

Werner, E. E. (1989a). Children of the Garden Island. *Scientific American, 260*, 106–111.

Werner, E. E. (1989b). High-risk children in young adulthood: A longitudinal study from birth to 32 years. *American Journal of Orthopsychiatry, 59*, 72–81.

Werner, E. E., & Smith, R. S. (1982). *Vulnerable but invincible: A longitudinal study of resilient children and youth*. New York, NY: McGraw-Hill.

Werner, E. E., & Smith, R. S. (1992). *Overcoming the odds: High risk children from birth to adulthood*. Ithaca, NY: Cornell University Press.

Werner, E. E., & Smith, R. S. (2001). *Journeys from childhood to midlife: Risk, resilience, and recovery*. Ithaca, NY: Cornell University Press.

Werner, H. (1957). The concept of development from a comparative and organismic point of view. In D. B. Harris (Ed.), *The concept of development: An issue in the study of human behavior*. Minneapolis, MN: University of Minnesota Press.

Werth, J. L., Jr., Blevins, D., Toussaint, K. L., & Durham, M. R. (2002). The influence of cultural diversity on end-of-life care and decisions. *American Behavioral Scientist, 46*, 204–219.

West, G. L., Anderson, A. A. K., & Pratt, J. (2009). Motivationally significant stimuli show visual prior entry: Evidence for attentional capture. *Journal of Experimental Psychology: Human Perception and Performance, 35*, 1032–1042.

Westefeld, J. S., Bell, A., Bermingham, C., Button, C., Shaw, K., Skow, C., et al. (2010). Suicide among preadolescents: A call to action. *Journal of Loss and Trauma, 15*, 381–407.

Westen, D., Gabbard, G. O., & Ortigo, K. M. (2008). Psychoanalytic approaches to personality. In O. P. John, R. W. Robins, & L. A. Pervin (Eds.), *Handbook of personality theory and research* (3rd ed.). New York, NY: Guilford.

Westerhof, G. J., Whitbourne, S. K., & Freeman, G. P. (2012). The aging self in a cultural context: The relation of conceptions of aging to identity processes and self-esteem in the United States and the Netherlands. *Journals of Gerontology: Series B: Psychological Sciences and Social Sciences, 67*, 52–60.

Westermann, G., Mareschal, D., Johnson, M. H., Sirois, S., Spratling, M. W., & Thomas, M. S. C. (2007). Neuroconstructivism. *Developmental Science, 10*, 75–83.

Westermann, G., Thomas, M S C., & Karmiloff-Smith, A. (2010). Neuroconstructivism. In U. Goswami (Ed.), *The Wiley-Blackwell handbook of childhood cognitive development* (2nd ed., pp. 723–748). Oxford, UK: Wiley Blackwell.

Weyandt, L. L. (2007). *An ADHD primer* (2nd ed.). Mahwah, NJ: Erlbaum.

Weyandt, L. L., & DuPaul, G. J. (2013). *College students with ADHD: Current issues and future directions.* New York, NY: Springer Science+Business Media.

Whalen, D. J., Dixon-Gordon, K., Belden, A. C., Barch, D., & Luby, J. L. (2015). Correlates and consequences of suicidal cognitions and behaviors in children ages 3 to 7 years. *Journal of the American Academy of Child & Adolescent Psychiatry, 54*, 926–37.

Whitbourne, S. K. Sneed, J. R., & Sayer, A. (2009). Psychosocial development from college through midlife: A 34-year sequential study. *Developmental Psychology, 45*, 1328–1340.

Whitbourne, S. K., & Tesch, S. A. (1985). A comparison of identity and intimacy statuses in college students and alumni. *Developmental Psychology, 21*, 1039–1044.

Whitbourne, S. K., & Whitbourne, S. B. (2014). *Adult development and aging: Biopsycholosocial perspectives* (5th ed.). Hoboken, NJ: Wiley.

White, A., & Hingson, R. (2014). The burden of alcohol use: Excessive alcohol consumption and related consequences among college students. *Alcohol Research: Current Reviews, 35*, 201–218.

White, J. B., Duncan, D. F., Nicholson, T., Bradley, D., & Bonaguro, J. (2011). Generational shift and drug abuse in older Americans. *Journal of Social, Behavioral, and Health Sciences, 5*, 58–66.

White, L., & Edwards, J. N. (1990). Emptying the nest and parental well-being: An analysis of national panel data. *American Sociological Review, 55*, 235–242.

White, L., & Rogers, S. J. (1997). Strong support but uneasy relationships: Coresidence and adult children's relationships with their parents. *Journal of Marriage and the Family, 59*, 62–76.

White, L., & Rogers, S. J. (2000). Economic circumstances and family outcomes: A review of the 1990s. *Journal of Marriage and the Family, 62*, 1035–1051.

White, R. M. B., Roosa, M. W., Weaver, S. R., & Nair, R. L. (2009). Cultural and contextual influences on parenting in Mexican American families. *Journal of Marriage and Family, 71*, 61–79.

Whitebread, D. (1999). Interactions between children's metacognitive abilities, working memory capacity, strategies and performance during problem-solving. *European Journal of Psychology of Education, 14*, 489–507.

Whitehead, B. D., & Popenoe, D. (2003). *The state of the unions. The social health of marriage in America 2003. Essay: Marriage and children: Coming together again?* The National Marriage Project, Rutgers University. Retrieved from www.marriage.rutgers.edu/Publications/Print/PrintSOOU2003.htm.

Whitehurst, G. J., & Lonigan, C. J. (1998). Child development and emergent literacy. *Child Development, 69*, 848–872.

Whitehurst, G. J., & Valdez-Menchaca, M. C. (1988). What is the role of reinforcement in early language acquisition? *Child Development, 59*, 430–440.

Whiteman, S. D., McHale, S. M., & Crouter, A. C. (2007). Longitudinal changes in marital relationships: The role of offspring's pubertal development. *Journal of Marriage and Family, 69*, 1005–1020.

Whiten, A. (2013). Social cognition: Making us smart, or sometimes making us dumb? Overimitation, conformity, nonconformity, and the transmission of culture in ape and child. In M. R. Banaji & S. A. Gelman (Eds.), *Navigating the social world: What infants, children, and other species can teach us* (pp. 150–154). New York, NY: Oxford University Press.

Whiting, B. B., & Edwards, C. P. (1988). *Children of different worlds: The formation of social behavior.* Cambridge, MA: Harvard University Press.

Wickremaratchi, M. M., & Llewelyn, J. G. (2006). Effects of ageing on touch. *Postgraduate Medical Journal, 82*, 301–304.

Widaman, K. F. (2009). Phenylketonuria in children and mothers. Genes, environments, behavior. *Current Directions in Psychological Science, 18*, 48–52.

Widén, S. E., & Erlandsson, S. I. (2004). The influence of socio-economic status on adolescent attitude to social noise and hearing protection. *Noise Health, 7*, 59–70.

Widén, S. E., Holmes, A. E., Johnson, T., Bohlin, M., & Erlandsson, S. I. (2009). Hearing, use of hearing protection, and attitudes towards noise among young American adults. *International Journal of Audiology, 48*, 537–545.

Widman, L., Choukas-Bradley, S., Noar, S. M., Nesi, J., & Garrett, K. (2016). Parent-adolescent sexual communication and adolescent safer sex behavior: A meta-analysis. *JAMA Pediatrics, 170*, 52–61.

Widmer, E. D., Treas, J., & Newcomb, R. (1998). Attitudes toward nonmarital sex in 24 countries. *Journal of Sex Research, 35*, 349–358.

Wiener-Megnazi, Z., Auslender, R., & Dirnfeld, M. (2012). Advanced paternal age and reproductive outcome. *Asian Journal of Andrology, 14*, 69–76.

Wiersema, J., Licklider, B., Thompson, J., Hendrich, S., Haynes, C., & Thompson, K. (2015). Mindset about intelligence and meaningful and mindful effort: It's not my hardest class any more! *Learning Communities Research and Practice, 3.* Retrieved from www.washingtoncenter.evergreen.edu/lcrpjournal/vol3/iss2/3.

Wigfield, A., Eccles, J. S., Fredricks, J. A., Simpkins, S., Roeser, R. W., & Schiefele, U. (2015). Development of achievement motivation and engagement. In R. M. Lerner (Ed.), *Handbook of child psychology and developmental science* (7th ed., pp. 1–44). Hoboken, NJ: Wiley.

Wigfield, A., Eccles, J. S., Yoon, K. S., & Harold, R. D. (1997). Change in children's competence beliefs and subjective task values across the elementary school years: A 3-year study. *Journal of Educational Psychology, 89*, 451–469.

Wijdicks, E. F. M., Varelas, P. N., Gronseth, G. S., & Greer, D. M. (2010). Evidence-based guideline update: Determining brain death in adults: Report of the quality standards subcommittee of the American Academy of Neurology. *Neurology, 74*, 1911–1918.

Wijngaards-de-Meij, L., Stroebe, M., Schut, H., Stroebe, W., van den Bout, J., van der Heijden, P., & Dijkstra, I. (2007). Neuroticism and attachment insecurity as predictors of bereavement outcome. *Journal of Research in Personality, 41*, 498–505.

Wikan, U. (1988). Bereavement and loss in two Muslim communities: Egypt and Bali compared. *Social Science and Medicine, 27*, 451–460.

Wikan, U. (1991). *Managing turbulent hearts.* Chicago, IL: University of Chicago Press.

Wilbur, J., Miller, A., & Montgomery, A. (1995). The influence of demographic characteristics, menopausal status, and symptoms on women's attitudes toward menopause. *Women and Health, 23*, 19–39.

Wilcock, A., Kobayashi, L., & Murray, I. (1997). Twenty-five years of obstetric patient satisfaction in North America: A review of the literature. *Journal of Perinatal and Neonatal Nursing, 10*, 36–47.

Wilcox, A. J., Weinberg, C. R., O'Connor, J. F., Baird, D. D., Schlatterer, J. P., Canfield, R. E., et al. (1988). Incidence of early loss of pregnancy. *New England Journal of Medicine, 319*, 189.

Wilcox, S., Evenson, K. R., Aragaki, A., Wassertheil-Smoller, S., Mouton, C. P., & Loevinger, B. L. (2003). The effects of widowhood on physical and mental health, health behaviors, and health outcomes: The Women's Health Initiative. *Health Psychology, 22*, 513–522.

Wilkie, C. (2013, February 27). Neil Heslin, father of Newtown victim, testifies at Senate assault weapons ban hearing. *Huffington Post.* Retrieved from www.huffingtonpost.com/2013/02/27/neil-heslin-assault-weapons-ban-newtown_n_2774598.html.

Willats, P. (1990). Development of problem solving strategies in infancy. In D. F. Bjorklund (Ed.), *Children's strategies.* Hillsdale, NJ: Erlbaum.

Willcox, D. C., Willcox, B. J., Rosenbaum, M., Sokolovsky, J., & Suzuki, M. (2009). Exceptional longevity and the quest for healthy aging: Insights from the Okinawa Centenarian Study. In J. Sokolovsky (Ed.), *The cultural context of aging* (3rd ed.). Westport, CT: Praeger.

Wille, B., Beyers, W., & De Fruyt, F. (2012). A transactional approach to person-environment fit: Reciprocal relations between personality development and career role growth across young to middle adulthood. *Journal of Vocational Behavior, 81*, 307–321.

Williams, J. E., & Best, D. L. (1990). *Measuring sex stereotypes: A multination study* (rev. ed.). Newbury Park, CA: Sage.

Williams, J. H., Waiter, G. D., Gilchrist, A., Perrett, D. I., Murray, A. D., & Whiten, A. (2006). Neural mechanisms of imitation and 'mirror neuron' functioning in autistic spectrum disorder. *Neuropsychologia, 44*, 610–621.

Williams, L. D., & Aber, J. L. (2016). Testing for plausibly causal links between parental bereavement and child socio-emotional and academic outcomes: A propensity-score matching model. *Journal of Abnormal Child Psychology, 44*, 705–718.

Williams, L. R., & Russell, S. T. (2013). Shared social and emotional activities within adolescent romantic and non-romantic sexual relationships. *Archives of Sexual Behavior, 42*, 649–658.

Williams, L. R., & Steinberg, L. (2011). Reciprocal relations between parenting and adjustment in a sample of juvenile offenders. *Child Development, 82*, 633–645.

Williams, M. E., Rogers, K. C., Carson, M. C., Sherer, S., & Hudson, B. O. (2012). Opportunities arising from transformation from treatment as usual to evidence-based practice. *Professional Psychology: Research and Practice, 43*, 9–16.

Williams, M. V., Baker, D. W., Parker, R. M., & Nurss, J. R. (1998). Relationship of functional health literacy to patients' knowledge of their chronic disease. *Archives of Internal Medicine, 158*, 166–172.

Williams, P. T. (1997). Evidence for the incompatibility of age-neutral overweight and age-neutral physical activity standards from runners. *American Journal of Clinical Nutrition, 65*, 1391–1396.

Williams, T. R., Alam, S., & Gaffney, M. (2015). Progress in identifying infants with hearing loss — United States, 2006–2012. Retrieved from www.cdc.gov/mmwr/preview/mmwrhtml/mm6413a4.htm.

Williams, T., Connolly, J., & Cribbie, R. (2008). Light and heavy heterosexual activities of young Canadian adolescents: Normative patterns and differential predictors. *Journal of Research on Adolescence, 18*, 145–172.

Williams, T., Connolly, J., Pepler, D., & Craig, W. (2003). Questioning and sexual minority adolescents: High school experiences of bullying, sexual harassment and physical abuse. *Canadian Journal of Community Mental Health, 22*, 47–58.

Williams, W. M., Blythe, T., White, N., Li, J., Gardner, H., & Sternberg, R. J. (2002). Practical intelligence for school: Developing metacognitive sources of achievement in adolescence. *Developmental Review, 22*, 162–210.

Willis, S. L., & Schaie, K. W. (1986). Training the elderly on the ability factors of spatial orientation and inductive reasoning. *Psychology and Aging, 1*, 239–247.

Willis, S. L., Tennstedt, S. L., Marsiske, M., Ball, K., Elias, J., Koepke, K. M., et al. (2006). Long-term effects of cognitive training on everyday functional outcomes in older adults. *Journal of the American Medical Association, 296*, 2805–2814.

Wilmoth, J. M., & Longino, C. F., Jr. (2006). Demographic trends that will shape U.S. policy in the twenty-first century. *Research on Aging, 28*, 269–288.

Wilson, C., & Hutchison, B. (2014). The foundations of career theory. Holland and Super theories. In G. Eliason, T. Eliason, J. Samide, & J. Patrick (Eds.), *Career development across the lifespan: Counseling for community, schools, higher education, and beyond* (pp. 17–43). Charlotte, NC: Information Age Publishing.

Wilson, R. S., Arnold, S. E., Tang, Y., & Bennett, D. A. (2006). Odor identification and decline in different cognitive domains in old age. *Neuroepidemiology, 26*, 61–67.

Wilson-Costello, D., Friedman, H., Minich, N., Siner, B., Taylor, G., Schluchter, M., & Hack, M. (2007). Improved neurodevelopmental outcomes for extremely low birth weight infants in 2000–2002. *Pediatrics, 119*, 37–45.

Wilt, J., Condon, D. M., & Revelle, W. (2012). Telemetrics and online data collection: Collecting data at a distance. In B. Laursen, T. D. Little, & N. A. Card (Eds.), *Handbook of developmental research methods* (pp. 163–180). New York, NY: Guilford.

Winerman, L. (2013, August 27). New prenatal tests reveal far more about fetuses. *The Washington Post*, p. E6.

Wingfield, A., & Lash, A. (2016). Audition and language comprehension in adult aging. In Schaie, K. W. & Willis, S. L. (Ed.), *Handbook of the psychology of aging* (8th ed., pp. 165–185). San Diego, CA: Elsevier.

Wingfield, A., Poon, L. W., Lombardi, L., & Lowe, D. (1985). Speed of processing in normal aging: Effects of speech rate, linguistic structure, and processing time. *Journal of Gerontology, 40*, 579–595.

Wink, P., & Dillon, M. (2002). Spiritual development across the adult life course: Findings from a longitudinal study. *Journal of Adult Development, 9*, 79–94.
Wink, P., & Dillon, M. (2003). Religiousness, spirituality, and psychosocial functioning in late adulthood: findings from a longitudinal study. *Psychology and Aging, 18*, 916–924.
Wink, P., & Dillon, M. (2008). Religiousness, spirituality, and psychosocial functioning in late adulthood: Findings from a longitudinal study. *Psychology of Religion and Spirituality*, S (1), 102–115.
Winner, E. (1996). *Gifted children: Myths and realities*. New York, NY: Basic Books.
Winsler, A., Carlton, M. P., & Barry, M. J. (2000). Age-related changes in preschool children's systematic use of private speech in a natural setting. *Journal of Child Language, 27*, 665–687.
Wischmann, T., Korge, K., Scherg, H., Strowitzki, T., & Verres, R. (2012). A 10-year follow-up study of psychosocial factors affecting couples after infertility treatment. *Human Reproduction, 27*, 3226–3232.
Witte, K. (2006, April 2). Untitled. *The Washington Post*, p. D1.
Wittmann, B. C., & D'Esposito, M. (2012). Functional magnetic resonance imaging. In H. Cooper (Editor-in-Chief), P. M. Camic, D. L. Long, A. T. Panter, D. Rindskopf, & K. J. Sher (Assoc. Eds.), *APA handbook of research methods in psychology: Vol. 1. Foundations, planning, measures, and psychometrics* (pp. 547–566). Washington, DC: American Psychological Association.
Wlodarczyk, B. J., Palacios, A. M., George, T. M., & Finnell, R. H. (2012). Antiepileptic drugs and pregnancy outcomes. *American Journal of Medical Genetics, Part A. 158A*, 2071–2090.
Wlodkowski, R. J. (1999). *Enhancing adult motivation to learn: A comprehensive guide for teaching all adults*. San Francisco, CA: Jossey-Bass Higher and Adult Education Series.
Wodrich, D. L. (2006). Sex chromosome anomalies. In L. Phelps (Ed.), *Chronic health–related disorders in children: Collaborative medical and psychoeducational interventions*. Washington, DC: American Psychological Association.
Wohlfahrt-Veje, C., Andersen, H. R., Jensen, T. K., Grandjean, P., Skakkebaek, N. E., & Main, K. M. (2012a). Smaller genitals at school age in boys whose mothers were exposed to non-persistent pesticides in early pregnancy. *International Journal of Andrology, 35*, 265–272.
Wohlfahrt-Veje, C., Andersen, H. R., Schmidt, I. M., Aksglaede, L., Sørensen, K., Juul, A., et al. (2012b). Early breast development in girls after prenatal exposure to non-persistent pesticides. *International Journal of Andrology, 35*, 273–282.
Wohlfahrt-Veje, C., Main, K. M., Schmidt, I. M., Boas, M., Jensen, T. K., Grandjean, P., et al. (2011). Lower birth weight and increased body fat at school age in children prenatally exposed to modern pesticides: A prospective study. *Environmental Health: A Global Access Science Source, 10*, 79.
Wolchik, S. A., West, S. G., Sandler, I. N., Tein, J. Y., Coatsworth, D., Lengua, L., Weiss, L., Anderson, E. R., Greene, S. M., & Griffin, W. A. (2000). An experimental evaluation of theory-based mother and mother–child programs for children of divorce. *Journal of Consulting and Clinical Psychology, 68*, 843–856.
Wolff, J. J., Gu, H., Gerig, G., Elison, J. T., Styner, M., Gouttard, S., et al. (2012). Differences in white matter fiber tract development present from 6 to 24 months in infants with autism. *American Journal of Psychiatry, 169*, 589–600.
Wolff, P. H. (1963). Observations on the early development of smiling. In B. M. Foss (Ed.), *Determinants of infant behavior: Vol. 2*. London, UK: Methuen.
Wolfner, G. D., & Gelles, R. J. (1993). A profile of violence toward children: A national study. *Child Abuse and Neglect, 17*, 197–212.
Wolfson, A. R., & Carskadon, M. A. (1998). Sleep schedules and daytime functioning in adolescents. *Child Development, 69*, 875–998.
Wolke, D., Copeland, W. E., Angold, A., & Costello, E. J. (2013). Impact of bullying in childhood on adult health, wealth, crime, and social outcomes. *Psychological Science, 24*, 1958–1970.
Women's Health Initiative. (2004). *The estrogen-plus-progestin study*. Retrieved from www.nhlbi.nih.gov/whi/estro_pro.htm.
Wong, B., Yin, B., & O'Brien, B. (2016). Neurolinguistics: Structure, function, and connectivity in the bilingual brain. *BioMed Research International*, 2016, Article ID 7069274.
Wong, E. (2012, July 23). Pressure grows in China to end one-child law. *The New York Times*, p. A1.
Wong, J. Y., & Earl, J. K. (2009). Towards an integrated model of individual, psychosocial, and organizational predictors of retirement adjustment. *Journal of Vocational Behavior, 75*, 1–13.
Wong, L. P. (2011). Attitudes toward menstruation, menstrual-related symptoms, and premenstrual syndrome among adolescent girls: A rural school-based survey. *Women & Health, 51*, 340–364.
Wong, P. T. P., & Watt, L. M. (1991). What types of reminiscence are associated with successful aging? *Psychology and Aging, 6*, 272–279.
Wong, W. I., Pasterski, V., Hindmarsh, P. C., Geffner, M. E., & Hines, M. (2013). Are there parental socialization effects on the sex-typed behavior of individuals with congenital adrenal hyperplasia? *Archives of Sexual Behavior, 42*, 381–391.
Woo, S. M., & Keatinge, C. (2008). *Diagnosis and treatment of mental disorders across the lifespan*. New York, NY: Wiley.
Woodhill, B. M., & Samuels, C. A. (2003). Positive and negative androgyny and their relationship with psychological health and well-being. *Sex Roles, 49*, 555–565.
Woodhill, B. M., & Samuels, C. A. (2004). Desirable and undesirable androgyny: A prescription for the twenty-first century. *Journal of Gender Studies, 13*, 15–28.
Woodward, A. L. (2009). Infants' grasp of others' intentions. *Current Directions in Psychological Science, 18*, 53–57.
Woodward, A. L., & Markman, E. M. (1998). Early word learning. In D. Kuhn & R. S. Siegler, (Vol. Eds.), W. Damon (Editor-in-Chief), *Handbook of child psychology: Vol. 2. Cognition, perception, and language* (5th ed., pp. 371–420). New York, NY: Wiley.
Woodward, A. T., Taylor, R. J., Bullard, K. M., Aranda, M. P., Lincoln, K. D., & Chatters, L. M. (2012). Prevalence of lifetime DSM-IV affective disorders among older African Americans, black Caribbeans, Latinos, Asians and non-Hispanic white people. *International Journal of Geriatric Psychiatry, 27*, 816–827.
Woodward, L., Fergusson, D. M., & Belsky, J. (2000). Timing of parental separation and attachment to parents in adolescence: Results of a prospective study from birth to age 16. *Journal of Marriage and the Family, 62*, 162–174.
Wooley, J. D. & Cornelius, C. A. (2013). Beliefs in magical beings and cultural myths. In M. Taylor (Ed.), *The Oxford handbook of the development of imagination* (pp. 61–74). Oxford University Press.
Woolley, J. D., Boerger, E. A., & Markman, A. B. (2004). A visit from the Candy Witch: Factors influencing young children's belief in a novel fantastical being. *Developmental Science, 7*, 456–468.
Worchel, F. F., Copeland, D. R., & Barker, D. G. (1987). Control-related coping strategies in pediatric oncology patients. *Journal of Pediatric Psychology, 12*, 25–38.
Worden, J. W., & Silverman, P. R. (1996). Parental death and the adjustment of school-age children. *Omega: Journal of Death and Dying, 33*, 91–102.
Worden, J. W., & Silverman, P. S. (1993). Grief and depression in newly widowed parents with school-age children. *Omega: Journal of Death and Dying, 27*, 251–261.
Worfolk, J. B. (2000). Heat waves: Their impact on the health of elders. *Geriatric Nursing, 21*, 70–77.
World Health Organization (2015). *Global Health Observatory (GHO) Data, Life expectancy at birth, 1990–2013*. Retrieved from www.gamapserver.who.int/gho/interactive_charts/mbd/life_expectancy/atlas.html.
Wortman, C. B., & Boerner, K. (2007). Beyond the myths of coping with loss: Prevailing assumptions versus scientific evidence. In H. S. Friedman & R. C. Silver (Eds.), *Foundations of health psychology*. New York, NY: Oxford University Press.
Wortman, C. B., & Silver, R. C. (2001). The myths of coping with loss revisited. In M. S. Stroebe, R. O. Hansson, W. Stroebe, & H. Schut (Eds.), *Handbook of bereavement research. Consequences, coping, and care*. Washington, DC: American Psychological Association.
Wright, W. E., & Shay, J. W. (2005). Telomere biology in aging and cancer. *Journal of the American Geriatrics Society, 53*, S292–S294.
Wrzus, C., Hänel, M., Wagner, J., & Neyer, F. J. (2013). Social network changes and life events across the life span: A meta-analysis. *Psychological Bulletin, 139*, 53–80.
Wrzus, C., Müller, V., Wagner, G. G., Lindenberger, U., & Riediger, M. (2013). Affective and cardiovascular responding to unpleasant events from adolescence to old age: Complexity of events matters. *Developmental Psychology, 49*, 384–397.
Wu, C. Y., Yu, T. J., & Chen, M. J. (2000). Age related testosterone level changes and male andropause syndrome. *Changgeng Yi Xue Za Zhi [Chinese Medical Journal], 23*, 348–353.
Wu, P., & Chiou, W. (2008). Postformal thinking and creativity among late adolescents: A post-Piagetian approach. *Adolescence, 43*, 237–251.
Wu, P., & Liu, H. (2014). Association between moral reasoning and moral behavior: A systematic review and meta-analysis. *Acta Psychologica Sinica, 46*, 1192–1207.
Wu, T., Mendola, P., & Buck, G. M. (2002). Ethnic differences in the presence of secondary sex characteristics and menarche among US girls: The third national health and nutrition examination survey, 1988–1994. *Pediatrics*, 110, 752–757.
Wu, Y., Barad, D. H., Kushnir, V., Lazzaroni, E., Wang, Q., Albertini, D. & Gleicher, N. (2015). Aging-related premature luteinization of granulosa cells is avoided by early oocyte retrieval. *Journal of Endocrinology, 226*, 167–180.
Wubbena, Z. C. (2013). Mathematical fluency as a function of conservation ability in young children. *Learning and Individual Differences, 26*, 153–155.
Wurmser, H., Rieger, M., Domogalla, C., Kahnt, A., Buchwald, J., Kowatsch, M., Kuehnert, N., Buske-Kirschbaum, A., Papousek, M., Pirke, K. M., & von Voss, H. (2006). Association between life stress during pregnancy and infant crying in the first six months of postpartum: A prospective longitudinal study. *Early Human Development, 82*, 341–349.
Wysocki, C. J., Louie, J., Leyden, J. J., Blank, D., Gill, M., Smith, L., et al. (2009). Cross-adaptation of a model human stress-related odor with fragrance chemicals and ethyl esters of axillary odorants: Gender-specific effects. *Flavour and Fragrance Journal, 24*(5), 209–218.
Yaffe, K., Barnes, D., Nevitt, M., Lui, L., & Covinsky, K. (2001). A prospective study of physical activity and cognitive decline in elderly women. *Archives of Internal Medicine, 161*, 1703–1708.
Yamazaki, K., & Beauchamp, G. K. (2007). Genetic Basis for MHC Dependent Mate Choice. In D. Yamamoto (Ed.), *Advances in genetics* (Vol. 59, pp. 129–145). New York, NY: Academic Press.
Yan, A. F., Voorhees, C. C., Clifton, K., Burnier, C., Voorhees, C. C., Clifton, K., et al. (2010). "Do you see what I see?—correlates of multidimensional measures of neighborhood types and perceived physical activity-related neighborhood barriers and facilitators for urban youth. *Preventive Medicine, 50 (Suppl 1), S18–S23*.
Yan, B., & Arlin, P. K. (1995). Nonabsolute/relativistic thinking: A common factor underlying models of postformal reasoning? *Journal of Adult Development, 2*, 223–240.
Yang, T. -C., Shoff, C., Noah, A. J., Black, N., & Sparks, C. S. (2014). Racial segregation and maternal smoking during pregnancy: A multilevel analysis using the racial segregation interaction index. *Social Science & Medicine, 107*, 26–36.
Yao Defen as Tallest Women in The World (2012). Retrieved from www.worldsmostamazingrecords.org/yao-defen-as-tallest-women-in-the-world/.
Yau, P. L., Castro, M. G., Tagani, A., Tsui, W. H., & Convit, A. (2012). Obesity and metabolic syndrome and functional and structural brain impairments in adolescence. *Pediatrics, 130*, 1–9.
Yavorsky, J. E., Kamp Dush, C. M., & Schoppe-Sullivan, S. (2015). The production of inequality: The gender division of labor across the transition to parenthood. *Journal of Marriage and Family, 77*, 662–679.
Yeager, D. S., Paunesku, D., Walton, G. M., & Dweck, C. S. (2013, May 10). How can we instill productive mindsets at scale? A review of the evidence and an initial R&D

agenda. White paper prepared for the White House meeting on *Excellence in education: The importance of academic mindsets*. Available at gregorywalton-stanford.weebly.com/uploads/4/9/4/4/49448111/yeagerpauneskuwaltondweck_-_white_house_r&d_agenda_-_5–9-13.pdf.

Yeager, D. S., Romero, C., Paunesku, D., Hulleman, C. S., Schneider, B., Hinojosa, C., ... Dweck, C. S. (2016). Using design thinking to improve psychological interventions: The case of the growth mindset during the transition to high school. *Journal of Educational Psychology, 108*, 374.

Yeates, K. O., & Selman, R. L. (1989). Social competence in the schools: Toward an integrative developmental model for intervention. *Developmental Review, 9*, 64–100.

Yeh, Y., & Wu, J. (2006). The cognitive processes of pupils' technological creativity. *Creativity Research Journal, 18*, 213–227.

Yendovitskaya, T. V. (1971). Development of attention. In A. V. Zaporozhets & D. B. Elkonin (Eds.), *The psychology of preschool children*. Cambridge, MA: MIT Press.

Yeung, W. J., & Pfeiffer, K. M. (2009). The black-white test score gap and early home environment. *Social Science Research, 38*, 412–437.

Yilmaz, G., Hizli, S., Karacan, C., Yurdakök, K., Coskun, T., & Dilmen, U. (2009). Effect of passive smoking on growth and infection rates of breast-fed and non-breast-fed infants. *Pediatrics International, 51*, 352–358.

Yonkers, K. A., & Casper, R. F. (2012). Epidemiology and pathogenesis of premenstrual syndrome and premenstrual dysphoric disorder. Retrieved from www.uptodate.com/contents/epideiology-and-pathogenesis-of-premenstrual-syndrome.

Yoo, H. (2015). Genetics of autism spectrum disorder: Current status and possible clinical applications. *Experimental Neurobiology, 24*, 257–272.

Yorifuji, T., Debes, F., Weihe, P., & Grandjean, P. (2011). Prenatal exposure to lead and cognitive deficit in 7- and 14-year-old children in the presence of concomitant exposure to similar molar concentration of methylmercury. *Neurotoxicology & Teratology, 33*, 205–211.

Youn, G. Y., Knight, B. G., Jeong, H. S., & Benton, D. (1999). Differences in familism values and caregiving outcomes among Korean, Korean American, and White American dementia caregivers. *Psychology and Aging, 14*, 355–364.

Young, J. C., & Widom, C. S. (2014). Long-term effects of child abuse and neglect on emotion processing in adulthood. *Child Abuse & Neglect, 38*, 1369–1381.

Young, L. R., & Nestle, M. (2002). The contribution of expanding portion sizes to the US obesity epidemic. *American Journal of Public Health, 92*, 246–249.

Young, W. C., Goy, R. W., & Phoenix, C. H. (1964). Hormones and sexual behavior. *Science, 143*, 212–218.

Youniss, J. (1980). *Parents and peers in social development. A Sullivan-Piaget perspective*. Chicago, IL: University of Chicago Press.

Youth Risk Behavior Survey (2009). *National trends in risk behaviors*. Retrieved from www.cdc.gov/HealthyYouth/yrbs/trends.htm.

Yu, Y., & Kushnir, T. (2016). When what's inside counts: Sequence of demonstrated actions affects preschooler's categorization by nonobvious properties. *Developmental Psychology, 52*, 400–410.

Yuenyong, S., O'Brien, B., & Jirapeet, V. (2010). Effects of labor support from close female relative on labor and maternal satisfaction in a Thai setting. *Journal of Obstetrics, Gynecology & Neonatal Nursing, 41*, 45–56.

Yuill, N. (1993). Understanding of personality and dispositions. In M. Bennett (Ed.), *The development of social cognition: The child as psychologist*. New York, NY: Guilford.

Zablotsky, B., Black, L. I., Maenner, M. J., Schieve, L.A., & Blumberg, S. J. (2015, November 13). Estimated prevalence of autism and other developmental disabilities following questionnaire changes in the 2014 National Health Interview Survey. *National Health Statistics Reports, no. 87*. Retrieved from www.cdc.gov/nchs/data/nhsr/nhsr087.pdf.

Zahn-Waxler, C., Friedman, R. J., Cole, P. M., Mizuta, I., & Himura, N. (1996). Japanese and United States preschool children's responses to conflict and distress. *Child Development, 67*, 2462–2477.

Zahn-Waxler, C., Radke-Yarrow, M., Wagner, E., & Chapman, M. (1992). Development of concern for others. *Developmental Psychology, 28*, 126–136.

Zajac, R., & Hayne, H. (2003). I don't think that's what really happened: The effect of cross-examination on the accuracy of children's reports. *Journal of Experimental Psychology: Applied, 9*, 187–195.

Zajonc, R. B. (2001a). Birth order debate resolved? *American Psychologist, 56*, 522–523.

Zajonc, R. B. (2001b). The family dynamics of intellectual development. *American Psychologist, 56*, 490–496.

Zaporozhets, A. V. (1965). The development of perception in the preschool child. *Monographs of the Society for Research in Child Development, 30*(2, Serial No. 100), 82–101.

Zaragoza, S. A., Salgado, S., Shao, Z., & Berntsen, D. (2015). Event centrality of positive and negative autobiographical memories to identity and life story across cultures. *Memory, 23*, 1152–1171.

Zarit, S. H. (2009). Empirically supported treatment for family caregivers. In S. H. Qualls & S. H. Zarit (Eds.), *Aging families and caregiving*. Hoboken, NJ: John Wiley.

Zarit, S. H., & Heid, A. R. (2015). Assessment and treatment of family caregivers. In P. A. Lichtenberg & B. T. Mast (Eds. in Chief) & B. D. Carpenter & J. L. Wetherell (Vol. Eds.), *APA handbook of clinical geropsychology: Vol. 2. Assessment, treatment, and issues of later life* (pp. 521–551). Washington, DC: American Psychological Association.

Zarit, S. H., & Talley, R. C. (Eds.). (2013). *Caregiving for Alzheimer's disease and related disorders: Research, practice, policy*. New York, NY: Springer Science+Business Media.

Zeanah, C. H. (Ed.). (2009). *Handbook of infant mental health* (3rd ed.). New York, NY: Guilford.

Zeanah, C. H., Berlin, L. J., & Boris, N. W. (2011). Clinical applications of attachment theory and research for infants and young children. *Journal of Child Psychology and Psychiatry, 52*, 819–833.

Zehr, J. L., Culbert, K. M., Siska, C. L., & Klump, K. L. (2007). An association of early puberty with disordered eating and anxiety in a population of undergraduate women and men. *Hormones and Behavior, 52*, 427–435.

Zeller, M. H., & Modi, A. C. (2006). Predictors of health-related quality of life in obese youth. *Obesity, 14*, 122–130.

Zemach, I., Chang, S., & Teller, D. Y. (2006). Infant color vision: Prediction of infants' spontaneous color preferences. *Vision Research, 47*, 1368–1381.

Zemach, I., Chang, S., & Teller, D. Y. (2007). Infant color vision: Prediction of infants' spontaneous color preferences. *Vision Research, 47*, 1368–1381.

Zemel, B. (2002). Body composition during growth and development. In N. Cameron (Ed.), *Human growth and development* (pp. 271–293). New York, NY: Academic Press.

Zendel, B. R., & Alain, C. (2012). Musicians experience less age-related decline in central auditory processing. *Psychology and Aging, 27*, 410–417.

Zenger, M., Brähler, E., Berth, H., & Stöbel-Richter, Y. (2011). Unemployment during working life and mental health of retirees: Results of a representative survey. *Aging & Mental Health, 15*, 178–185.

Zero to Three (2005). *Diagnostic classification of mental health and developmental disorders of infancy and early childhood* (rev. ed.). Washington, DC: Zero to Three Press.

Zetterberg, M. (2016). Age-related eye disease and gender. *Maturitas, 83*, 19–26.

Zhai, Y., Yi, H., Shen, W., Xiao, Y., Fan, H., He, F., ... Lin, J. (2015). Association of empty nest with depressive symptom in a Chinese elderly population: A cross-sectional study. *Journal of Affective Disorders, 187*, 218–223.

Zhang, H. (2009). The new realities of aging in contemporary China: Coping with the decline in family care. In J. Sokolovsky (Ed.), *The cultural context of aging* (3rd ed.). Westport, CT: Praeger.

Zhang, L. (2002). Thinking styles and cognitive development. *Journal of Genetic Psychology, 163*, 179–195.

Zhang, T., & Meaney, M. J. (2010). Epigenetics and the environmental regulation of the genome and its function. *Annual Review of Psychology, 61*, 439–466.

Zhou, M., & Lee, J. (2014). Assessing what is cultural about Asian Americans' academic advantage. *Proceedings of the National Academy of Sciences, 111*, 8321–8322.

Zhu, H., Belcher, M. and van der Harst, P. (2011) Healthy aging and disease: role for telomere biology? *Clinical Science, 120*, 427–440.

Zigler, E. (1995). Can we "cure" mild mental retardation among individuals in the lower socioeconomic stratum? *American Journal of Public Health, 85*, 302–304.

Zigler, E., Abelson, W. D., Trickett, P. K., & Seitz, V. (1982). Is an intervention program necessary to improve economically disadvantaged children's IQ scores? *Child Development, 53*, 340–348.

Zigman, W. B. (2013). Atypical aging in Down syndrome. *Developmental Disabilities Research Reviews, 18*, 51–67.

Zimmerman, F. J., Christakis, D. A., & Meltzoff, A. N. (2007). Associations between media viewing and language development in children under age 2 years. *Journal of Pediatrics, 151*, 364–368.

Zimmermann, M. B. (2007). The adverse effects of mild-to-moderate iodine deficiency during pregnancy and childhood: A review. *Thyroid, 17*, 829–835.

Zimprich, D., & Martin, M. (2002). Can longitudinal changes in processing speed explain longitudinal age changes in fluid intelligence? *Psychology and Aging, 17*, 690–695.

Zinke, K., Zeintl, M., Rose, N. S., Putzmann, J., Pydde, A., & Kliegel, M. (2014). Working memory training and transfer in older adults: Effects of age, baseline performance, and training gains. *Developmental Psychology, 50*, 304–315.

Zissimopoulos, J. M., & Karoly, L. A. (2009). Labor-force dynamics at older ages. Movements into self-employment for workers and nonworkers. *Research on Aging, 31*, 89–111.

Zosuls, K. M., Ruble, D. N., Bornstein, M. H., & Greulich, F. K. (2009). The acquisition of gender labels in infancy: Implications for gender-typed play. *Developmental Psychology, 45*, 688–701.

Zucker, A. N., Ostrove, J. M., & Stewart, A. J. (2002). College-educated women's personality development in adulthood: Perceptions and age differences. *Psychology and Aging, 17*, 236–244.

Zvoch, K., & Stevens, J. J. (2006). Longitudinal effects of school context and practice on middle school mathematics achievement. *Journal of Educational Research, 99*, 347–356.

Zwaigenbaum, L., Bryson, S., Rogers, T., Roberts, W., Brian, J., & Szatmari, P. (2005). Behavioral manifestations of autism in the first year of life. *International Journal of Developmental Neuroscience, 23*, 143–152.

Zych, I., Ortega-Ruiz, R., & Del Rey, R. (2015). Systematic review of theoretical studies on bullying and cyberbullying: Facts, knowledge, prevention, and intervention. *Aggression and Violent Behavior, 23*, 1–21.

Name Index

A

Aanerud, J., 152
AAP Task Force on Circumcision, 177
Aarons, S. J., 48
ABC News, 253
Abdi, H., 175
Abele, A. E., 367, 393
Aber, J. L., 547
Aber, L., 8
Ablard, K. E., 315
Abma, J. C., 32, 53, 389, 492
Abramov, I., 182
Abrams, J. M., 382
Abreau, K. A., 451, 452
Abshier, D. W., 247
Acevedo, B. P., 459, 460
Achenbach, T. M., 85, 509, 511
Ackerman, B. P., 434
Ackerman, P. L., 328
Adam, K., 378
Adams, G. R., 356
Adams, M., 96, 378
Adams, P. F., 155
Adams, R. E., 383
Adams, R. G., 24, 462
Adams, R. J., 169
Adamsons, K., 473
Addington, A. M., 502
Adelman, R. D., 489
Aderman, D., 540
Adler, J. M., 357
Adolph, K. E., 138, 171, 179, 180, 181, 381
Adolphs, R., 403
Adrian, V., 478
Afifi, T. D., 494
Ageton, S. S., 422
Agnew, R., 420, 495
Aguiar, A., 214, 215, 241
Ahadi, S. A., 339
Ahlgrim, C. J., 382
Ahluwalia, I. B., 119
Ahmetoglu, G., 459
Ai, A. L., 428, 429
Ainsworth, M. D. S., 440, 441, 443–444, 445
Ajrouch, K. J., 458
Akande, K., 389
Akers, K. G., 247

Akhtar, N., 303
Akinbami, L. J., 101
Akincigil, A., 526
Akiyama, H., 458
Aknin, L. B., 413
Aksan, N., 407, 414, 418
Aksglaede, L., 146
Akshoomoff, N., 508
Alba, J. W., 187
Albert, D., 437, 518
Albuquerque, S., 553
Alessandri, S. M., 337
Alexander, G. M., 371, 378
Alexander, K. W., 248
Alexander, P. A., 209, 251
Alfieri, T., 384
Alink, L. R. A., 21
Alio, A. P., 110
Alisat, S., 428
Alladi, S., 313
Allen, J., 536
Allen, J. P., 56, 454, 475, 482
Allen, M. C., 96
Allen, R. E. S., 492
Alliey-Rodriguez, N., 68, 72, 78
Allison, C. M., 148
Alloway, T. P., 251
Almeida, D. M., 384, 525
Almli, C. R., 369
Almond, D., 105
Almond, E., 158
Alpass, F. M., 360
Altermatt, E. R., 377
Altschul, I., 43
Alvarez, A., 219
Amani, R., 154
Amato, P. R., 82, 471, 475, 493, 494, 495
Ambady, N., 290
Ambrose, A. F., 191
American Academy of Neurology, 144
American Academy of Pediatrics, 21, 102
American Association on Intellectual and
    Developmental Disabilities, 291
American Psychiatric Association, 153, 369,
    502, 507, 512, 513, 518, 526, 529, 552
Amitay, S., 184
Amone-P'Olak, K., 511

Amstutz, D. D., 328
Anand, K. J., 177
Anastasi, A., 79
Andercheck, B., 387
Anderson, A. N., 69
Anderson, C. A., 423
Anderson, D. A., 378
Anderson, D. R., 21
Anderson, J., 253, 319
Anderson, P. J., 121
Anderson, R. M., 160
Anderson-Fry, E., 519
Ando, J., 342
Andrade, J. Q., 104
Angell, M., 526, 536
Angold, A., 512
Anim-Soumuah, M., 114
Anisfeld, E., 445
Annese, J., 237
Antebi, A., 160
Anthis, K., 345
Antonucci, T. C., 458
Apfel, N. H., 56
Apgar, V., 105
Apperly, I. A., 403
Appollonio, I., 196
Aquilino, W. S., 486
Aquino, K., 419
Arain, M., 131
Aratani, L., 520
Araya, R., 146
Arbeit, M. R., 56
Arber, S., 396
Arbona, C., 342, 454
Archer, A. H., 21
Archer, J., 376, 440
Archer, K. J., 146
Archer, S. L., 345–346
Ardelt, M., 285, 428, 429
Arenberg, D., 286
Arens, A. K., 323
Ariel, R., 251
Ariès, P., 8, 537
Arjmand, O., 377
Arking, R., 157, 159, 160
Arlin, P. K., 227
Armstrong, D., 556, 557

Boles, S., 518
Bolger, K. E., 497
Boloh, Y., 313
Bolton, P., 509
Bombard, Y., 71
Bonanno, G. A., 537, 543, 550–551, 552, 554, 555, 556, 559
Bond, M. H., 423
Bond, M. K., 423
Bong, M., 314, 315
Bongers, I. L., 511
Bono, J. E., 358
Bonoti, F., 548
Bonvillain, N., 366
Bonvillian, J. D., 303, 305
Booij, L., 80
Booth, A., 219, 475, 478, 491
Booth-LaForce, C., 446, 448
Borgstrom, K., 308
Boris, N. W., 447, 510
Borkenau, P., 353
Borman, W. C., 360
Born, J., 136, 186, 235
Bornovalova, M., 325
Bornstein, M. H., 306, 307, 468, 474
Borradaile, K. E., 140
Borst, G., 218
Bosak, J., 370
Bosch, A. M., 146
Bosse, R., 360
Boston Retinal Implant Project, 192
Bostrom, P. K., 292
Bottino, P. J., 67
Bouchard, G., 486, 487, 490
Bouchard, T. J., 369
Bouchard, T. J., Jr., 59, 76, 79, 82
Bowen, B. A., 328
Bowen, M., 17, 468
Bower, T. G. R., 182
Bowers, E. P., 423
Bowers, M., 302
Bowker, J. C., 453
Bowlby, J., 435, 440, 441, 442, 443, 447, 450, 460, 541–543, 544, 554
Bowman, M. S., 558
Boxer, P., 420
Boyatzis, C. J., 428, 429
Boyce, C. J., 355
Boyce, T., 81
Boyce, W. T., 83, 85, 98, 99
Boyle, D. E., 448
Boytchev, H., 63
Brabyn, J. A., 191
Bracey, J. R., 346
Bradbard, M. R., 380

Bradbury, T., 488
Bradbury, T. N., 484, 497
Bradley, R. H., 288, 477
Bradley-Geist, J., 483
Brady, C., 475
Brady, S. S., 389
Brähler, E., 359
Braine, M. D. S., 313
Brainerd, C. J., 247
Braithwaite, V., 351
Bramlett, H. M., 144
Brand, C. R., 266
Brand, J. E., 359
Brandão, S., 117
Brandt, J., 256
Brandtstadter, J., 350
Brandtstädter, J., 350
Branje, S. J. T., 482
Brant, A. M., 293
Bratberg, G. H., 147
Bratko, D., 77
Braun, N., 496
Braungart-Rieker, J., 473
Braver, S. L., 494
Bray, N. W., 243
Brazelton, T. B., 118
Breast-feeding Report Card, 119
Bredemeier, K., 505
Brehmer, Y., 250
Bremner, J. D., 256
Bremner, J. G., 172, 214
Brendgen, M., 73, 79
Brenick, A., 378
Brent, D., 516, 548, 549
Brent, S. B., 545
Bretherton, I., 441, 443
Bridge, J. A., 549
Bridges, L. J., 436
Briley, D. A., 76, 282
Britto, P. R., 475
Broadbent, D., 234
Broadbridge, C. L., 255
Broberg, M., 292
Brod, M., 513
Broderick, V., 318
Brody, D. J., 146
Brody, E. B., 278
Brody, E. M., 489, 490
Brody, G., 80, 81
Brody, G. H., 80, 418, 481
Brody, J. A., 154
Brody, N., 278
Broesch, T., 338
Bromley, D. B., 341, 404, 405
Bromnick, R. D., 225

Bronfenbrenner, U., 19, 31–32, 50–57, 140, 166, 212, 424, 468–469, 471, 499
Bronstad, P. M., 187
Brooks-Gunn, J., 147, 291, 337, 475
Brophy, J., 314, 316, 317
Broughton, J. M., 182, 205, 227
Brown, A. L., 244
Brown, A. M., 169
Brown, B. B., 322, 342, 455, 456–457, 482
Brown, D., 63
Brown, D. A., 144
Brown, I. T., 429
Brown, J. D., 45
Brown, R., 303, 304
Brown, R. D., 248
Brown, S. L., 484, 485, 489, 491
Browne, J. V., 173
Browne, M., 555
Brownell, C. A., 338, 449
Bruce, J., 447, 510
Bruck, M., 319
Brueckner, L., 172
Brummelman, E., 342
Bruner, J. S., 205, 208, 305
Brunskill, P. J., 376
Bryant, P., 319
Bryant, R. A., 254
Bryant-Waugh, R., 518
Brynie, F. H., 196
Buchanan, C. M., 147
Buchanan, N. R., 449
Buchanan, T., 483
Buchi, S., 553
Buchtel, E. E., 336, 351, 352
Buck, G. M., 145
Buckner, R. L., 252
Buddin, B., 436
Buehler, C. A., 493, 494
Buettner, D., 158
Bugental, D. B., 496, 497, 498
Buhrmester, D., 441, 450, 454, 480
Buil, J. M., 81
Buitelaar, J. K., 109
Buka, S. L., 509
Bukowski, W. M., 383, 442, 449, 453
Bulanda, J. R., 491
Bulanda, R. E., 472
Bullard, L., 495
Bullinger, A., 176
Bullock, M., 222, 223, 224, 274
Bundy, D. A., 275
Burack, J. A., 184
Burak, L., 185, 186
Bureau of Labor Statistics, 358, 370, 470, 564, 565, 566

Foos, P. W., 257
Foran, H. M., 496
Fordham, S., 322
Forgatch, M. S., 43, 494, 498
Forman, Y., 423
Forssell, S. L., 493
Forssman, L., 214
Fortenbaugh, F., 192
Foster, J. D., 23, 187
Foster, S. N., 108
Fouquet, M., 75
Fouts, H. N., 118
Fowler, J., 394, 428
Fowler, L. M., 226
Fowler, R. C., 210
Fowles, D. C., 418
Fox, E., 251
Fox, M. K., 141
Fox, S. E., 303
Fraga, M., 83
Fragouli, E., 91
Fraley, R. C., 446, 448, 460, 461, 555
Francis, D., 84
Franck, K. L., 493
Frank, J. A., 384
Frank, S. M., 197
Frankenmolen, N. L., 258
Frankland, P. W., 247
Franklin, C., 56
Franklin, S., 224
Franklin, Z., 169
Franko, D. L., 519
Frans, E. M., 67
Franzetta, K., 387
Fraser, M. W., 122, 424
Fraser, S. L., 102
Fratiglioni, L., 527, 528
Frattarelli, J. L., 110
Frayling, T., 157
Freedman, D. H., 43
Freedman, J., 303
Freeman, G. P., 350
Freeman, S. F. N., 292
Freud, A., 38, 39
Freud, E., 36
Freud, H., 36
Freud, S., 31–32, 35–41, 45, 48, 53–57,
    335–336, 342, 371–372, 382, 407–409,
    411–413, 428, 430, 440–441, 444–445,
    447, 503, 544, 554
Freund, A. M., 350, 354, 357, 358
Freund, L. S., 210
Frey, K. S., 341, 377
Freyd, J. J., 383

Frick, P. J., 421
Fried, E. I., 550
Friedland, D. S., 359
Friedlmeier, W., 435, 437
Friedman, H., 158
Friedman, H. S., 355
Friedman, L. J., 38, 39
Friedman, M. C., 258
Friedman, S. L., 448
Frieswijk, N., 350
Frisen, J., 152
Frith, U., 400
Froehlich, T. E., 513
Fry, C. L., 6
Fry, P. S., 361, 553
Fry, R., 486
Fryar, C. D., 143
Fryer, R., Jr., 317
Fu, G., 416
Fu, R., 354, 504
Fuglenes, D., 114
Fukumoto, A., 414
Fulcher, M., 374
Fuligni, A. J., 51, 143, 151, 424, 482, 486, 488
Furman, E., 544
Furman, W., 441, 450, 454, 455, 456, 457, 480
Furstenberg, F., 389
Furstenberg, F. F., Jr., 6, 8, 486

G

Gabbard, G. O., 35
Gage, F., 152
Gage, F. H., 152
Gaither, S. E., 346
Galambos, N. L., 384
Galanaki, E., 225
Galatzer-Levy, I., 550, 551
Galdo-Alvarez, S., 259
Galenson, E., 372
Gallagher, M., 488
Gallese, V., 403
Gallimore, R., 480
Gallo, L. C., 139
Gallup, G. G., Jr., 337
Galupo, M. P., 228
Galvan, A., 143
Gamé, F., 170
Gamiero, S., 92
Ganahl, D. J., 378
Ganiban, J. M., 497
Ganong, L., 492, 493, 494
Gao, X., 178
Gao, Y., 490
Garber, H. L., 312

Garber, J., 146, 505, 506, 510, 515, 522
Garcia, F., 482
García-Faura, Á., 172
Garciaguirre, J. S., 181
Garcia-Preto, N., 468
Garcia-Sierra, A., 309
Gardener, H., 509
Gardner, A., 433
Gardner, C. O., 503
Gardner, F., 498
Gardner, H., 269–270
Gardner, M., 130
Gardner, R. J. M., 26, 68
Garmezy, N., 512
Garnham, A., 380
Garofalo, R., 384
Garthe, A., 134
Gartstein, M. A., 339
Garvey, C., 451
Gatz, M., 75, 526, 527, 528
Gavrilov, L. A., 158
Gavrilova, N., 394, 396
Gavrilova, N. S., 158
Gayer, C., 7
Gazzaniga, M. S., 138
Ge, X., 477, 479, 523
Geda, Y. E., 256
Geddes, L., 72
Geier, C. F., 143
Geithner, C. A., 143
Geldmacher, D. S., 527
Gelles, R. J., 496, 497
Gelman, R. S., 172, 220
Gelman, S. A., 172, 308, 404
Geneser, A., 528
Gentaz, E., 182, 183
George, C., 497
George, J. B. E., 519
George, L. G., 356, 358
Gerena, M., 489
Gergely, G., 241
Germine, L. T., 5, 12
Gershoff, E. T., 42, 43
Gershon, E. S., 68, 72, 78
Gerstein, E. D., 292
Gerstel, N., 489
Gerst-Emerson, K., 463
Gerstorf, D., 488
Gervai, J., 377, 379
Gervain, J., 301, 306
Gest, S. D., 453
Getchell, N., 138, 139
Getzels, J. W., 275
Geurten, M., 244, 245

Geuze, R. H., 183
Gewirtz, A. H., 498
Ghatala, E. S., 251
Ghetti, S., 242
Giambra, L. M., 396
Giarrusso, R., 470, 471, 489
Gibbs, J. C., 399–400, 405, 407, 413, 418, 419, 421, 423, 425, 427, 428
Gibbs, N., 539
Gibson, E., 166, 167, 169, 171, 179–180
Gibson, J., 166, 167, 169
Giedd, J. N., 143, 420
Gifted Development Center, 293
Gil, D. G., 497
Gilbert, L., 437
Gilissen, C., 292
Gill, S. J., 153
Gillen, M., 389
Gillen-O'Neel, C., 151
Gini, G., 411
Ginn, J., 396
Ginsburg, A. P., 170
Ginzberg, E., 347
Giordano, P., 482
Giordano, P. C., 456
Girard, A., 73
Girard, C., 523
Gizer, I. R., 514
Glascock, A., 536, 537
Glascock, J., 378
Glaser, B. G., 540
Glaser, R., 253
Glass, G. V., 21
Glatt, S. J., 508
Gleason, J. B., 308
Gleason, P. M., 141
Gleason, T. R., 216
Glenberg, A. M., 403
Glenzer, N., 319
Glick, J. C., 229
Glick, M., 341
Gloth, F. M., 197
Glowinski, A. L., 522
Gluckman, P. D., 146
Glucksberg, S., 313
Gnepp, J., 404–405
Godar, S. P., 174
Gogate, L. J., 170
Goh, J. O., 16, 152
Gohlke, B., 146
Gold, A. L., 498
Gold, H. T., 558
Goldberg, A. E., 492, 493
Goldberg, A. P., 156
Goldberg, S., 442

Goldfield, G., 127
Goldhaber, D., 9, 33, 52
Golding, C., 210
Goldin-Meadow, S., 304, 307
Goldman, B., 394, 395
Goldman, S., 152
Goldsmith, H. H., 435
Goldstein, M. H., 306
Goldstein, S., 70
Goldstein, S. E., 456, 482
Golinkoff, R. M., 21, 306, 307, 311, 452
Golombok, S., 371, 374, 387, 493
Gong, Y., 253
Gonzaga, G. C., 488
Gonzales, N. A., 424
Gonzales-Backen, M. A., 346
Good, C., 290
Good, M., 428
Goodlett, C. R., 102
Goodluck, H., 302
Goodman, G. S., 248
Goodman, S. H., 511
Goodvin, R., 337, 341, 434, 436
Goodwin, J., 553
Goodz, N., 307
Gooren, L., 387
Gopnik, A., 5, 204, 401
Gorchoff, S. M., 486
Gordon, B. N., 382
Gordon, D. H., 222
Gordon, L. L., 247
Gori, M., 182
Gorman-Smith, D., 495, 496
Gorrese, A., 457
Gostin, L. O., 536
Goswami, U., 319
Gotlib, I. H., 5, 505, 510, 515, 516
Gottesman, I. I., 77, 78
Gottfredson, L., 267
Gottfredson, L. S., 279, 280, 281, 347
Gottfried, A. W., 275, 288, 293
Gottlieb, G., 65, 118
Gottman, J. M., 437, 484, 487
Goubet, N., 176
Gouin, K., 103
Gould, D. C., 155
Gould, M. S., 524
Govarts, E., 106
Goy, R. W., 376
Goyal, N., 27, 446
Graaf, P. M., 552
Graber, J. A., 147, 148
Gracia, E., 482
Grady, C. L., 313
Graesch, A., 4

Graham, M., 535
Graham-Bermann, S. A., 453
Grandin, T., 401, 507
Grandjean, P., 107
Granrud, C., 171
Grant, K. E., 506
Grasgruber, P., 128
Graven, S. N., 173
Gray, S. W., 312
Gray-Little, B., 344, 347
Grayman-Simpson, N., 429
Graziano, P. A., 452
Grbich, C., 541
Green, C., 256
Green, J. G., 513
Green, M., 547
Greenberg, J., 534
Greenberg, R. P., 40
Greenberger, E., 326, 485
Greene, J. D., 427
Greene, J. G., 154
Greene, K., 225
Greenfield, E. A., 429, 486
Greenfield, P. M., 302
Greenfield, R. A., 105
Greenhalgh, R., 117
Greenough, W. T., 134, 161, 275
Greer, D. M., 534
Gregory, E. C., 107
Greif, G. L., 488
Grello, C. M., 388
Greve, F., 278
Greve, W., 350
Greydanus, D. E., 520
Grieco, T. M., 174
Griffin, B., 359
Griffin, C. E., 175
Griffin, P., 559
Griffin, Z. M., 327
Griffiths, T. L., 5
Grigorenko, E. L., 275
Grijalva, E., 23
Grilo, C. M., 78, 520
Groark, C. J., 447
Grodsky, A., 396
Grogan-Kaylor, A., 141
Groh, A. M., 446, 461
Grolnick, W. S., 436, 475
Gromoske, A. N., 43
Grontved, A. M., 196
Gropman, A., 292
Grose-Fifer, J., 172, 175
Gross, C. L., 485
Gross, J. J., 246, 434, 436
Gross-Loh, C., 119

Grossman, A. H., 384, 385
Grossman, A. W., 503, 506
Grossmann, I., 5, 406
Grossmann, K. E., 446, 461
Grotevant, H. D., 347–348, 447
Gruber-Baldini, A. L., 283
Grundy, E., 489
Grunendahl, M., 525
Grusec, J. E., 418, 474
Grych, J., 494, 496
Gu, Q., 143
Guarnaccia, C. A., 558
Guay, F., 342
Gudsnuk, K. M. A., 109
Guerin, D. W., 339, 340
Guerra, N. G., 421, 422, 423
Guerreiro, M., 256
Guilamo-Ramos, V., 392
Guimond, A. B., 346
Gulko, J., 372
Gullone, E., 437
Gundersen, C., 140
Güngör, D., 354
Gunnar, M., 510
Gunnar, M. R., 447, 448
Gunnarson, A. D., 178
Guo, G., 422
Gurba, E., 227
Gurung, R. A. R., 462
Gur-Yaish, N., 444
Gus, L., 437
Gutiérrez, I. T., 545
Gutman, L. M., 322
Gutmann, D., 392, 393
Guxens, M., 106
Guyenet, S., 150
Gweon, H., 403

H
Ha, J., 556
Haber, D., 357
Hack, M., 273
Haddow, J. E., 130
Haegerstrom-Portnoy, G., 191
Hafdahl, A. R., 344, 347
Hafetz, J., 369
Hagan, L. K., 377
Hagan, M. J., 559
Hagan, R., 373
Hagberg, J. M., 156
Hagekull, B., 342
Hagen, E. W., 120
Hagestad, G. O., 487
Hagl, M., 559
Hahm, H. C., 389

Haidt, J., 427
Haight, B. K., 357
Haight, B. S., 357
Haight, W. L., 451
Haimovitz, K., 315
Haine, R. A., 556
Hainline, L., 169, 170, 182
Halberstadt, A. G., 437
Hales, S., 558
Haley, M., 77
Haley, W. E., 535
Halim, M. L., 367, 373, 374, 378, 379
Hall, C. S., 35
Hall, G. H., 517
Hall, G. S., 11–12
Hall, J., 78
Hall, L., 509
Hall, T., 197
Hallgren, A., 117
Halligan, S. L., 117
Halliwell, E., 519
Hallmayer, J., 509
Halmi, K. A., 519
Halpern, C. J. T., 388
Halpern, C. T., 65, 383
Halpern-Fisher, B. L., 389
Halpern-Meekin, S., 492
Halverson, C. F., Jr., 369, 379, 380
Ham, M., 438
Hambleton, L., 69
Hamer, R. D., 168
Hamilton, J. L., 523
Hamilton, M., 378
Hamlin, J. K., 401, 412, 413
Hamm, M. P., 13
Hammen, C. L., 5, 515
Hammer, J., 68
Hammer, M., 259
Hampson, S. E., 355
Handelsman, D. J., 155
Hänel, M., 458
Hanish, L. D., 374
Hankin, B. L., 80, 523
Hanlon, C., 304
Hannon, E. E., 166, 168
Hans, J. D., 389
Hansen, D. J., 497
Hansen, T., 492
Hanson, D. R., 78
Hanson, J. D., 423
Hanson, J. L., 8, 134
Hanson, M. A., 146
Hansson, R. O., 359, 360, 542, 556
Hanushek, E., 320
Hanushek, E. A., 320

Hanwella, R., 553
Hany, E. A., 283
Hardan, A. Y., 510
Harden, K. P., 53, 76, 77
Hardison, C. M., 289
Hardy, S. A., 419, 428
Harju, B. J., 327
Harley, A. E., 437
Harlow, H., 445
Harman, D., 160
Harmon, R. J., 338
Harold, G. T., 506
Harold, R. D., 370
Harpalani, V., 346
Harper, G., 328
Harper, H. J., 372
Harper, L. M., 113
Harper, M. S., 388
Harrington, D. M., 276
Harris, E., 467, 468
Harris, M., 38
Harris, M. A., 146
Harris, M. B., 371
Harris, M. J., 76
Harris, P. L., 217, 451
Harris, R. A., 102
Harris, T., 547
Hart, B., 275, 308–309
Hart, D., 341, 343, 419
Hart, H. M., 356
Hart, M. A., 108
Harter, S., 334, 338, 341, 342, 343, 344, 352, 436
Hartig, J., 559
Hartley, A., 259
Hartshorn, K., 239
Hartshorne, J. K., 5, 12
Hartung, P. J., 347
Hartup, W. W., 453
Hasegawa, J., 114
Haskett, M. E., 496
Hastings, P. D., 413
Hatch, T., 219
Hatfield, E., 459
Hattenschwiler, N., 254
Haught, P. A., 259
Haun, D. B. M., 44, 417, 449
Hausdorff, J. M., 191, 350
Haverstick, K., 360
Havighurst, R. J., 361
Havighurst, S. S., 437
Havlicek, J., 187
Hawkins, R. L., 325
Hawkley, L. C., 157
Haworth, C. M. A., 293

Hooker, K., 328
Hooper, F. H., 229
Hooper, J. O., 229
Hooper, S. R., 68
Hooper, S. R.., 68
Hooven, C., 437
Hopkins, M., 152
Hopmeyer, A., 455
Horn, J. L., 266, 267
Horn, K. H., 102
Horn, M. C., 525
Horn, S. P., 320
Horner, V., 44
Horney, K., 38
Horowitz, A., 192
Horowitz, L. M., 460
Horowitz, P., 478
Houdé, O., 206, 218
House, J. D., 322
Houser, J. J., 455
Houshyar, S., 498
Houston, D. M., 306
Houx, P. J., 259
Howard, L. H., 428
Howe, D., 444, 461
Howe, G. W., 359
Howe, M. L., 247, 248
Howe, N., 480
Howes, C., 374, 449, 451
Howlin, P., 509
Howson, C. P., 68
Hoy, W., 320, 321
Hoyer, W. J., 258, 259
Hrdy, S. B., 469
Hsia, Y., 149
Hsiao, C., 489
Hsin, A., 323–324, 325
Hsu, L. K. G., 519
Hsu, L. M., 351
Hu, V. W., 507
Huang, C-M, 152
Huang, M., 289
Hubbard, J., 17
Hubel, D., 177
Hudson, A., 437
Hudson, J., 248
Hudson, J. A., 247, 248
Hudziak, J. J., 422
Huesmann, L. R., 420
Huff, S. M., 558
Hughes, C., 401, 403, 404
Hughes, D., 346
Hughes, E. K., 437
Hughes, F., 381

Hughes, J. P., 146
Huguley, S., 495
Hui, D., 208
Huizink, A. C., 340
Hull, J., 473
Hulme, C., 319
Hultman, C. M., 509
Hultsch, D. F., 259
Hummert, M. L., 350
Humphries, T., 174
Hung, L., 254
Hunt, C., 113
Hunt, E., 325
Hunter, J. E., 279
Huntington, R., 537
Hurd, R. C., 556
Hurst, A. J., 157
Hurst, K., 520
Hurst, S., 414
Hurt, E., 514
Huston, A. C., 371
Huston, M., 492
Huston, T. L., 484
Hutchison, B., 347
Huynh, V., 151
Hwang, P., 292
Hwang, S., 424
Hybels, C. F., 525
Hyde, J. S., 113, 148, 368, 369, 384, 388, 484
Hyde, L. W., 503
Hyson, M. C., 311

I

Iacoboni, M., 403
Iacono, W. G., 78, 519
Imel, S., 328
Imperato-McGinley, J., 381
Imuta, K., 241
Inceoglu, I., 328
Infurna, F., 551
Ingersoll, B., 508
Ingoldsby, B. B., 483
Ingram, R. E., 505
Inhelder, B., 47, 219, 220, 249
Institute of Medicine, 496, 497, 498
Insurance Institute for Highway Safety, 194
International Human Genome Sequencing
    Consortium, 63
International Labor Organization, 51
Inzlicht, M., 290
Ippolito, M., 384
Ippolito, M. R., 384
Isaacs, K. R., 161
Isabella, R. A., 445

Islam, N., 18
Ittel, A., 481
Ive, S., 519
Iyengar, S. D., 116
Izard, C. E., 434, 435
Izquierdo, C., 3, 4, 8

J

Jaakkola, R., 545
Jaccard, J., 325
Jack, F., 246, 247
Jacklin, C. N., 374
Jackson, C., 392
Jackson, J. J., 355, 488
Jackson, J. S., 429
Jackson, P. W., 275
Jacob, B. A., 320
Jacobs, H. S., 155
Jacobs, J. E., 226, 370
Jacobs, R. J., 394
Jacobs, S. C., 54, 542
Jacobson, J. L., 102
Jacobson, S. W., 102
Jacobvitz, D., 555
Jacques, S., 437
Jadva, V., 371
Jaeger, G. J., 272
Jaffe, J., 443
Jaffee, S. R., 423, 496
Jager, T., 439
Jakub, D. K., 553
Jalmsell, L., 546, 547
Jambon, M., 416, 417
James, J., 53, 146
James, J. B., 357
James, S., 494
James, W., 167
Jamison, K. R., 550
Jampol, N. S., 455
Janevic, M. R., 458
Jankowiak, W. R., 459
Jankowski, J. J., 274
Jansen, M. D., 492
Janus, C. L., 382
Janus, J. S., 382
Jaquish, G. A., 286
Jarvis, P., 460
Jasiⓧska, K. K., 313
Jastrzembski, T. S., 254
Jaswal, R., 113
Jauregui, A., 185
Jayawardena, K. M., 496
Jayawardhana, J., 463
Je, J. H., 157

Keller, B., 479

Keller, H., 299, 308, 338

Keller, K. L., 140

Kelley, E., 509

Kellman, P. J., 169

Kellogg, N. D., 382

Kelly, D. J., 346

Kelly, J., 486, 493, 494

Kelsall, D. C., 196

Kember, D., 328

Kemp, S., 254

Kempe, C. H., 496

Kempe, R. S., 496

Kemper, S., 327

Kempermann, G., 134, 152

Kemtes, K. A., 327

Kendall-Tackett, K. A., 383

Kendeou, P., 319

Kendler, K. S., 82, 386, 503

Kendrick, C., 479

Keniston, K., 5

Kennedy, D. P., 269

Kennedy, J. F., 23

Kenney, E. L., 140

Kenny, L. C., 107

Kenny, M. E., 454

Kenny, S. L., 205, 227

Kensinger, E. A., 138

Kenward, B., 310

Kenyon, D. B., 423

Keppler, A., 446

Keppler, H., 186

Keren, M., 510

Kerig, P. K., 462

Kerka, S., 328

Kermoian, R., 171

Kern, M. L., 355

Kerns, K. A., 448, 450

Kerr, M., 456

Kessler, R. C., 513, 516, 518, 525

Kett, J. F., 8

Kettlewell, H. B. D., 61

Key, A. C., 385

Khaleque, A., 475

Kho, Y., 555

Khurana, A., 143, 251

Kidd, C., 415

Kiecolt, K. J., 495–496

Kiely, K. M., 193

Killen, M., 416, 417, 455

Kilmer, R. P., 557

Kim, G., 435

Kim, J., 480

Kim, J. M., 373

Kim, K., 172

Kim, K. H., 275, 278

Kim, M., 175

Kim, P., 8, 450, 477

Kim, S., 369, 446

Kim, S. Y., 476

Kim, T., 356

Kim, Y. D., 110

Kim, Y. S., 424

Kimber, M., 520

Kimbro, R. T., 140

Kim-Cohen, J., 498

Kimmel, D. C., 492

King, P. E., 428, 429

King, S., 78

King, V., 494, 495

Kingston, H. M., 70

Kingstone, A., 183

Kinney, D., 455

Kinsella, K. G., 157

Kintsch, W., 253

Kinzler, C. D., 428

Kipp, K., 221

Kirby, D., 56

Kirchhoff, B. A., 252

Kirchmeyer, C., 358

Kirkup, G., 369

Kirmeyer, S. E., 109

Kisilevsky, B. S., 175, 177

Kissane, D. W., 550, 559

Kitayama, S., 351, 352

Kitson, G. C., 493

Kitzmann, K. M., 473

Kjerulff, K., 114

Klaczynski, P. A., 222, 224, 226, 247, 261

Klass, D., 537, 555

Klaus, R. A., 312

Klebanov, P., 291

Klebold, D., 467, 468

Klebold, S., 467–468, 478

Klein, D., 313

Klein, S. I., 543

Kleinman, R. E., 514

Kliegel, M., 439

Klin, A., 507, 508

Kline, D. W., 194, 195

Klinger, R. L., 279, 280

Klipker, K., 438

Klump, K. L., 519

Knaapila, A., 176

Knafo-Noam, A., 413

Knapp, C., 548

Knecht, S., 138

Knee, D. O., 558

Knerr, W., 498

Knight, B. G., 489, 525

Knight, G. P., 346, 423

Knight, J. A., 160

Knopf, I., 185

Knopik, V. S., 102, 103

Knott, L. M., 248

Knudsen, D. D., 495

Kobak, R. R., 462

Kobayashi, L., 115

Kobor, M. S., 83, 85, 98, 99

Kochanska, G., 407, 408, 414, 418, 419, 427, 446, 448

Kochkin, S., 186

Kodama, K., 105

Kodish, E., 27, 28

Koehler, K., 553

Koehoorn, M., 146

Koerber, S., 224

Kogan, N., 276

Kogan, S. M., 383

Kohlberg, L., 35, 378–379, 407–410, 412–413, 416–419, 423, 425–430

Kohn, M. L., 359, 478

Kojima, H., 6

Kokkinos, C. M., 455

Kokko, K., 24

Kolb, B., 134

Kolstad, V., 241

Kong, A., 67

Koocher, G. P., 545, 548

Kopp, C. B., 51, 435

Koppel, J., 255

Korbin, J. E., 497

Korbut, O., 278

Korf, B. R., 70

Koropeckyj-Cox, T., 492

Kosberg, J. I., 490

Kosciw, J. G., 386

Kosloski, K., 360

Koss, M. P., 496

Kost, K., 391

Kotilahti, K., 138

Kotter-Grühn, D., 350, 351

Kovshoff, H., 184

Kowal, A., 480

Kowalski, R. M., 13

Krakow, J. B., 51

Kramer, D. A., 228

Krause, N., 429, 462, 463

Kraushaar, J. M., 185

Kravetz, S., 545

Kreager, D. A., 388

Krebs, C. P., 390

Krebs, D. L., 411

Kreicbergs, U., 546

Kretch, K. S., 171

Krettenauer, T., 419
Krile, D., 405
Kristen-Antonow, S., 337–338
Kroger, J., 345, 348, 356
Krogh, K. M., 327, 328
Krokstad, S., 195
Krowitz, A., 171
Krucoff, C., 156
Krueger, L. E., 258
Krueger, R. F., 77, 82, 353
Kruse, J., 559
Ku, S. Y., 146
Kübler-Ross, E., 539–541, 558
Kuczynski, L., 479
Kuebli, J., 247, 377
Kuehner, C., 525
Kuh, D., 154
Kuhl, P., 173, 306
Kuhl, P. K., 173, 309
Kuhn, D., 222, 224
Kuk, L. S., 348
Kulathilaka, S., 553
Kull, R. M., 386
Kumar, P., 106
Kuncel, N. R., 279
Kunter, M., 320
Kuny-Slock, A. V., 422
Kunz, J. A., 357
Kupersmidt, J. B., 290, 452, 453
Kurdek, L. A., 405, 486, 492
Kurowski, C. O., 436
Kushnir, T., 218
Kwak, J., 535
Kwak, K., 435
Kwan, V. S. Y., 353

L

Labouvie-Vief, G., 227, 229, 438
Lachance, J. A., 368
Lachman, M., 21–22, 24
Lachman, M. E., 22, 261
Ladd, G. W., 453
Laflamme, D., 473
LaFranchi, S. H., 130
LaFreniere, L., 547
Lagercrantz, H., 173, 306
Lahav, A., 173
Lai, E. R., 251
Lai, M., 509
Laird, R. D., 475
Lalande, K. L., 555
Lamb, M. E., 118, 469, 472, 473
Lambert, S. R., 178
Lamborn, S. D., 475, 482
Lamm, C., 403

Lammlein, S. E., 360
Lampinen, P., 157
Lampl, M., 134
Lampman-Petraitis, C., 438
Landen, J., 150
Landreth, G., 452
Landrigan, P. J., 107
Landry, S. H., 122, 123, 288
Lane, J. D., 416
Lane, M. A., 160
Lang, F. R., 350, 359, 439, 458
Lange, G., 493
Langer, A., 171
Langer, E., 351
Langer, E. J., 351
Langley, K., 111
Langley, L. K., 192
Langley-Evans, A. J., 110
Langley-Evans, S. C., 110
Långström, N., 387
Lanpher, B., 292
Lansford, J. E, 53, 421, 422, 423
Lansford, J. E., 423, 470, 475, 494, 497
Lantos, J., 27
Laopaiboon, M., 107
Laplante, D. P., 109
Lappin, S., 303
Lapsley, D. K., 416
Laris, B. A., 56
Larkina, M., 254
Larose, S., 454
Larsen, J. T., 436
Larson, R., 324, 438
Larson, R. W., 480
Larsson, H., 82, 422
Larsson, I., 382
Larsson, M., 196
La Rue, A., 526, 528, 530
Lash, A., 195
Latack, J. A., 556
Laucht, M., 514
Laughon, S. K., 113
Laungani, P., 536
Laureau, A., 309
Laurens, K. R., 78
Laursen, B., 346, 456, 481, 482
Lauzen, M. M., 378
Lavner, J. A., 484
LaVoie, J. C., 345
Law, R. W., 493
Lawson, K. R., 183
Lazarus, R. S., 436, 438
Leader, L. R., 239
Leaper, C., 370, 371, 374, 377
Lears, M., 378

LeBlanc, A. G., 141
Le Blanc, M., 352
Lechner, C. M., 553
Leckman, J. F., 441
LeCompte, D. C., 259
Lederberg, A. R., 304
Lederman, S. A., 106
Lee, G. R., 491
Lee, G. Y., 175
Lee, J., 323, 324, 389
Lee, J. K., 242
Lee, J. M., 146
Lee, K., 404
Lee, K. S., 492
Lee, N. Y. L., 427
Lee, S. J., 43
Lee, S. W., 152
Lee, S. Y., 324
Leeder, E. J., 468
Leenarts, L. E. W., 498
Leerkes, E. M., 340, 446
Lee-Shin, Y., 451
Lefkowitz, E. S., 389
Legare, C. H., 548
Leggett, E. L., 315
Lehman, D. R., 556
Lehman, H., 285
Leichtman, M. D., 247
Leiden Conference, 447
Leinbach, M. D., 371, 373, 376, 377
Lemanski, N., 324
LeMare, L. J., 405
Lemire, R. J., 102, 103
Lemke, L., 269
LeMoyne, T., 483
Leng, L., 504
L'Engle, K. L., 392
Lenhart, A., 13
Lenze, S., 517
Leo, A. J., 171
Leon, D. A., 280
Leon, G. R., 518
Leonard, K. E., 103
Leong, D. J., 209, 210
Leopold, T., 553
Lepore, J., 11
LePore, P. C., 326
Lerner, J. V., 423
Lerner, M. J., 488
Lerner, R. M., 32, 50, 52, 228, 423
Leslie, A., 400
Lester, D., 523
Lester, P., 447
Lettre, G., 128
Leudar, I., 555

Leutwyler, B., 251
LeVay, S., 387
Leve, L. D., 377
Levenkron, S., 519
Levenson, R. W., 438, 487
Leventhal, B., 424
Levin, J. R., 251
Levine, C. G., 348
Levinson, D., 357–358, 497
Levit-Dori, T., 224
Levitt, H. M., 384
Levitt, M. J., 462
Levitt, P., 303
Levkoff, S., 360
Levy, B., 351
Levy, B. R., 258, 350, 351
Levy, G. D., 372
Levy, M. L., 359
Levy, S., 462
Levy-Shiff, R., 484, 485
Lew, A. R., 214
Lewin-Bizan, S., 494
Lewinter-Suskind, L., 309
Lewis, B. A., 103
Lewis, C., 469, 472
Lewis, D. A., 338
Lewis, G. J., 286
Lewis, M., 337, 434, 435, 441, 443, 503
Lewis, P. G., 547
Lewis, R., 67, 68, 85, 435
Lewis, T., 178
Lewis, T. L., 178
Lewontin, R., 290
Li, D., 354
Li, K. Z. H., 258
Li, N., 369
Li, R. Y. H., 372
Li, S., 261
Li, W., 490
Liao, S., 496
Liben, L., 381
Liben, L. S., 347, 380
Libertus, K., 177
Lick, D. J., 492
Lickliter, R., 61, 65, 73, 83, 170
Lidz, J., 303
Lieberman, A. F., 462, 547
Lieberman, M. A., 494, 559
Liégeois, F., 138
Light, L. L., 327
Liker, J. K., 12
Lillard, A. S., 452
Lim, F., 423
Lim, S., 140
Limber, S. P., 424

Lincoln, C. R., 485
Lindahl, K. M., 469
Lindau, S. T., 394, 396
Lindberg, S. M., 384
Lindell, S. G., 84
Lindenberger, U., 12, 25, 197, 220, 258, 260, 261, 360, 438
Lindgren, M., 308
Lindin, M., 259
Lindsey, D. T., 169
Lindsey, E. W., 473
Lindstrom, R., 495
Linehan, C., 292
Ling, J. M., 144
Linn, M. C., 368
Lintern, V., 373, 374
Lipina, S. J., 275, 287, 288
Lippa, R. A., 387
Lippman, J. G., 547
Lipshultz, L. I., 153
Lipsitt, L. P., 11
Liptak, G. S., 93, 94, 103
Lipton, A. M., 528
Lisdahl, K. M., 520
Listfield, E., 521
Litman, L., 240
Litovsky, R. Y., 174
Little, M., 547
Little, T. D., 294
Litwin, H., 462
Liu, C., 394
Liu, D., 402, 403, 404
Liu, H., 428
Liu, L., 137
Livesley, W. J., 341, 404, 405
Livingston, G., 470, 473
Livson, F., 354
Llewelyn, J. G., 197
Lloyd, M. E., 236, 238
Lobjois R., 156
Lobo, S. A., 181
LoBue, V., 171
Lockheed, M. E., 381
Lockl, K., 245
Lodi-Smith, J., 352, 353
Loehlin, J. C., 73, 77, 80, 81
Loewenstein, G., 389
Lofthouse, N., 514
Loh, V., 359
Lohan, J., 552
Lohan, J. A., 553
Lohaugen, G. C., 251
Lohman, B. J., 56
Lohr, M. J., 456
London, K., 373

Longino, C. F., Jr., 470
Longmore, M. A., 482
Longoria, N., 447
Lonigan, C. J., 318, 319
Loovis, E. M., 181
Lopata, H. Z., 550, 556, 557
Lopez, O. L., 256
López-Teijón, M., 172
LoPresti, M. A., 558
Lorber, M. F., 484
Lord, S., 323
Loree, M., 492
Lorenz, F. O., 486
Lorenz, K., 440–441
Lorsbach, T. C., 251
Losada, A., 489
Loudenberg, R., 102
Lougheed, J. P., 438
Lourenço, O., 49, 205, 210
Lovaas, O. I., 509
Lövdén, M., 260
Lovegreen, L. D., 486
Lovén, J., 369
Lovett, B. J., 421
Lövgren, M., 553
Lowe, J. C., 7
Lu, P. H., 152
Lu, T., 447
Lubin, A., 220
Lubinski, D., 294
Luby, J. L., 510, 515, 516, 517
Lucas, C. G., 5
Lucas, R. E., 355
Lucas, T., 449
Lucio, R., 325
Lucki, I., 152
Lüdtke, O, 354
Luecken, L. J., 547, 559
Luk, G., 313
Luke, C., 347
Luke, M. A., 461
Luking, K. R., 516
Lukowski, A. F., 241
Luo, Y., 463
Luong, G., 439
Lupsakko, T. A., 196
Luria, A., 207
Luria, Z., 370
Lustig, J. L., 494
Luthar, S. S., 486, 551
Lyketsos, C. G., 526, 527
Lykken, D. T., 78, 79
Lynam, D., 420, 423
Lynch, M. E., 384
Lynch, M. P., 189

McAdams, D. P., 334, 342, 346, 356, 357
McAdams, R. M., 104
McAlister, A., 403
McCabe, E. R. B., 64
McCabe, J. E., 116
McCabe, L. L., 64
McCabe, M., 342
McCabe, M. P., 147, 519
McCall, R. B., 19, 274, 447
McCarroll, B., 510
McCarthy, J. R., 548
McCartney, K., 76, 80, 82
McCarton, C. M., 123
McCartt, A. T., 194
McCarty, C. A., 516
McCarty, F., 392
McCaul, E. J., 325
McClain, L., 484, 485
McClintock, M., 130, 382–383
McClintock, M. K., 130
McCloskey, L. A., 496
McCormick, M. C., 123
McCoy, S., 195
McCoyd, J. L. M., 540, 544, 548, 553
McCrae, R. R., 286, 335, 336, 352–353, 354
McCullough, B. M., 24
McCune, L., 306
McDevitt-Murphy, M., 556
McDonald, A., 95, 105
McDonald, R., 496
McDonough, C., 308
McDowell, E. E., 535
McDowell, M. A., 146
McElhaney, K. B., 475, 482
McEvoy, J., 292
McFall, R. M., 11
McFarland, D., 455
McGaugh, J. L., 235
McGaw, B., 21
McGillivray, S., 258
McGinley, M., 414
McGoldrick, M., 468, 470, 494, 537, 550, 556
McGowan, P. O., 84, 496
McGue, M., 76, 79, 482, 519, 522
McGuire, S., 480
McHale, J., 469
McHale, J. P., 469
McHale, S. J., 322
McHale, S. M., 377, 475, 480, 484, 485–486
McInnes, R. R., 66, 70
McIntosh, D. N., 403
McIsaac, C., 456, 457
McKenna, L., 309
McKinney, C., 428
McKitrick, L. A., 261

McKnew, D. H., Jr., 516
McKusick, V. A., 67
McLanahan, S. S., 7, 525
McLean, K. C., 346
McLoyd, V. C., 475
McMahon, E., 173
McMenamy, J. M., 436
McNair, J. L., 487
McNeill, D., 305
McShane, K., 413
Meade, C. S., 389
Meadows-Orlans, K. P., 196
Mealey, L., 503
Meaney, M. J., 65, 79, 83, 84, 85
Meck, S., 234, 237, 246
Medina, J., 160, 536
Medina, R. A., 261
Meeus, W. H. J., 482
Mehler, J., 306
Meier, R. P., 304
Meijer, S., 56
Meilman, P., 344, 345
Meins, E., 216, 403
Meir, E. I., 348
Melby-Lerväg, M., 319
Melchior, J., 228
Melhem, N. M., 548, 549
Mellinger, J. C., 328
Meltzoff, A. N., 240, 311, 403
Melz, H., 484
Melzer, D., 157
Melzi, G., 313
Menacker, F., 114
Menaghan, E. G., 494
Mendel, G., 66, 67
Mendle, J., 147, 457, 518
Mendola, P., 101, 145
Mendoza, B. L., 553
Mennella, J. A., 175, 176, 187, 188
Menon, U., 358
Ment, L. R., 122
Merikangas, K. R., 516, 518
Mernitz, S. E., 484
Mertesacker, B., 436
Meschke, L. L., 389
Mesquita, B., 437
Messer, D. J., 311
Messinger-Rapport, B. J., 194
Metcalf, P., 537
Metcalfe, J., 251
Meulemans, T., 244
Meulenbroek, O., 259
Meydani, M., 160
Meyer, F., 442, 453

Meyer, H., 300
Meyer, S., 414
Meyer-Bahlburg, H. F. L., 368, 376, 387
Meyerhoefer, C., 155
Meyer-Schiffer, P., 96
Mezulis, A. H., 523
Micali, N., 520
Micalizzi, L., 77, 340
Michael, S. L., 142
Michalska, K. J., 428
Miche, M., 350
Michel, M. K., 436
Michelangelo, 285
Mickelson, K., 350
Middleton, F., 514
Midgley, C., 323
Miech, R., 521
Mikulincer, M., 460, 555
Milaniak, I., 496
Milgram, J. I., 488
Milgram, S., 28
Milkie, M. A., 484, 486
Miller, G. E., 453
Miller, I. J., 188
Miller, J., 495
Miller, J. G., 27, 425, 426, 446
Miller, J. K., 236, 238
Miller, J. W., 496
Miller, N. B., 475
Miller, P., 250, 251
Miller, P. H., 32, 53, 55, 167, 185, 201, 203, 205
Miller, P. J., 545
Miller, R. A., 159
Miller, S. A., 14, 15, 17, 27, 288, 402, 403, 404
Miller, T. R., 524
Miller-Johnson, S., 453
Mills, C. J., 315
Milofsky, E., 356
Milos, G., 518
Mineka, S., 46
Miniño, A. M., 538
Minkin, M. J., 154
Minnes, S., 103
Mireault, G., 547
Misa, T. J., 369
Mischel, W., 336, 415
Mishori, R., 174
Mishra, G. D., 154
Misra, S., 27
Mistry, J., 6
Mitchell, A. A., 99
Mitchell, B. A., 486
Mitchell, J. E., 520
Mitchell, K. J., 13

Mitnick, D. M., 484
Mitzner, T. L., 327
Mo, Y., 459
Mock, S. E., 386
Modell, B., 68
Moen, P., 8, 358
Moffitt, T., 415
Moffitt, T. E., 342, 420, 488, 505
Mohammed, A. H., 275
Mohd Salleh, S. B., 208
Mok, K., 313
Molaison, H., 236, 237
Molenaar, P. C. M., 50, 52
Molfese, V. J., 288
Molina, B. S. G., 147, 515
Molina, G. B., 56
Mollborn, S., 7
Molteni, R., 150
Monahan, K. C., 420, 456
Mondloch, C. J., 178, 183
Mondschein, E. R., 381
Money, J., 375, 376, 381, 387
Monk, C. E., 172, 175
Monroe, S. M., 506
Monsour, A., 343
Montemayor, R., 343
Monti, M. M., 535
Moog, N. K., 130
Moon, C., 173, 306
Moon, S., 294
Moor, N., 552
Moore, A. B., 427
Moore, D. R., 184
Moore, D. S., 65, 83, 84, 85, 496
Moore, E. G. J., 289, 290
Moore, J. W., 7
Moore, K. L., 100
Moore, M. K., 182, 240
Moors, A. C., 388
Morales, J., 313
Moran, J. M., 406
Morasch, K. C., 240
Morelli, G., 446, 447
Morelli, G. A., 450
Moreno, M. A., 185
Morgan, E., 386
Morgan, G. A., 443
Morgan, M., 116–117
Morgan, P. L., 308
Morin, A. J. S., 344
Morin, R., 26
Morina, N., 555
Morizot, J., 352
Morley, G., 156

Morris, A. T., 553
Morris, J. T., 378
Morris, P., 8
Morris, P. A., 50, 51, 52, 469
Morris, R., 376
Morrison. L. A., 154
Morrongiello, B., 377
Morrow, D. G., 327
Morse, C. A., 154
Morse, J. Q., 461, 490
Morsella, E., 39
Mortimer, J. T., 326
Mory, M. S., 455
Moser, J. S., 314
Mosher, W. D., 389, 394
Moskey, E. G., 387
Moskovic, D. J., 153
Moskowitz, J. T., 552
Moss, M. S., 553
Moss, P., 509
Motzoi, C., 442, 453
Moxley, J. H., 253
Mroczek, D. K., 352, 438
Mueller, E., 449
Mueller, M. K., 423
Muir, D. W., 177
Mulatu, M. S., 359
Mullally, P. R., 351, 352
Müller, V., 438
Mundy, L., 414
Munro, E. R., 448
Munroe, R. L., 450
Murayama, K., 316
Murdoch, A., 317
Murdock, C., 347
Murnen, S. K., 378, 519
Murphy, E. M., 496
Murphy, G., 292
Murphy, M. L. M., 453
Murphy, S. A., 552, 553, 559
Murphy, S. L., 538
Murray, C., 289, 290
Murray, I., 115
Murray, L., 117, 435
Murray-Close, D., 369
Musil, C. M., 487
Mustanski, B., 384, 457
Myers, J. K., 525
Myrskylä, M., 485

N

Na, H. R., 529, 530
Nagel, S. K., 485
Nagy, G., 354

Naigles, L. G., 308
Naigles, L. R., 307
Naito, E., 254
Nakamura, J., 285
Nanayakkara, A. R., 315
Nanez, J. E., 171
Napoli, D. J., 174
Narayan, M., 256
Narciso, I., 553
Nash, A., 449
Nass, C., 186
National Center for Chronic Disease Prevention and Health Promotion, 149, 150
National Center for Education Statistics, 325, 328
National Center for Health Statistics, 8–9, 107, 109, 140
National Eye Institute, 193
National Human Genome Research Institute, 69, 70
National Institute of Child Health and Human Development, 448
National Institute of General Medical Sciences, 63
National Institute on Aging, 154, 528
National Institute on Deafness and Other Communication Disorders, 186, 193
National Institutes of Health, 193
National Osteoporosis Foundation, 155
National Research Council, 496, 497, 498
National Safety Commission, 194
National Sleep Foundation, 150
National Vital Statistics System, 107, 109, 139, 140
Natsuaki, M. N., 523
Neale, M. C., 78
Nebes, R. D., 255
Neblett, E. W. J., 346
Nederend, S., 384
Needham, A., 177, 182
Needle, E., 325
Negri, R., 188
Neiderhiser, J., 82
Neiderhiser, J. M., 479
Neighbors, H. W., 526
Neil, A., 110
Neimark, E. D., 226
Neimeyer, R. A., 551, 555, 557, 559
Neisser, U., 278, 279, 289, 290
Nelson, C. A., 134, 238, 303
Nelson, G., 403
Nelson, J. M., 428, 429
Nelson, K., 209, 247, 248

Pinhas, L., 518
Pinker, S., 302, 305, 308
Pinquart, M., 462, 489
Piontelli, A., 96, 97
Piopiunik, M., 320
Piper, W. E., 555, 556
Pipp, S., 338
Pipp, S. L., 205, 211, 227
Pittinsky, T. L., 290
Pittman, J. F., 347
Planalp, E. M., 473
Plassman, B., 256
Pleck, J. H., 472
Plomin, R., 10, 34, 63, 67, 72, 73, 74, 75, 76, 77, 78, 79, 80, 82, 276, 286, 287, 511
Ploughman, M., 142
Plucker, J. A., 272
Pluhar, E. I., 392
Poehlmann, J., 446
Pogue-Geile, M. F., 78
Polakowski, L. L., 101
Polderman, T. J. C., 78
Pomerantz, E. M., 341, 352, 377, 475, 476, 482
Pomerleau, A., 370, 473
Ponirakis, A., 147
Ponton, L., 388
Ponton, M. K., 347
Ponzone, A., 177
Poon, H. F., 159
Popenoe, D., 470, 471
Popli, G., 288
Poppie, K., 489
Porcher, N., 529
Porfeli, E. J., 347
Porter, R. H., 176
Portes, A., 320
Portley, R. M., 493
Posada, G., 447
Potter, L., 68
Poulin-Dubois, D., 307, 371
Powdhavee, N., 357
Powell, M. P., 68
Power, F. C., 423
Power, L., 428
Power, T. G., 342, 454
Powers, C. J., 453
Powers, H. J., 110
Powers, S. I., 463
Powlishta, K. K., 372
Pozzoli, T., 411
Prats-Galino, A., 172
Pratt, H. D., 520
Pratt, J., 368
Pratt, M. W., 209, 346, 409, 419, 425, 428

Premack, D., 413
Prescott, C., 522
Prescott, C. A., 503
Presnell, K., 520
Pressley, M., 244, 250, 251
Price, J. M., 505
Price, R. H., 359
Prieler, M., 378
Priess, H. A., 384, 484
Prigerson, H. G., 541, 542, 550, 552
Prinsen, T. J., 378
Prinstein, M. J., 389, 453
Prior, E., 113
Prior, J. C., 146
Pritchard, D. J., 70
Provenzano, F. J., 370
Pruden, S. M., 307
Pruett, J. H., 553
Pudrovska, T., 491, 492
Pulkkinen, L., 24
Puma, M., 312
Purifoy, F. E., 396
Putnam, f. w., 383
Putnam, F. W., 383
Putnam, R., 475
Putnam, S. P., 339
Pyszczynski, T., 534, 537, 548

Q

Qin, j., 105
Qin, L., 352
Qu, Y., 143
Qualls, S. H., 490
Qualter, P., 463
Queen, T. L., 406
Quevedo, K., 510
Qui, C., 527, 528
Quigley, B. A., 328
Quigley, M. A., 119
Quinn, P. C., 371
Quinsey, V. L., 421

R

Rabbani, A., 146
Raby, K. L., 446, 461
Racine, S. E., 519
Rackham, D. D., 428
Raggi, V. L., 515
Ragow-O'Brien, D., 558
Ramachandran, V. S., 403
Ramani, G. B., 449
Ramirez-Esparza, N., 309
Rampell, C., 486
Ramsey, B. K., 312

Ramsey, E., 421
Ramvi, E., 114
Rana, N., 113
Rando, T. A., 541
Rangmar, J., 102
Rantanen, T., 156
Raphael, B., 548
Rapkin, B. D., 328
Rapoport, J. L., 502
Rapson, R. L., 459
Rasch, B., 235
Rasoulinejad, S. A., 192
Ratey, J. J., 157
Rattaz, C., 176
Rauch, J., 357
Raver, C., 8
Ray, L. A., 489
Raymo, J. M., 490
Raynor, R., 41
Re, L., 68
Read, S., 520
Reagan, R., 527
Ream, G. L., 386
Rebacz, E., 146
Rebok, G., 258
Reczek, C., 492
Redekop, F., 347
Reed, A., 43, 419, 423
Reed, A. E., 439
Reed, D. R., 188
Reed, M. J., 310
Reed, T., 157
Rees, M., 146
Reese, E., 247, 338
Reese, H. W., 11, 53
Reeves, R. V., 42, 43
Regan, P. C., 458, 459, 483
Regier, D. A., 525
Rehnman, J., 369
Reich, S. M., 13
Reichow, B., 509
Reid, L. M., 255
Reid, M. W., 506
Reid, T. R., 7, 360
Reilly, D., 368
Reimer, J. F., 251
Reingold, E. M., 253
Reinhardt, J. P., 192
Reinherz, H. Z., 518
Reis, H. T., 458, 459, 460, 461, 487
Reis, S. M., 293
Reiser, L. W., 147
Reiss, D., 73, 78, 82, 479
Reiter, A. R., 176

Silventoinen, K., 146
Silver, R. C., 554
Silverman, I. W., 407
Silverman, L. R., 454
Silverman, P. R., 547, 548, 550, 556
Silvers, J. A., 438
Silverstein, M., 470, 471, 487, 489
Sim, L. A., 520
Simcock, G., 240, 246–247
Simion, F., 170
Simmons, R. G., 148, 323, 344
Simon, G., 218
Simon, H. A., 234
Simon, L. S., 279, 280
Simon, T., 267
Simons, L. G., 390
Simons-Morton, B. G., 522
Simonton, D. K., 272, 276, 285–286, 358
Simpson, J. A., 146, 448, 461
Sinan, B., 556
Sinclair, D. A., 91
Singer, D. G., 452
Singer, T., 283
Singh, D., 187
Singh, F., 156
Singh, P., 424
Sinigaglia, C., 403
Sinnott, J. D., 227, 228
Sionean, C., 389, 394
Sisler, A., 481
Skinner, B. F., 31, 32, 40–41, 43–46, 54–57, 255, 416, 421, 547
Skinner, E. A., 547
Skoe, E., 173
Skoog, T., 148
Slaby, R. G., 421, 423
Slade, M. D., 350
Slade, P., 117
Slaten, E., 488
Slater, A., 169, 214
Slater, C. L., 356
Slater, R., 177
Slatin, B., 269
Slaughter, V., 402, 403, 545
Slavich, G. M., 453
Slavkin, M., 394
Sloane, S., 413
Slobin, D. I., 309
Sloboda, Z., 522
Slotkin, T. A., 101
Slusarcick, A. L., 325
Slykerman, R. F., 109
Small, B. J., 259
Small, M., 118

Small, S. L., 302
Smart, D., 478
Smetana, J., 417
Smetana, J. G., 416, 417
Smith, A. D., 256
Smith, A. K., 487
Smith, C. H., 383
Smith, G. E., 527, 528
Smith, G. J. W., 451–452
Smith, G. T., 390
Smith, J., 285
Smith, J. T., 69
Smith, K. E., 122, 288
Smith, L. B., 180
Smith, M. L., 21
Smith, P., 251
Smith, P. J., 114, 137
Smith, P. K., 424
Smith, R. L., 378, 455
Smith, R. S., 122
Smith, S., 483
Smith, T., 509
Smith Slep, A. M., 484, 495
Smitsman, A. W., 180
Smolak, L., 519
Smolkowski, K., 518
Smyer, M. A., 526
Snarey, J. R., 425–426
Sneed, J. R., 356
Sneed, L., 120
Snider, J. B., 475
Snow, D., 307
Snowdon, D., 161
Sobolewski, J. M., 493, 494
Soderstrom, M., 306
Sodian, B., 224, 245, 401
Soederberg, L. M., 327
Søfting, G. H., 547
Sohrabvand, F., 91
Sokol, B. W., 416
Solomon, B. C., 488
Solomon, F., 547
Solomon, J., 444
Solomon, S., 534
Solso, S., 508
Soltys, F. G., 357
Somerville, L. H., 143, 344
Sommer, G., 130
Sommerville, J. A., 413, 414
Song, H., 152
Song, J., 360, 480
Sonksen, P. H., 130
Sookoian, S., 99
Sorbring, E., 475

Sorensen, A. B., 7, 525
Sorensen, L. C., 423
Sorensen, S., 489
Sorenson, S., 462
Soriano, F. I., 423
Sorkhabi, N., 475, 476
Sorokowska, A., 189
Sorri, M., 196
Sostek, A. M., 27
Soto, C. J., 342
Sotomayor, S., 333, 334
Soubry, A., 111
Soulsby, L. K., 552
Soussignan, R., 176
Span, P., 486
Sparks, A., 504, 508
Sparks, R. L., 317
Sparks, T. A., 311
Spear, L. P., 145, 520
Spearman, C., 266
Speece, D. L., 319
Speece, M. W., 545
Spelke, E. J., 172
Spelke, E. S., 169, 171, 172
Spence, I., 368
Spence, J. T., 327, 393
Spence, M., 175
Spencer, D., 376
Spencer, J. P., 441
Spencer, M. B., 27, 180, 181, 346
Spencer, P. E., 304
Spencer, S., 290
Spenser, K. A., 421
Sperling, M. B., 454
Sperling, S. A., 528
Spiby, H., 117
Spiegelman, D., 509
Spieler, D. H., 327
Spilman, S. K., 429
Spinath, B., 315
Spinrad, T. L., 338, 413
Spitz, R. A., 510
Spitze, G., 486
Spokane, A. R., 348
Spoth, R., 522
Springer, S., 138
Spruyt, K., 136
Spunt, R. P., 403
Squire, L. R., 236, 269
Squires, B., 304
Sroufe, A., 503
Sroufe, L. A., 443, 448, 449, 496, 503
Stacey, J., 473
Staff, J., 326, 388

Wiseman, R. A., 114
Witte, K., 347
Wittenborn, A. K., 462
Wittlinger, R. P., 257
Wittmann, B. C., 16
Wlodkowski, R. J., 327
Wodrich, D. L., 68
Woehr, D. J., 358
Woelfle, J., 146
Woerner, A., 96
Wohlfahrt-Veje, C., 107
Wojciszke, B., 367
Wolchik, S. A., 494
Wolery, M., 509
Wolfe, C. D., 243
Wolff, J. J., 508
Wolff, P. H., 442
Wolfner, G. D., 496, 497
Wolfson, A. R., 150
Wolke, D., 424
Women's Health Initiative, 154
Wong, B., 313
Wong, J. Y., 361
Wong, L. P., 153
Wong, P. T P., 328
Wong, P. T. P., 357
Wong, W. I., 372
Woo, S. M., 521, 524, 525
Wood, A. M., 355
Wood, D., 353, 354
Woodhill, B. M., 394
Woods, R., 371
Woodward, A. L., 401
Woodward, A. T., 526
Woodward, L., 494
Wooley, J. D., 217
Woolley, J. D., 217
Woolley, M. E., 488
Worchel, F. F., 546
Worden, J. W., 547, 548, 556
Worfolk, J. B., 197
World Health Organization (WHO), 514
Wortman, C. B., 550–551, 554, 556
Wright, F. L., 285
Wright, W. E., 159
Wrosch, C., 350
Wrzus, C., 438, 458
Wu, C. Y., 155
Wu, H., 489
Wu, J., 278

Wu, P., 228, 428
Wu, T., 145
Wu, Y., 91
Wubbena, Z. C., 220
Wurmser, H., 109
Wyatt, T., 436
Wynn, K., 401
Wysocki, C. J., 187
Wyss, N., 184

X

Xie, Y., 323–324, 325

Y

Yaffe, K., 157
Yahirun, J. J., 487
Yamazaki, K., 187
Yan, A. F., 149
Yan, B., 227
Yang, F., 354
Yang, T.-C., 101
Yassa, M. A., 242
Yau, P. L., 149
Yavorsky, J. E., 484
Yeager, D. S., 314, 315, 317
Yeates, K. O., 405
Yeh, Y., 278
Yendovitskaya, T. V., 183
Yeung, W. J., 289
Yilmaz, G., 119
Yin, B., 313
Yokum, S., 520
Yonas, A., 169, 171, 176
Yonkers, K. A., 153
Yoo, H., 509
Yoo, R. I., 217
Yorifuji, T., 106
Youn, G. Y., 490
Young, B., 536
Young, J. C., 497
Young, L. R., 150
Young, W. C., 376
Youngman, L., 110
Youngs, P., 320
Youniss, J., 441
Youth Risk Behavior Surveillance
    System, 149
Yu, T. J., 80, 155
Yu, Y., 218
Yuill, N., 404

Z

Zablotsky, B., 507
Zacher, H., 358
Zagoory-Sharon, O., 441
Zahn-Waxler, C., 413, 414, 423
Zaitchik, D., 49
Zajac, R., 248
Zajonc, R. B., 288
Zanjani, F. A. K., 282, 283
Zapfe, J. A., 142
Zaporozhets, A. V., 184
Zaragoza, S. A., 255
Zarit, S. H., 283, 489, 490
Zarratt, N. R., 314
Zarrett, N. R., 357
Zeanah, C. H., 447, 462, 510
Zehr, J. L., 148
Zelazo, D., 214
Zemach, I., 168, 169
Zemel, B., 132
Zenger, M., 359
Zero to Three, 510
Zerwas, S., 449
Zetterberg, M., 191
Zhai, Y., 490
Zhang, H., 490
Zhang, L., 228
Zhang, T., 65, 84
Zhou, M., 323, 324
Zhou, W., 119
Zhu, J., 114
Ziegler, A., 388
Zigler, E., 289, 292, 322, 341
Zigman, W. B., 68
Zimmer-Gembeck, M. J., 547
Zimmerman, F. J., 19–20, 130, 311
Zimmerman, R., 445
Zinbarg, R., 46
Zinke, K., 258
Zissimopoulos, J. M., 360
Zonderman, A. B., 525
Zosuls, K. M., 378, 379
Zucker, A. N., 345
Zukowski, A., 310
Zuvekas, S. H., 516
Zvoch, K., 320
Zwaigenbaum, L., 508
Zych, I., 424

Subject Index

Androgenized female, 376
Androgens, 130
Androgyny, 393–394
Andropause, 155
Anencephaly, 94
Anger, data collection methods for measuring, 17
Anorexia nervosa, 518–519
A-not-B error, 214
Anoxia, 113
Anterograde amnesia, 236
Anticipatory grief, 541
Antidepressant drugs, prenatal exposure to, 103
Antiepileptic drugs, prenatal exposure to, 103
Anti-Müllerian hormone, 154
Antioxidant, 159–160
Antisocial behavior
    adolescents, 420–424
    bullying, 423, 424
    coercive family environments, 421, 422
    conduct disorder, 420
    defined, 408
    Dodge's social information-processing model, 421
    genetics and, 78
    hostile attribution bias, 421
    infants, 413–414
    juvenile delinquency, 420
    nature–nurture issue, 422–423
    Patterson's model of development of, 421–422
    prevention, 423
    treatment, 423
Apgar test, 119–120
Aphasia, 302
Apolipoprotein E (APOE4) gene, 75
Applied behavior analysis (ABA), 509
Artificial insemination, 91
Asperger syndrome, 507
Asphyxia, 113
Assimilation, 203, 204
Assisted reproductive technologies (ARTs), 91
Assisted suicide, 535–536
Associative play, 451
At-risk infants
    identifying, 119–122
    newborns, 119–123
    skills for parenting, 123
Attachment. See also Relationships
    adult styles, 460–461, 462
    avoidant, 444
    bonding, 442
    caregiver's, to infant, 442–443
    caregiver's contributions, 444, 445
    cultural context, 446–447
    day care, 448
    defined, 440
    disorganized–disoriented, 444
    early, implications of, 447–449
    exploratory behavior, 443
    fears related to, 443
    infants, 441, 442–449
    insecure, 448–449
    internal working models of, 461
    later development, 441, 448–449
    nature–nurture issue, 440–441
    parent-adolescent, 454
    parent-child, 450
    quality of, 444–447
    resistant, 444
    secure, 444, 448–449, 462
    separations, 447–448
    social deprivation, 447
    temperament of infant, 446
Attachment theory, 440–441
Attention
    in adolescents, 185–186
    in children, 183–184
    defined, 183

multitasking, 185–186
    selective, 183–184
    span, 183–184
    systematic, 184
    visual search and, 192–193
Attention deficit hyperactivity disorder (ADHD),
        512–515
    causes, suspected, 513–514
    developmental course, 513
    genetics and, 68, 78
    recognizing, 514
    treatment, 514–515
Attention span, 183–184
Authoritarian parenting, 474, 475
Authoritative parenting, 474, 475, 476
Authority morality, 409
Autism spectrum disorder (ASD), 506–510
    Asperger syndrome, 507
    brain functioning, 508–509
    causes of, suspected, 509
    characteristics of, 508
    developmental outcomes and treatment, 509–510
    genetics and, 68, 68, 78
    rates of, 507–508
Autobiographical memory, 246–248
Automatization, 271
Autonomy, 482–483
Autonomy vs. shame and doubt, 37, 39, 355
Avoidant attachment, 444

B

Babbling, 307
Babinski reflex, 135, 136
Baby biographies, 11–12
Baby boom generation, 23
Baby boomlet. See Millennials
Bandura, Albert
    on sexual risk behavior, 45
    social cognitive theory, 43–45
Bayley Scales of Infant Development (BSID), 273
Behavior. See also Antisocial behavior; Sexual
        behavior
    after birth, developmental research on, 118
    exploratory, 443
    gender-typed, in children, 373–375
    moral, 410–411
    physical, in children, 138–139
    problem, in adolescents, 518
    prosocial, 407–408, 413
    risky, during adolescence, 143
Behavioral geneticists, 73, 74, 78, 79
Behavioral genetics, 72–79. See also Genetic
        influence
    adoption studies, 73
    breeding studies, 73
    defined, 72
    family studies, 73
    heritability, 73
    intellectual abilities, 76–77
    molecular genetics and, 75
    personality and, 77–78
    psychological disorders and, 78
    temperament and, 77–78
    twin studies, 73, 74, 75
Behavioral observations, 15–16, 17
Behavioral states
    infants, 136–137
Behaviorism, 41
Belief–desire psychology, 402, 403
Bereavement, 541–543
    among partners of gay men with HIV/AIDS, 552
    child, 547
    dual-process model of, 542–543
    dying, 559
    Family Bereavement Program, 559
    Parkes/Bowlby attachment model of, 541–542

posttraumatic growth, 557
    posttraumatic growth and, 557
Beta-amyloid, 527
Big Five trait dimensions, 335–336
Bilingual, 313–314
Binge eating disorder, 518–519
Bioecological model, 50–52
    environmental systems, 50–52
    in perspective, 54
    to reduce sexual risk behavior among teens, 56
    strengths and weaknesses of, 52
Biological aging, 5
Biological death, 534–535
Biological sex, 366–367
Biosocial theory, 375–376
Bipolar disorder, 68
Birth control pills, prenatal exposure to, 103
Blastocyst, 92
Body mass index (BMI), 140–141
Bonding, 442
Bonding phase of dating, 456
Bottle-feeding, 118–119
Brain
    adolescent development, 142–143
    adult, 151–153
    autism spectrum disorder, 508–509
    childhood development, 137–138
    damage, sports and, 144
    early experiences and, 177–178
    fetal development, 95, 96–97, 131
    hemispheres, 138
    infant development, 133–134, 177–178
    lateralization, 138
    neurogenesis, 151–152
    plasticity, 134
    regions associated with language
        development, 301–302
    theory of mind, 403
Breast-feeding, 118–119
Breathing reflex, 135, 136
Breech presentation, 113
Breeding studies, 73
Bronfenbrenner, Urie
    bioecological model, 32, 50–52
    on sexual risk behavior, 53
Bulimia nervosa, 518–519
Bullying, 423, 424

C

Caffeine consumption, prenatal exposure to, 103
Caloric restriction, 160
Careers
    aging worker, 359–360
    establishing, 358–359
    in human development (See Human
        development, careers in)
    job loss, 359
    retirement, 360–361
    success, academic achievement and, 325
    unemployment, 359
Caregiver
    attachment to infant, 442–443
    burden, 489–490
    contributions to attachment, 444, 445
    infant's attachment to, 443
Carrier, 69
Cascade model of substance use, 521–522
Case study, 17
Cataract, 178
Catch-up growth, 129
Categorical self, 337
Celiac disease, 128–129
Centenarians, 158
Central executive, 236
Centration, 217
Cephalocaudal principle, 132

I

Id, 36
Ideal self, 341–342
Ideational fluency, 272
Identical twins, 64
Identification, 37, 38
Identity
  adolescent, 344–348
  defined, 334
  developmental trends, 344–346
  ethnic, 346–347
  formation, 348
  narrative, 346
  vocational, choice and, 347–348
Identity achievement status, 345
Identity *vs.* role confusion, 37, 39, 344
Imaginary audience, 224
Imaginary companion, 216
Imitation, 401
Impairments, hearing, 174
Implicit memory, 236–237
Imprinting, 440–441
Independent variable, 18–19
Indirect effects, 473
Individualistic culture, 338
Individual rights, morality of, 409
Induction, 417
Industry *vs.* inferiority, 37, 39, 355
Infant Health and Development Program, 123
Infants, 133–137. *See also* Newborns
  antisocial behavior, 413–414
  attachment, 441, 442–449
  autism spectrum disorder, 506–510
  babbling, 307
  behavioral states, 136–137
  bonding, 442
  brain development, 133–134
  cognitive development, 213–215
  congenital malformations, 137
  contact comfort, 445
  cooing, 306–307
  day care, 448
  death of, 543–544
  depression, 510
  depth perception, 170–171
  differential treatment, 370–371
  early education, 311–312
  early experience and brain, 177–178
  early learning, gender differences in, 371
  early moral training, 414–415
  emotional development, 434–436
  emotion regulation, 435–436
  empathy, 413
  exploratory behavior, 443
  face perception, 170
  in family, 472–473
  fast mapping, 308
  fathers of, 472–473
  first emotions, 434–435
  functional grammar, 308
  gender differences, 370–372
  gender identity, 371
  grasping, 182
  growing healthier babies, 108
  habituation, 168
  health and wellness, 137
  hearing, 172–175
  holophrases, 307–309
  intuitive theories, 171–172
  joint attention, 307
  language, mastering, 306–307
  mastery motivation, 310–311
  memory, 239–242
  moral development, 412–415
  mothers of, 472–473
  needs of, 179
  newborn capabilities, 134–137

object permanence, 213–215
objects, organizing, 169–170
operant conditioning, 168
overextension, 308
overregularization, 310
peer relations, 449
personality, 337–340
preferential looking, 168
prosocial behavior, 413
psychological disorders, 506–511
rapid growth, 134
reaching, 182
reflexes, 134–136
self-awareness, 337–338
sensory and perceptual capacities, 167–179
separations, 447–448
sexual self, beginnings of, 371–372
sibling relationships, 479–481
smell, 175–176
social deprivation, 447
somaesthetic senses, 176–177
Strange Situation, 444, 445
symbols, emergence of, 215
syntactic bootstrapping, 307
taste, 175–176
telegraphic speech, 309–310
temperament, 338–340, 446
theory of mind, 401
transformational grammar, 310
underextension, 308
vision, 168–172
vocabulary spurt, 308
word segmentation, 306
Infant states, 97
Infertility, 91
Information-processing approach
  defined, 49
  educational recommendations based on, 329
  intelligence and, 295
  memory and, 234
  research on, 329
Informed consent, in developmental research, 27–28
Inheritance, mechanisms of, 66–67. *See also* Heredity
  polygenic inheritance, 67
  sex-linked inheritance, 67
  single gene-pair inheritance, 66–67
Initiation phase of dating, 456
Initiative *vs.* guilt, 37, 39, 355
Insecure attachment, 448–449
Instinct, 36
Instrumental hedonism, 409
Integrity, old-age, 357
Integrity *vs.* despair, 37, 39, 357
Intellectual competence, 448
Intellectual disability, 68, 70, 71, 291–293
Intelligence
  adolescent, 277–279
  adult, 279–286
  automatization, 271
  changes in, with age, 282–283
  child, 274–276
  cognitive approaches to, comparison of, 294–295
  constructivist approach and, 203–204
  crystallized, 267
  decline, predictors of, 283, 284
  defined, 203
  development of, 203–204
  educational recommendations based on, 329–330
  environmental influences, 290–291
  extremes of, 291–294
  factor analysis, 267
  fluid, 266, 267
  genetic factors, 290
  giftedness, 293–294
  infant, 273–274
  intellectual disability, 291–293

knowledge of, 267
older adult, 282–286
Piaget's definition of, 203
psychometric approach, 266, 267–269
research on, 329–330
successful, 271–272
theory of multiple intelligences, 269–270
training for aging adults, 284
triarchic theory of, 270–272
two-factor theory of, 266
Intelligence quotient (IQ) scores
  calculating, 268
  during childhood, stability of, 274–275
  ethnicity and, 289–291
  factors that influence, 286–291
  Flynn effect, 277–278
  gain in, causes of, 275
  genes and, 286–289
  genetics and, 76–77
  health and, 280, 281–282
  loss in, causes of, 275
  normal distribution, 268–269
  occupational success and, 279–280
  race and, 289–291
  standard deviation, 269
Intelligence quotient (IQ) tests
  Bayley Scales of Infant Development, 273
  biased, 289
  infant intelligence as predictor of later intelligence, 274–275
  motivational differences, 289–290
  school achievement and, 278
  Stanford–Binet Intelligence Scale, 268
  stereotype threat, 290
  test norms, 268
  Wechsler Scales, 268
Intentions
  of children, 416
  understanding, 401
Interactional mode, 479
Intergenerational transmission of parenting, 496
Internalizing problem, 511
Internal working model, 441
Internet addiction, 17
Intimacy
  early adult, 356
  in triangular theory of love, 459
Intimacy *vs.* isolation, 37, 39, 356
Intuitive theories, 172
Invariant sequence, 47
Investment theory, 272
In vitro fertilization (IVF), 91

J

Jaundice, 113
Job loss, 359
Joint attention, 307, 401
Jung, Carl, 38
Juvenile delinquency, 420

K

Kangaroo care, 121, 122
Karyotype, 64
Kinkeeper, 489
Klinefelter syndrome, 68
Knowledge base
  adolescents, 251
  children, 245
  older adults, 257
Kohlberg, Lawrence
  mercy-killing dilemma, 409, 410
  moral development, 408–410
  moral reasoning, 408–409
  moral thinking, 409, 410
  moral understandings, 416
Kübler-Ross's five "stages of dying," 539–541

Reversibility, 217, 218
Reversible dementia, 528–529
Rhythmic stereotypes, 180
Risk, in prenatal or perinatal period, 122–123
Rite of passage, 7–8
RNA, 63, 83
Role reversal, 489
Role-taking skills. *See* Perspective-taking skills
Romantic relationships, 458–460
    love, 459–460
    partner choice, 458–459
Rooting reflex, 135
Rubella, 104
Rule assessment approach, 249
Ruminative coping, 523

S

Safe haven, 443
Sample, 15
Santa Claus, children's beliefs in, 217
Savant syndrome, 269
Scaffolding, 208
Scaffolding theory of aging and compensation
    (STAC), 153
Schema processing theory, 379–380
Schematic-processing model, 379–380
Schemes, 203
    coordination of secondary, 213
Schizophrenia, 68, 78
Schools
    effective, 319–321
    high school dropouts, identifying, 325
Scientific method, 14–15
Scientific reasoning, 221–222
Script, 247–248
Secondary circular reaction, 215
Secular trend, 146
Secure attachment, 444, 448–449, 462
Secure base, 443
Selective attention, 183–184
Selective optimization with compensation (SOC), 261
Self
    emerging, in infants, 337–338
    gap between ideal and real self, reducing, 350
    sense of, in children, 341
Self-concept
    adolescent, 343–344
    adult, 349–352
    age and, 343
    cultural differences, 350, 351–352
    defined, 334
    gender differences and, 349–350
    older adults, 349–352
Self-conscious emotion, 435
Self-control, 414–415
Self-efficacy, 44
Self-esteem
    adolescent, 344
    adult, 349–352
    age differences and, 349–350
    child, 341–342
    cultural differences, 350, 351–352
    defined, 334
    gender differences and, 349–350
    older adults, 349–352
Self-evaluation, goals and standards of, 350
Self-recognition, 337, 338
Self-regulatory mechanisms, 410
Self-stereotyping, 350
Semantic memory, 236
Semantics, 301
Semenarche, 146
Sensation, 166
Sensitive period, 178
Sensorimotor stage, 47–48, 204, 213
Sensory and perceptual capacities
    adolescents, 185–189

children, 179–184
cultural variation in, 187, 188–189
defined, 166
educational recommendations based on, 330
evoked potentials, 168, 174
habituation, 168
infants, 167–179
nativist and constructivist positions on, 166–167
older adults, 190–198
operant conditioning, 168
perspectives on, 166–167
preferential looking, 168
research on, 330
Sensory information, integrating, 182–183
Sensory register, 234
Sensory threshold, 190
Separation anxiety, 443
Sequential design, 24–25
Seriation, 220
Sex
    determination of, 64–65
    understanding of, 366
Sex chromosome abnormality, 68
Sex hormones, prenatal exposure to, 103
Sex-linked inheritance, 67
Sex organs formed during fetal period, 96
Sexual abuse, 383
Sexual assault, 390
Sexual behavior. *See also* Sexual risk behavior
    adolescents, 388–389, 390–392
    children, 382–383
Sexuality
    adolescents, 385–392
    adults, 394–396
    children, 382–383
    infants, 371–372
Sexually transmitted infections (STIs)
    adolescents, 388, 389, 390, 391–392
    adults, 394–395
    causes, symptoms, and treatments, 391
    prenatal exposure to, 105
Sexual maturation, of adolescent, 143, 145–148
    adrenarche, 143, 145
    early *vs.* late development, 147–148
    menarche, 145, 146
    psychological implications, 146–147
    secular trend, 146
    semenarche, 146
    Tanner Scale, 145
Sexual orientation, in adolescents, 386–387
Sexual risk behavior. *See also* Sexually transmitted
    infections (STIs)
    among teens, developmental theories
      to reduce, 55–56
    Bronfenbrenner on, 53
    Freud and Erikson on, 38
    learning theorists on, 45
    Piaget on, 48
Shared environmental influences, 74, 76–77, 78
Short-term memory, 234
Sibling relationships, 479–481, 488
    ambivalence in, 480
    arrival of new baby, 479–480
    influences on development, 480–481
    interactions in, 403
Sibling rivalry, 480
Sickle-cell disease, 69, 70
Single gene-pair inheritance, 66–67
Singles, 491–492
Size constancy, 171
Skill, 212
Skinner, B. F.
    operant conditioning, 41–43
    on sexual risk behavior, 45
Sleep, adolescent, 150–151
Sleeper effect, 178
Slow-to-warm-up temperament, 339

Smell
    infant, 175–176
    older adults, 196, 197
Social clock, 7
Social cognition
    in adults, 405–406
    defined, 400
    perspective-taking skills, 405
    theory of mind, 400–404
    trait perception, 404–405
Social cognitive theory, 43–45
    gender roles, 376–378
    human agency, 44–45
    moral behavior, 410–411, 412
    observational learning, 43–44, 45
    personality, 335, 336
    reciprocal determinism, 44–45
    strengths and weaknesses of, 46
Social comparison, 341
Social competence, 448
Social context
    of attachment, 446–447
    of childbirth, 112
Social–conventional rules, 417
Social deprivation, 447
Social information-processing model, 421
Social interaction
    in infants, 337–338
    thought and, 208
Socialization goals of parents/parenting, 478
Social learning theory. *See* Social cognitive theory
Social media, adolescent development
    affected by, 13
Social networks
    adolescents, 455–456
    adults, 458
Social norm, 504
Social order–maintaining morality, 409
Social pretend play, 451
Social referencing, 435
Social-role theory, 369–370
Sociocultural perspective, 49, 52, 207–211
    cognitive developmental theory
      compared to, 211
    culture and thought, 207–208
    dynamic system view compared to, 212
    educational recommendations based on, 329
    to improve cognitive functioning, 210
    intelligence and, 295
    social interaction and thought, 208
    tools of thought, 208–209
Socioeconomic status (SES), 7–8
Socioemotional selectivity theory, 439
Sociometric popularity, 455
Sociometric techniques, 452
Solitary play, 451
Somaesthetic senses
    infants, 176–177
    older adults, 197
Somatic symptoms, 503
Species heredity, 60
Speech perception
    infants, 173, 175
    older adults, 195–196
Spillover effects, 485
Spina bifida, 93–94, 110
Spirituality, 428–429
Spontaneous abortion, 92
Sports and brain damage, 144
Spouse, death of, 550–552
    complicated grief, 551–552
    depression, 550–551
    resilience, 550, 551
Standard deviation, 269
Stanford–Binet Intelligence Scale, 268
Static thought, 217
Status phase of dating, 456

Summary of Physical, Cognitive, Personal, and Social Development Across the Life

Period	Physical Development	Cognitive Development
Infant (Birth to 2 years) 	Physical growth is rapid; neuronal connections in the brain rapidly expand and undergo pruning. Reflexes are followed by more voluntary motor control; walking occurs at 1 year. Functioning senses are available at birth; early ability to understand sensory information is impressive.	Sensorimotor period: Through senses and actions, infants acquire symbolic capacity and object-permanence concept. Cooing and babbling are followed by one-word and two-word sentences. Learning capacity and recognition memory are present from birth; recall improves with age.
Preschool child (2 to 5 years) 	Rapid brain development continues. Coordination and fine motor skills improve. Perceptual abilities are good; attention span is short.	Preoperational stage: Thought is guided by perceptions rather than logic. Symbolic capacity (language acquisition and pretend play) blossoms. There are some limits in information-processing capacity, use of memory strategies, and reasoning.
School-age child (6 to 10 years) 	Physical growth is slow; motor skills gradually improve. Children have increased ability to control attention and use the senses intelligently.	Concrete operations stage: Logical actions are carried out in the head; children master conservation. They also master fine points of language; memory strategies and problem-solving with concrete objects improve. IQs begin to stabilize.
Adolescent (10 to 18 years) 	Adolescents experience a brain spurt, a growth spurt, and attainment of sexual maturity. Physical functioning improves. Concern with body image is common.	Formal operations stage: Hypothetical and abstract thought emerge; scientific problem-solving improves. Attention and information-processing skills continue to improve, linked to brain growth spurt.
Emerging and young adult (18 to 39 years) 	This is the time of peak functioning, but a gradual decline in physical and perceptual capacities begins.	Brain development is completed, improving executive control; intellectual functioning is at a peak and mostly stable.
Middle-aged adult (40 to 64 years) 	Physical declines become noticeable (e.g., some loss of endurance, need for reading glasses). Chronic illness increases. Menopause and male andropause occur.	Sophisticated cognitive skills develop, especially in areas of expertise. There is the possibility of growth beyond formal thought and gains in knowledge. Fluid intelligence may begin to decline, but crystallized knowledge is maintained well. Often a peak time for creative achievement.
Older adult (65 years and older) 	Physical decline continues; more chronic disease, disability, and sensory impairment are common; and reaction time slows. But there is also continued plasticity and reorganization of the brain in response to intellectual stimulation.	Declines in cognition are common but not inevitable. Slower learning, memory problems, declines in IQ and problem-solving may occur, especially if skills are rarely exercised, but crystallized intelligence survives longer than fluid.